CHESHIRE, NORTH & FAWCETT

PRIVATE INTERNATIONAL LAW

FIFTEENTH EDITION

Edited By

PAUL TORREMANS

Consultant Editor

JAMES J. FAWCETT

Authors

UGLJEŠA GRUŠIĆ

CHRISTIAN HEINZE

LOUISE MERRETT

ALEX MILLS

CARMEN OTERO GARCÍA-CASTRILLÓN

ZHENG SOPHIA TANG

KATARINA TRIMMINGS

LARA WALKER

OXFORD

UNIVERSITY PRESS

OXFORD
UNIVERSITY PRESS

Great Clarendon Street, Oxford, OX2 6DP,
United Kingdom

Oxford University Press is a department of the University of Oxford.
It furthers the University's objective of excellence in research, scholarship,
and education by publishing worldwide. Oxford is a registered trade mark of
Oxford University Press in the UK and in certain other countries

Fifteenth Edition published in 2017
Impression: 1

Published in the United States of America by Oxford University Press
198 Madison Avenue, New York, NY 10016, United States of America

British Library Cataloguing in Publication Data
Data available

Library of Congress Control Number: 2017945333

ISBN 978–0–19–967899–0 (pbk.)
ISBN 978–0–19–967898–3 (hbk.)

Printed in Italy by
L.E.G.O. S.p.A.

Cheshire, North & Fawcett

PRIVATE INTERNATIONAL LAW

PREFACE TO THE FIFTEENTH EDITION

It was at the same time a privilege and a challenge to write this new fifteenth edition of Cheshire, North & Fawcett, *Private International Law*, and to follow in the footsteps of its illustrious former editors. We are first of all extremely grateful to James Fawcett, who accepted to stay on as consulting editor and who, in that capacity, has made a major contribution to this new edition. As general editor I had the support of a great team of authors: Prof. Carmen Otero-Garcia Castrillon (Universidad Complutense de Madrid, first drafts of chapters 1, 3–7, 29 with Paul Torremans), Prof. Christian Heinze (Leibnitz Universität Hannover, first drafts of chapters 19 and 20), Dr. Katarina Trimmings (University of Aberdeen, first drafts of chapters 21–23 and 25–27), Dr. Uglješa Grušić (UCL, first drafts of chapters 2, 8, 14–18 and 11 (with Alex Mills)) and Dr. Alex Mills (UCL, first drafts of chapters 10, 12, 13, 30–32, and 11 (with Uglješa Grušić)) each took on board several chapters, whilst Prof. Sophia Tang (Newcastle University, first drafts of chapters 28 and 35), Dr. Lara Walker (University of Sussex, first drafts of chapters 9, 24, 36 and 37) and Dr. Louise Merrett (University of Cambridge, first draft of chapter 38) provided specialist chapters. We each provided our detailed expertise, but James Fawcett and I made sure that each chapter reflects the specific and focussed approach that has made Cheshire, North & Fawcett's reputation in the field of private international law.

Private international law remains a rapidly evolving subject area. Many of the new developments have a European and international character, which is entirely fitting for an area of law that by definition crosses borders and involves an international element. That international element is also reflected in the group of authors, but for all of us our experience is also strongly anchored in the United Kingdom. The Brexit vote intervened during the preparation of this new edition. In consultation with our publishers we have decided to ignore it (for now). One should not try to read any political content into this decision though. The impact of the Brexit vote is simply not known yet and that uncertainty also affects private international law. It is not clear at all how private international law in the United Kingdom will be affected and looking at the complexity of the matters at hand it is likely to take several years before the changes to private international law become clear.

We therefore focus on the law as it stands on 31st January 2017. The existing chapters have been thoroughly updated and, in part, been rewritten. We have also added new chapters on surrogacy, corporations and insolvency and in the area of recognition and enforcement the basic elements, as they apply both to judgments and arbitral awards, have been developed further and this has also seen the addition of another chapter.

We also wish to express our gratitude towards our publishers for their support throughout the preparation of this new edition, especially for the preparation of the various tables and the index.

Nottingham
January 2017
Paul L.C. Torremans

PREFACE TO THE FIRST EDITION

Convention demands that in the preface to a new book the author should excuse his temerity in adding to the literature on the subject and should also state the objects he hopes to attain. My excuse is the fascination, perhaps my readers will say the fatal fascination, of the subject. Of all the departments of English law, Private International Law offers the freest scope to the mere jurist. It is the perfect antithesis of such a topic as real property law. It is not overloaded with detailed rules; it has been only lightly touched by the paralysing hand of the Parliamentary draftsman; it is perhaps the one considerable department in which the formation of a coherent body of law is in course of process; it is, at the moment, fluid not static, elusive not obvious; it repels any tendency to dogmatism; and, above all, the possible permutations of the questions that it raises are so numerous that the diligent investigator can seldom rest content with the solution that he proposes. Despite its value as a subject of academic study it is curiously neglected in the legal education of this country, a fact which is remarkable if regard is had to the number of different legal systems that the British Empire comprises. On the Continent and in the United States of America, Private International Law is one of the major subjects of study at the Universities but in England it cannot claim a professorship of its own and it forms only an insignificant part of the chief law examinations.

The purpose of this book, however, is not merely to indulge my own fancy, but to provide students with a shorter account of the subject than most of those already published. Further, my object has been not to remain satisfied with mere exposition but to approach the more controversial topics in a spirit of constructive criticism. There are many instances in which I have found it impossible to agree with the views of such great masters as Dicey and Westlake, and in which I have ventured, perhaps rashly, to suggest that the relevant authorities indicate a somewhat different principle, but in all such cases I have been careful to present the reader with what may be called the generally accepted textbook view of each matter. Some of the mild strictures contained in this book may not be well founded, but even so they can do little harm, for there is no doubt that the subject in general sorely needs criticism. It may be doubted, indeed, whether all is well with the English system of Private International Law. Instances are numerous in the last thirty years in which the Courts have adopted some plausible principle, without serious investigation of its merits and without considering what the effect will be if it is applied to a case with slightly different facts. There are other cases in which it is difficult to extract the *ratio decidendi*, or indeed any clear principle, from the judgments. Private International Law, in fact, presents a golden opportunity, perhaps the last opportunity, for the judiciary to show that a homogeneous and scientifically constructed body of law, suitable to the changing needs of society, can be evolved without the aid of the legislature, and, though the task must necessarily be performed by the judges, there seems no reason why the jurist should stand aside in cloistered inactivity.

The book contains no account of the law relating to British nationality. This is a subject which should be dealt with solely in works on Constitutional Law, for it clearly has little, if any, connexion with Private International Law. Whether a person is a national of a particular country is relevant neither to the question of choice of law nor, it is submitted, for purposes of jurisdiction.

Oxford
1 January 1935
G.C.C.

SUMMARY CONTENTS

Selected Bibliography   xix
Table of Statutes   xxix
Table of Cases   lxxiii

I INTRODUCTION

1. Definition, Nature and Scope of Private International Law   3
2. Historical Development and Current Theories   17

II PRELIMINARY TOPICS

3. Classification   41
4. The Incidental Question   51
5. Renvoi   57
6. Substance and Procedure   73
7. The Proof of Foreign Law   105
8. Exclusion of Foreign Law   114
9. Domicile, Nationality and Residence   145

III JURISDICTION, FOREIGN JUDGMENTS AND AWARDS

10. Jurisdiction of the English Courts—An Introduction   187
11. Jurisdiction Under the Brussels/Lugano System   191
12. The Competence of the English Courts Under—The Traditional Rules   323
13. Stays and the Management of Parallel Proceedings   391
14. Limitations on Jurisdiction   483
15. Recognition and Enforcement of Foreign
    Judgments and Arbitral Awards in England—An Introduction   520
16. Recognition and Enforcement of Foreign Judgments—The Traditional Rules 525
17. Recognition and Enforcement of Judgments Under
    the Brussels/Lugano System   608
18. Foreign Arbitral Awards   666

IV THE LAW OF OBLIGATIONS

19. Contracts   681
20. Non-Contractual Obligations   776

V FAMILY LAW

21. Marriage and Other Adult Relationships   891

22. Matrimonial and Related Causes   951

23. Declarations   1049

24. Financial Relief   1059

25. Children   1087

26. Cross-border Surrogacy   1179

27. Legitimacy, Legitimation and Adoption   1193

28. Mental Incapacity   1232

VI THE LAW OF PROPERTY

29. The Distinction Between Movables and Immovables   1251

30. Immovables   1255

31. The Transfer of Tangible Movables   1263

32. The Assignment of Intangible Movables   1280

33. Corporations   1306

34. Insolvency   1312

35. Administration of Estates   1325

36. Succession   1338

37. Matrimonial Property   1365

38. Trusts   1382

Index   1397

CONTENTS

Selected Bibliography   xix
Table of Statutes   xxix
Table of Cases   lxxiii

I INTRODUCTION

1. **Definition, Nature and Scope of Private International Law**   3
   1. Introduction   3
   2. Space and Time   5
   3. Scope of Private International Law   6
   4. Meaning of "Foreign Law"   8
   5. International Variety of Private International Law Rules   8
   6. Avoiding Conflicts   9
   7. The Name of the Subject   15
2. **Historical Development and Current Theories**   17
   1. Development of English Private International Law   17
   2. Modern Theories and Developments   21

II PRELIMINARY TOPICS

3. **Classification**   41
   1. Introduction   41
   2. Classification of the Cause of Action   42
   3. Classification of a Rule of Law   45
4. **The Incidental Question**   51
   1. What is an Incidental Question?   51
   2. The Elements of an Incidental Question   52
   3. The Problem Illustrated   52
   4. A Way Forward   54
   5. Dépeçage   55
5. **Renvoi**   57
   1. The Problem Stated   57
   2. Possible Solutions   58
   3. Scope of the Application of Renvoi   69
6. **Substance and Procedure**   73
   1. Difference Between Substance and Procedure   73
   2. Particular Issues   77

7. **The Proof of Foreign Law**   105
   1. Foreign Law: A Question of Fact   105
   2. How Foreign Law Is Proved   108
   3. Witnesses Who Can Prove Foreign Law   110
   4. The Role of the Court   111

8. **Exclusion of Foreign Law**   114
   1. Foreign Revenue, Penal and Other Public Laws   115
   2. Foreign Expropriatory Legislation   126
   3. Foreign Laws Repugnant to English Public Policy   132
   4. Mandatory Rules   143

9. **Domicile, Nationality and Residence**   145
   1. Introduction   145
   2. General Rules   147
   3. The Acquisition of a Domicile of Choice   148
   4. Domicile of Origin and Domicile of Choice Contrasted   162
   5. Domicile of Dependent Persons   165
   6. Domicile of Married Women   168
   7. Domicile and Nationality   170
   8. Concepts of Residence   172

III JURISDICTION, FOREIGN JUDGMENTS AND AWARDS

10. **Jurisdiction of the English Courts—An Introduction**   187
    1. Jurisdiction Under the Brussels/Lugano System   187
    2. Jurisdiction Under the Modified Regulation   189
    3. Jurisdiction Under the Traditional Rules   189
    4. The Hague Convention on Choice of Court Agreements   190

11. **Jurisdiction Under the Brussels/Lugano System**   191
    1. Introduction   191
    2. History and Interpretation   191
    3. The Brussels I Recast   198
    4. The Brussels Convention   312
    5. The Lugano Convention   313
    6. The Hague Convention on Choice of Court Agreements   315
    7. Allocating Jurisdiction within the United Kingdom: The Modified
       Regulation   317

12. **The Competence of the English Courts Under—The Traditional Rules**   323
    1. Actions in Personam   323
    2. Actions in Rem   382

13. **Stays and the Management of Parallel Proceedings**   391
    1. Introduction   391
    2. Stays of English Proceedings Under the Common Law   392
    3. Restraining Foreign Proceedings Under the Common Law:
       The Anti-Suit Injunction   422
    4. Parallel Proceedings Under the Brussels I Recast: Lis Pendens
       and Related Actions   442
    5. Stays of Proceedings Under the Brussels I Recast   459
    6. Restraining Foreign Proceedings and the Brussels I Recast   475

14. **Limitations on Jurisdiction**   483
    1. Introduction   483
    2. Jurisdiction in Respect of Foreign Property   484
    3. Jurisdiction Over the Parties   496
    4. Statutory Limitations on Jurisdiction   518

15. **Recognition and Enforcement of Foreign
    Judgments and Arbitral Awards in England—An Introduction**   520
    1. The Effect Given to Foreign Judgments and Arbitral Awards   520
    2. The Different Regimes Governing Recognition
       and Enforcement of Foreign Judgments   521
    3. Foreign Arbitral Awards   524

16. **Recognition and Enforcement of Foreign Judgments—The Traditional Rules** 525
    1. Introduction   525
    2. Recognition and Enforcement at Common Law   527
    3. Direct Enforcement of Foreign Judgments by Statute   588
    4. Inter-relation of the Common Law and Statutes   605
    5. The Recast of the Brussels I Regulation   607

17. **Recognition and Enforcement of Judgments Under
    the Brussels/Lugano System**   608
    1. The Brussels I Recast   608
    2. The EC/Denmark Agreement   652
    3. The Brussels Convention   652
    4. The Lugano Convention   653
    5. The European Enforcement Order Regulation   656
    6. The European Order for Payment Procedure Regulation   660
    7. The European Small Claims Procedure Regulation   663

18. **Foreign Arbitral Awards**   666
    1. Enforcement At Common Law   667
    2. Enforcement Under the Civil Jurisdiction and Judgments Act 1982 669
    3. Enforcement Under the Arbitration Act 1950   670

    4. Enforcement Under the Arbitration Act 1996   670

    5. Enforcement Under the Administration of Justice Act 1920 and the
       Foreign Judgments (Reciprocal Enforcement) Act 1933   677

    6. Enforcement Under the Arbitration (International
       Investment Disputes) Act 1966   677

IV THE LAW OF OBLIGATIONS

19. Contracts   681

    1. Introduction   681

    2. The Rome Convention   683

    3. The Rome I Regulation   686

20. Non-Contractual Obligations   776

    1. Introduction   776

    2. The Rome II Regulation   780

    3. Maritime Non-Contractual Obligations   875

    4. Mixed Issues Relating to Non-Contractual Obligations and Contract   879

    5. Non-Contractual Obligations Outside the Scope
       of the Rome II Regulation   883

V FAMILY LAW

21. Marriage and Other Adult Relationships   891

    1. The Meaning of "Marriage"   891

    2. Formalities of Marriage   893

    3. Capacity to Marry   909

    4. Reform of General Rules   927

    5. Polygamous Marriages   928

    6. Same Sex Relationships: Civil Partnership and Same Sex Marriage   946

    7. De Facto Cohabitation   949

22. Matrimonial and Related Causes   951

    1. Introduction   951

    2. Polygamous Marriages and Matrimonial Relief   952

    3. Divorce, Nullity and Judicial Separation   954

    4. Presumption of Death and Dissolution of Marriage   1037

    5. Dissolution, Nullity and Separation of Civil Partnerships   1039

    6. Divorce, Nullity and Separation of Same Sex Marriages   1045

23. Declarations   1049

    1. Introduction   1049

    2. Family Law Act 1986, Part III   1050

3. Child Abduction and Custody Act 1985 — 1056
4. Civil Partnership Act 2004 — 1057
5. Marriage (Same Sex Couples) Act 2013 — 1057
6. Presumption of Death Act 2013 — 1058

24. **Financial Relief** — 1059
 1. Jurisdiction of the English Court — 1059
 2. Financial Relief After a Foreign Divorce/Dissolution, Annulment or Legal Separation — 1071
 3. Choice of Law — 1078
 4. Recognition and Enforcement of Foreign Orders — 1078

25. **Children** — 1087
 1. Introduction — 1087
 2. Jurisdiction in Matters of Parental Responsibility — 1089
 3. Choice of Law — 1125
 4. Recognition and Enforcement — 1126
 5. Other Developments — 1177

26. **Cross-border Surrogacy** — 1179
 1. Introduction — 1179
 2. UK Approach to Surrogacy — 1183
 3. Human Rights Considerations — 1189

27. **Legitimacy, Legitimation and Adoption** — 1193
 1. Introduction — 1193
 2. Legitimacy — 1194
 3. Legitimation — 1202
 4. Adoption — 1205

28. **Mental Incapacity** — 1232
 1. Introduction — 1232
 2. Mental Capacity Act 2005 — 1233
 3. Cases Outside the Mental Capacity Act — 1245

VI THE LAW OF PROPERTY

29. **The Distinction Between Movables and Immovables** — 1251
 1. Introduction — 1251
 2. Classification by the Law of the Situs — 1252
 3. Some Examples — 1252
 4. Relevance of Distinction Between Realty and Personalty — 1254
 5. Distinction Between Tangible and Intangible Movables — 1254

30. **Immovables**   1255
    1. Jurisdiction   1255
    2. Choice of Law   1255

31. **The Transfer of Tangible Movables**   1263
    1. Introduction   1263
    2. The Various Theories   1264
    3. The Modern Law   1267

32. **The Assignment of Intangible Movables**   1280
    1. Introduction   1280
    2. Debts   1280
    3. Negotiable Instruments   1294
    4. Shares and Securities   1298

33. **Corporations**   1306
    1. Domicile   1306
    2. Residence   1307
    3. Status and Capacity   1307
    4. Internal Management   1308
    5. Winding Up   1309

34. **Insolvency**   1312
    1. Scope   1312
    2. Jurisdiction   1313
    3. Choice of Law   1319
    4. Recognition of Insolvency Proceedings   1323
    5. Groups of Companies and Their Members   1324

35. **Administration of Estates**   1325
    1. Introduction   1325
    2. English Grants   1330
    3. Choice of Law   1333
    4. Foreign Administrators   1335

36. **Succession**   1338
    1. Introduction   1338
    2. Movables   1339
    3. Immovables   1351
    4. European Harmonisation Concerning Succession and Wills   1358
    5. Powers of Appointment Exercised by Will   1359

37. **Matrimonial Property**   1365
    1. Introduction   1365
    2. Assignment Where There is no Ante-nuptial Contract   1366

3. Assignment Where There is an Ante-nuptial Contract   1372
4. Matrimonial Property Rights and Divorce   1378
5. Property Rights Arising from Other Adult Relationships   1379
6. European Proposals for Reform   1380

38. Trusts   1382
1. Introduction   1382
2. Preliminary Issues   1383
3. Choice of Law   1386
4. Recognition   1391
5. Mandatory Rules and Public Policy   1392
6. Variation of Trusts and Settlements   1393

Index   1397

SELECTED BIBLIOGRAPHY

Andenas *Liber Amicorum Guido Alpa: Private Law Beyond the National Systems*, M Andenas *et al* (eds) (2007)

Andenas and Jacobs *European Community Law in the English Courts*, by M Andenas and F Jacobs (1998)

Anton *Private International Law: A Treatise from the Standpoint of Scots Law*, by A E Anton, 2nd edn (1990)

Audit *Droit International Privé*, by B Audit (1991)

Barnett *Res Judicata, Estoppel, and Foreign Judgments*, by P R Barnett (2001)

Basedow and Kono *An Economic Analysis of Private International Law*, by J Basedow and T Kono (in co-operation with G Rühl) (2006)

Batiffol and Lagarde *Droit International Privé*, by H Batiffol and P Lagarde, 7th edn (1981–1983), 8th edn, Vol I (1993)

Baty *Polarized Law*, by T Baty (1914)

Beale *The Conflict of Laws*, by J H Beale (1935)

Beaumont and McEleavy *The Hague Convention on International Child Abduction*, by P Beaumont and P McEleavy (1999)

Beaumont and McEleavy *Anton's Private International Law*, by P Beaumont and P McEleavy, 3rd edn (2011)

Beaumont, Trimmings, Danov and Yüksel *Cross-Border Litigation in Europe*, P Beaumont, M Danov, K Trimmings and B Yüksel (eds) (2017)

Bell *Forum Shopping and Venue in Transnational Litigation*, by A S Bell (2003)

Benjamin *Interests in Securities: A Proprietary Law Analysis of the International Securities Markets*, by J Benjamin (2000)

Berman *Global Legal Pluralism: A Jurisprudence of Law Beyond Borders*, by P Berman (2012)

Binchy *Irish Conflicts of Law*, by W Binchy (1988)

Boele-Woelki *Perspectives for the Unification and Harmonisation of Family Law in Europe*, by K Boele-Woelki (2003)

Boele-Woelki and Beilfuss *Brussels II bis: Its Impact and Application in the Member State*, by K Boele-Woelki and C Beilfuss (2007)

Bogdan *Private International Law as a Component of the Law of the Forum, General Course in Private International Law*, by M Bogdan (2010)

Borras *E Pluribus Unum*, A Borras (ed) (1996)

Bos and Brownlie *Liber Amicorum for Lord Wilberforce*, by M Bos and I Brownlie (1987)

Briggs *Agreements on Jurisdiction and Choice of Law*, by A Briggs (2008)

Briggs *Private International Law in English Courts*, by A Briggs (2014)

Briggs *Civil Jurisdiction and Judgments*, by A Briggs, 6th edn (2015)

Briggs *The Conflict of Laws*, by A Briggs, 3rd edn (2013)

Brilmayer *Conflict of Laws: Foundations and Future Directions*, by L Brilmayer, 2nd edn (1995)

Broude and Shany *Multi-Sourced Equivalent Norms in International Law*, by T Broude and Y Shany (2011)

Cabeza, Bhutta and Braier *International Adoption*, R Cabeza, A Bhutta and J Braier (eds) (2012)

Cafaggi *The Institutional Framework of European Private Law*, F Cafaggi (ed) (2006)

Cafaggi and Muir Watt *Making European Private Law: Governance Design*, F Cafaggi and H Muir Watt (eds) (2008)

Cafaggi and Muir Watt *The Regulatory Function of European Private Law*, F Cafaggi and H Muir Watt (eds) (2009)

Calliess *Rome Regulations: Commentary on the European Rules of the Conflict of Laws*, by G-P Calliess, 2nd edn (2015)

Cansacchi *The Choice and Adaptation of Foreign Law in the Conflict of Laws*, by G Cansacchi (1953)

Carruthers *The Transfer of Property in the Conflict of Laws*, by J M Carruthers (2005)

Castel and Walker *Canadian Conflict of Laws*, by J Walker, 6th edn (2006)

Cavers *The Choice of Law Process*, by D F Cavers (1965)

Cavers: Essays *The Choice of Law: Selected Essays 1933–1983*, by D F Cavers (1985)

Cheong *Current Issues in International Commercial Litigation*, by C Cheong *et al* (1977)

Cheshire, Fifoot and Furmston's *Law of Contract*, by M Fifoot, 16th edn (2012)

Clarkson and Hill *The Conflict of Laws*, by J Hill and M Ní Shúilleabháin, 5th edn (2016)

Clive *The Law of Husband and Wife in Scotland*, by E Clive, 4th edn (1997)

Collier *Conflict of Laws*, by J G Collier and P Rogerson, 4th edn (2013)

Collins *The Civil Jurisdiction and Judgments Act 1982*, by L Collins (1983)

Collins *Essays in International Litigation and the Conflict of Laws*, by L Collins (1994)

Cook *Logical and Legal Bases of the Conflict of Laws*, by W W Cook (1942)

Crawford and Carruthers *International Private Law: A Scots Perspective*, by E Crawford and J Carruthers, 4th edn (2015)

Crawford and Carruthers *International Private Law in Scotland*, by E B Crawford and J M Carruthers, 2nd edn (2006)

Currie *Selected Essays on the Conflict of Laws*, by B Currie (1963)

De Boer *Beyond Lex Loci Delicti*, by T M De Boer (1987)

de Nova *Historical and Comparative Introduction to Conflicts of Laws*, by R de Nova (1966)

Dicey, Morris and Collins *The Conflict of Laws*, by Sir Lawrence Collins *et al*, 15th edn (2012)

Dickinson *The Rome II Regulation*, by A Dickinson (2008)

Dickinson and Lein *Brussels I Regulation Recast*, by A Dickinson and E Lein (2015)

Ehrenzweig *Private International Law* Vols I–III, by A A Ehrenzweig and E Jayme (1967–1977)

Ehrenzweig: Treatise *A Treatise on the Conflict of Laws*, by A A Ehrenzweig (1962)

Esplugues, Iglesias and Palao *Application of Foreign Law*, by C Esplugues, J-L Iglesias and G Palao (2011)

Falconbridge *Essays on the Conflict of Laws*, by J D Falconbridge, 2nd edn (1954)

Fawcett *Declining Jurisdiction in Private International Law*, J J Fawcett (ed) (1995)

Fawcett *Reform and Development in Private International Law: Essays in Honour of Sir Peter North*, by J J Fawcett (2002)

Fawcett, Harris and Bridge *International Sale of Goods in the Conflict of Laws*, by J J Fawcett, J M Harris and M Bridge (2005)

Fawcett, Ní Shúilleabháin and Shah, *Human Rights and Private International Law*, by J J Fawcett, M Ní Shúilleabháin and S Shah (2016)

Fawcett and Torremans *Intellectual Property and Private International Law*, by J J Fawcett and P Torremans, 2nd edn (2011)

Felix and Whitten *American Conflicts Law*, by R L Felix and R U Whitten, 6th edn (2011)

Fentiman *Foreign Law in English Courts*, by R Fentiman (1998)

Fentiman *International Commercial Litigation*, by R Fentiman, 2nd edn (2015)

Fenton-Glynn *Children's Rights in Intercountry Adoption: A European Perspective*, by C Fenton-Glynn, (2014)

Fenton-Glynn and Scherpe *Eastern and Western Perspectives on Surrogacy*, C Fenton-Glynn and J Scherpe (eds) (2017)

Fletcher *Conflict of Laws and European Community Law*, by I F Fletcher (1982)

Fletcher *Insolvency and Private International Law*, by I F Fletcher, 2nd edn (2005)

Francescakis *La Théoirie du Renvoi*, by Ph Francescakis (1958)

Garnett *Substance and Procedure in Private International Law*, by R Garnett (2012)

Gaudemet-Tallon *Competence et Execution Des Jugements En Europe*, by H Gaudemet-Tallon, 3rd edn (2002)

Geeroms *Foreign Law in Civil Litigation*, by S Geeroms (2004)

George *Relocation Disputes: Law and Practice in England and New Zealand*, by R George (2014)

Gillies *Electronic Commerce and International Private Law: A Study of Electronic Consumer Contracts*, by L Gillies, (2008)

Gration, Curry-Sumner, Williams, Setright and Wright *International Issues in Family Law: The 1996 Hague Convention on the Protection of Children and Brussels IIa*, by M Gration, I Curry-Sumner, D Williams, H Setright and M Wright (2015)

Graveson *Conflict of Laws: Private International Law*, by R H Graveson, 7th edn (1974)

Grušić *The European Private International Law of Employment*, by U Grušić (2015)

Harris *The Hague Trusts Convention*, by J Harris (2002)

Hartley *Civil Jurisdiction and Judgments*, by T C Hartley (1984)

Hartley *Choice-of-Court Agreements under the European and International Instruments*, by T C Hartley (2013)

Hartley *International Commercial Litigation* Hartley, by T C Hartley, 2nd edn (2015)

Hartley *Le droit international privé: esprit et methodes (Melanges en l'honneur de Paul Lagarde)*, by T C Hartley (2005)

Hay, Borchers and Symeonides *Conflict of Laws*, by P Hay, P J Borchers and S C Symeonides, 5th edn (2010)

Hayton *European Succession Laws*, by D Hayton, 2nd edn (2002)

Hayton *The International Trust*, D Hayton (ed) (2011)

Helfand *Negotiating State and Non-State Law: The Challenges of Global and Local Legal Pluralism*, by M Helfand (ed) (2015)

Hill *Cross-Border Consumer Contracts*, by J Hill (2008)

Hill *International Commercial Disputes*, by J Hill, 3rd edn (2005)

Hill and Chong *International Commercial Disputes*, by J Hill and A Chong, 4th edn (2010)

Hood *Conflict of Laws within the UK*, by K J Hood (2007)

Jackson *The "Conflicts" Process*, by D C Jackson (1975)

Jackson *The Enforcement of Maritime Claims*, by D C Jackson, 4th edn (2005)

Jaffey *Topics in Choice of Law*, by A J E Jaffey (1996)

Kahn-Freund *The Growth of Internationalism in English Private International Law, Lectures* by O Kahn-Freund (1960)

Kaye *The New Private International Law of Contract of the European Community*, by P Kaye (1993)

Kaye *Law of the European Judgments Convention*, Vols One–Five, by P Kaye (1999)

Kennett *The Enforcement of Judgments in Europe*, by W Kennett (2000)

Kruger *Civil Jurisdiction Rules of the EU and Their Impact on Third States*, by T Kruger (2008)

Kruger *International Child Abduction*, by T Kruger (2011)

Kuipers *EU Law and Private International Law: The Interrelationship in Contractual Obligations*, by J-J Kuipers (2012)

Lalive *The Transfer of Chattels in the Conflict of Laws*, by P A Lalive (1955)

Lasok and Stone *Conflict of Laws in the European Community*, by D Lasok and P A Stone (1987)

Layton and Mercer *European Civil Practice*, by A Layton and H Mercer *et al*, 2nd edn (2004)

Leflar *American Conflicts Law*, by R A Leflar, 4th edn (1986)

Leible *General Principles of European Private International Law*, by S Leible (2016).

Leible *Rome I Regulation: The Law Applicable to Contractual Obligations in Europe*, by S Leible and F Ferrari (2009)

Levontin *Choice of Law and Conflict of Laws*, by A V Levontin (1976)

Lindskoug, Maunsbach, Millqvist, Samuelsson and Vogel *Essays in Honour of Michael Bogdan*, by P Lindskoug, U Maunsbach, G Millqvist, P Samuelsson and H-H Vogel (2013)

Lipstein *Harmonization of Private International Law by the E.E.C.*, (ed) K Lipstein (1978)

Lloyd *Public Policy*, by D Lloyd (1953)

Lorenzen *Selected Articles on the Conflict of Laws*, by E G Lorenzen (1947)

Lowe *The New Brussels II Regulation*, by N Lowe *et al* (2005)

Lowe and Douglas *Bromley's Family Law*, N Lowe and G Douglas, 11th edn (2015)

Lowe and Nicholls *The 1996 Hague Convention on the Protection of Children*, by N Lowe and M Nicholls (2012)

Lowe and Nicholls *International Movement of Children: Law, Practice and Procedure*, by N Lowe and M Nicholls, 2nd edn (2016)

Magnus and Mankowski *Brussels I Regulation*, (eds) U Magnus and P Mankowski, 3rd edn (2015)

Magnus and Mankowski *European Commentaries on Private International Law*: Brussels II bis Regulation, by U Magnus and P Mankowski, Vol II (2017)

Mandaraka-Sheppard *Modern Maritime Law*, by A Mandaraka-Sheppard, 3rd edn, vol 1 (2013)

Mann *Foreign Affairs in English Courts*, by F A Mann (1986)

Mann: Money *The Legal Aspect of Money*, by F A Mann, 6th edn (2005)

Marsh *Marital Property in the Conflict of Laws*, by H Marsh (1952)

McClean *Recognition of Family Judgments in the Commonwealth*, by J D McClean (1983)

McLachlan *Foreign Relations Law*, by C McLachlan (2014)

McLachlan *Lis Pendens in International Litigation*, by C McLachlan (2009)

McLachlan and Nygh *International Tort Litigation*, by C McLachlan and P Nygh (1996)

McLean *Compensation for Damage: An International Perspective*, by S McLean (1993)

McLeod *The Conflict of Laws*, by J G McLeod (1983)

McParland *The Rome I Regulation on the Law Applicable to Contractual Obligations*, by M McParland (2015)

Meeusen, Pertegas, Straetmans and Swennen *International Family Law for the European Union*, by J Meeusen, M Pertegas, G Straetmans and F Swennen (2007)

Melchior *Die Grundlagen des deutschen internationalen Privatrechts*, by G Melchior (1971)

Merrett *Employment Contracts in Private International Law*, by L Merrett (2011)

Miller *International Aspects of Succession*, by G Miller (2000)

Mills *The Confluence of Public and Private International Law*, by A Mills (2009)

Morris: Essays *Contemporary Problems in the Conflict of Laws*, Essays in Honour of J H C Morris, K R Simmonds (ed) (1978)

Morris *The Conflict of Laws*, by D McClean and V Ruiz Abou-Nigm, 9th edn (2016)

Morris and North *Cases and Materials on Private International Law*, by J H C Morris and P M North (1984)

Morse *Torts in Private International Law*, by C G J Morse (1978)

Muir Watt and Arroyo *Private International Law and Global Governance*, (eds) H Muir Watt and F Arroyo (2014)

Nadelmann *Conflict of Laws: International and Interstate*, by K Nadelmann (1972)

North *The Private International Law of Matrimonial Causes in the British Isles and the Republic of Ireland*, by P M North (1977)

North *Contract Conflicts*, P M North (ed) (1984)

North *Private International Law Problems in Common Law Jurisdictions*, by P M North (1993)

North *Essays in Private International Law*, by P M North (1993)

Nygh *Autonomy in International Contracts*, by P Nygh (1999)

Nygh and Davies *Conflict of Laws in Australia*, by M Davies, A Bell and P Brereton, 9th edn (2014)

O'Hara *Economics of Conflict of Laws*, by E O'Hara (2007)

O'Hara and Ribstein *The Law Market*, by E O'Hara and L Ribstein (2009)

Ooi *Shares and Other Securities in the Conflict of Laws*, by M Ooi (2003)

Palsson *Marriage and Divorce in Comparative Conflict of Laws*, by L Palsson (1974)

Palsson *Marriage in Comparative Conflict of Laws: Substantive Conditions*, by L Palsson (1981)

Panagopoulos *Restitution in Private International Law*, by G Panagopoulos (2000)

Patchett *Recognition of Commercial Judgments and Awards in the Commonwealth*, by K W Patchett (1984)

Pertegas Sender *Cross-Border Enforcement of Patent Rights*, by M Pertegas Sender (2002)

Plender *The European Contracts Convention*, by R Plender and M Wilderspin, 2nd edn (2001)

Plender *Legal History and Comparative Law: Essays in Honour of Albert Kiralfy*, by R Plender (1990)

Plender and Wilderspin *European Private International Law of Obligations*, by R Plender and R Wilderspin, 4th edn (2015)

Rabel *The Conflict of Laws: A Comparative Study*, by E Rabel, 2nd edn (1958–1964)

Rains *The 1980 Hague Abduction Convention: Comparative Aspects*, R Rains (ed) (2014)

Rammeloo *Corporations in Private International Law*, by S Rammeloo (2001)

Raphael *The Anti-Suit Injunction*, by T Raphael (2008)

Read *Recognition and Enforcement of Foreign Judgments*, by H E Read (1938)

Restatement 2d *American Law Institute Restatement of the Law 2d: Conflict of Laws* (1971)

Robertson *Characterization in the Conflict of Laws*, by A H Robertson (1940)

Roodt *Private International Law, Art and Cultural Heritage*, by C Roodt (2015)

Rose *Lex Mercatoria: Essays in International Commercial Law in Honour of Francis Reynolds*, F Rose (ed) (2000)

Rose *Restitution and the Conflict of Laws*, F Rose (ed) (1995)

Rubino-Sammartano and Morse *Public Policy in Transnational Relationships*, by M Rubino-Sammartano and C G J Morse (1992)

Ruiz Abou-Nigm *The Arrest of Ships in Private International Law*, by V Ruiz Abou-Nigm (2011)

Sack *Conflicts of Laws in the History of the English Law*, in *Law: A Century of Progress 1835–1935*, by V Sack, Vol III (1937)

Savigny *A Treatise on the Conflict of Laws*, by F C Von Savigny, translated into English by W Guthrie (all references are to the 1st edn, 1869)

Schuz *The Hague Child Abduction Convention: A Critical Analysis*, by R Schuz (2013)

Scoles, Hay, Borchers and Symeonides *Conflict of Laws*, by E F Scoles, P Hay, P J Borchers and S C Symeonides, 4th edn (2004)

Shapira *The Interest Approach to Choice of Law*, by A Shapira (1970)

Shúilleabháin *Cross-Border Divorce Law: Brussels II Bis*, by M Ní Shúilleabháin (2010)

Symeonides *The American Choice-of-Law Revolution: Past, Present and Future*, by S C Symeonides (2006)

Symeonides and Perdue *Cases and Materials on Conflict of Laws: American, Comparative and International*, by S C Symeonides and W Collins Perdue, 3rd edn (2012)

Symeonides *Codifying Choice of Law Around the World: An International Comparative Analysis*, by S C Symeonides (2014)

Symeonides *Choice of Law*, by S C Symeonides (2016)

Stark *International Family Law*, by B Stark (2005)

Story *Commentaries on the Conflict of Laws*, by M M Bigelow, 8th edn (1883)

Sykes and Pryles *Australian Private International Law*, by E I Sykes and M C Pryles, 3rd edn (1991)

Sykes and Pryles: Casebook *Conflict of Laws Commentary and Materials*, by E I Sykes and M C Pryles, 3rd edn (1988)

Symeonides *The American Choice-of-Law Revolution: Past, Present and Future*, by S C Symeonides (2006)

Takahashi *Claims for Contribution and Reimbursement in an International Context*, by K Takahashi (2000)

Tang *Electronic Consumer Contracts in the Conflict of Laws*, by Z S Tang, 2nd edn (2015)

Trimmings *Child Abduction within the European Union*, by K Trimmings (2013)

van Calster *European Private International Law*, by G van Calster, 2nd edn (2016)

Van Hecke and K Lenaerts *Internationaal Privaatrecht*, by G Van Hecke and K Lenaerts, 2nd edn (1989)

Vischer *Die Rechtsvergleichenden Tatbestände im internationalen Privatrecht*, by F Vischer (1953)

von Hoffmann *European Private International Law*, by B von Hoffmann (1998)

Walker *Maintenance and Child Support in Private International Law*, by L Walker (2015)

Wengler *Zeitschrift für ausländisches und internationales Privatrecht*, by W Wengler (1934)

Weintraub *Commentary on the Conflict of Laws*, by R J Weintraub, 4th edn (2001)

Westlake *A Treatise on Private International Law*, by J Westlake (1858), 7th edn by N Bentwich (1925)

Wharton *Conflict of Laws*, by F Wharton, 3rd edn (1905)

Whincop and Keyes *Policy and Pragmatism in the Conflict of Laws*, by M J Whincop and M Keyes (2001)

Wolff *Private International Law*, by M Wolff, 2nd edn (1950)

Wood *English and International Set-off*, by P Wood (1989)

Yang *State Immunity in International Law*, by X Yang (2015)

Yeo *Choice of Law for Equitable Doctrines*, by T M Yeo (2004)
Zaphiriou *The Transfer of Chattels in Private International Law*, by G A Zaphiriou (1956)

BOOK CHAPTERS

H Baker and M Groff, 'The Impact of the Hague Conventions on European Family Law', in J Scherpe (ed), *European Family Law, Vol I*, (2016), 163–77

P Beaumont and K Trimmings, 'Recent Jurisprudence of the European Court of Human Rights in the Area of Cross-Border Surrogacy: Is There Still a Need for Global Regulation of Surrogacy?', in G Biagioni and F Ippolito (eds), *Migrant Children in the XXI Century. Selected Issues of Public and Private International Law*, (2017), 109–32

D Martiny, 'The Impact of the EU Private International Law Instruments on European Family Law', in J Scherpe (ed), *European Family Law, Vol I*, (2016), 262–92

K Trimmings and P Beaumont, 'General Report on Surrogacy', in K Trimmings and P Beaumont (eds), *International Surrogacy Arrangements: Legal Regulation at the International Level*, (2013), 439–549

K Trimmings and P Beaumont, 'Parentage and Surrogacy in a European Perspective', in J Scherpe (ed), *European Family Law, Vol III*, (2016), 232–83

K Trimmings, 'The Interface between Maintenance and Cross-Border Surrogacy', in P Beaumont, B Hess, L Walker and S Spancken (eds), *The Recovery of Maintenance in the EU and Worldwide*, (2014), 261–74

M Wells-Greco, 'National Report on Surrogacy: United Kingdom', in K Trimmings and P Beaumont (eds), *International Surrogacy Arrangements: Legal Regulation at the International Level*, (2013), 367–86

JOURNAL ARTICLES

A Bainham, 'Is Legitimacy Legitimate?', [2009] *Family Law* 673

I Bantekas, 'The Pitfalls of Lis Pendens in Transnational Matrimonial Jurisdiction Disputes Before English Courts', [2014] *International Family Law* 30

P Beaumont, K Trimmings, L Walker and J Holliday, 'Child Abduction: Recent Jurisprudence of the European Court of Human Rights', (2015) 64 *International and Comparative Law Quarterly* 39

P Beaumont, L Walker and J Holliday, 'Parental Responsibility and International Child Abduction in the Proposed Recast of Brussels IIa Regulation and the Effect of Brexit on Future Child Abduction Proceedings', [2016] *International Family Law* 307

P Beaumont, L Walker and J Holliday, 'Conflicts of EU Courts on Child Abduction: The Reality of Article 11(6)-(8) Brussels IIa Proceedings across the EU', (2016) 12 *Journal of Private International Law* 211

H Blackburn, 'Habitual Residence: *Re LC*', [2014] *International Family Law* 8

P Jiménez Blanco, 'Unmarried Fathers and Child Abduction in European Union Law', (2012) 8 *Journal of Private International Law* 135

C Bruch, 'The Unmet Needs of Domestic Violence Victims and their Children in Hague Abduction Cases', (2004) 38 *Family Law Quarterly* 529

R Cabeza, 'International Surrogacy: An English Perspective', [2014] *Family Law* 1444

A Caffrey, 'Surrogacy-Genetics v Gestation: The Determination of "Mother" in Irish Law', [2013] *Medico-Legal Journal of Ireland* 34

J Carruthers, 'International Family Relocation: Recent UK Experience', (2012) 3 *Juridical Review* 187

J P Costa, 'The Best Interests of the Child: Recent Case-law from the European Court of Human Rights', [2011] *International Family Law* 183

E Crawford and J Carruthers, 'Speculation on the Operation of the Succession Regulation 650/2012: Tales of the Unexpected', (2014) 22 *European Review of Private Law* 847

D Cullen, 'Surrogacy: "Commissioning" Parents not Domiciled in UK—Matters to Be Borne in Bind by those Contemplating Surrogacy Arrangements', (2008) 32 *Adoption & Fostering* 1

G Cuniberti and I Reuda, 'Abolition of Exequatur—Addressing the Commissions Concerns', (2011) 75 *Rabels Zeichshrift* 286

E Devereux and R George, 'When Will the Supreme Court Put Us Out of Our Payne?', [2014] *Family Law* 1586

E Devereux, '*Re J:* the 1996 Hague Convention in the Supreme Court', [2016] *International Family Law* 21

D Eaton and M Reardon, 'Relocation after *K v K*', [2011] *Family Law* 1093

D Eaton and M Reardon, '*K v K*: The End of the Road for Payne?', [2011] *International Family Law* 308

C Fenton-Glynn, 'The Regulation and Recognition of Surrogacy under English Law: An Overview of the Case-law', (2015) 27 *CFLQ* 83

A Fiorini, 'Rome III—Choice of Law in Divorce: Is the Europeanization of Family Law Going Too Far?', (2008) 22 *International Journal of Law, Policy and Family* 178

A Fiorini, 'Harmonising the Law Applicable to Divorce and Legal Separation—Enhanced Co-operation as the Way Forward?', (2010) 59 *International & Comparative Law Quarterly* 1143

B Frankle, 'It Is Ok to Be Inappropriate: *Mittal v Mittal*', [2014] *International Family Law* 17

M Freeman, 'International Family Mobility: Relocation and Abduction: Links and Lessons', [2013] *International Family Law* 41

M Freeman, 'Relocation Research: Where Are We Now?', [2011] *International Family Law* 131

M Freeman and Nicola Taylor, 'International Research Evidence on Relocation: Past, Present, and Future', (2010) 44 *Family Law Quarterly* 317

R Gaffney-Rhys, 'The Legal Response to Polygamous Marriages in England and Wales', [2011] *International Family Law* 319

R Gaffney-Rhys, 'Same-sex Marriage but not Mixed-sex Partnerships: Should the Civil Partnership Act 2004 be Extended to Opposite Sex Couples?', (2014) 26 *Child and Family Law Quarterly* 173

R Gaffney-Rhys, 'The Legal Status of Forced Marriages: Void, Voidable or Non-Existent?', [2010] *International Family Law* 336

C Geekie, 'Relocation and Shared Residence: One Route or Two?', [2008] *Family Law* 446

R George and O Cominetti, 'International Relocation in English Law: Thorpe LJ's Discipline and its Application', [2013] *International Family Law* 149

R George, 'Reviewing Relocation? *Re W (Relocation: Removal Outside Jurisdiction)*', [2011] EWCA Civ 345 and '*K v K (Relocation: Shared Care Arrangement)*', [2011] EWCA Civ 793 (2012) 24 *Child and Family Law Quarterly* 110

R George, 'How Do Judges Decide International Relocation Cases?', (2015) 27 *Child and Family Law Quarterly* 377

R George, 'Children's State of Mind and Habitual Residence in Abduction Cases', (2014) *Journal of Social Welfare and Family Law* 311

S Gilmore, 'The Payne Saga: Precedent and Family Law Cases', [2011] *Family Law* 970

J Herring, 'The Divorce Debacle', (2014) 164 *The New Law Journal* 12

D Hill 'The Continuing Refinement of Habitual Residence: *R, Petitioner*', (2016) *Edinburgh Law Review* 82

D Hodson, 'What Is Jurisdiction for Divorce in the EU? The Contradictory Law and Practice around Europe', [2014] *International Family Law* 170

K Horsey, 'Challenging Presumptions: Legal Parenthood and Surrogacy Arrangements', (2010) 22 *Child and Family Law Quarterly* 449

N Hyder, 'Couple Request Surrogate Mum to Abort over Disability', *BioNews*, 11 October 2010

E Isaacs, 'Parental Order Time Limits: Policy—What Policy?', [2014] *Family Law* 1723

M Jones, 'The Inherent Jurisdiction: What Place Does it Have in the Future of Family Justice?', [2015] *Family Law* 1371

I Karsten, 'The State of International Family Law Issues: A View from London', [2009] *International Family Law* 35

M Kaye, 'The Hague Convention and the Flight from Domestic Violence: How Women and Children are Being Returned by a Coach and Four', (1999) 13 *International Journal of Law, Policy and the Family* 191

T Kruger and L Samyn, 'Brussels II bis: Successes and Suggested Improvements', (2016) 12 *Journal of Private International Law* 132

T Kruger, 'Brussels II bis: Successes and Suggested Improvements', (2016) 12 *Journal of Private International Law* 132

A Laing, 'Adopting Foreign Children: Part II: A Counter-Argument; Choice of Laws', [2015] *Family Law* 703

A Laing, 'Adopting Foreign Children: Part I: Jurisdiction', [2015] *Family Law* 565

N Lowe, 'The Applicable Laws Provisions of the 1996 Hague Convention and the Impact of the Convention on International Child Abduction', [2010] *International Family Law* 51

N Lowe, 'The Enforcement of Custody and Access Decisions under the Revised Brussels II Regulation', [2011] *International Family Law* 121

N Lowe, 'A Supra-national Approach to Interpreting the 1980 Hague Child Abduction Convention – A Tale of Two European Courts: Part 2: The Substantive Impact of the Two European Courts' Rulings upon the Application of the 1980 Convention', [2012] *International Family Law* 170

Y Margalit, 'From Baby M to Baby M (Anji): Regulating International Surrogacy Agreements', (2016) 24 *Brooklyn Journal of Law and Policy* 41

J Masson, 'Recognition of Adoption Orders: A Problem for the Courts of England and Wales?', [2016] *Family Law* 1113

L-M Möller, 'No Fear of Talāq: A Reconsideration of Muslim Divorce Laws in Light of the Rome III Regulation', (2014) 10 *Journal of Private International Law* 461

K Norrie, 'Recognition of Foreign Relationships under the Civil Partnership Act 2004', (2006) 2 *Journal of Private International Law* 137

J Paton, 'The Correct Approach to the Examination of the Best Interests of the Child in Abduction Convention Proceedings Following the Decision of The Supreme Court in *RE E (Children) (Abduction: Custody Appeal)*', (2012) 8 *Journal of Private International Law* 547

C Marin Pedreno, David Williams and Michael Gration, 'Prorogation under Art 12 BIIR: The Death-knell of Advance Prorogation?', [2015] *International Family Law* 35

J Pirrung, 'Improvements to International Child Protection as a Result of the 1996 Hague Child Protection Convention', [2012] *International Family Law* 70

F Pocar, 'The European Harmonisation of Conflict of Law Rules on Divorce and Legal Separation: Is Enhanced Cooperation a Correct Approach?', [2012] *International Family Law* 24

R Probert, 'When Are We Married? Void, Non-existent and Presumed Marriages', (2002) 22 *Legal Studies* 398

R Probert, 'The Evolving Concept of the "Non-marriage"', [2013] *Child and Family Law Quarterly* 314

R Probert, '"Hanging on the Telephone: *City of Westminster v IC*"', [2008] *Child and Family Law Quarterly* 395

G Puppinck and C de la Hougue, 'ECHR: Towards the Liberalisation of Surrogacy: Regarding the Mennesson v. France and Labassee v. France Cases (N°65192/11 & N°65941/11)', [2014] *Revue Lamy de Droit Civil* 78

B Roche, 'International Relocation: Case for a Payne-Less Future?', [2010] *Family Law* 978

C Sanders, 'No Early Closing for Forum Shopping: *Mittal v Mittal*', [2013] *International Family Law* 1618

A Schulz, 'The Enforcement of Child Return Orders in Europe: Where Do We Go from Here', [2012] *International Family Law* 43

R Schuz, 'In Search of a Settled Interpretation of Article 12 (2) of the Hague Child Abduction Convention', [2008] *Child and Family Law Quarterly* 64

R Schuz, 'Habitual Residence of the Child Revisited: A Trilogy of Cases in the UK Supreme Court', (2014) 26 *Child and Family Law Quarterly* 342

R Schuz, 'The Hague Abduction Convention and Children's Rights Revisited', [2012] *International Family Law* 35

H Setright, E Devereux and A-M Hutchinson, 'Discretion, Settlement and Child's Objections: Re M (Abduction)', [2008] *Family Law* 230

S Shakargy, 'Marriage by the State or Married to the State? On Choice of Law in Marriage and Divorce', (2013) 9 *Journal of Private International Law* 499

U Rengachary Smerdon, 'Crossing Bodies, Crossing Borders: International Surrogacy between the United States and India (2008–2009)', 39 *Cumberland Law Review* 15

L Theis, 'Natalie Gamble and Louisa Ghevaert, Re X and Y (Foreign Surrogacy): "A Trek Through a Thorn Forest"', [2009] *Family Law* 239

L Trackman, 'Domicile of Choice in English Law: An Achilles Heel?' (2015) 11 *Journal of Private International Law* 317.

K Trimmings and P Beaumont, 'Article 20 of the 1980 Hague Abduction Convention', (2014) 9 *The Journal of Comparative Law* 66

K Trimmings, 'Transfer of Jurisdiction and the Best Interests of the Child', (2016) 75 *Cambridge Law Journal* 471

K Trimmings, 'Six Month Deadline for Applications for Parental Orders Relaxed by the High Court', (2015) 37 *Journal of Social Welfare and Family Law* 241

I Viarengo, 'The Rome III Regulation in Legal Practice: Case Law and Comments', (2014) 15 *ERA Forum* 547

L Walker, 'The Impact of the Hague Abduction Convention on the Rights of the Family in the Case-Law of the European Court of Human Rights and the UN Human Rights Committee: The Danger of *Neulinger*', (2010) 6 *Journal of Private International Law* 649

E Walsh, 'Habitual Residence: *Re B*', [2016] *Family Law* 14

D Watkins, 'Intercountry Adoption and the Hague Convention: Article 22 and Limitations upon Safeguarding', [2012] *Child and Family Law Quarterly* 389

M Weiner, 'International Child Abduction and the Escape from Domestic Violence', (2000) 69 *Fordham Law Review* 593

M Welstead, 'The Hurdles Fall: Surrogacy and Parental Orders', [2015] *Family Law* 1415

M Welstead, 'A Judicial Glide through the Minefield of International Surrogacy', [2014] *Family Law* 1299

David Wheeler, '*Re E (Children)*: Understanding the Implications of *Neulinger* and *Maumousseau*', [2011] *International Family Law* 224

D Williams, 'The Supreme Court Trilogy: A New Habitual Residence Rises!', [2014] *International Family Law* 84

D Williams, Michael Gration and Maria Wright, 'Habitual Residence and the "Parens Patriae" Jurisdiction after Re B', [2016] UKSC 4, [2016] *International Family Law* 239

D Williams, Michael Gration and Maria Wright, 'Habitual Residence and the "Parens Patriae" Jurisdiction after *Re B*', [2016] UKSC 4 [2016] [2016] *International Family Law* 239

TABLE OF STATUTES

INTRODUCTORY NOTE

This Table is set out in the following sections (in this order): UK (including Scotland and Northern Ireland) Statutes, followed by UK Statutory Instruments; EU Legislation (primary and secondary, excluding conventions); European Conventions; International Conventions; Bilateral Treaties; National Legislation of Other Countries (subdivided by country). Alphabetical order is followed within sections/subsections.

STATUTES

Access to Justice Act 1999
  Sch 13 para 71 1063
  para 76 1063
  Sch 15, Pt V 1063
Administration of Estates
  Act 1925 . . . . 57–8, 59, 942
  s 1 1333
  s 33 1333
  s 46 58
  s 46(1)(i), para 3 1351
  s 46(1)(vi) 49
Administration of Estates
  Act 1971
  s 1 1336
  s 2(1)–(2) 1336
  s 3(1) 1336
  s 11 1336
Administration of Estates Act
  (Northern Ireland) 1955
  s 7 1351
Administration of Estates (Small
  Payment s)Act 1965 1326
Administration of Justice
  Act 1920 . . . . . 521–2, 524, 571, 591–2,
                        593, 595, 602, 607, 677
  Pt II 521, 554, 585, 588
  s 9(1) 591
  (2) 591
  (2)(e) 592
  (3)(a)–(b) 592
  (5) 592
  s 10 591
  s 12(1) 591, 677
  s 13 591
  s 14 591
  s 15 109
Administration of Justice Act 1925
  s 42 1384
Administration of Justice Act 1956
  s 40(b) 592

Administration of Justice Act 1970
  s 44A 99
Administration of Justice Act 1977
  s 3 1079
  s 4 (2)(a) and (b) 677
  s (2)(b) 594, 601
  Sch 3 1079
  Sch 5 100
Administration of Justice Act 1982
  s 15 97
  s 18 1350
  ss 23–26 1344
  s 27 1344
  s 28(1) 1344
  Sch 1 97
Adoption Act 1958
  s 1(1) 1210
  s 7(1)(b) 1211
  Adoption Act 1968 11
Adoption Act 1976 1206
  s 11 1221
  s 38(1)(c) 1054, 1223
  s 39 1054
  s 56A 1208, 1219
  s 57 1221
  s 60 1223
Adoption and Children
  Act 2002 . . . . 11, 172, 1054
  Ch 6 1207
  Pt 1 1207
  Pt 2 1207
  s 1 . . . . 1184, 1184, 1204, 1206
  (1) . . . . 1209 , 1211
  ss 2 . . . . 1204, 1206
  s 7 1204
  s 21 1208–9
  s 22 1208
  s 26 . . . . 1091, 1108
  ss 42(1)–(6) 1209
  s 46 1206
  (1) 1206
  (8)–(9) 1206

s 49
  (1) 1208, 1227
  (2) 1227
  (3) 1227
s 50(1)–(2) 1208
s 51 (1). 1208
  (2) 1208, 1229
  (3)–(4) 1208
s 51A 1091, 1108
s 52(3) 1086
s 55 1204
s 66(1) 1054, 1225
s 67 . . . . 165, 166, 1054, 1204, 1229
  (1) 1207
  (2) and (5) 1229
  (3) 1239
s 83
  (1) 1219
  (4) 1207
  (5) 1207, 1219
  (6) 1207
s 84 . . . . 1218, 1220
  (3) 1207
  (4) 1220
  (6) 1207
s 85 1220
  (4) 1220
s 87 1225
  (1)(b) 1224
s 88 1229
s 89 1225
  (2) 1225
s 91 1225
s 91A 1219
ss 105–108 . . . . 1054, 1223
s 140(7)–(8) 1207
s 142(4)–(5) 1207
s 144 (1) 1204, 1224
  (4)–(5) 1208
Sch 1 1206
Sch 3 para 42 1088
  para 51 1195
  para 52 915
Sch 4, para 12 1219
Adoption (Intercountry Aspects)
  Act 1999 . . . . 1206, 1207
  s 1(1) and (3)–(5) 1207
Adoption of Children Act 1926 1207
  s 5(2) 1226
Age-Related Payments Act 2004
  s 8(2) 943
Aliens Restriction Act 1914 497
Anti- Social Behaviour, Crime and Policing
  Act 2014
  s 120 991

s 121 991
s 121(2) 990
s 121(7) 991
Arbitration Act 1950 . . . . 524, 670, 673
Pt II 670
s 4 416
  (1) 415
s 35 671
  (1) 670
s 37(1) 673
s 40 670
  (b) 670
Sch 1, para 1 670
Arbitration Act 1975 670
s 1 420
s 2 416
s 7(1) 417
Arbitration Act 1996 . . . . 419–20, 524, 670–76
Pt I 420
Pt III 420
s 1(c) 420
s 2 306
s 2(2)(a) 417
s 5 . . . . 417, 420, 669
s 6 417
s 7 . . . . .418 , 667
s 9 . . . . . . 370, 385, 393, 416–17, 420, 677
  (1) 417
  (2) 417
  (3) 417
  (4) 418
s 11 . . . . 306, 385
s 12 417
s 13(1)(4)(a) 78
s 46(1)(b) 715
s 66 . . . . 612, 646, 669, 670, 677
  (1) 669
s 81 420
  (a) and (c) 669
s 82(2) 417
s 99 670
s 100
  (1) 671
  (2) 671
  (2)(b) 671
  (3) 671
s 101
  (1) 672
  (3) 671
s 102 672
s 103 (1) 672
  (2) 672
  (2)(d) 673
  (3) 673
  (4) 673

s 104 676
s 105 671
Arbitration Acts 1889 to 1934 670
Arbitration (International Investment
  Disputes) Act 1966 . . . . 524, 677
ss 1–2 677
s 3(2) 677
Sch
  Art 1 677
  Art 25 677
  Art 55 677
Arms Control and Disarmament
  (Privileges and Immunities)
  Act 1988 . . . . 511, 512
Army Act 1955. 80
Asylum and Immigration (Treatment of
  Claimants, etc) Act 2004 894
s 19–24 992
s 19 992
  (2) 992
Atomic Energy Act 1989
Sch. 511
Bills of Exchange Act 1882 . . . . 699, 1294, 1295
s 4 1297
s 72 1295
  (1) 1295, 1296, 1297
  (2) 1295, 1296, 1297
  (4) 100
British Law Ascertainment Act 1859 109
British Nationality Act 1981 . . . . . 944 , 1110
s 1 1193
  (5)(a)–(b)) 1230
  (6) 1231
s 3(1) 1231
s 23(3)(b) 505
s 50(5) 174
s 50(9) 1193
s 52(6) 505
Sch 7 505
British Overseas Territories Act 2002
s 1(2) 174
Carriage by Air Act 1961 . . . . 9, 380, 518
s 4(4) 100
Sch 1
  Art 1(2) 518
  Art 22(5) 100
  Art 28(1) 518
Carriage by Air (Supplementary
  Provisions) Act 1962 . . . . 9, 380, 518
Sch, Art VIII 518
Carriage of Goods by Road
  Act 1965 . . . . 9, 380, 518
s 4 594
Sch,
  Art 27(2) 100

Art 31(1) 518, 597
Art 31(3) 594
Carriage of Goods by Sea Act 1924 9
Carriage of Goods by Sea
  Act 1971 . . . . 9, 416, 691
Sch, Art III, para 8 416
Carriage of Goods by Sea Act 1992
s2 693
Carriage of Passengers by Road
  Act 1974 9
Child Abduction Act 1984 1088
Child Abduction and Custody
  Act 1985 . . . . 1163, 1172
s 1(3) 1157, 1172
s 3 . . . . 1136, 1139
s 4 1040
s 8 . . . . 1056, 1137
s 9 1143
Sch 1 1089
Sch 2 1089
  Art 1 1167
Child Benefit Act 1976 943
Child Support Act 1991
s 27 1052
Child Support, Pensions and Social
  Security Act 2000
s 83 (2). 1052, 1053
Children Act 1989 . . . . 1089, 1091, 1207
Pts I–II and IV 1090
s 1 . . . . 1161, 1171, 1172, 1176
  (1) 1125, 1126, 1168
  (3) 1171
s 2 . . . . 1108, 1194
s 3 . . . . 1108, 1167
s 4 . . . . 1107, 1108
s 4A 1107, 1108
s 4ZA 1108
s 5 . . . . 1090, 1112
  (11)–(13) 1112
s 6 1090
s 8 . . . . 1068, 1087, 1090, 1091, 1092,
                                       1106–7, 1157
  (1) 1090
  (3) 1090
  (3)(a) 1090, 1109
  (3)(b) 1090
  (4) 1090
  (4)(g) 1072
s 9 1090
  (7) 1090
s 10 1090
s 11 1090
  (7) 1168
s 13 . . . . 1088, 1168
s 31(8) 173

s 91(4) 1110
s 105(6) 173
Sch 12, paras 37–40 1088
Sch 13 1088
   para 57 1134
Sch 15 . . . . 1088, 1134, 1143,
Children and Adoption Act 2006 1222
   Pt 2 1222
   s 9 1222
      (2) 1219, 1222
      (3)–(4), (7) and (10) (a) 1222
   s 10 1222
   s 11 (1)–(2) and (4) 1222
   s 12 1222
   s 13 . . . . 1219, 1222
   s 14 1222
Children and Families Act 2014
   s 12 109-
   s 12(3) 1087
   Sch 2(1), para 3 1087
Children and Young Persons Act 1963
   s 2 945
Children (Scotland) Act 1995
   s 14(3) 1125
   s 33 1133
Civil Aviation Act 1982 380
Civil Evidence Act 1972
   s 4 (1) 111
      (2) 108, 109, 112
      (3)–(5) 109
Civil Evidence Act 1995
   s 7 81
Civil Jurisdiction and Judgments
     Act 1991 . . . . 379, 588
Civil Jurisdiction and Judgments
     Act 1982 . . . . 12, 101, 189, 310,
        522, 523, 524, 534, 588–91,
        602, 603, 669–70, 1007
   s 2(1) 312
   s 4 652
   s 4A 653
   s 4(3) 623
   s 5A(1) and (3) 1084
   s 7(1) 1084
   s 8 . . . . 101, 1084
   s 16 . . . . 194, 317
      (1) 317
      (1)(a) 318
      (1)(b) 318, 320
      (3)(a) 195
      (3)(b) 197
   s 17 317
   s 18 . . . . 588–9, 613, 669
      (2) 588
      (2)(e) 669

      (3) 588
      (3)(ba) 589
      (4) 589
      (4A) 589
      (5) 589
      (5)(a) 589
      (5)(b) 589
      (6)–(7) 589, 589
      (8) 588
   s 19 . . . . 613, 670
      (1) 590
      (2) 590
      (3) 590
      (3)(b) 670
   s 24 . . . . 340, 380
   s 25 . . . . 305–7, 341, 349, 380
      (1) 306, 340
      (2) 307, 341
      (3)(b) 307
      (7) 306
   s 26 . . . . 306, 385, 390, 412
   s 30 . . . . 334, 493, 495, 1255
      (1) 492
      (2) 492
   s 31 505
      (1) 602
      (2), (3) and (5) 602
   s 32 . . . . 585–7, 592, 593, 597, 598,
        601, 644–5
      (1) 585–6
      (1)(a) 585, 586
      (1)(b)–(c) 585, 587
      (2) 586
      (3) 585, 587
      (4)(b) 586, 597
   s 33 . . . . 333, 535, 536, 538,
        585, 587, 593
      (1) 534–5
      (1)(a) 535–6, 537
      (1)(b) 535–6, 585
      (1)(c) 537
      (2)
   s 34 . . . . . . 355, 384, 556–7, 591, 599, 667
   s 35 591
      (1) 596
      (3) 592
   s 38 555
   s 41 . . . . 199, 319
      (2) 318–19
      (3)–(5) 319–20
      (6) 319
   s 41A 313
   s 42 201
      (4) 319
      (7) 201

s 43A 313
s 44A 313
s 46 202
s 47 (1)(b) 195
s 49 . . . . 314, 321
s 50 . . . . 317, 535, 585
s 54 . . . . 536, 537, 595, 597, 606
Sch 2
    para 2 101
    para 4 101
    para 14 586
    para 15 535
Sch 3C 194
Sch 4 . . . . 194, 317–22, 492
    r 1 319
    r 3 319
    r3–13 319
    r 3(a) 320
    r 3(h) 320
    r 4 320
    r 11(a)(i) 319
    r 12 . . . . 319, 320–21
Sch 5 317
    para (2) 321
Sch 6 . . . . 589, 590, 669
    para 3 590
    paras 2–6 589
    para 7, 8, 9 590
    para 10 590
Sch 7 . . . . 590, 669
    paras 1–4 590
    para 5 590
    para 5(5) 590
    para 7(2) 590
Sch 8 r 2(h) 381
Sch 10 593
    para 1 594
    para 1(2) 671
    para 4 . . . . 594, 677
    para 5 594
Sch 11 para 2 1079
    para 12 1063
    para 17 1064
Sch 13 Pt I, para 2 585
Pt II, paras 8, 8(1) and 9(1) 585
Sch 14 . . . . 536, 537, 595, 597, 606
Civil Jurisdiction and Judgments
    Act 1991 334
s 1(1) 194
Sch 2
    para 13 334
    para 24 314
Civil Liability (Contribution)
    Act 1978 . . . . 342, 867
s 1 113

Civil Partnership Act 2004 . . . . . . 900, 946–8,
                   949, 1048, 1379–80
Pt 1 946–7
Pt 2 947
    Ch 1 947
    Ch 2 1039
Pts 3–4 947
Pt 5 947
    Ch 1 947
    Ch 2 . . . . 947, 1043
    Ch 3 . . . . 1039, 1043, 1045
Pt 20 288
s 1 946–7
s 1(3) 947
s 2(1) and (5) 947
ss 3(1), 5(1), 8, 18 and 19 947
s 4 947
s 20 947
    (1) 947
s 21 947
ss 37–64 1039
s 37 1039
    (1) 1039
    (4)(b) 1039
    (5) 1039
s 44 1039
ss 44–48 1042
s 49 . . . . 1039, 1043
s 50 . . . . 1039, 1043
    (1)(a) 1043
    (1)(b) 1043
    (1)(c) 1043
    (1)(d) 1043
    (1)(e) 1043
s 51 1043
ss 52–53 1043
s 54 . . . . 1039, 1043
    (1)–(3) 1043
    (4) 1043
    (6) 1043
    (7) 1043
    (8) 1043
    (9) 1043
    (10) 72, 1043
s 55 . . . . 1039, 1042
s 56 . . . . 1039, 1042
s 57 1042
s 58 1057
s 59 1057
s 60 1057
s 61 1057
s 72(4) 1060, 1072
s 124 (10) 72
s 174 1043
s 177 (10) 72

s 210 901
s 211 902
s 212 . . . . 948, 1043
  (1A) 948
  (2) 948
  (2) 900, 922
s 213 1043
  (1) 947
s 214 . . . . 947, 1043
s 215 1043
  (1) 900, 922
  (1)(a) 919
  (2) 948
ss 216 and 218 . . . . 948, 1043
s 217(2) 948
s 218 948
ss 219–224 1039
ss 219–238 . . . . 1039, 1043
s 219 . . . . 1039–40, 1044, 1048
  (a) 1040
  (1)(b) 1044
  (3) 1040
s 220 1041
s 221
  (1) 1040, 1041
  (1)(a) 1040
  (1)(b) 1040
  (1)(c) 1040, 1041, 1046, 1058
  (2) 1041, 1043
  (2)(a) 1041
  (2)(b) 1041, 1047
  (2)(c) 1041, 1047, 1058
  (3) 1041, 1047
s 222 . . . . 1038, 1041, 1047, 1058
  (1) (c) 1041
s 223 1042
  (2) 1044
  (3) 1044
s 233 . . . . 1043, 1048
s 234 . . . . 1044, 1045, 1048
  (2) 1045
s 235 . . . . 1044, 1045, 1048
  (1) 1045
  (1A) 1045
  (2) 1044, 1045
  (2A) 1045
s 236 . . . . 1044, 1045, 1048
  (3)(b) 1044
s 237 . . . . 1044, 1045, 1048
s 238 1048
ss 240–241 948
Sch 1 947
  Pt 1 939
Sch 2 947
  Pt 1 947

Schs 5 and 6 1090
Sch 7 . . . . 1060, 1072
Sch 20 947
Sch 24, (3), para 40 943
Sch 27, para 125 925
Colonial and Other Territories
  (Divorce Jurisdiction) Act 1926 1012
Colonial and Other Territories
  (Divorce Jurisdiction)
  Act 1950 1012
Colonial Probates Act 1892 . . . . . . 1336, 1337
Colonial Probates (Protected States and
  Mandated Territories) Act 1927
  s 1 1337
Common Law Procedure Act 1852 372
Commonwealth Secretariat
  Act 1966 . . . . 506, 514
Companies Act 1948
  s 106 329
Companies Act 1985 . . . . 328, 331
Companies Act 2006 . . . . 327, 328–31,
                                  1306, 1307
  Pt 34 329–30
  Pt 37 328–9
  s 129 1298
  s 133(2)–(3) 1298
  s 1044 329
  s 1046 (2)(c) 329
    (2)(b) 365
  s 1139
    (1) 328
    (2) 329
    (2)(a) 331
    (4) 328
  s 1140 328
Consular Conventions Act 1949
  s 1(1) 1332
Consular Relations Act 1968 . . . . 509, 516
  s 1(2) 516
  ss 2–3 516
  s 12 516
  Sch I Arts 1, 41, 43, 45, 48–51
    and 57 516
Consumer Credit Act 1974 s 192 1268
  Sch 4, Pt 1 1268
Consumer Rights Act 2015 . . . . 233, 296
  ss 31, 47, and 57 . . . . 741, 747
  s 32 741
    (1) 747
  s 65(1) 879
  s 74 . . . . 741, 744, 747, 772
    (1) 747
  Pt 1 747
  Pt II 712, 741, 747, 855
Continental Shelf Act 1964 878

Contracts (Applicable Law)
    Act 1990 . . . . 4, 13, 70, 73, 74, 78,
        93, 96, 172, 682, 684–5, 1372
  s 2 690
    (1) 685
    (2) 685, 694, 745, 839
    (3) 685, 696
  s 3 685
    (1) 688
    (3) 689
  Sch 1, Art 1(2)(h). 73, 85, 97
  Sch 1, Art 3(1) 55
  Sch 1, Art 10(1)(c) 92, 96, 97
  Sch 1, Art 14(1) 85
  Sch 1, Art 14(2) 80
  Sch 1, Art 16 92
see also European Conventions/Resolutions;
    Rome Convention on the law
    applicable to contractual obligations
Contracts (Rights of Third Parties)
    Act 1999 342
Courts Act 2003
  Sch 8 para 68 1063
    para 69(3)(b) 1080
    para 88(2) 1079
    para 153. 1063
    paras 158 1063
  Sch 10 1063
    para 1. 1063
Courts and Legal Services Act 1990
  Sch 16, para 41 589
  Sch 20 589
Crime and Courts Act 2013
  Sch 11(1)
    para 42, 68 and 81(3). 1062
    para 88. 1072
    Sch 11(1), para 43(a) 1064
Crime and Disorder Act 1998
  ss 11–12. 1090
Criminal Justice Act 1988
  s 23 516
  Pt VI 361
  s 97 . . . . 552, 580
    (1)(c) 580
Criminal Justice Act 2003 516
  Pt II, Ch 2 516
Dealing in Cultural Objects (Offences)
    Act 2003 1277
Defamation Act 2013. . . . . 350, 353–5
  s 1(1) 351, 354
  s 9 . . . . 354, 378, 398, 519
    (1) 354
    (2) 354–5
Diplomatic and Consular Premises
    Act 1987 . . . . 510, 511

Diplomatic and Other Privileges
    Act 1971 . . . . 510, 514
Diplomatic Immunities (Commonwealth
    Countries and Republic of Ireland)
    Act 1952
  s 1(1) 510
Diplomatic Immunities Restriction
    Act 1955 514
Diplomatic Privileges Act 1708 . . . . . 498, 510
  s 3 510
Diplomatic Privileges Act 1964 . . . . . 509, 516
  s 1 510
  s2(3). 513
  s2(4). 513
  s2(6). 511
  s 3(1) 514
  s 4 510
  s 7(1) 514
  s 8(4) 510
  Sch 1
    Art 1 512
    Art 1(a)–(e) 511
    Art 1(g) 512
    Art 31(1) 511, 512
    Art 31(3) 512
    Art 32(2) 513
    Art 32(3)–(4) 514
    Art 33 . . . . 512, 513
    Arts 34 and 36 512
    Art 37 513
    Art 37(1)–(2) 512
    Art 38(1) 511
    Art 39(2) 513
  Sch 2 510
Divorce (Scotland) Act 1976 s 3A 1012
Divorce (Religious Marriages)
    Act 2002 1012
Domestic Proceedings and Magistrates'
    Courts Act 1978
  Pt I. 952
  s 1 1062
  s 2 1062
  s 30 (1), (3) 1063
  s 30(5) 1062
  ss 54–61. 1063
  s 63 1062
  Sch 2, para 39 952
Domicile and Matrimonial Proceedings
    Act 1973 . . . . 21, 169, 967, 975,
        977, 978, 980, 1052
  Pt II 954, 1001, 1007
  Pt III 952, 987, 1001
  s 1 . . . . 168, 172, 912, 931, 1351
    (2) 169
    (2)(b) 954

s 2 1022
s 3 .... 165, 172
  (1) 165
s 4 .... 165, 167, 172
  (1) 166
  (2) 172, 954
  (2)(a) 166
  (2)(b) 166
  (3) 166
  (4) 166, 167
s 5 .... 172, 1073
  (1)(a) 954
  (1A) 954
  (1)(b) 954
  (2) 177, 956, 965, 1379
  (2)(a) 954–62, 1060
  (2)(b) 960, 962, 977, 1068
  (3) 964, 965, 1051
  (3)(a) 964, 1060
  (3)(b) 965, 1008
  (3)(b)(ii) 965
  (5) 965, 967, 1041
  (5A) 967
  (6) 967, 1042, 1047
s 6 172
s 7(3A) 964
s 7(3B) 964
s 16 .... 1013, 1024
  (1) 1019
  (2) 1024
  (3) 1020
s 17 (2) 173, 980, 1038
Sch 1 .... 967, 1047
  para 2 .... 967, 972
  para 3 1061
  para 3(2) 967
  para 4(1) 967, 974
  paras 5–6 .... 967, 972
  para 7 967
  para 8 .... 967, 968
  para 8(1) 967
  para 8(2) 967
  para 9 .... 971, 972, 973, 976
  para 9(1) 968, 973, 975
  para 9(2) 973, 975
  para 9(3) 973
  para 9(4) 974
  para 10(1)–(2) 978
  para 11 978
  para 11(2)(b)–(c) and (3) 1061
Sch 1B 1045, 1048
Sch 6 173
Sch A1 1057
  para 1(a)–(c) 1046
  para 2(1) and 2(2) 1047

  para 2(1)(b) 1040, 1041, 1046, 1058
  para 2(1)(c) 1040, 1046
  para 2(2)(b) 1047
  para 2(2)(c) 1058
  para 3 .....1038, 1041, 1042, 1047, 1058
  para 3(a) 1051
  para 4 1057–8
  para 4(a) and (b) 1058
  para 5 1046
Domicile and Recognition of Foreign
  Divorces Act 1986
  s 1 169
Drug Trafficking Offences Act 1994 361
Emergency Powers (Defence) Act 1939
  s 3(1) 747
Employment Rights Act 1996
  s 204 .... 143, 747
Enduring Powers of Attorney
  Act 1985 .... 1232, 1239
European Communities
  Act 1972 .... 588, 601
  s 2(1) 503
  s 2(2) 601, 1102
  s 3 105
  s 4(1) 514
  Sch 3, Pt IV 514
Evidence Act 1938
  s 1 81
Evidence (Foreign Dominion and
  Colonial Documents) Act 1933 81
Evidence (Proceedings in Other
  Jurisdictions) Act 1975 .... 11, 83–4, 117
Factors Act 1889 ss 2, 8 and 9 1268
Family Law Act 1986 .... 21, 577, 583,
                917, 926, 1009
  Pt I 172, 1088–90, 1090–1,
                1126, 1132
    Ch V 1132
  Pt II 11, 52, 172, 924, 1000,
         1001, 1003, 1005–6, 1008,
      1009, 1011, 1013, 1018, 1020,
       1024, 1025, 1034, 1038–9,
           1044, 1050–56
  Pt III 172, 952, 1025, 1050
  s 1 1133
    (1)(a) 1091, 1106, 1110
    (1)(aa), (ab) and(ac) 1091
    (1)(b) 1091
    (1)(d) 1091, 1108–9, 1109, 1110
  s 2 .... 1006, 1017, 1091, 1110
    (1) 1092
    (1)(b) 1105–6
    (2A) 1108
    (2C) 1108
    (3) 1108, 1120

(3)(a) 1120
(3)(b)(ii) 1109
s 2A 1092, 1106
  (1) 1106
  (2) 1106
  (4) 1107
s 3 .... 1006, 1017, 1107, 1108, 1109
s 4 .... 1006, 1017
s 5 .... 1006, 1017, 1023, 1052,
                             1113, 1119
  (1) 1113
s 6 1017
  (1)–(2) 1112
  (3)(a) 1023
  (3)(b) 1023
  (3) and (5) 1112
s 7 (a) 1090
  (aa) 1106
  (c) .... 1107, .1109
ss 8–18 1106
s 17A 1133
s 19 1050
s 25(1) and (3) 1133
s 27 1133
s 28 1132
  (1) 1133
  (2) 1132
s 29 1133
s 30 (3) 1134
s 31 1134
s 32(1) 1133
ss 33–37 1088
s 39 1113
s 41 .... 1107, 1108
s 42 (2) 1002
s 43 .... 1090, 1132
s 44 .... 1001, 1013, 1015
  (1) 1001, 1008, 1016, 1017, 1019,
                           1024, 1043
  (2) 1001, 1010
  (7) 1113
s 45 .... 1006, 1013, 1024
  (1)(b) 1006, 1012
s 46 .... 1010, 1015, 1045
  (1) 1006, 1014, 1016, 1017, 1018,
              1020, 1021, 1024, 1025,
                 1032, 1037, 1045
  (1)(a) 1008, 1010, 1020, 1020
  (1)(b) 1007, 1009, 1020
  (1)(b)(i) 1007
  (1)(b)(ii) 1006
  (1)(b)(iii) 1008, 1010, 1020
  (2) 1007, 1014, 1017, 1018,
              1022, 1023, 1025, 1032,
              1045, 1077, 1079

(2)(a) 1023
(2)(b) 1009, 1032
(2)(c) 1023
(2)(b)(i)–(ii) 1033
(3)(a) 1006, 1008, 1020
(3)(b) 1022
(4) 1008, 1020
(5) 148, 168, 1007, 1023, 1045
s 46(a)(i) 1031
s 47 .... 1010, 1044
  (1) 1010, 1016, 1020, 1022
  (1)(a)–(b) 1008
  (2) 1009, 1010, 1022
s 48 .... 1010, 1020, 1022, 1044
  (1) 1016
  (1)(a) and (b) 1010
  (2) 1010
  (3) 1010
s 49 .... 1009 , 1010, 1020, 1044
  (1) 1009, 1022
  (2) 1009, 1010
  (3) 1009
  (3)(a) and (b) 1010
  (4) 1009, 1010, 1022
  (5) 1009, 1010
s 50 ..... 52, 923, 925–6, 992, 1010, 1045
s 51 .... 1001, 1010, 1020, 1024,
                1025, 1026, 1037, 1045
  (1) 583, 1026, 1027, 1033, 1034
  (1)(a) 1001
  (2) .... 1025, 1026, 1033 , 1034
  (2)(a) 1001
  (3) 1001, 1009, 1016, 1028, 1034
  (3)(a) 141, 1031, 1033
  (3)(a)(i) 1027
  (3)(a)(ii) 142, 1029
  (3)(b)(i) .... 1023 , 1033
  (3)(b)(ii) 1023, 1033
  (3)(c) 141, 1030, 1033
  (4) 1009, 1033
  (5) 1002, 1010, 1037
s 52 .... 1006, 1010, 1020
  (1) 1006
  (1)(a) 1001
  (3) 1001, 1009
  (4) .... 1009 , 1020
  (5) 1008
  (5)(a) 1021
  (5)(b) 1007, 1023
  (5)(c) 1012, 1023
  (5)(d) 1012
s 54 1006
  (1) 1001, 1010, 1017, 1020
s 55 .... 15, 1025, 1052, 1057
  (1) 1051, 1055

(2) 1051, 1058
(2)(c) 1052
(3) 1052
(5)(a) 1052
s 55A 1052
(1) 1052
(2) 1053
(3) 1052, 1053
(4) 1052, 1053
(5) 1053
(7) 1055
s 56 . . . . 1052, 1053
(2) 1055
(3) 1053
(4) 1055
(5) 1053
s 57
(1) 1054, 1055
(1)(a) and (b) 1054
(2) 1054
(3) 1054
s 58 1057
(1) 1055
(2) 1055
(3) 1054, 1055
(4) 1050, 1054
(5) 1054
(5)(b) 1053
(6) 1052
s 59 . . . . 1055, 1057
(2) 1055
s 60 . . . . 1055, 1057
ss 61–62 1054
s 65 1088
s 67 1134
s 68 1134
(1) 1012, 1013
(1) 1049
s 69 . . . . 1013, 1049
s 237(1) 1045
s 239 1045
Sch 1
para 14 952
para 28 1134
Sch 2 . . . . 1012, 1013, 1049
Family Law Act 1996 1048
Pt 4A 990
Pt IV 943
s 63 (5) 943
s 63A (1)–(3) 991
s 63A (4)–(6) 990
s 63B (1) 991
s 63B (2)(a) 991
s 63B (2)(b) and (3) 992
s 63C 991

s 63CA, (3) and (4) 991
63M(1) 990
and 63N. 977
s 63R 991
s 63S 990
Sch 8 1350
Family Law Reform Act 1969
Sch 3, para 3 1110
Family Law Reform Act 1987 . . . . . . 165, 1193
s 1 . . . . 1193, 1229, 1375
s 18 1229
s 19 . . . . 915 , 1229
s 22 1053
s 27 1199
s 28 944
(1)–(2) 1199
Sch 2, para 52 1062
Family Law (Scotland)
Act 2006 . . . . 900, 919, 949
s 2 . . . . 985, 992
s 3 1201
s 15 1012
ss 21 and 41 . . . . 1194, 1201
s 22 . . . . 165, 166
s 25–30 950
s 25(1) and (1)(a) 950
s 38 . . . . 927, 992
(1) 898
(1)(b) 989
(2) 918, 920
(2)(a) 910
(3) 919, 920, 992
(4) 921, 992
(5) 49, 899
s 39 (1) 1371
(5) 1370
(6)(b) 1371
s 41 1202
Fatal Accidents Act 1976 . . . . 867, 878,
882, 945
Finance Act 2009
Sch, paras 1, and 2(d). 944
Finance Act 2011
s 87 and Sch 25 126
Financial Services and Markets
Act 2000 361
Forced Marriage (Civil Protection)
Act 2007 990–92
Forced Marriage etc. (Protection and
Jurisdiction) (Scotland) Act 2011 990
Foreign Judgments (Reciprocal
Enforcement) Act 1933 . . . . . . 325, 521,
522, 524, 535, 548, 554, 574, 582,
585, 586, 588, 593–600, 604,
606, WA23–7, 609, 617, 677, 1012

s 1 593
  (1)–(2) 594
  (2A) 594
  (2)(b) 594
  (2)(c) 671
  (3) 594
s 2 . . . . 100, 594
  (1) 594, 601
  (1)(b) 596
  (2) 598
  (5) 594
s 4 . . . . 598, 599
  (1)(a) 598
  (1)(a)(ii) 598, 600
  (1)(b) 598
  (2) 600, 606
  (2)(a) 595, 606, 607
  (2)(a)(i) 535, 536, 537, 595
  (2)(a)(iii) 596
  (2)(a)(iv) 595
  (2)(a)(v) 597, 607
  (2)(b) 601
  (3) 597
  (3)(a) 597
  (3)(b) 586, 597
  (3)(c) 602
s 6 . . . . 599, 677
s 7 593
s 7(2) 593
s 8 . . . . 599, 600
  (1) 599, 600
  (2) 599
  (2)(b) 600
  (3) 599
s 10A 594, 677
s 11
  (1) 594
  (2) 597
Foreign Jurisdiction Act 1890
s 5, Sch 1 109
s 69(5) 109
Foreign Limitation Periods
  Act 1984 . . . . 21, 78–9, 768, 865
s 1 78
s 1 (1)(a). 78
  (2) 78
  (3)–(4) 79
  (5) 78
s 1A 78
s 1B 78
s 2 79
s 2(2) 79, 865
s 2(3) 79
s 3 . . . . 79, 562, 600
s 4(3) 79

Foreign Marriage
  Act 1892 . . . . 901, 908, 928, 997
Foreign Marriage Act 1947. . . . . 908, 997
Foreign Marriage (Amendment)
  Act 1988 . . . . 908, 928, 997
Gender Recognition
  Act 2004 . . . . 922, 948, 993, 1043
s 1 922
s 11A(3)(a) 922
s 11A(3)(b) 922
s 11A(4) 922
s 25(1) 922
Greek Marriages Act 1884 1054
Guardianship of Minors Act 1971 1112
Hire Purchase Act 1964
s 27 1268
Human Fertilisation and Embryology
  Act 2008 . . . . 1183, 1189–92, 1194
s 33(1) 1181, 1183
s 33(3) 1181
s 35(1) 1183
s 54 . . . . 1183, 1184, 1187
  (2) 1185
  (3) 1186
  (4) (a). 1182, 1185, 1186
  (4) (b) 1182, 1184, 1185
  (6) 1186
  (8) 1187, 1188
  Sch 6(1), para 16 and 17 1203
Human Fertilisation and Embryology
  Act 1990 1183
s 30(7) 1187
Human Rights Act 1998 . . . . 13, 137,
                          581, 1162–3
s 2(1) 14
s 3(1) and (2)(a) 14
s 4 15
  (1) 1185
  (2) 14, 503
s 6 582
  (1) 13–14
  (3) 14
Immigration Act 1971 . . . . 161, 992
  Sch 2 361
Immigration and Asylum Act 1999
  Pt II 361
Income and Corporation Taxes
  Act 1970 944
s 8(1) 944
Income and Corporation Taxes
  Act 1988
  749(1) 1306, 1307
Income Tax (Earnings and Pensions)
  Act 2003
s 10 146

Income Tax (Trading and Other Income)
  Act 2005
  s 636 146
Indian Independence Act 1947 509
Inheritance (Provision for Family and
  Dependants) Act 1975 . . . . 172, 361,
                                    943, 1353
  s 1(1) 1353
  s 25(4) 943
Inheritance Tax Act 1984
  s 267 146
Insolvency Act 1986 1310
  Pt IV, Ch VI 1313
  s 117 1309
    (2) 1309
    (7) 1309
  s 122(g) 1309
  s 124A 1309
  s 125 1309
  s 175(2)(b) 1321
  s 220 1310
  s 221(1)(2), and (3) 1310
  s 221(5) 1310
  s 238 207
  s 239 207
  s 420 1313
  s 421(1A) 1313
  s 423 207
  s 426 589
  Sch B1 1313
International Criminal Court
  Act 2001
  Sch 1, para 1 515
International Organisations
  Act 1968
  s 1 514
  s 2 . . . . 514, 515
  s3 514
  s 4 515
  s 4A 515
  s 4 515
  s 5 515
  s 5A 515
  s 6 515
  s 12(5) and (6) 514
  Sch 1, Pt III 515
  Sch 2, Pt II 515
International Organisations
  Act 1981 . . . . 514, 515
  s 2 515
  ss 3–5 515
International Organisations
  Act 2005 514
  s 5 515
  ss 6–8 515

International Organisations (Immunities
  and Privileges) Act 1950 514
International Transport Conventions
  Act 1983 . . . . 9, 518
Late Payment of Commercial Debts
  (Interest) Act 1998
  s 12 97
Law of Property Act 1925
  ss 34–36 1384
  s 136 1289
  s 184 1345
Law of Property (Miscellaneous Provisions)
  Act 1989
  s 2 . . . . 74, 1373
Law Reform (Enforcement of Contracts)
  Act 1954
  s 1 74
Law Reform (Miscellaneous Provisions)
  Act 1934 882
  s 1(1) 864
Law Reform (Miscellaneous Provisions)
  Act 1949
  s 1(1) and (4) 980
Law Reform (Miscellaneous Provisions)
  Act 1970
  s 1 891
Law Reform (Personal Injuries)
  Act 1948 . . . . 748, 880
  s 1(3) 867, 879, 882
Law Reform (Succession) Act 1995
  s 3 1350
Legal Aid Act 1988
  31(1)(b) 401
Legitimacy Act 1926 . . . . 67, 1202, 1203,
                                 1204, 1205
  (2) 67, 1203
Legitimacy Act 1959 . . . . 1194, 1199
  s 1 67
  s 2 1199
Legitimacy Act 1976 1203–4
  s 1 . . . . 1200, 1203
    (1) 944, 1199
    (2) 1199, 1203
  s 2 1203
  s 2A 1203
  s 3 71
    1203
    (2) 1203
  s 10(1) 1200, 1205
  s 11 1203
  Sch 1, para 1 1203
Limitation Act 1980 . . . . 135, 666
  s 3 78
  s 7 666
  s 17 78

s 24(1) 551
s 35 830

Limited Liability Partnerships Act 2000
s 1(2) and (5) 327
s 15 327

Maintenance Enforcement Act 1991
Sch 1 para 1 1080
  para 14 1063
Sch 2 para 16 1063

Maintenance Orders Act 1950
Pt II 1079
s 16 589
s 18(1) 1079

Maintenance Orders Act 1958 1079
s 2A 1072

Maintenance Orders (Facilities
  for Enforcement) Act 1920 1063–4,
                              1078 , 1079–80
ss 1–2 1080
s 3 1063
s 4 1080

Maintenance Orders (Reciprocal
  Enforcement) Act 1972 1063–4,
                              1078, 1080–1
Pts I and II 1064, 1080
s 1 1080
s 2 1080
s 5 1063
  (5) 1080
s 6 1080
s 9 1063
s 16 101
s 21 1063
s 25(1) 1063
s 26(3) and (6) 1063
ss 27B and 28A 1064
s 40 . . . . 1064, 1080
Sch 1 Pts I and II 1063

Maintenance Orders (Reciprocal
  Enforcement) Act 1992
Sch 1 Pt I 1063
  para 2 1080
Pt II 1063
  para 13 1064

Marriage Act 1753 903
Marriage Act 1949 . . . . 894, 896
Pt III 895
s 49 895
s 75(2) 942

Marriage and Civil Partnership (Scotland)
  Act 2014
s 4(2) and (3) 250

Marriage (Enabling) Act 1960 . . . . . . 917, 919
s 1 (1) 917
  (3) 923

Marriage (Prohibited Degrees of
  Relationship) Act 1986
s 1(7) 997

Marriage (Same Sex Couples)
  Act 2013 . . . . .892, 901, 922, 946,
                              948–9, 1057–8
s 1(1) 948
s 9
  (1) 946, 947
  (6) 946
s 10(1) 949
  (1)(a) and (b) 949
s 10(2) 949
s 11(1) 948
s 13 901
s 13(2) 901, 928
Sch 3
  Pt 1 . . . . 948, 950
  (1), para 1 1048
Sch 4(4) 1047
  para 8 1046
Sch 6 . . . . 901, 902
Sch 6, Pt 1 901
s 1 901
s 2 902
s 5 901
Sch 6, Pt 2 901
Sch 6, Pt 3 . . . . 901, 902
s 11 901
s 12(1)(a) 902
s 12(1)(b) 902, 909
s 12(1)(c) 902
s 12(2) 902

Marriage (Scotland) Act 1977
s 1 (1) 917
  (2) 920
s 2 (1) 917
  (1)(a) and (3)(a) 920
s 3(5) 917, 922
s 5(4) 917
s 20A 985, 992
  (1)–(5) 992

Married Women's Property
  Act 1882 1340
s 17 943

Married Women's Property (Scotland)
  Act 1920
s 7 1369

Matrimonial and Family Proceedings
  Act 1984
Pt III 21, 974, 1014, 1031, 1032,
                    1060, 1072, 1074, 1075,
                              1076, 1077
Pt IV 1072
s 4 1062

s 12 (1).........................1077
   (1)(a) 1077
   (1)(b).......................1077
   (2)–(3)......................1077
s 13 ....1073, 1076
   (2) 1075
   (3) 1076
s 14 ....1074 , 1076
   (2) 1074
s 15 ....1074, 1076
   (1) 1073, 1075
   (2) 1074, 1075
s 15(1)(A).................1073, 1075
s 16 1076
s 17 1072
s 18 ....1073, 1078
   (6) 1073
s 19 1072
s 20 1074
s 21 ....1072, 1076
s 22 1072
s 27 ....1072, 1073
s 38(2)(b).....................1109
s 46(1) 1079
Sch 1 paras 4 and 5 1079
   para 15........................952
Matrimonial Causes Act 1937
s 13 980
Matrimonial Causes Act 1973 ...... 15, 953,
   982, 1038
s 1 953
   (1) 1036
   (2)(a) 953
   (2)(b).......................953
   (2)(c) 953, 1036
s 4(3) 1037
s 7(3) 1037
s 11 ....933, 938–40, 985, 996, 997
   (b) 940
   (d) 918, 938–40
s 12 ....985, 993, 996
   (1)(f) 997
s 13(2) ....991 , 996
s 14 ....938, 982
   (1) 996–7
   (2) 997
s 16 ....985, 1035
s 18 (1).......................1036
   (2) 1036, 1037
s 19(5) 1038
s 20 1072
s 22.........................1060
s 23 ....1061, 1065, 1072
   (1) 1061
   (1)(a)–(f) 1060

s 24 ....1061, 1065, 1379
   (1) 1061
   (1) (a) and (b) 1060
   (1)(c) ....1060 , 1394
   (1)(d)..................1060 , 1394
s 25 ....1065, 1073, 1372
                    1373, 1379
   (2) 1379
25A 1073
s 27 ....1062, 1077
   (1) 1062
   (2) 1062
s 35 1062
   (1) 1062
   (1A)(a) 1062
   (1A)(b) 1062
s 36 1062
s 37 1060
s 45 ....1049, 1050, 1051, 1053, 1056
s 46 (1)(a)....................980
   (1)(b) 173, 980
   (2) 980
s 47 ....929, 934, 941, 952
   (1) 952
   (2) and (3) 952
   (4) 952, 953
Matrimonial Causes (War Marriages)
   Act 1944
s 4 1012
Matrimonial Proceedings (Polygamous
   Marriages) Act 1972
s 1 929
s 4 938
Medical Act 1983....................80
Mental Capacity Act 2005 ..... 168, 1232–45
s2 1234
ss 9–14......................1239
ss 15–21.....................1245
s 16(A) 1244
s 18(4) 1244
s 21 1235
ss 50–51.....................1244
s 63 ....1232, 1233
s 66 ....1232, 1239
   (3) 1384
s 67 ....1232, 1239
   (1) 1384
s 68 1233
Sch 1 1239
Sch 2 , para 7 1244
Sch 3 ....1233, 1233
   para 4........................1232
   para 5........................1242
   para 5(1) 1235
   para 5(1)(e)–(f) and (l)..........1235

para 6. 1238
para 7(1)–1(a) 1235
para 7(1)(c) 1236
para 7(2) 1236
para 8 (1) and (2). 1233, 1237
para 8(3) 1237
para 11. 1237
para 12. 1239
para 13(1)–(5) 1240
para 14(1) 1241
para 16. 1241
para 16(2) 1241
para 16(3) 1241
para 16(4) 1241
para 16(5)(b) 1241
paras 17–18 1241
para 19(1) 1242
para 19(2) 1233, 1242
para 19(3) 1242
para 19(4) 1243
para 19(5) 1233, 1245
paras 20(1) and 21 1242
para 22(1) and (3) 1244
para 24. 1242
paras 26–29 1245
para 30. 1233
Pt 4 1242
Sch 5 Pt 1. . . . . 1232, 1239, .1384
Pt 2 . . . . 1232, 1239
Sch 6 . . . . 1232, 1239
Sch 7 1384
Mental Health Act 1983. 1232
Pt VI 1232
Pt VII. 1232
ss 45–46. 1235
ss 80–85. 1246
s 86 1246
s 96 (1)(d) 1384
(1)(e) 1246
s 97(4) 1246
s 100 1248
Mental Health (Care and Treatment)
(Scotland) Act 2003
ss 289, 290 and 309 1246
Merchant Shipping Act 1894
s 240(6) 908
s 253(1)(viii) 908
Merchant Shipping Act 1970
s 100(3) 908
s 101(4) 908
Sch 5 908
Merchant Shipping
Act 1995 . . . . 9, 361, 380, 867
ss 153–154. 361
s 175 361

s 176A 361
s 183 101
s 185 . . . . 860, 867
Sch 6, Pt 1 101
Art 9 101
Sch 7 . . . . 860, 867
Misrepresentation Act 1967
s 2(1)–(2). 851
Nationality, Immigration and Asylum
Act 2002
Pt 1 1193
s 9(1) 1193
Northern Ireland, Forced Marriage
(Civil Protection) Act 2007
Sch 1, para 2(2)(a) 991
Nuclear Installations Act 1965 361
s 17(1) 518
Nullity of Marriage Act 1971
s 4 938
Oaths and Evidence (Overseas Authorities
and Countries) Act 1963
s 50 81
Oil and Gas (Enterprise)
Act 1982 878
Pakistan Act 1990
Sch, para 8 593
Patents Act 1977
s 44 748
(1) 883
(2) 883
Pensions Act 2004 361
Pensions Act 1995 361
Prescription Act 1832. 78
Prescription and Limitation (Scotland)
Act 1984
s 4 78
Presumption of Death Act 2013
s 1 . . . . 1037–8, 1041–2, 1047
ss 1(3) and (4) 954, 1058
s 3(2) (b) 954, 1038, 1051, 1058
s 5(1) 1038
s 6(2) 1038
Sch 2, para 2(a) 954
Presumption of Death Act (Northern
Ireland) 2009
s 1(2) 1038
Presumption of Death (Scotland)
Act 1977
s 1(3) 1038
Private International Law (Miscellaneous
Provisions) Act 1995 21
Pt II. 940
Pt III 93, 778, 884, 885
s 1(1) 99
s 5 . . . . 938, 940–41, 942, 945

(2) 938, 940, 941
s 6 945
   (1)–(2) and (3)–(5). 940
   (6) 941, 942
s 8 (2). 929, 934, 938, 941, 943
s 9 (2). 43
   (5) 69
   (6) 778
s 11 (1). 778
   (2) 778
   (2)(a) 778
s 12 . . . . 778, 858
s 13 . . . . 78, 778, 884
   (2) 885
   (2)(a)–(b). 884
s 14 (3). 95
   (3)(a)(i) 870
   (3)(a)(ii). 115, 125
   (3)(b) 73, 93
   (4) 866
Sch para 2 . . . . . . 918, 929, 934, 938, 941
   para 2(3) 952
   para 4. 943
Protection from Harassment
   Act 1997 991
Protection of Trading Interests
   Act 1980 . . . . 83–4, 380, 553–5,
                    564, 575, 627
   s1–4. 554
   s 2 84
   s 4 84
   s 5 . . . . 119, 434, 555
      (1) 869
      (2) 554, 869
      (2)(b). 554
      (3) 554, 869
      (4) 554
   s 6 555
      (1)and (3)–(5) 555
   s 7 . . . . 555, 593
Recognition of Divorces and Legal
   Separations Act 1971 . . . . 52, 924, 1000,
           1001, 1006, 1008, 1013,
           1017, 1025, 1026
   s 1 1013
   ss 2–5. 1032
   s 2 . . . . 1013, 1022
      (b) 1008
   s 3 . . . . 1013, 1037
      (2) 1007
   ss 4–5. . . . . 1006, 1013
   s 6 . . . . 1013, 1014, 1022
      (3)(b) 1007, 1024
   s 7. 913
   s 8 1037

(1) 1025, 1026
   (1)(a) 1001
   (2) 1027
   (2)(a) 1031
   (2)(a)(ii) 142
   (3) 1037
Recognition of Divorces, etc. Act
   1987 (Isle of Man) 1001
Recognition of Trusts Act 1987 . . . . . 11, 797,
         840–41, 1372, 1382, 1383, 1395
   s 1 (1). 1382
      (2) 1384
      (4) 1384
Requirements of Writing (Scotland)
   Act 1995
   s 1(2)(a)(i) 1261
Revenue Act 1889
   s 19 1326
Royal Marriages Act 1772 921
Sale and Supply of Goods Act 1994
   Sch 2 9
Sale of Goods Act 1979 250
   s 25 1268
Scotland Act 1998
   s 126(4)(a) 8
Senior Courts Act 1981 . . . . 386, 388
   s 20 382
   s 20 (2)(h) 382
   s 21 382
      (4) 384, 385
      (4)(i)-(4)(ii) 385
      (8) 384
   s 23 518
   s 25 1330
      1330
   s 37 . . . . 336, 340, 422
   s 41(1)(1) 1109
   s 41(2) 1110
   s 41(2A) 1110
   s 41(3) 1110
   s 49(3) 393, 417, 421
   s 51 . . . . 243, 289, 360
   s 114(2) 1332
   s 116 1331
   Sch 1, paras 1 and 3 1330
Settled Land Act 1882 1253
   s 22(5) 1253
Settled Land Act 1925
   s 75(5) 1253
Social Security Act 1975. 943
Social Security Act 1986. 944
Social Security Contributions and
   Benefits Act 1992. . . . . 361, 943
   s 121(1)(b) 943
   s 147(5) 943

State Immunity Act 1978. . . . . 497–511, 516, 588, 601–2
  Pt I. 500
  s 1 . . . . 500, 602
  s 2
    (1) 506
    (2) 506
    (3) 132, 507
    (3)(a) 506
    (3)(b) 506
    (4) 506
    (5) 507
    (6) 506, 507
    (7) 507
  s 3 500
    (1)(a) 503
    (2) 504
  s 4 503
    (1) 504–5
    (2) 505
    (2)(b) 503, 505
    (3) and (5) 505
  s 5 505
  s 6
    (1) 505
    (2) 505
    (4) 508
  s 7 505
  s 8 505
  s 9 (1)–(2) 506
  s 10 508
    (1) 506
  s 11 505
  s 12 508
  s 13 508
    (2)(a) 508
    (5) 509
  s 14
    (1) 498
    (2) 518
    (3) 508
    (4) 508–9
    (5) 508
  s 15 509
  s 16
    (1) 510, 516
    (1)(a) 503, 505
    (1)(b) 505, 511
    (2) 500
  s 18(1)–(3) 602
  s 19 602
    (1) 505
  s 20 . . . . 509, 510, 516
    (1)(a) 498
    (2) 516

  s 21(a) 509
  s 23 (3)(a). 506
State Pension Credit Act 2002
  s 12 943
Statute Law (Repeals) Act 2004
  Sch 1(14), para 1 . . . . 586, 602
Statute of Frauds 47, 1259
  s 4 . . . . 74, 76
Succession (Scotland) Act 1964 1369
Supreme Court Act 1981 . . . . 289, 382
  s 35A 97
Supreme Court of Judicature (Consolidation)
  Act 1925
  s 102 109
Surrogacy Arrangements Act 1985 1183
Tax Credits Act 2002
  s 43 943
Third Parties (Rights against Insurers)
  Act 2010 290
Trade Union and Labour Relations
  Act 1974
  s 18 75
Tribunals, Courts and Enforcement
  Act 2007
  Pt 6 1278
  s 134 (2). 1278
  s 135
    (1) 1278
    (3) 1278
  ss 136–138. 1278
Trustee Act 2000
  Sch 2(II), para 27 1333
Unfair Contract Terms
  Act 1977 . . . . 233, 712, 744
  s 2(1) 879
  s 26 733
  s 27 (2). 143, 712, 744, 747
Variation of Trusts Act 1958. 1393–4
  s 1 1393
Welfare Reform Act 2007
  Sch 1, para 6(7) 943
Welfare Reform and Pensions
  Act 1999 1072
Wills Act 1837
  s 18 1350
    (2) 1364
  ss 18A, 18B 1350
  s 20 1349
  s 27 1364
Wills Act 1861 . . . . 1341, 1343
  s 2 68
Wills Act 1963. . . . . . 10, 66, 172, 1341, 1342, 1343, 1349, 1362
  s 1 . . . . 1341, 1342
  2 (1)(a). 1341

(1)(b) 1352, 1364
(1)(c) 1349
(1)(d) 1362, 1364
(2) 1362
s 3 1343
s 4 1274
s 6 (1) 1343
(2) 1342
(2)(b) 1342
(3) 1343
s 7 (1)–(4) 1341

STATUTORY INSTRUMENTS

Adopted Children and Adoption Contact
    Register Regulations 2005 1207
Adoption Agencies (Miscellaneous
    Amendments) Regulations
    2013. 2016
Adoption Agencies Regulations
    2005. . . . . 1207, 1216
Adoption (Bringing Children into the
    United Kingdom) Regulations
    2003. . . . . 1207, 1219
Adoption of Children from Overseas
    Regulations 2001
    reg 7 1219
Adoption (Recognition of Overseas
    Adoptions) Order 2013 1224
Adoption (Recognition of Overseas
    Adoptions) (Scotland) Order 2013 . . 1224
Adoptions with a Foreign Element
    Regulations 2005 . . . . 1207–9, 1213,
                                    1216–21
Pt 2, Ch 1 1219
Pt 3, Ch 1 1216
Pt 3, Ch 2 . . . . 1216, 1220
    reg 1 1207
    reg 10 1220
    reg 13 1216
    (4) 1217
    regs 16–33 1217
    reg 18 1217
    reg 19 1217
    reg 20 1217
    reg 21 1217
    reg 22 1217
    reg 24–27 1217
    reg 31 1217
    reg 38 1217
    regs 42–44 1218
    reg 47 (1) 1218
    reg 50 1218
Asylum and Immigration (Treatment
    of Claimants, etc) Act 2004
    (Remedial) Order, 2011 . . . . 894, 992

Civil Jurisdiction and Judgments
    (Amendment) Regulations 2014
Sch 1 para 3(11). 145
Civil Jurisdiction and Judgments (Hague
    Convention on Choice of Court
    Agreements 2005) Regulations,
    2015. 586, 604
reg 16 586
reg 17 535
Civil Jurisdiction and Judgments
    (Maintenance) Regulations, 2011
    Sch 1
    para 4(1)(a) 1083
    para 6(1)(a) 1083
    para 6(2)(a) 1083
    para 6(3) 1083
    para 7, 8 and 9 1083
    Sch 4
    para 9. 586
    para 10. 535
    Sch 6 1062
    Sch 7
    para 6(2) 1062
    para 6(3)(b) 1062
    para 10. 1073
    para 10(2)(b) 1073, 1075
    para 10(2)(c) 1073
Civil Jurisdiction and Judgments
    Order 2001 . . . . 145, 149, 199, 356,
                            358, 360, 607, 622
Art 3 . . . . . 202, 296, 618, 622, 623, 624, 625
Art 4 . . . . 306, 317
Sch 1
    para 2. 623
    para 2(1) 623
    para 2(2) 623
    para 3. 623
    para 4. . . . . 623, 624
    para 5. 623
    para 6. 623
    para 7. 296
    para 8(1)(a) 618
    para 8(1)(b) 621, 625
    para 9. . . . . . 145, 199–200, 213, 244, 336
    para 9(2) 199, 223
    para 9(3) 199
    para 9(4) 199
    para 9(5) 199
    para 9(6) 210
    para 9(7) 210, 214
    para 10. 336
    para 11. 336
    para 12. . . . . 202, 336
Sch 2
    Pt II, para 3 317

Pt II, para 4 317
Pt IV, para 9 306
Pt IV, para 10 . . . . 306, 307
Pt IV, para 13 . . . . 334, 498
Pt IV, para 14 586
Pt IV, para 15 535
Civil Jurisdiction and Judgments
    Regulations 2007 315
  Sch 1(1) para 13 1075
Civil Partnership (Armed Forces)
    Order 2005 902
Civil Partnership (Jurisdiction and
    Recognition of Judgments)
    Regulations 2005 . . . . . 1040, 1041, 1044
  regs 3–5 1040
  regs 6–12 . . . . 1044, 1048
  reg 6 (1)–(3) 1044
  reg 7 1045
  reg 8 1045
    (3) 1044, 1045
    (3)(b) 1044
  regs 9–12 1044
Civil Partnership (Registration Abroad and
    Certificates) Order 2005 901
Civil Procedure Rules 315, 331, 335, 347,
                    356, 448, 622, 1308
  Pt 6 . . . . 325–6, 331–2
  Pt 11 363
  Pt 17 830
  Pt 24 . . . . 333–4, 419, 551
  Pt 62 666
  Pt 74 . . . . 619, 622
    paras 74.14–74.18 589
    para 74.16 590
  r 1.1 334
  r 3
    1 421
    1(f) 392
    1(2)(a) 228, 332
    1 (2)(f) 421
    10 . . . . *361*
  r 6
    3(1) 326
    3(2) 328, 331
    3(3) 327
    3(6) 213, 273, 287, 324, 334
    4(1) 326
    4(1)(b) 326
    4(2) 326
    5(3) 326, 332
    5(3)(c) 327
    6 326
    6 (1) 326
    7 . . . . 326, 327, 331, 333
    8 . . . . 308, 326, 327, 331

9 . . . . 213, 308, 326, 327
9(2) 327, 331–2
10 . . . . 326, 327
11 . . . . 326, 333
11(2) 327
12 344
15 . . . . 326, 332, 381
15(2) 326
16 . . . . 326, 332
19(1A) 306
20(1) 173
20(5)(c) 719
20(9) 668
31(1) 336, 360, 379
32 . . . . 327, 334, 337
33 . . . . 213, 308, 327, 334, 337, 380
33(1) 379
33(1)(a) 380
33(1)(b) 380
33(2)(b)(i) 379
33(2) 308, 379
33(2)(a) 380
33(2)(b) 380
33(2)(b)(i) 379
33(2A) 380
33(3) 380, 555
34 . . . . 308, 379
35 380
36 . . . . 327, 328, 333, 334, 337, 364–81,
                400, 405, 414, 423, 469,
                    486, 542, 556, 654
36(9) 355
37(1)(b) 363
37(2) 337
37(3) 335, 363, 365
40–46 381
41 308
42 308
43 308
r 7
  2A 327
  3 338
r 11 333
  (3) 332
  (4) 228, 332
  (5) 332
  (6) 392
  (8) 333
r 17.4 830
r 19 338
r 20
  (1) 339
  (4) 333
r 25(1) 340
r 26.4 421

r 35 3(1). 111
    3(2). 111
    4 –7 and 12 111
r 58 7. . . . . 228, 332
r 61
    4(7) 361
    11(5) 361
r 72.1(1). 1293
r 74
    7A(2–5) 624
    7A1 624
    7B 624
    7C 619
    11A 618
    11A(2) 623
    11A(4) 623
Commercial Agents (Council Directive)
    Regulations 1993 . . . . 144, 348, 749
Commonwealth Countries and Republic
    of Ireland (Immunities and
    Privileges) Order 1985 516
Commonwealth Countries and Republic
    of Ireland (Immunities and Privileges)
    Order 2005 516
Consular Marriages and Marriages under
    Foreign Law (No 2) Order 2014 901
Consumer Rights Act 2015 (Consequential
    Amendments Order) 2015/1726 9
Crime and Courts Act 2013 (Family
    Court: Consequential Provision)
    (No 2) Order 2014
    Pt 2
    Art 128(a) and (b) 1082
    Art 129(a) and (b) 1083
    Art 129 (c)(i)(aa) and (bb) 1083
    Art 138(a) and (b) 1086
    Art 138(c)(i)and (ii) 1086
Defence (Finance) Regulations 1939
    reg 2. 747
Divorce (Religious Bodies) (Scotland)
    Regulations 2006 1012
Divorce (Religious Marriages) Act 2002
    (Commencement) Order 2003. 1012
Electronic Commerce (EC Directive)
    Regulations 2002 873
    Arts 3(1) and (2) 873
European Communities (Definition of
    Treaties) (1996 Hague Convention
    on Protection of Children etc)
    Order 2010 1102
European Communities (Enforcement of
    Community Judgments) Order
    1972. . . . . 523, 524, 601
European Communities (Jurisdiction and
    Judgments in Matrimonial and Parental

Responsibility Matters) Regulations
    2005. 1089
European Communities (Matrimonial
    Jurisdiction and Judgments)
    Regulations 2001 954
Family Procedure (Adoption) Rules
    2005. 1206
Family Proceedings (Civil Partnership:
    Staying of Proceedings)
    Rules 2005. . . . . 1042, 1047
    r 1 (2). 1042
    (2)(c) 1042
    rs 2–5 and 7–8 1042
Family Procedure Rules 2010 . . . . . . 953, 1206
    rr 3.17– 3.19 1972
    r 6.41 965
    r 6.43(2). 966
    r 6.44. 966
    rr 6.45(1) and 6.46. 966
    r 7.27 967
    r 7.27(1). 967
    r 8.18 . . . . 1051, 1052, 1053, 1054
    r 8.19 . . . . 1051, 1052
    r8.20 . . . . 1051, 1052, 1053, 1054
    r 8.21 . . . . 1051, 1052, 1053, 1054
    r 8.22. 1052
    r 12.3. 1156
    rr 12.44– 12.57 1134
    r 12.60. 1162
    r 12.62– 12.64. 1114
    rr 12.66–12.67. 1113
    r 12.68. . . . . 1117, 1121
    r 14.22. 1225
    r 23.7. 1210
    r 31.7 –31.8 1130
    r 31.17 1130
    Pt VI, C.4 966
    Part 6 1208
    Part 12 1056
    Part 13 1183
    Part 14 1206
    Part 31 . . . . 1127, 1130
    Part 31, C4. 1132
Family Proceedings Rules 1991
    r 3.17–19 1072
Financial Collateral Arrangements
    (No 2) Regulations 2003 1302
    r 19 1302
Human Fertilisation and Embryology
    (Parental Order) Regulations
    2010. . . . . 1179, 1183, 1188
Immigration (Procedure for Marriage)
    Regulations 2011 . . . . 894, 992
Income Support (General) Regulations
    1987. 172

Intercountry Adoption (Hague Convention)
Regulations 2003 . . . . 1206, 1207
International Interests in Aircraft
Equipment (Cape Town Convention)
Regulations 2015 (SI 2015/912) 89
International Recovery of Maintenance
(Hague Convention 2007 etc)
Regulations, 2012
Sch 1, paras 3, 4 and 6 1086
Sch 4
para 2(1)–(8) 1086
para 5(3) 586
para 5(4) 535
Law Applicable to Non- Contractual
Obligations (England and Wales
and Northern Ireland) Regulations
2008 788
Law Applicable to Non-Contractual
Obligations (Scotland) Regulations
2008 788
Limited Liability Partnerships (Application
of Companies Act 2006) Regulations
2009 . . . . 327, 330
MARD Regulations (SI 2011/2931) 127
Marriage (Same Sex Couples) Act 2013
(Conversion of Civil Partnership)
Regulations 2014 946
Marriage (Same Sex Couples) (Jurisdiction
and Recognition of Judgments)
Regulations 2014 . . . . 1046, 1048
rr 3–9 . . . . 1044, 1048
Marriage (Same Sex Couples) (Jurisdiction
and Recognition of Judgments)
(Scotland) Regulations 1045, 1048
Matrimonial Causes (Northern Ireland)
Order 1978 1001
Art 18 1036
Mental Capacity Act 2005
(Commencement No 2) Order
2007 1233
Ministry of Justice, Explanatory
Memorandum to the Parental
Responsibility and Measures for the
Protection of Children (International
Obligations) (England and Wales and
Northern Ireland) Regulations 2010
Annex A, para 4 1102
Non-Contentious Probate Rules 1987
r 30 (1)(a)–(c) 1331
(2) 1332
(3)(a)(i)–(ii) 1331
(3)(b) 1332
r 31 1331
r 32 1332
r 39(3) and (6) 1337

Overseas Companies Regulations 2009 329
reg 7 329
reg 7 329
reg 7(1)(e) 329
Overseas Marriage (Armed Forces)
Order 2014 901
Parental Responsibility and Measures for the
Protection of Children (International
Obligations (England and Wales
and Northern Ireland) Regulations
2010 1102
r 7 1125
Proceeds of Crime Act 2002 (Investigation
in different part sof the United
Kingdom) Order 2003
Pt 6, Art 34 589
Protection of Trading Interests
(Australian Trade Practices)
Order 1988 554
Protection of Trading Interests
(Hong Kong) Order 1990 554
Protection of Trading Interests
(US Antitrust Measures)
Order 1983 554
Protection of Trading Interests (US
Cuban Assets Control Regulations)
Order 1992 554
Reciprocal Enforcement of Foreign
Judgments (Australia) Order 1994
Sch, Art 3 643
Reciprocal Enforcement of Foreign
Judgments (Canada) Order 1987
Sch, Art IX 643
Reciprocal Enforcement of Judgments
(Administration of Justice Act 1920,
Part II) (Amendment) Order
1994 522
Return of Cultural Objects Regulations
1994 . . . . 1277, 1278
Rules of the Supreme Court
Ord 11 335
r 1(1) 363, 469
r 1(1)(a) 363
r 1(1)(c) 173
r 1(1)(d) 341
r 1(1)(d)(ii) 344
r 1(1)(e) 347
r 1(1)(f) 347, 351
r 1(1)(g) 356
r 1(1)(h) 356
r 1(1)(i) 356, 357
r 1(1)(m) 668
r 1(1)(q)–(s) 363
r 1(1)(t) 359
r 1(2) 380

r 4 365
Ord 14. 419
Ord 15, r 16. 1049
Unfair Terms in Consumer Contracts
Regulations 1999 296
reg 9. 772
US Reexport Control Order 1982 554
Vienna Document 1992 (Privileges and
Immunities) Order 1992 511

EU LEGISLATION

Charter of Fundamental Rights of the
European Union. 35, 984
Art 2 1138
Art 47 . . . . 503, 505, 622
Civil Jurisdiction and Judgments
Act 1982 189
Annex II to Council Regulation (EC)
No 44/2001 12
Commission Regulation (EC) 261/2004
of 11 February 2004 establishing
common rules on compensation
and assistance to passengers in the
event of denied boarding and of
cancellation or delay of flights 260
Art 3(1) 774
Commission Regulation (EC) No 2245/
2004 amending Annexes I, II, III and
IV to Council Regulation (EC) No
44/2001 12,
Council Decision 2001/470/EC
establishing a European Judicial
Network in civil and commercial
matters. 193, 984
Council Decision 2002/762/EC in
relation to the Bunkers
Convention 203, 775, 875
Council Decision of 19 December 2002
authorising the Member States in the
interest of the Community to sign
the Convention 1101
Council Decision 2006/719/EC on the
accession of the Community to
the Hague Conference on Private
International Law. 13
Council Decision 2013/434/EU
authorising certain Member States to
ratify, or to accede to, the Protocol
amending the Vienna Convention on
Civil Liability for Nuclear Damage
of 21 May 1963, in the interest of
the European Union, and to make
a declaration on the application
of the relevant internal rules of
Union law 797

Council Decision of 4 December 2014
on the approval, on behalf of the
European Union, of the Hague
Convention of 30 June 2015
on Choice of Court
Agreements 552, 604
Council Directive 76/308/EEC on mutual
assistance for the recovery of claims
relating to certain levies, duties, taxes
and other measures. 361
Council Directive 85/374/EEC on
the approximation of the laws,
regulations and administrative
provisions of the Member States
concerning liability for defective
products. 820–21
Art 2 820
Art 3 822
Art 6 820
Art 9 820
Council Directive 86/653/EEC on the
coordination of the laws of the
Member States relating to self-
employed commercial agents 144
Art 17 749
Art 17 749
Art 18 749
Council Directive 90/314/EEC on
package travel, package holiday and
package tours 295
Council Directive 93/7/EEC on the
return of cultural objects unlawfully
removed from the territory of a
Member State. 1277
Art 1 279
Art 5 773
Council Directive 93/13/EEC on
unfair terms in consumer
contracts. 296, 855
Art 3(2). 855
Art 6(2) 773
Council Directive 99/44/EC on certain
aspects of the sale of consumer goods
and associated guarantees
Arts 1(2)(b) and 1(4) 256
Council Directive 2010/24/EU on mutual
assistance for the recovery of claims
relating to taxes, duties and other
measures. 125
Council Directive 2014/60/EU of the
European Parliament and of the
Council of 15 May 2014 on the
return of cultural objects unlawfully
removed from the territory of a
Member State. 121, 1277

Council Directive 2014/67/EU of the
European Parliament and of the
Council on the enforcement of the
Posted Workers Directive 297
Council Regulation (EC) No 6/2002 on
Community designs 601, 833
  Arts 27–34 693
  Arts 88(2), (3), 89(1), 89(1)(d) and
    89(2) 834
Council Regulation (EC) No 40/94 on
the Community trade mark 601
Council Regulation (EC) No 44/2001 on
jurisdiction and the recognition and
enforcement of judgments in civil
and commercial matters (Brussels
I Regulation) 12–13, 51,
          187–8, 189,191–322, 341, 351,
          457, 479–80, 518, 523, 603, 610,
              634, 637, 643, 652, 653–4,
                              684, 690
  Recital (11) 1064
  Recital (20) 700
  Art 1
    (1) 795
    (2)(e)–(f) 690
    (2) 192
  Art 4 . . . . 214 , 230
  Art 5
    (1) 690
    (2) 1064, 1065
    (3) 263, 785
    (4) 279
    (5) 279
    (6) 283
    (7) 283
  Art 6
    (1) 283, 456
    (2) 288
    (3) 288
    (4) 288
  Art 7 288
    (1) 695
    (2) 695, 692
  Arts 8–14 289
  Arts 15–17 292
  Art 15 294
    (1)(c) 293
  Art 22 . . . . 217, 218, 473–4
    (1) 51, 219, 1255
    (2) 494
    (3) 494
    (4) 314
  Art 23 . . . . 229, 230, 451, 473–4, 1067
    (3) 230
  Art 24 226

Art 27 . . . . . 443, 446, 451, 452, 474, 479,
                                480, 978
Art 28 . . . . 474, 479
Art 29 . . . . 450, 1068
Art 30 1068
Art 31 . . . . 303, 305
Art 34 (4) 641
Art 35 642
Art 45 (1)(d) 1128
Art 48 . . . . 615, 619
Art 63 (1) 237
Art 68(1) 192, 1064
Art 70
  (2) 614
Art 71 315
Art 72 315
Ch II 192, 195
  Section 5 481
Council Regulation (EC) No 1206/2001
on co-operation between the courts
of the Member States in the taking
of evidence in civil or commercial
matters 81–3, 193
Recitals (2) and (8) 81
Recitals (10)–(12) 82
Recital (14) 82
Recitals (15) 81
Art 1(2) 83
Art 3 81
Arts 4–6 82
Art 8 82
  (1) 82
Art 10 (1)–(2) 82
  (4) 82
Art 11 82
Art 12 82
  (4) 82
Art 13 82
Art 14 82
  (1) 82
  (2)(a)–(d) 82
  (3) 82
Art 17(2)–(6) 83
Art 18 82
  (2)–(3) 82
Art 21 81–2
Art 23 81
Ch II 82
Council Regulation (EC) No 1346/
2000 on insolvency
proceedings 193, 207,
                                548, 1312
Art 4(2)(i) 89
Art 7 1273
Art 39 552

Council Regulation (EC) No 1347/2000
  on jurisdiction and the recognition
  and enforcement of judgments in
  matrimonial matters and in matters
  of parental responsibility for children
  of both spouses (Brussels II) 627,
           954, 1000, 1051, 1052,
               1088, 1090
  Recital (6) 954
  Recital (10) 1061
  Recital (11) 1092
  Art 1 1002
  Art 2 949
  Art 3(3) 1099
  Art 11 957
    (1)–(2) 957
  Art 12 959
  Art 15(1)(a) 627
Council Regulation (EC) No 1348/
  2000 on the service in the Member
  States of judicial and extrajudicial
  documents in civil or commercial
  matters 193, 308, 309, 635, 966
Council Regulation (EC) No 861/2007
  of the European Parliament and
  Council establishing a European
  Small Claims Procedure 295, 523,
                 662, 663–5
  Recital (1) 663
  Recital (4) 663
  Art 1 663
  Art 2 663
    (1) 663
    (2) (a) –(j) 663
  Art 4(1) and (2) 664
  Art 5
    (1) –(4) 664
    (6) 664
  Art 7(1) 664
  Art 15(1) and () 664
  Art 18 664
  Art 23 664
  Art 20(1) 664
  Art 21
    (1) 664
    (2) 665
  Art 22(1) 664
  Art 23 664
  Art 25(1)(a) 664
  Annex 1 664
  Annex 4 665
Council Regulation (EC) No 1393/2007
  of the European Parliament and
  Council on the service in the Member
  States of judicial and extrajudicial

documents in civil or commercial
  matters 193, 308–9, 381,
                    449, 966
  Recital (2) 308
  Art 1 310
    (1)–(2) 309
  Art 2 309
  Arts 4–15 309
  Art 18 309
  Art 19 309
  Art 20
    (1) 308–9, 966
    2. 309
Council Regulation (EC) No 2201/
  2003 concerning jurisdiction and
  the recognition and enforcement of
  judgments in matrimonial matters and
  the matters of parental responsibility
  (Brussels II *bis*) 172, 177,
      583, 627, 803, 925, 954, 962–4,
      982, 993, 1000–1, 1003, 1030,
      1034, 1038, 1039, 1048, 1052,
          1088–9, 1090–1105
  Recital (1) 1002
  Recital (5) 1092
  Recital (7) 1002
  Recital (8) 1078
  Recital (9) 1061, 1093
  Recital (10) 1093, 1193
  Recital (11) 1078
  Recital (12) 1094
  Recital (13) 1115
  Recital (16) 971, 1119
  Recital (17) 1160
  Recitals (19) 1159
  Recital (20) 1159
  Recital (21) 1003, 1127, 1128
  Recital (25) 1130
  Recital (31) 954
  Art 1 . . . . 1003, 1093, 1102
    (1) 960, 1002
    (1)(a) 993
    (1)(b) 1093
    (2) 1110
    (2)(e) 1093
    (3) 1093
    (3)(a) 956–9, 1193
    (3)(b) 957–8, 1193
    (3)(e) 1078
  Art 2 .
    (1) 1003, 1127
    (4) 960, 1003, 1127
    (7) 1093
    (9) 1093
    (10) 1093, 1130

(11) .1138, 1157
Art 3 . . . . 175, 954–62, 960,
961, 962, 963, 965, 968,
975, 976, 979, 1005, 1040,
1046, 1060,
1094, 1098
(1) 976
(1)(a) 961, 962. 963
(1)(a) 5 and 6 179
Art 3(b) 1066
Art 4 . . . . . . 960, 961, 962, 963, 965, 1005
Art 5 . . . . . . 960, 961, 962, 963, 965, 1005
Art 6 . . . . 961, 962, 963, 1005
Art 7 . . . . 965, 975, 977, 979, 1005
(1) 960–2, 1105
(2) 961
Arts 8–20 1100
Art 8 . . . . 175, 1066, 1094, 1100,
1101, 1105, 1111, 1114, 1117,
1121, 1127
(1) 1094, 1104
Art 9 . . . 1094, 1097–8, 1100, 1101, 1105,
1111, 1114, 1117, 1121, 1127
(2) 1098
Art 10 . . . . 1094, 1098, 1100, 1101, 1103,
1104, 1105, 1111, 1114, 1117,
1127, 1157, 1161
(b)(iv) 1158
Art 11 . . . . 968, 1105, 1111, 1114,
1117, 1127
(1) 968, 1158
(2) 968, 1144, 1158
(3) 1158
(4) 1155, 1158, 1159
(5) 1159
(6) 183, 1160, 1162
(7) 183, 1157, 1158, 1160,
1161, 1162
(8) 183, 1130, 1158, 1160,
1161, 1162
Art 12 . . . . . 963, 1094, 1098–1100, 1101,
1103, 1105, 1111, 1114, 1115,
1117, 1127
(1) 1098–9, 1105
(1)(b) 1099
(2) 1105
(3) 1099, 1100, 1105
(3)(b) 1099
(4) 1099, 1100
Art 13 . . . . . 179, 1094, 1100, 1105, 1105,
1111, 1114, 1117, 1119, 1127
(2) 1100
Art 14 . . . . 1105, 1105, 1111, 1114,
1117, 1127
(1) 1105

Art 15 . . . . 975, 1100, 1103, 1113–16,
1124, 1129
(1) 1113
(2) 1114
(2)(c) 1118
(3) 1114, 1117, 1118
(3)(d) 1114
(4) 1114
(6) 1115
Art 16 . . . . 969, 970, 1118
Art 17 . . . . 962, 969, 1118
Art 19 . . . . 959, 967, 968, 969, 970,
972, 977, 978, 1004, 1042,
1061, 1100, 1103,
1117–18, 1120, 1124. 1132
(2) 1118, 1120, 1124
Art 20 . . . . . . 971–2, 1118, 1119–21, 1123
Art 21 . . . . 1003, 1127, 1132
Art 22 . . . . 141, 583, 584, 1004, 1005
(a) 141, 1002, 1004, 1005
(b) 141, 1028
(d) 1004
Art 23 . . . . 1127–8, 1129
(a) 1128, 1129
(b) 1128, 1158
Art 24 . . . . 1004, 1005, 1034, 1045,
1128, 1129
Art 25 . . . . 1004, 1005, 1011, 1045
Art 26 . . . . . 1004, 1005, 1045, 1128, 1129
Art 27 . . . . 1045, 1127
Art 28(1) and (2) 1129
Art 40 . . . . 1098, 1159, 1162
Art 41 . . . . 1098, 1130, 1159, 1162
(2) 1130
Art 42 . . . . 1161, 1162
(1) 1162
(2) 1162
Arts 40–45 . . . . 1130, 1132
Art 46 1003
Art 47 1161
(1) 1130
Art 48 1130
Art 53 1115
Art 55 1131
Art 60 1157
Art 61 1092
(b) 1130
Art 64 1003
Art 66 . . . . 1001, 1099, 1100,
1101, 1132
(d) 1132
Art 72 1003
Ch II
s 2 . . . . 1094, 1100
s3 1100

Ch III
  s 1 1044
  s 4 1130
Ch III. 1130
Council Regulation (EC) 4/2009 of
  18 December 2008 on jurisdiction,
  applicable law, recognition and
  enforcement of decisions and
  cooperation in matters relating to
  maintenance obligations [2009]
  OJ l 7/1 (Maintenance
  Regulation) 211–12, 586, 698,
                793, 794, 1059, 1060, 1062,
                1063, 1074, 1078–9, 1081–4
Recital (11) 1074
Recital (17) 1069
Recital (21) 1064
Recital (29) 1081
Art 1 1064
Art 2(3) 1066, 1067
Art 3 . . . . 175, 1066, 1068, 1070, 1074
  (a) 1066, 1070, 1071
  (b) 1066
  (c) 1060, 1065, 1066, 1068,
                      1074, 1079
  (d) 1065, 1066
Art 4 . . . . 1067, 1068, 1069, 1070
  (1)(a) 1067
  (1)(b) 1067
  (1)(c) 1067
  (c)(i). 1065
  (2) 1067
  (3) 1067
  (4) 1067, 1070
Art 5 . . . . 1067, 1068, 1069
Art 6 . . . . 1068, 1070
Art 7 . . . . 1068, 1069, 1070
Art 8 . . . . 1061, 1069
  (1) 1069
  (2)(a) – (d) 1069
Art 9 1068
Art 12 . . . . 1068, 1075, 1083
Art 13 . . . . 1068, 1083
Art 15 . . . . 698, 793
Art 17 1078
  (1) 1081
  (2) 1081
Art 19(1) – (2) 1081
Art 21(1)–(3) 1081
Arts 22–23. 1082
Art 24(a)–(d) 1082
Art 41 1081
Art 69
  (1) 1070, 1071
  (2) 1070

Art 75 1081
Council Regulation (EC) 207/2009 of
  26 February on the Community trade
  mark, as amended by Regulation
  (EU) 2015/2424 of the European
  Parliament and of the Council of
  16 December 2015 . . . . .274, 833
Arts 9–13. 834
Arts 16–24(a). 693
Art 97(5) 834
Art 101 834
Art 102(1) 834
Art 102(2) 834
Council Regulation (EU) No 1259/2010
  implementing enhanced cooperation
  in the area of the law applicable
  to divorce and legal separation
  (Rome III) 982–4, 993
Recital (6) 983
Recital (10) 983, 993
Recital (12) 983
Recital (13) 983
Recital (15) 983
Recital (16) 983, 984
Recital (19) 983
Recital (23) 983
Recital (24) 984
Recital (25) 984
Recital (26) 984
Recital (27) 983
Recital (29) 983
Recital (25) 984
Recital (30) 984
Art 1(1) 983, 993
Art 1(2) 983
Art 1(2)(c) 983, 993
Art 2 983
Art 4 983
Art 5(1) 983
Arts 6 and 7 983
Art 8 983
Art 9 983
Art 10 984
Art 11 983
Art 12 984
Art 13 984
Art 14 983
Art 15 983
Art 21 984
Directive 96/71/EC of the European
  Parliament and the Council
  concerning the posting of workers
  in the framework of the provision
  of services. 749, 773
Art 6 297

Directive 98/26/EC of the European
  Parliament and of the Council
  on settlement finality in payment
  and securities settlement
  systems.................. 1301, 1302
Directive 1999/44/EC of 25 May 1999
  on certain aspects of the sale of
  consumer goods and associated
  guarantees
  Art 7(2) 773
Directive 2000/31/EC of the European
  Parliament and of the Council on
  certain legal aspects of information
  society services, in particular
  electronic commerce, in the Internal
  Market.................... 873, 887
  Art 3 .... 278, 887, 888
  (3) 774
  Annex........................... 774
Directive 2002/47/EC of the European
  Parliament and of the Council
  on financial collateral
  arrangements 1301, 102
  Preamble (6)–(7) 1302
  Art 9(1) 1302
Directive 2002/65/EC of the European
  Parliament and of the Council
  concerning the distance marketing of
  consumer financial services 12(2) 773
Directive 2002/83/EC of the European
  Parliament and of the Council
  concerning life assurance 703
  Art 2 704
  Art 3(3) 704
  Art 51(1) and (2) (b) 704
Directive (EC) No 2004/35 of 21 April
  2004 on environmental liability
  with regard to the prevention
  and remedying of environmental
  damage
  Art 1(1) 829
  Art 3(3) 828
Directive 2006/123/EC of the European
  Parliament and of the Council on
  services in the internal market
  Art 3(2) and 17 774
Directive 2008/48/EC of 23 April 2008
  on credit agreements for consumers
  Art 22(4) 773
Directive 2008/122/EC of 14 January 2009
  on the protection of consumers in
  respect of certain aspects of timeshare,
  long- term holiday product, resale and
  exchange contracts
  Art 12(2) 773

Directive (EC) No 2009/22 of 23
  April 2009 on injunctions for the
  protection of consumers' interests
  Art 1 825
EC/Denmark Agreement.... 125, 188–9, 192,
          195, 197, 308, 379, 492, 607,
              652, 653–4, 781, 954
  (2)(c) 652
EC Treaty
  Art 50 256
  Art 192(2) 79
  Art 220 684
  Art 299 188
Eleventh Council Directive 89/666/EEC
  concerning disclosure requirements
  in respect of branches opened in a
  Member State by certain types of
  company governed by the law
  of another
  State........................... 329
Implementing Regulation (EU)
  2016/1823 303
Modified Regulation *see* Statutes, Civil
  Jurisdiction and Judgments Act
  1982, Sch 4
Protocol on the position of Denmark
  annexed to the Treaty on European
  Union and to the Treaty establishing
  the European Community 192
Protocol on the position of the United
  Kingdom and Ireland annexed to the
  Treaty on European Union and to
  the Treaty establishing the European
  Community
  Art 3 192
Regulation (EEC) No 3118/93 of 25
  October 1993 laying down the
  conditions under which non-resident
  carriers may operate national road
  haulage services within a
  Member State
  Art 6(1) 774
Regulation (EC) No 805/2004 of the
  European Parliament and of the
  Council creating a European
  Enforcement Order for uncontested
  claims.......... 193, 523, 655–9, 1083
  Recitals (1), (4), (5) 656
  Recital (6) 657
  Recital (8) 657
  Recital (9) 1084
  Recitals (10)–(13)................. 658
  Recital (14) 659
  Recital (18) 658
  Art 1 .... 656, 1084

Art 2 656
  (3) 656
Art 3 (1)........................ 657
  (1)(a) 657
  (1)(b) 657, 658
  (1)(c) 657, 658
  (1)(d) 657, 658
Art 4 (1) and (3)............. 656, 1084
  (5) 656, 1084
  (6) 657
Art 5 657
Art 6 .... 656, 657
  (1) 657
  (1)(d) 658
Art 9 657
Art 10 657
Art 12 (1)....................... 658
Art 13 658
  (1)(a)–(d) 658
  (2)........................... 659
Art 14 659
Arts 15–19 659
Art 20 (1) –(2) 659
Art 21 (1)................... 659, 665
  (2) 659
Arts 22–23 659
Arts 26 and 33 640
Art 27 656
Ch III........................... 658
Regulation (EC) No 2100/94 of 1
  September 1994 on Community
  plant variety rights 833
Arts 97(2), (3), and 103 834
Regulation (EC) No 864/2007 of the
  European Parliament and of the
  Council on the law applicable
  to non-contractual obligations
  (Rome II)........ 13, 95, 96, 115, 125,
             267, 348, 686, 690, 693,
             776, 780–875
Recital (6) 782, 784
Recital (7) ... 785, 792, 804, 857, 860, 881
Recital (8) 784, 792
Recital (9) 784, 793
Recital (10) 784, 793, 794–5
Recital (11) 783, 788, 790
Recital (12) 796, 866
Recital (13) 782, 784
Recital (14) 784, 784, 809
Recital (16) 784, 810, 813
Recital (17) 811, 825
Recital (18) 809, 814
Recital (19) 809, 819–20
Recital (20) 820, 821
Recital (21) 823, 825

Recital (22) 827
Recital (23) 783, 827
Recital (24) 783, 829
Recital (25) 830
Recital (26) 783, 831, 832
Recital (27) 835, 836
Recital (28) 836
Recital (30) ..... 694, 702, 783 , 850, 852
Recital (31) 854–5
Recital (32) 866, 868, 869
Recital (33) 819, 863
Recital (34) 871
Recital (35) .... 773 , 873
Recital (37) 875
Recitals (39)
Recital (40) 780
Art 1 .... 786, 793
  (1)...... 125, 692, 750, 789, 792, 874
  (2)............... 693, 789, 790, 793
  (2)(a) 697, 793, 794, 795, 816
  (2)(b) 697, 789, 794
  (2)(c) 699
  (2)(d) 700, 791, 796
  (2)(e) 791, 796
  (2) (f)........................ 797
  (2)(g) 702, 791, 797, 798,
              831, 883
  (3) 94, 787, 790, 793, 799,
        800, 832, 834, 856, 862
  (4) 780
Art 2 .... 789, 791, 820
  (1) 788, 803, 812, 821, 852
  (2) 788, 804, 821
  (3)(a) 810
  (3)(b) 803, 813, 821, 852
Art 3 .... 786, 801
Arts 4–14...................... 807
Art 4 .... 802, 807,
        809–10, 819, 822, 826,
       827, 842, 845, 846, 854,
         872, 875, 881
  (1) 785, 810–11, 812, 813, 814,
       818, 822, 823, 825, 826,
       828, 829, 845, 853, 854,
       863, 875, 877, 881
  (2) 810, 813–14, 818, 822,
       823, 826, 829, 835, 836,
       845, 846, 854, 875, 877
  (3) .... 792 , 793, 810, 812, 813,
       814–19, 823, 826, 836, 843,
       847–8, 854, 856, 875, 881,
       882, 883
  (4) 826–7
Art 5 .... 802, 809, 810, 819–23
  (1) 821, 822–3

(1)(a) 821, 822, 823
(1)(b) 821–2, 823
(1)(c) 822, 823
(2) 821, 823, 827
Art 6 .... 809, 810, 819, 823–8, 884
(1) 799, 810, 823–6, 868
(2) 826, 827
(3) 810, 827–8, 883
(3)(a) 828
(3)(b) 825, 828
(4) 828, 855, 858
Art 7 .... 809, 810, 819, 828–31
(5) 803
Art 8 ..... 809, 810, 819, 831–5, 837, 883
(1) 831, 832–3, 834, 868
(2) 831, 832, 833–4
(3) 827, 834–5, 855, 858
Art 9 ...... 80, 809, 810, 819, 835–6, 875
Art 10 .... 802, 806, 807,
837–8, 839, 840, 841, 843,
844, 846, 847, 848, 849, 852, 854
(1) 694, 793, 837, 839, 842,
843–5, 848, 856
(2) 845–6, 848
(3) 846–7, 848
(4) 845, 847, 848
Art 11 .... 802, 848–9, 852, 854, 879
(1) 694, 793, 856, 878–9
(2) 849, 878–9
(3)–(4) 879
Art 12 .... 702, 704, 802, 844, 849–54
(1) 704, 850, 851, 852–3, 854, 856
(2) 853–4
(2)(a) 854
(2)(b)–(c) 854
Art 13 .... 831, 837
Art 14 .... 810, 826, 828, 834, 854,
855, 856, 857–8
(1) 855, 856
(1)(a)–(b) 855
(2) 787, 857, 866
(3) 714, 857
Art 15 .... 94, 785, 800, 801, 858–66
(a) 88, 796, 807, 827, 832, 858,
859, 861
(b) 94, 95, 792, 801, 807, 858,
859, 860, 861, 862, 867, 881,
882, 883
(c) 88, 93, 94, 95, 766, 819,
858, 861–2, 863, 868
(d) 766, 801, 858, 861, 863, 864
(e) 858, 861, 864
(f) 88, 813, 858, 861, 864
(g) 88, 858, 861, 865, 866
(h) 78, 801, 858, 861, 865

Art 16 ....743, 810, 857, 866, 874, 882, 883
Art 17 .... 785, 830–31, 858, 871
Art 18 .... 704, 858, 872
Arts 19..... 704, 789, 807, 858, 872, 1292
Art 20 .... 789, 807, 858, 1292
Art 21 .... 80, 799–801, 858, 858, 873
Art 22 .... 799–801, 858
(1) 85
(2) 80
Art 20 872
Art 22 872
Art 23 .... 740, 803, 813, 846
(1) 802–3, 826
Art 24 .... 69, 70, 802
Art 25 875
(1)–(2) 788
Art 26 .... 810, 868–71
Art 27 .... 772, 773, 786, 834, 873
Art 28 .... 774, 806, 820, 860, 874
(1) 797, 819, 841, 867, 874
(2) 875
Art 29 .... 780, 786
(1) 874
Art 30 782
(1) 804
(1)(i) 803, 819
(2) 786, 797
Art 31 786
Art 32 .... 780, 786
Ch II 789, 790, 791, 802, 804–6, 809,
836–7, 842, 844, 849, 850,
852, 858, 875
Ch III......... 790, 791, 802, 806, 807,
808, 836–7, 844, 849, 850,
852, 858
Ch IV............. 790, 802, 854, 858
Regulation (EC) No 1896/2006 of the
European Parliament and of the
Council creating a European order
for payment procedure 193, 295,
523, 660–62
Recital (1) 660
Recital (13) 661
Recital (16) 661
Art 1
(1) 660
(2) 660
Art 2 (1)................. 660
(2)(a)–(c) 660
(2)(d) 661
(3) 660
Art 3(1) 660
Art 4 661
Art 6(1) and (2) 661
Art 7(1) 661

Arts 8–11 661
Art 12(1), (3) and (5) 661
Arts 13–15 661
Arts 16–20 661
Art 16(1) and (2)
Art 16(3) 662
Art 17(1) 662
  paras 2–5 662
Art 18(1) 662
Art 19 662
Art 20 662
Art 21(1) 662
Art 22(1) and (2) 662
Art 23 662
Arts 28–31 644
Ann VI 645
RegulatIon (EC) No 593/2008 of the
  European Parliament and of the
  Council of 17 June 2008 on the law
  applicable to contractual obligations
  (Rome I) [2008] OJ L 177/6 . . . . 13, 75,
        95, 233, 236, 262, 344, 416,
               419, 682–775
Recitals (4) 686
Recital (6) 686, 688
Recital (7) 688, 690, 692, 1287
Recital (8) 698
Recital (9) 699
Recital (10) 702
Recital (12) 700, 719, 720, 856
Recital (13) 696, 715
Recital (14) 716
Recital (15) 711
Recital (16) 726
Recital (17) 257, 727
Recital (18) 290
Recital (19) 290, 726, 734
Recital (21) 735
Recital (22) 731, 742
Recital (23) 741
Recital (24) 741, 742
Recital (25) 741, 742
Recitals (26)–(31) 742
Recitals (33) 742
Recitals (34) 742, 749
Recitals (35) 741, 742
Recital (36) 742
Recital (37) 143, 745
Recital (38) 693, 1285
Recital (39) 740
Recital (40) 692, 773, 774
Recital (42) 775
Art 1 883
  (1) 125, 690, 692, 696, 703, 787,
                  788–9, 864

  (2) 685, 697
  (2)(a) 88, 697, 761, 1261
  (2)(b) 697, 698, 702, 793
  (2)(c) 697, 794, 795
  (2)(d) 699, 795
  (2)(e) 586, 700
  (2)((f) 694, 697, 701, 704, 761, 796
  (2)(g) 701
  (2)(h) 702, 797
  (2)(i) 694, 702, 704, 743
  (2)(j) 703
  (3) 696, 697, 704, 710, 712
  (4) 683, 686
Art 2 . . . . 703, 705, 802
Art 3 . . . . 706–18, 728, 740, 743, 746,
         750, 751, 756, 764, 772, 856
  (1) 700, 706, 707, 709, 711,
       715, 717, 720, 722, 723, 856
  (2) 706, 709, 710, 716, 759,
                   855, 856
  (3) 695, 707, 711–13, 714, 715,
       718, 743, 744, 745, 785, 857
  (4) 713–14, 743, 744, 745
  (5) 717, 723–4, 755, 856
Art 4 . . . . . . 707, 708, 709, 716, 720, 723,
       724, 725, 726, 727, 728, 731,
    740, 743, 750, 751, 764, 772, 853
  (1) 349, 725, 726–40
  (1)(a) 690, 727, 728, 733, 735
  (1)(b) 690, 727, 728, 733, 735
  (1)(c) 257, 726, 728, 729, 735
  (1)(d) 726, 729, 735
  (1)(e) 726, 727, 729, 730, 735
  (1)(f) 726, 727, 729, 735
  1(g)–(h) 726, 735
  (2) 725, 726, 727, 731–9
  (3) 725, 735–8, 853
  (4) 725, 727, 730, 735
  (5) 725, 736, 737
Art 5 . . . . . . 706, 723, 726, 731, 742, 751,
                 764, 853
  (1) 731, 739, 741, 742
  (2) 706, 731, 739, 741, 742, 743
  (3) 731, 742, 853
Art 6 . . . . . . 706, 723, 741, 742, 747, 751,
              760, 764, 853
  (1) 739, 742, 743
  (2) 706, 712, 714, 741, 743, 744,
              745, 747, 880
  (4)(d) 742
Art 7 . . . . 703, 706, 723, 728, 741, 742–3,
       751, 774, 764, 853, 872
  (1) 743, 745
  (2) 739, 743, 745
  (3) 706, 714

(3)(b) 739
(3)(e)......................... 739
Art 8 ...... 300, 706, 723, 741, 742, 751,
764, 853, 882
(1) 706, 714, 743, 744, 745,
880, 882
(2) 741, 742, 880
(3) 301
(4) 853
Art 9 ...... 685, 711, 714, 741, 747, 743,
745, 746, 750, 773, 866
(1) 143, 712, 745, 746, 750, 866
(2) 713, 745, 746, 747–9, 750–1,
774, 880
(3) 143, 744, 745, 751–2, 754, 769,
770–72, 868
(6) 743, 745
Art 10 ..... 232, 345, 587, 724, 754, 755,
756, 856, 1278
(1) 54, 415, 419, 710, 717,
755, 756, 757, 764, 769,
770, 840, 851, 856
(2) 739, 755, 757–8
Art 11 .... 710, 724, 755, 756,
758, 764, 1278
(1) 758, 759, 760, 873
(2) 739. 758, 759–60
(3) 739, 758, 760
(4) 739, 741, 760
(5) 714, 740, 742, 745, 760, 761
Art 12 .... 693, 694, 755,
764–5, 767, 858
(1) 764–5
(1)(a) 718, 764
(1)(b) 765
(1)(c) 92, 96, 705, 764, 765,
769, 767–8, 840, 842,
861, 862, 863
(1)(d) 78, 705, 765, 768, 769, 865
(1)(e) 694, 768, 818, 839,
840, 844, 851
(1)(i) 850, 851
(2) 765, 769, 771
Art 13 .... 697, 724, 755, 756, 763,
1261, 1286
Art 14 .... 693, 755, 1285, 1291
(1) 1285, 1291
(2) 785, 864, 1285, 1287, 1289,
1291, 1294
(3) 1285
Arts 15................ 755, 1291, 1292
Art 16 .... 755, 1292
Art 17 772
Art 18 .... 85, 755, 799
Art 18 (2)......................... 80

Art 19
(1) 739–40, 802, 803
(2) 739, 769, 772
(3) 740
Art 20 .... 70, 706, 773, 802
Art 21 .... 92, 142–3, 714, 749, 752,
769, 771–2, 775, 869
Art 22 735
(1) 696, 714, 715
(2) 696
Art 23 .... 685, 692, 747, 749, 750,
773, 774, 775
Art 24 .... 686, 775
(1) 683
Art 25 .... 691, 696, 731, 775
(1) 774
(2) 775
Art 26(1) 774
Art 28 .... 686, 691
Art 29 786
Regulation 650/2012 of the European
Parliament and the Council
on jurisdiction, applicable law,
recognition and enforcement
of decisions and acceptance
and enforcement of authentic
instruments in matters of
succession and on the creation of
a European Certificate
of Succession 60, 212,
698, 795, 1327–9, 1359
Recital (25) 1328
Recital (42) 1328
Recital (69) 1328
Recital (71) 1328
Art 4 .... 175, 1328, 1359
Art 5 .... 1328, 1359
Art 6 .... 1328, 1359
Art 67 1359
Art 20 Art 6.................... 1359
Art 21 .... 1328, 1359
Art 22 .... 1328, 1359
1359
(2) 1359
Art 23...................... 1359
Art 23(2)(f) 1328
Art 29 1329
(1)–(3) 1329
Art 34(2) 1359
Art 36(2)(b) 1329
Art 62(2)–(3) 1328
Art 63 1328
Art 69 1328
1328
Art 83 and 84.................... 1359

Regulation (EU) No 1151/2012 of 21
November 2012 on quality schemes
for agricultural products and
foodstuffs Recital (12) 833
Regulation (EU) No 1215/2012 of the
European Parliament and of the
Council of 12 December 2012 on
jurisdiction and the recognition and
enforcement of judgments in civil
and commercial matters OJ 2012
L 351/1, amended by Regulation
(EU) No 542/2014 of the European
Parliament and of the Council of 15
May 2014 as regards the rules to be
applied with respect to the Unified
Patent Court and the Benelux Court
of Justice OJ 2014 L 163/1, and
Commission Delegated Regulation
(EU) 2015/281 of 26 November
2014 replacing Annexes I and
I (Brussels I Recast) 13, 125,
187–8, 190, 191–322, 324,
325, 328, 329, 332, 333, 335,
337, 341, 343, 347, 349, 354,
358, 379, 386, 399, 421, 443,
523, 572, 603, 604, 605,
607, 608–55, 684, 977
Recital (2) 619
Recital (3) 193, 609
Recital (4) 193, 609, 619
Recital (6) 609
Recital (10) 212
Recital (11) 611
Recital (12) 208, 211, 444, 480, 645
Recital (14) 296, 300
Recital (15) 200, 244, 464
Recital (16) 244
Recital (18) 296, 300
Recital (19) 200, 226, 296, 300
Recital (20) 232
Recital (22) 243, 453
Recital (23) 458
Recital (24) 458, 493
Recital (25) 304
Recital (26) 527, 619
Recital (27) 611
Recital (28) 618, 622
Recital (29) 619, 625
Recital (30) 643
Recital (31) 624, 647
Recital (32) 619, 621, 623
Recital (33) 303, 304–5, 616
Recital (34) 195, 617
Art 1 ... 201, 204, 206, 318, 612, 613, 614
    (1) 125, 491, 517, 692, 794

(1)(d) 612
(2) 661
(2)(a) 660, 697, 698
(2)(b) 660
(2)(c) 660
(2)(e) 304
(2)(f) 660, 698
Arts 2–7 213
Art 2 611
Art 2(2) 316
Art 2(4) 316
Art 2(a) 303, 611–12, 615, 616,
617, 639, 640
Art 2(d) 611
Art 2(e) 611
Art 2(f) 611
Art 3 482
(2) 618
Art 4 ...... 125, 203, 213, 216, 225, 230,
236, 243–4, 269, 278, 280,
303, 318, 386–7, 388, 389,
443, 457, 462, 463, 464,
465, 466, 467, 468, 482, 494, 617
Art 5 .... 213, 381, 482, 609
(1) 213, 297
Art 6 .... 125, 195, 214, 215, 227,
289, 296, 299, 388, 389, 392,
458, 468, 469, 470, 471, 661, 664
(1) 227, 291, 296, 297, 299
(2) 215, 651
Arts 7–9 .... 319, 457, 465–6
Arts 7–26 .... 303, 617
Art 7 .... 194, 216, 230, 244–5, 265,
318, 319, 389, 465, 609
(1) 233, 234, 242, 245–6,
247–9, 251, 255, 257, 262,
264–5, 267–9, 292, 347, 446,
518, 690, 692, 693, 766, 785,
788, 792, 804, 827, 833
(1)(a) 252–4, 256, 261, 262, 320
(1)(b) 196, 252, 255–62, 298, 727
(1)(c) 261–3
(2) 225, 246, 250, 251, 263–79,
318, 348, 349, 351, 443, 785,
788, 792, 804, 805, 806, 808,
810–11, 812, 876
(3) 206, 267, 279
(4) 267, 279
(5) 279–82, 289, 296, 299,
301, 530
(6) 283, 318
(7) 203, 283
Art 8 .... 216, 230, 283–7, 389, 465
(1) 283–7, 299, 337, 389,
456, 461, 466, 465

(2) 288
(3) 288
(4) 219, 287
Art 9 . . . . 203, 288, 389
Art 10 289
Arts 10–16 321
Art 11 289
(1) 290, 1260
(1)(b) 215
(2) 215, 289
Art 12 290
Art 13 290
(2) 290
(3) 290
Art 14 . . . . 289, 290
Art 15 . . . . 242–3, 289, 290–91, 855
Art 15(3) 199
Art 16 291
Arts 17–26 319
Art 17 . . . . 293, 294, 295
(1) 292, 296
(1)(a) 293
(1)(b) 293
(1)(c) 293–5
(2) 215, 296
(3) 295
(5) 297
Art 18 296
(1) 213, 214, 215, 296, 460,
            468, 481, 664
(2) 215, 296, 658, 661
(3) 296
Art 19 . . . . 242–3, 296, 297, 855
Art 19(3) 199
Art 20
(1) 283, 299
(2) 215, 299, 301
Art 21 . . . . 300, 302
(1)(b) 299, 301
(2) 213, 214, 215, 299, 460,
            468, 481, 664
Art 22
(1) 301
(2) 301
(5) 225
Art 23 . . . . 242–3, 299, 302, 855
Art 24 . . . . 213, 214, 215, 217, 218,
        224, 226, 227, 229, 236, 242,
    244, 316, 318–19, 380, 388, 450,
    453–4, 457, 458, 460, 466, 467,
        468, 473–4, 481, 482, 657,
                664, 1060
(1) 219, 220-23, 233, 491,
        492, 493, 494, 729, 1255
(2) 201, 224, 320, 494, 1309

(3) 224, 494
(4) 218, 225, 314, 321
Art 25 . . . . 203, 214, 215, 216, 226,
        227, 229, 230, 231, 233–9,
        240, 241, 242–4, 258, 261,
        262, 291, 296, 297, 302,
        318, 320, 345, 367, 369,
        370, 380, 387, 388, 398,
    410, 436, 450–53, 454, 457,
        458, 460, 462, 466, 468,
        473–4, 475, 481, 645, 664
(1) 494
(2) 239
(4) 242
(5) 233, 234
Art 26 . . . . 217, 226-9, 243, 289,
        296, 297, 299, 302, 318,
        452, 466, 627, 662
(2) 289, 291, 296, 297, 299, 302
(3) 229
Art 27 . . . . . . 217, 218, 311, 454, 459, 492
Art 28 . . . . 251, 609, 633, 651
(1) 217, 309
(2) 310, 632
(3) 310
(4) 310
Art 29 . . . . 203, 243, 321, 389–30,
        407, 443–8, 450, 452, 455,
        457, 469, 470, 476, 479,
        650, 968, 978, 1117
(3) 469
Art 30 . . . . 203, 285, 286, 389, 421,
        445, 446, 447, 448, 454–7,
    469, 470, 472, 475, 479, 494
(3) 288
Art 31 . . . . 235, 448, 452
(1) 311, 450, 454, 456, 459
(2) 243, 291, 297, 302, 392, 444,
        453, 454, 456
(3) 291, 297, 302
(4) 291, 297, 302, 452
Art 32 . . . . 196, 448, 457, 969
(1) 390
(1)(b) 449
Art 33 . . . . . 203, 389, 421, 457, 458, 459,
    460, 467, 470, 472, 473, 474,
        475, 493, 976
(1)(a) 458
(1)(b) 458
(2) 458
(3) 458
Art 34 . . . . 203, 389, 421, 457,
        458–9, 460, 467, 470,
    472, 473, 474, 475, 493, 976
(1)(a) 458

(1)(b) 458
(1)(c) 458
(2) 458
(2)(a) 458
(3) 458
Art 35 . . . . 209, 270, 303–7, 341, 616, 644
Art 36 . . . . 611, 613, 617, 649, 650
(3) 619
Art 37
(1) 617
(2) 618, 619
Art 38(a) 617, 647–9, 1003
Art 38(b) 619
Art 39 . . . . 611, 612, 613,
621, 622, 647
Art 40 620
Art 41
(1) 622
(2) 621, 625, 626, 643
(3) 622
Art 42 622
(1) 620
(1)(b) 621, 625
(2) 620
(3) 620
(4) 620
Art 43
(1) 621, 623
(2) 621, 623
(3) 623
Art 44
(1) 624
(2) 621, 647
Art 45 . . . . 619, 620, 622, 625, 626–45
(1) 619
(1)(a) 626–7, 632, 1004
(1)(b) 311, 615, 632–7, 639,
655, 1004, 1128, 1130
(1)(c) 285, 639, 640, 641,
642, 646, 1004, 1128
(1)(c)(ii) 454
(1)(d) 584, 640–42, 1004
(1)(e) 642, 644
(1)(e)(i) 642
(1)(e)(ii) 218
(2) 642
(3) 617, 631, 642, 643,
644, 646, 1005, 1129
(4) 619
Art 46 . . . . 622, 625
Art 47
(1) 623
(2) 624
(3) 624
Art 48 624

Art 49
(1) 624
(2) 624
Art 50 624
Art 51 647–9
(2) 648, 649
Art 52 . . . . 622, 627, 644, 649,
1005, 1129
Art 53 . . . . 615, 616, 618, 620, 621,
622, 625, 632, 634
Art 54
(1) 618, 622
(2) 618, 623
Art 56 622
Art 57 . . . . 618, 620, 622
Art 61 . . . . 618, 620
Art 62 . . . . 145, 198, 213, 244, 658,
660, 663
Art 63 . . . . 196, 198, 200, 201,
214, 215, 244, 660, 663, 802
(1) 200, 740
(1)(b) 802
(1)(c) 803
(2) 200, 214
(3) 201, 283
Art 64 206
Art 65 288
(2) 618
Art 66 192
Art 66(1) 523
Art 66(2) 610
Art 67 203
Art 68(1) 523, 603
Art 69 203
Art 70 614
Art 76 . . . . 192, 203
Art 71 . . . . 203, 309, 314, 386–7, 388,
389, 444, 461, 471–5, 613,
614, 655
(2)(a) 202
Art 72 . . . . 214, 625, 626, 643,
644, 652, 654
Art 73(2) 646
Art 75 609
Art 75(b) 624
Art 75(c) 624
Art 76 609
Art 76(1) 213
Art 81 192
Art 2325(1) 242
Annex I 615, 618, 621, 622,
625, 632
Ch II 195, 215, 611
s 1–7 . . . . 212, 216
s 1, Art 4 216

s 2, Arts 7–8 216
s 3, Arts 10–16 . . . . 216, 289–91,
465-6, 482, 642, 657
s 4, Arts17–19 . . . . 216, 292–7,
465-6, 482, 642
s 5, Arts 20–23 . . . . 216, 280,
283, 297–302, 465-6, 642
s 6, Art 24 . . . . 216, 642, 657
s 7, Arts 25–26 216
s 9, Arts 29–32 639
Ch III 212, 611, 613, 615, 616,
652, 654, 657
s 1 . . . . 617, 618
s 2 . . . . 618, 619, 622
s3 622
s 4 . . . . 619, 622
Regulation (EU) No 1257/2012 of 17
December 2012 implementing
enhanced cooperation in the area
of the creation of unitary patent
protection 833
Regulation (EU) No 542/2014 of
the European Parliament and of
the Council of 15 May 2014 as
regards the rules to be applied
with respect to the Unified Patent
Court and the Benelux Court
of Justice 191, 286
Regulation (EU) 655/2014 of the
European Parliament and of the
Council of 15 May 2014 establishing
a European Account Preservation
Order Procedure to facilitate cross-
border debt recovery in civil and
commercial matters 193, 303
Regulation (EU) 2015/848 of the
European Parliament and of
the council of 20 May 2015
on insolvency
proceedings 89, 126, 138,
193, 207, 1309, 1312
Art 1 1312
(1) 1313
(2) 1313
Art 2(1) 1312
Art 2(7) 1314
Art 2(8) 1314
Art 2(9) 1316
Art 2(10) 1315
Art 3(1) 1314
Art 3(2) 1315, 1323–4
Art 3(3) 1316, 1317
Art 3(4) 1317
Art 3(4)(b)(i) 1314
Art 4(1) 1317

Art 4(2) 1317
Art 5 1318
Art 6(1) 1318
Art 6(2) 1318
Art 6(3) 1318
Art 7
(1) 1319
(2) 1319
(2)(a) 1319
(2)(b)–(f) 1320
(2)(g)–(m) 1321
Art 8 1322
Art 9 1320
(2) 1320
Art 10 1322
Art 11 1320
Art 12 1322
Art 13 1320
Art 14 1323
Art 15 1323
Art 16 1322
Art 17 1323
Art 19 1323
Art 20 . . . . 1320, 1323
(1)–(2) 1323–4
Art 32 1319
Art 33 1323
Art 35 1319
Art 52 1319
Ch 4 1321
Annex A 1313
Regulation (EU) 2015/2421 193
Recital (26) 623
Regulation (EU) 2016/679 on the
protection of natural persons with
regard to the processing of personal
data and on the free movement of
such data
Art 82 798
Regulation (EU) 2016/1103
implementing enhanced cooperation
in the area of jurisdiction,
applicable law and the recognition
and enforcement of decisions in
matters of matrimonial property
regimes 698, 794, 795
Recital (18) 794
Regulation (EU) 2016/1104
implementing enhanced cooperation
in the area of jurisdiction, applicable
law and the recognition and
enforcement of decisions in matters
of the property consequences of
registered partnerships 698, 795
Art 3(1)(a) – (b) 795

Second Council Directive 88/357/EEC on
the coordination of laws, regulations
and administrative provisions relating
to direct insurance other than life
assurance and laying down provisions
to facilitate the effective exercise of
freedom to provide services
and amending
Directive 73/239/EEC 703
Treaty of Amsterdam 193
Arts 61–67 11
Art 65 11
Treaty of Lisbon
Art 65 12
(1) 12
Title IV 12
Treaty on European Union 12, 507
Art 3(2) 193, 782
Art 20(2) 982
Art 61(c) 686, 782
Art 65 782
Art 67 193
(5) . . . . 669, 771 A
Art 81 . . . . 193, 827
Art 82 827
Art 174 830
Title V 193
Treaty on the Functioning of the
European Union
Art 5(c) 612
Art 54 100
Art 67(1) 782
Art 67(4) 609, 656, 660, 663, 782
Art 81 . . . . 35, 609, 656, 664, 663, 782
(2)(c) 686, 782
(2) 34, 782
Art 101, 102 827
Art 191 830
Art 267 . . . . 194, 632, 686, 783
(2)and (3). 687, 783
Art 288 659
Art 297(1) 786
Arts 326–334. 982
Art 340 805
Art 355 . . . . 523, 602, 653
(2) 6683
(3) 612
Annex II. 683
Working Time Regulation 1998 503

EUROPEAN CONVENTIONS/
RESOLUTIONS

Agreement on the European Economic
Area 992

Austrian, Finnish and Swedish Accession
Convention (Brussels Convention)
1996. . . . . 193, 198, 205,
Austrian, Finnish and Swedish Accession
Convention (Rome Convention) 685
Brussels Convention on jurisdiction and
the enforcement of judgments in civil
and commercial matters 12–13, 125,
187, 188–9, 191, 192–3,
195–8, 201, 202, 203, 208, 212,
223, 227, 232, 235, 243, 270,
273, 284, 290, 296, 301, 306,
310, 311, 312, 313, 317, 321,
322, 351, 379, 386, 457, 460,
477–9, 523, 571, 589, 603–4,
610, 613, 614, 617, 637,
650, 652–3, 655
Art 1 125
(1) 491
Art 2 . . . . . 386, 388, 460, 462–5, 468, 494
Art 3 (2). 643
Art 4 . . . . 230, 469, 471
Art 5 465
(1) 242, 245–6, 252, 254, 258–9,
261, 301, 690, 766
(2) 212, 288
(3) 263, 276
(4) 279
(5) 279
(6) 283
(7) 283
Art 6 465
(1) 283, 460–61
(2) 288
(4) 288
Arts 7–12A. 289
Art 7 288
Art 12 465
Arts 13–15. 292
Art 13
(3) 292, 293, 294
(3)(b) 295
Art 16 . . . . . . 218, 388, 454, 466, 467, 468
(1) 219, 220, 221, 222
(1)(a) 219, 491, 492, 493
(1)(b) 223, 1255
(4) 225
Art 17 . . . . . 229, 229, 230, 235, 240, 241,
242, 243, 388, 410, 450,
451, 466
(5) 302
Art 18 . . . . . . 226, 227, 228, 229, 243, 627
Art 19 492
Art 21 . . . . . . 407, 443, 445, 447, 451, 476
Art 22 . . . . 285, 286

(1) 454
Art 23 450–51
Art 24 .... 270 , 303, 304, 306, 616
Art 27
    (2) 634, 635, 637
    (3) 285
    (4) 615
    (5) 584
Art 28 642
Art 34 625
Art 53 201
    (1) 200
Art 57 .... 386–7, 388, 389, 461, 518, 614
(1) 203
Art 59 .... 603, 604, 625, 643, 651–2
Art 68 196
    (1) 653
    Section 3 465
    Section 4 465
Title II 643
Convention on Contact concerning
    Children. 1089, 1177–8
Recital (16) 1177
Art 2 (c) 1177
Arts 4 and 19 1178
Art 20(1) and (3) 1178
Art 22(1) 1177
Convention on the Rights of the Child
    (UNCRC) 1221
    Art 3(1). 1165
    Art 12 1144
Convention on the service in the
    Member States of the European
    Union of judicial and extrajudicial
    documents in civil and commercial
    matters 308
Council of Europe Convention on
    Recognition and Enforcement of
    Decisions concerning Custody of
    Children and on the Restoration of
    Custody of Children. 1089, 1134,
                             1135, 1166
European Convention on
    Human Rights 13–14, 515, 639,
                     870, 1163–7, 1243
Art 4 .... 503, 511
Art 6 .... 13–14, 395, 422, 452, 502,
              503, 505, 511, 551, 575,
         580–82, 628, 629–30, 1163–4
    (1) 13–14, 178, 500, 503
Art 8 .... 14–15, 1157, 1164,
                     1185, 1189–90
Art 10 15
Art 12 .... 15, 992
Art 14 .... 15, 992, 1185, 1366

First Protocol, Art 1 ... 15, 602, 1278, 1279
Protocol 4 Art 2 1168
European Convention on Information
    on Foreign Law (London
    Convention). 109
European Convention on Recognition
    and Enforcement of Decisions
    concerning Custody of Children and
    on the Restoration of Custody of
    Children. 1089
European Convention on State
    Immunity. 497, 499
Art 20(3) 505
Art 28 492
European Patent Convention
    Art 64(3) 831
First Protocol on interpretation of the
    Rome Convention 685
Art 2 672
Greek Accession Convention (Brussels
    Convention) 1982 .... 192, 198
Greek Accession Convention (Rome
    Convention). 683
Lugano Conventions on jurisdiction and
    the enforcement of judgments in civil
    and commercial matters (1988 and
    2007) 189, 191, 192, 194–9,
               223, 298, 306, 313–14, 318,
            321, 322, 324, 332, 341, 379,
            386, 422, 523, 589, 603–4,
                653–5, 1059, 1060
Art 1(1) 491
Art 1(3) 314
Art 2 .... 494, 1069
Art 5 314
    (1) 248, 851
    (2) 314
    (2)(a) – (c) 1069
    (5) 282
Art 16
    (1)(b) 223
Art 22 .... 313, 388
    (1) 1255
    (4) 314
Art 23 .... 313, 388, 410
Art 26 314
Art 27 .... 313, 389, 407
    (2) 655
Art 28 .... 313, 389
Art 34 1084
    (1) 655
Art 35(1) 654
Art 50(2) 655
Art 54B(3) 654, 655
Art 59 .... 313, 654

Art 60 313
Art 63(1) and (2) 653
Art 64 (1) 313, 654
  (2)(a)–(b) 313
  (2)(c) 653
  (3) 654
Art 67 . . . . 386–7, 388, 389
  (1) 313, 314, 518
  (4) 655
Art 68
  (1) 654
  (2) 654
Art 70 (1)(a)–(c) 313
Art 71 313
Art 72 313
Protocol 1
  Art I 314
Protocol 2
  Preamble 195
  Art 2 195
Protocol 3(1) 313
Protocol on Interpretation (Brussels
  Convention) 312
Rhine Navigation Convention 518
Rome Convention on the law applicable
  to contractual obligations 13, 74,
          344, 415, 419, 682–5, 686
  Preamble para 2 684
  Art 1
    (1) 690, 695, 696
    (2) 685
    (2)(a) 697
    (2)(b) 794, 1372
    (2)(c) 699, 795
    (2)(e) 694, 796
    (2)(g) 797
    (2)(h) 704, 799
    (3) 685, 703
    (4) 685, 703
  Art 2 983
  Art 3 . . . . 703, 706
    (1) 707
    (3) 711, 744, 857
  Art 4 . . . . 703, 724–5, 724–5, 737
    (1) 707, 725, 730
    (2) 172, 725, 727, 730, 738, 739,
                        740, 744
    (3) 725, 726, 727, 729
    (4) 725, 726, 731, 742
    (5) 738
  Art 5 . . . . 172, 703, 726, 741, 742
    (2) 744
  Art 6 . . . . 726, 741, 742
    (1) 744
    (2) 301

Art 7 . . . . 857 685, 744, 744, 751
  (1) 868
  (1)(e) 839
  (2) 713, 744, 745, 746, 865
Art 8 755
  (1) 419
Art 9 758
  (1) 873
  (3) 758
  (4) 760
  (6) 744, 745
Art 10 . . . . 764, 767
  (1)(c) 96, 767, 862
  (1)(d) 78, 865
  (1)(e) 685, 694, 768, 839
Art 12 . . . . 1285, 1290, 1291
  (2) 807, 1287, 1290, 1291
Art 13 1126,
Art 14 . . . . 711, 799
Art 15 . . . . 70, 706
Art 16 752
Art 17 691
Art 18 . . . . 689, 690
Art 19
  (1) 696
  (2) 685, 696
Art 20 . . . . 692, 773
Art 21 . . . . 389, 691, 874
Art 22 . . . . 389, 685
  (1)(b) 694, 768, 817
Art 23 692
Arts 24 . . . . 683, 692
Art 28(1) 683
Art 33 690
Second Protocol on interpretation of
  the Rome Convention 684
Spanish and Portuguese Accession
  Convention (Brussels
  Convention) 1989 . . . . 192, 198
  Art 7 241
United Kingdom, Danish and Irish
  Accession Convention (Brussels
  Convention) 1978 . . . . 198, 240

INTERNATIONAL CONVENTIONS

Agreement on Trade-Related Aspects of
  Intellectual Property Rights (TRIPS)
  Arts 3 and 4 831
Athens Convention on the Carriage of
  Passengers by Sea 101
Berne Convention for the Protection of
  Literary and Artistic Works 9
  Art 5(2) 831
Brussels Convention on Immunity of
  State-owned Ships 498

ss 10(3-6) 506
s 17(1) 506
Protocol 498
Brussels Protocol (Visby
    Amendment) 9
Convention concerning the Powers of
    Authorities and the Law Applicable
    in respect of the Protection
    of Minors 1089, 1101
Convention on Adoption 1213
Convention on Celebration and
    Recognition of the Validity of
    Marriage. 927
Convention on Choice of Court
    Agreements 190, 192, 202, 229,
                314–16, 333, 345, 369,
                370, 380, 398, 399, 410,
                521, 522, 586, 588,
                604–5, 652
    Art 1(1)–(3) 316
    Art 2 416
    (1)(a)–(p) 316
    Art 3 . . . . 316, 604
    (b)–(c) 316
    Art 5(1)–(2) 317
    Art 6 317
    Art 8 . . . . 317, 604, 652
    Art 9 . . . . 317, 604, 652
    (a)–(e) 605
    (f)–(g) 605
    Art 11 575
    Art 11(1) 605
    Art 22 316
    Art 26(6) 229
    (a) 315
    (b) 652
Convention on International Wills
    (Washington Convention) 1344
    Arts 1–5 and 10 1344
    Ann 1344
Convention on Jurisdiction, Applicable
    Law, Recognition, Enforcement and
    Co-operation in respect of Parental
    Responsibility and Measures for
    the Protection of Children 172,
                1077, 1101–5
    Art 1(2) 1093, 1102
    Art 2 1094
    Art 3 . . . . 1093, 1102, 1103, 1112
    (b) 1102
    Art 4 . . . . 1093, 1103
    Arts 5–10 . . . . 1121, 1122, 1123
    Art 5 . . . . 1094, 1103–4
    Art 6 . . . . 1100, 1105, 1122
    (1) and (2). 1105

Art 7 . . . . 1098, 1103, 1104–5
    (3). 1123
Art 8 . . . . 1103, 1113, 1116–17, 1121
    (1), (2) and (4). 1117
Art 9 . . . . 1103, 1116–17, 1121
    (1)and (3). 1117
Art 10 . . . . 1098, 1103, 1105
Art 11 . . . . 1103, 1109, 1119,
                1120, 1121–4
    (1) 1121
    (2) 1123
Art 12 . . . . 1103, 1109, 1119, 1123
    (1) 1124
Art 13 . . . . 1103, 1121–4
    (1) 1121
    (2) 1121
Arts 15–22 1125
Art 15 (1), (2)–(3) 1125
Art 16 1125
    (1)–(2) 1125
Art 17 1126
Art 19
    (1) 1126
    (2) 1125
Art 21 1125
    (2) 1125
Art 23
    (1) 1131
    (2) 1131
    (2) (a) 1131
Art 24 1131
Art 25 1131
Art 26(1) and (2) 1132
Art 28 . . . . 1129, 1130, 1132
Art 33 1131
Art 53(1) 1103
Ch II 1103
Convention on Protection of Children
    and Co-operation in respect of
    Intercountry Adoption 1089, 1102,
              1206, 1207, 1213–16, 1223
    Arts 1–3 1214
    Art 4 . . . . 1214, 1216, 1230
    Art 5(a) 1215
    Art 14 1215
    Art 15 . . . . 1215, 1216
    (2) 1215
    Art 16 . . . . 1215, 1216
    Art 17 1216
    Art 18 1216
    Arts 23–27 . . . . 1223, 1230
    Art 24 1224
    Art 28 1216
    Art 30 1216
    (2) 1216

Art 32 1216
Art 41 1214
Ch IV. 1215
Convention on State Immunity 498
Art 2(2) 504
Art 6(2)(b) 502
Convention on the Civil Aspects of
 International Child Abduction 69,
  72, 1089, 1102, 1122, 1134–76,
  1163–7, 1215
Art 3 . . . . 1056, 1136–7, 1148
Art 4 1135
Art 5 (a) 1138
 (b) 1137
Art 7 1139–40
Arts 8–10 1139
Art 11 1139–40
Art 12 . . . . 1140, 1142, 1159
Art 13 . . . . 1141, 1142, 1143, 1144–9,
  1153, 1159, 1160, 1161,
  1162, 1166
 (2) 1145–7
Art 13 (b) 1151–2, 1154, 1155,
  1156, 1159
Art 14 1137
Art 15 . . . . 1056–7, 1137
Art 16 1143
Art 18 1142
Art 19 1140
Art 20 . . . . 1142, 1163, 1166
Art 21 1135
Arts 22 and 26 1108
Convention on the Conflicts of Laws
 Relating to the Form of Testamentary
 Dispositions 1358 1270, 1286
Convention on the Contract for the
 International Carriage of Goods by
 Road (CMR) 203, 389,
Convention on the International
 Administration of the Estates of
 Deceased Persons 1326
Arts 1–3 1326
Art 13(1)–(2) 1327
Art 14(1–(2). 1327
Art 15 1327
Art 16 1327
Art 17 1327
Art 30 1327
Art 31 1326
Convention on the International
 Protection of Adults 1232, 1233
Art 1 1232
Art 2(a) 1233
Arts 3–4 . . . . 1233, 1245
Arts 5–11 1235

Art 5 1235
Art 6 1236
Art 7
 (1) 1237, 1238
 (2)–(3) 1238
Art 8 1238
Art 10 1236
Art 11 (2) 1237
Art 13(1)–(2) 1238
Art 14 1239
Art 15(1)–(3) 1240
Art 17 1241
Art 22(2)(b)–(d). 1243
Arts (31)–(35) 1244
Art 33 . . . . 1244, 1245
Art 34 1245
Art 57 1180
Chs III–V. 1233
Convention on the International Recovery
 of Child Support and other Forms
 of Family Maintenance. 1060,
  1070–71, 1084–6
Art 18 . . . . 1061, 1085
Art 20 . . . . 1084, 1085
 (1)(a) 1084
 (1)(b) 1084
 (1)(c) 1084, 1085
 (1)(d) 1084
 (1)(e) 1084, 1085
 (1)(f) 1084, 1085
 (2)–(5. . . . . 1084, 1085
Art 22 1084
 (a)–(f) 1085
Art 23(4) 1085, 1086
Art 23(7) 1085
Arts 51 and 52 1070
Convention on International Recovery
 of Maintenance 586
Convention on the International
 Regulations for Preventing
 Collisions at Sea 387, 388, 389, 461
Convention on the International Return
 of Stolen or Illegally Exported
 Cultural Objects. 120, 1277
Convention on the Law Applicable to
 Certain Rights in respect of Securities
 Held with an Intermediary 1302–5
Art 1(1)(b) and (e) 1304
Art 2 (1). 1304
 (2)–(3) 1303
Art 4 . . . . 718, 1303, 1304
 (1)(a)–(b) 1304
Art 5
 (1) 1304
 (3) 1305

Art 6 1305
Art 7 1304
Arts 9–10...................... 1303
Art 11(1)–(3)................... 1305
Art 12(2)(b) and (3).............. 1303
Arts 18........................ 1303
Convention on the Law Applicable to
    International Sales of Goods
Art 2 721
Art 10(1) 724
Convention on the Law Applicable to
    Products Liability......... 820, 858, 874
Art 7 823
Art 8 858
    (8) 858
Art 9 871
Convention on the Law Applicable to
    Traffic Accidents............ 819, 858,
                                860, 874
Art 7 871
Art 8 858
2............................ 860
Convention on the Law Applicable
    to Trusts and on their
    Recognition 797, 806, 841, 874,
                             1382, 1383
Arts 2–3....................... 1384
Art 4 1385
Art 5 1388
Art 6 .... 1386, 1387, 1394
Art 7 .... 1387, 1388, 1391,
                         1393, 1394
    (b) 1388
Art 8 .... 1389, 1390, 1394
    (2)(h)...................... 1395
    (h)........................ 1393
Art 9 .... 1388, 1389, 1390
Art 10 1390
Arts 11........................ 1391
Art 13 .... 1387, 1392
Art 14 1391
Art 15 .... 1386, 1387, 1389, 1392,
                         1393, 1395
Art 16 .... 1387, 1388, 1392, 1393
Art 17 1386
Art 18 ...... 1387, 1388, 1392, 1393
Art 20 1384
Convention on the Means of Prohibiting
    and Preventing the Illicit Import,
    Export and Transfer of Ownership
    of Cultural Property........ 1277, 1278
Convention on the Recognition
    of Divorces and Legal
    Separations.............. 1000, 1006
Art 1 1033

Art 3 1007
Art 9 1025
Art 10 1030
Convention on the Service Abroad
    of Judicial and Extrajudicial
    Documents in Civil
    or Commercial Matters 310,
                             381, 966–7
Art 15 310
Art 20(1) 308
Convention on the Taking of Evidence
    Abroad in Civil or Commercial
    Matters..................... 81
Guadalajara Convention Supplementary
    to the Warsaw Convention for the
    Unification of Certain Rules Relating
    to International Carriage by Air
    Performed by a Person other than the
    Contracting Carrier 9, 518, 655
Hague Conventions 9, 12
see also titles of individual conventions
    (excluding Hague)
Inter-American Convention on the
    Law Applicable to International
    Contracts 683
International Convention Relating to the
    Arrest of Sea-Going Ships......203, 283,
                             386–7, 388, 389
Montreal Convention for the Unification
    of Certain Rules relating to
    International Carriage by Air 9, 518
New York Convention on the
    Recognition and Enforcement of
    Foreign Arbitral Awards 69, 208,
                         646, 670, 671, 672, 676
Art II 416, 524
Art II (3) 646
Paris Convention for the Protection of
    Industrial Property............... 797
Art 2 831
Protocol on the Law Applicable to
    Maintenance Obligations......... 1078
United Nations Convention on
    Contracts for the International
    Sale of Goods............... 9–10, 255
Art 3(1) 256
Art 7 689
    (1) 718
Art 37 689
United Nations Convention on the Law
    of the Sea (UNCLOS)
Art 33 877
Arts 55–75..................... 877
Art 56(1) 877
Arts 76–85..................... 877

United Nations Convention on
the Limitation Period in the
International Sale of Goods
Art 6(2) 256
United Nations Convention on the
Recovery Abroad of
Maintenance 1063–4
Vienna Convention on Consular
Relations 516
Vienna Convention on Diplomatic
Intercourse and Immunities 510
Art 29 511
Warsaw Convention for the Unification
of Certain Rules Relating
to International Carriage
by Air 9, 203, 518

BILATERAL TREATIES

UK- Australia Agreement
Art 2(2) 555
UK/Australia Judgments Convention 651
UK/Canada Judgments Convention 651
UK/US Judgments Convention 651

NATIONAL LEGISLATION
OF OTHER COUNTRIES

Australia

Domicile Act 1982 . . . . 162, 195
s 5(1) and (2) 169
s 7 164
s 9 . . . . 165, 166, 167
s 10 151
s 11 147
Family Law Act 1975
s 4(3) 147
s 39(3)(b) 147
s 104 1013
Foreign Anti-Trust Judgments
(Restriction of Enforcement)
Act 1979 553
Foreign Judgments Act 1991 s 7(5) 534
Foreign States Immunities Act 1985 497
Marriage Amendment Act 1985 927
Matrimonial Causes Act 1959 147
Motor Accidents Compensation Act
1999 (New South Wales) 95

Belgium

Belgian Code on Private International Law
art 19§1 54

Canada

Charter of Rights and Freedoms 580

Civil Code (Quebec) Art 3148 410
Divorce Act 1968
s 5(1) 147
Divorce and Corollary Relief
Act 1985 147
Foreign Extraterritorial Measures
Act 1985 553

France

Civil Code 717, 719
Art 14 . . . . 611, 651
Art 148 . . . . 47–8, 49
Code Napoléon 5
Code of Civil Procedure
Articles 1448, 1455, 1465 421

Germany

Civil Code 68–9
Art 38(3) 846
Art 41(2) 815
ZPO s 23 381

India

Hindu Marriage Act 1955 934
Iraq
Resolution 369 138–9
Ireland: Jurisdiction of Courts and
Enforcement of Judgments
(European Communities)
Act 1988
Sch 5, Pt I 199

Italy

Civil Code 23, 59, 64
Art 1337 . . . . 265, 850
Japan Civil Code Art 763 1012

Netherlands

Royal Decree of 1887 10

New Zealand

Domicile Act 1976 162
s 4 169
s 5 169
(2) 168
s 6 . . . . 165, 166, 167
s 9 151
s 10 147
s 11 164
Status of Children Act 1969 1201
s5 (3) 1181
Pakistan Muslim Family Laws Ordinance
1961 . . . . . . 984, 1013, 1017, 1021, 1024
Russia Marriage Code 997

South Africa Foreign States Immunities
    Act 1981 497
Switzerland Federal Statute on Private
    International Law 1987
    Art 117 732
    Art 128(2) 846
    Art 132 855

United States

Bankruptcy Code 533
Foreign Sovereign Immunities
    Act 1976 497

Restatement of the Conflict of
    Laws, First
    § 453 847
Restatement of the Conflict of Laws,
    Second 29–31, 820
    § 2d 382
    § 6 29
    § 102, comment d 491, 546
    § 223 1259
Uniform Acknowledgement
    Act 1957 1259

TABLE OF CASES

The full alphabetical list of cases is followed by a list of Court of Justice of the European Union cases ordered by year and case number.

1st Mover APS v Direct Hedge SA [2003] IL Pr 31 . . . . .257, 728
243930 Alberta Ltd v Wickham (1990) 73 DLR (4th) 474 104
345 (Comm) [2011] 1 Lloyd's Rep 510 422
472900 BC Ltd v Thrifty Canada Ltd (1999) 168 DLR (4th) 602. .408
699; [2017] UKSC 13, [2017] 2 WLR 853 . . . . .275–6, 292, 478
7E Communications Ltd v Vertex Antennentechnik GmbH [2007] EWCA
    Civ 140, [2007] 1 WLR 2175 . . . . .238, 259, 262
A (A Child) (Abduction: Rights of Custody: Imprisonment), Re [2004] 1 FLR 1 1136
A (A Child) (Adoption of a Russian Child), Re [2000] 1 FLR 539. 1214
A (A Child) (Custody Decision after Maltese Non-Return Order), Re [2006] 1160–61
A (A Child) (Foreign Contact Order: Jurisdiction), Re [2003] EWHC 2911,
    [2004] 1 FLR 641 1099
A (A Child) (Temporary Removal from Jurisdiction), Re [2004] EWCA Civ 1587, [2005] 1
    FLR 639. 1167–9
A (A Child) (Wardship: Habitual Residence), Re [2006] EWHC 3338 (Fam), [2007] 1
    FCR 390 1110
A (A Child), Re [2016] EWCA Civ 572. 1135
A (A Minor) (Abduction), Re [1988] 1 FLR 365, [1988] Fam Law 54. . . . . .1140, 1153
A (A Minor) (Wardship: Jurisdiction), Re [1995] 1 FLR 767 1107
A (A Minor) (Wrongful Removal of Child), Re [1988] Fam Law 383 1153
A (Abduction: Child's Objections to Return), Re [2014] EWCA Civ 554 1145
A (Abduction: Consent: Habitual Residence: Consent), Re [2005] EWHC 2998,
    [2006] 2 FLR 1 . . . . .1149, 1153
A (Abduction: Custody Rights), Re [1992] Fam 106 1150
A (Abduction: Declaration of Wrongful Removal), Re [2002] NI 114 1056
A (Abduction: Habitual Residence), Re [1998] 1 FLR 497 . . . . .176, 180–1, 1097
A (An Infant), Re [1963] 1 WLR 231 1211
A (Children) (Abduction: Objections: Non-Return), Re [2013] EWCA Civ 1256. 1146
A (Children) (Brussels II Revised: Article 15), Re [2014] EWFC 40 . . . . .1114, 1116
A (Children), Re [2015] EWCA Civ 133. 1052
A (Leave to Remove: Cultural and Religious Considerations), Re [2006] EWHC 421,
    [2006] 2 FLR 572 1169
A (Minors) (Abduction: Custody Rights), Re (No 2) [1993] Fam 1 . . . . .1143 . . . . .
A (Minors) (Abduction: Custody Rights), Re [1992] Fam 106. . . . . .1149–50, 152
A (Minors) (Abduction: Habitual Residence), Re [1996] 1 WLR 25 . . . . .176, 181–2
A (Parental Order: Domicile), Re [2013] EWHC 426 (Fam) 1184, 1188
A (Permission to Remove Child from Jurisdiction: Human Rights), Re [2000]
    2 FLR 225 1168
A (Wardship: Jurisdiction), Re [1995] 1 FLR 767 . . . . .177, 183, 1107
A and B (Children: Surrogacy: Parental Orders: Time limit) [2015] EWHC 911. 1186
A and B (Parental Order: Domicile), Re [2013] EWHC 426. 156
A and B v C and D [1982] 1 Lloyd's Rep 166 370
A Child (Hague Convention Proceedings), Re [2014] EWCA Civ 375 1157
A Co Ltd v B Co Ltd and Republic of Z, 1993 (unreported) 506
A Company Ltd v Republic of X [1990] 2 Lloyd's Rep 520 . . . . .506, 513
A County Council v M & Others (No 4) (Foreign Adoption: Refusal of
    Recognition) [2013] EWHC 1501. . . . . .1225, 1227–8
A Debtor, Re (No 11 of 1939) [1939] 2 All ER 400 595

A J Smeman Car Sales v Richardsons Pre-Run Cars (1969) 63 QJPR 150 1272
A LBC v Department for Children, Schools and Families [2009] EWCA Civ 41 1218
A Local Authority v MGM [2014] EWHC 1221 1115
A Local Authority v X [2013] EWHC 3274 . . . . .910, 916, 923, 986, 991, 1050–1
A Ltd v B Bank and Bank of X [1997] FSR 165 . . . . .349, 505
A v A (Attorney General Intervening) [2012] EWHC 2219 1051
A v A (Child Abduction) [1993] 2 FLR 225 . . . . .1107, 1143, 1150
A v A (Child: Removal from Jurisdiction), Re [1979] 1 FLR 380 1168
A v A (Children: Habitual Residence) (Reunite International Child Abduction . . . .
A v A (Forum Conveniens) [1999] 1 FLR 1 . . . . .373, 431
A v A and Another (Children: Habitual Residence) (Reunite International
    Child Abduction Centre and Others Intervening) [2013] UKSC 60 1158
A v A, 2 February 2004 (unreported) 736, 1168
A v B (C-112/13) EU:C:2014:2195 . . . . .227, 628, 634
A v B (C-184/14) 16 July 2015, ECLI:EU:C:2015:479 . . . . .1066, 1074, 1083
A v B (Jurisdiction) [2011] EWHC 2752 1117–18
A v B (No 2) [2007] EWHC 54 (Comm), [2007] 1 Lloyd's Rep 358 . . . . .232, 355, 437, 479, 506
A v B [2006] EWHC 2006 (Comm), [2007] 1 Lloyd's Rep 237 . . . . .420, 460, 479
A v B [2015] EWHC 1562 . . . . .1148, 1151
A v C [2016] EWFC 42 1186
A v D [2014] EWHC 3851 1115
A v H [2009] EWHC 636 . . . . .1137, 1199
A v K [2011] CSOH 101 898
A v L (Overseas Divorce) [2010] EWHC 460 .1011, 1019, 1027, 1029–30
A v L [2010] EWHC 460 (Fam), [2010] 2 FLR 1418 574
A v P [2011] EWHC 1738 1185
A v S (Financial Relief after Overseas US Divorce) [2002] EWHC 1157,
    [2003] 1 FLR 431 1076–8
A v T (Abduction: Consent) [2011] EWHC 3882 . . . . .1148, 1151
A, HA v MB (Brussels II Revised: Article 11(7) Application), Re [2007]
    EWHC 2016 . . . . .1158, 1160, 1161
A, Re [1970] Ch 665 1110
A, Re [2015] EWFC 25 15
A, Re [2015] EWHC 1756 1184–7
A, Re [2015] EWHC 2080 1186
A/S Nyborg Plast v Lameque Quality Group Ltd (2001) 213 DLR (4th) 301 411
A/S Svendborg v Ali Hussein Akar [2003] EWHC 797 (Comm) 437
A/S Svendborg v Wansa [1997] 2 Lloyd's Rep 183 . . . . .235, 439, 440, 534, 560, 573
AA v BB, [2015] EWCA Civ 1138 1074–5
AA v TT (Recognition and Enforcement) [2014] EWHC 3488 .1167
AAA v Unilever plc [2017] EWHC 371 (QB) 366, 373, 471
Aannemingsbedrijf Aertssen NV and Aertssen Terrassements SA v VSB
    Machineverhuur BV (C-523/14) EU:C:2015:722, [2016] IL Pr 16 . . . . .206, 448
Aaronson Bros Ltd v Maderera del Tropico SA [1967] 2 Lloyd's Rep 159 . . . . .343, 372
AB and Another v GH [2016] EWHC 2063 . . . . .1184–6, 1188
AB Bank Ltd, Off-Shore Banking Unit (OBU) v Abu Dhabi Commercial
    Bank PJSC [2016] EWHC 2082 (Comm), 2082 (Comm), [2017]
    1 WLR 810; Bushell (2017) 133 LQR 188 . . . . .306, 340
AB v CB (Divorce and Maintenance: Discretion to Stay) [2013] EWCA Civ 1255 976
AB v CB [2013] EWCA Civ 1255, [2014] 2 WLR 1033 474
AB v CD [2000] Fam LR 91 1172
AB v CD [2015] EWFC 12 1185–7
AB v JJB [2015] EWHC 192 1081
Abbassi v Abbassi [2006] EWCA Civ 355, [2006] 2 FLR 415, [2006] 2 FLR 648 . . . . .1027, 1051
Abbott v Abbott, 130 S Ct 1983 (2010) 109

ABCI (Formerly Arab Business Consortium International Finance and
    Investment Co) v Banque Franco-Tunisienne [2003] EWCA Civ 205, [2003]
    2 Lloyd's Rep 146. . . . . .342–3, 349, 351–2, 508
ABCI v BFT [1996] 1 Lloyd's Rep 485, [1997] 1 Lloyd's Rep 531. . . . . .559, 612, 669
Abela v Baadarani [2013] UKSC 44, [2013] 1 WLR 2043. . . . . .326, 376, 381
Abidin Daver, The [1984] AC 398 . . . . .393, 397, 400, 402–3, 406–9, 412
ABKCO Music & Records Inc v Music Collection International Ltd [1995] RPC 657 217
Abouloff v Oppenheimer (1882) 10 QBD 295 570
Abu Dhabi Investment Co v H Clarkson & Co Ltd [2006] EWHC 1252
    (Comm), [2006] 2 Lloyd's Rep 381 . . . . .107, 111, 419
Abusabib v Taddese [2013] ICR 603, EAT. 511, 513
Accentuate Ltd v Asigra Inc [2009] EWHC 2655 (QB), [2010] 2 All ER (Comm) 738 676
Ace Insurance SA-NV (Formerly Cigna Insurance Co of Europe SA NV)
    v Zurich Insurance Co [2001] EWCA Civ 173, [2001] 1 Lloyd's. 227, 369, 371,
                                                                                398, 414, 461, 473
Achillopoulos, Re [1928] Ch 433. . . . . .1325, 1334
Ackerman v Logan's Executor (No 1) 2002 SLT 37 893
Ackerman v Synergy Capital [2013] EWHC 887 (Ch) 1386
Actavis Group HF v Eli Lilly & Co [2013] EWCA Civ 517, [2013] RPC 985 331
Actavis UK Ltd v Eli Lilly & Co [2014] EWHC 1511. 832–3
Actavis UK Ltd v Eli Lilly & Co [2015] EWCA Civ 555. . . . . 88, 94, 799–801,
                                                                                858–9, 861, 864
Actial Farmaceutica Lda v De Simone [2016] EWCA Civ 1311. 275
Adams v Adams [1971] P 188 . . . . .168, 216, 565
Adams v Cape Industries plc [1990] Ch 433 . . . . 141, 329–30, 520, 526, 528–9,
                                                                                540–1, 565, 568, 573, 576
Adams v Clutterbuck (1883) 10 QBD 403 1259
Adams v National Bank of Greece and Athens [1958] 2 QB 59 50
Adams, Re [1967] IR 424 . . . . .71, 161–2
Addax BV Geneva Branch v Coral Suki SA [2004] EWHC 2882 (Comm), [2005]
    2 All ER (Comm). 381
Adderson v Adderson (1987) 36 DLR (4th) 631 179
Addison v Addison [1955] NI 1. 994
Addison v Brown [1954] 1 WLR 779 134
Adhiguna Meranti, The [1988] 1 Lloyd's Rep 384 . . . . .394, 402
ADM Asia-Pacific Trading Pte Ltd v PT Budi Semesta Satria [2016]
    EWHC 1427 (Comm). 439
Adolf Warski, The [1976] 2 Lloyd's Rep 241 412
Adria Services YU v Grey Shipping Co Ltd 30 July 1993 (unreported). 395
Advanced Cardiovascular Systems Inc v Universal Specialties Ltd [1997] 1 NZLR 186 371
Advanced Portfolio Technologies Inc v Ainsworth [1996] FSR 217 .429
Advent Capital plc v Ellinas Imports-Exports Ltd [2005] EWHC 1242
    (Comm), [2005] 2 Lloyd's Rep 607 478
Advent Capital plc v GN Ellinas Importers-Exporters Ld [2003] EWHC 3330,
    [2004] IL Pr 23 . . . . .439, 450, 478, 481
Aeroflot— Russian Airlines v Berezovsky [2013] EWCA Civ 784, [2013]
    2 Lloyd's Rep 242. 232
AES Ust-Kamenogorsk Hydropower Plant LLP v AES Ust-Kamenogorsk
    Hydropower Plant JSC [2011] EWCA Civ 647, [2012] 1 WLR 920 . . . . .538, 584, 587
AES Ust-Kamenogorsk Hydropower Plant LLP v Ust-Kamenogorsk
    Hydropower Plant JSC [2013] UKSC 35, [2013] 1 WLR 1889. . . . . .436, 441–2
AF (Father) v T (Mother) [2011] EWHC 1315. 1160
Afala, The [1995] 2 Lloyd's Rep 286 384
Affymetrix Inc v Multilyte Ltd [2004] EWHC 291 (Ch),
    [2005] IL Pr 34 392

Africa Express Line Ltd v Socofi SA [2009] EWHC 3223 (Comm), [2010] 2 All ER
  (Comm) 1085 234
African Fertilizers and Chemicals NIG Ltd (Nigeria) v BD Shipsnavo GmbH & Co
  Reederei KG [2011] EWHC 2452 (Comm), [2011] 2 Lloyd's Rep 531 . . . . .639, 646
Afza Mussarat v Secretary of State for the Home Department [1972] Imm AR 45 937
A-G (UK) v Heinemann Publishers Australia Pty Ltd (1987) 75 ALR 353 . . . . .115, 123, 780
A-G (UK) v Heinemann Publishers Australia Pty Ltd (No 2) (1988) 165 CLR 30 . . . . . . .115, 123
A-G for England and Wales v R [2002] 2 NZLR 91 105
A-G for the United Kingdom v Wellington Newspapers Ltd [1988] 1 NZLR 129 . . . . . . .115, 123
A-G for Victoria v Commonwealth of Australia (1961–1962) 107 CLR 529 1198
A-G for Zambia v Meer Care & Desai (A fi rm) [2005] EWHC 2120 (Ch), [2006]
  EWCA Civ 390, [2006] 1 CLC 436 . . . . .14, 366, 372
A-G of Ceylon v Reid [1965] AC 720 . . . . .934, 936–7, 953
A-G of New Zealand v Ortiz [1984] AC 1 . . . . .115, 117–23, 126
A-G of Zambia v Meer Care and Desai (A firm) [2005] EWHC 2102 (Ch) 14, 366, 372
A-G v Arthur Andersen & Co (United Kingdom) [1989] ECC 224 408
A-G v Bouwens (1838) 4 M & W 171 1298
A-G v Campbell (1872) LR 5 HL 524 . . . . .1386, 1388
A-G v Donaldson Lufkin and Jenrette Inc [1990] 1 QB 391 . . . . .78, 347–51,
                                                             359, 364, 373, 405, 777–8
A-G v Guardian Newspapers Ltd (No 2) [1990] 1 AC 109, 264–5, HL 123
A-G v Jewish Colonization Association [1901] 1 KB 123 1386
A-G v Kent (1862) 31 LJ Ex 391, 397 160
A-G v Lady Rowe (1862) 1 H & C 31 160
A-G v Lord Sudeley [1896] 1 QB 354 1280
A-G v Mill (1827) 3 Russ 328, 2 Dow and Clark 393 1347
A-G v Nissan [1970] AC 179, HL 114
A-G v Parsons [1956] AC 421 1258
A-G v Pottinger (1861) 30 LJ Ex 284, 292 152
A-G v Prince Ernest Augustus of Hanover [1957] AC 436 1050
A-G v Yule (1931) 145 LT 9 . . . . .149, 152, 162
A-G v Yule and Mercantile Bank of India (1931) 145 LT 9 162
Aganoor's Trusts, Re (1895) 64 LJ Ch 521 . . . . .1339, 1386
Agbaje v Akinnoye-Agbaje [2010] UKSC 13 1075–7
AGF Kosmos Assurances Générales v Surgil Trans Express [2007] IL Pr 24 640
AGF v Chiyoda [1992] 1 Lloyd's Rep 325 455
Aggeliki Charis Compañía Marítima SA v Pagnan SpA, The Angelic Grace
  [1995] 1 Lloyd's Rep 87 . . . . .424, 436–7, 440–1
Agnew v Lansforsakringsbolagens AB [2001] 1 AC 223 . . . . .247–8, 250, 252,
                                                                263, 264, 851
Agnew v Usher (1884) 14 QBD 78, 51 LT 752 356
Agosi v United Kingdom (1986) A 108 1278
Agrafax Public Relations Ltd v United Scottish Society Inc [1995] IL Pr 753 . . . . .346, 364
Agromet Motoimport v Maulden Engineering Co (Beds) Ltd [1985] 1 WLR 762 . . . . . . .666, 673
Aguilar Quila v Secretary of State for the Home Department [2011] UKSC 45 992
Ah Chong, Re (1913) 33 NZLR 384 930
AH v PH (Scandinavian Marriage Settlement) [2014] 2 FLR 251 1379
AH v Secretary of State for the Home Department [2006] UKIAT 38, [2006]
  INLR 517 893
Ahmed Mahamdia v République algérienne démocratique et populaire (C-154/11)
  EU:C:2012:491, [2014] All ER (EC) 96 . . . . .204, 280, 299, 302, 517
Ahmed v Habib Bank Ltd [2001] EWCA Civ 1270, [2002] 1 Lloyd's
  Rep 444 . . . . .551, 569, 594, 598
Ahuja v Politika Novine I Magazini Doo [2015] EWHC 3380 (QB),
  [2016] 1 WLR 1414 . . . . .14, 355

AIC Ltd v Federal Government of Nigeria [2003] EWHC 1357 (QB),
  [2003] All ER (D) 190 . . . . .500, 504, 509, 591–2, 602
AIG Capital Partners Inc v Republic of Kazakhstan [2005] EWHC 2239 (Comm),
  [2006] 1 All ER 284 . . . . .498, 509
AIG Europe v The Ethniki [1998] 4 All ER 301, [2000] 2 All ER 566 252–3
AIG v Ethniki [1998] 4 All ER 301, [2000] 2 All ER 566, CA 234, 252–3
AIG v QBE International Insurance Ltd [2001] 2 Lloyd's Rep 268 234
Aiglon v Gau Shan [1993] 1 Lloyd's Rep 164 461
Air Crash Disaster Near Chicago Illinois on May 25, Re, 1979 644 F 2d 594 (1981) 31
Air Foyle Ltd v Center Capital Ltd [2002] EWHC 2535 (Comm), [2003]
  2 Lloyd's Rep 753 . . . . .545, 559, 560, 563, 1252, 1267
Air India Ltd v CaribjetInc [2002] 2 All ER (Comm) 76 117
Air Link Pty Ltd v Paterson (2005) 218 ALR 700 42
Air Nauru v Niue Airlines Ltd [1993] 2 NZLR 632 411
Airbus Industrie GIE v Patel [1999] 1 AC 119 . . . . 424–6, 428, 431,
                                                                                435, 437, 978
Airey v Ireland, Judgment of 9 October 1979, Series A, No 32; (1979) 2 EHRR 305 14
Aitchison v Dixon (1870) LR 10 Eq 589 156
AJ (A Minor) (Brussels II Revised), Re [2011] EWHC 3450 1161
AJ v JJ [2011] EWCA Civ 1448 1145
AK Investment CJSC v Kyrgyz Mobil Tel Ltd [2011] UKPC 7 .217
Akai Pty Ltd v People's Insurance Co Ltd [1998] 1 Lloyd's Rep 90 . . . . 398, 408, 413, 416,
                                                                    438–9, 538–40, 700, 754
Akande v Balfour Beatty Construction Ltd [1998] IL Pr 110 . . . . .528–9, 531, 539, 591
Akers v Samba Financial Group [2014] EWCA Civ 1516; [2015] Ch 451 . . . . . .1385, 1387, 1393
Akhtar v Rafiq [2006] 1 FLR 27 966
Akram v Adam [2004] EWCA 1601 . . . . .987, 992
Akram v Akram 1979 SLT (Notes) 87 987
Al Amoudi v Brisard [2006] EWHC 1062 (QB) 351, 887
Al Attiya v Bin-Jassim Bin-Jaber Al Thant [2016] EWHC 212 (QB) 498, 508, 510
Al Battani, The [1993] 2 Lloyd's Rep 219 . . . . .397, 405
Al Habtoor v Fotheringham [2001] EWCA Civ 186, [2001] 1 FLR 951 . . . . .176, 181–2
AL, Petitioner [2007] CSOH 55 1153
Al-Adsani v Government of Kuwait (No 2) (1996) 107 ILR 536 .501
Al-Adsani v United Kingdom (2001) 34 EHRR 273 501
Al-Bassam v Al-Bassam [2004] EWCA Civ 857, [2004] WTLR 757 . . . . .14, 105, 1344
Alberta Inc v Katanga Mining Ltd [2008] EWHC 2679 (Comm), [2009] IL Pr 14 201
Alberta Ltd v Wickham (1990) 73 DLR (4th) 474 104
Albon v Naza Motor Trading [2007] EWHC 9 (Ch), [2007] 1 Lloyd's
  Rep 297 . . . . 341–2, 377, 418, 420,
                                                                                422, 429, 728
Albon v Naza Motor Trading Sdn Bhd (No 3) [2007] EWHC 327 (Ch),
  [2007] 2 Lloyd's Rep 1 . . . . .341–2, 377, 418, 420, 422, 429, 728
Alcock v Smith [1892] 1 Ch 238 . . . . .1266, 1268, 1282, 1295, 1297
Alcom Ltd v Republic of Colombia [1984] AC 580 .504–6, 509
Alder v Orlowska (C-325/11) EU:C:2012:824 308
Aldington Shipping Ltd v Bradstock Shipping Corpn and Mabanaft GmbH,
  The Waylink and Brady Maria [1988] 1 Lloyd's Rep 475 . . . . .394, 403
Aldrich v A-G [1968] P 281 . . . . .1049, 1330
Alfonso-Brown v Milwood [2006] EWHC 642, [2006] 2 FLR 265 898
Alfred Dunhill Ltd v Diffusion Internationale de Maroquinerie de Prestige [2002]
  IL Pr 13 . . . . .263, 273, 277
Alhaji Mohamed v Knott [1969] 1 QB 1 165
Ali Ebrahim v Ali Ebrahim [1983] 1 WLR 1336 966
Ali v Ali [1968] P 564 . . . . .913, 929, 931, 935, 937

Al-Jedda v Secretary of State for Defence [2010] EWCA Civ 758 114
Al-Koronky v Time Life Entertainment Group Ltd [2006] EWCA Civ 1123. 403
All ER 372. 368
Allen v Kemble (1848) 6 Moo PCC 314 96
Allen's Estate, Re [1945] 2 All ER 264 1355
Alliance Bank JSC v Aquanta Corporation [2012] EWCA Civ 1588, [2013]
    1 Lloyd's Rep 175. . . . . .342, 721
Allianz v West Tankers [2009] ECR I-663 (C-185/07) [2009] 1 AC 1138. . . . . .444, 479
Allison, Re (1979) 96 DLR (3d) 342 1110
Alloway v Phillips [1980] 1 WLR 888 1281
Alltrans Inc v Interdom [1991] 2 Lloyd's Rep 571 306
Al-Malki v Reyes [2015] EWCA Civ 32, [2016] 1 WLR 1785. . . . . .501, 503, 511–13
Al-Midani v Al-Midani [1999] 1 Lloyd's Rep 923 670
Al-Naimi v Islamic Press Agency Inc [2000] 1 Lloyd's Rep 522 418
Alpenhof GesmbH v Heller [2010] ECR I-12527 . . . . .294, 295, 688
Alpha Laval Tumba AB v Separator Spares International Ltd [2012] EWCA
    Civ 1569, [2013] 1 WLR 1110 298
Al-Saedy v Musawi [2010] EWHC 3293 894–6
Altertext Inc v Advanced Data Communications Ltd [1985] 1 WLR 457 . . . . .340, 486
Altimo Holdings and Investments Ltd v Kyrgiz Mobil Tel Ltd [2011] UKPC 7,
    [2012] 1 WLR 1804 . . . . .571, 574, 577
Alton v Alton 207 F 2d 667 981
Aluminium Industrie Vaassen BV v Romalpa Aluminium Ltd [1976] 1 WLR 676 1272
Al-Wazir v Islamic Press Agency Inc [2001] EWCA Civ 1276, [2002] 1 Lloyd's
    Rep 410 105
Amalgamated Metal Trading Ltd v Baron [2010] EWHC 3207 (Comm), [2012]
    1 CLC 920. 381
Amalgamated Wireless (Australasia) Ltd v McDonnell Douglas Corpn (1988) 77
    ALR 537 330
Amaltal Corpn Ltd v Maruha (NZ) Corpn Ltd [2004] 2 NZLR 614. 674
Amanuel v Alexandros Shipping Co, The Alexandros P [1986] 1 QB 464 366
Amazone, The [1940] P 40. 510
Amazonia, The [1990] 1 Lloyd's Rep 236. 108
Ambrose v Ambrose (1961) 25 DLR (2d) 1 897
Amchem Products Inc v Workers' Compensation Board (1993) 102
    DLR (4th) 96. . . . . .394, 395, 425, 428, 430
American International Specialty Lines Insurance Co v Abbott Laboratories [2002]
    EWHC 2714 (Comm), [2003] 1 Lloyd's Rep 267 . . . . .436, 720
American Motorists Insurance Co v Cellstar Corpn [2002] EWHC 421, [2002]
    2 Lloyd's Rep 216, [2003] EWCA Civ 206, [2003] 367, 369, 375, 462,
                                                                                                        718, 721, 728, 736
American Surety Co of New York v Wrightson (1910) 16 Com Cas 37 89
Amin Rasheed Shipping Corpn v Kuwait Insurance Co [1984] AC 50 . . . . 4, 70, 345, 366,
                                                                                                        375, 403, 719
Amin v Brown [2005] EWHC 1670 (Ch), [2006] IL Pr 5 496
Amlin Corporate Member Ltd v Oriental Assurance Corp [2012] EWCA Civ 1341, [2013]
    Lloyd's Rep IR 131. 421
Amoco (UK) Exploration Co v British American Offshore Ltd [1999]
    2 Lloyd's Rep 772. . . . . .336–7, 342, 367, 423–4
Amopharm Inc v Harris Computer Corpn (1992) 93 DLR (4th) 524 537
AMS Neve Ltd v Heritage Audio SL [2016] EWHC 2563 (IPEC). 264, 275–6, 278
AMT Futures Ltd v Grundmann [2016] EWHC 3606 (QB). 292
AMT Futures Ltd v Marzillier, Dr Meier & Dr Guntner Rechtsanwaltsgesellschaft
    mbH [2014] EWHC 1085 (Comm), [2015] 2 WLR 187, revd [2015] EWCA
    Civ 143, [2015] QB

AmTrust Europe Ltd v Trust Risk Group SpA [2015] EWCA Civ 437, [2016] 1 All ER
    (Comm) 325 237
An English Local Authority v SW [2014] EWCOP 43. 1235
Analog Devices BV v Zurich Insurance Co [2002] 2 ILRM 366 . . . . .338, 346
Anan Kasei Co Ltd v Molycorp Chemicals & Oxides (Europe) Ltd [2016]
    EWHC 1722 (Pat), [2016] Bus LR 945. . . . . .217, 225
ANCAP v Ridgley [1996] 1 Lloyd's Rep 570 . . . . .334, 377
Anchor Line (Henderson Bros) Ltd, Re [1937] Ch 483 489
Anderson v Equitable Assurance Society of the United States (1926) 134 LT 557 47
Anderton v Clwyd CC (No 2) [2002] EWCA Civ 933, [2002] 1 WLR 3174 326
Andre & Cie SA v Ets Michel Blanc & Fils [1979] 2 Lloyd's Rep 427 108
Andreas Kainz v Pantherwerke AG (C-45/13) EU:C:2014:7, [2015]
    QB 34 . . . . .248, 263, 267, 272, 785
Andromeda Marine SA v OW Bunker & Trading A/S (The Mana) [2006]
    EWHC 777 (Comm), [2006] 2 Lloyd's Rep 319 242
Andros, Re (1883) 24 Ch D 637 . . . . .1195, 1198, 1201, 1203
Angba v Marie (2006) 263 DLR (4th) 562 576
Anglo-Austrian Bank, Re [1920] 1 Ch 69 724
Anglo-Iranian Oil Co v Jaffrate (The Rose Mary) [1953] 1 WLR 246, Sup Ct of Aden 130
Anna H, The [1995] 1 Lloyd's Rep 11 386
Annesley, Re [1926] Ch 692 . . . . .59, 61, 66, 71, 168, 1345, 1385
Anstruther v Adair (1834) 2 My & K 513 1372
Antec International Ltd v Biosafety USA Inc [2006] EWHC 47 . . . . .370, 466
Anton Durbeck GmbH v Den Norske Bank ASA [2002] EWHC 1173 (Comm),
    [2003] QB 1160 . . . . .263, 272, 282
Anton Schlecker v Melitta Josefa Boedeker (C-64/12) ECLI:EU:C:2013:551 . . . . .737, 741
Anton v Bartolo (1891) Clunet 1171 42
Antonio Gramsci Shipping Corp v Stepanovs [2011] EWHC 333 (Comm), [2012]
    1 All ER (Comm) 293 242
Antonis P Lemos, The [1985] AC 711 382
Anziani, Re [1930] 1 Ch 407 . . . . .1268, 1282, 1287
AP Moller-Maersk A/S v Sonaec Villas Cen Sad Fadoul [2010] EWHC 355
    (Comm), [2010] 2 All ER (Comm) 1159 234
AP v TD (Relocation: Retention of Jurisdiction) [2010] EWHC 2040 . . . . .1098, 1106
Apcoa Parking (UK) Ltd, Re [2014] EWHC 997. 709
Apex Global Management Ltd v Fi Call Ltd [2013] EWCA Civ 642 . . . . .512, 516
Apis AS v Fantazia Kereskedelmi [2001] 1 All ER (Comm) 348. 673
Apostolides v Orams (C-420/07) [2009] ECR I-3571 . . . . 523, 612, 618, 627–8,
    631–2, 638, 642
Apple Computer Inc v Apple Corps SA [1990] 2 NZLR 598. 411
Apple Corps Ltd v Apple Computer Inc [1992] FSR 431 . . . . .136, 364, 367, 733, 752
Apple Corps Ltd v Apple Computer Inc [2004] EWHC 768 (Ch), [2004]
    IL Pr 34 . . . . .136, 343, 364, 367–8, 733–5
Apt v Apt [1948] P 83 . . . . .898, 987–8
Aquavita International SA v Ashapura Minecham Ltd [2014] EWHC 2806 721
AR (A Child: Relocation), Re [2010] EWHC 1346. 1170
AR v RN [2015] UKSC 35 . . . . .175, 179, 181, 183, 1095–6
Arab Bank Ltd v Barclays Bank (Dominion, Colonial and Overseas) [1954]
    AC 495 1292
Arab Business Consortium International Finance and Investment Co v Banque
    Franco Tunisienne [1996] 1 Lloyd's Rep 485 208
Arab Business Consortium International Finance and Investment Co v Banque
    Franco-Tunisienne [1996] 1 Lloyd's Rep 485. . . . . .342–3, 349, 351, 352, 508
Arab Monetary Fund v Hashim (No 3) [1991] 2 AC 114 . . . . .4, 514
Arab Monetary Fund v Hashim (No 4) [1992] 1 WLR 1176. .338

Arab Monetary Fund v Hashim (No 6) (1992) Times, 24 July 428
Arab Monetary Fund v Hashim (No 8) (1993) Times, 17 June 107, 428, 779
Arab Monetary Fund v Hashim (No 9) (1994) Times, 11 October 107, 808, 867
Arab Monetary Fund v Hashim [1996] 1 Lloyd's Rep 589 . . . . .78–9, 107, 515, 779, 867
Arab Republic of Egypt v Gamal-Eldin [1996] 2 All ER 237 504–5
Aratra Potato Co Ltd v Egyptian Navigation Co, The El Amria [1981] 2 Lloyd's
  Rep 119 403
Arblade (C-369/96) [1999] ECR I-8453 and (C-374/96) [1998] ECR I-8385 . . . . .746, 866
Arbuthnot Latham & Co Ltd v M3 Marine Ltd [2013] EWHC 1019 449
Arcadia Petroleum Ltd v Bosworth [2016] EWCA Civ 818 . . . . .43, 268, 298
Archer v Preston, undated 487
Ardila Investments NV v ENRC NV [2015] EWHC 1667 (Comm), [2015]
  2 BCLC 560 432
Arglasse v Muschamp (1682) 1 Vern 76 487–8
Ark Therapeutics plc v True North Capital Ltd [2005] EWHC 1585 (Comm),
  [2006] 1 All ER (Comm) 138 . . . . .732, 734
Arkwright Mutual Insurance Co v Bryanston Insurance [1990] 2 QB 649 . . . . 408, 460,
                                                                                    467, 494
ARM Asset Backed Securities SA (No 2), Re [2014] EWHC 1310 . . . .
ARM Asset Backed Securities SA, Re [2013] EWHC 3351 (Ch) 1097 . . . .
Armar Shipping Co Ltd v Caisse Algérienne d'Assurance et de Réassurance,
  The Armar [1980] 2 Lloyd's Rep 450, [1981] 1 WLR 207 .344, 716
Armitage v A-G [1906] P 135 . . . . .69, 1007, 1019, 1021, 1023
Armitage v Nanchen (1983) 4 FLR 293 . . . . .1064, 1081
Armour v Thyssen Edelstahlwerke AG [1991] 2 AC 339 1272–3
Armstrong International Ltd v Deutsche Bank Securities Inc QBD,
  11 July 2003 (unreported) 736
Armstrong v Armstrong [2003] EWHC 777 (Fam), [2003] 2 FLR 375 . . . . 177, 180,
                                                                                    955, 958, 974
Armytage v Armytage [1898] P 178 980
Arnott v Redfern (1825) 2 C & P 88 20
Arros Invest Ltd v Rafik Nishanov [2004] EWHC 576 (Ch), [2004] IL Pr 22 . . . . .112, 381
Arrowmaster Inc v Unique Forming Ltd [1995] IL Pr 505 550
Arsanovia Ltd v Cruz City 1 Mauritius Holdings [2012] EWHC 3702 (Comm),
  [2013] 2 All ER (Comm) 1 667
Artic Fish Sales Co Ltd v Adam (No 2) 1996 SLT 970 . . . . .625, 628, 632, 637
Arum, The [1921] P 12 876
Asaad v Kurter [2013] EWHC 3852 . . . . .893, 895–6, 998–9
ASB and KBS v MQS (Secretary of State for the Home Department Intervening)
  [2009] EWHC 2491 1230
Asbestos Insurance Coverage Cases, Re [1985] 1 WLR 331, HL 83
Ascherberg Hopwood and Crew v Casa Musicale Sonzogno [1971] 1 WLR 173 106
Asefa Yesuf Import and Export v AP Moller Maersk A/ S [2016] EWHC 1437 308
Ash v Corpn of Lloyd's [1993] IL Pr 330 404
Ashingdane v United Kingdom, Judgment of 28 May 1985, Series A, No 93, para 57;
  (1985) 7 EHRR 528 14
Ashley v Tesco Stores Ltd [2015] EWCA Civ 414, [2015] 1 WLR 5153 328
Ashton Investments Ltd v OJSC Russian Aluminium RUSAL [2006] EWHC 2545
  (Comm), [2007] 1 Lloyd's Rep 311 . . . . .350–1, 357, 360, 363
Ashurst v Pollard [2001] Ch 595 . . . . .208, 219–20, 1255
Askew, Re [1930] 2 Ch 259 . . . . .8, 21, 59–60, 65–7, 71
Askin v Absa Bank Ltd [1999] IL Pr 471 397
ASML Netherlands BV v Semiconductor Industry Services GmbH (SEMIS)
  (C-283/05) [2007] IL Pr 4 . . . . .198, 633, 635, 639, 1082
Aspinall's Club Ltd v Fouad Al-Zayat [2007] EWHC 362 (Comm) 1295–6

Assunzione, The [1954] P 150 724
Astilleros Zamakona SA v MacKinnons 2002 SLT 1206 242
Astra SA Insurance and Reinsurance Co v Sphere Drake Insurance Ltd [2000]
    All ER (D) 672 109
AstraZeneca UK Ltd v Albemarle International Corp [2010] EWHC 1028 (Comm),
    [2010] 2 Lloyd's Rep 61 360
Astro Valiente Compañía Naviera SA v Pakistan Ministry of Food and Agriculture
    (No 2) [1982] 1 WLR 1096 418
Astro Venturoso Compañía Naviera v Hellenic Shipyards SA, The Mariannina [1983]
    1 Lloyd's Rep 12 . . . . .419, 716
AT v SS [2015] EWHC 2703 . . . . .1151–5, 1159
Athenee, The (1922) 11 Lloyd's Rep 6 385
Atkinson Footwear Ltd v Hodgskin (1995) 31 IPR 186 494
Atlanska Plovidba v Consignaciones Asturianas SA (The Lapad) [2004] EWHC
    1273 (Comm), [2004] 2 Lloyd's Rep 109 442
Atlantic Star, The [1974] AC 436 . . . . .384–5, 393, 402, 405
Atlantic Telecom GmbH, Noter 2004 SLT 1031 . . . . .43, 692, 694,
                                                                                         728, 1283, 1299
Atlas Shipping v Suisse Atlantique [1995] 2 Lloyd's Rep 188 246
Attock Cement Co Ltd v Romanian Bank for Foreign Trade [1989] 1 WLR 1147 344
Attorney-General for England and Wales v R [2002] 2 NZLR 91 CA 105
Audrain v Aero Photo Inc (1983) 138 DLR (3d) 177 549
Auerbach v Resorts International Hotel Inc (1991) 89 DLR (4th) 688 . . . . .136, 574
Augustus v Permanent Trustee Co (Canberra) Ltd (1971) 124 CLR 245 1386
Australian Broadcasting Corpn v Lenah Game Meats Pty Ltd (2001) 185 ALR 1 . . . . . . .425, 428
Australian Broadcasting Corpn v Waterhouse (1991) 25 NSWLR 519 888
Australian Commercial Research and Development Ltd v ANZ McCaughan
    Merchant Bank Ltd [1989] 3 All ER 65 408–9
Austro-Mechana Gesellschaft zur Wahrnehmung mechanisch-musikalischer
    Urheberrechte Gesellschaft mbH v Amazon EU Sàrl (C-572/14) EU:C:
    2016:286, [2016] ECDR 23 . . . . .264, 267, 790, 792, 805
Auten v Auten 308 NY 155, 124 NE 2d 99 (1954) 682
AVH v SI (Abduction: Child's Objection) [2014] EWHC 2938 . . . . .1143, 1146–7
AWB (Geneva) SA v North America Steamships Ltd [2007] EWCA Civ 739,
    [2007] 2 Lloyd's Rep 315 437
AXA Corporate Solutions Assurance SA v Weir Services Australia Pty Limited [2016]
    EWHC 904 (Comm) 421
Axa v Ace [2006] EWHC 216, [2006] Lloyd's Rep IR 683 235
Ayerst v Jenkins (1873) LR 16 Eq 275 135
Ayres v Evans (1981) 39 ALR 129 117
AZ (A Minor) (Abduction: Acquiescence), Re [1993] 1 FLR 682 . . . . .1136, 1150
Azad v Entry Clearance Officer (Dhaka) [2001] Imm AR 318, [2001]
    INLR 109 . . . . .897, 940, 1194, 1199–1200
Aziz v Aziz [2007] EWCA Civ 712 . . . . .498, 516
Aziz v Republic of Yemen [2005] EWCA Civ 745 506

B (A Child) (Abduction: Acquiescence), Re [1999] 2 FLR 818 .1149
B (A Child) (Care Proceedings: Diplomatic Immunity), Re [2002] EWHC 1751 (Fam),
    [2003] 1 WLR 168 511–12
B (A Child) (Care Proceedings: Jurisdiction), Re [2013] EWCA Civ 1434 . . . . .1115, 1118
B (A Child) (Parentage: Knowledge of Proceedings), Re [2003] EWCA Civ 1842,
    [2004] 1 FLR 473 1052
B (A Minor) (Abduction), Re [1994] 2 FLR 249 . . . . .1137, 1149
B (A Minor) (Adoption Order: Nationality), Re [1999] 2 AC 136 1230
B (Abduction) (Rights of Custody), Re [1997] 2 FLR 594 1137

B (Abduction: Article 13 Defence), Re [1997] 2 FLR 573 1148
B (Abduction: Children's Objections), Re [1998] 1 FLR 667 182–3
B (Abduction: False Immigration Information), Re [2000] 2 FLR 835. 1141
B (Child Abduction: Habitual Residence), Re [1994] 2 FLR 915. . . . . 175, 177, 180, 182,
                                                                    183, 1107, 1135–7, 1149–50
B (Children) (Foreign Adoption: Refusal of Recognition), Re [2013] EWHC 1501. 1054–5
B (Children) (Leave to Remove: Impact of Refusal), Re [2004] EWCA Civ 956,
    [2005] 2 FLR 239 1169
B (Children) (Removal from Jurisdiction), S (Children) (Removal from Jurisdiction),
    Re [2003] EWCA Civ 1149, [2003] 2 FLR 1043 . . . . .1056, 1088, 1167–8
B (Children), Re [2005] EWCA Civ 643. . . . . .181, 1167, 1169
B (Infants), Re [1971] NZLR 143 1172
B (Minors) (Abduction), Re (No 2) [1993] 1 FLR 993 .176, 179, 1135
B (S) (An Infant), Re [1968] Ch 204, 208 .166, 1209, 1211, 1228
B v A (Wasted Costs Order) [2012] EWHC 3127 1139
B v A-G [1967] 1 WLR 776. 1049
B v B (Abduction: Custody Rights) [1993] Fam 32 . . . . .176, 1138, 1152
B v B (Divorce: Northern Cyprus) [2001] 3 FCR 331 1030
B v B (Divorce: Stay of Foreign Proceedings) [2002] EWHC 1711, [2003]
    1 FLR 1 . . . . .970, 973–4, 978
B v B (Minors: Enforcement of Access Abroad) [1988] 1 WLR 526. 1135–6
B v B (Relinquishment of Jurisdiction: Brussels II Revised Art 12) [2012]
    EWHC 1924 1099
B v B (Scottish Contact Order: Jurisdiction to Vary) [1996] 1 FLR 688. 1107
B v B [2014] EWHC 1804 . . . . .1102, 1122
B v B [2014] EWHC 4857 1067–8
B v El-B (Abduction: Sharia Law: Welfare of Child) [2003] 1 FLR 811 1172
B v H (Habitual Residence: Wardship) [2002] 1 FLR 388 182
B v I (Forced Marriage) [2010] FLR 1721 . . . . .986, 991, 1050
B v K (Child Abduction) [1993] 1 FCR 382 1156
B v S (Financial Remedy: Matrimonial Property Regime) [2012] 2 FLR 502. 1379
B v United Kingdom [2000] 1 FLR 1 1139
B, Re (1982) 4 FLR 492. . . . . .1169, 1175
B's Settlement, Re [1940] Ch 54 1173
Babanaft International Co SA v Bassatne [1990] Ch 13 . . . . .306, 615–16, 621
Babcock v Jackson [1963] 2 Lloyd's Rep 286, 12 NY 2d 473, 240 NYS 2d 743. 816
Babcock v Jackson 12 NY 2d 473, 191 NE 2d 279 (1963) 25, 30
Baccus SRL v Servicio Nacional del Trigo [1957] 1 QB 438. 503
Bachchan v India Abroad Publications Inc 588 NYS 2d 661 (Sup Ct NY 1992) 137
Bachy SA v Belbetoes Fundacoes E Betoes Especiais LDA [1999] IL Pr 743. 304
Backman v The Queen (1999) 178 DLR (4th) 126 105
Baden v Société Générale SA [1993] 1 WLR 509. . . . . .570, 572
Bader v Purdom 841 F 2d 38 (1988) 28
Baelz v Public Trustee [1926] Ch 863. 1298
Baghlaf v PNSC (No 2) [2000] 1 Lloyd's Rep 1 . . . . .402, 405, 412
Baghlaf v PNSC [1998] 2 Lloyd's Rep 229. . . . . .405, 412–13, 416
Baig v Entry Clearance Officer, Islamabad [2002] INLR 117. 1018
Bailet v Bailet (1901) 17 TLR 317 900
Bailey, Re [1985] 2 NZLR 656 . . . . .71, 491, 1353
Bain v Whitehaven Rly Co (1850) 3 HL Cas 1 80
Baindail v Baindail [1946] P 122 . . . . .53, 761–2, 934, 941–2
Baker v Ian McCall International Ltd [2000] CLC 189 . . . . .560, 563
Baldry (Deceased), Re [2004] WTLR 609 (Fam Div) 1331, 1349, 1358
Baldry v Jackson [1976] 1 NSWLR 19, [1976] 2 NSWLR 415, [1977]
    1 NSWLR 494. . . . . .325, 808

Balfour v Scott (1793) 6 Bro Parl Cas 550 1351
Balkanbank v Taher (No 2) [1995] 1 WLR 1067 . . . . .306, 333
Ballantyne v Mackinnon [1896] 2 QB 455 563
Balmoral Group Ltd v Borealis [2006] 2 Lloyd's Rep 629, [2006] EWHC 1900 105
Baltic Real Estate Ltd, Re [1992] BCC 629 336
Balts v Balts 273 Minn 419, 142 NW 2d 6 (1966) 816
Bamgbose v Daniel [1955] AC 107 . . . . .942, 1198
Banca Carige v BNC [2001] 2 Lloyd's Rep 147 356
Banco Atlantico SA v British Bank of the Middle East [1990] 2 Lloyd's Rep 504 . . . . .397, 402
Banco de Honduras SA v East West Insurance Co [1996] 1 LRLR 74 413
Banco de Vizcaya v Don Alfonso de Borbón y Austria [1935] 1 KB 140 . . . . .120, 126
Banco Nacional de Comercio Exterior SNC v Empresa de Telecomunicaciones
    de Cuba SA [2007] EWHC 2322 (Comm), [2007] IL Pr 59 . . . . .628, 649
Banco Nacional de Cuba, Re [2001] 1 WLR 2039 356
Banco, The [1971] P 137 384
Bangladesh Export Import Co Ltd v Sucden Kerry SA [1995] 2 Lloyd's Rep 1 770
Bangoura v Washington Post (2004) 258 DLR (4th) 350
Bank Handlowy w Warszawie SA and PPHU "ADAX"/Ryszard Adamiak
    v Christianapol sp z o o, (C-116/11) ECLI:EU:C:2012:739 . . . . .1316, 1321, 1323
Bank Mellat v Helliniki Techniki SA [1984] QB 291 . . . . .341, 670–1
Bank of Africa Ltd v Cohen [1909] 2 Ch 129 . . . . .1262, 1375
Bank of Australasia v Harding (1850) 9 CB 661 . . . . .87, 532, 564
Bank of Australasia v Nias (1851) 16 QB 717 . . . . .532, 564
Bank of Baroda v Vysya Bank Ltd [1994] 2 Lloyd's Rep 87 . . . . .335, 343–4, 364,
                                                                            366–7, 375, 733, 736, 739
Bank of Credit and Commerce International (Overseas) Ltd v Gokal
    [1995] IL Pr 316 543
Bank of Credit and Commerce International SA (In Liquidation) v
    Wajih Sirri Al-Kaylani [1999] IL Pr 278 199
Bank of Dubai Ltd v Abbas [1997] IL Pr 308, [1998] IL Pr 391 . . . . .199, 336, 443
Bank of Ireland v Meeneghan [1995] 1 ILRM 96 . . . . .115, 118–19, 121–2
Bank of Montreal v Snoxell (1982) 143 DLR (3d) 349 573
Bank of New South Wales v Commonwealth Steel Co Ltd [1983] 1 NSWLR 69 337
Bank of Scotland v Investment Management Regulatory Organisation Ltd 1989
    SLT 432 . . . . .224, 245
Bank of Scotland v SA Banque Nationale De Paris 1996 SLT 103 . . . . .447, 451, 454, 471
Bank of Scotland v Seitz 1990 SLT 584 263
Bank of St Petersburg OJSC v Arkhangelsky [2014] EWCA Civ 593, [2014]
    1 WLR 4360 487
Bank of Swaziland v Hahn [1986] 1 WLR 506 325
Bank of Tokyo Ltd v Karoon [1987] AC 45 . . . . .403, 406, 423, 426
Bank of Tokyo-Mitsubishi Ltd v Baskan Gida Sanayi Ve Pazalarma AS [2004]
    EWHC 945 (Ch), [2004] 2 Lloyd's Rep 394 231
Bank of Tokyo-Mitsubishi Ltd v Baskan Gida Sanayi Ve Pazarlama AS [2004]
    EWHC 945 (Ch), [2004] 2 Lloyd's Rep 395; 216, 231
Bank St Petersburg v Arkhangelsky [2014] EWCA Civ 593, [2014] 1 WLR 4360 422
Bank voor Handel en Scheepvaart NV v Slatford [1953] 1 QB 248 . . . . .128, 131–2, 1269
Bankers Trust International plc v RCS Editori SpA [1996] CLC 899 . . . . .233, 713
Bankes, Re [1902] 2 Ch 333 1377
Bankhaus H Aufhauser v Scotboard Ltd 1973 SLT (Notes) 87 . . . . .1284, 1287
Bannios and Sanchez's Marriage, Re (1989) 96 FLR 336 1174
Banque Cantonale de Geneve v Polevent Ltd [2015] EWHC 1968 . . . . .843, 845
Banque Cantonale v Waterlily [1997] 2 Lloyd's Rep 347 235
Banque Cantonale v Waterlily Maritime Inc [1997] 2 Lloyd's Rep 347 . . . . .235, 422
Banque des Marchands de Moscou (Koupetschesky), Re [1958] Ch 182 112

Banque Paribas v Cargill International SA [1992] 1 Lloyd's Rep 96, [1992]
    2 Lloyd's Rep 19. . . . . .346, 367, 374, 1284
Banque Privée Edmond de Rothschild Europe v Mme X, Cour de Cassation,
    1st Civil Chamber, 26 September 2012, No 11–26.022. .235
Barber & Sons v Lloyd's Underwriters [1986] 2 All ER 845, [1987] QB 103. 83
Barber v Lamb (1860) 8 CBNS 95. 556
Barclay v Sweeney [1999] IL Pr 288. 278
Barclays Bank International Ltd v Levin Bros (Bradford) Ltd [1977] QB 270 99
Barclays Bank Ltd v Piacun [1984] 2 Qd R 476. .549, 598, 599
Barclays Bank Plc v Ente Nazionale di Previdenza [2016] EWCA Civ 1261. . . . . . . .455, 457, 446
Barclays Bank plc v Glasgow City Council [1994] QB 404 286
Barclays Bank plc v Homan [1993] BCLC 680 . . . . .426–8, 432, 434
Barclays Bank plc v Kenton Capital Ltd et al (1994–95) Cayman Islands
    Law Reports 489 394
Barclay-Watt v Alpha Panareti Public Ltd, 23 November 2012, HC. 263, 273, 277
Barford v Barford [1918] P 140 111
Bariatinski, Re Princess (1843) 1 Ph 375 1245
Baring Bros & Co Ltd v Cunninghame District Council [1997] CLC 108, (1998)
    Times, 30 September 779, 847–8
Barings plc v Coopers & Lybrand [1997] IL Pr 12, [1997] IL Pr 576. . . . . .338, 364
Barker, Re [1995] 2 VR 439. 84
Barking and Dagenham LBC v C [2014] EWHC 2472. . . . . .1114, 1116
Barlow Clowes International Ltd v Henwood [2008] EWCA Civ 577 . . . . 150–1, 157, 159,
    161–4, 178
Barlow's Will, Re (1887) 36 Ch D 287. 1246
Barnard, Barnard v White, Re (1887) 56 LT 9 1377
Barnett's Trusts, Re [1902] 1 Ch 847 . . . . .49, 1339
Baron Penedo v Johnson (1873) 29 LT 452 511
Baroness von Eckhardstein v Baron von Eckhardstein (1907) 23 TLR 539. 978
Barony of Moynihan, Re [2000] 1 FLR 113. 1199
Barratt International Resorts Ltd v Martin 1994 SLT 434 . . . . .220, 613
Barrett v Universal-Island Records Ltd [2006] EWHC 1009 (Ch). 559
Barretto v Young [1900] 2 Ch 339. 1362
Barrie's Estate, 240 Iowa 431, 35 NW 2d 658 (1949) 1358
Barros Mattos Junior v General Securities and Finance Ltd [2004] EWHC 1188
    (Ch), [2004] 2 Lloyd's Rep 475 . . . . .753, 769
Barros Mattos Junior v MacDaniels [2005] EWHC 1323, [2005]
    IL Pr 630 . . . . .64, 70, 397, 847
Barry v Bradshaw [2000] IL Pr 706 . . . . .253, 257, 268
Barton (Deceased), Tod v Barton, Re [2002] EWHC 264 (Ch), [2002]
    WTLR 469 . . . . .1339, 1344, 1386–9, 1393, 1394
Barton v Golden Sun Holidays Ltd [2007] 151 SJLB 1128, [2007] IL Pr 57 288
BAS Capital Funding Corpn v Medfinco Ltd [2003] EWHC 1798 (Ch), [2004]
    1 Lloyd's Rep 652. . . . . .307, 326, 363, 367, 369, 381
Baschet v London Illustrated Standard [1900] 1 Ch 73 90
Base Metal Trading Ltd v Shamurin [2004] EWCA Civ 1316, [2005]
    1 WLR 1157 . . . . .690, 693–4, 701, 791, 796, 1308–9
Bastone & Firminger Ltd v Nasima Enterprises (Nigeria) Ltd [1996] CLC 1902. . . . . . . .343, 349
BAT Industries Plc v Windward Prospects Ltd [2013] EWHC 4087 366
Bat v Germany [2011] EWHC 2029 (Admin), [2013] QB 349. . . . . .499, 510
Bata v Bata [1948] WN 366, 92 Sol Jo 574 886
Batavia Times Publishing Co v Davis (1978) 88 DLR (3d) 144 . . . . .101, 594
Bater v Bater [1951] P 35. 569
Bath v British and Malayan Trustees Ltd [1969] 2 NSWLR 114 1331
Battalion Investment & Trust Co Ltd v Clifford, 2002 (unreported) 359

Baturina v Chistyakov [2014] EWCA Civ 1134, [2014] 2 CLC 209 430
Bavaria Fluggesellschaft Schwabe v Eurocontrol (9 and 10/77) [1977] ECR 1517 614
Bazias 3, The [1993] QB 673 383
BCCHK v Sonali [1995] 1 Lloyd's Rep 227 . . . . .399, 403
BCCI v Price Waterhouse [1997] 4 All ER 108 . . . . .498, 499, 512, 516
BCEN-Eurobank v Vostokrybprom Co Ltd (The Phoenix) [2014] 1 Lloyd's Rep 449 547
Beals v Saldanha [2003] 3 SCR 416, (2003) 234 DLR (4th) 1 136
Beals v Saldanha 2003 SCC 72 . . . . .136, 526, 543–4, 571, 574–5, 577–8, 580
Beamish v Beamish (1861) 9 HL Cas 274 903
Beatty v Beatty [1924] 1 KB 807 . . . . .108, 550, 552, 1078
Beaumont, Re [1893] 3 Ch 490 167
Beazley v Horizon Offshore Contractors Inc [2004] EWHC 2555 (Comm),
    [2005] IL Pr 11 . . . . .438, 440
Becker v Hainan Airlines Co Ltd Barkan v Air Nostrum LAM SA (C-448/16)
    and (C-447/16) OJ 2016 C 428/5 260
Beckford v Kemble (1822) 1 Sim & St 7 489
Becquet v MacCarthy (1831) 2 B & Ad 951 542
Beecham Group plc v Norton Healthcare Ltd [1997] FSR 81 . . . . .334, 349
Begum v Entry Clearance Officer, Dacca [1983] Imm AR 163 .156, 924
Beijing Jianlong Heavy Industry Group v Golden Ocean Group Ltd [2013]
    EWHC 1063 754
Beldis, The [1936] P 51 384
Belhaj v Straw [2014] EWCA Civ 1394 106
Belhaj v Straw [2017] UKSC 3, [2017] 2 WLR 456 . . . . .114, 498, 507, 1256, 1267
Bell v Graham (1859) 13 Moo PCC 242 987
Bell v Kennedy (1868) LR 1 Sc & Div 307, 319 . . . . .150, 157, 163
Belletti v Morici [2009] EWHC 2316 (Comm), [2009] ILPr 57 . . . . .307, 338
Bellinger v Bellinger [2003] UKHL 21, [2003] 2 AC 467 . . . . .892, 1051
Belton v Belton [1987] 2 FLR 343 1168
Bempde v Johnstone (1796) 3 Ves 198 168
Benarty, The [1984] 2 Lloyd's Rep 244 413
Benatti v WPP Holdings Italy srl [2007] EWCA Civ 263, [2007]
    1 WLR 2316 . . . . .216–17, 231, 241–2, 246, 257, 298, 301, 309, 448–9, 805
Benefit Strategies Group Inc v Prider [2005] SASC 194, (2005) 91 SASR 544 . . . . 119, 136, 553,
                                                                                              565, 569, 575
Benfield Holdings Ltd v Elliot Richardson [2007] EWHC 171 (QB) 433
Benincasa v Dentalkit Srl (C-269/95) [1997] ECR I-3767 . . . . .232–3, 237, 292
Benkharbouche v Embassy of Sudan [2015] EWCA Civ 33, [2015] 3 WLR 301 . . . . .503, 505
Benko, Re [1968] SASR 243 147
Ben-Rafael v Iran [2015] EWHC 3203 505
Ben-Rafael v Iran [2015] EWHC 3203 602
Bentinck v Bentinck [2007] EWCA Civ 175, [2007] IL Pr 391 308
Berchtold, Re [1923] 1 Ch 192 45
Berezovsky v Abramovich [2010] EWHC 647, [2011] EWCA Civ 153; [2011]
    1 WLR 2290 . . . . .830, 1384, 1386, 1388
Berezovsky v Michaels [2000] 1 WLR 1004 . . . . .335, 350, 365
Bergen, The (No 2) [1997] 2 Lloyd's Rep 710 412–13
Bergen, The [1997] 1 Lloyd's Rep 380 . . . . .203, 387
Berisford v New Hampshire [1990] 1 Lloyd's Rep 454 . . . . .235, 370, 399, 460, 467
Berkeley Administration Inc v McClelland [1995] IL Pr 201, [1996] IL Pr 72 650
Berkovits v Grinberg [1995] Fam 142 .1012, 1016–17, 1021, 1051–2
Berliner Industriebank AG v Jost [1971] 2 QB 463 . . . . .527, 549–51
Bernhard v Harrah's Club 546 P 2d 719 (1976) 26–7
Bernkrant v Fowler 55 Cal 2d 558, 360 P 2d 906 (1961) 47, 74
Berny, The [1979] QB 80 384

Berthiaume v Dastous [1930] AC 79 . . . . .893, 906–7, 920, 997, 1199
Bertrand v Ott (150/77) [1978] ECR 1431 . . . . .293, 295
Besix SA v Wasserreinigungsbau Alfred Kretzschmar GmbH & Co KG
    (WABAG) (C-256/00) [2002] ECR I-1699 . . . . .249, 254, 261, 263
Bethell, Re (1888) 38 Ch D 220 942
Bethlehem Steel Corpn v Universal Gas and Oil Co Inc (1978) Times, 3 August. 329
Betty Ott, The Ship v General Bills Ltd [1992] 1 NZLR 655. 89
BF (Children) (Abduction: Child's Objections), Re [2010] EWHC 2909 . . . . .1145–7, 1156
B-G (A Child) (Parental Orders: Domicile), Re [2014] EWHC 444 .1185
BG Group plc v Republic of Argentina, 572 US _ (2014) 419
Bharmal v Bharmal [2011] EWHC 1092. 489
Bhatia Shipping v Alcobex Metals [2004] EWHC 2323 (Comm), [2005]
    2 Lloyd's Rep 336. . . . . .345, 375, 716
Bheekhun v Williams [1999] 2 FLR 229, 232–233, CA 148, 151, 155–6, 486
BHP Billiton Ltd v Schultz (2004) 221 CLR 400 . . . . .325, 351, 394
BHP Petroleum Pty Ltd v Oil Basins Ltd [1985] VR 725 357
Bianca Purrucker v Guillermo Vallés Pérez (C-256/09) [2010] ECR I-07353. . . . . 1120, 1123,
                                                                                      1127, 1131
Bianca Purrucker v Guillermo Vallés Pérez (No 2) (C-296/10) [2010]
    ECR I-11163. . . . . .1118, 1120, 1123
Bibi v Chief Adjudication Officer [1998] 1 FLR 375 944
Bier BV v Mines de Potasse D'Alsace SA (21/76) [1978] QB 708, [1976]
    ECR 1735 . . . . .270, 830
Bio-Medical Research Ltd v Delatex SA [2001] 2 ILRM 51 . . . . .237, 252
Birang v Birang (1977) 7 Fam Law 172 898
Birch v Birch [1902] P 130 569
Birtwistle v Vardill (1840) 7 Cl & Fin 895 1256
Bischoffsheim, Re [1948] Ch 79 . . . . .915, 1195, 1198–9
Bitwise Ltd v CPS Broadcast Products BV 2003 SLT 455 252–3
Black Gold Potato Sales Inc v Joseph Garibaldi [1996] IL Pr 171. 586
Black v Yates [1992] QB 526 . . . . .558, 560
Black-Clawson International Ltd v Papierwerke Waldhof-Aschaffenburg AG
    [1975] AC 591. . . . . .78, 600
Blackett v Darcy [2005] NSWSC [13]. 150
Blaga v Romania [2014] ECHR 54443/ 10 1165
Blair v Chung (2006) 271 DLR (4th) 311 174
Blanckaert and Willems v Trost (139/80) [1981] ECR 819 280
Bliersbach v McEwen 1959 SC 43 . . . . .899, 911, 914
Blinds To Go Inc v Harvard Private Capital Holdings Inc (2003) 232 DLR (4th) 340. 408
Bloch v Soc Lima SpA (Versailles 14e ch, 6 February 1991) [1992] JCP 21972 736
Block Bros Realty Ltd v Mollard (1981) 122 DLR (3d) 323 . . . . .77, 133
Blohn v Desser [1962] 2 QB 116. 532–3
Blomqvist v Zavarco Plc [2015] EWHC 1898 (Ch), [2016] Ch 128 .224
Bloom v Harms Offshore AHT [2009] EWCA Civ 632 1310
Blue Sky One v Mahan Air [2010] EWHC 631. 1274
Blue Tropic Ltd v Chkhartishvili [2014] EWHC 2243 (Ch), [2014] IL Pr 33 . . . . . .224, 471, 494
Blue Wave, The [1982] 1 Lloyd's Rep 151 . . . . .412, 714
Blunden v Commonwealth (2004) 218 CLR 330 878
B-M (Wardship Jurisdiction), Re [1993] 1 FLR 979 183
BMG Trading Ltd v AS McKay [1998] IL Pr 691 . . . . .365, 396, 402, 405
BNP Paribas SA v Anchorage Capital Europe LLP [2013] EWHC 3073 . . . . .262, 282, 738
Boardwalk Regency Corpn v Maalouf (1992) 88 DLR (4th) 612. . . . . .136, 574
Bodley Head Ltd v Flegon [1972] 1 WLR 680. 136
Bodo Community v Shell Petroleum Development Co of Nigeria Ltd [2014]
    EWHC 1973. 485

Boeing Co v PPG Industries Inc [1988] 3 All ER 839 83
Boele v Norsemeter Holding AS [2002] NSWCA 363 577
Boettcher v Boettcher [1949] WN 83 926
Bohez v Wiertz (C-4/14) EU:C:2015:563, [2015] IL Pr 43 206
Boissevain v Weil [1949] 1 KB 482, CA, [1950] AC 327 747
Boissière and Co v Brockner & Co (1889) 6 TLR 85 538
Boks & Co and Peters, Rushton & Co Ltd, Re [1919] 1 KB 491 669
Bolagsupplysningen OÜ, Ingrid Ilsjan v Svensk Handel AB (C-194/16) OJ
    2016 C 211/35 278
Boldrini v Boldrini [1932] P 9 160–1
Bolmer v Edsell 90 NJ Eq 299 (1919) 908
Bols Distilleries v Superior Yacht Services Ltd [2006] UKPC 45, [2007]
    1 WLR 12 . . . . .216–17, 231–2, 240, 335
Bolton v Marine Services Ltd [1996] 2 NZLR 15 574
Bonacina, Le Brasseur v Bonacina, Re [1912] 2 Ch 394 133
Bonacina, Re [1912] 2 Ch 394 . . . . .4, 133
Bonaparte v Bonaparte [1892] P 402 . . . . .158, 1035
Bond v Graham (1842) 1 Hare 482 1336
Bondholders Securities Corpn v Manville [1933] 4 DLR 699 762
Bonelli's Goods, Re (1875) 1 PD 69 110
Bonhams 1793 Ltd v Lawson [2015] EWHC 3257 1267
Bonneval v De Bonneval, Re (1838) 1 Curt 856 158
Bonnier Media Ltd v Greg Lloyd Smith and Kestrel Trading Corpn 2003 SC 36,
    [2002] ETMR 86 . . . . .264, 336, 352
Booth v Phillips [2004] EWHC 1437, [2004] 2 Lloyd's Rep 457 . . . . .337, 349, 366
Bord Na Mona Horticulture Ltd v British Polythene Industries Plc [2012]
    EWHC 3346 273–4
Borealis AB v Stargas Ltd [1999] QB 863, [2002] 2 AC 205 339
Borg-Warner (Australia) Ltd v Zupan [1982] VR 437 808
Boss Group v Boss France SA [1997] 1 WLR 351 . . . . .244, 251–3, 255,
                                                                                                                     347, 443, 471, 559, 650
Boswell v Coaks (No 2) (1894) 86 LT 365 569
Boucher v Boucher 553 A 2d 313 (1988) 31
Boughton v Boughton (1750) 2 Ves Sen 12 1356
Bourdon v Stelco Inc (2006) 259 DLR (4th) 34 394
Bouygues Offshore SA v Caspian Shipping Co (Nos 1, 3, 4 and 5) [1998]
    2 Lloyd's Rep 461 . . . . .230, 412, 481
Bouygues Offshore SA v Caspian Shipping Co [1997] IL Pr 472 414
Bouygues v Caspian Shipping Co (No 2) [1997] 2 Lloyd's Rep 485 . . . . .338, 412, 414, 428
Bouzari v Iran (Islamic Republic) (2004) 243 DLR (4th) 406 504–5
Bowen's Estate, Re 351 NYS 2d 113 (1973) 1378
Bowie (or Ramsay) v Liverpool Royal Infirmary [1930] AC 588, 598 . . . . .149, 152–3, 162
Bowles and Phillips (1976) 39 MLR 196 99
Bowles and Whelan (1982) 45 MLR 434 98
Boyes v Bedale (1863) 1 Hem & M 798 . . . . .1198, 1202
Boyle v Sacker (1888) 39 Ch D 249 333
Boys v Chaplin [1968] 2 QB 1 94
Boyse v Colclough (1854) 1 K & J 124 546
BP Exploration Co (Libya) Ltd v Hunt (1980) 47 FLR 317 . . . . .106, 342
BP Exploration Co (Libya) Ltd v Hunt (No 2) [1979] 1 WLR 783, [1983]
    2 AC 352 . . . . .96, 99, 104
BP Exploration Co (Libya) Ltd v Hunt (No 2) [1983] 2 AC 352 . . . . .96, 99, 104
BP Exploration Co (Libya) Ltd v Hunt [1976] 1 WLR 788 . . . . .99, 342–3, 606
BP plc v Aon Ltd [2005] EWHC 2554 (Comm), [2006] 1 Lloyd's Rep 549 371
BP v DP (Children: Habitual Residence) [2016] EWHC 633 (Fam) 1135

Bradfield v Swanton [1931] IR 446 161
Bradlaugh v De Rin (1868) LR 3 CP 538 1295
Brailey v Rhodesia Consolidated Ltd [1910] 2 Ch 95. 111
Branco v Veira (1995) 9 ETR (2d) 49 1388
Brassard v Smith [1925] AC 371 1298
Braun v Custodian [1944] 4 DLR 209. 1298
Brealey v Board of Management of Royal Perth Hospital (1999) 21 WAR 79 333
Breams Trustees Ltd v Upstream Downstream Simulation Services Inc
    [2004] EWHC 211 (Ch) 370
Breavington v Godleman (1988) 169 CLR 41 93
Breen v Breen [1964] P 144. . . . . .53, 920
Breen v Breen [1964] P 144; Gotlieb (1977) 26 ICLQ 734 at 771. 53
Bremer v Freeman (1857) 10 Moo PCC 306 . . . . .59, 65, 1340, 1343
Brenner and Noller v Dean Witter Reynolds Inc (C-318/93) [1994]
    ECR I-4275 . . . . .202, 226, 296–7
Brennero v Wendel GmbH (258/83) [1984] ECR 3971 624
Breuning v Breuning [2002] EWHC 236 (Fam), [2002] 1 FLR 888 . . . . . . .163, 166, 180–1, 958
Bridgend CBC v GM [2012] EWHC 3118. 1100
Briggs v Briggs (1880) 5 PD 163 159
Brinkerhoff Maritime Drilling Corpn v PT Airfast Services Indonesia [1992] 2 SLR 776 394
Brinkibon Ltd v Stahag Stahl und Stahlwarenhandelsgesellschaft GmbH [1983]
    2 AC 34. . . . . .343, 346
Brinkley v A-G (1890) 15 PD 76. 929
Bristol City Council v AA and HA [2014] EWHC 1022 1114–16
Bristow Helicopters Ltd v Sikorsky Aircraft Corpn [2004] EWHC 401 (Comm),
    [2004] 2 Lloyd's Rep 150. . . . . .375, 400
Bristow v Sequeville (1850) 5 Exch 275 . . . . .110, 375, 400
Britannia Steamship Insurance Association Ltd v Ausonia Assicurazioni SpA [1984] 2
    Lloyd's Rep 98 373
Brite Strike Technologies Inc v Brite Strike Technologies SA (C-230/15)
    EU:C:2016:560, [2016] IL Pr 37. . . . . .203, 389
British Aerospace plc v Dee Howard Co [1993] 1 Lloyd's Rep 368 . . . . .235, 370, 399
British Airways Board v Laker Airways Ltd [1984] QB 142, [1985]
    AC 58 . . . . .84, 119, 426, 434, 554
British American Tobacco Denmark A/ S v Kazemier BV [2015] UKSC 65,
    [2016] AC 262. 389
British Arab Commercial Bank Plc v National Transitional Council of Libya
    [2011] EWHC 2274 497
British Linen Co v Drummond (1830) 10 B & C 903. . . . . .73, 78
British Nylon Spinners Ltd v ICI Ltd [1953] Ch 19, [1955] Ch 37. . . . . .136, 553
British South Africa Co v Companhia de Moçambique [1892] 2 QB 358,
    [1893] AC 602. . . . . .484, 491, 1255
British South Africa Co v De Beers Consolidated Mines Ltd [1910] 2 Ch
    502, [1912] AC 52. . . . . .487, 724, 1256
British Steel Corpn v Allivane International Ltd 1989 SLT (Sh Ct) 57. . . . . .228, 236, 320
British Sugar plc v Babbini [2004] EWHC 2560 (TCC), [2005] 1 Lloyd's Rep 332 288
British Sugar plc v Fratelli [2004] EWHC 2560, [2005] 1 Lloyd's Rep 332 202
Britto v Secretary of State for the Home Department [1984] Imm AR 93 173–4
Brixton Prison Governor, ex p Caldough [1961] 1 All ER 606. 106
Broadmayne, The [1916] P 64 507
Brockley Cabinet Co Ltd v Pears (1972) 20 FLR 333 598
Brodin v A R Seljan 1973 SC 213 . . . . .748, 882
Broit v Broit 1972 SLT (Notes) 32 . . . . .1008, 1012, 1017
Brokaw v Seatrain UK Ltd [1971] 2 QB 476. 118
Brook v Brook (1861) 9 HL Cas 193. . . . . .892, 913, 923

Brooks Associates Inc v Basu [1983] QB 220 . . . . .1281, 1292
Brower v Sunview Solariums Ltd (1998) 156 DLR (4th) 752. .591
Brown v Brown (1982) 3 FLR 212, 218, 220. . . . . .148, 157, 162–3
Brown v Gregson [1920] AC 860. . . . . .1260, 1357
Brown v Innovatorone Plc (In Liquidation) [2010] EWHC 2281 (Comm),
    [2011] IL Pr 9 287
Brown v Kalal (1986) 7 NSWLR 423 1110
Brown v Thornton 1837) 6 Ad & E1 185 80
Brown's Trust, Re (1865) 12 LT 488. 1176
Brownlie v Four Seasons Holdings Incorporated [2015] EWCA Civ 665,
    [2016] 1 WLR 1814 . . . . .343, 349, 710–11, 738, 856
Bryant v Bryant (1980) 11 Fam Law 85. . . . . .978, 1072
Buchanan v Rucker (1808) 9 East 192. . . . . .542, 576
Buckland v Buckland [1968] P 296 985–8
Buckle v Buckle [1956] P 181 926
Buehler AG v Chronos Richardson Ltd [1998] 2 All ER 960. . . . . .559, 560
Buenaventura v Ocean Trade Co [1984] ECC 183. 767
Buerger v New York Life Assurance Co (1927) 96 LJKB 930. 108
Bullock v Caird (1875) LR 10 QB 276 87
Bulmer v A-G [1955] Ch 558 1050
Bulova Watch Co Inc v Hattori and Co Ltd 508 F Supp 1322. 531
Bumbesti, The [2000] QB 559. 382–3
Bumper Development Corpn Ltd v Metropolitan Police Comr [1991]
    1 WLR 1362 . . . . .86, 112
Burbidge, Re [1902] 1 Ch 426. 1245
Burchell v Burchell (1928) 58 QLR 527 573
Burke v Burke 1983 SLT 331. 893
Burnham v Superior Court of California 109 L Ed 2d (1990) .325
Burns-Anderson v Wheeler [2005] EWHC 575, [2005] 1 Lloyd's Rep 580 327
Burrows v Jamaica Private Power Co Ltd [2002] CLC 255. . . . . .333, 343–4, 369, 371, 376
Burton v Dolben (1756) 2 Lee 312, 318 158
Burton v Fisher (1828) Milw 183. 158
Buswell v IRC [1974] 1 WLR 1631, 1637. . . . . .151, 157
Butler v Butler [1997] 2 All ER 822. 973
Butterley v Butterley (1974) 48 DLR (3d) 351. . . . . .1013, 1021
Buttes Gas and Oil Co v Hammer (No 3) [1982] AC 888 . . . . .114, 127, 485, 491
Buttes Gas and Oil Co v Hammer [1971] 3 All ER 1025, [1975] QB 557 376
BVG v JPMorgan Chase Bank SA (C-144/10) [2011] ECR I-3961 224

C (A Child) (Abduction: Grave Risk of Physical or Psychological Harm),
    Re (No 1) [1999] 2 FLR 478. 1152
C (A Child) (Abduction: Residence and Contact), Re [2005] EWHC 2205, [2006]
    2 FLR 277 . . . . .15, 1136, 1140, 1141, 1164, 1168
C (A Child) (Abduction: Residence and Contact), Re [2006] 2 FLR 277. 15
C (A Child) (Child Abduction: Settlement), Re [2006] EWHC 1229 (Fam), [2006] 2 FLR
    797. 1140–1
C (A Child) (Foreign Adoption: Natural Mother's Consent: Service), Re [2006]
    1 FLR 318 . . . . .1214, 1228
C (A Child) (Internal Relocation), Re [2015] EWCA Civ 1305. 1171
C (A Child) v Plymouth County Council [2000] 1 FLR 875. . . . . .173, 175
C (A Child); Saudi Arabia, Re [2015] EWHC 3440 1174
C (A Minor) (Adoption: Illegality), Re [1999] 1 FLR 370 1214
C (Abduction: Consent), Re [1996] 1 FLR 414. . . . . .183, 1149
C (Abduction: Interim Directions: Accommodation by Local Authority), Re [2003]
    EWHC 3065, [2004] 1 FLR 653. 1152

C (Abduction: Settlement), Re (No 2) [2005] 1 FLR 938 1140
C (An Infant), Re [1959] Ch 363. 512
C (Child Abduction) (Unmarried Father: Rights of Custody), Re [2002]
    EWHC 2219, [2003] 1 FLR 252. .183, 1056, 1138–9, 1180
C (Children), Re [2015] EWHC 2082. 1101
C (Leave to Remove from Jurisdiction), Re [2000] 2 FLR 457. .1168
C (Minors) (Abduction: Grave Risk of Psychological Harm), Re [1999] 1 FLR 1145 1152–3
C (Parental Order), Re [2013] EWHC 2413 1188
C and D (Children) (Fact finding Hearing), Re [2015] EWHC 1059 1180
C Czarnikow Ltd v Rolimpex [1979] AC 351 499
C Inc plc v L [2001] 2 All ER (Comm) 446. . . . . .334, 337–8, 341, 370, 412, 446
C v B (Abduction: Grave Risk) [2005] EWHC 2988, [2006] 1 FLR 1095 1144
C v C (Abduction: Rights of Custody) [1989] 1 WLR 654 . . . . .1137, 1153–4
C v C (Ancillary Relief: Nuptial Settlement) [2004] EWCA Civ 1030, [2005]
    Fam 250. 1393–5
C v C (Brussels II: French Conciliation and Divorce Proceedings) [2005] EWCA
    Civ 68, [2005] 1 WLR 469 970
C v C (Divorce: Stay of English Proceedings) [2001] 1 FLR 624 .974
C v C (Minors) (Child Abduction) [1992] 1 FLR 163. 1135–7
C v C [1942] NZLR 356. 986
C v C 2003 SLT 793 . . . . .1149, 1153
C v D (Abduction: Grave Risk of Harm) [2013] EWHC 2989 (Fam)— 1155
C v D [2015] EWHC 3990. 1148–9
C v FC (Brussels II: Free Standing Application For Parental Responsibility) [2004]
    1 FLR 317 . . . . .177, 180, 183
C v H (Abduction: Consent) [2009] EWHC 2660 (Fam) 1148–9
C v K (Children: Application for Temporary Removal to Algeria) [2014]
    EWHC 4125 1167
C v S [2006] EWHC 2891 1169
C v S [2010] EWHC 2676 . . . . .955–6, 959, 970
C v V [2016] EWHC 559 (Fam) 1146
C v W [2007] EWHC 1349 (Fam) 1145, 1148, 1150, 1155, 1159
C, Re [1978] Fam 105. 1174
C, Re [2012] EWHC 907 . . . . .1099, 1117
Cable, Lord see Lord Cable, Re Cable & Wireless plc v IBM United Kingdom
    Ltd [2002] EWHC 2059 (Comm), ...417
Cablevision Systems Development Co v Shoupe (1986) 39 WIR 1 .573
Cadogan Properties Ltd v Mount Eden Land Ltd [2000] IL Pr 722. 325
Cadre SA v Astra Asigurari SA [2004] EWHC 2504 (QB), [2005] EWHC 2626
    (Comm), [2006] 1 Lloyd's Rep 560 . . . . .373, 425, 428, 430, 719
Caisse Régional du Crédit Agricole Nord de France v Ashdown [2007]
    EWCA Civ 574 621
Caithness, Re (1891) 7 TLR 354 . . . . .1251, 1358
Caledonia Subsea Ltd v Micoperi SRL 2002 SLT 1022 . . . . .726, 728, 734, 736–8
Caledonian Contracting Partnership Ltd v Thomas Rodger [2004] EWHC 851 224
Callaghan, Re [1948] NZLR 846. 1201
Callwood v Callwood [1960] AC 659 . . . . .108, 1371, 1374
Caltex Singapore Pte Ltd and Ors v BP Shipping Ltd [1996]
    1 Lloyd's Rep 286. . . . . .801, 860, 862, 867
Caltex Trading Pte Ltd v Metro Trading International Inc [1999]
    2 Lloyd's Rep 724. . . . . .227, 288, 338
Caltex Trading Pte Ltd v Metro Trading International Inc and Ors and Glencore
    International AG and Ors (Third Parties) and Sea VictoryShipping
    Corp Procopiou and Baker Services Inc (Fourth Parties) [1999] 2
    Lloyd's Rep 724 227

Caltex v BP [1996] 1 Lloyd's Rep 286 . . . . .404, 860, 867
Cambridge Credit Corpn Ltd v Lissenden (1987) 8 NSWLR 411 1282
Cambridge Gas Transportation Corpn v Official Committee of
    Unsecured Creditors of Navigator Holdings plc [2006] UKPC 26,
    [2007] 1 AC 508 . . . . .526, 528, 544
Camdex International Ltd v Bank of Zambia (No 2) (1997) CLC 714 . . . . .115, 122–3
Camera Care Ltd v Victor Hasselblad AB (1986) Times, 6 January, [1986] ECC 373 377
Cameron v Cameron 1996 SLT 306; (No 2) 1997 SLT 206. . . . . .179–81, 1097, 1143, 1146
Camilla Cotton Oil Co v Granadex SA [1976] 2 Lloyd's Rep 10 406
Cammell v Cammell [1965] P 467. . . . . .1060–1, 1395
Cammell v Sewell (1858) 3 H & N 617, 5 H & N 728 . . . . .1267–8, 1276
Campbell Connelly & Co Ltd v Noble [1963] 1 WLR 252 1288
Campbell International Trading House Ltd v Peter Van Aart [1992] 2 IR 305 . . . . .228, 253
Campbell v Beaufoy (1859) John 320 1344–5
Campbell v Campbell (1866) LR 1 Eq 383 1348
Campbell v Campbell 1977 SLT 125. 1088
Campbell v MGN Ltd [2004] UKHL Ltd, [2002] 2 AC 457 798
CAN Insurance Co Ltd v Office Depot International (UK) Ltd [2005]
    EWHC 456 (Comm). 332–3, 465, 468, 471
Canada Post Corp v Lépine 2009 SCC 16, [2009] 1 SCR 549. 544
Canada Trust Co v Stolzenberg (No 2) [1998] 1 WLR 547, [2002]
    1 AC 1 . . . . .216, 243, 284, 335, 346
Canada Trust v Stolzenberg (No 2) [2002] 1 AC 1. . . . . .199, 213
Canadian Commercial Bank v Belkin (1990) 73 DLR (4th) 678 1336
Canadian National Steamship Co v Watson [1939] 1 DLR 876
Canadian Pacific Railway v Parent [1917] AC 195. 882
Canadian Transport, The (1932) 43 Lloyd's Rep 409 102
Cannon v Cannon [2004] EWCA Civ 1330, [2005] 1 FLR 169 1141
Canterbury Corpn v Wyburn and Melbourne Hospital [1895] AC 89 1386
Cantieri Navali Riuniti SpA v NV Omne Justitia, The Stolt Marmaro [1985]
    2 Lloyd's Rep 428. . . . . .346, 716, 724
Canyon Offshore Ltd v GDF Suez E&P Nederland BV [2014] EWHC 3810
    (Comm), [2015] IL Pr 8 . . . . .251, 254, 261
Cap Bon, The [1967] 1 Lloyd's Rep 543 385
Cape Moreton, The [2005] 219 ALR 48 . . . . .106, 385
Capelloni v Pelkmans (119/84) [1985] ECR 3147. 620
Capital Sarl v OJSC Rosneft Oil Co [2012] EWCA Civ 855, [2014] QB 458. 114
Capital Trust Investments Ltd v Radio Design TJ AB [2002] CLC 787 418
Capon, Re (1965) 49 DLR (2d) 675 1036
Car Trim GmbH v KeySafety Systems Srl (C-381/08) [2010] ECR I-1255 . . . . . . .255, 258, 727
Carapiet's Trust, The Armenian Patriarch of Jerusalem v Sonsino, Re [2002]
    EWHC 1304 (Ch), [2002] WTLR 989 . . . . .1383, 1388
Carey Group plc and others v AIB Group (UK) plc [2011] EWHC 567 (Ch),
    [2012] Ch 304. 115
Caribbean Gold Ltd v Alga Shipping Co Ltd [1993] 1 WLR 1100 .333
Carl Stuart Ltd v Biotrace Ltd [1994] IL Pr 554. 252–3
Carl Zeiss Stiftung v Rayner and Keeler Ltd (No 2) [1967] 1 AC 853 . . . . . .77, 127, 556, 558–61
Carlson v Rio Tinto plc [1999] CLC 551. 401
Carmichael v Director-General of Social Welfare [1994] 3 NZLR 477. 175
Carmona v White (1980) 25 SASR 525. 165
Carnegie v Giessen and Ors [2005] EWCA Civ 191, [2005] 1 WLR 2510 . . . . .100, 552
Carnival Cruise Lines Inc v Shute 111 S Ct 1614 (1991) 413
Carnoustie Universal SA v International Transport Workers' Federation [2002]
    EWHC 1624 (Comm), [2002] 2 All ER (Comm) 657, ...216, 231, 237, 284, 444, 461
Carrick Estates Ltd and Young, Re (1988) 43 DLR (4th) 161 .529, 539

Carrick v Hancock (1895) 12 TLR 59 . . . . .325, 529
Carron v Germany (198/85) [1986] ECR 2437 . . . . .622, 624
Cartel Damage Claims Hydrogen Peroxide SA (CDC) v Evonik Degussa
    GmbH (C-352/13) EU:C:2015:335, [2015] QB 906 . . . . 237, 264, 271, 274,
                              275, 284, 287, 811, 827–8, 856
Carter (1983) 54 BYBIL 207 89
Cartier International AG v British Sky Broadcasting Ltd [2016] EWCA Civ
    658, [2016] ETMR 43. 324
Cartier Parfums-Lunettes SAS v Ziegler France SA (C-1/13) EU:C:2014:109,
    [2014] IL Pr 25 444
Cartwright v Pettus (1676) 2 Cas in Ch 214 485
Carvalho v Hull, Blyth (Angola) Ltd [1979] 1 WLR 1228. 412
Carvill America Inc v Camperdown UK Ltd [2005] EWCA Civ 645, [2005]
    2 Lloyd's Rep 457. . . . . .335, 338, 363
Casdagli v Casdagli [1919] AC 145, 178 155
Casey v Arnott (1876) 2 CPD 24. 357
Casey v Casey [1949] P 420. . . . . .914, 998
Casey v Casey 1968 SLT 56 175
Casio Computer Co Ltd v Sayo [2001] EWCA Civ 661, [2001] IL Pr 43, [2001]
    IL Pr 164 . . . . .286, 805
Caspian Basin v Bouygous (No 4) [1997] 2 Lloyd's Rep 507, [1998]
    2 Lloyd's Rep 461. 404
Castanho v Brown and Root (UK) Ltd [1981] AC 557 . . . . .402, 423, 426, 427
Castree v Squibb [1980] 1 WLR 1248. 352
Castrique v Imrie (1870) LR 4 HL 414 . . . . .383, 546–8, 564
Catalyst Investment Group Ltd v Lewinsohn [2009] EWHC 1964 (Ch), [2010]
    2 WLR 839, [2010] Ch 218. . . . . .474, 494
Catania v Giannattasio (1999) 174 DLR (4th) 170 490
Caterpillar Financial Services Corpn v SNC Passion [2004] EWHC 569 (Comm),
    [2004] 2 Lloyd's Rep 99. . . . . .706, 711, 744
Catlin Syndicate Ltd v Adams Land & Cattle Co [2006] EWHC 2065 (Comm). 371, 373
Catterall v Catterall (1847) 1 Rob Eccl 580 903
Catterall v Sweetman (1845) 1 Rob Eccl 304 903
Cavani v Hungary [2014] ECHR 5493/ 13 1165
Cavell Insurance Co Ltd, Re (2006) 269 DLR (4th) 679 577
Caylon v Michailidis [2009] UKPC 34 617–18
CB v CB [2013] EWHC 2092 (Fam); 1147
CC and DD [2014] EWHC 1307 1184–5
Cecil v Bayat [2010] EWHC 641 (Comm), [2011] EWCA Civ 135, [2011]
    1 WLR 3086 . . . . .326, 360, 381
CEF Holdings Ltd v Mundey [2012] EWHC 1524 (QB),
    [2012] IRLR 912. 297–8
Celtic Salmon Atlantic (Killary) v Aller Acqua (Ireland) Ltd [2014] IEHC 421.244 559
Centrax v Citibank NA [1999] 1 All ER (Comm) 557. 708
Centre Intervening) [2014] AC 1. 1236
Centro Internationale Handelsbank AG v Morgan Grenfell Trade Finance Ltd
    [1997] CLC 870 456–7
Century Credit Corpn v Richard (1962) 34 DLR (2d) 291 .1271
Česká podnikatelská pojišťovna as, Vienna Insurance Group v Bilas (C-111/09)
    [2010] ECR I-4545 . . . . .229, 291, 642
Česká spořitelna as v Feichter (C-419/11) EU:C:2013:165 [2013]
    IL Pr 22 . . . . .246–7, 249–50, 261–2, 292
Ceskoslovenska Obchodni Banka AS v Nomura International plc
    [2003] IL Pr 20 . . . . .402, 403, 404
CFEM Façades SA v Bovis Construction Ltd [1992] IL Pr 561 . . . . .196, 612

CGU International Insurance plc v Szabo [2002] 1 All ER
   (Comm) 83 . . . . .367–8, 375, 708, 716, 725
CH Offshore Ltd v PDV Marina SA [2015] EWHC 595 338
Chadha v Dow Jones & Co Inc [1999] IL Pr 829 . . . . .350–1, 354
Chai v Peng (Jurisdiction: Forum Conveniens) (No 2) [2014] EWHC 3518 . . . . .955, 959
Chai v Peng [2014] EWHC 3518 (Fam), [2015] 2 FLR 42467283 . . . . .177, 560
Chalkley v Chalkley (1995) 10 RFL (4th) 442 1156
Chamberlain v Chamberlain 43 NY 424 (1870) 1346
Chamberlain v de la Mare [1982] 4 FLR 434 1168
Chandler v Chandler [2011] EWCA Civ 143 955
Chaney v Murphy [1948] WN 130, 64 TLR 489 339
Channel Tunnel Group Ltd v Balfour Beatty Construction Ltd [1993]
   AC 334 . . . . .306, 340–1, 417, 419, 420
Chantier de l'Atlantique SA v Gaztransport & Technigaz SAS [2011] EWHC 3383 560
Chaparral, The [1972] 2 Lloyd's Rep 315 345
Chaplin v Boys [1971] AC 356 . . . . 31, 73, 90, 93–4, 141,
                                         405, 777, 814, 861, 877
Chapman Estate v O'Hara [1988] 2 WWR 275 . . . . .491, 546
Chappell's Estate, Re 124 Wash 128, 213 P 684 (1923) 1346
Charkieh, The (1873) LR 4 A & E 59 505
Charles T Dougherty Co Inc v Krimke 144 A 617 (1929) 1272
Charm Maritime Inc v Minas Xenophon Kyriakou and David John Mathias
   [1987] 1 Lloyd's Rep 433 . . . . .400, 405
Charman v WOC [1993] 2 Lloyd's Rep 551 291
Charron v Montreal Trust (1958) 15 DLR (2d) 240 . . . . .762, 1336
Chartered Mercantile Bank of India v Netherlands India Steam Navigation Co
   (1883) 10 QBD 521 877–8
Charterers Mutual Assurance Association Ltd v British and Foreign
   [1998] IL Pr 838 . . . . .291, 446, 455
Chase Manhattan Bank NA v Israel-British Bank (London) Ltd [1981] Ch 105 76–7
Chase v Ram Technical Services Ltd [2000] 2 Lloyd's Rep 418 . . . . .337, 367–8, 375
Chatard's Settlement, Re [1899] 1 Ch 712 1176
Chatfield v Berchtoldt (1872) 7 Ch App 192 1254
Chaudhary v Chaudhary [1985] Fam 19, 26 157
Chaudhry v Chaudhry [1976] Fam 148 . . . . .942–3, 1017, 1020
Cheang Thye Phin v Tan Ah Loy [1920] AC 369 943
Chebaro v Chebaro [1987] Fam 127 1072
Chellaram v Chellaram (No 2) [2002] EWHC 632 (Ch), [2002]
   3 All ER 17 . . . . 199, 216, 283, 325, 335, 337, 345, 358,
                               369, 373, 376–7, 402, 1388, 1391
Chelleram v Chelleram [1985] Ch 409 1390
Chemische Fabrik Vormals Sandoz v Badische Anilin und Soda Fabriks
   (1904) 90 LT 733 363
Cheni v Cheni [1965] P 85 . . . . .141, 910, 921, 923, 930, 933–6
Cherney v Deripaska [2007] EWHC 965 (Comm), [2007] IL Pr 49 . . . . .149, 199
Chesterman's Trusts, Re [1923] 2 Ch 466 6
Chetti v Chetti [1909] P 67 . . . . .919, 921, 932
Chevron Corp v Yaiguaje 2015 SCC 42 . . . . .544, 551
Chief Adjudication Officer v Bath [2000] 1 FLR 8 . . . . .893, 895
Child and Family Agency v J. D. (C-428/15) [2016] All ER (D)
   24 (Nov) 1093, 1114, 1116
China Agribusiness Development Corpn v Balli Trading [1998]
   2 Lloyd's Rep 76 . . . . .672, 673
Chiron Corpn v Evans Medical Ltd [1996] FSR 863 . . . . .225, 286
Chiron Corpn v Organon Teknika Ltd (No 10) [1995] FSR 325 .303

Chiwell v Carlyon (1897) 14 SC 61 1374
Choice Investments Ltd v Jeromnimon [1981] All ER 225., [1981] QB 149 100
Chopra v Bank of Singapore Ltd [2015] EWHC 1549 332
Choudhary v Bhattar [2009] EWHC 314 (Ch), [2009] IL Pr 51, [2009]
    EWCA Civ 1176 466
Choudhary v Bhatter [2009] EWCA Civ 1176, [2010] 2 All ER 1031 217
Chris Sawyer v Atari Interactive Inc [2005] EWHC 2351 (Ch),
    [2006] IL Pr 8 . . . . .363, 366, 368
Christian v Christian (1897) 78 LT 86 978
Chung Chi Cheung v R [1939] AC 160 876
Chunilal v Merrill Lynch International Incorporated [2010] EWHC 1467 343
Church of Scientology of California v Metropolitan Police Comr (1976)
    120 Sol Jo 690 . . . . .777, 814, 865
CHW v GJH (25/81) [1982] ECR 1189 . . . . .207, 228, 305
Cienvik, The [1996] 2 Lloyd's Rep 395 337
Citadel Insurance Co v Atlantic Union Insurance Co SA [1982]
    2 Lloyd's Rep 543 . . . . .243, 344, 346
Citibank NA v Rafidian Bank [2003] EWHC 1950, [2003] IL Pr 49 629
Citi-March Ltd v Neptune Orient Lines Ltd [1997] 1 Lloyd's Rep 72 . . . . .345, 371, 412, 413
City & County Properties v Kamali [2006] EWCA Civ 1879, [2007] 1 WLR 1219 326
City of Gotha v Sotheby's, 9 September 1998, HC 115, 123, 129
City of Mecca, The (1879) 5 PD 28 548
CK v JK [2004] IR 224 1035
Clare & Co v Dresdner Bank [1915] 2 KB 576 1281
Clare Taverns v Charles Gill [2000] ILRM 98 . . . . .237, 240–1
Clare, Re (No 2) [1984] STC 609 148
Clark (A Child), Re [2006] EWCA Civ 1115 1113
Clark v Clark 1967 SC 269 1001
Clark v Clark 222 A 2d 205 (1966) 31
Clark's Estate, Re 21 NY 2d 478, 236 NE 2d 152 (1968) 1356
Clarke v Fennoscandia (No 3) [2007] UKHL 56; 2008 SC .520, 573
Clarke v Fennoscandia Ltd (No 2) 2001 SLT 1311 572
Clarke v Fennoscandia Ltd 1998 SLT 1014 589
Claxton Engineering Services Ltd v TXM Olaj-Es Gazkutato Kft [2011] EWHC . . . .
Cleveland Museum of Art v Capricorn Art International SA [1990] 2 Lloyd's
    Rep 166 . . . . .329–30, 408
Clinton v Ford (1982) 137 DLR (3d) 281 . . . . .534, 537, 594
Clodagh Daly v Irish Group Travel Limited Trading as "Crystal Holidays"
    [2003] IL Pr 38 287
Clore, Re [1982] Fam 113, [1982] Ch 456 1330
Club Mediterranee NZ v Wendell [1989] 1 NZLR 216 394
Clyne v Federal Comr of Taxation (No 2) (1981) 57 FLR 198 110
CNA Insurance Co Ltd v Office Depot International (UK) Ltd [2005]
    EWHC 456 (Comm) 332–3, 465, 468, 471
Coast Lines Ltd v Hudig and Veder Chartering NV [1972] 2 QB 34 . . . . .373–4, 597, 721, 725
Cochrane v Moore (1890) 25 QBD 57 1277
Cohen v Rothfield [1919] 1 KB 410 . . . . .427, 431
Cohn, Re [1945] Ch 5 . . . . .47, 50, 85, 112, 1345
Coin Controls Ltd v Suzo International (UK) Ltd [1999]
    Ch 33 . . . . .217–18, 225, 285, 307, 456, 492, 495–6
Coleman v Shang [1961] AC 481 942
Collens, Re [1986] Ch 505 . . . . .1338, 1352
Collett v Collett [1968] P 482 . . . . .904, 1049
Collier v Rivaz (1841) 2 Curt 855 . . . . .65–6, 71, 1343
Collins v A-G (1931) 145 LT 551 67

Collister v Collister [1972] 1 WLR 54 1063
Colonia Versicherung AG v Amoco Oil, The "Wind Star", 1993 (unreported). 370
Colonial Bank v Cady (1890) 15 App Cas 267 1300
Color Drack GmbH v LEXX International Vertriebs GmbH (C-386/05)
    [2007] IL Pr 35 . . . . .244, 254–5, 257, 259
Colquitt v Colquitt [1948] P 19. 67
Colt Industries Inc v Sarlie (No 2) [1966] 1 WLR 1287. . . . . .549, 550
Colt Industries Inc v Sarlie [1966] 1 WLR 440 .325, 374, 549, 550
Colt Telecom Group plc, Re (No 2) [2002] EWHC 2815 (Ch), [2003]
    BPIR 324. . . . . .133, 753
Comet Group plc v Unika Computer SA [2004] IL Pr 1 . . . . .257, 304
Comité d'entreprise de Nortel Networks SA and Others v Cosme Rogeau
    (qualitate qua) and Cosme Rogeau (qualitate qua) v Alan Robert Bloom,
    Alan Michael Hudson, Stephen John Harris and Christopher
    John Wilkinson Hill, (C-649/13) ECLI:EU:C:2015:384 .1316–17
Commercial Innovation Bank Alfa Bank v Kozeny [2002] UKPC 66. . . . . .573, 577
Commercial Marine Piling Ltd v Pierse Contracting Ltd [2009] EWHC 2241 (TCC),
    [2009] IL Pr 54 261
Commerzbank Aktiengesellschaft v Liquimar Tankers Management Inc [2017] EWHC 161
    (Comm), [2017] 1 Lloyd's Rep 273 . . . . .236, 453
Commonwealth Bank of Australia v White (No 4) [2001] VSC 511 440
Commonwealth Bank of Australia v White [1999] 2 VR 681. . . . . .330, 344
Commune De Macot La Plagne v SA Sebluxl [2007] IL Pr 12. 640
Compagnie Commercial Andre SA v Artibell Shipping Co Ltd 1999 SLT 1051 286
Compagnie d'Armement Maritime SA v Cie Tunisienne de Navigation SA [1971] AC 572. . . .724
Compagnie Française v Thorn Electrics [1981] FSR 306 593
Compañía Naviera Micro SA v Shipley International Inc, The Parouth
    [1982] 2 Lloyd's Rep 351. . . . . .344, 723, 756
Compañía Naviera Vascongada v SS Cristina [1938] AC 485. . . . . .131, 507
Concept Oil Services Limited (a company incorporated in Hong Kong) v EN-GIN Group
    LLP (a limited liability partnership under the law of Kazakhstan), EN-GIN Production
    LLP (a limited liability partnership under the law of Kazakhstan), and others [2013]
    EWHC 1897 (Comm). 1306
Concha v Murrietta (1889) 40 Ch D 543 112
Concord Trust v The Law Debenture Trust Corpn plc [2005] UKHL 27, [2005] 1 WLR 1591.105
Concurrent Claims (Royalties), Re (Case 4 Ob 66/01), [2003] IL Pr 30 265
Conductive Inkjet Technology Ltd v Uni-Pixel Displays Inc [2013] EWHC 2968 (Ch),
    [2014] 1 All ER (Comm) 654 . . . . .336, 343, 471–2, 826
Confirmation of a European Enforcement Order (Case 5 W 29/ 07),
    Re [2010] IL Pr 44. 658
Congreso del Partido [1983] 1 AC 244 . . . . .126, 499, 504
Conlon v Mohamed [1989] ILRM 523 . . . . .902, 905, 921, 941
Connelly v Connelly (1851) 7 Moo PCC 438 1013
Connelly v RTZ Corpn plc [1998] AC 854, [1999] CLC 533. . . . . .373, 394, 397, 401, 403
Connor v Connor [1974] 1 NZLR 632 . . . . .116, 553
Conocophillips (UK) Ltd v Partnereederei Ms Jork [2010] EWHC 1214 (Comm) 270
Continental Bank NA v Aeakos Compañía Naviera SA [1994]
    1 WLR 588 . . . . .235, 237, 436, 440, 451, 476
Continental Enterprises Ltd v Shandong Zhucheng Foreign Trade
    Group Co [2005] EWHC 92 (Comm) 701, 755, 769
Controller and Auditor-General v Davison [1996] 2 NZLR 278 497
Cood v Cood (1863) 33 LJ Ch 273 . . . . .487, 490
Cook Industries Inc v Galliher [1979] Ch 439. . . . . .486, 488, 490, 1255
Cook v Virgin Media Ltd [2015] EWCA Civ 1287, [2016] 1 WLR 1672 322
Cooke's Trusts, Re (1887) 56 LJ Ch 637 . . . . .761, 1375

Cool Carriers AB v HSBC Bank USA [2001] 2 Lloyd's Rep 22 342
Cooper Tire & Rubber Co Europe Ltd v Shell Chemicals UK Ltd [2010]
    EWCA Civ 864, [2010] 2 CLC 104 . . . . .273–4, 285, 444, 456
Cooper Tire & Rubber Co v Shell Chemicals UK Ltd [2009] EWHC 2609
    (Comm) 273–4
Cooper v Cooper (1888) 13 App Cas 88 . . . . .761–2, 911, 1375, 1376
Cooper v Crane [1891] P 369 988
Cooper-King v Cooper-King [1900] P 65 110
Copin v Adamson (1875) 1 Ex D 17 . . . . .532, 577
Coppin v Coppin (1725) 2 P Wms 291 . . . . .1256, 1259, 1352
Coral Isis, The [1986] 1 Lloyd's Rep 413 408–9
Corbet v Waddell (1879) 7 R (Ct of Sess) 200 1366
Corbett v Corbett (otherwise Ashley) [1971] P 83 892
Corbett v Corbett [1957] 1 WLR 486 . . . . .997, 1012, 1035
Corcoran v Corcoran [1974] VR 164. . . . . .55, 816
Corcoz v Molina, 9 July 2015, HC 638
Cordoba Shipping Co Ltd v National State Bank, Elizabeth, New Jersey,
    The Albaforth [1984] 2 Lloyd's Rep 91 . . . . .351–2, 367
Cordova Land Co Ltd v Victor Bros Inc [1966] 1 WLR 793 .366, 376
Coreck Maritime GmbHv Handelsveem BV (C-387/98) [2000] ECR I-9337 234
Corman-Collins SA v La Maison du Whisky SA (C-9/12) EU:C:2013:860
    [2014] QB 431 . . . . 256 729–30
Corps Ltd v Apple Computer Inc [1992] FSR 431. 136
Cortes v Yorkton Securities Inc (2007) 278 DLR (4th) 740 . . . . .559, 577
Cortese v Nowsco Well Service Ltd [2001] IL Pr 196. 404
Coty Germany GmbH v First Note Perfumes NV (C-360/12) EU:C:2014:1318,
    [2015] IL Pr 13 . . . . .264, 274, 276, 279, 834
Coupland v Arabian Gulf Oil Co [1983] 1 WLR 1136 881
Courtney, Re (1840) Mont 8 Ch 239. 489
Couzens v Negri [1981] VR 824 491
Coventry City Council v A [2014] EWHC 2033. 1100
Cox v Ergo Versicherung AG (formerly Victoria) [2014] UKSC 22 . . . . .45, 73, 786
Cox v Ergo Versicherung AG [2012] EWCA Civ 1001 864
Craignish, Re [1892] 3 Ch 180 . . . . .155, 157
Cramer v Cramer [1987] 1 FLR 116 . . . . .151–2, 162
Crane Accessories Ltd v Lim Swee Hee [1989] 1 NZLR 221 394
Cranstown v Johnston (1796) 3 Ves 170 . . . . .486, 488
Craven's Estate, Re [1937] Ch 423. 1276
Crédit Agricole Indosuez v Chailease Finance Corpn [2000] 1 Lloyd's Rep 348 . . . . . . .253–4, 261
Crédit Agricole Indosuez v Unicof Ltd [2003] EWHC 2676 (Comm),
    [2004] 1 Lloyd's Rep 196. . . . . .335, 337–8, 350, 374, 402–3
Crédit Chimique v James Scott Engineering Group Ltd 1979 SC 406, 1982 SLT 131. 393
Crédit Lyonnais v New Hampshire Insurance Co [1997] 2 Lloyd's Rep 1 . . . . .724, 728, 736
Crédit Suisse Fides Trust SA v Cuoghi [1998] QB 818, [1998] 1 WLR 474. 306–7
Crédit Suisse Financial Products v Société Générale d'Enterprises [1997]
    CLC 168, [1997] IL Pr 165 . . . . .234, 238
Crédit Suisse First Boston (Europe) Ltd v Seagate Trading Co Ltd [1999]
    1 Lloyd's Rep 784. . . . . .415, 436
Crédit Suisse First Boston (Europe) v MLC (Bermuda) Ltd [1999] 1 All ER
    (Comm) 237 . . . . .412, 438
Crescent Oil and Shipping Services Ltd v Importang UEE [1998] 1 WLR 919 508
Cressington Court (Owners) v Marinero (Owners), The Marinero [1955] 1 All ER 676 106
Crichton v Successor of Crichton 232 So 2d 109 (1970) 1368
Crichton's Estate, Re 20 NY 2d 124, 228 NE 2d 799 (1967). 1368
Crichton's Trust, Re (1855) 24 LTOS 267 1176

Crick v Hennessy [1973] WAR 74 543
Crickmay v Crickmay (1967) 60 DLR (2d) 734 917
Criminal Proceedings against Titus Alexander Jochen Donner (C-5/11)
    ECLI:EU:C:2012:370 832–3
Crociani v Crociani [2014] UKPC 40, [2015] WTLR 975 371
Croft v King [1893] 1 QB 419. 337
Croll v Croll, 229 F 3d 133 (2d Cir, 2000) 109
Cronos Containers NV v Palatin [2002] EWHC 2819 (Comm), [2003]
    2 Lloyd's Rep 489. . . . . .263, 266, 272, 455
Crosstown Music Co I LLC v Rive Droit Music Ltd [2010] EWCA Civ
    1222, [2012] Ch 68 495
Crowe v Kader [1968] WAR 122 937
Crucial Music Corpn v Klondyke Management AG [2007] EWHC 1782
    (Ch), [2007] IL Pr 54. . . . . .249, 277
Cruh v Cruh [1945] 2 All ER 545 160
Cruikshanks v Cruikshanks [1957] 1 WLR 564. 160
Cruse v Chittum [1974] 2 All ER 940 . . . . .1007, 1010
Cruz City 1 Mauritius Holdings v Unitech Ltd [2014] EWHC 3704
    (Comm), [2015] 1 Lloyd's Rep 191 304
CSR Ltd v Cigna Insurance Australia Ltd (1997) 189 CLR 345. . . . . .425, 428–9
Cube Lighting and Industrial Design Ltd v Afcon Electra Romania SA
    [2011] EWHC 2565 . . . . .216, 335
Cuccolini SRL v Elcan Industries Inc [2013] EWHC 2994 370
Cudak v Lithuania, Judgment of 23 March 2010; (2010) 51 EHRR 15. . . . . .501, 503
Cukurova Holding SA v Sonera Holding BV [2014] UKPC 15, [2015]
    2 All ER 1061 . . . . .672–3, 676
Culling v Culling [1896] P 116 909
Cunnington, Re [1924] 1 Ch 68 1348
Curati v Perdoni [2012] EWCA Civ 1381 156
Currie v Bircham (1822) 1 Dowl & Ry KB 35. 1333
Curtis v Hutton (1808) 14 Ves 537 1260
CW v NT & Anor [2011] EWHC 33 1180
Cyganik v Agulian [2006] EWCA Civ 129, [2006] 1 FCR 406 . . . . 148, 151,
                                                                      156, 162, 172, 1345, 1353
Czepek v Czepek [1962] 3 All ER 990 982

D (A Child) (Abduction: Rights of Custody), Re [2006] UKHL 51, [2007]
    1 AC 619 . . . . .1056–7, 1136–8, 1144–5, 1148, 1151, 1155–6, 1163, 1166
D (A Child) (Recognition and Enforcement of Romanian Order), Re [2016]
    EWCA Civ 12 1128
D (A Child), Re [2016] UKSC 34 1128
D (A Minor) (Child Abduction), Re [1988] FCR 585, [1989] 1 FLR 97 . . . . .1134–6, 1140, 1154
D (Abduction: Acquiescence), Re [1998] 2 FLR 335 1150
D (Abduction: Acquiescence), Re [1999] 1 FLR 36 1149
D (Abduction: Custody Rights), Re [1999] 2 FLR 626 .1139, 1144
D (Abduction: Discretionary Return), Re [2000] 1 FLR 24. . . . . .1136, 1150
D (Adoption: Foreign Guardianship), Re [1999] 2 FLR 865 .1214
D (Children) (Article 13(b): Non-Return), Re [2006] EWCA Civ 146, [2006]
    2 FLR 305 1154
D (Children) (Parental Order: Foreign Surrogacy), Re [2012] EWHC 2631 1187
D and L (Surrogacy) [2012] EWHC 2631. 1188
D v D (Child Abduction: Non-Convention Country), Re [1994] 1 FLR 137 1174
D v D (Custody: Jurisdiction) [1996] 1 FLR 574. 1108
D v D (Fertility Treatment: Paperwork Error) [2016] EWHC 2112. 1052
D v D (Parent and Child: Residence) 2001 SLT 1104 . . . . .179, 183

D v D [1994] 1 FLR 38 . . . . .175, 892–3, 1021, 1028
D v D 2001 SLT 1104 . . . . .176, 183
D v N v D (By her Guardian ad Litem) [2011] EWHC 471 1161
D v O [2011] EWCA Civ 128 1142
D, Re [1943] Ch 305 1110
D'Almeida Araujo Lda v Becker & Co Ltd [1953] 2 QB 329 92–3
D'Etchegoyen v D'Etchegoyen (1888) 13 PD 132 . . . . .155, 166
D'Hoker v Tritan Enterprises [2009] EWHC 949 (QB) 630
D'Orleans's (Duchess) Goods, Re (1859) 1 Sw & Tr 253 1332
Dadourian Group International Inc v Simms [2006] EWCA Civ 399, [2006]
    1 All ER (Comm) 709 284
Dagi v BHP (No 2) [1997] 1 VR 428 . . . . .484–5, 492
Dakota Lumber Co v Rinderknecht (1905) 6 Terr LR 210 541
Dallah Real Estate and Tourism Co v Ministry of Religious Affairs of the
    Government of Pakistan [2010] UKSC 46, [2011] 1 AC 763 . . . . .419, 670
Dallah Real Estate and Tourism Holding Company v Government of Pakistan [2010]
    UKSC 46, [2011] AC 763 419
Dallal v Bank Mellat [1986] QB 441 . . . . .563, 567, 672
Dalmia Cement Ltd v National Bank of Pakistan [1975] QB 9 668
Dalmia Dairy Industries Ltd v National Bank of Pakistan [1978]
    2 Lloyd's Rep 223 . . . . .108, 137, 573, 667–8
Dalrymple v Dalrymple (1811) 2 Hag Con 54, 161 ER 665 .20–1, 893
Damberg v Damberg [2001] 52 NSWLR 492 106
Daniel v Foster 1989 SLT 90 . . . . .150, 319
Danosa v LKB Lizings SIA (C-232/09) [2010] ECR I-11405 299
Dansommer A/S v Gotz (C-8/98) [2000] ECR I-393 221–2
Danvaern Production A/S v Schuhfabriken Otterbeck GmbH & Co (C-341/93) [1995]
    ECR I-2053 288
Danziger v Ford Motor Co 402 F Supp 2d 236 (DDC 2005) 25
Dar Al Arkan Real Estate Development Co v Refai [2014] EWCA Civ 715, [2015]
    1 WLR 135 217
Dardana Ltd v Yukos Oil Co [2002] EWCA Civ 543, [2002] 2 Lloyd's Rep 326 671–3
David Steel J in Knauf UK GmbH v British Gypsum Ltd [2001] EWCA Civ 1570 231
Davidsson v Hill [1901] 2 KB 606 878
Davies v Davies (1915) 24 DLR 737 1358
Davison v Sweeney (2005) 255 DLR (4th) 757 105
Dawson v Broughton, 31 July 2007 (unreported), Manchester County Court 778, 800
Dawson v Broughton, 31 July 2007 (unreported) 95
De Beéche v South American Stores Ltd and Chilian Stores Ltd [1935] AC 148 . . . . .110, 112
De Bloos v Bouyer (14/76) [1976] ECR 1497 . . . . .262, 280
De Brimont v Penniman (1873) 10 Blatch 436 91
De Cavel v De Cavel (143/78) [1979] ECR 1055 . . . . .212, 305, 612, 614, 1065
De Cavel v De Cavel (No 2) (120/79) [1980] ECR 731 . . . . .212, 612, 614, 1065
De Cosse Brissac v Rathbone (1861) 6 H & N 301 537
De Dampierre v De Dampierre [1988] AC 92 . . . . .402, 408–9, 973–4
De L v Director-General, New South Wales Department of Community
    Services (1996) 139 ALR 417, (1997) 21 Fam LR 413 1145
De L v H [2009] EWHC 3074 . . . . .1145, 1146, 1150
De la Vega v Vianna (1830) 1 B & Ad 284 . . . . .73, 104
De Larragoiti, Re [1907] 2 Ch 14 . . . . .1246, 1248
De Linden, Re [1897] 1 Ch 453 1246–7
De Massa v De Massa [1939] 2 All ER 150 . . . . .894, 1012
De Molestina v Ponton [2002] 1 Lloyd's Rep 271 . . . . .337, 363
De Nicols v Curlier [1900] AC 21 . . . . .44, 1369, 1372
De Nicols, Re (No 2) [1900] 2 Ch 410 . . . . .1256, 1372–3

De Nova (1964) 8 Am JLH 136, 141. 4
De Pina v MS Birka ICG [1994] IL Pr 694 456
De Reneville v De Reneville [1948] P 100 . . . . .106, 140, 914, 985, 995–6, 998
de Santis v Russo [2002] 2 Qd R 230. 534
De Thoren v A-G (1876) 1 App Cas 686 85
De Thoren v Wall (1876) 3 R (HL) 28. 1009
De Virte, Re [1915] 1 Ch 920 1357
De Wilton, Re [1900] 2 Ch 481 913
De Wolf v Cox BV (42/76) [1976] ECR 1759. . . . . .443, 556, 617–18, 618
De Wutz v Hendricks (1824) 2 Bing 314. 136
Deaville v Aeroflot [1997] 2 Lloyd's Rep 67 . . . . .203, 428, 476
Debaecker v Bouwman (49/84) [1985] ECR 1779 . . . . .636–8, 637, 638
Debt Collect London Ltd v SK Slavia Praha-Fotbal AS [2010] EWCA Civ
    1250, [2011] 1 WLR 866 . . . . .112, 449
Definitely Maybe (Touring) Ltd v Marek Lieberberg Konzertagentur GmbH
    (No 2) [2001] 1 WLR 1745. . . . . .262, 346, 725, 728, 736, 738, 1280
Degaramo's Estate, Re 33 NYS 502 (1895) 53
Degazon v Barclays Bank International Ltd [1988] 1 FTLR 17 .1336
Deichland, The [1990] 1 QB 361 . . . . .203, 214, 386
Delaire v Delaire [1996] 9 WWR 469 1293
Delhi Electric Supply and Traction Co Ltd, Re [1954] Ch 131 1335
Delisle, Re (1988) 52 DLR (4th) 106. 1271
Dellar v Zivy [2007] EWHC 2266 (Ch), [2007] IL Pr 60 . . . . .155, 358, 367, 408
Delos, The [2001] 1 Lloyd's Rep 703 417
Demirel v Tasarruff [2007] EWCA Civ 799, [2007] 1 WLR 2508, [2007]
    1 WLR 3066 . . . . .115–16, 335, 355, 374
Dent v Smith (1869) LR 4 QB 414 564
Deo Antoine Homawoo v GMF Assurances SA (C-412/10) ECLI:EU:
    C:2011:747 . . . . .783–4, 786
Department of Health and Community Services v Casse (1995) 19 Fam
    LR 474. 1150
Derby and Co Ltd v Larsson [1976] 1 WLR 202 337
Deripaska v Cherney [2009] EWCA Civ 849, [2009] CP Rep 48 . . . . .342, 372–3
Desarrollo Immobiliario Y Negocios Industriales De Alta v Kader
    Holdings Co Ltd [2014] EWHC 1460 . . . . .531–2, 538
Deschamps v Miller [1908] 1 Ch 856 . . . . .484, 487, 490
Desert Sun Loan Corpn v Hill [1996] 2 All ER 847. . . . . .534, 536, 550, 556, 559, 560, 563
Deshais, In the Goods of (1865) 4 Sw & Tr 13 1343
Despina GK, The [1983] 1 QB 214. 548
Deutsche Bahn AG v Morgan Advanced Materials Plc (formerly Morgan
    Crucible Co Plc) [2013] EWCA Civ 1484, [2014] CP Rep 10 . . . . .264, 276
Deutsche Bank AG London Branch v Petromena ASA [2013] EWHC 3065, [2015]
    EWCA Civ 226, [2015] 1 WLR 4225 . . . . .229, 249, 260, 272, 333
Deutsche Bank und Gesellschaft v Banque des Marchands de Moscou (1930)
    (unreported), CA. 1282
Deutsche Bank v Asia Pacific Broadband [2008] EWCA Civ 1091 233
Deutsche Bank v Highland Crusader [2009] EWCA Civ 725 . . . . .427, 429, 441
Deutsche Bank v Murtagh [1995] 1 ILRM 381 . . . . .173, 199
Deutsche Genossenschaftsbank v Brasserie du Pecheur SA (148/84) [1985] ECR 1981 624–5
Deutsche National Bank v Paul [1898] 1 Ch 283. 357
Deutsche Ruckversicherung AG v La Fondiara Assicurazioni SpA [2001]
    2 Lloyd's Rep 621. . . . . .216, 251
Deutsche Schachtbau v Shell International Petroleum Co Ltd [1990]
    1 AC 295 1293
Deutz Engines Ltd v Terex Ltd 1984 SLT 273 1272

Deverall v Grant Advertising Inc [1955] Ch 111 329
Devos v Devos (1970) 10 DLR (3d) 603 1368
Devrajan v District Judge Ballagh [1993] 3 IR 381 228
Dewar v Maitland (1866) LR 2 Eq 834 1355
Dexter Ltd (In Administrative Receivership) v Harley (2001) Times, 2 April 267, 276
DFDS Torline v SEKO (C-18/02) [2004] ECR I-1417, [2004] IL Pr 10 . . . . . .267, 272, 835, 876
Dharamal v Lord Holm-Patrick [1935] IR 760 1176
DHL GBS (UK) Ltd v Fallimento Finmatica SpA [2009] EWHC 291
    (Comm), [2009] 1 Lloyd's Rep 430 . . . . .211, 480, 648
Dhost Aly Khan's Goods, Re (1880) 6 PD 6 110
Di Ferdinando v Simon, Smits & Co Ltd [1920] 3 KB 409 102
Di Rollo v Di Rollo 1959 SC 75, 1959 SLT 278 . . . . .989, 1013
Di Savini, Savini v Lousada (1870) 18 WR 425 1176
Di Sora v Phillips (1863) 10 HL Cas 624 112
Diag Human SE v Czech Republic [2013] EWHC 3190, [2014] EWHC
    1639 (Comm), [2014] 2 Lloyd's Rep 244, 283 .559–60, 671, 673
Diageo Brands BV v Simiramida-04 EOOD (C-681/13) EU:C:2015:471 . . . . .628, 631
Diamond v Bank of London and Montreal [1979] QB 333 352
Dickinson v Del Solar [1930] 1 KB 376 511
Dickson v Dickson 1990 SCLR 692, 703 180
Didisheim v London and Westminster Bank [1900] 2 Ch 15 . . . . .87, 1246, 1247
Dimskal Shipping Co SA v International Transport Workers Federation
    (The Evia Luck No 2) [1990] 1 Lloyd's Rep 319, [1992] 2 AC 152 . . . . .70, 135
Dinwoodie's Executrix v Carruthers' Executrix (1895) 23 R 234 1284
Direct Energy Marketing Ltd v Hillson [2000] IL Pr 102 352
Director-General of Family and Community Services v Davis (1990) 14 Fam
    LR 381 1151–2
Disney Enterprises Inc v Click Enterprises Inc (2006) 267 DLR (4th) 291 530
Distillers Co (Biochemicals) Ltd v Thompson [1971] AC 458 348
Divall v Divall [2014] EWHC 95 . . . . .161, 163, 955
DL v EL [2013] 2 FLR 163 175
DL v EL [2013] EWCA Civ 865 1103
DM v SJ [2016] EWHC 270 (Fam) 1186
Do Carmo v Ford Excavations Pty Ltd (1984) 52 ALR 231 42
Doe and Birtwhistle v Vardill (1835) 2 Cl & Fin 571 1195
Doe v Armour Pharmaceutical Co Inc [1995] IL Pr 148 408
Doe v Howard [2015] VSC 75 . . . . .553, 575
Doetsch, Re [1896] 2 Ch 836 . . . . .50, 87–8
Doglioni v Crispin (1866) LR 1 HL 301 1343
Doiron v Bugge (2005) 258 DLR (4th) 716 349
Dollfus Mieg & Cie v CDW International Ltd [2004] IL Pr 12 288
Dollfus Mieg et Compagnie SA v Bank of England [1949] Ch 369 546
Dolphin Maritime & Aviation Services Ltd v Sveriges Angfartygs Assurans
    Forening [2009] EWHC 716 (Comm), [2009] 2 Lloyd's Rep 123 275
Domansa v Derin Shipping and Trading Co Inc [2001] 1 Lloyd's Rep 362 . . . . .329, 412
Domicrest v Swiss Bank Corpn [1999] QB 548 . . . . .272, 349, 792
Don v Lippmann (1837) 5 Cl & Fin 1 73–4
Don's Estate, Re (1857) 4 Drew 194 . . . . .1195, 1201
Donaldson v Donaldson [1949] P 363 . . . . .156, 160
Donegal International Ltd v Zambia [2007] EWHC 197 (Comm), [2007]
    1 Lloyd's Rep 397 506
Donlam v Maggurn 55 P 3d 74 893
Donofrio v Burrell 1999 GWD 12–528, 2000 SLT 1051 1135
Donohue v Armco Inc [2001] UKHL 64, [2002] 1 All ER 749 . . . . 362, 367, 370,
    410, 422–3, 428, 430, 436–7

Dooney, Re [1993] 2 Qd R 362...549
Doran v Power [1997] IL Pr 52 387
Dornach Ltd v Mauritius Union Assurance Co Ltd [2006] EWCA Civ 389,
    [2006] 2 Lloyd's Rep 475..................................719, 721, 723, 728, 734
Dornoch Ltd v Westminster International BV [2009] EWHC 1782 (Admlty),
    [2009] 2 Lloyd's Rep 420..112, 1267
Dornoch Ltd v Westminster International BV [2009] EWHC 889 (Admlty), [2009] 2
    Lloyd's Rep 191 1267
Dorward v Dorward 1994 SCCR 928 1107
Doucet v Geoghegan (1878) 9 Ch D 441 152
Douglas v Douglas (1871) LR 12 Eq 617......................................157
Douglas v Forrest (1828) 4 Bing 686 540
Douglas v Hello! [2007] UKHL 21, [2008] 1 AC 798
Douglas v Hello! Ltd (No 2) [2003] EWCA Civ 139, [2003] EMLR 28 ....360, 362
Douglas v Hello! Ltd (No 3) [2005] EWCA Civ 595, [2006] QB 125........360, 780, 806, 884
Douglas Webber Events Pty Ltd, Re [2014] NSWSC 1544 1308–9
Dow Jones & Co Inc v Gutnick (2002) 210 CLR 575....................350, 394, 398
Dow Jones & Co Inc v Jameel [2005] EWCA (Civ) 75, [2005] QB 946 ......14, 350–1353, 887
Dow Jones & Co Inc v Yousef Abdul Latif Jameel [2005] QB 946................14
Dowans Holding SA v Tanzania Electric Supply Co Ltd [2011] EWHC 1957 (Comm),
    [2011] 2 Lloyd's Rep 275...673
Dowdale's case (1604) 6 Co Rep 46b 1333
Dowis v Mud Slingers Inc 621 SE 2d 413 (Ga 2005)............................30
Downing v Al Tameer Establishment [2002] EWCA 721, [2002] 2 All ER (Comm) 545 344
Downtown v Royal Trust Co (1972) 34 DLR (3d) 403 1035
Doyle v Doyle (1974) 52 DLR (3d) 143 325
DR Insurance Co v Central National Insurance Co [1996]
    1 Lloyd's Rep 74....................................347, 364, 367, 744
Draka NK Cables Ltd v Omnipol Ltd (C-167/08) [2009] ECR I-3477.............625
Drammeh v Drammeh (1970) 78 Ceylon Law Weekly 55 ....936, 953
Drax Holdings Ltd, Re [2003] EWHC 2743 (Ch), [2004] 1 WLR 1049............224
Drevon v Drevon (1864) 34 LJ Ch 129, 133 155
Drew Brown v The Orient Trader (1972) 34 DLR (3d) 339......................92
Drouot Assurances SA v Consolidated Metallurgical Industries 485 (C-351/96)
    [1999] QB 497 446–7
Drozd and Janousek v France and Spain Series, A No 240, (1992) 14 EHRR 745 580–1
DSG International Sourcing Ltd v Universal Media Corp (Slovakia) SRO [2011]
    EWHC 1116 (Comm), [2011] IL Pr 33 308
DSG Retail Ltd v Mastercard Inc [2015] CAT 7 264
DT v FL [2004] 1 ILRM 509, [2006] IEHC 98, [2007] IL Pr 56 ....163, 640
DT v LBT (Abduction: Domestic Abuse) [2010] EWHC 3177....................1165
Du Moulin v Druitt (1860) 13 ICLR 212 908
Duarte v Black and Decker Corp [2007] EWHC 2720 (QB), [2008] 1 All ER
    (Comm) 401 133
Dubai Bank Ltd v Abbas [1997] IL Pr 308, [1998] IL Pr 391 ....336, 443
Dubai Electricity Co v Islamic Republic of Iran Shipping Lines, The Iran Vojdan
    [1984] 2 Lloyd's Rep 380...404, 716
Dubai Islamic Bank PJSC Energy Holding BSC [2013] EWHC 3186..............715
Dubai Islamic Bank PJSC v PSI Energy Holding Co BSC [2011] EWHC 1019
    (Comm), [2011] 1 CLC 595 234
Dubai Islamic Bank PJSC v PSI Energy Holding Company BSC [2013] EWHC
    3186 (Comm) 1256
Dubai Paymentech [2001] 1 Lloyd's Rep 65....................................417
Duchess of Kingston's case (1776) 20 State Tr 355............................488
Duff Development Co Ltd v Kelantan Government [1924] AC 797 506

Duhur-Johnson v Duhur-Johnson [2005] 2 FLR 1042 .1008, 1025, 1027
Duijnstee v Goderbauer (288/82) [1983] ECR 3663 . . . . .217–18, 309
Dukali v Lamrani (Attorney-General Intervening) [2012] EWHC 1748 . . . . . . .893–6, 900, 1026
Duke of Marlborough v A-G [1945] Ch 78 . . . . .1388, 1391
Duke of Wellington, Re [1947] Ch 506, [1948] Ch 118 . . . . .63, 65, 68, 71, 1256
Duke v Andler [1932] SCR 734 . . . . .491, 546
Dukov v Dukov (1968) 13 FLR 149 906–7
Dulaney v Merry & Son [1901] 1 KB 536 1274
Dulles' Settlement, Re (No 2) [1951] Ch 842 . . . . .333, 543
Dunbee Ltd v Gilman & Co (Australia) Pty Ltd [1968] 2 Lloyd's Rep 394 542
Duncan v Lawson (1889) 41 Ch D 394 . . . . 1251, 1258, 1260,
                                                                                                      1351, 1353
Duncan v Neptunia Corpn (2001) 199 DLR (4th) 354 349
Duncombe v Secretary of State for Children, Schools and Families [2011] UKSC 36,
    [2011] 4 All ER 1020 143
Dundas v Dundas (1830) 2 Dow & Cl 349 1356
Dunhill v Sunoptic [1979] FSR 337 106
Dunne v Byrne [1912] AC 407 1347
Duran v Beaumont (2d Cir, 2008) 534 F 3d 142 . . . . . 109Duran v Beaumont
    (2d Cir, 2010), 622 F 3d 97 109
Duran v Beaumont, 130 S Ct 3318 (2010) 109
Durie's Trustees v Osborne 1960 SC 444 . . . . .1347, 1363
Duyvewaardt v Barber (1992) 43 RFL (3d) 139 1372
DVA v Voest Alpine [1997] 2 Lloyd's Rep 279 . . . . .341, 427, 437, 439
Dymocks Franchise Systems (NSW) Pty Ltd v Todd [2002] UKPC 50,
    [2004] 1 NZLR 289 108
Dymocks Franchise Systems (NSW)) Pty Ltd v Todd [2002] UKPC 50,
    [2004] 1 NZLR 289 108
Dynamics Corpn of America, Re [1976] 1 WLR 757 99–100
Dynamit Actien-Gesellschaft v Rio Tinto Co Ltd [1918] AC 260 .136

E (A Child) (Abduction: Rights of Custody), Re [2005] EWHC 848, [2005] 2 FLR 759 1137
E (A Child) (Care Proceedings: Jurisdiction), Re [2014] EWHC 6 1115
E (A Minor) (Abduction), Re [1989] 1 FLR 135, [1989] Fam Law 105 . . . . .1143, 1153
E (Child: Abduction), Re [1991] FCR 631, [1992] 1 FCR 541 . . . . .179, 1107, 1143
E (Child: Abduction), Re [1992] 1 FCR 541 177
E (Children) (Abduction: Custody Appeal), Re [2011] UKSC 27 . . . . 1138, 1143,
                                                                                                  1152–6, 1160, 1166
E Pfeiffer Weinkellerei-Weineinkauf GmbH & Co v Arbuthnot Factors Ltd [1988]
    1 WLR 150 1273
E v B (C-436/13) 1099
E v F [1974] 2 NZLR 435 1174
E(D), Re [1967] Ch 761, [1967] 2 WLR 1370 1175
EA v AP [2013] EWHC 2344 1066
East India Trading Co Inc v Carmel Exporters and Importers Ltd [1952]
    1 All ER 1053 101
East India Trading Co Inc v Carmel Exporters and Importers Ltd [1952] 2 QB 439,
    [1952] 1 All ER 1053 . . . . .101, 666
East West Corpn v DKBS 1912 [2002] EWHC 83 (Comm), [2002] 2 Lloyd's Rep
    182, [2003] EWCA Civ 83, [2003] 1 Lloyd's Rep 239 765
Easterbrook v Easterbrook [1944] 1 All ER 90 . . . . .985, 994
Eastern Power Ltd v Azienda Comunale Energia e Ambiente [2001] IL Pr 6 343
Eastern Trader, The [1996] 2 Lloyd's Rep 585 . . . . .537, 539, 587
EC-L v DM (Child Abduction) [2005] EWHC 588, [2005]
    2 FLR 772 1139

Eco Cosmetics GmbH & Co KG v Dupuy and Raiffeisenbank St Georgen reg,
    Gen mbH v Bonchyk (C-119/13) and (C-120/13) EU:C:2014:2144,
    [2015] 1 WLR 678 661
Ecobank Transnational Inc v Tanoh [2015] EWCA Civ 1309, [2016]
    1 Lloyd's Rep 360...422, 439, 442
Ecobank Transnational Incorporated v Mr Thierry Tanoh [2015] EWHC 1874............584
Ecom Agroindustrial Corp Ltd v Mosharaf Composite Textile Mill Ltd [2013]
    EWHC 1276 (Comm), [2013] 2 Lloyd's Rep 196..............................422
ED & F Mann (Sugar) Ltd v Yani Haryanto (No 2) [1991] 1 Lloyd's Rep 161,
    [1991] 1 Lloyd's Rep 429...............................567, 574, 583
ED (Jurisdiction: Undertaking to Return), Re [2014] EWHC 2731 1099
eDate Advertising GmbH v X and Olivier Martinez and Robert Martinez v MGN
    Limited (C-161/10) [2011] ECR I-10269.............263, 270–1, 275, 278, 873, 887–8
eDate Advertising GmbH v X and Olivier Martinez and Robert Martinez v MGN
    Limited (C-509/09) and (C-161/10) [2011] ECR I-10269 .... 263, 270, 271,
                                                            275, 278, 873, 887, 888
Eddie v Alpa Srl 2000 SLT 1062 ....247, 257
EDG v RR [2014] EWHC 816 1081–2
Edinburgh Castle, The [1999] 2 Lloyd's Rep 362........................382
Edmunds v Simmonds [2001] 1 WLR 1003 ....93–4, 778, 800, 814, 863
Edwards v Carter [1893] AC 360.....................................1375–6
Edwards, Edwards v Edwards, Re (1969) 113 Sol Jo 108 ....148, 151
EF Hutton & Co (London) Ltd v Mofarrij [1989] 1 WLR 488...............342, 344
Effer v Kantner (38/81) [1982] ECR 825.............................221
Egbert v Short [1907] 2 Ch 205.....................................393
Egerton's Will Trusts, Re [1956] Ch 593 1366
Egmatra AG v Marco Trading Corpn [1999] 1 Lloyd's Rep 862................107
Egon Oldendorff v Liberia Corpn [1995] 2 Lloyd's Rep 64 ....344, 368, 369, 415,
                                                419, 587, 700, 720, 723, 756
Ehrenclou v MacDonald 12 Cal Rptr 3d 411 (Cal App 2004)..............1229
EI du Pont de Nemours & Co v I C Agnew and K W Kerr [1987] 2 Lloyd's Rep 585,
    [1988] 2 Lloyd's Rep 240..................367, 372, 402, 408–9, 716
Eider, The [1893] P 119...263, 346
Eilon v Eilon 1965 (1) SA 703.....................................152
Ekins v East-India Co (1717) 1 P Wms 395...........................96
El Ajou v Dollar Land Holdings plc [1993] 3 All ER 717, [1994]
    2 All ER 685 ....105, 108
El Ajou v Dollar Land Holdings plc [1994] 2 All ER 685 105
El Amria and El Minia, The [1981] 2 Lloyd's Rep 539....................412
El Amria, The [1981] 2 Lloyd's Rep 119 ....403, 411, 412
El Condado, The (1939) 63 Ll L Rep 330, 1939 SC 413..................132
El Fadl v El Fadl [2000] 1 FCR 685...........941, 1012, 1018, 1021, 1027–8, 1030–3
El Gamal v Al-Maktoum [2011] EWHC B27 894
El Majdoub v CarsOnTheWeb.Deutschland GmbH (C-322/14) EU:C:2015:334,
    [2015] 1 WLR 3986 239
El Nasharty v J Sainsbury [2003] EWHC 2195 (Comm), [2004] 1 All ER
    (Comm) 728 ....418, 420
Electrosteel Europe SA v Edil Centro SpA (C-87/10) [2011] ECR I-4987.................258
Elefanten Schuh GmbH v Jacqmain (150/80) [1981] ECR 1671............... 196, 226, 237,
                                                243, 456, 538, 690
Eleftheria, The [1970] P 94.......................................385, 411, 438
Elektrim SA v Vivendi Holdings 1 Corp [2008] EWCA Civ 1178, [2009]
    1 Lloyd's Rep 59...436
Elektrim SA v Vivendi Universal SA (No 2) [2007] EWHC 571 (Comm),
    [2007] 2 Lloyd's Rep 8.......................................422

Eleonore Prüller-Frey v Norbert Brodnig and Axa Versicherung AG (C-240/14)
ECLI:EU:C:2015:567 872
Elftherotria (Owners of) v Despina R, The Despina R [1979] AC 685. 99
Eli Lilly and Co v Novo Nordisk A/S [2000] IL Pr 73 . . . . .398, 409
Ella v Ella [2007] EWCA Civ 99 1075
Ellerman Lines Ltd v Read [1928] 2 KB 144 . . . . .436, 487, 569
Elliniko Dimosio v Stefanos Stroumpoulis and Others (C-292/14)
ECLI:EU:C:2016:116 . . . . .692, 876
Elliot v Joicey [1935] AC 209 . . . . .109, 433, 1201
Ellis v M'Henry (1871) LR 6 CP 228 567
Elwyn (Cottons) Ltd v Pearle Designs Ltd [1989] IR 9 620
EM (Lebanon) v Secretary of State for the Home Department [2006] EWCA
Civ 1531, [2007] 1 FLR 991 1163
Emanuel v Symon [1908] 1 KB 302 . . . . .529, 532, 540, 542, 606
Embassy of Brazil v de Castro Cerqueira [2014] 1 WLR 3718 508
Embiricos v Anglo-Austrian Bank [1904] 2 KB 870, [1905] 1 KB 677 1295–7
Emerald Stainless Steel Ltd v South Side Distribution Ltd 1983 SLT 162 1272
Emery v Emery 45 Cal 2d 421, 289 P 2d 218 (1955) 816
Emery's Investment Trusts, Re [1959] Ch 410 . . . . .118, 137
EMI Records Ltd v Modern Music Karl-Ulrich Waltebach GmbH [1992]
QB 115 616
Emin v Yeldag [2002] 1 FLR 956. . . . . .14, 1009, 1077
Employers' Liability Assurance Corpn v Sedgwick, Collins & Co [1927] AC 95 . . . . . . .528, 529
Empresa Exportadora de Azúcar v Industria Azucarera Nacional SA, The
Playa Larga [1983] 2 Lloyd's Rep 171 . . . . .118, 137, 504
Empresa Nacional de Telecomunicaciones SA v Deutsche Bank AG [2009]
EWHC 2579 (QB); [2010] 1 All ER (Comm) 649 130
Empson v Smith [1966] 1 QB 426. . . . . .510, 512
Emre II, The [1989] 2 Lloyd's Rep 182 385
Emrek v Sabranovic (C-218/12) EU:C:2013:666, [2014] IL Pr 39 295
Enercon GmbH v Enercon (India) Ltd [2012] EWHC 689 (Comm), [2012]
1 Lloyd's Rep 519, [2012] 1 Lloyd's Rep 519 550
Enforcement of a Judgment (Date Error in Translated Summons), Re (Case IX ZB 14/00)
[2003] IL Pr 32 632
Enforcement of a Portuguese Judgment, Re The (Case IX ZB 2/03) [2005] IL Pr 28 638
Enforcement of a United States Judgment for Damages, Re (Case IX ZR 149/91) [1994] IL
Pr 602 . . . . .119, 575
Enforcement of an Austrian Judgment, Re (Case 3 W 91/03) [2005] IL Pr 29. 635
Enforcement of an English Anti-Suit Injunction, Re [1997] IL Pr 320. 440
Eng Liat Kiang v Eng Bak Hern [1995] 3 SLR 97 394
Engdiv Ltd v G Percy Trentham Ltd 1990 SLT 617 249
English v Donnelly 1958 SC 494. 748
Enichem Anic Spa v Ampelos Shipping Co Ltd, The Delfini [1988] 2 Lloyd's Rep 599,
[1990] 1 Lloyd's Rep 252. 345
Ennstone Building Products Ltd v Stanger Ltd [2002] EWCA Civ 916, [2002]
1 WLR 3059 . . . . .688, 690, 728, 736, 739, 777
Enohin v Wylie (1862) 10 HL Cas 1 . . . . .1334, 1339, 1343
Entry Clearance Officer, Dhaka v Ranu Begum [1986] Imm AR 461 924
Equitas Ltd v Allstate Insurance Co [2008] EWHC 1671 (Comm), [2009] Lloyd's
Rep IR 227 . . . . .466, 471
Equitas Ltd v Allstate Insurance Company [2008] EWHC 1671 (Comm), [2009]
1 All ER (Comm) 1137 345
Equitas Ltd v Wave City Shipping Co Ltd [2005] EWHC 923 (Comm), [2005]
2 All ER (Comm) 301 267
Eras Eil Actions, The [1992] 1 Lloyd's Rep 570 . . . . .338, 350

ERGO Insurance SE v If P&C Insurance AS and Gjensidige Baltic AAS v PZU
   Lietuva UAB DK (C-359/14) and (C-475/14) ECLI:EU:C:2016:40 689–90,
                                                                         692–3, 743, 773,
                                                              783, 785, 788–9, 859, 872
Erich Gasser GmbH v Misat Srl (C-116/02) [2003] ECR I-4207 . . . . .195, 232, 243, 446, 476
Erie Beach Co v A-G for Ontario [1930] AC 161 1298
Erny v Estate of Merola 792 A 2d 1208 (NJ 2002) 26
Eroglü v Eroglü [1994] 2 FLR 287 . . . . .142, 1024, 1030–1
Erste Group Bank AG London Branch v JSC 'VMZ Red October' [2015]
   EWCA Civ 379 . . . . .338, 349, 361
Erste Group Bank AG v JSC "VMZ Red October" [2015] EWCA Civ 379 811
Ertel Bieber & Co v Rio Tinto Co [1918] AC 260 497
Esdale v Bank of Ottawa (1920) 51 DLR 485 539
Essar Shipping Ltd v Bank of China [2015] EWHC 3266 439
Esso Malaysia, The [1975] QB 198 878
Este v Smyth (1854) 18 Beav 112 1372
Et Plus SA v Welter [2005] EWHC 2115 (Comm), [2006] 1 Lloyd's Rep 251 . . . . .284, 287, 471
ET v TZ (Recognition and Enforcement of a Foreign Residence Order) [2013]
   EWHC 2621 1128
ETI Euro Telecom International NV v Republic of Bolivia [2008] EWCA Civ
   880, [2009] 1 WLR 665 . . . . .306, 508
Eurobank Ergasias SA v Kalliroi Navigation Company Ltd [2015]
   EWHC 2377 770
Euro-Diam Ltd v Bathurst [1990] 1 QB 1, [1987] 1 Lloyd's Rep 178 . . . . .118, 771
Eurodis Electron plc, Re [2011] EWHC 1025 1307
Eurofood IFSC Ltd (C-341/04) [2006] IL Pr 23 628
European Asian Bank AG v Punjab and Sind Bank [1982] 2 Lloyd's Rep 356 . . . . .397, 400
European Gateway, The [1987] QB 206 559
Eustace v Eustace [1924] P 45 980
Eva-Maria Painer v Standard Verlags GmbH (C-145/10) EU:C:2011 285
Evans Marshall & Co Ltd v Bertola SA [1973] 1 WLR 349 . . . . .235, 370, 371, 410
Evans v Burrell (1859) 28 LJP & M 82 1330
Evans, Re [1947] Ch 695 . . . . .158, 162
Evia Luck, The (No 2) see Dimskal Shipping Co SA v International Transport
   Workers Federation (The Evia Luck No 2) 70, 135
Evialis SA v SIAT [2003] EWHC 863, [2003] 2 Lloyd's Rep 377 . . . . 111–12, 196,
                                                                     216, 231, 234–5, 237
Evpo Agnic, The [1988] 1 WLR 1090 384
EWHC 328 (Comm), [2013] 2 Lloyd's Rep 104 368
Ewin, Re (1830) 1 Cr & J 151 1264
Ewing v Orr Ewing (1883) 9 App Cas 34 . . . . .486, 489
Ewins v Carlton [1997] 2 ILRM 223 270
Excalibur Ventures LLC v Texas Keystone Inc [2011] EWHC 1624 (Comm), [2011] 2
   Lloyd's Rep 289 422
Excalibur Ventures LLC v Texas Keystone Inc [2013] EWHC 2767 . . . . .702, 767
Excess Insurance Co Ltd v Allendale Mutual Insurance Co, CA, 8 March 1995
   (unreported) 371
Exchange Control and a Greek Guarantor, Re [1993] IL Pr 298 231
Exchersheim, The [1976] 1 All ER 920 385
Excomm Ltd v Ahmed Abdul-Qawi Bamordah, The St Raphael [1985]
   1 Lloyd's Rep 403 417
Exfin Shipping Ltd v Tolani Shipping Co Ltd [2006] EWHC 1090 (Comm),
   [2006] 2 Lloyd's Rep 389 417
Exmek Pharmaceuticals SAC v Alkem Laboratories Ltd [2015] EWHC 3158
   (Comm), [2016] 1 Lloyd's Rep 239 538

F (A Child) (Abduction: Art 13(b): Psychiatric Assessment), Re [2014] EWCA Civ 275 1152
F (A Child) (Abduction: Refusal to Order Summary Return), Re [2009] EWCA
 Civ 416 1058
F (A Child) (Application for Child Party Status), Re [2007] EWCA Civ 393. . . . . .1145, 1159
F (A Child) (International Relocation Cases), Re [2015] EWCA Civ 882 1171
F (A Child) (Permission to Relocate), Re [2012] EWCA Civ 1364 1170–1
F (A Minor) (Abduction: Custody Rights Abroad), Re [1995] Fam 224. . . . . . .1137–8, 1143, 1154
F (A Minor) (Abduction: Custody Rights), Re [1991] Fam 25. . . . . 176, 1137, 1143,
                            1152, 1154, 1172–4
F (A Minor) (Child Abduction), Re [1992] 1 FLR 548, 555 . . . . .179, 183, 1137, 1143
F (Abduction: Unborn Child), Re [2006] EWHC 2199 (Fam), [2007] 1 FLR 627 183
F (Abduction: Unmarried Father: Sole Carer), Re [2002] EWHC 2896, [2003]
 1 FLR 839 1138
F (Child's Objections), Re [2015] EWCA Civ 1022. 1146–7
F (Children) (Paternity: Registration), Re [2011] EWCA Civ 1765. 1052
F (Children) (Thai Surrogacy: Enduring Family Relationship), Re [2016]
 EWHC 1594 (Fam) 1185
F (Children), Re [2016] EWCA Civ 546 1145
F (Habitual Residence: Peripatetic Existence), Re [2014] EWFC 26 1100
F (Residence Order: Jurisdiction), Re [1995] 2 FLR 518 1125
F v F (Abduction: Habitual Residence) [1993] Fam Law 199. . . . . 176–7, 179, 182,
                             183, 1102, 1107–8
F v F (Divorce: Jurisdiction) [2009] EWHC 1448. 960
F v M [2015] EWHC 3300 . . . . .1152, 1155
F v R [2007] EWHC 64 (Fam) 1168
F v S (Wardship: Jurisdiction) [1993] 2 FLR 686. . . . . .177, 1107
Fagin's Bookshop plc, Re [1992] BCLC 118 224
FAI General Insurance v Ocean Marine Mutual (1996–1997) 41 NSWLR 117. 235
Faial, The [2000] 1 Lloyd's Rep 473. 385
Fairfield Sentry Ltd v Sitco Bank Nederland NV [2012] IEHC 81. 1318
Fairmays v Palmer [2006] EWHC 96 (Ch) 325
Falcke v Scottish Imperial Insurance Co (1887) 57 LT 39 569
Falco Privatstiftung and Thomas Rabitsch v Gisela Weller-Lindhorst (C-533/07)
 [2009] ECR I-3327 . . . . .261–2, 728, 730
Fall v Eastin 215 US 1 (1909) 491, 546
Falstria, The [1988] 1 Lloyd's Rep 495 402
Far Eastern Shipping Co v AKP Sovcomfl ot [1995] 1 Lloyd's Rep 520 671
Faraday Reinsurance Co Ltd v Howden North America Inc [2012] EWCA Civ 980 374
Farnell & Anor and Chanbua [2016] FCWA 17 1179
Faye v IRC (1961) 40 TC 103 162
Fayed v Al-Tajir [1988] QB 712. 513
Federal Commerce and Navigation Co Ltd v Tradax Export SA [1977]
 QB 324, [1978] AC 1 . . . . .99, 103
Federal Commerce and Navigation Co Ltd v Tradax Export SA [1978] AC 1 103
Federal Republic of Yugoslavia v Croatia [2000] IL Pr 591. 509
Fehmarn, The [1957] 1 WLR 815, [1958] 1 WLR 159 . . . . .385, 412
Feiner v Demkowicz (1973) 42 DLR (3d) 165. 988
Feliks Frisman v Finnair Oyj (C-533/15) OJ 2016 C 48/8. 260
Felixstowe Dock and Rly Co v United States Lines Inc [1989] QB 360 543
Fender v St John-Mildmay [1938] AC 1 139
Fenston's Settlement, Re [1971] 1 WLR 1640 1363
Fenton v Livingstone (1859) 33 LTOS 335 1260
Ferdinand Wagner v Laubscher Bros & Co [1970] 2 QB 313 . . . . .564, 593, 599
Ferguson Shipbuilders Ltd v Voith Hydro GmbH & Co KG 2000 SLT 229 . . . . . . .257, 727, 737
Ferguson's Trustee v Ferguson 1990 SLT (Sh Ct) 73. 220

Fergusson v Fyffe (1841) 8 C1 & Fin 121 96
Fergusson's Will, Re [1902] 1 Ch 483 1348
Fern Computer Consultancy Ltd v Intergraph Cadworx & Analysis Solutions
    Inc [2014] EWHC 2908 (Ch), [2015] 1 Lloyd's Rep 1 .348, 368
Fern Computer Consultancy v Intergraph Cadworx & Analysis Solutions Inc [2014]
    EWCA 2908 751
Ferndale Films Ltd v Granada Television Ltd [1994] IL Pr 180 252–3
Ferrari v Romania [2015] ECHR 1714/ 10, [2015] 2 FLR 303 1165
Ferrexpo AG v Gilson Investments Ltd [2012] EWHC 721 (Comm), [2012] 1 Lloyd's. . . . .
Ferrier-Watson & McElrath, In the Marriage of [2000] FamCA 219 150
Feyerick v Hubbard (1902) 71 LJKB 509. 532
FFSB Ltd v Seward & Kissel LLP [2007] UKPC 16. . . . . .348, 362, 808
FG Hemisphere Associates LLC v Congo [2005] EWHC 3103 (QBD). 1294
Fidelitas Shipping Co Ltd v V/O Exporteklab [1966] 1 QB 630 558
Fielden v IRC (1965) 42 TC 501, 507. 162
Findlay v Findlay (No 2) 1995 SLT 492. . . . . .182, 1135
Findlay v Findlay 1994 SLT 709 . . . . .177, 180
Findlay v Matondo and Secretary of State for the Home Department [1993]
    Imm AR 541 1108
Finnegan v Cementation Co [1953] 1 QB 688 1335
Finnish Marine Insurance Co Ltd v Protective National Insurance Co [1990]
    1 QB 1078. . . . . .333, 344, 347
Fiona Trust & Holding Corp v Privalov [2010] EWHC 3199 .780
Fiona Trust & Holding Corpn v Privalov [2007] EWCA Civ 20, [2007]
    2 Lloyd's Rep 267. . . . . .234, 237, 410, 415, 418, 420
Fiona Trust & Holding Corpn v Privalov [2007] UKHL 40, [2007] 2 All ER
    (Comm) 1053 . . . . .234, 237
Firebrace v Firebrace (1878) 4 PD 63. 160
Firma P v Firma K (178/83) [1984] ECR 3033 . . . . .611, 620
First American Corpn v Zayed [1999] 1 WLR 1154 83
First Laser Ltd v Fujian Enterprises (Holdings) Co [2012] HKCU 1397, (2012)
    HKFCAR 154 . . . . .559, 682, 725
First National Bank in Fort Collins v Rostek 514 P 2d 314 (1973) 28
First National Bank of Boston v Union Bank of Switzerland [1990] 1 Lloyd's Rep 32 407
First National Bank of Houston v Houston E & C Inc [1990] 5 WWR 719 534
Fisher v Fisher 250 NY 313 (1929) 908
Fisher v Unione Italiana de Riassicurazione SpA [1998] CLC 682 252
Fitzgerald, Re [1904] 1 Ch 573 . . . . .1372, 1378, 1386, 1388
Fitzgerald, Surman v Fitzgerald, Re [1904] 1 Ch 573. 1378
Fitzpatrick v International Rly 252 NY 127 (1929) 85
FKI Engineering Ltd v Dewind Holdings Ltd [2007] EWHC 72 (Comm),
    [2007] IL Pr 17 224
FKI Engineering Ltd v Dewind Holdings Ltd [2008] EWCA Civ 316. . . . . .284–5, 287
FKI Engineering Ltd v Stribog Ltd [2011] EWCA Civ 622, [2011] 2 Lloyd's Rep 387 455
Flaherty v Girgis (1987) 71 ALR 1. 349
Flecha, The [1999] 1 Lloyd's Rep 612 342
Fletcher v Ashburner (1779) 1 Bro CC 497 1252
Flight Refund Ltd v Deutsche Lufthansa AG (C-94/14) EU:C:2016:148, [2016]
    1 WLR 3567 662
Flightlease, Re [2012] IESC 12 544
Florin Lazar, représenté légalement par Luigi Erculeo v Allianz SpA (C-350/14)
    ECLI:EU:C:2015:802, [2016] 1 WLR 835 . . . . .349, 688, 783–4,
                                                                                                811, 813, 864
Flower v Lloyd (1877) 6 Ch D 297 . . . 569Flower v Lloyd (No 2) (1879)
    10 Ch D 327 569

flyLAL-Lithuanian Airlines AS v Starptautiskā lidosta Rīga VAS and Air Baltic
    Corporation AS (C-302/13) EU:C:2014:2319, [2015] IL Pr 2 . . . . .205, 629, 631, 827–8
Flynn, Flynn v Flynn, Re [1968] 1 WLR 103, 107. . . . . .155, 163
Flynn, Re (No 2) [1969] 2 Ch 403 551
Flynn, Re [1968] 1 WLR 103 . . . . .148, 155, 163
FMC Corpn v Russell 1999 SLT 99. . . . . .86, 428–30
FN and the Mental Health Act 1958, Re [1984] 3 NSWLR 520 . . . . .1247.
Fogarty v United Kingdom [2002] 34 EHRR 12 501
Fokas v Fokas [1952] SASR 152. 906
Folien Fischer AG and Fofitec AG v Ritrama SpA (C-133/11) EU:C:2012:664,
    [2013] QB 523 . . . . .251, 267
Fondation Solomon v Guggenheim v D Helion [1997] IL Pr 457, French Sup Ct. 220
Fondazione Enascarco v Lehman Brothers Finance SA [2014] EWHC 34 1319
Food Corpn of India v Carras (Hellas) Ltd [1980] 2 Lloyd's Rep 577 102
Football Association Premier League Ltd and Others v QC Leisure and Others and
    Karen Murphy v Media Protection Services Ltd (C-403/08) and (C-429/08)
    [2011] ECR I-9083 . . . . .688, 784
Football Dataco Ltd and Others v Sportradar GmbH and Sportradar AG
    (C-173/11) ECLI:EU:C:2012:642. 832
Football Dataco Ltd v Sportradar GmbH [2011] EWCA Civ 330, [2011]
    1 WLR 3044 445
Foote Cone & Belding Reklin Hizmetleri v Theron [2006] EWHC 1585 199
Forbes v Cochrane (1824) 2 B & C 448. 137
Forbes v Forbes (1854) Kay 341. . . . . .156, 160, 165, 1200
Force India Formula One Team Ltd v 1 Malaysia Racing Team Sdn Bhd [2012]
    EWHC 616 (Ch), [2012] RPC 29. 357
Ford v Stier [1896] P 1. 986
Fordyce v Bridges (1848) 2 Ph 497 1346–7
Forgo's case (1883) 10 Clunet 63 59
Forsyth v Forsyth [1891] P 363 . . . . .1061, 1395
Forsyth v Forsyth [1948] P 125 540
Fort Dodge Animal Health Ltd v Akzo Nobel NV [1998] FSR 222. . . . . 225, 285, 303,
                                                305, 476, 492, 496
Forum Craftsman, The [1984] 2 Lloyd's Rep 102, [1985] 1 Lloyd's Rep 291. . . . . .397, 414
Foster v Driscoll [1929] 1 KB 470, CA 122
Foster v Driscoll [1929] 1 KB 470 . . . . .122, 136, 753–4
Four Embarcadero Center Venture v Mr Greenjeans Corpn (1988) 64 OR (2d)
    746, 65 OR (2d) 160. 550
Fourie v Le Roux [2007] UKHL 1, [2007] 1 WLR 320. . . . . .187, 306–7, 324, 340–1
Fox v Henderson Investment Fund Ltd [1999] 2 Lloyd's Rep 303 772
Fox v Taher [1997] IL Pr 441 455
FR Lürssen Werft GmbH & Co Kg v Halle [2009] EWHC 2607 (Comm); 368
Fracis Times & Co v Carr (1900) 82 LT 698 544
Frahuil SA v Assitalia SPA (C-265/02) [2004] ECR I-1543 . . . . .204, 205, 249
Frank Pais, The [1986] 1 Lloyd's Rep 529 . . . . .411, 413, 415
Frankel's Estate v The Master 1950 (1) SA 220 (AD) 1367–8
Frankfurther v WL Exner Ltd [1947] Ch 629 . . . . .118, 120, 131
Frans Maas Logistics (UK) Ltd v CDR Trucking BV [1999] 2 Lloyd's Rep 179 203
Fraser v Buckle [1996] 1 IR 1, SC 134
Freccia Del Nord, The [1989] 1 Lloyd's Rep 388 . . . . .384, 390
Freehold Land Investments v Queensland Estates Ltd 123 CLR 418 712
Freeport plc v Olle Arnoldsson (C-98/06) [2007] IL Pr 58. 285–6
Freistaat Bayern v Jan Blijdenstein (C-433/01) [2004] ECR I-981, [2004] IL Pr 8. . . . . . .205, 245
Freke v Carbery (1873) LR 16 Eq 461 . . . . .1251, 1260, 1353, 1388
Fremont Insurance Ltd v Fremont Indemnity Co [1997] CLC 1428 338

Frere v Frere (1847) 5 Notes of Cases 593 . . . . .65, 71
Frisancho Perea v Slovakia [2016] 1 FLR 267. 1165
Fromovitz v Fromovitz (1977) 79 DLR (3d) 148 1035
Front Comor, The see West Tankers Inc v RAS Riunione Adriatica di Sicurta SpA
    (The Front Comor) 210, 440–1
Frymer v Brettschneider [1996] IL Pr 138 544
F-Tex SIA v Lietuvos-Anglijos UAB "Jadecloud-Vilma" (C-213/10) EU:C:2012:215,
    [2012] IL Pr 24 208
Fujifilm Kyowa Kirin Biologics Company Limited v Abbvie Biotechnology
    Limited [2016] EWHC 2204 (Pat) 348, 357, 422
Fuld's Estate, Re (No 3) [1968] P 675 . . . . .47, 68, 76, 80, 85, 112, 133, 148, 151, 154, 156
Fullemann v McInnes's Executor 1992 SLT 259. 104
Funabashi, The [1972] 1 WLR 666 97
Furse, Re [1980] 3 All ER 838. 151–2
Future Investments SA v Federation Internationale de Football Association [2010]
    EWHC 1019 (Ch), [2010] IL Pr 34 . . . . .272, 275

G & H Montage GmbH v Irvani [1990] 1 WLR 667 . . . . .44, 74, 758
G (A Child) (Adoption: Placement Outside Jurisdiction), Re [2008] EWCA Civ 105,
    [2008] WLR (D) 56. . . . . .1218, 1220
G (A Minor) (Abduction), Re [1989] 2 FLR 475, [1989] Fam Law 473 . . . . .1144, 1154
G (A Minor) (Abduction), Re [1990] FCR 189, [1989] 2 FLR 475. 1144
G (A Minor) (Child Abduction: Enforcement), Re [1990] FCR 973, [1990] 2 FLR 325. . .1135–6
G (A Minor) (Enforcement of Access Abroad), Re [1993] Fam 216. 179
G (A Minor) (Wrongful Removal of Child), Re [1990] FCR 189, [1989]
    2 FLR 475 . . . . .1056, 1135–6, 1144, 1154
G (A Minor; Enforcement of Access Abroad), Re [1993] Fam 216. 179
G (Abduction: Rights of Custody), Re [2002] 2 FLR 703, [2002] Fam Law 732
    (Fam Div) 1056, 1137
G (Abduction: Striking Out Application), Re [1995] 2 FLR 410. 1150
G (An Infant), Re [1968] 3 NSWR 483. 1211
G (Children) (Abduction: Children's Objections), Re [2010] EWCA Civ 1232. 1144
G (Children) (Foreign Contact Order: Enforcement), Re [2003] All ER (D) 144 . . . . .1089, 1178
G (Children) (Foreign Contact Order: Enforcement), Re [2004] 1 FLR 378. 1135
G (Children) (Recognition of Brazilian Adoption), Re [2014] EWHC 2605 1054–5
G (Children) (Residence: Same Sex Partner), Re [2006] EWCA Civ 372, [2006]
    2 FLR 614 1088
G (Foreign Adoption: Consent), Re [1995] 2 FLR 534 . . . . .1137, 1228
G (JDM), Re [1969] 1 WLR 1001 1172–3
G (Jurisdiction: Art 19 BIIR), Re [2014] EWCA Civ 680 1117
G (Parental Orders), Re [2014] EWHC 1561 . . . . .149–50, 156, 1184–6
G (Recognition of Brazilian Adoption), Re [2014] EWHC 2605. . . . . .1225, 1227, 1230–1
G (Removal from Jurisdiction), Re [2005] EWCA Civ 170, [2005] 2 FLR
    166. . . . . .499, 1056, 1088, 1154, 1167–9, 1220
G v Caledonian Newspapers Ltd 1995 SLT 559. 590
G v De Visser EU:C:2012:142 (C-292/10) [2013] QB 168. . . . . .200, 324, 659
G v G (Minors) (Abduction) [1991] 2 FLR 506 1174
G v G [1984] IR 368 1078
G v G [2014] EWHC 4182. 1131
G v G [2015] EWHC 2101 (Fam), [2016] 4 WLR 22. 283
G v G [2016] EWCA Civ 1292 219
G v United Kingdom (Children: Rights of Contact) [2001] 1 FLR 153,
    (2001) 33 EHRR 1 1164
G, Re (1983) 5 FLR 268 1175
G, Re [1966] NZLR 1028 167–8

Gabriel v Schlanck & Schick GmbH (C-96/00) [2002] ECR I-6367 294
Gadd v Gadd [1984] 1 WLR 1435 . . . . .973, 974, 978
Gaetano and Maria, The (1882) 7 PD 137 878
Gaffney v Gaffney [1975] IR 133 . . . . .1002, 1035
Gaillard v Chekili (C-518/99) [2001] ECR I-2771 219
Gajraj v DeBernardo (2002) 213 DLR (4th) 651 349
Galaxy Special Maritime Enterprise v Prima Ceylon Ltd (The Olympic Galaxy)
    [2006] EWCA Civ 528, [2006] 2 Lloyd's Rep 27 .365, 367–9, 408
Galene v Galene (otherwise Galice) [1939] P 237 . . . . .894, 1012
Gallo Africa Ltd v Sting Music (Pty) Ltd 2010 (6) SA 329, Sup Ct of
    Appeal of South Africa 494
Galloway v Goldstein [2012] EWHC 60 . . . . .894, 1051
Gambazzi v DaimlerChrysler Canada Inc and CIBC Mellon Trust Co (C-394/07)
    [2009] ECR I-2563 . . . . .612, 616, 626–8, 633
Gamlestaden plc v Casa de Suecia SA [1994] 1 Lloyd's Rep 433 443
Gamlestaden plc v CDS [1994] 1 Lloyd's Rep 433 235
Gan Insurance Co Ltd v Tai Ping Insurance Co Ltd [1999] IL Pr 729 719
Gandhi v Patel [2002] 1 FLR 603 . . . . .893–4, 898, 906, 943, 985
Gantner Electronic GmbH v Basch Exploitatie Maatschappij BV (C-111/01) [2003]
    ECR I-4207 445
Gard Marine and Energy Ltd v Tunnicliffe [2010] EWCA Civ 1052, [2011]
    2 All ER (Comm) 208 285
Garden Cottage Foods v Milk Marketing Board [1984] AC 130 827
Garnier, Re (1872) LR 13 Eq 532 1247
Garthwaite v Garthwaite [1964] P 356 . . . . .483, 1049
Gascoigne v Pyrah [1994] IL Pr 82 286
Gater Assets Ltd v Nak Naftogaz Ukrainiy [2007] EWCA Civ 988, [2007]
    2 Lloyd's Rep 588 671
Gateshead Metropolitan Borough Council v L [1996] 3 All ER 264 174
Gatoil International Inc v Arkwright-Boston Manufacturers Mutual Insurance Co
    [1985] AC 255 . . . . .382, 386
Gavin Gibson & Co v Gibson [1913] 3 KB 379 540
Gazdasági Versenyhivatal v Siemens Aktiengesellschaft Österreich (C-102/15)
    EU:C:2016:225 at [70], [2016] IL Pr 33 . . . . .265, 267, 694, 828
Gazprom OAO v Lithuania (C-536/13) EU:C:2015:316, [2015] 1 WLR 4937 . . . . .208, 480
GE v KE and AE (Nigerian Customary Marriage and Divorce) [2013]
    EWHC 1938 1051
Gelley v Shepherd [2013] EWCA Civ 1172 569
Gemeente Steenbergen v Baten (C-271/00) [2002] ECR I-10489, [2003]
    1 WLR 1996 . . . . .197, 205, 208, 784
General Motors Corpn v Royal & Sun Alliance Insurance Group [2007]
    EWHC 2206 (Comm) 436
General Motors-Holdens Ltd v The Ship Northern Highway (1982) 29
    SASR 138 383
General Star v Stirling Cooke [2003] EWHC 3 (Comm), [2003] IL Pr 19 429
General Steam Navigation Co v Guillou (1843) 11 M & W 877 . . . . .50, 87–8
George Monro Ltd v American Cyanamid and Chemical Corpn [1944] KB 432 366
George Veflings Rederi A/ S v President of India [1979] 1 WLR 59 . . . . .100, 103–4
George Veflings Rederi A/S v President of India [1978] 1 WLR 92, [1979]
    1 WLR 59 104
Gereis v Yagoub [1997] 1 FLR 854 . . . . .894–5, 985
Gerling v Italian Treasury (201/82) [1983] ECR 2503 . . . . .228, 291
German Graphics Graphische Maschinen GmbH v Alice van der Schee (C-292/08)
    [2009] ECR I-8421 . . . . .208, 1320
Gersten v The Law Society of New South Wales [2002] NSWCA 344 119

Gesellschaft für Antriebstechnik mbH & Co KG (GAT) v Luk Lamellen und
Kupplungsbau Beteiligungs KG (C-4/03) [2006] ECR I-6509 . . . . .225, 314, 466, 833
Geyer v Aguilar (1798) 7 Term Rep 681 525
Ghosh v D'Rozario [1963] 1 QB 106 513
Gibbon v Commerz und Creditbank Aktiengesellschaft [1958] 2 Lloyd's Rep 113 344
Gibbs v Fremont (1853) 9 Exch 25 96
Gibson v Holland (1865) LR 1 CP 1 74
Gienar v Meyer (1796) 2 Hy Bl 603 707
Gilbert v Seton Hall University 332 F 3d 105 (2d Cir 2003) 27
Giles v Thompson [1994] 1 AC 142, HL 134
Gill and Duffus Landauer Ltd v London Export Corpn GmbH [1982]
2 Lloyd's Rep 627 . . . . .344, 346
Girven, Petitioner 1985 SLT 92 1088
Glasgow City Council v M 2001 SLT 396 183
Glasson v Scott [1973] 1 NSWLR 689 1110
Glencore International AG v Exter Shipping Ltd [2002] EWCA Civ
528, [2002] All ER (Comm) 1 . . . . .333, 423, 425, 432–3, 437
Glencore International AG v Metro Trading International Inc (No 1) [1999]
2 Lloyd's Rep 632 . . . . .227, 231, 241, 445–7
Glencore International AG v Metro Trading International Inc (No 2) [2001]
1 Lloyd's Rep 284 .106, 111, 227, 231, 446, 1266, 1269–70
Global 5000 Ltd v Wadhawan [2012] EWCA Civ 13, [2012] 1 Lloyd's Rep 239 342
Global Garden Products Italy SpA, Re [2016] EWHC 1884 (Ch) .285
Global Multimedia v ARA Media Services [2006] EWHC 3107 (Ch), [2007]
1 All ER (Comm) 1160 106
GMC v Brauwers [2010] EWHC 106 (Admin) 361, 380
GN v Poland [2016] ECHR 667 1165
Godfrey v Demon Internet Ltd [2001] QB 201 . . . . .350, 353, 887
Godwin v Swindon BC [2001] EWCA Civ 1478, [2002] 1 WLR 997 325
Goenaga's Estate, Re [1949] P 367 1331
Goff v Goff [1934] P 107 . . . . .1061, 1396
Gold Reserve Inc v Venezuela [2016] EWHC 153 (Comm), [2016] 1 WLR 2829 . . . . . . .506, 508
Goldbet Sportwetten GmbH v Massimo Sperindeo (C-144/12) EU:C:2013:393,
[2014] IL Pr 1 . . . . .227, 662
Golden Acres Ltd v Queensland Estates Pty Ltd [1969] Qd R 378 712
Golden Endurance Shipping SA v RMA Watanya SA [2014] EWHC 3917 (Comm),
[2015] 1 Lloyd's Rep 266 . . . . .367, 428, 430
Golden Endurance Shipping SA v RMA Watanya SA [2016] EWHC 2110 (Comm); 537–8
Golden Ocean Group Ltd v Salgaocar Mining Industries PVT Ltd [2012]
EWCA Civ 265 721
Golden Trader, The [1975] QB 348 385
Golder v UK, Judgment of 21 February 1975, Series A, No 18; (1975)
1 EHRR 524 14
Goldman Sachs International v Novo Banco SA [2015] EWHC 2371 242
Goliath Portland Cement Co Ltd v Bengtell (1994) 33 NSWLR 414 405
Gollogly and Owen's Marriage, Re (1989) 13 Fam LR 622 1135
Golubovich v Golubovich [2010] EWCA Civ 810, [2010] 3 WLR 1607, [2011]
Fam 88 . . . . .142, 574, 1030–1
Gomez v Gomez-Monche Vives [2008] EWCA Civ 1065, [2009] Ch 245 . . . . . .202, 283, 466
Good Challenger Navegante SA v Metalexportimport SA (The Good Challenger)
[2003] EWCA Civ 1668, [2004] 1 Lloyd's Rep 67 . . . . .559–60, 563–4, 666–7
Goodman's Trusts, Re (1881) 17 Ch D 266 . . . . .1198, 1203, 1348
Google Inc v Vidal-Hall [2015] EWCA Civ 311, [2015] 3 WLR 409 . . . . .348, 362
Gordon Pacific Developments Pty Ltd v Conlon [1993] 3 NZLR 760 . . . . .526, 543, 606
Gordon v Australian Broadcasting Commission (1973) 22 FLR 181 886

Gorgeous Beauty Ltd v Liu [2014] EWHC 2952. 1387–8
Gorjat v Gorjat [2010] EWHC 1537. . . . . .692, 761, 763
Goshawk Dedicated Ltd v ROP Inc [2006] EWHC 1730 (Comm), [2006]
    Lloyd's Rep IR 711. 441
Goshawk Dedicated Receivables Ltd v Life Receivables Ireland Ltd [2009]
    IESC 7, [2009] IL Pr 26. 474
Gotha City v Sotheby's (No 2) (1998) Times, 8 October 133, 135, 137, 808
Gothaer Allgemeine Versicherung AG v Samskip GmbH EU:C:2012:719
    (C-456/11) [2013] QB 548 . . . . .478, 612, 650
Gould v Gould 1968 SLT 98 151
Goulder v Goulder [1892] P 240 152
Gourmet Resources International Inc v Paramount Capital Corpn [1993]
    IL Pr 583 537–8
Government of India v Taylor [1955] AC 491 . . . . .116–17, 1335
Government of the Islamic Republic of Iran v The Barakat Galleries Ltd
    [2007] EWCA Civ 1374 . . . . .1267, 1269, 1278
Government of the United States of America v Montgomery (No 2) [2004]
    UKHL 37, [2004] 3 WLR 2241 . . . . .14, 552, 580–1
Governor of Pitcairn v Sutton [1995] 1 NZLR 426 497
Gow v Grant [2012] UKSC 29 1380
Grace v Revenue and Customs Commissioners [2009] EWCA Civ 1082. 173–4
Granarolo SpA v Ambrosi Emmi France SA (C-196/15)
    EU:C:2016:559 . . . . .245–7, 256, 258, 264, 694, 703, 806, 808, 850–1
Grant v Easton (1883) 13 QBD 302 . . . . .526, 551
Grant's Trustees v Ritchie's Executor (1886) 13 R 646 1288
Grassi, Stubberfield v Grassi, Re [1905] 1 Ch 584 1260
Gray (otherwise Formosa) v Formosa [1963] P 259 . . . . .141, 168, 921
Graziano v Daniels (1991) 14 Fam LR 697 1140
GreCon Dimter Inc v JR Normand Inc (2005) 255 DLR (4th) 257 410
Green v Montagu [2011] EWHC 1856 1198
Green, Re (1909) 25 TLR 222 893
Greene Wood & McLean LLP v Templeton Insurance Ltd [2009] EWCA
    Civ 65, [2009] 1 WLR 2013 342
Greenfield, Re [1985] 2 NZLR 662 . . . . .1251, 1345
Greenwich LBC v S [2007] EWHC 820 (Fam) 1217–18
GREP GmbH v Freistaat Bayern (C-156/12) EU:C:2012:342, [2015] IL Pr 29 622
Gresham Corpn Pty Ltd, Re [1990] 1 Qd R 306 100
Grey's Trusts, Re [1892] 3 Ch 88 1198
Grimaldi Compagnia di Navigazione SpA v Sekihyo Line Ltd [1998] 3 All ER 943. 417
Grimwood v Bartels (1877) 46 LJ Ch 788 1247
Gronlund v Hansen (1969) 4 DLR (3d) 435 876–7
Groos, Groos v Groos, Re [1915] 1 Ch 572 1345
Groos, In the Estate of [1904] P 269 1350
Group Seven Ltd v Allied Investment Corp Ltd [2014] EWHC 2046 869
Grove, Re (1888) 40 Ch D 216 . . . . .1201, 1203
Grovit v De Nederlandsche Bank [2005] EWHC 2944 (QB), [2006] 1 Lloyd's Rep 636,
    [2007] EWCA Civ 953, [2008] 1 WLR 51 . . . . .205, 499, 517
Gruber v Bay Wa AG (C-464/01) [2006] QB 204 293
Grupo Torras SA and Torras Hostench London Ltd v Sheikh Fahad Mohammed Al-Sabah
    [1996] 1 Lloyd's Rep 7 . . .105, 107–8, 112–13, 199, 217, 350, 364, 377, 417, 419, 443, 456
Grupo Torras SA v Al-Sabah (No 5) [2001] Lloyd's Rep Bank 36. . . . . .105, 199, 350, 780
Grzybowicz v Grzybowicz [1963] SASR 62 906
GS v Georgia [2015] 2 FLR 647, [2015] ECHR 2361/ 13 1165
Gsponer's Marriage, Re (1988) 94 FLR 164. 1152–3
Guaranty Trust Co of New York v Hannay & Co [1918] 2 KB 623 108

Guardian Trust and Executors Co of New Zealand Ltd v Darroch [1973] 2 NZLR 143 1349
Gubisch Maschinenfabrik KG v Giulio Palumbo (144/86) [1987] ECR 4861 445
Guépratte v Young (1851) 4 De G & Sm 217 . . . . .106, 1377
Guerin v Proulx (1982) 37 OR (2d) 558 110
Guiard v De Clermont and Donner [1914] 3 KB 145 533
Guió v Slovakia [2014] ECHR 10280/ 12 1165
Guiseppe di Vittorio, The [1998] 1 Lloyd's Rep 136 . . . . .385, 509
Gulbenkian v Gulbenkian [1937] 4 All ER 618, 627 . . . . .152, 156
Gulf Bank KSC v Mitsubishi Heavy Industries Ltd [1994] 1 Lloyd's Rep 323 . . . . .346, 370
Gulf Consolidated v CSFB Ltd [1992] 2 Lloyd's Rep 301 112
Gulf Oil Corpn v Gilbert (1947) 330 US 501 407
Gulf Venture, The [1984] 2 Lloyd's Rep 445 384
Gunn v Diaz [2017] EWHC 157 (QB), [2017] 1 Lloyd's Rep 165 .349
Gur Corpn v Trust Bank of Africa Ltd [1987] QB 599 497
Gyonyor v Sanjenko [1971] 5 WWR 381 541

H (A Child) (Abduction: Habitual Residence: Consent), Re [2000]
    2 FLR 294 . . . . .182, 183, 1136, 1137, 1150, 1214
H (A Child) (Child Abduction), Re [2006] EWCA Civ 1247, [2007]
    1 FLR 242 . . . . .1145, 1158–9
H (A Child), Re [2013] EWCA Civ 148 1110
H (A Minor) (Abduction: Rights of Custody), Re [2000] 2 AC 291 1137–8
H (A Minor) (Foreign Custody Order: Enforcement), Re [1994] Fam 105 . . . . .1135, 1136, 1174
H (Abduction), Re [2009] EWHC 1735 (Fam) 1152, 1154
H (Abduction: Acquiescence), Re [1998] AC 72 . . . . .1137, 1150
H (Abduction: Child of 16), Re [2000] 2 FLR 51 . . . . .175, 181–3, 1135, 1145, 1150
H (Abduction: Dominica: Corporal Punishment), Re [2006] EWHC 199
    (Fam), [2006] 2 FLR 314 1174
H (Abduction: Habitual Residence: Consent), Re [2000]
    2 FLR 294 . . . . .182–3, 1135, 1137, 1150, 1214
H (Abduction: Jurisdiction), Re [2009] EWHC 2280 1160
H (An Infant), Re (1973) 4 Fam Law 77 . . . . .1223, 1226
H (Application to Remove from Jurisdiction), Re [1998] 1 FLR 848 1168
H (Child Abduction) (Unmarried Father: Rights of Custody), Re [2003] EWHC 492,
    [2003] 2 FLR 153 . . . . .183, 1056, 1138–9, 1180
H (Children) (Child Abduction: Grave Risk), Re [2003] EWCA Civ 355,
    [2003] 2 FLR 141 . . . . .1152–4, 1156
H (Children) (Child Abduction: Objections to Return), Re [2005] EWCA
    Civ 319, (2005) 149 SJLB 178 . . . . .182, 1156
H (Children) (Jurisdiction: Habitual Residence), Re [2014] EWCA Civ 1101 . . . . . .1057, 1095–6
H (Children), Re [2011] CLY 1350 . . . . .1140–1, 1150
H (Children: Residence Order: Relocation), Re [2001] EWCA Civ 1338, [2001]
    2 FLR 1277 . . . . .1098, 1167–9
H (Minors) (Abduction: Custody Rights), Re [1991] 2 AC 476 1135–6
H (Residence Order: Placement out of Jurisdiction), Re [2004] EWHC 3243, [2006]
    1 FLR 1140 1106
H and L (Abduction: Acquiescence), Re [2010] EWHC 652 . . . . .1140–1, 1150
H Gautzsch Großhandel GmbH & Co KG v Münchener Boulevard Möbel
    Joseph Duna GmbH (C-479/12) ECLI:EU:C:2014:75 834
H v D [2007] EWHC 802 (Fam) 1109
H v F [2005] EWHC 2705, [2006] 1 FLR 776 1169
H v H (Child Abduction: Stay of Domestic Proceedings) [1994] 1 FLR 530 . . . . . .177, 182, 1143
H v H (Child Abduction: Stay of Proceedings) [1994] 1 FLR 530 . . . . .177, 182
H v H (Protective Order: Exercise of Jurisdiction) [2016] EWHC 1252 (Fam) 1112
H v H (Talaq Divorce) [2007] EWHC 2945 . . . . .1019, 1029

H v H (Validity of Japanese Divorce) [2006] EWHC 2989 (Fam), [2007]
    1 FLR 1318 . . . . .1012, 1017, 1019, 1029–31
H v H [1954] P 258. 986
H v H [2004] EWHC 2111. 1136
H v H 2005 SLT 1025. . . . . .986–8, 992, 998
H v HK (C-295/13) ECLI:EU:C:2014:2410. 1318
H, Re [1966] 1 WLR 381 . . . . .1088, 1174
H's Marriage, Re (1985) FLC 80 1174
HA (A Child) (Brussels IIA Art 15), Re [2015] EWHC 1310 .1116
Haas v Atlas Assurance Co Ltd [1913] 2 KB 209 1326
Habaş Sinai ve Tibbi Gazlar Istihsal Endüstrisi AŞ v VSC Steel Co Ltd [2013]
    EWHC 4071 (Comm), [2014] 1 Lloyd's Rep 479 667–8
Habas Sinai Ve Tibbi Gazlar Istihsal Endustrisi AS v VSC Steel Co Ltd [2013]
    EWHC 4071 . . . . .667, 700, 720, 756
Habib Bank Ltd v Central Bank of Sudan [2006] EWHC 1767 (Comm), [2006]
    2 Lloyd's Rep 412. . . . . .381, 736
Habib Bank Ltd v Central Bank of Sudan [2014] EWHC 2288 . . . . .355, 551
Hack v Hack (1976) 6 Fam Law 177 1075
Hacker Kuchen GmbH v Bosma Huygen Meubelimpex BV (Case 14.197)
    [1992] IL Pr 379 252
Hadmor Productions Ltd v Hamilton [1983] 1 AC 191 365
Haeger & Schmidt GmbH v Mutuelles du Mans assurances IARD (MMA IARD)
    (C-305/13) ECLI:EU:C:2014:2320. . . . . .731, 737–8
Hagen, The [1908] P 189. . . . . .367, 376
Haines v Mid-Century Insurance Co 177 NW 2d 328 (1970). 682
Haji-Ioannou (Deceased), Re [2009] EWHC 2310 (QB), [2009] Il Pr 56 . . . . .619, 1339
Haji-Ioannou v Frangos [1999] 2 Lloyd's Rep 337 . . . . 199, 206, 216, 337, 405,
                                     445, 450, 456, 461, 469, 470
Haji-Ioannou (Deceased) v Frangos [2009] EWHC 2310 (QB) 1333–4, 1336
Hakeem v Hussain 2003 SLT 515 . . . . .986–7, 998
Halcyon Isle, The [1981] AC 221. . . . . .89, 90
Halcyon Skies, The (No 2) [1977] 1 Lloyd's Rep 22. 100
Haldane v Eckford (1869) LR 8 Eq 631. 155
Halki Shipping Corpn v Sopex Oils Ltd [1998] 1 WLR 726 . . . . .416–17, 420
Hall, Re (1901) 61 App D 266 1196
Hallam v Hallam (Minors) (Forum Conveniens) (Nos 1 and 2) [1993] 1 FLR 958 1125
Halpern v Halpern [2007] EWCA Civ 291, [2007] 2 Lloyd's Rep 56 . . . . .715–16, 734
Hamburg Star, The [1994] 1 Lloyd's Rep 399 400
Hamilton v Dallas (1875) 1 Ch D 257 59
Hamlin v Hamlin [1986] Fam 11 . . . . .487, 1060, 1073, 1256
Hamlyn & Co v Talisker Distillery [1894] AC 202 668
Hammer and Sohne v HWT Realisations Ltd 1985 SLT (Sh Ct) 21 1272
Hanbury Brown, In the Marriage of (1996) FLC 92–671 959
Hanchett-Stamford v Attorney General and Anor (Barclays Bank Trust
    Co Ltd Intervening) [2008] EWHC 330 (Ch). 49
Hanley's Estate, Re [1942] P 33 49
Hannema's Marriage, Re (1981) 54 FLR 79. . . . . .1372, 1378
Hapag Lloyd Container Line GmbH v La Réunion Européenne [2003] IL Pr 51 241
Happy Fellow, The [1998] 1 Lloyd's Rep 13. . . . . .443, 455–6
Haque v Haque (1962) 108 CLR 230 . . . . .53, 1251
Haque v Haque (No 2) (1965) 114 CLR 98 1251
Harada Ltd T/A Chequepoint UK Ltd v Turner [2000] IL Pr 574, [2003]
    EWCA Civ 1695 . . . . .228–9, 280, 300
Harald Kolassa v Barclays Bank plc (C-375/13) EU:C:2015:37, [2016]
    1 All ER (Comm) 733 . . . . .46, 246–7, 249–50, 277, 292, 296, 812

Harb v Aziz (No 1) [2005] EWCA Civ 632, [2005] 2 FLR 1108. . . . . 498, 511,
516, 1060, 1062
Harb v Aziz (No 2) [2005] EWCA Civ 1324, [2005] 1 FLR 825. 1062
Harb v Aziz [2015] EWCA Civ 481, [2016] Ch 308 516
Harben v Harben [1957] 1 WLR 261 1110
Harding v Wealands [2004] EWCA Civ 1735, [2005] 1 WLR 1539, [2006]
UKHL 32, [2007] 2 AC 1 . . . . .778, 862–3, 867
Harding v Wealands [2006] UKHL 32, [2007] 2 AC 1 . . . . .77, 80, 93–5
Hardwick Game Farm v Suffolk Agricultural Poultry Producers Association [1966]
1 WLR 287, [1969] 2 AC 31 . . . . .1267, 1276
Harley v Smith [2009] EWHC 56 (QB) 79
Harold Meyers Travel Service Ltd v Magid (1975) 60 DLR (3d) 42 105
Harriman v Harriman [1909] P 123 1037
Harris Investments Ltd v Smith [1934] 1 DLR 748 1386
Harris v Murray (1995) 11 RFL (4th) 450 978
Harris v Quine (1869) LR 4 QB 653 . . . . .78, 562
Harris v Taylor [1915] 2 KB 580 . . . . .528, 534
Harrison v Harrison [1953] 1 WLR 865 . . . . .149, 165, 167
Harrison v Sterry (1809) 5 Cranch 289 89
Harrods (Buenos Aires) Ltd, Re [1992] Ch 72 . . . . .380, 461
Harrods Ltd v Dow Jones & Co Inc [2003] EWHC 1162 (QB) 329, 331, 351, 353, 887
Harrop v Harrop [1920] 3 KB 386 549–50
Har-Shefi v Har-Shefi (No 2) [1953] P 220 . . . . .1008, 1012, 1019
Har-Shefi v Har-Shefi [1953] P 161 1049
Hartley (1996) 45 ICLQ 271, 285–9 106
Hartley v Fuld [1968] P 675 112
Harty v Sabre International Security Ltd [2011] EWHC 852 349
Harvey v Farnie (1882) 8 App Cas 43 . . . . .893, 1197
Hasberry v Steele, 25 November 2011, HC 636
Hashmi v Hashmi [1972] Fam 36 . . . . .941–2, 1195, 1201
Hassan v Hassan [1978] 1 NZLR 385 . . . . .931, 937
Hassan v Hassan, Re (1976) 69 DLR (3d) 224 935
Haugesund Kommune v Depfa ACS Bank [2010] EWCA Civ 579 1308
Haumschild v Continental Casualty Co 7 Wis 2d 130, 95 NW 2d 814 (1959) 816
Havhelt, The [1993] 1 Lloyd's Rep 523 . . . . .385, 412
Hawke Bay Shipping Co Ltd v The First National Bank of Chicago,
The Efthimis [1986] 1 Lloyd's Rep 244 . . . . .403, 407–8, 559
Hawthorne, Graham v Massey, Re (1883) 23 Ch D 743 490
Hays v Hays [2015] EWHC 3825 1353
Hayward, Re [1997] Ch 45 . . . . .207, 212, 219
Hazell v Hammersmith and Fulham Borough Council [1992] 2 AC 1, HL 247
HB (Abduction: Children's Objections), Re [1997] 1 FLR 392 1156
Health Service Executive of Ireland v PA [2015] EWCOP 38; [2015]
3 WLR 1923 1242
Health Service Executive v SC and AC (C-92/12) [2012] 2 FLR 1040 . . . . . .1093, 1119–20, 1123
Healy's Will, Re 125 NYS 2d 486 (1953). 1386
Hearle v Greenbank (1749) 1 Ves Sen 298 1356–7
Heath Lambert Ltd v Sociedad de Corretaje de Seguros [2003] EWHC 2269
(Comm) 716
Hedley Byrne v Heller [1964] AC 465 850
Heidberg, The [1994] 2 Lloyd's Rep 287 . . . . .586, 612, 645, 756
Heiko Koelzsch v État du Grand Duchy of Luxemburg (C-29/10) [2011]
ECR I-1595 . . . . .684, 688–90, 741
Heiser v Iran [2012] EWHC 2938. . . . . .505, 602
Helbert Wagg & Co Ltd's Claim, Re [1956] Ch 323 . . . . .130, 1281–2

Helene Roth, The [1980] QB 273 384
Hellenic Steel Co v Svolamar Shipping Co Ltd; The Komninos S [1991]
    1 Lloyd's Rep 370. 718
Hellmann's Will, Re (1866) LR 2 Eq 363. . . . . .1176, 1340
Helmsing Schiffahrts GmbH & Co KG v Malta Drydocks Corpn
    [1977] 2 Lloyd's Rep 444 . . . . .97, 99
Hemain v Hemain [1988] 2 FLR 388 . . . . .428, 431, 978
Henaff v Henaff [1966] 1 WLR 598 81
Henderson v Henderson (1844) 6 QB 288 . . . . .552, 564, 567
Henderson v Henderson [1967] P 77, [1965] 1 All ER 179. . . . . .146, 148, 151, 167
Henderson v Jaouen [2002] EWCA Civ 75, [2002] 1 WLR 2971 812
Hendrikman v Magenta Druck & Verlag GmbH (C-78/95) [1997]
    QB 426 . . . . .627, 632–4, 644
Hengst Import BV v Campese (C-474/93) [1995] ECR I-2113. 636
Henrich Björn, The (1886) 11 App Cas 270 384
Henry v Geoprosco International Ltd [1976] QB 726 . . . . .543, 596, 606
Henry v Henry (1995) 185 CLR 571. 409
Henwood v Barlow Clowes International Ltd (in Liquidation) [2007]
    EWHC 1579 155
Her Majesty's Revenue & Customs v Sunico ApS (C-49/12) EU:C:2013:231,
    [2014] QB 391 . . . . .125, 195, 204, 206
Herbert (Lady) v Herbert (Lord) (1819) 3 Phillim 58 893
Herceg Novi v Ming Galaxy [1998] 4 All ER 238 404
Hercules Aktieselskabet Dampskib v Grand Trunk Pacific Rly Co [1912]
    1 KB 222 330
Hermann Lutz v Elke Bäuerle (C-557/13) ECLI:EU:C:2015:227 . . . . .773, 1322
Hernando, Hernando v Sawtell, Re (1884) 27 Ch D 284. 1352
Heron v National Trustees Executors and Agency Co of Australasia Ltd
    [1976] VR 733. 1204
Herron, Re [1941] 4 DLR 203. 1345
Hertfordshire CC v LC [2015] EWHC 1617. 1115
Hesperides Hotels Ltd v Aegean Turkish Holidays Ltd [1979] AC 508 492
Heung Won Lee, Re (1963) 36 DLR (2d) 177. 1370
Hewden Tower Cranes Ltd v Wolffkran GmbH [2007] EWHC 857 (TCC),
    [2007] 2 Lloyd's Rep 138. . . . . .231, 237, 242, 265, 808
Hewit's Trustees v Lawson (1891) 18 R 793. 1258
Hewitson v Hewitson [1995] Fam 100. 1076
Hewitson v Hewitson [1999] 2 FLR 74 373
Hewitt's Settlement, Re [1915] 1 Ch 228. . . . . .1378, 1388
Hi Hotel HCF SARL v Uwe Spoering (C-387/12) EU:C:2014:215, [2014]
    1 WLR 1912 . . . . .264, 274, 276, 279
Hicks v Powell (1869) 4 Ch App 741. 490
Hida Maru, The [1981] 2 Lloyd's Rep 510. . . . . .377, 398
High Commissioner for Pakistan in the United Kingdom v National
    Westminster Bank [2015] EWHC 55 507
High Tech International AG v Deripaska [2006] EWHC 3276 (QB). 149, 199
Hill v Hill 1990 SCLR 238 1124
Hill's Goods, Re (1870) LR 2 P & D 89 1332
Hillside (New Media) Ltd v Baasland [2010] EWHC 3336 (Comm), [2010]
    2 CLC 986. . . . . .811–12, 1280–1
Hilton v Guyot 159 US 113 (1895). 526
Hindocha and Ors v Gheewala and Ors [2003] UKPC 77, [2004] 1 CLC 502 . . . .395, 400, 1330
Hinkley v Hinkley (1984) 38 RFL (2d) 337. 1080
Hipperson v Newbury District Electoral Registration Officer [1985] QB 1060 174
Hiscox v Outhwaite [1992] 1 AC 562 671

Hispano Americana Mercantil SA v Central Bank of Nigeria [1979]
2 Lloyd's Rep 277..504
HIT Entertainment Ltd v Gaffney International Licensing Pty Ltd [2007]
EWHC 1282 (Ch)..370, 466
HJ (Transfer of Proceedings), Re [2013] EWHC 1867............................1114
HJ Heinz Co Ltd v EFL Inc [2010] EWHC 1203 (Comm), [2010] 1 CLC 868...........560
Hlynski v Hlynski (1999) 176 DLR (4th) 132....................................487
HM (Vulnerable Adult: Abduction), Re [2010] 2 F.L.R. 1057...................1235–6
HN v Poland [2005] 3 FCR 85..1164
Hobbs v Australian Press Association [1933] 1 KB 1.............................328
Hobohm v Benedikt Kampik Ltd & Co KG (C-297/14) EU:C:2015:844,
[2016] QB 616..293, 295
Hodgson v De Beauchesne (1858) 12 Moo PCC 285, 329, 330..............149–50, 156
Hoffman v Sofaer [1982] 1 WLR 1350.....................................99, 102–3
Hoffmann v Krieg (145/86) [1988] ECR 645.......................618, 622, 632
Holden v Holden [1968] NI 7, [1968] VR 334.....................148, 1110
Holland v Holland 1973 (1) SA 897..........................980, 982
Holland v Lampen-Wolfe [2000] 1 WLR 1573......................498, 500–2, 504
Hollandia, The [1983] 1 AC 565...........................416, 775, 867
Holliday v Musa [2010] EWCA Civ 335........................151–2
Holman v Johnson (1775) 1 Cowp 341, 98 ER 1120..........20, 22, 116, 118
Holmes v Holmes [1989] Fam 47..................485, 1075–6, 1256
Holmes, Re (1861) 2 John & H 527.........................485
Holt Cargo Systems Inc v ABC Containerline NV (Trustees of) (2001)
207 DLR (4th) 577.....................................394
Holterman Ferho Exploitatie BV and Others v Friedrich Leopold Freiherr Spies
von Büllesheim (C-47/14) EU:C:2015:574, [2015] IL Pr 44........ 246, 257, 260, 268–9,
272, 297–8, 701
Homawoo v GMF Assurance SA [2010] EWHC 1941...........................786
Honeywell International Middle East Ltd v Meydan Group LLC [2014]
EWHC 1344 (TCC), [2014] 2 Lloyd's Rep 133...........................675
Hoop, The (1799) 1 Ch Rob 196................................497
Hooper v Hooper [1959] 1 WLR 1021, [1959] 2 All ER 575................71, 900
Hope v Hope (1854) 4 De G M & G 328........................1110, 1112
Hope v Hope [1968] NI 1....................................166
Hopkins v Hopkins [1951] P 116, 121–2.......................173
Horn Linie GmbH & Co v Panamericana Formas E Impresos SA (The Hornbay)
[2006] EWHC 373 (Comm), [2006] 2 Lloyd's Rep 44...........438–9, 700, 756, 757
Horn v Horn [1985] FLR 984..................................1080
Hornett v Hornett [1971] P 255..............................1027, 1035
Hoskins v Matthews (1856) 8 De GM & G 13, 28..................159
Hoszig Kft v Alstom Power Thermal Services (C-222/15) EU:C:2016:525,
[2016] IL Pr 36......................................234, 239
Hough v P & O Containers [1999] QB 834.....................288
House of Spring Gardens Ltd v Waite [1991] 1 QB 241............560, 563, 572
Houston, Re (1826) 1 Russ 312..............................1246
Howard Houlder and Partners Ltd v Marine General Transporters Corpn,
The Panaghia P [1983] 2 Lloyd's Rep 653....................343
Howden North America Inc v ACE European Group Ltd [2012] EWCA
Civ 1624, [2012] CLC 969................................376
Howe Louis, Re (1970) 14 DLR (3d) 49......................897
Hoy v Hoy 1968 SC 179.....................................1088
Hoyles, Re [1910] 2 Ch 333, [1911] 1 Ch 179................1252
Hoystead v Taxation Comr (1921) 29 CLR 537, [1926] AC 155..........558
HRH Maharanee Seethaderi Gaekwar of Baroda v Wildenstein [1972] 2 QB 283...........325

HSE Ireland v SF [2012] EWHC 1640 1120
Huber v Steiner (1835) 2 Bing NC 202 . . . . .73, 78
Hudson Trail Outfitters v District of Columbia Department of Employment
    Services 801 A 2d 987 893
Hudson v Leigh [2009] EWHC 1306 . . . . .893–4, 985, 1050
Hughes v Hannover [1997] 1 BCLC 497 . . . . .428, 589
Hull v Wilson (1996) 128 DLR (4th) 403 530
Hulse v Chambers [2001] 1 WLR 2386 . . . . .94, 863–4
Humphries's Estate, Re [1934] P 78 1332
Hunt v BP Exploration Co (Libya) Ltd (1979) 144 CLR 565, [1980]
    1 NZLR 104 . . . . .106, 595, 606
Hunt v T & N plc (1993) 109 DLR (4th) 16 . . . . .112, 526, 543
Hunter v Blom-Cooper [2000] IL Pr 229 275
Hunter v Hunter [1944] P 95 . . . . .985, 1073, 1396
Hunter v Hunter and Waddington [1962] P 1 1061
Hunter v Murrow (Abduction: Rights of Custody), Re [2005] EWCA Civ 976,
    [2005] 2 FLR 1119 1056–7
Huntington v Attrill (1892) 146 US 657 50
Huntington v Attrill [1893] AC 150 . . . . .50, 118–19, 121, 552
Hurtado v Superior Court 522 P 2d 666 (1974) 25
Hussein v Hussein [1938] P 159 986
Hutter v Hutter [1944] P 95 994
Hyde v Agar (1998) 45 NSWLR 487 376
Hyde v Hyde (1866) LR 1 P & D 130 . . . . .892, 929, 929–30, 932–3,
                                                        941–2, 945, 952
Hyland v Hyland (1971) 18 FLR 461 162
Hypoteční banka as v Lindner (C-327/10) EU:C:2011:745 . . . . .200, 202, 296, 324

I (A Child) (Contact Application: Jurisdiction), Re [2009] UKSC 10 . . . . . . .1057, 1098–9, 1111
I (Abduction: Acquiescence), Re [1999] 1 FLR 778 1150
I (Minors), Re, 23 April 1999 unreported, CA 15
I Congreso del Partido [1983] 1 All ER 1092, [1983] 1 AC 244 126
I, Petitioner [1999] Fam LR 126 1153
IB v MM (2015) EWHC 1502 . . . . .1148, 1151–2, 1156
IBS Technologies (PVT) Ltd v APM Technologies SA, 7 April 2003 (unreported) 227
ICL Shipping Ltd & Steamship Mutual Underwriting Association (Bermuda)
    Ltd v ChinTai Steel Enterprise Co Ltd [2003] EWHC 2320 (Comm) 361
ICL Shipping Ltd v Chin Tai Steel Enterprise Co Ltd [2004] 1 All ER (Comm) 246 289
Iglesias Gil v Spain [2005] 1FLR 190, (2005) 40 EHRR 3 1163
Igra v Igra [1951] P 404 . . . . .137, 142, 1027
IH (A Child) (Permission to Apply for Adoption), Re [2013] EWHC 1235 . . . . .1219, 1231
IJ (A Child), Re [2011] EWHC 921 . . . . .1179, 1182, 1184, 1186
Ikarian Reefer, The (No 2) [1999] 2 Lloyd's Rep 621 337
Ikimi v Ikimi [2001] EWCA Civ 873, [2001] 3 WLR 672, [2001] 2 FLR 1288 176–7,
    180–1, 958, 1097
Ikin (deceased), Re [2009] EWHC 3340 1350
Ilonka Sayn-Wittgenstein v Landeshauptstadt von Wien (C-208/09) [2010] ECR I-13693 35
Ilyssia Cia Naviera SA v Ahmed Abdul Qawi Bamaodah, The Elli 2 [1985]
    1 Lloyd's Rep 107 345
Iman Din v National Assistance Board [1967] 2 QB 213 . . . . .932, 944
Immigration Appeal Tribunal v Chelliah [1985] Imm AR 192 174
Immunity of Special Rapporteur, Re (1999) Times, 19 May 515
Import-Export Metro Ltd v Compañía Sud Americana de Vapores SA [2003] EWHC 11
    (Comm), [2003] 1 Lloyd's Rep 405 . . . . .94, 329, 370, 398–9, 413–14
Imrie v Castrique (1860) 8 CBNS 405 . . . . .383, 547, 564

Imtech Marine Belgium NV v Radio Hellenic SA (C-300/14) EU:C:2015:825,
  [2016] 1 WLR 1625 . . . . .657, 659
In re S (Hospital Patient: Foreign Curator) [1996] Fam 23, 31 151
in rem: The Deichland [1990] 1 QB 361 . . . . .203, 214
In the Marriage of Ferrier-Watson & McElrath [2000] FamCA 219 [78]–[80]. 150, 155
In the Matter of A (Children) [2013] UKSC 60. . . . . 175, 177–8, 180, 182–3,
                                              1095–6, 1103–4, 1110–12
In the Matter of B (A Child) [2016] UKSC 4 . . . . .176–80, 182, 1095, 1097, 1111–12
In the Matter of D (Habitual residence) 2014 WL 7254970 1118
In the Matter of H, R and E (Children) [2013] EWHC 3857 . . . . .1148, 1155
In the Matter of LC (Children) [2014] UKSC 1 .176–7, 180–3, 1095–6
In the Matter of M (Children) [2016] EWCA Civ 942 1155
In the Matter of S (A Child) [2010] EWCA Civ 465 1110
Inco Europe v First Choice Distribution [1999] 1 WLR 270, [2000] 1 WLR 586. 417–418
Incorporated Broadcasters Ltd v Canwest Global Communications Corpn
  (2003) 223 DLR (4th) 627 399
Independent Trustee Services Ltd v Morris [2010] NSWSC 1218, (2010)
  79 NSWLR 425. . . . . .540, 552
Indian Fortune, The [1985] 1 Lloyd's Rep 344. 412
Industrial Diamond Supplies v Riva (43/77) [1977] ECR 2175. . . . . .646, 648
Indyka v Indyka [1969] 1 AC 33 . . . . 544, 924, 1011,
                                              1026, 1038, 1228
Ines, The [1993] 2 Lloyd's Rep 492 339
Ingenieurburo Michael Weiss und Partner GbR v Industrie und Handelskammer Berlin
  (C-14/07). 309
Ingenium Technologies Corp v McGraw-Hill Companies, Inc (2005) 255 DLR
  (4th) 499 409
Inglis v Commonwealth Trading Bank of Australia (1972) 20 FLR 30 489
Inglis v Robertson [1898] AC 616 1275
Inland Revenue Comrs v Lysaght [1928] AC 234 173
Innes v Dunlop (1800) 8 Term Rep 595. . . . . .86, 1290
Innovia Films Ltd v Frito-Lay North America, Inc [2012] EWHC 790 . . . . . . .471, 805, 824, 826
Insurance Co "Ingosstrakh" Ltd v Latvian Shipping Co [2000] IL Pr 164 . . . . 359, 369,
                                              371, 410, 412
Insurance Co of the State of Pennsylvania v Equitas Insurance Ltd [2013] EWHC
  3713 (Comm), [2014] Lloyd's Rep IR 195. 409
Insured Financial Structures Limited v Elektrocieplownia Tychy SA [2003] EWCA
  Civ 110, [2003] QB 1280 234–5
Integral Petroleum SA v SCU-Finanz AG [2015] EWCA Civ 144 . . . . .45, 70, 758, 1308
Intel Corp. v European Commission (T-296/09) ECLI:EU:T:2014:547 827
Intercare Ltd, In the Matter of [2004] 1 ILRM 351. . . . . .455, 461
Intercontainer Interfrigo SC (ICF) v Balkenende Oosthuizen BV and MIC
  Operations BV (C-133/08) [2009] ECR I-9687 . . . . .684, 706–8, 725, 731, 737, 740
Interdesco SA v Nullifire Ltd [1992] 1 Lloyd's Rep 180 . . . . .572, 627–8, 648
Interedil Srl v Fallimento Interedil Srl en Intesa Gestione Crediti SpA (C-396/09)
  ECLI:EU:C:2011:671 1315
Intermetal Group Ltd & Trans-World (Steel) Ltd v Worslade Trading Ltd
  [1998] IL Pr 765 . . . . .394, 462
International Alltex Corp v Lawler Creations Ltd [1965] IR 264 666
International Association of Science and Technology for Development v Hamza
  (1995) 122 DLR (4th) 92 86
International Business Machines Corpn v Phoenix Intercontinental (Computers)
  Ltd [1994] RPC 251 106
International Commercial Bank plc v Insurance Corpn of Ireland plc
  [1989] IR 453 . . . . .400, 409

International Credit and Investment Co (Overseas) Ltd v Shaikh Kamal
  Adham [1999] IL Pr 302 . . . . .374, 405
International Group Ltd Trans-World (Steel) Ltd v Worstade Trading Ltd
  [1998] IL Pr 765 405
International Marine Services Inc v National Bank of Fujairah [1997]
  IL Pr 468 . . . . .339, 351, 372
International Nederlanden v CAA [1997] 1 Lloyd's Rep 80 443
International Tank and Pipe SAK v Kuwait Aviation Fuelling Co KSC
  [1975] QB 224 668
Interpool Ltd v Galani [1988] QB 738 1293
Inter-Tel Inc v Ocis Plc [2004] EWHC 2269 (QB) 405
Interview Ltd, Re [1975] IR 382 1272
Intpro Properties (UK) Ltd v Sauvel [1983] QB 1019 . . . . .505, 511
Iosub Caras v Romania [2007] 1 FLR 661 1165
IP Metal Ltd v Ruote OZ SpA [1993] 2 Lloyd's Rep 60 .455–6
IPCO (Nigeria) Ltd v Nigerian National Petroleum Corpn [2005] EWHC 726
  (Comm), [2005] 2 Lloyd's Rep 326 . . . . .670, 673–4
IPCO (Nigeria) Ltd v Nigerian National Petroleum Corpn [2008] EWCA Civ
  1157, [2009] 1 All ER (Comm) 611 670
IPCO (Nigeria) Ltd v Nigerian National Petroleum Corpn [2017] UKSC 16,
  [2017] 1 WLR 970 673
Iran Continental Shelf Oil Co v IRI International Corpn [2002] EWCA Civ
  1024, [2004] 2 CLC 696 . . . . .727, 733, 736, 739
Iran Vojdan, The [1984] 2 Lloyd's Rep 380 . . . . .404, 411, 415, 716
IRC v Bullock [1976] 1 WLR 1178, 1184 .147, 150–2, 155–6
IRC v Duchess of Portland [1982] Ch 314, 318–9 . . . . .149, 162–3, 169
IRC v Lysaght [1928] AC 234 173
IRC v Muller & Co's Margarines Ltd [1901] AC 217 1254
IRC v Stype Investments (Jersey) Ltd [1982] Ch 456 . . . . .1331, 1333, 1335
Irini A, The (No 2) [1999] 1 Lloyd's Rep 189 559
Irini A, The [1999] 1 Lloyd's Rep 196 430
Irish Shipping Ltd v Commercial Union Assurance Co plc [1991] 2 QB 206 . . . . . .368, 409, 748
Irvani v Irvani [2000] 1 Lloyd's Rep 412 672
Irvin v Irvin [2001] 1 FLR 178, 194 . . . . .156, 163
ISC v Guerin [1992] 2 Lloyd's Rep 430 . . . . .337, 338, 351, 359, 365, 396
ISC v Radcliff, 7 December 1990 (unreported) 359
Ishiodu v Entry Clearance Officer, Lagos [1975] Imm AR 56 . . . . .937, 939
Isis Investments Ltd v Oscatello Investments Ltd [2013] EWCA Civ 1493 . . . . .1308–9, 1320
Islamic Arab Insurance Co v Saudi Egyptian American Reinsurance Co [1987]
  1 Lloyd's Rep 315 . . . . .344, 376, 403
Islamic Republic of Iran v Barakat [2007] EWCA Civ 1374, [2009] QB 22 . . . . .121, 123–4
Islamic Republic of Iran v Berend [2007] EWHC 132 (QB), [2007] 2 All ER
  (Comm) 132 . . . . .71, 108, 1252, 1274, 1278
Ismail v Secretary of State for the Home Department [2013] EWHC 663 (Admin), [2013]
  ACD 76 581
Ispahani v Bank Melli Iran [1998] Lloyd's Rep Bank 133, (1997) Times, 29 December 753
Israel Discount Bank of New York v Hadjipateras [1984] 1 WLR 137 . . . . . .135, 532–3, 568, 574
ISS Machinery Services Ltd v Aeolian Shipping SA (the Aeolian) [2001] EWCA Civ 1162,
  [2001] 2 Lloyd's Rep 641 . . . . .709, 721
Italian Leather SpA v WECO Polstermobel GmbH & Co (C-80/00) [2002]
  ECR I-4995 . . . . .616, 640, 654
Ivan Zagubanski see Navigation Maritime Bulgare v Rustal Trading Ltd (The Ivan
  Zagubanski) Iveagh v IRC [1954] Ch 364 . . . . .209, 440
Iveco SpA v Magna Electronics Srl (formerly Italamec Srl) [2015] EWHC 2887 (TCC),
  [2016] IL Pr 18 . . . . .239, 265, 277, 288

Ivenel v Schwab (133/81) [1982] ECR 1891 . . . . .300, 690
Ivleva v Yates [2014] EWHC 554. . . . . .1011, 1027–8
Iwona Szyrocka v SiGerTechnologie GmbH (C-215/11) EU:C:2012:794 661

J (A Child) (1996 Hague Convention: Morocco), Re [2015] UKSC 70;
     [2015] EWCA Civ 329 . . . . .1092, 1103, 1121–3
J (A Child) (Adoption: Consent of Foreign Public Authority), Re [2002]
     EWHC 766, [2002] 2 FLR 618. 1214
J (A Child) (Return to Foreign Jurisdiction: Convention Rights), Re [2005]
     UKHL 40, [2005] 3 WLR 14, [2006] 1 AC 80 .15, 1056, 1172–4
J (A Child) (Return to Foreign Jurisdiction: Convention Rights), Re [2005]
     UKHL 40, [2005] 3 WLR 14 15
J (A Child: Brussels II Revised: Art 15: Practice and Procedure), Re
     [2014] EWFC 41 1115
J (A Minor) (Abduction: Custody Rights), Re [1990] 2 AC 562, 578 . . . . .176, 1135–9, 1143
J (A Minor) (Abduction: Custody Rights), Re [1999] 1 WLR 1937 578 182
J (A Minor) (Abduction: Ward of Court), Re [1989] Fam 85, [1990] Fam
     Law 177. . . . . .1056, 1136–7, 1139
J (Abduction: Acquiring Custody Rights by Caring for Child), Re [2005] 2 FLR 791 1153
J (Abduction: Rights of Custody), Re [1999] 3 FCR 577. 1056
J (Children) (Abduction: Child's Objections to Return), Re [2004] EWCA
     Civ 428, [2004] 2 FLR 64 . . . . .183, 1138, 1145–6
J (Children), Re [2006] EWCA Civ 1897, [2007] 2 FCR 149. .1168
J (Recognition of Foreign Adoption Order), Re [2012] EWHC 3353 . . . . .1225, 1227
J and S (Care Proceedings: Appeal), Re [2014] EWFC 4 1114–16
J H Rayner (Mincing Lane) Ltd v Bank für Gemainwirtschaft AG [1983]
     1 Lloyd's Rep 462. 563
J H Rayner (Mincing Lane) Ltd v Department of Trade and Industry [1989]
     Ch 72, [1990] 2 AC 418 . . . . .498, 504
J v C (Void Marriage: Status of Children) [2006] EWCA Civ 551, [2006]
     2 FLR 1098 . . . . .892, 1051, 1199
J v C [1970] AC 668 . . . . .13, 15, 1110, 1172–3, 1212
J v G (Parental Orders) [2013] EWHC 1432. 1188
J v K (Child Abduction: Acquiescence), Re 2002 SC 450. 1142
J v P [2007] EWHC 704 (Fam) 447, 455–6
J v U [2016] EWHC 2481. . . . . .1106, 1112
JA v TH [2016] EWHC 2535 1116
Jabbour (F & K) v Custodian of Israeli Absentee Property [1954] 1 WLR 139 . . . . .108, 131
Jabbour v Custodian of Israeli Absentee Property [1954] 1 WLR 139 . . . . .108, 131, 1281
Jablonowski v Jablonowski (1972) 28 DLR (3d) 440 160
Jacob Engineering Group Inc v Matthew [2014] CSIH 18, 2014 SC 579 807
Jacobs & Turner Ltd v Celsius sarl [2007] CSOH 76. 445
Jacobs v Crédit Lyonnais (1884) 12 QBD 589. . . . . .722, 724
Jacobs v Motor Insurers Bureau [2010] EWHC 231 . . . . .784, 811
Jacobson v Frachon (1927) 138 LT 386. . . . . .564, 576
Jaffe v Miller (1993) 103 DLR (4th) 315 . . . . .498, 506
Jakob Handte & Co GmbH v Traitements Mecano-Chimiques des Surfaces
     SA (TMCS) (C-26/91) [1992] ECR I-3967. 245–6
Jalakrishna, The [1983] 2 Lloyd's Rep 628 403
Jalamatsya, The [1987] 2 Lloyd's Rep 164 385
James (An Insolvent), Re [1977] Ch 41 565
James Hardie & Co v Hall (1998) 43 NSWLR 554. 112
James Miller & Partners Ltd v Whitworth Street Estates (Manchester) Ltd
     [1970] AC 583. . . . . .668, 735
James North & Sons Ltd v North Cape Textiles Ltd [1984] 1 WLR 1428 . . . . .336, 349

James Rhodes v OPO [2015] UKSC 710, 856
James, Re (1908) 98 LT 438. 159
Jamieson v Northern Electricity Supply Corpn (Private) Ltd 1970 SLT 113. . . . . .593, 596
Janred Properties Ltd v Ente Nazionale Italiano per il Turismo [1989] 2 All ER 444 701
Jaroszonek v Jaroszonek [1962] SASR 157 906
Jarrett v Barclays Bank plc [1999] QB 1. . . . . .221, 223
Jasmin Solar Pty Ltd v Trina Solar Australia Pty Ltd [2015] FCA 1453 757
Jayaretnam v Mahmood (1992) Times, 21 May 375, 403
JB (Child Abduction: Rights of Custody: Spain), Re [2003] EWHC 2130,
    [2004] 1 FLR 796 . . . . .72, 1139
JB v D [2016] EWHC 1607 (Fam) 1111
JEB Recoveries LLP v Binstock [2016] EWCA Civ 1008. . . . . .257, 260
Jefferson v O'Connor [2014] EWCA Civ 38 969
Jeffery v M'Taggart (1817) 6 M & S 126 86
Jenic Properties Ltd v Andy Thornton Architectural Antiques 1992 SLT (Sh Ct) 5 320
Jenner v Sun Oil Co [1952] 2 DLR 526 886
Jepson v General Cas Co of Wisconsin 513 NW 2d 467, 473 (Minn 1994) 31
Jeske v Jeske (1982) 29 RFL (2d) 348 484
Jet Holdings Inc v Patel [1990] 1 QB 335 568–9
Jewish National Fund Inc v Royal Trust Co (1965) 53 DLR (2d) 577 1347
JK v KC [2011] EWHC 1284 1107
JKN v JCN [2010] EWHC 843 (Fam), [2011] 1 FLR 826 . . . . .474, 975
JLM v Director General, NSW Dept of Community Services (2001) 180 ALR 402 403
Joachimson v Swiss Bank Corpn [1921] 3 KB 110. 1281
Joanna V, The [2003] EWHC 1655 (Comm), [2003] 2 Lloyd's Rep 617 . . . . .583, 676
Jocelyne, The [1984] 2 Lloyd's Rep 569 558–9
Johann Friedrich, The (1839) 1 Wm Rob 36 878
John Pfeiffer Pty Ltd v Rogerson (2000) 203 CLR 503 .80, 94, 325
John Pfeiffer Pty Ltd v Rogerson [2000] HCA 36 94
John Russell & Co Ltd v Cayzer, Irvine & Co Ltd [1916] 2 AC 298 324
John Sanderson & Co (NSW) Pty Ltd v Giddings [1976] VR 421 .325
Johnson v Coventry Churchill International Ltd [1992] 3 All ER 14. . . . . .777, 814
Johnson v Smith (1968) 70 DLR (2d) 374. . . . . .986, 987
Johnson v Taylor Bros [1920] AC 144 . . . . .346, 376
Johnson v Wallis 112 NY 230 (1889). 1336
Johnston, Re [1903] 1 Ch 821. . . . . .53, 171
Johnstone v Baker (1817) 4 Madd 474. 1252
Johnstone v Beattie (1843) 10 Cl & Fin 42, 139 . . . . .159, 167, 1088, 1176
Johnstone v Pedlar [1921] 2 AC 262 . . . . .114, 497
Joint Administrators of Heritable Bank plc v Winding up Board of Landsbanki
    Islands hf [2013] UKSC 13 1320
Joint Administrators of Rangers Football Club Plc, Notes 2012 SLT 599. 1385
Joint Stock Asset Management Co Ingosstrakh-Investments v BNP Paribas SA [2012]
    EWCA Civ 644, [2012] 1 Lloyd's Rep 649, [2012] 2 CLC 312. . . . . .337, 561
Joint Stock Co 'Aeroflot-Russian Airlines' v Berezovsky [2014] EWCA Civ 20, [2014] 1
    CLC 53 . . . . .14, 287, 548, 551, 559, 579, 581
Jones v Assurances Generales de France (AGF) SA [2010] IL Pr 4 290
Jones v Ministry of the Interior of the Kingdom of Saudi Arabia [2005] QB
    699, [2006] UKHL 26, [2007] 1 AC 270 . . . . .350, 498, 502, 507–8
Jones v United Kingdom, Judgment of 14 January 2014; (2014) 59 EHRR 1 . . . . .498, 501–2
Jones, Re (1961) 25 DLR (2d) 595 1198
Jones' Estate, Re (1921) 192 Iowa 78, 182 NW 227 164
Jonesco v Beard [1930] AC 298 569
Jong v HSBC Private Bank (Monaco) SA [2015] EWCA Civ 1057 . . . . .367, 371, 471
Jopp v Wood (1865) 4 De GJ & Sm 616. . . . . .149, 152

Jordan Grand Prix v Baltic Insurance Group [1998] 1 WLR 1049, [1999]
2 AC 127 . . . . .288, 290
Jordan v Jordan [2000] 1 WLR 210 1075–6
Jordan v Schatz (2000) 189 DLR (4th) 62 333
Joseph v Joseph [1953] 1 WLR 1182 1035
Joyce v Joyce [1979] Fam 93 . . . . .142, 1007, 1027, 1029, 1031
JP Morgan Europe Ltd v Primacom AG [2005] EWHC 508 (Comm), [2005]
2 Lloyd's Rep 665 . . . . .303, 445–6, 450–1, 455, 457
JP Morgan Securities Asia Private Ltd v Malaysian Newsprint Industries SDN
BHD [2001] 2 Lloyd's Rep 41 377
JS (Private International Adoption), Re [2000] 2 FLR 638 . . . . .1137, 1218
JSC BTA Bank v Ablyazov [2011] EWHC 202 (Comm), [2011] 2 All ER
(Comm) 10 . . . . .115, 124
JSC BTA Bank v Ablyazov [2017] EWCA Civ 40 272
JSC BTA Bank v Granton Trade Ltd [2010] EWHC 2577 (Comm), [2011] 2 All ER
(Comm) 542 366
JSC VTB Bank v Skurikhin [2014] EWHC 271 . . . . .119, 128, 551, 553, 573, 575
JSC Zestafoni v Ronly Holdings Ltd [2004] EWHC 245 (Comm), [2004]
2 Lloyd's Rep 335 . . . . .137, 720
Juan Ysmael & Co Inc v Indonesian Government [1955] AC 72 507
Jubert v Church Comrs for England 1952 SC 160 491
Jugoslavenska Oceanska Plovidba v Castle Investment Co Inc [1974]
QB 292 . . . . .98, 100, 103, 669
Jupiter, The (No 3) [1927] P 122 131
Jurisdiction in a claim based on a prize draw notification, Re [2007]
IL Pr 15 292
Jurisdiction in Internal Company Matters, Re [1995] IL Pr 425 231
Jurisdictional Immunities of the State (Germany v Italy; Greece intervening)
2012 ICJ Rep 99 501–2

K (A Child) (External Relocation: Judge's Evaluation), Re [2016] EWCA Civ 931 1171
K (A Child), Re [2013] EWCA Civ 895 1116
K (A Child), Re [2014] EWCA Civ 1364 1142
K (A Child), Re [2015] EWCA Civ 352 1124
K (A Minor) (Abduction), Re [1990] FCR 524, [1990] 1 FLR 387 1134
K (A Minor) (Adoption Order: Nationality), Re [1995] Fam 38 1230
K (A Minor) (Adoption: Foreign Child), Re [1997] 2 FLR 221 . . . . .1137, 1214
K (A Minor: Wardship: Jurisdiction: Interim Order), Re [1991] 2 FLR 104, [1991]
Fam Law 226 1112
K (Abduction: Child's Objections), Re [1995] 1 FLR 977 . . . . .1143, 1146, 1149
K (Abduction: Consent), Re [1997] 2 FLR 212 1149
K (Abduction: Consent: Forum Conveniens), Re [1995] 2 FLR 211 1137
K (Abduction: Inchoate Rights), Re [2014] UKSC 29 1137–8
K (Abduction: Psychological Harm), Re [1995] 2 FLR 550 1155
K v K (Abduction: Consent) [2009] EWHC 2721 .1149, 1151
K v K (Relocation: Shared Care Arrangement) [2011] EWCA Civ 793 1170–1
K v K [1986] 2 FLR 411 973
K v K [2006] EWHC 2685, [2007] 1 FCR 355 . . . . .1144, 1148
K v K [2007] EWCA Civ 533 1142
K v M, M and L (Financial Relief: Foreign Orders) [1998] 2 FLR 59, 75 173
K(E) v K(D) (2004) 257 DLR (4th) 549 134
KA Finanz AG v Sparkassen Versicherung AG Vienna Insurance Group (C-483/14)
ECLI:EU:C:2016:205 701
Kahan v Pakistan Federation [1951] 2 KB 1003 . . . . .503, 506
Kahler v Midland Bank Ltd [1950] AC 24 . . . . .117, 135, 769

Kalfelis v Schroder (189/87) [1988] ECR 5565 284
Kallang, The [2006] EWHC 2825 (Comm), [2007] 1 Lloyd's Rep 160 441
Kalogeropoulou v Greece and Germany, 12 December 2002 501
Kamouh v Associated Electrical Industries International Ltd, Re [1980] QB 199 . . . . .87, 1247
Kanani, Re (1978) 122 Sol Jo 611 1341
Kanoria v Guinness [2006] EWCA Civ 222, [2006] 1 Lloyd's Rep 701 672
Kapferer v Schlank & Schick GmbH (C-234/04) [2006] IL Pr 17 . . . . .250–1, 261
Kapitan Shvetsov, The [1998] 1 Lloyd's Rep 199 . . . . .394, 404
Kapur v Kapur [1984] FLR 920 . . . . .966, 973
Karadzic v Croatia [2006] 1 FCR 36, (2007) 44 EHRR 45 1165
Karafarin Bank v Mansoury-Dara [2009] EWHC 1217 (Comm), [2009]
    2 Lloyd's Rep 289 . . . . .430, 539, 556, 563
Kareem v Secretary of State for the Home Department [2014] UKUT 00024 898
Karnenas, Re (1978) 3 RFL (2d) 213 . . . . .1195, 1198
Karpov v Browder [2013] EWHC 3071 350
Kassim v Kassim [1962] P 224 . . . . .931, 987–8, 1049, 1052, 1055
Kaufman v Gerson [1903] 2 KB 114, [1904] 1 KB 591 . . . . .134–5, 682, 748
Kaufman v Gerson [1904] 1 KB 591, CA 134–5
Kaufman's Goods, Re [1952] P 325 1331
Kaur v Ginder (1958) 13 DLR (2d) 465 937
Kaverit Steel and Crane Ltd v Kone Corpn (1992) 87 DLR (4th) 129 418
Kay's Leasing Corpn Pty Ltd v Fletcher (1964) 116 CLR 124 748
Kaye v Sutherland (1887) 20 QBD 147 356
Kazakhstan Kagazy Plc v Arip [2014] EWCA Civ 381 307
KB v RT [2016] EWHC 760 (Fam) 1179, 1184, 1186–7
Kearly v Kearly [2009] EWHC 1876 962
Kebbeh v Farmer and others [2015] EWHC 3827 151
Keefe v Mapfre Mutualidad Cia De Seguros Y Reaseguros SA [2015] EWCA
    Civ 598, [2016] 1 WLR 905 . . . . .88, 290
Keele v Findley (1990) 21 NSWLR 444 571
Kefalonia Wind, The [1986] 1 Lloyd's Rep 292 99
Kehr, Re [1952] Ch 26 . . . . .1333, 1384, 1390
Kellman v Kellman [2000] 1 FLR 785 . . . . .142, 1008, 1009
Kelly v Cruise Catering Ltd [1994] 2 ILRM 394 343
Kelly v Ireland [1996] 2 ILRM 364 987
Kelly v McCarthy [1994] IL Pr 29 287
Kelly v Selwyn [1905] 2 Ch 117 . . . . .1284, 1289
Kelowna and District Credit Union and Perl, Re (1984) 13 DLR (4th) 756 529
Kenburn Waste Management Ltd v Bergmann [2002] EWCA Civ 98,
    [2002] CLC 644 252
Kendall v Kendall [1977] Fam 208 . . . . .1007, 1009, 1027, 1031, 1049
Kennedy v Kennedy [2009] EWCA Civ 986 . . . . .1057, 1137
Kenneth Allison Ltd v A E Limehouse & Co [1992] 2 AC 105 327
Kent CC v C [2014] EWHC 604 1156
Kent County Council v PA-K and IA (a child) [2013] EWHC 578 (Fam) 1220
Kent v Burgess (1840) 11 Sim 361 904
Kenward v Kenward [1951] P 124 . . . . .893, 914, 931, 937, 988, 997
Kenya Railways v Antares Co Pte Ltd, The Antares (Nos 1 and 2) [1987]
    1 Lloyd's Rep 424 775
Kernot, Re [1965] Ch 217 1174
Kerr's Settlement Trusts, Re [1963] Ch 553 1393
Key v Key [2010] EWHC 408 1339
Khaled Salam Racy v Salah Jacques Hawila [2004] EWCA Civ 209 409
Khalij Commercial Bank Ltd v Woods (1985) 17 DLR (4th) 358 . . . . .91, 139
Khan v Ahmad [2014] EWHC 3850 . . . . .893, 921, 1051

Khan v Khan (1959) 21 DLR (2d) 171 900
Khoo Hooi Leong v Khoo Hean Kwee [1926] AC 529 1201
Khyentse Hope [2005] 3 NZLR 501 358
Kianta Osakeyhtio v Britain and Overseas Trading Co Ltd [1954] 1 Lloyd's Rep 247 668
Kidd v van Heeren [1998] 1 NZLR 324, [2006] 1 NZLR 393 411
Kidron v Green (2000) 48 OR 3rd 775 577
Kildare v Eustace (1686) 1 Vern 437 488
Kilgour v Kilgour 1987 SLT 568 1135
Killen v Killen 1981 SLT (Sh Ct) 77 1063
Kinderis v Kineriene (No 2) [2014] EWHC 693 . . . . .1146–7, 1159
King of Spain v Machado (1827) 4 Russ 225 106
King of the Hellenes v Brostrom (1923) 16 Lloyd's Rep 167, 190 116
King v Brandywine Reinsurance Co (UK) Ltd [2004] EWHC 1033 (Comm), [2004] 2
    Lloyd's Rep 670, [2005] EWCA Civ 235, [2005] 1 Lloyd's 655 . . . . .112, 716, 719
King v Brandywine Reinsurance Co [2005] 1 Lloyd Rep 655, [2005] EWCA
    Civ 655 . . . . .107, 112
King v Crown Energy Trading AG [2003] EWHC 163 (Comm), [2003] IL
    Pr 28 . . . . .201, 216, 284, 456
King v King [1954] P 55 1062
King v Lewis [2004] EWCA (Civ) 1329, [2005] IL Pr 16 . . . . 336, 350, 352, 354,
                                                                          365, 373, 777, 887
Kingspan Environmental Ltd v Borealis A/ S [2012] EWHC 1147 . . . . .756, 851
Kirin-Amgen Inc v Boehringer Mannheim GmbH [1997] FSR 289 . . . . .559, 560, 563
Kislovodsk, The [1980] 1 Lloyd's Rep 183 412
Kitechnology BV v Unicor GmbH Plastmaschinen [1994] IL Pr 568 . . . . 237, 265, 275, 277,
                                                                          304, 307, 805
KJ v Poland [2016] 2 FCR 539; [2016] Fam Law 554 1165
KL (Abduction: Habitual Residence: Inherent Jurisdiction), Re [2013]
    UKSC 75 . . . . .1095–6, 1104, 1110
Klein v Rhodos Management Ltd [2005] ECR I-8667, [2006] IL Pr 2 . . . . .218, 221
Kleinwort Benson Ltd v Glasgow City Council (C-346/93) [1996] QB 57 . . . . .195, 247, 266
Kleinwort Benson Ltd v Glasgow City Council [1999] 1 AC 153 . . . . .195, 247, 266, 694
Kloebe, Re (1884) 28 Ch D 175 1334
Kloeckner & Co AG v Gatoil Overseas Inc [1990] 1 Lloyd's Rep 177 . . . . .373, 445, 456
Klomps v Michel (166/80) [1981] ECR 1593 . . . . .311, 633, 635, 637
Knauf UK GmbH v British Gypsum Ltd (No 2) [2002]
    2 Lloyd's Rep 416 . . . . .231–2, 243, 288, 308, 326, 381
Knauf UK GmbH v British Gypsum Ltd [2001] 2 All ER, [2001] EWCA
    Civ 1570, [2002] 1 Lloyd's Rep 199, [2002] 1 WLR 907 . . . . .231, 232, 243, 308
Knight v Knight (1995) 16 RFL (4th) 48 1035
Knight, Re [1898] 1 Ch 257 1248
Kochanski v Kochanska [1958] P 147 904–5
Koechlin et Cie v Kestenbaum [1927] 1 KB 616, [1927] 1 KB 889 . . . . .1294–5, 1297
Kohnke v Karger [1951] 2 KB 670 558
Kolden Holdings Ltd v Rodette Commerce Ltd [2007] EWHC 1597 (Comm),
    [2007] IL Pr 50 . . . . .216, 445, 448
Kolden Holdings Ltd v Rodette Commerce Ltd [2008] EWCA Civ 10, [2008]
    3 All ER 612 216
Komninos S, The [1990] 1 Lloyd's Rep 541 79
Komu v Komu (C-605/14) EU:C:2015:833, [2016] 4 WLR 26 .219
Konamaneni v Rolls-Royce Industrial Power (India) Ltd [2002]
    1 WLR 1269 . . . . .338, 367–8, 373, 377, 402
Konkola Copper Mines plc v Coromin Ltd (No 2) [2006] EWHC 1093 (Comm),
    [2006] 2 Lloyd's Rep 446 . . . . 231, 235, 370, 412,
                                                                          421, 467, 468, 494

Konkola Copper Mines PLC v Coromin Ltd [2005] EWHC 898 (Comm),
[2005] 2 Lloyd's Rep 555 235
Konkola Copper Mines plc v Coromin Ltd [2006] EWCA Civ 5, [2006]
1 Lloyd's Rep 410 . . . . .231, 235, 370, 412, 421, 467–8, 494
Konkola Copper Mines plc v Coromin Ltd [2006] EWCA Civ 5, [2006]
1 Lloyd's Rep 410 . . . . .216, 231
Kontic v Ministry of Defence [2016] EWHC 2034 498
Kornberg v Kornberg (1991) 76 DLR (4th) 379 . . . . .430, 973, 978
Korner v Witkowitzer [1950] 2 KB 128 84
Korvine's Trusts, Levashoff v Block, Re [1921] 1 Ch 343 50
Kostanjevec v F&S Leasing GmbH (C-185/15) EU:C:2016:397 .248, 288
Kraus's Administrators v Sullivan 1998 SLT 963 106
Kraut AG v Albany Fabrics Ltd [1977] QB 182 . . . . .99, 101, 103
Krejci Lager & Umschlagbetriebs GmbH v Olbrich Transport und Logistik
GmbH (C-469/12) EU:C:2013:788, [2014] IL Pr 8 . . . . .222, 257
Kremen v Agrest [2012] EWHC 45 1065
Krenge v Krenge [1999] 1 FLR 969 . . . . .967, 978
Krohn GmbH v Varna Shipyard [1998] IL Pr 607 336
Krombach v Bamberski (C-7/98) [2001] QB 709, [2000] ECR I-1935 631
Krombach v Bamberski [2001] QB 709 14
Kronhofer v Maier (C-168/02) [2004] IL Pr 27 . . . . .245, 277
Krupp Uhde GmbH v Weir Westgarth Ltd, 31 May 2002 (unreported) 737
Kruppa v Benedetti [2014] EWHC 1887 (Comm), [2014] 2 All ER (Comm) 617 667
Kruppstaal AG v Quitmann Products Ltd [1982] ILRM 551 1272
Kubacz v Shah [1984] WAR 156 507
Kuklycz v Kuklycz [1972] VR 50 904–5
Kupelyants (2016) 75 CLJ 216 533
Kurnia Dewi, The [1997] 1 Lloyd's Rep 552 . . . . .334, 339
Kurz v Stella Musical Veranstaltungs GmbH [1992] Ch 196 .228, 236
Kutchera v Buckingham International Holdings Ltd [1988] IR 61, (1988)
9 ILRM 501 . . . . .70, 106, 374, 411
Kuwait Airways Corpn v Iraqi Airways Co (Nos 4 and 5) [2002] UKHL 19,
[2002] 2 AC 883 . . . . .14–15, 114, 128, 132–3, 135, 137–8, 499, 508
Kuwait Airways Corpn v Iraqi Airways Co [1995] 1 Lloyd's Rep 25, [1995]
1 WLR 1147 . . . . .132, 499–500, 506, 508
Kuwait Airways Corpn v Iraqi Airways Co [2002] 2 AC 883 15–16
Kuwait Asia Bank EC v National Mutual Life Nominees Ltd [1991]
1 AC 187, [1990] 3 All ER 404 334
Kuwait Finance House (Bahrain) BSC v Teece [2014] NZHC 3162 527
Kuwait Oil Co (KSC) v Idemitsu Tankers KK, The Hida Maru [1981] 2 Lloyd's
Rep 510 377
Kuwait Oil Tanker Co SAK v Al Bader (No 3) [2000] 2 All ER (Comm)
271 . . . . .96, 105, 337, 840
Kuwait Oil Tanker Co SAK v Al Bader [1997] 1 WLR 1410, [2000]
2 All ER (Comm) 271 . . . . .105, 337
Kuwait Oil Tanker Co SAK v Qabazard [2003] UKHL 31, [2004] 1 AC 300 226
Kwok Chi Leung Karl v Comr of Estate Duty [1988] 1 WLR 1035 1281

L (A Child) (Abduction: Jurisdiction), Re [2002] EWHC 1864, [2002]
2 FLR 1042 . . . . .1154, 1157
L (A Child) (Contract: Domestic Violence), Re [2001] Fam 260 1168
L (A Child) (Human Fertilisation and Embryology Act 2008: Declaration of Non-
parentage), Re [2016] EWHC 2266 (Fam) 1052
L (A Child) (Recognition of Foreign Order), Re [2012] EWCA Civ 1157 1128
L (A Child), Re [2005] EWHC 1237, [2006] 1 FLR 843 . . . . .1136, 1152

L (A Minor), Re [2010] EWHC 3146 1188
L (Abduction: Pending Criminal Proceedings), Re [1999] 1 FLR 433 . . . . .1136, 1141, 1154
L (Child Abduction: European Convention), Re [1992] 2 FLR 178 1136
L (Children) (Abduction: Declaration), Re [2001] 2 FCR 1. . . . . .1056, 1136
L (HK), Re [1989] 1 WWR 556 1212
L v C (Applications by a Non-Biological Mother) [2014] EWFC 1280 . . . . .1093, 1118
L v M (C-656/13) 1099
L v Regional Government of X [2015] EWHC 68 (Comm), [2015] 1 WLR 3948 508
L, Re (1982) 4 FLR 368. 1175
L, Re [1974] 1 WLR 250. . . . . .1088, 1174, 1175
L'Oréal v eBay (C-324/09) [2011] ECR I-6011 832
LA Gear Inc v Gerald Whelan & Sons Ltd [1991] FSR 670. .456
La Generale des Carrieres et des Mines v FG Hemisphere Associates LLC
  [2012] UKPC 27, [2013] 1 All ER 409 499
LAB v KB (Abduction: Brussels II Revised) [2009] EWHC 2243 (Fam); 1128
Labassee v France [2014] ECHR 185. 1189
Lacroix Goods, Re (1877) 2 PD 94 65
Lacroix, In the Goods of (1877) 2 PD 94. . . . . .65, 1343
Ladgroup Ltd v Euroeast Lines SA 1997 SLT 916 . . . . .203, 386
Laemthong International Lines Co Ltd v BPS Shipping Ltd (1997) 190 CLR 181 385
Lafarge Plasterboard Ltd v Fritz Peters & Co KG [2000] 2 Lloyd's Rep 689. . . . . .238, 240
Lafi Office and International Business SL v Meriden Animal Health Ltd [2001]
  1 All ER (Comm) 54 . . . . .232, 238, 446, 461
Lakah Group v Al Jazeera Satellite Channel [2003] EWHC 1297, [2003]
  EWCA (Civ) 1781. . . . . .326, 330–2
Lake Avery, The [1997] 1 Lloyd's Rep 540 . . . . .208–9, 374
Lamagni v Lamagni [1995] 2 FLR 452 1077
Lamothe v Lamothe [2006] EWHC 1387, [2006] WTLR 1431 . . . . .1331, 1349, 1358
Lancray v Peters (C-305/88) [1990] I-2725 635
Land Berlin v Ellen Mirjam Sapir (C-645/11) EU:C:2013:228 [2013]
  IP Pr 29 . . . . .205, 287
Land Oberosterreich v CEZ AS (C-343/04) [2006] IL Pr 25 . . . . .217–18, 220, 486
Landhurst Leasing plc v Marcq [1998] IL Pr 822. . . . . .612, 640
Landis & Gyr Ltd v Scaleo Chip ET [2007] EWHC 1880 (QB), [2007] IL Pr 53. 455
Landry v Lachapelle [1937] 2 DLR 504. 1259
Laneuville v Anderson (1860) 2 Sw & Tr 24 1331
Langley's Settlement Trusts, Re [1961] 1 WLR 41, [1962] Ch 541 140
Laserpoint Ltd v Prime Minister of Malta [2016] EWHC 1820 (QB. 629, 638
Lash Atlantico, The [1987] 2 Lloyd's Rep 114 103
Lashley v Hog (1804) 4 Pat 581. 1369–70
Latchin (t/a Dinkha Latchin Associates) v General Mediterranean Holdings
  SA [2002] CLC 330. . . . . .216, 282, 286, 728
Laurie v Carroll (1958) 98 CLR 310 325
Lavitch, Re (1985) 24 DLR (4th) 248 1174
Law Debenture Trust v Elektrim Finance [2005] EWHC 1412 (Ch), [2005] 2 All ER
  (Comm) 476 . . . . .418, 420
Law v Gustin [1976] Fam 155 1049
Lawlor v Sandvik Mining and Construction Mobile Crushers and Screens Ltd [2013]
  EWCA Civ 365 . . . . .718–19, 721
Lawrence v Lawrence [1985] Fam 106 . . . . 52, 147–8, 152, 911–12, 915,
                                                                   923–6, 1007–8, 1011, 1049
Lawson v Serco Ltd, Botham v Ministry of Defence, Crofts v Veta Ltd
  [2006] UKHL 3, [2006] 1 All ER 823, [2006] ICR 250 143
Lazard Bros & Co v Midland Bank [1933] AC 289 . . . . .108, 112
Lazarewicz v Lazarewicz [1962] P 171 906

Lazarus-Barlow v Regent Estates Co Ltd [1949] 2 KB 465. 544
LBI HF v Stanford [2014] EWHC 3921 (Ch). 91
LC (Children) (International Abduction: Child's Objections to Return),
   Re [2013] EWCA Civ 1058. 1156
LC (Children) (International Abduction: Child's Objections to Return),
   Re [2014] UKSC 1). 1144–5, 1156
Le Feuvre v Sullivan (1855) 10 Moo PCC 1. 1289
Le Mesurier v Le Mesurier [1895] AC 517. 979
Leal v Dunlop Bio-Processes Ltd [1984] 2 All ER 207. 377
Lear v Lear (1973) 51 DLR (3d) 56. 108
Leathertex Divisione Sinetici SpA v Bodetex BVBA (C-420/97) [1999]
   ECR I-6747. . . . . .253, 446, 456
Leaton Leather & Trading Co v Ngai Tak Kong (1997) 147 DLR (4th) 377 577
Lebek v Domino (C-70/15) EU:C:2016:524, [2016] 1 WLR 4221. 638
Lebel v Tucker (1867) LR 3 QB 77. 1295
Lechouritou v Germany (C-292/05) [2007] IL Pr 14. 205
Lecouturier v Rey [1910] AC 262 131
Ledra Fisheries Ltd v Turner [2003] EWHC 1049 (Ch). 409
Lee v Abdy (1886) 17 QBD 309 . . . . .1282, 1286–7
Lee v Lau [1967] P 14 . . . . .930, 1018
Leeds Teaching Hospital NHS Trust v A and Ors [2003] EWHC 259 (QB),
   [2003] All ER (D) 374. 1052
Leffler v Berlin Chemie AG (C-433/03) [2006] IL Pr 6. .309
Lehman Brothers Bankhaus AG I Ins v CMA CGM [2013] EWHC 171
   (Comm), [2013] 2 All ER (Comm) 557 . . . . .446, 456
Lehman Brothers Finance AG v Klaus Tschira Stiftung GmbH [2014]
   EWHC 2782 (Ch), [2014] 2 CLC 242 448
Leibinger v Stryker Trauma GmbH [2005] EWHC 690 (Comm) 559
Leicester City Council v S [2014] EWHC 1575 1115
Lemenda Trading Co Ltd v African Middle East Petroleum Co Ltd [1988]
   QB 448 . . . . .136, 674, 752, 771
Lemmex v Bernard (2002) 213 DLR (4th) 627 349
Lendrum v Chakravarti 1929 SLT 96. . . . . .920, 932, 937, 953, 997
Lennon Scottish Daily Record [2004] EWHC 359 (QB). 322, 398
Leo Laboratories v Crompton BV [2005] 2 ILRM. 237, 455
Leon v Leon [1967] P 275. 960
Leon, The (1881) 6 PD 148. 878
Lepre v Lepre [1965] P 52 .141, 921, 986, 1049, 1052
Leroux v Brown (1852) 12 CB 801 . . . . .46–7, 74–5, 77, 80, 758
Les Verreries De Saint-Gobain SA v Martinswerk GmbH [1999] IL Pr 296. 232
Lesotho Highlands Development Authority v Impregilo SpA [2003]
   2 Lloyd's Rep 497. 97
Leufkens v Alba Tours International Inc (2002) 213 DLR (4th) 614 349
Levene v Inland Revenue Comrs [1928] AC 217 173–4
Levene v Inland Revenue Comrs [1928] AC 217 173–4
Levick's Will Trusts, Re [1963] 1 WLR 311 . . . . .1344, 1348, 1390
Lewal's Settlement Trusts, Re [1918] 2 Ch 391 . . . . .1339, 1362, 1364
Lewis v Balshaw (1935) 54 CLR 188 1332
Lewis v Eliades [2003] EWCA Civ 1758, [2004] 1 WLR 692, [2004]
   1 WLR 1393 .119, 120, 526, 550, 552–4
Lewis v Eliades [2003] EWCA Civ 1758 119–20
Lewis v Lewis [1956] 1 WLR 200 175
Lexi Holdings plc v Shaid Luqman, 22 October 2007 (unreported). 327
Lexmar v Nordisk [1997] 1 Lloyd's Rep 289 209
Leyland Daf Ltd, Re [1994] 1 BCLC 264; [1994] 2 BCLC 106 . . . . .237, 241

Leyvand v Barasch, (2000) Times, 23 March 173
Liaw v Lee [2015] EWHC 1462 . . . . .1027–8, 1079
Libertas-Kommerz GmbH v Johnson 1977 SC 191. 1288
Libyan Arab Foreign Bank v Bankers Trust Co [1989] QB 728 . . . . .740, 771
Liddell's Settlement Trusts, Re [1936] Ch 365 . . . . .335, 486
Liddell-Grainger's Will Trusts, Dormer v Liddell-Grainger,
    Re [1936] 3 All ER 173 . . . . .149, 156–7
Liew v Official Receiver 685 F 2d 1192 (1982) 27
Lifestyle Equities CV v Sportsdirect.com Retail Ltd [2017] EWHC 154 (Ch) 285
Lightbody v West (1903) 18 TLR 526 903
Lilienthal v Kaufman 395 P 2d 543 (1964) 682
Lim v Lim [1973] VR 370 160
Limerick v Limerick (1863) 32 LJPM & A 92 904
Limit (No 3) Ltd v PDV Insurance Co [2005] EWCA Civ 383,
    [2005] 2 All ER (Comm) 347 . . . . .333, 365–6, 368, 372
Lincoln National Life Insurance Co v Employers Reinsurance Corpn
    [2002] EWHC 28, [2002] Lloyd's Rep IR 853 344
Linda, The [1988] 1 Lloyd's Rep 175 . . . . .389, 457
Lindsay v Miller [1949] VLR 13 . . . . .1386, 1389
Lines Bros Ltd (No 2), Re [1984] Ch 438 99–100
Lines Bros Ltd, Re [1983] Ch 1 99–100
Linsen International Limited v Humpuss Transportasi Kimia [2011]
    EWCA Civ 1042 . . . . .355, 551
Linuzs v Latmar Holdings Corp [2013] EWCA Civ 4, [2013] IL Pr 19. 285
Littauer Glove Corpn v F W Millington (1920) Ltd (1928) 44 TLR 746. 530
Littrell v United States of America (No 2) [1995] 1 WLR 82. 500
Liverpool Marine Credit Co v Hunter (1867) LR 4 Eq 62. 1275
Livesley v Horst [1925] 1 DLR 159 94
L-K v K (Brussels II Revised: Maintenance Pending Suit) [2006] EWHC
    153 (Fam), [2006] 2 FLR 1113 . . . . .955, 969, 970, 1118
L-K v K (No 2) [2006] EWHC 3280 (Fam) 955, 956, 959
LL v PL, 29 March 2007 (unreported) (Fam Div) 1155
Lloyd Evans, Re [1947] Ch 695 . . . . .148, 156
Lloyd Pacifico, The [1995] 1 Lloyd's Rep 54. 382
Lloyd v Guibert (1865) LR 1 QB 115 . . . . .722, 724, 878, 1276
Lloyd v Lloyd [1961] 2 FLR 349 147
LM v DR [2016] EWHC 1943 (Fam). 1174
Lodge v Lodge (1963) 107 Sol Jo 437 . . . . .49, 899
Logan v Bank of Scotland (No 2) [1906] 1 KB 141 393
Logan v Fairlie (1825) 2 Sim & St 284. 1336
Lolley's case (1812) Russ & Ry. 1197
Lombard-Knight v Rainstorm Pictures Inc [2014] EWCA Civ 356, [2014]
    2 Lloyd's Rep 74. 672
London and South American Investment Trust v British Tobacco Co (Australia)
    [1927] 1 Ch 107 1298
London Borough of Greenwich v Ms S, Mr A, B, C, D, E (by their Children's
    Guardian), Z [2007] EWHC 820 (Fam), [2007] 2 FCR 141. 179
London Branch of the Nigerian Universities Commission v Bastians [1995]
    ICR 358. 506
London Branch v Kommunale Wasserwerke Leipzig GmbH [2010] EWHC
    2566 (Comm), [2010] 2 CLC 499. 224
London Helicopters Ltd v Heliportugal LDA-INAC [2006] EWHC 108, [2006]
    IL Pr 28 . . . . .263, 273, 277
London Steam-Ship Owners' Mutual Insurance Association Ltd v The Kingdom
    of Spain [2013] EWHC 3188 (Comm), [2014] 1 Lloyd's Rep 309 . . . . .639, 646

Long Beach Ltd v Global Witness Ltd [2007] EWHC 1980 (QB) 530
Lonrho plc v Fayed [1992] 1 AC 448 . . . . .347–8, 350, 359, 372–3, 777–8
Lonslow v Hennig [1986] 2 FLR 378 1168
Looiersgracht, The [1995] 2 Lloyd's Rep 411 385
Loon Energy Inc v Integra Mining [2007] EWHC 1876 (Comm) 417
Lord Advocate v Jaffrey [1921] 1 AC 146 979
Lord Advocate, Petitioner 1998 SLT 835 83
Lord Cable, Re [1977] 1 WLR 7 . . . . .117, 118, 1334, 1386, 1388
Lord Cloncurry's case (1811) 904
Lord v Colvin (1859) 4 Drew 366 . . . . .154, 161
Lorentzen v Lydden & Co [1942] 2 KB 202 131–2
Lorillard, Re [1922] 2 Ch 638 1334
Lothschutz v Vogel [2014] EWHC 473 659
Loucks v Standard Oil Co of New York 224 NY 99 133
Loutchansky v Times Newspapers Ltd [2001] EWCA Civ 1805, [2002] QB 783 350
Lowenstein v Allen [1958] CLY 491 1286
LR (A Child), Re [2014] EWCA Civ 1624 1099
LTU v Eurocontrol [1976] ECR 1541 204
Lu Schan, The [1993] 1 Lloyd's Rep 259 100
Lubbe v Cape plc [1999] IL Pr 113, [2000] 1 WLR 1545 . . . . 14, 373, 394, 397,
                                                                            399–403, 406, 462
Lucasfilm Ltd v Ainsworth [2008] EWHC 1878 (Ch), [2009] FSR 2 . . . . .495–6, 554
Lucasfilm Ltd v Ainsworth [2009] EWCA Civ 1328, [2010] 3 WLR 333, [2010]
        Ch 503; [2011] UKSC 39, [2012] 1 AC 208 . . . . .219, 484, 494–6, 530
Luccioni v Luccioni [1943] P 49 966
Luck's Settlement Trusts, Re [1940] Ch 864 1210
Luis Marburg & Söhne GmbH v Società Ori Martin SpA [1987] ECC 424 228
Luiz Vincente Barros Mattos v Macdaniels Ltd [2003] EWHC 1173 (Ch) 400
Lungowe v Vedanta Resources Plc [2016] EWHC 975 (TCC), [2016] BLR 461 . . . . .366, 471
Lupofresh Ltd v Sapporo Breweries Ltd [2013] EWCA Civ 948 . . . . .719, 721–2, 757
Luther v Sagor [1921] 3 KB 532 . . . . .127–30, 135, 140
Luton Borough Council v SB and another [2015] EWHC 3534 . . . . .909, 986, 991, 1050–1
Luxe Holding Ltd v Midland Resources Holding Ltd [2010] EWHC 1908 1267
Lynch v Provisional Government of Paraguay (1871) LR 2 P & D 268 . . . . .1339, 1343
Lysaght Ltd v Clark & Co [1891] 1 QB 552 328

M (A Child) (Abduction: Brussels II Revised), Re [2006] EWCA Civ 630,
        [2006] 2 FLR 1180 . . . . .1098, 1142, 1145, 1154, 1158, 1159
M (A Child) (Abduction: Intolerable Situation), Re [2000] 1 FLR 930 . . . . . .1141, 1151, 1154–6
M (A Child) (Adoption: Placement outside Jurisdiction), Re [2010] EWHC 1694 1220
M (A Child), Re [2007] EWCA Civ 260, (2007) 151 SJLB 434 1154
M (A Minor) (Abduction: Child's Objections), Re [1994] 2 FLR 126 . . .182–3, 1138, 1144, 1146
M (A Minor) (Abduction: Leave to Appeal), Re [1999] 2 FLR 550 .1154
M (Abduction Non-Convention Country), Re [1995] 1 FLR 89 1174
M (Abduction: Conflict of Jurisdiction), Re [2000] 2 FLR 372 1136
M (Abduction: Consent: Acquiescence), Re [1999] 1 FLR 171 1148–9
M (Abduction: Habitual Residence), Re [1996] 1 FLR 887, 895 . . . . .177, 182–3
M (Abduction: Paternity: DNA Testing), Re [2013] EWCA Civ 1131 1136
M (Adoption: International Adoption Trade), Re [2003] EWHC 219, [2003]
        1 FLR 1111 . . . . .1214, 1216
M (Brussels II Revised: Art 15), Re [2014] EWCA Civ 152 1114–16
M (Child Abduction) (European Convention), Re [1994] 1 FLR 551 . . . . 1134–5, 1138,
                                                                            1154, 1156
M (Children) (Abduction), Re [2007] UKHL 55, [2007]
        3 WLR 975 1141

M (Children) (Abduction: Child's Objections: Joinder of Children as
 Parties to Appeal), Re [2015] EWCA Civ 26 1144–7
M (Minors) (Child Abduction: Undertakings), Re [1995] 1 FLR 1021 1155
M (Minors) (Custody: Jurisdiction), Re [1992] 2 FLR 382 1134
M (Minors) (Residence Order: Jurisdiction), Re [1993] 1 FLR 495, 501, CA 182
M (Minors) (Residence Order: Jurisdiction), Re [1993] 1 FLR 495 . . . . 179, 182–3,
 1107, 1125, 1138
M and J (Children) (Abduction: International Judicial Collaboration), Re
 [2000] 1 FLR 803 1137
M v An tArd Chláraitheoir [2013] IEHC 91 1180
M v B (Residence: Forum Conveniens) [1994] 2 FLR 819. 1125
M v F [2016] EWHC 3194 1171
M v H (Custody: Residence Order), 27 July 2005 (unreported) (Fam Div) 1091
M v H [2005] EWHC 1186 . . . . .180, 196, 909
M v L (Financial Relief after Overseas Divorce) [2003] EWHC 328,
 [2003] 2 FLR 425 . . . . .967, 1075–8
M v M (Abduction: England and Scotland) [1997] 2 FLR 263 . . . . .180–1, 1148
M v M (Divorce: Jurisdiction: Validity of Marriage) [2001] 2 FLR 6 . . . . 15, 893–5, 929–30,
 932, 941, 1017
M v M (Domicile: Divorce) [2010] EWHC 982 962
M v M (Financial Provision After Foreign Divorce) [1994] 1 FLR 399 . . . . . . .974, 1073, 1075–6
M v M (Stay of Proceedings: Return of Children) [2005] EWHC 1159 (Fam),
 [2006] 1 FLR 138 . . . . .182, 1125, 1141
M v M [2007] EWHC 1404 (Fam), [2007] EWHC 1820 (Fam). 1150, 1151
M v M [2010] EWHC 3350 1148
M v Secretary of State for Work and Pensions [2006] 2 AC 91. 947
M v T [2010] EWHC 1479. 1160–1
M v V [2010] EWHC 1453. 1067
M v V [2014] EWHC 925. 1076
M v W (Application after New Zealand Financial Agreement) [2014]
 EWHC 1074
M, Petitioner 2000 GWD 32–1242. 1134
M, Petitioner 2005 SLT 2 181
M, Petitioner 2007 SLT 433 1154
M, Re [2011] EWHC 3590. 1233
M.R. and D.R. (suing by their father and next friend O.R.) & ors -v-An
 t-Ard-Chláraitheoir & ors [2014] IESC 60. 1180
M'Elroy v M'Allister 1949 SC 110. 69
MA v Austria [2015] ECHR 4097/ 13. 1165
MA v SK [2015] EWHC 887 1073
Mabey and Johnson Ltd v Danos [2007] EWHC 1094 (Ch). .418, 421
Macalpine v Macalpine [1958] P 35. 1027
Macartney, Re [1921] 1 Ch 522. . . . . .91, 139, 549, 573
Macaulay v Guaranty Trust Co of New York (1927) 44 TLR 99 87
Macaulay v Macaulay [1991] 1 WLR 179 . . . . .640, 1064, 1083
MacDonald v FIFA [1999] SLT 1129 286
Macdonald v Macdonald (1872) LR 14 Eq 60. 1344
Macdonald v Macdonald 1932 SC (HL) 79. 1252
MacDougall v Chitnavis 1937 SC 390. . . . . .919, 932, 997
Machinale Glasfabriek de Maas BV v Emaillerie [1985] 2 CMLR 281. 727
Maciej Rataj, The [1991] 2 Lloyd's Rep 458. . . . . .387, 399
Mackay Refined Sugars (NZ) Ltd v New Zealand Sugar Co Ltd [1997] 3 NZLR 476 409
Mackays Stores Ltd v Topward Ltd 2006 SLT 716. 237
Mackender v Feldia AG [1967] 2 QB 590 . . . . .118, 133, 343, 371, 376, 415
Mackie v Darling (1871) LR 12 Eq 319. 1176

Mackinnon v Iberia Shipping Co Ltd [1954] 2 Lloyd's Rep 372, 1955 SLT 49,
  1955 SC 20 876
Mackinnon v Iberia Shipping Co Ltd 1955 SC 20 93
Mackintosh v Townsend (1809) 16 Ves 330 1347
Maclaine Watson & Co Ltd v International Tin Council [1989] Ch 253 505
Maclean v Cristall (1849) Perry's Ori Cas 75 909
Macmillan Inc v Bishopsgate Investment Trust plc (No 3) [1995] 1 WLR 978,
  [1996] 1 WLR 387 ....105, 488, 838
Macmillan Inc v Bishopsgate Investment Trust plc (No 4) [1999] CLC 417 ....105, 107, 112–13
Macmillan Inc v Bishopsgate Trust (No 3) [1996] 1 WLR 387 ....43, 71
MacMillan v MacMillan 1989 SLT 350 ....1153, 1154
Macnichol (1874) LR 19 Eq 81 1336
Macreight, Paxton v Macreight, Re (1885) 30 Ch D 165 160
MacShannon v Rockware Glass Ltd [1978] AC 795 ....393, 397, 402
Macsteel Commercial Holdings (Pty) Ltd v Thermasteel V (Canada) Inc [1996]
  CLC 1403 368
Madoff Securities International Ltd v Raven [2011] EWHC 3102 (Comm), [2012]
  2 All ER (Comm) 634 ....284, 287
Maersk Olie & Gas v Firma M de Haan en W de Boer (C-39/02) [2004]
  ECR I-9657 ....612, 633–6
Magnesium Elektron Ltd v Molycorp Chemicals & Oxides (Europe) Ltd [2015]
  EWHC 3596 336
Magnier v Magnier (1968) 112 Sol Jo 233 994
Magyar BV, Re [2013] EWHC 3800 768
Mahadervan v Mahadervan [1964] P 233 ....46, 74, 76, 80, 85, 896–7
Maher v Grouprama Grand Est [2009] EWCA Civ 1191, [2010] 1 WLR 1564 ......88, 96, 290
Maher v Maher [1951] P 342 ....932, 1028
Mahkutai, The [1996] AC 650 414
Mahme Trust v Lloyds TSB Bank plc [2004] EWHC 1931, [2004] IL Pr 43 461
Mahmood v Mahmood 1993 SLT 589 ....986, 992
Mahmud v Mahmud 1994 SLT 559 ....986, 992
Mahonia Ltd v JP Morgan Chase Bank [2003] EWHC 1927 (Comm), [2003]
  2 Lloyd's Rep 911 ....137, 753
Mahtani v Sippy [2013] EWHC 285 485
Mail Order Promise of Win in a Draw, Re [2003] IL Pr 46 264
Maimann v Maimann [2001] IL Pr 27 237
Maire v Portugal [2004] 2 FLR 653, (2006) 43 EHRR 13 1163–4
Makefjell, The [1976] 2 Lloyd's Rep 29 414
Maksymec v Maksymec (1955) 72 WNNSW 522 905
Maldonado's Estate, Re [1954] P 223 ....15, 47, 49
Male v Roberts (1790) 3 Esp 163 762
Maletic v lastminute.com GmbH and TUI Österreich GmbH (C-478/12)
  EU:C:2013:735, [2014] QB 424 296
Malicorp Ltd v Government of the Arab Republic of Egypt [2015] EWHC
  361 (Comm), [2015] 1 Lloyd's Rep 423 ....550, 564, 574, 577, 672–3
Man Chiu Yu v Secretary of State for the Home Department [1981] Imm
  AR 1651 173
Mandani v Mandani [1984] FLR 699 1011
Manifold, Re [1962] Ch 1 1334–5
Mann (1976) 92 LQR 165, 166 98
Manners v Pearson & Son [1898] 1 Ch 581 97
Manning v Manning [1958] P 112 ....1012, 1020
Manolopoulos v Pnaiffe [1930] 2 DLR 169 564
Mansel v A-G (1877) 2 PD 265, 4 PD 232 1049
Mansour v Mansour [1990] FCR 17, [1989] 1 FLR 418 356

Manta Line Inc v Sofianites and Midland Bank plc [1984] 1 Lloyd's Rep 14 333
Manufacturers Life Insurance Co v Guarantee Co of North America (1988)
    62 OR (2d) 147 409
Maple Leaf Macro Volatility Master Fund v Rouvroy [2009] EWHC 257
    (Comm) 263, 277, 292
Maples v Maples [1988] Fam 14 . . . . .599–600, 1012, 1020
Maraver, In the Goods of (1828) 1 Hag Ecc 498 1340
Marazura Navegación SA v Oceanus Mutual Underwriting Association
    (Bermuda) Ltd [1977] 1 Lloyd's Rep 283 385
Marc Brogsitter v Fabrication de Montres Normandes EURL and Karsten Fräßdorf
    (C-548/12) EU:C:2014:148, [2014] QB 753 . . . . 46, 250, 265, 268, 693,
                                       789–90, 792, 805–6
Marc Rich & Co AG v Società Italiana Impianti PA (The "Atlantic Emperor")
    (No 2) [1992] 1 Lloyd's Rep 624 . . . . .208–9, 226, 228, 645
Marc Rich & Co AG v Societa Italiana Impianti PA, The Atlantic Emperor [1989]
    1 Lloyd's Rep 548 . . . . .226, 228, 419, 645
Marconi v PT Pan Indonesia Bank Ltd TBK [2004] EWHC 129 (Comm), [2004]
    1 Lloyd's Rep 594, [2005] EWCA 105, 326, 343–4, 346, 373,
                                        381, 402, 733, 736, 755
Mareva Cia Naviera SA v International Bulk Carriers SA [1980] 1 All ER 213 336
Marginson v Blackburn Borough Council [1939] 2 KB 426 558
Marinari v Lloyds Bank plc (Zubaidi Trading Co Intervener) (C-364/93)
    [1996] QB 217 812
Marine Contractors Inc v Shell Petroleum Development Co of Nigeria [1984]
    2 Lloyd's Rep 77 238
Marinos v Marinos [2007] EWHC 2047(Fam) 176, 180
Maritime Investment Holdings Inc v Underwriting Members of Syndicate 1183
    at Lloyd's [2015] EWHC 2190 1308
Maritime Trader, The [1981] 2 Lloyd's Rep 153 385
Mark v Mark [2005] UKHL 42, [2006] 1 AC 98 . . . . 14, 145, 147, 149, 151,
                      160–1, 174, 176–8, 180, 182–4, 956, 958
Markandu v Benaroch (2004) 242 DLR (4th) 101 398
Markel International Insurance Co Ltd v La República Compañía Argentina de Seguros
    Generales SA [2004] EWHC 1826 (Comm), [2005] Lloyd's Rep IR 90 . . . . . .351, 367, 719
Maronier v Larmer [2002] EWCA Civ 774, [2003] QB 620 14
Marren v Echo Bay Mines Ltd (2003) 226 DLR (4th) 622 382
Marrett, Chalmers v Wingfield, Re (1887) 36 Ch D 400 . . . . .149, 154
Marseilles Extension Rly and Land Co, Re (1885) 30 Ch D 598 . . . . .108, 1295
Marsh v Marsh 2002 SLT 87, Sh Principal 156–7
Marshall Rankine v Maggs [2006] EWCA Civ 20 326–7
Marshall v Motor Insurers Bureau [2015] EWHC 3421 . . . . .799, 813–14, 818
Marshall, Re [1957] Ch 507 . . . . .1054, 1223, 1229
Martelli v Martelli (1983) 148 DLR (3d) 746 567
Martin Blomqvist v Rolex SA and Manufacture des Montres Rolex SA (C-98/13)
    ECLI:EU:C:2014:55 833
Martin v Buret 1938 SLT 479 1009
Martin v Martin (1831) 2 Russ & M 507 490
Martin v Nadel [1906] 2 KB 26 1293
Martin, Loustalan v Loustalan, Re [1900] P 211 . . . . .42, 50, 158, 1350, 1367
Martin, Re [1900] P 211 . . . . .157, 168
Marubeni Hong Kong and South China Ltd v Mongolian Government [2002] 2 All ER
    (Comm) 873, [2005] EWCA Civ 395, [2005] 344–5, 369, 720, 722, 762
Marvin Safe Co v Norton 48 NJL 410, 7 A 418 (1886) 1272
Mary Moxham, The (1876) 1 PD 107 . . . . .491, 876
Maschinenfabric v Altikar Pty Ltd [1984] 3 NSWLR 152 99

Masri v Consolidated Contractors International (UK) Ltd [2005]
  EWCA Civ 1436, [2006] 1 WLR 830 . . . . .216, 243, 261, 284, 303, 432, 473
Masri v Consolidated Contractors International Company SAL [2008]
  EWCA Civ 303, [2009] QB 450 . . . . .226, 243
Masri v Consolidated Contractors International Company Sal [2008]
  EWCA Civ 625, [2009] QB 503 . . . . .303, 423, 432
Massey v Heynes & Co (1888) 21 QBD 330 338
Mastaka v Midland Bank Executor and Trustee Co Ltd [1941] Ch 192 1345
Masters v Leaver [2000] IL Pr 387 . . . . .560, 578, 579
Matchnet plc v William Blair & Co LLC [2002] EWHC 2128 (Ch), [2003] 2
  BCLC 195 329
Materiel Auxiliaire d'Informatique v Printed Forms Equipment Ltd [2006]
  IL Pr 803 . . . . .630, 640
Mathieu v Entry Clearance Officer, Bridgetown [1979–1980] Imm AR 157 1223
Mattar and Saba v Public Trustee [1952] 3 DLR 399 542
Mattenklott v Germany (Admissibility) (2007) 44 EHRR SE 12 .1164
Matthews v Kuwait Bechtel Corpn [1959] 2 QB 57 . . . . .343, 362
Matusevitch v Telnikoff [1996] IL Pr 181 137
Maudslay, Sons and Field, Re [1900] 1 Ch 602 1280
Maumousseau and Washington v France (2010) 51 EHRR 55 1165
Mauritius Commercial Bank Limited v Hestia Holdings Limited [2013]
  EWHC 1328 (Comm), [2013] 2 All ER (Comm) 898 236
Mauritius Commercial Bank Ltd v Hestia Holdings Ltd [2013] EWHC 1328 . . . . .709, 716
Mawan, The [1988] 2 Lloyd's Rep 459 384
Mawji v R [1957] AC 126 942
Maxter Catheters SAS v Medicina Ltd [2015] EWHC 3076 (Comm), [2016]
  1 WLR 349 448
Maxwell v Maxwell (1852) 16 Beav 106 1357
May v May [1943] 2 All ER 146, (1943) 169 LT 42 . . . . .158, 160
May's Marriage, Re (1987) 90 FLR 134 101
Mayo-Perrott v Mayo-Perrott [1958] IR 336 573
Mazur Media Ltd v Mazur Media GmbH [2004] EWHC 1566 (Ch),
  [2004] 1 WLR 2966 . . . . .268, 277, 460–1, 1320
MB v GK [2015] EWHC 2192 1124
Mbasogo v Logo Ltd [2006] EWCA Civ 1370, [2007] QB 846 . . . . .115, 123–4
MBM Fabri-Clad Ltd v Eisen-Und Huttenwerke Thale AG [2000] IL Pr 505 . . . . .252–3, 257
MC Pearl, The [1997] 1 Lloyd's Rep 566 412
McAllister v General Medical Council [1993] AC 388 80
McC v McC [1994] 1 IR 293 . . . . .549, 1078
McCabe v McCabe [1994] 1 FCR 257 . . . . .893, 898
McCarthy v Abowall (Trading) Ltd 1992 SLT (Sh Ct) 65 320
McCarthy v McCarthy 1994 SLT 743 1153–4
McCarthy v Pillay [2003] 2 ILRM 284 394
McConnell Dowell Constructors Ltd v Lloyd's Syndicate 396 [1988] 2 NZLR 257 . . . . . .394, 409
McCormick v Garnett (1854) 23 LJ Ch 777 108
McCulloch v Bank of Novia Scotia [2006] EWHC 790 (Ch), [2006]
  2 All ER (Comm) 714 381
McElhinney v Ireland [2002] 34 EHRR 13 501
McElhinney v Williams [1994] 2 ILRM 115 505
McElroy v McAllister 1949 SC 110 93
McEwan v McEwan 1969 SLT 342 160
McFee Engineering Pty Ltd v CBS Construction Pty Ltd (1980)
  44 FLR 340 342
McGee v Arkel Int'l, LLC, 671 F 3d 539, 543 (5th Cir 2012) 60
McGowan v Summit at Lloyds 2002 SLT 1258 . . . . .105, 235

McGraw-Hill International (UK) Ltd v Deutsche Apotheker-und
    Arztebank EG [2014] EWHC 2436 (Comm),
    [2014] 2 Lloyd's Rep 523 . . . . .273, 277, 282, 288
McGregor (1970) 33 MLR 1, 21 95
McKee v McKee [1951] AC 352 1087
McKenna v EH [2002] 2 ILRM 117 336
McKennitt v Ash [2006] EWCA Civ 1714, [2007] 3 WLR 194 884
McKenzie, Re (1951) 51 SRNSW 293 147
McLean v McLean [1979] 1 NSWLR 620 550
McLean v Shields (1885) 9 OR 699 . . . . .539, 550
McM v C (No 2) [1980] 1 NSWLR 27 1110
McM v C [1980] 1 NSWLR 1 1110
McMorran, Re [1958] Ch 624 . . . . .1347, 1362–4
McMullen v Wadsworth (1889) 14 App Cas 631 156
McNeilly v Imbree [2007] NSWCA 156 . . . . .95, 800
McOwan, In the Marriage of (1993) 17 Fam LR 377 1155
McShane v Duryea [2006] Fam LR 15 1169
McTavish & Hampton Securities and Investments Ltd, Re (1983)
    150 DLR (3d) 27 529
MD v CT [2014] EWHC 871 1128
Meadows Indemnity Co Ltd v Insurance Corpn of Ireland Ltd and International
    Commercial Bank plc [1989] 1 Lloyd's Rep 181, [1989] 2 Lloyd's Rep 298 . . . . .400, 409
Meatyard's Goods, Re [1903] P 125 1332
Mecklermedia Corpn v DC Congress GmbH [1998] Ch 40 . . . . .217, 264, 275, 446, 455–6
Medhurst v Markle (1995) 17 RFL (4th) 428 . . . . .1150, 1154
Mediterranean Shipping Co SA v Trafigura Beheer BV [2007] EWCA Civ 794 747
Medway Council v JB and others [2015] EWHC 3064 1114–15
Medway Packaging Ltd v Meurer Maschinen GmbH & Co KG [1990]
    2 Lloyd's Rep 112, CA 251–3
Meeth v Glacetal Sarl (23/78) [1978] ECR 2133 450
Mégret, Re [1901] 1 Ch 547 1363
Mehta v Mehta [1945] 2 All ER 690 930
Meisenhelder v Chicago and North Western Rly Co 170 Minn 317 (1927) 53
Melbourn, Re (1870) 6 Ch App 64 89
Melzer v MF Global UK Ltd (C-228/11) EU:C:2013:305, [2013] QB 1112 274
Mengel's Will Trusts, Re [1962] Ch 791 1355
Mengiste v Endowment Fund for the Rehabilitation of Tigre [2013]
    EWHC 599 (Ch); [2014] EWHC 4196 (Ch) 402
Mennesson v France [2014] ECHR 185 1189
Merak, The [1965] P 223 418
Mercantile Investment and General Trust Co v River Plate Trust, Loan
    and Agency Co [1892] 2 Ch 303 490
Mercedes Benz AG v Leiduck [1996] AC 284 . . . . .336, 340, 356
Merchant International Co Ltd v Natsionalna Aktsionerna Kompaniya
    Naftogaz Ukrayiny [2011] EWHC 1820 (Comm), [2011] 2 All ER (Comm)
    75, [2012] EWCA Civ 196, [2012] 1 WLR 3036 550–1
Merchant International Co Ltd v Natsionalna Aktsionerna Kompaniya Naftogaz
    Ukrayiny [2012] EWCA Civ 196, [2012] 1 WLR 3036 . . . . .14, 578, 582
Merck KGaA v Merck Sharp & Dohme Corp [2014] EWHC 3867 682
Mercury Bell, The v Amosin (1986) 27 DLR (4th) 641 106
Mercury Communications Ltd v Communication Telesystems International [1999]
    2 All ER (Comm) 33 . . . . .308, 369, 462
Mercury Publicity Ltd v Wolfgang Loerke GmbH [1993] IL Pr 142 . . . . .262, 299–300
Mercury v Communication Telesystems [1999] 2 All ER (Comm) 33 . . . .308, 369, 399, 413, 462
Meridien Biao GmbH v Bank of New York [1997] 1 Lloyd's Rep 437 409

Merker v Merker [1963] P 283 . . . . 564, 566, 894, 903, 906–8,
    998, 1006, 1009
Merrill Lynch v RAFFA [2001] IL Pr 31 409
Messer Griersheim GmbH v Goyal MG Gases PVT Ltd [2006] EWHC 79 (Comm),
    [2006] 1 CLC 283 557
Messier-Dowty v Sabena SA (No 2) [2000] 1 WLR 2040 . . . . .375, 456
Messina v Petrococchino (1872) LR 4 PC 144 564
Messina v Smith [1971] P 322, 330 . . . . .148, 582, 1025
Messiniaki Tolmi, The [1983] 1 Lloyd's Rep 666, [1984] 1 Lloyd's Rep 266 . . . . .333, 407
Metaalhandel JA Magnus BV v Ardfields Transport Ltd [1988] 1 Lloyd's Rep 197 103
Metal Industries (Salvage) v Owners of the S T Harle 1962 SLT 114 . . . . .50, 116, 121
Metal Scrap Trade Corpn v Kate Shipping Co Ltd [1990] 1 WLR 115 399
Metall und Rohstoff AG v Donaldson Lufkin and Jenrette Inc
    [1990] 1 QB 391 . . . . .78, 347–50, 359, 364, 373, 405, 777–8
Mette v Mette (1859) 1 Sw & Tr 416 . . . . .913, 923, 1351
Meyer v Dresser (1864) 16 CBNS 646 91
Meyer, Re [1971] P 298 . . . . .137, 1049, 1052
Meyers Travel Service Ltd v Magid (1975) 60 DLR (3d) 42 105
MF v An Bord Vehtala [1991] ILRM 399 1226
MG Probud Gdynia sp z o o, (C-444/07) ECLI:EU:C:2010:24 1323
MH v GP (Child: Emigration) [1995] 2 FLR 106 1168
Micallef's Estate, Re [1977] 2 NSWLR 929 1350
Michael Wilson and Partners Ltd v Sinclair [2015] EWHC 2847 592
Micula v Romania [2017] EWHC 31 (Comm) 677
Middle East Banking Co SA v Al-Haddad (1990) 70 OR (2d) 97 402
Middle East Tankers & Freighters Bunker Services SA v Abu Dhabi Container
    Lines PJSC [2002] EWHC 957 (Comm), [2002] 2 Lloyd's Rep 643 239–40
Middlemiss and Gould v Hartlepool Corpn [1972] 1 WLR 1643 669
Middleton v Middleton [1967] P 62 141
Midgulf International Ltd v Groupe Chimiche Tunisien [2010] EWCA Civ 66,
    [2010] 2 Lloyd's Rep 543 479
Midland Bank plc v Laker Airways Ltd [1986] QB 689 . . . . .423, 426, 434
Midland International Trade Services Ltd v Sudairy (1990) Financial
    Times, 2 May 96, 377, 527
Midland Resources Ltd v Gonvarri Industrial SA [2002] IL Pr 8 332
Mid-Ohio Imported Car Co v Tri-K Investments Ltd (1995) 129 DLR (4th) 181 . . . . . . .533, 538
Mietz v Intership Yachting Sneek BV [1996] IL Pr 661 303
Mighell v Sultan of Johore [1894] 1 QB 149 509
Mikado, The [1992] 1 Lloyd's Rep 163 336
Mike Trading and Transport Ltd v R Pagnan and Fratelli, The Lisboa [1980]
    2 Lloyd's Rep 546 436
Mikelson v United Services Auto Association 111 P 3d 601 (Hawaii 2005) 30
Milder v Milder [1959] VR 95 907
Miles Platts Ltd v Townroe Ltd [2003] EWCA Civ 145, [2003] 1 All ER
    (Comm) 561 . . . . .304, 443, 455–6
Milford, The (1858) Sw 362 89
Miliangos v George Frank (Textiles) Ltd (No 2) [1977] QB 489 96–101
Miliangos v George Frank (Textiles) Ltd [1976] AC 443 . . . . .98–102, 552, 669
Miller v Miller, McFarlane v McFarlane [2006] UKHL 24, [2006] 2 AC 618 1065
Miller v Teale (1954) 92 CLR 406 . . . . .919, 926
Miller, Bailie v Miller, Re [1914] 1 Ch 511 1355
Minalmet v Brandeis (C-123/91) [1992] ECR 1–5661 633
Minera Aquiline Argentina SA v IMA Exploration Inc and Inversiones Mineras
    Argentinas SA 2006 BCSC 1102 1384

Minister for Agriculture, Food and Forestry v Alte Leipziger Versicherüng
    Aktiengesellschaft [2002] 1 ILRM 306. 291
Minister of Employment and Immigration v Narwal (1990) 26 RFL (3d) 95. 925
Minister of Public Works of the Government of the State of Kuwait v Sir Frederick
    Snow & Partners [1983] 1 WLR 818, [1984] AC 426 . . . . .666, 670–1, 676
Ministry of Defence and Support of the Armed Forces for the Islamic Republic of Iran v
    FAZ Aviation Ltd [2007] EWHC 1042 (Comm), [2007] IL Pr 42 . . . . .201–2, 213, 243
Minmetals Germany GmbH v Ferco Steel Ltd [1999] CLC 647 . . . . .672–3, 676
Minna Craig Steamship Co v Chartered Bank of India [1897]
    1 QB 55, [1897] 1 QB 460 384
Minories v Afribank [1995] 1 Lloyd's Rep 134. 343
Minster Investments Ltd v Hyundai Precision and Industry Co
    Ltd [1988] 2 Lloyd's Rep 621. 273
Misland (Cyprus) Investments Ltd v McKillen [2014] EWHC 3859. 287
Mitchell and Baxter v Davies (1875) 3 R 208. 1363
Mitchell v Craft 211 So 2d 509 (1968) 31
Mitchell v McCulloch 1976 SC 1. 93
Mitchell v Mitchell 1993 SLT 123 . . . . .409, 973
Mitchell, ex p Cunningham, Re (1884) 13 QBD 418 160
Mitchell, Hatton v Jones, Re [1954] Ch 525, [1954] 2 All ER 246 . . . . .49, 1339
Mitchell's Trustee v Rule 1908 SLT 189 1348
Mitchner, Re [1922] St R Qd 252 1346
Mitford v Mitford [1923] P 130. . . . . .987, 997, 1012, 1029
Mitsubishi Corpn v Alafouzos [1988] 1 Lloyd's Rep 191 . . . . .136, 344, 368, 402
Mittal v Mittal [2013] EWCA Civ 1255 976
ML and AL (Children) (Contact Order: Brussels II Regulation), Re (No 1) [2006]
    EWHC 2385 (Fam), [2007] 1 FCR 475 . . . . .1098, 1119, 1130
MN (Recognition and Enforcement of Foreign Protective Measures), Re [2010]
    COPLR Con Vol 893. 1236
MO v RO [2013] EWHC 392. 1051
Modus Vivendi Ltd v British Products Sanmex Co Ltd [1996] FSR 790 . . . . .264, 275
Mohamed v Knott [1969] 1 QB 1 . . . . .165, 910, 921, 931
Mohammed v Bank of Kuwait and the Middle East KSC [1996] 1 WLR 1483 . . . . .365, 396, 404
Mohsin v The Commonwealth Secretariat [2002] EWHC 377 (Comm) 506, 514
Molins plc v GD SpA [2000] 1 WLR 1741 . . . . .326, 381
Mölnlycke AB v Procter & Gamble Ltd (No 4) [1992] 1 WLR 1112. 287
Molnlycke Health Care AB v BSN Medical Ltd [2009] EWHC 3370 (Pat), [2010] IL Pr 9. . . .448
Molony v Gibbons (1810) 2 Camp 502. 533
Molton Street Capital LLP v Shooters Hill Capital Partners LLP [2015] EWHC 3419 738
Monaco v Monaco (1937) 157 LT 231 1176
Mondial Trading Pty Ltd v Interocean Marine Transport Inc (1985) 65 ALR 155 325
Monory v Romania (2005) 41 EHRR 37. 1164
Monrose Investments v Orion Nominees [2002] IL Pr 21 332
Monterosso Shipping Co Ltd v International Transport Workers' Federation [
    1982] 3 All ER 841 . . . . .75, 85
Montgomery v Zarifi 1918 SC (HL) 128, (1919) 88 LJPC 20. . . . . .1372, 1378
Montreal Trust Co v Stanrock Uranium Mines Ltd (1965) 53 DLR (2d) 594 96
Moodey v Field, 13 February 1981 (unreported) 1168
Moore v Bull [1891] P 279 1071
Moore v Moore [2007] EWCA Civ 361, [2007] IL Pr 36 . . . . 207, 443, 969,
                                                            1064–5, 1075–7, 1118
Moorhouse v Lord (1863) 10 HL Cas 272, 285–6. . . . . .152, 155, 159, 161
Mora Shipping Inc v Axa Corporate Solutions Assurance SA [2005] EWCA
    Civ 1069, [2005] 2 Lloyd's Rep 769. . . . . .254, 261–2
Moran v Moran 1997 SLT 541 . . . . .176, 181–2

Morgan Grenfell & Co Ltd v Istituto per I Servizi Assicurativi del Commercio [2001]
   EWCA Civ 1932 . . . . .105, 107
Morgan Stanley & Co International Ltd v Pilot Lead Investments Ltd [2006]
   4 HKC 93 559
Morgan v Cilento [2004] EWHC 188 (Ch), [2004] All ER (D) 122 . . . . .155, 163
Morguard Investments Ltd v De Savoye (1991) 76 DLR (4th) 256 . . . . .526, 543, 603
Morin v Bonhams & Brooks Ltd [2003] EWHC 467 (Comm), [2003] IL Pr 25,
   [2003] EWCA Civ 1802, [2004] 1 Lloyd's Rep 702 . . . . .337, 350, 363–4, 755, 811
Morley v Reiter Engineering GmbH & Co KG [2011] EWHC 2798 (Ch),
   [2012] IL Pr 6 . . . . .251, 260
Morris v Baron & Co [1918] AC 1 74
Morris v Davies [2011] EWHC 1773 1339
Morris v Morris 1993 SCLR 144 1107
Morrison v Panic Link Ltd 1993 SLT 602, 1994 SLT 232 393
Morrison v The Society of Lloyd's [2000] IL Pr 92 415
Morse (1996) 45 ICLQ 888 93–4
Morson v Second National Bank of Boston 306 Mass 589, 29 NE 2d 19 (1940) 1277
Morviken [1983] 1 Lloyd's Rep 1 416
Moses v Shore Boat Builders Ltd (1993) 106 DLR (4th) 654 543–4
Moss v Moss [1937] QSR 1 1061
Mostyn v Fabrigas (1774) 1 Cowp 161, 98 ER 1021 . . . . .20, 894
Motala v A-G [1990] 2 FLR 261, [1990] Fam Law 340, [1992]
   2 AC 281 . . . . .52, 1050, 1053, 1195
Motorola Credit Corpn v Uzan (No 2) [2003] EWCA Civ 752, [2004]
   1 WLR 113 . . . . .307, 577
Motture v Motture [1955] 3 All ER 242n, [1955] 1 WLR 1066 .81
Mount Albert Borough Council v Australasian Temperance and General Mutual Life
   Assurance Society [1938] AC 224 . . . . .96, 766
Mount Cook (Northland) Ltd v Swedish Motors Ltd [1986] 1 NZLR 720 . . . . .106, 109
Moynihan v Moynihan (Nos 1 and 2) [1997] 1 FLR 59 158–9
MR v HS [2015] EWHC 234 . . . . .1147, 1154
MRG (Japan) Ltd v Engelhard Metals Japan Ltd [2003] EWHC 3418
   (Comm), [2004] 1 Lloyd's Rep 731 . . . . .363, 377
MS v PS (C-283/16) ECLI:EU:C:2017:104 1082
MS v PS [2015] EWHC 2880 1155
MS v PS [2016] EWHC 88 1081–2
Muduroglu Ltd v TC Ziraat Bankasi [1986] QB 1225 404
Muhammad v Suna 1956 SC 366 . . . . .911, 952
Mühlleitner v Yusufi (C-190/11) EU:C:2012:542, [2012] IL Pr 46 294
Mukoro v European Bank for Reconstruction and Development [1994] ICR 897 514
Mulhern's Estate, Re 297 NYS 2d 485 (1969) 1356
Mulox IBC Ltd v Geels (C-125/92) [1993] ECR I-4075 298
Multimedia v ARA Media Services [2006] EWHC 3107 (Ch), [2007] 1 All ER
   (Comm) 1160 106
Multinational Gas and Petrochemical Co v Multinational Gas and
   Petrochemical Services Ltd [1983] Ch 258 . . . . .338, 339, 378
Munchener Ruckversicherungs Gesellschaft v Commonwealth Insurance Co [2004]
   EWHC 914 (Comm) 344
Mund & Fester v Hatrex International Transport (C-398/92) [1994] ECR I-467 197
Municipal Council of Sydney v Bull [1909] 1 KB 7 116–18
Munro v Munro (1840) 7 Cl & Fin 842 .146–7, 149, 956–7, 959
Murphy v Deichler [1909] AC 446 1362
Murphy v Staples UK Ltd [2003] EWCA Civ 656, [2003] 1 WLR 2441 331
Murray and Tam, In the Marriage of (1993) 16 Fam LR 982 1135
Murray v Champernowne [1901] 2 IR 232 . . . . .1253, 1363

Murthy v Sivajothi [1999] 1 All ER 721, [1999] 1 WLR 467 543
Muscutt v Courcelles (2002) 213 DLR (4th) 577 . . . . .349, 543
Music Sales Ltd v Shapiro Bornstein & Co Inc [2005] EWHC 759 (Ch),
    [2006] 1 BCLC 371. 369
Musurus's Estate, Re [1936] 2 All ER 1666 . . . . .42, 49
Mutual Life Assurance Co of Canada v Peat Marwick (1998) 172 DLR (4th) 379. 398
Mutual Shipping Corpn of New York v Bayshore Shipping Co of Monrovia,
    The Montan [1985] 1 WLR 625 . . . . .672, 676
MV Kapitan Labunets, In the Matter of [1995] 1 ILRM 430 384
MV Turquoise Bleu, The [1996] 1 ILRM 406 456
Myerson v Martin [1979] 1 WLR 1390. 325
Mytton v Mytton (1977) 7 Fam Law 244. 974

N (A Child) (Abduction: Appeal), Re [2012] EWCA Civ 1086. 1111–12
N (A Child) (Adoption: Foreign Guardianship), Re [2000] 2 FLR 431 1214
N (A Minor) (Abduction: Brussels II Revised), Re [2014] EWHC 749 1129
N (Abduction: Habitual Residence), Re [2000] 2 FLR 899 181–2
N (Child Abduction: Habitual Residence), Re [1993] 2 FLR 124 . . . . 176, 177, 179, 181, 182–3,
                                                                    1107–8, 1140, 1152, 1214
N (Child Abduction: Habitual Residence), Re [2000]
    2 FLR 899 . . . . 175, 181–3, 1108, 1140 1214
N (Child Abduction: Jurisdiction), Re [1995] Fam 96 . . . . 177, 182–3, 1056, 1097,
                                                                    1107, 1140, 1174
N (Children) (Adoption: Jurisdiction) (AIRE Centre and others
    intervening, Re [2016] UKSC 15. . . . . .1115–16, 1209
N (Children) (Adoption: Jurisdiction), Re [2014] EWFC 45. 1115
N (Children) (Adoption: Jurisdiction), Re [2015] EWCA Civ 1112 1209–12
N (Children), Re [2015] EWCA Civ 1076 1145
N (Human Fertilisation Embryology Act 2008), Re [2016] EWHC
    1329 (Fam) 1052
N (Jurisdiction), Re [2007] EWHC 1274 (Fam Div). 955
N (Minors) (Abduction), Re [1991] 1 FLR 413, [1991] Fam Law 367 . . . . .1140, 1152
N (Recognition of Foreign Adoption Order), Re [2010] 1 FLR. 1102;
    [2010] Fam. Law 12. 1225
N v D (Customary Marriage) [2015] EWFC 28 . . . . .893, 896, 1051
N V Handel Maatschappij J Smits Import-Export v English Exporters Ltd [1955]
    2 Lloyd's Rep 69. 94
N v N (Abduction: Article 13 Defence) [1995] 1 FLR 107 1153–4
N v N (Foreign Divorce: Financial Relief) [1997] 1 FLR 900 . . . . .974, 978, 1076–7
N v N [1957] P 385. . . . . .966, 1038
NABB Brothers Ltd v Lloyds Bank International (Guernsey) Ltd [2005]
    EWHC 405 (Ch), [2005] IL Pr 37 . . . . .359–60, 363
Nabi v Heaton [1981] 1 WLR 1052 . . . . .936, 944
Nachimson v Nachimson [1930] P 217 . . . . .892, 930, 952
Nacional De Comercio Exterior SNC v Empresa De Telecommunicaciones
    De Cuba SA [2007] EWCA Civ 662, [2007] IL Pr 51. . . . . .304, 307, 620
Naftalin v London, Midland and Scottish Rly Co 1933 SC 259 93
Nane v Sykiotis (1966) 57 DLR (2d) 118 988
Nanglegan v Royal Free Hampstead NHS Trust [2002] 1 WLR 1043 326
Napoleon Bonaparte, Re the late Emperor (1853) 2 Rob Eccl 606. .158
Napp Laboratories v Pfizer Inc [1993] FSR 150. 225
Naraji v Shelbourne [2011] EWHC 3298 . . . . .560, 563
Naraji v The First National Bank of Chicago, The Efthimis [1986] 1 Shelbourne
    [2011] EWHC 3298 559
Nash v Nash [1973] 2 All ER 704 1168

National and Provincial Building Society and Ors v United Kingdom
  [1997] STC 1466. 1278
National Auto Glass Supplies v Nielsen & Moller Autoglass [2007] FCA 1625 106
National Grid Indus BV v Inspecteur van de Belastingdienst Rijnmond/kantoor
  Rotterdam (C-371/10) [2011] ECR I-12273. 35
National Justice Compañía Naviera SA v Prudential Assurance Co Ltd (No 2)
  [2000] 1 WLR 603, [2000] 1 Lloyd's Rep 129. . . . . .243, 288–9, 360
National Mortgage and Agency Co of New Zealand Ltd v Gosselin (1922)
  38 TLR 832. 344
National Navigacion v Endesa (The Wadi Sudr) [2009] EWCA Civ 1397,
  [2010] 2 All ER (Comm) 1243 . . . . .211, 444, 480, 630, 645
National Organisation Systems SA, Re An Application By (Decision 3265/2003)
  [2005] IL Pr 52, the One Member First Instance Court of Athens. 618
National Shipping Corpn v Arab [1971] 2 Lloyd's Rep 363. . . . . .106, 352
National Surety Co v Larsen [1929] 4 DLR 918 134
National Westminster Bank v Rabobank Nederland [2007] EWHC 1742 (Comm), [2008]
  1 All ER (Comm) 266 437
National Westminster Bank v Utrecht-America Finance Co [2001] EWCA
  Civ 658, [2001] 3 All ER 733 . . . . .421, 436–7, 439
Nationwide News Pty v University of Newlands, 9 December 2005, unreported 350
Naviera Amazonica Peruvia Sa v Cia International de Seguros del Peru
  [1988] 1 Lloyd's Rep 116. 668
Navig8 Pte Ltd v Al-Riyadh Co for Vegetable Oil Industry (The Lucky Lady) [2013] . . . .
Navigation Maritime Bulgare v Rustal Trading Ltd (The Ivan Zagubanski)
  [2002] 1 Lloyd's Rep 106. . . . . .209, 440
Navigators Insurance Co v Atlantic Methanol Production Co LLC [2003]
  EWHC 1706 (Comm), [2004] Lloyd's Rep IR 418 . . . . .363, 369
Navigators Insurance Co v Mohammed [2015] EWHC 1137 533
Nazym Khikmet, The [1996] 2 Lloyd's Rep 362. 385
NB Three Shipping Ltd v Harebell Shipping Ltd [2004] EWHC 2001
  (Comm), [2005] 1 Lloyd's Rep 509 417
NCF and AG v Italy (1995) 111 ILR 153 501
Negrepontis-Giannisis v Greece [2011] ECHR 56759/ 08. 1229
Neilson v Overseas Projects Corpn of Victoria Ltd (2005) 221 ALR 213, [2005] HCA 54
  . . . . .61, 69, 70, 106, 107, 777
Neilson v Overseas Projects Corpn of Victoria Ltd [2005] HCA 54. . . . . .69–70, 106–7
Nelson v Bridport (1846) 8 Beav 547. . . . . . . .105, 108, 491, 1256, 1260, 1339, 1351, 1353, 1355
Nesheim v Kosa [2007] EWHC 2710 (Ch) 334
Nessa v Chief Adjudication Officer [1998] 2 All ER 728, [1999] 1 WLR 1937 . . .172, 176,
  178–9, 181
Neste Chemicals SA v DK Line SA, The Sargasso [1994] 3 All ER 180 . . . . .306, 390
Netherlands State v Rüffer (814/79) [1980] ECR 3807 205
Network Telecom (Europe) Ltd v Telephone Systems International Inc [2003] EWHC 2890
  (QB), [2004] 1 All ER (Comm) 418 . . . . .347, 376–7
Neulinger and Shuruk v Switzerland [2010] ECHR 41615/ 07 . . . . .1153, 1165
Neumeier v Kuehner 286 NE 2d 454 (1972). 28
New Cap Reinsurance Corp Ltd v Grant [2011] EWCA Civ 971 .1311
New Hampshire Insurance Co v Aerospace Finance Ltd [1998] 2 Lloyd's Rep 539 . . . . . .337, 407
New Hampshire Insurance Co v Phillips Electronics North America Corpn [1998] IL Pr
  256. . . . . .368, 375–7
New Hampshire Insurance Co v Strabag Bau AG [1990] 2 Lloyd's Rep 61, [1992] 1 Lloyd's
  Rep 361 . . . . .281, 365, 367, 532
New Hampshire Insurance Co v Strabag Bau AG [1992] 1 Lloyd's Rep 361 237
New v Bonaker (1867) LR 4 Eq 655 1347
New York Breweries Co v A-G [1899] AC 62 . . . . .87, 1326, 1335

New York Life Insurance Co v Public Trustee [1924] 2 Ch 101 1281
New York Security and Trust Co v Keyser [1901] 1 Ch 666...........................1246–7
Newmarch v Newmarch [1978] Fam 79............................1029–31, 1034, 1071
Newsat Holdings Ltd v Zani [2006] EWHC 342 (Comm), [2006] 1 Lloyd's
   Rep 707 ....263, 273, 349, 351
Newtherapeutics Ltd v Katz [1991] Ch 226.....................196, 224, 377, 690
NF v EB [2014] EWHC 484...1155
Ng Ping On v Ng Choy Fund Kam [1963] SRNSW 782 930
NH (1996 Child Protection Convention: Habitual Residence), Re [2015]
   EWHC 2299...1105
Niboyet v Niboyet (1878) 4 PD 1 980
Niche Products Ltd v MacDermid Offshore Solutions LLC [2013] EWHC
   1493 (Ch), [2014] FSR 21..408
Nickel & Goeldner Spedition GmbH v "Kintra" UAB (C-157/13) EU:C:2014:2145,
   [2015] QB 96 ....207, 1318
Nielsen v Nielsen (1970) 16 DLR (3d) 33 1110
Nigeria v Ogbonna [2012] 1 WLR 139 505
Nike European Operations Netherlands BV v Sportland Oy, (C-310/14)
   ECLI:EU:C:2015:690 1322
Nile Rhapsody, The [1992] 2 Lloyd's Rep 399, [1994] 1 Lloyd's Rep 382 ....413, 414, 461
Nilon Ltd v Royal Westminster Investments SA [2015] UKPC 2, [2015] 3.....................
Nima Sarl v Deves Insurance Public Co Ltd (The Prestrioka) [2002]
   EWCA Civ 1132, [2003] 2 Lloyd's Rep 327 ....364, 366, 368, 373, 412–13
Nimrod, The [1973] 2 Lloyd's Rep 91 377
Nipponkoa Insurance Co (Europe) Ltd v Inter-Zuid Transport BV (C-452/12)
   EU:C:2013:858, [2014] IL Pr 10, [2014] 1 All ER (Comm) 288 ....203, 389, 613
Nissany v Michelson, 24 November 2016 253
NML Capital Ltd v Argentina [2011] UKSC 31, [2011] 2 AC 495.........498, 504, 506, 602
Noble Assurance Co v Gerling-Konzern General Insurance Co [2007]
   EWHC 253 (Comm)...433
Noirhomme v Walklate [1992] 1 Lloyd's Rep 427 ....623, 647
Nominal Defendant v Bagot's Executor and Trustee Co Ltd [1971] SASR 347, (1971) 124
   CLR 179 808
Nomura International Plc v Banca Monte Dei Paschi Di Siena SpA [2013] EWHC 3187
   (Comm), [2014] 1 WLR 1584...456
Nonus Asia Ltd v Standard Chartered Bank [1990] 1 HKLR 396 123
Nordea Bank Norge ASA v Unicredit Corporate Banking SPA [2011] EWHC 30...........449
Norden Steamship Co v Dempsey (1876) 1 CPD 654............................766
Nordglimt, The [1988] QB 183...........................385, 387, 390, 444, 455
Nore Challenger, The [2001] 2 Lloyd's Rep 103..............................382
Norfolk CC v VE [2015] EWFC 30 1115
Norman v Norman (No 2) (1968) 12 FLR 39 570
Norris v Chambers (1861) 29 Beav 246, 3 De G F & J 583..........................490
Norris, Re (1888) 4 TLR 452..174
Norsk Hydro ASA v State Property Fund of Ukraine (Note) [2002] EWHC 2120 (Comm),
   [2009] Bus LR 558 508
Norske Atlas Insurance Co Ltd v London General Insurance Co Ltd (1927) 43 TLR 541 ...667–8
North and Matheson, Re (1974) 52 DLR (3d) 280 892
North Scottish Helicopters Ltd v United Technologies Corpn Inc (No 2) 1988 SLT 778......103
North v North (1936) 52 TLR 380 81
North v Skipton Building Society 2002 WL 1039545 152
North Western Bank v Poynter [1895] AC 56 1276
North Yorkshire County Council v Wiltshire County Council [1999] 2 FLR 560 173
Northcote's Will Trusts, Re [1949] 1 All ER 442 1333
Northumberland City Council v Z, Y, X [2009] EWHC 498 (Fam) 1219

Norton v Florence Land Co (1877) 7 Ch D 332 490
Norton's Settlement, Re [1908] 1 Ch 471 393
Nottingham County Council v KB [2010 IEHC 9 1163
Nouvion v Freeman (1889) 15 App Cas 1 548
Nova (Jersey) Knit Ltd v Kammgarn Spinnerei GmbH [1977] 1 WLR 713............417, 419
Nova v Grove (1982) 140 DLR (3d) 527..1336
Novatrust Ltd v Kea Investments Ltd [2014] EWHC 4061 1309
Novelli v Rossi (1831) 2 B & Ad 757...531
Novello & Co Ltd v Hinrichsen Edition Ltd [1951] Ch 595 131
Novontech-Zala kft v Logicdata Electronic and Software Entwicklungs
    GmbH (C-324/12) EU:C:2013:205 662
Novoship (UK) Ltd v Mikhaylyuk [2012] EWHC 1352 430
Novus Aviation Ltd v Onur Air Tasimacilik AS [2009] EWCA Civ 122, [2009]
    1 Lloyd's Rep 576....................................345, 366, 368, 378
NP v JP [2015] EWHC 2551 ....1146–7, 1156, 1159
NP v KRP (Foreign Divorce) [2013] EWHC 694 ....1019, 1030–1
NR v AB [2016] EWHC 277 (Fam) 1065
NS v MI [2006] EWHC 1646 (Fam), [2007] 1 FLR 444 991
Nugent v Vetzera (1866) LR 2 Eq 704 1176
Nunneley v Nunneley and Marrian (1890) 15 PD 186 ....1061, 1395
Nurnberger Allgemeine Versicherungs AG v Portbridge Transport International BV (C-148/
    03) [2004] ECR I-10327 ....203, 217, 309
NV Handel Maatschappij J Smits Import-Export v English Exporters Ltd [1955] 2 Lloyd's
    Rep 69 94
Nycal (UK) Ltd v Lacey [1994] CLC 12 ....347, 359

O (A Minor) (Abduction: Habitual Residence), Re [1993]
    2 FLR 594 ....176, 179, 182, 183, 1107, 1140, 1150, 1214
O (Abduction: Consent and Acquiescence), Re [1997] 1 FLR 924................1138
O (Child Abduction: Custody Rights), Re [1997] 2 FLR 702 ....176, 182–3, 1138
O (Child Abduction: Undertakings), Re [1994] 2 FLR 349....................1155
O T M Ltd v Hydronautics [1981] 2 Lloyd's Rep 211 ....400, 419
O v O (Appeal against Stay: Divorce Petition) [2002] EWCA Civ 949,
    [2003] 1 FLR 192 974
O v O (Child Abduction: Return to Third Country) [2013] EWHC 2970 (Fam) 1140
O v O (Jurisdiction: Jewish Divorce) [2000] 2 FLR 147 1012
O, Re [2014] 3 WLR 453 1235
O, Re [2014] Fam. 197 1236
O'Callaghan v Thomond (1810) 3 Taunt 82 ....86, 1290
O'Daly v Gulf Oil Terminals (Ireland) Ltd [1983] ILRM 163 876
O'Keefe, Re [1940] Ch 124...64, 71, 171
O'Neill, Re [1922] NZLR 468..1251
Oakley v Ultra Vehicle Design Ltd (In Liquidation) [2005] EWHC 872
    (Ch), [2005] IL Pr 55.............................207, 240, 284, 287, 706
Obikoya v Silvernorth Ltd (1983) Times, 6 July...........................333
Ocarina Marine Ltd v Marcard Stein & Co [1994] 2 Lloyd's Rep 524 237
Ocean Industries v Steven C (1991) 104 ALR 353...........................385
Oceanic Sun Line Special Shipping Co Inc v Fay (1988) 165 CLR 197 880
Oceano Grupo Editorial SA v Rocio Murciano Quintero (C-240/98) [2000]
    ECR I-4941...232, 296
Ochsenbein v Papelier (1873) 8 Ch App 695 569
Odiase v Odiase [1965] NMLR 196..147
ÖFAB, Östergötlands Fastigheter AB v Frank Koot and Evergreen Investments
    BV (C-147/12) EU:C:2013:490, [2015] QB 20 ....245, 265, 272, 274
Official Solicitor v Stype Investments (Jersey) Ltd [1983] 1 All ER 629 357–8

Official Solicitor v Yemoh and others [2010] EWHC 3727 943
Offshore Rental Co Inc v Continental Oil Co 583 P 2d 721 (1978) 27
Ogden v Folliott (1790) 3 Term Rep 726, 100 ER 825 ....118, 120, 122
Ogden v Ogden [1908] P 46 ....47–9, 893, 899, 918–19
Ogelegbanwei v Nigeria [2016] EWHC 8 ....498, 501, 591
Ogilvie, Re [1918] 1 Ch 492 ....1345, 1355, 1357
Ohochuku v Ohochuku [1960] 1 All ER 253 ....932, 934–5
OJSC Oil Company Yugraneft v Abramovich [2008] EWHC 2613....................199
OJSC TNK-BP Holding v Lazurenko [2012] EWHC 3286 ....768, 847
Okpabi v Royal Dutch Shell plc [2017] EWHC 89 (TCC), [2017] BLR 136 337
Olafisoye v Olafisoye [2010] EWHC 3539 ....955–6, 959–60, 962, 1027–30
Olafsson v Gissurarson [2008] EWCA Civ 152 ....308, 326, 381
Old North State Brewing Co v Newlands Services Inc (1998) 155 DLR (4th)
    250, [1999] 4 WWR 573............................119, 136, 554
Oleszko v Pietrucha (1963) Times, 22 March............................907
Oleynikov v Russia, Judgment of 14 March 2013; (2013) 57 EHRR 15, ECtHR 501
Oliphant v Hendrie (1784) 1 Bro CC 571..............................1347
Olsen v Gearbulk Services Ltd [2015] IRLR 818 299
Olympia Productions Ltd v Mackintosh [1992] ILRM 204..........................252
Omega Group Holdings Ltd v Kozeny [2002] CLC 132 434
Omerri v Uganda High Commission (1973) 8 ITR 14 511
Onobrauche v Onobrauche (1978) 8 Fam Law 107..........................935, 952–3
Ontario Court v M and M (Abduction: Children's Objections) [1997]
    1 FLR 475....................1138, 1144, 1156
Ontulmus v Collett [2013] EWHC 980 885
Open Joint Stock Co Alfa-Bank v Trefilov [2014] EWHC 1806 573
Ophthalmic Innovations International (United Kingdom) Ltd v Ophthalmic Innovations
    International Inc [2004] EWHC 2948 (Ch), [2005] 345, 363, 365, 377
OPO v (1) MLA (2) SLT [2014] EWCA Civ 1277 ....710–11, 856
Oppenheim & Co v Mahomed Haneef [1922] 1 AC 482 668
Oppenheimer v Cattermole [1976] AC 249, 278, 283....................13, 127, 137–8, 171
Oppenheimer v Louis Rosenthal and Co AG [1937] 1 All ER 23 372
Optelec v Midtronics [2003] IL Pr 4 730
Orams v Apostolides [2006] EWHC 2226 (QB), [2007] 1 WLR 241 ....14–15, 632
Orascom Telecom Holding SAE v Chad [2008] EWHC 1841 (Comm), [2009]
    1 All ER (Comm) 315..............................508
Oriel Ltd, Re [1985] 1 WLR 180..............................329
Oriental Insurance Co Ltd v Bhavani Stores Pte Ltd [1998] SLR 253 394
Orphanos v Queen Mary College [1985] AC 761 173
Orrell v Orrell (1871) 6 Ch App 302..............................1355, 1357
Orr-Lewis v Orr-Lewis [1949] P 347..............................978
Osman v Elasha [2000] Fam 62..............................1172
Osman v United Kingdom, Judgment of 28 October 1998; (2000) 29 EHRR 245 14
Osoba, Osoba v Osoba, Re [1979] 1 WLR 247..............................1354
Österreichische Länderbank v S'Elite Ltd [1981] QB 565 106
Osvath-Latkoczy v Osvath-Latkoczy (1959) 19 DLR (2d) 495..........................152
OT Africa Line Ltd v Hijazy (The Kribi) [2001] 1 Lloyd's Rep 76 ....14, 240, 422, 440
OT Africa Line Ltd v Magic Sportswear Corpn [2004] EWHC 2441 (Comm), [2005]
    EWCA Civ 710, [2005] 2 Lloyd's 338, 348, 369, 398, 415–16, 425,
                                                              436, 439, 700, 754, 756
Oteri v R [1976] 1 WLR 1272..............................908
OTM Ltd v Hydronautics [1981] 2 Lloyd's Rep 211 400
OTP Bank Nyilvánosan Működő Részvénytársaság v Hochtief Solution AG (C-519/12)
    EU:C:2013:674, [2015] IL Pr 30..............................245, 265
OTV v Hilmarton [1999] 2 Lloyd's Rep 222 ....674, 675

Oundjian v Oundjian (1979) 1 FLR 198, 202 . . . . .169, 177, 958
Overseas Food Importers & Distributors Ltd and Brandt, Re (1981)
    126 DLR (3d) 422 533
Overseas Union Insurance Ltd v AA Mutual International Insurance Co Ltd
    [1988] 2 Lloyd's Rep 63 . . . . .386, 419, 444, 455
Overseas Union Insurance Ltd v Incorporated General Insurance Ltd [1992]
    1 Lloyd's Rep 439. 367
Overseas Union Insurance Ltd v New Hampshire Insurance Co (C-351/89)
    [1992] 1 QB 434 444
Owens Bank Ltd v Bracco (No 2) (C-129/92) [1994] QB 509 . . . . 204, 225, 443,
                                           456, 571, 611, 618
Owens Bank Ltd v Bracco [1992] 2 AC 443 . . . . .456, 526, 528, 560,
                                     571–3, 592, 598, 607, 641
Owens Bank Ltd v Etoile Commerciale SA [1995] 1 WLR 44 . . . . .563, 571–2
Owners of Eleftherotria v Despina R, The Despina R [1979] AC 685 . . . . .98–100, 102–3
Owners of the Stolt Kestrel v Owners of the Niyazi S [2015] EWCA Civ 1035,
    [2016] 1 Lloyd's Rep 125 . . . . .383–4, 387
Oxnard Financing SA v Rahn (Legal Personality of Swiss Partnership) [1998]
    1 WLR 1465 (CA) 87, 327–8
Ozalid Group (Export) Ltd v African Continental Bank Ltd [1979]
    2 Lloyd's Rep 231. 102

P (A Child) (Abduction: Custody Rights), Re [2004] EWCA Civ 971,
    [2004] 2 FLR 1057 . . . . .1057, 1148
P (A Child) (Mirror Orders), Re [2000] 1 FLR 435. 1108
P (A Minor) (Child Abduction: Declaration), Re [1995] 1 FLR 831,
    [1995] Fam Law 398 1056
P (Abduction: Declaration), Re [1995] 1 FLR 831. 1056
P (Abduction: Non-Convention Country), Re [1997] 1 FLR 780 1174
P (Children Act: Diplomatic Immunity), Re [1998] 1 FLR 624. . . . . .510, 512–13, 1056
P (Diplomatic Immunity: Jurisdiction), Re [1998] 1 FLR 1026. . . . . .498, 511, 1056
P (Forced Marriage), Re [2010] EWHC 3467 . . . . .986, 991, 1050–1
P (GE) (An Infant), Re [1965] Ch 568 166
P (LE) v P (JM) [1971] P 318 1072
P (Recognition and Registration of Orders under the 1996 Hague Child Protection
    Convention), Re [2014] EWHC 2845. 1131
P v A [2015] EWHC 3818 1138
P v B (Child Abduction: Undertakings) [1994] 3 IR 507. 1155
P v P (Minors) (Child Abduction), Re [1992] 1 FLR 155 . . . . .1143, 1154
P v P [2006] EWHC 2410 (Fam), [2007] 2 FLR 439 182
P v R (Forced Marriage: Annulment: Procedure) [2003] 1 FLR 661 . . . . .986, 1051
P v S (Child Abduction: Wrongful Removal) [2002] Fam LR 2 . . . . .1056, 1141
PA, Re [2016] Fam 47 177
Pace Europe v Dunham [2012] EWHC 852 553–4
Pacific Brands Sport Leisure Pty Ltd v Underworks Pty Ltd (2006) 149 FCR 395, [2006]
    FCAFC 40. 1285
Pacific International Sports Clubs Limited v Soccer Marketing International Ltd [2009]
    EWHC 1839 (Ch), [2010] EWCA Civ 753. . . . . .366, 369, 403, 471
Padolecchia v Padolecchia [1968] P 314. . . . . .53, 917, 920, 923
Paget v Ede (1874) LR 18 Eq 118 489
Paget's Settlement, Re [1965] 1 WLR 1046 1393–4
Pain v Holt (1919) 19 SRNSW 105. . . . . .1345, 1353
Paine, Re [1940] Ch 46 . . . . .913, 915–16, 923, 1197
Paley, Princess Olga v Weisz [1929] 1 KB 718 127
Pammer v Reederei Karl Schlüter GmbH & Co. KG and Hotel (C-585/08) and (C-144/09)

Pammer v Reederei Karl Schlüter GmbH & Co. KG and Hotel Alpenhof
    GesmbH v Heller (C-144/09) [2010] ECR I-12527 .294, 295, 688
Pan American World Airways Inc v Andrews 1992 SLT 268 . . . . .428, 430
Pan Indonesia Bank Ltd TBK v Marconi Communications International Ltd [2005]
    EWCA Civ 422 105
Panagaki v Apostolopoulos [2015] EWHC 2700 (QB) 199
Panaghia P, The see Howard Houlder and Partners Ltd v Marine General
    Transporters Corpn, The Panaghia P 343
Pancotto v Sociedade de Safaris de Mocambique SARL 422 F Supp 405 (1976) 30
Panseptos, The [1981] 1 Lloyd's Rep 152 411
Paolantonio v Paolantonio [1950] 2 All ER 404 966
Papadopoulos v Papadopoulos [1930] P 55 . . . . .565, 921, 1009, 1079
Papanicolaou v Thielen [1997] IL Pr 37 224
Paquette v Galipean [1981] 1 SCR 29 1212
Paragon Finance v DB Thakerar and Co [1999] 1 All ER 400 840
Paramount Airways Ltd (In Administration), Re [1992] Ch 160 334
Pardo v Bingham (1868) LR 6 Eq 485 89
Park's Estate, Re [1954] P 89, [1953] 2 All ER 1411 987
Parkasho v Singh [1968] P 233 . . . . .107–8, 112–13, 934–6
Parkes v MacGregor [2011] CSIH 69 589
Parlement Belge, The (1880) 5 PD 197 . . . . .507, 510
Parojcic v Parojcic [1958] 1 WLR 1280 . . . . .986, 987, 988
Partenreederei MS Tilly Russ v Haven and Vervaebedriff Nova NV (71/83)
    [1985] QB 931, [1984] ECR 2417 238
PAS v AFS [2005] 1 ILRM 306 182
Patel v Patel [2000] QB 551 417
Patel v Visa Officer, Bombay [1990] Imm AR 297 1226
Pathe Screen Entertainment v Handmade Films 1989 attached to Tonicstar Ltd
    v American Home [2004] EWHC 1234 (Comm), [2012] 1 CLC 271 235
Patrick v Shedden (1853) 2 E & B 14 550
Patten's Goods, Re (1860) 6 Jur NS 151 160
Patterson v D'Agostino (1975) 58 DLR (3d) 63 . . . . .541, 546
Patterson v Vacation Brokers Inc [1998] IL Pr 482 594
Pattni v Ali and Dinky International SA [2006] UKPC 51, [2007] 2 AC 85 . . . . 533, 544,
                                                                                    546–7, 1267
Patton v Reed (1972) 30 DLR (3d) 494 550
Paul v National Life 352 NE 2d 550 (1986) 31
Paulin, Re [1950] VLR 462 1353
Payam Tamiz v Google Inc [2013] EWCA Civ 68 887
Payne v Payne [2001] EWCA Civ 166, [2001] Fam 473 1167–9
Pazpena de Vire v Pazpena de Vire [2001] 1 FLR 460 . . . . .896, 898
PC (A Child) (Brussels II Revised: Jurisdiction within United Kingdom),
    Re [2013] EWHC 2336 1100–1
Peabody v Kent 153 App Div 286, 13 NYS 32 (1912), 213 NY 154,
    107 NE 51 (1914) 1388
Pearce v Brooks (1866) LR 1 Ex 213 135
Pearce v Ove Arup Partnership Ltd [1997] Ch 293, [2000] Ch 403 . . . . .220, 495–6
Pearl Petroleum Co Ltd v Kurdistan Regional Government of Iraq [2015]
    EWHC 3361 (Comm), [2016] 4 WLR 2 . . . . .499–500, 508
Pearson Education Ltd v Prentice Hall of India Private Ltd [2005]
    EWHC 655 (QB) 363, 377
Pebros Servizi Srl v Aston Martin Lagonda Ltd (C-511/14) EU:C:2016:448, [2016]
    4 WLR 138 657
PEC Ltd v Golden Asia Rice Co Ltd [2014]
    EWHC 1583 702

Peer International Corpn v Termidor Music Publishers Ltd [2003]
    EWCA Civ 1156, [2004] Ch 212 . . . . .128, 131–2, 144
Pei v Bank Bumiputra Malaysia Berhad (1998) 41 OR (3d) 39 .366, 373
Peillon v Brooking (1858) 25 Beav 218 1386
Pélégrin v Coutts & Co [1915] 1 Ch 696. 1247
Pellegrini v Italy (2001) 35 EHRR 44 580
Pemberton v Hughes [1899] 1 Ch 781. . . . . .528, 564–6, 1009, 1025
Pemberton, Re (1966) 59 DLR (2d) 44 . . . . .1336, 1340
Pena Copper Mines Ltd v Rio Tinto Co Ltd (1911) 105 LT 846 436
Pencil Hill Ltd v US Citta Di Palermo SpA, 19 January 2016, HC 552, 575
Pender v Commercial Bank of Scotland 1940 SLT 306 1287–8
Pendy Plastic Products BV v Pluspunkt Handelsgesellschaft mbH (228/81)
    [1982] ECR 2723 310
Penhas v Tan Soo Eng [1953] AC 304 . . . . .904, 929
Penn v Baltimore (1750) 1 Ves Sen 444, 27 ER 1132. . . . . .19, 1336
Pepin v Bruyère [1900] 2 Ch 504. 1352
Perella Weinberg Partners UK LLP v Codere SA [2016] EWHC 1182 (Comm) 453
Perlak Petroleum Maatschappij v Deen [1924] 1 KB 111. 110
Permanent Trustee Co (Canberra) Ltd v Finlayson (1967) 9 FLR 424, (1968) 122 CLR 338. . .117
Permanent Trustee Co (Canberra) Ltd v Permanent Trustee Co of New South Wales Ltd
    (1969) 14 FLR 246 1390
Perpetual Executors and Trustees Association of Australia Ltd v Roberts
    [1970] VR 732. . . . . .1201, 1388, 1390
Perpetual Trustee Co Ltd v Montuori [1982] 1 NSWLR 710. . . . . .1223, 1226
Perrin v Perrin 1994 SC 45 . . . . .1137, 1140, 1254, 1281
Perrin v Revenue and Customs Commissioners [2014] UKFTT 223 . . . . .1254, 1281
Perrini v Perrini [1979] Fam 84 919
Perry v Zissis [1977] 1 Lloyd's Rep 607 . . . . .336, 355, 551, 593
Persian v Persian [1970] 2 NSWR 538. 905
Pertreis v Tondear (1790) 1 Hag Con 136 900
Peter Buchanan Ltd and Macharg v McVey [1955] AC 516 n, [1954] IR 89 116–17
Peter Pinckney v KDG Mediatech AG (C-170/12) EU:C:2013:635,
    [2014] IL Pr 7 . . . . .264, 276, 279, 833
Peter Rehder v Air Baltic Corporation (C-204/08) [2009] ECR I-6073. 259–60
Petereit v Babcock International Holdings Ltd [1990] 1 WLR 350 649
Peters v Peters (1968) 112 Sol Jo 311 934
Peterson v Bezold (1970) 17 DLR (3d) 471 1336
Petra Engler v Janus Versand GmbH (C-27/02) [2005] ECR I-481 264–5
Petrofina SA v AOT Ltd [1992] QB 571 382
Petroleo Brasiliero SA v Mellitus Shipping Inc (The Baltic Flame) [2001] EWCA Civ 418,
    [2001] 2 Lloyd's Rep 203 . . . . .335, 338–9, 365, 378
Petromin SA v Secnav Marine Ltd [1995] 1 Lloyd's Rep 603 441
Petrotrade Inc v Smith [1998] 2 All ER 346, [1999] 1 WLR 457. . . . . .173, 284
Petter v EMC Europe Ltd [2015] EWHC 1498 (QB), [2015] EWCA Civ 828,
    [2016] IL Pr 3 . . . . .299, 301, 482
Pez Hejduk v EnergieAgentur.NRW GmbH (C-441/13) EU:C:2015:28, [2015]
    Bus LR 560 . . . . .264, 272, 276, 279
Pfunder Shull 1999 CanLII 6625, BC SC 122
Phelan v Phelan 2007 (1) SA 483 (C) 920
Philip Alexander Securities and Futures Ltd v Bamberger [1997] IL Pr 73 209–10,
                                                                              439–40, 630
Philippi v IRC [1971] 1 WLR 684. 159
Philippine Admiral, The [1977] AC 373 504
Philipson-Stow v IRC [1961] AC 727 . . . . .1252, 1260, 1344, 1348, 1354–5, 1390
Phillip Alexander Securities and Futures Ltd v Bamberger [1997] IL Pr 73 . . . . .210, 423

Phillips v Batho [1913] 3 KB 25 . . . . .541, 545, 1078
Phillips v Eyre (1870) LR 6 QB 1 . . . . .20, 777, 877
Phillips v Nussberger [2008] UKHL, [2008] 1 WLR 181 . . . . .308, 326, 381
Phillips v Phillips (1921) 38 TLR 150 903–4
Phillips v Symes [2002] 1 WLR 863, [2003] EWHC 1172 (Ch) 224, 326
Phoenix Marine Inc v China Ocean Shipping Co [1999] CLC 478 109
PHP Tobacco Carib Sarl v BAT Caribbean SA [2016] EWHC 3377 (Comm), ...288
Phrantzes v Argenti [1960] 2 QB 19 . . . . .90–1, 139, 573
Pia Vesta, The [1984] 1 Lloyd's Rep 169. 411
Pierce v Helz 314 NYS 2d 453 (1970) 816
Piercy, Re [1895] 1 Ch 83 . . . . .491, 1260
Pierson v Garnet (1786) 2 Bro CC 38 1348
Pike v Hoare (1763) Amb 428 485
Pike v The Indian Hotels Company Ltd [2013] EWHC 4096 349
Pilcher v Pilcher [1955] P 318 1080
Pilinski v Pilinska [1955] 1 All ER 631 897
Pilkington's Will Trusts, Re [1937] Ch 574 1390
Pillai v Sarkar (1994) The Times, 21 July 400
Pindling v National Broadcasting Corpn (1984) 14 DLR (4th) 391. 886
Pini v Romania [2005] 2 FLR 596, (2005) 40 EHRR 13. 1214
Pink v Perlin & Co (1898) 40 NSR 260 1370
Pioneer Container, The [1994] 2 AC 324. 411
Piper Aircraft Co v Reno 454 US 235 (1981). 393
Piper, Re [1927] 4 DLR 924 1246
Pipon v Pipon (1744) Amb 25, 27 ER 14. 21 . . . . .20, 1339
Pitt v Pitt (1864) 4 Macq 627 159
P-J (Children) (Abduction: Consent), Re [2009] EWCA Civ 588 1148–9
PK v TK [2002] IR 186 (Sup Ct). 1035
PL v An tArd Chlaraitheoir [1995] 2 ILRM 241 . . . . .150, 157
Place of Performance of an FOB Contract, Re (156/ 07) [2010] IL Pr 17 258
Planmount Ltd v Republic of Zaire [1981] 1 All ER 1110. 504
Plastus Kreativ AB v Minnesota Mining and Manufacturing Co [1995] RPC 438 496
Plaza BV v Law Debenture Trust Corp Plc [2015] EWHC 43 . . . . .471, 474–5, 494
Pletinka v Pletinka (1964) 109 Sol Jo 72 152
Plozza v South Australian Insurance Co. Ltd. [1963] SASR 122. 808
Plumex v Young Sports NV (C-473/04). 309
Plummer v IRC [1988] 1 WLR 292. . . . . .150, 162
P-M (Parental Order: Payments to Surrogacy Agency), Re [2013] EWHC 2328 (Fam) 1188
PO, Re [2013] EWHC 3932 (COP); [2013] WLR (D) 495 (CP) 1236
Po, The [1991] 2 Lloyd's Rep 206 .386–7, 400, 403, 461, 471
Pocket Kings Ltd v Safenames Ltd [2009] EWHC 2529 (Ch), [2010]
    Ch 438. . . . . .115, 122, 124, 499–500, 552
Poel v Poel [1970] 1 WLR 1469. 1168
Polessk [1996] 2 Lloyd's Rep 40. . . . . .405, 413
Police Comr of South Australia v Temple (1993) 17 Fam LR 144 1155
Polly Peck International plc (In Administration), Re (No 2) [1998]
    3 All ER 812 . . . . .217, 489, 492
Polly Peck International plc v Nadir (1992) The Independent, 2 September. 359
Ponticelli v Ponticelli [1958] P 204 . . . . .898, 914, 994–6
Poon v Tan (1973) 4 Fam Law 161 . . . . .934, 953
Pordea v Times Newspapers Ltd [2000] IL Pr 763 630
Porter v Freudenberg [1915] 1 KB 857 . . . . .325, 497
Porzelack KG v Porzelack (UK) Ltd [1987] 1 WLR 420 .593, 607
Potinger v Wightman (1817) 3 Mer 67 167
Potter v Broken Hill Pty Co Ltd (1906) 3 CLR 479. 494

Pouey v Hordern [1900] 1 Ch 492...1362
Povse v Austria [2014] 1 FLR 944 1165
Powell Duffryn plc v Petereit (C-214/89) [1992] ECR I-1745................237, 239, 245
Powell v Cockburn (1976) 68 DLR (3d) 700................................1025
Powell v OMV Exploration & Production Ltd [2014] ICR 63...................299–300
Power Curber International Ltd v National Bank of Kuwait SAK [1981]
    1 WLR 1233 ....402, 1281
Poyser v Minors (1881) 7 QBD 329 75
PP v White (1940) 9 MLJ 214..149, 152, 936
PPU C v M (C-376/14) [2014] All ER (D) 160 (Oct)............1094–5, 1104, 1118
PPU, Aguirre Zarraga v Simone Pelz (C-491/10) [2010] ECR I-14247.........1162
PPU, Detiček v Sgueglia (C-403/09) [2009] ECR I-12193 1120
PPU, J McB v LE (C-400/10) [2010] ECR I-08965 ....1093, 1138
PPU, Mercredi v Chaffe (C-497/10) [2010] ECLI:EU:C:
    2010:829 ....175–8, 182, 803, 956, 1094–5, 1104, 1242
PPU, P v Q (C-455/15) [2015] All ER (D) 181 (Nov) 1128–9
PPU, Povse v Alpago (C-211/10) [2010] ECR I– 6673 ....1158, 1161–2
PPU, Rinau v Rinau (C-195/08) [2008] ECR I-05271 ....1130, 1162
Practice Direction (Foreign Law Affidavit) [1972] 1 WLR 1433 111
Practice Direction (Judgments: Foreign Currency) (1992) PD 11 ....98, 100
Practice Direction [1966] 1 WLR 395 98
Practice Direction [1976] 1 WLR 83 100
Practice Direction [1977] 1 WLR 197 100
Pratt v Pratt [1939] AC 417 982
Pratt, Re 8 NY 2d 855, 168 NE 2d 709 (1960) 1386
Prazic v Prazic [2006] EWCA Civ 497, [2006] 2 FLR 1125...........220, 446, 455
Premium Nafta Products Ltd v Fili Shipping Co Ltd [2007] UKHL 40, [2007]
    2 All ER (Comm) 1053 ....410, 415, 418, 420
Preservatrice Fonciere TIARD SA v Staat der Nederlanden (C-266/01)
    [2003] ECR I-4867 204–6
President of India v Taygetos Shipping Co SA [1985] 1 Lloyd's Rep 155 104
President of the State of Equatorial Guinea v Royal Bank of Scotland International
    [2006] UKPC 7 ....115, 124
Preston v Melville (1841) 8 Cl & Fin 1 1334
Preston v Preston [1963] P 411 ....904, 906–7
Price Mobile Homes Centres Inc v National Trailer Convoy of Canada (1974)
    44 DLR (3d) 443..1271
Price v Dewhurst (1837) 8 Sim 279....................................569, 576
Price, Tomlin v Latter, Re [1900] 1 Ch 442 1348
PricewaterhouseCoopers v Saad Investments [2014] UKPC 35 1310
Pride Shipping Corpn v Chung Hwa Pulp Corpn [1991]
    1 Lloyd's Rep 126..374
Priest, Re [1944] Ch 58 ....47, 1345
Prifti on behalf of Lloyds Syndicates v Musini Sociedad Anonima de
    Segouras y Reaseguros [2003] EWHC 2796 (Admin), [2004] 1 CLC 517..............234
Princess Olga Paley v Weisz [1929] 1 KB 718, CA............................127
Print Concept GmbH v GEW (EC) Ltd [2001] EWCA Civ 352, [2002]
    CLC 352 ....727, 729, 733
Prism Investment BV v Jaap Anne van der Meer (C-139/10) [2011]
    ECR I-9511..621, 626
Pro Swing Inc v Elta Golf Inc [2006] SCR 612, (2007) 273 DLR (4th) 663 ....118–19, 137
Pro Swing Inc v Elta Golf Inc 2006 SCC 52, (2007) 273 DLR (4th) 663 ....119, 137, 552
Proceedings Brought by A (C-523/07) [2009] ECR I-02805, [2010]
    Fam 42 - -Korkein hallinto-oikeus 175–8, 182–3, 956, 1093–5, 1102,
                                                    1104, 1118–20, 1123, 1242

Procureur-generaal bij het hof van beroep te Antwerpen V Zaza Retail BV, (C-112/10)
    ECLI:EU:C:2011:743 1317
Proes v Revenue Commissioners [1998] 4 IR 176 . . . . .152, 163
Profit Investment SIM SpA v Stefano Ossi EU:C:2016:282, (C-366/13)
    [2016] 1 WLR 3832 . . . . .240, 242, 248, 251, 285
Propend Finance Pty Ltd v Sing (1997) 111 ILR 611. 498
Prostar Management Ltd v Twaddle 2003 SLT (Sh Ct) 11 292
Protea Leasing Ltd v Royal Air Cambodia [2002] 2 All ER 224 811
Protector Alarms Ltd v Maxim Alarms Ltd [1978] FSR 442. 486
Provimi Ltd v Roche Products Ltd [2003] EWHC 961 (Comm), [2003]
    2 All ER (Comm) 683 . . . . .231–3, 237
Provimi Ltd v Roche Products Ltd, Provimi v Aventis Animal Nutrition SA [2003]
    EWHC 961 (Comm), [2003] 2 All ER (Comm) 683 . . . . .202, 231–2, 237, 264
Provimiv Aventis Animal Nutrition SA [2003] EWHC 961 202
Prudential Assurance Co Ltd v Prudential Insurance Co of America (No 2) [2003]
    EWCA Civ 1154, [2004] ETMR 29 .15, 218, 333, 443, 453, 642
Prudential Assurance Co Ltd v Prudential Insurance Co of America [2003] EWCA Civ 327,
    [2003] 1 WLR 2295, [2003] FSR 97 .15, 217–18, 333, 443, 453, 642
Pryce, Re [1911] 2 Ch 286. 1362–3
PT Hutan Domas Raya v Yue Xiu Enterprises [2001] 2 SLR 49. 394
PT Pan Indonesia Bank Ltd TBK v Marconi Communications International Ltd [2005]
    EWCA Civ 422 . . . . .105, 343, 344, 691, 733, 736–7, 755
PT Royal Bali Leisure v Hutchinson & Co Trust Co Ltd [2004] EWHC 1014 (Ch) 111
PTKF Kontinent v VMPTO Progress 1994 SLT 235. 400
Public Service Co of New Hampshire v Voudonas 84 NH 387, 157 A 81 (1930) 1252
Public Trustee v Vodjdani (1988) 49 SASR 236 1353–4
Pugh v Pugh [1951] P 482. . . . . .913, 916, 920
Pugliese v Finmeccanica SpA (C-437/00) [2003] ECR I-10829 .302
Pula Parking d o o v Tederahn (C-551/15) EU:C:2017:193, [2017] IL Pr 15. . . . . . .206, 611, 657
Pulgrave, Brown & Son Ltd v SS Turid [1922] 1 AC 397. 766
Purcell v Khayat (1987) The Times, 23 November 402
Purdom v Pavey & Co (1896) 26 SCR 412 106
Purpose AS v Transnav Purpose Navigation Ltd [2017] EWHC 719 (Comm) 441
Puttick v A-G [1980] Fam 1, 17. . . . . .148–9, 159, 169, 1056
Pye Ltd v BG Transport Service Ltd [1966] 2 Lloyd's Rep 300. . . . . .118, 137

Q, Petitioner 2001 SLT 243. . . . . .1154, 1156
Qatar Petroleum v Shell International Petroleum [1983] 2 Lloyd's Rep 35 . . . . .338, 370
Qioptiq Ltd v Teledyne Scientific & Imaging LLC [2011] EWHC 229 401
QRS 1 ApS v Frandsen [1999] 1 WLR 2169 . . . . .117, 125, 204
QS v RS [2016] EWHC 2470 (Fam). 1054
Quazi v Quazi [1980] AC 744 . . . . 1007–8, 1013, 1015, 1017–18, 1021,
    1029, 1032–3, 1072
Queensland Mercantile and Agency Co, Re [1891] 1 Ch 536, [1892] 1 Ch 219 1294
Quoraishi v Quoraishi [1985] FLR 780. . . . . .952, 954, 982
Qureshi v Qureshi [1972] Fam 173 . . . . 141, 152, 155–7, 163, 895, 932–3,
    943, 1013, 1019, 1021, 1034, 1071

R (A Child) (Prohibited Steps Order), Re [2013] EWCA Civ 1115 1167
R (A Child), Re [2003] EWCA Civ 182, [2003] Fam 129 1053
R (A Minor) (Inter-Country Adoptions: Practice) (No 1) [1999] 1 FLR 1014 1214
R (A Minor: Abduction), Re [1992] 1 FLR 105. 1152
R (Abduction: Consent), Re [1999] 1 FLR 828 . . . . .1143, 1149
R (Abduction: Habitual Residence), Re [2003] EWHC 1968 (Fam), [2004]
    1 FLR 216 181

R (Abduction: Habitual Residence), Re [2003] EWHC 1968 (Fam) 181
R (Abduction: Hague and European Conventions), Re [1997] 1 FLR 663.................11
R (Abduction: Immigration Concerns), Re [2004] EWHC 2042, [2005] 1 FLR 33 1155
R (Adoption), Re [1967] 1 WLR 34 1211
R (Al-Jedda) v Secretary of State for Defence [2006] EWCA Civ 327, [2007] QB 621,
    [2007] UKHL 58...778, 814, 819
R (Baiai and others) v Secretary of State for the Home Department [2008]
    UKHL 53, [2009] AC 287...992
R (Child Abduction: Acquiescence), Re [1995] 1 FLR 716 ....1143, 1150
R (Children) (Temporary Leave to Remove from Jurisdiction), Re [2014] EWHC 643 1167
R (Haqq) v Knapman [2003] EWHC 3366 (Admin)................................155
R (Minors) (Abduction), Re [1994] 1 FLR 190 1152
R (Minors) (Abduction: Consent), Re [1999] 1 FCR 87 ....1143, 1149
R (Minors: Child Abduction), Re [1995] 1 FLR 716...................1143, 1146, 1150
R (on the application of Baiai and Ors) v Secretary of State for the Home Department
    [2006] EWHC 823 (Admin), [2007] 1 WLR 693, [2006] EWHC 1454 (Admin),......992
R (on the application of Davies) v Revenue and Customs Commissioners [2010] EWCA
    Civ 83 174
R (on the application of Freedom and Justice Party) v Secretary of State for Foreign and
    Commonwealth Affairs [2016] EWHC 2010 (Admin) 510
R (on the application of Kibris Turk Hava Yollari) v Secretary of State for Transport
    [2009] EWHC 1918 (Admin), [2010] 1 All ER (Comm) 253.....................497
R (on the application of Montana) v Secretary of State for the Home Department
    [2001] 1 FLR 449 1194
R (on the application of Sultan of Pahang) v Secretary of State for the Home
    Department [2011] EWCA Civ 616, (2011) Times, 13 June.....................509
R (on the application of Thomson) v Minister of State for Children [2005] EWHC 1378,
    [2006] 1 FLR 175 1220–1
R (on the application of Tigere) v Secretary of State for Business, Innovation and Skills
    [2015] UKSC 57 173–4
R (On the application of W) v Secretary of State for Health [2015] EWCA Civ 1034.........173
R (on the application of Williams) v France [2012] EWHC 2128 (Admin) 15
R (Recognition of Indian Adoption), Re [2012] EWHC 2956.....................1225, 1227
R (Shamsun Nahar) v The Social Security Commissioners [2001] EWHC Admin 1049,
    [2002] 1 FLR 670 944
R (Williams) v Horsham District Council [2004] EWCA Civ 39, [2004] 1 WLR 1137 150
R and McDonnell v Leong Ba Chai [1954] 1 DLR 401...........................1204
R and S S Hanbury-Brown, In the Marriage of (1996) 20 Fam LR 334.................1097
R Griggs Group Ltd v Evans [2004] EWHC 1088 (Ch), [2005] Ch 153.............488, 495
R v Ali Mohamed [1964] 2 QB 350...894, 942
R v Anderson (1868) LR 1 CCR 161...876, 908
R v Atakpu [1993] 4 All ER (Ch D) 215 1271
R v Barnet London Borough Council, ex p Shah see Shah v Barnet London Borough R v
    Bottrill [1947] KB 41..176, 1096
R v Bow Street Magistrate, ex p Pinochet (No 1) [2000] 1 AC 61 ....499, 516
R v Bow Street Magistrate, ex p Pinochet (No 3) [2000] 1 AC 147 ....499, 516
R v Brentwood Superintendent Registrar of Marriages, ex p Arias [1968] 2 QB 956 . 52, 53,
    71, 917, 919
R v Brixton Prison Governor, ex p Caldough [1961] 1 All ER 606.....................106
R v Cambridge County Court, ex p Ireland [1985] Fam Law 23 101
R v Carmenza Jiminez-Paez (1993) 98 Cr App Rep 239.............................516
R v Carr (1882) 10 QBD 76 908
R v D [2016] EWHC 1154 1160
R v Department of Health, ex p Misra [1996] 1 FLR 129 943
R v Forsyth (1997) Times, 8 April, CA...83

R v Gordon-Finlayson, ex p an Officer [1941] 1 KB 171 908
R v Governor of Pentonville Prison, ex p Osman (No 2) [1989] COD 446 510
R v Governor of Pentonville Prison, ex p Teja [1971] 2 QB 274 510
R v Hammer [1923] 2 KB 786 109
R v Hammersmith Superintendent Registrar of Marriages, ex p Mir-Anwarrudin
    [1917] 1 KB 634 1013
R v Harrow Crown Court, ex p UNIC Centre Sarl [2000] 1 WLR 2122 205
R v Humphrys [1977] AC 1 568
R v Ilich [1935] NZLR 90 110
R v Immigration Appeal Tribunal, ex p Asfar Jan [1995] Imm AR 440 ....937, 1023
R v Immigration Appeal Tribunal, ex p Hasna Begum [1995] Imm AR 249 943
R v Immigration Appeal Tribunal, ex p Rafika Bibi [1989] Imm AR 1 924
R v Immigration Appeal Tribunal, ex p Siggins [1985] Imm AR 14 174
R v Junaid Khan (1987) 84 Cr App Rep 44 ....940, 942
R v Kent County Council, ex p S [2000] 1 FLR 155 175
R v Keyn (1876) 2 Ex D 63 876
R v Lambeth Justices, ex p Yusufu [1985] Crim LR 510 510
R v Lancashire County Council, ex p Huddleston [1986] 2 All ER 941 173
R v M (Validity of Foreign Marriage) [2011] EWHC 2132 ....893, 896, 898
R v Madan [1961] 2 QB 1 513
R v Millis (1844) 10 Cl & Fin 534 903
R v Naguib [1917] 1 KB 359 932
R v Okolie (2000) Times, 16 June, CA 108
R v Okolie (2000) Times, 16 June 108
R v R (Divorce: Hemain Injunction) [2003] EWHC 2113, [2005] 1 FLR 386 978
R v R (Divorce: Jurisdiction: Domicile) [2006] 1 FLR 389 ....148–9, 155–6
R v R (Divorce: Stay of Proceedings) [1994] 2 FLR 1036 974
R v R (Leave to Remove) [2004] EWHC 2572, [2005] 1 FLR 687 1167–8
R v R (Residence Order: Child Abduction) [1995] Fam 209 .... 177, 182–3, 1056,
    1107, 1143
R v Rathbone, ex p Dikko [1985] QB 630 83
R v Registrar General of Births, Deaths and Marriages, ex p Minhas [1977] QB 1 1013
R v Sagoo [1975] QB 885 941
R v Sarwan Singh [1962] 3 All ER 612 941
R v Savage (1876) 13 Cox CC 178 110
R v Secretary of State for the Home Department, ex p Bagga [1991] 1 QB 485 510
R v Secretary of State for the Home Department, ex p Bibi [1985] Imm AR 134 171
R v Secretary of State for the Home Department, ex p Brassey [1989] FCR 423, [1989] 2
    FLR 486 ....1198, 1226, 1229
R v Secretary of State for the Home Department, ex p Fatima [1985] QB 190,
    [1986] AC 527 ....1013, 1015, 1017, 1021, 1024
R v Secretary of State for the Home Department, ex p Margueritte
    [1983] QB 180 173
R v Secretary of State for the Home Department, ex p Mohammed
    Butta [1994] Imm AR 197 175
R v Secretary of State for the Home Department, ex p Zahir Chugtai [1995]
    Imm AR 559 175
R v Turnbull, ex p Petroff (1971) 17 FLR 438 899
R v West London Magistrates' Court, ex p Emmett [1993] 2 FLR 663 ....1064, 1080
R v Williams [1942] AC 541, [1942] 2 All ER 95 1298
R, Petitioner' (2016) Edin L R 82 175
R, Re (1981) 2 FLR 416 1174
Raban v Romania [2011] 1 FLR 1130, [2010] ECHR 1625 1165
Radmacher (formerly Granatino) v Granatino [2010] UKSC 42 ....1372, 1379
Radmacher v Granatino [2010] UKSC 42 1394

Radwan v Radwan (No 2) [1973] Fam 35 . . . . 899–900, 909, 914, 916–17, 919, 923, 931, 937–8, 940
Radwan v Radwan [1973] Fam 24 . . . . 899–900, 935, 1013, 1017
Raffenel's Goods, Re (1863) 3 Sw & Tr 49 162
Rafferty's Restaurant Ltd v Sawchuk [1983] 3 WWR 261 529
Rafidain Bank, Re [1992] BCLC 301 505
Rahimtoola v Nizam of Hyderabad [1958] AC 379 507
Rahmatullah v Secretary of State for Defence [2017] 2 WLR 287, UKSC 1 114
Raiffeisen Zentral Bank Österreich Aktiengesellschaft v National Bank of Greece SA [1999]
    1 Lloyd's Rep 408 253
Raiffeisen Zentralbank Österreich AG v Alexander Tranos [2001] IL Pr 9,
    [2001] IL Pr 85 . . . . 263, 273, 277, 854
Raiffeisen Zentralbank Österreich AG v Five Star General Trading LLC and Ors [2001]
    EWCA Civ 68, [2001] QB 825 . . . . 43, 45, 50, 70, 688, 690–3, 1282, 1289–90, 1299
Raiffeisen Zentralbank Österreich AG v National Bank of Greece SA [1999]
    1 Lloyd's Rep 408 . . . . 253, 263, 268, 273, 277
Rainford v Newell Roberts [1962] IR 95 540
Rakusens Ltd (A Company) v Baser Ambalaj Plastik Sanayi Ticaret AS [2001]
    EWCA Civ 1820, [2002] 1 BCLC 104 329
Ralli Bros v Cia Naviera Sota y Aznar [1920] 2 KB 287 769–70
Ralph Schmid v Lilly Hertel, (C-328/12) ECLI:EU:C:2014:6 .1318
Ralston, Re [1906] VLR 689 1351
Ramos v Ramos (1911) 27 TLR 515 894
Ramsamy v Babar [2003] EWCA Civ 1252, [2005] 1 FLR 113 941
Rank Film Distributors Ltd v Lanterna Editrice SRL [1992] IL Pr 58 251–3
Rank Film Distributors v Lanterna Editrice Srl [1992] IL Pr 58 . . . . .251–3, 455
Rapisarda v Colladon (Irregular Divorces) [2014] EWFC 35 984
Rastelli Davide e C Snc v Jean-Charles Hidoux (qualitate qua) (C-191/10)
    ECLI:EU:C:2011:838 . . . . .1315, 1318
Ratanachai v Ratanachai [1960] CLY 480 1018
Raulin v Fischer [1911] 2 KB 93 553
Ravat v Halliburton Manufacturing & Services Ltd [2012] UKSC 1, [2012]
    2 All ER 905 143
Ray v Sekhri [2014] EWCA Civ 119 . . . . 157, 165, 955
Rayner v Davies [2002] EWCA Civ 1880, [2003] IL Pr 15 . . . . 268, 294, 741
Razelos v Razelos (No 2) [1970] 1 WLR 392 . . . . .324, 333, 486, 488–9, 1073, 1256
RB v DB [2015] EWHC 1817 . . . . .1102, 1122
RC and BC (Child Abduction) (Brussels II Revised: Article 11(7)),
    Re [2009] 1 FLR 574 1160
RD (Child Abduction) (Brussels II Revised: Arts 11(7) and 19), Re [2009] 1 FLR 586 1160
Realchemie Nederland BV v Bayer CropScience AG (C-406/09) [2011]
    ECR I-9773 . . . . 126, 195, 205, 613
Recognition of a Default Judgment, Re (Case 16 W 12/02) [2005] IL Pr 23 637
Red Sea Insurance Co Ltd v Bouygues SA [1995] 1 AC 190 . . . . .777, 818
Reddington v Riach's Executor 2002 SLT 537 . . . . .148, 155–7
Redhead v Redhead and Crothers [1926] NZLR 131 . . . . .333, 546
Reed v Clark [1986] Ch 1 173
Reed v Reed (1969) 6 DLR (3d) 617 921
Reefer Creole, The [1994] 1 Lloyd's Rep 584 380
Reeve v Plummer [2014] EWHC 4695 (QB), [2015] IL Pr 19 .638
Reeves v One World Challenge LLC [2006] 2 NZLR 184 574
Reeves v Sprecher [2007] EWHC 117 (Ch) 379
Refco Inc v ETC [1999] 1 Lloyd's Rep 159 . . . . .307, 341

Refcomp SpA v Axa Corporate Solutions Assurance SA (C-543/10) EU:C:2013:62,
    [2013] 1 Lloyd's Rep 449 . . . . .242, 246
Regas Ltd v Plotkins (1961) 29 DLR (2d) 282 . . . . .86, 1290
Regazzoni v K C Sethia (1944) Ltd [1956] 2 QB 490, [1958] AC 301 . . . . .118, 137, 753
Régie National des Usines Renault SA v Zhang [2002] 187 ALR 1 94
Régie Nationale des Usines Renault SA v Zhang [2002] HCA 10, (2003) 210
    CLR 491 . . . . .94, 394, 398, 777
Regina (Williams) v Horsham District Council [2004] EWCA Civ 39, [2004]
    1 WLR 1137 150
Regina and Palacios, Re (1984) 45 OR (2d) 269 513
Reichert v Dresdner Bank (No 2) (C-261/90) [1992] ECR I-2149 . . . . .225, 266
Reichhold Norway ASA v Goldman Sachs International [2000] 1 WLR 173 . . . . .417, 421
Reichling v Wampach [2002] IL Pr 42 288
Reid, In the Goods of (1866) LR 1 P & D 74 1350
Reid, Re (1970) 17 DLR (3d) 199 118
Reiner v Marquis of Salisbury (1876) 2 Ch D 378 485
Reinsurance Australia Corporation Ltd v HIH Casualty and General Insurance (in
    Liquidation) [2003] FCA 56 395
Reisch Montage AG v Kiesel Baumaschinen Handels GmbH (C-103/05) [2006] ECR I-
    6827 . . . . .284, 287
Relational LLC v Hodges [2011] EWCA Civ 774, [2012] IL Pr 4 .551
Relfo Ltd v Varsani [2009] EWHC 2297 . . . . .116, 559
Reliance Globalcom Ltd v OTE International Solutions SA [2011] EWHC 1848 261
Reliance Industries Ltd v Enron Oil and Gas India Ltd [2002] 1 Lloyd's Rep 645 107
Rellis v Hart 1993 SLT 738 . . . . .176–7, 182
Rena K, The [1979] QB 377 . . . . .385, 418–19
Renate Ilsinger v Martin Dreschers (Administrator in the Insolvency of
    Schlank & Schick GmbH) (C-180/06) [2009] ECR I-3961 . . . . .250, 292, 294
Rep 398 480
Rep 588 . . . . .473–5, 494
Republic of Ecuador v Occidental Exploration and Production Co [2005] EWCA Civ
    1116, [2006] QB 432 502
Republic of Haiti v Duvalier [1990] 1 QB 202 . . . . .305–6, 380
Republic of India v India Steamship Co Ltd (No 2) [1998] AC 878 . . . . .384, 390, 447, 557, 560
Republic of India v India Steamship Co Ltd [1993] AC 410 . . . . .557, 560, 583
Republic of Kazakhstan v Istil Group Inc [2006] EWHC 448 (Comm), [2006] 2 Lloyd's
    Rep 370 559
Republic of Pakistan v Zardari [2006] EWHC 2411 (Comm), [2006]
    2 CLC 667 . . . . .356, 357–9, 363, 377
Republic of Somalia v Woodhouse Drake & Carey (Suisse) SA [1993] QB 54 497
Republica de Guatemala v Nunez [1927] 1 KB 669 . . . . .140, 761, 1282,
                                                                                    1285, 1287, 1289
Republik Griechenland v Grigorios Nikiforidis (C-135/15)
    ECLI:EU:C:2016:774 . . . . .687, 689, 751, 754, 772
Resort Condominiums International Inc v Bolwell (1994) 118 ALR 655 674
Reuben v Time Inc [2003] EWCA Civ 06, [2003] EWHC 1430 QB 329, 331, 351
Revenue Comrs v Pelly [1940] IR 122 1386
Rewia, The [1991] 1 Lloyd's Rep 69, [1991] 2 Lloyd's Rep 325 . . . . .201, 214, 287, 412
RHSP v EIH [1999] 2 Lloyd's Rep 249 402–5
Ricardo v Garcias (1845) 12 Cl & Fin 368 556
Richard SA v Pavan [1998] IL Pr 193 238
Richard West & Partners (Inverness) Ltd v Dick [1969] 2 Ch 424 . . . . .488, 489
Richardson v Schwarzenegger [2004] EWHC 2422 (QB) .352–4, 887
Richman v Ben-Tovim 2007 (2) SALR 283 529

Riddell, Re (1888) 20 QBD 512 548
Ripon City, The [1897] P 226 383
Risk v Risk [1951] P 50 . . . . .932, 937, 952
Ritchie, Re [1942] 3 DLR 330. 1251
River Rima, The [1988] 1 WLR 758 382
Robb Evans v European Bank Ltd (2004) 61 NSWLR 75 553
Robb Evans v European Bank Ltd [2004] NSWCA 82 122–3
Roberdeau v Rous (1738) 1 Atk 543 485
Robert v Robert [1947] P 164 993–6
Roberta, The (1937) 58 Lloyd's Rep 159 85
Roberts v Soldiers, Sailors, Airmen and Families Association-Forces Help
    [2016] EWHC 2744 288
Roberts, Re [1978] 1 WLR 653 1351
Robertson v Jackson (1845) 2 CB 412 766
Robertson, Re (1885) 2 TLR 178. 159
Robey v Snaefell Mining Co (1887) 20 QBD 152 346
Robinson & Co v Continental Insurance Co of Mannheim [1915] 1 KB 155 497
Robinson v Bland (1760) 1 Wm Bl 234, 2 Burr 1077 . . . . .19, 136
Robinson v Fenner [1913] 3 KB 835 576–7
Robson v Premier Oil and Pipe Line Co [1915] 2 Ch 124 136
Roche Nederland BV v Primus (C-539/03) [2007] IL Pr 9 . . . . .285, 454, 456
Rocklea Spinning Mills Pty Ltd v Consolidated Trading Corpn [1995] 2 VR 181 407
Rockware Glass Ltd v MacShannon [1978] AC 795. .393, 397, 402
Rodenstock GmbH, Re [2011] EWHC 1104 . . . . .1309, 1313
Roerig v Valiant Trawlers [2002] EWCA Civ 21, [2002]
    1 WLR 2304 . . . . .95, 778, 800, 862, 867, 876
Roerig v Valiant Trawlers Ltd [2002] 1 Lloyd's Rep 681 94
Rogers v Markel Corpn [2004] EWHC 1375, [2004] EWHC 2046 97
Rogers-Headicar v Rogers-Headicar [2004] EWCA Civ 1867, [2005]
    2 FCR 1 . . . . .969–70, 1118
Rome v Punjab National Bank (No 2), [1989] 1 WLR 1211 329
Romeyko v Whackett (No 2) (1980) 25 SASR 531 1110
Roneleigh Ltd v MII Exports Inc [1989] 1 WLR 619 .374–5, 405
Rosler v Hilbery [1925] Ch 250. . . . . .336, 339
Rösler v Rottwinkel (241/83) [1986] QB 33 . . . . .218, 222–3, 493
Ross Smith v Ross Smith [1963] AC 280 . . . . .985, 995
Ross v Ross (1894) 25 SCR 307 62
Ross v Ross [1930] AC 1, 6 157
Ross, Re [1930] 1 Ch 377 . . . . .59, 61, 65–6, 68, 71, 491, 1256–7, 1260, 1353, 1385
Rossano v Manufacturers' Life Insurance Co Ltd [1963] 2 QB 352 . . . . .111, 117, 541, 606, 1281
Rotherham Metropolitan Borough Council v J and others [2016] EWHC 1844 (Fam) 1103
Rothnie, The [1996] 2 Lloyd's Rep 206 . . . . .371, 399, 413, 414
Rothwells v Connell (1993) 119 ALR 538 116
Rousillon v Rousillon (1880) 14 Ch D 351 . . . . .133, 529, 532, 540
Rouyer Guillet et Cie v Rouyer Guillet & Co Ltd [1949] 1 All ER 244 112
Rowan v Rowan [1988] ILRM 65, 67 . . . . .148, 162
Rowe v Silverstein [1996] 1 VR 509 484
Royal & Sun Alliance Insurance plc v MK Digital FZE (Cyprus) Ltd [2006]
    EWCA Civ 629, [2006] 2 All ER (Comm) 145 [2006] 2 Lloyd's Rep 110. . . . . 201, 203,
                                                                                216–17, 231, 253
Royal Bank of Canada v Cooperative Centrale Raiffeisen-Boerenleenbank BA [2004]
    EWCA Civ 7, [2004] 1 Lloyd's Rep 471 . . . . .424–5, 428
Royal Bank of Scotland Plc v Highland Financial Partners LP [2013] EWCA Civ 328,
    [2013] 1 CLC 596. 439
Royal Bank of Scotland v Hicks [2010] EWHC 2579 432

Royal Boskalis Westminster NV v Mountain [1999] QB 674–5. . . . . .105, 135–6, 753
Royal Exchange Assurance Co Ltd v Compañía Naviera Santi SA, The Tropaioforos
    [1962] 1 Lloyd's Rep 410 423
Royal v Cudahy Packing Co (1922) 190 NW 427 946
RPS Prodotti Siderurgici Srl v Owners and/or demise charterers of the Sea Maas,
    The Sea Maas [1999] 2 Lloyd's Rep 281, [2000] 1 All ER 536 253
RS v Poland [2015] 2 FLR 848 1165
RSA, Re [1901] 2 KB 32 1247
Rubin v Eurofinance SA [2010] EWCA Civ 895 1311
Rubin v Eurofinance SA [2012] UKSC 46, [2013] 1 AC 236 . . . . 526–7, 529, 539, 543,
                                        545, 594–5, 599, 1311
Rudd v Rudd [1924] P 72 576
Ruding v Smith (1821) 2 Hag Con 371 . . . . .900, 904
Runevič-Vardyn & Wardyn v Vilniaus miesto savivaldybès administacija
    (C-391/09) [2011] ECR I-3787 35
Rush v Savchuck 444 US 320 (1980) 382
Russ v Russ [1964] P 315 . . . . .139, 931–2, 1013
Russell v Smyth (1842) 9 M & W 810 525
Russian Bank for Foreign Trade, Re [1933] Ch 745 . . . . .112, 131
Russian Commercial and Industrial Bank v Comptoir d'Escompte
    de Mulhouse [1923] 2 KB 630 112
Russo-Asiatic Bank, Re [1934] Ch 720 1281
Rutten v Cross Medical Ltd (C-383/95) [1997] ECR I-57, [1997] All ER (EC) 121 196
Ryan v Friction Dynamics Ltd (2000) Times, 14 June 307
Ryanair Ltd v Esso Italiana Srl [2013] EWCA Civ 1450, [2015] 1 All ER
    (Comm) 152 . . . . .237, 410
Ryder Industries Ltd v Chan [2015] HKCFA 32 . . . . .753, 771
Rylands v Fletcher (1868) LR 3 HL 330 829
RZB v NBG [1999] 1 Lloyd's Rep 408 733

S (A Child) (Abduction: Custody Rights), Re [2002] EWCA Civ 908, [2002] 2 FLR 815
    . . . . .176, 182, 1056, 1134, 1152, 1153–4, 1166
S (A Child) (Abduction: Hearing the Child), Re [2014] EWCA Civ 1557 1175
S (A Child) (Abduction: Residence Order), Re [2002] EWCA Civ 1949, [2003] 1 FLR
    1008 . . . . .182, 1056, 1088, 1108, 1134, 1142
S (A Child) (Abduction: Rights of Custody), Re [2012] UKSC 10 . . . . . . .1152–3, 1156, 1065–6
S (A Child) (Enforcement of Foreign Judgment), Re [2009] EWCA Civ 993 1129
S (A Child) (Habitual Residence and Child's Objections) (Brazil), Re [2015] EWCA Civ 2 . . .1147
S (A Child), Re [2015] EWFC 86 1171
S (A Minor) (Abduction), Re [1991] 2 FLR 1, 20, CA 176, 179
S (A Minor) (Abduction), Re [1991] FCR 656, [1991] 2 FLR 1 . . . . .1136, 1141, 1143
S (A Minor) (Abduction: Custody Rights), Re [1993] Fam 242 . . . . . . 176, 182–3, 1136–9,
    1142–6, 1148, 1150–2
S (A Minor) (Abduction: European Convention), Re [1998] AC 750 1136
S (A Minor) (Custody: Habitual Residence), Re [1998] AC 750 . . . . .179, 1136
S (A Minor) (Jurisdiction to Stay Application), Re [1995] 1 FLR 1093 1107
S (A Minor) (Stay of Proceedings), Re [1993] 2 FLR 912 1125
S (Abduction: Acquiescence), Re [1998] 2 FLR 115 1150
S (Abduction: Intolerable Situation: Beth Din), Re [2000] 1 FLR 454 1173
S (Abduction: Return into Care), Re [1999] 1 FLR 843 1148
S (Brussels II: Recognition: Best Interests of Child) (No 1), Re [2003] EWHC 2115, [2004]
    1 FLR 571 . . . . .1128, 1213
S (Child Abduction: Delay), Re [1998] 1 FLR 651 . . . . .1135, 1143, 1145
S (Child Abduction: Joinder of Sibling: Child's Objections), Re [2016]
    EWHC 1227 (Fam) 1156

S (Children) (Child Abduction: Asylum Appeal), Re [2002] EWCA Civ 843,
    [2002] 2 FLR 465 1175
S (Children: Application for Removal from Jurisdiction), Re [2004] EWCA
    Civ 1724, [2005] 1 FCR 471 . . . . .183, 1167–9, 1220
S (H), Re (1995) 13 RFL (4th) 301 1212
S (Hospital Patient: Foreign Curator), Re [1996] Fam 23. . . . . .149, 151, 1176, 1245, 1246
S (Jurisdiction: Prorogation), Re [2013] EWHC 647 . . . . .1115–16, 1099
S (Minors) (Abduction), Re [1994] 1 FLR 297 1173
S (Minors) (Abduction: Acquiescence), Re [1994] 1 FLR 819 . . . . .1146, 1150
S (Minors) (Abduction: Wrongful Retention), Re [1994] Fam 70 . . . . .182, 183, 1136, 1155
S (Parental Order), Re [2009] EWHC 2977 1187
S (S M) v A(J) (1990) 65 DLR (4th) 222. 1138
S (Violent Parent: Indirect Contact), Re [2000] 1 FLR 481 1168
S (Wardship: Summary Return: Non-Convention Country), Re [2015] EWHC 176 1174
S v B (Abduction: Human Rights) [2005] 2 FLR 878 15
S v B (Abduction: Human Rights) [2005] EWHC 733, [2005] 2 FLR 878 . . . . .1153, 1157, 1164
S v D 2007 SLT (Sh Ct) 37 1100–1
S v H (Abduction: Access Rights) [1997] 1 FLR 970 . . . . .1135, 1137
S v S (Abduction: Wrongful Retention) [2009] EWHC 1494 . . . . .1135–6, 1141
S v S (Brussels II Revised: Articles 19(1) and (3): Reference to ECJ) [2014]
    EWHC 3613 . . . . .964, 969–70
S v S (Child Abduction: Custody Rights: Acquiescence) 2003 SLT 344 1136
S v S (Custody: Jurisdiction) [1995] 1 FLR 155 . . . . .1112, 1134
S v S (Hemain Injunction) [2009] EWHC 3224 (Fam) 978–9
S v S [1997] 2 FLR 100 . . . . .895, 973–4, 985, 1076
S&T Bautrading v Nordling [1997] 3 All ER 718 612
S&W Berisford plc and NGI Precious Metals Inc v New Hampshire Insurance Co
    [1990] 1 Lloyd's Rep 454 370
S&W Berisford plc v New Hampshire Insurance Co [1990] 2 All ER 321 . . . . .235, 289, 460, 467
S(M), Re [1971] Ch 621 1174
S, Re (Hospital Patient: Foreign Curator) [1996] Fam 23. . . . . .149, 151, 1176, 1245–6
S, Re (Residence Order: Forum Conveniens) [1995] 1 FLR 314 . . . . .1112, 1125
SA (Vulnerable Adult with Capacity: Marriage), Re [2005] EWHC 2942 (Fam),
    [2006] 1 FLR 867 909
SA Consortium General Textiles v Sun and Sand Agencies Ltd [1978] QB 279,
    [1978] 2 All ER 339. . . . . .119, 243, 532, 539, 552, 575, 594–6, 598
SA Marie Brizzard et Roger International v William Grant & Sons Ltd (No 2)
    2002 SLT 1365 . . . . .14, 630
Saab v Saudi American Bank [1999] 1 WLR 1861 . . . . .329, 331, 343, 350
Saba Molnlycke AS v Procter & Gamble Scandinavia Inc [1997] IL Pr 704 . . . . .264, 275
Sabah Shipyard (Pakistan) Ltd v Islamic Republic of Pakistan [2002] EWCA Civ 1643,
    [2003] 2 Lloyd's Rep 571 . . . . .422, 424–5, 441, 506, 508
Sabbagh v Khoury [2014] EWHC 3233 287
Sabbagh v Sabbagh [1985] FLR 29 . . . . .142, 1011, 1027, 1029, 1061, 1077
Sabeh El Leil v France, Judgment of 29 June 2011; (2012) 54 EHRR 14. . . . . .501, 503
Sachs v Standard Chartered Bank (Ireland) Ltd [1987] ILRM 297 . . . . .1064, 1078
Sadler v Robins (1808) 1 Camp 253 551–2
Sahar v Tsitsekkos [2004] EWHC 2659 (Ch) 356
Said Ajami v Customs Comptroller [1954] 1 WLR 1405 110
Saipem Spa v Dredging V02 BV and Geosite Surveys Ltd, The Volvox Hollandia [1988] 2
    Lloyd's Rep 361 407
Salaman, Re [1908] 1 Ch 4 1201
Salfinger v Niugini Mining (Australia) Pty Ltd (No 3) [2007] FCA 1532. . . . . .1285, 1288
Salvesen v Administrator of Austrian Property [1927] AC 641 . . . . .528, 545, 894, 898
Salvesen's Trs 1993 SC 14. 1229

Salzgitter Mannesmann Handel GmbH v SC Laminorul SA (C-157/12) EU:C:2013:597,
    [2014] 1 WLR 904 641
Samcrete Egypt Engineers and Contractors SAE v Land Rover Exports Ltd [2001] EWCA
    Civ 2019, [2002] CLC 533 ....344, 369, 715, 721–2, 725, 733, 736
Samengo-Turner v J & H Marsh & McLennan (Services) Ltd [2007] EWCA Civ 723,
    [2007] IL Pr 52 ....299, 301, 426, 482
Sanders v Van der Putte (73/77) [1977] ECR 2383 ....218, 251
SanDisk Corpn v Koninklijke Philips Electronics [2007] EWHC 332 (Ch), [2007] IL Pr 22
    ....264, 272, 275, 304
Sandra Nogueira v Crewlink Ltd Miguel José Moreno Osacar v Ryanair Ltd (C-168/16) and
    (C-169/16) EU:C:2017:312. 300
Sandwell Metropolitan Borough Council v RG [2013] EWHC 2373 ....987, 991
Sangha v Mander (1985) 47 RFL (2d) 212 ....994, 995
Sanicentral GmbH v Collin (25/79) [1979] ECR 3423 ....204, 233
Sar Schotte GmbH v Parfums Rothschild Sarl (218/86) [1987] ECR 4905 ....280, 282
Sara v Sara (1962) 31 DLR (2d) 566, 36 DLR (2d) 499 937
Sarrio SA v Kuwait Investment Authority [1997] 1 Lloyd's Rep 113, [1999] 1 AC 32 . . 446,
    454–7, 468–70, 977
Saudi Arabia v Nelson [1993] IL Pr 555. 504
Saunders v Drake (1742) 2 Atk 465 1348
Saunders v Saunders 796 So 2d 1253 (Fla App 2001) 1353
Savelieff v Glouchkoff (1964) 45 DLR (2d) 520 996
Savenis v Savenis [1950] SASR 309 905
Saxby v Fulton [1909] 2 KB 208 105
Sayce v Ameer Ruler Sadig Mohammad Abbasi Bahawalpur State [1952] 2 QB 390 509
Sayers v International Drilling Co NV [1971] 1 WLR 1176 ....748, 876, 879
SB (Bangladesh) v Secretary of State for the Home Department [2007]
    EWCA Civ 28, [2007] Fam Law 494. 944
Scania Finance SA v Rockinger Spezialfabrik Fur Anhangerkupplungen
    GmbH & Co (C-522/03) [2006] IL Pr 1 ....633, 635
Scappaticci v A-G [1955] P 47. 155–6
Scarfe v Matthews [2012] EWHC 3071. 1352
Scarpetta v Lowenfeld (1911) 27 TLR 509. 577
SCB v PNSC [1995] 2 Lloyd's Rep 365 412
SCET v Extrucable (Societe) [2013] IL Pr 25. 658
SCF Finance Co Ltd v Masri (No 3) [1987] QB 1028. 1293
Schaffenius v Goldberg [1916] 1 KB 284. 497
Schapira v Ahronson [1998] IL Pr 587. ....106, 351, 400
Scheer v Rockne Motors Corpn 68 F 2d 942 (1934) 25
Scheffer v Scheffer [1967] NZLR 466 1110
Schemmer v Property Resources Ltd [1975] Ch 273 ....87, 119, 543
Schering Ltd v Stockholms Enskilda Bank Aktiebolag [1946] AC 219. 497
Scherrens v Maenhout (158/87) [1988] ECR 3791 219
Schibsby v Westenholz (1870) LR 6 QB 155 ....526, 529, 531, 540–2
Schintz, Re [1926] Ch 710. 339
Schlesinger, In the Goods of [1950] CLY 1549 1039
Schmidt v Government Insurance Office of New South Wales [1973] 1 NSWLR 59. .....55, 816
Schmidt v Schmidt (C-417/15) EU:C:2016:881 ....206, 220, 246, 261, 809
Schnabel v Yung Lui [2002] NSWSC 115 ....119, 136, 549–50, 553, 575
Schnapper, Re [1928] Ch 420 1340
Schneider's Estate, Re, 96 NYS 2d 652 (Surr Ct 1950) 71
Scholefield, Re [1905] 2 Ch 408 1364
Schorsch Meier GmbH v Hennin [1975] QB 416. 98
Schreiber v Canada (Attorney General) (2002) 216 DLR (4th) 513. 505–6
Schreiber v Federal Republic of Germany (2001) 196 DLR (4th) 281 506

Schreter and Gasmac Inc, Re (1992) 89 DLR (4th) 365 675
Schwartz v Schwartz 103 Ariz 562, 447 P 2d 254 (1968). 816
Schwebel v Schwebel (1970) 10 DLR (3d) 742 1035–6
Schwebel v Ungar (1963) 42 DLR (2d) 622, (1964) 48 DLR (2d) 644 . . . . .53, 917, 920
SCOR v Eras EIL (No 2) [1995] 2 All ER 278 . . . . .429, 430, 554
Scott v A-G (1886) 11 PD 128 927
Scott v Avery (1856) 5 HL Cas 811 535
Scott v Bentley (1855) 1 K & J 281 1247
Scott v Pilkington (1862) 2 B & S 11 550
Scott, Re (1874) 22 WR 748 1245
Scottish & Newcastle International Ltd v Othon Ghalanos Ltd [2008]
    UKHL 11, [2008] 1 Lloyd's Rep 462 258
Scottish National Orchestra Society Ltd v Thomson's Executor 1969 SLT 325. . . . . . . .118, 1334
Scottish Provident Institution v Cohen (1888) 16 R 112 1284
Scottish Provident Institution v Robinson (1892) 29 SLR 733. . . . . .1284, 1288
Scotts of Greenock Ltd and Lithgows Ltd v United Kingdom (1986) A 102 1278
Scrimshire v Scrimshire (1752) 2 Hag Con 395, 161 ER 782 .20, 893
SCT Industri (C-111/08) [2009] ECR I-5655. . . . . .207, 1321
Scullion v Scullion 1990 SCLR 577. 1107
Sea Assets Ltd v PT Garuda Indonesia [2000] 4 All ER 371. 331
Sea Maas, The see RPS Prodotti Siderurgici srl v Owners and/or demise
    charterers of the Sea Maas, The Sea Maas 253
Sea Trade Maritime Corpn v Hellenic Mutual War Risks Association (Bermuda)
    Ltd (The Athena) (No 2) [2006] EWHC 2530 (Comm), [2007] 1 Lloyd's Rep 280 235
Seaconsar Far East Ltd v Bank Markazi Jomhouri Islami Iran [1994] 1 AC 438. . . . . . . .335, 363
Sealey (otherwise Callan) v Callan [1953] P 135 978
Seashell Shipping Corpn v Mutualidad de Seguros Del Instituto Nacional De
    Industria, The Magnum ex Tarraco Augusta [1989] 1 Lloyd's Rep 47. . . . . .368, 373
Seat Pagine Gialle Spa, Re [2012] EWHC 3686. 1310
Sebba, Re [1959] Ch 166. 108
Secret Hotels 2 Ltd v EA Traveller Ltd [2010] EWHC 1023 (Ch), [2010] IL Pr 33. 445
Secretary of State for the Home Department v Lofthouse [1981] Imm AR 166 1223
Secretary of State for Work and Pensions v Jones (2003) Times, 13 August 1052
Secure Capital SA v Credit Suisse AG [2015] EWHC 388 (Comm) 45
Seedat's Executors v The Master 1917 AD 302. 1196
Seismic Shipping Inc v Total E&P UK plc (The Western Regent) [2005]
    EWCA Civ 985, [2005] 2 Lloyd's Rep 359 . . . . .425, 427–8, 432, 801, 860, 862, 867
Sell v Miller 11 Ohio State 331 (1860). 1258
Sellars v Sellars 1942 SC 206 160
Selot's Trusts, Re [1902] 1 Ch 488 139–40
Sembawang Salvage Pte Ltd v Shell Todd Oil Services Ltd [1993] 2 NZLR 97 382
Senator Hanseatische, Re [1996] 2 BCLC 562. . . . . .205, 224
Sengupta v Republic of India [1983] ICR 221. 505
Sennar, The (No 2) [1984] 2 Lloyd's Rep 142, [1985] 1 WLR 490 . . 411–12, 414–15, 470,
    559–62 588, 600
Serge Caudron v Air Zaire [1986] ILRM 10. . . . . .336, 382
Serious Fraud Office v Saleh [2015] EWHC 2119 (QB), [2015] Lloyd's Rep
    FC 629. . . . . .544, 547, 560, 563
Seroka v Bellah 1995 SLT 304 1138
SerVaas Inc v Rafidain Bank [2012] UKSC 40, [2013] 1 AC 595 509
Service Temps Inc v MacLeod [2013] CSOH 162, 2014 SLT 375 . . . . .120, 539, 554, 575–6
Services Europe Atlantique Sud v Stockholms Rederiaktiebolag SVEA, The Folias [1979]
    AC 685; [1979] QB 491 . . . . .99, 101–2, 104
SET Select Energy GmbH v F&M Bunkering Ltd [2014] EWHC 192 (Comm), [2014] 1
    Lloyd's Rep 652 446

Sethi v Sethi 1995 SLT 104 1080
Settebello Ltd v Banco Toto and Acores [1985] 1 WLR 1050, 1056, CA 13, 130
Seven Arts Entertainment Ltd v Content Media Corp Plc [2013] EWHC 588 . . . . .551, 560
Seven Licensing Co Sarl v FFG-Platinum SA [2011] EWHC 2967 (Comm),
    [2012] IL Pr 7 455
Sextum, The [1982] 2 Lloyd's Rep 532 385
SF v HL [2015] EWHC 2891 . . . . .1107, 1124
Sfeir & Co v National Insurance Co of New Zealand Ltd [1964] 1 Lloyd's
    Rep 330 . . . . .532, 591
SH v HH [2011] EWCA Civ 796 1110
SH v NB [2009] EWHC 3274 . . . . .986, 989, 991, 1050–1
Shaffer v Heitner 433 US 186 (1977) 382
Shagroon v Shabartly [2012] EWCA Civ 1507 . . . . .894–5, 985, 1077
Shah v Barnet London Borough [1983] 2 AC 309, 342 . . . . .173–6, 181
Shahar v Tsitsekkos [2004] EWHC 2659 .224, 334, 339, 348, 357, 1298
Shahnaz v Rizwan [1965] 1 QB 390 . . . . .139, 943
Shaker v El-Bedrawi [2002] EWCA Civ 1452, [2003] Ch 350 106
Shami v Shami [2012] EWHC 664 (Ch), [2013] EWCA Civ 227 . . . . .491, 546, 597
Shamil Bank of Bahrain EC v Bexico Pharmaceuticals Ltd [2004] 1 WLR 1784,
    [2004] EWCA Civ 19 105
Shamil Bank of Bahrain v Beximco Pharmaceuticals Ltd [2004] EWCA Civ 19,
    [2004] 1 WLR 1784 . . . . .714–15, 717
Shanks v Shanks 1965 SLT 330 . . . . .160, 166
Shannon v Global Tunnelling Experts UK Ltd [2015] EWHC 1267 285
Shanshal v Al-Kishtaini [2001] EWCA Civ 264 at [50]–[62], [2001] 2 All ER (Comm) 601 . . .15
Shanshal v Al-Kishtaini [2001] EWCA Civ 264, [2001] 2 All ER (Comm) 601 15
Sharab v Prince Al-Waleed Al-Saud [2009] EWCA Civ 353, [2009]
    2 Lloyd's Rep 160 . . . . .343, 346, 366, 374, 376, 396
Sharab v Prince Al-Waleed Al-Saud [2012] EWHC 1798 (Ch),
    [2012] 2 CLC 612 342
Sharif v Azad [1967] 1 QB 605 . . . . .112, 118
Sharif v Sharif (1980) 10 Fam Law 216 . . . . .1013, 1017, 1022, 1024, 1029–30
Sharp v Ministry of Defence [2007] EWHC 224 (QB) 105–6
Sharpe v Crispin (1869) LR 1 P & D 611 . . . . .160, 168
Sharps Commercials Ltd v Gas Turbines Ltd [1956] NZLR 819 .606
Shaw v Gould (1868) LR 3 HL 55 . . . . .52, 917, 1195–7
Shaw v Hungary [2012] 2 FLR 1314, [2011] ECHR 6457/ 09 1165
Shaw v Shaw [1979] Fam 62 . . . . .511, 513
Shearson Lehman Bros Inc v Maclaine Watson & Co Ltd (International
    Tin Council intervening) (No 2) [1988] 1 WLR 16 507
Sheffield City Council v E [2004] EWHC 2808, [2005] 1 FLR 965 909
Shekleton v Shekleton [1972] 2 NSWR 675 165
Shell International Petroleum Co Ltd v Coral Oil Co Ltd (No 2) [1999]
    2 Lloyd's Rep 606 . . . . .430, 713
Shell International Petroleum Co Ltd v Coral Oil Co Ltd [1999] 1 Lloyd's Rep 72 . . . . . .430, 713
Shell Tankers (UK) Ltd v Astro Comino Armadora SA [1981] 2 Lloyd's Rep 40 . . . . .97, 99
Shell UK Exploration and Production Ltd v Innes 1995 SLT 807 . . . . .428, 430
Shelling v Farmer (1725) 1 Stra 646, 93 ER 756 20
Shemshadfard v Shemshadfard [1981] 1 All ER 726 973–4
Shenavai v Kreischer (266/85) [1987] ECR 239 . . . . .247, 298, 734
Sherdley v Nordea Life and Pensions SA [2012] EWCA Civ 88, [2013] IL Pr 26 . . . . .291, 302
Shergill v Khaira [2014] UKSC 33, [2015] AC 359 114
Shetty v Al Rushaid Petroleum Investment Co [2011] EWHC 1460 288
Shevill v Presse Alliance SA (C-68/93) [1995] 2 AC 18 . . . . .217, 263
Shiblaq v Sadikoglu [2004] EWHC 1890 (Comm), [2004] IL Pr 51 . . . . .111–12, 326, 381

Shipowners' Mutual Protection and Indemnity Association (Luxembourg) v
  Containerships Denizcilik Nakliyat ve Ticaret AS [2016] EWCA Civ 386,
  [2016] 1 Lloyd's Rep 641 441–2
Shoesmith, Re [1938] 2 KB 637 75
Short v British Nuclear Fuels plc [1997] IL Pr 747. 204
Short v Ireland [1997] 1 ILRM 161 348
Showlag v Mansour [1995] 1 AC 431 . . . . .583, 676
Shrichand & Co v Lacon (1906) 22 TLR 245 96
Sibir Energy Ltd v Tchigirinski [2012] EWHC 1844 (QB), [2012] 2 All ER (Comm) 1285 . . .287
Siboti K/ S v BP France SA [2003] EWHC 1278 (Comm), [2003] 2 Lloyd's
  Rep 364 . . . . .234, 241, 239
Siegfried János Schneider (C-386/12) EU:C:2013:633, [2014] 2 WLR 1048 . . . . .51, 206
Sierra Leone Telecommunications Co Ltd v Barclays Bank plc [1998]
  2 All ER 821 . . . . .497, 733, 739, 1308–9
Sigurdson v Farrow (1981) 121 DLR (3d) 183. . . . . .104, 134
Sill v Worswick (1791) 1 Hy Bl 665. 1264
Silver Athens, The (No 2) [1986] 2 Lloyd's Rep 583 385
Silver v Silver [1955] 1 WLR 728. 987
Sim v Robinow (1892) 19 R 665 395
Simon Engineering plc v Butte Mining plc (No 2) [1996] 1 Lloyd's Rep 91. . . . . .430, 554
Simon v Byford [2014] EWCA Civ 280. 1339
Simona Kornhaas v Thomas Dithmar (qualitate qua), (C-594/14)
  ECLI:EU:C:2015:806 . . . . .1319, 1321
Simonin v Mallac (1860) 2 Sw & Tr 67 . . . . .48–9, 761, 899
Simons v Simons [1939] 1 KB 490, [1938] 4 All ER 436 1079
Simpson v Fogo (1863) 1 Hem & M 195 . . . . .564, 1271
Simpson v Intralinks Ltd [2012] ICR 1343 302
Simpson, Re [1916] 1 Ch 502 1364
Sinclair v Cracker Barrel Old Country Store Inc (2002) 213 DLR (4th) 643 349
Sinclair v Sinclair [1968] P 189 1062
Sinclair v Sinclair 1988 SLT 87 1174
Sindh, The [1975] 1 Lloyd's Rep 372. 414
Sinfra Akt v Sinfra Ltd [1939] 2 All ER 675 112
Singh (Pawandeep) v Entry Clearance Officer (New Delhi) [2004]
  EWCA Civ 1075, [2005] QB 608 1224–5
Singh v Singh 2005 SLT 749 . . . . .960–1, 964, 986, 989, 992
Singularis Holdings SA v PricewaterhouseCoopers [2014] UKPC 36. 1310
Sinha Peerage Claim (1939) 171 Lords Journals 350, [1946] 1 All ER 348 934
Sinochem International Oil (London) Co Ltd v Mobil Sales and Supply Corp
  (No 2) [2000] 1 Lloyd's Rep 670 . . . . .235, 366, 398, 410, 412, 462
Sinocore International Co Ltd v RBRG Trading (UK) Ltd [2017] EWHC 251 (Comm),
  [2017] 1 Lloyd's Rep 375. 676
Siporex Trade SA v Comdel Commodities Ltd [1986] 2 Lloyd's Rep 428. 560
Sirdar Gurdyal Singh v The Rajah of Faridkote [1894] AC 670 . . . . .528–9, 532
Siskina (Cargo Owners) v Distos Cia Naviera SA, The Siskina [1979] AC 210. . . . . . . .336, 382
Sit Woo-tung, Re [1990] 2 HKLR 410 . . . . .1198, 1201
Six Constructions Ltd v Humbert (32/88) [1989] ECR 341 . . . . .298, 301
Six Widows' case (1908) 12 Straits Settlements LR 120 943
SK (India) v Secretary of State for the Home Department [2007] Imm A R 142 1230
SK v KP [2005] 3 NZLR 590 . . . . .176, 178
Skogvik v Sveriges Television AB [2003] IL Pr 417. 270
Skrine & Co v Euromoney Publications plc (2000) Times, 10 November 403
Skrine & Co v Euromoney Publications plc [2002] EMLR 15. . . . . .15, 137
Skype Technologies SA v Joltid Ltd [2009] EWHC 2783 (Ch), [2011] IL Pr 8 . . . . .466, 471, 481
Slater v Mexican National Rly Co 194 US 120 (1904). 91–2

SMAY Investments Ltd v Sachdev (Practice Note) [2003] EWHC 474 (Ch),
  [2003] 1 WLR 1973 ....334, 369
SMI Group Ltd v Levy [2012] EWHC 3078 ....264, 276
Smijth v Smijth (1918) 1 SLR 156 1194
Smit Tak International Zeesleepen Berginsbedrijk BV v Selco Salvage Ltd
  [1988] 2 Lloyd's Rep 398 100
Smith Kline & French Laboratories Ltd v Bloch [1983] 1 WLR 730 430
Smith v Huertas [2015] EWHC 3745 630
Smith v Hughes [2003] EWCA Civ 656, [2003] 1 WLR 2441 327
Smith v Nicolls (1839) 5 Bing NC 208 564
Smith v Smith 1962 (3) SA 930 160
Smith, Lawrence v Kitson, Re [1916] 2 Ch 206 ....487, 1259
Smith's Goods, Re (1850) 2 Rob Eccl 332 160
Smith's Trustees v Macpherson 1926 SC 983 1348
Smyth v Behbehani [1999] IL Pr 584 407
Smyth, Re [1898] 1 Ch 89 1390
Šneersone and Kampanella v Italy [2011] 2 FLR 1322 1165
Snookes v Jani-King (GB) Ltd [2006] EWHC 289 (QB), [2006]
  IL Pr 19 ....202, 233, 237, 319, 412
Société Commerciale de Réassurance v Eras International Ltd (No 2) [1995]
  2 All ER 278 482
Société Cooperative Sidmetal v Titan International Ltd [1966] 1 QB 828 ....543, 597, 606
Société d'Informatique Service Réalisation Organisation (SISRO) v
  Ampersand Software BV (C-432/93) [1994] IL Pr 55, [1996]
  QB 127 ....621, 624, 628, 647, 649
Société des Hôtels Réunis SA v Hawker (1913) 29 TLR 578 135
Société Eram [2001] 2 Lloyd's Rep 394 106
Société Eram Shipping Co Ltd v Compagnie Internationale de Navigation [2001] EWCA
  Civ 1317, [2001] 2 Lloyd's Rep 627, [2003] UKHL 30, [2004] 105, 131, 1281, 1293–4
Société Eram Shipping Co Ltd v Compagnie Internationale de Navigation
  [2003] UKHL 30, [2004] 1 AC 260 ....105, 131
Société Financière & Industrielle du Peloux v Société AXA Belgium (C-112/03)
  [2006] QB 251 241
Société Francaise Bunge SA v Belcan NV [1985] 3 All ER 378 102
Société Générale de Paris v Dreyfus Bros (1885) 29 Ch D 239 366
Societe Generale v Goldas Kuyumculuk Sanayi Ithalat Ihracat AS [2017]
  EWHC 667 (Comm) 381
Société Nationale Industrielle Aérospatiale v Lee Kui Jak [1987] AC 871 at 895 4
Société Nationale Industrielle Aérospatiale v United States District Court
  for the Southern District of Iowa 107 S Ct 2542 (1987) 4, 83, 423, 426–7
Société ND Conseil SA v Société Le Meridien Hotels [2007] IL Pr 39 ....257, 543
Société Nouvelle des Papeteries de l'Aa v Machinefabriek BOA 25 September,
  NJ (1992) No 750, RvdW (1992) No 207 736
Society of Lloyd's v Fraser [1999] Lloyd's Rep IR 156 ....137, 753
Society of Lloyd's v Hyslop [1993] 3 NZLR 135 ....394, 411
Society of Lloyd's v Price; Society of Lloyd's v Lee 2006 5 SA 393 (SCA) 78
Society of Lloyd's v Romahn 2006 4 SA 23 78
Society of Lloyd's v Saunders (2001) 210 DLR (4th) 519 ....574, 577, 598
Society of Lloyd's v Tropp [2004] EWHC 33 (Comm) 326
Society of Lloyd's v White (No 1) [2002] IL Pr 10, (No 2) [2002] IL Pr 11 ....439, 440
Society of Lloyd's v X [2009] IL Pr 12 630
Sohio Supply Co v Gatoil (USA) Inc [1989] 1 Lloyd's Rep 588 ....235, 407, 430
Sohrab v Kahn 2002 SLT 1255 ....986, 992
Soinco SACI v Novokuznetsk Aluminium Plant [1998] 2 Lloyd's Rep 337 ....671, 675
Sokha v Secretary of State for the Home Department 1992 SLT 1049 393

Soleh Boneh International Ltd v Government of the Republic of Uganda and National
    Housing Corpn [1993] 2 Lloyd's Rep 208 673
Soleimany v Soleimany [1998] 3 WLR 811 574
Soleimany v Soleimany [1999] QB 785, CA 137
Solo Kleinmotoren GmbH v Boch (C-414/92) [1994] ECR I-2237 . . . . .612, 626, 639
Solomon v Solomon (1912) 29 WN NSW 68 160
Solomon v Walters (1956) 3 DLR (2d) 78 986
Solomons v Ross (1764) 1 Hy Bl 131 n 20
Solovyev v Solovyeva [2014] EWFC 1546 1001
Solvalub Ltd v Match Investments Ltd [1998] IL Pr 419 . . . . .333, 341
Solvay SA v Honeywell Fluorine Products Europe BV (C-616/10)
    EU:C:2012:445 . . . . .218, 286, 305
Somafer v Saar-Ferngas (33/78) [1978] ECR 2183. . . . . .196, 280
Somers v Fournier (2002) 214 DLR (4th) 611, CA (Ont), [2002] OJ No 2543 (CA) 73
Sommersett's case (1772) 20 State Tr 1. 137
Sonatrach Petroleum Corpn v Ferrell International Ltd [2002] 1 All ER
    (Comm) 627 . . . . .418, 716
Sonntag v Waidmann (C-172/91) [1993] ECR I-1963 . . . . .196, 205–6, 625, 631, 633, 636
Sony Computer Entertainment Ltd v RH Freight Services Ltd [2007]
    EWHC 302 (Comm), [2007] IL Pr 21 . . . . .390, 455
Sottomaior, Re (1874) 9 Ch App 677 1245
Sottomayor v De Barros (1877) 3 PD 1 . . . . .761, 913, 918, 923, 994, 997
Sottomayor v De Barros (No 2) (1879) 5 PD 94 . . . . .761, 918–19, 921, 926, 928, 990
Soucie v Soucie 1995 SLT 414. 1140
Source Ltd v TUV Rheinland Holding AG [1998] QB 54. . . . . .253, 268, 791
South Carolina Co v Assurantie NV [1987] AC 24 . . . . .424–6, 432
South India Shipping Corpn Ltd v Import-Export Bank of Korea [1985] 1 WLR 585. 329
Southcote, Ex p (1751) 2 Ves Sen. 1245
SOVAG— Schwarzmeer und Ostsee Versicherungs-Aktiengesellschaft v If
    Vahinkovakuutusyhtiö Oy (C-521/14) EU:C:2016:41, [2016] QB 780. 288
Sovracht (vo) v Van Udens Scheepvart en Agentuur Maatschappij (NV Gebr)
    [1943] AC 203. 497
Sowa v Sowa [1961] P 70. . . . . .930–1, 933–4, 941
Soya Margareta, The [1961] 1 WLR 709 384
Spalenkova v Spalenkova [1954] P 141 966
Span Terza, The [1982] 1 Lloyd's Rep 225 384–5
Spar Aerospace Ltd v American Mobile Satellite Corpn (2002) 220 DLR (4th) 54 . . . . . .394, 397
Spargos Mining NL v Atlantic Capital Corpn (1995) Times, 11 December 377
Speed Investments Ltd v Formula One Holdings Ltd (No 2) [2004]
    EWCA Civ 1512, [2005] 1 WLR 1936 . . . . .196, 218, 224, 453, 1308–9
Speed Investments Ltd v Formula One Holdings Ltd (No 2) [2004]
    EWCA Civ 1512 . . . . .196, 218, 224
Spence v Spence 1995 SLT 335 . . . . .148, 151, 157
Spence, Re [1989] 2 All ER 679. 1199
Spencer's Trustees v Ruggles 1982 SLT 165 . . . . .1223, 1390
Sperling v Sperling 1975 (3) SA 707 (AD). 1367
Sphere Drake Insurance plc v Gunes Sigorta Anonim Sirketi [1987] 1 Lloyd's Rep 139 333
Spiliada Maritime Corpn v Cansulex Ltd [1987] AC 460 . . . . .4, 335, 345, 365–7, 372, 376,
                                       378–9, 385, 393–4, 399–403, 412, 973, 1124
Spinazzi, Ex p 1985 (3) SA 650 1377
Spitzley v Sommer Exploitation SA (48/84) [1985] ECR 787 227
Spivack v Spivack (1930) 99 LJP 52. 929
Spliethoff's Bevrachtingskantoor BV v Bank of China Ltd [2015] EWHC 999 (Comm);
    [2016] 1 All ER (Comm) 1034; [2015] 2 Lloyd's Rep 123 . . . . .538, 574, 584
Sporting Index Ltd v O'Shea [2015] IEHC 407. 631

SPRL Arcado v SA Haviland (9/87) [1988] ECR 1539 . . . . .250, 688
Srini Vasan v Srini Vasan [1946] P 67 941
SS Celia v SS Volturno [1921] 2 AC 544 . . . . .97, 102
SS Pacific Star v Bank of America National Trust and Savings Association
    [1965] WAR 159 548
SSL International Plc v TTK LIG Ltd [2011] EWCA Civ 1170, [2012]
    1 WLR 1842 . . . . .326, 330, 332
SSQ Europe SA v Johann & Backes OHG [2002] 1 Lloyd's Rep 465. . . . . .228, 231, 240
St Paul Dairy Industries NV v Unibel Exser BVBA (C-104/03) [2005]
    ECR I-3481, [2005] IL Pr 31. 304
St Pierre v South American Stores (Gath and Chaves) Ltd [1936] 1 KB 382 . . . . . . .485, 487, 492
St Vincent European General Partner Ltd v Robinson [2016] EWHC 2920
    (Comm). 612
Stahlwerk Becker Aktiengesellschaft's Patent, Re [1917] 2 Ch 272. .497
Stamps Comrs v Hope [1891] AC 476. 1280
Standard Bank London Ltd v Apostolakis (No 1) [2002] CLC 933 . . . . .232, 235, 292, 297
Standard Bank London Ltd v Apostolakis (No 2) [2002] CLC 939 .232
Standard Bank Plc v EFAD Real Estate Company WLL [2014] EWHC
    1834 (Comm), [2014] 2 All ER (Comm) 208 . . . . .338, 363
Standard Bank Plc v Just Group LLC [2014] EWHC 2687 338
Standard Chartered Bank (Hong Kong) Ltd v Independent Power Tanzania Ltd
    [2016] EWCA Civ 411, [2016] 2 Lloyd's Rep 25. 421
Standard Chartered Bank Ltd v IRC [1978] 1 WLR 1160 1298
Standard Chartered Bank v Zungeru Power Ltd [2014] EWHC 4714 591
Standard Steamship Owners' Protection and Indemnity Association (Bermuda)
    Ltd v Gann [1992] 2 Lloyd's Rep 528 . . . . .231, 240, 291
Standard Steamship Owners' Protection and Indemnity Association (Bermuda)
    Ltd v GIE Vision Bail [2004] EWHC 2919 (Comm), [2005] 1 All ER
    (Comm) 618 . . . . .231, 240, 291
Stanley v Bernes (1830) 3 Hag Ecc 373 149
Star of Luxor, The [1981] 1 Lloyd's Rep 139 411
Star Reefers Pool Inc v JFC Group Co Ltd [2012] EWCA Civ 14, [2012]
    1 Lloyd's Rep 376. . . . . .422, 427–30, 435
Star Texas, The [1993] 2 Lloyd's Rep 445. . . . . .430, 716, 720
Stark v Stark (1979) 94 DLR (3d) 556. . . . . .550, 573
Stark v Stark (1988) 16 RFL (3d) 257 1372
Starkowski v A-G [1954] AC 155. 897
Starlight International Inc v AJ Bruce [2002] EWHC 374, [2002] IL Pr 35 . . . . . . .538, 539, 549
Starr v Starr 1999 SLT 335. 1154
State Bank of India v Murjani Marketing Group Ltd, 27 March 1991(unreported) 529
State of Brunei Darussalam v Bolkiah (2000) Times, September 5 307
State of New York v Fitzgerald (1983) 148 DLR (3d) 176 540
State of Norway's Application, Re (Nos 1 & 2) [1990] 1 AC 723. . . . . .83, 115, 204
State of Norway's Application, Re [1987] QB 433 . . . . .115, 123, 204
State of Norway's Applications (Nos 1 and 2), Re [1990] 1 AC 723. . . . . .83, 115–17, 204
Steadman v Steadman [1976] AC 536, 563 148
Steel and Morris v United Kingdom, Judgment of 15 February 2005. 14
Steer, Re (1858) 3 H & N 594. 157
Steiner v IRC (1973) 49 TC 13 156
Steinhardt & Son Ltd v Meth (1961) 105 CLR 440. 494
Stephan J, The [1985] 2 Lloyd's Rep 344 384
Stevens v Hamed [2013] EWCA Civ 911 [2013] IL Pr 37. . . . . .485, 488, 493
Stevens v Head (1993) 176 CLR 433. . . . . .93–4, 800
Stevenson v Masson (1873) LR 17 Eq 78. 155–6
Stewart v Honey (1972) 2 SASR 585 808

Stewart v Royal Bank of Scotland 1994 SLT (Sh Ct) 27 1292
Stewart v Trafalgar House Steamship Co Ltd 2013 SLT 834 284
Stichting Shell Pensioenfonds v Krys [2014] UKPC 41, [2015] AC 616 . . . . .423, 540, 1310
Stirling, Re [1908] 2 Ch 344 1197
Stirling-Maxwell v Cartwright (1879) 11 Ch D 522 1333
Stolzenberg v Daimler Chrysler Canada Inc [2005] IL Pr 24 629
Stone v Stone [1958] 1 WLR 1287 160
Stonebridge Underwriting Ltd v Ontario Municipal Insurance Exchange [2010]
      EWHC 2279 (Comm), [2011] Lloyd's Rep IR 171 366–8
Stransky v Stransky [1954] P 428 175
Strathaird Farms Ltd v GA Chattaway & Co 1993 SLT 36 . . . . .195, 228, 247
Stryker Corpn v Sulzer Metco AG [2006] IEHC 60, [2007] IL Pr 47 238
Studd v Cook (1883) 8 App Cas 577 1355
Stylianou v Toyoshima [2013] EWHC 2188 . . . . .96, 349
Suarez, Suarez v Suarez, Re [1918] 1 Ch 176 514
Submarine Telegraph Co v Dickson (1864) 15 CBNS 759 878
Sulaiman v Juffali [2002] 1 FLR 479, [2002] 2 FCR 427 . . . . .955, 960, 1014, 1016, 1018
Sulamérica Cia Nacional de Seguros SA v Enesa Engelharia SA [2012]
      EWCA Civ 638, [2013] 1 WLR 102 . . . . .419, 667, 700
Sundelind Lopez v Lopez Lizazo (C-68/07) [2008] IL Pr 4 960–2
Sunderland Marine Mutual Insurance Co Ltd v Wiseman [2007] EWHC
      1460 (Comm) 263, 273, 277, 322
Superior Composite Structures LLC v Parrish [2015] EWHC 3688 . . . . .567, 579
Surety Co of New York v Wrightson (1910) 16 Com Cas 37 89
Suria's Marriage, Re (1977) 29 FLR 308 988
Surrey (UK) Ltd v Mazandaran Wood & Paper Industries [2014] EWHC 3165 342
Surzur Overseas Ltd v Koros [1999] 2 Lloyd's Rep 611 217
Sussex Peerage case (1844) 11 Cl & Fin 85 . . . . .110, 904
Sutherland v German Property Administrator (1933) 50 TLR 107 1281
Sutton LBC v K [2016] EWHC 1375 (Fam) 14
Svendborg v Wansa [1997] 2 Lloyd's Rep 183 . . . . .235, 439, 440, 534, 560, 573
Svenska Petroleum Exploration AB v Republic of Lithuania (No 2) [2005] EWHC 2437
      (Comm), [2006] 1 Lloyd's Rep 181, [2006] EWCA Civ 1529 . . . . .112, 504, 506,
                                                                                         559, 670, 672
Svenska Petroleum Exploration AB v Republic of Lithuania [2005]
      EWHC 9 (Comm), [2005] 1 Lloyd's Rep 515 . . . . .112, 504, 506, 559, 670, 672
Svenska Petroleum Exploration v Government of the Republic of Lithuania (No 2) [2005]
      EWHC 2437 (Comm) 112
Svirskis v Gibson [1977] 2 NZLR 4 573
Swaddling v Adjudication Officer (C-90/97) [1999] ECR I-1075 . . . . .179, 803
Swain v Hillman [2001] 1 All ER 91 338
Swan, In the Will of (1871) 2 VR (IE & M) 47 913–14
Sweedman v Transport Accident Commission [2006] HCA 8 42
Swiss Bank Corpn v Boehmische Industrial Bank [1923] 1 KB 673 1281
Swiss Bank Corpn v State of New South Wales (1993) 33 NSWLR 63 97
Swiss Life AG v Kraus [2015] EWHC 2133 539
Swiss Reinsurance Company Ltd v United India Insurance Co [2002] EWHC 741
      (Comm), [2004] IL Pr 4 363
Swissair Schweizerische Luftverkehr-Aktiengesellschaft, Re [2009] EWHC
      2099 (Ch) 1310
Swissmarine Services SA v Gupta Coal India Private Limited [2015] EWHC 265 437
Swithenbank Foods Ltd v Bowers [2002] EWHC 2257 (QB), [2002]
      2 All ER (Comm) 974 . . . . .297–8, 308
Syal v Heyward [1948] 2 KB 443 . . . . .568, 573, 598, 607
Syarikat Bumiputra Kimonis v Tan Kok Voon [1988] 3 MLJ 315 .394

Sydney Express [1988] 2 Lloyd's Rep 257 228–9
Sydney Municipal Council v Bull [1909] 1 KB 7 116
Sykeham, Re (1823) Turn & R 537 1246
Sylvester v Austria [2003] 2 FLR 210, (2003) 37 EHRR 17 .1164
Syska v Vivendi Universal SA [2009] EWCA Civ 677 1319–20
Szalatnay-Stacho v Fink [1947] KB 1 777
Szechter v Szechter [1971] P 286 . . . . .160, 917, 986, 988, 990, 995, 998
Szemik v Gryla (1965) 109 Sol Jo 175 1038

T & N Ltd and Ors (No 2), Re [2006] 1 WLR 1792 94
T (A Child) (Abduction: Appointment of Guardian ad Litem), Re [1999] 2 FLR 796 1145
T (A Child) (Application for Parental Responsibility), Re [2001] EWCA
    Civ 1067 . . . . .177, 180, 1098, 1133
T (A Child) (Care Proceedings: Request to Assume Jurisdiction), Re [2013]
    EWCA Civ 895 1113
T (A Child), Re [2015] EWHC 4050 1110
T (A Child: Art 15, Brussels II Revised), Re [2013] EWHC 521 1115
T (Brussels II Revised: Art 15), Re [2013] EWCA Civ 895 1115
T (Children) (Abduction: Child's Objections to Return), Re [2000]
    2 FLR 192 . . . . .182, 183, 1145, 1146, 1156
T (Minors) (Hague Convention: Access), Re [1993] 2 FLR 617, [1993] 1 WLR 1461 1135
T and J (Children) (Abduction: Recognition of Foreign Judgment), Re [2006]
    EWHC 1472, [2006] 2 FLR 1290 1160–1
T and M (Adoption), Re [2010] EWHC 964 1225–6
T v E [2016] EWHC 3148 (Fam), ...1152, 1155, 1156
T v K and others [2016] EWHC 2963 (Fam) 15
T v T (Child Abduction: Consent) [1999] 2 FLR 912 1148–9
T v T (Custody: Jurisdiction) [1992] 1 FLR 43 . . . . .967, 1106, 1112, 1133
T v T (Hemain Injunction) [2012] EWHC 3462 979
T v T (Jurisdiction) [2012] EWHC 2877 1101
T v T 2004 SC 323 . . . . .1148, 1150
T, Petitioner 2007 SLT 543, 2007 GWD 11–200 1138
T, Re [1968] Ch 704, [1969] 1 WLR 1608 . . . . .1056, 1174
Taczanowska v Taczanowski [1957] P 301 . . . . .71, 904, 948
Tadros (deceased), Re [2014] EWHC 2860 1341
Tagus, The [1903] P 44 89
Tahir v Tahir 1993 SLT 194 . . . . .1030, 1032
Tallack v Tallack and Broekema [1927] P 211 . . . . .333, 1061, 1073, 1396
Tallinna Laevaushisus (A/ S) v Estonian State Steamship Line (1947)
    80 Lloyd's Rep 99 . . . . .112, 131
Tamil Nadu Electricity Board v St CMS Electricity Co [2007] EWHC 1713
    (Comm), [2007] 2 All ER (Comm) 701 . . . . .106, 770
Tan v Choy [2014] EWCA Civ 251 . . . . .176, 180, 955–7, 959
Tang Lai Sau-kiu v Tang Loi [1987] HKLR 85 930
Tasarruff v Demirel [2006] EWHC 3354 (Ch), [2007] IL Pr 8, [2007] EWCA Civ 799,
    [2007] 1 WLR 2508, [2007] 1 WLR 3066 .115–16, 335, 363
Taser International Inc v SC Gate 4 Business SRL and Cristian Mircea
    Anastasiu (C-175/15) EU:C:2016:176, [2016] QB 887 . . . . .226, 229
Tassell v Hallen [1892] 1 QB 321 . . . . .356, 362
Taurus Petroleum Limited v State Oil Company of the Ministry of Oil, Republic of Iraq
    [2013] EWHC 33494 (Comm), [2015] EWCA Civ 835 [2016] 1 Lloyd's Rep 42 509,
    733, 1281
Tavoulareas v Tsavliris [2006] EWCA Civ 1772 198
Taylor v Best (1854) 14 CB 487 512
Taylor v Chester (1869) LR 4 QB 309 135

Taylor v Ford 1993 SLT 654 1137
Taylor v Giovani Developers Ltd [2015] EWHC 328 292
Taylor v Hollard [1902] 1 KB 676 556
Taylor v Lovegrove (1912) 18 ALR (CN) 22 1272
Taylor's Marriage, Re (1988) 92 FLR 172 1174
TB v JB (Abduction: Grave Risk of Harm) [2001] 2 FLR 515 1155
TC and JC (Children: Relocation), Re [2013] EWHC 292 (Fam) 1171
TDI Hospitality Management Consultants Inc v Browne (1995) 117 DLR
    (4th) 289 530
Tee v Tee [1974] 1 WLR 213 162–3
Teekay Tankers Ltd v STX Offshore & Shipping Co [2014] EWHC 3612
    (Comm), [2015] 2 All ER (Comm) 263 . . . . .331, 368
Tehrani v Secretary of State for the Home Department [2006] UKHL 47,
    [2007] 1 AC 521 . . . . .187, 202, 393, 395
Tekron Resources Ltd v Guinea Investment Co Ltd [2003] EWHC 2577
    (QB), [2004] 2 Lloyd's Rep 26 . . . . .136, 753
Telnikoff v Matusevitch 702 A2d 230 573
Temperance and General Mount Albert Borough Council v Australasian
    Mutual Life Assurance Society [1938] AC 224 . . . . .96, 766
Terry, Re [1951] NZLR 30 1345
Tesam Distribution Ltd v Shuh Mode Team GmbH [1990] IL Pr 149 . . . . .244, 251
Tessili v Dunlop (12/76) [1976] ECR 1473 . . . . .262, 460
Texaco Melbourne, The [1994] 1 Lloyd's Rep 473 . . . . .99, 103
Texan Management Ltd v Pacific Electric Wire & Cable Company [2009]
    UKPC 46 . . . . .333, 392
Tezcan v Tezcan (1992) 87 DLR (4th) 503 . . . . .42, 58, 1371, 1373–4
Thai-Lao Lignite (Thailand) and Hongsa Lignite (Lao PDR) v Government of the Lao
    People's Democratic Republic [2012] EWHC 3381 673
Thai-Lao Lignite (Thailand) Co Ltd v Laos [2013] EWHC 2466 (Comm), [2013]
    2 All ER (Comm) 883 509
Tharsis Sulphur and Copper Co Ltd v Société Industrielle et Commerciale
    des Métaux (1889) 58 LJQB 435 326
The Acrux [1965] P 391 . . . . .89, 116
The Alexandros T [2013] UKSC 70, [2014] 1 All ER 590 . . . . .195, 228
The Alexandros T [2013] UKSC 70, [2014] 1 Lloyd's Rep 223 . . . . 443, 446, 449,
                                                                                                                    455, 457, 478, 480
The Alexandros T [2014] EWCA Civ 1010, [2014] 2 Lloyd's Rep 544 . . . . .437, 478
The Amazonia [1990] 1 Lloyd's Rep 236 108
The Baarn [1933] P 251 95
The Canadian Transport (1932) 43 Lloyd's Rep 409 102
The Colorado [1923] P 102 89–90
The El Condado (1939) 63 Lloyd's Rep 330, 1939 SC 413 132
the Enforcement of a United States Judgment for Damages, Re (Case IX ZR 149/
    91) [1994] IL Pr 602 119
The Eva [1921] P 454 116
The Evia Luck (No 2) [1990] 1 Lloyd's Rep 319 70
The Funabashi [1972] 1 WLR 666 97
The Gaetano and Maria (1882) 7 PD 137 84
The Halcyon Isle [1981] AC 221 89–90
The Halcyon Skies (No 2) [1977] 1 Lloyd's Rep 22 100
The Islamic Republic of Iran v Berend [2007] EWHC 132 (QB), [2007]
    2 All ER (Comm) 132 71
The Jupiter (No 3) [1927] P 122 131
The Kefalonia Wind [1986] 1 Lloyd's Rep 292 n 99
The King of Spain v Machado (1827) 4 Russ 225 106

The Komninos S [1990] 1 Lloyd's Rep 541 79
The Komninos S [1991] 1 Lloyd's Rep 370 236
The Lash Atlantico [1987] 2 Lloyd's Rep 114 103
the late Emperor Napoleon Bonaparte, Re (1853) 2 Rob Eccl 606 .158
The London Steam Ship Owners Mutual Insurance Association Ltd v Spain
    Prestige [2015] EWCA Civ 333, [2015] 2 Lloyd's Rep 33 506
The Lu Schan [1993] 1 Lloyd's Rep 259 100
The Mercury Bell v Amosin (1986) 27 DLR (4th) 641 106
The Milford (1858) Sw 362 89
The Playa Larga [1983] 2 Lloyd's Rep 171, 190, CA 13
The Rewia [1991] 2 Lloyd's Rep 325 214
The Roberta (1937) 58 Lloyd's Rep 159 85
The Royal Bank of Scotland Plc v FAL Oil Company Ltd [2012] EWHC 3628 307
The Ship Betty Ott v General Bills Ltd [1992] 1 NZLR 655 89
The Sydney Express [1988] 2 Lloyd's Rep 257 228
The Tagus [1903] P 44 89
The Texaco Melbourne [1994] 1 Lloyd's Rep 473 . . . . .99, 103
The Transoceanica Francesca and Nicos V [1987] 2 Lloyd's Rep 155 (tort) 100
The Xing Su Hai [1995] 2 Lloyd's Rep 15 209
The Zigurds [1932] P 113 89
Thiele v Thiele (1920) 150 LT Jo 387 160
Thierry Morin v Bonhams & Brooks Ltd [2003] EWHC 467 (Comm), [2003]
    IL Pr 25, [2003] EWCA Civ 1802, [2004] IL Pr 24 755
Thiery v Chalmers Guthrie & Co, Re [1900] 1 Ch 80 1247
Thoday v Thoday [1964] P 181 558
Thom, Re (1987) 40 DLR (4th) 184 . . . . .71, 1351
Thomas Cook Belgium NV v Thurner Hotel GmbH (C-245/14) EU:C:2015:715,
    [2016] 1 WLR 878 662
Thomas v Penna [1985] 2 NSWLR 171 349
Thomson v Harding (1853) 2 E & B 630 1335
Thomson v Thomson (1994) 119 DLR (4th) 253 1138
Thomson, Petitioner 1980 SLT (Notes) 29 1088
Thorne v Dryden-Hall (1995) 18 RFL (4th) 15 1153
Thorne, Ernst & Whinney Inc v Sulpetro Ltd (1987) 47 DLR (4th) 315 87
Thornton v Curling (1824) 8 Sim 310 1344–5
Through Transport Mutual Insurance Association (Eurasia) Ltd v New India Assurance
    Association Co Ltd [2004] EWCA (Civ) 1598, [2005] 1 Lloyd's Rep 67 209
Through Transport Mutual Insurance Association (Eurasia) Ltd v New India Assurance
    Association Co Ltd [2004] 209, 430, 440–2, 444, 476, 478, 630
Thurn and Taxis (Princess) v Moffit [1915] 1 Ch 58 497
Thwaites v Aviva Assurances [2010] IL Pr 47 290
Thynne v Thynne [1955] P 272 934
Thyssen-Bornemisza v Thyssen-Bornemisza [1986] Fam 1 . . . . .967, 972, 974
Tiang Shen No 8, The [2000] 2 Lloyd's Rep 430 384
Tiernan v The Magen Insurance Co Ltd [2000] IL Pr 517 . . . . .368, 377, 719, 728
Timms v Nicol 1968 (1) SA 299 133
Tinkler, Re [1990] 1 NZLR 621 1330
Tipperary Developments Pty Ltd v The State of Western Australia [2009] WASCA 126 80
Tisand v Owners of the Ship MV Cape Moreton (Ex Freya) [2005] FCAFC 68,
    (2005) 219 ALR 48 106
Tito v Waddell (No 2) [1977] Ch 106 . . . . .485, 487, 489
Tjaskemolen, The (No 2) [1997] 2 Lloyd's Rep 476 383
Tjaskemolen, The [1997] 2 Lloyd's Rep 465 385
TNT Express Nederland BV v Axa Versicherung AG (C-533/08) [2010]
    ECR I-4107 . . . . .203, 389, 613–14, 646

Todd Shipyards Corpn v Altema Compania Maritima SA (1972) 32 DLR (3d) 571 89–90
Todd v Armour (1882) 9 R 901 1269
Toepfer International GmbH v Molino Boschi Srl [1996] 1 Lloyd's Rep
    510. . . . . .208, 228, 439, 446, 455
Toepfer International GmbH v Société Cargill France [1997] 2 Lloyd's
    Rep 98, [1998] 1 Lloyd's Rep 379 . . . . .208, 305, 427, 441–2, 444
Toller v Carteret (1705) 2 Vern 494 489
Tolofson v Jensen (1994) 120 DLR (4th) 289 . . . . .78, 777
Tolten, The [1946] P 135 491
Tonicstar Ltd v American Home [2004] EWHC 1234 (Comm), [2005] Lloyd's
    Rep IR 32 235
Toome Eel Fishery (Northern Ireland) v Jangaard and Butler [1960] CLY 1297 485
Toomey (Syndicate 2021) v Banco Vitalicio de España SA de Seguros y Reaseguros
    [2003] EWHC 1102 (Comm), [2004] EWCA Civ 622, [2004] 1 CLC 965 112
Topolski v R (1978) 90 DLR (3d) 66 1366
Toprak v Finagrain [1979] 2 Lloyd's Rep 98 . . . . .136, 770–1
Torok v Torok [1973] 1 WLR 1066 . . . . .171, 1008–10, 1072
Touchburn v O'Brien (2002) 210 DLR (4th) 668 349
Tower Hamlets LBC v MK [2012] EWHC 426 1157
Toyota Tsusho Sugar Trading v Prolat SRL [2014] EWHC 3649 (Comm), [2015]
    1 Lloyd's Rep 344 640
Tracomin SA v Sudan Oil Seeds Co Ltd (Nos 1 and 2), [1983] 1 Lloyd's Rep 560,
    [1983] 1 WLR 662, [1983] 419, 423, 436, 558–9, 562, 565, 567, 584, 586–7
Trade Agency Ltd v Seramico Investments Ltd (C-619/10) EU:C:2012:531 311,
                                                                                629, 630, 633–4, 637
Trade Indemnity v Försäkrings AB Njord [1995] 1 All ER 796 . . . . .367, 375
Trade Practices Commission v Australia Meat Holdings Pty Ltd (1988)
    83 ALR 299 . . . . .123, 554
Trademark Licensing Co Ltd v Leofelis SA [2009] EWHC 3285 (Ch), [2010] IL Pr 16 444
Tradigrain SA v SIAT SpA [2002] EWHC 106 (Comm), [2002]
    2 Lloyd's Rep 553 . . . . .234, 291, 456
Trafalgar Tours Ltd v Alan James Henry [1990] 2 Lloyd's Rep 298 377
Trafigura Beheer BV v Kookmin Bank Co (No 2) [2006] EWHC 1921 (Comm),
    [2007] 1 Lloyd's Rep 669 . . . . .430, 736, 815
Trafigura Beheer BV v Kookmin Bank Co (Preliminary Issue) [2006] EWHC 1450 43
Trafigura Beheer BV v Kookmin Bank Co [2005] EWHC 2350 (Comm) 430, 736
Trafigura Beheer BV v Kookmin Bank Co [2006] EWHC 1921 (Comm),
    [2006] 2 Lloyd's Rep 455 . . . . .430, 736, 815
Train v Train's Executor (1899) 2 F 146 1351
Trans-Continental Textile Recycling v Partenreederei MS Erato [1998] IL Pr 129 333
Transocean Towage Co Ltd v Hyundai Construction Co Ltd [1987] ECC 282 227
Transoceanica Francesca and Nicos V, The [1987] 2 Lloyd's Rep 155 100
Trasporti Castelletti Spedizioni Internazionali SpA v Hugo Trumpy SpA
    (C-159/97) [1999] ECR I-1597 . . . . .240, 242
Traube v Perelman, 2001 (unreported) 419
Traugutt, The [1985] 1 Lloyd's Rep 76 403
Travelers Casualty and Surety Co of Europe Ltd v Sun Life Assurance Co of
    Canada (UK) Ltd [2004] EWHC 1704 (Comm) 119
Travelers Casualty and Surety Co of Europe Ltd v Sun Life Assurance Co of
    Canada (UK) Ltd [2004] EWHC 1704, [2004] IL Pr 50 . . . . .119, 372, 375
Travers v Holley [1953] P 246 . . . . .543, 1035
Traversi's Estate, Re 189 Misc 251, 64 NYS 2d 453 (1946) 1349
Trawnik v Lennox [1985] 1 WLR 532 . . . . .492, 509
Treasurer of Ontario v Blonde [1947] AC 24 1298
Trendtex Trading Corpn v Central Bank of Nigeria [1977] QB 529 . . . . .499, 504

Trendtex Trading Corpn v Crédit Suisse [1982] AC 679 . . . . 134, 397, 399,
403, 411–15, 1285, 1287–8
Trepanier v Kloster Cruise Ltd (1995) 23 OR (3d) 398 413
Trepca Mines Ltd, Re [1960] 1 WLR 1273 . . . . .543, 546, 606
Trillium (Nelson) Properties Ltd v Office Metro Ltd [2012] EWHC 1191 1315
Trimbey v Vignier (1834) 1 Bing NC 151 . . . . .86, 112
Trinidad Shipping Co v Alston [1920] AC 888 137
Trotter v Trotter (1992) 90 DLR (4th) 554 174
Trufort, Trafford v Blanc, Re (1887) 36 Ch D 600. 548
Trumann Investment Group Ltd v Société Générale SA [2004] EWHC 1769 (Ch). 338
Trussler v Trussler [2003] EWCA Civ 1830 . . . . .967, 970
Trustees Executors and Agency Co Ltd v Margottini [1960] VR 417. 1390
Trustees of Olympic Airlines SA Pension and Life Insurance Scheme v
    Olympic Airlines SA [2015] UKSC 27. 1315
Trustor AB v Barclays Bank plc (2000) Times, 22 November 2000 308
Tryg Baltica International (UK) Ltd v Boston Compañía de Seguros SA [2004]
    EWHC 1186 (Comm), [2005] Lloyd's Rep IR 40 . . . . .369, 375, 417, 719, 728
Trygg Hansa v Equitas [1998] 2 Lloyd's Rep 439 417
Tseitline v Mikhelson [2015] EWHC 3065 326
TSN Kunststoffrecycling GmbH v Jurgens [2002] EWCA Civ 11, [2002] 1 WLR 2459. 637
Tubantia, The [1924] P 78. 877–8
Tucker, In the Goods of (1864) 34 LJPM & A 29 1330
Tullow Uganda Ltd v Heritage Oil and Gas Ltd, Heritage Oil plc [2013]
    EWHC 1656 (Comm). 117
Turcotte v Ford Motor Co 494 F 2d 173 (1974) 31
Turczak v Turczak [1970] P 198. 1071
Turczynski v Wilde and Partners [2003] IL Pr 64. 628
Turiddu, The [1998] 2 Lloyd's Rep 278 384
Turnbull v Walker (1892) 67 LT 767. 543
Turner v Grovit [2000] QB 345, [2001] UKHL 65, [2002] 1 WLR 107. . . . . .437, 448
Turner, Re [1906] WN 27 110
Tursi v Tursi [1958] P 54 1036
Tyburn Productions Ltd v Conan Doyle [1991] Ch 75 494
Tychy, The (No 2) [2001] 2 Lloyd's Rep 403 385
Tychy, The [1999] 2 Lloyd's Rep 11 385
Tyler v Bell (1837) 2 My & Cr 89 1336
Tyler v Judges of the Court of Registration (1900) 175 Mass 71 323
Tyler v Tyler [1989] 2 FLR 158 1168
Tyndall, Re [1913] SASR 39 1390

U v U [2010] EWHC 1179 (Fam). 1174
U-B (A Child) Re [2015] EWCA Civ 60 1147
UBS AG v Omni Holding AG (In Liquidation) [2000] 1 WLR 916 . . . . .207, 398
UBS Ltd v Regione Calabria [2012] EWHC 699 (Comm), [2012] IL Pr 22 . . . . .449, 455
UBS v HSH Nordbank AG [2009] EWCA Civ 585 1 All ER (Comm) 727 . . . . .237, 410
Udny v Udny (1869) LR 1 Sc & Div 441, 455, 457 . . . . 147, 149, 151, 159,
161–3, 165, 170, 1200
Ulf Kazmierz Radziejewski v Kronofogdemyndigheten i Stockholm (C-461/11)
    ECLI:EU:C:2012:704. 1313
Ullee, Re (1885) 53 LT 711. 937
Ultisol v Bouygues [1996] 2 Lloyd's Rep 140. 230
Underwriting Members of Lloyd's Syndicate 980 v Sinco SA [2008]
    EWHC 1842 (Comm), [2009] Lloyd's Rep IR 365 445–6
Ungar v Ungar [1967] 2 NSWR 618 917
Unibank A/S v Christensen (C-260/97) [1999] ECR I-3715. 612

Union Carbide Corpn Gas Plant Disaster at Bhopal, India, Re 634 F Supp
    842 (SDNY 1986) 406
Union de Remorquage et de Sauvetage SA v Lake Avery Inc, The Lake Avery
    [1997] 1 Lloyd's Rep 540 . . . . .208, 374
Union International Insurance Co Ltd v Jubilee Insurance Co Ltd [1991]
    1 WLR 415 344
Union Nationale des Cooperatives Agricoles de Céréales v Catterall [1959] 2 QB 44 668
Union Transport plc v Continental Lines SA [1992] 1 WLR 15 .209, 253
United Antwerp Maritime Agencies (Unamar) NV v Navigation
    Maritime Bulgare (C-184/12) EU:C:2013:663, [2014] 1 Lloyd's
    Rep 161 . . . . .144, 706, 746, 749–50, 866
United City Merchants (Investments) Ltd v Royal Bank of Canada [1982] QB 208, [1983]
    1 AC 168 770–1
United Film Distribution Ltd v Chhabria [2001] EWCA Civ 416, [2001]
    2 All (Comm) 865 338–1
United Rlys of the Havana and Regla Warehouses Ltd, Re [1960] 2 All ER 332 98
United Rlys of the Havana and Regla Warehouses Ltd, Re [1960] Ch 52, [1961]
    AC 1007 . . . . .70, 97–8
United States of America and Republic of France v Dollfus Mieg et Cie SA
    and Bank of England [1952] AC 582 . . . . .505, 507
United States of America v Abacha [2014] EWCA Civ 1291, [2015]
    1 WLR 1917 . . . . .119, 307, 545, 552
United States of America v Friedland (1999) 182 DLR (4th) 614 505–6
United States of America v Harden (1963) 41 DLR (2d) 721 .116, 552
United States of America v Inkley [1989] QB 255 . . . . .115–16, 121
United States of America v Ivey (1995) 130 DLR (4th) 674, (1996) 139
    DLR (4th) 570 123–4
United States of America v Ivey (1996) 139 DLR (4th) 570, Ont CA 123–4
United States of America v Nolan [2015] UKSC 63, [2016] AC 463 505–6
United States Securities and Exchange Commission v Cosby 2000 BCSC 338 122
United States Securities and Exchange Commission v Manterfield [2009]
    EWCA Civ 27, [2010] 1 WLR 172 . . . . .115, 122, 553
United States Surgical Co v Hospital Products International Pty Ltd [1982] 2 NSWLR 780
Universal General Insurance Co (UGIC) v Group Josi Reinsurance Co SA (C-412/98)
    [2001] QB 68 . . . . .215, 226, 289
Universal Music International Holding BV v Michael Tétreault Schilling
    (C-12/15) EU:C:2016:449, [2016] QB 967 . . . . .263, 277, 811–12
Unterweser Reederei GmbH v Zapata Off-Shore Co, The Chaparral [1968]
    2 Lloyd's Rep 158 . . . . .345, 371–2
Upton v National Westminster Bank plc [2004] EWHC 1962, [2004] WTLR 1339 915
Urness v Minto 1994 SC 249 . . . . .1144, 1156
Urquhart v Butterfield (1887) 37 Ch D 357 . . . . .165, 168
US Mortgage Finance II LLC v Dew [2015] EWHC 3621 . . . . .532, 542
USA v Harden [1963] SCR 366, (1963) 41 DLR (2d) 721 116
USF Ltd (t/ a USF Memcor) v Aqua Technology Hanson NV/ SA [2001]
    1 All ER (Comm) 856 252
USF Ltd (t/a USF Memcor) v Aqua Technology Hanson NV/SA [2001]
    1 All ER (Comm) 856 . . . . .252, 471

V (Abduction: Habitual Residence), Re [1995] 2 FLR 992 . . . . .959, 1097
V v B (A Minor) (Abduction), Re [1991] FCR 451, [1991] 1 FLR 266 . . . . .179, 1136, 1153
V v V (Divorce: Jurisdiction) [2011] EWHC 1190 955–9
V v V [2006] EWHC 3374 (Fam), [2007] Fam Law 304 .1106, 1125
Vadala v Lawes (1890) 25 QBD 310 . . . . .564, 569
Vak Estate v Dukelow (1994) 117 DLR (4th) 122 1351

Vale Do Rio Doce Navegacao SA v Shanghai Bao Steel Ocean Shipping Co
    Ltd (T/ A Bao Steel Ocean Shipping Co) [2000] 2 Lloyd's Rep 1 208–9
VALE Építési kft (C-378/10) EU:C:2012:440 [2013] 1 WLR 294 . . . . .35, 1307
Valentine's Settlement, Re [1965] Ch 831 . . . . .1054, 1223, 1226, 1228–9
Valier v Valier (1925) 133 LT 830 986
Vallée v Dumergue (1849) 4 Exch 290. . . . . .532, 577
Vamvakas v Custodian of Enemy Property [1952] 2 QB 183. 497
Van Dalfsen v Van Loon (C-183/90) [1991] ECR I-4743 . . . . .624, 649
Van de Mark and Toronto-Dominion Bank, Re (1989) 68 OR (2d) 379 118
Van den Boogard v Laumen (C-220/95) [1997] QB 759, [1997] ECR I-1147 . . . . . . .1065, 1074
Van Dooselaere v Holt Cargo Systems Inc [1999] IL Pr 634 404
Van Grutten v Digby (1862) 31 Beav 561 1377
Van Uden Maritime BV (t/a Van Uden Africa Line) v Kommanditgesellschaft in Firma
    Deco-Line (C-391/95) [1999] QB 1225 . . . . .208–9, 303, 617
Vander Donckt v Thellusson (1849) 8 CB 812. 110
Vanessa Ann, The [1985] 1 Lloyd's Rep 549. 383
Vanquelin v Bouard (1863) 15 CBNS 341. . . . . .564, 566, 1326, 1333, 1335–6
Varanand v Varanand (1964) 108 Sol Jo 693 . . . . .141, 1018
Vardinoyannis v Vardinoyannis [2011] EWCA Civ 1369. 955
Varna, The (No 2) [1994] 2 Lloyd's Rep 41 . . . . .383, 405, 408, 556
Varna, The [1993] 2 Lloyd's Rep 253 383
Varsani v Relfo Ltd (In Liquidation) [2010] EWCA Civ 560, [2011] 1 WLR 1402. 327
Vassis, Re (1986) 64 ALR 407 174
Vasso, The (formerly Andria) [1984] 1 Lloyd's Rep 235. . . . . .383, 418
V-B (Abduction: Rights of Custody), Re [1999] 2 FLR 192. 1138
VC v GC (Jurisdiction: Brussels II Revised Art 12) [2012] EWHC 1246. 1098
Velasco v Coney [1934] P 143 . . . . .1349, 1364
Veracruz I, The [1992] 1 Lloyd's Rep 353. 340
Verdoliva v JM Van der Hoeven BV (C-3/05) [2006] IL Pr 31. 623
Verein für Konsumenteninformation v Amazon EU Sàrl (C-191/15)
    ECLI:EU:C:2016:612 . . . . .688, 741, 783, 789, 804, 824, 825
Verein Für Konsumenteninformation v K H Henkel (C-167/00) [2002]
    ECR I-8111. . . . . .205, 245, 266, 293
Vervaeke v Smith [1981] Fam 77, [1983] 1 AC 145. . . . . .919, 1025, 1049
Vervaeke v Smith [1983] 1 AC 145 . . . . .133, 135, 139, 142
Viccari v Viccari (1972) 7 RFL 241 1021
Vickers, In the Estate of (2001–2) 4 ITELR 584 . . . . .1349, 1358
Vida v Vida (1961) 105 Sol Jo 913. 916
Vidal-Hall v Google Inc [2014] EWHC 13 798
Vidal-Hall v Google Inc [2015] EWCA Civ 311 . . . . .780, 805–6, 885
Viditz v O'Hagan [1899] 2 Ch 569, [1900] 2 Ch 87. 1375–7
Vien Estate v Vien Estate (1988) 49 DLR (4th) 558 . . . . .163, 1368
Viking Line ABP v The International Transport Workers' Federation
    [2005] EWHC 1222, [2006] IL Pr 4 . . . . .35, 450, 461, 465–6, 631
Vile v Von Wendt Zurich Insurance Co (1979) 103 DLR (3d) 356 .349
Ville De Bauge v China [2014] EWHC 3975 . . . . .960, 970
Viola v Viola 1988 SLT 7. 1154
Virgin Atlantic Airways Ltd v Zodiac Seats UK Ltd (formerly
    Contour Aerospace Ltd) [2013] UKSC 46, [2013] 3 WLR 299. 563
Virgin Aviation v CAD Aviation [1991] IL Pr 79. 457
Vishva Abha [1990] 2 Lloyd's Rep 312. 400
Vishva Ajay, The [1989] 2 Lloyd's Rep 558 . . . . .375, 385, 402, 405
Vishva Prabha, The [1979] 2 Lloyd's Rep 286 411
Viskase Ltd v Paul Kiefel GmbH [1999] 1 WLR 1305. . . . . .252, 257
Visser, Re [1928] Ch 877. 116

Viswalingham v Viswalingham (1979) 1 FLR 15 . . . . .1011, 1018
Vitol Bahrain EC v Nasdec General Trading LLC [2013] EWHC 3359. 435
Vizcaya Partners Ltd v Picard [2016] UKPC 5; [2016] 3 All ER 181 . . . . .533, 542
VK v JV (Abduction: Consent) [2012] EWHC 4033. 1149
Vladi v Vladi (1987) 39 DLR (4th) 563. . . . . .62, 71, 1366
Vogel v R and A Kohnstamm Ltd [1973] QB 133 .530, 532, 541, 606
Vogler v Szendroi 2008 NSCA 18 79
Voinet v Barrett (1885) 55 LJQB 39 537
Volger v Szendroi 2008 NSCA 18 . . . . .73, 79
Volvox Hollandia, The [1987] 2 Lloyd's Rep 520, [1988] 2 Lloyd's Rep 61 398
Von Horn v Cinnamond (C-163/95) [1998] QB 214 473
Von Lorang v Administrator of Austrian Property [1927] AC 641 1035
Von Rocks, The [1998] 2 Lloyd's Rep 198 382
Von Wyl v Engeler [1998] 3 NZLR 416 539
Voogsgeerd v Navimer SA (C-384/10) [2011] ECR I-13275 . . . . .301, 741
Vorarlberger Gebietskrankenkasse v WGV-Schwäbische Allgemeine
    Versicherungs AG (C-347/08) [2009] ECR I-8661 . . . . .289, 690
Voth v Manildra Flour Mills Pty Ltd (1990) 171 CLR 538 . . . . .353, 365, 367, 394
VTB Capital v Nutritek [2013] UKSC 5 at [44], [2013] 2 WLR 398 . . . . . .366-7, 372, 378, 395
Vuong v Hoang [1999] CLY 3734 . . . . .893, 896

W (A Child) (Abductions: Conditions for Return), Re [2004] EWCA Civ 1366,
    [2005] 1 FLR 727 1155
W (Abduction: Child's Objections), Re [2010] EWCA Civ 520 1146
W (Abduction: Procedure), Re [1995] 1 FLR 878 . . . . .1136, 1149
W (Jurisdiction: Mirror Order), Re [2011] EWCA Civ 703. 1099
W (Minors) (Abduction: Father's Rights), Re [1998] 2 FLR 146 . . . . .183, 1138-9
W (V) v S(D) (1996) 134 DLR (4th) 481 1138
W and B v H (Child Abduction: Surrogacy) (No 1) [2002] 1 FLR 1008 . . . . .176, 1097, 1180
W and B v H (Child Abduction: Surrogacy) [2002] 1 FLR 1008. 176
W and W v H (Child Abduction: Surrogacy) (No 2) [2002] 2 FLR 252 . . . . .176, 1097, 1180
W H Martin Ltd v Felbinder Spezialfahrzeugwerke GmbH [1998] IL Pr 794 252
W v H [2016] EWCA Civ 176, [2017] Fam 35. . . . . .510-11, 515
W v H [2016] EWHC 213 (Fam), [2017] 1 FLR 669 511
W v W (Child Abduction: Acquiescence) [1993] 2 FLR 211 . . . . .1141, 1143, 1150, 1156
W v W (Financial Relief: Appropriate Forum) [1997] 1 FLR 257 . . . . .978, 1076-7
W v W (Foreign Custody Order: Enforcement) [2005] EWHC 1811 . . . . .1091, 1128
W v W (Preliminary Issue: Stay of Petition) [2002] EWHC 3049, [2003]
    1 FLR 1022. . . . . .966, 969-70, 974, 1118
W v W [1989] 1 FLR 22 . . . . .1075, 1141
W v W [2009] EWHC 3288 1156
W v W [2010] EWHC 332 . . . . .1141, 1146, 1150
W v W 2003 SCLR 478. 1156
W, Re [2013] EWHC 3570 (Fam). 1188
W: B (Child Abduction: Unmarried Father), Re [1998] 2 FLR 146. .183
WA (A Child) (Abduction) (Consent; Acquiescence; Grave Risk of Harm
    or Intolerability), Re [2015] EWHC 3410. . . . . .1151, 1156
Wagner v Luxembourg [2007] ECHR 76240/ 01 1229
Wagner v Tettweiler [1985] ECC 258 1229
Wah (aka Alan Tang) v Grant Thornton International Ltd [2012] EWHC 3198 419
Wahl v A-G (1932) 147 LT 382. . . . . .152, 156-7, 161-2
Waite and Kennedy v Germany (1999) 30 EHRR 261. 501
Waite's Settlement, Re [1958] Ch 100 . . . . .1362, 1364
Walanpatrias Stiftung v Lehman Brothers International (Europe) [2006]
    EWHC 3034 (Comm). 357

Walker (Litigation Guardian of) v Bank of New York (1994) 111 DLR (4th) 186 498
Walker v Roberts 1998 SLT 1133 893
Walker v Walker [1950] 4 DLR 253 1021
Walker, Re [1908] 1 Ch 560 1363
Walkinshaw v Diniz [2000] 2 All ER (Comm) 237 417
Wall v Mutuelle de Poitiers Assurances [2014] EWCA Civ 138 . . . . .94, 799–800, 862–3
Wall v Wall [1950] P 112 1038
Walley v Walley [2005] EWCA Civ 910, [2005] 3 FCR 35 1155
Walsall MBC v K [2013] EWHC 3192 . . . . .1114, 1116
Walter Vapenik v Josef Thurner (C-508/12) EU:C:2013:790, [2014]
     1 WLR 2486 . . . . .293, 658, 741
Walton, Petitioner [2012] CSIH 54 595
War Eagle Mining Co v Robo Management Co [1996] 2 WWR 504 1251
Ward v Coffin (1972) 27 DLR (3d) 58 488
Ward v Revenue and Customs Commissioners [2016] UKFTT 114 173
Ward v Ward (1923) 39 TLR 440 980
Warner Bros v Nelson [1937] 1 KB 209 . . . . .106, 134
Warner v B&M Europe Ltd, 13 July 2016, EAT 515
Warren v Warren [1972] Qd R 386 . . . . .55, 816
Warrender v Warrender (1835) 2 Cl & Fin 488 . . . . .893, 911, 913, 920, 929, 931
Warter v Warter (1890) 15 PD 152 926–7
Waterford Wedgwood plc v David Nagli Ltd [1999] IL Pr 9 . . . . .272, 276, 288
Waterhouse v Australian Broadcasting Corpn (1989) 86 ACTR 1 93
Waterhouse v Reid [1938] 1 KB 743 362
Waterhouse v Stansfield (1851) 9 Hare 234 489–90
Watkins v North American Land and Timber Co Ltd (1904) 20 TLR 534 325
Watkins, Ex p (1752) 2 Ves Sen 470 1176
Watson v First Choice Holidays [2001] EWCA Civ 972, [2001] 2 Lloyd's
     Rep 339 . . . . .263, 286–7
Watts v Shrimpton (1855) 21 Beav 97 1377
Waung v Subbotovsky [1968] 121 CLR 337 87
Waung v Subbotovsky [1968] 3 NSWR 499, 121 CLR 337 87
Waverley Asset Management Ltd v Saha 1989 SLT (Sh Ct) 87 . . . . .252, 293
Way v Way [1950] P 71, [1951] P 124 . . . . .987–8, 994, 996
Wayland, In the Estate of [1951] 2 All ER 1041 . . . . .1330–1, 1349
Waziristan, The [1953] 1 WLR 1446 876
W-B (Family Jurisdiction: Appropriate Jurisdiction within the UK), Re [2012]
     EWCA Civ 592 1101
Wealands v CLC Contractors [1999] 2 Lloyd's Rep 739 .417–18
Webb v Webb [1991] 1 WLR 1410 219
Webb, In the Estate of (1992) 57 SASR 193 1390
Weber v Universal Ogden Services Ltd (C-37/00) [2002] QB 1189 300
Weber v Weber (C-438/12) EU:C:2014:212, [2015] Ch 140 . . . . .219, 453
Wegmann v Elsevier Science Ltd [1999] IL Pr 379 272
Weiner v Weiner [2010] EWHC 1843 970
Weir v Lohr (1967) 65 DLR (2d) 717 116
Weiss, In the Estate of [1962] P 136 1334
Weissfisch v Julius [2006] EWCA Civ 218, [2006] 1 Lloyd's Rep 716 . . . . .419, 422
Welex AG v Rosa Maritime Ltd (The Epsilon Rosa) (No 1) [2002] EWHC 762
     (Comm), [2002] 2 Lloyd's Rep 81, [2003] EWCA Civ 938, [2003] 756–7
Welex AG v Rosa Maritime Ltd (The Epsilon Rosa) (No 2) [2002] EWHC 2035 (Comm),
     [2002] 2 Lloyd's Rep 701, [2003] EWCA Civ 938, [2003] 2 Lloyd's Rep 509 756–7
Wellamo, The [1980] 2 Lloyd's Rep 229 400
Weller v Associated Newspapers Ltd [2015] EWCA Civ 1176 15
Wendel v Moran 1993 SLT 44 . . . . .529, 541

Wermuth v Wermuth [2003] EWCA Civ 50, [2003] 1 WLR 942 . . . . .968–70, 971
West of England Steamship Owners Protection and Indemnity Association Ltd v John
    Holman & Sons [1957] 1 WLR 1164 . . . . .328, 369
West Tankers Inc v Allianz SpA (The Front Comor) [2011] EWHC 829
    (Comm), [2011] 2 All ER (Comm) 1 . . . . .639, 646, 669
West Tankers Inc v Allianz SpA [2011] EWHC 829 (Comm), [2011] 2 All ER
    (Comm) 1, affd [2012] EWCA Civ 27, [2012] 2 All ER (Comm) 113 . . . . .639, 646
West Tankers Inc v Allianz SpA [2012] EWCA Civ 27, [2012] 1 Lloyd's . . . .
West Tankers Inc v RAS Riunione Adriatica di Sicurta SpA (The Front Comor)
    [2005] EWHC 454 (Comm), [2005] 2 Lloyd's Rep 257 . . . . .210, 440–1
West Tankers Inc v RAS Riunione Adriatica di Sicurta SpA [2007] UKHL 4,
    [2007] 1 Lloyd's Rep 391 . . . . .210–11, 440–1, 478–9
Westacre Investments Inc v Jugoimport-SDPR Holding Co Ltd [2000] 1 QB 288,
    [1999] 1 WLR 1999 . . . . .674, 753
Westacre v Jugoimport [2000] 1 QB 288 136
Westdeutsche Landesbank Girozentrade v Islington Borough Council [1996] AC 669 841
Westec Aerospace Inc v Raytheon Aircraft Co (1999) 173 DLR (4th) 498, (2001) 197
    DLR (4th) 211 . . . . .403–4, 408
Western Union Insurance Co v Re-Con Building Products Inc (2001) 205 DLR
    (4th) 184 408–9
Western's Goods, Re (1898) 78 LT 49 1330
Westerton, Re [1919] 2 Ch 104 1287
Westfal-Larsen & Co A/S v Ikerigi Compañía Naviera SA [1983] 1 All ER 382 . . . . .558, 560
Westinghouse Electric Corpn Uranium Contract, Re [1978] AC 547 . . . . .83, 553, 601
Westland Ltd v AOI [1995] QB 282 127
Westminster City Council v C [2008] EWCA Civ 198 141
Westminster City Council v Government of the Islamic Republic of Iran [1986]
    1 WLR 979 508
Westminster City Council v IC (A Protected Party by this Litigation Friend)
    and Ors [2008] EWCA Civ 198, [2008] WCR (D) 92 . . . . .898, 909, 986, 991, 1051
Westpac Banking Corpn v Commonwealth Steel Co Ltd [1983] 1 NSWLR 735 337
Westpac Banking Corpn v Dempsey [1993] 3 IR 331 644
WH Martin Ltd v Felbinder Spezialfahrzeugwerke GmbH [1998] IL Pr 794 252
Whicker v Hume (1858) 7 HL Cas 124 . . . . .146, 161
Whitaker v Forbes (1875) 1 CPD 51 485
White Sea & Onega Shipping Co Ltd v International Transport Workers
    Federation [2001] 1 Lloyd's Rep 421 . . . . .70, 85, 461
White v Damon (1802) 7 Ves 30 140
White v Hall (1806) 12 Ves 321 488
White v Tennant 31 W Va 790, 8 SE 596 (1888) 150
White v Verkouille [1990] 2 Qd R 191 87
Whitehead v Whitehead [1963] P 117 966
Whitelegg's Goods, Re [1899] P 267 111
Whyte v Rose (1842) 3 QB 493 1333
Whyte v Whyte [2005] EWCA Civ 858 533
Wicken v Wicken [1999] Fam 224, [1999] 1 FLR 293 . . . . .80, 893, 896, 910,
                                                        1018, 1021, 1023, 1033
Wicks' Marriage Settlement, Re [1940] Ch 475 67
Wier's case (1607) 1 Roll Abr 530 K 12 19
Wight v Eckhardt Marine GmbH [2003] UKPC 37, [2004] 1 AC 147 . . . . .126, 768
Wild Ranger, The (1862) Lush 553 878
Wilhelm Finance Inc v Ente Administrador Del Astillero Rio Santiago [2009]
    EWHC 1074 (Comm), [2009] 1 CLC 867 499
Wilkinson v Kitzinger [2007] EWHC 2022 (Fam), [2007] 1 FLR 295 15
Wilkinson v Kitzinger and Ors [2006] EWHC 2022 (Fam) 15

Wilkinson's Settlement, Re [1917] 1 Ch 620 1364
Wilks, Re [1935] Ch 645. . . . . .50, 1333, 1390
Wille v Farm Bureau Mutual Insurance Co 432 NW 2d 784 (1988) 31
William Grant & Sons International Ltd v Marie Brizard et Roger International
    SA [1997] IL Pr 391. . . . . .263, 443, 446, 454, 737
William Grant & Sons International Ltd v Marie Brizard et Roger
    International SA 1998 SC 536. . . . . .263, 443, 446, 454, 737
Williams & Humbert Ltd v W & H Trade Marks (Jersey) Ltd [1986]
    AC 368 . . . . .13, 115–17, 119, 126–8, 131
Williams and Glyn's Bank Ltd v Boland [1981] AC 487 207
Williams and Humbert Ltd v W and H Trade Marks (Jersey) Ltd
    [1986] AC 368. . . . . .115–17, 126–30
Williams v A-G [1987] 1 FLR 501. 1049
Williams v Colonial Bank (1888) 38 Ch D 388. 1300
Williams v Rawlings Truck Line Inc 357 F 2d 581 (1965) 25
Williams v Society of Lloyd's [1994] 1 VR 274 343
Williams v Wheeler (1860) 8 CBNS 299 74
Williams, Petitioner 1977 SLT (Notes) 2 166
Willis Australia Group Services Pty Ltd v Giggs [2012] NSWSC 659 106
Willoughby, Re (1885) 30 Ch D 324. . . . . .1110, 1112
Wilson v Jones (Preliminary Issue), 8 June 2000 (unreported), Ch D. 1345, 1353
Wilson v Wilson [1903] P 157. 111
Wilson, Re [1954] Ch 733. . . . . .1054, 1197, 1223
Wilson's Trusts, Re (1865) LR 1 Eq 247. 1197
Winans v A-G (1901) 85 LT 508, 510. 158
Winans v A-G [1904] AC 287 . . . . .148–9, 152–3, 158, 162
Wink v Croatio Osiguranje DD [2013] EWHC 1118. 349
Winkler v Shamoon [2016] EWHC 217 212
Winkworth v Christie, Manson and Woods Ltd [1980] Ch 496 . . . . .71, 1267–9, 1273, 1275
Winnetka Trading Corp v Julius Baer International Ltd [2008]
    EWHC 3146 (Ch), [2009] 2 All ER (Comm) 735 . . . . .473, 494
Winrow v Hemphill & Anor [2014] EWHC 3164 . . . . .802–3, 814, 818
Winter v Winter [1894] 1 Ch 421 358
Winter, The [2000] 2 Lloyd's Rep 298 . . . . .377, 390, 443, 445
Wintersteiger AG v Products 4U Sondermaschinenbau GmbH (C-523/10)
    EU:C:2012:220, [2012] IL Pr 23. . . . . .264, 272, 276, 278
Witkowska v Kaminski [2006] EWHC 1940 (Ch), [2007] 1 FLR 1547 956
WMS Gaming Inc v B Plus Giocolegale Ltd [2011] EWHC 2620 (Comm),
    [2012] IL Pr 5 446–7
Wokuri v Kassam [2012] EWHC 105 (Ch), [2013] Ch 80 .511, 513
Wolf 's Goods, Re [1948] P 66, [1947] 2 All ER 841. 1039
Wolf Naturprodukte GmbH v SEWAR spol sro (C-514/10) EU:C:2012:367
    [2012] IL Pr 37 610
Wolfenden v Wolfenden [1946] P 61. . . . . .903, 908–9
Wolff v Oxholm (1817) 6 M & S 92, 105 ER 1177. . . . . .86, 118
Wood Floor Solutions Andreas Domberger GmbH v Silva Trade SA (C-19/09)
    [2010] ECR I-2121 . . . . .257, 259, 260
Wood v Wood [1957] P 254 . . . . .1034, 1071
Woodcock v Woodcock 1990 SLT 848 1133
Wood-Cutting Machine, Re [1995] IL Pr 191 232
Woodger v Federal Capital Press of Australia Pty Ltd (1996) 107 ACTR 1 888
Worcester City and County Banking Co v Firbank, Pauling & Co [1894] 1 QB 784. 327
Word Publishing Co Ltd, Re [1992] 2 Qd R 336. 606
World Star, The [1986] 2 Lloyd's Rep 274 385

Worldview Capital Management SA v Petroceltic International Plc [2015]
EWHC 2185 (Comm), [2015] IL Pr 46 ....253, 261
Worms v De Valdor (1880) 49 LJ Ch 261 139–40
Woyno v Woyno [1960] 1 WLR 986..1049
WP v FP [2007] EWHC 779 (Fam), [2007] 2 FLR 129 ....178, 182
WPP Holdings Italy Srl v Benatti [2006] EWHC 1641 (Comm), [2006]
2 Lloyd's Rep 610...241, 298, 301, 448
Wright v Deccan Chargers Sporting Ventures Ltd [2011] EWHC 1307 (QB),
[2011] IL Pr 37 ....299, 397
Wright's Trs v Callender 1993 SC (HL) 13..................................1195
Wright's Trusts, Re (1856) 2 K & J 595 165
Wright's Trusts, Re (1856) 25 LJ Ch 621 159
WT (A Child), Re [2014] EWHC 1303 ....1184–6, 1188
Wyatt v Fulrath 16 NY 2d 169, 211 NE 2d 673 (1965)......................1368
Wyler v Lyons [1963] P 274, [1963] 1 All ER 821....................1061, 1396
Wynn, Re [1984] 1 WLR 237 ....1341, 1348

X (A Child) (Surrogacy: Time Limit), Re [2014] EWHC 3135 1186
X (Children), Re [2011] EWHC 3147..1188
X (Court of Protection Practice), Re [2015] EWCA Civ 599.................1243
X (Foreign Surrogacy: Child's Name), Re [2016] EWHC 1068 (Fam), ...1179–80
X City Council v MB [2006] EWHC 168......................................909, 1050
X County Council v B (Abduction: Rights of Custody in the Court) [2009]
EWHC 2635...1138, 1056
X v Fountaine Pajot (Societe) [2011] IL Pr 21 575
X v Latvia (first instance) [2012] 1 FLR 860, [2011] ECHR 27853/ 09 1165
X v Latvia [2013] ECHR 27853/ 09, [2014] 1 FLR 1135.............1153, 1165–6
X v Y [1990] 1 QB 220 306
X, Y and Z (Children) (Retrospective Leave to Remove from the Jurisdiction),
Re [2016] EWHC 2439 (Fam) 1157
X, Y and Z v The Bank [1983] 2 Lloyd's Rep 535 118
X's Marriage, Re (1983) 65 FLR 132.......................................893, 905
XAG v A Bank [1983] 2 Lloyd's Rep 535....................................724
XCC v AA [2012] EWHC 2183 ....909, 986, 990–1, 1050–1
Xin Yang, The [1996] 2 Lloyd's Rep 217 ....351, 388, 397, 404, 450, 468–70
Xing Su Hai, The [1995] 2 Lloyd's Rep 15.................209, 287, 333, 337
Xiong v Xiong 648 NW 2d 900...893
XL Insurance Co SE (formerly XL Insurance Co Ltd) v AXA Corporate Solutions Assurance
[2015] EWHC 3431 (Comm), [2016] Lloyd's Rep IR 420 ....249, 267
XN Corpn Ltd v Point of Sale Ltd [2001] IL Pr 35 409

Y (Abduction: Undertakings Given for Return of Child), Re [2013] EWCA
Civ 129 ....1102, 1159
Y (Leave to Remove from Jurisdiction) , Re [2004] 2 FLR 330 1167–9
Y (Minors) (Adoption: Jurisdiction), Re [1985] Fam 136....................166
Yates v Thompson (1835) 3 Cl & Fin 544 ....80, 1348
Yoon v Song [2000] NSWC 1147 571
Youell v Kara Mara Shipping Co [2000] 2 Lloyd's Rep 102 341
Youell v La Reunion Aerienne [2008] EWHC 2493 (Comm), [2009] IL Pr 23, [2009]
EWCA Civ 175, [2009] 2 All ER (Comm) 1071............................289
Youell v La Reunion Aerienne [2009] EWCA Civ 175, [2009] 2 All ER
(Comm) 1071 ....210, 251
Young v Anglo American South Africa Ltd [2014] EWCA Civ 1130, [2014]
2 Lloyd's Rep 606...200–1
Young v Phillips [1984] STC 520...1298

Yuen Tse v Minister of Employment and Immigration (1983)
  32 RFL (2d) 274 . . . . .942, 1200
Yukon Consolidated Gold Corpn v Clark [1938] 2 KB 241. 592
Yukos Capital Sarl v OJSC Oil Co Rosneft [2014] EWHC 2188 (Comm) 108
Yukos Capital Sarl v OJSC Rosneft Oil Co (No 2) [2011] EWHC 1461 559
Yukos Capital Sarl v OJSC Rosneft Oil Co (No 2) [2012]
  EWCA Civ 855, [2014] QB 458 . . . . .560, 564, 568, 571, 574
Yukos Capital Sarl v OJSC Rosneft Oil Co [2014] EWHC 2188 (Comm),
  [2014] 2 Lloyd's Rep 435. . . . . .574, 668, 673
Yula Bondarovskaya, The [1998] 2 Lloyd's Rep 357 383
Yuninshing v Edward Mondong [2002] 2 SLR 506 394

Z (A Child) (Surrogate Father: Parental Order), Re [2015] EWFC 73 1185
Z (A Child) (Surrogate Father: Parental Order), Re [2016] EWHC 1191 (Fam),. 1185
Z (A Child), Re [2006] EWCA Civ 1291 1174
Z (A Child), Re [2014] EWHC 2147 1099
Z (Abduction: Non-Convention Country), Re [1999] 1 FLR 1270 .1174
Z (Foreign Surrogacy: Allocation of Work: Guidance on Parental Order
  Reports), Re [2015] EWFC 90. . . . . .1179, 1184, 1186
Z and another v C and another [2011] EWHC 3181. . . . . .149, 156, 1184
Z v Z (Abduction: Children's Views) [2005] EWCA Civ 1012, [2006]
  1 FLR 410 1142
Z v Z (Divorce Jurisdiction) [2009] EWHC 2626 (Fam), ...955–6, 958–9
Z v Z (Financial Provision: Overseas Divorce) [1992] 2 FLR 291 .1076
Z v Z (No 2) (Financial Remedy: Marriage Contract) [2012] 1FLR 1100 1379
Z v Z (Recognition of Brazilian Adoption Order) [2013] EWHC 747. . . . . . . .1054, 1225, 1227
Zaal v Zaal (1982) 4 FLR 284 . . . . .1013, 1017, 1032, 1034
Zahnrad Fabrik Passau GmbH v Terex Ltd 1986 SLT 84 1272–3
Zahra v Visa Officer, Islamabad [1979–80] Imm AR 48. 938
Zair v Eastern Health and Social Services Board [1999] IL Pr 823 .287
Zambia Steel v Clark and Eaton [1986] 2 Lloyd's Rep 225. 417
Zanelli v Zanelli (1948) 64 TLR 556 . . . . .160, 980
Zavarco Plc, Re [2015] EWHC 1898 (Ch), [2016] Ch 128. 457
Zebrarise Ltd and Anor v De Nieffe [2004] EWCA 1842, [2005]
  1 Lloyd's Rep 154. 1295–7
Zelger v Salinitri (56/79) [1980] ECR 89. . . . . .234, 245, 262
Zellner v Phillip Alexander Securities and Futures Ltd [1997] IL Pr 730 209–10
Zenel v Haddow 1993 SLT 975; 1993 SCLR 872 181
ZI Pompey Industrie v Ecu-Line NV [2000] IL Pr 600, [2000] IL Pr 608 415
Zigurds, The [1932] P 113. 89
Ziraat Muduroglu Ltd v TC Bankasi [1986] QB 1225. 404
Zivlin v Baal Taxa [1998] IL Pr 106 400
Zoernsch v Waldock [1964] 1 WLR 675 . . . . .513, 515
Zollverein, The (1856) Sw 96. 878
Zoneheath Associates Ltd v China Tianjin International Economic and
  Technical Co-operative Corpn [1994] CLC 348 1293
ZP v PS (1994) 122 CLR 639 1174
Zuid-Chemie BV v Philippo's Mineralenfabriek NV/SA (C-189/08) [2009]
  ECR I-6917. . . . . .263, 272, 277
Zulfikarpašić v Gajer (C-484/15) EU:C:2017:199, [2017] IL Pr 16. . . . . .611, 657
Zumax Nigeria Limited v First City Monument Bank plc [2016] EWCA Civ 567. 333–4

COURT OF JUSTICE OF THE EUROPEAN UNION CASES,
BY YEAR AND NUMBER

1976

12/76 Tessili v Dunlop [1976] ECR 1473 ....254, 262, 460
14/76 De Bloos v Bouyer [1976] ECR 1497 ....247, 252, 262, 280–1
21/76 Bier BV v Mines de Potasse D'Alsace SA [1978] QB 708, [1976]
    ECR 1735 ....270, 348, 830
24/76 Colzani v Rüwa [1976] ECR 1831 ....234, 238
25/76 Galeries Segoura Sprl v Bonakdarian [1976] ECR 1851....................232, 239
29/76 Lufttransportunternehmen GmbH v Organisation Européenne
    pour la Securité de la Navigation Aérienne (Eurocontrol) [1976]
    ECR 1541 ....196, 204, 614
42/76 De Wolf v Cox BV [1976] ECR 1759 ....443, 460, 556, 617–19, 649

1977

9 and 10/77 Bavaria Fluggesellschaft Schwabe v Eurocontrol [1977]
    ECR 1517 614
43/77 Industrial Diamond Supplies v Riva [1977] ECR 2175 ....646, 648
73/77 Sanders v Van der Putte [1977] ECR 2383 ....218, 221–2, 233, 251
150/77 Bertrand v Ott [1978] ECR 1431 ....293, 295

1978

23/78 Meeth v Glacetal Sarl [1978] ECR 2133 ....235, 237, 450
33/78 Somafer v Saar-Ferngas [1978] ECR 2183.............................196, 280
133/78 Gourdain v Nadler [1979] ECR 733 207
143/78 De Cavel v De Cavel [1979] ECR 1055...............206, 212, 305, 612, 614, 1065

1979

25/79 Sanicentral GmbH v Collin [1979] ECR 3423 ....204, 233
56/79 Zelger v Salinitri [1980] ECR 89....................................234, 245, 262
120/79 De Cavel v De Cavel (No 2) [1980] ECR 731...................212, 612, 614, 1065
125/79 Denilauler SNC v Couchet Frères [1980]
    ECR 1553 ....609, 615–16, 620
814/79 Netherlands State v Rüffer [1980] ECR 3807 205

1980

139/80 Blanckaert and Willems v Trost [1981] ECR 819..........................280
150/80 Elefanten Schuh GmbH v Jacqmain [1981]
    ECR 1671 ....196, 226–9,
                          237, 243, 456, 538, 690, 752
157/80 Rinkau [1981] ECR 1391 206

1981

25/81 CHW v GJH [1982] ECR 1189 ....207, 228, 305
27/81 Röhr v Ossberger [1981] ECR 2431 ....228, 627, 631–2
38/81 Effer v Kantner [1982] ECR 825....................................221, 251
133/81 Ivenel v Schwab [1982] ECR 1891 ....300, 688, 690
166/80 Klomps v Michel [1981] ECR 1593 ....303, 311, 633, 635–7
228/81 Pendy Plastic Products BV v Pluspunkt Handelsgesellschaft mbH
    [1982] ECR 2723 ....310, 633

1982

34/82 Peters v Zuid Nederlandsee Aannemers Vereniging [1983] ECR 987 245
201/82 Gerling v Italian Treasury [1983] ECR 2503 . . . . .228, 241, 291
288/82 Duijnstee v Goderbauer [1983] ECR 3663 . . . . .217–18, 225, 309

1983

71/83 Partenreederei MS Tilly Russ v Haven and Vervaebedriff Nova NV [
    1985] QB 931, [1984] ECR 2417 . . . . .238, 241
129/83 Zelger v Salinitri (No 2) [1984] ECR 2397 445
178/83 Firma P v Firma K [1984] ECR 3033 . . . . .611, 620
241/83 Rösler v Rottwinkel [1986] QB 33 .276, 218, 222, 493
258/83 Brennero v Wendel GmbH [1984] ECR 3971 624

1984

48/84 Spitzley v Sommer Exploitation SA [1985] ECR 787 226–7
49/84 Debaecker v Bouwman [1985] ECR 1779 636–8
119/84 Capelloni v Pelkmans [1985] ECR 3147 620
148/84 Deutsche Genossenschaftsbank v Brasserie du Pecheur SA
    [1985] ECR 1981 625
220/84 AS Autoteile Service GmbH v Malhé [1985] ECR 2267 225
221/84 F Berghoefer GmbH and Co Kg v ASA SA [1985] ECR 2699 239

1985

22/85 Anterist v Crédit Lyonnais [1986] ECR 1951 236
198/85 Carron v Germany [1986] ECR 2437 . . . . .622, 624
266/85 Shenavai v Kreischer [1987] ECR 239 . . . . .247, 253, 298, 734
313/85 Iveco Fiat SpA v Van Hool NV [1986] ECR 3337 239

1986

144/86 Gubisch Maschinenfabrik KG v Giulio Palumbo
    [1987] ECR 4861 445
145/86 Hoffmann v Krieg [1988] ECR 645 . . . . 618, 622, 627,
                                                                                      632, 640, 1083
218/86 Sar Schotte GmbH v Parfums Rothschild Sarl [1987] ECR 4905 . . . . . . .280–2, 330, 531

1987

9/87 SPRL Arcado v SA Haviland [1988] ECR 1539 . . . . .250, 688, 766
158/87 Scherrens v Maenhout [1988] ECR 3791 219
189/87 Kalfelis v Schroder [1988] ECR 5565 . . . . .263–4, 266, 284

1988

C-32/88 Six Constructions Ltd v Humbert [1989] ECR 341 .298, 301
C-115/88 Reichert v Dresdner Bank [1990] ECR I-27 493
C-220/88 Dumez France and Tracoba v Hessische Landesbank
    [1990] ECR I-49 . . . . .276, 812
C-305/88 Lancray v Peters [1990] ECR I-2725 635
C-365/88 Kongress Agentur Hagen GmbH v Zeehaghe BV
    [1990] ECR I-1845 . . . . .288, 464, 472, 477

1989

C-190/89 Marc Rich & Co v Società Italiana Impianti PA
    [1991] ECR I-3855 . . . . .209, 215, 618

C-214/89 Powell Duffryn plc v Petereit [1992] ECR I-1745 . . . . .231–3, 237, 239, 245
C-351/89 Overseas Union Insurance Ltd v New Hampshire Insurance Co [1992] 1 QB 434
. . . . .444, 450

1990

C-183/90 Van Dalfsen v Van Loon [1991] ECR I-4743 . . . . .624, 647, 649
C-261/90 Reichert v Dresdner Bank (No 2) [1992] ECR I-2149. . . . . .225, 266, 304
C-280/90 Hacker v Euro-Relais [1992] ECR I-1111 221

1991

C-26/91 Jakob Handte & Co GmbH v Traitements Mecano-Chimiques
    des Surfaces SA (TMCS) [1992] ECR I-3967 . . . . .245–6, 249, 269
C-89/91 Shearson Lehman Hutton v TVB Treuhandgesellschaft für
    Vermogensverwaltung und Beteiligungen mbH [1993] ECR I-139 . . . . . .265, 267, 281, 293
C-123/91 Minalmet v Brandeis [1992] ECR 1–5661. . . . . .633, 638
C-172/91 Sonntag v Waidmann [1993] ECR I-1963. . . . . 46, 196, 205–6,
                                                      279, 614, 625, 631, 633–4, 636

1992

C-125/92 Mulox IBC Ltd v Geels [1993] ECR I-4075 . . . . .298, 300
C-129/92 Owens Bank Ltd v Bracco (No 2) [1994]QB 509 . . . . 204, 225, 443,
                                                      456, 571, 611, 613, 618
C-288/92 Custom Made Commercial Ltd v Stawa Metallbau
    GmbH [1994] ECR I-2913. . . . . .232, 240, 244, 254, 460
C-294/92 Webb v Webb [1994] QB 696. . . . . .220, 486
C-398/92 Mund & Fester v Hatrex International Transport [1994] ECR I-467. 197
C-406/92 Owners of cargo lately laden on board Tatry v Owners
    of Maciej Rataj,
The Tatry [1994] ECR I-5439 . . . . .203, 215, 384, 387, 389, 445, 447
C-414/92 Solo Kleinmotoren GmbH v Boch [1994] ECR I-2237. . . . . .612, 626, 639

1993

C-68/93 Shevill v Presse Alliance SA [1995] 2 AC 18 . . . . .217, 263
C-292/93 Lieber v Göbel [1994] ECR I-2535. 220
C-318/93 Brenner and Noller v Dean Witter Reynolds Inc [1994]
    ECR I-4275. . . . . .202, 226, 296–7
C-341/93 Danvaern Production A/S v Schuhfabriken Otterbeck
    GmbH & Co [1995] ECR I-2053. 288
C-346/93 Kleinwort Benson Ltd v Glasgow City Council [1996] QB 57 . . . . .195, 247, 266
C-364/93 Marinari v Lloyds Bank plc (Zubaidi Trading Co Intervener)
    [1996] QB 217 . . . . .276, 812
C-432/93 Société d'Informatique Service Réalisation Organisation (SISRO)
v Ampersand Software BV [1994] IL Pr 55, [1996] QB 127 . . . . .621, 624, 647, 649
C-439/93 Lloyd's Register of Shipping v Société Campenon Bernard
    [1995] ECR I-961 . . . . .280, 282, 289, 296
C-474/93 Hengst Import BV v Campese [1995] ECR I-2113 . . . . .615, 633, 636, 644

1995

C-78/95 Hendrikman v Magenta Druck & Verlag GmbH [1997] QB 426 . . . . . 534, 627, 632–4,
    638, 644
C-106/95 MSG v Graviéres Rhénanes [1997] ECR I-911 . . . . .234, 240, 259, 262
C-163/95 Von Horn v Cinnamond [1998] QB 214. 473
C-220/95 Van den Boogard v Laumen [1997] QB 759, [1997] ECR I-1147. . . . .207, 1065, 1074
C-269/95 Benincasa v Dentalkit Srl [1997] ECR I-3767 . . . . .232–3, 237, 292

C-295/95 Farrell v Long [1997] QB 842, [1997] ECR I-1683. 196
C-383/95 Rutten v Cross Medical Ltd [1997] ECR I-57, [1997]
    All ER (EC) 121 196
C-391/95 Van Uden Maritime BV (t/a Van Uden Africa Line) v
    Kommanditgesellschaft in Firma Deco-Line [1999] QB 1225 . . . . .208–9, 303, 617

1996

C-99/96 Mietz v Intership Yachting Sneek BV [1999] ECR I-2277 . . . . .293, 303–4, 616, 642
C-126/96 - Marie Brizard et Roger International SA, Re Petition
    of [1997] IL Pr 373 . . . . .631, 633
C-351/96 Drouot Assurances SA v Consolidated Metallurgical
    Industries 485 [1999] QB 497 446–7
C-369/96 Ardblade [1999] ECR I-8453 and (C-374/96) [1998] ECR I-8385. . . . . .746, 866

1997

C-51/97 Réunion Européenne SA v Spliethoff's Bevrachtingskantoor
    BV [2000] QB 690 . . . . .245, 249, 265, 273,
                                                                                    279, 284, 286, 811
C-90/97 Swaddling v Adjudication Officer [1999] ECR I-1075 .179, 803
C-159/97 Trasporti Castelletti Spedizioni Internazionali SpA v Hugo
    Trumpy SpA [1999] ECR I-1597. . . . . .229, 232, 240, 242
C-260/97 Unibank A/S v Christensen [1999] ECR I-3715 612
C-420/97 Leathertex Divisione Sinetici SpA v Bodetex BVBA [1999]
    ECR I-6747 . . . . .253, 446, 456
C-440/97 GIE Groupe Concorde v The Master of the Vessel Suhadiwarno
    Panjan [1999] ECR I-6307 . . . . .254, 730

1998

C-7/98 Krombach v Bamberski [2001] QB 709, [2000] ECR I-1935 . . . . 143, 206, 279,
                                                                                627–8, 631, 639, 642,
                                                                                644, 753, 869, 1082
C-38/98 Régie Nationale des Usines Renault SA v Maxicar SpA
    [2000] ECR I-2973 . . . . .627–8, 631–2, 644, 753, 869
C-240/98 Oceano Grupo Editorial SA v Rocio Murciano
    Quintero [2000] ECR I-4941 . . . . .232, 296
C-387/98 Coreck Maritime GmbH v Handelsveem BV [2000]
    ECR I-9337 . . . . .230, 234, 241, 467
C-412/98 Universal General Insurance Co (UGIC) v Group Josi
    Reinsurance Co SA [2001] QB 68 . . . . .215, 226, 289

1999

C-267/97 Coursier v Fortis Bank [1999] ECR I-2543 621
C-518/99 Gaillard v Chekili [2001] ECR I-2771. 219

2000

C-8/98 Dansommer A/S v Gotz [2000] ECR I-393. 221–2
C-37/00 Weber v Universal Ogden Services Ltd [2002] QB 1189 . . . . .300, 877
C-80/00 Italian Leather SpA v WECO Polstermobel GmbH & Co [2002]
    ECR I-4995. . . . . .616, 639–40, 654
C-96/00 Gabriel v Schlanck & Schick GmbH [2002] ECR I-6367 . . . . .292, 294
C-167/00 Verein Für Konsumenteninformation v K H Henkel [2002]
    ECR I-8111 . . . . .205, 245, 249, 265–6, 293
C-256/00 Besix SA v Wasserreinigungsbau Alfred Kretzschmar GmbH & Co
    KG (WABAG) [2002] ECR I-1699 .249, 254, 258, 261, 263, 463

C-271/00 Gemeente Steenbergen v Baten [2002] ECR I-10489, [2003]
1 WLR 1996 . . . . .197, 205, 208, 688, 784
C-334/00 Fonderie Offi cine Meccaniche Tacconi SpA v Heinrich
Wagner Sinto Maschinenfabrik GmbH (HWS) [2002] ECR I-7357 . . . . 246, 249–50,
265, 298, 806, 850
C-437/00 Pugliese v Finmeccanica SpA [2003] ECR I-10829 302

2001

C-111/01 Gantner Electronic GmbH v Basch Exploitatie Maatschappij
BV [2003] ECR I-4207 . . . . .194, 445
C-266/01 Preservatrice Fonciere TIARD SA v Staat der Nederlanden [2003]
ECR I-4867 . . . . .125, 204–6
C-433/01 Freistaat Bayern v Jan Blijdenstein [2004] ECR I-981, [2004] IL Pr 8 . . . . .205, 245
C-464/01 Gruber v Bay Wa AG [2006] QB 204 293

2002

C-18/02 DFDS Torline v SEKO [2004] ECR I-1417, [2004] IL Pr 10 . . . . . . .267, 272, 835, 876
C-24/02 - Marseille Fret SA v Seatrano Shipping Co Ltd [2002] ECR I-3383 207
C-27/02 Petra Engler v Janus Versand GmbH [2005]
ECR I-481 . . . . .245, 247, 249–50, 264–5, 292, 294
C-39/02 Maersk Olie & Gas v Firma M de Haan en W de Boer [2004]
ECR I-9657 . . . . .444–5, 447, 455, 612, 615, 633–6
C-116/02 Erich Gasser GmbH v Misat Srl [2003] ECR I-4207 . . . . 195, 232, 243,
446, 450, 476
C-159/02 Turner v Grovit [2004] ECR I-3565, [2005] 1 AC 101 . . . . 433, 450, 463–4,
472, 477, 630, 979
C-168/02 Kronhofer v Maier [2004] IL Pr 27 . . . . .245, 277
C-265/02 Frahuil SA v Assitalia SPA [2004] ECR I-1543 . . . . .125–6, 204–5, 249
C-281/02 Owusu v Jackson [2005] ECR I-1383, [2005] QB 801 . . . . 195, 202, 215,
217, 243, 289, 296, 366, 388,
450, 458, 460–2, 494, 706

2003

C-4/03 Gesellschaft für Antriebstechnik mbH & Co KG (GAT) v Luk Lamellen
und Kupplungsbau Beteiligungs KG [2006] ECR I-6509 . . . . 51, 225, 314,
463, 466, 833
C-104/03 St Paul Dairy Industries NV v Unibel Exser BVBA [2005]
ECR I-3481, [2005] IL Pr 31. 304
C-112/03 Société Financière & Industrielle du Peloux v Société AXA
Belgium [2006] QB 251 . . . . .241, 291
C-148/03 Nurnberger Allgemeine Versicherungs AG v Portbridge
Transport International BV [2004] ECR I-10327 .203, 217, 309
C-433/03 Leffler v Berlin Chemie AG [2006] IL Pr 6 309
C-522/03 Scania Finance SA v Rockinger Spezialfabrik Fur Anhangerkupplungen
GmbH & Co [2006] IL Pr 1 . . . . .633, 635
C-539/03 Roche Nederland BV v Primus [2007] IL Pr 9. . . . . .285, 454, 456, 463
C-555/03 - Magali Warbecq v Ryanair Ltd. 207, 274

2004

C-77/04 GIE Réunion Européenne v Zurich España [2005] IL Pr 456 288–9
C-234/04 Kapferer v Schlank & Schick GmbH [2006] IL Pr 17 . . . . .250–1, 261
C-341/04 Eurofood IFSC Ltd [2006] IL Pr 23 . . . . .138, 628, 1313–15, 1318, 1323–4

C-343/04 Land Oberosterreich v CEZ AS [2006] IL Pr 25 ....217–18, 220, 486
C-473/04 Plumex v Young Sports NV 309

2005

C-3/05 Verdoliva v JM Van der Hoeven BV [2006] IL Pr 31 623
C-103/05 Reisch Montage AG v Kiesel Baumaschinen Handels GmbH
    [2006] ECR I-6827 ....284, 287
C-283/05 ASML Netherlands BV v Semiconductor Industry Services
    GmbH (SEMIS) [2007] IL Pr 4.......................633, 635, 639, 1082
C-292/05 Lechouritou v Germany [2007] IL Pr 14.........................205, 517, 793
C-386/05 Color Drack GmbH v LEXX International Vertriebs GmbH
    [2007] IL Pr 35 ....244, 254–5, 257, 259

2006

C-98/06 Freeport plc v Olle Arnoldsson [2007] IL Pr 58............................285–6
C-180/06 Renate Ilsinger v Martin Dreschers (Administrator in the Insolvency of
    Schlank & Schick GmbH) [2009] ECR I-3961 250, 292, 294-C-435/06 -
    Korkein hallinto-oikeus (Re C) OJ 2006 C 326/33, 2008 IL Pr 1 ....1093, 1102
C-463/06 FBTO Schadeverzekeringen NV v Jack Odenbreit...........................290

2007

C-14/07 Ingenieurburo Michael Weiss und Partner GbR v Industrie und
    Handelskammer Berlin...309, 636
C-68/07 Sundelind Lopez v Lopez Lizazo [2008] IL Pr 4.........................960–2
C-185/07 Allianz v West Tankers [2009] ECR I-663, [2009] 1 AC 1138..............444, 479
C-394/07 Gambazzi v DaimlerChrysler Canada Inc and CIBC Mellon
    Trust Co [2009] ECR I-2563................................612, 616, 626–8, 633
C-413/07 Haase v Superfast Ferries SA 300
C-420/07 Apostolides v Orams [2009] ECR I-3571 .... 523, 612, 618,
    627–8, 631–2, 638, 642
C-444/07 MG Probud Gdynia sp z o o, ECLI:EU:C:2010:24.........................1323
C-523/07 Proceedings Brought by A [2009] ECR I-02805,
    [2010] Fam 42- 175–8, 182–3, 956, 1093–5, 1102,
    1104, 1118–20, 1123, 1242
C-533/07 Falco Privatstiftung and Thomas Rabitsch v Gisela
    Weller-Lindhorst [2009] ECR I-3327 ....261–2, 728, 730

2008

C-111/08 SCT Industri [2009] ECR I-5655 ....207, 1321
C-133/08 Intercontainer Interfrigo SC (ICF) v Balkenende Oosthuizen BV
    and MIC Operations BV [2009] ECR I-9687 ....684, 706–8, 725, 731, 737, 740
C-167/08 Draka NK Cables Ltd v Omnipol Ltd [2009] ECR I-3477 625
C-168/08 [2009] ECR I-6871 955
C-189/08 Zuid-Chemie BV v Philippo's Mineralenfabriek NV/SA [2009]
    ECR I-6917..263, 272, 277
C-195/08 PPU, Rinau v Rinau, [2008] ECR I-05271 ....1130, 1162
C-204/08 Peter Rehder v Air Baltic Corporation [2009] ECR I-6073 259–60
C-292/08 *German Graphics Graphische Maschinen GmbH v Alice van*
    der Schee [2009] ECR I-8421...208, 1320
C-347/08 Vorarlberger Gebietskrankenkasse v WGV-Schwäbische Allgemeine
    Versicherungs AG [2009] ECR I-8661...................................289, 690
C-381/08 Car Trim GmbH v KeySafety Systems Srl [2010] ECR I-1255 ....255, 258, 727

C-403/08 and C-429/08 Football Association Premier League Ltd and Others v QC
Leisure and Others and Karen Murphy v Media Protection Services Ltd [2011]
ECR I-9083 . . . . .688, 784
C-533/08 TNT Express Nederland BV v Axa Versicherung AG [2010]
ECR I-4107 . . . . .203, 389, 613–14, 646
C-585/08 and C-144/09 Pammer v Reederei Karl Schlüter GmbH & Co.
KG and Hotel Alpenhof GesmbH v Heller [2010] ECR I-12527 . . . . .294, 295, 688

2009

C-19/09 Wood Floor Solutions Andreas Domberger GmbH v Silva Trade SA
[2010] ECR I-2121 . . . . .257, 259, 260
C-111/09 Česká podnikatelská pojišťovna as, Vienna Insurance Group v Bilas
[2010] ECR I-4545 . . . . .229, 291, 642
C-144/09 Pammer v Reederei Karl Schlüter GmbH & Co. KG and Hotel
Alpenhof GesmbH v Heller [2010] ECR I-12527 . . . . .294, 295, 688
C-208/09 Ilonka Sayn-Wittgenstein v Landeshauptstadt von Wien [2010]
ECR I-13693 35
C-232/09 Danosa v LKB Lizings SIA [2010] ECR I-11405 299
C-256/09, Bianca Purrucker v Guillermo Vallés Pérez, [2010] ECR I-07353 . . . . 1120, 1123,
1127, 1131
T-296/09 Intel Corp. v European Commission ECLI:EU:T:2014:547 827
C-324/09 L'Oréal v eBay [2011] ECR I-6011 832
C-391/09 Runevič-Vardyn & Wardyn v Vilniaus miesto savivaldybès
administacija [2011] ECR I-3787 35
C-396/09 Interedil Srl v Fallimento Interedil Srl en Intesa Gestione
Crediti SpA, ECLI:EU:C:2011:671 1315
C-403/09 PPU, Detiček v Sgueglia [2009] ECR I-12193 1120
C-406/09 Realchemie Nederland BV v Bayer CropScience AG [2011]
ECR I-9773 . . . . .126, 195, 205, 613
C-509/09 and C-161/10 eDate Advertising GmbH v X and Olivier Martinez
and Robert Martinez v MGN Limited [2011] ECR I-10269 . . . . . . 263, 270, 271, 275, 278,
873, 887, 888

2010

C-29/10 Heiko Koelzsch v État du Grand Duchy of Luxemburg [2011]
ECR I-1595 . . . . .684, 688–90, 741
C-87/10 Electrosteel Europe SA v Edil Centro SpA [2011] ECR I-4987 258
C-112/10 Procureur-generaal bij het hof van beroep te Antwerpen V Zaza Retail BV, ...
ECLI:EU:C:2011:743 1317
C-139/10 Prism Investment BV v Jaap Anne van der Meer [2011] ECR I-9511 . . . . .621, 626
C-144/10 BVG v JPMorgan Chase Bank SA [2011] ECR I-3961 224
C-145/10 Eva-Maria Painer v Standard Verlags GmbH EU:C:2011 285
C-161/10 eDate Advertising GmbH v X and Olivier Martinez and Robert Martinez v
MGN Limited [2011] ECR I-10269 . . . . .263, 270–1, 275, 278, 873, 887–8
C-191/10 Rastelli Davide e C Snc v Jean-Charles Hidoux (qualitate qua),
ECLI:EU:C:2011:838 . . . . .1315, 1318
C-211/10 PPU, Povse v Alpago [2010] ECR I– 6673 . . . . .1158, 1161–2
C-213/10 F-Tex SIA v Lietuvos-Anglijos UAB "Jadecloud-Vilma" EU:C:2012:215,
[2012] IL Pr 24 208
C-292/10 G v De Visser EU:C:2012:142, [2013] QB 168 . . . . .200, 324, 659
C-296/10, Bianca Purrucker v Guillermo Vallés Pérez (No 2), [2010]
ECR I-11163 . . . . .1118, 1120, 1123
C-327/10 Hypoteční banka as v Lindner EU:C:2011:745 . . . . .200, 202, 296, 324
C-371/10 National Grid Indus BV v Inspecteur van de Belastingdienst
Rijnmond/kantoor Rotterdam [2011] ECR I-12273 35

C-378/10 VALE Építési kft EU:C:2012:440, [2013] 1 WLR 294 . . . . .35, 1307
C-384/10 Jan Voogsgeerd v Navimer SA ECLI:EU:C:2011:842 741
C-384/10 Voogsgeerd v Navimer SA [2011] ECR I-13275 301
C-400/10 PPU, J McB v LE [2010] ECR I-08965. . . . . .1093, 1138
C-412/10 Deo Antoine Homawoo v GMF Assurances SA ECLI:EU:
    C:2011:747 . . . . .783–4, 786
C-491/10 PPU, Aguirre Zarraga v Simone Pelz [2010] ECR I-14247 1162
C-497/10 PPU, Mercredi v Chaffe [2010] ECLI:EU:C:2010:829 . . . . 175–8, 182,
    803, 956, 1094–5, 1104, 1242
C-514/10 Wolf Naturprodukte GmbH v SEWAR spol sro EU:C:2012:367,
    [2012] IL Pr 37 610
C-523/10 Wintersteiger AG v Products 4U Sondermaschinenbau GmbH
    EU:C:2012:220, [2012] IL Pr 23. . . . . .264, 272, 276, 278
C-543/10 Refcomp SpA v Axa Corporate Solutions Assurance SA
    EU:C:2013:62, [2013] 1 Lloyd's Rep 449 . . . . .242, 246
C-616/10 Solvay SA v Honeywell Fluorine Products Europe BV EU:C:2012:445 . . .218, 286, 305
C-619/10 Trade Agency Ltd v Seramico Investments Ltd
    EU:C:2012:531 . . . . .311, 629, 630, 633–4, 637

2011

C-5/11 Criminal Proceedings against Titus Alexander Jochen Donner
    ECLI:EU:C:2012:370 832–3
C-116/11 Bank Handlowy w Warszawie SA and PPHU "ADAX"/Ryszard
    Adamiak v Christianapol sp z o o, ECLI:EU:C:2012:739 . . . . .1316, 1321, 1323
C-133/11 Folien Fischer AG and Fofitec AG v Ritrama SpA EU:C:2012:664,
    [2013] QB 523 . . . . .251, 267
C-154/11 Ahmed Mahamdia v République algérienne démocratique et
    populaire EU:C:2012:491, [2014] All ER (EC) 96 . . . . .204, 280, 299, 302, 517
C-173/11 Football Dataco Ltd and Others v Sportradar GmbH and
    Sportradar AG ECLI:EU:C:2012:642 832
C-190/11 Mühlleitner v Yusufi EU:C:2012:542, [2012] IL Pr 46 294
C-215/11 Iwona Szyrocka v SiGerTechnologie GmbH EU:C:2012:794 661
C-228/11 Melzer v MF Global UK Ltd EU:C:2013:305, [2013] QB 1112. 274
C-325/11 Alder v Orlowska EU:C:2012:824. 308
C-419/11 Česká spořitelna as v Feichter EU:C:2013:165 at [46], [2013] IL
    Pr 22 . . . . .246–7, 249–50, 261–2, 292
C-456/11 Gothaer Allgemeine Versicherung AG v Samskip GmbH EU:C:2012:719,
    [2013] QB 548 . . . . .478, 612, 650
C-461/11 Ulf Kazmierz Radziejewski v Kronofogdemyndigheten i Stockholm,
    ECLI:EU:C:2012:704 1313
C-645/11 Land Berlin v Ellen Mirjam Sapir EU:C:2013:228, [2013] IP Pr 29 . . . . .205, 287

2012

C-9/12 Corman-Collins SA v La Maison du Whisky SA EU:C:2013:860,
    [2014] QB 431 . . . . 256 729–30
C-49/12 Her Majesty's Revenue & Customs v Sunico ApS EU:C:2013:231,
    [2014] QB 391 . . . . .125, 195, 204, 206
C-64/12 Anton Schlecker v Melitta Josefa Boedeker ECLI:EU:C:2013:551. . . . . .737, 741
C-92/12, Health Service Executive v SC and AC, [2012] 2 FLR 1040. . . . . .1093, 1119–20, 1123
C-144/12 Goldbet Sportwetten GmbH v Massimo Sperindeo
    EU:C:2013:393, [2014] IL Pr 1. . . . . .227, 662
C-147/12 ÖFAB, Östergötlands Fastigheter AB v Frank Koot and Evergreen
    Investments BV EU:C:2013:490, [2015] QB 20 .245, 265, 272, 274
C-156/12 GREP GmbH v Freistaat Bayern EU:C:2012:342,
    [2015] IL Pr 29 622

C-157/12 Salzgitter Mannesmann Handel GmbH v SC Laminorul SA
EU:C:2013:597, [2014] 1 WLR 904 641
C-170/12 Peter Pinckney v KDG Mediatech AG EU:C:2013:635,
[2014] IL Pr 7 . . . . .264, 276, 279, 833
C-184/12 United Antwerp Maritime Agencies (Unamar) NV v Navigation
Maritime Bulgare EU:C:2013:663, [2014] 1 Lloyd's Rep 161 . . . . 144, 706, 746,
749–50, 866
C-218/12 Emrek v Sabranovic EU:C:2013:666, [2014] IL Pr 39 295
C-324/12 Novontech-Zala kft v Logicdata Electronic and Software Entwicklungs
GmbH EU:C:2013:205 662
C-328/12 Ralph Schmid v Lilly Hertel, ECLI:EU:C:2014:6 1318
C-360/12 Coty Germany GmbH v First Note Perfumes NV EU:C:2014:1318,
[2015] IL Pr 13 . . . . .264, 274, 276, 279, 834
C-386/12 Siegfried János Schneider EU:C:2013:633, [2014] 2 WLR 1048 . . . . .51, 206
C-387/12 Hi Hotel HCF SARL v Uwe Spoering EU:C:2014:215, [2014]
1 WLR 1912 . . . . .264, 274, 276, 279
C-438/12 Weber v Weber EU:C:2014:212, [2015] Ch 140 . . . . .219, 453
C-452/12 Nipponkoa Insurance Co (Europe) Ltd v Inter-Zuid Transport BV
EU:C:2013:858, [2014] IL Pr 10, [2014] 1 All ER (Comm) 288 . . . . .203, 389, 613
C-469/12 Krejci Lager & Umschlagbetriebs GmbH v Olbrich Transport und
Logistik GmbH EU:C:2013:788, [2014] IL Pr 8 . . . . .222, 257
C-478/12 Maletic v lastminute.com Gmbh and TUI Österreich GmbH
EU:C:2013:735, [2014] QB 424 296
C-479/12 H Gautzsch Großhandel GmbH & Co KG v Münchener
Boulevard Möbel Joseph Duna GmbH ECLI:EU:C:2014:75 834
C-508/12 Walter Vapenik v Josef Thurner EU:C:2013:790, [2014]
1 WLR 2486 . . . . .293, 658, 741
C-519/12 OTP Bank Nyilvánosan Működő Részvénytársaság v Hochtief
Solution AG EU:C:2013:674, [2015] IL Pr 30 . . . . .245, 265
C-548/12 Marc Brogsitter v Fabrication de Montres Normandes EURL
and Karsten Fräßdorf EU:C:2014:148, [2014] QB 753 . . . . 46, 250, 265,
268, 693, 789–90, 792, 805–6

2013

C-1/13 Cartier Parfums-Lunettes SAS v Ziegler France SA EU:C:2014:109,
[2014] IL Pr 25 444
C-45/13 Andreas Kainz v Pantherwerke AG EU:C:2014:7 at [20],
[2015] QB 34 . . . . .248, 263, 267, 272, 785
C-98/13 Martin Blomqvist v Rolex SA and Manufacture des Montres
Rolex SA ECLI:EU:C:2014:55 833
C-112/13 A v B EU:C:2014:2195 . . . . .227, 628, 634
C-119/13 and C-120/13 Eco Cosmetics GmbH & Co KG v Dupuy and
Raiffeisenbank St Georgen reg, Gen mbH v Bonchyk
EU:C:2014:2144, [2015] 1 WLR 678 661
C-157/13 Nickel & Goeldner Spedition GmbH v "Kintra" UAB EU:C:2014:2145,
[2015] QB 96 . . . . .207, 1318
C-295/13 H v HK, ECLI:EU:C:2014:2410 1318
C-302/13 flyLAL-Lithuanian Airlines AS v Starptautiskā lidosta Rīga VAS and
Air Baltic Corporation AS EU:C:2014:2319, [2015] IL Pr 2 . . . . .205, 629, 631, 827–8
C-305/13 Haeger & Schmidt GmbH v Mutuelles du Mans assurances IARD
(MMA IARD) ECLI:EU:C:2014:2320 . . . . .731, 737–8
C-352/13 Cartel Damage Claims Hydrogen Peroxide SA (CDC) v Evonik
Degussa GmbH EU:C:2015:335, [2015] QB 906 . . . . 237, 264, 271, 274, 275,
284, 287, 811, 827–8, 856

C-366/13 Profit Investment SIM SpA v Stefano Ossi EU:C:2016:282,
  [2016] 1 WLR 3832 . . . . .240, 242, 248, 251, 285
C-375/13 Harald Kolassa v Barclays Bank plc EU:C:2015:37, [2016]
  1 All ER (Comm) 733 . . . . 46, 246–7, 249–50,
                                                                                        277, 292, 296, 812
C-436/13, E v B. 1099
C-441/13 Pez Hejduk v EnergieAgentur.NRW GmbH EU:C:2015:28
  at [24], [2015] Bus LR 560 . . . . .264, 272, 276, 279
C-536/13 Gazprom OAO v Lithuania EU:C:2015:316, [2015] 1 WLR 4937. . . . . .208, 480
C-557/13 Hermann Lutz v Elke Bäuerle ECLI:EU:C:2015:227 . . . . .773, 1322
C-649/13 Comité d'entreprise de Nortel Networks SA and Others v Cosme
  Rogeau (qualitate qua) and Cosme Rogeau (qualitate qua) v Alan Robert
  Bloom, Alan Michael Hudson, Stephen John Harris and Christopher John
  Wilkinson Hill, ECLI:EU:C:2015:384 1316–17
656/13, L v M 1099
C-681/13 Diageo Brands BV v Simiramida-04 EOOD EU:C:2015:471 . . . . .628, 631

2014

C-4/14 Bohez v Wiertz EU:C:2015:563, [2015] IL Pr 43 206
C-47/14 Holterman Ferho Exploitatie BV and Others v Friedrich Leopold Freiherr Spies von
  Büllesheim EU:C:2015:574, [2015] IL Pr 44. . . . . . .246, 257, 260, 268–9, 272, 297–8, 701
C-94/14 Flight Refund Ltd v Deutsche Lufthansa AG EU:C:2016:148, [2016] 1 WLR 3567. .662
C-184/14 A v B, 16 July 2015, ECLI:EU:C:2015:479. . . . . .1066, 1074, 1083
C-240/14 Eleonore Prüller-Frey v Norbert Brodnig and Axa Versicherung AG
  ECLI:EU:C:2015:567 872
C-245/14 Thomas Cook Belgium NV v Thurner Hotel GmbH EU:C:2015:715,
  [2016] 1 WLR 878 662
C-292/14 Elliniko Dimosio v Stefanos Stroumpoulis and Others
  ECLI:EU:C:2016:116 . . . . .692, 876
C-297/14 Hobohm v Benedikt Kampik Ltd & Co KG EU:C:2015:844,
  [2016] QB 616 . . . . .293, 295
C-300/14 Imtech Marine Belgium NV v Radio Hellenic SA EU:C:2015:825,
  [2016] 1 WLR 1625 . . . . .657, 659
C-310/14 Nike European Operations Netherlands BV v Sportland Oy,
  ECLI:EU:C:2015:690 1322
C-322/14 El Majdoub v CarsOnTheWeb.Deutschland GmbH EU:C:2015:334,
  [2015] 1 WLR 3986 239
C-350/14 Florin Lazar, représenté légalement par Luigi Erculeo v Allianz SpA
  ECLI:EU:C:2015:802, [2016] 1 WLR 835 . . . . 349, 688, 783–4,
                                                                                        811, 813, 864
C-359/14 and C-475/14 ERGO Insurance SE v If P&C Insurance AS and
  Gjensidige Baltic AAS v PZU Lietuva UAB DK ECLI:EU:
  C:2016:40 . . . . 689–90, 692–3, 743, 773,
                                                                                        783, 785, 788–9, 859, 872
C-376/14 PPU C v M [2014] All ER (D) 160 (Oct) .1094–5, 1104, 1118
C-483/14 KA Finanz AG v Sparkassen Versicherung AG Vienna
  Insurance Group ECLI:EU:C:2016:205. 701
C-489/14, OJ 2015 C 389/12 971
C-511/14 Pebros Servizi Srl v Aston Martin Lagonda Ltd EU:C:2016:448,
  [2016] 4 WLR 138 657
C-521/14 SOVAG— Schwarzmeer und Ostsee Versicherungs-Aktiengesellschaft
  v If Vahinkovakuutusyhtiö Oy EU:C:2016:41, [2016] QB 780 288
C-523/14 Aannemingsbedrijf Aertssen NV and Aertssen Terrassements SA
  v VSB Machineverhuur BV EU:C:2015:722, [2016] IL Pr 16 . . . . .206, 448

C-559/14 EU:C:2016:349, [2017] QB 85 629
C-572/14 Austro-Mechana Gesellschaft zur Wahrnehmung mechanisch-musikalischer
Urheberrechte Gesellschaft mbH v Amazon EU Sàrl EU:C:2016:286,
[2016] ECDR 23 . . . . .264, 267, 790, 792, 805
C-594/14 Simona Kornhaas v Thomas Dithmar (qualitate qua),
ECLI:EU:C:2015:806 . . . . .1319, 1321
C-605/14 Komu v Komu EU:C:2015:833, [2016] 4 WLR 26 219

2015

C-12/15 Universal Music International Holding BV v Michael Tétreault
Schilling EU:C:2016:449, [2016] QB 967 . . . . .263, 277, 811–12
C-70/15 Lebek v Domino EU:C:2016:524, [2016] 1 WLR 4221 638
C-102/15 Gazdasági Versenyhivatal v Siemens Aktiengesellschaft Österreich
EU:C:2016:225 at [70], [2016] IL Pr 33 . . . . .265, 267, 694, 828
C-135/15 Republik Griechenland v Grigorios Nikiforidis
ECLI:EU:C:2016:774 . . . . .687, 689, 751, 754, 772
C-175/15 Taser International Inc v SC Gate 4 Business SRL and Cristian
Mircea Anastasiu EU:C:2016:176, [2016] QB 887 . . . . .226, 229
C-185/15 Kostanjevec v F&S Leasing GmbH EU:C:2016:397 .248, 288
C-191/15 Verein für Konsumenteninformation v Amazon EU Sàrl
ECLI:EU:C:2016:612 . . . . 688, 741, 783,
789, 804, 824, 825
C-196/15 Granarolo SpA v Ambrosi Emmi France SA
EU:C:2016:559 . . . . 245–7, 256, 258,
264, 694, 703, 806, 808, 850–1
C-222/15 Hoszig Kft v Alstom Power Thermal Services
EU:C:2016:525, [2016] IL Pr 36 . . . . .234, 239
C-230/15 Brite Strike Technologies Inc v Brite Strike Technologies SA
EU:C:2016:560, [2016] IL Pr 37 . . . . .203, 389
C-417/15 Schmidt v Schmidt EU:C:2016:881 . . . . .206, 220, 246, 261, 809
C-428/15, Child and Family Agency v J. D., [2016] All ER (D)
24 (Nov) 1093, 1114, 1116
C-455/15 PPU, P v Q, [2015] All ER (D) 181 (Nov) 1128–9
C-484/15 Zulfikarpašić v Gajer EU:C:2017:199, [2017] IL Pr 16 . . . . .611, 657
C-533/15 Feliks Frisman v Finnair Oyj OJ 2016 C 48/8 260
C-551/15 Pula Parking d o o v Tederahn EU:C:2017:193, [2017] IL Pr 15 . . . . .206, 611, 657

2016

C-168/16 Sandra Nogueira v Crewlink Ltd and C-169/16 Miguel José
Moreno Osacar v Ryanair Ltd EU:C:2017:312 300
C-194/16 Bolagsupplysningen OÜ, Ingrid Ilsjan v Svensk Handel AB OJ
2016 C 211/35 278
C-283/16 MS v PS ECLI:EU:C:2017:104 1082
C-447/16 Becker v Hainan Airlines Co Ltd and C-448/16 Barkan v Air
Nostrum LAM SA OJ 2016 C 428/5 260

PART I

INTRODUCTION

1. Definition, Nature and Scope of Private
   International Law   3
2. Historical Development and Current Theories   17

1

DEFINITION, NATURE AND SCOPE
OF PRIVATE INTERNATIONAL LAW

1. Introduction	3	4. Meaning of "Foreign Law"		8
2. Space and Time	5	5. International Variety of Private		
(a) Space	5	International Law Rules		8
(b) Time	5	6. Avoiding Conflicts		9
3. Scope of Private International Law	6	(a) Unification of internal laws		9
(a) Jurisdiction	6	(b) Unification of private		
(b) Recognition	7	international law		10
(c) Choice of law	7	7. The Name of the Subject		15

1. INTRODUCTION

Private international law is that part of English law which comes into operation whenever the court is faced with a claim that contains a foreign element. It is only when this element is present that private international law has a function to perform. It has three main objects.

First, to prescribe the conditions under which the court is competent to entertain such a claim.

Secondly, to determine for each class of case the particular municipal system of law by reference to which the rights of the parties must be ascertained.

Thirdly, to specify the circumstances in which (a) a foreign judgment can be recognised as decisive of the question in dispute; and (b) the right vested in the judgment creditor by a foreign judgment can be enforced by action in England.

The *raison d'être* of private international law is the existence in the world of a number of separate municipal systems of law—a number of separate legal units—that differ greatly from each other in the rules by which they regulate the various legal relations arising in daily life. Courts in one country must frequently take account of some rule of law that exists in another. A sovereign is supreme within his own territory and, according to the universal maxim of jurisprudence, he has exclusive jurisdiction over everybody and everything within that territory and over every transaction that is effected there. He can, if he chooses, refuse to consider any law but his own. Although the adoption of this policy of indifference might have been common enough in other ages, it is impracticable in the modern civilised world. Consequently, nations have long found that they cannot, by sheltering behind the principle of territorial sovereignty, afford to disregard foreign rules of law merely because they happen to be different from their own internal system of law. Moreover, as will be shown later, it is no derogation of sovereignty to take account of foreign law.

The recognition of a foreign law in a case containing a foreign element may be necessary for at least two reasons. In the first place, the invariable application of the law of the forum, ie the local law of the place where the court is situated, would often lead to gross injustice. Suppose that a person engaged in English litigation is required to prove that she is the lawful widow of a man who has just died, the marriage having taken place abroad many years ago. The marriage ceremony, though regular according to the law of the place where it was performed, did not perhaps satisfy the formal requirements of English law, but nevertheless to apply the English Marriage Act 1949 to such a union, and thereby to deny that the couple were man and wife, would be nothing but a travesty of justice.

Secondly, if the court is to carry out in a rational manner the policy to which it is now committed—that of entertaining actions in respect of foreign claims—it must, in the nature of things, take account of the relevant foreign law or laws. A claimant,[1] for instance, seeks damages for breach of a contract that was both made and to be performed in France. Under the existing practice the court is prepared to create and to enforce in his favour, if he substantiates his case, an English right corresponding as nearly as possible to that which he claims. However, neither the nature nor the extent of the relief to which he is rightly entitled nor, indeed, whether he is entitled to any relief can be determined if the law of France is disregarded. This is because to consider English law alone might reverse the legal obligations of the parties as fixed by the law to which their transaction, both in fact and by intention, was originally subjected. A promise, for instance, made by an Englishman in Italy and to be performed there, if valid and enforceable by Italian law, would not be held void by an English court merely because it was unsupported by consideration.[2]

In justifying this reference to a foreign law, English judges and textbook writers have frequently used[3] the term *comity of nations*, "a phrase which is grating to the ear, when it proceeds from a court of justice".[4] Although the term has been often used, analysis of it reveals that it has been employed in a meaningless or misleading way. The word itself is incompatible with the judicial function, for comity is a matter for sovereigns, not for judges required to decide a case according to the rights of the parties.[5] Again, if the word is given its normal meaning of courtesy it is scarcely consistent with the readiness of English courts to apply enemy law in time of war. Moreover, if courtesy formed the basis of private international law a judge might feel compelled to ignore the law of Utopia on proof that Utopian courts apply no law but their own, since comity implies a bilateral, not a unilateral, relationship. If, on the other hand, comity means that no foreign law is applicable in England except with the permission of the sovereign, it is nothing more than a truism. The fact is, of course, that the application of a foreign law implies no act of courtesy, no sacrifice of sovereignty. It merely derives from a desire to do justice.

Private international law, then, is that part of law which comes into play when the issue before the court affects some fact, event or transaction that is so closely connected with a foreign system of law as to necessitate recourse to that system. It has, accordingly, been described as meaning "the rules voluntarily chosen by a given State for the decision of cases which have a foreign complexion".[6] The legal systems of the world consist of a variety of territorial systems, each dealing with the same phenomena of life—birth, death, marriage, divorce, bankruptcy, contracts, wills and so on—but in most cases dealing with them differently. The moment that a case is seen to be affected by a foreign element, the court must look beyond its own internal

---

[1] Following the reforms to civil procedure introduced in 1999, the term "claimant" is now used in place of "plaintiff". It needs to be borne in mind that the latter term was used in earlier English decisions and is still used in other common law jurisdictions.

[2] *Re Bonacina* [1912] 2 Ch 394; and see now the Contracts (Applicable Law) Act 1990.

[3] Eg *Amin Rasheed Shipping Corpn v Kuwait Insurance Co* [1984] AC 50 at 65; *Spiliada Maritime Corpn v Cansulex Ltd* [1987] AC 460 at 477; *Société Nationale Industrielle Aérospatiale v Lee Kui Jak* [1987] AC 871 at 895; and *Arab Monetary Fund v Hashim (No 3)* [1991] 2 AC 114 at 136.

[4] De Nova (1964) 8 Am JLH 136, 141, citing the early American author, Livermore.

[5] Nadelmann, *Conflict of Laws: International and Interstate*, p 8; for further discussion see Wolff, pp 14–15; Yntema (1966) 65 Mich LR 1; Khan-Freund (1974) III Hague Recueil 147, 164.

[6] Baty, *Polarized Law*, p 148.

law, lest the relevant rule of the internal system to which the case most appropriately belongs should happen to be in conflict with that of the forum. The forms in which this foreign element may appear are numerous. One of the parties may be foreign by nationality or domicile; a businessman may be declared bankrupt in England, having numerous creditors abroad; the action may concern property situated abroad or a disposition made abroad of property situated in England; if the action is on a bill of exchange, the foreign element may consist in the fact that the drawing or acceptance or endorsement was made abroad; a contract may have been made in one country to be performed in another; two persons may resort to the courts of a foreign country where the means of contracting or of dissolving a marriage are more convenient than in the country of their domicile. It is the existence of such foreign elements as these that has caused the courts to frame a number of different *rules for the choice of law* which demonstrate the most appropriate legal system to govern the issue that has arisen.

2. SPACE AND TIME

(a) Space

It is frequently stressed that the function of private international law is to indicate the area over which a rule of law extends—that it "deals primarily with the application of laws in space".[7] The essence of this is that a rule of substantive law, eg the English rule that every simple contract must be supported by consideration, is generally expressed in universal terms and seems to have no dimension in space, for according to its wording it applies to all contracts wherever made. But its dimension in space, ie its sphere of authority, is the very thing that is fixed by private international law, because a sovereign is free to provide, if he chooses, that the area over which a rule of substantive law, whether domestic or foreign, is to prevail shall be wider than the territorial jurisdiction in which it originated. If, for instance, an English court decides that the goods situated in England belonging to a man who died intestate and domiciled in France shall be distributed according to the provisions of the Code Napoléon, what it decides in effect is that the rule of the French internal law relating to intestacy is, in the case of persons domiciled in France, to be given effect outside the territorial limits of the French law-maker, provided of course that French law so permits. In the words of Savigny:

> It is this diversity of positive laws which makes it necessary to mark off for each, in sharp outline, the area of its authority, to fix the limits of different positive laws in respect to one another.[8]

This method of expressing the function of the subject does not mean that the sphere of application of each rule of law is, or can be, determined once and for all for every situation to which it may be relevant.[9] The area over which any given rule of law extends will vary with the particular circumstances in which its operation is under consideration. Consequently, the English rules governing contractual capacity will apply to certain transactions effected by domiciled Englishmen abroad, but not to others.

(b) Time

There are certain circumstances in which the factor of time as well as that of space may require consideration.[10] In the dimension of space, for instance, the rights of a husband and

---

[7] Beale, p 1; see especially, Unger (1957) 43, Grotius Society 87, 94 et seq.

[8] *Private International Law*, Guthrie's translation, p 6.

[9] Cook, *Logical and Legal Bases of Conflict of Laws*, p 7.

[10] On this topic, see F A Mann (1954) 31 BYBIL 317; Grodecki (1959) 35 BYBIL 58; Spiro (1960) 9 ICLQ 357; Kahn-Freund (1974) III Hague Receuil 147, 441–6; Fassberg (1990) 38 ICLQ 956; Grodecki,

wife to each other's property are usually governed, in the absence of a marriage settlement, by the law of the domicile. But does this rule of selection refer to domicile at the time of the marriage or to domicile as it may change from time to time?[11] Again, whether a will has been effectively revoked by the execution of a later will or by its destruction is determinable by the law of the testator's domicile, but if his domicile does not remain constant this selective rule will produce no decision until it has been decided whether the reference is to the law of the domicile at the time of the execution, or of the act of destruction, or at the time of the testator's death.[12]

Another type of case in which the factor of time is relevant arises where, subsequently to the transaction in issue, there has been a change in the foreign law selected to govern the rights of the parties. Here, it is essential to ascertain whether the English court must apply the foreign law as it stood at the time of the transaction or as it now exists after the change.[13] Generally, courts prefer the latter solution.[14]

A variety of situations in which the factor of time is pertinent will be considered at later stages in this book.

3. SCOPE OF PRIVATE INTERNATIONAL LAW

Private international law is not a separate branch of law in the same sense as, say, the law of contract or of tort. It is all-pervading.

> It starts up unexpectedly in any court and in the midst of any process. It may be sprung like a mine in a plain common law action, in an administrative proceeding in equity, or in a divorce case, or a bankruptcy case, in a shipping case or a matter of criminal procedure. . . . The most trivial action of debt, the most complex case of equitable claims, may be suddenly interrupted by the appearance of a knot to be untied only by Private International Law.[15]

Nevertheless, private international law is a separate and distinct unit in the English legal system just as much as the law of tort or of contract, but it possesses this unity, not because it deals with one particular topic, but because it is always concerned with one or more of three questions, namely:

(a) Jurisdiction of the English court.
(b) Recognition and enforcement of foreign judgments.
(c) The choice of law.

We must be prepared to consider almost every branch of private law, but only in connection with these three matters.

(a) Jurisdiction

The basic rule at common law is that the English court has no jurisdiction to entertain an action *in personam* unless the defendant has been personally served with a claim form in England or Wales. This rule, which cannot be satisfied while the defendant is abroad, applies,

---

3 *International Encyclopedia of Comparative Law*, Chapter 8; Dicey, Morris and Collins, pp 63–76; Morris, paras 20-034–20-045.

[11] See infra, pp 1367 and 1368.
[12] See infra, pp 1348–50.
[13] See for instance, infra, pp 897–8.
[14] *Re Chesterman's Trusts* [1923] 2 Ch 466 at 478.
[15] Frederic Harrison, *Jurisprudence and the Conflict of Laws*, pp 101–2.

of course, whether the case has a foreign complexion or not, but there are three reasons which require the question of jurisdiction to be separately treated in a book on private international law. First, there are certain circumstances in which the court is empowered by statute to assume jurisdiction over absent defendants, a power which naturally is of greater significance in foreign than in domestic cases.[16] Secondly, there are certain types of action, such as a petition for divorce, where the mere presence of the defendant in the country does not render the court jurisdictionally competent.[17] Thirdly, there is a separate regime of jurisdictional rules in the case of a defendant domiciled (in a specially defined sense) in a Member State of the European Union.[18]

(b) Recognition

Where there has been litigation abroad, but the defendant has most of his assets in England, it will be important to ascertain whether English law will recognise or permit the enforcement of the foreign judgment. Provided that the foreign court had jurisdiction to adjudicate on the case, according to English private international law, the English court will generally recognise the foreign judgment as if one of its own and it can be enforced accordingly.[19] Again, our membership of the European Union has led to the introduction of important specific rules for the recognition of judgments from courts of the Member States.[20]

(c) Choice of law

If the English court decides that it possesses jurisdiction, then a further question, as to the choice of law, must be considered; ie which system of law, English or foreign, must govern the case?[21] The action before the English court, for instance, may concern a contract made or a tort committed abroad or the validity of a will made by a person who died domiciled abroad. In each case that part of English law which consists of private international law directs what legal system shall apply to the case, ie, to use a convenient expression, what system of internal law shall constitute the applicable law. English private international law, for instance, requires that the movable property of a British subject who dies intestate domiciled in Italy shall be distributed according to Italian law. These rules for the choice of law, then, indicate the particular legal system by reference to which a solution of the dispute must be reached. This does not necessarily mean that only one legal system is applicable, for different aspects of a case may be governed by different laws, as is the case with marriage where formal and essential validity are governed by different laws.[22]

The function of private international law is complete when it has chosen the appropriate system of law. Its rules do not furnish a direct solution of the dispute, and it has been said that this department of law resembles the inquiry office at a railway station where a passenger may learn the platform at which his train starts. If, for instance, the defence to an action for breach of contact made in France is that the formalities required by French law have not been observed, private international law ordains that the formal validity of the contract shall be determined by French law. But it says no more. The relevant French law must then be proved by a witness expert in the subject.

---

[16] Infra, p 334.
[17] Infra, p 954 et seq.
[18] See infra, Chapter 11.
[19] Infra, p 525 et seq.
[20] Infra, p 608 et seq.
[21] For the view that this question is becoming less significant in comparison with jurisdictional issues, see Briggs (1989) 9 OJLS 251, 252–7; Fawcett [1991] Current Legal Problems 39.
[22] Infra, p 893 et seq.

It is generally said that the judge at the forum "applies" or "enforces" the chosen law, or alternatively that the case is "governed" by the foreign law. These expressions are convenient to describe loosely what happens, but they are not accurate. Neither is it strictly accurate to say that the judge enforces not the foreign law, but a right acquired under the foreign law.[23] The only law applied by the judge is the law of the forum, the only rights enforced by him are those created by the law of the forum. But owing to the foreign element in the case, the foreign law is a fact that must be taken into consideration, and what the judge attempts to do is to create and to enforce a right as nearly as possible similar to that which would have been created by the foreign court had it been seised of a similar case which was purely domestic in character.[24]

4. MEANING OF "FOREIGN LAW"

For the purposes of private international law the expression "foreign system of law" means a distinctive legal system prevailing in a territory other than that in which the court functions. It therefore includes, not merely the law existing in a state under a foreign political sovereignty, but also the law prevailing in a sub-division of the political state of which the forum is part. Thus, for the purpose of private international law and so far as English courts are concerned, the law of Scotland, of the Channel Islands, of Northern Ireland, or of one of the member countries of the Commonwealth or European Union is just as much a foreign law as the law of Japan or Brazil.

5. INTERNATIONAL VARIETY OF
PRIVATE INTERNATIONAL LAW RULES

Private international law is not the same in all countries. There is no one system that can claim universal recognition, though there has been a significant movement in recent years towards the harmonisation of private international law rules between groups of countries. This book is concerned solely with the English rules, ie with the rules that guide an English court whenever it is seised of a case that contains some foreign element. A writer on public international law may perhaps claim with some justification that the doctrines which he propounds are entitled to universal recognition. Thus, in theory at any rate, a German and a French jurist should agree as to what constitutes an effective blockade. But the writer on private international law can make no such claim. This branch of law as found, for instance, in Japan shows many striking contrasts with its English counterpart, and though the English and American rules show considerable similarity they are fundamentally different on a number of points. The many questions relating to the personal status of a party depend in England on the law of his domicile, but in France, Italy, Spain and most other Continental European countries on the law of his nationality. Again, the principles applied by various legal systems to divorce jurisdiction may so conflict that the same two persons are deemed married in one jurisdiction but unmarried in another. On the other hand, though Scottish internal law differs substantially from that of England, the principles of private international law are so similar in both countries that an English decision is usually, though not invariably, followed in Scotland and vice versa.[25]

---

[23] *Re Askew* [1930] 2 Ch 259 at 267.

[24] Infra, pp 23–4, and see Lorenzen (1920) 20 Col LR 247, 259.

[25] By virtue of the Scotland Act 1998, Scottish civil law (being a reference to the general principles of private law, including private international law—s 126(4)(a)) falls within the legislative competence of the

6. AVOIDING CONFLICTS

There are two possible ways in which this lack of unanimity among the various systems of private international law may be ameliorated.[26]

(a) Unification of internal laws

The first is to secure by international conventions the unification of the *internal* laws of the various countries on as many legal topics as possible. When attention is paid to the fundamental and basic differences in principle that distinguish one legal system from another, especially in the common law systems as contrasted with their civil law counterparts, it is obvious that this form of unification holds out no great prospect of success. Nevertheless, a certain amount of progress has been made in the few departments of law where this unity is imperative and possible.

An important example of unification is the Warsaw Convention of 1929 as amended at The Hague, 1955, and supplemented by the Guadalajara Convention, 1961,[27] which makes the international carriage of persons or goods by aircraft for reward subject to uniform rules as regards both jurisdiction and the law to be applied. It also provides that any agreement by the parties purporting to alter the rules on these matters shall be null and void. The Convention has been made binding in England by the Carriage by Air Act 1961. Further examples of the unification of internal laws are the Carriage of Goods by Sea Act 1924,[28] the Carriage of Goods by Road Act 1965, the Carriage of Passengers by Road Act 1974, the International Transport Conventions Act 1983 and the Merchant Shipping Act 1995, all of which give effect to conventions made at international conferences. Mention may also be made of the Berne Convention of 1886, since amended several times, by which an international union for the protection of the rights of authors over their literary and artistic works was formed. The Council of the League of Nations entrusted to the Institute for the Unification of Private Laws (UNIDROIT), established by the Italian Government in Rome, the task of indicating the lines along which further unification might be attained.[29] An important result of its labours, in conjunction with those of the Hague Conference,[30] was the conclusion at The Hague in 1964 of a convention which establishes a uniform set of rules on international sales of goods and also on the formation of contracts for such sales. These conventions were accepted by the United Kingdom and incorporated in the Uniform Laws on International Sales Act 1967[31] which, when its provisions apply, excludes the rules of private international law.[32] There is now a successor to the 1964 Convention, the United Nations Convention on Contracts for the International Sale of Goods of 1980,[33] prepared under the auspices of another body

---

Scottish Parliament. However, the private international law aspects of reserved matters (s 29(3)) are reserved to the Westminster Parliament. See Crawford and Carruthers, para 2-04.

[26] For an excellent account of the various methods of seeking unanimity, and an assessment of their success, see David, 2 *International Encyclopedia of Comparative Law*, Chapter 5.

[27] This was made part of the law of the United Kingdom by the Carriage by Air (Supplementary Provisions) Act 1962. The Warsaw Convention was modernised by the Montreal Convention for the Unification of Certain Rules relating to International Carriage by Air 1999.

[28] The Hague Rules which are contained in the Act were amended by a Brussels Protocol of 1968 which is embodied in the Carriage of Goods by Sea Act 1971, which came into force in 1977.

[29] See David, op cit, pp 133–41.

[30] Infra, pp 10–11.

[31] As amended by the Sale and Supply of Goods Act 1994, Sch 2 and the Consumer Rights Act 2015 (Consequential Amendments Order) 2015/1726.

[32] Graveson, Cohn and Graveson, *Uniform Laws on International Sales Act 1967*.

[33] See Honnold, *Uniform Law for International Sales Act under the 1980 United Nations Convention* (3rd edn, 1999).

concerned with the unification of law, the United Nations Committee on International Trade Law (UNCITRAL). The United Kingdom is not a party to the 1980 Convention. On a smaller scale, the Scandinavian countries,[34] and a number of Latin-American countries,[35] have adopted conventions unifying various areas of their laws.

(b) Unification of private international law

The second method by which the inconvenience that results from conflicting national rules may be diminished is to unify the rules of private international law, so as to ensure that a case containing a foreign element results in the same decision irrespective of the country of its trial.[36] Several attempts have been made in the Hague Conference on Private International Law[37] to reduce the number of topics on which the rules for choice of law in different countries conflict, thus indicating the desirability of having a code of private international law common to the civilised world. Prior to the seventh session in 1951, the sessions were confined to the Continental states of Europe, for, owing to the fundamental differences between the common law and the civil law which forms the basis of most European systems, there seemed little prospect of agreement being reached between the two groups. The British delegates, however, attended the seventh and subsequent sessions, no longer as mere observers but as full members of the conference[38] and they have since been joined by delegations from other common law jurisdictions, including Australia, Canada and the USA.[39]

A step of great significance taken in 1951 was the drafting of a charter designed to place the Hague Conference on a lasting footing by the establishment of a permanent bureau. This charter has been accepted by many countries, including the United Kingdom, and the Bureau, consisting now of a Secretary-General, a Deputy Secretary-General, three First Secretaries and a small team of Legal Officers belonging to different countries, was established at The Hague. Its mission is to be a forum for the Member States for the development and implementation of common rules of private international law in order to co-ordinate the relationships between different private law systems in international situations and to promote international judicial and administrative co-operation in the fields of protection of the family and children, civil procedure and commercial law. Its chief functions are to examine and prepare proposals for the unification of private international law and to keep in touch with the Council of Europe and with governmental and non-governmental organisations, such as the Commonwealth Secretariat and the International Law Association.[40] The Bureau works under the general direction of the Standing Government Commission of the Netherlands, which was established by Royal Decree in 1897, with the object of promoting the codification of private international law. Fairly recent English statutes relating to private international law problems which owe their existence, at least in part, to acceptance by the United Kingdom of the Hague Conventions,[41] include the Wills Act 1963,[42] the

---

[34] David, op cit, pp 181–8.

[35] Ibid, pp 148–50; and see Parra-Aranguren (1979) III Hague Recueil 55; Maekelt (1982) IV Hague Recueil 193; Juenger (1994) 42 AJCL 381.

[36] Vitta (1969) I Hague Recueil 111–232; van Loon, in *Forty Years On: The Evolution of Postwar Private International Law in Europe* (1990), pp 101–22; Pfund (1994) V Hague Recueil 9.

[37] See generally <http://www.hcch.net> accessed 14 April 2017.

[38] Van Hoogstraten (1963) 12 ICLQ 148.

[39] Nadelmann (1965) 30 Law & Contemporary Problems 291; Pfund (1985) 19 Int Lawyer 505; Reese (1985) 19 Int Lawyer 881; McClean in Borras (ed), *E Pluribus Unum* (1996), p 205.

[40] On the work of the Hague Conference generally, see Nadelmann (1972) 20 AJCL 323; David, op cit, pp 141–8; Droz (1980) III Hague Recueil 123; Overbeck (1992) Hague Recueil 9; Boggiano, ibid, 99; McClean, ibid, 267; TMC Asser Institute, *The Influence of the Hague Conference on Private International Law* (1993); (1994) 57 Law & Contemporary Problems, No 3.

[41] See North, *Essays in Private International Law* (1993), pp 225–6.

[42] Infra, pp 1341–51.

Adoption Act 1968,[43] the Evidence (Proceedings in Other Jurisdictions) Act 1975,[44] the Child Abduction and Custody Act 1985,[45] Part II of the Family Law Act 1986[46] and the Recognition of Trusts Act 1987.[47]

In addition to the conventions mentioned above, many similar arrangements have been made between individual countries, as for example the bilateral conventions on civil procedure concluded by the United Kingdom with a large number of foreign states. An example of a limited multilateral convention is that concluded in 1969 between the Benelux states— Belgium, the Netherlands and Luxembourg—which unified the rules of private international law on the more important matters, such as capacity and status, succession to property on death and the essential validity of contracts.[48]

(i) Europeanisation of private international law

A modern feature of private international law is the Europeanisation of the subject,[49] by which is meant the assimilation of Member States' private international law rules, and the creation of a European "area of freedom, security and justice". The legal basis for this development is the Treaty of Amsterdam,[50] Articles 61 to 67, in terms of which the subject of judicial co-operation in civil matters became a matter of European Union law rather than one merely of inter-governmental co-operation. By virtue of Article 65, measures in the field of judicial co-operation in civil matters having cross-border implications may be taken *in so far as necessary for the proper functioning of the internal market*, and shall include improving and simplifying the recognition and enforcement of decisions in civil and commercial cases; promoting the compatibility of the rules applicable in the Member States concerning the conflict of laws and of jurisdiction; and eliminating obstacles to the good functioning of civil proceedings, if necessary by promoting the compatibility of the rules on civil procedure applicable in the Member States. There followed, in 1998, the Vienna Action Plan[51] of the European Council and Commission on how best to implement the Amsterdam provisions, and subsequently, in 1999, there was convened in Tampere, Finland, an Extraordinary European Council Meeting, which produced a programme of work for the period 1999–2004, devoted to the development of the European judicial area. The results of the five-year Tampere programme were presented by the European Commission in June 2004, and in November that year, a new programme, termed the "Hague Programme",[52] was adopted by the European Council, with a view to strengthening and developing the EU Justice and Home Affairs legislative portfolio over the period 2005–09. Then followed the "Stockholm Programme" in

---

[43] See now Adoption and Children Act 2002, infra, p 1156 et seq.

[44] Infra, pp 83–4.

[45] Infra, p 1134 et seq.

[46] Infra, p 1005 et seq.

[47] Infra, pp 1382–3.

[48] For discussion of the activities of the seven Inter-American Specialised Conferences on Private International Law, see http://www.oas.org/en/sla/dil/private_international_law.asp> accessed 14 April 2017. Also Parra-Aranguren, in *Conflicts and Harmonisation* (1990) 155–75; and see Burman (1995) 28 Vand J of Transnational L 367; Parra-Aranguren in Borras (ed), *E Pluribus Unum* (1996), p 299.

[49] See generally Crawford and Carruthers (2005) 3 Jur Rev 251.

[50] Signed in 1997 and in force on 1 May 1999.

[51] OJ 1999 C 19.

[52] The Hague Programme: Strengthening Freedom, Security and Justice in the European Union (OJ 2003 C 53/1) and the Council and Commission Action Plan Implementing the Hague Programme on Strengthening Freedom, Security and Justice in the European Union (OJ 2005 C 198/1). See European Council 4/5 November 2004, Presidency Conclusions (Press Release, Brussels, December 8, 2004, 14292/1/04 REV1 CONCL3), and Communication from the Commission to the Council and the European Parliament: Report on the Implementation of the Hague Programme for 2006 (COM (2007) 373 final).

December 2009, which covered the period 2010–14,[53] and which was replaced in June 2014 by the European Council's strategic guidelines in the area of freedom, security and justice.[54]

Title IV ("Area of Freedom, Security and Justice") of the Treaty of Lisbon, amending the Treaty on European Union and the Treaty establishing the European Community,[55] replaces the pre-existing provision on visas, asylum, immigration and other policies related to free movement of persons. Article 65 in Chapter 3 of Title IV of the Lisbon Treaty concerns judicial co-operation in civil matters, and provides that:

1. The Union shall develop judicial cooperation in civil matters having cross-border implications, based on the principle of mutual recognition of judgments and of decisions in extrajudicial cases. Such cooperation may include the adoption of measures for the approximation of the laws and regulations of the Member States.

The wording of the new Article 65(2) is noteworthy:

2. For the purposes of paragraph 1, the European Parliament and the Council, acting in accordance with the ordinary legislative procedure, shall adopt measures, *particularly when necessary for the proper functioning of the internal market,*[56] aimed at ensuring:
   (a) the mutual recognition and enforcement between Member States of judgments and of decisions in extrajudicial cases;
   (b) the cross-border service of judicial and extrajudicial documents;
   (c) the compatibility of the rules applicable in the Member States concerning conflict of laws and of jurisdiction;
   (d) cooperation in the taking of evidence;
   (e) effective access to justice;
   (f) the elimination of obstacles to the proper functioning of civil proceedings, if necessary by promoting the compatibility of the rules on civil procedure applicable in the Member States;
   (g) the development of alternative methods of dispute settlement;
   (h) support for the training of the judiciary and judicial staff.

Accordingly, the European Union has proved to be, and looks set to continue to be, a major force for the creation of uniform law within the Community and for the unification of private international law among EU Member States.[57] European harmonisation efforts have generated, for example and of note, in the area of civil and commercial jurisdiction, the 1968 Brussels Convention on jurisdiction and the enforcement of judgments in civil and commercial matters[58] (almost entirely replaced by Council Regulation (EC) No 44/2001 on jurisdiction and the recognition and enforcement of judgments in civil and commercial

---

[53] Adopted by the European Council on 2 December 2009, The Stockholm Programme—An open and secure Europe serving and protecting the citizens, OJ 2010 C 115/1, see <https://ec.europa.eu/anti-trafficking/eu-policy/stockholm-programme-open-and-secure-europe-serving-and-protecting-citizens-0_en.> accessed 14 April 2017.

[54] See <http://register.consilium.europa.eu/doc/srv?l=EN&f=ST%2079%202014%20INIT#page=2> accessed 14 April 2017. A mid-term review is planned for 2017.

[55] Signed in Lisbon on 13 December 2007 and entered into force 1 December 2009.

[56] Emphasis added. This requirement is less stringent than that which applies under Art 65 of the Treaty of Amsterdam.

[57] *Harmonisation of Private International Law by the EEC* (ed Lipstein); Fletcher, *Conflict of Laws and European Community Law* (1982); Lasok and Stone, *Conflict of Laws in the European Community* (1987); North, in *Forty Years On: The Evolution of Postwar Private International Law in Europe* (1990), pp 29–48; Duintjer Tebbens, ibid, pp 49–69; Stone, *EU Private International Law Harmonisation of Laws* (2006).

[58] Implemented in the UK by means of the Civil Jurisdiction and Judgments Act 1982. See infra, Chapter 10.

matters and the Recast Brussels I Regulation[59]),[60] and in choice of law, the 1980 Rome Convention on contractual obligations[61] (now the Rome I Regulation),[62] implemented in the United Kingdom by means of the Contracts (Applicable Law) Act 1990 and the Rome II Regulation.[63] There now exist many EU directives, regulations and proposed regulations containing private international law measures, concerned not only with the allocation of jurisdiction and enforcement of judgments, but also with choice of law and matters of procedure. These will be identified and examined in context throughout the book.

For the European Union, there is an important, and sometimes difficult, balance to strike between securing regional harmonisation of laws, and participating in projects which seek to bring about global harmonisation of laws.[64] By virtue of membership of the European Union, Member States have lost the power to act autonomously in matters concerning judicial co-operation in civil matters which fall within European Union competence. In 2006, the European Union decided to accede to the Hague Conference on Private International Law, by means of declaration of acceptance of the Statute of the Hague Conference.[65] The Accession of the Community to the Hague Conference took place on 3 April 2007.[66] The admission of the European Union to the Hague Conference is in addition to the individual membership of the Conference of the various European Union Member States.[67]

(ii) Impact of European Convention on Human Rights on private international law[68]

The Human Rights Act 1998 incorporates into the law of the United Kingdom the European Convention on Human Rights (ECHR). Human rights concerns were aired in private international law cases in the United Kingdom long before the passing of the 1998 Act,[69] but since its entry into force instances of this phenomenon have increased dramatically.

The rights incorporated are referred to under the Act as "Convention rights". In terms of section 6(1) of the 1998 Act, it is unlawful for a public authority, which includes a court

---

[59] Regulation (EU) No 1215/2012 of the European Parliament and of the Council of 12 December 2012 on jurisdiction and the recognition and enforcement of judgments in civil and commercial matters (recast) [2012] OJ L 351/1.

[60] See, infra, Chapter 11.

[61] OJ 1980 L 266; North, *Contract Conflicts* (1982). See infra, Chapter 19.

[62] Regulation (EC) No 593/2008 of the European Parliament and of the Council of 17 June 2008 on the law applicable to contractual obligations (Rome I) [2008] OJ L 177/6.

[63] Regulation (EC) No 864/2007 of the European Parliament and of the Council of 11 July 2007 on the law applicable to non-contractual obligations (Rome II) [2007] OJ L199/40.

[64] See H van Loon and A Schulz, 'The European Community and the Hague Conference on Private International Law' in B Martenczuk and S van Thiel (eds), *Justice, Liberty, Security: New Challenges for the External Relations of the European Union* (Institute for European Studies of the Free University of Brussels, 2007).

[65] Council Decision (EC) 2006/719 of 5 October 2006 on the accession of the Community to the Hague Conference on Private International Law OJ 2006 L 297/1. Membership of the Conference is open to Regional Economic Integration Organisations to which the member states thereof have transferred competence over matters of private international law (Art 3 of the amended version (1 January 2007) of the Statute of the Hague Conference).

[66] See Schulz (2007) 56 ICLQ 939.

[67] On the distribution of competences between the Regional Economic Integration Organisation and its Member States, see Schulz (2007) 56 ICLQ 939, 945.

[68] See, generally, J J Fawcett, M Ní Shúilleabháin and S Shah, *Human Rights and Private International Law*, (2016); Fawcett (2007) 56 ICLQ 1; and Bell in Bottomley and Kinley (eds), *Commercial Law and Human Rights*, 115.

[69] Eg *J v C* [1970] AC 668, HL; *Oppenheimer v Cattermole* [1976] AC 249, 278 (per Lord Cross), 283 (per Lord Salmon), HL; *Williams & Humbert Ltd v W & H Trade Marks (Jersey) Ltd* [1986] AC 368, 428 (per Lord Templeman); *The Playa Larga* [1983] 2 Lloyd's Rep 171, 190, CA; *Settebello Ltd v Banco Toto and Acores* [1985] 1 WLR 1050, 1056, CA.

or tribunal,[70] to act in a way which is incompatible with a Convention right. A court or tribunal determining a question which has arisen in connection with a Convention right must "take into account"[71] any judgment, decision, declaration or advisory opinion of the European Court of Human Rights (ECtHR), whenever made or given, so far as, in the opinion of the court or tribunal, it is relevant to the proceedings in which that question has arisen.[72] Moreover, in so far as it is possible to do so, primary legislation and subordinate legislation, whenever enacted,[73] must be read and given effect in a way which is compatible with the Convention rights.[74] If a court[75] is satisfied that a provision is incompatible with a Convention right, it may make a declaration of that incompatibility.[76]

In the context of private international law, discussion of the ECHR has most commonly focused upon the effect of Article 6, which provides the right to a fair trial.[77] Article 6 has been considered not only in the context of rules of jurisdiction,[78] but also in relation to recognition and enforcement of foreign judgments.[79] Decisions of the ECtHR have made clear the point that denial of access to national courts may amount to a breach of Article 6,[80] but it is equally clear that the right of access to a court is not absolute, and may be subject to restrictions, provided that these pursue a legitimate aim and are proportionate.[81]

With regard to other provisions of the Convention, United Kingdom courts have been required to consider, in a private international law context, the implications of Article 8

---

[70] S 6(3).

[71] Though not necessarily follow.

[72] S 2(1).

[73] S 3(2)(a).

[74] S 3(1).

[75] Meaning, for this purpose, the House of Lords; the Judicial Committee of the Privy Council; the Courts-Martial Appeal Court; in England and Wales or Northern Ireland, the High Court or the Court of Appeal; and in Scotland, the High Court of Justiciary sitting otherwise than as a trial court, or the Court of Session (s 4(5)).

[76] S 4(2).

[77] For full analysis of the impact of Art 6 on private international law rules, see J J Fawcett, M Ní Shúilleabháin and S Shah, *Human Rights and Private International Law*, (2016), Chapters 3–8.

[78] In relation to jurisdiction in civil and commercial matters, see, eg, *OT Africa Line Ltd v Hijazy (The Kribi)* [2001] 1 Lloyd's Rep 76. The UK judicial response to arguments based on Art 6 sometimes has been fairly dismissive, eg *Lubbe v Cape plc* [2000] 1 WLR 1545; *Dow Jones & Co Inc v Yousef Abdul Latif Jameel* [2005] QB 946; and *AG of Zambia v Meer Care and Desai (A firm)* [2005] EWHC 2102 (Ch). See, in detail, infra, p 628. In relation to jurisdiction in matrimonial matters, see, eg, *Mark v Mark* [2005] UKHL 42 (infra, Chapter 22).

[79] Eg *Joint Stock Co 'Aeroflot—Russian Airlines' v Berezovsky and another* [2014] EWCA Civ 20; *Merchant International Co Ltd v Natsionalna Aktsionerna Kompaniya Naftogaz Ukrayiny* [2012] EWCA Civ 196; *Ahuja v Politika Navine/Magazini Doo* [2015] EWHC 3380 (QB); *Sutton LBC v K* [2016] EWHC 1375 (Fam); *Kuwait Airways Corpn v Iraqi Airways Co (Nos 4 and 5)* [2002] UKHL 19, [2002] 2 AC 883; *Maronier v Larmer* [2002] EWCA Civ 774, [2003] QB 620; *SA Marie Brizzard et Roger International v William Grant & Sons Ltd (No 2)* 2002 SLT 1365; *Al-Bassam v Al-Bassam* [2004] EWCA Civ 857; *Government of the United States of America v Montgomery (No 2)* [2004] UKHL 37, [2004] 3 WLR 2241; and *Orams v Apostolides* [2006] EWHC 2226 (QB). As regards the operation of public policy as a defence to recognition and enforcement, see *Krombach v Bamberski* [2001] QB 709; further, infra, pp 626–32. In relation to matrimonial matters, see, eg, *Emin v Yeldag* [2002] 1 FLR 956 (concerning the grant of ancillary relief dependent upon recognition by the English court of a divorce obtained in the Turkish Republic of Northern Cyprus, a country not recognised by the British Government).

[80] Eg *Airey v Ireland*, Judgment of 9 October 1979, Series A, No 32; (1979) 2 EHRR 305; *Golder v UK*, Judgment of 21 February 1975, Series A, No 18; (1975) 1 EHRR 524; and *Osman v United Kingdom*, Judgment of 28 October 1998; (2000) 29 EHRR 245.

[81] *Ashingdane v United Kingdom*, Judgment of 28 May 1985, Series A, No 93, para 57; (1985) 7 EHRR 528; *Steel and Morris v United Kingdom*, Judgment of 15 Feb 2005, para 62.

(right to respect for private and family life),[82] Article 10 (freedom of expression);[83] Article 12 (right to marry);[84] Article 14 (prohibition of discrimination);[85] and Article 1 of the First Protocol (protection of property).[86]

More detailed examination of particular Convention rights in their private international law context will be included in subsequent chapters, as appropriate.

7. THE NAME OF THE SUBJECT

The issue of the name or title of the subject may seem to be of little importance, but needs to be addressed, largely because there is no name which commands universal approval. The expression "Private International Law", coined by Story in 1834,[87] was adopted by the earlier English authors, such as Westlake and Foote, and is used in most civil law countries. The chief criticism directed against its use is its tendency to confuse private international law with the law of nations or public international law, as it is usually called. There are obvious differences between the two. The latter primarily governs the relations between sovereign states and it may perhaps be regarded as the common law of mankind in an early state of development;[88] the former is designed to regulate disputes of a private nature, notwithstanding that one of the parties may be a sovereign state.[89] There is, at any rate in theory, one common system of public international law, consisting of the "customary and treaty rules which are considered legally binding by States in their intercourse with each other",[90] but, as we have seen, there are as many systems of private international law as there are systems of municipal law. Moreover, as often as not a question of private international law arises between two persons of the same nationality, as, for instance, where the issue is the validity of a divorce between two English persons in a foreign country.

---

[82] Eg *Weller v Associated Newspapers Ltd* [2015] EWCA Civ 1176; *T v K and others* [2016] EWHC 2963 (Fam); *Re A* [2015] EWFC 25; *R (on the application of Williams) v France* [2012] EWHC 2128 (Admin); *J v C* [1970] AC 668, HL; *Re I (Minors)* 23 April 1999 unreported, CA; *Re J (A Child) (Return to Foreign Jurisdiction: Convention Rights)* [2005] UKHL 40, [2005] 3 WLR 14; *S v B (Abduction: Human Rights)* [2005] 2 FLR 878; and *Re C (A Child) (Abduction: Residence and Contact)* [2006] 2 FLR 277. See J J Fawcett, M Ní Shúilleabháin and S Shah, *Human Rights and Private International Law*, (2016), Chapter 13.

[83] Eg *Weller v Associated Newspapers Ltd* [2015] EWCA Civ 1176; *Skrine & Co v Euromoney Publications plc* [2002] EMLR 15; and *Prudential Assurance Co Ltd v Prudential Insurance Co of America (No 2)* [2003] EWCA Civ 1154, [2004] ETMR 29. See J J Fawcett, M Ní Shúilleabháin and S Shah, *Human Rights and Private International Law*, (2016), Chapter 10.

[84] Eg *Wilkinson v Kitzinger and Ors* [2006] EWHC 2022 (Fam), in which the petitioner, an English domiciliary, sought a declaration as to her marital status in terms of the Family Law Act 1986, s 55, failing which, a declaration of incompatibility, under s 4 of the 1998 Act, in relation to s 11(c) of the Matrimonial Causes Act 1973, which specifies that a marriage shall be void on the ground that parties are not respectively male and female. Dismissing the petition, the court concluded that neither Art 8 nor Art 12 of the ECHR guaranteed the petitioner the right to have her foreign same sex marriage recognised as having the status of a marriage in English law. See J J Fawcett, M Ní Shúilleabháin and S Shah, *Human Rights and Private International Law*, (2016), Chapter 11.

[85] Eg *Re J (A Child) (Return to Foreign Jurisdiction: Convention Rights)* [2005] UKHL 40, [2005] 3 WLR 14. See J J Fawcett, M Ní Shúilleabháin and S Shah, *Human Rights and Private International Law*, (2016), Chapter 9.

[86] Eg *Shanshal v Al-Kishtaini* [2001] EWCA Civ 264 at [50]–[62], [2001] 2 All ER (Comm) 601; *Kuwait Airways Corpn v Iraqi Airways Co* [2002] 2 AC 883; and *Orams v Apostolides* [2006] EWHC 2226 (QB), [36]. See Carruthers, paras 8.71–8.76 and J J Fawcett, M Ní Shúilleabháin and S Shah, *Human Rights and Private International Law*, (2016), Chapter 15.

[87] *Commentaries on the Conflict of Laws* (1st edn), S 9.

[88] Jenks, *The Common Law of Mankind*; Jessup, *Transnational Law*.

[89] See, eg, *Re Maldonado's Estate* [1954] P 223; infra, pp 49–50.

[90] Oppenheim, *International Law* (1967) 8th edn, Vol I, pp 4–5.

It would, of course, be a fallacy to regard public and private international law as totally unrelated. Some principles of law, such as requirements of natural justice, are common to both; some rules of private international law, as for example the traditional common law doctrine of the "proper law" of a contract, have been adopted by a court in the settlement of a dispute between sovereign states; equally, some rules of public international law are applied by a municipal court when hearing a case containing a foreign element.[91]

An equally common title to describe the subject, and one generally used in the USA, is "The Conflict of Laws".[92] This is innocuous if it is taken as referring to a difference between the internal laws of two countries on the same matter. When, for instance, a question arises regarding whether the assignment in France of a debt due from a person resident in England ought to be governed by English or by French internal law, it may be said that these two legal systems are in conflict with each other in the sense that they can each put forward claims to govern the validity of the assignment. But the title is misleading if it is used to suggest that two systems of law are struggling to govern a case. If an English court decides that the assignment must be governed by French law, it does not do so because English law has been worsted in a conflict with the law of France, but because it is held by the law of England, albeit another part of the law of England, ie private international law, that in the particular circumstances it is expedient to refer to French law. In fact, the very purpose of private international law is to avoid conflicts of law. The one case where a genuine conflict arises is where two territorial systems, differing in themselves, both seek to regulate the same matter, as, for example, where the bequest of a Greek citizen dying domiciled in England is governed by the law of his domicile according to the English doctrine, but by the national law according to the Greek view.

The fact is that no title can be found that is accurate and comprehensive,[93] and the two titles "Private International Law" and "The Conflict of Laws" are so well known to, and understood by, lawyers that no possible harm can ensue from the adoption of either of them. It might be argued that the latter title is preferable, because it is a little unrealistic to speak in terms of international law if the facts of the case are concerned with England and some other part of the British Isles. However, the former is the title most widely used throughout the world and, significantly for this country, it is the description used in the European Union and most other international bodies of which the United Kingdom is a member.

---

[91] Eg the doctrine of sovereign immunity, infra, p 491 et seq. The interaction of public and private international law has been fully canvassed by Wortley (1954) I Hague Recueil 245; Hambro (1962) I Hague Recueil 1–68. See also Vallindas (1959) 8 ICLQ 620–4; Lipstein (1972) I Hague Recueil 104, 167–94; Kahn-Freund (1974) III Hague Recueil 147, 165–96; Lowenfeld (1979) II Hague Recueil 311; Mann, *Foreign Affairs in English Courts* (1986) and A Mills, *The Confluence of Public and Private International Law* (2009). See, for the interesting interface between private international law and public international law, *Kuwait Airways Corpn v Iraqi Airways Co* [2002] 2 AC 883, and comment thereon in Carruthers and Crawford (2003) 52 ICLQ 761.

[92] For criticism of this title in the USA, see Maiea (1993) 56 Albany LR 753, 754.

[93] Other terms which have been used to describe the subject are "International Private Law", "Intermunicipal Law", "Comity", and the "Extra-territorial Recognition of Rights".

2

HISTORICAL DEVELOPMENT AND CURRENT THEORIES

1. Development of English Private		(a) Theory of acquired rights	21
International Law	17	(b) Local law theory	23
(a) Early history	17	(c) The American revolution	24
(b) Later development	19	(d) The European (r)evolution	33
2. Modern Theories and Developments	21	(e) The English approach	36

Private international law as found in England is a substantive part of English law and was, until the last four or five decades, almost entirely the result of judicial decisions; though it is now the case that much of this field of law has been embodied in legislation, some of which is of purely domestic and some of European or international origin. The writings of jurists in other countries have influenced its growth to a considerable extent, especially through those doctrines that have found acceptance on the Continent. Twentieth-century analyses of the basis of the subject, particularly those carried out in the USA, have also been of influence. Most recently, English private international law has been reshaped through the impact of European Union law. It is difficult to study the subject without at any rate a slight acquaintance with the historical development of the earlier and current trends of thought. It is proposed, therefore, to start by giving a short sketch of the historical development of this branch of law[1] in England,[2] before moving on to look briefly at the varied approaches to the subject in the twentieth and early twenty-first centuries.

1. DEVELOPMENT OF ENGLISH PRIVATE INTERNATIONAL LAW

(a) Early history

Given that private international law issues had exercised the minds of civil lawyers for centuries, and given the growth of English activity as a trading nation, it seems at first sight surprising that English lawyers did not find it necessary to deal with choice of law problems until a couple of centuries ago. This, however, was the case and it was only in the eighteenth century that an awareness of the problems developed. Blackstone did not mention them and it was the middle of the nineteenth century before an English treatise on private international law was written, by

---

[1] For an account of the historical development of the subject more generally since Roman times and with particular emphasis on developments in Continental Europe, see the 12th edn of this book (1992), pp 15–23.

[2] The only separate work in English of an historical nature is Sack, *Conflicts of Laws in the History of the English Law*, in *Law: A Century of Progress 1835–1935* (1937), Vol III, pp 342–454. Beale gives a full and valuable outline of the general history of the subject in *Conflict of Laws* (1935), pp 1881–975. See also Wolff, pp 19–51; Westlake, pp 1–22; Yntema (1953) 2 AJCL 297; de Nova (1966) II Hague Recueil 435, 441–77; Lipstein (1972) I Hague Recueil 97, 104–66; Mills (2006) 55 ICLQ 1; and see Kegel (1964) II Hague Recueil 91, 103–11; Juenger (1985) IV Hague Recueil 119, 136–69.

Westlake. Sack has traced this tardiness of development to the special features of the common law and to the English system of administration of justice.[3] His explanation in brief is as follows.

The intra-national conflicts, that had long been inevitable on the Continent owing to the existence of different legal systems within the territory of a single nation, could not arise in England after the whole country had been brought under the sway of a single common law. International conflicts were precluded by the rule, established at an early date, that the common law courts were unable to entertain foreign causes. This rule was the necessary result of the practice by which the members of the jury were summoned from the place where the operative facts had occurred, since their function was to decide according to their knowledge of the facts. The sheriff could scarcely summon a jury from a foreign country in which the dispute between the parties had arisen. It is true that special courts were set up to deal with cases that might contain foreign elements. The King established courts to deal with complaints made by foreigners whom he had invited to England and who were, therefore, entitled to his protection. The staple courts and the piepowder courts decided mercantile disputes. But in each of these cases the law administered was the law merchant which, at any rate in theory, was regarded as a universally binding system. There was no question of applying a foreign law at variance with the law of England.

When English traders began to extend their commercial activities beyond the seas, it was inevitable that they would occasionally suffer from this inability to obtain redress in respect of transactions effected abroad. A remedy ultimately became available to them in the Court of Admiralty, which extended its jurisdiction to foreign causes as early as the middle of the fourteenth century. By the middle of the sixteenth century it was competent to try disputes arising out of mercantile dealings abroad.[4] Again, however, there was no question of choice of law, for the court dispensed the general law maritime or, in cases of purely commercial matters, the general law merchant.[5]

By the end of the sixteenth century the common law courts had begun to compete for this jurisdiction. The technical difficulty that formerly stood in their way had disappeared, for the jury relied no longer on its own knowledge but on the testimony of witnesses. The initial step was to deal with "mixed" cases, ie those in which some of the operative facts occurred in England, others abroad, as, for example, where the defendant failed to perform in Spain a charter-party that had been made in England.[6] The final step, that of trying cases connected solely with a foreign country, was facilitated by the new division of actions into local and transitory. In transitory actions, ie where the cause of action might have arisen anywhere, there was no necessity to summon the jury from one particular neighbourhood. The plaintiff could sue the defendant where he was to be found, and could lay the *venue* (ie the place from which the jury was summoned) where he liked. By Coke's time it was settled that the courts at Westminster could entertain all actions that were of a transitory nature, such as actions for breach of contract or on bills of exchange, notwithstanding that the relevant facts were connected with a foreign country.[7]

Thus the stage was reached at which it should have been necessary to deal with the familiar problem of choice of law. But in the case of mercantile disputes, which must have formed the bulk of those brought to court, the problem was avoided for many generations, since such disputes were decided according to the general law merchant common to European nations. By the nineteenth century, when the international nature of this law had ceased and it had been incorporated as one

---

[3] See Sack, *Conflicts of Laws in the History of English Law*, in *Law: A Century of Progress, 1835–1935* (1937), Vol III, pp 342–454; and see Anton (1956) 5 ICLQ 534; Nygh (1961) 1 U Tas LR 555; (1964) 2 U Tas LR 28.

[4] Sack, ibid, pp 353–5.

[5] Ibid, p 355.

[6] Ibid, pp 359–60.

[7] Ibid, pp 370–1.

of the municipal branches of English law, the modern doctrines of private international law had already taken root in England.[8] Moreover, although the common law courts had expressed their willingness to take cognisance of foreign law, they were reluctant to entertain actions in which this would be necessary.[9] When the necessity became pressing, their first reaction was to require foreign cases to be tried by the appropriate court abroad, and to accompany this with a readiness to enforce the foreign judgment in England. This recognition of foreign judgments, which dates at least from 1607,[10] has never involved a reference to the foreign municipal law. All the English courts have ever done in this connection is to inquire whether the foreign court had jurisdiction in the international sense and whether its judgment was final.[11]

(b) Later development

The growth of the British Empire inevitably led to increased links between British subjects owing obedience to a variety of laws, and consequently to an increase in the number of disputes that required, if justice were to be done, a reference to something more than the common law of England. Yet the emergence of anything approaching a connected system of private international law proved to be a slow and laborious process.

The first hesitant steps are to be seen in *Robinson v Bland*[12] in 1760. This involved the question, which was discussed but not decided, whether a contract valid by the law of France where it was made, though void by English law, could be sued on in England.

> The plaintiff had lent £300 to X in Paris, which X immediately lost to the plaintiff by gaming, together with an additional £372. X gave the plaintiff a bill of exchange payable in England for the whole amount. It was found that in France "money lost at play between gentlemen may be recovered as a debt of honour before the Marshals of France, who can enforce obedience to their sentences by imprisonment".[13] After the death of X the plaintiff brought assumpsit against his administrator on three counts: on the bill of exchange, for money lent, and for money had and received. It was held that the bill of exchange was void and that no action lay for the recovery of the money won at play. The plaintiff, however, was held entitled to recover on the loan.

The reason for the decision given by two of the three judges was that the laws of France and of England were the same on all these points, and that therefore it was unnecessary to consider which law would apply had there been a difference between them. The judges, however, expressed their opinions on the question. Wilmot J considered it "a great question", but inclined to the belief that a claim contrary to public policy could not be pursued in England. Denison J felt that English law would govern since the plaintiff had chosen an English forum. It was left to Lord Mansfield to give a more modern flavour to the discussion.

> The general rule, established *ex comitate et jure gentium*, is that the place where the contract is made, and not where the action is brought, is to be considered in expounding and enforcing the contract. But this rule admits of an exception when the parties at the time of making the contract had a view to a different kingdom.[14]

He amplified his remark as to the exception in these words: "The law of the place can never be the rule, where the transaction is entered into with an express view to the law of another

---

[8] Ibid, pp 375–7.
[9] Ibid, p 381.
[10] *Wier's Case* (1607) 1 Roll Abr 530 K 12.
[11] The cases such as *Penn v Baltimore* (1750) 1 Ves Sen 444, 27 ER 1132, in which equity exercises personal jurisdiction in respect of acts occurring abroad, do not involve the application of foreign law; infra, p 486 et seq.
[12] (1760) 1 Wm Bl 234, 2 Burr 1077.
[13] Wilmot J described it as "this wild, illegal, fantastic Court of Honour"! 2 Burr 1077 at 1083.
[14] 1 Wm Bl 234 at 258–9.

country, as the rule by which it is to be governed."[15] Although this was the first mention of the doctrine that the law to govern a contract is the law intended by the parties, what is more noteworthy about the decision is that as late as 1760 the rules on so important a matter were completely unsettled.

In 1775 in *Mostyn v Fabrigas*,[16] Lord Mansfield also adumbrated part of the rule that governed liability in tort until very recently,[17] though it was not finally settled until 1869.[18] He laid down that what was a justification by the law of the place of the tort could be pleaded as a defence to an action in England. Other principles suggested or established in the eighteenth century were that the law of the place of celebration governs the formal validity of a marriage,[19] that movables are subject to the law of the domicile of the owner for the purpose of succession[20] and bankruptcy distribution,[21] and that actions relating to foreign immovables are not sustainable in England.[22] It was not, however, until nearly the close of the century that a clear acknowledgment was made of the duty of English courts to give effect to foreign laws. It was made, once again, by Lord Mansfield.

> Every action here must be tried by the law of England, but the law of England says that in a variety of circumstances, with regard to contracts legally made abroad, the laws of the country where the cause of action arose shall govern.[23]

Thus the eighteenth century represents the embryonic period of private international law, a period which extended to at least the middle of the next century. As late as 1825, Best CJ felt justified in remarking that "these questions of international law do not often occur",[24] and though the era of development was at hand, a considerable time had yet to pass before the main rules were determined. Thus, although rules to govern contracts, torts and legitimation were laid down in 1865, 1869 and 1881 respectively, it was not until 1895 that the dependence of divorce jurisdiction on domicile was established. Such matters as capacity to marry, choice of law in nullity and legitimacy are still unsettled. The formative period is not yet at an end.[25] There are still transactions and events common in daily life that are governed by comparatively ancient decisions, and there are others on which the decisions are so hesitating and vacillating that it is difficult to extract the governing principle with assurance. An important fact, and one that should never be overlooked either by the student or the practitioner, is that many of the older decisions are faulty and dangerous guides, and especially so when the point at issue has been the subject of more recent adjudication. Moreover, the number of decisions on choice of law issues is still relatively small[26] in comparison with the case law that surrounds such topics as contracts and torts. Indeed, this general state of the authorities, coupled with the movement in favour of unification by conventions,[27] the establishment of

---

[15] 2 Burr 1077 at 1078.

[16] (1774) 1 Cowp 161, 98 ER 1021.

[17] Infra, pp 777–8.

[18] *Phillips v Eyre* (1870) LR 6 QB 1, infra, p 777 et seq.

[19] *Scrimshire v Scrimshire* (1752) 2 Hag Con 395, 161 ER 782.

[20] *Pipon v Pipon* (1744) Amb 25, 27 ER 14.

[21] *Solomons v Ross* (1764) 1 Hy Bl 131 n.

[22] *Shelling v Farmer* (1725) 1 Stra 646, 93 ER 756.

[23] *Holman v Johnson* (1775) 1 Cowp 341, 98 ER 1120. Lord Stowell spoke to the same effect in *Dalrymple v Dalrymple* (1811) 2 Hag Con 54, 161 ER 665.

[24] *Arnott v Redfern* (1825) 2 Car & P 88 at 90, 172 ER 40.

[25] See Fentiman, in Krawietz and Summers (eds), *Prescriptive Formality and Normative Rationality in Modern Legal Systems* (1994) 443.

[26] One area where there is a substantial number of reported decisions is that relating to jurisdictional disputes, infra, Chapters 11–14.

[27] Supra, pp 10–11.

the Law Commissions,[28] and Europeanisation of the subject area[29] has led in recent years to increasing legislative intervention in the field of private international law.[30]

2. MODERN THEORIES AND DEVELOPMENTS[31]

The development of, and theoretical interest in, private international law did not end with the nineteenth century and more recent developments must now briefly be surveyed. Whilst the early theoretical development of the subject was very much a task undertaken by civil lawyers,[32] in the twentieth century the mantle of theoretical analysis passed to the common lawyers and, in particular, to theorists in the USA. Much of the most recent developments, however, have been occurring in Europe and have been caused by the Europeanisation of the subject area.

(a) Theory of acquired rights

The theory of vested or acquired rights[33] originated with the Dutch jurist Huber,[34] but it was elaborated in the early twentieth century by common lawyers; by Dicey[35] in England and by Beale[36] in the USA. This theory is based on the principle of territoriality. A judge cannot directly recognise or sanction foreign laws nor can he directly enforce foreign judgments, for it is his own territorial law which must exclusively govern all cases that require his decision. The administration of private international law, however, raises no exception to the principle of territoriality, for what the judge does is to protect rights that have already been acquired by a claimant under a foreign law or a foreign judgment. Extra-territorial effect is thus given, not to the foreign law itself, but merely to the rights that it has created.[37]

Support for this theory is claimed from the judgment of Sir William Scott in *Dalrymple v Dalrymple*,[38] where the question at issue was whether Miss Gordon was the wife of Mr Dalrymple. Sir William Scott said:

> The cause being entertained in an English court it must be adjudicated according to the principles of English law applicable to such a case . . . the validity of Miss Gordon's marriage

---

[28] See, eg, Domicile and Matrimonial Proceedings Act 1973; Matrimonial and Family Proceedings Act 1984, Part III; Foreign Limitation Periods Act 1984; Family Law Act 1986; Private International Law (Miscellaneous Provisions) Act 1995.

[29] Supra, pp 11–13.

[30] See North (1982) 46 RabelsZ 490, 500 et seq; Reese (1987) 35 AJCL 395; North (2001) 50 ICLQ 477; Forsyth (2005) 1 J Priv Int L 93.

[31] See also Anton, Chapter 2; *Nygh's Conflict of Laws in Australia* (2014), Chapter 12; Morris, Chapter 2; Mills (2013) 23 Duke J Comp and Int L 445.

[32] Civil lawyers' energies have more recently been directed to the formulation of new or replacement codes. Many of the recent national private international law codes have been reported in the Yearbook of Private International Law. See generally on codification, Jayme (1982) IV Hague Recueil 9; a symposium in (1990) 38 AJCL 423 et seq; Symeonides, in Brown and Snyder (eds), *General Reports of the XVIIIth Congress of the International Academy of Comparative Law* (2012) 167; Symeonides, *Codifying Choice of Law Around the World: An International Comparative Analysis* (2014).

[33] See Morris, para 2-006.

[34] For translations of the title *De Conflictu Legum*, and for accounts of Huber's influence, see Lorenzen, *Selected Articles on the Conflict of Laws* (1947), Chapter 6; Llewelfryn Davies (1937) 18 BYBIL 49; and see Lipstein (1972) I Hague Recueil 97, 121–31.

[35] *Conflict of Laws* (1932) 5th edn, pp 17, 43; see Nadelmann, *Conflict of Laws: International and Interstate* (1972), pp 14–18; Lipstein [1972B] CLJ 67–71.

[36] *Conflict of Laws* (1935), pp 1967–9.

[37] Holland, *Jurisprudence* (1900) 9th edn, pp 398–9; *Re Askew* [1930] 2 Ch 259 at 267.

[38] (1811) 2 Hag Con 54, 161 ER 665.

rights must be tried by reference to the law of the country where, if they exist at all, they had their origin.[39]

This theory of acquired rights receives scant support at the present day and it has, indeed, been devastatingly criticised.[40] It no doubt stresses one of the principal objects of private international law, for, as we have already seen, one of the elementary duties of a civilised court is impartially to protect existing rights even though they originated abroad. Nevertheless, it must be observed that to protect a right is to give effect to the legal system to which it owes its origin, for a right is not a self-evident fact, but a conclusion of law.[41] The theory is open to several objections. First, it is advanced in explanation of the difficulty of reconciling the recognition of a foreign law with the general principle that the laws of a sovereign state have force only within its own territorial jurisdiction. But this difficulty is only an imagined one because it assumes too narrow a meaning of the expression "territorial law", which is not confined to the positive rules that regulate acts and events occurring within the jurisdiction, but includes also rules for the choice of the applicable law.[42] English choice of law rules are part of the law of England and when a court, for instance, tests the substantial validity of a contract made by two foreigners in Paris by reference to French law, it applies a rule of English law and it may accurately be described as putting into force part of the territorial law of England.

Secondly, the theory is futile if its supposed objective is to indicate what legal system governs each legal relation, for it begs the question and produces a vicious circle. A judge who is merely directed to protect a foreign acquired right is not far advanced on his journey, for he still needs to identify the particular legal system, out of perhaps several possible choices, which is entitled to determine whether acquisition is complete. Such a search is not facilitated by the bald statement that a right once vested is inviolable. Once the appropriate law to govern a case has been determined, the rights that it has vested in the litigant ought certainly to be recognised as far as possible, but that fact can scarcely be called "the foundation of judicial decisions" on private international law.[43] As Cook has shown, there are no fundamental and logical principles which infallibly indicate in any given situation what court has jurisdiction and what law is applicable.[44]

Thirdly, the theory is untrue in fact, since the choice of law rules current in much of the common law world can require the enforcement of a right that is unrecognised, or even repudiated, by the chosen law.[45]

> A French widow, for instance, claims a share of her husband's English land. This claim raises a question either of succession or of the mutual property rights of husband and wife. If the English judge classifies the issue as one concerned with the mutual property rights of spouses, he must enforce whatever right is granted to a widow by that particular part of French law. But if French law would have classified the case as one of succession, it may well be that the English judge will enforce a right that would not have been admitted in France.

The theory as advocated by Beale is open to a difficulty of a different nature. He insisted that the municipal law of the country under which a right has been acquired must be followed *to the exclusion of its choice of law rules*. This no doubt is correct as a general principle;[46] but

---

[39] Ibid, at 58.
[40] Arminjon (1933) II Hague Recueil 1; Cook, *Logical and Legal Bases of the Conflict of Laws* (1942), passim; Carswell (1959) 8 ICLQ 268; Kahn-Freund (1974) III Hague Recueil 139, 464–5.
[41] Carswell (1959) 8 ICLQ 268, 285.
[42] Arminjon (1933) II Hague Recueil 1, 27; see also Lord Mansfield in *Holman v Johnson* (1775) 1 Cowp 341 at 343, 98 ER 1120.
[43] Dicey, *Conflict of Laws* (1932) 5th edn, p 18.
[44] *Logical and Legal Bases of the Conflict of Laws* (1942), pp 18–9.
[45] Arminjon (1933) II Hague Recueil 1, 32–3, 47–8.
[46] Infra, pp 57 and 69–70.

if so, the result will frequently be that the right enforced by the court of the forum will not correspond with that recognised by the relevant foreign law. The logic of the vested rights theory requires that the court of the forum shall apply not merely the domestic rules but also the choice of law rules of the legal system under which the right is said to have been acquired. If, for instance, an American citizen were to die intestate domiciled in Italy, some American courts would apply the law of his domicile and would grant to the relatives such rights to the movable property of the deceased as would have been granted to them by the relevant provisions of the Italian Civil Code had the deceased been an Italian with no foreign connections. But Italian private international law, in its insistence that intestacy is governed by the law of the patriality, would deny that the relatives possess any such rights.

Again it was said by Dicey in his lifetime that, "the incidents of a right of a type recognised by English law acquired under the law of any civilised country must be determined in accordance with the law under which the right is acquired".[47] This is not completely true, for the incidents and consequences attached to a foreign right when enforced in England may differ from those recognised in its country of origin. An English court, for instance, may exact maintenance from a husband living in England, although he and his wife are domiciled in a country where no such obligation is recognised.

The theory of vested rights is analytically defective and is inadequate as an explanation of the pattern of rules of private international law. On the other hand, it may have performed a useful role in the development of the subject. As has already been pointed out, the theory stresses one of the primary objectives of private international law. It serves to emphasise the need to find solutions with an international flavour. The notion that a foreign right is vested and as such requires respect, although analytically a fiction, tends to induce the correct psychological background for the formulation of choice of law rules. The fiction of vested rights is a fiction inimical to insular prejudices.

(b) Local law theory

Another theory is that which has been called the *local law theory*.[48] This was expounded by Walter Wheeler Cook, who differed from earlier jurists with regard to the value of so-called fundamental principles. His method, congenial to English lawyers, was to derive the governing rules, not from the logical reasoning of philosophers and jurists, but by observing what the courts have actually done in dealing with cases involving private international law issues. He stressed that what lawyers investigate in practice is how judges have acted in the past, in order that it may be prophesied how they will probably act in the future. A statement of law is "true", not because it conforms to an alleged "inherent principle", but because it represents the past, and therefore the probable future, judicial attitude.

The gist of the local law theory as formulated by Cook is that the court of the forum recognises and enforces a local right, ie one created by its own law. This court applies its own rules to the total exclusion of all foreign rules. But, since it is confronted with a foreign-element case, it does not necessarily apply the rule of the forum that would govern an analogous case purely domestic in character. For reasons of social expedience and practical convenience, it takes into account the laws of the foreign country in question. It creates its own local right, but fashions it as nearly as possible on the law of the country in which the decisive facts have occurred.

---

[47] Dicey, *Conflict of Laws* (1932) 5th edn, p 43, General Principle No V.
[48] Cook, especially Chapter I; Lorenzen, *Selected Articles on the Conflict of Laws* (1947), I; de Sloovère (1928) 41 Harv LR 421; Cheatham (1945) 58 Harv LR 361; Falconbridge (1937) 53 LQR 537, 556; Falconbridge, *Essays on the Conflict of Laws* (1954) 2nd edn, pp 30–7; Morris, para 2-007.

Since the court of the forum adopts the view that the chosen law would have taken not of the actual case, but of an equivalent domestic case, it does not necessarily recognise the right that would in fact have been vested in the claimant according to the chosen law. If the court of the chosen law had tried the actual case, it would not have regarded it as a domestic case. Owing to the presence of foreign elements, it would have been guided by its own choice of law rules, and therefore it might well have applied some law other than its own domestic system. Cook sums up the theory in these words:

> The forum, when confronted by a case involving foreign elements, always applies its own law to the case, but in doing so adopts and enforces as its own law a rule of decision identical, or at least highly similar though not identical, in scope with a rule of decision found in the system of law in force in another state or country with which some or all of the foreign elements are connected, the rule so selected being in many groups of cases, and subject to the exceptions to be noted later, the rule of decision which the given foreign state or country would apply, not to the very group of facts now before the court of the forum, but to *a similar but purely domestic group of facts involving for the foreign court no foreign element*. .... The forum thus enforces, not a foreign right, but a right created by its own law.[49]

It is scarcely deniable, however, that this local law theory is little more than what one writer has stigmatised as a sterile truism—sterile because it affords no basis for the systematic development of private international law.[50] To remind an English judge, about to try a case containing a foreign element, that whatever decision he gives he must enforce only the law of the forum is a technical quibble that explains nothing and solves nothing. It provides no guidance whatever as to the limits within which he must have regard to the foreign law.

(c) The American revolution[51]

Some of the most important theoretical developments of private international law took place in the USA in the second half of the twentieth century. Indeed they have been described as a new American revolution.[52] Whilst a variety of ways of tackling choice of law problems has been put forward in the USA, they tend to have a similar basic characteristic—an analysis of the issues arising in a particular case with a concern to devise the appropriate rule for this more narrowly formulated problem as compared with the far more broadly based conventional choice of law rules.[53] This analysis of issues in individual cases requires the court to examine the particular substantive rules of law in conflict in the case, to identify the policies at issue and to resolve any conflict so identified by choice of law rules appropriate to that narrowly defined conflict.

In order to examine briefly these developments, we shall have to look first at two general approaches common to most of the "revolutionaries" before looking at the main theoretical approaches put forward.

---

[49] Cook, pp 20–1.

[50] Yntema (1953) 2 AJCL 297, 317.

[51] See De Boer, *Beyond Lex Loci Delicti* (1987); Brilmayer, *Conflict of Laws: Foundations and Future Directions* (1995) 2nd edn; (1995) 252 Hague Recueil 9; Symeonides, *The American Choice-of-Law Revolution: Past, Present and Future* (2006); Symeonides and Perdue, *Cases and Materials on Conflict of Laws: American, Comparative and International* (2012) 3rd edn; Hay, Borchers and Symeonides, *Conflict of Laws* (2010) 5th edn; Symeonides, *Choice of Law* (2016). Also, from 1987 onwards, Annual Surveys of American Choice-of-Law Cases, cited in Symeonides (2016) 64 AJCL 221 at n 1.

[52] See Kegel (1964) II Hague Recueil 91.

[53] For a comparison of the two approaches, see Hay (1991) I Hague Recueil 282; Bliesener (1994) 42 AJCL 687.

(i) Two general approaches

(a) Rule selection or jurisdiction selection?

English choice of law rules cover a wide variety of matters—such as the rule that the formal validity of a marriage is governed by the law of the place of celebration, that the essential validity of a contract is governed by the law chosen by the parties or by certain other considerations in the absence of choice, or that succession to movables is governed by the law of the testator's domicile. All these rules, however, have one thing in common. They are, in the terminology of the American writers, "jurisdiction-selecting" rules. They require the court to apply the law of the country chosen by the choice of law rule irrespective of the content of the particular rule of law thereby selected. This is to be compared with the technique of "rule-selection" favoured in the USA, which emphasises a choice between different substantive rules of law which in turn leads to a balancing of the respective "interests" involved in the application of a particular substantive rule of one legal system rather than a different substantive rule of another legal system.

The choice between a jurisdiction-selecting or a rule-selecting approach has been put thus:

> Should a court in dealing with a claim that a foreign law is applicable to the case before it or to an issue in that case choose between its own and the foreign legal system or, instead, choose between its own rule and the foreign rule?[54]

Rule-selection is preferred by the American writers and in some fields by the courts, but such an approach can take a variety of forms. Before attempting to outline some of these forms, it is necessary to examine a further general issue which may eradicate the need for any choice at all, namely the question whether there is a true or false conflict.

(b) True and false conflicts[55]

A jurisdiction-selecting approach to choice of law leads to the application of the rules of law of the chosen jurisdiction irrespective of which of the rules of substantive law of two or more apparently involved legal systems is to be applied. There is a basic assumption here that rules from two or more legal systems do have a claim to be applied. If they do not, and on analysis only one has such a claim, there is no choice to be made. This latter situation has been described as a "false conflict";[56] the former case where more than one set of rules has a legitimate claim to application, thereby necessitating the development of rules for choosing between them, is a "true conflict". There is a third possibility,[57] which has been described as a "no-interest" case,[58] where a conflict of decision may result from the application of the laws of the different states, but where neither state has an interest in its law being applied.[59]

> The classic "no interest" case is one in which the plaintiff's state has a law favourable to the defendant and the defendant's state has a law favourable to the plaintiff . . .. The plaintiff's state has no interest in protecting the defendant who comes from another state and the defendant's state has no reason to give the plaintiff more compensation than he would get under the law of his own state.[60]

---

[54] Cavers (1970) III Hague Recueil 75, 122.

[55] Pryles (1987) 11 Sydney LR 284.

[56] This term covers the case where the laws of the two states are the same or would produce the same result, eg *Scheer v Rockne Motors Corpn* 68 F 2d 942 (1934) and where the laws are different but only one has an interest in being applied; eg *Babcock v Jackson* 12 NY 2d 473, 191 NE 2d 279 (1963); *Williams v Rawlings Truck Line Inc* 357 F 2d 581 (1965). See *Danziger v Ford Motor Co* 402 F Supp 2d 236 (DDC 2005).

[57] For a range of seven possibilities, see Westen (1967) 55 Calif LR 74.

[58] Eg Currie, *Selected Essays on the Conflict of Laws* (1963), pp 152–6.

[59] *Hurtado v Superior Court* 522 P 2d 666 (1974).

[60] Weintraub (1977) 41 Law and Contemporary Problems 146, 153.

It will be apparent that in this whole area a two-stage analysis is involved. First, does the case concern a true or a false conflict? This question is to be answered by a proper interpretation of the rules in issue in the light of their respective purposes and the facts of the case.[61] Indeed, it is said that if, after such a test has been applied, a true conflict is seen to exist, the test should be applied more carefully again in the hope that on truer analysis the conflict will prove to be false and the need for choice of law rules that much the less.[62]

If, despite re-analysis, the choice of law problem still remains in the form of a "true" conflict, the next stage of analysis is reached, ie the selection between the various rules which have a legitimate claim to application. On this, American writers have put forward a variety of rule-selection techniques, which we must now examine.

(ii) Rule-selection techniques

(a) Governmental interest analysis

Currie, described as the father[63] of the governmental interest analysis approach, proposed[64] that the court should examine the policies expressed in the rules of substantive law in apparent conflict and assess the interests of the respective states in having the policies embodied in their rules applied in a fact situation not restricted to the one state. If, on careful assessment, the rules, policies and interests are found to be in conflict, a "true" conflict, then the law of the forum is to be applied. This is so notwithstanding the fact that the other state has an interest in the application of its own contrary policy.

The main role of interest analysis is to determine whether the conflict is true or false, but applying the law of the forum, without more, to a true conflict is, in truth, an abandonment of the internationalism of private international law.[65] Furthermore, the technique of interest analysis, particularly in a country like England where choice of law problems are more likely to be international than inter-state,[66] suffers from major defects.[67] The weighing of interests is limited to the identification of whether the conflict is true or false; it plays no part at the crucial stage of determining the applicable law. The latter is as important as the former. Furthermore, any weighing of interests is limited to state interests. This may be thought legitimate in the field of public international law; but in the context of private international law, the court should seek "conflicts justice"[68] and this requires due regard to be paid to the interests of the parties in the individual case.

Another disadvantage of governmental interest analysis is that it assumes a willingness and ability on the part of judges to identify and to evaluate the policies and interests expressed in the substantive laws under review. There are real difficulties here. How is the court to determine the policy underpinning a statutory rule;[69] and is the policy evident at the time

---

[61] Cavers (1970) III Hague Recueil 75, 129.

[62] Currie (1963) 63 Col LR 1233, 1241–2.

[63] *Bernhard v Harrah's Club* 546 P 2d 719 at 722 (1976).

[64] Currie, *Selected Essays on the Conflict of Laws* (1963), especially Chapters 4 and 12; (1963) 63 Col LR 1233.

[65] Eg *Erny v Estate of Merola* 792 A 2d 1208 (NJ 2002).

[66] See Shapira, *The Interest Approach to Choice of Law* (1970), pp 34–44.

[67] For criticism of Currie's views, see Kegel (1964) II Hague Recueil 91, 180–207; Reese (1965) 16 UTLJ 228; Shapira, *The Interest Approach to Choice of Law* (1970), pp 175–85; Cavers (1970) III Hague Recueil 75, 147–8; Kahn-Freund (1974) III Hague Recueil 139, 413–5; Reese (1976) II Hague Recueil 1, 44–62, 181–91; Hancock (1977) 26 ICLQ 799; North (1980) I Hague Recueil 9, 33–8; Juenger (1984) 32 AJCL 1, 25–50. For defence of Currie's views, see Weintraub (1984) 35 Mercer LR 629; Posnak (1988) 36 AJCL 681; (1994) 40 Wayne LR 1121; Kay (1989) II Hague Recueil 9; Shaman (1997) 45 Buffalo LR 329. See also the symposium in [2015] U Ill L Rev 1847 et seq.

[68] Kegel (1964) II Hague Recueil 91, 181–9.

[69] See Brilmayer (1980) 78 Mich LR 392.

the statute was passed still one that justifies its retention? There are similar problems caused by the passage of time in relation to judge-made law and the policies justifying the rule may never have been clearly articulated. The problems are compounded when the policy assessment has to be made in relation to the law of a foreign country whose legal system and law-making processes are very different from ours.[70] It is no answer to these difficulties to say that American courts have, mainly in the areas of tort and contract, applied interest analysis for several decades. Most of the relevant cases have involved inter-state rather than international conflicts[71] and, more often than not, no real attempt has been made to discover the policy basis of the rules in conflict. There tends to be merely a statement, without evidence, as to what the policies of the rules must be—very much a forum oriented assessment.

There are further difficulties with this approach. Not only is it inherently uncertain, but it also normally requires a judicial determination of where the balance of interests lies. This inhibits lawyers from giving advice and it suggests (as has proved to be the case) that the approach may best be used in areas such as the law of tort where "the function of the law is substantially pathological and the view of the court is essentially retrospective".[72] It has been little used in family law and in property matters where the law's function may more often be prospective, involving advice as to the future. A final disadvantage concerns what Currie described as "the disinterested third State".[73] This is the case where the interests of three states have to be assessed, where the forum has no interest in its law being applied but where there is a true conflict between the interests of the two other states. The Currie analysis breaks down; there is no merit in applying the law of the forum and no rule for deciding which other law to apply.

(b) Comparative impairment

There is a body of opinion in the USA which, though prepared to go much of the way with Currie's interest analysis and the identification, and thus elimination, of false conflicts, is not willing to accept that the law of the forum automatically be applied in cases of true conflicts. In contrast to Currie's views, such opinion believes that courts are able to and ought to weigh the conflicting interests. The criterion for such evaluation is suggested as that of "comparative impairment". This approach, first propounded in 1963 by Baxter[74] and since supported by the Supreme Court of California,[75] requires the court to determine which of the conflicting states' interests would be more impaired if its policy were subordinated to the policy of the other state. The essence of the comparative impairment approach has been summed up thus:

> the comparative impairment approach to the resolution of true conflicts attempts to determine the relative commitment of the respective states to the laws involved. The approach incorporates several factors for consideration: the history and current status of the states' laws: the function and purpose of those laws.[76]

Though this approach is open to all the objections that may be made against any rule-selection approach, with its underlying premise that the identification of governmental interests or state policies implicit in the conflicting rules is easy to accomplish, it does meet some

---

[70] Fawcett (1982) 31 ICLQ 150.

[71] See Kegel (1979) 27 AJCL 615.

[72] North (1980) I Hague Recueil 9, 37. Eg *Gilbert v Seton Hall University* 332 F 3d 105 (2d Cir 2003).

[73] (1963) 28 Law and Contemporary Problems 754.

[74] (1963) 16 Stan LR 1; and see Horowitz (1974) 21 UCLALR 719, 748–58.

[75] *Bernhard v Harrah's Club* 546 P 2d 719 (1976); *Offshore Rental Co Inc v Continental Oil Co* 583 P 2d 721 (1978); and see *Liew v Official Receiver* 685 F 2d 1192 (1982).

[76] *Offshore Rental Co Inc v Continental Oil Co* 583 P 2d 721 at 727 (1978). For criticisms of this approach, see Bradley (1976) 29 Stan LR 127, 146; Weintraub (1977) 41 Law and Contemporary Problems 146, 158; North (1980) I Hague Recueil 9, 38–40; Kay (1980) 68 Calif LR 577; and Juenger (1999) 73 Tul LR 1309.

of the criticisms of Currie's mechanistic forum-oriented approach and of his failure to solve the problem of the disinterested third state.

(c) Principles of preference

As long ago as 1933 Cavers advocated[77] the abandonment of a jurisdiction-selecting approach in favour of rule-selection. Later, he developed[78] his choice of law rules as "principles of preference". He and Currie have much in common. They were both supporters of rule-selection: both would utilise this analysis to identify cases of true and false conflict. Resolution of false conflicts is easy—there is no conflict. The parting of the ways comes with true conflicts. Cavers did not accept "Currie's stern rejection of all choice-of-law rules".[79] Instead, he sought to develop choice of law rules for the resolution of true conflicts. Accepting that the detailed development of rule-selection rules may be a long process, he suggested that the courts should develop broad principles of preference:

> The court is to seek a rule for choice of law or a principle of preference which would either reflect relevant multistate policies or provide the basis for a reasonable accommodation of the laws' conflicting purposes. A principle of preference would be applicable to all cases having the same general pattern of law and fact and would identify a preferred result on choice-of-law grounds. If the case could not thus be generalised, the court should state the reasons leading it to prefer one result to the other on choice-of-law grounds. In either case it should apply the law leading to the preferred result.[80]

This is the gradualist approach. It involves the introduction of broad principles of preference, worked out by Cavers in some fields, namely torts, contracts and conveyances, but not developed at all in others. The main objective is to do justice between the parties and, from these just principles, it is envisaged that more specific detailed rules will emerge as a result of judicial development.[81]

The main appeal of Cavers' approach is that it attempts a solution to the true conflict, but in the process it attracts all the criticisms of any rule selection approach.[82] It is still necessary to identify and evaluate state policies or interests. Uncertainty and unpredictability remain, even with principles of preference. This is because their evolution is seen in terms of judicial development, and choice of law rules based on principles of such detail as is necessary to accommodate so many varied policies will take a very long time to develop. This may be easier in a federal state, as Cavers himself admitted,[83] than with the type of international conflicts with which English courts tend to be faced.

(d) Interpretation of forum policy

Criticism of both the traditional jurisdiction-selecting approaches and more recent governmental interests analysis is found in the writings of Ehrenzweig.[84] In his view, a court, in searching for the appropriate choice of law rule, should give pre-eminence to the law of the

---

[77] (1933) 47 Harv LR 173.

[78] *The Choice-of-Law Process* (1965); (1970) III Hague Recueil 75; (1977) 26 ICLQ 703; *The Choice of Law, Selected Essays* (1985).

[79] *The Choice-of-Law Process* (1965), p 94.

[80] Ibid, p 64.

[81] The courts have, in some cases, attempted to develop such detailed rules; see *Neumeier v Kuehner* 286 NE 2d 454 (1972); *First National Bank in Fort Collins v Rostek* 514 P 2d 314 (1973); *Bader v Purdom* 841 F 2d 38 (1988).

[82] For criticisms, see de Nova (1966) II Hague Recueil 435, 597–603; Lipstein (1972) I Hague Recueil 97, 157–61.

[83] (1933) 47 Harv LR 173, 203.

[84] *A Treatise on the Conflict of Laws* (1962); *Private International Law*, Vols I–III (1967–1977); (1960) 58 Mich LR 637; (1961) 49 Cal LR 240; (1968) II Hague Recueil 167, 178.

forum—an approach described as "interpretation of forum policy".[85] He maintained that, in practice, the courts have applied the law of the forum as the general rule, and suggested that foreign law was not to be regarded as "applicable" to govern a case, merely that it should be "tolerated".[86] Reference to a foreign law is only to be made in exceptional circumstances where application of the law of the forum would be unfair to the parties or contrary to their intentions. Application of the law of the forum has the obvious advantages for all concerned in litigation that it is easy and cheap to apply; but it depends on knowing what the forum is going to be. Ehrenzweig's approach is a recipe for "forum-shopping", with the claimant seeking to sue in the country with the law most favourable to him. It is hardly satisfactory that the merits of his approach to choice of law issues depend on the availability of controls over jurisdictional rules. Furthermore, a forum-oriented approach cannot provide choice of law decisions in the absence of litigation.[87]

(e) Choice of law factors

There are two, fairly similar, American approaches to choice of law problems under which the applicable law is determined by reference to a variety of choice of law factors. The first of these is the American Law Institute's Second Restatement of the Conflict of Laws, which adopts as its basic criterion for choice of law the application of the law of the state which has the most significant relationship to the particular issue under principles laid down in paragraph 6 of the Restatement. This requires the court to follow a statutory directive of its own state on choice of law but, in the absence of such a directive, the factors relevant to the choice of the applicable law include:

(a) the needs of the inter-state and international systems;
(b) the relevant policies of the forum;
(c) the relevant policies of other interested states and the relative interests of those states in the determination of the particular issue;
(d) the protection of justified expectations;
(e) the basic policies underlying the particular field of law;
(f) certainty, predictability and uniformity of result; and
(g) ease in the determination and application of the law to be applied.

The most significant relationship test, with these choice influencing factors, is applied to a whole variety of conflicts issues, ranging from contract and tort to marriage and property.

Reese, the Reporter of the Second Restatement and architect of this approach,[88] would describe the test provided in the Restatement as an "approach" to choice of law and not as providing in itself rules for the solution of specific choice of law problems.[89] Nevertheless, it is perceived as a means to the end of development of clear, precise rules:

> I believe that one ultimate goal, be it ever so distant, should be the development of hard-and-fast rules of choice of law. I believe that in many instances these rules should be directed, at least initially, at a particular issue. And I believe that in the development of these rules consideration should be given to the basic objectives of choice of law, to the relevant local law rules of the potentially interested states and, of course, to the contacts of the parties and of the occurrence with these states.[90]

---

[85] Cavers (1970) III Hague Recueil 75, 150.
[86] *A Treatise on the Conflict of Laws* (1962), p 311.
[87] For other criticisms, see Shapira, *The Interest Approach to Choice of Law* (1970), pp 205–8; Kegel (1964) II Hague Recueil 91, 224–36; Lipstein (1972) I Hague Recueil 97, 144–7.
[88] Cheetham and Reese (1952) 52 Col LR 959. See Symeonides (1997) 56 Maryland LR 1248.
[89] Reese (1976) II Hague Recueil 1, 44–65.
[90] Ibid, p 180.

The attraction of this approach is that, in reality, it attempts to have the best of all worlds. It provides specific choice of law rules, unlike the forum-oriented approach of Currie and Ehrenzweig. It does not require an analysis into true and false conflicts with its difficulties of determining in detail the interests of the states whose laws are competing, or the policies underlying the creation or retention of such rules; yet it provides some consolation, in the reference to "the relevant policies of other interested states and the relative interests of those states in the determination of the particular issue", to those who are supporters of interest analysis. It acknowledges the desirability of certainty and ease of application of the law, surely very necessary elements in the formulation of new rules of law. It requires a new look at the old choice of law rules, and encourages that new look to be issue-oriented rather than aimed at whole areas of the law such as "contract", "tort" or "marriage". Indeed, it is both jurisdiction selecting and rule selecting at the same time.[91] The purpose of indicating that regard should be had to the policies of the interested states and their relative interests in the determination of the particular issue must be in order to aid the selection of the more appropriately applicable rule—a form of interest analysis or rule-selection. In giving consideration, as Reese does in the passage just quoted, to the contacts of the parties and of the occurrence with the interested states, Reese relies on a "grouping of contacts" approach which is predominantly jurisdiction-selecting.

Although the Second Restatement has had a significant impact on the decision of tort cases in the USA involving choice of law issues,[92] it does not escape criticisms,[93] which are of two main kinds. The first is that "the factors often point in different directions and carry in themselves no measure of their significance".[94] You cannot point in rule selection and jurisdiction selection directions at one and the same time. Secondly, it is hard to be certain as to the purpose of the Restatement's choice influencing factors. They read like an exhortation to a law reformer, as criteria to be weighed in formulating new rules. Their effectiveness depends both on litigation and on judicial creativity, on a willingness of judges to cast aside old rules in a search for better ones, despite any uncertainty that may bring. It is not surprising that their main impact has been in the field of choice of law in tort, where the role of the law is far more retrospective than prospective.

The second approach involving choice of law factors is that of Leflar who has advocated that courts resolve choice of law issues by reference to five "choice-influencing considerations". In no particular order of priority, he lists them[95] as:

(a) Predictability of result;
(b) Maintenance of interstate and international order;
(c) Simplification of the judicial task;
(d) Advancement of the forum's governmental interests;
(e) Application of the better rule of law.

All but the last of these essentially mirror factors to be found in the list in the Second Restatement. They have the same attractions and are subject to the same criticisms; but the

---

[91] See Shapira, *The Interest Approach to Choice of Law* (1970), p 214.

[92] Eg *Babcock v Jackson* 191 NE 2d 279 (1963); *Pancotto v Sociedade de Safaris de Mocambique SARL* 422 F Supp 405 (1976).

[93] See the symposium in (1997) 56 Maryland LR 1193. Also *Dowis v Mud Slingers Inc* 621 SE 2d 413 at 417–8 (Ga 2005).

[94] Cavers (1970) III Hague Recueil 75, 145.

[95] Leflar, *American Conflicts Law* (1986) 4th edn, pp 277–9. For an assessment of Leflar's work, see the symposium in (1980) 34 Ark LR 199. Also *Mikelson v United Services Auto Association* 111 P 3d 601 (Hawaii 2005).

fifth factor, that of "the better rule of law", calls for separate comment. It is a factor which has proved attractive to the judiciary, though one which is more likely to lead to a court concluding that its own, the forum's, rule of law is the better rule.[96] Nevertheless, it is a dangerous factor to use in the choice of law process because it confuses the issue of the reform of the substantive law of one country with that of choosing the most appropriate law to govern a dispute with links with two or more countries. It is certainly not the task of a judge in one country to try to reform the law in another.[97]

(iii) Impact of the revolution

Whilst the direct influence of these American developments of private international law theory is essentially limited to the USA,[98] writers from, for example, France,[99] Italy,[100] Germany[101] and Switzerland[102] have welcomed the developments as, at least, providing an impetus for reappraisal of the civil lawyer's[103] approach to choice of law problems. At the same time, however, the voices of American critics[104] of interest analysis and the like are strong, concerned with many of the criticisms of the "revolution" which have been mentioned earlier. Few, however, are as robust as this:

> Conflicts of law has become a veritable playpen for judicial policymakers . . . . [The] courts are saddled with a cumbersome and unwieldy body of conflicts law that creates confusion, uncertainty and inconsistency, as well as complication of the judicial task. The approach has been like that of the misguided physician who treated a case of dandruff with nitric acid, only to discover that the malady would have been remedied with medicated shampoo. Neither the doctor nor the patient need have lost his head.[105]

In truth, the impact of the new ideas has been limited. Whilst its effects on choice of law have been substantial in the area of tort law,[106] and have been significant in the context of contract

---

[96] Eg *Clark v Clark* 222 A 2d 205 (1966); *Turcotte v Ford Motor Co* 494 F 2d 173 (1974); *Wille v Farm Bureau Mutual Insurance Co* 432 NW 2d 784 (1988); cf *Boucher v Boucher* 553 A 2d 313 (1988).

[97] Cavers (1971) 49 Texas LR 211, 215; but contrast Juenger (1985) IV Hague Recueil 119, 253–318. See Symeonides (2001) 49 AJCL 1, 8 et seq; and *Jepson v General Cas Co of Wisconsin* 513 NW 2d 467, 473 (Minn 1994).

[98] Though some direct influence in England can be seen, on what were our choice of law rules in tort, in *Chaplin v Boys* [1971] AC 356, HL, infra, pp 777–8.

[99] Audit (1979) 27 AJCL 589.

[100] Vitta (1982) 30 AJCL 1.

[101] Kegel (1979) 27 AJCL 615.

[102] Siehr (2000) 60 La LR 1353.

[103] See further the symposium papers collected in (1982) 30 AJCL 1–146; Jayme, in de Boer (ed), *Forty Years On: The Evolution of Postwar Private International Law in Europe* (1990) 15; Vischer, in Nafziger and Symeonides (eds), *Law and Justice in a Multistate World* (2002) 459.

[104] Eg Juenger (1984) 32 AJCL 1; (1985) 46 Ohio State LJ 509; (1985) IV Hague Recueil 119, 227–52; (1988) 21 UC Davis LR 515; Rosenberg (1981) 81 Col LR 946; Korn (1983) 83 Col LR 772; Reppy (1983) 34 Mercer LR 645; Brilmayer (1985) 46 Ohio State LJ 459; (1984) 35 Mercer LR 555; Dane (1987) 96 Yale LJ 1191; Brilmayer (1989) 98 Yale LJ 1277; and see Baxter (1987) 36 ICLQ 92; Whitten (2001) 37 Willamette LR 259; Maltz (2005) 36 Rutgers LJ 527; cf Weintraub (1984) 35 Mercer LR 629; Posnak (1988) 36 AJCL 681; (1994) 40 Wayne LR 1121; Kay (1989) II Hague Recueil 9; Shaman (1997) 45 Buffalo LR 329. Also, the symposium in (2000) 75 Ind LJ 399, including comment by Juenger (at 403), Symeonides (at 437), Simson (at 649) and Weintraub (at 679); Symeonides (2001) 37 Willamette LR 1; Symeonides, *The American Choice-of-Law Revolution: Past, Present and Future* (2006); Levin (2007) 60 Stan LR 247; and the symposium in [2015] U Ill L Rev 1847 et seq.

[105] *Paul v National Life* 352 NE 2d 550 at 551, 553 (1986).

[106] It is often the case that a court may be influenced by more than one approach, as in *Mitchell v Craft* 211 So 2d 509 (1968). For a striking example of a federal court applying a variety of approaches to different claims arising from one accident, see *Re Air Crash Disaster Near Chicago Illinois on May 25, 1979* 644 F 2d 594 (1981).

rules, interest analysis and its progeny have been little discussed in the context of family law[107] or property matters and have had little impact on judicial decisions in those fields.

(iv) Post-revolutionary developments

The decline of American conflicts scholarship, the result of an awareness that the vigour of the American "revolution" has subsided, has been followed by a revival in recent years.[108] Interesting developments in conflict of laws thinking, primarily in the USA but also in other countries, have emerged from interdisciplinary interest in this field of law, most importantly from the perspectives of economics, political science and anthropology.

The most important interdisciplinary movement is "law and economics",[109] which, as Ralf Michaels explains, has come up with three broad types of economic model.[110] A first set of "private-law" models focus on the interests of individuals as rational actors.[111] The goal is either to achieve greater efficiency among individuals or to maximise global social welfare, perceived as the sum of the utilities of all individuals. This type of model favours private ordering, party autonomy and predictable rules. A second set of "international-law" models are also oriented towards efficiency and welfare, but with the focus on the conduct of states as rational agents and the maximisation of their preferences.[112] Important considerations are the effectiveness of state policies and cooperation between states. Party autonomy plays a very limited role in this second set of models. "Combined" models combine the previous two, as the focus is on the incentives created by choice-of-law rules for both individuals and states as regulators.[113] The novelty of this third set of models lies in the fact that they emphasise regulatory competition between states and the role of party autonomy in incentivising states to pass efficient domestic substantive laws.[114] These types of economic model are, of course, ideal types and individual economic models developed by different scholars may fall into more than category.[115]

Other interdisciplinary approaches of importance for conflict of laws include "law and political science" and "law and anthropology". The most important modern representative of the former approach is the private international law and global governance movement.[116] This

---

[107] North (1980) I Hague Recueil 9.

[108] See Knop, Michaels and Riles (2008) 71(3) Law and Contemporary Problems 1; Michaels (2009) 11 YBPIL 11.

[109] See, generally, Whincop and Keyes, *Policy and Pragmatism in the Conflict of Laws* (2001); Basedow and Kono (eds, in cooperation with Rühl), *An Economic Analysis of Private International Law* (2006); Kono (2013) 369 Hague Recueil 361; and O'Hara (ed), *Economics of Conflict of Laws* (2007).

[110] Michaels, in Basedow and Kono (eds) 143; (2008) 71 Law and Contemporary Problems 73; (2009) 11 YBPIL 11, 23–4.

[111] See, eg, Whincop and Keyes; O'Hara and Ribstein, *The Law Market* (2009); (2000) 67 U Chi L Rev 1151.

[112] See, eg, Brilmayer, *Conflict of Laws: Foundations and Future Directions* (1995) 2nd edn, pp 169–218; Kramer (1990) 90 Col L Rev 277; Trachtman, *The Economic Structure of International Law* (2008); (1994) 26 Vand J Transnat L 975; (2001) 42 Va J Int L 1.

[113] See, eg, Guzman (2002) 90 Geo LJ 883; see also Muir Watt (2003) 9 Col J Eur L 383; (2004) 307 Hague Recueil 25; (2004) 39 Tex Int L J 429; (2005) 9 Edinburgh L Rev 6; Wai (2002) 40 Col J Transnat L 209.

[114] See, eg, Garcimartín Alférez (1999) 8 Eur J L & Econ 251.

[115] For other economic models see, eg, Solimine (1989) 24 Georgia LR 49; Stephan (2002) 90 Geo LJ 957; Rühl (2006) 24 Berkeley J Int L 801; Rühl, in Gottschalk, Michaels, Rühl and von Hein (eds), *Conflict of Laws in a Globalized World* (2007) 153; (2010) 6 J Priv Int L 59. See also O'Hara and Parisi, 'Conflict of Laws', in Newman (ed), *The New Palgrave Dictionary of Economics and the Law* (1998), Vol 1, 387; Parisi and Ribstein, 'Choice of Law', in Newman (ed), *The New Palgrave Dictionary of Economics and the Law* (1998), Vol 1, 236; O'Hara and Ribstein, 'Conflict of Laws and Choice of Law', in de Geest (ed), *Encyclopedia of Law and Economics* (2012), Vol 8, Chapter 5.

[116] See, eg, Muir Watt and Fernandez Arroyo (eds), *Private International Law and Global Governance* (2014); Wai, in Mueller and Lederer (eds), *Criticizing Global Governance* (2005) 243; Buxbaum (2006) 46

movement focuses on the role played by private international law, including that of freedom of choice as a foundational principle of this field, in supporting transnational private ordering, even to an extent that enables transnational private economic actors to effectively escape domestic public policy regulation in a way that harms global collective goods. An important question is whether private international law can, and if so to what extent, be a countervailing force. Another interdisciplinary approach translates insights from legal pluralism, a concept formulated mainly within anthropology, into private international law.[117] A major question for conflict of laws is how to deal with non-state normative orders.

Whilst the mentioned approaches incorporate insights from other disciplines into conflict of laws, some scholars have emphasized the virtue of conflict of laws as technique, as an intellectual style,[118] and applied a conflict of laws analysis to the problems of delineation of several potentially applicable normative orders that are facing other disciplines such as the fragmentation of public international law[119] or the treatment of international law in domestic courts.[120]

(d) The European (r)evolution

Whilst most, if not all, private international lawyers would agree that private international law in the European Union has changed considerably in the last several decades as a result of the Europeanisation of the subject area, there is a disagreement over the nature, extent and depth of the change. For some, European Union private international law is undergoing a revolution of its own, very different but equally, if not more, radical in comparison to its American counterpart.[121] For others, the developments in the European Union represent a culmination of various evolutionary processes.[122]

The disagreement largely stems from different conceptions of private international law that the participants in this debate adopt. European "revolutionaries" deal not only with the rules of jurisdiction, choice of law and recognition and enforcement of judgments that are contained in European Union private international law instruments but broaden the concept of private international law to include functional equivalents such as the European Union law principles of mutual recognition and country of origin.[123] A justification for this approach is that, ultimately, all of these rules are based on the principle of mutual trust, which is one of

---

Va J Int L 251; Whytock (2009) 84 Tul LR 67; (2009) 84 NYU L Rev 719; (2012) 2 St John's J Int & Comp L 55; Muir Watt (2010) 6 Eur Rev Contract L 250; (2011) 2 Transnat Legal Theory 347. See also contributions to (2011) 2 Transnat Legal Theory 153 et seq.

[117] See, eg, Berman, *Global Legal Pluralism: A Jurisprudence of Law Beyond Borders* (2012); (2005) 153 U Pa LR 1819; (2005) 51 Wayne LR 1105; (2009) 5 Annual Review of Law and Social Science 225; Michaels (2005) 51 Wayne LR 1209; (2009) 5 Annual Review of Law and Social Science 243; Riles (2008) 71 Law and Contemporary Problems 273; Wai (2008) 71 Law and Contemporary Problems 107. See also Helmand (ed), *Negotiating State and Non-State Law: The Challenges of Global and Local Legal Pluralism* (2015).

[118] Michaels, in Muir Watt and Fernandez Arroyo (eds), *Private International Law and Global Governance* (2014) 54.

[119] Michaels and Pauwelyn, in Broude and Shany (eds), *Multi-Sourced Equivalent Norms in International Law* (2011) 19.

[120] Knop, Michaels and Riles (2009) 103 Am Soc Int L Proc 269. See also Knop, Michaels and Riles (2012) 64 Stan LR 589 for the relevance of conflict of laws technique for the feminism/culture debate.

[121] See Michaels (2008) 82 Tul LR 1607; Mills (2013) 23 Duke J Comp and Int L 445; Meeusen (2007) 9 Eur J Migration and L 287; see also contributions to the symposium in (2008) 82 Tul LR 1607 et seq.

[122] See North (1990) I Hague Recueil 9; Symeonides (2008) 82 Tul LR 1741; von Hein (2008) 82 Tul LR 1663; Hay [2015] U Ill L Rev 2053.

[123] See Michaels (2006) 2 J Priv Int L 195; Kuipers (2009) 2 Eur J L Studies 66; Kuipers, *EU Law and Private International Law: The Interrelationship in Contractual Obligations* (2012), Chapter 6; see also Fallon and Meeusen (2002) 4 YBPIL 37; de Baere (2004) 11 Maastricht J of Eur and Comp L 287.

the foundational principles of European Union law.[124] Moreover, European "revolutionaries" are interested in the way the system created by private international law rules interacts with other legal systems such as human rights law.

Private international law in the European Union is undeniably going through a process of federalization. An ever increasing amount of private international law rules is now contained in European Union legal instruments, mostly regulations and to a lesser extent also in directives (and domestic implementing measures) and primary European Union law.[125] But even more important than the move of private international law regulation from the domestic to the European Union level is the fact that the nature and role of private international law rules in the European Union has changed. All European Union private international law instruments are derived from the European Treaties and are based on provisions laying down the competences of the European Union. Consequently, all European Union private international law rules are directly connected to, and influenced by, substantive policies pursued by the European Union. Among those policies, by far the most important is the proper functioning of the internal market;[126] but other policies are of importance too, for example, the protection of employees, consumers and the environment.[127] This link between European Union private international law and substantive European Union policies means that private international law in the European Union is now an instrument of European integration, which makes this field of law very different from classical private international law that was traditionally perceived as a private, apolitical and value neutral discipline. Another important consequence of this process of federalisation pertains to the interests pursued by European Union private international law rules. The rules of classical private international law, conceived of as a branch of domestic law and, therefore, a matter of domestic regulation, pursued purely domestic interests. Admittedly, some private international law matters were dealt with in international treaties,[128] but the adoption of treaties was within the discretion of individual states which would accede to a treaty only when it was in their best interest. The conferral on the European Union of competence over private international law matters means that European Union private international law rules do not have to be, and are frequently not, in line with the interests of individual Member States. European Union private international law rules pursue European interests. These rules perform an important function of distributing the regulatory, ie jurisdictional, legislative and enforcement authority in civil and commercial matters among the Member States.[129] In doing so, European Union private international law is an important supplement of the key European Union law principles of subsidiarity, proportionality and effectiveness and an important tool for the management of legal diversity that exists in the European Union.[130]

---

[124] See Weller (2015) 11 J Priv Int L 64.

[125] Supra, pp 11–13; see von Hoffmann, in von Hoffmann (ed), *European Private International Law* (1998) 19; Beaumont (1999) 48 ICLQ 223; Basedow (2000) 37 CMLR 687; Basedow, in Andenas *et al* (eds), *Liber Amicorum Guido Alpa: Private Law Beyond the National Systems* (2007) 168; (2008) 82 Tul LR 2119; Israel (2000) 7 Maastricht JECL 81; Remien (2001) 38 CMLR 53; Boele-Wolki and van Ooik (2002) 4 YBPIL 1; D'Oliveira, in Fawcett (ed), *Reform and Development of Private International Law: Essays in Honour of Sir Peter North* (2002) 111; Crawford and Carruthers (2005) 3 Juridical Review 251; Dickinson (2005) 1 J Priv Int L 197; Fiorini (2008) 57 ICLQ 969; Kuipers, *EU Law and Private International Law: The Interrelationship in Contractual Obligations* (2012). For an early analysis see Drobnig (1967) 15 AJCL 204.

[126] Treaty on the Functioning of the European Union, Art 81(2).

[127] See Muir Watt, in Cafaggi (ed), *The Institutional Framework of European Private Law* (2006) 107; Cafaggi and Muir Watt, 'Introduction', in Cafaggi and Muir Watt (eds), *Making European Private Law: Governance Design* (2008); Cafaggi and Muir Watt (eds), *The Regulatory Function of European Private Law* (2009); Muir Watt (2003) 9 Col J Eur L 383; (2005) 9 Edinburgh L Rev 6.

[128] Supra, pp 10–11.

[129] Mills, *The Confluence of Public and Private International Law* (2009); (2010) 32 U Pa J Int Law 369.

[130] Mills, ibid; Remien (2001) 38 CMLR 53; Liukkunen (2012) 20 Eur Rev Priv L 1045.

Private international law in the European Union is also undergoing a related process of constitutionalisation.[131] The described process of federalization itself represents a form of constitutionalisation, in the sense that European Union private international law is taking on a "public" role of distributing regulatory authority in a quasi-federal context. Apart from the rules of jurisdiction, choice of law and recognition and enforcement of judgments contained in European Union private international law instruments, this distributive function is also performed by the principles of mutual recognition and country of origin.[132] It is this interplay between, on the one hand, the rules of jurisdiction, choice of law and recognition and enforcement of judgments and, on the other, the rules of primary and secondary European Union law on the free movement of goods, services, people and capital that is one of the defining features of European Union private international law. But there is also another, arguably deeper, process of constitutionalisation of private international law taking place in the European Union. The rules of jurisdiction, choice of law and recognition and enforcement of judgments are based on Article 81 of the Treaty on the Functioning of the European Union, which provides that such rules can be adopted by the European Parliament and the European Council "particularly when necessary for the proper functioning of the internal market". Similarly, the Treaty provisions on the fundamental economic freedoms and the related case-law of the CJEU pursue economic interests of opening up the internal market. A countervailing force to the economic logic of European Union private international law is to be found in the areas of non-discrimination and human rights, which have recently been given a strong impetus through the introduction of citizenship of the European Union and by granting the Charter of Fundamental Rights of the European Union the same legal value as the European Treaties. Human rights, and in particular the right to a fair trial, have had an important role in the field of recognition and enforcement of judgments and have arguably contributed to the emergence of a European legal culture.[133] Human rights and the principle of non-discrimination, which are inherent in European Union citizenship, have had an even greater impact and have led in the area of family law and personal status to the setting aside of choice-of-law rules that interfered with the recognition and protection of personal identity.[134] These processes of constitutionalisation of European Union private international law through federalisation and interplay with human rights and the principle of non-discrimination put this legal discipline right in the middle of modern developments and debates concerning the identity and responsibilities of the European Union.

These processes of federalization and constitutionalisation inevitably lead to a different treatment of two categories of private international law situation: those that are connected solely

---

[131] See generally Bomhoff, in Muir Watt and Fernandez Arroyo (eds), *Private International Law and Global Governance* (2014) 262.

[132] See, eg, in the area of company law, Case C-212/97 *Centros Ltd v Erhvervs-og Selskabsstyrelsen* [1999] ECR 1-1459; Case C-208/00 *Uberseering BV Nordic Construction Co Baumanagement GmbH (NCC)* [2002] ECR 1-9919; Case C-167/01 *Kamer van Koophandel en Fabrieken voor Amsterdam v Inspire Art Ltd* [2003] ECR 1-10155; Case C-411/03 *SEVIC Systems AG* [2005] ECR I-10805; Case C-210/06 *Cartesio Oktató és Szolgáltató bt* [2008] ECR I-9641; Case C-371/10 *National Grid Indus BV v Inspecteur de Belastingdienst Rijnmond/kantoor Rotterdam* [2011] ECR I-12273; Case C-378/10 *VALE Építési kft* EU:C:2012:440, [2013] 1 WLR 294; in the area of labour law, Case C-438/05 *International Transport Workers' Federation and Finnish Seamen's Union v Viking Line ABP and OÜ Viking Line Eesti* [2007] ECR I-10779; Case C-341/05 *Laval un Partneri Ltd v Svenska Byggnadsarbetareförbundet, Svenska Byggnadsarbetareförbundets avdelning 1, Byggettan and Svenska Elektrikerförbundet* [2007] ECR I-11767.

[133] Muir Watt (2001) 36 Tex Int LJ 539.

[134] See, eg, Case C-148/02 *Garcia Avello v Belgium* [2003] ECR I-11613; Case C-353/06 *Grunkin-Paul* [2008] ECR I-7639; Case C-208/09 *Ilonka Sayn-Wittgenstein v Landeshauptstadt von Wien* [2010] ECR I-13693; Case C-391/09 *Runevič-Vardyn & Wardyn v Vilniaus miesto savivaldybès administacija* [2011] ECR I-3787; cf Muir Watt (2008) 82 Tul L Rev 1983.

with the European Union and those that are connected with one or more third states. Intra-EU conflicts come in three different forms: "vertical" conflicts between European Union law and the Member States' domestic laws, "horizontal" conflicts that arise in horizontal relationships between private actors, and "diagonal" conflicts that arise in situations where the European Union is competent to regulate one aspect of the private international law situation (eg fundamental economic freedoms) and the Member States remain competent to regulate another aspect (eg areas that remain within the exclusive competence of individual Member States such as industrial action).[135] Intra-EU conflicts are resolved not only by the application of the rules of jurisdiction, choice of law and recognition and enforcement of judgments, but also by the application of the European Union law principles of supremacy of European Union law, mutual recognition and country of origin. Furthermore, in intra-EU conflicts party autonomy is used as a tool of regulatory competition, and the doctrines of public policy and mandatory rules play a limited role. With regard to external conflicts,[136] European Union private international law has developed somewhat different techniques that are aimed at safeguarding the European Union interests and values from non-European elements. This is achieved by the application of European Union law whenever a particular private international law situation has a sufficient connection with the European Union.[137] The differentiation between the different techniques applicable in intra-EU and external conflicts represents yet another defining feature of European Union private international law.

One may disagree with the thesis that these developments amount to a revolution in European Union private international law, but it cannot be disputed that the nature, extent and depth of the changes in this field in the last several decades has been significant. Although this book adopts a traditional view of private international law and regards it as encompassing rules of jurisdiction, choice of law and recognition and enforcement of judgments, whilst leaving aside the principles of mutual recognition and country of origin, as well as the detail of the impact of human rights and other legal systems on private international law, to specialized works,[138] it must be acknowledged that an understanding of the context in which private international law in England today operates is crucial to a proper understanding of this field of law. This conclusion will remain valid even after the Brexit, the forthcoming withdrawal of the United Kingdom from the European Union, whose precise shape is hard to predict at this stage,[139] at least until the legislation in this field of law that is derived from European Union law is repealed and replaced.

(e) The English approach

What, in the light of the theories and approaches discussed above, is the theoretical or doctrinal basis of English private international law? In considering its nature do we find ourselves perplexed by the enigma that apparently it subordinates the sovereignty of the law of the forum to that of a foreign country? To answer this last question first, the position surely is that for the forum of its own volition to give effect to a foreign law or to enforce a right that is the creature of that law involves no abdication of sovereignty. The forum's recognition of the foreign right is not based on an admission that it has any force in itself, but on the forum's realisation that its own positive rules of law, though in its view

---

[135] Joerges (1998) 18 Legal Studies 146; (2004) 14 Duke J Comp and Int L 149; (April 2013) LEQS Paper No 28/2010.

[136] More generally, on private international law and EU external relation see Mills (2016) 65 ICLQ 541.

[137] See Case C-381/98 *Ingmar GB Ltd v Eaton Leonard Technologies Inc* [2000] ECR I-9305; Francq (2006) 8 YBPIL 333.

[138] On the impact of human rights see Fawcett, Ní Shúilleabháin and Shah, *Human Rights and Private International Law* (2016).

[139] See Dickinson (2016) 12 J Priv Int L 195.

best suited for matters solely connected with its own country, are not always the right and proper rules for the regulation of matters that contain some foreign element. It therefore provides its own special rules for dealing with such cases—rules which specify when its courts shall be competent to try a foreign-element case, and which indicate the particular legal system that shall guide the courts in their exercise of this jurisdiction. These rules are as much part of its own territorial law as those that regulate the conveyance of land in its own country.

But on what principle are the rules constructed? Is there one overriding principle from which they can all be deduced? Must they conform to a single doctrine? Are there certain maxims or axioms by reference to which the correct solution of all the diverse cases that arise in practice can be discovered? Do our difficulties disappear if we are reminded that all laws are personal, or that they are all real, or that every right duly established under the law of a foreign country must in general be sanctioned by an English judge? Clearly, such theoretical analyses are unsupported in English private international law. They are alien to the common law tradition and if offered in argument would be a matter of surprise to an English judge. The instinct of the English lawyer is to test a proposed rule by its practical bearing on normal human activities and expectations. It is by this method that in his opinion the purpose of law, which at bottom is to promote justice and convenience, can best be furthered. He is nothing if not an empiricist and a pragmatist. This is the spirit in which our choice of law rules have been conceived until the stage has been reached at which it is possible to extract a general principle from the existing stream of authority. In so doing, regard will be had to the policy objectives of choice of law rules. This task is undertaken not, as in the USA,[140] to provide individual choice of law solutions for each case that arises, but in order to develop clear rules properly applicable to the generality of cases in a particular field.

There is no sacred principle that pervades all decisions, but when the circumstances indicate that the internal law of a foreign country will provide a solution more just, more convenient and more in accord with the expectations of the parties than the internal law of England, the English judge does not hesitate to give effect to the foreign rules. What particular foreign law shall be chosen depends on different considerations in each legal category. Neither justice nor convenience is promoted by rigid adherence to any one principle; it is preferable that the various principles should fit the needs of the different legal relations, and should harmonise with the social, legal and economic traditions of England. Thus, for instance, the law to govern capacity will vary according to whether the matter under consideration is a commercial contract, a contract of marriage or a disposition of property. Again, the law to govern the essential validity of a contract is, in the absence of choice, determined by a number of rules and the possibility of departing from them in favour of the country with which the contract is manifestly more closely connected. All objective factors are to be considered and weighed in the course of this exercise. Private international law is no more an exact science than is any other part of the law of England; it is not scientifically founded on the reasoning of jurists, but it is beaten out on the anvil of experience.

In the text that follows regard will be had, where appropriate, to the developments in European Union private international law, which, as has been argued, envisages a more administrative role for the judges of European Union Member States.[141]

---

[140] Supra, p 24 et seq.
[141] See Fentiman (2008) 82 Tul LR 2021; Harris (2008) 4 J Priv Int L 347.

Part II

PRELIMINARY TOPICS

3. Classification   41
4. The Incidental Question   51
5. Renvoi   57
6. Substance and Procedure   73
7. The Proof of Foreign Law   105
8. Exclusion of Foreign Law   114
9. Domicile, Nationality and Residence   145

3

CLASSIFICATION[1]

1. Introduction	41	3. Classification of a Rule of Law	45
2. Classification of the Cause of Action	42	(a) The problem described	45
(a) Meaning of classification	42	(b) Basis on which classification is made	46
(b) Difficulties	42		
(c) Basis on which classification is made	43		

1. INTRODUCTION

In a case containing a foreign element, the English court will have to examine various matters in sequence. First, it will have to be determined that the English court has jurisdiction both over the parties and the cause of action. The detailed rules on jurisdiction are discussed later.[2] Suffice it to say at this stage that different jurisdiction rules may apply depending on the cause of action. That cause of action needs therefore to be classified, eg as a contractual or tortious cause of action, to determine which rule of jurisdiction should apply to the case. Then, having satisfied itself that it possesses jurisdiction, the court must next determine the juridical nature of the question that requires decision. Is it, for instance, a question of breach of contract or the commission of a tort? Until this is determined, it is obviously impossible to apply the appropriate rule for the choice of law and thus to ascertain the applicable law. This is the first issue of classification to be discussed in this chapter—classification of the cause of action. The court, having done this, must next select the legal system that governs the matter. This selection will be conditioned by what has aptly been called a connecting factor,[3] ie some outstanding fact which establishes a natural connection between the factual situation before the court and a particular system of law. The connecting factor varies with the circumstances. If, for instance, a British subject dies intestate, domiciled in France, leaving movables in

---

[1] An alternative English word for classification is "characterization". In French it is called *qualification*. The problems that it raises, since their discovery by Kahn in 1891 and Bartin in 1897, have been widely discussed both in England and abroad. The following are the chief contributions in English: Beckett (1934) 15 BYBIL 46; Robertson, *Characterization in the Conflict of Laws* (1940); Falconbridge, pp 51–123; Cook, pp 211 et seq; Lorenzen (1920) 20 Col LR 247; Unger (1937) 19 Bellyard 3; Lederman (1951) 29 Can Bar Rev 3, 168; Inglis (1958) 74 LQR 493, 503 et seq; Lipstein, [1972B] CLJ 67, 77–83; Ehrenzweig, *XXth Century Comparative and Conflicts Law*, pp 395 et seq; Kahn-Freund (1974) III Hague Recueil 147, 367 et seq; Dine [1983] Jur Rev 73; Forsyth (1998) 114 LQR 141; Jackson, *The "Conflicts" Process*, Chapters 5 and 6; Levontin, *Choice of Law and Conflict of Laws*, Chapter 5; Anton, pp 65–75; Wolff, pp 146–67; Morris, paras 20-001–20-010; Briggs, paras 3.48-3.63; Dicey, Morris and Collins, paras 2-001–2-047; J Meeusen, 'Conflict of Laws and the Area of Freedom, Security and Justice after the Treaty of Lisbon', in P Lindskoug *et al* (eds), *Essays in Honour of Michael Bogdan*, pp 307–17.

[2] Infra, p 187 et seq.

[3] Falconbridge (1937) 53 LQR 235, 236, adopted by Robertson, *Characterization in the Conflict of Laws*, p 92.

England and land in Scotland, his movables will be distributed according to the law of France because of his domicile in that country; but Scots law, as being the law of the situs, will determine the succession to the land. This raises the second issue of classification to be examined here—classification of a rule of law. This is the identification of the department of law under which a particular legal rule falls, in order to ascertain whether it falls within the department with regard to which the chosen law is paramount.[4]

2. CLASSIFICATION OF THE CAUSE OF ACTION

(a) Meaning of classification

The "classification of the cause of action" means the allocation of the question raised by the factual situation before the court to its correct legal category. Its object is to reveal the relevant rule for the choice of law.[5] The rules of any given system of law are arranged under different categories, some being concerned with status, others with succession, procedure, contract, tort and so on, and until a judge, faced with a case involving a foreign element, has determined the particular category into which the question before him falls, he can make no progress, for he will not know what choice of law rule to apply. He must discover the true basis of the claim being made.[6] He must decide, for instance, whether the question relates to the administration of assets or to succession, for in the case of movables left by a deceased person, the former is governed by the law of the forum, the latter by the law of the domicile. Whether undertaken consciously or unconsciously, this process of classification must always be performed. It is usually done automatically and without difficulty. If, for instance, the defendant is sued for the negligent damaging in France of the claimant's goods, the factual situation before the court clearly raises a question of tort.

(b) Difficulties

Occasionally, however, the matter is far from simple. In the first place, it may be a case near the line in which it is difficult to determine whether the question falls naturally within this or that judicial category. Secondly, it may be a case where English law and the relevant foreign law hold diametrically opposed views on the correct classification. There may, in other words, be a conflict of classification, as, for instance, where the question whether a will is revoked by marriage may be regarded by the forum as a question of matrimonial law, but by the foreign legal system as a testamentary matter.[7]

These two difficulties are well illustrated by the historic *Maltese Marriage* case,[8] decided by the Court of Appeal at Algiers in 1889, which made the problem of classification a fashionable subject of study.

> A husband and wife, who were domiciled in Malta at the time of their marriage, acquired a French domicile. The husband bought land in France. After his death his widow brought an

---

[4] The fact that this is done slightly differently in each national system of private international law may give rise to problems, see H Heiss and E Kaufmann-Mohi, 'Classification: A Subject Matter for a Rome 0 Regulation?' in S Leible, (ed), *General Principles of European Private International Law*, (2016), pp 87–100.

[5] See *Tezcan v Tezcan* (1992) 87 DLR (4th) 503 at 509–11; and *Sweedman v Transport Accident Commission* [2006] HCA 8, per Gleeson CJ, Gummow, Kirby and Hayne JJ, at [25]–[32], and per Callinan J, at [110]–[116].

[6] *Re Musurus's Estate* [1936] 2 All ER 1666 at 1667; *Do Carmo v Ford Excavations Pty Ltd* (1984) 52 ALR 231, per Wilson J at 239–40; and *Air Link Pty Ltd v Paterson* (2005) 218 ALR 700, per Callinan J at 230.

[7] Cf *Re Martin, Loustalan v Loustalan* [1900] P 211.

[8] *Anton v Bartolo* (1891) *Clunet* 1171. For a fuller and more detailed account see Robertson, *Characterization in the Conflict of Laws*, pp 158–62; Beckett (n 1), 50; Wolff, p 149.

action in France claiming a usufruct in one quarter of this land. There was uniformity in the rules for the choice of law of both countries: succession to land was governed by the law of the situs, but matrimonial rights were dependent on the law of the domicile at the time of the marriage.

The first essential, therefore, was to decide whether the facts raised a question of succession to land or of matrimonial rights. At this point, however, a conflict of classification emerged. In the French view the facts raised a question of succession; in the Maltese view a question of matrimonial rights. When a conflict of this nature arises it is apparent that, *if a court applies its own rule of classification*, the ultimate decision on the merits will vary with the country in which the action is brought. On this hypothesis, the widow would have failed in France but have succeeded in Malta.[9]

The crucial question, therefore, is: on what principles do English judges classify the cause of action? Or, to put it in another way, according to what system of law must the classification be made? Must it be made according to the internal law of England, on the ground that the internal rules and the rules of private international law in any country are based on the same legal conceptions?[10] It is arguable, for instance, that when English private international law submits intestate succession to movables to the law of the deceased's domicile, the expression "intestate succession" must be given the meaning that it bears in English internal law and not a more extensive meaning than may be attributed to it in the foreign domicile. In opposition to this view, which had wide support, it has been suggested that classification must be based on the "essential general principles of professedly universal application" of analytical jurisprudence and comparative law.[11] But, although it may be desirable to solve the problem in this scientific manner, it is scarcely practicable to do so whilst there are no commonly agreed general jurisprudential principles.

(c) Basis on which classification is made

There can be little doubt that, in practice, classification of the cause of action is effected on the basis of the law of the forum. Thus, by application of the principles of English law, an English judge makes an analysis of the question before him and, after determining its juridical nature in accordance with those principles, assigns it to a particular legal category.[12] Or, as Auld LJ put it in *Macmillan v Bishopsgate*[13]: "the proper approach is to look beyond the formulation of the claim and to identify according to the lex fori the true issue or issues thrown up by the claim and defence".

Although English law principles are being applied here, the case is in fact one which contains a foreign element, and so the classification which is made will not necessarily be the same as that which would be made in a purely domestic case.[14] In this context, its object is to serve

---

[9] In fact the French court applied the matrimonial law of Malta.

[10] Cf Jackson, *The "Conflicts" Process*, pp 72–82.

[11] Beckett (n 1), 59.

[12] Statutory provision to this effect is made, in relation to tort claims, by the Private International Law (Miscellaneous Provisions) Act 1995, s 9(2), in respect of the interpretation of which, see *Trafigura Beheer BV v Kookmin Bank Co (Preliminary Issue)* [2006] EWHC 1450: "the words 'for the purposes of private international law' in s 9(2) indicate that Parliament intended that the court should examine relevant issues to decide whether they would be characterised as 'relating to tort' not only by reference to English legal concepts and classifications, but by taking a broad 'internationalist' view of legal concepts. It followed that the word 'tort' in s 9 was to be construed broadly, so as to embrace non-contractual civil wrongs that gave rise to a remedy." (Aikens J, at [68]). See further, infra, pp 776–8 and 778–91.

[13] *Macmillan Inc v Bishopsgate Trust (No 3)* [1996] 1 WLR 387, at 407; and see *Arcadia Petroleum Ltd v Bosworth* [2016] EWCA Civ 818.

[14] See *Macmillan Inc v Bishopsgate Trust (No 3)* [1996] 1 WLR 387; and see Forsyth (1998) 114 LQR 141; infra, pp 837–8—Characterisation as restitution and pp 1298–9—Shares. Also *Raiffeisen Zentralbank Österreich AG v Five Star General Trading LLC and Ors* [2001] QB 825, per Mance LJ at [26], and *Atlantic Telecom GmbH, Noter* 2004 SLT 1031, per Lord Brodie at p [1044].

the purposes of private international law and, since one of the functions of this department of law is to formulate rules applicable to a case that impinges on foreign laws, it is obviously incumbent on the judge to take into account the accepted rules and institutions of foreign legal systems. It follows, therefore, that the judge must not rigidly confine himself to the concepts or categories of English internal law for, if he were to adopt this parochial attitude, he might be compelled to disregard some foreign concept merely because it was unknown to his own law. The concepts of private international law, such as "contract", "tort", "corporation", "bill of exchange",[15] must be given a wide meaning in order to embrace "analogous legal relations of foreign type".[16] In the words of one author:

> The various legal categories, into one of which the judge must decide that the question falls before he can select his conflicts rule, must be wider than the categories of the internal law, because otherwise the judge in a conflicts question will be unable to make provision for any rule or institution of foreign law which does not find its counterpart in his own internal law, and thus one of the reasons for the existence of the science of conflict of laws will be defeated.[17]

Two examples will show that English judges have been prepared to solve the problem of classification in this broad spirit. In *De Nicols v Curlier*[18] the facts were as follows:

> A couple, French by nationality and by domicile, were married in Paris without making an express contract as to their proprietary rights. Their property, both present and future, thus became subject by French law to the system of community of property. The husband died domiciled in England, leaving a will which disregarded his widow's rights under French law. The widow took proceedings in England to recover her community share.

The rule of English private international law is that the proprietary rights of a spouse to movables are governed primarily by any contract, express or implied, that the parties may have made before marriage. Failing a contract, the rights are determined by the law of the matrimonial domicile of the parties. Thus the problem of classification was whether the right claimed by the widow was to be treated as contractual or testamentary, for only after that had been decided would it be possible to choose between the French law governing the contract and the English law governing testamentary questions. It was clear that in the eyes of English internal law no contract had been made, but the House of Lords held that according to French law a husband and wife are bound by an implied contract to adopt the system of community, despite the absence of an express agreement to that effect. Thus the court, by its readiness to recognise a foreign concept, widened the category of contracts as understood by English internal law.

A second illustration of the international spirit in which English judges fulfil the task of classification is that, when required to determine whether or not the property in dispute is to be regarded as land and thus subject to the law of the situs, they abandon the distinction between realty and personalty in favour of the more universal distinction between movables and immovables.[19] Thus land in England, subject to a trust for sale but not yet sold, is regarded under the domestic doctrine of conversion as already possessing the character of personalty. If, therefore, the owner dies intestate domiciled abroad, it is arguable that he has died entitled not to land, but to pure personalty, and that the relevant intestacy rules are those

---

[15] *G & H Montage GmbH v Irvani* [1990] 1 WLR 667 at 678.
[16] Nussbaum (1940) 40 Col LR 1461, 1470.
[17] Robertson, op cit, p 33.
[18] [1900] AC 21.
[19] Discussed, infra, Chapter 29. See also Carruthers (2005), Chapter 1.

of the law of his domicile, not of the law of the situs. Despite this, it is held that his right must be classified as a right to an immovable to be governed by the law of the situs.[20]

There is, however, one type of case in which the English judge will probably not make the classification on the basis of English law as the law of the forum. This is where the only possible applicable law is either the law of country X or the law of country Y and both these laws classify the question in the same manner, though in a manner different from that usual in English law.[21]

3. CLASSIFICATION OF A RULE OF LAW

(a) The problem described

Once the main legal category has been determined the next step is to apply the correct choice of law rule in order that the governing law may be ascertained. As we have seen, the correct rule will depend on some connecting factor, such as domicile or the situation of immovables, which links the question to a definite legal system. X, for instance, dies intestate domiciled in France, leaving movables in England. Since he has been connected by domicile with France, the operative rule for the choice of law is, therefore, that the question of intestate succession must be governed by French law. However, at this stage the second process of classification has to be gone through. It may be necessary to identify the legal category into which some particular rule falls, in order to discover whether it falls within a category with regard to which the law selected by our choice of law rules is paramount. That law has a certain sphere of control, ie it governs some, but not all, aspects of the juridical question as classified by the English court in the sense already indicated. Thus, for instance, in an action brought in England for breach of a contract made and performable in France, French law governs matters of formal and essential validity, but all questions of procedure are subject to English law. A French procedural rule is outside the sphere of control of the chosen French law relating to matters of substance. If, therefore, a particular French rule is pleaded and if it is doubtful whether it relates to procedure or to substance, its true nature must obviously be determined. It must be ignored if it is procedural in character, otherwise it must be applied. Likewise, an English domestic rule is excluded if it relates to form or substance, but is applicable if it is procedural in nature.[22]

It should be kept in mind that in this context the term used for a legal category is merely a useful way of referring to a bundle of issues that are regarded as appropriate for determination by a certain law. The boundaries are therefore flexible and the court should consider the rational of the English conflict rule, as well as the purpose of the substantive rule that is to be classified when deciding whether or not the conflict rule covers the substantive rule at issue. In case there is no appropriate conflicts rule that can cover the substantive rule a new conflict rule should be created.[23]

---

[20] *Re Berchtold* [1923] 1 Ch 192.

[21] Robertson, op cit, pp 76–8; Lorenzen (1920) 20 Col LR 247, 281; Beckett (n 1), 62.

[22] See *Cox v Ergo Versicherung AG (formerly Victoria)* [2014] UKSC 22 where a German rule on damages was held to be substantive rather than procedural as it dealt with the scope of liability. Had it been procedural the court would not have applied it. See also infra Chapter 6 for the impact of the distinction between substance and procedure, which is clearly in origin a classification issue.

[23] *Raiffeisen Zentralbank Österreich AG v Five Star General Trading LLC and Ors* [2001] QB 825 (CA); see also *Integral Petroleum SA v SCU-Finanz SA* [2015] EWCA Civ 144, and *Secure Capital SA v Credit Suisse AG* [2015] EWHC 388 (Comm).

This kind of classification is also found in EU law and it is important to note that the CJEU often resorts to the principle of autonomous interpretation to determine the exact meaning and scope of a term used in EU legislation.[24] The same term may therefore get another scope for the purposes of classification.[25] The EU private international law Regulations[26] are good examples. Sometimes they include their own definitions of certain concepts and on other occasions it is left to the CJEU to provide autonomous interpretations of them and of their scope.[27] International conventions also often include their own definitions of certain concepts, which can influence or even determine the classification issue.

(b) Basis on which classification is made

The critical and controversial question is the basis on which the classification should be made, and illustrations from the authorities will now be given to show how English judges have dealt with the matter. It is, however, essential to appreciate that a rule either of the foreign chosen law or of English law itself may require to be classified and that the line of reasoning is not necessarily the same in each of these situations.

(i) Classification of an English rule

Leroux v Brown[28] illustrates the process applied to an English rule:

> By an oral agreement, made in France, the defendant, resident in England, undertook to employ the plaintiff in France for a period longer than a year. The substantive validity of the contract was governed by French law, by which the contract was valid as to substance. The defendant pleaded, however, that the plaintiff's claim to recover damages was unenforceable in England, since the Statute of Frauds provided that "no action shall lie upon a contract not to be performed within the space of one year from the making thereof" unless the agreement or some note thereof was in writing signed by the defendant.

This plea required the court to decide whether the statutory rule was of a procedural character.[29] If so it was fatal to the plaintiff, for being a rule of English procedure it was necessarily binding in an English action. Unfortunately, the members of the court took the line of least resistance and, ignoring the larger issues involved, confined their attention to the literal wording of the statute. The reasoning of Maule J, for instance, lacked nothing in simplicity: the statute provides that no action shall be brought on an agreement not to be

---

[24] See, eg, Case C-172/91 *Volker Sonntag v Hand Waidmann and others* [1993] ECR I-1963 where the CJEU gave an interpretation to the concept of civil and commercial matters that departed from the one in use in the Member State concerned and applied that for classification purposes in a Brussels I context.

[25] EU law also has an impact on the use of certain connecting factors and in particular on the use of nationality as a connecting factor, see M Bogdan, 'The EC Treaty and the Use of Nationality and Habitual Residence as Connecting Factors in International Family Law', in J Meeusen *et al* (eds), *International Family Law for the European Union*, (2007) pp 303–7, and J Meeusen, 'Conflict of Laws and the Area of Freedom, Security and Justice after the Treaty of Lisbon', in P Lindskoug *et al* (eds), *Essays in Honour of Michael Bogdan*, pp 307–17.

[26] Their different nature and approach are also highlighted by R Hausmann, 'General Issues in European Private International Law—Le questioni generali nel diritto internazionale private europeo', 51 (2015) Rivista di diritto internazionale private e processuale 3, pp 499–522: '[. . .] the primary objective of the European legislation in the field of private international law is not to identify the closest factual connecting element of a case to the law of a certain country but, rather, to accelerate and improve the legal protection of European citizens and to reduce the costs in cross-border disputes by allowing parties and courts to opt for the lex fori and thus to avoid, to a large extent, the application of foreign law'.

[27] See, eg, Case C-375/13 *Harald Kolassa v Barclays Bank plc* ECLI:EU:C:2015:37, where prospectus liability was classified as tortious in nature and Case C-548/12 *Marc Brogsitter v Fabrication de Montres Normandes EURL and Karsten Fräßdorf* ECLI:EU:C:2014:148, where the EU used a contractual classification, despite a tort classification being applicable under national law.

[28] (1852) 12 CB 801; and see *Mahadervan v Mahadervan* [1964] p 233.

[29] For the present law, see infra, Chapter 6.

performed within a year, unless it is evidenced by a written memorandum; the present agreement is of this nature and there is no memorandum; "the case, therefore, plainly falls within the distinct words of the statute".[30]

The defect of this reasoning lay in basing classification on English internal law instead of on private international law. The court failed to appreciate that the classification of the statutory rule was required for an international case, not for a purely domestic one. The issues are different. The fact that a rule has been classified, or that it ought properly to be classified, in a particular way for a domestic transaction containing no foreign element, does not preclude an entirely different approach when a question of private international law is involved. In this latter type of case, a condition precedent to the classification of an English rule is to ascertain the policy that the rule is designed to serve. Was it, for instance, the policy of the Statute of Frauds that no oral contract of guarantee should be actionable in England, irrespective of the law by which it was governed or of the country in which it was performable? Unless this was clearly the policy of the Act, it was an unfortunate application of mechanical jurisprudence to read the words—*no action shall be brought*—in a rigid and literal sense and thus to deprive the plaintiff in that case of a right recognised as valid and enforceable by the law with which it was alone connected. To do this is to strike at the roots of private international law and to defeat one of its fundamental objects. At the present day, when the principles of this part of the law are more mature and its purpose better understood, it is believed that a court, if required to classify a rule of English law, would have regard to the foreign features of the case and would solve the problem more appropriately than the Court of Common Pleas did in *Leroux v Brown*.[31]

(ii) Classification of a foreign rule
(a) Parental consent to marry
The law reports contain several examples of the classification of a foreign rule. The best introduction to this issue, however, is provided by the controversial Court of Appeal decision in *Ogden v Ogden*:[32]

> This concerned a domiciled Frenchman, aged nineteen, who married a domiciled Englishwoman, in England, without first obtaining the consent of his parent, as required by Article 148 of the French Code. The husband obtained an annulment of this marriage in a French court on the ground of want of consent. The wife subsequently went through a ceremony of marriage in England with a domiciled Englishman, who, in the present action, petitioned for a decree of nullity on the ground that at the time of the ceremony the respondent was still married to the Frenchman.

The factual situation, therefore, raised the question of the validity of the French marriage. There were two connecting factors: the husband was domiciled in France; the marriage was solemnised in England. Guided by these factors, English private international law indicated two rules: "firstly, the essential validity of the marriage, including the capacity of the husband, must be governed by French law; secondly, the formal validity of the marriage ceremony must be tested by English law".

---

[30] (1852) 12 CB 801.
[31] Cf *Bernkrant v Fowler* 55 Cal 2d 558, 360 P 2d 906 (1961). Among other examples of the classification of an English rule, see *Anderson v Equitable Assurance Society of the United States* (1926) 134 LT 557, at 566; *Re Cohn* [1945] Ch 5 (the Law of Property Act 1925, s 184, dealing with *commorientes* classified as part of the substantive, not procedural, law, infra, pp 50 and 1345); *Re Priest* [1944] Ch 58 (rule that a gift to an attesting witness to a will renders the gift void goes to essential validity, not to form); *Re Maldonado's Estate* [1954] P 223, infra, pp 49–50, *Re Fuld's Estate (No 3)* [1968] P 675 at 697, 698 (rule as to knowledge and approval in the proof of wills is evidential and thus procedural).
[32] [1908] P 46.

Only the essential validity of the marriage was controlled by French law. It followed, therefore, that if the purpose of Article 148 was to incapacitate the husband from matrimony unless he complied with its provisions, it affected the essential validity of any marriage that he might contract and should be granted extra-territorial recognition.

So far all is straightforward. Moreover, there is no difficulty if both English and French law agree on the juridical nature of the consent rule and therefore on its sphere of application. Complications arise, however, when the true nature of the rule is doubtful. The difficulty then is to discover the reasoning by which a solution must be reached. Is, for instance, the French classification to be followed blindly? Again, is the English view of an analogous rule in the internal law of England, presuming that one exists, to be adopted? Neither alternative is satisfactory. The rational method is for the English judge to examine the rule in its foreign setting, in order to ascertain its intended scope, the policy by which it has been dictated and the part that it is designed to play by the French legislature.

Only by this process can full and proper effect be given to the English choice of law rule. French law, having been chosen to govern essential validity, must be allowed within reason to determine which of its domestic rules are essential rather than formal. To take the opposite course and to uphold a marriage, which is essentially void under the personal law of the parties, by attributing a merely ceremonial character to a rule regarded as essential by that law would not only be the negation of so-called comity, but would incongruously debilitate the English choice of law rule. The only reservation is that a foreign classification must be repudiated, if to adopt it would contravene the English doctrine of public policy or be repugnant to some fundamental principle of English law.

In *Simonin v Mallac*,[33] decided forty-eight years before *Ogden v Ogden*, the court was confronted with a different French provision that was obviously not intended to affect capacity in the strict sense of the word.

> Two domiciled French persons came to England and went through a ceremony of marriage in the English form, returning to Paris two or three days later. The wife subsequently petitioned the English court for a decree of nullity on the ground of want of parental consent. By French law, the parties were capable of inter-marriage, but they were required to ask advice of their parents, a request which had to be repeated each month for three months if the parents were adverse to the marriage. At the end of the fourth month, the marriage might take place despite parental disapproval.

It was clear that absence of the consent required by this rule did not render the parties incapable of inter-marriage. The obtaining of consent was in essence an additional formality and, since the form of the ceremony is a matter solely for the law of the place of celebration, the marriage was rightly adjudged to be valid.[34]

In *Ogden v Ogden*, however, the relevant French rule was to this effect: "the son who had not reached the age of twenty-five could not contract marriage without the consent of his father and mother".

Although it seems almost unarguable that the object of this provision was to impose a total incapacity on the parties unless they obtained parental consent, the Court of Appeal held the marriage to be valid, since the ceremony had been performed in accordance with the requirements of English law, the law of the place of celebration. The latter marriage between the respondent and the Englishman was therefore bigamous. It is submitted that this case was

---

[33] (1860) 2 Sw & Tr 67.
[34] Infra, Chapter 21.

not on the same footing as *Simonin v Mallac*, and that it is opposed to established principles. For the English court to classify the rule as formal was in effect to infringe the principle that the essential validity of a marriage falls to be determined by the law of the domicile.[35] The most unfortunate feature of *Ogden v Ogden* is its suggestion that every rule requiring parental consent to a marriage must be classified as formal.[36]

(b) *Bona vacantia*

Re Maldonado's Estate[37] provides an outstanding example of a foreign rule being construed in its context, with a view to deciding whether it fell within the sphere of control of the foreign governing law. The facts were these: a person died intestate domiciled in Spain leaving assets to the extent of some £26,000 in England. By Spanish law those assets passed to the Spanish state, since the deceased left no relatives entitled to take them by way of succession.

The English choice of law rule applicable to this factual situation is that intestate succession to movables must be determined according to Spanish law as being the law of the domicile. Therefore, the sphere of control of Spanish law in the instant case was confined to matters of succession, and the problem was whether the Spanish rule under which the assets passed to the state was to be classified as a rule of succession.

At this point it is pertinent to notice that, though the movables of a deceased owner who dies intestate without leaving recognised successors pass to the state in the great majority of countries, yet the capacity in which the state takes is not uniform throughout the world. In some countries, such as Italy and Germany, it has been regarded as an heir taking by way of succession; in others, such as Turkey, Austria and formerly England, the State has been held to act in its capacity as the paramount sovereign authority and confiscates the movables as being *bona vacantia*, ownerless goods.[38] If, for example, the deceased died domiciled in Turkey, the Turkish law, since it governs only questions of succession and since it does not regard the State as a successor, has been considered to have no say in the matter and movables found in England passed to the Crown.[39]

The provision of the Spanish code applicable to the facts of the *Maldonado* case was that "The State shall inherit" movables. Moreover, the expert evidence accepted by the court showed that in the Spanish view this was a true case of taking by way of succession, not a case of seizing ownerless goods. Thus the rule under which movables, failing relatives, pass to the state is classified as a rule of succession in Spain but as a confiscatory rule in England, and the short question was whether in an English action this foreign conception of the relationship between the State and the deceased was to prevail with regard to movables found in England. Could the law of the domicile dictate to the English court what meaning should be attributed to heirship?

---

[35] The Court of Appeal in *Ogden v Ogden* refused to recognise the French annulment of the marriage, with the result that the parties possessed the status of married persons in England, but of unmarried persons in France. Infra, Chapter 22.

[36] In *Lodge v Lodge* (1963) 107 Sol Jo 437, Hewson J, after hearing expert evidence, held that a contravention of Art 148 of the French Code rendered the marriage voidable, and he followed *Ogden v Ogden*. The Law Commission has left any reform to judicial development: Law Com No 165 (1987). In contrast, see, for Scots law, Family Law (Scotland) Act 2006, s 38(5) (in respect of which, see Crawford and Carruthers, para 11-32).

[37] [1954] P 223; Lipstein [1954] CLJ 22.

[38] See Wolff, p 157. Under s 46(1)(vi) of the Administration of Estates Act 1925 it is arguable that the Crown takes by succession and not by virtue of a prerogative right to ownerless property: *Re Mitchell, Hatton v Jones* [1954] Ch 525; cf *Re Hanley's Estate* [1942] P 33; but see Ing, *Bona Vacantia*, pp 57–62. See also *Hanchett-Stamford v Attorney General and Anor (Barclays Bank Trust Co Ltd Intervening)* [2008] EWHC 330 (CH).

[39] *Re Musurus's Estate* [1936] 2 All ER 1666 (Turkey); *Re Barnett's Trust* [1902] 1 Ch 847 (Austria).

It was argued for the Crown that the English rules of private international law are dominant so far as property in England is concerned, and that no one can be described as a "successor" in the eyes of English law unless he has a personal nexus with the deceased, a connection which certainly cannot be claimed by a sovereign state to which the property passes. This argument, however, did not prevail. It was held, both by Barnard J and by the Court of Appeal, that the Spanish law of the domicile, which admittedly governed all questions of intestate succession, must be allowed to determine the sense and scope of the term "succession". Further, the alleged requirement of a personal nexus between the deceased and the heir was dismissed as a fallacy, for in the words of Jenkins LJ: "The heir or successor is surely the person, whether related to the deceased or not, who under the relevant law is entitled to inherit or to succeed."[40]

Finally, there was nothing contrary to public policy or repugnant to English law in allowing a sovereign state to take property in the capacity of an heir.

(c) Other examples

In an earlier case, of *commorientes*, the question was whether the relevant rule of the German law of the domicile was to be applied as affecting substance or to be rejected as being procedural in nature. Uthwatt J followed the same process of construing the rule in its foreign setting and, therefore, accepted the German classification.[41] In the later case of *Adams v National Bank of Greece and Athens*[42] Diplock J found it necessary to decide whether a certain Greek decree related to status or to the discharge of contractual liabilities, and he was insistent that for this purpose he was bound "to look at the substance of the law, not merely at its form".[43] There is no need at this stage to discuss other cases in which English courts have classified foreign rules, since examples will appear from time to time in the course of the following pages.[44]

---

[40] [1954] P 223 at 249.

[41] *Re Cohn* [1945] Ch 5.

[42] [1958] 2 QB 59.

[43] [1958] 2 QB 59 at 75.

[44] *General Steam Navigation Co v Guillou* (1843) 11 M & W 877, infra, pp 87–8 (whether a French rule affected procedure or the substantive law of tort); *Re Doetsch* [1896] 2 Ch 836 and other similar cases, infra, p 87 (whether a rule regulating the order in which parties must be sued affected procedure or substance); *Huntington v Attrill* [1893] AC 150, infra, p 121 (whether a New York statutory rule was penal or remedial); *Re Martin, Loustalan v Loustalan* [1900] P 211, infra, pp 1350–1 (whether revocation of a will by marriage was a testamentary or matrimonial question); *Re Wilks* [1935] Ch 645 (whether the time at which shares forming part of an estate must be sold was a question of succession or administration); *Re Korvine's Trusts, Levashoff v Block* [1921] 1 Ch 343 (whether a gift in the event of death is to be classed as a bequest or a gift *inter vivos*); *Metal Industries (Salvage) Ltd v S T Harle (Owners)* 1962 SLT 114; and *Raiffeisen Zentralbank Österreich AG v Five Star General Trading LLC and Ors* [2001] QB 825 (whether an assignee's claim under the assignment of a marine insurance policy, made with French insurers, but governed by English law, was to be treated as contractual or proprietary).

4

THE INCIDENTAL QUESTION

1. What is an Incidental Question?	51	4. A Way Forward	54
2. The Elements of an Incidental Question	52	5. Dépeçage	55
3. The Problem Illustrated	52		

1. WHAT IS AN INCIDENTAL QUESTION?

A case involving private international law may place a subsidiary issue, as well as a main question, before the court. Once the relevant choice of law rule has been applied and the law to govern the main issue thereby determined, a further choice of law rule may be required to answer the subsidiary question affecting the main issue.[1]

This problem may be illustrated as follows:

> Suppose that W claims rights of intestate succession to H's immovables in Italy. According to English rules of private international law, this falls to be determined by Italian law as the law of the situs.[2] Assume further that, under English conflict rules, W is recognised as H's widow, but not under Italian rules, because, for instance, Italian law does not recognise H's divorce from his first wife. The main problem, whether W can succeed to H's estate, is clearly determinable by Italian law, but must the subsidiary problem of the validity of the marriage also be referred to that law?

A question of this nature has been aptly termed the "incidental question" by Wolff,[3] though the less satisfactory expression "the preliminary question" is also used.[4]

---

[1] This chapter looks at the incidental questions from a choice of law angle, which is how the issue is looked at mainly. But a similar issue may also arise in a jurisdiction case, eg when in a Brussels I context case that is mainly concerned with the capacity of a natural person the 'incidental' question of the exclusive jurisdiction of the court of the place of the immovable property that is to be disposed of arises. The application of article 22(1) Brussels I Regulation needed to be rejected before the jurisdiction of the court for the main issue could be established. Case C-386/12 *Siegfried János Schneider* ECLI:EU:C:2013:633. A similar scenario arises when validity is raised in a patent infringement case, see Case C-4/03 *Gesellschaft für Antriebstechnik mbH & Co KG v Lamellen und Kupplungsbau Beteiligungs KG* ECLI:EU:C:2006:457.

[2] Infra, pp 1351–2.

[3] Op cit, p 206. The problem has been described by Ehrenzweig, p 340, as "another miscreant of a conceptualism gone rampant".

[4] For discussion of this problem, see Robertson, Chapter 6; Dicey, Morris and Collins, Chapter 2; Levontin, *Choice of Law and Conflict of Laws*, Chapter 4; Gotlieb (1955) 33 Can Bar Rev 523; de Nova (1966) II Hague Recueil 443, 557–69; Kahn-Freund (1974) III Hague Recueil 147, 437–40; Gotlieb (1977) 26 ICLQ 734; Juenger (1985) IV Hague Recueil, 123, 195–7; Wengler, Vol III *International Encyclopedia of Comparative Law*, Chapter 7; Schmidt (1992) II Hague Recueil 305; Cansacchi, 'The Choice and Adaptation of Foreign Law in the Conflict of Laws', 83 (1953) II Hague Recueil 79–161; see G Mäsch, 'Preliminary Question', in S Leible, *General Principles of European Private International Law*, (2016), Chapter 6; Dannemann, 'Adaptation', in ibid Chapter 15; Bogdan, 'Private International Law as a Component of the Law of the Forum, General Course in Private International Law' (2010) 348 Recueil des Cours, 221; Melchior, *Die Grundlagen des deutschen internationalen Privatrechts* (1971), Wengler, Zeitschrift

2. THE ELEMENTS OF AN INCIDENTAL QUESTION

An incidental question properly so-called presumes the existence of three facts.[5] The main issue should, under the English rules of private international law,[6] be governed by a foreign law. There should be a subsidiary question involving a foreign element which could have arisen separately and which has its own independent choice of law rule. This choice of law rule should lead to a conclusion different from that which would have been reached had the law governing the main question been applied. Without these prerequisites there is no "incidental question",[7] and in most of the cases where a true problem has arisen the court has not appreciated that a determination of the law to govern the incidental question is required. This is an issue on which the support of jurists may be found for a variety of solutions. Some support the law governing the main issue,[8] others the choice of law rules of the forum,[9] and others consider that the determination of the problem will depend on the nature of the individual case and the policy of the forum thereto.[10]

3. THE PROBLEM ILLUSTRATED

The way in which an incidental question arises may be illustrated by two decisions, one English, the other Canadian, on the inter-relation of the choice of law rules for divorce recognition and for capacity to marry.[11] The English case is *Lawrence v Lawrence*:[12]

> The first husband and his wife married in Brazil and lived there until 1970. In that year the wife obtained a divorce in Nevada, USA, which was not recognised in Brazil; but the next day she married the second husband in Nevada. Later, the second husband petitioned for a declaration as to the validity of this second marriage. An incidental question arose from the fact that, under Brazilian law, being that of the wife's domicile to which English choice of law rules referred capacity to marry, she lacked capacity to marry the second husband. On the other hand, the Nevada divorce was recognised in England under our divorce recognition rules.[13]

The Court of Appeal, by a variety of reasoning, upheld the validity of the second marriage.[14] The effect of this was to give primacy to the divorce recognition issue at the expense of that of capacity to marry.[15]

---

für ausländisches und internationales Privatrecht (1934), p 148 [2008] OJ L 177/6. See G. van Calster, European Private International Law, Hart (2nd edn), 2016; see also P Beaumont and P McEleavy, *Anton's Private International Law*, (3rd edn, 2011), 4.71–9 and Crawford and Carruthers, 4.07.

[5] See Dicey, Morris and Collins, para 2-049 and M Bogdan, 'Private International Law as a Component of the Law of the Forum, General Course in Private International Law' (2010) 348 Recueil des Cours, pp 221 et seq.

[6] Including any EU Regulations on private international law.

[7] See the discussion of *Shaw v Gould* (1868) LR 3 HL 55, infra, pp 1143–6, by Webb and Davis, *Casebook on the Conflict of Laws in New Zealand*, pp 86–7; cf Gotlieb (1955) 33 Can Bar Rev 523, 535–7. In the context of legitimacy, contrast *Motala v A-G* [1990] 2 FLR 261, [1990] Fam Law 340, infra, pp 1198–9.

[8] Wolff, p 206; Robertson, p 141; Lipstein [1972B] CLJ 67, 90–6.

[9] Breslauer, pp 18–21; Nussbaum, pp 104–9; Falconbridge (1939) 17 Can Bar Rev 369, 377–8.

[10] Dicey, Morris and Collin para 2-049; Crawford and Carruthers para 4-07; and see Gotlieb (1955) 33 Can Bar Rev 523, 555.

[11] Infra, pp 925–6.

[12] [1985] Fam 106. Infra, p 926.

[13] Recognition of Divorces and Legal Separations Act 1971; see now Family Law Act 1986, Part II, infra, p 1005 et seq.

[14] For a converse approach, see *R v Brentwood Superintendent Registrar of Marriages, ex p Arias* [1968] 2 QB 956.

[15] This result would now be reached by statute under the Family Law Act 1986, s 50.

The Canadian decision in *Schwebel v Ungar*[16] provides a converse example of the incidental question, where the capacity rule prevailed over that of divorce recognition. The facts were these:

> A Jewish husband and wife, domiciled in Hungary, decided to settle in Israel. When they were in Italy, en route to Israel, the husband divorced his wife by "gett". Under Hungarian law, the law of their domicile, and under Italian law this divorce was invalid, but it was effective according to Israeli law. They then acquired an Israeli domicile and whilst so domiciled the wife later visited Ontario and married a second husband who ultimately petitioned the Ontario court for a decree of nullity on the ground of his "wife's" bigamy.

The Canadian court had not only to consider the question of the wife's capacity to marry, governed under Ontario choice of law rules by Israeli law, but also the question of the validity of the wife's divorce by gett. Under the Ontario rules of private international law the divorce would not be recognised, but it would under the Israeli rules. The Supreme Court of Canada upheld the validity of the second marriage. It was valid by the law of Israel, the law governing capacity to marry, and this prevailed over the Ontario rule denying recognition to the divorce.[17] Here, capacity was regarded as the main question, to which divorce recognition was incidental.

The majority of the decisions in which an incidental question has arisen have applied the law applicable to the main issue, though often without an apparent realisation that an incidental question was involved.[18] So unthinking and mechanical an approach cannot be justified and the determination of this issue must vary according to the class of case under review. If it is one, such as succession to movables, in which the doctrine of total renvoi[19] requires the whole law of the foreign country to be followed, then both the main and incidental questions should, probably, be referred to that law.[20] Where, on the other hand, it is one in which the court is referred to the internal law of the foreign country, as perhaps in the case of a question of torts,[21] then there should be a greater likelihood of the court's separating the incidental from the main question and applying the appropriate English choice of law rule to each. However, as *Schwebel v Ungar*[22] illustrates, even in this type of case the court may still apply the law governing the main question on the grounds that "to hold otherwise would be to determine the personal status of a person not domiciled in Ontario by the law of Ontario instead of by the law of that person's country of domicile".[23] However, if one turns the issue round and asks why, in a question of status, should the law of the forum subordinate its own choice of law rules to those of some other jurisdiction, then any real justification for the decision in that case is harder to find.[24]

---

[16] (1963) 42 DLR (2d) 622; affd 48 DLR (2d) 644; Lysyk (1965) 43 Can Bar Rev 363; Webb (1965) 14 ICLQ 659.

[17] This approach is approved in *Padolecchia v Padolecchia* [1968] P 314 at 338–40, though on the facts as found no true incidental question arose.

[18] Eg *Re Johnston* [1903] 1 Ch 821; *Baindail v Baindail* [1946] P 122 at 127; *Haque v Haque* (1962) 108 CLR 230; *Schwebel v Ungar*, supra; *R v Brentwood Superintendent Registrar of Marriages, ex p Arias*, supra; and see *Breen v Breen* [1964] P 144; Gotlieb (1977) 26 ICLQ 734 at 771 et seq.

[19] See infra p 60 et seq. (Ch5).

[20] See, eg, *Re Johnson*, supra; *Baindail v Baindail*, supra; *Haque v Haque*, supra; Gotlieb (1955) Can Bar Rev 523, 545, 547; and see the interesting problem posed by Webb and Davis, *Casebook on the Conflict of Laws in New Zealand* p 88.

[21] Cf *Re Degaramo's Estate* 33 NYS 502 (1895); and see *Meisenhelder v Chicago and North Western Rly Co* 170 Minn 317 (1927); Webb and Davis, op cit, pp 84–5; cf de Nova (1966) II Hague Recueil 443, 566–7.

[22] Supra, and see *Padolecchia v Padoleccha*, supra.

[23] (1963) 42 DLR (2d) 622 at 633.

[24] Lysyk (1965) 43 Can Bar Rev 363 at 379; though cf *Breen v Breen* [1964] P 144.

4. A WAY FORWARD

The courts have dealt with the issue of preliminary questions in a haphazard way and legal scholars have not (yet) come up with a single approach, but it is clear that a correct application of classification and choice of law rules can lead to very different outcomes in cases where a preliminary question arises, depending on how the preliminary question is approached.[25] It is therefore suggested that the following could provide a coherent and predictable approach. On cannot simply take the law applicable to the main question and decide both questions under that substantive law. That would undo the principles of classification and choice of law through the operation of a connecting facto. The classification and choice of law stage needs therefore to be gone through also and separately for the incidental question, but as it is the main question that is essentially before the court it is proposed to do so on the basis of the conflict rules of the law applicable to the main question.[26] This should re-enforce the consistency of the solution and it is also in line with the approach most often taken by English courts. Further support is found in EU instruments, eg in Article 10(1) Rome I Regulation[27] where existence and validity are submitted to the substantive law, rather than to the law of the forum. It is also arguable that the scope of the applicable law in EU Regulations dealing with choice of law can provide answers as to whether the incidental question is covered by the law applicable to the principal issue or not. This might eventually hint at a departure from the rule that the law applicable to the main question is to be applied to the incidental question of the latter falls clearly outside the scope of the applicable law.

This approach avoids relying on the nature of the individual case and provides predictability. There may however be a need for a correction mechanism in specific cases. But here the one criterion that could (also in the existing cases) lead to a different applicable law is when the circumstances of the case demonstrate on the one hand a weak link with the law applicable to the preliminary question and on the other hand a close link with the law of another country. The law of that other country will also be clearly visible, so the risk for predictability and legal certainty is minimal.[28] The law of that other more closely connected country will then be applied to the preliminary question. In determining whether there is such a close connection in a specific case the court will also be able to give a role to the substantial legal considerations involved in the case and to the value judgments they give rise to.[29] Public policy can then play its proper rule as the ultimate safeguard, mainly for the interests of the forum.

---

[25] The importance of the incidental question in practice is well demonstrated in relation to same sex relationships and Muslim marriages in M Jänterä-Jareborg, 'The Incidental Question of Private International Law, Formalised Same-Sex Relationships and Muslim Marriages', in P Lindskoug, U Maunsbach, G Millqvist, P Samuelsson and H-H Vogel (eds), *Essays in Honour of Michael Bogdan* (date) pp 149–64.

[26] G Melchior, *Die Grundlagen des deutschen internationalen Privatrechts*, De Gruyter (1971) pp 245–65 and W Wengler (1934) Zeitschrift für ausländisches und internationales Privatrecht p 148.

[27] [2008] OJ L 177/6. See G van Calster, *European Private International Law*, (2nd edn, 2016), p 7.

[28] A similar exception clause is found in the Belgian Code on Private International Law, art 19§1, see <http://www.ejustice.just.fgov.be/cgi_loi/change_lg.pl?language=nl&la=N&cn=2004071631&table_name=wet> accessed 14 April 2017, and in English see Clijmans and Torremans (2006) RabelsZ 358 and 6 Ybk Priv Int L 319 (2004).

[29] Taking on board the essence of de Nova's approach, R de Nova, 'Historical and Comparative Introduction to Conflicts of Laws' (1966) Rec Cours II, 557–69.

5. DÉPEÇAGE

A problem related to that of the incidental question is that of "picking and choosing"[30] or '*dépeçage*'. A case involving foreign elements may give rise to issues which involve different choice of law rules. To take the simplest example,[31] if a husband and wife, both domiciled in England, marry in France, then any dispute as to the validity of their marriage may have to be referred to English or French law. In fact, if the dispute is as to the formal validity of the marriage, reference will be made to French law as the law of the place of celebration, and if the issue is one of capacity, it will be determined according to English law as the ante-nuptial domiciliary law of the parties.[32] Here it is clear that the one general issue of the validity of the marriage has to be analysed into two separate sub-issues referable to different laws. The court will pick and choose between these two sub-issues. A similar example is provided in the law of contract where the parties are free to choose different laws to govern different parts of their contract.[33]

In other cases the question whether there are two issues referable to different laws or but one single issue is less easy to determine. Although a failure to distinguish separate issues may produce an unjust and distorted result, it might also be said that the decision to pick and choose may be motivated by a desire to avoid the application of a rule that is regarded as undesirable. The most commonly cited example relates to interspousal immunity in tort.[34] If a husband and wife, both domiciled in a foreign country, are involved in a motor accident in England in which the husband negligently injures the wife, this would be classified as a tort problem to which the appropriate choice of law rules would be applied, pointing as a general rule towards the application of English law,[35] though with the possibility of this being displaced in favour of the law of another country.[36] Let us assume, however, that although an action will lie between husband and wife under English law, it will not so lie under the law of their domicile. Are we to say that the question of interspousal immunity arising in a tort claim is a tort issue,[37] or should we adopt a more subtle categorisation and suggest that the interspousal immunity issue is a matter of status to be segregated from the tort context in which it arose and to be referred to the law of the domicile?[38] The latter is the better approach.

The problem can become more complex, as where the law of the domicile would permit the spouses to sue, but its substantive tort rules would deny the wife recovery, for example, because she was guilty of contributory negligence, whilst under the law governing liability in tort a wife cannot sue her husband but, apart from that, she has a good claim in tort.[39] If one picks and chooses, then the law governing the tort issue may only be applied to the tort elements of the wife's claim, whilst the law of the domicile is applied to the question of interspousal immunity. The result is that the wife can recover by picking and choosing different

---

[30] Cavers (1970) III Hague Recueil 137–40; Ehrenzweig, *Private International Law* pp 119–21; Reese (1973) 73 Col LR 58.

[31] Lipstein (1972) I Hague Recueil 214.

[32] Infra, p 892.

[33] Contracts (Applicable Law) Act 1990, Sch 1, Art 3 (1), infra, pp 707–9; but see Mclachlan (1990) 61 BYBIL 311.

[34] Cavers (1970) III Hague Recueil 138.

[35] Infra, p 816 et seq.

[36] Which could be the law of the country of their common domicile.

[37] Eg *Schmidt v Government Insurance Office of New South Wales* [1973] 1 NSWLR 59; *Corcoran v Corcoran* [1974] VR 164, infra, p 816 et seq.

[38] Eg *Warren v Warren* [1972] Qd R 386.

[39] Cavers (1970) III Hague Recueil 138.

laws to govern different issues, though had any one law been applied to all issues, she would have failed.

Dépeçage scenarios also often lead to the application of a technique known as adaptation.[40] This occurs and is needed when two or more legal systems are being used to resolve a private international law problem, typically in a situation with a central issue and dépeçage.[41] Classification then means that two laws are applicable to different parts of the issue, eg marriage and inheritance. The legal concepts and figures used in one system do not necessarily correspond with, or seamlessly fit into, the other, and there may be contradictions, inconsistencies or gaps. There may need some adaptation before they can operate as part of the answer to the complete issue in the case. One approach to adaptation will try to bring the whole case under a single classification[42] and therefore a single law[43], whilst another approach will slightly modify the content of one of the applicable laws.[44]

---

[40] See G Dannemann, 'Adaptation', in S Leible, *General Principles of European Private International Law* (2016) Chapter 15; and G Cansacchi, 'The Choice and Adaptation of Foreign Law in the Conflict of Laws', 83 (1953) II Hague Recueil, 79–161.

[41] But it can also occur in a situation comprised of incidental and central issues that are resolved through the application of different legal systems.

[42] Wolff (1950).

[43] One could even apply a single law without resorting to a single classification, Kegel, *Internationales Privaterecht* (1987) at 222.

[44] Eg one legal system governing the legal status of a natural person may know a sui generis contract whereby foreign foster parents accept to raise the child as their own until the age of eighteen, at which stage all links are severed, on the side of a full scale adoption (which merely applies in the country), whereas the country whose law applies to the main issue does not know the *sui generis* legal figure. Adaptation then allows the *sui generis* figure to be treated as adoption when it is slotted into the law applicable to the main issue to decide the whole case. It is adapted to the closest equivalent if that is needed to allow it to operate. See also F Vischer, *Die Rechtsvergleichenden Tatbestände im internationalen Privatrecht* (1953).

5

RENVOI[1]

1. The Problem Stated   57
2. Possible Solutions   58
   (a) Apply internal law only   58
   (b) Doctrine of single renvoi   59
   (c) Doctrine of total renvoi   60

3. Scope of the Application of Renvoi   69
   (a) Renvoi inapplicable in many cases 69
   (b) Issues to which renvoi may apply   71

1. THE PROBLEM STATED

Once it is decided that a court has jurisdiction, how the issue before it is to be characterised in terms of private international law and what choice of law rules are applicable, it might be thought that the judge's task was reaching its conclusion. Nothing remains for him to do but apply the chosen law. If this is English law there is no doubt that what he is required to do is to give effect to English internal law. Thus, where a person dies intestate domiciled in England leaving movables here the rules of distribution contained in the Administration of Estates Act 1925 must be applied. There can be no question of paying any further regard to the private international law of England. The function of that department of the law is purely selective and its selection of English law as the applicable law must perforce refer to English internal law, ie to the rules applicable to a purely domestic situation having no foreign complexion.

If, however, the applicable law is that of a foreign country the situation may be more complex. The difficulty is to determine what is meant by the applicable "law". If, for example, the English rule for the choice of law refers to the law of Italy, what meaning must be attributed to "the law of Italy"? The difficulty is not obvious at first sight, but it can be demonstrated by a simple illustration: X, a British subject, dies intestate, domiciled in Italy, and an English court is required to decide how his movables in England are to be distributed. It is clearly desirable that the mode of distribution should be the same everywhere, in the sense that no matter what

---

[1] The literature on the subject is immense; among the contributions in English see: Bate, *Notes on the Doctrine of Renvoi*; Mendelssohn-Bartholdy, *Renvoi in Modern English Law*; Rabel, Vol I, 75 et seq; Lorenzen (1910) 10 Col LR 190, 327; Abbot (1908) 24 LQR 133; Falconbridge, pp 137–263; Lorenzen (1917) 27 Yale LJ 509; Schreiber (1917) 31 Harv LR 523; Griswold (1938) 51 Harv LR 1165; Morris (1937) 18 BYBIL 32; Cowan (1938) 87 U of Pa LR 34; Griswold, ibid 257; Falconbridge (1953) 6 Vanderbilt Law Review 708; Inglis (1958) 74 LQR 493; Von Mehren, *XXth Century Comparative and Conflicts Law*, 360; de Nova (1966) II Hague Recueil 443, 478–577; Kahn-Freund (1974) III Hague Recueil 147, 392–7, 431–437; Sauveplanne, *International Encyclopaedia of Comparative Law*, Vol III, Chapter 6 (1990); Briggs (1998) 47 ICLQ 877; Levontin, *Choice of Law and Conflict of Laws*, Chapter 3; Dicey, Morris and Collins, Chapter 4; Crawford and Carruthers, Chapter 5; Morris, paras 20-016–20-033; Briggs, *Private International Law in English Courts* (2014) paras 3.64–3.79; Anton, 4.40–70; J von Hein, 'Renvoi in European Private International Law', in S Leible, *General Principles of European Private International Law* (2016) Ch 12; and Harder (2011) 60 ICLQ 659. See also A Davì, 'Le renvoi en droit international privé contemporain', (2010) 352 Hague Receuil 9, and E Agostini, 'Le mécanisme du renvoi', (2013) 3 Rev Crit DIP 545.

national court deals with the matter there ought to be universal agreement as to what particular legal system shall indicate the actual beneficiaries. The fact, however, that there are different systems of private international law militates against this ideal solution. Thus, according to the English rules for the choice of law, the question of intestate succession to movables is governed by Italian law as being the law of X's domicile at the time of death, but according to the Italian rules it must be referred to the law of England as being the law of his nationality. In the above example, for instance, an English court has no option but to refer the question of succession to Italian law; while an Italian judge if faced with this issue is under an equal necessity to apply the national law. The English judge, of course, is exclusively governed by his own system of private international law, and must therefore decide that X's goods shall be distributed according to Italian law. Despite this obvious conclusion, however, we are still confronted with the question—what is meant by Italian law? Does it mean Italian internal law, ie the rules enacted by the Italian Code analogous to section 46 of the Administration of Estates Act 1925 which regulate the distribution of an intestate's property? Or does it mean the whole of Italian law, including in particular the rules of private international law as recognised in Italy? If the latter is the correct meaning, a further difficulty is caused by the difference between the English and Italian rules of the choice of law; for on referring to Italian private international law we find ourselves referred back to English law. This being so, the question is whether we are to ignore the divergent Italian rule or to accept the reference back that it makes. If we accept the reference back, are we to stop finally at that point and to distribute X's goods according to the Administration of Estates Act?

2. POSSIBLE SOLUTIONS

When a case is complicated in this fashion, owing to a difference in the private international law of two countries, there are three possible solutions.[2] These are as follows:

The judge who is faced with this issue and who is referred by English private international law to, say, the law of Italy, may

(i) take "the law of Italy" to mean the internal/substantive law of Italy; *or*
(ii) decide the case on the assumption that the doctrine of single renvoi is recognised by English law; *or*
(iii) take "the law of Italy" to mean the law which an Italian judge would administer if he were seised of the matter, ie the doctrine of double renvoi.

These possible courses will now be discussed to show that in some types of case the third solution, whether rightly or wrongly, has been frequently adopted by the judges.

(a) Apply internal law only

The first solution, and the one which is in general correct and desirable, is to read the expression "the law of the country" as meaning only the internal rules of that law. The following would seem to represent the sensible view:

> If England chooses the law of a person's domicile as the best one to apply to a certain relationship, does she mean the ordinary law for ordinary people, his friends and neighbours, in that domicile? Or does she include that country's rules for the choice of law? Common sense could answer that the last alternative is absurd and otiose: a rule for the choice of an

---

[2] See *Tezcan v Tezcan* (1992) 87 DLR (4th) 503 at 519–21.

appropriate law has already been applied, namely our own. To proceed to adopt a foreign rule is to decide the same question twice over.[3]

This would seem to be in accord with the intention of the propositus. If, for instance, a man voluntarily abandons England and acquires a domicile in Italy where he permanently resides until his death many years later, the natural inference is that he willingly submits himself to the internal law of that country. This seems also to be the obvious answer in those cases, such as contract,[4] where the parties are allowed expressly to choose the law to govern their relationship. Few businessmen would voluntarily choose the doctrine of renvoi. This approach has been definitely adopted in at least two early English decisions, one by a court of first instance,[5] the other by the Privy Council.[6] It is, and always has been, unconsciously adopted in a multitude of decisions.[7]

(b) Doctrine of single renvoi

The second solution is to apply the doctrine of renvoi, in the form of single renvoi. Such doctrine is to this effect: if a judge in country A is referred by his own rule of the choice of a law to the "law" of country B, but the rule of the choice of law in B refers such a case to the "law" of A, then the judge in A must apply the internal law of his own country. The operation of this famous but regrettable doctrine, which demands that a reference to the law of a country shall mean a reference to the whole of its law, including its private international law, is best explained by the example already given: X, a British subject, dies intestate, domiciled in Italy, and an English court is required to decide how his movables in England are to be distributed. The English court is directed by its own private international law to refer this question of distribution to Italian law as being the law of the deceased's domicile. When, however, it examines the provision relating to the choice of the applicable law contained in the Italian Code, it finds that in the case of succession to movables the Code prefers the law of the deceased's nationality to that of his domicile, and that if an Italian court had been hearing this matter in the first instance it would have resorted to the law of England. Thus, the English court finds itself referred back to English law as being the law of X's nationality. There is a renvoi or remission to English law.

If the court accepts this remission and distributes the property according to the Administration of Estates Act 1925, it is true to say that the doctrine of renvoi is part of English law. Italian law has been allowed, not to give a direct solution to the problem under consideration, but to indicate what legal system shall furnish the final solution. Where the court that is hearing the matter accepts the remission and applies its own municipal law it recognises the doctrine in its simplest form. Renvoi, properly so called, is best exemplified by the well-known decision of the French Cour de Cassation in *Forgo's* case.[8]

> Forgo, a Bavarian national, died intestate in France, where he had lived since the age of five. The question before the French court was whether his movables in France should be distributed according to the internal law of France or of Bavaria. Collateral relatives were entitled to succeed by Bavarian law, but under French law the property passed to the French government to the exclusion of collaterals. French private international law referred the matter of succession to Bavarian law, but Bavarian private international law referred it to French law.

---

[3] Baty, *Polarised Law* (1914), p 116.

[4] Infra, p 706.

[5] *Hamilton v Dallas* (1875) 1 Ch D 257.

[6] *Bremer v Freeman* (1857) 10 Moo PCC 306; see also *Re Annesley* [1926] Ch 692 at 709; *Re Askew* [1930] 2 Ch 259 at 278; cf *Re Ross* [1930] 1 Ch 377 at 402.

[7] Infra, pp 71–2.

[8] (1883) 10 Clunet 63; and see Juenger (1985) IV Hague Recueil 123, 197–9.

The Cour de Cassation in France accepted the remission and applied the succession provisions of French law.

Where, as in *Forgo's* case, there are only two legal systems concerned—where the reference is merely from country A to country B and back from B to A—the doctrine of renvoi appears in its simplest form. It can best be described as *remission*. Internationally it is known as first degree renvoi.[9] A case may occur, however, where the reference is from A to B, and from B to C. Suppose, for instance, that an Italian testator dies domiciled in France leaving movables in England, English law will refer the question of succession to movables to the law of his domicile, French law. If, however, France were to refer the same question to the law of his nationality, Italian law, this would be a case of reference from B to C, best described as *transmission*. Internationally this is known as second degree renvoi.[10]

This particular doctrine of renvoi, whether in the form of remission or transmission, which is now generally called *partial* or *single* renvoi,[11] is not part of English law.[12] That is to say, if English law refers a matter to the law of the domicile and if the latter remits the question to English law, the judge does not automatically accept the remission and apply English internal law. He does not act as the French court did in *Forgo's* case. It seems unnecessary, therefore, to elaborate the objections to which the doctrine is open.[13]

(c) Doctrine of total renvoi

(i) The doctrine stated

The third possible solution is to adopt what may be called the *foreign court theory* or the "doctrine of double renvoi" or total renvoi,[14] or "the English doctrine of renvoi". This demands that an English judge, who is referred by his own law to the legal system of a foreign country, must apply whatever law a court in that foreign country would apply if it were hearing the case. Let us assume, for example, a question arises concerning the testamentary dispositions of a British subject who dies domiciled and habitually resident in Belgium, leaving assets solely in England (and having moved back to England on a trial basis, whilst holding on to his rented house in Belgium three months before his death). A Belgian judge dealing with this matter would be referred by his rules of private international law to English law,[15] but he would then find that the case was remitted to him by English law. Evidence must therefore be adduced in the English proceedings to show what the Belgian judge would in fact do. He might accept the remission and apply his own internal law, and this would be his course if renvoi in the *Forgo* sense (single renvoi) is recognised in Belgium, or he might reject the remission and apply English internal law. Whatever he would do inexorably determines the

---

[9] Or Rückverweisung. See G Van Hecke and K Lenaerts, *Internationaal Privaatrecht* (2nd edn, 1989), para 312.

[10] Or Weiterverweisung. See ibid.

[11] Dicey, Morris and Collins, para 4-009. Although the term 'partial' is a mere English reflection on renvoi in the light of the English approach and the term is not generally accepted.

[12] *Re Askew* [1930] 2 Ch 259 at 268: "An English court can never have anything to do with it [renvoi], except so far as foreign experts may expound the doctrine as being part of the *lex domicilii*", per Maugham J.

[13] Rabel, Vol I, 81.

[14] *Dallah Real Estate and Tourism Holding Company v The Ministry of Religious Affairs, Government of Pakistan* [2010] UKSC 46, paras 123–125. See also Dicey, Morris and Collins, para 4-010; Falconbridge, p 170, and cf the US case *McGee v Arkel Int'l, LLC*, 671 F 3d 539, 543 (5th Cir 2012).

[15] The Belgian judge would have jurisdiction the basis of article 4 of the succession Regulation (Regulation (EU) No 650/2012 of the European Parliament and of the Council on jurisdiction, applicable law, recognition and enforcement of decisions and acceptance and enforcement of authentic instruments in matters of succession and on the creation of a European Certificate of Succession, [2012] OJ 201/107) and would be referred to English law by article 21(2) of the Regulation (the escape clause). The UK does not participate in the Regulation.

decision of the English judge.[16] If this third solution is adopted, it is vital to realise that the decision given by the English judge will depend on whether the doctrine of single renvoi is recognised by the particular foreign law to which he is referred. The doctrine, for instance, is repudiated in Italy but recognised in France. Therefore, if the issue in England is the intrinsic validity of a will made by a British subject domiciled in Italy, the judge, if he is to make an imaginary judicial journey to Italy, will reason as follows: an Italian judge would refer the matter to English law, as being the national law of the propositus. English law remits the question to Italian law as being the law of his domicile. Italian law does not accept this remission, since it repudiates the single renvoi doctrine. Therefore an Italian judge would apply English internal law.[17] A French domicile, however, would produce the opposite result, since a court sitting in France would accept the remission from England and would ultimately apply French internal law.[18]

(ii) Objections to the doctrine

This third solution does not lack support in England, North America and Australia.[19] Certain English decisions, which will be discussed later, may be cited in its favour; throughout his life Dicey maintained its truth; the editor of his fifth edition was equally strong in advocating its merits;[20] and an American jurist sums up his conclusions in these words: "When a court is referred by its own conflicts rule to a foreign law, it should, as a matter of course, look to the entire foreign law as the foreign court would administer it."[21]

Before estimating the value of the English decisions, therefore, it is appropriate to consider a few of the objections that may be raised to this total renvoi doctrine. The burden of the following pages—that it is objectionable in principle—is based on unconvincing authority and cannot be said to represent the general rule of English law. It is submitted that, subject to certain well-defined exceptions, an English judge, when referred by a rule for the choice of law to the legal system of a foreign country, is not required to consider whether the renvoi doctrine is recognised by the private international law of either country, but must administer the internal law of the legal system to which he has been referred.

The following objections, among others, may be directed against the doctrine:[22]

(a) The total renvoi doctrine does not necessarily ensure uniform decisions

The laudable objective of those who favour the doctrine either of single or of total renvoi is to ensure that the same decision shall be given on the same disputed facts, irrespective of the country in which the case is heard. In truth, however, the doctrine of renvoi, in whatever form it is expressed, will produce this uniformity only if it is recognised in one of the countries concerned and rejected in the other—not if it is recognised in both. If, for example, the law of the domicile, to which the English judge is referred, ordains that the case is to be decided exactly as the national (English) court would decide it, what is the judge to do on finding that by English law his decision is to be exactly what it would be in the country of the domicile?[23] Where is a halt to be called to the process of passing the ball from one judge

---

[16] The doctrine is ambiguous in the sense that the grounds on which the English judge must arrive at the Belgian decision are far from clear. Must he reason on the basis of the actual circumstances of the case, especially the presence of the assets in England? Or, must he reason on a false assumption, namely, that the assets are in Belgium? There is judicial authority for both views. See Dobrin (1934) 15 BYBIL 36, 37–45.

[17] *Re Ross* [1930] 1 Ch 377, infra, pp 66–7.

[18] *Re Annesley* [1926] Ch 692, infra, p 66.

[19] *Neilson v Overseas Projects Corpn of Victoria Ltd* (2005) 221 ALR 213; infra, p 69.

[20] Dicey, *Conflict of Laws* (5th edn), pp 863 et seq; Keith (1942) 24 JCL 69.

[21] Griswold (1938) 51 Harv LR 1165, 1183.

[22] See also Morris, paras 20-029–20-032.

[23] Morris (n 1), 37; and see Schreiber (1917) 31 Harv LR 523.

to another? There is no apparent way in which this inextricable circle can be broken—or in which this international game of tennis can be terminated.

Uniformity will, indeed, be attained if the law of the domicile repudiates the doctrine of total renvoi, ie if, instead of seeking guidance from a foreign judge, it categorically provides that the national (English) law shall govern the matter, for in this case English internal law will apply and harmony will prevail. It is true that the total renvoi doctrine is apparently unrecognised in countries outside the Commonwealth, but nonetheless it is difficult "to approve a doctrine which is workable only if the other country rejects it".[24] The fact is, of course, that uniformity of decisions is unattainable[25] on any consistent principle with regard to matters that are determined in some countries by the law of the nationality, in others by the law of the domicile.

A second obstacle to uniformity of decisions is that the foreign court doctrine does not require, in fact does not allow, the English judge to don the mantle of his foreign colleague without any reservations. Matters that are classified as procedural in England must be submitted to English internal law, even though the foreign judge might have regarded them as substantive.[26] This may well lead to a discrepancy of result. Moreover, the application of a rule of foreign law will sometimes be excluded on grounds of public policy or because it is considered to be a penal, revenue or other public law matter.[27]

(b) The total renvoi doctrine signifies the virtual capitulation of the English rules for choice of law

Stripped of its verbiage, the doctrine involves nothing less than a substitution of the foreign for the English choice of law rules. In the case, for instance, of the British subject who dies intestate domiciled in Italy, the English rule selects the law of Italy as the governing law, but the equivalent Italian rule selects the law of England. When, therefore, the English judge defers to the decision that an Italian judge would have given, he applies the internal law of England and thus shows a preference for the Italian selective rule. The English rule is jettisoned, since it does not meet with the approval of the law-maker in Italy. This, indeed, is the apotheosis of comity.[28] Moreover, a rule for the choice of the applicable law is essentially selective in nature,[29] and that it should have no other effect than to select another and contradictory rule of selection savours of incompatibility and paradox. Furthermore, the application of the law selected by the foreign country's choice of law rules may be unacceptable in public policy terms.[30]

One acute critic, however, finds nothing strange in this surrender to a foreign rule for the choice of law.[31] He denies that there is any logical reason why an English rule of this nature should not be taken to indicate the private international law of a foreign country rather than its internal law. To regard a reference to the law of the domicile as a reference to the internal law is, he says, merely to beg the question. This argument, it is submitted, ignores

---

[24] Lorenzen (1941) 50 Yale LJ 743, 753.

[25] H Batiffol, *Aspects philosophiques du droit international privé* (1956), pp 214–15.

[26] Infra, Chapter 6.

[27] Infra, Chapter 8.

[28] See the dissenting judgment of Taschereau J in the Canadian case of *Ross v Ross* (1894) 25 SCR 307; and see Schreiber (1917) 31 Harv LR 523, 561, 564.

[29] Ibid, 533.

[30] In such circumstances a Canadian court has applied the internal law of the country chosen by the forum's choice of law rules, ie ignored the doctrine of renvoi on public policy grounds: *Vladi v Vladi* (1987) 39 DLR (4th) 563.

[31] Griswold (1938) 51 Harv LR 1165, 1176, 1178.

both the nature and genesis of a rule for the choice of the applicable law. The truth is that such a rule is based on substantial grounds of national policy. It represents what appears to the enacting authority to be right and proper, having regard to the sociological and practical considerations involved. The English principle, for instance, that an intestate's movables shall be distributed according to the law of his last domicile is founded on the reasoning that rights of succession should depend on the law of the country where the deceased established his permanent home. Having voluntarily become an inhabitant of the country, it is the view of English law that in this matter he should be on the same footing as other inhabitants. Moreover, the natural inference is that he submits himself to the law which binds his friends and neighbours. This would seem to be his presumed intention. Thus, if the reference to the law of his domicile is regarded as a reference to whatever internal system the private international law of the domicile may choose, then not only is the deliberate policy of English law reversed, but the probable intention of the propositus is ignored. Indeed, his expectations may be flouted. He may, for instance, have refrained from making a will, having been content with the local rules governing intestacy, the substance of which it will have been a simple matter for him to ascertain. A quite different set of rules, however, may operate if the private international law of his domicile is to have effect.

(c) The total renvoi doctrine is difficult to apply

The doctrine obliges the English judge to ascertain as a fact the precise decision that the foreign court would give. This confronts him with two difficulties. First, he must ascertain what view prevails in the foreign country with regard to the doctrine of single renvoi. Secondly, where the foreign rule for the choice of law selects the national law of the propositus, the judge must ascertain what is meant by national law.

As we have already seen, the chosen law that emerges from an application of the doctrine depends, inter alia, on whether the doctrine of single renvoi is recognised by the law of the domicile.[32] If the court of the domicile would accept the remission made to it by English law, it would determine the case according to its own internal law; otherwise it would apply the internal law of England. This dependence of the rights of the parties on the attitude of the law of the domicile to the renvoi doctrine is a cause of acute embarrassment. There are few matters on which it is more difficult to obtain reliable information, not least because of the undue influence of expert witnesses over the process. Alternatively, the English judge may be confronted with a somewhat arduous and invidious task, as witness the following remarks of Wynn-Parry J:

> It would be difficult to imagine a harder task than that which faces me, namely, of expounding for the first time either to this country or to Spain the relevant law of Spain as it would be expounded by the Supreme Court of Spain, which up to the present time has made no pronouncement on the subject, and having to base that exposition on evidence which satisfies me that on this subject there exists a profound cleavage of legal opinion in Spain and two conflicting decisions of courts of inferior jurisdiction.[33]

The second difficulty that may arise is to ascribe a definite meaning to the expression "national law". When the private international law rules of the country in which the English judge is presumed to sit select the nationality of a person as the connecting factor, it becomes necessary to correlate the national law with some precise system of internal law by which the issue before the court may be determined. This is a simple matter when the person is a national of

---

[32] Supra, pp 59–60.
[33] *Re Duke of Wellington* [1947] Ch 506 at 515; infra, p 68.

some country, such as Sweden, which has a unitary system of territorial law.[34] There is a single body of internal law applicable throughout the territory known as Sweden. The position is far different where the country of nationality comprises several systems of territorial law, as is true for example of the United Kingdom and the USA. What, for instance, is the national law of a British subject? For an English court, the question is really pointless, because the law that governs a British subject in personal matters varies according to the territory of the foreign country in which he is domiciled. It is one system in England, another in Scotland, and so on. The case of *Re O'Keefe*[35] will serve to illustrate both the nature of the difficulty and the speciousness of the total renvoi doctrine. The facts were these:

> The question before the English court was the way in which the movables of X, a spinster who died intestate, were to be distributed. X's father was born in 1835 in Ireland, but at the age of 22 he went to India, and except for various stays in Europe lived there throughout his life and died in Calcutta in 1885. X was born in India in 1860; from 1867 to 1890 she lived in various places in England, France and Spain; but in 1890 she settled down in Naples and resided there until her death 47 years later in 1937. About the year 1878 she had made a short tour in Ireland with her father. She never lost her British nationality, but it was held that she had acquired a domicile in Italy.

The law selected by English private international law to govern the question of distribution was, therefore, the law of her domicile. Had an Italian judge been hearing the case, however, he would have been referred to her national law by the Italian Civil Code. He would have rejected any remission made to him by the national law, since the single renvoi doctrine had not been adopted in Italy. The Civil Code used the general expression "national law" and failed to define what this means when the country of nationality contains more than one legal system. Which system of internal law, then, out of those having some relation to X, would be regarded by an Italian court as applicable? The issue raised in the case was whether it was the law of England, Ireland or India. Which of these systems would be selected by a court in Italy? The expert witnesses agreed that it would be the law of the country to which X "belonged" at the time of her death. She certainly did not "belong", whatever that may mean, to England in the sense of attracting to herself English internal law, for she had spent no appreciable time in the country. She might perhaps, by reason of her birth in Calcutta, be regarded as belonging to India, though she had not been there for seventy years. The reasonable man might even be excused for thinking that she most properly belonged to Italy, the country where she had continuously spent the last forty-seven years of her life.[36] Crossman J, however, would have none of these. He reverted to X's domicile of origin, and held that she belonged to Ireland because that was the country where her father was domiciled at the time of her birth. In the result, therefore, the succession to her property was governed by the law of the country which she had never entered except during one short visit some sixty years before her death; which was not even a separate political unit until sixty-two years after her birth; of whose succession laws she was no doubt profoundly and happily ignorant; and under the law of which it was impossible in the circumstances for her to claim citizenship. The convolutions by which such a remarkable result is reached are interesting. First, the judge is referred by the English rule to the law of the domicile, which in the instant case means the law of the domicile of choice; then he bows to the superior wisdom of a foreign legislator and allows the law

---

[34] For a stimulating exposé of the present difficulty, see Falconbridge, pp 202–16. See also Morris (1940) 56 LQR 144. For judicial comment on the onerous nature of the doctrine, see *Barros Mattos Junior v MacDaniels Ltd* [2005] IL Pr 45, per Lawrence Collins J, at [108].

[35] [1940] Ch 124. See Nadelmann (1969) 17 AJCL 418, 443–8.

[36] Morris points out (n 34 at 46) that the originating summons did not suggest Italian law as a possible choice, and he assumes that the decision is no authority against the view that the internal law of the domicile should have been applied.

of the domicile to be supplanted by the law of the nationality; then, upon discovering that the law of the nationality is meaningless, he throws himself back on the domicile of origin; and thus determines the rights of the parties by a legal system which is neither the national law nor the law of the domicile as envisaged by the English rule for choice of law.[37] Comment is surely superfluous.

(iii) Analysis of decisions supporting the doctrine

Although a number of cases are often cited in support of the total renvoi doctrine, they are far from satisfactory. The first of these is *Collier v Rivaz*,[38] where the facts were as follows:

> A British subject, who according to English law was domiciled in Belgium at the time of his death, had executed seven testamentary instruments, a will and six codicils. The will and two of the codicils had been executed in accordance with the formalities required by Belgian internal law. The remaining four codicils, though formally valid according to the Wills Act 1837, were not made in the form required by Belgian internal law. According to the law of Belgium the testator had never acquired a domicile in that country, since he had not obtained the necessary authorisation from the government. The question was whether the instruments could be admitted to probate in England.

Sir Herbert Jenner, after propounding the theory that he must sit as a Belgian judge, admitted the will and two codicils to probate because they satisfied the formalities of the internal law of the country in which the testator was domiciled in the English sense. He extended the same indulgence to the remaining codicils on the ground that, since the testator had not acquired a domicile in Belgium in the Belgian sense, a judge in Brussels would apply Belgian private international law, under which the formal validity of the instruments would be tested by English internal law.

This decision is open to many criticisms.[39] It is obvious that, when a choice of law rule selects a particular legal system as the one to govern a given question, it is necessary to decide whether this means the internal law or the private international law of the selected system. It cannot mean both, for the private international law rules may indicate some other legal system, the internal law of which differs from the internal law of the selected system. If the question in *Collier v Rivaz* had been, not the formal, but the essential, validity of the testamentary instruments, and if, for instance, some of them had been lawful by English internal law but unlawful by Belgian internal law, while others had been lawful in Belgium but unlawful in England, it would have been impossible to uphold them in their totality. Sir Herbert Jenner, however, had it both ways. He held that the formal validity of a will cannot be denied if it satisfies either the internal law or the private international law of the selected legal system. There is much to be said for this benevolent rule in the one case of formal validity, since it is obviously desirable that the intention of a testator, clearly expressed and not intrinsically objectionable, should be respected if reasonably possible.[40] What is impossible is that the rule should be allowed a wider general operation.[41]

---

[37] The difficulty of identifying the law to which a British national is subject was ignored in *Re Ross* [1930] 1 Ch 377, infra, pp 66–7; *Re Askew* [1930] 2 Ch 259, infra, p 67; and *Re Duke of Wellington* [1947] Ch 506, infra, p 68. In these cases English law was chosen without argument.

[38] (1841) 2 Curt 855; see also *Frere v Frere* (1847) 5 Notes of Cases 593; cf *Bremer v Freeman* (1857) 10 Moo PCC 306, infra, pp 1340–1.

[39] See especially: Abbot (1908) 24 LQR 133, 143; Falconbridge, pp 143–5, 151–2; Morris (n 1), 43–4; Mendelssohn-Bartholdy, *Renvoi in English Law*, pp 58–64.

[40] Choice of law rules relating to wills are discussed infra, pp 1339 et seq and 1352 et seq.

[41] *Re Lacroix Goods* (1877) 2 PD 94 was another case where the English judge seems to have applied both the private international law rules and the internal law of the domicile; see Morris (n 39), 42. The operation of any renvoi doctrine in matters concerning the formal validity of wills has now been virtually excluded by the

In contrast to *Collier v Rivaz, Re Annesley*[42] was concerned with the essential validity of a will.

An Englishwoman was domiciled at the time of her death in France according to the principles of English law, but was domiciled in England in the eyes of French law. This was because she had never obtained the authorisation of the French government which, before 1927, was necessary for the acquisition of domicile. Her testamentary dispositions were valid by English internal law, but invalid by French internal law, since she had failed to leave two-thirds of her property to her children.

Russell J held that the validity of the dispositions must be determined by French law. His actual decision, therefore, was in accordance with the view that a reference to the law of a given country is a reference to its internal law,[43] but he did not reach his conclusion in this simple fashion. He preferred the total renvoi theory. Although the judge's reasoning is not altogether clear, it seems that he ultimately arrived at the application of French internal law by the following route:

> English private international law refers the matter to French law as being the law of the domicile.
>
> A French judge would be referred by his own rules to English law. He would, however, find himself referred back by English private international law to French law.
>
> Single renvoi is recognised in France.
>
> Therefore, a French court would accept the remission, and in the result would apply French internal law.

It is to be noted, however, that, had the judge not thought himself bound by previous authorities, he would have preferred to have based his decision on an alternative and simpler ground. This, the direct antithesis of the approach that we have just considered, was that the natural meaning of the expression "the law of a country" is the internal law of the country in question. "When we say that French law applies to the administration of the personal estate of an Englishman who dies domiciled in France, we mean that French municipal law which France applies in the case of Frenchmen."[44]

Another case concerned with the essential validity of a will is *Re Ross*.[45]

> The testatrix, a British subject, who was domiciled in Italy, both in the English and the Italian sense, disposed of her property by a will which excluded her son from the list of beneficiaries. This exclusion was justifiable by English internal law, but contrary to Italian internal law which required that one-half of the property should go to the son as his *legitima portio*. She left land in Italy and movable property both in England and Italy.

Luxmoore J held with regard to the movables that in accordance with the English rule of the choice of law the claim of the son to his *legitima portio* must be determined by Italian law as being the law of the testatrix's domicile. He then put the question: what is meant by the law of the domicile? Does it refer merely to the municipal law of the domicile or does it include its rules of private international law?[46]

Wills Act 1963 which governs wills of testators dying after 1963, and under which there is a variety of systems of internal law by which the formal validity of a will may be tested; infra, pp 1340–2.

[42] [1926] Ch 692.
[43] Supra, p 59.
[44] [1926] Ch 692 at 709. This view was rejected by Luxmoore J in *Re Ross* [1930] 1 Ch 377 at 402; in a later case, *Re Askew* [1930] 2 Ch 259 at 278, Maugham J considered that there was "much to be said for it".
[45] [1930] 1 Ch 377.
[46] Ibid, at 388, 389.

In the result the judge applied English internal law and disallowed the claim of the son. This was the conclusion which an Italian judge would have reached. He would have referred the matter to the law of the nationality and would have rejected the remission made to him by English law. As regards the land, the English rule for the choice of law referred the judge to Italian law as being the law of the situs. The expert evidence showed that an Italian court would again turn to the law of the nationality and would adopt the rule of English internal law applicable to land situated in England and belonging to an English testator. It was held once more, therefore, that the claim of the son failed. In this way Mrs Ross was allowed to evade one of the cardinal rules of the legal system, the protection of which she had enjoyed for the last fifty-one years of her life.

The next case, *Re Askew*,[47] raised an issue of legitimacy.

By an English marriage settlement made on the marriage of X, a British subject domiciled in England, to his first wife, Y, it was provided that X, if he married again, might revoke in part the settled trusts and make a new appointment to the children of *such subsequent marriage*. Some time before 1911, X, who had long been separated from Y, acquired a German domicile. In 1911, having obtained a divorce from a competent German court, he married Z, in Berlin. Some time *before the divorce* a daughter had been born to X and Z in Switzerland. In 1913 X exercised his power of revocation and made an appointment in favour of his daughter.

The question before the English court concerned the validity of this appointment. A short answer to this question, and one that would have involved no reference to private international law, was that the daughter of Z was in no sense a child of the "subsequent marriage", for the only marriage subsisting at the time of her birth was that between X and Y. She might be legitimate, but she could not possibly be the child of a non-existing marriage.[48] This fact, however, was not brought to the notice of Maugham J, who insisted that the validity of the appointment depended on whether the daughter was legitimate. She could not claim legitimacy under the Legitimacy Act 1926[49] since at the time of her birth her father was married to someone other than her mother.[50] By English private international law, however, her legitimacy depended on whether German law, being that of her father's domicile both at the time of her birth and also at the time of his marriage to Z, recognised legitimation by subsequent marriage. In such a case, German private international law referred the matter to the law of the father's nationality. Moreover, the doctrine of single renvoi was generally accepted in Germany. If, therefore, a German court were required to pronounce on the legitimacy of Z's daughter, it would first refer to English law, and then, on finding a remission made by English law to the law of the domicile, would accept this and apply German internal law. In other words, if the English reference to the law of the domicile was a reference to the private international law rules of the domicile, the daughter would be legitimate. Maugham J felt that both on principle and on the authorities he was obliged to consider the private international law of Germany. He therefore decided in favour of the legitimacy of the daughter and the validity of the appointment.

---

[47] [1930] 2 Ch 259, followed in *Collins v A-G* (1931) 145 LT 551.

[48] *Re Wicks' Marriage Settlement* [1940] Ch 475; cf *Colquitt v Colquitt* [1948] P 19 at 25 where it was suggested that no difference should be drawn between phrases such as a "legitimate child" and a "child of a subsisting marriage".

[49] Now replaced by the Legitimacy Act 1976.

[50] Section 1(2) of the 1926 Act. This rule was abrogated by the Legitimacy Act 1959, s l; see now the Legitimacy Act 1976, infra, pp 1203–4.

The facts of *Re Duke of Wellington*,[51] another relevant case, were as follows:

> The Duke of Wellington, a British subject domiciled in England, left two wills, one dealing with his Spanish, the other with his English, property. By the former he left his land in Spain to the person who would succeed both to his English dukedom and to his Spanish dukedom of Ciudad Rodrigo.[52] He died a bachelor, with the result that by the internal law of England his English dukedom passed to his uncle, while by the internal law of Spain his sister succeeded to the Spanish dukedom. Therefore, the Spanish land remained undisposed of, since there was no one person qualified to take both dukedoms.

The problem, therefore, was to identify the person to whom the Spanish land passed, and this depended on whether the solution was to be found in the internal law of Spain or of England. By the former, the testator was entitled to devise only half of his land, the other half passing as on intestacy;[53] by English internal law, the land would pass to the next Duke of Wellington under the residuary gift contained in the English will.

Wynn-Parry J decided in favour of English internal law for the following reasons: the English choice of law rule referred him in the first instance to Spanish law, which, having regard to such cases as *Re Ross*,[54] included the private international law of Spain; the Spanish code provided that testate and intestate succession was to be determined by the national law of the deceased, whatever be the country in which the property was situated; therefore, the question was whether a Spanish court, having thus been referred to the national (English) law, would accept the remission made by that law to the law of the situs. In short, was the doctrine of single renvoi recognised in Spain? After considering the conflicting evidence of the expert witnesses and the conflicting decisions of two Spanish courts of first instance, the judge reached the conclusion that a court in Spain would not accept the remission made by the national law. Therefore, the Duke of Wellington was entitled to the land under the English will.

A further case to be considered is *Re Fuld's Estate (No 3)*[55] where the facts were as follows:

> The testator, a German by origin, had acquired Canadian nationality when resident in Ontario, but he died domiciled in Germany. His will and its second codicil were executed in England and were considered formally valid in England.[56] The three other codicils to his will were executed in Germany and, thus, according to English private international law, German law, as the law of his domicile, governed their formal validity. The last two of these codicils were invalid as to form under German domestic law, but valid under English and Ontario domestic law.

What had to be determined was whether reference to German law was to German internal law or the whole of German law, including its rules of private international law. This involved a difficult problem of the interpretation of the German Civil Code which allowed reference in such cases to either the law governing validity or that of the place of execution. Scarman J construed this latter reference as a reference to the internal law of Germany. However, the reference under German law to the law governing validity was to the law of Ontario as the law of the nationality. This was considered to be a reference to the whole of Ontario law,

---

[51] [1947] Ch 506.
[52] This will also dispose of his movables in Spain.
[53] This difference is not brought out in the report, see Morris (1948) 64 LQR 264, 266.
[54] Supra, p 68.
[55] [1968] P 675; Graveson (1966) 15 ICLQ 937, 941–4.
[56] Under the Wills Act 1861, s 2.

including its rules of private international law. These led to a reference back to German law, as the law of the domicile, and this reference back was accepted by German law under the Civil Code. German internal law was applied and, consequently, the codicils were invalid.

The nature and application of the renvoi doctrine was the focus of an important recent Western Australian case, *Neilson v Overseas Projects Corporation of Victoria Ltd*,[57] the facts of which were as follows:

> Mrs Neilson, an Australian citizen, domiciled in Western Australia, moved with her husband to China, he having accepted a position with the defendant Victoria corporation, which required him to work there. Subsequently, Mrs Neilson was injured at the couple's place of residence in China, and so sued her husband's employer, in contract and in tort, in Western Australia.

The point in issue was whether application of the Chinese law of the place where the tort was committed should include the Chinese choice of law rules, which, in the circumstances of the case, conferred a discretion on the forum to apply Australian substantive law, which had a more generous limitation period than domestic Chinese law. By majority,[58] the High Court of Australia held that where the law of the place where the tort was committed rule requires an Australian court to apply foreign law, the court must, ordinarily at least, apply foreign choice of law rules, and whichever law those rules yield. While three judges were of the view that, in resolving the appeal, it was "unnecessary to postulate a single theory of renvoi to govern all proceedings in Australian courts requiring reference to foreign substantive law",[59] it is worthy of note that total renvoi was accepted by a majority of five judges.[60]

3. SCOPE OF THE APPLICATION OF RENVOI

(a) Renvoi inapplicable in many cases

This review of the principal decisions[61] discloses that the total renvoi doctrine is not of general application.[62] Its scope appears to be limited to certain matters concerning either status or the disposition of property on death. In countless cases dealing with such matters as torts,[63]

---

[57] (2005) 221 ALR 213. For commentary, see Keyes (2005) 13 Torts Law Journal 1; Lu and Carroll (2005) 1 J Priv Int L 35; and Mortensen (2006) 2 J Priv Int L 1.

[58] McHugh J, dissenting.

[59] Per Kirby J, at [175]; see also Gummow and Hayne JJ, at [99].

[60] Per Gummow and Hayne JJ, at [90]; Gleeson CJ, at para 13; Kirby J, at [176] and [191]; Heydon J, at [271]. See Mortensen, (2006) 2 J Priv Int L 1, 10. Nevertheless, Mortensen, at 12, remarks that *Neilson*, ". . . reinforces our understanding of the shortcomings of the doctrine of renvoi, and especially of double renvoi".

[61] It is thought that *Armitage v A-G* [1906] P 135 was not a case on renvoi, but rather a decision on the jurisdiction of the courts: Falconbridge, p 745; Lipstein [1972b] CLJ 66, 84–6.

[62] At the international level there are instruments that exclude renvoi (the New York Convention on the Recognition and Enforcement of Foreign Arbitral Awards 1958 is an example, see *Dallah Real Estate and Tourism Holding Company v The Ministry of Religious Affairs, Government of Pakistan* [2010] UKSC 46, at para 124), whilst others, such as the 1980 Hague Convention on the Civil Aspects of International Child Abduction, embrace it.

[63] *M'Elroy v M'Allister* 1949 SC 110 at 126. See now the Private International Law (Miscellaneous Provisions) Act 1995, s 9(5), infra, p 778. The Rome II Regulation contains an exclusion of renvoi clause (Art 24). See, in contrast, however, *Neilson v Overseas Projects Corpn of Victoria Ltd* [2005] HCA 54, supra, p 69; see, for a statement of principle, Callinan J, at [261]. Also Keyes (2005) 13 Torts Law Journal 1; Lu and Carroll (2005) 1 J Priv Int L 35; and Mortensen (2006) 2 J Priv Int L 1.

insurance, sale of movables, gifts *inter vivos* or *mortis causa*, mortgages, negotiable instruments, partnerships, dissolution of foreign companies and so on, the English courts, when referred to "the law" of a foreign country, have never had the slightest hesitation in applying the internal law of that country. One of the clearest rejections of any renvoi doctrine is to be found in the field of contract, it being thought that no sane businessman or his lawyers would choose the application of renvoi. Not only was the rejection made clear at common law,[64] but this position has been confirmed by Article 15 of the (1980) Rome Convention on the law applicable to contractual obligations to which effect is given by the Contracts (Applicable Law) Act 1990.[65] The general principle is reiterated in the Rome I Regulation in Article 20. The clear terms of Article 15 of the Convention and Article 20 of the Regulation are that the application of the law of any country specified by this Convention/Regulation means the application of the rules of law in force in that country other than its rules of private international law.[66]

There are, however, as we have seen, decisions which do apply renvoi in certain limited areas. These cases perhaps show that the judges, in considering whether the reference may not be to the private international law of the chosen country, have taken the view that "the various categories of cases merit individual consideration in the light of expediency"[67] and that the entire problem is not to be decided on *a priori* reasoning. One writer, who has done much to illuminate the subject, suggests that the renvoi doctrine cannot be rejected in toto, since it has proved to be a useful and justifiable expedient for the solution of at least certain special questions.[68] Renvoi has recently been allocated a supporting role in bringing about the goals of the choice of law rule involved in the case by the High Court of Australia, in case it is necessary to depart from the rigid application of the choice of law rule and the applicable law it determines to achieve the goals of the choice of law rule.[69] The conclusion, in fact, is that generally a reference made by an English rule for choice of law to a foreign legal system is to the internal law, not to the private international law, of the chosen system, but that this general principle is subject to a number of exceptions.

As regards unjust enrichment, in *Barros Mattos Junior v MacDaniels Ltd*[70] counsel for the claimant argued that the applicable law should be construed as being that law, including its rules of private international law. Lawrence Collins J, while judging the argument to be premature, nevertheless opined that, although there is no authority directly in point, "the claim to the application of renvoi in restitution claims is weak".[71]

---

[64] *Re United Rlys of the Havana and Regla Warehouses Ltd* [1960] Ch 52 at 97; *The Evia Luck (No 2)* [1990] 1 Lloyd's Rep 319 at 327, affd sub nom *Dimskal Shipping Co SA v International Transport Workers Federation* [1992] 2 AC 152; *Amin Rasheed Shipping Corpn v Kuwait Insurance Co* [1984] AC 50 at 61–2; and *see Kutchera v Buckingham International Holdings Ltd* [1988] IR 61 at 68; cf Briggs (1989) 9 OJLS 251, 254–6.

[65] Infra, p 706. See *Integral Petroleum SA v Scu-Finanz AG* [2015] EWCA Civ 144.

[66] Cf Rome II Regulation, Art 24; infra, p 802.

[67] Rabel, Vol I, 77.

[68] Falconbridge (1953) 6 Vanderbilt LR 708. For a more recent defence, see Briggs (1998) 47 ICLQ 877.

[69] *Neilson v Overseas Projects Corpn of Victoria Ltd* [2005] HCA 54. Cf in a context of classification *Raiffeisen Zentralbank Österreich AG v Five Star General Trading LLC and Ors* [2001] QB 825 (CA), supra, p 43.

[70] [2005] IL Pr 45.

[71] Para 121. See also Rome II Regulation, Art 24; infra, p 802.

(b) Issues to which renvoi may apply

(i) Validity of bequests

Where the essential validity of a will[72] or intestate succession to movables[73] is determinable by the law of a foreign country, the view that would be taken of the matter by the foreign judge, if he were hearing the case, must be adopted. Also, in cases in which the testator died before 1964 and in cases in which, although he died after 1963, the formal validity of his will is considered under the old common law rule of reference to the law of the domicile, a grant of probate will not be denied on the ground of formal invalidity if the will is formally valid according to the private international law, though not according to the internal law, of the governing legal system.[74]

(ii) Claims to foreign immovables

Where a question arises of the right to foreign immovables, as in *Re Ross*,[75] the English court will apply the private international law rules of the country where the immovables are situated, if they would be applied by a court of the situs hearing the same question.[76] This may be justified on the ground that it promotes the security of title.[77]

(iii) Some cases of movables

If the English choice of law rule refers a disputed title to movables to the law of their situs at the time when the alleged title was said to have been acquired, it is probable that the court will apply the internal system of law that a court of the situs would apply in the particular circumstances of the case.[78]

(iv) Family law issues

The one area of family law where there is clear authority for the application of renvoi is that of the recognition, at common law, of legitimation by subsequent marriage.[79] There is also some authority for the application of the doctrine of renvoi to matrimonial property issues[80] and to both formal[81] and essential[82] validity of marriage.[83] What is not wholly clear is whether

---

[72] *Re Annesley* [1926] Ch 692, supra, p 66; *Re Ross* [1930] 1 Ch 377, supra, p 66; *Re Adams* [1967] IR 424. Proposed European harmonisation of choice of law rules concerning the essential validity of wills would "obviate the need for renvoi where all the connecting factors are situated in a Member State". See EU Green Paper, "Succession and Wills" COM (2005) 65 final, para 2.7; infra, Chapter 36.

[73] *Re O'Keefe* [1940] Ch 124, supra, p 64; cf *Re Thom* (1987) 40 DLR (4th) 184.

[74] *Collier v Rivaz* (1841) 2 Curt 855, supra, p 66; *Frere v Frere* (1847) 5 Notes of Cases 593; and see Wills Act 1963, infra, pp 1340–2.

[75] [1930] 1 Ch 377, supra, p 66.

[76] *Re Ross*, supra, p 66; *Re Duke of Wellington* [1947] Ch 506, supra, p 68; *Re Bailey* [1985] 2 NZLR 656; *Re Schneider's Estate* 96 NYS 2d 652 (Surr Ct 1950), discussed by Morris (1951) 4 ILQ 268; Falconbridge (1953) 6 Vanderbilt LR 708, 725–31. See Carruthers, paras 1.43–1.45, and pp 276 and 293. Contractual issues are dealt with separately, without renvoi, under the Rome I Regulation.

[77] Yntema (1957) 35 Can Bar Rev 721, 740.

[78] See *The Islamic Republic of Iran v Berend* [2007] EWHC 132 (QB), [2007] 2 All ER (Comm) 132, and note by Knight (2007) Conveyancer and Property Lawyer 564. In *Macmillan Inc v Bishopsgate Trust (No 3)* [1996] 1 WLR 387, Staughton LJ said (at p 405) that renvoi did not apply to the choice of the law to determine who has title to shares in a company. But see *Winkworth v Christie, Manson and Woods Ltd* [1980] Ch 496 at 514; and infra, p 1269.

[79] *Re Askew* [1930] 2 Ch 259, supra, p 67. It is doubtful whether the doctrine of renvoi applies to recognition of a foreign legitimation under the Legitimacy Act 1976, s 3, infra, pp 1203–5.

[80] *Vladi v Vladi* (1987) 39 DLR (4th) 563.

[81] *Taczanowska v Taczanowski* [1957] P 301; see also *Hooper v Hooper* [1959] 2 All ER 575, infra, p 900.

[82] *R v Brentwood Superintendent Registrar of Marriages, ex p Arias* [1968] 2 QB 956, infra, p 925. The actual decision in this case would now be different by reason of the Family Law Act 1986, s 50, infra, pp 925–6.

[83] This view was provisionally supported in Law Commission Working Paper No 89 (1985), paras 2.39, 3.39; but not all commentators agreed, see Law Com No 165 (1987), paras 2.5–2.6. Similarly, use of renvoi is

renvoi allows the validity of a marriage to be upheld if it is valid either under the internal law of the country to which English choice of law rules refer or under that country's private international law rules—a rule of alternative reference.[84]

So too in relation to children, the Peréz-Vera Report on the 1980 Hague Convention on the Civil Aspects of International Child Abduction indicates that the applicable law in terms of the Convention includes its rules of private international law.[85]

---

expressly permitted by the Civil Partnership Act 2004, s 54(10) in relation to testing the validity of civil partnerships registered outside England and Wales (cf s 124(10), for Scotland, and s 177(10) for Northern Ireland).

[84] Infra, pp 925–6.

[85] Explanatory Report (1981), paras 66 and 67. Infra, Chapter 25. See, eg, *Re JB (Child Abduction) (Rights of Custody: Spain)* [2003] EWHC 2130, [2004] 1 FLR 796, discussed by Beevers and Perez Milla (2007) 3 J Priv Int L 201.

6

SUBSTANCE AND PROCEDURE

1. Difference Between Substance and Procedure	73	(b) Evidence	80
		(c) Parties	86
(a) Procedure governed by the law of the forum	73	(d) Priorities	89
		(e) The nature and extent of the remedy	90
(b) Importance of distinction between substance and procedure	74	(f) Damages	91
		(g) Judgments in foreign currency	97
(c) How is the distinction to be made?	75	(h) Execution	104
2. Particular Issues	77		
(a) The time within which an action must be brought	78		

1. DIFFERENCE BETWEEN SUBSTANCE AND PROCEDURE

(a) Procedure governed by the law of the forum

One of the eternal truths of every system of private international law is that a distinction must be made between substance and procedure[1], between right and remedy.[2] The substantive rights of the parties to an action may be governed by a foreign law, but all matters appertaining to procedure are governed exclusively by the law of the forum.[3]

At first sight the principle seems almost self-evident. A person who resorts to an English court for the purpose of enforcing a foreign claim cannot expect to occupy a different procedural position from that of a domestic litigant. The field of procedure constitutes perhaps the most technical part of any legal system, and it comprises many rules that would be unintelligible to a foreign judge and certainly unworkable by a machinery designed on different lines. A party to litigation in England must take the law of procedure as he finds it. He cannot by virtue of some rule in his own country enjoy greater advantages than other parties here; neither must he be deprived of any advantages that English law may confer upon a litigant in the particular form of action.[4] To take an old example, an English creditor who sued his debtor in Scotland could not insist on trial by jury, nor, in the converse case, could a Scottish creditor suing in

---

[1] See generally R Garnett, *Substance and Procedure in Private International Law*, (2012).

[2] Cf Cook (1932–33) 42 Yale LJ 333; Szaszy (1966) 15 ICLQ 436, 455–6; and see Spiro (1969) 18 ICLQ 949. This distinction is, in principle, drawn by the Contracts (Applicable Law) Act 1990, infra, p 704 (article 18 Rome I Regulation), which excludes (in Sch 1, Art 1(2) (h)) from its rules for determining the law applicable to a contract matters of evidence and procedure, subject to a number of limited exceptions, discussed infra. Similar provision is made in the case of tort by the Private International Law (Miscellaneous Provisions) Act 1995, s 14(3)(b).

[3] *British Linen Co v Drummond* (1830) 10 B & C 903; *De la Vega v Vianna* (1830) 1 B & Ad 284; *Huber v Steiner* (1835) 2 Bing NC 202; *Don v Lippmann* (1837) 5 Cl & Fin 1 at 13; *Chaplin v Boys* [1971] AC 356 at 378–9, 381–2, 392–3, 394, *Cox v Ergo Versicherung AG (formerly Victoria)* [2014] UKSC 22, paras 13–14. Cf, in Canada, *Somers v Fournier* (2002) 214 DLR (4th) 611, CA (Ont); and *Volger v Szendroi* 2008 NSCA 18.

[4] *De la Vega v Vianna* (1830) 1 B & Ad 284 at 288; *Chaplin v Boys* [1971] AC 356 at 394.

England refuse the intervention of a jury, on the ground that in Scotland, where the debt arose, the case would have been tried by a judge alone.[5]

(b) Importance of distinction between substance and procedure[6]

Although the principle is certain and universal, its application can give rise to considerable difficulty, especially when trying to establish a test by which a procedural rule can be distinguished from a substantive one. Unless the distinction is made with a clear regard to the underlying purpose of private international law, the inevitable result will be to defeat that purpose. So intimate is the connection between substance and procedure that to treat an English rule as procedural may defeat the policy which demands the application of a foreign substantive law. A glaring example of this is afforded by section 4 of the Statute of Frauds, which formerly provided that no action should be brought on certain contracts unless they were evidenced by a note or memorandum signed by the party to be charged or by his lawfully authorised agent. In *Leroux v Brown*:[7]

> An oral agreement was made in France by which the defendant, resident in England, agreed to employ the plaintiff, resident in France, for a period that was longer than a year. The contract was valid and enforceable by French law, which was the law by which it was to be governed, but had it been an English domestic contract it would, though valid, nevertheless have been unenforceable under the Statute of Frauds. An action brought in England for its breach failed on the ground that the statute imposed a rule of procedure which was binding on all litigants suing in England.

Although this decision might, possibly, be based on an intelligible principle of domestic law, it is repugnant to the principles on which English private international law is founded. That law exists to fulfil foreign rights, not to destroy them. The law governing the contract in *Leroux v Brown* undoubtedly entitled the plaintiff to recover damages for the breach of the undertaking and, had he obtained judgment in France in an action to which the defendant voluntarily appeared, nothing would have prevented him from succeeding in an action brought on the judgment in England. Moreover, he would have succeeded had he done something in furtherance of the contract that constituted an act of part performance in the eyes of English law.[8] To refuse him a right of action in England on the contract was tantamount to denying that the contract, admittedly governed as to substance by French law, conferred a right on him. It is a stultification of private international law to refuse recognition to a foreign right substantively valid under its governing law, unless its recognition will conflict with some rule of public policy so insistent as to override all other considerations. Willes J attacked the decision in two later cases, and evidently thought that in the circumstances the statutory rule should not have been treated as procedural.[9]

---

[5] *Don v Lippmann* (1837) 5 Cl & Fin 1 at 14.

[6] See Fentiman, *Foreign Law in English Courts* (1998), pp 35–41, 92–4; and Carruthers (2004) 53 ICLQ 691.

[7] (1852) 12 CB 801; and see *Morris v Baron & Co* [1918] AC 1 at 15. The statute now just applies to a contract of guarantee: Law Reform (Enforcement of Contracts) Act 1954, s 1. In the case of contracts concerning land they need to be made by signed writing. If not, the contract is invalid: Law of Property (Miscellaneous Provisions) Act 1989, s 2.

[8] *Mahadervan v Mahadervan* [1964] P 233 at 242.

[9] *Williams v Wheeler* (1860) 8 CBNS 299 at 316; *Gibson v Holland* (1865) LR 1 CP 1 at 8. This view has been adopted in the USA; *Bernkrant v Fowler* 55 Cal 2d 588, 360 P 2d 906 (1961). However, in *G & H Montage GmbH v Irvani* [1990] 1 WLR 667 it was suggested that the reasoning in *Leroux v Brown* was "unassailable" and that only the House of Lords could overrule the decision: [1990] 1 WLR 667 at 684, and see at 690. On the other hand, in considering the Contracts (Applicable Law) Act 1990 and the Rome Convention on the Law Applicable to Contractual Obligations (infra, pp 758–9) it should be borne in mind that it has been suggested that whether a contract has to be in writing may be regarded as a matter of the substantive

The Court of Appeal took a somewhat different approach in *Monterosso Shipping Co Ltd v International Transport Workers' Federation*.[10]

The plaintiff, a Maltese company, owned a ship which was managed by a Norwegian company with Norwegian officers and a Spanish crew. The defendants were an international federation of trade unions with whom the plaintiff had purported to enter into a collective agreement in 1980. However, the defendants "blacked" the ship when it started a regular run between Swedish ports, because the Swedish seamen's union objected to the use of a Spanish and not a Swedish crew. The plaintiff claimed damages for breach of the 1980 collective agreement, and the issue was raised of whether the law governing the agreement was English or Spanish. The Court of Appeal held that it was Spanish; but the court also had to consider whether to give effect to section 18 of the Trade Union and Labour Relations Act 1974, which declared that a collective agreement "shall be conclusively presumed not to have been intended by the parties to be a legally enforceable contract unless the agreement . . . states that the parties intend that the agreement shall be a legally enforceable contract". It was argued by the defendants that this section was procedural in effect so that an English court should apply the section irrespective of the law governing the contract.

The Court of Appeal held that section 18 was to be classed as substantive and not procedural. In so doing dissatisfaction was expressed[11] with the reasoning in *Leroux v Brown*[12] and, in holding section 18 of the 1974 Act to be substantive, Lord Denning MR had this to say:

It seems to me that the true distinction is between the existence of a contract (which is substantive law) and the remedies for breach of it (which is the procedural law). The right course is to analyse the statute and see whether it negatives the existence of a contract or not. If there is no contract, but the statute says it cannot be enforced (except in writing or within a stated period) that is procedural law. It is governed by the *lex fori*. In this present case, as I construe s 18 of the 1974 Act, it negatives the existence of any contract at all.[13]

(c) How is the distinction to be made?

It remains to consider further how the line between substance and procedure is to be drawn for the purposes of private international law.[14] Only the most general definitions of "the law of procedure" have been given by the English judges. Perhaps the best known is that of Lush LJ: "The mode of proceeding by which a legal right is enforced, as distinguished from the law which gives or defines the right, and which by means of the proceeding the court is to administer the machinery as distinguished from its product."[15] This substitution of "mode of proceeding" for "procedure" does not carry us far. Nor does the definition ensure a just and convenient solution. It implies that, since the owner has chosen to fashion his foreign-acquired right into a new form through the instrumentality of English machinery, he must rest content with the design and movement of that machine. This sounds sensible but if, as in *Leroux v Brown*, the machinery refuses to move, one part of private international law is nullified by another. Nor shall we arrive at a solution if we change the metaphor and concentrate

---

formal validity of a contract: Giuliano and Lagarde Report OJ 1980 C 282/31. This line is continued in the Rome I Regulation.

[10] [1982] 3 All ER 841.

[11] Ibid, at 846.

[12] And with the leading cases on limitation of actions, see *infra*, p 78 et seq.

[13] [1982] 3 All ER 841 at 846; and see at 848–9, per May LJ.

[14] Carruthers, op cit, 696.

[15] *Poyser v Minors* (1881) 7 QBD 329 at 333; adopted in *Re Shoesmith* [1938] 2 KB 637. See Carruthers, op cit, pp 694–6.

on the contrast between right and remedy. They do not always admit of contrast in law. Historically they are inseparably connected. As Goulding J has said:

> Within the municipal confines of a single legal system, right and remedy are indissolubly connected and correlated, each contributing in historical dialogue to the development of the other, and save in very special circumstances, it is as idle to ask whether the court vindicates the suitor's substantive right or gives the suitor a procedural remedy as to ask whether thought is a mental or cerebral process. In fact the court does both things by one and the same act.[16]

The truth is that substance and procedure cannot be relegated to clear-cut categories. There is no preordained dividing line between them which can be discovered by logic alone. Determining the nature of a rule as procedural or substantive cannot be done in the abstract. Although the two must be distinguished, the line between them should be drawn by having regard to the relativity of legal terms and the exact purpose for which the distinction is being made.

This problem was clearly faced by Scarman J in *Re Fuld's Estate (No 3)*[17] when he asked: "When is a question one of substantive law? When is a question merely one of evidence or procedure? I attempt no general answer to these questions; for answer can only be made after an analysis of the specific questions calling for decision, its legal background and factual context." This shows that the line should not be drawn in the same place for all purposes.[18] It should be drawn in the light of the relevant circumstances, one of which is that the purposes of private international law as distinct from municipal law require fulfilment. Thus it is at least arguable that whether section 4 of the Statute of Frauds is of a procedural or substantive nature should be decided differently according to whether a foreign or purely English transaction is involved. The crux of the matter is: Why is the distinction between substance and procedure made in private international law? The answer presumably is: For the convenience of the court. The court, when faced with a conflict of laws problem, though bound to apply the law selected by the choice of law rules, cannot be expected to import all the relevant rules of the foreign law. To apply, for instance, the foreign rules concerned with such matters as service of process, evidence and methods of enforcing judgments would be not only inconvenient but impracticable. Nevertheless, the overriding policy is to apply the foreign substantive law, and if this will be defeated by a slavish adherence to the domestic distinction between substance and procedure, the court should consider whether in the circumstances such adherence is necessary. For: "It is not everything that appears in a treatise on the law of evidence that is to be classified internationally as adjective law, but only provisions of a technical or procedural character—for example rules as to the admissibility of hearsay evidence or what matters may be noticed judicially."[19]

"If we admit", says Cook, "that the 'substantive' shades off by imperceptible degrees into the 'procedural', and that the 'line' between them does not 'exist', to be discovered merely by logic and analysis, but is rather to be drawn so as best to carry out our purpose, we see that our problem resolves itself substantially into this: How far can the court of the forum go in applying the rules taken from the foreign system of law without unduly hindering or inconveniencing itself?"[20] One critic has replied, "Not much farther than we have already gone";[21]

---

[16] *Chase Manhattan Bank NA v Israel-British Bank (London) Ltd* [1981] Ch 105 at 124.

[17] [1968] P 675 at 695.

[18] Cook, op cit, at 344, 352 and 356.

[19] *Mahadervan v Mahadervan* [1964] P 233 at 243.

[20] Cook, *Logical and Legal Bases of the Conflict of Laws*, p 166. A more radical solution has been suggested by Cavers, *The Choice-of-Law Process*, p 289, that "Before trial each party could move . . . for the use of one or more specifically identified procedural rules, to be drawn from the law of the state supplying the substantive law of the case relevant to the issue or issues to which the procedural rules related and to be used for specified purposes in the trial or other proceedings in the case. If the motions were granted, the rules thereby allowed to be used would take the place of the rules of the forum that would otherwise be applied for the same purposes."

[21] Ailes (1941) 39 Mich LR 392, 418.

but at least it would be possible to go far enough to avoid such decisions as *Leroux v Brown*,[22] and a Canadian court has suggested that legislation should be categorised as procedural only if the question is beyond doubt.[23]

It should be borne in mind that the issue whether a rule is one of substance or procedure may arise in more than one context. The most common context, as illustrated by *Leroux v Brown*, is the determination of the nature of a rule of English law in circumstances where the governing law is foreign. If the English rule is procedural, it is applied notwithstanding the foreign governing law. If the English rule is substantive, it is ignored and the foreign law applied. The problem can, however, arise in circumstances where, although the applicable law is foreign, there is some doubt as to whether the rules of that country's law are procedural (and to be ignored in England) or substantive (and to be applied in England).[24] In *Chase Manhattan Bank NA v Israel-British Bank (London) Ltd*:[25]

> The plaintiff, a New York bank, sought to trace and recover in equity £2 million paid by mistake to the account of the defendant bank. The issue was whether the plaintiff bank was entitled to trace the proceeds. Although the court held that there was no significant difference between the two relevant laws, English and New York law, on the right to trace, Goulding J asked the question "whether the equitable right of a person who pays money by mistake to trace and claim such money under the law of New York is conferred by substantive law or is of a merely procedural character".[26] He concluded[27] that the view of an English court would be that the plaintiff New York bank had, under New York law, an equitable interest as a *cestui que* trust which was substantive in nature.

Why did the judge ask the question as to the nature of the equitable right to trace? Presumably, because if he had found the New York rule to be procedural, he would have been unwilling to apply it in England.

2. PARTICULAR ISSUES

Authority is scarcely needed for the proposition that all routine matters arising in the successive stages of litigation must be governed exclusively by English law as being the law of the forum. Such routine matters are generally said to include: service of process; the form that the action must take and whether any special procedure is permissible; the title of the action, eg by what persons and against what persons it should be brought; the competency of witnesses and questions as to the admissibility of evidence; the respective functions of judge and jury; the right of appeal, and, according to some writers, the burden of proof.[28]

It is necessary to consider separately certain issues whose classification as substantive or procedural raises difficulties.

---

[22] Supra, p 74 et seq.
[23] *Block Bros Realty Ltd v Mollard* (1981) 122 DLR (3d) 323 at 328.
[24] Eg *Harding v Wealands* [2007] 2 AC 1.
[25] [1981] Ch 105.
[26] Ibid, at 122.
[27] Ibid, at 127.
[28] Lord Reid has said in *Carl Zeiss Stiftung v Rayner and Keeler Ltd (No 2)* [1967] 1 AC 853 at 919 that "estoppel is a matter for the *lex fori* but the *lex fori* ought to be developed in a manner consistent with good sense," see infra, Chapter 15.

(a) The time within which an action must be brought

Until 1984, English law was committed to the view that statutes of limitation, if they merely specified a certain time after which rights could not be enforced by action, affected procedure and not substance.[29] This meant that limitation was governed by English law, as the law of the forum, and any limitation provision of the applicable law was ignored.[30] Where, however, it could be shown that the effect of a statute of limitation of the foreign applicable law was not just to bar the plaintiff's remedy, but also to extinguish his cause of action,[31] then the English courts would be prepared to regard the foreign rule as substantive and to be applied in England.[32]

The common law rule, which has been criticised in a number of common law jurisdictions,[33] tends to have no counterpart in civil law countries which usually treat statutes of limitation as substantive.[34] Furthermore, the Contracts (Applicable Law) Act 1990, implementing the European Community Convention on the Law Applicable to Contractual Obligations (1980),[35] provides that the law which governs the essential validity of a contract is to govern "the various ways of extinguishing obligations, and prescription and limitation of actions".[36] In 1982 the Law Commission concluded that "there is a clear case for the reform of the present English rule"[37] and their recommendations formed the basis of the Foreign Limitation Periods Act 1984.[38]

The general principle of the 1984 Act abandons the common law approach which favoured the application of the domestic law of limitation.[39] Instead, the English court is to apply the law which governs the substantive issue according to English choice of law rules, and this new approach is applied to both actions[40] and arbitrations[41] in England. In the case of those few tort claims, such as defamation, to which the common law choice of law rules still apply,[42] English law, as the law of the forum, will remain relevant[43] because of the choice of law rule which requires actionability both by the law of the forum and by the law of the place of the tort.[44] The corollary of the main rule is that English law is no longer automatically to

---

[29] *Black-Clawson International Ltd v Papierwerke Waldhof-Aschaffenburg AG* [1975] AC 591 at 630.

[30] *British Linen Co v Drummond* (1830) 10 B & C 903; *Huber v Steiner* (1835) 2 Bing NC 202; *Don v Lippmann* (1837) 5 C1 & Fin 1; *Harris v Quine* (1869) LR 4 QB 653. Contrast *Tolofson v Jensen* (1994) 120 DLR (4th) 289.

[31] Examples in English law are provided by acquisitive prescription under the Prescription Act 1832 or express extinction of the former owner's title under the Limitation Act 1980, ss 3 and 17.

[32] *Harris v Quine* (1869) LR 4 QB 653 at 656.

[33] Law Com No 114 (1982), paras 3.3–3.8.

[34] See Law Commission Working Paper No 75 (1980), paras 25–6. But see, in South Africa, *Society of Lloyd's v Price; Society of Lloyd's v Lee* 2006 5 SA 393 (SCA), discussed by Forsyth (2006) 2 J Priv Int L 169, and (2006) 2 J Priv Int L 425, and by Neels 2007 Journal of South African Law 178. See also *Society of Lloyd's v Romahn* 2006 4 SA 23 (C).

[35] Infra, p 667.

[36] Sch 1, Art 10(1)(d); and see North, *Contract Conflicts* (1982), p 16. Cf Rome I Regulation, Art 12 (1) (d) and Rome II Regulation, Art 15(h), examined infra, p 865. On the impact of the Rome I and II Regulations on the distinction between substance and procedure see Schoeman [2010] LMCLQ 81; Briggs (2009) 125 LQR 1291, at 195; Illmer (2009) CJQ 237.

[37] Law Com No 114 (1982), para 3.10.

[38] Carter (1985) 101 LQR 68; Stone [1985] LMCLQ 497. Cf, for Scotland, Prescription and Limitation (Scotland) Act 1984, s 4.

[39] S 1(5); but the doctrine of renvoi may be relevant in determining, under s 1(1), the relevant foreign substantive law; see Law Com No 114 (1983), para 4.33; Stone [1985] LMCLQ 497, 506–7.

[40] S 1(1)(a).

[41] Arbitration Act 1996, s 13(1)(4)(a). See also Foreign Limitation Periods Act 1984, ss 1A and 1B.

[42] Under the Private International Law (Miscellaneous Provisions) Act 1995, s 13, infra, p 885.

[43] S 1(2), of the 1984 Act.

[44] *Metall und Rohstoff AG v Donaldson Lufkin & Jenrette Inc* [1990] 1 QB 391 at 438; *Arab Monetary Fund v Hashim* [1996] 1 Lloyd's Rep 589; and see, infra, pp 777–8.

be applied. There is, of course, a significant difference between a rule under which a claim is to be held to be statute barred in England if statute barred under the governing law, a reform which seems widely to be welcomed, and a further rule that, if the claim is not statute barred abroad, it must be allowed to proceed in England. This is more controversial and the question whether any, and if so what, restriction should be placed on the application of the foreign rule was examined at length by the Law Commission.[45] At the end of the day, they decided not to adopt, for example, any "long-stop" provision such as that an action could not proceed after, say, fifty years;[46] but concluded that the courts had adequate power under the doctrine of public policy to disapply either an extremely long or a very short foreign limitation period. Such a public policy exception to the general rule is to be found in section 2(1) of the 1984 Act; but it is worth noting that it is reinforced by a provision,[47] not found in the Law Commission's draft Bill, to the effect that the causing of undue hardship to a party by the application of the foreign period would be contrary to public policy.[48] Such hardship has been held to arise where the defendants had agreed to an extension of time which proved to be ineffective under the governing law, the basis of the hardship being the parties' unawareness that that law would apply.[49]

There are some practical limits to the application of a foreign limitation rule. For example, it is for English law to determine the time at which the limitation period stops running against the claimant, eg when he commences litigation[50]—to do otherwise might involve the English court in detailed matters of foreign procedure. For similar reasons, the English court will ignore foreign rules as to the interruption of the running of the period because of the absence of a party from the jurisdiction.[51] On the other hand, if there is a discretion under the foreign law, eg to suspend the running of the period, the English court must attempt to exercise it in the same way as it would be exercised in the foreign courts.[52] The rule that equitable relief may be refused apart from a statute of limitation, if for example the claimant has been guilty of delay, has been preserved. Yet still, where there is a foreign applicable law, the English court must exercise its discretion by having regard to the relevant rules of any foreign applicable law.[53]

In 2006, the Legal Affairs Committee of the European Parliament[54] requested that the European Commission should submit a legislative proposal on limitation periods in relation to cross-border personal injury and fatal accident claims. The view of the Committee is that, given current divergences among Member States as regards limitation periods, there may be sufficient justification for the setting of common minimum requirements throughout Europe, by means of legislation, at least in respect of cross-border litigation cases.[55] A consultation followed in 2012.

---

[45] Law Com No 114 (1982), paras 4.35–4.50.

[46] It might be noted that the Scottish Law Commission, having toyed with a similar idea, rejected it as inappropriate and undesirable; Scot Law Com No 74 (1983), para 7.8; cf Carter (1985) 101 LQR 68, 70.

[47] S 2(2); and see *Arab Monetary Fund v Hashim* [1996] 1 Lloyd's Rep 589 at 599–600.

[48] See *Harley v Smith* [2009] EWHC 56 (QB), at 94. The test was approved on appeal [2010] EWCA Civ 78.

[49] *The Komninos S* [1990] 1 Lloyd's Rep 541.

[50] S 1(3).

[51] S 2(3); and see Law Com No 114 (1982), paras 4.26–4.32.

[52] S 1(4).

[53] S 4(3). Section 3 of the 1984 Act which deals with foreign judgments on limitation points is discussed infra, Chapter 15. Cf, in Canada, *Vogler v Szendroi* 2008 NSCA 18.

[54] Having recourse to the special powers conferred on it by Art 192(2) of the EC Treaty.

[55] European Parliament, Legal Affairs Committee, Draft Report 2006/2014 (INI), PE 367.972v03-00 (May 2006).

(b) Evidence[56]

(i) Evidence a matter for the law of the forum

Every system of law has its own principles for deciding the way in which the truth of facts, acts and documents shall be ascertained, and it is obvious that those principles must usually apply whether the question at issue is domestic or foreign in origin. If another system of evidence were admissible it would be equally reasonable to permit another mode of trial.[57] "Whether a witness is competent or not", said Lord Brougham "whether a certain matter requires to be proved by writing or not, whether certain evidence proves a certain fact or not, that is to be determined by the law of the country where the question arises."[58]

Leroux v Brown[59] is an outstanding example of the rule that the law of the forum determines whether written evidence is required. There is, however, in the case of contracts an important statutory exception to the rule that proof of facts is for the law of the forum. Under the Contracts (Applicable Law) Act 1990,[60] a contract or an act intended to have legal effect may be proved in any way allowed by the law of the forum or by reference to any law governing the formal validity of the contract or act,[61] provided that the mode of proof under such law can be administered in the courts of the forum. This provision is echoed, in respect of non-contractual obligations, in Article 22(2) of the Rome II Regulation,[62] which provides that acts intended to have legal effect may be proved by any mode of proof recognised by the law of the forum or by any of the laws governing the formal validity of the act,[63] provided that such mode of proof can be administered by the forum.

(ii) Distinction between interpretation and proof of document

With regard to the evidence necessary to prove a certain fact, an important distinction exists where a document is in issue, in that the interpretation of the document must be distinguished from its proof. The foreign document must be interpreted according to the system of law by which it is governed, but it must be proved in accordance with the requirements of the law of the forum.[64] The English court that is hearing the matter must investigate the governing law as a fact and must take such expert evidence as shows what the construction would be in the foreign country, but at that point the reference to the foreign law must stop. What evidence that law admits or rejects is irrelevant.[65] For example, the meaning of technical expressions used in a charter-party must be ascertained by reference to the governing law, but the existence of the charter-party itself must be proved in the manner required by English law. Thus, in *Brown v Thornton*:[66]

---

[56] See generally Layton and Mercer, Chapter 7. See also Anton, 27.14-19 and Crawford and Carruthers, Ch 8.

[57] *Yates v Thomson* (1835) 3 Cl & Fin 544 at 587.

[58] *Bain v Whitehaven Rly Co* (1850) 3 HL Cas 1 at 19; and see *Mahadervan v Mahadervan* [1964] P 233 at 243; *Re Fuld's Estate (No 3)* [1968] P 675 at 697–8.

[59] (1852) 12 CB 801, supra, p 76. See now the Contracts (Applicable Law) Act 1990 and the Giuliano and Lagarde Report OJ 1980 C 282/31, infra, Chapter 19. The Australian Courts explicitly rejected the approach in *Leroux v Brown*, see *Tipperary Developments Pty Ltd v The State of Western Australia* [2009] WASCA 126, endorsing *John Pfeiffer Pty Ltd v Rogerson* (2000) 203 CLR 503. The English courts however refused to follow the latter decision, see *Harding v Wealands* [2006] UKHL 32.

[60] Sch 1, Art 14(2). Cf Rome I Regulation, Art 18(2). For further statutory exceptions, see the Army Act 1955, the Medical Act 1983 and *McAllister v General Medical Council* [1993] AC 388.

[61] Art 9.

[62] Infra, Chapter 20.

[63] Art 21.

[64] Eg *Wicken v Wicken* [1999] Fam 224.

[65] *Yates v Thomson* (1835) 3 Cl & Fin 544 at 586.

[66] (1837) 6 Ad & El 185.

An action was brought in England to cover freight due under a charter-party that had been made in Batavia, by means of the instrument being written in the book of a notary, and signed by the parties. Each party received a copy, signed and sealed by the notary, and counter-signed by the principal governmental officer of Java. A charter-party was sufficiently proved in a Javanese court by production of the notary's book, but, since such books were not allowed to be removed from Java, courts in other parts of the Dutch dominions admitted the copies as evidence.

The plaintiff was nonsuited owing to his failure to prove the charter-party in the manner required by English law. The original contract contained in the notary's book was not produced. Secondary evidence would have been admissible had it been given in the form either of a copy made by the public officer of a court, or of a copy made by some person authorised by each party to give a binding copy, but neither of these ways was available.

The Crown, however, has power under the Evidence (Foreign Dominion and Colonial Documents) Act 1933[67] to issue Orders in Council providing that entries contained in the public registries of other countries, whether part of the Commonwealth or not, shall be admissible evidence in English proceedings, and that they shall be proved by means of duly authenticated official certificates.[68]

(iii) Taking of evidence within the EU:[69] Council Regulation (EC) No 1206/2001

This matter is regulated by Council Regulation (EC) No 1206/2001 on co-operation between the courts of the Member States in the taking of evidence in civil or commercial matters.[70] In order to facilitate the proper functioning of the internal market, it was thought necessary to improve co-operation between the courts of Member States in the taking of evidence; in particular to simplify and accelerate relevant procedures for the transmission and execution of requests for taking evidence,[71] and also to allow a court in one Member State (the requesting court), in accordance with its own law, to take evidence directly in another Member State (the requested court), if accepted by the latter State and subject to such conditions as the requested court may determine.[72] Each Member State is required to designate a "central body" to assist in the operation of the European scheme,[73] but it is expected that the transmission and execution of requests for the taking of evidence generally should be made directly and by the most rapid means possible between the courts of the Member States.

In terms of Article 21, the Regulation shall prevail over other provisions contained in bilateral or multilateral agreements concluded by Member States, including, in particular, the 1970 Hague Convention on the Taking of Evidence Abroad in Civil or Commercial Matters (to which the United Kingdom is a party), in relations between the Member States party thereto.

---

[67] As amended by the Oaths and Evidence (Overseas Authorities and Countries) Act 1963, s 5; Fentiman, *Foreign Law in English Courts* (1998), p 225. Evidence of documents may also be admitted under s 7 of the Civil Evidence Act 1995 (see formerly, s 1 of the Evidence Act 1938: *Henaff v Henaff* [1966] 1 WLR 598). See Dicey, Morris and Collins, para 17-039 et seq.

[68] See *North v North* (1936) 52 TLR 380; *Motture v Motture* [1955] 3 All ER 242n, [1955] 1 WLR 1066.

[69] Except Denmark: Council Regulation (EC) No 1206/2001, recital (22).

[70] Entered into force on 1 July 2001, and having effect throughout the EU, with the exception of Denmark, as from 1 January 2004. See Report from the Commission to the Council, the European Parliament and the European Economic and Social Committee on the application of Regulation (EC) No 1206/2001 (COM (2007) 769 final), prepared in accordance with Art 23 of the Regulation. See also Practice Guide for the application of the Regulation, drawn up by the Commission Services, and available at: http://ec.europa.eu/civiljustice/evidence/evidence_ec_guide_en.pdf.

[71] Recitals (2) and (8).

[72] Recital (15).

[73] Art 3. The central body for England and Wales is the Senior Master, Queen's Bench Division, Royal Courts of Justice.

(a) Evidence by means of request

Chapter II of the Regulation deals with the transmission and execution of requests for the taking of evidence. Article 4 lays down strict rules regarding the form and content of requests, which must be presented in an official (or accepted) language of the requested state.[74]

The requested court is required to execute the request expeditiously[75] and in accordance with its own law.[76] If it is not possible for the request to be executed by the requested court within ninety days of the court's receipt thereof, the court should inform the requesting court, stating reasons for the delay in execution.[77] If the request cannot be executed because it does not contain all information required in terms of Article 4, the requested court shall inform the requesting court thereof without delay, and shall request that it send the missing information.[78]

If permitted by the law of the requesting court, parties and their representatives are entitled to be present at the taking of evidence,[79] and it is competent also for representatives of the requesting court to be present at the taking of evidence, if compatible with the law of the Member State of that court (and subject to such conditions as may be imposed by the requested court),[80] in order to enhance the evaluation of the evidence.[81] Alternatively, the requesting court may ask the requested court to utilise communications technology, such as video conferencing or teleconferencing.[82]

Where necessary in executing a request, the requested court shall apply the appropriate coercive measures in the instances and to the extent as are provided for by the law of the Member State of the requested court for the execution of a request made for the same purpose by its national authorities or one of the parties concerned.[83]

Possibilities for the requested court to refuse the request are confined to strictly limited, exceptional situations,[84] such as where a person claims the right to refuse to give evidence, or to be prohibited from giving evidence, under the law of the State of the requested court, or under the law of the State of the requesting court (subject to confirmation by the requesting court);[85] or where the request falls outside the scope of the Regulation, or where execution of the request falls outside the functions of the judiciary of the requested court.[86] Significantly, Article 14.3 provides that execution of the request cannot be refused solely on the ground that under the law of the State of the requested court that court has exclusive jurisdiction over the subject matter of the action, or because the law of the State of the requested court would not admit the right of action on it.

As regards costs, Article 18 provides that the execution of a request for the taking of evidence shall not give rise to a claim for any reimbursement of taxes or costs. Nevertheless, the requested court may require the requesting court to ensure the prompt reimbursement of experts' and interpreters' fees, and costs occasioned by use of communications technology.[87]

---

[74] Art 5.
[75] Recital (10), and Art 6.
[76] Recital (12), and Art 10(2).
[77] Art 10(1).
[78] Art 8(1).
[79] Art 11.
[80] Art 12(4).
[81] Recital (14); and Art 12.
[82] Art 10(4).
[83] Art 13.
[84] Recital (11), and Art 14.
[85] Art 14(1).
[86] Art 14(2)(a) and (b). Additionally, the request may be refused if the requesting court does not comply within thirty days with the request by the requested court to supply information pursuant to Art 8 (Art 14(2)(c)), or if a deposit or advance asked for in accordance with Art 18.3 has not been made within sixty days (Art 14(2)(d)).
[87] Art 18(2) and (3).

(b) <u>Direct taking of evidence by the requesting court</u>

A request by the court of one Member State for the direct taking of evidence may be made in relation to judicial proceedings, commenced or contemplated.[88] Direct taking of evidence can take place only if it can be performed voluntarily, without need of coercive measures.[89] The taking of such evidence shall be performed by a member of the judicial personnel, or by a designated expert, in accordance with the law of the Member State of the requesting court.[90]

As with the taking of evidence by means of request, the requested court is required to act expeditiously and in accordance with its own law.[91] The central body of the requested Member State must inform the requesting court within thirty days of receipt if the request is accepted, and, if necessary, under what conditions the performance is to be carried out.[92] Similarly, the grounds for refusal to allow the direct taking of evidence are restricted to cases where the request does not fall within the scope of the Regulation; or where the request does not contain all the necessary information pursuant to Article 4; or where the direct taking of evidence requested is contrary to fundamental principles of law in its Member State.[93]

(iv) *Taking of evidence outside the EU: Evidence (Proceedings in Other Jurisdictions) Act 1975; Protection of Trading Interests Act 1980*

The Evidence (Proceedings in Other Jurisdictions) Act 1975[94] gives effect to the Hague Convention on the Taking of Evidence Abroad in Civil and Commercial Matters (1970).[95] It empowers the High Court to order the taking of evidence (including its video recording)[96] in England when requested to do so by a foreign court, if the evidence is to be obtained for the purpose of actual or contemplated proceedings in any civil or commercial matter[97] or actual criminal proceedings.[98] In general, the court has a discretion whether or not to order such taking of evidence and it will refuse permission where the request amounts to a "fishing expedition";[99] but under the Protection of Trading Interests Act 1980 it must refuse to make an order

---

[88] Art 1(2).

[89] Art 17(2).

[90] Art 17(3).

[91] Art 17(6).

[92] Art 17(4). The central body may assign a court of its Member State to take part to ensure the proper application of Art 17.

[93] Art 17(5).

[94] See Sutherland (1982) 31 ICLQ 784; Collins (1986) 35 ICLQ 765.

[95] The English courts regard their jurisdiction hereunder as wholly statutory: *Boeing Co v PPG Industries Inc* [1988] 3 All ER 839. However, the US Supreme Court has held that the procedures of the Hague Convention are optional, not mandatory: *Société Nationale Industrielle Aérospatiale v United States District Court for the Southern District of Iowa* 107 S Ct 2542 (1987); Slomanson (1988) 37 ICLQ 391; Minch (1988) 22 Int Lawyer 511; Prescott and Alley, ibid, 939; Born and Hoing (1990) 24 Int Lawyer 393; Griffin and Bravin (1991) 25 Int Lawyer 331; Black (1991) 40 ICLQ 901. For a comparative analysis, see Morse in Plender (ed), *Legal History and Comparative Law: Essays in Honour of Albert Kiralfy* (1990), p 159.

[96] *Barber & Sons v Lloyd's Underwriters* [1987] QB 103, [1986] 2 All ER 845; and *R v Forsyth* (1997) Times, 8 April, CA. For implications of the use of video and audio conferencing technology in transnational litigation, see Davies (2007) 55 AJCL 205.

[97] *Re State of Norway's Application (Nos 1 and 2)* [1990] 1 AC 723; Carter [1989] BYBIL 494; Lipstein (1990) 39 ICLQ 120. The House of Lords held that the proceedings had to be so classified under the law of both the requesting and requested states and, on this basis, included fiscal proceedings. A Special Commission (1989) of the Hague Conference on Private International Law has preferred an autonomous interpretation of the phrase; see Mann (1990) 106 LQR 354.

[98] *Re Westinghouse Electric Corpn Uranium Contract* [1978] AC 547; *Re Asbestos Insurance Coverage Cases* [1985] 1 WLR 331, HL; *R v Rathbone, ex p Dikko* [1985] QB 630; and see Sutherland (1982) 31 ICLQ 784.

[99] *Re State of Norway's Application (Nos 1 & 2)* [1990] 1 AC 723 at 766–767, 810; *First American Corpn v Zayed* [1999] 1 WLR 1154; cf *Lord Advocate, Petitioner* 1993 SC 638; and *Lord Advocate, Petitioner* 1998 SLT 835.

if the request by the foreign court infringes the jurisdiction of the United Kingdom or is otherwise prejudicial to the United Kingdom.[100] The 1980 Act was passed because of concern over the effect of American anti-trust litigation involving British companies[101] and it also permits[102] the Secretary of State to give directions prohibiting compliance with an order of a foreign court requiring a person in the United Kingdom to produce commercial documents, not within the territorial jurisdiction of the foreign court, or to provide commercial information from such documents if it appears to the Secretary of State that the request infringes United Kingdom jurisdiction, or is otherwise prejudicial to the United Kingdom, or if compliance would be prejudicial to the security of the United Kingdom or its relations with other governments.[103]

(v) Interpretation distinguished from evidence

Evidence must be distinguished from interpretation.[104] The rule of English law, for instance, that if a contract is written, "the writing is the grand criterion of what terms are intended to be contractual and what not"[105] and that therefore oral evidence is inadmissible to add to, vary or contradict the writing, is a rule of evidence properly so called that must be applied in every English action.[106] But, despite its deceptive similarity, the rule which admits oral evidence to show that the parties intended to incorporate a certain condition customarily included in a contract of a particular kind is a rule of interpretation that is not necessarily applicable merely because the action is in England. It concerns interpretation, not proof.[107] Owing to the imperfect manner in which the contract has been drafted, the intention of the parties is not clear and the object of the particular rule is to explain what they meant.

A distinction must also be made between facts that are relevant and the evidence by which such facts are proved, for the former fall to be decided according to the law governing the transaction, while the latter is a matter of procedure for the law of the forum. This was considered in *The Gaetano and Maria*.[108]

> An action was brought in England on a bottomry bond given at the Azores by the master of a ship flying the Italian flag, without any communication with his owners. By Italian law the bond was valid; by English law its validity depended on proof that at the time it was given the ship was in distress and in need of repair and that the circumstances were such as to render it impossible for the master to communicate with the cargo-owners. It was argued that, since proof of the necessity of immediate repairs is a matter of evidence, the question of the validity of the bond must be determined by English law, being the law of the forum. The flaw in this argument was exposed by the Court of Appeal.

The sole fact in issue was one of substance, namely, whether the master had authority to give a valid bond. This was a question that fell to be determined by Italian law, the law of the flag. The equivalent English rule on this question no doubt differed from that under Italian law, but since it affected substance, not procedure, it was not to be invoked merely because the action was brought in England.

---

[100] S 4.

[101] Huntley (1981) 30 ICLQ 213; for rather different American perspectives, see Batista (1983) 17 Int Lawyer 61; Blythe (1983) 31 AJCL 99.

[102] S 2. For the effect of the 1980 Act on the recognition and enforcement of foreign judgments, see infra, Chapter 15.

[103] See *British Airways Board v Laker Airways Ltd* [1984] QB 142 at 195–8; affd on this issue [1985] AC 58 at 87–92.

[104] See *Re Barker* [1995] 2 VR 439.

[105] *Korner v Witkowitzer* [1950] 2 KB 128 at 162.

[106] [1950] 2 KB 128 at 162–3.

[107] [1950] 2 KB 128 at 163.

[108] (1882) 7 PD 137.

(vi) Presumptions and burden of proof

A controversial question is whether presumptions and burden of proof are matters that affect procedure or substance.[109] The classification of presumptions will depend on their nature and effect.[110] Presumptions of fact pose no problem for they raise no legal issue. Presumptions of law may be either irrebuttable or rebuttable. The former would appear to be substantive in effect,[111] but it is not clear how the latter should be classified. It has been suggested[112] that those which apply to a restricted class of case should be treated as substantive, but that it is uncertain how presumptions of general application, such as the presumptions of death or validity of marriage, should be classified. There is authority for treating the presumption as to the validity of a marriage as substantive so that a marriage may be upheld under the presumption of the foreign governing law.[113] But if the English law presumption favoured the validity of marriage whilst the foreign one did not, it is tempting to conclude that the public policy of the forum in favour of validity would prevail.

Whilst there may be much to be said for the view that the burden of proof is regulated by the law governing matters of substance,[114] the contrary view has been voiced.[115] Indeed, in *Re Fuld's Estate (No 3)*[116] Scarman J concluded that the English Probate Court "must in all matters of burden of proof follow scrupulously its own *lex fori*".[117]

The question whether a rule distributing the burden of proof affects substance or procedure has arisen in the USA on a plea of contributory negligence. There is authority for the view that the burden of proving contributory negligence is a question of substantive law, to be determined by the law governing such substantive issues.[118]

Again, in the case of contractual and non-contractual obligations, there are special legislative rules. The Contracts (Applicable Law) Act 1990 provides[119] that the rules of the law governing the substance of the contract which "raise presumptions of law or determine the burden of proof" shall be applied. It is only if these rules are to be classified as ones of substance that they are to be applied in place of the law of the forum. If they are merely procedural, they are inapplicable.[120] As regards non-contractual obligations, Article 22(1) of the Rome II Regulation[121] provides an equivalent rule, to the effect that the law governing a non-contractual obligation under the Regulation shall apply to the extent that, in matters of non-contractual obligations, it contains rules which raise presumptions of law or determine the burden of proof.

---

[109] See Wolff, pp 234–6.

[110] Dicey, Morris and Collins, paras 7-036–7-037.

[111] *Re Cohn* [1945] Ch 5; see *Monterosso Shipping Co v International Transport Workers Federation* [1982] 3 All ER 841.

[112] Dicey, Morris and Collins, paras 7-036–7-037; and see Morse, *Torts in Private International Law*, pp 178–9.

[113] *De Thoren v A-G* (1876) 1 App Cas 686; *Mahadervan v Mahadervan* [1964] P 233.

[114] Dicey, Morris and Collins, para 7-034.

[115] *The Roberta* (1937) 58 Lloyd's Rep 159.

[116] [1968] P 675.

[117] Ibid, at 697; and see at 698–9.

[118] See *Fitzpatrick v International Rly* 252 NY 127 (1929); Hancock, *Torts in the Conflict of Laws*, 159 et seq; Webb and Brownlie (1962) 50 Can Bar Rev 79, 87–9; Morse, *Torts in Private International Law*, pp 174–8.

[119] Sch 1, Art 14(1). Cf Rome I Regulation, Art 18.

[120] Indeed they fall outside the legislation altogether: Art 1(2)(h), infra, Chapter 19.

[121] Infra, Chapter 20.

(c) Parties

Two questions need to be considered in connection with the identity of the parties to the action. The first is the determination of the appropriate person to sue,[122] and the second concerns the identity of the person to be sued.[123]

(i) *The proper claimant*

The first question is whether the name in which an action may be brought falls to be determined exclusively by the law of the forum on the ground that it is a mere matter of procedure. It is a question that arises principally where the claimant is not the original owner of the subject matter of the dispute, but has acquired it derivatively from the original owner, as, for instance, in the case of the assignment of a debt or other intangible movable. In those cases where English law requires the assignee to sue in the name of the assignor, it has been said,[124] and indeed on one occasion held,[125] that the requirement must be observed in an action in this country, even though it is not necessary by the law governing the transaction.

But on principle it is doubtful whether every rule that regulates the name in which an action must be brought is merely procedural in character. It would seem to be an unwarranted extension of the province of procedure, at any rate in cases falling within the sphere of private international law, to regard a rule as procedural if the effect is to deprive the claimant of a right which he has definitely acquired under the governing legal system.[126] If, for instance, English law still regarded a contractual right as so essentially personal as to be actionable only at the suit of the original contracting party, it would surely be the negation of principle, and indeed of justice, to enforce such a rule indiscriminately as being one of procedure, and thus to defeat a claimant who had acquired a contractual right derivatively under some legal system that regarded the transaction as valid. To adopt this attitude would be to mistake substance for procedure. There is little authority on the matter, but the early case of *O'Callaghan v Thomond*[127] at least shows that the English courts have not always adopted this attitude: the assignee of an Irish judgment brought an action of debt in his own name in England to recover the amount of the judgment. He was entitled so to sue by Irish law. The argument of counsel for the defendant was instructive. Though admitting the general principle that the law of one country would recognise and enforce obligations raised by the law of another country, he contended that the principle applied only to the substance of the contract, and could neither affect the form of enforcing an obligation in another country nor be allowed to contravene the general rule of English law that intangible movables were unassignable. He therefore argued that no action could be maintained in the present circumstances except in the name of the person who recovered the judgment. The court, however, was unanimous that the rule was a matter of substance, not procedure.

One problem which can arise in determining who is a proper claimant is whether a person will be permitted to sue in England in a representative capacity, relying on an appointment

---

[122] See Crawford (2000) 6 Jur Rev 347; Anton, 27.08-10 and *FMC Corpn v Russell* 1999 SLT 99.

[123] See Prott (1989) V Hague Recueil 215, 245–54; *International Association of Science and Technology for Development v Hamza* (1995) 122 DLR (4th) 92 and Anton, 27.11-13.

[124] *Wolff v Oxholm* (1817) 6 M & S 92 at 99.

[125] *Jeffery v M'Taggart* (1817) 6 M & S 126.

[126] In *Bumper Development Corpn v Metropolitan Police Comr* [1991] 1 WLR 1362, the Court of Appeal, whilst accepting that the issue of whether a foreigner (here a ruined Indian Hindu temple recognised in India as a juristic person) could sue in England was a matter for English law as the law of the forum, took the broad view that it would not be contrary to public policy so to permit it.

[127] (1810) 3 Taunt 82. See also *Innes v Dunlop* (1800) 8 Term Rep 595; *Trimbey v Vignier* (1834) 1 Bing NC 151 at 160; cf *Regas Ltd v Plotkins* (1961) 29 DLR (2d) 282.

made under a foreign law. In *Kamouh v Associated Electrical Industries International Ltd*[128] the plaintiff was Lebanese and, because his brother had disappeared, he caused himself to be appointed by a court in Beirut as his brother's "judicial administrator" and, in that capacity, sought to bring an action in England on a contract made between his brother and the defendants. Parker J refused to recognise his title to sue, observing[129] that, in such cases, there are two conflicting principles to be examined: first, that these courts should as a matter of comity give effect to the curator's or tuteur's right under foreign law to sue in his own name; secondly, that municipal procedure should be applied. The first principle prevails in the case of bankruptcy,[130] receivership[131] and the curatorship of the mentally ill;[132] whilst the second holds sway in respect of an administrator of the property of a deceased[133] or absent[134] person.

(ii) The appropriate defendant

The second question relates to the party sued. It has to be decided whether a foreign rule determining the identity of the party to be sued, or prescribing the order in which parties must be sued, is one of substance or of procedure. In order to do this, it is necessary to classify the exact nature and effect of the rule according to the legal system of which it forms a part.

The question is of special importance in partnership cases.[135] The doctrine, for instance, of English law that any one partner may be sued alone for the totality of the partnership debts is in sharp contrast with the rule, obtaining in many other jurisdictions, that a creditor cannot sue an individual partner until he has first sued the partners jointly and the assets of the firm have been exhausted. If a rule of this nature is pleaded as a bar to an English action, it has to be classified in its foreign context. It must not be dismissed as procedural, if the result will be to impose a liability that does not exist by the law governing the transaction; but if it merely requires the enforcement in a particular manner of an admitted liability, it must be dismissed as a rule affecting only the mode of process. The principle applied by the courts appears to be as follows:

> If the law governing matters of substance considers there to be no doubt as to the defendant's liability, even though the action is conditional on other parties being sued first, then this is a rule of procedure which, unless it obtains in England, is ignored in English proceedings. If, on the other hand, the governing law regards the defendant as being under no liability whatever unless other parties are sued first, it imposes a rule of substance that must be observed in English proceedings.[136]

Thus in an action brought against the executors of a deceased member of a Spanish firm, a claim that, according to Spanish law, creditors could not institute a suit against the separate estate of a deceased partner until they had had recourse to and had exhausted the property

---

128 [1980] QB 199.
129 Ibid, at 206.
130 *Macaulay v Guaranty Trust Co of New York* (1927) 44 TLR 99.
131 *Schemmer v Property Resources Ltd* [1975] Ch 273, where it is emphasised, at 287, that recognition will depend on there being sufficient connection between the defendant and the country in which the receiver was appointed; and see *Thorne, Ernst & Whinney Inc v Sulpetro Ltd* (1987) 47 DLR (4th) 315; *White v Verkouille* [1990] 2 Qd R 191.
132 *Didisheim v London and Westminster Bank* [1900] 2 Ch 15, infra, pp 1247–8.
133 *New York Breweries Co v A-G* [1899] AC 62.
134 *Kamouh v Associated Electrical Industries Ltd* [1980] QB 199.
135 Eg *Oxnard Financing SA v Rahn (Legal Personality of Swiss Partnership)* [1998] 1 WLR 1465 (CA). It may also arise in cases where, under the foreign law, a creditor must sue the principal debtor before he can sue a surety. This rule has been held to be procedural: *Waung v Subbotovsky* [1968] 3 NSWR 499; affd on other grounds 121 CLR 337.
136 *General Steam Navigation Co v Guillou* (1843) 11 M & W 877; *Bank of Australasia v Harding* (1850) 9 CB 661; *Bullock v Caird* (1875) LR 10 QB 276; *Re Doetsch* [1896] 2 Ch 836. The suggested principle is criticised by Wolff, p 240.

of the firm was not upheld because the rule in question merely determined the mode of procedure.[137]

The distinction was neatly raised in the leading case of *General Steam Navigation Co v Guillou*,[138] where the facts were as follows:

> The plaintiffs brought an action in England to recover damages for injury caused to one of their ships by the negligent navigation of a French ship which at the time of the accident was under the direction and management of the defendant's servants. The offending ship belonged to a French company of which the defendant was a shareholder and acting director.

The third plea to the action stated that:

> By the law of France the defendant . . . was not . . . responsible for or liable to be sued . . . individually, or in his own name or person, in any manner whatsoever, in respect of the said causes of action, . . . but by the law of France the said company alone . . . or the master in command for the time being of the said ship, was . . . responsible for, and liable to be sued . . . for, the said causes of action.

The one question, therefore, that fell to be decided here was whether the French law, as disclosed in the plea, absolved the defendant from all liability in any circumstances, or whether it imposed on him an undoubted, though a joint, liability. Although the court unanimously took this distinction,[139] the judges of the Court of Exchequer were equally divided on the question on the facts, although the plea clearly alleged a denial of liability by French law. Lord Abinger and Alderson B held that French law merely required the defendant to be sued jointly with his co-owners in the name of the company; while Barons Parke and Gurney considered that according to the plea the defendant incurred no responsibility whatsoever, joint or several, for the acts of the master. This judicial difference of opinion on the question of fact is of no great moment, for the importance of the decision lies in the clearness with which the general principle is stated.

A different approach is applied if the Rome II Regulation applies.[140] Its article 15(a)[141] provides for the application of the substantive applicable law (lex causae) to "the determination of persons who may be held liable for acts performed by them"[142] and this also encompasses the question of capacity to incur liability.[143] Article 15(c) then goes on to apply the law applicable to the non-contractual obligation to the question whether "a right to claim damages or a remedy may be transferred, including by inheritance". And finally that law also applies to determine the persons who are entitled to compensation for damage they sustained personally[144] and the liability for the acts of another person.[145] This restricts the scope of the law of the forum as the procedural law in this area greatly.

---

[137] *Re Doetsch*, supra.

[138] Supra.

[139] (1843) 11 M & W 877 at 895.

[140] Beaumont and Tang (2008) 12 Edin L Rev 131.

[141] See *Actavis UK Ltd v Eli Lilly & Co* [2015] EWCA Civ 555, paras 130–45.

[142] Direct actions against the insurer in cases of road accidents are dealt with in Article 18. See also *Maher v Groupama Grand Est* [2009] EWCA Civ 1191 and already in a pre-Rome II setting *Keefe v Mapfre Mutualidad Compania de Seguros y Reaaseguros SA* [2015] EWCA Civ 598, paras 76–86.

[143] A Dickinson, *The Rome II Regulation*, (2008), paras 14.09–14.12. But contrast this with the approach under the Rome I Regulation, Art 1(2)(a).

[144] Article 15(f).

[145] Article 15(g).

(d) Priorities

It has consistently been held that the order in which property in the possession of the court is distributable among creditors must be governed by English law. The priority of creditors in such a case is a procedural matter that is determinable by the law of the forum;[146] though it does not necessarily follow that the forum's rule as to priorities should be the same in an international claim as in a purely domestic case.[147] The law of the forum governs because the issue of priority forms no part of the transaction under which a creditor has acquired his right. It is extrinsic and comprises in effect a privilege dependent on the law of the country where the remedy is sought.[148] Thus priorities of creditors claiming in bankruptcy or in the administration of a deceased insolvent's estate are governed exclusively by the law of the forum.[149] It is the same in the case of liens. Where, for instance, two or more persons prosecute claims against a ship that has been arrested in England, the order in which they are entitled to be paid is governed exclusively by English law.[150]

In the case of a right *in rem* such as a lien, however, this principle must not be allowed to obscure the rule that the substantive right of the creditor depends on the governing law. The validity and nature of the right must be distinguished from the order in which it ranks in relation to other claims. Before it can determine the order of payment, the court should examine the law governing the transaction upon which the claimant relies in order to verify the validity of the right and to establish its precise nature. Once the nature of the right is ascertained in this way, then the principle of procedure should come into play and determine that the order of payment prescribed by English law for a right of that particular kind shall govern.

Whilst this is the basis on which courts ought to proceed, decisions in relation to maritime liens have not consistently followed this line.[151] A clear and, it is suggested, correct illustration of the approach to be adopted is provided by *The Colorado*.[152]

At least one earlier decision[153] had failed[154] to draw the crucial distinction between the substance of the right, an issue for the governing law, and the question of priorities, a remedial matter for the law of the forum. A similar failure is evident in the decision of the majority in the Privy Council in *The Halcyon Isle*.[155]

---

[146] *Pardo v Bingham* (1868) LR 6 Eq 485; *Re Melbourn* (1870) 6 Ch App 64; *The Colorado* [1923] P 102; *The Halcyon Isle* [1981] AC 221; distinguish priority of assignees of intangible movables, infra, Chapter 30.

[147] Carter (1983) 54 BYBIL 207, 211–12.

[148] *Harrison v Sterry* (1809) 5 Cranch 289 at 298; approved in *The Colorado* [1923] P 102 at 107.

[149] See Council Regulation (EC) No 1346/2000 on Insolvency Proceedings, Art 4(2)(i), now Regulation (EU) 2015/848 of the European Parliament and of the Council of 20 May 2015 on insolvency proceedings [2015] OJ L 141/19, Art 7(2)(i).

[150] *The Milford* (1858) Sw 362 at 366; *The Tagus* [1903] P 44; *American Surety Co of New York v Wrightson* (1910) 16 Com Cas 37; *The Colorado* [1923] P 102; *The Halcyon Isle* [1981] AC 221. In relation to aircraft there is now a substantive priority rule benefitting international interests, see International Interests in Aircraft Equipment (Cape Town Convention) Regulations 2015 (SI 2015/912).

[151] Carter (1983) 54 BYBIL 207.

[152] [1923] P 102, in which the Court of Appeal held that while French law determined the substance of a mortgagee's right to a ship, English law determined whether the right ranked before or after an opposing claim. See also *The Acrux* [1965] P 391 at 404. In *The Zigurds* [1932] P 113, German necessaries men sought reimbursement from the proceeds of sale of a ship but failed to gain priority over the English mortgagee because, although they enjoyed such priority under German law, that was as a matter of German procedural (and not substantive) law; and it was for English procedural law to determine priorities. Also *The Ship Betty Ott v General Bills Ltd* [1992] 1 NZLR 655.

[153] *The Tagus* [1903] P 44.

[154] As is pointed out by the Supreme Court of Canada in *Todd Shipyards Corpn v Altema Compania Maritima SA* (1972) 32 DLR (3d) 571 at 575–6.

[155] [1981] AC 221.

An English bank had a mortgage on the *Halcyon Isle*, a British registered ship being repaired in the USA by American ship repairers. The repair bill was unpaid and the ship was arrested in Singapore and ordered by the court to be sold, but the proceeds were insufficient to satisfy the claims of both the bank and the repairers. So a question of priorities arose. Under Singapore law (which was the same as English law), the mortgagees had priority because the ship repairers were not regarded as having a maritime lien. Under US law, the repairers were regarded as having such a lien as would give them priority.

The Singapore Court of Appeal held in favour of the repairers,[156] but was reversed by a majority in the Privy Council who gave priority to the English bank. Whilst both the majority and the dissenting minority in the Privy Council agreed that matters of priority are procedural and to be governed by the law of the forum, they disagreed as to the analysis of the claims to be ranked in order of priority. Lord Diplock, for the majority, concluded that the issue of priority depended "upon whether or not if the repairs to the ship had been done in Singapore, the repairers would have been entitled under the law of Singapore to a maritime lien on the *Halcyon Isle* for the price of them. The answer to that question is that they are not. The mortgagees are entitled to priority."[157]

This approach fails to give due consideration to the law of the USA. It is for that law, as the governing law, to consider both whether the claim by the repairers was valid and whether it would lead to the creation, *under US law*, of a maritime lien. The basis of the majority judgment seems to be that whether the repairs are entitled to a lien is solely a procedural matter, and Lord Diplock claimed that such analysis is consistent with the decision in *The Colorado*.[158]

Much to be preferred is the analysis of the minority,[159] who found in favour of the ship repairers. The essence of their approach is succinctly expressed thus:

> The question is—does English law, in circumstances such as these, recognise the maritime lien created by the law of the United States of America, ie the *lex contractus* where no such lien exists by its own internal law? In our view the balance of authorities, the comity of nations, private international law and natural justice all answer this question in the affirmative. If this be correct then English law (the *lex fori*) gives the maritime lien created by the *lex loci contractus* precedence over the mortgagees' mortgage. If it were otherwise, injustice would prevail. The ship-repairers would be deprived of their maritime lien, valid as it appeared to be throughout the world, and without which they would obviously never have allowed the ship to sail away without paying a dollar for the important repairs.[160]

(e) The nature and extent of the remedy

It is obvious that a claimant who seeks to enforce a foreign claim in England can demand only those remedies recognised by English law. Even then, he cannot demand such remedies unless they harmonise with the right according to its nature and extent as fixed by the foreign law.[161] "Put in another way", to quote Lord Parker CJ, in *Phrantzes v Argenti*,[162] "if the machinery by way of remedies here is so different from that in Greece as to make the right

---

[156] Following the decision of the Supreme Court of Canada in *Todd Shipyards Corpn v Altema Compania Maritima SA* (1972) 32 DLR (3d) 571.

[157] [1981] AC 221 at 241.

[158] Supra. See [1981] AC 221 at 238. He also, thereby, disapproved of the Supreme Court of Canada's decision in *Todd Shipyards Corpn v Altema Compania Maritima SA*, supra: [1981] AC 221 at 241–2.

[159] Lord Salmon and Lord Scarman.

[160] [1981] AC 221 at 246–7.

[161] *Chaplin v Boys* [1971] AC 356 at 381–2, 394; and see *Baschet v London Illustrated Standard* [1900] 1 Ch 73.

[162] [1960] 2 QB 19 at 35–6.

sought to be enforced a different right, that right would not, in my judgment, be enforced in this country". *Phrantzes* was concerned with the Greek law relating to the obligation of a man to provide a dowry for his son-in-law.[163] By that law, a father was obliged to establish a dowry for his daughter on her marriage, the amount of which depended, inter alia, on his finances, the number of his children and the social position of himself and his son-in-law. If a father failed to fulfil this obligation, his daughter, and she alone, had a cause of action to compel him to enter into a dowry contract not with herself, but with her husband. If the father was abroad, he could be directed by the Greek court to conclude the contract, wherever he might happen to be, in the presence either of a public notary or the Greek consul. It was against this background that Mrs Phrantzes brought an action in England against her father, claiming a declaration that she was entitled to be provided with a dowry and petitioning that the amount properly due to her should be assessed. All parties were Greek nationals, and it was assumed that the father was domiciled in Greece.

Lord Parker was satisfied that the obligation of a man to establish a dowry in favour of his son-in-law was one that on general principles was enforceable in England. It could not be excluded on the ground that the right of the beneficiary was unknown to English law.[164] Nevertheless, he held that for at least two reasons the action must fail.

> First, there was no remedy at common law appropriate to enforce the exact right vested in the plaintiff by Greek law, namely, "a right to obtain an order condemning someone to enter into a contract in a particular form with a person not even a party to the proceedings".[165]

> Secondly, the daughter did not come to the English court possessed of a right to a definite sum of money. What she was entitled to was such sum as, failing agreement, a court in its discretion might assess; and this assessment depended on a wide variety of factors such as the social position of the parties in a Greek environment.

> All these enquiries and decisions are essentially matters for the domestic courts, and matters largely for the discretion of those courts and not our courts.[166]

It is established that a claim to set-off affects procedure, not substance, since the issue that it raises is whether the relief claimed by the defendant shall be granted in the claimant's action or whether it is obtainable only by a counter-action.[167] If the court, in accordance with its own procedural code, refuses the privilege of set-off, it makes no attack on the substance of the defendant's claim, but, without adjudging the merits of the claim, merely rules that it must be put in suit in separate proceedings.[168]

(f) Damages[169]

The subject of damages raises a problem of some difficulty in private international law, not because the principles are obscure but because the English authorities are scanty.

---

[163] For an American example, see *Slater v Mexican National Rly Co* 194 US 120 (1904).

[164] Distinguishing in this respect such decisions as *Re Macartney* [1921] 1 Ch 522, and *De Brimont v Penniman* (1873) 10 Blatch 436, where a New York court refused to enforce the duty, recognised by French law, of a father-in-law to support his son-in-law, infra, Chapter 15.

[165] [1960] 2 QB 19 at 35.

[166] Ibid, per Lord Parker; cf *Khalij Commercial Bank Ltd v Woods* (1985) 17 DLR (4th) 358.

[167] *Meyer v Dresser* (1864) 16 CBNS 646; and see Wood, *English and International Set-off* (1989), Chapter 23. One can distinguish another type of set-off that amounts to an equity directly attaching to the claim. Here the link with the claim will prevail and the substantive law that applies to it will also apply to the set-off. See *LBI HF v Stanford* [2014] EWHC 3921 (Ch), para. 2013.

[168] But see Wolff, pp 233, 234, where it is shown that under Continental laws set-off is extra-judicial and is regarded as a matter of substance; and see Wood, op cit, Chapter 24.

[169] See, generally, Carruthers, op cit.

Various questions must be segregated. In brief, remoteness of damage and heads of damage must be distinguished from measure of damages. The rules relating to remoteness indicate what kind of loss actually resulting from the commission of a tort or from a breach of contract is actionable; the rules for the measure of damages show the method by which compensation for an actionable loss is calculated. There is one principle of remoteness in tort, another in contract, with similar variations between the two causes of action as to the heads of damage or loss for which recovery may be made. However, the rule that regulates the measure of damages is the same for contracts as it is for torts. It requires *restitutio in integrum*.

(i) Remoteness of damage

There can be no doubt, at least in principle, that remoteness of damage must be governed by the law governing the obligation that rests on the defendant. Both the existence and the extent of an obligation, whether it springs from a breach of contract or the commission of a wrong, must be determined by the system of law from which it derives its source.[170] The governing law admittedly determines the nature and content of the right created by a contract, and it is clear that the kind of loss for which damages are recoverable on breach forms part of that content. Both the nature and the content of a contractual right depend in part on the question whether certain consequential loss that may ensue if the contract is unperformed will be too remote in the eye of the law. If the governing law determines what constitutes a breach, it also determines the consequences of a breach.[171]

> Suppose, for the sake of argument, that by French law a purchaser who sues a seller for non-delivery of goods is entitled to recover for the loss that he has suffered through failure to carry out any sub-contracts he may have made.

On this hypothesis, a purchaser under a French contract for the sale of goods acquires a right of perfectly definite extent. Furthermore, the principles of private international law as embodied in the Contracts (Applicable Law) Act 1990[172] require that his position in this respect shall be neither improved nor prejudiced by the fact that he happens to bring his action in England. If the court applies the rule of internal English law, that compensation cannot be recovered for sub-contract losses, the result is to diminish the content of the right as fixed by the governing law. The law applicable to the contract will therefore govern the issue of remoteness of damage. Of course, an exception must be made when the type of loss for which recovery may be had in the foreign country is contrary to the distinctive policy of the law of the forum.[173]

In *D'Almeida Araujo Lda v Becker & Co Ltd*, a case of breach of contract, Pilcher J based his decision on the distinction between remoteness of damage and measure of damages.[174] The facts were these:

> By a contract, made on 20 March and governed by Portuguese law, the plaintiffs, merchants in Lisbon, agreed to sell 500 tons of palm oil to the defendants, a British company carrying on business in London. With a view to the fulfilment of their undertaking, the plaintiffs agreed to buy 500 tons of palm oil from one Mourao, a Portuguese dealer. This contract provided that, in the event of its breach, the party in default should indemnify the other to the extent of 5 per cent of the total value of the contract, a sum that in fact amounted to

---

[170] *Slater v Mexican National Rly Co* 194 US 120 (1904).
[171] Contracts (Applicable Law) Act 1990, Sch 1, Art 10(1)(c) and cf Rome I Regulation, Art 12(1)(c), infra, Chapter 19; and see *Drew Brown v The Orient Trader* (1972) 34 DLR (3d) 339.
[172] Ibid.
[173] 1990 Act, Sch 1, Art 16. Cf Rome I Regulation, Art 21.
[174] [1953] 2 QB 329.

the equivalent of £3,500. The plaintiffs were forced into the payment of this sum, since the defendants broke the contract of 20 March.

In the present action, the plaintiffs claimed to recover by way of damages the £3,500 which they had been obliged to pay under the indemnity. It was admitted that according to English law the loss suffered by reason of this payment would found no claim to damages, since it was not the kind of loss that ensued in the usual course of things from such a breach of contract. The judge, however, held that English law was irrelevant, concluding that the question whether the plaintiffs were entitled to claim from the defendants the £3,500 which they paid to Mourao, depended on whether such damage were too remote, a question which fell to be determined in accordance with Portuguese law.[175]

It should logically follow from the *D'Almeida* case that remoteness of damage in tort is also a matter of substance to be determined by the governing law,[176] for to rule otherwise would permit a claimant to exact compensation for what did not constitute a ground of liability under that law. This principle has been given legislative effect in Article 15(c) of the Rome II Regulation.[177]

(ii) Heads of damage

A further issue in which the distinction between substance and procedure has arisen is that of deciding whether a particular head of damage is recoverable, ie whether this is a matter of the quantification of the measure of damages and thus procedural, or whether it raises a substantive issue. Whilst there seems little doubt that, in the field of contract, this is a substantive issue for the law governing the contract, tort claims caused more difficulty because of the basic choice of law rule that the claim had to be actionable both by English law as the law of the forum and by the law of the place of the tort.[178] Although tort choice of law rules have now been placed on a statutory basis,[179] the determination of whether an issue is a matter of procedure or of substance is left to the common law.[180] It seems clear that, at common law, a claim for damages for pain and suffering or,[181] in a fatal accidents claim, for solatium,[182] is to be classed as substantive. Similarly, the question whether recovery may be had in a tort action for heads of economic loss is a matter of substance and not of procedure,[183] as is a claim for exemplary damages.[184] The position is less certain in relation to statutory caps on damages.[185]

---

[175] [1953] 2 QB 329 at 338, [1953] 2 All ER 288 at 293. The case would be decided the same way under the Contracts (Applicable Law) Act 1990.

[176] See Morse, *Torts in Private International Law*, pp 197–200; Morse (1996) 45 ICLQ 888 at 895–6; and *Edmunds v Simmonds* [2001] WLR 1003 at 1009.

[177] Infra, Chapter 20.

[178] Infra, p 778.

[179] Private International Law (Miscellaneous Provisions) Act 1995, Part III, infra, p 778.

[180] Ibid, s 14(3)(b), in respect of the interpretation of which, see *Harding v Wealands* [2007] 2 AC 1.

[181] See the majority in *Chaplin v Boys* [1971] AC 356, at 379 (per Lord Hodson), 393 (per Lord Wilberforce), 394–5 (per Lord Pearson).

[182] Eg *Naftalin v London, Midland and Scottish Rly Co* 1933 SC 259; *McElroy v McAllister* 1949 SC 110; and see *Mackinnon v Iberia Shipping Co Ltd* 1955 SC 20; but cf Walker, *The Law of Delict in Scotland* (2nd edn), pp 67–8.

[183] *Mitchell v McCulloch* 1976 SC 1; *Breavington v Godleman* (1988) 169 CLR 41.

[184] *Waterhouse v Australian Broadcasting Corpn* (1989) 86 ACTR 1.

[185] See *Stevens v Head* (1993) 176 CLR 433 at 458; Morse (1996) 45 ICLQ 888 at pp 895–6; and *Harding v Wealands* [2007] 2 AC 1, per Lord Hoffman at [42]–[46]. Also, in *Harding*, per Lord Rodger at [72]: "Lord Hoffman has analysed the passage in *Dicey & Morris, The Conflict of Laws* [7th edn, 1958, p 1092], to the effect that 'statutory provisions limiting a defendant's liability are *prima facie* substantive; but the true construction of the statute may negative this view'. I respectfully agree with his analysis. In any event, as the passage recognises, in any given case the answer to the question must depend on the construction of the relevant provision in the context of the particular statute." See Dicey, Morris and Collins, paras 7-040–7-043.

One should also note that the Rome II Regulation now deals with the classification of damages for matters that fall within its scope.[186] The Regulation does not deal with procedure,[187] but its concept of scope is very wide and it treats the availability of a certain head of damages as a substantive matter, as it does with the issue of remoteness discussed above.[188]

(iii) Measure of damages

The next question is by what law is the measure of damages governed?[189] A rule as to the measure of damages in the narrow sense is a mere rule of calculation. Its function is to quantify in terms of money the sum payable by the defendant in respect of the injury, whether it be a tort or breach of contract, for which his liability has already been determined by the governing law. A claimant who seeks to recover compensation in England in respect of an obligation that is governed as to substance by a foreign law has already acquired a right the nature and extent of which have been fully determined. His object is that his right as established shall be converted by the English court into a right to receive a definite sum of money. He is entitled to be paid in full for the injury suffered and he takes advantage of the English process and machinery in order to exact this payment.

It would seem, therefore, that all questions that arise in the course of this quantification of the amount payable should be governed by English law as the law of the forum. This has been the approach, traditionally, of courts in the United Kingdom. Although Pilcher J has said that, "the quantification of damage, which according to the proper law is not too remote, should be governed by the *lex fori*",[190] some opposition has been expressed.[191] Indeed McNair J found, "the greatest possible difficulty in appreciating the distinction . . . between remoteness of damage and measure of damage".[192] Moreover, if the quantification of damages is considered to be a matter of procedure, to be governed by the law of the forum (*lex fori*), "difficulties will arise if the applicable law recognises a cause of action which is unknown to English domestic law [the *lex fori*], for the simple reason that there will be no English domestic rules on quantification and assessment for the English court to apply as the *lex fori*".[193] Nevertheless, the distinction has long been held both valid and valuable by the House of Lords.[194]

Opportunity for the House of Lords to revisit the distinction, and to review its merits, arose in *Harding v Wealands*,[195] the facts of which were as follows:

> The claimant, Giles Harding, an English national, domiciled in England, was rendered tetraplegic as a result of a motor accident in New South Wales in February 2003. The defendant

---

[186] Article 15.

[187] Article 1(3), see *Wall v Mutuelle de Poitiers Assurances* [2014] EWCA Civ 138.

[188] Articles 15(b) and (c), see *Actavis UK Ltd v Eli Lilly & Co* [2015] EWCA Civ 555.

[189] See *Edmunds v Simmonds* [2001] WLR 1003; *Roerig v Valiant Trawlers Ltd* [2002] 1 Lloyd's Rep 681; *Hulse v Chambers* [2001] 1 WLR 2386; and *Harding v Wealands* [2007] 2 AC 1. Also Carruthers, op cit; Panagopoulos (2005) 1 J Priv Int L 69; and Carruthers (2005) 1 J Priv Int L 323.

[190] The *D'Almeida Case* [1953] 2 QB 329 at 336.

[191] See the minority in *Stevens v Head* (1993) 176 CLR 433. Also *John Pfeiffer Pty Ltd v Rogerson* [2000] HCA 36; *Régie National des Usines Renault SA v Zhang* [2002] 187 ALR 1; and *Re T & N Ltd and Ors (No 2)* [2006] 1 WLR 1792 at [63].

[192] *N V Handel Maatschappij J Smits Import-Export v English Exporters Ltd* [1955] 2 Lloyd's Rep 69 at 72. This is a view with which Lord Upjohn has sympathised, in *Boys v Chaplin* [1968] 2 QB 1 at 31; and see *Livesley v Horst* [1925] 1 DLR 159 at 164.

[193] Morse (1996) 45 ICLQ 888 at 895–896. See Carruthers (2004) 53 ICLQ 691, 699–700.

[194] *Chaplin v Boys* [1971] AC 356 at 378–9, 382–3, 392–3, 394. Cf, in Australia, the majority in *Stevens v Head* (1993) 176 CLR 433.

[195] [2007] 2 AC 1. See Carruthers (2005) 1(2) J Priv Int L 323; Dougherty and Wyles (2007) 56 ICLQ 443; and Weintraub (2007) 43 Texas Int LJ 311.

was Mr Harding's partner, Tania Wealands, an Australian national who had lived in Australia until June 2001, at which time she moved to England to live with the claimant in a settled relationship. Ms Wealands conceded liability, but a preliminary issue arose before Elias J concerning the law applicable to the assessment of damages. Elias J held in favour of the claimant, concluding, inter alia, that the New South Wales statutory damages provisions were to be treated as procedural in nature, and subject, therefore, to the English *lex fori*.

Upon Ms Wealand's appeal, the Court of Appeal, by a majority,[196] reversed the decision of the judge at first instance,[197] and upheld Ms Wealand's contention that the claim for damages was to be determined in accordance with the law of New South Wales. The House of Lords, however, allowed Mr Harding's appeal, restoring the judgment of Elias J and affirming the "damages principle", holding that the question of the assessment of damages in tort, in terms of section 14(3) of the Private International Law (Miscellaneous Provisions) Act 1995, is to be regarded as a matter of procedure, governed by the law of the forum. In the instant case, the provisions of the New South Wales Motor Accidents Compensation Act 1999[198] were characterised as procedural, meaning that the claimant's damages were to be quantified in accordance with English law.

Reference of the issue of measure of damages to the law of the forum will mean that if, for instance, the defendant pleads a tender of the amount due, he must prove that the tender is in accordance with English law. This is because if the task of the court is to fix the amount payable it must also be competent to decide whether in its view payment has in effect already been made.[199] Furthermore, the question whether the damages should be paid in a lump sum or by means of periodic payments is a procedural matter for the law of the forum.[200] The question whether collateral benefits accruing from the death of a deceased person ought to be deducted in calculating an award of damages for loss of dependency has been judged to be a matter of procedure, to be determined by the law of the forum.[201] Conversely, the question whether a claimant is contributorily negligent, leading to a reduction in the award of damages payable, has been held to be a factor relevant to the scope of the defendant's liability for the victim's injuries and the identification of actionable damage, and thus a substantive issue, rather than merely an aspect of the assessment of damages.[202]

This traditional approach of the English courts to the matter of quantification of damages has now been superseded by the provisions of the Rome I and Rome II Regulations and it is therefore now confined to those areas of law not covered by the Regulations, such as defamation. By virtue of Article 15(c) of Rome II, not only the existence and the nature of damage, but also the assessment of damage are matters to be determined by the law applicable to the non-contractual obligation.[203] There is no role left for the law of the forum. This provision represents a major change in English private international law. Article 15(c) adopts the position taken in most Member States, which regard assessment of damages as a substantive matter to be determined by the applicable law, and it has the virtue of

---

[196] Arden LJ and Sir Wm Aldous; Waller LJ, dissenting.

[197] See [2005] 1 WLR 1539, per Arden LJ at [52].

[198] In respect of which, see also *McNeilly v Imbree* [2007] NSWCA 156.

[199] *The Baarn* [1933] P 251.

[200] McGregor (1970) 33 MLR 1, 21 et seq.

[201] *Roerig v Valiant Trawlers Ltd* [2002] 1 WLR 2304 at [25]–[26]. The court indicated that the question of deductions is closely tied to policy considerations, and "with the way in which damages under the particular head are to be assessed overall" (at [26]).

[202] *Dawson v Broughton*, 31 July 2007 (unreported), considered at (2007) Journal of Personal Injury Law C186. See now Rome II Regulation, Art 15(b) ("division of liability"), examined, infra, Chapter 20.

[203] Infra, Chapter 20.

preventing forum shopping within the European Union for an assessment of damages advantage.[204] In looking at the provisions of the substantive law the English courts will also need to consider the relevant judicial practices and guidelines that come with them in order to be able to award the level of damages that would be awarded in the country whose law is applicable.[205]

In this sense the Rome II Regulation broadly follows Article 10(1)(c) of the Rome Convention on the Law Applicable to Contractual Obligations, now Article 12(1)(c) Rome I Regulation. This means that both under the Contracts (Applicable Law) Act 1990 and the Rome I Regulation the law governing the substance of the contract also governs "the consequences of breach, including the assessment of damages in so far as it is governed by rules of law", provided that the court of the forum has these powers according to its procedural law.[206] This is intended only to apply rules of law for the assessment of damages to be found in the governing law, since "questions of fact will always be for the court hearing the action".[207] This 'governed by rules of law' restriction is however absent from the provisions of the Rome II Regulation,[208] which is therefore even more wide ranging on this point.

(iv) Payment of interest

The issue as to whether interest is payable necessitates consideration of whether interest is claimed by virtue of a term in a contract or as damages and whether what is in issue is the right to interest or the rate at which it is payable. It was well established at common law that whether interest was payable on a contractual debt, and if so at what rate, was a matter to be determined by the law governing the essential validity of the contract.[209] This would still appear to be the case under the Contracts (Applicable Law) Act 1990.[210] This rule has been applied in the case of dishonour of a bill of exchange. So, whether interest is recoverable on dishonour depends on the law governing the contract under which the defendant rendered himself liable.[211] Where damages for breach of contract are being claimed, rather than a debt, then the right to interest on the damages is governed by the law applicable to the contract.[212] There is authority for the conclusion that the right to interest on damages in tort is governed by the law applicable to the substantive tort issue.[213]

Turning now to the rate at which interest is to be paid, or whether the interest is to be compound or simple, there seems little doubt again that, in the case of a contractual claim for interest, these matters are governed by the law applicable to the contract.[214] There is less

---

[204] For possible difficulties in application, see, infra, Chapter 20.

[205] A Dickinson, *The Rome II Regulation*, para. 14.19.

[206] Sch 1, Art 10(1)(c). Cf Rome I Regulation, Art 12(1)(c).

[207] Giuliano and Lagarde Report, OJ 1980 C 282/33.

[208] *Stylianou v Toyoshima* [2013] EWHC 2188 (QB).

[209] *Montreal Trust Co v Stanrock Uranium Mines Ltd* (1965) 53 DLR (2d) 594; and see *Shrichand & Co v Lacon* (1906) 22 TLR 245; *Mount Albert Borough Council v Australasian Temperance and General Mutual Life Assurance Society* [1938] AC 224; Law Com No 124 (1983), para 2.29.

[210] Sch 1, Art 10(1)(c).

[211] *Allen v Kemble* (1848) 6 Moo PCC 314; *Gibbs v Fremont* (1853) 9 Exch 25.

[212] See, at common law, *Miliangos v George Frank (Textiles) Ltd (No 2)* [1977] QB 489; cf *Midland International Trade Services Ltd v Sudairy* (1990) Financial Times, 2 May. Similarly, in a claim for restitutionary relief based on frustration, the law governing the frustrated contract has been applied to determine a claim to interest: *BP Exploration Co (Libya) Ltd v Hunt (No 2)* [1979] 1 WLR 783 at 845–50; affd [1983] 2 AC 352.

[213] *Maher v Groupama Grand Est* [2009] EWCA Civ 1191; see also *Ekins v East-India Co* (1717) 1 P Wms 395. But see *Kuwait Oil Tanker Co SAK v Al Bader (No 3)* [2000] 2 All ER (Comm) 271, per Moore-Bick J at 339–44.

[214] This was clearly the position at common law: *Fergusson v Fyffe* (1841) 8 Cl & Fin 121 at 140 (compound interest); *Mount Albert Borough Council v Australasian Temperance and General Mutual Life Assurance Society* [1938] AC 224 (rate of interest).

certainty as to the law to determine the rate of interest payable on damages. In an action for damages for breach of contract, it was decided in *Miliangos v George Frank (Textiles) Ltd (No 2)*[215] that the question of the rate of interest is a matter relating to measure of damages, and thus a matter of procedure governed by the law of the forum.[216] This has been dissented from by Kerr J: "Both the right to interest and its amount should be determined by the proper law. The proper law results from the express or implied choice of both parties or from the nature of the transaction."[217]

There are no clear answers to be discerned from the Contracts (Applicable Law) Act 1990 which simply excludes matters of procedure from its scope, without defining them.[218] So we are thrown back on the common law decisions for guidance. There are difficulties with Kerr J's approach in the case, for example, of contractual claims for damages in foreign currency. The currency of the law governing the contract may be different from the currency of account, the currency of the loss and the currency of the forum.[219] The rates of interest relevant to each may well reflect the strength and weaknesses of the various currencies. If the rate of interest is governed by the law of the forum,[220] this means that, in England, the court has a discretion as to the rate[221] and it has been made clear by the Court of Appeal that, prima facie, interest should be awarded at the rate applicable to the currency of the judgment.[222] This might not be possible if the governing law of the contract determined the rate. The Law Commission has considered this issue and concluded, though without proposing legislation on the matter, that the practical arguments in favour of the application of the law of the forum should prevail.[223]

(g) Judgments in foreign currency[224]

(i) Old rule: judgment must be in sterling

It was accepted in England for many years that an English court could not order payment of debts or damages except in English currency.[225] The amount due to the plaintiff in foreign currency had to be converted into sterling and the appropriate exchange rate was that at the date the cause of action arose, eg the date of the breach of a contract[226] or the commission of a tort.[227]

---

[215] [1977] QB 489; and see *The Funabashi* [1972] 1 WLR 666 at 671.

[216] See now Contracts (Applicable Law) Act 1990, Sch 1, Art 10(1)(c). Also Late Payment of Commercial Debts (Interest) Act 1998, s 12.

[217] *Helmsing Schiffahrts GmbH & Co KG v Malta Drydocks Corpn* [1977] 2 Lloyd's Rep 444 at 450.

[218] Sch 1, Art 1(2)(h).

[219] Infra, p 101 et seq.

[220] See *Lesotho Highlands Development Authority v Impregilo SpA* [2003] 2 Lloyd's Rep 497, per Brooke LJ, at para 50; and *Rogers v Markel Corpn* [2004] EWHC 1375, per Treacy J, at [77]–[81], and [2004] EWHC 2046. See Dicey, Morris and Collins, at paras 33-397–33-400.

[221] Supreme Court Act 1981, s 35A (added by the Administration of Justice Act 1982, s 15 and Sch 1).

[222] *Shell Tankers (UK) Ltd v Astro Comino Armadora SA* [1981] 2 Lloyd's Rep 40 at 45–7; and see *Miliangos v George Frank (Textiles) Ltd (No 2)* [1977] QB 489; *Swiss Bank Corpn v State of New South Wales* (1993) 33 NSWLR 63. The prima facie rule was displaced in *Helmsing Schiffahrts GmbH & Co KG v Malta Drydocks Corpn*, supra.

[223] Working Paper No 80, *Foreign Money Liabilities* (1981), paras 4.23–4.27; Law Com No 124, *Foreign Money Liabilities* (1983), paras 3.55–3.56.

[224] Mann, *The Legal Aspect of Money*, (2005) 6th edn, Chapter 4; Goode, *Payment, Obligations and Financial Transactions* (1983), Chapter V; Bowles, *Law and the Economy* (1982), Chapter 9. The whole question of foreign money liabilities was considered by the Law Commission in Law Com No 124 (1983).

[225] *Manners v Pearson & Son* [1898] 1 Ch 581.

[226] Eg *Re United Rlys of the Havana and Regla Warehouses Ltd* [1961] AC 1007.

[227] Eg *SS Celia v SS Volturno* [1921] 2 AC 544.

(ii) Miliangos v George Frank (Textiles) Ltd

The rule that judgment must be in sterling came under increasing attack, culminating in the decision of the House of Lords in *Miliangos v George Frank (Textiles) Ltd.*[228]

> By means of a contract governed by Swiss law, the plaintiff, a Swiss national, had agreed to sell a quantity of polyester yarn to the English defendants. The yarn was delivered in 1971. The money of account and of payment was Swiss francs. The defendant having failed to pay, the plaintiff sought payment of the sterling equivalent of the sum due in Swiss francs, at the date when payment should have been made. However, after a decision of the Court of Appeal allowing judgment to be given in a foreign currency,[229] the plaintiff in *Miliangos* was given leave to amend his claim so as to claim the amount due to him in Swiss francs.

The problem facing the House of Lords was a fairly simple one. Were they to act on the Practice Direction of 1966[230] and reverse an earlier but fairly recent decision of their own[231] and accept the line already taken by the Court of Appeal, or were they to confirm the well-established rule that judgment could only be given in sterling with a conversion date as of the date of breach? The significance of the decision to the plaintiff, in an era of rapidly fluctuating interest rates, was very considerable and especially given that the Swiss franc was strong and sterling weak. Judgment in Swiss francs, converted into sterling as at the date of judgment, would give him almost 50 per cent more in sterling than conversion as at the date of the breach. Their Lordships decided to abandon the old rule and allow judgment to be given in foreign currency, here Swiss francs.[232] This was a decision of major commercial and financial significance but it left a whole range of further issues undecided, many of which have since been resolved by judicial decision. The most important of them are: how far beyond judgments for debts expressed in foreign currency does the *Miliangos* decision go? And in what currency may a court give judgment?

(iii) Claims to which the Miliangos rule applies

The first issue to be considered is the scope of the *Miliangos* decision. Their Lordships were very careful to limit their new principle to the type of case before them, leaving it to future decisions to work out the further implications of it. Indeed, Lord wilberforce said:

> I would confine my approval at the present time . . . to claims such as those with which we are here concerned, ie, to foreign money obligations, sc. obligations of a money character to pay foreign currency arising under a contract whose proper law is that of a foreign country and where the money of account and payment is that of that country, or possibly of some other country, but not of the United Kingdom.[233]

Development came very rapidly. It started with cases of debt, then extended to liquidated damages for breach of contract and eventually to claims for unliquidated damages.[234] The result is

---

[228] [1976] AC 443. It had already been decided that an arbitral award (*Jugoslavenska Oceanska Plovidba v Castle Investment Co Inc* [1974] QB 292) and a judgment for a debt (*Schorsch Meier GmbH v Hennin* [1975] QB 416) could be made in foreign currency. For Scots law on this issue, see Moran (1995) 44 ICLQ 72.

[229] *Schorsch Meier GmbH v Hennin* [1975] QB 416.

[230] [1966] 1 WLR 395. See now *Practice Direction (Judgments: Foreign Currency)* (1992) PD 11.

[231] *Re United Rlys of the Havana and Regla Warehouses Ltd* [1961] AC 1007, [1960] 2 All ER 332.

[232] Lord Simon of Glaisdale dissented, believing that such a revolutionary change should only be made by Parliament; [1976] AC 443 at 470. However, the Law Commission subsequently examined the whole question of foreign money liabilities and concluded that "the principle underlying the decision in *Miliangos* and the consequences which flow from it are greatly to be preferred to the rules which that decision superseded": Law Com No 124 (1983), para 3.8; cf Bowles and Whelan (1982) 45 MLR 434.

[233] [1976] AC 443 at 467–8; and see 497–8, 503; see *Owners of Eleftherotria v Despina R, The Despina R* [1979] AC 685 at 695. But see Mann (1976) 92 LQR 165, 166.

[234] For discharge of foreign currency obligations, especially debts, other than where there is a judgment, see Dicey, Morris and Collins, paras 37R-051–37-060.

that it is now established that the court can give judgment for a sum in foreign currency as damages for breach of contract[235] and as damages in tort.[236] Furthermore, the principle applies in contractual claims whether the law governing the contract is English law[237] or foreign law.[238] It also extends to restitutionary claims,[239] winding up orders[240] and voluntary liquidations,[241] and it also seems clear that it will apply to salvage claims.[242]

In all these cases it has normally been the claimant who sought payment in a currency other than sterling because of the depreciation of sterling. There is now much greater variation in exchange rates. "Sterling is no longer a stable currency, nor are US dollars, nor French francs. No currency is stable. They all swing about with every gust that blows."[243] So what happens when sterling appreciates? In the case of an action for a debt it seems clear that the claimant ought to be entitled to judgment in the currency of the debt, converted into sterling as at the date of payment, and not judgment in sterling converted from the currency of the debt as at the date of breach. As was said in *Miliangos*, "the creditor has no concern with pounds sterling: for him what matters is that a Swiss franc for good or ill should remain a Swiss franc".[244] A similar rule ought to apply to claims for damages in foreign currency. The claimant should be entitled to judgment in the currency of his loss[245] and not in sterling calculated as at the date the cause of action arose. In this way the claimant is protected against changes in the value of his currency as against sterling, but is not, and should not be, protected against changes in the internal value of his own currency.[246]

(iv) Interest

Interest may be allowed in an action for payment of a debt or damages in foreign currency at a rate which may be different from the English rate for sterling.[247] The rate of interest to be paid on a judgment given in a foreign currency is within the discretion of the court, and is not confined to the English statutory rate for judgment debts.[248]

---

[235] *Services Europe Atlantique Sud v Stockholms Rederiaktiebolag SVEA, The Folias* [1979] AC 685; and see *Kraut AG v Albany Fabrics Ltd* [1977] QB 182; *Federal Commerce and Navigation Co Ltd v Tradax Export SA* [1977] QB 324 at 341–2; revsd on other grounds [1978] AC 1; *The Texaco Melbourne* [1994] 1 Lloyd's Rep 473.

[236] *Owners of Elftherotria v Despina R, The Despina R* [1979] AC 685; *Hoffman v Sofaer* [1982] 1 WLR 1350.

[237] Eg *Services Europe Atlantique Sud v Stockholms Rederiaktiebolag SVEA, The Folias*, supra; *Barclays Bank International Ltd v Levin Bros (Bradford) Ltd* [1977] QB 270; *Federal Commerce and Navigation Co Ltd v Tradax Export SA*, supra, at 341–2.

[238] *Miliangos v George Frank (Textiles) Ltd (No 2)* [1977] QB 489.

[239] *BP Exploration Co (Libya) Ltd v Hunt (No 2)* [1979] 1 WLR 783, affd [1983] 2 AC 352.

[240] *Re Dynamics Corpn of America* [1976] 1 WLR 757.

[241] *Re Lines Bros Ltd* [1983] Ch 1; *Re Lines Bros Ltd (No 2)* [1984] Ch 438.

[242] *Services Europe Atlantique Sud v Stockholms Rederiaktiebolag SVEA, The Folias* [1979] QB 491 at 516; affd [1979] AC 685; and see *Miliangos v George Frank (Textiles) Ltd* [1976] AC 443 at 468.

[243] [1979] QB 491 at 513.

[244] [1976] AC 443 at 466.

[245] Discussed, infra, p 101 et seq.

[246] *Owners of Eleftherotria v Despina R, The Despina R* [1979] AC 685 at 697.

[247] *Miliangos v George Frank (Textiles) Ltd (No 2)* [1977] QB 489; *Helmsing Schiffahrts GmbH & Co KG v Malta Drydocks Corpn* [1977] 2 Lloyd's Rep 444; *Shell Tankers (UK) Ltd v Astro Comino Armadora SA* [1981] 2 Lloyd's Rep 40; *Maschinenfabric v Altikar Pty Ltd* [1984] 3 NSWLR 152; *The Kefalonia Wind* [1986] 1 Lloyd's Rep 292 n; and see Bowles and Phillips (1976) 39 MLR 196.

[248] Private International Law (Miscellaneous Provisions) Act 1995, s 1(1), inserting a new s 44A to that effect into the Administration of Justice Act 1970. This provision implements a recommendation of the Law Commission, in Law Com No 124 (1983), para 4.15.

(v) Procedural nature of the Miliangos rule

The rule propounded in the *Miliangos* decision is a rule of procedure and not of substance;[249] thus English law is applied as the law of the forum. This can be seen from the fact that the rule has been applied where the law governing the substance of the contract in question was foreign,[250] and without reference, at common law in tort, to the law of the place of the tort.[251]

(vi) Date for conversion of currency

Although judgment may be given in foreign currency, a question of conversion into sterling may still arise. The judgment may be satisfied by payment of the sum in foreign currency[252] but, failing such satisfaction, the claimant will seek to enforce the judgment and this will necessitate conversion of the judgment into sterling.[253] In fact in *Miliangos* itself, the House of Lords considered that the claim could be in the alternative, either for the foreign currency or the sterling equivalent at "the date of payment". It has been stated in the Court of Appeal that the conversion should be made "as close as practicable to the date of payment, having regard to the realities of enforcement procedures".[254] In normal cases, the "date of payment" at which conversion must be made will be the date at which the court authorises enforcement of the judgment in terms of sterling,[255] and this also applies to the case of an arbitrator's award.[256] In the case of the winding up of a company (both compulsory and voluntary), the appropriate date will be the date of the winding-up order.[257]

There are various cases where it has been provided by statute that the conversion into sterling shall be made according to the rate of exchange prevailing at the time of judgment and, of course, these are unaffected by the *Miliangos* decision. The judgment-date rule applies to carriage by air[258] but not to carriage of goods by road.[259] In the case of foreign judgments expressed in foreign currency and registered in England under the Foreign Judgments (Reciprocal Enforcement) Act 1933[260] for the purposes of recognition and enforcement, they were to be registered in the foreign currency with conversion at the date of payment[261] just

---

[249] *Owners of Eleftherotria v Despina R, The Despina R* [1979] AC 685 at 704.
[250] Eg *Miliangos v George Frank (Textiles) Ltd* [1976] AC 443.
[251] *Owners of Eleftherotria v Despina R, The Despina R* [1979] AC 685.
[252] See *Practice Direction* [1976] 1 WLR 83, as amended by *Practice Direction* [1977] 1 WLR 197; and *Practice Direction (Judgments: Foreign Currency)* (1992) PD 11.
[253] *Miliangos v George Frank (Textiles) Ltd* [1976] AC 443 at 497, 501.
[254] *Carnegie v Giessen and Ors* [2005] EWCA Civ 191; [2005] 1 WLR 2510, per Carnworth LJ, at [12].
[255] Ibid, at 468–9, 497–8, 501–2; and see *Practice Direction* [1976] 1 WLR 83, as amended by *Practice Direction* [1977] 1 WLR 197; *The Halcyon Skies (No 2)* [1977] 1 Lloyd's Rep 22; *George Veflings Rederi A/S v President of India* [1979] 1 WLR 59. The Law Commission re-examined this rule and supported its retention, but also made a number of detailed proposals for changes to the relevant procedural laws: Law Com No 124 (1983), Part V. On garnishee orders against foreign currency bank accounts, see *Choice Investments Ltd v Jeromnimon* [1981] QB 149, [1981] All ER 225; and now, Third Party Debt Orders *per* Civil Procedure Rules, Pt 72, in respect of which see Dicey, Morris and Collins, paras 24R-080–24-084. In the case of set-off, see *The Transoceanica Francesca and Nicos V* [1987] 2 Lloyd's Rep 155 (tort); *Smit Tak International Zeesleepen Berginsbedrijk BV v Selco Salvage Ltd* [1988] 2 Lloyd's Rep 398 (contract); and see *The Lu Schan* [1993] 1 Lloyd's Rep 259.
[256] Ibid, at 469; Law Com No 124 (1983), para 2.43; cf *Jugoslovenska Oceanska Plovidba v Castle Investment Co* [1974] QB 292.
[257] *Re Dynamics Corpn of America* [1976] 1 WLR 757; cf *Miliangos v George Frank (Textiles) Ltd* [1976] AC 443 at 469, 498 (compulsory); *Re Lines Bros Ltd* [1983] Ch 1; *Re Lines Bros (No 2)* [1984] Ch 438 (voluntary); and see *Re Gresham Corpn Pty Ltd* [1990] 1 Qd R 306.
[258] Carriage by Air Act 1961, Sch 1, Art 22(5), and see s 4(4).
[259] Carriage of Goods by Road Act 1965, Sch, Art 27(2).
[260] S 2, for the main provisions see infra, Chapter 15.
[261] Repealed by the Administration of Justice Act 1977, ss 4, 32(4), Sch 5, which also repeals the Bills of Exchange Act 1882, s 72(4).

as if the claimant had sued on the original cause of action, or, it is assumed, as if there was an action on the judgment at common law.[262] There is no provision in the Civil Jurisdiction and Judgments Act 1982,[263] which governs the recognition and enforcement of judgments given in European Union States,[264] indicating the date for converting into sterling the currency in which the foreign judgment was given. It is assumed,[265] however, that the same principles will apply. The rules are different for the enforcement of foreign maintenance orders,[266] where the conversion date is not that, under the *Miliangos* rule, of actual payment or when enforcement is authorised, but rather the earlier date of the registration of the order.[267] This difference of approach can be justified on grounds of convenience.[268] It is quite impracticable for the sums due under a foreign maintenance order, often payable weekly, to vary from week to week in the light of currency fluctuations.[269] In the case of claims for damages falling within section 183 of the Merchant Shipping Act 1995[270] the rate of exchange is either that at the date of judgment or at the date agreed by the parties.[271]

(vii) In what currency should the court give judgment?

We have seen that the question whether damages can be given in a foreign currency is a procedural issue. This leads to a further issue of classification. Given that an English court can award damages in a foreign currency, is it for English law as the procedural law of the forum to provide the legal rules for deciding in which currency this is to be done, or is the question of the identification of the currency a matter of substantive law? For example, if the governing law of a contract is French, and the English court is prepared to give damages in a foreign currency, does the court use the English or the French rules for deciding which is the appropriate currency? This issue would appear to be a matter of substance. In the field of contract, the currency in which damages are to be calculated has been held to be a matter for the law governing substantive issues,[272] as in *Kraut AG v Albany Fabrics Ltd*,[273] in which the facts were as follows:

> The plaintiff, a Swiss company, sold cloth to the English defendants, by means of contract governed by Swiss law. The defendant failed to pay and the plaintiff sought payment of various sums owing to it and damages for breach of contract. The issue before the court was whether judgment could be given in Swiss francs.

This was the first case after *Miliangos v George Frank (Textiles) Ltd*[274] where the court had to consider whether the principle of that decision extended to a claim for damages for breach of

---

[262] *East India Trading Co Inc v Carmel Exporters and Importers Ltd* [1952] 2 QB 439, [1952] 1 All ER 1053 would, it is suggested, be decided differently after *Miliangos*; see *Batavia Times Publishing Co v Davis* (1978) 88 DLR (3d) 144 especially at 151–4; and see Law Com No 124 (1983), para 2.38.

[263] Except in the case of maintenance orders, infra.

[264] Infra, Chapter 16.

[265] Collins, *The Civil Jurisdiction and Judgments Act 1982* (1983), p 116; Law Com No 124 (1983), paras 2.38–2.42, 3.45–3.46.

[266] Infra, Chapter 24.

[267] Maintenance Orders (Reciprocal Enforcement) Act 1972, s 16; Civil Jurisdiction and Judgments Act 1982, s 8; Civil Jurisdiction and Judgments Act 1991, Sch 2, para 2; cf *Re May's Marriage* (1987) 90 FLR 134.

[268] Law Com No 124 (1983), paras 2.48–2.51, 3.47–3.49.

[269] English maintenance orders may be made in foreign currency (eg *R v Cambridge County Court, ex p Ireland* [1985] Fam Law 23) but in such cases conversion is effected at the date the enforcement procedure is initiated: see Law Com No 124 (1983), para 2.52.

[270] Giving effect to the Athens Convention on the Carriage of Passengers by Sea, contained in Sch 6, Part I of the 1995 Act.

[271] 1995 Act, Sch 6, Part I, Art 9.

[272] *Services Europe Atlantique Sud v Stockholms Rederiaktiebolag SVEA, The Folias* [1979] AC 685 at 700; and see *Miliangos v George Frank (Textiles) Ltd* [1976] AC 443 at 465.

[273] [1977] QB 182.

[274] [1976] AC 443.

contract, rather than a claim for the payment of a debt. In allowing the claim in Swiss francs, Eveleigh J relied on Swiss law, the law governing the contract, under which law the defendant was treated as if it was a debtor. This justified the application of the *Miliangos* principle that judgment may be given in a foreign currency, but also indicated that the currency in which the loss is to be calculated should be determined by the governing law. The questions whether, in a contract action, judgment should be given in a foreign currency and, in a case where there is more than one possible currency, in which currency, have been held to depend on general principles of the law of contract and on rules of private international law:

> The former require application, as nearly as possible of the principle of *restitutio in integrum*, regard being had to what was in the reasonable contemplation of the parties. The latter involve ascertainment of the proper law of the contract, and application of that law. If the proper law is English, the first step must be to see whether, expressly or by implication, the contract provides an answer to the currency question.[275]

It ought logically to follow that, if the determination of the currency in which damages for breach of contract are to be calculated is a matter of substance for the law governing the contract, it should also be a matter of substance so far as claims in tort are concerned. The tort position is less clear because in the one relevant decision, *The Despina R*,[276] English law was applied without reference to the fact that the tort in question was committed in China. One can argue that, where foreign law is not pleaded, it is deemed to be the same as English law.[277]

Turning now to the English rules for determining the currency in which damages should be assessed, the House of Lords has taken the view[278] that, once the obligation to give judgment in sterling has been abandoned, any rule[279] that, where damages consisted of loss incurred directly in a foreign currency, the damages must be assessed in that currency, should also be abandoned. Instead the court must identify the currency of the claimant's loss for:

> a plaintiff, who normally conducts his business through a particular currency, and who, when other currencies are immediately involved, uses his own currency to obtain those currencies, can reasonably say that the loss he sustains is to be measured not by the immediate currencies in which the loss first emerges but by the amount of his own currency, which in the normal course of operation, he uses to obtain those currencies. This is the currency in which his loss is felt, and is the currency which it is reasonably foreseeable he will have to spend.[280]

Guidance in determining the currency of loss in claims for damages is provided by two decisions, which were consolidated on appeal to the House of Lords in 1979, one in contract, the other in tort. In *Services Europe Atlantique Sud v Stockholms Rederiaktiebolag SVEA, The Folias*[281] the facts were as follows:

> By contract governed by English law, the plaintiff, a French company, chartered a Swedish ship from the defendants. Owing to defective refrigeration, the cargo was damaged on arrival in Brazil. The plaintiff settled a claim by the receiver of the cargo, paying him in Brazilian

---

[275] *Services Europe Atlantique Sud v Stockholms Rederiaktiebolag SVEA, The Folias* [1979] AC 685 at 700.

[276] [1979] AC 685, infra, p 103. In *Hoffman v Sofaer* [1982] 1 WLR 1350, another tort case, both the law of the place where the tort was committed and the law of the forum were English.

[277] Infra, p 105 et seq.

[278] *Services Europe Atlantique Sud v Stockholms Rederiaktiebolag SVEA, The Folias* [1979] AC 685.

[279] Eg *Di Ferdinando v Simon, Smits & Co Ltd* [1920] 3 KB 409; *SS Celia v SS Volturno* [1921] 2 AC 544; *The Canadian Transport* (1932) 43 Lloyd's Rep 409.

[280] [1979] AC 685 at 697.

[281] [1979] AC 685; Bowles and Whelan (1979) 42 MLR 452; and see *Ozalid Group (Export) Ltd v African Continental Bank Ltd* [1979] 2 Lloyd's Rep 231; *Food Corpn of India v Carras (Hellas) Ltd* [1980] 2 Lloyd's Rep 577; *Société Francaise Bunge SA v Belcan NV* [1985] 3 All ER 378.

currency. In arbitration proceedings, the defendants admitted liability, but maintained that they should reimburse the plaintiff in Brazilian currency, the currency the plaintiff had used to settle the claim, and not in French francs, the currency used by the plaintiff to buy the Brazilian cruzeiros.

Judgment was given in French francs as the currency most truly expressing the plaintiff's loss. Again, the significance of the decision lies in inflation, because the Brazilian currency had weakened greatly against the French franc between the date of settling the claim and the date of judgment. The decision, therefore, protected the plaintiff from the effects of this fluctuation.

Where a contract is governed by English law, the determination of the currency in which payment is to be made is ascertained in the first instance by reference to the terms of the contract. If it provides expressly or impliedly for the currency in which damages are to be calculated[282] then judgment should be given in that currency. In the absence of such provision in the contract, where the claimant incurs expenditure as a consequence of the defendant's breach of contract, judgment for damages should be in the currency most truly expressing the claimant's loss,[283] provided the parties can be taken reasonably to have this in contemplation.[284] This will not necessarily be the currency of the expenditure which may[285] or may not[286] be the currency of the contract.

The other 1979 House of Lords decision is in the tort field, *The Despina R.*[287]

> The plaintiff's ship and the defendants' ship, both Greek, were in collision in Shanghai harbour. The plaintiff's ship received temporary repairs in Shanghai and then went to Japan and eventually to the USA for further repairs. The plaintiff, having expended sums on repairs and other expenses in Chinese and Japanese currencies, in US dollars and in sterling, sought payment of these sums as damages for the harm negligently done to its ship, arguing that they should be expressed in US dollars, that being the currency in which it carried on its business.

Their Lordships held that damages in tort, as in contract, are payable in the currency of the plaintiff's loss, here US dollars, being the currency which the plaintiff is able to show is that in which he normally conducts trading operations.[288]

Reference to the currency of the claimant's loss must be qualified. This is because, if the claimant has exacerbated his loss by use of his own currency, he runs the risk that the use of his own currency may be too remote a consequence of the defendant's conduct as to justify quantifying his loss by reference to it.[289] The principle laid down in *The Despina R* is of general application, whatever the basis of the tort claim, even though that case only related to the torts of negligence and damage to property.[290] In *Hoffman v Sofaer*[291] the court was prepared to award the plaintiff, an American, damages in dollars for loss of earnings stemming from negligent medical treatment suffered in England. Damages for pain, suffering and loss of

---

[282] Ibid, at p 700; and see *Jugoslavenska Oceanska Plovidba v Castle Investment Co Inc* [1974] QB 292 at 298.

[283] [1979] AC 685, 701–3, 705; and see *The Texaco Melbourne* [1994] 1 Lloyd's Rep 473.

[284] Ibid at p 701; see *Metaalhandel JA Magnus BV v Ardfields Transport Ltd* [1988] 1 Lloyd's Rep 197.

[285] *Federal Commerce and Navigation Co Ltd v Tradax Export SA* [1977] QB 324 at 341–2; revsd on other grounds [1978] AC 1.

[286] [1979] AC 685 at 702.

[287] [1979] AC 685; Knott (1980) 43 MLR 18; and see *The Lash Atlantico* [1987] 2 Lloyd's Rep 114.

[288] *Per* Lord Wilberforce at 698.

[289] See the Court of Appeal, [1978] QB 396 at 437; and see [1979] AC 685 at 697–9.

[290] Cf *North Scottish Helicopters Ltd v United Technologies Corpn Inc (No 2)* 1988 SLT 778.

[291] [1982] 1 WLR 1350; and see *Kraut AG v Albany Fabrics Ltd* [1977] QB 182 at 189.

amenity were given in sterling, however, on the ground that it would be impossible to assess them in dollars.[292]

We have seen that judgments, other than for unliquidated damages, may be given in foreign currency. In the case of a debt or claim for liquidated damages, the contract may provide for the currency in which the debt is to be paid; and judgment should be given in that currency.[293] In other cases, where the money of account (the currency in which the obligation is measured) is different from the money of payment (the currency in which the obligation is discharged), judgment should normally be given in the former.[294] If, however, the contract provides an agreed rate of exchange between the two, judgment should be given in the money of payment.[295] In the case of a restitutionary claim,[296] the award should be related not to the claimant's loss, but to the currency of the defendant's benefit. Where the benefit is money, the award should normally be for repayment by the defendant in the same currency as that in which he received payment. If the benefit is other than money, then the award should be in the currency in which the benefit can be "most fairly and appropriately valued".[297]

(h) Execution

Judgments and the execution of judgments, being integral parts of the process which the claimant has elected to adopt, are necessarily subject to the law of the forum. The particular mode of execution admitted by that law, whether more or less favourable to the claimant than that recognised by the law governing the transaction, has exclusive application. This principle covers such matters as whether the judgment may be satisfied out of land or goods;[298] whether debts in the hands of third parties can be attached by third party debt order; whether a receiver may be appointed; whether a writ *ne exeat regno* is procurable; or whether personal constraint is permissible. Thus, where a Portuguese, who had been arrested in the course of English proceedings for non-payment of a debt which was due to a Spaniard under a Portuguese contract, applied to be discharged from custody on the ground that he was not liable to arrest by the law governing the contract, the application was refused.[299]

---

[292] Ibid at 1357. Cf *Fullemann v McInnes's Executor* 1992 SLT 259.

[293] *Services Europe Atlantique Sud (SEAS) v Stockholms Rederiaktiebolag SVEA, The Folias* [1979] QB 491 at 514.

[294] *George Veflings Rederi A/S v President of India* [1978] 1 WLR 92; affd [1979] 1 WLR 59; cf *BP Exploration Co (Libya) Ltd v Hunt (No 2)* [1979] 1 WLR 783 at 840–1.

[295] *President of India v Taygetos Shipping Co SA* [1985] 1 Lloyd's Rep 155.

[296] *BP Exploration Co (Libya) Ltd v Hunt (No 2)* [1979] 1 WLR 783 at 837–45 (affd [1983] 2 AC 352); see infra, Chapter 20.

[297] Ibid at 840.

[298] But where, in the case of a mortgage, the governing law provides that both the property mortgaged and other property of the debtor are liable for the debt, this amounts to a substantive rule, applicable even though the law of the forum restricts the claim to the property mortgaged; *Sigurdson v Farrow* (1981) 121 DLR (3d) 183; and see *243930 Alberta Ltd v Wickham* (1990) 73 DLR (4th) 474.

[299] *De la Vega v Vianna* (1830) 1 B & Ad 284.

7

THE PROOF OF FOREIGN LAW[1]

1. Foreign Law: A Question of Fact   105   3. Witnesses Who Can Prove Foreign Law   110
2. How Foreign Law Is Proved   108   4. The Role of the Court   111

1. FOREIGN LAW: A QUESTION OF FACT

The established rule is that knowledge of foreign law[2] is not to be imputed to an English judge.[3] Judicial notice is on the other hand taken of European Community law, which, of course, is not technically foreign law.[4] The same does however not apply to foreign law. Even though the foreign law is notorious, it has been said that the court cannot take judicial notice of it.[5] Unless the foreign law with which a case may be connected is pleaded by the party relying thereon, it is assumed that it is the same as English law.[6] Foreign principles of public policy are also presumed to be the same as English ones.[7] The presumption, that the content of the foreign law is the same as the content of English law has, is however not uncontested

---

[1] Fentiman, *Foreign Law in English Courts* (1998), (1992) 108 LQR 142; Geeroms, *Foreign Law in Civil Litigation* (2004)—for a comparative study; Hartley (1996) 45 ICLQ 271; Lando (1995) 2 Maastricht JECL 359, at 367–372; Hood (2006) 2 J Priv Int L 181, C Esplugues, J-L Iglesias and G. Palao (eds), *Application of Foreign Law* (2011) and Crawford and Carruthers, 8.24-38; Esplugues Mota, 'Harmonisation of Private International Law in Europe and Application of Foreign Law: The Madrid Principles of 2010', in (2011) *Yearbook of Private International Law*, Vol 13, 273–97; E M Kieninger, 'Ascertaining and Applying Foreign Law', in S Leible (ed), *General Principles of European Private Law* (2016), pp 357–73.

[2] This can include Sharia law: *Shamil Bank of Bahrain EC v Bexico Pharmaceuticals Ltd* [2004] EWCA Civ 19, [2004] 1 WLR 1784; *Al-Bassam v Al-Bassam* [2004] EWCA Civ 857.

[3] *Nelson v Bridport* (1846) 8 Beav 547, though cf *Saxby v Fulton* [1909] 2 KB 208 at 211; *Harold Meyers Travel Service Ltd v Magid* (1975) 60 DLR (3d) 42 at 44; *El Ajou v Dollar Land Holdings plc* [1993] 3 All ER 717 at 736; revsd by the Court of Appeal [1994] 2 All ER 685 but not on this point; *Grupo Torras SA and Torras Hostench London Ltd v Sheikh Fahad Mohammed Al-Sabah* [1996] 1 Lloyd's Rep 7 at 18, CA.

[4] See the European Communities Act 1972, s 3.

[5] *El Ajou v Dollar Land Holdings plc* [1993] 3 All ER 717 at 736; revsd by the Court of Appeal [1994] 2 All ER 685 but not on this point. For criticism of this see *Morgan Grenfell & Co Ltd v Istituto per I Servizi Assicurativi del Commercio* [2001] EWCA Civ 1932 at [53]. See generally Fentiman, *Foreign Law in English Courts* (1998), pp 248–51.

[6] *Macmillan Inc v Bishopsgate Investment Trust plc (No 4)* [1999] CLC 417, CA; *El Ajou v Dollar Land Holdings plc*, supra; *Kuwait Oil Tanker Co SAK v Al Bader* [2000] 2 All ER (Comm) 271 at 336, CA; *Al -Wazir v Islamic Press Agency Inc* [2001] EWCA Civ 1276 at [20], [42]–[43], [2002] 1 Lloyd's Rep 410; *Société Eram Shipping Co Ltd v Compagnie Internationale de Navigation* [2001] EWCA Civ 1317 at [45], [2001] 2 Lloyd's Rep 627; revsd [2003] UKHL 30, [2004] 1 AC 260 without discussion of this point; *Concord Trust v The Law Debenture Trust Corpn plc* [2005] UKHL 27 at [44], [2005] 1 WLR 1591; *PT Pan Indonesia Bank Ltd TBK v Marconi Communications International Ltd* [2005] EWCA Civ 422 at [70]; *Balmoral Group Ltd v Borealis* [2006] EWHC 1900 (Comm) at [427]–[435], [2006] 2 Lloyd's Rep 629; *Sharp v Ministry of Defence* [2007] EWHC 224 (QB). See also *McGowan v Summit at Lloyds* 2002 SLT 1258 at 1263; *Attorney-General for England and Wales v R* [2002] 2 NZLR 91 CA; *Backman v The Queen* (1999) 178 DLR (4th) 126, Fed CA; *Davison v Sweeney* (2005) 255 DLR (4th) 757.

[7] *Royal Boskalis Westminster NV v Mountain* [1999] QB 675 at 725 (per Phillips LJ), 689 (per Stuart-Smith LJ), CA.

and has been criticised in a defamation case[8] and where the Court's process of execution was sought to be invoked[9] and more generally where the foreign legal system is very different from the forum.[10] This presumption may not be applied where the claimant asks for summary judgment[11] or in a case where an injunction is sought preventing acts of passing off[12] or acts of infringement abroad.[13] Finally, it should be pointed out that there are a number of cases where an English court has not assumed the foreign law to be the same as English statute law.[14] The onus of proving that the foreign law is different from English law, and of proving what it is, lies on the party who pleads the difference.[15] If there is no such plea, or if the difference is not satisfactorily proved,[16] the court must give a decision according to English law, even though the case may be connected solely with some foreign country,[17] and the law of that foreign country is applicable according to English choice of law rules.[18] The difficulty that there can sometimes be in applying this presumption is illustrated by a decision of the High Court of Australia[19] where, although there was proof that there was a flexible exception to the general tort choice of law rule that exists under Chinese law, there was inadequate evidence as to how this was applied and whether it would be applied in the circumstances of the present case. The majority applied the presumption and asked how an Australian court would

---

[8] *Schapira v Ahronson* [1998] IL Pr 587 at 599, CA. *Société Eram* [2001] 2 Lloyd's Rep 394 at 398 (per Toulson J) but cf the Court of Appeal, op cit, at [55]–[56].

[9] *Société Eram* [2001] 2 Lloyd's Rep 394 at 398 (per Toulson J) but cf the Court of Appeal, op cit, at [55]–[56].

[10] *Neilson v Overseas Projects Corpn of Victoria Ltd* [2005] HCA 54 at [203] (per Kirby J). See generally on exceptions to the presumption, Fentiman, *Foreign Law in English Courts* (1998), pp 146–8; *Damberg v Damberg* [2001] 52 NSWLR 492 at [119]–[162], NSWCA; *Shaker v El-Bedrawi* [2002] EWCA Civ 1452 at [64]–[72], [2003] Ch 350.

[11] *National Shipping Corpn v Arab* [1971] 2 Lloyd's Rep 363.

[12] *Dunhill v Sunoptic* [1979] FSR 337.

[13] *International Business Machines Corpn v Phoenix Intercontinental (Computers) Ltd* [1994] RPC 251. Nor has it been applied in a tax case involving German law, which is not a common law based system: *Damberg v Damberg*, supra, at [162], distinguished in *Tisand v Owners of the Ship MV Cape Moreton (Ex Freya)* [2005] FCAFC 68, (2005) 219 ALR 48. Nor has it been applied where the proper law of a contract was foreign and there was no proof of that law: *Global Multimedia v ARA Media Services* [2006] EWHC 3107 (Ch) at [37]–[40], [2007] 1 All ER (Comm) 1160. Nor has it been applied where there was only proof of part of the foreign law: *Tamil Nadu Electricity Board v St CMS Electricity Co* [2007] EWHC 1713 (Comm) at [97]–[98], [2007] 2 All ER (Comm) 701.

[14] *R v Brixton Prison Governor, ex p Caldough* [1961] 1 All ER 606; *Osterreichische Länderbank v S'Elite Ltd* [1981] QB 565 at 569; and see *Purdom v Pavey & Co* (1896) 26 SCR 412; *BP Exploration Co (Libya) Ltd v Hunt* (1980) 47 FLR 317; *The Mercury Bell v Amosin* (1986) 27 DLR (4th) 641; *Shaker v El-Bedrawi*— possibly where an English statute cannot be applied without significant modification; see also *Belhaj v Straw* [2014] EWCA Civ 1394 and *Willis Australia Group Services Pty Ltd v Giggs* [2012] NSWSC 659; cf *De Reneville v De Reneville* [1948] P 100; for Australia see *National Auto Glass Supplies v Nielsen & Moller Autoglass* [2007] FCA 1625 at [33]–[45]. See also Hartley (1996) 45 ICLQ 271, 285–9 who mentions exceptions in relation to criminal proceedings, international obligations not to enforce a contract and, without judicial authority to support this, status and illegality.

[15] *The King of Spain v Machado* (1827) 4 Russ 225 at 239; *Ascherberg Hopwood and Crew v Casa Musicale Sonzogno* [1971] 1 WLR 173, affd ibid at 1128; *Kutchera v Buckingham International Holdings Ltd* [1988] IR 61 at 68; *Kraus's Administrators v Sullivan* 1998 SLT 963; *Glencore International AG v Metro Trading International Inc (No 2)* [2001] 1 Lloyd's Rep 284 at [55]; the *PT Pan Indonesia Bank* Case, supra, at [70].

[16] In the latter situation, it is not necessary for the opposing party to adduce his own contradictory evidence: the *PT Pan Indonesia Bank* Case, supra, at [70].

[17] *Warner Bros v Nelson* [1937] 1 KB 209; *Cressington Court (Owners) v Marinero (Owners), The Marinero* [1955] 1 All ER 676; *Mount Cook (Northland) Ltd v Swedish Motors Ltd* [1986] 1 NZLR 720; cf *Guépratte v Young* (1851) 4 De G & Sm 217 at 224–5. As to the alternatives open to a court when a party fails to prove foreign law, see Kahn-Freund (1974) III Hague Recueil 139, 422–6. See generally North, *Essays*, pp 179–81.

[18] For torts see, infra, pp 803–4; Fentiman, *Foreign Law in English Courts* (1998), p 106. For the position in relation to contract see, infra, pp 710–11, n 257; Fentiman, op cit, pp 87 et seq. See also *Sharp v Ministry of Defence* [2007] EWHC 224 (QB) at [11]–[12].

[19] *Neilson v Overseas Projects Corpn of Victoria Ltd* [2005] HCA 54; Briggs [2006] LMCLQ 1.

construe an Australian statute, concluding, in the light of this, that this exception would be applied by a Chinese court.[20] There is much force in a critical dissenting judgment which pointed out that Australian law had no such flexible exception and argued that construction could not be divorced from what was being construed.[21]

The presence of the procedural rule that in the absence of proof (of the content of the foreign law) the judge is obliged to assume that the content of the foreign law is the same as English law and decide the case on that basis presupposes that the English choice of law rule is mandatory.[22] One can after all only get to this procedural rule if the choice of law rule[23] has been applied by the judge, irrespective of the case put forward by the parties. Other legal systems, such as the German legal system and to a large extent also the Swiss and Belgian legal systems to pick just a few examples,[24] derive from the mandatory application of the choice of law rule that the court has to ascertain the content of the foreign law so determined and apply it. The fact that the English approach is very different is based on our very different procedural traditions and shows how non-harmonised procedural rules can undermine the consistent application of EU choice of law rules.[25] Hence the idea to establish a Rome 0 Regulation to deal with the underlying issues.[26]

Foreign law is, therefore, treated as a question of fact but it is "a question of fact of a peculiar kind".[27] To describe it as one of fact is no doubt apposite, in the sense that the applicable law must be ascertained according to the evidence of witnesses, yet there can be no doubt that what is involved is at bottom a question of law. This has been recognised by the courts.[28] The rule, for instance, in a purely domestic case is that an appellate court will disturb a finding of fact by the trial judge only with the greatest reluctance, but this is not so when the "fact" that has been found in the court below is the relevant rule of a foreign legal system.[29] In such

---

[20] *Neilson v Overseas Projects Corpn of Victoria Ltd*, supra, at [125]–[127] (per Gummow and Hayne JJ), [249] (per Callinan J), [267] (per Heydon J).

[21] Ibid at [36] (McHugh J). Kirby J at [203] and Gleeson CJ at [16] also found the presumption of no assistance.

[22] As it is in Germany, but not all countries follow this line, eg in France they are discretional in the areas where the parties' rights at issue are disposable.

[23] This includes EU Regulations. Fentiman (supra note 16) has argued that the imperative character of the choice of law rules in Regulations also flows from their origin in an international instrument, but he stands alone with this argument.

[24] There is a kind of international consensus on this point, see Esplugues Mota, 'Harmonisation of Private International Law in Europe and Application of Foreign Law: The Madrid Principles of 2010', in (2011) *Yearbook of Private International Law*, Vol 13, pp 273–97. E M Kieninger would add the concept of proportionality and take into consideration issues of time and cost and give the judge a discretion to apply the law of the forum if the parties agree: E M Kieninger, 'Ascertaining and Applying Foreign Law', in S Leible (ed), *General Principles of European Private Law*, (2016), pp 357–73.

[25] T Hartley, 45 (1996) ICLQ 2, pp 271–92.

[26] S Leible (ed), *General Principles of European Private Law*, (2016).

[27] *Parkasho v Singh* [1968] P 233 at 250; *Macmillan Inc v Bishopsgate Investment Trust plc (No 4)* [1999] CLC 417, CA; *Morgan Grenfell & Co Ltd v Istituto per I Servizi Assicurativi del Commercio* [2001] EWCA Civ 1932 at [45]; *King v Brandywine Reinsurance* Co [2005] EWCA Civ 655 at [66]–[67], [2005] 1 Lloyd's Rep 655, Briggs (2005) BYBIL 660; *Abu Dhabi Investment Co v H Clarkson & Co Ltd* [2006] EWHC 1252 (Comm) at [26], [2006] 2 Lloyd's Rep 381. Propositions of foreign law which a claimant advances in order to succeed against a person claiming contribution under the Civil Liability (Contribution) Act 1978, s l, are not properly to be regarded as part of the factual basis of the claim against such person: *Arab Monetary Fund v Hashim (No 8)* (1993) Times, 17 June; see also *Arab Monetary Fund v Hashim (No 9)* (1994) Times, 11 October.

[28] See, eg, *Egmatra AG v Marco Trading Corpn* [1999] 1 Lloyd's Rep 862; *Reliance Industries Ltd v Enron Oil and Gas India Ltd* [2002] 1 Lloyd's Rep 645—Arbitration Act 1996, s 69 (appeals on a question of law) cases.

[29] *Grupo Torras SA and Torras Hostench London Ltd v Sheikh Fahad Mohammed Al-Sabah* [1996] 1 Lloyd's Rep 7 at 18, CA.

a case the role of the appellate court has been described in terms of a "duty . . . to examine the evidence of foreign law which was before the justices and to decide for ourselves whether that evidence justifies the conclusion to which they came".[30] Nevertheless, the courts have concluded that a mistake as to foreign law is to be regarded as a mistake of fact.[31]

2. HOW FOREIGN LAW IS PROVED[32]

It is clear that the relevant foreign law on some particular matter must be proved, like other matters of which no knowledge is imputed to the judge,[33] "by appropriate evidence, ie by properly qualified witnesses",[34] unless both parties agree to leave the investigation to the judge and to dispense with the aid of witnesses.[35] This is by no means a universal law though. By German, Belgian and Netherlands law, for instance, foreign law is regarded as law, not fact, and is commonly ascertained by personal research by the court itself.[36] The method of proof by way of expert witnesses has been criticised on the basis that it can involve a vast amount of oral and written evidence, leading to inordinate delay and expense.[37] Efforts have been made under the civil procedure rules to remedy this by giving the courts power to control expert evidence;[38] even so, it remains the case that, subject to section 4(2) of the Civil Evidence Act 1972,[39] foreign law cannot be proved, for instance, by citing a previous decision of an English court in which the same foreign rule was in issue,[40] or by merely presenting the judge with the text of the foreign law and leaving him to draw his own conclusions,[41] or by referring to a decision in which a court of the foreign country has stated the meaning and effect of the law in question.[42] A fortiori, it cannot be proved by referring to a decision as to the law of the foreign country in question given in the courts of some other foreign country.[43]

---

[30] *Parkasho v Singh,* supra; *Dalmia Dairy Industries Ltd v National Bank of Pakistan* [1978] 2 Lloyd's Rep 223 at 286; and see Webb (1967) 16 ICLQ 1152, 1155–6; Fentiman, *Foreign Law in English Courts* (1998), pp 201–2. Proof of foreign law in an appellate court is discussed further, infra, p 113.

[31] *The Amazonia* [1990] 1 Lloyd's Rep 236, CA; and see *Andre & Cie SA v Ets Michel Blanc & Fils* [1979] 2 Lloyd's Rep 427, CA.

[32] See generally Fentiman, *Foreign Law in English Courts* (1998), Chapter VI.

[33] A good overview on how the foreign law is proved as a matter of fact is provided in *Yukos Capital Sarl v OJSC Oil Co Rosneft* [2014] EWHC 2188 (Comm), paras 24–31; see also *Islamic Republic of Iran v Berend* [2007] EWHC 132, para 50.

[34] *Nelson v Bridport* (1845) 8 Beav 527 at 536; *Beatty v Beatty* [1924] 1 KB 807 at 814; *Lazard Bros & Co v Midland Bank* [1933] AC 289; *El Ajou v Dollar Land Holdings plc* [1993] 3 All ER 717 at 736; revsd by the Court of Appeal [1994] 2 All ER 685 but not on this point; *Grupo Torras SA and Torras Hostench London Ltd v Sheikh Fahad Mohammed Al-Sabah* [1996] 1 Lloyd's Rep 7 at 17 et seq, CA; *R v Okolie* (2000) Times, 16 June, CA. Cf *Lear v Lear* (1973) 51 DLR (3d) 56.

[35] *Jabbour (F & K) v Custodian of Israeli Absentee Property* [1954] 1 WLR 139 at 147–8; *Dalmia Dairy Industries Ltd v National Bank of Pakistan* [1978] 2 Lloyd's Rep 223 at 236; *Islamic Republic of Iran v Berend* [2007] EWHC 132 (QB) at [35], [2007] 2 All ER 132.

[36] Geeroms, *Foreign Law in Civil Litigation* (2004), paras 2.132–2.175, Hartley, op cit, pp 275–6. In New Zealand, the court has power to decide a question of foreign law in the absence of other expert evidence: Evidence Act, 1908, s 40; *Dymocks Franchise Systems (NSW) Pty Ltd v Todd* [2002] UKPC 50, [2004] 1 NZLR 289.

[37] *Grupo Torras SA and Torras Hostench London Ltd v Sheikh Fahad Mohammed Al-Sabah,* supra n 34, at 17.

[38] Discussed infra, pp 111–12.

[39] Infra.

[40] *Lazard Bros & Co v Midland Bank Ltd,* supra; *McCormick v Garnett* (1854) 23 LJ Ch 777; *Re Marseilles Extension Rly and Land Co* (1885) 30 Ch D 598 at 602. But in *Re Sebba* [1959] Ch 166, Danckwerts J considered that in the circumstances he was justified in departing from this rule.

[41] *Buerger v New York Life Assurance Co* (1927) 96 LJKB 930 at 940.

[42] *Beatty v Beatty* [1924] 1 KB 807 at 814–15; *Guaranty Trust Co of New York v Hannay & Co* [1918] 2 KB 623 at 638, 667.

[43] *Callwood v Callwood* [1960] AC 659; Webb (1960) 23 MLR 556; Carter (1960) 36 BYBIL 408.

Nor can it be proved by the assertion of an opinion as to the effect of the foreign law without reference to the relevant authorities.[44] However, the parts of the United Kingdom form an exception to these rules in cases coming before the Supreme Court as the ultimate appellate tribunal in civil matters. Thus Scottish law must be proved by evidence in the courts inferior to the Supreme Court, but in the Supreme Court itself, which is the common forum of both England and Scotland, it is a matter of which their Lordships have judicial knowledge.[45]

However, proof of foreign law, including Scots and Northern Irish law, is rendered easier by section 4(2) of the Civil Evidence Act 1972. It provides that, when any question of foreign law has been determined in civil or criminal proceedings in the High Court, the Crown Court, certain other courts or in appeals therefrom, or in proceedings before the Judicial Committee of the Privy Council on appeal from courts abroad,[46] any finding made or decision given in such proceedings shall, if reported in citable form,[47] be admissible in later civil proceedings as evidence of the foreign law.[48] Indeed, the foreign law shall be taken to be in accordance with such finding or decision unless the contrary is proved, provided it does not conflict with another finding of foreign law adduced in the same proceedings.[49]

The English courts have not adopted the practice in civil law systems according to which a government may be requested to give an official statement of the law on some particular matter. By the British Law Ascertainment Act 1859, however, a court within Her Majesty's Dominions, which is of the opinion that it is necessary or expedient for the disposal of a case to ascertain the law of some part of Her Majesty's Dominions, may remit to a superior court in the latter place the question of law on which a ruling is required.[50] The provisions of this Act may be extended by Order in Council to other British territories.[51]

Foreign law had formerly to be proved to the satisfaction of the jury, but the Supreme Court Act 1981[52] has now provided as follows:

> Where . . . it is necessary to ascertain the law of any other country which is applicable to the facts of the case, any question as to the effect of the evidence given with respect to that law shall, instead of being submitted to the jury, be decided by the judge alone.

---

[44] *Mount Cook (Northland) Ltd v Swedish Motors Ltd* [1986] 1 NZLR 720. See also *Astra SA Insurance and Reinsurance Co v Sphere Drake Insurance Ltd* [2000] All ER (D) 672. An extreme example is found in the US case *Duran v Beaumont* (2d Cir, 2008) 534 F 3d 142, 147, where the 2nd Circuit rejected an affidavit on Chilean law from the Chilean Central Authority under the Hague Abduction Convention and instead preferred a conflicting interpretation in one of its own prior cases, *Croll v Croll*, 229 F 3d 133 (2d Cir, 2000). Both decisions were overturned and vacated by the Supreme, see *Abbott v Abbott*, 130 S Ct 1983 (2010) and *Duran v Beaumont*, 130 S Ct 3318 (2010). The 2nd Circuit remanded the case to the District court *Duran v Beaumont* (2d Cir, 2010), 622 F 3d 97.

[45] *Elliot v Joicey* [1935] AC 209 at 236. This rule is unaffected by the Civil Evidence Act 1972, s 4(2), infra.

[46] S 4(4).

[47] S 4(5).

[48] See *Phoenix Marine Inc v China Ocean Shipping Co* [1999] CLC 478.

[49] Findings or decisions as to foreign law in earlier proceedings may only be adduced if notice is given to all other parties: s 4(3).

[50] S 1. The European Convention on Information on Foreign Law, sometimes referred to as the London Convention, Treaty Series No 117 (1969) (Cmnd 4229) sets out to achieve the same aims as the 1859 Act in respect of foreign countries generally. The Convention has been ratified by the United Kingdom, but has never been implemented. See Fentiman, *Foreign Law in English Courts* (1998), pp 239–44; Geerooms, *Foreign Law in Civil Litigation* (2004), paras 2.256–2.257; Dicey, Morris and Collins, para 9-024; Rodger and Van Doorn (1997) 46 ICLQ 151; Rodger 1998 SLT 80.

[51] Foreign Jurisdiction Act 1890, s 5, Sch 1.

[52] S 69(5), replacing Administration of Justice Act 1920, s 15 and Supreme Court of Judicature (Consolidation) Act 1925, s 102. The Act applies to criminal trials: *R v Hammer* [1923] 2 KB 786.

3. WITNESSES WHO CAN PROVE FOREIGN LAW[53]

It is obvious that no witness can speak to a question of law as a fact and that all he can do is to express his opinion. The rule is, therefore, that he must be an expert. The question as to who is a sufficient expert in this matter has not been satisfactorily resolved by the English decisions.[54] Though no doubt the court has a discretion in the matter, the general principle has been that no person is a competent witness unless he is a practising lawyer in the particular legal system in question, or unless he occupies a position or follows a calling in which he must necessarily acquire a practical working knowledge of the foreign law. In other words, practical experience is a sufficient qualification. Thus, in accordance with this principle:

A Roman Catholic bishop was allowed to testify to the matrimonial law of Rome, since a knowledge of its provisions was essential to the performance of his official duties.[55]

A hotel-keeper in London, a native of Belgium, who had formerly been a commissioner of stocks in Brussels, was admitted to prove the Belgian law of promissory notes, on the ground that his business had made him conversant with commercial law.[56]

An ex-Governor of Hong Kong was held competent to prove the marriage law of that colony.[57]

A secretary to the Persian Embassy was allowed to depose to the law of Persia, on it being shown that there were then no professional lawyers in that country, but that all diplomatic officials had to be thoroughly versed in the law.[58]

Where it was necessary to ascertain the meaning of a bill of exchange given in Chile, the evidence of a London bank director with long experience of banking in South America was preferred to that of a young man who had been at the Chilean Bar for four years.[59]

An experienced police officer from Quebec was able to prove the road traffic law of that Province before an Ontario court.[60]

The view taken by the courts was that a mere academic knowledge of foreign law scarcely qualified a person as an expert witness. Thus in *Bristow v Sequeville*[61] where it was necessary to prove the law in force at Cologne, a witness was called who stated that he was a jurist and legal adviser to the Prussian consul in England, and that having studied law at Leipzig University, but never practised in Prussia, he knew from his studies there that the Code Napoléon applied in Cologne. It was held that he was not a competent witness. But although it has been said that study alone is not sufficient qualification,[62] the courts did not consistently observe the requirement of practical experience. Thus the Reader in Roman-Dutch law to the Council of Legal Education, who had made a special study of that law

---

[53] See generally Fentiman, *Foreign Law in English Courts* (1998), pp 178–82.

[54] Falconbridge, op cit, pp 833–8.

[55] *The Sussex Peerage Case* (1844) 11 Cl & Fin 85; distinguish *R v Savage* (1876) 13 Cox CC 178; see also *R v Ilich* [1935] NZLR 90.

[56] *Vander Donckt v Thellusson* (1849) 8 CB 812; distinguish *Perlak Petroleum Maatschappij v Deen* [1924] 1 KB 111.

[57] *Cooper-King v Cooper-King* [1900] P 65. The only lawyer who could be found to give such expert evidence had demanded "a prohibitive fee of fifteen guineas".

[58] *Re Dhost Aly Khan's Goods* (1880) 6 PD 6.

[59] *De Beéche v South American Stores* [1935] AC 148. The evidence of a bank manager was also accepted in *Said Ajami v Customs Comptroller* [1954] 1 WLR 1405; distinguished in *Clyne v Federal Comr of Taxation (No 2)* (1981) 57 FLR 198.

[60] *Guerin v Proulx* (1982) 37 OR (2d) 558.

[61] (1850) 5 Exch 275; *Re Bonelli's Goods* (1875) 1 PD 69.

[62] *Re Turner* [1906] WN 27.

for the purpose of his lectures, was admitted to testify to Rhodesian law;[63] an English barrister, who in the course of his profession had made researches into the marriage laws of Malta, was held competent to prove the validity of a marriage that had been solemnised at Valetta;[64] evidence as to the law of Chile was admitted from an English solicitor who, though never a practitioner in that country, stated that he had considerable experience of its laws;[65] and, in another case,[66] evidence as to Egyptian law was admitted from an English barrister who had practised before the mixed courts and British consular courts in Egypt until they ceased to function, thirteen years earlier. Since then he had had no right of audience in Egyptian courts, though he had done his best to keep his knowledge of Egyptian law up to date. It has now been made clear, by section 4(1) of the Civil Evidence Act 1972, that evidence as to foreign law may be given by a person who is qualified to do so on account of his knowledge and experience "irrespective of whether he has acted or is entitled to act as a legal practitioner there".[67] Subsequently, a Dutch academic lawyer who had undertaken extensive research and had wide contact with Indonesian lawyers and practice was qualified to give evidence as to the land law of Indonesia[68] and an academic lawyer has given evidence on UAE law.[69]

4. THE ROLE OF THE COURT[70]

Under the Civil Procedure Rules the courts have the power to control expert evidence for the purpose of reducing costs and delay. No party may call an expert or put in evidence an expert's report without the court's permission.[71] Expert evidence is to be given in a written report unless the court directs otherwise.[72] A party may put written questions to an expert instructed by another party about his report.[73] The court may, at any stage, direct a discussion between experts with a view to identifying issues and their reaching an agreed opinion on these issues.[74] Where two or more parties wish to submit expert evidence on a particular issue, the court may direct that the evidence on that issue is to be given by one expert only.[75] The court may give permission for oral evidence on a case management occasion. An expert has an overriding duty to help the court on the matters within his expertise.[76] This overrides any duty to the person from whom he has received instructions or by whom he is paid.[77]

---

[63] *Brailey v Rhodesia Consolidated Ltd* [1910] 2 Ch 95; and see *Barford v Barford* [1918] P 140.

[64] *Wilson v Wilson* [1903] P 157.

[65] *Re Whitelegg's Goods* [1899] P 267.

[66] *Rossano v Manufacturers' Life Insurance Co Ltd* [1963] 2 QB 352.

[67] See in relation to evidence given by affidavit, *Practice Direction (Foreign Law Affidavit)* [1972] 1 WLR 1433.

[68] *PT Royal Bali Leisure v Hutchinson & Co Trust Co Ltd* [2004] EWHC 1014 (Ch) at [107].

[69] *Glencore International AG v Metro Trading International Inc (No 2)* [2001] 1 Lloyd's Rep 284 at [52]. See also *Evialis SA v SIAT* [2003] EWHC 863, [2003] 2 Lloyd's Rep 377 at [43]; *Shiblaq v Sadikoglu* [2004] EWHC 1890 (Comm) at [4]–[12], [2004] IL Pr 51; *Abu Dhabi Investment Co v H Clarkson & Co Ltd* [2006] EWHC 1252 (Comm), [2006] 2 Lloyd's Rep 381.

[70] Fentiman, *Foreign Law in English Courts* (1998), pp 188–202.

[71] CPR, r 35.4.

[72] CPR, r 35.5.

[73] CPR, r 35.6.

[74] CPR, r 35.12.

[75] CPR, r 35.7.

[76] CPR, r 35.3(1).

[77] CPR, r 35.3(2).

Although he must state his opinion as based on his knowledge or practical experience of the foreign law, the expert may refer to codes, decisions or treatises for the purpose of refreshing his memory, but in such an event the court is at liberty to examine the law or passage in question in order to arrive at its correct meaning.[78] If the expert witnesses disagree the court must look at the sources of the foreign law.[79] Even if the expert witness is uncontradicted by other expert testimony, the court may examine the texts in order to reach its own conclusions on the foreign law, though where the expert evidence is uncontradicted, the court should be reluctant to reject it,[80] unless it is absurd.[81] However, the power to reject the expert's opinion is not confined to instances of absurdity in at least one situation, namely where the English court interprets a foreign statute in accordance with English rules of construction, there being no evidence that different rules would govern the foreign court's interpretation.[82] Essentially the judge's finding is as to statutory interpretation and as such is one of law. The court should not examine texts which have not been relied on by the expert or by counsel.[83] Again, if there is a conflict of testimony between the expert witnesses on either side, the court must place its own interpretation on the foreign law in the light of all the evidence given,[84] having regard to the preponderance of legal opinion before it.[85] The evidence of one expert may be accepted as a whole over that of another but is, nevertheless, not accepted on a particular issue.[86] It may be necessary to find the proper construction of a particular foreign provision by inference from the evidence of one or both of the experts, applying the rules of construction under the foreign law.[87] The expert proves the foreign rules of construction and the court itself, in the light of these rules, determines the meaning of contractual documents.[88] In all cases, in fact, it is the right and duty of the court to examine and criticise the evidence.[89]

---

[78] *Concha v Murrietta* (1889) 40 Ch D 543; *Russian Commercial and Industrial Bank v Comptoir d'Escompte de Mulhouse* [1923] 2 KB 630 at 643; *Re Cohn* [1945] Ch 5; see 61 LQR 340; *De Beéche v South American Stores Ltd and Chilian Stores Ltd* [1935] AC 148 at 158–9; *Parkasho v Singh* [1968] P 233 at 250–2, 254.

[79] *Arros Invest Ltd v Rafik Nishanov* [2004] EWHC 576 (Ch) at [22], [2004] IL Pr 22.

[80] *Sharif v Azad* [1967] 1 QB 605 at 616; *Grupo Torras SA and Torras Hostench London Ltd v Sheikh Fahad Mohammed Al-Sabah* [1996] 1 Lloyd's Rep 7 at 18, CA; *James Hardie & Co v Hall* (1998) 43 NSWLR 554 at 573. A lack of plausibility or independence on the side of the witness may be good reasons to reject the evidence: *Dornoch Ltd v Westminster International BV* [2009] EWHC 1782 (Admlty), para 49; *Debt Collect London Ltd v SK Slavia Praha Fotbal AS* [2010] EWCA Civ 1250, paras 31–6.

[81] The *Grupo Torras* case, supra. Contrast the view of expert evidence taken in *Re Russian Bank for Foreign Trade* [1933] Ch 745 with the view taken of the same expert's evidence in *Re Banque des Marchands de Moscou (Koupetschesky)* [1958] Ch 182 and see Civil Evidence Act 1972, s 4(2), supra, p 114.

[82] *Macmillan Inc v Bishopsgate Investment Trust plc (No 4)* [1999] CLC 417, CA; *Hunt v T & N plc* (1993) 109 DLR (4th) 16 at 29–30 (Sup Ct Can).

[83] *Bumper Development Corpn Ltd v Metropolitan Police Comr* [1991] 1 WLR 1362.

[84] *Trimbey v Vignier* (1834) 1 Bing NC 151; *Di Sora v Phillips* (1863) 10 HL Cas 624 at 636–42; *Lazard Bros & Co v Midland Bank Ltd* [1933] AC 289 at 298; *Sinfra Akt v Sinfra Ltd* [1939] 2 All ER 675; *Parkasho v Singh* [1968] P 233; *Grupo Torras SA and Torras Hostench London Ltd v Sheikh Fahad Mohammed Al-Sabah* [1996] 1 Lloyd's Rep 7 at 18, CA; *Macmillan Inc v Bishopsgate Investment Trust plc (No 4)* [1999] CLC 417, CA; *Gulf Consolidated v CSFB Ltd* [1992] 2 Lloyd's Rep 301 at 303; Fentiman, *Foreign Law in English Courts* (1998), pp 200–1.

[85] *Shiblaq v Sadikoglu* [2004] EWHC 1890 (Comm) at [10], [2004] IL Pr 51.

[86] *Gulf Consolidated v CSFB Ltd*, supra, at 303–4.

[87] Ibid.

[88] Dicey, Morris and Collins, para 9-019; *King v Brandywine Reinsurance Co* [2005] EWCA Civ 655 at [68], [2005] 1 Lloyd's Rep 655; *Evialis SA v SIAT* [2003] EWHC 863 (Comm) at [44], [2003] 2 Lloyd's Rep 377; *Toomey (Syndicate 2021) v Banco Vitalicio de España SA de Seguros y Reaseguros* [2003] EWHC 1102 (Comm) at [37], appeal dismissed without discussion of this point [2004] EWCA Civ 622 at [37], [2004] 1 CLC 965; *Svenska Petroleum Exploration v Government of the Republic of Lithuania (No 2)* [2005] EWHC 2437 (Comm) at [29], [2006] 1 Lloyd's Rep 181, appeal dismissed without discussion of this point [2006] EWCA Civ 1529.

[89] *Tallinna Laevaushisus (A/S) v Estonian State Steamship Line* (1947) 80 Lloyd's Rep 99 at 108; *Rouyer Guillet et Cie v Rouyer Guillet & Co Ltd* [1949] 1 All ER 244 n; *Re Fuld's Estate (No 3), Hartley v Fuld* [1968] P 675 at 700–3; as to the question of the court examining the constitutionality of foreign legislation, see Mann

The question of proof of foreign law in an appellate court has been examined by Sir Jocelyn Simon P who said:

> Foreign law is, it is true, regarded in English courts as a question of fact; and appellate courts are slow to interfere with trial courts on questions of fact; but that only applies with particular force as regards the assessment of relative veracity and the judgment of matters of degree. Where the inference of fact depends on the consideration of written material, an appellate court is at no particular disadvantage compared to a trial court and will regard itself as freer to review the decision of the trial court.[90]

The Court of Appeal has interfered with the judge's finding of fact in the situation where this was contrary to the views of both side's experts.[91] The Court of Appeal is entitled and bound to form its own view, independently of the trial judge's view, on the issue of construction of a foreign statute, where its interpretation has been in accordance with English rules of construction, there being no evidence that different rules would govern the foreign court's interpretation.[92] Due regard must, however, be paid to the relevant circumstances as found by the judge.

(1943) 59 LQR 155; Lipstein (1967) 42 BYBIL 265; Kahn-Freund (1974) III Hague Recueil 139, 449–52; Kahn-Freund, *Festschrift für F A Mann*, p 207.

[90] *Parkasho v Singh*, supra, at 254. See also *Grupo Torras SA and Torras Hostench London Ltd v Sheikh Fahad Mohammed Al-Sabah* [1996] 1 Lloyd's Rep 7 at 18, CA.

[91] *Grupo Torras SA and Torras Hostench London Ltd v Sheikh Fahad Mohammed Al-Sabah*, supra, at 23.

[92] *Macmillan Inc v Bishopsgate Investment Trust plc (No 4)* [1999] CLC 417, CA.

8

EXCLUSION OF FOREIGN LAW

1. **Foreign Revenue, Penal and Other Public Laws** 115
   (a) Foreign revenue laws 116
   (b) Foreign penal laws 118
   (c) Other foreign public laws 123
   (d) Effect of European Union private international law 125
2. **Foreign Expropriatory Legislation** 126
   (a) Property within the foreign jurisdiction at time of decree 127
   (b) Property outside the foreign jurisdiction at time of decree 130
   (c) Requisition of property 132

3. **Foreign Laws Repugnant to English Public Policy** 132
   (a) General principles 132
   (b) Summary of cases where distinctive policy is affected 135
   (c) Cases involving a foreign status 139
   (d) Recognition of foreign divorces, etc 141
   (e) Effect of European Union private international law 142
4. **Mandatory Rules** 143

It is obvious that circumstances will occasionally arise in which the law of the forum must be preferred to the foreign law that would normally be applicable to the case. An outstanding example of this is the civil law doctrine of *ordre public* under which any domestic rule designed to protect the public welfare must prevail over an inconsistent foreign rule. The danger of a doctrine so vague as this is that it may be interpreted to embrace such a multitude of domestic rules as to provide a fatally easy excuse for the application of the law of the forum and thus to defeat the underlying purpose of private international law. The analogous English doctrine, though less unruly, is indeed not above suspicion in this respect. Summarily stated, it withholds all recognition from any foreign law or judgment which is repugnant to the distinctive policy of English law, and it refuses to enforce any foreign law or judgment which is of a penal, revenue or other public law nature.[1] Furthermore, foreign expropriatory laws will, in some circumstances, not be recognised, and, in other circumstances, although recognised, will not be enforced. Finally, the mandatory rules of the forum may be applied, with the result that, to that extent, a foreign law is excluded.

We will now deal separately with these four[2] cases. Before we proceed, it is worth recalling that much of private international law in England is now of European origin. European

---

[1] See Holder (1968) 17 ICLQ 926; FA Mann (1971) I Hague Recueil 115, 172–81; Carter (1984) 55 BYBIL 111; Carter (1989) 48 CLJ 417; Lipstein, in Banakas (ed), *United Kingdom Law in the 1980s* (1988) 38 and Forsyth, in ibid, 94; Collins (2007) 326 Hague Recueil 9.

[2] There are also the doctrines of Crown Act of State and foreign Act of State, which are beyond the scope of this book. On Crown Act of State see, eg, *Johnstone v Pedlar* [1921] 2 AC 262, HL; *A-G v Nissan* [1970] AC 179, HL; *Al-Jedda v Secretary of State for Defence* [2010] EWCA Civ 758, [2011] QB 773; *Rahmatullah v Secretary of State for Defence* [2017] UKSC 1, [2017] 2 WLR 287. On foreign Act of State see, eg, *Buttes Gas and Oil Co v Hammer (No 3)* [1982] AC 888, HL; *Kuwait Airways Corpn v Iraqi Airways Co (Nos 4 and 5)* [2002] UKHL 19, [2002] 2 AC 883; *Yukos Capital Sarl v OJSC Rosneft Oil Co* [2012] EWCA Civ 855, [2014] QB 458; *Belhaj v Straw* [2017] UKSC 3, [2017] 2 WLR 456. See generally Dicey, Morris and Collins, paras 5-043–5-053; McLachlan, *Foreign Relations Law* (2014). See also *Shergill v Khaira* [2014] UKSC 33, [2015] AC 359, [41]–[43].

Union private international law instruments, generally speaking, apply in civil and commercial matters, and allow English courts, within certain limits, to refuse to recognise any foreign law or judgment which is contrary to English public policy and to apply English overriding mandatory provisions. While there is a degree of similarity in this area between the traditional English doctrines and rules and the related doctrines and rules of European Union private international law, these do not necessarily have the same meaning and effect.

1. FOREIGN REVENUE, PENAL AND OTHER PUBLIC LAWS

Dicey, Morris and Collins[3] employs a three-fold classification of foreign laws which will not be enforced, either directly or indirectly, by English courts, ie revenue laws, penal laws and other public laws. This classification, which was adopted by Lord Denning in *A-G of New Zealand v Ortiz*,[4] has been endorsed by the Court of Appeal on a number of occasions,[5] has been given the support of the House of Lords in *Re State of Norway's Applications (Nos 1 and 2)*,[6] and was enshrined in statutory form for the area of tort choice of law by the Private International Law (Miscellaneous Provisions) Act 1995.[7] The same classification has also been adopted by the High Court of Australia,[8] the Court of Appeal in New Zealand[9] and in the High Court in Ireland.[10] "Public laws" is, seemingly, the umbrella concept which encompasses both revenue and penal laws, but also allows for a category of "other public laws".[11] The common thread running through the exclusionary rule in relation to revenue, penal and other public laws is that laws will not be enforced if they involve an exercise or assertion of sovereign authority by one state within the territory of another.[12] If the exclusionary rule

---

[3] Dicey, Morris and Collins, para 5R-019.

[4] [1984] AC 1 at 20 et seq, CA. Cf Ackner LJ at 34 and O'Connor LJ at 35. The House of Lords decided the case on a narrow point of construction: infra, p 120, n 56.

[5] See *Williams and Humbert Ltd v W and H Trade Marks (Jersey) Ltd* [1986] AC 368 at 394, 401; see also in the House of Lords the judgment of Lord Mackay at 437, cf Lord Templeman at 428; *Re State of Norway's Application* [1987] QB 433 at 477–8; *United States of America v Inkley* [1989] QB 255 at 265–6; *Camdex International Ltd v Bank of Zambia (No 2)* (1997) CLC 714; *Mbasogo v Logo Ltd* [2006] EWCA Civ 1370 at [51], [2007] QB 846; *United States Securities and Exchange Commission v Manterfield* [2009] EWCA Civ 27 at [11], [2010] 1 WLR 172.

[6] [1990] 1 AC 723.

[7] S 14(3)(a)(ii); the 1995 Act is discussed infra, p 778. Choice of law for non-contractual obligations is now largely governed by the Rome II Regulation; discussed infra, pp 780–875.

[8] *A-G (UK) v Heinemann Publishers Australia Pty Ltd (No 2)* (1988) 165 CLR 30.

[9] *A-G for the United Kingdom v Wellington Newspapers Ltd* [1988] 1 NZLR 129.

[10] *Bank of Ireland v Meeneghan* [1995] 1 ILRM 96 at 101.

[11] *United States of America v Inkley* [1989] QB 255 at 264–5, CA.

[12] *Re State of Norway's Applications (Nos 1 and 2)* [1990] 1 AC 723 at 807–8, HL. See also *Camdex International Ltd v Bank of Zambia (No 2)* (1997) CLC 714 at 723, 734, CA; *City of Gotha v Sotheby's*, 9 September 1998, HC; *Mbasogo v Logo Ltd* [2006] EWCA Civ 1370 at [27], [41], [42], [50], [51], [2007] QB 846; Briggs (2006) 77 BYBIL 554 and (2007) 123 LQR 182; Knight (2008) 19 KLJ 176; Mills (2007) 66 CLJ 3; Scott [2007] LMCLQ 296 and (2007) 2 J Priv Int L 309; Whomersley (2009) 125 LQR 227; *Tasarruff v Demirel* [2006] EWHC 3354 (Ch) at [63], [2007] IL Pr 8; affd without discussion of this point [2007] EWCA Civ 799, [2007] 1 WLR 2508, leave to appeal to the House of Lords dismissed [2007] 1 WLR 3066; *United States Securities and Exchange Commission v Manterfield* [2009] EWCA Civ 27 at [11], [2010] 1 WLR 172; *Pocket Kings Ltd v Safenames Ltd* [2009] EWHC 2529 (Ch) at [34]–[40], [2010] Ch 438; *JSC BTA Bank v Ablyazov* [2011] EWHC 202 (Comm) at [18], [2011] 2 All ER (Comm) 10. See also *President of the State of Equatorial Guinea v Royal Bank of Scotland International* [2006] UKPC 7 at [23]–[28]; Briggs (2006) 77 BYBIL 554; Dickinson (2006) 122 LQR 569. But an English court will not restrain voluntary compliance with a foreign public law, provided it does not involve committing any wrong under English law: *Carey Group plc and others v AIB Group (UK) plc* [2011] EWHC 567 (Ch), [2012] Ch 304.

applies it has been said that, in conceptual terms, what the court is doing is declining to exercise its jurisdiction.[13] Whether the claim brought in the English courts is one which involves the enforcement of a foreign revenue, penal or other public law is an issue to be determined according to the criteria of English law.[14] It is irrelevant whether a foreign law so regards it.[15] The three related concepts of revenue, penal and other public laws will now be examined.

(a) Foreign revenue laws[16]

(i) *The prohibition on enforcement*

Although it has been generally accepted, at any rate since the time of Lord Mansfield,[17] that no action lies in England for the enforcement of a foreign revenue law, authority for the proposition long remained a little nebulous, with the issue only being raised clearly on just one or two occasions.[18] All doubts were, however, stilled in 1955 by the decision of the House of Lords in *Government of India v Taylor*,[19] where, after a company, registered in England but carrying on business in India, had gone into voluntary liquidation, a demand was made on it by the Indian Commissioner of Income Tax for the payment of a large sum of income tax in respect of the capital gain derived from the earlier sale of the business. The Commissioner claimed to prove for this debt in the liquidation, but his claim was rejected by the liquidator and by the lower courts. It was argued for the appellants in the House of Lords that the alleged rule excluding the recognition of foreign revenue laws did not extend to taxes similar to those imposed in England, but was confined to penal laws, and that in any event it demanded modification in the case of a foreign country belonging to the Commonwealth. Further, it was said that the rule, even if accepted in toto, did not apply to liquidation proceedings, for a liquidator is under a statutory duty to discharge all the "liabilities" of the company, which is a word of wide import not confined to debts directly enforceable by action.

These arguments were rejected. Their Lordships were unanimous in holding that the rule expressed by Lord Mansfield rested on a solid basis of authority and convenience.[20] They also

---

[13] *Re State of Norway's Applications (Nos 1 and 2)* [1990] 1 AC 723 at 807–8, HL. The practical consequence is that the claim will be struck out as not justiciable. This means that the test in relation to the issue of exclusion is whether the claimant has a real prospect of succeeding (a serious issue to be tried) on the claim, rather than showing a good arguable case: *Tasarruff v Demirel* [2006] EWHC 3354 (Ch) at [62], [2007] IL Pr 8; affd without discussion of this point [2007] EWCA Civ 799, [2007] 1 WLR 2508, leave to appeal to the House of Lords dismissed [2007] 1 WLR 3066. It also means that a decision by a court to decline to exercise jurisdiction to enforce, directly or indirectly, foreign revenue, penal or other public laws is not a determination of the cause of action on the merits: *Relfo Ltd v Varsani* [2009] EWHC 2297 (Ch); affd without discussion of this point [2010] EWCA Civ 560, [2011] 1 WLR 1402.

[14] *United States of America v Inkley* [1989] QB 255 at 265, CA.

[15] *Tasarruff v Demirel* [2006] EWHC 3354 (Ch) at [65], [2007] IL Pr 8; affd without discussion of this point [2007] EWCA Civ 799, [2007] 1 WLR 2508, leave to appeal to the House of Lords dismissed [2007] 1 WLR 3066.

[16] See especially M Mann (1954) 3 ICLQ 465 and (1955) 4 ICLQ 564, and the judgment of Kingsmill Moore J in the Irish case of *Peter Buchanan Ltd and Macharg v McVey* [1955] AC 516 n, [1954] IR 89, SC. See also Albrecht (1953) 30 BYBIL 454, 459–65; Castel (1964) 42 Can Bar Rev 277; Stoel (1967) 16 ICLQ 663, 671 et seq; Smart (1986) 35 ICLQ 704; Briggs [2001] Sing JLS 280; Basedow and others (2004) 6 YBPIL 1.

[17] *Holman v Johnson* (1775) 1 Cowp 341 at 343, 98 ER 1120.

[18] See, eg, *Municipal Council of Sydney v Bull* [1909] 1 KB 7; *Re Visser* [1928] Ch 877. See also *The Eva* [1921] P 454; *King of the Hellenes v Brostrom* (1923) 16 Lloyd's Rep 167 and 190; *Metal Industries (Salvage) v Owners of the S T Harle* 1962 SLT 114; cf *The Acrux* [1965] P 391; Webb (1965) 28 MLR 591.

[19] [1955] AC 491; see also *Williams and Humbert Ltd v W and H Trade Marks (Jersey) Ltd* [1986] AC 368 at 428, HL; discussed infra, pp 128–30; *USA v Harden* [1963] SCR 366, (1963) 41 DLR (2d) 721; *Rothwells v Connell* (1993) 119 ALR 538 at 548–9, QCA.

[20] But the rule will only operate if the English court classifies the claim as a tax or revenue claim, eg, *Weir v Lohr* (1967) 65 DLR (2d) 717, Man QB; *Connor v Connor* [1974] 1 NZLR 632, NZSC; the former case also

held, with one dissentient,[21] that the duty of a liquidator in the winding up of a company is confined to the discharge of such liabilities as are legally enforceable.

(ii) Indirect enforcement

The rule that no action lies to recover foreign taxes is not affected by the identity of the claimant or by the form in which the action is brought. "In every case the substance of the claim must be scrutinised, and if it then appears that it is really a suit brought for the purpose of collecting the debts of a foreign revenue it must be rejected."[22] That an indirect evasion of the rule will not be tolerated is well illustrated by *Rossano v Manufacturers' Life Insurance Co Ltd*:[23]

> The plaintiff was an Egyptian national resident in Alexandria, who brought an action to recover money due under three policies of life insurance issued by the defendant, an insurance company with a head office in Toronto and branches in many other countries. The first two policies required payment in London in pounds sterling; the third directed payment at New York in dollars.

One defence raised by the defendant was that two garnishee orders[24] had been served on three of its branches in Cairo which would render it responsible for the payment of certain taxes alleged to be due from the plaintiff to the Egyptian government if it paid him before he had satisfied this fiscal liability. The defence failed, for to allow the garnishee orders, which related solely to taxation debts, to defeat the plaintiff's cause of action would constitute an indirect enforcement of a foreign revenue law. The obvious result of dismissing the action would be the recovery of the taxes by the Egyptian government.[25]

However, the prohibition on indirect enforcement of foreign revenue laws does not prevent an English court from assisting a foreign state to obtain evidence against one of that state's taxpayers. Thus an English court will accede to a request by a foreign state that witnesses in England give oral evidence pursuant to the Evidence (Proceedings in Other Jurisdictions) Act 1975,[26] even though this is in connection with proceedings in the foreign state against one of its taxpayers.[27] Seemingly, this is the case regardless of whether the taxpayer supports the request.

It is questionable whether the general ban on indirect enforcement is not too rigid. If, for instance, in the *Rossano* case the defendants had in fact paid the taxes due to the government, would not an action based upon the unjust enrichment of the plaintiff have succeeded? It

---

indicates that the rule may well not operate between the states of a federal country; see also *Permanent Trustee Co (Canberra) Ltd v Finlayson* (1967) 9 FLR 424, ACT SC; revsd on another point (1968) 122 CLR 338.

[21] Lord Keith.

[22] *Peter Buchanan Ltd and Macharg v McVey* [1955] AC 516 n at 529, [1954] IR 89 at 107, SC; approved by the House of Lords in *Government of India v Taylor* [1955] AC 491; *QRS 1 ApS v Frandsen* [1999] 1 WLR 2169, CA; *Air India Ltd v CaribjetInc* [2002] 2 All ER (Comm) 76; see also *Tullow Uganda Ltd v Heritage Oil and Gas Ltd, Heritage Oil plc* [2013] EWHC 1656 (Comm) at [115], [2014] 1 All ER (Comm) 22. But see on the first two of these cases *Williams and Humbert Ltd v W and H Trade Marks (Jersey) Ltd* [1986] AC 368 at 440, HL. In *Re Lord Cable* [1977] 1 WLR 7 at 13 it is suggested that proceedings in England by a foreign government for direct enforcement of that government's currency control regulations, even against a citizen of that country, would be contrary to the principle of non-enforcement of foreign revenue laws; but cf *Kahler v Midland Bank Ltd* [1950] AC 24 at 46–7, 57, HL; see also *A-G of New Zealand v Ortiz* [1984] AC 1 at 24 (per Lord Denning MR in the Court of Appeal).

[23] [1963] 2 QB 352.

[24] As to garnishment (third party debt orders), see infra, pp 1292–3.

[25] See, eg, *Peter Buchanan Ltd and Mackay v McVey* [1955] AC 516 n, [1954] IR 89, SC; *Williams and Humbert Ltd v W and H Trade Marks (Jersey) Ltd* [1986] AC 368 at 437–41, HL; cf *Ayres v Evans* (1981) 39 ALR 129, FCA.

[26] Supra, pp 83–4.

[27] *Re State of Norway's Applications (Nos 1 and 2)* [1990] 1 AC 723, HL.

may even be questioned whether such a decision as that reached in *Municipal Council of Sydney v Bull*,[28] where the plaintiff failed in its bid to recover a contribution imposed by a local statute in respect of certain street improvements effected in the area where the defendant owned property, accords with the practice of states and their subordinate bodies to furnish services in return for payment.

The narrow dividing line is illustrated by *Brokaw v Seatrain UK Ltd*:[29]

> In this case goods were shipped from the USA to England in an American ship. Whilst the ship was at sea, the US Treasury served a notice of levy, in respect of taxes unpaid by the owners of the goods, on the shipowners demanding that the goods should be surrendered. When the ship arrived at Southampton, the shipowners refused to deliver the goods to the consignee, who claimed delivery or their value.

By reason of interpleader proceedings, the court had to consider the claim of the US Treasury, which was rejected on the basis that to allow it amounted to indirect enforcement of a foreign revenue law by seizure of goods. However, had the notice of levy been effective to reduce the goods into the possession of the US Treasury, their claim would have been upheld, for the court would then have been enforcing a possessory title rather than a revenue law.

(iii) Recognition of a foreign revenue law

This rule that no action will lie at the instance of a foreign state to enforce a revenue law does not mean, despite what Lord Mansfield said in *Holman v Johnson*,[30] that such a law is to be totally ignored.[31] Refusal to enforce it implies no disclaimer of its lawful existence, and circumstances may require that its existence be recognised. Thus, on the ground that public policy demands the maintenance of harmonious relations with other nations, the courts will not countenance any transaction, such as a fraudulent tax-evasion scheme, which is knowingly designed to violate a revenue law of a foreign and friendly state.[32] If personal representatives have had personally to pay taxes on a foreign estate under foreign revenue laws, those foreign laws will be recognised here so as to enable the personal representatives to be indemnified from assets of the estate situated here.[33] Furthermore, in such cases the personal representatives should be given leave to remit the assets to the foreign country for payment of the taxes.[34]

(b) Foreign penal laws[35]

It is well settled that an English court will not lend its aid to the enforcement, either directly or indirectly, of a foreign penal law.[36] The imposition of a penalty normally reflects the

---

[28] [1909] 1 KB 7.

[29] [1971] 2 QB 476, CA; see *A-G of New Zealand v Ortiz* [1984] AC 1 at 31–2 (per Ackner LJ in the Court of Appeal). See also *Re Van de Mark and Toronto-Dominion Bank* (1989) 68 OR (2d) 379, Ont SC.

[30] (1775) 1 Cowp 341 at 343, 98 ER 1120 at 1121: "No country takes notice of the revenue laws of another."

[31] *Regazzoni v KC Sethia (1944) Ltd* [1956] 2 QB 490 at 515, CA; affd [1958] AC 301 at 319, HL; *X, Y and Z v The Bank* [1983] 2 Lloyd's Rep 535 at 546–7; cf *Sharif v Azad* [1967] 1 QB 605 at 617, CA; *Mackender v Feldia AG* [1967] 2 QB 590 at 601, CA. See also *Bank of Ireland v Meeneghan* [1995] 1 ILRM 96.

[32] *Re Emery's Investment Trusts* [1959] Ch 410; *Pye Ltd v BG Transport Service Ltd* [1966] 2 Lloyd's Rep 300 at 308–9. See also *Euro-Diam Ltd v Bathurst* [1990] 1 QB 1 at 39–40, CA.

[33] *Re Lord Cable* [1977] 1 WLR 7 at 25–6; and see *Re Reid* (1970) 17 DLR (3d) 199, BC CA.

[34] *Re Lord Cable* [1977] 1 WLR 7 at 25–6; and see *Scottish National Orchestra Ltd v Thomson's Executor* 1969 SLT 325.

[35] See especially FA Mann (1954) 40 Grotius Society 25; M Mann (1956) 42 Grotius Society 133; Stoel (1967) 16 ICLQ 663.

[36] *Ogden v Folliott* (1790) 3 Term Rep 726, 100 ER 825; *Wolff v Oxholm* (1817) 6 M & S 92, 105 ER 1177; *Huntington v Attrill* [1893] AC 150, PC; *Frankfurther v WL Exner Ltd* [1947] Ch 629; *Empresa Exportadora de Azúcar v Industria Azucarera Nacional SA, The Playa Larga* [1983] 2 Lloyd's Rep 171, CA; *X,*

exercise by a state of its sovereign power, and it is an obvious principle that an act of sovereignty can have no effect in the territory of another state.

(i) *The meaning of a penalty*

The word "penalty" is equivocal, and if understood without qualification it comprises penalties to the enforcement of which there can be no objection, as for example one incorporated in a commercial contract with the object of securing its performance.[37] What, therefore, is the meaning of the word in the present context? The answer given by the Privy Council in *Huntington v Attrill*,[38] the leading English authority on the subject, is that it is limited to a fine or other exaction imposed by the state for some violation of public order of a criminal complexion.[39] Applying this definition, an order made pursuant to a criminal statute confiscating a convicted person's assets will not be enforced,[40] nor will a restraint order,[41] nor will an order committing a person to prison for contempt of court.[42] Nor will an order for contempt of court arising out of an action between private parties be enforceable.[43] Lord Denning MR has indicated[44] that, in the context of recognition of foreign judgments, a judgment for exemplary damages or damages for "resistance abusive" under French law is not to be denied recognition as being in respect of "a penalty". The courts in many common law countries have come to the same conclusion in relation to a judgment for punitive damages.[45] It may well be, therefore, that a foreign law as to exemplary or punitive damages will be applied here and will not be castigated as a penal law.[46] On the other hand, there is a statutory prohibition on the enforcement of foreign judgments for multiple damages,[47] such as treble damages under the USA anti-trust laws. These laws have been described as penal at common law.[48] More recently, the

---

Y and Z v The Bank [1983] 2 Lloyd's Rep 535; *A-G of New Zealand v Ortiz* [1984] AC 1, CA; *Williams and Humbert Ltd v W and H Trade Marks (Jersey) Ltd* [1986] AC 368, HL. For Canada see *Pro Swing Inc v Elta Golf Inc* [2006] SCR 612, (2007) 273 DLR (4th) 663.

[37] *Huntington v Attrill* [1893] AC 150 at 156, PC.

[38] [1893] AC 150.

[39] See also *Lewis v Eliades* [2003] EWCA Civ 1758 at [50], [2004] 1 WLR 692, leave to appeal to the House of Lords refused [2004] 1 WLR 1393—a penalty "normally means a sum payable to the state, and not to a private plaintiff", referring to *SA Consortium General Textiles v Sun and Sand Agencies Ltd* [1978] QB 279 at 299–300 (per Lord Denning MR), CA; *Schemmer v Property Resources Ltd* [1975] Ch 273.

[40] See *United States of America v Abacha* [2014] EWCA Civ 1291, [2015] 1 WLR 1917 (concerning proceedings in the USA to forfeit assets which had allegedly been involved in money laundering offences within its jurisdiction).

[41] *Bank of Ireland v Meeneghan* [1995] 1 ILRM 96.

[42] *Gersten v The Law Society of New South Wales* [2002] NSWCA 344.

[43] *Pro Swing Inc v Elta Golf Inc* [2006] SCR 612, (2007) 273 DLR (4th) 663.

[44] *SA Consortium General Textiles v Sun and Sand Agencies Ltd* [1978] QB 279 at 299–300, CA; see also *Pencil Hill Ltd v US Citta Di Palermo SpA*, 19 January 2016, HC—foreign arbitration award enforced where the arbitrators awarded the claimant a reduced additional sum in place of a contractual penalty, representing 25 per cent of the penalty claimed; cf *JSC VTB Bank v Skurikhin* [2014] EWHC 271 (Comm) at [94]—arguable that an excessive award of interest in a Russian judgment between private parties was not recoverable on the ground that it was punitive in effect. Discussed infra, pp 574–5.

[45] *Old North State Brewing Co v Newlands Services Inc* (1998) 155 DLR (4th) 250; *Benefit Strategies Group Inc v Prider* [2005] SASC 194, (2005) 91 SASR 544; *Doe v Howard* [2015] VSC 75; cf *Schnabel v Yung Lui* [2002] NSWSC 15—punitive damages constituting a penal award because of a public element (failure to comply with a US court order). Compare *Re the Enforcement of a United States Judgment for Damages* (Case IX ZR 149/91) [1994] IL Pr 602, German Federal Supreme Court—enforcement of a foreign judgment awarding a sum in respect of exemplary and punitive damages contrary to German public policy.

[46] Cf *Travelers Casualty and Surety Co of Europe Ltd v Sun Life Assurance Co of Canada (UK) Ltd* [2004] EWHC 1704 (Comm) at [77], [2004] IL Pr 50.

[47] Protection of Trading Interests Act 1980, s 5; discussed infra, pp 553–5. Under the 1980 Act the Secretary of State can make orders prohibiting persons in the United Kingdom from complying with foreign extra-territorial measures which are damaging to United Kingdom trading interests; see ss 1–3.

[48] *British Airways Board v Laker Airways Ltd* [1984] QB 142 at 163 (per Parker J), and in the Court of Appeal at 201 (per Donaldson MR); Paterson [1995] UBCLR 241. But cf *Old North State Brewing Co v*

Court of Appeal has accepted, obiter, that this is arguable but found it unnecessary to decide the point.[49]

(ii) Examples of the prohibition on indirect enforcement of a penal law

An example of an attempt to enforce a foreign penalty indirectly is *Banco de Vizcaya v Don Alfonso de Borbón y Austria*[50] where the facts were these:

> The former King of Spain had bought certain securities with his own money and had instructed that they should be held by a London bank to the order of his agents, the Banco de Vizcaya, a Spanish concern. The Spanish Republican Government later decreed that all his property, wherever situated, should be confiscated and that anything deposited with Spanish banks should be delivered to the Treasury. The plaintiffs claimed delivery of the securities from the London bank on the ground that they had a contractual right of recovery by virtue of the instructions given by King Alfonso at the time of the original deposit.

Lawrence J held that the plaintiffs were not in reality asserting their own contractual rights as they originally existed, but the rights of the Spanish Republic. Therefore their claim failed, since to countenance it would in effect be to enforce an admittedly penal law of the Republic.

A more recent case to discuss the question of enforcement of a foreign penal law is *A-G of New Zealand v Ortiz*:[51]

> A Maori carved door was removed from New Zealand without permission of the appropriate authorities and was eventually offered for sale by the first defendant by auction in London. The Attorney-General of New Zealand (the plaintiff) alleged that the state was the owner of the door and sought an injunction in the English courts restraining the sale and an order for delivery up of the door. The basis of this claim was a New Zealand statute which, in certain circumstances, provided for the forfeiture, without compensation, of historic articles.

Staughton J, at first instance, gave judgment for the plaintiff. The Court of Appeal allowed an appeal on the basis of a point of construction of the New Zealand statute.[52] It was held that the statute only provided for the forfeiture of historic articles when the goods had been seized by the appropriate New Zealand authorities, and this had not happened in the present case. However, the Court of Appeal went on to discuss the wider point of the nature of the New Zealand statute. Lord Justices Ackner and O'Conner held, obiter, that the New Zealand statute was a penal law and, therefore, would not be enforced in England.[53] The claim was made by the Attorney-General on behalf of the state, the cause of action concerned a public right—the preservation of historic articles within New Zealand, and vindication of the right was sought through forfeiture of the property without compensation.[54] Lord Denning expressed himself in different terms; he regarded the New Zealand statute as coming within the category of an "other public law"[55] rather than a penal law.[56]

Newlands Services Inc (1998) 155 DLR (4th) 250, BC CA (treble damages based on an unfair and deceptive trade practice statute not anti-trust).

[49] *Lewis v Eliades* [2003] EWCA Civ 1758 at [50], [2004] 1 WLR 692; see also *Service Temps Inc v MacLeod* [2013] CSOH 162 at [39]–[41], 2014 SLT 375; Scott (2013) 84 BYBIL 523. Discussed infra, pp 554–5.

[50] [1935] 1 KB 140. A similar case is *Frankfurther v W L Exner Ltd* [1947] Ch 629. For an early example, see *Ogden v Folliott* (1790) 3 Term Rep 726, 100 ER 825.

[51] [1984] AC 1, CA; Nott (1984) 33 ICLQ 203. See generally on claims by foreign states for return of their property, Collins, *Essays*, pp 118–29; Collins (2007) 326 Hague Recueil 9, Chapter 5.

[52] [1984] AC 1 at 17–18, 29, 35, CA.

[53] Ibid, at 31–4, 35.

[54] Ibid, at 33–4 (per Ackner LJ).

[55] Ibid, at 20–4; see infra, pp 123–5.

[56] On appeal to the House of Lords, the decision of the Court of Appeal was upheld solely on the narrow point of construction of the New Zealand statute. The Law Lords, at 45–9 (per Lord Brightman), having

(iii) Characterisation of the foreign law/right of action

It is undeniable that the English court must itself characterise the alleged penal, revenue or other public law, but regard will be had to the attitude adopted in the courts in the foreign jurisdiction.[57] According to the Privy Council in *Huntington v Attrill*[58] nothing can be regarded as a penalty unless it is "recoverable at the instance of the State, or of an official duly authorised to prosecute on its behalf, or of a member of the public in the character of a common informer".[59] The facts of the case were as follows:

> A New York statute, designed, inter alia, to protect the public against company promoters, provided that the directors of a corporation should be personally liable for its debts on proof that false reports of its financial condition had been published. Sums recoverable under this provision were payable to creditors in satisfaction pro tanto of their claims. A creditor instituted a suit under the statute in a New York court and obtained judgment for a large sum. He later brought an action on the judgment in Ontario. The New York courts had decided that actions brought under the statute were of a penal character.

The Privy Council held, first, that it was for the Ontario court to put its own interpretation on the statutory provision; and, secondly, that the statute was remedial, not penal, since it permitted a subject to enforce a liability in his own interests and for the protection of his own private rights.[60]

In *United States of America v Inkley*,[61] the Court of Appeal was faced with a more complex case involving an action by a foreign state, but which was clothed in civil form.

> An action was brought by the US government for enforcement of a judgment for the amount of an appearance bond plus interest obtained in a federal court in Florida, sitting as a civil court, against the defendant who had been released on bail but had subsequently failed to appear to answer criminal charges.

The Court of Appeal refused to enforce the judgment on the basis that this was an action by a foreign state to enforce the execution of its own public/penal law. Dicey, Morris and Collins's three-fold classification of the exclusionary rule was adopted. "Public laws" was seen as the wide overall exclusionary category, and a foreign penal law will necessarily also be a foreign public law. Whether the right of action which it is sought to have enforced in England is public or private was said to depend on three considerations: the party in whose favour the

---

heard no argument on the point relating to the enforcement of a penal law, declined to express any opinion on the correctness of the obiter dicta on this matter in the Court of Appeal. The result of the case is to leave a problem over the return of unlawfully exported cultural heritage. But see now *Islamic Republic of Iran v Barakat* [2007] EWCA Civ 1374, [2009] QB 22; Briggs (2007) 78 BYBIL 628; Knight (2008) 19 KLJ 176; Rogerson (2008) 67 CLJ 246; Rushworth [2008] LMCLQ 123—claim to allow recovery of Iranian cultural heritage allowed in the situation where, under the foreign law, the claimant enjoyed both title to and an immediate right to possession of the historic artefacts without having to seize them. For attempts to solve the problem by international arrangements, see the Commonwealth Scheme for the Protection of the Material Cultural Heritage, 1993; O'Keefe (1995) 44 ICLQ 147; the UNIDROIT Convention on the International Return of Stolen or Illegally Exported Cultural Objects (1995) 34 ILM 1322. For the position within the European Union see Directive 2014/60/EU of the European Parliament and of the Council of 15 May 2014 on the return of cultural objects unlawfully removed from the territory of a Member State and amending Regulation (EU) No 1024/2012 (Recast) OJ L 159/1, implemented in the United Kingdom by SI 1994/501, SI 1997/1719, SI 2001/3972 and SI 2015/1926. See generally Roodt, *Private International Law, Art and Cultural Heritage* (2015).

[57] *United States of America v Inkley* [1989] QB 255 at 265, CA.

[58] [1893] AC 150; and see *Metal Industries (Salvage) Ltd v Owners of S T Harle* 1962 SLT 114 at 116.

[59] [1893] AC 150 at 157, 158. See *A-G of New Zealand v Ortiz* [1984] AC 1 at 32 (per Ackner LJ), CA. See also *Bank of Ireland v Meeneghan* [1995] 1 ILRM 96.

[60] The Supreme Court of the US reached the same conclusion: (1892) 146 US 657.

[61] [1989] QB 255; Carter (1988) BYBIL 347.

right is created; the purpose of the law on which the right is based; the general context of the case as a whole. The Court of Appeal held[62] that the action was concerned with the right of the US government to ensure the due observance of its criminal law; the purpose of the action was part of a public law process aimed to ensure the attendance of persons accused of crime before the criminal courts; the general context was criminal or penal. The essentially public/penal law nature of the action was not affected by the fact that it was dressed up in civil form. Applying these considerations to the facts of the case it was concluded that: "Notwithstanding its civil clothing, the purpose of the action initiated by the writ issued in this case was the due execution by the United States of America of a public law process aimed to ensure the attendance of persons accused of crime before the criminal courts."[63]

In *United States Securities and Exchange Commission v Manterfield*[64] the Court of Appeal addressed the question whether a worldwide freezing order, obtained by a US regulatory body in support of US proceedings for, *inter alia*, the recovery of money allegedly misappropriated by the defendant and its return to defrauded investors, fell within the exclusionary rule.[65] The court held that the substance of the claim for disgorgement was not penal in nature and that the worldwide freezing order should be continued. This case is an example of a wider rule that when a public or regulatory body brings civil proceedings on behalf of a group or class of victims, it is not seeking to enforce a foreign penal or other public law.[66]

(iv) Recognition of foreign penal laws

The enforcement of a foreign penal law must be distinguished from its application or recognition.[67] Although enforcement will not be allowed, it is going too far to assert that "the penal laws of one country cannot be taken notice of in another".[68] This is scarcely true for, subject to the possible intervention of the doctrine of public policy,[69] such a law must be regarded as operative even in English proceedings if it is part of the foreign legal system which, according to the relevant rule for the choice of law, governs the transaction that is sub judice.[70] If, for example, a Ruritanian statute makes the export of certain raw materials a crime punishable by fine and confiscation of property, in no circumstances will the fine be recoverable by an action in England. Nevertheless, if a Ruritanian businessman, by a contract that falls to be governed by the law of that country, agrees to sell the prohibited materials to an Englishman, an action brought against him in England for non-delivery must necessarily fail. The illegality of the contract according to its governing law, though springing from a crime and from a penal law devoid of extraterritorial effect, cannot be ignored. The same is true for a penal law of the place of performance of a contract which prohibits the performance of the contract.[71]

---

[62] [1989] QB 255, at 265–6.

[63] Ibid, at 266.

[64] [2009] EWCA Civ 27, [2010] 1 WLR 172; Briggs (2009) 80 BYBIL 628. Distinguished in *Pocket Kings Ltd v Safenames Ltd* [2009] EWHC 2529 (Ch), [2010] Ch 438—a civil order from a Kentucky court for the forfeiture of an Internet domain name used for illegal online gambling in that state held to be penal in nature.

[65] The claimant in the US proceedings also sought a civil monetary penalty; it also gave an undertaking that, if successful at trial in the USA, it would not seek to enforce in England any judgment relating to penalties. The court accepted this undertaking and was concerned with the disgorgement aspect of the claim alone.

[66] See also *Robb Evans v European Bank Ltd* [2004] NSWCA 82; Thomas (2005) 121 LQR 380; *United States Securities and Exchange Commission v Cosby* 2000 BCSC 338; *Pfunder Shull* 1999 CanLII 6625, BC SC.

[67] M Mann (1956) 42 Grotius Society 133, 135–6.

[68] *Ogden v Folliott* (1790) 3 Term Rep 726 at 733, 100 ER 825 at 829.

[69] Infra, pp 132–43.

[70] See *A-G of New Zealand v Ortiz* [1984] AC 1 at 31 (per Ackner LJ in the Court of Appeal). See also *Bank of Ireland v Meeneghan* [1995] 1 ILRM 96.

[71] *Foster v Driscoll* [1929] 1 KB 470, CA. The same principles affect a foreign revenue law, supra, p 118.

(c) Other foreign public laws[72]

Judicial and statutory adoption[73] of Dicey, Morris and Collins's three-fold classification of foreign laws which will not be enforced means that this third category is now firmly established. What we are concerned with here are public laws which are not revenue or penal ones. It is not difficult to find examples of "other public laws": import and export regulations; trading with the enemy legislation; price control regulations; and anti-trust legislation.[74] However, it is much more difficult to give a precise definition to the concept of "public laws", since the common law does not as yet recognise any clear distinction between public and private laws.[75] In *A-G of New Zealand v Ortiz*[76] Lord Denning admitted that the concept of "other public laws" was very uncertain, but went on to explain that they are laws which are eiusdem generis with penal or revenue laws.[77] He found a common thread underlying these three categories in the principles applied in international law; in particular, in the principle that laws will not be enforced if they involve an exercise by a government of its sovereignty beyond the limits of its authority, ie beyond its own frontiers.[78] He concluded that legislation providing for the automatic forfeiture to the state of works of art should they be exported would come within this principle, and, accordingly, within the category of other public laws. In *Camdex International Ltd v Bank of Zambia (No 2)*,[79] the Court of Appeal held that the English courts would not entertain proceedings to enforce a civil cause of action that, it was argued,[80] the Bank of Zambia had under Zambian law against a Zambian mining company to recover foreign exchange due under a direction issued by the bank, on the basis that this would constitute enforcement of Zambian public law. In giving the direction the bank was exercising its authority under a Zambian statute as the agent responsible for administering exchange control. That legislation was part of the public law of Zambia enforceable by right of the authority of the Zambian state rather than by way of a private right in the bank.

The exclusion of other public laws has been accepted by the High Court of Australia and the Court of Appeal in New Zealand in the *Spycatcher* cases,[81] which involved the important issues of confidentiality and state security. The Attorney-General of the United Kingdom sought, inter alia, injunctions in Australia and New Zealand to prevent publication in those respective countries of the whole or parts of *Spycatcher*, the memoirs of Peter Wright—a former intelligence officer of the British Security Services. The Attorney-General's argument,

---

[72] See generally Baade, in Lipstein (ed), *International Encyclopedia of Comparative Law* (1986), Vol 3, Chapter 12; (1995) 30 Texas Int LJ 429. For an exception in Australia and the USA see the Australia-United States Free Trade Agreement, Art 14.7, Hogan-Doran (2006) 80 ALJ 361.

[73] Supra, p 115. But cf *United States of America v Ivey* (1996) 139 DLR (4th) 570, Ont CA; discussed infra, p 124.

[74] Anti-trust laws may be penal, see supra, pp 119–20.

[75] *Re State of Norway's Application* [1987] QB 433 at 475, CA; affd by the House of Lords without discussion of this specific point [1990] 1 AC 723, 458.

[76] [1984] AC 1, CA.

[77] Ibid, at 20.

[78] See also the authorities cited in fn 12. But cf *Islamic Republic of Iran v Barakat* [2007] EWCA Civ 1374, [2009] QB 22.

[79] (1997) CLC 714, CA; Briggs (1997) 68 BYBIL 369. The issue of enforcement of a foreign public law arose in the context of garnishment (now called a third party debt order) of a debt, see infra, pp 1292–3.

[80] This argument was rejected by the Court of Appeal.

[81] In Australia: *A-G (UK) v Heinemann Publishers Australia Pty Ltd (No 2)* (1988) 165 CLR 30, HCA; see also *Trade Practices Commission v Australia Meat Holdings Pty Ltd* (1988) 83 ALR 299 at 360–3, FCA; *Robb Evans v European Bank Ltd* [2004] NSWCA 82. In New Zealand: *A-G for the United Kingdom v Wellington Newspapers Ltd* [1988] 1 NZLR 129, NZCA. Criticised by FA Mann (1988) 104 LQR 497; Carter (1989) 48 CLJ 417, 430–1; Collier (1989) 48 CLJ 33; see also Lord Keith in *A-G v Guardian Newspapers Ltd (No 2)* [1990] 1 AC 109, 264–5, HL. The exclusion of "other public laws" has also been accepted in Hong Kong in a different context: *Nonus Asia Ltd v Standard Chartered Bank* [1990] 1 HKLR 396.

that Wright was acting in breach of duties of confidence (fiduciary and contractual) owed to the United Kingdom government, was assumed to be correct. One of the defences in both cases was that the Australian and New Zealand courts will not enforce a foreign penal or other public law.

Both the Australian and New Zealand courts refused to grant the relief sought, albeit on different grounds. The High Court of Australia regarded the action as one whereby the United Kingdom government sought to protect the efficiency of its Security Services as part of the defence of the country; as such, it fell within the exclusion of "other public laws". The majority of the court also suggested that rather than referring to "public laws", it would be more apt to refer to "public interests" or "governmental interests" to signify that the exclusionary rule applies to claims enforcing the interests of a foreign sovereign which arise from the exercise of certain powers peculiar to government, and that the rule rendered unenforceable actions to enforce the governmental interests of a foreign state. The Court of Appeal in *Government of Iran v Barakat*[82] held that the test laid down by the High Court of Australia is not only consistent with the English authorities but is "a helpful and practical test".[83] The New Zealand Court of Appeal, however, took a different view in the *Spycatcher* case. The duty of confidentiality was said to arise from the relationship between the parties as employer and employee. An action for damages (an injunction having earlier been refused on the basis that the contents of the book were already in the public domain) was therefore not barred by the exclusionary rule in relation to foreign penal or other public laws. Nonetheless, this was not thought to be a proper case for protecting the United Kingdom's security secrets since there had been prior publication abroad of the information in *Spycatcher*; moreover, the New Zealand public interest justified publication.

In contrast, the Ontario Court of Appeal has regarded the public law exception as resting on a rather shaky foundation, without though closing the door on such an exception.[84] On the assumption that there was such an exception, a US law which allows the US government to bring an action for compensation under a US statute for the cost of cleaning up environmental damage was not regarded as being a public law.[85] There were two reasons for this. First, the claim was concerned with clearing up damage in the USA.[86] Secondly, although asserted by a public authority the action was said to be so close to a claim for nuisance that it was in substance of a commercial or private law character. Relevant to this was the fact that such an action could be brought between private parties or against the government.

There is some controversy over whether an English court "will refuse to enforce all public laws . . . or whether the court should only refuse to enforce a foreign public law if enforcement is contrary to public policy".[87] The uncertainty over this is reflected in the wording of

---

[82] [2007] EWCA Civ 1374, [2009] QB 22.

[83] Ibid, at [125]. See also *Pocket Kings Ltd v Safenames Ltd* [2009] EWHC 2529 (Ch) at [40], [2010] Ch 438; *JSC BTA Bank v Ablyazov* [2011] EWHC 202 (Comm) at [18], [2011] 2 All ER (Comm) 10. In an earlier case, *Mbasogo v Logo Ltd* [2006] EWCA Civ 1370 at [52], [2007] QB 846, the Court of Appeal found it unnecessary to express a view as to whether the decision of the Australian High Court would be correct as a matter of English law. In *President of the State of Equatorial Guinea v Royal Bank of Scotland International* [2006] UKPC 7 at [23]–[28], the Privy Council approved, at least tentatively, the approach of the High Court of Australia.

[84] *United States of America v Ivey* (1996) 139 DLR (4th) 570, Ont CA.

[85] As a result, judgments granted in the USA were enforceable, see infra, p 553.

[86] The Ontario Court of Appeal approved the reasoning of Sharpe J (1995) 130 DLR (4th) 674, who stressed this point at 689. See also *City of Gotha v Sotheby's*, 9 September 1998, HC.

[87] Collins, Proceedings of the Special Public Bill Committee, Private International Law (Miscellaneous Provisions) Bill, Further Memorandum *HL Paper* 36 (1995), p 68. The former view is seemingly supported by Lord Denning in the *Ortiz* case; the latter by Staughton J in the same case, by Brennan J in the High

the Private International Law (Miscellaneous Provisions) Act 1995.[88] This does not simply provide an exception to the normal statutory tort choice of law rules for cases involving a foreign penal, revenue or other public law. It qualifies this by referring to a foreign penal, revenue or other public law "as would not otherwise be enforceable under the law of the forum". This deliberately does not answer the question when such a foreign law would not be enforceable at common law.

(d) Effect of European Union private international law

It is now necessary to consider the extent to which the rule against the enforcement of foreign revenue, penal and other public laws has been affected by the United Kingdom membership of the European Union. European Union private international law instruments apply in "civil and commercial matters"; revenue, customs and administrative matters are often expressly mentioned as matters that are not civil and commercial and, therefore, outside the scope of these instruments.[89] These concepts are given an autonomous meaning, and do not necessarily correspond to the traditional English concepts of foreign revenue, penal and others public laws. This is clear if one compares the traditional English rule against the indirect enforcement of foreign revenue laws with the approach of European Union private international law.

In *QRS 1 ApS v Fransden*[90] the Court of Appeal held that the English exclusionary rule had not been affected by the United Kingdom becoming a Contracting State to the Convention on Jurisdiction and the Enforcement of Judgments in Civil and Commercial Matters of 1968 (the Brussels Convention), now replaced for virtually all purposes by the Brussels I Regulation Recast.[91] The facts of this case were as follows:

> The plaintiffs, Danish companies, were owned by the defendant who stripped their assets, which led to the plaintiffs being put into liquidation. The Danish tax authorities claimed against the plaintiffs substantial sums in respect of taxes and interest. As the only creditors, the tax authorities appointed a liquidator and funded the action brought by the plaintiffs against the defendant in England. The claims were for restitution of the value of their assets and, in the alternative, for damages arising out of the defendant's negligence in allowing the plaintiffs to suffer loss as a result of asset stripping.

This claim undeniably fell foul of the English exclusionary rule. The Court of Appeal held that this was a revenue matter within the meaning of Article 1 of the Brussels Convention.[92] As such, it fell outside the scope of that Convention.[93] Moreover, the English exclusionary rule was held to be not incompatible with the EEC Treaty.[94]

But this case cannot be regarded as a good authority any more because it goes against the recent decision of the Court of Justice of the European Union in *HMRC v Sunico ApS*.[95]

Court of Australia in the *Spycatcher* case at 50–2, and by the Court of Appeal in *Islamic Republic of Iran v Barakat* [2007] EWCA Civ 1374, [2009] QB 22. See generally Vischer (1992) I Hague Recueil 9, 150–3.

[88] S 14 (3)(a)(ii); the 1995 Act is discussed infra, p 778. Choice of law for non-contractual obligations is now largely governed by the Rome II Regulation, infra, pp 780–875.

[89] See, eg, Brussels I Regulation Recast, Art 1(1); Rome I Regulation, Art 1(1); Rome II Regulation, Art 1(1).

[90] [1999] 1 WLR 2169; Briggs (1999) BYBIL 341; Smart (2000) 116 LQR 360.

[91] And by the EC/Denmark Agreement, see infra, pp 191–312.

[92] Discussed infra, p 204.

[93] The Court of Appeal also held that if it had been a matter within the scope of the Convention, the English exclusionary rule could not be invoked because it would impair the effectiveness of the Convention, [1999] 1 WLR 2169 at 2177–8, CA.

[94] In particular Art 59, [1999] 1 WLR 2169 at 2178–80, CA.

[95] Case C-49/12 EU:C:2013:545, [2014] QB 391; Collins (2014) 130 LQR 353. See also Case C-266/01 *Préservatrice foncière TIARD SA v Netherlands* [2003] ECR I-4867 and Case C-265/02 *Frahuil SA v*

Here, the United Kingdom tax authorities brought proceedings in England against a number of persons domiciled in Denmark, alleging that they had been involved in a VAT fraud which had led to the evasion of output VAT to the detriment of the United Kingdom Treasury. Since the defendants had not incurred liability under United Kingdom VAT legislation, the action was based on tortious conspiracy to defraud, and the amount of damages claimed was equal to the unlawfully evaded tax.

The CJEU held that the concept of "civil and commercial matters" covered an action whereby a public authority of one Member State claimed in another Member State damages for loss caused by a tortious conspiracy to defraud. This was essentially because the action was based on ordinary private law of tort.

Another example of the English exclusionary rule being affected by European Union law is the Insolvency Regulation.[96] Article 2(12) of the Regulation provides that the term "foreign creditor" includes tax authorities and social security authorities of Member States, who are thereby given the right to lodge their claims in insolvency proceedings conducted in other Member States, provided that the proceedings come within the scope of the Regulation.[97] Another striking example is provided by European Union Directives providing for mutual assistance and recovery as between Member States in relation to duties and taxes.[98]

2. FOREIGN EXPROPRIATORY LEGISLATION

A somewhat troublesome question is the extent to which foreign expropriatory legislation is recognised in England when it is directed, not against a particular person, as in *Don Alfonso's* case,[99] or a particular item, as in the *Ortiz* case,[100] but against national property generally. It would seem that legislation of this nature may take four forms.[101]

First, *requisition*, which term is generally confined to the seizure of property in the public interest for a limited period, usually until the end of some emergency, and in return for compensation.

Secondly, *nationalisation*, which is the permanent absorption of property into public ownership in furtherance of some political aim and in return for compensation.

Thirdly, *compulsory acquisition*, which is the permanent seizure of property in fulfilment of some economic or social aim, and in exchange for compensation.

Fourthly, *confiscation*, which is the permanent seizure of private property without payment of compensation.[102]

Assitalia SpA [2004] ECR I-1543 (both cases concerned guarantee of payment of customs duties); Case C-406/09 *Realchemie Nederland BV v Bayer CropScience AG* [2011] ECR I-9773 (concerning the recognition and enforcement of an order imposing a fine); discussed infra, pp 204–6.

[96] Regulation (EU) 2015/848 of the European Parliament and of the Council on insolvency proceedings OJ 2015 L 141/19.

[97] See Fletcher, *Insolvency in Private International Law* (2005) 2nd edn, para 2.94.

[98] Council Directive 2010/24/EU of 16 March 2010 concerning mutual assistance for the recovery of claims relating to taxes, duties and other measures OJ 2010 L 84/1; implemented in the United Kingdom by Finance Act 2011, s 87 and sch 25 and MARD Regulations SI 2011/2931.

[99] Supra, p 120.

[100] Supra, p 120.

[101] See *I Congreso del Partido* [1981] 1 All ER 1092 at 1103, CA; revsd on a different point [1983] 1 AC 244; *Williams and Humbert Ltd v W and H Trade Marks (Jersey) Ltd* [1986] AC 368, HL; infra, pp 128–9.

[102] See in relation to discharge of a debt by governmental act, *Wight v Eckhardt Marine GmbH* [2003] UKPC 37, [2004] 1 AC 147.

The main question of private international law in this connection is the extent to which, in the eyes of English law, a decree of a foreign state implementing one of these forms of expropriation affects property belonging either to nationals of that state or to aliens.

The general principles that have a bearing on the question defy simple harmonisation, for against the principles that neither foreign legislation nor foreign penal laws have extraterritorial effect, stands the equally fundamental doctrine that a foreign sovereign cannot normally be impleaded.[103] If, for instance, the Ruritanian government obtains possession of jewellery held by a London bank on the ground that it falls within the scope of a Ruritanian decree of confiscation and if the decree is not regarded by English law as applicable to property in England, how can this view be rendered effective against a sovereign power that is immune from the jurisdiction?

Another obstacle to a simple generalisation of the law is the doubt whether all forms of property stand on the same footing for the purpose of determining the effect of expropriation. The suggestion, for instance, by no means unsupported by authority, has been made that a merchant ship stands in a category of its own, since it has a permanent situs in the country to which it belongs.[104] If this is correct, a state which requisitions or confiscates its national ships exercises a quasi-territorial, not an extra-territorial, act of authority.

If an English judge is required to determine the effect of foreign expropriatory legislation, his decision will depend on three main factors, namely the interpretation of the foreign legislation; the situs of the property at the time of the legislative decree; and the question whether the foreign sovereign was in actual possession or control of the property outside his territory at the time when the facts giving rise to the litigation occurred. The present law appears to be as follows.

(a) Property within the foreign jurisdiction at time of decree

The English courts recognise without hesitation that the ownership of property is conclusively and finally determined by the terms of the foreign decree of expropriation if the property is situated within the jurisdiction of the sovereign at the time of the decree, notwithstanding that it is later brought to England and is still there at the time of the action. For instance, in *Luther v Sagor*:[105]

> Timber, situated in Russia and belonging to the plaintiff, a private company incorporated according to the law of Russia, was seized by the Soviet authorities under a decree that had nationalised all profits belonging to industrial and commercial establishments. Part of the timber was later brought to England and there sold to the defendants by a Soviet agent. The plaintiff sued for damages in what is now called conversion (formerly trover) on the ground that the ownership of the timber was still vested in it.

The Court of Appeal, on grounds which were not identical, found for the defendant.

In the view of Warrington LJ, no sovereign state must sit in judgment upon the acts of another foreign state affecting property within its own territory.[106] Bankes LJ found it impossible to

---

[103] Infra, pp 497–509.

[104] McNair (1945) 31 Grotius Society 30.

[105] [1921] 3 KB 532 at 548, CA. Followed in *Princess Olga Paley v Weisz* [1929] 1 KB 718, CA; and see *Oppenheimer v Cattermole* [1976] AC 249 at 282–3, HL; *Buttes Gas and Oil Co v Hammer (No 3)* [1982] AC 888 at 931, HL; *Williams and Humbert Ltd v W and H Trade Marks (Jersey) Ltd* [1986] AC 368, HL; *Westland Ltd v AOI* [1995] QB 282. Cf *Carl Zeiss Stiftung v Rayner and Keeler Ltd (No 2)* [1967] 1 AC 853, HL. Quaere whether the decision would be the same if the owner escaped with his property from the country after the decree but before he had been deprived of possession by the local authorities.

[106] [1921] 3 KB 532 at 548–9.

ignore the law of Russia, the law of the situs at the time of the decree, under which the seller had acquired a good title to the goods.[107] Scrutton LJ, following perhaps a more doubtful line of reasoning, argued that, since the doctrine of immunity would have prevented any investigation of the Russian sovereign's title had the timber been found in England in the possession of a Russian official, it followed that no such investigation was possible where possession had been given to a private purchaser. "What the court cannot do directly, it cannot do indirectly."[108]

But surely the simple and decisive justification of the decision is the rule that a title to movables, valid according to the law of the situs at the time of its acquisition, is recognised by English law.[109] The law of the situs must prevail in such circumstances unless the rule of that law under which the title has been acquired is so immoral or so alien to the principles of justice as understood in England that it must be disregarded as being contrary to public policy. The Court of Appeal considered this objection, but found it impossible to regard the nationalisation decree as anything else but the expression of a policy designed, whether mistakenly or not, to promote the best interests of Russians. This can be contrasted with *Kuwait Airways Corpn v Iraqi Airways Co (Nos 4 and 5)*[110] where an Iraqi resolution divesting the Kuwaiti owners of aircraft situated in Iraq of their title was not simply a governmental expropriation of property within its territory, but was part of an attempt to extinguish every vestige of Kuwait as a separate state. The House of Lords held that enforcement or recognition of the resolution would be manifestly contrary to the public policy of English law.[111]

The principle of *Luther v Sagor* was followed by the House of Lords in *Williams and Humbert Ltd v W and H Trade Marks (Jersey) Ltd*.[112] One point that should be noted from the outset about this case is that at first instance and in the Court of Appeal the case was regarded as one of confiscation of property, ie expropriation *without* payment, whereas the House of Lords treated it as a case of compulsory acquisition, ie expropriation *with* payment. Nonetheless, the principle in *Luther v Sagor* was still applied in all three courts. The facts of the case, according to the House of Lords, were as follows:

> The Spanish government compulsorily acquired all the shares of a company incorporated in Spain, Rumasa, and of the subsidiary companies of Rumasa incorporated in Spain, including two banks—"Jerez" and "Norte". Rumasa also held all the shares in an English company, Williams and Humbert; this company was now, therefore, indirectly controlled by the Spanish government. The plaintiffs, the English company and the three above-named Spanish companies, at the instigation of the Spanish government, brought actions in England against the defendants, the original owners of the Spanish companies, the Mateos family, and a Jersey company, for the return of property (in the form of trade marks and money), which it was alleged had been improperly diverted from the English company and one of the Spanish companies, and for damages. The defendants argued that the proceedings were an attempt to enforce a foreign penal law and/or it would be contrary to public policy to grant the relief sought.

---

[107] Ibid, at 545.

[108] Ibid, at 555–6.

[109] See the remarks of Devlin J in *Bank voor Handel en Scheepvaart NV v Slatford* [1953] 1 QB 248 at 260. See also *Peer International Corpn v Termidor Music Publishers Ltd* [2003] EWCA Civ 1156, [2004] Ch 212.

[110] [2002] UKHL 19, [2002] 2 AC 883; Briggs (2002) 73 BYBIL 400 and 490; Carruthers and Crawford (2003) 52 ICLQ 761; O'Keefe (2002) 61 CLJ 499; Peel (2003) 119 LQR 1; Rogerson (2003) 265 CLP 265; discussed further infra, pp 138–9; distinguished in *Peer International Corpn v Termidor Music Publishers Ltd* [2003] EWCA Civ 1156, [2004] Ch 212.

[111] Public policy operated as an exception to tort choice of law rules, but if there had been an action asserting title to the aircraft, public policy would have operated as an exception to the lex situs rule, [2002] UKHL 19 at [192] (per Lord Scott), [2002] 2 AC 883.

[112] [1986] AC 368; FA Mann (1986) 102 LQR 191; (1987) 103 LQR 26; (1988) 104 LQR 346; (1985) 56 BYBIL 316; Carter (1986) 57 BYBIL 439. See also *JSC VTB Bank v Skurikhin* [2014] EWHC 271 (Comm).

Nourse J ordered that the defence be struck out, as disclosing no reasonable defence, and this was upheld by a majority of the Court of Appeal. There were appeals to the House of Lords.

The House of Lords unanimously dismissed the appeals. Lord Templeman, with whom the other Law Lords concurred, examined the decision in *Luther v Sagor* and then stated the principle that "an English court will recognise the compulsory acquisition law of a foreign state and will recognise the change of title to property which has come under the control of a foreign state and will recognise the consequences of that change of title".[113] Here, the property was the shares in the Spanish companies and this property was situated in Spain, the companies being incorporated there. The change in ownership of the shares was, accordingly, recognised. The Spanish government would have no right to confiscate the English property, ie the shares in Williams and Humbert; but, according to Lord Templeman, it did not purport to do so, since this property would remain in the ownership of Rumasa, one of the Spanish companies.[114] In reality though, the Spanish government would control Williams and Humbert. The Spanish government would, therefore, be able to achieve by indirect means (confiscation of Rumasa) what it could not achieve by direct confiscation.

When it came to the specific allegation that what was involved was enforcement of a foreign penal law, Lord Templeman doubted if the Spanish law could be regarded as penal.[115] Even if it was accepted that it was a penal law there was no attempt directly to enforce this law in England,[116] since the objective of the law, to acquire and control various companies, had already been achieved in Spain. Nor was there an attempt indirectly to enforce the Spanish law, since the actions were brought by the companies, and under well-established principles of company law these were distinct entities from the Spanish government which owned the companies.[117] If the argument that it was a penal law were to be accepted, it would produce the anarchic result that none of the companies could pursue actions outside Spain and wrongdoers vis à vis the companies would be released from liability.[118]

The *Williams and Humbert* case is also interesting for its discussion at first instance[119] and in the Court of Appeal[120] of foreign confiscatory laws. The Court of Appeal[121] agreed with Nourse J, at first instance, that confiscatory laws should be classified as follows:

Class 1 laws, which the English courts will not recognise:

A. Foreign confiscatory laws which, by reason of their being discriminatory on grounds of race, religion or the like, constitute so grave an infringement of human rights that they ought not to be recognised as laws at all.

B. Foreign laws which discriminate against nationals of this country in time of war by purporting to confiscate their moveable property situated in the foreign state.

Class 2 laws,[122] which will be recognised, but to which effect will not be given:

A. Foreign laws confiscating property situated in the foreign state, if they are penal.

B. Foreign laws which purport to confiscate property situated in this country.

---

[113] [1986] AC 368 at 431.

[114] Ibid, at 428, 433.

[115] Ibid, at 428; see also 437 (per Lord Mackay).

[116] Ibid, at 428–9; see also 437–41 (per Lord Mackay).

[117] Ibid, at 429.

[118] Ibid, at 429–30. Lord Templeman rejected the suggestion that a receiver should be appointed to deal with English assets and to recover debts; cf FA Mann (1962) 11 ICLQ 471; (1986) 102 LQR 191.

[119] [1986] 1 AC 375 at 379.

[120] [1986] 1 AC 389; Forsyth (1985) 44 CLJ 376.

[121] [1986] 1 AC 389, at 392, 414.

[122] On which see *City of Gotha v Sotheby's*, 9 September 1998, HC.

Class 3 laws, to which effect will be given provided they do not fall within Class 1: Foreign laws which confiscate property in the foreign state and where title has been perfected there.[123]

It was argued, at first instance, by counsel for the defence that there was a further category within Class 1 of foreign confiscatory laws which are aimed at confiscating the property of particular individuals or classes of individuals,[124] but Nourse J denied the existence of any such category. It was at this point that it was argued, unsuccessfully,[125] that on the facts of the case there was an attempt to enforce a foreign confiscatory law which was penal or a public law (Class 2A).

One final point to note about the *Williams and Humbert* case is that, seemingly, it introduces a principle that, for reasons of comity, a party cannot plead in a case of compulsory acquisition that the foreign government has acted in an oppressive way.[126] Neither will the English courts consider the merits of the compulsory acquisition or the motives of the foreign government.[127] What is new is the suggestion that such matters cannot even be pleaded by a party.

The last question which has to be asked is whether the principle of *Luther v Sagor* applies where the confiscated property, though situated within the jurisdiction of the confiscating state, belongs to aliens. This was the main issue raised in *Anglo-Iranian Oil Co v Jaffrate*, better known as *The Rose Mary*,[128] where the court took the view that *Luther v Sagor* does not condone the confiscation of movables belonging to an owner who is not a national of the confiscating state unless adequate compensation is paid to him in return. It has subsequently been held by Upjohn J, however, that neither the nationality of the dispossessed owner nor the payment of compensation to him affects the general principle laid down in *Luther v Sagor* and other cases.[129] The principle is that English law recognises the extra-territorial effectiveness of confiscatory legislation passed by a foreign state in respect of movables situated within its territory or of contracts governed by its law, unless the doctrine of public policy intervenes.

(b) Property outside the foreign jurisdiction at time of decree

If the property was outside the territory of the confiscating or requisitioning sovereign at the time of the decree, whether in England, in a foreign country or on the high seas, the first task of the judge is to construe the decree in order to ascertain whether it is in terms confined to property within the jurisdiction or whether it purports to affect property outside the territory. It is for the judge to form his own opinion on this question after hearing the evidence of expert witnesses.

If he comes to the conclusion that the decree was neither expressly nor implicitly directed against property in other countries or on the high seas, then the question is no longer

---

[123] This quotation is from *Settebello Ltd v Banco Totta* [1985] 1 WLR 1050 at 1056 where the Court of Appeal adopted the classification of Nourse J in the *Williams and Humbert* case.

[124] [1986] 1 AC 375 at 381.

[125] See the judgment of Nourse J ibid, at 382–6; the argument was also rejected in the Court of Appeal, Lloyd LJ dissenting; for the House of Lords see supra, pp 128–9.

[126] [1986] AC 368 at 431, 434, 436, HL.

[127] See also *Settebello Ltd v Banco Totta* [1985] 1 WLR 1050, CA—a case involving the issue of letters of request.

[128] [1953] 1 WLR 246, Sup Ct of Aden.

[129] *Re Helbert Wagg & Co Ltd* [1956] Ch 323; see also *Empresa Nacional de Telecomunicaciones SA v Deutsche Bank AG* [2009] EWHC 2579 (QB), [2010] 1 All ER (Comm) 649. However, see O'Connell (1955) 4 ICLQ 267, 270; Wortley, *Expropriation in Public International Law* (1959), pp 33–6, 95; FA Mann (1954) 70 LQR 181, 188–90.

significant. This was the substantial basis of the House of Lords decision in *Lecouturier v Rey*.[130] Under a French statute, the Carthusian monks had been expelled from France and deprived of their property. They continued, but now in Spain, to manufacture the liqueur known as Chartreuse, according to its original secret formula. Their Lordships held that the monks, rather than the French liquidator, were still free to exploit in England the reputation which Chartreuse had obtained there. The statute neither expressly nor by implication affected property outside France.

If, on the other hand, the judge comes to the conclusion that the foreign legislation is intended to have extra-territorial operation, the first general principle to be considered is that legislation has no extra-territorial effect. Broadly speaking, jurisdiction is coincident with power, and how can power be exerted within the territory of another sovereign?[131]

The clear implication of the territorial principle is that property situated, say, in England cannot be affected by a foreign decree of expropriation and that the rights of the owner remain unimpaired. Thus a Cuban law purporting to confiscate the copyright (situated in England) in certain Cuban musical works has been held to be ineffective.[132] The only doubt is whether the decree is effective against a national of the foreign state, since historical authority is not lacking for the view that the right to expropriate property may be based on the allegiance of its owner as well as upon its situs.[133] Whether this view is justifiable or not, it has found few adherents.[134] Thus in one case Maugham J held that a Soviet confiscatory decree was ineffective with regard to property in England although the owner was a Soviet subject at the time of the decree.[135] The application of the principle, however, that the legislative power of a state is only territorial, may be frustrated by the impact of the equally well-established principle[136] that a foreign state or sovereign cannot normally be impleaded, for if the sovereign is in possession or control of the expropriated property, even though it may be in England, the owner is unable to enforce his rights.[137]

If property is not in the possession or control of the foreign state at the time of the proceedings and if it was outside the territorial jurisdiction of that state at the time of the expropriatory decree, it is now established that the rights of the owner are unaffected.[138] A contrary rule would conflict not only with the principle that legislative power is territorial, but also in the particular case of confiscation with the doctrine that the penal laws of another country will not be indirectly enforced in England.[139] Since the foreign state is not in possession at the time of the proceedings, the principle that the state is immune from the jurisdiction of the

---

[130] [1910] AC 262; *The Jupiter (No 3)* [1927] P 122.

[131] *Jabbour (F & K) v Custodian of Israeli Absentee Property* [1954] 1 WLR 139 at 150, and authorities there cited; *Williams and Humbert Ltd v W and H Trade Marks (Jersey) Ltd* [1986] AC 368 at 427–8, HL.

[132] *Peer International Corpn v Termidor Music Publishers Ltd* [2003] EWCA Civ 1156, [2004] Ch 212; Osborne (2004) 63 CLJ 567. See also *Société Eram Shipping Co Ltd v Cie Internationale de Navigation* [2003] UKHL 30 at [54], [80], [2004] 1 AC 260.

[133] McNair (1946) 31 Grotius Society 30, 35 et seq.

[134] But see *Lorentzen v Lydden & Co* [1942] 2 KB 202, infra.

[135] *Re Russian Bank for Foreign Trade* [1933] Ch 745.

[136] Governed now by the State Immunity Act 1978, infra, pp 497–509.

[137] Eg *Compañía Naviera Vascongado v SS Cristina* [1938] AC 485, HL; though there would now not appear to be immunity in such a case involving a ship used for commercial purposes, by reason of the State Immunity Act 1978, s 10(2).

[138] *Tallinna Laevauhisus (A/S) v Estonian State Steamship Line* (1947) 80 Lloyd's Rep 99, CA; *Novello & Co Ltd v Hinrichsen Edition Ltd* [1951] Ch 595; *Bank voor Handel en Scheepvaart NV v Slatford* [1953] 1 QB 248.

[139] *Frankfurther v W L Exner Ltd* [1947] Ch 629 at 636–7.

court has no application, for if the foreign state commences the proceedings this amounts to submission and there is no immunity.[140]

(c) Requisition of property

Owing to the decision of Atkinson J in *Lorentzen v Lydden & Co*,[141] it was for some time doubtful whether an extra-territorial effect should not be attributed to the requisition, as distinct from the confiscation, of property by a foreign state. In that case the public policy exception was used in a positive way to give effect to a foreign government's act of requisition in relation to property situated in England. However, in *Bank voor Handel en Scheepvaart NV v Slatford*,[142] Devlin J followed an earlier Scots decision[143] in preference to that of Atkinson J. Devlin J favoured "the simple rule that generally property in England is subject to English law and to none other".[144] The position is now finally settled by the Court of Appeal in *Peer International Corpn v Termidor Music Publishers Ltd*,[145] where this simple rule was applied and *Lorentzen v Lydden* was overruled. It was held that the public policy exception could not be used in a positive way to give effect to a foreign government's confiscatory act in relation to property situated in England, ie to give that act a validity that it would not otherwise have. The Court distinguished *Kuwait Airways Corpn v Iraqi Airways Co (Nos 4 and 5)*,[146] which was concerned with the very different situation where public policy was used in a negative way to deny recognition to a foreign government's confiscatory act in relation to property situated in that country, ie to deny that act a validity that it would otherwise have. The *Peer* case involved confiscation but it supports the wider principle that English law will not enforce foreign laws that purport to have extra-territorial effect, a principle that applies equally to non-confiscatory cases as it does to confiscatory cases.

3. FOREIGN LAWS REPUGNANT TO ENGLISH PUBLIC POLICY[147]

(a) General principles

It is a well-established principle that any action brought in this country is subject to the English doctrine of public policy. Certain heads of the domestic doctrine of public policy command such respect, and certain foreign laws and institutions seem so repugnant to English notions and ideals, that the English view must prevail in proceedings in this country, for Scarman J has said that "an English court will refuse to apply a law which outrages its

---

[140] State Immunity Act 1978, s 2(3).
[141] [1942] 2 KB 202.
[142] [1953] 1 QB 248.
[143] *The El Condado* (1939) 63 Lloyd's Rep 330, 1939 SC 413.
[144] [1953] 1 QB 248 at 260.
[145] [2003] EWCA Civ 1156, [2004] Ch 212.
[146] [2002] UKHL 19, [2002] 2 AC 883; discussed further supra, p 128 and infra, pp 138–9.
[147] On this subject see Kahn-Freund (1953) 39 Grotius Society 39; Lloyd, *Public Policy* (1953), Chapter 5; Nygh (1964) 13 ICLQ 39; Kahn-Freund (1974) IV Hague Recueil 139, 426–31; FA Mann, *Foreign Affairs in English Courts* (1986), Chapter 8; Sammartano and Morse, *Public Policy in Transnational Relationships* (1992); Lagarde, in Lipstein (ed), *International Encyclopedia of Comparative Law* (1986), Vol 3, Chapter 11; Bucher (1993) II Hague Recueil 13; Carter (1993) 42 ICLQ 1; Enonchong (1996) 45 ICLQ 633; Leslie [1995] Jur Rev 477; Blom (2003) 50 NILR 373; Meidanis (2005) 30 ELR 95; Mills (2008) 4 J Priv Int L 201; Kramberger-Škerl (2011) 7 J Priv Int L 461; Chong (2012) 128 LQR 88; Oster (2015) 11 J Priv Int L 542. See also *Application of the Convention of 1902 Governing the Guardianship of Infants (Netherlands v Sweden)* [1958] ICJ Reports 55.

sense of justice and decency".[148] However, he also struck a note of caution in suggesting that "before it exercises such power it must consider the relevant foreign law as a whole".[149]

The occasional exclusion of a foreign law on the grounds of public policy is no doubt inevitable, but the English domestic doctrine of public policy covers a multitude of sins varying in their degree of turpitude, and it is essential to resist the suggestion that an action concerning a transaction governed by a foreign law must necessarily fail because it would have failed had the governing law been English. Judges in the past have now and then expressed somewhat extravagant views on the matter. Thus, for instance, in a restraint of trade case,[150] Fry J seemed to suggest that every limb of the domestic doctrine must apply in every action in England. This can scarcely be so. The conception of public policy is, and should be, narrower and more limited in private international law than in internal law.[151] A transaction that is valid by its foreign governing law should not be nullified on this ground unless its enforcement would offend some moral, social or economic principle so sacrosanct in English eyes as to require its maintenance at all costs and without exception. In the words of Cardozo J in a New York case:

> We are not so provincial as to say that every solution of a problem is wrong because we deal with it otherwise at home . . . The courts are not free to refuse to enforce a foreign right at the pleasure of the judges, to suit the individual notion of expediency or fairness. They do not close their doors unless help would violate some fundamental principle of justice, some prevalent conception of good morals, some deep-rooted tradition of the common weal.[152]

English courts should not invoke public policy save in cases where foreign law is manifestly incompatible with public policy.[153]

The particular rule of public policy that the defendant invokes may be of this overriding nature and therefore enforceable in all actions. Or it may be local in the sense that it represents some feature of internal policy. If so, it must be confined to cases where the governing law is English.[154] The mere fact that, for example, a contract, governed by a foreign law, infringes some rule of English domestic law such as the need for consideration to support a simple contract will not prevent its enforcement in England.[155]

To ascertain whether it is all-pervading or merely local, it must be examined "in the light of its history, the purpose of its adoption, the object to be accomplished by it, and the local conditions".[156] Perhaps the most important question to ask in each case is—what is the rule designed to prevent?[157] Presumably, for instance, the policy underlying the rule which invalidates a promise by an employee not to compete against his employer in the future is to further the economic well-being of the country by enabling every person freely to exploit

---

[148] *Re Fuld's Estate (No 3)* [1968] P 675 at 698. See also *Kuwait Airways Corpn v Iraqi Airways Co (Nos 4 and 5)* [2002] UKHL 19 at [16] (per Lord Nicholls), [2002] 2 AC 883.

[149] *Re Fuld's Estate (No 3)* [1968] P 675 at 698.

[150] *Rousillon v Rousillon* (1880) 14 Ch D 351 at 369. Actually the governing law in the circumstances of the case was English law. Therefore, of course, the domestic doctrine applied. Cf *Duarte v Black and Decker Corp* [2007] EWHC 2720 (QB), [2008] 1 All ER (Comm) 401; *Timms v Nicol* 1968 (1) SA 299, Rhod HC.

[151] *Vervaeke v Smith* [1983] 1 AC 145 at 164 (per Lord Simon), HL; *Kuwait Airways Corpn v Iraqi Airways Co (Nos 4 and 5)* [2002] UKHL 19 at [114] (per Lord Steyn), [2002] 2 AC 883.

[152] *Loucks v Standard Oil Co of New York* 224 NY 99 at 111 (1918); quoted in *Kuwait Airways Corpn v Iraqi Airways Co (Nos 4 and 5)* [2002] UKHL 19 at [16] (per Lord Nicholls), [2002] 2 AC 883.

[153] *Gotha City v Sotheby's (No 2)* (1998) Times, 8 October, CA.

[154] Cf *Mackender v Feldia AG* [1967] 2 QB 590 at 601, CA; *Re Colt Telecom Group plc (No 2)* [2002] EWHC 2815 (Ch) at [76]–[77], [2003] BPIR 324.

[155] *Re Bonacina, Le Brasseur v Bonacina* [1912] 2 Ch 394, CA. See now the Rome I Regulation, discussed *infra*, pp 752–4.

[156] Wharton, *Conflict of Laws* (1905), 3rd edn, Vol I, 16.

[157] See, eg, *Block Bros Realty Ltd v Mollard* (1981) 122 DLR (3d) 323, BC CA.

in England the trade that he has learnt. If so, only a rigid doctrinaire would claim that this particular rule is of universal application, designed to control relations between employers and employees in other countries. The English prohibition of contracts in restraint of trade is only concerned with freedom of trade in *England*.[158]

If the court decides that, having regard to the particular circumstances, the distinctive policy of English law is in truth affected, then the incompatible foreign rule must, indeed, be totally excluded. Some of the older decisions, however, have perhaps tended to invoke the domestic doctrine of public policy in all its ramifications with remorseless determination.

Kaufman v Gerson[159] provides a striking example of insularity.

> The husband of the defendant had misappropriated money entrusted to him by the plaintiff. By a contract made and to be performed in France the defendant agreed to pay to the plaintiff by instalments out of her own money the full amount misappropriated, in consideration that the plaintiff would refrain from prosecuting the husband for what was a crime by French law. Both the plaintiff and defendant were French nationals domiciled in France; the misappropriation had occurred in France; the contract was valid by French law.

This contract could scarcely be regarded as offensive to some fundamental principle of justice, for there is nothing particularly reprehensible in allowing a person to escape criminal proceedings at the price of paying full compensation to the sufferer. Nevertheless, an action for the recovery of instalments still due was dismissed on the ground that "to enforce a contract so procured would be to contravene what by the law of this country is deemed an essential moral interest".[160]

In *Addison v Brown*,[161] however, a less insular interpretation was put on the reservation of public policy.

> A wife sued her husband to recover arrears of maintenance due under a contract that was governed by Californian law. It was expressly agreed that neither party would apply to any court for the variation of the contract and that if in fact it were varied by any court in subsequent divorce proceedings it would nevertheless remain in force as written. Ten years later the husband obtained a divorce in California, and the contract, far from being varied, was incorporated in the judgment.

The contract, since it contained an agreement by the parties to oust the jurisdiction of the court, was contrary to the doctrine of public policy as understood in England, and it was therefore pleaded that the action was not maintainable. Streatfield J, however, refused to treat this particular segment of the doctrine as being of universal application. He said that there could be no objection in England to an agreement that purports to oust the jurisdiction of a foreign court.[162]

The principle that emerges in *Addison v Brown* is that, in order to apply the English domestic rules on public policy to an agreement, it must be shown that the agreement relates to England, in some important way. The same principle was applied, in a different context, in *Trendtex Trading Corpn v Crédit Suisse*.[163] There, the House of Lords held that, since an

---

[158] *Warner Bros v Nelson* [1937] 1 KB 209.
[159] [1904] 1 KB 591, CA, reversing Wright J [1903] 2 KB 114. The decision was not followed in the Canadian case of *National Surety Co v Larsen* [1929] 4 DLR 918, BC CA; but see *K(E) v K(D)* (2004) 257 DLR (4th) 549, BC CA.
[160] [1904] 1 KB 591 at 599–600.
[161] [1954] 1 WLR 779.
[162] Ibid, at 784.
[163] [1982] AC 679, HL; Thornley (1982) 41 CLJ 29. See also *Sigurdson v Farrow* (1981) 121 DLR (3d) 183, Alta QB; *Fraser v Buckle* [1996] 1 IR 1, SC. For the changing English domestic law attitude towards some instances of champerty see *Giles v Thompson* [1994] 1 AC 142, HL.

assignment of a cause of action savoured of champerty, it was contrary to public policy and therefore void. A crucial point in the case was that the assignment related to an *English* cause of action.

(b) Summary of cases where distinctive policy is affected

It is no easy matter to classify those cases in which the English court will refuse to enforce a foreign acquired right, on the ground that its enforcement would affront some moral principle the maintenance of which admits of no possible compromise. However, the following is suggested as the probable classification.

(i) Where the basic principles of English justice and fairness are affronted

Lord Nicholls in *Kuwait Airways Corpn v Iraqi Airways Co (Nos 4 and 5)*[164] has said that "the courts of this country must have a residual power, to be exercised exceptionally and with the greatest circumspection, to disregard a provision in the foreign law when to do otherwise would affront basic principles of justice and fairness which the courts seek to apply in the administration of justice in this country".[165] Two particular instances of this, namely a breach of human rights and a fundamental breach of international law, will be considered below. However, this principle cannot be confined to one particular category of unacceptable laws.[166] The established rule, which will be stated later,[167] that a foreign judgment cannot be recognised in England if it offends the principles of natural justice, as, for example, if the defendant was denied the opportunity of presenting his case to the foreign court, exemplifies this aspect of English public policy. Another example is the rule that a contract obtained by a class of duress so unconscionable that it will cause the English court, as a matter of public policy, to override the law governing the contract, is unenforceable in England.[168] Consistent with this, a foreign judgment granted in respect of a contract entered into under undue influence, duress or coercion may be refused enforcement in England on the ground of public policy.[169] As a final example, to permit a party which has not acted in good faith in relation to the purchase of stolen goods to benefit from a foreign limitation period as against a party who had no knowledge of the whereabouts of stolen goods and no possibility of recovering them, was against English public policy as expressed in the Limitation Act 1980.[170]

(ii) Where the English conceptions of morality are infringed

It cannot be doubted that a contract or other transaction which is objectionable in English eyes on the ground that it tends to promote sexual immorality,[171] such as a contract for prostitution, will receive no judicial recognition in England, though it may be innocuous according

---

[164] [2002] UKHL 19, [2002] 2 AC 883 .

[165] Ibid, at [18]. (Lord Hoffmann concurred with this judgment, as did Lord Scott on the public policy/recognition and enforcement point).

[166] Ibid.

[167] Infra, pp 576–8.

[168] *Royal Boskalis Westminster NV v Mountain* [1999] QB 674 at 729 (per Phillips LJ), CA. See, eg, *Kaufman v Gerson* [1904] 1 KB 591, CA, supra, p 134. Cf *Dimskal Shipping Co SA v International Transport Workers Federation* [1992] 2 AC 152, HL involving a different type of duress (ie economic). See also *Société des Hôtels Réunis SA v Hawker* (1913) 29 TLR 578; *Kahler v Midland Bank Ltd* [1950] AC 24 at 44–5, HL; cf *Luther v Sagor* [1921] 3 KB 532 at 558–9, CA.

[169] *Israel Discount Bank of New York v Hadjipateras* [1984] 1 WLR 137, CA; infra, p 574. For public policy as a defence to recognition and enforcement of foreign judgments under the traditional English rules see *Vervaeke v Smith* [1983] 1 AC 145, HL; generally infra, pp 573–6. For public policy as a defence to recognition and enforcement of foreign judgments under the Brussels I Regulation Recast see generally infra, pp 626–32.

[170] *Gotha City v Sotheby's (No 2)* (1998) Times, 8 October, CA.

[171] See, eg, *Pearce v Brooks* (1866) LR 1 Ex 213; *Ayerst v Jenkins* (1873) LR 16 Eq 275; *Taylor v Chester* (1869) LR 4 QB 309.

to its foreign governing law.[172] Similarly, an agreement to be performed abroad involving payment for the use of personal influence in securing a contract will not be enforced in England, at least not in the situation where the foreign place of performance applies the same public policy.[173] Neither, in this age of commercial fraud, will a contract drafted to deceive third parties be enforced.[174] On the other hand, Canadian courts have held that the enforcement of contracts relating to gambling debts would not violate Canadian concepts of essential judicial morality,[175] nor would enforcement of a foreign judgment for treble or punitive damages,[176] or for excessive damages.[177]

(iii) *Where a transaction prejudices the interests of the United Kingdom or its good relations with foreign powers*

An example of the first part of the above statement is the prohibition of business with an alien enemy.[178] In one case, for instance, an English company, owning mines in Spain, made a contract in 1910 for the delivery by instalments spread over a number of years of minerals to a German company.[179] The contract contained a suspensory clause which provided that in the event of war the obligations of the parties should be suspended during hostilities. The English company brought an action in 1916 claiming a declaration that the contract was not merely suspended but was abrogated by the existence of a state of war between Great Britain and Germany. The objection was taken that this was a German contract and that therefore it fell to be governed by German law. It was argued that illegality according to English law was irrelevant. What had to be shown was that the contract was illegal by German law. It was held, however, that the German character of the contract had no bearing on this question. "It is illegal for a British subject to become bound in a manner which sins against the public policy of the King's realm",[180] and it has long been established that the prohibition of trading with an alien enemy rests on public policy. It seems that payment in breach of United Nations sanctions as enacted in the relevant domestic law is akin to trading with the enemy for the purposes of public policy.[181]

Support for the second part of our statement may be derived from the rule that it is contrary to public policy for persons in England to enter into an engagement with the avowed object of causing injury to a friendly government,[182] as, for example, by raising a loan to further a revolt,[183] by an agreement to import liquor contrary to a prohibition law,[184] to defraud its

---

[172] *Robinson v Bland* (1760) 2 Burr 1077 at 1084, 97 ER 717.

[173] *Lemenda Trading Co Ltd v African Middle East Petroleum Co Ltd* [1988] QB 448; Carter (1988) BYBIL 356. See also *Westacre v Jugoimport* [2000] 1 QB 288, CA discussed further infra, pp 674–5; *Apple Corps Ltd v Apple Computer Inc* [1992] FSR 431; *Tekron Resources Ltd v Guinea Investment Co Ltd* [2003] EWHC 2577 (QB), [2004] 2 Lloyd's Rep 26.

[174] *Mitsubishi Corpn v Alafouzos* [1988] 1 Lloyd's Rep 191.

[175] *Boardwalk Regency Corpn v Maalouf* (1992) 88 DLR (4th) 612, Ont CA; *Auerbach v Resorts International Hotel Inc* (1991) 89 DLR (4th) 688, Que CA. These cases involved enforcement of foreign judgments, see infra, pp 573–6.

[176] *Old North State Brewing Co v Newlands Services Inc* [1999] 4 WWR 573, BC CA; discussed infra, p 575. See also *Benefit Strategies Group Inc v Prider* [2005] SASC 194, (2005) 91 SASR 544; cf *Schnabel v Yung Lui* [2002] NSWSC 15.

[177] *Beals v Saldanha* [2003] 3 SCR 416, (2003) 234 DLR (4th) 1—damages in Florida were considerably larger than those that would be granted in a comparable case in Canada; discussed infra, p 575.

[178] *Robson v Premier Oil and Pipe Line Co* [1915] 2 Ch 124 at 136, CA.

[179] *Dynamit Actien-Gesellschaft v Rio Tinto Co Ltd* [1918] AC 260, HL.

[180] Ibid, at 294.

[181] *Royal Boskalis Westminster NV v Mountain* [1999] QB 674 at 693 (per Stuart-Smith LJ), CA.

[182] *British Nylon Spinners Ltd v ICI Ltd* [1955] Ch 37 at 52; *Bodley Head Ltd v Flegon* [1972] 1 WLR 680 at 687–8.

[183] *De Wutz v Hendricks* (1824) 2 Bing 314, 130 ER 326.

[184] *Foster v Driscoll* [1929] 1 KB 470, CA; cf *Toprak v Finagrain* [1979] 2 Lloyd's Rep 98, CA; *Tekron Resources Ltd v Guinea Investment Co Ltd* [2003] EWHC 2577 (QB), [2004] 2 Lloyd's Rep 26.

revenue[185] or to export a prohibited commodity.[186] Such conduct is a breach of international comity and tends to injure the relations of the British government with friendly powers. It is not, however, contrary to public policy to enforce a contract which is illegal and/or void by the law of a foreign and friendly state when the contract was made in England and involved the performance exclusively in England of acts entirely lawful under English law.[187] Nor is it against public policy to enforce a contract, judgment or arbitral award between nationals of two foreign countries, both friendly to the United Kingdom, even though the two foreign states are enemies of each other.[188] A court in this country cannot set itself up as a judge of the rights and wrongs of a controversy between two countries friendly to us.[189]

(iv) A gross infringement of human rights

Gross infringements of human rights are one instance, and an important instance, of a provision of a foreign law, which if recognised or enforced would affront basic principles of justice and fairness which the courts seek to apply in the administration of justice in this country.[190] A German decree during the Nazi era depriving Jewish émigrés of their German nationality and, consequentially, leading to the confiscation of their property is an example of a law which constitutes so grave an infringement of human rights that the English courts ought to refuse to recognise it as a law at all.[191] An English court will not apply a foreign law that involves such a grave infringement of human rights.[192] Nowadays, human rights are protected under the European Convention on Human Rights.[193] In recent years human rights law has been used to cast light on the public policy defence to recognition and enforcement of foreign judgments.[194]

---

[185] *Re Emery's Investments Trusts* [1959] Ch 410; *Pye Ltd v BG Transport Service Ltd* [1966] 2 Lloyd's Rep 300 at 308–9.

[186] *Regazzoni v K C Sethia (1944) Ltd* [1958] AC 301, HL. For a critical study of this decision, see FA Mann (1958) 21 MLR 130. Cf *Trinidad Shipping Co v Alston* [1920] AC 888, PC; *Dalmia Dairy Industries Ltd v National Bank of Pakistan* [1978] 2 Lloyd's Rep 223 at 267–8, CA; *Soleimany v Soleimany* [1999] QB 785, CA; *Mahonia Ltd v JP Morgan Chase Bank* [2003] 2 Lloyd's Rep 911—extended to where the illegal purpose is known to just one party.

[187] *JSC Zestafoni v Ronly Holdings Ltd* [2004] EWHC 245 (Comm) at [75], [2004] 2 Lloyd's Rep 335. See also *Society of Lloyd's v Fraser* [1999] Lloyd's Rep IR 156, CA.

[188] *Dalmia Dairy Industries Ltd v National Bank of Pakistan* [1978] 2 Lloyd's Rep 223, at pp 299–301.

[189] *Empresa Exportadora De Azúcar v Industria Azucarera Nacional SA, The Playa Larga* [1983] 2 Lloyd's Rep 171, CA; Carter (1983) 54 BYBIL 297.

[190] *Kuwait Airways Corpn v Iraqi Airways Co (Nos 4 and 5)* [2002] UKHL 19 at [18] (per Lord Nicholls, Lords Hoffmann and Scott concurring), [114] (per Lord Steyn), [137] (per Lord Hope), [2002] 2 AC 883.

[191] *Oppenheimer v Cattermole* [1976] AC 249 at 277–8, HL. This proposition was cited with approval in *Kuwait Airways Corpn v Iraqi Airways Co (Nos 4 and 5)* at [18] (per Lord Nicholls), [114] (per Lord Steyn), [137] (per Lord Hope). For other cases arising out of the Nazi era contrast *Re Meyer* [1971] P 298 with *Igra v Igra* [1951] P 404. For early examples of foreign laws or status offending English conceptions of human liberty and freedom of action see in relation to slavery, see *Sommersett's Case* (1772) 20 State Tr 1; *Forbes v Cochrane* (1824) 2 B & C 448 at 467, 107 ER 450; *Regazzoni v K C Sethia (1944) Ltd* [1956] 2 QB 490 at 524, CA; cf *Santos v Illidge* (1860) 8 CBNS 861. See also *Gotha City v Sotheby's (No 2)* (1998) Times, 8 October, CA. US courts have refused to enforce English libel judgments on the basis that English libel law provides inadequate freedom of speech: *Bachchan v India Abroad Publications Inc* 588 NYS 2d 661 (Sup Ct NY 1992); *Matusevitch v Telnikoff* [1996] IL Pr 181, US District Ct for the District of Columbia; Maltby (1994) 94 Col LR 1978; Devgun (1994) 23 Anglo-Am LR 195. For the link between constitutional guarantees and public policy in Canada see *Pro Swing Inc v Elta Golf Inc* [2006] SCR 612 at [59]–[62], (2007) 273 DLR (4th) 663.

[192] See the parallel situation where there was a fundamental breach of international law, discussed below. See also *Skrine & Co v Euromoney Publications plc* [2002] EMLR 15, CA—a contribution action following settlement of claims abroad.

[193] For enforcement of the Convention rights in the United Kingdom see the Human Rights Act 1998.

[194] Both under the Brussels/Lugano system (discussed infra, pp 628–30), and the traditional English rules on recognition and enforcement (discussed infra, pp 576 and 580–2). See also the use of human rights law when

(v) A fundamental breach of international law

As far back as 1973, the House of Lords accepted that it is part of English public policy that our courts should give effect to clearly established rules of international law.[195] The leading case developing this category of public policy is *Kuwait Airways Corpn v Iraqi Airways Co (Nos 4 and 5)*.[196]

> Following the Iraq invasion of Kuwait in 1990, aircraft belonging to the claimant, Kuwait Airways Corporation, were seized and flown by the defendant, Iraqi Airways Company, to Iraq. The Revolutionary Command Council of Iraq (RCC) passed Resolution 369 which purported to divest the claimant of its title to its aircraft and transfer this to the defendant. This was part and parcel of the Iraqi seizure of Kuwait and its assets and the assimilation of these assets into the structure of Iraq. The claimant brought proceedings in England for return of the aircraft or payment of their value, and damages.

Mance J gave judgment for the claimant on liability. The Court of Appeal dismissed the defendant's appeal against this decision. The House of Lords, affirming this decision, held that in appropriate circumstances it is legitimate for an English court to have regard to the content of international law when deciding whether to recognise a foreign law.[197] The judiciary does not have to shut its eyes to a breach of international law when the breach is plain and, indeed, acknowledged.[198] The acceptability of a foreign law must be judged by contemporary standards.[199] This was not simply a governmental expropriation of property within its territory, it was part of an attempt to extinguish every vestige of Kuwait as a separate state. Expropriation in such circumstances was not acceptable in today's world. Iraq's invasion of Kuwait and seizure of its assets were gross violations of established rules of international law of fundamental importance. Enforcement or recognition of Resolution 369 therefore would be manifestly contrary to the public policy of English law.[200] In the case of a fundamental breach of international law, no connection with England is needed for the public policy exception to operate, since it is not based on a principle of English public policy which is domestic in character.[201] In this case public policy operated as an exception to the tort choice of law rules.[202] The House of Lords then applied the tort choice of law rules on the footing that the transfer of title purportedly made by Resolution 369 was to be disregarded.[203] This was because it was contrary to public policy to apply Iraqi law as the lex situs to exclude

---

considering the public policy defence under the EU Insolvency Regulation (Reg 2015/848) in C-341/04 *Eurofood IFSC Ltd* [2006] ECR I-3813 at [67].

[195] *Oppenheimer v Cattermole* [1976] AC 249 at 277–8, HL.

[196] [2002] UKHL 19, [2002] 2 AC 883. Their Lordships, at [28] (per Lord Nicholls, with whose judgment Lord Hoffmann concurred, as did Lord Scott on the public policy/recognition and enforcement point), at [114] (per Lord Steyn), [138] (per Lord Hope) placed reliance on *Oppenheimer v Cattermole* [1976] AC 249, HL. The *Kuwait Airways* case also involved important points in relation to tort choice of law, which are discussed infra, pp 870–1.

[197] [2002] UKHL 19 at [26] (per Lord Nicholls), [2002] 2 AC 883.

[198] The non-justiciable principle under the Act of State doctrine does not require this, ibid, at [26] (per Lord Nicholls), at [112]–[113] (per Lord Steyn), at [135]–[149] (per Lord Hope).

[199] Ibid, at [28] (per Lord Nicholls).

[200] Ibid, at [29] (per Lord Nicholls), at [114] (per Lord Steyn), at [149] (per Lord Hope). It would also be contrary to United Kingdom obligations under the UN Charter: Lord Nicholls at [29]; Lord Steyn at [114], at [141] (per Lord Hope).

[201] Ibid, at [166]–[167] (per Lord Hope). There was a clear connection between Resolution 369, which was part of the law of the place where the tort was committed (which is what the court was concerned with in a tort choice of law case), and the breach of international law.

[202] Ibid, at [33] (per Lord Nicholls), [114] (per Lord Steyn), [165]–[166] (per Lord Hope). Public policy would have operated as an exception to the lex situs rule if there had been an action asserting title to the aircraft, at [192] (per Lord Scott).

[203] Ibid, at [37] (per Lord Nicholls), at [117]–[118] (per Lord Steyn), [168]–[170]. Lord Scott dissenting at [172], [191]–[194].

claims it would otherwise have under Iraqi law as the law of the place where the tort was committed.[204] In other words, the court applied the law of the place where the tort was committed minus that part of it which was against public policy to recognise. The upshot was that there was actionability under the law of Iraq.

(c) Cases involving a foreign status

Any attempt to classify the foreign laws that are offensive to the English concept of public policy is not easy to reconcile with decisions on the measure of recognition to be given to a foreign status. The short answer, no doubt, is that, though the court must recognise the existence of a person's status as fixed by the law of his foreign domicile, it need not necessarily give effect to the results or incidents attributed to it by that law, including the capacities and incapacities of the person affected.[205] The problem, however, is to determine what incidents may be accepted, what must be repudiated. Obviously an incident must be repudiated if it is contrary to a positive rule of English internal law. Again, a remedy permitted by the foreign law of the status will not be granted if English law is not adapted to its enforcement. Thus, an English court was quite prepared to recognise that under Greek law a father should provide his daughter with a dowry, though the nature of the daughter's right was such that it should not be enforced here.[206] Finally, a foreign status or incident of status will be disregarded if it offends the English doctrine of public policy. So far as English internal law is concerned, it has long been settled that a judge is no longer free to invent new heads of public policy. He may expound, but must not expand, this branch of the law.[207] In the field of private international law, however, exposition has gradually blossomed into expansion to such an extent that apparently the judges now feel free to exclude the law of the domicile whenever[208] they feel it proper to do so in the circumstances.

The ancestry of this extreme view may be traced back to *Worms v De Valdor*[209] in 1880. That case was concerned with the French status of prodigality which arises when a court appoints an adviser, a *conseil judicaire*, to safeguard the interests of an adult person of extravagant habits. The court may prohibit him from compromising claims, borrowing or receiving money, alienating or mortgaging property and bringing or defending actions without the collaboration of his adviser. The question in *Worms v De Valdor* was whether an action for the cancellation of certain bills of exchange, brought by a prodigal in his own name and without the assistance of his *conseil judiciaire*, could succeed. Fry J, unaided by expert evidence, made his own researches into French law and concluded that the appointment of a *conseil judiciaire* neither changed the status of a prodigal nor subjected him to a personal disqualification. Had it done so, the judge intimated that he would have disregarded the disqualification as being penal in nature. He did in fact allow the action to proceed, but on the ground, it would seem, that whether the prodigal could sue in England in his own name was a procedural question determinable by English law as that of the forum.

In the case of *Re Selot's Trusts*,[210] the question was whether the status of prodigality, imposed on the plaintiff by the French law of his domicile, precluded his recovery of a legacy bequeathed

---

[204] Ibid, at [31]–[33] (per Lord Nicholls).

[205] Allen (1930) 46 LQR 277, 293 et seq; Inglis (1957) 6 ICLQ 202, 220–4; Falconbridge, p 751.

[206] *Phrantzes v Argenti* [1960] 2 QB 19; supra, pp 90–1; Webb (1960) 23 MLR 446; Carter (1960) 36 BYBIL 412; and see *Shahnaz v Rizwan* [1965] 1 QB 390—recognition of deferred dower; cf *Re Macartney* [1921] 1 Ch 522; *Khalij Commercial Bank Ltd v Woods* (1985) 17 DLR (4th) 358, Ont SC.

[207] *Fender v St John-Mildmay* [1938] AC 1 at 40, HL; *Vervaeke v Smith* [1983] 1 AC 145 at 164, HL— existing principles can be applied to new circumstances.

[208] *Russ v Russ* [1964] P 315, CA.

[209] (1880) 49 LJ Ch 261.

[210] [1902] 1 Ch 488.

to him by an English will. Farwell J, affecting to follow *Worms v De Valdor*, held that the disability of the prodigal to bring an action without the assistance of his legal adviser was a penal restriction that had no effect in English proceedings. What the judge overlooked was that this was not the ratio decidendi of Fry J in the earlier case.[211]

A later case concerned with a status of incompetence is *Re Langley's Settlement Trusts*.[212] The Court of Appeal held that the joint exercise of a power to withdraw part of settled funds by the settlor and his wife was effective, even though the settlor was disqualified as incompetent by the law of his residence and domicile, California. The exercise complied with English law which governed the settlement that created the power, since the document had been signed by a man who was not incompetent in the eyes of English internal law. It also complied with the law that governed the man's status, for the wife in signing the document had obeyed the express directions of the Californian court.

What, however, is more pertinent to the present discussion is that the Court of Appeal gave an alternative reason for the decision. The principle, it was said, is that it is a matter of judicial discretion whether a foreign status shall be recognised.[213] Had the only facet of the Californian law requiring investigation in the present case been the ban placed on the settlor's right to withdraw the settled funds, the court would have exercised its discretion against the recognition of his status of incompetence. But in order that the law may be reasonably certain and predictable it has long been established that judicial discretion must be exercised in accordance with settled rules, not in an arbitrary or capricious manner. It is not an unfettered discretion, but one, as Lord Eldon said in a specific performance case, that "must be regulated upon grounds that will make it judicial".[214] What, therefore, was the particular head of public policy that justified the rejection of the Californian status? The Court of Appeal, affirming Buckley J in the court below, classified the status as penal since it deprived the settlor of his power to deal with a valuable interest. The word "penal", said Buckley J, "means law of a kind which deprives the person affected of his rights or property in a way which adversely affects his interests".[215] But this is to attribute to the word a meaning that is warranted neither by the dictionary nor by the nature of the particular status. The object of the Californian order was not to penalise the invalid, but to protect him against the machinations of "artful or designing persons".[216] Similarly, the subjection of a spendthrift to the status of prodigality is designed to protect him against his own extravagance. It would seem, therefore, that to stigmatise as penal any law which deprives him of a valuable interest is to invent a new head of public policy that is supported by no authority except the doubtful decision of Farwell J in *Re Selot's Trusts*. It is a proposition that scarcely accords with the views expressed in *Luther v Sagor*.[217]

Moreover, the proposition that a judge has a free discretion to exclude a foreign status or its incidents if he considers that in the particular circumstances it will adversely affect a person's right to deal with his property cannot be accepted with any degree of complacency. Its impact

---

[211] The two decisions have sometimes been said to support the proposition that a foreign status unknown to English law will not be recognised in England. See, eg, *Republica de Guatemala v Nunez* [1927] 1 KB 669 at 701, CA. The proposition is unfounded. For example, the married status of the parties to a polygamous marriage is recognised and, indeed, English courts will grant matrimonial relief to the parties to such a marriage. So also was the status arising from a foreign adoption or a foreign legitimation *per subsequens matrimonium* recognised before those institutions were accepted by English internal law.

[212] [1961] 1 WLR 41; affd [1962] Ch 541; Grodecki (1962) 11 ICLQ 578.

[213] See *De Reneville v De Reneville* [1948] P 100 at 109, CA.

[214] *White v Damon* (1802) 7 Ves 30 at 35, 32 ER 13.

[215] [1961] 1 WLR 41 at 46.

[216] Californian Probate Code, s 1466.

[217] [1921] 3 KB 532, CA; supra, pp 127–8.

on the doctrine of public policy would, at first sight, be disastrous, for what has been laboriously shaped into a reasonably ordered form would become once more amorphous and indeterminate. It is difficult to disagree with the criticism that it is "a revolutionary innovation in our private international law",[218] and that "the courts might just as well abandon any attempt to formulate and apply defined rules of law if these can be overridden by an undefinable discretion".[219]

However, this whole problem of a free discretion is perhaps, at the moment, more apparent than real. The most common situation where the recognition of a foreign status arises is in cases involving the effect of a foreign divorce, annulment or legal separation. But, as will be seen below, the whole area of recognition of foreign divorces, etc is now put on a legislative basis and it is clear that recognition cannot be refused on the ground of a lack of substantial justice.

(d) Recognition of foreign divorces, etc[220]

At one time, the discretion to refuse to recognise a foreign status applied in the context of recognition of foreign divorces, annulments and legal separations. It was said that there was a power to refuse to recognise a foreign divorce "which offends against English ideas of substantial justice".[221] The inherent difficulty in defining this concept was a cause for concern, as was the width of the doctrine.[222] However, in the case of divorces, etc granted in a European Union Member State, recognition is now dealt with by a Union Regulation and, in the case of divorces granted outside a European Union Member State, is now put on a statutory basis. Under the relevant Regulation[223] recognition has to be given to foreign divorces, etc unless one of a limited list of grounds of non-recognition applies. Similarly, under the relevant statute[224] recognition has to be given to foreign divorces, etc unless the court exercises its discretion on a limited listed number of grounds to deny recognition. With both Regulation and statute these grounds do not contain any provision allowing the courts to refuse recognition on the basis of want of substantial justice. It is possible, though, to refuse recognition in cases where there has been, in effect, a denial of natural justice,[225] and in cases where recognition would be "manifestly contrary to public policy".[226] It is not entirely clear whether

---

[218] Nygh (1964) 13 ICLQ 39, 50.

[219] Ibid, 51; and see *Chaplin v Boys* [1971] AC 356 at 378, HL.

[220] Public policy as a defence in cases of recognition of foreign divorces, etc is dealt with more fully, infra, pp 1004–5 and 1030–3.

[221] *Middleton v Middleton* [1967] P 62 at 69; see also *Gray (otherwise Formosa) v Formosa* [1963] P 259, CA; *Lepre v Lepre* [1965] P 52. For the reintroduction of this concept, but now in the area of enforcement of foreign commercial judgments, see *Adams v Cape Industries plc* [1990] Ch 433 at 557 et seq, CA; discussed infra, p 578.

[222] See Carter (1962) 38 BYBIL 497; Lewis (1963) 12 ICLQ 298; Blom-Cooper (1963) 26 MLR 94; Carter (1965–1966) 41 BYBIL 445; Unger (1966) 29 MLR 327. See also *Varanand v Varanand* (1964) 108 Sol Jo 693, cited in *Qureshi v Qureshi* [1972] Fam 173 at 201.

[223] Council Regulation (EC) No 2201/2003 of 27 November 2003 concerning jurisdiction and the recognition and enforcement of judgments in matrimonial matters and the matters of parental responsibility OJ 2003 L 338/1 (Brussels II *bis*), Art 22; discussed infra, pp 1002–5.

[224] The Family Law Act 1986; see s 51.

[225] Brussels II *bis*, Art 22(b); Family Law Act 1986, s 51(3)(a).

[226] Brussels II *bis*, Art 22(a); Family Law Act 1986, s 51(3)(c). There are a number of other circumstances in which public policy issues arise, in the context of family law. A foreign law of domicile governing capacity to marry may not be recognised if it is repugnant to English public policy: *Cheni v Cheni* [1965] P 85 at 98–9, infra, p 921; see also *Westminster City Council v C* [2008] EWCA Civ 198, [2009] Fam 11. Restraint on remarriage after a foreign divorce may be regarded as penal, so that the restriction will be regarded as inoperative outside the jurisdiction in which it was imposed, see infra, pp 926–7.

the use of the common law concept of public policy as one of the statutory grounds of non-recognition and the exclusion of the concept of substantial justice represents a shift in substance or merely one of terminology.[227] However, it is clear that the courts have been willing to use public policy as a ground for non-recognition of foreign divorces in circumstances where one might have expected a reluctance to do so. Thus in *Joyce v Joyce*[228] public policy was used as a ground[229] for non-recognition of a Quebec divorce, even though this involved criticism of the laws and procedure of a foreign and friendly country as being unfair to the respondent. In *Vervaeke v Smith*[230] a foreign nullity decree was refused recognition in the House of Lords on the basis of public policy, where there was no unfairness to the respondent. No criticism was made of the foreign law.[231] Rather, their Lordships were concerned to uphold the English policy of maintaining the validity of sham marriages, which was to be preferred to the Belgian policy, and that this policy should not be avoided by petitioners going abroad to obtain a nullity decree,[232] especially when the petitioner had previously put forward a bogus case in England which had failed. A policy of upholding sham marriages is odd enough, but to give this policy overriding force in an international context is even stranger. More recently, however, in *Golubovich v Golubovich*[233] the Court of Appeal allowed the appeal against a judgment refusing recognition to a Russian divorce on the grounds that the husband had fraudulently misled the English court by forging the divorce and had disregarded orders, in particular an interim injunction, made by the English court. The Court of Appeal held that the judge's task was to determine whether it would be manifestly contrary to public policy to grant recognition. The divorce was recognized because it had been validly made by the Russian court and, furthermore, the wife would be able to pursue her claim for financial relief in England following the recognition of the divorce. The court further stated that, absent a breach of the rules of natural justice, to refuse recognition of a decree of divorce pronounced by a court in another jurisdiction within the Council of Europe must be regarded as truly exceptional.

(e) Effect of European Union private international law

Most European Union private international law instruments allow the English courts to refuse to recognise any foreign law or judgment which is contrary to English public policy. But this does not mean that the English courts would have necessarily reached the same results in the cases discussed above had those cases fell to be decided under the private international law rules of European Union law. European Union private international law instruments emphasise the exceptional nature of the doctrine of public policy. For example, the Rome I Regulation on the law applicable to contractual obligations states, in Article 21, that "[t]he application of a provision of the law of any country specified by this Regulation may be refused only if such application is manifestly incompatible with the public policy (*ordre public*) of the forum". The meaning

---

[227] See *Vervaeke v Smith* [1983] 1 AC 145 at 164 (per Lord Simon, who seems to regard the two concepts as being, in substance, the same), HL. The Law Commission regards the courts' treatment of the two concepts as involving the same approach, Law Com No 137 (1984), para 2.26.

[228] [1979] Fam 93; cf *Igra v Igra* [1951] P 404 at 412. The public policy defence did not succeed in *Sabbagh v Sabbagh* [1985] FLR 29; *Eroglu v Eroglu* [1994] 2 FLR 287; *Kellman v Kellman* [2000] 1 FLR 785.

[229] It was also decided that there had been a denial of the opportunity to take part in the proceedings under s 8(2)(a)(ii) of the Recognition of Divorces and Legal Separations Act 1971; now s 51(3)(a)(ii) of the Family Law Act 1986.

[230] [1983] 1 AC 145, HL; Smart (1983) 99 LQR 24; Jaffey (1983) 32 ICLQ 500.

[231] See [1983] 1 AC 145 at 156 (per Lord Hailsham).

[232] Ibid, at 156–7, 163–7.

[233] [2010] EWCA Civ 810, [2010] 3 WLR 1607.

and effect of this provision is clarified in Recital 37, according to which public policy is engaged only "in exceptional circumstances".[234] Furthermore, in *Krombach v Bamberski*,[235] the leading decision on public policy as a defence to recognition and enforcement of foreign judgments under the Brussels/Lugano system, the European Court of Justice held that national courts must give public policy a meaning which is appropriate in the context of European Union private international law, and the Court of Justice may intervene if they fail to do so. Thus we are left with the position whereby the courts of the Member States determine, according to their own conceptions, what public policy requires, but there are limits to that concept which are subject to review by the Court of Justice. These limits are a matter for interpretation of European Union private international law. Furthermore, some of the cases discussed above, especially those concerning transactions that prejudice the relations of the United Kingdom with foreign powers, now fall within Article 9(3) of the Rome I Regulation which is concerned with the application of overriding mandatory provisions of the law of the place of performance. The operation of this Article, and its relationship with the doctrine of public policy, is uncertain and discussed in more detail in the chapter dealing with choice of law for contractual obligations.[236]

4. MANDATORY RULES

The concept of mandatory rules has only recently been introduced into English law. Mandatory rules of the forum have been described by the Law Commissions as domestic rules which "are regarded as so important that as a matter of construction or policy they must apply in any action before a court of the forum, even where the issues are in principle governed by a foreign law selected by a choice of law rule".[237] A useful definition is also provided in Article 9(1) of the Rome I Regulation on the law applicable to contractual obligations according to which "overriding mandatory provisions are provisions the respect for which is regarded as crucial by a country for safeguarding its public interests, such as its political, social or economic organisation, to such an extent that they are applicable to any situation falling within their scope, irrespective of the law otherwise applicable". The statutory and European Union rules on choice of law in respect of trusts,[238] contracts[239] and torts[240] all have rules providing for the application of the mandatory rules of the forum. Some mandatory rules are of purely domestic origin; others implement European Union law. An example of English mandatory rules is provided by the controls on exemption clauses contained in the Unfair Contract Terms Act 1977; the Act itself stipulates[241] that, in certain circumstances, these controls shall apply despite the parties' choice of a foreign law to govern the contract. Another example of English mandatory rules is provided by the Employment Rights Act 1996; the Act provides[242] that the governing law of the employment contract is immaterial for the purposes of the Act; the exact territorial scope of this employment legislation is left to be determined by the courts.[243] An example of

---

[234] The public policy exception under the Rome I Regulation is discussed infra, pp 752–4.

[235] Case C-7/98 [2000] ECR I-1935 at [22]–[23], discussed infra, pp 628–30.

[236] Infra, pp 751–2.

[237] Law Com Working Paper No 87 (1984), Scot Law Com Consultative Memorandum No 62 (1984), para 4.5.

[238] Infra, pp 1392–3.

[239] Infra, pp 746–51.

[240] Infra, pp 866–8.

[241] S 27(2).

[242] S 204.

[243] See *Lawson v Serco Ltd* [2006] UKHL 3, [2006] 1 All ER 823; *Duncombe v Secretary of State for Children, Schools and Families* [2011] UKSC 36, [2011] 4 All ER 1020; *Ravat v Halliburton Manufacturing & Services Ltd* [2012] UKSC 1, [2012] 2 All ER 905.

English mandatory rules of European origin is provided by the Commercial Agents (Council Directive) Regulations 1993,[244] certain provisions of which have been held by the European Court of Justice in the *Ingmar* case to be of a mandatory nature and applicable whenever the legal relationship in question has a sufficient connection with the European Union.[245] The concept of mandatory rules is a positive one; the concern is to apply a particular mandatory rule. This contrasts with the exclusionary rules previously examined in this chapter where the concern is that a foreign rule should not be applied, ie they are negative concepts.[246] However, the effect of the application of a mandatory rule of English law is that a foreign domestic law, which would otherwise govern under choice of law rules, is not applied. To that extent application of mandatory rules can be regarded as an exclusionary concept. At the same time, and this brings out the essentially different nature of mandatory rules, there can be circumstances where the concern is to apply the mandatory rules of a foreign country, rather than those of the forum. The statutory rules on choice of law for trusts and contracts[247] provide for the application of foreign mandatory rules. Naturally, under these particular provisions it is not a case of the exclusion of a foreign law, but of its application.

---

[244] SI 1993/3053, implementing Council Directive 86/653/EEC of 18 December 1986 on the coordination of the laws of the Member States relating to self-employed commercial agents OJ L 382/17 into United Kingdom law.

[245] Case C-381/98 *Ingmar GB Ltd v Eaton Leonard Technologies Inc* [2000] ECR I-9305. See also Case C-184/12 *United Antwerp Maritime Agencies (Unamar) NV v Navigation Maritime Bulgare* EU:C:2013:663, [2014] 1 Lloyd's Rep 161.

[246] See *Peer International Corpn v Termidor Music Publishers Ltd* [2003] EWCA Civ 1156, [2004] Ch 212; discussed supra, p 131. But see the argument that public policy in contract cases sometimes operates as a positive concept, the concern being to apply English law, infra, pp 748–9. See generally Blom (2003) 50 NILR 373, 379–82.

[247] Infra, pp 1392–3 and 751–2. Cf the position in relation to torts, see infra, p 868.

9

DOMICILE, NATIONALITY AND RESIDENCE[1]

1. Introduction	145	(b) Abandonment of an existing domicile	162
2. General Rules	147	(c) Revival of the domicile of origin	163
3. The Acquisition of a Domicile of Choice	148	5. Domicile of Dependent Persons	165
		(a) Children	165
(a) Residence	149	(b) Mental disorder or mental incapacity	168
(b) The requisite intention	151	(c) Capacity to acquire a domicile	168
(c) Voluntary residence	158	6. Domicile of Married Women	168
(d) Precarious residence	160	(a) The abolition of dependency	168
(e) The burden of proof	161	(b) Transitional problems	169
(f) Change of domicile and change of nationality	161	7. Domicile and Nationality	170
		(a) Nationality and domicile contrasted	170
4. Domicile of Origin and Domicile of Choice Contrasted	162	8. Concepts of Residence	172
		(a) Ordinary residence	173
(a) Tenacity of the domicile of origin	162	(b) Habitual residence	175

1. INTRODUCTION

It has been universally recognised that questions affecting the personal status of a human being should be governed constantly by one and the same law, irrespective of where he may happen to be or of where the facts giving rise to the question may have occurred.[2] But unanimity goes no further. There is disagreement on two matters. What is the scope of this "personal law", as it is called, and should its criterion be domicile or nationality?[3] In England, however, it has long been settled that questions affecting status are determined by the law of the domicile of the *propositus* and that, broadly speaking, such questions are those affecting family relations and family property.[4] To be more precise, the following are some of the matters that are to a greater or lesser extent governed by the personal law:[5] the essential validity of a marriage; the effect of marriage on the proprietary rights of husband and wife; jurisdiction in divorce and nullity of marriage, though only to a limited degree; legitimacy,

---

[1] Kahn, *South African Law of Domicile of Natural Persons* (1972); North (1990) I Hague Recueil 13, 26–48.

[2] Rabel, i, 109; and see Kahn-Freund (1974) III Hague Recueil 139, 334–5, 391–492.

[3] On the respective merits of nationality and domicile see infra, pp 170–1.

[4] It will be seen, infra, pp 198–201, that domicile is an important basis of jurisdiction in the very different context of jurisdiction in civil and commercial matters, where domicile is given a special meaning, see the Civil Jurisdiction and Judgments Order, SI 2001/3929, para 9 of Sch I, as substituted by Civil Jurisdiction and Judgments (Amendment) Regulations 2014/2947 Sch 2 para 3(11) and Art 62 of Regulation (EU) No 1215/2012 of the European Parliament and of the Council of 12 December 2012 on jurisdiction and the recognition and enforcement of judgments in civil and commercial matters (the Brussels I recast), discussed infra, pp 198–312.

[5] See further *Mark v Mark* [2005] UKHL 42 [38], [2006] 1 AC 98.

legitimation and adoption; wills of movables, intestate succession to movables, and inheritance by a dependant.

When it comes to a definition of domicile, this is no easy matter. The concept of domicile is not uniform throughout the world. To a civil lawyer it means habitual residence, but at common law it is regarded as the equivalent of a person's permanent home.[6] Such a definition gives a misleading air of simplicity to the English concept of domicile. It fails to mention, for example, that there are two main classes of domicile; the *domicile of origin* that is communicated by operation of law to each person at birth, ie the domicile of his father or his mother, according as he is legitimate or illegitimate;[7] and the *domicile of choice* which every person of full age is free to acquire in substitution for that which he at present possesses. This distinction relates merely to the acquisition and loss of domicile, not to its effects. It also fails to point out that the acquisition of a domicile of choice requires not only residence in a territory subject to a distinctive legal system,[8] but also an intention by the *propositus* to remain there permanently. "There must be the act and there must be the intention."[9] But, as will be seen,[10] both the concept of permanency and the ascertainment of a person's intentions are fraught with difficulty.

The English concept of domicile is bedevilled by rules; these are complex, often impossible to justify in policy terms, and lead to uncertainty of outcome. Before looking at these rules in detail, one preliminary matter should be considered. This is the question of whether the same test for domicile applies, regardless of the context in which the matter is raised.

According to what WW Cook called the "single conception theory", English law takes the view that the test which determines the place of a person's domicile must remain constant no matter what the nature of the issue may be before the court. Cook,[11] however, denied that this was true in practice. He regarded "domicile" as a relative term which varies in meaning according to the different situations (eg taxation, divorce, intestate succession) to which it is applicable. A judge, he said, must inevitably focus his attention on the concrete problem before him, otherwise he will neglect the "social and economic" requirements of the situation. Although there appears to have been a tendency in the USA to adopt this view,[12] the conventional approach in England has been to reject it.[13] However, it should be noted that under the Inheritance Tax Act 1984[14] there is a special definition whereby, for certain purposes, persons are treated as domiciled in the United Kingdom. Also it is hard to believe that judges in this country have not been influenced by an awareness of the consequences of the finding as to domicile in the particular case before them.[15] There is evidence[16] that the courts wish to achieve a number of policy objectives: in particular, to validate wills, or to grant parental orders in cross border surrogacy cases. It is easy for courts to achieve the right result by manipulating the process for ascertaining the domicile, and this is a likely explanation of many cases which are otherwise hard to reconcile on their facts.

---

[6] *Whicker v Hume* (1858) 7 HL Cas 124, 160.

[7] Infra, p 147.

[8] *Henderson v Henderson* [1967] P 77, 79.

[9] *Munro v Munro* (1840) 7 Cl & Fin 842.

[10] Infra, p 151 et seq.

[11] *Logical and Legal Bases of the Conflict of Laws*, pp 194 et seq; Kahn-Freund (1974) III Hague Recueil 139, 404–5.

[12] Reese (1955) 55 Col LR 589; Restatement 2d, section 11(2).

[13] Eg 7th Report of the Private International Law Committee, 1963 (Cmnd 1955), para 12.

[14] S 267; see the Income Tax (Earnings and Pensions) Act 2003, s 10; Income Tax (Trading and Other Income) Act 2005, s 636.

[15] See Fawcett (1985) 5 OJLS 378.

[16] Fawcett, ibid.

2. GENERAL RULES

There are five general rules that may be briefly discussed.

It is a settled principle that nobody shall be without a domicile,[17] and in order to make this effective the law assigns what is called a domicile of origin to every person at his birth, namely, to a legitimate child the domicile of the father, to an illegitimate child the domicile of the mother,[18] and to a foundling the place where he is found.[19] This domicile of origin prevails until a new domicile has been acquired,[20] so that if a person leaves the country of his origin with an undoubted intention of never returning to it again, nevertheless his domicile of origin adheres to him until he actually settles with the requisite intention in some other country.[21]

Secondly, a person cannot have two domiciles.[22] Since the object of the law in insisting that no person shall be without a domicile is to establish a definite legal system by which certain of his rights and obligations may be governed, and since the facts and events of his life frequently impinge upon several countries, it is necessary on practical grounds to hold that he cannot possess more than one domicile at the same time, at least for the same purpose.[23]

Domicile signifies connection with what has conveniently been called a "law district",[24] ie a territory subject to a single system of law. In the case of a federation, where the legislative authority is distributed between the state and federal legislatures, this law district is generally represented by the particular state in which the *propositus* has established his home.[25] A resident in the USA for instance, is not normally domiciled in the USA as such, but in one of its states. Nevertheless, the doctrine of unity of domicile—one man, one domicile—may be modified by federal legislation. Thus the Family Law Act 1975, which has force throughout the Commonwealth of Australia, provides, inter alia, that proceedings for a decree of dissolution of marriage may be instituted if either party to the marriage is "domiciled in Australia".[26] Thus, the effect within a limited field is to create an Australian, as distinct from a state, domicile and, indeed, one that, because of statutory amendments in this limited context,[27] is different from domicile in a state for other purposes, eg succession.[28]

Thirdly, the fact that domicile signifies connection with a single system of territorial law does not necessarily connote a system that prescribes identical rules for all classes of persons. It may well be that in a unit such as India different legal rules apply to different classes of the population according to their religion, race or caste, but nonetheless it is the territorial law of

---

[17] *Mark v Mark* [2005] UKHL 42 [37], [2006] 1 AC 98.
[18] *Udny v Udny* (1869) LR 1 Sc & Div 441, 457.
[19] Westlake, s 248; Dicey, Morris and Collins, para 6R-025. See also *Re McKenzie* (1951) 51 SRNSW 293.
[20] *Munro v Munro* (1840) 7 Cl & Fin 842, 876.
[21] Infra, pp 148–61.
[22] *Mark v Mark* [2005] UKHL 42 [37], [2006] 1 AC 98. See also *IRC v Bullock* [1976] 1 WLR 1178, 1184; *Lawrence v Lawrence* [1985] Fam 106, 132.
[23] Cf supra, p 146, and see Restatement 2d, § 11(2).
[24] Dicey, Morris and Collins, para 6-016.
[25] Cf Nigeria: *Odiase v Odiase* [1965] NMLR 196.
[26] Family Law Act 1975, s 39(3)(b).
[27] Ibid, s 4(3); see Nygh (1976) 25 ICLQ 674.
[28] *Lloyd v Lloyd* [1961] 2 FLR 349; and see *Re Benko* [1968] SASR 243 (both decisions on the earlier Matrimonial Causes Act 1959); but now see the Domicile Act 1982, s 11 (adopted uniformly in Australia), and in New Zealand the Domicile Act 1976, s 10. The Canadian Divorce Act 1968 provided similarly that divorce jurisdiction could be exercised over a petitioner "domiciled in Canada": s 5(1); however, domicile is no longer used as a connecting factor in cases of divorce jurisdiction: Divorce and Corollary Relief Act 1985.

India that governs each person domiciled there, notwithstanding that Hindu law may apply to one case, Muslim to another.

Fourthly, there is a presumption in favour of the continuance of an existing domicile. Therefore the burden of proving a change lies in all cases on those who allege that a change has occurred.[29] This presumption may have a decisive effect, for if the evidence is so conflicting or indeterminate that it is impossible to elicit with certainty what the resident's intention is, the court will decide in favour of the existing domicile.[30]

The standard of proof necessary to rebut the presumption is that adopted in civil actions, which requires the intention of the *propositus* to be proved on a balance of probabilities, not beyond reasonable doubt as is the case in criminal proceedings.[31] It has been said that there is a heavy burden of proof of loss of a domicile of origin[32] and Sir Jocelyn Simon P has gone further and suggested that, when the displacement of a domicile of origin by a domicile of choice is alleged, "the standard of proof goes beyond a mere balance of probabilities".[33] This observation no doubt stems from such cases as *Winans v A-G*[34] which appear to regard the intention in favour of retaining the domicile of origin as an almost irrebuttable presumption. Scarman J, however, after observing that the language used in such cases emphasises as much the nature and quality of the intention to be proved as the standard of proof required, observed that: "Two things are clear—first that unless the judicial conscience is satisfied by evidence of change, the domicile of origin persists; and secondly, that the acquisition of a domicile of choice is a serious matter not to be lightly inferred from slight indications or casual words."[35] The Court of Appeal when endorsing this approach has actually disapproved of the use of the phrase "heavy burden".[36]

The fifth and final rule[37] is that, subject to certain statutory exceptions,[38] the domicile of a person is to be determined according to the English and not the foreign concept of domicile.[39]

3. THE ACQUISITION OF A DOMICILE OF CHOICE[40]

The two requisites for the acquisition of a fresh domicile are residence and intention. It must be proved that the person in question established his residence in a certain country with the intention of remaining there permanently. Such an intention, however unequivocal it may be, does

---

[29] *Winans v A-G* [1904] AC 287, 289; *Re Lloyd Evans* [1947] Ch 695; *Messina v Smith* [1971] P 322, 330; *Puttick v A-G* [1980] Fam 1, 17; *Spence v Spence* 1995 SLT 335; *Bheekhun v Williams* [1999] 2 FLR 229, 234, CA; *Reddington v Riach's Executor* 2002 SLT 537 [27], OH.

[30] See, eg, *Winans v A-G*, supra, Lord Halsbury's speech.

[31] *Re Fuld's Estate (No 3)* [1968] P 675, 685–6; *Re Flynn* [1968] 1 WLR 103, 115; *Re Edwards, Edwards v Edwards* (1969) 113 Sol Jo 108; *Buswell v IRC* [1974] 1 WLR 1631, 1637; but see *Lawrence v Lawrence* [1985] Fam 106, 110, 111, where the matter was left open by Lincoln J; affd by the Court of Appeal, ibid, 120, without discussion of this point.

[32] *Holden v Holden* [1968] NI 7.

[33] *Henderson v Henderson* [1967] P 77, 80; *Steadman v Steadman* [1976] AC 536, 563; *R v R (Divorce: Jurisdiction: Domicile)* [2006] 1 FLR 389 [26].

[34] [1904] AC 287, infra, pp 152–3.

[35] *Re Fuld's Estate (No 3)* [1968] P 675, 686; approved in *Cyganik v Agulian* [2006] EWCA Civ 129 [7], [2006] 1 FCR 406. See also *Re Clare (No 2)* [1984] STC 609, 614.

[36] *Brown v Brown* (1982) 3 FLR 212, 218, 220.

[37] See infra, p 168.

[38] Family Law Act 1986 s 46(5), infra, p 1006.

[39] See *Lawrence v Lawrence* [1985] Fam 106, 132; *Rowan v Rowan* [1988] ILRM 65, 67.

[40] The question of capacity to acquire a fresh domicile is discussed infra, p 168.

not per se suffice.[41] These two elements of residence and intention must concur,[42] but this is not to say that there need be unity of time in their concurrence. The intention may either precede or succeed the establishment of the residence. The emigrant forms his intention before he leaves England for Australia; the émigré who flees from persecution may not form it until years later.

(a) Residence

Residence and intention are separate but inter-related concepts. "Residence in a country for the purposes of the law of domicile is physical presence in that country as an inhabitant of it."[43] In one case[44] a taxpayer who spent ten to twelve weeks each year in Quebec for the purpose of maintaining her links with that Province with a view ultimately to returning to live was held not to be a resident of Quebec during her presence there since she was not there as an inhabitant. A Russian multi-millionaire who owned twenty houses round the world and used his two houses in England as mere stop-overs whilst on business trips was not resident in England.[45] Normally though, the requirement of residence is easy to establish. Residence is regarded as being a question of fact and one can be resident in a place where one has no right to be.[46]

Residence and intention are inter-related in that, strictly speaking, residence is a fact, though a necessary one, from which intention may be inferred.[47] Older cases adopted a presumption in favour of domicile which grew in strength with the length of the residence and was hard to rebut.[48] However, more recent cases,[49] including House of Lords authorities,[50] have attached less weight to the length of residence, and have taken the view that, although a material consideration, it is rarely decisive. In *Re G*, a surrogacy case, an English domicile was found where the parties had been residing in England for one year.[51] It has been suggested that domicile could be acquired in a few days or even upon arrival in a country.[52]

Whatever weight is given to the length of residence it is undeniable that time is not the sole criterion of domicile.[53] Long residence does not constitute, nor does brief residence negative, domicile. Everything depends on the attendant circumstances, for they alone disclose the nature of the person's presence in a country. In short, the residence must answer "a qualitative as well as a quantitative test".[54] Thus in *Jopp v Wood*[55] it was held that a residence of twenty-five years in India did not suffice to give a certain John Smith an Indian domicile because of

---

[41] *Harrison v Harrison* [1953] 1 WLR 865.

[42] *Mark v Mark* [2005] UKHL 42 [39], [2006] 1 AC 98.

[43] *IRC v Duchess of Portland* [1982] Ch 314, 318–9. See, eg, *Re S (Hospital Patient: Foreign Curator)* [1996] Fam 23, 31.

[44] *IRC v Duchess of Portland*, supra.

[45] *High Tech International AG v Deripaska* [2006] EWHC 3276 (QB)—a case on domicile for the purposes of the Civil Jurisdiction and Judgments Order 2001, discussed infra, p 199. See also *Cherney v Deripaska* [2007] EWHC 965 (Comm), [2007] IL Pr 49.

[46] *Mark v Mark* [2005] UKHL 42 [47] (Baroness Hale), [13] (Lord Hope), [2006] 1 AC 98.

[47] *Munro v Munro* (1840) 7 Cl & Fin 842, 877.

[48] *Stanley v Bernes* (1830) 3 Hag Ecc 373; *Re Marret, Chalmers v Wingfield* (1887) 36 Ch D 400; *Hodgson v De Beauchesne* (1858) 12 Moo PCC 285 at 329; *Udny v Udny* (1869) LR 1 Sc & Div 441, 455; *Re Liddell-Grainger's Will Trusts, Dormer v Liddell-Grainger* [1936] 3 All ER 173.

[49] Eg *Puttick v A-G* [1980] Fam 1, 17.

[50] *Winans v A-G* [1904] AC 287, 297–298; *Bowie (or Ramsay) v Liverpool Royal Infirmary* [1930] AC 588; both cases are discussed, infra, pp 152–4.

[51] *Re G (Parental Orders)* [2014] EWHC 1561 (Fam).

[52] Ibid [43]; *Z and another v C and another* [2011] EWHC 3181 (Fam) [29]–[31].

[53] Ibid; *Hodgson v De Beauchesne* (1858) 12 Moo PCC 285, 329, 330.

[54] *Bowie (or Ramsay) v Liverpool Royal Infirmary* [1930] AC 588, 598. See *R v R (Divorce: Jurisdiction: Domicile)* [2006] 1 FLR 389 [24], [26].

[55] (1865) 4 De GJ & Sm 616. See also *A-G v Yule* (1931) 145 LT 9.

his alleged intention ultimately to return to Scotland, the land of his birth. Again, in *IRC v Bullock*[56] a Canadian who had a domicile of origin in Nova Scotia was held not to have become domiciled in England, despite the fact that he had either served in the RAF or lived in England for over forty years. He retained his domicile in Nova Scotia because he intended to return there should his wife predecease him.

Conversely, brevity of residence is no obstacle to the acquisition of a domicile if the necessary intention exists. If a man clearly intends to live in another country permanently, as, for example, where an emigrant, having wound up his affairs in the country of his origin, flies off with his wife and family to Australia, his mere arrival there will satisfy the element of residence.[57] A striking example of this truth occurred in the United States.[58]

> A man abandoned his home in State X and took his family to a house in State Y, about half a mile from X, intending to live there permanently. Having deposited his belongings there, he and his family returned to X, in order to spend the night with a relative. He fell ill and died there. It was held that his domicile at death was in Y.

In *Re G* an English domicile was found after one year because it was clear that the parties intended to live in England permanently. They had sold their family home in France to purchase a property in England, both applicants were employed in England and paid both tax and national insurance there, and they asserted that they did not want to return to France as they did not like how they were treated there due to their sexual orientation.[59] It is possible for a person to be resident in several countries at the same time. In such a case of dual or multiple residence a domicile of choice can only be acquired in a country if this can be shown to be the chief residence.[60] This was established in *Plummer v IRC*.[61] The taxpayer had an English domicile of origin. She spent the majority of each year in England, where she was being educated. However, she spent more than three months of each year in Guernsey, which had become her family home. Hoffmann J held that, despite the taxpayer's retention of residence in England, her domicile of origin, she could acquire a domicile of choice in Guernsey if she could show that this was her chief residence. This she was unable to do. She had not yet settled in Guernsey. Accordingly she retained her English domicile. The case could, though, have been decided on the much simpler ground that she lacked the requisite intention for acquisition of a Guernsey domicile of choice.[62]

Problems in relation to residence would disappear if this concept were to be replaced by the simpler concept of presence.[63]

---

[56] [1976] 1 WLR 1178.

[57] *Hodgson v de Beauchesne* (1858) 12 Moo PCC 285, 330; *Bell v Kennedy* (1868) LR 1 Sc & Div 307, 319; *PL v An tArd Chlaraitheoir* [1995] 2 ILRM 241; *In the Marriage of Ferrier-Watson & McElrath* [2000] FamCA 219 [78]–[80]; *Blackett v Darcy* [2005] NSWSC [13].

[58] *White v Tennant* 31 W Va 790, 8 SE 596 (1888).

[59] *Re G (Parental Orders)* [2014] EWHC 1561 (Fam).

[60] See *Barlow Clowes International Ltd v Henwood* [2008] EWCA Civ 577. For the meaning of main residence for the purpose of liability to council tax, see *Regina (Williams) v Horsham District Council* [2004] EWCA Civ 39, [2004] 1 WLR 1137.

[61] [1988] 1 WLR 292; Kunzlik [1988] CLJ 187; Carter [1988] 59 BYBIL 350; Smart (1990) 10 OJLS 572. However, dual residence can lead to a dual domicile for the purposes of the Civil Jurisdiction and Judgments Order 2001; cf *Daniel v Foster* 1989 SLT 90.

[62] But see Fentiman [1991] CLJ 445.

[63] This was one of the proposals of the Law Commissions, set out in Law Com No 168 (1987), Scot Law Com No 107 (1987), para 5.7. However, these proposals have been rejected, Law Com No 239 (1995) p 10, n 24. For Australia see *In the Marriage of Ferrier-Watson & McElrath* [2000] Fam, CA 219 [80].

(b) The requisite intention

(i) *The nature of the intention*

(a) An intention to reside permanently

As has already been mentioned,[64] the acquisition of a domicile of choice requires an intention by the *propositus* to remain permanently in the territory in which he resides. This is not difficult to understand if the word permanent is used in its correct sense as signifying the opposite of "temporary". According to the *Shorter Oxford English Dictionary* it means "lasting or designed to last indefinitely without change", and this indeed is the definition that most of the judges have recognised when required to consider the nature of the intention necessary for a change of domicile. In *Udny v Udny*,[65] for instance, Lord Westbury described the intention as being one to reside "for an unlimited time". A more modern statement to the same effect is that of Baroness Hale who referred to an intention to reside "permanently or indefinitely".[66]

The essence, therefore, of these and many other similar statements is that the intended residence must not be for a limited period, whether the limitation is expressed in terms of time or made dependent on the occurrence of a contingency, such as the accomplishment of a definite task, that will occur if at all during the life of the *propositus*.

It is also clear that a conditional intention will not suffice. Thus in *Cramer v Cramer*[67] a woman with a French domicile of origin who came to England intending to remain here and marry an Englishman, who was already married, did not acquire an English domicile of choice. Her intention to remain was conditional on both herself and her proposed husband obtaining divorces and on their relationship continuing. It would, no doubt, have been different if she had intended to remain here come what may, but this was not her intention.

(b) Unlikely contingencies

In cases where the termination of residence is dependent on the occurrence of a contingency this will not prevent the acquisition of a domicile unless the contingency is itself unambiguous and realistic. In the words of Scarman J:

> If a man intends to return to the land of his birth upon a clearly foreseen and reasonably anticipated contingency, eg the end of his job, the intention required by law is lacking; but, if he has in mind only a vague possibility, such as making a fortune (a modern example might be winning a football pool) . . . such a state of mind is consistent with the intention required by law.[68]

Subsequently, a distinction has been drawn between the question whether a contingency itself is clear and the question whether a contingency which is clear will happen.[69]

---

[64] Supra, p 148.

[65] (1869) LR 1 Sc & Div 441 at 458; followed in *Re Fuld's Estate (No 3)* [1968] P 675; *Bheekhun v Williams* [1999] 2 FLR 229, 232-233, CA; *Spence v Spence* 1995 SLT 335.

[66] *Mark v Mark* [2005] UKHL 42 [39], [2006] 1 AC 98; *Cyganik v Agulian* [2006] EWCA Civ 129 [45] (Mummery LJ), [2006] 1 FCR 406; *Barlow Clowes International Ltd v Henwood* [2008] EWCA Civ 577 [140], [147]; *Kebbeh v Farmer and others* [2015] EWHC 3827 (Ch) [20]. For use of "indefinitely" see also *Re Fuld's Estate (No 3)* [1968] P 675, 684; and see *Re Edwards, Edwards v Edwards* (1969) 113 Sol Jo 108; *Cramer v Cramer* [1987] 1 FLR 116; *In re S (Hospital Patient: Foreign Curator)* [1996] Fam 23, 31; *Holliday v Musa* [2010] EWCA Civ 335 [3]. For Australia see Domicile Acts 1982, s 10. For New Zealand see Domicile Act 1976, s 9.

[67] [1987] 1 FLR 116.

[68] *Re Fuld's Estate (No 3)* [1968] P 675, 684–5. See also *Henderson v Henderson* [1967] P 77, 80–1; *Buswell v IRC* [1974] 1 WLR 1631, 1637; *IRC v Bullock* [1976] 1 WLR 1178, 1186; *Re Furse* [1980] 3 All ER 838; *Cyganik v Agulian* [2006] EWCA Civ 129[6], [2006] 1 FCR 406; *Gould v Gould* 1968 SLT 98.

[69] *IRC v Bullock* [1976] 1 WLR 1178, 1186.

If a contingency is not sufficiently clear to be identified then it cannot operate to prevent the acquisition of a domicile of choice. Thus in *Re Furse*[70] evidence that the *propositus*, who had a Rhode Island domicile of origin, would leave England, where he had lived for nearly forty years, if he was no longer able to live an active physical life on his farm was not fatal to a change of domicile, and it was held that the *propositus* had acquired an English domicile of choice. Similarly the vague possibility that in some undefined circumstances a person might decide to move to another country does not weigh against him.[71]

On the other hand, if the contingency can be identified, it has to be asked whether there is a substantial possibility of the contingency happening; if there is, this will prevent the acquisition of a domicile of choice. Thus in *IRC v Bullock*,[72] where a husband intended to return to Canada to live permanently if his wife predeceased him, it was held that the husband did not acquire an English domicile of choice, since there was a real possibility, in view of their ages, of this happening. In contrast, in *Holliday v Musa* the deceased had stated that he would return to Cyprus on his retirement, therefore he considered he had not lost his domicile of origin in Cyprus. However when he died aged seventy-four, still resident in England, the Court of Appeal considered that if he had not retired to Cyprus by the age of seventy-four, then it was unlikely that this was ever going to happen had he remained alive.[73] If there is no substantial possibility of a contingency happening, the evidence evincing a desire to leave the residence will not prevent the acquisition of a domicile of choice.[74]

(c) The former attitude towards contingencies: *Winans v A-G,*
Ramsay v Liverpool Royal Infirmary

That a contingency must be something more than a vague possibility if it is to prevent the acquisition of a domicile in the country of residence has not been invariably accepted by the courts. It has several times been affirmed, and more than once by the House of Lords, that the present residence of a man is not to be equated with domicile if he contemplates some remote or uncertain event, whose occurrence at some indeterminate time in the future might cause him to leave his country of residence. If this possibility is present to his mind, even an intention to reside indefinitely in the country is said to be ineffective.[75] This view appears to equate the word "permanent" with "perpetual", and to require for a change of domicile an irrevocable intention never to abandon the present place of domicile. Yet it is no part of the law that the intention to maintain the residence should be irrevocable,[76] for such a requirement would virtually exclude the acquisition of a domicile of choice.[77] Nevertheless, in *Winans v A-G*[78]

---

[70] [1980] 3 All ER 838. See also *Doucet v Geoghegan* (1878) 9 Ch D 441; *Lawrence v Lawrence* [1985] Fam 106, 110–11; affd by the Court of Appeal without discussion on this point. Distinguished in *Proes v Revenue Commissioners* [1998] 4 IR 176, where the contingency of "if no longer able to look after herself" was held to be clear.

[71] *North v Skipton Building Society* 2002 WL 1039545 at [21].

[72] [1976] 1 WLR 1178; Carter (1976–77) 48 BYBIL 362; *Cramer v Cramer* [1987] 1 FLR 116. See also *Qureshi v Qureshi* [1972] Fam 173.

[73] *Holliday v Musa* [2010] EWCA Civ 335 [67]. There were also other factors which indicated that the deceased had acquired a domicile of choice in England.

[74] *Pletinka v Pletinka* (1964) 109 Sol Jo 72; see also *Osvath-Latkoczy v Osvath-Latkoczy* (1959) 19 DLR (2d) 495.

[75] *Moorhouse v Lord* (1863) 10 HL Cas 272, 285–6; *Jopp v Wood* (1865) 4 De GJ & Sm 616; *Goulder v Goulder* [1892] P 240; *Winans v A-G* [1904] AC 287; *Bowie (or Ramsay) v Liverpool Royal Infirmary* [1930] AC 588; *A-G v Yule* (1931) 145 LT 9; *Wahl v A-G* (1932) 147 LT 382. The rigorous theory adopted in these decisions has been rejected in South Africa: *Eilon v Eilon* 1965 (1) SA 703, 708–9.

[76] *Gulbenkian v Gulbenkian* [1937] 4 All ER 618, 627; *IRC v Bullock* [1976] 1 WLR 1178, 1184; *Lawrence v Lawrence* [1985] Fam 106, 110–11; affd by the Court of Appeal, without discussion of this point.

[77] See *A-G v Pottinger* (1861) 30 LJ Ex 284, 292.

[78] [1904] AC 287.

and in *Bowie (or Ramsay) v Liverpool Royal Infirmary*,[79] the House of Lords came very near to regarding a vague possibility as if it were, to cite the words of Scarman J again, "a clearly foreseen and reasonably anticipated contingency".[80] The facts of the former case were these:

> Winans was born in 1823 in the USA, where he was continuously engaged in his father's business until 1850. From 1850 to 1859 he resided in Russia. He married a British subject and appears never to have set foot again in the USA. In 1859 he showed signs of consumption, and, being advised by the doctors to winter in Brighton in England, he reluctantly took rooms at a hotel there, and in 1860 leased two adjoining houses. He still held these houses at the time of his death. From 1860 to 1893 he spent time each year in England but also time in Scotland, Germany or Russia. From 1893 until he died in 1897 he lived entirely in England. The Crown claimed legacy duty on a comparatively small amount of property abroad. Such duty was payable only if he had acquired an English domicile at the time of his death.

The fact that he had resided principally in England for the last thirty-seven years of his life raised a very strong presumption in favour of an English domicile, but there was no direct evidence as to what his intention was. Lord Macnaghten analysed with some particularity the hopes, projects and daily habits of Mr Winans. He found that, in addition to the care of his health, Mr Winans had two objects in life. The first was the construction in Baltimore of a large fleet of spindle-shaped vessels, which would give the USA superiority at sea over Britain. The second object was to develop a large property of about 200 acres in Baltimore. On this, wharves and docks were to be constructed for the spindle-shaped vessels, and a large house built in which Mr Winans intended to live in order that he might take personal command of the whole undertaking. He succeeded in getting control of the property only at the very end of his life, and at the time of his death he was working day and night on the scheme.

Lord Macnaghten reached the conclusion that the domicile of origin in New Jersey had not been lost. He said that "up to the very last he had an expectation or hope of returning to America and seeing his grand scheme inaugurated".[81] Lord Halsbury found it impossible to infer from the evidence what Mr Winans' intention was, and he held therefore that the Crown had not discharged its duty of proving a change of domicile. Lord Lindley vigorously dissented. In his view Winans had given up all serious idea of returning to America.[82]

Bowie (or Ramsay) v Liverpool Royal Infirmary[83] concerned one George Bowie, who had left a will that was formally valid if his domicile at death was Scottish but invalid if it was English. The story of his life was uneventful.

> He was born in Glasgow in 1845 with a Scottish domicile of origin. He gave up his employment as a commercial traveller at the age of thirty-seven and refused to do any more work during the remaining forty-five years of his life. But even the idle must be fed, and after residing with his mother and sisters in Glasgow, he moved his residence to Liverpool in 1892 in order to live on the bounty of his brother. At first he lived in lodgings, but moved to his brother's house when the latter died twenty-one years later, and resided there with his sole surviving sister until she died in 1920. He remained there until his own death in 1927.

Thus George lived in England for the last thirty-six years of his life. During that time he left the country only twice, once on a short visit to the USA, on the second occasion to take a holiday in the Isle of Man. Though he often said he was proud to be a Glasgow man, he

---

[79] [1930] AC 588.

[80] Supra, p 151.

[81] [1904] AC 287, 298.

[82] [1904] AC 287, 300. The decision against the acquisition of an English domicile was virtually that of Lord Macnaghten alone. In the courts below, Kennedy J, Phillimore J (83 LT 634), Collins MR, Stirling LJ and Mathew LJ (85 LT 508), reached the opposite conclusion without any hesitation.

[83] [1930] AC 588.

resolutely refused on several occasions to return to Scotland, even for the purpose of attending his mother's funeral. On the contrary, he had expressed his determination never to set foot in Glasgow again and had arranged his own burial in Liverpool.

Thus evidence was completely lacking of any inclination, either by words or actions, to disturb a long and practically uninterrupted residence in England. Nevertheless the House of Lords held unanimously that George died domiciled in Scotland. Their Lordships denied that his prolonged residence disclosed an intention to choose England as his permanent home. Rather, they inferred that had his English source of supply failed he would have retreated to Glasgow.

(d) Evaluation of judicial statements and decisions

It would, however, be a mistake to exaggerate the importance of judicial pronouncements or decisions which on the surface appear to distort the character of the intention that is necessary for the acquisition of a domicile. Scarman J has stressed that the difficulty of reconciling the numerous statements arises not from lack of clarity of judicial thought, but from the nature of the subject. The cases involve a detailed examination of the facts and it is not surprising that different judicial minds concerned with different factual situations have chosen different language to describe the law.[84] Scarman J would regard the difference between the statements of judges in earlier cases as showing a difference of emphasis and therefore as being of no great moment.[85]

It may well be, then, that to construct a formula which describes the precise intention required by English law for the acquisition of a domicile of choice is an impossibility, but perhaps the most satisfactory definition was that offered nearly a hundred and fifty years ago by Kindersley V-C:

> That place is properly the domicile of a person in which he has voluntarily fixed the habitation of himself and his family, not for a mere special and temporary purpose, but with a present intention of making it his permanent home, unless and until something (which is unexpected or the happening of which is uncertain) shall occur to induce him to adopt some other permanent home.[86]

(e) Time at which intention is relevant

The traditional statement that there must be a *present* intention of permanent residence merely means that so far as the mind of the person at the relevant time was concerned he possessed the requisite intention. The relevant time varies with the nature of the inquiry. It may be past or present. If, for example, the inquiry relates to the domicile of a deceased person, it must be ascertained whether at some period in his life he had formed and retained a fixed and settled intention of residence in a given country. Once this is established, evidence of his subsequent fluctuations of opinion as to whether he would or would not move elsewhere will be ignored.[87] If, on the other hand, the essential validity of a proposed marriage depends on the law of X's domicile and if the identity of this law is in doubt, what must be examined is his immediate intention.

(f) A bona fide intention

The intention must be bona fide "in the sense of being genuine and not pretended for some other purpose, such as getting a divorce to which one would not be entitled by the law of the true domicile".[88]

---

[84] *Re Fuld's Estate (No 3)* [1968] P 675, 682–3.
[85] Ibid, 684.
[86] *Lord v Colvin* (1859) 4 Drew 366, 376.
[87] *Re Marrett, Chalmers v Wingfield* (1887) 36 Ch D 400.
[88] *Mark v Mark* [2005] UKHL 42[47], [2006] 1 AC 98.

(ii) Evidence of intention

The question whether a person has formed the requisite intention is one of fact.[89] It is impossible to lay down any positive rule with respect to the evidence necessary to prove intention. All that can be said is that every conceivable event and incident in a man's life is a relevant and an admissible indication of his state of mind. Everything said and done during the whole of a person's life should be considered, taking account of things said and done after as well as before the time when it is alleged that the chosen domicile has been acquired.[90] It may be necessary to examine the history of his life with the most scrupulous care, and to resort even to hearsay evidence where the question concerns the domicile that a person, now deceased, possessed in his lifetime.[91] Nothing must be overlooked that might possibly show the place which he regarded as his permanent home at the relevant time.[92] No fact is too trifling to merit consideration.[93] Indeed, one of the defects of English law is that the evidence adduced in a disputed case of domicile is often both voluminous and difficult to assess. This is due to the over-scrupulous manner in which the courts attempt to discover a man's exact intention. The tendency is to investigate his actual state of mind, rather than to rest content with the natural inference of his long-continued residence in a given country. This, indeed, is to set sail on an uncharted sea. Nothing must be neglected that can possibly indicate the bent of the resident's mind. His aspirations, whims, *amours*, prejudices, health, religion, financial expectations—all are taken into account.[94]

Having regard, therefore, to the roving commission imposed on the courts, it is not surprising that their decisions exhibit a multiplicity of different factors that have been regarded as *indicia* of intention. Without attempting to give an exhaustive list, it may be useful to observe that at one time or another the following have been regarded as relevant criteria of intention: naturalisation,[95] retention of citizenship,[96] obtaining a passport,[97] purchase[98] or building of a house,[99] where income is earned,[100] purchase of a burial ground,[101] directions in a will as to burial in a particular country,[102] a long period of residence in a country,[103] the exercise of political rights,[104] such as voting,[105] not learning the language of the country in

---

[89] Ibid.

[90] *Bheekhun v Williams* [1999] 2 FLR 229, 237, CA.

[91] *Scappaticci v A-G* [1955] P 47.

[92] See, eg, the voluminous evidence considered by Chitty J in *Re Craignish* [1892] 3 Ch 180.

[93] *Drevon v Drevon* (1864) 34 LJ Ch 129, 133; and see *Re Flynn, Flynn v Flynn* [1968] 1 WLR 103, 107; *Morgan v Cilento* [2004] EWHC 188 (Ch), [2004] All ER (D) 122.

[94] *Casdagli v Casdagli* [1919] AC 145, 178.

[95] *D'Etchegoyen v D'Etchegoyen* (1888) 13 PD 132; *Qureshi v Qureshi* [1972] Fam 173, 190–1.

[96] *IRC v Bullock* [1976] 1 WLR 1178; *Bheekhun v Williams* [1999] 2 FLR 229, 235, CA; *R v R (Divorce: J urisdiction: Domicile)* [2006] 1 FLR 389 [26]; *Dellar v Zivy* [2007] EWHC 2266 (Ch) [35], [2007] IL Pr 60.

[97] *Bheekhun v Williams*, supra.

[98] *D'Etchegoyen v D'Etchegoyen* (1888) 13 PD 132; *Moorhouse v Lord* (1863) 10 HL Cas 272; for the history of this case see Thompson and Mackie [1979] Jur Rev 138; *Stevenson v Masson* (1873) LR 17 Eq 78; *Re Craignish* [1892] 3 Ch 180. See also *Henwood v Barlow Clowes International Ltd (in Liquidation)* [2007] EWHC 1579 (Ch), renting for thirteen years.

[99] *Morgan v Cilento* [2004] EWHC 188 (Ch), [2004] All ER (D) 122.

[100] *R v R (Divorce: Jurisdiction: Domicile)* [2006] 1 FLR 389 [24]; *Dellar v Zivy* [2007] EWHC 2266 (Ch) [35], [2007] IL Pr 60.

[101] *Stevenson v Masson*, supra; *Haldane v Eckford* (1869) LR 8 Eq 631.

[102] *Reddington v Riach's Executor* 2002 SLT 537 [29], OH.

[103] *Bheekhun v Williams* [1999] 2 FLR 229, 237, CA; *Reddington v Riach's Executor* 2002 SLT 537 [29], OH; *R (On the Application of Haqq) v Knapman* [2003] EWHC 3366 [51] (Admin); *Henwood v Barlow Clowes International Ltd (in Liquidation)* [2007] EWHC 1579 (Ch). See also *In the Marriage of Ferrier-Watson & McElrath* [2000] Fam, CA 219 [83].

[104] *Drevon v Drevon* (1864) 34 LJ Ch 129, 137.

[105] *Morgan v Cilento* [2004] EWHC 188 (Ch), [2004] All ER (D) 122; *R v R (Divorce: Jurisdiction: Domicile)* [2006] 1 FLR 389 [24].

which you are living,[106] not acquiring a bank account or credit cards in that country,[107] the establishment of children in business,[108] the statutory declaration made by a candidate for naturalisation that he intends to reside permanently in the United Kingdom,[109] the place where a man's wife and family reside,[110] statements by an elderly person that the move would be his last,[111] departure from a country owing to compulsion of war,[112] the refusal of a foreign *fiancée* to leave her own country,[113] statements as to his domiciliary intentions made by a deceased person in his lifetime,[114] a statement by the *propositus* that the marriage should be dissolved in England because this was where he and his wife resided,[115] the effect of racial intolerance on domiciliary intention,[116] the effect of treatment on the basis of sexual orientation on domiciliary intention,[117] the fact that a family is split between England and abroad,[118] choosing on separation to come to a country rather than returning to one's homeland,[119] and remaining in a country after a spouse has died.[120]

Undue stress must not be laid on any single fact however impressive it may appear when viewed out of its context, for its importance as a determining factor may well be minimised when considered in the light of other qualifying events. Again, no one fact is of constant value, for every case varies in its circumstances, and what is of decisive importance in one may be of little weight in another.[121]

It is for this reason that it is impossible to formulate a rule specifying the weight to be given to particular evidence. All that can be gathered from the authorities in this respect is that more reliance is placed on conduct rather than declarations of intention, especially if they are oral.[122] This kind of evidence, however, especially when given long after the conversation occurred, is suspect, for witnesses may lie or forget.[123] Little weight should be given to this kind of evidence.[124] Declarations should contain "a real expression of intention",[125] for it only too frequently happens that they cannot be taken at their face value. They may be interested statements designed to flatter or to deceive the hearer; they may represent nothing more than vain expectations unlikely to be fulfilled; and the very facility with which they can

---

[106] *Irvin v Irvin* [2001] 1 FLR 178, 194; cf *Curati v Perdoni* [2012] EWCA Civ 1381.

[107] *R v R (Divorce: Jurisdiction: Domicile)* [2006] 1 FLR 389 [24].

[108] *Stevenson v Masson* (1873) LR 17 Eq 78.

[109] *Gulbenkian v Gulbenkian* [1937] 4 All ER 618; distinguish *Wahl v A-G* (1932) 147 LT 382 and see *Steiner v IRC* (1973) 49 TC 13.

[110] *Forbes v Forbes* (1854) Kay 341; *Aitchison v Dixon* (1870) LR 10 Eq 589; cf *IRC v Bullock* [1976] 1 WLR 1178, 1185; *Cyganik v Agulian* [2006] EWCA Civ 129 [46], [2006] 1 FCR 406.

[111] *Reddington v Riach's Executor* 2002 SLT 537 [29], OH.

[112] *Re Lloyd Evans* [1947] Ch 695.

[113] *Donaldson v Donaldson* [1949] P 363.

[114] *Scappaticci v A-G* [1955] P 47.

[115] *Bheekhun v Williams* [1999] 2 FLR 229, 238, CA.

[116] *Qureshi v Qureshi* [1972] Fam 173, 193.

[117] *Z and another v C and another* [2011] EWHC 1381 (Fam) [7]; *Re A and B (Parental Order: Domicile)* [2013] EWHC 426 (Fam) [10], [26]; *Re G (Parental Orders)* [2014] EWHC 1561 (Fam).

[118] *Begum v Entry Clearance Officer, Dacca* [1983] Imm AR 163.

[119] *Marsh v Marsh* 2002 SLT 87, Sh Principal.

[120] *Reddington v Riach's Executor* 2002 SLT 537 [29], OH.

[121] *Hodgson v De Beauchesne* (1858) 12 Moo PCC 285, 330; *Doucet v Geoghegan* (1878) 9 Ch D 441, 445; *Wahl v A-G* (1932) 147 LT 382.

[122] *McMullen v Wadsworth* (1889) 14 App Cas 631, 636, PC.

[123] *Hodgson v De Beauchesne* (1858) 12 Moo PCC 285; *Re Liddell-Grainger's Will Trusts* [1936] 3 All ER 173; *Re Fuld's Estate (No 3)* [1968] P 675, 691–2.

[124] *Cyganik v Agulian* [2006] EWCA Civ 129 [13], [2006] 1 FCR 406.

[125] *Hodgson v De Beauchesne, supra*, 325.

be made requires their sincerity to be manifested by some active step taken in furtherance of the expressed intention. The circumstances in which the statement is made need to be considered, and any declaration must be backed up by conduct consistent with the declared intention.[126]

Even lower in the scale of values is evidence given in the course of the trial by the person himself not of his past declarations, but of his past intention. This must be accepted with very considerable reserve, for on such a personal issue as his own place of domicile he is under a bias that is likely to influence his mind, perhaps even his veracity.[127] It is different, and some significance will be attached to the evidence, in the situation where the person whose domicile is in issue has nothing to be gained from the outcome of the present proceedings and his actions are consistent with this evidence.[128]

In at least two respects, motive, in the sense of the antecedent desire that determines the will to act, is one of the *indicia* of the intention requisite for the acquisition of a domicile of choice. First, it may throw light on the question whether the removal to another country was intended to be permanent. It will serve, for instance, to contrast the case of a man who flees to England to escape political persecution in his own country with that of a retired officer who goes to Jersey to avoid heavy taxation. Secondly, it may provide means of testing the sincerity of a declaration of intention. Thus, if a widower testifies that at the time of his wife's death he and she regarded Scotland as their permanent home, the fact that by Scots law he is entitled to one-half of his wife's property may make his testimony a little suspect.[129] Both of these points arose in *Spence v Spence*,[130] where the dominant reason for a couple's departure from Spain had been to avoid tax liability. It was held that the husband had not acquired a domicile of choice in Spain, where he had lived for nine years. The court was wary of his statement of an intention to remain in Spain in the future. It was also relevant that he had not registered as a Spanish resident, paid no taxes there, and his business ventures had links with a number of other countries.

It is important to realise that the only intention relevant to a change of domicile is an intention to settle permanently in a country. This will effect a change of domicile even if the *propositus* intended to retain his former personal law.[131] One of the legal consequences of an intention to settle in country X is that the person in question becomes subject to the law of X whether this is his wish or not. It is the inevitable effect of his residence in that country coupled with his intention to remain there without any limit of time.[132]

---

[126] *Ross v Ross* [1930] AC 1, 6; and see *Qureshi v Qureshi* [1972] Fam 173, 192–3; *Spence v Spence* 1995 SLT 335, 340; *Marsh v Marsh* 2002 SLT 87; *Reddington v Riach's Executor* 2002 SLT 537 [29], OH. In several cases even written declarations have been disregarded: *Re Martin* [1900] P 211—declaration in mortgage deed; *Re Liddell-Grainger's Will Trusts* [1936] 3 All ER 173—declaration in a will; *Wahl v A-G* (1932) 147 LT 382—declaration in naturalisation papers; *Buswell v IRC* [1974] 1 WLR 1631—declaration on an Inland Revenue form.

[127] *Bell v Kennedy* (1868) LR 1 Sc & Div 307, 313; *Re Craignish* [1892] 3 Ch 180, 190; *Chaudhary v Chaudhary* [1985] Fam 19, 26, affd by CA, ibid 33; *Spence v Spence* 1995 SLT 335, 340; *Barlow Clowes International Ltd v Henwood* [2008] EWCA Civ 577 [81]–[82]; *Ray v Sekhri* [2014] EWCA Civ 119 [65].

[128] *PL v An tArd Chlaraitheoir* [1995] 2 ILRM 241. See also *Brown v Brown* (1982) 3 FLR 212, 214–15 where the declaration was consistent with conduct.

[129] Cf *Re Craignish* [1892] 3 Ch 180.

[130] 1995 SLT 335.

[131] *Douglas v Douglas* (1871) LR 12 Eq 617 at 644, 645; *Re Steer* (1858) 3 H & N 594. To the same effect, *Re Liddell-Grainger's Will Trusts* [1936] 3 All ER 173.

[132] *Re Craignish* [1892] 3 Ch 180, 188–9.

(c) Voluntary residence

It is a commonplace that to constitute domicile a residence must be voluntary—a matter of free choice,[133] not of constraint. In several cases, the circumstances may raise a doubt as to whether such freedom exists.

(i) Prisoners

A clear example of constraint preclusive of this freedom is imprisonment in a foreign country, and there is no doubt that a prisoner, except perhaps one transported or exiled for life, retains the domicile that he possessed before his confinement.[134]

(ii) Refugees/persons seeking asylum

It cannot be predicated that refugees necessarily retain their former domicile. The motive that induced the flight no doubt militates against the inference that there was an intention of permanent residence in the chosen asylum. There is a presumption against a change of domicile, but "what is dictated by necessity in the first instance may afterwards become a matter of choice",[135] and the presumption may well be reversed by subsequent circumstances, as, for example, by the continued retention of the residence after a return to the original country has become safe and practicable.[136]

(iii) Fugitives from justice

Another example of involuntary residence in a new country is that of the fugitive from justice. Nevertheless, if a man leaves his domicile in order to escape the consequences of crime, the natural inference is that he has left for ever and that a presumption arises in favour of the acquisition of a fresh domicile in the country of refuge. His departure, has indeed, been forced upon him, yet this does not necessarily mean that he intends it to be temporary. For example, in *Moynihan v Moynihan (Nos 1 and 2)*[137] it was held that the *propositus*, who had left the United Kingdom to avoid arrest on serious fraud charges, had, at his death, acquired a domicile of choice in the Philippines, where he had lived for twenty years, built up a thriving business, acquired properties, married and had children. In *Re Martin, Loustalan v Loustalan*,[138] however, Lindley LJ suggested that the "all-important" factor is whether there is a definite period after which a wrongdoer may return home in safety. In other words, if the crime ceases to be punishable or the sentence to be enforceable after a given number of years, residence in another country, unless fortified by other facts, does not effect a change of domicile; but if the fugitive remains perpetually liable to proceedings, then the new place of residence becomes the new domicile.[139] This view was not adopted by the other members of the court, Rigby LJ remarking that to suggest that the fugitive in question intended at the time of his escape from France to return as soon as he could safely do so (twenty years in the particular case) was "so irrational that, in default of the strongest evidence, it ought not to be imputed to him".[140] It is, indeed, difficult to agree with Lindley LJ, except possibly where

---

[133] It may perhaps be more accurate to say that in all cases physical presence in a country satisfies the requirement of residence, and that constraint is relevant only to the question of intention; see McClean (1962) 11 ICLQ 1156–60.

[134] *Burton v Fisher* (1828) Milw 183; *Burton v Dolben* (1756) 2 Lee 312, 318; *Re the late Emperor Napoleon Bonaparte* (1853) 2 Rob Eccl 606.

[135] *Winans v A-G* (1901) 85 LT 508, 510.

[136] *De Bonneval v De Bonneval* (1838) 1 Curt 856; *May v May* [1943] 2 All ER 146; cf *Re Evans* [1947] Ch 695.

[137] [1997] 1 FLR 59.

[138] [1900] P 211.

[139] Ibid, 232.

[140] Ibid, 235.

the offence is trifling and the term of prescription short. The judgment of Lindley LJ was not referred to in the judgment of Sir Stephen Brown P in *Moynihan v Moynihan (Nos 1 and 2)*.

Re Martin was concerned with the possibility of a fugitive from justice being free to return to his domicile abroad; more recently, the entirely different problem has arisen of the possibility of a fugitive being forced to return to face justice abroad under an extradition treaty. If the fugitive never set up a home and has no affection for England, merely seeing it as a place of refuge, and is ready to move on if detection and arrest is imminent, a domicile of choice will not be acquired.[141]

(iv) Fugitive debtors

Freedom of choice is also affected when a man finds it desirable to flee the country to avoid his creditors.[142] Whether this raises a presumption against an intention to return to his own country must obviously depend on a variety of circumstances, such as the amount of the debts, the possibility of meeting them, the imminence of legal proceedings, the activities of the debtor in his new residence and so on. It certainly cannot be said that the adoption of the new residence per se effects a change of domicile,[143] particularly where the debtor does not acquire a new chief or principal residence.[144]

(v) Invalids

The case of an invalid who settles in a foreign country for the sake of his health, not merely for the purpose of convalescence, should on principle cause no difficulty. The principle is that unless a man is a free agent his adoption of a new residence does not effect a change of domicile. He must have an alternative—either to stay or to go. But it would seem that an alternative is open to every invalid. To take even the extreme case, if a man, being assured by his doctors that he has only a few months to live, decides to spend the short remainder of his life in a country where the climate may alleviate his suffering, it would seem clear, if all sentiment of pity is dismissed, that of his own volition he has chosen a new and permanent home, since he intends to continue his new residence until death. The residence and intention essential for a change of domicile are present. Yet, this suggestion has been stigmatised by Lord Kingsdown as "revolting to common sense and the common feelings of humanity".[145] No doubt it is, and no doubt a court would in fact declare against a change of domicile in such circumstances, but nevertheless the decision would be difficult to reconcile with strict principle unless, perhaps, it could be buttressed by the argument that the invalid contemplated a return to his former home if the medical verdict should prove to be unfounded.

The case just put, however, is an extreme one. Where the necessity of selecting a different climate is of a less compelling nature, where there is no immediate danger,[146] the normal principle is consistently applied and the fact that the invalid's sole reason for departure is a desire to enjoy better health or to retard the progress of a disease cannot per se be regarded as excluding an intention to remain permanently in the chosen place. In such a case it has been said that the *propositus "was exercising a preference, and not acting upon a necessity"*, and the judge refused to hold that the domicile cannot be changed.[147]

---

[141] *Puttick v A-G* [1980] Fam 1, 18.

[142] *Barlow Clowes International Ltd v Henwood* [2008] EWCA Civ 577.

[143] Eg see *Pitt v Pitt* (1864) 4 Macq 627; *Udny v Udny* (1869) LR 1 Sc & Div 441; *Briggs v Briggs* (1880) 5 PD 163; *Re Robertson* (1885) 2 TLR 178; *Re Wright's Trusts* (1856) 25 LJ Ch 621, 624.

[144] *Barlow Clowes International Ltd v Henwood* [2008] EWCA Civ 577.

[145] *Moorhouse v Lord* (1863) 10 HL Cas 272. See also *Johnstone v Beattie* (1843) 10 Cl & Fin 42, 139.

[146] *Hoskins v Matthews* (1856) 8 De GM & G 13, 28.

[147] Ibid, 28–29 emphasis added. See also *Philippi v IRC* [1971] 1 WLR 684; cf *Re James* (1908) 98 LT 438.

(vi) Miscellaneous cases

There are various other cases, somewhat analogous to those just discussed, in which the reason to which a change of residence is due has a rather more decisive effect on the question of intention. Thus, if a person resides abroad in pursuance of his duties as a public servant of his own government, as, for example, an ambassador, a military or naval officer or a consul, or if he is an employee under contract to go where sent, the inference to be drawn from the cause of the residence is that it is not intended to be permanent.[148]

In such cases the existing domicile is retained unless there are additional circumstances from which a contrary intention can be determined.[149] Thus, to take an extreme case, it has been held that even a member of the armed forces may acquire a domicile in a foreign country where he is compulsorily resident and whence he is liable to be removed at any moment by higher authority, if there is sufficient evidence of his intention to settle there permanently as soon as he once more becomes a free agent.[150] The fact that the area of his new home coincides with his area of service does not per se preclude him from acquiring a new domicile. It has also been held that, if the requisite residence and intention are satisfactorily proved, he may acquire a domicile in a country other than that in which he is compulsorily serving.[151] It would seem that a person who enters the armed forces of a foreign power, in such circumstances as to necessitate his indefinite residence in the foreign country, acquires a new domicile there.[152]

(d) Precarious residence

A person can form an intention to remain in a place despite considerable uncertainty as to whether this will be possible.[153] The mere fact than an alien living in England under a certificate of registration is liable to deportation does not prevent him from acquiring an English domicile of choice,[154] or deprive him of a domicile already acquired.[155] Indeed, a domicile of choice may even continue after deportation if re-entry is lawful.[156] Neither the permissive nor the precarious character of his residence nullifies his intention to settle in England.[157] A domicile of choice in England can be acquired, even though that person's presence in the United Kingdom is unlawful. The House of Lords so decided in *Mark v Mark*[158]

---

[148] *Re Patten's Goods* (1860) 6 Jur NS 151 (naval); *A-G v Lady Rowe* (1862) 1 H & C 31 (Chief Justice of Ceylon); *Firebrace v Firebrace* (1878) 4 PD 63 (army officer); *Re Mitchell, ex p Cunningham* (1884) 13 QBD 418 (army officer); *Re Macreight, Paxton v Macreight* (1885) 30 Ch D 165 (Jerseyman serving in British Army); *A-G v Kent* (1862) 31 LJ Ex 391, 397 (attaché to Portuguese Embassy); *Sharpe v Crispin* (1869) LR 1 P & D 611 (consul).

[149] *Re Smith's Goods* (1850) 2 Rob Eccl 332; and see *McEwan v McEwan* 1969 SLT 342.

[150] *Donaldson v Donaldson* [1949] P 363; *Cruikshanks v Cruikshanks* [1957] 1 WLR 564. So held also in Scotland: *Sellars v Sellars* 1942 SC 206.

[151] *Stone v Stone* [1958] 1 WLR 1287.

[152] *Re Mitchell, ex p Cunningham* (1884) 13 QBD 418, 421, as qualified by the earlier remarks of Page Wood V-C in *Forbes v Forbes* (1854) Kay 341, 356.

[153] *Mark v Mark* [2005] UKHL 42 [47], [2006] 1 AC 98.

[154] *Boldrini v Boldrini* [1932] P 9; *May v May* (1943) 169 LT 42; *Zanelli v Zanelli* (1948) 64 TLR 556; *Szechter v Szechter* [1971] P 286; *Lim v Lim* [1973] VR 370. See also *Mark v Mark* [2005] UKHL 42 [39], [2006] 1 AC 98.

[155] *Cruh v Cruh* [1945] 2 All ER 545; *Mark v Mark* [2005] UKHL 42 [39], [2006] 1 AC 98.

[156] *Thiele v Thiele* (1920) 150 LT Jo 387; and see Dicey, Morris and Collins, para 6-060.

[157] *Zanelli v Zanelli*, supra. See also *Mark v Mark* [2005] UKHL 42 [49], [2006] 1 AC 98.

[158] [2005] UKHL 42, [2006] 1 AC 98; Briggs (2005) 76 BYBIL 675. See to the same effect in Canada, *Jablonowski v Jablonowski* (1972) 28 DLR (3d) 440. Cf in Australia, *Solomon v Solomon* (1912) 29 WN NSW 68 and in South Africa, *Smith v Smith* 1962 (3) SA 930; discussed by Spiro (1963) 12 ICLQ 680; Kahn, *South African Law of Domicile of Natural Persons* (1972) pp 62–4.

where the issue was whether a person can be habitually resident or domiciled in England for the purpose of jurisdiction to grant a divorce when that person's presence was a criminal offence under the Immigration Act 1971. Their Lordships held that there was no reason of public policy to deny acquisition of a domicile in England in such a case.[159] Indeed, if a person has chosen to make his home in a new country for an indefinite period of time, it is appropriate that he should be connected to that country's system of law for the kind of purposes for which domicile is relevant.[160] Neither is legality an essential element in either presence or in the formation of the requisite intention, both of which are issues of fact.[161] However, the legality of a person's presence is not completely irrelevant. As in the other cases of precarious residence, it may well be relevant as to whether that person had formed the requisite intention.[162]

(e) The burden of proof

The burden of proof that lies on those who allege a change of domicile varies with the circumstances. In this connection there are two observations that may be made. First, English judges have taken the view that it requires far stronger evidence to establish the abandonment of a domicile of origin in favour of a fresh domicile than to establish a change from one domicile of choice to another.[163] However where a domicile of origin has merely been revived by operation of law, the weight of evidence required to displace it is no greater than that required to displace an existing domicile of choice.[164] Secondly, and by way of contrast, there is authority for the view that a change of domicile from one country to another under the same sovereign, as from Jersey or Scotland to England, is more easily proved than a change to a foreign country.[165] It is not lightly to be inferred that a man intends to settle permanently in a country where he will possess the status of an alien, with all the difficulties and conflict of duties that such a status involves.

(f) Change of domicile and change of nationality

It is important to emphasise that nationality and domicile are two different conceptions and that a man may change the latter without divesting himself of his nationality.[166] An Englishman may remain an Englishman in the sense that his allegiance renders him subject to certain duties to the Crown, and yet he may so change his residence that many of his legal rights and obligations will be determinable by a foreign system of law, as being the law of his domicile.[167] In the same regard a change of nationality or citizenship is not always determinative of a change in domicile.[168]

---

[159] *Mark v Mark*, supra [44]–[47] (Baroness Hale, Lords Hope, Nicholls, Hoffmann and Phillips concurring).

[160] Ibid [46].

[161] Ibid [47]–[49] (Baroness Hale), [13] (Lord Hope).

[162] Ibid [50] (Baroness Hale), [13] (Lord Hope).

[163] Infra, pp 162–3.

[164] *Barlow Clowes International Ltd v Henwood* [2008] EWCA Civ 577 [141].

[165] *Lord v Colvin* (1859) 4 Drew 366, 422–3; *Whicker v Hume* (1858) 7 HL Cas 124, 159; *Moorhouse v Lord* (1863) 10 HL Cas 272, 287.

[166] *Boldrini v Boldrini* [1932] P 9, 15; *Bradfield v Swanton* [1931] IR 446; *Re Adams* [1967] IR 424, 447–8. For the converse case of a change of nationality without a change of domicile, see *Wahl v A-G* (1932) 147 LT 382. See the discussion by Westlake, *Private International Law* (7th edn), pp 348–54.

[167] *Udny v Udny* (1869) LR 1 Sc & Div 441, 452.

[168] *Barlow Clowes International Ltd v Henwood* [2008] EWCA Civ 577 [18] (Arden LJ); *Divall v Divall* [2014] EWHC 95 (Fam) [31] and [51].

4. DOMICILE OF ORIGIN AND DOMICILE OF CHOICE CONTRASTED

As compared with the views held in civil law countries, in the USA, in New Zealand and Australia,[169] the domicile of origin is regarded by English law as fundamentally different from a domicile of choice. It differs in its character, in the conditions necessary for its abandonment and in its capacity for revival.

(a) Tenacity of the domicile of origin

There is the strongest possible presumption in favour of the continuance of a domicile of origin. As contrasted with the domicile of choice, it has been said by Lord Macnaghten that "its character is more enduring, its hold stronger and less easily shaken off".[170] In fact, decisions such as *Winans v A-G*[171] and *Bowie (or Ramsay) v Liverpool Royal Infirmary*[172] warrant the conclusion that almost overwhelming evidence is required to shake it off. In the latter of these cases evidence was completely lacking of the slightest indication, either by words or actions, that George Bowie intended to live anywhere else than in England. Yet it was held that the tenacity of his Scottish domicile of origin had not yielded. Much more recently, in *Cramer v Cramer* Stephen Brown and Balcombe LJJ held that the burden of proving a change of domicile from one of origin to one of choice was a heavy one.[173]

(b) Abandonment of an existing domicile

Since a domicile of choice is voluntarily acquired if there is the requisite intention and residence, so it is extinguishable in the same manner, ie merely by a removal from the country with an intention not to return and even without acquiring a fresh domicile of choice.[174] In such cases the domicile of origin shall revive by operation of law, regardless of any intention to return to the domicile of origin, until a new domicile of choice is established.[175] In cases of dual or multiple residence what is necessary is that the country ceases to be the chief residence[176] with, presumably, an intention not to reside there as the chief residence. The only distinction between acquisition and abandonment is that the latter requires less evidence than the former.[177] There cannot be abandonment by intention alone.[178]

But it has been objected by Megarry J, obiter, that to require proof of an intention not to return is too rigorous a test, since it denies effect to a departure from a country without an intention of returning. In his view, it is unnecessary to prove a positive intention not to

---

[169] See the New Zealand Domicile Act 1976 and the Australian Domicile Acts 1982; Nygh and Davies, paras 13.10–13.11.
[170] *Winans v A-G* [1904] AC 287, 290; and see *A-G v Yule and Mercantile Bank of India* (1931) 145 LT 9; *Wahl v A-G* (1932) 147 LT 382; *Hyland v Hyland* (1971) 18 FLR 461; *Cyganik v Agulian* [2006] EWCA Civ 129 [56], [2006] 1 FCR 406.
[171] Supra, pp 152–4.
[172] [1930] AC 588.
[173] [1987] 1 FLR 116; cf the attitude towards the domicile of origin shown in *Brown v Brown* (1982) 3 FLR 212, infra, p 163.
[174] *Udny v Udny* (1869) LR 1 Sc & Div 441, 450; *Fielden v IRC* (1965) 42 TC 501, 507; *Tee v Tee* [1974] 1 WLR 213, 215.
[175] *Barlow Clowes International Ltd v Henwood* [2008] EWCA Civ 577 [140]. Since nobody can be without a domicile, if no substitute domicile of choice is acquired then the domicile of origin must be revived.
[176] *Plummer v IRC* [1988] 1 WLR 292, 295.
[177] *Re Evans* [1947] Ch 695.
[178] *Re Raffenel's Goods* (1863) 3 Sw & Tr 49; *Faye v IRC* (1961) 40 TC 103; *Re Adams* [1967] IR 424, 452; *IRC v Duchess of Portland* [1982] Ch 314 discussed infra, p 169; *Rowan v Rowan* [1988] ILRM 65.

return, since the "merely negative absence of any intention"[179] to resume the residence will suffice to effect an abandonment of the domicile. This negative test would cover the situation where a person departs from their domicile of choice and initially intends to return to live there. Gradually this resolve withers and eventually dies. At that point there would be the necessary intention for abandonment,[180] even though there might not yet be a definite resolve not to return. Literally, the negative test would also cover the situation where, at the time of departure, the person in question has not thought about whether to return or not. But it is questionable whether such an absence of thought would be enough for abandonment. A person who has thought about whether to return, but is in two minds, would not have the requisite intention for abandonment.[181] What is uncontroversial is that there will be no abandonment where there is a positive intention to return.[182]

But the domicile of origin, which in its inception is not a matter of free will but is communicated to a person by operation of law, is not extinguished by mere removal with an intention not to return. It cannot be lost by mere abandonment. It endures until supplanted by a fresh domicile of choice. *Bell v Kennedy*[183] is the leading authority for this rule.

> The domicile of origin of Bell was in Jamaica. In 1837, he left the island without any intention of returning, resided in Scotland, and occupied himself in looking for an estate in that country on which to settle down. He had not been successful in this when his wife died in 1838.

It was held that his domicile at that moment was in Jamaica. Although he had abandoned the island for good in 1837 and was resident in Scotland, he had not at that time decided to make his permanent residence there. The evidence showed that in 1838 his mind was vacillating with regard to his future home. Therefore, since he had not acquired a Scottish domicile of choice, he retained his domicile of origin.

A modern instance of removal from the domicile of origin with an intention not to return is *Brown v Brown*.[184] In this case there was evidence of a willingness by the court to infer the intention necessary for the acquisition of a domicile of choice, on the basis that the person in question, who worked for a multinational oil company, had severed his links with his domicile of origin in the USA, and the nature of his work meant that he had opportunities for the acquisition of a new domicile abroad.[185]

(c) Revival of the domicile of origin

If the domicile of origin is displaced as a result of the acquisition of a domicile of choice, the rule of English law is that it is merely placed in abeyance for the time being. It remains in the background ever ready to revive and to fasten upon the *propositus* immediately he abandons his domicile of choice.[186] In *Barlow Clowes* the appellants had presented a bankruptcy petition against Mr Henwood on 19 December 2005, and they were seeking to show

---

[179] *Re Flynn* [1968] 1 WLR 103, 113; approved in *Qureshi v Qureshi* [1972] Fam 173, 191; *Morgan v Cilento* [2004] EWHC 188 (Ch) [15], [2004] All ER (D) 122. A negative test was used in *IRC v Duchess of Portland* [1982] Ch 314, 318; *Proes v Revenue Commissioners* [1998] 4 IR 176. But cf *Irvin v Irvin* [2001] 1 FLR 178, 185; *Breuning v Breuning* [2002] EWHC 236 (Fam), [2002] 1 FLR 888, 904; *Divall v Divall* [2014] EWHC 95 (Fam) [35]. See generally Crawford (2005) 54 ICLQ 829, 851.

[180] See *Morgan v Cilento* [2004] EWHC 188 (Ch) [15], [76], [2004] All ER (D) 122.

[181] Ibid, [15].

[182] *Irvin v Irvin* [2001] 1 FLR 178.

[183] (1868) LR 1 Sc & Div 307.

[184] (1982) 3 FLR 212. Cf *DT v FL* [2004] 1 ILRM 509, SC of Ireland—no immediate intention of returning. See also *Vien Estate v Vien Estate* (1988) 49 DLR (4th) 558.

[185] (1982) 3 FLR 212, 215, 217.

[186] *Udny v Udny* (1869) LR 1 Sc & Div 441; *Tee v Tee* [1974] 1 WLR 213, 215–16. See also Wade (1983) 32 ICLQ 1, 12 et seq.

that Mr Henwood was domiciled in England and Wales on that date.[187] Mr Henwood's domicile of origin was in England,[188] however he acquired a domicile of choice in the Isle of Man in 1977.[189] In 1992 he left the Isle of Man, abandoned his domicile of choice there and leased a fully furnished villa in Mauritius.[190] However he continued to travel, and only spent an average of eighty-seven days per year at the property in Mauritius.[191] He and Mrs Henwood spent substantially more time at their property in France between 1992 and 2006.[192] Mr Henwood had no attachment to his domicile of origin in England.[193] Mr Henwood argued that he was domiciled in Mauritius, however the Court of Appeal questioned whether he had the intention to reside there permanently and the number of days he spent in Mauritius appeared inconsistent with the acquisition of a domicile there. He did not have a work permit for Mauritius, he had not tried to gain permanent residence there and the facts indicated that he enjoyed living in France.[194] Mr Henwood had failed to establish a domicile of choice in Mauritius by the relevant date in 2005, consequently his domicile of origin in England had revived despite the fact that he had no attachment to England.[195]

Nobody can be without a domicile, so the revival of the domicile of origin could be considered to be the most logical approach given the endurance and tenacity of a domicile of origin. This rule creates certainty where a *propositus* has abandoned a domicile of choice and failed to create a new intention to reside permanently elsewhere. However this approach has been criticised, as revival of the domicile of origin can be artificial where the link between this state and the *propositus* is negligible.[196] In such circumstances the advantages of preferring the domicile of origin are not particularly conspicuous. The country that determines his personal law might be one that he has never visited, or has not lived for many years, and for which he feels a repugnance. Nevertheless, if he wishes to marry, his capacity will be determined by reference to that law. A comparative analysis indicates that the doctrine of revival is not accepted in the USA,[197] and was rejected in New Zealand[198] and in Australia.[199] Instead the old domicile of choice remains until a new one is selected. Both approaches have similar problems as each one could be said to create an artificial link. In *Barlow Clowes* it was clear that Mr Henwood had no connection with neither England nor the Isle of Man, hence raising the question whether domicile is the correct approach in a world where our movements are increasingly fluid.

---

[187] *Barlow Clowes International Ltd v Henwood* [2008] EWCA Civ 577, as required by Insolvency Act 1986, s 265.

[188] Ibid [26].

[189] Ibid [27].

[190] Ibid [29] and [118].

[191] Ibid [30].

[192] Ibid.

[193] Ibid [117].

[194] Ibid [119]–[126].

[195] Ibid [127]–[128].

[196] L Trackman, 'Domicile of Choice in English Law: An Achilles Heel?' (2015) 11 J Priv Int L 317, 325–6.

[197] *Re Jones' Estate* (1921) 192 Iowa 78, 182 NW 227.

[198] Domicile Act 1976, s 11; see Webb (1977) 26 ICLQ 194; but see generally for the position in Commonwealth countries, McClean, *Recognition of Family Judgments in the Commonwealth* (1983), Chapter 1.

[199] Domicile Acts 1982, s 7; Nygh and Davies, 13.11.

5. DOMICILE OF DEPENDENT PERSONS

There are two classes of dependent persons—children[200] and mentally disordered persons.

(a) Children

(i) A child's domicile of origin

A child acquires at birth a domicile of origin by operation of law, namely, if legitimate and born in his father's lifetime, the domicile of his father,[201] if illegitimate[202] or born after his father's death,[203] the domicile of his mother.[204] A foundling is domiciled in the country where he is found.[205] If a child is born illegitimate, but is later legitimated, his father's domicile will be communicated to him from the date of legitimation, but it is probable that his domicile of origin remains that of his mother, presuming that at his birth his parents were domiciled in different countries.[206] It is important to note that a domicile of origin once acquired remains constant throughout life.[207]

(ii) When an independent domicile can be acquired

Before reaching the age of sixteen, an unmarried child is incapable of acquiring by his own act an independent domicile of choice.[208] He is powerless to alter his civil status. Once that age is reached, then a child, whether male or female, is fully capable of having an independent domicile.[209] Furthermore, any child below that age who is validly married can acquire an independent domicile. Although this will not affect the status of English domiciled children, who are incapable of marriage until the age of sixteen, it does mean that any child below that age whose foreign marriage is recognised here[210] will be regarded as capable of having an independent domicile.

---

[200] Palmer (1974) 4 Fam Law 35; Binchy (1979) 11 Ottowa LR 279; Blaikie [1984] Jur Rev 1.

[201] *Forbes v Forbes* (1854) Kay 341 at 353; *Udny v Udny* (1869) LR 1 Sc & Div 441 at 457; *Ray v Shekhri* [2014] EWCA Civ 119. According to the Adoption and Children Act 2002, s 67 an adopted person is to be treated in law as if they were born as the child of the adoptive parent(s), suggesting they would take the domicile of the adoptive parent(s) on the date of adoption.

[202] *Udny v Udny*, supra; *Re Wright's Trusts* (1856) 2 K & J 595; *Urquhart v Butterfield* (1887) 37 Ch D 357; *Carmona v White* (1980) 25 SASR 525. See Law Com No 168 (1987) and Scot Law Com No 107 (1987) for proposals for reform, which have unfortunately been rejected; for New Zealand, see the Domicile Act 1976, s 6; for Australia the Domicile Acts 1982, s 9.

[203] There appears to be no English authority for this.

[204] Though see discussion of legitimacy, infra, pp 1194–202. Although the Family Law Reform Act 1987 very largely assimilates the rights of children, regardless of whether they are legitimate or illegitimate, the concept of legitimacy is still relevant for domicile purposes. See, however, now in Scotland, Family Law (Scotland) Act 2006, s 22, which effects a change in the rules of Scots law concerning the domicile of persons under 16.

[205] Westlake, s 248; Dicey, Morris and Collins, para 6R-025.

[206] Wolff, pp 118–19.

[207] Except perhaps in the case of adoption, supra.

[208] *Forbes v Forbes* (1854) Kay 341, 353.

[209] Domicile and Matrimonial Proceedings Act 1973, s 3(1). A child who was over sixteen or was married but was incapable of having an independent domicile before 1 January 1974 is regarded as capable from that date. Sections 3 and 4 of the 1973 Act are not retrospective, and, therefore, in considering the domicile of a child as at any time before 1 January 1974 (which it may be necessary to do when tracing that person's domicile up to the present day), the old law is still applicable. Under such rules a child is incapable of acquiring an independent domicile until reaching full age whether or not married: *Harrison v Harrison* [1953] 1 WLR 865. A female married child takes the domicile of her husband but if widowed reverts to that of her father until majority: *Shekleton v Shekleton* [1972] 2 NSWR 675.

[210] Eg *Alhaji Mohamed v Knott* [1969] 1 QB 1.

(iii) The effect of a change in the parent's domicile

Although an unmarried child under sixteen[211] is unable to acquire a domicile of choice by his own act there is nothing to prevent the acquisition of a domicile of choice *for* him by the act of one of his parents. This may be effected either by the father or by the mother. The primary rule is that the domicile of a legitimate child[212] automatically changes with any change that occurs in the domicile of the father.[213] This unity is not destructible at the will of the father. It is not terminated if he purports to create a separate domicile for his son, for instance, by setting him up in business abroad.[214] At one time, as between a living father and his legitimate child, there was a necessary unity of domicile, even though they may have resided in different countries, and even after a divorce and the mother had custody.[215] But this has been altered by the Domicile and Matrimonial Proceedings Act 1973[216] in the one case where both parents[217] are alive but are living apart. In such a case the child's domicile is that of the mother, if the child has his home with her and no home with his father,[218] or if he has acquired his mother's domicile in this way and has not since then had a home with his father.[219] This latter provision means that a child who has his home with his mother keeps her domicile, though he ceases to live with her, provided he does not later have a home with his father. Furthermore, a child who has his mother's domicile by reason of these provisions continues to retain it after her death unless and until he has a home with his father.[220]

Two points should be stressed in relation to these statutory provisions. They apply only to the determination of a child's dependent domicile and do not appear to affect the determination of his domicile of origin. Thus, a child born of parents who are married but living apart at the time of his birth would appear to acquire his father's domicile as his domicile of origin but, immediately thereafter, a domicile of dependence with his mother, where his home is.[221] Secondly, these provisions apply only to the case where both parents are alive and are living apart, and provided the child is legitimate.[222] It is unfortunate that other cases giving rise to problems relating to a child's dependent domicile are left to be dealt with by the common law.[223] If a father, on the death of his wife, abandons his children and acquires a fresh domicile elsewhere, and the children are left to be cared for by grandparents, their domicile is still decided by obscure common law rules. However, it seems most unlikely that a court would affirm the inevitability of the application of the father's domicile. This was the view at common law, taken by Lord MacDermott LCJ in the Northern Ireland case of *Hope v Hope*,[224] of the situation where the mother was alive, where he characterised the capacity of a father to change the domicile of his minor child as "a manifestation of parental authority

---

[211] Hereafter described as a "child".

[212] An adopted person is treated as the legitimate child of the adopters or adopter: Adoption and Children Act 2002, s 67.

[213] *D'Etchegoyen v D'Etchegoyen* (1888) 13 PD 132. As to whether a change in a guardian's domicile is communicated to his ward, see Spiro (1956) 5 ICLQ 196 et seq.

[214] Wolff, p 117.

[215] *Breuning v Breuning* [2002] EWHC 236 (Fam), [2002] 1 FLR 888, 902 (discussing the pre-1974 law).

[216] S 4(1); see *Williams, Petitioner* 1977 SLT (Notes) 2. The equivalent in Australia is the Domicile Acts 1982, s 9; in New Zealand the Domicile Act 1976, s 6.

[217] Including adoptive parents: Adoption and Children Act 2002, s 67.

[218] S 4(2)(a). On the meaning of "home", see *Re P (GE) (An Infant)* [1965] Ch 568 at 585–6; *Re Y (Minors) (Adoption: Jurisdiction)* [1985] Fam 136; and cf Family Law (Scotland) Act 2006, s 22.

[219] S 4(2)(b).

[220] S 4(3).

[221] See Palmer (1974) 4 Fam Law 35, 36; Dicey, Morris and Collins, para 6-028.

[222] S 4(4). This includes adopted: Adoption and Children Act 2002, s 67.

[223] See Palmer (1974) 4 Fam Law 35, 36–8.

[224] [1968] NI 1; not following the Scottish decision in *Shanks v Shanks* 1965 SLT 330; cf *Re B (S) (An Infant)* [1968] Ch 204, 208.

and responsibility". Therefore he asked: "why should it apply to tie the domicile of the child to the will of a father who has abjured his responsibility by walking out of his child's life?"[225] It is suggested that this view is still valid in those cases unaffected by the Domicile and Matrimonial Proceedings Act 1973.

The domicile that a child acquires by reason of his father or mother moving to another country is a domicile of choice, or better perhaps of quasi-choice,[226] and his domicile of origin continues to be that imposed upon him at birth.[227] This rule may become important at a later stage in his life. For instance, a father, domiciled in England at the time of his son's birth, acquires a domicile of choice in France and retains it until after his son reaches the age of sixteen. At the age of twenty-five, the son acquires a domicile of choice in Italy, but later abandons that country for good and dies without having acquired another permanent home. In these circumstances, the English domicile will revive on the loss of his Italian domicile and English law will govern testamentary or intestate succession to his movables.

A child acquires, on the death of his father, the domicile of his mother.[228] The question that has arisen here is whether such a child's domicile continues to follow that of the mother, or whether there are any circumstances in which it will remain unaffected by her acts. The general doctrine is that, if after the death of the father the child continues to live with the mother, then any new domicile acquired by the mother is prima facie to be regarded as communicated to the child.[229] But this is not necessarily so. It is recognised that the mother is empowered to change her children's domicile either by taking them to a new domicile acquired by her, or by leaving them where their father was domiciled at the time of his death[230] or even, it would seem, by placing them in another country under the care of a competent person. But this power must be exercised bona fide and with the sole object of promoting the welfare of the children. Thus, even the prima facie rule, that a new domicile acquired by the mother is communicated to her children, is displaced if this is disadvantageous to them or if the change of domicile is due to some fraudulent design on her part, as, for example, where her motive is to take advantage of a law of succession more beneficial to herself.[231]

(iv) Criticism of the existing law

It is hard to disagree with the criticism by the Law Commissions of the present rules, namely that they "discriminate between legitimate and illegitimate children and between their fathers and mothers. They also fail to deal adequately with the cases where a child is abandoned, his parents die, the child is fostered or is taken into the care of a local authority".[232] However, finding acceptable new rules to replace the present rules is not so easy.[233]

---

[225] [1968] NI 1, 5; and see Carter (1968–69) 43 BYBIL 239.
[226] *Harrison v Harrison* [1953] 1 WLR 865, suggested by counsel at 866.
[227] *Henderson v Henderson* [1967] P 77, [1965] 1 All ER 179.
[228] *Potinger v Wightman* (1817) 3 Mer 67. The domicile of a child whose father is dead, or of an illegitimate child, is unaffected by s 4 of the Domicile and Matrimonial Proceedings Act 1973: s 4(4). For Australia see the Domicile Acts 1982, s 9; for New Zealand the Domicile Act 1976, s 6.
[229] *Johnstone v Beattie* (1843) 10 Cl & Fin 42, 138.
[230] *Re Beaumont* [1893] 3 Ch 490; *Re G* [1966] NZLR 1028; Blaikie [1984] Jur Rev 1, 4 et seq. This power would have gone if the Law Commissions' proposals, Law Com No 168 (1987), Scot Law Com No 107 (1987), had been accepted.
[231] *Potinger v Wightman* (1817) 3 Mer 67, 79, 80.
[232] Law Com No 168 (1987), Scot Law Com No 107 (1987), para 3(2)(d).
[233] See Law Com No 168 (1987), Scot Law Com No 107 (1987), for the Law Commissions' proposals in relation to children, which were rejected.

(b) Mental disorder or mental incapacity

Although there is no direct authority, it is generally agreed that the domicile of a mentally disordered or mentally incapacitated person cannot be changed either by himself, since he is incapable of forming an intention, or by the person to whose care he has been entrusted.[234] Of course, in accordance with the general principle applicable to children, the domicile of the father will be communicated to a child of unsound mind during the childhood of the latter, but a somewhat irrational distinction has been suggested as regards an adult who is mentally disordered or mentally incapacitated. If he has been continuously disordered or incapacitated both during childhood and after the age of sixteen, it is said that his domicile will continue to change with that of his father; but that if he first becomes disordered or incapacitated after reaching the age of sixteen, his then domicile becomes indelible, for if the power of changing it were vested in the father great danger might be done to "the interests of others".[235] There are two possible solutions, though neither is supported by authority in England. First, as the paramount consideration is the interest of the mentally disordered or mentally incapacitated person, not of others, it might be advisable that the Court of Protection should be entitled to change his domicile if this appears to be for his benefit. Secondly, a rule could be adopted to the effect that an adult who is mentally disordered or mentally incapacitated should be domiciled in the country with which he is for the time being most closely connected.[236]

(c) Capacity to acquire a domicile

It has been suggested that the capacity of a dependent person to acquire a fresh domicile is not always governed by English law, the law of the forum. Such a possibility was adumbrated obiter in an English case in 1887,[237] and subsequently it has been canvassed by Graveson.[238] It is submitted, however, that this thesis is based upon a fundamental misconception, since it overlooks the fact that domicile is no more than a connecting factor. Its acquisition is not *itself* a problem for the solution of which a rule for the choice of law is required. For the connecting factor in any English choice of law rule must logically always be interpreted according to English notions.[239]

6. DOMICILE OF MARRIED WOMEN[240]

(a) The abolition of dependency

Until 1974, the rule was that the domicile of a husband was communicated to his wife immediately on marriage and it was necessarily and inevitably retained by her for the duration of the marriage. This rule was much criticised as "the last barbarous relic of a wife's servitude"[241] and was abolished by section 1 of the Domicile and Matrimonial Proceedings Act 1973.[242]

---

[234] *Urquhart v Butterfield* (1887) 37 Ch D 357, 382. See also *Bempde v Johnstone* (1796) 3 Ves 198; *Sharpe v Crispin* (1869) LR 1 P & D 611; Westlake, p 251; cf *Re G* [1966] NZLR 1028. Nor probably can it be altered by the Court of Protection in exercise of its powers under the Mental Capacity Act 2005, see Dicey, Morris and Collins, paras 6R-107, 6-108-6-110.

[235] *Sharpe v Crispin* (1869) LR 1 P & D 611, 618.

[236] See the rejected proposals of the Law Commissions: Law Com No 168 (1987), Scot Law Com No 107 (1987), Part IV.

[237] *Urquhart v Butterfield* (1887) 37 Ch D 357, 384.

[238] (1950) 3 ILQ 149. See also Mendes de Costa, *Studies in Canadian Family Law* (1972), Vol II, pp 914–16; cf Nygh and Davies, 13.25; New Zealand Domicile Act 1976, s 5(2).

[239] *Re Martin* [1900] P 211, 227; *Re Annesley* [1926] Ch 692, 705. But see Family Law Act 1986, s 46(5).

[240] Palmer (1974) 124 NLJ 49, 73, 95.

[241] *Gray v Formosa* [1963] P 259, 267; and see *Adams v Adams* [1971] P 188, 216.

[242] S 1.

The domicile of a married woman as at any time on or after 1 January 1974 "shall, instead of being the same as her husband's by virtue only of marriage, be ascertained by reference to the same factors as in the case of any other individual capable of having an independent domicile".

This means that a married woman is to be treated as capable of acquiring a separate domicile; though in the vast majority of cases she and her husband will, independently, acquire the same domicile. It is, however, quite possible for happily married spouses to have separate domiciles as where, for example, a student at an English university who is domiciled in New York marries a fellow student domiciled in England, both intending at the end of their studies to go and live in New York.[243]

(b) Transitional problems

The 1973 Act deals also with the transitional problem of the domicile of dependence of a wife acquired before 1974.[244] A woman, married before 1974, who, therefore, acquired her husband's domicile on marriage, is to be treated as retaining that domicile as a domicile of choice if it was not the wife's own domicile of origin, until it is changed by acquisition of a new domicile of choice or revival of the domicile of origin on or after 1 January 1974.[245] This means that, after that date, the wife's domicile is not to be treated as dependent on her husband but as her own domicile of origin, or of choice, until she acquires a new domicile of choice or until her domicile of origin revives.[246] The operation of these transitional provisions is shown in *IRC v Duchess of Portland*:[247]

> The taxpayer, who had a domicile of origin in Canada, married her husband, an English domiciliary, in 1948, thereby acquiring an English domicile of dependency. The couple set up home in England. However, the taxpayer, throughout her marriage, maintained close links with Canada, including retaining a bank account, owning a house and returning for visits for ten to twelve weeks each year. It was agreed that when her husband retired they would both live permanently in Canada.

Nourse J held that the taxpayer had not reacquired her domicile of origin in Canada and retained her domicile of choice in England during the period in question. He reasoned as follows: the 1973 Act turned the taxpayer's domicile of dependency into one of choice; she had not abandoned this English domicile of choice, notwithstanding her intention to return to Canada, since she had not ceased to reside in England.[248] The judge regarded the language of the transitional provisions as clear and said that the above construction "does not . . . lead to any result which is unjust and anomalous or absurd".[249]

---

[243] See *Puttick v A-G* [1980] Fam 1, 17; *IRC v Duchess of Portland* [1982] Ch 314, 319–20.

[244] In considering the domicile of a married woman as at any time before 1 January 1974, the old law will apply, so that she will be regarded as incapable of acquiring a domicile independent from that of her husband. Cf the position in Ireland where the Supreme Court has held the wife's dependent domicile rule to be unconstitutional, and a wife's domicile has to be worked out like that of any other independent person whether before or after 1986, when the domicile of dependency was abolished by the Domicile and Recognition of Foreign Divorces Act 1986, s 1: *W v W* [1993] 2 IR 476.

[245] Domicile and Matrimonial Proceedings Act 1973, s 1(2).

[246] For a different interpretation of s 1(2) of the 1973 Act, see Wade (1983) 32 ICLQ 1, particularly at 6 et seq.

[247] [1982] Ch 314; Wade, op cit, 3 et seq; Thompson (1983) 32 ICLQ 237; Carter (1982) 53 BYBIL 295.

[248] The same approach was applied earlier in *Oundjian v Oundjian* (1979) 1 FLR 198, 202.

[249] *Duchess of Portland*, supra, 320. However, the New Zealand Domicile Act 1976, ss 4 and 5 and the Australian Domicile Acts 1982, s 5(1) and (2) give a different solution. The English and Scottish Law Commissions in their rejected proposals set out in Law Com No 168 (1987) and Scot Law Com No 107 (1987) Part VIII, favoured the Australian and New Zealand solution, and the reversal of *IRC v Duchess of Portland*.

7. DOMICILE AND NATIONALITY

(a) Nationality and domicile contrasted[250]

Nationality is a possible alternative to domicile as the criterion of the personal law. These are two different conceptions. Nationality represents a person's political status, by virtue of which he owes allegiance to some particular country; domicile indicates his civil status and it provides the law by which his personal rights and obligations are determined.[251] Nationality depends, apart from naturalisation, on the place of birth or on parentage; domicile, as we have seen, is constituted by residence in a particular country with the intention of residing there permanently. It follows that a person may be a national of one country but domiciled in another.

If one looks at the historical development, it will appear that, over the last two centuries, the ascertainment of the personal law, which ought to be governed by legal and practical considerations, has in fact been influenced by varying political and economic factors. The French Revolution, the struggles of Italy to win independence, the wave of nationalism that swept Europe in the nineteenth century, the desire of the poorer countries to share in the prosperity of their emigrants—these and other similar circumstances have led to a widespread idolatry of the principle of nationality. At present many countries in Europe and South America adopt nationality as the criterion of personal law, whilst the common law jurisdictions of the Commonwealth and the USA, among others, still stand by the test of domicile. As immigration has increased in Western Europe since the Second World War, domicile has gained ground at the expense of nationality.[252]

It may be asked, what are the respective merits of domicile and nationality as a determinant of the law to govern status and personal rights generally? Each has its merits and demerits.[253]

(i) The merits and demerits of domicile

The English preference for domicile is based on two main grounds. First, domicile means the country in which a person has established his permanent home, and what can be more natural or more appropriate than to subject him to his home law? It is difficult to agree that he should be excommunicated from that law merely because technically he is a citizen of some state that he may have abandoned years ago.[254] Secondly, domicile furnishes the only practicable test in the case of such political units as the United Kingdom, Canada, Australia and the USA where the same nationality embraces a number of, sometimes diverse, legal systems. The expression "national law" when applied to a British subject is meaningless. It is one system for England, another in Scotland; similarly for a Canadian, there is one system in Ontario and a quite different one in Quebec.

In the course of its development in England, however, the law relating to domicile has acquired certain vices. A short mention of these will suffice here, as they have already been discussed in this chapter. First, it will not infrequently happen that the legal domicile of a person is out of touch with reality, for the exaggerated importance attributed to the domicile of origin, coupled with the technical doctrine of its revival, may well ascribe to a person a

---

[250] de Winter (1969) III Hague Recueil 357–503; Nadelmann (1969) 17 AJCL 418; and see Pålsson, *Marriage and Divorce in Comparative Conflict of Laws*, Chapter 3; North, *Private International Law of Matrimonial Causes*, pp 5–15.

[251] *Udny v Udny* (1869) LR 1 Sc & Div 441, 457.

[252] Pålsson (1986) IV Hague Recueil 316, 332 et seq.

[253] See de Winter, op cit, pp 400–18; Kahn-Freund (1974) III Hague Recueil 139, 314, 389–91, 467–8.

[254] Of course, if a country which adopts the principle of nationality also accepts the doctrine of renvoi, the practical result may be the substitution of the law of the domicile for the law of nationality, supra, pp 57–61.

domicile in the country which by no stretch of the imagination can be called his home.[255] Secondly, an equally irrational result may ensure from the view, sometimes accepted by the English courts, that long residence is not equivalent to domicile if accompanied by the contemplation of some uncertain event the occurrence of which will cause a termination of the residence.[256] Thirdly, the ascertainment of a person's domicile depends to such an extent on proof of his intention, the most elusive of all factors, that only too often it will be impossible to identify it with certainty without recourse to the courts.[257]

(ii) The merits and demerits of nationality

Nationality, as compared with domicile, enjoys the advantages that it is relatively easy to understand as a concept and normally it is easily ascertainable.[258] Nevertheless, it is objectionable as a criterion of the personal law on at least three grounds.[259]

First, it may point to a country with which the person in question has lost all connection, or with which perhaps he has never been connected. It is a strange notion, for instance, that a Neapolitan, who has emigrated to California in his youth without becoming naturalised in the USA, should throughout his life remain subject to Italian law with regard to such matters as marital and testamentary capacity. Secondly, nationality is sometimes a more fallible criterion than domicile. In the eyes of English law no person can be without a domicile, no person can have more than one domicile at the same time. On the other hand, the person may be stateless or may simultaneously be a citizen of two or more countries.[260] Thirdly, nationality cannot always determine the internal law to which a person is subject. This is the case, as we have seen, when one political unit such as the USA comprises a variety of legal systems. Similarly, nationality breaks down as a connecting factor in the case of the United Kingdom where, for many purposes, there is no such thing as United Kingdom law. The application of the concept of nationality in such circumstances will lead to eccentric decisions such as that given in *Re O'Keefe*.[261]

Perhaps a fair conclusion, speaking very generally, is to say that, as determinants of the personal law, nationality yields a predictable but frequently an inappropriate law; domicile yields an appropriate but frequently an unpredictable law.

This division of the world into those countries that adopt the principle of nationality and those that prefer the test of domicile is unfortunate, since it obstructs the movement for the unification of rules of private international law; the reconciliation of the opposing views is highly desirable. Moreover, whilst there has been a tendency on the Continent to substitute domicile for nationality as the test of personal law, there has been a natural reluctance to absorb the English principles *in toto*.[262] This has led to international efforts to reach agreement on the meaning of both domicile and also residence as connecting factors.[263]

---

[255] Supra, p 163 et seq.

[256] Supra, p 151 et seq.

[257] Supra, p 155 et seq.

[258] See generally Law Com No 168 (1987), Scot Law Com No 107 (1987), para 3.9. It is ascertained by reference to the law of the state of the nationality concerned; eg *Oppenheimer v Cattermole* [1976] AC 249; *R v Secretary of State for the Home Department, ex p Bibi* [1985] Imm AR 134.

[259] North, *Private International Law of Matrimonial Causes*, pp 9–10. See also Law Com No 168 (1987), Scot Law Com No 107 (1987), paras 3.10–3.11.

[260] Eg *Torok v Torok* [1973] 1 WLR 1066.

[261] [1940] Ch 124, discussed supra, pp 64–5, and *Re Johnson* [1903] 1 Ch 821.

[262] Folke Schmidt (1951) 4 ILQ 39–52; Cheshire, ibid, 52–9; de Winter (1969) III Hague Recueil 357, 419–23.

[263] Eg Council of Europe Resolution (72)1 on the Standardisation of the Legal Concepts of "Domicile" and of "Residence".

8. CONCEPTS OF RESIDENCE

Dissatisfaction with nationality as a connecting factor has led to a realisation of the defects of domicile also. This has had several consequences. There has been attempts in England to reform the concept of domicile,[264] but these have been successful only in relation to the dependent domicile of children and married women.[265] Problems in the basic definition of domicile remain. The failure, over many years, to reform domicile has led, in its turn, to a tendency to reject it as a connecting factor in favour of residence.[266] One of the main forces in this direction has been the fact that the Hague Conventions have relied on "habitual residence" as a connecting factor.[267] The Rome I Regulation on contract choice of law[268] also utilises this concept, but now in the commercial sphere. This has resulted in the concept being introduced into English law as legislation is passed to implement these conventions.[269] The wheel has been turned full circle as purely domestic legislation has also adopted "habitual residence" as a major connecting factor in matrimonial jurisdiction.[270] It is also used as a condition for eligibility for income support, housing benefit and council tax benefit.[271] Nonetheless, although habitual residence is increasingly being used as an alternative connecting factor, it would be wrong to introduce a general substitution of habitual residence for domicile.[272] For the connection between a person and a country provided by habitual residence is not sufficiently strong to justify that person's affairs always being determined by the law of that country. Take the example of English expatriates working abroad, in countries such as Saudi Arabia, on long-term contracts. Their personal affairs, such as their capacity to enter a marriage, should be determined by the law of England, their domicile, not by the law of Saudi Arabia, their habitual residence.

---

[264] Law Com No 168 (1987) and Scot Law Com No 107 (1987).

[265] Domicile and Matrimonial Proceedings Act 1973, ss 1, 3, 4, supra, pp 166–9.

[266] North, *Private International Law of Matrimonial Causes*, pp 10–15.

[267] de Winter (1969) III Hague Recueil 357, 419–54; Cavers (1972) 21 Am ULR 475.

[268] See Arts 4 and 19, infra, pp 726–31 and pp 739–40.

[269] Eg Wills Act 1963, infra, p 1341 et seq; Adoption and Children Act 1976, infra, p 1208; Child Abduction and Custody Act 1985, infra, p 1134; Family Law Act 1986, Pt II, infra, p 1007 et seq; Contracts (Applicable Law) Act 1990, infra, pp 684–6; The Hague Convention on Jurisdiction, Applicable Law, Recognition, Enforcement and Co-operation in respect of Parental Responsibility and Measures for the Protection of Children of 1996, also makes extensive use of habitual residence, see infra, pp 1103–4; Clive [1998] Jur Rev 169.

[270] Domicile and Matrimonial Proceedings Act 1973, ss 5, 6, infra, pp 954–60; Family Law Act 1986, Parts I and III, infra, pp 1052–4 and 1056–8. See also the Child Support Act 1991, s 44(1). Council Regulation (EC) No 2201/2003 of 27 November 2003 concerning jurisdiction and the recognition and enforcement of judgments in matrimonial matters and the matters of parental responsibility OJ 2003 L 338/1 (Brussels II bis), discussed infra, pp 1094–7 and 1107–8, uses habitual residence as an alternative connecting factor for jurisdiction. See generally the comments of Thorpe LJ in *Nessa v Chief Adjudication Officer* [1998] 2 All ER 728, 737, CA; affd [1999] 1 WLR 1937, HL.

[271] See, eg, Income Support (General) Regulations, 1987 SI 1987/1967. See generally Hardy (1997) 19 JSW and FL 73.

[272] Law Com No 168 (1987), Scot Law Com No 107 (1987), paras 3.5–3.8. The proposals that the Law Commissions did put forward for reform have been rejected. Cf Irish Law Reform Commission's Report on Domicile and Habitual Residence as Connecting Factors in the Conflict of Laws of 1983; Binchy, *Irish Conflicts of Law*, pp 98–100. Cf *Cyganik v Agulian* [2006] EWCA Civ 129 [58] (Longmore LJ), [2006] 1 FCR 406 suggesting consideration of replacing domicile by habitual residence in the Inheritance (Provision for Family and Dependants) Act 1975.

(a) Ordinary residence[273]

"Ordinary residence" has been known as a connecting factor in English law for some time. It used to form a basis for service of a claim form out of the jurisdiction;[274] it used to be a basis of jurisdiction in matrimonial causes in the case of a petitioning wife;[275] it used to be a criterion for obtaining security for costs;[276] it is a significant connecting factor for the purposes of immigration[277] and social security law;[278] it is an important connecting factor in taxation statutes;[279] it has been the criterion used for determining eligibility for a mandatory student award from the local authority;[280] used as the basis for determining whether a student is a home or overseas student for the purpose of payment of university fees[281] and access to student loans,[282] accessing the NHS,[283] and for designating the local authority to be responsible in a care order.[284]

There is some authority on the meaning of "ordinary residence", though its precise meaning has caused difficulty.[285] One judge went so far as to say that the adjective adds nothing to the noun.[286] However, Lord Scarman in giving the judgment of the House of Lords in *Shah v Barnet London Borough*,[287] said that this adjective brings out two important features of ordinary residence, namely residence must be adopted voluntarily, ie not by virtue of kidnapping or imprisonment,[288] and for settled purposes, which can include for the purposes

---

[273] Smart (1989) 38 ICLQ 175. For the meaning of residence, simpliciter, see *K v M, M and L (Financial Relief: Foreign Orders)* [1998] 2 FLR 59, 75. For residence as a component of domicile, see supra, pp 149–50.

[274] Ord 11, r 1(1)(c), of the old Rules of the Supreme Court, replaced by what is now r 6.20(1) of the CPR; see infra, pp 326–7. In Ireland, domicile for the purposes of jurisdiction in civil and commercial matters is defined in terms of ordinary residence, see *Deutsche Bank v Murtagh* [1995] 1 ILRM 381.

[275] Matrimonial Causes Act 1973, s 46(1)(b), repealed by the Domicile and Matrimonial Proceedings Act 1973, s 17(2), Sch 6.

[276] See *Leyvand v Barasch*, (2000) Times, 23 March. This has been replaced by residence: CPR, r 25.13(2)(a).

[277] *Man Chiu Yu v Secretary of State for the Home Department* [1981] Imm AR 1651; it must be questionable whether the case would now be decided the same way in the light of the decisions in *Shah v Barnet London Borough Council* [1983] 2 AC 309; *R v Secretary of State for the Home Department, ex p Margueritte* [1983] QB 180 (acquisition of UK citizenship); *Britto v Secretary of State for the Home Department* [1984] Imm AR 93.

[278] Eg National Insurance Decision No R (P) 1/72; Wikeley, Ogus and Barendt, *The Law of Social Security* (5th edn), pp 231–2.

[279] See *Levene v Inland Revenue Comrs* [1928] AC 217; *Inland Revenue Comrs v Lysaght* [1928] AC 234; *Reed v Clark* [1986] Ch 1; *Grace v Revenue and Customs Commissioners* [2009] EWCA Civ 1082; *Ward v Revenue and Customs Commissioners* [2016] UKFTT 114 (TC).

[280] *Shah v Barnet London Borough Council* [1983] 2 AC 309; *R v Lancashire County Council, ex p Huddleston* [1986] 2 All ER 941.

[281] See *Orphanos v Queen Mary College* [1985] AC 761.

[282] The Supreme Court held that settlement might be sufficient in cases where the individual has had a long residence in England which was not lawful, however still required that residence be lawful in order for there to be ordinary residence. *R (on the application of Tigere) v Secretary of State for Business, Innovation and Skills* [2015] UKSC 57.

[283] National Health Service (Charges to Overseas Visitors) Regulations 2011 (SI 2011/1556); *R (On the application of W) v Secretary of State for Health* [2015] EWCA Civ 1034.

[284] The Children Act 1989, s 31(8); *C (A Child) v Plymouth County Council* [2000] 1 FLR 875, CA. See also s 105(6) of the 1989 Act; *North Yorkshire County Council v Wiltshire County Council* [1999] 2 FLR 560.

[285] McClean (1962) 11 ICLQ 1153, 1161–6.

[286] *Hopkins v Hopkins* [1951] P 116, 121–2.

[287] [1983] 2 AC 309, 342. Lord Scarman was referring to the adverb "habitually" but he equated this with "ordinarily".

[288] Cf *Petrotrade Inc v Smith* [1998] 2 All ER 346 at 350–351—involuntary residence in situation where arrested and given bail on condition did not leave.

of "education, business or profession, employment, health, family or merely love of the place".[289] The words "ordinary residence" should be given their natural and ordinary meaning, and not an artificial legal construction,[290] which will be the same regardless of the context, unless it can be shown that the statutory framework requires a different meaning.[291] Ordinary residence does not connote continuous physical presence, but physical presence with some degree of continuity, notwithstanding occasional temporary absences.[292] It is possible to have more than one ordinary residence and the time spent in the residence can be relatively minimal.[293] There must, however, be some physical presence. Intention to reside is not, alone, sufficient.[294] Ordinary residence is primarily a matter of fact,[295] the principles are derived from case law and were summarised by the Court of Appeal in *Grace*.[296] However it is a question of construction of a statute whether the word "lawful" should be implied so as to qualify the ordinary residence.[297] In *Shah* it was said obiter that a person cannot rely on his unlawful presence in breach of the immigration laws to constitute *ordinary* residence.[298] However, this is regarded as a rule of construction of the relevant statute which uses the ordinary residence criterion.[299] Thus for the purpose of United Kingdom tax laws there is no requirement that the ordinary residence must be lawful.[300] On the other hand, unlawful residence cannot be relied upon for the purposes of acquiring citizenship;[301] or accessing a student loan.[302] The difference between these examples is that a person may benefit from being ordinarily resident in the United Kingdom for immigration purposes whereas a person will not so benefit for taxation purposes.[303] The state does have an interest in whether a person is ordinarily resident in the United Kingdom or not.[304] Moreover, it can be argued that, as a matter of general principle, a person should not benefit from his own unlawful conduct.

Each case must, of course, depend on its own peculiar facts, but the authorities show that even absence for a considerable time will not terminate a person's ordinary residence if it

---

[289] *Shah v Barnet London Borough Council* [1983] 2 AC 309, 344; *Britto v Secretary of State for the Home Department* [1984] Imm AR 93. For Canada see *Trotter v Trotter* (1992) 90 DLR (4th) 554.

[290] *Gateshead Metropolitan Borough Council v L* [1996] 3 All ER 264 at 267.

[291] The *Shah* case, supra, 341–3.

[292] *Levene v Inland Revenue Comrs* [1928] AC 217, 232; *Shah v Barnet London Borough Council* [1983] 2 AC 309, 341–342; *R v Immigration Appeal Tribunal, ex p Siggins* [1985] Imm AR 14; *Re Vassis* (1986) 64 ALR 407.

[293] *Re: Norris* (1888) 4 TLR 452 *Levene v Commissioners of Inland Revenue* (1928) 13 TC 486, 505; *Grace v Revenue and Customs Commissioners* [2009] EWCA Civ 1082; *R (on the application of Davies) v Revenue and Customs Commissioners* [2010] EWCA Civ 83.

[294] National Insurance Decision No R(P) 1/72.

[295] *Grace v Revenue and Customs Commissioners* [2009] EWCA Civ 1082 [4].

[296] Ibid [6]–[7]; *R (on the application of Davies) v Revenue and Customs Commissioners* [2010] EWCA Civ 83[15].

[297] *Mark v Mark* [2005] UKHL 42 [31], [2006] 1 AC 98.

[298] *Shah v Barnet London Borough Council* [1983] 2 AC 309, 343–4, 349; *Mark v Mark*, supra, [32]. See also *R v Secretary of State for the Home Department, ex p Marguerrite* [1983] QB 180; British Nationality Act 1981, s 50(5) as amended by British Overseas Territories Act 2002, s 1(2); *Immigration Appeal Tribunal v Chelliah* [1985] Imm AR 192. On the lawfulness of a person's residence and the qualification to vote, see *Hipperson v Newbury District Electoral Registration Officer* [1985] QB 1060.

[299] *Mark v Mark* [2005] UKHL 42 [31], [2006] 1 AC 98. See for Canada, *Blair v Chung* (2006) 271 DLR (4th) 311, illegal residence can in some circumstances constitute ordinary residence.

[300] Ibid.

[301] Ibid, [32].

[302] *R (on the application of Tigere) v Secretary of State for Business, Innovation and Skills* [2015] UKSC 57 [43]–[46] and [56].

[303] *Mark v Mark* [2005] UKHL 42 [36].

[304] Ibid [45].

is due to some specific and unusual cause, as for instance when a wife accompanies her husband during his employment in a foreign country,[305] or a man is looking after his sick mother abroad.[306] Again, the significance of a comparatively prolonged absence will be weakened if, during the relevant period, the *propositus* has maintained a house or flat in England ready for immediate occupation.[307] However, a person who, after living in England for seven years, returned to Pakistan and then sought unsuccessfully to re-enter England over a six-year period was not ordinarily resident in England during that period.[308] The ordinary residence of a new-born baby necessarily has to be dependent on the residence of its mother.[309] The ordinary residence of a small child or an adult who is too handicapped to form an intention is prima facie that of the parents.[310]

(b) Habitual residence[311]

Habitual residence is predominantly a question of fact, therefore the concept can be easily manipulated by the courts. There are a number of factors a court can take into account when examining the question of habitual residence. The weight given to each factor will vary depending on the facts of the case and the area of law. Habitual residence is the main connecting factor in various EU Regulations,[312] and the CJEU has noted that the concept must be given an autonomous and uniform meaning throughout the EU in light of the objective of the legislation in question.[313]

The English courts have held that the concept of habitual residence should be treated consistently in respect of children,[314] and stated that "the test adopted by the European Court is preferable to that earlier adopted by the English courts".[315] In order for an individual to be habitually resident in a particular place or country there must be a degree of stability or regularity in their residence, in the sense that it must not be temporary or intermittent.[316] There is no need for permanence or an intention to reside indefinitely.[317] There must be some degree

---

[305] *Stransky v Stransky* [1954] P 428; *Lewis v Lewis* [1956] 1 WLR 200; *Shah v Barnet London Borough Council*, supra, at 343.

[306] *R v Secretary of State for the Home Department, ex p Zahir Chugtai* [1995] Imm AR 559.

[307] The *Stransky* case, supra; *Casey v Casey* 1968 SLT 56. But cf *Carmichael v Director-General of Social Welfare* [1994] 3 NZLR 477—keeping chattels in a room in a daughter's house.

[308] *R v Secretary of State for the Home Department, ex p Mohammed Butta* [1994] Imm AR 197.

[309] *C (A Child) v Plymouth County Council* [2000] 1 FLR 875, 879, CA.

[310] *R v Kent County Council, ex p S* [2000] 1 FLR 155.

[311] de Winter (1969) III Hague Recueil 357; Hall (1975) 24 ICLQ 1; Clive [1997] Jur Rev 137; Leslie 1996 SLT 145; Crawford [1992] Jur Rev 177 and [2000] Jur Rev 89; Rogerson (2000) 49 ICLQ 86; Stone (2000) 29 Anglo-Am LR 342; R George, 'Children's State of Mind and Habitual Residence in Abduction Cases' (2014) Journal of Social Welfare and Family Law 311; D Hill 'The Continuing Refinement of Habitual Residence: *R, Petitioner*' (2016) Edin L R 82 and see Council of Europe Resolution 72(1): Standardisation of the Legal Concepts of "Domicile" and "Residence".

[312] Such as Brussels II*bis* Arts 3 and 8; Council Regulation (EC) 4/2009 of 18 December 2008 on jurisdiction, applicable law, recognition and enforcement of decisions and cooperation in matters relating to maintenance obligations [2009] OJ l 7/1 (Maintenance Regulation) Art 3; Regulation (EU) No 650/2012 of the European Parliament and of the Council of 4 July 2012 on jurisdiction, applicable law, recognition and enforcement of decisions and acceptance and enforcement of authentic instruments in matters of succession and on the creation of a European Certificate of Succession (Succession Regulation) Art 4.

[313] Case C-523/07 *A* [2009] ECR I-2805 [34]–[35].

[314] *In the Matter of A (Children)* [2013] UKSC 60 [35], [54](ii) (Lady Hale); B [31].

[315] Ibid, [54](v).

[316] Case C-523/07 *A* [2009] ECR I-2805 [38]; Case C-497/10 PPU, *Mercredi v Chaffe* [2010] ECLI:EU:C:2010:829 [44], [49].

[317] *DL v EL* [2013] 2 FLR 163 [71] et seq; *In the Matter of A (Children)* [2013] UKSC 60 [51]; *AR v RN* [2015] UKSC 35 [16].

of integration into the social and family environment in the state,[318] and it is necessary to look at the whole factual situation including the reason why a person is an a particular place at a particular time.[319]

Habitual residence has also been described as the habitual centre of an adult's interests.[320] However, in *Mercredi* the CJEU held that the integration of a very young child into the social and family environment was to be determined in part by the integration of the adult into that social and family environment;[321] suggesting that an adult's "habitual centre of interests" can be determined by examining their degree of integration into the social and family environment in a particular state. When assessing the degree of integration it is relevant to take account of the person's state of mind at the relevant time,[322] in addition to the factual situation.

Habitual residence, under European law, differs from the concept of ordinary residence because a person can only have one habitual residence,[323] although they might have more than one ordinary residence. It is also likely that the term "habitual" connotes something different than ordinary residence, given the deliberate decision by the Law Commissions to use different terminology.[324] Recent jurisprudence indicates that the test developed in *Shah*[325] should be abandoned,[326] at least in respect of children,[327] and consigned to legal history.[328] Unlike domicile, it is possible for a person to have no habitual residence.[329] Whether a person is habitually resident in a particular country is predominantly a question of fact, to be decided by reference to all the circumstances of any particular case.[330] Habitual residence is a concept without the various legal artificialities of domicile, such as the doctrine of revival, and analogies with that concept are not appropriate.[331] Nonetheless, determination of

---

[318] Case C-523/07 *A* [2009] ECR I-2805 [38], [39], [44]; Case C-497/10 PPU *Mercredi v Chaffe* [2010] ECLI:EU:C:2010:829 [47]; *In the Matter of A (Children)* [2013] UKSC 60 [47]; *In the Matter of LC (Children)* [2014] UKSC 1 [34]; *In the Matter of B (A Child)* [2016] UKSC 4 [39].

[319] Case C-523/07 *A* [2009] ECR I-2805 [39]; Case C-497/10 PPU *Mercredi v Chaffe* [2010] ECLI:EU:C:2010:829 [48], [56]; *In the Matter of A (Children)* [2013] UKSC 60 [54].

[320] *Marinos v Marinos* [2007] EWHC 2047(Fam); *Tan v Choy* [2014] EWCA Civ 251 [29]; A Borras, 'Explanatory Report on the Convention on Jurisdiction and the Recognition and Enforcement of Judgments in Matrimonial Matters' [1998] OJ C 221/27 [32].

[321] *Mercredi v Chaffe* [2010] ECLI:EU:C:2010:829 [55].

[322] *In the Matter of LC (Children)* [2014] UKSC 1 [37] et seq.

[323] *Marinos v Marinos* [2007] EWHC 2047 (Fam) [40]–[41]; *Tan v Choy* [2014] EWCA Civ 251; *In the Matter of B (A Child)* [2016] UKSC 4 [45]. Cf *Ikimi v Ikimi* [2001] EWCA Civ 873.

[324] *In the Matter of A (Children)* [2013] UKSC 60 [38] (Lady Hale).

[325] *R v Barnet London Borough Council, ex p Shah* [1983] 2 AC 309.

[326] *In the Matter of A (Children)* [2013] UKSC 60 [54](v); *In the Matter of LC (Children)* [2014] UKSC 1 [30](ii).

[327] *In the Matter of A (Children)* [2013] UKSC 60 [54](v).

[328] *In the Matter of LC (Children)* [2014] UKSC 1 [37] (Lord Wilson).

[329] Case C-523/07 *A* [2009] ECR I-2805; Case C-497/10 PPU, Case C-497/10 PPU *Mercredi v Chaffe* [2010] ECLI:EU:C:2010:829; *In the Matter of A (Children)* [2013] UKSC 60. However it has since been stated that this should only happen in exceptional situations. *In the Matter of B (A Child)* [2016] UKSC 4 [42], [44] (Lord Wilson).

[330] *Re J (A Minor) (Abduction: Custody Rights)* [1990] 2 AC 562, 578 (Lord Brandon); *Re A (Minors) (Abduction: Habitual Residence)* [1996] 1 WLR 25; *Re A (Abduction: Habitual Residence)* [1998] 1 FLR 497; *Nessa v Chief Adjudication Officer* [1999] 1 WLR 1937, 1942; *Al Habtoor v Fotheringham* [2001] EWCA Civ 186, [2001] 1 FLR 951; *Mark v Mark* [2005] UKHL 42 [36], [2006] 1 AC 98; *In the Matter of A (Children)* [2013] UKSC 60 [54](i); *AR v RN* [2015] UKSC 35 [17]; *In the Matter of B (A Child)* [2016] UKSC 4 [46]. For Scotland see *Rellis v Hart* 1993 SLT 738; *Moran v Moran* 1997 SLT 541; *D v D* 2001 SLT 1104 [19], First Division. For New Zealand see *SK v KP* [2005] 3 NZLR 590, CA.

[331] *Re S (A Minor) (Abduction)* [1991] 2 FLR 1, 20, CA. See also *Re B (Minors) (Abduction) (No 2)* [1993] 1 FLR 993; *Al Habtoor v Fotheringham* [2001] EWCA Civ 186 [42], [2001] 1 FLR 951; *W and B v H (Child Abduction: Surrogacy)* [2002] 1 FLR 1008.

a person's habitual residence, particularly that of a child, has perhaps inevitably also become partly a question of law,[332] and the law on habitual residence has become increasingly complex. The burden of proof is upon the person seeking to show a change of habitual residence to establish this.[333]

(i) Acquisition of a new habitual residence

A new habitual residence can be acquired where there is a degree of integration into the social and family environment in the new state and presence in that state is not temporary or intermittent.[334]

(a) Residence

Before a child or adult can be habitually resident in a country he must be resident there.[335] This does not necessarily require physical presence at all times. Temporary absence, for example on holiday[336] or for educational purposes[337] or for an attempt to effect a reconciliation with an estranged spouse,[338] will not bring an end to habitual residence. Indeed it can continue despite considerable periods of absence.[339] In an extreme example, a petitioner was held to be habitually resident in England for the whole of the preceding year, despite spending 204 days of that year in a concurrent habitual residence in Nigeria.[340] A habitual residence in England has been held to continue despite a period of some two years and nine months residing in Hong Kong.[341] It has also been held that an adult will retain their habitual residence in state A when they are placed in a medical institution in state B as a result of a court order made in state A, reviewable by that court.[342] In *OL v QP* the CJEU held that the baby could not be considered to be habitually resident in Italy, a state she had never been present.[343] The fact that the baby had an uninterrrupted residence in Greece for several months, as agreed by the parents, meant that she could not be habitually resident in Italy despite the original intentions of the parents that the mother and baby would return to Italy a few months after the birth.[344]

Habitual residence for the purpose of divorce jurisdiction under section 5(2) of the Domicile and Matrimonial Proceedings Act 1973[345] need not be lawful residence and can be acquired by a person who is in England illegally.[346] However, it is a question of statutory construction

---

[332] *In the Matter of B (A Child)* [2016] UKSC 4 [57] (Lady Hale and Lord Toulson).

[333] *F v S (Wardship: Jurisdiction)* [1993] 2 FLR 686, CA. See also *Re E (Child: Abduction)* [1992] 1 FCR 541, CA (Parker LJ).

[334] Case C-523/07 *A* [2009] ECR I-2805 [38], [39], [44]; Case C-497/10 PPU *Mercredi v Chaffe* [2010] ECLI:EU:C:2010:829 [47]; *In the Matter of A (Children)* [2013] UKSC 60 [47]; *In the Matter of LC (Children)* [2014] UKSC 1 [34]; *In the Matter of B (A Child)* [2016] UKSC 4 [39].

[335] *Re M (Abduction: Habitual Residence)* [1996] 1 FLR 887, 895 (Sir John Balcombe), 896 (Millet LJ), CA.

[336] *Findlay v Findlay* 1994 SLT 709; *Rellis v Hart* 1993 SLT 738.

[337] *Re A (Wardship Jurisdiction)* [1995] 1 FLR 767.

[338] *Re B (Child Abduction: Habitual Residence)* [1994] 2 FLR 915; *H v H (Child Abduction: Stay of Proceedings)* [1994] 1 FLR 530.

[339] *Oundjian v Oundjian* (1979) 1 FLR 198, where over one-third of the period was spent abroad.

[340] *Ikimi v Ikimi* [2001] EWCA Civ 873, [2001] 3 WLR 672. Cf *Armstrong v Armstrong* [2003] EWHC 777 (Fam), [2003] 2 FLR 375.

[341] *C v FC (Brussels II: Free Standing Application For Parental Responsibility)* [2004] 1 FLR 317.

[342] *Re PA* [2016] Fam 47 [53]–[54].

[343] C-111/17, 8 June 2017, ECLI:EU:2017:436.

[344] Ibid [71] and see the Opionion of AG Wahl, ECLI:EU:C:2017:375, paras 17–31.

[345] Amended in the light of Council Regulation (EC) No 2201/2003 of 27 November 2003 concerning jurisdiction and the recognition and enforcement of judgments in matrimonial matters and the matters of parental responsibility OJ 2003 L 338/1 (Brussels II *bis*), discussed infra, pp 1002–5, which gives pre-eminence to the jurisdiction rules contained therein.

[346] *Mark v Mark* [2005] UKHL 42 [35], [2006] 1 AC 98; *Chai v Peng* [2014] EWHC 3518 (Fam) [27]–[28].

whether the word "lawfully" should be implied into a statutory provision which uses the concept of habitual residence.[347] There was no reason to imply this in the case of a statute dealing with divorce jurisdiction. Indeed, it is only right that persons with long-standing links with England should have their personal affairs dealt with in England and subject to English law.[348] This would not necessarily work to their benefit; it may be a disadvantage, so there is no question of benefiting from unlawful residence. But there are other statutory provisions, in particular those conferring entitlement to some benefit from the state where it would be proper to imply a requirement that the residence be lawful.[349] Even where the word "lawfully" cannot be implied into a statute, the fact that the residence is unlawful might still be relevant to the factual question of whether that residence is "habitual".[350] Thus a person who went on the run after a deportation order might find it hard to establish that the residence was habitual.[351]

(b) A period of time

In order for residence to be habitual there must be a stability in that residence and there must be a degree of integration into society in the place of that residence. The longer someone remains in a place then the deeper that integration is likely to be. However a variety of factors may affect the speed at which integration into the new state occurs, and therefore a new habitual residence can be established.[352] If the relevant factors make it clear that a degree of integration is relatively simple a new habitual residence could be gained relatively quickly. Lady Hale has stated that she "does not accept that it is impossible to become habitually resident in a single day".[353] In *Nessa v Chief Adjudication Officer*,[354] it was held that a woman who arrived in England from Bangladesh was not habitually resident for the purpose of entitlement to income support on the day that she arrived.[355] It follows that there may be a gap between habitual residence in one state and acquisition of habitual residence in another, but this should be the exception rather than the rule.[356] A person may have no habitual residence at all.[357] However, it may be that for the purposes of making particular legislation effective, an example being the founding of jurisdiction, it may be necessary that a person is habitually resident in some state. In other words there would not be a gap. A move in this regard, although what *In the Matter of B* may be understood as implying,[358] would be contentious because it removes the factual nature of the concept and may create tenuous links with a state; as the doctrine of revival does for domicile.[359] In *B* the majority were trying to enforce a policy argument and they adapted the concept of habitual residence to reach a desired result. The case involved a second female parent who had not sought a parental order, so she

---

[347] *Mark v Mark* [2005] UKHL 42 [31].

[348] Ibid, [31]–[34]. Cf the reasoning of the Court of Appeal, [2004] EWCA Civ 168, [2005] Fam 267, which was based on a denial of access to the English courts contrary to Art 6(1) of the ECHR.

[349] Ibid, [36]. See also the discussion in relation to ordinary residence, supra, p 174.

[350] Ibid.

[351] Ibid.

[352] *In the Matter of B (A Child)* [2016] UKSC 4 [46].

[353] *In the Matter of A (Children)* [2013] UKSC 60 [44]; *In the Matter of B (A Child)* [2016] UKSC 4 [76].

[354] [1999] 1 WLR 1937, HL; Crawford [2000] Jur Rev 89.

[355] Ibid.

[356] *In the Matter of B (A Child)* [2016] UKSC 4 [45], where Lord Wilson considers a change in habitual residence as akin to a "see-saw" effect.

[357] *Mark v Mark* [2005] UKHL 42 [37], [2006] 1 AC 98; Case C-523/07 *A* [2009] ECR I-2805; Case C-497/10 PPU *Mercredi v Chaffe* [2010] ECLI:EU:C:2010:829; *In the Matter of A (Children)* [2013] UKSC 60 [54]; *In the Matter of B (A Child)* [2016] UKSC 4. See also *SK v KP* [2005] 3 NZLR 590 [48], CA; *WP V FP* [2007] EWHC 779 (Fam), [2007] 2 FLR 129.

[358] *In the Matter of B (A Child)* [2016] UKSC 4 [67] et seq.

[359] *Barlow Clowes International Ltd v Henwood* [2008] EWCA Civ 577, discussed supra pp 163–4.

was not considered as a legal parent of the child and she did not have parental responsibility. The English courts sought to retain jurisdiction as it was unlikely that the courts in Pakistan would recognise any relationship between the applicant and the child.[360]

Courts should be wary of imposing an artificial habitual residence on individuals simply in order to make legislation effective, or to find an effective remedy for a particular party. The European Regulations, generally, provide additional bases of jurisdiction that can apply where the individual in question does not have a habitual residence, such as presence.[361] However the importance of context when determining the meaning of habitual residence is shown in *Swaddling v Adjudication Officer*,[362] where the European Court of Justice held that a community Regulation concerned with income support for employed persons precluded the United Kingdom from adopting a definition of habitual residence (on which entitlement to the benefit was based) that looked to the length of residence, requiring an appreciable period of residence.[363]

It is a question of fact whether and when the requisite period has been established. This depends very much on the circumstances of the particular case.[364] The requisite period is not a fixed one.[365] The period may in some circumstances be short.[366] Butler-Sloss LJ has said that a month can be sufficient for these purposes[367] and Lord Slynn has said that, if a person leaves one country to go to another with the established intention of settling there permanently, habitual residence may change very quickly.[368] In *V v B (A Minor) (Abduction)*[369] a habitual residence was acquired after less than three months' residence in Australia, the parties, according to the plaintiff, having decided to settle there. In *AR v RN* the children were found to be habitually resident in Scotland after spending five months there with their mother, notwithstanding the agreement between the mother and father that the move was for a temporary basis (twelve months).[370] This is consistent with the factual nature of habitual residence. It would have been artificial to find that the children had retained their French habitual residence during their period in Scotland when they had integrated into the new social environment within the five month period, and there was stability in their residence during that period. In *D v D* a few days was not enough.[371] In a difficult case, such as a local authority placing a child overseas without a final plan, even one or two years' residence may not be enough for losing an existing habitual residence and replacement by a new one abroad.[372] The position where someone is resuming a habitual residence that they previously had is different from that where they are coming to England for the first time.[373] It might still be possible for

---

[360] *In the Matter of B (A Child)* [2016] UKSC 4 [66] (Lord Sumption) dissenting.

[361] Art 13 Brussels II *bis*. The common law also provides other rules.

[362] Case C-90/97 [1999] ECR I-1075.

[363] Ibid, [30] and [34].

[364] *Nessa v Chief Adjudication Officer* [1999] 1 WLR 1937, 1942.

[365] Ibid, 1943. See *Cameron v Cameron* 1996 SLT 306, 313, no minimum period is required. Though see Brussels II *bis*, Art 3.1(a), indents 5 and 6, discussed infra, pp 956–8.

[366] *Nessa v Chief Adjudication Officer* [1999] 1 WLR 1937, 1943.

[367] *Re F (A Minor) (Child Abduction)* [1992] 1 FLR 548, 555, CA; *Re G (A Minor) (Enforcement of Access Abroad)* [1993] Fam 216, CA.

[368] *Re S (A Minor) (Custody: Habitual Residence)* [1998] AC 750, HL. See also *Re B (Minors) (Abduction) (No 2)* [1993] 1 FLR 993, 995.

[369] [1991] FCR 451, [1991] 1 FLR 266. See also *Re S (A Minor) (Abduction)* [1991] 2 FLR 1; *Cameron v Cameron* 1996 SLT 306. Cf *Adderson v Adderson* (1987) 36 DLR (4th) 631, Alberta CA—two short periods of a few months each not enough to establish a habitual residence in Hawaii.

[370] *AR v RN* [2015] UKSC 35.

[371] 2001 SLT 1104.

[372] *London Borough of Greenwich v Ms S, Mr A, B, C, D, E (by their Children's Guardian), Z* [2007] EWHC 820 (Fam), [2007] 2 FCR 141.

[373] *Nessa v Chief Adjudication Officer*, op cit, 1943, referring to Case C-90/97 *Swaddling v Adjudication Officer* [1999] ECR I-1075, ECJ.

an adult to have more than one habitual residence at a time,[374] where English common law is applicable. A person could be habitually resident in England for the whole of a one-year period despite also being habitually resident in another country.[375] However, in such a case the person must have spent an appreciable part of the year in England, 161 days being sufficient[376] and seventy-one days insufficient.[377] In the context of certain European Regulations a person can only have one habitual residence at a time,[378] and often these Regulations have 'universal application' so they can apply beyond intra-EU cases as long as, for example, one of the parties is habitually resident in an EU Member State.[379] A child can only ever have one habitual residence, regardless of the context, because it is desirable to have a uniform understanding of the concept.[380] Less dramatically, it is possible, for example, to be habitually resident for part of the year in London and for the rest of the year in Corfu.[381]

(c) The role of intentions when determining a factual concept

A person's state of mind is also relevant for determining whether they have acquired a habitual residence in a particular place.[382] This used to be described as a "settled intention" but the Supreme Court has since questioned the suitability of this term, because habitual residence is meant to be a question of fact.[383] Lady Hale has stated that habitual residence is "not a matter of intention: one does not acquire a habitual residence merely by intending to do so; nor does one fail to acquire one merely by not intending to do so".[384] Despite this subjective factors are still one of many relevant factors when determining habitual residence, such as an individual's perception of being in a place or their state of mind while being there.[385] However terms like "'wishes', 'views', 'intentions' and 'decisions' are not the right words, whether we are considering the habitual residence of a child or indeed an adult".[386] It is unclear what relevance "settled intention" currently has because in *B* the term was revived; Lord Wilson's judgment suggesting that an adult can still form a settled intention,[387] but this will not be determinative of a child's habitual residence.[388]

The question of a person's state of mind, or perceptions, is relevant in the assessment of whether that person has a sufficient degree of integration in the social and family environment

---

[374] *Mark v Mark* [2005] UKHL 42 [37], [2006] 1 AC 98; *Ikimi v Ikimi* [2001] EWCA Civ 873, [2001] 3 WLR 672; *Breuning v Breuning* [2002] EWHC 236 (Fam), [2002] 1 FLR 888, 900; *M v H* [2005] EWHC 1186 (Fam). Cf *Marinos v Marinos* [2007] EWHC 2047 (Fam) [40]–[41]; *Tan v Choy* [2014] EWCA Civ 251. Cf also the position in Scotland: *Dickson v Dickson* 1990 SCLR 692, 703; *Findlay v Findlay* 1994 SLT 709; *Cameron v Cameron* 1996 SLT 306. Cf Blom (1973) 22 ICLQ 109, 136; Clive [1997] Jur Rev 137, 144; Leslie 1996 SLT 145, 147–8.

[375] *Ikimi v Ikimi* [2001] EWCA Civ 873, [2001] 3 WLR 672. See also *C v FC (Brussels II: Free Standing Application For Parental Responsibility)* [2004] 1 FLR 317.

[376] *Ikimi v Ikimi*, supra.

[377] *Armstrong v Armstrong* [2003] EWHC 777 (Fam).

[378] *Marinos v Marinos* [2007] EWHC 2047 (Fam) [40]–[41]; *Tan v Choy* [2014] EWCA Civ 251.

[379] See infra Chapter 24.

[380] *In the Matter of A (Children)* [2013] UKSC 60 [35].

[381] *Re V (Abduction: Habitual Residence)*, supra; *Re A (Abduction: Habitual Residence)* [1998] 1 FLR 497, 505.

[382] *In the Matter of LC (Children)* [2014] UKSC 1 [37] et seq.

[383] Ibid.

[384] Ibid [59].

[385] Ibid [37] et seq (Lord Wilson); [60] (Lady Hale).

[386] Ibid [60] (Lady Hale). Although Lady Hale is dissenting she agrees with the key factors behind Lord Wilson's leading judgment and the shift of focus to state of mind. She disagrees that this should only apply to adults and adolescents, considering that younger children's states of mind could also be considered [61].

[387] *In the Matter of B (A Child)* [2016] UKSC 4[1], [36], [38].

[388] Ibid [47].

in that state,[389] or has the "habitual centre of their interests" there. Thus if a person's mind is somewhat absent from the new environment, still yearning for a previous residence, this will affect their degree of integration in the new state despite objective factors which suggest integration. In essence habitual residence as a question of fact is a very malleable concept and judges can give importance to different factors depending on the circumstances of the case, and the result that they wish to achieve.

A move can be for a limited period.[390] The period may be limited by the immediate purpose such as employment, even short-term employment of no more than six months.[391] A person can be habitually resident in a country even though he intends at some future date to move to another country.[392] For example, a serviceman who is posted abroad, anticipating at least a three-year stay, can acquire a habitual residence there.[393] A move on a trial or temporary basis can result in a new habitual residence.[394] However where an individual's "mind was in a state of rebellious turmoil that would be inconsistent with any degree of integration on her part".[395]

Where there is a long period of residence in a particular state the objective facts will then point to this being the habitual residence.[396] The objective facts spoke for themselves where a child had been in a country for fifteen months.[397] In relation to the new terminology, a person is likely to have a greater degree of integration into the social and family environment the longer he remains in the new state, unless their state of mind suggests otherwise. Conversely, if the residence has been for a short period only, their state of mind, or the degree of integration reflected by all the relevant facts, becomes crucial.

(d) Voluntarily

There is a further requirement in relation to adults that the residence must have been voluntary.[398] A serviceman who is stationed on a base abroad can be regarded as voluntarily resident in that country (he could have left the armed forces if he did not want to accept the posting) and, having made the family home there, he and his family will take this country as their habitual residence.[399]

---

[389] *In the Matter of LC (Children)* [2014] UKSC 1 [39].

[390] *Moran v Moran* [1997] SLT 541; *Al Habtoor v Fotheringham* [2001] EWCA Civ 186 [37], [2001] 1 FLR 951; *Re R (Abduction: Habitual Residence)* [2003] EWHC 1968 (Fam), [2004] 1 FLR 216; *AR v RN* [2015] UKSC 35.

[391] *Re R (Abduction: Habitual Residence)* supra.

[392] *M v M (Abduction: England and Scotland)* [1997] 2 FLR 263, CA.

[393] *Re A (Abduction: Habitual Residence)* [1996] 1 FLR 1.

[394] *Al Habtoor v Fotheringham* [2001] EWCA Civ 186, [2001] 1 FLR 951; *Cameron v Cameron* 1996 SC 17; *M, Petitioner* 2005 SLT 2; *AR v RN* [2015] UKSC 35. Cf *Re N (Abduction: Habitual Residence)* [2000] 2 FLR 899.

[395] *In the Matter of LC (Children)* [2014] UKSC 1 [37].

[396] *Zenel v Haddow* 1993 SLT 975; 1993 SCLR 872. See also *Leslie* 1996 SLT 145, 147. But see *M v M (Abduction: England v Scotland)* [1997] 2 FLR 263, 267 (Butler-Sloss LJ)—two years was not necessarily conclusive of habitual residence. See also *Breuning v Breuning* [2002] EWHC 236 (Fam), [2002] 1 FLR 888, 899—evidence going back over a long period of time should be discouraged.

[397] *Zenel v Haddow*, supra.

[398] *Shah v Barnet London Borough Council* [1983] 2 AC 309, 342; *Nessa v Chief Adjudication Officer* [1999] 1 WLR 1937, 1943, HL; *M v M (Abduction: England and Scotland)*, supra; *Ikimi v Ikimi* [2001] EWCA Civ 873 [34], [2001] 3 WLR 672. But cf *Cameron v Cameron* 1996 SLT 306, 311; Clive [1997] Jur Rev 137, 141; Leslie 1996 SLT 145, 146; Crawford and Carruthers, para 6-43.

[399] *Re A (Minors) (Abduction: Habitual Residence)* [1996] 1 WLR 25, 32–3.

(ii) Abandonment

A person can cease to be habitually resident in a country in a single day if he or she leaves it with a settled intention not to return to it but to take up long-term residence in another country instead.[400] For example in *Moran v Moran*[401] the parents, who were habitually resident in California, agreed that the mother and child should return to Scotland for a year, whilst the father remained in California to deal with business problems. It was held that the child's habitual residence ceased as from the date of departure from California. However, habitual residence in one jurisdiction does not necessarily come to an end merely because the person concerned leaves for a short period or for a temporary purpose,[402] such as formal education.[403] The abandonment of a habitual residence can take place without acquisition of another habitual residence elsewhere,[404] with the inevitable result that a person has no habitual residence.[405]

(iii) Children[406]

The habitual residence of a child is not fixed and can change when their family, or primary carer, moves. However, as discussed above, the child itself would have to be integrated into the new social and family environment, as determined by all relevant objective and subjective facts, before gaining a new habitual residence.[407] If the parents are living together and the child is living with them, the child will most likely take the parents' habitual residence.[408] This is particularly true in the case of very young children, who are wholly dependent on their primary carer.[409] Older children can obtain a habitual residence which is independent of their primary carer.[410] There is authority to the effect that a newborn child takes this habitual residence immediately on birth, rather than having to reside for an appreciable period in that country before doing so.[411]

If both parents have joint parental responsibility, neither parent can unilaterally change the child's habitual residence by removing or retaining it wrongfully and in breach of the other party's rights.[412] A father can, for example, consent to the child being with the mother and

---

[400] *Re J (A Minor) (Abduction: Custody Rights)* [1999] 1 WLR 1937 578 (Lord Brandon). See also *Re M (Minors) (Residence Order: Jurisdiction)* [1993] 1 FLR 495, 501, CA; *F v F (Abduction: Habitual Residence)* [1993] Fam Law 199; *Re N (Abduction: Habitual Residence)* [2000] 2 FLR 899; *Al Habtoor v Fotheringham* [2001] EWCA Civ 186 [25], [2001] 1 FLR 951.

[401] 1997 SLT 541.

[402] *Rellis v Hart* 1993 SLT 738, 741.

[403] *P v P* [2006] EWHC 2410 (Fam), [2007] 2 FLR 439.

[404] *Re M (Abduction: Habitual Residence)* [1996] 1 FLR 887; *WP v FP* [2007] EWHC 779 (Fam), [2007] 2 FLR 129.

[405] *Mark v Mark* [2005] UKHL 42 [37], [2006] 1 AC 98; *In the Matter of A (Children)* [2013] UKSC 60 [54]; *In the Matter of B (A Child)* [2016] UKSC 4. See supra pp 178–9.

[406] Crawford [1992] Jur Rev 177; Stone (1992) 4 JCL 170.

[407] Case C-523/07 *A* [2009] ECR I-2805 [38], [39], [44]; *Mercredi v Chaffe* [2010] ECLI:EU:C:2010:829 [47]; *In the Matter of A (Children)* [2013] UKSC 60 [47]; *In the Matter of LC (Children)* [2014] UKSC 1 [34]; *In the Matter of B (A Child)* [2016] UKSC 4 [39].

[408] *Re A (Minors) (Abduction: Habitual Residence)* [1996] 1 WLR 25.

[409] *Mercredi v Chaffe* [2010] ECLI:EU:C:2010:829.

[410] *In the Matter of LC (Children)* [2014] UKSC 1.

[411] *B v H (Habitual Residence: Wardship)* [2002] 1 FLR 388, 403; *PAS v AFS* [2005] 1 ILRM 306, 317, SC of Ireland. See also Clive [1997] Jur Rev 137, 146. Cf *In the Matter of A (Children)* [2013] UKSC 60.

[412] *Re M (Abduction: Habitual Residence)* [1996] 1 FLR 887, 896, (Millet LJ), CA. See also *H v H (Child Abduction: Stay of Domestic Proceedings)* [1994] 1 FLR 530; *Re S (Minors) (Abduction: Wrongful Retention)* [1994] Fam 70; *Findlay v Findlay* 1994 SLT 709; *Findlay v Findlay (No 2)* 1995 SLT 492; *Moran v Moran* 1997 SLT 541; *Re B (Abduction: Children's Objections)* [1998] 1 FLR 667; *Re N (Abduction: Habitual Residence)* [2000] 2 FLR 899; *B v H (Habitual Residence: Wardship)* [2002] 1 FLR 388.

therefore to a change of habitual residence.[413] However if the father simply consented to a move by the mother and children for a limited period, this would not prevent a change in the children's habitual residence if the facts suggested it had changed in that time and the children were integrated into their new environment.[414] The father's "intentions" as to the children's habitual residence are irrelevant. A court order determining rights of residence and custody can also change the child's habitual residence.[415] However, commonsense would suggest that if, for example, a child has been living with its mother for ten years it would take the same habitual residence as the mother, even though during this period the mother has been acting in defiance of a court order to return the child.[416] A child subject to a supervision requirement probably remains habitually resident at the home of his or her parent.[417]

Generally before a child can be habitually resident in a country it must be resident there.[418] Thus for a child's habitual residence to change to that of another country the child has to leave the country in which he is resident and reside in that other country.[419] The previous two sentences should not be regarded as statements of law but rather as assertions of fact.

If a child has been made a ward of court, a parent cannot then change its habitual residence without leave of the court.[420]

(iv) Does habitual residence have different meanings in different contexts?

It is likely that habitual residence can have slightly different meanings in different contexts where required by statute. The CJEU has held that the meaning of habitual residence needs to be interpreted within the context of the objective pursued by the particular legislation in question.[421]

In recent years the case law on the habitual residence of children has developed significantly. It is clear that the habitual residence of children has the same meaning regardless of the context and this is predominantly derived from the case law of the CJEU.[422] This does not create any difficulties in the context of child abduction because you simply look to the habitual residence prior to the removal rather than a new habitual residence. The same factors can be used to determine whether a child was or is habitually resident in a place. However this wealth of case law from the Supreme Court has caused some difficulty because the court has rejected previous case law, which relates to both children and adults. It is unclear whether this rejection of the earlier case law is just in the context of children, meaning that habitual residence has a different meaning for children than it does for adults, or if the rejection goes further than this. *In LC* Lord Wilson suggested the latter, stating that *Shah* should be consigned to legal history.[423] Unfortunately there has been limited case law on the habitual residence of adults, in recent times, so the concept has not developed in the same manner in this context.

---

[413] *Re F (A Minor) (Child Abduction)* [1992] 1 FLR 548, CA; *Re H (Abduction: Habitual Residence: Consent)* [2000] 2 FLR 294; *D v D* 2001 SLT 1104 [27]–[28] (Lord Carloway), overturned by the First Division without discussion of this point; *C v FC (Brussels II: Free Standing Application For Parental Responsibility)* [2004] 1 FLR 317.

[414] *AR v RN* [2015] UKSC 35.

[415] *Re F (A Minor) (Child Abduction)* supra; *Re S (Minors) (Abduction: Wrongful Retention)* [1994] Fam 70.

[416] *Re B (Abduction: Children's Objections)* [1998] 1 FLR 667, 671. See also Clive [1997] Jur Rev 137, 145. However this is somewhat diluted by Brussels II*bis* Art 11(6)-(8), infra pp 1159–62.

[417] *Glasgow City Council v M* 2001 SLT 396, 400.

[418] *Re M (Abduction: Habitual Residence)* [1996] 1 FLR 887, 895 (Sir John Balcombe), CA.

[419] Ibid (disapproving of *Re A (Wardship: Jurisdiction)* [1995] 1 FLR 767, 773). See also *Re F (Abduction: Unborn Child)* [2006] EWHC 2199 (Fam), [2007] 1 FLR 627.

[420] *Re B-M (Wardship Jurisdiction)* [1993] 1 FLR 979; *Re W: Re B (Child Abduction: Unmarried Father)* [1998] 2 FLR 146, 159.

[421] Case C-523/07 *A* [2009] ECR I-2805 [34]–[35].

[422] *In the Matter of A (Children)* [2013] UKSC 60.

[423] *In the Matter of LC (Children)* [2014] UKSC 1 [37] (Lord Wilson).

In *Mark v Mark* Baroness Hale, stated that "habitual residence may have a different meaning in different statutes according to their context and purpose".[424] This difference in meaning in different contexts comes out in two different aspects of the concept of habitual residence. First, it comes out in relation to whether there is a requirement that the residence must be lawful. As has been seen,[425] this does indeed depend on the statute and its context and purpose. Secondly, it comes out in relation to the requisite period of residence. Normally, there can be a gap between habitual residence in one state and acquisition of habitual residence in another. However, it may be that for the purposes of making particular legislation effective, an example being the founding of jurisdiction, it may be necessary that a person is habitually resident in some state and so there will be no gap. This departs from evaluating habitual residence as a matter of fact, therefore judges should be very cautious of this approach. Removing the gap between habitual residences, in certain cases, will result in habitual residence becoming a legal, and sometimes artificial construct, like domicile. Although habitual residence is subject to manipulation as a factual construct, adding an artificial legal gloss will also create difficulties when it is clear from the facts of the case that the individual is habitually resident in a different state or nowhere at all.

---

[424] [2005] UKHL 42 [15], [37], [2006] 1 AC 98.
[425] Supra, pp 177–8.

PART III

JURISDICTION, FOREIGN JUDGMENTS AND AWARDS

10. Jurisdiction of the English Courts—An Introduction   187
11. Jurisdiction Under the Brussels/Lugano System   191
12. The Competence of the English Courts Under—
    The Traditional Rules   323
13. Stays and the Management of Parallel Proceedings   391
14. Limitations on Jurisdiction   483
15. Recognition and Enforcement of Foreign Judgments
    and Arbitral Awards in England—An Introduction   520
16. Recognition and Enforcement of Foreign
    Judgments—The Traditional Rules   525
17. Recognition and Enforcement of Judgments
    Under the Brussels/Lugano System   608
18. Foreign Arbitral Awards   666

10

JURISDICTION OF THE ENGLISH COURTS—AN INTRODUCTION

1. Jurisdiction Under the Brussels/Lugano System	187	3. Jurisdiction Under the Traditional Rules	189
(a) The Brussels I Regulation and Brussels I Recast	187	(a) Whether the English courts have power to hear the case	190
(b) The EC/Denmark Agreement	188	(b) Whether the court will decline jurisdiction or stay the proceedings, or restrain foreign proceedings	190
(c) The Brussels Convention	188		
(d) The Lugano Convention	189	(c) Whether there is a limitation upon the exercise of jurisdiction	190
2. Jurisdiction Under the Modified Regulation	189	4. The Hague Convention on Choice of Court Agreements	190

"Jurisdiction" is a word susceptible of several different meanings, but in the present account it is used to refer to the question of whether an English court will hear and determine an issue upon which its decision is sought.[1] The position is complicated by the fact that there are numerous separate sets of rules determining the jurisdiction of English courts. First, there are four different sets of rules under the Brussels/Lugano system, ie the rules contained in the Brussels I Regulation as amended in the Brussels I Recast, the EC/Denmark Agreement, the Brussels Convention, and the Lugano Convention. Second, there are the rules contained in a modified version of the Brussels I Regulation (the Modified Regulation), giving effect to the Regulation as between the component legal orders of the United Kingdom. Third, there are the traditional English rules on jurisdiction. Fourth, there are the rules in the Hague Convention on Choice of Court Agreements 2005, which the European Union has ratified on behalf of all the Member States (except Denmark).

1. JURISDICTION UNDER THE BRUSSELS/LUGANO SYSTEM

(a) The Brussels I Regulation and Brussels I Recast

The Brussels I Regulation was adopted in 2001, to replace the earlier Brussels Convention (discussed below). For proceedings commenced on or after 10 January 2015, the Brussels

---

[1] *Tehrani v Secretary of State for the Home Department* [2006] UKHL 47 at [66] (per Lord Scott, [2007] 1 AC 521; *Fourie v Le Roux* [2007] UKHL 1 at [25] (per Lord Scott, [2007] 1 WLR 320.

I Regulation has been replaced by the Brussels I Recast. In broad terms, the rules on jurisdiction contained in the Brussels I Recast apply where:

(a) the matter is within the scope of the Brussels I Recast (most civil and commercial matters); and

(b) the defendant is domiciled in a European Union Member State, apart from Denmark (ie in Austria, Belgium, Bulgaria, Croatia, Cyprus,[2] the Czech Republic, Estonia, Finland, France, Germany, Greece, Hungary, Ireland, Italy, Latvia, Lithuania, Luxembourg, Malta, the Netherlands, Poland, Portugal, Romania, Slovakia, Slovenia, Spain, Sweden and the United Kingdom). Even if the defendant is not so domiciled, certain provisions in the Brussels I Recast will still apply, eg where the case involves title to land in a Member State or where there is an agreement conferring jurisdiction on the courts of a Member State.

The Brussels I Regulation and Brussels I Recast are discussed in Chapter 11, aside from those aspects dealing with stays and the management of parallel proceedings, which are discussed in Chapter 13.

(b) The EC/Denmark Agreement

In broad terms, the rules on jurisdiction contained in the EC/Denmark Agreement apply where:

(a) the matter is within the scope of the Brussels I Recast (most civil and commercial matters); and

(b) the defendant is domiciled in Denmark. Even if the defendant is not so domiciled, certain provisions in the Brussels I Recast will still apply, eg where the case involves title to land in Denmark or where there is an agreement conferring jurisdiction on the courts of Denmark.

The EC/Denmark Agreement initially applied by international law the provisions of the Brussels I Regulation, with minor amendments. Pursuant to the Agreement, Denmark has formally decided to apply the Brussels I Recast.[3] Accordingly, the EC/Denmark agreement is also discussed in Chapter 11.

(c) The Brussels Convention

In broad terms, the rules on jurisdiction contained in the Brussels Convention are applied where:

(a) the matter is within the scope of the Convention (most civil and commercial matters); and

(b) the defendant is domiciled in one of the territories of the Contracting States[4] which fall within the territorial scope of the Brussels Convention and are excluded from the Brussels I Regulation and Brussels I Recast.[5] The territories in question are (in relation to France) the French overseas territories, such as New Caledonia and Mayotte, and (in relation to the Netherlands) Aruba.[6] Even if the defendant is not so domiciled, certain provisions in the Convention will still apply, eg where the case involves title to land in one of the French overseas territories or Aruba, or where there is an agreement conferring jurisdiction on the courts of one of the French overseas territories or Aruba.

---

[2] Including the territory of the so-called 'Turkish Republic of Northern Cyprus': *Apostolides* [2009] EUECJ C-420/07; Hartley (2009) 58 ICLQ 1013; De Baere (2010) 47 CMLR 1123.

[3] OJ 2013 L 79/4.

[4] At the moment the Contracting States to the Brussels Convention are the original fifteen Member States.

[5] Art 68(1). Territories are excluded from the Brussels I Regulation and Brussels I Recast pursuant to Art 299 of the EC Treaty.

[6] See Layton and Mercer, paras 11.061–11.071. See also Kruger, paras 1.026–1.037.

The Brussels Convention is discussed in Chapter 11.

(d) The Lugano Convention

In broad terms, the rules on jurisdiction contained in the Lugano Convention are applied in the United Kingdom and in other European Union Member States where:

(a) the matter is within the scope of the Convention (most civil and commercial matters); and

(b) the defendant is domiciled in an EFTA State other than Liechtenstein[7] (ie Iceland, Norway or Switzerland).[8] Even if the defendant is not so domiciled, certain provisions in the Convention will still apply, eg where the case involves title to land in an EFTA State other than Liechtenstein or where there is an agreement conferring jurisdiction on the courts of an EFTA State other than Liechtenstein.

The terms of the Lugano Convention have been aligned with those of the Brussels I Regulation (but not, at present, the Brussels I Recast) and are accordingly also discussed in detail in Chapter 11.

2. JURISDICTION UNDER THE MODIFIED REGULATION

The Civil Jurisdiction and Judgments Act 1982 applies a modified version of the Brussels I Regulation in cases where:

(a) the matter is within the scope of the Brussels I Regulation (most civil and commercial matters); and

(b) the defendant is domiciled in the United Kingdom or the proceedings are of a kind where jurisdiction is allocated to the courts of a part of the United Kingdom regardless of domicile, eg the case involves title to land in part of the United Kingdom.

The modified version of the Brussels I Regulation rules serves to allocate jurisdiction between the component legal orders of the United Kingdom (England and Wales, Scotland, and Northern Ireland). Because of its close links with the Brussels I Regulation, the Modified Regulation is also discussed in detail in Chapter 11.

3. JURISDICTION UNDER THE TRADITIONAL RULES

The traditional rules on jurisdiction are still applicable, in practical terms,[9] in cases falling outside the Brussels/Lugano system and the Modified Regulation. Before the advent of the Brussels/Lugano system and the Modified Regulation the traditional rules were applied in all cases, and their historical roots make it appropriate to refer to them as the traditional rules.

---

[7] Liechtenstein became an EFTA State in 1991, but has not become a party to the Lugano Convention.

[8] It is possible for non-EFTA/European Union States to become parties to the Convention.

[9] In terms of theory the position is more difficult since Art 6 of the Brussels I Recast provides that, if the defendant is not domiciled in a Member State, the jurisdiction of the courts of each Member state shall, subject to Arts 18(1), 21(2), 24 and 25, be determined by the national private international law rules of that Member State. This has led to the idea that there is only one source of jurisdiction rules, namely the Brussels I Recast (and previously the Brussels I Regulation), at least for cases falling within its scope. See Opinion of the Court of Justice 1/03 Competence of the Community to conclude the new Lugano Convention [2006] ECR-I1145 at para 148 and generally Kruger, paras 1.052–1.057.

Jurisdiction under the traditional rules involves three major issues:

(a) Whether the English courts have power to hear the case

As will be seen in Chapter 12, the competence of the courts to hear a case is a procedural matter and is dependent on the service of a claim form on the defendant. A claim form can be served on the defendant if he is present within the jurisdiction, if he submits to the jurisdiction of the English courts, or if the courts authorise service of a claim form out of the jurisdiction under rule 6.36 and Practice Direction 6B of the Civil Procedure Rules. Whether a court will permit service out of the jurisdiction is a matter of discretion pursuant to the doctrine of *forum conveniens*.

(b) Whether the court will decline jurisdiction or stay the proceedings, or restrain foreign proceedings

Notwithstanding that it is competent to hear the case, the court can decline jurisdiction or stay the proceedings in cases where the doctrine of *forum non conveniens* applies or where a decision to proceed with the case would be contrary to an exclusive jurisdiction clause, and the court must decline jurisdiction if proceeding would be contrary to an arbitration clause. The courts' powers to refuse to exercise jurisdiction will be discussed in Chapter 13. If the English courts determine that they should exercise jurisdiction, the courts may issue an anti-suit injunction to restrain a party from commencing or continuing foreign proceedings—the circumstances in which such an order can and will be made are also discussed in Chapter 13.

(c) Whether there is a limitation upon the exercise of jurisdiction

Even where there has been service of process, the jurisdiction of the courts is subject to certain limitations, the effect of which is to render the court incompetent to determine the issue. These limitations relate to the subject matter of the issue (eg the case involves foreign land); the kind of relief sought (eg the case involves granting a divorce); and the persons between whom the issue is joined (eg the defendant is a foreign sovereign state). There are also certain statutory limitations on jurisdiction which derive from international conventions (eg the case involves international carriage by air). These limitations will be discussed in Chapter 14.

4. THE HAGUE CONVENTION ON CHOICE OF COURT AGREEMENTS

In 2015, the European Union ratified the Hague Convention on Choice of Court Agreements 2005, both in its own right and on behalf of each of the Member States (excluding Denmark). The Convention overrides both European Union and national law rules of jurisdiction to the extent of any inconsistency, although does not affect the Brussels I Recast for disputes which are internal to the European Union. The purpose of the Convention is to give greater effectiveness to jurisdiction agreements in favour of the courts of Convention states. At present, Mexico and Singapore have also ratified the Convention, and the USA and Ukraine have signed but not yet ratified. Although not strictly part of the Brussels/Lugano System, the Convention forms part of European Union law on jurisdiction and is therefore also discussed in Chapter 11.

11

JURISDICTION UNDER THE BRUSSELS/LUGANO SYSTEM

1. Introduction	191	5. The Lugano Convention	313
2. History and Interpretation	191	(a) When does the Lugano Convention	
(a) Emergence of the Brussels/Lugano		apply?	313
System and the Modified Regulation	191	(b) The terms of the Lugano Convention	314
(b) Interpretation of the Brussels/Lugano		(c) Stays of action	314
system and the Modified Regulation	194	6. The Hague Convention on Choice	
3. The Brussels I Recast	198	of Court Agreements	315
(a) A special definition of domicile	198	7. Allocating Jurisdiction within the	
(b) When does the Brussels I Recast apply?	202	United Kingdom: The Modified	
(c) Bases of jurisdiction	216	Regulation	317
(d) Provisional measures	303	(a) When does the Modified Regulation	
(e) Service and notice of the claim	308	apply?	317
(f) Stays and parallel proceedings	311	(b) The terms of the Modified Regulation	319
4. The Brussels Convention	312	(c) Stays of action	321

1. INTRODUCTION

This chapter examines jurisdiction under the Brussels/Lugano system (ie the Brussels I Recast, the EC/Denmark Agreement, the Brussels Convention, and the Lugano Convention) and under the Modified Regulation, which deals with the allocation of jurisdiction within the United Kingdom. It also considers the effect of the Hague Convention on Choice of Court Agreements, which has been ratified by the European Union on its own behalf and on behalf of each of the Member States (except Denmark).

2. HISTORY AND INTERPRETATION

(a) Emergence of the Brussels/Lugano System and the Modified Regulation

One of the key pillars of European Union private international law is the effort to unify jurisdiction rules in civil and commercial matters and to ensure rapid and simple recognition and enforcement of judgments given in Member States. The current version of the EU rules on these matters is set out in the Brussels I Recast,[1] which applies to proceedings commenced on

---

[1] Regulation (EU) No 1215/2012 of the European Parliament and of the Council of 12 December 2012 on jurisdiction and the recognition and enforcement of judgments in civil and commercial matters OJ 2012 L 351/1, amended by Regulation (EU) No 542/2014 of the European Parliament and of the Council of 15 May 2014 as regards the rules to be applied with respect to the Unified Patent Court and the Benelux Court of Justice OJ 2014 L 163/1, and Commission Delegated Regulation (EU) 2015/281 of 26 November 2014 replacing Annexes I and II OJ 2015 L 54/1. See generally Dickinson and Lein (eds), *Brussels I Regulation Recast* (2015); Fentiman, *International Commercial Litigation* (2015) 2nd edn; Briggs, *Civil Jurisdiction and Judgments* (2015) 6th edn; Briggs, *Private International Law in English Courts* (2014); Magnus and Mankowski (eds), *Brussels Ibis Regulation* (2015) 3rd edn; Wilke (2015) J Priv Int L 128.

or after 10 January 2015.[2] References in this chapter are to the rules in the Brussels I Recast, unless otherwise specified. The Brussels I Recast replaced the Brussels I Regulation,[3] which itself had come into force on 1 March 2002.[4]

The Brussels I Recast directly applies in all the EU Member States,[5] with the exception of Denmark.[6] However, under the EC/Denmark Agreement[7] the provisions of the Brussels I Regulation, with minor modifications, were applied by international law to the relations between the European Union and Denmark. For the purposes of the Agreement the application of the provisions of the Regulation were modified, but there were no modifications in relation to Chapter II (Jurisdiction) of the Regulation.[8] Pursuant to the Agreement, Denmark has now agreed to apply the Brussels I Recast.[9]

The Brussels I Regulation was based on, and updated, the earlier Brussels Convention,[10] which it replaced in virtually all cases.[11] That Convention came into force in 1973 and applied (as an additional treaty arrangement) as between the original six members of the European Economic Community. The Brussels Convention was subsequently amended by four separate Accession Conventions, as the then European Community was enlarged.[12]

---

[2] Arts 66 and 81.

[3] Council Regulation (EC) No 44/2001 of 22 December 2000 on jurisdiction and the recognition and enforcement of judgments in civil and commercial matters OJ 2001 L 12/1. For commentaries see Briggs and Rees, *Civil Jurisdiction and Judgments* (2009) 5th edn; Layton and Mercer, Vol 1, chapters 11–23; Dicey, Morris and Collins, paras 11-001R–11-100 and 11R-247–11-417; Magnus and Mankowski (eds), *Brussels I Regulation* (2012) 2nd edn; Ancel (2001) 3 YBPIL 101; Hartley (2006) 319 Hague Recueil 9, ch VI. The Regulation is referred to as "Brussels I" to avoid confusing it with "Brussels II", ie Council Regulation (EC) No 1347/2000 of 29 May 2000 on jurisdiction and the recognition and enforcement of judgments in matrimonial matters and in matters of parental responsibility for children of both spouses OJ 2000 L 160; replaced by Council Regulation (EC) No 2201/2003 of 27 November 2003 concerning jurisdiction and the recognition and enforcement of judgments in matrimonial matters and the matters of parental responsibility OJ 2003 L 338/1 (Brussels II *bis*); discussed infra, pp 954–64 and 1002–5.

[4] Art 76.

[5] The United Kingdom and Ireland "opted in" to the Brussels I Regulation and Brussels I Recast, in accordance with Art 3 of the Protocol (No 21) on the position of the United Kingdom and Ireland in respect of the area of freedom, security and justice annexed to the Treaty on European Union. If or when the United Kingdom leaves the European Union in light of the June 2016 "Brexit" referendum, all EU law instruments including the Brussels I Recast will no longer apply in the UK. The negotiations over the terms of Brexit may lead to a variety of potential outcomes, including a fall back to the common law jurisdictional rules examined in Chapter 12, accession to the 2007 Lugano Convention (see infra, p 313), and/or accession to the Hague Convention on Choice of Court Agreements (see infra, p 315). See generally Dickinson (2016) 12 J Priv Int L 195.

[6] See the Protocol (No 22) on the position of Denmark (the Danish opt-out) annexed to the Treaty on European Union.

[7] OJ 2005 L 299/61. For consequential amendments in the UK see SI 2007/1655. Prior to the entry into force of this Agreement, the Brussels Convention applied in relation to Denmark.

[8] Art 2(2). The modifications related to: Ch III (Recognition and Enforcement), Art 50 (legal aid and decisions given by an administrative authority in Denmark in respect of maintenance); Ch V (General Provisions), Art 62 (in matters relating to maintenance, court to include Danish administrative authorities; Art 64 (notification of consular officer in certain disputes involving ships registered in Denmark); Ch VI (Transitional Provisions), Art 66; Relations with Other Instruments (Ch VII), Arts 70(2), 72; (Ch VIII) Final Provisions, Art 76; and Annexes I,II, III and IV.

[9] OJ 2013 L 79/4.

[10] Convention on Jurisdiction and the Enforcement of Judgments in Civil and Commercial Matters of 1968. There was also a Protocol on Interpretation in 1971, which came into force in 1975. Both the original Convention and the Protocol are to be found in OJ 1978 L 304/77 and 97.

[11] Art 68(1) of the Brussels I Regulation and now Brussels I Recast.

[12] These are as follows: first, the United Kingdom, Danish and Irish Accession Convention of 1978 (OJ 1978 L 304/1); secondly, the Greek Accession Convention of 1982 (OJ 1982 L 388/1); thirdly, the Spanish and Portuguese Accession Convention of 1989—the San Sebastian Convention (OJ 1989 L 285/1); fourthly,

Although it has been replaced in virtually all cases by the Brussels I Regulation and now Brussels I Recast, unfortunately the Brussels Convention has not been consigned entirely to history. It still applies in relation to certain territories of Member States and will be examined later on in this chapter.[13]

The Treaty of Amsterdam, which entered into force in 1999, established Community competence in private international law, which enabled the Brussels Convention to be converted to a Regulation.[14] The great advantages of a Regulation are that it is directly applicable in the Member States, automatically binding on new Member States, and may be readily modified through EU legislative procedures. In contrast, the Brussels Convention had to be ratified and in some cases separately implemented by each Contracting State. The legal basis for the Brussels I Recast is now set out in Title V of the Treaty on European Union, in particular Article 67, which authorises the adoption of measures in the field of judicial co-operation in civil matters. Article 81 specifically mentions "the compatibility of the rules applicable in the Member States concerning conflict of laws and of jurisdiction" and "the mutual recognition and enforcement between Member States of judgments and of decisions in extrajudicial cases". The Brussels I Recast is one of a number of measures[15] relating to judicial co-operation in civil matters having cross-border implications which have been adopted to promote the sound operation of the internal market.[16] Such measures fall within the wider objective the European Union has set itself[17] of establishing an area of freedom, security and justice, in which the free movement of persons is ensured.[18]

---

the Austrian, Finnish and Swedish Accession Convention of 1996 (OJ 1997 C 15/1). A consolidated version of the 1968 Convention and 1971 Protocol, as amended by the four Accession Conventions, is set out in OJ 1998 C 27/1. All references to the "Brussels Convention" (or the "Convention") and the "1971 Protocol" are to the latest version amended by the four Accession Conventions.

13 See infra, p 312.

14 See Beaumont (1999) 48 ICLQ 223; Basedow (2000) 37 CMLR 687; Israel (2000) 7 Maastricht JECL 81; Remien (2001) 38 CMLR 53.

15 Note also eg Council Regulation (EC) No 1348/2000 of 9 May 2000 on the service in the Member States of judicial and extra-judicial documents in civil or commercial matters OJ 2000 L 160/37, replaced by Council Regulation (EC) No 1393/2007 OJ 2007 L 324/79, discussed infra, pp 308–9; Council Regulation (EC) No 1346/2000 of 29 May 2000 on insolvency proceedings OJ 2000 L 160/1, now Recast Regulation (EU) 2015/848 OJ 2015 L 141/19, discussed supra, p 126; Council Regulation (EC) No 1206/2001 of 28 May 2001 on co-operation between the courts of the Member States in the taking of evidence in civil or commercial matters OJ 2001 L 174/1, discussed supra, p 81; Regulation (EC) No 805/2004 of the European Parliament and of the Council of 21 April 2004 creating a European Enforcement Order for uncontested claims OJ 2004 L 143/15, discussed infra, p 656 et seq; Regulation (EC) No 1896/2006 of the European Parliament and of the Council of 12 December 2006 creating a European order for payment procedure OJ 2006 L 399 (amended by Regulation (EU) 2015/2421 OJ 2015 L 341), discussed infra, p 660 et seq; Regulation (EC) No 861/2007 of the European Council and of the Parliament of 11 July 2007 establishing a European Small Claims Procedure OJ 2007 L 199 (amended by Regulation (EU) 2015/2421 OJ 2015 L 341), discussed infra, p 663 et seq; Regulation (EU) No 655/2014 of the European Parliament and of the Council of 15 May 2014 establishing a European Account Preservation Order Procedure to facilitate cross-border debt recovery in civil and commercial matters OJ 2014 L 189, discussed infra, p 303. A number of regulations on family law matters including property consequences of marriages and registered partnerships have also been proposed or adopted: see infra Chapter 22. See more generally Council Decision of 28 May 2001 establishing a European Judicial Network in civil and commercial matters OJ 2001 L 174/25; 'Action Plan Implementing the Stockholm Programme: Delivering an area of freedom, security and justice for Europe's citizens' (COM/2010/0171 final). On European harmonisation of private international law see generally Crawford and Carruthers [2005] Jur Rev 251; Dickinson (2005) 1 J Priv Int L 197; Fiorini (2008) 57 ICLQ 969; Mills (2013) 23 Duke J Comp & Intl L 445.

16 See Recitals (3) and (4) of the Brussels I Recast.

17 See Art 3(2) of the Treaty on European Union.

18 See Art 67 of the Treaty on European Union and the discussion in Chapter 1, supra, pp 11–13.

The European Free Trade Association (EFTA) bloc was at one time the single most import-ant trading partner of the European Community, and the need for legal and economic co-operation between the two blocs was recognised. A convention on jurisdiction and the recognition and enforcement of judgments was seen as part of this process of cooperation, and was agreed at Lugano in 1988.[19] The 1988 Lugano Convention mirrored the Brussels Convention by adopting the same fundamental principles but there were some crucial differ-ences in the terms of the two Conventions. The EFTA bloc has since contracted as its con-stituent states have acceded to the European Community and now European Union, being confined for the purposes of Lugano to just Iceland, Norway and Switzerland.[20] With the replacement of the Brussels Convention in virtually all cases by the Brussels I Regulation it was desirable for the terms of the Lugano Convention to be amended to bring them into line so far as possible with the Regulation. A new Lugano Convention was concluded in 2007, which replaces the 1988 Convention.[21] The European Community (now European Union) had exclusive competence to conclude this new Convention.[22]

The Brussels I Recast assigns jurisdiction to the courts of Member States. The United Kingdom is the Member State under the Brussels I Recast; this raises the particular problem of whether the courts of England and Wales, Scotland or Northern Ireland are to have juris-diction. Section 16 of the Civil Jurisdiction and Judgments Act 1982, as amended,[23] solved this problem by introducing a modified version of the Brussels I Regulation,[24] which allo-cates jurisdiction within the United Kingdom. With some of the provisions in the Brussels I Recast it is possible to identify a part or place in the United Kingdom which is to have juris-diction.[25] It is not possible to do so where, for example, jurisdiction is allocated to the United Kingdom on the basis that the defendant is domiciled within the United Kingdom under Article 4 of the Brussels I Recast. The Modified Regulation is examined in detail towards the end of this chapter.[26]

(b) Interpretation of the Brussels/Lugano System and the Modified Regulation

(i) Referrals to the Court of Justice

Article 267 of the Treaty on the Functioning of the European Union authorises the Court of Justice, at the request of a Member State court, to give preliminary rulings on the validity and interpretation of acts of the institutions, bodies, offices or agencies of the Union, which obvi-ously includes interpretation of the Brussels I Recast.[27] A court can only request a preliminary ruling "if it considers that a decision on the question is necessary to enable it to give judg-ment".[28] As such, no reference is necessary or possible if the meaning of the Brussels I Recast is clear (known in EU law as the *acte clair* doctrine). The English courts have on occasion

---

[19] OJ 1988 L 391/9. This is set out in Sch 3C to the Civil Jurisdiction and Judgments Act 1982, added by s 1(1) of the Civil Jurisdiction and Judgments Act 1991. See generally the 13th edn of this book (1999), pp 278–83.

[20] Liechtenstein is an EFTA State but not a Contracting State to Lugano.

[21] Art 69(6) of the 2007 Lugano Convention OJ 2007 L 339/3. A further Report was produced by Professor Fausto Pocar to assist in interpreting this updated Convention: OJ 2009 C 319/1.

[22] Opinion of the Court of Justice 1/03 Competence of the Community to conclude the new Lugano Convention [2006] ECR I-1145. See generally Mills (2016) 65 ICLQ 541.

[23] By SI 2001/3929, Art 4 and Sch 2, Part II, para 3.

[24] Set out in Sch 4 to the 1982 Act, as substituted by SI 2001/3929, Art 4 and Sch 2, Part II, para 4.

[25] Eg under Art 7. See infra, p 224 et seq.

[26] Infra, pp 317–22.

[27] In exceptional circumstances the Court can refuse to rule on a question referred to it, see Case C-111/01 *Gantner Electronic GmbH v Basch Exploitatie Maatschappij BV* [2003] ECR I-4207 at [33]–[41].

[28] See further Case C-419/11 *Česká spořitelna, as v Gerald Feichter* EU:C:2013:165, [2013] IL Pr 22. The procedure for references from English courts is contained in CPR, Part 68 and Practice Direction 68.

relied on this doctrine in matters which might be considered slightly controversial,[29] but in general have made numerous references to the Court of Justice in relation to the interpretation of the Brussels Convention and Regulation. If a matter of interpretation of the Brussels I Recast is not *acte clair* and raised in a court other than the Supreme Court, a reference to the Court of Justice is optional. A reference must be made as a matter of EU law if the matter is not *acte clair* and is raised in the UK Supreme Court (as the national court of final appeal). Under the EC/Denmark Agreement, the Danish courts are required to request a ruling from the European Court of Justice in the same circumstances as the courts of another Member State are required to do so in relation to the Brussels I Recast.[30]

The Lugano Convention is part of EU law and, accordingly, the Court of Justice also has jurisdiction to give rulings on the interpretation of its provisions.[31] However, a reference for such a ruling can only be made from a court or tribunal of a European Union Member State, not from the courts of one of the three EFTA contracting parties. Where a reference to the Court of Justice is made for such a ruling, the EFTA States are entitled to submit statements of case or written observations.[32] Any court applying and interpreting the Convention is required to pay due account to the principles laid down in any relevant decision of the Court of Justice.[33] This obligation covers not only the courts in the Member States but also the courts in the three EFTA States.[34]

The Court of Justice does not, however, have jurisdiction to give a preliminary ruling on a question of interpretation of the Modified Regulation.[35] Even though this is modelled on the Brussels I Regulation, the allocation of jurisdiction within the United Kingdom is not a matter of EU law. Section 16(3)(a) of the Civil Jurisdiction and Judgments Act 1982 requires the English courts to pay regard to the decisions of the Court of Justice and to the relevant principles followed by it in relation to the jurisdictional provisions in Title II of the Brussels Convention or Chapter II of the Brussels I Regulation and Brussels I Recast.[36] However, if the Court of Justice interprets the Brussels I Regulation or Brussels I Recast in a way of which the United Kingdom disapproves, the United Kingdom can alter the Modified Regulation to nullify such decisions in relation to allocating jurisdiction within the United Kingdom.[37]

*(ii) The principles and decisions laid down by the Court of Justice in respect of the Brussels
      I Regulation and Brussels Convention*

The Brussels I Recast should be interpreted in the light of the substantial body of case law decided under the Brussels I Regulation and the Brussels Convention.[38] Many of the rules in

---

A national court when making a referral can rely on submissions of one party to the main proceedings of which it has not yet examined the merits: Case C-116/02 *Erich Gasser GmbH v Misat Srl* [2003] ECR I-4207.

[29] See, eg, *The Alexandros T* [2013] UKSC 70, [2014] 1 All ER 590.

[30] Art 6. See further Case C-49/12 *Her Majesty's Revenue & Customs v Sunico ApS* EU:C:2013:231, [2014] QB 391.

[31] See the Preamble to Protocol 2 attached to the Convention.

[32] Protocol 2, Art 2.

[33] Art 1(1), Protocol 2.

[34] Ibid.

[35] Case C-346/93 *Kleinwort Benson Ltd v Glasgow City Council* [1995] ECR I-615; Briggs (1995) 15 YEL 492; Turkki (1996) 21 ELR 419; Peel [1996] LMCLQ 9; Collins (1995) 111 LQR 541; Bishop (1995) 20 ELR 495; Betlem (1996) 33 CMLR 137.

[36] See, eg, *Kleinwort Benson Ltd v Glasgow City Council* [1999] 1 AC 153, discussed infra, pp 247–8. See also *Strathaird Farms Ltd v G A Chattaway & Co* 1993 SLT (Sh Ct) 36.

[37] S 47(1)(b) of the 1982 Act.

[38] See Brussels I Recast, Recital (34); note also the opinion of AG Leger in Case C-281/02 *Owusu v Jackson* [2005] I-1383 at [193]–[194]; Case C-406/09 *Realchemie Nederland* [2009] ECR I-9773 at [38].

the Brussels I Recast are the same as those in the Brussels I Regulation or Brussels Convention and their meaning has previously been explained by the Court of Justice. Even where the rules have been modified, an understanding of the previously applicable rules may assist in contextualising and interpreting the changes.

Other decisions by the Court of Justice may also be relevant in so far as they lay down principles of interpretation. These principles are important not only when interpreting rules in the Brussels I Recast which have been directly borrowed from the Brussels I Regulation or Brussels Convention but also when interpreting new rules introduced by the Brussels I Recast. The principles laid down by the Court of Justice when interpreting the Brussels I Regulation and Brussels Convention are as follows:

(i) The meaning of a provision should be ascertained in the light of its purpose rather than by taking its literal meaning.[39] This approach was adopted under the Convention,[40] and the objectives of the Brussels I Regulation and Brussels I Recast are broadly the same as those of the Convention.[41] The Recitals of the Brussels I Recast are intended to serve as particularly important aids to its interpretation, including by setting out its object and purpose. The context of a provision, including its relationship with other provisions in the Brussels I Recast, may also assist in its interpretation.[42]

(ii) As a general principle, the terms of the Brussels I Recast should be interpreted autonomously,[43] rather than by reference to national law. The reason for this is that many of the concepts in the Brussels I Recast have different meanings under the separate national laws of the Member States and reference to national law inevitably leads to a lack of uniformity in interpretation. The objectives of the Brussels I Recast therefore require that it should be given a uniform application throughout the Community where possible. A number of important changes introduced by the Brussels I Regulation replaced rules which under the Convention had been interpreted as requiring a reference to national law with autonomous definitions.[44] As an implication of this interpretive principle, another source of authority for the English courts is the decisions of the courts of other Member States in relation to the Brussels I Recast, the Brussels I Regulation and the Brussels Convention. English courts should also always be prepared to consider the texts of the Brussels I Recast in other languages, which is what they have done with the Brussels I Regulation and Brussels Convention.[45]

Under the Lugano Convention, due account must similarly be paid by the courts of both Member States and the three EFTA States to the principles laid down by any relevant decision rendered by the national courts of the states bound by the Convention.[46] A relevant decision, whether of the Court of Justice or a national court, may concern not just a provision of the Lugano Convention (2007) but also any similar provision of

---

[39] *Speed Investments Ltd v Formula One Holdings Ltd (No 2)* [2004] EWCA Civ 1512 at [22]–[28], [2005] 1 WLR 1936. See also *M v H* [2005] EWHC 1186 (Fam) at [85]—a Brussels II *bis* case.

[40] Case 29/76 *Lufttransportunternehmen GmbH v Organisation Européenne pour la Securité de la Navigation Aérienne (Eurocontrol)* [1976] ECR 1541; Case C-172/91 *Sonntag v Waidmann* [1993] ECR I-1963.

[41] *Evialis SA v SIAT* [2003] EWHC 863 (Comm) at [93], [2003] 2 Lloyd's Rep 377.

[42] Case 33/78 *Somafer v Saar-Ferngas* [1978] ECR 2183.

[43] Case C-383/95 *Rutten v Cross Medical Ltd* [1997] ECR I-57 at 74; Case C-295/95 *Farrell v Long* [1997] ECR I-1683 at 1704.

[44] See Art 7(1)(b) of the Brussels I Recast, discussed infra, p 255 et seq, Art 32, discussed infra, pp 448–9, and Art 63, discussed p 198 et seq.

[45] See Art 68 of the Brussels Convention; Case 150/80 *Elefanten Schuh GmbH v Jacqmain* [1981] ECR 1671; *Newtherapeutics Ltd v Katz* [1991] Ch 226 at 243–5; *CFEM Façades SA v Bovis Construction Ltd* [1992] IL Pr 561.

[46] Art 1(1), Protocol 2.

the Brussels I Regulation, the Brussels Convention or the EC/Denmark Agreement.[47] A relevant decision of a national court may also concern the 1988 Lugano Convention.[48]

(iii) In ascertaining the meaning of concepts used in the Brussels I Recast, regard should be had to the meaning of cognate concepts to be found in the EU Treaties or in secondary legislation.[49] The need for such an interpretation, which was warranted under the Brussels Convention,[50] is even more pertinent now that the Convention has been replaced by a Regulation and has therefore been integrated into the Community legal order in a more systematic and direct manner.[51]

(iv) As discussed in various places below, there are more specific principles where the Court of Justice has identified the purpose underlying a particular provision and has laid down policy considerations to be taken into account, in particular, whether a particular provision is to be narrowly or widely interpreted.

(iii) Aids to interpretation

The interpretation of the Brussels I Recast, Brussels I Regulation, and Brussels Convention may also be assisted by reference to various reports which form part of the negotiating or drafting history of each of these instruments. These reports may also be relied on in interpreting the Modified Regulation which is modelled on the Brussels I Regulation and allocates jurisdiction within the United Kingdom.[52]

As noted above, the Brussels I Recast was adopted in 2012. The Brussels I Regulation had required the Commission, no later than five years after the entry into force of the Regulation, to present a Report on the application of the Regulation,[53] accompanied by proposals for such changes as thought necessary. In pursuance of this obligation, the *Report on the Application of Regulation Brussels I in the Member States* was prepared by the Institute of Private International Law at the University of Heidelberg (the Hess, Pfeiffer and Schlosser Report).[54] This Report was an empirical study based on questionnaires sent out by the general reporters to national contributors, who, after addressing stakeholders, collecting statistical information, and conducting interviews with the profession and other interested parties, produced National Reports. In the light of these National Reports, and the research of the general reporters themselves, the Hess, Pfeiffer and Schlosser Report identified problems with the operation of the Regulation and indicated possible solutions. This Report forms part of the context for the emergence of a Recast Regulation, although a degree of caution should be exercised before relying on it to interpret the Brussels I Recast, as the changes finally

---

[47] Ibid.

[48] Ibid. No reference could be made to the ECJ in relation to interpretation of the 1988 Lugano Convention.

[49] Case C-271/00 *Gemeente Steenbergen v Baten* [2002] ECR I-10489 at [43].

[50] The Brussels Convention has been held to be "linked" to the EC Treaty, and the provisions of the latter apply to matters within the scope of the Convention: Case C-398/92 *Mund & Fester v Hatrex International Transport* [1994] ECR I-467; Briggs (1994) 14 YEL 557; Beaumont (1995) 44 ICLQ 220.

[51] See the opinion of AG Tizzano in *Gemeente Steenbergen v Baten*, supra, at [44]. See also JJ Forner Delaygua 'Internet Jurisdiction in Business to Business On-Line Performed Contracts: Lessons From The Hague?' in JJ Barcelo III and KM Clermont (eds), *A Global Law of Jurisdiction and Judgments: Lessons from The Hague*.

[52] S 16(3)(b) of the 1982 Act.

[53] Art 73.

[54] Study JLS/C4/2005/03, Final Version September 2007. A second *Study on Residual Jurisdiction* was prepared by Nuyts (the Nuyts Report), Study JLS/C4/2005/07-30, Final Version September 2007. This was concerned with jurisdiction under traditional national rules of jurisdiction. It contains a comparative analysis of these national jurisdictional rules and options for their possible future harmonisation. The harmonisation of residual national jurisdictional rules was proposed by the European Commission for the Brussels I Recast (COM(2010) 748 final), but this proposal was not adopted.

adopted may not reflect those proposed in the Report. The European Commission proposal for a Recast Brussels I Regulation[55] may also be considered helpful interpretive context, but only to the extent that the Commission proposals were actually adopted in the final Brussels I Recast, which is certainly not true in all respects, and even then only reflects the view of the Commission which is not necessarily determinative.

An Explanatory Memorandum from the Commission of the European Communities was also produced at the time of the proposal for a Regulation to replace the Brussels Convention.[56] This is, however, fairly brief and again only represents the view of the Commission.[57] There was no official report accompanying the Brussels I Regulation itself. This contrasts with the position in relation to the Brussels Convention, the draft of which was accompanied by the Jenard Report.[58] This is a commentary prepared by the rapporteur of the committee of experts which drew up the draft Convention. Each of the first three Accession Conventions to the Brussels Convention is also accompanied by a Report,[59] as was the 1988 Lugano Convention.[60] The Court of Justice has not infrequently referred to the Jenard Report and to the subsequent Reports in order to ascertain the meaning of provisions in the Brussels Convention. As noted above, these Reports are still relevant to interpreting the many provisions in the Brussels I Regulation and now Brussels I Recast which have been taken unaltered from the Convention. There is, however, no authoritative Report explaining the changes introduced by the Brussels I Regulation or the Brussels I Recast.

3. THE BRUSSELS I RECAST

(a) A special definition of domicile

Extensive use is made of the concept of domicile for the purpose of deciding when the Brussels I Recast applies, and, where it does, of allocating jurisdiction to particular Member States. However, despite the importance of this concept, it is only partially defined in the Brussels I Recast. This raises a significant problem since the meaning of the concept differs in some respects from one Member State to another.

(i) Natural persons

Article 62 of the Brussels I Recast[61] deals with the question of which Member State's definition of domicile is to be used—in practice, this rule applies only for natural persons because Article 63, discussed below, covers companies and other legal persons. The first paragraph states that the courts of the Member State seised of the matter shall apply their own definition of domicile to determine whether a party is domiciled in that Member State. According to the second paragraph, in order to determine whether a party is domiciled in another Member State, a court must apply the law of that State; eg if the United Kingdom courts want to know whether the defendant is domiciled in France, they must apply the French definition of domicile used

---

[55] COM(2010) 748 final.

[56] COM (1999) 348 final.

[57] For cases using the Explanatory Memorandum, see, eg, the Opinion of AG Colomer in Case C-283/05 *ASML Netherlands BV v Semiconductor Industry Services GmbH (SEMIS)* [2006] ECR I-12041 at [50]–[51] of the opinion; *Tavoulareas v Tsavliris* [2006] EWCA Civ 1772 at [4], [2006] 1 All ER (Comm) 109.

[58] OJ 1979 C 59.

[59] The Schlosser Report OJ 1979 C 59; the Evrigenis and Kerameus Report OJ 1986 C 298/1; the Almeida Cruz, Desantes Real, Jenard Report OJ 1990 C 189/06. There is no report accompanying the Austrian, Finnish and Swedish Accession Convention of 1996.

[60] The Jenard and Möller Report OJ 1990 C 189/57.

[61] Article 59 of the Brussels I Regulation.

for these purposes.[62] For natural persons, the meaning of "domicile" for the purposes of the Brussels I Recast therefore varies for each Member State. This alone should not lead to inconsistent decisions on jurisdiction because the varied meanings are applied identically by the courts of every Member State, although it does mean that a natural person may be domiciled in more than one Member State, or even, more problematically, that a person living in several different Member States may at least in theory not be domiciled in any of them.[63]

What English law usually means by "domicile" is far removed from what civil law means.[64] To aid in harmonisation of the law on jurisdiction, the Civil Jurisdiction and Judgments Order 2001[65] therefore contains special provisions on the meaning of the domicile of an individual for the purposes of the Brussels I Regulation and now Brussels I Recast. The simplest solution, which would have been to equate an individual's habitual residence with his domicile,[66] would have been problematic because of the separate references in the Brussels I Regulation to habitual residence.[67] Paragraph 9 of Schedule 1 of the Civil Jurisdiction and Judgments Order 2001 adopts a complicated solution, with different rules for each of the contexts under the Brussels I Regulation and now Brussels I Recast in which an individual's domicile has to be ascertained. Thus, the rules[68] determine when an individual is domiciled: (i) in the United Kingdom, (ii) in a particular part of the United Kingdom, (iii) in a particular place in the United Kingdom and (iv) in a state other than a Brussels I Recast State. For most of these purposes[69] domicile is equated with the state where (a) a person is resident[70] and (b) the nature and circumstances of his residence indicate that he has a substantial connection with it.[71] Under some of these rules, but not others, a rebuttable presumption of a substantial connection arises where there has been a period of residence for three months or more.[72] The onus is on the claimant to show a good arguable case that the defendant is domiciled in a particular State.[73] If the defendant's current domicile is

---

[62] *Haji-Ioannou v Frangos* [1999] 2 Lloyd's Rep 337, 344, CA; *Bank of Credit and Commerce International SA (In Liquidation) v Wajih Sirri Al-Kaylani* [1999] IL Pr 278, CA—interrogatories can be administered to ascertain whether a person comes within the foreign definition. See also Layton and Mercer, Vol 2, chapters 47–64 at .051 in each of these chapters (for the definition of domicile in other European Union Member States).

[63] The Hess, Pfeiffer and Schlosser Report pointed out that the determination of the domicile of natural persons is, in some cases, rather complex, and suggested that there should be discussion on whether an acceptable autonomous definition can be found: See Study JLS/C4/2005/03, Final Version September 2007, para 873.

[64] See the Schlosser Report, pp 95–7.

[65] SI 2001/3929, amended by SI 2007/1655. See previously the Civil Jurisdiction and Judgments Act 1982, s 41.

[66] In Ireland domicile is, however, equated with ordinary residence: Sch 5, Part I of the Jurisdiction of Courts and Enforcement of Judgments (European Communities) Act 1988; *Deutsche Bank v Murtagh* [1995] 1 ILRM 380.

[67] See now, eg, Arts 15(3), 19(3) of the Brussels I Recast.

[68] See para 9(2) to (7), infra, pp 213–15 and 317–19.

[69] But not when domicile in a particular place in the United Kingdom is being ascertained, see para 9(4).

[70] "Resident" is given its ordinary English meaning, discussed supra, pp 149–50: *Bank of Dubai Ltd v Abbas* [1997] IL Pr 308, CA. See also *Grupo Torras SA and Torras Hostench London Ltd v Sheikh Fahad Mohammed Al-Sabah* [1995] 1 Lloyd's Rep 374 at 444–6; *Chellaram v Chellaram (No 2)* [2002] EWHC 632 (Ch) at [21], [2002] 3 All ER 17; *Foote Cone & Belding Reklin Hizmetleri v Theron* [2006] EWHC 1585 (Ch); *High Tech International AG v Deripaska* [2006] EWHC 3276 (QB); *Cherney v Deripaska* [2007] EWHC 965 (Comm), [2007] IL Pr 49; *OJSC Oil Company Yugraneft v Abramovich* [2008] EWHC 2613 (Comm)—regular visits to London to watch Chelsea FC win football matches did not establish residence.

[71] A person may be resident in England but lack the substantial connection: *Petrotrade Inc v Smith* [1999] 1 WLR 457 at 461–2—one factor being that the defendant was unable to leave because of a bail condition. See also *Panagaki v Apostolopoulos* [2015] EWHC 2700 (QB).

[72] The presumption is contained in para 9(6). It can be used for the purposes of para 9(2) and (3), but not para 9(4) and (7).

[73] *Canada Trust v Stolzenberg (No 2)* [2002] 1 AC 1.

unknown and cannot be determined, the defendant may be treated as domiciled at their last known place of domicile.[74]

(ii) Companies and other legal persons; trusts

Since the adoption of the Brussels I Regulation, a different approach has been taken towards determining the domicile of companies and other legal persons.[75] In order "to make the common rules more transparent and to avoid conflicts of jurisdiction",[76] Article 63 of the Brussels I Recast[77] gives an autonomous definition to the concept of the domicile of a company. It provides in paragraph (1) that, "for the purposes of this Regulation, a company or other legal person or association of natural or legal persons is domiciled at the place where it has its:

(a) statutory seat,

(b) central administration, or

(c) principal place of business.

Because these are alternatives, a company or other legal person can, in principle, be domiciled in more than one Member State.

Article 63 does not eliminate all the definitional problems that can arise in relation to the domicile of a company. What is the definition of the terms "statutory seat", "central administration" and "principal place of business"? Given that Article 63 is concerned to give an autonomous meaning to the concept of the domicile of a company, these terms should also be given an autonomous meaning. The three alternative criteria used in Article 63(1) correspond to the three criteria (registered office, central administration or principal place of business) used in Article 54 of the Treaty on the Functioning of the European Union, which deals with the right of establishment of companies within the Community. Regard should be had to the case law on these Article 54 terms when ascertaining the meaning of the terms used in Article 63.[78]

One immediate difficulty is that the concept of the statutory seat of a company is well known in civil law systems,[79] but would be difficult to apply to companies established in common law jurisdictions. Article 63(2) caters for this difference by stating that:

> For the purposes of Ireland, Cyprus and the United Kingdom, "statutory seat" means the registered office or, where there is no such office anywhere, the place of incorporation or, where there is no such place anywhere, the place under the law of which the formation took place.

This provision only applies "For the purposes of Ireland, Cyprus and the United Kingdom." It is somewhat unclear from the text whether "for the purposes of" is supposed to mean "when determining whether a company is domiciled in" these jurisdictions, or "when the domicile of a company is being determined by a court in" one of these jurisdictions. The former would mean, for example, that an English or German court determining whether a company is domiciled in England should apply the revised test. The latter would mean that an English court would apply the revised test when determining whether a company is domiciled in either England or Germany, but the test would never be applied by a German

---

[74] Case C-327/10 *Hypoteční banka as v Lindner* EU:C:2011:745; see further Case C-292/10 *G v De Visser* EU:C:2012:142, [2013] QB 168.

[75] Cf Art 53, para 1 of the Brussels Convention, discussed infra, p 312. See generally Benedettelli [2005] EBLR 55.

[76] Recital (15) of the Brussels I Recast.

[77] Article 60 of the Brussels I Regulation.

[78] See, eg, *Young v Anglo American South Africa Ltd* [2014] EWCA Civ 1130, [2014] 2 Lloyd's Rep 606.

[79] See Weser (1961) 10 AJCL 323, 329–30; Rammeloo, *Corporations in Private International Law* (2000), p 323 et seq.

court. The latter approach would, however, mean that different Member State courts would apply different tests for domicile for the same jurisdiction, and should be rejected. Although the drafting is not clear, this was the apparent intended effect of section 42 of the Civil Jurisdiction and Judgments Act 1982 in relation to the Brussels Convention.[80] Thus the modified test should apply in the situation where an English court is determining whether it has jurisdiction on the basis of the company being domiciled in England, or where a German court is determining whether a company is domiciled in England, but not where the English courts are considering whether a company is domiciled in Germany.

As regards the meaning of "central administration", this cannot be identified simply by looking at where important personnel, such as the chief executive officer and various departmental heads, are located.[81] A court may take into account whether the activities of a company office are subject to the control of senior management located elsewhere,[82] but the search should not necessarily be for the highest level of control, but rather "the place where the company concerned, through its relevant organs according to its own constitutional provisions, takes the decisions that are essential for that company's operations" or "conducts its entrepreneurial management".[83]

Central administration is a different concept from "central management and control", which is a concept used by the United Kingdom in the context of the Brussels Convention (which did not itself contain a definition of "seat" for the purposes of common law jurisdictions).[84] In ascertaining where a company has its central management and control it is relevant to look at where the directors are resident, hold meetings and decide major policy issues,[85] and whether the company has just started.[86] This focus on the board of directors is different from the entrepreneurial emphasis of the concept of central administration.

As regards the meaning of the "principal place of business", this is a concept with which the English courts are already familiar. Leggatt LJ in *The Rewia* held, in the context of a choice of jurisdiction clause providing for trial in the principal place of business, that this referred to the "chief" or "most important" place of business, rather than the "main" place of business.[87] It is not necessarily the place where most of the business is carried out. This case has been described as "an essential tool" in deciding on the principal place of business for the purposes of Article 63 of the Brussels I Recast.[88] It has been suggested that the principal place of business may be identified by looking at where important personnel, such as the chief executive officer and various departmental heads, are located,[89] although that may overlap extensively

---

[80] Note in particular s 42(7): "A corporation or association shall not be regarded as having its seat in a Contracting State other than the United Kingdom if it is shown that the courts of that state would not regard it as having its seat there."

[81] *Young v Anglo American South Africa Ltd* [2014] EWCA Civ 1130 at [44], [2014] 2 Lloyd's Rep 606, disapproving of *King v Crown Energy Trading AG* [2003] EWHC 163 (Comm), [2003] IL Pr 28.

[82] *889457 Alberta Inc v Katanga Mining Ltd* [2008] EWHC 2679 (Comm), [2009] IL Pr 14.

[83] *Young v Anglo American South Africa Ltd* [2014] EWCA Civ 1130 at [45], [2014] 2 Lloyd's Rep 606.

[84] Art 53; Civil Jurisdiction and Judgments Act 1982, s 42; see infra, p 312; *Young v Anglo American South Africa Ltd* [2014] EWCA Civ 1130 at [44], [2014] 2 Lloyd's Rep 606.

[85] See *The Rewia* [1991] 1 Lloyd's Rep 69 at 74; this point was not disputed in the appeal which overruled the decision on other grounds [1991] 2 Lloyd's Rep 325, CA.

[86] *Royal & Sun Alliance Insurance plc v MK Digital FZE (Cyprus) Ltd* [2006] EWCA Civ 629 at [85]–[86], [2006] 2 Lloyd's Rep 110.

[87] [1991] 2 Lloyd's Rep 325 at 334, CA.

[88] *King v Crown Energy Trading AG* [2003] EWHC 163 (Comm) at [14], [2003] IL Pr 28. See also *Ministry of Defence and Support of the Armed Forces for the Islamic Republic of Iran v FAZ Aviation Ltd* [2007] EWHC 1042 (Comm), [2007] IL Pr 42.

[89] *Ministry of Defence and Support of the Armed Forces for the Islamic Republic of Iran v FAZ Aviation Ltd* [2007] EWHC 1042 (Comm) at [29], [2007] IL Pr 42.

with the meaning of "central administration", and the better view is probably that central administration and principal place of business should be given more distinctive definitions, with the latter focusing more on the activities rather than administration of the company. The domicile of a company is tested at the time of commencement of proceedings, so a company may have no "principal place of business" if it has ceased all activities when proceedings are commenced against it.[90]

When it comes to the domicile of a trust, under Article 63(3) the courts seised of the matter are instructed to apply their rules of private international law to determine whether the trust is domiciled in their jurisdiction.[91] The courts of a Member State must do likewise when ascertaining the seat of a company for the purposes of exclusive jurisdiction under Article 24(2) of the Brussels I Recast.[92]

(b) When does the Brussels I Recast apply?

(i) *The matter must be within the scope of the Brussels I Recast*

None of its provisions, whether on jurisdiction or on recognition and enforcement of judgments, will apply unless the matter is within the scope of the Brussels I Recast.

Article 1 is designed to deal with the scope of the Brussels I Recast. But before looking at this, various other limitations on the operation of the Brussels I Recast must be mentioned. First, the Brussels I Recast is only concerned with the *international jurisdiction* of Member States. This limitation was spelt out in the preamble to the Brussels Convention[93] but has been held to apply also in relation to the Brussels I Regulation, even though it is not mentioned in the Recitals.[94] It follows that the Brussels I Recast should not apply where a dispute involves no foreign element or where the foreign element only involves another part of the United Kingdom. It is, perhaps, unclear if a foreign element is established merely because the parties have chosen a foreign court in a jurisdiction agreement, or because the dispute could otherwise be litigated before a foreign court, although the better view is probably that this is sufficient.[95] The foreign element can clearly be satisfied by connections with a non-Member State.[96] Thus the Brussels I Recast will apply where there are connections with two States, one of which is a Member State and the other a non-Member State, as, for example, where both parties are domiciled in a Member State and the events at issue occurred in a non-Member

---

[90] *Ministry of Defence and Support of the Armed Forces for the Islamic Republic of Iran v FAZ Aviation Ltd* [2007] EWHC 1042 (Comm) at [32], [53], [2007] IL Pr 42.

[91] For the domicile of a trust for the purposes of the Brussels I Recast under English private international law see the Civil Jurisdiction and Judgments Order, SI 2001/3929, Art 3 and Sch 1, para 12; *Gomez v Gomez-Monche Vives* [2008] EWCA Civ 1065, [2009] Ch 245. For domicile of the Crown see Civil Jurisdiction and Judgments Act 1982, s 46 and *Tehrani v Secretary of State for the Home Department* [2006] UKHL 47, [2006] 3 WLR 699.

[92] See infra, p 224.

[93] See the Jenard Report, pp 8, 37–8; the Schlosser Report, p 123. See also Case C-281/02 *Owusu v Jackson* [2005] ECR I-1383 at [25], and the opinion of AG Leger at [102]; the opinion of AG Darmon in Case C-318/93 *Brenner and Noller v Dean Witter Reynolds Inc* [1994] ECR I-4275 at 4282.

[94] Opinion of the Court of Justice 1/03 Competence of the Community to conclude the new Lugano Convention [2006] ECR I-1145 at [143]–[145].

[95] There is support for the argument that a jurisdiction agreement or other possibility of proceedings in another state is enough: *Provimiv Aventis Animal Nutrition SA* [2003] EWHC 961 (Comm) at [74]–[75]— obiter, [2003] 2 All ER (Comm) 683; *Snookes v Jani-King (GB) Ltd* [2006] EWHC 289 (QB) at [39]–[45]— a provisional view, but perhaps wrongly applied to an intra-UK case, [2006] IL Pr 19; cf *British Sugar plc v Fratelli* [2004] EWHC 2560 at [34]—ratio, [2005] 1 Lloyd's Rep 332. Foreign nationality is relevant to this question even if it cannot affect the application of the rules on jurisdiction: Case C-327/10 *Hypoteční banka as v Lindner* EU:C:2011:745.

[96] *Owusu v Jackson*, supra, at [26].

State.[97] Despite its justification being linked to improving the functioning of the internal market, the Brussels I Recast does not require connections with two Member States.

Second, the Brussels I Recast does not affect certain other conventions on jurisdiction or recognition and enforcement which Member States have *in the past* entered into,[98] or statutes implementing them.[99] There is no provision, as there is under the Brussels Convention[100] for conventions entered into by Member States *in the future*. The European Union does, however, have the power to enter into international agreements which may override the rules in the Brussels I Recast,[101] and this power has been exercised in ratifying the Hague Convention on Choice of Court Agreements.[102]

In England, admiralty jurisdiction and carriage by road are examples of areas which are left largely untouched because of conventions entered into in the past.[103] Nonetheless, some of the provisions in the Brussels I Recast will still apply. The application of the Brussels I Recast is precluded solely in relation to questions governed specifically by the specialised convention in question.[104] In so far as the latter is silent on a jurisdictional matter, the Brussels I Recast will still apply.[105] Further, the Court of Justice has suggested that prior conventions are only preserved to the extent that their rules are consistent with the principles and objectives of the Brussels I Regulation (and now Brussels I Recast),[106] which may affect how those conventions can permissibly be interpreted.[107]

---

[97] Ibid.

[98] Art 71. Where the defendant does not enter an appearance the court must verify of its own motion whether it has jurisdiction under the specialised convention: Art 71(2)(a); Case C-148/03 *Nurnberger Allgemeine Versicherungs AG v Portbridge Transport International BV* [2004] ECR I-10327. The European Council can authorise Member States' accession to international conventions, see, eg, Council Decision (EC) No 2002/762 of 19 September 2002 in relation to the Bunkers Convention OJ 2002 L 256/7.

[99] Arts 71 and 67: Case C-406/92 *The Tatry (Owners of the cargo) v Owners of Maciej Rataj* [1994] ECR I-5439, discussed infra, p 447; Arts 69 and 76 require production of a list of the bilateral conventions which are superseded by the Brussels I Recast; a previous list was included in Article 69 of the Brussels I Regulation. For the effect of these provisions on recognition and enforcement of foreign judgments in England see infra, pp 613–14.

[100] Art 57(1) of the Brussels Convention.

[101] See the Opinion of the Court of Justice 1/03 Competence of the Community to conclude the new Lugano Convention [2006] ECR I-1145 at [148]. See more generally on external competence of the Community and private international law: Kotuby [2001] NILR 1; Beaumont in Fawcett (ed), *Reform and Development of Private International Law* (2002), pp 25–9; Kruger, Chapter 7; Mills (2016) 65 ICLQ 541.

[102] Infra, p 315 et seq.

[103] See infra, pp 386–90, for the effect of the Brussels I Recast on admiralty jurisdiction. The provisions in the Brussels I Recast affecting this are Arts 7(7) and 9; see in relation to the Brussels Convention the Schlosser Report, pp 108–11, 139–42. In cases where the Brussels I Recast does apply, Art 4 will operate in relation to an action *in rem: The Deichland* [1990] 1 QB 361. For the position in Scotland see *Ladgroup Ltd v Euroeast Lines SA* 1997 SLT 916. For carriage by road see the CMR Convention; *Royal & Sun Alliance Insurance plc v MK Digital FZE (Cyprus) Ltd* [2006] EWCA Civ 629, [2006] 2 All ER (Comm) 145; Case C-533/08 *TNT Express Nederland BV v Axa Versicherung AG* [2010] ECR I-4107.

[104] *The Tatry*, supra.

[105] Ibid. The Arrest Convention of 1952 is silent on *lis pendens* and therefore Arts 29–30 and 33–4 of the Brussels I Recast (infra, p 443 et seq) will apply. See Briggs [1995] LMCLQ 161. The principle in *The Tatry* has been followed in relation to the CMR Convention on carriage by road: *Frans Maas Logistics (UK) Ltd v CDR Trucking BV* [1999] 2 Lloyd's Rep 179. But see the misapplication of this principle in *The Tatry* in *The "Bergen"* [1997] 1 Lloyd's Rep 380, discussed infra, p 387, in relation to what is now Art 25 of the Brussels I Recast; *Deaville v Aeroflot* [1997] 2 Lloyd's Rep 67—a Warsaw Convention case.

[106] Case C-533/08 *TNT Express Nederland BV* [2010] ECR I-4107; Case C-230/15 *Brite Strike Technologies Inc v Brite Strike Technologies SA* EU:C:2016:560, [2016] IL Pr 37.

[107] Case C-452/12 *Nipponkoa Insurance Co (Europe) Ltd v Inter-Zuid Transport BV* EU:C:2013:858, [2014] IL Pr 10. But see also *British American Tobacco Denmark A/S v Kazemier BV* [2015] UKSC 65, [2016] AC 262, suggesting that this should be narrowly confined, particularly where non-Member States are parties to the relevant convention; Briggs [2016] LMCLQ 197.

Thirdly, the rules on jurisdiction and recognition and enforcement make it clear that they do not apply to proceedings, or issues arising in proceedings, in Member States concerning the recognition and enforcement of judgments given in non-Member States.[108]

(a) Civil and commercial matters

Article 1 of the Brussels I Recast declares that "This Regulation shall apply in civil and commercial matters whatever the nature of the court or tribunal."

No definition is given of "civil and commercial matters",[109] although it is clear that "civil" extends coverage to non-commercial claims such as torts and employment disputes.[110] Article 1 goes on to say that it does not include "revenue,[111] customs[112] or administrative matters",[113] or "the liability of the State for acts and omissions in the exercise of State authority (*acta iure imperii*)".[114] These words are there to make it clear that public law matters are excluded. The difficulty for English lawyers is that in domestic law the distinction between private and public law is not sharply drawn.[115] In civil law jurisdictions there is a clearer distinction between the two, although the same criteria are not always applied when drawing the distinction. Some guidance on this definitional problem was given by the Court of Justice in the leading case of *LTU v Eurocontrol*[116] where it was held that a Community meaning had to be given to "civil and commercial matters", with the result that the Brussels Convention did not apply to the situation where a public authority was acting in the exercise of its powers. The public authority was an international organisation concerned with air safety; it was acting in the exercise of its powers when it sought to collect charges from an airline for the use of its services, the use of the services being obligatory and the rate of charge being fixed unilaterally.

The difficulty with requiring the public authority to be acting in the exercise of its powers, before the matter can be excluded from the Brussels I Recast, is that it is often hard to tell whether a public authority is acting in a private capacity or in the exercise of its powers.[117]

---

[108] Case C-129/92 *Owens Bank Ltd v Bracco (No 2)* [1994] QB 509 at 544–6; Hartley (1994) 19 ELR 545.

[109] See the Jenard Report, p 9; the opinion of the Advocate General in Case 29/76 *LTU v Eurocontrol* [1976] ECR 1541; Betlem and Bernasconi (2006) 122 LQR 124.

[110] See the Jenard Report, pp 9, 24; the Schlosser Report, p 82; the opinion of the Advocate General in *Netherlands v Rüffer*, supra; Case 25/79 *Sanicentral GmbH v Collin* [1979] ECR 3423 (on which see Collins, p 8).

[111] It was at one time thought that this excludes both direct and indirect attempts to enforce the revenue law of another State: *QRS 1 ApS v Frandsen* [1999] 1 WLR 2169, CA. It now appears that revenue law may be enforced indirectly through private law claims, as through for example a tort claim for conspiracy to defraud the tax office: Case C-49/12 *Her Majesty's Revenue & Customs v Sunico ApS* EU:C:2013:231, [2014] 1 QB 391; Collins (2014) 130 LQR 353.

[112] This does not encompass where a guarantor has paid customs duties and seeks reimbursement from a third party, their relationship being governed by private law: Case C-265/02 *Frahuil SA v Assitalia SPA* [2004] ECR I-1543. Nor where a State seeks payment from the guarantor: Case C-266/01 *Preservatrice Fonciere TIARD SA v Staat der Nederlanden* [2003] ECR I-4867 at [44].

[113] See the Schlosser Report, p 82. See also *Re State of Norway's Application* [1987] QB 433 at 473–4, affd in *Re State of Norway's Application (Nos 1 and 2)* [1990] 1 AC 723, HL; *Short v British Nuclear Fuels plc* [1997] IL Pr 747, Irish Sup Ct.

[114] This final exclusion, essentially codifying the case law discussed below, was added in the Brussels I Recast. There had been some uncertainty about whether the Brussels I Regulation had any impact on questions of state or diplomatic immunity in civil proceedings, but this exclusion should preclude that possibility. See further Case C-154/11 *Ahmed Mahamdia v République algérienne démocratique et populaire* EU:C:2012:491, [2014] All ER (EC) 96.

[115] See the Advocate General's opinion in *LTU v Eurocontrol*, supra; the Schlosser Report, p 82; *Re State of Norway's Application*, supra. See also Philip (1978) II Hague Recueil 1, 63–72.

[116] Case 29/76 *Lufttransportunternehmen GmbH v Organisation Européene pour la Securité de la Navigation Aérienne (Eurocontrol)* [1976] ECR 1541; see Hartley (1977) 2 ELR 61. The decision is criticised by Giardina (1978) 27 ICLQ 263, 272–4; and by Fletcher, *Conflict of Laws and European Community Law* (1982), p 112.

[117] See the Schlosser Report, pp 83–4.

In *Netherlands State v Rüffer*[118] the Court of Justice held that a public authority, in this case the Dutch State, was acting in the exercise of its powers in respect of a public waterway when it sought to recover from a German shipowner the costs of removing a wreck, even though under Dutch law (the Dutch courts being seised of the matter) the action was classified as one in tort. The action arose from international treaty obligations and would be regarded by many Member States as an administrative one, the common core of the national legal systems being an important consideration when giving a Community meaning to this concept. Similarly, an action in tort by Greek nationals against Germany to obtain compensation for damage caused by the German armed forces when occupying the territory of Greece was held not to constitute a civil and commercial matter, as operations conducted by armed forces are one of the characteristic emanations of state sovereignty.[119]

In other cases, however, the concept of civil and commercial matters appears to be interpreted expansively. A teacher, although the holder of a public office, was held not to be acting in the exercise of public authority powers when supervising a pupil who was killed in an accident, even though this was covered under a social insurance scheme.[120] Nor was a public body acting in the exercise of public powers when it sought recovery under rules of civil law from a person of sums paid by the state by way of social assistance to the divorced spouse and child of that person,[121] or when a public body sought, using principles of private law, to recover money inadvertently overpaid in the exercise of its public authority,[122] or when a state-owned airline brought a competition law claim.[123] An action brought by a consumer protection organisation against a trader was similarly held to be a civil matter.[124] The former was a private body not acting in the exercise of public powers since its action was concerned with making relationships governed by private law subject to review by the courts. Likewise forfeiture proceedings for infringement of a trade mark brought by a Trading Standards Office in the Magistrates Court were a civil matter because they were for the benefit of a private individual.[125] An action brought by a state by which it sought to enforce a private law guarantee contract was also similarly determined to be a civil and commercial matter.[126] Where an action was brought by a guarantor (A) against an importer (F) after A had paid customs duties owed by F, the action fell within the concept of civil and commercial matters based on an examination of the legal relationship between the parties to the dispute and the basis of the action.[127] A fine imposed by a court to enforce orders made in a commercial dispute was considered civil and commercial, even though not payable to a private party, because the underlying dispute concerned private rights.[128] Similarly, a claim by a local authority for an

---

[118] Case 814/79 [1980] ECR 3807. For criticism see Hartley, pp 11–15; (1981) 6 ELR 215. See also *LTU v Eurocontrol*, supra; *Re Senator Hanseatische* [1996] 2 BCLC 562; *Grovit v De Nederlandsche Bank* [2007] EWCA Civ 953, [2008] 1 WLR 51—a State bank was acting in the exercise of its public law powers when it sent out a letter which contained libellous material.

[119] Case C-292/05 *Lechouritou v Germany* [2007] ECR I-1519; Lyons (2007) ELR 563; Gartner (2007) 8 German LJ 417.

[120] Case C-172/91 *Sonntag v Waidmann* [1993] ECR I-1963; Briggs (1993) 13 YEL 517; Hartley (1994) 19 ELR 538; Plender (1993) 64 BYBIL 555.

[121] Case C-271/00 *Gemeente Steenbergen v Baten* [2002] ECR I-10489. See also Case C-433/01 *Freistaat Bayern v Jan Blijdenstein* [2004] ECR I-981 at [21]. It is different if the public body is acting under a prerogative of its own, specifically conferred on it by the legislature (in this case to ignore an agreement between spouses limiting maintenance after divorce), see *Gemeente Steenbergen v Baten* at [36].

[122] Case C-645/11 *Land Berlin v Ellen Mirjam Sapir* EU:C:2013:228, [2013] IP Pr 29.

[123] Case C-302/13 *flyLAL-Lithuanian Airlines AS v Starptautiskā lidosta Rīga VAS and Air Baltic Corporation AS* EU:C:2014:2319, [2015] IL Pr 2.

[124] Case C-167/00 *Verein Für Konsumenteninformation v K H Henkel* [2002] ECR I-8111 at [30].

[125] *R v Harrow Crown Court, ex p UNIC Centre Sarl* [2000] 1 WLR 2122.

[126] Case C-266/01 *Preservatrice Fonciere TIARD SA v Staat der Nederlanden* [2003] ECR I-4867 at [36].

[127] Case C-265/02 *Frahuil SA v Assitalia SPA* [2004] ECR I-1543 at [20].

[128] Case C-406/09 *Realchemie Nederland* [2009] ECR I-9773; Schlosser Report, p 84.

unpaid parking ticket was held to be civil and commercial, on the basis that the underlying relationship was contractual and the authority was not exercising public powers in pursuing the debt.[129] Even a claim brought by the UK tax authorities against third parties outside the UK for conspiracy to evade UK VAT was considered to be civil and commercial (and not covered by the revenue exclusion), because the action was a claim in tort governed by private law and did not require the exercise of any special public powers.[130]

Article 1 states that the Brussels I Recast shall apply "whatever the nature of the court or tribunal". It follows that a decision of a criminal court or administrative tribunal is within the Brussels I Recast provided that it relates to a civil or commercial matter.[131] An example is provided by the decision where a criminal court awarded damages to the family of a pupil negligently killed by a teacher.[132]

(b) Exclusions

Article 1 sets out a number of matters which are excluded from the scope of the Brussels I Recast, even though they are civil and commercial matters. In principle these matters should only be excluded where they are the main subject of the proceedings,[133] although as discussed below this has raised particular difficulties in relation to the exclusion of arbitration.

(i) "The status or legal capacity of natural persons, rights in property arising out of
    a matrimonial relationship or out of a relationship deemed by the law applicable
    to such relationship to have comparable effects to marriage"

The Court of Justice has held that this exclusion should not apply where the relevant question arises as an incidental or preliminary matter, such as where a party contests a contractual obligation on the grounds of incapacity.[134] For English lawyers there are no real problems in understanding what is meant by status[135] or legal capacity of natural persons,[136] although it should be noted that these must be given an autonomous EU meaning. The same cannot be said in respect of the concept of rights in property arising out of a matrimonial or comparable relationship.[137] No guidance is given in the Brussels I Recast as to the meaning of this expression. According to the Schlosser Report it is designed to exclude the matrimonial regime used in civil law countries whereby special rules on separation or community of property are established in respect of family assets.[138] The Court of Justice in the first *De Cavel*[139] case held that rights in property arising out of a matrimonial relationship covered not only matrimonial regimes but also any proprietary relationship resulting directly from the marital relationship or its dissolution. It meant the exclusion of protective measures (freezing of assets) relating to

---

[129] Case C-551/15 *Pula Parking d o o v Tederahn* EU:C:2017:193, [2017] IL Pr 15.

[130] Case C-49/12 *Her Majesty's Revenue & Customs v Sunico ApS* EU:C:2013:231, [2014] 1 QB 391.

[131] See, eg, Case 157/80 *Rinkau* [1981] ECR 1391, Hartley (1981) 6 ELR 483; Case C-7/98 *Krombach v Bamberski* [2000] ECR I-1935 at [30]; Case C-523/14 *Aannemingsbedrijf Aertssen NV and Aertssen Terrassements SA v VSB Machineverhuur BV* EU:C:2015:722, [2016] IL Pr 16. See also Arts 7(3) and 64 of the Regulation.

[132] Case C-172/91 *Sonntag v Waidmann* [1993] ECR I-1963. See also *Haji-Ioannou v Frangos* [1999] 2 Lloyd's Rep 337 at 351, CA.

[133] See the Jenard Report, p 10; Case C-266/01 *Preservatrice Fonciere TIARD SA v Staat der Nederlanden* [2003] ECR I-4867 at [42].

[134] Case C-417/15 *Schmidt v Schmidt* EU:C:2016:881, at [25], [2017] IL Pr 6.

[135] This encompasses the exercise of parental responsibility over the person of a child, including access or custody rights: see Case C-4/14 *Bohez v Wiertz* EU:C:2015:563, [2015] IL Pr 43.

[136] See the Schlosser Report, p 89; Case C-386/12 *Schneider* EU:C:2013:633, [2014] 2 WLR 1048. See also the discussion of Brussels II *bis*, infra, pp 954 et seq.

[137] See generally on matrimonial property, infra, Chapter 37.

[138] See the Schlosser Report, p 87. See also Collins, pp 25–6; Hartley, pp 17–19.

[139] Case 143/78 [1979] ECR 1055.

the property of the spouses pending divorce proceedings before a French court. The Court of Justice has also held that an action in respect of the husband's management of his wife's property must be considered to be closely connected with the proprietary relationship of the parties flowing from the marriage and was therefore excluded.[140]

There are great difficulties in applying these principles in a common law context. There is no English equivalent of the Continental matrimonial regime. In English law, a dispute concerning matrimonial property may simply be concerned with general property law principles, and the Brussels I Recast will apply, for example, where there is a dispute between a wife and a mortgagee bank in respect of a matrimonial home mortgaged by the husband.[141] Prior to the exclusion of maintenance from the Brussels I Recast, difficulties also arose in determining whether a payment or transfer of property arising out of divorce proceedings was for maintenance or concerned "rights in property arising out of a matrimonial relationship",[142] but as maintenance is now also excluded[143] this should no longer matter for present purposes.

(ii) *"Bankruptcy, proceedings relating to the winding up of insolvent companies or other legal persons, judicial arrangements, compositions and analogous proceedings"*[144]

It is intended that only proceedings arising directly from, and closely connected with, a bankruptcy should be excluded from the Brussels I Recast.[145] In *Gourdain v Nadler*[146] the Court of Justice held that a French provision, under which a manager of a company in liquidation could be ordered to pay money to form part of the assets of the company, came within the bankruptcy exclusion, the legal foundation of this action being the French law of bankruptcy and it being very closely connected with the winding-up proceedings. It has been said, obiter, that claims in a compulsory liquidation by a liquidator under section 238 (transactions at an undervalue) or section 239 (preferences) of the Insolvency Act 1986 would be within the exception.[147]

The Court of Justice has, however, emphasised the need to interpret this provision strictly. A claim by a trustee in bankruptcy to recover from a third party assets said to belong to the bankrupt's estate did not, it was held, have bankruptcy as its principal subject matter, and thus fell outside the bankruptcy exclusion,[148] as did a claim against an insolvent purchaser

---

[140] Case 25/81 *CHW v GJH* [1982] ECR 1189.

[141] See *Williams and Glyn's Bank Ltd v Boland* [1981] AC 487.

[142] Case C-220/95 *Van Den Boogaard v Laumen* [1997] ECR I-1147. For the propositions to be derived from the case see *Moore v Moore* [2007] EWCA Civ 361 at [80], [2007] IL Pr 36.

[143] Infra, pp 211–12.

[144] A question has been referred by the Bundesgerichtshof Germany to the Court of Justice in relation to this provision in Case C-339/07 *Rechtsanwalt Christopher Seagon v Deko Marty Belgium NV*. Private international law issues in insolvency are dealt with by Council regulation (EC) No 1346/2000 of 29 May 2000 on insolvency proceedings OJ 2000 L 160, now recast as Regulation (EU) 2015/848 OJ 2015 L 141; discussed infra, p 126. See generally Fletcher, *Insolvency in Private International Law* (2007) 2nd edn.

[145] See the Jenard Report, pp 11–12; the Schlosser Report, pp 89–92. See generally Fletcher, *Conflict of Laws and European Community Law* (1982), Chapter 6. This does not encompass a dispute over rights under pre-liquidation transactions: *UBS AG v Omni Holding AG (In Liquidation)* [2000] 1 WLR 916.

[146] Case 133/78 [1979] ECR 733; Hartley (1979) 4 ELR 482. See also Case C-111/08 *SCT Industri* [2009] ECR I-5655; Case C-339/07 *Deko Marty Belgium* [2009] ECR I-767.

[147] *UBS AG v Omni Holding AG (In Liquidation)* [2000] 1 WLR 916, at 922. See also *Oakley v Ultra Vehicle Design Ltd (In Liquidation)* [2005] EWHC 872 (Ch) at [42], [2005] IL Pr 55. In contrast, it has been suggested that an action under s 423 of the Insolvency Act 1986 (transactions prejudicial to creditors) falls outside the exception, Smart [1998] CJQ 149 at 153–60.

[148] *Re Hayward* [1997] Ch 45 at 53–5; Briggs (1996) 67 BYBIL 1577; Harris (1997) ELR 179; approved in *UBS AG v Omni Holding AG (In Liquidation)* [2000] 1 WLR 916 at 922. See also the *Oakley* case, supra, at [42]; Case C-157/13 *Nickel & Goeldner Spedition GmbH v "Kintra" UAB* EU:C:2014:2145, [2015] QB 96.

based on a retention of title clause,[149] and even proceedings brought by an assignee of a liquidator's right to have a transaction set aside in exercise of that right.[150] Likewise a claim by a trustee in bankruptcy for an order for the sale of the bankrupt's villa did not have bankruptcy as its principal subject matter.[151] It was a property claim that happened to be brought by a trustee in bankruptcy.

(iii) "Social Security"[152]

A claim directly relating to social security brought by or against administrative authorities would not be covered by the Brussels I Recast. A claim brought by a state authority to recover money paid as social security to a divorced person, from their former partner, was held not to be covered by this exclusion, but was still not covered by the Brussels Convention because it involved the exercise of public powers to override the settlement agreement between the partners.[153]

(iv) "Arbitration"

The essential purpose of the arbitration exclusion is to preserve the functioning of the New York Convention 1958, which regulates the effectiveness of arbitration agreements and the recognition and enforcement of arbitral awards.[154] The exact scope of the arbitration exclusion from the Brussels Convention, Brussels I Regulation, and now Brussels I Recast has, however, been one of its most contentious issues.[155] Some aspects of the exclusion are clear. It has been held that the Brussels Convention does not apply to proceedings and decisions concerning applications for the revocation, amendment, recognition and enforcement of arbitration awards.[156] Also clearly excluded, according to the Court of Justice, are proceedings which are ancillary to arbitration proceedings, such as the appointment or dismissal of arbitrators, the fixing of the place of arbitration or the extension of the time limit for making awards.[157] Recital (12) to the Brussels I Recast now provides, in part, that:

> This Regulation should not apply to any action or ancillary proceedings relating to, in particular, the establishment of an arbitral tribunal, the powers of arbitrators, the conduct of an arbitration procedure or any other aspects of such a procedure, nor to any action or judgment concerning the annulment, review, appeal, recognition or enforcement of an arbitral award.

The English courts have similarly referred to the exclusion of judicial proceedings which are integral to the arbitration process,[158] and of proceedings directed to the regulation and

---

[149] Case C-292/08 *German Graphics Graphische Maschinen GmbH v Alice van der Schee* [2009] ECR I-8421.

[150] Case C-213/10 *F-Tex SIA v Lietuvos-Anglijos UAB "Jadecloud-Vilma"* EU:C:2012:215, [2012] IL Pr 24.

[151] *Ashurst v Pollard* [2001] Ch 595, CA.

[152] See the Schlosser Report, p 92; Case C-271/00 *Gemeente Steenbergen v Baten* [2003] 1 WLR 1996—action by the administration acting under rules of the ordinary civil law to recover from a person benefits paid by way of social assistance to the divorced spouse of that person not within this exclusion, [48]–[49]. See the Schlosser Report, p 92.

[153] Case C-271/00 *Gemeente Steenbergen v Baten* [2002] ECR I-10489.

[154] See infra, Chapter 18; *Marc Rich & Co AG v Società Italiana Impianti PA (The "Atlantic Emperor") (No 2)* [1992] 1 Lloyd's Rep 624; Coleman J in *Toepfer International GmbH v Société Cargill France* [1997] 2 Lloyd's Rep 98 at 103.

[155] See the Schlosser Report, p 92.

[156] Case C-391/95 *Van Uden Maritime BV (t/a Van Uden Africa Line) v Kommanditgesellschaft in Firma Deco-Line* [1998] ECR I-7091; see also *Arab Business Consortium International Finance and Investment Co v Banque Franco Tunisienne* [1996] 1 Lloyd's Rep 485; Case C-536/13 *Gazprom OAO v Lithuania* EU:C:2015:316, [2015] 1 WLR 4937.

[157] Case C-391/95 *Van Uden Maritime BV (t/a Van Uden Africa Line) v Kommanditgesellschaft in Firma Deco-Line* [1998] ECR I-7091.

[158] *Toepfer International GmbH v Molino Boschi srl* [1996] 1 Lloyd's Rep 510 at 513; *Union de Remorquage et de Sauvetage SA v Lake Avery Inc, The Lake Avery* [1997] 1 Lloyd's Rep 540 at 549. For an example of what

support of arbitration proceedings and awards, such as for security for the costs of an arbitration.[159] However, provisional measures granted by a court using Article 35 of the Brussels I Recast[160] in support of arbitration proceedings are not ancillary to those proceedings but in parallel to them and are therefore not excluded.[161] They do not concern arbitration as such but the protection of the substantive rights of the parties.

The difficult issues concern proceedings in which the validity of the arbitration agreement is itself contested. This may arise in three ways.

First, the proceedings may have as their sole object the determination of whether the arbitration agreement is valid or invalid, such as where a claim is brought for declaratory relief in the English courts, or where the English courts are asked to restrain a party from commencing or continuing foreign proceedings by way of ordering specific performance of an English arbitration agreement.[162] In *Marc Rich & Co v Società Italiana Impianti PA*[163] the Court of Justice did not decide whether, when the issue of the existence or validity of the arbitration agreement arises on its own (ie not as a preliminary issue), this comes within the arbitration exclusion,[164] but the Advocate General supported the view that this is also excluded.[165] In *Van Uden Maritime*, the Court of Justice suggested that the Brussels Convention does not apply to judgments solely focused on determining whether an arbitration agreement is valid or not or, because it is invalid, ordering the parties not to continue the arbitration proceedings,[166] and this was confirmed (in relation to the Brussels I Regulation) in the *West Tankers* decision,[167] discussed further below.

Second, the proceedings may have as their main object a matter which would fall within the scope of the arbitration exclusion, such as the appointment of an arbitrator, but the validity of the arbitration agreement must be determined as a preliminary question to that issue. In the *Marc Rich* case the Court of Justice held that whether a dispute is excluded from the scope of the Brussels Convention should be determined by reference solely to the subject matter of the dispute.[168] The fact that, during the course of the dispute, there has to be determined a preliminary issue, whatever that issue may be, cannot affect the exclusion. It followed that

---

is not encompassed, see: *Vale Do Rio Doce Navegacao SA v Shanghai Bao Steel Ocean Shipping Co Ltd (T/A Bao Steel Ocean Shipping Co)* [2000] 2 Lloyd's Rep 1.

[159] *Lexmar v Nordisk* [1997] 1 Lloyd's Rep 289. Contrast *The Xing Su Hai* [1995] 2 Lloyd's Rep 15 at 21.

[160] Infra, p 303 et seq.

[161] The *Van Uden* case, supra.

[162] A party may not, however, be restrained from commencing or continuing proceedings in another Member State which fall within the scope of the Brussels I Recast: see infra, p 476 et seq.

[163] Case C-190/89 [1991] ECR I-3855; Hartley (1991) 16 ELR 529; Briggs (1991) 11 YEL 527; Davidson 1992 SLT 267. The Court of Appeal's decision referring the matter to the Court of Justice is reported at [1989] 1 Lloyd's Rep 438. See also *Union Transport plc v Continental Lines SA* [1992] 1 WLR 15 at 17–18; *Through Transport Mutual Insurance Association (Eurasia) Ltd v New India Assurance Association Co Ltd* [2004] EWCA (Civ) 1598 at [38]–[51], [2005] 1 Lloyd's Rep 67; *Navigation Maritime Bulgare v Rustal Trading Ltd (The Ivan Zagubanski)* [2002] 1 Lloyd's Rep 106; *Toepfer v Cargill*, supra, at 102–5.

[164] *Marc Rich & Co AG v Società Italiana Impianti PA (The "Atlantic Emperor") (No 2)* [1992] 1 Lloyd's Rep 624 at 628, 632, CA; Kaye [1993] CJQ 359.

[165] See AG Darmon's opinion in the *Marc Rich* case, supra, at 3875–6.

[166] Case C-391/95 *Van Uden Maritime BV (t/a Van Uden Africa Line) v Kommanditgesellschaft in Firma Deco-Line* [1998] ECR I-7091; the Schlosser Report, para 64; *The Lake Avery* [1997] 1 Lloyd's Rep 540 at 549; *The Ivan Zagubanski*, supra, at [100]; *Philip Alexander Securities and Futures Ltd v Bamberger* [1997] IL Pr 73 at 100 (Waller J—regardless of whether invalidity was ruled on at a preliminary stage or together with a judgment on the substance of the dispute); but cf Leggat LJ in the Court of Appeal [1997] IL Pr 104 at 115, CA; Audit (1993) 9 Arb Int 1. See generally Hascher (1997) 13 Arb Int 33.

[167] Case C-185/07 *Allianz SpA v West Tankers* [2009] ECR I-663 at [23].

[168] For the problem of recognition and enforcement of foreign judgments where a court has taken jurisdiction despite an arbitration clause, see infra, pp 644–6.

the entire litigation concerning the appointment of an arbitrator was excluded, even though the existence or validity of the arbitration agreement was raised as a preliminary issue in that litigation.

Third, the proceedings may have as their main object a matter which would fall within the scope of the Brussels I Recast, such as an ordinary claim for breach of contract, but the defendant claims that the court should not take jurisdiction because the proceedings would be in breach of an arbitration agreement. Here the approaches in the first two types of cases above would seem in tension with one another. Under the first, the determination of the validity of an arbitration agreement should not fall within the scope of the Brussels I Recast, while under the second, the main subject matter of the proceedings should determine that they do fall within the scope of the Brussels I Recast. It was long accepted that the mere fact that the invalidity of the arbitration clause is dealt with as a preliminary issue does not bring the judgment as to the substance of the claim within the exclusion.[169] But this does not resolve the question of what status should be given to a decision by the courts of a Member State regarding the invalidity of an arbitration clause, which is made incidental to a decision on the merits which falls within the scope of the Brussels I Recast.

This precise issue arose in relation to the Brussels I Regulation in the case of *Allianz SpA v West Tankers*.[170]

> West Tankers owned a ship, the *Front Comor*, which was chartered by Erg Petroli. The charter contract contained an English arbitration agreement. The ship was involved in a collision with a jetty in Italy owned by Erg. Erg claimed against its insurance policy with Allianz up to the limit of its insurance cover, and commenced arbitral proceedings in London against West Tankers for the excess. Allianz was also later added as a party to the English arbitration. Allianz commenced proceedings in the Italian courts against West Tankers, exercising rights of subrogation to Erg's claims, seeking to recover the sums paid to Erg. West Tankers commenced proceedings in the English courts asking for a declaration that Allianz was bound by the arbitration agreement in the charter contract, and an injunction to require Allianz to cease the Italian proceedings.

The House of Lords confidently expressed the view that proceedings for an injunction restraining a person from commencing or continuing proceedings abroad on the ground that such proceedings are in breach of an arbitration agreement are excluded since they "are entirely to protect the contractual right to have the dispute determined by arbitration".[171] The Court of Justice determined, however, that the House of Lords had focused on the wrong set of proceedings. The key question was not whether the English proceedings fell within the scope of the Brussels I Regulation (as proceedings solely concerned with the validity of an arbitration agreement, they did not), but whether the Italian proceedings did so. The court held that the Italian proceedings fell within the scope of the Brussels I Regulation, even though they would require the Italian court to determine (as a preliminary question) whether the claim was covered by the arbitration agreement. Thus, the court determined that proceedings whose substance falls within the scope of the Brussels I Regulation do so in their entirety, even if they require determination of the validity of an arbitration agreement as a preliminary question. As discussed further elsewhere, a key consequence of this was that an anti-suit injunction could not be awarded, as it would be contrary to the principle of mutual

---

[169] *Zellner v Phillip Alexander Securities and Futures Ltd* [1997] IL Pr 730. See also *The Atlantic Emperor (No 2)*, supra, at 632–3; *Philip Alexander Securities and Futures Ltd v Bamberger*, supra, at 94–102; *Youell v La Reunion Aerienne* [2009] EWCA Civ 175, [2009] 2 All ER (Comm) 1071.

[170] Case C-185/07 [2009] ECR I-663.

[171] *West Tankers Inc v RAS Riunione Adriatica di Sicurta SpA* [2007] UKHL 4 at [14], [2007] Lloyd's Rep 391.

trust between the courts of Member States to interfere with the ability of the Italian courts to determine the question of their own jurisdiction under the Brussels I Regulation.[172] A second consequence was that if the Italian courts did decide that the arbitration agreement was inapplicable, that decision, as a judgment under the Brussels I Regulation, would be binding on the English courts.[173]

The decision in *West Tankers* was controversial,[174] principally for the reason that the second consequence undermined the effectiveness of arbitration agreements, because it gave priority to the Italian courts rather than the English courts (the courts of the seat of the arbitration) in determining this question. Parties entering into an exclusive English arbitration agreement are likely to anticipate that any judgment as to whether the arbitration can continue will be given by the English courts (although this argument does somewhat presume the validity of the arbitration agreement), and giving priority to the Italian courts could promote abusive litigation tactics designed to frustrate the effectiveness of the arbitration agreement. As a result of these criticisms, the issue was much discussed in the negotiations for the Brussels I Recast.[175] The Hess, Pfeiffer and Schlosser Report and the European Commission advocated bringing at least some proceedings relating to arbitration within the scope of the Brussels I Recast, giving priority to the courts of the seat of arbitration (or the tribunal itself if established) in case of parallel proceedings.[176] In the end, however, this approach was not adopted, and a new Recital (12) was added providing (in part) as follows:

> This Regulation should not apply to arbitration. Nothing in this Regulation should prevent the courts of a Member State, when seised of an action in a matter in respect of which the parties have entered into an arbitration agreement, from referring the parties to arbitration, from staying or dismissing the proceedings, or from examining whether the arbitration agreement is null and void, inoperative or incapable of being performed, in accordance with their national law.

> A ruling given by a court of a Member State as to whether or not an arbitration agreement is null and void, inoperative or incapable of being performed should not be subject to the rules of recognition and enforcement laid down in this Regulation, regardless of whether the court decided on this as a principal issue or as an incidental question.

Although a Recital is not the most satisfactory way of achieving this outcome,[177] the clear intention here is to reverse the second consequence of the *West Tankers* judgment (but not the first[178]). Where a decision on the validity of an arbitration agreement arises as an incidental question to a claim which falls within the scope of the Brussels I Recast, it is now clear that the decision as to the validity of the arbitration agreement itself does not fall within the scope of the Brussels I Recast, and does not bind other Member State courts.

(v) *"Maintenance obligations arising from a family relationship, parentage, marriage or affinity"*

Maintenance obligations are (newly) excluded from the scope of the Brussels I Recast, following the adoption of Council Regulation (EC) No 4/2009 of 18 December 2008 on

---

[172] Infra, p 479 et seq.

[173] Confirmed in *National Navigacion v Endesa (The Wadi Sudr)* [2009] EWCA Civ 1397, [2010] 2 All ER (Comm) 1243; Fentiman [2010] CLJ 242; *DHL GBS (UK) Ltd v Fallimento Finmatica SpA* [2009] EWHC 291 (Comm), [2009] 1 Lloyd's Rep 430. See further infra, p 480.

[174] See eg Fentiman [2009] CLJ 278; Briggs [2009] LMCLQ 161; Peel (2009) 125 LQR 365; Radicati di Brozolo (2011) 7 J Priv Int L 423.

[175] See generally Hartley (2014) 63 ICLQ 843.

[176] Study JLS/C4/2005/03, Final Version September 2007, paras 862–70; Proposal for a Regulation of the European Parliament and of the Council on jurisdiction and the recognition and enforcement of judgments in civil and commercial matters (Recast), COM(2010) 748 final.

[177] As a Recital is merely an aid to interpretation. But the effect of the Recital is also assisted by Article 73(2).

[178] See infra, p 480.

jurisdiction, applicable law, recognition and enforcement of decisions and cooperation in matters relating to maintenance obligations.[179] The Brussels I Regulation and Brussels Convention had both included rules dealing with jurisdiction over maintenance claims.[180]

Maintenance is not defined in the Brussels I Recast and was not defined in the Brussels I Regulation or Brussels Convention, which raised some difficulties,[181] although the 2008 Maintenance Regulation and the case law arising thereunder is likely to provide greater clarity. Under the Convention, it was held that maintenance can include lump sum as well as periodical payments.[182] The subject of maintenance was discussed by the Court of Justice in the second *De Cavel* case,[183] where it was held that interim compensatory payments payable on a monthly basis by one spouse to another as part of a French judgment dissolving a marriage were in the nature of maintenance, a crucial point being that they were designed to support that spouse and were based on need. This meant that the case fell within the terms of the Brussels Convention, but would now mean that it fell outside the scope of the Brussels I Recast. The application of these criteria to the financial orders that can be made by English courts is dealt with later on in the book, where maintenance is considered in detail.[184]

(vi) *"Wills and succession, including maintenance obligations arising by reason of death"*
The concept of wills and succession is well understood in English law,[185] although once again it must be noted that it should be given an autonomous meaning for the purposes of the Brussels I Recast. The exclusion of these matters from the Brussels I Recast is motivated in part by the adoption in 2012 of a Regulation dealing specifically with jurisdiction and applicable law in matters of succession,[186] and the jurisprudence on the Succession Regulation should aid in interpretation.[187] The United Kingdom has, however, not opted in to the Succession Regulation, and thus these matters remain governed by common law jurisdictional rules.[188]

(ii) *Whether the defendant is domiciled in a Member State*

When examining the scope of the Brussels I Recast, it is necessary to distinguish between: (a) bases of jurisdiction (Chapter II, Sections 1–7); (b) other provisions on jurisdiction in Chapter II; (c) provisions on recognition and enforcement in Chapter III. It is only in the first of these, the bases of jurisdiction under the Brussels I Recast, that an initial basic distinction is drawn between the situation where the defendant is and is not domiciled in a Member State.[189] Section 1 of Chapter II notes certain exceptions where this basic distinction does not operate. The position can be summarised as follows:

---

[179] Recital (10). See infra, p 1064 et seq.

[180] Art 5(2).

[181] See generally the Schlosser Report, pp 101–5.

[182] See ibid, p 102.

[183] Case 120/79 *De Cavel v De Cavel (No 2)* [1980] ECR 731. It does not matter whether it is an interim or final order, see the first *De Cavel* case, Case 143/78 [1979] ECR 1055; Hartley (1979) 4 ELR 222. The wording of Art 5(2) of the Brussels Convention was altered expressly to include payments ancillary to divorce proceedings, see the Schlosser Report, pp 84–7.

[184] Infra, Chapter 24.

[185] See *Re Hayward* [1997] Ch 45 at 53–4. See generally infra, Chapter 36.

[186] Regulation (EU) No 650/2012 of the European Parliament and of the Council of 4 July 2012 on jurisdiction, applicable law, recognition and enforcement of decisions and acceptance and enforcement of authentic instruments in matters of succession and on the creation of a European Certificate of Succession OJ 2012 L 201/107.

[187] See *Winkler v Shamoon* [2016] EWHC 217 (Ch).

[188] See infra, Chapter 36.

[189] For the position under the Brussels I Recast as regards other provisions on jurisdiction, see infra, p 444; for recognition and enforcement, see infra, p 611.

(a) Where the defendant is domiciled in a Member State the bases of jurisdiction under the Brussels I Recast will apply and not the traditional rules of jurisdiction of the forum.

(b) Where the defendant is not domiciled in a Member State, in general, the traditional rules of jurisdiction of the forum will apply.

(c) There are exceptions to (b), ie some of the bases of jurisdiction under the Brussels I Recast (Articles 18(1), 21(2), 24 and 25) will apply to defendants, even though they are not domiciled in a Member State.

Each of these will be looked at in more detail.

(a) Where the defendant is domiciled in a Member State

Article 4 contains the most important basis of jurisdiction under the Brussels I Recast, that a defendant domiciled in a Member State is subject to the jurisdiction of the courts of that State. If the defendant is to be sued in the courts of a Member State other than that of his domicile, Article 5(1) provides that this can only be done by virtue of the bases of jurisdiction set out in Sections 2 to 7. This prevents national courts from using their traditional rules on jurisdiction, including their exorbitant rules, against a defendant who is domiciled in a Member State.[190] In the United Kingdom's case this means that, against such a defendant, jurisdiction can no longer be founded on presence of the defendant in the forum or through service out of the jurisdiction under rule 6.36 and Practice Direction 6B of the Civil Procedure Rules.[191] (Where there is a basis of jurisdiction under the Brussels I Recast, the claim form may be served (without the permission of the court) on a defendant with a place of business in the territory under CPR rule 6.9 or outside the territory pursuant to CPR rule 6.33.)[192] Article 5(1) does not refer to the domicile of the *claimant*. It follows that, for example, a Japanese domiciliary, although not domiciled in a Member State, would have to use the bases of jurisdiction under the Brussels I Recast if he wished to sue in a Member State a defendant who was so domiciled.

Articles 4 and 5 require courts to decide whether a defendant is domiciled in a Member State. At least for English purposes, it is the defendant's domicile at the moment of the issue of proceedings which matters, rather than at the time of their subsequent service on the defendant.[193] As discussed previously, Paragraph 9 of Schedule 1 to the Civil Jurisdiction and Judgments Order 2001[194] contains a provision for determining, for the purposes of the Brussels I Recast, when an individual is domiciled in the United Kingdom.[195] He is so domiciled if and only if (a) he is resident in the United Kingdom, and (b) the nature and circumstances of his residence indicate that he has a substantial connection with the United Kingdom, with a period of three months residence giving rise to a presumed substantial connection. If the individual is not domiciled in the United Kingdom it then has to be seen whether he is domiciled in another Member State. Paragraph 9 has no provisions for determining this. This is consistent with Article 62 of the Brussels I Recast, which, it will be recalled,[196] provides that, in order to determine whether a party is domiciled in another Member State, the courts shall apply the law of that state.

---

[190] These rules were formerly listed in Annex I to the Brussels I Regulation; see now Article 76(1) of the Brussels I Recast and OJ 2015 C 4/2.

[191] See the Schlosser Report, p 100. CPR, r 6.36 and PD6B is discussed infra, p 334 et seq.

[192] See further infra, p 308.

[193] *Canada Trust Co v Stolzenberg (No 2)* [2002] 1 AC 1. See also *Ministry of Defence and Support of the Armed Forces for the Islamic Republic of Iran v FAZ Aviation Ltd* [2007] EWHC 1042 (Comm) at [5], [52], [53], [2007] IL Pr 42. For the position where proceedings are brought in Scotland see *Canada Trust*, per Lord Hope at 23–6.

[194] SI 2001/3929, amended by SI 2007/1655.

[195] Para 9(2). The Modified Regulation will also apply if he is. See further supra, p 199.

[196] See supra, p 198.

As regards the domicile of companies, recourse must be had to the autonomous definition contained in Article 63 of the Brussels I Recast. Accordingly, a company will be domiciled in the United Kingdom if it has its statutory seat, or central administration, or principal place of business there. In the situation where a court in the United Kingdom (or indeed a court in another Member State) is deciding whether a company is domiciled in the United Kingdom,[197] "statutory seat" means the registered office or, where there is no such office anywhere, the place of incorporation or, where there is no such place anywhere, the place under the law of which the formation took place. Article 63 will likewise apply in order to determine whether a company is domiciled in another Member State, although the special provision equating the "statutory seat" with the registered office will only apply if the other Member State is Cyprus or Ireland. Under Article 63 a company may be domiciled in more than one State. For example, it may have its statutory seat in Panama but its central administration in Germany. In such a case the company undoubtedly has a domicile in a Member State. The bases of jurisdiction contained in the Brussels I Recast will apply and the company cannot be sued in a Member State under that State's traditional rules on jurisdiction.[198]

(b) The defendant is not domiciled in a Member State

Where the defendant is not domiciled in a Member State, Article 6 states that the jurisdiction of the courts of each Member State shall, subject to Article 18(1), Article 21(2) and Articles 24 and 25, be determined by the law of that Member State. If, to take an example, an Englishman wishes to sue a Californian domiciliary in England, he would generally have to do so under the traditional English rules on jurisdiction (examined in Chapter 12), which are, by and large, more generous to the claimant than their equivalent under the Brussels I Recast, although consider jurisdiction to be discretionary. Article 6 therefore recognises the use of exorbitant jurisdiction by Member States in certain circumstances. This has far-reaching consequences when it comes to enforcing judgments and declining jurisdiction in cases of *lis pendens* between Member States, which are matters governed by the Brussels I Recast regardless of domicile.[199]

Article 6 requires the courts of Member States to ascertain when a defendant is not domiciled in any Member State. In practice, this usually does not require identifying the domicile of the defendant, but only deciding that an individual defendant is not domiciled in the United Kingdom or in any other Member State under the respective applicable definitions of domicile. In the rare situations where the particular non-Member State in which the defendant is domiciled has to be ascertained,[200] this is done by applying paragraph 9(7) of Schedule 1 to the Civil Jurisdiction and Judgments Order 2001, which provides that an individual is domiciled in a state other than a Regulation State if and only if (a) he is resident in that state, and (b) the nature and circumstances of his residence indicate that he has a substantial connection with that state.[201] In this particular context there is no presumption to aid in showing the required substantial connection, and it is possible, in rare cases, that an individual may not have a substantial connection with any one state at all. Where this happens one would have to be resigned to saying that the individual is domiciled in a non-Regulation

---

[197] The better view is that this is what "for the purposes of the United Kingdom" means, as required by Art 63(2). See *supra*, p 200.

[198] *The Deichland* [1990] 1 QB 361, CA; *The Rewia* [1991] 2 Lloyd's Rep 325, CA.

[199] See the Jenard Report, pp 20–1, and *infra*, pp 444 and 611.

[200] It may be necessary to ascertain the particular non-Regulation State because of Art 72, discussed *infra*, p 643.

[201] It may be queried whether "State" is here referring to the political unit, eg the USA, or to a law district, eg New York. When para 9(7) refers to a Regulation State this means a political unit; it is arguable that "a state other than a Regulation State" likewise means a political unit. On the other hand, the normal meaning of a state in English private international law is that of a law district.

State but it is not clear in which particular one.[202] As regards corporate defendants, Article 63 of the Brussels I Recast will be applied to determine whether a company is domiciled in a non-Member State.

The Hess, Pfeiffer and Schlosser Report identified a problem with Article 4 of the Brussels I Regulation (now Article 6 of the Brussels I Recast) in that it results in an unequal system of access to justice for European Community (now European Union) plaintiffs.[203] This comes about because the national rules of jurisdiction in some Member States are open to plaintiffs, regardless of their domicile, whereas in other Member States they are only available to plaintiffs domiciled in that Member State.[204] In the negotiations of the Brussels I Recast, it was decided not to extend the rules to cover claims against non-Member State domiciled defendants,[205] which would have addressed this issue.

(c) The exceptions
Article 6 mentions four exceptions to the rule that national bases of jurisdiction apply where the defendant is not domiciled in a Member State: Article 18(1), Article 21(2) and Articles 24 and 25. Article 18(1) gives jurisdiction to the courts of the domicile of a consumer in certain circumstances, regardless of the domicile of the defendant.[206] Article 21(2) may similarly give jurisdiction to the courts of the place of work of an employee regardless of the domicile of the defendant.[207] Article 24 gives exclusive jurisdiction in certain circumstances, regardless of the defendant's domicile, based on subject matter connections between the dispute and a particular Member State. Article 25 is concerned with agreements on jurisdiction, and since the Brussels I Recast does not require either party to be domiciled in a Member State—previously, at least one party had to be so domiciled for the rule to apply.[208] It may be noted in addition that some other provisions—in particular, Articles 11(2), 17(2) and 20(2)—deem a defendant to be domiciled in a Member State in circumstances which would ordinarily not satisfy the relevant requirements.[209]

(d) Claimant's domicile
There is no requirement for the application of Chapter II of the Brussels I Recast that the claimant is domiciled in a Member State.[210] Thus the Brussels I Recast will apply in a dispute between a claimant domiciled in a non-Member State and a defendant domiciled in a Member State.[211] There are some bases of jurisdiction which presuppose that the claimant is domiciled in a Member State, because they permit a claimant to sue in the Member State court of their own domicile.[212] If the claimant is not so domiciled these bases cannot be used. But it remains open to the claimant to use other bases of jurisdiction.

---

[202] See, supra, n 200.

[203] Study JLS/C4/2005/03, Final Version September 2007, para 875 and paras 155–65.

[204] Jurisdictional rules may not, however, be restricted based on the nationality of the plaintiff: see Brussels I Recast, Art 6(2).

[205] See supra, p 191; Gillies (2012) 8 J Priv Int L 489.

[206] See infra, p 296.

[207] See infra, p 301.

[208] See infra, p 230.

[209] See infra, pp 289, 296 and 299.

[210] Case C-412/98 *Universal General Insurance Co (UGIC) v Group Josi Reinsurance Co SA* [2000] ECR I-5925; Peel [2001] YEL 354.

[211] Case C-412/98 Universal General Insurance Co (UGIC) v Group Josi Reinsurance Co SA [2000] ECR I-5925, at [61]. See also Case C-190/89 *Marc Rich & Co v Società Italiana Impianti PA* [1991] ECR I-3855; Case C-406/92 *The Tatry* [1994] ECR I-5439. See also Case C-281/02 *Owusu v Jackson* [2005] I-1383 at [27].

[212] Arts 11(1)(b) and 18(2).

(c) Bases of jurisdiction

The first seven Sections of Chapter II set out the bases of jurisdiction under the Brussels I Recast, with each Section containing one or more bases of jurisdiction. The division into Sections emphasises that different types of jurisdiction are being dealt with. The Brussels I Recast provides for: (i) general jurisdiction (Section 1, Article 4); (ii) special jurisdiction (Section 2, Articles 7–9); (iii) jurisdiction in matters relating to insurance (Section 3, Articles 10–16); (iv) jurisdiction over consumer contracts (Section 4, Articles 17–19); (v) jurisdiction over individual contracts of employment (Section 5, Articles 20–23); (vi) exclusive jurisdiction (Section 6, Article 24); and (vii) prorogation of jurisdiction (Section 7, Articles 25–26).

In this Chapter the various grounds of jurisdiction will be dealt with in order of hierarchy (based on precedence and generality) rather than in the order of the Brussels I Recast itself. First, the most powerful grounds of jurisdiction, those of exclusive jurisdiction, will be examined. Second, the rules on prorogation of jurisdiction, which are the next most powerful rules, will be considered. Third, the rules on general jurisdiction, based on the domicile of the defendant, will be set out. Fourth, the rules on special jurisdiction, permitting claims to be brought in other Member States based on subject matter connections, will be examined. Finally, the special rules on matters relating to insurance, consumer contracts, and individual contracts of employment will be considered.

In some situations, the claimant will have to sue the defendant in the courts of a Member State which is allocated exclusive jurisdiction under the Brussels I Recast. In other situations, the courts of more than one Member State will have jurisdiction and the claimant will be able to choose the Member State in which to sue the defendant. With the harmonisation of rules on jurisdiction in the different Member States, lawyers in the United Kingdom can now advise many clients on whether they can sue or be sued not only in the United Kingdom but also in other Member States.

When the issue comes to trial in England under the Brussels I Recast, it is well established that the claimant has to show a good arguable case that the terms of the relevant jurisdictional rule is satisfied, whether under Article 4,[213] 7 or 8,[214] 25,[215] or any other basis of jurisdiction.[216] A good arguable case has a certain flexibility and suggests that one party has a much better argument on the evidence available.[217] The

---

[213] *Haji-Ioannou v Frangos* [1999] 2 Lloyd's Rep 337, 348, CA; in *Royal & Sun Alliance Insurance plc v MK Digital FZE (Cyprus) Ltd* [2006] EWCA Civ 629 at [86], [2006] 2 Lloyd's Rep 110. See also *Latchin (t/a Dinkha Latchin Associates) v General Mediterranean Holdings SA)* [2002] CLC 330, 336–9; *Chellaram v Chellaram (No 2)* [2002] EWHC 632 (Ch) at [23], [2002] 3 All ER 17; *King v Crown Energy Trading AG* [2003] EWHC 163 (Comm) at [4], [2003] IL Pr 28.

[214] *Canada Trust Co v Stolzenberg (No 2)* [1998] 1 WLR 547 at 553–9, CA, approved by the House of Lords [2002] 1 AC 1 at 13 (per Lord Steyn, with whom the other Law Lords concurred); Briggs (2000) 71 BYBIL 446; Look Chan Ho (2001) 50 ICLQ 632; *Masri v Consolidated Contractors International (UK) Ltd* [2005] EWCA Civ 1436 at [15], [2006] 1 WLR 830. See also in *Deutsche Ruckversicherung AG v La Fondiara Assicurazioni SpA* [2001] 2 Lloyd's Rep 621 at 622. This adopts the same test as applies for service out of the jurisdiction with the permission of the courts under the traditional rules, infra, p 335.

[215] *Bols Distilleries v Superior Yacht Services Ltd* [2006] UKPC 45 at [27]–[28], [2007] 1 WLR 12. See also *Carnoustie Universal v International Transport Workers Federation* [2002] EWHC 1624 (Comm) at [47], [2003] IL Pr 7; *Evialis SA v SIAT* [2003] EWHC 863 (Comm) 377 at [70]–[71], [2003] 2 Lloyd's Rep 377; *Bank of Tokyo-Mitsubishi Ltd v Baskan Gida Sanayi Ve Pazarlama AS* [2004] EWHC 945 (Ch) at [193], [2004] 2 Lloyd's Rep 395; *Cube Lighting And Industrial Design Ltd v Afcon Electra Romania SA* [2011] EWHC 2565 (Ch).

[216] *Bank of Tokyo-Mitsubishi* case, supra, at [193]; *Kolden Holdings Ltd v Rodette Commerce Ltd* [2008] EWCA Civ 10, [2008] 3 All ER 612.

[217] *Masri v Consolidated Contractors International (UK) Ltd* [2005] EWCA Civ 1436, [2006] 1 WLR 830; the *Bols Distilleries* case, supra, at [28]; the *Bank of Tokyo-Mitsubishi* case, supra, at [193]; *Konkola Copper*

requirement of a good arguable case is intended to encapsulate the rule that the court must be as satisfied as it can be, having regard to the limitations of the interlocutory process, that factors exist which allow the court to take jurisdiction.[218] The application of the test may vary from case to case, both in order to take account of any relevant policy underlying the Brussels I Recast and in order to take account of the limitations imposed by the interlocutory process.[219] Moreover, there is a threshold requirement, at least in cases of special jurisdiction, which the claimant has to satisfy before the defendant can be subjected to jurisdiction. The claimant's case must establish that there is a serious issue on the merits to be tried.[220] Common sense would suggest that the same requirement should apply in respect of the other bases of jurisdiction.[221]

If a defendant domiciled in one Member State is sued in the court of another Member State and does not enter an appearance,[222] the court is required to examine its own jurisdiction and declare of its own motion that it has no jurisdiction unless its jurisdiction is derived from the provisions of the Brussels I Recast.[223] This is a fundamental change of procedure for English courts, which had, in the past, only acted after submissions from the parties.[224]

(i) Exclusive subject-matter jurisdiction

Article 24[225] allocates jurisdiction to the courts of a Member State[226] which is thought to be uniquely well placed to deal with the subject matter listed in that Article. So strong is this connection that Article 24 expressly provides that it applies regardless of domicile. Despite Court of Appeal authority to the contrary,[227] it is clearly therefore an exception to the normal rule that the bases of jurisdiction under the Brussels I Recast only apply where the defendant is domiciled in a Member State.[228] Where jurisdiction is assigned to the United Kingdom

---

Mines plc v Coromin Ltd [2006] EWCA Civ 5 at [86], [2006] 1 Lloyd's Rep 410; *Benatti v WPP Holdings Italy srl* [2007] EWCA Civ 263 at [42]–[44] (per Toulson LJ), [2007] 1 WLR 2316. But see also *Konkola* at [96] where Rix LJ suggests a different test where a jurisdictional issue goes to the heart of the merits. See also Rix LJ in *Royal & Sun Alliance Insurance PLC v MK Digital FZE (Cyprus) Ltd* [2006] EWCA Civ 629 at [62], [2006] 2 Lloyd's Rep 110.

[218] *Benatti v WPP Holdings*, supra, at [41]; the *Bols Distilleries* case, supra, at [28].

[219] *Benatti v WPP Holdings*, supra, at [41].

[220] *AK Investment CJSC v Kyrgyz Mobil Tel Ltd* [2011] UKPC 7. See also *ABKCO Music & Records Inc v Music Collection International Ltd* [1995] RPC 657, CA; *Mecklermedia Corpn v DC Congress GmbH* [1998] Ch 40 at 46; *Grupo Torras SA and Torras Hostench London Ltd v Sheikh Fahad Mohammed Al-Sabah* [1995] 1 Lloyd's Rep 374. Cf *Surzur Overseas Ltd v Koros* [1999] 2 Lloyd's Rep 611 at 613 CA, where the standard was wrongly described as being a good arguable case. The standard of proof as to the merits is a matter for national courts as part of determining their own jurisdiction: Case C-68/93 *Shevill v Presse Alliance SA* [1995] ECR I-415.

[221] The argument against is based on the analogy with the traditional rules, where there is no such requirement in relation to defendants within the jurisdiction; see in support of this argument the *Mecklermedia* case, supra.

[222] As in the context of Art 26 prorogation (discussed below), contesting jurisdiction is not entering an appearance, see Case C-148/03 *Nurnberger Allgemeine Versicherungs AG v Portbridge Transport International BV* [2004] ECR I-10327.

[223] Art 28(1).

[224] See the Schlosser Report, pp 81–2. See also Art 27 and Case 288/82 *Duijnstee v Goderbauer* [1983] ECR 3663. See generally Kohler (1985) 34 ICLQ 563, 573–4.

[225] Art 22 of the Brussels I Regulation and Art 16 of the Brussels Convention.

[226] For discussion of what should happen if there is an equivalent connection with a non-Member State, see infra, p 473 et seq.

[227] *Choudhary v Bhatter* [2009] EWCA Civ 1176, [2010] 2 All ER 1031. But see *Dar Al Arkan Real Estate Development Co v Refai* [2014] EWCA Civ 715, [2015] 1 WLR 135.

[228] Case C-343/04 *Land Oberosterreich v CEZ AS* [2006] ECR I-4557 at [21]; Case C-73/04 *Klein & Klein* [2005] ECR I-8667 at [14]. See generally supra, pp 214–15. Both the claimant and defendant could be domiciled in a non-Member State, see Case C-281/02 *Owusu v Jackson* [2005] ECR I-1383 at [28].

under Article 24, the Modified Regulation will apply to allocate jurisdiction to a part of the United Kingdom. For example, where the proceedings concern the ownership of land in England, the English courts will have exclusive jurisdiction.

The jurisdiction under Article 24 is exclusive in the sense that a Member State other than the one which has been allocated jurisdiction under it is deprived of jurisdiction, even though it would otherwise have had it under one of the other bases of jurisdiction such as the domicile of the defendant. Article 24 therefore trumps other bases of jurisdiction, even jurisdiction based on the agreement of the parties.[229] Exceptionally, jurisdiction under Article 24 is not subject to the *lis pendens* rules in the Brussels I Recast, because breach of Article 24 operates as a defence to the recognition and enforcement of foreign judgments.[230] The courts of Member States are required by Article 27 to declare of their own motion that they do not have jurisdiction where they are seised of a claim which is "principally concerned" with a matter over which the courts of another Member State have exclusive jurisdiction by virtue of Article 24. This perhaps suggests that Article 24 should also only apply where the proceedings are "principally concerned" with one of the identified matters,[231] an approach which is generally supported by the case law. The requirement under Article 27 applies to Member States regardless of their own rules on procedure, and regardless of what steps have been taken by the defendant.[232] Where more than one Member State is allocated jurisdiction under Article 24, Article 31 provides that any court other than the one first seised shall decline jurisdiction.[233]

Article 24 has five heads: (i) immovable property; (ii) certain company law matters; (iii) validity of entries in public registers; (iv) certain matters involving intellectual property; (v) enforcement of judgments. The reported cases on the corresponding provisions in the Brussels I Regulation (Article 22) and Brussels Convention (Article 16), have given a Community meaning to its terms and have interpreted the heads in the light of their purpose and their place within the scheme of the Convention. It has repeatedly been emphasised that this provision must not be given a wider interpretation than is required by its objective.[234] This has often led to what is now Article 24 of the Brussels I Recast being given a narrow interpretation (because it is an exception to the general rules on jurisdiction and restricts party autonomy), but on some occasions a wide interpretation has been adopted to give effect to the purposes of Article 24 and to avoid splitting closely related proceedings.[235] The head which has the most contentious repercussions is the first one and this will be examined in detail; the remaining four heads will be set out more briefly.

---

[229] See Recital (19) of the Brussels I Recast. Note, however, that this does not affect whether other courts may award provisional measures: see Case C-616/10 *Solvay SA v Honeywell Fluorine Products Europe BV* EU:C:2012:445; infra, p 305.

[230] Art 45(1)(e)(ii); see infra, p 642.

[231] See, eg, the opinion of the Advocate General in the *Duijnstee* case, supra; *Re Polly Peck International plc (No 2)* [1998] 3 All ER 812 at 828, CA; *Coin Controls Ltd v Suzo International (UK) Ltd* [1999] Ch 33 at 50–1; *Prudential Assurance Co Ltd v Prudential Insurance Co of America* [2003] EWCA Civ 327, [2003] 1 WLR 2295; *Anan Kasei Co Ltd v Molycorp Chemicals & Oxides (Europe) Ltd* [2016] EWHC 1722 (Pat), [2016] Bus LR 945.

[232] Case 288/82 *Duijnstee v Goderbauer* [1983] ECR 3663; Hartley (1984) 10 ELR 64.

[233] See *Prudential Assurance Co Ltd v Prudential Insurance Co of America* [2003] EWCA Civ 327 at [25], [2003] 1 WLR 2295.

[234] Case 73/77 *Sanders v van der Putte* [1977] ECR 2383 at [17]–[18]; Case C-73/04 *Klein v Rhodos Management Ltd* [2005] ECR I-8667 at [15]; Case C-343/04 *Land Oberosterreich v CEZ AS* [2006] ECR I-4557 at [26]–[27].

[235] Cf *Duijnstee v Goderbauer*, supra (on what is now Art 24(4)); Case 73/77 *Sanders v van der Putte* [1977] ECR 2383; Case 241/83 *Rösler v Rottwinkel* [1985] ECR 99; *Speed Investments Ltd v Formula One Holdings Ltd (No 2)* [2004] EWCA Civ 1512, [2005] 1 WLR 1936.

Article 24 provides that the following courts shall have exclusive jurisdiction, regardless of domicile:

> **Article 24(1)** in proceedings which have as their object rights *in rem* in immovable property or tenancies of immovable property, the courts of the Member State in which the property is situated.[236]

This rule is comparable to the common law rule that disputes concerning title to foreign immovable property are non-justiciable.[237] For Article 24(1) to apply (at least directly), the immovable property must be situated in a Member State or States. It is somewhat unclear whether the common law rule is compatible with the Brussels I Recast;[238] if not, this raises difficulties when dealing with claims against Member State domiciled defendants concerning title to immovable property in a non-Member State.[239]

If the dispute relates to property situated in two Member States (eg it concerns the existence of a lease over such property) the Court of Justice in *Scherrens v Maenhout*[240] has held that normally each Member State has exclusive jurisdiction over the property situated in the territory of the state. Nonetheless, in certain exceptional circumstances one State may be given exclusive jurisdiction over the entire property. An example given of where this might happen would be where property is subject to a single lease, the land in one Member State is adjacent to the land in the other Member State and the property is situated almost entirely in one of those two Member States. In cases where the property is situated in the United Kingdom, the Modified Regulation will apply to allocate jurisdiction to a part of the United Kingdom. Article 24(1) covers two sorts of proceedings: ones which have as their object (ie are based upon) rights *in rem* in immovable property and ones which have as their object tenancies of immovable property.

(a) Rights *in rem*

The proceedings must have as their object a right which is enforceable against the whole world (a right *in rem*), not a right which is merely enforceable against a particular person (a right *in personam*). Thus proceedings involving a claim to legal ownership of one-half of a villa in Minorca, together with an order that steps be taken to rectify the Minorcan property register and an order for the sale of the villa and division of proceeds, had as their object a right *in rem*.[241] The essence of the proceedings was an attempt by the trustee to establish, protect and perfect his title.[242] Proceedings involving the disputed exercise of a right of pre-emption attached to property and effective against third parties have also been considered to fall within this rule.[243]

In contrast, the following have as their object a right *in personam*, and are accordingly outside the scope of Article 24(1):[244] proceedings for rescission of a contract of sale of land and for consequential damages;[245] proceedings to determine the validity of a contract for the

---

[236] Art 22(1) of the Brussels I Regulation; Art 16(1)(a) of the Brussels Convention, prior to that Art 16(1).

[237] See infra, p 484 et seq.

[238] See *Lucasfilm v Ainsworth* [2009] EWCA Civ 1328, [2010] Ch 503; [2011] UKSC 39 at [113], [2012] 1 AC 208; Rogerson [2010] CLJ 245; Dicey, Morris and Collins, para 23-026 et seq.

[239] See infra, p 473 et seq.

[240] Case 158/87 [1988] ECR 3791; Hartley (1989) 11 ELR 57.

[241] *Re Hayward* [1997] Ch 45 at 56–7. See further *Webb v Webb* [1991] 1 WLR 1410; Case C-605/14 *Komu v Komu* EU:C:2015:833, [2016] 4 WLR 26; *G v G* [2016] EWCA Civ 1292.

[242] *Re Hayward*, supra, at 48; distinguished in *Ashurst v Pollard* [2001] Ch 595, 608, CA, on which see Carruthers, paras 2.39–2.50.

[243] Case C-438/12 *Weber v Weber* EU:C:2014:212, [2015] Ch 140.

[244] But note Article 8(4)—see infra, p 288.

[245] Case C-518/99 *Gaillard v Chekili* [2001] ECR I-2771.

transfer of land;[246] proceedings for a declaration that the defendant holds property on trust for the claimant and for an order requiring him to execute documents vesting legal title in the claimant;[247] proceedings for a declaration that a person is an equal owner in equity of property;[248] proceedings brought by a trustee in bankruptcy for an order for the sale of a villa with vacant possession (which did not involve establishing, protecting or perfecting his title to the land);[249] proceedings for compensation for the use of a flat, otherwise than under a tenancy and the ownership of which was not in dispute;[250] proceedings to determine the existence or scope of an easement;[251] proceedings for the restoration of property to its original condition;[252] and an action to terminate the appointment of a manager of a timeshare development in Spain and eject him from the property.[253]

According to the Court of Justice in *Reichert v Dresdner Bank*[254] Article 16(1) of the Brussels Convention (Article 24(1) of the Brussels I Recast) is only concerned with actions which determine "the extent, content, ownership or possession of immovable property or the existence of other rights *in rem* therein and to provide the holders of those rights with the protection of the powers which attach to their interest". Applying this narrow Community definition the Court held that an action whereby a creditor sought to have set aside a gift of the legal ownership of immovable property which he alleged was made by the debtor to defraud his creditors (an *action paulienne*) did not come within the scope of Article 16(1) of the Brussels Convention. This action did not concern the rules and customs of the situs and accordingly there was no reason why it should come within the exclusive jurisdiction of the courts of the situs.

Likewise, applying this narrow Community definition, the Court of Justice held in *Land Oberosterreich v CEZ AS* that Article 16(1) of the Brussels Convention does not apply to an action, possibly preventative, for cessation of a nuisance.[255] Although the basis of such an action was the interference with a right *in rem* in immovable property, the real and immovable nature of that right was, in that context, of only marginal significance.[256] Moreover, considerations of the sound administration of justice which underlie exclusive jurisdiction under Article 16(1) (now Article 24(1)) did not apply to this particular case of nuisance, which involved a claimant and defendant with land in different states, requiring an assessment of facts relating to both States.[257] Finally, this narrow definition would exclude actions for damages based on infringement of rights *in rem* or on damage to property in which rights *in rem* exist, since the existence and content of such rights *in rem*, usually rights of ownership, are of only marginal significance.[258]

---

[246] Case C-417/15 *Schmidt v Schmidt* EU:C:2016:881, [2017] IL Pr 6.

[247] Case C-294/92 *Webb v Webb* [1994] ECR I-1717; Briggs (1994) 110 LQR 526; (1994) 14 YEL 563; Hartley (1994) 19 ELR 547; Rogerson [1994] CLJ 462; Birks (1994) 8 Trust Law Int 99; MacMillan [1996] Conv 125.

[248] *Prazic v Prazic* [2006] EWCA Civ 497, [2006] 2 FLR 1125.

[249] *Ashurst v Pollard* [2001] Ch 595, CA; Briggs (2000) 71 BYBIL 443; Harris [2001] LMCLQ 205.

[250] Case C-292/93 *Lieber v Göbel* [1994] ECR I-2535; Briggs (1994) 14 YEL 572.

[251] Case C-343/04 *Land Oberosterreich v CEZ AS* [2006] ECR I-4557, opinion of AG Maduro at [82].

[252] *Fondation Solomon v Guggenheim v D Helion* [1997] IL Pr 457, French Sup Ct.

[253] *Barratt International Resorts Ltd v Martin* 1994 SLT 434.

[254] Case 15/88 [1990] ECR I-27; Hartley (1991) 16 ELR 69. See also the earlier Scots case of *Ferguson's Trustee v Ferguson* 1990 SLT (Sh Ct) 73.

[255] Case C-343/04 *Land Oberosterreich v CEZ AS* [2006] ECR I-4557.

[256] Ibid, at [34].

[257] Ibid, at [37]–[38].

[258] Ibid, at [33]. See similarly *Pearce v Ove Arup Partnership* [1997] Ch 293 at 302 (the case related to intellectual property; the court held that even if such property were covered by the provision, infringement proceedings would not be); revsd by CA on a different point [2000] Ch 403.

(b) Tenancies

Article 24(1) also applies to proceedings which have as their object tenancies of immovable property. Leases involve complex social legislation and the courts of the Member State where this is in force are best able to apply their own law and are accordingly given exclusive jurisdiction.[259] A tenancy does not include a claim for compensation for the use of a property, where a transfer in ownership has been annulled.[260] The difficulty with including tenancies under Article 24(1) is that in some cases a dispute between a landlord and a tenant may relate essentially to the land itself (this is within Article 24(1)); whereas, in other cases, the issue may relate more obviously to the contractual rights and obligations between the parties (which are less obviously within the ambit of Article 24(1)).

In *Sanders v Van der Putte*[261] the Court of Justice held that, where the dispute relates to the existence or interpretation of the lease, compensation for damage caused by the tenant[262] or for giving up possession of the premises, it was within Article 16(1) of the Brussels Convention (the corresponding provision to Article 24(1) of the Brussels I Recast). The effect of including disputes relating to the existence of the lease is that a court's jurisdiction under Article 16(1) of the Brussels Convention cannot be defeated by an allegation that the lease is void.[263] The Court of Justice, which was not prepared to give Article 16(1) of the Brussels Convention a wider ambit than was required by its objectives, went on to hold that Article 16(1) of the Brussels Convention did not apply to a dispute between an original tenant and a sub-lessee as to the existence of an agreement under which the sub-lessee agreed to rent and run the original tenant's retail business, the emphasis in the agreement being on this latter aspect.[264]

By analogy with this decision, the Court of Justice in *Hacker v Euro-Relais*[265] held that there was no tenancy agreement within Article 16(1) of the Brussels Convention (Article 24(1) of the Brussels I Recast) where a travel agent and a client entered into a contract for a travel package involving the provision of a number of different services, including making reservations for the journey, for an inclusive price, even where one of these services was the use of holiday accommodation. Likewise the Court of Justice has held that there was no tenancy agreement where there was a type of timeshare involving a membership contract enabling the member to acquire, for a user fee, the right to use an apartment (within a complex but not individually designated) but also enabling the member to exchange their holiday accommodation (plus the right to further services at the complex). There was a separate membership fee and user fee, the former costing nearly five times the latter.[266] By contrast, Article 24(1) of the Brussels I Recast will apply where there are services, such as insurance in the event of cancellation or a guarantee of reimbursement in the event of the tour operator's insolvency, which are merely ancillary to a contract's principal status as a tenancy agreement.[267] Such

---

[259] See the Jenard Report, pp 34–5.

[260] *Lieber v Göbel*, supra.

[261] [1977] ECR 2383; see Hartley (1978) 3 ELR 164.

[262] See also Case C-8/98 *Dansommer A/S v Gotz* [2000] ECR I-393.

[263] See also Case 38/81 *Effer v Kantner* [1982] ECR 825.

[264] Because part of the dispute fell within the rules on exclusive jurisdiction and part fell without, the proceedings were split up.

[265] [1992] ECR I-1111; Briggs (1992) 12 YEL 657; Plender (1992) 63 BYBIL 607; Hartley (1992) ELR 17.

[266] Case C-73/04 *Klein v Rhodos Management Ltd* [2005] ECR I-8667, [2006] IL Pr 2. Contrast *Jarrett v Barclays Bank plc* [1999] QB 1 (finding that a simpler timeshare arrangement was a tenancy for the purposes of the provision, but that it did not cover disputes concerning financing of the timeshare); Briggs (1996) 67 BYBIL 577.

[267] Case C-8/98 *Dansommer A/S v Gotz* [2000] ECR I-393; Peel (2001) YEL 357.

services cannot alter the status of the tenancy agreement, especially when these are not in issue before the court.[268] Moreover Article 24(1) is not rendered inapplicable because the dispute is between a professional tour operator who is subrogated to the rights of the owner and the tenant who had rented the accommodation from the tour operator.[269]

Sanders only dealt with a limited range of the issues that can arise in disputes between a landlord and a tenant. For example, the Court of Justice gave no answer as to whether claims for the payment of rent and other outgoings were within Article 16(1) of the Brussels Convention. Subsequently, the Court of Justice in *Rösler v Rottwinkel*[270] departed from the spirit of narrow interpretation in *Sanders* by holding that Article 16(1) of the Brussels Convention (Article 24(1) of the Brussels I Recast) applies to disputes concerning the respective obligations of the landlord and tenant under the agreement.[271] This would cover, for instance, a simple action for unpaid rent or other outgoings, an action in respect of repairs and decoration of property, and an action in respect of damage to movable property caused by the tenant.[272]

Such disputes are accordingly subject to the exclusive jurisdiction of the Member State in which the immovable property is situated. In favour of this, it can be said that one Member State will be allocated jurisdiction in respect of most of the disputes that can arise between a landlord and a tenant. This is preferable to having an action which involves, for example, a claim for possession and for unpaid rent split up between different Member States. Also the rationale of Article 24(1) of the Brussels I Recast may suggest a wide interpretation, since many Member States have social legislation in respect of rents and therefore ought to be able to hear a case which involves a claim for rent in respect of property situated in their territory.

The *Rösler* case also establishes, by way of contrast, that proceedings which only indirectly concern the use of the property, such as a claim by a landlord for damages for lost enjoyment of a holiday in the property let (and for travel expenses) following the alleged breach by a tenant of a user clause in the lease, do not have as their object the tenancy of immovable property and accordingly fall outside the scope of Article 24(1). A dispute concerning a contract to rent storage space has similarly been viewed as falling outside this provision.[273]

The Hess, Pfeiffer and Schlosser Report voiced concern over the necessity for exclusive jurisdiction in contracts relating to the rental of office space and recommended making Article 24(1) narrower and more flexible,[274] but the provision was not amended in the adoption of the Brussels I Recast.

(c) Short-term holiday lets

The *Rösler* case involved a short-term holiday let. Such lets (ie ones for a maximum period of six months) are now subject to the second paragraph of Article 24(1),[275] which provides as follows:

---

[268] Case C-8/98 *Dansommer A/S v Gotz* [2000] ECR I-393 at [34].

[269] Ibid, at [38].

[270] Case 241/83 [1985] ECR 99. Criticised by FA Mann (1985) 101 LQR 329 and Hartley (1985) 10 ELR 361.

[271] See also the opinion of the Advocate General in *Sanders v Van der Putte*, supra; Anton and Beaumont's *Civil Jurisdiction in Scotland*, para 7.10. Cf the Jenard Report, p 35.

[272] It is not clear whether the damage to property mentioned in *Sanders* was only referring to the immovable property.

[273] Case C-469/12 *Krejci Lager & Umschlagbetriebs GmbH v Olbrich Transport und Logistik GmbH* EU:C:2013:788, [2014] IL Pr 8.

[274] Study JLS/C4/2005/03, Final Version September 2007, para 879.

[275] Art 16(1)(b) of the Brussels Convention; Art 22(1) of the Brussels I Regulation.

However, in proceedings which have as their object tenancies of immovable property concluded for temporary private use for a maximum period of six consecutive months, the courts of the Member State in which the defendant is domiciled shall also have jurisdiction, provided that the tenant is a natural person and that the landlord and the tenant are domiciled in the same Member State

This provision[276] is designed to deal with criticisms levelled at *Rösler v Rottwinkel*. In this case the Court of Justice held, inter alia, that a claim by a plaintiff landlord against a defendant tenant in respect of outgoings, such as water and gas, in relation to the short-term holiday let of a villa in Italy, had to be tried in Italy where the property was situated. This was despite the fact that both parties were resident in Germany and that therefore trial in Italy would be very inconvenient to them. Moreover, the drafters of the Brussels Convention did not intend to give exclusive jurisdiction to the Contracting State in which the property was situated in cases involving short-term holiday lets.[277]

The second paragraph of Article 24(1) meets these criticisms by providing that in a case like this the Member State in which the defendant is domiciled shall also have jurisdiction. The plaintiff in the *Rösler* case could now therefore, if he wanted to, sue in Germany. On the other hand, if he preferred, he could still sue in Italy under the first paragraph of Article 24(1). Both the Member State in which the defendant is domiciled and the Member State in which the property is situated have exclusive jurisdiction under Article 24(1). This could result in concurrent proceedings in two different Member States; eg one party may sue in Italy and the other party in Germany. In such a situation Article 31 will operate so that the court other than the one first seised must decline jurisdiction.[278]

The first requirement that has to be satisfied before jurisdiction is given to the Member State in which the defendant is domiciled is that the proceedings have as their object tenancies of immovable property. The meaning of this has been examined above in relation to the first paragraph of Article 24(1). The other requirements are largely, but not exclusively, geared to the facts of the *Rösler* case. The second requirement is that it must be a short-term let (for a maximum period of six consecutive months). The third requirement is that the tenant must be a natural person. Legal persons, such as companies, are excluded on the basis that they are generally engaged in commercial transactions. This involves a relaxation from the predecessor wording under the Brussels Convention,[279] which required that the landlord must also be a natural person,[280] a requirement based on the facts of the *Rösler* case. Fourthly, both parties must be domiciled in the same Member State.[281]

At the same time, the second paragraph of Article 24(1) is wide enough to cover a dispute between the landlord and tenant that relates (unlike in the *Rösler* case) to the land itself, so that inspection of the land may be necessary. The most appropriate place for trial in such a case is the Member State in which the land is situated; nonetheless, the Member State in

---

[276] See the Almeida Cruz, Desantes Real and Jenard Report, para 25. The introduction of this provision into the Brussels Convention followed the 1988 Lugano Convention (on which see the Jenard and Möller Report OJ 1990 C 189/57) with some modifications. The 1988 Convention has been replaced by the 2007 Lugano Convention.

[277] See the Jenard and Möller Report, p 75; the Schlosser Report, para 164.

[278] Infra, p 450.

[279] Art 16(1)(b) of the Brussels Convention. But followed Art 16(1)(b) of the 1988 Lugano Convention (replaced by Art 22(1) of the 2007 Lugano Convention), infra, pp 313–14.

[280] The Almeida Cruz, Desantes Real and Jenard Report, para 25; see also *Jarrett v Barclays Bank plc* [1999] QB 1 at 13–14.

[281] See the *Dansommer* case, supra, where this requirement was not met but the first para of Art 24(1) applied.

which the defendant is domiciled also has jurisdiction, provided that the above requirements are met, and will have priority if first seised. It was again suggested in the Hess, Pfeiffer and Schlosser Report that this might justify a more flexible approach,[282] but no changes were adopted in the Brussels I Recast.

Article 24(2) in proceedings which have as their object the validity of the constitution, the nullity or the dissolution of companies[283] or other legal persons or associations of natural or legal persons,[284] or the validity of the decisions of their organs,[285] the courts of the Member State in which the company, legal person or association has its seat. In order to determine that seat, the court shall apply its rules of private international law;

The Brussels I Recast (and previously Brussels I Regulation) differs from the Brussels Convention (at least in its drafting) in making it clear that this provision is only concerned with the *validity* of the decisions of organs, etc. It covers proceedings *principally concerned with* the validity of directors' exercise of their powers,[286] but not an action concerning misappropriation of the company's money by the directors[287] or contractual claims.[288] In the United Kingdom there is a special statutory definition of the seat of a company for the purposes of this rule.[289] Like the other rules in Article 24 of the Brussels I Recast, this rule gives exclusive jurisdiction to the designated courts regardless of any jurisdiction agreement between the disputing parties, including as set out in a shareholders agreement.[290] In practice, this rule has been interpreted narrowly,[291] thus excluding a dispute over whether a power of a legal person had been exercised properly (which did not challenge the existence of the power).[292] If in a contractual dispute one party (a company) argues that it should not be bound by the contract because the decision of its directors was *ultra vires*, that on its own should not be sufficient to bring the dispute within this rule, unless the *ultra vires* issue is the main subject matter of the dispute.[293]

Article 24(3) in proceedings which have as their object the validity of entries in public registers, the courts of the Member State in which the register is kept.[294]

---

[282] Study JLS/C4/2005/03, Final Version September 2007, para 879.

[283] See *Re Senator Hanseatische* [1996] 2 BCLC 562 at 577; affd by CA at 597 without discussion of this point. This is concerned with the dissolution of solvent companies: *Re Drax Holdings Ltd* [2003] EWHC 2743 (Ch) at [28], [2004] 1 WLR 1049.

[284] This covers a partnership: *Phillips v Symes* [2002] 1 WLR 853; Schlosser Report, p 120.

[285] *Speed Investments Ltd v Formula One Holdings Ltd (No 2)* [2004] EWCA Civ 1512 at [22]–[34], [2005] 1 WLR 1936—dispute about the composition of the Board; Briggs (2004) 75 BYBIL 543; *Shahar v Tsitsekkos* [2004] EWHC 2659 (Ch) at [47]–[50]. An "organ" can include a court appointed officer: *Papanicolaou v Thielen* [1997] IL Pr 37, Irish HC. See also *Bank of Scotland v Investment Management Regulatory Organisation Ltd* 1989 SLT 432.

[286] Case C-144/10 *BVG v JPMorgan Chase Bank SA* [2011] ECR I-3961. See also the *Phillips* case, supra, at [44]–[50]; *Newtherapeutics Ltd v Katz* [1991] Ch 226; Kaye (1991) 10 CJQ 220; Carter (1990) 61 BYBIL 397; *UBS AG, London Branch v Kommunale Wasserwerke Leipzig GmbH* [2010] EWHC 2566 (Comm), [2010] 2 CLC 499.

[287] *Grupo Torras SA v Sheikh Fahad Mohammed Al-Sabah* [1996] 1 Lloyd's Rep 7, CA.

[288] *FKI Engineering Ltd v Dewind Holdings Ltd* [2007] EWHC 72 (Comm), [2007] IL Pr 17.

[289] SI 2001/3929, Art 3, Sch 1, para 10.

[290] Article 25(4), discussed infra p 242; *Speed Investments Ltd v Formula One Holdings Ltd (No 2)* [2004] EWCA Civ 1512, [2005] 1 WLR 1936.

[291] Note Recital (15); see, eg, Case C-144/10 *BVG v JPMorgan* [2011] ECR I-3961 at [30].

[292] Case C-372/07 *Hassett v South Eastern Health Board* [2008] ECR I-7403.

[293] Case C-144/10 *BVG v JPMorgan* [2011] ECR I-3961; Fentiman (2011) 70 CLJ 513. See also *Blue Tropic Ltd v Chkhartishvili* [2014] EWHC 2243 (Ch), [2014] IL Pr 33; *Blomqvist v Zavarco Plc* [2015] EWHC 1898 (Ch), [2016] Ch 128.

[294] *Re Fagin's Bookshop plc* [1992] BCLC 118; *Re Hayward* [1997] Ch 45 at 55–7; *Caledonian Contracting Partnership Ltd v Thomas Rodger* [2004] EWHC 851 (Ch); *Blomqvist v Zavarco Plc* [2015] EWHC 1898 (Ch), [2016] Ch 128.

This is properly a matter of exclusive jurisdiction because public registers are, like immovable property, a matter within the sovereign control of a single state.

Article 24(4) in proceedings concerned with the registration or validity of patents, trade marks, designs, or other similar rights required to be deposited or registered, irrespective of whether the issue is raised by way of an action or as a defence, the courts of the Member State in which the deposit or registration has been applied for, has taken place or is under the terms of an instrument of the Union or an international convention deemed to have taken place.

Without prejudice to the jurisdiction of the European Patent Office under the Convention on the Grant of European Patents, signed at Munich on 5 October 1973, the courts of each Member State shall have exclusive jurisdiction in proceedings concerned with the registration or validity of any European patent granted for that Member State.[295]

This provision covers only questions of registration or validity, such as proceedings for revocation of a patent,[296] but not issues concerning ownership of a patent involving an invention of an employee.[297] Actions for infringement or a declaration of non-infringement are governed by the general rules in the Brussels I Recast, including Articles 4 and 7(2), not by Article 24(4).[298] However, where invalidity is raised as a defence to infringement or a declaration is sought of non-infringement on the basis of invalidity the Court of Justice in *GAT* has ruled that Article 16(4) of the Brussels Convention (Article 24(4) of the Brussels I Recast) will apply.[299] The court hearing an infringement action will not have the power to determine validity as an incidental question—an interpretation which appears at odds with the approach to other provisions under the Regulation. The words "irrespective of whether the issue is raised by way of an action or as a defence", which were added in the Brussels I Recast (and Lugano Convention 2007), confirm this result.

Article 24(5) in proceedings concerned with the enforcement of judgments,[300] the courts of the Member State in which the judgment has been or is to be enforced.[301]

As enforcement proceedings involve the potential exercise of powers to seise assets, they are territorially limited. The provision does not cover a set-off between the right whose enforcement is being sought and a claim over which the courts of the Member State would have no jurisdiction if it were raised independently,[302] nor does it cover equitable

---

[295] See generally the Schlosser Report, p 124; the Jenard Report, p 36; Case 288/82 *Duijnstee v Goderbauer* [1984] ECR 3363; Fawcett and Torremans, pp 15–27, 66–7; Wadlow (1985) 10 ELR 305.

[296] *Napp Laboratories v Pfizer Inc* [1993] FSR 150; *Chiron Corpn v Evans Medical Ltd* [1996] FSR 863 at 866.

[297] *Duijnstee v Goderbauer*, supra.

[298] Case C-4/03 *Gesellschaft für Antriebstechnik mbH & Co KG (GAT) v Luk Lamellen und Kupplungsbau Beteiligungs KG* [2006] ECR I-6509 at [16]; Briggs [2006] LMCLQ 447; the *Chiron* case, supra, at 866–7; see generally infra, p 264, n 636.

[299] See Torremans (2007) 29 EIPR 195–203. Where invalidity is raised as a defence, English courts had come to the same conclusion: *Coin Controls Ltd v Suzo International (UK) Ltd* [1999] Ch 33; *Fort Dodge Animal Health Ltd v Akzo Nobel NV* [1998] FSR 222, CA; *Anan Kasei Co Ltd v Molycorp Chemicals & Oxides (Europe) Ltd* [2016] EWHC 1722 (Pat), [2016] Bus LR 945. See generally on the issue of invalidity as raised in different ways during infringement proceedings, Fawcett and Torremans, Chapter 7 and Fawcett in Fawcett (ed), *Reform and Development of Private International Law* (2002), Chapter 6. For suggestions for reform of Art 24(4) and more generally for intellectual property cases, see the Hess, Pfeiffer and Schlosser Report, paras 917–25.

[300] See Art 39, infra, p 622 et seq: Case C-129/92 *Owens Bank Ltd v Bracco* [1994] QB 509 at 545.

[301] On provisional measures in support of proceedings for enforcement of a judgment, see infra, p 303.

[302] See Case 220/84 *AS Autoteile Service GmbH v Malhé* [1985] ECR 2267; Hartley (1986) 11 ELR 98. Nor does it cover an *action paulienne* under French law: Case C-261/90 *Reichert v Dresdner Bank (No 2)* [1992] ECR I-2149.

orders which may lead to enforcement,[303] but it does apply to a third party debt (garnishee) order.[304]

(ii) Prorogation of jurisdiction

Jurisdiction selected by the parties may take the form of either an agreement on jurisdiction (Article 25), or the defendant's submission to the forum by appearing before its courts (Article 26). In both cases the Brussels I Recast respects the wishes of the parties, subject to exclusive jurisdiction under Article 24 which trumps the jurisdiction under Articles 25 and 26.[305] Article 26 is in practice hierarchically superior to Article 25, because submission essentially constitutes a waiver of any prior rights under a jurisdiction agreement,[306] and so will be considered first.

(a) Submission to the forum

Article 26[307] provides that "a court of a Member State before which a defendant enters an appearance shall have jurisdiction". This means that where the defendant submits to the courts of a Member State he will give those courts jurisdiction even though they would not otherwise have had it under the Brussels I Recast, and regardless of whether there is any connection between the parties or their dispute and that Member State. Once the defendant has submitted, this covers the whole of the proceedings, including any earlier orders or decisions in the proceedings.[308] Because of the *lis pendens* rules under the Brussels I Recast,[309] the effect of submission to a particular court is to give that court exclusive jurisdiction—once a Member State court has been seized of the dispute, no other Member State court may hear it.

Where the appearance is before a court in the United Kingdom the familiar problem of allocating jurisdiction within the United Kingdom arises.[310] Where the Modified Regulation applies, this will allocate jurisdiction to a part of the United Kingdom. Where it does not, the Brussels I Recast itself can be regarded as allocating jurisdiction to the courts of England and Wales, Scotland or Northern Ireland, depending on in which court the defendant actually appears.

For Article 26 to apply there are two conditions. First, it is strongly arguable that in principle the defendant must be domiciled in a Member State.[311] There is nothing in the wording of Article 26 to indicate that it is intended to apply regardless of domicile. The wording of this

---

[303] *Masri v Consolidated Contractors International Company SAL* [2008] EWCA Civ 303, [2009] QB 450.

[304] *Kuwait Oil Tanker Co SAK v Qabazard* [2003] UKHL 31, [2004] 1 AC 300; Briggs [2003] LMCLQ 418; Rogerson [2003] CLJ 576.

[305] See Recital (19) of the Brussels I Recast.

[306] Case 150/80 *Elefanten Schuh GmbH v Jacqmain* [1981] ECR 1671; Case 48/84 *Spitzley v Sommer Exploitation SA* [1985] ECR 787. This is not expressly set out in the Brussels I Recast, but is implicitly confirmed in Article 31(2). The waiver analysis suggests the same result should arise even if the defendant is not domiciled in an EU Member State (and thus, as argued below, Article 26 does not apply), or where Article 26 does apply but the jurisdiction agreement is in favour of the courts of a non-Member State (and thus Article 25 does not apply): see Case C-175/15 *Taser International Inc v SC Gate 4 Business SRL and Cristian Mircea Anastasiu* EU:C:2016:176, [2016] QB 887.

[307] Article 24 of the Brussels I Regulation; Article 18 of the Brussels Convention.

[308] *Marc Rich & Co AG v Società Italiana Impianti PA, The Atlantic Emperor (No 2)* [1992] 1 Lloyd's Rep 624 at 633, CA—a case involving enforcement under the traditional English rules, discussed infra, p 527 et seq.

[309] See infra, p 443 et seq.

[310] Infra, p 317 et seq.

[311] See supra, p 215. See also the Jenard Report, p 38; Gaudemet-Tallon, point 79; Hartley, p 76. Cf Collins, p 51; Briggs 2015, para 2.85; Layton and Mercer, para 20.120. But see Case C-318/93 *Brenner and Noller v Dean Witter Reynolds Inc* [1994] ECR I-4275 at 4280 (Advocate General Darmon); Case C-412/98 *Universal General Insurance Co (UGIC) v Group Josi Reinsurance Co SA* [2000] ECR I-5925 at [44]. The point

provision can be contrasted with that of Article 25 which does indicate that it is intended to apply regardless of the parties' domicile. It is true that the fact that Article 25 applies regardless of domicile might be a basis for arguing that Article 26 also should, since both articles are dealing with prorogation of jurisdiction;[312] indeed (as noted above) Article 26 can override Article 25. A strong counter-argument to this is that Article 26 must be read in the light of Article 6, and Article 6(1) expressly spells out that the application of traditional national jurisdictional rules to non-Member State domiciled defendants is subject to Articles 24 and 25, but omits Article 26.

Secondly, the defendant must enter an appearance before a court of a Member State. The Brussels I Recast does not define the meaning of entering an appearance. According to the Jenard Report, referring to the Brussels Convention, it will be for the court seised of the proceedings to determine this in accordance with its own rules of procedure,[313] although the Court of Justice has suggested that this is subject to EU limitations.[314] Article 26 also only refers to the *defendant* entering an appearance; it would not appear to cover the case where a claimant enters an appearance to contest a set-off sought by the defendant in response to the claimant's original claim. However, the Court of Justice in *Spitzley v Sommer Exploitation SA*[315] held that a court of a Member State, which would not otherwise have had jurisdiction in respect of the set-off, had it under Article 18 of the Brussels Convention (corresponding to Article 26 of the Brussels I Recast) because of the plaintiff's appearance before the court. Whilst this interpretation flies in the face of the wording of Article 18 (Article 26 of the Brussels I Recast), it is not unfair to the parties who have both (one by seeking the original claim, the other by seeking a set-off) elected for trial in that Member State. There is also economy of procedure if both the claim and set-off are dealt with in the same Member State.[316]

There are two limits on the application of Article 26.

First, Article 26 does not apply where the appearance was entered to contest jurisdiction. The defendant must be extremely careful as to how he conducts his defence where proceedings are commenced against him in a Member State. Where the defendant enters an appearance and fights the action on its merits (eg denies he is in breach of contract), the court of the Member State before which he appears will have jurisdiction.[317] Where the defendant merely denies that the court of a Member State has jurisdiction over him (eg he points out that it is using a traditional exorbitant basis of jurisdiction against him and that this is prohibited by the Brussels I Recast), the court of the Member State before which he appears will not have jurisdiction. A defendant does not submit to the jurisdiction of the English courts merely by acknowledging

---

is not often raised in English practice because the rules governing submission under the common law are, in any case, very similar to those under Article 26.

[312] See *Transocean Towage Co Ltd v Hyundai Construction Co Ltd* [1987] ECC 282, Netherlands Sup Ct.

[313] At p 38. See also the opinion of the Advocate General in *Elefanten Schuh v Jacqmain*, supra. See in relation to English procedure for defending a claim: *Ace Insurance SA-NV (Formerly Cigna Insurance Co of Europe SA NV) v Zurich Insurance Co* [2001] EWCA Civ 173 at [14], [2001] 1 Lloyd's Rep 618; *IBS Technologies (PVT) Ltd v APM Technologies SA*, 7 April 2003 (unreported) at [16]–[29]. See also *Caltex Trading Pte Ltd v Metro Trading International Inc and Ors and Glencore International AG and Ors (Third Parties) and Sea Victory Shipping Corp Procopiou and Baker Services Inc (Fourth Parties)* [1999] 2 Lloyd's Rep 724, 730–2—issuing a summons for discovery of documents.

[314] Case C-112/13 *A v B* EU:C:2014:2195 (absent defendant did not submit merely because their court-appointed representative appeared).

[315] Case 48/84 [1985] ECR 787; Hartley (1986) 11 ELR 98.

[316] See similarly Article 8(3), dealing with counter-claims, discussed infra, p 288.

[317] But not where a defendant merely opposes an application for a European order for payment (under Regulation (EC) No 1896/2006), even on the merits: Case C-144/12 *Goldbet Sportwetten GmbH v Massimo Sperindeo* EU:C:2013:393, [2014] IL Pr 1.

service and applying to stay the action.[318] The distinction between fighting on the merits and contesting jurisdiction is well known to English lawyers,[319] and is easy to apply where the defendant acts in only one of these ways. What if the defendant appears before the courts of a Member State and argues in the alternative, that there is no jurisdiction over him and that, even if there is, he did not, for instance, break the contract?

The corresponding provision under the Brussels Convention (Article 18) refers (in the English language version) to the submission rule not applying where appearance was entered *solely* to contest jurisdiction. A literal interpretation of Article 18 of the Brussels Convention would therefore suggest that the court before which the defendant has appeared is given jurisdiction in this situation, because the defendant has not appeared *solely* to contest jurisdiction. This interpretation of Article 18 of the Brussels Convention was rejected by the Court of Justice in *Elefanten Schuh v Jacqmain*.[320] The Court held that one of the objectives of the Convention is to give the defendant the right to defend himself, and he should not be handicapped from going into matters of substance by this having the effect of destroying his arguments as to jurisdiction. It may actually be necessary for him to go into matters of substance in order to protect his property from seizure. The defendant, therefore, does not submit if he argues in the alternative. This result is, if anything, strengthened under the Brussels I Recast because Article 26 now omits the word "solely". A defendant cannot, therefore, contest a default judgment on the basis that he was unable to argue on the merits for fear of submission (even if jurisdiction was being contested separately in an appellate court).[321]

There can be no objections to this principle when it is applied in the situation where the primary purpose of the defence is to challenge the jurisdiction.[322] But the principle would also appear to cover the situation where the primary purpose of the defence is to fight the action on its merits. Spurious arguments as to a lack of jurisdiction may be added on to what is, in essence, a defence based on substance, in order to avoid the application of Article 26 of the Brussels I Recast. The Court of Justice has stopped the defendant from tacking on arguments as to jurisdiction at a late stage,[323] holding that it must be clear to the claimant and the court from the time of the defendant's first defence on the merits that it is intended to contest the court's jurisdiction; if not, Article 26 will give jurisdiction to the courts of the Member State before which the defendant has appeared.[324] In other words, the challenge to jurisdiction must be made before or at the same time as the defendant's appearance or argument on

---

[318] CPR, Part 11; *The Sydney Express* [1988] 2 Lloyd's Rep 257. See also *Kurz v Stella Musical Veranstaltungs GmbH* [1992] Ch 196 at 201–2; *British Steel Corpn v Allivane International Ltd* 1989 SLT (Sh Ct) 57.

[319] Infra, pp 533–40; Collins, pp 92–3.

[320] Supra. Followed in Case 25/81 *CHW v GJH* [1982] ECR 1189; Case 27/81 *Röhr v Ossberger* [1981] ECR 2431; Case 201/82 *Gerling v Italian Treasury* [1983] ECR 2503. See also *Luis Marburg & Söhne GmbH v Società Ori Martin SpA* [1987] ECC 424, Italian Supreme Court; *Campbell International Trading House Ltd v Peter Van Aart* [1992] 2 IR 305, Supreme Court of Ireland.

[321] *Harada Ltd (t/a Chequepoint UK) v Turner* [2003] EWCA Civ 1695.

[322] See *Marc Rich & Co AG v Società Italiana Impianti PA, The Atlantic Emperor (No 2)* [1992] 1 Lloyd's Rep 624 at 633, CA; *Toepfer v Molino Boschi* [1996] 1 Lloyd's Rep 510 at 514–15.

[323] As a matter of English procedure, a defendant can in any case ordinarily (subject to CPR, r 3.1(2)(a)) only dispute the court's jurisdiction within 14 days of filing an acknowledgment of service: CPR, r 11(4) (or 28 days in the Commercial Court: CPR, r 58.7). The Supreme Court has held that this is compatible with the Brussels I Recast: *The Alexandros T* [2013] UKSC 70 at [121], [2014] 1 All ER 590.

[324] *Elefanten Schuh v Jacqmain*, supra. Where the challenge to jurisdiction is not a preliminary matter see the Advocate General's opinion in *CHW v GJH*, supra. See also *Devrajan v District Judge Ballagh* [1993] 3 IR 381, Supreme Court of Ireland; *Strathaird Farms Ltd v GA Chattaway & Co* 1993 SLT (Sh Ct) 36; *SSQ Europe SA v Johann & Backes OHG* [2002] 1 Lloyd's Rep 465—intention to contest jurisdiction clear despite a counterclaim as well as a defence on merits.

the merits.[325] This does nothing to stop the well-advised defendant who, at an early stage of the proceedings, includes a specious defence which contests jurisdiction. A defendant who contests jurisdiction at the right stage can (if no preliminary trial on jurisdiction is ordered) participate in a full trial on the merits and still maintain his objection to jurisdiction.[326]

Secondly, Article 26 also does not apply where another court has exclusive jurisdiction by virtue of Article 24. The Court of Justice has confirmed that Article 26 is not, however, subject to Article 25 by holding that an appearance under Article 18 of the Brussels Convention (Article 26 of the Brussels I Recast) overrides an agreement conferring jurisdiction under Article 17 of the Convention (Article 25 of the Brussels I Recast).[327] This is only right and proper; both Articles 25 and 26 are dealing with selection of jurisdiction by the parties and a later selection by appearance should take precedence over an earlier selection by agreement. Submission under Article 26 thus equally establishes jurisdiction even if there is an exclusive jurisdiction agreement in favour of the courts of a non-Member State.[328] Similarly, because Article 26 only mentions that it is subject to Article 24, a weaker party protected by the special jurisdictional rules relating to consumers, employees and insurance may nevertheless submit to the courts of another Member State.[329] But where the policyholder, the insured, a beneficiary of the insurance contract, the injured party, the consumer or the employee is the defendant, the court shall, before assuming jurisdiction on the basis of submission by entering an appearance, ensure that the defendant is informed of his right to contest the jurisdiction of the court and of the consequences of entering or not entering an appearance.[330]

(b) An agreement on jurisdiction

Article 25[331] is concerned with jurisdiction agreements, also known as choice of court agreements or forum selection clauses, in favour of the courts of Member States. (An agreement in favour of the courts of a Member State is, however, covered by the Hague Convention on Choice of Court Agreements 2005 (discussed below)[332] if one party to the agreement is resident in a Hague Convention contracting state which is not a Member State.)[333] This section considers (i) the relevance of the domicile of the parties; (ii) the requirements in relation to the agreement, both substantive and formal; (iii) the potential effect of jurisdiction agreements on third parties; and (iv) the limitations on the effectiveness of jurisdiction agreements.

Where there is an agreement conferring jurisdiction under Article 25, the courts of the Member State selected by the parties have jurisdiction (without any discretionary power to refuse to take jurisdiction[334]). There is no requirement for any connection between the parties or their dispute and the chosen court.[335] As discussed further below, such jurisdiction shall be exclusive unless the parties have agreed otherwise.[336] The consequence of the courts of a Member State being allocated exclusive jurisdiction is that the courts of other

---

[325] *Harada Ltd (t/a Chequepoint) v Turner* [2003] EWCA Civ 1695 at [29] (per Simon Brown LJ); *Deutsche Bank AG London Branch v Petromena ASA* [2015] EWCA Civ 226, [2015] 1 WLR 4225.

[326] *Harada* at [38] (per Simon Brown LJ), [50] (per Mance LJ).

[327] *Elefanten Schuh v Jacqmain*, supra. See also *The Sydney Express* [1988] 2 Lloyd's Rep 257.

[328] Case C-175/15 *Taser International* EU:C:2016:176, [2016] QB 887.

[329] Case C-111/09 *Česká podnikatelská pojišťovna as, Vienna Insurance Group v Bilas* [2010] ECR I-4545.

[330] Art 26(2).

[331] Art 23 of the Brussels I Regulation; Art 17 of the Brussels Convention. See generally Hartley, *Choice of Court Agreements Under the European and International Instruments* (2013).

[332] See infra, pp 315–17.

[333] Hague Convention on Choice of Court Agreements 2005, Article 26(6).

[334] See infra, p 459 et seq.

[335] Case C-159/97 *Transporti Castelletti Spedizioni Internazionali SpA v Hugo Trumpy SpA* [1999] ECR I-1597 at [50].

[336] See infra, pp 234–5.

Member States[337] are deprived of jurisdiction.[338] The consequence of a non-exclusive jurisdiction agreement is that jurisdiction is conferred on the chosen court, but the courts of other Member States are not deprived of jurisdiction. In this case, Article 25 operates as a non-exclusive basis of jurisdiction (alongside, generally, Articles 4, 7 and 8) giving a claimant an additional choice of where to commence proceedings. Some jurisdiction agreements may not be clearly either exclusive or non-exclusive, or may combine elements of both.[339]

(i) The domicile of the parties
Under the Brussels I Recast, Article 25 applies regardless of the domicile of the parties.[340] This is an extension of the scope of the rule, which previously (under the Brussels I Regulation and Brussels Convention) had a different effect depending on whether one or more parties was domiciled in a Member State.

Under Article 23 of the Brussels I Regulation (Article 17 of the Brussels Convention), an agreement could only confer jurisdiction if one or more of the parties was domiciled in a Member State (Contracting State).[341] It was clear from Article 4 of the Regulation that it did not matter whether this was the defendant or claimant, because it specified that Article 23 applied regardless of the domicile of the defendant. The omission of Article 17 from mention in Article 4 of the Convention had previously left the point slightly uncertain.

Under the Brussels I Regulation (and the Brussels Convention), whether the courts of a Member State could or would take jurisdiction under a jurisdiction agreement between two non-EU Member State domiciled parties was thus a matter for the residual national jurisdictional rules of that Member State. However, Article 23(3) of the Regulation (and Article 17 of the Brussels Convention)[342] provided that where neither party[343] is domiciled in a Member State "the courts of other Member States shall have no jurisdiction over their disputes unless the court or courts chosen have declined jurisdiction". Thus, under the Regulation (and the Brussels Convention), an exclusive jurisdiction agreement between two non-EU Member State domiciled parties in favour of the courts of a Member State did, at least provisionally, preclude the courts of other Member States from having jurisdiction.[344] The extension of Article 25 of the Brussels I Recast to apply regardless of the domicile of the parties has made this provision unnecessary, and thus there is no equivalent in the Brussels I Recast.

(ii) The requirements in relation to the agreement
For an agreement to come within Article 25 two requirements, dealt with in turn below, must be satisfied: (a) the parties must, substantively, have agreed that a court or the courts of a Member State are to have jurisdiction to settle any disputes which have arisen or which may arise in connection with a particular legal relationship; (b) the agreement must satisfy certain requirements as to form.

---

[337] The jurisdiction of non-Member States is not precluded by Art 25: *Ultisol v Bouygues* [1996] 2 Lloyd's Rep 140; appeal allowed on a different point in *Bouygues Offshore SA v Caspian Shipping (Nos 1, 3, 4 and 5)* [1998] 2 Lloyd's Rep 461, CA.

[338] According to the Schlosser Report (p 81), the courts of other Member States must of their own motion consider if what is now Art 25 applies.

[339] See generally Keyes and Marshall (2015) 11 J Priv Int L 345; Briggs [2012] LMCLQ 364.

[340] Where both parties are domiciled in the same Member State, and particularly where the parties also agree on jurisdiction in that State, there is a basic problem of whether the dispute is international in character, and thus whether it falls within the scope of the Brussels I Recast: see supra, p 202.

[341] Case C-387/98 *Coreck Maritime GmbHv Handelsveem BV* [2000] ECR I-9337—in a case involving third parties one of the parties to the original contract must be so domiciled.

[342] As amended.

[343] This is referring to the original contracting parties.

[344] See the Schlosser Report, p 124.

A claimant who seeks to establish the jurisdiction of the English courts under Article 25 must show a good arguable case that its terms have been met.[345] However, if the defendant claims that an English court, which would otherwise have jurisdiction, has no jurisdiction because of a clause providing for the exclusive jurisdiction of the courts of another Member State (or on some other similar basis),[346] it has been suggested that the burden lies on the defendant.[347]

(a) The parties[348] must have agreed that a court or the courts of a Member State[349] are to have jurisdiction to settle any disputes which have arisen or which may arise in connection with a particular legal relationship

An agreement The concept of an "agreement" is to be given an autonomous meaning.[350] Normally, the parties will have agreed contractually on the court which is to have jurisdiction; however, it can also be conferred by a trust instrument.[351] A choice of jurisdiction clause contained in the statutes of a company can constitute an agreement for the purposes of Article 25, which is binding on all the shareholders.[352] It does not matter that the shareholder has not specifically agreed to the clause; by becoming and remaining a shareholder he agrees to be bound by the contents of the statutes of the company.[353] This takes a relaxed view of the concept of an "agreement". Formal requirements for jurisdiction agreements are discussed further below.

---

[345] *Bols Distilleries v Superior Yacht Services Ltd* [2006] UKPC 45 at [28] (per Lord Rodger), [2007] 1 WLR 12. See also *Glencore International AG v Metro Trading International Inc (No 1)* [1999] 2 Lloyd's Rep 632 at 642; *Carnoustie Universal v International Transport Workers Federation* [2002] EWHC 1624 (Comm) at [47], [2003] IL Pr 7; *SSQ Europe SA v Johann & Backes OHG* [2002] 1 Lloyd's Rep 465 at 476; *Evialis SA v SIAT* [2003] EWHC 863 (Comm) 377 at [70]–[71], [2003] 2 Lloyd's Rep 377; the *Bank of Tokyo-Mitsubishi* case, supra, at [193]. But see *Standard Steamship Owners' Protection and Indemnity Association (Bermuda) Ltd v GIE Vision Bail* [2004] EWHC 2919 (Comm) at [27], [2005] 1 All ER (Comm) 618—standard of proof is on a balance of probabilities where facts have to be decided at the jurisdictional stage and will not be decided later.

[346] *Benatti v WPP Holdings Italy Srl* [2007] EWCA Civ 263 at [37]–[44] (per Toulson LJ), [2007] 1 WLR 2316 (defendant arguing that there was a contract of employment).

[347] *Konkola Copper Mines plc v Coromin Ltd* [2006] EWCA Civ 5 at [95], [101], [2006] 1 Lloyd's Rep 410—not finally deciding the issue; *Hewden Tower Cranes Ltd v Wolffkran GmbH* [2007] EWHC 857 at [46] (TCC), [2007] 2 Lloyd's Rep 138. See the judgment of David Steel J in *Knauf UK GmbH v British Gypsum Ltd* [2001] EWCA Civ 1570 at [41], [2002] 1 Lloyd's Rep 199—the Court of Appeal did not comment on whether this was correct; *Bank of Tokyo-Mitsubishi Ltd v Baskan Gida Sanayi Ve Pazalarma AS*, supra, at [193]. But cf the *Carnoustie* case, supra, at [46]; *Provimi Ltd v Roche Products Ltd* [2003] EWHC 961 (Comm) at [55], [2003] 2 All ER (Comm) 683. The standard of proof is not settled but there has been a tendency to apply a flexible good arguable case test (consistent with the idea of one side having a much better argument on the material available), *Konkola* at [75]–[96]; *Hewden* at [46]; *Bols Distilleries*, supra, at [28]; *Benatti v WPP Holdings Italy SRL* [2007] EWCA Civ 263 at [42]–[44], [2007] 1 WLR 2316. But see the suggestion of Rix LJ in *Konkola* at [96] for a different test, at least where a jurisdictional issue goes to the heart of the merits. See also Rix LJ in *Royal & Sun Alliance Insurance plc v MK Digital FZE (Cyprus) Ltd* [2006] EWCA Civ 629 at [62], [2006] 2 Lloyd's Rep 110.

[348] An agent can agree: see *Standard Steamship Owners' Protection and Indemnity Association (Bermuda) Ltd v GIE Vision Bail* [2004] EWHC 2919 (Comm) at [52]–[55], [2005] 1 All ER (Comm) 618.

[349] Art 25 will not apply where the clause confers jurisdiction on a state which at the time the action is begun is not a Member State: *Re Exchange Control and a Greek Guarantor* [1993] IL Pr 298, German Federal Supreme Court.

[350] Case C-214/89 *Powell Duffryn v Petereit* [1992] ECR I-1745. The better view is that this question (what may constitute an "agreement") should be considered distinct from the question of the validity of any such agreement (whether an agreement has been successfully established in the particular case), which is a matter for national law under the Brussels I Recast, as discussed below.

[351] Art 25(3).

[352] *Powell Duffryn v Petereit*, supra, at 1772–5; Briggs (1992) 12 YEL 664; Hartley (1993) 18 ELR 225; Polak (1993) 30 CMLR 406. See also *Re Jurisdiction in Internal Company Matters* [1995] IL Pr 425, German Federal Supreme Court.

[353] *Powell Duffryn v Petereit*, supra, at 1772–5.

A question may arise as to the material validity of the "agreement" (ie the jurisdiction clause).[354] Material validity encompasses issues of formation and consent to the agreement.[355] For example, there may be a jurisdiction clause in writing but it is alleged that this is not incorporated into the contract between the parties or that the "contract" containing the jurisdiction clause was never concluded.[356] It might be alleged that, as a result of mistake, misrepresentation, duress or undue influence, there was no consent to the clause.

Under the Brussels I Regulation and Brussels Convention, the authorities were split on whether the material validity of the "agreement" was to be determined by reference to national substantive law as identified by the relevant private international law rules for determining the applicable law,[357] or by developing the autonomous concept of an "agreement" to identify when genuine consent arises.[358] The weight of authority favoured the latter view, although it would have appeared to necessitate the Court of Justice essentially developing principles of European contract law on a case-by-case basis, purely for the purposes of jurisdiction agreements, which would have meant significant uncertainty for the foreseeable future.[359]

Happily, the issue has been addressed directly in the Brussels I Recast,[360] which specifies that an agreement on the jurisdiction of the courts of a Member State is effective "unless the agreement is null and void as to its substantive validity under the law of that Member State". Recital (20) further clarifies that:

> Where a question arises as to whether a choice-of-court agreement in favour of a court or the courts of a Member State is null and void as to its substantive validity, that question should be decided in accordance with the law of the Member State of the court or courts designated in the agreement, including the conflict-of-laws rules of that Member State.

---

[354] The Schlosser Report, p 125. See generally: Briggs 2015, para 2.146; Dannemann in Rose (ed), *Lex Mercatoria-Essays on International Commercial Law in Honour of Francis Reynolds* (2000) Chapter 11.

[355] See Art 10 of the Rome I Regulation, discussed infra, pp 755–8.

[356] *Bols Distilleries v Superior Yacht Services Ltd* [2006] UKPC 45 at [14], [2007] 1 WLR 12.

[357] Case C-214/89 *Powell Duffryn v Petereit* [1992] ECR I-1745 at [32], [33]—the questions whether the dispute arose out of the legal relationship in connection with which the jurisdiction agreement was made and whether the scope of the clause applied to the dispute are both a matter for the national court applying national laws. However, the Court at [14] also said that the concept of an agreement conferring jurisdiction must be regarded as an independent one, and see *Provimi Ltd v Roche Products Ltd* [2003] EWHC 961 (Comm) at [83], [2003] 2 All ER (Comm) 683. For national support for this solution see: *Lafi Office and International Business SL v Meriden Animal Health Ltd* [2001] 1 All ER (Comm) 54; *Les Verreries De Saint-Gobain SA v Martinswerk GmbH* [1999] IL Pr 296, Cour de Cassation; *Re a Wood-Cutting Machine* [1995] IL Pr 191, Oberlandesgericht, Dusseldorf.

[358] Case C-288/92 *Custom Made Commercial Ltd v Stawa Metallbau GmbH* [1994] ECR I-2913 at 2946–2948 (AG Lenz, who expressly discusses the matter); Case C-269/95 *Benincasa v Dentalkit Srl* [1997] ECR I-3767 at [25], criticised by Harris (1998) 23 ELR 279; Case C-159/97 *Transporti Castelletti Spedizioni Internazionali SpA v Hugo Trumpy SpA* [1999] ECR I-1597 at [49], [51], Hartley (2000) 25 ELR 178, Peel (2001) YEL 340; Case C-116/02 *Erich Gasser v Misat Srl* [2003] ECR I-4207 at [51] and more explicitly by AG Leger at [78], [81]. For national support see: *Knauf UK GmbH v British Gypsum Ltd* [2001] 2 All ER (Comm) 332, the Court of Appeal left this point open [2001] EWCA Civ 1570 at [61], [2002] 1 Lloyd's Rep 199; *Provimi Ltd v Roche Products Ltd* [2003] EWHC 961 (Comm) at [82], [2003] 2 All ER (Comm) 683; *Aeroflot—Russian Airlines v Berezovsky* [2013] EWCA Civ 784, [2013] 2 Lloyd's Rep 242. See also Case 25/76 *Galeries Segoura Sprl v Bonakdarian* [1976] ECR 1851 at 1860. In any event, jurisdiction agreements are always subject to the requirements of European law. So a jurisdiction clause must not, for example, infringe the EU law derived elements of the Consumer Rights Act 2015; Case C-240/98 *Oceano Grupo Editorial SA v Rocio Murciano Quintero* [2000] ECR I-4941; Staudenmayer (2000) 8 ERPL 547; *Standard Bank London Ltd v Apostolakis (No 2)* [2002] CLC 939.

[359] But see the Hess, Pfeiffer and Schlosser Report, Study JLS/C4/2005/03, Final Version September 2007, para 881. See further discussion in Merrett (2009) 58 ICLQ 545; Camilleri (2011) 7 J Priv Int L 297.

[360] See generally Hartley, *Choice-of-Court Agreements under the European and International Instruments* (2013); Herranz Ballesteros (2014) 10 J Priv Int L 291; Garcimartin, in Dickinson and Lein (eds), *Brussels I Regulation Recast* (2015).

Thus, if the English courts are determining the validity of a jurisdiction agreement in favour of the French courts, they should apply French choice of law rules to determine which law governs that issue. Jurisdiction agreements are notably excluded from the scope of the Rome I Regulation, and so these will be national choice of law rules rather than harmonised EU rules.[361] This approach should ensure that, for any given jurisdiction agreement, the same test for validity is applied in the courts of each Member State, while leaving the question of the choice of law rules for jurisdiction agreements as well as the applicable substantive contract law standards to national law. The disadvantages of this approach are first, that jurisdiction agreements in favour of the courts of different Member States may have different standards of material validity; and second, that an English court deciding on jurisdiction may have to receive evidence of both foreign choice of law rules and also foreign substantive contract law, which is likely to add time and expense to jurisdictional hearings.

Where national laws go beyond matters of form and consensus and, as a matter of public policy, have a rule prohibiting agreements conferring jurisdiction in certain cases, for example, in contracts of employment, this national law is overridden by the Brussels I Recast and the agreement will have full effect provided, of course, that it complies with all the other requirements under Article 25.[362]

It may be alleged that under national law the contract containing the jurisdiction clause is void. Consistently with the prior jurisprudence of the courts, Article 25(5) of the Brussels I Recast now expressly states that:

> An agreement conferring jurisdiction which forms part of a contract shall be treated as an agreement independent of the other terms of the contract.
>
> The validity of the agreement conferring jurisdiction cannot be contested solely on the ground that the contract is not valid.

The courts of the Member State with exclusive jurisdiction under Article 25 thus also have exclusive jurisdiction in relation to disputes covering the validity of the contract as a whole,[363] provided that, according to the national court, the jurisdiction clause covers this dispute.[364] Only if the jurisdiction clause is specifically challenged by allegations of, for example, duress or mistake, will this affect whether the court has jurisdiction under Article 25.[365] This solution is consistent with that adopted in relation to Articles 7(1) and 24(1).[366] According to the Court of Justice, any other solution would mean that a party could frustrate the operation of what is now Article 25 simply by claiming that the whole of the contract was void.

---

[361] See infra, pp 700–1.

[362] Case 25/79 *Sanicentral GmbH v Collin* [1979] ECR 3423; Hartley, pp 72–3, and in (1980) 5 ELR 73. See also Case C-269/95 *Benincasa v Dentalkit Srl* [1997] ECR I-3767 at 3797; *Bankers Trust International plc v RCS Editori SpA* [1996] CLC 899. *Snookes v Jani-King (GB) Ltd* [2006] EWHC 289 (QB) at [13]–[32], [2006] IL Pr 19, accepting, obiter, that a jurisdiction clause in breach of the Unfair Contract Terms Act 1977 (now part of the Consumer Rights Act 2015) is unenforceable appears to be wrong. More complex issues arise where jurisdiction agreements are apparently contrary to international conventions: see Baatz [2011] LMCLQ 208.

[363] *Benincasa v Dentalkit*, supra, at 3798–9. See further *Deutsche Bank v Asia Pacific Broadband* [2008] EWCA Civ 1091 at [24], [2009] 2 All ER (Comm) 129.

[364] *Benincasa v Dentalkit*, supra, at 3798–9; Case C-214/89 *Powell Duffryn plc v Petereit* [1992] ECR I-1745, discussed infra, p 237.

[365] *Deutsche Bank v Asia Pacific Broadband* [2008] EWCA Civ 1091 at [24], [2009] 2 All ER (Comm) 129. It is somewhat unclear how this principle should be applied if the contract as a whole is (potentially) invalidated, including the jurisdiction agreement—for example, if it is argued that no contract at all would have been signed but for duress. The better view is that the validity of the jurisdiction agreement is challenged in such cases, even if the challenge also extends to the substantive contractual terms, although Article 25(5) might suggest otherwise. See similarly in relation to arbitration agreements, infra, p 418.

[366] *Effer v Kantner*, discussed infra, p 251; *Sanders v Van der Putte*, discussed supra, p 221.

A jurisdiction agreement may similarly survive the rescission of the substantive terms of an initially valid contract,[367] unless the jurisdiction agreement itself is repudiated.[368]

It is possible for a jurisdiction clause to be incorporated by reference to another document or contract.[369] For example, a contract may refer to general conditions of trading, a reinsurance contract may incorporate the terms of an insurance contract and a bill of lading may incorporate the terms of a charter-party. Issues may arise concerning whether the body of terms to be incorporated is sufficiently clearly identified to establish a consensus. The law governing these questions should, in accordance with Article 25, be determined by the choice of law rules of the Member State whose court has been chosen.

Conferring jurisdiction The agreement must confer jurisdiction on the courts of a Member State. It is not necessary for the jurisdiction clause to be phrased in such a way that the competent court can be identified on its wording alone.[370] It is sufficient that the clause states the objective factors on the basis of which the parties have agreed to choose a court to which they wish to submit disputes.

In general, Article 25 does not apply where the parties merely specify the Member State which is the place of performance of a contractual obligation, even though the effect of this is to give a Member State jurisdiction under Article 7(1).[371] However, the requirements of Article 25 cannot be evaded by an agreement on a fictitious place of performance. If the agreement on the place of performance is designed solely to establish jurisdiction, not to determine the place where the person liable is actually to perform the obligations incumbent on him, then the requirements of Article 25 must be met.[372]

Non-exclusive jurisdiction agreements The parties may agree to confer either exclusive or non-exclusive jurisdiction on the courts of a Member State. Under the Brussels I Recast, Article 25 provides that the jurisdiction allocated "shall be exclusive unless the parties have agreed otherwise". This clarifies that non-exclusive jurisdiction agreements are also covered by Article 25 (the point was not entirely clear under the Brussels Convention[373]), and will be given their intended effect. The fact that the jurisdiction conferred is exclusive unless agreed otherwise means that the effect of a jurisdiction agreement is determined not only by its governing law, but also in part by Article 25 itself.[374]

---

[367] *Fiona Trust & Holding Corpn v Privalov* [2007] UKHL 40, [2007] 2 All ER (Comm) 1053; *AP Moller-Maersk A/S v Sonaec Villas Cen Sad Fadoul* [2010] EWHC 355 (Comm), [2010] 2 All ER (Comm) 1159.

[368] *Dubai Islamic Bank PJSC v PSI Energy Holding Co BSC* [2011] EWHC 1019 (Comm), [2011] 1 CLC 595.

[369] Case 24/76 *Colzani/Salotti v RUWA* [1976] ECR 1831; *Crédit Suisse Financial Products v Société Générale d'Enterprises* [1997] CLC 168, CA; *AIG v Ethniki* [1998] 4 All ER 301, [2000] 2 All ER 566, CA; *AIG v QBE International Insurance Ltd* [2001] 2 Lloyd's Rep 268; Briggs (2001) 71 BYBIL 452; *Evialis SA v SIAT* [2003] EWHC 863 (Comm) 377 at [25]–[36] and [74]–[80], [2003] 2 Lloyd's Rep 377; *Tradigrain SA v SIAT SpA* [2002] EWHC 106 (Comm), [2002] 2 Lloyd's Rep 553; *Siboti K/S v BP France SA* [2003] 2 Lloyd's Rep 364; *Prifti on behalf of Lloyds Syndicates v Musini Sociedad Anonima de Segouras y Reaseguros* [2003] EWHC 2796 (Admin), [2004] 1 CLC 517; *Africa Express Line Ltd v Socofi SA* [2009] EWHC 3223 (Comm), [2010] 2 All ER (Comm) 1085.

[370] Case C-387/98 *Coreck Maritime GmbHv Handelsveem BV* [2000] ECR I-9337 at [15]—jurisdiction was allocated to the country where the carrier had its principal place of business; noted by Peel (2001) YEL 340. See also Case C-222/15 *Hoszig Kft v Alstom Power Thermal Services* EU:C:2016:525, [2016] IL Pr 36.

[371] Case 56/79 *Zelger v Salinitri* [1980] ECR 89, discussed infra, p 262.

[372] Case C-106/95 *Mainschiffahrts-Genossenschaft eG (MSG) v Les Gravières Rhénanes Sarl* [1997] ECR I-911. See further infra, p 259.

[373] See, eg, *Insured Financial Structures Limited v Elektrocieplownia Tychy SA* [2003] EWCA Civ 110, [2003] QB 1280.

[374] Cf supra, p 232.

Under the Brussels Convention, by contrast, it was a matter for national law to determine whether a jurisdiction agreement was exclusive or non-exclusive. As far as English law was concerned, the law governing the jurisdiction agreement, rather than the agreement as a whole, determined as a matter of construction[375] whether the clause was "exclusive" or not.[376] The burden of proving that a clause was exclusive was said to rest on the party who relied on it.[377]

On the courts of a Member State Article 25 only refers to an agreement that the courts of a "Member State", in the singular, are to have jurisdiction. However, the Court of Justice in *Meeth v Glacetal Sarl*[378] held that an agreement giving jurisdiction to the courts of two Member States was within what is now Article 25. The agreement provided that the parties, who were domiciled in different Member States, could only be sued in the courts of their respective domiciles. This could result in two Member States having exclusive jurisdiction under Article 25 if each party decided to sue the other. Article 31 would then apply and the court seised of the matter second would defer to the court first seised.

Another form of asymmetrical jurisdiction agreement is one entered into for the benefit of only one party—thus regulating only the possible forum selection of the other party. Article 17 of the Brussels Convention specified that "If the agreement conferring jurisdiction was concluded for the benefit of only one of the parties, that party shall retain the right to bring proceedings in any other court which has jurisdiction by virtue of this Convention." Although this wording is not part of the Brussels I Recast, there is little doubt that such agreements would continue to be given effect.[379]

A further form of asymmetrical jurisdiction clause, commonly used in loan agreements, is exclusive for one party (the borrower) but non-exclusive for the other (the lender). This also comes within Article 25.[380] Recent French case law,[381] which has held that such jurisdiction

---

[375] *Evans Marshall v Bertola SA* [1973] 1 WLR 349; *Sohio Supply Co v Gatoil (USA) Inc* [1989] 1 Lloyd's Rep 588 at 591, CA; *S&W Berisford plc v New Hampshire Insurance Co* [1990] 2 All ER 321 at 326; *Continental Bank NA v Aeakos Compania Naviera SA*, supra, at 592–4; *Svendborg v Wansa* [1997] 2 Lloyd's Rep 183 at 186, CA; *Insured Financial Structures Ltd v Elektrocieplownia Tychy SA* [2003] EWCA Civ 110 at [8], [2003] QB 1280; *Standard Bank London Ltd v Apostolakis (No 1)* [2002] CLC 933; *Pathe Screen Entertainment v Handmade Films* 1989 attached to *Tonicstar Ltd v American Home* [2004] EWHC 1234 (Comm), [2012] 1 CLC 271; *Konkola Copper Mines PLC v Coromin Ltd* [2005] EWHC 898 (Comm) at [69]–[73], [2005] 2 Lloyd's Rep 555; affd without discussion of this point [2006] EWCA Civ 5, [2006] 1 Lloyd's Rep 410; *Konkola Copper Mines plc v Coromin Ltd (No 2)* [2006] EWHC 1093 (Comm) at [22]–[24], [2006] 2 Lloyd's Rep 446. See also *FAI General Insurance v Ocean Marine Mutual* (1996–1997) 41 NSWLR 117.

[376] For the effect of there also being an English choice of law clause cf *British Aerospace plc v Dee Howard Co* [1993] 1 Lloyd's Rep 368, *Sinochem International Oil (London) Co Ltd v Mobil Sales and Supply Corp (No 2)* [2000] 1 Lloyd's Rep 670 at 676 with *Axa v Ace* [2006] EWHC 216 at [29]–[30], [2006] Lloyd's Rep IR 683; *Sea Trade Maritime Corpn v Hellenic Mutual War Risks Association (Bermuda) Ltd (The Athena) (No 2)* [2006] EWHC 2530 (Comm), [2007] 1 Lloyd's Rep 280. See generally Peel [1998] LMCLQ 182 at 182–5. The clause does not have to provide in express terms that the chosen court is to be the exclusive forum. Nor does a non-exclusive agreement have to be express: *Evialis SA v SIAT* [2003] EWHC 863 (Comm) 377 at [68], [2003] 2 Lloyd's Rep 377. For the similar if not identical principles of construction under Scots law see *McGowan v Summit at Lloyds* 2002 SLT 1258.

[377] *Evans Marshall v Bertola SA*, supra, at 361.

[378] Case 23/78 [1978] ECR 2133; Hartley (1979) 4 ELR 125.

[379] It might be argued that this should be a matter left for national law, pursuant to the choice of law in Article 25(1). The better view, however, is that national law may not impose general restrictions on the types of jurisdiction agreements which may be valid, as this would not genuinely be a rule concerning substantive validity but a restriction on the scope of Article 25. Clarification from the Court of Justice on this point is likely to be required.

[380] *Continental Bank v Aeakos* [1994] 1 WLR 588; *Anterist v Crédit Lyonnais*, supra. See also *Banque Cantonale v Waterlily* [1997] 2 Lloyd's Rep 347; *Gamlestaden plc v CDS* [1994] 1 Lloyd's Rep 433. The comments in the footnote immediately preceding are also applicable here.

[381] *Soc Banque Privée Edmond de Rothschild Europe v Mme X,* Cour de Cassation, 1st Civil Chamber, 26 September 2012, No 11-26.022 (English translation [2013] IL Pr 12); Fentiman (2013) 72 CLJ 24; Briggs [2013] LMCLQ 137; Keyes and Marshall (2015) 11 J Priv Int L 345.

agreements are contrary to the object and purpose of Article 25 and thus invalid, is unlikely to be approved by the Court of Justice and has been doubted by the English courts.[382] The object and purpose of Article 25 is to give effect to agreements as to jurisdiction freely entered into by the parties, not to protect the equality of rights of the parties.

The contractual clause in *Meeth* did not give the parties a choice of forum in which to sue. Nonetheless, it is clear that a clause providing, for example, that "the courts of England and Germany are to have exclusive jurisdiction in any proceedings brought by either party" comes within Article 25.[383] Such a clause is exclusive in the sense that it precludes the jurisdiction of the courts of other Member States, but non-exclusive in preserving a degree of choice for the claimant.

Allocating jurisdiction within the United Kingdom   Where the Member State whose courts are given jurisdiction under Article 25 is the United Kingdom, there is the usual problem of allocating jurisdiction within the United Kingdom. Where the Modified Regulation applies[384]—ie (a) the subject matter of the proceedings is within the scope of the Brussels I Recast and (b) the defendant is domiciled in the United Kingdom or the proceedings are of a kind mentioned in Article 24 (exclusive jurisdiction regardless of domicile)—this will provide the answer.[385] Where the Modified Regulation does not apply, the position is less straightforward. It will be necessary to interpret Article 25 as giving jurisdiction not merely to the courts of the United Kingdom, but to the courts of a part of the United Kingdom. This is easy enough where the parties have specifically agreed on trial in England and Wales, Scotland, or Northern Ireland. It is not so easy in the unlikely event of the parties merely agreeing on trial in "the United Kingdom", without any further specification.[386] The courts of England and Wales have, however, on occasion presumed that a reference to "British courts" was a reference to themselves.[387]

Conferring jurisdiction on the courts of a non-Member State   Where the parties confer jurisdiction on the courts of a non-Member State, Article 25 will not apply.[388] Other bases of jurisdiction under the Brussels I Recast may, however, still be applicable, eg Article 4. A court in a Member State must assess the validity of such a jurisdiction clause according to its own rules for determining the applicable law.[389] The effect to be given to such a clause, if it is valid, is less clear. In particular, can such a clause be used as a ground for declining jurisdiction under the Regulation? This raises the question of whether the exercise of jurisdiction under the Regulation is mandatory, which is considered in Chapter 13.[390]

To settle any disputes which have arisen or which may arise in connection with a particular legal relationship The agreement must be to settle any disputes "which have arisen or which may arise".[391] It follows that an agreement as to jurisdiction may be made after the dispute

---

[382] See, eg, *Mauritius Commercial Bank Limited v Hestia Holdings Limited* [2013] EWHC 1328 (Comm), [2013] 2 All ER (Comm) 898; *Commerzbank Aktiengesellschaft v Liquimar Tankers Management Inc* [2017] EWHC 161 (Comm), [2017] 1 Lloyd's Rep 273.

[383] *Kurz v Stella Musical Veranstaltungs GmbH* [1992] Ch 196. See also Case 22/85 *Anterist v Crédit Lyonnais* [1986] ECR 1951 at 1962–3.

[384] See infra, pp 317–19.

[385] See infra, pp 317–22.

[386] See Briggs 2015, para 2.142.

[387] *The Komninos S* [1991] 1 Lloyd's Rep 370.

[388] The *Coreck* case, supra, para 19.

[389] Ibid. Note that jurisdiction agreements are excluded from the scope of the Rome I Regulation: see infra, pp 700–1.

[390] Infra, p 459 et seq.

[391] See *British Steel Corpn v Allivane International Ltd* 1989 SLT (Sh Ct) 57.

has arisen, as well as beforehand. It is for the national court to interpret the clause conferring jurisdiction invoked before it in order to determine whether the dispute in question comes within its scope.[392] This raises a question of construction of the clause, which must be determined by its governing law.[393] In English law, this means the law applicable to the clause, which is not necessarily the law applicable to the agreement as a whole. Where English law governs, the relevant English principles of construction will apply,[394] under which jurisdiction clauses are construed expansively (and are thus likely to include, for example, non-contractual claims relating to the contract).[395] Complex issues of interpretation may also arise where related contracts contain inconsistent jurisdiction agreements, and the court must determine which prevails.[396]

The disputes which the agreement is dealing with must be "in connection with a particular legal relationship".[397] This has not been interpreted strictly—for example, it has been held that if the courts of a Member State have exclusive jurisdiction under what is now Article 25, the same courts are not precluded from considering a set-off by the defendant against the plaintiff, thereby cutting out superfluous procedure.[398] It is not clear, however, whether it imposes other limitations on the scope of a jurisdiction agreement, so that it may not, for example, encompass non-contractual claims which are not connected to the contractual relationship between the parties as part of which the jurisdiction clause was agreed.[399]

(b) The form of the agreement
Article 25 stipulates the form which a choice of court agreement must take, and the Court of Justice has held that requirements as to form under national law are no longer applicable.[400]

---

[392] Case C-214/89 *Powell Duffryn plc v Petereit* [1992] ECR I-1745; Case C-269/95 *Benincasa v Dentalkit Srl* [1997] ECR I-3767 at 3798. See *Hewden Tower Cranes Ltd v Wolffkran Gmbh* [2007] EWHC 857 at [34]–[39] (TCC), [2007] 2 Lloyd's Rep 138.

[393] *Continental Bank NA v Aeakos Compañía Naviera SA* [1994] 1 WLR 588 at 592, CA. See also *Re Leyland Daf Ltd* [1994] 1 BCLC 264; affd [1994] 2 BCLC 106, CA, without discussion of this point; *Ocarina Marine Ltd v Marcard Stein & Co* [1994] 2 Lloyd's Rep 524; *Maimann v Maimann* [2001] IL Pr 27; *Carnoustie Universal v International Transport Workers Federation* [2002] EWHC 1624 (Comm) at [92]–[106], [2003] IL Pr 7; *Provimi Ltd v Roche Products Ltd* [2003] EWHC 961 (Comm) at [57], [2003] 2 All ER (Comm) 683; *Evialis SA v SIAT* [2003] EWHC 863 (Comm) 377 at [60]–[61], [2003] 2 Lloyd's Rep 377; *Snookes v Jani-King (GB) Ltd* [2006] EWHC 289 (QB) at [52], [2006] IL Pr 19; *Clare Taverns v Charles Gill* [2000] ILRM 98 at 109–11; *Bio-Medical Research Ltd v Delatex SA* [2001] 2 ILRM 51, SC of Ireland; *Leo Laboratories v Crompton BV* [2005] 2 ILRM, SC of Ireland. For Scotland see *Mackays Stores Ltd v Topward Ltd* 2006 SLT 716.

[394] Set out in the *Continental Bank* case, supra, at 592–3; see also *Kitechnology BV v Unicor GmbH Plastmaschinen* [1994] IL Pr 568 at 574–7, CA.

[395] *Fiona Trust & Holding Corpn v Privalov* [2007] EWCA Civ 20 at [18], [2007] 1 All ER (Comm) 891, appeal dismissed [2007] UKHL 40, [2007] 2 All ER (Comm) 1053, discussed infra, p 418; *UBS v HSH Nordbank AG* [2009] EWCA Civ 585 at [82], [2010] 1 All ER (Comm) 727. But see *Ryanair Ltd v Esso Italiana Srl* [2013] EWCA Civ 1450, [2015] 1 All ER (Comm) 152.

[396] See Dicey, Morris and Collins, para 12-110; *AmTrust Europe Ltd v Trust Risk Group SpA* [2015] EWCA Civ 437, [2016] 1 All ER (Comm) 325.

[397] Case C-214/89 *Powell Duffryn plc v Petereit* [1992] ECR I-1745 at 1777–8.

[398] Case 23/78 *Meeth v Glacetal* [1978] ECR 2133. For counterclaims see the Advocate General's opinion in that case and Art 8(3).

[399] See *Powell Duffryn plc v Petereit*, supra; Case C-352/13 *Cartel Damage Claims (CDC) Hydrogen Peroxide SA v Akzo Nobel NV* EU:C:2015:335, [2015] QB 906.

[400] Case 150/80 *Elefanten Schuh GmbH v Jacqmain* [1981] ECR 1671; Hartley (1983) 8 ELR 237. The Court of Justice classified the Belgian requirement as to the language of the contract as one of form. Specific national requirements were, however, adopted for Luxembourg under the Brussels I Regulation (Art 63(2)) and Brussels Convention (Protocol, Article I). The Court of Appeal suggested that the question whether a choice of jurisdiction should be implied in a contract governed by English law is a matter of English law, which did not recognise an implied choice: *New Hampshire Insurance Co v Strabag Bau AG* [1992] 1 Lloyd's Rep 361 at 371–2; perhaps the better view is that this result should follow from the form requirements under the Brussels I Recast.

The purpose of these formal requirements is to establish the genuine consensus of the parties.[401] The agreement must be:

(a) in writing[402] or evidenced in writing;

(b) in a form which accords with practices which the parties have established between themselves; or

(c) in international trade or commerce, in a form which accords with a usage of which the parties are or ought to have been aware and which in such trade or commerce is widely known to, and regularly observed by, parties to contracts of the type involved in the particular trade or commerce concerned.

The attitude of the Court of Justice towards the interpretation of these provisions has not always been a model of clarity. On the one hand, the Court of Justice has considered that the purpose of the requirements as to form and the place of Article 25 in the Brussels I Recast should lead to a strict interpretation. On the other hand, the Court of Justice has also noted that the need to uphold normal commercial practices necessitates that the formal requirements be not unduly onerous.

In writing or evidenced in writing   The *in writing* requirement is clearly satisfied where there is a written contract which contains a choice of jurisdiction clause in the text and the contract is signed by both parties. Any variant of this causes problems. Where the choice of jurisdiction clause is contained in general conditions on the back of a written and signed contract there is a danger that, although it is in writing, it will still go unnoticed. Accordingly, the Court of Justice has held that the text of the contract must contain an express reference to these general conditions.[403] The text of the contract[404] does not have to contain an express reference to the jurisdiction clause, it is enough that it refers to the general conditions containing this clause.[405] The fact that the other party does not have a copy of these general conditions is not necessarily decisive.[406] Similarly, where the contract refers to earlier offers which had general conditions on the back, the text of the contract must refer expressly to the earlier offers.[407] Where the written contract contains the choice of jurisdiction clause in the text but has only been signed by one party, there is, again, a danger of it going unnoticed by the other party. The Court of Justice has held that the consent of the other party has also to be in writing, either in the document itself or in a separate document.[408]

---

[401] Case 24/76 *Colzani/Salotti* v *RUWA* [1976] ECR 1831.

[402] For the classification of a requirement as to writing under English private international law, see *supra*, pp 74–5.

[403] Case 24/76 *Colzani/Salotti* v *Rüwa* [1976] ECR 1831. See also *Marine Contractors Inc v Shell Petroleum Development Co of Nigeria* [1984] 2 Lloyd's Rep 77; *Richard SA v Pavan* [1998] IL Pr 193, French Sup Ct (illegible choice of jurisdiction clause—Art 17 of the Brussels Convention not satisfied); *Lafarge Plasterboard Ltd v Fritz Peters & Co KG* [2000] 2 Lloyd's Rep 689 at 697; *Lafi Office and International Business SL v Meriden Animal Health Ltd* [2001] 1 All ER (Comm) 54—party sending terms and conditions cannot argue it did not consent; *7E Communications Ltd v Vertex Antennentechnik GmbH* [2007] EWCA Civ 140, [2007] 1 WLR 2175; *Stryker Corpn v Sulzer Metco AG* [2006] IEHC 60, [2007] IL Pr 47.

[404] The contract may be contained in two documents, see *7E Communications Ltd v Vertex Antennentechnik GmbH* [2007] EWCA Civ 140 at [33]–[37], [2007] 1 WLR 2175.

[405] *7E Communications*, *supra*, at [30]–[32].

[406] *Crédit Suisse Financial Products v Société Générale d'Entreprises* [1997] IL Pr 165, CA.

[407] The *Colzani* case, *supra*, at [12]. The conditions must have been expressly referred to in the offer and must have been communicated to the other party.

[408] Case 71/83 *Partenreederei MS Tilly Russ v Haven and Vervaebedriff Nova NV* [1985] QB 931, [1984] ECR 2417; see the notes by Wilderspin (1984) 9 ELR 456, and North [1985] LMCLQ 177.

The effect of these cases is that not only must the choice of jurisdiction clause be in writing but also the consensus on its application must be in writing. Although this strict approach remains good law,[409] subsequent cases raising different issues have taken a more liberal line. The mere fact that a written agreement containing a choice of jurisdiction clause has expired is not fatal if it can be shown that under the relevant applicable law the parties can validly extend the initial contract without observing the requirements of writing.[410] In the case of a shareholder, the requirement of form is complied with if the statutes containing the jurisdiction clause are lodged in a place to which the shareholder may have access or in a public register.[411]

Article 25(2) provides that: "Any communication by electronic means which provides a durable record of the agreement shall be equivalent to 'writing'." This provision (added in the Brussels I Regulation) ensures that the need for the agreement to be in writing or evidenced in writing does not invalidate a jurisdiction agreement that is not written on paper but is accessible in an electronic form.[412] To provide a "durable record" it is sufficient if the electronic display of terms and conditions could potentially be saved or printed.[413]

The *evidenced in writing* alternative is designed to deal with the situation where there is an oral contract which is confirmed in writing.[414] In *Galeries Segoura Sprl v Firma Rahim Bonakdarian*[415] the Court of Justice held that, where an oral agreement is made subject to general conditions of sale, the confirmation in writing (accompanied in that case by notification of the general conditions of sale which contained a clause conferring jurisdiction) must be accepted in writing by the other party. It was reasoned that in such a case there is no initial oral agreement as to a clause conferring jurisdiction which is capable of being evidenced by the confirmation in writing. Subsequently, the Court of Justice has shown a concern that the requirements as to form should not be so onerous as to impede normal commercial practices, and has adopted a rather more liberal line. In *Partenreederi MS Tilly Russ v Haven and Vervaebedriff Nova NV*[416] it held that where the choice of jurisdiction clause is in writing (in the instant case, in printed conditions in a bill of lading[417]) this can be regarded as written confirmation of an earlier communicated oral agreement between the parties expressly referring to that clause.

The same willingness to recognise that there has been confirmation in writing is evident in the decision of the Court of Justice in *F Berghoefer GmbH and Co Kg v ASA SA*.[418] Here it was held that, in the situation where there is an oral agreement expressly dealing with

---

[409] *Siboti K/S v BP France SA* [2003] EWHC 1278 (Comm) at [39], [2003] 2 Lloyd's Rep 364. Case C-222/15 *Hoszig Kft v Alstom Power Thermal Services* EU:C:2016:525, [2016] IL Pr 36.

[410] Case 313/85 *Iveco Fiat SpA v Van Hool NV* [1986] ECR 3337; Allwood (1987) 12 ELR 461.

[411] Case C-214/89 *Powell Duffryn plc v Petereit* [1992] ECR I-1745.

[412] See the Explanatory Memorandum in the Proposal for a Council Regulation COM (1999) 348 final, p 18.

[413] Case C-322/14 *El Majdoub v CarsOnTheWeb.Deutschland GmbH* EU:C:2015:334, [2015] 1 WLR 3986; Dickinson and Ungerer [2016] LMCLQ 15.

[414] But see *Middle East Tankers & Freighters Bunker Services SA v Abu Dhabi Container Lines PJSC* [2002] EWHC 957 (Comm), [2002] 2 Lloyd's Rep 643 at 651–2.

[415] Case 25/76 [1976] ECR 1851.

[416] Supra.

[417] The bill of lading may come into existence after the creation of the contract of carriage to which the jurisdiction clause relates; however, Art 25 does not require the agreement on jurisdiction to be contemporaneous with the original contract. See on this aspect of the case, North [1985] LMCLQ 177.

[418] Case 221/84 [1985] ECR 2699; Hartley (1986) 11 ELR 470. For an English case taking this liberal line, see *Middle East Tankers & Freighters Bunker Services SA v Abu Dhabi Container Lines PJSC* [2002] EWHC 957 (Comm), [2002] 2 Lloyd's Rep 643. See also Case 313/85 *Iveco Fiat SpA v Van Hool NV* [1986] ECR 3337.

jurisdiction,[419] the formal requirements of Article 17 of the Brussels Convention (the corresponding provision to Article 25 of the Brussels I Recast) were satisfied if written confirmation of the agreement by one of the parties was received by the other and the latter raised no objection.[420] It was not required that the confirmation comes from the party who stands to lose from the clause. Thus in the instant case it was a German plaintiff who confirmed the oral agreement that the German courts should have exclusive jurisdiction.

In a form which accords with practices which the parties have established between themselves This provision gives effect to the idea developed by the Court of Justice that the consensus of the parties may be shown by a continuous business relationship between them which was subject to the general conditions containing the jurisdiction clause.[421]

In international trade or commerce, in a form which accords with a usage of which the parties are or ought to have been aware and which in such trade or commerce is widely known to, and regularly observed by, parties to contracts of the type involved in the particular trade or commerce concerned[422] This provision on trade usage was introduced[423] because of fears that the Court of Justice had interpreted the original requirements on writing or evidenced in writing so restrictively that businessmen would find it hard to meet them.[424] This relaxation of the formal requirements has repercussions on the issue of the reality of the consensus of the parties to the jurisdiction clause. Consensus is presumed to exist where there are commercial usages in the relevant branch of international trade or commerce of which the parties are or ought to have been aware.[425] An established usage in international trade or commerce must be shown to exist and to have been followed.[426] This is assessed solely in the light of commercial usages, not by national requirements.[427] No independent requirements are laid down for this, such as that the jurisdiction clause is contained

---

[419] See *Bols Distilleries v Superior Yacht Services Ltd* [2006] UKPC 45 at [38], [2007] 1 WLR 12—not evidenced in writing where no evidence jurisdiction agreement ever discussed and agreed.

[420] See also Case C-106/95 *Mainschiffahrts-Genossenschaft eG (MSG) v Les Gravières Rhénanes Sarl* [1997] ECR I-911.

[421] *Tilly Russ*, supra; *Segoura v Bonakdarian*, supra. See also *O T Africa Line Ltd v Hijazy (The Kribi)* [2001] 1 Lloyd's Rep 76 at 89; *SSQ Europe SA v Johann & Backes OHG* [2002] 1 Lloyd's Rep 465—a good arguable case established that the defendant had traded for a long period (with 672 invoices) in the knowledge that the claimant was only willing to deliver on its standard terms and the defendant knew the content of these terms and never once objected to them; *Middle East Tankers & Freighters Bunker Services SA v Abu Dhabi Container Lines PJSC* [2002] EWHC 957 (Comm), [2002] 2 Lloyd's Rep 643, 652; *Lafarge Plasterboard Ltd v Fritz Peters & Co KG* [2000] 2 Lloyd's Rep 689 at 698; *Standard Steamship Owners' Protection and Indemnity Association (Bermuda) Ltd v GIE Vision Bail* [2004] EWHC 2919 (Comm) at [45], [2005] 1 All ER (Comm) 618; *Oakley v Ultra Vehicle Design Limited (In Liquidation)* [2005] EWHC 872 (Ch) at [54], [2005] IL Pr 55.

[422] Case C-106/95 *Mainschiffahrts-Genossenschaft eG (MSG) v Les Gravières Rhénanes Sarl* [1997] ECR I-911; Seatzu (1998) 49 NILQ 327; AG Lenz's opinion in Case C-288/92 *Custom Made Commercial Ltd v Stawa Metallbau GmbH* [1994] ECR I-2913 at 2934–48; Case C-159/97 *Transporti Castelletti Spedizione Internatzionali SpA v Hugo Trumpy SpA* [1999] ECR I-1597; Case C-366/13 *Profit Investment SIM SpA v Stefano Ossi* EU:C:2016:282, [2016] 1 WLR 3832.

[423] See the 1978 Accession Convention to the Brussels Convention.

[424] See the Schlosser Report, p 125. It may be that both the *Colzani* and *Segoura* cases would now come within this, as would the *Tilly Russ* case (see *SSQ Europe SA v Johann & Backes OHG* [2002] 1 Lloyd's Rep 465 at 481).

[425] Case C-106/95 *Mainschiffahrts-Genossenschaft eG (MSG) v Les Gravières Rhénanes Sarl*, supra, at 201–2; Case C-159/97 *Trasporti Castelletti Spedizioni Internazionali SpA v Hugo Trumpy SpA* [1999] ECR I-1597.

[426] The *Trasporti Castelletti* case, supra, at [30]; *Standard Steamship Owners' Protection and Indemnity Association (Bermuda) Ltd v GIE Vision Bail* [2004] EWHC 2919 (Comm) at [44], [46], [2005] 1 All ER (Comm) 618. See also *Clare Taverns v Charles Gill* [2000] ILRM 98, 109.

[427] See the *Trasporti Castelletti* case, supra, at [39]. The Hess, Pfeiffer and Schlosser Report suggested that some degree of Community harmonisation of the substantive law on formation of contracts would assist in relation to determining usages: Study JLS/C4/2005/03, Final Version September 2007, para 882.

in a written document. The parties must have been or ought to have been aware of the usage.[428] There is an additional requirement[429] that this usage must, on the one hand, be widely known to, and, on the other hand, regularly observed by, parties to contracts of the type involved in the particular trade or commerce concerned.[430]

Which party can allege that the requirements relating to form have not been met? Clearly the party who did not have notice of the choice of jurisdiction clause can do so. This was the position in the *Colzani* and *Segoura* cases. But if this party wishes to rely on the clause, can the other party, who knew about it from the outset, challenge the clause on the basis of lack of compliance with the requirements as to form? Since the purpose of these requirements is to prevent choice of jurisdiction clauses going unnoticed by one of the parties, it is arguable that only the party who did not have notice of the clause should be able to challenge it. On the other hand, if, as the Schlosser Report suggested in relation to the Brussels Convention,[431] the courts of Member States must of their own motion determine whether Article 17 (Article 25 of the Brussels I Recast) operates to prevent them from having jurisdiction, these are requirements which apply regardless of the arguments of the parties, and it should be irrelevant which party raises the issue.

(iii) Third parties and jurisdiction agreements

Difficult questions can arise concerning when jurisdiction agreements may be enforced by or against third parties. In *Gerling v Italian Treasury*[432] the Court of Justice held that a third party beneficiary would be entitled to rely on a choice of jurisdiction clause inserted for his benefit in a contract (which satisfied Article 17 of the Brussels Convention requirements) between an insurer and a policyholder, even though the third party had not satisfied the requirements as to form. The Court pointed out that the provisions on insurance in the Convention were designed to protect the policyholder. It would be pointless to require a third party to go through these formalities; and in those cases where the beneficiary was not told of the jurisdiction clause, impossible for him to do so. Consistent with this, in the later *Tilly Russ*[433] case it was held that a third party who, under the applicable national law, stood in the shoes of an original shipper, succeeding to his rights and obligations under a bill of lading (which did comply with Article 17 of the Brussels Convention, corresponding to Article 25 of the Brussels I Recast), could not avoid the obligations in respect of jurisdiction under this by arguing that he did not consent to the jurisdiction clause.[434] Similarly, according to the Court of Justice in *Coreck Maritime GmbH v Handelsveem BV*,[435] a jurisdiction clause is

---

[428] *Trasporti Castelletti*, supra, at [45]. See also *The Kribi*, supra, at 90; *Clare Taverns v Charles Gill* [2000] ILRM 98, 109.

[429] Originally added to the Brussels Convention by the 1989 Accession Convention, Art 7.

[430] See *The Kribi*, supra, at 90.

[431] Schlosser Report, p 21; see also the *Colzani* case.

[432] Case 201/82 [1983] ECR 2503; Hartley (1983) 8 ELR 264 Applied in: *Re Leyland Daf Ltd* [1994] 2 BCLC 106, CA—involving a receiver of a company; *Glencore International AG v Metro Trading International Inc (No 1)* [1999] 2 Lloyd's Rep 632—involving an assignee of a debt. See also Case C-112/03 *Société Financière & Industrielle du Peloux v Société AXA Belgium* [2005] ECR I-3707, discussed infra, p 291.

[433] Case 71/83 [1984] ECR 2417.

[434] Under English law a third party holder of a bill of lading will so succeed: *The Kribi*, supra, at 90. A receiver of a company is bound by an agreement on jurisdiction entered into by the company: *Re Leyland Daf Ltd* [1994] 2 BCLC 106, CA; *Glencore International AG v Metro Trading International Inc (No 1)*, supra. See also *WPP Holdings Italy Srl v Benatti* [2006] EWHC 1641 (Comm) at [102]–[108], [2006] 2 Lloyd's Rep 610; it was not necessary to discuss this point on appeal in *Benatti v WPP Holdings Italy SRL* [2007] EWCA Civ 263, [2007] 1 WLR 2316—appeal allowed in relation to one claimant and dismissed in relation to other claimants.

[435] Case C-387/98 [2000] ECR I-9337. See also *Siboti K/S v BP France SA* [2003] 2 Lloyd's Rep 364; *Hapag Lloyd Container Line GmbH v La Réunion Européenne* [2003] IL Pr 51, French Cour de Cassation.

valid as against a third party who succeeded by virtue of the applicable national law to the shipper's rights and obligations. If the third party bearer of the bill of lading, succeeded by virtue of the applicable law to the shipper's rights and obligations when he acquired the bill of lading there is no need to ascertain whether he accepted the jurisdiction clause in the original contract.[436] However, if, under the applicable national law, the party not privy to the original contract did not succeed to the rights and obligations of one of the original parties, the court seised must ascertain, having regard to the requirements laid down in the first paragraph of Article 17 of the Brussels Convention, whether he actually accepted the jurisdiction clause relied on against him.[437]

Coreck suggests that the crucial question whether a party not privy to the original contract has succeeded to the rights and obligations of one of the original parties (so that it is not necessary to demonstrate the consent of the third party) must be determined according to the applicable national law.[438] However, in *Refcomp SpA v Axa Corporate Solutions Assurance SA*[439] the Court of Justice suggested that the rule in *Coreck* was based on "the very specific nature of bills of lading",[440] which are internationally accepted as establishing a substitution of one party for another in a legal relationship. In *Refcomp*, the French doctrine under which a sub-buyer replaces the original buyer of goods in a chain of contracts was considered not to establish such a substitution, in part because the contractual terms may vary, and in part because this was not a matter on which there was agreement between Member States. As a result, the court held that the issue should not be governed by national law, which would introduce different outcomes among the Member States, and it would be necessary to demonstrate that the third party (sub-buyer) has actually consented to the jurisdiction agreement in accordance with the requirements of Article 25 of the Brussels I Recast.

The principles set out above apply equally to the situation where neither party is privy to the original contract.[441] The original contracting parties must have consented to the jurisdiction clause (which includes satisfying the formal requirements) and each new party must have succeeded to the rights and obligations of an original party.

(iv) Limitations on the effectiveness of the agreement
First, Article 25(4) provides that the courts which have exclusive jurisdiction under Article 24 cannot be deprived of it by an agreement under Article 25, and any agreement which purports to do so shall have no legal force. It also provides that agreements conferring jurisdiction are of no legal force if they are contrary to either Article 15, Article 19 or Article 23.[442] This means that in matters relating to insurance, in consumer contracts and in individual

---

[436] The *Coreck* case, supra, at [25]. Cf the attitude of the Court of Justice towards the use of Art 5(1) of the Brussels Convention, (equivalent to Art 7(1) of the Brussels I Recast), see infra, pp 244–5.

[437] Ibid, at [26]. See *Astilleros Zamakona SA v MacKinnons* 2002 SLT 1206; *Andromeda Marine SA v OW Bunker & Trading A/S (The Mana)* [2006] EWHC 777 (Comm), [2006] 2 Lloyd's Rep 319; *Hewden Tower Cranes Ltd v Wolffkran Gmbh* [2007] EWHC 857 at [52]–[60] (TCC), [2007] 2 Lloyd's Rep 138. Regard must also be had to the formalities under Art 25(1) of the Brussels I Recast.

[438] The *Coreck* case, supra, at [24]. The national court must apply its rules of private international law to determine this law: ibid, at [30]. See also Case C-366/13 *Profit Investment SIM SpA v Stefano Ossi* EU:C:2016:282, [2016] 1 WLR 3832; *Goldman Sachs International v Novo Banco SA* [2015] EWHC 2371 (Comm) at [76] (reversed on other grounds at [2016] EWCA Civ 1092); *Antonio Gramsci Shipping Corp v Stepanovs* [2011] EWHC 333 (Comm), [2012] 1 All ER (Comm) 293.

[439] Case C-543/10 EU:C:2013:62, [2013] 1 Lloyd's Rep 449.

[440] At [35].

[441] Case C-159/97 *Trasporti Castelletti Spedizioni Internazionali SpA v Hugo Trumpy SpA* [1999] ECR I-1597. See the opinion of AG Leger at 1617 [79].

[442] For the burden of proof see *Benatti v WPP Holdings Italy Srl* [2007] EWCA Civ 263 at [37]–[44] (per Toulson LJ), [2007] 1 WLR 2316; discussed supra, p 216 et seq.

contracts of employment, any agreement conferring jurisdiction must comply with both the requirements of Article 25 and of Article 15, Article 19 or Article 23.

Secondly, there is another limitation on the effectiveness of the agreement, which is not mentioned in Article 25. As noted previously, the Court of Justice has held that the defendant's submission to the courts of a Member State under Article 18 of the Brussels Convention (Article 26 of the Brussels I Recast) overrides an agreement conferring jurisdiction under Article 17 of the Convention (Article 25 of the Brussels I Recast).[443] Equally, submission to the courts of a Member State by a non-Member State domiciled party (which would not strictly be covered by Article 26, assuming that this provision only applies to Member State domiciled parties) should override Article 25.[444]

Under the Brussels I Regulation and Brussels Convention, the rules on *lis pendens* operated as a third limitation on the effectiveness of an agreement on jurisdiction. A party who did not wish to be bound by an agreement providing, for example, for the exclusive jurisdiction of the English courts could bring pre-emptive proceedings before the courts of another Member State (known colloquially as an "Italian torpedo" action), and the court chosen in the agreement could not take jurisdiction until (and unless) the court first seised determined that it did not have jurisdiction.[445] The Brussels I Recast has introduced an amendment to the *lis pendens* rules (Article 31(2)) which strengthens the position of jurisdiction agreements, giving priority to the court chosen by the parties in the case of parallel proceedings concerning the validity of a jurisdiction agreement.[446]

(iii) General jurisdiction

Article 4 provides that "persons domiciled in a Member State shall, whatever their nationality, be sued in the courts of that Member State". Article 4 is concerned with the domicile of the defendant at the time of commencement of proceedings, which in England means the issue of proceedings rather than the time of their subsequent service on the defendant.[447]

The Brussels I Recast adopts the principle that, in general, persons should be sued[448] in the courts of the Member State where they are domiciled.[449] The words "shall . . . be sued" must not be taken literally.[450] The defendant may, and, in some circumstances, must, be sued in the courts of a Member State other than that of his domicile.[451] Article 4 is thus a basis of

---

[443] Case 150/80 *Elefanten Schuh GmbH v Jacqmain* [1981] ECR 1671.

[444] Supra, p 226.

[445] C-116/02 *Erich Gasser v Misat Srl* Case [2003] ECR I-4207; discussed infra, pp 450–3.

[446] See infra, pp 452–3; Recital (22).

[447] *Canada Trust Co v Stolzenberg (No 2)* [2002] 1 AC 1, HL. See also *Ministry of Defence and Support of the Armed Forces for the Islamic Republic of Iran v FAZ Aviation Ltd* [2007] EWHC 1042 (Comm) at [5], [52], [53], [2007] IL Pr 42. For the position where proceedings are brought in Scotland see *Canada Trust*, per Lord Hope at 23–6.

[448] *National Justice Compañia Naviera SA v Prudential Assurance Co Ltd (The Ikarian Reefer (No 2)* [2000] 1 WLR 603, CA; Briggs (2000) 71 BYBIL 450—this does not include an application under s 51 of the Senior Courts Act 1981 to recover costs from a non-party. Followed in *Masri v Consolidated Contractors International (UK) Ltd* [2008] EWCA Civ 876, [2009] 2 WLR 699, which concerned an application for an order for an officer of a corporate judgment debtor to attend court to provide information; reversed by the House of Lords without discussion of this point [2009] UKHL 3, [2010] 1 AC 90.

[449] See the Jenard Report, pp 13 and 18–19. See also *SA Consortium General Textiles v Sun and Sand Agencies Ltd* [1978] QB 279 at 295, CA; *Citadel Insurance Co v Atlantic Union Insurance Co SA* [1982] 2 Lloyd's Rep 543 at 549, CA; *Knauf UK GmbH v British Gypsum Ltd* [2001] EWCA Civ 1570 at [49], [2002] 1 Lloyd's Rep 199.

[450] Although they are not without effect: see Case C-281/02 *Owusu v Jackson* [2005] ECR I-1383 at [37]; infra, pp 462–4.

[451] Where Art 29 (*lis pendens*) applies it also requires the courts of Member States, including that of the defendant's domicile, to decline jurisdiction.

non-exclusive jurisdiction, unlike, for example, Article 24, or Article 25 where the parties have entered into an exclusive jurisdiction agreement. Where Article 4 applies, other Articles under the Brussels I Recast may give the claimant alternative places in which to commence proceedings, but according to Recital (15), the Brussels I Recast is "founded on the principle that jurisdiction is generally based on the defendant's domicile", which means that other grounds of jurisdiction tend to be interpreted restrictively. Article 4 is, by contrast, a basis of general jurisdiction—there is no requirement for the dispute to have any connection with the Member State in which the defendant is domiciled (or indeed with any other Member State).

In order to ascertain whether the defendant is domiciled in a Member State under Article 4, reference must be made (if an individual) to Article 62 of the Brussels I Recast and paragraph 9 of Schedule 1 to the Civil Jurisdiction and Judgments Order 2001, and (if a company) to Article 63 of the Brussels I Recast, which have already been discussed.[452] Where the Member State in which the defendant is domiciled is the United Kingdom, the Modified Regulation will apply to allocate jurisdiction between the courts of England and Wales, Scotland and Northern Ireland.[453]

(iv) Special jurisdiction

In some cases trial is permitted in the courts of a Member State other than the one in which the defendant is domiciled; this is known as special jurisdiction and the relevant provisions are found in Section 2 of Chapter II of the Brussels I Recast. This alternative form of jurisdiction is justified on the basis of a close connection between the court and the action or in order to facilitate the sound administration of justice.[454] It is left to the claimant to decide whether he wishes to sue the defendant in the latter's domicile under Article 4 or whether he wishes to sue him in another Member State under Section 2. Where the Member State given special jurisdiction is the United Kingdom, the claimant will want to know whether he is to sue in England, Scotland or Northern Ireland or has the choice of suing in any of these. The modified version of the Brussels I Regulation will not apply[455] to allocate jurisdiction within the United Kingdom. It has no need to. The provisions on special jurisdiction are designed to give local as well as international jurisdiction[456] and can be regarded as giving jurisdiction to the courts of a part of the United Kingdom and not merely to the courts of the United Kingdom as a whole. Many of the provisions give jurisdiction to the courts of a place in a Member State, and the place in the United Kingdom would be in England, Scotland or Northern Ireland, as indicated by the particular provisions. Other provisions give jurisdiction to the courts or a court of a Member State, but the context readily identifies which part of the United Kingdom is the appropriate one to have jurisdiction.

(a) Special jurisdiction under Article 7

This is the most important of the three articles in Section 2. Article 7 provides that a person domiciled in a Member State may be sued in another Member State in seven specified situations. Before looking at these, it is important to realise that the use of the words "may be sued" is not intended to confer on courts a discretion to refuse to take jurisdiction.[457]

---

[452] Supra, pp 198–202.

[453] Infra, pp 317–22.

[454] Recital (16) of the Brussels I Recast. See also Case C-386/05 *Color Drack GmbH v LEXX International Vertriebs GmbH* [2007] ECR I-3699 at [22]. It may not be the court with the closest connection, Case C-288/92 *Custom Made Commercial Ltd v Stawa Metallbau GmbH* [1994] ECR I-2913.

[455] Infra, p 318.

[456] See the Schlosser Report, p 98; Hartley, p 40.

[457] *Tesam Distribution Ltd v Schuh Mode Team GmbH* [1990] IL Pr 149, CA; *Boss Group Ltd v Boss France SA* [1997] 1 WLR 351, CA; see infra, p 459 et seq.

Rather it emphasises that the claimant is allowed (but not required) to sue the defendant in a Member State other than where the defendant is domiciled. Nonetheless, the defendant's domicile is the normal place for trial. Article 7 is an exception to this general rule,[458] and its provisions must not be given an interpretation going beyond the situations envisaged by the Brussels I Recast.[459] It is less clear whether this means that all its provisions should be given a restrictive interpretation.[460]

The seven situations where the defendant can be sued in a Member State other than that of his domicile are set out in Article 7(1) to (7) as follows:

Article 7(1)[461]

(a) in matters relating to a contract, in the courts for the place of performance of the obligation in question;

(b) for the purpose of this provision and unless otherwise agreed, the place of performance of the obligation in question shall be:

- in the case of the sale of goods, the place in a Member State where, under the contract, the goods were delivered or should have been delivered,

- in the case of the provision of services, the place in a Member State where, under the contract, the services were provided or should have been provided,

(c) if point (b) does not apply then point (a) applies.

(i) What are matters relating to a contract?

In order for Article 7(1) to apply there must be a matter relating to a contract. The Court of Justice has given an autonomous meaning to this concept, rather than applying the classification adopted under the national law of a Member State.[462]

A contractual relationship   There must be a contractual relationship between the parties.[463] In certain circumstances this can present a problem, with no consensus under the substantive law of the Member States over whether there is such a relationship, and the Court of Justice has had to resolve the question. In the *Peters* case[464] the Court has had to consider the relationship between an association and its members. Not all Member States regard this as a contractual relationship. Nonetheless, the Court held that this came within Article 5(1) of the Brussels Convention, the predecessor of Article 7(1) of the Brussels I Recast. The

---

[458] Case 56/79 *Zelger v Salinitri* [1980] ECR 89.

[459] Case C-26/91 *Jakob Handte & Co GmbH v Traitements Mecano-chimiques des Surfaces SA (TMCS)* [1992] ECR I-3967 at [14]; Case C-433/01 *Freistaat Bayern v Blijdenstein* [2004] ECR I-981 at [25]; Case C-168/02 *Kronhofer v Maier* [2004] ECR I-6009 at [14]; the opinion of AG Jacobs in Case C-167/00 *Verein Für Konsumenteninformation v K H Henkel* [2002] ECR I-8111 at [33].

[460] Cf the *Kronhofer* case with the denials by AG Jacobs in *Verein* and the Court of Justice in Case C–27/02 *Engler v Janus Versand GmbH* [2005] ECR I-481 at [48] (following AG Jacobs at [38] of his opinion).

[461] Art 5(1) of the Brussels I Regulation; Art 5(1) of the Brussels Convention.

[462] Case 34/82 *Peters v Zuid Nederlandse Aannemers Vereniging* [1983] ECR 987; Case C-26/91 *Jakob Handte & Co GmbH v Traitements Mecano-Chimiques des Surfaces SA (TMCS)* [1992] ECR I-3967.

[463] Case C-26/91 *Jakob Handte & Co GmbH v Traitements Mecano-Chimiques des Surfaces SA (TMCS)* [1992] ECR I-3967; Case C-51/97 *Réunion Européenne SA v Spliethoff's Bevrachtingskantoor BV* ECR I-3967 at [19]; Case C-196/15 *Granarolo SpA v Ambrosi Emmi France SA* EU:C:2016:559 at [25], [2016] IL Pr 32.

[464] Case 34/82 [1983] ECR 987; Hartley (1983) 8 ELR 262. See also Case C-214/89 *Powell Duffryn plc v Wolfgang Petereit* [1992] ECR I-1745; *Bank of Scotland v Investment Management Regulatory Organisation Ltd* 1989 SLT 432. Cf Case C-147/12 *ÖFAB, Östergötlands Fastigheter AB v Frank Koot and Evergreen Investments BV* EU:C:2013:490, [2015] QB 20; Case C-519/12 *OTP Bank Nyilvánosan Működő Részvénytársaság v Hochtief Solution AG* EU:C:2013:674, [2015] IL Pr 30.

autonomous definition of matters relating to a contract includes relationships which involve close links of the same kind as are created between the parties to a contract.[465] In *Jakob Handte & Co GmbH v Traitements Mecano-Chimiques des Surfaces SA (TMCS)*[466] the Court of Justice had to consider the relationship between a manufacturer and a sub-buyer who brings a claim in respect of damage to the product itself. Under French law there was liability in contract, whereas under English law, and that of many other Member States, usually there is no liability at all, either in contract or tort. The Court held that it was irrelevant how the relevant national court classified the matter or how it was classified under the applicable law; "matters relating to a contract" had to be given an independent meaning. The action did not relate to a contractual matter since there was no contractual relationship between the parties[467] because the manufacturer had not undertaken any contractual obligation towards the sub-buyer,[468] and the nature of the manufacturer's liability was not regarded by the overwhelming majority of Contracting States to the Brussels Convention as being contractual. However, such liability (ie that imposed under French law) should be regarded as falling within the scope of Article 7(2) of the Brussels I Recast,[469] even though such liability is not regarded in Member States as being tortious in the strict sense.[470] In *Česká spořitelna as v Feichter*[471] the Court of Justice held that the relationship between the payee of a promissory note and the giver of a guarantee (an aval) is contractual in nature. But the relationship between the issuer of a bearer bond and the person who has acquired the bond from a third party, where the issuer has not freely assumed an obligation towards the acquirer, is not.[472] In *Schmidt v Schmidt*[473] the Court of Justice assumed that a contract of gift of immoveable property falls within Article 7(1). A contractual relationship between the parties can be tacit, as in the case of a long-standing business relationship which has formed without a contract in writing.[474] The existence of a tacit contractual relationship must be demonstrated by a body of consistent evidence such as the existence of a long-standing business relationship, good faith between the parties, regularity of transactions and their development over time in terms of quantity and value, any agreements as to prices and discounts, and the correspondence exchanged.[475]

An identifiable obligation   The Court of Justice in *Fonderie Officine Meccaniche Tacconi SpA v Heinrich Wagner Sinto Maschinenfabrik GmbH (HWS)*[476] has said that "while Article 5(1) of the Brussels Convention does not require a contract to have been concluded, it is nevertheless essential, for that provision to apply, to identify an obligation, since the jurisdiction of the national court is determined, in matters relating to a contract, by the place of performance

---

[465] Followed in Case C-47/14 *Holterman Ferho Exploitatie BV and Others v Friedrich Leopold Freiherr Spies von Büllesheim* EU:C:2015:574, [2015] IL Pr 44—the relationship between a company and its former manager contractual in nature.

[466] Case C-26/91 [1992] ECR I-3967; Briggs (1992) 12 YEL 667; Decker (1993) 42 ICLQ 366; Hartley (1993) 18 ELR 506; Fawcett (1993) I Hague Recueil 13 at 76–8. See also Case C-543/10 *Refcomp SpA v Axa Corporate Solutions Assurance SA* EU:C:2013:62, [2013] 1 Lloyd's Rep 449.

[467] Cf *Atlas Shipping v Suisse Atlantique* [1995] 2 Lloyd's Rep 188—a contract between A and B to pay C held to be within Art 5(1) of the Brussels Convention, and to the same effect see *Benatti v WPP Holdings Italy SRL* [2007] EWCA Civ 263 at [52] (per Toulson LJ), [2007] 1 WLR 2316.

[468] The obligation must be freely assumed by one party towards the other, see infra, pp 249–50.

[469] AG Jacobs at 3989. In principle, this would not stop a national court from then classifying the action as contractual for choice of law purposes, AG Jacobs at 3984.

[470] The wide scope of Art 7(2) is discussed infra, pp 263–6.

[471] Case C-419/11 EU:C:2013:165, [2013] IL Pr 22.

[472] Case C-375/13 *Harald Kolassa v Barclays Bank plc* EU:C:2015:37, [2016] 1 All ER (Comm) 733.

[473] Case C-417/15 EU:C:2016:881 at [38], [2017] IL Pr 6.

[474] Case C-196/15 *Granarolo SpA v Ambrosi Emmi France SA* EU:C:2016:559, [2016] IL Pr 32; Grušić (2016) 12 ERCL 395; McParland [2016] LMCLQ 500.

[475] Case C-196/15 *Granarolo SpA v Ambrosi Emmi France SA* EU:C:2016:559 at [26], [2016] IL Pr 32.

[476] Case C-334/00 [2002] ECR I-7357.

of the obligation in question".[477] In that particular case there were negotiations that gave rise to expectations but the stage had not yet been reached when there were obligations.[478] The House of Lords in *Agnew v Lansforsakringsbolagens AB*[479] has held that the requirement of an identifiable obligation[480] is separate from the requirement that there be a matter relating to a contract.[481] The nature of this obligation has been examined by the House of Lords in both the *Agnew* case and in the earlier case of *Kleinwort Benson Ltd v Glasgow City Council*.[482]

In *Kleinwort Benson* a majority of the House of Lords, influenced by the allocation of jurisdiction to the place of performance of the obligation in question, adopted a principle that a claim can only come within Article 5(1) of the Modified Convention (now the Modified Regulation),[483] allocating jurisdiction within the United Kingdom, if it is based on a particular contractual obligation, ie the obligation whose performance is sought in the judicial proceedings.[484] This suggests that the obligation must be a contractual one and that it must also be a performance obligation. Support for both propositions can be found in terminology used by the Court of Justice in a number of cases.[485] The *Kleinwort Benson* case concerned a claim for restitution of money paid under a purported contract subsequently accepted by both parties, in the light of an earlier judgment,[486] as being void *ab initio*. This claim was based on the concept of unjust enrichment, not on a particular contractual obligation and, accordingly, fell outside the scope of Article 5(1) of the Modified Convention (now Modified Regulation).[487] Moreover, since it was accepted that the contract was void *ab initio*, there was no obligation and Article 5(1) could not apply.[488] This does not mean that all claims for restitution would fall outside what is now Article 7(1) of the Brussels I Recast. A restitutionary

---

[477] Ibid, at [22]. See also Case C–27/02 *Petra Engler v Janus Versand GmbH* [2005] ECR I-481 at [50]; Case C-419/11 *Česká spořitelna as v Feichter* EU:C:2013:165 at [46], [2013] IL Pr 22; Case C-375/13 *Harald Kolassa v Barclays Bank plc* EU:C:2015:37 at [39], [2016] 1 All ER (Comm) 733; Case C-196/15 *Granarolo SpA v Ambrosi Emmi France SA* EU:C:2016:559 at [24], [2016] IL Pr 32.

[478] See the opinion of AG Geelhoed in the *Fonderie* case at [81]–[83].

[479] [2001] 1 AC 223.

[480] Ibid, at 240 (per Lord Woolf), 246 (per Lord Cooke—an obligation so intimately connected with contract that it falls within Art 5(1) of the Lugano Convention), 250 (per Lord Hope), 262–6, (per Lord Millett), 233–4 (per Lord Nicholls).

[481] Ibid, at 240 (per Lord Woolf), 246 (per Lord Cooke), 250 (per Lord Hope). Lord Millett (262–6) accepted this requirement but regarded it as falling within the concept of matters relating to a contract, as, seemingly, did Lord Nicholls (233–4). The latter was the view in the earlier House of Lords case of *Kleinwort Benson Ltd v Glasgow City Council* [1999] 1 AC 153.

[482] [1999] 1 AC 153; Briggs (1997) 68 BYBIL 331; Dickinson [1998] RLR 104; Maher [1998] Jur Rev 131; McGrath (1999) 18 CJQ 41; Virgo (1998) 114 LQR 386; Peel [1997] LMCLQ 22; Pitel (1998) 57 CLJ 19. See generally Peel, in Rose (ed) *Restitution and the Conflict of Laws* (1995), Chapter 1.

[483] It appears from their Lordships' judgments that these would have been exactly the same if it had been a case on the Brussels Convention. See also *Eddie v Alpa Srl* 2000 SLT 1062 at 1068. The Court of Justice in Case C-346/93 *Kleinwort Benson Ltd v Glasgow City Council* [1995] ECR I-615, infra, p 266, declined to give a ruling on the Art 5(1) point on the basis that it arose in the context of an intra-United Kingdom dispute under the Modified Convention, rather than in order to apply the Brussels Convention itself.

[484] At 167–71 (per Lord Goff), 181 (per Lord Clyde), 189 (per Lord Hutton). See the powerful and convincing dissent of Lord Nicholls at 174–6, with whom Lord Mustill, at 174 et seq, concurred.

[485] Both Case 14/76 *De Bloos v Bouyer* [1976] ECR 1497 at [11], [14] and Case 266/85 *Shenavai v Kreischer* [1987] ECR 239 at [18] refer to a contractual obligation. The latter also refers to "the contractual obligation whose performance is sought in the judicial proceedings". See also the opinion of AG Geelhoed in the *Fonderie* case at [38]–[39].

[486] *Hazell v Hammersmith and Fulham Borough Council* [1992] 2 AC 1, HL.

[487] It also fell outside Art 5(3) of the Modified Convention (now Modified Regulation), see infra, p 266. See also *Strathaird Farms Ltd v G A Chattaway & Co* 1993 SLT (Sh Ct) 36 and *Eddie v Alpa Srl* 2000 SLT 1062—claim for restitution for overpayment outside Art 5(1) of the Modified Convention and the Brussels Convention, respectively.

[488] At 169 (per Lord Goff), 181 and 183 (per Lord Clyde), 195–6 (per Lord Hutton). But cf the judgment of Millet LJ in the Court of Appeal [1996] QB 678 at 698–9.

claim that is based on a contractual obligation will not do so.[489] A claim to recover money paid under a valid contract, on the ground of a failure of consideration following a breach of contract by the defendant, is capable of being classified under some systems as contractual and the concept of a contractual obligation is broad enough to encompass this.[490] In *Profit Investment SIM SpA v Stefano Ossi*[491] the Court of Justice has held that actions seeking the annulment of a contract and the restitution of sums paid but not due under the contract fall within Article 7(1). This is because, if there had not been a contractual relationship freely assumed between the parties, the obligation would not have been performed and there would have been no right to restitution. It is this causal link between the right to restitution and the contractual relationship that brings the action for restitution within Article 7(1).[492] The *Kleinwort Benson* case can be reconciled with *Profit Investment* by confining it to its exceptional set of facts where the parties accepted that the contract was void *ab initio*.

The requirement that the claim has to be based on the performance of a particular contractual obligation raised concerns that what is now Article 7(1) might not apply where the claim arises out of a pre-contractual obligation. However, these concerns were put to rest[493] by the House of Lords in *Agnew v Lansforsakringsbolagens AB*,[494] which held by a majority[495] that a claim for a declaration that the plaintiffs were entitled to avoid (ie rescind) insurance contracts on the basis of misrepresentations and non-disclosure fell within Article 5(1) of the Lugano Convention. In other words, an "obligation", which in this case could variously be described as being to make a fair presentation of the risk, not to misrepresent the risk, or to disclose facts material to the risk,[496] included a pre-contractual obligation which if not fulfilled gave the plaintiffs the right to set aside the contract.[497] Doubts were expressed in the *Agnew* case as to whether it would be appropriate to refer to an "obligation" not to be guilty of duress, or undue influence or inducing a contract by mistake in a case of a person seeking to rely on duress, etc.[498] Moreover, there could be no place of performance of such a negative obligation.[499] In contrast, where the negative obligation was not to commit yourself to other partners this was regarded by the Court of Justice as an obligation but the problem was that there was a multiplicity of

---

[489] Fawcett, Harris and Bridge paras 8.13–8.27.

[490] *Kleinwort Benson*, supra, Lord Goff at 167 and 171.

[491] Case C-366/13 EU:C:2016:282, [2016] 1 WLR 3832. See also the opinion of AG Kokott in Case C-185/15 *Kostanjevec v F&S Leasing GmbH* EU:C:2016:397 at [58]–[61], [2017] 4 WLR 7.

[492] The *Profit Investment* case, at [55].

[493] It remains to be seen whether the adoption of the Rome II Regulation on the law applicable to non-contractual obligations, which provides in Art 12 choice-of-law rules for *culpa in contrahendo* which apply regardless of whether the contract was actually concluded or not, will affect the rule laid down in the *Agnew* case; discussed infra, pp 849–54. The Court of Justice has expressed a view that the provisions of the Brussels I Regulation need not be interpreted in the light of Rome II, see Case C-45/13 *Andreas Kainz v Pantherwerke AG* EU:C:2014:7 at [20], [2015] QB 34. See also Art 1(2)(i) of the Rome I Regulation, discussed infra, pp 702–3.

[494] [2001] 1 AC 223; Briggs (2000) 71 BYBIL 451; Pester [2000] LMCLQ 289; Hemsworth [2001] LMCLQ 509.

[495] Lords Hope and Millett dissenting.

[496] Per Lord Cooke at 246. According to Lord Woolf, at 239, the obligation was to disclose. Lord Nicholls, at 233–4, concurred with both Lords Cooke and Woolf, which leaves the precise nature of the obligation uncertain.

[497] Cf the *Fonderie* case, which concerned pre-contractual liability but no contract was ever concluded and the obligation was therefore based on a rule of law.

[498] [2001] 1 AC 223 at 241 (per Lord Woolf, with whom Lord Nicholls concurred), 265 (per Lord Millett, who, after examining the nature of the so-called obligation according to the applicable national law, thought there was no obligation in such cases).

[499] The requirement of an identifiable place of performance is discussed infra, p 250.

places of performance in different Member States and therefore what is now Article 7(1)(a) could not be used.[500]

We must turn now to the statement in the *Fonderie* case that no contract need have been concluded.[501] This makes clear that what is now Article 7(1) can apply where there is agreement on the main parts of the contract but not on all terms and conditions and there is no signed contract.[502] At this late stage, when there is almost a complete contract, it can be inferred from the circumstances that obligations have been assumed by the parties.

An obligation that is freely assumed   The Court of Justice has repeatedly held that, in order for there to be a matter relating to a contract, there must be an obligation freely assumed by one party towards another.[503] This requirement has come into play in three different situations.

The first is where there is no direct contractual relationship between the parties. This is illustrated by the *Jakob Handte* case[504] where, although there was no direct contractual relationship between a sub-buyer and the manufacturer, under French law the sub-buyer had a contractual claim against the manufacturer.[505] The Court of Justice said that the manufacturer "undertakes no contractual obligation to that [sub]buyer whose identity and domicile may, quite reasonably, be unknown to him".[506] Neither was this requirement met where a guarantor (A), who paid customs duties under a guarantee obtained by the forwarding agent (V), sought reimbursement from the owner of goods (F), who was not a party to the contract of guarantee.[507] It would, however, be met if F authorised the conclusion of the contract of guarantee.[508] There was also no contractual relationship freely entered into between the consignee of goods and a sub-carrier which was a third party to a transport contract between the consignee and another company which issued the bill of lading.[509]

---

[500] Case C-256/00 *Besix SA v Wasserreinigungsbau Alfred Kretzschmar GmbH & Co KG (WABAG)* [2002] ECR I-1699; discussed infra, pp 254–5. See also in relation to a negative obligation *Crucial Music Corpn v Klondyke Management AG* [2007] EWHC 1782 (Ch), [2007] IL Pr 54, which held that the obligation can also be a warranty as to an existing state of affairs.

[501] At [22]. See also Case C–27/02 *Petra Engler v Janus Versand GmbH* [2005] ECR I-481 at [45], [50]; Case C-419/11 *Česká spořitelna as v Feichter* EU:C:2013:165 at [46], [2013] IL Pr 22; Case C-375/13 *Harald Kolassa v Barclays Bank plc* EU:C:2015:37 at [38], [39], [2016] 1 All ER (Comm) 733.

[502] See the opinion of AG Geelhoed in the *Fonderie* case at [83].

[503] The *Jakob Handte* case at [15]; Case C-51/97 *Réunion Européenne SA v Spliethoff's Bevrachtingskantoor BV* [1998] ECR I-6511 at [17], [19]; Case C-334/00 *Fonderie Officine Meccaniche Tacconi SpA v Heinrich Wagner Sinto Maschinenfabrik GmbH (HWS)* [2002] ECR I-7357 at [23]; Case C-265/02 *Frahuil SA v Assitalia SPA* [2004] ECR I-1543 at [24]; the *Petra Engler* case at [50]; Case C-419/11 *Česká spořitelna as v Gerald Feichter* EU:C:2013:165 at [46], [47], [2013] IL Pr 22; Case C-375/13 *Harald Kolassa v Barclays Bank plc* EU:C:2015:37 at [39], [2016] 1 All ER (Comm) 733. For the problems raised by this requirement in the case of an action between a carrier and a third party holder of a bill of lading see Fawcett, Harris and Bridge, paras 5.21–5.26.

[504] Case C-26/91 [1992] ECR I-3967. For a different illustration see Case C-167/00 *Verein Für Konsumenteninformation v K H Henkel* [2002] ECR I-8111 at [38]–[40]. See also *Deutsche Bank AG London Branch v Petromena ASA* [2013] EWHC 3065 (Comm); but see [2015] EWCA Civ 226, [2015] 1 WLR 4225; *Iveco SpA v Magna Electronics Srl (formerly Italamec Srl)* [2015] EWHC 2887 (TCC), [2016] IL Pr 18; *XL Insurance Co SE (formerly XL Insurance Co Ltd) v AXA Corporate Solutions Assurance* [2015] EWHC 3431 (Comm), [2016] Lloyd's Rep IR 420, appeal pending; cf *Engdiv Ltd v G Percy Trentham Ltd* 1990 SLT 617.

[505] This is based on the theory that the intermediate supplier transmits to the sub-buyer his contractual rights against the manufacturer (or against a previous intermediary) as an accessory of the goods.

[506] At [20].

[507] Case C-265/02 *Frahuil SA v Assitalia SPA* [2004] ECR I-1543.

[508] Ibid.

[509] Case C-51/97 *Réunion Européenne SA v Spliethoff's Bevrachtingskantoor BV* [1998] ECR I-6511; Peel (1998) 18 YEL 700; Briggs [1999] LMCLQ 333; Hartley (2000) 25 ELR 89; Takahashi [2001] LMCLQ 107. However, the action came within the scope of what is now Art 7(2).

The second situation where this requirement came into play arose in the *Fonderie* case.[510] There was no identifiable contractual obligation, the negotiations not having reached the stage where contractual obligations arose. The obligation in that case to make good the damage allegedly caused by the unjustified breaking off of negotiations could derive only from rules of law, in particular the rule which requires the parties to act in good faith in negotiations with a view to the formation of a contract.[511] Accordingly, there was no obligation freely assumed by one party towards another.[512]

The third situation where this requirement came into play arose in *Česká spořitelna as v Feichter*[513] where the Court of Justice held that the giver of an aval (a kind of guarantee), by signing a promissory note, voluntarily consents to act as the guarantor of the obligations of the issuer of the promissory note. This is even if the promissory note was incomplete at the date of its signature and was subsequently completed by the payee, pursuant to an agreement on the right to complete the note which was also signed by the giver of the aval. By contrast, in *Harald Kolassa v Barclays Bank plc*[514] the Court found that, if there were no obligations freely assumed in the relationship between the issuer of a bearer bond and the person who has acquired the bond from a third party, Article 7(1) was not engaged.

Where there are contractual obligations, these can arise both by virtue of the terms of the contract and under the general law (such as the obligations imposed on the seller by the Sale of Goods Act 1979). Contractual obligations arising by virtue of the terms of the contract are undeniably freely assumed by one party towards another. As regards obligations that arise by virtue of the general law, it can be said that by voluntarily entering into a contract the parties freely assume the legal incidents of the contract.[515] This means that the source of the obligation, whether it is the general law or the express terms of the contract, does not matter.[516] Neither is there any problem in meeting this requirement where there is a unilateral undertaking by a commercial body to award a prize.[517]

An identifiable place of performance   Not only must there be an identifiable obligation, there must also be an identifiable place of performance.[518] This, like the requirement of an identifiable obligation, was regarded by the majority of Law Lords in the *Agnew* case as a separate requirement from there being a matter relating to a contract.[519]

---

[510]   Case C-334/00 [2002] ECR I-7357.

[511]   Ibid, at [24]–[25].

[512]   Ibid. However, this pre-contractual liability will come within what is now Art 7(2), discussed infra, pp 263–79.

[513]   Case C-419/11 EU:C:2013:165, [2013] IL Pr 22.

[514]   Case C-375/13 EU:C:2015:37, [2016] 1 All ER (Comm) 733.

[515]   *Agnew v Lansforsakringsbolagens AB* [2001] 1 AC 223, 264 (per Lord Millett), HL.

[516]   Ibid, at 240–4 (per Lord Woolf), 233–4 (per Lord Nicholls), 253 (per Lord Hope), 264 (per Lord Millett). See also Case 9/87 *SPRL Arcado v SA Haviland* [1988] ECR 1539; Allwood (1988) 13 ELR 366; Briggs (1988) 8 YEL 269; Stone [1988] LMCLQ 383—statutory claim for damages for the wrongful repudiation of a commercial agency agreement. For concurrent actions in tort and contract see Case C-548/12 *Marc Brogsitter v Fabrication de Montres Normandes EURL and Karsten Fräßdorf* EU:C:2014:148, [2014] QB 753; infra, pp 268–9.

[517]   Case C–27/02 *Petra Engler v Janus Versand GmbH* [2005] ECR I-481 at [51]–[60]; Case C-234/04 *Kapferer v Schlank & Schick GmbH* [2006] ECR I-2585 at [45]–[50] of the opinion of AG Tizzano; Case C-180/06 *Ilsinger v Dreschers (Administrator in the Insolvency of Schlank & Schick GmbH)* [2009] ECR I-3961 at [57].

[518]   See the opinion of AG Jacobs in the *Petra Engler* case at [33]; *Agnew v Lansforsakringsbolagens AB* [2001] 1 AC 223 at 240 (per Lord Woolf), 246 (per Lord Cooke), 250 (per Lord Hope), 233–4 (per Lord Nicholls), HL.

[519]   [2001] 1 AC 223 at 240 (per Lord Woolf), 246 (per Lord Cooke), 250 (per Lord Hope). Lord Millett (262–6) accepted this requirement but regarded it as falling within the concept of matters relating to a

(ii) Disputes relating to the existence of the agreement

In *Effer v Kantner*[520] the Court of Justice held that jurisdiction under what is now Article 7(1) may be invoked by the plaintiff even where there is a dispute between the parties over the existence of the contract on which the claim is based. Courts would be too easily deprived of jurisdiction if an allegation by the defendant that no contract existed was sufficient to prevent the dispute falling within Article 7(1). The court seised of the matter may end up deciding that no contract exists but this is neither here nor there. All that matters is that this court is satisfied that the requirements of Article 7(1) are satisfied, including that it is a matter relating to a contract. When it comes to trial in England it has to be shown that there is a good arguable case, ie a better or much better argument on the material available, that a contract exists, which may well involve going into the merits of the case.[521] Where a negative declaration is sought denying the existence of the contract the claimant can rely upon the fact that the defendant is seeking to enforce a contract against him.[522] The court whose jurisdiction is invoked under Article 7(1) may, of its own motion, examine its jurisdiction,[523] including the question of the existence of the contract, and decide that it does not have jurisdiction.

The *Effer* case involved an action for the enforcement of the performance of a contractual obligation, during the course of which the question of the existence of the contract arose as a preliminary issue.[524] Similarly, in *Boss Group Ltd v Boss France SA*[525] the Court of Appeal used what is now Article 7(1) to take jurisdiction to grant the plaintiff a negative declaration that no contract existed in circumstances where the defendant was seeking to enforce a contractual obligation against the plaintiff. What would happen though if the question of the existence of the contract is the only matter in issue between the parties? This question arose in *Profit Investment SIM SpA v Stefano Ossi*[526] which concerned actions seeking the annulment of a contract and the restitution of sums paid but not due under the contract. The Court of Justice held that the national court's jurisdiction to determine questions relating to a contract includes the power to consider the existence of the constituent parts of the contract itself.[527]

---

contract, as, seemingly, did Lord Nicholls (233–4). The latter was the view of the House of Lords in the earlier *Kleinwort Benson* case.

[520] Case 38/81 [1982] ECR 825; Hartley (1982) 7 ELR 235. See Art 24, Case 73/77 *Sanders v van der Putte* [1977] ECR 2383; Case C-234/04 *Kapferer v Schlank & Schick GmbH* [2006] ECR I-2585 at [60] of the opinion of AG Tizzano.

[521] *Tesam Distribution Ltd v Schuh Mode Team GmbH* [1990] IL Pr 149, CA; *Medway Packaging Ltd v Meurer Maschinen GmbH & Co KG* [1990] 2 Lloyd's Rep 112, CA; *Rank Film Distributors Ltd v Lanterna Editrice SRL* [1992] IL Pr 58; *Deutsche Ruckversicherung AG v La Fondiara Assicurazioni SPA* [2001] 2 Lloyd's Rep 621; *Morley v Reiter Engineering GmbH & Co KG* [2011] EWHC 2798 (Ch), [2012] IL Pr 6; *Canyon Offshore Ltd v GDF Suez E&P Nederland BV* [2014] EWHC 3810 (Comm), [2015] IL Pr 8.

[522] *Boss Group Ltd v Boss France SA* [1997] 1 WLR 351 at 356–7, CA. For negative declarations under Art 7(2) see Case C-133/11 *Folien Fischer AG and Fofitec AG v Ritrama SpA* EU:C:2012:664, [2013] QB 523.

[523] Where Art 28 of the Brussels I Recast applies the court will be under a duty to do so, see infra, p 309.

[524] This was used by Lords Clyde and Goff in the *Kleinwort Benson* case at 182 and 170, to reconcile the principle adopted by the majority of the House of Lords, that the claim must be based on a particular contractual obligation, with the decision in the *Effer* case allowing jurisdiction in relation to a dispute over the existence of the contract. But cf Lord Nicholls, Lord Mustill concurring, at 174. Lord Hutton, at 193–4, although in favour of the above principle did not attempt to reconcile it with the *Effer* case which he distinguished on the basis that it did not involve a contract accepted as being void *ab initio*.

[525] [1997] 1 WLR 351; Briggs (1996) 67 BYBIL 583; Forsyth [1996] LMCLQ 329; Peel (1996) 112 LQR 541; Crawford (2005) 54 ICLQ 829, 840. The decision was approved by Lord Clyde in the *Kleinwort Benson* case at 182. See also *Youell v La Reunion Aerienne* [2009] EWCA Civ 175, [2009] 2 All ER (Comm) 1071; Briggs (2009) 80 BYBIL 595. See also Case C-133/11 *Folien Fischer AG and Fofitec AG v Ritrama SpA* EU:C:2012:664, [2013] QB 523.

[526] Case C-366/13 EU:C:2016:282, [2016] 1 WLR 3832.

[527] Ibid, at [54].

(iii) The general rule

Article 7(1)(a) lays down the general rule of jurisdiction for matters relating to a contract, according to which jurisdiction is given to the courts for the place of performance of the obligation in question. This rule is based on Article 5(1) of the Brussels Convention, although there is one difference between the two provisions: employment contracts, which were dealt with in Article 5(1) of the Brussels Convention, are now the subject of a separate section.[528] In order to avoid the problems of interpretation surrounding this general rule, the Brussels I Regulation introduced, in what is now Article 7(1)(b), special rules of jurisdiction for two most important types of contract, namely contracts for the sale of goods and the provision of services.[529] All other contracts are subject to the general rule.

The obligation in question   A multiplicity of obligations (which may have different places of performance) can arise in complex contractual cases, yet the Brussels I Recast gives no indication in Article 7(1)(a) as to which obligation is being referred to.

In *De Bloos v Bouyer*[530] the Court of Justice went some way towards an autonomous definition for the obligation in question. It held that Article 5(1) of the Brussels Convention is referring not to any obligation under the contract but to the contractual obligation forming the basis of the legal proceedings, the one which the contract imposes on the defendant, the non-performance of which is relied upon by the plaintiff. Thus an English court had jurisdiction in a case where German defendants broke their obligation to give reasonable notice of termination of an exclusive distribution agreement to an English company in England.[531] There is a problem in identifying the obligation in question in cases where the claimant is seeking a negative declaration, ie a declaration that he is not liable to perform an obligation under the contract, on the basis that the other party has not performed a term of the contract. It has been suggested that the obligation in question is that term and not the claimant's obligation to perform the contract.[532] With certain contracts it is by no means easy to ascertain precisely what the obligations of the parties are.[533] It may also be necessary to ascertain whether an agreement has been superseded by a further agreement imposing separate contractual obligations, one of which is being relied upon.[534] Moreover, if the claimant is seeking compensation

---

[528] Discussed infra, pp 297–302.

[529] Infra, pp 255–63. See Fawcett, Harris and Bridge, paras 3.143–3.235, 3.298–3.301; Takahashi (2002) 27 ELR 530.

[530] Case 14/76 [1976] ECR 1497. See Giardina (1978) 27 ICLQ 263, 269–71; Hartley (1977) 2 ELR 60.

[531] *Medway Packaging Ltd v Meurer Maschinen GmbH & Co KG* [1990] 2 Lloyd's Rep 112, CA. See also *Waverley Asset Management Ltd v Saha* 1989 SLT (Sh Ct) 87; *Bitwise Ltd v CPS Broadcast Products BV* 2003 SLT 455.

[532] *AIG Europe (UK) Ltd v The Ethniki* [2000] 2 All ER 566 at [27], CA. See also *Boss Group Ltd v Boss France SA* [1997] 1 WLR 351, CA; *Fisher v Unione Italiana de Riassicurazione SpA* [1998] CLC 682; *USF Ltd (t/a USF Memcor) v Aqua Technology Hanson NV/SA* [2001] 1 All ER (Comm) 856. The *Agnew* case would tend to support this.

[533] See generally on the parties' obligations where there is a distribution agreement: *Ferndale Films Ltd v Granada Television Ltd* [1994] IL Pr 180, Irish Supreme Court; *Boss Group Ltd v Boss France SA* [1997] 1 WLR 351, CA; *Carl Stuart Ltd v Biotrace Ltd* [1994] IL Pr 554, Irish High Court; *USF Ltd (t/a USF Memcor) v Aqua Technology Hanson NV/SA* [2001] 1 All ER (Comm) 856; *Bio-Medical Research Ltd v Delatex SA* [2001] 2 ILRM 51, Irish Supreme Court. For a concession agreement, see *Hacker Kuchen GmbH v Bosma Huygen Meubelimpex BV (Case 14.197)* [1992] IL Pr 379, Dutch Hoge Raad. For licences, see *Rank Film Distributors v Lanterna Editrice Srl* [1992] IL Pr 58; *Olympia Productions Ltd v Mackintosh* [1992] ILRM 204, Irish High Court. See generally on the above agreements, Fawcett and Torremans, pp 84–99. There can also be problems with a sale of goods contract: see *Viskase Ltd v Paul Kiefel GmbH* [1999] 1 WLR 1305, CA; Briggs (1999) 70 BYBIL 336; *MBM Fabri-Clad Ltd v Eisen-Und Huttenwerke Thale AG* [2000] IL Pr 505, CA, Fawcett, Harris and Bridge, paras 3.109–3.141; and with a settlement contract, see *Kenburn Waste Management Ltd v Bergmann* [2002] EWCA Civ 98, [2002] CLC 644, CA.

[534] *W H Martin Ltd v Felbinder Spezialfahrzeugwerke GmbH* [1998] IL Pr 794, CA.

a decision then has to be made as to whether this claim involves an independent contractual obligation (and therefore falls within Article 7(1)(a)), or whether it involves a new obligation replacing the unperformed contractual obligation (which would be outside Article 7(1)(a)). There is no consensus among the legal systems of the different Member States as to which of these two is the source of the right to claim compensation. The national court where trial is sought is therefore left to decide this in the light of the law applicable to the contract under its private international law rules. If English law applies, an obligation to pay unliquidated damages cannot form the basis of jurisdiction under Article 7(1)(a) since this obligation is remedial in character, not an independent contractual obligation.[535]

A particular difficulty with the *De Bloos* approach is that the claimant may make several claims involving different obligations to be performed in different states. This problem was solved by the Court of Justice in *Shenavai v Kreischer*.[536] The judge dealing with the case is to be guided by the maxim *accessorium sequitur principale* and is to identify the principal obligation on which the claimant's action is based and jurisdiction is to be determined in accordance with this. Thus, if the defendant shipowners are in breach of obligations under a charter-party to, first, nominate a vessel (this obligation to be performed in London) and, secondly, provide a vessel for the carriage of cargo (this obligation to be performed in Florida) the first obligation is the principal one, since it is the performance of this obligation that triggers other obligations.[537] The plaintiff is not allowed to camouflage the principal obligation by relegating it to a subordinate role by the way he chooses to express his claim.[538] If all the obligations are to be performed in the same country, there is no need to identify the principal obligation.[539] In the situation where the action is founded on two obligations of equal rank arising from the same contract, one obligation to be performed in one Member State and the other in another Member State, the same court does not have jurisdiction to hear the whole of an action.[540] For the purposes of Article 7(1)(a) the claims are split up and tried before the courts of different Member States. However, the claimant can avoid this by bringing the whole of the action in the Member State in which the defendant is domiciled.

---

[535] *Medway Packaging Ltd v Meurer Maschinen GmbH & Co KG* [1990] 1 Lloyd's Rep 383 at 389, Hobhouse J at first instance. The Court of Appeal did not discuss this point.

[536] Case 266/85 [1987] ECR 239; Allwood (1988) 13 ELR 60. See also *Campbell International Trading House Ltd v Peter Van Aart* [1992] 2 IR 305, Irish Supreme Court; *Ferndale Films Ltd v Granada Television Ltd* [1994] IL Pr 180, Irish Supreme Court; *Carl Stuart Ltd v Biotrace Ltd* [1994] IL Pr 554, Irish High Court; *Raiffeisen Zentral Bank Österreich Aktiengesellschaft v National Bank of Greece SA* [1999] 1 Lloyd's Rep 408; *Rank Film Distributors v Lanterna Editrice Srl* [1992] IL Pr 58; *AIG Europe v The Ethniki* [1998] 4 All ER 301, affd [2000] 2 All ER 566, CA; *Bitwise Ltd v CPS Broadcast Products BV* 2003 SLT 455.

[537] *Union Transport plc v Continental Lines SA* [1992] 1 WLR 15, HL; Briggs (1992) 108 LQR 186. For characterisation of the principal obligation in cases of: a bill of lading, see *RPS Prodotti Siderurgici srl v Owners and/or Demise Charterers of the Sea Maas, The Sea Maas* [2000] 1 All ER 536; carriage by road, see *Royal & Sun Alliance Insurance plc v MK Digital FZE (Cyprus) Ltd* [2006] EWCA Civ 629 at [87]–[105], [2006] 2 Lloyd's Rep 110; reinsurance, see *AIG Europe (UK) Ltd v The Ethniki* [2000] 2 All ER 566, CA; supply and delivery of goods, see *MBM Fabri-Clad Ltd v Eisen-Und Huttenwerke Thale AG* [2000] IL Pr 505, CA; a letter of credit, see *Crédit Agricole Indosuez v Chailease Finance Corpn* [2000] 1 Lloyd's Rep 348, CA; accountancy services, see *Barry v Bradshaw* [2000] IL Pr 706, CA; quality control inspection services, see *Source Ltd v TUV Rheinland Holding AG* [1998] QB 54, CA; agreement between an investor in a company and the company, see *Worldview Capital Management SA v Petroceltic International Plc* [2015] EWHC 2185 (Comm), [2015] IL Pr 46.

[538] *The Ethniki* at [25], CA.

[539] *Boss Group Ltd v Boss France SA* [1997] 1 WLR 351, CA.

[540] Case C-420/97 *Leathertex Divisione Sinetici SpA v Bodetex BVBA* [1999] ECR I-6747; Panagopoulos [2000] LMCLQ 150; Peel (2001) 20 YEL 331; distinguished in *The Ethniki* at [26], CA. See also *Nissany v Michelson*, 24 November 2016, HC.

The place of performance of the obligation in question   Article 7(1)(a) does not contain
an autonomous definition of the place of performance of the obligation in question, and the
Court of Justice has not been prepared to provide one. Instead, the place of performance
of the obligation in question under Article 7(1)(a) is determined by the forum applying its
rules of private international law. In *Tessili v Dunlop*[541] the Court of Justice held that the
national court before which the matter is brought "must determine in accordance with its
own rules of conflict of laws what is the law applicable to the legal relationship in question
and define in accordance with that law the place of performance of the contractual obligation
in question".[542] The shortcomings in the *Tessili* approach were criticised by academics[543] and
by Advocates General.[544] Criticisms include the fact that it leads to a lack of harmonisation
in the law of jurisdiction[545] and that the process that has to be gone through is undeniably
complex and difficult to apply.[546] The Court of Justice has accepted that this approach can
lead to jurisdiction being allocated to a forum which is not the one that has the closest connection with the dispute.[547]

In *Besix SA v Wasserreinigungsbau Alfred Kretzschmar GmbH & Co KG (WABAG)*,[548] the
Court of Justice held that Article 5(1) of the Brussels Convention (now Article 7(1)(a) of the
Brussels I Recast) had to be interpreted as meaning that, in the event that the relevant contractual obligation under the law applicable to the contract has been, or is to be, performed
in a number of places, jurisdiction to hear and determine the case cannot be conferred on
the court within whose jurisdiction any one of those places of performance happens to be
located.[549] Instead, jurisdiction had to be based on the rule of general jurisdiction. It was clear
from the wording of the provision, which is in the singular (the place of performance), that
a single place of performance for the obligation in question must be identified.[550] The Court
was concerned to avoid a multiplicity of competent courts and the risk that the plaintiff is
able to choose the place of performance which he judges to be most favourable to his interests. The *Besix* case concerned the situation where the place of performance of the obligation
in question could not be determined because it consisted of an undertaking by the defendants not to do something (not to commit themselves to other partners) which was not subject
to any geographical limit and was therefore characterised by a multiplicity of places of its

---

[541] Case 12/76 [1976] ECR 1473. See Giardina (1978) 27 ICLQ 263, 271–2; Hartley (1977) 2 ELR 59.
This decision was confirmed by the Court of Justice in: Case C-288/92 *Custom Made Commercial Ltd v Stawa
Metallbau GmbH* [1994] ECR I-2913; Briggs (1994) 14 YEL 573; Case C-440/97 *GIE Groupe Concorde v
The Master of the Vessel Suhadiwarno Panjan* [1999] ECR I-6307; Peel (2001) 20 YEL 331; the *Leathertex*
case; Case C-256/00 *Besix SA v Wasserreinigungsbau Alfred Kretzschmar GmbH & Co KG (WABAG)* [2002]
ECR I-1699.

[542] The *Tessili* case at [13].

[543] See Kennett (1995) 15 YEL 193; Anton and Beaumont's, *Civil Jurisdiction in Scotland* (1995) 2nd edn,
p 101; Hill (1995) 44 ICLQ 591, 618; Reed [1997] NILQ 243; Ancel (2001) 3 YBPIL 101.

[544] AG Leger in the *Leathertex* case, AG Lenz in the *Custom Made* case and AG Ruiz-Jarabo Colomer in
the *GIE* case. See also AG Bot in Case C-386/05 *Color Drack GmbH v LEXX International Vertriebs GmbH*
[2007] ECR I-3699 at [54]–[77].

[545] AG Leger in the *Leathertex* case at [128].

[546] See AG Ruiz-Jarabo Colomer in the *GIE* case at 874–5. This has led to resistance from national courts,
particularly in France, to applying the *Tessili* approach, see Droz [1997] Rec Dalloz 351; AG Ruiz-Jarabo
Colomer in the *GIE* case at 878.

[547] Case C-288/92 *Custom Made Commercial Ltd v Stawa Metallbau GmbH* [1994] ECR I-2913 at
2956–7.

[548] Case C-256/00 [2002] ECR I-3699.

[549] Ibid, at [28]. See also *Mora Shipping Inc v Axa Corporate Solutions Assurance SA* [2005] EWCA Civ
1069 at [21], [2005] 2 Lloyd's Rep 769; cf *Crédit Agricole Indosuez v Chailease Finance Corpn* [2000] 1 Lloyd's
Rep 348, CA; *Canyon Offshore Ltd v GDF Suez E&P Nederland BV* [2014] EWHC 3810 (Comm), [2015]
IL Pr 8.

[550] The *Besix* case at [29], [32].

performance.[551] The place of performance, in effect, was in any place in the world, including all the Contracting States to the Convention.

(iv) Special rule for sales and services contracts

The Brussels I Regulation introduced two major innovations in the rule of jurisdiction for contractual matters. First, what is now Article 7(1)(b) provides that for the contracts for the sale of goods and the provision of services the obligation in question is the obligation to deliver the goods and perform the service, regardless of the obligation on which the claim is based. Second, there is now an autonomous definition of the place of performance of the obligation in question for these two types of contract.[552] These innovations were introduced to remedy the shortcomings in the *De Bloos/Tessili* approach.[553] They are designed to reinforce the unification of the rules of jurisdiction whilst ensuring their predictability.[554] Article 7(1) (b) represents a compromise between the Member States, some of which wanted to retain the existing rule and others to abolish Article 7(1) altogether.[555]

The scope of Article 7(1)(b)   There are two clear limitations on the scope of Article 7(1) (b).[556] First, it is explicitly provided that the case must be one of the "sale of goods" or the "provision of services". Neither concept is defined in the Brussels I Recast. It is easier to say what each concept does not cover than what it does. We know from other provisions in the Brussels I Recast that "sale of goods" and "provision of services" do not cover insurance contracts, individual contracts of employment and consumer contracts. Neither, when working out the meaning of "sale of goods", does this cover the provision of services and vice versa.

Turning to what "sale of goods" does cover, it is important to note that twenty-three of the twenty-seven European Union Member States subject to the Brussels I Recast are parties to the UN Convention on the International Sale of Goods (CISG) of 1980 (the Vienna Convention). The concept of sale of goods under that Convention represents the corpus of most of the legal systems of the Member States. One should therefore turn to the meaning of "sale of goods" under the Vienna Convention to answer the question of what is covered by the words "sale of goods" in Article 7(1)(b). This is helpful in determining whether a contract for the supply of goods to be manufactured is one for the "sale of goods". It also tells us that "goods" should be given a broad meaning to include minerals and crops and should also encompass the sale of software, whether contained on a disk or transferred over the internet.[557] On the other hand, "sale of goods" should not cover the sale of things that are excluded from the Vienna Convention. The leading case on the concept of the "sale of goods" is the *Car Trim* case.[558]

> A German supplier of components used in the manufacture of airbag systems entered into several contracts with an Italian manufacturer of those systems. The German company was to manufacture or produce airbags following precise requirements and individual specifications of the purchaser.

---

[551] The earlier decision of the Court of Appeal in *Boss Group Ltd v Boss France SA* [1997] 1 WLR 351, where jurisdiction was taken under Art 5(1) of the Brussels Convention in a case involving a negative obligation performable "everywhere", including in England and France, can no longer be followed.

[552] See Kadner Graziano (2014) 16 YBPIL 167.

[553] See the Explanatory Memorandum in the Proposal for a Council Regulation COM (1999) 348 final, p 14.

[554] Case C-386/05 *Color Drack GmbH v LEXX International Vertriebs GmbH* [2007] ECR I-3699 at [24].

[555] See Beaumont, in Fawcett (ed), *Reform and Development of Private International Law* (2002) 9, p 15 et seq.

[556] For these and other possible limitations, see Fawcett, Harris and Bridge, paras 3.146–3.170.

[557] See Reymond (2014) 16 YBPIL 219. For business to business e-commerce, see Fawcett, Harris and Bridge, paras 10.42–10.53. For licensing agreements, see infra, p 261.

[558] Case C-381/08 *Car Trim GmbH v KeySafety Systems Srl* [2010] ECR I-1255.

The contracts between the parties involved both the sale of goods and the provision of services. But, for the purposes of what is now Article 7(1)(b), the Court of Justice held that it was necessary to classify the contracts as falling within either the former or the latter category. The Court stated that, since what is now Article 7(1)(b) identifies as a connecting factor the obligation which characterises the contract in question, the classification of the contract depends on the nature of its characteristic obligation. Classification should be performed by reference to the Vienna Convention[559] and other relevant instruments of EU law and international law, namely the Directive on certain aspects of the sale of consumer goods and associated guarantees[560] and the UN Convention on the Limitation Period in the International Sale of Goods of 1974.[561] These instruments indicate that the key factors to be taken into account are the origin of the raw materials, ie whether or not those materials have been supplied by the purchaser, and the responsibilities of the supplier. The fact that all the raw materials, or most of them, have been supplied by the purchaser is an indication that the contract should be classified as one for the provision of services. The fact that the supplier is responsible only for the correct implementation of the purchaser's requirements and instructions, as opposed to being responsible for the quality of the goods and their compliance with the contract, is another indication that the contract is one for the provision of services. In a subsequent case, the Court of Justice held that a long-standing business relationship between two parties can be classified as a relationship for the sale of goods where that relationship is limited to successive agreements each having the object of the delivery and collection of goods.[562]

The concept of the "provision of services" should also be given an autonomous meaning. The starting point in this respect is *Falco Privatstiftung, Thomas Rabitsch v Gisela Weller-Lindhorst*,[563] which concerned the classification of a contract for the assignment of intellectual property rights. The Court of Justice held that the concept of service implies, at the least, that the party who provides the service carries out a particular activity in return for remuneration. Since no such activity is involved in a contract for the assignment of intellectual property rights, such contract falls outside the scope of Article 7(1)(b) and within the scope of the general rule of jurisdiction for contractual matters in Article 7(1)(a). The Court also held that this analysis could not be called into question by arguments based on the concept of services within the meaning of other secondary EU law or the freedom to provide services set out in Article 50 EC (now Article 57 TFEU) because the Brussels I Regulation and these other instruments of EU law pursue different aims and objectives. The Court refined the definition of the concept of service for the purposes of Article 7(1)(b) of the Brussels I Recast in a number of subsequent cases. With regard to the existence of an activity, this criterion requires the performance of positive acts, to the exclusion of mere omissions.[564] With regard to the provision of remuneration as consideration for an activity, this criterion covers not only the payment of a sum of money but also any other economic benefit.[565] The Court has thus held that an exclusive distribution agreement,[566]

---

[559] Art 3(1).

[560] Directive 1999/44/EC of 25 May 1999 OJ 1999 L 171/12, Arts 1(2)(b) and 1(4).

[561] Art 6(2).

[562] Case C-196/15 *Granarolo SpA v Ambrosi Emmi France SA* EU:C:2016:559, [2016] IL Pr 32; Grušić (2016) 12 ERCL 395; McParland [2016] LMCLQ 500. If the relationship is regarded as a distribution agreement, the contract will be one for the provision of services.

[563] Case C-533/07 [2009] ECR I-3327; McGuire (2009) 11 YBPIL 453.

[564] Case C-196/15 *Granarolo SpA v Ambrosi Emmi France SA* EU:C:2016:559 at [38], [2016] IL Pr 32.

[565] Ibid, at [40], [41].

[566] Case C-9/12 *Corman-Collins SA v La Maison du Whisky SA* EU:C:2013:860, [2014] QB 431; see also Case C-196/15 *Granarolo SpA v Ambrosi Emmi France SA* EU:C:2016:559, [2016] IL Pr 32. But individual contracts for the sale of goods concluded under the framework distribution agreement should be classified as falling under the first indent of Art 7(1)(b).

a contract for the warehouse storage of goods[567] and a contract between a company and its former manager[568] may satisfy these two requirements and should therefore be regarded as contracts for the provision of services. The concept of service covers not only professional services such as contracts for accountancy advice,[569] to restructure one's business interests,[570] to design a website,[571] devising advertising material,[572] or contracts to act as commercial agent for someone,[573] but also the separate autonomous contracts under a letter of credit,[574] reinsurance contracts,[575] contracts of carriage, contracts for the inspection of goods, and franchise contracts.[576] However, the "provision of services" should be interpreted as not covering contracts relating to a right *in rem* or a tenancy of immovable property.[577] Further guidance on the meaning of services can be found by looking at examples of contracts held to fall outside Article 7(1)(b) generally.[578]

The second clear limitation on the scope of Article 7(1)(b) is implicit from the part of Article 7(1)(b) that allocates jurisdiction. This is that the goods were delivered or should have been delivered/services were provided or should have been provided in *a place in a Member State*.

One final observation that should be made about the scope of Article 7(1)(b) relates to its width. It "applies regardless of the obligation in question, even where this obligation is the payment of the financial consideration for the contract. It also applies where the claim relates to several obligations".[579] This means that if goods are delivered in England the English courts will have jurisdiction under Article 7(1), even though the claim is for payment for the goods.[580] The width of the rule can be justified on the basis that delivery characterises the contract of sale,[581] and providing the service characterises the contract for the provision of services. At first sight this might suggest that it is no longer necessary to identify the obligation in question in cases of sale of goods or the provision of services. However, this is still necessary because of the possibility of displacement of the place of delivery/provision of services rule.[582]

---

[567] Case C-469/12 *Krejci Lager & Umschlagbetriebs GmbH v Olbrich Transport und Logistik GmbH* EU:C:2013:788, [2014] IL Pr 8.

[568] Case C-47/14 *Holterman Ferho Exploitatie BV and Others v Friedrich Leopold Freiherr Spies von Büllesheim* EU:C:2015:574, [2015] IL Pr 44. This is on the assumption that the contract in question is not an employment contract.

[569] See *Barry v Bradshaw* [2000] IL Pr 706, CA. But cf *Benatti v WPP Holdings Italy SRL* [2007] EWCA Civ 263 at [56]–[57] (per Toulson LJ)—contract to act as a consultant not covered, [2007] 1 WLR 2316.

[570] *JEB Recoveries LLP v Binstock* [2016] EWCA Civ 1008.

[571] *1st Mover APS v Direct Hedge SA* [2003] IL Pr 31, Eastern Court of Appeal, Denmark.

[572] *Société ND Conseil SA v Société Le Meridien Hotels* [2007] IL Pr 39, French Cour de Cassation.

[573] Case C-19/09 *Wood Floor Solutions Andreas Domberger GmbH v Silva Trade SA* [2010] ECR I-2121. See also Mankowski (2008) 10 YBPIL 19.

[574] But cf Beaumont, in Fawcett (ed), *Reform and Development of Private International Law* (2002) 9, pp 22–3.

[575] These fall outside Section 3 and therefore within Art 7(1), see infra, pp 289–91.

[576] See Recital (17) of the Rome I Regulation.

[577] See Art 4(1)(c) of the Rome I Regulation.

[578] Infra, p 261.

[579] See the Explanatory Memorandum, in the Proposal for a Council Regulation COM (1999) 348 final, p 14; the opinion of AG Bot in Case C-386/05 *Color Drack GmbH v LEXX International Vertriebs GmbH* [2007] ECR I-3699 at [88] and the Court of Justice at [26].

[580] See the opinion of AG Bot in Case C-386/05 *Color Drack GmbH v LEXX International Vertriebs GmbH* [2007] ECR I-3699 at [89]; *Comet Group plc v Unika Computer SA* [2004] IL Pr 1.

[581] The *Color Drack* case at [38], Court of Justice; AG Mayras in the *Tessili* case; Takahashi (2002) 27 ELR 530, 534. See also the importance attached to delivery by the Court of Appeal in the *MBM Fabri-Clad* and *Viskase* cases and by the Court of Session House in Scotland in *Ferguson Shipbuilders Ltd v Voith Hydro GmbH & Co KG* 2000 SLT 229 and in *Eddie v Alpa Srl* 2000 SLT 1062.

[582] Discussed infra, p 261.

The place in a Member State where, under the contract, the goods were delivered or should have been delivered   Article 7(1)(b) allocates jurisdiction to the place where, "under the contract", the goods were delivered or should have been delivered. This means that, when ascertaining this place, recourse must be had to all the relevant terms and clauses of the contract. The sales contract may, for example, expressly provide for delivery ex works or for delivery at frontier or contain other terms and clauses which are capable of clearly identifying the place of delivery of the goods. Of particular importance in this respect are the international commercial terms known as Incoterms drawn up by the International Chamber of Commerce, which reflect the usages of international trade and commerce.[583] The parties, by agreeing on the place of delivery, are effectively choosing the place to be allocated jurisdiction. Nonetheless there is no requirement that the formalities under Article 25 have to be met. In the absence of such an express agreement by the parties on the place of delivery, it may be possible to imply an agreement from the terms of the contract. It should also be possible to imply an agreement from the circumstances of the case, such as from the fact that the parties have contracted before and delivery has always been to one particular place. In the absence of an express or implied agreement as to the place of delivery, this place is to be determined without reference to the substantive law applicable to the contract[584] and is considered to be the place where the physical transfer of the goods took place, as a result of which the purchaser obtained, or should have obtained, actual power of disposal over those goods at the final destination of the sales transaction.[585]

Numerous problems arise with the place of delivery rule.[586] Two of the most obvious are as follows. First, what happens if goods are delivered to more than one place and these are in different Member States?[587]

> For example, assume that there is a contract for the sale of 10,000 tons of grain, 3,000 tons to be delivered to England and 7,000 tons to Germany. All 10,000 tons are rendered defective by contact with a previous cargo. The claimant wishes to sue in one Member State in respect of the whole 10,000 tons.

It will be remembered that in *Besix SA v Wasserreinigungsbau Alfred Kretzschmar GmbH & Co KG (WABAG)*,[588] the Court of Justice held that Article 5(1) of the Brussels Convention had to be interpreted as meaning that, in the event that the relevant contractual obligation has been, or is to be, performed in a number of places, jurisdiction to hear and determine the case cannot be conferred on the court within whose jurisdiction any one of those places of performance happens to be located. Instead, jurisdiction had to be based on the rule of general jurisdiction. The Court was concerned to avoid a multiplicity of competent courts and the risk that the plaintiff is able to choose the place of performance which he judges to be most favourable to his interests. But it is questionable whether the *Besix* case should be

---

[583] See Case C-87/10 *Electrosteel Europe SA v Edil Centro SpA* [2011] ECR I-4987. See also Case C-196/15 *Granarolo SpA v Ambrosi Emmi France SA* EU:C:2016:559 at [36], [2016] IL Pr 32. See also *Scottish & Newcastle International Ltd v Othon Ghalanos Ltd* [2008] UKHL 11, [2008] 1 Lloyd's Rep 462; *Place of Performance of an FOB Contract, Re* (156/07) [2010] IL Pr 17, German Bundesgerichtshof.

[584] In *Scottish & Newcastle International Ltd v Othon Ghalanos Ltd* [2008] UKHL 11, [2008] 1 Lloyd's Rep 462, the House of Lords interpreted the meaning of the commercial terms used by reference to English law. The reference to a domestic substantive law must now be regarded as erroneous. See Briggs (2008) 79 BYBIL 508; Hare and Hinks [2008] LMCLQ 353; Merrett (2008) 67 CLJ 244.

[585] Case C-381/08 *Car Trim GmbH v KeySafety Systems Srl* [2010] ECR I-1255; Case C-87/10 *Electrosteel Europe SA v Edil Centro SpA* [2011] ECR I-4987.

[586] See Fawcett, Harris and Bridge, paras 3.204–3.226 and, for the place of delivery in cases of e-commerce, paras 10.55–10.75.

[587] See Grušić (2011) 7 J Priv Int L 321.

[588] Case C-256/00 [2002] ECR I-3699; discussed supra, pp 254–5.

applied in cases falling within what is now Article 7(1)(b) of the Brussels I Recast. An alternative way of achieving a single court with jurisdiction over the whole of the goods would be to allocate jurisdiction to the court of the principal place of delivery, determined on the basis of economic criteria. This was the solution adopted by the Court of Justice in the *Color Drack* case, which involved several places of delivery within the same Member State.[589] Although the Court has not had the opportunity to extend the solution from *Color Drack* to cases involving delivery in several Member States, it has applied this case by analogy in cases concerning provision of services in several Member States.[590] It would appear that consistent interpretation of the two indents of Article 7(1)(b) requires the extension of the solution from the *Color Drack* case to cases involving delivery in several Member States. The position is more difficult in the situation where the claim relates to all the deliveries and economic criteria do not disclose a principal place of delivery,[591] or where the claimant wishes to sue in England for merely the 3,000 tons delivered there, or in cases involving delivery partly within and partly outside the EU. One will have to wait for further clarifications from the Court of Justice before definitive answers can be given.

Secondly, what happens if there is a fictitious place of delivery, ie the contract provides for delivery in a place when this is designed not to determine where delivery will actually take place, but solely to establish that the courts for a particular place have jurisdiction? That this is the aim can be shown by the fact that a place of delivery has been designated which has no connection with the reality of the contract and the obligations under the contract, obligations which, because of their very nature or because of geographical fact, can only be performed in some other country.[592] Goods may then be delivered to this other country (Member State A), rather than to the fictitious place of delivery (Member State B). An attempt may be made to bring an action in the fictitious place of delivery (Member State B) on the basis that, under the contract, goods "should have been delivered" there within the wording of Article 7(1)(b). The Court of Justice has held that where there is a fictitious place of performance, this is governed not by Article 5(1) of the Brussels Convention but by Article 17 (Article 25 of the Brussels I Recast) and the requirements of that provision must be met.[593] In other words, the fictitious place of performance is treated as an attempted jurisdiction clause. The same approach should be adopted towards a fictitious place of delivery, given that the place of delivery rule is being used to determine the place of performance of the obligation in question.

There are also problems where there is: delivery to alternative places; a deemed place of delivery; constructive delivery; a floating place of delivery; an agreement on the place of delivery entered into after the contract was made; a refusal to accept delivery; and identifying the place of delivery in cases of e-commerce.[594]

Jurisdiction is allocated to the place where the goods were delivered or *should have been delivered*. This deals with cases of non-delivery and mis-delivery. Thus if goods are delivered to

---

[589] Case C-386/05 *Color Drack GmbH v LEXX International Vertriebs GmbH* [2007] ECR I-3699; Gardella (2007) 9 YBPIL 439; Harris (2007) 123 LQR 522. This was without prejudice to the position where the places of delivery are in several Member States (at [16]). Where the principal place cannot be determined, the claimant may sue in the place of delivery of its choice (at [46]).

[590] See Case C-204/08 *Peter Rehder v Air Baltic Corporation* [2009] ECR I-6073; Case C-19/09 *Wood Floor Solutions Andreas Domberger GmbH v Silva Trade SA* [2010] ECR I-2121.

[591] The *Color Drack* case would suggest that the claimant may sue in the place of delivery of its choice (at [46]).

[592] Case C-106/95 *Mainschiffahrts-Genossenschaft eG (MSG) v Les Gravières Rhénanes Sarl* [1997] ECR I-911; Hartley (1997) 22 ELR 360.

[593] The *MSG* case. See also *7E Communications Ltd v Vertex Antennentechnik GmbH* [2007] EWCA Civ 140 at [50], [2007] 1 WLR 2175.

[594] See Fawcett, Harris and Bridge, paras 3.142–3.301.

England when, under the contract, they should have been delivered to France, the place of performance of the obligation in question under Article 7(1)(b) will be France, rather than England.[595]

The place in a Member State where, under the contract, the services were provided or should have been provided   Everything said in the previous section about the meaning of "under the contract" applies equally to this provision. Likewise the reference to the place where services should have been provided deals with cases of non-provision of services and mis-provision in the sense of a party providing services in the wrong place. When it comes to identification of the place in a Member State where, under the contract, the services were provided or should have been provided, the situation is analogous to that of identification of the place in a Member State where, under the contract, the goods were delivered or should have been delivered. Analogous problems can arise. For example, services may be provided in more than one place and these are in different Member States. The Court of Justice dealt with this situation in two cases. The *Rehder* case[596] concerned a claim for compensation[597] under a contract for the provision of air transport services from one Member State to another. The Court referred to the *Color Drack* case and held that, since the services in the case at hand were provided in an identical and indivisible manner in both the place of departure and the place of arrival of the aircraft and, therefore, no place of the main provision of services existed, the claimant could choose to commence proceedings in the courts for either the place of departure or the place of arrival of the aircraft. In the *Wood Floor* case[598] the Court of Justice dealt with the place of performance of a commercial agency contract. It confirmed that the court which has jurisdiction to hear and determine all the claims arising from the contract is the court in whose jurisdiction the place of the main provision of services is situated. For a commercial agency contract, that place is the place of the main provision of services by the agent, as it appears from the provisions of the contract or, in the absence of such provisions, the actual performance of that contract or, where it cannot be established on that basis, the place where the agent is domiciled. The operation of the rule of jurisdiction for services contracts may throw up certain problems that may not arise or are less likely to arise under the sale of goods rule. A letter of credit, payment under which should be regarded as the provision of a service, may provide that "we shall pay you as per your instructions". This is a floating place of payment; there is no identifiable place of payment as at the time the contract is concluded but there is a mechanism for identifying this place and this place will crystallise later, when the beneficiary gives his instructions. Effect

---

[595]   See *Morley v Reiter Engineering GmbH & Co KG* [2011] EWHC 2798 (Ch), [2012] IL Pr 6.

[596]   Case C-204/08 *Peter Rehder v Air Baltic Corporation* [2009] ECR I-6073; George and Harris (2010) 126 LQR 30. This case concerned air transport carried out on the basis of a contract with only one airline as the operating carrier. It is not entirely clear how *Rehder* should be applied in cases involving connecting flights and more than one airline: see the references for a preliminary ruling from the German Supreme Court in Case C-533/15 *Feliks Frisman v Finnair Oyj* OJ 2016 C 48/8, which case was subsequently settled OJ 2016 C 279/24, and in Cases C-447/16 *Becker v Hainan Airlines Co Ltd* and C-448/16 *Barkan v Air Nostrum LAM SA* OJ 2016 C 428/5, and the reference for a preliminary ruling by the Amtsgericht Düsseldorf in Case C-274/16 *flightright GmbH v Air Nostrum, Líneas Aéreas del Mediterráneo SA* OJ 2016 C 343/22.

[597]   Based on Regulation (EC) 261/2004 of 11 February 2004 establishing common rules on compensation and assistance to passengers in the event of denied boarding and of cancellation or long delay of flights OJ 2004 L 46/1.

[598]   Case C-19/09 *Wood Floor Solutions Andreas Domberger GmbH v Silva Trade SA* [2010] ECR I-2121, applied in *JEB Recoveries LLP v Binstock* [2016] EWCA Civ 1008. See also Case C-47/14 *Holterman Ferho Exploitatie BV and Others v Friedrich Leopold Freiherr Spies von Büllesheim* EU:C:2015:574, [2015] IL Pr 44 concerning the place of provision of services under a contract between a company and its former manager. See also *Deutsche Bank AG London Branch v Petromena ASA* [2013] EWHC 3065 (Comm) at [58], where the court held that the focus is where the relevant work was done by the provider of the service. The location of the recipient of the service is insignificant; affd [2015] EWCA Civ 226 at [96], [2015] 1 WLR 4225.

has been given by the Court of Appeal to a floating place of payment in a letter of credit for the purposes of identifying the place of performance of the obligation in question under Article 5(1) of the Brussels Convention.[599]

Displacement where it is otherwise agreed   The special rule that operates in the case of the sale of goods and in the case of the provision of services is subject to the proviso that it applies "unless otherwise agreed". Let us assume that goods have been delivered in Spain but it has been agreed that payment shall be made in England. The claimant wishes to sue in England for non-payment. The question arises whether the place of performance of the obligation to pay will be in England by virtue of the displacement rule. It seems that the answer is in the negative and that the "unless otherwise agreed" proviso requires an agreement specifically on the displacement of Article 7(1)(b) and, therefore, on the application of Article 7(1)(a) and the *De Bloos/Tessili* approach to a contract for the sale of goods or the provision of services. Admittedly, rational parties are unlikely to agree to such a clause, especially in the light of the availability of jurisdiction agreements under Article 25. Nevertheless, the interpretation under which a mere agreement on the place of payment would lead to the displacement of Article 7(1)(b) and would implicitly allocate jurisdiction to the place of payment would threaten to undermine the objectives pursued by this provision.[600]

Cases falling outside the scope of Article 7(1)(b)   Article 7(1)(c) is concerned with the situation where Article 7(1)(b) does not apply. Examples of contracts which are neither for the sale of goods nor the provision of services are a contract for the assignment of intellectual property rights,[601] a relationship between the payee of a promissory note and the giver of a guarantee (an aval),[602] a contract of gift of immoveable property,[603] a licensing agreement, an agreement to provide a joint tender for a construction project,[604] a contract for the payment of a prize,[605] a contract whereby a person received a percentage participation in an oil concession,[606] a contract in the form of a guarantee,[607] a contract for the purchase of capacity on a fiber optic submarine cable network,[608] a contract whereby an employer agrees to make payments to a sub-contractor provided that the latter continues to perform its obligations under the sub-contract,[609] a contract whereby an investor in a company agreed to support a share-placing on an investments market in exchange for commitments given by the company to make changes to its corporate structure and to review its strategy and business.[610] It has been assumed that Article 7(1)(c) will apply to an average guarantee entered into between

---

[599] *Crédit Agricole Indosuez v Chailease Finance Corpn* [2000] 1 Lloyd's Rep 348, CA. See also *Canyon Offshore Ltd v GDF Suez E&P Nederland BV* [2014] EWHC 3810 (Comm), [2015] IL Pr 8—place of performance equally England or Scotland. Cf Case C-256/00 *Besix SA v Wasserreinigungsbau Alfred Kretzschmar GmbH & Co KG (WABAG)* [2002] ECR I-1699; *Mora Shipping Inc v Axa Corporate Solutions Assurance SA* [2005] EWCA Civ 1069 at [21], [2005] 2 Lloyd's Rep 769.

[600] See also Briggs 2015, para 2.173; cf Fentiman 2015, para 9.54.

[601] Case C-533/07 *Falco Privatstiftung, Thomas Rabitsch v Gisela Weller-Lindhorst* [2009] ECR I-3327.

[602] Case C-419/11 *Česká spořitelna as v Feichter* EU:C:2013:165, [2013] IL Pr 22.

[603] Case C-417/15 *Schmidt v Schmidt* EU:C:2016:881, [2017] IL Pr 6.

[604] See the opinion of AG Alber in Case C-256/00 *Besix SA v Wasserreinigungsbau Alfred Kretzschmar GmbH & Co KG (WABAG)* [2002] ECR I-1699 at [48].

[605] Case C-234/04 *Kapferer v Schlank & Schick GmbH* [2006] ECR I-2585 at [64] of the opinion of AG Tizzano.

[606] *Masri v Consolidated Contractors International (UK) Ltd* [2005] EWHC 944 (Comm) at [74] and [99], [2005] 1 CLC 1125, affd without discussion of this point [2005] EWCA Civ 1436, [2006] 1 WLR 830.

[607] *Commercial Marine Piling Ltd v Pierse Contracting Ltd* [2009] EWHC 2241 (TCC), [2009] IL Pr 54.

[608] *Reliance Globalcom Ltd v OTE International Solutions SA* [2011] EWHC 1848 (QB).

[609] *Canyon Offshore Ltd v GDF Suez E&P Nederland BV* [2014] EWHC 3810 (Comm), [2015] IL Pr 8.

[610] *Worldview Capital Management SA v Petroceltic International Plc* [2015] EWHC 2185 (Comm), [2015] IL Pr 46.

shipowners and cargo insurers,[611] and a loan agreement under a salvage agreement.[612] A further example is a contract relating to a right *in rem* or to a tenancy of immovable property.[613] Moreover, a contract for the sale of goods or provision of services would fall outside the scope of Article 7(1)(b) in the situation where the performance of the characteristic obligation is made or should have been made in a non-Member State.[614]

Article 7(1)(c) provides that if 7(1)(b) does not apply then Article 7(1)(a) applies, including the *De Bloos/Tessili* approach.[615] This approach requires the national court: first, to determine the contractual obligation in question;[616] secondly, to determine in accordance with its own rules of conflict of laws[617] what is the law applicable to the legal relationship in question; and, thirdly, to define in accordance with that law the place of performance of the obligation in question.[618] Examination of the substantive domestic law of Member States shows that the same general approach towards determining the place of performance is applied throughout the European Union.[619] First, effect is given to an express stipulation as to the place of performance in the contract. It is common to find such an express stipulation. This can be done in an informal way without the formalities required for an agreement as to jurisdiction under Article 25,[620] even though the effect of such a contractual provision is to lead indirectly, by reason of Article 7(1)(a), to a particular court having jurisdiction.[621] However, there is a qualification to this in the case of a fictitious place of performance.[622] If the agreement on the place of performance is designed not to determine the place where the person liable is actually to perform the obligations incumbent on him, but solely to establish that the courts for a particular place have jurisdiction, this is governed not by Article 7(1) but by Article 25, and the requirements of that provision must be met.[623] The only other proviso is that the clause specifying the place of performance must be valid under the law applicable to the contract.[624] Secondly, in the absence of an express stipulation, it may be possible to imply a choice by the parties. This is a question of contractual interpretation. Thirdly, if this does not produce an answer each Member State has residual rules which determine the place of performance. It is at this stage that the question of the applicable law may become crucial, since these national rules sometimes provide different solutions.[625] For example, Member States differ on whether, in the absence of a stipulation on the due place of payment, the obligation to pay must be performed in the creditor's place of business

---

[611] *Mora Shipping Inc v Axa Corporate Solutions Assurance SA* [2005] EWCA Civ 1069 at [21], [2005] 2 Lloyd's Rep 769.

[612] *Tavoulareas v Tsavliris* [2005] EWHC 2140 (Comm) at [48]–[55], [2006] 1 All ER (Comm), 109.

[613] Supra, p 257.

[614] *BNP Paribas SA v Anchorage Capital Europe LLP* [2013] EWHC 3073 (Comm).

[615] Case C-533/07 *Falco Privatstiftung, Thomas Rabitsch v Gisela Weller-Lindhorst* [2009] ECR I-3327; Case C-419/11 *Česká spořitelna as v Feichter* EU:C:2013:165, [2013] IL Pr 22.

[616] Case 14/76 *De Bloos v Bouyer* [1976] ECR 1497.

[617] See the Rome I Regulation, discussed infra, pp 686–775; Forsyth and Moser (1996) 45 ICLQ 190; Tang (2008) 4 J Priv Int L 35.

[618] Case 12/76 *Tessili v Dunlop* [1976] ECR 1473 at [13].

[619] See Kennett (1995) 15 YEL 193.

[620] Art 25 is discussed supra, pp 237–41.

[621] Case 56/79 *Zelger v Salinitri* [1980] ECR 89; Hartley (1981) 6 ELR 61.

[622] Discussed supra, p 259.

[623] Case C-106/95 *Mainschiffahrts-Genossenschaft eG (MSG) v Les Gravières Rhénanes Sarl* [1997] ECR I-911. See also *7E Communications Ltd v Vertex Antennentechnik GmbH* [2007] EWCA Civ 140 at [50], [2007] 1 WLR 2175.

[624] The *Zelger* case. See generally on the law applicable to the contract, infra, pp 686–775.

[625] See *Definitely Maybe (Touring) Ltd v Marek Lieberberg Konzertagentur GmbH (No 2)* [2001] 1 WLR 1745; *Mercury Publicity Ltd v Wolfgang Loerke GmbH* [1993] IL Pr 142, CA; Forsyth and Moser (1996) 45 ICLQ 190, 193.

or in the debtor's.[626] If the obligation in question under the law applicable to the contract has been, or is to be, performed in a number of places, jurisdiction to hear and determine the case cannot be conferred on the court within whose jurisdiction any of those places of performance happens to be located.[627] A single place of performance for the obligation in question must be identified.

Article 7(2)[628]

in matters relating to tort, delict or quasi-delict, in the courts for the place where the harmful event occurred or may occur.

(i) What are matters relating to tort, delict or quasi-delict?
The Court of Justice in *Kalfelis v Schröder*[629] has held that the concept of "matters relating to tort, *delict* or *quasi-delict*" must be given an autonomous definition. The question then arises of how widely or narrowly this concept is to be interpreted. In many cases this has not been regarded as problematic. So, for example, it has been held that actions for infringement of "personality rights" (defamation and privacy),[630] negligent misstatement,[631] negligent and fraudulent misrepresentation;[632] negligence,[633] product liability,[634] conversion,[635]

---

[626] See the *Definitely Maybe* case; *Bank of Scotland v Seitz* 1990 SLT 584; *Tavoulareas v Tsavliris* [2005] EWHC 2140 (Comm) at [52], [2006] 1 All ER (Comm) 109. Under English law, the default place of payment is in the creditor's place of business: *The Eider* [1893] P 119.

[627] Case C-256/00 *Besix SA v Wasserreinigungsbau Alfred Kretzschmar GmbH & Co KG (WABAG)* [2002] ECR I-1699.

[628] Art 5(3) of the Brussels I Regulation; Art 5(3) of the Brussels Convention.

[629] Case 189/87 [1988] ECR 5565; Hartley (1989) 14 ELR 172; Briggs (1988) 8 YEL 272.

[630] Case C-68/93 *Shevill v Presse Alliance SA* [1995] ECR I-415; Joined cases C-509/09 and C-161/10 *eDate Advertising GmbH v X and Olivier Martinez and Robert Martinez v MGN Limited* [2011] ECR I-10269.

[631] *Domicrest Ltd v Swiss Bank Corp* [1999] QB 548; *Alfred Dunhill Ltd v Diffusion Internationale de Maroquinerie de Prestige SARL* [2002] IL Pr 13; *Newsat Holdings Ltd v Zani* [2006] EWHC 342 (Comm), [2006] 1 Lloyd's Rep 707; *London Helicopters Ltd v Heliportugal LDA-INAC* [2006] EWHC 108 (QB), [2006] IL Pr 28. See also the obiter dicta in the Court of Appeal in *ABCI v Banque Franco-Tunisienne* [2003] EWCA Civ 205 at [41], [2003] 2 Lloyd's Rep 146 (per Mance LJ). For Scotland see *William Grant & Sons International Ltd v Marie Brizard et Roger International SA* [1997] IL Pr 391.

[632] For negligent misrepresentation see: *Raiffeisen Zentral Bank Österreich AG v National Bank of Greece SA* [1999] 1 Lloyd's Rep 408—negligent misrepresentation under Greek law; the *Alfred Dunhill* case— negligent misrepresentation under s 2(1) of the Misrepresentation Act 1967. For fraudulent misrepresentation see: *Agnew v Lansforsakringsbolagens AB* [2001] 1 AC 223 at 259, 252–3 (obiter dicta per Lord Hope), HL; *Raiffeisen Zentral Bank Österreich AG v Tranos* [2001] IL Pr 9—the claim was based on fraudulent or negligent misrepresentations; *ABCI v Banque Franco-Tunisienne* [2003] EWCA Civ 205 at [41], [2003] 2 Lloyd's Rep 146; *Bank of Tokyo-Mitsubishi Ltd v Baskan Gida Sanayi Ve Pazarlama AS* [2004] EWHC 945 (Ch) at [223], [2004] 2 Lloyd's Rep 395—a claim based on deceit and what was sometimes described as negligent misstatement and at other times as negligent misrepresentation; *Sunderland Marine Mutual Insurance Co Ltd v Wiseman* [2007] EWHC 1460 (Comm), [2007] 2 Lloyd's Rep 308; *Barclay-Watt v Alpha Panareti Public Ltd*, 23 November 2012, HC; *Maple Leaf Macro Volatility Master Fund v Rouvroy* [2009] EWHC 257 (Comm), [2009] 1 Lloyd's Rep 475; Briggs (2009) 80 BYBIL 616.

[633] *Watson v First Choice Holidays & Flights Ltd* [2001] EWCA Civ 972 at [26], [2001] 2 Lloyd's Rep 339; Case C-12/15 *Universal Music International Holding BV v Michael Tétreault Schilling* EU:C:2016:449, [2016] QB 967—a claim based on professional (lawyer's) negligence.

[634] Case C-189/08 *Zuid-Chemie BV v Philippo's Mineralenfabriek NV/SA* [2009] ECR I-6917; Case C-45/13 *Andreas Kainz v Pantherwerke AG* EU:C:2014:7, [2015] QB 34.

[635] *Anton Durbeck GmbH v Den Norske Bank ASA* [2002] EWHC 1173 (Comm), varied [2003] QB 1160, CA, without an appeal on this point; the *Bank of Tokyo-Mitsubishi Ltd v Baskan Gida Sanayi Ve Pazarlama AS* case at [218]; *Cronos Containers NV v Palatin* [2002] EWHC 2819 (Comm), [2003] 2 Lloyd's Rep 489. See also *Re: Action for a Prohibitory Injunction* (II ZR 329/03) [2006] IL Pr 39, German Bundesgerichtshof.

infringement of intellectual property rights,[636] passing off,[637] unfair competition,[638] and actionable breaches of EU law giving rise to a claim for damages[639] come within Article 7(2). The crucial question is whether the concept of "tort, delict or quasi-delict" extends to cover an action in respect of a non-contractual obligation which is not characterised in the substantive domestic law of Member States as one in tort, such as one in unjust enrichment or non-contractual breach of confidence.[640]

The Court of Justice in *Kalfelis* also held that the term matters relating to tort, delict or quasi-delict "must be regarded as an independent concept covering all actions which seek to establish the liability of a defendant and which are not related to a 'contract' within the meaning of [Article 7(1)]".[641] This statement has been repeated and approved in numerous subsequent decisions of that Court[642] and has been followed in national courts.[643] The Court of Justice in these subsequent cases has interpreted this statement as setting out the scope of Article 7(2). The technique adopted by the Court of Justice for determining whether Article 7(2) applies is as follows.[644] The first question asked is whether there is a matter relating to a contract under Article 7(1).[645] If there is, that is the end of the matter and Article 7(2) cannot apply.[646] Once it has been decided that there is not, the question arises of whether it must be held that it is a matter relating to tort, delict or quasi-delict. Some cases, especially older ones, seem to suggest that Article 7(2) is a residual category literally covering all cases which seek to establish the liability of a defendant and which are not related to a "contract" within

---

[636] Case C-523/10 *Wintersteiger AG v Products 4U Sondermaschinenbau* GmbH EU:C:2012:220, [2012] IL Pr 23; Case C-170/12 *Peter Pinckney v KDG Mediatech AG* EU:C:2013:635, [2014] IL Pr 7; Case C-387/12 *Hi Hotel HCF SARL v Uwe Spoering* EU:C:2014:215, [2014] 1 WLR 1912; Case C-441/13 *Pez Hejduk v EnergieAgentur.NRW GmbH* EU:C:2015:28 at [24], [2015] Bus LR 560; *AMS Neve Ltd v Heritage Audio SL* [2016] EWHC 2563 (IPEC). See also Case C-572/14 *Austro-Mechana Gesellschaft zur Wahrnehmung mechanisch-musikalischer Urheberrechte Gesellschaft mbH v Amazon EU Sàrl* EU:C:2016:286, [2016] ECDR 23—damages for breach of domestic law implementing the "fair compensation" system provided for in Directive 2001/29/EC on the harmonization of certain aspects of copyright and related rights in the information society OJ 2001 L 167/10; *SMI Group Ltd v Levy* [2012] EWHC 3078 (Ch)—damages for infringement of database rights. For the problem where invalidity is raised as a defence, see supra, p 225. See generally, Fawcett and Torremans, p 150 et seq.

[637] *Modus Vivendi Ltd v British Products Sanmex Co Ltd* [1996] FSR 790; *Mecklermedia Corpn v DC Congress GmbH* [1998] Ch 40; *Bonnier Media Ltd v Greg Lloyd Smith and Kestrel Trading Corpn* 2003 SC 36, [2002] ETMR 86; *AMS Neve Ltd v Heritage Audio SL* [2016] EWHC 2563 (IPEC).

[638] *Saba Molnlycke AS v Procter & Gamble Scandinavia Inc* [1997] IL Pr 704, Tonsberg Court of Appeal—a Lugano Convention case; Case C-360/12 *Coty Germany GmbH v First Note Perfumes NV* EU:C:2014:1318, [2015] IL Pr 13.

[639] Case C-352/13 *Cartel Damage Claims (CDC) Hydrogen Peroxide SA v Akzo Nobel NV* EU:C:2015:335, [2015] QB 906—damages for breach of EU competition law; *Deutsche Bahn AG v Morgan Advanced Materials Plc (formerly Morgan Crucible Co Plc)* [2013] EWCA Civ 1484, [2014] CP Rep 10 and *DSG Retail Ltd v Mastercard Inc* [2015] CAT 7—claims for "follow on" damages under the Competition Act 1998; *Provimi Ltd v Roche Products Ltd* [2003] EWHC 961 (Comm) at [126], [2003] 2 All ER (Comm) 683. See also Withers [2002] JBL 250, 259–64. See also *SanDisk Corpn v Koninklijke Philips Electronics NV* [2007] EWHC 332 (Ch), [2007] IL Pr 22—abuse of dominant position.

[640] The classification of this cause of action is, as a matter of substantive law, unclear, see Fawcett and Torremans, pp 511–12.

[641] Case 189/87 [1988] ECR 5565 at [18].

[642] Most recently in Case C-196/15 *Granarolo SpA v Ambrosi Emmi France SA* EU:C:2016:559 at [20], [2016] IL Pr 32.

[643] See, eg, *Re Mail Order Promise of Win in a Draw* [2003] IL Pr 46, German Bundesgerichtshof.

[644] See, eg, Case C-572/14 *Austro-Mechana Gesellschaft zur Wahrnehmung mechanisch-musikalischer Urheberrechte Gesellschaft mbH v Amazon EU Sàrl* EU:C:2016:286 at [32]–[51], [2016] ECDR 23.

[645] Ibid, at [33].

[646] Case C-27/02 *Petra Engler v Janus Versand GmbH* [2005] ECR I-481 at [60]; *Agnew v Lansforsakringsbolagens AB* [2001] 1 AC 223 at 244–5 (per Lord Woolf), 233–4 (per Lord Nicholls), 247 (per Lord Cooke), 259 (per Lord Hope), 267 (per Lord Millett), HL.

the meaning of Article 7(1).[647] This seems to go too far.[648] In some recent cases, the Court of Justice has asked whether there is a "harmful event" and a causal connection between the damage and the event in which that damage originates.[649] There are therefore Article 7 cases falling outside both Article 7(1) and 7(2), such as non-contractual cases where the requirement that there is a harmful event has not been met.[650] One such example, according to AG Wahl in *Gazdasági Versenyhivatal v Siemens Aktiengesellschaft Österreich*,[651] are claims for restitution on the ground of unjust enrichment.

Nevertheless, Article 7(2) is given a very wide scope. The Court of Justice has not inquired into whether under the law of the various Member States there was a tort in the substantive domestic law sense and it has applied Article 7(2) in the situation where there was no such tort. This is shown most graphically in *Fonderie Officine Meccaniche Tacconi SpA v Heinrich Wagner Sinto Maschinenfabrik GmbH (HWS)*.[652] The Court of Justice held that a claim based on pre-contractual liability under Article 1337 of the Italian Civil Code, which provides that, in the context of the negotiation and formation of a contract, the parties must act in good faith, did not relate to a contract and in the light of this was a matter relating to tort, delict or quasi-delict within what is now Article 7(2).[653] Article 1337 sets out a non-contractual obligation which is not regarded under Italian law as delictual.[654] There was no evidence that it was regarded as being delictual under the law of other Member States. Another example is provided by *ÖFAB, Östergötlands Fastigheter AB v Frank Koot and Evergreen Investments BV*,[655] where the Court of Justice held that what is now Article 7(2) covered actions brought by the creditors of a limited company seeking to hold liable for its debts a director and a shareholder of the company. This means that other non-contractual obligations which are not characterised as tortious in the substantive domestic law sense may fall within the scope of Article 7(2),[656] provided, of course, that the other requirements (set out below) for coming within this provision are met.

---

[647] See Case C-51/97 *Réunion Européenne SA v Spliethoff's Bevrachtingskantoor BV* [1998] ECR I-6511 at [23]–[24]; AG Geelhoed in Case C-334/00 *Fonderie Officine Meccaniche Tacconi SpA v Heinrich Wagner Sinto Maschinenfabrik GmbH (HWS)* [2002] ECR I-7357 at [73]; Case C-548/12 *Marc Brogsitter v Fabrication de Montres Normandes EURL and Karsten Fräßdorf* EU:C:2014:148 at [27], [2014] QB 753. See also Case C-167/00 *Verein Fur Konsumenteninformation v K H Henkel* [2002] ECR I-8111 at [40]–[41].

[648] See AG Wahl in Case C-102/15 *Gazdasági Versenyhivatal v Siemens Aktiengesellschaft Österreich* EU:C:2016:225 at [70], [2016] IL Pr 33; AG Jacobs in Case C-27/02 *Petra Engler v Janus Versand GmbH* [2005] ECR I-481 at [57].

[649] See the *Austro-Mechana Gesellschaft* case at [39]–[41]; Case C-147/12 *ÖFAB, Östergötlands Fastigheter AB v Frank Koot and Evergreen Investments BV* EU:C:2013:490 at [34]–[38], [2015] QB 20; see also AG Wahl in Case C-102/15 *Gazdasági Versenyhivatal v Siemens Aktiengesellschaft Österreich* EU:C:2016:225 at [59]–[60], [2016] IL Pr 33.

[650] See infra, p 267.

[651] Case C-102/15 EU:C:2016:225, [2016] IL Pr 33; the unjust enrichment point was not discussed by the CJEU, which held that the action did not fall within the scope of the Brussels I Regulation; cf AG Darmon in Case C-89/91 *Shearson Lehman Hutton Inc v TVB* [1993] ECR I-139 at [102].

[652] Case C-334/00 [2002] ECR I-7357.

[653] Ibid, at [27].

[654] Benatti, *La Responsabilita precontracttuale* (1963), p 133 et seq.

[655] Case C-147/12 EU:C:2013:490, [2015] QB 20. See also Case C-519/12 *OTP Bank Nyilvánosan Müködö Részvénytársaság v Hochtief Solution AG* EU:C:2013:674, [2015] IL Pr 30.

[656] See the decision of the Austrian Supreme Court in *Re Concurrent Claims (Royalties)* (4 Ob 66/01) [2003] IL Pr 30—a non-contractual claim based on "any conceivable legal ground" held to fall within what is now Art 7(2). See also *Kitechnology BV v Unicor GmbH Plastmaschinen* [1994] IL Pr 568, CA—a claim for non-contractual breach of confidence; *Hewden Tower Cranes Ltd v Wolffkran GmbH* [2007] EWHC 857 (TCC), [2007] 2 Lloyd's Rep 138 and *Iveco SpA v Magna Electronics Srl (formerly Italamec Srl)* [2015] EWHC 2887 (TCC), [2016] IL Pr 18—claims for contribution between tortfeasors, the classification of which is unclear under English domestic law.

A leading English authority on the issue is *Kleinwort Benson Ltd v Glasgow City Council*,[657] in which the House of Lords has given a narrow interpretation to what is now Article 7(2), holding unanimously that a claim for restitution based on unjust enrichment did not fall within this provision.[658] Reliance was placed on another passage in the *Kalfelis* case[659] which states that "a court which has jurisdiction under [Article 7(2)] over an action in so far as it is based on tort or delict does not have jurisdiction over that action in so far as it is not so based". The House of Lords interpreted the first key passage, which has been relied upon so much by the Court of Justice, as merely being concerned with whether an independent meaning should be given to the term "tort", not with the question of scope, which in their Lordships' view was dealt with in the second passage.[660] This may have been a tenable interpretation at the time the *Kleinwort* case was decided but it cannot be reconciled with the more recent decision in the *Fonderie* case, nor with other later decisions of that Court which have not asked whether there is a tort in the substantive domestic law sense. In any event, as far as a claim for restitution based on unjust enrichment is concerned there was another reason given for excluding this from the scope of what is now Article 7(2), namely there was no harmful event.[661]

An action which seeks to establish the liability of a defendant   According to the Court of Justice in *Kalfelis*, to come within Article 7(2) the action must seek to establish the *liability* of a defendant.[662] In *Reichert v Dresdner Bank (No 2)*,[663] the Court of Justice held that an action whereby a creditor sought to set aside a gift of property made by a debtor, which allegedly defrauded him of his rights (an *action paulienne* under French law) did not seek to establish the liability of a defendant in the sense understood in what is now Article 7(2). There was no question of making good the damage done to the creditor by the debtor's fraudulent act and the action was not just directed at the defendant debtor but also at the third party beneficiary of the disposition by the debtor.[664] "Liability" has been widely defined to encompass types of legal liability other than the obligation to make financial reparation, such as refraining from certain types of unlawful conduct.[665] Thus a claimant may seek to establish liability not just by claiming compensation. He could equally do so by seeking an injunction to prevent damage[666] or by seeking a declaration that certain conduct

---

[657] [1999] 1 AC 153.

[658] Ibid, at 172 (per Lord Goff), 185 (per Lord Clyde), 196 (per Lord Hutton), 172 (per Lord Mustill), 177 (per Lord Nicholls). See also *Compagnie Commerciale Andre SA v Artibell Shipping Co Ltd* 1999 SLT 1051. The Court of Justice in Case C-346/93 *Kleinwort Benson Ltd v Glasgow City Council* [1995] ECR I-615 declined to give a ruling on the question whether what is now Article 7(2) has an extended meaning in relation to restitutionary claims on the basis that this question arose in the context of an intra-UK dispute under the Modified Convention (now the Modified Regulation), rather than in order to apply the Brussels Convention itself. It was left to the English courts to solve this difficult question of interpretation.

[659] Case 189/87 [1988] ECR 5565 at [19].

[660] [1999] 1 AC 153 at 196 (per Lord Hutton). The more obvious explanation for the second passage is that it is dealing with concurrent actions in tort and contract (as well as unjust enrichment), ie the situation that actually arose in the *Kalfelis* case, see the *Réunion Européenne SA* case, Peel [1998] LMCLQ 22 at 26. Concurrent actions are discussed infra, pp 268–70.

[661] See infra, p 267.

[662] For the difficulties caused by this requirement see Briggs 2015, para 2.188.

[663] Case C-261/90 [1992] ECR I-2149; Briggs (1992) 12 YEL 660.

[664] Cf *Cronos Containers NV v Palatin* [2002] EWHC 2819 (Comm) at [15], [2003] 2 Lloyd's Rep 489—a conversion case where proprietary restitution of money was sought. The claim was based on a wrongful act, ie the denial of title, and damages are payable for this.

[665] AG Jacobs in Case C-167/00 *Verein Für Konsumenteninformation v K H Henkel* [2002] ECR I-8111 at [35]. See also AG Geelhoed in the *Fonderie* case at [76], who said that what is now Art 7(2) covered a failure to comply with a legal rule regulating conduct.

[666] As in the *Verein* case.

is unlawful as an essential precursor to an action for damages.[667] Each of these has been held to come within the scope of Article 7(2). It has also been held that an action for a declaration that that person is under no liability because no tort has been committed falls within Article 7(2).[668] The liability can be in respect of a non-contractual obligation, ie one that is not in a strict sense tortious or delictual.[669]

A harmful event There must be a "harmful event" for an action to come within Article 7(2).[670] Other than in exceptional circumstances, a claim based on unjust enrichment does not presuppose such an event. This was the second line of reasoning used by the House of Lords in *Kleinwort Benson* to explain their decision that the action did not come within Article 5(3) of the Modified Convention (now the Modified Regulation).[671] The same line of reasoning has recently been adopted by AG Wahl in *Gazdasági Versenyhivatal v Siemens Aktiengesellschaft Österreich*,[672] adding further that non-contractual liability, unlike restitution on the basis of unjust enrichment, requires that there is some ground for holding the defendant responsible for the damage or loss sustained by the claimant, be it in the form of intent, negligence or strict liability[673] and referring to the treatment of unjust enrichment under the Rome II Regulation.[674] In *Casio Computer Co Ltd v Sayo*,[675] the Court of Appeal held that a constructive trust claim based on dishonest assistance fell within what is now Article 7(2), distinguishing *Kleinwort Benson* on the basis that, in the case in front of them, there was a harmful event. Whilst the result looks right, this ignored the narrow interpretation of the *Kalfelis* case adopted by the House of Lords. The separate issue of whether there was a matter relating to tort, delict or quasi-delict, and what that means, was not examined. The concept of a harmful event is a wide one and with regard to consumer protection it covers situations other than where an individual has personally suffered damage.[676]

---

[667] Case C-18/02 *DFDS Torline v SEKO* [2004] ECR I-1417 at [19]–[28].

[668] Case C-133/11 *Folien Fischer AG and Fofitec AG v Ritrama SpA* EU:C:2012:664, [2013] QB 523; *Equitas Ltd v Wave City Shipping Co Ltd* [2005] EWHC 923 (Comm), [2005] 2 All ER (Comm) 301, by analogy with the position under Art 7(1), supra, p 251.

[669] The *Fonderie* case, supra, p 265, n 654.

[670] See Case C-572/14 *Austro-Mechana Gesellschaft zur Wahrnehmung mechanisch-musikalischer Urheberrechte Gesellschaft mbH v Amazon EU Sàrl* EU:C:2016:286 at [39]–[41], [2016] ECDR 23; see also AG Wahl in Case C-102/15 *Gazdasági Versenyhivatal v Siemens Aktiengesellschaft Österreich* EU:C:2016:225 at [60], [2016] IL Pr 33; *XL Insurance Co SE (formerly XL Insurance Co Ltd) v AXA Corporate Solutions Assurance* [2015] EWHC 3431 (Comm), appeal pending—no harmful event where the claimant insurer's entitlement to a contribution from the defendant co-insurer arose by operation of law and arose once it had overpaid the insured.

[671] [1999] 1 AC 153.

[672] Case C-102/15 EU:C:2016:225, [2016] IL Pr 33; the unjust enrichment point was not discussed by the CJEU, which held that the action did not fall within the scope of the Brussels I Regulation; cf AG Darmon in Case C-89/91 *Shearson Lehman Hutton Inc v TVB* [1993] ECR I-139 at [102].

[673] The *Gazdasági Versenyhivatal v Siemens Aktiengesellschaft Österreich* case, AG opinion, at [62].

[674] Ibid, at [72]; see infra, pp 837–48. For a view that the provisions of the Brussels I Regulation need not be interpreted in the light of Rome II, see Case C-45/13 *Andreas Kainz v Pantherwerke AG* EU:C:2014:7 at [20], [2015] QB 34; AG Wahl in *Gazdasági Versenyhivatal v Siemens Aktiengesellschaft Österreich* also compared the wording of Art 7(2) of the Brussels I Recast with that of Arts 7(3) and (4), which apply to civil claims "for damages or restitution which is based on an act giving rise to criminal proceedings" and "for the recovery, based on ownership, of a cultural object", respectively; see infra, p 279.

[675] [2001] EWCA Civ 661, [2001] IL Pr 43; Briggs (2001) 72 BYBIL 470; Yeo (2001) 117 LQR 560. See also in relation to jurisdiction over constructive trustees *Dexter Ltd (In Administrative Receivership) v Harley* (2001) Times, 2 April; See also *Benatti v WPP Holdings Italy SRL* [2007] EWCA Civ 263 at [58] (per Toulson LJ), [2007] 1 WLR 2316—breach of fiduciary duty assumed to come within what is now Art 7(2).

[676] The *Verein* case at [42]. In the instant case, the concept of a "harmful event" covered the undermining of legal stability by the use of unfair terms which it was the task of associations such as the Consumers' Association to prevent.

(ii) Concurrent actions in tort and contract[677]

We are concerned here with the situation where, for example, the claimant commences proceedings in one court involving parallel claims in contract and tort for failure to take care. Such actions raise particularly difficult problems in relation to the scope of Article 7(2) and to some extent Article 7(1). It is well established that an action cannot fall within both Article 7(1) and 7(2).[678] These two provisions are mutually exclusive.[679] The matter will have to be classified as either one relating to a tort or as one relating to a contract, but not both. And the claimant is unable to choose which it is. This follows from the principle in *Kalfelis* that Article 7(2) covers all actions which seek to establish the liability of a defendant and which are not related to a "contract" within the meaning of Article 7(1) and its corollary that if a case falls within Article 7(1) it does not fall within Article 7(2).[680] The *Kalfelis* case involved claims in tort and contract as well as for unjust enrichment and, in the second key passage in the case,[681] appears to be saying that in an action in tort and contract a court which has jurisdiction in respect of the former does not by that fact have jurisdiction in respect of the latter.[682] *Kalfelis* was followed by the Court of Appeal in *Source Ltd v TUV Rheinland Holding AG*,[683] where there were allegations of breach of contract and breach of a duty of care in failing to exercise reasonable skill and care in the preparation and supply of reports as to the quality of goods purchased by the plaintiffs. The Court of Appeal held that both causes of action were excluded from the scope of what is now Article 7(2) because both related to a contract within Article 7(1).[684] Whilst the result looked to be right, the process of reasoning was hard to square with the requirement stressed by the House of Lords in the subsequent *Kleinwort Benson* case that the claim was based on a particular contractual obligation. The tort claim could not be so regarded. In the light of the *Kleinwort Benson* case, Tuckey J said, obiter, that he did not regard *Source* as still being good law.[685] But *Source* was approved, without discussion of this point, in obiter dicta by Morison J[686] and in another case by Ward LJ in the Court of Appeal.[687]

The much needed clarification was given by the Court of Justice in the *Brogsitter* case.[688]

> A German seller of luxury watches concluded a contract with a French master watchmaker for the development of two watch movements. In parallel to developing the two movements, the French watchmaker also developed and marketed other watch movements, cases and watch faces. The German party invoked the jurisdiction of the German courts under what is now Article 7(2), arguing that this amounted to a breach of the exclusivity clause in the contract and gave rise to tortious liability under German law.

---

[677] See, generally, Zogg (2013) 9 J Priv Int L 39.

[678] AG Geelhoed in the *Fonderie* case at [71]; the *Agnew* case at 244–5 (per Lord Woolf), 233–4 (per Lord Nicholls), 247 (per Lord Cooke), 267 (per Lord Millett).

[679] The *Agnew* case at 267 (per Lord Millett).

[680] AG Geelhoed in the *Fonderie* case at [41].

[681] Supra, p 266.

[682] See Peel [1998] LMCLQ 22 at 26; Briggs 2015, para 2.188.

[683] [1998] QB 54.

[684] Ibid, at 63 (per Staughton LJ, Waite and Aldous LJs concurring).

[685] *Raiffeisen Zentral Bank Österreich AG v National Bank of Greece SA* [1999] 1 Lloyd's Rep 408 at 411.

[686] *Rayner v Davies* [2003] IL Pr 14 at [18]–[19], affd without discussion of this point [2002] EWCA Civ 1880, [2003] IL Pr 15.

[687] *Barry v Bradshaw* [2000] IL Pr 706 at [10]. See also *Mazur Media Ltd v Mazur Media GMBH* [2004] EWHC 1566 (Ch) at [30], [2004] 1 WLR 2966.

[688] Case C-548/12 *Marc Brogsitter v Fabrication de Montres Normandes EURL and Karsten Fräßdorf* EU:C:2014:148, [2014] QB 753; Dickinson [2014] LMCLQ 466. This case has been followed in Case C-47/14 *Holterman Ferho Exploitatie BV and Others v Friedrich Leopold Freiherr Spies von Büllesheim* EU:C:2015:574, [2015] IL Pr 44; *Arcadia Petroleum Ltd v Bosworth* [2016] EWCA Civ 818 (in the context of an employment dispute), appeal pending.

The Court of Justice rejected the argument that the mere fact that one contracting party brought a civil liability claim against the other was sufficient to consider that the claim concerned "matters relating to the contract".[689] It went on to say[690] that this was the case only where the conduct complained of may be considered a breach of contract, which may be established by taking into account the purpose of the contract. This will a priori be the case where the interpretation of the contract which links the parties is indispensable to establish the lawfulness of the conduct complained of. It is for the domestic court to determine whether the purpose of the claims is to seek damages. the legal basis for which can reasonably be regarded as a breach of the rights and obligations set out in the contract, which would make its taking into account indispensable in deciding the action. The decisions in the *Kalfelis, Source* and *Brogsitter* cases raise three questions. First, in the *Source* and *Brogsitter* cases would Article 7(2) still not have applied if the action had been pleaded only in tort, with no mention of contract; and would the matter still be regarded as related to a contract simply because the parties have a contractual relationship and the claim could have been brought in contract? There are indications that the Court of Appeal would have answered this first question in the affirmative.[691] It follows from the *Brogsitter* case that the parties who are bound by a contract can invoke Article 7(2) in respect of a related tort only if the interpretation of the contract is not "indispensable" to establish the lawfulness of the defendant's conduct, that is, only if the taking into account of the contract is not "indispensable" in deciding the action.[692] Secondly, if the tort claim is not a matter relating to contract can the court with jurisdiction under Article 7(1) over the contract claim also try the claim in so far as it is based on tort? The opinion of the Advocate General in the *Kalfelis* case, that the whole of the action should be channelled into the court with contract jurisdiction, appears to have been rejected by the Court of Justice in the second key passage in that case.[593] The decision of the Court indicates that the tort claim disappears altogether as far as Article 7(1) and 7(2) are concerned. The action is regarded for jurisdictional purposes as one solely in contract. The claimant is, of course, free to use some other basis of jurisdiction, such as Article 4, which is not concerned with whether the matter relates to tort or contract. Thirdly, if jurisdiction is based on Article 7(1) and the tort claim has disappeared for the purposes of that provision, does it follow that, as the proceedings unfold, the claimant is confined to a claim in contract? In particular, can the claimant rely on tort choice of law rules, rather than those in contract? In principle, this should be possible.[694]

In *Domicrest v Swiss Bank Corpn*,[695] Rix J distinguished the *Source* case on the basis that not only were the claims in contract and tort not parallel but they were also premised on opposite lines of argument.[696] The claim in contract was based on the argument that payment was due from the defendant bank under a payment order; the claim in tort on the basis that an employee of the bank was wrong to tell the plaintiff that a payment order was as good as cash.

---

[689] The *Brogsitter* case, at [23].

[690] Ibid, at [24]–[26].

[691] The *Source* case at 63–4. See also *Burke v Uvex Sports GmbH* [2005] IL Pr 26, Irish HC.

[692] See also Case C-47/14 *Holterman Ferho Exploitatie BV and Others v Friedrich Leopold Freiherr Spies von Büllesheim* EU:C:2015:574 at [70]–[71], [2015] IL Pr 44.

[693] The *Kalfelis* case at [19] (the second key passage) and [20]. See also Lords Goff and Clyde in the *Kleinwort Benson* case at 166–7, 183–4, who interpreted the judgment of the Court of Justice as rejecting the Advocate General's opinion.

[694] See the opinion of AG Jacobs in Case C-26/91 *Jacob Handte & Co GmbH v Société Traitements Mécano-Chimiques des Surfaces SA (TMCS)* [1992] ECR I-3967 at 3984. It would be necessary to meet the criteria for the application of tort choice of law rules, see infra, pp 786–802.

[695] [1999] QB 548.

[696] Ibid, at 561.

The two claims were entirely separate and accordingly had to be treated as such under what is now Article 7. Article 7(1) would have to be satisfied in relation to the claim in contract and Article 7(2) in relation to the claim in tort.

(iii) Threatened wrongs

Article 7(2) provides that the defendant may be sued in the courts for the place where the harmful event occurred *or may occur*. This reference to where the harmful event may occur was added to the Brussels I Regulation to make it clear that what is now Article 7(2) covers an action to prevent a threatened wrong.[697] This is an important clarification since with certain torts, such as infringement of intellectual property rights, it is common to seek an injunction in the Member State in which the threat exists.[698]

(iv) Where is the place[699] where the harmful event occurred?

The Jenard Report deliberately left open the question of whether "the place where the harmful event occurred" referred to the place where the event giving rise to the damage occurred or the place where the damage occurred. The Court of Justice provided the answer in *Bier BV v Mines de Potasse D'Alsace SA*.[700] This provides a classic example of the situation in which the elements in a tort are split up among different states.

> It was alleged that the French defendants had polluted the waters of the Rhine in France. These waters flowed into the Netherlands, where damage was caused to a Dutch horticultural business. The Dutch plaintiffs wished to sue in the Netherlands; so it was necessary to decide on the place where the harmful event occurred.

The Court of Justice, on a reference from the Dutch courts, held that Article 5(3) of the Brussels Convention, now Article 7(2) of the Brussels I Recast, was intended to cover both the place where the damage occurred and the place of the event giving rise to it, where the two are not identical. The claimant therefore has the option of suing in either place. The Court of Justice justified this wide interpretation in three ways. First, Article 7(2) is concerned to give jurisdiction to an appropriate forum. Both the place of acting and of damage are appropriate places for trial. Secondly, it is designed to give the claimant the option of suing elsewhere than in the state where the defendant is domiciled. Applying a place of acting rule on its own would not normally allow this. Applying a place of damage rule on its own would ignore cases where the act took place somewhere other than in the state where the defendant is domiciled. Thirdly, there is artificiality in concentrating on one element in a tort or delict to the exclusion of the other elements.

The *Bier* rule was applied by the Court of Justice in the very different context of multi-state defamation in *Shevill v Presse Alliance SA*.[701]

---

[697] For the position under the Brussels Convention, which lacks this additional wording see infra, p 312.

[698] It was possible even under the Brussels Convention to obtain an injunction in such cases by using Art 24 of the Convention (Art 35 of the Brussels I Recast), discussed infra, pp 303–5. See Fawcett and Torremans, pp 153, 243.

[699] The concept of "place" includes a platform or installation within the continental shelf adjacent to the Member State: *Conocophillips (UK) Ltd v Partnereederei Ms Jork* [2010] EWHC 1214 (Comm).

[700] Case 21/76 [1976] ECR 1735; Hartley (1977) 2 ELR 143.

[701] [1995] ECR I-415; Briggs (1995) 15 YEL 487; Forsyth (1995) 54 CLJ 515; Carter, in McLachlan and Nygh, Chapter 7, pp 118–21; Reed and Kennedy [1996] LMCLQ 108. See also *Ewins v Carlton* [1997] 2 ILRM 223, Irish High Court; *Skogvik v Sveriges Television AB* [2003] IL Pr 24, Norwegian Supreme Court—libel on cable television; Joined cases C-509/09 and C-161/10 *eDate Advertising GmbH v X and Olivier Martinez and Robert Martinez v MGN Limited* [2011] ECR I-10269—infringement of personality rights over the internet. On "libel tourism" see further infra, pp 353–5.

The first plaintiff was an English resident working at a bureau de change in Paris. She alleged that an article which appeared in "France Soir", published by a French incorporated company, suggested that she was involved in laundering drugs money. Proceedings were brought in England for libel. The House of Lords sought guidance, inter alia, on the interpretation of "the place where the harmful event occurred".

The Court of Justice held that the definition in the *Bier* case applied equally in the case of damage other than physical or pecuniary, and, in particular, applied to injury to reputation and good name. Accordingly, the plaintiff had the option of suing either in the courts for the place where the damage occurred or in the courts for the place of the event which gave rise to and was at the origin of that damage. There is a question, which is examined below, of where these places are in a case of multi-state defamation. There is also a question that arises where, for example, the claimant bases jurisdiction on damage in England of whether there has been such damage in England and of who is to decide this. The Court of Justice held that the criteria for assessing whether the event in question is harmful and the evidence required of the existence and extent of the harm alleged by the victim of the defamation are governed by the substantive law determined by the national private international law rules of the court seised, provided that the effectiveness of the Convention (now the Brussels I Recast) is not thereby impaired.[702] Moreover, the fact that damage is presumed under national law does not preclude the operation of Article 7(2). The case was referred back to the House of Lords which, applying the decision of the Court of Justice, held that where English law[703] presumed that the publication of a defamatory statement was harmful to the person defamed without specific proof thereof, that was sufficient for the application of what is now Article 7(2).[704] Accordingly, the plaintiff was able to invoke the jurisdiction of the English courts under this Article.

The place of the event giving rise to the damage[705]   In *Shevill*, the Court of Justice gave an autonomous meaning to the concept of the place of the event giving rise to the damage, rather than ascertaining this in the light of the elements of the tort under the substantive law of the forum or the applicable law. It held that, in the case of a libel by a newspaper article distributed in several Contracting States, the giving rise to the damage "can only be the place where the publisher of the newspaper in question is established, since that is the place where the harmful event originated and from which the libel was issued and put into circulation".[706] The court of this place has jurisdiction to hear the action for damages for all the harm caused by the unlawful act.

The *Shevill* case has been followed in the *eDate Advertising and Olivier Martinez* case[707] which concerned an alleged infringement of personality rights over the internet.

This judgment concerned two separate cases that were joined by the Court of Justice. In the first case, the claimant, a German domiciliary, commenced proceedings in Germany against

---

[702] The *Shevill* case at [34]–[41].

[703] English law was applied as the substantive law of the forum: [1996] AC 959 at 983. However, according to the Court of Justice in *Shevill* it should only be applied if it is the governing law according to national private international law rules.

[704] [1996] AC 959; Leslie 1997 SLT (News) 133; Briggs (1996) 67 BYBIL 586.

[705] Recently, the Court of Justice has started to refer to this place as the "causal event": eg Case C-352/13 *Cartel Damage Claims (CDC) Hydrogen Peroxide SA v Akzo Nobel NV* EU:C:2015:335 at [43] et seq, [2015] QB 906.

[706] *Shevill* at [24].

[707] Joined cases C-509/09 and C-161/10 *eDate Advertising GmbH v X and Olivier Martinez and Robert Martinez v MGN Limited* [2011] ECR I-10269; Bogdan (2011) 13 YBPIL 483; Gillies (2012) 61 ICLQ 1007; Hartley (2012) 128 LQR 197; Kuipers (2012) 49 CMLR 1211; Nagy (2012) 8 J Priv Int L 251; Reymond (2011) 13 YBPIL 493. For internet torts generally, see Bigos (2005) 54 ICLQ 585; Fawcett, Harris and Bridge, paras 10.137–10.161.

an Austrian defendant which operated an internet portal that published a report about a crime committed by the claimant. The defendant was requested to refrain from using his full name when reporting about the crime. In the second case, two French claimants commenced proceedings in France against an English defendant which published the website of the "Sunday Mirror". The claim concerned the interference with the claimants' private lives and infringement of the right to image by reason of the posting online of an article.

The Court of Justice held that the same considerations as in the *Shevill* case may be applied to media and means of communication other than newspapers and may cover a wide range of infringements of personality rights recognised in various legal systems. The place of the event giving rise to the damage was therefore held to be the place where the publisher of the online content was established.

The same principles as in the *Shevill* and *eDate Advertising and Olivier Martinez* cases have been applied in the analogous situation of infringement of intellectual property rights.[708] In a case of allegedly unlawful industrial action by a trade union leading to the immobilising of a ship, the event giving rise to the damage was the notice of industrial action given and publicised by the union at its head office.[709] As regards actions brought by the creditors of a limited company against a director and a shareholder, the relevant place is the place where the activities carried out by that company, and where the director and the shareholder failed to discharge their monitoring duties, took place.[710] In product liability cases, the place of the event giving rise to the damage is in principle the place where the defective product was manufactured, not where it was marketed.[711]

The analogy of defamation has also been applied by the English courts in a case of negligent misstatement.[712] In *Domicrest Ltd v Swiss Bank Corpn*,[713] Rix J held that in such a case the place where the harmful event giving rise to the damage occurs is where the misstatement originates, rather than where it is received and relied upon. In the case of a telephone conversation between persons in different countries, this is where the words constituting the

---

[708] *Wegmann v Elsevier Science Ltd* [1999] IL Pr 379, French Cour de Cassation—copyright infringement involving publications in several Member States; Case C-523/10 *Wintersteiger AG v Products 4U Sondermaschinenbau GmbH* EU:C:2012:220, [2012] IL Pr 23—trade mark infringement over the internet; Case C-441/13 *Pez Hejduk v EnergieAgentur.NRW GmbH* EU:C:2015:28 at [24], [2015] Bus LR 560—copyright infringement over the internet.

[709] Case C-18/02 *DFDS Torline v SEKO* [2004] ECR I-1417 at [41].

[710] Case C-147/12 *ÖFAB, Östergötlands Fastigheter AB v Frank Koot and Evergreen Investments BV* EU:C:2013:490, [2015] QB 20; see also Case C-47/14 *Holterman Ferho Exploitatie BV and Others v Friedrich Leopold Freiherr Spies von Büllesheim* EU:C:2015:574 at [76], [2015] IL Pr 44.

[711] Case C-45/13 *Andreas Kainz v Pantherwerke AG* EU:C:2014:7, [2015] QB 34; see also Case C-189/08 *Zuid-Chemie BV v Philippo's Mineralenfabriek NV/SA* [2009] ECR I-6917 at [25], [27].

[712] For conversion, see *Cronos Containers NV v Palatin* [2002] EWHC 2819 (Comm) at [19], [2003] 2 Lloyd's Rep 489. For abuse of a dominant position, see *SanDisk Corpn v Koninklijke Philips Electronics NV* [2007] EWHC 332 (Ch), [2007] IL Pr 22. For unlawful means conspiracy implemented in England to wrongfully deal with assets located abroad in breach of a worldwide freezing order, see *JSC BTA Bank v Ablyazov* [2017] EWCA Civ 40—a Lugano Convention case. For interference with third party's freedom of action, see *Future Investments SA v Federation Internationale de Football Association* [2010] EWHC 1019 (Ch), [2010] IL Pr 34—a Lugano Convention case. For breaches of duties of loyalty, confidentiality and to act as financial advisor, see *Deutsche Bank AG London Branch v Petromena ASA* [2013] EWHC 3065 (Comm)—a Lugano Convention case; the Court of Appeal did not discuss this point. For the problem of identifying this in the situation where an indemnity is sought from a third party, see *Waterford Wedgwood plc v David Nagli Ltd* [1999] IL Pr 9. This is not the place where a decision to commit a tort is reached: *Anton Durbeck GmbH v Den Norske Bank ASA* [2002] EWHC 1173 (Comm), varied [2003] QB 1160, CA, without an appeal on this point.

[713] [1999] QB 548; Reed (1999) 18 CJQ 218.

misstatement are spoken (in the instant case, this was in Switzerland), rather than where they are heard (in the instant case, this was in England). Accordingly, the English court had no jurisdiction. There is no difference for these purposes between oral or other instant-aneous communication and a written document. Rix J refused to follow the earlier negligent misstatement case of *Minster Investments Ltd v Hyundai Precision and Industry Co Ltd*.[714] In this case, which was decided before *Shevill*,[715] Steyn J decided to use a traditional English formula,[716] and ask "where in substance the cause of action in tort arises, or what place the tort is most closely connected with". The essence of the action for negligent misstatement was said to be the negligent advice and reliance on it. Certificates negligently produced in France and Korea were received and relied upon in England, and accordingly there was jurisdiction in England. However, as Rix J pointed out, the "substance" test "does not reflect either the wording or the philosophy of the Brussels Convention as laid down in the European Court's decisions".[717] Moreover, the plaintiff always has the option of suing in the place where the damage occurred, which is quite likely to be the place of receipt and reliance.[718] The *Domicrest* approach has been preferred to that in *Hyundai* by other judges at first instance,[719] including in a case involving certificates,[720] and by Mance LJ in obiter dicta in the Court of Appeal.[721]

The Court of Justice in *Réunion Européenne v Spliethoff's Bevrachtingskantoor BV*[722] acknowledged that in certain cases it may be difficult or indeed impossible to determine the place where the event giving rise to the damage occurred. Such impossibility is illustrated by the facts of the case. Pears were shipped in refrigerated containers by the defendant maritime carrier from Australia to the Netherlands, then taken by road to France where the consignee discovered that the goods were damaged. There had been a breakdown in the cooling system in the containers. In such circumstances the claimant will have to rely on bringing the defendant maritime carrier before the courts for the place where the damage occurred.

An issue that has arisen recently concerns the identification of the place where the event giving rise to the damage occurred in a case where there are multiple alleged perpetrators

---

[714] [1988] 2 Lloyd's Rep 621; Hartley (1988) 13 ELR 217. See also *Modus Vivendi Ltd v Sanmex Co Ltd* [1996] FSR 790.

[715] And before the decisions of the Court of Justice on the place where damage occurred, infra, pp 275–9.

[716] Taken from cases on the old tort head of Ord 11, RSC (now CPR, r 6.36 and CPR Practice Direction 6B, para 3.1(9)), infra, p 348, n 286.

[717] The *Domicrest* case at 566–7.

[718] Ibid, at 567–8. But not in the *Domicrest* case, see infra, p 277.

[719] *Raiffeisen Zentral Bank Österreich AG v Tranos* [2001] IL Pr 9; *Alfred Dunhill Ltd v Diffusion Internationale de Maroquinerie de Prestige SARL* [2002] IL Pr 13 at [31]; *Newsat Holdings Ltd v Zani* [2006] EWHC 342 (Comm) at [43]–[44], [2006] 1 Lloyd's Rep 707; *Sunderland Marine Mutual Insurance Co Ltd v Wiseman* [2007] EWHC 1460 (Comm), [2007] 2 Lloyd's Rep 308; *Barclay-Watt v Alpha Panareti Public Ltd*, 23 November 2012, HC at [58]; *McGraw-Hill International (UK) Ltd v Deutsche Apotheker- und Arztebank EG* [2014] EWHC 2436 (Comm), [2014] 2 Lloyd's Rep 523. But see *Raiffeisen Zentral Bank Österreich AG v National Bank of Greece SA* [1999] 1 Lloyd's Rep 408 where Tuckey J refrained from expressing a view on which approach was correct and *Bank of Tokyo-Mitsubishi Ltd v Baskan Gida Sanayi Ve Pazarlama AS* [2004] EWHC 945 (Ch), [2004] 2 Lloyd's Rep 395, where Lawrence Collins J said at [223] that it was not necessary to decide whether *Domicrest* applied to fraudulent and negligent misrepresentation, or whether it was rightly decided.

[720] *London Helicopters Ltd v Heliportugal LDA-INAC* [2006] EWHC 108 (QB), [2006] IL Pr 28—where misstatement was put into circulation.

[721] *ABCI v Banque Franco-Tunisienne* [2003] EWCA Civ 205 at [41], [2003] 2 Lloyd's Rep 146.

[722] Case C-51/97 [1998] ECR I-6511. See also *Cooper Tire & Rubber Co v Shell Chemicals UK Ltd* [2009] EWHC 2609 (Comm) at [65], [2009] 2 CLC 619, revd by CA, [2010] EWCA Civ 864, [2010] Bus LR 1697 without discussion of this point; *Bord Na Mona Horticulture Ltd v British Polythene Industries Plc* [2012] EWHC 3346 (Comm) at [86].

who are established in and act in different countries. In *Melzer v MF Global UK Ltd*[723] a German private investor brought a tortious claim in Germany against an English broker trading in futures on the basis that he had been solicited as a client in Germany by a German company, which managed the claimant's file and opened an account for the claimant with the defendant. The defendant seems to have been sued both for its own alleged wrongdoing in England and for assisting the German company's alleged wrongdoing in Germany. Furthermore, it seems to have been conceded that the only viable jurisdictional basis was with respect to the German company's alleged wrongdoing in Germany, which the defendant had allegedly assisted. The Court of Justice adopted an autonomous and strict interpretation of what is now Article 7(2) and refused to allow the German courts to assume jurisdiction over the English co-perpetrator on the ground that the place where the event giving rise to the damage occurred cannot be a place where the defendant has not itself acted. The same reasoning was applied in two subsequent cases which dealt with alleged infringements of copyright[724] and unlawful comparative advertising or unfair imitation of a sign protected by a Community trade mark, prohibited by the law against unfair competition[725] committed by multiple perpetrators.

A more complex case is *Cartel Damage Claims (CDC) Hydrogen Peroxide SA v Akzo Nobel NV*.[726] Here, an action for damages and disclosure of information was brought by a Belgian claimant who was the transferee of claims of multiple individual victims against multiple defendants domiciled in various Member States. The defendants had participated in a cartel found by the European Commission to be contrary to EU competition law. The Court of Justice held that in the case at hand, which concerned a single and continuous infringement of EU competition law in which the defendants had participated in several Member States, at different times and in different places, the event giving rise to the damage occurred in relation to each alleged victim on an individual basis and each of the victims could choose to bring an action against all the defendants before the courts of the place in which the cartel was definitively concluded[727] or, as the case may be, the place in which one agreement in particular was concluded which is identifiable as the sole causal event giving rise to the loss allegedly suffered. In reaching this conclusion, the Court held that the transfer of claims by the initial creditors cannot, by itself, have an impact on the application of what is now Article 7(2).[728]

It is unclear whether the preceding decisions apply to vicarious liability. It seems that at least in cases concerning employment relationships where vicarious liability is universally accepted, the place where the employee or another person for whom the defendant is vicariously liable acts or fails to act should be the place of the event giving rise to the damage.[729]

---

[723] Case C-228/11 EU:C:2013:305, [2013] QB 1112.

[724] Case C-387/12 *Hi Hotel HCF SARL v Uwe Spoering* EU:C:2014:215, [2014] 1 WLR 1912.

[725] Case C-360/12 *Coty Germany GmbH v First Note Perfumes NV* EU:C:2014:1318, [2015] IL Pr 13. The jurisdiction to hear claims in relation to EU Trade Marks is governed by Council Regulation (EC) No 207/2009 of 26 February on the Community trade mark OJ 2009 L 78/1, as amended by Regulation (EU) 2015/2424 of the European Parliament and of the Council of 16 December 2015 OJ 2015 L 341/21. The application of Art 7(2) is expressly precluded.

[726] Case C-352/13 EU:C:2015:335, [2015] QB 906; Wurmnest (2016) 53 CMLR 225. See, generally, on jurisdiction in EU competition law claims: Danov (2012) 61 ICLQ 27.

[727] This might be impossible to determine: the *CDC* case, at [45]; *Cooper Tire & Rubber Co v Shell Chemicals UK Ltd* [2009] EWHC 2609 (Comm) at [65], [2009] 2 CLC 619, revd by CA, [2010] EWCA Civ 864, [2010] Bus LR 1697 without discussion of this point; *Bord Na Mona Horticulture Ltd v British Polythene Industries Plc* [2012] EWHC 3346 (Comm) at [86].

[728] See also Case C-147/12 *ÖFAB, Östergötlands Fastigheter AB v Frank Koot and Evergreen Investments BV* EU:C:2013:490 at [56]–[59], [2015] QB 20.

[729] Also Briggs 2014, fn 393 on p 280.

The place where the damage occurred   A number of problems arise in relation to this concept. First, it is not easy to ascertain what the damage is and hence where it occurs in cases where the damage is other than physical or pecuniary.[730] "In the case of an international libel through the press, the injury caused by a defamatory publication to the honour, reputation and good name of a natural or legal person occurs in the places where the publication is distributed, when the victim is known in these places."[731] In the case of infringement of personality rights over the internet, damage occurs wherever the online content is or has been accessible and also in the place where the alleged victim has his or her centre of interests.[732] With passing off, damage occurs where the goodwill is damaged.[733] With unfair competition it is the place where direct economic loss to the claimant, in the form of loss of sales, was sustained.[734] With breach of EU competition law that results in additional costs incurred because of artificially high prices, damage occurs at the victim's registered office.[735] It has been held in a case of non-contractual breach of confidence, that damage occurs where there is damage directly caused to the claimant's commercial interests in that state.[736] With interference with third party's freedom of action, damage occurs where the contract with the claimant would have been made if there had been no interference.[737] With unlawful means conspiracy and inducing a breach of contract/wrongful interference with contractual relations, damage occurs where the claimant did not receive the money which, if the contract had been performed, it should have received[738] or where the goods under the contract interfered with should have been delivered.[739] Where the claim is for wrongfully inducing third parties to breach exclusive English jurisdiction clauses contained in contracts that these third parties entered into with the claimant, damage occurs where the proceedings violating the jurisdiction clauses were commenced and where the claimant incurred the expenditure occasioned by those proceedings.[740] But what of a tort, such as infringement of intellectual property rights, where damage is not one of the elements of the tort? The concept of damage becomes

---

[730] Locating the place where financial loss occurred is not always easy, see Case C-18/02 *DFDS Torline v SEKO* [2004] ECR I-1417 at [42]–[45]—damage caused by immobilising a ship located in flag state. See generally Lehmann (2011) 7 J Priv Int L 527.

[731] The *Shevill* case at [29]. See also *Hunter v Blom-Cooper* [2000] IL Pr 229, Irish High Court—a republication case.

[732] Joined cases C-509/09 and C-161/10 *eDate Advertising GmbH v X and Olivier Martinez and Robert Martinez v MGN Limited* [2011] ECR I-10269.

[733] *Mecklermedia Corpn v DC Congress GmbH* [1998] Ch 40 at 51–2; *Modus Vivendi Ltd v British Products Sanmex Co Ltd* [1996] FSR 790 at 802–3. See also *AMS Neve Ltd v Heritage Audio SL* [2016] EWHC 2563 (IPEC) at [25]—with regard to a claim of passing off based on UK registered trade marks, damage occurs where the right subsisted.

[734] *Saba Molnlycke AS v Procter & Gamble Scandinavia Inc* [1997] IL Pr 704, Tonsberg Court of Appeal. See for abuse of dominant position *SanDisk Corpn v Koninklijke Philips Electronics NV* [2007] EWHC 332 (Ch), [2007] IL Pr 22.

[735] Case C-352/13 *Cartel Damage Claims (CDC) Hydrogen Peroxide SA v Akzo Nobel NV* EU:C:2015:335, [2015] QB 906. See also *DSG Retail Ltd v Mastercard Inc* [2015] CAT 7.

[736] *Kitechnology BV v Unicor GmbH Plastmaschinen* [1994] IL Pr 568 at 581–2, CA. This is assuming that such an action comes within the scope of Art 7(2).

[737] *Future Investments SA v Federation Internationale de Football Association* [2010] EWHC 1019 (Ch), [2010] IL Pr 34.

[738] *Dolphin Maritime & Aviation Services Ltd v Sveriges Angfartygs Assurans Forening* [2009] EWHC 716 (Comm), [2009] 2 Lloyd's Rep 123; Briggs (2009) 80 BYBIL 616.

[739] *Actial Farmaceutica Lda v De Simone* [2016] EWCA Civ 1311; see also *AMT Futures Ltd v Marzillier, Dr Meier & Dr Gunter Rechtsanwaltsgesellschaft mbH* [2014] EWHC 1085 (Comm) at [34](6), [2015] 2 WLR 187; revd [2015] EWCA Civ 143, [2015] QB 699 and [2017] UKSC 13, [2017] 2 WLR 853 without discussion of this point.

[740] *AMT Futures Ltd v Marzillier, Dr Meier & Dr Gunter Rechtsanwaltsgesellschaft mbH* [2017] UKSC 13, [2017] 2 WLR 853. The *Dolphin Maritime* case was distinguished, at [26], on the basis that it concerned the positive obligation to pay money into the claimants' bank account in England.

highly artificial and difficult to ascertain in such a case.[741] The Court of Justice has held, in a case of infringement of a trade mark registered in a Member State, that damage occurs where the trade mark is registered.[742] With respect to infringements of copyrights, damage occurs where the copyright is protected, provided that the alleged damage occurred or may occur within the jurisdiction of the court seised, eg by means of a website being accessible within that jurisdiction.[743]

Secondly, is this referring just to the place where direct damage occurs or does it also allow jurisdiction where indirect damage occurs? This question has first arisen in the context of financial harm. In *Dumez France and Tracoba v Hessische Landesbank*[744] the immediate victims of the alleged harmful act (of cancelling certain bank loans) committed in Germany were German subsidiary companies, which suffered financial loss in Germany, but as a consequence of this the parent companies also suffered financial loss in France where their head offices were situated. The Court of Justice held that Article 5(3) of the Brussels Convention, now Article 7(2) of the Brussels I Recast, could not be construed as allowing the parent companies to bring proceedings in France against the German defendants. The *Bier* case, although allowing jurisdiction to be assumed in the state where the harm occurs, was concerned with cases where a direct consequence was felt in a Member State (this would be in Germany), not an indirect consequence, as occurred in France.[745] The *Dumez* case was followed in *Marinari v Lloyds Bank plc (Zubaidi Trading Co Intervener)*,[746] which was a simpler case involving direct and indirect damage to the same person.

> The Italian domiciled plaintiff was arrested in England and promissory notes were sequestrated. The plaintiff subsequently brought an action in Italy, inter alia, for compensation for the damage he claimed to have suffered as a result of his arrest, the breach of several contracts and injury to his reputation.

The Court of Justice held that the place of damage was to be interpreted as not referring to the place where the victim claimed to have suffered financial loss consequential upon initial damage arising and suffered by him in another Member State. The Court of Justice was concerned to keep what is now Article 7(2) within certain bounds so as to avoid multiplication of competent fora. It also wanted to avoid the situation where the plaintiff was able to sue in the place where he was domiciled. These principles were applied to the situation where there is financial loss which has simultaneous and co-extensive consequences in a Member State (X), where the victim was domiciled and his assets were concentrated, other than that

---

[741] See Fawcett and Torremans, pp 163–6.

[742] Case C-523/10 *Wintersteiger AG v Products 4U Sondermaschinenbau* GmbH EU:C:2012:220, [2012] IL Pr 23. See also *AMS Neve Ltd v Heritage Audio SL* [2016] EWHC 2563 (IPEC).

[743] Case C-170/12 *Peter Pinckney v KDG Mediatech AG* EU:C:2013:635, [2014] IL Pr 7. See also Case C-387/12 *Hi Hotel HCF SARL v Uwe Spoering* EU:C:2014:215, [2014] 1 WLR 1912; C-441/13 *Pez Hejduk v EnergieAgentur NRW GmbH* EU:C:2015:28, [2015] Bus LR 560. See also Case C-360/12 *Coty Germany GmbH v First Note Perfumes NV* EU:C:2014:1318, [2015] IL Pr 13—a case concerning an allegation of unlawful comparative advertising or unfair imitation of a sign protected by a Community trade mark, prohibited by the law against unfair competition; *SMI Group Ltd v Levy* [2012] EWHC 3078 (Ch)—a case concerning a claim for infringement of database rights.

[744] Case 220/88 [1990] ECR I-49; Hartley (1991) 16 ELR 71.

[745] See also *Deutsche Bahn AG v Morgan Advanced Materials Plc (formerly Morgan Crucible Co Plc)* [2013] EWCA Civ 1484, [2014] CP Rep 10, refusing permission to appeal, with reasons, the judgment in [2013] CAT 18: what is now Art 7(2) does not contain a requirement that the claimant is an immediate victim; Scott (2013) 84 BYBIL 510.

[746] Case C-364/93 [1995] ECR I-2719; Briggs [1996] LMCLQ 27 and (1995) 15 YEL 511; Collier (1996) 55 CLJ 216; Hartley (1996) 21 ELR 164. See also *Waterford Wedgwood plc v David Nagli Ltd* [1999] IL Pr 9 at 22–3; *Dexter Ltd (In Administrative Receivership) v Harley* (2001) Times, 2 April.

in which it arises and is suffered by the victim.[747] There is no jurisdiction in Member State X. But in *Harald Kolassa v Barclays Bank plc*,[748] a case which concerned the purchase by a claimant domiciled in one Member State of a financial instrument in the form of a bearer bond issued by a bank in another Member State from an intermediary bank established in a third Member State, the Court of Justice held that the courts where the claimant is domiciled have jurisdiction to hear and determine an action against the bank for prospectus liability and breach of obligations to protect and advise, particularly when the damage alleged occurred directly in the claimant's bank account held with a bank established within the jurisdiction of those courts.[749] Consistently with the *Marinari* case, it was held by the English High Court in the *Domicrest* case that the damage occurred in Switzerland and Italy where, on the strength of the alleged negligent misstatement by the defendant bank, goods stored in those countries were released by the English plaintiff without prior payment.[750] It follows that, in a case of breach of confidence, there is no jurisdiction in the Member State where there is financial loss consequent on the damage to the claimant's commercial interests.[751] The reasoning in *Marinari* applies equally to cases of product liability and personal injury. In *Zuid-Chemie BV v Philippo's Mineralenfabriek NV/SA*,[752] the defendant produced a chemical that was contaminated during manufacture. The chemical was delivered to the claimant which used it to produce fertilizer. The Court of Justice held that the place where the damage occurred was the place where the initial damage occurred as a result of the normal use of the product for the purpose for which it was intended, which, in the case at hand, was the factory where the contaminated chemical was processed and unusable fertilizer produced.[753] In *Henderson v Jaouen*,[754] initial damage had been suffered by the claimant in a road traffic accident in France but his medical condition had deteriorated whilst living in England. The Court of Appeal held that there was no "harmful event" in England under what is now Article 7(2) of the Brussels I Recast. This concept is to be given an autonomous meaning. The decision was therefore unaffected by the fact that under French law deterioration constitutes a separate cause of action from the original injury.

---

[747] Case C-168/02 *Kronhofer v Maier* [2004] ECR I-6009.

[748] Case C-375/13 EU:C:2015:37, [2016] 1 All ER (Comm) 733; Lehmann (2016) 12 J Priv Int L 318.

[749] Compare Case C-12/15 *Universal Music International Holding BV v Michael Tétreault Schilling* EU:C:2016:449, [2016] QB 967, a case concerning purely financial loss suffered in one Member State as a result of alleged negligent drafting of a contract negotiated and concluded in another Member State, which follows the *Marinari* and *Kronhofer* cases in finding that the courts for the place of the claimant's domicile, where the bank account from which money was paid, do not have jurisdiction. The *Kolassa* case was distinguished, rather unpersuasively, and confined to its specific facts.

[750] The *Domicrest* case at 568. See also *Raiffeisen Zentral Bank Österreich AG v National Bank of Greece SA* [1999] 1 Lloyd's Rep 408 at 414; *Bank of Tokyo-Mitsubishi Ltd v Baskan Gida Sanayi Ve Pazarlama AS* [2004] EWHC 945 (Ch) at [223], [2004] 2 Lloyd's Rep 395; *Raiffeisen Zentral Bank Österreich AG v Tranos* [2001] IL Pr 9; *Alfred Dunhill Ltd v Diffusion Internationale De Maroquinerie De Prestige SARL* [2002] IL Pr 13 at [53]–[55]; *London Helicopters Ltd v Heliportugal LDA-INAC* [2006] EWHC 108 (QB) at [21], [27], [2006] IL Pr 28; *Crucial Music Corpn v Klondyke Management AG* [2007] EWHC 1782 (Ch), [2007] IL Pr 54; *Maple Leaf Macro Volatility Master Fund v Rouvroy* [2009] EWHC 257 (Comm) at [214], [2009] 1 Lloyd's Rep 475; *Barclay-Watt v Alpha Panareti Public Ltd*, 23 November 2012, HC at [58]; *McGraw-Hill International (UK) Ltd v Deutsche Apotheker- und Arztebank EG* [2014] EWHC 2436 (Comm) at [53], [2014] 2 Lloyd's Rep 523. See on these cases Fawcett, Harris and Bridge, paras 6.93–6.95.

[751] *Kitechnology BV v Unicor GmbH Plastmaschinen* [1994] IL Pr 568 at 581–582, CA. See also in relation to inability to exploit a copyright: *Mazur Media Ltd v Mazur Media GmbH* [2004] EWHC 1566 (Ch) at [44]–[52], [2004] 1 WLR 2966. And in relation to payment under a fraudulent insurance claim: *Sunderland Marine Mutual Insurance Co Ltd v Wiseman* [2007] EWHC 1460 (Comm), [2007] 2 Lloyd's Rep 308.

[752] Case C-189/08 [2009] ECR I-6917.

[753] See also *Iveco SpA v Magna Electronics Srl (formerly Italamec Srl)* [2015] EWHC 2887 (TCC), [2016] IL Pr 18—place where damage occurred for a claim under Civil Liability (Contribution) Act 1978.

[754] [2002] EWCA Civ 75, [2002] 1 WLR 2971; Briggs (2002) 73 BYBIL 458.

Thirdly, in the situation where there is direct damage in more than one Member State, does Member State A which has jurisdiction on the basis of damage in that state also have jurisdiction in relation to the damage sustained in other Member States? This problem is especially acute in the context of torts committed over the internet.[755] This starting point is the *Shevill* case, which concerned multi-state defamation through the press. The Court of Justice held that each Member State in which the defamatory publication was distributed and in which the victim claims to have suffered injury to his reputation (in that state) only has jurisdiction to rule on the injury caused in that state to the victim's reputation in that state.[756] It is obviously undesirable to have different aspects of the same dispute tried before different courts. However, the claimant can avoid this by bringing the entire claim in the Member State where the defendant is domiciled (using Article 4) or in the Member State where the publisher is established (using Article 7(2)), where this is different. The problem arose again in the *eDate Advertising and Olivier Martinez* case[757] which concerned an alleged infringement of personality rights over the internet. The Court of Justice held that the usefulness of the criterion relating to distribution is reduced in the context of the internet because online content is in principle ubiquitous and universal. Moreover, it is not always technically possible to quantify the distribution in different Member States or, therefore, to assess the damage caused in different Member States. This contrasts with the serious nature of the harm which may be suffered by the holder of a personality right which is infringed online. The Court therefore held that the claimants in the case at hand could commence proceedings not only in each Member State in which the online content is or has been accessible, in respect of the damage caused in the respective Member State, but also, in respect of all the damage caused,[758] in the Member State in which the victim's centre of interest is based. This place corresponds in general to the victim's habitual residence, although a person may also have the centre of his or her interests in another Member State, insofar as other factors, such as the pursuit of a professional activity, may establish the existence of a particularly close link with that State.[759] The connecting factor of the victim's centre of interest has not been adopted in cases concerning infringement of intellectual property rights. Where a trade mark registered in one Member State (Austria) has been allegedly infringed through the use, by an advertiser, of a keyword identical to that trade mark on a search engine website operating under a top-level domain different from that of the Member State where the trade mark is registered (Google.de), the courts of the Member State where the trade mark is registered have jurisdiction to determine all the damage allegedly caused to the proprietor of the trade mark and to hear an application for an injunction in respect of all infringements of that trade mark.[760] In cases of copyright infringement,

---

[755] For internet torts generally, see Bigos (2005) 54 ICLQ 585; Fawcett, Harris and Bridge, paras 10.137–10.161.

[756] [1995] ECR I-415 at [33]. See also *Barclay v Sweeney* [1999] IL Pr 288, Cour d'Appel, Paris—invasion of privacy and the infringement by the press of the right to one's image.

[757] Joined cases C-509/09 and C-161/10 *eDate Advertising GmbH v X and Olivier Martinez and Robert Martinez v MGN Limited* [2011] ECR I-10269. See also the request to the Court of Justice for a preliminary ruling in Case C-194/16 *Bolagsupplysningen OÜ, Ingrid Ilsjan v Svensk Handel AB* OJ 2016 C 211/35.

[758] It is uncertain if this refers only to the damage caused within the European Union or worldwide: see the *eDate Advertising and Olivier Martinez* case, at [48].

[759] The wide choice given to the claimant in the *eDate Advertising and Olivier Martinez* case is balanced by the second part of the judgment which concerned the effect of Article 3 of Directive 2000/31/EC on certain legal aspects of information society services, in particular electronic commerce, in the Internal Market OJ 2000 L 178/1. The Court of Justice held that in relation to the coordinated field, Member States must ensure that the provider of an electronic commerce service is not subject to stricter requirements than apply under the law of the Member State of origin, which is normally the country where the provider is established.

[760] Case C-523/10 *Wintersteiger AG v Products 4U Sondermaschinenbau* GmbH EU:C:2012:220, [2012] IL Pr 23. See also *AMS Neve Ltd v Heritage Audio SL* [2016] EWHC 2563 (IPEC).

jurisdiction is given to the court of the Member State in which the copyright is protected, provided that the alleged damage occurred or may occur within the jurisdiction of the court seised, eg by means of a website being accessible within that jurisdiction; that court has jurisdiction only to rule on the damage caused in the Member State in which it is situated.[761]

Fourthly, can the place where the damage is discovered be regarded as the place where the damage occurred? This question arose in *Réunion Européenne SA v Spliethoff's Bevrachtingskantoor*.[762] The Court of Justice held that the place (France) where the plaintiff consignee merely discovered the existence of the damage to the goods delivered to it could not constitute the place where the damage occurred.[763] This is consistent with the decisions in *Dumez* and *Marinari*; to decide otherwise would often mean attributing jurisdiction to the place of the plaintiff's domicile. In the case of an international transport operation of the kind in question, the place where the damage occurs can only be that where the actual maritime carrier was to deliver the goods, not the place of final delivery or where the consignee discovered the damage.

> **Article 7(3)**[764] as regards a civil claim for damages or restitution which is based on an act giving rise to criminal proceedings, in the court seised of those proceedings, to the extent that that court has jurisdiction under its own law to entertain civil proceedings.[765]

> **Article 7(4)**[766] as regards a civil claim for the recovery, based on ownership, of a cultural object[767] initiated by the person claiming the right to recover such an object, in the courts for the place where the cultural object is situated at the time when the court is seised.

> **Article 7(5)**[768] as regards a dispute arising out of the operations of a branch, agency or other establishment, in the courts for the place where the branch, agency or other establishment is situated.

There are two requirements under Article 7(5): first, the defendant domiciled in a Member State must have a branch, agency or other establishment in another Member State. Secondly, the dispute must arise out of the operations of the branch, agency or other establishment.

(i) A branch, agency or other establishment

A literal interpretation would suggest that these three terms encompass different situations and are there to give width to Article 7(5). The Court of Justice has, instead, applied a

---

[761] Case C-170/12 *Peter Pinckney v KDG Mediatech AG* EU:C:2013:635, [2014] IL Pr 7; Case C-387/12 *Hi Hotel HCF SARL v Uwe Spoering* EU:C:2014:215, [2014] 1 WLR 1912; C-441/13 *Pez Hejduk v EnergieAgentur NRW GmbH* EU:C:2015:28, [2015] Bus LR 560. See also Case C-360/12 *Coty Germany GmbH v First Note Perfumes NV* EU:C:2014:1318, [2015] IL Pr 13—a case concerning an allegation of unlawful comparative advertising or unfair imitation of a sign protected by a Community trade mark, prohibited by the law against unfair competition.

[762] Case C-51/97 [1998] ECR I-6511. See also the subsequent decision of the French Cour de Cassation in [1999] IL Pr 613.

[763] The *Réunion* case at [37].

[764] Art 5(4) of the Brussels I Regulation; Art 5(4) of the Brussels Convention.

[765] See generally Case C-172/91 *Sonntag v Waidmann* [1993] ECR I-1963; Case C-7/98 *Krombach v Bamberski* [2000] ECR I-1935.

[766] Art 7(4) is a new provision introduced in the Brussels I Recast. See Roodt, *Private International Law, Art and Cultural Heritage* (2015) Chapter 4; Gillies (2015) 11 J Priv Int L 295. The Hess, Pfeiffer and Schlosser Report recommended the introduction of a new wide jurisdictional rule for cases where the object of the dispute is moveable property, which would allocate jurisdiction to the courts of the Member State in which the property is situated: Study JLS/C4/2005/03, Final Version September 2007, para 876.

[767] As defined in point 1 of Article 1 of Council Directive 93/7/EEC on the return of cultural objects unlawfully removed from the territory of a Member State OJ 1993 L74/74.

[768] Art 5(5) of the Brussels I Regulation; Art 5(5) of the Brussels Convention. See Fawcett (1984) 9 ELR 326; Bogdan (2006) 17 KCLJ 97.

teleological interpretation to this provision and has reached a different conclusion.[769] After looking at the purpose of the Brussels Convention and the place within it of what is now Article 7(5) as an exception to what is now Article 4, the Court of Justice has decided that this provision should be interpreted narrowly. The "branch", "agency" and "other establishment" are identified by characteristics which are said to be common to all three.[770] These are as follows: the branch, agency or other establishment must (a) have a fixed permanent place of business, (b) be subject to the direction and control of the parent, (c) have a certain autonomy[771] and (d) act on behalf of and bind the parent. These are the characteristics of a typical branch office. Any other method of carrying on business is likely to fall outside the ambit of Article 7(5). The one characteristic that does separate the three terms is that of legal personality. A branch will not have a separate legal personality, whereas an establishment or agent can be a legally independent entity.

The Court of Justice has examined this matter in four cases. The *Somafer*[772] case concerned a sales representative.

> A French company (Somafer) carried on business in Germany by means of a sales representative who was one of their employees. There was no office or furniture in Germany and Somafer was not entered in a commercial register as a branch. A German company wished to sue Somafer in Germany and the question was whether Somafer had a branch, agency or other establishment in that country.

The Court of Justice held that the concept of branch, agency or other establishment implies a place of business which has the appearance[773] of permanency, such as the extension of the parent, has a management and is materially equipped to negotiate business with third parties so that the latter, although knowing that there will if necessary be a legal link with the body, the head office of which is abroad, do not have to deal directly with the parent but may transact business at the place of business constituting the extension. It stressed the need for a fixed permanent place of business in Germany and the sales representative having the power to act on behalf of and to bind his parent,[774] neither of which would appear to be satisfied on the above facts.

Blanckaert v Trost[775] involved a company carrying on business abroad by means of a commercial agent.

> A Belgian manufacturer of furniture appointed a German independent commercial agent to set up a sales network in Germany. The agent was free to arrange its own work, was not prevented from representing several other firms competing in the same sector, and transmitted orders to the parent without being involved in either their terms or their execution.

---

[769] Case 14/76 *De Bloos v Bouyer* [1976] ECR 1497; Case 33/78 *Somafer v Saar-Ferngas* [1978] ECR 2183; Case 139/80 *Blanckaert and Willems v Trost* [1981] ECR 819; Case 218/86 *Sar Schotte GmbH v Parfums Rothschild Sarl* [1987] ECR 4905. See also Case C-439/93 *Lloyd's Register of Shipping v Société Campenon Bernard* [1995] ECR I-961. See also Case C-154/11 *Ahmed Mahamdia v République algérienne démocratique et populaire* EU:C:2012:491, [2014] All ER (EC) 96, a case on Section 5 of Chapter II concerning individual contracts of employment—an embassy may be an establishment in a claim against a foreign state arising from the activities of its embassy.

[770] The approach in *Harada Ltd T/A Chequepoint UK Ltd v Turner* [2000] IL Pr 574 at [23], EAT, which simply looked at the fact that there was a registered branch in England must be regarded as being wrong.

[771] The Advocate General in the *De Bloos* case gave his opinion that the autonomy of an agency is less marked than that of a branch.

[772] Case 33/78 [1978] ECR 2183; Hartley (1979) 4 ELR 127.

[773] See also the *Blanckaert* case at [12].

[774] Cf the *Harada* case at [23], which must be regarded as wrong.

[775] Case 139/80 [1981] ECR 819; Hartley (1981) 6 ELR 481.

The Court of Justice, emphasising the need for the intermediary to be under the direction and control of the parent, held that such an agent did not have the character of a branch, agency or other establishment.[776]

The requirement of direction and control had first been introduced in *De Bloos v Bouyer*[777] which concerned an exclusive distributor rather than a commercial agent.

> The defendant French company granted exclusive distribution rights in Belgium for its products to the plaintiff Belgian company. The question arose of whether the plaintiff could sue the defendant in Belgium on the basis that the plaintiff was a Belgian branch, agency or other establishment of the defendant.

The Court of Justice held that it could not do so where the grantee of the concession was not subject to the direction and control of the parent. This would be the situation with a typical grantee. The Court of Justice also made it clear that "an establishment" is based on the same essential characteristics as a branch or agency. Finally, it emerges from the case that Article 7(5) is designed for third parties who wish to sue the parent. It is doubtful whether an intermediary can ever rely on its own presence within a Member State to found jurisdiction in an action brought by it against the parent.[778] To allow this would, in effect, give the claimant the right to sue in his own domicile whenever Article 7(5) is applicable. A third party claimant who wishes to found jurisdiction on Article 7(5) will not necessarily be suing in the state where he is domiciled.

The Court of Justice was faced with a case involving a subsidiary company carrying on business through its parent in *Sar Schotte GmbH v Parfums Rothschild Sarl*.[779]

> The plaintiff German company provided atomisers to the defendant French company (French Rothschild). The defendant company was a wholly-owned subsidiary of a German company (German Rothschild). The plaintiff wished to sue the French defendant in Germany for the price of the atomisers supplied, and argued that German Rothschild was an "establishment" of French Rothschild.

The Court of Justice held that what is now Article 7(5) would apply, even though under company law German Rothschild was an independent company with a separate legal personality.[780] German Rothschild and French Rothschild had the same name and identical management, and German Rothschild negotiated and conducted business in the name of French Rothschild, which used German Rothschild as an extension of itself and would appear as such to third parties.[781] The place of business of the branch, etc does not have to be owned by the defendant. The same principles will doubtless also apply in the more common situation where a parent carries on business through its subsidiary. This case shows that an "establishment" under Article 7(5) has a different meaning from a "branch" in so far as it covers a body with a separate legal personality. However, this is not much of an advance. German Rothschild only came within Article 7(5) because it acted, in effect, as if it were a branch of French Rothschild. The case is unusual in that a typical parent or subsidiary will act for

---

[776] See also *New Hampshire Insurance Co v Strabag Bau AG* [1990] 2 Lloyd's Rep 61 at 68–9; appeal dismissed [1992] 1 Lloyd's Rep 361, CA.

[777] Case 14/76 [1976] ECR 1497; Hartley (1977) 2 ELR 61.

[778] See the Advocate General's opinion at 1519.

[779] Case 218/86 [1987] ECR 4905; Allwood (1988) 13 ELR 213. See *Zellner v Philip Alexander Securities and Futures Ltd* [1997] IL Pr 716, District Court Krefeld.

[780] There was previously considerable uncertainty over this situation: see the opinion of the Advocate General in *De Bloos, Somafer* and *Blanckaert*.

[781] See also Case C-89/91 *Shearson Lehman Hutton Inc v TVB Treuhandgesellschaft für Vermögensverwaltung und Beteiligungen mbH* [1993] ECR I-139 at 169–72 (per AG Darmon).

itself and not on behalf of its subsidiary or parent, and will thus be outside the ambit of Article 7(5).

(ii) The dispute must arise out of the operations of the branch, agency or other establishment
This provision ensures that the Member State given jurisdiction under Article 7(5) is an appropriate one for trial. It presupposes that the branch, agency or other establishment has power to carry out activities itself (albeit on behalf of the parent); this ties in with the requirement, already mentioned, that the intermediary must have a certain autonomy. In the *Somafer* case the Court of Justice identified three sorts of actions comprised within the concept of a dispute arising out of the operations of a branch, agency or other establishment.[782] First, there are actions concerning the management of the intermediary "such as those concerning the situation of the building . . . or the local engagement of staff to work there".[783] Secondly, there are actions relating to undertakings entered into in the name of the parent in the place where the intermediary is situated.[784] The Court of Justice subsequently, in *Lloyd's Register of Shipping v Société Campenon Bernard*,[785] held that the undertakings given by the intermediary might be performed outside the Member State where the intermediary was established, possibly by another ancillary establishment such as another branch office. The Court of Appeal in *Anton Durbeck GmbH v Den Norske Bank Asa*[786] regarded the *Lloyd's Register* case as demonstrating that there must be such nexus between the branch, etc and the dispute as to render it natural to describe the dispute as one that has arisen out of the activities of the branch.[787] Where the claim is in contract, that nexus can be derived from the negotiations between the claimant and the branch, etc which give rise to the contractual obligation, the alleged breach of which is the subject of the dispute.[788] This would include a case where the branch, etc conducts all the negotiations but the final contract is signed by the parent.[789] Thirdly, there are non-contractual actions arising from the activities of the intermediary. The Court of Appeal in *Anton Durbeck* has held, in the light of the *Lloyd's Register* case, that these activities do not have to be carried out at the place where the branch, etc is established.[790] Nor must the activities bring about the harmful event within the jurisdiction.[791] The same broad flexible criterion that applies in contract cases is equally applicable in tort cases, namely that there must be such nexus between the branch, etc and the dispute as to render it natural to describe the dispute as one that has arisen out of the activities of the branch.[792] It was not thought by

---

[782] But cf the *Harada* case at [22] which seems to have ignored this.

[783] [1978] ECR 2183 at 2192–3.

[784] See *Latchin (t/a Dinkha Latchin Associates) v General Mediterranean Holdings SA)* [2002] CLC 330 at [50]–[51].

[785] Case C-439/93 [1995] ECR I-961; Briggs (1995) 15 YEL 496; Hartley (1996) 21 ELR 162; Hill [1996] CJQ 94. See also the Advocate General in the *Sar Schotte* case at 4914–15. Cf the Court of Justice in the *Somafer* case at 2192–3.

[786] [2003] EWCA Civ 147, [2003] QB 1160—a case on Art 5(5) of the Lugano Convention. An appeal to the House of Lords on the question of a stay of the English proceedings was withdrawn, see infra, p 314. See also *McGraw-Hill International (UK) Ltd v Deutsche Apotheker- und Arztebank EG* [2014] EWHC 2436 (Comm) at [57]–[69], [2014] 2 Lloyd's Rep 523.

[787] The *Anton Durbeck* case, at [40].

[788] Ibid. The *Lloyd's Register* case at [20] supports this. See also *BNP Paribas SA v Anchorage Capital Europe LLP* [2013] EWHC 3073 (Comm) at [78].

[789] But cf the opinion of AG Slynn in Case 218/86 *SAR Schotte GmbH v Parfums Rothschild SARL* [1987] ECR 4905 at 4914. However, this was a case decided before the *Lloyd's Register* case with its wide view of the requirement that the dispute arises out of the operations of the branch, etc. Moreover, AG Slynn would have preferred to interpret the requirement widely to encompass this situation.

[790] The *Anton Durbeck* case at [40].

[791] Ibid, at [38]–[40].

[792] Ibid, at [40].

the Court of Appeal to be desirable to formulate any more specific test to determine whether a tortious dispute has arisen out of the activities of a branch.[793] The answer must depend on the facts of the individual case. In the instant case there was a tortious claim for wrongful interference with a bill of lading following the arrest of a ship, as a consequence of which its cargo perished. The Court of Appeal held that the dispute arose out of the activities of the defendants' London branch.[794] The loan in respect of which security over a ship was given was negotiated by the London branch of the defendant Norwegian bank. The decision to enforce the security by arresting the ship was taken in London and the instructions and power of attorney to arrest the ship were given by the London branch.

Article 7(6)[795] as regards a dispute brought against a settlor, trustee or beneficiary of a trust created by the operation of a statute, or by a written instrument, or created orally and evidenced in writing, in the courts of the Member State in which the trust is domiciled.[796]

Article 7(7)[797] as regards a dispute concerning the payment of remuneration claimed in respect of the salvage of a cargo or freight, in the court under the authority of which the cargo or freight in question:

(a) has been arrested to secure such payment, or

(b) could have been so arrested, but bail or other security has been given;

provided that this provision shall apply only if it is claimed that the defendant has an interest in the cargo or freight or had such an interest at the time of salvage.[798]

(b) Special jurisdiction under Article 8
Under Article 8 there are four further situations where the defendant may be sued in a Member State other than that of his domicile, as follows:

Article 8(1)[799] where he is one of a number of defendants, in the courts for the place where any one of them is domiciled, provided the claims are so closely connected that it is expedient to hear and determine them together to avoid the risk of irreconcilable judgments resulting from separate proceedings;[800]

A person domiciled in a Member State cannot be sued before the courts of another Member State in which an action has been brought against a co-defendant who is not domiciled in

---

[793] Ibid, at [41].

[794] Ibid, at [46].

[795] Art 5(6) of the Brussels I Regulation; Art 5(6) of the Brussels Convention.

[796] It does not apply to constructive or implied trusts. In order to determine where the trust is domiciled for the purposes of the Brussels I Recast, see Art 63(3) and SI 2001/3929, Art 3, Sch 1, para 12. English courts have jurisdiction in relation to trust disputes where the trust is governed by English law: *Gomez v Gomez-Monche Vives* [2008] EWHC 259 (Ch), [2009] Ch 245; Briggs (2008) 79 BYBIL 533. Domicile is tested as at the date of the proceedings: *Chellaram v Chellaram (No 2)* [2002] EWHC 632 (Ch), [2002] 3 All ER 17. For allocation within the United Kingdom, see para 7 of Sch 1 to SI 2001/3929. For the nature of the proceedings falling within Art 7(6) see the *Gomez* case. See also *G v G* [2015] EWHC 2101 (Fam) at [34], [2016] 4 WLR 22.

[797] Art 5(7) of the Brussels I Regulation; Art 5(7) of the Brussels Convention.

[798] See the Schlosser Report, pp 108–9. Salvage of a ship is dealt with under the Brussels Convention of 1952 on the Arrest of Seagoing Ships and the Brussels I Recast does not apply.

[799] Art 6(1) of the Brussels I Regulation; Art 6(1) of the Brussels Convention.

[800] See generally Fawcett (1995) 44 ICLQ 744, pp 749–54; Tang (2009) 34 ELR 80. Art 6(1) of the Brussels I Regulation was not available in matters relating to individual contracts of employment falling within Section 5 of Chapter II: Case C-462/06 *GlaxoSmithKline and Laboratories GlaxoSmithKline v Rouard* [2008] ECR I-3965; Harris (2008) 124 LQR 523. But now Art 20(1) of the Brussels I Recast states that it is without prejudice, in the case of proceedings brought against an employer, to Art 8(1).

any of the Member States.[801] The proceedings must be brought before the courts for the place in a Member State where one of the defendants (so-called anchor defendant) is domiciled.[802] It is not sufficient if the proceedings against the first defendant are brought on another basis of jurisdiction. If trial[803] is sought in England, the claimant has to establish a good arguable case that the first defendant was domiciled in England. The relevant time for determining domicile is that of process being issued, rather than at the time of its service on the first defendant[804] or at the time at which it was sought to join the additional defendants or at the time at which they were actually joined.[805] Article 8(1) does not require service on the first defendant prior to the issue or service of proceedings on other defendants.[806] Neither does it require that the defendants are defendants in the same set of proceedings; there can be separate actions in the same Member State.[807] Article 8(1) can apply even though an action is regarded under a national provision as inadmissible, eg because of bankruptcy acting as a procedural bar, from the time it is brought against the first defendant.[808] It can also apply where the action against the first defendant is withdrawn, eg because of an out-of-court settlement.[809] Article 8(1) is limited to cases where the same claimant or claimants bring proceedings against a locally domiciled defendant and a non-domiciliary defendant, and does not apply where one claimant sues a locally domiciled defendant and another claimant sues a non-domiciliary defendant.[810]

However, there is a danger of misuse of this provision with proceedings being brought against a number of defendants solely with the object of ousting the jurisdiction of the courts of the Member State in which one of the defendants is domiciled. Accordingly, the Brussels I Recast contains a proviso that "the claims are so closely connected that it is expedient to hear and determine them together to avoid the risk of irreconcilable judgments resulting from separate proceedings".[811] There is though no further need to establish separately that the claims were

---

[801] Case C-51/97 *Réunion Européenne SA v Spliethoff's Bevrachtingskantoor BV* [1998] ECR I-6511.

[802] Ibid, at [44]. The Hess, Pfeiffer and Schlosser Report, Study JLS/C4/2005/03, Final Version September 2007, para 878, recommended that consideration should be given to extending Art 8(1) so that other bases of jurisdiction are sufficient.

[803] There is no restriction in Art 8 on the type of action. It can include a claim for an anti-suit injunction: *The Eras EIL Actions* [1995] 1 Lloyd's Rep 64.

[804] *Canada Trust Co v Stolzenberg (No 2)* [2002] 1 AC 1 at 8–12 (per Lord Steyn), 22–3 (per Lord Hoffmann), 23 (per Lord Cooke), 23 (per Lord Hope), 26 (per Lord Hobhouse), HL. For the position where proceedings are brought in Scotland see Lord Hope at 23–6.

[805] *Petrotrade Inc v Smith* [1999] 1 WLR 457.

[806] The *Canada Trust* case at 12–13 (per Lord Steyn), 23 (per Lord Hoffmann), 23 (per Lord Cooke), 23 (per Lord Hope), 26 (per Lord Hobhouse).

[807] *Masri v Consolidated Contractors International (UK) Ltd* [2005] EWCA Civ 1436, [2006] 1 WLR 830.

[808] Case C-103/05 *Reisch Montage AG v Kiesel Baumaschinen Handels GmbH* [2006] ECR I-6827; Briggs [2006] LMCLQ 447.

[809] Case C-352/13 *Cartel Damage Claims (CDC) Hydrogen Peroxide SA v Akzo Nobel NV* EU:C:2015:335, [2015] QB 906. See also *Linuzs v Latmar Holdings Corp* [2013] EWCA Civ 4, [2013] IL Pr 19; *Stewart v Trafalgar House Steamship Co Ltd* 2013 SLT 834, a case on the Modified Regulation.

[810] *Madoff Securities International Ltd v Raven* [2011] EWHC 3102 (Comm), [2012] 2 All ER (Comm) 634.

[811] Under the Brussels Convention this requirement was laid down by the Court of Justice in Case 189/87 *Kalfelis v Schröder* [1988] ECR 5565, rather than being contained in the Convention. For example of where there was the requisite connection see Case C-352/13 *Cartel Damage Claims (CDC) Hydrogen Peroxide SA v Akzo Nobel NV* EU:C:2015:335, [2015] QB 906; see also *Carnoustie Universal SA v International Transport Workers' Federation* [2002] EWHC 1624 (Comm) at [120]–[134], [2002] 2 All ER (Comm) 657; *The Bank of Tokyo-Mitsubishi Ltd v Baskan Gida Sanayi Ve Pazarlama AS* [2004] EWHC 945 (Ch) at [216], [2004] 2 Lloyd's Rep 395; *King v Crown Energy Trading AG* [2003] EWHC 163 (Comm), [2003] IL Pr 28; *Oakley v Ultra Vehicle Design Ltd (In Liquidation)* [2005] EWHC 872 (Ch) at [55]–[56], [2005] IL Pr 55; *Et Plus SA v Welter* [2005] EWHC 2115 (Comm), [2006] 1 Lloyd's Rep 251; *Dadourian Group International Inc v Simms* [2006] EWCA Civ 399 at [34], [2006] 1 WLR 2499; *FKI Engineering Ltd v De Wind Holdings*

not brought with the sole object of ousting the jurisdiction of the courts of the Member State where one of the defendants was domiciled.[812]

The Court of Justice in *Roche Nederland BV v Primus* has left open the question whether "irreconcilable" should be widely construed as being equivalent to "contradictory".[813] Nevertheless, the Court of Justice went on to hold that in order that decisions may be regarded as contradictory it is not sufficient that there be a divergence in the outcome of the dispute, but that divergence must also arise in the context of the same situation of fact and law.[814] Thus, even under this broad definition, Article 8(1) was held not to apply where infringement proceedings are brought in a number of courts in different Member States in respect of a European patent granted in each of those States, against defendants domiciled in those States in respect of acts allegedly committed in their territory, since any divergences between the decisions given by the courts concerned would not arise in the context of the same factual and legal situation.[815] In this scenario, Article 8(1) was held not to apply even though the defendant companies belong to the same group and have acted in an identical or similar manner in accordance with a common policy elaborated by one of them.[816] The Court of Justice dealt with similar factual circumstances in two recent cases. *Eva-Maria Painer v Standard Verlags GmbH*[817] concerned a claim for copyright infringement by a freelance photographer against a number of newspaper and magazine publishers, one of which was domiciled in Austria, the others in Germany. Some of the newspapers and magazines were distributed in both Austria and Germany, others only in one of the two countries. Some of the defendants run websites on the internet. In these circumstances, the Court of Justice held that the application of Article 8(1) is not precluded solely because actions against several defendants for substantially identical copyright infringements are brought on national legal grounds which vary according to the Member States concerned, provided that it was foreseeable by the defendants that they might be sued in the Member State where at least one of them is domiciled.[818] When assessing whether there is the requisite connection, the national court may take into

---

Ltd [2008] EWCA Civ 316, [2009] 1 All ER (Comm) 118; *Cooper Tire & Rubber Co Europe Ltd v Shell Chemicals UK Ltd* [2010] EWCA Civ 864, [2010] Bus LR 1697; *Gard Marine and Energy Ltd v Tunnicliffe* [2010] EWCA Civ 1052, [2011] 2 All ER (Comm) 208; *Linuzs v Latmar Holdings Corp* [2013] EWCA Civ 4, [2013] IL Pr 19; *Shannon v Global Tunnelling Experts UK Ltd* [2015] EWHC 1267 (QB); *Global Garden Products Italy SpA, Re* [2016] EWHC 1884 (Ch); *Lifestyle Equities CV v Sportsdirect.com Retail Ltd* [2017] EWHC 154 (Ch). There was no requisite connection in Case C-366/13 *Profit Investment SIM SpA v Stefano Ossi* EU:C:2016:282, [2016] 1 WLR 3832—the mere fact that the result of one of the procedures may have an effect on the result of the other does not suffice. The concern is whether there is the requisite connection as at the time of institution of the proceedings: the *Kalfelis* case at [12]; *Messier Dowty Ltd v Sabena SA* [2000] 1 WLR 2040 at [50], CA, noted by Briggs (2000) 71 BYBIL 455.

[812] Case C-98/06 *Freeport plc v Olle Arnoldsson* [2007] ECR I-8319 at [54].

[813] Case C-539/03 [2006] ECR I-6535 at [22]–[25]; Briggs [2006] LMCLQ 447. "Irreconcilable" for the purposes of Art 22 of the Brussels Convention (Art 30 of the Brussels I Recast) is defined in terms of "contradictory", see infra, pp 454–5. "Irreconcilable" for the purposes of Art 27(3) of the Brussels Convention (Art 45(1)(c) of the Brussels I Recast) is defined as entailing mutually exclusive legal consequences, see infra, pp 639–40. AG Leger at [71]–[106] gave his opinion that a narrower definition should be given to "irreconcilable" in the context of what is now Art 8(1); cf Case C-145/10 *Eva-Maria Painer v Standard Verlags GmbH* EU:C:2011, Opinion of AG Trstenjak at [58]–[71].

[814] However, there is no requirement that the legal bases of the claims against the two defendants are the same, see Case C-98/06 *Freeport plc v Olle Arnoldsson* [2007] ECR I-8319, infra, pp 286–7.

[815] Case C-539/03 *Roche Nederland BV v Primus* [2006] ECR I-6535—factually, the defendants were different and the infringements allegedly committed in different Member States were not the same, and legally each patent was governed by different national laws ([27]–[32]). See also *Fort Dodge Animal Health Ltd v Akzo Nobel NV* [1998] FSR 222, CA; *Coin Controls Ltd v Suzo International (UK) Ltd* [1999] Ch 33 at 52. See generally Fawcett and Torremans, pp 181–3.

[816] The *Roche Nederland BV v Primus* case.

[817] Case C-145/10 EU:C:2011:798; Torremans [2014] IPQ 1.

[818] The *Painer* case, at [81], [84].

account whether or not the defendants acted independently.[819] In *Solvay SA v Honeywell Fluorine Products Europe BV*,[820] unlike in the *Roche* case, the defendants domiciled in different Member States were each separately accused before the courts of one of those states of committing an infringement of the same national part of a European patent, which was in force in yet another Member State, by virtue of their performance of reserved actions with regard to the same product. In these circumstances, the Court of Justice held that potential divergences in the outcome of the proceedings are likely to arise in the same situation of fact and law, so that it is possible that they will culminate in irreconcilable judgments from separate proceedings.[821] It is for the national court to assess whether such a risk exists.[822] But with the entry into force of the Agreement on a Unified Patent Court,[823] disputes pertaining to European patents will be submitted to this court.[824]

According to earlier English case law, judgments may be irreconcilable because they involve inconsistent findings of fact, or inconsistent legal conclusions drawn from those facts.[825] This appears to fit in with what was later said in the *Roche* case. However, English case law providing that judgments may be irreconcilable because they involve contradictory remedies[826] falls foul of the statement in *Roche* that a mere divergence in the outcome of the dispute is not enough. If the claims against the various defendants are substantially the same in law and fact, such as where the defendants are joint debtors or joint tortfeasors,[827] there is an obvious risk of irreconcilable judgments. Even where the claims are largely based on different facts, there can be a risk of an inconsistent finding of fact in relation to a particular central matter.[828] In contrast, there is no such risk if the case just concerns England and Scotland and is going to go on appeal to the House of Lords, whose judgment would be binding on both law districts.[829] The Court of Justice has held that the fact that claims brought against a number of defendants have different legal bases does not preclude the application of Article 8(1).[830] An example of this would be where the claim against one defendant is based on contractual liability and the claim against the other defendant is based on liability in tort or delict.[831] It is

---

[819] Ibid, at [83].

[820] Case C-616/10 EU:C:2012:445; Torremans [2014] IPQ 1.

[821] The *Solvay* case, at [27].

[822] For factors that the national court should take into account see ibid at [28], [29].

[823] OJ 2013 C175/1.

[824] European Parliament and Council Regulation (EU) No 542/2014 amending Regulation (EU) No 1215/2012 as regards the rules to be applied with respect to the Unified Patent Court and the Benelux Court of Justice OJ 2014 L163/1, which keeps the existing jurisdictional rules in relation to claims against defendants domiciled in a Member State, whilst submitting defendants domiciled outside the European Union to the jurisdictional rules of the Brussels I Recast.

[825] *Gascoigne v Pyrah* [1994] IL Pr 82, CA; *Casio Computer Co Ltd v Sayo* [2001] EWCA Civ 661, [2001] IL Pr 43—applying the analogy of Art 22 of the Brussels Convention (Art 30 of the Brussels I Recast), discussed infra, pp 454–5; *Latchin (t/a Dinkha Latchin Associates) v General Mediterranean Holdings SA* [2002] CLC 330. See also *MacDonald v FIFA* 1999 SLT 1129; *Compagnie Commercial Andre SA v Artibell Shipping Co Ltd* 1999 SLT 1051. But see *Watson v First Choice Holidays* [2001] EWCA Civ 972, [2001] 2 Lloyd's Rep 339, which referred to the Court of Justice the question whether judgments can be irreconcilable when this is based on irreconcilable findings of fact but the case was subsequently removed from the register.

[826] *The Eras EIL Actions* [1995] 1 Lloyd's Rep 64 at 78–9—an English court would grant an anti-suit injunction against a defendant when a foreign court, faced with essentially the same facts, would not.

[827] See, eg, *Pearce v Ove Arup Partnership Ltd* [2000] Ch 403, CA. See also *Chiron Corpn v Evans Medical Ltd* [1996] FSR 863, involving a licensee under a patent.

[828] The *Gascoigne* case.

[829] *Barclays Bank plc v Glasgow City Council* [1994] QB 404, CA.

[830] Case C-98/06 *Freeport plc v Olle Arnoldsson* [2007] ECR I-8319 at [47].

[831] The *Freeport* case. Earlier obiter dicta in Case C-51/97 *Réunion Européenne SA v Spliethoff's Bevrachtingskantoor BV* [1998] ECR I-6511 at [50], that have been interpreted as laying down a requirement that the legal bases were the same, were regarded in *Freeport* at [42]–[46] (and see AG Mengozzi at [32]–[46]),

for the national court to assess whether there is a risk of irreconcilable judgments if the claims are tried separately and to take into account all the necessary factors in the case file.[832] This may lead it to take into consideration the legal bases of the actions. In some circumstances, a claim against one defendant in contract and the other in tort can, if the claims are tried separately, lead to the risk of irreconcilable judgments.[833] In such a case, Article 8(1) will apply.

Again to prevent abuse, English courts have held that there are additional requirements to be satisfied before this provision can be used,[834] although the Court of Appeal has questioned recently whether this is consistent with the autonomous interpretation of Article 8(1).[835] First, English courts have held that there must be a valid claim[836] against the defendant domiciled in the forum.[837] The Court of Justice has effectively confirmed this requirement by saying that Article 8(1) cannot be interpreted in such a way as to allow a plaintiff to make a claim against a number of defendants for the sole purpose of removing one of them from the jurisdiction of the courts of the Member State in which that defendant is domiciled.[838] The national court can find that Article 8(1) has potentially been circumvented only where there is firm evidence to support the conclusion that the applicant artificially fulfilled, or prolonged the fulfilment of, that provision's applicability.[839] Secondly, English courts have held that the second defendant must be a necessary or proper party to the action against the first defendant.[840] This was not satisfied where a German domiciled defendant was added merely in order to obtain discovery of documents.[841]

---

as being confined to the facts of that case and interpreted (somewhat unconvincingly) as just reinforcing the point that Art 8(1) only applies where proceedings are brought in a Member State where one of the defendants is domiciled. See also Case C 645/11 *Land Berlin v Ellen Mirjam Sapir* EU:C:2013:228, [2013] IL Pr 29, in particular [47].

[832] The *Freeport* case at [41].

[833] See *Watson v First Choice Holidays* [2001] EWCA Civ 972 at [31], [2001] 2 Lloyd's Rep 339. Cf *Messier Dowty Ltd v Sabena SA* [2000] 1 WLR 2040 at [50], CA. If the claims against both defendants are in both contract and tort it may be possible to show the requisite connection, see *Clodagh Daly v Irish Group Travel Limited Trading as "Crystal Holidays"* [2003] IL Pr 38, Irish High Court.

[834] Requirements to be found under the multi-defendant provision under the traditional rules, CPR, r 6.36 and CPR Practice Direction 6B, para 3.1(3), discussed infra, pp 336–9.

[835] *Joint Stock Co Aeroflot Russian Airlines v Berezovsky* [2013] EWCA Civ 784 at [101]–[110], [2013] 2 Lloyd's Rep 242; but the scope of the *Aeroflot* decision has been interpreted restrictively in *Misland (Cyprus) Investments Ltd v McKillen* [2014] EWHC 3859 (Ch) at [45]–[58], with reference to *Sabbagh v Khoury* [2014] EWHC 3233 (Comm) at [88]–[99], appeal pending.

[836] As at the date of the issue of the claim form: *Zair v Eastern Health and Social Services Board* [1999] IL Pr 823, CA.

[837] The *Rewia* [1991] 2 Lloyd's Rep 325 at 335–6, CA; the *Gascoigne* case; *Gannon v B & I Steam Packet Co Ltd* [1994] IL Pr 405, Irish Supreme Court; *Kelly v McCarthy* [1994] IL Pr 29, Irish High Court; *The Xing Su Hai* [1995] 2 Lloyd's Rep 15; *Andrew Weir Shipping Ltd v Wartsila UK Ltd* [2004] EWHC 1284 (Comm), [2004] 2 Lloyd's Rep 377; *Nokia Corp v AU Optronics Corp* [2012] EWHC 731 (Ch); *Et Plus SA v Welter* [2005] EWHC 2115 (Comm) at [59], [2006] 1 Lloyd's Rep 251; *FKI Engineering Ltd v Dewind Holdings Ltd* [2008] EWCA Civ 316 at [18], [2009] 1 All ER (Comm) 118; *Madoff Securities International Ltd v Raven* [2011] EWHC 3102 (Comm) at [83]–[125], [2012] 2 All ER (Comm) 634; *Bord Na Mona Horticulture Ltd v British Polythene Industries Plc* [2012] EWHC 3346 (Comm) at [75]–[83]—a real or serious issue to be tried or real prospect of success. There must also be a serious issue to be tried against the non-domiciliary defendant: *Brown v Innovatorone Plc (In Liquidation)* [2010] EWHC 2281 (Comm) at [25], [2011] IL Pr 9.

[838] Case C-103/05 *Reisch Montage AG v Kiesel Baumaschinen Handels GmbH* [2006] ECR I-6827 at [32].

[839] Case C-352/13 *Cartel Damage Claims (CDC) Hydrogen Peroxide SA v Akzo Nobel NV* EU:C:2015:335 at [29], [2015] QB 906. See also *Sibir Energy Ltd v Tchigirinski* [2012] EWHC 1844 (QB) at [30]–[31], [2012] 2 All ER (Comm) 1285.

[840] *Mölnlycke AB v Procter & Gamble Ltd (No 4)* [1992] 1 WLR 1112, CA; *Oakley v Ultra Vehicle Design Ltd (In Liquidation)* [2005] EWHC 872 (Ch) at [56], [2005] IL Pr 55; *Misland (Cyprus) Investments Ltd v McKillen* [2014] EWHC 3859 (Ch) at [61], [69].

[841] The *Mölnlycke* case at 1116–7. Cf *Messier Dowty Ltd v Sabena SA* [2000] 1 WLR 2040 at [49], CA.

Article 8(2)[842] as a third party in an action on a warranty or guarantee or in any other third-party proceedings,[843] in the court seised of the original proceedings, unless these were instituted solely with the object of removing him from the jurisdiction of the court which would be competent in his case.[844]

Article 8(3)[845] on a counterclaim[846] arising from the same contract or facts on which the original claim was based,[847] in the court in which the original claim is pending.

Article 8(4)[848] in matters relating to a contract, if the action may be combined with an action against the same defendant in matters relating to rights *in rem* in immovable property, in the court of the Member State in which the property is situated.[849]

(c) Special jurisdiction under Article 9

Article 9[850] provides that:

Where by virtue of this Regulation a court of a Member State has jurisdiction in actions relating to liability from the use or operation of a ship, that court, or any other court substituted

---

[842] Art 6(2) of the Brussels I Regulation; Art 6(2) of the Brussels Convention.

[843] For England, see CPR, Part 20.

[844] See also Art 65. See Case C-365/88 *Kongress Agentur Hagen GmbH v Zeehaghe BV* [1990] ECR I-1845; Hartley (1991) 16 ELR 73; North, in *Nouveaux itinéraires en droit: Hommage à Rigaux* (1993), p 373. See also *Kinnear v Falconfilms NV* [1996] 1 WLR 920; *Waterford Wedgwood plc v David Nagli Ltd* [1999] IL Pr 9; *Caltex Trading Pte Ltd v Metro Trading International Inc* [1999] 2 Lloyd's Rep 724; *National Justice Compania Naviera SA v Prudential Assurance Co Ltd (No 2)* [2000] 1 WLR 603, CA; *Knauf UK GmbH v British Gypsum Ltd (No 2)* [2002] EWHC 739 (Comm), [2002] 2 Lloyd's Rep 416; *British Sugar plc v Babbini* [2004] EWHC 2560 (TCC), [2005] 1 Lloyd's Rep 332; *Barton v Golden Sun Holidays Ltd* [2007] EWHC 3455 (QB), [2007] IL Pr 57; *Shetty v Al Rushaid Petroleum Investment Co* [2011] EWHC 1460 (Ch); *McGraw-Hill International (UK) Ltd v Deutsche Apotheker- und Arztebank EG* [2014] EWHC 2436 (Comm) at [39]–[45], [2014] 2 Lloyd's Rep 523; *Iveco SpA v Magna Electronics Srl (formerly Italamec Srl)* [2015] EWHC 2887 (TCC) at [48], [2016] IL Pr 18; *Roberts v Soldiers, Sailors, Airmen and Families Association-Forces Help* [2016] EWHC 2744 (QB); *PHP Tobacco Carib Sarl v BAT Caribbean SA* [2016] EWHC 3377 (Comm), appeal pending. On the proviso under Art 8(2), see *Hough v P & O Containers Ltd* [1999] QB 834. Art 25 takes priority over Art 8(2): the *Hough* case. Art 8(2) is applicable to third-party proceedings between insurers based on multiple insurance, in so far as there is a sufficient connection between the original proceedings and the third party proceedings to support the conclusion that the choice of forum does not amount to an abuse: Case C-77/04 *GIE Réunion Européenne v Zurich España* [2005] IL Pr 456. Art 8(2) is also applicable to an action brought by a third party, in accordance with national law, against the defendant in the original proceedings, where that action is closely linked to the original proceedings and seeks reimbursement of compensation paid by that third party to the claimant in the original proceedings: Case C-521/14 *SOVAG—Schwarzmeer und Ostsee Versicherungs-Aktiengesellschaft v If Vahinkovakuutusyhtiö Oy* EU:C:2016:41, [2016] QB 780.

[845] Art 6(3) of the Brussels I Regulation; Art 6(3) of the Brussels Convention.

[846] This does not cover set-off as a defence: Case C-341/93 *Danvaern Production A/S v Schuhfabriken Otterbeck GmbH & Co* [1995] ECR I-2053; Briggs (1995) 15 YEL 498; Hartley (1996) 21 ELR 166. This does cover a counterclaim for reimbursement on the ground of unjust enrichment of a payment made under an extrajudicial settlement reached following a judgment that was subsequently set aside: Case C-185/15 *Kostanjevec v F&S Leasing GmbH* EU:C:2016:763, [2017] 4 WLR 7. See also *Dollfus Mieg & Cie v CDW International Ltd* [2004] IL Pr 12—counterclaim does not include a cross-claim by a person not an original defendant, on which see also *Jordan Grand Prix v Baltic Insurance Group* [1999] 2 AC 127, HL, concerning Art 14(2), discussed, infra, p 290. For criticism of a restrictive German interpretation, see Sturner [2007] IPRax 41.

[847] This is not to be construed in the same way as "related actions" under Art 30(3) of the Brussels I Recast (infra, pp 454–6): the Opinion of AG Léger in the *Danvaern* case at 2068–70. The question whether it is a more restrictive concept was referred to the Court of Justice by the District Court in Luxembourg in *Reichling v Wampach* [2002] IL Pr 42 but the Court of Justice in Case C-69/02 [2002] ECR I-3393 held that that court was not authorised to request a reference. See also Case C-185/15 *Kostanjevec v F&S Leasing GmbH* EU:C:2016:763, [2017] 4 WLR 7—a counterclaim for reimbursement on the ground of unjust enrichment arises from the leasing contract from which the lessor's original action originated.

[848] Art 6(4) of the Brussels I Regulation; Art 6(4) of the Brussels Convention.

[849] See the Almeida Cruz, Desantes Real and Jenard Report, para 24.

[850] Art 7 of the Brussels I Regulation; Art 7 of the Brussels C\onvention.

for this purpose by the internal law of that Member State, shall also have jurisdiction over claims for limitation of such liability.[851]

(v) Jurisdiction in matters relating to insurance

Scope of Section 3 of Chapter II   Section 3 of Chapter II of the Brussels I Recast (Articles 10 to 16)[852] deals with matters relating to insurance,[853] although it does not define the term. Section 3 does not apply to disputes between a reinsurer and a reinsured in connection with a reinsurance contract because neither party is in a weaker position vis à vis the other, but it does apply to disputes between the policy-holder, the insured or a beneficiary and the reinsurer.[854] It also does not apply where the claim is brought by a social security institution, acting as the statutory assignee of the rights of the injured party.[855] Generally, it only applies in the situation where the defendant is domiciled in a Member State,[856] although there is the exception of the situation where there is an agreement as to jurisdiction under Article 15. An extended meaning is given to domicile in this context.[857] Where an insurer not domiciled in a Member State has a branch, agency or other establishment in a Member State, and the dispute arises out of the latter's operations,[858] the insurer is deemed to be domiciled in that State.[859] Unlike some of the provisions concerning consumer and individual employment contracts, the international scope of the rules of jurisdiction in Section 3 has not been extended to cover claims against the typically stronger party, ie the insurer, not domiciled in a Member State. The provisions contained in Section 3 are exclusive.[860] Where they apply it is not possible to rely on other bases of jurisdiction under the Brussels I Recast.[861] It differs from exclusive jurisdiction under Section 6 in two important respects. First, jurisdiction is not assigned to a single Member State under Section 3; instead the claimant, where he is the weaker party, is allowed a limited choice of forum. Secondly, the parties may in certain

---

[851]   See the Schlosser Report, pp 109–10; the Hess, Pfeiffer and Schlosser Report, paras 253–78. For service out of the jurisdiction see *ICL Shipping Ltd v Chin Tai Steel Enterprise Co Ltd* [2004] 1 All ER (Comm) 246.

[852]   Arts 8–14 of the Brussels I Regulation; Arts 7–12A of the Brussels Convention (on which see the Schlosser Report, pp 112–17).

[853]   This does not include third-party proceedings between insurers based on alleged multiple insurance: Case C-77/04 *GIE Réunion européenne v Zurich España* [2005] ECR I-4509; *Youell v La Reunion Aerienne* [2008] EWHC 2493 (Comm), [2009] IL Pr 23, affd without discussion of this point in [2009] EWCA Civ 175, [2009] 2 All ER (Comm) 1071. "Insurance" does not cover an application by insurers for costs against a non-party under the Supreme Court Act 1981 (now Senior Courts Act 1981), s 51 even though there were main proceedings relating to insurance: *National Justice Compañía Naviera SA v Prudential Assurance Co Ltd (No 2)* [2000] 1 WLR 603 at 616, CA.

[854]   Case C-412/98 *Group Josi Reinsurance Co SA v Universal General Insurance Co UGIC* [2000] ECR I-5925. See also *Agnew v Lansförsäkringsbolagens AB* [2001] 1 AC 223 at 238–9 (per Lord Woolf), 233–4 (per Lord Nicholls), 245–6 (per Lord Cooke), 249 (per Lord Hope), 262 (per Lord Millett), HL.

[855]   Case C-347/08 *Vorarlberger Gebietskrankenkasse v WGV-Schwäbische Allgemeine Versicherungs AG* [2009] ECR I-8661; this rule does not apply where the claim is brought by the heirs of the injured party: ibid at [44].

[856]   See Art 10, which says that Section 3 is without prejudice to Art 6; see also Arts 11 and 14.

[857]   Art 11(2). For the application of this provision within the United Kingdom (the Modified Regulation does not have such a provision), see SI 2001/3929, Art 3, Sch 1, para 11.

[858]   For the interpretation of this phrase see the opinion of AG Elmer in Case C-439/93 *Lloyd's Register of Shipping v Société Campenon Bernard* [1995] ECR I-961 at 971.

[859]   See the opinion of AG Léger in Case C-281/02 *Owusu v Jackson* [2005] ECR I-1383 at [132]–[134]. See, eg, *S & W Berisford plc v New Hampshire Insurance Co* [1990] 2 QB 631. The appointment of a claims representative does not in itself constitute an establishment: Art 21(6) of European Parliament and Council Directive 2009/103/EC relating to insurance against civil liability in respect of the use of motor vehicles, and the enforcement of the obligation to insure against such liability OJ 2009 L 263/11.

[860]   Art 10, which is without prejudice to Arts 6 and 7(5).

[861]   Art 26 is an exception to this: Art 26(2).

limited circumstances depart from the provisions of Section 3. These two aspects of Section 3 will be examined in more detail.

Jurisdictional rules in Section 3 of Chapter II   Section 3 contains protective provisions, designed to protect the party in a weaker position.[862] In a dispute between the policyholder (ie the other party to the contract of insurance),[863] the insured or a beneficiary, on the one hand, and the insurer, on the other, this will be the policyholder, the insured or a beneficiary.[864] The claimant is given a choice of forum when suing the defendant insurer. According to Article 11(1), where the insurer is the defendant he can be sued: (a) in the Member State where he is domiciled; or (b) in another Member State, in the case of actions brought by the policyholder, the insured or a beneficiary, in the courts for the place where the claimant is domiciled; or (c) if he is a co-insurer, in the courts of a Member State in which proceedings are brought against the leading insurer.[865] Where the insurer is the claimant, he is given no choice of forum. According to Article 14 he may bring proceedings only in the courts of the Member State in which the defendant is domiciled,[866] whether he is the policyholder, the insured or a beneficiary.[867] Article 14 can be used by a claimant insurer who is not domiciled in any Member State.[868]

The policy of favouring the insured party has been strongly criticised by English lawyers; it gives an unwarranted opportunity for the insured to forum-shop, and is based on the erroneous assumption that the insured is always the weaker party, whereas, in reality, the insured may be a wealthy enterprise which is every bit as strong as the insurer.[869] Nonetheless, Section 3 will still operate.[870]

Jurisdiction Agreements and Submission   The validity of this criticism is lessened to some extent by the fact that Section 3 can be departed from by an agreement on jurisdiction. Article 15 requires the agreement to satisfy one of five alternatives set out in that

---

[862] Recitals (18) and (19) of the Brussels I Recast.

[863] See the Jenard Report, p 31; the Schlosser Report, p 117.

[864] The right (granted under the Brussels Convention) of the policyholder as claimant to sue in his domicile was extended to the insured and to a beneficiary by the Brussels I Regulation.

[865] The options are extended in cases of liability insurance, or insurance of immovable property, see Arts 12 and 13. Art 13(2) allows the injured party to bring an action directly against the insurer (eg in England under the Third Parties (Rights Against Insurers) Act 2010) before the courts for the place in a Member State where that injured party is domiciled, provided that such a direct action is permitted and the insurer is domiciled in a Member State: Case C-463/06 *FBTO Schadeverzekeringen NV v Odenbreit* [2007] ECR I-11321; see also *Maher v Grouprama Grand Est* [2009] EWCA Civ 1191, [2010] 1 WLR 1564; Briggs (2009) 80 BYBIL 619; *Jones v Assurances Generales de France (AGF) SA* [2010] IL Pr 4, Mayor's and City of London Court; *Thwaites v Aviva Assurances* [2010] IL Pr 47, Mayor's and City of London Court; *Keefe v Mapfre Mutualidad Cia De Seguros Y Reaseguros SA* [2015] EWCA Civ 598, [2016] 1 WLR 905, appeal pending; Ulfbeck [2011] LMCLQ 293.

[866] Or, in the case of a counterclaim (which means a counterclaim against the original claimant, ie not one involving new parties) in the Member State in which, in accordance with Section 3, the original claim is pending, see *Jordan Grand Prix Ltd v Baltic Insurance Group* [1999] 2 AC 127, HL. See also Art 13(3) for specific provision for the joinder of the policyholder or insured as a party to the action brought by the injured party directly against the insurer; *Maher v Grouprama Grand Est* [2009] EWCA Civ 1191 at [14]–[21], [2010] 1 WLR 1564; *Keefe v Mapfre Mutualidad Cia De Seguros Y Reaseguros SA* [2015] EWCA Civ 598, [2016] 1 WLR 905, appeal pending.

[867] This is not an exhaustive list, and Art 14 can apply to other defendants provided that the claim relates to insurance: *Jordan Grand Prix Ltd v Baltic Insurance Group* [1998] 1 WLR 1049, CA, affd by HL [1999] 2 AC 127, which found it unnecessary to discuss this point; Briggs (1998) 69 BYBIL 346.

[868] *Jordan Grand Prix Ltd v Baltic Insurance Group* [1999] 2 AC 127, HL.

[869] Collins, p 68, and in Lipstein (ed), *Harmonization of Private International Law by the EEC* (1978) 91, pp 99–100; Kerr (1978) 75 LS Gaz 1190, 1191.

[870] See *New Hampshire Insurance Co v Strabag Bau AG* [1992] 1 Lloyd's Rep 361, CA.

Article. These are as follows: (i) the agreement is entered into after the dispute has arisen; (ii) the agreement allows the policyholder, the insured or a beneficiary to bring proceedings in courts other than those indicated in Section 3;[871] (iii) the agreement is concluded between a policyholder and an insurer, both of whom are at the time of conclusion of the contract domiciled or habitually resident in the same Member State, and confers jurisdiction on the courts of that state even if the harmful event were to occur abroad, provided that such an agreement is not contrary to the law of that state;[872] (iv) the agreement is concluded with a policyholder who is not domiciled in a Member State except in so far as the insurance is compulsory or relates to immovable property in a Member State; (v) the agreement relates to a contract of insurance in so far as it covers one or more of the risks set out in Article 16.[873] The agreement would also have to satisfy the requirements relating to agreements as to jurisdiction under Article 25 of the Brussels I Recast.[874] Under Article 25, neither party has to be domiciled in a Member State.[875] Article 15 allows all the other provisions in Section 3 (including any requirement as to the defendant being domiciled in a Member State) to be departed from. It therefore appears that an agreement conferring jurisdiction in a matter relating to insurance does not require that the parties are domiciled in a Member State.[876] Articles 31(2) and 31(3) which provide for an exception to the general *lis pendens* rule in cases involving exclusive agreements on jurisdiction are not applicable to matters relating to insurance where the policyholder, the insured, a beneficiary of the insurance contract or the injured party is the claimant and the agreement is not valid under Article 15.[877] Section 3 can also be departed from by the defendant submitting to the courts of a Member State by entering an appearance under Article 26.[878] However, where the policyholder, the insured, a beneficiary of the insurance contract or the injured party is the defendant, the court shall, before assuming jurisdiction on the basis of submission by entering an appearance, ensure that the defendant is informed of his right to contest the jurisdiction of the court and of the consequences of entering or not entering an appearance.[879]

---

[871] See *Sherdley v Nordea Life and Pensions SA* [2012] EWCA Civ 88, [2013] IL Pr 26, which suggests that an exclusive jurisdiction agreement, entered into before the dispute has arisen, cannot be effective in an insurance dispute because it is not an agreement which "allows" (but requires) the weaker party to bring proceedings in courts other than those indicated in Section 3; Rushworth and Scott (2012) 83 BYBIL 293.

[872] The jurisdiction agreement cannot be relied upon against a beneficiary under the insurance contract who has not expressly subscribed to that clause and is domiciled in a Member State other than that of the policyholder and the insurer: Case C-112/03 *Société financière et industrielle du Peloux v Axa Belgium* [2005] ECR I-3707.

[873] See generally *Charman v WOC* [1993] 2 Lloyd's Rep 551, CA; *Charterers Mutual Assurance Association Ltd v British and Foreign* [1998] IL Pr 838 at 850; *Tradigrain SA v SIAT SpA* [2002] EWHC 106 (Comm) at [39]–[43], [2002] 2 Lloyd's Rep 553; *Minister for Agriculture, Food and Forestry v Alte Leipziger Versicherüng Aktiengesellschaft* [2002] 1 ILRM 306, Irish Supreme Court; *Standard Steamship Owners' Protection and Indemnity Association (Bermuda) Ltd v GIE Vision Bail* [2004] EWHC 2919 (Comm) at [58]–[64], [2005] 1 All ER (Comm) 618. The Brussels I Recast in Art 16(5) extends the risks to cover "large risks" as defined in European Parliament and Council Directive 2009/138/EC on the taking-up and pursuit of the business of insurance and reinsurance (Solvency II) OJ 2009 L 335/1.

[874] Case 201/82 *Gerling Konzern Speziale Kreditversicherungs-AG v Italian Treasury Administration* [1983] ECR 2503. For the need for an "agreement" under Art 25, see *Evialis SA v SIAT* [2003] EWHC 863 (Comm) at [59]–[69], [2003] 2 Lloyd's Rep 377. See also *Tradigrain SA v SIAT SpA* [2002] EWHC 106 (Comm) at [44]–[62], [2002] 2 Lloyd's Rep 553.

[875] Art 6(1).

[876] See Collins, p 51.

[877] Art 31(4).

[878] Art 26(2). For the same position under the Brussels I Regulation see Case C-111/09 *Česká podnikatel-ská pojišťovna as, Vienna Insurance Group v Bilas* [2010] ECR I-4545; Grušić (2011) 48 CMLR 947.

[879] Art 26(2).

(vi) Jurisdiction over consumer contracts[880]

Scope of Section 4 of Chapter II   Section 4 of Chapter II of the Brussels I Recast (Articles 17 to 19)[881] applies in matters relating to a contract concluded by a person, the consumer, for a purpose which can be regarded as being outside his trade or profession. This provision has been interpreted by the Court of Justice and domestic courts on many occasions. It has been held that, in order to fall within Section 4, the claim must be contractual in nature, but also that Section 4 extends to claims which are so closely linked to the consumer contract as to be indivisible. Thus a claim for a prize to be awarded on condition that the consumer ordered goods, which he did, fell within Section 4.[882] A contract has to have been concluded. Section 4 does not therefore ordinarily extend to a claim for a prize whose award is not conditional on placing an order, unless the trader has undertaken in law to pay that prize to the consumer or the consumer has in fact placed an order.[883] Nor does it extend to an action brought by a consumer who has acquired a bearer bond from a professional intermediary against the issuer of the bond, without a contract having been concluded between the consumer and the issuer.[884] But even if the claimant cannot rely on Section 4 where a contract has not been concluded, it may still be possible for him to rely on the general rule of jurisdiction in contractual matters in Article 7(1).[885] A consumer is regarded to be a person who concludes a contract for a purpose outside and independently of his present or future[886] trade or profession, ie solely for the purpose of satisfying his own needs in terms of private consumption.[887] The concept of "satisfying one's own needs in terms of private consumption" has been given a broad meaning by the English courts who regard as consumers private investors entering into foreign exchange contracts or purchasing property as investment.[888] But these decisions have been questioned and not followed in some recent cases.[889] The concept of "satisfying one's own needs in terms of private consumption" is in any event not so broad as to enable a natural person with close professional links to a company, ie its managing director or majority shareholder, to rely on Section 4 when he guarantees the obligations of the company.[890] Where a contract is concluded for purposes partly within and partly outside a trade or profession,

---

[880] Hill, *Cross-Border Consumer Contracts* (2008), Chapters 3 and 4; Cachia (2009) 34 ELR 476.

[881] Arts 15–17 of the Brussels I Regulation; Arts 13–15 of the Brussels Convention (on which see the Schlosser Report, pp 117–20).

[882] Case C-96/00 *Gabriel v Schlank & Schick GmbH* [2002] ECR I-6367 at [53]–[59].

[883] Case C-180/06 *Ilsinger v Dreschers (Administrator in the Insolvency of Schlank & Schick GmbH)* [2009] ECR I-3961. Cf Case C–27/02 *Engler v Janus Versand GmbH* [2005] ECR I-481 at [36]–[43]; *Re Jurisdiction in a claim based on a prize draw notification* [2007] IL Pr 15, German Bundesgerichtshof—the latter two cases are on Art 13(3) of the Brussels Convention that is worded differently from Art 17(1)(c) of the Brussels I Recast.

[884] Case C-375/13 *Kolassa v Barclays Bank Plc* EU:C:2015:37, [2016] 1 All ER (Comm) 733.

[885] The *Engler* case; the *Ilsinger* case; discussed supra, p 250.

[886] Case C-269/95 *Benincasa v Dentalkit Srl* [1997] ECR I-3767.

[887] Art 17(1); the *Benincasa* case.

[888] *Standard Bank London Ltd v Apostolakis (No 1)* [2002] CLC 933 at 936–7; cf the decision to the contrary of a Greek court when faced with the same facts in *Standard Bank London v Apostolakis* (Decision 8032/2001) [2003] IL Pr 29, Multi-Member First Instance Court Athens; *Taylor v Giovani Developers Ltd* [2015] EWHC 328 (Comm) at [40].

[889] *Maple Leaf Macro Volatility Master Fund v Rouvroy* [2009] EWHC 257 (Comm) at [202]–[209], [2009] 1 Lloyd's Rep 475; *AMT Futures Ltd v Marzillier, Dr Meier & Dr Guntner Rechtsanwaltsgesellschaft mbH* [2014] EWHC 1085 (Comm) at [56]–[59], [2015] 2 WLR 187, revd [2015] EWCA Civ 143, [2015] QB 699 and [2017] UKSC 13, [2017] 2 WLR 853 without discussion of this point; *AMT Futures Ltd v Grundmann* [2016] EWHC 3606 (QB). See also *Prostar Management Ltd v Twaddle 2003* SLT (Sh Ct) 11, a case on the Modified Convention (now Modified Regulation).

[890] Case C-419/11 *Česká spořitelna as v Feichter* EU:C:2013:165, [2013] IL Pr 22.

Section 4 applies if the business purpose is negligible.[891] The other party to the contract must be engaged in commercial or professional activities.[892] Where a consumer assigns his rights to a non-consumer, the latter cannot rely on Section 4 even if the consumer could have relied on it.[893] Similarly, a consumer protection organisation which brings an action on behalf of consumers cannot rely on Section 4.[894]

Furthermore, Section 4 applies only if the contract is one of the three alternative types listed in Article 17. The first type (Article 17(1)(a)) is a contract for the sale of goods[895] on instalment credit terms, a concept which has been given an autonomous meaning by the Court of Justice.[896] The second type (Article 17(1)(b)) is a contract for a loan repayable by instalments, or for any other form of credit, made to finance the sale of goods. The third type (Article 17(1)(c)) applies in all other cases and encompasses two alternatives. The first is where "the contract has been concluded with a person who pursues commercial or professional activities in the Member State of the consumer's domicile". The second alternative is where the contract has been concluded with a person who "by any means, directs such activities to that Member State or to several States including that Member State". In both cases the contract must fall within the scope of such activities. Art 17(1)(c) may even be applied to a contract concluded between a consumer and a professional which on its own does not come within the scope of the commercial or professional activities "directed" by that professional "to" the Member State of the consumer's domicile, but which is closely linked to a contract concluded beforehand by those parties in the context of such activities. The court should take into account whether the parties to both contracts are identical in law or in fact, whether the economic objectives of those contracts are identical, and whether the second contract complements the first contract in that it seeks to make it possible for the economic objective of the first contract to be achieved.[897]

Article 17(1)(c) is worded differently from its predecessor under the Brussels Convention[898] because of concerns over new means of communication and the development of electronic commerce.[899] The new wording involves three major changes when compared with its predecessor.

---

[891] Case C-464/01 *Gruber v Bay Wa AG* [2005] ECR I-439. The court cannot take account of facts or circumstances of which the other party may have been aware when the contract was concluded, unless the person wishing to rely on Section 4 behaved in such a way as to give the other party the legitimate impression that he was acting for the purposes of his business.

[892] Case C-508/12 *Vapenik v Thurner* EU:C:2013:790, [2014] 1 WLR 2486, a case on European Parliament and Council Regulation (EC) No 805/2004 creating a European Enforcement Order for uncontested claims OJ 2004 L 143/15; discussed infra, pp 656–9.

[893] Case C-89/91 *Shearson Lehman Hutton Inc v TVB Treuhandgesellschaft für Vermogensverwaltung und Beteiligungen mbH* [1993] ECR I-139; Briggs (1993) 13 YEL 511; Hartley (1994) 19 ELR 537; Plender (1993) 64 BYBIL 557.

[894] Case C-167/00 *Verein Für Konsumenteninformation v K H Henkel* [2002] ECR I-8111 at [33].

[895] This does not include sale of unit trusts: *Waverley Asset Management Ltd v Saha* 1989 SLT (Sh Ct) 87, a case on the Modified Convention (now Modified Regulation).

[896] Case 150/77 *Bertrand v Ott* [1978] ECR 1431; Hartley (1979) 4 ELR 47. This does not encompass a contract involving manufacture and payment in full (by instalments) before possession is transferred: Case C-99/96 *Mietz v Intership Yachting Sneek BV* [1999] ECR I-2277; Peel (2001) YEL 359.

[897] Case C-297/14 *Hobohm v Benedikt Kampik Ltd & Co KG* EU:C:2015:844, [2016] QB 616, concerning a transaction-management contract designed to achieve the economic objective of a brokerage contract concluded beforehand between the same parties.

[898] Art 13(3) of the Brussels Convention. The new wording was introduced by Art 15(1)(c) of the Brussels I Regulation.

[899] See generally on Art 17(1)(c) and e-commerce: Oren (2003) 52 ICLQ 665; Farah (2008) 33 ELR 257. See also Gillies, *Electronic Commerce and International Private Law: A Study of Electronic Consumer Contracts* (2008), Chapter 5; Tang, *Electronic Consumer Contracts in the Conflict of Laws* (2015) 2nd edn, Chapter 2.

First, Article 17(1)(c) just refers to "in all other cases" whereas its predecessor referred to "any other contract for the supply of goods or a contract for the supply of services".[900]

The second change is to introduce the concept of activities pursued in (under the first alternative) or directed towards (under the second alternative) a Member State. This replaces a requirement that in the state of the consumer's domicile the conclusion of the contract was preceded by a specific invitation addressed to him or by advertising. The old provision was very specific in naming the activities of the defendant in the consumer's domicile that would subject him to trial there. The new provision is much more general, merely referring to "activities" (without specifying what these are) pursued in or directed towards a Member State. However, the requirement, under the old provision, of positive conduct by the seller or provider of services, normally preceding the involvement of the consumer,[901] still applies in relation to the new provision under the Brussels I Recast.[902] The idea also remains that the trader must have taken steps to market his goods or services in the country where the consumer resides.[903] "Directing activities" towards a Member State can be "by any means". In order to determine whether the activities of a trader, which are presented on its website or on a website of an intermediary, have been directed towards a Member State, the court should ascertain whether it is apparent from those websites and the trader's overall activities that it has manifested its intention to conclude contracts with consumers domiciled in one or more Member States, including that Member State.[904] The Court of Justice has provided the following non-exhaustive list of relevant factors: the international nature of the activities, description of itineraries from other Member States to the place where the trader is established, use of a language or a currency not generally used in the Member State in which the trader is established, mention of a telephone number with an international code, disbursement of expenditure on an internet referencing service, use of a top-level domain name other than that of the Member State in which the trader is established or of a neutral top-level domain, and mention of an international clientele composed of customers domiciled in various Member States.[905] The mere accessibility of the trader's or the intermediary's website in a Member State is not sufficient;[906] nor is the mention of an email address, geographical address, telephone number without an international code, or the use of a language or a currency generally used in the Member State in which the trader is established.[907] Article 17(1)(c) does not require the contract between the consumer and the trader to be concluded in the Member State of the consumer's domicile or at a distance.[908] Nor does it require the existence

[900] For the importance of this difference in wording compare Case C-180/06 *Ilsinger v Dreschers (Administrator in the Insolvency of Schlank & Schick GmbH)* [2009] ECR I-3961 with Case C–27/02 *Engler v Janus Versand GmbH* [2005] ECR I-481 at [36]–[43].

[901] See *Rayner v Davies* [2002] EWCA Civ 1880 at [24] (per Mummery LJ), [2003] IL Pr 15—a case on Art 13(3) of the Brussels Convention of a consumer going to Italy where a surveyor was domiciled and negotiations carried on there but fax sent by surveyor to England with a formal offer, held no invitation by surveyor to consumer in England. Art 17(1)(c) of the Brussels I Recast would doubtless not be met either.

[902] See Joined Cases C-585/08 and C-144/09 *Pammer v Reederei Karl Schlüter GmbH & Co. KG and Hotel Alpenhof GesmbH v Heller* [2010] ECR I-12527 at [76].

[903] See Case C-96/00 *Gabriel v Schlanck & Schick GmbH* [2002] ECR I-6367 at [40]–[44]—a case on Art 13(3) of the Brussels Convention.

[904] Joined Cases C-585/08 and C-144/09 *Pammer v Reederei Karl Schlüter GmbH & Co. KG and Hotel Alpenhof GesmbH v Heller* [2010] ECR I-12527; Bogdan (2010) 12 YBPIL 565; Gillies (2011) 60 ICLQ 557.

[905] The *Pammer/Hotel Alpenhof* case.

[906] The Joint Statement by the Council and Commission on Arts 15 and 73 of the Brussels I Regulation (Art 15 is now Art 17 of the Brussels I Recast); cf the Explanatory Memorandum in the Proposal for a Council Regulation COM (1999) 348 final, p 16 (hereinafter "the Explanatory Memorandum").

[907] The *Pammer/Hotel Alpenhof* case.

[908] Case C-190/11 *Mühlleitner v Yusufi* EU:C:2012:542, [2012] IL Pr 46. Cf Explanatory Memorandum, p 16; the Joint Statement by the Council and Commission.

of a causal link between the means employed to direct the activities to the Member State of the consumer's domicile, ie a website, and the conclusion of the contract with that consumer.[909] But the conclusion of the contract at a distance and the existence of a causal link may constitute strong evidence that the trader's activities have been directed to the Member State in which the consumer is domiciled.

The third major change is to get rid of the condition in the predecessor provision[910] that the consumer must have taken necessary steps for the conclusion of the contract in his home state. This condition precluded the consumer from relying on Section 4 when he had been induced by the trader to leave his home state to conclude the contract.[911] The change was also prompted by a consideration of the position where contracts are concluded via an interactive website.[912] For such contracts the place where the consumer takes these steps was seen as being difficult or impossible to determine, and they might in any event be irrelevant to creating a link between the contract and the consumer's state.[913] The philosophy of Article 17 is that the co-contractor creates the necessary link when directing his activities towards the consumer's state.[914]

Article 17(1)(c) is a contentious provision. As an alternative to international litigation, the European Commission is pursuing initiatives on alternative consumer dispute resolution schemes.[915] This is to be welcomed. For all the attention paid to Article 17 of the Brussels I Recast, international litigation is not the best way of solving cross-border consumer disputes. Also welcome is the introduction of a European Small Claims Procedure.[916]

It is expressly provided that Section 4 on consumer protection shall not apply to contracts of transport other than a contract which, for an inclusive price, provides for a combination of travel and accommodation (package holidays).[917]

Jurisdictional Rules in Section 4 of Chapter II Section 4 adopts the same general approach towards allocating jurisdiction as does Section 3: the normal rules on jurisdiction do not apply (Section 4 should therefore be interpreted so as to be strictly limited to its objectives);[918] the claimant, where he is the weaker party, is given a choice of forum; and the provisions of Section 4 can be departed from by agreement in certain limited circumstances. But Sections 3 and 4 are very different in terms of their international scope. When the consumer is the defendant, Section 4, like Section 3, only applies (apart from agreements as

---

[909] Case C-218/12 *Emrek v Sabranovic* EU:C:2013:666, [2014] IL Pr 39.

[910] Art 13(3)(b) of the Brussels Convention.

[911] See the Explanatory Memorandum, p 16.

[912] Ibid.

[913] Ibid.

[914] Ibid.

[915] See European Parliament and Council Directive 2008/52/EC on certain aspects of mediation in civil and commercial matters OJ 2008 L 136/3.

[916] European Parliament and Council Regulation (EC) No 861/2007 establishing a European Small Claims Procedure OJ 2007 L 199/1; discussed infra, pp 663–5. This introduces a cheaper and simplified procedure. It is optional and covers claims of up to 5,000 Euros. Jurisdiction is still needed in accordance with the Brussels I Recast. See also European Parliament and Council Regulation (EC) No 1896/2006 creating a European Order for payment procedure OJ 2006 L 399/1, discussed infra, pp 660–3.

[917] Art 17(3). This should be interpreted in accordance with the provisions of Council Directive 90/314/EEC on package travel, package holiday and package tours OJ 1990 L 158/59. A contract concerning a voyage by freighter may be a contract for transport which, for an inclusive price, provides for a combination of travel and accommodation: Joined Cases C-585/08 and C-144/09 *Pammer v Reederei Karl Schlüter GmbH & Co. KG and Hotel Alpenhof GesmbH v Heller* [2010] ECR I-12527.

[918] 150/77 *Bertrand v Ott* [1978] ECR 1431; Case C-297/14 *Hobohm v Benedikt Kampik Ltd & Co KG* EU:C:2015:844 at [32], [2016] QB 616.

to jurisdiction under Article 19) where the defendant is domiciled in a Member State.[919] Where the trader is the defendant, Section 4 also applies where the defendant is domiciled in a Member State, but the notion of domicile is extended to cover a defendant trader with a branch, agency or other establishment in one of the Member States, provided that the dispute arises out of the latter's operations.[920] A novelty introduced by the Brussels I Recast is that the rule of jurisdiction laid down in Article 18(1) (based on the consumer's domicile) may also be invoked against a trader not domiciled in a Member State.[921] Where the provisions in Section 4 apply it is not possible to rely on other bases of jurisdiction under the Brussels I Recast.[922]

Section 4 is, like Section 3, a protective provision; in this case it is the consumer who is in the weaker position.[923] Under Article 18 the consumer is given the choice of suing the other party to a contract[924] either in the defendant's domicile or, regardless of the domicile of the other party, in his own domicile.[925] Where the roles are reversed, the other party can only sue the defendant consumer in the latter's domicile.[926] The right to bring a counterclaim is not affected.[927]

Jurisdiction Agreements and Submission   Section 4 can be departed from by an agreement which complies with one of the three alternatives under Article 19 (an agreement which is entered into after the dispute has arisen, or an agreement which allows the consumer to bring proceedings in courts other than those indicated in the Section, or an agreement which confers jurisdiction on the courts of the common domicile or habitual residence of the parties at the time of conclusion of the contract) and also complies with Article 25. One further limitation on the use of jurisdiction agreements in consumer cases is that the agreement must not infringe the Consumer Rights Act 2015.[928] A jurisdiction clause which has not been individually negotiated and which confers exclusive jurisdiction on the seller's or supplier's principal place of business must be regarded as being unfair,[929] as must a clause which involves an imbalance of convenience (alternative jurisdictions available

---

[919] Art 17(1) is without prejudice to Art 6; see also Art 18(2); Case C-318/93 *Brenner and Noller v Dean Witter Reynolds Inc* [1994] ECR I-4275; Briggs (1994) 14 YEL 578—a case on the Brussels Convention.

[920] Art 17(2); see the opinion of AG Leger in Case C-281/02 *Owusu v Jackson* [2005] ECR I-1383 at [132]–[134]. For the application of this provision within the United Kingdom (the Modified Regulation does not contain such a provision), see SI 2001/3929, Art 3, Sch 1, para 11. If, as a result of using the deemed domicile provision under Art 17(2), both parties are now domiciled in the same Member State, AG Darmon has given his opinion that the Brussels Convention will not apply since there is no issue of international jurisdiction, Case C-318/93 *Brenner and Noller v Dean Witter Reynolds Inc* [1994] ECR I-4275 at 4282. For interpretation of the phrase "branch . . . operations", see the opinion of AG Elmer in Case C-439/93 *Lloyd's Register of Shipping v Société Campenon Bernard* [1995] ECR I-961 at 971.

[921] Arts 6(1) and 18(1).

[922] Art 17(1), which is without prejudice to Arts 6 and 7(5). Art 26 is another exception to this: Art 26(2).

[923] See Recitals (14), (18) and (19).

[924] This may also cover the contracting partner of the travel operator with which a consumer concluded a contract and which has its registered office in the Member State in which the consumer is domiciled: Case C-478/12 *Maletic v lastminute.com Gmbh and TUI Österreich GmbH* EU:C:2013:735, [2014] QB 424, distinguished in Case C-375/13 *Kolassa v Barclays Bank Plc* EU:C:2015:37, [2016] 1 All ER (Comm) 733.

[925] For allocation within the United Kingdom, see the Civil Jurisdiction and Judgments Order, SI 2001/3929, Art 3 and Sch 1, para 7.

[926] Art 18(2). Where the consumer defendant's domicile is unknown, the courts of the Member State in which the defendant had his last known domicile have jurisdiction: Case C-327/10 *Hypoteční banka as v Lindner* EU:C:2011:745.

[927] See Art 18(3).

[928] This Act replaces the Unfair Terms in Consumer Contracts Regulations SI 1999/2083, which implemented Council Directive 93/13/EEC on unfair terms in consumer contracts 1993 OJ L 95/29.

[929] Case C-240/98 *Oceano Grupo Editorial SA v Rocio Murciano Quintero* [2000] ECR I-4941.

to the claimant but not to the defendant consumer), which took the consumer by surprise (no translation and no careful explanation).[930] Under Article 25, neither party has to be domiciled in a Member State.[931] The position is arguably the same in Section 4 cases.[932] Articles 31(2) and 31(3) which provide for an exception to the general *lis pendens* rule in cases involving exclusive agreements on jurisdiction are not applicable to matters relating to consumer contracts where the consumer is the claimant and the agreement is not valid under Article 19.[933] Section 4 can also be departed from under Article 26, ie where the defendant submits to the courts of a Member State by entering an appearance.[934] However, where the consumer is the defendant, the court shall, before assuming jurisdiction on the basis of submission by entering an appearance, ensure that the defendant is informed of his right to contest the jurisdiction of the court and of the consequences of entering or not entering an appearance.[935]

(vii) Jurisdiction over individual contracts of employment[936]

Scope of Section 5 of Chapter II   Section 5 of Chapter II of the Brussels I Recast (Articles 20–23) is concerned with matters relating to individual contracts of employment. The Brussels Convention contained certain provisions designed to protect the employee,[937] as the weaker party to the contract. The Brussels I Regulation took things a stage further by introducing a Section[938] devoted entirely to individual contracts of employment, putting such contracts on the same footing as insurance and consumer contracts. The Brussels I Recast continues to lay down the rules of jurisdiction in employment matters in a separate Section. It should also be noted that in cases involving the posting of workers within the European Union, the posted worker can rely on Article 6 of the Posted Workers Directive.[939]

"Matters relating to individual contracts of employment" refers to the situation where claims arise out of an employment relationship. Section 5 is engaged whenever a claim that is related to an individual contract of employment is advanced by a party to such a contract,[940] regardless of whether it is advanced during or after the termination of employment and regardless of whether it concerns employment in the private or the public sector. Thus a claim against an employee for conspiracy to harm the employer's business by soliciting fellow employees is a matter relating to an individual contract of employment.[941] So is a claim for breach of copyright, misuse of confidential information and unfair competition against

---

[930] *Standard Bank London Ltd v Apostolakis (No 2)* [2002] CLC 939. But see Hill and Chong, para 5.8.35.

[931] Art 6(1).

[932] See Collins, p 60; Layton and Mercer, para 16.003; see the argument on this point in relation to insurance, supra, p 291. But cf the opinion of AG Darmon in Case C-318/93 *Brenner and Noller v Dean Witter Reynolds Inc* [1994] ECR I-4275 at 4282.

[933] Art 31(4).

[934] Art 26(2).

[935] Ibid.

[936] Grušić, *The European Private International Law of Employment* (2015), Chapter 4; Merrett, *Employment Contracts in Private International Law* (2011), Chapter 4.

[937] See Arts 5(1) and 17(5).

[938] Section 5 of Chapter II, Arts 18–21.

[939] European Parliament and Council Directive 96/71/EC concerning the posting of workers in the framework of the provision of services OJ 1997 L 18/1. See also Directive 2014/67/EU of the European Parliament and of the Council on the enforcement of the Posted Workers Directive OJ 2014 L 159/11.

[940] See Case C-47/14 *Holterman Ferho Exploitatie BV v Spies von Bullesheim* EU:C:2015:574, [2015] IL Pr 44.

[941] *CEF Holdings Ltd v Mundey* [2012] EWHC 1524 (QB), [2012] IRLR 912, disapproving *Swithenbank Foods Ltd v Bowers* [2002] EWHC 2257 (QB), [2002] 2 All ER (Comm) 974. *CEF Holdings Ltd v Mundey* is a case on the Modified Regulation.

an employee who obtained the employer's design drawings by bribing a fellow employee for the purpose of facilitating unlawful competition against the employer.[942] But claims for unlawful means conspiracy brought against the former CEO and CFO for siphoning off sums from the employers for their own benefit and to the detriment of the employers was held to be outside the scope of the protective jurisdictional rules of the Lugano Convention 2007, as were claims for breach of fiduciary duty occurring other than for the periods when the defendants were employed.[943] A claim that concerns pre-contractual liability, such as discrimination for not offering employment, does not seem to be covered by Section 5.[944] Section 5 does not define "individual contracts of employment". However, it is clear that "individual" "contracts of employment" are to be contrasted with collective agreements between employers and workers' representatives[945] and with contracts for the provision of services.[946] Moreover, guidance can be found in the decisions of the Court of Justice in *Shenavai v Kreischer*,[947] and *Holterman Ferho Exploitatie BV v Spies von Bullesheim*.[948] In *Shenavai v Kreischer* the Court of Justice had to decide in the context of Article 5(1) of the Brussels Convention whether the case involved a contract of employment. *Shenavai* involved a claim by an architect for fees in connection with the drawing up of plans for the building of houses. The Court of Justice held that this was not a contract of employment. It was said[949] that contracts of employment had certain peculiarities, distinguishing them from other types of contract: they created a lasting bond bringing the worker to some extent within the organisational framework of the business of the employer; "they are linked to the place where the activities are pursued, which determines the application of mandatory rules and collective agreements". The relationship of the parties in a contract of employment has also been described as one of subordination of the employee to the employer.[950] The *Holterman* case involved a claim by four companies against a defendant concerning the latter's liability as manager of those companies. The defendant was also a director and held a minority share in one of those companies, the holding company of the group. After confirming that "individual contracts of employment" is an autonomous concept,[951] the Court of Justice referred to the decision in *Shenavai* and added that "the essential feature

---

[942] *Alpha Laval Tumba AB v Separator Spares International Ltd* [2012] EWCA Civ 1569, [2013] 1 WLR 1110, also disapproving *Swithenbank Foods Ltd v Bowers* [2002] EWHC 2257 (QB), [2002] 2 All ER (Comm) 974.

[943] *Arcadia Petroleum Ltd v Bosworth* [2016] EWCA Civ 818, appeal pending, distinguishing *CEF Holdings Ltd v Mundey* [2012] EWHC 1524 (QB), [2012] IRLR 912 and *Alpha Laval Tumba AB v Separator Spares International Ltd* [2012] EWCA Civ 1569, [2013] 1 WLR 1110. The test to be applied was held to be, at [66], "whether the reality and substance of the conduct relates to the individual contract of employment, having regard to the social purpose of [protective jurisdictional rules]".

[944] See Case C-334/00 *Fonderie Officine Meccaniche Tacconi SpA v Heinrich Wagner Sinto Maschinenfabrik GmbH* [2002] ECR I-7357. Cf *Gerhard Fahey v McKinsey & Co Inc* EE/2001/146, Irish Equality Tribunal.

[945] See the Jenard and Möller Report, which accompanied the 1988 Lugano Convention (replaced by the 2007 Lugano Convention), p 73.

[946] See Art 7(1)(b).

[947] Case 266/85 [1987] ECR 239.

[948] Case C-47/14 EU:C:2015:574, [2015] IL Pr 44. See also *WPP Holdings Italy Srl v Benatti* [2007] EWCA Civ 263 at [45]–[51] (per Toulson LJ), [75]–[82] (Buxton LJ), [98]–[100] (per Clarke MR), [2007] 1 WLR 2316; Briggs (2007) 78 BYBIL 611.

[949] [1987] ECR 239 at 255–6. See also Case 32/88 *Six Constructions Ltd v Humbert* [1989] ECR 341; Hartley (1989) 14 ELR 236; Case C-125/92 *Mulox IBC Ltd v Hendrick Geels* [1993] ECR I-4075; Hartley (1994) 19 ELR 540; Plender (1993) 64 BYBIL 558.

[950] The Jenard and Möller Report, p 73; *WPP Holdings Italy Srl v Benatti* [2006] EWHC 1641 (Comm) at [69], [2006] 2 Lloyd's Rep 610; affd in [2007] EWCA Civ 263, [2007] 1 WLR 2316.

[951] EU:C:2015:574 at [36]–[37], [2015] IL Pr 44.

of an employment relationship is that for a certain period of time one person performed services for and under the direction of another in return for which he receives remuneration".[952] In order to assess whether the defendant was an employee, the referring court was instructed to examine all the circumstances of the case, and in particular the extent to which the defendant, in his capacity as a shareholder, was able to influence the will of the administrative body of the company of which he was the manager and who had authority to issue him with instructions and monitor their implementation. The Court of Appeal has held that a contract appointing an advertising agency as a sole commercial agent was not one of employment.[953] Nor was a contract one of employment where a person had his hours expressed in maximum, not minimum, terms, was paid a low retainer plus commission, was allowed to spend a substantial amount of time on other business interests and, if he used a financial adviser in the performance of his duties, had to pay for this himself.[954] But a bonus agreement was held to be an employment contract.[955]

If the employee is the defendant, Section 5 only applies (apart from agreements as to jurisdiction under Article 23) where the defendant is domiciled in a Member State.[956] If the employer is the defendant, Section 5 also applies where the defendant is domiciled in a Member State,[957] but the notion of domicile is extended to cover a defendant employer with a branch, agency or other establishment in one of the Member States, provided that the dispute arises out of the latter's operations.[958] A novelty introduced by the Brussels I Recast is that the rules of jurisdiction laid down in Article 21(1)(b) (based on the habitual place of work and on the engaging place of business) may also be invoked against an employer not domiciled in a Member State.[959] Where the provisions in Section 5 apply it is not possible to rely on other bases of jurisdiction under the Brussels I Recast.[960]

---

[952] Ibid, at [41]; see also [42]. The Court of Justice referred to its interpretation of the term "employee" in primary and substantive EU law in Case 66/85 *Lawrie-Blum v Land Baden-Wurttemberg* [1986] ECR 2121 and Case C-232/09 *Danosa v LKB Lizings SIA* [2010] ECR I-11405.

[953] *Mercury Publicity Ltd v Wolfgang Loerke GmbH* [1993] IL Pr 142, CA.

[954] The *Benatti* case.

[955] *Samengo-Turner v J & H Marsh & McLennan (Services) Ltd* [2007] EWCA Civ 723, [2007] IL Pr 52; *Duarte v Black & Decker Corp* [2007] EWHC 2720 (QB), [2008] 1 All ER (Comm) 401; *Petter v EMC Europe Ltd* [2015] EWCA Civ 828, [2016] IL Pr 3.

[956] Art 20(1) is without prejudice to Art 6; see also Art 22. In *Samengo-Turner v J & H Marsh & McLennan (Services) Ltd* [2007] EWCA Civ 723, [2007] IL Pr 52, the Court of Appeal interpreted Section 5 as giving the employee a statutory right to be sued exclusively in the Member State of their domicile, which right—if the employee is domiciled in England and the employer has commenced or intends to commence proceedings in a non-Member State—may be protected by an anti-suit injunction; Briggs (2007) 78 BYBIL 615; see also *Petter v EMC Europe Ltd* [2015] EWCA Civ 828, [2016] IL Pr 3; Raphael [2016] LMCLQ 256; discussed, infra, pp 481–2.

[957] See *Powell v OMV Exploration & Production Ltd* [2014] ICR 63, EAT.

[958] Art 20(2). See Case C-154/11 *Ahmed Mahamdia v République algérienne démocratique et populaire* EU:C:2012:491, [2014] All ER (EC) 96 (the term "branch, agency or other establishment" must be interpreted in accordance with Art 7(5); an embassy is an establishment for this purpose); *Wright v Deccan Chargers Sporting Ventures Ltd* [2011] EWHC 1307 (QB) at [47]–[56], [2011] IL Pr 37; *Olsen v Gearbulk Services Ltd* [2015] IRLR 818 at [52]–[58], EAT. For the application of this provision within the United Kingdom (the Modified Regulation does not contain such a provision), see SI 2001/3929, Art 3, Sch 1, para 11.

[959] Arts 6(1) and 21(2). See, eg, *Petter v EMC Europe Ltd* [2015] EWHC 1498 (QB), affd on this point in [2015] EWCA Civ 828, [2016] IL Pr 3.

[960] Art 20(1), which is without prejudice to Arts 6, 7(5) and, in the case of proceedings brought against an employer, Art 8(1) (for the position under the Brussels I Regulation, under which the equivalent of Art 8(1) was not available to claimant employees, see Case C-462/06 *GlaxoSmithKline and Laboratories GlaxoSmithKline v Rouard* [2008] ECR I-3965; Harris (2008) 124 LQR 523). Art 26 is another exception to this: Art 26(2).

Jurisdictional Rules in Section 5 of Chapter II   Section 5, like Sections 3 and 4, contains rules of protective jurisdiction: in this case it is the employee who is the weaker party.[961] Under Article 21 the employee may sue the employer in the Member State where the employer is domiciled. Alternatively, and regardless of whether or not the employer is domiciled in a Member State, the employee may commence proceedings in another Member State in the courts for the place[962] where or from where the employee habitually carries out his work or in the courts for the last place where he did so. Allocation of jurisdiction to the courts for the habitual place of work has been justified[963] on the basis that this points to the courts of the Member State which were closely connected with the dispute and whose law may well be applicable,[964] and on the basis that this best protects the employee as the weaker party. However, a rule based on this place is not without its problems. In the situation where an employee works in several Member States, where is the habitual place of work? In *Rutten v Cross Medical*,[965] the Court of Justice held that this is the place where the employee has established the effective centre of his working activities and where, or from which, he in fact performs the essential part of his duties vis-à-vis his employer.[966] The identification of this place is a matter for the national court. However, it is necessary to take into account whether the employee spent most of his working time[967] in one of the Member States and whether the employee has an office where he organises his business activities and to which he returns after each business trip abroad. In the instant case, the employee spent approximately two-thirds of his working hours in the Netherlands and the remaining one-third in four other countries. Moreover, he carried out his work from an office in his home in the Netherlands to which he returned after each business trip. It cannot be open to doubt that he habitually carried out his work in the Netherlands. However, the employee may not have an office that constitutes the effective centre of his working activities. In such a case, the habitual place of work is where, taking account of all the circumstances of the case, he actually performs the essential part of his duties.[968] If the employee performs the same activities in several countries, failing other criteria, he will habitually work where he has worked the longest. This place is to be determined by looking at the whole period of employment. Applying these criteria it may still be impossible to identify the habitual place of work either because there are two places of work of equal importance or because there is no place with a sufficiently strong connection to be regarded

---

[961] See Recitals (14), (18) and (19).

[962] Work carried out on fixed or floating installations positioned on or above the Continental shelf adjacent to a Member State is regarded as work in that state: Case C-37/00 *Weber v Universal Ogden Services Ltd* [2002] ECR I-2013.

[963] See Case 133/81 *Ivenel v Schwab* [1982] ECR 1891; Hartley (1983) 8 ELR 328. The decision is criticised by McClellan and Kremlis (1983) 20 CMLR 529, 542. It was distinguished in *Mercury Publicity Ltd v Wolfgang Loerke GmbH* [1993] IL Pr 142, CA.

[964] The Rome I Regulation, Art 8, discussed, infra, pp 741–2.

[965] Case C-385/95 [1997] ECR I-57. See also *Powell v OMV Exploration & Production Ltd* [2014] ICR 63 at [26]–[42], EAT.

[966] This takes into account their earlier decision in Case C-125/92 *Mulox IBC Ltd v Geels* [1993] ECR I-4075.

[967] Rather than looking just at where he works at the point of dismissal: *Harada Ltd t/a Chequepoint UK Ltd v Turner* [2000] IL Pr 574 at [26], EAT.

[968] Case C-37/00 *Weber v Universal Ogden Services Ltd* ECR I-2013 at [58]. See also the opinion of AG Øe in Cases C-168/16 *Sandra Nogueira v Crewlink Ltd* and C-169/16 *Miguel José Moreno Osacar v Ryanair Ltd* EU:C:2017:312: cabin crew members habitually carry out their work at the place where or from which they principally carry out their obligations vis-à-vis their employer. The Provincial Labour Court of Appeal, Mecklenberg-Vorpommern, Germany, has referred several questions to the Court of Justice in relation to employees working on a ship: Case C-413/07 *Haase v Superfast Ferries SA* OJ 2008 C 54/40. The Court of Justice had no jurisdiction to decide the matter in this case.

as the main link. Article 21(2)(b), which applies regardless of whether or not the employer is domiciled in a Member State, provides that "if the employee does not or did not habitually carry out his work in any one country," the employer can be sued "in the courts for the place where the business which engaged the employee is or was situated". This rule ensures that jurisdiction is not given to a multiplicity of different Member States.[969] This rule is inapplicable where there is a habitual place of work outside the European Union.[970] Furthermore, the law of the country in which the engaging place of business is situated will normally be applied, at least in the absence of a choice of the applicable law by the parties.[971] The leading case on the meaning of the concept of the engaging place of business is *Voogsgeerd v Navimer SA*.[972] A place of business, in this context, is intended to be understood in a broad sense: it refers not only to the employer's domicile but also to any establishment, regardless of whether it possesses legal personality, over which the employer exercises effective control so that its actions are attributable to the employer, which possesses a sufficient degree of permanence, and which has been set up in accordance with the relevant provisions of the country in which it has been established.[973] In other words, it encompasses the employer's domicile and "branch, agency and other establishment" in the sense of Articles 7(5) and 20(2).[974] The term "engaged" refers to active engagement of employees, manifested by the conclusion and negotiation of the employment contract.[975] If the engaging place of business changes between the time of engagement of the employee and the time when proceedings are brought, the employee can bring proceedings in either place. Under the Brussels Convention the employee was also given the same choice of places in which to sue the employer.[976] What is different under the Brussels I Regulation and now Brussels I Recast is that the position where the employer[977] sues the employee is spelt out. He can only do so in the Member State where the employee is domiciled.[978] He does not have the option, which he had under the Brussels Convention, of suing in the place where the employee habitually carries out his work.[979]

The question can arise of where is the habitual place of work in the situation where an employee works for more than one employer. A contract of employment may be suspended

---

[969] The Jenard and Möller Report, p 73.

[970] Case 32/88 *Six Constructions Ltd v Humbert* [1989] ECR 341; *Shell International Ltd v Liem* [2004] IL Pr 18, French Cour de cassation; Cruz, Real and Jenard Report, which accompanied the Convention on the accession of Spain and Portugal to the Brussels Convention OJ 1990 C 189/35, p 45; cf Briggs 2015, para 2.120, fn 731; Merrett, *Employment Contracts in Private International Law* (2011), para 4.84 (for a different view from the same author see Merrett in Dickinson and Lein (eds), *The Brussels I Regulation Recast* (2015) 239, para 7.37, fn 79).

[971] Art 8(3) of the Rome I Regulation, infra, pp 741–2.

[972] Case C-384/10 [2011] ECR I-13275, criticised by Grušić (2013) 62 ICLQ 173. This case concerned the interpretation of Art 6(2) of the Rome Convention, the predecessor of Art 8(3) of the Rome I Regulation.

[973] The *Voogsgeerd* case, at [54]–[57]; opinion of AG Trstenjak at [78]–[81]. See also the Jenard and Möller Report, p 73.

[974] The *Voogsgeerd* case, AG opinion at [83]; Cruz, Real and Jenard Report, p 45, fn 1.

[975] The *Voogsgeerd* case, Court of Justice judgment at [45]–[50]; AG opinion at [65]–[70].

[976] See Art 5(1) of the Brussels Convention.

[977] For the meaning of employer, see Case C-384/10 *Voogsgeerd v Navimer SA* [2011] ECR I-13275 at [59]–[65]; AG opinion at [86]–[91]; *WPP Holdings Italy Srl v Benatti* [2006] EWHC 1641 (Comm) at [109], [2006] 2 Lloyd's Rep 610; this point was not addressed by the Court of Appeal in *WPP Holdings Italy Srl v Benatti* [2007] EWCA Civ 263, [2007] 1 WLR 2316; *Samengo-Turner v J & H Marsh & McLennan (Services) Ltd* [2007] EWCA Civ 723 at [32]–[35], [2007] IL Pr 52; *Petter v EMC Europe Ltd* [2015] EWCA Civ 828 at [13]–[23], [2016] IL Pr 3.

[978] Art 22(1). However, the employer has the right to bring a counterclaim in the court in which, in accordance with Section 5, the original claim is pending: Art 22(2).

[979] But if the employee did not habitually carry out his work in any one country the employer had to sue him in his domicile and could not sue in the engaging place of business.

whilst the employee works for another employer in a different place. The place where the employee habitually carries out his work under the first contract can be the latter place, provided that at the time of the conclusion of the second contract the first employer has an interest in the employee's performance for the second employer.[980] In determining whether the requisite interest exists it is relevant to consider such factors as whether the second contract was envisaged when the first contract was concluded; the first contract was amended on account of the second; there were organisational or economic links between the two employers; there was an agreement between the two employers providing a framework for the coexistence of the two contract; the first employer retained management powers in respect of the employee; the first employer was able to decide the duration of the employee's performance for the second employer.[981]

Jurisdiction Agreements and Submission   Section 5 may be departed from by an agreement which complies with one of the two alternatives under Article 23 (an agreement which is entered into after the dispute has arisen, or one which allows the employee to bring proceedings in courts other than those indicated in Section 5). It does not matter whether the designated court is in a Member State or not.[982] The latter alternative means that a claimant employee can rely on an agreement conferring jurisdiction entered into before the dispute has arisen. In this situation the agreement does not confer exclusive jurisdiction since the claimant employee, instead of suing in the Member State agreed upon, could opt to sue under Article 21 in the Member State of the employer defendant's domicile or in another Member State in the courts for the habitual place of work, etc.[983] On the other hand, an employee in the position of defendant cannot rely on an agreement entered into before the dispute has arisen. An employer, whether acting as claimant or defendant, can only rely on an agreement conferring jurisdiction entered into after the dispute has arisen.[984] The same two alternatives were to be found in the Brussels Convention.[985] The agreement must also comply with Article 25.[986] Articles 31(2) and 31(3) which provide for an exception to the general *lis pendens* rule in cases involving exclusive agreements on jurisdiction are not applicable to matters relating to individual contracts of employment where the employee is the claimant and the agreement is not valid under Article 23.[987] Section 5 can also be departed from under Article 26, ie where the defendant submits to the courts of a Member State by entering an appearance.[988] However, where the employee is the defendant, the court shall, before assuming jurisdiction on the basis of submission by entering an appearance, ensure that the defendant is informed of his right to contest the jurisdiction of the court and of the consequences of entering or not entering an appearance.[989]

---

[980]   Case C-437/00 *Pugliese v Finmeccanica SpA* [2003] ECR I-10829.
[981]   Ibid, at [24].
[982]   Case C-154/11 *Ahmed Mahamdia v République algérienne démocratique et populaire* EU:C:2012:491, [2014] All ER (EC) 96.
[983]   But see *Sherdley v Nordea Life and Pensions SA* [2012] EWCA Civ 88, [2013] IL Pr 26.
[984]   *Samengo-Turner v J & H Marsh & McLennan (Services) Ltd* [2007] EWCA Civ 723 at [37], [2007] IL Pr 52.
[985]   Art 17(5) of the Brussels Convention.
[986]   The Schlosser Report, p 120; *Simpson v Intralinks Ltd* [2012] ICR 1343 at [32], EAT.
[987]   Art 31(4).
[988]   Art 26(2).
[989]   Ibid.

(d) Provisional measures[990]

(i) Jurisdiction as to the substance

A court which has jurisdiction[991] as to the substance of a case in accordance with Articles 4 and 7 to 26 of the Brussels I Recast also has jurisdiction to order any provisional or protective measures which may prove necessary.[992] This is not subject to any further conditions, such as that the measure sought must be capable of enforcement in the state of that court. Thus it would allow a Dutch court, using its Kort-geding (summary) procedure, to grant an interim injunction prohibiting the infringement of a patent outside the Netherlands[993] or an English court to grant a world-wide freezing injunction. However, a court of a Member State has no power to order a provisional or protective measure on the above basis if the parties have referred the settlement of their dispute to arbitration, since the effect of this is to deprive the court of jurisdiction under the Regulation as to the substance of the case.[994] It is now clear from the Brussels I Recast that provisional measures ordered by a court with jurisdiction over the substance of the case may benefit from the rules on recognition and enforcement under the Regulation, provided certain conditions are met.[995]

(ii) Article 35 of the Brussels I Recast

In addition there is Article 35,[996] which allows a court to order provisional or protective measures even if it does not have jurisdiction as to the substance of the case.[997] This provides that: "Application may be made to the courts of a Member State for such provisional, including protective, measures as may be available under the law of that State, even if, under this Regulation, the courts of another Member State have jurisdiction as to the substance of the matter."

---

[990] Collins, *Essays*, Chapter 1; (1981) 1 YEL 249; Matthews [1995] CJQ 190; Kennett (1993) 56 MLR 342; Maher and Rodger (1999) 48 ICLQ 302; Hartley (1999) 24 ELR 674; Petrochilos [2000] LMCLQ 99; Aird (2002) 21 CJQ 271; Hill and Chong, Chapter 10; Fentiman 2015, Chapter 17; Briggs 2015, Chapter 6. Regulation (EU) No 655/2014 of the European Parliament and of the Council of 15 May 2014 OJ 2014 L 189, established a European Account Preservation Order procedure, which is a harmonised form of protective order for freezing bank accounts in other Member States. The United Kingdom and Denmark have, however, not opted in to this Regulation. Such orders may not therefore be made in respect of UK bank accounts, or obtained by UK domiciled claimants, but UK parties with accounts in other Member States and UK banks with branches in other Member States may be affected. See also Implementing Regulation (EU) 2016/1823 OJ 2016 L 283/1.

[991] A court will still have jurisdiction, even though it has stayed its proceedings under Art 29(1): *JP Morgan Europe Ltd v Primacom AG* [2005] EWHC 508 (Comm) at [70]–[73], [2005] 2 Lloyd's Rep 665.

[992] Case C-391/95 *Van Uden Maritime BV (t/a Van Uden Africa Line) v Kommanditgesellschaft in Firma Deco-Line* [1998] ECR I-7091; Peel (1998) YEL 693; Rodger (1999) 18 CJQ 199; *Masri v Consolidated Contractors International Company SAL* [2008] EWCA Civ 303, [2009] QB 450.

[993] See the criticism of this in *Chiron Corpn v Organon Teknika Ltd (No 10)* [1995] FSR 325 at 338. For the circumstances where an injunction was granted by an English court restraining the Dutch proceedings, see *Fort Dodge Animal Health Ltd v Akzo Nobel NV* [1998] FSR 222, CA; this is no longer possible, see infra, pp 475–81. See also the more general criticism of the Kort-geding procedure in *Mietz v Intership Yachting Sneek BV* [1996] IL Pr 661, German Federal Supreme Court. However, the Court of Justice has held that this procedure is of a type envisaged by Art 24 of the Brussels Convention (Art 35 of the Brussels I Recast): Case C-99/96 *Mietz v Intership Yachting Sneek BV* [1999] ECR I-2277, at [43].

[994] The *Van Uden* case, supra. Recourse can, however, be had to Art 35 of the Brussels I Recast, discussed infra. The arbitration exclusion is discussed supra, pp 208–11.

[995] Recital (33); Art 2(a) (definition of "judgment"); discussed infra, pp 611–13.

[996] Art 31 of the Brussels I Regulation, and 24 of the Brussels Convention.

[997] The *Van Uden* case, supra.

According to the Court of Justice, "provisional or protective measures" under Article 24 of the Brussels Convention, which corresponds to Article 35 of the Brussels I Recast, are ones which are intended to maintain a legal or factual situation in order to safeguard rights.[998] This encompasses the English freezing (Mareva) injunction[999] and search (Anton Piller) order, the Continental *saisie conservatoire*, an ordinary interlocutory injunction under English law[1000] and a French process of appointing a judicial expert, who investigated and protected evidence of facts but could not impose any final solution of the dispute on the parties, regarded by French law as interim proceedings.[1001] Provisional payments of money owed under a contract can fall within Article 35 subject to certain conditions. The interim payment of a sum of money claimed to be due under a contract under the Dutch Kort-geding procedure does not constitute a provisional measure within the meaning of Article 35 unless, first, repayment to the defendant of the sum awarded is guaranteed if the claimant is unsuccessful as regards the substance of his claim and, secondly, the measure sought relates only to specific assets of the defendant located or to be located within the confines of the territorial jurisdiction of the court to which application is made.[1002] An order for maintenance[1003] pending trial has been held not to be a provisional measure because, on the facts, of the lack of a realistic prospect of repayment.[1004] "Provisional or protective measures" do not encompass an *action paulienne* under French law, which, rather than maintaining the status quo, allows a disposition of property to be set aside.[1005] Moreover, it finally determines the position. Neither does the phrase cover a measure ordering the hearing of a witness for the purpose of enabling the applicant to decide whether to bring the case.[1006]

The granting of provisional or protective measures on the basis of Article 35 is conditional on, inter alia, the existence of a real connecting link between the subject matter of the measures sought and the territorial jurisdiction of the Member State of the court before which those measures are sought.[1007] This requirement will be met if the assets subject to the measures sought are located in the Member State in which those measures are sought. Under the Brussels I Regulation, the precise significance of this condition was, however, otherwise unclear. It was uncertain if it could be met if a world-wide freezing injunction were sought,[1008] or if assets were not within the territory, whether it was necessary or sufficient that the defendant was subject to the personal jurisdiction of the English courts.[1009] Recital (33)

---

[998] Case C-261/90 *Reichert v Dresdner Bank (No 2)* [1992] ECR-I 2149; the *Van Uden* case, supra. See also now Recital (25) of the Brussels I Recast.

[999] For recognition and enforcement of freezing injunctions, see infra, pp 615–17.

[1000] See *Kitechnology BV v Unicor GmbH Plastmaschinen* [1994] IL Pr 568, CA; infra, p 307 but not an injunction restraining foreign proceedings; but cf Briggs [1994] LMCLQ 158 at 162.

[1001] *Miles Platts Ltd v Townroe Ltd* [2003] EWCA Civ 145, [2003] 1 All ER (Comm) 561.

[1002] The *Van Uden* case, supra. See also Case C-99/96 *Mietz v Intership Yachting Sneek BV* [1999] ECR I-2277 at [43]. On the second requirement see *Bachy SA v Belbetoes Fundacoes E Betoes Especiais LDA* [1999] IL Pr 743, French Cour de cassation.

[1003] But note now the exclusion of maintenance from the Brussels I Recast, Art 1(2)(e)—see supra, p 211.

[1004] *Wermuth v Wermuth* [2003] EWCA Civ 50 at [31] (per Henry LJ) and [43] (per Lawrence Collins J), [2003] 1 WLR 942—neither was it a protective measure. See also *Comet Group plc v Unika Computer SA* [2004] IL Pr 1 at [23].

[1005] The *Reichert* case, supra.

[1006] Case C-104/03 *St Paul Dairy Industries NV v Unibel Exser BVBA* [2005] ECR I-3481, [2005] IL Pr 31.

[1007] The *Van Uden* case, supra. See *Banco Nacional De Comercio Exterior SNC v Empresa De Telecommunicaciones De Cuba SA* [2007] EWCA Civ 662, [2007] IL Pr 51; Merrett [2007] CLJ 495; *SanDisk Corpn v Koninklijke Philips Electronics* [2007] EWHC 332 (Ch), [2007] IL Pr 22.

[1008] It is unclear whether it is enough if there are assets in England as well as abroad, and the freezing injunction relates to the former as well as the latter. See further Briggs [2003] LMCLQ 418; Merrett [2008] LMCLQ 71; Hartley (2010) 126 LQR 194; Dickinson (2010) 6 J Priv Int L 519.

[1009] See, eg, *Cruz City 1 Mauritius Holdings v Unitech Ltd* [2014] EWHC 3704 (Comm), [2015] 1 Lloyd's Rep 191.

of the Brussels I Recast now states (*inter alia*) that "Where provisional, including protective, measures are ordered by a court of a Member State not having jurisdiction as to the substance of the matter, the effect of such measures should be confined, under this Regulation, to the territory of that Member State". This suggests that provisional measures made pursuant to the authority of Article 35 must be strictly territorially limited, and it will be necessary for there to be assets within the territory.

Article 35 has been interpreted by the Court of Justice as only applying to provisional measures which relate to matters within the scope of the Brussels I Recast.[1010] It has to be asked what rights a provisional measure seeks to protect and, if these rights are outside the scope of the Brussels I Recast, a provisional measure cannot be granted under Article 35. Provisional measures may, however, be granted under Article 35 even though the proceedings as to the substance of the case are to be conducted before arbitrators, despite the fact that arbitration is excluded from the scope of the Brussels I Recast.[1011] There is no requirement that the main proceedings in the other Member State must have actually started when the interim relief is sought, or that they will start in the future. All that is required is that the possibility of substantive proceedings exists under national law.[1012] Article 35 obviously allows a provisional measure to be granted in support of proceedings as to the substance of the case in another Member State, even if the courts of the other Member State have exclusive jurisdiction.[1013] However, it does not appear to preclude a provisional measure being granted in support of proceedings as to the substance of the case in the same Member State in which the provisional measure is sought.[1014] The court granting the provisional measure can base its jurisdiction to do so on traditional national rules of jurisdiction, including exorbitant rules prohibited under Article 5 of the Brussels I Recast.[1015]

The Hess, Pfeiffer and Schlosser Report reserved its strongest criticism of the Brussels I Regulation for Article 31 (the predecessor to Article 35).[1016] It was highly critical of the lack of any provision which would allow a court having jurisdiction over the substance of the dispute to set aside or modify in pursuance with their own law a provisional or protective order granted by a court of another Member State. It recommended that such a provision should be introduced, but no such modification was made in the Brussels I Recast.

(iii) Section 25 of the 1982 Act

Article 35 does not allow provisional measures to be granted where none were available beforehand. It authorises the courts of the Member State before which an application is made to grant the provisional measures which are available under the law of that State.[1017] If none

---

[1010] Case 143/78 *De Cavel v De Cavel* [1979] ECR 1055; Case 25/81 *CHW v GJH* [1982] ECR 1189; the *Reichert* case, supra; the *Van Uden* case, supra. For the special problem with matrimonial property of not knowing at the time of the interim order what substantive rights are going to be enforced later, see Hartley, pp 17–18.

[1011] The *Van Uden* case, supra. See also *Toepfer v Cargill* [1997] 2 Lloyd's Rep 98 at 107–8. For the reasons for this, see supra, pp 208–11.

[1012] The *Van Uden* case, supra: it was enough that proceedings "may be commenced"; see also the opinion of AG Leger in the same case. But cf *Fort Dodge Animal Health Ltd v Akzo Nobel NV* [1998] FSR 222 at 245, CA.

[1013] Case C-616/10 *Solvay SA v Honeywell Fluorine Products Europe BV* EU:C:2012:445.

[1014] No objection was made by the Court of Justice in the *Van Uden* case, which involved provisional measures sought before the Dutch courts, to the fact that proceedings as to substance took place in the Netherlands where arbitration proceedings were instituted.

[1015] The *Van Uden* case.

[1016] Study JLS/C4/2005/03, Final Version September 2007, paras 907–16; see further Dickinson (2010) 6 J Priv Int L 519.

[1017] *Republic of Haiti v Duvalier* [1990] 1 QB 202 at 212, CA.

are available in the particular circumstances,[1018] Article 35 would not help. There was a danger of this happening under English law. A freezing injunction was regarded as being an ancillary order which was only available where the English courts had jurisdiction over the main action.[1019] If this rule had remained, Article 24 of the Brussels Convention (Article 35 of the Brussels I Recast) would have been of no practical effect in England. Section 25[1020] of the 1982 Act altered the rule to prevent this happening.[1021] It provides that English courts can grant interim relief[1022] where proceedings[1023] have been or are to be commenced[1024] in another state. This could be in a Regulation State, a Brussels Convention or Lugano Convention Contracting State or in a non-Member/non-Contracting State.[1025] It could be in another part of the United Kingdom. Although this is a wide provision, it does require that the provisional measure is used in support of *foreign* proceedings (actual or imminent[1026]), which will resolve the merits of the dispute.[1027] It has been held that it only permits orders obtained against a party to the foreign proceedings, and thus may not be used to obtain a *Norwich Pharmacal* order against a third party in support of foreign proceedings.[1028] An English court could, for example, grant a world-wide freezing injunction over assets in England (and perhaps also abroad), pending trial in France, the object being to preserve the English assets for when the French judgment is enforced in England under the Brussels I Recast.[1029] The usefulness of section 25 goes beyond this. It also allows an interlocutory injunction to be granted stopping a wrong in England or abroad, such as the infringement of an intellectual property right or a breach of confidence, or a threatened wrong, even though the English courts are unable to try the substantive dispute because they lack jurisdiction under the Brussels I Recast or

---

[1018] Eg it may not be available under the law of X, if the parties confer jurisdiction on Member State Y and intended provisional measures to be sought there, see Collins, p 90.

[1019] *The Siskina* [1979] AC 210; *Mercedes-Benz AG v Leiduck* [1996] AC 284, PC. See McLachlan (1987) 36 ICLQ 669.

[1020] As extended by SI 1997/302 and amended by SI 2001/3929, Art 4, Sch 2, Part IV, para 10, and SI 2014/2947, Art 2, Sch 1.

[1021] *Babanaft International Co SA v Bassatne* [1990] Ch 13 at 30; *Republic of Haiti v Duvalier*, supra, at 210; *X v Y* [1990] 1 QB 220 at 227–8. See generally Hogan (1989) 14 ELR 191. S 25 is discussed infra. See also s 24, as amended by SI 2001/3929, Art 4, Sch 2, Part IV, para 9 (interim relief in cases of doubtful jurisdiction) and s 26 (security in Admiralty proceedings), as amended by s 11 of the Arbitration Act 1996. S 25 also applies in relation to the Brussels and Lugano Conventions.

[1022] See s 25(7). A claim form for an interim remedy under s 25(1) may be served out of the jurisdiction with the permission of the court: CPR, r 6.36 and PD6B, para 3.1(5)—see infra, pp 340–1. But where the defendant is domiciled in a Member State it would appear that the claim form can be served out of the jurisdiction without the permission of the court by virtue of CPR, r 6.33 (see infra p 308). But cf Dicey, Morris and Collins, paras 8.031, 11.249 n 667. An English court granting interim relief can consider a counterclaim: *Balkanbank v Taher (No 2)* [1995] 1 WLR 1067, CA.

[1023] This does not cover arbitration proceedings: *ETI Euro Telecom International NV v Republic of Bolivia* [2008] EWCA Civ 880, [2009] 1 WLR 665. However, s 2 of the Arbitration Act 1996 provides that the power to grant interim relief in support of arbitration applies even if the seat of the arbitration is outside England and Wales or Northern Ireland and even if no seat has been determined or designated.

[1024] See *Alltrans Inc v Interdom* [1991] 2 Lloyd's Rep 571.

[1025] See SI 1997/302. See also Capper [1998] CJQ 35; IRS [1997] CJQ 185. For Scotland see Maher 1998 SLT 225; Crawford and Carruthers, paras 7.57–7.58.

[1026] *Fourie v Le Roux* [2007] UKHL 1, [2007] 1 WLR 320.

[1027] *Channel Tunnel Group Ltd v Balfour Beatty Construction Ltd* [1993] AC 334 at 365; *Balkanbank v Taher (No 2)* [1995] 1 WLR 1067 at 1073; *Neste Chemicals SA v DK Line SA The Sargasso* [1994] 3 All ER 180 at 187–8; *Crédit Suisse Fides Trust SA v Cuoghi* [1998] QB 818 at 825, CA.

[1028] *AB Bank Ltd, Off-Shore Banking Unit (OBU) v Abu Dhabi Commercial Bank PJSC* [2016] EWHC 2082 (Comm), [2017] 1 WLR 810; Bushell (2017) 133 LQR 188.

[1029] See *Republic of Haiti v Duvalier* [1990] 1 QB 202, CA. The object may be, as in this case, to discover where the assets are. This has to be read now in the light of the *Van Uden* case, discussed supra, p 303.

otherwise.[1030] There is no requirement under section 25 that the subject matter of the proceedings is within the scope of the Brussels I Recast[1031] or that the defendant be domiciled in a European Union Member State.[1032] It follows that interim relief can be granted, for example, in support of foreign insolvency proceedings.[1033]

The court may refuse to grant interim relief if the fact that it is exercising an ancillary jurisdiction in support of substantive proceedings elsewhere makes it inexpedient to grant it.[1034] Five considerations should be born in mind when determining whether it is inexpedient to grant relief: (i) whether the order would interfere with the management of the case in the primary court; (ii) whether it was the policy in the primary jurisdiction not itself to make world-wide freezing/disclosure orders; (iii) whether there was a danger that the orders made would give rise to disharmony and/or risk of inconsistent orders in other jurisdictions; (iv) whether there was likely to be a potential conflict as to jurisdiction; (v) whether the court would be making an order it could not enforce.[1035] A freezing order will ordinarily not be granted in support of foreign proceedings which would not give rise to a judgment capable of recognition and enforcement in England.[1036] A good arguable case on the merits must also be established.[1037] A sufficient connection with England is necessary to justify the order,[1038] and where the case falls under Article 35 of the Brussels I Recast, account should also be taken of the need[1039] for the existence of a real connecting link between the subject matter of the measures sought and the territorial jurisdiction of the Member State of the court before which those measures are sought.[1040] Where there was reason to suppose that the order made against a foreign defendant would be disobeyed and that, in this eventuality, no sanction would exist, then the court should refrain from making the order.[1041] Relief is not limited to remedies which could be granted by the court trying the substantive dispute.[1042] Thus the Court of Appeal has approved the grant of a world-wide freezing injunction in support of proceedings in Switzerland, even though the Swiss courts had no power to make such an order.[1043]

[1030] *Kitechnology BV v Unicor GmbH Plastmaschinen* [1994] IL Pr 568, CA; *Coin Controls Ltd v Suzo International (UK) Ltd* [1999] Ch 33 at 53. See also Fawcett and Torremans, pp 236–46. Recourse can be had to traditional exorbitant national bases of jurisdiction according to the Court of Justice in the *Van Uden* case, supra.

[1031] See s 25(3)(b) (as amended by Art 4, Sch 2, Part IV, para 10), and SI 1997/302.

[1032] *X v Y*, supra, at 229.

[1033] See Smart [1998] CJQ 149 at 150–3; *Fourie v Le Roux* [2007] UKHL 1, [2007] 1 WLR 320.

[1034] S 25(2); *Motorola Credit Corpn v Uzan (No 2)* [2003] EWCA Civ 752, [2004] 1 WLR 113; *Crédit Suisse Fides Trust SA v Cuoghi* [1998] QB 818; petition for leave to appeal to the House of Lords dismissed: [1998] 1 WLR 474; *Refco Inc v ETC* [1999] 1 Lloyd's Rep 159, CA; *Ryan v Friction Dynamics Ltd* (2000) Times, 14 June; *State of Brunei Darussalam v Bolkiah* (2000) Times 5 September; *Bas Capital Funding Corpn v Medfinco Ltd* [2003] EWHC (Ch), [2004] 1 Lloyd's Rep 652 at [201]; *Banco Nacional de Comercio Exterior SNC v Empresa de Telecommunicaciones De Cuba SA* [2007] EWCA Civ 662, [2007] IL Pr 51.

[1035] The *Motorola* case, supra. See in relation to (b) and (c), *Banco Nacional De Comercio Exterior SNC*, supra.

[1036] In *United States of America v Abacha* [2014] EWCA Civ 1291, the court held that a freezing order could not be granted over assets in England for this reason, even though the property might ultimately be subject to seizure pursuant to the Proceeds of Crime Act 2002 (External Requests and Orders) Order 2005.

[1037] See, eg, *Kazakhstan Kagazy Plc v Arip* [2014] EWCA Civ 381.

[1038] See, eg, the *Motorola* case, supra; *Mobil Cerro Negro Ltd v Petroleos De Venezuela SA* [2008] EWHC 532 (Comm), [2008] 1 Lloyd's Rep 684; cf *The Royal Bank of Scotland Plc v FAL Oil Company Ltd* [2012] EWHC 3628 (Comm).

[1039] The *Van Uden* case, supra, p 303.

[1040] *Banco Nacional De Comercio Exterior SNC v Empresa de Telecommunicaciones de Cuba SA* [2007] EWCA Civ 662 at [29], [2007] IL Pr 51.

[1041] The *Motorola* case, supra; *Belletti v Morici* [2009] EWHC 2316 (Comm), [2009] IL Pr 57.

[1042] The *Crédit Suisse* case, supra, at 829.

[1043] Ibid.

(e) Service and notice of the claim

(i) Service of the claim form

Under the traditional English rules on jurisdiction, service of a claim form performs the dual functions of providing the basis of jurisdiction and giving the defendant notice of the proceedings. The Brussels I Recast has bases of jurisdiction which do not depend on service of a claim form. Procedure is largely left as a matter for national law, rather than being dealt with by the Brussels I Recast. The procedure under English law where the Brussels I Recast applies is as follows. A claim form can be served on a defendant present in the jurisdiction in accordance with the usual English rules, without the permission of the court.[1044] A claim form can also be served out of the jurisdiction[1045] without the permission of the court, provided that each claim[1046] included in the claim form is one which the court has power to determine under the Brussels I Recast and the *lis pendens* rules under the Brussels I Recast do not preclude the court taking jurisdiction.[1047]

As regards the practicalities of service, where service is to be effected in another Member State, Regulation (EC) No 1393/2007 of the European Parliament and Council on the service in the Member States of judicial and extrajudicial documents in civil or commercial matters[1048] applies,[1049] precluding alternative methods of service for cases falling within its scope.[1050] The Service Regulation is concerned to improve and expedite the transmission of documents for service between the Member States[1051] and, in relation to matters to which it applies, replaces the Hague Convention of 1965 on the Service Abroad of Judicial and Extrajudicial Documents in Civil or Commercial Matters and any bilateral or regional instruments between Member States.[1052] The Court of Justice has power to give a ruling on the interpretation of the Service Regulation, on the matter being referred to it by a national court. The Regulation

---

[1044] See infra, p 324 et seq.

[1045] CPR, r 6.33. For the accompanying statement required by r 6.34 see also PD6B, para 2.1; *Trustor AB v Barclays Bank plc* (2000) Times, 22 November 2000; *DSG International Sourcing Ltd v Universal Media Corp (Slovakia) SRO* [2011] EWHC 1116 (Comm), [2011] IL Pr 33.

[1046] See *Shahar v Tsitsekkos* [2004] EWHC 2659 (Comm) at [96].

[1047] *Swithenbank Foods Ltd v Bowers* [2002] EWHC 2257, [2002] 2 All ER (Comm) 974; *Mercury Communications Ltd v Communication Telesystems International* [1999] 2 All ER (Comm) 33—a Brussels Convention case. The conditions for establishing jurisdiction are set out in CPR, r 6.33(2).

[1048] OJ 2007 L 324/79 (the "Service Regulation"). This replaced Council Regulation (EC) No 1348/2000 OJ 2000 L 160/37 (the 2000 Service Regulation). The United Kingdom and Ireland have "opted in" to the 2007 Service Regulation. The Regulation is not directly applicable to Denmark. However, by virtue of an Agreement between the European Community and Denmark (OJ 2005 L 300/55), as from 1 July 2007 the provisions in the original Service Regulation were applied by international agreement to the relations between the Community and Denmark (this is a separate Agreement from the EC/Denmark Agreement extending the Brussels I Regulation to Denmark). This was updated to cover the 2007 Service Regulation in 2008—see OJ 2008 L331/21. The 2000 Service Regulation was based on the 1997 Convention on the service in the Member States of the European Union of judicial and extrajudicial documents in civil and commercial matters OJ 1997 C 261/1. The Explanatory Report accompanying the Service Convention is set out at OJ 1997 C 261/26. See generally on the Service Convention, Kennett [1998] CJQ 284. For English procedural rules, see CPR r 6.41.

[1049] As from 13 November 2008.

[1050] Case C-325/11 *Alder v Orlowska* EU:C:2012:824; *Asefa Yesuf Import and Export v AP Moller Maersk A/S* [2016] EWHC 1437 (Admlty). The Regulation cannot be subverted by using an alternative method of service (as authorised by CPR, r 6.8) such as by serving the defendant's English lawyers within the jurisdiction: *Knauf UK GmbH v British Gypsum Ltd* [2001] EWCA Civ 1570 at [47] and [58], [2002] 1 Lloyd's Rep 199; *Bentinck v Bentinck* [2007] EWCA Civ 175 at [49] (per Lawrence Collins LJ), [2007] IL Pr 391; or by dispensing with service (CPR, r 6.9): *Phillips v Nussberger* [2008] UKHL 1 at [39], [2008] 1 WLR 181. Dispensing with service may be allowed in a Brussels/Lugano case in exceptional circumstances where there is no such subverting: *Olafsson v Gissurarson* [2008] EWCA 152.

[1051] Recital (2).

[1052] Art 20(1). However, Member States are not precluded from concluding between themselves arrangements to expedite further or simplify the transmission of documents, provided that they are compatible

applies in civil and commercial matters where a judicial or extra-judicial document has to be transmitted from one Member State to another for service there.[1053] However, it does not apply where the address of the person to be served with the document is not known.[1054] The Regulation provides for the establishment of a transmitting agency and a receiving agency in each Member State[1055] and for the direct transmission of documents between agencies in different Member States.[1056] This is designed to avoid the delays which, in the past, have built up due to transmission being effected through a chain of intermediaries. The receiving agency is under a duty to serve a document or have it served on the defendant as soon as possible, and in any event within one month of receipt.[1057] The addressee can refuse to accept a document if it is not written in, or accompanied by a translation into, a language which the addressee understands or the official language of the state addressed.[1058] Member States are free to use certain other specified means of transmission and service of documents,[1059] including service by post directly to persons residing in another Member State.[1060] The Regulation sets up a Committee which assists the Commission in implementing the Regulation.[1061] The Service Regulation is also concerned with the notice of the proceedings that is given to the defendant and, as will be seen later in this chapter,[1062] has provisions designed to safeguard his interests.

(ii) Safeguarding the rights of the defendant

The Brussels I Recast safeguards the rights of the defendant in two ways, which are now examined in turn.

(a) The duty to examine jurisdiction where the defendant does not enter an appearance

A court of a Member State before which a defendant (domiciled in another Member State) is sued, but in circumstances where he does not enter an appearance,[1063] is required to examine its own jurisdiction and declare of its own motion that it has no jurisdiction unless this is derived from the provisions of the Brussels I Recast.[1064] Hitherto, an English court acted on the basis of the submissions of the parties; review of these issues by the court of its own motion presents a challenge to traditional English procedure.[1065]

---

with the Regulation: Art 20(2). The United Kingdom is a party to the 1965 Hague Convention and has also entered into various bilateral Civil Procedure Conventions. See generally CPR, rr 6.42 and 6.43. It will continue to use these arrangements in cases where the Regulation does not apply.

[1053] Art 1(1). The Regulation does not extend to revenue, customs or administrative matters or to liability of the State for actions or omissions in the exercise of state authority (*acta iure imperii*).

[1054] Art 1(2).

[1055] Art 2.

[1056] Art 4.

[1057] Art 7. After one month the receiving agency must continue to take all necessary steps to serve: Art 7(2)(b).

[1058] Art 8. See in relation to sending the translation required: Case C-433/03 *Leffler v Berlin Chemie AG* [2005] ECR I-9611; Mankowski (2006) 43 CMLR 1689. See also *Benatti v WPP Holdings Italy SRL* [2007] EWCA Civ 263 at [68]–[69] (per Toulson LJ), [86]–[90] (per Buxton LJ), [97] (per Clarke MR), [2007] 1 WLR 2316; Case C-14/07 *Ingenieurbüro Michael Weiss und Partner GbR v Industrie und Handelskammer Berlin* [2008] ECR I-3367.

[1059] Arts 12–15.

[1060] Art 14; *Benatti v WPP Holdings Italy SRL*, supra, at [88] (per Buxton LJ). These are alternatives to service under Arts 4 to 11 and both may be used, see Case C-473/04 *Plumex v Young Sports NV* [2006] ECR I-1417.

[1061] Art 18.

[1062] Infra.

[1063] Contesting jurisdiction is not entering an appearance, see Case C-148/03 *Nurnberger Allgemeine Versicherungs AG v Portbridge Transport International BV* [2004] ECR I-10327.

[1064] Art 28(1). For application of this requirement where jurisdiction is based on a special convention under Art 71 see the *Nurnberger* case, supra.

[1065] See the Schlosser Report, pp 81–2. See also Art 27 and Case 288/82 *Duijnstee v Goderbauer* [1983] ECR 3663. See generally Kohler (1985) 34 ICLQ 563, 573–4.

(b) Minimum standards in relation to notice

A court of a Member State "shall stay the proceedings so long as it is not shown that the defendant has been able to receive the document instituting the proceedings or an equivalent document in sufficient time to enable him to arrange for his defence, or that all necessary steps have been taken to this end".[1066] It is intended that this will only apply where the defendant is domiciled in one Member State, is sued in another, and does not enter an appearance.[1067] This provision was introduced with civil law systems in mind, under some of which there is a danger of a defendant having a judgment entered against him in default of appearance without having any knowledge of the action. Where the defendant does not enter an appearance, the court of a Member State before which an action is brought is required to consider its own procedure, to see that it conforms with these minimum standards, before entering a default judgment.

This is not likely to lead to stays of proceedings in Member States for three reasons. First, the minimum standards in relation to notice set out in Brussels I Recast are replaced by those in Article 19 of the 2007 Service Regulation if the document instituting the proceedings has to be transmitted from one Member State to another pursuant to this Regulation.[1068] Article 19 of the Service Regulation provides that, if the defendant did not appear, judgment shall not be given unless it is established that either the document was served in compliance with the law of the State addressed, or the document was actually delivered to the defendant or to his residence by another method provided for by the Service Regulation. In either case, it must also be shown that service or delivery was effected in sufficient time to enable the defendant to defend. The Hess, Pfeiffer and Schlosser Report pointed out that the interaction of the Brussels I Recast and Article 19 of the Service Regulation is very difficult for practitioners to understand and that it may be advisable to find a more simple solution.[1069] Secondly, where the provisions of the Service Regulation are not applicable,[1070] eg the document is not to be transmitted to another Member State, Article 15 of the Hague Convention of 1965 on the Service Abroad of Judicial and Extrajudicial Documents in Civil or Commercial Matters applies if the document instituting the proceedings or an equivalent document had to be transmitted abroad pursuant to that Convention.[1071] The minimum standards for notice contained in Article 15 are the same as those contained in Article 19 of the Service Regulation. The latter effectively incorporated the terms of the former. Article 15 of the Hague Service Convention, like Article 19 of the Service Regulation, does not apply where the address of the person to be served is not known. Thirdly, in cases falling outside both the Service Regulation and the Hague Service Convention, eg where the address of the person to be served is not known, Member States will use their own rules for service abroad. English courts are likely to assume that their procedure for service abroad[1072] will comply with the minimum standards for notice set out in the Brussels I Recast since the procedure for service abroad was introduced after the Civil Jurisdiction and Judgments Act 1982 (implementing the Brussels Convention with the same minimum standards) was passed.[1073]

[1066] Art 28(2).

[1067] See the Jenard Report, pp 39–40. Also Case 228/81 *Pendy Plastic Products BV v Pluspunkt Handelsgesellschaft mbH* [1982] ECR 2723; Anton and Beaumont's, *Civil Jurisdiction in Scotland* (1995) 2nd edn, para 7.33.

[1068] Art 28(3) of the Brussels I Recast.

[1069] Study JLS/C4/2005/03, Final Version September 2007, para 872.

[1070] See Art 1 of the Service Regulation.

[1071] Art 28(4) of the Brussels I Recast; see also *Pendy Plastic Products v Pluspunkt*, supra.

[1072] See supra, p 308 et seq.

[1073] See Collins, p 96.

The English procedure will come in for scrutiny from the courts of other Member States which are asked to recognise or enforce a judgment of an English court.[1074] Conversely, English courts will have to consider foreign procedure when asked to recognise the judgments of courts in other Member States.[1075]

(f) Stays and parallel proceedings

Various issues arise under the Brussels I Recast concerning stays and the management of parallel proceedings—these are briefly introduced here, and examined in detail in Chapter 13.

As examined earlier in this chapter, in some cases the Brussels I Recast identifies a single court which is given exclusive jurisdiction. In such cases, if proceedings are commenced in the courts of any other Member State, the court seised must (of its own motion) stay those proceedings.[1076] If more than one court has exclusive jurisdiction, any court other than the court first seised must similarly decline jurisdiction.[1077]

In other circumstances, however, a number of different courts may potentially have jurisdiction under the Brussels I Recast, and in many cases covered by the Brussels I Recast it is also possible that non-Member State courts will have jurisdiction. The Brussels Convention, Brussels I Regulation and now Brussels I Recast have always contained rules dealing with issues of *lis pendens* (the existence of prior proceedings between the same parties dealing with the same subject matter) as well as related proceedings, as they may arise between the courts of Member States.[1078] Essentially, for cases of *lis pendens*, the court first seised has priority to hear the case and any court second seised must stay its proceedings; for cases of related proceedings the court second seised has a discretion to stay its proceedings. Under the Brussels I Recast, further rules have been added dealing with the same issues as they arise where the prior proceedings are in a non-Member State.[1079] The *lis pendens* rules apply not only to the merits, but also to jurisdictional questions. A court first seised under the Brussels I Recast thus normally has the power to determine whether it has a basis of jurisdiction, and any court second seised must stay its proceedings even if it considers that the court first seised lacks jurisdiction, at least until such time as the court first seised has determined that question.

Aside from these rules, there has been a long-running issue whether proceedings commenced under the Brussels I Recast may be stayed in other circumstances, which will be examined in Chapter 13.[1080] The English courts traditionally used the doctrine of *forum non conveniens* to stay proceedings commenced under the Brussels Convention and Brussels I Regulation rules, but this has now been directly rejected by the Court of Justice.[1081] It remains contested, however, whether under the Brussels I Recast itself there is a residual power or obligation to stay proceedings (other than pursuant to the *lis pendens*/related proceedings rules or where another Member State court has exclusive jurisdiction).[1082] The English courts have held that such a power may exist, for example, where the dispute has strong subject matter connections with a non-Member State, or where there is an exclusive jurisdiction agreement in favour of the courts of a non-Member State.

[1074] See, eg, Case C–619/10 *Trade Agency Ltd v Seramico Investments Ltd* EU:C:2012:531.
[1075] See Art 45(1)(b); Case 166/80 *Klomps v Michel* [1981] ECR 1593; Hunnings [1985] JBL 303; infra, p 632 et seq.
[1076] Art 27; supra, p 218.
[1077] Art 31(1); infra, p 450.
[1078] Infra, p 442 et seq.
[1079] Infra, p 457 et seq.
[1080] Infra, p 459 et seq.
[1081] Infra, p 462 et seq.
[1082] Infra, p 464 et seq.

A further issue concerning the management of parallel proceedings relates to the power of the English courts to issue an anti-suit injunction, which restrains a party from commencing or continuing foreign proceedings.[1083] The English courts traditionally viewed this power as unaffected by the Brussels/Lugano System, but again the Court of Justice has directly rejected this approach.[1084] As examined further in Chapter 13, in cases falling within the scope of the Brussels I Recast, an injunction may not be awarded to restrain proceedings in another Member State, because this would interfere with the ability of the foreign court to determine its own jurisdiction. The power to restrain proceedings in a non-Member State does not appear to be restricted by the Brussels I Recast—indeed, there is an argument that the Brussels I Recast may promote the exercise of such a power in certain circumstances.[1085]

4. THE BRUSSELS CONVENTION

The Brussels Convention on Jurisdiction and the Enforcement of Judgments in Civil and Commercial Matters of 1968,[1086] as amended by four Accession Conventions,[1087] has been replaced in virtually all cases by the Brussels I Regulation and now Brussels I Recast. However, one has to say "virtually" because the Convention continues to apply in relation to the territories of the Contracting States[1088] which fall within the territorial scope of that Convention and are excluded from the Brussels I Recast.[1089] The territories in question are (in relation to France) the French overseas territories, such as New Caledonia and Mayotte, and (in relation to the Netherlands) Aruba.[1090] The rules on jurisdiction contained in the Brussels Convention are therefore applied in the United Kingdom and in the other Contracting States in the situation where the matter is within the scope of the Convention (a civil and commercial matter) and the defendant is domiciled in one of these territories, or Article 16 (exclusive jurisdiction) or Article 17 (an agreement on jurisdiction) of the Convention allocates jurisdiction to the courts of one of these territories. The rules on jurisdiction under the Brussels Convention are significantly different from those of the Brussels I Recast. The former are described fully in previous editions of this book[1091] and the reader is referred to what is said there for further details.

[1083] Infra, p 422 et seq.

[1084] Infra, p 476 et seq.

[1085] Infra, p 481–2.

[1086] There is also a Protocol on Interpretation in 1971, which came into force in 1975.

[1087] Both the original Convention and the Protocol are to be found in OJ 1978 L 304/77 and 97. The four Accession Conventions are listed supra, p 192, n 12. All references to the "Brussels Convention" (or the "Convention") and the "1971 Protocol" are to the latest version amended by the four Accession Conventions. For implementation of the Convention in the United Kingdom, see s 2(1) of the Civil Jurisdiction and Judgments Act 1982, as amended. The latest version of the Convention is to be found in OJ 1998 C 27/1 and also in the latest United Kingdom implementing legislation, SI 2000/1824, which implements the fourth Accession Convention.

[1088] At the moment the Contracting States to the Brussels Convention are the fifteen Member States who were parties after the fourth Accession Convention in 1996. There has been some speculation that the Brussels Convention may revive in the United Kingdom if or when it leaves the European Union in light of the June 2016 "Brexit" referendum, although this would clearly be unsatisfactory (not least because post-1996 EU accession states are not parties to the Brussels Convention); Dickinson (2016) 12 J Priv Int L 195.

[1089] Art 68(1). Territories are excluded from the Brussels I Recast pursuant to Art 299 of the EC Treaty.

[1090] See Layton and Mercer, paras 11.061–11.071. See also Kruger, paras 1.026–1.037.

[1091] See the 13th edn of this book (1999), pp 182–262.

5. THE LUGANO CONVENTION

As noted previously,[1092] a convention on jurisdiction and the recognition and enforcement of judgments has long been part of the process of cooperation between the European Community (now European Union) and European Free Trade Area. A new Lugano Convention was concluded in 2007 to mirror the terms of the Brussels I Regulation, replacing the previous 1988 Convention which mirrored the terms of the Brussels Convention. The Lugano Convention has not, however, been updated to reflect the changes introduced in the Brussels I Recast. The states bound by the Lugano Convention 2007 are the twenty-eight European Union Member States and three EFTA States—Iceland, Norway and Switzerland. The Convention allows for the accession of future EFTA Member States,[1093] European Community Member States acting on behalf of non-European territories that are part of their territory[1094] and even for third states to accede to the Convention.[1095]

(a) When does the Lugano Convention apply?

A matter of concern to European Union Member States, including the United Kingdom, is the relationship of the Lugano Convention to the Brussels I Recast, the Brussels Convention[1096] and the EC/Denmark Agreement. The Lugano Convention provides that these instruments continue to apply in the circumstances previously outlined in this chapter, unaffected by the Lugano Convention.[1097] The Lugano Convention is applied by courts in the Member States, including the United Kingdom, in relation to jurisdiction in the situation where the matter is within the scope of the Convention and the defendant is domiciled[1098] in Iceland, Norway or Switzerland, or Article 22 (exclusive jurisdiction) or Article 23 (agreement as to jurisdiction) of the Convention gives jurisdiction to the courts of Iceland, Norway or Switzerland.[1099] As far as the Member States are concerned, the provisions in the Lugano Convention on *lis pendens* and related actions[1100] will apply if there are concurrent proceedings in a European Union Member State and in Iceland, Norway or Switzerland.[1101] The Convention does not affect any conventions by which the contracting parties and/or the states bound by the Convention are bound and which in relation to particular matters govern jurisdiction or the recognition or enforcement of judgments.[1102]

[1092] Supra, p 194.

[1093] Arts 70(1)(a) and 71 of the Lugano Convention (all references to "the Lugano Convention" refer to the 2007 Convention).

[1094] Arts 70(1)(b) and 71 of the Lugano Convention.

[1095] Arts 70(1)(c) and 72 of the Lugano Convention. Poland, prior to becoming a European Community Member State, acceded to the 1988 Lugano Convention. There has been some speculation that the United Kingdom may accede to the 2007 Lugano Convention if or when it leaves the European Union in light of the June 2016 "Brexit" referendum; Dickinson (2016) 12 J Priv Int L 195.

[1096] And the Protocol on interpretation of that Convention.

[1097] Art 64(1) of the Lugano Convention.

[1098] See Arts 59 and 60 of the Convention; ss 41A, 43A, 44A of the Civil Jurisdiction and Judgments Act 1982 (introduced by SI 2009/3131).

[1099] Art 64(2)(a) of the Lugano Convention. As far as the three EFTA States are concerned, their courts will apply Lugano where the matter is within the scope of the Convention and the defendant is domiciled in the territory of a state where the Convention applies (ie a Member State or EFTA State) or Art 22 or Art 23 of the Convention confer jurisdiction on the courts of such a state.

[1100] Arts 27 and 28.

[1101] Art 64(2)(b) of the Lugano Convention. As far as the three EFTA States are concerned, Arts 27 and 28 of the Convention will apply if there are concurrent proceedings in an EFTA State and a Member State/EFTA State.

[1102] Art 67(1) of the Lugano Convention. Provisions on jurisdiction or recognition or enforcement in acts of the institutions of the European Community (now European Union) are treated in the same way as conventions: Protocol 3(1).

This covers conventions entered into in the past. The position is the same under the Brussels I Recast.[1103] The Convention goes on to provide that it does not prevent contracting parties from entering into such conventions in the future.[1104]

(b) The terms of the Lugano Convention

The Lugano Convention has been aligned with the Brussels I Regulation and the terms of the two are very similar. Indeed, these are much closer than the 1988 Lugano Convention was to the parallel Brussels Convention. There are obvious differences in terminology between the Lugano Convention and the Brussels I Regulation. Thus all references in the latter to "a Member State" are replaced by a reference to "a State bound by this Convention".[1105] But as far as jurisdiction is concerned,[1106] there are only two differences of substance.[1107] First, Article 5(2) of the Lugano Convention (special jurisdiction in matters relating to maintenance) sets out an additional alternative State (bound by the Convention) in which a person domiciled in a State bound by the Convention may be sued, namely:

> (c) in the court which, according to its own law, has jurisdiction to entertain proceedings concerning parental responsibility, if the matter relating to maintenance is ancillary to those proceedings, unless that jurisdiction is based solely on the nationality of one of the parties.

Secondly, Article 22(4) (exclusive jurisdiction in proceedings concerned with the registration or validity of patents etc) expressly provides that this provision applies "irrespective of whether the issue is raised by way of an action or as a defence". Article 22(4) of the Brussels I Regulation does not say this, but that provision was been interpreted by the Court of Justice to so provide,[1108] and the additional wording in the Lugano Convention has now been included in Article 24(4) of the Brussels I Recast.

(c) Stays of action

An English court must not act in a way which is inconsistent with the Convention.[1109] The question of when a stay of English proceedings is inconsistent with the Brussels Convention (and the Brussels I Recast), already noted above, will be discussed in detail in Chapter 13, and what is said there need not be duplicated here. It is likely that the English courts will apply the same principles in relation to the Lugano Convention as are applied in relation to the Brussels Convention/Regulation and Brussels I Recast. This would mean, for example, that if, in a case involving a Swiss defendant, an English court has been allocated jurisdiction under Article 5 of the Lugano Convention, that court is precluded from declining jurisdiction on the ground that a court of a state bound by the Convention or even a state which is not bound would be more appropriate for the trial of the action.[1110]

[1103] Art 71 of the Brussels I Recast.

[1104] Art 67(1) of the Lugano Convention.

[1105] As defined in Art 1(3). The 1988 Lugano Convention referred to "a Contracting State".

[1106] Title 2, Arts 2–31 of the Lugano Convention. For service of documents see Protocol 1, Art I.

[1107] Art 26 has been altered but not seemingly in substance.

[1108] Case C-4/03 *Gesellschaft für Antriebstechnik mbH & Co KG (GAT) v Luk Lamellen und Kupplungsbau Beteiligungs KG* [2006] ECR I-6509 (a Brussels Convention case); supra, p 225, n 298.

[1109] S 49 of the Civil Jurisdiction and Judgments Act 1982, as amended by Sch 2, para 24 of the Civil Jurisdiction and Judgments Act 1991 so provided in relation to the 1988 Lugano Convention.

[1110] The correctness of the *Re Harrods* principle was due to be considered by the House of Lords in the context of the Lugano Convention in *Anton Durbeck GmbHv Den Norske Bank Asa* but the appeal was withdrawn. The decision of the Court of Appeal is reported at [2003] EWCA Civ 147, [2003] 2 WLR 1296.

6. THE HAGUE CONVENTION ON CHOICE OF COURT AGREEMENTS

In 2005, a Convention on Choice of Court Agreements was adopted by the Hague Conference on Private International Law.[1111] The purpose of the Convention is to give greater effectiveness to jurisdiction agreements in favour of the courts of Convention states. The European Community (now European Union) became a member of the Hague Conference in 2007[1112] and ratified the Convention in 2015 on its own behalf and on behalf of all the Member States (excluding Denmark).[1113] At present, Mexico and Singapore have also ratified the Convention, while the USA and Ukraine have signed but not yet ratified, and the Hague Conference has reported that a number of other states are considering ratification. The Convention only applies to agreements in favour of a particular state court which are entered into after the Convention comes into force for that state.

The Convention overrides both European Union and national law rules of jurisdiction to the extent of any inconsistency.[1114] However, its effect on the Brussels I Recast is limited for two reasons. First, the Convention will only prevail over the Brussels I Recast where one of the parties to a jurisdiction agreement is resident in a Contracting State to the Convention that is not a European Union Member State.[1115] This appears to mean that exclusive jurisdiction agreements between French and English parties or Hong Kong and English parties in favour of the courts of Singapore will not be covered by the Convention,[1116] and thus the Hague Convention will leave unresolved much of the uncertainty around the effect

---

[1111] See <https://www.hcch.net/en/instruments/conventions/specialised-sections/choice-of-court>. See the Explanatory Report (2007) by Hartley and Dogauchi, available on this website; Hartley (2006) 31 ELR 414; Hartley (2006) 319 Hague Recueil 137–41, *Choice of Court Agreements Under the European and International Instruments* (2013); Fentiman 2015, para 2.29ff; Kruger (2006) 55 ICLQ 447; Teitz (2005) 53 AJCL 543; Tu (2007) 55 AJCL 347; Beaumont (2009) 5 J Priv Int L 125; Garnett (2009) 5 J Priv Intl L 161; Keyes and Marshall (2015) 11 J Priv Int L 345. Attempts at a much wider Hague jurisdiction and judgments convention failed, see McClean in Fawcett (ed), *Reform and Development of Private International Law*, (2002), Chapter 11; O'Brian (2003) 66 MLR 491; Schulz (2006) 2 J Priv Int L 243. But these have since been revived: see <https://www.hcch.net/en/projects/legislative-projects/judgments>.

[1112] See Schulz (2007) 56 ICLQ 915.

[1113] In the light of Opinion 1/03 of the Court of Justice holding that the Community had exclusive competence to conclude the new Lugano Convention; on which see Lavranos (2006) 43 CMLR 1087. Negotiations at the Hague were carried out on the pragmatic basis of a shared competence with Member States; see the Joint Statement by the Council and the Commission on Articles 71 and 72 [of the Brussels I Regulation] and on the negotiations within the framework of the Hague Conference on Private International Law, ST 14139 2000 INIT, 14 December 2000. Importantly, however, the fact that accession to the Hague Convention was ultimately determined to be within the exclusive competence of the EU means that the EU is the sole party which acceded to the Hague Convention. If or when the United Kingdom leaves the European Union in light of the June 2016 "Brexit" referendum, the Hague Convention on Choice of Court Agreements would not continue to apply to the UK unless the UK separately accedes to the Convention. See generally Dickinson (2016) 12 J Priv Int L 195.

[1114] The Civil Procedure Rules have been amended to reflect the requirements of the Hague Convention: SI 2015/1644. Where jurisdiction is based on the Hague Convention, a claim form may be served outside the jurisdiction without the permission of the court: see CPR 6.33(2B).

[1115] Art 26(6)(a).

[1116] Assuming (as is the case at the present date) that the UK, France and Singapore are all parties to the Convention, and Hong Kong is not. There is an argument that the Brussels I Recast rules should be considered not to cover jurisdiction in such cases (because there are no rules dealing directly with non-Member State jurisdiction agreements), which would leave them regulated by the Hague Convention—this would be sensible, although it would also be a contentious interpretation of the Brussels I Recast, particularly in light of Recital (24). See infra, p 458.

of non-Member State jurisdiction agreements under the Brussels I Recast.[1117] Second, even where the Convention does prevail, the rules which apply are very similar to those in the Brussels I Recast. Indeed, one objective of the Brussels I Recast reforms was to ensure that the application of the Hague Convention would not affect the position which would otherwise apply under EU law.[1118] However, the ratification by the European Union also has the effect that the United Kingdom is bound by the Convention even in cases not covered by the Brussels I Recast, and the Convention has a considerable impact on the traditional English rules of jurisdiction.

The Convention applies in international cases[1119] to exclusive choice of court agreements concluded in civil or commercial matters.[1120] There are, though, various exclusions from its scope.[1121] It does not apply to exclusive choice of court agreements to which a natural person acting primarily for personal, family or household purposes (a consumer) is a party.[1122] Nor does it apply to exclusive choice of court agreements where they relate to contracts of employment, including collective agreements.[1123] There is also a long list of matters excluded from the scope of the Convention.[1124] Many are familiar to us, being matters that are either also excluded from the scope of the Brussels I Recast[1125] or matters in respect of which exclusive jurisdiction is allocated under Article 24 of the Brussels I Recast.[1126] But the Convention goes beyond this and, for instance, also excludes claims for personal injury brought by or on behalf of natural persons[1127] and tort or delict claims for damage to tangible property that do not arise from a contractual relationship.[1128]

The Convention is, in general, confined to "exclusive" choice of court agreements.[1129] If it had included non-exclusive agreements, there would have been the risk of parallel proceedings in different states, which would have necessitated a *lis pendens* provision. An exclusive choice of court agreement is defined by Article 3, which requires the agreement to be concluded or documented in writing, or by any other means of communication which renders information accessible so as to be usable for subsequent reference.[1130] A choice of court agreement which designates the courts of one Contracting State or one or more specific courts of one Contracting State shall be deemed to be exclusive unless the parties have expressly provided otherwise.[1131] The courts of a Contracting State designated by such an agreement have jurisdiction to decide a dispute to which the agreement applies, unless the agreement is null and void under the law of that state (including its choice of law rules which may refer to the

---

[1117] See further infra, pp 467–8.

[1118] See the Hess, Pfeiffer and Schlosser Report Study JLS/C4/2005/03, Final Version September 2007, para 884.

[1119] As defined in Art 1(2) and (3).

[1120] Art 1(1).

[1121] Art 2.

[1122] Art 2(1)(a).

[1123] Art 2(1)(b).

[1124] Art 2 (2)(a)–(p). See also Art 2(4).

[1125] See Art 2(2): (a) status and legal capacity of natural persons; (c) family law matters, including matrimonial property regimes; (d) wills and succession; (e) insolvency; and Art 2(4) arbitration. The scope of the Brussels I Recast is discussed supra, pp 202–12.

[1126] See Art 2(2): (l) rights in rem in immovable property and tenancies; (m) validity, nullity or dissolution of legal persons; (n) validity of intellectual property rights; (p) validity of entries in public registers. Art 24 of the Brussels I Recast is discussed supra, pp 217–26.

[1127] Art 2(2)(j).

[1128] Art 2(2)(k).

[1129] Recognition and enforcement can be extended to non-exclusive agreements by reciprocal declarations made by Contracting States, see Art 22.

[1130] Art 3(c).

[1131] Art 3(b).

substantive law of some other state),[1132] and are forbidden to decline to exercise jurisdiction on the ground that the dispute should be tried in a court of another state.[1133]

A court in a Contracting State other than that of the chosen court is required to suspend or dismiss proceedings to which the agreement applies unless one of five alternative limitations operates.[1134] These are that: (a) the agreement is null and void under the law of the state of the chosen court (including its choice of law rules); (b) a party lacked the capacity to conclude the agreement under the law of the state of the court seised; (c) giving effect to the agreement would lead to a manifest injustice or would be manifestly contrary to the public policy of the state of the court seised; (d) for exceptional reasons beyond the control of the parties, the agreement cannot reasonably be performed; or (e) the chosen court has decided not to hear the case.

A judgment given by a court of a Contracting State designated in the agreement will be recognised and enforced in other Contracting States,[1135] subject to limited grounds of refusal.[1136] Recognition of judgments under the Convention is discussed further in Chapter 16.[1137]

7. ALLOCATING JURISDICTION WITHIN THE UNITED KINGDOM: THE MODIFIED REGULATION[1138]

(a) When does the Modified Regulation apply?

Section 16 of the Civil Jurisdiction and Judgments Act 1982[1139] is headed "allocation within UK of jurisdiction in certain civil proceedings". Section 16(1) states that the Modified version of Chapter II of the Brussels I Regulation set out in Schedule 4 of the 1982 Act:[1140]

> shall have effect for determining, for each part of the United Kingdom,[1141] whether the courts of law of that part . . . have . . . jurisdiction in proceedings where:

> (a) the subject-matter of the proceedings is within the scope of the Regulation[1142] as determined by Article 1 of the Regulation (whether or not the Regulation has effect in relation to the proceedings); and

> (b) the defendant . . . is domiciled in the United Kingdom or the proceedings are of a kind mentioned in Article 24 of the Regulation (exclusive jurisdiction regardless of domicile).

It follows from section 16 that for the Modified Regulation to apply three conditions must be satisfied.

(i) *The situation must concern allocation of jurisdiction within the United Kingdom*

This presupposes that courts in the United Kingdom have jurisdiction. There are two situations where this will be so: first, in cases where the Brussels I Recast, the Brussels Convention

---

[1132] Art 5(1). See the Hartley and Dogauchi Report, para 125.
[1133] Art 5(2).
[1134] Art 6.
[1135] Art 8.
[1136] Art 9.
[1137] Infra, pp 652–3.
[1138] Sch 4 to the Civil Jurisdiction and Judgments Act 1982; as substituted by SI 2001/3929, art 4 and Sch 2, Part II, para 4. See generally Hood, *Conflict of Laws Within the UK* (2007), paras 5.12–5.33.
[1139] As amended by SI 2001/3929, Art 4 and Sch 2, Part II, para 3; and SI 2014/2947, Art 2 and Sch 1.
[1140] For the limited exclusions from Sch 4, see s 17 and Sch 5 (as amended). For special provisions with respect to trusts and consumer contracts, see s 10, as substituted by SI 2001/3929, Art 3 and Sch 1, para 7.
[1141] S 50 defines this as England and Wales, Scotland or Northern Ireland.
[1142] The definition of "Regulation" has been updated to refer to the Brussels I Recast: see SI 2014/2947, Sch 1.

or the Lugano Convention has allocated jurisdiction to courts in the United Kingdom;[1143] secondly, in internal United Kingdom cases, where for example a Scotsman sues an Englishman in respect of land in England. Rules are needed to determine which part of the United Kingdom should have jurisdiction, although it would have been quite possible to leave the traditional English rules on jurisdiction to do this. The Brussels I Recast and the Brussels and Lugano Conventions themselves are inapplicable in internal United Kingdom cases.[1144]

(ii) *The subject matter of the proceedings must be within the scope of the Brussels I Recast as determined by Article 1*

The scope of the Brussels I Recast has already been dealt with.[1145] Section 16(1)(a) of the Civil Jurisdiction and Judgments Act 1982 provides that the Modified Regulation will apply "whether or not the [Brussels I Recast] has effect in relation to the proceedings". In an internal United Kingdom case the proceedings may be within the provisions on the scope of the Brussels I Recast set out in Article 1 (ie a civil and commercial matter), yet the Brussels I Recast would not be applied. It will be recalled that the Brussels I Recast is only concerned with the international jurisdiction of Member States.[1146] This additional wording in section 16(1)(a) gets over this particular problem.

(iii) *The defendant must be domiciled in the United Kingdom or the proceedings must be of a kind mentioned in Article 24 of the Brussels I Recast*

The Modified Regulation is only concerned with proceedings where the defendant is domiciled in the United Kingdom or the proceedings are of a kind mentioned in Article 24 of the Brussels I Recast (exclusive jurisdiction regardless of domicile). Where jurisdiction is allocated under Article 4 (the defendant is domiciled in a Member State) or under Article 24 (exclusive jurisdiction regardless of domicile), this refers to international jurisdiction (ie jurisdiction is conferred on the United Kingdom) and not local jurisdiction (ie jurisdiction conferred on a part of the United Kingdom).[1147] Where jurisdiction is assigned to the courts in the United Kingdom under other articles, it is necessary to regard jurisdiction as being allocated to the courts in a part of the United Kingdom. In general, there is no problem where Article 7 applies, as this is designed to give local jurisdiction.[1148] Most of the heads of Article 7 are phrased in terms of the courts for a "place" in a Member State having jurisdiction.[1149] For example, Article 7(2) refers to the courts for the place where the harmful event occurred; ascertaining the "place" where the harmful event occurred inevitably pinpoints a part of the United Kingdom whose courts are to have jurisdiction. Where Articles 25 and 26 of the Brussels I Recast apply, as has already been seen,[1150] there may be more difficulty in allocating jurisdiction to a part of the United Kingdom.

The requirement under section 16(1)(b) of the 1982 Act that the defendant be domiciled in the United Kingdom causes the usual definitional problems. In principle, a person is domiciled in England and Wales, Scotland, or Northern Ireland, not in the United Kingdom. Section 41(2) of the 1982 Act solves this difficulty by defining, for the purposes of the Act, whether an individual is domiciled in the United Kingdom. This is only so if (a) he is resident

---

[1143] See the Schlosser Report, p 98; infra, p 317 et seq.
[1144] Supra, p 194.
[1145] Supra, p 202 et seq.
[1146] See supra, pp 202–3.
[1147] See the Schlosser Report, p 98.
[1148] Ibid.
[1149] There is, however, a problem with Art 7(6) which gives jurisdiction to the courts of the Member State in which a trust is domiciled and does not refer to "the place".
[1150] Supra, pp 217–18 and 226.

in the United Kingdom, and (b) the nature and circumstances of his residence indicate that he has a substantial connection with the United Kingdom. Showing this substantial connection is made easier by the introduction of a presumption under section 41(6), according to which, where an individual (a) is resident in the United Kingdom, or in a particular part; and (b) has been so resident for the last three months or more, the requirement as to a substantial connection is presumed to have been fulfilled, unless the contrary is shown. With corporations, section 42(3) basically provides that for the purposes of the 1982 Act a corporation has its domicile (referred to as its seat) in the United Kingdom if (a) it was incorporated and has its registered office in the United Kingdom, or (b) its central management and control is exercised in the United Kingdom.

(b) The terms of the Modified Regulation

Although there was no necessity for the allocation of jurisdiction within the United Kingdom to be based on the Brussels Convention or Brussels I Regulation, this is the form it was decided it should take.[1151] The effect of this can be seen in two examples. In the first example, the defendant is domiciled in the United Kingdom; the claimant will be able to sue him in England (if he is domiciled there),[1152] or in Scotland (if special jurisdiction under rule 3 of the Modified Regulation[1153] gives jurisdiction to Scotland), or in Northern Ireland (if there is an agreement on jurisdiction under rule 12 of the Modified Regulation giving jurisdiction to Northern Ireland—under this provision the jurisdiction given is not exclusive[1154]). In the second example, the dispute concerns the ownership of land in England; the claimant will have to sue in England (under rule 11(a)(i) of the Modified Regulation).

The Modified Regulation is based on the Brussels I Regulation, but differs in certain respects which will now be examined.

(i) The modifications

Some of these modifications are necessary to allocate jurisdiction within the United Kingdom. Where the Regulation refers to a *Member State*, the Modified Regulation instead refers to a *part of the United Kingdom*. Thus, under rule 1 "persons domiciled in a part of the United Kingdom shall be sued in the courts of that part". According to rule 3 they "may be sued in the courts of another part of the United Kingdom only by virtue of rules 3 to 13 of this Schedule [which correspond to Articles 7–9 and Articles 17–26 of the Brussels I Recast]".

In order to determine whether an individual is domiciled in a particular part of the United Kingdom one must refer to section 41(3) of the 1982 Act. This uses the same criteria as are used under section 41(2) when ascertaining whether an individual is domiciled in the United Kingdom, ie it looks for residence and a substantial connection with that part. The presumption under section 41(6) based on three months' residence is also applicable. Even if the presumption can be rebutted, this is not the end of the matter. Section 41(5) declares that, where the substantial connection cannot be shown in relation to any particular part of the United Kingdom, an individual shall be treated as domiciled in the part of the United Kingdom in which he is resident. Applying these rules, a person could be domiciled in two

---

[1151] See Anton and Beaumont's *Civil Jurisdiction in Scotland* (1995) 2nd edn, paras 1.33, 9.01–9.04. Originally when it was decided to base the Modified Convention on the Brussels Convention this was, in part, because Scotland wished to replace its traditional rules on jurisdiction with rules based on the Brussels Convention. See also Crawford and Carruthers, paras 7.53–7.54.

[1152] Under s 41 of the 1982 Act a person may have a dual domicile in different parts of the United Kingdom, so the claimant can sue in either part: *Daniel v Foster* 1989 SLT 90.

[1153] This is the equivalent to Art 7 of the Brussels I Recast.

[1154] *Snookes v Jani-King (GB) Ltd* [2006] EWHC 289 (QB) at [56]–[62], [2006] IL Pr 19.

parts of the United Kingdom at the same time (eg a person has a home in England where he lives all winter but he has spent the previous three months of the summer at his home in Scotland), and both parts would have jurisdiction.[1155] As far as companies are concerned, section 42(4) provides in broad terms that a company has a seat in a particular part of the United Kingdom only if it has its registered office in that part, or its central management and control is exercised in that part, or it has a place of business in that part. It may also be necessary in the case of some bases of jurisdiction to ascertain the place in the United Kingdom where an individual is domiciled. Section 41(4) provides a definition for determining this.[1156]

There are also modifications of substance, the most important of which are as follows. Rule 3(a) of the Modified Regulation starts off like Article 7(1)(a) of the Brussels I Recast by providing special jurisdiction "in matters relating to a contract, in the courts for the place of performance of the obligation in question". However, it does not go on to define the place of performance of the obligation in question for contracts for the sale of goods or the provision of services.

The Modified Regulation contains two additional bases of special jurisdiction. Rule 3(h) deals, inter alia, with proceedings concerning debts secured on immovable property and gives jurisdiction to the courts of the part of the United Kingdom in which the property is situated. Rule 4 of the Modified Regulation deals with proceedings which have as their object a decision of an organ of a company and gives jurisdiction to the courts of the part of the United Kingdom in which the company has its seat. This rule is treated as one of special jurisdiction. In contrast, the Brussels I Recast deals with such proceedings by allocating exclusive jurisdiction to the courts of the seat of the company.[1157]

Rule 12 of the Modified Regulation, which deals with jurisdiction agreements, differs from Article 25 of the Brussels I Recast in a number of respects. First, the effect of an agreement on jurisdiction may be different. Rule 12 of the Modified Regulation provides that, if the parties have chosen the courts of a part of the United Kingdom (eg the English courts) as the forum for trial, those courts will have jurisdiction. However, in contrast to Article 25 of the Brussels I Recast, Rule 12 does not expressly say that such an agreement is presumed to give or even can give exclusive jurisdiction,[1158] and there is some authority which suggests that, despite such an agreement, a claimant will be able to use the other bases of jurisdiction set out in the Modified Regulation to sue in another part of the United Kingdom.[1159] Secondly, for jurisdiction to be conferred by Rule 12 of the Modified Regulation there is a requirement that the defendant is domiciled in the United Kingdom.[1160] For jurisdiction to be conferred by Article 25 of the Brussels I Recast it is not necessary for either party to be domiciled in a Member State (under the Brussels I Regulation it was sufficient if one party were domiciled in a Member State). Thirdly, if the parties have not specified which part of the United Kingdom has jurisdiction conferred on it (ie the agreement just says that trial is to take place in the United Kingdom), Rule 12 of the Modified Regulation will not apply, and the other

---

[1155] For stays of action, see infra, pp 321–2.

[1156] For example, s 41(4) has to be used where Art 8 is applicable. For companies, see s 42(5).

[1157] Art 24(2) of the Brussels I Recast. See supra, p 224.

[1158] Under Art 25 of the Brussels I Recast jurisdiction is exclusive unless the parties have agreed otherwise. See supra, p 234.

[1159] See *British Steel Corpn v Allivane International Ltd* 1989 SLT (Sh Ct) 57. But see *Jenic Properties Ltd v Andy Thornton Architectural Antiques* 1992 SLT (Sh Ct) 5, and *McCarthy v Abowall (Trading) Ltd* 1992 SLT (Sh Ct) 65—if it is an exclusive jurisdiction clause, effect will be given to this and jurisdiction is precluded in another part of the United Kingdom.

[1160] See s 16(1)(b) of the Civil Jurisdiction and Judgments Act 1982, as amended by SI 2001/3929 Art 4, Sch 2, Part II, para 3.

bases of jurisdiction under the Modified Regulation will have to be used to allocate jurisdiction within the United Kingdom. Fourthly, there is no requirement in respect of the form of agreement, though there must still be a real agreement between the parties.[1161] Fifthly, the agreement, however, must be effective to confer jurisdiction under the law of that part of the United Kingdom whose courts the parties have agreed are to have jurisdiction.

Finally, the provisions on jurisdiction in matters relating to insurance and exclusive jurisdiction in relation to patents,[1162] which are contained in the Brussels I Recast,[1163] are omitted from the Modified Regulation. This means that other bases of jurisdiction under the Modified Regulation will have to be used in these cases. There is also no provision on *lis pendens* in the Modified Regulation.

(c) Stays of action

(i) Lis pendens

The absence of a provision on *lis pendens* from the Modified Regulation does not cause any problems. Where the Brussels I Recast is applicable, Article 29 is worded in such a way as to require all courts in the United Kingdom, whether in England and Wales, Scotland or Northern Ireland, to decline jurisdiction where the courts of another Member State are first seised of the action. In internal United Kingdom cases, the Brussels I Recast is inapplicable and the traditional English rules on the discretion to stay,[1164] including those relating to parallel proceedings, can be used.

(ii) A general discretion to stay

The wording of the Modified Regulation, being based on the Brussels I Regulation, contains no suggestion that there is a discretion to stay proceedings on the basis of *forum non conveniens*. Section 49 of the 1982 Act merely provides that a stay of action must not be inconsistent with the Brussels Convention or the Lugano Convention. As a matter of EU law, a stay of action must also not be inconsistent with the Brussels I Recast. It would, therefore, appear that a discretion to stay actions on the basis of *forum non conveniens* exists under the Modified Regulation, where its use is not inconsistent with the Brussels I Recast, the Brussels Convention or the Lugano Convention. In deciding whether its use is inconsistent it is important to distinguish between, on the one hand, situations where the Brussels I Recast, the Brussels Convention or the Lugano Convention applies (as well as the Modified Regulation) and, on the other hand, situations where the Modified Regulation applies on its own (internal United Kingdom cases).

Where the Brussels I Recast, the Brussels Convention or the Lugano Convention applies, there is no discretion to stay proceedings on the basis of *forum non conveniens*, even where the alternative forum is a non-European Union/EFTA State.[1165] Thus, an English court cannot stay proceedings on the basis that a more appropriate alternative forum is, for example, France or New York.[1166] However, where the Modified Regulation then applies to allocate jurisdiction within the United Kingdom, it is likely that there is a discretion to stay on this

---

[1161] *British Steel Corpn v Allivane International Ltd*, supra.

[1162] For the more general exclusion of patent proceedings from the Modified Regulation see Sch 5, para (2) of the 1982 Act, on which see generally (in relation to the earlier Modified Convention) Anton and Beaumont's *Civil Jurisdiction in Scotland* (1995) 2nd edn, para 9.12.

[1163] Arts 10–16 and 24(4).

[1164] Infra, p 392 et seq.

[1165] See infra, p 460 et seq.

[1166] Unless provided for under the Brussels I Recast, either expressly or through reflexive effect—see further infra, p 471 et seq.

basis. It can be argued that the allocation of jurisdiction within the United Kingdom is a purely internal matter, and other Member or Contracting States can have no objection to a discretion to stay being used to transfer actions from one part of the United Kingdom to another.[1167] A stay will only be granted if there is an alternative forum with jurisdiction elsewhere in the United Kingdom. This avoids the danger of all the parts of the United Kingdom staying the proceedings, thereby denying the claimant his right, under the Brussels I Recast, the Brussels Convention or the Lugano Convention to sue the defendant domiciled in the United Kingdom in that Member State.

In internal United Kingdom cases the Brussels I Recast, Brussels Convention and Lugano Convention are inapplicable and therefore courts in the United Kingdom can use a discretion to stay on the basis of *forum non conveniens* without having to concern themselves with whether this is inconsistent with any of these instruments.[1168]

[1167] See the Schlosser Report, p 98; Briggs 2015, para 2.312; Hartley, p 80; Collins, pp 45–6; Stone (1983) 29 ICLQ 477, 496–9.

[1168] *Cumming v Scottish Daily Record and Sunday Mail Ltd* [1995] EMLR 538; *Lennon v Scottish Daily Record* [2004] EWHC 359 (QB); Collins (1995) 111 LQR 541; *Ivax Pharmaceuticals UK Ltd v Akzo Nobel BV* [2005] EWHC 2658 (Ch), [2006] FSR 43; *Sunderland Marine Mutual Insurance Company Ltd v Wiseman* [2007] EWHC 1460 (Comm) at [38], [2007] 2 All ER (Comm) 937; *Cook v Virgin Media Ltd* [2015] EWCA Civ 1287, [2016] 1 WLR 1672. Drake J in *Cumming* departed from his earlier decision in *Foxen v Scotsman Publications Ltd* [1995] 3 EMLR 145; criticised by Collins and Davenport (1994) 110 LQR 325. See also *Kelly Banks v CGU Insurance plc*, Outer House Court of Session, 5 November 2004 (unreported), per Lady Smith. But for a contrary view, see Hood, *Conflict of Laws Within the UK* (2007), paras 5.16–5.17.

12

THE COMPETENCE OF THE ENGLISH COURTS UNDER— THE TRADITIONAL RULES[1]

1. Actions in Personam	323	2. Actions in Rem	382
(a) Service of a claim form on a defendant present within the jurisdiction	324	(a) An action against a ship as defendant	382
(b) Submission to the jurisdiction	332	(b) An action against a ship other than the primary ship	384
(c) Service of a claim form on a defendant out of the jurisdiction	334	(c) A stay of proceedings which is subject to conditions	385
(d) Are there other bases of competence?	381	(d) The effect of the Brussels/Lugano system	386

1. ACTIONS IN PERSONAM

An action in personam is designed to settle the rights of the parties as between themselves,[2] eg an action for damages for breach of contract, an action for an injunction in a tort case, or an action for possession of tangible property. The most striking feature of the English common law rules relating to competence in actions in personam is their purely procedural character. Anyone may invoke or become amenable to the jurisdiction, provided only that the defendant has been properly served with a claim form.[3]

This procedural approach has meant that, apart from cases where matrimonial relief is sought,[4] the courts have traditionally not been concerned with the connection that the parties or their dispute have with England, but only with whether the defendant can be served. Two important consequences stem from this. First, the mere service of a claim form will give the English courts power to try actions which may be inappropriate for trial in England; eg the defendant may be a foreigner who is only transiently in England and the cause of action may have no factual connection with England. The development of a wide, flexible discretion to stay actions on the basis of *forum non conveniens* is an effective solution to this problem. This allows courts, although competent to try the case, to refuse to do so where there is a clearly more appropriate forum for trial abroad.[5]

---

[1] See generally Hartley (2006) 319 Hague Recueil, Ch IV; Briggs 2015, Chapters 4 and 5; Fentiman 2015, para 8.26ff. For Scots residual national rules see Sch 8 to the Civil Jurisdiction and Judgments Act 1982, as substituted by Civil Jurisdiction and Judgments Order, SI 2001/3929, Sch 2(III), para 7.

[2] *Tyler v Judges of the Court of Registration* (1900) 175 Mass 71.

[3] For the procedure for disputing the English court's jurisdiction see CPR, Part 11. Prior to April 1999, the defendant had to be served with a writ of summons, or its equivalent, eg an originating summons.

[4] Infra, p 954 et seq.

[5] Infra, p 392 et seq.

The second consequence of this procedural approach is the converse of the first. If the defendant is not present within the jurisdiction, the English courts were traditionally denied power to try actions in many cases in which it would be appropriate for trial to be held here, such as when a tort has been committed in England or when the defendant is domiciled, but not physically present, in England. This defect was recognised many years ago and was remedied by statute so as to give a discretionary power to the courts (now contained in the Civil Procedure Rules[6]) to authorise service of a claim form on a defendant abroad in certain cases. Another exception to the normal principle that the courts have no power to entertain an action against a defendant who is outside the jurisdiction was found to be necessary to deal with cases where the defendant submitted to the English court's jurisdiction.

The result of these developments is that the English courts are now competent under common law rules to try an action in personam in three situations:

(a) where there has been service of a claim form on a defendant present within the jurisdiction;
(b) where the defendant has submitted to the English court's jurisdiction;
(c) where there has been service of a claim form out of the jurisdiction under rule 6.36 of the Civil Procedure Rules.

It should be noted that these rules only apply where the claim is not covered by the jurisdictional rules set out in Chapter 11, as explained further in Chapter 10. The common law rules apply in cases which fall outside the scope of the Brussels/Lugano rules, as well as to some cases involving defendants who are not domiciled in a Brussels/Lugano state. Most claims against defendants domiciled in England, another part of the United Kingdom, or in another Member State will therefore not be covered by these rules. If the defendant's current domicile is unknown and cannot be determined, under the Brussels I Recast the defendant is treated as domiciled at their last known place of domicile—if this was in the European Union, national rules of jurisdiction may therefore not be applied unless there is firm evidence that the defendant has now left the European Union.[7]

(a) Service of a claim form on a defendant present within the jurisdiction

(i) Individuals

As has already been seen, at common law "whoever is served with the King's writ [now called a claim form] and can be compelled consequently to submit to the decree made is a person over whom the courts have jurisdiction".[8] Jurisdiction accordingly may be established on the basis of the presence of the defendant in England. This is a basis of general jurisdiction—there is no requirement that the claim relate in any way to activities of the person within the territory, although that will be taken into account in determining whether to stay the proceedings.[9] Once the court has asserted its power by service of process on the defendant it is not rendered incompetent by his subsequent departure from the country.[10] The corollary to this is that if a defendant escapes service, by reason of his absence abroad, no proceedings

---

[6] CPR, r 6.36.

[7] Case C-327/10 *Hypoteční banka as v Lindner* EU:C:2011:745; see further Case C-292/10 *G v De Visser* EU:C:2012:142, [2013] QB 168.

[8] *John Russell & Co Ltd v Cayzer, Irvine & Co Ltd* [1916] 2 AC 298 at 302, HL.

[9] See infra, p 392 et seq. The question of jurisdiction must, however, be distinguished from the question of whether the court has the power to make the particular order sought by the claimant: *Fourie v Le Roux* [2007] UKHL 1 at [25], [2007] 1 WLR 320; *Cartier International AG v British Sky Broadcasting Ltd* [2016] EWCA Civ 658, [2016] ETMR 43.

[10] *Razelos v Razelos (No 2)* [1970] 1 WLR 392; cf the American case of *Michigan Trust Co v Ferry* 228 US 346 (1913).

could traditionally be brought against him,[11] although permission may now be given to serve outside the jurisdiction in various circumstances.[12]

Even the mere transient presence of a person in England suffices to render him amenable to the jurisdiction of the courts. If a claim form is served, eg, on a Japanese person during a visit of a few hours to London, an action may then be brought against him in his absence concerning a matter totally unrelated to anything that has occurred in England.[13] Not only is the justice of this exercise of power suspect, but in many cases it will be ineffective, for in this example a judgment given in the action will be of no use to the claimant unless followed by proceedings in Japan for its enforcement, and a Japanese court can scarcely be expected to recognise a jurisdiction based on such flimsy grounds. This English doctrine is inevitable in domestic law because of the procedural significance of the claim form, but it is unfortunate from the point of view of private international law that jurisdiction is founded merely on presence and not on a stronger connection such as residence.[14] Nevertheless, it has been twice confirmed by the Court of Appeal, holding that the court had jurisdiction over a defendant who was served whilst visiting England for a few days unconnected with the litigation,[15] or even whilst visiting England for Ascot races.[16] Similarly service on a defendant who has been brought within the jurisdiction in police custody or who has come in answer to a witness summons has been held to be good and to confer jurisdiction on the court.[17] If, however, a defendant is enticed within the jurisdiction fraudulently or improperly, then service of the claim form may be set aside.[18]

Part 6 of the Civil Procedure Rules sets out rules on the method of service of a claim form[19] and other documents[20] within the jurisdiction. In principle, Part 6 should not alter the fundamental rule that a defendant may only be served with originating process within the jurisdiction if he is present within the jurisdiction at the time of service or deemed service.[21] It is only concerned with the *method* of service. However, the Court of Appeal has (controversially) disagreed, holding that service can be effected using a method authorised by Part 6

---

[11] *Laurie v Carroll* (1958) 98 CLR 310; *Myerson v Martin* [1979] 1 WLR 1390, CA; *Mondial Trading Pty Ltd v Interocean Marine Transport Inc* (1985) 65 ALR 155; cf *Porter v Freudenberg* [1915] 1 KB 857 at 887–8.

[12] See infra, p 334 et seq.

[13] Cf *Carrick v Hancock* (1895) 12 TLR 59, infra, p 529.

[14] The Foreign Judgments (Reciprocal Enforcement) Act 1933, whose object it is to facilitate the enforcement in England of judgments obtained abroad, specifies the residence, not the mere presence, of the defendant in the country as one of the circumstances sufficient to found the jurisdiction of a court of that country, infra, p 595. For the position under the common law rules on recognition and enforcement, see infra, p 529. Note however that residence with a substantial connection would establish domicile for the purposes of the Brussels I Recast, meaning that the common law rules would generally no longer apply: see supra, p 199.

[15] *Colt Industries Inc v Sarlie* [1966] 1 WLR 440, following *Carrick v Hancock* (1895) 12 TLR 59 at 60.

[16] *HRH Maharanee Seethaderi Gaekwar of Baroda v Wildenstein* [1972] 2 QB 283, CA. The presence rule has been accepted by the US Supreme Court in *Burnham v Superior Court of California* 109 L Ed 2d (1990); Collins (1991) 107 LQR 10. See for Australia: *John Pfeiffer Pty Ltd v Rogerson* (2000) 203 CLR 503 at [13], HC of Australia; *BHP Billiton Ltd v Schultz* (2004) 221 CLR 400 at [17], HC of Australia.

[17] *Doyle v Doyle* (1974) 52 DLR (3d) 143; *John Sanderson & Co (NSW) Pty Ltd v Giddings* [1976] VR 421; *Baldry v Jackson* [1976] 1 NSWLR 19; affd without discussion of this issue [1976] 2 NSWLR 415.

[18] *Watkins v North American Land and Timber Co Ltd* (1904) 20 TLR 534, HL; *Colt Industries Inc v Sarlie*, supra, at 443–4.

[19] Section II.

[20] Section III. See *Godwin v Swindon BC* [2001] EWCA Civ 1478, [2002] 1 WLR 997.

[21] *Bank of Swaziland v Hahn* [1986] 1 WLR 506, HL; *Chellaram v Chellaram (No 2)* [2002] EWHC 632 (Ch) at [47], [2002] 3 All ER 17; *Fairmays v Palmer* [2006] EWHC 96 (Ch). But see the criticism by Zuckerman (2006) 25 CJQ 127. Service by an alternative method (formerly called substituted service), discussed infra, cannot be used to get round this: *Cadogan Properties Ltd v Mount Eden Land Ltd* [2000] IL Pr 722, CA.

(leaving a claim form at the defendant's place of business[22]) to serve a defendant who was temporarily abroad at the time of service, and that there is no longer any such fundamental rule.[23] Part 6 provides[24] that a claim form may be served on an individual by any of the following methods: (a) personal service (ie leaving it with that individual[25]); (b) first class post, document exchange or other service which provides for delivery on the next business day; (c) leaving the claim form at a place specified in rule 6.7, 6.8, 6.9 or 6.10; (d) by fax or other means of electronic communication.[26] The court may make an order permitting service by an alternative method[27] and can dispense with service.[28] The court will serve a claim form within the jurisdiction, subject to a number of exceptions,[29] one of which is where the claimant notifies the court that he wishes to serve it himself.[30] Where the court is to serve the claim form, it is for the court to decide which of the methods of service specified above is to be used.[31]

Rule 6.6 provides that a claim form must be served within the jurisdiction, except as provided by the rules on service out of the jurisdiction.[32] If the defendant has given the business address of a solicitor as an address for service, or a solicitor has notified the claimant that they are authorised to accept service on behalf of the defendant, service must be at the address of the solicitor.[33] A defendant may alternatively designate an address at which they reside or carry on business as the address for service,[34] or agree to another method of service contractually.[35] For example, the parties may agree in a contract that service is to be effected on an agent of the defendant in England. The defendant out of the jurisdiction will be deemed to have been served by service on his agent within the jurisdiction.[36] However, if the parties

---

[22] See CPR, r 6.9; discussed infra, p 327. Service other than personal service, eg by post, was available prior to the CPR.

[23] *City & County Properties v Kamali* [2006] EWCA Civ 1879, [20007] 1 WLR 1219. The decision of the House of Lords in *Bank of Swaziland* was distinguished as one simply of construction of the then procedural rule. See also *SSL International Plc v TTK LIG Ltd* [2011] EWCA Civ 1170, [2012] 1 WLR 1842.

[24] CPR, r 6.3(1).

[25] CPR, rule 6.5(3). See *Tseitline v Mikhelson* [2015] EWHC 3065 (Comm). There is an exception where a solicitor is authorised to accept service, r 6.7, discussed infra.

[26] See further PD6A; *Molins plc v GD SpA* [2000] 1 WLR 1741, CA; *BAS Capital Funding Corpn v Medfinco Ltd* [2003] EWHC 1798 (Ch) at [167], [2004] 1 Lloyd's Rep 652.

[27] CPR, r 6.15. Previously this could not be made retrospectively (*Anderton v Clwyd CC (No 2)* [2002] EWCA Civ 933, [2002] 1 WLR 3174 at 3185), but this is now permitted under r 6.15(2). It may also be used for defendants outside the territory (*Abela v Baadarani* [2013] UKSC 44, [2013] 1 WLR 2043), but it may not be used to avoid conventions providing the mechanism for service out of the jurisdiction (*Knauf UK GmbH v British Gypsum Ltd* [2002] 1 WLR 907, CA; distinguished in *Phillips v Nussberger* [2008] UKHL 1 at [39], [2008] 1 WLR 180); see also *Cecil v Bayat* [2011] EWCA Civ 135, [2011] 1 WLR 3086. For examples of "good reason" for alternative service: see *Marconi v PT Pan Indonesia Bank Ltd TBK* [2004] EWHC 129 (Comm) at [39]–[45], [2004] 1 Lloyd's Rep 594—very extensive delay under Indonesian procedure; appeal on a different point dismissed [2005] EWCA Civ 422; *Phillips v Symes* [2003] EWHC 1172 (Ch) (Peter Smith J)—speed was essential.

[28] CPR, r 6.16. See *Phillips v Nussberger* [2008] UKHL 1 at [34]–[35], [2008] 1 WLR 180; *Olafsson v Gissurarson* [2008] EWCA Civ 152. This power should not be used to circumvent the requirements of a service convention: *Shiblaq v Sadikoglu* [2004] EWHC 1890 (Comm) at [57], [2004] IL Pr 51. See also *Lakah Group v Al Jazeera Satellite Channel* [2003] EWCA Civ 1781 at [10]–[13].

[29] CPR, r 6.4(1).

[30] CPR, r 6.4(1)(b).

[31] CPR, 6.4(2).

[32] CPR, r 6.6(1). In a case where service within the jurisdiction is problematic, this appears to suggest that a claimant who goes straight for service out of the jurisdiction may fall foul of this provision.

[33] CPR, r 6.7. See *Marshall Rankine v Maggs* [2006] EWCA Civ 20; *Nanglegan v Royal Free Hampstead NHS Trust* [2002] 1 WLR 1043.

[34] CPR, r 6.8.

[35] CPR, r 6.11; *Society of Lloyd's v Tropp* [2004] EWHC 33 (Comm).

[36] This follows the common law rule in *Tharsis Sulphur and Copper Co Ltd v Société Industrielle et Commerciale des Métaux* (1889) 58 LJQB 435.

agree on a method of service which involves service out of the jurisdiction, the claim form shall not be deemed to have been duly served abroad unless permission has been granted under rule 6.36 or service of the claim form is allowed without permission under rule 6.32 or 6.33.[37] Where no solicitor is acting for the party to be served and the party has not given an address for service, the claim form must be sent or transmitted to, or left at, the place shown in a table set out in rule 6.9(2).[38] In the case of an individual, this is the usual or last known residence.[39] In the case of an individual who is being sued in the name of a business, it is the usual or last known residence, or the principal or last known place of business.[40]

(ii) Partnerships

In the case of a partnership,[41] the claimant may serve the claim form on an individual partner who is present in England, or on the partnership firm.[42] Where the claim is against the partnership, the Civil Procedure Rules provide that co-partners carrying on business in England must be sued in the name of the firm, unless it is inappropriate to do so.[43] The Civil Procedure Rules also deal with the method of service and state that, where partners are being sued in the name of their firm, a claim form is served personally on a partnership by leaving it with a partner, or a person who, at the time of service, has the control or management of the partnership at its principal place of business.[44] It is also possible to serve a claim form on a partnership by first class post or document exchange or other next business day delivery service, leaving it at a place specified in rule 6.7, 6.8, 6.9 or 6.10,[45] or by fax or other means of electronic communication.[46] Therefore, service which is effected on the person who has the control or management of the English business operates as a valid service on all the partners, even in the case of a foreign firm all the members of which are resident abroad.[47] Similarly, service on one partner present in England is effective against the co-partners out of

---

[37] CPR, r 6.11(2); *McCulloch v Bank of Nova Scotia* [2006] EWHC 790 (Ch) at [33], [2006] 2 All ER (Comm) 714.

[38] In the case of a natural person, the table sets out alternative methods of service, more than one of which may be used: *Phillips v Symes* [2002] 1 WLR 863 at [26] (Hart J).

[39] Even if the defendant did not receive it: *Akram v Adam* [2004] EWCA 1601; *Smith v Hughes* [2003] EWCA Civ 656, [2003] 1 WLR 2441. The latter case also establishes that it does not matter that the claimant knows or believes that the defendant was no longer living at that address. *Smith v Hughes* was distinguished in *Marshall Rankine v Maggs*, supra. See also *Burns-Anderson v Wheeler* [2005] EWHC 575, [2005] 1 Lloyd's Rep 580; *Varsani v Relfo Ltd (In Liquidation)* [2010] EWCA Civ 560, [2011] 1 WLR 1402.

[40] See, eg, *O'Hara v McDougall* [2005] EWCA Civ 1623.

[41] The nature and status of an entity is a matter for the law under which it is created: *Oxnard Financing SA v Rahn* [1998] 1 WLR 1465, CA.

[42] CPR, r 7.2A and PD 7A.

[43] CPR, PD 7A, 5A. Where an individual foreigner carries on a business here in a name other than his own name, a claim may be brought against the business name: CPR, PD 7A, 5C. Valid service can be effected on a person acting on a partner's instructions to accept service: *Kenneth Allison Ltd v A E Limehouse & Co* [1992] 2 AC 105, HL.

[44] CPR, r 6.5(3)(c). This provision will not apply to a limited liability partnership. The partnership is a separate entity and the *partners* are not being sued in the name of the firm. Such a partnership is a body corporate according to s 1(2) of the Limited Liability Partnerships Act 2000 (partnership law is also disapplied by s 1(5)). By virtue of CPR, r 6.9, an LLP can be sued at the principal office of the partnership or any place of business of the partnership within the jurisdiction which has a real connection with the claim. The Companies Act 2006 provisions in relation to service (discussed infra, pp 328–31) have been extended to cover limited liability partnerships (see s 15 of the Limited Liability Partnerships Act 2000) allowing service at its registered office: The Limited Liability Partnerships (Application of Companies Act 2006) Regulations 2009, SI 2009/1804, s 75.

[45] See infra. Rule 6.9 specifies that an individual being sued in the business name of a partnership may be served at the usual or last known residence of the individual, or the principal or last known place of business of the partnership. See, eg, *Lexi Holdings plc v Shaid Luqman*, 22 October 2007 (unreported).

[46] CPR, r 6.3(3).

[47] *Worcester City and County Banking Co v Firbank, Pauling & Co* [1894] 1 QB 784, CA.

the jurisdiction,[48] and service effected with the permission of the court under rule 6.36[49] on one partner out of the jurisdiction is a good service on all the other partners out of the jurisdiction.[50] Service on the partnership in England will allow the claimant to seek permission to serve a partner abroad as a "necessary or proper party to that claim".[51] In the situation where there is a foreign partnership which does not carry on business within the jurisdiction, it is permissible to sue the partnership in England by naming as defendants the individual partners being sued in their capacity as partners.[52] Service of the claim form on these individuals will have to be effected within the jurisdiction or out of the jurisdiction using rule 6.36.

(iii) Companies[53]

The same principle applies for corporate defendants as for individual defendants: the defendant is subject to the jurisdiction of the English court if he is present in England. Of course, a company cannot literally be present in England. It is therefore necessary to give an artificial presence to a corporate defendant, according to which a foreign company can be present and thus subject to service in England by virtue of the transaction of business.

Rule 6.3(2) of the Civil Procedure Rules specifies that a company may be served (alternatively) pursuant to the Companies Act 2006 or the Civil Procedure Rules themselves.

(a) The Companies Act 2006

The Companies Act 2006, which replaced the old Companies Act 1985, made important changes to the rules on service of proceedings. The rules under the 1985 Act were unclear in various respects,[54] and the Companies Act 2006 has made fundamental changes.

(i) A company registered in the United Kingdom[55]

Part 37 of the Companies Act 2006 deals with service on companies. A document may be served on a company registered under the Act by leaving it at, or sending it by post to, the company's registered office.[56] This also permits English proceedings to be commenced against a Scottish company through service on the Scottish registered office.[57] There is a special rule for the situation where a company registered in Scotland or Northern Ireland carries on business in England and Wales. The process of any court in England and Wales may be served on the company by leaving it at, or sending it by post to, the company's principal place of business in England and Wales, addressed to the manager or other head officer in England and Wales of the company, as well as sending a copy by post to the registered office.[58]

Provision is also made for service of documents on a director or secretary of a company.[59] There is no suggestion that this can be used to bring an action against the company.

---

48 *Lysaght Ltd v Clark & Co* [1891] 1 QB 552.
49 Discussed, infra, p 334 et seq.
50 *Hobbs v Australian Press Association* [1933] 1 KB 1, CA.
51 *West of England Steamship Owners Protection and Indemnity Association Ltd v John Holman & Sons* [1957] 1 WLR 1164; infra, pp 336–9.
52 *Oxnard Financing SA v Rahn* [1998] 1 WLR 1465, CA.
53 See generally Enonchong (1999) 48 ICLQ 921; Rogerson (2000) 3 CFILR 272.
54 See the previous edition of this book for discussion.
55 It should be noted that jurisdiction for most civil and commercial claims against a company with its registered office, central administration, or principal place of business in the United Kingdom will be determined by the Brussels I Recast: see supra, p 200. In such cases, these rules only determine the correct means of service.
56 Companies Act 2006, s 1139(1).
57 *Ashley v Tesco Stores Ltd* [2015] EWCA Civ 414, [2015] 1 WLR 5153.
58 S 1139(4).
59 S 1140.

(ii) An overseas company[60]

The Companies Act 2006 also deals with service on an overseas company, defined as a company incorporated outside the United Kingdom.[61] Part 34 requires an overseas company to register certain particulars[62] if the company opens a branch[63] or other establishment[64] in the United Kingdom, including the "name and service address of every person resident in the United Kingdom authorised to accept service of documents on behalf of the company in respect of the establishment, or a statement that there is no such person".[65] Part 37 then provides that a document may be served on an overseas company whose particulars have been so registered by leaving it at, or sending it by post to, the registered address of a person authorised to accept service.[66] If there is no such person, or if service cannot be effected on the nominated person, a document may be served at any place of business of the company.[67]

Establishment of a place of business is deliberately different from merely carrying on business.[68] Ultimately it is a question of fact whether a place of business has been established.[69] The place of business test has long been used under the Companies Act, and the older cases can still be used as guidance.[70] There is conflicting authority on whether the requirement for a place of business means a place of business that is still established at the time of service, or whether service on a former place of business that has ceased to function is adequate.[71] The case law indicates that it is relevant to see whether the business is carried on from a fixed and definite place (although a stand open for nine days at an exhibition has been held sufficient[72]) and whether the company uses an agent that can bind it contractually.[73] Indeed, the latter factor should be regarded as being a powerful one, albeit not determinative.[74] The business premises do not have to be owned or leased by the company.[75] If the foreign company

---

[60] It should be noted that jurisdiction for most civil and commercial claims against a company with its registered office, central administration, or principal place of business in a European Union Member State will be determined by the Brussels I Recast: see supra, p 200. In such cases, these rules only determine the correct means of service.

[61] S 1044.

[62] Specified in the Overseas Companies Regulations 2009, SI 2009/1801, reg 7.

[63] This means a branch within the meaning of the Eleventh Company Law Directive (EEC) No 89/666. The Directive does not, however, contain a definition of a branch; recourse should arguably be had to the definition used under the Brussels I Recast (see supra, p 279 et seq), but see *Saab v Saudi American Bank* [1999] 1 WLR 1861, 1871, CA.

[64] Pursuant to s 1046(2)(c) of the Companies Act 2006 and the definition of "establishment" in the Overseas Companies Regulations 2009, supra, reg 2.

[65] Overseas Companies Regulations 2009, supra, reg 7(1)(e).

[66] Section 1139(2).

[67] Ibid.

[68] *Rakusens Ltd (A Company) v Baser Ambalaj Plastik Sanayi Ticaret AS* [2001] EWCA Civ 1820 at [33] (per Arden LJ), [2002] 1 BCLC 104.

[69] The *Rakusens* case, supra. See also *Reuben v Time Inc* [2003] EWHC 1430 QB at [33].

[70] See *South India Shipping Corpn Ltd v Import-Export Bank of Korea* [1985] 1 WLR 585, CA; *Re Oriel Ltd* [1985] 1 WLR 180, CA; *Adams v Cape Industries plc* [1990] Ch 433 at 530–1; *Cleveland Museum of Art v Capricorn Art International SA* [1990] 2 Lloyd's Rep 166; the *Rakusens* case, supra; *Domansa v Derin Shipping And Trading Co Inc* [2001] 1 Lloyd's Rep 362, 365–6; *Matchnet plc v William Blair & Co LLC* [2002] EWHC 2128 (Ch) at [7], [2003] 2 BCLC 195; *Harrods Ltd v Dow Jones & Co Inc* [2003] EWHC 1162 (QB).

[71] *Deverall v Grant Advertising Inc* [1955] Ch 111, CA; and see *Bethlehem Steel Corpn v Universal Gas and Oil Co Inc* (1978) Times, 3 August, HL; but see *Rome v Punjab National Bank (No 2)* [1989] 1 WLR 1211.

[72] *Dunlop Pneumatic Tyre Co Ltd v AG Cudell & Co* [1902] 1 KB 342, CA.

[73] The *Rakusens* case, supra, at [17] (per Buxton LJ), [39] (per Arden LJ); *Harrods Ltd v Dow Jones & Co Inc* [2003] EWHC 1162 (QB) at [21]. Note that CPR, r 6.12 also permits a defendant out of the jurisdiction to be served through its local agent when the claim relates to a contract entered into in the jurisdiction with or through the agent.

[74] The *Adams* case, supra, at 531; followed by Arden LJ in the *Rakusens* case, supra, at [40], [41] and in *Reuben v Time Inc* [2003] EWHC 1430 QB at [40], [41].

[75] *Re Oriel Ltd* [1986] 1 WLR 180, CA, a case under s 106 of the Companies Act 1948.

carries on business in England by means of an independent commercial "agent", the latter will doubtless own or lease the business premises. Nonetheless, the foreign company may have established a place of business in England.[76] On the other hand, it is not enough for the company to have an office if it does not carry on any business at that place.[77] Nor is it enough merely to own land in England; it has to be shown that the business of the foreign company is habitually carried on from that land.[78] However, a private residence of one of the directors of the company can constitute a place of business if the company transacts business from there,[79] but occasional board meetings will not be sufficient.[80] The lack of some external manifestation of the defendant company, such as a nameplate or its modern equivalent (a website setting out its business address[81]) at the premises, although a relevant factor, is not a decisive one. Statements on the company's website have to be treated with caution because they are not designed to be legal statements.[82] It is not necessary to show that the activities in England constitute a substantial part of the foreign company's business; and no objection has been made to the fact that activities in London were merely incidental to the defendant's main objects.[83]

In cases where a foreign company carries on business in England by means of a wholly-owned subsidiary company,[84] jurisdiction over each legal entity is analysed separately, and if litigation is pursued against the parent company the question will arise whether the English subsidiary is carrying on its own business or that of its parent. The ability of the former to bind the latter contractually will be an important factor in determining this. Frequently, the English subsidiary will carry on its own business and not that of the parent,[85] with the result that the foreign parent company will not be present in England. It has been argued that it would be better to look at the economic realities of the situation, and that if the parent and subsidiary form one economic unit it should be possible to found jurisdiction against the foreign parent on the basis of the presence of its subsidiary in England, or indeed against a foreign subsidiary on the basis of the presence of the parent in England,[86] or more generally on the basis of a corporate defendant's economic presence within the jurisdiction rather than on the establishment of a place of business.[87]

As noted above, the Regulations adopted under the Companies Act 2006 require the address of a person authorised to accept service "on behalf of the company *in respect of the establishment*" (emphasis added). The Companies Act 2006 itself, however, permits service on any

---

[76] *Cleveland Museum of Art v Capricorn Art Internationals A* [1990] 2 Lloyd's Rep 166. The English proceedings were, however, stayed, see infra, p 408.

[77] The *Matchnet* case, supra.

[78] *Re Oriel Ltd*, supra, at 223.

[79] Ibid, at 222.

[80] *SSL International Plc v TTK LIG Ltd* [2011] EWCA Civ 1170, [2012] 1 WLR 1842.

[81] *Commonwealth Bank of Australia v White* [1999] 2 VR 681, 692.

[82] The *Matchnet* case, supra; *Lakah Group v Al Jazeera Satellite Channel* [2003] EWHC 1231 (QB) at [32], [46]–[47]; affd [2003] EWCA Civ 1781 without discussion of this point.

[83] The *South India Shipping* case, supra, per Ackner LJ who followed a case decided under the common law: *Hercules Aktieselskabet Dampskib v Grand Trunk Pacific Rly Co* [1912] 1 KB 222, CA.

[84] See *Adams v Cape Industries plc* [1990] Ch 433, a case on enforcement of a foreign judgment, discussed infra, pp 529–31.

[85] See, eg, the *Matchnet* case, supra; *Lakah Group v Al Jazeera Satellite Channel* [2003] EWHC 1231 (QB). But for an example where the parent acted on behalf of the subsidiary, see Case 218/86 *Sar Schotte GmbH v Parfums Rothschild* [1987] ECR 4905, a case concerned with jurisdiction under Art 5(5) of the Brussels Convention, discussed supra, p 281; *Amalgamated Wireless (Australasia) Ltd v McDonnell Douglas Corpn* (1988) 77 ALR 537 at 540.

[86] See Fawcett (1988) 37 ICLQ 645 at 663 et seq. Such an approach was rejected in *Adams v Cape Industries plc* [1990] Ch 433 at 532 et seq, CA.

[87] Fawcett, op cit. Cf *Ets Soules et Cie v Handgate Co Ltd SA, The Handgate* [1987] 1 Lloyd's Rep 142.

person authorised to "accept service of documents on the company's behalf".[88] On this basis, it has been held that there is no requirement that the claim relate to the company's establishment or activities within the jurisdiction.[89] As with service of proceedings on a natural person within the territory, mere presence is sufficient to establish a basis of general jurisdiction, although the connection between the claim and the territory will be taken into account in determining whether to stay proceedings.[90] On this issue, the position under the Companies Act 1985 was somewhat unclear.[91]

(b) Part 6 of the Civil Procedure Rules

As has been seen, the Companies Act 2006 sets out methods of service in relation to UK and overseas companies. However, as an alternative to these methods of service a company may be served by any method permitted under Part 6 of the Civil Procedure Rules.[92] There was traditionally some uncertainty as to the relationship between Part 6 of the Civil Procedure Rules and the rules under the Companies Act 1985.[93] The issue was significant for two main reasons. First, under the Civil Procedure Rules, it is clear that there is no requirement that the claim relate to the activities of a company (including an overseas company) within the territory,[94] whereas the position under the Companies Act 1985 was less clear. Second, the Companies Act 1985 and now Companies Act 2006 both refer to an "establishment" of an overseas company, where the Civil Procedure Rules refer only to a "place of business"—if the former were intended to set a requirement of formality and permanence in order for an overseas company to be subject to service, it would arguably be undermined by the latter. The argument that Part 6 is ultra vires in providing these alternative methods of service was, however, rejected by Longmore J in *Sea Assets Ltd v PT Garuda Indonesia*.[95] Since there is (apparently) no requirement under the Companies Act 2006 that a claim relate to the activities of the company within the territory,[96] there would be less scope to argue that the Civil Procedure Rules are inconsistent with the Act. It has always been uncontroversial that the methods of service set out in Part 6 of the Civil Procedure Rules can be used if a foreign company fails to register a business establishment as required under the Companies Act.

One of the methods of service set out under the Civil Procedure Rules is leaving the document at a specified place. If a defendant has given a business address as an address for service, or agreed to be served at the business address of their solicitors, then they may be served by leaving the document at that address.[97] If a defendant has not given any such address, the document must be sent or transmitted to, or left at, the place shown in the table set out in

---

[88] Companies Act 2006, s 1139(2)(a).

[89] *Teekay Tankers Ltd v STX Offshore & Shipping Co* [2014] EWHC 3612 (Comm), [2015] 2 All ER (Comm) 263.

[90] See infra, p 393 et seq.

[91] See further, eg, *Saab v Saudi American Bank* [1999] 1 WLR 1861; *Sea Assets Ltd v PT Garuda Indonesia* [2000] 4 All ER 371.

[92] CPR, r 6.3(2). See *Murphy v Staples UK Ltd* [2003] EWCA Civ 656, [2003] 1 WLR 2441 (service under the Companies Act was possible even if the defendant had given the address of solicitors for service under the CPR).

[93] *Lakah Group v Al Jazeera Satellite Channel*, [2003] EWHC 1297 at [39]–[41]; affd [2003] EWCA Civ 1781; *Harrods Ltd v Dow Jones & Co Inc* [2003] EWHC 1162 (QB); *Reuben v Time Inc* [2003] EWHC 1430 (QB).

[94] See, eg, *Saab v Saudi American Bank* [1999] 1 WLR 1861; *Sea Assets Ltd v PT Garuda Indonesia* [2000] 4 All ER 371.

[95] [2000] 4 All ER 371.

[96] *Teekay Tankers Ltd v STX Offshore & Shipping Co*, supra.

[97] CPR, r 6.7 and 6.8. On the interpretation of an agreement to accept service see *Actavis Group HF v Eli Lilly & Co* [2013] EWCA Civ 517, [2013] RPC 985.

rule 6.9(2). For a company registered in England and Wales,[98] the specified place of service is the principal office of the company, or any place of business of the company within the jurisdiction which has a real connection with the claim. For any other company it is any place within the jurisdiction where the corporation carries on its activities, or any place of business of the company within the jurisdiction. Service on an address with which the company has no more than a transient or irregular connection will not be valid.[99] It must be the defendant's place of business; what is needed is evidence of actual business activity on the part of the defendant. Business activity on the part of an associated company is not enough.[100]

Another method is that of personal service. A document is served personally on a company or other corporation by leaving it with a person holding a senior position within the company or corporation,[101] such as a director. There is some uncertainty over whether this provision can be used in relation to a foreign company. The accompanying Practice Direction[102] is phrased in narrower terms than the rule itself. It states that personal service on a "registered company or corporation" (ie one registered in England) is effected by leaving a document with a person holding a senior position. When it defines what is meant by a person holding a senior position it again refers to a "registered company or corporation".[103] The intention is seemingly that this method of service cannot be used with a foreign company, and this must be the correct interpretation.[104] It would be absurd if service on a director of a foreign company (which may have no branch or other established place of business or even carry on business in England) who happens to be transiently present in England were to regarded as being effective service on that company. As with service on an individual, the court may make an order permitting service by an alternative method[105] and can dispense with service.[106]

(b) Submission to the jurisdiction

Despite the fundamental principle that the court cannot entertain an action against a defendant who is absent from England, it has long been recognised that an absent defendant may confer jurisdiction on the court by submitting to it. (In cases where the defendant is domiciled in a European Union Member State or contracting state to the Lugano Convention, submission will now be governed by the Brussels I Recast or Lugano Convention and not the common law.)[107] This may be done in a variety of ways, such as by the defendant acknowledging service or entering an appearance without contesting the jurisdiction of the court.[108]

---

[98] This does not include an overseas company, see the *Sea Assets* case, supra. But note that most civil and commercial claims against a company with its registered office, central administration or principal place of business in England will be governed by the Brussels I Recast and not these rules. In such cases, these rules only determine the correct means of service. See infra, p 200.

[99] *Lakah Group v Al Jazeera Satellite Channel* [2003] EWCA Civ 1781 at [8].

[100] *Lakah Group v Al Jazeera Satellite Channel* [2003] EWHC 1297 at [48]; affd without discussion of this point [2003] EWCA Civ 1781; *Chopra v Bank of Singapore Ltd* [2015] EWHC 1549 (Ch).

[101] CPR, r 6.5(3). See PD6A, 6.2 for the definition of "a person holding a senior position".

[102] PD6A, 6.1.

[103] It does, though, have a definition of such a person in respect of a "corporation which is not a registered company": PD6A, 6.2(2).

[104] See *SSL International Plc v TTK LIG Ltd* [2011] EWCA Civ 1170, [2012] 1 WLR 1842; but see *Lakah Group v Al Jazeera Satellite Channel* [2003] EWHC 1231 (QB), affd [2003] EWCA Civ 1781.

[105] CPR, r 6.15; supra p 326.

[106] CPR, r 6.16; supra p 326.

[107] See infra, pp 226–9.

[108] CPR, r 11(5). There is no submission by acknowledging service but failing to tick the box indicating an intention to contest jurisdiction, and the defendant ordinarily (subject to CPR, r 3.1(2)(a)) has 14 days to make his application: CPR, r 11(3), (4) (or 28 days in the Commercial Court: CPR, r 58.7); *IBS Technologies (PVT) Ltd v APM Technologies SA* 2003 (unreported); *Monrose Investments v Orion Nominees* [2002] IL Pr 21; *Midland Resources Ltd v Gonvarri Industrial SA* [2002] IL Pr 8; *CAN Insurance Co Ltd v Office Depot International (UK) Ltd* [2005] EWHC 456 (Comm) at [26]. An extension may be granted,

If a foreign defendant agrees (contractually or otherwise) that they can be served within the jurisdiction (including for example through an English solicitor), without reserving the right to subsequently contest jurisdiction, this may also be considered to constitute submission.[109] A jurisdiction agreement in favour of the English courts does not on its own constitute submission, although (particularly if it is exclusive) it is likely to be a weighty factor in any exercise of jurisdictional discretion.[110] A foreign claimant who commences an action in England also submits willingly to the jurisdiction and is subject to all the incidents of litigation in England, including amenability to a related counterclaim.[111] In contrast, a foreign defendant who is brought to jurisdiction by answering a claim within rule 6.36 of the Civil Procedure Rules is brought to England unwillingly and can limit his submission to the jurisdiction; prima facie he is regarded as submitting only on a claim-by-claim basis.[112] Although a defendant who acknowledges service and contests the case on its merits will be held to have submitted to the jurisdiction,[113] an acknowledgment of service merely to protest that the court does not have jurisdiction will not constitute submission,[114] even if the defendant also seeks a stay of proceedings pending the outcome of proceedings abroad.[115] Nor will the retention of the claim form and acknowledgment of service, by themselves, amount to a waiver of any irregularity.[116] The question is whether the defendant has taken action which is inconsistent with contesting the jurisdiction of the court. Where a defendant has complied with Part 11 of the Civil Procedure

even retrospectively—*Texan Management Ltd v Pacific Electric Wire and Cable Co Ltd* [2009] UKPC 46; *Zumax Nigeria Limited v First City Monument Bank plc* [2016] EWCA Civ 567. However, if the jurisdictional challenge fails at first instance, filing a second acknowledgment of service will indicate submission, even if the defendant later appeals the jurisdictional decision: CPR, r 11(8); *Deutsche Bank AG London Branch v Petromena ASA* [2015] EWCA Civ 226, [2015] 1 WLR 4225. An extension of time to file the second acknowledgement of service should instead be sought in these circumstances.

[109] The Civil Procedure Rules provide that service within the territory according to a contractually agreed method is valid (CPR, r 6.7, 6.11), without specifying that it establishes submission; it is not clear that the authorities actually support the proposition (stated in previous editions of this book) that submission is established in this way (as opposed to merely a right to serve in the territory) unless the agreement to accept service is unconditional and relates to a particular dispute. See *Carmel Exporters (Sales) Ltd v Sea-Land Services* [1981] 1 WLR 1068; *Manta Line Inc v Sofianites and Midland Bank plc* [1984] 1 Lloyd's Rep 14, CA; *Sphere Drake Insurance plc v Gunes Sigorta Anonim Sirketi* [1988] 1 Lloyd's Rep 139; *Burrows v Jamaica Private Power Co Ltd* [2002] 1 All ER (Comm) 374; *Jordan v Schatz* (2000) 189 DLR (4th) 62, BC Court of Appeal.

[110] See infra, pp 398–9. Note that the effect of a jurisdiction agreement in favour of the English courts is, however, now generally governed by the Brussels I Recast, regardless of the domicile of the parties (see supra, p 230) unless the case is covered by the Hague Convention on Choice of Court Agreements (see supra, p 315).

[111] CPR, r 20(4). See also *High Commissioner for India v Ghosh* [1960] 1 QB 134; *Balkanbank v Taher (No 2)* [1995] 1 WLR 1067, CA; *Glencore International AG v Exter Shipping Ltd* [2002] EWCA Civ 528 at [45]–[56], [2002] All ER (Comm) 1.

[112] *Glencore International*, supra.

[113] *Boyle v Sacker* (1888) 39 Ch D 249, CA; cf *Redhead v Redhead and Crothers* [1926] NZLR 131; *Obikoya v Silvernorth Ltd* (1983) Times, 6 July; *Brealey v Board of Management of Royal Perth Hospital* (1999) 21 WAR 79; *Global Multimedia International Ltd v ARA Media Services* [2006] EWHC 3612 (Ch), [2007] 1 All ER (Comm) 1160. Consenting to an order of the court may constitute submission, see *Esal (Commodities) Ltd v Mahendra Pujara* [1989] 2 Lloyd's Rep 479; as will a counterclaim, see *CAN Insurance Co Ltd v Office Depot International (UK) Ltd* [2005] EWHC 456 (Comm) at [26].

[114] CPR, r 11, see supra, p 332. See generally *Re Dulles' Settlement* (No 2), *Dulles v Vidler* [1951] Ch 842, CA; *Tallack v Tallack and Broekema* [1927] P 211; *Razelos v Razelos (No 2)* [1970] 1 WLR 392 at 403; *Air Nauru v Nive Airlines Ltd* [1993] 2 NZLR 632; cf *Solvalub Ltd v Match Investments Ltd* [1998] IL Pr 419 (going beyond a protest as to jurisdiction and into the merits constituted submission), Jersey CA; *Trans-Continental Textile Recycling v Partenreederei MS Erato* [1998] IL Pr 129, Federal Court of Canada. The principle is the same when it comes to enforcement of foreign judgments: Civil Jurisdiction and Judgments Act 1982, s 33, as amended, discussed infra, pp 534–7.

[115] *Williams and Glyns Bank plc v Astro Dinamico Cia Naviera SA* [1984] 1 WLR 438, HL; cf *The Messiniaki Tolmi* [1984] 1 Lloyd's Rep 266, CA; *Finnish Marine Insurance Co Ltd v Protective National Insurance Co* [1990] 1 QB 1078; *Prudential Assurance Co Ltd v Prudential Insurance Co of America* [2003] FSR 97 at 101–5.

[116] *Caribbean Gold Ltd v Alga Shipping Co Ltd* [1993] 1 WLR 1100. See also on waiver *The Xing Su Hai* [1995] 2 Lloyd's Rep 15.

Rules with a view to challenging the jurisdiction, and the time for making his application has not expired, any conduct on his part must be wholly unequivocal to amount to a submission to the jurisdiction and a waiver of that right of challenge.[117] Seeking to obtain evidence through discovery which may support a challenge to jurisdiction does not therefore constitute submission.[118] Any submission must not have been induced by misrepresentation.[119]

It must be noted that the parties cannot by submission confer jurisdiction on the court to entertain proceedings beyond its authority.[120] Submission will not, for example, confer jurisdiction in divorce or nullity proceedings,[121] or over proceedings principally concerned with a question of title to foreign land.[122]

(c) Service of a claim form on a defendant out of the jurisdiction[123]

The traditional rule at common law, that no action in personam will lie against a defendant unless he has been served with a claim form while present in England, would often preclude a claimant from enforcing a claim in the most appropriate forum. Because of this an entirely different kind of jurisdiction, generally called "assumed" jurisdiction, was introduced many years ago,[124] which gave the courts a discretionary power to summon absent defendants, whether English or foreign. The exercise of this jurisdiction is now governed by rule 6.36 of the Civil Procedure Rules, and Practice Direction 6B. The overriding objective of these rules is to enable the court to deal with cases justly.[125]

Rules 6.32, 6.33 and 6.36 permit service of a claim form on a defendant who is out of the jurisdiction (ie not to be found in England or Wales) in the circumstances that will be considered below. In some cases service is allowed without the permission of the court. However, in many cases service is only allowed with the permission of the court. This contrasts with the position in a number of common law jurisdictions in which this requirement has been dispensed with altogether.[126] There is something to be said for the latter approach.[127] An amendment to the English rules on service out of the jurisdiction to reflect this has been considered but has not been introduced.

(i) Service of a claim form out of the jurisdiction with the permission of the court

Rule 6.36 empowers the court, upon an application being made to it,[128] to permit service[129] of a claim form[130] on a defendant who is abroad. However, permission will only

---

[117] *SMAY Investments Ltd v Sachdev* [2003] EWHC 474 (Ch), [2003] 1 WLR 1973.

[118] *Zumax Nigeria Limited v First City Monument Bank plc* [2016] EWCA Civ 567.

[119] *Beecham Group plc v Norton Healthcare Ltd* [1997] FSR 81 at 88.

[120] *Re Paramount Airways Ltd (In Administration)* [1992] Ch 160 at 171.

[121] Infra, p 954 et seq.

[122] Civil Jurisdiction and Judgments Act 1982, s 30, as amended by the Civil Jurisdiction and Judgments Act 1991, Sch 2, para 13 and the Civil Jurisdiction and Judgments Order 2001/3929 Sch 2(IV), para 13; infra, p 492.

[123] Collins (1972) 21 ICLQ 656; reprinted in *Essays*, p 226.

[124] By the Common Law Procedure Act 1852.

[125] CPR, r 1.1.

[126] For Canada, see Castel and Walker, *Canadian Conflict of Laws* (6th edn), para 11.5; Blom in Fawcett (ed), *Declining Jurisdiction*, pp 121–4. For New Zealand, see NZ High Court Rule 219; *Kuwait Asia Bank EC v National Mutual Life Nominees Ltd* [1991] 1 AC 187, [1990] 3 All ER 404 (service can nonetheless be set aside on the application of the defendant); Barnard in Fawcett (ed), *Declining Jurisdiction*, pp 343–5.

[127] Infra, p 377.

[128] For the requirement of supporting written evidence see r 6.37; *ANCAP v Ridgley* [1996] 1 Lloyd's Rep 570; *The Kurnia Dewi* [1997] 1 Lloyd's Rep 552 at 562–3.

[129] For retrospective permission see *Nesheim v Kosa* [2007] EWHC 2710 (Ch).

[130] A counterclaim should be treated as a claim form: *Shahar v Tsitsekkos* [2004] EWHC 2659 (Ch) at [92]. For service out of the jurisdiction of documents other than claim forms see CPR, r 6.38; *C Inc plc v L* [2001] 2 All ER (Comm) 446.

be given if England and Wales is the proper place in which to bring the claim.[131] The court has to be satisfied: first, that there is a good arguable case that one of the grounds of paragraph 3.1 of Practice Direction 6B is satisfied; secondly, that there is a reasonable prospect of success (a serious issue to be tried on the merits); thirdly, that the discretion should be exercised to permit service out of the jurisdiction. The onus is on the claimant to satisfy these three points.[132]

(a) The grounds of Practice Direction 6B

The Civil Procedure Rules, introduced in 1999, aimed to produce a list of grounds for service out of the jurisdiction which was clearer and simpler than the list under the predecessor Rules of the Supreme Court, Order 11.[133] Although there were a number of drafting changes introduced by the Civil Procedure Rules, and there have been further subsequent amendments, many of the principles expounded in former authorities relating to the old grounds remain applicable.[134] The claimant must show a good arguable case that one of the grounds set out in paragraph 3.1 of Practice Direction 6B is satisfied.[135] The standard for a good arguable case is less stringent than a balance of probabilities but more than that of a real prospect of success.[136] A good arguable case is a concept with a certain flexibility and suggests that one party has a much better argument on the evidence available.[137] The court must not appear to pre-try the central issue in the case but at the same time must carefully scrutinise the factor which gives jurisdiction.[138] However, where jurisdiction depends on a question of law or construction, the court will decide it rather than apply the good arguable case test.[139] The following are the cases where the service of a claim form out of the jurisdiction is allowed with the permission of the court.

(i) General grounds

(1) Where "a claim is made for a remedy against a person domiciled within the jurisdiction".[140] This ground is an extensive departure from common law principles. It renders jurisdiction possible over practically any kind of claim[141] against an absent person (including a corporation), provided that he is domiciled in England. In this context, domicile is now determined in accordance with the definition contained in the Brussels I Recast and the Civil

---

[131] CPR, r 6.37(3).

[132] See generally *AK Investment CJSC v Kyrgyz Mobil Tel Ltd* [2011] UKPC 7, [2012] 1 WLR 1804. On the first two points see *Seaconsar Far East Ltd v Bank Markazi Jomhouri Islami Iran* [1994] 1 AC 438 at 454 et seq, HL; on the third see *Spiliada Maritime Corpn v Cansulex Ltd* [1987] AC 460 at 481 and *Berezovsky v Michaels* [2000] 1 WLR 1004, HL. See further Rogerson (2013) 9 J Priv Int L 387.

[133] See the Lord Chancellor's Department Consultation Paper on the Civil Procedure Rules—Service of Court Process Abroad, para 23.

[134] *Petroleo Brasiliero SA v Mellitus Shipping Inc (The Baltic Flame)* [2001] EWCA Civ 418 at [31], [2001] 2 Lloyd's Rep 203. Cf *Crédit Agricole Indosuez v Unicof Ltd* [2003] EWHC 2676 (Comm) at [16], [2004] 1 Lloyd's Rep 196.

[135] *Seaconsar Far East Ltd v Bank Markazi Jomhouri Islami Iran* [1994] 1 AC 438 at 453–4, 456–7, HL. See also *Bank of Baroda v Vysya Bank Ltd* [1994] 2 Lloyd's Rep 87 at 90.

[136] *Carvill America Inc v Camperdown UK Ltd* [2005] EWCA Civ 645 at [45], [2005] 2 Lloyd's Rep 457.

[137] *Canada Trust Co v Stolzenberg (No 2)* [1998] 1 WLR 547 at 555–6 (per Waller LJ), approved by HL [2002] 1 AC 1 at 13 (per Lord Steyn with whom the other Law Lords agreed). See also *Bols Distilleries v Superior Yacht Services Ltd* [2006] UKPC 45, [2007] 1 WLR 12; *Tasarruff v Demirel* [2006] EWHC 3354 (Ch) at [40], [2007] IL Pr 8, affirmed without discussion of this point [2007] EWCA Civ 799, [2007] 1 WLR 2508, leave to appeal to the House of Lords dismissed [2007] 1 WLR 3066; *Cube Lighting and Industrial Design Ltd v Afcon Electra Romania SA* [2011] EWHC 2565 (Ch); supra, p 216. See the application of this principle in relation to PD6B, 3.1(6) infra, p 346. See generally Crawford (2005) 54 ICLQ 829, 840–1.

[138] *Canada Trust Co v Stolzenberg (No 2)*, supra, 555–6 (per Waller LJ).

[139] *Chellaram v Chellaram (No 2)* [2002] EWHC 632 (Ch) at [136], [2002] 2 All ER 17.

[140] CPR, PD6B, 3.1(1).

[141] *Re Liddell's Settlement Trusts* [1936] Ch 365, CA.

Jurisdiction and Judgments Order 2001.[142] This definition is used in cases arising within the Brussels I Recast, and as has been seen,[143] is a very complex one. Of course, the jurisdiction rules contained in the Brussels I Recast and/or the Modified Regulation will apply in a case where the defendant is domiciled in England provided that the dispute concerns international jurisdiction and it is a civil and commercial matter. This ground is therefore concerned only with cases which fall outside the scope of the Brussels/Lugano system.[144]

(2) Where "a claim is made for an injunction ordering the defendant to do or refrain from doing an act within the jurisdiction".[145] The courts refuse to grant permission under this ground unless the substantial and genuine dispute between the parties is whether an injunction against some act in England[146] ought to be granted. It follows that this ground cannot be used in the case of an anti-suit injunction restraining a defendant from pursuing proceedings abroad,[147] nor where an injunction is sought which is worldwide in scope or would ordinarily not be complied with in England.[148] The claimant cannot found the jurisdiction of the English court by claiming an injunction that is only incidental to the remedy that he in fact desires.[149] This ground is wide enough to cover a permanent injunction restraining threatened breaches of contract and torts within the jurisdiction.[150] However, it does not cover the issue of a freezing injunction (previously known as a "Mareva"[151] injunction), ie an *interlocutory* injunction[152] to restrain a defendant from removing his assets from the jurisdiction or from dissipating them pending the trial of an action against him. There is no power to order the issue of a claim form out of the jurisdiction under this ground merely because a freezing injunction is sought.[153] There is, however, a separate ground under Practice Direction 6B which permits this.[154]

(3) Where "a claim is made against a person ('the defendant') on whom the claim form has been or will be served (otherwise than in reliance on this paragraph) and: (a) there is between the claimant and the defendant a real issue which it is reasonable for the court to try; and (b) the claimant wishes to serve the claim form on another person who is a necessary or proper party to that claim".[155] Permission to serve a person abroad may be obtained under

---

[142] CPR, r 6.31(1) referring to the Judgments Regulation and paras 9–12 of Sch 1 of the 2001 Order.
[143] Supra, pp 198–202.
[144] See, eg, *Bank of Dubai v Abbas* [1997] IL Pr 308, CA.
[145] CPR, PD6B, 3.1(2). See *Re Baltic Real Estate Ltd* [1992] BCC 629 at 635.
[146] See *King v Lewis* [2004] EWCA Civ 1329 at [2], [2005] IL Pr 16—no act in England where an injunction was sought against publication on a website controlled abroad. Cf the differently worded Scots interdict provision and *Bonnier Media Ltd v Greg Lloyd Smith and Kestrel Trading Corpn* [2002] ETMR 86.
[147] *Amoco (UK) Exploration Co v British American Offshore Ltd* [1999] 2 Lloyd's Rep 772 at 778. But PD6B, 3.1(5) can be used, see infra, pp 340–1.
[148] *Conductive Inkjet Technology Ltd v Uni-Pixel Displays Inc* [2013] EWHC 2968 (Ch).
[149] *Rosler v Hilbery* [1925] Ch 250, CA.
[150] *James North & Sons Ltd v North Cape Textiles Ltd* [1984] 1 WLR 1428, CA; *Magnesium Elektron Ltd v Molycorp Chemicals & Oxides (Europe) Ltd* [2015] EWHC 3596 (Pat).
[151] *Mareva Cia Naviera SA v International Bulk Carriers SA* [1980] 1 All ER 213 n, CA.
[152] Under s 37 of the Senior Courts Act 1981.
[153] *Siskina (Cargo Owners) v Distos Cia Naviera SA, The Siskina* [1979] AC 210, HL; applied by the Privy Council in *Mercedes Benz AG v Leiduck* [1996] AC 284; Collins (1996) 112 LQR 8; Andrew [1996] CLJ 12; Smart (1996) 112 LQR 397; and see *Perry v Zissis* [1977] 1 Lloyd's Rep 607 at 616–17, CA; *Serge Caudron v Air Zaire* [1986] ILRM 10, Supreme Court of Ireland, distinguished in *McKenna v EH* [2002] 2 ILRM 117. But cf the dissent of Lord Nicholls in the *Mercedes-Benz* case, supra, at 312–14; followed in *Krohn GmbH v Varna Shipyard* [1998] IL Pr 614, Royal Court Jersey. Cf also an injunction under s 30 of the Merchant Shipping Act 1894, re-enacted in Merchant Shipping Act 1995, Sch 1, para 6: *The Mikado* [1992] 1 Lloyd's Rep 163.
[154] See CPR, PD6B, 3.1(5); discussed infra, pp 340–1.
[155] CPR, PD6B, 3.1(3). See generally Fawcett (1995) 44 ICLQ 744, 746–9.

this ground in circumstances that are not covered by any of the other heads—for instance, when a tort has been committed in a foreign country by two persons jointly, only one of whom is subject to the court's jurisdiction.[156] This provision is thus concerned with the situation where there are two defendants:[157] a first (or anchor) defendant, who has actually been served or will be served; and a second defendant whom the claimant now wishes to serve out of the jurisdiction. The claims against each defendant do not have to be based on the same cause of action.[158] There are separate requirements in respect of each defendant.

It is a condition of the grant of permission in respect of the second defendant that the first defendant has already been validly served[159] or will be served.[160] The service can be within the jurisdiction or out of the jurisdiction under rule 6.32, 6.33 or 6.36, provided this is not in reliance on Practice Direction 6B, paragraph 3.1(3). This means that this rule may be used to add a second defendant where a claim has been brought against the first defendant under the Brussels I Recast as well as under other common law rules. For claims falling within the scope of the Brussels I Recast, the rule cannot, however, be used where the second defendant is domiciled in a Member State—jurisdiction over the second defendant would in that case be governed by the Brussels I Recast, including the more restrictive rule on joining additional parties under Article 8(1).[161]

It must also be shown that a claim is made against the defendant who has been served or will be served. However, it need no longer be shown, as was the case with its predecessor, that the first defendant was "duly served".[162] There is, though, a separate requirement under paragraph 3.1(3)(a) that there is between the claimant and the first defendant a real issue which it is reasonable for the court to try.[163] The claimant's application for service out of the jurisdiction under paragraph 3.1(3) must be supported by written evidence stating the grounds for the witness's belief that there is a real issue between the claimant and the first defendant.[164] This merits threshold test[165] protects the first defendant, who can be served with a claim

---

[156] *Croft v King* [1893] 1 QB 419.

[157] They do not need to be joint or even alternative defendants: *Bank of New South Wales v Commonwealth Steel Co Ltd* [1983] 1 NSWLR 69; *Westpac Banking Corpn v Commonwealth Steel Co Ltd* [1983] 1 NSWLR 735.

[158] See, eg, *Owusu v Jackson* [2002] EWCA Civ 877, [2002] IL Pr 45.

[159] *Kuwait Oil Tanker Co SAK v Al Bader* [1997] 1 WLR 1410, CA; *The Xing Su Hai* [1995] 2 Lloyd's Rep 15; *The Cienvik* [1996] 2 Lloyd's Rep 395; *Amoco (UK) Exploration Co v British American Offshore Ltd* [1999] 2 Lloyd's Rep 772, 779; *Chellaram v Chellaram (No 2)* [2002] EWHC 632 (Ch), [2002] 3 All ER 17. It is possible to validate the purported leave with retrospective effect under CPR, r 3.10; this is criticised by Briggs (1997) 68 BYBIL 360.

[160] Service on the first defendant can be retrospectively permitted by alternative means: *Joint Stock Asset Management Co Ingosstrakh-Investments v BNP Paribas SA* [2012] EWCA Civ 644, [2012] 1 Lloyd's Rep 649. This ground cannot however be used if the action against the first defendant has been stayed: *Haji-Ioannou v Frangos* [1999] 2 Lloyd's Rep 337, 361, CA.

[161] See supra, p 283 et seq.

[162] On which see *Derby and Co Ltd v Larsson* [1976] 1 WLR 202, HL.

[163] *Morin v Bonhams & Brooks Ltd* [2003] EWHC 467 (Comm), [2003] IL Pr 25, the Court of Appeal affirmed the decision at first instance that Monegasque law governed the tort claim [2003] EWCA Civ 1802, [2004] 1 Lloyd's Rep 702; *Chase v Ram Technical Services Ltd* [2000] 2 Lloyd's Rep 418 at [11]–[13]; *C Inc plc v L* [2001] 2 All ER (Comm) 446 at [94]; *Crédit Agricole Indosuez v Unicof Ltd* [2003] EWHC 2676 (Comm) at [16], [2004] 1 Lloyd's Rep 196; *Booth v Phillips* [2004] EWHC 1437 at [11]–[23], [2004] 2 Lloyd's Rep 457. For cases on the requirement under Ord 11, r 1(1)(c) RSC that there was a serious issue on the merits in respect of the first defendant: see, eg, *New Hampshire Insurance Co v Aerospace Finance Ltd* [1998] 2 Lloyd's Rep 539 at 542; *The Ikarian Reefer (No 2)* [1999] 2 Lloyd's Rep 621 at 627.

[164] See CPR, r 6.37(2); *ISC v Guerin* [1992] 2 Lloyd's Rep 430 at 432.

[165] *De Molestina v Ponton* [2002] 1 Lloyd's Rep 271 at [37]; *Okpabi v Royal Dutch Shell plc* [2017] EWHC 89 (TCC), [2017] BLR 136.

form, from spurious claims being brought against him solely in order to obtain jurisdiction over the second defendant who is outside the jurisdiction. It also, of course, protects the second defendant. There will not be "a real issue which it is reasonable for the court to try" if the claimant has no real prospect of succeeding on that issue.[166] "Real" is to be contrasted with "fanciful".[167] This requirement will not be met if the claim against the first defendant is bound to fail. If the claim against the first defendant is not a bona fide one, ie the first defendant is joined with the sole object of subjecting the second defendant to the jurisdiction of the English courts, this may affect whether this requirement is satisfied,[168] or may be taken into account in exercising the discretion whether or not to permit service outside the territory.[169] Proceedings brought against the first defendant solely for provisional measures in support of foreign substantive proceedings will not constitute a claim against the first defendant for the purposes of this rule.[170]

The claimant must establish a good arguable case[171] that the second defendant, whom the claimant wishes to serve out of the jurisdiction, is "a necessary or proper party"[172] to the claim against the first defendant. In determining whether a person is a proper party the courts have been very much influenced by English procedural rules on joinders of parties.[173] Generally a person who may be joined in proceedings in accordance with the English rules as to joinder of parties is a "proper party".[174] The focus is on whether there are common questions of law or fact arising out of the same transaction or series of transactions in the claims against each

---

[166] *Owusu v Jackson* [2002] EWCA Civ 877 at [32], [2002] IL Pr 45.

[167] Ibid. The Court said that CPR, PD6B, 3.1(3) invokes the language of r 24.2(a)(i) (summary judgment may be awarded against the claimant where there is "no real prospect of succeeding on the claim or issue") and in that context "real" contrasts with "fanciful", citing *Swain v Hillman* [2001] 1 All ER 91 at [10]. This approach was approved in *AK Investment CJSC v Kyrgyz Mobil Tel Ltd* [2011] UKPC 7, [2012] 1 WLR 1804; see also eg *Hague v Nam Tai Electronics Inc* [2008] UKPC 13.

[168] *Konamaneni v Rolls-Royce Industrial Power (India) Ltd* [2002] 1 WLR 1269 at [44]; *Erste Group Bank AG London Branch v JSC 'VMZ Red October'* [2015] EWCA Civ 379.

[169] *AK Investment CJSC v Kyrgyz Mobil Tel Ltd* [2011] UKPC 7 at [79], [2012] 1 WLR 1804.

[170] *Belletti v Morici* [2009] EWHC 2316 (Comm), [2009] ILPr 57.

[171] *Carvill America Incorporated v Camperdown UK Ltd* [2005] EWCA Civ 645 at [45], [2005] 2 Lloyd's Rep 457.

[172] CPR, PD6B, 3.1(3)(b). See generally *Massey v Heynes and Co* (1888) 21 QBD 330; *Qatar Petroleum v Shell International Petroleum* [1983] 2 Lloyd's Rep 35; *ISC v Guerin* [1992] 2 Lloyd's Rep 430; *Barings plc v Coopers & Lybrand* [1997] IL Pr 12 at 23–4; affd by CA [1997] IL Pr 576 at 585; *Bouygues Offshore SA v Caspian Shipping Co (No 3)* [1997] 2 Lloyd's Rep 493; *C Inc plc v L* [2001] 2 All ER (Comm) 446 at [94]; *McCarthy v Pillay* [2003] 2 ILRM 284; *Crédit Agricole Indosuez v Unicof Ltd* [2003] EWHC 2676 (Comm), [2004] 1 Lloyd's Rep 196; *Caltex Trading Pte Ltd v Metro Trading International Inc* [1999] 2 Lloyd's Rep 724, 737; *OT Africa Line Ltd v Magic Sportswear Corpn* [2005] EWCA Civ 710 at [14], [2005] 2 Lloyd's Rep 170; *Standard Bank Plc v EFAD Real Estate Company WLL* [2014] EWHC 1834 (Comm), [2014] 2 All ER (Comm) 208; *Standard Bank Plc v Just Group LLC* [2014] EWHC 2687 (Comm); *CH Offshore Ltd v PDV Marina SA* [2015] EWHC 595 (Comm).

[173] *Massey v Heynes & Co* (1888) 21 QBD 330 at 338 (per Lord Esher MR), quoted by May LJ in *Multinational Gas and Petrochemical Co v Multinational Gas and Petrochemical Services Ltd* [1983] Ch 258 at 274, CA; *The Eras Eil Actions* [1992] 1 Lloyd's Rep 570, CA; *Arab Monetary Fund v Hashim (No 4)* [1992] 1 WLR 1176, CA; *Barings plc v Coopers & Lybrand* [1997] IL Pr 12 at 18; affd by CA [1997] IL Pr 576 at 585; *Fremont Insurance Ltd v Fremont Indemnity Co* [1997] CLC 1428. See also *Analog Devices BV v Zurich Insurance Co* [2002] 2 ILRM 366, SC of Ireland. See also *Konamaneni v Rolls-Royce Industrial Power (India) Ltd* [2002] 1 WLR 1269 at [44].

[174] *Petroleo Brasiliero SA v Mellitus Shipping Inc (The Baltic Flame)* [2001] EWCA Civ 418 at [33], [2001] 2 Lloyd's Rep 203; Takahashi (2002) 51 ICLQ 127. See also *United Film Distribution Ltd v Chhabria* [2001] EWCA Civ 416 at [32]–[38], [2001] 2 All (Comm) 865; the *Owusu* case, supra, at [9]; *Trumann Investment Group Ltd v Société Générale SA* [2004] EWHC 1769 (Ch); *Carvill America Inc v Camperdown UK Ltd* [2005] EWCA Civ 645 at [48]–[49], [2005] 2 Lloyd's Rep 457. The English rules on joinder are contained in CPR, r 19. CPR, r 7.3 provides that a claimant may use a single claim form to start all claims which can be conveniently disposed of in the same proceedings.

defendant, requiring a "single investigation".[175] There is nothing to suggest that the power of the court to give permission for service out under Practice Direction 6B, paragraph 3.1(3) is narrower than under its predecessor or that the circumstances in which a person may properly be joined as a defendant are narrower under the Civil Procedure Rules than under their predecessor.[176] The second defendant will not be a necessary or proper party if he has a good defence in law to the claim and therefore it is bound to fail;[177] nor will it be the case if the claimant's rights are predominantly against the first defendant.[178] If the claim should have been principally brought against the *second defendant*, the requirements of the rule may also not be satisfied because of the need for a real issue between the claimant and the first defendant, discussed above.[179]

When it comes to the exercise of the discretion to serve out of the jurisdiction, special care is needed with this ground, "in the sense that the court will give careful examination to the cause of action relied on, both as to its substance and its prospects (is it bound or very likely to fail?), whether it is brought in good faith or with some improper motive or ulterior purpose, and whether or not full and fair disclosure has been made".[180] Establishing that England is the clearly appropriate forum for trial will not be easy because the rule applies to cases where there is no territorial connection between the claim which is the subject of the relevant action and the jurisdiction of the English courts.[181] Nevertheless, this is a good provision in terms of litigational convenience, allowing for the consolidation of litigation in one state, promoting efficient dispute resolution and reducing the risk that inconsistent decisions of law or fact may arise in separate proceedings. These are factors which may properly encourage a judge to lean in favour of allowing service out of the jurisdiction in the absence of positive counter-indications.[182] Permission has not been granted where there are substantial defendants who are subject to the jurisdiction and there is no real advantage to the claimant in joining further defendants who are abroad.[183]

(4) Where "a claim is an additional claim under Part 20 and the person to be served is a necessary or proper party to the claim or additional claim".[184] Additional claims under Part 20 include counterclaims by a defendant and claims by a defendant for contribution or indemnity.[185] In determining whether to permit service out of the jurisdiction under this

---

[175] *AK Investment CJSC v Kyrgyz Mobil Tel Ltd* [2011] UKPC 7, [2012] 1 WLR 1804; *Barings plc v Coopers & Lybrand*, supra, at [20].

[176] *United Film Distribution Ltd v Chhabria*, supra, at [38].

[177] *Multinational Gas and Petrochemical Co v Multinational Gas and Petrochemical Services Ltd* [1983] Ch 258 at 273, 287, CA. See also *The Ines* [1993] 2 Lloyd's Rep 492 at 494; *The Kurnia Dewi* [1997] 1 Lloyd's Rep 552 at 564; *Borealis AB v Stargas Ltd* [1999] QB 863, CA, affd by the House of Lords on different grounds [2002] 2 AC 205.

[178] *Re Schintz* [1926] Ch 710.

[179] *Rosler v Hilbery* [1925] Ch 250, CA; *Multinational Gas and Petrochemical Co v Multinational Gas and Petrochemical Services Ltd*, supra, at 279.

[180] *Petroleo Brasiliero SA v Mellitus Shipping Inc (The Baltic Flame)* [2001] EWCA Civ 418 at [21], [2001] 2 Lloyd's Rep 203.

[181] *Multinational Gas and Petrochemical Co v Multinational Gas and Petrochemical Services Ltd* [1983] Ch 258 at 271 (per May LJ), CA.

[182] The *Petroleo Brasiliero* case, supra, at [22].

[183] *Chaney v Murphy* [1948] WN 130, 64 TLR 489. See also *International Marine Services Inc v National Bank of Fujairah* [1997] IL Pr 468, CA.

[184] CPR, PD6B, 3.1(4). See, eg, *Petroleo Brasiliero SA v Mellitus Shipping Inc (The Baltic Flame)* [2001] EWCA Civ 418, [2001] 2 Lloyd's Rep 203 (a contribution case).

[185] CPR, r 20.2. For counterclaims against a non-party see *Shahar v Tsitsekkos* [2004] EWHC 2659 (Ch) at [85]–[92].

ground the court should, as with other grounds, be influenced by the interests of the parties and practical justice.[186]

(4A) Where "a claim is made against the defendant in reliance on one or more of paragraphs (2), (6) to (16), (19) or (21) and a further claim is made against the same defendant which arises out of the same or closely connected facts".[187] This is a new rule which (since October 2015) permits additional related claims to be brought against a defendant subject to the jurisdiction of the court on one of the other listed grounds, where there would otherwise be no basis of jurisdiction for those claims. Previously, each claim had to be separately justified under one of the different jurisdictional gateways in Practice Direction 6B. This rule will be of great practical assistance to claimants seeking to ensure that a number of related claims against a defendant can be heard in the English courts, even if some of those claims are unconnected with England. The consolidation of related claims against a single defendant promotes the efficiency of litigation and the avoidance of conflicting judgments, but the discretion to permit service of a claim form outside the jurisdiction on this basis is likely to be exercised cautiously because it encompasses claims with no connection to England. The "anchor claim" which permits jurisdiction to be exercised on this basis will no doubt be scrutinised to ensure that it is not a device to bring the proceedings within the jurisdiction of the English courts. It is expected that the principles developed to constrain this basis of jurisdiction will be analogous to those developed for proceedings brought under Paragraph 3.1(3), discussed above, where jurisdiction is based on a claim against a separate "anchor defendant".

(ii) Claims for interim remedies

(5) Where "a claim is made for an interim remedy under section 25(1) of the Civil Jurisdiction and Judgments Act 1982".[188] The English courts may make a variety of interim remedies, including orders freezing assets, orders to preserve or inspect property, and orders to provide information or disclose documents.[189] An English court automatically has power to make such orders in support of English proceedings, as part of its inherent jurisdiction,[190] and Section 24 of the 1982 Act provides that interim relief can be granted pending trial in England even where the initial issue to be tried is whether the court has jurisdiction to entertain the proceedings. This provision is therefore concerned with orders in support of (actual or imminent[191]) foreign proceedings. It has been held that it only permits orders obtained against a party to the foreign proceedings, and thus may not be used to obtain a *Norwich Pharmacal* order against a third party in support of foreign proceedings.[192]

At one time a freezing injunction could not be granted in support of foreign proceedings.[193] However, this restriction on the issue of freezing injunctions was subsequently

---

[186] The *Petroleo Brasiliero* case, supra, at [38].

[187] CPR, PD6B, 3.1(4A).

[188] CPR, PD6B, 3.1(5). For the need for such a provision see *Mercedes Benz AG v Leiduck* [1996] 1 AC 284 at 304–5 (per Lord Mustill), PC.

[189] CPR, r 25.1.

[190] Senior Courts Act 1981, s 37.

[191] *Fourie v Le Roux* [2007] UKHL 1, [2007] 1 WLR 320.

[192] *AB Bank Ltd, Off-Shore Banking Unit (OBU) v Abu Dhabi Commercial Bank PJSC* [2016] EWHC 2082 (Comm).

[193] *The Siskina*, supra, at 255; *Channel Tunnel Group Ltd v Balfour Beatty Construction Ltd* [1993] AC 334, at 362, HL. For the position in respect of a search order, see *Altertext Inc v Advanced Data Communications Ltd* [1985] 1 WLR 457 at 463. The general question of jurisdiction over movables is discussed infra, pp 356–8 and 381–2. *The Siskina* is still relevant where a freezing injunction is used in support of domestic proceedings. For a separate aspect of the legacy of *The Siskina*, see *The Veracruz I* [1992] 1 Lloyd's Rep 353, CA; criticised by Collins (1992) 108 LQR 175; Marshall [1992] LMCLQ 161; Wilde [1993] LMCLQ 309.

doubted[194] and was eventually swept aside by section 25[195] of the Civil Jurisdiction and Judgments Act 1982 as extended.[196] Section 25 now allows an English court to grant "interim relief",[197] such as a freezing injunction, in respect of proceedings which have been or are to be commenced[198] in another state (regardless of whether this is a Brussels I Recast State,[199] Brussels/Lugano Convention Contracting State or a non-Regulation/Convention State) or in another part of the United Kingdom. The court may refuse to grant an interim remedy if the fact that it is exercising an ancillary jurisdiction in support of substantive proceedings elsewhere makes it inexpedient to grant it.[200] The approach towards the exercise of this power is the same in non-Regulation/Convention cases as it is in Regulation/Convention cases.[201]

(iii) Claims in relation to contracts

(6) Where "a claim is made in respect of a contract" in four alternative specified cases.[202] The predecessor of this ground was much more detailed, requiring that "the claim is brought to enforce, rescind, dissolve, annul or otherwise affect a contract, or to recover damages or obtain any other remedy in respect of the breach of a contract".[203] It is unlikely that this drafting change was intended to have any narrowing effect on the court's powers.[204] Cases that fell within the predecessor ground will doubtless fall within the new ground. Thus, for example, a claim for an anti-suit injunction to uphold an exclusive jurisdiction agreement in favour of the English court came within the predecessor provision because it was one to "enforce" the contract[205] and should now be regarded as a claim made in respect of a contract. More significantly, however, the new simpler wording can be interpreted as bringing within the new ground cases that were not within its predecessor. Thus the Court of Appeal held in relation to a predecessor of this rule that it was necessary to assert that there was a contract and that the cause of action was based upon this contract.[206] The new wording, which merely requires that a claim is made *in respect of* a contract (ie it relates to or is connected with the contract),[207] given its natural meaning, leads to the result that

---

[194] *Channel Tunnel Group Ltd v Balfour Beatty Construction Ltd* [1993] AC 334 at 340–2 (per Lords Browne-Wilkinson, Keith and Goff), HL; Collins (1993) 19 LQR 342; Hill [1993] LMCLQ 465. See also the majority of the Privy Council in *Mercedes Benz AG v Leiduck*, supra, at 304 which expressed no conclusion on whether there was such power; cf the dissent of Lord Nicholls at 305–10. There is power to grant interim relief in support of foreign arbitration proceedings: *Channel Tunnel Group Ltd v Balfour Beatty Construction Ltd* [1993] AC 334, HL; see also Arbitration Act 1996, s 2. See generally Capper [1996] CJQ 211. See also *C Inc plc v L* [2001] 2 All ER (Comm) 446 at [75]—claim for substantive relief made abroad. The restriction has been rejected in Jersey, *Solvalub Ltd v Match Investments Ltd* [1998] IL Pr 419, CA Jersey, following the dissent of Lord Nicholls in the *Mercedes Benz* case, supra, at 305–10.

[195] As amended to reflect the introduction of the Lugano Convention, the Brussels I Regulation, and now the Brussels I Recast.

[196] SI 1997/302. S 25(3) authorises this extension.

[197] It has been doubted whether this includes security for costs, see *Bank Mellat v Helliniki Techniki SA* [1984] QB 291.

[198] See *Fourie v Le Roux* [2007] UKHL 1, [2007] 1 WLR 320; Devonshire (2007) 123 LQR 361.

[199] This jurisdiction is permitted under the Brussels I Recast, Article 35; supra, p 303 et seq.

[200] S 25(2) of the Civil Jurisdiction and Judgments Act 1982.

[201] *Refco Inc v ETC* [1999] 1 Lloyd's Rep 159 at 172, 174, CA. See supra, pp 305–7.

[202] CPR, PD6B, 3.1(6).

[203] Ord 11, r 1(1)(d) RSC.

[204] This particular drafting change probably stems from the objective of producing a list of grounds for service out of the jurisdiction which is clearer and simpler: see the Lord Chancellor's Department Consultation Paper on the Civil Procedure Rules—Service of Court Process Abroad, para 23.

[205] The term "contract" refers to the English concept of a contract: *Youell v Kara Mara Shipping Co* [2000] 2 Lloyd's Rep 102.

[206] *DVA v Voest Alpine* [1997] 2 Lloyd's Rep 279 at 287 (per Hobhouse LJ), 291 (per Morritt LJ), CA.

[207] *Albon v Naza Motor Trading* [2007] EWHC 9 (Ch), [2007] 1 Lloyd's Rep 297.

the cause of action does not have to be based on the contract.[208] The Court of Appeal has thus held that the expression "in respect of a contract" should be construed broadly, and should encompass a claim for a constructive trust arising out of a contract.[209] Similarly, a restitutionary claim for the return of an overpayment of money by one contracting party to another, which is based on unjust enrichment, has been held to fall within the new provision.[210] This was despite the fact that there is now a restitution ground which would encompass cases that are so based.[211] The claimant in the above circumstances therefore has overlapping alternatives under Practice Direction 6B. However, a claim in quantum meruit presuming the absence of a contract is not a claim in respect of a contract, and would need to be based on the restitution head of jurisdiction.[212] A claim for damages for fraudulent misrepresentation inducing the claimant to enter a contract[213] and a claim for tortious interference with a contract[214] did not fall within the predecessor provision. It is unclear whether such claims would now be viewed as made "in respect of" a contract. A claim in respect of a contract should not encompass a claim for a declaration that no contract exists since a new ground for service out of the jurisdiction has been added to the list of grounds to cover such a claim.[215] Neither does it encompass a claim for interpleader relief since this involves a claim to be released from proceedings, not a claim for a substantive right.[216] This is authority that this ground only covers claims which relate to a contract entered into between the claimant and defendant to the proceedings,[217] although this has subsequently been rejected,[218] and the position appears to be that only the defendant needs to be a party to the contract.[219] The claim must, however, relate to the particular contract which satisfies the basis of jurisdiction.[220]

---

[208] Compare this with the tort ground, discussed infra, p 347 which requires that the claim is "made" in tort, ie based on a tort.

[209] *Deripaska v Cherney* [2009] EWCA Civ 849, [2009] CP Rep 48.

[210] *Albon v Naza Motor Trading* [2007] EWHC 9 (Ch), [2007] 1 Lloyd's Rep 297. The predecessors of PD6B, 3.1(6) encompassed restitutionary claims arising out of what was then regarded as an implied contract: see, eg, *McFee Engineering Pty Ltd v CBS Construction Pty Ltd* (1980) 44 FLR 340. That was before the development of unjust enrichment, which did not satisfy the former requirement that the claim was based on a contract. In so far as restitutionary claims are still in some instances based on contract, it is uncontroversial that they would come within PD6B, 3.1(6). See in relation to claims that a contract is frustrated and for consequent relief: *BP Exploration Co (Libya) Ltd v Hunt* [1976] 1 WLR 788. See generally Fawcett, Harris and Bridge, paras 8.64–8.81.

[211] CPR, PD6B, 3.1(16).

[212] *Sharab v Prince Al-Waleed Al-Saud* [2012] EWHC 1798 (Ch), [2012] 2 CLC 612.

[213] *Arab Business Consortium International Finance and Investment Co v Banque Franco-Tunisienne* [1996] 1 Lloyd's Rep 485 at 492.

[214] *Amoco (UK) Exploration Co v British American Offshore Ltd* [1999] 2 Lloyd's Rep 772 at 779.

[215] CPR, PD6B, 3.1(8); discussed infra, p 347.

[216] *Cool Carriers AB v HSBC Bank USA* [2001] 2 Lloyd's Rep 22.

[217] *The Flecha* [1999] 1 Lloyd's Rep 612.

[218] *Greene Wood & McLean LLP v Templeton Insurance Ltd* [2009] EWCA Civ 65 at [18], [2009] 1 WLR 2013; Dickinson [2010] LMCLQ 1 (dealing with a claim for contribution under the Civil Liability (Contribution) Act 1978, and also suggesting that this basis of jurisdiction could be available for claims pursuant to the Contracts (Rights of Third Parties) Act 1999).

[219] *Alliance Bank JSC v Aquanta Corporation* [2012] EWCA Civ 1588, [2013] 1 Lloyd's Rep 175. If the claim is for breach of contract, whether the claimant is a party is also evidently important for the question of whether there is a reasonable prospect of success on the merits: see, eg, *Surrey (UK) Ltd v Mazandaran Wood & Paper Industries* [2014] EWHC 3165 (Comm).

[220] *ABCI (Formerly Arab Business Consortium International Finance and Investment Co) v Banque Franco-Tunisienne* [2003] EWCA Civ 205 at [17], [2003] 2 Lloyd's Rep 146; *Global 5000 Ltd v Wadhawan* [2012] EWCA Civ 13, [2012] 1 Lloyd's Rep 239; Dickinson [2012] LMCLQ 181. But see *EF Hutton (London) v Mofarrij* [1989] 1 WLR 488.

The four alternative cases specified in paragraph 3.1(6) are as follows:

(a) Where the contract "was made within the jurisdiction".[221] In general, the English rules on formation of a contract should be used to ascertain whether the contract was made within the jurisdiction since the place where a contract is made is a connecting factor and, as such, should be defined by English law.[222] Thus, a contract is formed through the postal services at the place where the acceptance is posted, but a contract is formed by an instantaneous communication (such as by telephone) at the place where the acceptance is received.[223] However, there is authority which assumes (doubtfully) that if a foreign law was applicable to the contract this will determine when and where the contract is made.[224] It is sufficient for this provision if the contract was substantially made within the jurisdiction,[225] although if a contract made in one location is subsequently revised in another, difficult questions may arise concerning whether the revised contract should be treated as a new agreement (made in a new place) or as a continuation of the old one.[226] In principle, it is possible to have a contract made in more than one country, such as where the parties' deliberately signed separate copies in different countries so as to avoid giving the other party an advantage in terms of where the contract was finalised.[227] If one of these countries is England, the terms of paragraph 3.1(6)(a) will be met. There is authority that a similar approach should be applied where a contract is entered into through an exchange of electronic communications, such that the traditional analysis of offer and acceptance would be artificial—instead, for jurisdictional purposes, the contract should be considered to have been entered into in the location of both parties.[228] English law provides that in the case of a contract of employment the employer may be sued either in tort or for breach of contract if he neglects his implied duty to take reasonable care for the safety of the employee. If, therefore, the contract is made in England for employment abroad, or, indeed, if the contract is governed by English law,[229] the employee may (in cases not covered by the Brussels I Recast[230]) invoke this part of the rule without being driven to rely on rule (9) given below which is confined to a tort where the damage was sustained, or resulted from an act committed, in England.[231]

---

[221] CPR, PD6B, 3.1(6)(a). Eg *Mackender v Feldia AG* [1967] 2 QB 590; *Aaronson Bros Ltd v Maderera del Tropico SA* [1967] 2 Lloyd's Rep 159; *Howard Houlder and Partners Ltd v Marine General Transporters Corpn, The Panaghia P* [1983] 2 Lloyd's Rep 653; *Bank of Baroda v Vysya Bank Ltd* [1994] 2 Lloyd's Rep 87 at 94; *Minories v Afribank* [1995] 1 Lloyd's Rep 134; *Kelly v Cruise Catering Ltd* [1994] 2 ILRM 394; *Bastone & Firminger Ltd v Nasima Enterprises (Nigeria) Ltd* [1996] CLC 1902; *Williams v Society of Lloyd's* [1994] 1 VR 274; *Saab v Saudi American Bank* [1999] 1 WLR 1861 at [6], CA; *Eastern Power Ltd v Azienda Comunale Energia e Ambiente* [2001] IL Pr 6, Ont CA; *Burrows v Jamaica Private Power Co Ltd* [2002] CLC 255; *ABCI (Formerly Arab Business Consortium International Finance and Investment Co) v Banque Franco-Tunisienne* [2003] EWCA Civ 205 at [23]–[27], [2003] 2 Lloyd's Rep 146.

[222] *Entores v Miles Far East Corp* [1955] QB 327. See also *Eastern Power Ltd v Azienda Comunale Energia e Ambiente* [2001] IL Pr 6, Ont CA.

[223] *Brinkibon Ltd v Stahag Stahl und Stahlwarenhandelsgesellschaft GmbH* [1983] 2 AC 34; *Chunilal v Merrill Lynch International Incorporated* [2010] EWHC 1467 (Comm); *Brownlie v Four Seasons Holdings Incorporated* [2015] EWCA Civ 665, [2016] 1 WLR 1814.

[224] *Marconi v PT Pan Indonesia Bank Ltd TBK* [2004] EWHC 129 (Comm), [2004] 1 Lloyd's Rep 594; affd [2005] EWCA Civ 422 at [70]–[71].

[225] *BP Exploration Co (Libya) Ltd v Hunt* [1976] 1 WLR 788 at 797–8.

[226] *Sharab v Prince Al-Waleed Al-Saud* [2009] EWCA Civ 353, [2009] 2 Lloyd's Rep 160.

[227] *Apple Corps Ltd v Apple Computer Inc* [2004] EWHC 768 (Ch), [2004] IL Pr 34.

[228] *Conductive Inkjet Technology Ltd v Uni-Pixel Displays Inc* [2013] EWHC 2968 (Ch), at [72]–[73]. For criticism of the traditional rules in the light of e-commerce see Fawcett, Harris and Bridge, paras 10.99–10.100; Hogan-Doran (2003) 77 ALJ 377.

[229] See (c) infra, pp 344–5.

[230] See supra, p 297 et seq.

[231] *Matthews v Kuwait Bechtel Corpn* [1959] 2 QB 57.

(b) Where the contract "was made by or through an agent trading or residing within the jurisdiction".[232] This ground is applicable even where the agent is a conduit with no authority to effect a completed contract. Thus in *National Mortgage and Agency Co of New Zealand Ltd v Gosselin*[233] the London agent of a Belgian firm, who was employed merely for the purpose of obtaining orders, sent the firm's price list to the plaintiff. The plaintiff gave an order which was forwarded by the agent and accepted through the post by the Belgian firm. It was held that the contract had been made "through" the agent, for, though the final acceptance did not lie with him, he had negotiated its terms. It is implicit that the agent is acting on behalf of the foreign defendant who is the principal.[234] The agent must not be acting as a broker on behalf of the claimant.[235]

(c) Where the contract "is governed by English[236] law".[237] This is determined by English choice of law rules; depending on the date of the contract, it is a matter for the rules contained in the Rome Convention of 1980 or the Rome I Regulation 2008.[238] Paragraph 3.1(6)(c) presupposes that one law governs the whole of the contract.[239] Yet under the Rome Convention and Rome I Regulation it is possible for different laws to govern different parts of the contract.[240] If the dispute only relates to part of the contract it should be enough that this part of the contract is governed by English law.

The court normally has only to reach a tentative or provisional conclusion that English law governs,[241] but this presupposes that there is room for further investigation of facts or law later on.[242] If the facts are before the court and not in dispute, a definite conclusion

---

[232] CPR, PD6B, 3.1(6)(b); formerly Ord 11, r 1(1)(d)(ii) RSC; on which see, eg, *Gibbon v Commerz und Creditbank Aktiengesellschaft* [1958] 2 Lloyd's Rep 113; *Burrows v Jamaica Private Power Co Ltd* [2002] CLC 255; *Munchener Ruckversicherungs Gesellschaft v Commonwealth Insurance Co* [2004] EWHC 914 (Comm) at [21] and [24]; *Marconi v PT Pan Indonesia Bank Ltd TBK* [2004] EWHC 129 (Comm), [2004] 1 Lloyd's Rep 594; affd [2005] EWCA Civ 422 at [72]. Cf *Bank of Baroda v Vysya Bank Ltd* [1994] 2 Lloyd's Rep 87 at 96. See also *Commonwealth Bank of Australia v White* [1999] 2 VR 681 at 694–6. This ground of jurisdiction provides for service on the principal; for jurisdiction over the principal by means of serving the agent see CPR, r 6.12.

[233] (1922) 38 TLR 832, CA. See also *Citadel Insurance Co v Atlantic Union Insurance Co SA* [1982] 2 Lloyd's Rep 543, CA; *Lincoln National Life Insurance Co v Employers Reinsurance Corpn* [2002] EWHC 28, [2002] Lloyd's Rep IR 853.

[234] This was explicit in Ord 11, r 1(1)(d)(ii) RSC.

[235] *Gill and Duffus Landauer Ltd v London Export Corpn GmbH* [1982] 2 Lloyd's Rep 627. See also *Union International Insurance Co Ltd v Jubilee Insurance Co Ltd* [1991] 1 WLR 415.

[236] See *Downing v Al Tameer Establishment* [2002] EWCA Civ 721, [2002] 2 All ER (Comm) 545—reference to "UK law" interpreted as referring to English law.

[237] CPR, PD6B, 3.1(6)(c).

[238] Discussed infra, Chapter 19. See, eg, *PT Pan Indonesia Bank Ltd TBK v Marconi Communications International Ltd* [2005] EWCA Civ 422 at [39] where this was common ground; *Egon Oldendorff v Liberia Corpn* [1995] 2 Lloyd's Rep 64 at 68; *Marubeni Hong Kong and South China Ltd v Mongolian Government* [2002] 2 All ER (Comm) 873; appeal on a different issue dismissed [2005] EWCA Civ 395, [2005] 1 WLR 2497. See also *Samcrete Egypt Engineers and Contractors SAE v Land Rover Exports Ltd* [2001] EWCA Civ 2019, [2002] CLC 533 (*forum non conveniens*). For an argument that the traditional English rules on the proper law of the contract should apply see Morse [1994] LMCLQ 560 at 561–3, for a counter-argument see the 13th edn of this book, p 304. On the question whether the Court of Justice would accept a reference from the English courts in relation to the interpretation of the Rome Convention when it arises in the jurisdictional context, see the 14th edn of this book, p 673.

[239] See *Armar Shipping Co Ltd v Caisse Algérienne d'Assurance et de Réassurance, The Armar* [1980] 2 Lloyd's Rep 450 at 456.

[240] Infra, pp 707–9.

[241] *Compañia Naviera Micro SA v Shipley International Inc, The Parouth* [1982] 2 Lloyd's Rep 351 at 354; *Mitsubishi Corpn v Aristidis Alafouzos* [1988] 1 Lloyd's Rep 191 at 193; *Attock Cement Co Ltd v Romanian Bank for Foreign Trade* [1989] 1 WLR 1147 at 1152–1156, CA; Collier [1990] CLJ 39; *Finnish Marine Insurance Co Ltd v Protective National Insurance Co* [1990] 1 QB 1078 at 1084.

[242] *E F Hutton & Co (London) Ltd v Mofarrij* [1989] 1 WLR 488 at 485, CA; *Islamic Arab Insurance Co v Saudi Egyptian American Reinsurance Co* [1987] 1 Lloyd's Rep 315 at 317, CA.

as to the applicable law should be reached at this jurisdictional stage of the action.[243] At one time the courts showed a considerable reluctance to exercise their discretion under this particular head.[244] Subsequently, this appeared to have been replaced by a more neutral attitude,[245] although the point is now somewhat unclear.[246] The better view is probably that the exercise of the discretion depends on the individual circumstances of the case.[247]

(d) Or where the contract "contains a term to the effect that the court shall have jurisdiction to determine any claim in respect of the contract".[248] Where there is a jurisdiction clause providing for trial in England, this will often be covered by one of two other jurisdictional regimes. First, it may be covered by the Hague Convention on Choice of Court Agreements, if the agreement is exclusive and at least one party to the agreement is resident in a Hague Convention contracting state which is not a European Union Member State.[249] Second, if the Hague Convention does not apply, a jurisdiction agreement (exclusive or non-exclusive) in favour of the English courts will often meet the requirements of Article 25 of the Brussels I Recast (particularly since it governs jurisdiction agreements in favour of the courts of a Member State regardless of the domicile of the parties)[250] and (mandatory[251]) jurisdiction will be allocated to the English courts by virtue of that provision.[252] Paragraph 3.1(6)(d) is concerned with the situation where Article 25 does not apply, because the dispute falls outside the scope of the Brussels I Recast. This is considered a strong basis of jurisdiction—where jurisdiction is available pursuant to paragraph 3.1(6)(d), the parties should generally be bound by the jurisdiction clause[253] to which they have agreed unless there is some strong reason to the contrary.[254] This provision encompasses not only clauses providing for the exclusive jurisdiction of the English courts but also clauses providing for the non-exclusive

---

[243] *Ilyssia Cia Naviera SA v Ahmed Abdul Qawi Bamaodah, The Elli 2* [1985] 1 Lloyd's Rep 107 at 114, CA; *Enichem Anic Spa v Ampelos Shipping Co Ltd, The Delfini* [1988] 2 Lloyd's Rep 599 at 602–3; appeal on other grounds dismissed [1990] 1 Lloyd's Rep 252; *Ophthalmic Innovations International (United Kingdom) Ltd v Ophthalmic Innovations International Inc* [2004] EWHC 2948 (Ch), [2005] IL Pr 10; *Chellaram v Chellaram (No 2)* [2002] EWHC 632 (Ch) at [136], [2002] 2 All ER 17; *Marubeni Hong Kong and South China Ltd v Mongolian Government* [2002] 2 All ER (Comm) 873 at [29]–[30]; appeal on a different issue dismissed [2005] EWCA Civ 395, [2005] 1 WLR 2497.

[244] *Amin Rasheed Shipping Corpn v Kuwait Insurance Co*, supra, at 68 (per Lord Diplock).

[245] *Spiliada Maritime Corpn v Cansulex Ltd* [1987] AC 460; following Lord Wilberforce in the *Amin Rasheed* case at 72.

[246] *Novus Aviation Ltd v Onur Air Tasimacilik AS* [2009] EWCA Civ 122, [2009] 1 Lloyd's Rep 576.

[247] *Spiliada Maritime*, supra, at 481–2; see infra, pp 367–9.

[248] CPR, PD6B, 3.1(6)(d). On the question of the law to be applied in order to determine whether the contract contains such a term see Art 10 of the Rome I Regulation, discussed infra, pp 755–8.

[249] See supra, p 315. Permission to serve outside the territory is not required where jurisdiction is based on the Hague Convention—see infra, p 380.

[250] Discussed supra, pp 229 et seq.

[251] See infra, p 459 et seq.

[252] See, eg, *Equitas Ltd v Allstate Insurance Company* [2008] EWHC 1671 (Comm), [2009] 1 All ER (Comm) 1137. For a case that appears to have ignored this point see *OT Africa Line Ltd v Magic Sportwear Corpn* [2006] EWCA Civ 710, [2005] 2 Lloyd's Rep 170.

[253] This can take an indirect form, see *Bhatia Shipping v Alcobex Metals* [2004] EWHC 2323 (Comm) at [17], [2005] 2 Lloyd's Rep 336—agreement on jurisdiction in the place of delivery of goods.

[254] *Unterweser Reederei GmbH v Zapata Off-Shore Co, The Chaparral* [1968] 2 Lloyd's Rep 158; *Citi-March v Ltd v Neptune Orient Lines Ltd* [1997] 1 Lloyd's Rep 72. See also the discussion of *forum conveniens* infra, pp 369–70, and of *forum non conveniens*, infra, pp 398–9. When proceedings were brought before the US courts an injunction was, originally, granted enjoining the parties from proceeding in England, but the US Supreme Court ruled that the English jurisdiction clause should be enforced unless such enforcement would be unreasonable or unjust: *The Chaparral* [1972] 2 Lloyd's Rep 315.

jurisdiction of the English courts (ie the parties are not precluded from commencing proceedings abroad).[255]

(7) Where "a claim is made in respect of[256] a breach of contract committed within the jurisdiction".[257] Permission cannot be granted under this ground unless the claimant establishes a good arguable case that three conditions are fulfilled: the alleged contract must in fact have been made; it must have been broken; and the breach must have occurred in England. If the central issue to be tried is as to whether there was a contract at all, the court must be careful not to give the appearance of pre-trying this issue, whilst at the same time carefully scrutinising whether there was a breach committed within the jurisdiction.[258] If the breach involves a failure to perform, it is necessary to look at where the performance was to take place.[259] It is not sufficient, however, that performance would have been possible in England—performance must have been required (or perhaps at least mutually understood) to take place in England.[260] The place of performance of a contractual obligation should not be viewed as a jurisdictional question (necessarily governed by English law), but rather as a matter of contractual interpretation governed by the law of the contract.[261] Thus, the general presumption in English law that a payment obligation is located at the place of the creditor should only apply if the contract is governed by English law.[262] This provision might establish a basis of jurisdiction for only some contractual claims in the situation where there are distinguishable and independent obligations, some of which have a place of performance within the jurisdiction and others of which have a place of performance outside the jurisdiction.[263] But what of the position where the obligations are not independent of each other? *Johnson v Taylor Bros & Co Ltd*[264] was such a case.

> Swedish sellers failed to ship goods that they had sold to English buyers under a contract cif Leeds. The shippers failed both to deliver the shipping documents and to ship the goods. The obligations are linked for if the goods have not been shipped, the shipping documents will never have come into existence. The former breach occurred in England but the latter occurred in Stockholm.

The English courts should now be regarded as having jurisdiction under Practice Direction 6B, paragraph 3.1(7) for breach of the obligation to deliver the shipping documents on the basis that the shippers failed to deliver these in England. The wording of the predecessor of this provision was amended[265] to specify that it applied irrespective of whether some other

---

[255] *Gulf Bank KSC v Mitsubishi Heavy Industries Ltd* [1994] 1 Lloyd's Rep 323; *Standard Steamship Owners' Protection and Indemnity v Gann* [1992] 2 Lloyd's Rep 528; Fawcett [2001] LMCLQ 234, 244–5.

[256] See discussion supra, pp 341–2.

[257] CPR, PD6B, 3.1(7). *Citadel Insurance Co v Atlantic Union Insurance Co SA* [1982] 2 Lloyd's Rep 543; *Cantieri Navali Riuniti SpA v NV Omne Justitia. The Stolt Marmaro* [1985] 2 Lloyd's Rep 428; *Banque Paribas v Cargill International SA* [1992] 2 Lloyd's Rep 19 at 23, CA; *Agrafax Public Relations Ltd v United Scottish Society Inc* [1995] IL Pr 753, CA; *Marconi v PT Pan Indonesia Bank Ltd TBK* [2004] EWHC 129 (Comm), [2004] 1 Lloyd's Rep 594; affd [2005] EWCA Civ 422 at [73]. See also *Analog Devices BV v Zurich Insurance Co* [2002] 2 ILRM 366, SC of Ireland. For the application of this ground in cases of international sale of goods see Fawcett, Harris and Bridge, para 4.51–4.89.

[258] *Canada Trust Co v Stolzenberg (No 2)* [1998] 1 WLR 547 at 555–6 (per Waller LJ), approved by HL [2002] 1 AC 1 at 13 (per Lord Steyn with whom the other Law Lords agreed).

[259] See *Brinkibon Ltd v Stahag Stahl und Stahlwarenhandelsgesellschaft GmbH* [1983] 2 AC 34, 49–50, HL; *Gill and Duffus Landauer Ltd v London Export Corpn GmbH* [1982] 2 Lloyd's Rep 627, 630.

[260] *Sharab v Prince Al-Waleed Al-Saud* [2009] EWCA Civ 353, [2009] 2 Lloyd's Rep 160.

[261] See Dicey, Morris and Collins, paras 11-194–11-203.

[262] *The Eider* [1893] P 119 at 136–7; see similarly *Definitely Maybe (Touring) Ltd v Marek Lieberberg Konzertagentur GmbH (No 2)* [2001] 1 WLR 1745 (a case under the Brussels Convention).

[263] *Rein v Stein* [1892] 1 QB 753 at 757 (per Lindley LJ), CA. See also *Robey v Snaefell Mining Co* (1887) 20 QBD 152; *The Eider* [1893] P 119 at 126 (per the President, Sir Francis H Jeune), at 126.

[264] [1920] AC 144.

[265] This was because the House of Lords in the *Johnson* case, which was faced with a differently worded breach provision, refused permission for service of process out of the jurisdiction on the basis that, although

breach was committed out of the jurisdiction,[266] thereby ensuring that this situation came within the breach ground. It was considered unnecessary to retain this additional wording in Practice Direction 6B. It has been argued that this turns the clock back so that the breach ground does not apply where, although there was a breach committed within the jurisdiction, the substantial breach was committed out of the jurisdiction.[267] But this change was one of the minor drafting changes introduced by the Civil Procedure Rules, designed to produce a list of grounds for service out of the jurisdiction which was clearer and simpler than its predecessor and was not intended to have any substantive effect on the court's powers.[268] The better view is therefore that any breach of contract in the territory may be sufficient to establish jurisdiction, irrespective of whether it is a substantial or the principal breach, although this will be relevant for the exercise of jurisdictional discretion. Claims for related breaches which did not take place in the territory may not be based on this gateway, but may come under another basis of jurisdiction, such as paragraph 3.1(4A).[269]

(8) Where "a claim is made for a declaration that no contract exists where, if the contract was found to exist, it would comply with the conditions set out in paragraph (6)".[270] This ground of jurisdiction, added by the Civil Procedure Rules, makes it clear that paragraph 3.1(6) applies where there is a claim for a negative declaration that no contract exists.[271] This ensures that the position under the traditional rules on jurisdiction[272] is the same as that under the Brussels I Recast.[273] Paragraph 3.1(8) does not cover a claim made for a declaration of non-liability which does not dispute the existence of the contract.

(iv) Claims in tort

(9) Where "a claim is made in tort where (a) damage was sustained, or will be sustained, within the jurisdiction; or (b) the damage which has been or will be sustained resulted from an act committed, or likely to be committed, within the jurisdiction".[274] A claim is "made" in tort when it is founded (ie based) on a tort,[275] ie there must be liability under English or

---

the failure to deliver the shipping documents represented a breach in England, the substantial breach was the non-shipment of the goods at Stockholm.

[266] Ord 11, r 1(1)(e) RSC said "and irrespective of the fact, if such be the case, that the breach was preceded or accompanied by a breach committed out of the jurisdiction that rendered impossible the performance of so much of the contract as ought to have been performed within the jurisdiction".

[267] See the argument of counsel in *Network Telecom (Europe) Ltd v Telephone Systems International Inc* [2003] EWHC 2890 (QB), [2004] 1 All ER (Comm) 418 at [101]–[103]—the court did not decide the point.

[268] See the Lord Chancellor's Department Consultation Paper on the Civil Procedure Rules—Service of Court Process Abroad, para 23.

[269] See supra, p 340.

[270] CPR, PD6B, 3.1(8).

[271] See the Lord Chancellor's Department Consultation Paper on the Civil Procedure Rules—Service of Court Process Abroad, para 21.

[272] The position previously was unclear. Cf *Finnish Marine Insurance Co Ltd v Protective National Insurance Co* [1990] 1 QB 1078—not within the contract head, with *DR Insurance Co v Central National Insurance Co* [1996] 1 Lloyd's Rep 74—within the head if agreement entered into with intent to create legal relations.

[273] For the use of Art 5(1) of the Brussels Convention (Art 7(1) of the Brussels I Recast) to take jurisdiction to grant a negative declaration that no contract existed, see *Boss Group Ltd v Boss France SA* [1997] 1 WLR 351, CA; see supra, p 251.

[274] CPR, PD6B, 3.1(9).

[275] Ord 11, r 1(1)(f) RSC so provided. The change in wording in paragraph 3.1(9) doubtless simply reflects the desire for simpler and clearer grounds. Claims founded on a constructive trust do not come within this ground: *Metall und Rohstoff AG v Donaldson Lufkin and Jenrette Inc* [1990] 1 QB 391 at 474; overruled on a different point in *Lonrho plc v Fayed* [1992] 1 AC 448, HL; *Nycal (UK) Ltd v Lacey* [1994] CLC 12. See also *ISC v Guerin* [1992] 2 Lloyd's Rep 430—equitable restitutionary remedies for breach of trust or fiduciary duty held to be not founded on a tort. It would include a claim for restitution for tortious wrongdoing but

foreign law which is to be classified as being tortious.[276] Although it is not clear from the text, this basis of jurisdiction has been held to encompass proceedings for a negative declaration, ie that no tort has been or will be committed.[277] A claim for misuse of private information has been held to be tortious for these purposes,[278] although a separate ground of jurisdiction for breach of confidence or misuse of private information has also recently been added[279]—it is unclear whether this will affect the previous characterisation, but in any case the new ground of jurisdiction is closely modelled on paragraph 3.1(9). A claim for breach of statutory duties relating to data protection has also been held to be a tort for these purposes.[280] If the claim is founded on what is, in English law, a tort then clearly it should be classified as tortious for jurisdictional purposes.[281] This encompasses the situation where the claimant relies on the English law of tort or on a foreign cause of action that is known to English law, such as negligence under New York law. However, the introduction of statutory tort choice of law rules, and now European Union choice of law rules for non-contractual obligations, means that the English courts will now be faced with actions for invasion of privacy under French law and the like.[282] With a cause of action like this, unknown to English law, how are the courts to determine whether the claim is founded on a tort?[283] The fact that the foreign state whose law is relied upon regards the cause of action as tortious (or delictual) should be regarded as persuasive evidence of this; the case for this becomes even stronger if it can be shown generally that other countries that have this cause of action also adopt this characterisation.[284]

Paragraph 3.1(9) makes it clear that jurisdiction can be taken in England if *either* damage was sustained[285] *or* damage resulted from an act committed in England.[286] The result is to make the tort head a very wide one,[287] and to bring tort cases under Practice Direction 6B at least broadly into line with tort cases under the jurisdiction rules to be found under the Brussels/Lugano system.[288] The references to prospective damage were added to paragraph 3.1(9) in

---

not if it is based on unjust enrichment, see Fawcett, Harris and Bridge, para 8.87–88, 8.93; Briggs in Rose (ed), *Restitution and the Conflict of Laws*, pp 57–60. It also includes a claim by a tortfeasor for contribution under a statute: *FFSB Ltd v Seward & Kissel LLP* [2007] UKPC 16.

[276] *OT Africa Line Ltd v Magic Sportswear Corpn* [2004] EWHC 2441 (Comm) at [24], [2005] 1 Lloyd's Rep 252; appeal dismissed without discussion of this point [2005] EWCA Civ 710, [2005] 2 Lloyd's Rep 170.

[277] *Fujifilm Kyowa Kirin Biologics Company Limited v Abbvie Biotechnology Limited* [2016] EWHC 2204 (Pat) at [106].

[278] *Google Inc v Vidal-Hall* [2015] EWCA Civ 311, [2015] 3 WLR 409 (permission granted to appeal to the Supreme Court, but settled before judgment).

[279] See infra, p 362.

[280] *Douglas v Hello! Ltd (No 2)* [2003] EWCA Civ 139. See also *Fern Computer Consultancy Ltd v Intergraph Cadworx & Analysis Solutions Inc* [2014] EWHC 2908 (Ch), [2015] 1 Lloyd's Rep 1 (claim for breach of statutory duty under the Commercial Agents (Council Directive) Regulations 1993 (SI 1993/3053) may be tortious).

[281] See *Metall und Rohstoff AG v Donaldson Lufkin and Jenrette Inc* [1990] 1 QB 391 at 449, CA; overruled on a different point in *Lonrho plc v Fayed* [1992] 1 AC 448.

[282] Infra, p 776 et seq.

[283] See generally Harris (1998) 61 MLR 33.

[284] Cf the position under the Rome II Regulation, infra, p 804 et seq.

[285] See, eg, *Short v Ireland* [1997] 1 ILRM 161.

[286] This avoids the definitional problem encountered under a predecessor provision, which referred to "a tort committed within the jurisdiction"; see *Distillers Co (Biochemicals) Ltd v Thompson* [1971] AC 458. The problem of where a tort is committed can still arise in the context of jurisdiction (infra, pp 350–3), as well as that of choice of law (infra, pp 885–8). Cf Kaye in McLean (ed), *Compensation for Damage: An International Perspective*, Chapter 8 1993. This old test is still used in the Bahamas, see *FFSB Ltd v Seward & Kissel LLP* [2007] UKPC 16.

[287] But for examples which do not come within either, see *ABCI v BFT* [1997] 1 Lloyd's Rep 531, CA; *Shahar v Tsitsekkos* [2004] EWHC 2659 (Ch) at [35]–[40].

[288] See Art 7(2) of the Brussels I Recast; Case 21/76 *Bier v Mines de Potasse* [1978] QB 708, supra, pp 253–8.

October 2015 to clarify that it encompasses injunctions to restrain threatened torts, also in line with the Brussels I Recast rule[289]—the position had previously been unclear.[290]

Damage was sustained, or will be sustained, within the jurisdiction A contentious issue has arisen over when damage should be considered to be sustained in England for the purposes of this rule. If the act and direct injury take place in State A, but the claimant is hospitalised in State B, is damage sustained there?[291] This raises the question whether the damage caused must be direct or whether it can include indirect damage. A number of recent first instance decisions have suggested that indirect damage in England is sufficient, relying on the fact that jurisdiction under the common law rules is discretionary and thus may be interpreted broadly.[292] The better view is, however, that damage refers to the direct damage sounding in monetary terms which the wrongful act produced upon the claimant.[293] This is the same definition of damage as that applied by the Court of Justice of the European Union for the purposes of Article 7(2) of the Brussels I Recast. The adoption of this European Union definition for the purposes of service out of the jurisdiction acknowledges the fact that the tort ground for service out of the jurisdiction was reworded to align with what is now Article 7(2).[294] It has also been argued that this interpretation should be preferred for consistency with Article 4(1) of the Rome I Regulation, which itself should be interpreted consistently with the Brussels I Recast.[295] It is still necessary, however, to identify the direct damage carefully. If a widow sues in her own right for loss of dependency the damage will be direct and located where she lives, rather than where her husband was killed abroad.[296] If a libel is

---

[289] See supra, p 266.

[290] See, eg, *Beecham Group plc v Norton Healthcare Ltd* [1997] FSR 81 at 97. Paragraph 3.1(2) was, however, potentially available as an alternative: see *James North and Sons Ltd v North Cape Textiles Ltd* [1984] 1 WLR 1428 at 1431, supra, p 336. It is also possible to use s 25 of the Civil Jurisdiction and Judgments Acts 1982, supra, p 340, to grant an interim injunction to prevent a threatened wrong in England.

[291] There is Canadian support for an affirmative answer: *Vile v Von Wendt Zurich Insurance Co* (1979) 103 DLR (3d) 356. See also in Canada (a significant connection under the real and substantial connection test): *Duncan v Neptunia Corpn* (2001) 199 DLR (4th) 354; *Muscutt v Courcelles* (2002) 213 DLR (4th) 577, Ont CA; *Doiron v Bugge* (2005) 258 DLR (4th) 716, Ont CA. But for a denial of jurisdiction in international cases (where it is more difficult to justify jurisdiction) as not satisfying the real and substantial connection test: see *Leufkens v Alba Tours International Inc* (2002) 213 DLR (4th) 614, Ont CA; *Lemmex v Bernard* (2002) 213 DLR (4th) 627, Ont CA; *Sinclair v Cracker Barrel Old Country Store Inc* (2002) 213 DLR (4th) 643, Ont CA; *Gajraj v DeBernardo* (2002) 213 DLR (4th) 651, Ont CA; distinguished in *Doiron*. Cf for inter-provincial cases (satisfying this test) the *Muscutt* case; *Touchburn v O'Brien* (2002) 210 DLR (4th) 668, Novia Scotia CA. For Australian support see *Thomas v Penna* [1985] 2 NSWLR 171, but now see *Flaherty v Girgis* (1987) 71 ALR 1, High Court of Australia.

[292] *Booth v Phillips* [2004] EWHC 1437 at [33]–[47], [2004] 1 WLR 3293; *Cooley v Ramsey* [2008] EWHC 129 (QB); *Harty v Sabre International Security Ltd* [2011] EWHC 852 (QB); *Wink v Croatio Osiguranje DD* [2013] EWHC 1118 (QB); *Stylianou v Toyoshima* [2013] EWHC 2188 (QB); *Pike v The Indian Hotels Company Ltd* [2013] EWHC 4096 (QB).

[293] *Brownlie v Four Seasons Holdings Incorporated* [2015] EWCA Civ 665, [2016] 1 WLR 1814; *Erste Group Bank AG London Branch v JSC 'VMZ Red October'* [2015] EWCA Civ 379 at [105]; *Gunn v Diaz* [2017] EWHC 157 (QB), [2017] 1 Lloyd's Rep 165; *Newsat Holdings Ltd v Zani* [2006] EWHC 342 (Comm) at [46]–[49], [2006] 1 Lloyd's Rep 707; *ABCI (Formerly Arab Business Consortium International Finance and Investment Co) v Banque Franco-Tunisienne* [2003] EWCA Civ 205 at [44], [2003] 2 Lloyd's Rep 146; *Beecham Group plc v Norton Healthcare Ltd* [1997] FSR 81 at 97–8; *Bastone & Firminger Ltd v Nasima Enterprises (Nigeria) Ltd* [1996] CLC 1902.

[294] *Brownlie v Four Seasons Holdings Incorporated*, supra; *Newsat Holdings Ltd v Zani* [2006] EWHC 342 (Comm) at [46]–[49], [2006] 1 Lloyd's Rep 707; *ABCI (Formerly Arab Business Consortium International Finance and Investment Co) v Banque Franco-Tunisienne* [2003] EWCA Civ 205 at [43], [2003] 2 Lloyd's Rep 146; *Domicrest Ltd v Swiss Bank Corporation* [1999] QB 548, 567; *Metall und Rohstoff v Donaldson Lufkin & Jenrette* [1990] 1 QB 391, 437.

[295] *Brownlie v Four Seasons Holdings Incorporated*, supra. But see Bergson [2016] LQR 42.

[296] *Booth v Phillips*, supra, at [45], which is correct on this point; *Brownlie v Four Seasons Holdings Incorporated*, supra. But note Case C-350/14, *Lazar* EU:C:2015:802, [2016] 1 WLR 835, arguably adopting a different approach in the context of choice of law under the Rome II Regulation: see infra, pp 812–13.

published in England and the claimant has a reputation in England it is accepted that paragraph 3.1(9) will apply.[297] This was on the basis that significant damage to reputation (sometimes expressed as a "real and substantial tort") was sustained within the jurisdiction[298]—for a claim to be actionable under English law, there is now a requirement for "serious harm", which will also affect whether the court gives permission to serve outside the jurisdiction because of the requirement for "a reasonable prospect of success".[299] As regards libel over the internet (discussed further below), where the libel is contained in text which is uploaded[300] abroad and downloaded[301] in England, publication takes place in England.[302]

Damage to the claimant might have been suffered in more than one country, particularly in a case involving an economic tort. The Court of Appeal in *Metall und Rohstoff AG v Donaldson Lufkin and Jenrette Inc*[303] held that it is not necessary that all the damage has been sustained within the jurisdiction; it is "enough if some significant damage has been sustained in England".[304] "Damage" can include the situation where the acts of the defendant expose the claimant to claims by others which are pursued in England, and if successful will result in judgment against the claimant.[305] But in a case of financial loss it is not enough to show that a company has its seat in England.[306] If damage has been suffered in multiple places, this basis of jurisdiction would only support a claim in respect of the damage suffered in England, but paragraph 3.1(4A) may support the addition of claims in respect of damage in other places.[307]

An act committed within the jurisdiction[308] The tortious act from which the damage resulted may have been committed partly within the jurisdiction and partly without. According to the Court of Appeal in the *Metall und Rohstoff* case,[309] it is not necessary that

---

[297] *King v Lewis* [2004] EWCA Civ 1329, [2005] IL Pr 16; *Dow Jones & Co Inc v Jameel* [2005] EWCA Civ 75 at [49], [2005] QB 946.

[298] In *Berezovsky v Michaels* [2000] 1 WLR 1004, HL, it was accepted by counsel that the tort ground of service out (at that time Ord 11, r 1(1)(f) RSC) was satisfied because significant damage (to the claimants' reputations in England) was sustained in England; see also *Chadha v Dow Jones & Co Inc* [1999] IL Pr 829, CA; *Dow Jones & Co Inc v Jameel* [2005] EWCA Civ 75; *Karpov v Browder* [2013] EWHC 3071 (QB). See also *Dow Jones & Co Inc v Gutnick* (2002) 210 CLR 575 at [46], HC of Australia; discussed infra, p 353.

[299] Defamation Act 2013, s 1(1). See infra, p 351. On the impact of the Defamation Act 2013, see further infra, p 353 et seq.

[300] Ie the information is made available over the internet by placing it in a storage area managed by a web-server.

[301] On to the computer of a person who has used a web-browser to pull the material from the web-server.

[302] *Godfrey v Demon Internet Ltd* [2001] QB 201 at 208–9; *Loutchansky v Times Newspapers Ltd* [2001] EWCA Civ 1805 at [58], [2002] QB 783; *King v Lewis*, supra, where this was common ground; *Dow Jones & Co Inc v Jameel* [2005] EWCA Civ 75 at [48]–[49], [2005] QB 946; *Dow Jones & Co Inc v Gutnick* (2002) 210 CLR 575, HC of Australia; discussed infra, p 353. For Canada see *Bangoura v Washington Post* (2004) 258 DLR (4th) 341; and for New Zealand *Nationwide News Pty v University of Newlands* CA, 9 December 2005. See also *Ashton Investments Ltd v OJSC Russian Aluminium RUSAL* [2006] EWHC 2545 (Comm) at [62], [2007] 1 Lloyd's Rep 311, damage in England by hacking (from Russia) into a server in England.

[303] [1990] 1 QB 391; overruled on a different point in *Lonrho plc v Fayed* [1992] 1 AC 448.

[304] [1990] 1 QB 391, at 437. See also *Morin v Bonhams & Brooks Ltd* [2003] EWHC 467 (Comm) at [61], [2003] I L Pr 25. The Court of Appeal affirmed the decision at first instance that Monegasque law governed the tort claim [2003] EWCA Civ 1802, [2004] 1 Lloyd's Rep 702. See also *Jones v Ministry of the Interior of the Kingdom of Saudi Arabia* [2005] QB 699 at [29], CA—psychological damage in England after torture abroad; reversed without discussion of this point, [2006] UKHL 26, [2007] 1 AC 270.

[305] *The Eras Eil Actions* [1992] 1 Lloyd's Rep 570. For another example of damage, see *Crédit Agricole Indosuez v Unicof Ltd* [2003] EWHC 2676 (Comm) at [20], [2004] 1 Lloyd's Rep 196.

[306] *The Eras Eil Actions*, supra. See also *Deuruneft v Bullen* [2004] 1 WWR 535 at [51]–[60].

[307] See supra, p 340. But note the impact of the Defamation Act 2013—see infra, p 353 et seq.

[308] See, eg, *Saab v Saudi American Bank* [1999] 1 WLR 1861 at [6], CA.

[309] Supra. See also *Grupo Torras SA and Torras Hostench London Ltd v Sheikh Fahad Mohammed Al-Sabah* [1995] 1 Lloyd's Rep 374 at 450, appeals to CA dismissed without discussion of this point [1996] 1 Lloyd's Rep 7, CA; *Morin v Bonhams & Brooks Ltd* [2003] EWHC 467 (Comm) at [61], [2003] IL Pr 25, the Court of Appeal affirmed the decision at first instance that Monegasque law governed the tort claim [2003] EWCA

all of the acts have been committed within the jurisdiction. It is enough if "substantial and efficacious acts" have been committed within the jurisdiction, even if substantial and efficacious acts have also been committed outside the jurisdiction. In determining where a tortious act was committed, regard should be had to the case law identifying the place of the event giving rise to the damage for the purpose of Article 7(2) of the Brussels I Recast or the earlier Brussels I Regulation and Brussels Convention.[310] It follows that, in a case of negligent or fraudulent misrepresentation, the damage sustained resulted from an act committed within the jurisdiction if the misstatement was made in England, rather than being received in England.[311]

Exercise of the discretion   The courts showed a distinct willingness to exercise their discretion to allow service out of the jurisdiction under the predecessor to paragraph 3.1(9). The House of Lords in *Berezovsky v Michaels*[312] followed earlier Court of Appeal cases[313] in holding that, when exercising the *forum conveniens* discretion, regard is to be had to the principle that the jurisdiction in which a tort was committed is prima facie the natural forum for the determination of the dispute.[314] Two Russian businessmen alleged that they were libelled by the editor and publishers of an American business magazine and claimed damages in England restricted to the injury to their reputations in England. There was publication of the libel in England because of the distribution of copies of the magazine there. This publication constituted a separate tort which was committed in England.[315] This meant that England was prima facie the natural forum for trial. The number of copies distributed in England (some 1,900 compared to over 785,000 in the USA and Canada) was said to be significant.[316] This was important because the tort committed within the jurisdiction must be substantial.[317]

Civ 1802, [2004] 1 Lloyd's Rep 702; *Ashton Investments Ltd v OJSC Russian Aluminium RUSAL* [2006] EWHC 2545 (Comm) at [63], [2007] 1 Lloyd's Rep 311.

[310] See *ABCI (Formerly Arab Business Consortium International Finance and Investment Co) v Banque Franco-Tunisienne* [2003] EWCA Civ 205 at [41], [2003] 2 Lloyd's Rep 146. This case law is discussed supra, pp 271–4.

[311] *Newsat Holdings Ltd v Zani* [2006] EWHC 342 (Comm), [2006] 1 Lloyd's Rep 707.

[312] [2000] UKHL 25, [2000] 1 WLR 1004, HL; Briggs (2000) 71 BYBIL 440; Hare [2000] CLJ 461; Harris (2000) 116 LQR 562. For other *forum conveniens* cases involving libel, see *Kroch v Rossell* [1937] 1 All ER 725, CA; *Schapira v Ahronson* [1998] IL Pr 587, CA; *Chadha v Dow Jones & Co Inc* [1999] IL Pr 829, CA; *Reuben v Time Inc* [2003] EWHC 1430 QB and, earlier, *Reuben v Time Inc* [2003] EWCA Civ 06 at [14]; *Harrods Ltd v Dow Jones & Co Inc* [2003] EWHC 1162 (QB). See more generally *Markel International Insurance Co Ltd v La República Compañía Argentina de Seguros Generales SA* [2004] EWHC 1826 (Comm) at [29], [2005] Lloyd's Rep IR 90 QBD (Comm).

[313] *Cordoba Shipping Co Ltd v National State Bank, Elizabeth, New Jersey, The Albaforth* [1984] 2 Lloyd's Rep 91; Fawcett [1985] LMCLQ 6; Carter (1984) 55 BYBIL 347; *AG v Donaldson Lufkin and Jenrette Inc* [1990] 1 QB 391 at 484. See also *ISC v Guerin* [1992] 2 Lloyd's Rep 430 at 435; *The Xin Yang* [1996] 2 Lloyd's Rep 217 at 223, CA; *International Marine Services Inc v National Bank of Fujairah* [1997] IL Pr 468 at 470, CA.

[314] But cf for Australia *BHP Billiton Ltd v Schultz* (2004) 221 CLR 400 at [18] (per Gleeson CJ, McHugh and Heydon JJ, HC of Australia). Callinan J at [259] adopts the same principle as in *Berezovsky*.

[315] In the House of Lords, it was accepted by counsel that the tort ground of service out (at that time Ord 11, r 1(1)(f) RSC) was satisfied because significant damage (to their reputations in England) was sustained in England.

[316] The *Berezovsky* case, supra, at 1013 (per Lord Steyn), 1033 (per Lord Hobhouse).

[317] Ibid, at 1014 (per Lord Steyn), 1033 (per Lord Hobhouse), following *Kroch v Rossell* [1937] 1 All ER 725, CA. See also *Reuben v Time Inc* [2003] EWHC 1430 QB at [53]—over 13,000 copies. Cf *Dow Jones & Co Inc v Jameel* [2005] EWCA Civ 75 at [70], [2005] QB 946; Briggs (2005) 76 BYBIL 668, service set aside where only five subscribers in England accessed the offending text. See also *Al Amoudi v Brisard* [2006] EWHC 1062 (QB). But note now the Defamation Act 2013, s 1(1), requiring "serious harm" for a claim to be actionable under English law—this will also affect whether the court gives permission to serve outside the jurisdiction on the basis of a tort committed in England, because of the requirement for "a reasonable prospect of success". See infra, pp 363–4.

Moreover, on conventional *Spiliada* principles the claimants had significant connections with England and reputations to protect in England.[318] It was also highly relevant that the claimants were only seeking damages for the loss of their reputation *in England*.[319] Trial in Russia would not redress damage to the plaintiffs' reputation in England.[320] In contrast, if the plaintiffs had had a reputation in the USA and were suing for damage to that reputation, this would point to trial in the USA. The majority[321] concluded that England was the appropriate forum for trial. In contrast, if publication takes place abroad there will be considerable difficulty in persuading the court to permit service out of the jurisdiction.[322]

The House of Lords in *Berezovsky* examined the relationship between the natural forum principle and the *forum conveniens* test laid down in the *Spiliada* case.[323] All the Law Lords agreed that the two were consistent with each other.[324] Lord Steyn went on to explain that the former went to the weight of evidence.[325] The latter was concerned with a high level of generality and the former with a much lower level of generality. Lord Hope added that the natural forum principle was no more than a starting point for identification of the most appropriate forum.[326] This idea has been repeated by the Court of Appeal in *King v Lewis*.[327] This subtle shift in emphasis has the potential for the presumption becoming a weak one.

This natural forum principle requires the court to ascertain where a tort is committed. Whilst it is easy enough to state and apply the rule as to where the tort of defamation is committed, namely where the defamation is published,[328] it is by no means always easy to state or apply the rule as to where many other torts are committed.[329] The identification of the place where a tort is committed when this has occurred over the internet is particularly problematic.[330]

The natural forum principle was introduced at the time when service out of the jurisdiction in tort cases was based on the commission of a tort within the jurisdiction[331] and when the

---

[318] The *Berezovsky* case, supra, at 1014 (per Lord Steyn), 1033 (per Lord Hobhouse), 1016 (per Lord Nolan).

[319] Ibid, at 1017 (per Lord Nolan), 1014–15 (per Lord Steyn), 1033 (per Lord Hobhouse).

[320] Ibid, at 1014–15 (per Lord Steyn), 1033 (per Lord Hobhouse).

[321] Lords Steyn, Nolan, and Hobhouse; Lords Hoffmann and Hope dissenting.

[322] *Reuben v Time Inc* [2003] EWCA Civ 06 at [14].

[323] See infra, p 365 et seq.

[324] The *Berezovsky* case, supra, at 1014 (per Lord Steyn), 1033 (per Lord Hobhouse), 1017 (per Lord Nolan), 1019–21 (per Lord Hoffmann), 1030–32 (per Lord Hope).

[325] Ibid, at 1014; at 1033 (per Lord Hobhouse).

[326] Ibid, at 1032.

[327] [2004] EWCA Civ 1329 at [26], [2005] IL Pr 16; Briggs (2004) 75 BYBIL 565. See also *Richardson v Schwarzenegger* [2004] EWHC 2422 (QB); Briggs (2004) 75 BYBIL 565 at 570.

[328] On the facts of the *Berezovsky* case, all the constituent elements of the tort were said to have occurred in England, per Lord Steyn at 1013, and so there was no difficulty over where the tort was committed. See also *Reuben v Time Inc* [2003] EWCA Civ 06 at [14]; *King v Lewis*, supra, at [27]. For Canada see *Direct Energy Marketing Ltd v Hillson* [2000] IL Pr 102, 114–15.

[329] See generally the cases decided under the old tort head of Ord 11, r 1(1) which required that a tort was committed within the jurisdiction: *Distillers v Thompson* [1971] AC 458; *Diamond v Bank of London and Montreal* [1979] QB 333; *Castree v Squibb* [1980] 1 WLR 1248; the *Cordoba* case, supra. See also the identification of the place of the tort under the common law tort choice of law rules discussed infra, pp 778 and 883–8. See for an example of the difficulty, the position in relation to negligent misstatements and negligent and fraudulent misrepresentations discussed in Fawcett, Harris and Bridge, paras 6.110–6.113. For fraudulent conspiracy see *ABCI (Formerly Arab Business Consortium International Finance and Investment Co) v Banque Franco-Tunisienne* [2003] EWCA Civ 205 at [41], [2003] 2 Lloyd's Rep 146.

[330] See, eg, *Bonnier Media Ltd v Greg Lloyd Smith and Kestrel Trading Corpn* [2002] ETMR 86 (trade mark infringement and passing off) and more generally Fawcett, Harris and Bridge, paras 10.169 (defamation); 10.185 (negligent misstatement); 10.198 (conversion); 10.212 (inducement of breach of contract); 10.220 (negligence).

[331] *Cordoba Shipping Co Ltd v National State Bank, Elizabeth, New Jersey (The Albaforth)* [1984] 2 Lloyd's Rep 91, CA.

tort choice of law rules also required this place to be ascertained.[332] However, it makes less sense now that the tort ground does not seek to find a single place which is where the tort was committed but, instead, looks at both the place of damage and the place where the act from which the damage resulted was committed. Neither do the tort choice of law rules require this place to be ascertained,[333] apart from in cases of defamation,[334] where the old common law rules still operate. We would be better served not having presumptions when exercising a discretion and not having a principle that the jurisdiction in which a tort was committed is prima facie the natural forum for the dispute. Instead, what we should look at in tort cases is the law applicable to the tort,[335] which is the idea underlying the presumption.[336] If the law applicable to the tort is English law, this should be recognised as strong evidence in favour of England clearly being the appropriate forum for trial.[337]

Libel tourism and the Defamation Act 2013   The application of these principles in the context of defamation potentially gives a claimant a significant degree of choice of forum when it comes to publications distributed around the world. This creates the potential for forum shopping, where a claimant selects the most advantageous forum rather than the one most suited to the resolution of the dispute, which raises concerns of both fairness and efficiency. In the early years of the twenty-first century, the English courts developed a reputation as an attractive destination for forum shopping in this area, which became colloquially known as "libel tourism".[338] This was facilitated by the jurisdictional rules discussed above, and encouraged by the fact that English choice of law rules[339] led to the application of English law (considered to be claimant friendly, particularly in comparison with the United States) where the defamation claim was based on publications in England, even if there were other publications elsewhere.

The perceived problems of libel tourism have been exacerbated because of the growth of the internet and social media which further facilitate cross-border communications.[340] In *Dow Jones & Co Inc v Gutnick*[341] the High Court of Australia held that ordinarily the place where the tort of defamation is committed is where the material alleged to be defamatory is downloaded on to the computer of a person who has used a web-browser to pull the material from the web-server. This was preferred to the place of uploading (ie the place where information is made available over the internet by placing it in a storage area managed by a web-server).[342] In England, it is now also well established that a libel is committed where publication takes place and that a text on the internet is published at the place where it is downloaded.[343] The

---

[332] The common law tort choice of law rules are discussed infra, pp 883–8.

[333] The statutory and EU tort choice of law rules are discussed infra, Chapter 20.

[334] See infra, pp 885–8.

[335] See *Ark v True North Capital* [2005] EWHC 1585 (Comm) at [68], [2006] 1 All ER (Comm) 138. It may be necessary to ascertain this at the jurisdictional stage to show that there is a reasonable prospect of success, see the *Metall und Rohstoff* case, supra, and pp 363–4.

[336] See *Voth v Manildra Flour Mills Pty Ltd* (1990) 171 CLR 538 at 566 et seq, High Court of Australia.

[337] Ibid.

[338] See generally Morse (2005) 58 CLP 13; Garnett and Richardson (2009) 5 J Priv Int L 471; Hartley (2010) 59 ICLQ 25; Nielsen (2013) 9 J Priv Int L 269; Auda (2016) 12 J Priv Int L 106.

[339] See infra, p 883 et seq.

[340] See further eg Mills (2015) 7 J Media L 1.

[341] (2002) 210 CLR 575, HC of Australia; Briggs (2003) 119 LQR 210; Kohl (2003) 52 ICLQ 1049; Rolph (2002) 24 Sydney LR 263; Fitzgerald (2003) 27 Melbourne ULR 590.

[342] *Dow Jones & Co v Gutnick*, supra.

[343] *Godfrey v Demon Internet Ltd* [2001] QB 201, 208–9; *Loutchansky v Times Newspapers Ltd* [2002] QB 783 at [58], CA; *Harrods Ltd v Dow Jones & Co Inc* [2003] EWHC 1162 (QB) at [36]; *King v Lewis*, supra (this was accepted by the parties); *Richardson v Schwarzenegger* [2004] EWHC 2422 (QB) at [19]; *Dow Jones & Co Inc v Jameel* [2005] EWCA Civ 75 at [48]–[49], [2005] QB 946. See also Lord Hoffmann in the *Berezovsky* case, supra, at 1024.

Court of Appeal in *King v Lewis*[344] said that a publisher who chooses the internet, which is a global medium, cannot be too fastidious about the part of the world where he is made a libel defendant.[345] The Court rejected the notion that the court should be more ready to stay proceedings where the defendants did not target their publications towards the jurisdiction in which they have been sued.[346] It was pointed out that a defendant targets every jurisdiction in which his text may be downloaded.

This approach is, however, arguably too simplistic. It is questionable whether the same attitude should be adopted where it is not a commercial on-line publisher (who could equally well publish in conventional form abroad, and would then be subject to jurisdiction there, as on-line) but instead a private individual who is not out to make a profit. Moreover, there are situations where the defendant commercial on-line publisher may not reasonably foresee the text being downloaded in England, such as where a defendant on-line publisher makes it clear that he will not contract with subscribers in England but an English resident lies or uses an anonymising technique to take out a subscription.[347]

Some safeguards against the dangers of libel tourism were, however, developed in the case law. In *Berezovsky*, Lord Hope dissented from the majority on the question whether England was the clearly appropriate forum (ie in his view the presumption that English was the natural forum was rebutted), because he disagreed with the majority finding that the claimants had significant connections with England.[348] Lord Hope's judgment, and other case law on international libel,[349] led the Court of Appeal in *King v Lewis* to state the following general proposition for such cases. The more tenuous the claimant's connection with England (and the more substantial any publication abroad) the weaker the consideration that England is the natural forum becomes.[350] With transnational libels (ie publication in many different States), including internet defamation, the global picture has to be considered.[351] With such libels the place where the tort is committed ceases to be very meaningful.[352]

These principles were not, however, perceived to be sufficient to respond to the concerns about libel tourism, and further forms were adopted in the Defamation Act 2013.[353] The major reforms are in section 9 of the Act,[354] which provides (in relevant part) that:

> (2) A court does not have jurisdiction to hear and determine an action to which this section applies unless the court is satisfied that, of all the places in which the statement complained of has been published, England and Wales is clearly the most appropriate place in which to bring an action in respect of the statement.

---

[344] Supra. *King v Lewis* [2004] EWCA Civ 1329, [2005] IL Pr 16.

[345] Ibid, at [31].

[346] Ibid, at [34]–[35].

[347] See Fawcett, Harris and Bridge, para 10.15–10.16.

[348] [2000] 1 WLR 1004, 1032–3. See also the dissent of Lord Hoffmann at 1023–4.

[349] In particular *Chadha v Dow Jones & Co Inc* [1999] IL Pr 829, CA.

[350] *King v Lewis*, supra, at [27]. See also *Richardson v Schwarzenegger* [2004] EWHC 2422 (QB) at [23]; *Chadha v Dow Jones* [1999] ILPr 829, CA, at [23].

[351] *King v Lewis*, supra, at [28], following Lord Steyn in the *Berezovsky* case, supra, at 1012.

[352] The *King v Lewis* case, supra.

[353] The Defamation Act 2013 applies only to cases covered by common law jurisdiction (it does not affect the exercise of jurisdiction under the Brussels I Recast—see s 9(1)), but it applies regardless of the basis of common law jurisdiction. It thus equally applies where a defamation claim is brought against a non-Member State domiciled company based on their presence in England through an English place of business—in that context affecting the potential exercise of the discretion to stay proceedings. See infra, p 398.

[354] But note also the substantive reform in section 1(1), discussed supra, p 350.

(3) The references in subsection (2) to the statement complained of include references to any statement which conveys the same, or substantially the same, imputation as the statement complained of.

The effect of subsection (2) is to clarify the test of jurisdictional discretion, so that the English courts will only hear the case where they are clearly the most appropriate forum.[355] The effect of subsection (3) is to confirm (in accordance with the case law noted above) that in making this determination, the court must take into account all publications of the material world-wide, not just those publications in England.[356] While the motivation behind these reforms may be applauded, some concerns may be raised regarding their potential effects.[357] The rule appears to preclude the English courts from exercising jurisdiction if they are not clearly the most appropriate forum regardless of whether an alternative forum is practically available, which may be inconsistent with the requirements of access to justice under the European Convention on Human Rights.[358] It also appears to preclude the English courts from exercising jurisdiction where a publication is distributed in a number of places including England and the English courts would be equally as appropriate as any other forum. There is no obvious reason why jurisdictional abstention is desirable in such circumstances, although for service out cases this is probably not a change from the position prior to the Act.

(v) Enforcement
(10) Where "a claim is made to enforce any judgment or arbitral award".[359] The identically worded predecessor of this ground was introduced in the light of the Civil Jurisdiction and Judgments Act 1982. The background to it is the rule that any action in England to enforce a foreign judgment at common law requires the English rules as to jurisdiction and service of claim forms to be satisfied.[360] If the claimant was unable to satisfy this requirement, he was always left with the option of bringing a new action on the original cause of action, with the possibility of using service out as the basis of jurisdiction. Section 34 of the Civil Jurisdiction and Judgments Act 1982 prevents the claimant from doing this,[361] hence the need for some basis for serving a claim form on a defendant in order to enforce the foreign judgment. Paragraph 3.1(10) provides the means for satisfying this requirement. The claimant must show a good arguable case that the foreign judgment would be enforced in England and ordinarily that he can reasonably expect a benefit from the English judgment.[362] However, there is no requirement under paragraph (10) that the defendant has assets in England.[363]

---

[355] On the *forum conveniens* test, see p 364 et seq. The change is more striking in relation to defendants who are present in the territory; the *forum non conveniens* test ordinarily only requires that there be no other clearly more appropriate forum. See p 395 et seq.

[356] See, eg, *Ahuja v Politika Novine I Magazini Doo* [2015] EWHC 3380 (QB), [2016] 1 WLR 1414, noting that the important issue is generally not the extent of publication in different jurisdictions but the extent of reputational damage.

[357] See further Mills (2015) 7 J Media L 1. It is notable that the statutory reforms are not particularly targeted at "libel tourists"—they apply equally to English resident claimants.

[358] See generally Fawcett, Ní Shúilleabháin, and Shah, *Human Rights and Private International Law* (2016) paras 10.95–10.197. The Explanatory Notes to s 9 of the Defamation Act 2013 do, however, suggest that a court should take into account "whether there is reason to think that the claimant would not receive a fair hearing elsewhere".

[359] CPR, r 6.36(9).

[360] *Perry v Zissis* [1977] 1 Lloyd's Rep 607, see infra, p 527.

[361] Infra, p 556.

[362] *Demirel v Tasarruff* [2007] EWCA Civ 799 at [29], [2007] 1 WLR 2508; leave to appeal to the House of Lords dismissed [2007] 1 WLR 3066.

[363] *Demirel v Tasarruff* [2007] EWCA Civ 799 at [10]–[25]; *Habib Bank Ltd v Central Bank of Sudan* [2014] EWHC 2288 (Comm). But see *Linsen International Limited v Humpuss Transportasi Kimia* [2011] EWCA Civ 1042, at [24], holding that this ground of jurisdiction does not support an order freezing assets outside England, because it only applies to "enforcement" within the jurisdiction.

Paragraph (10) also applies in respect of arbitral awards. An action for a pre-judgment freezing injunction in support of foreign proceedings does not, however, come within this provision.[364] A freezing injunction does not "enforce" anything and there is no "judgment" to be enforced.

(vi) Claims about property within the jurisdiction

(11) Where "the subject matter of the claim relates wholly or principally to property within the jurisdiction, provided that nothing under this paragraph shall render justiciable the title to or the right to possession of immovable property outside England and Wales".[365] This rule was newly formulated in the Civil Procedure Rules, in place of three earlier rules.[366] It embraces and extends beyond the contents of those rules.[367] In considering the application of this provision it is necessary to examine how the case was put, and what in substance it involved.[368] The elements of this ground for service out of the jurisdiction are as follows.

A claim that relates to property This provision extends to any claim for relief, whether for damages or otherwise, so long as it relates to property located within the jurisdiction.[369] This phrase "relates to" has been widely construed so that the claim does not have to have a direct effect on the property itself, its possession or title. It cannot be construed as being confined to claims relating to the ownership or possession of property,[370] such as one for the recovery of land,[371] although these will commonly be the sort of claims where this ground will be invoked. Thus this provision applied where a declaration was sought that a transfer of shares constituted a transaction at an undervalue within the meaning of the Insolvency Act 1986.[372] It is enough that the claim relates to a transaction affecting the property, rather than as to the property or some interest therein. In principle therefore, it can extend to, for example, a claim for damages arising from a breach of contract or a tort relating to property located within the jurisdiction. If, for example, a buyer sues the seller for damages for breach of contract alleging that the goods situated in England are defective, the claim "relates to" property located within the jurisdiction.[373] This is because compensation is sought in respect of the diminished value of that property arising out of its defective state. A predecessor, and more restrictively worded, property ground[374] encompassed an action against the assignee of a lease for breach of covenant to repair,[375] a claim by a tenant of a farm to recover compensation for improvements,[376]

---

[364] *Mercedes-Benz AG v Leiduck* [1996] AC 284 at 298–9 (per Lord Mustill), PC; see also *Mansour v Mansour* [1990] FCR 17, [1989] 1 FLR 418.

[365] CPR, PD6B, 3.1(11).

[366] *Re Banco Nacional de Cuba* [2001] 1 WLR 2039, 1254, 1255. The case is also reported as *Banca Carige v BNC* [2001] 2 Lloyd's Rep 147. The three earlier rules are RSC, Ord 11, r 1(1)(g), (h), (i). These provided as follows: (g) the whole subject matter of the action is land situate within the jurisdiction (with or without rents or profits) or the perpetuation of testimony relating to land so situate; (h) the claim is brought to construe, rectify, set aside or enforce an act, deed, will, contract, obligation or liability affecting land situate within the jurisdiction; (i) the claim is made for a debt secured on immovable property or is made to assert, declare or determine proprietary or possessory rights, or rights of security, in or over *movable* property, or to obtain authority to dispose of *movable* property, situate within the jurisdiction.

[367] *Re Banco Nacional de Cuba*, supra, 2055.

[368] *Sahar v Tsitsekkos* [2004] EWHC 2659 (Ch) at [41]–[42]; *The Republic of Pakistan v Zardari* [2006] EWHC 2411 (Comm) at [157], [2006] 2 CLC 667.

[369] *Re Banco Nacional de Cuba*, supra, 2055.

[370] Ibid.

[371] *Agnew v Usher* (1884) 14 QBD 78; affd 51 LT 752. This came within a predecessor of Ord 11, r 1(1)(g) RSC.

[372] *Re Banco Nacional de Cuba*, supra.

[373] Ibid.

[374] Ord 11, r 1(1)(h) and its predecessors.

[375] *Tassell v Hallen* [1892] 1 QB 321.

[376] *Kaye v Sutherland* (1887) 20 QBD 147.

and an action to enforce obligations under a declaration of trust in respect of land which had been sold at the time of the action.[377] These actions would all come within paragraph 3.1(11). An action for the recovery of rent[378] and one concerning royalties in respect of the production of oil[379] were not covered in the past[380] but would be now since they "relate to" property in the wide sense which has been given to this phrase.

Property   This provision is not limited to land, but extends to personal property.[381] In conflict of laws terminology, this is not limited to immovable property but extends to movable property. This could be tangible movable property, such as physical goods, or intangible movable property, such as shares.[382] Property may include confidential information,[383] and certainly includes money,[384] including money representing the proceeds of sale of land.[385] So disputed funds paid into a bank account in England would come within paragraph 3.1(11) but permission for service out of the jurisdiction would very likely be refused where the connection with England was so tenuous.[386] An action in relation to a life policy assigned to a lender as security for a loan was covered by a previous property ground[387] and would now come within paragraph 3.1(11).

Wholly or principally located within the jurisdiction[388]   Immovable property is easily located. However, movable property obviously may be moved from one country to another. We should be concerned with location at the time of the commencement of the proceedings, which should be regarded as being the moment when permission is sought for service out of the jurisdiction.[389] Whilst there is normally no difficulty in fixing the location of tangible movable property, this can be problematic with intangible movable property, such as shares.[390] This rule previously required that the property be wholly within the jurisdiction, which was potentially problematic if, for example, the claim related to a trust fund which included some foreign assets. It was amended in October 2015 to extend to property wholly or principally located in England, but with the qualification that jurisdiction is not extended to disputes concerning title to foreign land, which have traditionally been viewed as non-justiciable under the common law.[391]

---

[377] *Official Solicitor v Stype Investments (Jersey) Ltd* [1983] 1 All ER 629.

[378] *Agnew v Usher* (1884) 14 QBD 78.

[379] *BHP Petroleum Pty Ltd v Oil Basins Ltd* [1985] VR 725.

[380] Under Ord 11, r 1(1)(h). The action had to directly affect the land itself: *Casey v Arnott* (1876) 2 CPD 24.

[381] *Re Banco Nacional de Cuba*, supra, 2055.

[382] Ibid. See also *Walanpatrias Stiftung v Lehman Brothers International (Europe)* [2006] EWHC 3034 (Comm) at [25].

[383] *Ashton Investments Ltd v OJSC Russian Aluminium RUSAL* [2006] EWHC 2545 (Comm) at [67], [2007] 1 Lloyd's Rep 311. But see *Force India Formula One Team Ltd v 1 Malaysia Racing Team Sdn Bhd* [2012] EWHC 616 (Ch), at [376], [2012] RPC 29.

[384] The *Walanpatrias* case, supra, at [25].

[385] *The Republic of Pakistan v Zardari* [2006] EWHC 2411 (Comm) at [157]–[159], [2006] 2 CLC 667.

[386] Ibid.

[387] See *Deutsche National Bank v Paul* [1898] 1 Ch 283, which held that such a claim did not fall within one of the contract heads. This led to the introduction of a new head of Ord 11 (eventually Ord 11, r 1(1) (i)) to deal with this.

[388] See *Shahar v Tsitsekkos* [2004] EWHC 2659 (Ch) at [42].

[389] We are concerned with domicile as at the moment of the issue of proceedings, rather than the subsequent service on the defendant, *Canada Trust Co v Stolzenberg (No 2)* [2002] 1 AC 1, HL. This approach was approved in *Fujifilm Kyowa Kirin Biologics Company Limited v Abbvie Biotechnology Limited* [2016] EWHC 2204 (Pat) at [97], although leaving open the question of whether the rule might apply if property is in transit to the jurisdiction at the time of commencement of proceedings.

[390] See infra, Chapter 32.

[391] See infra, p 484 et seq.

Exercise of the discretion   Where there is a dispute about title to real property in England, depending on English law, it is almost impossible to envisage where England would not be the clearly appropriate forum for trial.[392] Where the dispute more broadly relates to the ownership of property (and the proceeds of sale) in England, England may still be the clearly appropriate forum.[393]

(vii)   Claims about trusts, etc (including restitution)

(12) Where "a claim is made in respect of a trust which is created by the operation of a statute, or by a written instrument, or created orally and evidenced in writing, and which is governed by the law of England and Wales". The question whether English law applies to a trust is tested as at the time when permission to serve out was sought.[394] This ground and that in paragraph 3.1(12A) were added or amended in April 2015. They are in terms concerned with express trusts and accordingly do not apply to constructive or resulting trusts.[395] There is a separate ground dealing with such trusts.[396] There is no need for the property subject to the trusts to be situated in England. So, for example, this ground will apply where a defendant trustee has sold the entire trust funds and has departed abroad with the proceeds.[397]

(12A) Where "a claim is made in respect of a trust which is created by the operation of a statute, or by a written instrument, or created orally and evidenced in writing, and which provides that jurisdiction in respect of such a claim shall be conferred upon the courts of England and Wales". This is a new basis of jurisdiction which permits service out on the basis of a jurisdiction clause in the trust instrument. See also the comments on paragraph 3.1(12) above.

(13) Where "a claim is made for any remedy which might be obtained in proceedings for the administration of the estate of a person who died domiciled[398] within the jurisdiction or whose estate includes assets within the jurisdiction".[399] This ground was amended in October 2015 so that it extends to estates with assets in the jurisdiction, not just to the estates of persons domiciled in the jurisdiction.

(14) "A probate claim or a claim for the rectification of a will".[400] This ground applies to an action for the grant of probate, or letters of administration of an estate, or for the revocation of such a grant, or for a decree pronouncing against the validity of a will, provided the action is not non-contentious or common form probate business. The Civil Procedure Rules added wording to make it clear that this ground includes a claim for the rectification of a will.

(15) Where "a claim is made against the defendant as constructive trustee, or as trustee of a resulting trust, where the claim arises out of acts committed or events occurring within the

---

[392] *The Republic of Pakistan v Zardari* [2006] EWHC 2411 (Comm) at [171], [2006] 2 CLC 667. See also *Khyentse Hope* [2005] 3 NZLR 501.

[393] *The Republic of Pakistan* case, supra, at [171]–[181].

[394] *Chellaram v Chellaram (No 2)* [2002] EWHC 632 (Ch) at [148]–[153], [2002] 3 All ER 17.

[395] *Chellaram*, supra, at [137], [138].

[396] CPR, PD6B, 3.1(15); set out infra.

[397] At one time, under a differently worded ground, the property subject to the trusts had to be situated in England (see *Winter v Winter* [1894] 1 Ch 421 and *Official Solicitor v Stype Investments (Jersey) Ltd* [1983] 1 All ER 629), but this limitation was removed.

[398] Domicile is now determined in accordance with the definition contained in the Brussels I Recast and the Civil Jurisdiction and Judgments Order 2001 (discussed supra, pp 198–202): CPR, r 6.31(1).

[399] CPR, PD6B, 3.1(13). See *Dellar v Zivy* [2007] EWHC 2266 (Ch), [2007] IL Pr 60. It is very debatable whether the discretion would be exercised in the case of foreign immovables; see Davis (1966) 2 NZULR 243 at 244–5.

[400] CPR, PD6B, 3.1(14).

jurisdiction or relates to assets within the jurisdiction".[401] This provision was amended in October 2015 to extend to resulting trusts—it had previously only applied to constructive trusts. At this time it was also amended to clarify that it applies to "events occurring" as well as "acts committed" in the jurisdiction, and also to claims which "relate to assets within the jurisdiction". The earlier provision under the Rules of the Supreme Court allowed for service out of the jurisdiction where "the claim is brought for money had and received or for an account or other remedy against the defendant as constructive trustee, and the defendant's alleged liability arises out of acts committed, whether by him or otherwise, within the jurisdiction". It was doubtless not intended that these changes should have any substantive effect on the court's powers,[402] and the subsequent changes will have only expanded the scope of the rule. It follows that recourse probably can be had to the old wording and to the authorities under that provision, at least for positive confirmation of cases covered by this ground. These authorities establish that the constructive trust ground will cover knowing participation in acts[403] in England in a fraudulent breach of trust committed in England.[404] Probably, it also covers knowing receipt abroad of the proceeds of such frauds, the knowledge having been acquired abroad.[405] The concept of a constructive trust is wide enough to cover a proprietary equitable claim.[406] Bribes and the property from time to time representing the bribe are held on a constructive trust for the person injured.[407] It is not necessary that all the acts have been committed within the jurisdiction.[408] It is enough that "substantial and efficacious acts" have been committed within the jurisdiction, even if substantial and efficacious acts have also been committed outside the jurisdiction.[409] There must be some link between the acts committed within the jurisdiction and the defendant but those acts do not have to be those of the defendant.[410] If the principal fraudster gives instructions for money in England to be paid abroad to a knowing recipient, it is not necessary for the recipient to have done anything in England for paragraph 3.1(15) to apply to allow service out of the jurisdiction against the recipient.[411]

---

[401] CPR, PD6B, 3.1(15); formerly Ord 11, r 1(1)(t) RSC, on which see *Insurance Co "Ingosstrakh" Ltd v Latvian Shipping Co* [2000] IL Pr 164, CA.

[402] See the Lord Chancellor's Department Consultation Paper on the Civil Procedure Rules—Service of Court Process Abroad, para 22, which notes that a number of minor drafting changes were proposed which did not affect the substance. This appears to be another of these changes.

[403] But probably not an omission: *Battalion Investment & Trust Co Ltd v Clifford*, 2002 (unreported).

[404] *ISC v Guerin* [1992] 2 Lloyd's Rep 430 at 433, Hoffman J; *ISC v Radcliff*, 7 December 1990 (unreported) (Millett J).

[405] *ISC v Guerin*, supra; *Polly Peck International plc v Nadir* (1992) The Independent, 2 September. Cf *ISC v Radcliff*, supra.

[406] *NABB Brothers Ltd v Lloyds Bank International (Guernsey) Ltd* [2005] EWHC 405 (Ch) at [68]–[73], [2005] IL Pr 37.

[407] *The Republic of Pakistan v Zardari* [2006] EWHC 2411 (Comm) at [164], [2006] 2 CLC 667.

[408] See in relation to constructive trusts *ISC v Guerin*, [1992] 2 Lloyd's Rep 430, 433, Hoffmann J; *Polly Peck International v Nadir* (1992) The Independent, 2 September, revsd by the Court of Appeal (1993). The Times, 22 March, but Hoffmann LJ said obiter that he adhered to his view in the *ISC* case. See also *The Republic of Pakistan v Zardari* [2006] EWHC 2411 (Comm) at [166]–[168], [2006] 2 CLC 667. Cf *ISC v Radcliff*, 7 December 1990 (unreported) (Millett J).

[409] *Nycal (UK) Ltd v Lacey* [1994] CLC 12, a case decided under Ord 11, r 1(1)(t) RSC. Substantial and efficacious acts committed within the jurisdiction between breach of duty and receipt of relevant property were acts out of which liability arose even where committed by persons other than the defendant. See also in relation to the tort ground *Metall und Rohstoff AG v Donaldson Lufkin and Jenrette Inc* [1990] 1 QB 391, CA; overruled on a different point in *Lonrho plc v Fayed* [1992] 1 AC 448.

[410] *NABB Brothers Ltd v Lloyds Bank International (Guernsey) Ltd* [2005] EWHC 405 (Ch) at [86], [2005] IL Pr 37; *The Republic of Pakistan v Zardari* [2006] EWHC 2411 (Comm) at [169], [2006] 2 CLC 667.

[411] *NABB Brothers*, supra, at [87].

(16) Where "a claim is made for restitution where—(a) the defendant's alleged liability arises out of acts committed within the jurisdiction; or (b) the enrichment is obtained within the jurisdiction; or (c) the claim is governed by the law of England and Wales".[412] This ground for service out of the jurisdiction was introduced by the Civil Procedure Rules, and parts (b) and (c) were added in October 2015. A claim for a restitutionary remedy that is based on unjust enrichment is undeniably a claim "made for restitution". However, this phrase would appear to go much wider than this and would cover all cases where a restitutionary remedy is sought, regardless of what the claim is based on.[413] It could be based on contract or on wrongdoing. It would cover an equitable proprietary claim.[414] Seemingly, it can also cover an action for equitable relief for breach of confidence,[415] although the position is less clear since a new basis of jurisdiction specifically for breach of confidence, paragraph (21), was added in October 2015.[416] Acts may have been committed partly within the jurisdiction and partly outside the jurisdiction. The same problem has arisen with both the tort ground[417] and the constructive and resulting trust ground.[418] The position adopted in relation to those grounds should also be adopted in relation to this ground. Thus it should not be necessary that all the acts have been committed within the jurisdiction. It should be enough that "substantial and efficacious acts" (or omissions) have been committed within the jurisdiction, even if substantial and efficacious acts have also been committed outside the jurisdiction.[419] For example, it has been held that there is no difficulty in coming within paragraph (16) where there are separate breaches of the equitable duty of confidentiality and one of these takes place in England by virtue of publication of photos (taken in New York in circumstances of breach of confidence).[420]

(viii) Claims by HM Revenue and Customs

(17) Where "a claim is made by the Commissioners for HM Revenue and Customs relating to duties or taxes against a defendant not domiciled[421] in Scotland or Northern Ireland".[422]

(ix) Claim for costs order in favour of or against third parties

(18) Where "a claim is made by a party to proceedings for an order that the court exercise its power under section 51 of the Senior Courts Act 1981 to make a costs order in favour of or against a person who is not a party to those proceedings; (Rule 46.2 sets out the procedure where the court is considering whether to exercise its discretion to make a costs order in favour of or against a non-party)".[423]

---

[412] CPR, PD6B, 3.1(16).

[413] See Fawcett, Harris and Bridge, paras 8.37–8.38. Contrast the wording of the tort ground, a claim "made *in* tort". Observe also the grouping of the restitution ground with other grounds concerned with the remedy sought.

[414] *NABB Brothers Ltd v Lloyds Bank International (Guernsey) Ltd* [2005] EWHC 405 (Ch) at [77], [2005] IL Pr 37.

[415] *Douglas v Hello! Ltd (No 2)* [2003] EWCA Civ 139 at [23]–[26], [2003] EMLR 28, where this was common ground for counsel. But not every such claim, see *Ashton Investments Ltd v OJSC Russian Aluminium RUSAL* [2006] EWHC 2545 (Comm) at [69], [2007] 1 Lloyd's Rep 311.

[416] See infra, p 362.

[417] Supra, p 350.

[418] Supra, p 359.

[419] See *Cecil v Bayat* [2010] EWHC 641 (Comm) (reversed on other grounds at [2011] EWCA Civ 135, [2011] 1 WLR 3086); *AstraZeneca UK Ltd v Albemarle International Corp* [2010] EWHC 1028 (Comm), [2010] 2 Lloyd's Rep 61.

[420] *Douglas v Hello! Ltd (No 2)*, supra, at [36].

[421] Domicile is determined in accordance with the definition contained in the Brussels I Recast and the Civil Jurisdiction and Judgments Order 2001: CPR, r 6.31(1); discussed supra, pp 198–202.

[422] CPR, PD6B, 3.1(17).

[423] CPR, PD6B, 3.1(18). For the need for this provision see *National Justice Compañía Naviera SA v Prudential Assurance Co Ltd (The Ikarian Reefer (No 2)* [2000] 1 Lloyd's Rep 129 at 137. See *OT Africa Line*

(x) Admiralty claims

(19) Where "a claim is—(a) in the nature of salvage and any part of the services took place within the jurisdiction; or (b) to enforce a claim under section 153, 154, 175 or 176A of the Merchant Shipping Act 1995".[424] Admiralty "other claims" (ie formerly called in personam claims)[425] are in general subject to the same rules for service out of the jurisdiction as any other claim.[426] However, paragraph 3.1(19) is a special rule providing for service out of the jurisdiction where the claim is in the nature of salvage or where the claim arises from oil pollution. The Civil Procedure Rules also provide that a claim form in a collision claim may not be served out of the jurisdiction unless there is a specified connection with England or the defendant has submitted to or agreed to submit to the jurisdiction of the court.[427]

(xi) Claims under various enactments

(20) Where "a claim is made—(a) under an enactment which allows proceedings to be brought and those proceedings are not covered by any of the other grounds referred to in this paragraph; or (b) under the Directive of the Council of the European Communities dated 15 March 1976 No. 76/308/EEC,[428] where service is to be effected in a Member State of the European Union".[429] Previously, a list of the enactments covered by part (a) of this rule was provided.[430] No list of these enactments is now given, making this ground of jurisdiction potentially applicable to any claim based on a statute, without any particular connection with England required—only that the court's permission must be obtained to commence the proceedings,[431] as discussed further below.[432] This is a very expansive approach to jurisdiction. If the claim relates to acts or events outside the jurisdiction, it would still, however, be necessary to determine whether a statutory cause of action was intended to have extraterritorial application in the circumstances of the case—if not, the claim would not satisfy the "reasonable prospect of success" test, discussed below.[433]

Ltd v Magic Sportswear Corpn [2004] EWHC 2441 (Comm) at [26]–[28], [2005] 1 Lloyd's Rep 252; appeal dismissed without discussion of this point [2005] EWCA Civ 710 at [15], [2005] 2 Lloyd's Rep 170; *Locabail (UK) Ltd v Bayfield Properties Ltd (No.3)* [2000] 2 Costs LR 169.

[424] CPR, PD6B, 3.1(19).

[425] See CPR, PD61, 12.1.

[426] Subject to CPR, Part 61 and PD61 provisions on limitation and collision claims, "other claims" proceed in accordance with Part 58 (Commercial Court).

[427] CPR, r 61.4(7). The permission of the court to serve outside the territory, in accordance with the usual rules under Part 6, is also required. See also in relation to limitation claims CPR, r 61.11(5), *ICL Shipping Ltd & Steamship Mutual Underwriting Association (Bermuda) Ltd v ChinTai Steel Enterprise Co Ltd* [2003] EWHC 2320 (Comm).

[428] Council Directive 76/308/EEC of 15 March 1976 on mutual assistance for the recovery of claims resulting from operations forming part of the system of financing the European Agricultural Guidance and Guarantee Fund, and of the agricultural levies and customs duties, OJ 1976 L 73. This Directive was previously in the list of enactments covered by this rule.

[429] CPR, PD6B, 3.1(20).

[430] These were listed in a previous version of PD6B, as follows: the Nuclear Installations Act 1965; Schedule 2 to the Immigration Act 1971; the Inheritance (Provision for Family and Dependents) Act 1975; Council Directive (EEC) No 76/308 dated 15 March 1976 (now part (b) of the rule); Part VI of the Criminal Justice Act 1988; the Social Security Contributions and Benefits Act 1992; the Drug Trafficking Offences Act 1994; The Pensions Act 1995; Part II of the Immigration and Asylum Act 1999; the Financial Services and Markets Act 2000; The Pensions Act 2004.

[431] See, eg, *GMC v Brauwers* [2010] EWHC 106 (Admin).

[432] See infra, p 364 et seq.

[433] See, eg, *Erste Group Bank AG London Branch v JSC 'VMZ Red October'* [2015] EWCA Civ 379.

(xii) Claims for breach of confidence or misuse of private information

(21) Where "a claim is made for breach of confidence or misuse of private information where—(a) detriment was suffered, or will be suffered, within the jurisdiction; or (b) detriment which has been, or will be, suffered results from an act committed, or likely to be committed, within the jurisdiction".[434] This basis of jurisdiction was added in October 2015 to respond to uncertainties regarding the proper jurisdictional basis for actions for breach of confidence and misuse of private information. There is previous authority supporting the view that actions for breach of confidence were to be classified as falling under the ground of jurisdiction dealing with restitution,[435] or potentially the ground of jurisdiction dealing with property (to the extent that confidential information may be classified as property),[436] and that actions for misuse of private information were to be classified as torts for jurisdictional purposes.[437] For misuse of private information, the change makes little difference, as this basis of jurisdiction is modeled on that for actions in tort. For breach of confidence, the difference is significant as the grounds of jurisdiction for claims in restitution (and property) are defined distinctively. For such claims, it is unclear whether paragraph 3.1(21) should be viewed as an additional basis of jurisdiction, or as reversing the previous classification of such actions as restitutionary (or proprietary). While this provision does address an existing uncertainty, it creates others, and further judicial clarification of the relationship between these grounds of jurisdiction and the principles to be applied in interpreting this new paragraph will be necessary.

(xiii) The interaction of the different grounds of Practice Direction 6B, paragraph 3.1

It should be pointed out that an overlap between the various paragraphs of paragraph 3.1 is possible, and one case may come within several grounds. At the same time, the grounds under paragraph 3.1 are to be read disjunctively and each paragraph is complete in itself and independent of the others.[438] This means, for example, that an employee, who has suffered personal injury abroad (following a negligent act there) during the course of his employment and who can sue his employer for damages either for breach of contract or in tort, can elect to frame his action in contract rather than in tort, thereby bringing his case within one of the grounds of paragraph 3.1.[439] A separate basis of jurisdiction is, however, required for each claim. This traditionally meant that if service abroad had been allowed under one of the grounds, the claimant was not allowed later to add to his particulars of claim a claim for another cause of action for which permission to serve a claim form out of the jurisdiction would not have been given.[440] However, since paragraph 3.1(4A)[441] now allows permission to be given for related claims which do not themselves have an independent jurisdictional basis, a more flexible approach to the late addition of related claims is likely to be possible.

---

[434] CPR PD6B, 3.1(21).

[435] *Douglas v Hello! Ltd (No 2)* [2003] EWCA Civ 139 at [23]–[26], [2003] EMLR 28; see supra, p 360.

[436] See supra, p 357.

[437] *Google Inc v Vidal-Hall* [2015] EWCA Civ 311, [2015] 3 WLR 409 (permission granted to appeal to the Supreme Court, but settled before judgment); supra, p 348.

[438] *Matthews v Kuwait Bechtel Corpn* [1959] 2 QB 57 at 62 (an Ord 11 RSC case); and see *Tassell v Hallen* [1892] 1 QB 321.

[439] *Matthews v Kuwait Bechtel Corpn*, supra.

[440] *Waterhouse v Reid* [1938] 1 KB 743; *The Siskina* [1979] AC 210 at 254–5; *Donohue v Armco Inc* [2001] UKHL 64 at [21], [2002] 1 All ER 749. Cf *FFSB Ltd v Seward & Kissel LLP* [2007] UKPC 16.

[441] See supra, p 340.

(b) A reasonable prospect of success

An application for permission to serve a claim form out of the jurisdiction under rule 6.36 (in accordance with Practice Direction 6B) must be supported by written evidence stating that the claimant believes that his claim has a reasonable prospect of success.[442] This is synonymous with "a real prospect of success".[443] "Real is to be contrasted with fanciful or imaginary".[444] The test is the same or substantially the same as that previously laid down by the House of Lords in *Seaconsar Far East Ltd v Bank Markazi Jomhouri Islami Iran*[445] in relation to service out of the jurisdiction under Order 11, rule 1(1) of the Rules of the Supreme Court, the predecessor of rule 6.36.[446] In that case, the House of Lords held that the claimant has to establish that there is a serious issue to be tried in that there is "a substantial question of fact or law or both, arising on the facts disclosed by the affidavits, which the [claimant] . . . bona fide desires to try . . .".[447] An issue that is imaginary or fanciful is not a serious issue to be tried.[448] Conversely, a claimant has a real prospect of success if his chances of success are not fanciful.[449]

The threshold test of a reasonable prospect of success (serious issue on the merits) is a low one.[450] It is a lower standard of proof than that of a good arguable case, the standard that previously applied to the merits. This inquiry is an element in the exercise of the court's discretion[451] but is separate and distinct from the *forum conveniens* element.[452] With many grounds of Practice Direction 6B, paragraph 3.1, eg paragraphs (1) and (20), once the ground is established there will have to be a separate inquiry into the merits.[453] It seems that this will also be necessary in respect of paragraph (2).[454] In contrast, with paragraph (7) this will not

---

[442] CPR, r 6.37(1)(b).

[443] *Swiss Reinsurance Company Ltd v United India Insurance Co* [2002] EWHC 741 (Comm) at [27], [2004] IL Pr 4 at 62; *Carvill America Inc v Camperdown UK Ltd* [2005] EWCA Civ 645 at [24], [2005] 2 Lloyd's Rep 457; *The Republic of Pakistan v Zardari* [2006] EWHC 2411 (Comm) at [136], [2006] 2 CLC 667; *Tasarruff v Demirel* [2006] EWHC 3354 (Ch) at [39], [2007] IL Pr 8, affd without discussion of this point [2007] EWCA Civ 799; *Standard Bank Plc v EFAD Real Estate Company WLL* [2014] EWHC 1834 (Comm). The wording "real prospect of success" is to be found in CPR, Part 24; see similarly Part 3.4(2)(a) ("no reasonable grounds for bringing or defending the claim").

[444] The *Swiss Reinsurance Co* case, supra; the *Carvill America* case, supra, at [24].

[445] [1994] 1 AC 438; Briggs [1994] LMCLQ 1; Carter (1993) BYBIL 464; Perkins [1994] CLJ 244.

[446] The *Swiss Reinsurance Company* case, supra (the same or substantially the same); *Navigators Insurance Co v Atlantic Methanol Production Co* [2003] EWHC 1706 (Comm) at [33] (treated as the same); *BAS Capital Funding Corpn v Medfinco Ltd* [2003] EWHC 1798 at [153] (no reason to believe differs in any material way), [2004] IL Pr 16; *MRG (Japan) Ltd v Engelhard Metals Japan Ltd* [2003] EWHC 3418 (Comm) at [7]–[10] (the same), [2004] 1 Lloyd's Rep 731; *Ophthalmic Innovations International (United Kingdom) Ltd v Ophthalmic Innovations International Inc* [2004] EWHC 2948 (Ch) at [39], [2005] IL Pr 109; *NABB Brothers Ltd v Lloyds Bank International (Guernsey) Ltd* [2005] EWHC 405 (Ch) at [53], [2005] IL Pr 37; *Pearson Education Ltd v Prentice Hall of India Private Ltd* [2005] EWHC 655 (QB); *Ashton Investments Ltd v OJSC Russian Aluminium (RUSAL)* [2006] EWHC 2545 (Comm), [2007] 1 Lloyd's Rep 311; *The Republic of Pakistan v Zardari* [2006] EWHC 2411 (Comm) at [136], [2006] 2 CLC 667. The merits threshold under CPR, r 6.36 should not differ in substance from that of summary judgment under r 24.2 (in other words, the court should not subject a foreign defendant to proceedings which the defendant would be entitled to have summarily dismissed): *De Molestina v Ponton* [2002] 1 Lloyd's Rep 271, 281; the *Carvill America* case, supra, at [24]; *Chris Sawyer v Atari Interactive Inc* [2005] EWHC 2351 (Ch) at [49]–[50], [2006] IL Pr 8.

[447] *Seaconsar Far East Ltd v Bank Markazi Jomhouri Islami Iran* [1994] 1 AC 438 at 452 (per Lord Goff), HL.

[448] The *Swiss Reinsurance Co* case, supra.

[449] The *Carvill America* case, supra, at [24].

[450] *Morin v Bonhams & Brooks Ltd* [2003] EWHC 467 (Comm) at [46], [2003] IL Pr 25; affd [2003] EWCA 1802, [2004] IL Pr 24; the *Carvill America* case, supra, at [24].

[451] See CPR, r 6.37(3), infra, p 364 et seq.

[452] The *Seaconsar* case, supra, at 455–6.

[453] Ibid, at 454, referring to Ord 11, r 1(1) (a), (q), (r) and (s).

[454] See *Chemische Fabrik Vormals Sandoz v Badische Anilin und Soda Fabriks* (1904) 90 LT 733 at 735; approved in the *Seaconsar* case.

be necessary.[455] In order to have invoked this ground the claimant will have had to establish the elements of contract, breach and place of breach; in effect, the claimant will have already established a good arguable case on the merits and no separate issue as to the merits to which a lower standard of proof is applicable will arise. The position in relation to paragraph (6) is more complex.[456] Sub-paragraphs (a), (b), (c) and (d) all require the relevant contract to be proved.[457] Once that is done, there arises a separate issue as to the merits of the claim relative to that contract.[458] The position under paragraph (3) is equally complex.[459] The claimant has to show that there is a serious issue which it is reasonable for the court to try in respect of the defendant who has been or will be served.[460] In deciding whether a person is a proper party it is necessary to identify the common questions of law or fact which arise in the claim against the person served (or to be served) and the other person sought to be served. This goes to establishing the ground, and the standard is that of a good arguable case. It is then necessary to be satisfied that these questions of law or fact raise a serious issue to be tried on the merits.[461] With paragraph (9), a separate inquiry is necessary, it being accepted in the *Seaconsar* case that the standard of proof for establishing negligence was a lesser one than that for establishing that the negligence occurred within the jurisdiction (which goes to establishing the terms of the ground).[462]

If the law is in issue but there is no serious issue to be tried in relation to the facts, the court may determine the point of law at the application to serve out stage and refuse permission for such service.[463] Establishing a reasonable prospect of success (a serious issue on the merits) can raise choice of law questions at the jurisdictional stage of the action. Thus in *Metall und Rohstoff AG v Donaldson Lufkin and Jenrette Inc*[464] the Court of Appeal applied the English common law tort choice of law rules to determine whether the claimant had established the case on the merits.[465] At that time,[466] for the claimant to succeed, actionability by English law had to be shown, which there was in respect of the claim for inducement of a breach of contract, but not in respect of the claim, as pleaded, for conspiracy.

(c) The exercise of the discretion under rule 6.36

The courts *may*, rather than *must*, allow service of a claim form out of the jurisdiction. Where the case falls within one of the grounds of Practice Direction 6B, paragraph 3.1, the exercise of

---

[455] The *Seaconsar* case, supra, at 453–4. See also *Agrafax Public Relations Ltd v United Scottish Society Inc* [1995] IL Pr 753.

[456] The *Seaconsar* case, supra, at 454–5.

[457] With sub-para (a) a good arguable case will also have to be shown that the contract was made within the jurisdiction, the *Seaconsar* case, supra. See also *Apple Corps Ltd v Apple Computer Inc* [2004] EWHC 768 (Ch) at [34]–[35], [2004] IL Pr 34; *Bank of Baroda v Vysya Ltd* [1994] 2 Lloyd's Rep 87 at 95.

[458] The *Seaconsar* case, supra, at 454–5. See also *DR Insurance Co v Central National Insurance Co* [1996] 1 Lloyd's Rep 74 at 80.

[459] The *Seaconsar* case, supra, at 455.

[460] *Grupo Torras SA and Torras Hostench London Ltd v Sheikh Fahad Mohammed Al-Sabah* [1995] 1 Lloyd's Rep 374 at 380; appeals to the CA dismissed without discussion of this point, [1996] 1 Lloyd's Rep 7.

[461] *Barings plc v Coopers & Lybrand (A Firm)* [1997] IL Pr 12 at 23–4; aff'd by CA [1997] IL Pr 576 at 585.

[462] The *Seaconsar* case, supra, at 455; approving the judgment of Lord Tucker in *Vitkovice Horni a Hutni Tezirstvro v Korner* [1951] AC 869 at 889, HL. See also *Barings plc v Coopers & Lybrand (A Firm)* [1997] IL Pr 12 at 25–6; aff'd by CA, [1997] IL Pr 576 at 585.

[463] The *De Molestina* case, supra, at 281; *Nima Sarl v Deves Insurance Public Co Ltd (The Prestrioka)* [2002] EWCA Civ 1132 at [18], [2003] 2 Lloyd's Rep 327; the *Carvill America* case, supra, at [25].

[464] [1990] 1 QB 391; overruled on a different point in *Lonhro plc v Fayed* [1992] 1 AC 448, HL; Fentiman [1989] CLJ 191; Fawcett [1991] Current Legal Problems 39, 42–3. See also *Morin v Bonhams & Brooks Ltd* [2003] EWHC 467 (Comm), [2003] IL Pr 25; aff'd [2003] EWCA 1802, [2004] IL Pr 24.

[465] At that time the standard was that of a good arguable case.

[466] See now the choice of law rules under the Rome II Regulation on non-contractual obligations, infra, Chapter 20.

assumed jurisdiction in any given case lies within the discretion of the court[467] and the court will not give permission for service out of the jurisdiction unless satisfied that England and Wales is the proper place in which to bring the claim.[468] The onus is on the claimant to show good reason why service out should be permitted.[469] The criterion for exercise of the rule 6.36 discretion is that of *forum conveniens*,[470] ie service out of the jurisdiction will only be allowed where England is clearly the most appropriate forum in the interests of the parties and the ends of justice. The law in this area has been exhaustively re-examined and restated by the House of Lords in *Spiliada Maritime Corpn v Cansulex Ltd*[471] where Lord Goff, with whom the other Law Lords concurred, set out the relevant principles for the exercise of the discretion.

(i) The basic principle

Lord Goff said that the underlying fundamental principle was "to identify the forum in which the case can be suitably tried for the interests of all the parties and for the ends of justice".[472] The same principle underlies the discretion to stay actions on the basis of *forum non conveniens* after the service of a claim form, which is examined in Chapter 13.[473] Lord Goff then went on to state a number of other principles which help to explain the basic principle. These principles relate to the following: the appropriate forum; considerations of justice and juridical advantage; the (possibly) exorbitant nature of rule 6.36 jurisdiction; and the particular ground of rule 6.36 being employed. A further question examined below is whether any significance should be attached to the fact that an action is for negative declaratory relief.

(ii) The appropriate forum

The burden of proof is on the claimant to show that England is the appropriate forum for trial,[474] and that this is clearly so.[475] Appropriateness comprises a wide range of

---

[467] For an appeal court's powers to review the discretion vested in a judge see *Hadmor Productions Ltd v Hamilton* [1983] 1 AC 191; *Spiliada Maritime Corpn v Cansulex Ltd* [1987] AC 460, HL; *Berezovsky v Michaels* [2000] 1 WLR 1004 at 1021 (per Lord Hoffmann); *Owusu v Jackson* [2002] EWCA Civ 877 at [30], [2002] IL Pr 45; *King v Lewis* [2004] EWCA Civ 1329 at [35], [2005] IL Pr 16; *Limit (No 3) Ltd v PDV Insurance Co* [2005] EWCA Civ 383 at [69], [2005] 2 All ER (Comm) 347; *Galaxy Special Maritime Enterprise v Prima Ceylon Ltd (The Olympic Galaxy)* [2006] EWCA Civ 528 at [30], [2006] 2 Lloyd's Rep 27.

[468] CPR, r 6.37(3). This is differently worded from its predecessor (Ord 11, r 4) but the principles expounded in former authorities relating to Ord 11 remain applicable: *Petroleo Brasiliero SA v Mellitus Shipping Inc (The Baltic Flame)* [2001] EWCA Civ 418 at [31], [2001] 2 Lloyd's Rep 203.Where the application is for permission to serve a claim form in Scotland or Northern Ireland and it appears that the claimant may also be entitled to a remedy there, the courts in deciding whether to grant permission shall compare the cost and convenience of proceeding there or in England: r 6.37(4).

[469] *Ophthalmic Innovations International (United Kingdom) Ltd v Ophthalmic Innovations International Inc* [2004] EWHC 2948 (Ch) at [41], [2005] IL Pr 10.

[470] This presupposes that there is an obvious alternative forum abroad available to the claimant in the sense that there is no barrier to taking proceedings there, even if the remedy sought is not available there, see *Petroleo Brasiliero* case, supra, at [35]. If there is not it is proper to allow service out of the jurisdiction: *Ets Soules et Cie v Handgate Co Ltd SA, The Handgate* [1987] 1 Lloyd's Rep 142. See also *New Hampshire Insurance Co v Strabag Bau AG* [1992] 1 Lloyd's Rep 361 at 369–70, CA.

[471] [1987] 1 AC 460. Confirmed in *Berezovsky v Michaels* [2000] 1 WLR 1004, HL.

[472] The *Spiliada* case, supra, at 480.

[473] Infra, p 395. This is entirely consistent with the overriding objective of the CPR to deal with cases justly. See also *Voth v Manildra Flour Mills Pty Ltd* (1990) 171 CLR 538 at 563–4, High Court of Australia. The Australian test for service out of the jurisdiction is, however, easier for the claimant to satisfy than the English one, only being concerned with whether the forum is clearly inappropriate, see Collins (1991) 107 LQR 182; Epstein in Fawcett (ed), *Declining Jurisdiction*, p 82 et seq.

[474] On an application by the defendant to set aside permission previously granted the onus is on the claimant to establish this is so as at the date on which the order granting permission was made: *ISC v Guerin* [1992] 2 Lloyd's Rep 430 at 434–5; *Mohammed v Bank of Kuwait and the Middle East KSC* [1996] 1 WLR 1483 at 1493, CA. But cf *BMG Trading Ltd v A S McKay* [1998] IL Pr 691 at 694, CA.

[475] *Spiliada Maritime Corpn v Cansulex Ltd* [1987] AC 460 at 481; the *Berezovsky* case, supra. Nonetheless, the defendant must identify clearly the issues where he alleges that it is appropriate that some of these should

considerations. These are all also relevant to the *forum non conveniens* discretion to stay proceedings, and some of them are discussed further in Chapter 13. "The court must take into account the nature of the dispute, the legal and practical issues involved, such questions as local knowledge, availability of witnesses and their evidence[476] and expense."[477] It also involves looking at the expense and inconvenience to a foreign defendant in having trial in England.[478] As well as these matters of litigational convenience, the courts have considered the connections that the parties and the cause of action have with the alternative fora,[479] but it has recently been emphasised by the Supreme Court that the primary focus should be on efficient dispute resolution, rather than evaluating the relative strength of the jurisdictional connections with different states.[480] It is, therefore, not particularly significant whether a contract was made within the jurisdiction, unless that affects the location of witnesses or other evidence.[481] It will, however, evidently be important to establish whether an alternative forum would have jurisdiction, although a defendant may in practice ensure this through a timely undertaking to submit to the foreign court.[482] Beyond this, the circumstances of an individual case may raise a range of other considerations. Three of the most significant factors are highlighted below.

Consolidation of claims and prior foreign proceedings   The fact that England is the only forum in which all of the claims against the defendant or defendants can be heard is a powerful factor in favour of trial in England.[483] This circumstance may now arise more frequently as a result of two developments. First, the fact that claims brought in England under the Brussels I Recast may not generally be stayed because a non-Member State court would be a clearly more appropriate forum[484]—thus, if one defendant is domiciled in England, claims against other non-Member State defendants may have to proceed in England to ensure their consolidation in a single forum, depending on the relative importance of the various defendants.[485] However, if some defendants have the benefit of

---

be tried abroad: *Limit (No 3) Ltd v PDV Insurance Co* [2005] EWCA Civ 383 at [72] (per Clarke LJ), [2005] All ER (Comm) 347; *Chris Sawyer v Atari Interactive Inc* [2005] EWHC 2351 (Ch) at [54], [2006] IL Pr 8; *Novus Aviation Ltd v Onur Air Tasimacilik AS* [2009] EWCA Civ 122 at [31], [2009] 1 Lloyd's Rep 576.

[476] *Abbassi v Abbassi* [2006] EWCA Civ 355; *VTB Capital v Nutritek* [2013] UKSC 5 at [62], [2013] 2 WLR 398. However, the increased availability of video-links may reduce the inconvenience of travelling to England: *Nima Sarl v Deves Insurance Public Co Ltd (The Prestrioka)* [2002] EWCA Civ 1132 at [76], [2003] 2 Lloyd's Rep 327; *Stonebridge Underwriting Ltd v Ontario Municipal Insurance Exchange* [2010] EWHC 2279 (Comm), [2011] Lloyd's Rep IR 171.

[477] Per Lord Wilberforce in *Amin Rasheed Corpn v Kuwait Insurance Co* [1984] AC 50 at 72.

[478] *Société Générale de Paris v Dreyfus Bros* (1885) 29 Ch D 239 at 242; *George Monro Ltd v American Cyanamid and Chemical Corpn* [1944] KB 432; *Cordova Land Co Ltd v Victor Bros Inc* [1966] 1 WLR 793 at 801–2.

[479] *Kroch v Rossell et Cie* [1937] 1 All ER 725; *Amanuel v Alexandros Shipping Co, The Alexandros P* [1986] 1 QB 464; *Spiliada Maritime Corpn v Cansulex Ltd* [1987] AC 460; *International Marine Services Inc v National Bank of Fujarah* [1997] IL Pr 468, CA.

[480] *VTB Capital v Nutritek* [2013] UKSC 5, [2013] 2 WLR 398.

[481] *Bank of Baroda v Vysya Bank Ltd* [1994] 2 Lloyd's Rep 87 at 96.

[482] See, eg, *Sharab v Prince Al-Waleed Al-Saud* [2009] EWCA Civ 353, [2009] 2 Lloyd's Rep 160.

[483] *Booth v Phillips* [2004] EWHC 1437 (Comm) at [51], [2004] 2 Lloyd's Rep 457. See also *Sinochem International Oil (London) Ltd v Mobil Sales and Supply Corpn Ltd (Sinochem International Oil Co Ltd, third party) (No 2)* [2000] 1 All ER (Comm) 758, 773; *Attorney General of Zambia v Meer Care & Desai (A Firm)* [2005] EWHC 2120 (Ch); appeal on other grounds dismissed [2006] EWCA Civ 390, [2006] 1 CLC 436. See also *Pei v Bank Bumiputra Malaysia Berhad* (1998) 41 OR (3d) 39.

[484] Case C-281/02, *Owusu v Jackson* [2005] QB 801; see infra, p 462. The exception, introduced in the Brussels I Recast, is that proceedings may now be stayed under certain conditions where a non-Member State court is first seised, pursuant to Articles 33 and 34: see infra, p 457 et seq.

[485] See, eg, *AAA v Unilever plc* [2017] EWHC 371 (QB) (appeal pending); *Lungowe v Vedanta Resources Plc* [2016] EWHC 975 (TCC); *BAT Industries Plc v Windward Prospects Ltd* [2013] EWHC 4087 (Comm); *JSC BTA Bank v Granton Trade Ltd* [2010] EWHC 2577 (Comm), [2011] 2 All ER (Comm) 542; but compare *Pacific International Sports Clubs Ltd v Soccer Marketing International Ltd* [2010] EWCA Civ 753.

foreign[486] exclusive jurisdiction clauses, the policy of consolidating proceedings may be counter-balanced by the desirability of holding the parties to their agreement.[487] Second, the addition of paragraph 3.1(4A) to Practice Direction 6B, permitting related claims against a defendant which would not otherwise have a jurisdictional basis.[488] This factor is particularly significant if there are related claims already before the English courts. Conversely, the interests of justice may be best served by submission of a whole suit to a single tribunal abroad which can adjudicate on all the matters in issue, rather than having trial continuing partly in England and partly abroad.[489] If trial in England would lead to a multiplicity of proceedings, with concurrent overlapping actions taking place in England and abroad, this would be a ground for exercising the discretion against allowing service out of the jurisdiction.[490]

With or without multiple claims or defendants, the appropriateness of a foreign court may be increased if foreign proceedings have already been commenced.[491] However, the weight to be attached to this factor depends on how far the proceedings have advanced abroad, and thus how much more efficient that court is likely to be in resolving the disputed issues.[492] The parties and issues do not have to be identical.[493] It is enough that there is a risk of inconsistent findings of law or fact.[494]

The applicable law   The fact that English law is applicable to the dispute in question may point towards England as being the appropriate forum for trial, depending on the circumstances.[495] Lord Goff in the *Spiliada* case[496] said that the law governing the contract

---

[486] Note that if a jurisdiction clause is in favour of the courts of another European Union Member State and satisfies the formal requirements of Article 25 of the Brussels I Recast, jurisdiction will in any event be governed by the Brussels I Recast: supra, p 229 et seq.

[487] See, eg, *Jong v HSBC Private Bank (Monaco) SA* [2015] EWCA Civ 1057; infra, p 369.

[488] See supra, p 340.

[489] See *Donohue v Armco Inc* [2001] UKHL 64, [2002] 1 All ER 749—a case involving breach of an English exclusive jurisdiction agreement; discussed infra, pp 437–9.

[490] *The Hagen* [1908] P 189; *EI du Pont de Nemours & Co v I C Agnew and K W Kerr* [1987] 2 Lloyd's Rep 585; *DR Insurance Co v Central National Insurance Co* [1996] 1 Lloyd's Rep 74; cf *The Bank of Baroda v The Vysya Bank Ltd* [1994] 2 Lloyd's Rep 87 at 97–8; *Chase v Ram Technical Services Ltd* [2000] 2 Lloyd's Rep 418; *American Motorists Insurance Co v Cellstar Corpn* [2003] EWCA Civ 206 at [48], [2003] IL Pr 370; *Galaxy Special Maritime Enterprise v Prima Ceylon Ltd (The Olympic Galaxy)* [2006] EWCA Civ 528, [2006] 2 Lloyd's Rep 27. Cf *Amoco (UK) Exploration Co v British American Offshore Ltd* [1999] 2 Lloyd's Rep 772, 780—no risk of inconsistent decisions; *Markel International Insurance Co Ltd v La República Compañía Argentina de Seguros Generales SA* [2004] EWHC 1826 (Comm) at [38], [2005] Lloyd's Rep IR 40, QBD. See also *Spiliada Maritime Corpn v Cansulex Ltd*, supra—a case involving third party proceedings.

[491] *New Hampshire Insurance Co v Strabag Bau AG* [1992] 1 Lloyd's Rep 361, CA. See also *Galaxy Special Maritime Enterprise v Prima Ceylon Ltd (The Olympic Galaxy)* [2006] EWCA Civ 528, [2006] 2 Lloyd's Rep 27. But cf *CGU v Szabo* [2002] 1 All ER (Comm) 83.

[492] *Ark v True North Capital* [2005] EWHC 1585 (Comm) at [70], [2006] 1 All ER (Comm) 138; *Stonebridge Underwriting Ltd v Ontario Municipal Insurance Exchange* [2010] EWHC 2279 (Comm), [2011] Lloyd's Rep IR 171. See further infra, pp 408–9.

[493] *BAS Capital Funding Corpn v Medfinco Ltd* [2003] EWHC 1798 at [107], [2004] IL Pr 16; *Konamaneni v Rolls-Royce Industrial Power (India) Ltd* [2002] 1 WLR 1269 at [172]–[173].

[494] The *BAS* and *Konamaneni* cases, supra.

[495] *Cordoba Shipping Co Ltd v National State Bank, Elizabeth, New Jersey, The Albaforth* [1984] 2 Lloyd's Rep 91 at 93–94, CA (involving tort); *Spiliada Maritime Corpn v Cansulex Ltd* [1987] AC 460, HL (contract), discussed infra, p 379; *Banque Paribas v Cargill International SA* [1992] 2 Lloyd's Rep 19, CA; *Overseas Union Insurance Ltd v Incorporated General Insurance Ltd* [1992] 1 Lloyd's Rep 439, CA; *CGU International Insurance plc v Szabo* [2002] 1 All ER (Comm) 83; *Apple Corps Ltd v Apple Computer Inc* [2004] EWHC 768 (Ch) at [68], [2004] IL Pr 34; *Dellar v Zivy* [2007] EWHC 2266 (Ch) at [46], [2007] IL Pr 60; *VTB Capital v Nutritek* [2013] UKSC 5 at [46], [2013] 2 WLR 398; *Golden Endurance Shipping SA v RMA Watanya SA* [2014] EWHC 3917 (Comm), [2015] 1 Lloyd's Rep 266. See further Rogerson (2013) 9 J Priv Int L 387. But cf *Trade Indemnity v Försäkrings AB Njord* [1995] 1 All ER 796—English law applicable outweighed by fact that focus of dispute was business practices of Swedish insurance co; see also *Voth v Manildra Flour Mills Pty Ltd* (1990) 171 CLR 538 at 566 et seq, High Court of Australia.

[496] *Spiliada Maritime Corpn v Cansulex Ltd* [1987] AC 460, 481, HL.

would in some cases be of very great importance, and, in others, of little importance.[497] On the facts of the case this was said to be by no means an insignificant factor[498] since the dispute was, inter alia, as to the nature of the obligation under the contract. The fact that English law governs a contract is of greater importance in cases raising an issue of English public policy,[499] or where the issues of English law are particularly complex.[500] By contrast, if a dispute is concerned largely with determining contested questions of fact, the applicable law is less significant as a connecting factor. The issues arising in the case may not raise significant points of law[501] and in so far as English law is applied it may be easy for a foreign court to state and apply this.[502] Where a case involves issues of both law and fact, it has been suggested that the appropriate forum for determining the facts should take priority,[503] although the better view is probably that this should depend on the significance of factual or legal questions in the particular dispute.

It has been held that the applicable law is a significant factor where there is evidence that the foreign court may not apply English law despite an express choice of this as the governing law, although this may be better analysed as a factor going to whether justice will be obtained in the foreign court, and applied restrictively.[504] Where the defendant seeks trial abroad so as to take advantage of foreign choice of law rules (or the application of foreign public policy to defeat an English law contract,[505] or to avoid the application of English or European Union mandatory rules[506]) this has similarly been regarded as a factor in favour of trial in England,[507] although it may be doubted whether mere differences in choice of law rules are sufficient to support a claim that justice would not be served in the foreign court.

In contrast, where no difference between the competing laws is shown, the fact that a foreign court would apply a different law is given little weight.[508] Nor is the applicable law given any

---

[497] See, eg, *Egon Oldendorff v Liberia Corpn* [1995] 2 Lloyd's Rep 64 at 76; *Teekay Tankers Ltd v STX Offshore & Shipping Co* [2014] EWHC 3612 (Comm), [2015] 2 All ER (Comm) 263.

[498] See also *CGU International Insurance plc v Szabo* [2002] 1 All ER (Comm) 83; *Apple Corps Ltd v Apple Computer Inc* [2004] EWHC 768 (Ch) at [68], [2004] IL Pr 34.

[499] *Mitsubishi Corpn v Aristidis I Alafouzos* [1988] 1 Lloyd's Rep 191 at 196; *E I Du Pont de Nemours and Co v I C Agnew* [1987] 2 Lloyd's Rep 585 at 594–5.

[500] See, eg, *FR Lürssen Werft GmbH & Co Kg v Halle* [2009] EWHC 2607 (Comm); *Teekay Tankers Ltd v STX Offshore & Shipping Co* [2014] EWHC 3612 (Comm), [2015] 2 All ER (Comm) 263.

[501] *Limit (No 3) Ltd v PDV Insurance Co* [2005] EWCA Civ 383 at [46]–[49], [2005] 2 All ER (Comm) 347; *Royal & Sun Alliance Insurance plc v Retail Brand Alliance Inc* [2004] EWHC 2139 (Comm) at [25], [2005] Lloyd's Rep IR 110, QBD (Comm); *Novus Aviation Ltd v Onur Air Tasimacilik AS* [2009] EWCA Civ 122, [2009] 1 Lloyd's Rep 576.

[502] *Nima SARL v Deves Insurance Public Co Ltd (The Prestrioka)* [2002] EWCA Civ 1132 at [73], [2003] 2 Lloyd's Rep 327; *Galaxy Special Maritime Enterprise v Prima Ceylon Ltd (The Olympic Galaxy)* [2006] EWCA Civ 528 at [23], [2006] 2 Lloyd's Rep 27. If issues of UK company law arise, it is arguable that these should have a greater influence on jurisdiction, based on the policy underlying Article 24(2) of the Brussels I Recast (see supra, p 224). See, eg, *Nilon Ltd v Royal Westminster Investments SA* [2015] UKPC 2, [2015] 3 All ER 372.

[503] *New Hampshire Insurance Co v Phillips Electronics North America Corpn* [1998] IL Pr 256, CA.

[504] See infra, p 372. See also *Chris Sawyer v Atari Interactive Inc* [2005] EWHC 2351 (Ch) at [62], [2006] IL Pr 8; *Stonebridge Underwriting Ltd v Ontario Municipal Insurance Exchange* [2010] EWHC 2279 (Comm), [2011] Lloyd's Rep IR 171; *Navig8 Pte Ltd v Al-Riyadh Co for Vegetable Oil Industry (The Lucky Lady)* [2013] EWHC 328 (Comm), [2013] 2 Lloyd's Rep 104.

[505] *Seashell Shipping Corpn v Mutualidad de Seguros Del Instituto Nacional De Industria, The Magnum ex Tarraco Augusta* [1989] 1 Lloyd's Rep 47.

[506] *Fern Computer Consultancy Ltd v Intergraph Cadworx & Analysis Solutions Inc* [2014] EWHC 2908 (Ch), [2015] 1 Lloyd's Rep 1.

[507] *Tiernan v The Magen Insurance Co Ltd* [2000] IL Pr 517 at [18]; *Irish Shipping Ltd v Commercial Union Assurance Co Plc* [1991] 2 QB 206 at 229–30.

[508] *Macsteel Commercial Holdings (Pty) Ltd v Thermasteel V (Canada) Inc* [1996] CLC 1403, CA; *Chase v Ram Technical Services Ltd* [2000] 2 Lloyd's Rep 418 at 421; *Konamaneni v Rolls-Royce Industrial Power (India)*

significant weight when a case combines issues arising under different legal systems, such as when a reinsurance contract governed by English law relates to liability under the law of Texas.[509] The fact that a dispute involves complex questions of foreign law will, however, generally be a strong pointer towards trial abroad in the country whose law governs.[510] This factor may be particularly strong where the dispute requires application of foreign company law.[511] But the governing law may be of little weight where it is not so complex that it cannot be dealt with easily by the English courts.[512]

Jurisdiction agreements   Cases falling under common law jurisdictional rules involving an exclusive jurisdiction clause providing for trial in England are now likely to be rare,[513] but in such cases the discretion, in the absence of strong reason to the contrary, will be exercised in favour of holding parties to their bargain.[514] The normal principle established in *Spiliada*, that the burden of proof is on the claimant to satisfy the court that England is clearly and distinctly the appropriate forum for trial, is replaced in cases where there is an agreement as to English jurisdiction.[515] This means that the court will ordinarily give effect to the jurisdiction agreement, although still retaining a discretion to refuse permission to commence proceedings if the defendant can show strong reasons against holding the parties to their bargain. A good reason for not granting permission may be some factor that could not have been foreseen at the time that the contract was made.[516] Instances where good reason can be shown are

---

Ltd [2002] 1 WLR 1269 at [170]; *Chellaram v Chellaram (No 2)* [2002] EWHC 632 (Ch) at [170], [2002] 3 All ER 17; *Navigators Insurance Co v Atlantic Methanol Production Co LLC* [2003] EWHC 1706 (Comm) at [48], [2004] Lloyd's Rep IR 418. See also *Galaxy Special Maritime Enterprise v Prima Ceylon Ltd (The Olympic Galaxy)* [2006] EWCA Civ 528 at [23], [2006] 2 Lloyd's Rep 27.

[509] *Ace Insurance SA-NV (Formerly Cigna Insurance Co of Europe SA NV) v Zurich Insurance Co* [2001] EWCA Civ 173 at [47], [2001] 1 Lloyd's Rep 618, CA—a *forum non conveniens* case.

[510] *American Motorists Insurance Co v Cellstar Corpn* [2002] EWHC 421, [2002] 2 Lloyd's Rep 216; affd [2003] EWCA Civ 206 at [48], [2003] IL Pr 370; *Tryg Baltica International (UK) Ltd v Boston Compañia de Seguros SA* [2004] EWHC 1186 (Comm) at [42], [2005] Lloyd's Rep IR 40, QBD; *Pacific International Sports Clubs Ltd v Soccer Marketing International Ltd* [2010] EWCA Civ 753. See also *Burrows v Jamaica Private Power Co Ltd* [2002] CLC 255—foreign law and jurisdiction. The parties may accept the importance of the applicable law: *Samcrete Egypt Engineers and Contractors SAE v Land Rover Exports Ltd* [2001] EWCA Civ 2019, [2002] CLC 533.

[511] *SMAY Investments Ltd v Sachdev* [2003] EWHC 474 (Ch), [2003] 1 WLR 1973; *Konamaneni v Rolls-Royce International Industrial Power (India) Ltd* [2002] 1 WLR 1269. This reflects the policy underlying the rule of exclusive jurisdiction which applies to companies domiciled in European Union Member States under Article 24(2) of the Brussels I Recast, supra, p 224.

[512] *Music Sales Ltd v Shapiro Bornstein & Co Inc* [2005] EWHC 759 (Ch) at [25], [2006] 1 BCLC 371. The English courts have on occasion noted their own expertise in dealing with complex international cases including questions of foreign law as a relevant consideration here.

[513] Where there is an English jurisdiction agreement, or one in favour of the courts of another Member State, generally Art 25 of the Brussels I Recast, discussed supra, p 229 et seq, will apply (particularly since under the Brussels I Recast it applies regardless of the domicile of the parties); in certain cases that will in turn be trumped by the Hague Convention on Choice of Court Agreements: see supra, p 315. We are concerned here with the situation where those rules do not apply. Normally, where there is an English jurisdiction clause English law will govern the contract as well, see infra, pp 719–21. For the significance to be attached to arbitration in England, see *Egon Oldendorff v Liberia Corpn* [1995] 2 Lloyd's Rep 64 at 76.

[514] *Unterweser Reederei GmbH v Zapata Off-Shore Co (The Chaparral)* [1968] 2 Lloyd's Rep 158 at 163 (per Willmer LJ).

[515] *The Standard Steamship Owners Protection and Indemnity Association (Bermuda) Ltd v Gann* [1992] 2 Lloyd's Rep 528. See also *Insurance Co "Ingosstrakh" Ltd v Latvian Shipping Co* [2000] IL Pr 164, CA; *Citi-March Ltd v Neptune Orient Lines Ltd* [1997] 1 Lloyd's Rep 72; *BAS Capital Funding Corpn v Medfinco Ltd* [2003] EWHC 1798 at [192], [2004] IL Pr 16; *OT Africa Line Ltd v Magic Sportswear Corporation* [2005] EWCA Civ 710 at [19], [2005] 2 Lloyd's Rep 170.

[516] *Marubeni Hong Kong and South China Ltd v Mongolian Government* [2002] 2 All ER (Comm) 873 at [43]; appeal on a different issue dismissed [2005] EWCA Civ 395. See also *Mercury Communications Ltd v Communication Telesystems International* [1999] 2 All ER (Comm) 33 at 41; *JP Morgan Securities Asia Private*

likely to be rare.[517] An example would be where the interests of parties other than the parties bound by the exclusive jurisdiction clause are involved or grounds of claim not the subject of the clause are part of the relevant dispute so that if the agreement is upheld there is a risk of parallel proceedings and inconsistent decisions.[518] However, if this risk was foreseeable, the contractual bargain will be upheld and service out refused.[519]

The position is less certain in cases where the parties have agreed on the non-exclusive jurisdiction of the English courts.[520] There are cases where the same principle has been applied as in cases involving an exclusive jurisdiction clause.[521] However, other cases have rightly regarded a non-exclusive jurisdiction clause differently from an exclusive one[522] and the Court of Appeal has applied the normal principle in the *Spiliada* case to a non-exclusive jurisdiction clause.[523] When applying this principle it is relevant to take into account the fact that the parties have implicitly agreed that England is *an* appropriate forum for trial.[524] However, they are not agreeing that it is *the* appropriate forum. A feature which may justify not taking jurisdiction in England would be where there are overlapping proceedings abroad.[525]

Where the parties have agreed to trial abroad,[526] they should be kept to their agreement and it takes a strong cause to permit the court to ignore a foreign exclusive jurisdiction

---

Ltd v Malaysian Newsprint Industries SDN BHD [2001] 2 Lloyd's Rep 41 at [51]; *Import-Export Metro Ltd v Compañia Sud Americana de Vapores SA* [2003] EWHC 11 (Comm), [2003] 1 Lloyd's Rep 405; *Antec International Ltd v Biosafety USA Ltd* [2006] EWHC 47 (Comm) at [7]. What matters is what was foreseeable, not what was foreseen: *Cuccolini SRL v Elcan Industries Inc* [2013] EWHC 2994 (QB). Cf *British Aerospace plc v Dee Howard Co* [1993] 1 Lloyd's Rep 368 at 376—this is the only factor providing good reason; the *BAS Capital Funding Corpn* case, supra, at [191]; *Konkola Copper Mines plc v Coromin Ltd (No 2)* [2006] EWHC 1093 (Comm) at [32], [2006] 2 Lloyd's Rep 446—a case concerning a foreign jurisdiction clause.

[517] The *Mercury Communications* case, supra, at 41.
[518] *Donohue v Armco Inc* [2001] UKHL 64, [2002] 1 All ER 749—an example of strong reasons for not upholding the agreement in the context of not granting an anti-suit injunction in relation to foreign proceedings and also in the context of stays of action on the basis of a foreign jurisdiction clause; infra, pp 410 and 437–40.
[519] *Konkola Copper Mines plc v Coromin Ltd (No 2)* [2006] EWHC 1093 (Comm), [2006] 2 Lloyd's Rep 446.
[520] See generally Fawcett [2001] LMCLQ 234, 245–8. For the identification of a clause as being nonexclusive, see supra, p 234 and Fawcett, ibid, at 235–41. For discussion of such clauses in the context of *forum non conveniens* see infra, p 399.
[521] The *Standard Steamship Owners* case, supra; *Gulf Bank KSC v Mitsubishi Heavy Industries Ltd* [1994] 1 Lloyd's Rep 323; the *Mercury Communications* case, supra, at 41; the *Marubeni* case, supra, at [63]–[64]; the *JP Morgan* case, supra, at [43]; *Breams Trustees Ltd v Upstream Downstream Simulation Services Inc* [2004] EWHC 211 (Ch); *Antec International Ltd v Biosafety USA Ltd* [2006] EWHC 47 (Comm) at [7]; *HIT Entertainment Ltd v Gaffney International Licensing Pty Ltd* [2007] EWHC 1282 (Ch).
[522] *Evans Marshall & Co v Bertola SA* [1973] 1 WLR 349 at 361 (Kerr J); the *Sinochem* case, supra. See also the *BAS Capital Funding Corpn* case, supra, at [192].
[523] *Colonia Versicherung AG v Amoco Oil, The "Wind Star"*, 1993 (unreported).
[524] *S & W Berisford plc and NGI Precious Metals Inc v New Hampshire Insurance Co* [1990] 1 Lloyd's Rep 454 at 463.
[525] The *BAS Capital Funding* case, supra, at [193]—especially if started abroad by the claimant in England.
[526] Note, however, that if the agreement is in favour of the courts of a European Union Member State, the English courts will normally (regardless of the domicile of the parties) be required not to exercise jurisdiction, pursuant to Article 25 of the Brussels I Recast: see supra, p 229 et seq. Where an agreement is in favour of a non-Member State which is a party to the Hague Convention on Choice of Court Agreements, that Convention is similarly likely to require the English courts not to exercise jurisdiction: see supra, p 315. Jurisdiction may also not be exercised if the parties have agreed on arbitration abroad in a case falling under section 9 of the Arbitration Act 1996: see infra, p 416; *A and B v C and D* [1982] 1 Lloyd's Rep 166, affd sub nom *Qatar Petroleum v Shell International Petroleum* [1983] 2 Lloyd's Rep 35, CA.

clause.[527] When the question is whether to give leave for service out of the jurisdiction, rather than to stay otherwise well founded proceedings, there is an even heavier burden to discharge upon the applicant who asks the court not to enforce a foreign exclusive jurisdiction clause.[528] If there are multiple defendants in English proceedings and only some have the benefit of such clauses, the policy of consolidating proceedings (discussed above) may be counter-balanced by the desirability of holding the parties to their agreement.[529] Where the issue arises of whether there is a foreign exclusive jurisdiction clause in a contract, the claimant has to establish a good arguable case that there was not.[530] The considerations material to the exercise of the discretion in such a case (ie a service out case where there is a foreign exclusive jurisdiction clause) are the same as in cases involving a stay of English proceedings where there is a foreign exclusive jurisdiction clause.[531] Where a clause in a trust deed confers exclusive jurisdiction on a foreign court, similar rules apply, although it has been held that less weight should be given to the clause because of the inherent jurisdiction of the court to supervise the administration of a trust.[532]

If the foreign jurisdiction clause is non-exclusive, there is no breach of agreement in commencing proceedings in England and the normal principle in the *Spiliada* case should apply.[533] As with a non-exclusive jurisdiction clause providing for trial in England, the parties have implicitly agreed that the foreign court is *an* appropriate forum for trial, but not *the* appropriate forum.[534] In determining whether England is the clearly appropriate forum, a relevant consideration is whether proceedings are pending in the forum abroad designated by the non-exclusive jurisdiction clause.[535] Where they are so pending, the continuance of the English proceedings has been regarded as involving a breach of the non-exclusive jurisdiction clause (by not agreeing to submit to that foreign court).[536] That clause has therefore been regarded as being akin to an exclusive jurisdiction clause and the claimant has had to show strong reasons justifying trial in England in preference to trial abroad in the designated forum.[537]

---

[527] *Mackender v Feldia AG* [1967] 2 QB 590 at 604; *Unterweser Reederei GmbH v Zapata Off-Shore Co, The Chaparral* [1968] 2 Lloyd's Rep 158 at 163–4; *Evans Marshall & Co Ltd v Bertola SA* [1973] 1 WLR 349; *Citi-March Ltd v Neptune Orient Lines Ltd* [1997] 1 Lloyd's Rep 72; the *Sinochem* case, supra, at 766; *Insurance Co "Ingosstrakh" Ltd v Latvian Shipping Co* [2000] IL Pr 164, 169, CA; *Burrows v Jamaica Private Power Co Ltd* [2002] 1 All ER (Comm) 374 at [9]; *Dornoch Ltd v Mauritius Union Assurance Co Ltd* [2006] EWCA Civ 389 at [12], [2006] 2 Lloyd's Rep 475; *Advanced Cardiovascular Systems Inc v Universal Specialties Ltd* [1997] 1 NZLR 186. Foreign choice of jurisdiction clauses are also important when it comes to stays of action, discussed infra, pp 414–16.

[528] The *Insurance Co "Ingosstrakh"* case, supra, at 169; The *Sinochem* case, supra, at 767.

[529] See, eg, *Jong v HSBC Private Bank (Monaco) SA* [2015] EWCA Civ 1057.

[530] *Dornoch Ltd v Mauritius Union Assurance Co Ltd* [2006] EWCA Civ 389 at [18], [2006] 2 Lloyd's Rep 475. The fact that the defendant can also establish a good arguable case does not matter.

[531] *Citi-March Ltd v Neptune Orient Lines Ltd*, supra; the *Insurance Co "Ingosstrakh"* case, supra, 169–70. See infra, pp 414–16.

[532] *Crociani v Crociani* [2014] UKPC 40, [2015] WTLR 975; Tan [2015] LMCLQ 278.

[533] *E D & F Man Ship Ltd v Kvaerner Gibraltar Ltd, The Rothnie* [1996] 2 Lloyd's Rep 206 at 211—a stay case; *BP plc v Aon Ltd* [2005] EWHC 2554 (Comm) at [21]–[22], [2006] 1 Lloyd's Rep 549; *Catlin Syndicate Ltd v Adams Land & Cattle Co* [2006] EWHC 2065 (Comm) at [19]. But cf *Excess Insurance Co Ltd v Allendale Mutual Insurance Co*, CA, 8 March 1995 (unreported)—involving a service of suit clause which is akin to a non-exclusive jurisdiction clause; *Burrows v Jamaica Private Power Co Ltd* [2002] CLC 255 at 258–9.

[534] *BP plc v Aon Ltd*, supra, at [23].

[535] Ibid at [31]; *Catlin Syndicate*, supra, at [47].

[536] *BP plc v Aon Ltd*, supra, at [23].

[537] Ibid; relying on *Ace Insurance SA-NV (Formerly Cigna Insurance Co of Europe SA-NV) v Zurich Insurance Co* [2001] EWCA Civ 173 at [62], [2001] 1 Lloyd's Rep 618, CA—a *forum non conveniens* case, infra, p 414.

(iii) Justice and juridical advantage

Identification of "the forum in which the case can be suitably tried for the interests of all the parties and for the ends of justice" involves looking not only at factors of appropriateness but at other considerations as well.[538] Guidance on the range of considerations to be taken into account when exercising the rule 6.36 discretion can be found in cases on the discretion to stay actions on the basis of *forum non conveniens* after the service of a claim form within the jurisdiction.[539] This follows from the fact that the same basic principle underlies the exercise of the discretion in both areas, although there are differences between the burdens of proof and in respect of the fact that rule 6.36 has (traditionally) been regarded as an exorbitant form of jurisdiction.[540] Two particular considerations, which have not been mentioned so far, need to be examined.

First, there is the question, which was asked even before the *Spiliada* case, of whether justice will be obtained in the foreign court.[541] As in *forum non conveniens*, this has commonly been described as a second stage of the test—the first seeking to identify whether the English courts are clearly the most appropriate forum, and if they are not, the second giving the claimant an opportunity to argue that the English courts should nevertheless exercise jurisdiction to prevent a denial of justice.[542] This 'two-stage' approach has, however, recently been doubted by the Supreme Court, and so *forum conveniens* (unlike *forum non conveniens*) is perhaps better viewed as a single test taking both aspects into consideration in determining whether the English courts are the most suitable forum.[543] If there is a "real risk"[544] that the claimant, owing to political or other reasons, will not receive a fair trial abroad, the court may well exercise its discretion in favour of the application for service out of the jurisdiction, even though both parties to the suit are foreigners and even though their rights fall to be governed by foreign law.[545] The English courts are, by contrast, unlikely to consider whether the defendant would receive a fair trial in England, particularly if this would require any critical evaluation of the adequacy of English procedures.[546]

Questions such as whether a foreign judicial system is corrupt or biased are justiciable in the English courts in this context, although such allegations have to be made out to a high standard of cogency.[547] The Court of Appeal has been prepared to take this idea of not

---

[538] *Metall Und Rohstoff AG v Donaldson and Jenrette Inc* [1990] 1 QB 391; overruled on a different point in *Lonrho plc v Fayed* [1992] 1 AC 448, HL.

[539] Infra, p 410 et seq.

[540] *Spiliada Maritime Corpn v Cansulex Ltd* [1987] AC 460 at 481; *AK Investment CJSC v Kyrgyz Mobil Tel Ltd* [2011] UKPC 7, [2012] 1 WLR 1804. See generally Edinger (1986) 64 Can Bar Rev 283. If a case involves some defendants outside the jurisdiction, and others within the jurisdiction, the case is looked at in the round: *EI Du Pont de Nemours & Co v I C Agnew and K W Kerr* [1987] 2 Lloyd's Rep 585 at 593; *Travelers Casualty and Surety Co of Europe Ltd v Sun Life Assurance Co of Canada (UK) Ltd* [2004] EWHC 1704, [2004] IL Pr 50.

[541] *Aaronson Bros Ltd v Maderera del Tropico SA* [1967] 2 Lloyd's Rep 159 at 162; and *Unterweser Reederei GmbH v Zapata Off-Shore Co, The Chaparral* [1968] 2 Lloyd's Rep 158.

[542] See, eg, *Deripaska v Cherney* [2009] EWCA Civ 849, [2009] CP Rep 48.

[543] *VTB Capital v Nutritek* [2013] UKSC 5 at [44], [2013] 2 WLR 398.

[544] *AK Investment CJSC v Kyrgyz Mobil Tel Ltd* [2011] UKPC 7 at [95], [2012] 1 WLR 1804; Briggs [2011] LMCLQ 329.

[545] *Oppenheimer v Louis Rosenthal and Co AG* [1937] 1 All ER 23. See generally on the modern attitude towards allegations of injustice abroad, infra, p 400 et seq.

[546] See *Attorney General for Zambia v Meer Care & Desai* [2006] EWCA Civ 390, [2006] 1 CLC 436—the fact that the defendants could not get to England to defend in person did not mean that trial would be unfair when alternative arrangements were made to hear their evidence. See similarly, in relation to *forum non conveniens*, infra, p 401.

[547] *International Marine Services Inc v National Bank of Fujairah* [1997] IL Pr 468 at 470, CA; *Limit (No 3) Ltd v PDV Insurance Co* [2005] EWCA Civ 383 at [63]–[66], [2005] 2 All ER (Comm) 347; *Deripaska*

receiving a fair trial abroad further and has held[548] that, where the foreign jurisdiction is "compelled to apply a law which is contrary to the general understanding of commercial men",[549] this is a good reason for the exercise of the discretion to allow service abroad, notwithstanding the inconvenience to the defendant. The House of Lords has held that substantial justice would not be done abroad in a country where no financial assistance was available, the nature and complexity of the case being such that it could not be tried at all without the benefit of financial assistance.[550] This has led to the suggestion that the level of injustice abroad must be such as to deprive the claimant of any remedy at all.[551] Thus evidence of delay in trial in India of between four and five years, or possibly up to ten years, was not enough to constitute substantial injustice.[552] But the case law does not establish clear guidelines—evidence that delay in trial in Indonesia of more than ten years was usual was held to be enough.[553]

Secondly, there is the question whether the claimant will obtain a legitimate personal or juridical advantage from trial in England. This has traditionally been one of the factors to be considered when exercising the discretion to stay on the basis of *forum non conveniens*. The effect of the *Spiliada* case is to introduce this factor as a consideration when exercising the discretion to allow service out of the jurisdiction in rule 6.36 cases.[554] Lord Goff said[555] that the court should not be deterred from refusing permission in what are now rule 6.36 cases simply because the claimant will be deprived of an advantage, such as higher damages or a more generous limitation period,[556] provided that the court is satisfied that substantial justice will be done in the available appropriate forum abroad. This may require consideration of whether the claimant has acted reasonably in allowing a foreign limitation period to expire.

---

v Cherney [2009] EWCA Civ 849, [2009] CP Rep 48; *AK Investment CJSC v Kyrgyz Mobil Tel Ltd* [2011] UKPC 7 at [97], [2012] 1 WLR 1804; *AAA v Unilever plc* [2017] EWHC 371 (QB) (appeal pending). Cf the rather more relaxed attitude in Ontario: *Pei v Bank Bumiputra Malaysia Berhad* (1998) 41 OR (3d) 39.

[548] *Coast Lines v Hudig and Veder Chartering NV* [1972] 2 QB 34. See also *Seashell Shipping Corpn v Mutualidad de Seguros Del Instituto Nacional De Industria, The Magnum ex Tarraco Augusta* [1989] 1 Lloyd's Rep 47 at 53 (the foreign court might not apply the law agreed by the parties); Carter (1989) 60 BYBIL 482; *Kloeckner & Co AG v Gatoil Overseas Inc* [1990] 1 Lloyd's Rep 177 at 207.

[549] *Coast Lines v Hudig and Veder Chartering NV,* supra, at 45; see also *Britannia Steamship Insurance Association Ltd v Ausonia Assicurazioni SpA* [1984] 2 Lloyd's Rep 98 at 102; *Cadre SA v Astra Asigurari* [2004] EWHC 2504 (QB) at [16]; cf *Catlin Syndicate Ltd v Adams Land & Cattle Co* [2006] EWHC 2065 (Comm) at [42]–[46].

[550] *Connelly v RTZ Corpn plc* [1998] AC 854, HL—a stay of proceedings case, discussed infra, p 401. See also *Lubbe v Cape* [2000] 1 WLR 1545, HL, infra, p 401. Cf *Hewitson v Hewitson* [1999] 2 FLR 74.

[551] *Konamaneni v Rolls-Royce Industrial Power (India) Ltd* [2002] 1 WLR 1269 at [175]–[177]. This constituted "no alternative forum" abroad, but compare the meaning of this phrase in cases of *forum non conveniens*, infra, pp 395–7.

[552] Ibid. See also *Chellaram v Chellaram (No 2)* [2002] EWHC 632 (Ch) at [177], [2002] 3 All ER 17. For similar cases in relation to *forum non conveniens*, see infra, p 402.

[553] *Marconi v PT Pan Indonesia Bank Ltd TBK* [2004] EWHC 129 (Comm) at [38], [2004] 1 Lloyd's Rep 594; affd [2005] EWCA Civ 422 at [77].

[554] Not to be taken into account in the initial search for the appropriate forum, see the *Metall und Rohstoff* case, supra, 488. But see the criticism of the Court of Appeal in *King v Lewis* [2004] EWCA Civ 1329, [2005] IL Pr 16.

[555] [1987] AC 460 at 482–4. See also the *Connelly* case, supra, at 872.

[556] If the English proceedings are set aside, this may be on condition that the defendant should waive its right to rely on the time bar in the foreign proceedings, per Lord Goff at 487–8; *Nima Sarl v Deves Insurance Public Co Ltd, The Prestrioka* [2002] EWCA Civ 1132 at [80], [2003] 2 Lloyd's Rep 327—only exceptionally will this not be required. See on time-bars, *Metall und Rohstoff AG v Donaldson Lufkin and Jenrette Inc* [1990] 1 QB 391 at 488; overruled on a different point in *Lonrho plc v Fayed* [1992] 1 AC 448, HL. Problems with time-bars have arisen in the context of foreign choice of jurisdiction agreements, see infra, p 412.

It is envisaged that the sort of advantage mentioned above, which is to the benefit of the claimant and to the detriment of the defendant, will not be decisive.[557] However, the position may be different in the situation where the advantage to the claimant is not to the disadvantage of the defendant. Thus, on the facts of the *Spiliada* case one crucial point was that the claimants obtained an advantage from trial in England in that similar proceedings involving the same defendant company, lawyers, expert witnesses and insurers had been commenced and eventually settled in England.[558] The advantage that this gave to the claimants in terms of "efficiency, expedition and economy" did not involve a countervailing disadvantage to the defendants. Indeed, it was in the objective interests of justice that trial should take place in England. The result was that the House of Lords allowed service out of the jurisdiction. The advantage that the claimant obtains from the award of costs in English proceedings has been taken into account on the basis that substantial justice would not be done in the foreign proceedings if the claimant would have to pay costs there,[559] as has the advantage of trial before an English court which would uphold an arbitration agreement, whereas the alternative forum abroad might not,[560] and the advantage of the availability of urgent interlocutory relief.[561]

There is no fixed list of the considerations that can be taken into account. Thus it has been held in a case involving connections with three states that it is not in the interests of the parties or of justice to refuse trial in England in the situation where there was another appropriate court in State X to which neither party wished to resort, producing the result that the case should be tried in State Y, which was clearly less appropriate for trial than England.[562] The fact that a claimant gets no legitimate benefit from trial in England is a relevant consideration. It will ordinarily not be just to permit service out of the jurisdiction unless there is a real prospect of a legitimate benefit to the claimant from the English proceedings.[563] If the only known assets to enforce the judgment are in England, this may point to the appropriateness of the forum, to avoid the need for separate enforcement proceedings if the trial takes place abroad.[564] If there are no English assets, the court may consider whether an English judgment is likely to be recognised and enforced in a place in which assets are located.[565] The ease with which an English judgment can be enforced in other European countries by virtue of what is now the Brussels I Recast may constitute a legitimate advantage to the claimant.[566]

On the other hand, it seems that certain considerations cannot be taken into account when exercising the discretion. The courts are not "to embark upon a comparison of the procedures,

---

[557] See also *King v Lewis*, supra, at [20]—fact that action could not be brought successfully abroad but could in England not to be taken into account.

[558] The *Spiliada* case, supra, at 484–6. See also *Crédit Agricole Indosuez v Unicof Ltd* [2003] EWHC 2676 (Comm) at [19], [2004] 1 Lloyd's Rep 196.

[559] *Roneleigh Ltd v MII Exports Inc* [1989] 1 WLR 619 at 623; cf *Pride Shipping Corpn v Chung Hwa Pulp Corpn* [1991] 1 Lloyd's Rep 126 at 135.

[560] *Union de Remorquage et de Sauvetage SA v Lake Avery Inc, The "Lake Avery"* [1997] 1 Lloyd's Rep 540.

[561] *Intermetal Group Ltd & Trans-World (Steel) Ltd v Worslade Trading Ltd* [1998] IL Pr 765, Irish Supreme Court.

[562] *Banque Paribas v Cargill International SA* [1992] 2 Lloyd's Rep 19 at 25, CA.

[563] *Demirel v Tasarruff* [2007] EWCA Civ 799 at [27], [2007] 1 WLR 2508, leave to appeal to the House of Lords dismissed [2007] 1 WLR 3066.

[564] See, eg, *Colt Industries Inc v Sarlie* [1966] 1 WLR 440.

[565] See, eg, *Faraday Reinsurance Co Ltd v Howden North America Inc* [2012] EWCA Civ 980.

[566] *International Credit and Investment Co (Overseas) Ltd v Shaikh Kamal Adham* [1999] IL Pr 302, CA; *Sharab v Prince Al-Waleed Al-Saud* [2009] EWCA Civ 353, [2009] 2 Lloyd's Rep 160. Cf *Coast Lines v Hudig and Veder Chartering NV* [1972] 2 QB 34 at 45, CA; Bissett-Johnson (1972) 21 ICLQ 53; cf Collins (1972) 21 ICLQ 656; Graupner (1963) 12 ICLQ 357. See also *Kutchera v Buckingham International Holdings Ltd* (1988) 9 ILRM 501 at 505–6, Sup Ct of Ireland.

or methods, or reputation or standing of the courts of one country as compared with those of another",[567] although it may be observed that this temptation occasionally proves difficult to resist entirely in practice.[568]

(iv) Negative declarations[569]

One important factor that may be taken into account in deciding whether the case is a proper one for service out of the jurisdiction, not mentioned by Lord Goff in the *Spiliada* case, is that the claimant seeks a negative declaration from the English courts. The modern approach towards the grant of negative declarations is set out in *Messier-Dowty v Sabena SA (No 2)*,[570] where Lord Woolf MR said that:

> The deployment of negative declarations should be scrutinised and their use rejected where it would serve no useful purpose. However, where a negative declaration would help to ensure that the aims of justice are achieved the courts should not be reluctant to grant such declarations. They can and do assist in achieving justice.[571]

No valid reason could be seen for taking an adverse view of negative declaratory relief.[572] The crucial question therefore is whether such a declaration would serve a useful purpose. An example of where it would do so is where the person against whom it is sought is "temporising" (ie was not prepared to come forward and make his claim).[573] Where the negative declaration would serve a useful purpose the normal *forum conveniens* principles (or *forum non conveniens*) will then apply.[574] The trend appears to be toward recognising that a party who may be subject to suit generally has a legitimate interest in clarifying its position and obtaining legal certainty through proceedings for negative declaratory relief. Where the negative declaration would serve no useful purpose, however, permission for service out of the jurisdiction should be refused or, in a case of *forum non conveniens*, a stay granted.[575] Careful scrutiny must be exercised to ensure that inappropriate forum shopping is not allowed.[576] If

---

[567] *Amin Rasheed Corpn v Kuwait Insurance Co* [1984] AC 50 at 72 (per Lord Wilberforce), at 67 (per Lord Diplock) See also *Jayaretnam v Mahmood* (1992) Times, 21 May; *New Hampshire Insurance Co v Strabag Bau AG* [1992] 1 Lloyd's Rep 361 at 371; *Bank of Baroda v Vysya Bank Ltd* [1994] 2 Lloyd's Rep 87 at 98; *Trade Indemnity v Försäkrings AB Njord* [1995] 1 All ER 796 at 809. See further infra, p 400 et seq.

[568] See, eg, *Lubbe v Cape* [2000] 1 WLR 1545 at 1560, HL; *The Vishva Ajay* [1989] 2 Lloyd's Rep 558; *Roneleigh Ltd v MII Exports Inc* [1989] 1 WLR 619.

[569] Collins, *Essays*, Chapter 5; Dicey, Morris and Collins, paras 12-048–12-050; Bell (1995) 111 LQR 674; Bell, *Forum Shopping and Venue in Transnational Litigation,* paras 3.106, 4.250–4.293.

[570] [2000] 1 WLR 2040, CA—a Brussels Convention case discussing the principles to be applied under the traditional English rules of jurisdiction; Briggs (2000) 71 BYBIL 455. See also *New Hampshire Insurance Co v Phillips Electronics North America Corpn* [1998] IL Pr 256, CA.

[571] The *Messier-Dowty* case, supra, at 2050.

[572] Ibid, at 2049.

[573] *Bristow Helicopters Ltd v Sikorsky Aircraft Corpn* [2004] EWHC 401 (Comm) at [25], [2004] 2 Lloyd's Rep 150—a *forum non conveniens* case. See also *Bhatia Shipping v Alcobex Metals* [2004] EWHC 2323 (Comm) at [24]–[26], [2005] 2 Lloyd's Rep 336.

[574] See *Swiss Reinsurance Co Ltd v United India Insurance Co* [2002] EWHC 741 (Comm) at [27], [2004] IL Pr 4—a case on service out of the jurisdiction; *Travelers Casualty and Surety Co of Europe Ltd v Sun Life Assurance Co of Canada (UK) Ltd* [2004] EWHC 1704 (Comm), [2004] IL Pr 50—a case involving both *forum conveniens* and *forum non conveniens*; *CGU International Insurance plc v Szabo* [2002] 1 All ER (Comm) 83; *Tryg Baltica International (UK) Ltd v Boston Compañía de Seguros SA* [2004] EWHC 1186 (Comm) at [10]–[40], [2005] Lloyd's Rep IR 40, QBD; *Ark v True North Capital* [2005] EWHC 1585 (Comm) at [72], [2006] 1 All ER (Comm) 138. In the *Messier-Dowty* case, supra, a negative declaration was refused because the joinder of the party against whom it was sought was improper.

[575] See *American Motorists Insurance Co v Cellstar Corpn* [2002] EWHC 421, [2002] 2 Lloyd's Rep 216; affd [2003] EWCA Civ 206, [2003] IL Pr 370—without discussion of this point; *Chase v Ram Technical Services Ltd* [2000] 2 Lloyd's Rep 418 at 420–1.

[576] *Travelers Casualty and Surety Co of Europe Ltd v Sun Life Assurance Co of Canada (UK) Ltd* [2004] EWHC 1704 (Comm) at [90]–[92], [2004] IL Pr 50.

the possibility exists that the claimant in the English proceedings will be sued by the defendant in an alternative forum abroad, the English court must be particularly careful to ensure that the negative declaration is sought for a valid and valuable purpose and not in an illegitimate attempt to pre-empt the jurisdiction in which the dispute between the parties is to be resolved.[577] Likewise, where there are existing proceedings abroad, if the negative declaration does serve a useful purpose, the court must consider whether it is proper to grant permission for service out of the jurisdiction notwithstanding the undesirability of concurrent proceedings.[578] The fact that an English court might rehearse arguments of English law which could arise in the foreign proceedings is unlikely to constitute a useful purpose where the foreign court could and would decide any such questions itself.[579]

(v) An exorbitant basis of jurisdiction?

The predecessor of what is now rule 6.36 and Practice Direction 6B has sometimes been regarded as being an "exorbitant" or "extraordinary" basis of jurisdiction.[580] It is a wider jurisdiction than we recognise in others, in that if a foreign court took jurisdiction in similar circumstances English courts would not be prepared to recognise that court's judgment.[581] Jurisdiction assumed on these grounds has been seen as conflicting with the general principles of comity between civilised nations, and, because of this, at one time it was said that the power to allow service out of the jurisdiction should be exercised with extreme caution.[582]

Such views now seem rather old fashioned, and have recently been expressly doubted by the Supreme Court.[583] It remains to be seen whether this will affect a number of traditional principles, all of which have operated against the exercise of assumed jurisdiction in this context. As has been seen,[584] the claimant must show that there is a reasonable prospect of success. The power conferred by what is now rule 6.36 has also been considered to be exercisable by the court only in cases "which seem to it to fall within the spirit as well as the letter of the various classes of case provided for" in Practice Direction 6B.[585] If, in the circumstances, the construction of the ground is at all doubtful it has been held that it should be resolved in favour of the defendant.[586] The claimant must also show that England is *clearly* the appropriate forum.[587] Moreover, since the application for permission is made without notice being

---

[577] *New Hampshire Insurance Co v Phillips Electronics North America Corpn* [1998] IL Pr 256, CA. See also *Burrows v Jamaica Private Power Co Ltd* [2002] 1 All ER (Comm) 374 at [7]; *Ark v True North Capital*, supra, at [73]–[78].

[578] *Ark v True North Capital*, supra, at [76].

[579] *Howden North America Inc v ACE European Group Ltd* [2012] EWCA Civ 1624, [2012] CLC 969.

[580] *Spiliada Maritime Corpn v Cansulex Ltd* [1987] AC 460 at 481. See generally De Winter (1968) 17 ICLQ 706; Collins (1991) 107 LQR 10.

[581] See infra, p 528 et seq. For the position under the Brussels I Recast, see supra, p 213.

[582] *Cordova Land Co Ltd v Victor Bros Inc* [1966] 1 WLR 793 at 796; *Mackender v Feldia AG* [1967] 2 QB 590 at 599; *Amin Rasheed Corpn v Kuwait Insurance*, supra, at 65. Cf *Hyde v Agar* (1998) 45 NSWLR 487.

[583] *Abela v Baadarani* [2013] UKSC 44, [2013] 1 WLR 2043, at [50], per Lord Sumption (with whom the other Justices agreed) ("It should no longer be necessary to resort to the kind of muscular presumptions against service out which are implicit in adjectives like 'exorbitant'. The decision is generally a pragmatic one in the interests of the efficient conduct of litigation in an appropriate forum."). See further, eg, Briggs [2013] LMCLQ 415; Dickinson (2014) 130 LQR 197; Collins (2014) 130 LQR 555.

[584] Supra, pp 363–4.

[585] *Johnson v Taylor Bros* [1920] AC 144 at 153; but see *Sharab v Prince Al-Waleed Al-Saud* [2009] EWCA Civ 353 at [35], [2009] 2 Lloyd's Rep 160.

[586] *The Hagen* [1908] P 189 at 201; *The Siskina* [1979] AC 210 at 254–5; cf *Buttes Gas and Oil Co v Hammer* [1971] 3 All ER 1025 (for later proceedings, see [1975] QB 557); *Chellaram v Chellaram (No 2)* [2002] EWHC 632 (Ch) at [153], [2002] 3 All ER 17; *Network Telecom (Europe) Ltd v Telephone Systems International Inc* [2003] EWHC 2890 (QB), [2004] 1 All ER (Comm) 418 at [53]–[55].

[587] *Spiliada Maritime Corpn v Cansulex Ltd* [1987] AC 460 at 481; *Islamic Arab Insurance Co v Saudi Egyptian American Reinsurance Co* [1987] 1 Lloyd's Rep 315 at 318–19.

served on any other party, full and fair disclosure of all the material facts,[588] such as that proceedings have been commenced abroad,[589] is necessary.[590] Any unreasonable delay by the claimant in seeking leave militates against leave being given.[591] Strict compliance with the procedural requirements under what is now rule 6.36 is usually required and irregularities cannot normally be cured at a later stage of the action.[592]

Whilst the traditional reluctance to exercise jurisdiction under what is now rule 6.36 is understandable, it should be tempered by a realisation that other countries have similar (and similarly 'exorbitant') bases of jurisdiction.[593] Moreover, we should not be overly critical of at least some of the grounds used under rule 6.36 and set out in Practice Direction 6B (and overly reluctant to exercise jurisdiction on these grounds). Many of the grounds of jurisdiction under Practice Direction 6B are also found in the Brussels/Lugano system, and under that system no permission is required to serve outside the jurisdiction,[594] and jurisdiction is required to be taken without any discretionary rule to decline to exercise that jurisdiction.[595] Now that we have a *forum non conveniens* discretion to stay actions once a claim form has been served, there is an argument that it would rationalise the English law on jurisdiction if service out of the jurisdiction was automatically available without the leave of the court (as in some other common law jurisdictions such as New Zealand).[596] The *forum non conveniens* discretion could then come into play once the claim form had been served. After all, this discretion is based on the same fundamental principle as the rule 6.36 discretion. However, the (traditional) notion that rule 6.36 is an exorbitant form of jurisdiction with the consequential placing of the burden of proof on the claimant, coupled with a fear of defendants being forced to respond to unmeritorious actions which would have been filtered out by a permission requirement, stands in the way of this change. The better approach (as suggested

---

[588] Ie material to showing that the claimant has a reasonable prospect of success and all the other matters the judge has to consider: *MRG (Japan) Ltd v Engelhard Metals Japan Ltd* [2003] EWHC 3418 (Comm) at [26]–[31], [2004] 1 Lloyd's Rep 731; *The Republic of Pakistan v Zardari* [2006] EWHC 2411 (Comm) at [140], [2006] 2 CLC 667.

[589] *Tiernan v The Magen Insurance Co Ltd* [2000] IL Pr 517 at [21]; *Network Telecom (Europe) Ltd v Telephone Systems International Inc*, supra; *Ophthalmic Innovations International (United Kingdom) Ltd v Ophthalmic Innovations International Inc* [2004] EWHC 2948 (Ch) at [45], [2005] IL Pr 10.

[590] *Kuwait Oil Co (KSC) v Idemitsu Tankers KK, The Hida Maru* [1981] 2 Lloyd's Rep 510; *Trafalgar Tours Ltd v Alan James Henry* [1990] 2 Lloyd's Rep 298; *Newtherapeutics Ltd v Katz* [1991] Ch 226, [1991] 2 All ER 151; *Grupo Torras SA and Torras Hostench London Ltd v Sheikh Fahad Mohammed Al-Sabah* [1995] 1 Lloyd's Rep 374 at 449, appeals to the Court of Appeal dismissed without discussion of this point, [1996] 1 Lloyd's Rep 7; *ANCAP v Ridgley* [1996] 1 Lloyd's Rep 570; *Konamaneni v Rolls-Royce Industrial Power (India) Ltd* [2002] 1 WLR 1269 at [179]–[187]; *Chellaram v Chellaram (No 2)* [2002] EWHC 632 (Ch) at [189]–[193], [2002] 3 All ER 17; the *Network Telecom* case, supra; *JP Morgan Securities Asia Private Ltd v Malaysian Newsprint Industries SDN BHD* [2001] 2 Lloyd's Rep 41 at [58]–[65]; the *BAS Capital Funding Corpn* case, supra, at [196]–[199]; *Pearson Education Ltd v Prentice Hall India PTE Ltd* [2005] EWHC 636 (QB), [2006] FSR 8; *Albon v Naza Motor Trading* [2007] EWHC 9 (Ch) at [34]–[38], [2007] 1 Lloyd's Rep 297.

[591] *The Nimrod* [1973] 2 Lloyd's Rep 91.

[592] *Ophthalmic Innovations International (United Kingdom) Ltd v Ophthalmic Innovations International Inc* [2004] EWHC 2948 (Ch) at [43], [2005] IL Pr 10 following *Camera Care Ltd v Victor Hasselblad AB* (1986) Times, 6 January, [1986] ECC 373—a case under Ord 11, RSC; *Leal v Dunlop Bio-Processes Ltd* [1984] 2 All ER 207. Cf *Midland International Trade Services Ltd v Sudairy* (1990) Financial Times, 2 May. Cf *Spargos Mining NL v Atlantic Capital Corpn* (1995) Times, 11 December. A fresh application for permission may be made: *Albon v Naza Motor trading* [2007] EWHC 9 (Ch) at [16], [2007] 1 Lloyd's Rep 297.

[593] See De Winter (1968) 17 ICLQ 706; for European Union Member States note Art 5 of the Brussels I Recast, discussed supra, p 213, and the *Study on Residual Jurisdiction* (the Nuyts Report), Study JLS/C4/2005/07-30, Final Version September 2007.

[594] See infra, pp 308–9.

[595] On the question whether an English court can use the traditional English doctrine of *forum non conveniens*, see infra, p 460 et seq.

[596] See NZ High Court Rule 219.

in the following section) is to take a more context-sensitive view on the grounds of jurisdiction under Practice Direction 6B, rather than to adopt broader characterisations of these grounds of jurisdiction as a whole.

(vi) The significance of the particular ground of Practice Direction 6B

Whilst accepting that what is now rule 6.36 is an exorbitant form of jurisdiction, Lord Goff pointed out that the circumstances specified under the different grounds vary greatly, and that this should affect the court's willingness to exercise the discretion in favour of allowing service out of the jurisdiction.[597] In cases coming under paragraph 3.1(3) of Practice Direction 6B (permitting service outside the jurisdiction on a defendant who would not otherwise be subject to the jurisdiction of the courts, if they are a necessary or proper party to English proceedings) special care is needed[598] because of the lack of connection, under this ground, between the claim and an English forum.[599] The same considerations will apply to the new paragraph 3.1(4A) (permitting multiple claims to be made against a single defendant arising out of the same or closely connected facts, where only one claim would otherwise have a connection sufficient to justify service outside the territory),[600] and perhaps also to paragraph 3.1(6)(c) (where jurisdiction is based on the fact that a contract is governed by English law).[601] In contrast to this, if the parties have agreed on trial in England by putting an English jurisdiction clause in their contract, the courts have been very willing to allow service out of the jurisdiction under paragraph 3.1(6)(d),[602] unless there was a strong reason to the contrary, since the parties should abide by their agreement and there is a strong prima facie case that the jurisdiction chosen is an appropriate one.[603] In tort cases the starting point for the operation of the discretion has been a willingness to allow service out of the jurisdiction. As has already been mentioned,[604] the House of Lords in *Berezovsky v Michaels*[605] endorsed the principle that the jurisdiction in which a tort was committed is prima facie the natural forum for the determination of the dispute, although it will be recalled that this is now subject to the modifications or clarifications in section 9 of the Defamation Act 2013.[606]

However, the real question, recently re-emphasised by the Supreme Court, is always whether it is appropriate *in the circumstances of the particular case* for a claim form to be served out of the jurisdiction.[607] It is certainly important to look at the relevant ground of Practice Direction 6B invoked by the claimant, to ask whether there is a close connection with England on the facts of the case, whether English law will apply and whether the parties have agreed on trial in England, but generalisations or presumptions about particular grounds of Practice Direction 6B do not help. Lord Goff in the *Spiliada* case said that the importance to be attached to any particular ground of what is now Practice Direction 6B may vary from case to case.[608] Thus, as has already been seen,[609] the fact that English law is the law

---

[597] *Spiliada Maritime Corpn v Cansulex Ltd* [1987] AC 460 at 481.

[598] *Petroleo Brasiliero SA v Mellitus Shipping Inc (The Baltic Flame)* [2001] EWCA Civ 418 at [21], [2001] 2 Lloyd's Rep 203; see supra, pp 336–9; *AK Investment CJSC v Kyrgyz Mobil Tel Ltd* [2011] UKPC 7 at [71], [2012] 1 WLR 1804.

[599] *Multinational Gas and Petrochemical Co v Multinational Gas and Petrochemical Services* [1983] Ch 258 at 271–2, CA.

[600] See supra, p 340.

[601] See *Novus Aviation Ltd v Onur Air Tasimacilik AS* [2009] EWCA Civ 122, [2009] 1 Lloyd's Rep 576.

[602] Supra, pp 345–6.

[603] Supra, pp 369–71.

[604] Supra, pp 351–3.

[605] [2000] 1 WLR 1004.

[606] See supra, pp 353–5.

[607] *VTB Capital v Nutritek* [2013] UKSC 5, [2013] 2 WLR 398.

[608] [1987] AC 460 at 481.

[609] Supra, pp 367–9.

governing the contract would, in some cases, be of very great importance, and, in others, of little importance, depending on the circumstances. In the *Spiliada* case itself it was by no means an insignificant factor.[610]

(vii) The operation of the principles
This can be best illustrated by examining the *Spiliada* case[611] itself.

> The plaintiff shipowners, a Liberian company, alleged that the *Spiliada* had been damaged by wet sulphur being loaded on it by order of the defendant shippers, a British Columbia company, and sought damages for breach of contract. A similar action had previously been started by different plaintiffs against, inter alia, the defendants, following damage to the ship *Cambridgeshire*. In the *Spiliada* action it was held at first instance that there was a contract governed by English law.

Although one of the grounds of what is now Practice Direction 6B was satisfied, the Court of Appeal held that it was not a proper case for exercising the discretion to allow service out of the jurisdiction and set aside the writ.

The House of Lords allowed the appeal. Lord Goff stated the principles to be applied in relation to the exercise of what is now the rule 6.36 discretion, as set out above.[612] The availability of witnesses and the risk of a multiplicity of proceedings were examined. However, the crucial point was the *Cambridgeshire* factor. If the *Spiliada* action also took place in England there would be teams of lawyers and experts available who had prepared for the *Cambridgeshire* action. This would contribute to the efficient administration of justice.[613] The court would be assisted in reaching a just decision, and the possibility of a settlement of the proceedings (as happened in the *Cambridgeshire* action) would be enhanced. Trial in England was not merely a matter of financial advantage to the plaintiff (without being to the disadvantage of the defendant) but was "in the objective interests of justice". Moreover, it was a relevant factor that the litigation was being fought under a contract governed by English law, and on the facts this was by no means an insignificant factor.[614]

(ii) Service of a claim form out of the jurisdiction without the permission of the court

Rule 6.33 allows service of a claim form out of the jurisdiction *without* the permission of the court in three situations. The first[615] is where the court has jurisdiction by virtue of the Brussels I Recast,[616] the Lugano Convention,[617] or the Civil Jurisdiction and Judgments Act 1982.[618] This statute, as amended by the Civil Jurisdiction and Judgments Act 1991, is concerned with cases coming within the Brussels Convention and the Modified Regulation; the question of service of the claim form in such cases has already been discussed.[619] For this rule to apply, the English courts must have jurisdiction under the Brussels I Recast or Brussels or Lugano Conventions. The rule thus applies to defendants domiciled in a Member State[620] or Contracting State[621] or where the jurisdictional rules apply regardless of domicile, as under

---

[610] Supra, pp 367–8.
[611] *Spiliada Maritime Corpn v Cansulex Ltd* [1987] AC 460.
[612] Supra, p 364 et seq.
[613] [1987] AC 460 at 485–6. See also *Reeves v Sprecher* [2007] EWHC 117 (Ch).
[614] Supra.
[615] A statement is required by CPR, r 6.34 of the grounds on which the claimant is entitled to serve the claim form out of the jurisdiction; for the form this takes see PD6B, 2.1, referring to practice form N510.
[616] CPR, r 6.33(2).
[617] CPR, r 6.33(1).
[618] CPR, r 6.33(1).
[619] Supra, pp 308–9.
[620] CPR, r 6.33(2)(b)(i). This includes Denmark, by virtue of the EC/Denmark agreement.
[621] CPR, r 6.33(1)(b)(i).

Articles 24 and 25 of the Brussels I Recast and in respect of certain claims by consumers and employees,[622] but subject to the rules on *lis pendens*,[623] including as modified by the Brussels I Recast.[624]

At one time a question was raised over whether the predecessor of this rule[625] was wide enough to cover the situation where an interim remedy, such as a freezing injunction, was sought in England in support of proceedings in another state or in another part of the United Kingdom by virtue of section 25 of the Civil Jurisdiction and Judgments Act 1982.[626] However, a special ground providing for service of the claim form out of the jurisdiction with the permission of the court has been introduced to deal with this situation.[627]

The second is where the court has power to determine the claim under the Hague Convention on Choice of Court Agreements. As discussed further in Chapter 11, this will be where there is an exclusive jurisdiction agreement in favour of the English courts, and at least one party to the agreement is resident in a Hague Convention contracting state which is not a European Union Member State.[628]

The third situation covered by this rule is where the court has power to hear and determine the claim by virtue of some other enactment which provides for jurisdiction even though the defendant is not within the jurisdiction or the facts giving rise to the claim did not occur within the jurisdiction.[629] An example of such an enactment is the Protection of Trading Interests Act 1980.[630] Rule 6.33(3) will also apply to actions brought under certain statutes passed as the result of international conventions which give a party the right to sue in England, such as the Carriage by Air Act 1961, the Carriage by Air (Supplementary Provisions) Act 1962, the Carriage of Goods by Road Act 1965, the Civil Aviation Act 1982 and the Merchant Shipping Act 1995.[631] This provision is, however, generally to be interpreted restrictively, otherwise it would undermine the usual requirement that the court's permission is required to commence proceedings against a non-present defendant, including for statutory causes of action.[632] In a multi-defendant case, each defendant is looked at separately so that service out of the jurisdiction may be effected on one defendant without permission, provided that the normal requirements for this are met, irrespective of whether the claims against the other defendants satisfy these requirements.[633] Where a claim form can be served under rule 6.33 it must be so served and the claimant does not have the option of seeking permission to serve under rule 6.36,[634] under which the period for responding to a claim form is calculated differently.[635] This can present a practical problem for claimants who are unsure which jurisdictional regime covers their claim, such as where the domicile of the defendant is not clearly ascertainable.

---

[622] CPR, r 6.33(1)(b) and (2)(b).
[623] CPR r 6.33(1)(a) and (2)(a).
[624] CPR r 6.33(2A).
[625] Ord 11, rule 1(2) RSC.
[626] Cf *Mercedes-Benz AG v Leiduck* [1996] AC 284 at 302, PC with *Republic of Haiti v Duvalier* [1990] 1 QB 202. S 25 is discussed supra, pp 305–7.
[627] CPR, PD6B, 3.1(5); discussed supra, pp 340–1.
[628] See supra, p 315.
[629] CPR, r 6.33(3). See *Re Harrods (Buenos Aires) Ltd* [1992] Ch 72 at 115–16.
[630] See infra, pp 553–5.
[631] See generally Dicey, Morris and Collins, Chapter 15.
[632] *In Re Harrods (Buenos Aires Ltd) (No 2)* [1992] Ch 72; *GMC v Brauwers* [2010] EWHC 106 (Admin). See CPR PD6B, 3.1(20), discussed supra, p 361.
[633] See SI 1996/2892, reg 2.
[634] *The Reefer Creole* [1994] 1 Lloyd's Rep 584 at 586.
[635] See CPR, r 6.35; PD6B, para 6.

(iii) Service of the claim form in practice

Where service of a claim form out of the jurisdiction is allowed, with or without the permission of the court, there is the practical problem of how this is to be effected on a defendant who is abroad. Service within the European Union is dealt with by the EU Service Regulation.[636] More complex rules apply for service outside the European Union.[637] Actions that contain a foreign element must frequently require the assistance of judicial and administrative officers in other countries, and the United Kingdom has therefore concluded conventions with a number of states in order to facilitate the conduct of legal proceedings in civil and commercial matters, and is a party to the Hague Convention[638] on the service abroad of judicial and extrajudicial documents in civil or commercial matters, which came into effect in 1969.[639] It is, however, not strictly necessary that service be in accordance with the usual legal requirements of the place of service, only that it brings the claim form properly to the attention of the defendant, and not be by a method prohibited under the law of the place of service.[640]

(d) Are there other bases of competence?

A doctrine of arrestment *ad fundandam jurisdictionem* operates in Scotland[641] and in certain civil law countries[642] under which an action may be brought against a person absent from the forum if movables[643] situated there and belonging to him have been taken into the custody of the law at the instance of the claimant.[644] The court can deal with a claim unconnected

---

[636] Supra, pp 308–9.

[637] See generally CPR, rr 6.40–6.46.

[638] (1964) Cmnd 1613; see (1965) 14 ICLQ 564–72. For alternative methods of service allowed under the Convention see: *Molins plc v GD SpA* [2000] 1 WLR 1741, CA; *Arros Invest Ltd v Rafik Nishanov* [2004] IL Pr 22. The parties can agree on a method of service: *McCulloch v Bank of Novia Scotia* [2006] EWHC 790 (Ch), [2006] 2 All ER (Comm) 714.

[639] CPR, r 6.15 (service by an alternative method not otherwise permitted by the CPR rules, on which see *Addax BV Geneva Branch v Coral Suki SA* [2004] EWHC 2882 (Comm), [2005] 2 All ER (Comm) 137) can be used for defendants outside the jurisdiction (*Abela v Baadarani* [2013] UKSC 44, [2013] 1 WLR 2043), but cannot be used to avoid application of the Hague Service Convention or a bilateral convention: *Knauf UK GmbH v British Gypsum Ltd* [2002] 1 WLR 907; distinguished in *Phillips v Nussberger* [2008] UKHL 1, [2008] 1 WLR 180; *Cecil v Bayat* [2011] EWCA Civ 135, [2011] 1 WLR 3086; *Marconi v PT Pan Indonesia Bank Ltd TBK* [2004] EWHC 129 (Comm) at [39]–[45], [2004] 1 Lloyd's Rep 594; appeal on a different point dismissed [2005] EWCA Civ 422. The principles in *Knauf* have been applied to CPR, r 6.16 (power to dispense with service) in *Shiblaq v Sadikoglu* [2004] EWHC 1890 (Comm) at [56]–[58], [2004] IL Pr 51. For service where the country abroad is not a party to the Hague Service Convention and with which there is no bilateral convention, see CPR, rr 6.42 and 6.43, *BAS Capital Funding Corpn v Medfinco Ltd* [2003] EWHC 1798 at [156]–[168], [2004] IL Pr 16; *Habib Bank Ltd v Central Bank of Sudan* [2006] EWHC 1767 (Comm), [2006] 2 Lloyd's Rep 412. For the use of CPR, rr 6.16 and 6.42 in a Lugano Convention case, see *Olafsson v Gissurarson* [2008] EWCA 152.

[640] *Abela v Baadarani* [2013] UKSC 44, [2013] 1 WLR 2043; *Amalgamated Metal Trading Ltd v Baron* [2010] EWHC 3207 (Comm), [2012] 1 CLC 920; CPR r 6.15(2) and r 6.40(4). But compliance with the law of the place of service is ordinarily required: *Societe Generale v Goldas Kuyumculuk Sanayi Ithalat Ihracat AS* [2017] EWHC 667 (Comm).

[641] This doctrine does not apply where the defendant is domiciled in the United Kingdom: Civil Jurisdiction and Judgments Act 1982, Sch 8, r 2(h). Nor does it apply where the case is within the scope of the Brussels I Recast or Brussels or Lugano Convention and the defendant is domiciled in a Regulation State, Contracting State to the Brussels Convention or a State bound by the Lugano Convention, Art 5 of the Brussels I Recast and Art 3 of the Conventions: discussed supra, pp 213–14.

[642] For Germany see s 23 ZPO; BGH 2.7.1991, NJW 1991, 3092 (a sufficient connection with Germany is required); Dannemann (1992) 41 ICLQ 632. A Regulation State or Contracting State to the Brussels Convention or State bound by the Lugano Convention cannot use this form of jurisdiction in the situation where the case is within the scope of the Brussels I Recast or either Convention and the defendant is domiciled in a Regulation State, Contracting State to the Brussels Convention or a State bound by the Lugano Convention: Art 5 of the Brussels I Recast and Art 3 of the Conventions, discussed supra, pp 213–14.

[643] Jurisdiction over immovables is discussed infra, p 484 et seq.

[644] For Scots law see Civil Jurisdiction and Judgments Act 1982, Sch 8, r 2(h); Beaumont and McEleavy, *Anton's Private International Law*, pp 188–93; Crawford and Carruthers, para 7-04.

with the movables and deliver a personal judgment against the owner that will be wholly or partially satisfied by their sale. Another instance is the jurisdiction *quasi in rem* that is recognised in the USA, which enables a personal claim against a defendant living abroad to be satisfied out of chattels owned by him but situated in the forum. Attachment of the chattels confers jurisdiction on the court of the situs, but any judgment that may be given is limited in its effect to the value of the property attached.[645]

English law stands aloof from this doctrine,[646] at least in cases where the claim is unrelated to the movables. An attempt in *The Siskina*[647] to introduce indirectly a ground based on the presence of assets in the forum was unsuccessful. However, where the claim is related to the movables the position is very different. Paragraph 3.1(11) of Practice Direction 6B of the Civil Procedure Rules allows a claim form to be served out of the jurisdiction with the permission of the court where the claim relates "wholly or principally" to property (and this includes movable property) located within the jurisdiction.[648]

It is not open to the courts to introduce new additional bases of competence.[649] Any extension of the jurisdiction of the courts over foreign defendants requires subordinate legislation by the rules committee if not primary legislation by Parliament itself.[650]

2. ACTIONS IN REM[651]

(a) An action against a ship as defendant

In Roman law an action in rem was one brought in order to vindicate a jus in rem, ie a right such as ownership available against all persons, but the only action in rem known to English law is that which lies in an Admiralty court against a particular res, namely a ship or some other res, such as cargo, associated with the ship.[652] The Senior Courts Act 1981 (originally called the Supreme Court Act 1981) lists the claims that lie within the Admiralty Court[653]

---

[645] Restatement 2d, Conflict of Laws, § 66; Hay (1986) 35 ICLQ 32; *Shaffer v Heitner* 433 US 186 at 210 (1977); *Rush v Savchuck* 444 US 320 (1980).

[646] See also in relation to Canada *Marren v Echo Bay Mines Ltd* (2003) 226 DLR (4th) 622, BC CA.

[647] *Siskina (owners of cargo lately laden on board) v Distos Cia Naviera SA, The Siskina* [1979] AC 210.

[648] Discussed supra, pp 356–8. If a claim is partly but not principally related to property in the jurisdiction it may be possible to use Paragraph 3.1(4A); discussed supra, p 340.

[649] *Siskina (owners of cargo lately laden on board) v Distos Cia Naviera SA* [1979] AC 210. See also *Serge Caudron v Air Zaire* [1986] ILRM 10, Supreme Court of Ireland.

[650] At 260 (Lord Diplock); see also at 262–3 (Lord Hailsham).

[651] See generally Mandaraka-Sheppard, *Modern Maritime Law* (2013) 3rd edn, vol 1; Ruiz Abou-Nigm, *The Arrest of Ships in Private International Law* (2011); Berlingieri, *Arrest of Ships* (2011) 5th edn; Jackson, *Enforcement of Maritime Claims* (2005) 4th edn, paras 2.31–2.239. For an examination of this whole subject in Australia, see (1986) ALRC 33; the Admiralty Act 1988 (Cth); Davenport [1987] LMCLQ 317; Crawford [1997] LMCLQ 519.

[652] "Ship" can include a dredger, *The Von Rocks* [1998] 2 Lloyd's Rep 198, Supreme Court of Ireland. For cargo, see *Sembawang Salvage Pte Ltd v Shell Todd Oil Services Ltd* [1993] 2 NZLR 97. The owner and other persons interested are also made defendants. The action also lies against an aircraft, Senior Courts Act 1981, s 21(3), or hovercraft, Hovercraft Act 1968, s 2(1).

[653] See Senior Courts Act 1981, s 20, as amended. This includes, eg, a claim "arising out of any agreement relating to the carriage of goods in a ship or to the use or hire of a ship": s 20(2)(h), on which see *The Antonis P Lemos* [1985] AC 711; *Petrofina SA v AOT Ltd* [1992] QB 571; *The Lloyd Pacifico* [1995] 1 Lloyd's Rep 54; *The Bumbesti* [2000] QB 559; see also *Gatoil International Inc v Arkwright-Boston Manufacturers Mutual Insurance Co* [1985] AC 255, HL. It also includes a claim "in respect of goods or materials supplied to a ship for her operation": s 20(2)(m), on which see *The River Rima* [1988] 1 WLR 758, HL; Jackson [1988] LMCLQ 423; *The Edinburgh Castle* [1999] 2 Lloyd's Rep 362; *The Nore Challenger* [2001] 2 Lloyd's Rep 103.

and goes on to make detailed provision as to when an action in rem may be brought.[654] To take one instance, the rule has long been that a maritime lien attaches to and remains enforceable against a ship that collides with and damages another, even if the ship is subsequently sold.[655] Such a lien "is a privileged claim upon a vessel in respect of service done to it or injury caused by it, to be carried into effect by legal process. It is a right acquired by one over a thing belonging to another—a *jus in re aliena*".[656]

That the ship is the defendant in an action brought to enforce the lien is underlined by the legal process available to the claimant. After the issue of an in rem claim form, service may be made by fixing a copy of the claim form on the outside of the ship.[657] The claimant is entitled to have the ship arrested, in which case the Admiralty Marshal will effect service, but (subject to the section below on the effects of the Brussels/Lugano system) this is not necessary to establish jurisdiction.[658]

The "person" against whom jurisdiction is exercised is the ship, and therefore it is essential that it should be "so situated as to be within the lawful control of the State under the authority of which the court sits".[659] In short, the court is competent to entertain the action if and only if the ship lies within the territorial waters of England—the claim form for an action in rem may not be served outside the territory.[660] It has been held that the issue of a warrant for the arrest of property in an Admiralty action in rem is no longer[661] a discretionary remedy.[662] So long as a claimant's case is not bound to fail, which means that he has an arguable case, he is entitled to proceed with it.[663] Accordingly, there is no duty of full and frank disclosure.[664] However, it is possible that the court might have a general discretion to set aside a warrant of arrest on the basis that its effects are unjust.[665] The court has power to release a ship under arrest,[666] and the shipowner can protect itself by giving security. The usual practice is that the ship will only be released on the provision of sufficient security to cover the amount of the claim plus costs.[667]

The granting of security aspect of the action in rem is underlined by the fact that the ship or other chattel can be sold under the authority of the court and the proceeds adjudged to the claimant

---

[654] S 21. For procedural rules see CPR, Part 61 and Practice Direction 61; Tsimplis and Gaskell [2002] LMCLQ 520.

[655] S 21 (3).

[656] *The Ripon City* [1897] P 226 at 242.

[657] CPR, PD61, 3.6. There are other alternative ways in which service can be made.

[658] *The Nautik* [1895] P 121.

[659] *Castrique v Imrie* (1870) LR 4 HL 414 at 429; *General Motors-Holdens Ltd v The Ship Northern Highway* (1982) 29 SASR 138.

[660] CPR, PD61, 3.6(7); *Owners of the Stolt Kestrel v Owners of the Niyazi S* [2015] EWCA Civ 1035, [2016] 1 Lloyd's Rep 125.

[661] See *The Vasso (formerly Andria)* [1984] 1 Lloyd's Rep 235.

[662] *The Varna* [1993] 2 Lloyd's Rep 253, CA; Dockray (1994) 110 LQR 382. This decision reflected changes to the procedural rules. Since *The Varna* these have been altered yet again (see now CPR, r 61.5) but this probably does not alter the position, see Tsimplis and Gaskell, op cit, at pp 522–6.

[663] *The Yula Bondarovskaya* [1998] 2 Lloyd's Rep 357 at 361.

[664] *The Varna*, supra. CPR, PD61, 5.3 sets out the particulars required in the declaration by the party making an application for arrest.

[665] *The Varna*, supra, at 258.

[666] See, eg, *The Bumbesti*, supra, 572–5 (adequate other security). Release can be made subject to conditions, see, eg, *The Vanessa Ann* [1985] 1 Lloyd's Rep 549. For subsequent arrest and subsequent provision of security, see Art 3(3) of the Arrest Convention; *The Tjaskemolen No 2* [1997] 2 Lloyd's Rep 476.

[667] *The Bazias 3* [1993] QB 673, CA—the usual practice applies even though the claim is subject to an arbitration clause. For retention of the ship for satisfaction of any arbitration award, see the Arbitration Act 1996, s 11, infra, p 385.

in satisfaction of his claim.[668] If a sale is ordered, the judgment operates in rem in the sense that it divests the property in the ship from the owners and confers an absolute title on the purchaser, good against all persons.[669]

The formal position is that the ship is the defendant. However, the House of Lords in *Republic of India v India Steamship Co (No 2)*[670] held that the reality is that an action in rem is also an action against the owner of the ship.[671] While the scope of the decision is not certain,[672] it appears to mean that the owner is a party to the action in rem,[673] reflecting the fact that in practice it will be the owner who appears to dispute jurisdiction or defend the merits.[674] This is important, inter alia, when it comes to the operation of section 34 of the Civil Jurisdiction and Judgments Act 1982, which is concerned with the estoppel effect of a foreign judgment.[675] The position is comparable under the *lis pendens* rules of the Brussels I Recast. According to the Court of Justice in *The Tatry*,[676] if one action is in personam and the other in rem, and the latter has subsequently continued both in rem and in personam, or solely in personam, the parties are to be considered the same.[677]

(b) An action against a ship other than the primary ship

Normally the action lies only against the primary ship (eg the offending ship in a collision case[678]) but in the case of certain claims that arise in connection with a ship for which "the relevant person" (ie the owner, charterer, person in possession or control of the ship) would be liable in an action in personam,[679] section 21(4) of the Senior Courts Act 1981 allows an action in rem to be brought against either (i) that ship (the primary ship) or (ii) another ship owned by "the relevant person,"[680] but not both.[681] However, it does not allow an action to be brought against a ship owned by a sister company of the owners of the primary ship.[682]

---

[668] *The Henrich Björn* (1886) 11 App Cas 270 at 276–7. For priority amongst creditors, see *The Turiddu* [1998] 2 Lloyd's Rep 278.

[669] *Minna Craig Steamship Co v Chartered Mercantile Bank of India, London and China* [1897] 1 QB 460.

[670] [1998] AC 878, HL; Briggs (1997) 68 BYBIL 355; Rose [1998] LMCLQ 27; Teare [1998] LMCLQ 33; Davenport (1998) 114 LQR 169.

[671] See also, eg, *Owners of the Cargo Laden on Board the Ship Tatry v Owners of the Tatry* [1992] 2 Lloyd's Rep 552, CA. This does not, however, mean that the proceedings are also in personam—a separate basis of jurisdiction is required for that purpose: *Owners of the Stolt Kestrel v Owners of the Niyazi S* [2015] EWCA Civ 1035, [2016] 1 Lloyd's Rep 125.

[672] It may not apply in cases involving a maritime lien (such as that arising from a collision), because in that context the claim against the ship does not necessarily imply a claim against the owner: *The Stolt Kestrel*, supra.

[673] But contrast the position in Australia: *Comandate Marine Corp v Pan Australia Shipping Pty Ltd* (2006) 157 FCR 45, [2008] 1 Lloyd's Rep 119.

[674] If the owner submits to the jurisdiction (which may be required as a condition for the release of the ship), they are then also subject to in personam proceedings: see, eg, *The August 8* [1983] 2 AC 450, PC.

[675] Infra, p 556 et seq.

[676] Case C-406/92 *Owners of Cargo lately laden on board Tatry v Owners of Maciej Rataj, The Tatry* [1994] ECR I-5439, [1999] QB 515.

[677] See infra, p 447.

[678] Eg *The Beldis* [1936] P 51; *The Atlantic Star* [1974] AC 436.

[679] See *The Gulf Venture* [1984] 2 Lloyd's Rep 445.

[680] Eg *The Soya Margareta* [1961] 1 WLR 709; *The Span Terza* [1982] 1 Lloyd's Rep 225; *The Mawan* [1988] 2 Lloyd's Rep 459. For ships flying the flag of a non-Contracting State, see *In the Matter of MV Kapitan Labunets* [1995] 1 ILRM 430, Sup Ct of Ireland.

[681] *The Banco* [1971] P 137; *The Stephan J* [1985] 2 Lloyd's Rep 344; *The Afala* [1995] 2 Lloyd's Rep 286. It is, however, possible to have claim forms issued against several ships and then to serve one of these claim forms on the ship which comes conveniently within the jurisdiction, see *The Berny* [1979] QB 80; Senior Courts Act 1981, s 21(8); see also *The Helene Roth* [1980] QB 273; *The Freccia Del Nord* [1989] 1 Lloyd's Rep 388.

[682] *The Evpo Agnic* [1988] 1 WLR 1090. See also *The Tiang Shen No 8* [2000] 2 Lloyd's Rep 430, HK CA.

In cases where the action is brought against the primary ship "the relevant person" must be, at the time when the action is brought, either the beneficial owner of that ship[683] or the charterer of it under a charter by demise,[684] under which he would have full possession and control but not ownership.

In cases where the action is brought against another ship it must be shown that "the relevant person" is the beneficial owner of that ship, "as respects all the shares in it". It is clear from the wording of section 21(4)[685] that it is not enough to show that "the relevant person" is a charterer under a charter by demise. However, if "the relevant person" does own another ship the ambit of section 21(4) is very wide. Since "the relevant person" can include a mere charterer, whether under a charter by demise or under some other type of charter,[686] of the primary ship, it follows that an action can be brought against another ship owned by a charterer of the primary ship[687] although this is not a sister ship.

(c) A stay of proceedings which is subject to conditions

A problem may arise, once an action in rem against a ship has been brought and the ship arrested or security for it given, if the defendant seeks to have the proceedings stayed. The court has a discretion to order the stay of the proceedings if the parties have agreed to submit their dispute to a foreign court[688] or if a foreign court would be a more appropriate forum.[689] If the case falls under section 9 of the Arbitration Act 1996,[690] a stay is mandatory. If the action in rem is stayed the arrested ship or other security can be retained as a security for the satisfaction of any arbitration award or judgment;[691] alternatively, the court can make the staying of the action conditional on the defendant giving some other security.[692] It is irrelevant whether or not the other proceedings have actually started.[693] However, it seems that these provisions in respect of security where Admiralty proceedings are stayed cannot apply if the proceedings are outside the jurisdiction of the Admiralty Court.[694]

---

[683] Cf for Australia *The Cape Moreton* [2005] 219 ALR 48; Hetherington [2005] LMCLQ 428.

[684] S 21(4). See *The Nazym Khikmet* [1996] 2 Lloyd's Rep 362, CA; *The Guiseppe di Vittorio* [1998] 1 Lloyd's Rep 136, CA; *The Looiersgracht* [1995] 2 Lloyd's Rep 411, Canada Federal Court Trial Division; *The Tjaskemolen* [1997] 2 Lloyd's Rep 465 (sham transfer ignored). Cf *Ocean Industries v Steven C* (1991) 104 ALR 353.

[685] Cf s 21(4)(i) with s 21(4)(ii).

[686] *The Span Terza* [1982] 1 Lloyd's Rep 225, CA (involving a time charterer); *The Tychy* [1999] 2 Lloyd's Rep 11, CA (slot charterers—the issue of their replacement was considered in *The Tychy (No 2)* [2001] 2 Lloyd's Rep 403, CA), Baughen [2006] LMCLQ 129; *The Faial* [2000] 1 Lloyd's Rep 473; *The Sextum* [1982] 2 Lloyd's Rep 532 (HK Supreme Court).

[687] *The Span Terza* [1982] 1 Lloyd's Rep 225, CA; *The Sextum* [1982] 2 Lloyd's Rep 532 (HK Supreme Court); *Laemthong International Lines Co Ltd v BPS Shipping Ltd* (1997) 190 CLR 181 High Court of Australia. Cf the obiter dicta by Lord Diplock in *The Jade*, sub nom *The Exchersheim* [1976] 1 All ER 920 at 925; and see *The Maritime Trader* [1981] 2 Lloyd's Rep 153.

[688] Infra, p 410 et seq; see *The Athenee* (1922) 11 Lloyd's Rep 6; *The Fehmarn* [1957] 1 WLR 815; *The Eleftheria* [1970] P 94.

[689] Infra, p 393 et seq; see *The Cap Bon* [1967] 1 Lloyd's Rep 543; *The Atlantic Star* [1974] AC 436; *The Vishva Ajay* [1989] 2 Lloyd's Rep 558.

[690] Infra, p 416 et seq; see *The Golden Trader* [1975] QB 348; *Marazura Navegación SA v Oceanus Mutual Underwriting Association (Bermuda) Ltd* [1977] 1 Lloyd's Rep 283 at 287–8; *The Rena K* [1979] QB 377.

[691] Civil Jurisdiction and Judgments Act 1982, s 26; Arbitration Act 1996, s 11. See *The Vasso* [1984] 1 Lloyd's Rep 235 at 243; *Spiliada Maritime Corpn v Cansulex Ltd* [1987] AC 460, HL; *The World Star* [1986] 2 Lloyd's Rep 274; *The Silver Athens (No 2)* [1986] 2 Lloyd's Rep 583; *The Emre II* [1989] 2 Lloyd's Rep 182.

[692] Conditions other than this can be imposed under the 1982 Act, s 26 (see *The Havhelt* [1993] 1 Lloyd's Rep 523) but not under the 1996 Act, s 11.

[693] *The Jalamatsya* [1987] 2 Lloyd's Rep 164; *The Nordglimt* [1988] 1 QB 183 at 204.

[694] *The Nordglimt*, supra.

(d) The effect of the Brussels/Lugano system[695]

(i) The basis of jurisdiction

The Brussels I Recast normally applies in cases where the defendant is domiciled in a European Union Member State and the matter in question is a civil and commercial matter.[696] The Brussels Convention normally applies in cases where the defendant is domiciled in one of the French overseas territories, such as New Caledonia and Mayotte, or (as regards the Netherlands) Aruba and the matter in question is a civil and commercial matter. The Lugano Convention normally applies in cases where the defendant is domiciled in an EFTA State (other than Liechtenstein) and it is a civil and commercial matter. However, Article 71 of the Brussels I Recast, Article 57 of the Brussels Convention and Article 67 of the Lugano Convention preserve other conventions relating to jurisdiction previously entered into by the United Kingdom, eg the Convention Relating to the Arrest of Sea-Going Ships of 1952 (the Arrest Convention[697]). The Court of Appeal in *The Anna H*[698] rejected the argument that Admiralty jurisdiction in cases of arrest had been altered or that the jurisdiction to entertain the claim and rule upon its merits had been taken away. It follows that English courts are still able to take jurisdiction under the provisions of the Senior Courts Act 1981, in so far as these provisions are derived from the Arrest Convention,[699] even if the defendant is domiciled in a Regulation State or a Contracting State to the Brussels Convention or a State bound by the Lugano Convention, and even if that State is not a party to the Arrest Convention.[700] To take an example, it is still possible to bring an action in rem against a ship, owned by a Frenchman, which is arrested in English waters following a collision at sea. On the other hand, in cases coming within the Brussels I Recast or the Brussels or Lugano Convention, jurisdiction has to be taken under the Brussels I Recast or that Convention, and cannot be taken under any provision in the Senior Courts Act 1981, if that provision is not derived from the Arrest Convention.

The Arrest Convention (but not the Collision Convention[701]) requires a ship actually to be arrested. In *The Deichland*[702] a writ in rem was served on a ship in England, but then, as is commonly the case, the demise charterers (Deich) gave undertakings as to security in consideration of the ship not being arrested. There was jurisdiction under the 1981 Act (ignoring for the moment the Brussels/Lugano system) but this was not based on the Arrest Convention, since the ship had not been arrested. Deich was domiciled in Germany and under Article 2 of the Brussels Convention (corresponding to Article 4 of the Brussels I Recast, which would now apply on the facts) had to be sued there. The Court of Appeal granted a declaration that

---

[695] See in relation to the Brussels/Lugano system: Jackson, *Civil Jurisdiction and Judgments—Maritime Claims* (1987); *The Enforcement of Maritime Claims* (2005) 4th edn, paras 6.1–6.63; Dicey, Morris and Collins, paras 13-022–13-035; Brice [1987] LMCLQ 281; Blackburn [1988] LMCLQ 91.

[696] Discussed supra, p 202 et seq.

[697] Also, rather confusingly, often referred to as the Brussels Convention. An updated version, the 1999 Arrest Convention, came into force in 2011. The United Kingdom has however not ratified the 1999 Convention.

[698] [1995] 1 Lloyd's Rep 11, CA; Hartley [1995] LMCLQ 31. For the position in Scotland see *Ladgroup Ltd v Euroeast Lines SA* 1997 SLT 916.

[699] *The Deichland* [1990] 1 QB 361; *The Sea Maas* [1999] 2 Lloyd's Rep 281 at 282. On the complex question of the extent to which the 1981 Act is based on the Arrest Convention, see *Gatoil International Inc v Arkwright-Boston Manufacturers Mutual Insurance Co* [1985] AC 255, HL; *The Deichland*, supra.

[700] Art 71 of the Brussels I Recast, Art 57 of the Brussels Convention and Art 67 Lugano Convention, supra, p 203. However, the Arrest Convention must, of course, apply in respect of that particular defendant, see Jackson, *The Enforcement of Maritime Claims* (4th edn 2005), paras 6.12–6.21.

[701] *The Po* [1991] 2 Lloyd's Rep 206.

[702] [1990] 1 QB 361; Carter (1989) 60 BYBIL 489. Cf *The Po* [1991] 2 Lloyd's Rep 206. Cf *The Anna H*, supra, where it was unsuccessfully argued that the arrest did not come within the Arrest Convention.

the English courts lacked jurisdiction. Although this was an action in rem, Deich was treated as the defendant for the purposes of Article 4 of the Brussels Convention.[703] However, a ship can be arrested under the Arrest Convention, which requires that the arrest is to secure a maritime claim, even though bail or other security has already been given.[704]

Moreover, in cases coming within the Brussels/Lugano system, it is not possible to take jurisdiction in rem against aircraft, hovercraft or against property connected with a ship, ie the cargo or freight, since the Arrest Convention only provides for jurisdiction against a ship.[705] Instead, jurisdiction has to be taken under the Brussels/Lugano system.[706]

Article 71 of the Brussels I Recast, Article 57 of the Brussels Convention and Article 67 of the Lugano Convention also preserve the 1952 International Convention on Certain Rules Concerning Civil Jurisdiction in Matters of Collision (the Collision Convention).[707] What matters is that the United Kingdom legislation, which was designed to implement the Collision Convention, is in accordance with that Convention. It does not matter that that Convention has not been directly implemented in the United Kingdom.[708]

In the situation where jurisdiction is derived from the Arrest Convention it has been held in *The Bergen*[709] that an English court is not deprived of jurisdiction by a foreign choice of jurisdiction clause coming within Article 17 of the Brussels Convention (corresponding to Article 25 of the Brussels I Recast, which would now apply on the facts). However, this decision appears to be wrong. The Brussels/Lugano system will continue to apply in so far as the Arrest Convention is silent on a jurisdictional matter,[710] and the latter says nothing about the effect of agreements on jurisdiction. Accordingly, Article 25 of the Brussels I Recast will still apply to deprive an English court of jurisdiction.

(ii) Stays of action

The power to stay an action in rem, unlike the action in rem itself, does not derive from an international convention. It is part of the English courts' inherent jurisdiction, but cannot be used in circumstances where to grant a stay would be inconsistent with the Brussels I Recast (or the Brussels or Lugano Conventions).[711] It is unclear, however, in what circumstances granting a stay of proceedings commenced pursuant to Article 71 of the Brussels I Recast (where there is jurisdiction in rem under the Arrest or Collision Conventions) would be inconsistent with the Brussels I Recast. Such a stay could arise in two different situations.

The first is a case which would, apart from Article 71 of the Brussels I Recast, fall under the Brussels I Recast jurisdictional rules, including where the defendant is domiciled in a Member State. A stay might be sought in favour of the courts of another Member State, or of a third state. In *The Po*[712] the Court of Appeal applied the doctrine of *forum non conveniens* to a case involving

---

[703] See further *Owners of the Stolt Kestrel v Owners of the Niyazi S* [2015] EWCA Civ 1035, [2016] 1 Lloyd's Rep 125.

[704] *The Anna H*, supra. See also *The Prinsengracht* [1993] 1 Lloyd's Rep 41.

[705] On the definition of 'ship' in this context see Rainey [2013] LMCLQ 50.

[706] See, in particular, Art 7(7) of the Brussels I Recast and Art 5(7) of the Brussels and Lugano Conventions, discussed supra, p 283.

[707] See *The Po* [1991] 2 Lloyd's Rep 206; Hartley [1991] LMCLQ 446. Cf *Doran v Power* [1997] IL Pr 52, Irish Supreme Court.

[708] *The Po*, supra, at 211.

[709] [1997] 1 Lloyd's Rep 380; Siig [1997] LMCLQ 362.

[710] Case C-406/92 *Owners of cargo lately laden on board Tatry v Owners of Maciej Rataj, The Tatry* [1994] ECR I-5439, [1999] QB 515n; discussed infra, p 447.

[711] See infra, p 459 et seq.

[712] [1991] 2 Lloyd's Rep 206. See also *The Nordglimt* [1988] 1 QB 183 at 205.

jurisdiction under the Collision Convention, despite the fact that the defendants were domiciled in Italy, which, at that time, brought the case within the Brussels Convention (now the Brussels I Recast would apply on the facts). It is important to note that the case was argued on the basis that the alternative forum for trial was Brazil.[713] This was a case decided before the landmark decision of the Court of Justice in *Owusu v Jackson*,[714] which held that where the jurisdiction of a court of a Contracting State is based on Article 2 of the Brussels Convention (now Article 4 of the Brussels I Recast), that court is precluded from declining jurisdiction on the ground that a court of a non-Contracting State would be a more appropriate forum for the trial of the action. However, in a case of jurisdiction in rem under, for example, the Arrest Convention or Collision Convention (as preserved by Article 71 of the Brussels I Recast, Article 57 of the Brussels Convention and Article 67 of the Lugano Convention) this is not based on Article 4 or, indeed, on any other of the bases of jurisdiction set out in the Brussels I Recast or Brussels or Lugano Conventions. This arguably means that the doctrine of *forum non conveniens* should still operate in this situation, so that the Brussels I Recast does not affect the taking of jurisdiction (broadly understood) under the applicable international conventions such as the Arrest Convention or Collision Convention.

Even where the alternative forum is that of another Member State, there is authority in *Sarrio SA v Kuwait Insurance Authority*[715] that the doctrine of *forum non conveniens* can operate where jurisdiction is based on common law rules under Article 6, and it might be argued that this should extend to Article 71 cases. It is as yet unclear how this is affected by the decision of the Court of Justice in *Owusu v Jackson* and another decision of that court is needed to clarify the matter.

The second situation is where there is jurisdiction in rem under the Arrest or Collision Conventions but the defendant is domiciled outside a Brussels I Recast State[716] and Articles 24 and 25 of the Brussels I Recast[717] do not apply. According to Clarke J in *The Xin Yang*,[718] Article 4 of the Brussels Convention (on these facts this would now be Article 6 of the Brussels I Recast) would apply. Jurisdiction is therefore to be determined by the law of each Member State and in the case of England this encompasses not only bases of jurisdiction (including the provisions in the Senior Courts Act 1981 dealing with actions in rem[719]) but also the discretion to stay on the ground of *forum non conveniens*.[720] As will be seen,[721] according to *Sarrio*, in cases covered by Article 4 of the Brussels Convention (now Article 6 of the Brussels I Recast) the doctrine of *forum non conveniens* can operate even where the alternative forum is another Member State.[722] Clarke J, following this line of authority, held that the Netherlands was the appropriate forum for trial and stayed the English proceedings in rem. This, though, is now subject to the decision of the Court of Justice in *Owusu v Jackson* and it is unclear whether *Sarrio* can still stand in the light of that decision. However, Advocate General Leger said in *Owusu* that where the jurisdiction of a court of a Contracting State is established pursuant to Article 4 of the Brussels Convention

---

[713] However, on the particular facts the first instance decision refusing a stay was upheld, the defendants having failed to show that Brazil was a clearly more appropriate forum.

[714] Case C-281/02 [2005] QB 801; discussed infra, pp 462–8.

[715] [1997] 1 Lloyd's Rep 113, CA; reversed by the House of Lords without discussion of this point.

[716] Or Brussels Convention Contracting State or state bound by the Lugano Convention.

[717] Arts 16 and 17 of the Brussels Convention, Arts 22 and 23 of the Lugano Convention.

[718] [1996] 2 Lloyd's Rep 217; Newton [1997] LMCLQ 337.

[719] *The Xin Yang*, supra, at 220.

[720] *The Xin Yang*, supra; *Sarrio SA v Kuwait Insurance Authority* [1996] 1 Lloyd's Rep 650 at 654; affd by the Court of Appeal [1997] 1 Lloyd's Rep 113; revsd by the House of Lords without discussion of this point [1999] 1 AC 32.

[721] Infra, pp 469–70.

[722] *Sarrio SA v Kuwait Insurance Authority* [1997] 1 Lloyd's Rep 113, CA; revsd by the House of Lords without discussion of this point.

(now Article 6 of the Brussels I Recast) this does not prevent the court in question from declining to exercise its jurisdiction, in accordance with the doctrine of *forum non conveniens* on the ground that a court of a non-Member State would be more appropriate to deal with the substance of the case.[723] It is notable that Articles 33 and 34 of the Brussels I Recast, dealing with stays of proceedings in favour of the courts of a non-Member State, apply only if jurisdiction is based on Article 4 or on Articles 7, 8 or 9. There is an argument that this same principle should apply even if the stay is in favour of the courts of another Member State.[724] There is also another way of analysing this situation. It is arguable that Article 6 of the Brussels I Recast should not apply to cases, of which *The Xin Yang* appears to be one, coming within Article 71 of the Brussels I Recast.[725] The latter preserves bases of jurisdiction set out in specialised conventions and thereby creates a regime which falls outside those provisions in the Brussels I Recast[726] concerned with bases of jurisdiction, such as Article 6. If the case is treated as an Article 71 case, rather than as an Article 6 case, the argument set out above applies—that Article 71 should be understood as not affecting the taking of jurisdiction (broadly understood) under the applicable international conventions such as the Arrest Convention or Collision Convention. In either case, there is a good argument that a stay on the ground of *forum non conveniens* should be available.

Whatever the position may be in relation to *forum non conveniens*, it is clear that Articles 29 (*lis pendens*) and 30 (related actions) of the Brussels I Recast[727] can apply in cases where jurisdiction has been brought under the Arrest Convention. (As noted above, the new Articles 33 and 34 dealing with prior proceedings in non-Member States[728] do not, however, apply, because they are limited to cases in which jurisdiction is based on Article 4 or on Articles 7, 8 or 9.) The application of the Brussels I Recast is precluded solely in relation to questions specifically governed by the specialised convention in question; in so far as the latter is silent on a jurisdictional matter,[729] the Brussels I Recast will continue to apply.[730] The Court of Justice has also suggested that prior conventions are only preserved to the extent that their rules are consistent with the principles and objectives of the Brussels I Recast,[731] which may affect how those conventions can permissibly be interpreted.[732] Whilst Article 71 of the Brussels I Recast[733] preserves the Arrest Convention, the latter says nothing about proceedings brought in two different jurisdictions and nothing about the question of which court is to decline jurisdiction.[734] It will be recalled that Article 29 requires that the two sets

---

[723] At [235].

[724] See infra, pp 469–70.

[725] Or Art 57 of the Brussels Convention or Art 67 of the Lugano Convention.

[726] Or Brussels or Lugano Convention.

[727] Supra, p 443 et seq. Arts 21 and 22 of the Brussels Convention and Arts 27 and 28 of the Lugano Convention.

[728] See supra, p 457 et seq.

[729] The Supreme Court has held that the CMR Convention should be viewed as exhaustive in terms of permissible grounds of jurisdiction, and thus recourse to the equivalent of Article 8(1) of the Brussels I Recast to add a further party to proceedings is not permitted: *British American Tobacco Denmark A/S v Kazemier BV* [2015] UKSC 65, [2016] AC 262.

[730] Case C-406/92 *Owners of Cargo lately laden on board Tatry v Owners of Maciej Rataj, The Tatry* [1994] ECR I-5439, [1999] QB 515 n; a case on the Brussels Convention discussed infra, p 447.

[731] Case C-533/08 *TNT Express Nederland BV* [2010] ECR I-4107; Case C-230/15 *Brite Strike Technologies Inc v Brite Strike Technologies SA* EU:C:2016:560.

[732] Case C-452/12 *Nipponkoa Insurance Co (Europe) Ltd v Inter-Zuid Transport BV* EU:C:2013:858, [2014] IL Pr 10. But see also *British American Tobacco Denmark A/S v Kazemier BV* [2015] UKSC 65, [2016] AC 262, suggesting that this should be narrowly confined, particularly where non-Member States are parties to the relevant convention.

[733] Art 57 of the Brussels Convention and Art 67 of the Lugano Convention.

[734] *The Tatry*, supra. See also *The Linda* [1988] 1 Lloyd's Rep 175 at 178. The position is the same in relation to the Geneva Convention on the Contract for the International Carriage of Goods by Road of 1956

of proceedings involve the same parties. It will also be recalled that, according to the Court of Justice in *The Tatry*,[735] if one action is in personam and the other in rem, and the latter has subsequently continued both in rem and in personam, or solely in personam, according to the distinctions drawn by the national law of that other Member State, the parties are the same. Moreover, the answer would be the same, even if the action in rem had continued as such according to national law,[736] since the distinction drawn by the law of a Member State between an action in personam and an action in rem is not material for the interpretation of Article 29. The court first seised of the action takes priority and any other court must decline jurisdiction once the jurisdiction of the court first seised has been established. With an action in rem an English court is seised of the proceedings from the moment when the document instituting the proceedings is lodged with the court[737] (ie on the date of the issue of the claim form) and not from the time of service of a claim form or arrest of a ship.[738] In the situation where an English court has declined jurisdiction under Article 29, the arrested ship can be retained as security and made available to meet a judgment in the foreign action in the court first seised of the proceedings.[739]

(the CMR Convention), *Sony Computer Entertainment Ltd v RH Freight Services Ltd* [2007] EWHC 302 (Comm) at [27].

[735] *The Tatry*, supra. See also *The Winter* [2000] 2 Lloyd's Rep 298 (on whether cause of action was the same).

[736] *Republic of India v India Steamship Co Ltd (No 2)* [1998] AC 878 at 913, HL (per Lord Steyn with whom the other Law Lords concurred).

[737] Art 32(1) of the Brussels I Recast.

[738] The position under the Lugano Convention is the same as under the Brussels I Recast. Under the Brussels Convention it is unclear whether an English court is seised from the moment of service (see *Neste Chemicals SA v DK Line SA, The Sargasso* [1994] 3 All ER 180, CA) or whether, as an alternative, it can be from the time of arrest when this is earlier (see *The Freccia del Nord* [1989] 1 Lloyd's Rep 388 and *The Sargasso*, supra, footnote d).

[739] Civil Jurisdiction and Judgments Act 1982, s 26; *The Nordglimt* [1988] 1 QB 183 at 203–4. The position is more problematical if security has been given to prevent arrest; Hartley (1989) 105 LQR 640 argued that Art 22 of the Brussels Convention (corresponding to Art 30 of the Brussels I Recast) has to be used in such a case.

13

STAYS AND THE MANAGEMENT
OF PARALLEL PROCEEDINGS

1. Introduction	391	5. Stays of Proceedings Under the Brussels I Recast	459
2. Stays of English Proceedings Under the Common Law	392	(a) A discretion to stay proceedings in the Brussels I Recast itself?	459
(a) Forum non conveniens	393	(b) Can the traditional English doctrine of forum non conveniens be used?	460
(b) Foreign jurisdiction clauses	410		
(c) Arbitration agreements	416	(c) Is there a residual discretion?	471
(d) Stays pending the determination of proceedings abroad	421	(d) Does the Brussels I Recast have "reflexive" effects?	473
3. Restraining Foreign Proceedings Under the Common Law: The Anti-Suit Injunction	422	6. Restraining Foreign Proceedings and the Brussels I Recast	475
(a) Underlying principles	423	(a) A discretion to restrain foreign proceedings in the Brussels I Recast itself?	475
(b) Categorisation of the cases	425		
4. Parallel Proceedings Under the Brussels I Recast: Lis Pendens and Related Actions	442	(b) Can the traditional English power to restrain foreign proceedings be used?	476
(a) Proceedings in another Member State	443		
(b) Proceedings in a non-Member State	457		

1. INTRODUCTION

It will be evident from Chapters 11 and 12 that in many cases the English courts will be one of a number of courts which might have jurisdiction over a particular dispute. Under the Brussels I Recast this may arise, for example, where the rules on non-exclusive jurisdiction apply, giving the claimant a choice between the courts of different Member States. Different courts may also have jurisdiction depending on which party commences proceedings—an English company might sue a French company in France for breach of contract, for example, or the French company might sue the English party in England for a declaration that the contract has been fully performed. It will also commonly be possible that non-Member State courts might be seised of disputes which could be litigated in England, such as where a claim against an English domiciled party relates to a tort committed in New York. These are all situations in which more than one court might legitimately be seised on the merits. It is also possible that any number of courts might be seised of jurisdictional questions. Even if, for example, two parties have entered into an exclusive jurisdiction agreement in favour of the English courts, that does not foreclose the possibility that proceedings may be commenced in one or more foreign courts, which might then have to decide on the validity of the jurisdiction agreement in order to determine their own jurisdiction.

The frequent possibility that proceedings could be brought in England or in a foreign court gives rise to two related issues. First, if proceedings are commenced in England, should the English courts exercise jurisdiction if a foreign court would be better placed to resolve the dispute? This is the question of stays of proceedings—as discussed below, it is generally possible for the English court to stay proceedings commenced pursuant to the common law rules on jurisdiction, but generally not (although subject to potential exceptions) where proceedings are commenced under the Brussels I Recast. Second, what should happen if proceedings are or might be commenced both in a foreign court and in the English courts? The risk that parallel proceedings might give rise to conflicting judgments, leaving parties subject to contradictory obligations in different jurisdictions, is one of the major concerns of private international law. As discussed below, where two courts are or might be seised of a dispute, the common law approach is (broadly speaking) to determine which court is better placed to resolve the dispute, while the Brussels I Recast generally[1] prioritises the court first seised. Where the English courts decide that they should hear the case, despite the existence of earlier, later or potential foreign proceedings, this also raises the issue of the anti-suit injunction—an order developed by the English courts restraining a party from commencing or continuing with foreign proceedings. This order has become an important part of the common law approach to reducing the risk of parallel proceedings; but, as we will see, its use in relation to proceedings in the courts of other Member States has been curtailed by the Court of Justice.

2. STAYS OF ENGLISH PROCEEDINGS UNDER THE COMMON LAW

Even though an English court has power to try a case under the common law rules,[2] ie a claim form has been served on the defendant in accordance with the rules set out in the previous chapter, it can, nonetheless, refuse to take jurisdiction and stay the English proceedings.[3] The court also has power to stay an action in which its own jurisdiction is in issue—the English courts may therefore take the view on occasion that it is not necessary to determine whether they have a basis of jurisdiction, because even if they did, the proceedings would be stayed.[4] Although the English court is technically only regulating its own jurisdiction, the effect of a stay is to force a claimant to go abroad to sue or, in some cases, to go to arbitration.[5] The court is therefore, in reality, choosing between alternative fora for trial, or between trial and arbitration.[6] The power to stay English proceedings is derived from the court's inherent jurisdiction,[7]

---

[1] The exception is Article 31(2) of the Brussels I Recast, which prioritises the court chosen in an exclusive jurisdiction agreement over the court first seised: see infra, pp 452–3.

[2] This includes cases in which the English court is applying the common law rules pursuant to Article 6 of the Brussels I Recast: see infra, p 468 et seq.

[3] The procedure for disputing the court's jurisdiction or arguing that the court should not exercise its jurisdiction is set out in Part 11 of the CPR. An application for a stay should ordinarily be made within the time limits for disputing the court's jurisdiction (see CPR, r 11(6); supra, pp 332–3), but if circumstances change a stay may also be sought at a later stage relying on the inherent power of the court. See *Texan Management Ltd v Pacific Electric Wire & Cable Company* [2009] UKPC 46.

[4] *Williams and Glyn's Bank plc v Astro Dinamico Compañía Naviera SA* [1984] 1 WLR 438.

[5] The arbitration may be in England or abroad; in cases where there is an arbitration agreement, a stay of proceedings will be mandatory. See infra, p 416 et seq.

[6] This is not to say that a claimant will necessarily take up an available alternative forum—in practice, many claims may not be pursued at all if they cannot be pursued in the English courts.

[7] There is a separate power to stay proceedings using general powers of case management under CPR, r 3.1(f). It may be difficult to persuade the court to exercise this power in an international case, see *Affymetrix Inc v Multilyte Ltd* [2004] EWHC 291 (Pat), [2005] IL Pr 34.

which is preserved by statute,[8] and from statutory provision on arbitration.[9] The power is exercised in three situations:

(a) where the doctrine of *forum non conveniens* applies;
(b) where there is a foreign choice of jurisdiction clause;
(c) where there is an agreement on arbitration.

Each of these three situations will be examined in turn. After which, a different sort of stay, namely one granted pending the determination of proceedings abroad, will be considered.

(a) Forum non conveniens[10]

It has already been seen that the discretionary power to allow service of a claim form out of the jurisdiction is exercised on the basis of *forum conveniens*.[11] There is also a general discretionary power to stay actions on the basis of *forum non conveniens* (ie where the clearly appropriate forum for trial is abroad).[12] Whilst there has been such a power in Scotland[13] and the USA[14] for a considerable length of time, it is only relatively recently that a general doctrine of *forum non conveniens* has been accepted in England.[15] The English discretion to stay is now indistinguishable from the Scottish doctrine of *forum non conveniens*.[16] That this is the case has been endorsed by the House of Lords in the leading authority on stays of action, *Spiliada Maritime Corpn v Cansulex Ltd*.[17] It is clear from this case that the same basic criterion applies in cases involving stays of action as in cases involving the exercise of the discretion to serve a claim form out of the jurisdiction.[18] The *Spiliada* case set off a chain reaction in a number of common law jurisdictions, and has been followed[19] in New

---

[8] See s 49(3) of the Senior Courts Act 1981.

[9] The Arbitration Act 1996, s 9; discussed infra, p 416 et seq.

[10] Bell, *Forum Shopping and Venue in International Litigation* (2003); Briggs 2015, para 4.13ff; Fentiman 2015, Chapter 13; Dicey, Morris and Collins, paras 12R-001–12-047; Fawcett, *Declining Jurisdiction*, especially pp 10–27 (for a comparative survey); Brand (2002) 37 Texas Int LR 467; International Law Association, Third Interim Report: Declining and Referring Jurisdiction in International Litigation; Briggs (1983) 3 LS 74; [1984] LMCLQ 227; [1985] LMCLQ 360; Barma and Elvin (1985) 101 LQR 48; Schuz (1986) 35 ICLQ 374; (for a comparison with Dutch law) Verheul (1986) 35 ICLQ 413; Robertson (1987) 103 LQR 398; Slater (1988) 104 LQR 554; Fawcett (1989) 9 OJLS 205; Beaumont, in Fawcett (ed), *Declining Jurisdiction*, pp 207–23; Peel (2001) 117 LQR 187; Arzandeh (2014) 10 J Priv Int L 89.

[11] Supra, p 364 et seq.

[12] For the application of this doctrine in the area of family law see infra, p 972 et seq.

[13] Crawford and Carruthers, paras 7-45–7-46. *Crédit Chimique v James Scott Engineering Group Ltd* 1979 SC 406, 1982 SLT 131.

[14] Hay, Borchers and Symeonides, paras 11.8–11.13; Felix and Whitten, *American Conflicts Law*, (2011) 6th edn, pp 111–17; *Gulf Oil Corpn v Gilbert* 330 US 501 (1946); *Piper Aircraft Co v Reno* 454 US 235 (1981).

[15] By Lord Diplock in *The Abidin Daver* [1984] AC 398 at 411. Lords Edmund-Davies, Keith and Templeman concurred with Lord Diplock. For earlier relaxation in the law see *The Atlantic Star* [1974] AC 436, at 454, 468; *MacShannon v Rockware Glass Ltd* [1978] AC 795. For much earlier cases confining the grant of a stay to cases of vexation and oppression, see *Logan v Bank of Scotland (No 2)* [1906] 1 KB 141; *Egbert v Short* [1907] 2 Ch 205; *Re Norton's Settlement* [1908] 1 Ch 471.

[16] *The Abidin Daver*, supra, at 411 (per Lord Diplock).

[17] [1987] AC 460; Briggs [1987] LMCLQ 1; Collier [1987] CLJ 33; Carter (1986) 57 BYBIL 429; Hill (2001) 54 CLP 439; Arzandeh (2014) 10 J Priv IL 89. See also *Connelly v RTZ Corpn plc* [1998] AC 854, HL; *Lubbe v Cape plc* [2000] 1 WLR 1545, HL; *Tehrani v Secretary of State for the Home Department* [2006] UKHL 47, [2007] 1 AC 521.

[18] Supra, p 364 et seq.

[19] For Scots reaction see *Sokha v Secretary of State for the Home Department* 1992 SLT 1049; *Morrison v Panic Link Ltd* 1993 SLT 602; reclaiming motion refused 1994 SLT 232; *PTKF Kontinent v VMPTO* 1994 SLT 235.

Zealand,[20] Canada,[21] Hong Kong,[22] Brunei,[23] Singapore,[24] Gibraltar,[25] the Caribbean[26] and Ireland,[27] but not in Australia,[28] where a majority of the High Court, in a very unclear and much criticised decision, required there to be vexation or oppression for the grant of a stay, but could not agree on what this meant. However, it has been established subsequently that this can be shown by the fact that the forum is a clearly inappropriate one for trial[29] (a formula loaded in favour of trial in the forum[30]).

(i) The principles on which the discretion to stay is exercised

The law was exhaustively considered and restated by the House of Lords in *Spiliada Maritime Corpn v Cansulex Ltd*,[31] where Lord Goff, giving the unanimous judgment of the Law Lords, set out a number of principles on which the discretion should be exercised. These principles have been affirmed and further explained by Lord Goff[32] in the House of Lords in *Connelly v RTZ Corpn plc*[33] and by Lord Bingham[34] in the House of Lords in *Lubbe v Cape plc*.[35] Before

---

[20] *McConnell Dowell Constructors Ltd v Lloyd's Syndicate 396* [1988] 2 NZLR 257, CA; *Club Mediterranee NZ v Wendell* [1989] 1 NZLR 216, CA; *Crane Accessories Ltd v Lim Swee Hee* [1989] 1 NZLR 221; Paterson (1989) 13 NZULR 337; *Society of Lloyd's v Hyslop* [1993] 3 NZLR 135, CA; see generally Barnard in Fawcett (ed), *Declining Jurisdiction*, pp 348–58.

[21] *Amchem Products Inc v Workers' Compensation Board* (1993) 102 DLR (4th) 96 at 107–12 (per Sopinka J), Sup Ct of Canada; Edinger [1993] Can BR 366; *Holt Cargo Systems Inc v ABC Containerline NV (Trustees of)* (2001) 207 DLR (4th) 577, Sup Ct of Canada; *Spar Aerospace Ltd v American Mobile Satellite Corpn* (2002) 220 DLR (4th) 54 at 80–5, Sup Ct of Canada; Walker (2003) 118 LQR 567; *Bourdon v Stelco Inc* (2006) 259 DLR (4th) 34, Sup Ct of Canada. For the differences between the Canadian and English doctrines, see Blom in Fawcett (ed), *Declining Jurisdiction*, p 127 et seq. The doctrine has been codified in some Canadian provinces: see Pitel (2011) 7 J Priv Int L 251.

[22] *The Adhiguna Meranti* [1988] 1 Lloyd's Rep 384, HK CA; *The Kapitan Shvetsov* [1998] 1 Lloyd's Rep 199, HK CA; Svantesson (2005) 35 HKLJ 395.

[23] *Syarikat Bumiputra Kimonis v Tan Kok Voon* [1988] 3 MLJ 315.

[24] *Brinkerhoff Maritime Drilling Corpn v PT Airfast Services Indonesia* [1992] 2 SLR 776; *Eng Liat Kiang v Eng Bak Hern* [1995] 3 SLR 97; *Oriental Insurance Co Ltd v Bhavani Stores Pte Ltd* [1998] SLR 253; *PT Hutan Domas Raya v Yue Xiu Enterprises* [2001] 2 SLR 49; *Yuninshing v Edward Mondong* [2002] 2 SLR 506.

[25] *Aldington Shipping Ltd v Bradstock Shipping Corpn and Mabanaft GmbH, The Waylink and Brady Maria* [1988] 1 Lloyd's Rep 475, Gibraltar CA.

[26] *Barclays Bank plc v Kenton Capital Ltd et al* (1994–95) Cayman Islands Law Reports 489; McDowell (2000) 49 ICLQ 108.

[27] *Intermetal Group Ltd & Trans-World (Steel) Ltd v Worslade Trading Ltd* [1998] IL Pr 765, Irish Sup Ct; *McCarthy v Pillay* [2003] 2 ILRM 284, Irish Sup Ct.

[28] *Oceanic Sun-Line Special Shipping Co Inc v Fay* (1988) 165 CLR 197, High Court of Australia. See Pryles (1988) 62 ALJ 774; Reynolds (1989) 105 LQR 4; Briggs (1989) 105 LQR 200; Briggs [1989] LMCLQ 216; Collins (1989) 105 LQR 364; Garner (1989) 38 ICLQ 361; Mclachlan [1990] CLJ 37. But see, however, Arzandeh (2016) 65 ICLQ 475, arguing that the Australian and English tests are no different in practice.

[29] *Voth v Manildra Flour Mills Pty Ltd* (1990) 171 CLR 538, HC of Australia: following Deane J in the *Oceanic Case*, supra, at 247–8. See Collins (1991) 107 LQR 182; Pryles (1991) 65 ALJ 442; Brereton (1991) 40 ICLQ 895; Epstein in Fawcett (ed), *Declining Jurisdiction*, p 82 et seq; Marasinghe (1993) 23 UWA LR 264; Prince (1998) 47 ICLQ 573; Garnett (1999) 23 Melbourne ULR 30. See also *Dow Jones & Company Inc v Gutnick* (2002) 210 CLR 575, HC of Australia; *Puttick v Tenon Limited (formerly called Fletcher Challenge Forests Limited)* [2008] HCA 54. Where a person has been served outside Australia there is a power under Reg 11.7 of the Uniform Civil Procedure Rules 2005 (NSW), to set service aside on the ground that the court is an inappropriate forum (a less emphatic test). However, this still requires the defendants to establish vexation or oppression: *Régie Nationale Des Usines Renault SA v Zhang* (2001) 210 CLR 491, HC of Australia.

[30] For the reasons for this formulation see *BHP Billiton Ltd v Schultz* (2004) 221 CLR 400 at [9]–[11], HC of Australia.

[31] [1987] AC 460. The facts of the case are discussed supra, p 379.

[32] With whom the other Law Lords concurred.

[33] [1998] AC 854, HL. Lord Hoffmann dissented on the application of those principles to the facts of the case.

[34] With whom the other Law Lords concurred.

[35] [2000] 1 WLR 1545, HL.

turning to examine these principles, one general point needs to be made. The decision on the exercise of the discretion is essentially one for the judge at first instance, and an appellate court should not interfere merely because it would give different weight to the factors involved.[36]

(a) The basic principle

The basic principle is that a stay will only be granted on the ground of forum non conveniens where the court is satisfied that there is some other available forum, having jurisdiction, which is the appropriate forum for trial of the action, ie in which the case may be tried more suitably for the interests of all the parties and the ends of justice.[37]

This is the most important of the principles and sums up the whole basis of the *forum non conveniens* discretion. Lord Goff, however, did lay down a number of other subordinate principles which have been frequently followed. He referred to a two-stage inquiry. The first stage is concerned with whether there is another available forum which is clearly more appropriate than the English forum; the second stage with the requirements of justice.[38]

(b) The two-stage inquiry

(i) The first stage: another available forum which is clearly more appropriate
The burden of proof is on the defendant to show that there is another available forum which is clearly or distinctly more appropriate than the English forum.[39] The defendant will find it all the easier to discharge this burden where it has only a tenuous connection with the forum.[40] The same has been said to apply where service was effected out of the jurisdiction, at least where the defendant did not earlier seek to set aside service out on the basis that the claimant had not shown that England was clearly the most appropriate forum.[41]

Another available forum   The defendant must show that there is another "available" forum abroad[42] in which the issues may be resolved.[43] In the *Spiliada* case availability refers to another court abroad having "competent jurisdiction" to try the case.[44] Lord Walker, delivering the judgment of the Privy Council in *Hindocha v Gheewala*,[45] has said that an alternative

---

[36] The *Spiliada* case, supra; *VTB Capital v Nutritek* [2013] UKSC 5, [2013] 2 WLR 398.

[37] The *Spiliada* case, supra, at 476. See also *Connelly v RTZ Corpn plc* [1998] AC 854 at 868–9, HL; the *Lubbe* case, supra, at 1554.

[38] Cf the Canadian doctrine which considers the juridical advantage when determining the appropriate forum: *Amchem Products Inc v Workers' Compensation Board* (1993) 102 DLR (4th) 96 at 110, Sup Ct of Canada. Although in practice a two stage inquiry has been followed both in cases of *forum non conveniens* and *forum conveniens*, it has recently been suggested by the Supreme Court that a two stage inquiry is not the correct approach in the latter: see *VTB Capital v Nutritek* [2013] UKSC 5 at [44], [2013] 2 WLR 398; discussed supra, p 372.

[39] The *Spiliada* case, supra, at 474; the *Lubbe Case*, supra, at 1554.

[40] The *Spiliada* case, supra, at 477.

[41] *Hindocha v Gheewala* [2003] UKPC 77 at [26]. But the claimant will have had to show that England was clearly the most appropriate forum in order to obtain permission for service out of the jurisdiction.

[42] This requirement may be considered as ensuring compliance with Article 6 of the European Convention on Human Rights—a stay should not mean that a claimant is denied access to any court. See further Fawcett (2007) 56 ICLQ 1; *Lubbe v Cape plc* [2000] 1 WLR 1545.

[43] It has also been held that there must be real issues to be tried between the parties. If there is no arguable defence, a stay will be refused: *Adria Services YU v Grey Shipping Co Ltd* 30 July 1993, (unreported), Clarke J.

[44] See the approval by Lord Goff of the classic statement of Lord Kinnear in *Sim v Robinow* (1892) 19 R 665. See also *Lubbe v Cape plc* [2000] 1 WLR 1545 at 1565–6 (per Lord Hope, the other Law Lords concurring); *Tehrani v Secretary of State for the Home Department* [2006] UKHL 47, [2007] 1 AC 521. Cf *Petroleo Brasiliero SA v Mellitus Shipping Inc* [2001] EWCA Civ 418 at [35] (per Potter LJ), [2001] 2 Lloyd's Rep 203. For Australia see *Reinsurance Australia Corporation Ltd v HIH Casualty and General Insurance (in Liquidation)* [2003] FCA 56.

[45] [2003] UKPC 77; Merrett [2004] CLJ 309 and (2005) 54 ICLQ 211.

forum is not available (in the relevant sense) unless it is open to the claimant to institute proceedings as of right in that forum.[46] Taken literally this might suggest that the defendant must be present in the forum abroad.[47] But this is not the case. The crucial point is that the foreign court has jurisdiction and the basis on which this is taken should not matter. This is borne out by the fact that a forum can be available abroad solely by virtue of the defendant's undertaking before the judge in England, when he was considering *forum non conveniens*, to submit to the jurisdiction of the foreign court.[48] It seems that, in principle, it is possible to have an implied undertaking to submit.[49] In carrying out this inquiry into availability the court is concerned with evidence as at the date of the defendant's application for a stay.[50] However, in exceptional and extreme cases a stay could be granted on the basis of a change of circumstances between that date and the date of the hearing.[51] The same principles in relation to the time element no doubt apply to all aspects of the *forum non conveniens* inquiry.[52]

Evans LJ, with whom Saville and Morritt LJJ concurred, in *Mohammed v Bank of Kuwait and the Middle East KSC*[53] gave "availability" a more complex and more questionable meaning. They said that this meant "available in practice to this plaintiff to have his dispute resolved", and that the question whether substantial justice is likely to be achieved is relevant to this issue.

> There was evidence in the case showing that the Iraqi plaintiff, who had worked in Kuwait for a Kuwait bank against which he commenced proceedings in England, was unable to visit Kuwait personally and there were perhaps diplomatic and legal restrictions which could affect his ability to have a legal representative of his choice whom he could fully and properly instruct for the purpose of proceedings there.

In the light of this evidence, it was held that Kuwait was not shown by the defendant to be available to the plaintiff in a practical sense as an alternative forum for trial, and the decision of the judge at first instance granting a stay was reversed.

The difficulty with this definition of "availability" is that it requires the court to distinguish between different types of injustice. One type goes to availability of the alternative forum and is considered at the first stage of the *Spiliada* inquiry; consequently the onus is on the defendant to show that there is no such injustice. The other type does not go to availability and is raised at the second stage of the inquiry; consequently the onus is on the claimant to show circumstances by reason of which justice demands that a stay should not be granted. This is not a distinction that it is easy to draw, and merely serves to complicate the law on *forum non conveniens*. In the *Mohammed* case, Evans LJ clearly regarded the evidence mentioned above as going to availability, whereas allegations that the plaintiff would not get a fair trial in Kuwait because of hostility to Iraqis following the Iraqi invasion of Kuwait were not so regarded and were said to be a matter to be raised at the second stage of the inquiry.[54] It would have been best if "availability" had been confined to the issue of whether the alternative forum abroad had jurisdiction to try the

---

[46] *Hindocha v Gheewala*, supra, at [22].

[47] Or has assets in the forum: *Lubbe v Cape plc* [2000] 1 WLR 1545 at 1565–6 (per Lord Hope, who was presumably thinking of when a Scots court has jurisdiction as of right).

[48] The *Lubbe* case, supra, *Hindocha v Gheewala*, supra, at [22]. See similarly *Sharab v Prince Al-Waleed Al-Saud* [2009] EWCA Civ 353, [2009] 2 Lloyd's Rep 160 (a *forum conveniens* case).

[49] *Hindocha v Gheewala*, supra, at [24]–[25].

[50] *Lubbe v Cape plc* [2000] 1 WLR 1545 at 1565–6 (per Lord Hope), 1556 (per Lord Bingham with whom the other Law Lords concurred); *Hindocha v Gheewala* supra, at [22]; *Mohammed v Bank of Kuwait and the Middle East KSC* [1996] 1 WLR 1483, CA. Cf *ISC v Guerin* [1992] 2 Lloyd's Rep 430 at 434.

[51] The *Mohammed* case, supra.

[52] *BMG Trading Ltd v AS McKay* [1998] IL Pr 691 at 694, CA.

[53] [1996] 1 WLR 1483, CA; Briggs (1996) 67 BYBIL 587.

[54] The *Mohammed* case, supra, at 1495.

case on the merits[55] and that substantial justice had been regarded as irrelevant at this stage of the inquiry. Given, though, that this distinction has been drawn, it would be best to confine the idea of injustice that goes to "availability" to the facts of the *Mohammed* case.

It is encouraging to note that a differently constituted Court of Appeal has accepted that there is substance in the criticisms of the *Mohammed* case, and that in a future case in which the onus of proof is vital it might be necessary to consider whether that decision can stand against the *Spiliada* case.[56] Moreover, the House of Lords in a subsequent case[57] regarded injustice that took the form of not being able to try the case at all abroad because financial assistance was not available there, and the nature and complexity of the case required such assistance, as arising at the second stage of the inquiry. There was no suggestion that this went to "availability", although the case would have been a stronger authority if this argument had been raised and rejected. This has been followed by another House of Lords case to the same effect.[58]

Clearly more appropriate   The other available forum must be clearly or distinctly more appropriate than the English forum.[59] Another way of putting it is to say the other available forum must be the "natural forum".[60] The terms "natural forum" and "appropriate forum" have been used synonymously.[61] It is, however, not enough just to show that England is not the natural or appropriate forum for trial. Neither is it enough to establish a mere balance of convenience in favour of the foreign forum.[62] This principle is designed to reflect the fact that, in cases where a stay is sought on the basis of *forum non conveniens*, jurisdiction will have been founded as of right, ie a claim form will have been served within the jurisdiction.[63]

In ascertaining whether there is a clearly more appropriate forum abroad, the search is for the country with which the action has the most real and substantial connection.[64] The court will look for connecting factors "and these will include not only factors affecting convenience or expense (such as availability of witnesses),[65] but also other factors such as the law governing the relevant transaction[66] . . ., and the place where the parties respectively reside or carry on business".[67]

---

[55] Likewise, if the foreign court refuses to exercise its jurisdiction and stays the action the alternative forum abroad is not available. If English proceedings have been stayed on the basis that the foreign court is available, they may in these circumstances be resumed.

[56] *Askin v Absa Bank Ltd* [1999] IL Pr 471 at [29]–[30], CA; Briggs (1999) 70 BYBIL 319.

[57] *Connelly v RTZ Corpn plc* [1998] AC 854, HL; infra, p 401.

[58] The *Lubbe* case, supra.

[59] For examples of where the natural forum was abroad, see *Rockware Glass Ltd v MacShannon* [1978] AC 795; *The Al Battani* [1993] 2 Lloyd's Rep 219; *The Xin Yang* [1996] 2 Lloyd's Rep 217.

[60] Ie the country with which the action has the most real and substantial connection: the *MacShannon* case, supra, at 829. See also *The Abidin Daver* [1984] AC 398 at 415 (Lord Keith); *The Forum Craftsman* [1984] 2 Lloyd's Rep 102 at 108 (Sheen J); affd by the Court of Appeal [1985] 1 Lloyd's Rep 291.

[61] See the *Spiliada* case, supra; *Rockware Glass Ltd v MacShannon* [1978] AC 795 at 812 (per Lord Diplock); see also *Trendtex Trading Corpn v Crédit Suisse* [1980] 3 All ER 721 at 734; *European Asian Bank AG v Punjab and Sind Bank* [1982] 2 Lloyd's Rep 356 at 364.

[62] The *Spiliada* case, supra, at 474; *Banco Atlantico SA v British Bank of the Middle East*, supra, at 508.

[63] See the *Lubbe* case, supra, at 1554. Contrast the approach under *forum conveniens*: see supra, p 365 et seq.

[64] The *Spiliada* case, supra, at 477–8.

[65] For location of documents see *Arab Banking Corpn v First Union National Bank*, 2001 (unreported).

[66] As in the context of *forum conveniens*, the significance of this factor will depend on the complexity and importance of the legal issues in the dispute. See, eg, *The Xin Yang* [1996] 2 Lloyd's Rep 217; *Luiz Vicente Barros Mattos Junior v Macdaniels Ltd* [2005] EWHC 1323 (Ch) at [138]; *Wright v Deccan Chargers Sporting Ventures Ltd* [2011] EWHC 1307 (QB), [2011] IL Pr 37. If there is a dispute as to the applicable law and this cannot be tried as a preliminary issue, this is a neutral factor: *Lubbe v Cape plc* [1999] IL Pr 113 at 126, CA (the first CA case); Briggs (1998) 67 BYBIL 336; affd without discussion of this point [2000] 1 WLR 1545, HL. Cf the treatment of choice of law on the facts of the case in the second Court of Appeal case, [2000] IL Pr 439, Briggs (1999) 68 BYBIL 319, revsd by the House of Lords on the injustice abroad point.

[67] The *Spiliada* case, supra, at 478. For Canada see *Spar Aerospace Ltd v American Mobile Satellite Corpn* (2002) 220 DLR (4th) 54, 80–5, Sup Ct of Canada; *Eastern Power Ltd v Azienda Communale Energia and*

These are the same factors considered when determining the *forum conveniens* for the purposes of service out of the jurisdiction. The weight to be attached to the fact that English law governs the contract or that a foreign law governs has been considered in that context[68] and what is said there need not be repeated here. Likewise, the significance of the fact that a tort was committed in England or was committed abroad has been considered previously.[69] The presumption that the natural forum for trial is where the tort was committed applies equally to cases of *forum non conveniens* as to cases of *forum conveniens*.[70] For defamation cases, however, it should be noted that this is now subject to the modifications or clarifications in section 9 of the Defamation Act 2013.[71]

When it comes to a stay of English proceedings on *forum non conveniens* grounds in a case where the parties have agreed on the exclusive jurisdiction of the English courts,[72] there has been a lack of consistency of approach by the courts. In most cases, it has been accepted that the courts retain their discretion to stay the English proceedings but there is no agreement on whether the normal principles of *forum non conveniens* apply (with the agreement operating as an important factor against the grant of a stay[73]) or whether a special rule should be adopted by analogy with the special rule that (at least arguably) operates in the situation where there is an exclusive jurisdiction clause providing for trial abroad (the court will uphold the agreement, requiring specific performance of the contractual obligation to sue in the chosen forum, unless strong reasons can be shown).[74] The unresolved issue is essentially whether a jurisdiction agreement should be considered as a factor in applying the procedural rules on jurisdiction, or as a matter of substantive contract law. As an example of the latter approach it has been said that, when it comes to showing the strong cause needed for a stay, this must go beyond matters of mere convenience and must enter into the interests of justice itself[75] or refer to some matter that was unforeseeable at the time of entering into the contract.[76]

Ambiente (1999) 178 DLR (4th) 409, Ontario CA; *Markandu v Benaroch* (2004) 242 DLR (4th) 101, Ont CA.

[68] Supra, pp 367–9.

[69] Supra, pp 351–3. For Australia see: *Dow Jones & Co Inc v Gutnick* (2002) 210 CLR 575 (tort committed in Victoria, no stay because Victoria not a clearly inappropriate forum); *Régie National des Usines Renault SA v Zhang* (2002) 210 CLR 491 at 521. For Ontario see *Mutual Life Assurance Co of Canada v Peat Marwick* (1998) 172 DLR (4th) 379, Ont CA.

[70] *Lennon Scottish Daily Record* [2004] EWHC 359 (QB) at [36]–[38]. See also *Reuben v Time Inc* [2003] EWCA Civ 06 at [14].

[71] See supra, pp 353–5.

[72] We are concerned with the situation where Article 25 of the Brussels I Recast (discussed supra, p 229 et seq) does not apply, and neither does the Hague Convention on Choice of Court Agreements 2005 (discussed supra, p 315). Where either does, which will almost always be the case (particularly now that Article 25 of the Brussels I Recast applies regardless of the domicile of the parties), the English courts have no power to stay the English proceedings on *forum non conveniens* grounds (see infra, p 460 et seq). For a case which did not discuss whether Art 25 applied in relation to an English jurisdiction clause see *OT Africa Line Ltd v Magic Sportswear Corpn* [2005] EWCA Civ 710, [2005] 2 Lloyd's Rep 170. For Canadian reaction to an English jurisdiction agreement see *OT Africa Line Ltd v Magic Sportswear Ltd* 2006 FCA 284, [2007] 1 Lloyd's Rep 85.

[73] *The Volvox Hollandia* [1987] 2 Lloyd's Rep 520 at 529, appeal on a separate point allowed [1988] 2 Lloyd's Rep 61, CA; *The Hida Maru* [1981] 2 Lloyd's Rep 510, CA; *Eli Lilly and Co v Novo Nordisk A/S* [2000] IL Pr 73 at 80, CA. See also *Bouygues v Caspian* [1997] IL Pr 472, CA.

[74] *Akai Pty Ltd v People's Insurance Co Ltd* [1998] 1 Lloyd's Rep 90 at 104–5; *UBS AG v Omni Holding AG (In Liquidation)* [2000] 1 WLR 916 at 925; *Import-Export Metro Ltd v Compañia Sud Americana De Vapores SA* [2003] EWHC 11 (Comm), [2003] 1 Lloyd's Rep 405. The special rule for foreign jurisdiction clauses is discussed infra, p 410 et seq.

[75] *Sinochem International Oil (London) Ltd v Mobil Sales and Supply Corpn Ltd (No 2)* [2000] 1 All ER (Comm) 758, 772. For the significance of this factor in cases of *forum conveniens* see supra, pp 372–5.

[76] See the *Import-Export Metro Ltd* case, supra. See the same approach applied in relation to a foreign service of suit clause in *Ace Insurance SA-NV (Formerly Cigna Insurance Co of Europe SA-NV) v Zurich Insurance Co* [2001] EWCA Civ 173 at [62], [2001] 1 Lloyd's Rep 618, CA, infra, p 414.

The disregarding of foreseeable matters assumes that the parties acted freely in adopting the clause.[77] An even more radical suggestion is that, where there is a clause providing for the exclusive jurisdiction of the English courts, the courts have no discretion to stay the English proceedings on the ground of *forum non conveniens*.[78] Where there is a non-exclusive jurisdiction agreement providing for trial in England there is still a discretion to stay the English proceedings but there is again no consistency as to how the agreement is to be factored into the exercise of the discretion. One approach has been to adopt a modified version of the *Spiliada* principles, whereby the parties are precluded from raising factors of appropriateness;[79] unless the factor could not have been foreseen by the defendant when the contract was entered into;[80] the other has been to apply the *Spiliada* principles in the normal way but to treat a non-exclusive jurisdiction clause as a very important factor.[81] Where there is a clause providing for the exclusive jurisdiction of a foreign court, a stay of the English proceedings will ordinarily be granted, not on the ground of *forum non conveniens*,[82] but on the separate ground that the court should uphold the agreement of the parties.[83] Where there is a clause providing for the non-exclusive jurisdiction of a foreign court similar principles have been adopted as in cases where there is a clause providing for the non-exclusive jurisdiction of an English court. Thus one approach has been to apply a modified version of the *Spiliada* principles precluding the consideration of any factors of appropriateness, even seemingly those the parties could not have foreseen at the time the contract was entered into;[84] another approach has been to apply the *Spiliada* principles in the normal way, treating the clause as a very important factor in ascertaining the appropriate forum. Turning to other factors of appropriateness, what has been said earlier about the significance of the fact that a negative declaration is sought[85] and the importance of the fact that all the litigation can be heard together in one state, rather than having to be split between states,[86] is equally applicable in the present context. Where the subject matter of a dispute concerns the internal management of a company, the location of the company is particularly important.[87]

Cases where there is no clearly more appropriate forum abroad In cases where there is no clearly more appropriate forum abroad, ie where either there is no country which is the natural forum or England is the natural forum, the courts will ordinarily refuse a stay of proceedings.[88] Examples of cases where there was no natural forum for trial and a stay was

---

[77] *Import-Export Metro Ltd* case, supra. See also *Mercury v Communication Telesystems* [1999] 2 All ER (Comm) 33.

[78] *Berisford v New Hampshire* [1990] 1 Lloyd's Rep 454, 458 (Hobhouse J—obiter). But cf the approach of Hobhouse LJ in *Bouygues v Caspian*, supra. This is also generally the case where the jurisdiction agreement is covered by the Brussels I Recast (see infra, p 460 et seq) or Hague Convention on Choice of Court Agreements (see supra, p 315).

[79] *British Aerospace plc v Dee Howard Co* [1993] 1 Lloyd's Rep 368.

[80] Ibid; *Mercury v Communication Telesystems* [1999] 2 All ER (Comm) 33; the *Import-Export Metro Ltd* case, supra, at [14]. See also *Sinochem (No 2)* [2000] 1 All ER (Comm) 758 (a case involving an exclusive English jurisdiction clause applying the foreseeability approach).

[81] *Berisford v New Hampshire* [1990] 1 Lloyd's Rep 454 at 463.

[82] Under that doctrine this is a strong indication that the appropriate forum is abroad: *Trendtex Trading Corpn v Crédit Suisse* [1980] 3 All ER 721 at 737 and in the Court of Appeal, at 758, affd by the House of Lords, [1982] AC 679.

[83] Infra, p 410 et seq.

[84] *The Rothnie* [1996] 2 Lloyd's Rep 206.

[85] Supra, pp 375–6.

[86] Supra, pp 366–7.

[87] *Incorporated Broadcasters Ltd v Canwest Global Communications Corpn* (2003) 223 DLR (4th) 627, Ont CA.

[88] *Spiliada Maritime Corpn v Cansulex Ltd* [1987] AC 460 at 478; *Lubbe v Cape plc* [2000] 1 WLR 1545 at 1554. See also *Metal Scrap Trade Corpn v Kate Shipping Co Ltd* [1990] 1 WLR 115 at 133 (per Lord Goff) HL; *The Maciej Rataj* [1991] 2 Lloyd's Rep 458 at 467; *BCCHK v Sonali* [1995] 1 Lloyd's Rep 227; *Dubai*

therefore refused are: where banks were in dispute over payment under a letter of credit;[89] and where there was a collision on the high seas.[90] A stay will likewise be refused in cases where it is possible to identify the natural forum and this is England.[91] In cases where the court has exercised its discretion to allow service out of the jurisdiction under rule 6.36 and Practice Direction 6B of the Civil Procedure Rules (and that exercise of discretion has not subsequently been set aside on application of the defendant), the court has already decided that England is clearly the most appropriate forum for trial.[92] It follows that a stay of proceedings will not usually be granted subsequently on the basis of *forum non conveniens*.[93] In practice, therefore, stays are normally sought in cases where a claim form has been served within the jurisdiction, rather than in cases where a claim form has been served out of the jurisdiction under rule 6.36.[94]

Since the *Spiliada* case, numerous cases have been decided on the basis that there was no clearly more appropriate forum abroad. But what is noticeable about these cases is that in virtually all of them the courts have considered all the circumstances of the case, including considerations going beyond those of appropriateness. This has often been on the basis that the ultimate question is what justice demands and all the factors for and against a stay have to be considered together.[95] As will be seen, in cases where there is a clearly more appropriate forum abroad the courts will necessarily go on to consider the other relevant circumstances in the case.

(ii) The second stage: the requirements of justice

Lord Goff has said that:

> if there is some other available forum which prima facie is clearly more appropriate for the trial
> of the action, it [the court] will ordinarily grant a stay unless there are circumstances by reason
> of which justice requires that a stay should nevertheless not be granted.[96]

Once it has been shown that there is a clearly more appropriate forum for trial abroad the burden of proof shifts to the claimant to justify coming to England.[97] The court is concerned

---

Bank Ltd v Abbas [1998] IL Pr 391; *PTKF Kontinent v VMPTO Progress* 1994 SLT 235; *Bristow Helicopters Ltd v Sikorsky Aircraft Corpn* [2004] EWHC 401 (Comm) at [27], [2004] 2 Lloyd's Rep 150.

[89] *European Asian Bank AG v Punjab and Sind Bank* [1982] 2 Lloyd's Rep 356. This was a pre-*Spiliada* case but one which was used by Lord Goff to illustrate his third principle. See also *Luis Vincente Barros Mattos v Macdaniels Ltd* [2003] EWHC 1173 (Ch).

[90] *Spiliada Maritime Corpn v Cansulex Ltd*, supra, at 477; *The Vishva Abha* [1990] 2 Lloyd's Rep 312 at 314. The position may be the same after a collision in territorial waters, see *The Po* [1990] 1 Lloyd's Rep 418; affd by the Court of Appeal [1991] 2 Lloyd's Rep 206. But cf *The Wellamo* [1980] 2 Lloyd's Rep 229; *The Abidin Daver* [1984] AC 398.

[91] *OTM Ltd v Hydronautics* [1981] 2 Lloyd's Rep 211; *The Hamburg Star* [1994] 1 Lloyd's Rep 399; *Meridien Biao Bank GmbH* [1997] 1 Lloyd's Rep 437, CA; *Zivlin v Baal Taxa* [1998] IL Pr 106; *Schapira v Ahronson* [1998] IL Pr 587, CA. Cf *Pillai v Sarkar* (1994) The Times, 21 July.

[92] Supra, p 365.

[93] A possible exception would be if there were a significant change in circumstances, eg, if the claimant subsequently commenced proceedings in a foreign court.

[94] A defendant who fails to ask for service out of the jurisdiction to be set aside on the basis that England is not the *forum conveniens* can, however, still seek a stay on grounds of *forum non conveniens*: *Hindocha v Gheewala* [2003] UKPC 77 at [26].

[95] See, eg, *Charm Maritime Inc v Minas Xenophon Kyriakou and David John Mathias* [1987] 1 Lloyd's Rep 433 at 447. See also *The Po* [1990] 1 Lloyd's Rep 418 at 424; affd by the Court of Appeal [1991] 2 Lloyd's Rep 206; *Arkwright Mutual Insurance Co v Bryanston Insurance Co Ltd* [1990] 2 Lloyd's Rep 70 at 83; cf *Meadows Indemnity Co Ltd v Insurance Corpn of Ireland Ltd and International Commercial Bank plc* [1989] 1 Lloyd's Rep 181 at 190; affd [1989] 2 Lloyd's Rep 298; *Saab v Saudi Arabian Bank* [1999] 1 WLR 1861, 1882, CA.

[96] *Spiliada Maritime Corpn v Cansulex Ltd*, supra, at 478; the *Lubbe* case, supra, at 1554.

[97] [1987] AC 460 at 476. This has been described as an evidential burden: *Charm Maritime Inc v Minas Xenophon Kyriakou and David John Mathias* [1987] 1 Lloyd's Rep 433 at 448.

with the question whether justice requires that a stay should not be granted.[98] (As in the case of *forum conveniens*, an English court is unlikely to consider whether the interests of justice might require granting a stay, particularly if this would require any critical evaluation of the adequacy of English procedures, although one possible exception is where certain evidence would not be available to the English courts.[99]) This second stage of the inquiry has been considered and further explained by Lord Goff in the House of Lords in *Connelly v RTZ Corpn plc*.[100]

> The plaintiff, who was domiciled in Scotland, worked in Namibia at a uranium mine operated by a Namibian subsidiary of the first defendant, an English company. After being found to be suffering from cancer, the plaintiff commenced proceedings in England against the first defendant and one of its English subsidiaries for negligence. No financial assistance was available to the plaintiff in Namibia, whereas it was available to the plaintiff in England, in the form either of legal aid or a conditional fee agreement. The defendants sought a stay of the English proceedings, which was granted by the judge at first instance. The Court of Appeal lifted the stay.[101] The defendants appealed to the House of Lords.

The House of Lords dismissed the defendants' appeal.[102] It was accepted by the plaintiff that Namibia was the jurisdiction with which the action had the closest connection, with the result that prima facie a stay should be granted.[103] The point at issue in the case was therefore whether a stay should nevertheless be refused because justice so required. Lord Goff, by way of further explanation of his classic statements in the *Spiliada* case, enunciated a principle that "if a clearly more appropriate forum overseas has been identified, generally speaking the plaintiff will have to take that forum as he finds it, even if it is in certain respects less advantageous to him than the English forum".[104] Applying this principle, it was said that as a general rule the court will not refuse to grant a stay simply because the plaintiff has shown that no financial assistance, eg in the form of legal aid, will be available to him in the appropriate forum, whereas such financial assistance will be available to him in England.[105] However, this was an exceptional case since it was clear that the nature and complexity of the case was such that it could not be tried at all without the benefit of financial assistance.[106] Accordingly, substantial justice would not be done in the particular circumstances of the case if the plaintiff had to proceed in the appropriate forum where no financial assistance was available.[107] Likewise, the circumstances in *Lubbe v Cape plc*[108] were special and unusual. If the English proceedings were stayed in favour of the more appropriate forum in South Africa the probability was that the plaintiffs would have no means of obtaining the professional

---

[98] *Spiliada Maritime Corpn v Cansulex Ltd* [1987] AC 460 at 478, HL.

[99] See, eg, *Qioptiq Ltd v Teledyne Scientific & Imaging LLC* [2011] EWHC 229 (Ch).

[100] [1998] AC 854, HL; Briggs (1997) 68 BYBIL 357. See also *Carlson v Rio Tinto plc* [1999] CLC 551.

[101] [1997] IL Pr 643, CA.

[102] The plaintiff also appealed to the House of Lords from a decision of a differently constituted Court of Appeal: [1996] QB 361; English [1996] CLJ 214, dismissing the plaintiff's appeal against the stay. This appeal to the House of Lords was upheld. For comment on both Court of Appeal decisions, see Briggs (1996) 67 BYBIL 587; Peel (1997) 113 LQR 43. The plaintiff's appeal was concerned with the availability of legal aid; the defendant's appeal was concerned with the impact of a conditional fee agreement. The House of Lords held that s 31(1)(b) of the Legal Aid Act 1988 did not preclude the court from taking the availability of legal aid into account in considering a stay.

[103] The *Connelly* case, supra, at 872.

[104] Ibid; *Lubbe v Cape plc*, supra, at 1554.

[105] The *Connelly* case, supra, at 873; *Lubbe v Cape plc*, supra, at 1554.

[106] The *Connelly* case, supra, at 873–4. It might have been different if it had been possible to put on a rudimentary presentation abroad and the plaintiff sought to put on a Rolls-Royce presentation in England, supra, at 874.

[107] Lord Hoffmann dissented on this point.

[108] [2000] 1 WLR 1545, HL; Briggs (2000) 71 BYBIL 435; Muchlinski (2001) 50 ICLQ 1; Peel (2001) 117 LQR 187; Sinclair [2001] LMCLQ 197.

representation and the expert evidence which would be essential if their claims were to be justly decided.[109] This would amount to a denial of justice.

In determining whether justice requires that a stay should not be granted, all the circumstances of the case will be taken into account. The court will consider the fact that a claimant may not obtain justice abroad because, for example, the judiciary is not independent.[110] It has also been held that it is not conducive to justice to require a claimant, who had an arguable claim under what we would regard as the governing law, to litigate abroad in a country which would summarily reject the claimant's action.[111] If the fairness or outcome of the foreign proceedings is unclear, English proceedings may be stayed in the understanding that they can be revived if necessary.[112] Inordinate delay of the order of magnitude of ten years before an action comes to trial abroad has also been held to be a denial of justice;[113] as has a derisory low limit on damages imposed by the foreign court.[114] In another case, doubts were expressed as to whether any foreign judge "could conscientiously resolve with any confidence that he was reaching a correct answer" to a question as to the effect of a contract as a matter of English public policy.[115] Neither is it just to stay proceedings in England when the claimant would be liable to imprisonment if he were to return to the alternative forum abroad.[116] Much more commonly, though, what is considered is whether, by staying the proceedings, the claimant will be deprived of some advantage that he would have obtained from trial in England.

Treatment of the advantage to the claimant   The mere fact that the claimant obtains a legitimate[117] personal[118] or juridical (ie substantive law[119] or procedural) advantage cannot be decisive.[120] The claimant will not ordinarily discharge the burden lying upon him by showing that he will enjoy procedural advantages, or a higher scale of damages or more generous rules of limitation if he sues in England.[121] As has been mentioned, generally

---

[109] The *Lubbe* case, supra, at 1559.

[110] *The Abidin Daver* [1984] AC 398 at 411. See cases cited infra, p 403, n 129. See also *Middle East Banking Co SA v Al-Haddad* (1990) 70 OR (2d) 97 (complete breakdown of the administration of justice because of civil war).

[111] *Banco Atlantico SA v British Bank of the Middle East* [1990] 2 Lloyd's Rep 504 at 509.

[112] See, eg, *Mengiste v Endowment Fund for the Rehabilitation of Tigre* [2013] EWHC 599 (Ch) and [2014] EWHC 4196 (Ch); *Baghlaf v PNSC (No 2)* [2000] 1 Lloyd's Rep 1, CA.

[113] *The Vishva Ajay* [1989] 2 Lloyd's Rep 558 at 560 (delay in India). Cf *Ceskoslovenska Obchodni Banka AS v Nomura International plc* [2003] IL Pr 20—four or even up to six years, delay in Czech Republic; *Crédit Agricole Indosuez v Unicof Ltd* [2004] 1 Lloyd's Rep 196 at 205 (delay in Kenya). It is not clear if delays in India are still such as to amount to a substantial injustice; see *RHSP v EIH* [1999] 2 Lloyd's Rep 249 at 253–4 and the following *forum conveniens* cases: *Konamaneni v Rolls-Royce Industrial Power (India) Ltd* [2002] 1 WLR 1269 at [175]–[177] (evidence of four to five years' or might be up to ten); *Chellaram v Chellaram(No 2)* [2002] EWHC 632 (Ch) at [177], [2002] 3 All ER 17 (evidence of four to five years). For a *forum conveniens* case similar to *The Vishva Ajay* see *Marconi v PT Pan Indonesia Bank Ltd TBK* [2004] EWHC 129 (Comm) at [38], [2004] 1 Lloyd's Rep 594— more than ten years' delay usual in Indonesia; affd [2005] EWCA Civ 422 at [77].

[114] *BMG Trading Ltd v A S McKay* [1998] IL Pr 691, CA; *The Adhiguna Meranti* [1988] 1 Lloyd's Rep 384 at 395–6, Hong Kong Court of Appeal; see also *The Falstria* [1988] 1 Lloyd's Rep 495.

[115] *E I Du Pont de Nemours & Co v Agnew and Kerr* [1987] 2 Lloyd's Rep 585 at 595; see also *Mitsubishi Corpn v Aristidis I Alafouzos* [1988] 1 Lloyd's Rep 191 at 196.

[116] *Purcell v Khayat* (1987) The Times, 23 November.

[117] *Rockware Glass Ltd v MacShannon* [1978] AC 795 at 812. Lord Scarman in *Castanho v Brown and Root (UK) Ltd* [1981] AC 557 at 575 said that time should not be spent in speculating about the meaning of "legitimate advantage".

[118] Ie the claimant is an English resident: *Rockware Glass Ltdv MacShannon* [1978] AC 795 at 819.

[119] *The Atlantic Star* [1974] AC 436 at 468 (per Lord Wilberforce); *Power Curber International Ltd v National Bank of Kuwait SAK* [1981] 1 WLR 1233.

[120] *Spiliada Maritime Corpn v Cansulex Ltd* [1987] AC 460 at 482. See also *De Dampierre v De Dampierre* [1988] AC 92 at 109–10.

[121] *Lubbe v Cape plc* [2000] 1 WLR 1545, at 1554 (per Lord Bingham with whom the other Law lords concurred), HL.

speaking the claimant will have to take the clearly more appropriate forum overseas as he finds it, even if it is in certain respects less advantageous to him than the English forum.[122]

Comparing the quality of justice The House of Lords has held that the courts should not engage in the invidious task of comparing the quality of justice obtained under the English common law system of procedure with that obtained under a civil law system.[123] A differently constituted House of Lords has held that the English courts should be careful to reject a procedural comparison between England and South Africa in relation to the handling of group actions.[124] The fact that trial in England would take place before the Commercial Court or the Admiralty Court, with their great experience and international standing, should no longer be taken into account as an advantage to the claimant.[125] When it comes to other forms of procedural advantage, the effect of this prohibition on making comparisons between different legal systems is less clear. The House of Lords in *Spiliada Maritime Corpn v Cansulex Ltd* was prepared to regard a more complete procedure for discovery (disclosure) as an advantage to the plaintiff,[126] along with other juridical advantages, but was not prepared to give decisive weight to such advantages when operating the discretion.[127] Certainly, when faced with *undisputed evidence* of a specific substantial procedural advantage to the claimant of trial in England, the courts have been willing to take this into account.[128] Similarly if there is positive and cogent evidence that the claimant, if forced to litigate abroad, would not obtain justice, eg because the judiciary is not independent, then this should be considered.[129] Inevitably whenever there is held to be injustice abroad the English court is making a comparison between the quality of justice there and in England, where there is no such injustice. English courts are concerned that a minimum standard of justice is available in the alternative forum and the Court of Appeal has warned that "the

---

[122] *Connelly v RTZ Corpn plc* [1998] AC 854, at 872, HL; *Lubbe v Cape plc* [2000] 1 WLR 1545, at 1554, HL.

[123] *Amin Rasheed Shipping Corpn v Kuwait Insurance Co* [1984] AC 50 at 67; *The Abidin Daver* [1984] AC 398 at 410. See also *Aratra Potato Co Ltd v Egyptian Navigation Co, The El Amria* [1981] 2 Lloyd's Rep 119 at 127, CA. See *BCCHK v Sonali* [1995] 1 Lloyd's Rep 227; *RHSP v EIH* [1999] 2 Lloyd's Rep 249 at 254.

[124] *Lubbe v Cape plc* [2000] 1 WLR 1545 at 1559 (per Lord Bingham with whom the other Law Lords concurred).

[125] *The Abidin Daver* [1984] AC 398 at 424–5; *Hawke Bay Shipping Co Ltd v The First National Bank of Chicago, The Efthimis* [1986] 1 Lloyd's Rep 244 at 260; *Ceskoslovenska Obchodni Banka AS v Nomura International plc* [2003] IL Pr 20. But see *Islamic Arab Insurance Co v Saudi Egyptian American Reinsurance Co* [1987] 1 Lloyd's Rep 315 at 319, 320; Slater (1988) 104 LQR 554.

[126] *Bank of Tokyo Ltd v Karoon* [1987] AC 45 n at 62–3 (per Goff LJ), CA. See also *Trendtex Trading Corpn v Crédit Suisse* [1980] 3 All ER 721 at 737—decided before the House of Lords cases forbidding the making of comparisons; *Metall Und Rohstoff AG v ACLI Metals (London) Ltd* [1984] 1 Lloyd's Rep 598—a case on restraining foreign proceedings. Cf *The Traugutt* [1985] 1 Lloyd's Rep 76 at 79.

[127] [1987] AC 460 at 482–3. See also *Ceskoslovenska Obchodni Banka AS v Nomura International plc* [2003] IL Pr 20 at [17].

[128] *The El Amria* [1981] 2 Lloyd's Rep 119 at 127; *The Jalakrishna* [1983] 2 Lloyd's Rep 628 at 630–1; *The Po* [1991] 2 Lloyd's Rep 206 at 213.

[129] *The Abidin Daver* [1984] AC 398 at 411; *Pacific International Sports Clubs Limited v Soccer Marketing International Ltd* [2010] EWCA Civ 753. See similarly the *forum conveniens* case law, supra, p 372. See also *Ziraat Muduroglu Ltd v TCBankasi* [1986] QB 1225; *Aldington Shipping Ltd v Bradstock Shipping Corpn and Mabanaft GmbH, The Waylink and Brady Maira* [1988] 1 Lloyd's Rep 475 at 482, Gibraltar Court of Appeal; *Crédit Agricole Indosuez v Unicof Ltd* [2004] 1 Lloyd's Rep 196 at 205—replacement of judges in Kenya; *Limit (No 3) Ltd v PDV Insurance Co* [2005] EWCA Civ 383 at [63]–[66]; *Al-Koronky v Time Life Entertainment Group Ltd* [2006] EWCA Civ 1123. But cf *Jayaretnam v Mahmood* (1992) Times, 21 May; *Skrine and Co (A Firm) v Euromoney Publications plc* (2000) Times, November 10. For Australia and Canada see *JLM v Director General, NSW Dept of Community Services* (2001) 180 ALR 402—acceptance that judges corrupt in Mexico seemingly without evidence, and *Pei v Bank Bumiputra Malaysia Bd* (1998) 41 OR (3d) 39, Ont Court (Gen Div). But compare *Westec Aerospace Inc v Raytheon Aircraft Co* (1999) 173 DLR (4th) 498, British Columbia Court of Appeal—cogent evidence needed.

court must not be too unworldly in its approach" and that "there are other parts of the world where things are badly wrong".[130] The courts are, however, not going to be easily convinced of the existence of such injustice. Thus the courts could not find any justification for holding that Kuwaiti judges would not have acted fairly if an Iraqi citizen appeared as plaintiff before them, despite the earlier Iraqi invasion and Gulf War.[131] This difficulty in convincing the court is particularly marked when it is alleged that injustice arises in a country which is one with which the United Kingdom has close ties, such as a fellow European Union Member State.[132] So far the discussion has been about a comparison of procedural matters; but neither will the English courts decide whether the substantive law of England is better than that of a foreign country.[133]

The weight to be attached to the advantage to the claimant   At one time great weight was attached to this factor, and if the claimant obtained a substantial advantage from trial in England the courts were unlikely to grant a stay of the English proceedings. The House of Lords in the *Spiliada* case sought to reduce the weight given to the advantage to the claimant when exercising the discretion to stay. Hence the principle that the mere fact that the claimant has a legitimate personal or juridical advantage in proceedings in England cannot be decisive.[134] Lord Goff gave an example:[135] an English court would not, in ordinary circumstances, hesitate to stay English proceedings even though the plaintiff would be deprived of a higher award of damages available here. The same example was given by Lord Goff in the *Connelly* case[136] when he enunciated the general principle that, normally speaking, the claimant will have to take the clearly more appropriate forum overseas as he finds it, even if it is in certain respects less advantageous to him than the English forum. The claimant may also have to do without the more generous English system of discovery (disclosure) of documents,[137] and accept the foreign forum's system of court procedure,[138] including rules of evidence. Trial abroad does not amount to an injustice.[139] The claimant will also normally have to accept the fact that financial assistance, eg in the form of legal aid, is not available abroad.[140] Neither can the claimant justify trial in England on the basis that there is a higher limit of liability here than abroad.[141] There was no injustice in trial abroad in such a case. Likewise there has been held to be no injustice in denying the claimant the advantage sought, if the action against the defendant was not stayed, of being able to join further defendants (the case against whom was

---

[130] *Muduroglu Ltd v TC Ziraat Bankasi* [1986] QB 1225 at 1248.

[131] *Mohammed v Bank of Kuwait and the Middle East KSC* [1996] 1 WLR 1483 at 1496, CA. See also *Cortese v Nowsco Well Service Ltd* [2001] IL Pr 196, CA of Alberta—attitude of Alberta court towards prosecution in Italy.

[132] *Dubai Electricity Co v Islamic Republic of Iran Shipping Lines, The Iran Vojdan* [1984] 2 Lloyd's Rep 380 at 388.

[133] *Herceg Novi v Ming Galaxy* [1998] 4 All ER 238 at 247, CA (leaving open, however, the possibility that a denial of justice might arise if foreign law violated an accepted international standard).

[134] Cf in Canada *Van Dooselaere v Holt Cargo Systems Inc* [1999] IL Pr 634, Canadian Fed CA.

[135] The *Spiliada* case, supra, at 482. See *RHSP v EIH* [1999] 2 Lloyd's Rep 249 at 254.

[136] [1998] AC 854 at 872, HL; the *Lubbe* case, supra, at 1554.

[137] The *Connelly* case, supra, at 872; *The Xin Yang* [1996] 2 Lloyd's Rep 217 at 224, CA; *Ceskoslovenska Obchodni Banka AS v Nomura International Plc* [2003] IL Pr 20 at [17]. See also *Lubbe* case, supra, at 1554. For Ontario see *Ash v Corpn of Lloyd's* [1993] IL Pr 330, Ont CA.

[138] See *Westec Aerospace Inc v Raytheon Aircraft Co* (1999) 173 DLR (4th) 498 at 514, British Columbia CA.

[139] The *Ceskoslovenska Obchodni Banka AS* case, supra.

[140] The *Connelly* case, supra, at 873.

[141] *Herceg Novi v Ming Galaxy* [1998] 4 All ER 238, CA; Briggs (1998) 69 BYBIL 340; disapproving of *Caltex v BP* [1996] 1 Lloyd's Rep 286, *Caspian Basin v Bouygous (No 4)* [1997] 2 Lloyd's Rep 507 at 530, appeal dismissed [1998] 2 Lloyd's Rep 461, CA. Cf *The Kapitan Shvetsov* [1998] 1 Lloyd's Rep 199, HK CA.

very weak) who were out of the jurisdiction using the multi-defendant ground under what is now rule 6.36 and Practice Direction 6B of the Civil Procedure Rules.[142] Neither, standing on its own, was there any injustice in trial in South Africa from the lack of established procedures for handling group actions.[143] Instead this involved the kind of procedural comparison which the courts should be careful to avoid. There are suggestions from Lord Goff that the attitude towards the advantage to the claimant may be different where jurisdiction has been founded on an exorbitant basis of jurisdiction such as the transient presence of the defendant in the forum.[144] In such a case, the court may be prepared to help the claimant by refusing a stay to enable him to keep the benefit of an advantage available to him in this country.

Nonetheless, Lord Goff was concerned to pay regard to the interests of all the parties and of the ends of justice. All the circumstances of the case have to be considered. Circumstances can arise which lead to a different conclusion and to the refusal of the grant of a stay. This is graphically illustrated by the *Connelly* case, where it will be recalled that substantial justice would not be done in the particular circumstances of the case if the plaintiff had to proceed in the appropriate forum abroad where no financial assistance was available, the nature and complexity of the case being such that it could not be tried at all without the benefit of financial assistance. Lord Goff also said in the *Spiliada* case that, in the situation where the claimant is time-barred from proceeding abroad but comes within the English limitation period, it would not be just to deprive him of the benefit of trial in England if he acted reasonably in commencing proceedings here and did not act unreasonably in failing to commence proceedings in the foreign jurisdiction.[145] Seemingly, if the claimant obtains an advantage from trial in England, which does not involve a corresponding disadvantage to the defendant (eg there is a similar action before the English courts involving the same defendant, expert witnesses, lawyers and insurers), there may be injustice to the claimant in depriving him of this advantage by staying the English action.[146] The fact that an English court can award costs to a successful litigant can be an important advantage and one that operates for the benefit of both parties.[147] An advantage to the claimant can include matters relevant to the aftermath of the trial such as the ease of enforcement of an English judgment elsewhere in Europe.[148]

The concern to reduce the weight to be attached to the advantage to the claimant is a development to be welcomed. Although there has been considerable judicial condemnation of the practice of forum shopping,[149] it appears in the past that the more the claimant had to gain

---

[142] *Haji-Ioannou v Frangos* [1999] 2 Lloyd's Rep 337 at 360–1, CA. Even if there was jurisdiction against the first defendant, service out against the further defendants would not have been permitted. Cf *Charm Maritime Inc v Minas Xenophon Kyriakou and David John Mathias* [1987] 1 Lloyd's Rep 433.

[143] The *Lubbe* case, supra, at 1559.

[144] The *Connelly* case, supra, at 873.

[145] The *Spiliada* case, at 483–4; the *Lubbe* case, supra, at 1554. See also *Metall Und Rohstoff AG v Donaldson Lufkin & Jenrette Inc* [1990] 1 QB 391 at 486–8; overruled on a different point in *Lonrho plc v Fayad* [1992] 1 AC 448, HL; *BMG Trading Ltd v A S McKay* [1998] IL Pr 691 at 700; *Baghlaf v PNSC* [1998] 2 Lloyd's Rep 229, CA; *Baghlaf v PNSC (No 2)* [2000] 1 Lloyd's Rep 1, CA; *Goliath Portland Cement Co Ltd v Bengtell* (1994) 33 NSWLR 414, CA. See also, infra, pp 411–12.

[146] The *Spiliada* case, supra, at 485–6; see also supra, p 379.

[147] *The Vishva Ajay* [1989] 2 Lloyd's Rep 558; *The Al Battani* [1993] 2 Lloyd's Rep 219; *Roneleigh Ltd v MII Exports Inc*[1989] 1 WLR 619; see also *International Group Ltd and Trans-World (Steel) Ltd v Worstade Trading Ltd* [1998] IL Pr 765, Irish Supreme Court—availability of urgent interlocutory relief; cf *The Varna (No 2)* [1994] 2 Lloyd's Rep 41 at 48; *The Polessk* [1996] 2 Lloyd's Rep 40; *RHSP v EIH* [1999] 2 Lloyd's Rep 249 at 254.

[148] *International Credit and Investment Co (Overseas) Ltd v Shaikh Kamal Adham* [1999] IL Pr 302, CA. See also *Dubai Bank Ltd v Abbas* [1998] IL Pr 391 at 404; *Inter-Tel Inc v Ocis Plc* [2004] EWHC 2269 (QB).

[149] *Chaplin v Boys* [1971] AC 356 at 406, 380, 383; *The Atlantic Star* [1974] AC 436 at 454; see Fawcett (1984) 35 NILQ 141; Schuz (1986) 35 ICLQ 374; Bell (1995) 69 ALJ 124. For robust defence of forum

from this practice the more likely he was to be allowed to continue his action in England.[150] The emphasis in the House of Lords is now very much on chauvinism being replaced by judicial comity.[151] However, the extent to which this new spirit has filtered down to lower courts is questionable. In many cases the courts have concluded that the interests of justice demand that a stay be refused, even though the clearly most appropriate forum is abroad. As has been seen, there are numerous recent examples of cases where English courts have held that there would be positive injustice in trial abroad or an important advantage to the claimant in trial in England.

(c) Public interest factors[152]

In *Lubbe v Cape plc*, the Court of Appeal held that public interest considerations supported trial in South Africa.[153] This referred to South Africa's interest in trying cases of personal injury following mining operations in South Africa which affected persons employed and resident there. The public interest was not directly spelt out but seemingly could lie in the fact that, for example, questions could be raised as to whether local regulations were ignored and whether these were stringent enough.[154] It was an opportunity for a developing country to pass judgment on behalf of its own people.[155] Although this was not mentioned, England could have been said to have a public interest in not trying the case in that there were at least three thousand foreign plaintiffs who would be legally aided, which could have had implications for the legal aid fund. However, this approach was disapproved by the House of Lords.[156] Lord Hope said that the basic principle on which the doctrine of *forum non conveniens* is exercised, which looks to the interests of the parties and the ends of justice, left no room for consideration of public interest or public policy which cannot be related to the private interests of the parties or the ends of justice.[157] This means that where the plea of *forum non conveniens* has failed (ie it cannot be shown that there is some other available forum in which the case may be tried more suitably for the interests of all the parties and the ends of justice) trial must take place in England however desirable on grounds of public interest or public policy that the litigation should be tried abroad. Conversely, there is a public interest in favour of trial in England in that when foreigners litigate in England, this forms a valuable invisible export[158] and reflects and confirms the reputation of the English legal system. Nonetheless, where the plea of *forum non conveniens* is successful a stay ought to be granted however desirable it may be on grounds of public interest or public policy that the action should be tried here.[159] Lord Hope explained that not only does the basic principle not allow for consideration of public interest factors but

---

shopping, see Slater (1988) 104 LQR 554; Juenger (1994) 16 Sydney LR 5, the reply by Opeskin at 14 and the rejoinder by Juenger at 28.

[150] Cf Goff LJ in *Bank of Tokyo Ltd v Karoon* [1987] AC 45 at 62–3, CA.

[151] See *The Abidin Daver* [1984] AC 398 at 411 (per Lord Diplock). See also *Owens Bank Ltd v Bracco* [1991] 4 All ER 833 at 858, CA in relation to litigation within the European Community in cases outside the Brussels Convention.

[152] See Morse (2002) 37 Texas Int LJ 541.

[153] [2000] 1 Lloyd's Rep 139, 161–2, (per Pill LJ, Aldous and Tuckey LJJ concurring), CA. This was the second Court of Appeal case. The first is reported at [1999] IL Pr 113, CA.

[154] This point was made in *Re Union Carbide Corpn Gas Plant Disaster at Bhopal, India* 634 F Supp 842 (SDNY 1986), which was quoted with approval at 161–2.

[155] *Re Union Carbide Corpn*, supra.

[156] [2000] 1 WLR 1545.

[157] Ibid at 1566; see also ibid at 1561 (per Lord Bingham with whom the other Law Lords concurred). But see CPR, r 1.1 (overriding objective), particularly r 1.1(2)(e).

[158] Kerr (1978) 41 MLR 1; Lord Devlin, *Samples of Lawmaking* (1962), pp 29–30. See also *Camilla Cotton Oil Co v Granadex SA* [1976] 2 Lloyd's Rep 10 at 14.

[159] The *Lubbe* case, op cit, at 1567 (per Lord Hope), 1561 (per Lord Bingham with whom the other Law Lords concurred).

also the English courts are not equipped to conduct the sort of enquiry that would be needed if such factors were to be considered.[160] This is an important point of contrast with the way in which *forum non conveniens* has developed in the United States.[161]

(ii) Multiplicity of proceedings

If litigation involving the same parties and the same issues is continuing simultaneously in two different countries, this is referred to as a case of *lis alibi pendens*, often abbreviated to *lis pendens*.[162] In such cases the issue facing the English court is not simply that of deciding to which of the alternative fora the claimant should have to go to bring his action. Instead, the choice is between, on the one hand, trial in England *plus* trial abroad[163] (if a stay is refused) and, on the other hand, trial abroad (if a stay is granted). It is highly undesirable to have concurrent actions in England and abroad: this involves more expense and inconvenience to the parties than if the trial were held in merely one country; it can also lead to two conflicting judgments, with an unseemly race by the parties to be the first to obtain a judgment and to subsequent problems of estoppel.[164] The objection to concurrent proceedings has been said to be even stronger if this involves in one of the two states proceedings for a negative declaration (a declaration that a person is not liable in an existing action).[165] But this was before the adoption by the courts of a more relaxed attitude towards the granting of such declarations.[166] If it is in the interest of justice, such a declaration may still be granted.[167] If there is a multiplicity of proceedings in England and abroad, but the parties or the issues are different in each of the actions, this is technically not a case of *lis alibi pendens*; nonetheless, it is undesirable to have this multiplicity of proceedings and some, if not all, of the objections inherent in cases of *lis alibi pendens* will still be applicable.[168]

In cases where the concurrent proceedings are in the United Kingdom and in another European Union Member State or in an EFTA State, the *lis alibi pendens* provision contained in Article 29[169] of the Brussels I Recast (or Article 21 of the Brussels Convention or Article 27 of the Lugano Convention) may be applicable. However, what we are concerned with in this section are cases which do not fall within these Articles, eg where there are concurrent proceedings in England and New York.

The common law has no separate *lis alibi pendens* rule.[170] Instead, the fact that the refusal of a stay of English proceedings will lead to a multiplicity of proceedings in England and

---

[160] Ibid, at 1567.

[161] See further *Gulf Oil Corpn v Gilbert* 330 US 501 (1947); *Piper Aircraft Co v Reyno* 454 US 235 (1981).

[162] See generally McLachlan, *Lis Pendens in International Litigation* (2009). On the significance of a multiplicity of proceedings in *forum conveniens* cases see supra, pp 366–7.

[163] This is of course subject to the possibility that the foreign court may stay its proceedings, or that they may be withdrawn pursuant to an anti-suit injunction against the foreign claimant: see infra, p 422 et seq.

[164] *The Abidin Daver* [1984] AC 398 at 412 (per Lord Diplock), 423–4 (per Lord Brandon). See also *The Messiniaki Tolmi* [1983] 1 Lloyd's Rep 666 at 672. On estoppel see infra, p 556 et seq.

[165] *First National Bank of Boston v Union Bank of Switzerland* [1990] 1 Lloyd's Rep 32 at 38–9. See also *Saipem Spa v Dredging V02 BV and Geosite Surveys Ltd, The Volvox Hollandia* [1988] 2 Lloyd's Rep 361 at 371, CA; *Sohio Supply Co v Gatoil (USA) Inc* [1989] 1 Lloyd's Rep 588 at 593.

[166] See supra, pp 375–6.

[167] *Smyth v Behbehani* [1999] IL Pr 584, CA—in the interest of justice that proceedings in relation to comparable transactions should all be tried at one and the same time.

[168] See *Metall Und Rohstoff AG v ACLI Metals (London) Ltd* [1984] 1 Lloyd's Rep 598, CA; *Hawke Bay Shipping Co Ltd v The First National Bank of Chicago, The Efthimis* [1986] 1 Lloyd's Rep 244, CA; *New Hampshire Insurance Co v Aerospace Finance Ltd* [1998] 2 Lloyd's Rep 539. But cf *Eli Lilly and Co v Novo NordiskA/S* [2000] IL Pr 73, 80, CA.

[169] Infra, p 443 et seq. Cf the position in Australia, on which see *Rocklea Spinning Mills Pty Ltd v Consolidated Trading Corpn* [1995] 2 VR 181.

[170] *Canada Trust Co v Stolzenberg (No 2)* [2002] 1 AC 1 at [20] (per Lord Hoffmann).

abroad is an important additional element to be taken into account under the doctrine of *forum non conveniens*. Lord Goff in the *Spiliada* case did not explain how the new restated principles in relation to *forum non conveniens* would operate in cases involving a multiplicity of proceedings. However, in *De Dampierre v De Dampierre*[171] he said that the "same principle is applicable whether or not there are other relevant proceedings already pending in the alternative forum".[172] The defendant[173] has to show that there is a clearly more appropriate forum abroad, ie *the* natural forum must be abroad.[174] This will be determined in the light of the fact that the case involves a multiplicity of proceedings.

The modern approach towards a multiplicity of proceedings can be illustrated by looking at *Cleveland Museum of Art v Capricorn Art International SA*,[175] where there were concurrent proceedings in Ohio and England between the same parties involving the same issues. Hirst J applied the basic principle used in the *Spiliada* case. He examined the factors in favour of trial in Ohio and England, took into account the fact that the action was now ready for trial in Ohio and the undesirable consequences of concurrent litigation, both in terms of expense and inconvenience to the parties and in terms of the possibility of conflicting judgments, and concluded that the Ohio court was clearly the more appropriate forum for trial of the action, in the sense of being the one in which the case may be tried more suitably for the interests of all the parties and the ends of justice. A stay of the English proceedings was accordingly granted.

In contrast to this, the operation of the same approach by the Court of Appeal led to the refusal of a stay, despite the undesirability of having concurrent proceedings, in a case where the contract was governed by English law.[176] Questions of English public policy would arise and doubts were expressed as to whether any foreign court could fairly resolve them. Similarly, an English choice of jurisdiction clause may outweigh the multiplicity of proceedings factor, with the result that a stay will be refused.[177] A stay will also be refused if there is no country which is a natural forum for trial, even if this may mean a multiplicity of proceedings. Thus a stay was refused in a case where a collision occurred in international waters between two ships of different nationalities.[178]

---

[171] [1988] AC 92. For Canada see: *472900 BC Ltd v Thrifty Canada Ltd* (1999) 168 DLR (4th) 602, British Columbia CA; *Westec Aerospace Inc v Raytheon Aircraft* Co (1999) 173 DLR (4th) 498, British Columbia CA; appeal dismissed (2001) 197 DLR (4th) 211, Sup Ct of Canada; *Western Union Insurance Co v Re-Con Building Products Inc* (2001) 205 DLR (4th) 184, British Columbia CA; *Blinds To Go Inc v Harvard Private Capital Holdings Inc* (2003) 232 DLR (4th) 340, New Brunswick CA.

[172] *De Dampierre v De Dampierre*, supra, at 108. See also *The Varna (No 2)* [1994] 2 Lloyd's Rep 41; *Niche Products Ltd v MacDermid Offshore Solutions LLC* [2013] EWHC 1493 (Ch), [2014] FSR 21. Cf the earlier position set out in *The Abidin Daver* [1984] AC 398. See *Galaxy Special Maritime Enterprise v Prima Ceylon Ltd (The Olympic Galaxy)* [2006] EWCA Civ 528 at [25]–[26], [2006] 2 Lloyd's Rep 27, which regards *The Abidin Daver* as being largely untouched. This must be regarded as being wrong.

[173] For cases involving the claimant seeking a stay of English proceedings, see *A-G v Arthur Andersen & Co (United Kingdom)* [1989] ECC 224; *Australian Commercial Research and Development Ltd v ANZ McCaughan Merchant Bank Ltd* [1989] 3 All ER 65; and see *Doe v Armour Pharmaceutical Co Inc* [1995] IL Pr 148, Irish SC.

[174] Cf Lord Diplock's formulation in the earlier case of *The Abidin Daver* [1984] AC 398. It is inappropriate now to use Lord Diplock's formulation, see *Arkwright Mutual Insurance Co v Bryanston Insurance Co Ltd* [1990] 2 QB 649 at 665; *Niche Products Ltd v MacDermid Offshore Solutions LLC* [2013] EWHC 1493 (Ch), [2014] FSR 21.

[175] [1990] 2 Lloyd's Rep 166.

[176] *E I Du Pont de Nemours & Co v Agnew and Kerr* [1987] 2 Lloyd's Rep 585. See also *Hawke Bay Shipping Co Ltd v The First National Bank of Chicago, The Efthimis* [1986] 1 Lloyd's Rep 244; *Dellar v Zivy* [2007] EWHC 2266 (Ch) at [45]–[48], [2007] IL Pr 60, concerning a will to be interpreted according to English law.

[177] *Akai Pty Ltd v People's Insurance Co Ltd* [1998] 1 Lloyd's Rep 90 at 107.

[178] *The Coral Isis* [1986] 1 Lloyd's Rep 413.

The weight to be attached to the factor of multiplicity of proceedings will depend on the circumstances of the case. It is not a decisive factor in the sense of automatically making a foreign forum clearly more appropriate and shifting the burden of proof to the claimant to justify trial in England.[179] It does not matter, in principle, whether the action was commenced first in England or abroad; this is merely an accident of timing.[180] But the date when trial would be held in each country has been taken into account.[181] It is also seemingly relevant whether it is a case of the same claimant starting proceedings in two different jurisdictions or a case where the claimant in one jurisdiction is the defendant in another jurisdiction and vice versa. In the former case the claimant will generally be forced to elect the country in which he wants trial.[182] If he elects for trial abroad the court will then dismiss the English proceedings. It is also relevant to look at the motivation behind the commencement of the foreign proceedings and the progress made in them. If an action is commenced abroad not because of a genuine desire for trial in that country but merely to avoid being time-barred and to demonstrate the possibility of trial in that country, the factor of multiplicity of proceedings will be given no weight.[183] Likewise, if no substantial progress has been made in the foreign proceedings, eg there has been no discovery,[184] or the foreign proceedings are unlikely to survive a jurisdictional challenge in that country,[185] the multiplicity of proceedings will be given little weight. On the other hand, if genuine proceedings have developed abroad to the stage where they have some impact upon the dispute, especially if this is likely to be of continuing effect, then this may be relevant.[186] In one case,[187] the fact that the dispute might come to trial abroad during the year made the multiplicity of proceedings a relevant factor. In *The Abidin Daver* one of the factors pointing towards Turkey as the natural forum for trial was the fact that proceedings were promptly started there soon after a collision in Turkish waters between a Cuban-owned vessel and a Turkish-owned vessel, and were proceeding with dispatch; indeed, the Turkish court had appointed a surveyor who had already interviewed relevant witnesses and prepared a report for the court.[188]

---

[179] *Meadows Indemnity Co Ltd v Insurance Corpn of Ireland Ltd and International Commercial Bank plc* [1989] 1 Lloyd's Rep 181 at 189; affd [1989] 2 Lloyd's Rep 298, CA.

[180] *The Coral Isis* [1986] 1 Lloyd's Rep 413; *E I Du Pont de Nemours & Co v Agnew and Kerr* [1987] 2 Lloyd's Rep 585 at 593; *Mitchell v Mitchell* 1993 SLT 123. Cf Art 29 of the Brussels I Recast, infra, p 443 et seq. See also *McConnell Dowell Constructors Ltd v Lloyd's Syndicate 396* [1988] 2 NZLR 257 at 273; *Western Union Insurance Co v Re-Con Building Products Inc* (2001) 205 DLR (4th) 184, British Columbia Court of Appeal; appeal dismissed (2001) 197 DLR (4th) 211, Sup Ct of Canada; *Ingenium Technologies Corp v McGraw-Hill Companies, Inc* (2005) 255 DLR (4th) 499, British Columbia CA.

[181] *Eli Lilly and Co v Novo Nordisk A/S* [2000] IL Pr 73, 80, CA; *XN Corpn Ltd v Point of Sale Ltd* [2001] IL Pr 35 (expedited trial in England).

[182] See *Australian Commercial Research and Development Ltd v ANZ McCaughan Merchant Bank Ltd* [1989] 3 All ER 65 at 70; *Ledra Fisheries Ltd v Turner* [2003] EWHC 1049 (Ch); *Khaled Salam Racy v Salah Jacques Hawila* [2004] EWCA Civ 209; *A-G v Arthur Andersen & Co* [1989] ECC 224. See also *Manufacturers Life Insurance Co v Guarantee Co of North America* (1988) 62 OR (2d) 147. Cf *Merrill Lynch v RAFFA* [2001] IL Pr 31; *Insurance Co of the State of Pennsylvania v Equitas Insurance Ltd* [2013] EWHC 3713 (Comm), [2014] Lloyd's Rep IR 195. See also Smart [1990] LMCLQ 326.

[183] *De Dampierre v De Dampierre*, supra, at 108. See also *Irish Shipping Ltd v Commercial Union Assurance Co plc* [1991] 2 QB 206 at 232, 245.

[184] *Arkwright Mutual Insurance Co v Bryanston Insurance Co Ltd* [1990] 2 Lloyd's Rep 70 at 80.

[185] *Meridien Biao GmbH v Bank of New York* [1997] 1 Lloyd's Rep 437 at 445, where Millett LJ did not dissent from the view of the trial judge on this point, CA.

[186] *De Dampierre v De Dampierre*, supra. See also *The Coral Isis*, supra; *Henry v Henry* (1995) 185 CLR 571, High Court of Australia; *Mackay Refined Sugars (NZ) Ltd v New Zealand Sugar Co Ltd* [1997] 3 NZLR 476.

[187] *Meadows Indemnity Co Ltd v Insurance Corpn of Ireland Ltd and International Commercial Bank plc* [1989] 1 Lloyd's Rep 181 at 189; affd [1989] 2 Lloyd's Rep 298, CA.

[188] [1984] AC 398 at 410, 421.

(b) Foreign jurisdiction clauses[189]

If parties have agreed on trial in a European Union or EFTA State, Article 25 of the Brussels I Recast, Article 17 of the Brussels Convention or Article 23 of the Lugano Convention is likely to be applicable,[190] according to which the European Union or EFTA State on which jurisdiction has been conferred by the parties is given exclusive jurisdiction. Similarly, if the parties have agreed to trial in a Contracting State to the Hague Convention on Choice of Court Agreements 2005, and at least one party is resident in a Contracting State which is not a European Union Member State, the Hague Convention may be applicable and mandate that exclusive jurisdiction be given to the chosen court.[191] What we are concerned with here, however, are cases where Article 25 of the Brussels I Recast and the Hague Convention are not applicable, eg where the parties have agreed on trial in New York. At present, we are also focused only on cases in which the jurisdiction of the English courts is based on the common law rules—the question of stays under the Brussels I Recast is examined later in this chapter.[192]

(i) *The exercise of the discretion to stay*[193]

As has been seen,[194] an English court will be most reluctant to permit service out of the jurisdiction in the face of an agreement by the parties to submit their disputes to the exclusive jurisdiction of a foreign court. In the situation where the English court has undoubted jurisdiction over actions properly instituted in England, there is an inherent discretion in the court to stay English proceedings brought in breach of an express foreign jurisdiction clause. This differs from the previous situation in so far as there is a heavier burden in the service out of the jurisdiction cases on the claimant to persuade the court not to give effect to the express clause.[195] The question may arise whether the dispute that has arisen falls within the scope of an exclusive jurisdiction clause. English courts give such clauses, as between the parties to them, a generous interpretation.[196] Lord Bingham in the House of Lords in *Donohue v Armco Inc*[197] summarised the principles that apply when exercising the discretion to stay English proceedings brought in breach of a foreign exclusive jurisdiction clause.[198] The

---

[189] Pryles (1976) 25 ICLQ 543; Kahn-Freund (1977) 26 ICLQ 825; Robertson (1982) 20 Alberta LR 296; Briggs [1984] LMCLQ 227 at 241–8; Barma and Elvin (1985) 101 LQR 48 at 65–7; Peel [1998] LMCLQ 182; Fawcett [2001] LMCLQ 234.

[190] Supra, p 229 et seq.

[191] Supra, pp 315–17.

[192] See infra, p 459 et seq.

[193] Cf Civil Code of Quebec, Art 3148, para 2, under which a Quebec court has no jurisdiction to decide a case if the parties have agreed to submit all disputes to a foreign court or arbitrator, unless the defendant submits to the Quebec court; *GreCon Dimter Inc v JR Normand Inc* (2005) 255 DLR (4th) 257, Sup Ct of Canada.

[194] Supra, pp 369–71.

[195] *Evans Marshall & Co Ltd v Bertola SA* [1973] 1 WLR 349 at 362; *Insurance Co "Ingosstrakh" Ltd v Latvian Shipping Co* [2000] IL Pr 164, 169; *Sinochem International Oil (London) Ltd v Mobil Sales and Supply Corpn Ltd (No 2)* [2000] 1 All ER (Comm) 758, 767.

[196] *Donohue v Armco Inc* [2001] UKHL 64 at [14] (per Lord Bingham, Lords Mackay and Nicholls concurring), [60]–[61] and [68] (per Lord Scott), [2002] 1 All ER 749. See also *Fiona Trust & Holding Corpn v Privalov* [2007] EWCA Civ 20 at [18] (per Longmore LJ), [2007] 2 Lloyd's Rep 267; appeal dismissed sub nom *Premium Nafta Products Ltd v Fili Shipping Co Ltd* [2007] UKHL 40, [2007] 2 All ER (Comm) 1053 without discussing choice of jurisdiction agreements; *UBS v HSH Nordbank AG* [2009] EWCA Civ 585 at [82], [2010] 1 All ER (Comm) 727. But see *Ryanair Ltd v Esso Italiana Srl* [2013] EWCA Civ 1450, [2015] 1 All ER (Comm) 152.

[197] [2001] UKHL 64, [2002] 1 All ER 749.

[198] Lords Mackay at [40] and Nicholls at [41] concurred with the judgment of Lord Bingham. Lords Hobhouse and Scott delivered judgments coming to the same conclusion as Lord Bingham and agreed that these were the principles to be applied.

case concerned an injunction sought to restrain proceedings brought abroad in breach of an English exclusive jurisdiction clause. But Lord Bingham widened the discussion to refer more generally to the principles that apply where there has been a breach of an exclusive jurisdiction clause, which includes the situation where proceedings are brought in England in breach of a foreign jurisdiction clause:

> If contracting parties agree to give a particular court exclusive jurisdiction to rule on claims between those parties, and a claim falling within the scope of the agreement is made in proceedings in a forum other than that which the parties have agreed, the English court will ordinarily[199] exercise its discretion (whether by granting a stay of proceedings in England, or by restraining the prosecution of proceedings in the non-contractual forum abroad, or by such other procedural order as is appropriate in the circumstances) to secure compliance with the contractual bargain, unless the party suing in the non-contractual forum (the burden being on him) can show strong reasons for suing in that forum.[200]

Whether a party can show strong reasons, sufficient to displace the other party's prima facie entitlement to enforce the contractual bargain, will depend on all the facts and circumstances of the particular case.[201] The House of Lords approved[202] the judgment of Brandon J in *The Eleftheria*,[203] a case on the stay of English proceedings brought in breach of a foreign exclusive jurisdiction clause which has been repeatedly cited and approved over the years.[204] Brandon J listed some of the matters which might properly be regarded by the court when exercising its discretion.[205]

> (a) In what country the evidence on the issues of fact is situated, or more readily available, and the effect of that on the relative convenience and expense of trial as between the English and foreign courts.[206] (b) Whether the law of the foreign court applies and, if so, whether it differs from English law in any material respects.[207] (c) With what country either party is connected, and how closely.[208] (d) Whether the defendants genuinely desire trial in the foreign country, or are only seeking procedural advantages.[209] (e) Whether the plaintiffs would be prejudiced by having to sue in the foreign court because they would: (i) be deprived of

---

[199] This recognises that it is a discretion. Also a party may lose its claim to equitable relief by dilatoriness or other unconscionable conduct, supra, at [24].

[200] Ibid, at [24].

[201] Ibid.

[202] Ibid.

[203] [1970] P 94.

[204] Most importantly, *The Eleftheria* was affirmed by the Court of Appeal in the *El Amria* [1981] 2 Lloyd's Rep 119, by the House of Lords in *The Sennar (No 2)* [1985] 1 WLR 490 at 500; see also *Trendtex Trading Corpn v Crédit Suisse* [1980] 3 All ER 721; affd by the House of Lords [1982] AC 679. They were also seemingly accepted by Lord Goff in *The Pioneer Container* [1994] 2 AC 324, PC; Toh [1995] LMCLQ 183. See also *Kutchera v Buckingham International Holdings Ltd* (1988) 9 ILRM 501, Supreme Court of Ireland; *Apple Computer Inc v Apple Corps SA* [1990] 2 NZLR 598; *Air Nauru v Niue Airlines Ltd* [1993] 2 NZLR 632; *Society of Lloyd's & Oxford Members Agency Ltd v Hyslop* [1993] 3 NZLR 135; *Kidd v van Heeren* [1998] 1 NZLR 324 and [2006] 1 NZLR 393. For New Brunswick see *A/S Nyborg Plast v Lameque Quality Group Ltd* (2001) 213 DLR (4th) 301, New Brunswick CA.

[205] [1970] P 94, at 99–100.

[206] *The Panseptos* [1981] 1 Lloyd's Rep 152.

[207] *Trendtex Trading Corpn v Crédit Suisse* [1980] 3 All ER 721 at 735; affd by the House of Lords, [1982] AC 679; *The Panseptos* [1981] 1 Lloyd's Rep 152.

[208] The courts have also looked more generally at the connections that the facts of the case have with the alternative fora. If there is no connection with England it has been said that only a perverse exercise of the discretion would lead to refusal of a stay: *The Sennar (No 2)* [1985] 1 WLR 490 at 501, HL (per Lord Brandon); see also *The Star of Luxor* [1981] 1 Lloyd's Rep 139.

[209] *The Vishva Prabha* [1979] 2 Lloyd's Rep 286; *The Atlantic Song* [1983] 2 Lloyd's Rep 394; *The Pia Vesta* [1984] 1 Lloyd's Rep 169; *The Iran Vojdan* [1984] 2 Lloyd's Rep 380; *The Frank Pais* [1986] 1 Lloyd's Rep 529.

security for their claim;[210] (ii) be unable to enforce any judgment obtained; (iii) be faced with a time bar not applicable in England;[211] or (iv) for political, racial, religious or other reasons be unlikely to get a fair trial.[212]

This list is not intended to be exhaustive.[213] After examining many of the authorities, Lord Bingham concluded that, where the dispute is between two contracting parties, and the interests of other parties are not involved, effect will in all probability be given to the exclusive jurisdiction clause.[214] In contrast, the English court may well decline to grant a stay (or grant an anti-suit injunction as the case may be) where the interests of parties other than the parties bound by the exclusive jurisdiction clause are involved or grounds of claim not the subject of the clause are part of the relevant dispute so that there is a risk of parallel proceedings and inconsistent decisions.[215] However, if this risk was foreseeable, a stay will be granted.[216] The above factors have been decisive in refusing a stay, although not fitting easily within any of the considerations set out in the *The El Amria*, which shows the non-exclusive nature of the list of considerations. In *The El Amria*[217] Brandon LJ added that judges should not be drawn into making comparisons between the two different systems of administering justice used by English courts on the one hand and foreign courts on the other.[218] It has been said in other cases that it ill behoves a party who has agreed to trial in a particular foreign country subsequently to argue that he would suffer some procedural disadvantage from trial there,[219]

---

[210] This factor appears to be no longer of importance because of s 26 of the Civil Jurisdiction and Judgments Act 1982 (stay subject to retention of security, etc), supra, p 385; *The Havhelt* [1993] 1 Lloyd's Rep 523 at 524. See also *The Bergen (No 2)* [1997] 2 Lloyd's Rep 710 at 721.

[211] See *The Adolf Warski* [1976] 2 Lloyd's Rep 241; *The El Amria and El Minia* [1981] 2 Lloyd's Rep 539; *The Blue Wave* [1982] 1 Lloyd's Rep 151; *The Sennar (No 2)* [1984] 2 Lloyd's Rep 142, CA; affd [1985] 1 WLR 490, HL; *The Indian Fortune* [1985] 1 Lloyd's Rep 344; *The Pioneer Container*, supra; *Citi-March Ltd v Neptune Orient Lines Ltd* [1997] 1 Lloyd's Rep 72; *The MC Pearl* [1997] 1 Lloyd's Rep 566; *The Bergen (No 2)* [1997] 2 Lloyd's Rep 710; *Baghlaf Al Zafer v PNSC* [1998] 2 Lloyd's Rep 229 at 237, CA; *Insurance Co "Ingosstrakh" Ltd v Latvian Shipping Co* [2000] IL Pr 164, CA. See also *Spiliada Maritime Corpn v Cansulex Ltd* [1987] AC 460, HL; *Nima Sarl v Deves Insurance Public Co Ltd (The Prestrioka)* [2002] EWCA Civ 1132 at [76], [2003] 2 Lloyd's Rep 327 (a *forum conveniens* case); *Snookes v Jani-King (GB) Ltd* [2006] EWHC 289 (QB) at [67]–[75], [2006] IL Pr 19.

[212] See *Carvalho v Hull, Blyth (Angola) Ltd* [1979] 1 WLR 1228. This can include delays in coming to trial: *Baghlaf Al Zafer v PNSC* [1998] 2 Lloyd's Rep 229 at 235–6, CA.

[213] The *Donohue* case, supra, at [24].

[214] Ibid, at [25]. An early exception is *The Fehmarn* [1958] 1 WLR 159. A more recent one is *Domansa v Derin Shipping and Trading Co Inc* [2001] 1 Lloyd's Rep 362.

[215] The *Donohue* case, supra, at [27] referring to the following stay cases: *The El Amria*, supra, *Citi-March Ltd v Neptune Orient Lines Ltd* [1997] 1 Lloyd's Rep 72 at 78; *The MC Pearl* [1997] 1 Lloyd's Rep 566. For similar refusal of stay cases not mentioned see *The Rewia* [1991] 1 Lloyd's Rep 69 at 75; overruled on a different point [1991] 2 Lloyd's Rep 325, CA; *SCB v PNSC* [1995] 2 Lloyd's Rep 365; *Sinochem International Oil (London) Ltd v Mobil Sales and Supply Corpn Ltd (No 2)* [2000] 1 All ER (Comm) 758, 772. Lord Bingham also referred to anti-suit injunction cases: *Bouygues Offshore SA v Caspian Shipping Co (Nos 1, 3, 4 and 5)* [1998] 2 Lloyd's Rep 461; Briggs (1998) 69 BYBIL 342; *Crédit Suisse First Boston (Europe) v MLC (Bermuda) Ltd* [1999] 1 All ER (Comm) 237 and to *Evans Marshal & Co Ltd v Bertola SA* [1973] 1 WLR 349 (a service out case). For post-*Donohue* cases see *Konkola Copper Mines plc v Coromin Ltd* [2006] EWCA Civ 5, [2006] 1 Lloyd's Rep 410—also taking into account that there was only a provisionally found foreign jurisdiction clause; *Konkola Copper Mines plc v Coromin Ltd(No 2)* [2006] EWHC 1093 (Comm), [2006] 2 Lloyd's Rep 446.

[216] *Konkola Copper Mines plc v Coromin Ltd (No 2)* [2006] EWHC 1093 (Comm), [2006] 2 Lloyd's Rep 446. See also on the significance of unforeseeability in the context of permitting service out of the discretion, supra, pp 369–70.

[217] [1981] 2 Lloyd's Rep 119.

[218] Ibid, at 127. See also *The Abidin Daver* [1984] AC 398, discussed supra, p 403; *The Bergen (No 2)* [1997] 2 Lloyd's Rep 710 at 715. But see in relation to delays in coming to trial: *Baghalf Al Zafer v PNSC* [1998] 2 Lloyd's Rep 229 at 235–6, CA.

[219] *Trendtex Trading Corpn v Crédit Suisse* [1980] 3 All ER 721 at 736–7; affd by the House of Lords, [1982] AC 679; *The Kislovodsk* [1980] 1 Lloyd's Rep 183 at 186; *Konkola Copper Mines plc v Coromin Ltd (No 2)* [2006] EWHC 1093 (Comm) at [31], [2006] 2 Lloyd's Rep 446.

or to argue that the substantive law which would be applied by the foreign court would be disadvantageous to him.[220] Even if one assumes that such disadvantages can be taken into account in the present context, they will be of considerably less weight than under the second stage of the *Spiliada* test.[221] There has been a tentative suggestion that the necessary strong cause to rebut the prima facie case for a stay is easier to find where the jurisdiction clause is a standard one incorporated into a contract (without any previous course of dealing between the parties) than where it has been specifically negotiated.[222] Another, and probably better, distinction that could be drawn is whether the parties acted freely in adopting the clause.[223]

The criteria listed in *The El Amria* encompass the same factors which are considered under the doctrine of *forum non conveniens*,[224] and the attitude towards individual factors is the same in both contexts.[225] Thus a stay should not be granted where a claimant has acted reasonably in commencing proceedings in England and not unreasonably in allowing time to expire in the agreed foreign jurisdiction.[226] Nonetheless, the law has not yet reached the stage where the two forms of discretion can be assimilated.[227] The principle that the parties should abide by their agreement—and that a stay is a means of giving specific performance to that agreement—is of great importance in cases involving an exclusive jurisdiction clause. The starting point is that the English proceedings should be stayed if there is such a clause providing for the exclusive jurisdiction of a foreign court, whereas under the *forum non conveniens* discretion the starting point is that an action properly commenced in England should be allowed to continue. This means that the burden of proof is different under each discretion.[228] In cases involving foreign exclusive jurisdiction clauses the burden is on the claimant to show why a stay should not be granted.[229] In cases of *forum non conveniens* the burden is on the defendant, at least as regards showing that the natural forum is abroad.[230] Moreover, a

---

[220] *The Benarty* [1984] 2 Lloyd's Rep 244 at 251, CA.

[221] *The Nile Rhapsody* [1992] 2 Lloyd's Rep 399 at 414; Briggs (1993) 109 LQR 382; appeal dismissed, [1994] 1 Lloyd's Rep 382, CA; *Banco de Honduras SA v East West Insurance Co* [1996] 1 LRLR 74 at 80.

[222] *The Bergen (No 2)* [1997] 2 Lloyd's Rep 710 at 715. See also *Akai Pty Ltd v People's Insurance Co Ltd* [1998] 1 Lloyd's Rep 90 at 105–6. In the USA, jurisdiction clauses are subject to judicial scrutiny for fairness: *Carnival Cruise Lines Inc v Shute* 111 S Ct 1614 (1991); Richman (1992) 40 AJCL 977; Purcell (1992) 40 UCLA LR 423. See also *Trepanier v Kloster Cruise Ltd* (1995) 23 OR (3d) 398.

[223] *Import-Export Metro Ltd v Compañía Sud Americana de Vapores SA* [2003] EWHC 11 (Comm), [2003] 1 Lloyd's Rep 405; *Mercury v Communication Telesystems* [1999] 2 All ER (Comm) 33—cases concerned with the exclusive jurisdiction of the English courts, supra, pp 398–9.

[224] See *The Frank Pais* [1986] 1 Lloyd's Rep 529 at 535; *Citi-March Ltd v Neptune Orient Lines Ltd* [1997] 1 Lloyd's Rep 72 at 74. These are also the same factors as in *forum conveniens*, supra, p 364 et seq.

[225] See *The Pioneer Container*, supra, at 348, where Lord Goff quoted his comments in the *Spiliada* case on time bars. See also *The Bergen (No 2)* [1997] 2 Lloyd's Rep 710 at 715, citing the *Spiliada* case; *Baghlaf Al Zafer v PNSC* [1998] 2 Lloyd's 229 at 237. But cf *Citi-March Ltd v Neptune Orient Lines Ltd* [1997] 1 Lloyd's Rep 72 at 76–7.

[226] *The Pioneer Container*, supra; *The Bergen (No 2)*, supra; *Baghlaf Al Zafer v PNSC*, supra—a stay can be granted on terms that the defendant waives the time bar; *Nima Sarl v Deves Insurance Public Co Ltd, The Prestrioka* [2002] EWCA Civ 1132 at [80], [2003] 2 Lloyd's Rep 327 (a *forum conveniens* case).

[227] *Baghlaf Al Zafer v PNSC*, supra; *Citi-March Ltd v Neptune Orient Lines Ltd*, supra; *The Polessk* [1996] 2 Lloyd's Rep 40 at 42; see also *The Rothnie* [1996] 2 Lloyd's Rep 206; *The Nile Rhapsody* [1992] 2 Lloyd's Rep 399, appeal dismissed [1994] 1 Lloyd's Rep 382, CA, where there were attempts to use the two tests in conjunction with each other. Cf Briggs [1984] LMCLQ 227 at 241–8; Barma and Elvin (1985) 101 LQR 48 at 65–7.

[228] *Trendtex Trading Corpn v Crédit Suisse* [1980] 3 All ER 721 at 734–5; affd by the House of Lords [1982] AC 679.

[229] If the plaintiff discharges this burden, a stay will not be granted to the defendant on the basis of *forum non conveniens*, see *The Frank Pais* [1986] 1 Lloyd's Rep 529 at 535.

[230] Supra, p 395.

claimant cannot complain of the procedure of the foreign court if that court has been chosen by the parties.[231]

So far we have been discussing foreign exclusive jurisdiction clauses. If the foreign jurisdiction clause is non-exclusive the position is very different.[232] There is no breach of agreement in commencing proceedings in England and in principle it looks to be wrong to apply the same principles in the case of a non-exclusive jurisdiction clause as are applied in the case of an exclusive one. The right approach in the case of a non-exclusive jurisdiction clause is to apply the principles of *forum non conveniens* and to grant a stay on that basis.[233] However, the Court of Appeal has applied the principles to be applied to a foreign exclusive jurisdiction clause to a foreign service of suit clause, which is akin to a non-exclusive jurisdiction clause.[234]

(ii) Reliance on, escape from, exclusive jurisdiction clauses

The impact of a foreign exclusive jurisdiction clause on service out of the jurisdiction under rule 6.36 of the Civil Procedure Rules and on stays of action is such that a defendant who does not wish to face trial in England will seek to rely on such a clause wherever possible, whereas a claimant who wishes to bring his action in England will seek to escape from such a clause.

(a) When can a defendant rely on an exclusive jurisdiction clause?

A defendant who is not a party to a contract containing an exclusive jurisdiction clause will not be able to rely on it, unless he can show that under the governing law he has an enforceable right to invoke the clause.[235] The issue of when a third party to a jurisdiction clause has such a right, or indeed is subject to an obligation under the clause, raises complex questions.[236]

(b) When can a claimant escape from an exclusive jurisdiction clause?

A claimant cannot avoid a foreign exclusive jurisdiction clause by simply framing his action in tort, since it is for the law governing (presumably) the agreement on jurisdiction, and not for English law as the law of the forum, to determine whether the claim lies in contract or in tort,[237] and in any event the jurisdiction agreement may be effective for non-contractual claims which fall within its scope. Furthermore, if a foreign court has given a judgment

---

[231] *Trendtex Trading Corpn v Crédit Suisse* [1980] 3 All ER 721 at 734–5; affd by the House of Lords [1982] AC 679. See also *The Nile Rhapsody* [1992] 2 Lloyd's Rep 399 at 414; appeal dismissed [1994] 1 Lloyd's Rep 382, CA.

[232] The rules for determining whether a clause is exclusive or non-exclusive are discussed supra, pp 234–5.

[233] *The Rothnie* [1996] 2 Lloyd's Rep 206; Fawcett [2001] LMCLQ 234, at 253–5. See also *Morrison v Panic Link Ltd* 1994 SLT 232.

[234] *Ace Insurance SA-NV (Formerly Cigna Insurance Co of Europe SA-NV) v Zurich Insurance Co* [2001] EWCA Civ 173 at [62], [2001] 1 Lloyd's Rep 618, CA. See also the obiter dicta in *Import-Export Metro Ltd v Compañía Sud Americana de Vapores SA* [2003] EWHC 11 (Comm) at [14], [2003] 1 Lloyd's Rep 405—applying the same principles as where there is an English non-exclusive jurisdiction agreement (for the latter see supra, p 399 for *forum non conveniens* and supra, p 370 for *forum conveniens*).

[235] *The Forum Craftsman* [1985] 1 Lloyd's Rep 291. Quaere whether this is the law governing the agreement on jurisdiction or of the contract as a whole. For the question under English law of whether shipowners can rely on an exclusive jurisdiction clause, see *The Mahkutai* [1996] AC 650, PC; *Bouygues Offshore SA v Caspian Shipping Co* [1997] IL Pr 472, CA.

[236] See generally Black and Pitel (2016) 12 J Priv Int L 26. See also in the context of the Brussels I Recast, supra, pp 241–2.

[237] *The Sindh* [1975] 1 Lloyd's Rep 372, CA; cf *The Makefjell* [1976] 2 Lloyd's Rep 29; Knight (1977) 26 ICLQ 664. See also *The Sennar (No 2)* [1984] 2 Lloyd's Rep 142 at 148–9, CA; although this decision was affd by the House of Lords [1985] 1 WLR 490, it was thought unnecessary to express any view on this particular matter, per Lord Brandon at 500.

deciding that the exclusive jurisdiction clause applies to the claim, this may create an issue estoppel preventing the claimant from denying this.[238]

However, a claimant can escape from a foreign exclusive jurisdiction clause by showing that it is void[239] and therefore of no effect.[240] It will only be in rare cases that the claimant will succeed in establishing this. It is not enough to show that part of the agreement between the parties is void, if the foreign choice of jurisdiction clause is still left intact.[241] Neither it appears will it necessarily be enough for the claimant to show that the *whole* agreement of which the jurisdiction agreement is a part is void. There is support for the idea that a jurisdiction agreement (whether foreign or English) should be regarded as severable from the main contract in which the jurisdiction agreement is contained (in a clause).[242] This is on the basis that the parties, when nominating a court to settle their disputes, may well have expected this court to try the issue of the validity of the main contract.[243] This draws an analogy with the position in relation to arbitration agreements, which can be void or voidable only on grounds which relate directly to the arbitration agreement.[244] Applying this analogy, where it is argued that there never was a main contract at all (eg because of forgery), that will also be an attack on the validity of the jurisdiction agreement contained within the main contract.[245] In contrast, an argument that the main contract can be rescinded because it was procured by bribery may affect the main contract but does not necessarily undermine the jurisdiction agreement.[246]

As regards the validity of the whole agreement, the existence and validity of a contract is generally governed by the rules on the applicable law set out in the Rome I Regulation.[247] A fundamental breach of contract may result in termination of the contract and the non-application of the clause therein, including a jurisdiction clause.[248] When it comes to the question of the validity of just the exclusive jurisdiction clause it has been held that this is to be decided by applying the governing law, and the clause will be struck down if it is void according to this law.[249] In principle, this should be the law governing the agreement on

---

[238] *The Sennar (No 2)* [1985] 1 WLR 490, discussed infra, pp 561–2.

[239] A final judgment is needed to this effect even where it is alleged the contract is *void ab initio: Morrison v The Society of Lloyd's* [2000] IL Pr 92, New Brunswick QB.

[240] It is not clear on which party the burden of proof lies in respect of the validity of the exclusive jurisdiction clause.

[241] *Trendtex Trading Corpn v Crédit Suisse* [1982] AC 679.

[242] See Dicey, Morris and Collins, para 12-112; approved obiter in *Fiona Trust & Holding Corpn v Privalov* [2007] EWCA Civ 20 at [27] (per Longmore LJ), [2007] 2 Lloyd's Rep 267; appeal dismissed sub nom *Premium Nafta Products Ltd v Fili Shipping Co Ltd* [2007] UKHL 40, [2007] 2 All ER (Comm) 1053. The House of Lords only discussed severability in relation to arbitration agreements. See generally on recent cases involving incorporation of jurisdiction and arbitration agreements into contracts, Briggs (2006) 77 BYBIL 581.

[243] Dicey, Morris and Collins, para 12-113.

[244] See infra, p 418.

[245] Ibid. See also *Mackender v Feldia AG* [1967] 2 QB 590 at 598 (per Lord Denning), 602–3 (per Diplock LJ); *Crédit Suisse First Boston (Europe) Ltd v Seagate Trading Co Ltd* [1999] 1 Lloyd's Rep 784— where the attack on the main contract also involved a direct attack on an English exclusive jurisdiction agreement.

[246] Infra, p 418.

[247] Art 10(1), infra, pp 755–8. The Rome Convention or common law choice of law rules may still apply to some contracts, depending on the date of formation of the contract. The issue of incorporation of a clause has been held to be one of material validity of the *contract* and hence to be determined by the application of Art 10(1): *Egon Oldendorff v Liberia Corpn* [1995] 2 Lloyd's Rep 64. For the treatment of this issue in Australia see *Oceanic Sun-Line Special Shipping Co Inc v Fay* (1988) 165 CLR 197, High Court of Australia.

[248] *ZI Pompey Industrie v Ecu-Line NV* [2000] IL Pr 600, and [2000] IL Pr 608, Fed Ct of Canada.

[249] *The Iran Vojdan* [1984] 2 Lloyd's Rep 380; *The Frank Pais* [1986] 1 Lloyd's Rep 529 at 530; *OT Africa Line Ltd v Magic Sportswear Corpn* [2005] EWCA Civ 710 at [58]–[61], [83], [2005] 2 Lloyd's Rep 170; Baatz [2006] LMCLQ 143; Briggs (2005) 76 BYBIL 650; *Horn Linie GmbH & Co v Panamericana Formas E Impresos SA* [2006] EWHC 373 (Comm) at [10], [2006] 2 Lloyd's Rep 44.

jurisdiction, not the contract as a whole.[250] In practice, however, the courts are likely to presume that (unless otherwise clearly indicated) the parties will have intended a single law to govern all terms of their contract, and thus find the jurisdiction agreement to be governed by the same law which governs the contract as a whole.[251]

An exclusive jurisdiction clause may also be void because of the terms of a statute.[252] In *The Hollandia*,[253] the House of Lords held that an exclusive jurisdiction clause providing for trial in the Netherlands was rendered null and void and of no effect by virtue of the Hague-Visby Rules, which are part of English law.[254] The Rules provide, inter alia, that any clause lessening the liability of the carrier otherwise than as provided for under the Rules shall be null and void.[255] The Dutch exclusive jurisdiction clause had the effect, albeit indirectly, of lessening the carrier's liability, since, if trial was held in the Netherlands, the Dutch courts would apply Dutch law which set a lower maximum limit on the carrier's liability than that provided for under the Rules.[256] In the absence of an exclusive jurisdiction clause and of any other basis for the granting of a stay, the shipper's action was allowed to proceed.[257]

In *The Hollandia* the continuance of the plaintiff's action depended ultimately on the wording of the Hague-Visby Rules. The same is true of the later case of *The Benarty*.[258] In that case the Court of Appeal held that an exclusive jurisdiction clause providing that actions should be brought in the Indonesian courts was not rendered void under the Hague-Visby Rules, since the case concerned a tonnage limitation (ie one calculated on the tonnage of the ship carrying the goods), and not a package limitation[259] as in the *The Hollandia* (ie one calculated on the number of packages or on their weight). In consequence, the principle that the parties should abide by their agreement was applied and a stay of the English[260] proceedings was granted.

(c) Arbitration agreements[261]

Section 9 of the Arbitration Act 1996[262] substantially gives effect to Article II of the New York Convention on the Recognition and Enforcement of Arbitral Awards (1958).[263] It applies to

---

[250] To be determined under traditional common law rules (the Rome I Regulation excludes agreements on jurisdiction from its scope, infra, pp 700–1): *OT Africa Line Ltd v Magic Sportswear Corpn* [2005] EWCA Civ 710 at [60] (per Rix LJ), [2005] 2 Lloyd's Rep 170. However, Longmore LJ, at [1]–[2] and [20]–[23], favoured the law governing the *contract as a whole*. Unhelpfully, Laws LJ agreed with both Rix LJ and Longmore LJ. Longmore LJ was followed in the *Horn Linie* case, supra, at [20].

[251] Dicey, Morris and Collins, paras 12-103 and 32-021.

[252] *The Hollandia* [1983] 1 AC 565; *Akai Pty Ltd v People's Insurance Co Ltd* (1996) 71 ALJR 156 High Court of Australia.

[253] [1983] 1 AC 565, [1982] 3 All ER 1141; sub nom *The Morviken* [1983] 1 Lloyd's Rep 1; Mann (1983) 99 LQR 376, 400–6. *The Hollandia* is unaffected by the Rome I Regulation, see infra, pp 774–5.

[254] See the Carriage of Goods by Sea Act 1971.

[255] See the Schedule to the Carriage of Goods by Sea Act 1971, Art III, para 8.

[256] [1983] 1 AC 565 at 574–5. Defendants can undertake not to take advantage of the lower limit, in which case the jurisdiction clause is no longer disregarded: *Baghlaf Al Zafer v PNSC* [1998] 2 Lloyd's Rep 229 at 238, CA.

[257] *The Hollandia*, supra, at 576–7.

[258] [1984] 2 Lloyd's Rep 244; Reynolds [1984] LMCLQ 545.

[259] Ibid, at 250–1, 253–4.

[260] Ibid, at 251, 255.

[261] Hill, paras 20.2.1–20.2.37.

[262] For interpretation of the 1996 Act, see Departmental Advisory Committee (DAC) Report on Arbitration Law, February 1996, on the relevance of which see *Halki Shipping Corpn v Sopex Oils Ltd* [1998] 1 WLR 726 at 732, CA.

[263] And replaces s 2 of the Arbitration Act 1975 and s 4 of the Arbitration Act 1950.

all written arbitration[264] agreements.[265] Section 9 applies even if the seat of the arbitration is outside England and Wales or Northern Ireland or no seat has been designated or determined.[266] Section 9 will doubtless also apply regardless of whether the arbitration agreement is governed by English or foreign law.[267]

A party[268] to an arbitration agreement against whom legal proceedings[269] are brought (whether by way of claim or counterclaim) in respect of a matter which under the agreement is to be referred to arbitration[270] may (upon notice to the other parties to the proceedings) apply to the courts in which the proceedings have been brought to stay the proceedings so far as they concern that matter.[271] Most arbitration clauses refer any "dispute" to arbitration. The question whether there is a "dispute" between the parties that they have agreed to refer to arbitration therefore arises. There is a "dispute" whenever there is a claim which the other party refused to admit or did not satisfy.[272] It does not matter whether there is an answer to the claim in fact or law.[273] The fact that an application may be made to stay a counterclaim, as well as a claim, represents a change to the previous statutory position. Another statutory provision provides that an application may be made notwithstanding that the matter is to be referred to arbitration only after the exhaustion of other dispute resolution procedures.[274] An application may not be made by a person before taking the appropriate procedural step (if any) to acknowledge the legal proceedings against him or after he has taken any step in those proceedings to answer the substantive claim.[275] The court must be satisfied that there was an

---

[264] *Walkinshaw v Diniz* [2000] 2 All ER (Comm) 237. For agreements on alternative dispute resolution see *Cable & Wireless plc v IBM United Kingdom Ltd* [2002] EWHC 2059 (Comm), [2002] 2 All ER (Comm) 1041.

[265] 1996 Act, s 5 (agreement to be in writing); s 6 (definition of arbitration agreement, which can include incorporation of arbitration clause from another document—on which see *Trygg Hansa v Equitas* [1998] 2 Lloyd's Rep 439; *The Delos* [2001] 1 Lloyd's Rep 703); replacing 1975 Act, s 7(1); *Excomm Ltd v Ahmed Abdul-Qawi Bamordah, The St Raphael* [1985] 1 Lloyd's Rep 403; *Zambia Steel v Clark and Eaton* [1986] 2 Lloyd's Rep 225.

[266] 1996 Act, s 2(2)(a). For the determination of the seat see *Dubai Paymentech* [2001] 1 Lloyd's Rep 65.

[267] See *Nova (Jersey) Knit Ltd v Kammgarn Spinnerei GmbH* [1977] 1 WLR 713.

[268] This includes any person claiming under or through a party to the agreement: 1996 Act, s 82(2). See in relation to the same phrase under the 1975 Act, *Grupo Torras SA and Torras Hostench London Ltd v Sheikh Fahad Mohammed Al-Sabah* [1995] 1 Lloyd's Rep 374 at 450–1; appeals dismissed [1996] 1 Lloyd's Rep 7, CA. See in relation to an assignee, *The League* [1984] 2 Lloyd's Rep 259. For a stay using s 49(3) of the Senior Courts Act 1981 pending arbitration abroad between a party to the litigation and a third party (not involved in the litigation), see *Reichhold Norway ASA v Goldman Sachs International* [2000] 1 WLR 173, CA; discussed infra, p 421.

[269] This includes where one party seeks declaratory relief from the court, including where the applicant seeks in the alternative an extension of time to come to arbitration: *Grimaldi Compagnia di Navigazione SpA v Sekihyo Line Ltd* [1998] 3 All ER 943.

[270] See *NB Three Shipping Ltd v Harebell Shipping Ltd* [2004] EWHC 2001 (Comm), [2005] 1 Lloyd's Rep 509. The matter must be capable of settlement by arbitration: 1996 Act, s 81(1)(a); Hill, paras 20.2.9–20.2.11.

[271] Arbitration Act 1996, s 9(1). The Court of Appeal will entertain an appeal against a decision as to whether to stay under s 9: *Inco Europe v First Choice Distribution* [2000] 1 WLR 586, HL. For the relationship between ss 9 and 12 (extension of time to come to arbitration), see *Grimaldi Compagnia di Navigazione SpA v Sekihyo Line Ltd* [1998] 3 All ER 943.

[272] *Halki Shipping Corpn v Sopex Oils Ltd* [1998] 1 WLR 726, CA; Whiteley [1998] LMCLQ 164; *Wealands v CLC Contractors* [1999] 2 Lloyd's Rep 739, CA; *Exfin Shipping Ltd v Tolani Shipping Co Ltd* [2006] EWHC 1090 (Comm), [2006] 2 Lloyd's Rep 389. See also *Loon Energy Inc v Integra Mining* [2007] EWHC 1876 (Comm) at [85]–[87].

[273] The *Halki* case, supra.

[274] Arbitration Act 1996, s 9(2). This deals with a point made by Lord Mustill in *Channel Tunnel Group Ltd v Balfour Beatty Construction Ltd* [1993] AC 334 at 354.

[275] Arbitration Act 1996, s 9(3). See *Patel v Patel* [2000] QB 551, CA—application for a default judgment to be set aside and for leave to defend and counterclaim was not such a step.

arbitration clause and that the subject of the action was within that clause.[276] Under English law, arbitration clauses in international commercial contracts are to be liberally construed.[277] Construction of the arbitration clause starts from the assumption that the parties, as rational businessmen, are likely to have intended any dispute arising out of the relationship into which they have entered or purported to enter to be decided by the same tribunal, unless the language makes it clear that certain questions were intended to be excluded from the arbitrator's jurisdiction.[278] Thus an arbitration clause was construed to cover a dispute as to whether the contract of which it formed part was procured by bribery.[279] The staying of the proceedings is mandatory[280] unless the court is satisfied that the arbitration agreement is null and void,[281] inoperative[282] or incapable of being performed.[283] Under English arbitration law an arbitration agreement is separable from the main contract of which it forms part.[284] It follows that the invalidity or rescission of the main contract does not necessarily entail the invalidity or rescission of the arbitration agreement.[285] The arbitration agreement is a distinct agreement and can be void or voidable only on grounds which relate directly to the arbitration agreement.[286] An argument that the main contract can be rescinded because it was procured by bribery may affect the main contract but does not necessarily undermine the arbitration agreement as a distinct agreement.[287] On the other hand, where it is argued that there never

---

[276] *Al-Naimi v Islamic Press Agency Inc* [2000] 1 Lloyd's Rep 522, CA; *Albon v Naza Motor Trading Sdn Bhd (No 3)* [2007] EWHC 665 (Ch), [2007] 2 Lloyd's Rep 1. See on the scope of the clause: *Wealands v CLC Contractors* [1999] 2 Lloyd's Rep 739, CA; *Capital Trust Investments Ltd v Radio Design TJ AB* [2002] CLC 787; *Sonatrach Petroleum Corpn v Ferrell International Ltd* [2002] 1 All ER (Comm) 627 at 639–40; *Anglia Oils Ltd v Owners of the Vessel "Marine Champion"* [2002] EWHC 2407 (Admiralty); *El Nasharty v J Sainsbury* [2003] EWHC 2195 (Comm) at [29], [2004] 1 Lloyd's Rep 309; *Law Debenture Trust v Elektrim Finance* [2005] EWHC 1412 (Ch), [2005] 2 All ER (Comm) 476 at [32]–[37]. For the use of the court's inherent jurisdiction where the court is not sure of this see infra, pp 420–1.

[277] *Fiona Trust & Holding Corpn v Privalov* [2007] EWCA Civ 20 at [18] (per Longmore LJ), [2007] 2 Lloyd's Rep 267; appeal dismissed sub nom *Premium Nafta Products Ltd v Fili Shipping Co Ltd* [2007] UKHL 40, [2007] 2 All ER (Comm) 1053. For explicit support in the House of Lords for the views of Longmore LJ see at [26] (per Lord Hope), [38] (per Lord Brown). See also *Mabey and Johnson Ltd v Danos* [2007] EWHC 1094 (Ch) at [12]–[15].

[278] *Fiona Trust & Holding Corpn v Privalov* sub nom *Premium Nafta Products Ltd v Fili Shipping Co Ltd* [2007] UKHL 40 at [13] (per Lord Hoffmann), [22] (per Lord Hope), [36] (per Lord Scott), [37] (per Lord Walker), [38] (per Lord Brown), [2007] 2 All ER (Comm) 1053.

[279] Ibid. With the result that a stay of the court proceedings for a declaration that the contracts had been rescinded was granted.

[280] And must be unconditional: *The Rena K* [1979] QB 377 at 400; see also supra, p 385. *The Vasso, formerly Andria* [1984] 1 Lloyd's Rep 235 at 242. However, security available in an action in rem can be retained: 1996 Act, s 11.

[281] See *Inco Europe v First Choice Distribution* [1999] 1 WLR 270, CA; affd on the question of the jurisdiction of the Court of Appeal to hear the appeal: [2000] 1 WLR 586, HL.

[282] See *The Merak* [1965] P 223 at 239, decided under s 4(2) of the Arbitration Act 1950; *Astro Valiente Compañía Naviera SA v Pakistan Ministry of Food and Agriculture (No 2)* [1982] 1 WLR 1096; *Kaverit Steel and Crane Ltd v Kone Corpn* (1992) 87 DLR (4th) 129.

[283] Arbitration Act 1996, s 9(4).

[284] Ibid, s 7.

[285] *Fiona Trust & Holding Corpn v Privalov* sub nom *Premium Nafta Products Ltd v Fili Shipping Co Ltd* [2007] UKHL 40 at [17] (per Lord Hoffmann), [22] (per Lord Hope), [36] (per Lord Scott), [37] (per Lord Walker), [38] (per Lord Brown), [2007] 2 All ER (Comm) 1053.

[286] Ibid.

[287] Ibid at [35] (per Lord Hope), [17]–[21] (per Lord Hoffmann), [36] (per Lord Scott), [37] (per Lord Walker), [38] (per Lord Brown). There is, however, some uncertainty as to the scope of this principle—the better view is that a challenge to the validity of the arbitration agreement is no less critical because it also affects substantive contractual terms. If the contract as a whole (including the arbitration agreement) would not have been signed but for the bribery, it is difficult to see how in principle the arbitration agreement should be considered binding. By contrast, if the bribery only affected the substantive terms negotiated, then it should not be considered to affect the validity of the arbitration agreement. See, eg, *Albon v Naza Motor Trading Sdn Bhd* [2007] EWCA Civ 1124, [2008] 1 Lloyd's Rep 1.

was a main contract at all (eg because of forgery), that will be an attack on the validity of the arbitration agreement contained within the main contract.[288] The relevant time for ascertaining the validity of the arbitration agreement and whether it is capable of being performed is as at the date of commencement of the proceedings to be stayed, rather than as at the date of the application for a stay.[289] The burden of proof is on the party alleging this.[290] No choice of law rule is provided for these issues in the Arbitration Act 1996.

The question whether an arbitration agreement is null and void is a matter for the law governing the arbitration agreement.[291] The same law governs the question whether a contract contains an arbitration clause.[292] The determination of the scope of an arbitration clause and whether it covers the matter in dispute between the parties is likewise an issue for the law governing the arbitration agreement.[293] "Inoperative" encompasses the situation where the arbitration agreement has come to an end.[294] The question whether the arbitration agreement is incapable of being performed relates not to whether one of the parties can satisfy any award that may be made but rather to whether the agreement can be performed up to the stage of an award being made.[295] Questions of admissibility, such as whether any procedural preconditions for arbitration have been satisfied, do not affect the validity of the arbitration agreement and are arguably therefore matters which should be left to the arbitral tribunal to determine,[296] although it is not clear whether the practice of the English courts follows this distinction.[297]

Under the previous statutory provision there was a further ground for not granting a stay, namely that there was not in fact any dispute between the parties with regard to the matter agreed to be referred to arbitration.[298] If the claimant could show that there was no defence to the claim, the court could at the same time refuse a stay and give a summary judgment[299] in favour of the claimant.[300] The Arbitration Act 1996 omits this ground for not granting a

---

[288] *Fiona Trust*, supra, at [17] (per Lord Hoffmann), [22] (per Lord Hope), [36] (per Lord Scott), [37] (per Lord Walker), [38] (per Lord Brown), [2007] 2 All ER (Comm) 1053.

[289] *Traube v Perelman*, 2001 (unreported).

[290] *Overseas Union Insurance Ltd v AA Mutual International Insurance Co Ltd* [1988] 2 Lloyd's Rep 63 at 70.

[291] See *Astro Venturoso Compañía Naviera v Hellenic Shipyards SA, The Mariannina* [1983] 1 Lloyd's Rep 12; *Weissfisch v Julius* [2006] EWCA Civ 218, [2006] 1 Lloyd's Rep 716; *Sulamerica Cia Nacional de Seguros SA v Enesa Engenharia SA* [2012] EWCA Civ 638, [2012] 1 Lloyd's Rep 671. This will be determined according to traditional common law rules; the Rome I Regulation and Rome Convention exclude arbitration agreements from their scope, infra, pp 700–1.

[292] *Marc Rich & Co AG v Societa Italiana Impianti PA, The Atlantic Emperor* [1989] 1 Lloyd's Rep 548; the case was referred to the European Court of Justice on a different point, see supra, p 209. See also *O T M Ltd v Hydronautics* [1981] 2 Lloyd's Rep 211. Cf *The Rena K* [1979] QB 377. However, the issue of incorporation of an arbitration clause has been held to be one of material validity of the *contract* and hence to be determined by the application of Art 8(1) of the Rome Convention (now Art 10(1) of the Rome I Regulation): *Egon Oldendorff v Liberia Corpn* [1995] 2 Lloyd's Rep 64. But where a foreign court gives a judgment on the question of incorporation this may create an estoppel, see *Tracomin SA v Sudan Oil Seeds Co Ltd (Nos 1 and 2)* [1983] 1 WLR 1026, discussed infra, pp 584–5.

[293] *Nova (Jersey) Knit Ltd v Kammgarn Spinnerei GmbH* [1977] 1 WLR 713 at 718–19, 730; *Abu Dhabi Investment Co v H Clarkson & Co Ltd* [2006] EWHC 1252 (Comm), [2006] 2 Lloyd's Rep 381.

[294] *Downing v Al Tameer* [2002] EWCA Civ 721, [2002] CLC 1291.

[295] *The Rena K* [1979] 1 QB 377 at 393. See also *Grupo Torras SA and Torras Hostench London Ltd v Sheikh Fahad Mohammed Al-Sabah* [1995] 1 Lloyd's Rep 374 at 451–2; appeals dismissed [1996] 1 Lloyd's Rep 7, CA.

[296] See, eg, *BG Group plc v Republic of Argentina*, 572 US __ (2014).

[297] *Dallah Real Estate and Tourism Holding Company v Government of Pakistan* [2010] UKSC 46, [2011] AC 763; *Wah (aka Alan Tang) v Grant Thornton International Ltd* [2012] EWHC 3198 (Ch).

[298] 1975 Act, s 1(1).

[299] See now CPR, Part 24; previously RSC, Ord 14.

[300] *Channel Tunnel Group Ltd v Balfour Beatty Construction Ltd* [1993] AC 334 at 356, HL.

stay on the basis that it is confusing and unnecessary.[301] The intention of the 1996 Act was to exclude this summary judgment jurisdiction based on an investigation of what was in fact disputable.[302] A stay will be granted and the claimant's application for summary judgment will be dismissed, even though the claimant claims that the defendant has no arguable defence.[303]

One final matter concerns the extent to which the courts can use their inherent jurisdiction to stay proceedings in cases involving arbitration. One of the general principles set out in the Arbitration Act 1996, in the light of which all the provisions in the Act must be read, is that "in matters governed by this Part [Part I, ie sections 1 to 84] the court should not intervene except as provided by this Part".[304] It follows that a court cannot use its inherent jurisdiction to stay proceedings where the matter is governed by Part I. Thus it cannot do so where the conditions for the application of Article 9 are satisfied but a stay is refused because the arbitration agreement is incapable of being performed. On the other hand, there is nothing in the 1996 Act to prevent a court from using its inherent jurisdiction where the matter is not governed by Part I. Moreover, to use its inherent jurisdiction in this situation is supported by House of Lords authority in relation to the statutory predecessor of section 9 of the 1996 Act, where it was held that, whether or not the procedure for resolving disputes agreed between the parties amounted to an arbitration agreement falling within section 1 of the Arbitration Act 1975, the court had an inherent jurisdiction to stay the proceedings.[305] This leaves the question: which matters are not governed by Part I of the 1996 Act? Two examples have been suggested.[306] The first is an oral arbitration agreement;[307] the second, an agreement to refer a dispute to an alternative dispute resolution mechanism other than arbitration.[308] Going beyond this, it has been suggested in the Court of Appeal that a stay under the inherent jurisdiction might be sensible in the situation where the court could not be sure that there was an arbitration agreement or that the subject of the action was within that agreement.[309] Thus recourse has been had to the inherent jurisdiction and a stay granted in relation to claims designed to impugn the validity of an arbitration agreement.[310] Traditionally it has been suggested that the case would have to be an exceptional one before the court would grant a stay, leaving these matters to an arbitrator, in circumstances where the court was uncertain as to whether there was an arbitration agreement.[311] However, there

---

[301] DAC Report (1996), para 55. See also *Hayter v Nelson* [1990] 2 Lloyd's Rep 265.

[302] *Halki Shipping Corpn v Sopex Oils Ltd* [1998] 1 WLR 726 at 750 (per Henry LJ), CA.

[303] Ibid. There must, of course, be a dispute between the parties that they have agreed to refer to arbitration, supra, p 417.

[304] Arbitration Act 1996, s 1(c).

[305] *Channel Tunnel Group Ltd v Balfour Beatty Construction Ltd* [1993] AC 334; Reymond (1993) 109 LQR 337. This involves a discretionary power which is based on the idea that the parties should abide by their agreement and is analogous to upholding foreign choice of jurisdiction agreements, discussed supra, p 410 et seq.

[306] Hill, para 20.2.39.

[307] See the Arbitration Act 1996, ss 5 (agreement to be in writing) and 81 (saving any rule of law, consistent with the provisions of Part I, as to the effect of an oral arbitration agreement).

[308] See *Channel Tunnel Group Ltd v Balfour Beatty Construction Ltd* [1993] AC 334, HL— a case decided in relation to the Arbitration Act 1975, s 1.

[309] *Al-Naimi v Islamic Press Agency Inc* [2000] 1 Lloyd's Rep 522 at 525 (per Waller LJ) and 528 (per Chadwick LJ), CA. See also *Fiona Trust & Holding Corpn v Privalov* [2007] EWCA Civ 20 at [37]–[38] (per Longmore LJ), [2007] 2 Lloyd's Rep 267; appeal dismissed sub nom *Premium Nafta Products Ltd v Fili Shipping Co Ltd* [2007] UKHL 40, [2007] 2 All ER (Comm) 1053; *Albon v Naza Motor Trading Sdn Bhd (No 3)* [2007] EWHC 665 (Ch) at [16], [2007] 2 Lloyd's Rep 1.

[310] *A v B* [2006] EWHC 2006 (Comm), [2007] 1 Lloyd's Rep 237.

[311] *El Nasharty v J Sainsbury* [2003] EWHC 2195 (Comm) at [29], [2004] 1 All ER (Comm) 728; *Albon v Naza Motor Trading Sdn Bhd (No 3)* [2007] EWHC 665 (Ch) at [24]–[25], [2007] 2 Lloyd's Rep 1; *Law Debenture Trust v Elektrim Finance* [2005] EWHC 1412 (Ch), [2005] 2 All ER (Comm) 476.

is some authority which supports the idea that the English courts should adopt a doctrine of 'negative competence-competence', like that followed in French law,[312] under which an arbitral tribunal is (at least usually) given the first opportunity to determine the validity of the arbitration agreement.[313] The means of achieving this would be a stay of the court's jurisdiction, pursuant to its inherent powers, without any finding as to the validity or effectiveness of the arbitration agreement. These questions could then be considered if an arbitral award is rendered, in an application to set aside or enforce the award.

(d) Stays pending the determination of proceedings abroad

So far, stays of English proceedings where the effect of the stay has been to force the claimant to go abroad to sue or to go to arbitration abroad have been considered. However, the English courts also have power[314] to stay English proceedings pending the final determination of arbitration or trial abroad,[315] in other words, to suspend temporarily the English proceedings.[316] This involves less of an interference with the claimant's right to bring his action in England—it affects only the timing of the proceedings, rather than whether jurisdiction will be exercised at all. (This does have an impact on jurisdiction, however, and it is unclear in what circumstances this power can be exercised where jurisdiction has been taken pursuant to the Brussels I Recast.)[317] It is a special case of the power of the English courts to order a stay of proceedings on case management grounds, as part of the courts' general powers of management of proceedings.[318] This general power is commonly used even in purely domestic cases, for example, to stay civil proceedings until the completion of related criminal proceedings, or to allow for settlement negotiations to take place.[319] Nevertheless, the power to stay proceedings pending the determination of proceedings abroad will only be exercised in rare and compelling circumstances, such as where there are related foreign proceedings which cannot or should not be consolidated with the English proceedings, and it would be in the interests of justice for those foreign proceedings to be concluded before the English proceedings are permitted to continue.[320] It was correctly exercised in *Reichhold Norway ASA v Goldman Sachs International*.[321]

> X began an action against Y before the English courts. X then commenced arbitration proceedings against Z in Norway. The two sets of concurrent proceedings overlapped to a significant degree. Y obtained a stay of the English proceedings pending the determination of the arbitration in Norway.

---

[312] French Code of Civil Procedure, Articles 1448, 1455 and 1465.

[313] *Fiona Trust v Privalov* [2007] EWCA Civ 20 at [34] (per Longmore LJ), [2007] 2 Lloyd's Rep 267 ("it will, in general, be right for the arbitrators to be the first tribunal to consider whether they have jurisdiction to determine the dispute").

[314] Under its inherent jurisdiction expressly preserved by s 49(3) of the Senior Courts Act 1981.

[315] *Reichhold Norway ASA v Goldman Sachs International* [2000] 1 WLR 173, CA; *Standard Chartered Bank (Hong Kong) Ltd v Independent Power Tanzania Ltd* [2016] EWCA Civ 411, [2016] 2 Lloyd's Rep 25.

[316] In cases covered by the Brussels I Recast, an equivalent power to stay proceedings pending the outcome of foreign litigation is provided where there are prior related proceedings in another Member State (Art 30, infra, p 454 et seq), or prior proceedings (related or identical) in a non-Member State (Arts 33–34, infra, p 457 et seq).

[317] See infra, pp 471–3.

[318] CPR, r 3.1—the power to stay proceedings is dealt with in 3.1(2)(f).

[319] See also CPR, r 26.4.

[320] *Reichhold*, supra, at 186 (per Lord Bingham delivering the judgment of the Court of Appeal); see also eg *AXA Corporate Solutions Assurance SA v Weir Services Australia Pty Limited* [2016] EWHC 904 (Comm). For refusal to grant a stay: see *Konkola Copper Mines plc v Coromin Ltd* [2006] EWCA Civ 5, [2006] 1 Lloyd's Rep 410; *Mabey and Johnson Ltd v Danos* [2007] EWHC 1094 (Ch); *Amlin Corporate Member Ltd v Oriental Assurance Corp* [2012] EWCA Civ 1341, [2013] Lloyd's Rep IR 131.

[321] [2000] 1 WLR 173, CA. Cf *National Westminster Bank v Utrecht-America Finance Co* [2001] EWCA Civ 658 at [24]–[25], [2001] 3 All ER 733.

3. RESTRAINING FOREIGN PROCEEDINGS UNDER THE COMMON LAW: THE ANTI-SUIT INJUNCTION

An English court cannot prohibit a foreign court from trying an action. However, it does have a discretionary power, in certain circumstances, to grant an injunction restraining a party from commencing or continuing as claimant in foreign proceedings, commonly known as an 'anti-suit injunction'.[322] If in the foreign proceedings themselves an anti-suit injunction is sought to restrain English judicial or arbitral proceedings, the restraint of such proceedings by the English courts is sometimes referred to as an 'anti-anti-suit injunction'.[323] (In unusual circumstances, a so-called 'domestic anti-suit injunction' may also be awarded by the English courts, restraining a party from commencing English proceedings.)[324] If foreign proceedings have continued to judgment, an order may also (exceptionally) be obtained restraining enforcement of the judgment, known as an 'anti-enforcement injunction'.[325]

The English courts have held that the power to make these orders is not restricted by the European Convention on Human Rights,[326] Article 6 of which is not concerned with *where* the right to a fair and public hearing is to be exercised by a litigant but rather with the fact that civil rights must be exercised *somewhere* by a hearing and before a tribunal in accordance with the provisions of that Article.[327] The power to grant an anti-suit injunction is, however, restricted by the Brussels/Lugano System, as explored later in this chapter.[328] For the purposes of this section, it should be assumed that the injunction relates to foreign proceedings which are not in a European Union Member State or a Lugano Convention state. The focus in this section is on restraining proceedings before a foreign court, although it should be noted that an English court may equally (under similar principles) restrain a party from commencing or continuing an arbitration, known as an 'anti-arbitration injunction'.[329]

---

[322] See generally Raphael, *The Anti-Suit Injunction*; Briggs 2015, para 5.32ff; Fentiman 2015, Chapter 16; Dicey, Morris and Collins, paras 12-078–12-090; Briggs in Rose (ed), *Lex Mercatoria: Essays in International Commercial Law in Honour of Francis Reynolds*, p 219; Fentiman in Cheong *et al* (eds), in *Current Issues in International Commercial Litigation*, pp 44–71; Collins in, Cheong *et al* (eds), *Current Issues in International Commercial Litigation*, pp 5–10; Wilson [1997] JBL 424; Bell and Gleeson (1997) 71 ALJ 955; Males [1998] LMCLQ 543; Hartley (1987) 35 AJCL 48; Ho (2003) 52 ICLQ 697. This power to restrain foreign proceedings is also referred to as enjoining foreign proceedings. For the powers of the High Court in respect of injunctions, see the Senior Courts Act 1981, s 37. For the powers of an appeal court to interfere with the exercise of the discretion by a lower court see *Donohue v Armco Inc* [2001] UKHL 64, [2002] 1 All ER 749 at [37]–[38]; *Star Reefers Pool Inc v JFC Group Co Ltd* [2012] EWCA Civ 14, [2012] 1 Lloyd's Rep 376. The terms of the injunction may take the form of not contesting certain matters in the foreign court, see *Banque Cantonale v Waterlily Maritime Inc* [1997] 2 Lloyd's Rep 347 at 357.
[323] See, eg, *Sabah Shipyard (Pakistan) Ltd v Islamic Republic of Pakistan* [2002] EWCA Civ 1643, [2003] 2 Lloyd's Rep 571; *Ecom Agroindustrial Corp Ltd v Mosharaf Composite Textile Mill Ltd* [2013] EWHC 1276 (Comm), [2013] 2 Lloyd's Rep 196.
[324] See *Fujifilm Kyowa Kirin Biologics Company Limited v Abbvie Biotechnology Limited* [2016] EWHC 2204 (Pat).
[325] See, eg, *Bank St Petersburg v Arkhangelsky* [2014] EWCA Civ 593, [2014] 1 WLR 4360; *Ecobank Transnational Inc v Tanoh* [2015] EWCA Civ 1309, [2016] 1 Lloyd's Rep 360.
[326] *OT Africa Line Ltd v Hijazy (The Kribi)* [2001] 1 Lloyd's Rep 76 at [41]–[44]; Fawcett, Ní Shúilleabháin, and Shah, *Human Rights and Private International Law* (2016) paras 6.182–6.242.
[327] But note the additional caution which applies in 'single forum' cases—see infra, p 433 et seq.
[328] See infra, p 475 et seq.
[329] See, eg, *Elektrim SA v Vivendi Universal SA (No 2)* [2007] EWHC 571 (Comm), [2007] 2 Lloyd's Rep 8; *Albon v Naza Motor Trading Sdn Bhd* [2007] EWCA Civ 1124, [2008] 1 Lloyd's Rep 1; *Excalibur Ventures LLC v Texas Keystone Inc* [2011] EWHC 1624 (Comm), [2011] 2 Lloyd's Rep 289. Some authorities suggest, however, that this power should only be exercised exceptionally—see *Weissfisch v Julius* [2006] EWCA Civ 218, [2006] 1 Lloyd's Rep 716; *Claxton Engineering Services Ltd v TXM Olaj-Es Gazkutato Kft* [2011] EWHC 345 (Comm) [2011] 1 Lloyd's Rep 510.

(a) Underlying principles

First, the restraining order is directed not against the foreign court but against the party proceeding or threatening to proceed in the foreign court.[330] It binds only that party, in personam.[331] If the order is disobeyed, the person against whom it is directed can be punished for contempt of court. However, the reality is that, if the defendant neither lives in England nor has substantial assets there, the injunction is unlikely to be enforceable except by the foreign court recognising and giving effect to the injunction, or, if it refuses to do so, as may well be the case, by the English court refusing to recognise or enforce the judgment of the foreign court.[332]

Secondly, an injunction will only be issued restraining a party who is amenable to the jurisdiction of the court, against whom an injunction will be an effective remedy.[333] Frequently, substantive proceedings will have been commenced in England—in such cases, the court necessarily has the power to make ancillary orders such as an anti-suit injunction.[334] If this is not the case, a jurisdictional basis must be found for the proceedings to obtain the injunction. There is no difficulty in a case where the person against whom the injunction is directed is an English resident. The position is more complicated in a case where he is a foreign resident. There is jurisdiction to grant the injunction if the person against whom it is directed has submitted to the English court's jurisdiction,[335] or if he has sufficient connection with England to justify this,[336] eg where he has brought an action abroad in breach of an agreement providing for arbitration in England.[337] Furthermore, if a claim form has been or could be served out of the jurisdiction on the defendant under rule 6.36 and Practice Direction 6B of the Civil Procedure Rules, the courts will thereby have power to grant an injunction restraining foreign proceedings.[338] If there is jurisdiction to grant the injunction, the courts, when deciding whether to exercise their discretion to grant this, will not consider the likelihood that a foreign defendant will not obey this order,[339] although they may refuse to make the order if it would be futile and unenforceable.[340] The grant of an injunction does not require the English court to make any finding as to the jurisdiction of the foreign court.[341]

---

[330] *Donohue v Armco Inc* [2001] UKHL 64, [2002] 1 All ER 749, 757; *Turner v Grovit* [2001] UKHL 65 at [23], [2002] 1 WLR 107; *Société Nationale Industrielle Aérospatiale v Lee Kui Jak* [1987] AC 871, 892.

[331] *Turner v Grovit*, supra, at [23].

[332] *Phillip Alexander Securities and Futures Ltd v Bamberger* [1997] IL Pr 73 at 117, CA. The German court in this case refused to permit the injunctions to be served in Germany, regarding them as an infringement of their sovereignty. For the refusal to enforce the foreign judgment, see infra, p 574.

[333] *Castanho v Brown and Root (UK) Ltd* [1981] AC 557, HL; *Midland Bank plc v Laker Airways Ltd* [1986] QB 689; *Bank of Tokyo Ltd v Karoon* [1987] AC 45 n at 59, CA; *Société Aérospatiale*, supra, at 892; *Donohue v Armco Inc*, supra, at 757; *Turner v Grovit*, supra, at [23]; Thomas [1983] LMCLQ 692.

[334] *Masri v Consolidated Contractors International Company Sal* [2008] EWCA Civ 625, [2009] QB 503.

[335] *Glencore International AG v Exter Shipping Ltd* [2002] EWCA Civ 528 at [52], [2002] 2 All ER (Comm) 1. See also *Royal Exchange Assurance Co Ltd v Compañía Naviera Santi SA, The Tropaioforos* [1962] 1 Lloyd's Rep 410; *Castanho v Brown and Root (UK) Ltd*, supra; *Masri v Consolidated Contractors International Company Sal* [2008] EWCA Civ 625, [2009] QB 503.

[336] *The Tropaioforos*, supra; *Castanho v Brown and Root (UK) Ltd*, supra.

[337] *Tracomin SA v Sudan Oil Seeds Co Ltd (Nos 1 and 2)* [1983] 1 WLR 1026, an agreement to arbitrate in England can alternatively be regarded as a submission to jurisdiction for these purposes.

[338] *Donohue v Armco Inc*, supra, at 758. See also *Royal Exchange Assurance v Compañía Naviera Santi SA, The Tropaioforos*, supra. The injunction ground under CPR, PD6B, 3.1(2) cannot be used: *Amoco (UK) Exploration Co v British American Offshore Ltd* [1999] 2 Lloyd's Rep 772.

[339] *Castanho v Brown and Root (UK) Ltd*, supra.

[340] *Stichting Shell Pensioenfonds v Krys* [2014] UKPC 41, [2015] AC 616.

[341] *Turner v Grovit*, supra, at [26].

Thirdly, although the claim form is directed at a person there is, nonetheless, an implicit interference with the jurisdiction of a foreign court whenever an English court grants an injunction restraining foreign proceedings. There are obvious comity problems inherent in the exercise of the power to restrain foreign proceedings; for this reason it has often been said that the power must be exercised with caution.[342] "Considerations of comity grow in importance the longer the foreign suit continues and the more the parties and the Judge have engaged in its conduct and management."[343]

Fourthly, and more specifically, an anti-suit injunction will not be granted in circumstances which amount to a breach of comity. In *Airbus Industrie GIE v Patel* Lord Goff, giving the unanimous judgment of the House of Lords, said that:

> As a general rule, before an anti-suit injunction can properly be granted by an English court to restrain a person from pursuing proceedings in a foreign jurisdiction in cases of the kind under consideration in the present case, comity requires that the English forum should have a sufficient interest in, or connection with, the matter in question to justify the indirect interference with the foreign court which an anti-suit injunction entails.[344]

This was stated "as a general rule", which inevitably begs the question of what the exception is to this. Lord Goff contemplated that there may be extreme cases, "for example where the conduct of the foreign state exercising jurisdiction is such as to deprive it of the respect normally required by comity", where no such limit is required to the exercise of the jurisdiction to grant an anti-suit injunction.[345]

Fifthly, different principles apply to cases where an injunction is sought to restrain a party from proceeding in a foreign court in breach of an arbitration agreement or a clause providing for exclusive jurisdiction in England.[346] In particular, there is not the same concern with comity. This affects the operation of the third and fourth principles.

Sixthly, the broad principle underlying the jurisdiction is that it is to be exercised when the ends of justice require it.[347]

Finally, judicial decisions limit when it may be considered just to grant an injunction.[348] The power to make the order is at least generally[349] dependent upon there being wrongful conduct of the party to be restrained of which the applicant is entitled to complain and has a legitimate interest in seeking to prevent.[350] The conduct in question should fit within the

---

[342] See, eg, *Castanho v Brown and Root (UK) Ltd*, supra; *British Airways Board v Laker Airways Ltd* [1985] AC 58 at 95 (per Lord Scarman), HL; *South Carolina Insurance Co v Assurantie NV* [1987] AC 24 at 40, HL (per Lord Brandon); *Société Aérospatiale*, supra, at 892; *Airbus Industrie GIE v Patel* [1999] 1 AC 119 at 133, HL; *Donohue v Armco Inc*, supra, at 757; *Sabah Shipyard (Pakistan) Ltd v Islamic Republic of Pakistan* [2002] EWCA Civ 1643 at [40], [2003] 2 Lloyd's Rep 571. On comity see also *Amoco (UK) Exploration Co v British American Offshore Ltd* [1999] 2 Lloyd's Rep 772 at 780.

[343] *Royal Bank of Canada v Cooperative Centrale Raiffeisen-Boerenleenbank BA* [2004] EWCA Civ 7 at [50], [2004] 1 Lloyd's Rep 471.

[344] *Airbus Industrie GIE v Patel, supra*, at 138.

[345] Ibid, at 140.

[346] *Aggeliki Charis Compañia Marítima SA v Pagnan SpA, The Angelic Grace* [1995] 1 Lloyd's Rep 87, CA; infra, pp 441–2.

[347] *Airbus Industrie GIE v Patel*, supra, at 133 (per Lord Goff), HL; *Société Aérospatiale* , supra, at 892, PC; *Donohue v Armco Inc*, supra, at 757; *Turner v Grovit*, supra, at [24].

[348] *Turner v Grovit*, supra, at [22].

[349] There are cases in which the focus appears to be less on the wrongful conduct of the foreign claimant and more on the unjust consequences for the foreign defendant, such as *Société Aérospatiale*, supra, discussed in further detail below. They may be reconciled with this principle by viewing the foreign claimant's choice of the foreign forum as unconscionable because of these unjust consequences.

[350] *Turner v Grovit*, supra, at [24]. For criticism of the legitimate interest of the applicant requirement see infra, p 435.

description of being unconscionable in the eye of English law.[351] The use of the word unconscionable makes the point that the remedy is a personal one for the wrongful conduct of an individual. It is essentially a fault-based remedial concept.[352] It is unconscionable conduct that founds the right, legal or equitable, for the protection of which an injunction can be granted; if the applicant has also acted unconscionably that may preclude the award of the injunction.[353]

(b) Categorisation of the cases

It is possible to divide up the cases where an injunction has been granted into various categories, and each category contains more specific criteria for the grant of an injunction. However, neither the judges in the leading cases[354] nor writers[355] are able to agree on what these categories are. This is partly because different attempts at categorisation emphasize different things: some focus on the conduct of the party to be restrained; others on the right of the applicant to complain. Lord Hobhouse giving the judgment in the most recent House of Lords case on the topic, *Turner v Grovit*,[356] was more concerned with identifying and explaining what he saw as being the requirement that runs through the case law than with identifying different categories of case. This is the requirement that there is wrongful conduct of the party to be restrained of which the applicant is entitled to complain and has a legitimate interest in seeking to prevent.[357] *Turner* has been interpreted by the Court of Appeal as laying down two categories[358] and this is the categorisation that will be applied here, namely:

(i)   where the conduct of the party to be restrained is unconscionable;

(ii) where the bringing of the proceedings abroad is in breach of an agreement.

It is upon these two categories (the second arguably being a special case of the first, also involving a breach of a legal right) that the present discussion will focus. But before doing so,

---

[351] Ibid; following *British Airways Board v Laker Airways Ltd* [1985] AC 58 at 81 (per Lord Diplock).

[352] *Turner v Grovit*, supra, at [24].

[353] *Glencore International AG v Exter Shipping Ltd* [2002] EWCA Civ 528 at [42], [2002] 2 All ER (Comm) 1; *OT Africa Line Ltd v Magic Sportswear Corpn* [2005] EWCA Civ 710 at [63] and [83], [2005] 2 Lloyd's Rep 170.

[354] Cf *South Carolina Co v Assurantie NV* [1987] AC 24 at 40, HL (three categories: invasion of a legal or equitable right not to be sued abroad; bringing of the proceedings abroad would be unconscionable; there is another forum which is more appropriate in the interests of justice) with *Airbus Industrie GIE v Patel* [1999] 1 AC 119, HL (vexation or oppression, breach of an agreement, unconscionability) and then *Turner v Grovit*, supra, at [24] (unconscionable conduct). Cf these English cases with *Amchem Products Inc v Workers' Compensation Board* (1993) 102 DLR (4th) 96, Sup Ct of Canada; *CSR Ltd v Cigna Insurance Australia Ltd* (1997) 189 CLR 345, High Court of Australia; *Australian Broadcasting Corpn v Lenah Game Meats Pty Ltd* (2001) 185 ALR 1.

[355] Dicey, Morris and Collins, paras 12R-001 and 12-080–12-089 (where the injunction is necessary in the interests of justice but with a separate section on single forum cases); Briggs 2015, paras 5.37–5.44 (breach of a legal right not to be sued abroad, or restraint of an equitable wrong; the latter means where this would be unconscionable conduct and the most important instance would be where it is vexatious or oppressive); Fentiman 2015, para 16.38ff (protecting substantive rights or protecting procedural rights); Hill, paras 11.2.2–11.2.22 (unconscionable behaviour, including vexation or oppression, or infringement of a legal or equitable right not to be sued abroad); Harris (1997) 17 OJLS 477, 485–8 (vexation or oppression, or possibly breach of contract). See also Ho (2003) 52 ICLQ 697.

[356] [2001] UKHL 65, [2002] 1 WLR 107; followed in *Glencore International AG v Exter Shipping Ltd* [2002] EWCA Civ 528 at [42], [2002] 2 All ER (Comm) 1.

[357] *Turner v Grovit*, supra, at [24].

[358] *Sabah Shipyard (Pakistan) Ltd v Islamic Republic of Pakistan* [2002] EWCA Civ 1643 at [39], [2003] 2 Lloyd's Rep 571, CA; *Royal Bank of Canada v Cooperative Centrale Raiffeisen-Boerenleenbank BA* [2004] EWCA Civ 7 at [8], [2004] 1 Lloyd's Rep 471; *Seismic Shipping Inc v Total E&P UK plc (The Western Regent)* [2005] EWCA Civ 985 at [44]–[46], [2005] 2 Lloyd's Rep 359; *OT Africa Line Ltd v Magic Sportwear Corpn* [2006] EWCA Civ 710 at [63], [83], [2005] 2 Lloyd's Rep 170. The restatement in *Seismic* of the principles to be applied was followed in *Cadre SA v Astra Asigurari SA* [2005] EWHC 2626 (Comm), [2006] 1 Lloyd's Rep 560.

---

it is important to stress that the power to grant injunctions is not restricted, and should not be restricted, to certain limited categories.[359] New categories should be capable of introduction where the ends of justice require it.[360] However, according to Lord Hobhouse the grant of an injunction is subject to the requirement that there is wrongful conduct of the party to be restrained of which the applicant is entitled to complain and has a legitimate interest in seeking to prevent.[361]

(i) Where the conduct of the party to be restrained is unconscionable

In *British Airways Board v Laker Airways Ltd*[362] the House of Lords held that:

> The power of the English court to grant the injunction exists, if the bringing of the suit in the foreign court is in the circumstances so unconscionable that in accordance with our principles of a "wide and flexible" equity it can be seen to be an infringement of an equitable right of the applicant.[363]

This is a very broad category and for the purposes of analysis it is important to divide it up into two very different sub-categories, which deal with very different situations and involve very different considerations. The first of these sub-categories is where the pursuit of proceedings abroad is vexatious or oppressive. This is the most important instance of unconscionable conduct. In this sub-category the right not to be sued derives from the inappropriateness of the forum abroad.[364] The second sub-category is what can be called other instances of unconscionable conduct. Here the right not to be sued derives from the conduct itself and not from the inappropriateness of the forum abroad.[365] These two categories are sufficiently different that it is legitimate to examine each separately in turn.

(a) Where the pursuit of proceedings abroad is vexatious or oppressive

The House of Lords in *South Carolina Insurance Co v Assurantie NV*[366] held that unconscionable conduct included "conduct which is oppressive or vexatious". Lord Goff in the House of Lords in *Airbus Industrie GIE v Patel* described the grant of an injunction on this ground as a particular application of the broad principle underlying the jurisdiction to grant an injunction restraining foreign proceedings, namely that this is to be exercised when the ends of justice require it.[367] According to Lord Hobhouse in *Turner v Grovit*, the terms "vexatious" and "oppressive" are other phrases used to criticise unconscionable

---

[359] *Castanho v Brown and Root (UK) Ltd* [1981] AC 557 at 573 (per Lord Scarman, with whom the other Law Lords concurred), HL; *British Airways Board v Laker Airways Ltd* [1985] AC 58 at 81, HL; *Société Nationale Industrielle Aérospatiale v Lee Kui Jak* [1987] AC 871 at 892; *Barclays Bank plc v Homan* [1993] BCLC 680 at 685–687 (Hoffmann J), [1993] BCLC 680 at 705, CA. Cf *South Carolina Insurance Co v Assurantie NV* [1987] AC 24 at 39–41 (per Lord Brandon—Lords Bridge and Brightman concurring, Lords Goff and Mackay dissented on this point), HL; Carter (1986) 57 BYBIL 434; note (1987) 103 LQR 157; Forsyth [1988] CLJ 177.

[360] *Castanho v Brown and Root (UK) Ltd*, supra, at 573; *British Airways Board v Laker Airways Ltd*, supra, at 81; *Société Aérospatiale*, supra, at 892; *Bank of Tokyo Ltd v Karoon* [1987] AC 45 n at 59, CA. This is also implicit in *Airbus Industrie GIE v Patel*, supra, with its statement of the underlying principle being the ends of justice.

[361] But for the introduction of what is in effect a new category which arguably ignores this requirement see *Samengo-Turner v J & H Marsh & McLennan (Services) Ltd* [2007] EWCA Civ 723 at [38]–[44], [2007] IL Pr 52; infra, p 482.

[362] [1985] AC 58, [1984] 3 All ER 39, HL; Collier [1984] CLJ 253; Carter (1984) 55 BYBIL 358.

[363] *British Airways Board v Laker Airways*, supra, at 95 (per Lord Scarman); see also 81 (per Lord Diplock); *Airbus Industrie GIE v Patel* [1999] 1 AC 119 at 134 (per Lord Goff), HL; *Midland Bank plc v Laker Airways Ltd* [1986] QB 689 at 701, 711–12.

[364] *Turner v Grovit*, supra, at [25].

[365] Ibid.

[366] [1987] AC 24.

[367] [1999] 1 AC 119 at 133, HL.

conduct.[368] But these are not to be taken as limiting definitions.[369] He too emphasised "the basic principle of justice".[370] What we are concerned with are English ideas of justice.[371] There is not and should not be any choice of law issue in relation to the right not to be sued abroad.[372] When discussing the grant of an injunction on this ground it is important to distinguish two different situations. The first is where there are two or more available fora for trial, one of which is England. The second is where trial is available in alternative fora abroad, but not in England. In the former situation an injunction will be granted where the pursuit of the proceedings abroad is vexatious or oppressive. In the latter situation, as a general rule an injunction will not be granted even though the pursuit of the proceedings abroad is vexatious or oppressive.

(i) *There are two or more available fora for trial (one of which is England)*

In this situation the courts are deciding whether trial should take place in England or abroad, for the effect of granting an injunction restraining foreign proceedings is to force the claimant to sue (or be sued) in England. For many years the courts exercised the power to restrain foreign proceedings on the basis of vexation or oppression.[373] The widening of the principles to be applied in respect of the stay of English proceedings soon filtered through to cases on restraining foreign proceedings. At one time it was said that the principle was the same, regardless of whether the remedy sought was a stay of English proceedings or a restraint of foreign proceedings.[374] Lord Goff in the *Spiliada* case[375] was careful to state the principles on *forum non conveniens* without reference to injunctions restraining foreign proceedings. Nonetheless, there was a danger after *Spiliada* that, in practice, injunctions restraining foreign proceedings would simply be granted on the basis that England was the natural forum for trial. This was recognised by the Privy Council in *Société Nationale Industrielle Aérospatiale v Lee Kui Jak*,[376] which held that it was no longer right, in the light of the *Spiliada* case, to apply the same criteria to restraining foreign proceedings as those applied when granting a stay of English proceedings. To do so would be against comity and would disregard the fundamental requirement that an injunction will only be granted where the ends of justice so require.

When it comes to the criteria to be applied for determining whether to grant an injunction, Lord Goff resurrected the old language of vexation and oppression:

> in a case such as the present where a remedy for a particular wrong is available both in the English . . . court and in a foreign court, the English . . . court will, generally speaking, only restrain the plaintiff from pursuing proceedings in the foreign court if such pursuit would be vexatious or oppressive.[377]

---

[368] *Turner v Grovit*, supra, at [24]. See also *DVA v Voest Alpine* [1997] 2 Lloyd's Rep 279 at 286, CA; *Toepfer v Société Cargill* [1998] 1 Lloyd's Rep 379 at 384, CA; Harris (1997) 17 OJLS 477 at 487; *Seismic Shipping Inc v Total E & P UK plc (The Western Regent)* [2005] EWCA Civ 985 at [44]–[46], [2005] 2 Lloyd's Rep 359; *Deutsche Bank v Highland Crusader* [2009] EWCA Civ 725; *Star Reefers Pool Inc v JFC Group Co Ltd* [2012] EWCA Civ 14, [2012] 1 Lloyd's Rep 376.

[369] *Turner v Grovit*, supra, at [24].

[370] Ibid; following Lord Goff in *Société Aérospatiale*, supra, at 893.

[371] *Barclays Bank plc v Homan* [1993] BCLC 680 at 687 (Hoffmann J), [1993] BCLC 680 at 705, CA.

[372] Cf Briggs [1997] LMCLQ 90. For a rebuttal see Harris [1997] LMCLQ 413. See in relation to foreign causes of action and the scope of a jurisdiction clause, infra, p 437, n 483.

[373] See *Cohen v Rothfield* [1919] 1 KB 410.

[374] *Castanho v Brown and Root (UK) Ltd* [1981] AC 557 at 574 (per Lord Scarman).

[375] [1987] AC 460 at 480. See also *Société Aérospatiale*, supra, at 896.

[376] [1987] AC 871; Kunzlik [1987] CLJ 406; Briggs [1987] LMCLQ 391; Carter (1988) 59 BYBIL 342.

[377] *Société Aérospatiale*, supra, at 896.

This old terminology was then combined with the modern terminology of the natural forum. According to Lord Goff, the vexation or oppression test that is now being adopted generally presupposes that the English court has first concluded that it provides the natural forum for trial.[378] If the only issue is whether an English or a foreign court is the more appropriate forum for trial of the action, that question should normally be decided by the foreign court applying the principle of *forum non conveniens*.[379] The English court preferably should not pre-empt the foreign court's decision as to its jurisdiction by granting an injunction before the decision is made.[380] But vexation or oppression requires more than that England is the natural forum (and hence is a more stringent test than that used prior to the *Société Aérospatiale* case).[381] It has to be shown that there would be injustice to the defendant if the claimant was allowed to pursue the foreign proceedings. Since the court is ultimately concerned with the ends of justice, account must also be taken of the claimant's position: "the court will not grant an injunction if, by doing so, it will deprive the plaintiff of advantages in the foreign forum of which it would be unjust to deprive him".[382] These principles have been applied by the House of Lords in *Donohue v Armco Inc*,[383] by the Court of Appeal in numerous cases[384] and have been accepted, obiter, by the House of Lords in *Airbus Industrie GIE v Patel*,[385] in which Lord Goff delivered the judgment of the House of Lords, and in *Turner v Grovit*.[386] They have also found broad acceptance in the Supreme Court of Canada,[387] have influenced the High Court of Australia[388] and been applied in Scotland.[389]

The application of these principles to particular facts can be seen by looking at the *Société Aérospatiale* case:

> The plaintiffs were the widow and administrators of the estate of a businessman, resident in Brunei, who was killed when the helicopter on which he was a passenger crashed in Brunei. The helicopter was manufactured by the defendant S, a French company, and operated by

---

[378] Ibid; *Airbus Industrie GIE v Patel* [1999] 1 AC 119 at 134 (per Lord Goff); *Donohue v Armco Inc* [2001] UKHL 64, [2002] 1 All ER 749 at [20]. See also *Amchem Products Inc v Workers' Compensation Board* (1993) 102 DLR (4th) 96 at 118 (per Sopinka J), Sup Ct of Canada. For examples of where an injunction was refused because England was not the natural forum, see the *Donohue* case, supra, *Bouygues v Caspian Shipping Co (No 2)* [1997] 2 Lloyd's Rep 485.

[379] *Barclays Bank plc v Homan* [1993] BCLC 680 at 701, CA; *Arab Monetary Fund v Hashim (No 6)* (1992) Times, 24 July

[380] *Amchem Products Inc v Workers' Compensation Board* (1993) 102 DLR (4th) 96 at 118 (per Sopinka J), Sup Ct of Canada; *Deaville v Aeroflot* [1997] 2 Lloyd's Rep at 67; *Pan American World Airways Inc v Andrews* 1992 SLT 268.

[381] *Société Aérospatiale*, supra; *Cadre SA v Astra Asigurari SA* [2005] EWHC 2626 (Comm) at [13], [2006] 1 Lloyd's Rep 560; *Star Reefers Pool Inc v JFC Group Co Ltd* [2012] EWCA Civ 14, [2012] 1 Lloyd's Rep 376; *Golden Endurance Shipping SA v RMA Watanya SA* [2014] EWHC 3917 (Comm), [2015] 1 Lloyd's Rep 266.

[382] *Société Aérospatiale*, supra, at 896.

[383] [2001] UKHL 64, [2002] 1 All ER 749 at 757–8 (per Lord Bingham, Lords Mackay and Nicholls concurring), at 768 (per Lord Hobhouse).

[384] *EI du Pont de Nemours & Co and Endo Laboratories Inc v Agnew (No 2)* [1988] 2 Lloyd's Rep 240; *Hemain v Hemain* [1988] 2 FLR 388; *Barclays Bank plc v Homan* [1993] BCLC 680, CA; *Hughes v Hannover* [1997] 1 BCLC 497, CA; *Royal Bank of Canada v Cooperative Centrale Raiffeisen-Boerenleenbank BA* [2004] EWCA Civ 7 at [37], [2004] 1 Lloyd's Rep 471; *Seismic Shipping Inc v Total E & P UK plc (The Western Regent)* [2005] EWCA Civ 985 at [44]–[46], [2005] 2 Lloyd's Rep 359.

[385] [1999] 1 AC 119 at 133, HL.

[386] Supra, at [23]–[29].

[387] *Amchem Products Inc v Workers' Compensation Board* (1993) 102 DLR (4th) 96, Sup Ct of Canada; Glenn (1994) 28 UBCLR 193.

[388] *CSR Ltd v Cigna Insurance Australia Ltd* (1997) 189 CLR 345; Briggs (1998) 114 LQR 27; *Australian Broadcasting Corpn v Lenah Game Meats Pty Ltd* (2001) 185 ALR 1.

[389] *Pan American World Airways Inc v Andrews* 1992 SLT 268; *Shell UK Exploration and Production Ltd v Innes* 1995 SLT 807; *FMC Corpn v Russell* 1999 SLT 99; and Brown 1995 SLT (News) 253.

the defendant BM, a Malaysian company. The plaintiffs instituted proceedings against S and BM both in Brunei and Texas (where S carried on business). S sought an injunction in Brunei restraining the plaintiffs from continuing with the Texas action. This was refused by the Court of Appeal of Brunei.

On appeal to the Privy Council it was held that an injunction should be granted. The natural forum for trial of the plaintiffs' action against S was held to be Brunei. This was on the basis of the strong connections with Brunei, including the fact that the accident happened there, Brunei law was applicable, the deceased was resident there and carried on his principal business there. However, this in itself was not enough to justify the grant of an injunction restraining the foreign proceedings. Generally speaking, what has to be shown is vexation or oppression. Trial in Texas would involve serious injustice to S amounting to oppression in that the company might be unable to claim a contribution from BM in the Texas proceedings. Instead, S might have to bring a separate action in Brunei against BM with attendant difficulties. At the same time, there was no injustice in depriving the plaintiffs of trial in Texas. Any advantages that the plaintiffs obtained from trial in Texas (such as superior means of gathering evidence to mount a case against S, availability of expert counsel, the contingency fee system, prospects of an early trial) were effectively neutralised by undertakings given by S that, for example, evidence already obtained in the Texas proceedings would be available in Brunei proceedings.

A number of problems arise out of this decision.

First, what is meant by vexation or oppression?[390] We know that these terms are another way of criticising unconscionable conduct.[391] Despite what was said in the Privy Council,[392] older cases can be of little value in ascertaining this. The problem faced by the courts nowadays is that of claimants forum shopping in countries where a very wide jurisdiction is taken, a very different sort of problem from that faced by courts in the nineteenth century.[393] The use of language from the nineteenth century only serves to obscure the basic considerations that should be taken into account in this area: the interests of the parties; the connections with the alternative fora; the dictates of comity and the need for caution before restraining foreign proceedings.[394]

Another example of oppression is provided by *Airbus Industrie GIE v Patel*.[395] As discussed further below, there were two appropriate fora for an action, but the plaintiffs sought to sue in a third forum, Texas, which was clearly inappropriate (none of the parties had any connection with Texas, none of the causes of action arose there, nor had any loss been suffered there, and the law of Texas was irrelevant to the settlement of the dispute). The conduct of the plaintiffs was prima facie oppressive.

To take another example, requiring the defendant to fight in two different jurisdictions can amount to substantial injustice,[396] unless this is necessary in the circumstances for the

---

[390] For a very narrow Australian view of this concept, see *CSR Ltd v Cigna Insurance Australia Ltd* (1997) 189 CLR 345 at 393–4, High Court of Australia.

[391] *Turner v Grovit*, supra, at [24].

[392] The *Société Aérospatiale* case, supra, at 896.

[393] Ibid at 894.

[394] See *Metall und Rohstoff AG v ACLI Metals (London) Ltd* [1984] 1 Lloyd's Rep 598; *Star Reefers Pool Inc v JFC Group Co Ltd* [2012] EWCA Civ 14, [2012] 1 Lloyd's Rep 376.

[395] [1997] 2 Lloyd's Rep 8, CA; reversed by the House of Lords [1999] 1 AC 119 but not on the oppression point. It was accepted, at 140, that the conduct in the case may properly be regarded as oppressive.

[396] *SCOR v Eras EIL (No 2)* [1995] 2 All ER 278; *Advanced Portfolio Technologies Inc v Ainsworth* [1996] FSR 217; Harris [1997] CJQ 279; *FMC Corpn v Russell* 1999 SLT 99 at 102; *General Star v Stirling Cooke* [2003] EWHC 3 (Comm), [2003] IL Pr 19; *Albon v Naza Motor Trading Sdn Bhd* [2007] EWCA Civ 1124, [2008] 1 Lloyd's Rep 1; but cf *Deutsche Bank v Highland Crusader* [2009] EWCA Civ 725.

claimant to ensure recovery of damages.[397] Other examples of the sort of material injustice amounting to oppression include such situations as where a party is prevented from properly preparing his case, or the foreign court is being misled, or a party is forced to incur expense not apparently connected with the case;[398] where the defendant would not have a fair trial abroad[399] or when the claim abroad is brought in bad faith, or is doomed to fail;[400] or where there was no good reason for seeking to have the dispute tried abroad (the action being started abroad as a defensive step to prevent other courts from taking jurisdiction).[401] Continuance of foreign proceedings brought in breach of a contractual clause providing for the exclusive jurisdiction of the English courts may well in itself be vexatious and oppressive.[402] On the other hand, the fact that there are concurrent proceedings does not in itself mean that there is oppression,[403] although the court recognises the undesirable consequences that may follow, namely conflicting judgments or a rush to obtain a judgment creating a situation of *res judicata*.[404] There is no oppression in suing a defendant abroad in a state with which the proceedings have very real connections, such as US plaintiffs, mostly US or non-English defendants, and a fraudulent scheme that allegedly arose in New York.[405] Foreign proceedings are equally not oppressive merely because the foreign court would apply a different law than the English court.[406]

Secondly, what is meant in the present context by an advantage to the claimant? As an example, it has been held that the fact that a ship has been arrested abroad to obtain security for a claim is an advantage for these purposes.[407] On the other hand, it is doubtful whether this would encompass the higher damages, eg punitive damages, available in the USA. Indeed, it seems to be suggested[408] that the fact that the plaintiffs sought this advantage in Texas might have had some relevance as evidence of oppression if this point had not been neutralised by undertakings given by the plaintiffs. Similarly, availability of contingency fees and pre-trial discovery proceedings abroad have been held not to be legitimate advantages unless the forum abroad is the single or natural forum.[409]

---

[397] *Karafarin Bank v Mansoury-Dara* [2009] EWHC 1217 (Comm), [2009] 2 Lloyd's Rep 289; *Novoship (UK) Ltd v Mikhaylyuk* [2012] EWHC 1352 (Comm).

[398] *FMC Corpn v Russell* 1999 SLT 99 at 102.

[399] *Al-Bassam v Al-Bassam* (2004) EWCA Civ 857.

[400] *SCOR v Eras EIL (No 2)* [1995] 2 All ER 278; *Shell International Petroleum Co Ltd v Coral Oil Co Ltd (No 2)* [1999] 2 Lloyd's Rep 606; *Baturina v Chistyakov* [2014] EWCA Civ 1134, [2014] 2 CLC 209. See also *Trafigura Beheer BV v Kookmin Bank Co (No 2)* [2006] EWHC 1921 (Comm) at [51], [52], [2007] 1 Lloyd's Rep 669; Briggs (2007) 123 LQR 18.

[401] *Cadre SA v Astra Asigurari SA* [2005] EWHC 2626 (Comm) at [18], [2006] 1 Lloyd's Rep 560.

[402] *Sohio Supply Co v Gatoil (USA) Inc* [1989] 1 Lloyd's Rep 588. See infra, p 436 et seq.

[403] *Société Aérospatiale*, supra, at 894; *Seismic Shipping*, supra, at [44]; *Star Reefers Pool Inc v JFC Group Co Ltd* [2012] EWCA Civ 14, [2012] 1 Lloyd's Rep 376.

[404] *Seismic Shipping*, supra, at [44].

[405] *Donohue v Armco Inc* [2001] UKHL 64, [2002] 1 All ER 749 at [20] (per Lord Bingham, Lords Mackay and Nicholls concurring), [45] (per Lord Hobhouse). For other examples see also *Kornberg v Kornberg* (1991) 76 DLR (4th) 379; *Pan American World Airways Inc v Andrews* 1992 SLT 268; *Through Transport Mutual Insurance Association (Eurasia) Ltdv New India Assurance Co Ltd* [2004] EWCA (Civ) 1598 at [96].

[406] See, eg, *Star Reefers*, supra; Fentiman (2012) 71 CLJ 273; *Golden Endurance Shipping SA v RMA Watanya SA* [2014] EWHC 3917 (Comm), [2015] 1 Lloyd's Rep 266.

[407] *The Irini A* [1999] 1 Lloyd's Rep 196.

[408] [1987] 1 AC 871 at 899. But cf *FMC Corpn v Russell* 1999 SLT 99 at 105.

[409] *Simon Engineering plc v Butte Mining plc* [1996] 1 Lloyd's Rep 104 n at 110–11; *Simon Engineering plc v Butte Mining plc (No 2)* [1996] 1 Lloyd's Rep 91 at 98–100; following *Smith Kline & French Laboratories Ltd v Bloch* [1983] 1 WLR 730, CA. See also *Shell UK Exploration and Production Ltd v Innes* 1995 SLT 807 at 824; *Amchem Products Inc v Workers' Compensation Board* (1993) 102 DLR (4th) 96 at 110–11 (Sopinka J), Sup Ct of Canada.

Thirdly, *Société Aérospatiale* was a case where the plaintiffs had started proceedings in two different fora. Nonetheless, the principles set out by the Privy Council are seemingly equally applicable in cases where the roles of the parties are reversed, ie the claimant in the foreign proceedings is the defendant in the English proceedings and vice versa.[410] It has been suggested that the courts should be even more cautious about granting an injunction in reversed role cases than in cases where a claimant has instituted proceedings in two different jurisdictions, on the ground that in the former case the claimant in the foreign proceedings has been compelled to appear in the English proceedings.[411] Moreover, an English court can grant an injunction enjoining foreign proceedings even if proceedings in respect of the main cause of action have not yet been commenced here. The only concern is that England is available as a forum.

Fourthly, what are the comity considerations in a case like the *Société Aérospatiale* case? The House of Lords has subsequently held that there is no infringement of comity where England is the natural forum for the resolution of the dispute.[412] This provides England with a sufficient interest in, or connection with, the matter in question to justify the interference with the foreign court that an anti-suit injunction entails.

(ii) Trial is available in alternative fora abroad (but not in England)
This is the situation that arose in *Airbus Industrie GIE v Patel*.[413]

> Following an aircraft crash in India, the defendants, English residents, brought proceedings in Texas against the plaintiffs, manufacturers of the aircraft. The plaintiffs sought from the English courts an injunction restraining the defendants from continuing with the Texas proceedings.

The House of Lords, reversing the decision of the Court of Appeal,[414] held that the grant of an injunction in the circumstances was inconsistent with comity. The English courts had no interest in, or connection with, the matter in question to justify such interference. This was despite the fact that the natural forum for trial was India; but the courts there were unable to grant effective injunctive relief in respect of the English defendants,[415] whereas the English courts could grant effective relief to prevent the pursuit of proceedings in Texas which may properly be regarded as oppressive. Nor was the fact that Texas, at that time, did not recognise and apply the doctrine of *forum non conveniens* so extreme as to deprive that state of the respect required by comity. Accordingly, there could be no exception to the general rule requiring a sufficient interest in, or connection with, the matter in question. Lord Hobhouse in *Turner v Grovit*[416] has caused some confusion by referring to the need for the *applicant* to have a legitimate interest in making his application[417] and interpreting *Airbus Industrie GIE v Patel* as being a case where the applicant had no such interest. According to Lord Hobhouse, what this case shows is that the necessary legitimate interest of the applicant must be the existence of proceedings in England which need to be protected by the grant of a restraining

---

[410] *E I Du Pont & Co v I C Agnew* [1988] 2 Lloyd's Rep 240. Cf the position in relation to stays of English proceedings in cases involving a multiplicity of proceedings.

[411] *Hemain v Hemain* [1988] 2 FLR 388, 390, quoting from *Cohen v Rothfield* [1919] 1 KB 410 at 414. The latter case was cited with approval in the *Société Aérospatiale* case at 892. For the significance of the *Hemain* case in relation to matrimonial causes see infra, p 978.

[412] *Airbus Industrie GIE v Patel* [1999] 1 AC 119 at 134, 138–9 (per Lord Goff), HL.

[413] [1999] 1 AC 119, HL; Briggs (1998) 69 BYBIL 332; Peel (1998) 114 LQR 543; approved in *Turner v Grovit*, supra, at [27].

[414] [1997] 2 Lloyd's Rep 8; Briggs (1996) 67 BYBIL 601; Fentiman [1997] CLJ 46.

[415] Coleman J refused to enforce at common law a judgment of the Indian court purporting to restrain the defendants from claiming damages other than in India, [1996] IL Pr 465.

[416] *Turner v Grovit*, supra, at [27].

[417] See Ambrose (2003) 52 ICLQ 401, 406.

order.[418] This misunderstands the reasoning in the case where the concern was with *England's* interest. Moreover, whilst the two different tests in relation to the relevant interest lead to the same result in a case like *Airbus Industrie GIE v Patel*, the legitimate interest of the applicant test causes real problems in single forum cases.[419]

(b) Other instances of unconscionable conduct

Lord Hobhouse in *Turner v Grovit* said that there were instances of unconscionable conduct where the right not to be sued abroad derives from the conduct itself and not from the inappropriateness of the forum abroad (eg as in the *Société Aérospatiale* case) or the breach of an agreement.[420] There is a judicial reluctance to define what is meant by "unconscionable" conduct.[421] In principle it simply means contrary to the rules of English equity.[422] What is unconscionable cannot and should not be defined exhaustively.[423] Guidance on the meaning of unconscionable conduct can also be found in *British Airways Board v Laker Airways Ltd*[424] where Lord Diplock said that unconscionable conduct encompasses the bringing of an action against a person who has a right not to be sued because a defence, such as estoppel in pais, promissory estoppel, election, waiver, standing by and laches, is available to him under English law.[425] In contrast, it is not unconscionable to continue with an action in Texas for damages following a collision at sea after an English court has granted a decree limiting the shipowner's liability.[426] The purpose of an injunction is not to ensure that a foreign court recognises an English judgment but to prevent unconscionable conduct.[427] However, it has been found unconscionable for a claimant to seek to obtain an order in foreign proceedings which has already been sought without success in the English courts.[428] This is sometimes also described as justified by the power of the English courts to protect their jurisdiction, which may extend to restraining a party from taking steps which would undermine the effectiveness of an (actual or anticipated) English judgment.[429] The House of Lords similarly in *South Carolina Insurance Co v Assurantie NV*[430] held that unconscionable conduct included not only conduct which is oppressive or vexatious but also conduct "which interferes with the due process of the court". The meaning of vexatious and oppressive has previously been examined. Attention will now turn to the concept of conduct which interferes with the due process of the court or, as it is sometimes called, abuse of process.

(i) *Interference with the due process of the court*

Turner v Grovit on its facts concerned abuse of process, which is another way of expressing the same general ideas as "unconscionable" conduct but with particular reference to the

---

[418] *Turner v Grovit*, supra, at [27].

[419] Infra, p 433 et seq.

[420] Supra, at [25].

[421] See *South Carolina Insurance Co v Assurantie NV* [1987] AC 24 at 41, HL.

[422] *Barclays Bank plc v Homan* [1993] BCLC 680 at 687 (Hoffmann J); [1993] BCLC 680 at 705, CA.

[423] *Glencore International AG v Exter Shipping Ltd* [2002] EWCA Civ 528 at [42], [2002] 2 All ER (Comm) 1.

[424] [1985] AC 58.

[425] Ibid, at 81.

[426] *Seismic Shipping Inc v Total E & P UK plc (The Western Regent)* [2005] EWCA Civ 985, [2005] 2 Lloyd's Rep 359, Briggs (2005) 76 BYBIL 663. There was no reason to think that the Texan court would not give full consideration to the English decree, at [49].

[427] The *Seismic Shipping* case, supra, at [48] (per Clarke LJ, Nourse LJ concurring).

[428] *Royal Bank of Scotland v Hicks* [2010] EWHC 2579 (Ch); *Masri v Consolidated Contractors International Company Sal* [2008] EWCA Civ 625, [2009] QB 503.

[429] *Masri v Consolidated Contractors International Company Sal* [2008] EWCA Civ 625 at [95], [2009] QB 503; *Ardila Investments NV v ENRC NV* [2015] EWHC 1667 (Comm), [2015] 2 BCLC 560. This principle extends also to English arbitral awards: *C v D* [2007] EWCA Civ 1282, [2008] 1 Lloyd's Rep 239.

[430] [1987] AC 24, HL.

effect of the unconscionable conduct upon pending English proceedings.[431] The facts of the case are examined in more detail later in this chapter.[432] The House of Lords held that it was proper for the Court of Appeal to grant an injunction on these facts because: (a) the applicant was a party to existing legal proceedings in England; (b) the defendants had in bad faith commenced and proposed to prosecute proceedings in another jurisdiction for the purpose of frustrating or obstructing the proceedings in England; (c) the court considered that it was necessary in order to protect the legitimate interest of the applicant in the English proceedings to grant the applicant a restraining order against the defendants.[433] However, the proceedings abroad were in another European Union Member State, Spain, and this raised the question, referred to the Court of Justice, whether it was inconsistent with the Brussels Convention to grant an injunction in such circumstances. As discussed in more detail later in this chapter, the Court of Justice held that it was, even where the party commencing proceedings before the court of another Member State was acting in bad faith with a view to frustrating the existing proceedings.[434] The House of Lords decision nevertheless stands as authority concerning the circumstances in which an anti-suit injunction restraining proceedings in a non-Member State may be awarded.

Lord Hobhouse in *Turner v Grovit* highlighted the need for there not only to be wrongful conduct of the party to be restrained but also for the applicant to be entitled to complain about this conduct and to have a legitimate interest in seeking to prevent it.[435] Lord Hobhouse went on to say that where there has been clearly unconscionable conduct on the part of the party sought to be restrained, as there was in the instant case, this is a sufficiently strong element to support the affected party's application for an order to restrain such conduct.[436] This is not based upon the complaint that the action has been brought in an inappropriate forum.[437] But where there was unconscionable conduct for some non-contractual reason, the necessary legitimate interest must be the existence of proceedings in England which need to be protected by the grant of a restraining order.[438] This latter requirement was met on the facts of the case.

Another and very obvious example of unconscionable conduct can be seen in *Glencore International AG v Exter Shipping Ltd*,[439] where the plaintiffs in an action in Georgia had no legitimate interest in pursuing claims in Georgia. This was part of a deliberate strategy of harassment and vexation, designed to wear down the applicant (a defendant in the Georgia action) by subjecting it to the burden of litigating on several fronts, and designed to put off the day when a conclusion was reached on the issues dividing the parties.[440] There was a clear need to protect existing English proceedings[441] and the appeal against the grant of an injunction was dismissed.

(ii) Single forum cases

Lord Hobhouse in *Turner v Grovit* did not discuss "single" forum cases. This phrase covers not only cases where an injunction is sought restraining proceedings in the only state which

---

[431] *Turner v Grovit* [2001] UKHL 65 at [24], [2002] 1 WLR 107.
[432] Infra, p 477.
[433] *Turner v Grovit*, supra, at [29].
[434] Case C-159/02 *Turner v Grovit* [2004] All ER (EC) 485; infra, p 477 et seq.
[435] *Turner v Grovit* [2001] UKHL 65 at [24], [2002] 1 WLR 107.
[436] Ibid, at [25].
[437] Ibid.
[438] Ibid, at [27].
[439] [2002] EWCA Civ 528 at [65]–[70], [2002] 2 All ER (Comm) 1; Briggs (2002) 73 BYBIL 463. See also *Noble Assurance Co v Gerling-Konzern General Insurance Co* [2007] EWHC 253 (Comm); *Benfield Holdings Ltd v Elliot Richardson* [2007] EWHC 171 (QB).
[440] The *Glencore* case, supra, at [69].
[441] Ibid at [62]–[64].

has jurisdiction[442] but also cases where there is only one state in which the claimant could bring a successful action.[443] The contrast has been made with alternative forum cases, ie the English court is choosing between two or more alternative fora for trial, such as in the *Société Aérospatiale* case. "Single" forum cases should be examined as a separate group of cases because of the need for extra caution before granting an injunction in such cases.

In the *South Carolina* case a party to an English action sought to obtain in the USA discovery of documents from a third party. US pre-trial procedure allows this evidence to be obtained, whereas English procedure does not. The House of Lords held that there was no unconscionable conduct. There was no interference with the due process of the English courts. The English courts still controlled their own procedure, since it is up to the parties to obtain, either in England or abroad, the relevant evidence.[444] Moreover, mere extra cost and inconvenience to the parties cannot be characterised as interference with the court's control of its own process.[445] In contrast, an injunction was granted preventing the obtaining of witness statements in the USA when it was intended to call those witnesses in England and they might be discouraged from attending if witness statements had been obtained in the USA.[446]

In *British Airways Board v Laker Airways Ltd*[447] the House of Lords unanimously allowed an appeal against the grant of an injunction restraining an action in the USA by Laker Airways Ltd (Laker), a Jersey company with its principal office in London, against British Airways and another British airline. The action was for multiple damages for breach of US anti-trust laws by conspiring to eliminate Laker as a competitor by fixing "predatory" air fare tariffs. There was no cause of action under English law, and the only country in which Laker could obtain a remedy was the USA. For this reason the case was distinguishable from cases where a choice is being made between alternative fora; those cases were of no assistance here.[448] Caution was said to be a "very necessary" in these single forum cases.[449] It was not unconscionable to allow the proceedings in the USA to continue, seemingly, because no complaint could be made about Laker's conduct. It had been argued that, since Laker was admitted to the scheduled airlines' club and submitted to the regulations required by the club, it could not complain about the conduct of fellow members of the club that was permitted by the club's rules in relation to fares. This argument was rejected on the basis that Laker's action was founded not on the actual fares charged but on the fact that the other airlines were allegedly in breach of US law.[450] It is to be noted that in exercising their discretion their Lordships did not give weight to the fact that it would be impossible to enforce in England an American judgment for multiple damages in an anti-trust case.[451]

On the other hand, in *Midland Bank plc v Laker Airways Ltd*[452] the Court of Appeal held it to be unconscionable conduct for Laker to bring an anti-trust suit in the USA against the Midland Bank and an injunction was allowed restraining those threatened proceedings. The alleged liability of the bank arose out of banking acts done in England and intended to be

---

[442] *Airbus Industrie GIE v Patel*, supra, at 134.
[443] See *Barclays Bank plc v Homan* [1993] BCLC 680 at 698, CA.
[444] *South Carolina Insurance Co v Assurantie NV*, supra, at 41–4.
[445] Ibid, at 42–3.
[446] *Omega Group Holdings Ltd v Kozeny* [2002] CLC 132.
[447] [1985] AC 58, HL.
[448] [1985] AC 58, at 80, 85.
[449] Ibid, at 95.
[450] [1985] AC 58, at 84–5.
[451] See the Protection of Trading Interests Act 1980, s 5, discussed infra, pp 553–5. See also the judgment of Parker J at first instance [1984] 1 QB 142 at 162–3.
[452] [1986] QB 689, CA. Distinguished in *Barclays Bank plc v Homan* [1993] BCLC 680 at 688, 692; [1993] BCLC 680 at 705, CA.

governed by English law; the bank had never submitted to US anti-trust law or US jurisdiction; and there was no claim against it in England.[453] It was also considered relevant that the evidence of conspiracy under US law was weak, although the court was reluctant to examine the question of the weight of the evidence too closely, and recent case law has suggested that in general the English courts should not take into consideration the strength of the case before the foreign court.[454] However, in rare cases where it is clear that the action abroad is bound to fail, this will make the claimant's foreign action frivolous and vexatious and therefore unconscionable.[455] But the fact that a party will be exposed to pre-trial discovery in the US proceedings is not a source per se of injustice.[456]

The requirement that, as a general rule, the English forum should have a sufficient interest in, or connection with, the matter in question to justify the interference with the foreign court that an anti-suit injunction entails, applies as much to single forum as to alternative forum cases.[457] The decision in the *Midland Bank* case has been described by Lord Goff as being consistent with this requirement in that the relevant transaction was overwhelmingly English in character.[458] In contrast, the grant of an injunction in the *British Airways Board* case could not be justified in this way.[459] Lord Hobhouse in *Turner v Grovit* has muddied the waters by introducing the requirement that the *applicant* has a legitimate interest in seeking to prevent the wrongful conduct and that where there was unconscionable conduct for some non-contractual reason, the necessary legitimate interest of the *applicant* must be the existence of proceedings in England which need to be protected by the grant of a restraining order.[460] There were no such English proceedings in the *Midland Bank* case. However, Lord Hobhouse was not referring to single forum cases and his words should not be taken as limiting the right to grant an injunction in such cases. He was thinking of *Airbus Industrie GIE v Patel* and seems not to have understood the concern in that case that *England* should have an interest. Looking at that requirement, what Lord Goff's comments (in *Airbus Industrie GIE v Patel*) in relation to the *Midland Bank* case show is that the requisite interest of the English forum can still be shown even where there are no proceedings in England which need to be protected.

In principle, there is even more need for caution in restraining foreign proceedings in cases where the claimant has only a single forum in which he is able to bring an action (ie which has jurisdiction) than there is in cases when there are alternative fora for trial, since the effect of granting the stay is to deny the claimant trial in any country at all. On the other hand, it is questionable whether the need for extra caution exists in those cases (such as the *Laker* cases) where the claimant is being denied the opportunity to bring a successful action, but does in fact have a choice of fora (ie two states have jurisdiction).[461]

The need for caution is even stronger if a judgment has actually been obtained in the forum abroad and a world-wide injunction is sought to restrain a party from relying on this

---

[453] [1986] QB 689 at 699–700, 704–5, 712–13.

[454] *Star Reefers Pool Inc v JFC Group Co Ltd* [2012] EWCA Civ 14, [2012] 1 Lloyd's Rep 376; *Vitol Bahrain EC v Nasdec General Trading LLC* [2013] EWHC 3359 (Comm).

[455] *Midland Bank*, supra, at 700, 702, 710, 712–13. See also *British Airways Board v Laker Airways Ltd* [1985] AC 58 at 86.

[456] [1986] QB 689 at 714.

[457] *Airbus Industrie GIE v Patel* [1999] 1 AC 119 at 134, 138 (per Lord Goff), HL.

[458] Ibid at 138.

[459] Ibid.

[460] *Turner v Grovit*, supra, at [27].

[461] The courts still refer to these as single forum cases, but are using the term in a different sense from that where only one state has jurisdiction.

judgment. Even if that party is acting unconscionably the court may exercise its discretion and refuse to grant the injunction.[462]

(ii) The bringing of the proceedings abroad would be in breach of an agreement

Where proceedings abroad would be in breach of a valid[463] exclusive jurisdiction clause[464] providing for trial in England,[465] the English courts have an inherent power to restrain a party from bringing or continuing the proceedings abroad, for that would constitute a breach of contract.[466] The same principles apply where proceedings abroad would be in breach of a valid arbitration clause.[467] Less commonly, the breach of an agreement is in *bringing the proceedings* abroad (in breach of, for example, an obligation to follow designated procedural steps before any legal proceedings may be commenced) rather than being in breach of an exclusive jurisdiction clause or arbitration clause, which relates to where the proceedings must be brought or what type of proceedings must be brought. Nonetheless the same principles will apply.[468] In cases where there would be a breach of an agreement, different principles in relation to the grant of an injunction apply from cases where there is no such agreement. First, the requirement that there is wrongful conduct of the party to be restrained of which the applicant is entitled to complain and has a legitimate interest in seeking to prevent[469] is easily met in such cases. The conduct of the party acting in breach of the agreement is at least prima facie unconscionable.[470] A contractual jurisdiction or arbitration clause will provide a right not to be sued in another forum.[471] This is independent of whether any substantive proceedings have been commenced or are pending before the English courts.[472] The applicant does not have to show that the contractual forum is more appropriate than any other; the contractual agreement does that for him. Where the applicant is relying upon a contractual

---

[462] *E D & F Man (Sugar) Ltd v Yani Haryanto (No 2)* [1991] 1 Lloyd's Rep 161 at 167–8.

[463] See supra, pp 415–16 on the validity of an exclusive jurisdiction clause. See specifically in the present context *Crédit Suisse First Boston (Europe) Ltd v Seagate Trading Co Ltd* [1999] 1 Lloyd's Rep 784; *OT Africa Line Ltd v Magic Sportwear Corpn* [2006] EWCA Civ 710, [2005] 2 Lloyd's Rep 170.

[464] An agreement on jurisdiction can take the form of a consent order in foreign proceedings whereby the parties agree not to challenge the jurisdiction of the English courts: *General Motors Corpn v Royal & Sun Alliance Insurance Group* [2007] EWHC 2206 (Comm).

[465] Such a clause will ordinarily fall within Art 25 of the Brussels I Recast, supra, p 229 et seq. It is submitted that this does not preclude the English courts from granting an injunction in relation to proceedings in a non-Member State, see infra, pp 481–2.

[466] This power has been recognised for many years see *Ellerman Lines Ltd v Read* [1928] 2 KB 144; *Mike Trading and Transport Ltd v R Pagnan and Fratelli, The Lisboa* [1980] 2 Lloyd's Rep 546, CA; *British Airways Board v Laker Airways Ltd* [1985] AC 58 at 81; *Continental Bank NA v Aeakos Compañía Naviera SA* [1994] 1 WLR 588, CA. It must be not merely arguable that there is a breach, but shown to a high degree of probability: *National Westminster Bank v Utrecht-America Finance Co* [2001] EWCA Civ 658, [2001] 3 All ER 733; *American International Specialty Lines Insurance Co v Abbott Laboratories* [2002] EWHC 2714 (Comm) at 275.

[467] *Aggeliki Charis Compañía Marítima SA v Pagnan SpA, The Angelic Grace* [1995] 1 Lloyd's Rep 87, CA. For earlier cases see *Pena Copper Mines Ltd v Rio Tinto Co Ltd* (1911) 105 LT 846; *Tracomin SA v Sudan Oil Seeds Co Ltd (Nos 1 and 2)* [1983] 1 WLR 1026.

[468] *National Westminster Bank v Utrecht-America Finance Co* [2001] EWCA Civ 658, [2001] 3 All ER 733; *Elektrim SA v Vivendi Holdings 1 Corp* [2008] EWCA Civ 1178, [2009] 1 Lloyd's Rep 59.

[469] *Turner v Grovit*, supra, at [24].

[470] Ibid, at [27]. See also *OT Africa Line Ltd v Magic Sportswear Corpn* [2005] EWCA Civ 710 at [63] and [83], [2005] 2 Lloyd's Rep 170. It is possible, however, that the foreign claimant could demonstrate the existence of circumstances which might justify their conduct. The existence of closely related foreign proceedings involving other parties might be one such consideration—as discussed earlier in this chapter, in rare cases this may justify the English courts refusing to exercise jurisdiction despite an English exclusive jurisdiction agreement.

[471] *Turner v Grovit*, supra, at [25]. See also *British Airways Board v Laker Airways Ltd* [1985] AC 58 at 81.

[472] *AES Ust-Kamenogorsk Hydropower Plant LLP v Ust-Kamenogorsk Hydropower Plant JSC* [2013] UKSC 35, [2013] 1 WLR 1889; *Donohue v Armco Inc* [2001] UKHL 64, [2002] 1 All ER 749.

right not to be sued in the foreign country then, in the absence of some special circumstance, he has by reason of his contract a legitimate interest in enforcing that right against the other party to the contract.[473] Secondly, a party to an exclusive English jurisdiction clause has a right to have the contract enforced and this can only be displaced by strong reasons being shown by the opposite party why an injunction should *not* be granted.[474] The same principle applies in relation to breach of an arbitration clause.[475] By contrast, where an anti-suit injunction is sought in the absence of a jurisdiction or arbitration clause the applicant has to show that justice requires that he should be granted an injunction.[476] Thirdly, the principle that the power to grant an injunction restraining foreign proceedings must be exercised with caution does not apply in breach cases.[477] Fourthly, there is not the same concern with comity in such cases.[478] This underlies the first and third of the above points. A separate point to note in relation to the breach of an agreement is that a claimant is able to recover as damages its reasonable expenses in litigating abroad (as defendant) where this was in breach of an exclusive jurisdiction clause.[479] This includes the costs of defending such part of the action abroad as fell within the clause.[480]

(a) Breach of an exclusive jurisdiction agreement

It will be recalled[481] that Lord Bingham in the House of Lords in *Donohue v Armco Inc*[482] summarised the principles to be applied where there has been a breach of an exclusive jurisdiction agreement as follows. Where contracting parties agree to give a particular court exclusive jurisdiction to rule on claims between those parties, and a claim falling within the scope of the agreement[483] is made in proceedings in a forum other than that on which the parties have agreed, the English court will ordinarily[484] exercise its discretion by restraining the prosecution of proceedings in the non-contractual forum abroad (or by granting a stay of proceedings in England, or by such other procedural order as is appropriate in the

---

[473] *Turner v Grovit*, supra, at [27]. See also *Airbus Industrie GIE v Patel* [1999] 1 AC 119, 138, HL.

[474] The *Donohue* case, supra, at [45] (per Lord Hobhouse).

[475] See infra, pp 441–2.

[476] The *Donohue* case, supra, at [45] (per Lord Hobhouse).

[477] *Aggeliki Charis Compañia Maritima SA v Pagnan SpA, The Angelic Grace* [1995] 1 Lloyd's Rep 87, 96, CA; *Glencore International AG v Exter Shipping Ltd* [2002] EWCA Civ 528 at [43], [2002] 2 All ER (Comm) 1. See also the *Donohue* case, supra, at 757, which only referred to this principle when discussing vexation or oppression.

[478] Infra, pp 439–40.

[479] *Union Discount Co Ltd v Zoller* [2001] EWCA Civ 1755, [2002] 1 WLR 1517; Briggs (2001) 72 BYBIL 446; *Donohue v Armco Inc* [2001] UKHL 64 at [75] (per Lord Scott), [48] (per Lord Hobhouse), [2002] 1 All ER 749; *A/S Svendborg v Ali Hussein Akar* [2003] EWHC 797 (Comm); *National Westminster Bank v Rabobank Nederland* [2007] EWHC 1742 (Comm), [2008] 1 All ER (Comm) 266; *The Alexandros T* [2014] EWCA Civ 1010, [2014] 2 Lloyd's Rep 544; *Swissmarine Services SA v Gupta Coal India Private Limited* [2015] EWHC 265 (Comm); Tan and Yeo [2003] LMCLQ 435; Tham [2004] LMCLQ 46; Ho (2003) 52 ICLQ 697, 707–10; Merrett (2006) 55 ICLQ 315; Ruddell [2015] LMCLQ 9. See in relation to damages for breach of an arbitration clause: *DVA v Voest Alpine* [1997] 2 Lloyd's Rep 279, 285; *A v B (No 2)* [2007] EWHC 54 (Comm), [2007] 1 Lloyd's Rep 358.

[480] *Donohue v Armco Inc* [2001] UKHL 64 at [75] (per Lord Scott), [48] (per Lord Hobhouse), [2002] 1 All ER 749. See also *A v B (No 2)* [2007] EWHC 54 (Comm), [2007] 1 Lloyd's Rep 358 (indemnity costs for breach of an arbitration agreement).

[481] See pp 410–12.

[482] [2001] UKHL 64, [2002] 1 All ER 749.

[483] An English court will decide whether claims brought abroad under a foreign cause of action fall within the scope of the exclusive jurisdiction clauses, see *Donohue v Armco Inc* [2000] 1 Lloyd's Rep 579 at 586–9; revd by the House of Lords [2001] UKHL 64, [2002] 1 All ER 749, where the scope of the clauses was not in issue. See also *National Westminster Bank v Utrecht-America Finance Co* [2001] EWCA Civ 658, [2001] 3 All ER 733; *AWB (Geneva) SA v North America Steamships Ltd* [2007] EWCA Civ 739, [2007] 2 Lloyd's Rep 315.

[484] This recognises that it is a discretion.

circumstances) to secure compliance with the contractual bargain, unless the party suing in the non-contractual forum (the burden being on him) can show strong reasons for suing in that forum.[485] These principles apply in both the contexts of an injunction restraining foreign proceedings brought in breach of an exclusive jurisdiction clause providing for trial in England and of a stay of English proceedings brought in breach of an exclusive jurisdiction clause providing for trial abroad.[486] The matters that might properly be regarded by the court when exercising its discretion in the latter context are equally relevant in the former context. It follows that the matters listed by Brandon J in *The Eleftheria*, set out earlier in this chapter when discussing stays of action,[487] should be considered when exercising the discretion to grant an injunction.[488] This is not intended to be an exhaustive list.[489] After examining many of the authorities from both areas, Lord Bingham concluded that, where the dispute is between two contracting parties, and the interests of other parties are not involved, effect will in all probability be given to the exclusive jurisdiction clause.[490] In contrast, the English court may well decline to grant an anti-suit injunction (or a stay as the case may be) where the interests of parties other than the parties bound by the exclusive jurisdiction clause are involved or grounds of claim not the subject of the clause are part of the relevant dispute so that there is a risk of parallel proceedings and inconsistent decisions.[491] The principle that applies in cases of *forum non conveniens* that, where there is a clause providing for the exclusive jurisdiction of the English courts, the courts should refuse to pay regard to matters of convenience that were foreseeable at the time the contract was concluded,[492] has been applied in the present context.[493]

The *Donohue* case concerned an injunction sought to restrain proceedings brought in New York in breach of English exclusive jurisdiction clauses contained in agreements relating to the sale of shares. The defendants in the English proceedings were able to show the requisite strong reasons, sufficient to displace the claimant's prima facie entitlement to enforce the contractual bargain, and an injunction restraining the proceedings in New York was refused. There were other defendants in the New York proceedings who were potential co-claimants in the English proceedings,[494] some of whom were not parties to the exclusive jurisdiction clauses. The strong reasons lay in the prospect, if the injunction were to be granted, of litigation between the defendants on the one side and the claimant and the potential co-claimants on the other continuing partly in England and partly in New York.[495] The interests of justice were best served by the submission of the whole suit to a single tribunal which could adjudicate on all the matters in issue, namely the New York courts.[496]

---

[485] The *Donohue* case, supra, at [24].

[486] On the latter see supra, p 410 et seq.

[487] Supra, p 411.

[488] *Beazley v Horizon Offshore Contractors Inc* [2004] EWHC 2555 (Comm) at [24], [2005] IL Pr 11.

[489] The *Donohue* case, supra, at [24].

[490] Ibid, at [25]. See *Horn Linie GmbH & Co v Panamericana Formas e Impresos SA (The Hornbay)* [2006] EWHC 373 (Comm), [2006] 2 Lloyd's Rep 44, a cargo insurer seeking to avoid the parties' bargain.

[491] The *Donohue* case, supra, at [27] referring to the following anti-suit injunction cases: *Bouygues Offshore SA v Caspian ShippingCo (Nos 1, 3, 4 and 5)* [1998] 2 Lloyd's Rep 461; *Crédit Suisse First Boston (Europe) v MLC (Bermuda) Ltd* [1999] 1 All ER (Comm) 237. The stay cases referred to are cited supra, p 412, n 215. See more generally on refusal to grant an injunction: *Akai Pty Ltd v People's Insurance Co Ltd* [1998] 1 Lloyd's Rep 90 at 104 et seq; *Shell v Coral Oil* [1999] 1 Lloyd's Rep 72 at 79.

[492] Supra, pp 398–9.

[493] The *Beazley case*, supra, at [29].

[494] They could not be joined to the English action as claimants because they had no cause of action entitling them to an anti-suit injunction on the ground of vexation or oppression, supra, at [17]–[22] (per Lord Bingham) and [45] (per Lord Hobhouse).

[495] The *Donohue* case, supra, at [33] (per Lord Bingham) and [75] (per Lord Scott).

[496] Ibid, at [34].

In contrast, the parties were held to their bargain and an injunction granted in relation to proceedings brought in Canada in breach of an agreement providing for the exclusive jurisdiction of the English courts, even though there were real connections with that country and there was also a Canadian statute which rendered a jurisdiction clause in a bill of lading, which provided for trial outside Canada, as being of no effect and which was equivalent to the internationally agreed Hamburg Rules.[497]

Lord Bingham in *Donohue* has said that a party may lose his claim to equitable relief by dilatoriness or other unconscionable conduct.[498] This is consistent with earlier statements that the longer the delay before the application was made the more likely it was that there would be good reason to refuse it, and that equally voluntary submission to the jurisdiction of the foreign court would very often amount to such good reason, especially where the proceedings have progressed for any period of time, a fortiori where an application for a stay of the foreign proceedings had been made and failed.[499] The mere fact that an applicant for an anti-suit injunction has disputed jurisdiction in the foreign court without success will not necessarily weaken their application, although making points on the merits before the foreign court may do so, and any delay in the application for an anti-suit injunction (even to dispute jurisdiction in the foreign court) may count against the applicant.[500]

The principles governing the grant of injunctions and stays are not entirely the same, a point acknowledged by Lord Bingham in the *Donohue* case,[501] in that considerations of comity arise in the former case but not in the latter. However, a concern with comity has not always been evident in cases where the ground for an injunction is that of a breach of an agreement.[502] Indeed, Lord Bingham did not think that this difference in the principles governing the grant of injunctions and stays needed to be explored in the instant case (one where there was a breach of an exclusive jurisdiction agreement).[503] The Court of Appeal has said that there is no reason in principle why comity should stand in the way of granting an injunction where proceedings are brought in breach of an English exclusive jurisdiction clause.[504] In *The Angelic Grace* it was thought that no court would be offended by the grant of an injunction to restrain a party from invoking a jurisdiction which he had promised not to invoke and

---

[497] *OT Africa Line Ltd v Magic Sportswear Corpn* [2005] EWCA Civ 710, [2005] 2 Lloyd's Rep 170. See also *Horn Linie GmbH & Co v Panamericana Formas e Impresos SA (The Hornbay)* [2006] EWHC 373 (Comm), [2006] 2 Lloyd's Rep 44.

[498] The *Donohue* case, supra, at [24]. See also, eg, *Royal Bank of Scotland Plc v Highland Financial Partners LP* [2013] EWCA Civ 328, [2013] 1 CLC 596.

[499] *Svendborg v Wansa* [1997] 2 Lloyd's Rep 183, Clarke J; the Court of Appeal said that there could be no criticism of the way that the judge had exercised the discretion, ibid. See generally on delay *Toepfer International GmbH v Molino Boschi Srl* [1996] 1 Lloyd's Rep 510 at 518; *Philip Alexander Securities and Futures Ltd v Bamberger*, supra, at 92–3 (Waller J), appeal to the Court of Appeal dismissed without discussion of this point; *Society of Lloyd's v White (No 1)* [2002] IL Pr 10; *Advent Capital plc v GN Ellinas Importers-Exporters Ld* [2003] EWHC 3330 at [26]–[27], [42]–[44], [2004] IL Pr 23; cf *Akai Pty Ltd v People's Insurance Co Ltd* [1998] 1 Lloyd's Rep 90 at 107–8; *DVA v Voest Alpine* [1997] 2 Lloyd's Rep 279 at 288, CA; *Verity Shipping SA v NV Norexa* [2008] EWHC 213 (Comm), [2008] 1 Lloyd's Rep 652; *Essar Shipping Ltd v Bank of China* [2015] EWHC 3266 (Comm).

[500] For a recent application and summary of the authorities see *ADM Asia-Pacific Trading Pte Ltd v PT Budi Semesta Satria* [2016] EWHC 1427 (Comm).

[501] Supra, at [24].

[502] Lord Goff in *Airbus Industrie GIE v Patel*, supra, when discussing comity stressed that he was not discussing cases where the choice of forum was the subject of an agreement between the parties (at 138).

[503] The *Donohue* case, supra, at [24].

[504] *National Westminster Bank v Utrecht-America Finance Co* [2001] EWCA Civ 658, [2001] 3 All ER 733. See also *OT Africa Line Ltd v Magic Sportswear Corpn* [2006] EWCA Civ 710 at [32], [83], [2005] 2 Lloyd's Rep 170. But cf *Ecobank Transnational Inc v Tanoh* [2015] EWCA Civ 1309, [2016] 1 Lloyd's Rep 360—the better view is that comity considerations are not irrelevant in this context.

which it was its own duty to decline.[505] This has proved to be unduly optimistic and the German courts have regarded the issue of anti-suit injunctions, in a case involving a consumer contract which provided for arbitration in London but where the German court did not regard itself as obliged to stay its proceedings in such circumstances, as an infringement of its sovereignty and refused to permit the injunctions to be served.[506] Waller J in *Philip Alexander Securities and Futures Ltd v Bamberger*, aware of the fact that the German courts were offended by the grant of an anti-suit injunction by the English courts, distinguished *The Angelic Grace*, inter alia, on this ground, and held that it was not a case where it was appropriate to grant an injunction.[507] The Court of Appeal in the *Bamberger* case, recognising the comity problem where effect needs to be given to the injunction by a foreign court,[508] thought that the English practice in relation to the grant of anti-suit injunctions may need reconsideration in the light of the facts of this case.[509] However, many subsequent cases have followed the principles in *The Angelic Grace*, ignoring the reaction of foreign courts to the grant of an injunction.[510] Nonetheless, it is submitted that where there is clear evidence that a foreign court would be offended[511] a degree of caution is desirable even in cases involving breach of an agreement. When it comes to whether a foreign court will be offended by the grant of an injunction it may be necessary to distinguish common law jurisdictions which are used to granting such an injunction themselves and are therefore not likely to be offended[512] and civil law jurisdictions which are not and are therefore likely to be offended. As noted previously and discussed further below,[513] anti-suit injunctions may not in any event be awarded to restrain a party from commencing or continuing proceedings in European Union Member States in cases which fall within the Brussels/Lugano System.

Where the agreement provides for the non-exclusive jurisdiction of the English courts there is no breach of agreement in bringing proceedings abroad and therefore an injunction will not be granted on the basis of breach of an agreement.[514] However, if one party (A) by way of a pre-emptive strike seeks an injunction abroad whereby the other party (B) will be permanently restrained from making any demand under a contract (containing a non-exclusive English jurisdiction clause) in the hope of preventing B from starting proceedings in

---

[505] *Aggeliki Charis Compañia Marítima SA v Pagnan SpA, The Angelic Grace* [1995] 1 Lloyd's Rep 87, CA. See also *Through Transport Mutual Insurance Association (Eurasia) Ltd v New India Assurance Co Ltd* [2004] EWCA (Civ) 1598; *West Tankers Inc v Ras Riunione Adriatica di Sicurta SpA (The Front Comor)* [2005] EWHC 454 (Comm), [2005] 2 Lloyd's Rep 257, Hill [2006] LMCLQ 166. As discussed infra, in the *West Tankers* case a related question was referred to the Court of Justice by the House of Lords.

[506] *Re the Enforcement of an English Anti-Suit Injunction* [1997] IL Pr 320; Harris [1997] CJQ 283.

[507] [1997] IL Pr 73 at 93–4.

[508] It may be doubted whether this was genuinely recognition of comity concerns, or merely of concerns regarding effectiveness.

[509] [1997] IL Pr 73 at 117, CA. See generally Males [1998] LMCLQ 543 at 547 et seq.

[510] *Through Transport Mutual Insurance Association (Eurasia) Ltd v New India Assurance Co Ltd* [2004] EWCA (Civ) 1598, [2005] 1 Lloyd's Rep 67; the *West Tankers Case*, supra, at [43]–[52]. See also *Navigation Maritime Bulgare v Rustal Trading Ltd (The Ivan Zagubanski)* [2002] 1 Lloyd's Rep 106 at [115]–[119]; *XL Insurance Ltd v Owens* [2000] 2 Lloyd's Rep 500. Cf *OT Africa Line ltd v Hijazy (The Kribi)* [2001] 1 Lloyd's Rep 76 at [83]; *Evialis SA v SIAT* [2003] 2 Lloyd's Rep 377 at 388–9.

[511] See *The Kribi*, supra, at [83].

[512] *Beazley v Horizon Offshore Contractors Inc* [2004] EWHC 2555 (Comm) at [40], [2005] IL Pr 11; *Society of Lloyd's v White (No 2)* [2002] IL Pr 11 at [54]–[56]. But see *Commonwealth Bank of Australia v White (No 4)* [2001] VSC 511, Moshinsky (2005) 79 ALJ 82, court refused to stay its proceedings, despite an English anti-suit injunction granted on the basis of breach of a jurisdiction agreement.

[513] See infra, p 475 et seq.

[514] *Royal Bank of Canada v Cooperative Centrale Raiffeisen-Boerenleenbank BA* [2004] EWCA Civ 7, [2004] 1 Lloyd's Rep 471, Briggs (2004) 75 BYBIL 558; *Continental Bank v Aeakos* [1994] 1 WLR 588, CA; *A/S Svendborg v Wansa* [1997] 2 Lloyd's Rep 183, CA; Fawcett [2001] LMCLQ 234 at 255–7.

England, this is a breach of contract and vexatious.[515] An injunction restraining A from continuing the proceedings abroad will then be granted on the basis of vexation or oppression.[516] Moreover, if English proceedings have been commenced on the basis of a non-exclusive jurisdiction clause, the nature of the clause may be such that, although not exclusive, it does not contemplate parallel proceedings and pursuing proceedings abroad would be vexatious or oppressive.[517] A non-exclusive jurisdiction agreement may contemplate the possibility of simultaneous trials in England and abroad and, if trial is pursued abroad, there will not only be no breach of such an agreement but also no vexatious or oppressive conduct.[518] It may be doubted, however, whether generally parties understand a non-exclusive jurisdiction agreement to contemplate parallel proceedings, rather than simply to create an option as to where proceedings may be commenced.

(b) Breach of an arbitration agreement

Where there is an agreement valid under its governing law to arbitrate and foreign court proceedings are pending, the English courts have an inherent power to restrain the parties from bringing or continuing the foreign proceedings, for that would constitute a breach of contract.[519] In such cases, the court need feel no diffidence in granting the injunction, provided that it is sought promptly and before the foreign proceedings are too far advanced.[520] The often expressed principle that the power to issue an anti-suit injunction must be exercised with caution was said to have no application in such a case. There has often been said to be no difference in principle between an injunction to restrain proceedings in breach of an arbitration clause and one to restrain proceedings in breach of an exclusive jurisdiction clause.[521] The justification for the grant of an injunction in either case is that, without it, the claimant will be deprived of his contractual rights in a situation in which damages are manifestly an inadequate remedy.[522] The ground for granting the injunction to restrain the foreign proceedings is the clear and simple one that the defendant has promised not to bring them.[523] The principles in the *Donohue* case[524] (a case concerned with exclusive jurisdiction clauses) have

---

[515] *Sabah Shipyard (Pakistan) Ltd v Islamic Republic of Pakistan* [2002] EWCA Civ 1643, [2003] 2 Lloyd's Rep 571, CA, Briggs (2003) 74 BYBIL 528.

[516] The *Sabah* case, supra.

[517] Ibid, [36]–[37] (per Waller LJ), [52] (per Pill LJ).

[518] *Royal Bank of Canada v Cooperative Centrale Raiffeisen-Boerenleenbank BA* [2004] EWCA Civ 7, [2004] 1 Lloyd's Rep 471; *Deutsche Bank v Highland Crusader* [2009] EWCA Civ 725.

[519] See *Aggeliki Charis Compañía Marítima SA v Pagnan SpA, The Angelic Grace* [1995] 1 Lloyd's Rep 87, CA; followed in, eg, *Bankers Trust Co v PT Jakarta International Hotels and Development* [1999] 1 Lloyd's Rep 910; approved most recently in *Through Transport Mutual Insurance Association (Eurasia) Ltd v New India Assurance Co Ltd* [2004] EWCA (Civ) 1598; the *West Tankers* case, supra; *AES Ust-Kamenogorsk Hydropower Plant LLP v Ust-Kamenogorsk Hydropower Plant JSC* [2013] UKSC 35, [2013] 1 WLR 1889; *Shipowners' Mutual Protection and Indemnity Association (Luxembourg) v Containerships Denizcilik Nakliyat ve Ticaret AS* [2016] EWCA Civ 386, [2016] 1 Lloyd's Rep 641, appeal pending. For where the sole purpose of proceeding abroad is to obtain arrest of a ship, see *Petromin SA v Secnav Marine Ltd* [1995] 1 Lloyd's Rep 603. See also *The Kallang* [2006] EWHC 2825 (Comm), [2007] 1 Lloyd's Rep 160—arrest abroad used to undermine arbitration clause; *Purpose AS v Transnav Purpose Navigation Ltd* [2017] EWHC 719 (Comm).

[520] The *Angelic Grace*, supra, at 96 (per Millett LJ); the *Through Transport* case, supra, at [90].

[521] The *Angelic Grace*, supra, at 96 and the *Through Transport* case, supra, at [90]. See also the *Natwest Bank* case, supra, at [32]; the *American International Specialty Lines Insurance Co* case, supra, at 275; *Goshawk Dedicated Ltd v ROP Inc* [2006] EWHC 1730 (Comm), [2006] Lloyd's Rep IR 711. In arbitration cases, the New York Convention does not provide a ground for refusal of an anti-suit injunction: *West Tankers Inc v Ras Riunione Adriatica Di Sicurta SpA (The Front Comor)* [2005] EWHC 454 (Comm) at [57], [2005] 2 Lloyd's Rep 257; affd on this point [2007] UKHL 4.

[522] *Aggeliki Charis Compañía Marítima SA v Pagnan SpA, The Angelic Grace* [1995] 1 Lloyd's Rep 87, CA.

[523] *Toepfer International GmbH v Société Cargill France* [1998] 1 Lloyd's Rep 379 at 384, CA; the *Through Transport* case, supra, at [90].

[524] Supra, pp 437–9.

thus been applied where an injunction was sought to restrain proceedings brought in breach of a clause providing for arbitration in England.[525] As noted previously (and similarly to the situation with respect to exclusive jurisdiction agreements), it is not necessary for there to be actual or pending English arbitral proceedings, as the injunction is to enforce a contractual right.[526] The party obtaining the injunction need not have been a party to the original contract containing the arbitration clause, if they have become a beneficiary of that clause.[527] It has been held that this extends to cases in which an arbitral award has been rendered, and an injunction is sought to restrain a party from foreign proceedings seeking to set it aside.[528] The award of an anti-suit injunction nevertheless remains discretionary, and comity considerations are not irrelevant.[529] In cases where the foreign court is likely to reach the conclusion that the dispute is covered by an English arbitration agreement, an anti-suit injunction may be considered unnecessary; by contrast, an injunction is likely to be awarded if a foreign court has refused to recognise the arbitration agreement on grounds that are not acceptable to the English courts.[530] The English court will normally form its own view as to whether the proceedings are covered by an arbitration agreement, although if this is the result of particular English rules, the court may accept that the principles in *The Angelic Grace* should not apply to foreign proceedings which would not be viewed by the foreign court as brought in breach of the arbitration agreement.[531]

4. PARALLEL PROCEEDINGS UNDER THE BRUSSELS I RECAST: LIS PENDENS AND RELATED ACTIONS

As examined earlier in this chapter, the common law has traditionally dealt with parallel proceedings through the exercise of the *forum conveniens* and *forum non conveniens* discretions—refusing to exercise jurisdiction or staying English proceedings where a foreign forum is better placed to resolve the dispute most efficiently and in the interests of justice. If there are prior identical or related foreign proceedings, particularly where they have advanced to the merits of the dispute, this may be an important factor in identifying the most appropriate forum, as there would be evident inefficiencies in requiring the parties to start the proceedings again in the English courts. The existence of prior foreign proceedings is, however, neither necessary nor sufficient for a stay to be granted or for permission to commence English proceedings

---

[525] *Welex AG v Rosa Maritime Ltd* [2003] EWCA Civ 938 at [47]–[52], [2003] 2 Lloyd's Rep 509; followed in *Through Transport Mutual Insurance Association (Eurasia) Ltdv New India Assurance Co Ltd* [2003] EWHC 3158 (Comm), [2004] 1 Lloyd's Rep 509; overruled in part but without disapproval of this point—[2004] EWCA (Civ) 1598; *C v D* [2007] EWHC 1541 (Comm), [2007] 2 Lloyd's Rep 367, appeal dismissed [2007] EWCA Civ 1282. Cf *Toepfer International GmbH v Société Cargill France* [1997] 2 Lloyd's Rep 98 at 110. The Court of Appeal at [1998] 1 Lloyd's Rep 379 at 386 held that Colman J did not err in principle in the exercise of his discretion. Effect will also be given to the arbitration agreement by appointing an arbitrator in England, despite proceedings abroad: *Atlanska Plovidba v Consignaciones Asturianas SA (The Lapad)* [2004] EWHC 1273 (Comm), [2004] 2 Lloyd's Rep 109.

[526] *AES Ust-Kamenogorsk Hydropower Plant LLP v Ust-Kamenogorsk Hydropower Plant JSC* [2013] UKSC 35, [2013] 1 WLR 1889; Fentiman (2013) 72 CLJ 521.

[527] See, eg, *Shipowners' Mutual Protection and Indemnity Association (Luxembourg) v Containerships Denizcilik Nakliyat ve Ticaret AS* [2016] EWCA Civ 386, [2016] 1 Lloyd's Rep 641, appeal pending.

[528] *C v D* [2007] EWCA Civ 1282, [2008] 1 Lloyd's Rep 239.

[529] See, eg, *Ecobank Transnational Inc v Tanoh* [2015] EWCA Civ 1309, [2016] 1 Lloyd's Rep 360.

[530] Ibid.

[531] *Through Transport Mutual Insurance Association (Eurasia) Ltd v New India Assurance Co Ltd* [2004] EWCA (Civ) 1598 at [95]–[97] (involving a statutory transfer of rights of action); see further *Shipowners' Mutual Protection and Indemnity Association (Luxembourg) v Containerships Denizcilik Nakliyat ve Ticaret AS* [2016] EWCA Civ 386, [2016] 1 Lloyd's Rep 641, appeal pending.

to be refused, merely an element in the exercise of jurisdictional discretion. The approach to dealing with parallel proceedings under the Brussels I Recast is strikingly different. As examined further below, the rules are only engaged if a foreign court has been seised prior to the English courts, and in some situations a stay is mandatory rather than discretionary. Different rules apply depending on whether the prior proceedings are in another Member State or a non-Member State, so these situations will be dealt with in turn.

(a) Proceedings in another Member State

(i) *Lis pendens*[532]

Article 29[533] of the Brussels I Recast provides that:

1. Without prejudice to Article 31(2),[534] where proceedings involving the same cause of action and between the same parties are brought in the courts of different Member States, any court other than the court first seised shall of its own motion stay its proceedings until such time as the jurisdiction of the court first seised is established.
2. In cases referred to in paragraph 1, upon request by a court seised of the dispute, any other court seised shall without delay inform the former court of the date when it was seised in accordance with Article 32.
3. Where the jurisdiction of the court first seised is established, any court other than the court first seised shall decline jurisdiction in favour of that court.

The Brussels I Recast will often give jurisdiction to the courts of more than one Member State in respect of a single dispute, eg an Italian claimant, who is injured in Italy by the negligent driving of a defendant domiciled in France, can sue either in Italy under Article 7(2) or in France under Article 4. There is an obvious need for a provision to deal with the problems of concurrent proceedings and the risk of conflicting judgments in the courts of different Member States.[535] Whilst Article 29 is limited to concurrent[536] proceedings[537] in Member States, it should be noted that it is not limited to proceedings

---

[532] See generally Fawcett *Declining Jurisdiction*, pp 27–46; Herzog (1995) 43 AJCL 379; Hartley (2006) 139 Hague Recueil 166–169; McLachlan, *Lis Pendens in International Litigation* (2009).

[533] Art 27 of the Brussels I Regulation; Art 21 of the Brussels Convention.

[534] See infra, p 450 et seq.

[535] See Case 42/76 *De Wolf v Cox BV* [1976] ECR 1759; Hartley (1977) 2 ELR 146; the case is discussed infra, pp 649–50.

[536] The proceedings must be pending, not concluded (*Berkeley Administration Inc v McClelland* [1995] IL Pr 201, CA; *Prudential Assurance Co Ltd v Prudential Insurance Co of America* [2003] EWCA Civ 327 at [26], [2003] 1 WLR 2295) or discontinued (*International Nederlanden v CAA* [1997] 1 Lloyd's Rep 80 at 93–4) or struck out on the basis that they are bound to fail (*QRS I Aps v Frandsen* [1999] IL Pr 432). See also *Gamlestaden plc v Casa de Suecia SA* [1994] 1 Lloyd's Rep 433; *Tavoulareas v Tsavliris (No 2)* [2005] EWHC 2643 (Comm), [2006] 1 All ER (Comm) 130, Art 29 does not apply where judgment is given in the court first seised at the time the court second seised makes its determination as to whether to decline—the rules on recognition and enforcement of judgments will apply instead. Art 29 will apply where the court first seised has declared that it is without jurisdiction but an appeal is pending (*Moore v Moore* [2007] EWCA Civ 361 at [102]–[103], [2007] IL Pr). It will also apply where the decision of the court first seised that it has jurisdiction is itself under appeal (*William Grant & Sons International Ltd v Marie Brizard et Roger International* SA 1998 SC 536).

[537] This does not include provisional proceedings: *Miles Platts Ltd v Townroe Ltd* [2003] EWCA Civ 145 at [21]–[22], [2003] 1 All ER (Comm) 561; *Boss Group Ltd v Boss France SA* [1997] 1 WLR 351, CA (but cf *The Winter* [2000] 2 Lloyd's Rep 298, 302—provisional measure raising substantive matters); nor those concerning the recognition and enforcement of judgments given in non-Contracting States, Case C-129/92 *Owens Bank Ltd v Bracco* [1994] QB 509; *Bank of Dubai Ltd v Abbas* [1998] IL Pr 391. Nor does it mean issues raised in proceedings: *The Happy Fellow* [1998] 1 Lloyd's Rep 13, CA; *The Alexandros T* [2013] UKSC 70, [2014] 1 Lloyd's Rep 223. Amended proceedings are treated as separate from original proceedings: *Grupo Torras SA and Torras Hostench London Ltd v Sheikh Fahad Mohammed Al-Sabah* [1995] 1 Lloyd's Rep 374 at

under the bases of jurisdiction set out in the Brussels I Recast.[538] Article 29 will apply where proceedings involving the same cause of action and parties have been commenced in two Member States under their traditional rules on jurisdiction (the bases of jurisdiction under the Brussels I Recast being inapplicable).[539] The Court of Justice, following a reference from the Court of Appeal, confirmed in *Overseas Union Insurance Ltd v New Hampshire Insurance Co* that there is no requirement that either party be domiciled in a Member State.[540] This is clear from the wording and purpose of Article 29. It is for this reason that the English courts have long understood that the *forum non conveniens* discretion may not be exercised to stay proceedings commenced under the Brussels I Recast jurisdictional rules where the alternative forum is the courts of another Member State. Of course, for Article 29 to apply, the proceedings have to be within the scope of the Brussels I Recast.[541] A court second seised can decide this question and does not have to stay its proceedings so that there can be a decision on this matter by the court first seised.[542]

It should be noted that Article 29 is a purely mechanical rule. The court of the Member State first seised of the matter takes priority (subject to the exception in Article 31(2), discussed below), and any court of another Member State must of its own motion decline jurisdiction, once the jurisdiction of the court first seised is established in that State.[543] Jurisdiction is established in the court first seised once the proceedings are at the stage where a substantive defence is submitted, if the court first seised has not declined its own jurisdiction and the parties have not contested its jurisdiction.[544] The court seised second normally cannot examine the jurisdiction of the court first seised.[545] Under Article 29, there is no discretion given to the courts of either Member State as to whether they should take jurisdiction. A mechanical rule tends to produce certainty, but this does not mean that there are no problems with Article 29—indeed the *lis pendens* rules have given rise to some of the most contentious questions concerning the Brussels/Lugano System.

431, this was not part of the appeal; affd [1996] 1 Lloyd's Rep 7, CA. Proceedings encompasses an application to a court to establish a liability limitation fund: Case C-39/02 *Maersk Olie & Gas AS v M De Haan en W De Boer* [2004] I-9657 at [33].

[538] See *The Nordglimt* [1988] QB 183.

[539] See Arts 5 and 6, supra, pp 214–15; the Jenard Report, pp 20–1.

[540] Case C-351/89 [1992] 1 QB 434; Briggs (1991) 11 YEL 521; Hartley (1992) 17 ELR 75; *Trademark Licensing Co Ltd v Leofelis SA* [2009] EWHC 3285 (Ch), [2010] IL Pr 16; *Cooper Tire & Rubber Co Europe Ltd v Shell Chemicals UK Ltd* [2010] EWCA Civ 864, [2010] 2 CLC 104.

[541] *Toepfer v Société Cargill* [1998] 1 Lloyd's Rep 379, CA; see further supra, p 202 et seq. If the Brussels I Recast is displaced by another international convention pursuant to Article 71, the *lis pendens* rules in the Brussels I Recast may still apply if there are no equivalent rules in the international convention. See supra, p 389.

[542] *Through Transport Mutual Insurance Association (Eurasia) Ltd v New India Assurance Association Co Ltd* [2004] EWCA (Civ) 1598 at [23]–[37], [2005] 1 Lloyd's Rep 67; although it is unclear whether this remains good authority in light of the decision of the Court of Justice in Case C-185/07 *Allianz v West Tankers* [2009] ECR I-663, [2009] 1 AC 1138; see also *National Navigacion v Endesa (The Wadi Sudr)* [2009] EWCA Civ 1397, [2010] 2 All ER (Comm) 1243, discussed infra, p 480; but note in respect of arbitration agreements the effect of Recital (12) of the Brussels I Recast, discussed infra, p 480 and supra, p 211. In any case, this does not permit the court second seised to issue an anti-suit injunction restraining the court first seised from determining its own jurisdiction, even if the court second seised believes that the matter falls outside the scope of the Brussels I Recast: see infra, p 479.

[543] See the Schlosser Report, p 125. See also *Carnoustie Universal SA v International Transport Workers' Federation* [2002] EWHC 1624 (Comm) 657 at [45]–[46], [2002] 2 All ER (Comm) 657—onus is on the claimant to show a good arguable case that the English court should take jurisdiction, ie that Art 29 does not apply. The court must be satisfied of this whether or not the defendant mounts a challenge. See also *Kolden Holdings Ltd v Rodette Commerce Ltd* [2008] EWCA Civ 10, [2008] 1 Lloyd's Rep 434.

[544] Case C-1/13 *Cartier Parfums-Lunettes SAS v Ziegler France SA* EU:C:2014:109, [2014] IL Pr 25.

[545] *Overseas Union Insurance Ltd v New Hampshire Insurance Co*, supra; *Haji-Ioannou v Frangos* [1999] 2 Lloyd's Rep 337 at 351, CA—a Brussels Convention case which summarises the principles to be applied.

(a) Same cause of action

The two sets of proceedings must involve the same cause of action. According to the Court of Justice in *Gubisch Maschinenfabrik KG v Giulio Palumbo*[546] this, like the other terms in Article 21 of the Brussels Convention (Article 29 of the Brussels I Recast) concerned with whether a situation of *lis pendens* exists, must be given an independent Community meaning. The cause of action refers to the "facts and the rule of law relied on as the basis of the action".[547] There is, though, a separate (albeit closely related) requirement, which does not appear in the English language version of Article 29: the *subject matter* or *object* of the proceedings, ie "the end the action has in view",[548] must be the same.[549] We are concerned with the subject matter (and other substantive requirements, namely the same cause of action and same parties) as at the time when the *lis pendens* comes into existence (ie from the moment when two courts of two Member States are seised of an action).[550] This happens at an early stage before the defendants have been able to put forward their arguments. It follows that in determining the subject matter (and other substantive requirements), account should be taken only of the claims of the respective applicants, not of the defence that may be raised by a defendant.[551] The Court of Justice in the *Gubisch* case held that the same subject matter requirement was satisfied in circumstances where one party brought an action in Italy for the rescission or discharge of an international sales contract whilst an action by the other party to enforce the same contract was pending before a court in Germany. The same question whether the contract was binding lay at the heart of both actions and it was not required that the two claims be entirely identical.[552] Whilst this broad interpretation is understandable, as otherwise Article 29 could be avoided by raising additional issues in the court second seised, it does tend to break down the distinction between this provision and Article 30, which deals with related actions. A broad interpretation was also followed in *The Tatry*,[553] where the Court of Justice held that an action seeking to have the defendant held liable for causing loss and to pay damages constituted the same cause of action and subject matter as earlier proceedings by that defendant for a

---

[546] Case 144/86 [1987] ECR 4861; Hartley (1988) 13 ELR 216.

[547] Case C-406/92 *The Owners of the Cargo Lately Laden on Board the Ship Tatry v The Owners of the Ship Maciej Rataj* [1994] ECR I-5439 at 5475; [1999] QB 515; Case C-39/02 *Maersk Olie & Gas AS v M De Haan en W De Boer* [2004] ECR I-9657 at [38]; *Haji-Ioannou v Frangos* [1999] 2 Lloyd's Rep 337 at 351, CA; *JP Morgan Europe Ltd v Primacom AG* [2005] EWHC 508 (Comm) at [39]–[49], [2005] 2 Lloyd's Rep 665. For examples where the cause of action was the same, see the *Carnoustie* case, supra, at [86]–[91]; *Glencore International AG v Metro Trading International Inc (No 1)* [1999] 2 Lloyd's Rep 632, 638; *The Winter* [2000] 2 Lloyd's Rep 298, 305; *Bank of Tokyo-Mitsubishi Ltd v Baskan Gida Sanayi Ve Pazarlama AS* [2004] EWHC 945 (Ch) at [207], [2004] 2 Lloyd's Rep 395; *JP Morgan Europe*, supra, at [39]–[49]; *Jacobs & Turner Ltd v Celsius sarl* [2007] CSOH 76 at [68]. See also *Kloeckner & Co AG v Gatoil Overseas Inc* [1990] 1 Lloyd's Rep 177, where each purchase and sale agreement stemming from a basic contract was treated as a separate cause of action.

[548] *The Tatry*, supra, at 5475; Case C-111/01 *Gantner Electronic GmbH v Basch Exploitatie Maatschappij BV* [2003] ECR I-4207 at [25]; *Haji-Ioannou v Frangos* [1999] 2 Lloyd's Rep 337 at 351, CA; *Underwriting Members of Lloyd's Syndicate 980 v Sinco SA* [2008] EWHC 1842 (Comm), [2009] Lloyd's Rep IR 365.

[549] For examples of where this requirement was satisfied, see the *Carnoustie* case, supra, at [88]; *The Winter*, supra, 305; *Bank of Tokyo-Mitsubishi*, supra, at [208]; *JP Morgan Europe*, supra, at [39]–[49]; *Jacobs & Turner Ltd*, supra, at [68]–[75]; *Kolden Holdings Ltd v Rodette Commerce Ltd* [2007] EWHC 1597 (Comm) at [60], [2007] IL Pr 50 (not challenged on appeal).

[550] The *Gantner* case, supra, at [27]; following Case 129/83 *Zelger v Salinitri (No 2)* [1984] ECR 2397; Hartley (1985) 10 ELR 56.

[551] The *Gantner* case, supra, at [32]; *Jacobs & Turner Ltd*, supra, at [70]; *Kolden Holdings Ltd v Rodette Commerce Ltd* [2008] EWCA Civ 10, [2008] 1 Lloyd's Rep 434.

[552] See also *Secret Hotels 2 Ltd v EA Traveller Ltd* [2010] EWHC 1023 (Ch), [2010] IL Pr 33; *Football Dataco Ltd v Sportradar GmbH* [2011] EWCA Civ 330, [2011] 1 WLR 3044.

[553] Case C-406/92 *The Owners of the Cargo Lately Laden on Board the Ship Tatry v The Owners of the Ship Maciej Rataj* [1994] ECR I-5439; [1999] QB 515; Briggs [1995] LMCLQ 161; and (1994) 14 YEL 579; Davenport (1995) 111 LQR 366; Fentiman [1995] CLJ 261.

negative declaration that he was not liable for that loss. Allowing negative declarations to come within Article 29[554] gives the green light to pre-emptive forum shopping by a party who fears that proceedings are going to be commenced against him.[555] The cause of action in one set of proceedings may be broader than that in the other. If the cause of action is broader in the court second seised, there is authority for the proposition that Article 29 will operate in respect of the element common to both sets of proceedings.[556] This would be consistent with the approach adopted by the Court of Justice in relation to multi-party cases, but would risk further fragmenting proceedings.[557] In *The Alexandros T*,[558] however, the Supreme Court held that Article 27 of the Brussels I Regulation (the equivalent to Article 29 of the Brussels I Recast) was not engaged when proceedings were first commenced in Greece and then in England, with the English proceedings including a claim for breach of an English jurisdiction agreement—the validity of the jurisdiction agreement being an issue which the Greek courts would also be required to determine. The Supreme Court did not consider it necessary to refer the question to the Court of Justice. The approach in *The Alexandros T* is consistent with other English authority preferring to examine the proceedings as a whole rather than each element when determining whether what is now Article 29 of the Brussels I Recast applies.[559]

A simple example of where the cause of action is not the same in the two sets of proceedings is where one cause of action is for infringement of a trade mark and the other is for passing off.[560] The object is not the same where one claim is for the recovery of money and the other is in large part the tracing of that money into the assets acquired with it and a claim to a beneficial interest.[561] Neither the cause of action nor the object were the same

---

[554] See also Case C-351/96 *Drouot Assurances SA v Consolidated Metallurgical Industries* 485 [1999] QB 497; Case C-116/02 *Erich Gasser v Misat Srl* [2003] ECR I-4207; *Messier Dowty Ltd v Sabena SA* [2000] 1 WLR 2040, at 2049, CA; *Kinnear v Falconfilms NV* [1996] 1 WLR 920.

[555] See generally the criticism by Collins (1992) 108 LQR 545; *Mélanges En L'Honneur De Jacques-Michel Grossen*, p 386 and *Essays*, p 274 and 283 et seq; more specifically in respect of the decision of the Court of Justice: Fentiman, op cit; Davenport, op cit. See also Lawrence Collins J in *Bank of Tokyo-Mitsubishi Ltd*, supra, at [198].

[556] See the opinion of AG Tesauro in *The Tatry*, supra; *William Grant & Sons International Ltd v Marie Brizard et Roger International* SA 1998 SC 536; *Glencore International AG v Metro Trading International Inc (No 1)* [1999] 2 Lloyd's Rep 632, 638–9; *Jacobs & Turner Ltd*, supra, at [46].

[557] See the discussion, infra, of *The Tatry*, supra.

[558] [2013] UKSC 70, [2014] 1 Lloyd's Rep 223; Baatz [2014] LMCLQ 159; Dickinson (2015) 131 LQR 186; Ahmed (2015) 11 J Priv Int L 406.

[559] See, eg, *Underwriting Members of Lloyd's Syndicate 980 v Sinco SA* [2008] EWHC 1842 (Comm), [2009] Lloyd's Rep IR 365; *WMS Gaming Inc v B Plus Giocolegale Ltd* [2011] EWHC 2620 (Comm), [2012] IL Pr 5; *Barclays Bank Plc v Ente Nazionale di Previdenza* [2016] EWCA Civ 1261.

[560] *Mecklermedia Corpn v DC Congress GmbH* [1998] Ch 40. For other examples, see: *Sarrio SA v Kuwait Investment Authority* [1997] 1 Lloyd's Rep 113, CA, revsd by the House of Lords [1999] 1 AC 32 without discussion of this point; *Berkeley Administration Inc v McClelland* [1996] IL Pr 72 at 786, CA; *Toepfer v Molino Boshci* [1996] 1 Lloyd's Rep 510 at 513; *Charterers Mutual Assurance Association Ltd v British and Foreign* [1998] IL Pr 838 at 855; *Glencore International AG v Shell Trading and Shipping Co Ltd* [1999] 2 All ER (Comm) 922; *Lafi Office and International Business SL v Meriden Animal Health Ltd* [2001] 1 All ER (Comm) 54 at 70–1; *JP Morgan Europe Ltd v Primacom AG* [2005] EWHC 508 (Comm) at [54]–[56], [2005] 2 Lloyd's Rep 665; *Prazic v Prazic* [2006] EWCA Civ 497 at [16], [2006] 2 FLR 1128; *Lehman Brothers Bankhaus AG I Ins v CMA CGM* [2013] EWHC 171 (Comm), [2013] 2 All ER (Comm) 557; *SET Select Energy GmbH v F&M Bunkering Ltd* [2014] EWHC 192 (Comm), [2014] 1 Lloyd's Rep 652. It is unclear whether the cause of action is the same in the situation where there are actions in two Member States under Art 7(1) of the Brussels I Recast, there being two obligations of equal weight each to be performed in the two different Member States. (See Case C-420/97 *Leathertex Divisione Sinetici SpA v Bodetex BVBA* [1999] ECR I-6747 at [36]; Panagopoulos [2000] LMCLQ 150. The European Commission assumed in their arguments that it would be, but this situation would appear more suited to Article 30 of the Brussels I Recast.)

[561] *Haji-Ioannou v Frangos* [1999] 2 Lloyd's Rep 337 at 351, CA. For other examples see *Glencore International AG v Shell Trading and Shipping Co Ltd*, op cit; *JP Morgan Europe Ltd v Primacom AG* [2005] EWHC 508 (Comm) at [51]–[53], [2005] 2 Lloyd's Rep 665.

where a shipowner sought to limit liability by establishing a liability limitation fund and a victim sought damages from the shipowner.[562] As regards the cause of action, the legal rule which formed the basis of each of these applications was different, one action being based on an international Convention and national law giving effect to it, the other being based on the law of non-contractual liability.[563] As regards the object, one action sought to have the defendant declared liable, whereas the other sought to limit liability in the event that that person was held liable.[564]

(b) Same parties

The two sets of proceedings must be between the same parties.[565] This requirement has raised problems in maritime actions. The Court of Justice in *The Tatry*[566] held that if one action is brought in personam (against a person) in one Contracting State and the other is brought in rem (against a ship) in another Contracting State, and has subsequently continued both in rem and in personam, or solely in personam, according to the distinctions drawn by the national law of that other Member State, the parties are the same. It was said that the distinction drawn under national law between an action in personam and one in rem is not material for the interpretation of Article 21 of the Brussels Convention (Article 29 of the Brussels I Recast). It follows that the result in the case would have been exactly the same if the action in rem had continued as such according to national law.[567] Multi-party cases have also raised problems. In *The Tatry*, the Court of Justice adopted a party-by-party approach, holding that "the second court seised is required to decline jurisdiction only to the extent to which the parties to the proceedings before it are also parties to the action previously commenced; it does not prevent the proceedings from continuing between the other parties".[568]

> Thus, if in the court first seised A, B and C sue X, and in the court second seised X sues A and B, the latter court must decline jurisdiction in relation to all the parties in the proceedings before it. Whereas in the converse situation, ie if in the court first seised A and B sue X, and in the court second seised X sues A, B and C, Article 29 will not operate in respect of the action brought against C.[569]

In ascertaining whether the parties are the same, it is possible to look beyond their strict formal identities. An insurer and an insured can be considered to be the same party for the purposes of Article 29 in the situation where their interests are the same, such as where an insurer, by virtue of its right of subrogation, brings or defends an action in the name of its insured, but not where their interests diverge.[570] It is for the national court to decide whether

---

[562] Case C-39/02 *Maersk Olie & Gas AS v M De Haan en W De Boer* [2004] ECR I-9657 at [42].

[563] Ibid, at [38].

[564] Ibid, at [35].

[565] For examples where the requirement was not met, see *Bank of Scotland v SA Banque Nationale De Paris* 1996 SLT 103; the *Lafi* case, supra, 70; *WMS Gaming Inc v B Plus Giocolegale Ltd* [2011] EWHC 2620 (Comm), [2012] IL Pr 5. Cf in the area of maintenance *J v P* [2007] EWHC 704 (Fam) at 48.

[566] Case C-406/92 *The Owners of the Cargo Lately Laden on Board the Ship Tatry v The Owners of the Ship Maciej Rataj* [1999] QB 515, [1994] ECR I-5439.

[567] See the judgment of Lord Steyn, with whom the other Law Lords concurred, in *Republic of India v India Steamship Co Ltd (No 2)* [1998] AC 878 at 910, 913.

[568] *The Tatry*, supra, at 5474. See also *Haji-Ioannou v Frangos* [1999] 2 Lloyd's Rep 337 at 351, CA; *Glencore International AG v Shell Trading and Shipping Co Ltd*, supra, 925; *Glencore International AG v Metro Trading International Inc (No 1)*, supra, 637.

[569] The court second seised is able, though, to use Art 30, discussed infra, p 454 et seq, to stay the proceedings against C on the ground that they are related, see *The Tatry*, supra, at 5477–80.

[570] Case C-351/96 *Drouot Assurances SA v Consolidated Metallurgical Industries* [1999] QB 497; Handley (2000) 116 LQR 191; Peel (1998) 18 YEL 689; Seatzu (1999) 24 ELR 540.

it is such a situation.[571] On a reference back to the French courts it was held on the facts that an insurer of a hull who does not cover fault on a shipowner's part is not the same party as the insured (ie the owner).[572] It may also be unreal to regard a wholly-owned subsidiary as being a different party from its parent.[573] The deployment of a related company in a group of companies as claimant in proceedings may be a sham to avoid the application of Article 29, in which case the court will look at the reality of the situation and the parties will be regarded as being the same.[574]

(c) Identifying when a court is seised

Article 29 can lead to a race between the parties,[575] the winner being the one who can show that the court where he brought the action is first seised of jurisdiction.[576] The Brussels I Recast (and previously Brussels I Regulation) filled what has been seen as a gap in the law[577] by defining in Article 32[578] the precise moment at which a court[579] is first seised for the purposes of Articles 29, 30 and 31. Arriving at a uniform definition which would apply in all Member States was not easy because of the different procedural systems adopted by different Member States. The solution adopted in Article 32 is to provide two alternative definitions. One is for Member States where the claim is lodged with the court before service of the document instituting the proceedings. This is what happens in England. The other is for Member States, such as France, where service precedes lodging with the court. In Member States where the claim is lodged with the court before service, a court is deemed to be seised "at the time when the document instituting the proceedings or an equivalent document is lodged with the court, provided that the claimant has not subsequently failed to take the steps he was required to take to have service effected on the defendant . . .".[580] In the case of England, the courts will be seised on the date of the issue of the claim form.[581] The steps the claimant is required to take to effect service will depend on the legal system in question. They may include transmission to the court of all material facts enabling it to serve notice, or the

---

[571] See, eg, *Kolden Holdings Ltd v Rodette Commerce Ltd* [2008] EWCA Civ 10, [2008] 1 Lloyd's Rep 434—assignee held to be same party as assignor. Cf *Molnlycke Health Care AB v BSN Medical Ltd* [2009] EWHC 3370 (Pat), [2010] IL Pr 9—licensee not the same party as patent owner.

[572] *Drouot Assurances SA v Consolidated Metallurgical Industries* [2000] IL Pr 421, French Cour de Cassation.

[573] See *Berkeley Administration Inc v McClelland* [1995] IL Pr 201 at 211 (per Dillon LJ), CA. But see *WMS Gaming Inc*, supra, suggesting (at [38]) that *Berkeley Administration Inc* may be confined to its facts.

[574] *Turner v Grovit* [2000] QB 345, CA. This point was not discussed by the House of Lords [2001] UKHL 651, [2002] 1 WLR 107.

[575] This is the opposite of the culture which the English CPR seek to promote, see *Messier Dowty v Sabena SA* [2000] 1 WLR 2040, 2047, CA. Particular problems may arise under the Pre-Action Protocols of the Civil Procedure Rules, pursuant to which the defendant will be notified of the potential claim well before proceedings can be commenced: see Morgan [2011] LMCLQ 275.

[576] The court must be seised of proceedings which could continue to the merits—a distinct action for protective measures would not establish seisure: *Maxter Catheters SAS v Medicina Ltd* [2015] EWHC 3076 (Comm), [2016] 1 WLR 349. In some legal systems this is satisfied where civil claims are attached to criminal proceedings: see Case C-523/14 *Aannemingsbedrijf Aertssen NV and Aertssen Terrassements SA v VSB Machineverhuur BV* EU:C:2015:722, [2016] IL Pr 16.

[577] See the views of the European Commission in the Explanatory Memorandum in the Proposal for a Council Regulation COM (1999) 348 final, p 20.

[578] Article 30 of the Brussels I Regulation.

[579] This may in some states include a conciliation authority: *Lehman Brothers Finance AG v Klaus Tschira Stiftung GmbH* [2014] EWHC 2782 (Ch), [2014] 2 CLC 242.

[580] Art 32(1)(a). See *Tavoulareas v Tsavliris* [2005] EWHC 2140 (Comm), [2006] 1 All ER (Comm) 109.

[581] See Dicey, Morris and Collins, para 12-067; *WPP Holdings Italy SRL v Benatti* [2006] EWHC 1641 (Comm) at [28], [2006] 2 Lloyd's Rep 610; Lesage (2006) EU Lp 157—this point was not mentioned on appeal in *Benattiv WPP Holdings Italy SRL* [2007] EWCA Civ 263, [2007] 1 WLR 2316 (appeal allowed in relation to one claimant and dismissed in relation to other claimants). This date is entered on the form by the court: CPR r 7.2.

handing over of the document already registered with the court to the competent authority for service, or payment of a fee.[582] In Member States where the document has to be served before being lodged with the court, such as France, a court is deemed to be seised "at the time when it is received by the authority responsible[583] for service, provided that the claimant has not subsequently failed to take the steps he was required to take to have the document lodged with the court".[584] It is to be noted that in this scenario the moment when a court is deemed to be seised is not the time of actual service,[585] it will be prior to that when the document is received by the authority responsible for service.[586] Being seised is different from having been properly served and so it does not matter that the service was invalid under the European Community Service Regulation,[587] nor that there were procedural irregularities with service in England if they are subsequently rectified by order of the court.[588] All that Article 32(1)(b) requires is that the claimant, after lodging the document with the authority responsible for service, must not have failed to take the steps he was required to take to have the document lodged with the court (which no doubt might include steps to facilitate service as a pre-requisite to lodgement with the court).[589] The fact that Member States will not all be applying the same definition runs the risk, in theory at least, that the race to become first seised is still going to be run on unequal terms. However, this risk is more apparent than real since both definitions take as the moment of being first seised the earliest practicable moment in the sequence of events under that procedural system. There is also a practical problem for an English court in determining when a foreign court is seised. Whether a document is effective to institute proceedings in another Member State should be for the national law of that foreign Member State to determine.[590] If claims are amended or added after proceedings have been commenced, this should not affect the date at which the court was seised.[591] If, however, the relevant party was added as a further defendant to existing proceedings, it will be the date at which that party was added rather than the date of commencement of the proceedings as a whole which is significant.[592]

(d) Application when jurisdiction is disputed

It may be perfectly clear which court of a Member State is first seised of the proceedings, but jurisdiction may be challenged in that court. The court seised second must of its own motion[593]

---

[582] *Debt Collect London Ltd v SK Slavia Praha-Fotbal AS* [2010] EWCA Civ 1250, [2011] 1 WLR 866. See also the views of the European Commission in the Explanatory Memorandum in the Proposal for a Council Regulation COM (1999) 348 final, p 20.

[583] There is uncertainty in Member States about the definition of responsible authority, see the Hesss, Pfeiffer and Schlosser Report, at para 897, which recommends clarification of its meaning.

[584] Art 32(1)(b). See, eg, *Arbuthnot Latham & Co Ltd v M3 Marine Ltd* [2013] EWHC 1019 (Comm), [2014] 1 WLR 190.

[585] *Benattiv WPP Holdings Italy SRL* [2007] EWCA Civ 263 at [96] (per Clarke MR), [2007] 1 WLR 2316.

[586] It is unclear whether this is referring to the transmitting agency or the receiving agency under the EC Service Regulation. Buxton LJ in *Benattiv WPP Holdings Italy Srl*, supra, at [85] assumes it is the former, but Hamblin J in *Arbuthnot Latham & Co Ltd*, supra, takes the view that it is the latter.

[587] *Benatti*, supra, at [66]–[67] (per Toulson LJ), [92]–[97] (per Clarke MR). Cf Buxton LJ in *Benatti* at [84]–[85] and *Tavoulareas v Tsavliris* [2004] EWCA Civ 48 at [31], [2004] 1 Lloyd's Rep 445.

[588] *Phillips v Symes* [2008] UKHL 1, [2008] 1 WLR 180.

[589] *Benatti*, supra, at [66] (per Toulson LJ), [92]–[97] (per Clarke MR).

[590] *Benatti*, supra, at [84] (per Buxton LJ); *UBS Ltd v Regione Calabria* [2012] EWHC 699 (Comm), [2012] IL Pr 22. But cf *Tavoulareas v Tsavliris* [2005] EWHC 2140 (Comm) at [60], [61], [2006] 1 All ER (Comm), 109; Briggs (2005) 76 BYBIL 654, 656.

[591] *The Alexandros T* [2013] UKSC 70, [2014] 1 Lloyd's Rep 223.

[592] See, eg, *Nordea Bank Norge ASA v Unicredit Corporate Banking SPA* [2011] EWHC 30 (Comm).

[593] For the effect on the burden of proof on the parties see *Benattiv WPP Holdings Italy Srl* [2007] EWCA Civ 263 at [62] (per Toulson LJ), [2007] 1 WLR 2316.

stay its proceedings[594] until such time as the jurisdiction of the court first seised is established.[595] Once it has been, the court seised second must then decline jurisdiction. This two-stage process avoids the danger of the court seised of the action second declining jurisdiction in favour of the court first seised; but, then the latter court decides subsequently that it has no jurisdiction. Both actions would have been dismissed and starting an action afresh might run into time-bar problems. It also reflects the principle that the courts of each Member State should determine their own jurisdiction, and avoids the danger of the court second seised exercising jurisdiction on a basis which is inconsistent with the decision on jurisdiction reached by the court first seised. Put simply, the rules on *lis pendens* apply to jurisdictional proceedings as well as merits proceedings— the court first seised of a jurisdictional question must be given the opportunity to determine that question, and thus to determine whether or not it can proceed to the merits.

(e) Application in exclusive jurisdiction cases

Article 29 is wide enough to cover cases where two Member States have exclusive jurisdiction. Nonetheless, the point is expressly covered by Article 31(1)[596] which, like Article 29, requires a court, other than the one first seised, to decline jurisdiction in favour of that court. Article 31(1) does not stipulate whether it is referring to exclusive jurisdiction under Article 24 or Article 25,[597] and must be assumed to cover both.

More problematical is the situation where a court in one Member State regards itself as having exclusive jurisdiction under Article 24 or 25, but a court in another Member State, nonetheless, has previously allowed the commencement of proceedings in that State.

(i) Court second seised claims exclusive jurisdiction under Article 25

This situation arose before the Court of Justice in *Erich Gasser v Misat Srl*,[598] which was the first of three important decisions[599] of that Court to hold that English practices in relation to international litigation were inconsistent with the Brussels Convention. The decision in *Gasser* has now, however, effectively been overturned in the Brussels I Recast. The issues arising under the Brussels Convention and Brussels I Regulation will first be examined, before considering this reform.

In *Gasser* the Court of Justice held that a court seised second whose jurisdiction has been claimed under an agreement conferring jurisdiction has nevertheless to stay proceedings until

---

[594] But can still make a provisional order: *JP Morgan Europe Ltd v Primacom AG* [2005] EWHC 508 (Comm) at [70]–[72], [2005] 2 Lloyd's Rep 665.

[595] The court first seised decides upon its jurisdiction: *Advent Capital plc v Ellinas Imports-Exports Ltd* [2005] EWHC 1242 (Comm) at [105], [2005] 2 Lloyd's Rep 607. The jurisdiction of an English court is not "established" if it has stayed its proceedings: *The Xin Yang* [1996] 2 Lloyd's Rep 217 at 222. But it may still be seised: *Viking Line ABP v The International Transport Workers' Federation* [2005] EWHC 1222, [2006] IL Pr 4 at [73]; but cf *Haji-Ioannou v Frangos* [1999] 2 Lloyd's Rep 337.

[596] Art 29 of the Brussels I Regulation; Art 23 of the Brussels Convention, on which see the Jenard Report, p 42.

[597] On the provision under the Brussels Convention (Art 17) corresponding to Art 25 of the Brussels I Recast, see Case 23/78 *Meeth v Glacetal Sarl* [1978] ECR 2133.

[598] Case C-116/02 [2003] ECR I-4207; Baatz [2004] LMCLQ 25; Fentiman [2004] CLJ 312, and (2005) 42 CMLR 241; Hartley in (2005) 54 ICLQ 813 and *Le droit international privé: esprit et methodes (Melanges en l'honneur de Paul Lagarde)* (Dalloz, Paris, 2005), p 383; Mance (2004) 120 LQR 357. In Case C-351/89 *Overseas Union Insurance Ltd v New Hampshire Insurance Co*, supra, the position in this situation was left open by the Court of Justice. See also *JP Morgan Europe Ltd v Primacom AG* [2005] EWHC 508 (Comm) at [36], [2005] 2 Lloyd's Rep 665; Briggs (2005) 76 BYBIL 641, 648–50.

[599] The other two cases were Case C-281/02 *Owusu v Jackson* [2005] ECR I-1383, [2005] QB 801, discussed infra, p 462 et seq, and Case C-159/02 *Turner v Grovit* [2004] ECR I-3565, [2005] 1 AC 101, discussed infra, p 477 et seq. See generally on all three cases, Hartley in (2005) 54 ICLQ 813 and in (2006) 319 Hague Recueil des cours, 169–84.

the court first seised has declared that it has no jurisdiction. It is for the court first seised to pronounce as to its jurisdiction in the light of the jurisdiction clause.[600] Prior to this decision, the English courts had taken a different view. The Court of Appeal in *Continental Bank NA v Aeakos Compañía Naviera SA*[601] held that a dispute brought first before the Greek courts came within an English exclusive jurisdiction clause, and that since the English court "second seised" had jurisdiction in relation to any such dispute conferred on it by the agreement of the parties under Article 17 of the Brussels Convention (Article 23 of the Brussels I Regulation), this took precedence over Article 21 of the Convention (Article 27 of the Brussels I Regulation).[602] This was on the basis that Article 17 deprives the courts of other Contracting States of jurisdiction in relation to disputes coming within the scope of the clause and therefore these courts cannot be "first seised". Likewise, Advocate General Leger in his opinion in the *Gasser* case was concerned to uphold the effectiveness of choice of jurisdiction agreements and proposed that Article 17 of the Convention (Article 23 of the Brussels I Regulation) should constitute an exception to Article 21 of the Convention (Article 27 of the Brussels I Regulation). But the Court of Justice decided that Article 21 of the Convention trumps Article 17.

In terms of the structure and objectives of the Convention and Brussels I Regulation this decision was clearly correct, but in terms of policy it was highly contentious. The *Continental Bank* approach was open to the criticism that the English court was making a decision on whether the Greek court had jurisdiction. As the Court of Justice in *Gasser* pointed out, "the court second seised is never in a better position than the court first seised to determine whether the latter has jurisdiction".[603] Under the Convention and Brussels I Regulation, this consideration was considered to outweigh the commercial importance of giving effect to jurisdiction agreements.[604] This approach was perhaps supported by the possibility that the English courts might later be able to award damages for breach of the jurisdiction agreement, at least in cases where the court first seised had not determined that the agreement was invalid or inapplicable.[605]

As a matter of policy, however, *Gasser* led to the very real practical problem that a party might adopt delaying tactics, commencing pre-emptive proceedings before a court which he knows lacks jurisdiction because of an exclusive jurisdiction clause, thereby preventing trial in the Member State agreed on until the court first seised has declared that it has no jurisdiction.[606] To make things worse, there are Member States, one of which is (or at least has been) Italy, in which in general the duration of proceedings (from commencement to obtaining a decision on jurisdiction) is excessively long.[607] (This form of strategic pre-emptive litigation has, as a consequence, become widely known as the 'Italian torpedo'.)[608] An excessive

---

[600] Distinguished in the *Through Transport* case, supra, at [36] on the basis that in the latter case there was a question whether the claim in England was within the Brussels I Regulation, but see now infra, pp 478–80.

[601] [1994] 1 WLR 588; Bell (1994) 10 LQR 204; Briggs [1994] LMCLQ 158; Hartley (1994) 19 ELR 549; Rogerson [1994] CLJ 241. *Continental Bank* was followed in many cases. The same approach was adopted in Scotland: *Bank of Scotland v SA Banque Nationale De Paris* 1996 SLT 103.

[602] The Court of Appeal went on to grant an injunction restraining proceedings in Greece. Such an injunction has since been held to be incompatible with the Brussels Convention, see infra, p 476 et seq.

[603] *Gasser*, supra, at [48].

[604] But cf the opinion of AG Leger, supra, at [67] and [83].

[605] See Merrett (2006) 55 ICLQ 315.

[606] See Hartley in Nafziger and Symeonides (eds), *Law and Justice in a Multistate World* (2002), p 73; *JP Morgan Europe Ltd v Primacom AG* [2005] EWHC 508 (Comm), [2005] 2 Lloyd's Rep 665.

[607] The *Gasser* case, supra, at [57].

[608] Franzosi [1997] 7 EIPR 382; see, eg, *Research In Motion UK Ltd v Visto Corporation* [2008] EWCA Civ 153, [2008] IL Pr 34.

delay would involve a breach of Article 6 of the European Convention on Human Rights (ECHR). Nevertheless, the Court of Justice in *Gasser* held that Article 21 of the Brussels Convention (Article 27 of the Brussels I Regulation) will still give priority to the court first seised, even where the duration of proceedings before the courts of the Contracting State in which the court first seised is established is excessively long.[609] The mutual trust which the Contracting States accord to each other's legal systems and judicial institutions, on which the Brussels Convention is based, was said to dictate this.[610] An alternative approach, which was advocated by the United Kingdom government, would have been to have an exception to the *Gasser* principle which would allow the court second seised to examine the jurisdiction of the court first seised where the claimant has brought an action before that court in bad faith (in order to block proceedings in another Contracting State) and that court has not decided the question of jurisdiction within a reasonable time.[611] The difficulty with this approach is that this exception would normally apply in every case where the court first seised is one where excessive delay is routine. The exception effectively becomes country specific, rather than case specific, hence the concern with mutual trust among Contracting States. Nonetheless, it was highly contentious whether a concern with mutual trust should outweigh both the commercial importance of giving effect to jurisdiction agreements and the human rights of the party seeking to uphold the jurisdiction agreement. There is perhaps even a risk that the Member State whose courts are seised second may find itself in breach of Article 6 of the ECHR for failing to try the case with reasonable dispatch.[612]

The Hess, Pfeiffer and Schlosser Report[613] advocated a different approach from that of the United Kingdom government, ie to allow parallel proceedings if the risk of conflicting decisions on jurisdiction could be minimised.[614] In the end, the Brussels I Recast adopted a more targeted reform. This was set out in Article 31, as follows:

2. Without prejudice to Article 26,[615] where a court of a Member State on which an agreement as referred to in Article 25 confers exclusive jurisdiction is seised, any court of another Member State shall stay the proceedings[616] until such time as the court seised on the basis of the agreement declares that it has no jurisdiction under the agreement.
3. Where the court designated in the agreement has established jurisdiction in accordance with the agreement, any court of another Member State shall decline jurisdiction in favour of that court.[617]

The intended effect of these reforms is evidently that the court chosen in an exclusive jurisdiction agreement is given priority (provided that it is actually seised), and even if another

---

[609] The *Gasser* case, supra, at [73]. On *Gasser* and human rights, see generally Fawcett, Ní Shúilleabháin, and Shah, *Human Rights and Private International Law* (2016) paras 4.131–4.200.

[610] Ibid, at [72]. See generally on mutual trust under the Brussels Convention, Blobel and Spath (2005) 30 ELR 528.

[611] The *Gasser* case, supra at [63].

[612] See Hartley, op cit.

[613] Study JLS/C4/2005/03, Final Version September 2007.

[614] At paras 888–91. One possibility they raise for achieving this was by introducing an additional mode for concluding an exclusive choice of forum agreement by way of a short and clear-cut standard form.

[615] The reference to Article 26 reflects the fact that a jurisdiction agreement will no longer be operative where the parties have submitted to another court: see supra, p 226.

[616] It appears that 'the proceedings' refers to cases covered by Article 29, but arguably not those covered by Article 30—see Kenny and Hennigan (2015) 64 ICLQ 197.

[617] Article 31(4) confirms that these rules do not apply to exclusive jurisdiction agreements which are invalid because of the special protective rules of jurisdiction dealing with insurance contracts, consumers and employees.

court is first seised it must give way.[618] To put this another way, party autonomy and the effectiveness of exclusive jurisdiction agreements is now considered to trump the principle of mutual trust in these circumstances.[619] This should apply equally to an asymmetrical jurisdiction agreement where only one party benefits from the exclusive jurisdiction clause, and that party commences proceedings in the designated court after being sued in the courts of another Member State.[620]

The rule is, however, less certain than it might at first appear to be. Although Article 31(2) is stated to apply only if a court is (second)[621] seised pursuant to an exclusive jurisdiction agreement, it goes on to contemplate the possibility that the court (second) seised might determine that it has no jurisdiction under the 'agreement'.[622] The intention is clearly that the court first seised should give way to the court designated in the 'agreement', without itself determining whether the jurisdiction clause is valid or applicable. What the reform leaves out, therefore, is the threshold for the application of this rule. It should not be sufficient that a party merely claims (without evidence) that the dispute is covered by an exclusive jurisdiction agreement, otherwise the rule would clearly be open to a variation on the tactical litigation experienced as a result of the *Gasser* decision, with parties spuriously claiming jurisdiction agreements in favour of, for example, the Italian courts, and commencing proceedings in Italy accordingly, in order to frustrate the jurisdiction of the English courts. Nor should it be necessary to establish that a jurisdiction agreement actually governs the dispute, otherwise this decision would need to be made by any court seised to determine whether the rule applies, which would defeat the objective of the rule.[623] For the rule to apply, there clearly must be some intermediate standard—an 'apparent' exclusive jurisdiction agreement, or a 'prima facie' exclusive jurisdiction agreement. This question will have to be clarified by the courts and eventually the Court of Justice, and it is unfortunate that it was not addressed more clearly in the Brussels I Recast. Nevertheless, the general effect of the reforms is to be welcomed for the policy reasons set out above.

(ii) Court second seised claims exclusive jurisdiction under Article 24
Gasser was concerned with the relationship between the provisions on choice of jurisdiction agreements and *lis pendens*. The position is different in a case involving Article 24 of the Brussels I Recast. In this situation the court seised second with exclusive jurisdiction under Article 24 is not required to stay its proceedings in favour of the court seised first, and this was also the case under the Brussels Convention and Brussels I Regulation.[624] Article 24

---

[618] See Recital (22).

[619] See Hartley (2013) 129 LQR 309; Ballesteros (2014) 10 J Priv Int L 291; Baatz [2014] LMCLQ 159; Bergson (2015) 11 J Priv Int L 1; Wilke (2015) 11 J Priv Int L 128. See also Recital (22) of the Brussels I Recast.

[620] See, eg, *Perella Weinberg Partners UK LLP v Codere SA* [2016] EWHC 1182 (Comm) at [18]; *Commerzbank Aktiengesellschaft v Liquimar Tankers Management Inc* [2017] EWHC 161 (Comm), [2017] 1 Lloyd's Rep 273; on asymmetrical jurisdiction agreements under the Brussels I Recast see further supra, p 235.

[621] If the court is first seised under an exclusive jurisdiction agreement, the usual rules on *lis pendens* will apply: see Recital (22).

[622] Recital (22) expressly states that "the designated court has priority to decide on the validity of the agreement and on the extent to which the agreement applies to the dispute pending before it".

[623] Although it should be noted that the designated court can continue with its proceedings regardless of whether the court first seised has determined if this rule applies: Recital (22).

[624] See the opinion of AG Leger in the *Gasser* case, supra, at [52]; the *Overseas Union Insurance* case, supra, at [26]; *Prudential Assurance Co Ltd v Prudential Insurance Co of America* [2003] EWCA Civ 327 at [22], [2003] 1 WLR 2295; *Speed Investments Ltd v Formula One Holdings Ltd* [2004] EWCA Civ 1512 at [35]–[38], [2005] 1 WLR 1936. This was confirmed in Case C-438/12 *Weber v Weber* EU:C:2014:212, [2015] Ch 140.

cases can be distinguished from Article 25 cases on two grounds. First, a court seised first is required to declare of its own motion that it has no jurisdiction if the courts of another Member State have exclusive jurisdiction under Article 24, but not under Article 25.[625] The jurisdiction of the court first seised is not capable of being established.[626] Secondly, a court in another Member State will not recognise a judgment if it conflicts with Article 24, but it will if it conflicts with Article 25.[627] This has not changed under the Brussels I Recast, although a party to an English exclusive jurisdiction agreement should be able to prevent a judgment from arising in the courts of another Member State simply by commencing proceedings in England, even if only for a declaration that the agreement is valid.

(ii) Related actions

Article 30 of the Brussels I Recast is concerned with related actions. Article 30(1) provides that: "Where related actions are pending[628] in the courts of different Member States, any court other than the court first seised may stay its proceedings." There is also power under Article 30(2) for the court seised second to decline jurisdiction if the court first seised has jurisdiction over the related actions in question and its law permits the consolidation thereof.[629]

Related actions are defined as ones which are so closely connected that it is expedient to hear them together to avoid irreconcilable judgments from separate proceedings[630] in the courts of different Member States.

The Court of Justice has held that this definition must be broadly interpreted[631] and covers all cases where there is a risk of conflicting decisions, even if, because the parties are different, the judgments can be separately enforced and their legal consequences are not mutually exclusive.[632] The concern is to prevent conflicting judgments, albeit only as regards their reasoning, and the court second seised should be able to use Article 30 whenever it considers that the reasoning of the court first seised may concern issues likely to be relevant to its own decision.[633] The House of Lords applied these principles in *Sarrio SA v Kuwait Investment Authority*[634] and, reversing the decision of the Court of Appeal,[635] held that no distinction is to be drawn between the primary or essential issues necessary to establish a cause of action and other matters not essential to the court's conclusion. Adopting this broad common sense approach, their Lordships affirmed the decision of Mance J, at first instance,[636] that the

---

[625] Art 27. This distinction was used by the Court of Justice to justify its decision in the *Gasser* case, supra, at [52]. See also the *Prudential Assurance* case, supra, at [22].

[626] The *Prudential Assurance* case, supra, at [22].

[627] Art 45(1)(e)(ii) of the Brussels I Recast. This point was made by the Commission in the *Gasser* case, which treated Art 16 of the Brussels Convention (Art 24 of the Brussels I Recast) cases differently from Art 17 of the Convention (Art 25 of the Brussels I Recast) cases, see [35]–[36]. See also the opinion of AG Leger in that case at [75].

[628] Cf Art 22(1) of the Brussels Convention, which requires both actions to be pending *at the first instance stage*. The Brussels I Recast is worded so as to avoid this requirement.

[629] Both actions must be pending at first instance, on which see *William Grant & Sons International Ltd v Marie Brizard et Roger International SA* [1997] IL Pr 391 at 401, Court of Session; *Bank of Scotland v SA Banque Nationale de Paris* 1996 SLT 103 at 131–2.

[630] Art 30(3).

[631] *The Tatry*, supra. See also *Sarrio SA v Kuwait Investment Authority* [1999] AC 32, HL; Briggs (1997) 68 BYBIL 331; Harris [1998] LMCLQ 145; *Prazic v Prazic* [2006] EWCA Civ 497 at [17].

[632] *The Tatry*, supra. It follows that "irreconcilable" under Art 30(3) has a different and wider meaning from that in the context of Art 45(1), infra, pp 639–41. On which see Case C-539/03 *Roche Nederland BV v Primus* [2007] IL Pr 9 at [23].

[633] See the opinion of AG Tesauro in *The Tatry*, supra.

[634] Supra.

[635] [1997] 1 Lloyd's Rep 113.

[636] [1996] 1 Lloyd's Rep 650.

actions were related[637] where there were allegations common to both sets of proceedings in relation to whether negotiations leading to a sale were conducted by or on behalf of the defendant. The risk of irreconcilable judgments may arise from both questions of jurisdiction and merits,[638] and from issues raised in claims as well as in defences or counter-claims.[639] As a consequence, Article 30 concerns may arise at any time during the course of proceedings, not just at their commencement, and should be evaluated by the court based on the circumstances as at the time the issue is being considered. Nevertheless, the application of Article 30 depends on which court is first seised of proceedings, not in which court a particular issue is first raised.[640]

Article 30 is concerned with situations that fall outside Article 29, ie the cause of action and subject matter, or the parties,[641] or even both[642] will not be the same.[643] There is no risk of irreconcilable judgments if there is no intention of pursuing the proceedings, commenced in two different Member States, anywhere other than in one Member State,[644] or if one set of proceedings has been definitively terminated,[645] or if one action is for provisional measures and the other is as to the merits.[646] It is not permissible to examine whether the courts of another Member State have exercised properly their jurisdiction under the Brussels I Recast when determining whether actions are related.[647] Although the point is contentious, it seems to be implicit from the part of the definition of related actions that refers to it being expedient to hear the two actions together[648] that the court first seised is able to try both actions

---

[637] See also as examples of related actions: *The Happy Fellow* [1998] 1 Lloyd's Rep 13, CA—collision and limitation actions related; *Toepfer v Molino Boschi* [1996] 1 Lloyd's Rep 510 at 513–14; *Glencore International AG v Metro Trading International Inc (No 1)*, supra, 646–7; *Cronos Containers NV v Palatin* [2002] EWHC 2819, [2003] 2 Lloyd's Rep 489; *Evialis v SIAT* [2003] EWHC 863 (Comm) at [123] and [125], [2003] 2 Lloyd's Rep 377; *Bank of Tokyo-Mitsubishi Ltd v Baskan Gida Sanayi Ve Pazarlama AS* [2004] EWHC 945 (Ch) at [226], [2004] 2 Lloyd's Rep 395; *In the Matter of Intercare Ltd* [2004] 1 ILRM 351; *Prazic v Prazic* [2006] EWCA Civ 497 at [18], [2006] 2 FLR 1128; *UBS Ltd v Regione Calabria* [2012] EWHC 699 (Comm), [2012] IL Pr 22. Cf *Mecklermedia Corpn v DC Congress GmbH* [1998] Ch 40 at 54; *Charterers Mutual Assurance Association Ltd v British and Foreign* [1998] IL Pr 838 at 855; the *Lafi* case, supra, 71; *Miles Platts Ltd v Townroe Ltd* [2003] EWCA Civ 145 at [28]–[34], [2003] 1 All ER (Comm) 561; *Bank of Tokyo-Mitsubishi*, supra, at [241]; *Leo Laboratories v Crompton* BV [2005] 2 IRLM 423—one action in tort, the other in contract following the delivery of contaminated defective product; *Jacobs & Turner Ltd*, supra, at [77]; *Sony Computer Entertainment Ltd v RH Freight Services Ltd* [2007] EWHC 302 (Comm) at [27]–[34], [2007] IL Pr 21; *J v P* [2007] EWHC 704 (Comm) at [49]–[52]; *Landis & Gyr Ltd v Scaleo Chip ET* [2007] EWHC 1880 (QB) at [46]–[50], [2007] IL Pr 53; *Seven Licensing Co Sarl v FFG-Platinum SA* [2011] EWHC 2967 (Comm), [2012] IL Pr 7.

[638] *IP Metal Ltd v Ruote OZ SpA* [1993] 2 Lloyd's Rep 60.

[639] *Research In Motion UK Ltd v Visto Corporation* [2008] EWCA Civ 153, [2008] IL Pr 34.

[640] *FKI Engineering Ltd v Stribog Ltd* [2011] EWCA Civ 622, [2011] 2 Lloyd's Rep 387; *The Alexandros T* [2013] UKSC 70, [2014] 1 Lloyd's Rep 223; *Barclays Bank Plc v Ente Nazionale di Previdenza* [2016] EWCA Civ 1261.

[641] *The Tatry*, supra; *The Nordglimt* [1988] 1 QB 183 at 201—if the facts were to occur now the parties would be regarded as being the same and Art 29 would apply.

[642] See *Sarrio SA v Kuwait Investment Authority*, supra.

[643] See the opinion of AG Tesauro in *The Tatry*, supra.

[644] *Fox v Taher* [1997] IL Pr 441, CA.

[645] Case C-39/02 *Maersk Olie & Gas AS v M De Haan en W De Boer* [2004] ECR I-9657 at [40].

[646] *Rank Film Distributors v Lanterna Editrice Srl* [1992] IL Pr 58. It might be different if the provisional measure raises issues as to the merits as it did in the *Miles Platts* case, although on the facts of that case there was little duplication of issues and therefore the actions were held not to be related.

[647] *AGF v Chiyoda* [1992] 1 Lloyd's Rep 325; following *Overseas Union Insurance Co v New Hampshire Insurance Co*, supra. For an exception to the principle prohibiting an examination of the jurisdiction of the court first seised, see supra, p 453.

[648] The actions may be connected but not capable of being heard together in a real sense because their basis is very different: *JP Morgan Europe Ltd v Primacom AG* [2005] EWHC 508 (Comm) at [57], [2005] 2 Lloyd's Rep 665.

together, not just in relation to Article 30(2), which makes this an express requirement, but also in relation to Article 30(1); where this is not the case the actions (under this view) cannot come within Article 30.[649] If this view is correct, then in such circumstances a temporary stay pending the resolution of the proceedings in the court first seised might, however, still be available on case management grounds.[650] It is important to note that Article 30 itself does not confer jurisdiction.[651] In particular, it does not accord jurisdiction to a court of a Member State to try an action which is related to another action in respect of which it has jurisdiction under the Brussels I Recast. One final observation on the definition of related actions is that the same wording is to be found in Article 8(1) of the Brussels I Recast.[652] Cases decided in the latter context have been relied on for guidance in the present context, and vice versa.[653] However, the Court of Justice has left open the question whether the same definition of "irreconcilable" should be used in these two different contexts,[654] or whether a narrower interpretation should be given in the context of Article 8(1).[655]

Any court other than the court first seised may (rather than must) stay its proceedings[656] or decline jurisdiction.[657] This gives a discretion,[658] in exercising which "regard may be had to the question of which court is in the best position to decide a given question".[659] The court may consider matters "such as the extent of the relatedness, the stage reached in each set of proceedings and the proximity of each Court to the subject matter of the case".[660] This involves considerations comparable to *forum conveniens*,[661] but there is one crucial additional consideration that is unique to this area, namely that there is a risk of irreconcilable

---

[649] *Haji-Ioannou v Frangos* [1999] 2 Lloyd's Rep 337 at 352, CA; *L A Gear Inc v Gerald Whelan & Sons Ltd* [1991] FSR 670; *De Pina v MS Birka ICG* [1994] IL Pr 694. But cf *Centro Internationale Handelsbank AG v Morgan Grenfell Trade Finance Ltd* [1997] CLC 870; *Lehman Brothers Bankhaus AG I Ins v CMA CGM* [2013] EWHC 171 (Comm), [2013] 2 All ER (Comm) 557; *Nomura International Plc v Banca Monte Dei Paschi Di Siena SpA* [2013] EWHC 3187 (Comm), [2014] 1 WLR 1584.

[650] See supra, p 421; but if jurisdiction is taken under the Brussels I Recast, the position is unclear: see infra, pp 471–3.

[651] Case C-420/97 *Leathertex Divisione Sinetici SpA v Bodetex BVBA* [1999] ECR I-6747, 6792 at [30].

[652] Article 6(1) of the Brussels I Regulation; supra, p 283 et seq.

[653] In considering Art 6(1) of the Brussels I Regulation, it has been said that it is necessary to have in mind the related actions provision: *Messier-Dowty v Sabena SA* [2000] 1 WLR 2040, 2053, CA; *Coin Controls v Suzo (UK) Ltd* [1999] Ch 33 at 46 and vice versa (*King v Crown Energy Trading AG* [2003] EWHC 163 (Comm) at [36], [2003] IL Pr 28).

[654] Case C-539/03 *Roche Nederland BV v Primus* [2007] IL Pr 9 at [23]–[25]—a case under Art 6(1) of the Brussels I Regulation.

[655] AG Leger was in favour of a narrower definition for what is now Art 8(1), see [79]–[105] of his opinion.

[656] Under Art 30(1). See *Kloeckner & Co AG v Gatoil Overseas Inc* [1990] 1 Lloyd's Rep 177 at 206; Case 150/80 *Elefanten Schuh GmbH v Jacqmain* [1981] ECR 1671.

[657] Under Art 30(2). See *Owens Bank Ltd v Bracco* [1992] 2 AC 443, [1992] 2 WLR 127, CA; *Sarrio SA v Kuwait Investment Authority*, supra; *Haji-Ioannou v Frangos* [1999] 2 Lloyd's Rep 337 at 352, CA.

[658] See *IP Metal Ltd v Ruote OZ SpA* [1993] 2 Lloyd's Rep 60; *The MV Turquoise Bleu* [1996] 1 ILRM 406; *Research In Motion UK Ltd v Visto Corporation* [2008] EWCA Civ 153, [2008] IL Pr 34. The discretion can be exercised on the application of just one claimant, even though there are several claimants in the court first seised: *The Happy Fellow* [1998] 1 Lloyd's Rep 13, CA.

[659] See the opinion of AG Lenz in Case C-129/92 *Owens Bank Ltd v Bracco (No 2)* [1994] QB 509 at 542.

[660] *Grupo Torras SA and Torras Hostench London Ltd v Sheikh Fahad Mohammed Al-Sabah* [1995] 1 Lloyd's Rep 374 at 418, 437; the Court of Appeal in [1996] 1 Lloyd's Rep 7 found it unnecessary to discuss this point following the opinion of AG Lenz in *Owens Bank Ltd v Bracco*, supra, at 541; see also *Cooper Tire & Rubber Co Europe Ltd v Shell Chemicals UK Ltd* [2010] EWCA Civ 864, [2010] 2 CLC 104.

[661] The *Grupo Torras* case, supra. See also *Mecklermedia Corpn v DC Congress GmbH* [1998] Ch 40 at 55–6; *Tradigrain v SIAT SpA* [2002] EWHC 106 (Comm) at [66], [2002] 2 Lloyd's Rep 553; *Miles Platts Ltd v Townroe Ltd* [2003] EWCA Civ 145 at [34], [2003] 1 All ER (Comm) 561; *Bank of Tokyo-Mitsubishi*, supra, at [228]. But cf *J v P* [2007] EWHC 704 (Comm) at [50], [71]–[73]. *Forum conveniens* is discussed infra, p 364 et seq.

judgments if a stay is not granted. There is a strong presumption in favour of granting a stay so as to avoid this.[662] However, this presumption is likely to be rebutted where the action in the court first seised was brought in breach of an agreement providing for the exclusive jurisdiction of the English courts.[663]

(b) Proceedings in a non-Member State

Articles 29 and 30 are limited to concurrent proceedings in different Member States. To take an example, they would not apply to concurrent actions in Japan and the United Kingdom. In many such cases (eg a Japanese domiciliary sues a United Kingdom domiciliary in Japan, and there are concurrent proceedings in the United Kingdom where the United Kingdom domiciliary sues the Japanese domiciliary) the Brussels I Recast would not apply to the action brought in the United Kingdom and the courts would use traditional bases of jurisdiction and can also use the accompanying rules on *forum conveniens* or *forum non conveniens*, which are used to deal with cases of *lis pendens*.[664] In other cases (eg a Japanese domiciliary sues a United Kingdom domiciliary in the United Kingdom, and there are concurrent proceedings in Japan where the United Kingdom domiciliary sues the Japanese domiciliary), the Brussels I Recast would apply to the action brought in the United Kingdom. The Brussels Convention and Brussels I Regulation did not contain rules dealing with this situation, and it was unclear whether proceedings could be stayed in these circumstances, as discussed later in this chapter.[665] The Brussels I Recast has added new provisions, Articles 33 and 34, which deal with *lis pendens* or related proceedings where the prior proceedings are in a non-Member State (referred to in the Brussels I Recast as a 'third State').[666]

Article 33, which is analogous to Article 29, deals with the situation where there are prior proceedings in a non-Member State "involving the same cause of action and between the same parties". Article 34, which is analogous to Article 30, deals with the situation where the non-Member State prior proceedings are "related". These key terms should be interpreted consistently with the authorities dealing with Articles 29 and 30. The definition of when a court should be considered to be seised, set out in Article 32 and discussed above,[667] also applies to determining when a non-Member State court is seised for the purposes of Articles 33 and 34.

Both Articles 33 and 34 apply only where jurisdiction is based on Article 4 or on Articles 7, 8 or 9. They therefore only permit English proceedings to be stayed where the English courts have non-exclusive jurisdiction under the general jurisdictional rules in the Brussels I Recast, not where jurisdiction is taken under Articles 24[668] or 25, or under the special rules dealing with insurance, consumers, and employment contracts. They also do not apply

---

[662] *Virgin Aviation v CAD Aviation* [1991] IL Pr 79 at 88; the opinion of AG Lenz in *Owens Bank Ltd v Bracco*, supra, at 541. See also *The Linda* [1988] 1 Lloyd's Rep 175 at 179; Mance J in the *Grupo Torras* case, supra—caution must be exercised before refusing a stay, and in *Sarrio Sa v Kuwait Investment Authority* [1996] 1 Lloyd's Rep 650 at 661—neither the Court of Appeal nor the House of Lords discussed this point; *Jacobs & Turner Ltd*, supra, at [78]. This has led to statements that the discretion is not one based on *forum non conveniens: The Linda*, supra; *Virgin Aviation v CAD Aviation*, supra; the *Miles Platts* case, supra, at [34]. Cf on the burden of proof *Centro Internationale Handelsbank AG v Morgan Grenfell Trade Finance Ltd* [1997] CLC 870.

[663] *JP Morgan Europe Ltd v Primacom AG* [2005] EWHC 508 (Comm) at [65]–[66], [2005] 2 Lloyd's Rep 665; *The Alexandros T* [2013] UKSC 70, [2014] 1 Lloyd's Rep 223; *Barclays Bank Plc v Ente Nazionale di Previdenza* [2016] EWCA Civ 1261.

[664] See infra, pp 468–70, and supra, pp 407–9 for the relevant English rules.

[665] See infra, pp 466–7.

[666] See generally, Fentiman 2015, para 12.04ff; Briggs 2015, para 2.290ff.

[667] See supra, pp 448–9.

[668] See, eg, *Re Zavarco Plc* [2015] EWHC 1898 (Ch), [2016] Ch 128.

where jurisdiction has been taken under the common law rules, pursuant to Article 6—the role of *forum conveniens* or *forum non conveniens* in those cases is preserved. Both Article 33 and 34 may be applied on application by a party to the proceedings or, where possible under national law, of the court's own motion. It is unclear whether English procedural law permits an English court to consider these points other than on application by a party.

Under both Articles 33 and 34, a stay is discretionary rather than mandatory. The exercise of the discretion is likely to be strongly shaped by the requirement that the court must be satisfied that "a stay is necessary for the proper administration of justice".[669] Recital (24) explains that in considering this question, the court should "assess all the circumstances of the case before it", which may include "connections between the facts of the case and the parties and the third State concerned, the stage to which the proceedings in the third State have progressed by the time proceedings are initiated in the court of the Member State and whether or not the court of the third State can be expected to give a judgment within a reasonable time". As discussed above, these are all factors traditionally taken into consideration in the exercise of the Article 30 discretion.[670] The court may also consider "whether the court of the third State has exclusive jurisdiction in the particular case in circumstances where a court of a Member State would have exclusive jurisdiction". The effect of this guidance is that Articles 24 and 25 are given a discretionary 'reflexive effect',[671] allowing a Member State court to decline jurisdiction based on strong subject matter connections with a non-Member State (equivalent to those under Article 24) or an exclusive jurisdiction agreement in favour of a non-Member State, but only if there are prior proceedings in that state. If the English courts are first seised, the problems created by the decision of *Owusu v Jackson*,[672] discussed further below,[673] are not addressed.

For a stay under either Article 33 or 34, the court must also be satisfied that the non-Member State proceedings will give "a judgment capable of recognition and, where applicable, of enforcement in that Member State".[674] The Brussels I Recast does not apply to the recognition and enforcement of non-Member State judgments, which means that the application of these rules will be based on national law, and will thus differ between the Member States.[675] This is not very satisfactory as a matter of European Union law and is likely to lead to pressure to harmonise those rules in the future.

Proceedings stayed pursuant to Articles 33 or 34 may be continued if the non-Member State proceedings are themselves stayed or discontinued, unlikely to conclude within a reasonable time, or if required for the proper administration of justice.[676] If the non-Member State proceedings conclude and give rise to a judgment capable of recognition and enforcement, the Member State proceedings "shall" be dismissed where the proceedings are identical (under Article 33(3), suggesting a mandatory rule), and "may" be dismissed where the proceedings are related (under Article 34(3), suggesting there is a discretion).

For the application of Article 34, dealing with prior related proceedings in a non-Member State, there is an additional requirement: that "it is expedient to hear and determine the related actions together to avoid the risk of irreconcilable judgments resulting from separate

---

[669] Art 33(1)(b); Art 34(1)(c). See (obiter) discussion in *Re Zavarco Plc*, supra.
[670] See supra, p 454 et seq.
[671] See further infra, p 473 et seq.
[672] Case C-281/02 [2005] ECR I-1383, [2005] QB 801.
[673] See infra, p 462 et seq.
[674] Art 33(1)(a); Art 34(1)(b).
[675] See also Recital (23).
[676] Art 33(2); Art 34(2).

proceedings".[677] This is likely to be interpreted consistently with the case law dealing with the same requirement under Article 30. In addition to the circumstances discussed above, proceedings stayed pursuant to Article 34 may also be continued if there no longer appears to be a risk of irreconcilable judgments.[678]

The addition of Articles 33 and 34 is in many ways to be welcomed, in reducing the risk of irreconcilable judgments arising between Member State and non-Member State courts, and more generally in recognising the external effects of the Brussels I Recast. However, the new rules inevitably raise a number of uncertain points which will require judicial clarification. It is also worth noting that the rules do not require reciprocity for their application—they do not depend on third States declining jurisdiction in equivalent circumstances, even if a Member State court is first seised—and thus they address the risk of conflicting judgments through unilateral jurisdictional abstention rather than coordination. For this reason, the external effects of the Brussels I Recast would be better addressed through multilateral efforts such as those being pursued at the Hague Conference on Private International Law.[679]

5. STAYS OF PROCEEDINGS UNDER THE BRUSSELS I RECAST

As examined in Chapter 11 and in the previous section of this Chapter, the Brussels I Recast contains various rules under which a Member State court either must or may stay proceedings which would ordinarily have a basis of jurisdiction, because priority is given to another court. For example, in some cases the Brussels I Recast identifies a single court which is given exclusive jurisdiction. In such cases, if proceedings are commenced in the courts of any other Member State, the court seised must (of its own motion) stay those proceedings.[680] If more than one court has exclusive jurisdiction, any court other than the court first seised must similarly decline jurisdiction.[681] If the case is not covered by the rules on exclusive jurisdiction, the rules on *lis pendens* and related proceedings in the Brussels I Recast establish that (in general) any court other than the court first seised either must or may stay its proceedings, giving priority to the court first seised.

Outside the circumstances covered by these rules, there has been a long-standing controversy over whether proceedings commenced under the Brussels Convention, Brussels I Regulation and now Brussels I Recast may be stayed, either pursuant to the doctrine of *forum non conveniens* or on some other similar basis.

(a) A discretion to stay proceedings in the Brussels I Recast itself?

A distinctive feature of the law relating to jurisdiction in common law systems is the presence of a discretionary power to refuse to take jurisdiction on the basis of *forum non conveniens*; ie the appropriate forum for trial is abroad.[682] There is no such power in civil law systems.[683] Given that the Brussels I Recast is based on the Brussels Convention which had civil law origins, it is not surprising to find that it contains no general discretion to stay actions on the

---

[677] Art 34(1)(a).

[678] Art 34(2)(a).

[679] See supra, p 315; Mills (2016) 65 ICLQ 541.

[680] Art 27; supra, p 443 et seq.

[681] Art 31(1); supra, p 450.

[682] See generally Fawcett, *Declining Jurisdiction*, pp 10–27. *Forum non conveniens* is discussed supra, p 393 et seq.

[683] See ibid, pp 10, 21–7; Kennett (1995) 54 CLJ 552.

basis of *forum non conveniens*.[684] The provisions requiring a court to stay proceedings (noted above) are generally mandatory rather than discretionary, with the exception of Article 30 dealing with related proceedings, and Articles 33 and 34 dealing with prior non-Member State proceedings.

(b) Can the traditional English doctrine of forum non conveniens be used?

An English court must not act in a manner which is inconsistent with the Brussels I Recast.[685] In answering the question whether, by using the doctrine of *forum non conveniens*, it is so acting, it is important to distinguish four different situations.

(i) *The Brussels I Recast is inapplicable*

In the situation where the Brussels I Recast is inapplicable (ie the matter is not within the scope of the Brussels I Recast)[686] the courts in the United Kingdom will be able to apply their rules on stays of action (whether these are based on *forum non conveniens*, or on a foreign choice of jurisdiction clause)[687] as well as their traditional bases of jurisdiction.

(ii) *The Brussels I Recast is applicable and the bases of jurisdiction set out therein come into play*

We are concerned here with the situation where the matter is within the scope of the Brussels I Recast and the bases of jurisdiction set out therein apply (where the defendant is domiciled in a Member State, or where Article 18(1), Article 21(2), Article 24 or Article 25 applies). In this situation, it has to be decided whether the court of the Member State which has been assigned jurisdiction by the Brussels I Recast is obligated to take it. If so, to grant a stay would be inconsistent with the Brussels I Recast. Continental lawyers[688] have long taken the view that any court of a Contracting State allocated jurisdiction under the Brussels Convention (replaced in virtually all cases by the Brussels I Recast) must try the case and that courts in the United Kingdom cannot use their *forum non conveniens* discretion in such circumstances. However, English lawyers, when discussing the Brussels Convention, were not prepared to give up their doctrine of *forum non conveniens* so easily, and distinguished between cases where the alternative forum is a Contracting State and those where it is a non-Contracting State. After examining the English authorities attention will turn to the decision of the Court of Justice in *Owusu v Jackson*,[689] which overturned the English law in this area.

(a) The English authorities

In *S & W Berisford plc v New Hampshire Insurance Co*[690] and *Arkwright Mutual Insurance Co v Bryanston Insurance Co Ltd*[691] it was held that there was no general discretionary power to stay the proceedings when jurisdiction had been allocated to England under Article 2 of the Brussels Convention, even if the alternative forum was a non-Contracting State.

---

[684] See the opinion of the Advocate General in Case 12/76 *Tessili v Dunlop* [1976] ECR 1473; Case 42/76 *De Wolf v Cox* [1976] ECR 1759. See also the hostile attitude of the Court of Justice towards the use of the idea of an appropriate forum in connection with the basis of jurisdiction in Case C-288/92 *Custom Made Commercial Ltd v Stawa Metallbau* [1994] ECR I-2913.

[685] *Mazur Media Ltd v Mazur Media GMBH* [2004] EWHC 1566 (Ch) at [69], [2004] 1 WLR 2966.

[686] Supra, p 202 et seq.

[687] See *A v B* [2006] EWHC 2006 (Comm), [2007] 1 Lloyd's Rep 237—claims designed to impugn the validity of an arbitration agreement fell outside the scope of the Lugano Convention.

[688] See the Schlosser Report, pp 97–9; Kohler (1985) 31 ICLQ 563, 571–4; Droz, *Compétence judicaire et effets des judgmentsdans le marché commun*, p 128; Tebbens in Sumampouw (ed), *Law and Reality: Essays on National and International Procedural Law in Honour of Voskuil*, p 47; Gaudemet-Tallon (1991) Rev crit dr int privé 491.

[689] Case C-281/02 [2005] ECR I-1383, [2005] QB 801.

[690] [1990] 2 QB 631.

[691] [1990] 2 QB 649; Collins (1990) 106 LQR 535; Briggs [1991] LMCLQ 10.

However, the Court of Appeal in *Re Harrods (Buenos Aires) Ltd*[692] disagreed. Proceedings were brought in England for, inter alia, the winding up of an English incorporated company. It was argued that the most appropriate forum for trial was Argentina, where the company exclusively carried on its business, and a stay was sought of the English proceedings. The Brussels Convention applied by virtue of the company's English domicile. Nonetheless, it was held that there was power to stay the English proceedings on the ground of *forum non conveniens* and a stay was granted. A fundamental distinction was drawn between cases where the alternative forum was, as here, in a non-Contracting State and cases where it was in a Contracting State. The *forum non conveniens* discretion could still be exercised in the former case, but not in the latter, which is regulated by the *lis pendens* and related proceedings rules under the Convention and now Regulation.[693] The Court of Appeal accepted the argument[694] that the Convention was intended to regulate jurisdiction as between Contracting States and not as between a Contracting and a non-Contracting State. Exercise of the discretion to stay in a case involving a non-Contracting State would therefore not be inconsistent with the Convention. Although a controversial decision,[695] *Re Harrods* was followed by differently constituted Courts of Appeal on a number of occasions.[696] These subsequent decisions showed that the principle in *Re Harrods* was not limited to cases where no other Member State was involved and it was applied in the situation where the defendant was domiciled not in England but in another Member State and the alternative forum abroad was a non-Member State.[697] The principle also looked to be applicable regardless of the basis of jurisdiction.[698] It was applied in cases where jurisdiction was based not on domicile but on special jurisdiction under Article 6(1) of the Convention,[699] on the insurance provisions

---

[692] [1992] Ch 72; Briggs (1991) 107 LQR 180; Kaye [1992] JBL 47; Hartley (1992) 17 ELR 553. For critical Continental reaction see Gaudemet-Tallon op cit; Tebbens, op cit.

[693] The unavailability of the discretionary power to stay in cases where the alternative forum was a Contracting State was confirmed in *Messier Dowty Ltd v Sabena SA* [2000] 1 WLR 2040, 2047, CA; *Aiglon v Gau Shan* [1993] 1 Lloyd's Rep 164; *Lafi Office and International Business SL v Meriden Animal Health Ltd* [2001] 1 All ER (Comm) 54; *Carnoustie Universal SA v The International Transport Workers Federation* [2003] EWHC 1108 (Comm) at [27], [2004] IL Pr 2; *Mahme Trust v Lloyds TSB Bank plc* [2004] EWHC 1931, [2004] IL Pr 43; *Mazur Media Ltd v Mazur Media Gmbh* [2004] EWHC 1566 (Ch) at [71], [2004] 1 WLR 2966. But cf *White Sea & Onega Shipping Co Ltd v International Transport Workers Federation* [2001] 1 Lloyd's Rep 421, disapproved by CA. For post-Case C-281/02 *Owusu v Jackson* [2005] ECR I-1383, [2005] QB 801 confirmation, see *Viking Line ABP v The International Transport Workers' Federation* [2005] EWHC 1222, [2006] IL Pr 4 at [73]–[75]; Briggs (2005) 76 BYBIL 641, 646–7.

[694] Put forward by Collins (1990) 106 LQR 535.

[695] Cf the criticism in the 13th edn of this book, pp (1999), 264–5; Briggs and Rees (2000) 3rd edn, para 2.216 and (2005) 4th edn, para 2.223; and Layton and Mercer, paras 13.023–13.026 with Dicey and Morris (2000) 13th edn, paras 12-017–12-018. See generally Fentiman [2000] Cambridge Yearbook of European Legal Studies 107.

[696] *The Po* [1991] 2 Lloyd's Rep 206, CA; *The Nile Rhapsody* [1994] 1 Lloyd's Rep 382, CA; *Haji-Ioannou v Frangos* [1999] 2 Lloyd's Rep 337 et 346, CA (which regarded itself as being bound as a matter of precedent), Briggs (1999) 70 BYBIL 474; *Ace Insurance SA-NV (Formerly Cigna Insurance Co of Europe SA NV) v Zurich Insurance Co* [2001] EWCA Civ 173 at [39] (which also regarded itself as being bound as a matter of precedent), [2001] 1 Lloyd's Rep 618, CA, Briggs (2001) 72 BYBIL 474. For Ireland see *In the Matter of Intercare Ltd* [2004] 1 ILRM 351, 358.

[697] *Eli-Lilly and Co v Novo Nordisk A/S* [2000] IL Pr 73, CA; *Ace Insurance*, supra, at [31]; *The Po* [1991] 2 Lloyd's Rep 206, where England had jurisdiction by virtue of the Collision Convention, preserved by Art 57 of the Brussels Convention (Art 71 of the Brussels I Recast), and not by virtue of the defendant's domicile in England. See also the restatement of the *Re Harrods* principle by Lord Bingham in The *Haji-Ioannou* case, supra, at 346. Cf the judgment of Dillon LJ in *Re Harrods*.

[698] See the restatement of the *Re Harrods* principle by Lord Bingham in The *Haji-Ioannou* case, supra, at 346.

[699] Article 8(1) of the Brussels I Recast. See *Aiglon v Gau Shan*, supra.

under Section 3,[700] on submission,[701] and on exclusive jurisdiction under Article 17 of the Convention (Article 25 of the Brussels I Recast).[702] The Court of Appeal[703] also applied the principle in the situation where the English courts were being asked to stay the proceedings not on the basis of *forum non conveniens* but on the closely related basis that the action had been brought in breach of an agreement conferring exclusive jurisdiction on the courts of a non-Member State,[704] the alternative forum being the courts of that state.

(b) The decision of the Court of Justice in *Owusu v Jackson*

When the Court of Appeal decision in *Re Harrods (Buenos Aires) Ltd* was appealed to the House of Lords, the issue of the correctness of the principle adopted in that case was referred to the Court of Justice;[705] but before the Court could consider the matter, the action was settled. In *Lubbe v Cape plc*, Lord Bingham, with whom the other Law Lords concurred, agreed that the law in this area was not clear and said obiter that this matter should be referred to the Court of Justice.[706] This finally happened in *Owusu v Jackson*,[707] where the claimant, domiciled in England, brought proceedings in England against the first defendant, who was also domiciled in England, after being injured in Jamaica whilst staying at a villa he had rented from the first defendant. The latter sought a stay of the proceedings on the basis of *forum non conveniens*. The Court of Appeal[708] referred to the Court of Justice the correctness of the principle in *Re Harrods*.

The Court of Justice held that Article 2 of the Brussels Convention[709] applied even though the claimant and one of the defendants were domiciled in the same Contracting State and even though the dispute had links with a non-Contracting State and not with another Contracting State.[710] It then went on to hold that the Brussels Convention precludes a court of a Contracting State from declining the jurisdiction conferred on it by Article 2 of that Convention on the ground that a court of a non-Contracting State would be a more

---

[700] *American Motorists Insurance Co (Amico) v Cellstar Corpn* [2003] EWCA Civ 206 at [49], [2003] IL Pr 22—it was accepted that *Re Harrods* would apply, if it was a correct decision.

[701] The *Ace Insurance* case, supra.

[702] The *Eli-Lilly* case, supra—it appears to have been a case of an exclusive jurisdiction clause; *Sinochem International Oil (London) Ltd v Mobil Sales and Supply Corp Ltd (No 2)* [2000] 1 Lloyd's Rep 670—an exclusive jurisdiction clause; *Mercury Communications Ltd v Communication Telesystems International* [1999] 2 All ER (Comm) 33—non-exclusive jurisdiction agreement.

[703] *The Nile Rhapsody* [1994] 1 Lloyd's Rep 382, CA. However, the Court of Appeal, at 392, was prepared to assume that a reference to the Court of Justice was needed to clarify the law on this point but that a reference should not be made in this particular case because of the expense and delay to the parties this would involve.

[704] See infra, p 410 et seq.

[705] Case C-314/92 *Ladenimor SA v Intercomfinanz SA*.

[706] [2000] 1 WLR 1545, 1562, HL. The House of Lords avoided the contentious matter of the correctness of the decision in *Re Harrods (Buenos Aires) Ltd* by finding that under *forum non conveniens* principles no stay would be granted. See also *Intermetal Group Ltd & Trans-World (Steel) Ltd v Worslade Trading Ltd* [1998] IL Pr 765, Irish Sup Ct.

[707] Case C-281/02 [2005] ECR I-1383, [2005] QB 801; Briggs (2005) 121 LQR 535 and [2005] LMCLQ 378; Fentiman [2005] CLJ 303 and (2006) 43 CMLR 705; Rodger (2006) 2 J Priv Int L 71; Cuniberti (2005) 54 ICLQ 973; Hare [2006] JBL 157; Harris (2005) 54 ICLQ 933; Hartley (2005) 54 ICLQ 813; Ibili [2006] NILR 127; Peel [2005] LMCLQ 363; Knight [2007] CLJ 288.

[708] [2002] EWCA Civ 877, [2002] IL Pr 45, CA; Briggs (2002) 73 BYBIL 453. See also *American Motorists Insurance Co (Amico) v Cellstar Corpn* [2003] EWCA Civ 206, [2003] IL Pr 22, where the Court of Appeal referred the same question to the Court of Justice in *Owusu* with a view to it being combined with the reference in that case.

[709] Article 4 of the Brussels I Recast.

[710] The *Owusu* case, supra, at [23]–[36].

appropriate forum for the trial of the action even if the jurisdiction of no other Contracting State is in issue or the proceedings have no connecting factors to any other Contracting State.[711]

The decision in *Owusu* on the declining jurisdiction point was based on three considerations[712] and the conclusion is entirely convincing even if the reasoning is not. First, Article 2 is "mandatory in nature and that, according to its terms, there can be no derogation from the principle it lays down except in the cases expressly provided for by the Convention".[713] The persuasiveness of this argument may, however, be doubted because *Owusu* applies equally to cases where jurisdiction is based on other provisions in the Convention (or Regulation), not only on Article 2 (Article 4 of the Brussels I Recast).[714] Nevertheless, the Court followed a theme that ran through their earlier decisions in *Gasser*[715] and *Turner v Grovit*,[716] which also held that English practices in relation to international litigation were incompatible with the Convention, and that the Convention lays down a compulsory system of jurisdiction which the courts in Contracting States are required to respect.[717]

Secondly, the authors of the Convention did not provide for an exception on the basis of *forum non conveniens*, although the question of so providing was discussed. This might, however, also be explained by the fact that no common law state was a party to the Convention at the time of its adoption.

Thirdly, application of the doctrine of *forum non conveniens* would undermine certain objectives of the Convention,[718] namely: respect for the principle of legal certainty;[719] the strengthening in the Community of the legal protection of persons established therein; and the laying down of common rules of jurisdiction to the exclusion of derogating national rules. When it comes to the first of these objectives, the discretionary nature of the doctrine of *forum non conveniens* is liable to undermine the predictability of the rules of jurisdiction, in particular of Article 2 (now Article 4 of the Brussels I Recast), and consequently the principle of legal certainty. As regards the second objective, the legal protection of persons established in the Community would also be undermined in that a defendant, who is generally better placed to conduct his defence before the courts of his domicile, would not be able reasonably to foresee before which other court he may be sued. (It may, however, be observed that in *Owusu*, there was nothing unforeseeable about suit in Jamaica, and in any case, it was Owusu the defendant seeking the stay of proceedings. The court here appears to confuse certainty about where a defendant *might be* sued, which would be unaffected by *forum non conveniens*, with certainty about where the case will be heard once the defendant *has been* sued, which would indeed be affected.) The legal protection of the claimant is also undermined in that, under this doctrine, it is for the claimant to establish that he would not obtain justice before the foreign

---

[711] Ibid, at [54]. This follows criticism of the use of *forum non conveniens* in the European Community context by AG Ruiz-Jarabo Colomer in Case C-159/02 *Turner v Grovit* [2004] ECR I-3565 at [35]; discussed infra, p 477 et seq.

[712] The *Owusu* case, supra, at [38]–[47]. AG Leger, at [235]–[259] of his opinion mentioned a fourth consideration, that the scheme of the Convention supported this conclusion.

[713] Ibid, at [37].

[714] See infra, pp 465–6.

[715] [2003] ECR I-14693, [2005] QB 1 at [72]; discussed supra, pp 450–2.

[716] Supra, at [24].

[717] The *Owusu* case, supra, at [38].

[718] This would in turn undermine the effectiveness of the Convention: AG Leger at [271].

[719] This principle has been described as the basis of the Convention, see Case C-539/03 *Roche Nederland BV v Primus*, supra, at [37]. See also Case C-256/00 *Besix*, supra, at [24]–[26] and Case C-4/03 *GAT*, supra, at [28].

court.[720] Finally, turning to the third objective, allowing *forum non conveniens* in the context of the Brussels Convention when this doctrine has developed only in the United Kingdom and Ireland, and not in the other Contracting States, would be likely to affect the uniform application of the rules contained in the Convention, thereby defeating the objective of laying down common rules of jurisdiction to the exclusion of derogating national rules. This final argument is the most persuasive for the outcome of the case. Concern that the objectives of the Convention may be undermined not only provides a positive reason for rejecting the doctrine of *forum non conveniens*, it also destroys what might be argued is a justification for the use of *forum non conveniens*. The Court of Justice in an earlier case had drawn a difficult distinction between jurisdiction (dealt with by the Convention) and procedure (which is for national law).[721] But application of procedural rules must not, according to the Court, impair the effectiveness of the Convention.[722] According to Advocate General Leger in *Owusu*, if it is assumed for the sake of argument that *forum non conveniens* is a procedural rule it is one that impairs the effectiveness of the Convention.[723]

Owusu was a Brussels Convention case but the reasoning of the Court of Justice is equally applicable to the Brussels I Regulation and now Brussels I Recast. Indeed, Advocate General Leger said[724] that the eleventh Recital in the Preamble to the Brussels I Regulation, which states that "the rules of jurisdiction must be highly predictable", confirmed his view that a court of a Contracting State is precluded from declining jurisdiction on the ground that a court of a non-Contracting State would be more appropriate for the trial of the action.[725]

(c) Altering the facts

The Court of Appeal referred a further question to the Court of Justice, namely, if the Court holds that the use of *forum non conveniens* is inconsistent with the Convention in the circumstances of the *Owusu* case itself, is the use of that doctrine ruled out in all circumstances or just in certain circumstances? The Court of Justice refused to answer this hypothetical question, pointing out that its function was confined to answering questions necessary for the effective resolution of a dispute.[726] This inevitably raises a number of questions relating to whether the result would be any different if the material facts were altered.

First, would the result be any different if the parties were not domiciled in the same Member State but instead one was domiciled in a Member State and the other in a non-Member State (and the events in issue occurred within that non-Member State or some other non-Member State)? This is materially no different from *Owusu*. This new situation involves the relationships between the court of a single Member State and those of a non-Member State(s) and, according to the Court of Justice, Article 2 of the Convention (now Article 4 of the Brussels I Recast) would apply.[727] This new situation would then fall squarely within the ruling of the

---

[720] The *Owusu* case, supra, at [43]. This would be at the second stage of the *forum non conveniens* process, discussed supra, p 400 et seq. AG Leger, at [268] of his opinion, pointed out that this plea may be raised by a defendant as a delaying tactic and, at [272], that a claimant by being denied trial in a Contracting State is also denied the benefit of the recognition and enforcement rules under the Convention.

[721] Case 365/88 *Kongress Agentur Hagen GmbH v Zeehaghe BV* [1990] ECR I-1845.

[722] Ibid.

[723] The *Owusu* case, at [260]–[261]. The same point has been made by the Court of Justice in Case C-159/02 *Turner v Grovit* [2004] ECR I-3565, [2005] 1 AC 101 at [29], discussed infra, p 477 et seq, in relation to injunctions restraining foreign proceedings.

[724] The *Owusu* case, supra, at [278].

[725] Now Brussels I Recast, Recital (15). See also Layton and Mercer, para 13.027.

[726] The *Owusu* case, supra, at [48]–[53]. The Advocate General's Opinion, at [64]–[81] and [217], deliberately keeps strictly to the facts of the *Owusu* case.

[727] Ibid, at [36].

Court of Justice that, in such cases, the use of *forum non conveniens* is precluded "even if the jurisdiction of no other Contracting State is in issue or the proceedings have no connecting factors to any other Contracting State".[728] But what would happen if the jurisdiction of another Member State is in issue or there is a connecting factor with another Member State? For example, let us assume that the parties were domiciled in different Member States (and the event at issue occurred in one of those Member States or in some other Member State) or the parties were domiciled in the same Member State (and the event at issue occurred in another Member State). This involves the relationships between the courts of different Member States and there is no question but that Article 2 (now Article 4 of the Brussels I Recast) will apply.[729] The objections raised by the Court of Justice to declining jurisdiction in favour of a court of a non-Member State apply equally to declining jurisdiction in favour of a court of a Member State and the English courts should not decline jurisdiction in the latter situation.[730] However, this situation is unlikely to come before the Court of Justice since it is accepted in England that there is no power to decline jurisdiction in favour of another Member State.[731]

Secondly, would the result be any different if the jurisdiction of a Member State was based not on Article 2 of the Convention (now Article 4 of the Brussels I Recast) but on some other basis set out in the Convention or Brussels I Recast? *Owusu* obviously applies where jurisdiction is based on Article 12 of the Convention (insurer suing in the defendant's domicile).[732] In *Owusu* Advocate General Leger said that where jurisdiction is based on Articles 5 and 6[733] and Sections 3 and 4 of the Convention the case will necessarily involve relations between two Contracting States and not relations between a Contracting State and a non-Contracting State[734] (with the unsaid but implicit result that the doctrine of *forum non conveniens* cannot be used). Although it is correct to note that in cases covered by Articles 5 and 6 of the Convention (Articles 7 and 8 of the Brussels I Recast) there are necessarily two Contracting States with potential jurisdiction, which perhaps strengthens the *Owusu* argument, this also oversimplifies the position. The case may involve two Member States and a non-Member State. For example, the English court's jurisdiction over a defendant domiciled in another Member State may be based on special jurisdiction under Article 8(1) of the Brussels I Recast but the alternative forum for trial is in a non-Member State, with which the dispute has strong connections. Prior to *Owusu* an English court has applied *Re Harrods* in this precise situation.[735] It is submitted that it should no longer do so. The objections to the use of the doctrine of *forum non conveniens* raised by the Court of Justice in terms of the authors of the Convention not providing for such an exception and its use undermining certain objectives of the Convention (the second and third considerations set out above) are equally applicable, regardless of which of the bases of jurisdiction set out in the Brussels I Recast is used by the English court. The only possible difference that the basis used can make is over the question whether that particular basis is, like Article 4 of the Brussels I Recast, mandatory (the first consideration). Admittedly the wording of special jurisdiction under Articles 7, 8 and 9 and jurisdiction under Sections 3, 4 and 5 of the Brussels I Recast is less obviously mandatory

---

[728] Ibid, at [54].

[729] Ibid, at [36].

[730] *Viking Line ABP v The International Transport Workers' Federation* [2005] EWHC 1222, [2006] IL Pr 4 at [73]–[75].

[731] Supra, p 461.

[732] *CNA Insurance Co Ltd v Office Depot International (UK) Ltd* [2005] EWHC 456 (Comm) at [26]. Now Article 14 of the Brussels I Recast.

[733] Now Articles 7 and 8 of the Brussels I Recast.

[734] The *Owusu* case, supra, at [24] of his opinion.

[735] *Aiglon v Gau Shan*, supra.

than the wording of Article 4 of the Brussels I Recast. Nonetheless, there is no hint in the wording of Articles 7, 8 and 9 and Sections 3, 4 and 5 that the principles laid down in these provisions can be derogated from. *Owusu* has been applied by the English courts where jurisdiction was based on what is now Articles 7 and 8(1) of the Brussels I Recast,[736] and it has been considered to apply equally whenever there is jurisdiction under the Brussels I Recast.[737] Where jurisdiction is based on Articles 24 or 25 of the Brussels I Recast[738] (Articles 16 and 17 of the Convention), this can involve, as in *Owusu*, the relationships between the courts of a Member State and a non-Member State.[739] Nonetheless these provisions will still apply.[740] Again, the wording of Articles 24 and 25 of the Brussels I Recast is less obviously mandatory than the wording of Article 4. But there is no hint in the wording of Articles 24 and 25 that the principles laid down in these provisions can be derogated from. Indeed, the case for regarding Articles 24 and 25 as being mandatory in nature is particularly compelling[741] and the Court of Justice has described jurisdiction under Article 24 as being mandatory in nature.[742] It has to be remembered that under these provisions the case for the courts of a particular Member State having jurisdiction is so strong that it is given exclusive jurisdiction. It would be extraordinary if a Member State could then decline jurisdiction when it cannot do so when jurisdiction is based on Article 4 (which does not give exclusive jurisdiction). Here too it is submitted that to decline jurisdiction in favour of the courts of a non-Member State would be inconsistent with the Brussels I Recast, and the English courts have adopted this approach.[743] In the situation where Article 25 gives non-exclusive jurisdiction (ie there is a non-exclusive jurisdiction clause), the position is essentially the same as where jurisdiction is based on Articles 7, 8 and 9 or Sections 3, 4 and 5 of the Brussels I Recast. As in those cases, declining jurisdiction in favour of the courts of a non-Member State would be inconsistent with the Brussels I Recast.[744]

Thirdly, can the principle in *Re Harrods* (and hence the doctrine of *forum non conveniens*) still be used in the situation where the jurisdiction of a Member State is based on Article 4 (or some other basis set out in the Brussels I Recast) but a court of a non-Member State has previously been seised of a claim liable to give rise to *lis pendens* or related actions. *Re Harrods* was used in the past in this situation.[745] The Court of Justice regarded the hypothetical question referred to them as to whether the use of *forum non conveniens* is precluded in all circumstances, which it refused to answer, as being asked in connection with, inter alia, this

---

[736] *Viking Line ABP v The International Transport Workers' Federation* [2005] EWHC 1222, [2006] IL Pr 4 at [70]–[72]; *Gomez v Gomez-Monche Vives* [2008] EWCA Civ 1065, [2009] Ch 245; *FKI Engineering Ltd v De Wind Holdings Ltd* [2008] EWCA Civ 316, [2008] IL Pr 33.

[737] *Viking Line*, supra, at [71].

[738] The position would be same in Art 26 of the Brussels I Recast cases. See generally on Art 25 and *Owusu*, Baatz [2006] LMCLQ 143 at 149.

[739] The *Owusu* case, supra, at [28].

[740] Ibid.

[741] With the possible exception that Article 24 might be given 'reflexive effect' (discussed below) to override an agreement under Article 25, on the basis that Article 24 trumps Article 25 under the Brussels I Recast. See supra, p 218.

[742] Case C-4/03 *Gesellschaft für Antriebstechnik mbH & Co KG (GAT) v Luk Lamellen und Kupplungsbau Beteiligungs KG* [2006] ECR I-6509 at [24].

[743] *Choudhary v Bhattar* [2009] EWHC 314 (Ch), [2009] IL Pr 51 (point not addressed on appeal at [2009] EWCA Civ 1176); *Equitas Ltd v Allstate Insurance Co* [2008] EWHC 1671 (Comm), [2009] Lloyd's Rep IR 227; *Skype Technologies SA v Joltid Ltd* [2009] EWHC 2783 (Ch), [2011] IL Pr 8.

[744] But see the doubts expressed, without deciding the point, in *Antec International Ltd v Biosafety USA Inc* [2006] EWHC 47 (Comm) at [17]–[26]. See also where it was unnecessary to decide the point because the criteria for a stay were not met, *HIT Entertainment Ltd v Gaffney International Licensing Pty* [2007] EWHC 1282 (Ch).

[745] The *Ace Insurance* case, supra.

situation.[746] Nonetheless, the reasoning of the Court of Justice that precluded the declining of jurisdiction on the ground that a court of a non-Contracting State would be more appropriate is equally applicable in this situation. The possibility of using *forum non conveniens* in this situation must now be understood to be definitively precluded by the new Articles 33 and 34 of the Brussels I Recast, which expressly deal with *lis pendens* or related prior proceedings in a non-Member State, discussed earlier in this Chapter.[747]

Fourthly, can the principle in *Re Harrods* (and hence the doctrine of *forum non conveniens*) still be used in the situation where the jurisdiction of a Member State is based on Article 4 (or some other basis set out in the Brussels I Recast) but the links connecting the dispute with a non-Member State are of a kind referred to in Article 24 of the Brussels I Recast (Article 16 of the Brussels Convention)? Even before *Re Harrods*, English courts were suggesting that there was a discretion to stay the English proceedings in this situation.[748] The Court of Justice regarded the hypothetical question referred to them as to whether the use of *forum non conveniens* is precluded in all circumstances, which it refused to answer, as also being asked in connection with this situation.[749] Advocate General Leger was also at pains to make clear that he was not dealing with this situation.[750] However, the reasoning of the Court of Justice that precluded the declining of jurisdiction on the basis of the *forum non conveniens* discretion is equally applicable in this situation.[751] But what is left open for a future decision is the possibility, in this situation, of the Brussels I Recast having "reflexive" effects.[752]

There is a separate question that arises in the situation where the links connecting the dispute with a non-Member State are of a kind referred to in Article 24 of the Brussels I Recast (Article 16 of the Brussels Convention). Will the traditional subject matter limitations on jurisdiction, which preclude an English court from trying a case, apply? This question is best answered below[753] when examining these limitations on jurisdiction.

Fifthly, what is the effect of *Owusu* in the situation where the jurisdiction of a Member State is based on Article 4 (or some other basis set out in the Brussels I Recast) but a court of a non-Member State has been designated by an agreement conferring jurisdiction? Even before *Re Harrods*, English courts were suggesting that there was a discretion to stay the English proceedings in this situation.[754] Under the English traditional rules on stays of actions the ground for obtaining a stay in this situation would not be *forum non conveniens* but the related ground that there has been a breach of an agreement providing for trial abroad.[755] This raises a question of principle of whether the result would be any different if a stay was granted on what is a discretionary basis other than *forum non conveniens*.[756] The Court of Justice was concerned with cases of *forum non conveniens* and never seems to have thought about this

---

[746] The *Owusu* case, supra, at [48]. The Court of Justice also said that the question was asked in connection with the situation where a "Convention" granted jurisdiction to the court of a non-Contracting State.

[747] See supra, p 457 et seq.

[748] *Arkwright Mutual Insurance Co v Bryanston Insurance Co Ltd*, supra, at 663.

[749] The *Owusu* case, supra, at [48].

[750] Ibid, at [70], [217] and [281].

[751] But see *Konkola Copper Mines plc v Coromin Ltd* [2005] EWHC 898 (Comm), [2005] Lloyd's Rep 555; affd without discussion of this point [2006] EWCA Civ 5, [2006] 1 Lloyd's Rep 410; discussed infra, p 468. See also Peel [2005] LMCLQ 363, 374–376; Briggs [2005] LMCLQ 378.

[752] Discussed infra, p 473 et seq.

[753] Infra, pp 492–4.

[754] See *S & W Berisford plc v New Hampshire Insurance Co* [1990] 2 QB 631 at 643; *Arkwright Mutual Insurance Co v Bryanston Insurance Co Ltd*, [1990] 2 QB 649 at 663. This approach appeared to be implicitly endorsed in Case C-387/98 *Coreck Maritime GmbH v Handelsveem BV* [2000] ECR I-9337.

[755] Supra, p 410 et seq.

[756] The question whether there is a residual discretion to stay is discussed infra, pp 471–3.

situation. Advocate General Leger was at pains to make clear that he was not dealing with this situation.[757] Nonetheless, the reasoning of the Court of Justice is equally applicable to it, and when it comes to achieving the objectives of the Brussels I Recast the same objections can be made to this national discretionary power to stay as were made to the *forum non conveniens* discretionary power. Accordingly, the grant of a stay on this basis should also be precluded in this situation.[758] But, as with the Article 24 situation, what is left open for a future decision is the possibility, in this situation, of the Brussels I Recast having "reflexive" effects.[759]

Unfortunately, Colman J in *Konkola Copper Mines Plc v Coromin Ltd*[760] said obiter that the English national law discretion to stay proceedings brought in breach of a choice of jurisdiction clause providing for trial abroad in a non-Contracting State can still be used in the situation where the English court's jurisdiction is based on Article 2 of the Brussels Convention (Article 4 of the Brussels I Recast). *Owusu* was distinguished on the unconvincing basis that that case involved use of the *forum non conveniens* discretion, whereas *Konkola* involved the discretion that applies where there is a breach of a foreign jurisdiction clause.[761] This entirely misses the point that the Court of Justice clearly regarded the use of national discretionary powers as being incompatible with the objectives of the Convention. Reliance was placed on pre-*Owusu* case law,[762] rather than on the reasoning in that case. Colman J appeared to regard the position where the links connecting the dispute with a non-Contracting State are of a kind referred to in Article 16 of the Brussels Convention (Article 24 of the Brussels I Recast) as being in principle the same as that where there was a clause conferring jurisdiction on the courts of a non-Contracting State.[763] Accordingly, he might have been prepared to allow a discretion in that situation as well.

(iii) The Brussels I Recast is applicable but refers the case to national rules of jurisdiction

We are concerned here with the situation where the matter is within the scope of the Brussels I Recast but none of the bases of jurisdiction set out therein come into play (the defendant is domiciled in a non-Member State and neither Article 18(1), Article 21(2), Article 24 nor Article 25 applies). According to Article 6 of the Brussels I Recast, in this situation jurisdiction is determined by the law of each Member State. The English law of jurisdiction includes not only bases of jurisdiction but also the discretion to stay on the ground of *forum non conveniens*.[764] But what if the alternative forum is a Member State? Can the doctrine of *forum non conveniens* still be used?

---

[757] The *Owusu* case, supra, at [69], [217] and [281].

[758] But cf Briggs 2015, para 2.307; Peel [2005] LMCLQ 363, 374–6; Briggs [2005] LMCLQ 378. See generally Harris (2005) 54 ICLQ 933, 943–5.

[759] Discussed infra, pp 473–5.

[760] [2005] EWHC 898 (Comm), [2005] Lloyd's Rep 555; affd [2006] EWCA Civ 5, [2006] 1 Lloyd's Rep 410 but without an appeal on this particular point; Briggs (2005) 76 BYBIL 641.

[761] Contrast *Konkola* with *CNA Insurance Co Ltd v Office Depot International (UK) Ltd* [2005] EWHC 456 (Comm) at [26], holding that *Owusu* precludes a stay on case management grounds (but in a case in which the case management stay would effectively be permanent rather than temporary).

[762] The *Arkwright* case, supra. Reliance was also placed on the Schlosser Report, para 176, which says that there is nothing in the Convention to support the conclusion that agreements conferring jurisdiction on courts of non-Contracting States must be inadmissible in principle. But as Colman J had to admit, there was nothing to suggest that the Report was thinking of the English discretion. Indeed what it may have been referring to was the reflexive effect of the Convention.

[763] The *Konkola* case, supra, at [98].

[764] The *Xin Yang* [1996] 2 Lloyd's Rep 217 at 220; *Sarrio SA v Kuwait Investment Authority* [1996] 1 Lloyd's Rep 650 at 654, affd by the Court of Appeal [1997] 1 Lloyd's Rep 113, revsd by the House of Lords without discussion of this point [1999] 1 AC 32.

(a) Alternative forum is a Member State

The Court of Appeal in *Sarrio SA v Kuwait Investment Authority*,[765] adopting the analysis of Mance J at first instance,[766] decided that, in the light of what Article 4 of the Convention (Article 6 of the Brussels I Recast) provides,[767] the doctrine of *forum non conveniens* can operate in cases where Article 4 (now Article 6) applies, even where the alternative forum is another Contracting State. Moreover, to separate out the inextricably linked concepts of bases of jurisdiction and the courts' discretion to decline jurisdiction on the ground of *forum non conveniens*, so that once a basis of jurisdiction was satisfied the English courts would have to try the case, would lead to an anomaly given that one of the bases of jurisdiction under the traditional rules, service of a claim form out of the jurisdiction, under what is now rule 6.36 of the Civil Procedure Rules,[768] is itself a discretionary form of jurisdiction.[769] A discretion would operate in rule 6.36 cases but not where the basis of jurisdiction is service of a claim form within the jurisdiction. While this argument is persuasive, it may, however, also be noted that the rules on *lis pendens* and related proceedings between Member States in the Brussels I Recast might be considered to regulate possible parallel proceedings between Member State courts exhaustively, and these apply even in cases where the courts of different Member States are taking jurisdiction under their national rules pursuant to the Brussels I Recast.[770] This could arguably restrict a stay on *forum non conveniens* grounds where there are identical or related proceedings in another Member State. For example, if the English courts are first seised, it might be considered that a *forum non conveniens* stay in favour of the courts of another Member State would undermine the effectiveness of Articles 29 and 30 of the Brussels I Recast, although an argument could also be made that the jurisdiction of the English courts is not "established" if proceedings are stayed.[771]

How is this affected by *Owusu*? Advocate General Leger in that case said that where jurisdiction of a court of a Contracting State is established pursuant to Article 4 of the Convention this does not prevent the court in question from declining to exercise its jurisdiction, in accordance with the doctrine of *forum non conveniens* on the ground that a court of a *non-Contracting State* would be more appropriate to deal with the substance of the case.[772] This is not dealing with the situation that arose in the *Sarrio* case, which concerned an alternative forum in a Contracting State. However, Advocate General Leger did accept that Article 4 cases are to be treated differently from Article 2 cases, and to that extent can be said to support the *Sarrio* case. Nonetheless, the position in the *Sarrio* situation is unclear and a reference is needed to the Court of Justice to resolve it.[773] Until there is such a decision, or one from the House of Lords, overruling the principle in *Sarrio*, that decision remains as a binding authority.

---

[765] [1997] 1 Lloyd's Rep 113; Briggs (1996) 67 BYBIL 592; revsd by the House of Lords without discussion of this point [1999] 1 AC 32, H. See also *Haji-Ioannou v Frangos* [1999] 2 Lloyd's Rep 337, CA; *The Xin Yang* [1996] 2 Lloyd's Rep 217; Harris (1997) 113 LQR 557; Newton [1997] LMCLQ 337.

[766] [1996] 1 Lloyd's Rep 650 at 654–6. See also Mance J in *Grupo Torras SA v Al Sabah* [1995] 1 Lloyd's Rep 374 at 441; the Court of Appeal [1996] 1 Lloyd's Rep 7 did not discuss this point.

[767] The *Sarrio* case, supra, (Mance J). See also *The Xin Yang*, supra, at 220.

[768] At that time Order 11, r 1(1) of the Rules of the Supreme Court. CPR, r 6.36 is discussed, supra, p 334 et seq.

[769] [1997] 1 Lloyd's Rep 113 at 123, CA.

[770] See supra, pp 443–4. This might also affect the possibility of a stay on case management grounds—see supra, p 421.

[771] See Art 29(3).

[772] The *Owusu* case, supra, at [235].

[773] This was recognised (prior to *Owusu*) in *Haji-Ioannou v Frangos* [1999] 2 Lloyd's Rep 337, 348, CA, and since *Owusu* in *Luiz Vicente Barros Mattos v Macdaniels Ltd* [2005] EWHC 1323 (Ch) at [137], [2005] IL Pr 630. See also Briggs 2015, para 2.310.

A practical problem arises if the English court exercises its discretion and stays the English proceedings in circumstances where the "alternative forum" is another Member State. The danger is that no Member State will end up trying the case. If the jurisdiction of the English courts is considered to be "established", the court in the other Member State, which is second seised, will have to decline jurisdiction because of Article 29 of the Brussels I Recast, assuming, of course, that the requirements of that provision have been met. However, this danger can be avoided in various ways: by the English court dismissing the action rather than merely staying it (which is the best solution),[774] by the foreign court regarding the jurisdiction of the English court as not being "established" in the situation where it has stayed its proceedings,[775] or by the English court refusing to stay its proceedings.[776]

(b) Alternative forum is a non-Member State

The *Sarrio* case involved the situation where the alternative forum was a Member State.[777] Where the alternative forum is a non-Member State it can be said with some confidence that the *forum non conveniens* discretion can still be used.[778] Articles 33 and 34 of the Brussels I Recast, dealing with prior proceedings in a non-Member State, expressly provide that they do not apply where jurisdiction is taken under national law pursuant to Article 6,[779] and thus there is no issue of whether *forum non conveniens* might be restricted in these circumstances by the rules on parallel proceedings. There is support for this in the Opinion of Advocate General Leger in the *Owusu* case[780] and in earlier obiter dicta in an English case, *The Xin Yang*.[781] What is less clear is the basis for the availability of *forum non conveniens*. Advocate General Leger took the view that the principle in *Re Harrods* can still be used in this situation. However, the better view is that cases under Article 6 of the Brussels I Recast are different from Article 4 cases for the reasons explained in *Sarrio* and, under this view, whether the alternative forum is a Member State or a non-Member State is irrelevant. In *The Xin Yang*, it is not entirely clear which of these two views underlay the support for the use of the *forum non conveniens* discretion.[782]

Once it has been decided that the English court should stay or decline jurisdiction under Articles 29 or 30 of the Brussels I Recast,[783] it becomes immaterial to consider whether England is the appropriate or inappropriate forum for trial.[784] To grant a stay on the grounds of *forum non conveniens* in this situation would evidently be inconsistent with the Brussels I Recast.[785]

(iv) *The knock on effect of Owusu in multi-defendant cases*

In the situation where there are two defendants, one domiciled in England and the other in a non-Member State, it is necessary to look separately at each defendant. There is no power

---

[774] See *Haji-Ioannou v Frangos* [1999] 2 Lloyd's Rep 337, 347–8, CA.

[775] *The Xin Yang*, supra; the *Sarrio* case in the Court of Appeal, supra, at 123.

[776] The *Sarrio* case in the Court of Appeal, supra, at 123.

[777] As did *The Xin Yang*, supra.

[778] Cf Briggs 2015, para 2.309. A stay on case management grounds should equally be unaffected by the Brussels I Recast in these circumstances.

[779] See supra, p 458.

[780] The *Owusu* case, supra, at [235].

[781] [1996] 2 Lloyd's Rep 217 at 222.

[782] Ibid.

[783] Supra, p 442 et seq.

[784] *Sarrio SA v Kuwait Investment Authority* [1996] 1 Lloyd's Rep 650 at 656, Mance J, whose analysis was adopted by the Court of Appeal [1997] 1 Lloyd's Rep 113; reversed by the House of Lords without discussion of this point. See *Haji-Ioannou v Frangos* [1999] 2 Lloyd's Rep 337, 347, CA.

[785] See in relation to the Brussels Convention the judgment of Kerr LJ in *The Sennar (No 2)* [1984] 2 Lloyd's Rep 142 at 154, CA.

to stay on the ground of *forum non conveniens* the proceedings against the English defendant. But there is power to stay the proceedings against the second defendant.[786] However, the English court when exercising the *forum non conveniens* discretion may be reluctant to grant a stay because this will involve splitting up the multi-defendant action, leading to concurrent proceedings in two different countries.[787] Indeed in the English first instance decision in *Owusu* a stay was refused against Jamaican co-defendants for this very reason.[788] These considerations may be countered where the second defendant has the benefit of an exclusive jurisdiction agreement in favour of a non-Member State court.[789]

(v) Article 71 of the Brussels I Recast applies

We are concerned here with the situation where the English court's jurisdiction is derived from an international Convention, and is accordingly preserved by Article 71 of the Brussels I Recast. The principle in *Re Harrods* has been applied in this situation.[790] However, the Article 71 situation is essentially the same as that in relation to Article 4 of the Convention (Article 6 of the Brussels I Recast) and everything said in the previous sections is equally applicable here.[791]

(c) Is there a residual discretion?

The English courts in the past have held that they have a residual discretion to decline jurisdiction in Brussels Convention cases so as to prevent an abuse of process,[792] as where the claimant's claim is purely speculative and is bound to fail.[793] Abuse of process has been explained in terms of preventing frivolous or vexatious actions.[794] It has similarly been held that in at least limited circumstances a stay should be available on case management grounds.[795]

---

[786] The same issue arises where the court's permission is required to commence proceedings against the second defendant. If the first defendant is domiciled in England those proceedings may not be stayed, and thus permission is more likely to be given to commence proceedings against a non-EU domiciled second defendant, to ensure consolidation of the proceedings in a single forum. The second defendant may be added purely on the basis that they are a necessary and proper party to the proceedings. See *Lungowe v Vedanta Resources Plc* [2016] EWHC 975 (TCC), [2016] BLR 461; *AAA v Unilever plc* [2017] EWHC 371 (QB) (appeal pending); supra, p 336 et seq.

[787] This consideration may also support the award of an anti-suit injunction: *Skype Technologies SA v Joltid Ltd* [2009] EWHC 2783 (Ch), [2011] IL Pr 8. But see *Golden Ocean Assurance Ltd v Martin (The Goldean Mariner)* [1990] 2 Lloyd's Rep 215, 222.

[788] Judge Bentley QC had earlier decided that he had no power to stay the proceedings against the English defendant.

[789] *Jong v HSBC Private Bank (Monaco) SA* [2015] EWCA Civ 1057.

[790] *The Po* [1991] 2 Lloyd's Rep 206. See in relation to in rem jurisdiction pp 387–90.

[791] See, eg, *Innovia Films Ltd v Frito-Lay North America Inc* [2012] EWHC 790 (Pat), [2012] RPC 24; *Conductive Inkjet Technology Ltd v Uni-Pixel Displays Inc* [2013] EWHC 2968 (Ch), [2014] 1 All ER (Comm) 654.

[792] *Boss Group Ltd v Boss France SA* [1997] 1 WLR 351 at 358, CA; *Pearce v Ove Arup Partnership Ltd* [1997] Ch 293 at 309; revsd by the Court of Appeal on the basis that the judge had been wrong to hold that the claim was bound to fail, [1997] 1 All ER 769, CA; *Bank of Scotland v SA Banque Nationale de Paris* 1996 SLT 103 at 133–4.

[793] The *Pearce* case, supra.

[794] The *Boss* case, supra. This does not include seeking a negative declaration where it serves no useful purpose: *USF Ltd (t/a USF Memcor) v Aqua Technology Hanson NV/SA* [2001] 1 All ER (Comm) 856 at [24]–[26].

[795] *Et Plus SA v Welter* [2005] EWHC 2115 (Comm) at [91], [2006] 1 Lloyd's Rep 251; *Equitas Ltd v Allstate Insurance Co* [2008] EWHC 1671 (Comm), [2009] Lloyd's Rep IR 227; *Pacific International Sports Clubs Limited v Soccer Marketing International Ltd* [2009] EWHC 1839 (Ch), approved at [2010] EWCA Civ 753; *Blue Tropic Ltd v Chkhartishvili* [2014] EWHC 2243 (Ch), [2014] IL Pr 33; *Plaza BV v Law Debenture Trust Corp Plc* [2015] EWHC 43 (Ch); *Lungowe v Vedanta Resources Plc* [2016] EWHC 975 (TCC), [2016] BLR 461; but cf *CNA Insurance Co Ltd v Office Depot International (UK) Ltd* [2005] EWHC 456 (Comm) at [26]; *Skype Technologies SA v Joltid Ltd* [2009] EWHC 2783 (Ch), [2011] IL Pr 8; *Conductive*

The justification that has been given for this residual discretion is as follows. The Brussels Convention is not concerned with questions of procedure except in so far as they impair the effectiveness of the Convention.[796] It has been argued that the doctrine of abuse of process and the discretion to stay on case management grounds are procedural rules that do not impair the effectiveness of the Convention.[797] However, it is doubtful whether such an argument would be accepted by the Court of Justice in such broad terms. In *Turner v Grovit*,[798] the Court of Justice has held that the Brussels Convention precludes the grant of an injunction whereby a court of a Contracting State prohibits a party to proceedings pending before it from commencing or continuing legal proceedings before a court of another Contracting State, even where that party is acting in bad faith with a view to frustrating the existing proceedings.[799] The procedural rule argument was raised in the *Turner* case but rejected on the basis that, even if an injunction was a procedural rule, it was one that impaired the effectiveness of the Convention.[800] The procedural argument was also rejected by Advocate General Leger in the *Owusu* case in the context of the English courts staying their own proceedings on the basis of *forum non conveniens*. He gave his Opinion that if it is assumed for the sake of argument that *forum non conveniens* is a procedural rule, it is one that impairs the effectiveness of the Convention.[801] The discretionary nature of *forum non conveniens* that goes to undermine the objective under the Convention/Regulation of achieving legal certainty[802] and consistent application in different Convention/Member States is equally a feature of a residual common law discretion to stay to prevent abuse of process or on case management grounds. This argument is, however, weaker in relation to case management stays, if the stay is merely temporary and does not affect which court ultimately hears the dispute. It is difficult to see any rational policy reason why, for example, the Brussels I Recast should restrict the power of the English courts to stay proceedings temporarily to allow the parties to attempt to negotiate a settlement. However, there is an argument that a temporary stay pending the resolution of foreign proceedings[803] should only be available in the circumstances provided by Articles 30[804] and 33–34[805] of the Brussels I Recast—a case management stay for this purpose but not covered by these provisions (such as where the English courts were first seised, but wished to stay the English proceedings pending the resolution of a related foreign claim) could arguably be precluded.[806] The better view may be that case management stays are indeed restricted by the Brussels I Recast, but only in situations in which they would impair the effectiveness of the Brussels I Recast, such as where the stay is in reality likely to be permanent, or where it is to defer English proceedings pending the resolution of related foreign proceedings in a situation covered by the Brussels I Recast rules on *lis pendens* or related proceedings. However, until there is a decision of the Court of Justice or the House of Lords

---

Inkjet Technology Ltd v Uni-Pixel Displays Inc [2013] EWHC 2968 (Ch), [2014] 1 All ER (Comm) 654; *AAA v Unilever plc* [2017] EWHC 371 (QB) (appeal pending). See Fentiman 2015, para 14.24ff. On case management stays in general, see supra, p 421.

[796] Case 365/88 *Kongress Agentur Hagen GmbH v Zeehaghe BV* [1990] ECR I-1845—a decision in relation to the Brussels Convention.

[797] See *Berkeley Administration Inc v McClelland* [1996] IL Pr 772, CA.

[798] Case C-159/02 [2004] ECR I-3565, [2005] 1 AC 101, discussed infra.

[799] Ibid, at [32].

[800] Ibid, at [29].

[801] The *Owusu* case, supra, at [260]–[261].

[802] See ibid, at [42]. AG Leger at [266], [272] mentioned that the objectives of the Convention were also undermined by the procedural consequences of a stay and the denial to the claimant of simplified recognition and enforcement.

[803] See supra, p 421.

[804] See supra, p 454 et seq.

[805] See supra, p 457 et seq.

[806] See, eg, the *Lafi* case, supra, 74.

providing to the contrary, the English courts are likely to continue exercising a residual discretion in the circumstances outlined above.

(d) Does the Brussels I Recast have "reflexive" effects?

Some continental lawyers and common lawyers alike have long argued that there is power to decline jurisdiction in certain limited situations on the basis that the Brussels Convention (and now Brussels I Recast) should have "reflexive" effects.[807] Reflexive effect refers to the possibility that certain provisions of the Brussels I Recast, which permit or require a court to stay proceedings based on connections which the dispute has with another Member State, might also be applied by extension (either as a matter of residual national law or as an implicit effect of the Brussels I Recast) where equivalent connections exist with non-Member States. There are three possible such circumstances. The first is where jurisdiction has been taken under the Brussels I Recast,[808] but the parties have agreed on trial exclusively in a non-Member State (in a manner which would satisfy Article 25 of the Brussels I Recast if the agreement were in favour of a Member State). The second situation is where jurisdiction has been taken under the Brussels I Recast,[809] but there are subject matter connections with a non-Member State of a kind referred to in Article 24 of the Brussels I Recast. The third is where a court in a non-Member State has previously been seised of a claim liable to give rise to *lis pendens* or related actions. As examined previously, this third situation is now covered by Articles 33 and 34 of the Brussels I Recast,[810] but the issue of reflexive effect in these circumstances arose under both the Convention and Brussels I Regulation.

The reflexive effect doctrine may be regarded either as coming from within the Brussels I Recast itself,[811] in which case it is very different from a national court granting a stay on the basis of a traditional ground of its own, as happened in *Re Harrods*. Alternatively, it might be considered as a residual application of national law, which to this extent remains compatible with the Brussels I Recast. The Court of Justice in the *Owusu* case refused to discuss the second and third situations mentioned above[812] and Advocate General Leger was at pains to make clear that he was not dealing with these three situations.[813] This appears to leave it open for a national court to decline jurisdiction in these three situations on the basis of the "reflexive" effects theory.[814] In the aftermath of *Owusu*, a number of English decisions have applied this doctrine in relation to Article 22[815] and 23[816] of the Brussels I Regulation (Articles 24

---

[807] See Gaudemet-Tallon (1991) Rev crit dr int privé 491; Droz, *Compétence judiciaire et effets des judgments dans le marchécommun*, p 108; Gothot and Holleaux, *La Convention de Bruxelles du 27 Septembre 1968*, pp 83–4; and generally Kennett (1995) 54 CLJ 552, 563–6. For English support, see Layton and Mercer, para 13.022; Fentiman 2015, para 12.44ff. See also Case C-163/95 *Von Horn v Cinnamond* [1998] QB 214, where the Commission raised the reflexive effect but the Court of Justice found it unnecessary to discuss this.

[808] Other than under Art 24.

[809] Even, arguably, under Art 25, through a reflexive effect of Art 25(4).

[810] Supra, p 457 et seq.

[811] See Kruger, paras 3.10–3.19; but cf Dicey, Morris and Collins, para 12-024; Fentiman 2015, para 12.54; Briggs 2015, para 2.305ff.

[812] The *Owusu* case, [48]–[52] and the discussion supra, p 464 et seq.

[813] Ibid, at [217].

[814] The Court of Appeal in *Ace Insurance SA-NV (formerly Cigna Insurance Co of Europe SA NV) v Zurich Insurance Co* [2001] EWCA Civ 173 at [42], [2001] 1 Lloyd's Rep 618, had found it unnecessary to decide whether Art 17 of the Brussels Convention had "reflexive" effect. See also the comments of Longmore J at first instance, [2000] 2 Lloyd's Rep 423 at [21].

[815] *Masri v Consolidated Contractors International Co SAL* [2008] EWCA Civ 303 at [127], [2008] 2 Lloyd's Rep 128; *Ferrexpo AG v Gilson Investments Ltd* [2012] EWHC 721 (Comm), [2012] 1 Lloyd's Rep 588; Smith, Lasserson, and Rymkiewicz (2012) 8 J Priv Int L 389.

[816] *Konkola Copper Mines plc v Coromin Ltd* [2005] EWHC 898 (Comm), [2005] Lloyd's Rep 555 (but for criticism of the reasoning see supra, p 468); *Winnetka Trading Corp v Julius Baer International Ltd* [2008] EWHC 3146 (Ch), [2009] 2 All ER (Comm) 735; *Masri v Consolidated Contractors International Co SAL*

and 25 of the Brussels I Recast), and also considered whether it should apply in relation to Articles 27 and 28 of the Brussels I Regulation[817] (although this is no longer necessary in light of Articles 33 and 34 of the Brussels I Recast). For cases not covered by Articles 33 and 34 of the Brussels I Recast, a decision of the Court of Justice is needed on whether these decisions are consistent with the Brussels I Recast.

There are two main arguments in favour of the reflexive effect doctrine. First, in response to one of the arguments relied on by the Court of Justice in *Owusu*, unlike *forum non conveniens* it does not compromise the consistent application of the Brussels I Recast between Member States. Depending on how the doctrine is understood, this is either because it is not a national law doctrine, or alternatively, because it only encompasses matters not covered by the Brussels I Recast. Second, it advances the policies adopted in the Brussels I Recast— recognising certain subject matter connections as giving rise to exclusive jurisdiction, and recognising party autonomy. It would be a strange outcome if the Brussels I Recast were to force Member State courts to hear claims brought against Member State domiciled parties concerning title to non-Member State immovable property, for example, because any judgment awarded would be likely to be ineffective—but without a reflexive effect doctrine, this would indeed be the consequence of *Owusu*. It would be equally strange if Member State domiciled parties were unable to enter into effective exclusive jurisdiction agreements in favour of non-Member State courts—but without a reflexive effect doctrine (and with the exception of cases covered by the Hague Convention on Choice of Court Agreements),[818] this would again be the consequence of *Owusu*.

There are, however, three strong arguments which may be raised against the reflexive effect doctrine. First, there is no textual support for it in the Brussels I Recast, so it requires a controversial degree of judicial activism, perhaps going beyond what is permissible interpretation of the Brussels I Recast (although such activism is not beyond the Court of Justice). Second, under the Brussels I Recast, one aspect of reflexive effect (*lis pendens* and related proceedings) is now addressed directly in the text, in Articles 33 and 34. There is an argument that this reduces the possibility that, through expansive interpretation of the rules, other aspects could be considered as implicitly addressed. This argument is strengthened because Recital (24) specifies that in applying Articles 33 and 34 of the Brussels I Recast, the court may take into account "whether the court of the third State has exclusive jurisdiction in the particular case in circumstances where a court of a Member State would have exclusive jurisdiction". If there were a reflexive effect doctrine for Articles 24 and 25 of the Brussels I Recast, this provision would appear redundant.[819] This is not to say that this position would be satisfactory. If exclusive jurisdiction considerations could only be taken into account as part of the rules addressing *lis pendens* and related proceedings, an English party who has entered into an exclusive jurisdiction agreement in favour of the courts of New York, for example, could still

---

[2008] EWCA Civ 303 at [125], [2008] 2 Lloyd's Rep 128; *Plaza BV v Law Debenture Trust Corp Plc* [2015] EWHC 43 (Ch).

[817] *Catalyst Investment Group Ltd v Lewinsohn* [2009] EWHC 1964 (Ch), [2010] Ch 218 (no reflexive effect); *Ferrexpo AG v Gilson Investments Ltd* [2012] EWHC 721 (Comm), [2012] 1 Lloyd's Rep 588 (reflexive effect); *Plaza BV v Law Debenture Trust Corp Plc* [2015] EWHC 43 (Ch) (obiter, reflexive effect). See also *Goshawk Dedicated Receivables Ltd v Life Receivables Ireland Ltd* [2009] IESC 7, [2009] IL Pr 26 (in which the question was referred to the Court of Justice, but the case subsequently settled). For a similar argument in favour of reflexive effect under the Brussels II Regulation (see generally infra, p 974 et seq) see *JKN v JCN* [2010] EWHC 843 (Fam), [2011] 1 FLR 826; *AB v CB* [2013] EWCA Civ 1255, [2014] 2 WLR 1033.

[818] See supra, p 315 et seq.

[819] Although it might alternatively be argued that this has the effect of recognising the importance of non-Member State exclusive jurisdiction connections, in a way which reinforces the reflexive effect doctrine.

be sued in England, provided that the English courts were first seised. There would, in effect, be the possibility of an 'EU torpedo' undermining non-Member State exclusive jurisdiction agreements.

The third argument against the reflexive effect doctrine is that it is not clear whether the authority to decline jurisdiction on this basis should be mandatory or discretionary, and neither approach seems entirely satisfactory. If the doctrine were mandatory, this would be more consistent with the objectives of legal certainty supported by the decision in *Owusu*, but the policy outcome would be unsatisfactory. For example, the strict requirement in Article 25 to stay proceedings where there is an exclusive jurisdiction agreement in favour of the courts of another Member State is premised on the assumption, grounded in mutual trust between Member States, that the chosen court will be available and able to deliver justice to the parties. But what if the parties chose the courts of a non-Member State, and because of a change in circumstances those courts are no longer available or would be biased against one of the parties? Giving mandatory effect to the jurisdiction agreement would not seem consistent with the requirements of access to justice in such circumstances.

If the reflexive effect doctrine were discretionary, it would be possible for the courts to take such matters into consideration. However, this would be more difficult to reconcile with the decision of the Court of Justice in *Owusu*, with its evident antipathy to discretion which is viewed as undermining the objectives of legal certainty.[820] Having said that, Articles 33 and 34 have introduced further discretion into the Brussels I Recast (in addition to that which existed already under Article 30), so there would be scope to reconsider whether legal certainty was indeed a necessary feature of the rules. The discretionary reflexive effect approach would be the most satisfactory outcome in policy terms (and is the approach favoured by most English authority),[821] but it remains to be seen whether the Court of Justice would be sufficiently open to reviewing certain aspects of the reasoning in its *Owusu* decision to endorse this approach.

6. RESTRAINING FOREIGN PROCEEDINGS AND THE BRUSSELS I RECAST[822]

(a) A discretion to restrain foreign proceedings in the Brussels I Recast itself?

As well as the power to stay proceedings, there is another distinctive feature of the law relating to the management of parallel proceedings in common law jurisdictions. This is the discretionary power, in certain circumstances, to grant an injunction restraining a party from commencing or continuing as claimant in foreign proceedings, known as an anti-suit injunction. The circumstances in which an anti-suit injunction may be awarded have been examined in detail earlier in this chapter.[823] In contrast, civil law jurisdictions, when faced with the same problem of forum shopping abroad, deal with it in an indirect way at the stage of recognition and enforcement of the foreign judgment obtained in an inappropriate forum for trial.[824] It is

---

[820] The *Owusu* case, supra, at [42].

[821] See, eg, *Ferrexpo AG v Gilson Investments Ltd* [2012] EWHC 721 (Comm), [2012] 1 Lloyd's Rep 588; but cf *Plaza BV v Law Debenture Trust Corp Plc* [2015] EWHC 43 (Ch) at [76].

[822] Briggs in Andenas and Jacobs (eds), *European Community Law in the English Courts*, pp 287–92; Briggs 2015, para 5.45; Fentiman 2015, para 16.131ff.

[823] See supra, p 422 et seq.

[824] Fawcett, *Declining Jurisdiction*, pp 66–7. But see now *Banque Worms v Brachot* 11 November 2002, 2003 Rev Crit 816.

not surprising, therefore, to find that the Brussels I Recast, with its civil law origins, contains no such power to restrain foreign proceedings.

(b) Can the traditional English power to restrain foreign proceedings be used?

There is an obligation on the courts of Member States not to act in a way that is incompatible with the Brussels I Recast. So the real question is whether the Brussels I Recast precludes the use of the traditional English power to restrain foreign proceedings. In cases falling outside its scope there can be no question of the Brussels I Recast precluding the use of this power,[825] and the traditional English power to restrain foreign proceedings, including proceedings in another Member State, can be used. What "falling outside the scope of the Brussels I Recast" means for the purposes of this rule has, however, been more contentious than it might at first appear—this is discussed further below. In cases falling within the scope of the Brussels I Recast the position is more complex. In such cases it is important to distinguish instances where proceedings in a Member State are being restrained from those where proceedings in a non-Member State are being restrained.

(i) *Restraining proceedings in a Member State*

(a) The English case law

In the past, the Court of Appeal held that it had power to restrain proceedings in another Contracting State to the Brussels Convention in situations where there had been a breach of a clause providing for the exclusive jurisdiction of the English courts,[826] and a breach of an arbitration clause.[827] This power was then extended by the Court of Appeal in *Turner v Grovit*[828] to the situation where, in the view of the English court, that court was first seised of the proceedings and, accordingly, Article 21 of the Convention (Article 29 of the Brussels I Recast) would apply. The *Turner* case also went on to extend the power to the situation where proceedings are launched in another Contracting State for no purpose other than to harass and oppress a party who was already a litigant in England.

(b) The effect of *Erich Gasser GmbH v Misat Srl*

The power to restrain foreign proceedings in another Member State in the situation where there had been a breach of a clause providing for the exclusive jurisdiction of the English courts was severely limited as a result of the decision of the Court of Justice in *Erich Gasser GmbH v Misat Srl*.[829] It will be recalled that the Court held that a court seised second whose jurisdiction has been claimed under an agreement conferring jurisdiction has nevertheless no power to stay proceedings until the court first seised has declared that it has no jurisdiction. It is for the court first seised to pronounce as to its jurisdiction in the light of the jurisdiction clause.[830] In such circumstances, an English court second seised cannot claim that there has been a breach of an exclusive jurisdiction clause providing for trial in England and is therefore unable to restrain on this basis the foreign proceedings in the Member State first seised.[831] Of

---

[825] *Deaville v Aeroflot* [1997] 2 Lloyd's Rep 67.

[826] *Continental Bank NA v Aeakos Compañía Naviera SA* [1994] 1 WLR 588, CA; followed in *Fort Dodge Animal Health Ltd v Akzo Nobel NV* 1998] FSR 222, CA—a case involving exclusive jurisdiction under Art 16 of the Brussels Convention (Art 24 of the Brussels I Recast).

[827] *The Angelic Grace* [1995] 1 Lloyd's Rep 87, CA.

[828] [2000] QB 345, CA; Briggs (1999) 70 BYBIL 332; Fentiman [2000] CLJ 45; Harris (1999) 115 LQR 576; Hartley (2000) 49 ICLQ 166. The decision of the House of Lords and Court of Justice are discussed infra.

[829] Case C-116/02 [2003] ECR I-4207; discussed supra, pp 450–2.

[830] Ibid.

[831] *Through Transport Mutual Insurance Association (Eurasia) Ltd v New India Assurance Association Co Ltd* [2004] EWCA (Civ) 1598 at [89], [2005] 1 Lloyd's Rep 67 (wrongly, however, refusing to extend this principle to arbitration agreements—see further below).

course, this did not affect the power to restrain proceedings in another Member State in the situation where the English court was first seised. Nor did it affect situations where the power has been exercised in situations other than where there had been a breach of a jurisdiction clause. The fatal blow to the power to restrain proceedings in other Member States came from the decision of the Court of Justice in *Turner v Grovit*,[832] which was the second (in time) of the three recent decisions of the Court of Justice to hold that English practices in relation to international litigation were inconsistent with the Brussels Convention.[833]

(c) *Turner v Grovit*

The facts of the case were simple.

> Turner brought an action in England against his employer (an English company) for unfair dismissal. A Spanish company (in the same group of companies) for which Turner had previously worked brought an action in Spain for damages. The Court of Appeal granted an injunction ordering the defendants, which included the English and Spanish companies, not to continue the Spanish action, having concluded that this action had been brought in bad faith to harass Turner. The defendants appealed to the House of Lords on the basis that there was no power to grant an injunction in such circumstances.

The House of Lords[834] referred to the Court of Justice the narrow question whether it is inconsistent with the Brussels Convention "to grant restraining orders against defendants who are threatening to commence or continue legal proceedings in another Convention country when those defendants are acting in bad faith with the intent and purpose of frustrating or obstructing proceedings properly brought before the English courts?". The Court of Justice[835] held that the Brussels Convention precludes the grant of an injunction whereby a court of a Contracting State prohibits a party to proceedings pending before it from commencing or continuing legal proceedings before a court of another Contracting State, even where that party is acting in bad faith with a view to frustrating the existing proceedings.[836] The Court said that any injunction restraining a party from commencing or continuing proceedings before a foreign court constituted an interference with the jurisdiction of the foreign court which, as such, was incompatible with the system of the Convention.[837] Arguments put forward by the House of Lords and by the United Kingdom government in support of the use of such injunctions were rejected. This interference could not be justified on the basis that it was only an indirect interference and was intended to prevent an abuse of process by the defendant in the proceedings in the forum state. A decision by an English court as to the abusive nature of the defendant's conduct involved an assessment of the appropriateness of bringing proceedings in another Contracting State which ran counter to the principle of mutual trust underpinning the Convention.[838] Even if one was prepared to accept for the sake of argument that the grant of an injunction was a procedural measure, it was one which impaired the effectiveness of the Convention.[839] The grant of injunctions did not contribute to minimising the risk of conflicting decisions and avoiding a multiplicity of proceedings.

---

[832] Case C-159/02 [2005] 1 AC 101.

[833] The first decision was the *Gasser* case, supra; discussed supra, pp 450–2. The third was *Owusu*, supra; discussed supra, p 462 et seq.

[834] [2001] UKHL 65, [2002] 1 WLR 107; Briggs (2001) 72 BYBIL 436; Ambrose (2003) 52 ICLQ 401.

[835] Case C-159/02 [2005] 1 AC 101; Briggs (2004) 120 LQR 529; Hare [2004] CLJ 570; Hartley (2005) 54 ICLQ 813; Kruger (2004) 53 ICLQ 1030.

[836] Case C-159/02 [2005] 1 AC 101 at [32].

[837] Ibid, at [27].

[838] Ibid, at [28]. For application of this principle in the context of setting aside a judgment subject to payment into court, see *Tavoulareas v Tsavliris* [2005] EWHC 2140 (Comm) at [44], [2006] 1 All ER (Comm) 109.

[839] Para 29; referring to Case C-365/88 *Kongress Agentur Hagen GmbHvZeehaghe BV* [1990] ECR I-1845.

Injunctions restraining foreign proceedings rendered ineffective the specific mechanisms provided by the Brussels Convention for cases of *lis pendens* and related actions.[840] Moreover, such injunctions could give rise to conflicts for which the Convention contained no rules.[841] An injunction could be issued in one Contracting State but a decision given in another. There could be two Contracting States issuing contradictory injunctions.

(d) Going beyond cases of bad faith

On its facts, the *Turner* case involved the situation where proceedings were launched in another Contracting State for no purpose other than to harass and oppress a party who was already a litigant in England and the reference from the House of Lords was a narrow one which referred specifically to this situation. However, the language and reasoning of the Court of Justice is not so confined. The Court of Justice regarded it as being axiomatic that any injunction restraining a party from bringing proceedings before a foreign court constituted an interference with the jurisdiction of that court. The grant of an injunction in the situation where, for example, there has been a breach of an exclusive jurisdiction clause would equally constitute an interference with the jurisdiction of the foreign court.[842] The English courts exercise the power to grant injunctions restraining foreign proceedings in a wide variety of different situations and, as discussed earlier in this chapter,[843] it is by no means easy to categorise the cases where such an injunction has been granted. The prohibition on the grant of an injunction restraining proceedings before a court of another Member State should apply regardless of the category of case involved.[844] The only remaining uncertainty following *Turner v Grovit* related to the situation where an injunction is granted to restrain a party from commencing or continuing proceedings brought in a breach of an arbitration agreement. This raises a question of the scope of the Brussels I Recast.

(e) Breach of an arbitration agreement

The Court of Appeal in *Through Transport Mutual Insurance Association (Eurasia) Ltd v New India Assurance Association Co Ltd*[845] held that the English courts have power to grant an

---

[840] *Turner v Grovit*, supra, at [30].

[841] Ibid.

[842] Many cases will be dealt with by the principles in the *Gasser* case, supra, pp 450–2. It may be possible to obtain damages for breach of the jurisdiction agreement, see Merrett (2006) 55 ICLQ 315; *The Alexandros T* [2014] EWCA Civ 1010, [2014] 2 Lloyd's Rep 544; supra, p 437. In certain cases it may even be possible to pursue a claim against foreign lawyers in tort for inducing foreign proceedings in breach of the jurisdiction agreement: *AMT Futures Ltd v Marzillier* [2017] UKSC 13, [2017] 2 WLR 853 (finding that for jurisdictional purposes the location of such a tort would be the place of the foreign proceedings, see supra, p 275). However it is difficult to see how these claims can be pursued if another Member State court has determined that the jurisdiction agreement is invalid or inapplicable (as was the case in *Marzillier*), as that decision will be binding on the English courts: see, eg, Case C-456/11 *Krones AG v Samskip GmbH* EU:C:2012:719, [2013] QB 548. Where the foreign court has not yet reached a decision on the point, there is an argument that such proceedings should also be precluded by Article 29 of the Brussels I Recast, for the same reason, but this was rejected in *The Alexandros T* [2013] UKSC 70, [2014] 1 Lloyd's Rep 223: see supra, p 446.

[843] Supra, p 425 et seq.

[844] But see the *Through Transport* case, supra, at [91] and [95], which seems to confine *Turner* to cases of vexation and oppression. Cf *Advent Capital plc v Ellinas Imports-Exports Ltd* [2005] EWHC 1242 (Comm) at [98], [2005] 2 Lloyd's Rep 607.

[845] [2004] EWCA (Civ) 1598 at [66]–[92], [2005] 1 Lloyd's Rep 67; Briggs (2004) 75 BYBIL 549; Merrett [2005] CLJ 308; Pengelley (2006) 2 J Priv Int L 397; *Through Transport Mutual Insurance Association (Eurasia) Ltd v New India Assurance Association Co Ltd* [2005] EWHC 455 (Comm), [2005] 2 Lloyd's Rep 378 (for the follow-up on the facts). The decision of the Court of Appeal was followed in *West Tankers Inc v Ras Riunione Adriatica di Sicurta SpA* [2005] EWHC 454 (Comm); Briggs (2005) 76 BYBIL 641, at 648; but see the reference from the House of Lords [2007] UKHL 4 to the Court of Justice (discussed infra). See also Ambrose (2003) 52 ICLQ 401, 419–21.

anti-suit injunction in a case where a party to an arbitration agreement begins proceedings in the courts of a Member State in breach of an arbitration clause in a contract. According to the Court of Appeal the crucial distinction between this situation and the ones that arose in the *Gasser*[846] and *Turner* cases was that a claim in England for such an injunction fell outside the scope of the Brussels I Regulation,[847] whereas those cases involved proceedings in two Member States both sets of which fell within the scope of what is now the Brussels I Recast.[848] But the more compelling point was surely that the proceedings in the Member State abroad could (and in the view of that court did) fall within the scope of what is now the Brussels I Recast.[849] It should have followed that the injunction undermined the jurisdiction granted to the courts of that state by what is now the Brussels I Recast, contrary to the *Turner* case.[850]

The House of Lords in *West Tankers Inc v RAS Riunione Adriatica di Sicurta SpA*[851] referred this question to the Court of Justice—whether it is consistent with the Brussels I Regulation for a court of a Member State to make an order to restrain a person from commencing or continuing proceedings in another Member State on the ground that such proceedings are in breach of an arbitration agreement. In its reference, the House of Lords confidently expressed the view that proceedings for an injunction restraining a person from commencing or continuing proceedings abroad on the ground that such proceedings are in breach of an arbitration agreement are excluded since they "are entirely to protect the contractual right to have the dispute determined by arbitration".[852] In its decision, reported as *Allianz Spa v West Tankers*,[853] the Court of Justice determined, however, that the House of Lords had focused on the wrong set of proceedings. The key question was not whether the English proceedings fell within the scope of the Brussels I Regulation (as proceedings solely concerned with the validity of an arbitration agreement, they did not), but whether the Italian proceedings did so. The court held that the Italian proceedings fell within the scope of the Brussels I Regulation, even though they would require the Italian court to determine (as a preliminary question) whether the claim was covered by the arbitration agreement. Thus, the court determined that proceedings whose substance falls within the scope of the Brussels I Regulation do so in their entirety, even if they require determination of the validity of an arbitration agreement as a preliminary question. A key consequence of this was that an anti-suit injunction could not be awarded, as it would be contrary to the principle of mutual trust between the courts of Member States to interfere with the ability of the Italian courts to determine the question of their own jurisdiction under the Brussels I Regulation. (The decision clearly should not affect the power of the English courts to restrain proceedings in a non-Member State brought in breach of an English arbitration agreement.)[854] A second consequence was that if the Italian

---

[846] The Court of Appeal had earlier held that the court second seised can decide whether the proceedings before it are within the scope of the Brussels I Regulation, see supra, p 444. The Court, at [83], accepted that if that were wrong the *Gasser* case would apply.

[847] [2004] EWCA (Civ) 1598 at [47], [2005] 1 Lloyd's Rep 67; supra, p 210. This meant that Arts 27 and 28 (Arts 29 and 30 of the Brussels I Recast) would not apply. For an analogous argument in relation to stays of action, see *A v B* [2006] EWHC 2006 (Comm), [2007] 1 Lloyd's Rep 237—claims designed to impugn the validity of an arbitration agreement fell outside the scope of the Lugano Convention and therefore a stay of the claims could be granted under the English courts' inherent jurisdiction.

[848] [2004] EWCA (Civ) 1598 at [83], [2005] 1 Lloyd's Rep 67.

[849] The Court of Appeal appears to have accepted this. The court of the Member State abroad held that the arbitration clause did not apply to a third party.

[850] See the *Turner* case, supra, at [27].

[851] [2007] UKHL 4, [2007] 1 Lloyd's Rep 391; Fentiman [2007] CLJ 493; Steinbruck [2007] CJQ 358.

[852] *West Tankers Inc v RAS Riunione Adriatica di Sicurta SpA* [2007] UKHL 4 at [14], [2007] Lloyd's Rep 391.

[853] Case C-185/07 [2009] ECR I-663, [2009] 1 AC 1138.

[854] *Midgulf International Ltd v Groupe Chimiche Tunisien* [2010] EWCA Civ 66, [2010] 2 Lloyd's Rep 543.

courts did decide that the arbitration agreement was inapplicable, that decision, as a judgment under the Brussels I Regulation, would be binding on the English courts.[855] The decision in *West Tankers* was controversial,[856] although principally for the second consequence rather than the first, which encourages tactical litigation. While a new Recital (12) was added to the Brussels I Recast, which appears to reverse this second consequence,[857] the better view is that it leaves unaltered the prohibition on anti-suit injunctions in these circumstances.[858]

Subsequent to the decision of the Court of Justice, the English courts have held that an arbitral tribunal may award damages for breach of the arbitration agreement occasioned by the Italian proceedings.[859] While this does not interfere with the power of the Italian courts to determine their own jurisdiction, there was an argument that under the Brussels I Regulation such a claim should have been precluded by the *lis pendens* provision, Article 27. This is because it requires the English courts to determine whether the arbitration agreement is valid and applicable, which is an issue before the first seised Italian courts.[860] This argument would, however, no longer apply under the Brussels I Recast, because the Italian decision on such matters is no longer binding on the English courts,[861] and thus damages for breach of an arbitration agreement should be available as partial compensation for the inability to restrain proceedings brought in another Member State.

An alternative approach would be for the arbitral tribunal to issue an anti-suit injunction to restrain proceedings in a Member State court brought in breach of the arbitration agreement. In *Gazprom*, the Court of Justice held that an arbitral tribunal is not bound by the obligations of mutual trust which apply between Member States, and its power to issue an anti-suit injunction is therefore not restricted by the Brussels I Regulation.[862] It remains unclear, however, whether it would be compatible with the Brussels I Recast for the courts of a Member State to enforce the order of the arbitral tribunal—mutual trust might arguably require the court to refuse enforcement on the basis of public policy. This point was not addressed in the *Gazprom* case.

(f) What if jurisdiction is not founded on a Brussels I Recast ground?

The Court of Justice was concerned to prevent interference with the jurisdiction of the foreign court. In the *Turner* case, the jurisdiction of the Spanish court was founded on one of the bases of jurisdiction under the Brussels Convention since the defendant in the Spanish proceedings was domiciled in the United Kingdom. Would the position be any different in the situation where the Brussels I Recast applies (ie the matter is within the scope of the Brussels I Recast) but none of the bases of jurisdiction set out in the Brussels I Recast apply to the proceedings which are being restrained (ie the defendant in the proceedings being restrained

---

[855] Confirmed in *National Navigacion v Endesa (The Wadi Sudr)* [2009] EWCA Civ 1397, [2010] 2 All ER (Comm) 1243; Fentiman (2010) 69 CLJ 242; Baatz [2010] LMCLQ 364; Knight [2009] LMCLQ 285; *DHL GBS (UK) Ltd v Fallimento Finmatica SpA* [2009] EWHC 291 (Comm), [2009] 1 Lloyd's Rep 430. See further infra, Chapter 17.

[856] See, eg, Fentiman (2009) 68 CLJ 278; Briggs [2009] LMCLQ 161; Peel (2009) 125 LQR 365; Santomauro (2010) 6 J Priv Int L 281; Radicati di Brozolo (2011) 7 J Priv Int L 423.

[857] See supra, p 211.

[858] See, eg, Hartley (2015) 64 ICLQ 965; Camilleri (2013) 62 ICLQ 899.

[859] *West Tankers Inc v Allianz SpA* [2012] EWHC 854 (Comm), [2012] 2 Lloyd's Rep 103.

[860] But cf the decision in *The Alexandros T* [2013] UKSC 70, [2014] 1 Lloyd's Rep 223; discussed supra, p 446. Similar issues were raised in *West Tankers Inc v Allianz SpA* [2012] EWCA Civ 27, [2012] 1 Lloyd's Rep 398.

[861] Recital (12).

[862] C-536/13 *Gazprom OAO* EU:C:2015:316, [2015] 1 WLR 4937; Kajkowska (2015) 74 CLJ 412; Briggs [2015] LMCLQ 284; Ojiegbe (2015) 11 J Priv Int L 267; Demirkol (2016) 65 ICLQ 379.

is domiciled in a non-Member State and neither Article 18(1), Article 21(2), Article 24 nor Article 25 applies)? Article 6 of the Brussels I Recast applies, according to which the jurisdiction of each Member State is determined by the law of that state. To take an example, a German court has taken jurisdiction under some traditional German basis of jurisdiction in an action brought against a New York defendant, and there is no question of Article 24 or 25 either giving the German courts jurisdiction or ousting their jurisdiction. The jurisdiction of the German court is directly derived from German national rules on jurisdiction, even if the authority for the German courts to use their national rules is derived from Article 6 of the Brussels I Recast. The Court of Justice in the *Turner* case referred to an injunction of the kind at issue limiting the application of the rules on jurisdiction "laid down by the Convention"[863] and this is referring to the bases of jurisdiction set out in the Convention.[864] Nonetheless, it is submitted that the Court of Justice should be concerned to prevent interference with the jurisdiction of the German courts in the above situation. One of the objections to injunctions restraining foreign proceedings made by the Court of Justice in the *Turner* case was that they rendered ineffective the specific mechanisms provided by the Brussels Convention for cases of *lis pendens* and related actions. Those mechanisms apply even where the jurisdiction of Member States is based on national rules on jurisdiction. So this criticism is equally valid in the present situation.

(g) An injunction preventing the commencement or continuation of proceedings

The injunction sought in the *Turner* case was to prevent the continuance of proceedings previously commenced. An injunction sought at an earlier stage which seeks to prevent the commencement of proceedings in another Member State would equally be prohibited by the decision in that case.

(ii) *Restraining proceedings in a non-Member State*

We are concerned here with the situation where an English court has jurisdiction under one of the bases of jurisdiction set out in the Brussels I Recast and the claimant in English proceedings seeks to restrain a party from commencing or continuing proceedings in a non-Member State. The injunction, if granted, constitutes an interference with the jurisdiction of the foreign court. But in this situation it is submitted that this would not be incompatible with the system of the Brussels I Recast. In the *Turner* case it was the fact that the injunction prohibited a party to proceedings pending before it from commencing or continuing legal proceedings *before a court of another Contracting State* that made the injunction incompatible with the Convention system. In the present situation, if anything, the injunction is being used to uphold the jurisdiction allocated under the Brussels I Recast and its grant should not be regarded as being incompatible with the Brussels I Recast. Accordingly, there is power to grant the injunction. Thus an injunction may be granted restraining proceedings brought in a non-Member State in breach of a clause which gives the English courts exclusive jurisdiction under Article 25 of the Brussels I Recast.[865]

There is, indeed, some controversial authority which suggests that the case for an anti-suit injunction to restrain non-Member State proceedings may be strengthened by the Brussels

---

[863] The *Turner* case, supra, at [30].

[864] Ibid, at [25].

[865] *Advent Capital plc v Ellinas Imports-Exports Ltd* [2005] EWHC 1242 (Comm) at [100], [2005] 2 Lloyd's Rep 607; *Skype Technologies SA v Joltid Ltd* [2009] EWHC 2783 (Ch), [2011] IL Pr 8. See also *Ultisol v Bouygues* [1996] 2 Lloyd's Rep 140—a Brussels Convention case. An appeal was allowed against the decision on the basis of changes in the position since the first instance judgment was given: *Bouygues Offshore SA v Caspian Shipping Co (Nos 1, 3, 4 and 5)* [1998] 2 Lloyd's Rep 461, CA. There was, however, no denial of the power to grant an injunction.

I Recast in certain circumstances. In *Samengo-Turner v J & H Marsh & McLennan (Services) Ltd*, an injunction was granted in relation to proceedings in New York in the situation where the defendant English domiciled employees who worked in London had the right to be sued only in England by virtue of Section 5 of the Brussels I Regulation.[866] The acceptance that there was power to grant an injunction in this situation must be right,[867] as there was no incompatibility with the Brussels I Regulation and nor would there be under the Brussels I Recast. What is more questionable, however, is the contention that, because there was the right under that section to be sued exclusively in England, this right provided the ground for granting the injunction.[868] This extends the grant of anti-suit injunctions by effectively creating a new category.[869]

Two criticisms can be levelled at this decision. First, it does not satisfy Lord Hobhouse's requirement in *Turner v Grovit* that there is wrongful conduct of the party to be restrained.[870] On the contrary, that party had commenced proceedings in New York acting in reliance on an agreement between the parties providing for the exclusive jurisdiction of the New York courts. Secondly, in terms of comity, New York courts cannot be expected to be sympathetic to an English assertion of exclusive jurisdiction under an EU Regulation to which New York is not a party or to the English courts striking out of the exclusive jurisdiction agreement by virtue of that Regulation. The situation is very different from one where there has been a breach of an exclusive jurisdiction agreement. Tuckey LJ accepted that the case for granting an injunction was not as strong as one where there had been a breach of an exclusive jurisdiction agreement.[871] But nonetheless, an injunction was granted.

If *Samengo-Turner* is correctly decided, the same reasoning would arguably apply to cases where the English courts are allocated exclusive jurisdiction under Article 24 or under Sections 3 and 4 of the Brussels I Recast. There is even an argument that it should extend to cases in which an English-domiciled defendant is sued in England on the basis of Article 4 of the Brussels I Recast. In the past, an injunction restraining proceedings in a non-Contracting State to the Brussels Convention has not been granted merely because those proceedings were brought outside the Contracting State in which the defendant was domiciled.[872] The reasoning behind this was that there was no "right" to be sued in the Contracting State in which the defendant was domiciled, at least in cases where the alternative forum was a non-Contracting State.[873] But now there is an argument that the *Owusu* case effectively establishes such a "right".[874] It would follow that an injunction could be granted for breach of this. This would extend even further the new category of anti-suit injunction created by *Samengo-Turner*, exacerbating the problems noted above. If the approach adopted in *Samengo-Turner* is to be applied in future, it may be better confined to cases in which the jurisdiction of the courts is established under the Brussels I Recast in order to protect a weaker party—that is, Sections 3, 4 and 5 of the Brussels I Recast[875]—with the possible addition of cases where a Member State court is given exclusive jurisdiction pursuant to Article 24.[876]

---

[866] [2007] EWCA Civ 723, [2007] IL Pr 52; Briggs [2007] LMCLQ 433. See also *Petter v EMC Europe Ltd* [2015] EWCA Civ 828, [2016] IL Pr 3; Raphael [2016] LMCLQ 256.

[867] This was common ground by counsel.

[868] It might be argued, however, that this made the foreign proceedings vexatious and oppressive: see infra, p 426 et seq.

[869] See supra, p 426.

[870] Supra, p 425.

[871] The *Samengo-Turner* case, supra, at [41].

[872] *Société Commerciale de Réassurance v Eras International Ltd (No 2)* [1995] 2 All ER 278 at 298–9.

[873] Reliance was placed on *Re Harrods*, supra.

[874] Supra, p 462 et seq.

[875] See supra, p 289 et seq.

[876] See supra, p 217 et seq.

14

LIMITATIONS ON JURISDICTION

1. Introduction   483
2. Jurisdiction in Respect of Foreign
   Property   484
   (a) Foreign immovables   484
   (b) Foreign intellectual property rights   494
3. Jurisdiction Over the Parties   496
   (a) Persons who cannot invoke the
        jurisdiction   496
   (b) Persons who may claim exemption
        from the jurisdiction   497
4. Statutory Limitations on Jurisdiction   518

1. INTRODUCTION

Jurisdiction under the traditional rules is subject to certain limitations, the effect of which is to render the court incompetent to try a case notwithstanding that the defendant has been properly served with a claim form. These limitations have been judicially classified into the following three types.[1]

(i) *Limitations that affect the subject matter of the issue* Broadly stated, these limitations preclude a right of action if the issue relates to foreign immovables,[2] validity of foreign intellectual property rights,[3] foreign taxes,[4] or the rights and liabilities arising under a foreign penal or other public law.[5]

(ii) *Limitations that affect the kind of relief sought* These restrict the power of the court to grant relief affecting the matrimonial status of the parties. In this type of case it is not enough that the respondent has been served with process. As will be seen in Chapter 22 on matrimonial and related causes, the competence of the court to proceed with the trial is conditioned by such factors as the habitual residence or domicile of the parties.[6]

(iii) *Limitations relating to persons between whom the issue is joined* There are certain persons against whom the jurisdiction cannot be enforced, and others by whom it cannot be invoked.[7]

There is one further limitation which should be added to this list.

(iv) *Limitations on jurisdiction imposed by certain statutes*[8]

It is intended in this chapter to deal with limitations in respect of foreign immovables and foreign intellectual property rights, limitations relating to the parties and limitations imposed

---

[1] *Garthwaite v Garthwaite* [1964] P 356 at 387, CA.
[2] Infra, pp 484–94.
[3] Infra, pp 494–6.
[4] Supra, p 116 et seq.
[5] Supra, p 118 et seq.
[6] Infra, pp 954–79.
[7] Infra, pp 496–518.
[8] Infra, pp 518–19.

by certain statutes. The other limitations mentioned above are more appropriately dealt with elsewhere in the book.

2. JURISDICTION IN RESPECT OF FOREIGN PROPERTY

(a) Foreign immovables[9]

The limitations on jurisdiction in relation to foreign immovables are derived from two sources: first, certain common law rules; secondly, the Brussels/Lugano system. Each of these limitations will be examined in turn.

(i) *The common law limitation*

(a) *The exclusionary rule*

An English court has no jurisdiction to adjudicate upon the right of property in, or the right to possession of, foreign immovables, even though the parties may be resident or domiciled in England.[10] The basis for this general rule is that controversies should be decided in the country of the situs of the property because the right of granting it was vested in that country's sovereign power, and the maintenance of comity and the avoidance of conflict with foreign jurisdictions.[11]

It was at one time thought, however, that as regards England the rule was not based on substantial grounds, but was due to the technicalities of the English law of procedure. A distinction was made between local and transitory actions. If a cause of action was one that might have arisen anywhere, it was *transitory*; if it was one that could have arisen only in one place, it was *local*. In local matters, such as claims to the ownership of land,[12] the *venue* had to be laid with accuracy, but in transitory matters the plaintiff was allowed to lay the *venue* where he pleased. However, local venues were abolished by the Judicature Act 1873. This removed the technical objection to the possibility of bringing an action in respect of foreign immovables before an English court, and it was not long before it was suggested, and indeed decided, that such actions could now be entertained. This argument was strongly pressed in *British South Africa Co v Companhia de Moçambique*.[13]

> This was an action of trespass brought against the defendants for having broken into and taken possession of large tracts of lands and mines in South Africa.

The Court of Appeal held that, local *venues* having been abolished, such an action could properly be brought here.[14] The House of Lords, however, reversed this decision and held that an English court has no jurisdiction to entertain a suit with respect to foreign immovables and, moreover, it finally dispelled the idea that this principle ever rested on a technical rule of procedure.[15] Stated more explicitly, what this decision now signifies is that the jurisdiction of the court is barred where the action raises the issue of the title to, or right to possession of, land abroad.

---

[9] On the distinction between movables and immovables, see infra, Chapter 29.

[10] *British South Africa Co v Companhia de Moçambique* [1893] AC 602, HL; *Deschamps v Miller* [1908] 1 Ch 856; *Hesperides Hotels Ltd v Muftizade* [1979] AC 508, HL; Merrills (1979) 28 ICLQ 523; Carter (1978) 49 BYBIL 286. For a Canadian and an Australian authority on this point, see *Jeske v Jeske* (1982) 29 RFL (2d) 348, BC SC; *Dagi v BHP (No 2)* [1997] 1 VR 428, VSC. Cf *Rowe v Silverstein* [1996] 1 VR 509, VSC.

[11] *Lucasfilm Ltd v Ainsworth* [2011] UKSC 39 at [106], [2012] 1 AC 208.

[12] The place from which the jury was summoned.

[13] [1893] AC 602, HL.

[14] [1892] 2 QB 358.

[15] [1893] AC 602 at 629, HL.

This exclusion of jurisdiction is justified on the basis that any judgment in rem that might be given would be totally ineffective unless it were accepted and implemented by the authorities in the situs.[16] However, this issue must be raised directly, for "it is the action *founded on* a disputed claim of title to foreign lands over which an English court has no jurisdiction, and . . . where no question of title arises, or only arises as a collateral incident of the trial of other issues, there is nothing to exclude the jurisdiction".[17] Examples of a refusal of jurisdiction on this ground are: proceedings for the partition of land in Ireland;[18] an action to test the validity of a devise of land situated in Pennsylvania;[19] an action[20] or a petition of right[21] to recover possession of Colonial land; a claim to obtain inspection of documents, possessed by the defendant in England, in aid of an action for the recovery of land that was pending in India;[22] an action for a declaration of title to fishery rights;[23] declaration of transfer of title to a foreign property.[24]

A question that has arisen is whether an action to recover arrears of rent charged on land abroad is maintainable in England. In *Whitaker v Forbes*:[25]

> An English testator devised land in Australia to the defendant, but charged it with the payment of an annuity of £500 to the plaintiff.

An action to recover arrears of this rentcharge inevitably failed, for it had been commenced before the abolition of the rules of *venue* by the Judicature Act, and thus the court had no option but to enforce the technical rule that the action was local and therefore not maintainable. Lord Cairns, however, remarked that it might possibly be maintainable in the future.[26] In this particular case, of course, the defendant, having assumed no contractual obligation, was liable solely on the ground of privity of estate arising from his possession of the land, and there can be no doubt that a liability which rests on privity of contract, as where a borrower charges his land with the repayment of the loan, will be enforceable in English proceedings.

(b) Exceptions to the exclusionary rule
There are two exceptions to the exclusion of jurisdiction under the rule in the *Moçambique* case.

(i) Action founded on a personal obligation[27]
If the conscience of the defendant is affected in the sense that he has become bound by a personal obligation to the claimant, the court, in the exercise of its jurisdiction in personam, will not shrink from ordering him to convey or otherwise deal with foreign land. For the

---

[16] This sentence was cited with approval in *Stevens v Hamed* [2013] EWCA Civ 911 at [16], [2013] IL Pr 37. It is unlikely that foreign judgments relating to title to English land will be recognised in this country, see infra, p 546.

[17] *St Pierre v South American Stores (Gath and Chaves) Ltd* [1936] 1 KB 382 at 397, CA, interpreting the speech of Lord Herschell in the *Moçambique* case [1893] AC 602 at 626; and see *Tito v Waddell (No 2)* [1977] Ch 106 at 262–4, 310; *Stevens v Hamed* [2013] EWCA Civ 911 at [14], [2013] IL Pr 37; *Bodo Community v Shell Petroleum Development Co of Nigeria Ltd* [2014] EWHC 1973 (TCC) at [161]–[166]. See also *Dagi v BHP (No 2)* [1997] 1 VR 428 at 441, VSC—the claim must essentially concern rights to or over foreign land. The rule in the *Moçambique* case will not apply where what is involved is more than a mere dispute between private individuals, see *Buttes Gas and Oil Co v Hammer (No 3)* [1982] AC 888.

[18] *Cartwright v Pettus* (1675) 2 Cas in Ch 214, 22 ER 916.

[19] *Pike v Hoare* (1763) Amb 428, 27 ER 286.

[20] *Roberdeau v Rous* (1738) 1 Atk 543, 26 ER 342.

[21] *Re Holmes* (1861) 2 John & H 527.

[22] *Reiner v Marquis of Salisbury* (1876) 2 Ch D 378.

[23] *Toome Eel Fishery (Northern Ireland) v Jangaard and Butler* [1960] CLY 1297.

[24] *Mahtani v Sippy* [2013] EWHC 285 (Ch).

[25] (1875) 1 CPD 51, CA.

[26] Ibid, at 52.

[27] See generally Yeo, *Choice of Law for Equitable Doctrines* (2004), paras 1.03–1.26.

argument that a court cannot, by its judgments or decrees, directly bind or affect land that lies within the confines of another state has no force where the issue before the court is not a right in rem relating to foreign immovables, but an obligation enforceable in personam against the defendant.[28]

The primary essential is that the defendant should be subject to the general jurisdiction of the court.[29] This jurisdiction, as we have seen, is founded on his presence in England, but as regards the power to pronounce a decree in personam against him it is equally well founded by service of a claim form under rule 6.36 of the Civil Procedure Rules and para 3.1 of the Civil Procedure Rules Practice Direction 6B.[30] Once the court is thus empowered to take cognizance of the matter, the doctrine that equity acts in personam may be freely and effectively applied. A decree may be issued which, though personal in form, will indirectly affect land abroad. The operation of this rule may readily be illustrated by decisions on the making of search orders, ie orders without notice for the inspection of property, in relation to property abroad. If the defendant has been properly served in England, the court has power to, and may well make, the order. It is, however, a discretionary order and though an order has been granted for the inspection of premises in one foreign state,[31] an order has been refused in relation to premises in another foreign state.[32] Furthermore, if the jurisdiction of the court is based on service of the claim form out of the jurisdiction following an application without notice under rule 6.36, execution of the search order abroad may be suspended until the defendant has had an opportunity to seek to set aside the service of the claim form.[33]

If, for instance, a mortgagee of land in New York refuses to reconvey on receipt of principal, interest and costs, there is no way by which a direct transfer of the property to the mortgagor can be effected at the instance of the English court. But the court can indirectly produce the desired result by saying to the recalcitrant mortgagee, "You are subject to our jurisdiction by reason of your presence in England, and if you refuse to take the steps required by the law of the situs for a reconveyance of the property to the mortgagor, we shall imprison you or sequestrate your English property until you comply." The distinction is that the court cannot act upon the land directly, but acts on the conscience of the defendant.[34]

This right to affect foreign land was finally established by the decision in *Penn v Baltimore*[35] in 1750. In that case:

> A contract had been made in England between the plaintiff and the defendant, by which a scheme was arranged for fixing the boundaries of Pennsylvania and Maryland. To a claim for specific performance brought in this country the defendant objected that the court had no jurisdiction, since it could neither make an effectual decree nor execute its own judgment.

Lord Hardwicke, while admitting that he could not make a decree in rem, granted specific performance, on the ground that the strict primary decree in a court of equity was in personam.

---

[28] *Ewing v Orr Ewing* (1883) 9 App Cas 34 at 40, HL. For the position under the Brussels/Lugano system, which reaches the same conclusion, see Case C-294/92 *Webb v Webb* [1994] ECR I-1717, supra, p 220; Case C-343/04 *Land Oberösterreich v Čez AS* [2006] ECR I-4557.

[29] *Razelos v Razelos (No 2)* [1970] 1 WLR 392 at 403. See also *Bheekhun v Williams* [1999] 2 FLR 229 at 242, CA.

[30] *Re Liddell's Settlement Trusts* [1936] Ch 365 at 374, CA. For CPR, r 6.36 and CPR Practice Direction 6B, para 3.1, see supra, pp 334–81.

[31] *Cook Industries Inc v Galliher* [1979] Ch 439.

[32] *Protector Alarms Ltd v Maxim Alarms Ltd* [1978] FSR 442.

[33] *Altertext Inc v Advanced Data Communications Ltd* [1985] 1 WLR 457.

[34] *Cranstown v Johnston* (1796) 3 Ves 170 at 182, 30 ER 952; *Companhia de Moçambique v British South Africa Co* [1892] 2 QB 358 at 364, HL.

[35] (1750) 1 Ves Sen 444, 27 ER 1132.

The exercise of this jurisdiction, of course, is not confined to questions concerning foreign land. It extends to any case where the defendant has been guilty of conduct that in the eyes of the court is contrary to equity and good conscience. An important example of the general jurisdiction occurs where a person who is amenable to the jurisdiction commences, or threatens to commence, legal proceedings abroad, the institution of which is inequitable. In such circumstances the court has a power to issue an injunction restraining the foreign proceedings and a power to award damages for costs incurred by reason of foreign proceedings, for decrees of this nature are not directed against the authority of the foreign court but merely commands a person within the English jurisdiction what he is to do. Even where a person has actually obtained judgment abroad, an injunction may be issued restraining him from reaping its fruits, if he has obtained it in breach of some contractual or fiduciary duty or in a manner contrary to the principles of equity and conscience.[36]

We must now, however, confine the discussion to the manner in which the exercise of this personal jurisdiction may affect foreign land. The fundamental requirement is that the defendant should be subject to some personal obligation arising from his own act, for it is only when his conscience is affected that the court is entitled to interfere. This personal obligation can arise "out of contract or implied contract, fiduciary relationship, or fraud, or other conduct which, in the view of the Court of Equity in this country, would be unconscionable, and [does] not depend for [its] existence on the law of the *locus* of the immovable property".[37] It will lead, perhaps, to a better appreciation of the subject if we attempt to tabulate the various circumstances that have been considered sufficient to raise the necessary personal equity. It should, however, be stressed that the courts may decide that a personal equity exists without going on to categorise the situation before them. Thus the Court of Appeal has held[38] that there is jurisdiction to grant a wife an order restraining her husband from disposing of a villa in Spain, since the right to financial relief arising from divorce proceedings is concerned with a personal equity and this is enough to give jurisdiction.

Contracts relating to foreign land It is clear that a party to a contract concerning foreign land is subject to a personal obligation which affects his conscience and which can be enforced by the personal process of a court of equity,[39] even if his contractual right can only be pursued by an uncontested assertion of his title to foreign land.[40] The existence of a contractual obligation was the ground of the decision in *Penn v Baltimore*.[41] In a very early case,[42] the defendant, who refused to perform a contract for the sale of land in Ireland, was successfully sued for specific performance while on a casual visit to England. Again, a decree for specific performance was made against the English executors of a testator who had agreed for valuable consideration to execute a legal mortgage of land in the island of Dominica;[43] and an action has lain in England for recovery of rent due under a lease of land in Chile.[44]

---

[36] *Ellerman Lines Ltd v Read* [1928] 2 KB 144, CA; *Bank of St Petersburg OJSC v Arkhangelsky* [2014] EWCA Civ 593, [2014] 1 WLR 4360.

[37] *Deschamps v Miller* [1908] 1 Ch 856 at 863. See also Westlake, s 173; Foote, p 224; Dicey, Morris and Collins, paras 23-042–23-051; *Companhia de Moçambique v British South Africa Co* [1892] 2 QB 358 at 364, HL.

[38] *Hamlin v Hamlin* [1986] Fam 11, CA. See also *Hlynski v Hlynski* (1999) 176 DLR (4th) 132, Sask CA.

[39] *Cood v Cood* (1863) 33 LJ Ch 273, 55 ER 388; *British South Africa Co v De Beers Consolidated Mines Ltd* [1910] 2 Ch 502 at 523, 524, CA; *St Pierre v South American Stores (Gath and Chaves) Ltd* [1936] 1 KB 382, CA.

[40] *Tito v Waddell (No 2)* [1977] Ch 106 at 264, 310; infra, p 489.

[41] (1750) 1 Ves Sen 444, 27 ER 1132.

[42] *Archer v Preston*, undated, but cited in *Arglasse v Muschamp* (1682) 1 Vern 75 at 77, 23 ER 322.

[43] *Re Smith, Lawrence v Kitson* [1916] 2 Ch 206.

[44] *St Pierre v South American Stores (Gath and Chaves) Ltd* [1936] 1 KB 382, CA.

More recently, specific performance of a contract for the sale of land in Scotland has been decreed against an English purchaser, notwithstanding the argument that there was considerable difference between Scots and English land law.[45] In Canada, specific performance has been granted by a New Brunswick court against a vendor who attempted to repudiate a contract for the sale of land in Quebec.[46] In a recent case, the Court of Appeal held that a claim for the reimbursement of money paid under a contract of sale of foreign property, where the defendant was said to have failed to perform the contract by transferring the title to the property, fell within the exception to the exclusionary rule.[47] It has been said *per curiam* that the fact that land is situated abroad should affect the choice of law, not jurisdiction, if the case is one in which it is sought to enforce an equitable claim in personam.[48] Thus a claim to have foreign land conveyed to the claimant, based on an English contract and made against a purchaser of the land with prior notice of that contract (who would be considered to be acting unconscionably), could in principle succeed, provided the foreign law would not overreach the English doctrine of notice.[49]

Fraud and other unconscionable conduct Fraud is an extrinsic, collateral act, violating all proceedings, even those of courts of justice,[50] and it always creates a right in the injured party to sue the defendant in personam wherever he can find him, no matter where the cause of action has arisen or where the subject matter of the action is situated. The leading case is *Cranstown v Johnston*.[51]

> The plaintiff was liable to pay to the defendant in London over £2,500 but was unable to make the payment at the required time. He was entitled to a plantation of great value in the island of St Christopher. The law of that island allowed a creditor to proceed against an absent debtor. After judgment had been obtained without any actual notice to the plaintiff, the plantation was seized and the plaintiff's interest therein sold to the defendant for £2,000, which was far less than its true value. The plaintiff filed a bill for relief in the English Court of Equity.

The Master of the Rolls decreed that on receipt of what was due for principal, interest and costs the defendant should reconvey the plantation to the plaintiff. He did not deny that what had been done was in accordance with the law of the situs, but he pointed out that the defendant had used the local law not to satisfy the debt, but to obtain an estate at an inadequate price. This was a "gross injustice" sufficient to justify the court in acting on the conscience of the defendant.

Fiduciary relationship A trust attached to foreign land may be enforced by the English court, provided that the trustee is present in this country.[52] This is so, even though the author of the

---

[45] *Richard West & Partners (Inverness) Ltd v Dick* [1969] 2 Ch 424; affd, [1969] 2 Ch 424 at 435, CA. In view of the general requirement of jurisdiction over the defendant, discussed supra, p 323 et seq, it is hard to see why Harman LJ [1969] 2 Ch 424 at 436 was unwilling to commit himself if the defendant was not domiciled in England.

[46] *Ward v Coffin* (1972) 27 DLR (3d) 58, New Brunswick CA.

[47] *Stevens v Hamed* [2013] EWCA Civ 911, [2013] IL Pr 37; Scott (2013) 84 BYBIL 515.

[48] *R Griggs Group Ltd v Evans* [2004] EWHC 1088 (Ch) at [110], [2005] Ch 153. See also *Macmillan Inc v Bishopsgate Investment Trust plc (No 3)* [1995] 1 WLR 978 at 989; affd on other grounds [1996] 1 WLR 387, CA; *Lightning v Lightning Electrical Contractors Ltd* [1998] NPC 71, CA; *Stevens v Hamed* [2013] EWCA Civ 911 at [20], [2013] IL Pr 37; Wass (2014) 63 ICLQ 103.

[49] The *R Griggs Group Ltd v Evans* case, at [111].

[50] *Duchess of Kingston's Case* (1776) 20 State Tr 355 at 544, 168 ER 175; *White v Hall* (1806) 12 Ves 321, 33 ER 122.

[51] (1796) 3 Ves 170, 30 ER 952. See also *Arglasse v Muschamp* (1682) 1 Vern 75, 23 ER 322; *Cook Industries Inc v Galliher* [1979] Ch 439.

[52] *Kildare v Eustace* (1686) 1 Vern 437, 23 ER 571; see also *Razelos v Razelos (No 2)* [1970] 1 WLR 392. It is not clear, in the latter case, whether jurisdiction was assumed on the basis of fraud or of a fiduciary relationship: Chesterman (1970) 33 MLR 209, 212–13.

trust is not subject to the English jurisdiction.[53] A declaration that foreign land is held by the defendant as a trustee and that the claimant has an equitable interest in the trust property can be sought from an English court if the defendant is amenable to the court's jurisdiction.[54] However, two different types of problem may arise in relation to a trust or other equitable obligation concerning foreign land. The first is where the dispute before the court concerns the enforcement of the trust. It may be that a beneficiary can only establish his right to benefit under the trust by asserting evidence of his title to foreign land. In that event, the question of title to the land, though relevant to the claimant's claim, is only incidental to the dispute before the court, namely the enforcement of the trust, such as a trust of royalties from the mining of land.[55] If, on the other hand, there are rival claimants to the land, then the claimant's assertion of title is part of the subject matter of the dispute and would come within the *Moçambique* rule, whether the claim related to a trust[56] or to a contractual obligation[57] concerning the foreign land. A claim that is based on legal ownership of immovable property abroad will come within the *Moçambique* rule, even though the remedy sought is that of a constructive trust.[58]

Mortgage and foreclosure   Again, a personal equity arising from a mortgage of foreign land may justify an action in this country. Thus, where the mortgagor of land in Jamaica had obtained a decree from the English court which directed certain accounts to be taken with a view to redemption, the court granted an injunction restraining the mortgagees, who were present in England, from instituting foreclosure proceedings in Jamaica.[59] The mortgagor had a clear equity to be protected from a double account. The same principle applies to foreclosure proceedings. In English proceedings a decree in a foreclosure action is merely a decree in personam since it destroys the right of redemption given by equity to the mortgagor, and it can therefore be made by an English court against a mortgagor who is within the jurisdiction, although the subject of the mortgage may be immovables situated abroad.[60] Whether a personal obligation is such as to affect the defendant's conscience is a matter to be determined solely by English law. According to *Re Courtney*,[61] the court does not refuse to exercise its equitable jurisdiction merely because the right, recognised by English law as springing from the personal relationship between the parties, is one that is not recognised by the law of the situs.

Limitations on the doctrine   The doctrine of *Penn v Baltimore*, however, is subject to two limitations. First, it must be possible for the decree issued by the English court to be carried into effect in the country where the land is situated.[62] This restriction requires no elaboration, for the futility of ordering the defendant to perform some act which would be forbidden by the law of the situs is obvious.[63]

---

[53] *Ewing v Orr Ewing* (1883) 9 App Cas 34, HL; and see *Chellaram v Chellaram* [1985] Ch 409 at 426–7.
[54] *Bharmal v Bharmal* [2011] EWHC 1092 (Ch).
[55] *Tito v Waddell (No 2)* [1977] Ch 106 at 262–4, 272, 310.
[56] Ibid, at 263, 310.
[57] Supra, pp 487–8.
[58] *Re Polly Peck International plc (In Administration) (No 2)* [1998] 3 All ER 812 at 828, CA.
[59] *Beckford v Kemble* (1822) 1 Sim & St 7, 57 ER 3; cf *Inglis v Commonwealth Trading Bank of Australia* (1972) 20 FLR 30, ACTSC; Pryles (1973) 22 ICLQ 756.
[60] *Toller v Carteret* (1705) 2 Vern 494, 23 ER 916; *Paget v Ede* (1874) LR 18 Eq 118.
[61] (1840) Mont & Ch 239 at 251; *Re Anchor Line (Henderson Bros) Ltd* [1937] Ch 483 at 488.
[62] *Waterhouse v Stansfield* (1851) 9 Hare 234, 68 ER 489; cf *Richard West & Partners (Inverness) Ltd v Dick* [1969] 2 Ch 424 at 429–30, 436; *Razelos v Razelos (No 2)* [1970] 1 WLR 392 at 403–5.
[63] *Re Courtney* (1840) Mont & Ch 239 at 250–1.

Secondly, the personal obligation which is the basis of the English court's jurisdiction must, to use an expression of Beale, "have run from the defendant to the plaintiff",[64] ie there must be privity of obligation between the parties to the action.

It is firmly established that the court acts only against the actual person who, as a result of his *own* conduct, is under a personal obligation to the claimant, and it stops short of exercising the jurisdiction against a third party, even though he may have acquired the land from one who is contractually, or otherwise personally, liable to the claimant.[65] There must be privity of obligation between claimant and defendant, and that privity must arise from some transaction effected by the claimant with the defendant.

> If A agrees to sell foreign land to B, there is no doubt that A incurs a personal liability that is justiciable in England. But if, in breach of his contract, A sells the land to X, there is no personal equity which B can enforce against X. There is no contract by X with B, no unconscionable conduct by X towards B personally.

What is involved in such a case is a claim of title to foreign land advanced by two contesting parties who are strangers to each other so far as mutual dealings are concerned. Such a question of title is, of course, determinable exclusively by the law of the situs and is subject exclusively to the jurisdiction of the courts at the situs.[66]

There may, of course, be exceptional circumstances in which an equity that has arisen between A and B can be enforced against C under the doctrine of *Penn v Baltimore*. It is always a question of personal obligation. Is the defendant, though not a party to the original transaction which gave rise to the dispute, contractually or otherwise personally bound? Thus where the defendants had agreed to take land in Mexico subject to an express obligation in favour of existing debenture-holders, it was clearly unconscionable that they should rely exclusively on the law of the situs.[67]

Concluding remarks on the doctrine   Such, then, is the doctrine that the English court invokes to justify an order which, though personal in form, may affect the title to foreign land. It is a doctrine that in some cases has undoubtedly been carried to an extent scarcely warranted by the principles of international law,[68] as, for instance, where an Englishman resident in Chile was ordered to carry out a contract concerning land, binding according to English law, which the Chilean courts had held not to be binding.[69] In fact, Lord Esher MR once went so far as to say that the decision in *Penn v Baltimore*, "seems to me to be open to the strong objection, that the Court is doing indirectly what it dare not do directly".[70]

An interesting question is whether a foreign judgment based on the same principle as that adopted in *Penn v Baltimore*, but affecting *English* land, will be granted extra-territorial effect.[71]

---

[64]   (1906) 20 HLR 382, 390.
[65]   *Martin v Martin* (1831) 2 Russ & M 507, 39 ER 487; *Waterhouse v Stansfield* (1851) 9 Hare 234, 68 ER 489; *Norris v Chambres* (1861) 29 Beav 246, 54 ER 621; affd 3 De G F & J 583, 45 ER 1004; *Hicks v Powell* (1869) LR 4 Ch App 741; *Norton v Florence Land Co* (1877) 7 Ch D 332; *Catania v Giannattasio* (1999) 174 DLR (4th) 170, Ont CA.
[66]   *Norris v Chambres* (1861) 29 Beav 246, 54 ER 621; affd (1861) 3 De G F & J 583, 45 ER 1004. Followed in *Deschamps v Miller* [1908] 1 Ch 856; and see *Re Hawthorne, Graham v Massey* (1883) 23 Ch D 743; *Cook Industries Inc v Galliher* [1979] Ch 439.
[67]   *Mercantile Investment and General Trust Co v River Plate Trust, Loan and Agency Co* [1892] 2 Ch 303.
[68]   Story, p 758.
[69]   *Cood v Cood* (1863) 33 LJ Ch 273, 55 ER 388.
[70]   *Companhia de Moçambique v British South Africa Co* [1892] 2 QB 358 at 404–5, CA.
[71]   Dicey, Morris and Collins, paras 14R-108–14-117.

If, for instance, a Californian court decrees that X, resident in California, shall reconvey English land to Y, from whom he had obtained it by fraud, will the English court, in proceedings brought by Y, compel X to carry the decree into effect?

Comity, if it means anything, would dictate an affirmative answer. However, any attempt by a foreign court to regulate the disposition of land outside its jurisdiction not unnaturally provokes a certain animosity in the state where the property is situated and it is doubtful whether in this particular context the English judges would be imbued with any spirit of reciprocity. The Supreme Court of Canada, indeed, has satisfied itself that English courts do not regard their own decrees in personam affecting land abroad as having any extra-territorial effect, and that therefore no recognition will be granted to similar decrees of foreign courts.[72]

(ii) Questions affecting foreign land arising incidentally in an English action

The second exception to the exclusion of jurisdiction under the rule in the *Moçambique* case, which lacks direct authority but which undoubtedly exists in practice, is apparent from such well-known cases as *Re Duke of Wellington*[73] and *Nelson v Bridport*,[74] to take only two examples.[75] In each of these cases jurisdiction was assumed although quite clearly the title to foreign land was the matter in dispute. Since parties cannot consent to the exercise of a jurisdiction which the court admittedly does not possess,[76] how is this divergence from the general principle to be explained? The usual explanation is that if an estate or a trust, which includes English property and foreign immovables, is being administered in English proceedings,[77] the court is prepared to determine a disputed title to the foreign immovables.[78] Perhaps Lord Herschell had this practice in mind when he accepted that the courts could take jurisdiction to determine incidental matters involving title to foreign land.[79] Although a stern critic might question whether the title to the Spanish land in *Re Duke of Wellington* was a mere incident in the proceedings, there is no doubt that in the course of dealing with such a matter as a trust or a will subject to English law the courts have in fact not hesitated to determine the title to foreign land. The jurisdictional difficulty that arises appears to have been canvassed only once,[80] and all that can be said is that the practice comes perilously near to destroying the supposedly universal principle that jurisdiction concerning the title to, or possession of, immovables resides only in the state in which the property is situated.

---

[72] *Duke v Andler* [1932] SCR 734, [1932] 4 DLR 529; see Gordon (1933) 49 LQR 547; Anderson (1999) 48 ICLQ 167; cf *Shami v Shami* [2012] EWHC 664 (Ch) at [30]–[35]; affd without discussing this point [2013] EWCA Civ 227; *Chapman Estate v O'Hara* [1988] 2 WWR 275, Sask CA. In the USA, although the Supreme Court in *Fall v Eastin* 215 US 1 (1909) held that recognition need not be given to judgments in personam concerning land, most states are prepared to recognise such judgments: Restatement 2d § 102, comment d.

[73] [1948] Ch 118, CA, supra, p 68.

[74] (1846) 8 Beav 547, 50 ER 215, infra, pp 1255–6.

[75] See also *Re Piercy* [1895] 1 Ch 83; *Re Hoyles* [1911] 1 Ch 179, CA; *Re Ross* [1930] 1 Ch 377, supra, pp 66–7. Cf *Buttes Gas and Oil Co v Hammer (No 3)* [1982] AC 888, HL.

[76] Duncan and Dykes, *Principles of Civil Jurisdiction* (1911), p 258; see also the doubt expressed by Somervell LJ in *The Tolten* [1946] P 135 at 166, CA.

[77] The jurisdiction of the English court to administer an *inter vivos* trust of land in a European Union or EFTA State is subject to Arts 1(1) and 24(1) of the Brussels I Regulation Recast (Arts 1(1) and 16(1)(a) of the Brussels Convention and Arts 1(1) and 22(1) of the Lugano Convention, supra, pp 219–20 and 312.

[78] *Jubert v Church Comrs for England* 1952 SC 160; *Re Bailey* [1985] 2 NZLR 656, NZHC; Morris (1948) 64 LQR 264, 268. Morris suggests that the English and foreign property must be subject to similar limitations, but is this right?

[79] *British South Africa Co v Companhia de Moçambique* [1893] AC 602, at 626, HL. See also Westlake, s 173.

[80] *Re Duke of Wellington* [1948] Ch 118 at 120, CA gives the misleading impression that if the parties consent the court can arrogate a jurisdiction that it does not possess. It must be admitted, however, that this was done in *The Mary Moxham* (1876) 1 PD 107, CA. See also *Couzens v Negri* [1981] VR 824, VSC.

(c) Damages for trespass to foreign land

Until fairly recently the limitations at common law extended to prevent jurisdiction in cases where the action raised the issue of the recovery of damages for trespass to foreign land, even though no question of title to the land arose.[81] This rule came in for much criticism and was abolished by section 30(1) of the Civil Jurisdiction and Judgments Act 1982,[82] which provides that:

> the jurisdiction . . . to entertain proceedings for trespass to, or any other tort affecting, immovable property shall extend to cases in which the property in question is situated outside [England] unless the proceedings are principally concerned with a question of the title to, or right to possession of, that property.

According to the Court of Appeal in *Re Polly Peck International plc (In Administration) (No 2)*,[83] "principally" is used in the ordinary sense of "for the most part" or "chiefly",[84] so that section 30(1) preserves the *Moçambique* rule only in cases where the real issue in the proceedings is the question of title to, or the right to possession of, foreign land, and all other questions are merely incidental thereto.[85] The applicants claimed to own and be entitled to immediate possession of land, buildings and other immovable property in the Northern part of Cyprus, properties which were expropriated after the 1974 Turkish invasion. The applicants' claim was undeniably concerned with a question of title to, and the right to possession of, that property. However, it was seriously arguable[86] that the proceedings were not principally so concerned because they raised substantial questions, such as whether Polly Peck International itself committed any acts of trespass and whether Polly Peck International could be liable for acts of trespass by its subsidiaries, which were not principally concerned with a question of title to, or the right to possession of, the property in Cyprus. It followed that the court could entertain the proceedings.

(ii) *The limitation under the Brussels/Lugano system*

The limitation on jurisdiction in respect of foreign immovables under the Brussels/Lugano system stems from Article 24(1) of the Brussels I Regulation Recast,[87] Article 22(1) of the Lugano Convention and Article 16(1)(a) of the Brussels Convention,[88] the effect of which is to prevent a court in the United Kingdom from taking jurisdiction in proceedings which have as their object rights in rem in, or tenancies of, immovable property situated in another European Union State or in an EFTA State,[89] since the courts of the European Union/EFTA State in which the property is situated are given exclusive jurisdiction over such proceedings.

---

[81] *St Pierre v South American Stores (Gath and Chaves) Ltd* [1936] 1 KB 382 at 396, CA; *Hesperides Hotels Ltd v Aegean Turkish Holidays Ltd* [1979] AC 508, HL. See also *Dagi v BHP (No 2)* [1997] 1 VR 428, 443, VSC (negligence).

[82] Applied in *Trawnik v Lennox* [1985] 1 WLR 532, CA.

[83] [1998] 3 All ER 812; Briggs (1998) 69 BYBIL 356; Dickinson [1998] LMCLQ 519.

[84] [1998] 3 All ER 812 at 828.

[85] Ibid, at 829. It was said, at 828, that this approach was consistent with the interpretation of Art 19 of the Brussels Convention (Art 27 of the Brussels I Regulation Recast), supra, pp 217–18, in *Fort Dodge Animal Health Ltd v Akzo Nobel* [1998] FSR 222, CA and *Coin Controls Ltd v Suzo International (UK) Ltd* [1999] Ch 33 at 50–1. But there, "principally" has been equated with "not arising incidentally" which is a much laxer test than "chiefly".

[86] It was not necessary to determine this matter definitively before the trial on the merits, [1998] 3 All ER 812 at 827.

[87] Under the EC/Denmark Agreement the provisions of the Regulation are applied by international law to the relations between the European Union and Denmark.

[88] See supra, pp 219–24.

[89] For the position where the immovable property is situated in Scotland or Northern Ireland, see para 11(a) of the Modified Regulation in the Civil Jurisdiction and Judgments Act 1982, Sch 4, discussed generally supra, p 319.

If Article 24(1) of the Brussels I Regulation Recast, or Article 22(1) of the Lugano Convention, or Article 16(1)(a) of the Brussels Convention, is applicable, the common law rules on jurisdiction in relation to foreign immovables are overridden by this Article.[90] It is important to note that the limitation under Article 24(1) is wider in two respects than that under the common law rules.[91] First, Article 24(1) is not confined to proceedings raising the issue of the title to, or the right to possession of, foreign immovables. The provision has been widely interpreted to encompass, for example, a simple action for unpaid rent in respect of a villa in Italy.[92] Secondly, apart from the case of short-term lets,[93] there are no exceptions to the limitation contained in Article 24(1). It follows that English courts will not be able to take jurisdiction, for example, in a case involving fraud or unconscionable conduct[94] if Article 24(1) is applicable. However, if the matter affecting the foreign land only arises incidentally, the proceedings will not come within Article 24(1) since they will not have rights in rem "as their object";[95] English courts will, accordingly, be able to take jurisdiction in such a case, as they can do at common law.[96]

What if Article 24(1) is not applicable as, for example, in a case where there is a dispute over the title to land in a non-European Union/EFTA State, such as New York? Can the exclusion in the *Moçambique* case be used to deny jurisdiction to English courts? In cases where the traditional bases of jurisdiction apply, clearly it can. But what if jurisdiction has been allocated to the United Kingdom under the Brussels/Lugano system[97] (eg the defendant is domiciled in the United Kingdom)? Articles 33 and 34 of the Brussels I Regulation Recast[98] allow the courts of European Union States to stay their proceedings, under certain conditions, if parallel or related proceedings are already pending in a non-European Union State. Recital 24 clarifies that, when deciding whether to stay their proceedings in such cases, the courts of the Member States may take into account, *inter alia*, "the question whether the court of the third State has exclusive jurisdiction in the particular case in circumstances where a court of a Member State would have exclusive jurisdiction". Thus if proceedings which have as their object rights in rem in, or tenancies of, immoveable property situated in New York are already pending in that state, English courts may stay any subsequent parallel or related proceedings which have been commenced in England. The basis for doing so is not the exclusion in the *Moçambique* case, but an express rule of the Brussels I Regulation Recast. But the Recast does not expressly allow the courts of the Member States to stay their proceedings where the court of a non-European Union State "has exclusive jurisdiction in the particular case in circumstances where a court of a Member State would have exclusive jurisdiction" if there are no prior parallel or related proceedings pending in that third State. The question arises whether the exclusion in the *Moçambique* case can be used to deny jurisdiction to English courts in this situation? The same question arises in cases where jurisdiction has been allocated to the

---

[90] *Pearce v Ove Arup Partnership Ltd* [1999] 1 All ER 769 at 793, CA. The Civil Jurisdiction and Judgments Act 1982, s 30 is also subject to the Brussels I Regulation Recast, the Lugano and Brussels Conventions and the Modified Regulation; see s 30(2) and the Civil Jurisdiction and Judgments Order, SI 2001/3929 Sch 2(IV), para 13.

[91] See *Stevens v Hamed* [2013] EWCA Civ 911 at [15]–[16], [2013] IL Pr 37, which suggests that the limitations under the Brussels/Lugano system and the common law should be aligned.

[92] See Case 241/83 *Rösler v Rottwinkel* [1985] ECR 99, discussed supra, pp 222–4.

[93] Art 24(1) of the Brussels I Regulation Recast; Art 22(1) of the Lugano Convention; Art 16(1)(b) of the Brussels Convention. This provision is, in substance, worded in the same way in the first two instruments but differently in the third instrument, supra, pp 222–4 and 312.

[94] See supra, p 488 for the common law position.

[95] Case 115/88 *Reichert v Dresdner Bank* [1990] ECR I-27, particularly at 35 (per the Advocate General).

[96] See supra, p 488.

[97] Supra, pp 216–302.

[98] See supra, pp 457–9. There are no equivalent rules under the Lugano and Brussels Conventions.

United Kingdom under the Lugano Convention or the Brussels Convention. Jurisdiction probably should not be denied on the basis of the exclusion contained in the *Moçambique* case.[99] The wording of Article 4 of the Brussels I Regulation Recast (Article 2 of the Lugano and Brussels Conventions) is mandatory and not optional.[100] In addition, the application by the English courts of the exclusion contained in the *Moçambique* case would undermine one of the objectives of the Recast, namely the uniform application of the rules contained in the Recast,[101] unless it can be shown that all the other Member States operate the same rule.[102] Moreover, an English court should not use its discretionary powers to stay the proceedings on the basis that New York is the appropriate forum for trial.[103] However, there are worrying indications that English courts are prepared to continue to use discretionary powers when they should not do so. Colman J has said, obiter, that discretionary powers to stay the English proceedings can still be used in a case involving an agreement providing for jurisdiction in a non-European Union State[104] and his reasoning indicates that in his view a discretionary power to stay would also still operate in a case where there is a dispute over land in a non-Member State.[105] This could spill over into continued use of the non-discretionary exclusionary rule contained in the *Moçambique* case. Rather than use this rule or *forum non conveniens*, a safer way for refusing to try the case would be to argue that jurisdiction can be declined by giving "reflexive" effect to Article 24(1).[106]

(b) Foreign intellectual property rights[107]

Although it had been initially assumed in England that the exception in the *Moçambique* case had been confined to cases involving foreign *immovable* property, in *Tyburn Productions Ltd v Conan Doyle*[108] Vinelott J applied the *Moçambique* case to exclude actions relating to

---

[99] See, however, for suggestions to the contrary: Droz, paras 165–9; Dicey, Morris and Collins, para 23-028; note by AM 1987 SLT 52; Briggs 2015, para 2.308; *Lucasfilm Ltd v Ainsworth* [2009] EWCA Civ 1328 at [103]–[134], [2010] Ch 503; the Supreme Court expressed no view on this issue in [2011] UKSC 39, [2012] 1 AC 208.

[100] Case 281/02 *Owusu v Jackson* [2005] ECR I-1383, discussed supra, pp 462–4. This was concerned with the discretionary doctrine of *forum non conveniens* but much of the reasoning of the ECJ would apply equally to the subject matter limitation on jurisdiction in the *Moçambique* case.

[101] See the reasoning in the *Owusu* case, supra, pp 462–4.

[102] France has no such rule.

[103] Supra, p 467. All the reasoning in the *Owusu* case applies in this situation.

[104] See *Konkola Copper Mines plc v Coromin* [2005] EWHC 898 (Comm), [2005] 2 Lloyd's Rep 555; affd [2006] EWCA Civ 5, [2006] 1 Lloyd's Rep 410 but with no appeal on this point, criticised supra, pp 467–8; cf *Catalyst Investment Group Ltd v Lewinsohn* [2009] EWHC 1964 (Ch), [2010] 2 WLR 839; *Goshawk Dedicated Ltd v Life Receivables Ireland Ltd* [2008] IEHC 90.

[105] See Coleman J's reliance on *Arkwright Mutual Insurance Co v Bryanston Insurance Co Ltd* [1990] 2 QB 649 at 663, a pre-*Owusu* case, which should now be regarded as wrong.

[106] Supra, pp 473–5. See *Ferrexpo AG v Gilson Investments Ltd* [2012] EWHC 721 (Comm), [2012] 1 Lloyd's Rep 588—the court gave "reflexive" effect to Art 22(2) and (3) of the Brussels I Regulation (Art 24(2) and (3) of the Brussels I Regulation Recast) and stayed proceedings brought against English domiciliaries in relation to a dispute regarding ownership of shares in a company from a non-European Union/EFTA State; Crawford and Carruthers (2013) 17 Edin LR 78; Goodwin (2013) 129 LQR 317; De Verneuil Smit, Lasserson and Rymkiewicz (2012) 8 J Priv Int L 389; see also *Blue Tropic Ltd v Chkhartishvili* [2014] EWHC 2243 (Ch) at [18], [2014] ILPr 33; *Plaza BV v Law Debenture Trust Corp Plc* [2015] EWHC 43 (Ch) ("reflexive" effect of what are now Arts 25(1) and 30 of the Brussels I Regulation Recast).

[107] Trooboff in McLachlan and Nygh, Chapter 8; Austin (1997) 113 LQR 321; Fentiman [1997] CLJ 503; Fawcett and Torremans, pp 298–316; Lipstein [2002] CLJ 295.

[108] [1991] Ch 75; Arnold [1990] 7 EIPR 254; Carter (1990) 61 BYBIL 400; following the High Court of Australia's decisions in *Potter v Broken Hill Pty Co Ltd* (1906) 3 CLR 479; *Steinhardt & Son Ltd v Meth* (1961) 105 CLR 440. See also *Atkinson Footwear Ltd v Hodgskin* (1995) 31 IPR 186, NZHC; *Gallo Africa Ltd v Sting Music (Pty) Ltd* 2010 (6) SA 329, Sup Ct of Appeal of South Africa; cf *KK Sony Computer Entertainment v Van Veen* (2006) 71 IPR 179, NZHC.

foreign intellectual property rights.[109] The historical distinction between *local* and *transitory* actions was resurrected. Any question of validity of title to, or infringement of,[110] a foreign copyright, patent or trade mark was a local one for the courts of the country by whose law the copyright, patent or trade mark was created, such rights being territorially limited to that country. It followed that the question raised in the case, namely whether the defendant was entitled to copyright under the law of the USA, was not justiciable in the English courts. This misunderstands the *Moçambique* case, which was decided on a point of substance as to whether an English court could give an effective judgment and not on the basis of a procedural distinction between *local* and *transitory* actions.[111]

Moreover, policy considerations for and against having such a limitation on jurisdiction were ignored.[112] The Court of Appeal in *Pearce v Ove Arup Partnership Ltd*[113] has said, in effect, that the views of Vinelott J should be confined to the facts of the case before him, ie a case where a declaration was sought and the issue was as to the existence and validity of the right, and that the *Tyburn* decision is of little or no assistance in the different situation where there is an action for infringement abroad of a foreign intellectual property right, the existence and validity of which are not in issue. However, the Court of Appeal found it unnecessary to decide whether such an action was justiciable in the English courts. Nor was *Tyburn* thought to be helpful in a case where it was held that the court in the exercise of its equitable in personam jurisdiction could order a person, who had acquired intellectual property situated abroad with sufficient notice of an earlier obligation to transfer the property to another, to assign that property to its equitable owner, provided that the English equity was not extinguished by foreign law. This was especially so where the original contract was governed by English law and the rights existed in manifold jurisdictions.[114] There were two other cases, decided at first instance, which supported the abolition of the limitation on jurisdiction in relation to the infringement of foreign intellectual property rights whose existence and validity had not been in question.[115]

But this welcome development was brought in question by the Court of Appeal in *Lucasfilm Ltd v Ainsworth*,[116] which held that there was a subject matter limitation in relation to infringement of a foreign, non-European Union (or Lugano) copyright. Although Jacob LJ's conclusion on non-justiciability only referred to copyrights, the judge also said that "there are good reasons for holding that foreign intellectual property rights, registered or not, should not be justiciable [in England]".[117] This case went to the Supreme Court, which has now settled the question.[118]

---

[109] Such rights are not classified as immovable property, accordingly s 30 of the 1982 Act does not apply: *Coin Controls Ltd v Suzo International (UK) Ltd* [1999] Ch 33; *Pearce v Ove Arup Partnership Ltd* [1997] Ch 293, (Lloyd J), appeal allowed on a different point [2000] Ch 403, CA; *R Griggs Group Ltd v Evans* [2004] EWHC 1088 (Ch) at [119], [2005] Ch 153; Fawcett and Torremans, pp 295–8, 301–2.

[110] For doubts over what Vinelott J decided in relation to infringement see *Lucasfilm Ltd v Ainsworth* [2009] EWCA Civ 1328, [2010] Ch 503.

[111] Supra, pp 484–5.

[112] Fawcett and Torremans, pp 308–12.

[113] [2000] Ch 403, CA; Briggs (1999) 70 BYBIL 337; Harris [1999] LMCLQ 360.

[114] *R Griggs Group Ltd v Evans* [2004] EWHC 1088 (Ch) at [139]–[140], [2005] Ch 153.

[115] *Satyam Computer Services Ltd v Unpaid Systems Ltd* [2008] EWHC 31 (Comm), [2008] Il Pr 29, appeal dismissed without discussion of the limitation point [2008] EWCA Civ 487, [2008] 2 All ER (Comm) 465; Briggs (2008) 79 BYBIL 537; *Lucasfilm Ltd v Ainsworth* [2008] EWHC 1878 (Ch), [2009] FSR 2.

[116] [2009] EWCA Civ 1328 at [138], [2010] Ch 503, distinguished in *Crosstown Music Co I LLC v Rive Droit Music Ltd* [2010] EWCA Civ 1222, [2012] Ch 68.

[117] Ibid, at [148].

[118] [2011] UKSC 39, [2012] 1 AC 208; Rushworth and Scott (2011) 81 BYBIL 641; Dickinson [2012] LMCLQ 21; Pila (2012) 128 LQR 15.

The defendant in *Lucasfilm Ltd v Ainsworth* was skilled in vacuum-moulding in plastic. He made the Imperial Stormtrooper helmet for the claimants to be used as a part of a costume for the Star Wars films. Subsequently, the defendant began producing replicas of the helmet for sale to the public, some of which were sold to buyers in the USA. The claimants brought proceedings in England for infringement of English and US copyright law.

The Supreme Court allowed the appeal on the jurisdictional issue and held that the exclusionary rule did not apply to a claim for infringement of a foreign copyright. Since there are no policy considerations which militated against the enforcement of foreign copyright and there is an interest in the international recognition and enforcement of copyrights, the Supreme Court held that the *Tyburn* decision was wrongly decided. Consequently, the claim in the *Lucasfilm* case, which was about the ownership and infringement of a foreign copyright rather than about its existence and validity, was justiciable.

What is now clear is that in cases where jurisdiction is based on the Brussels/Lugano system there is no limitation in relation to the infringement of foreign intellectual property rights,[119] at least where invalidity is not raised as a defence and these rights are created in a European Union/EFTA State and probably also even where they are created outside such a State.[120] In cases where jurisdiction is based on the traditional English rules, it is also clear that there is no limitation on jurisdiction in relation to the infringement of a foreign copyright. What is less clear is whether the decision of the Supreme Court in the *Lucasfilm* case extends to actions involving either the infringement of foreign intellectual property rights other than copyright or the validity of foreign intellectual property rights. It is submitted that the answer is in the affirmative. It is understandable that judges should be reluctant to decide whether a person has infringed a foreign patent and other intellectual property right dependent on the grant or authority of a foreign state or whether a foreign intellectual property right is a valid one,[121] but it is always possible for a stay of the proceedings to be granted using the doctrine of *forum non conveniens*.[122] An inflexible blanket limitation on jurisdiction is both unnecessary and undesirable.

3. JURISDICTION OVER THE PARTIES

(a) Persons who cannot invoke the jurisdiction

The one person precluded from suing in an English court is an alien enemy. Before a person can bear this character there must, of course, be a state of war between the United Kingdom and an enemy country at the time of the attempted proceedings, and whether the countries are still at war despite the cessation of hostilities is conclusively settled by a certificate from the Secretary of State for Foreign and Commonwealth Affairs.[123] Given a state of war, however, the question whether a person is an alien enemy does not depend on his nationality but

---

[119] *Fort Dodge Animal Health Ltd v Akzo Nobel NV* [1998] FSR 222, CA; Dutson [1998] LMCLQ 505; *Coin Controls Ltd v Suzo International (UK) Ltd* [1999] Ch 33; *Pearce v Ove Arup Partnership Ltd* [2000] Ch 403, CA; Fawcett and Torremans, pp 213–8; supra, p 225.

[120] Fawcett and Torremans, pp 218–21; Briggs (1997) 113 LQR 364 at 366; Dutson (1997) 46 ICLQ 918 at 921; cf *Lucasfilm Ltd v Ainsworth* [2009] EWCA Civ 1328 at [103]–[134], [2010] Ch 503; the Supreme Court expressed no view on this issue in [2011] UKSC 39, [2012] 1 AC 208.

[121] See *Plastus Kreativ AB v Minnesota Mining and Manufacturing Co* [1995] RPC 438.

[122] While Mance J in *Lucasfilm Ltd v Ainsworth* [2008] EWHC 1878 (Ch) at [269], [2009] FSR 2 saw the doctrine of *forum non conveniens* as the appropriate vehicle for dealing with actions relating to foreign intellectual property rights, the Court of Appeal took a different view on appeal [2009] EWCA Civ 1328 at [185], [2010] Ch 503.

[123] *R v Bottrill* [1947] KB 41, CA; *Amin v Brown* [2005] EWHC 1670 (Ch), [2006] IL Pr 5.

on where he resides or carries on business. A British subject or a neutral who is voluntarily resident, or who is carrying on business, in enemy territory or in territory under the effective control of the enemy is treated as an alien enemy and is in the same position as a subject of hostile nationality resident in hostile territory.[124] A person of hostile nationality who is within the Queen's peace, as, for example, when he is resident in England under a cartel[125] or by permission of the Crown,[126] is temporarily free from his enemy character and may invoke the jurisdiction.[127] An alien enemy can neither initiate an action nor continue one that was commenced before hostilities.[128] The disability of suing is based on public policy, but there are no considerations of public policy that make it desirable to suspend actions *against* alien enemies, and it is now well established that they may be sued.[129] Moreover, when sued they can plead a set-off in diminution of the claim of the claimant; they can take all the usual procedural steps, and they are at liberty to challenge an adverse judgment by appealing to a higher tribunal.[130]

(b) Persons who may claim exemption from the jurisdiction[131]

(i) Sovereigns and sovereign states[132]

The basic rule at common law was that a foreign sovereign or sovereign foreign state was immune from the jurisdiction of the English courts, though the court would take jurisdiction if the sovereign submitted thereto. This immunity extended both to direct actions against the sovereign and to indirect actions involving his property. However, this whole question was the subject of the European Convention on State Immunity (1972)[133] which led to the law being placed on a statutory basis by the State Immunity Act 1978.[134] Legislative authority for

---

[124] *Porter v Freudenberg* [1915] 1 KB 857 at 869, CA; *Sovracht (vo) v Van Udens Scheepvart en Agentuur Maatschappij (NV Gebr)* [1943] AC 203, HL. See McNair (1942) 58 LQR 191. For the purposes of the Trading with the Enemy Act 1939, which penalises persons trading with the enemy, *de facto* residence, though not voluntary, is sufficient: *Vamvakas v Custodian of Enemy Property* [1952] 2 QB 183.

[125] *The Hoop* (1799) 1 Ch Rob 196 at 201, 165 ER 146.

[126] Eg when he was registered under the Aliens Restriction Act 1914: *Princess Thurn and Taxis v Moffit* [1915] 1 Ch 58; *Schaffenius v Goldberg* [1916] 1 KB 284, CA.

[127] *Johnstone v Pedlar* [1921] 2 AC 262, HL.

[128] *Porter v Freudenberg* [1915] 1 KB 857, CA. An alien enemy, respondent to a petition for the revocation of a patent, has been allowed, however, to amend his specification by way of disclaimer, since this constitutes a defence to the petition: *Re Stahlwerk Becker Aktiengesellschaft's Patent* [1917] 2 Ch 272. His right of action is generally abrogated, but sometimes merely suspended; see *Ertel Bieber & Co v Rio Tinto Co* [1918] AC 260, HL; *Schering Ltd v Stockholms Enskilda Bank Aktiebolag* [1946] AC 219, HL.

[129] *Robinson & Co v Continental Insurance Co of Mannheim* [1915] 1 KB 155; *Porter v Freudenberg* [1915] 1 KB 857, CA.

[130] *Porter v Freudenberg* [1915] 1 KB 857, CA.

[131] See Fox and Webb, *The Law of State Immunity* (2013) 3rd edn; Lewis, *State and Diplomatic Immunity* (1989) 3rd edn; McLachlan, *Foreign Relations Law* (2014), Chapter 10; Yang, *State Immunity in International Law* (2015); Sinclair (1980) II Hague Recueil 114; Trooboff (1986) V Hague Recueil 235; Watts (1994) III Hague Recueil 13; Marasinghe (1991) 54 MLR 664.

[132] We are concerned here with recognised states. On the question whether an unrecognised state can sue or be sued in an English court, see *Gur Corpn v Trust Bank of Africa Ltd* [1987] QB 599, CA; Warbrick (1987) 50 MLR 84; Mann (1987) 36 ICLQ 348; *R (on the application of Kibris Turk Hava Yollari) v Secretary of State for Transport* [2009] EWHC 1918 (Admin), [2010] 1 All ER (Comm) 253. On the recognition of a foreign regime as the government of a state, see *Republic of Somalia v Woodhouse Drake & Carey (Suisse) SA* [1993] QB 54; Kingsbury (1993) 109 LQR 377; Leslie [1997] Jur Rev 110; Crawford [1993] CLJ 4; *Sierra Leone Telecommunications Co Ltd v Barclays Bank plc* [1998] 2 All ER 821; *British Arab Commercial Bank Plc v National Transitional Council of Libya* [2011] EWHC 2274 (Comm); Warbrick (2012) 61 ICLQ 247.

[133] Cmnd 5081; Sinclair (1973) 22 ICLQ 254; Mann (1973) 36 MLR 18.

[134] See Bowett [1978] CLJ 193; White (1979) 42 MLR 72; Mann (1979) 50 BYBIL 43; Delaume (1979) 73 AJIL 185; Lewis [1980] LMCLQ 1. For similar legislation abroad see Foreign States Immunities Act 1981 (South Africa); Foreign Sovereign Immunities Act 1976 (USA); State Immunity Act 1982 (Canada); Foreign States Immunities Act 1985 (Australia). See, though, for New Zealand, where the common law still applies: *Governor of Pitcairn v Sutton* [1995] 1 NZLR 426, NZCA; *Controller and Auditor-General v Davison*

immunity is essential.[135] An argument that the European Union should have an independent claim to sovereign immunity by analogy to a foreign state has been rejected because of the lack of legislative authority for this.[136] When a question of immunity arises under the 1978 Act this must be tried as a preliminary issue before the substantive action can proceed.[137] Before turning to the provisions of the 1978 Act, it must be mentioned that there is now a United Nations Convention on State Immunity.[138] This Convention has not yet entered into force. The United Kingdom signed this Convention on 30 September 2005, but has not ratified it. Related to this is the question whether ratification would require amendment to the 1978 Act. In the meantime, the Convention is regarded by the English courts as powerfully demonstrating international thinking on state immunity.[139]

(a) Scope of the State Immunity Act 1978

The immunity conferred by the 1978 Act is not limited to those states which are parties to the 1972 Convention but is world-wide in effect.[140] It applies to any foreign or Commonwealth state, other than the United Kingdom, to the sovereign or other head of that state[141] in his public capacity,[142] to the government of that state and to any department thereof.[143] An official or agent of a foreign state enjoys state immunity *ratione materiae* in respect of his acts of a sovereign or governmental nature.[144] Applying this principle, there is an absolute right to

---

[1996] 2 NZLR 278, NZCA. The 1978 Act also implements the provisions of the 1926 Brussels Convention on Immunity of State-owned Ships, together with the Protocol thereto of 1934.

[135] For a case where the immunity of the defendant under the foreign law applicable to the claim operated to prevent action against the defendant in England, see *Kontic v Ministry of Defence* [2016] EWHC 2034 (QB).

[136] *J H Rayner (Mincing Lane) Ltd v Department of Trade and Industry* [1989] Ch 72 at 198–203, 223, 252–3, CA; affd [1990] 2 AC 418, 516, HL without deciding this point.

[137] Ibid, at 194, 252; affd by HL without deciding this point. The trial should be public: *Harb v Aziz* [2005] EWCA Civ 632, [2005] 2 FLR 1108. See also *Al Attiya v Bin-Jassim Bin-Jaber Al Thani* [2016] EWHC 212 (QB).

[138] United Nations Convention on Jurisdictional Immunities of States and Their Property of 2004; O'Keefe, Tams and Tzanakopoulos, *United Nations Convention on Jurisdictional Immunities of States and Their Property: A Commentary* (2013); Denza (2006) 55 ICLQ 395; Fox (2006) 55 ICLQ 399; Gardiner (2006) 55 ICLQ 407. Criticised by Hall (2006) 55 ICLQ 411; McGregor (2006) 55 ICLQ 437. The International Law Commission produced in 2001 draft articles on the Responsibility of States for Internationally Wrongful Acts.

[139] *Jones v Ministry of the Interior of the Kingdom of Saudi Arabia* [2006] UKHL 26 at [8], [2007] 1 AC 270, following *AIG Capital Partners Inc v Republic of Kazakhstan* [2005] EWHC 2239 (Comm) at [80], [2006] 1 WLR 1420; *NML Capital Ltd v Argentina* [2011] UKSC 31 at [126], [2011] 2 AC 495. Cf *Belhaj v Straw* [2017] UKSC 3 at [25]–[26], [2017] 2 WLR 456.

[140] For the provisions as to recognition of foreign judgments see, infra, pp 601–2.

[141] For proposals for reform, see the Resolution of the Institute of International Law of 2001 on "The Immunities from Jurisdiction and Execution of Heads of State and Heads of Government in International Law", on which see Fox (2002) 51 ICLQ 119.

[142] A sovereign, or head of state, when acting outside his public capacity, is entitled to immunity under the Diplomatic Privileges Act 1964 (infra, pp 509–10) with some modifications: 1978 Act, s 20(1)(a); *BCCI v Price Waterhouse* [1997] 4 All ER 108; Hopkins [1998] CLJ 4; *Harb v Aziz* [2005] EWCA Civ 632, [2005] 2 FLR 1108; *Aziz v Aziz* [2007] EWCA Civ 712 at [57], [2008] 2 All ER 501.

[143] 1978 Act, s 14(1). For the immunity of a department see *Jones v Ministry of the Interior of the Kingdom of Saudi Arabia* [2006] UKHL 26, [2007] 1 AC 270.

[144] *Propend Finance Pty Ltd v Sing* (1997) 111 ILR 611, CA; *Jones v Ministry of the Interior of the Kingdom of Saudi Arabia* [2006] UKHL 26, [2007] 1 AC 270 and *Jones v United Kingdom*, Judgment of 14 January 2014; (2014) 59 EHRR 1, ECtHR, discussed infra, p 502; *Grovit v De Nederlandsche Bank* [2005] EWHC 2944 (QB), [2006] 1 WLR 3323; affd by the Court of Appeal without any discussion of the state immunity point [2007] EWCA Civ 953, [2008] 1 WLR 51; *Ogelegbanwei v Nigeria* [2016] EWHC 8 (QB); *Re P (Diplomatic Immunity: Jurisdiction)* [1998] 1 FLR 1026. See also *Walker (Litigation Guardian of) v Bank of New York* (1994) 111 DLR (4th) 186, Ont CA; *Jaffe v Miller* (1993) 103 DLR (4th) 315, Ont CA. See also Art 2(1)(b)(iv) of the UN Convention of 2004. For the immunity of an official at common law see *Holland v Lampen-Wolfe* [2000] 1 WLR 1573, HL. See further Douglas (2011) 82 BYBIL 281.

claim immunity, even in respect of civil claims against state officials for systematic torture committed outside the country of suit.[145] Provision is made for the application of the Act by Order in Council to the constituent territories of a federal state.[146] This is because such constituent territories do not automatically enjoy immunity under the 1972 Convention but only if the federal state so declares.[147] A difficult question before the passing of the 1978 Act was to determine whether a state corporation such as a state bank, or the US Shipping Board, could properly claim to be an emanation of the foreign state and thus entitled to immunity.[148] This problem is dealt with in the 1978 Act through the use of the concept of "a separate entity".[149] Such an entity, being distinct from the executive organs of the government of the foreign state and being capable of suing or being sued, is not entitled to immunity unless the proceedings relate to something done by the "separate entity" in the exercise of sovereign authority and the circumstances were such that the state would have been immune.[150] The question of when a "separate entity" is exercising sovereign authority came before the House of Lords[151] where it was held that this term refers to the common law concept of *acta jure imperii*,[152] and that Iraqi Airways was so acting when it removed aircraft from Kuwait following the Iraqi invasion. The airline was closely involved with the State of Iraq in the last stage of an enterprise which entailed both the seizure and removal of the aircraft.[153] However, the subsequent retention and use of the aircraft did not amount to so acting, even though this was done in consequence of a legislative decree vesting the aircraft in the airline.[154] Indeed, once this decree was passed the situation changed, and the acts of Iraqi Airways were no longer in the exercise of sovereign authority but were commercial acts. In subsequent proceedings, it was held that perjured evidence had been given to the House of Lords and that Iraqi Airways had even earlier than this done acts which were no longer in the exercise of

---

[145] The *Jones* case. See also obiter dicta in *R v Bow Street Magistrate, ex p Pinochet (No 3)* [2000] 1 AC 147, 264 (per Lord Hutton), 278 (per Lord Millett), 280–1 (per Lord Phillips), HL. The human rights concerns involved are discussed infra, pp 501–3. See generally Fox [2006] EHRLR 142. For the position where extradition of a former head of state is sought for criminal offences of torture, see *R v Bow Street Magistrate, ex p Pinochet (No 1)* [2000] 1 AC 61, HL; *R v Bow Street Magistrate, ex p Pinochet (No 3)* [2000] 1 AC 147, HL; for the position where extradition of a state official or agent is sought see *Bat v Germany* [2011] EWHC 2029 (Admin), [2013] QB 349.

[146] 1978 Act, s 14(5); SI 1979/457; SI 1993/2809. For the situation where an order has not been made, see s 14(6); *BCCI v Price Waterhouse* [1997] 4 All ER 108; *Pocket Kings Ltd v Safenames Ltd* [2009] EWHC 2529 (Ch), [2010] Ch. 438; *Pearl Petroleum Co Ltd v Kurdistan Regional Government of Iraq* [2015] EWHC 3361 (Comm), [2016] 4 WLR 2.

[147] Art 28, see Sinclair (1973) 22 ICLQ 254, 279–80.

[148] *Trendtex Trading Corpn v Central Bank of Nigeria* [1977] QB 529, CA; *C Czarnikow Ltd v Rolimpex* [1979] AC 351, HL; *I Congreso del Partido* [1983] 1 AC 244 at 258, HL.

[149] This probably refers to a "separate entity" of a state: *Kuwait Airways Corpn v Iraqi Airways Co* [1995] 1 WLR 1147 at 1158, HL. See also *Wilhelm Finance Inc v Ente Administrador Del Astillero Rio Santiago* [2009] EWHC 1074 (Comm), [2009] 1 CLC 867; *The Altair* [2008] EWHC 612 (Comm), [2008] 2 Lloyd's Rep 90.

[150] 1978 Act, ss 14(1), (2). Employees of the separate entity are also entitled to immunity, subject to the same provisos: *Grovit v De Nederlandsche Bank* [2005] EWHC 2944 (QB), [2006] 1 WLR 3323; affd by the Court of Appeal without any discussion of the state immunity point [2007] EWCA Civ 953, [2008] 1 WLR 51. See also *La Generale des Carrieres et des Mines v FG Hemisphere Associates LLC* [2012] UKPC 27, [2013] 1 All ER 409 where the test from the 1978 Act, ss 14(1), (2) was used for the purposes of liability and enforcement of debts under arbitral awards.

[151] *Kuwait Airways Corpn v Iraqi Airways Co* [1995] 1 WLR 1147; Fox (1996) 112 LQR 186; reversing in part [1995] 1 Lloyd's Rep 25, CA; Staker (1994) 66 BYBIL 496; Fox (1994) 110 LQR 199; Marks [1994] CLJ 213; Talmon (1995) 15 OJLS 295; for criticism of the first instance decision of Evans J denying immunity, see Fox (1994) 43 ICLQ 193 at 196.

[152] The *Kuwait Airways* case at 1156.

[153] Ibid, at 1163.

[154] Lords Mustill and Slynn dissenting. For the subsequent conversion action see *Kuwait Airways Corpn v Iraqi Airways Co (Nos 4 and 5)* [2002] UKHL 19, [2002] 2 AC 883.

sovereign authority, namely engaging in the process of the absorption of the Kuwaiti aircraft into the Iraqi Airways fleet by registration, repainting and insurance of some of the aircraft with a view to their subsequent commercial use.[155] More recently, a state's central bank was held by the Court of Appeal to have acted in the exercise of sovereign authority when it had exported some gold, which had been deposited by the claimant for safe custody and sale on certain terms, to a refinery and then placed it in a bank in London with the purpose of increasing the state's currency reserves.[156] In two other recent cases[157] the High Court held that the defendants, constituent territories of two federal states to which the 1978 Act had not been extended by Order in Council, were not states for the purposes of the Act; being "separate entities" within the meaning of the Act, the defendants were not entitled to state immunity because they had exercised they own authority and not the sovereign authority of the federal states.

Part I of the 1978 Act (proceedings in the United Kingdom by or against other states) does not apply to proceedings relating to anything done by or in relation to the armed forces of another state whilst present in the United Kingdom.[158] In such cases immunity depends upon common law principles, including the one referred to above, namely that a foreign sovereign is only entitled to immunity in respect of acts within the sphere of sovereign activity, ie *acta jure imperii*.[159] There is no single test for determining this. It requires consideration of the whole of the context in which the claimant's claim was made.[160] Relevant factors can include where the act happened, whom it involved and what kind of act it was (ie whether it was wholly military or primarily private or commercial).[161] After considering these factors it was held that the US Government was immune from suit in an action for personal injury brought by a US serviceman who was treated at a US military hospital in England, the operation of which was required for the maintenance of the US armed forces in the United Kingdom.[162] Similarly, there was immunity from suit in an action for defamation brought by a US citizen, a civilian instructor at a US military base in England, against another US citizen, who was a civilian education services officer at the base, the provision within a military base of education for military personnel being part of a state's sovereign function of maintaining its armed forces.[163]

The basic principle of the 1978 Act is that a foreign state is immune from the jurisdiction[164] of the English courts and effect is to be given to that immunity whether or not the state appears in the proceedings.[165]

---

[155] *Kuwait Airways Corpn v Iraqi Airways Co (No 11)* [2003] EWHC 31, [2003] 1 Lloyd's Rep 448. This separate fraud action follows *Kuwait Airways Corpn v Iraqi Airways Co (No 8) (Petition for Variation of Order)* [2001] 1 WLR 429, HL.

[156] *KOO Golden East Mongolia v Bank of Nova Scotia* [2007] EWCA Civ 1443, [2008] QB 717.

[157] *Pocket Kings Ltd v Safenames Ltd* [2009] EWHC 2529 (Ch), [2010] Ch. 438; *Pearl Petroleum Co Ltd v Kurdistan Regional Government of Iraq* [2015] EWHC 3361 (Comm), [2016] 4 WLR 2.

[158] The 1978 Act, s 16(2).

[159] *Littrell v United States of America (No 2)* [1995] 1 WLR 82, CA; Staker (1994) 66 BYBIL 491; Collier [1995] CLJ 7; applied in *Holland v Lampen-Wolfe* [2000] 1 WLR 1573, HL.

[160] The *Littrell v United States of America (No 2)* case, at 95 (per Hoffmann LJ).

[161] Ibid.

[162] Ibid.

[163] *Holland v Lampen-Wolfe* [2000] 1 WLR 1573, HL; Tomonori (2001) 64 MLR 472; Yang [2001] CLJ 17. The immunity was claimed by the USA on behalf of the defendant.

[164] This includes English proceedings for recognition of a foreign judgment against a foreign state granted in that state: *AIC Ltd v Federal Government of Nigeria* [2003] EWHC 1357 (QB).

[165] 1978 Act, s 1. See *Mauritius Tourism Promotion Authority v Wong Min*, 24 November 2008, EAT—a court is under a duty when state immunity issues arise to consider the position carefully and make appropriate enquiries to satisfy itself that it can properly exercise jurisdiction.

(b) State immunity and human rights[166]

The European Court of Human Rights (ECtHR) in *Al-Adsani v United Kingdom* has accepted that, in cases of sovereign immunity, the right of access to a court under Article 6(1) of the European Convention on Human Rights is engaged.[167] It follows that, to be compatible with Article 6(1), the limitation on jurisdiction under the doctrine of sovereign immunity has to pursue a legitimate aim and be proportionate.[168] The ECtHR considered the application of these criteria in the context of a civil claim against the State of Kuwait alleging torture in that state. A majority of the ECtHR said that "the grant of sovereign immunity to a State in civil proceedings pursues the legitimate aim of complying with international law to promote comity and good relations between States through the respect of another State's sovereignty".[169] Moreover, the restriction is proportionate to the aim pursued since state immunity reflects "a generally accepted rule of international law".[170] The majority of the ECtHR concluded that the use of state immunity, even in these circumstances, does not constitute an unjustified restriction on the claimant's right of access to the courts as laid down by Article 6(1).[171] This confirms the correctness of an earlier decision of the Court of Appeal that state immunity applies even where the sovereign acts outside the law of nations by violating fundamental human rights by torturing prisoners.[172] According to the ECtHR in *McElhinney v Ireland*, neither was there a breach of Article 6(1) where state immunity was used to deny access to the Irish courts in a case involving a civil claim in tort brought against the British government following acts by its agent (a soldier) within the sphere of *de jure imperii*.[173] The same Court in *Fogarty v United Kingdom* decided that there was no breach of Article 6(1) where state immunity was used to deny access to the English courts in a case involving a civil claim for discrimination brought against the US government by an applicant for re-employment at the US embassy.[174]

---

[166] Fawcett, Ní Shúilleabháin and Shah, *Human Rights and Private International Law* (2016), paras 6.244–6.279; Kloth, *Immunities and the Right of Access to Court under Article 6 of the European Convention on Human Rights* (2010); Garnett (2002) 118 LQR 367; Lloyd Jones (2003) 52 ICLQ 463; Voyiakis (2003) 52 ICLQ 297; Yang (2003) 74 BYBIL 333.

[167] Judgment of 21 November 2001 at [52]; (2001) 34 EHRR 273, ECtHR. See also *McElhinney v Ireland*, Judgment of 21 November 2001 at [26]; (2002) 34 EHRR 13, ECtHR; *Fogarty v United Kingdom*, Judgment of 21 November 2001 at [28]; (2002) 34 EHRR 12, ECtHR; App No 50021/00, *Kalogeropoulou v Greece and Germany*, 12 December 2002; *Cudak v Lithuania*, Judgment of 23 March 2010; (2010) 51 EHRR 15, ECtHR; *Sabeh El Leil v France*, Judgment of 29 June 2011; (2012) 54 EHRR 14, ECtHR; *Oleynikov v Russia*, Judgment of 14 March 2013; (2013) 57 EHRR 15, ECtHR; *Jones v United Kingdom*, Judgment of 14 January 2014; (2014) 59 EHRR 1, ECtHR.

[168] The *Al-Adsani* case, at [53]; following *Waite and Kennedy v Germany*, Judgment of 18 February 1999; (1999) 30 EHRR 261—immunity granted to an international organisation (the European Space Agency). See also *NCF and AG v Italy* (1995) 111 ILR 153, European Commission on Human Rights.

[169] The *Al-Adsani* case, at [54]. See also the *McElhinney* case, at [35]; the *Fogarty* case, at [34]; the *Jones* case, at [188].

[170] The *Al-Adsani* case, at [56]–[57]. See also the *McElhinney* case, at [35]–[40]; the *Fogarty* case, at [38]; the *Jones* case, at [189]; and *Holland v Lampen-Wolfe* [2000] 1 WLR 1573 at 1578–9 (per Lord Hope), 1581 (per Lord Clyde), HL; *Entico Corp Ltd v United Nations Educational Scientific and Cultural Association* [2008] EWHC 531 (Comm), [2008] 2 All ER (Comm) 97; *Al-Malki v Reyes* [2015] EWCA Civ 32, [2016] 1 WLR 1785, appeal pending; *Ogelegbanwei v Nigeria* [2016] EWHC 8 (QB). See further the decision of the International Court of Justice in *Jurisdictional Immunities of the State (Germany v Italy; Greece intervening)* 2012 ICJ Rep 99; Barker (2013) 62 ICLQ 741; Ranganathan (2015) 74 CLJ 16.

[171] The *Al-Adsani* case.

[172] *Al-Adsani v Government of Kuwait (No 2)* (1996) 107 ILR 536, CA; Fox (1994) 138 SJ 854.

[173] Judgment of 21 November 2001; (2002) 34 EHRR 13, ECtHR.

[174] Ibid, at 12, ECtHR.

The English courts in *Jones v Ministry of the Interior of the Kingdom of Saudi Arabia*[175] were faced with a more complex case than *Al-Adsani*. Following alleged torture abroad, civil claims for damages were brought against both a foreign state, the Kingdom of Saudi Arabia, and individual defendants who were officials of that state.[176] The House of Lords agreed with the Court of Appeal[177] that the Kingdom was entitled to immunity.[178] But, unlike the Court of Appeal,[179] it regarded the position of individual defendants as being the same as that of the Kingdom[180] with the result that immunity also applied in relation to the claims against the individual defendants. On a straightforward application of the State Immunity Act 1978, immunity would apply in relation both to the Kingdom and to the individual defendants.[181] The claimants argued that to apply the 1978 Act would be incompatible with the right of access to the English courts provided by Article 6. Their Lordships expressed doubts[182] as to the correctness of the unanimous decision of the ECtHR in *Al-Adsani* that Article 6 was engaged in a case of state immunity but were prepared to assume that it was.[183] The claimants sought to show that the restriction imposed by the law of State immunity was disproportionate by arguing that the proscription of torture by international law, having the authority of a peremptory norm,[184] precludes the grant of immunity to states or individuals sued for committing acts of torture since such acts cannot be governmental acts or exercises of state authority entitled to protection of state immunity *ratione materiae*.[185] The House of Lords was unable to accept that torture cannot be a governmental or official act.[186] Immunity under the 1978 Act was not disproportionate as inconsistent with a peremptory norm of international law and, accordingly, there was no infringement of the claimants' rights under Article 6.[187] The *Jones* case eventually went to the ECtHR, which confirmed that there had been no violation of Article 6(1).[188]

In a much easier case, immunity granted to employees of the Dutch Central Bank, who were sued, along with the Bank, for defamation, was not disproportionate where there was an effective remedy in the Netherlands and the gravity of the allegations against the defendants was much less than in the *Jones* case.[189]

---

[175] [2006] UKHL 26, [2007] 1 AC 270; Seymor (2006) 65 CLJ 479; Tomonori (2008) 71 MLR 734; Wright (2010) 30 OJLS 143. See also *Grovit v De Nederlandsche Bank* [2005] EWHC 2944 (QB), [2006] 1 WLR 3323; affd without discussion of the state immunity point [2007] EWCA Civ 953, [2008] 1 WLR 51; *Republic of Ecuador v Occidental Exploration and Production Co* [2005] EWCA Civ 1116 at [49], [2006] QB 432.

[176] Under the UN Convention on State Immunity it is unclear whether such a claim would attract immunity, see Art 6(2)(b).

[177] [2004] EWCA Civ 1394, [2005] QB 669; Fox (2005) 121 LQR 353 and (2006) EHRLR 142; Yang (2005) 64 CLJ 1. Distinguished in *Republic of Ecuador v Occidental Exploration and Production Co* [2005] EWCA Civ 1116 at [49], [2006] QB 432.

[178] [2006] UKHL 26 at [29] (per Lord Bingham), at [36] (per Lord Hoffmann), [2007] 1 AC 270. Lords Rodger at [103], Walker at [104] and Carswell at [105] concurred with these two speeches.

[179] [2004] EWCA Civ 1394 at [92], [2005] QB 669.

[180] [2006] UKHL 26 at [10]–[13] (per Lord Bingham), [66] (per Lord Hoffmann), [2007] 1 AC 270.

[181] Ibid, at [13] (per Lord Bingham). See also Lord Hoffmann at [66].

[182] Approving the obiter dicta of Lord Millett in *Holland v Lampen-Wolfe* [2000] 1 WLR 1573 at 1588, HL. Cf Mance LJ in the Court of Appeal in the *Jones* case, at [82].

[183] [2006] UKHL 26 at [14] (per Lord Bingham), [64] (per Lord Hoffmann), [2007] 1 AC 270.

[184] It was common ground that this was so, ibid, at [13] (per Lord Bingham).

[185] Ibid, at [17] (per Lord Bingham).

[186] [2006] UKHL 26 at [19], [27] (per Lord Bingham), at [85] (per Lord Hoffmann), [2007] 1 AC 270.

[187] Ibid, at [28] (per Lord Bingham).

[188] *Jones v United Kingdom*, Judgment of 14 January 2014; (2014) 59 EHRR 1, ECtHR, applying *Jurisdictional Immunities of the State (Germany v Italy; Greece intervening)* 2012 ICJ Rep 99.

[189] *Grovit v De Nederlandsche Bank* [2005] EWHC 2944 (QB), [2006] 1 WLR 3323; affd without discussion of the state immunity point [2007] EWCA Civ 953, [2008] 1 WLR 51. See also *Holland v Lampen-Wolfe* [2000] 1 WLR 1573 at 1578–9 (per Lord Hope), 1581 (per Lord Clyde), HL.

In *Benkharbouche v Embassy of Sudan*[190] the English courts were faced with two employment claims against foreign states. The first claim was brought by a Moroccan national who was employed as a cook at the Sudanese embassy in London. The second claim was brought by another Moroccan national who worked as a member of domestic staff at the Libyan embassy in London and was not habitually resident in the United Kingdom at the time when the employment contract was made. The claimants brought a number of claims for, inter alia, unfair dismissal and breach of the Working Time Regulations 1998. Both claims were met by an assertion of state immunity. Although the 1978 Act lays down an exception to state immunity in regard to contracts of employment,[191] this exception does not apply if at the time when the employment contract was made the employee was neither a United Kingdom national nor habitually resident there[192] and to proceedings concerning the employment of the members of a diplomatic mission.[193] The Court of Appeal held that, in considering state immunity and Article 6(1) of the European Convention for Human Rights, the court was concerned essentially with the single test of whether the grant of immunity was required by international law. The court found that international law did not require the United Kingdom to adopt the two restrictions to the exception to state immunity in regard to contracts of employment. The limitations of Article 6(1), therefore, could not be justified and the court granted declarations, pursuant to section 4(2) of the Human Rights Act 1998, that the two restrictions breached Article 6(1). Since the employment claims were based, in part, on the Working Time Regulations 1998, they came within the material scope of European Union law and the rights of access to justice under Article 47 of the Charter of Fundamental Rights of the European Union was engaged. The court found that the two restrictions to the exception to state immunity in regard to contracts of employment also breached Article 47. Since this article, being a provision which reflected a general principle of European Union law, has horizontal direct effect, the court had to disapply the two restrictions pursuant to section 2(1) of the European Communities Act 1972 in order to give effect to the claimant's claims which fell within the scope of European Union law. Interestingly, in a case decided on the same day as the *Benkharbouche* case the Court of Appeal, composed of the same judges who decided the *Benkharbouche* appeal, held that Articles 4 and 6 of the European Convention on Human Rights had not been breached by the grant of diplomatic immunity in proceedings brought against a foreign diplomatic agent by domestic workers who had worked in an official diplomatic residence and were victims of trafficking.[194]

(c) Exceptions from immunity

The State Immunity Act 1978 provides a substantial list of exceptions from state immunity. Section 3 provides an exception of major significance. A foreign state is not immune as respects any proceedings relating to a commercial transaction entered into by that state,[195] bearing in mind the wide definition of state already discussed. Until fairly recently, the position at common law was that a foreign state was immune even with regard to its purely commercial activities.[196] However, this wide immunity was rejected in a series of cases,

---

[190] [2015] EWCA Civ 33, [2015] 3 WLR 301, appeal pending; Garnett (2015) 64 ICLQ 783; Sanger (2016) 65 ICLQ 213. See also *Cudak v Lithuania*, Judgment of 23 March 2010; (2010) 51 EHRR 15, ECtHR; *Sabeh El Leil v France*, Judgment of 29 June 2011; (2012) 54 EHRR 14, ECtHR; Webb (2016) 27 EJIL 745.

[191] S 4; infra, pp 504–5.

[192] S 4(2)(b).

[193] S 16(1)(a).

[194] *Al-Malki v Reyes* [2015] EWCA Civ 32, [2016] 1 WLR 1785, appeal pending.

[195] S 3(1)(a).

[196] Eg *Kahan v Pakistan Federation* [1951] 2 KB 1003, CA; *Baccus SRL v Servicio Nacional del Trigo* [1957] 1 QB 438, CA.

culminating in two decisions of the House of Lords.[197] Instead, the "restrictive"[198] doctrine of immunity was applied, both to actions in rem and in personam, under which a foreign state was entitled to immunity in respect of its governmental acts but not in respect of its commercial transactions.

These common law developments are now, in substance, embodied in the 1978 Act.[199] "Commercial transaction" is defined[200] to include not only contracts for the supply of goods or services but also the provision of finance through loans and the like, and any guarantee or indemnity in respect of such transactions. Even more widely it extends to "any other transaction or activity (whether of a commercial, industrial, financial, professional or other similar character) into which a state enters or in which it engages otherwise than in the exercise of sovereign authority".[201] Indeed, this commercial exception from immunity extends further to include any obligation of the foreign state which by virtue of a contract, whether or not a commercial transaction, falls to be performed in whole or in part in the United Kingdom.[202] This would include contracts made in the exercise of sovereign authority to be performed here, such as contracts for the building of warships. There must also be "proceedings relating to" a commercial transaction. This refers to claims arising out of the transaction.[203] These will usually be contractual claims. It does not cover tortious claims arising independently of the transaction but in the course of its performance.[204]

There is a variety of other exceptions to immunity. In the case of contracts of employment, there is no immunity in respect of proceedings between the state and an individual where the contract was made in the United Kingdom or the work is to be wholly or partly performed here.[205]

---

[197] *The Philippine Admiral* [1977] AC 373; *Trendtex Trading Corpn v Central Bank of Nigeria* [1977] QB 529, CA; Lewis [1979] LMCLQ 460; *Hispano Americana Mercantil SA v Central Bank of Nigeria* [1979] 2 Lloyd's Rep 277, CA; *Planmount Ltd v Republic of Zaire* [1981] 1 All ER 1110; *I Congreso del Partido* [1983] 1 AC 244, HL; Fox (1982) 98 LQR 94; Mann (1982) 31 ICLQ 573; *Alcom Ltd v Republic of Colombia* [1984] AC 580, HL; Ghandi (1984) 47 MLR 597; Lloyd Jones [1984] CLJ 222; Crawford (1984) 55 BYBIL 340; Fox (1985) 34 ICLQ 115. See also *Empresa Exportadora de Azúcar v Industria Azucarera Nacional SA, The Playa Larga* [1983] 2 Lloyd's Rep 171, CA.

[198] See generally, Sornarajah (1982) 31 ICLQ 661; Crawford (1983) 54 BYBIL 75.

[199] See *Planmount Ltd v Republic of Zaire* [1981] 1 All ER 1110; *I Congreso Del Partido* [1983] 1 AC 244 at 260, HL; *Alcom Ltd v Republic of Colombia* [1984] AC 580, HL.

[200] S 3(3). See *Alcom Ltd v Republic of Colombia* [1984] AC 580 at 601–3, HL; *Arab Republic of Egypt v Gamal-Eldin* [1996] 2 All ER 237 at 247, EAT; *Svenska Petroleum Exploration AB v Government of the Republic of Lithuania (No 2)* [2006] EWCA Civ 1529 at [129]–[131], [2007] QB 886; Kawharu [2007] LMCLQ 136. Cf the definition under Art 2(2) of the UN Convention on State Immunity. On the relevance of the common law cases, see Fox (1982) 98 LQR 94. For the position in the USA, see *Saudi Arabia v Nelson* [1993] IL Pr 555, SC.

[201] S 3(3)(c). See *Svenska Petroleum Exploration AB v Government of the Republic of Lithuania (No 2)* [2006] EWCA Civ 1529 at [132]–[133], [2007] QB 886. Special provision is made in s 10 for ships that are used for commercial purposes.

[202] S 3(1)(b). See *J H Rayner (Mincing Lane) Ltd v Department of Trade and Industry* [1989] Ch 72 at 194–5, 222, 252, CA; affd by HL [1990] 2 AC 418 without discussion of this point. The exception from immunity provided by s 3 is inapplicable if the parties to the dispute are states or have otherwise agreed in writing or if the contract (not being a commercial transaction) was made in the territory of the foreign state and the obligation is governed by its administrative law: s 3(2).

[203] *Holland v Lampen-Wolfe* [2000] 1 WLR 1573 at 1587 (per Lord Millett), HL; *Svenska Petroleum Exploration AB v Government of the Republic of Lithuania (No 2)* [2006] EWCA Civ 1529 at [134]–[137], [2007] QB 886. See also *Bouzari v Iran (Islamic Republic)* (2004) 243 DLR (4th) 406, Ont CA.

[204] *Holland v Lampen-Wolfe* [2000] 1 WLR 1573, HL. Proceedings for registration or enforcement of a foreign judgment relate to the judgment and not to a commercial transaction, even if the transaction underlying the judgment was commercial: *AIC Ltd v Federal Government of Nigeria* [2003] EWHC 1357 (QB); *NML Capital Ltd v Argentina* [2011] UKSC 31, [2011] 2 AC 495.

[205] S 4(1); see generally Fox (1995) 66 BYBIL 97; Garnett (2005) 54 ICLQ 705. This is subject to exception in the case of contrary agreement in writing or where the employee is a national of the foreign state or is

There is no immunity as regards proceedings for death or personal injury or damage to or loss of tangible property caused by an act or omission in the United Kingdom;[206] nor is there immunity in the case of proceedings relating to United Kingdom patents, trade marks, and similar rights belonging to the state, or to the alleged infringement in the United Kingdom by the foreign state of such rights, including copyright.[207]

Immunity is excluded in the case of proceedings relating to the state's interest in immovables in England or to an obligation arising from such an interest.[208] Thus the French government, who were tenants of a house in London which was not being used for the purpose of a diplomatic mission,[209] did not have immunity in respect of an action by the landlords for damages for loss sustained as a result of an alleged refusal by the tenants to permit entry to carry out repairs.[210] Furthermore, the state has no immunity in the case of proceedings relating to its interest in other immovable or movable property by way of succession, gift or *bona vacantia*.[211] There is no requirement that the property be situated in England but the circumstances in which a judgment based on this exception must be recognised elsewhere are limited.[212] In the case of the administration of estates or trusts, or insolvency, the court's jurisdiction is unaffected by the fact that a foreign state may claim an interest in the property.[213] There is also an exception to immunity in the case of a state which is a member of a corporate or unincorporated body, or a partnership, which has members other than states and which is incorporated or constituted under United Kingdom law or is controlled from or has its principal place of business in the United Kingdom.[214] There is no immunity as regards proceedings for VAT, customs or excise duties, or rates on commercial premises.[215]

An important practical exception from immunity is that relating to ships in use, or intended for use, for commercial purposes. In the case of such ships, there is no immunity in Admiralty

---

neither a United Kingdom national nor habitually resident there: s 4(2), (3) and (5), as amended by British Nationality Act 1981, s 52(6) and Sch 7 and see the transitional provision in s 23(3)(b), applied in *Sengupta v Republic of India* [1983] ICR 221, EAT. See *Arab Republic of Egypt v Gamal-Eldin* [1996] 2 All ER 237, EAT S 4(1) is also subject to s 16(1)(a) (diplomatic and consular immunity). In *Benkharbouche v Embassy of Sudan* [2015] EWCA Civ 33, [2015] 3 WLR 301, appeal pending, the court held that the application ss 4(2)(b) and 16(1)(a) breached Art 6 of the European Convention on Human Rights and Art 47 of the Charter of Fundamental Rights of the European Union; discussed supra, p 503. See also *United States v Nolan* [2015] UKSC 63, [2016] AC 463.

[206] S 5. See *Caramba-Coker v Military Affairs Office of the Kuwait Embassy*, 10 April 2003, EAT and *Nigeria v Ogbonna* [2012] 1 WLR 139, EAT (these two cases concerned a claim for personal injury by an employee and concerned the relationship between ss 4 and 5 of the 1978 Act); *Heiser v Iran* [2012] EWHC 2938 (QB) and *Ben-Rafael v Iran* [2015] EWHC 3203 (QB) (these two cases dealt with actions to enforce US judgments against the defendant state for damages with regard to death or personal injury suffered after terrorist attacks and whether s 5 would have applied had the case arisen in the UK). See also *United States of America v Friedland* (1999) 182 DLR (4th) 614, Ont CA; *Schreiber v Canada (Attorney General)* [2002] 3 SCR 269, (2002) 216 DLR (4th) 513; *Bouzari v Iran (Islamic Republic)* (2004) 243 DLR (4th) 406, Ont CA. For the position in Ireland see *McElhinney v Williams* [1994] 2 ILRM 115.

[207] S 7. See *A Ltd v B Bank and Bank of X* [1997] FSR 165, CA.

[208] S 6(1); and see *The Charkieh* (1873) LR 4 A & E 59 at 97; *Alcom Ltd v Republic of Colombia* [1984] AC 580 at 603, HL.

[209] See s 16(1)(b); discussed infra, p 511.

[210] *Intpro Properties (UK) Ltd v Sauvel* [1983] QB 1019.

[211] S 6(2).

[212] See 1978 Act, s 19(3) for the limitations on the recognition here of foreign judgments involving this exemption; and see Art 20(3) of the European Convention on State Immunity (1972) and s 31 of the Civil Jurisdiction and Judgments Act 1982, discussed infra, p 602.

[213] S 6(3); *Re Rafidain Bank* [1992] BCLC 301; cf *United States of America and Republic of France v Dollfus Mieg et Cie SA and Bank of England* [1952] AC 582 at 617–8, HL.

[214] S 8. See *Maclaine Watson & Co Ltd v International Tin Council* [1989] Ch 253 at 282–3, CA.

[215] S 11.

proceedings (or proceedings on a claim which could be made the subject of Admiralty proceedings) relating to an action in rem against a ship belonging to the foreign state or to an action in personam for enforcing a claim in connection with such a ship.[216]

Finally, there is no immunity if the state has submitted to the jurisdiction of the courts;[217] and there is a related exception in the case where a state has agreed in writing to submit a dispute to arbitration,[218] for there is then no immunity with regard to court proceedings which relate to the arbitration.[219] This includes proceedings for enforcement of a foreign arbitration award.[220] There are detailed rules as to what constitutes submission by the foreign state. Submission may be by prior written agreement[221] or after the dispute has arisen;[222] but a provision in an agreement that the law of a part of the United Kingdom is to govern does not constitute submission.[223] Any intervention by a foreign state for the purpose only of claiming immunity or asserting an interest in property in circumstances such that the state would have been entitled to immunity had the proceedings been brought against that state does not amount to submission.[224] A state is, however, deemed to submit if it has instituted

---

[216] S 10(1), (2). Cf *The Guiseppe Di Vitorio* [1998] 1 Lloyd's Rep 136, CA. Special provision is made for actions in rem against one ship in connection with another ship, actions concerning cargo, or proceedings where the foreign state is a party to the Brussels Convention covering the Immunity of State-owned Ships (1926): ss 10(3)–(6), 17(1).

[217] S 2(1); *Svenska Petroleum Exploration AB v Government of the Republic of Lithuania (No 2)* [2006] EWCA Civ 1529 at [124]–[128], [2007] QB 886; *Donegal International Ltd v Zambia* [2007] EWHC 197 (Comm), [2007] 1 Lloyd's Rep 397; *United States of America v Nolan* [2015] UKSC 63, [2016] AC 463. A state is deemed to have submitted if it has instituted the proceedings (s 2(3)(a), *Schreiber v Canada (Attorney General)* (2002) 216 DLR (4th) 513, Sup Ct of Canada) or has taken any step in the proceedings (s 2(3)(b), *The London Steam Ship Owners Mutual Insurance Association Ltd v Spain Prestige* [2015] EWCA Civ 333, [2015] 2 Lloyd's Rep 33) and this would include where it seeks a stay on the grounds of *forum non conveniens: A Co Ltd v B Co Ltd and Republic of Z*, 1993 (unreported); *Kuwait Airways Corpn v Iraqi Airways Co* [1995] 1 Lloyd's Rep 25, CA; revsd, but not on this point, by the House of Lords [1995] 1 WLR 1147; cf *Jaffe v Miller* (1993) 103 DLR (4th) 315, Ont CA. For the purposes of s 2(3)(b) action taken by a member of the mission or its solicitors must be authorised by the head of mission: *Aziz v Republic of Yemen* [2005] EWCA Civ 745, [2005] ICR 1391. For counterclaims see s 2(6); *United States of America v Friedland* (1999) 182 DLR (4th) 614, Ont CA; *Schreiber v Federal Republic of Germany* (2001) 196 DLR (4th) 281, Ont CA; affd by SC of Canada in *Schreiber v Canada (Attorney General)* (2002) 216 DLR (4th) 513. Submission does not imply submission to the enforcement jurisdiction of the courts; see s 13(3), and *Alcom Ltd v Republic of Colombia* [1984] AC 580 at 600.

[218] *Svenska Petroleum Exploration AB v Government of the Republic of Lithuania (No 2)* [2006] EWCA Civ 1529 at [114]–[116], [2007] QB 886.

[219] S 9(1). This is subject to contrary provision in the arbitration agreement. See also in relation to the Commonwealth Secretariat Act 1966, *Mohsin v The Commonwealth Secretariat* [2002] EWHC 377 (Comm). Nor does it apply to an arbitration agreement between states: s 9(2).

[220] *Svenska Petroleum Exploration AB v Government of the Republic of Lithuania (No 2)* [2006] EWCA Civ 1529 at [117]–[122], [2007] QB 886; *The London Steam Ship Owners Mutual Insurance Association Ltd v Spain Prestige* [2015] EWCA Civ 333, [2015] 2 Lloyd's Rep 33; *Gold Reserve Inc v Venezuela* [2016] EWHC 153 (Comm), [2016] 1 WLR 2829 (enforcement of an arbitration award rendered under a bilateral investment treaty); *L R Avionics Technologies Ltd v Nigeria* [2016] EWHC 1761 (Comm), [2016] 4 WLR 120 (proceedings for enforcement of a foreign judgment entered by way of enforcement of an award).

[221] See, eg, *A Company Ltd v Republic of X* [1990] 2 Lloyd's Rep 520; *Sabah Shipyard (Pakistan) Ltd v Islamic Republic of Pakistan* [2002] EWCA Civ 1643 at [18]–[27] (per Waller LJ), [48]–[51] (per Pill LJ), [2003] 2 Lloyd's Rep 571; *NML Capital Ltd v Argentina* [2011] UKSC 31, [2011] 2 AC 495; Dickinson [2011] LMCLQ 581; Fox (2012) 128 LQR 10 and, on the High Court judgment, (2009) 125 LQR 544. See also s 17(2).

[222] S 2(2); and see the transitional provision in s 23(3)(a); cf *Duff Development Co Ltd v Kelantan Government* [1924] AC 797, HL; *Kahan v Pakistan Federation* [1951] 2 KB 1003, CA. The head of the state's diplomatic mission in the United Kingdom is deemed to have authority to submit, as is any person who entered into a contract on behalf of the state in matters relating to that contract: s 2(7); cf *Baccus SLR v Servicio Nacional del Trigo* [1957] 1 QB 438 at 473, CA.

[223] S 2(2).

[224] S 2(4); see generally, *London Branch of the Nigerian Universities Commission v Bastians* [1995] ICR 358, EAT.

the proceedings or, subject to what has just been said, if it intervenes in the proceedings,[225] unless it does so in reasonable ignorance of facts entitling it to immunity, and immunity is claimed as soon as is reasonably practicable.[226]

(d) Indirect impleading

It has been assumed so far that the question of the immunity to which a sovereign state is entitled arises in the course of proceedings in which the state is named as defendant, ie direct impleading. In practice, however, what is far more common is "indirect impleading". In this type of case the issue of state immunity arises either because of interpleader proceedings by the state or because one party to the proceedings claims, for example, that the goods in issue[227] are subject to the power of a foreign state and that to proceed with the claim would indirectly implead that state. Before the State Immunity Act 1978 a variety of issues had been held to implead a foreign sovereign, such as an action which put his title to goods in issue or which related to property in the possession of the foreign state[228] or which the state had the right to possess,[229] or even property "in the control" of the foreign sovereign.[230] Most cases of indirect impleading involved chattels but the doctrine of immunity was extended to cases where the subject matter of the action was a chose in action to which title was claimed by a foreign state.[231] Finally, the foreign state did not have to prove its title to the property in issue. It was sufficient for evidence to be adduced that the claim of the foreign state was not illusory or founded on a manifestly defective title.[232] It had to be an arguable issue.[233] Another example of indirect impleading is the situation where a civil claim for damages is brought against individual state officials, following alleged official torture or abuse of public power abroad.[234] The foreign state is indirectly impleaded since the acts of the officials are attributable to it. If these claims against individual defendants were to proceed and be upheld, the interests of the foreign state would obviously be affected, even though it is not a named party.

The question of "indirect impleading" is not dealt with, as such, in the State Immunity Act 1978 even though it is the most likely circumstance in which the issue of sovereign immunity will arise. Nevertheless, this aspect of sovereign immunity is very substantially regulated. First, it is clear that the immunity, and the exceptions thereto, provided by the 1978 Act are intended to apply whether the foreign state is a party to the action or intervenes by means of interpleader proceedings. This is apparent from section 2(4) which provides that a state does not submit to the jurisdiction merely by intervening in proceedings to assert an interest in property in circumstances such that the state would have been immune if directly impleaded.

---

[225] S 2(3). See *Fusco v O'Dea* [1994] 2 ILRM 389.

[226] S 2(5). Any submission extends to an appeal, but not to a counterclaim unless it arises out of the same legal relationship or facts as the original claim: s 2(6). See also *Kubacz v Shah* [1984] WAR 156, WASC.

[227] Eg *The Parlement Belge* (1880) 5 PD 197, CA.

[228] Eg *Compañía Naviera Vascongada v SS Cristina* [1938] AC 485, HL.

[229] Eg *United States of America and Republic of France v Dollfus Mieg et Cie SA and Bank of England* [1952] AC 582, HL.

[230] Eg *The Broadmayne* [1916] P 64, CA.

[231] *Rahimtoola v Nizam of Hyderabad* [1958] AC 379, HL. See also *High Commissioner for Pakistan in the United Kingdom v National Westminster Bank* [2015] EWHC 55 (Ch).

[232] *Juan Ysmael & Co Inc v Indonesian Government* [1955] AC 72 at 88–90, PC. Cf *Shearson Lehman Bros Inc v Maclaine Watson & Co Ltd (International Tin Council intervening) (No 2)* [1988] 1 WLR 16, 29–31, HL—a sovereign asserting a right of property in a document in the possession of a third party.

[233] *Rahimtoola v Nizam of Hyderabad* [1958] AC 379 at 410, HL.

[234] *Jones v Ministry of the Interior of the Kingdom of Saudi Arabia* [2006] UKHL 26 at [31], [2007] 1 AC 270. Compare *Belhaj v Straw* [2017] UKSC 3, [2017] 2 WLR 456—state immunity cannot be invoked where a claim for alleged serious violations of human rights abroad against the United Kingdom government and its officials and agents necessarily requires findings of illegality in respect of acts on the part of officials of foreign states for which they could claim immunity if they or the foreign states concerned were sued directly.

Secondly, the problems of indirect impleading surface in section 6(4) which provides that a court may entertain proceedings against a person other than a state notwithstanding that the proceedings relate to property in the possession or control of a state or in which a state claims an interest. This is the indirect impleading situation where the state does not necessarily intervene; but the court's power to entertain such proceedings depends on the state not being immune if the proceedings were brought directly against it and, in the case where the proceedings relate to property in which the state claims an interest, the state's claim must be neither admitted nor supported by prima facie evidence.

The result is that in a case of indirect impleading the law is much as before. There will be immunity unless the case falls within an exception under the 1978 Act, and it is unlikely that the exceptions in the 1978 Act would have altered the decisions in favour of immunity in many of the cases, other than those relating to ships,[235] decided at common law,[236] for there is no statutory exception to immunity in most cases involving movables. The requirement of property being in the possession or control of the foreign state indicates little change; though the need to adduce prima facie evidence in support of a claim to an interest in the goods perhaps imposes a heavier burden than at common law. Finally, the reference in section 6(4) of the 1978 Act to "property", without qualification, suggests that the provision covers both corporeal and incorporeal property, ie choses in action.

In the situation where the indirect impleading arises out of a claim against individual officials following alleged torture abroad, the 1978 Act has been applied to provide immunity for these individuals.[237]

(e) Procedural and other miscellaneous matters in the 1978 Act
There are a number of other miscellaneous, but significant, matters dealt with by the State Immunity Act 1978. Provision is made for the service of process on a foreign state and for a number of other procedural matters.[238] These include immunity from injunctive relief[239] and from the processes of execution except with the state's written consent or in respect of property in use or intended for use for commercial purposes.[240] It has been held that a credit balance in a bank account kept for the purpose of meeting the day-to-day expenditure of a

---

[235] See the exceptions to immunity in the 1978 Act, s 10.

[236] Mann (1973) 36 MLR 18, 23–4.

[237] *Jones v Ministry of the Interior of the Kingdom of Saudi Arabia* [2006] UKHL 26, [2007] 1 AC 270; discussed supra, p 502; *Al Attiya v Bin-Jassim Bin-Jaber Al Thani* [2016] EWHC 212 (QB).

[238] 1978 Act, ss 12, 13, 14(3)–(5); see *Kuwait Airways Corpn v Iraqi Airways Co* [1995] 1 WLR 1147, HL—service has to be transmitted through the Foreign and Commonwealth Office to the Ministry of Foreign Affairs in the state in question; *ABCI (Formerly Arab Business Consortium International Finance and Investment Co) v Banque Franco-Tunisienne* [2002] 1 Lloyd's Rep 511, appeals dismissed [2003] 2 Lloyd's Rep 146, CA—service in an agreed way; *Westminster City Council v Government of the Islamic Republic of Iran* [1986] 1 WLR 979; *Crescent Oil and Shipping Services Ltd v Importang UEE* [1998] 1 WLR 919; *Norsk Hydro ASA v State Property Fund of Ukraine (Note)* [2002] EWHC 2120 (Comm), [2009] Bus LR 558; *Embassy of Brazil v de Castro Cerqueira* [2014] 1 WLR 3718, EAT; *L v Regional Government of X* [2015] EWHC 68 (Comm), [2015] 1 WLR 3948; cf *Gold Reserve Inc v Venezuela* [2016] EWHC 153 (Comm), [2016] 1 WLR 2829.

[239] *ETI Euro Telecom International NV v Bolivia* [2008] EWCA Civ 880, [2009] 1 WLR 665. See also *Soleh Boneh International Ltd v Government of the Republic of Uganda* [1993] 2 Lloyd's Rep 208, CA (an order for provision of security for an arbitral award not an injunction); *Pearl Petroleum Co Ltd v Kurdistan Regional Government of Iraq* [2015] EWHC 3361 (Comm), [2016] 4 WLR 2 (an application for enforcement of a peremptory order under s 42 of the Arbitration Act 1996, not being an application for a mandatory injunction, does not engage s 13(2)(a) of the State Immunity Act 1978).

[240] 1978 Act, s 13; *Sabah Shipyard (Pakistan) Ltd v Islamic Republic of Pakistan* [2002] EWCA Civ 1643 at [18]–[27] (per Waller LJ), [48]–[51] (per Pill LJ), [2003] 2 Lloyd's Rep 571; Wilkes (2004) 53 ICLQ 512; *NML Capital Ltd v Argentina* [2011] UKSC 31 at [89] (per Lord Mance), [2011] 2 AC 495; *L R Avionics Technologies v Nigeria* [2016] EWHC 1761 (Comm), [2016] 4 WLR 120. See also *Coreck Maritime GmbH v Sevrybokholodflot* 1994 SLT 893. See in relation to the property of a state's Central Bank: s 14(4), *AIC Ltd v*

foreign embassy was not used for commercial purposes and was therefore immune from the processes of execution.[241] Some of the expenditure would no doubt come within the concept of commercial purposes under the Act, but other expenditure clearly did not, and the bank balance was one and indivisible; it was not susceptible of dissection to reflect the different expenditure. It is the commercial purpose of the use, or intended use, of the state's property that is relevant, and the fact that the origin of the property is in, or that the property is related to, a commercial transaction is irrelevant.[242] The head of a state's diplomatic mission in the United Kingdom is deemed to have authority to give, on behalf of the state, consent to execution, and his certificate to the effect that any property is not in use or intended for use for commercial purposes is accepted as sufficient evidence of that fact unless the contrary is proved.[243] Power is given to provide by Order in Council for the restriction or extension of the Act's immunities and privileges. They may be restricted where they exceed those accorded by the foreign state in relation to the United Kingdom; and they may be extended where they are less than those required by any international agreement between the United Kingdom and the foreign state.[244] Nothing in the list of exceptions to the general principle of immunity is to affect the immunities and privileges conferred by the Diplomatic Privileges Act 1964 or the Consular Relations Act 1968;[245] but the 1964 Act is extended to apply to a head of state, his family and his private servants.[246]

One final issue which may arise is whether the party in question is a foreign state for the purposes of the 1978 Act. This is an issue which arose in relation to sovereign immunity before this Act and the position is, in effect, unchanged. The status of a foreign sovereign is a matter of which the court takes judicial notice, that is to say it is a matter that the court is either assumed to know or to have the means of discovering without embarking upon a contentious inquiry.[247] Where it was doubtful whether a person enjoyed sufficient independence to entitle him to immunity, as, for instance, in the case of a ruler in Malaya[248] or in a case after the Indian Independence Act 1947 of a former ruler of an independent state in India,[249] the court applied to the Secretary of State for Foreign and Commonwealth Affairs whose answer was final and conclusive, and this rule is embodied in the 1978 Act.[250]

(ii) Ambassadors and other diplomatic officers[251]

It has long been recognised that the representatives in the United Kingdom of a foreign state are sent on the understanding that they shall have an immunity from the civil and criminal

---

Federal Government of Nigeria [2003] EWHC 1357 (QB) at [44]–[59]; *AIG Capital Partners Inc v Republic of Kazakhstan* [2005] EWHC 2239 (Comm), [2006] 1 WLR 1420; *Thai-Lao Lignite (Thailand) Co Ltd v Laos* [2013] EWHC 2466 (Comm), [2013] 2 All ER (Comm) 883; *Taurus Petroleum Ltd v State Oil Marketing Co of the Ministry of Oil, Iraq* [2015] EWCA Civ 835, [2016] 1 Lloyd's Rep 42.

[241] *Alcom Ltd v Republic of Colombia* [1984] AC 580, HL; Ghandi (1984) 47 MLR 597; Lloyd Jones [1984] CLJ 222; Crawford (1984) 55 BYBIL 340; Fox (1985) 34 ICLQ 115. The onus is on the judgment creditor to show the commercial purpose. See also *Orascom Telecom Holding SAE v Chad* [2008] EWHC 1841 (Comm).

[242] *SerVaas Inc v Rafidain Bank* [2012] UKSC 40, [2013] 1 AC 595.

[243] S 13(5).

[244] 1978 Act, s 15. See in relation to the USSR/Russian Federation, SI 1978/1524, SI 1997/2591; *Coreck Maritime GmbH v Sevrybokholodflot* 1994 SLT 893; *The Guiseppe Di Vittorio* [1998] 1 Lloyd's Rep 136, CA.

[245] Infra.

[246] 1978 Act s 20, discussed infra, pp 515–16.

[247] *Mighell v Sultan of Johore* [1894] 1 QB 149 at 161, CA. See also *Federal Republic of Yugoslavia v Croatia* [2000] IL Pr 591, French cour de Cassation.

[248] *Mighell v Sultan of Johore* [1894] 1 QB 149, CA; *R (on the application of Sultan of Pahang) v Secretary of State for the Home Department* [2011] EWCA Civ 616, (2011) Times, 13 June; see also *R (on the application of Alamieyeseigha) v Crown Prosecution Service* [2005] EWHC 2704 (Admin).

[249] *Sayce v Ameer Ruler Sadig Mohammad Abbasi Bahawalpur State* [1952] 2 QB 390, CA.

[250] S 21(a). See *Trawnik v Lennox* [1985] 1 WLR 532.

[251] For a discussion of the historical development, see Young (1964) 40 BYBIL 141.

jurisdiction of the local courts which reflects that enjoyed by the sovereign whom they represent.[252] The Diplomatic Privileges Act 1708,[253] which was declaratory though not exhaustive of the common law,[254] provided in accordance with this principle that "all writs and processes" against a foreign ambassador or other public minister should be "utterly null and void".[255] At common law the immunity is shared by the members of the foreign envoy's family, if living with him; by his diplomatic family, as it is sometimes called, such as his counsellors, secretaries and clerks; and by his domestic staff, such as chauffeurs.

This principle of immunity is a feature of all systems of law, but since its application has been far from uniform, especially as regards the position of domestic servants, the law on the subject was ultimately codified in 1961 by the Vienna Convention on Diplomatic Intercourse and Immunities.[256] Effect has been given to this Convention by the Diplomatic Privileges Act 1964,[257] which, in respect of the matters dealt with therein, replaces any previous enactment or rule of law. It applies not only to diplomatic representatives of foreign countries but also to the diplomatic representatives of Commonwealth countries and the Republic of Ireland and their staffs.[258] Furthermore the Act is retrospective in operation and applies to actions begun before the date on which it came into force.[259] The Act does not regulate or replace the common law on special missions.[260]

(a) The persons entitled to privileges

The persons entitled to immunity are allocated to three categories, and the particular privileges allowed them vary according to the category to which they belong. Any doubt as to whether a person is entitled to a privilege is conclusively settled by a certificate given by the Secretary of State.[261] No immunity is conferred until the representative of the foreign state has been accepted or received in this country.[262] The three categories are as follows:

---

[252] *The Parlement Belge* (1880) 5 PD 197 at 207, CA.

[253] See Blackstone's Commentaries, i, 255.

[254] *The Amazone* [1940] P 40, CA.

[255] S 3.

[256] See generally Denza, *Diplomatic Law* (2008) 3rd edn.

[257] S 1. See Samuels (1964) 27 MLR 689; Buckley (1965–1966) 41 BYBIL 321; and see Hardy, *Modern Diplomatic Law* (1968), pp 52–68; Brown (1988) 37 ICLQ 53. The Act has been amended in minor respects by the Diplomatic and Other Privileges Act 1971, and the Diplomatic and Consular Premises Act 1987; and see the State Immunity Act 1978, ss 16(1), 20.

[258] Diplomatic Privileges Act 1964, s 8(4), Sch 2, repealing the Diplomatic Immunities (Commonwealth Countries and Republic of Ireland) Act 1952, s 1(1), and thereby limiting the immunity in the case of the staff of Commonwealth High Commissions, eg *Empson v Smith* [1966] 1 QB 426, CA.

[259] *Empson v Smith* [1966] 1 QB 426, CA.

[260] *R (on the application of Freedom and Justice Party) v Secretary of State for Foreign and Commonwealth Affairs* [2016] EWHC 2010 (Admin), appeal pending—the common law gives effect to the customary international law rule requiring the inviolability and immunity from criminal jurisdiction of special mission members.

[261] Diplomatic Privileges Act 1964, s 4. See, eg, *R v Governor of Pentonville Prison, ex p Teja* [1971] 2 QB 274; *R v Governor of Pentonville Prison, ex p Osman (No 2)* [1989] COD 446; *Bat v Germany* [2011] EWHC 2029 (Admin), [2013] QB 349; Sanger (2013) 62 ICLQ 193; *Al Attiya v Bin-Jassim Bin-Jaber Al Thani* [2016] EWHC 212 (QB); *W v H* [2016] EWCA Civ 176, [2017] Fam 35; *R (on the application of Freedom and Justice Party) v Secretary of State for Foreign and Commonwealth Affairs* [2016] EWHC 2010 (Admin), appeal pending. However, such a certificate whilst conclusively settling that a child is a dependant will not settle that the child is a member of the household of the diplomat, which is what is required, see infra: *Re P (Children Act: Diplomatic Immunity)* [1998] 1 FLR 624 at 626.

[262] *R v Governor of Pentonville Prison, ex p Teja* [1971] 2 QB 274; *R v Lambeth Justices, ex p Yusufu* [1985] Crim LR 510; *R v Governor of Pentonville Prison, ex p Osman (No 2)* [1989] COD 446. However, the position appears to be different in immigration cases: *R v Secretary of State for the Home Department, ex p Bagga* [1991] 1 QB 485 at 496–7, 508–9.

(i) Diplomatic agents

These comprise the head of the mission and the members of his diplomatic staff,[263] as for instance, the secretaries, counsellors and attachés. Arms control inspectors and observers are now included in the definition.[264]

Such a person is exempt from the civil[265] and criminal jurisdiction of the English courts[266] in respect both of his official and private acts, and, though he himself may institute proceedings,[267] no remedy is enforceable against him in the United Kingdom at the instance of either a private citizen or the state. Thus no action will lie against a High Commissioner for unfair dismissal.[268] Nor will an action for compensation lie against a foreign diplomatic agent by a domestic worker who works in a diplomatic mission or an official diplomatic residence and is a victim of trafficking;[269] this was held not to breach Articles 4 and 6 of the European Convention on Human Rights.[270] But this immunity does not import immunity from legal liability.[271] Thus, if a diplomatic agent commits a tort against which he has insured himself he can claim to be indemnified by the insurer. If a diplomatic agent is a citizen of the United Kingdom and Colonies or if he is permanently resident in the United Kingdom,[272] his immunity from the civil jurisdiction is limited to official acts performed in the exercise of his functions.[273] The diplomatic agent must be treated with due respect and all appropriate steps must be taken to prevent any attack on his person, freedom or dignity.[274]

By way of exception to the exemption from civil jurisdiction there are three types of action that lie against a diplomatic agent, namely:

(a) a real action relating to private immovable property in England, unless it is held on behalf of the sending state for the purposes of the mission[275]—it has been decided that a diplomatic agent's private residence was not held for the purposes of the mission;[276]

(b) an action relating to succession in which the diplomatic agent is involved as executor, administrator, heir or legatee in his capacity as a private person;

---

[263] Diplomatic Privileges Act 1964, Sch1, Art 1(a)–(e).

[264] Arms Control and Disarmament (Privileges and Immunities) Act 1988. See also the Vienna Document 1999 (Privileges and Immunities) Order, SI 2003/2621. For the position of foreign personnel assisting after a nuclear accident see the Atomic Energy Act 1989, Sch.

[265] Including a divorce petition: *Shaw v Shaw* [1979] Fam 62.

[266] 1964 Act, Sch 1, Art 31(1). Furthermore, the private residence of a diplomatic agent is inviolable, as are the premises of the mission. But see *Re B (A Child) (Care Proceedings: Diplomatic Immunity)* [2002] EWHC 1751 (Fam), [2003] 2 WLR 168; *Al-Malki v Reyes* [2015] EWCA Civ 32, [2016] 1 WLR 1785, appeal pending. On diplomatic and consular premises, see generally the Diplomatic and Consular Premises Act 1987.

[267] *Baron Penedo v Johnson* (1873) 29 LT 452.

[268] *Omerri v Uganda High Commission* (1973) 8 ITR 14.

[269] *Al-Malki v Reyes* [2015] EWCA Civ 32, [2016] 1 WLR 1785, appeal pending; cf *Wokuri v Kassam* [2012] EWHC 105 (Ch), [2013] Ch 80; *Abusabib v Taddese* [2013] ICR 603, EAT.

[270] The *Al-Malki v Reyes* case.

[271] *Dickinson v Del Solar* [1930] 1 KB 376 at 380; *Re P (Diplomatic Immunity: Jurisdiction)* [1998] 1 FLR 1026.

[272] See *W v H* [2016] EWCA Civ 176, [2017] Fam 35.

[273] Diplomatic Privileges Act 1964, s 2(6); Sch 1, Art 38(1). This limited immunity may, however, be extended by Order in Council.

[274] Art 29 of the Vienna Convention. On which see *Harb v Aziz* [2005] EWCA Civ 632; *Aziz v Aziz* [2007] EWCA Civ 712, [2005] 2 FLR 1108.

[275] See State Immunity Act 1978, s 16(1)(b).

[276] *Intpro Properties (UK) Ltd v Sauvel* [1983] QB 1019; *W v H* [2016] EWHC 213 (Fam), [2017] 1 FLR 669. Even if the premises are held for professional purposes, for the immunity to apply there must be proceedings concerning a state's title to or its possession of property.

(c) an action relating to any professional or commercial activity pursued by him in the United Kingdom[277] outside his official functions.[278]

This last exception reverses the previous law, under which a person of diplomatic rank was not liable to be sued in respect of his commercial or private transactions.[279]

No writ of execution may be issued against a diplomatic agent, except where judgment has been given against him in an action relating to immovable property, to succession or to any private commercial transaction, and even then no measure may be taken that will infringe the inviolability of his person or residence.[280]

The general rule is that a diplomatic agent is exempt from all dues and taxes, personal or real, national, regional or municipal.[281]

The above privileges granted to a diplomatic agent are also possessed by the members of his family forming part of his household,[282] provided that they are of alien nationality.[283]

(ii) Members of the administrative and technical staff [284]

This category includes such persons as clerks, typists, archivists and radio or telephone operators. Such members of the staff, together with the members of their families, provided that they are neither citizens of the United Kingdom and Colonies nor permanently resident in the United Kingdom, are immune from the civil jurisdiction, but only in respect of acts done within the scope of their duties.[285] They are also on the same footing as diplomatic agents with regard to the exemption from taxes and other dues.[286]

(iii) Members of the service staff

Members of the service staff, who are defined by the Convention as "members of the staff of the mission in the domestic staff of the mission",[287] include such persons as butlers, cooks, maids and chauffeurs. These enjoy no privileges if they are either citizens of the United Kingdom and Colonies or if they are permanently resident in the United Kingdom. Otherwise, they enjoy immunity from the civil jurisdiction of the courts, but only in respect of acts performed in the course of their duties; and they are exempt from income tax on the

---

[277] But not outside, see *BCCI v Price Waterhouse* [1997] 4 All ER 108 at 111–2; *Apex Global Management Ltd v Fi Call Ltd* [2013] EWCA Civ 642, [2014] 1 WLR 492.

[278] Diplomatic Privileges Act 1964, Sch 1, Art 31(1). A contract for the provision of services which are incidental to family or domestic life of a foreign diplomatic agent does not fall within the "commercial activity" exception: *Al-Malki v Reyes* [2015] EWCA Civ 32, [2016] 1 WLR 1785, appeal pending.

[279] *Taylor v Best* (1854) 14 CB 487, 139 ER 201.

[280] Diplomatic Privileges Act 1964, Sch 1, Art 31(3).

[281] Ibid, Sch 1, Arts 33, 34, 36.

[282] A dependent child, although a member of the diplomat's family, may not form part of his household: *Re P (Children Act: Diplomatic Immunity)* [1998] 1 FLR 624 at 626. See also *Apex Global Management Ltd v Fi Call Ltd* [2013] EWCA Civ 642, [2014] 1 WLR 492—"members of the family forming part of the household" includes the spouse, civil partner, dependent children and a dependent parent of a diplomat normally resident with him or her.

[283] The 1964 Act, Sch 1, Art 37(1); see also *Re C (An Infant)* [1959] Ch 363; Wilson (1965) 14 ICLQ 1265; O'Keefe (1976) 25 ICLQ 329.

[284] Diplomatic Privileges Act 1964, Sch 1, Art 1; eg *Empson v Smith* [1966] 1 QB 426, CA. See also Arms Control and Disarmament (Privileges and Immunities) Act 1988.

[285] *Re B (A Child) (Care Proceedings: Diplomatic Immunity)* [2002] EWHC 1751 (Fam), [2003] 2 WLR 168.

[286] Diplomatic Privileges Act 1964, Sch 1, Art 37(2).

[287] Ibid, Sch 1, Art 1(g).

emoluments paid to them by the sending state and from liability to pay contributions under social security legislation.[288]

(b) Cessation of immunities and privileges

The immunities and privileges enjoyed by any person normally cease at the moment when he leaves the United Kingdom[289] or on the expiry of a reasonable time within which to do so, provided that his functions have come to an end. Nevertheless, his immunity continues to endure in respect of acts already done by him in the exercise of his official duties.[290] On the other hand his immunity in respect of acts already done in his private capacity no longer avails him.[291] However, diplomatic immunity which comes into existence after an action has been started will necessitate a stay of those proceedings until such time as the immunity may cease to be enjoyed.[292]

(c) Waiver of privileges

It was recognised at common law that a diplomatic agent or other member of the diplomatic staff might waive his immunity from the civil and criminal jurisdiction of the local courts, either by expressly consenting through his solicitor to the proceedings, or by entering an appearance to the writ or by commencing proceedings as plaintiff. Since, however, the privilege is the privilege of the sending state, not of the individual diplomat, it was essential that consent to its waiver should have been given by the sending state in the case of proceedings against the head of the mission, and by the head of the mission where the proceedings were against a subordinate member of the state. It followed that, even if a subordinate member had waived the privilege, he might later obtain a stay of proceedings by showing that he had not acted with the consent of his superior.[293]

These rules have been little affected by the Act of 1964. In the first place, the authority of the sending state to waive the privilege is retained;[294] and it is enacted that a waiver by the head of the mission shall be deemed to be a waiver by that state.[295] The words of this last provision are wide enough to embrace the case where the head of the mission waives his own privilege, not merely that of a subordinate member of the staff.[296] It is enacted that a waiver must always be express.[297] It is possible to waive personal immunity, but at the same time to maintain immunity in respect of a diplomatic document.[298]

---

[288] Ibid, s 2(4); Sch 1, Arts 33, 37.

[289] *Shaw v Shaw* [1979] Fam 62; see also *Re Regina and Palacios* (1984) 45 OR (2d) 269, Ont CA.

[290] Diplomatic Privileges Act 1964, Sch 1, Art 39(2).

[291] *Zoernsch v Waldock* [1964] 1 WLR 675 at 692, CA; *Re P (Diplomatic Immunity: Jurisdiction)* [1998] 1 FLR 1026—taking children from the jurisdiction at the end of a posting; *Wokuri v Kassam* [2012] EWHC 105 (Ch), [2013] Ch 80 and *Abusabib v Taddese* [2013] ICR 603, EAT—former diplomats did not have immunity in relation to claims by domestic workers; cf *Al-Malki v Reyes* [2015] EWCA Civ 32, [2016] 1 WLR 1785, appeal pending.

[292] *Ghosh v D'Rozario* [1963] 1 QB 106, CA.

[293] *R v Madan* [1961] 2 QB 1, CA and authorities there cited.

[294] Diplomatic Privileges Act 1964, Sch 1, Art 32(1). See *Propend Finance v Sing* (1997) 111 ILR 611, CA; *Re P (Children Act: Diplomatic Immunity)* [1998] 1 FLR 624.

[295] Diplomatic Privileges Act 1964, s 2(3).

[296] For the difficulties involved in such a waiver, see *Fayed v Al-Tajir* [1988] QB 712 at 733, 737, CA. Kerr LJ appears to doubt whether the head of the mission can waive his own privilege (at 737), whereas Mustill LJ appears to accept this (at 733).

[297] Diplomatic Privileges Act 1964, Sch 1, Art 32(2). See *A Company Ltd v Republic of X* [1990] 2 Lloyd's Rep 520, which held that the waiver must be given to the court itself; Mann (1991) 107 LQR 362.

[298] *Fayed v Al-Tajir* [1988] QB 712, CA.

Where, under the former law, a person entitled to immunity waived his privilege and commenced an action as claimant, it was doubtful whether it was permissible for the defendant to plead a counterclaim. The Act now settles this doubt by providing that:

> the initiation of proceedings by . . . a person enjoying immunity from jurisdiction . . . shall preclude him from invoking immunity from jurisdiction in respect of any counterclaim directly connected with the principal claim.[299]

The rule at common law that a judgment given against a foreign diplomat cannot be executed, notwithstanding that he has waived his immunity from the jurisdiction,[300] has been confirmed. There can be no enforcement of a judgment unless there has been a separate waiver of the immunity from execution.[301] Failing a separate waiver, the judgment remains unenforceable until the defendant has ceased to be a member of the foreign mission.

(d) Restriction of privileges and immunities

It sometimes happens that the privileges granted to a British mission in a particular foreign state are less than those enjoyed by the mission of that state in the United Kingdom. In that event, an Order in Council may be made withdrawing the statutory immunities and privileges to such extent or in respect of such persons as appears to Her Majesty to be proper.[302] Furthermore, reciprocal arrangements for wider immunities than those contained in the 1964 Act may be continued.[303]

(e) International organizations[304]

It is clear, then, that immunity from jurisdiction is enjoyed by the diplomatic representatives of foreign states who reside in the United Kingdom during the performance of their duties. The International Organisations Act 1968[305] provides that certain privileges may be conferred on persons who are present for a limited time in the United Kingdom as the representatives of some organisation of which the United Kingdom and one or more Sovereign Powers are members.[306] What organisations are eligible and what particular immunities they are to enjoy must be specified by Order in Council.[307] Examples of organisations that have been specified are the United Nations, the Commission of the European Union, the European Bank for Reconstruction and Development,[308] the Council of

---

[299] Diplomatic Privileges Act 1964, Sch 1, Art 32(3).

[300] *Re Suarez, Suarez v Suarez* [1918] 1 Ch 176, CA.

[301] Diplomatic Privileges Act 1964, Sch 1, Art 32(4).

[302] Diplomatic Privileges Act 1964, s 3(1); re-enacting the Diplomatic Immunities Restriction Act 1955.

[303] Ibid, s 7(1).

[304] See generally Gaillard and Pingel-Lenuzza (2002) 51 ICLQ 1; Reinisch, *The Privileges and Immunities of International Organizations in Domestic Courts* (2013). In certain circumstances, an international organisation may sue in England, see *Arab Monetary Fund v Hashim (No 3)* [1991] 2 AC 114, CA; Mann (1991) 107 LQR 357; Carter (1991) 62 BYBIL 447; Hill (1992) 12 OJLS 135.

[305] As amended by the Diplomatic and Other Privileges Act 1971; the European Communities Act 1972, s 4(1), Sch 3, Part IV; the International Organisations Act 1981, and the International Organisations Act 2005.

[306] Replacing the International Organisations (Immunities and Privileges) Act 1950, as amended by the Diplomatic Privileges Act 1964. The 1968 Act has been extended to Commonwealth organisations; see International Organisations Act 1981, s 1. See also the Commonwealth Secretariat Act 1966, as amended by the International Organisations Act 2005, ss 1–3; *Mohsin v The Commonwealth Secretariat* [2002] EWHC 377 (Comm).

[307] International Organisations Act 1968, s 1. Orders in Council made under the 1950 Act are to continue to have effect: s 12(5), (6).

[308] *Mukoro v European Bank for Reconstruction and Development* [1994] ICR 897, EAT.

Europe,[309] the International Labour Organisation, the World Health Organisation, the International Court of Justice, the International Criminal Court, the European Court of Human Rights and the International Tribunal for the Law of the Sea.

The maximum immunities that may be granted to an organisation or to a representative thereof vary with each case. Thus, high officers and members of committees and missions may be put on the same footing as heads of diplomatic missions with regard to immunity from suit and legal process, inviolability of residence and exemption from taxes and privileges as to the importation of certain articles, and there is the like inviolability of official premises as is accorded in respect of the premises of a diplomatic agent;[310] but the maximum privileges of other officers and representatives are limited to immunity from suit and legal process in respect of things done in the course of their employment, to exemption from income tax on their official salaries, to exemption from certain other customs duties and taxes and to privileges as to the importation of certain articles.[311] Although an officer of an international organisation has immunity, this is granted for the benefit of the organisation and may be waived by it. Accordingly, there is no limitation on jurisdiction in an action by the organisation against the officer.[312] The immunity of an officer only extends to official acts and cannot include the situation where the officer is accepting a bribe for his own benefit.[313]

Special provision is made in the International Organisations Act 1968 for conferring diplomatic exemptions and privileges on officers of specialised agencies of the United Nations,[314] and also on other organisations, including international commodity organisations, of which the United Kingdom is not a member,[315] on bodies established under the Treaty on European Union,[316] on persons involved in international judicial proceedings[317] and on representatives at international conferences in the United Kingdom.[318]

(f) Immunity of foreign sovereigns

In placing the whole question of sovereign immunity on a statutory basis, the State Immunity Act 1978[319] has limited the immunity formerly enjoyed by a foreign sovereign or head of state. In so far as the immunities conferred by the Diplomatic Privileges Act 1964 are wider

---

[309] Of which the European Commission of Human Rights is an organ: *Zoernsch v Waldock* [1964] 1 WLR 675, CA. For immunities for United Kingdom representatives to the Consultative Assembly of the Council of Europe, see s 4 of the International Organisations Act 1981.

[310] International Organisations Act 1968, Sch I, Pt II; as amended by s 5 of the International Organisations Act 1981.

[311] The 1968 Act, Sch I, Pt III; as amended by the International Organisations Act 1981, s 5.

[312] *Arab Monetary Fund v Hashim* [1996] 1 Lloyd's Rep 589, CA.

[313] Ibid.

[314] The 1968 Act, s 2. See *W v H* [2016] EWCA Civ 176, [2017] Fam 35. The immunity enjoyed by specialised agencies of the United Nations is not incompatible with the European Convention on Human Rights: *Entico Corp Ltd v United Nations Educational Scientific and Cultural Association* [2008] EWHC 531 (Comm), [2008] 2 All ER (Comm) 97. Similarly, *Warner v B&M Europe Ltd*, 13 July 2016, EAT (European Patent Office). See also *Re Immunity of Special Rapporteur* (1999) Times, 19 May, ICJ.

[315] International Organisations Act 1968, s 4; and s 4A, added by s 2 of the International Organisations Act 1981.

[316] International Organisations Act 1968, s 4B, added by s 5 of the International Organisations Act 2005.

[317] The 1968 Act, s 5; extended by ss 7 and 8 of the International Organisations Act 2005. See in relation to the International Tribunal for the Law of the Sea, SI 2005/2047. See also the International Criminal Court Act 2001, Sch 1, para 1, extended by the International Organisations Act 2005, s 6.

[318] International Organisations Act 1968, s 6; see also s 5A added by the International Organisations Act 1981, s 3.

[319] Supra, p 497 et seq.

than those under the 1978 Act, it has been thought desirable to apply the appropriate immunities of the 1964 Act to a sovereign or other head of state, the members of his family forming part of his household and his private servants;[320] though without the qualifications in the 1964 Act relating to residence or nationality.[321]

(g) Consular immunities

The regulation of consular immunity, so far as foreign consuls and their staffs are concerned,[322] is governed by the Consular Relations Act 1968,[323] giving effect to the Vienna Convention on Consular Relations 1963. Consular officers[324] are not liable to arrest, save in the case of a grave crime,[325] and are only subject to restrictions on personal freedom in execution of judicial decisions of final effect.[326] In the case of civil proceedings, consular officers and employees are not amenable to the jurisdiction of the courts of this country in respect of acts performed in the exercise of consular functions except, in the case of a contractual action, where such officer or employee does not contract expressly or impliedly as an agent of his sending state, and in the case of an action by a third party for damage arising from an accident in the United Kingdom caused by a vessel, vehicle or aircraft.[327] There is power for these various exemptions to be waived by the sending state.[328]

There are provisions dealing also with exemption from social security provisions, taxation, customs and estate duties.[329] Special provision is made for the fact that the varied privileges and immunities shall not be accorded to consular employees and the families of members of a consular post who carry on private gainful occupations in the United Kingdom.[330] Again, as with the Diplomatic Privileges Act 1964, there is provision for those cases where there is already agreement for additional or reduced privileges[331] and for the withdrawal of privileges.[332]

---

[320] State Immunity Act 1978, s 20. See *BCCI v Price Waterhouse* [1997] 4 All ER 108; *Harb v Aziz* [2005] EWCA Civ 632, [2005] 2 FLR 1108; *Aziz v Aziz* [2007] EWCA Civ 712, [2008] 2 All ER 501. The half-brother and nephew of the King of Saudi Arabia were held not to be "members of his family forming part of his household" in *Apex Global Management Ltd v Fi Call Ltd* [2013] EWCA Civ 642, [2014] 1 WLR 492. A former head of state has immunity from criminal jurisdiction for acts done in his official capacity as head of state: *R v Bow Street Magistrate, ex p Pinochet (No 3)* [2000] 1 AC 147, HL. However, this does not extend to official acts of torture committed after ratification of the International Convention against Torture and Other Cruel, Inhuman or Degrading Treatment or Punishment 1984. The estate of a former head of state has no immunity in respect of a suit regarding a private act done whilst head of state regardless of whether he ceased to be head of state because he died in office or because he left office: *Harb v Aziz* [2015] EWCA Civ 481, [2016] Ch 308.

[321] State Immunity Act 1978, s 20(2).

[322] For the position of consular officers from the Commonwealth and the Republic of Ireland see the Consular Relations Act 1968, s 12, as amended by the Diplomatic and Other Privileges Act 1971 and the Commonwealth Countries and Republic of Ireland (Immunities and Privileges) Order 1985, SI 1985/1983, as amended by the Commonwealth Countries and Republic of Ireland (Immunities and Privileges) Order 2005, SI 2005/246.

[323] See Woodliffe (1969) 32 MLR 59; and see the State Immunity Act 1978, s 16(1).

[324] Defined in Sch I, Art 1.

[325] Defined in s 1(2).

[326] Sch I, Art 41. A consular official is within the United Kingdom for the purposes of the hearsay rule and s 23 of the Criminal Justice Act 1988, repealed by Criminal Justice Act 2003, for hearsay evidence now see ss Pt 11, Ch 2 of the 2003 Act; see *R v Carmenza Jiminez-Paez* (1994) 98 Cr App Rep 239, CA.

[327] Sch I, Art 43. See Lee, *Vienna Convention on Consular Relations* (1966), pp 143–6.

[328] Sch I, Art 45.

[329] Sch I, Arts 48–51.

[330] Sch I, Art 57.

[331] S 3.

[332] S 2.

(iii) The Brussels/Lugano system

To what extent are these rules on sovereign and diplomatic immunity affected by the Brussels/ Lugano system? It will be recalled that this system only applies in relation to civil and commercial matters. If the action concerns the commercial transactions of a foreign state or diplomat this would appear to relate to a civil and commercial matter. However, where an action involves the governmental acts of a foreign state or the official acts of a diplomat (ie the situation where immunity is granted) it will fall outside this concept. This is because Article 1(1) of the Brussels I Regulation Recast provides that the Regulation does not extend to "the liability of the State for acts and omissions in the exercise of State authority (*acta iure imperii*)".[333] Moreover, as has been seen, the Court of Justice of the European Union has held on many occasions that actions involving a public authority acting in the exercise of its powers fall outside the scope of the Brussels/ Lugano system.[334]

The leading case on the relationship between state immunity and the scope of the Brussels/ Lugano system, is *Lechouritou v Germany*.[335] The Court of Justice held that an action by natural persons of a Contracting State to the Brussels Convention against another Contracting State to obtain compensation for damage caused by the armed forces of the latter Contracting State when invading the territory of the first State did not constitute a civil and commercial matter. The reasoning of the Court is highly instructive in the present context. It was said that operations conducted by armed forces are one of the characteristic emanations of state sovereignty.[336] It followed that the acts complained of must be regarded as resulting from the exercise of public powers on the part of the state on the date when those acts were perpetrated.[337] The question whether the acts carried out in the exercise of these public powers were lawful made no difference.[338] In the light of this finding the Court held that there was no need to discuss the second question referred to the Court, namely whether a plea of state immunity is compatible with the Brussels Convention.[339] In *Mahamdia v People's Republic of Algeria*[340] the CJEU dealt with an employment claim brought before the German courts by an employee of the Algerian state who worked as a driver at this state's embassy in Berlin. The Court held that under the generally accepted principles of international law concerning immunity from jurisdiction a state could not be sued before the courts of another state in a dispute such as that which arose in this case.[341] But the Court also held that immunity from jurisdiction is not absolute, and that it may be excluded if the legal proceedings relate to the acts of state performed *iure gestionis* which do not fall within the exercise of public power and if the proceedings are not likely to interfere with the security interests of the State.[342] Whether or not this is the case is for the court seised with the dispute to determine.[343] In in *Grovit v De Nederlandsche Bank*,[344] the Court of Appeal held that a claim for defamation brought against the Dutch Central Bank and two of its employees, all of whom were entitled

---

[333] An equivalent wording does not exist in the Brussels and Lugano Conventions.

[334] Supra, pp 204–6.

[335] Case C-292/05 [2007] ECR I-1519.

[336] Ibid, at [37].

[337] Ibid, at [38].

[338] Ibid, at [43].

[339] Ibid, at [47].

[340] Case C-154/11 EU:C:2012:491, [2012] IL Pr 41.

[341] Ibid, at [54]. The Court clarified that such immunity is based on the principle *par in parem non habet imperium*, as a state cannot be subjected to the jurisdiction of another state.

[342] Ibid, at [55], [56].

[343] Ibid, at [56], [57].

[344] [2007] EWCA Civ 953, [2008] 1 WLR 51, affirming [2005] EWHC 2944 (QB), [2006] 1 Lloyd's Rep 636.

to immunity,[345] was not a civil one within the meaning of the Brussels I Regulation. The first defendant was a public authority and the defamation was contained in a letter written during the exercise of public powers.

4. STATUTORY LIMITATIONS ON JURISDICTION

There are a number of statutes, most of which implement international conventions,[346] which preclude the jurisdiction of the English courts over actions in rem and in personam in particular situations. The situations may be defined either by reference to ministerial decision or by the statutes and conventions themselves. The first case may be illustrated by the Senior Courts Act 1981, section 23 of which provides that no court in England shall have jurisdiction to entertain any claim certified by the Secretary of State to be such as falls to be determined under the Rhine Navigation Convention.[347] Similarly, the jurisdiction of any court in the United Kingdom is excluded under the Nuclear Installations Act 1965 in the case of any claim certified by the Minister to be one which, under any relevant international agreement, falls to be determined by some other United Kingdom or foreign court.[348]

Other statutes, mainly those implementing international transport conventions, stipulate that actions may be brought only under the jurisdictional rules stated in the conventions. For example, the Carriage by Air Act 1961 requires that in the case of international carriage[349] any action for damages must be brought in the territory of one of the High Contracting Parties to the convention,[350] either before the court at the place of destination or before the court having jurisdiction where the carrier ordinarily resides or has his principal place of business or has an establishment by which the contract has been made.[351] Similar jurisdictional rules are prescribed under the Carriage by Air (Supplementary Provisions) Act 1962,[352] the Carriage of Goods by Road Act 1965,[353] and the International Transport Conventions Act 1983.[354]

---

[345] See s 14(2) of the 1978 Act.

[346] These conventions are not affected by the Brussels I Regulation Recast, Danish Agreement and the Brussels/Lugano Conventions; see Art 71(1) of the Brussels I Regulation Recast (which preserves existing agreements, which in relation to particular matters govern jurisdiction, but does not allow for the United Kingdom entering into such agreements), Art 57 of the Brussels Convention and Art 67(1) of the Lugano Convention, supra, pp 203 and 312.

[347] See Jackson, *Enforcement of Maritime Claims* (2005) 4th edn, para 12.153.

[348] S 17(1).

[349] Sch 1, Art 1(2).

[350] The Warsaw Convention 1929, as amended at The Hague in 1955, supplemented by the Guadalajara Convention 1961, and modernised by the Montreal Convention for the Unification of Certain Rules relating to International Carriage by Air 1999.

[351] Carriage by Air Act 1961, Sch 1, Art 28(1).

[352] Sch, Art VIII.

[353] Sch, Art 31(1).

[354] S 1 and Appendix A of the Convention concerning International Carriage by Rail, Cmnd 8535 (1982) which is given the force of law by the 1983 Act. Most of the 1983 Act is repealed and replaced by the Railways (Convention on International Carriage by Rail) Regulations, SI 2005/2092. Other statutes containing specific jurisdictional rules based upon or by reference to international conventions are the Senior Courts Act 1981, ss 20–22, amended by the Merchant Shipping (Salvage and Pollution) Act 1994, s 1(6), Sch 2, para 6, Merchant Shipping Act 1995, s 314(2), Sch 13, para 59(2)(a), (b), (c) and (d), and SI 2006/1265; and the Merchant Shipping Act 1995, Part VI, Chapter III (ss 152–171, as amended by SI 2006/1244), s 183(1).

The only statute which removes the subject matter jurisdiction of the English courts and does not implement an international convention is the Defamation Act 2013. Section 9 of the Act[355] prescribes that the English court has no jurisdiction to hear and determine the action unless the court is satisfied that, of all the places in which the statement complained of has been published, England and Wales is clearly the most appropriate place in which to bring an action in respect of the statement. This rule is only applicable to defamation claims against a person not domiciled in a Member State of the European Union.

---

[355] Discussed supra, pp 353–5.

15

RECOGNITION AND ENFORCEMENT OF FOREIGN JUDGMENTS AND ARBITRAL AWARDS IN ENGLAND—AN INTRODUCTION

1. The Effect Given to Foreign Judgments and Arbitral Awards	520	(b) Judgments from a European Union or EFTA State	522
2. The Different Regimes Governing Recognition and Enforcement of Foreign Judgments	521	(c) Judgments from other parts of the United Kingdom	524
		(d) Insolvency	524
(a) Judgments from outside the European Union and EFTA	521	(e) Family law	524
		(f) Wills and successions	524
		3. Foreign Arbitral Awards	524

1. THE EFFECT GIVEN TO FOREIGN JUDGMENTS AND ARBITRAL AWARDS

Unsatisfied foreign judgments and arbitral awards give rise to complicated questions of private international law. If a claimant fails to obtain satisfaction of a judgment or an award in the country where it has been granted, the question arises as to whether it is enforceable in another country where the defendant or his assets are found. It is clear at the outset that owing to the principle of territorial sovereignty a judgment delivered in one country cannot, in the absence of international agreement, have a direct operation of its own force in another. Levy of execution, for instance, cannot issue in England in respect of a judgment delivered in New York. Nevertheless, the common law systems have long permitted the enforcement of foreign judgments and awards within certain defined limits, since otherwise some of the essential objects of private international law, eg the protection of rights acquired under a foreign system of law and international cooperation, would not be fully attained.[1] The common law systems have also long given recognition to foreign judgments and awards as *res judicata* by "treating the relevant claim as having been decided once and for all".[2]

Recognition and enforcement are in some cases governed not by the common law rules, but by a statute that is in force in England. Some statutes have the aim of implementing a recognition and enforcement treaty that the United Kingdom has entered into with a foreign country or countries. The United Kingdom is for the time being a Member State of the European Union and, therefore, bound by the rules of the Brussels/Lugano system, whose

---

[1] See *Adams v Cape Industries plc* [1990] Ch 433 at 552–3, CA.
[2] *Clarke v Fennoscandia (No 3)* [2007] UKHL 56; 2008 SC (HL) 122 at [21], citing Briggs, *The Conflict of Laws* (2002), p 116.

objective is to achieve the free circulation of judgments within the European Union and the EFTA States other than Liechtenstein[3] (ie Iceland, Norway and Switzerland). As a European Union Member State, the United Kingdom is for the time being also bound by the rules of the Hague Convention on Choice of Court Agreements of 2005, which the European Union has ratified on behalf of all the Member States.

The interplay between and among the common law, statutes, international treaties and European Union legal instruments is what makes the English private international law in this area, as well as the presentation of the law, complicated. This introductory chapter aims to list the different regimes that govern the recognition and enforcement of foreign judgments and awards in England and to briefly describe the situations in which these different regimes apply.

2. THE DIFFERENT REGIMES GOVERNING RECOGNITION AND ENFORCEMENT OF FOREIGN JUDGMENTS

Distinction should be made between the recognition and enforcement of: 1) judgments from outside the European Union and EFTA, excluding Liechtenstein; 2) judgments from a European Union or an EFTA State other than Liechtenstein; and 3) judgments from another part of the United Kingdom. A further distinction should be made between separate sets of rules that govern the recognition and enforcement of foreign judgments in general and those that apply to foreign judgments given in specialised subject matters such as insolvency, family law and wills and successions.

(a) Judgments from outside the European Union and EFTA

The majority of judgments originating from outside the European Union and EFTA are recognised and enforced at common law. So are the majority of judgments from a European Union or EFTA State which fall outside the scope of the legal instruments that form part of the Brussels/Lugano system.

Enforcement (and sometimes recognition) of certain non-EU/EFTA judgments, as well as of certain EU/EFTA judgments that fall outside the scope of the Brussels/Lugano system, is governed by statute. The two main statutes in England which are concerned with such foreign judgments are the Administration of Justice Act 1920, Part II and the Foreign Judgments (Reciprocal Enforcement) Act 1933.

The Administration of Justice Act 1920, Part II applies to the enforcement within the United Kingdom of certain judgments obtained in a superior court of most of the countries and territories forming part of the Commonwealth, ie Anguilla, Antigua and Barbuda, Bahamas, Barbados, Belize, Bermuda, Botswana, British Indian Ocean Territory, British Virgin Islands, Cayman Islands, Christmas Island, Cocos (Keeling) Island, Republic of Cyprus, Dominica, Falkland Islands, Fiji, The Gambia, Ghana, Grenada, Guyana, Jamaica, Kenya, Kiribati, Lesotho, Malawi, Malaysia, Malta, Mauritius, Montserrat, New Zealand, Nigeria, Norfolk Island, Papua New Guinea, St Christopher and Nevis, St Helena, St Lucia, St Vincent and the Grenadines, Seychelles, Sierra Leone, Singapore, Solomon Islands, Sovereign Base Areas of Akrotiri and Dhekelia in Cyprus, Sri Lanka, Swaziland, Tanzania, Trinidad and Tobago,

---

[3] Liechtenstein became an EFTA State in 1991, but has not become a party to the Lugano Convention.

Turks and Caicos Islands, Tuvalu, Uganda, Zambia and Zimbabwe.[4] The vast majority of judgments from Cyprus and Malta are now recognised and enforced under the Brussels/Lugano system. But if a judgment from one of these two countries falls outside the scope of the Brussels/Lugano system, the 1920 Act may apply to it. Enforcement under the 1920 Act is optional: the judgment creditor can choose to either register the judgment for enforcement under the provisions of the Act or bring an action for enforcement of the judgment at common law. The 1920 Act does not apply to the recognition of judgments, which continues to be governed by the rules of the common law.

The Foreign Judgments (Reciprocal Enforcement) Act 1933 applies to the recognition and enforcement within the United Kingdom of certain judgments obtained in a number of foreign countries and territories, some of which form part of the Commonwealth. The countries to which the 1933 Act has been extended are Australia, Austria, Belgium, Canada (excluding Quebec), France, Germany, Guernsey, India, the Isle of Man, Israel, Italy, Jersey, the Netherlands, Norway, Pakistan, Suriname and Tonga. The vast majority of judgments from Austria, Belgium, France, Germany, Italy, the Netherlands and Norway are now recognised and enforced under the Brussels/Lugano system. But if a judgment from one of these countries falls outside the scope of the Brussels/Lugano system, its recognition and enforcement may be governed by the 1933 Act. The Act applies on an exclusive basis. A judgment debtor whose judgment is registrable under the 1933 Act cannot resort to common law for its enforcement. The extension of the 1933 Act to a certain country is preceded by the United Kingdom entering into a recognition and enforcement treaty with that country. Since the treaties on the basis of which the 1933 Act has been extended to different countries are not uniform, one must refer to the provisions of these treaties in order to get the full picture of the legal framework that governs the recognition and enforcement of judgments from a country to which the 1933 Act has been extended.

In 2015, the Hague Convention on Choice of Court Agreements 2005 entered into force. The European Union ratified this Convention,[5] both in its own right and on behalf of each of the Member States (excluding Denmark). At present, the only other Contracting Parties are Mexico and Singapore, while the USA and Ukraine have signed but not yet ratified. In cases where the rules on recognition and enforcement of foreign judgments of this Convention apply, these rules supersede all other rules on recognition and enforcement. This Convention is implemented in the United Kingdom by the Civil Jurisdiction and Judgments Act 1982.

The recognition and enforcement of judgments originating from outside the European Union and EFTA is examined in Chapter 16 of this book.

(b) Judgments from a European Union or EFTA State

Judgments from a European Union or EFTA State that fall within the scope of the legal instruments that form part of the Brussels/Lugano system are recognised and enforced under the rules of these instruments. The traditional English rules, both of common law and

---

[4] See Reciprocal Enforcement of Judgments (Administration of Justice Act 1920, Part II) (Amendment) Order, SI 1985/1994. The 1920 Act used to apply to the enforcement of certain judgments from Australia, Canada, Gibraltar and Hong Kong. Australian and Canadian (excluding Quebec) judgments are now recognised and enforced under the Foreign Judgments (Reciprocal Enforcement) Act 1933. Judgments from Gibraltar are now recognised and enforced under the Civil Jurisdiction and Judgments Act 1982. Hong Kong is now part of China, whose judgments are recognised and enforced at common law.

[5] Council Decision of 4 December 2014 on the approval, on behalf of the European Union, of the Hague Convention of 30 June 2015 on Choice of Court Agreements OJ 2014 L 353/5.

statutory origin, do not apply to such judgments.[6] There are a number of instruments that form part of the Brussels/Lugano system.

The main instrument is the Recast of the Brussels I Regulation, which has repealed and replaced the earlier Brussels I Regulation. The Brussels I Regulation Recast applies to judgments given in civil and commercial matters in legal proceedings instituted on or after its entry into force on 10 January 2015.[7] Judgments from all European Union Member States, with the exception of Denmark, fall within the Recast, ie from Austria, Belgium, Bulgaria, Croatia, Cyprus,[8] the Czech Republic, Estonia, Finland, France, Germany, Greece, Hungary, Ireland, Italy, Latvia, Lithuania, Luxembourg, Malta, the Netherlands, Poland, Portugal, Romania, Slovakia, Slovenia, Spain, Sweden and the United Kingdom. Under the EC/Denmark Agreement the provisions of the Brussels I Regulation applied, with minor amendments, by international law to the relations between the European Union and Denmark. Pursuant to the Agreement, Denmark has formally decided to apply the Brussels I Regulation Recast.[9]

Other important instruments of European Union law in this area are the European Enforcement Order Regulation, the European Order for Payment Procedure Regulation and the European Small Claims Procedure Regulation, which apply to certain judgments given in uncontested and small claims proceedings. All European Union Member States, with the exception of Denmark, are bound by these regulations.

The Brussels I Regulation, the predecessor of the Brussels I Regulation Recast, replaced the earlier Brussels Convention in virtually all cases after its entry into force in March 2002. One has to say "virtually" because the Brussels Convention continued to apply and still applies to judgments given in the territories of the Contracting States[10] which fall within the scope of the Convention and are excluded from the Brussels I Regulation Recast.[11] The territories in question are (in relation to France) the French overseas territories, such as New Caledonia and Mayotte, and (in relation to the Netherlands) Aruba. The Brussels Convention is implemented in the United Kingdom by the Civil Jurisdiction and Judgments Act 1982.

The system of free circulation of judgments within the European Union has been extended to the EFTA States other than Liechtenstein (ie Iceland, Norway and Switzerland) by the 2007 Lugano Convention, which repealed and replaced the earlier 1988 Lugano Convention. The terms of the 2007 Lugano Convention have been aligned with those of the Brussels I Regulation (but not, at present, the Brussels I Regulation Recast). The 2007 Lugano Convention is implemented in the United Kingdom by the Civil Jurisdiction and Judgments Act 1982.

Finally, it should be mentioned that the enforcement within the United Kingdom of judgments of the courts and institutions of the European Union is governed by the European Communities (Enforcement of Community Judgments) Order 1972.

---

[6] The only exception are the common law rules on recognition of foreign judgments which continue to apply even with respect to judgments falling within the Brussels/Lugano system, see infra, pp 649–50.

[7] Art 66(1).

[8] Even if the judgment given by a Cypriot court sitting in the government-controlled area concerns land situated in the northern area: Case C-420/07 *Apostolides v Orams* [2009] ECR I-3571; De Baere (2010) 47 CMLR 1123; Hartley (2009) 58 ICLQ 1013.

[9] OJ 2013 L 79/4.

[10] At the moment the Contracting States to the Brussels Convention are the original fifteen Member States.

[11] Art 68(1). Territories are excluded from the Regulation pursuant to Art 355 of the TFEU.

The recognition and enforcement of EU/EFTA judgments is examined in Chapter 17 of this book, with the exception of the European Communities (Enforcement of Community Judgments) Order 1972 which is examined in Chapter 16.

(c) Judgments from other parts of the United Kingdom

Judgments originating in one part of the United Kingdom (ie England and Wales, Scotland and Northern Ireland) are recognised and enforced in another part under the Civil Jurisdiction and Judgments Act 1982. The 1982 Act also applies to the recognition and enforcement of judgments from Gibraltar. The Act applies on an exclusive basis. It is examined in Chapter 16 of this book.

(d) Insolvency

There are special rules dealing with the effects of foreign judgments in insolvency proceedings. These rules are examined later in Chapter 34 of this book.

(e) Family law

There are special rules dealing with the recognition of foreign divorces, annulments and legal separations, foreign maintenance orders, and foreign orders relating to children. These rules are examined later in Part V of this book, on family law, and in Chapter 37, on matrimonial property.

(f) Wills and successions

There are special rules dealing with the effects of foreign judgments relating to wills and successions. These rules are examined later in Chapter 36 of this book.

3. FOREIGN ARBITRAL AWARDS

The recognition and enforcement of foreign arbitral awards is also complicated by the fact that it is governed by numerous separate sets of rules. For now, it is sufficient to mention that the vast majority of foreign arbitral awards are given effect in the United Kingdom under the rules of the 1958 New York Convention on the recognition and enforcement of foreign arbitral awards, which is implemented in England and Wales and Northern Ireland by the Arbitration Act 1996. Awards rendered under the 1965 Convention on the settlement of investment disputes between states and nationals of other states are given effect in the United Kingdom by the Arbitration (International Investment Disputes) Act 1966. Recognition and enforcement of arbitral awards may in some cases take place at common law or under the rules of the Administration of Justice Act 1920, the Foreign Judgments (Reciprocal Enforcement Act) 1933, the Arbitration Act 1950 or the Civil Jurisdiction and Judgments Act 1982. Foreign arbitral awards are discussed in Chapter 18 of this book.

16

RECOGNITION AND ENFORCEMENT OF FOREIGN JUDGMENTS—THE TRADITIONAL RULES

1. Introduction	525
(a) The theory underlying recognition and enforcement at common law	525
(b) Enforcement under statute	527
2. Recognition and Enforcement at Common Law	527
(a) Jurisdiction of the foreign court: judgments in personam	528
(b) Judgments in rem	544
(c) Final and conclusive judgment	548
(d) Enforcement of foreign judgments in personam	551
(e) Recognition of foreign judgments	556
(f) Defences to recognition and enforcement	564
3. Direct Enforcement of Foreign Judgments by Statute	588
(a) The Civil Jurisdiction and Judgments Act 1982: recognition and enforcement within the United Kingdom	588
(b) Administration of Justice Act 1920	591
(c) Foreign Judgments (Reciprocal Enforcement) Act 1933	593
(d) European Union judgments	601
(e) Judgments against states	601
(f) The Brussels and Lugano Conventions	603
(g) The Hague Convention on Choice of Court Agreements 2005	604
4. Inter-relation of the Common Law and Statutes	605
5. The Recast of the Brussels I Regulation	607

1. INTRODUCTION

(a) The theory underlying recognition and enforcement at common law[1]

The attitude adopted by English law from the earliest days has been to permit the successful litigant to rely on the foreign judgment in England as *res judicata* or to bring an action in England on the foreign judgment. But over the years the courts have changed their view as to the ground upon which this privilege is based. The older cases put it solely on the ground of comity.[2] It is unnecessary, however, to consider this historical theory further, for it has been supplanted by a far more defensible principle that has been called "the doctrine of obligation".[3] This doctrine, which was laid down in 1842, is that, where a foreign court of competent jurisdiction has adjudicated a certain sum to be due from one person to another, the liability to pay that sum becomes a legal obligation that may be enforced in this country by an action of debt.[4] Once the judgment is proved the burden lies on the defendant to show why he should not perform the obligation.

---

[1] Briggs 2015, para 7.46; Briggs (1987) 36 ICLQ 240, (2004) 8 Sing YBIL 1 and (2013) 129 LQR 87; Harris (1997) 17 OJLS 477; Ho (1997) 46 ICLQ 443.

[2] See *Geyer v Aguilar* (1798) 7 Term Rep 681 at 697, 101 ER 1196; Piggott, *Foreign Judgments* (1908), p 10 et seq.

[3] Piggott, *Foreign Judgments* (1908), p 10 et seq.

[4] *Russell v Smyth* (1842) 9 M & W 810 at 819, 152 ER 343. See also *Williams v Jones* (1845) 13 M & W 628 at 633, 153 ER 262; *Godard v Gray* (1870) LR 6 QB 139 at 148; *Adams v Cape Industries plc* [1990]

The judgment of a court of competent jurisdiction over the defendant imposes a duty or obligation on the defendant to pay the sum for which judgment is given, which the courts in this country are bound to enforce; and consequently that anything which negatives that duty, or forms a legal excuse for not performing it, is a defence to the action.[5]

In other words, a new right[6] has been vested in the creditor and a new obligation imposed on the debtor at the instance of the foreign court, which right supersedes the underlying cause of action and may be directly enforced in England. Lord Esher once said that "the liability of the defendant arises upon an implied contract to pay the amount of the foreign judgment".[7] This does not mean that the justification for the enforcement of the obligation is an implied contract, but that for procedural purposes the debtor is regarded as having implicitly promised to pay.[8]

The doctrine of obligation has in turn come in for criticism in that it fails to reveal the policy considerations underlying the rules on recognition and enforcement.[9] It is more concerned with explaining in theoretical terms why we recognise and enforce foreign judgments than with explaining in theoretical terms which foreign judgements should be recognised and enforced. The Supreme Court of Canada has considered the latter. It has referred to a modern and more clearly defined concept of comity which is concerned with "justice, necessity and convenience".[10]

> Comity in the legal sense is neither a matter of absolute obligation, on the one hand, nor of mere courtesy and good will, upon the other. But it is the recognition which one nation allows within its territory to the legislative, executive or judicial acts of another nation, having due regard both to international duty and convenience, and to the rights of its own citizens or of other persons who are under the protection of its laws.[11]

This allows for the adoption of rules in the light of modern conditions. Old common law rules that were based on an outmoded view of the world that emphasised sovereignty and independence often at the cost of fairness have been rejected.[12] "Greater comity is required in our modern era when international transactions involve a constant flow of products, wealth and people across the globe."[13] The end result is a new Canadian rule which provides for recognition and enforcement when the judgment granting state has properly or appropriately exercised jurisdiction,[14] a test which is near to one of jurisdictional reciprocity.

Ch 433 at 513, 552–3, CA; *Owens Bank Ltd v Bracco* [1992] 2 AC 443 at 484, HL; *Murthy v Sivajothi* [1999] 1 WLR 467 at 476, CA; *Lewis v Eliades* [2003] EWCA Civ 1758 at [48], [2004] 1 WLR 692; *Rubin v Eurofinance SA* [2012] UKSC 46 at [9], [2013] 1 AC 236; *Gordon Pacific Developments Pty Ltd v Conlon* [1993] 3 NZLR 760. In *Rubin*, the Supreme Court confirmed, at [9], that the doctrine of obligation was based on the mode of pleading an action on a foreign judgment in debt, not merely as evidence of the obligation to pay the underlying liability.

[5] *Schibsby v Westenholz* (1870) LR 6 QB 155 at 159.

[6] See *Adams v Cape Industries plc* [1990] Ch 433 at 552, CA; *Cambridge Gas Transportation Corpn v Official Committee of Unsecured Creditors of Navigator Holdings plc* [2006] UKPC 26 at [13], [2007] 1 AC 508.

[7] *Grant v Easton* (1883) 13 QBD 302 at 303, CA. See also *Williams v Jones* (1845) 13 M & W 628 at 630, 153 ER 262.

[8] Read, *Recognition and Enforcement of Foreign Judgments* (1938), pp 112–13.

[9] Ho (1997) 46 ICLQ 443.

[10] *Morguard Investments Ltd v De Savoye* [1990] 3 SCR 1077, (1991) 76 DLR (4th) 256; discussed infra, pp 543–4. See also *Beals v Saldanha* [2003] 3 SCR 416, (2003) 234 DLR (4th) 1; discussed infra, pp 543–4.

[11] The *Morguard* case at 269. This adopts the definition in *Hilton v Guyot* 159 US 113 at 163–4, 16 S Ct 139 (1895).

[12] *Hunt v T & N plc* [1993] 4 SCR 289, (1993) 109 DLR (4th) 16.

[13] Ibid.

[14] For identifying this see infra, pp 543–4.

(b) Enforcement under statute

The doctrine of obligation provides the theoretical and historical basis for giving effect to foreign judgments at common law. It does not apply to enforcement under statute.[15] In the United Kingdom, there are several statutes under which the enforcement of a foreign judgment occurs by way of registration of the judgment. These statutes either implement a recognition and enforcement treaty that the United Kingdom (or the European Union on behalf of its Member States) has entered into with a foreign country or countries or apply where reciprocity has been considered to in fact exist between the United Kingdom and a foreign country in the area of enforcement of judgments. There is also a statute that governs the recognition and enforcement of judgments within the United Kingdom.

One very important recent development is the adoption and entry into force of the Recast of the Brussels I Regulation on jurisdiction and the recognition and enforcement of judgments in civil and commercial matters. The Recast has introduced a system of automatic recognition and enforcement of judgments within the European Union. According to Recital 26 of the Recast, a judgment given by the courts of one Member State is treated as if it had been given in the Member State where the recognition and enforcement of the judgment is sought. As far as the United Kingdom is concerned, this is achieved by eliminating the requirement that a judgment from another European Union Member State can be enforced only after it has been registered for enforcement. If a foreign judgment falls within the scope of the Recast, the judgment creditor can request directly enforcement measures in the Member State addressed. While the place of the Recast within the existing framework of rules on recognition and enforcement of foreign judgments is considered briefly later on in this chapter, the relevant rules of the Recast are considered in detail in the next chapter.

This chapter firstly sets out the common law rules on recognition and enforcement, after which direct enforcement of foreign judgments by statute is examined, as well as the interrelation of the common law and statutes.[16]

2. RECOGNITION AND ENFORCEMENT AT COMMON LAW

We must now consider the principles on which the successful litigant may take advantage of a foreign judgment at common law.[17] A foreign judgment creditor has an alternative. He may either sue on the obligation created by the judgment, or he may plead the judgment as *res judicata* in proceedings which involve the same cause of action or raise the same issue. It is important to emphasise that it is never a foreign judgment as such which is enforced in England under the common law rules. What is enforceable is an English judgment given on

---

[15] *Rubin v Eurofinance SA* [2012] UKSC 46 at [9], [2013] 1 AC 236.

[16] For useful summaries of the law on recognition and enforcement of foreign judgments in some other common law countries see (2014) 15 YBPIL 255 et seq, including Australia at p 255 (report written by Harder), Canadian common law provinces at 313 (by Saumier), Hong Kong at 349 (by Lu and Fan), Commonwealth African countries at 365 (by Oppong), Singapore at 451 (by Yeo) and South Africa at 467 (by Bäder and Kruger).

[17] The foreign decision must, of course, always be one that is regarded as a judgment: *Berliner Industriebank AG v Jost* [1971] 2 QB 463, CA—entry of a debt in the record as a judgment in bankruptcy proceedings; *Midland International Trade Services Ltd v Sudairy*, Financial Times, 2 May 1990—a decision of the Saudi Arabian Chamber for Settlement of Commercial Paper Disputes held to be a judgment; *Midtown Acquisitions LP v Essar Global Fund Ltd* [2017] EWHC 519 (Comm)—a New York "judgment by confession" held to be a judgment. See also *Kuwait Finance House (Bahrain) BSC v Teece* [2014] NZHC 3162—a decision of the Bahrain Chamber for Dispute Resolution not a judgment of a court.

an action on the foreign judgment. The expression "enforcement of foreign judgments" is thus somewhat misleading but will nevertheless be adopted for the sake of convenience. We start by setting out the two requirements that every foreign judgment—be it in personam or in rem—has to meet in order to be recognised or enforced in England (jurisdiction of the foreign court; finality and conclusiveness). This is followed by the description of the method of, and requirements for, enforcement of foreign judgments in personam in England and how the common law recognises foreign judgments by regarding them as *res judicata*. The defences to recognition and enforcement are then set out.

(a) Jurisdiction of the foreign court:[18] judgments in personam

A judgment in personam determines the existence of rights against a person.[19] The first and overriding essential for the effectiveness of a foreign judgment in personam in England is that the adjudicating court should have had jurisdiction in the international sense over the defendant. A foreign court may give a judgment which, according to the system of law under which it sits, is conclusively binding on the defendant, but unless the circumstances are such as in the eyes of English law to justify the court in having assumed jurisdiction, the judgment does not create a cause of action that is actionable in England.[20] In other words, in the view of English law, the foreign court must have been entitled to summon the defendant and subject him to judgment.[21]

Since a foreign judgment is effective only because it imposes an obligation on the defendant, it follows that any fact which negatives the existence of that obligation is a bar to the recognition and enforcement of the judgment. One of the negative facts must necessarily be that the defendant owes no duty to obey the command of the tribunal which has purported to create the obligation. There must be a correlation between the legal obligation of the defendant and the right of the tribunal to issue its command. The tests that determine whether obedience is due to an English court should, on grounds of reciprocity, also be adopted when the inquiry relates to the competence of a foreign court. Personal jurisdiction in this country under the traditional rules depends on the right of a court to summon the defendant. Apart from special powers conferred by statute,[22] it is obvious that, since the right to summon depends on the power to summon, jurisdiction is in general exercisable only against those persons who are present in England.[23] If the defendant is absent from a country, then, whether he be a citizen or an alien, he would appear to be immune from the jurisdiction, unless he has voluntarily submitted to the decision of the court.[24] The burden of proof is on the person invoking the judgment of a foreign court to establish that the court had jurisdiction in the international sense over the defendant.[25]

Let us now consider, in more detail, what are the criteria of jurisdiction in the international sense.

---

[18] Clarence Smith (1953) 2 ICLQ 510; Pryles (1972) 21 ICLQ 61; Von Mehren (1980) II Hague Recueil 9 at 55 et seq; Briggs (1987) 36 ICLQ 240.

[19] *Cambridge Gas Transportation Corpn v Official Committee of Unsecured Creditors of Navigator Holdings plc* [2006] UKPC 26 at [13], [2007] 1 AC 508. Judgments in rem will be considered infra, p 544.

[20] See, eg, *Sirdar Gurdyal Singh v The Rajah of Faridkote* [1894] AC 670, PC.

[21] *Pemberton v Hughes* [1899] 1 Ch 781 at 790 et seq, CA; *Salvesen v Austrian Property Administrator* [1927] AC 641 at 659, HL.

[22] Supra, pp 334–81.

[23] *Employers' Liability Assurance Corpn v Sedgwick, Collins & Co* [1927] AC 95 at 114, HL.

[24] *Harris v Taylor* [1915] 2 KB 580 at 589, CA.

[25] *Adams v Cape Industries plc* [1990] Ch 433 at 550, CA; *Owens Bank Ltd v Bracco* [1992] 2 AC 443 at 489, HL; *Akande v Balfour Beatty Construction Ltd* [1998] IL Pr 110 at 113.

(i) Residence and presence of defendant in the foreign country at the time of the suit

<u>(a) An individual defendant</u>

The residence of the defendant within the foreign country is sufficient for jurisdiction.[26] What is more debatable is whether the mere presence of the defendant in the foreign country for a short time will suffice.[27] The argument in favour of jurisdiction on such a basis is that persons who happen to be within a territorial dominion owe obedience to its sovereign power—obedience, that is to say, to the jurisdiction of its courts and in certain respects to its laws. "By making himself present he contracts-in to a network of obligations, created by the local law and by the local courts."[28] This duty of obedience results from mere presence in the territory, and therefore the length of time for which the presence continues is immaterial.[29] Furthermore, the jurisdiction of the English court may be based on the mere presence of the defendant within the jurisdiction.[30]

This view is supported by *Carrick v Hancock*:[31]

> A domiciled Englishman appeared after a writ was served on him in Sweden while he was on a short visit to that country. It was held that despite his fleeting stay in Sweden an action on the judgment lay against him in this country.

It has been endorsed, obiter, by the Court of Appeal in *Adams v Cape Industries plc*.[32] The temporary presence must be voluntary, ie not induced by compulsion, fraud or duress.[33] The date of service of process in the foreign country is probably the relevant one for examining whether the defendant is present abroad, rather than the date of issue of proceedings.[34] It is not the date of the cause of action arising.[35]

There is, however, much to be said for the view that casual presence, as distinct from residence, is not a desirable basis of jurisdiction. Where, for instance, both parties are foreigners and the cause of action is based entirely on facts occurring abroad and subject to foreign law, it is strange that the defendant should be bound by the decision of a court in whose jurisdiction he may by chance have been temporarily present. "The court is not a convenient one for either of the parties, nor is it in a favourable position to deal intelligently either with the facts or with the law."[36] Furthermore, any analogy based on the jurisdiction of the English courts is not particularly convincing, since the rules on jurisdiction are operated in conjunction with

---

[26] *Schibsby v Westenholz* (1870) LR 6 QB 155 at 161; *Rousillon v Rousillon* (1890) 14 Ch D 351 at 371; *Sirdar Gurdyal Singh v The Rajah of Faridkote* [1894] AC 670 at 684, PC; *Emanuel v Symon* [1908] 1 KB 302 at 309, CA; *Employers' Liability Assurance Corpn v Sedgwick, Collins & Co* [1927] AC 95 at 104, HL. Residence without presence at the date of commencement of proceedings is seemingly enough: *State Bank of India v Murjani Marketing Group Ltd*, 27 March 1991, CA; *Martyn v Graham* [2003] QDC 447 at [22]. Cf, however, *Adams v Cape Industries plc* [1990] Ch 433 at 518, CA; *Rubin v Eurofinance SA* [2012] UKSC 46 at [10], [89], [2013] 1 AC 236; Briggs 2014, para 6.153; Briggs 2015, para 7.47–7.48.

[27] See generally Oppong (2007) 3 J Priv Int L 321.

[28] The *Adams* case at 553.

[29] *Carrick v Hancock* (1895) 12 TLR 59; the *Adams* case at 517–18.

[30] Supra, pp 324–32. See also *Wendel v Moran* 1993 SLT 44.

[31] (1895) 12 TLR 59.

[32] [1990] Ch 433 at 517–18, CA. See also *Richman v Ben-Tovim* 2007 (2) SALR 283, South African Sup Ct. Cf *Carrick Estates Ltd v Young* (1988) 43 DLR (4th) 161, Sask CA.

[33] The *Adams* case at 517–18.

[34] Ibid. But cf *Akande v Balfour Beatty Construction Ltd* [1998] IL Pr 110 at 117.

[35] The *Emanuel v Symon* case; see also *Wendel v Moran* 1993 SLT 44; *McTavish and Hampton Securities v Investments Ltd* (1983) 150 DLR (3d) 27, Alta Ct of QB; *Rafferty's Restaurant Ltd v Sawchuk* [1983] 3 WWR 261, Manitoba Co Ct; *Kelowna and District Credit Union v Perl* (1984) 13 DLR (4th) 756, Alta CA; *Hull v Wilson* (1995) 128 DLR (4th) 403, Alta CA.

[36] Dodd (1929) 23 Ill LR 427, 437–8.

a discretion to stay the proceedings, and the exercise of the discretion is likely to be an issue when jurisdiction is founded on mere presence.

(b) A corporate defendant

A company cannot literally be resident or present in a foreign country. It may, though, carry on business abroad. The circumstances in which this can amount to an artificial residence or presence in a foreign country were set out by the Court of Appeal in *Adams v Cape Industries plc*.[37] It has to be shown that: (i) the corporation has its own fixed place of business (a branch office) there, from which it has carried on its own business for more than a minimal time, or a representative has carried on the corporation's business for more than a minimal time from a fixed place of business;[38] and (ii) the corporation's business is transacted from that fixed place of business. This second requirement is unlikely to cause any difficulties if a branch office is established.[39] However, if business is carried on abroad by a representative the question will arise of whether this person is carrying on the corporation's business or no more than his own. It will then be necessary to look into the functions which this representative has been performing and his relationship with the overseas corporation. This will involve looking at such things as acquisition of business premises, payment of the representative, reimbursement of expenses, the degree of control by the corporation, and display of the corporation's name. The representative's power to bind the corporation contractually is of particular importance. If the representative lacks this power this is a powerful factor counting against the presence or residence of the overseas corporation.

In the *Adams* case these principles were applied to the situation where the corporation carried on business abroad by means of a subsidiary company.

> The defendants, an English company concerned with mining asbestos, and its world-wide marketing subsidiary, another English company, carried on business in the USA through its US marketing subsidiary, NAAC and its successor CPC, companies incorporated in Illinois. Asbestos mined by the defendants was sold for use in an asbestos factory in Texas. The 206 plaintiffs, who were mainly employees injured whilst working at this factory, commenced proceedings for damages in the US Federal District Court at Tyler, Texas. The defendants took no part in these proceedings (the Tyler 2 actions), although they had taken part in earlier asbestos-related proceedings involving different plaintiffs (the Tyler 1 actions),[40] and a default judgment was awarded against them by the US court.

Scott J dismissed the action to enforce the default judgment in England, and this was affirmed by the Court of Appeal. It was held that the defendants were not present in Illinois, since NAAC and CPC, the representatives of the defendants, were carrying on exclusively their own business and not that of the defendants.[41] Relevant to this was the fact that, inter alia, NAAC leased premises itself, bought and stored asbestos, paid taxes on its profits and had its

---

[37] [1990] Ch 433 at 530–1, CA; Collier [1990] CLJ 416; Carter (1990) 61 BYBIL 402. Cases on the jurisdiction of English courts over claims against foreign companies are relevant in this context: see supra, pp 328–32.

[38] Following *Littauer Glove Corpn v F W Millington (1920) Ltd* (1928) 44 TLR 746 and *Vogel v R and A Kohnstamm Ltd* [1973] QB 133. See also *TDI Hospitality Management Consultants Inc v Browne* (1995) 117 DLR (4th) 289, Manitoba CA; *Hull v Wilson* (1996) 128 DLR (4th) 403, Alta CA. See also *Long Beach Ltd v Global Witness Ltd* [2007] EWHC 1980 (QB), website accessible from judgment granting state not enough; also, *Lucasfilm Ltd v Ainsworth* [2009] EWCA Civ 1328 at [187]–[195], [2010] 3 WLR 333; cf the position in Canada, *Disney Enterprises Inc v Click Enterprises Inc* (2006) 267 DLR (4th) 291, Ont Sup Ct of Justice.

[39] There is no requirement, as under the Brussels/Lugano system, that the branch has a certain autonomy, see the discussion of Art 7(5) of the Recast of the Brussels I Regulation supra, pp 279–82.

[40] This raises arguments in relation to submission, discussed infra, p 539.

[41] [1990] Ch 433 at 545 et seq, CA.

own creditors/debtors. The position of CPC was even weaker since it was an independently owned company and not even a subsidiary of either of the defendants. Moreover, whilst NAAC and CPC performed valuable services for the defendants as intermediaries, neither had power to, and never did, bind the defendants contractually.

A subsidiary will normally act just for itself and not for the overseas parent.[42] Counsel for the plaintiffs tried to get round this difficulty by arguing that the defendants and NAAC were all part of a single economic unit.[43] This radical idea, which is based on the economic reality of the situation and has found favour in the USA,[44] was rejected by the Court of Appeal, who emphasised the traditional company law notion that parent and subsidiary are separate legal entities. This means that an English company can set up its business abroad in such a way that it is not present or resident there. Provided that the company does not submit to the jurisdiction of the foreign court and that the subsidiary is not a "mere façade concealing the true facts",[45] judgments against it in that country will not be enforced in England. The principles in the *Adams* case apply equally to the situation where a defendant company carries on business abroad by means of companies in the same group, which are not subsidiaries, and by means of companies in which it has a shareholding.[46] Normally, these associated companies will act for themselves and not for the defendant company.

(c) Residence and presence and non-unitary states

The trial in the *Adams* case took place in Texas. One of the questions that arose was whether the relevant territorial connection had to exist between the defendant and the state in which the trial took place or whether it would have been enough if the defendant had been present or resident in another US state, eg Illinois? Without expressing a final decision on this issue, there are some surprising suggestions, albeit rather hesitant ones, from the Court of Appeal that the existence of the relevant connection with Illinois would have been sufficient.[47] This was on the basis that the trial took place in a federal district court (ie a US court) rather than a state of Texas court. This was despite the fact that a federal court judge sitting in Texas has to apply that state's rules on both jurisdiction in personam and choice of law, and a federal judgment is itself a foreign judgment when it comes to its enforcement within the USA. This rule applies *mutatis mutandis* where the jurisdiction of the foreign court is said to derive from a submission of the defendant.

(ii) Submission to the foreign court

(a) Submission by virtue of being the claimant or counterclaimant in the foreign action

It is perfectly clear that, if a person voluntarily and unsuccessfully submits his case as claimant or counterclaimant to the decision of a foreign tribunal, he cannot afterwards, if the judgment is invoked against him in England, aver that he was not subject to the jurisdiction of that tribunal.[48]

---

[42] But see Case 218/86 *Sar Schotte Gmbh v Parfums Rothschild* [1987] ECR 4905, which is concerned with jurisdiction under Art 5(5) of the Brussels Convention (identical to Art 7(5) of the Recast of the Brussels I Regulation), discussed supra, pp 279–83.

[43] [1990] Ch 433 at 532 et seq, CA; Fawcett (1988) 37 ICLQ 645.

[44] See *Bulova Watch Co Inc v K Hattori and Co Ltd* 508 F Supp 1322 at 1342 (EDNY, 1981).

[45] [1990] Ch 433 at 539, CA.

[46] *Akande v Balfour Beatty Construction Ltd* [1998] IL Pr 110.

[47] [1990] Ch 433 at 550 et seq, CA. Cf the *Akande* case at 122.

[48] *Schibsby v Westenholz* (1870) LR 6 QB 155 at 161; *Novelli v Rossi* (1831) 2 B & Ad 757, 109 ER 1326; *Desarrollo Immobiliario Y Negocios Industriales De Alta v Kader Holdings Co Ltd* [2014] EWHC 1460 (QB) at [58]–[90].

(b) Agreements to submit

What may be regarded as a particular example of submission arises where the defendant has previously contracted to submit himself to the foreign jurisdiction,[49] as, for instance, in *Feyerick v Hubbard*,[50] where a domiciled British subject resident in London agreed to sell his patent rights to a Belgian, the contract of sale containing a provision that all disputes should be submitted to the jurisdiction of the Belgian courts.[51] A less explicit agreement was held to be sufficient in *Copin v Adamson*,[52] where it was held that the articles of association of a company, which provided that all disputes that might arise during liquidation should be submitted to the jurisdiction of a French court, constituted a contract on the part of every shareholder that he should be bound by a judgment so obtained. "It appears to me", said Lord Cairns, "that, to all intents and purposes, it is as if there had been an actual and absolute agreement by the defendant [shareholder]."[53] If the agreement was entered into under undue influence it will not constitute submission, but the defendant cannot raise in England the issue of undue influence if this defence was available to him in the foreign proceedings and he failed to raise it there.[54]

In *Copin v Adamson* and other cases[55] the agreement to accept the foreign jurisdiction was express and the weight of authority was in favour of the view that an agreement to submit cannot be implied.[56] Despite this body of opinion, DiplockJ held in *Blohn v Desser*[57] that a partner in an Austrian firm who was resident in England and took no part in the conduct of the business would be held impliedly to have agreed to submit to the jurisdiction of the Austrian courts.[58] This conclusion has been strongly criticised, extra-judicially,[59] and was rejected by Ashworth J in *Vogel v R and A Kohnstamm Ltd*,[60] who refused to countenance an implied agreement to submit. The Court of Appeal in *New Hampshire Insurance Co Ltd v Strabag Bau AG*[61] expressed a preference for this view rather than that of Diplock J in *Blohn v Desser*.

In *Adams v Cape Industries plc*[62] it was argued that the defendants, by their conduct in participating in the earlier asbestos-related actions (the Tyler 1 actions) in the same court, had

---

[49] *Copin v Adamson* (1874) LR 9 Ex 345 at 354, affd (1875) 1 Ex D 17; *Rousillon v Rousillon* (1880) 14 Ch D 351 at 371; *Emanuel v Symon* [1908] 1 KB 302 at 309, CA.

[50] (1902) 71 LJKB 509. See also *Desarrollo Immobiliario Y Negocios Industriales De Alta v Kader Holdings Co Ltd* [2014] EWHC 1460 (QB) at [9]–[57]. Distinguish an agreement which merely selects the law of a foreign country as the governing law of a contract: *US Mortgage Finance II LLC v Dew* [2015] EWHC 3621 (Comm), affd without discussing this point by the Court of Appeal in an unreported judgment of 1 March 2017; infra, p 717.

[51] But if the parties agree that a specific court will have jurisdiction and the claimant obtains judgment from another court in the same country, that court will not be the court of competent jurisdiction for the purposes of English private international law: *SA Consortium General Textiles v Sun and Sand Agencies Ltd* [1978] QB 279, CA. This case is also an authority on submission by voluntary appearance, discussed infra, pp 533–7.

[52] (1874) LR 9 Ex 345, affd (1875) 1 Ex D 17; *Vallée v Dumergue* (1849) 4 Ex 290, 154 ER 1221.

[53] (1875) 1 Ex D 17 at 19.

[54] *Israel Discount Bank of New York v Hadjipateras* [1984] 1 WLR 137, CA; discussed infra, pp 567–8 and 574.

[55] *Bank of Australasia v Harding* (1850) 9 CB 661, 137 ER 1052; *Bank of Australasia v Nias* (1851) 16 QB 717, 117 ER 1055.

[56] *Sirdar Gurdyal Singh v The Rajah of Faridkote* [1894] AC 670 at 685–6, PC; the *Emanuel v Symon* case at 305, 313–14.

[57] [1962] 2 QB 116; and see *Sfeir & Co v National Insurance Co of New Zealand Ltd* [1964] 1 Lloyd's Rep 330 at 339–40.

[58] In the event, however, the defendant was held not to be liable, since the judgment was not final and conclusive; infra, pp 548–51.

[59] Lewis (1961) 10 ICLQ 910; Cohn (1962) 11 ICLQ 583; Abel (1962) 11 ICLQ 587; Carter (1962) 38 BYBIL 493; and see the 8th edn of this book (1970), pp 627–8.

[60] [1973] QB 133; Cohn (1972) 21 ICLQ 157.

[61] [1992] 1 Lloyd's Rep 361 at 372, CA.

[62] [1990] Ch 433 at 463–7. The first instance decision in relation to submission was not challenged on appeal.

represented that they would similarly participate in future claims (ie the Tyler 2 actions) brought in that court, and in that sense had impliedly agreed to submit to the jurisdiction. Scott J, speaking obiter, seemed to accept that an implied agreement to submit might suffice. However, a clear indication of consent to the exercise of the foreign court's jurisdiction was needed. Furthermore, in the case of a representation, as opposed to a contractual agreement, this would have to be acted upon by the claimants in some way.

The possibility of implied submission was thus uncertain until the Privy Council cast away any doubts in *Vizcaya Partners Ltd v Picard*.[63] The background to the dispute was the fraudulent Ponzi scheme operated by one Mr Madoff in New York. The trustee in the liquidation of the scheme commenced proceedings in New York under the anti-avoidance provisions of the US Bankruptcy Code against investors who had been repaid before the fraud was discovered. The trustee obtained a default judgment against the absent judgment debtor and sought to enforce the judgment in Gibraltar. The question was whether the judgment debtor impliedly agreed to submit to the jurisdiction of the New York court on the basis that the contract with Mr Madoff's company contained a New York choice of law clause and some other factors. Lord Collins, who gave the judgment for the Board, stated that the real question is whether the judgment debtor actually contractually agreed or consented in advance to the jurisdiction of the foreign court. Such contractual agreement or consent may be implied or inferred, either as a matter of fact from the circumstances in order to give effect to the intention of the parties or as a matter of law as a necessary incident of the contractual relationship. However, the mere fact of being a shareholder in a foreign company or a member of a foreign partnership,[64] or that the contract which was the subject of the foreign proceedings was governed by a foreign law or was made or was to be performed in a foreign country, or that the foreign governing law conferred jurisdiction on the foreign court under its own law, was not sufficient. Whether there is an implied or inferred agreement to submit depends on the governing law, which governs questions of interpretation and construction and supplies the relevant background of implied statutory and other terms. On the facts of *Vizcaya Partners Ltd v Picard*, no such agreement existed.

(c) Submission by voluntary appearance[65]

(i) An appearance to fight on the merits

The defendant submits to the jurisdiction of the foreign court by voluntary appearance if he has fought the action on its merits, and so taken his chance of obtaining a judgment in his own favour.[66] A person's submission in respect of a claim against him can also be taken as a submission, first, in respect of claims concerning the same subject matter, and, secondly, in respect of related claims which might properly be brought against him under the foreign court's rules of procedure, either by the original claimant or by others who were parties to the proceedings (eg co-defendants who subsequently brought a cross-claim) at the time he submitted.[67] It is suggested that if the defendant is represented by a lawyer who has no authority

---

[63] [2016] UKPC 5, [2016] 3 All ER 181; Kupelyants (2016) 75 CLJ 216.

[64] *Blohn v Desser* [1962] 2 QB 116 was held to be wrongly decided on this point.

[65] For the position where there has been undue influence, see *Israel Discount Bank of New York v Hadjipateras* [1984] 1 WLR 137, CA; discussed infra, at pp 567–8 and 574.

[66] *Molony v Gibbons* (1810) 2 Camp 502, 170 ER 1232; *Guiard v De Clermont and Donner* [1914] 3 KB 145; *The Atlantic Emperor (No 2)* [1992] 1 Lloyd's Rep 624 at 633, CA; *Pattni v Ali and Dinky International SA* [2006] UKPC 51 at [39], [2007] 2 AC 85; *Navigators Insurance Co v Mohammed* [2015] EWHC 1137 (Comm). On what amounts to an appearance, see *Overseas Food Importers & Distributors Ltd v Brandt* (1981) 126 DLR (3d) 422, British Columbia CA; *Mid-Ohio Imported Car Co v Tri-K Investments Ltd* (1995) 129 DLR (4th) 181, British Columbia CA.

[67] *Murthy v Sivajothi* [1999] 1 WLR 467, CA; Briggs (1998) 69 BYBIL 349; *Whyte v Whyte* [2005] EWCA Civ 858, [2005] Fam Law 863.

to act for him this should not be regarded as a submission.[68] The finding of a foreign court that the defendant had authorised a lawyer to act on his behalf, and had accordingly submitted to the jurisdiction, may create an issue estoppel preventing this issue of authority being relitigated in England.[69]

(ii) An appearance to protest against jurisdiction

The case that for many years caused difficulty was where a defendant entered an appearance with the sole object of protesting against the jurisdiction of the foreign court.

At common law an illogical distinction was drawn between a protest as to the existence of jurisdiction and as to the exercise of a discretion in relation to jurisdiction. In *Henry v Geoprosco International Ltd*:[70]

> The defendant, a company registered in Jersey, appeared before a court in Alberta and argued, unsuccessfully, that service out of the jurisdiction should be set aside, on the ground, inter alia, that the court was not the *forum conveniens*.

When it came to enforcement of the Alberta judgment in England, the Court of Appeal held that an appearance, such as this, to ask the court to use its discretion not to exercise its jurisdiction constituted submission. However, the court left open the question of whether an appearance solely to protest against the existence of the jurisdiction of a foreign court constituted submission. Not only was the above distinction unjustifiable, but also its application led to the absurd result that, in certain circumstances, a defendant who appeared before a foreign court to protest that it had no jurisdiction over him would be deemed to have submitted to that court's jurisdiction.

The old law has been replaced by section 33 of the Civil Jurisdiction and Judgments Act 1982,[71] which is designed to get rid of this absurdity; but, as will be seen, there are still some problems which are caused by the wording of this section.

Section 33(1) provides that:

> For the purposes of determining whether a judgment given by a court of an overseas country should be recognised or enforced in England and Wales or Northern Ireland, the person against whom the judgment was given shall not be regarded as having submitted to the jurisdiction of the court by reason only of the fact that he appeared (conditionally or otherwise) in the proceedings for all or any one or more of the following purposes, namely:
>
> (a) to contest the jurisdiction of the court;
> (b) to ask the court to dismiss or stay the proceedings on the ground that the dispute in question should be submitted to arbitration or to the determination of the courts of another country;
> (c) to protect, or obtain the release of, property seized or threatened with seizure in the proceedings.

---

[68] This point was left open in *First National Bank of Houston v Houston E & C Inc* [1990] 5 WWR 719 at 725, British Columbia CA. But see under the Brussels Convention, Case C–78/95 *Hendrikman v Magenta Druck & Verlag GmbH* [1996] ECR I-4943.

[69] *Desert Sun Loan Corpn v Hill* [1996] 2 All ER 847, CA; cf *A/S D/S Svendborg v Wansa* [1997] 2 Lloyd's Rep 183 at 188, CA.

[70] [1976] QB 726, CA, following *Harris v Taylor* [1915] 2 KB 580, CA; Carter (1974–1975) 47 BYBIL 379; Collier [1975] CLJ 219; Collins (1976) 92 LQR 268; Solomons (1976) 25 ICLQ 665. *Henry v Geoprosco* has not been followed in Canada, see *Clinton v Ford* (1982) 137 DLR (3d) 281, Ont CA; Lange (1983) 61 Can Bar Rev 637.

[71] For Australia see s 7(5) of the Foreign Judgments Act 1991 (Cth); *de Santis v Russo* [2002] 2 Qd R 230, CA.

Section 33 only applies to a judgment given by a court of an "overseas country", ie "any country or territory outside the United Kingdom".[72] It does not distinguish between recognition and enforcement at common law and by statute[73] and can, therefore, apply to both, except in so far as section 33(2) applies.

Section 33(2)[74] provides that:

> Nothing in this section shall affect the recognition or enforcement in England and Wales or Northern Ireland of a judgment which is required to be recognised or enforced there under the 1968 Convention or the Lugano Convention or the [Brussels I] Regulation or the Maintenance Regulation or the 2007 Hague Convention or the 2005 Hague Convention.

This means that, although, in principle, section 33 applies to judgments covered by the Brussels/Lugano system and other legal instruments mentioned in section 33(2), it remains subject to this system and these other instruments.[75]

Section 33(1) is a negative provision; it does not define what amounts to submission to the jurisdiction of a foreign court, but merely states that an appearance for one or more specified purposes does not amount to submission. *Henry v Geoprosco*[76] shows that a defendant may, in fact, put in an appearance to argue:

(1) that the foreign court has no jurisdiction because no basis of jurisdiction is applicable;
(2) that the foreign court should use its discretionary powers to set aside service out of the jurisdiction on the basis that it is not the *forum conveniens*;
(3) that the foreign court should use its discretionary powers to stay the proceedings on the basis of *forum non conveniens*;
(4) that the foreign court should dismiss or stay the proceedings because of an agreement on jurisdiction;
(5) that the foreign court should dismiss or stay the proceedings because of an arbitration agreement;
(6) that the foreign court should dismiss or stay the proceedings because of a *Scott v Avery*[77] arbitration clause, ie one which provides not merely for arbitration but that an action cannot be maintained until the matter in dispute has first been referred to and decided by arbitrators.

If a defendant puts in an appearance for any one of these purposes, how is this treated under section 33? The answer is to be found by looking at the six categories above and considering them in relation to the three sub-sections under section 33(1).

The three purposes of appearance, specified under section 33(1), which do not amount to submission are as follows:

Section 33(1)(a) *an appearance "to contest the jurisdiction of the court"*

---

[72] S 50 of the 1982 Act. For judgments given within the United Kingdom, see infra, pp 588–91.

[73] As far as enforcement under the Foreign Judgments (Reciprocal Enforcement) Act 1933 is concerned, s 33 of the 1982 Act merely replaces a similarly worded provision under the 1933 Act (s 4(2)(a)(i)), discussed infra, p 595.

[74] As amended by the Civil Jurisdiction and Judgments Act 1991, Sch 2, para 15, Civil Jurisdiction and Judgments Order, SI 2001/3929, Sch 2(IV), para 15, Civil Jurisdiction and Judgments (Maintenance) Regulations, SI 2011/1484, Sch 4, para 10, International Recovery of Maintenance (Hague Convention 2007 etc) Regulations, SI 2012/2814, Sch 4, para 5(4) and the Civil Jurisdiction and Judgments (Hague Convention on Choice of Court Agreements 2005) Regulations, SI 2015/1644, reg 17.

[75] In cases coming within the Brussels/Lugano system, recognition and enforcement are not dependent on whether the defendant has submitted to the foreign court (see infra, pp 608–9) and therefore s 33 is irrelevant, see Collins, *The Civil Jurisdiction and Judgments Act 1982* (1983), p 144.

[76] [1976] QB 726, CA; discussed supra, p 534.

[77] *Scott v Avery* (1856) 5 HL Cas 811, 10 ER 1121, HL.

Section 33(1)(a) is of the same effect as, and virtually identical in wording to, the end part of section 4(2)(a)(i) of the Foreign Judgments (Reciprocal Enforcement) Act 1933, which it replaces.[78] It follows that, although section 33(1)(a) will be significant in relation to both recognition and enforcement at common law and under the 1933 Act, it only introduces a major change in the law in respect of common law.

Section 33(1)(a) follows the 1933 Act in not defining what is meant by contesting the jurisdiction. Given the history of this area of law it is to be regretted that this concept was not clearly spelled out in the 1982 Act. Category (1), of the six categories set out above, clearly comes within section 33(1)(a).[79] There is more difficulty with category (2). A narrow interpretation of section 33(1)(a) would be that only arguments as to the bases of jurisdiction (category (1)) come within it. The distinction drawn in *Henry v Geoprosco* between the existence of jurisdiction and the exercise of a discretion, with category (2) coming within the latter, could still be followed under section 33(1)(a), due to the imprecise wording of this provision. However, it would be better to give a wide interpretation to section 33(1)(a) so that it encompasses any argument in relation to jurisdiction, whether as to the existence of jurisdiction or as to the exercise of a discretion. The wording of the provision allows this interpretation. Moreover, the distinction drawn in *Henry v Geoprosco* was strongly criticised at the time[80] and section 33(1) was intended to overrule that decision.[81] If this wide interpretation of section 33(1)(a) is accepted, it would also encompass category (3).

> **Section 33(1)(b)** *an appearance "to ask the court to dismiss or stay the proceedings on the ground that the dispute in question should be submitted to arbitration or to the determination of the courts of another country"*

It was necessary to have a separate provision in section 33(1) to deal with the situation set out in section 33(1)(b) because of a line of reasoning adopted by the Court of Appeal in *Henry v Geoprosco*.[82] There, the defendant appeared and sought a stay of proceedings abroad on the basis, inter alia, that there was a *Scott v Avery* type of arbitration clause in the contract between the parties. According to the Court of Appeal,[83] this defence involved an assertion that the plaintiff had no accrued cause of action, and this meant that the defendants were voluntarily asking the court to adjudicate on the merits of that part of the defence. The defendants had, therefore, submitted to the jurisdiction of the court. Section 33(1)(b) makes it clear that there is no submission in this situation (ie category 6).[84]

It was not entirely clear whether section 33(1)(b) could also be said to cover category (5).[85] In the first reported decision on section 33, *Tracomin SA v Sudan Oil Seeds Co Ltd*,[86] Staughton J held that Sudanese sellers who appeared before the Swiss courts to ask for a stay of proceedings because of an arbitration clause, which provided that disputes should

---

[78] See s 54 and Sch 14 of the 1982 Act, and infra, p 595.

[79] See *Desert Sun Loan Corpn v Hill* [1996] 2 All ER 847 at 861, CA (per Roch LJ). But cf Evans LJ and Stuart-Smith LJ who ignored this provision.

[80] See the 10th edn of this book (1979), p 640; Collins (1976) 92 LQR 268, 287; cf Carter (1974–1975) 47 BYBIL 379, 381.

[81] This becomes even more apparent when one looks at s 33(1)(b), discussed infra.

[82] [1976] QB 726, CA; discussed supra, p 534.

[83] Ibid, at 732–5, 750.

[84] The Court of Appeal, ibid, at 750, said that this defence could be raised as a plea in bar and not merely where a stay is sought; hence s 33(1)(b) refers to an appearance to ask the court to "dismiss" the proceedings, as well as referring to an appearance to ask the court to stay the proceedings.

[85] In the *Henry v Geoprosco* case a stay was sought in Alberta on the basis of both categories (5) and (6).

[86] [1983] 1 WLR 662 at 670–2, affd by the Court of Appeal [1983] 1 WLR 1026; the only point raised on appeal was whether s 33, which came into force during the course of the first instance hearing, could apply to an action commenced and a judgment given before the 1982 Act came into force or had been passed.

be submitted to arbitration in London, had not submitted to the jurisdiction of the Swiss courts. The judge did not say whether this situation came within section 33(1)(a) or (1)(b). But in a recent case, in which the defendant in proceedings in Morocco had asked the Moroccan court to dismiss or stay the proceedings in favour of arbitration, the court treated this as falling within section 33(1)(b).[87] Section 33(1)(b) does not just deal with agreements on arbitration; it also appears from the context to be designed to deal with agreements on the choice of court (category 4).

Section 33(1)(c) *an appearance "to protect, or obtain the release of, property seized or threatened with seizure in the proceedings"*

Under the common law rules, a defendant who possessed property abroad was placed in a particularly awkward situation. If he ignored the foreign proceedings, he stood to lose his property in the event of a default judgment being granted. On the other hand, if he put in an appearance in order to safeguard his foreign property he stood to lose not only his foreign property but also his English property as well because his appearance would, in some circumstances, amount to a submission to the foreign court and that court's judgment would accordingly be enforceable in England. Section 33(1)(c) enables the defendant to appear abroad to safeguard his property without running this risk.

Like section 33(1)(a), this provision is closely modelled on the end part of section 4(2)(a)(i) of the Foreign Judgments (Reciprocal Enforcement) Act 1933 which it replaces.[88] Although section 33(1)(c) applies to both recognition and enforcement at common law and under the 1933 Act, it will only effect a major change in the law in respect of common law, and is a development to be welcomed as bringing uniformity to these two different types of recognition and enforcement.

Section 33(1)(c) follows section 4(2)(a)(i) of the 1933 Act in applying regardless of whether the defendant is seeking to protect property that has already been seized in the proceedings, or whether he is acting with foresight to protect property that is merely threatened with seizure.[89] It thus gets rid of the distinction under the common law between the situation where property had already been seized (an appearance to protect this property would not amount to submission)[90] and where the property was merely threatened with seizure (an appearance to protect this property would amount to submission).[91] Now, in neither case is there submission to the foreign court.

(iii) Arguing in the alternative

There is no submission if the defendant merely raises an initial plea on the merits at the same time as his defence that the foreign court lacks jurisdiction, but does not go on actually to fight on the merits.[92] A defendant may do this because he is required under some legal

---

[87] *Golden Endurance Shipping SA v RMA Watanya SA* [2016] EWHC 2110 (Comm), [2017] 1 All ER (Comm) 438—the fact that under Moroccan law a challenge based on an arbitration agreement was regarded as an "admissibility", not "jurisdiction", challenge, which necessitated serving a defence on the merits, did not disengage s 33.

[88] See s 54 of and Sch 14 to the 1982 Act and infra, p 595.

[89] See *The Eastern Trader* [1996] 2 Lloyd's Rep 585 at 600—a counterclaim to obtain the release of property threatened with seizure did not amount to a submission.

[90] *Henry v Geoprosco* [1976] QB 726 at 746–7, CA. See also *Clinton v Ford* (1982) 137 DLR (3d) 281, Ont CA; *Amopharm Inc v Harris Computer Corpn* (1992) 93 DLR (4th) 524, Ont CA.

[91] *De Cosse Brissac v Rathbone* (1861) 6 H & N 301, 158 ER 123; *Voinet v Barrett* (1885) 55 LJQB 39, CA; *Guiard v De Clermont* [1914] 3 KB 145.

[92] *The Atlantic Emperor (No 2)* [1992] 1 Lloyd's Rep 624 at 633, CA; *The Eastern Trader* [1996] 2 Lloyd's Rep 585 at 601; Collins, *The Civil Jurisdiction and Judgments Act 1982* (1983), p 144. But cf *Gourmet Resources*

systems to plead a defence on the merits at the outset if he is to raise this defence later on, and he may wish to keep alive this possibility.[93] After the defence as to lack of jurisdiction fails, the defendant may then decide to take no further part in the proceedings. The defendant should not be regarded as having submitted in this situation. According to the Court of Appeal in *The Atlantic Emperor (No 2)*,[94] section 33 should not be construed too narrowly. Even if the defendant is not required to plead a defence on the merits at the outset, where he does so he will not be regarded as having submitted in the situation where he makes it abundantly clear that his primary purpose is to challenge the foreign court's jurisdiction and takes no further part in the proceedings after the defence of lack of jurisdiction fails.

Where the defendant's plea that the foreign court lacked jurisdiction fails and he then goes on to fight the action on its merits, he will have usually submitted to the foreign court's jurisdiction.[95] The courts have, however, recently adopted a more flexible approach to submission and held that the party concerned must not be put in the position of having to choose between losing his right to challenge the jurisdiction of the foreign court and losing the right to defend himself. If he has no option but to participate in the hearing of the substance of the dispute, under protest, and to wait to appeal a decision on jurisdiction only after the decision on the merits has been reached, his appearance at the substantive hearing will not, without more, be characterised as voluntary.[96] In *AES Ust-Kamenogorsk Hydropower Plant LLP v AES Ust-Kamenogorsk Hydropower Plant JSC*,[97] a case concerning a challenge to the jurisdiction of the foreign court on the basis of an arbitration agreement, the Court of Appeal held that the defendant in the original proceedings, otherwise within the jurisdiction of the foreign court, had no other choice than to defend the merits of the case. This was because, unless it had done so, the defendant would have been precluded, under the law of the foreign court, from appealing against the court's decision on jurisdiction. But a foreign judgment will be recognised and enforced where a party who unsuccessfully defended the merits in the hope of getting a judgment in his favour then challenges the validity of the judgment on the basis that the foreign court was not one of competent jurisdiction.[98]

(iv) Appeals against judgments in default

A foreign judgment that is given against an absent defendant in default of his appearance is clearly not effective in England, but is this so if he later moves to have the default judgment set aside and is unsuccessful? The answer would seem to depend on the grounds for the appeal. If the appeal is as to the merits of the claim, then this will constitute

---

International Inc v Paramount Capital Corpn [1993] IL Pr 583, Ont Ct of Justice; *Mid-Ohio Imported Car Co v Tri-K Investments Ltd* (1995) 129 DLR (4th) 181, British Columbia CA.

[93] See, eg, Case 150/80 *Elefanten Schuh GmbH v Jacqmain* [1981] ECR 1671; discussed supra, p 228. See also *The Eastern Trader* case at 600.

[94] [1992] 1 Lloyd's Rep 624 at 633, CA. See also *Starlight International Inc v AJ Bruce* [2002] EWHC 374 at [14], [2002] IL Pr 35.

[95] *Boissière and Co v Brockner & Co* (1889) 6 TLR 85; *The Atlantic Emperor (No 2)* case at 633; *Akai Pty Ltd v People's Insurance Co Ltd* [1998] 1 Lloyd's Rep 90 at 96–8; *Spliethoff's Bevrachtingskantoor BV v Bank of China Ltd* [2015] EWHC 999 (Comm) at [121]–[125], [2016] 1 All ER (Comm) 1034.

[96] *AES Ust-Kamenogorsk Hydropower Plant LLP v AES Ust-Kamenogorsk Hydropower Plant JSC* [2011] EWCA Civ 647 at [166]–[190], [2012] 1 WLR 920; Rushworth and Scott (2011) 82 BYBIL 651; *Desarrollo Immobiliario Y Negocios Industriales De Alta v Kader Holdings Co Ltd* [2014] EWHC 1460 (QB) at [58]–[90]; *Exmek Pharmaceuticals SAC v Alkem Laboratories* Ltd [2015] EWHC 3158 (Comm), [2016] 1 Lloyd's Rep 239; *Golden Endurance Shipping SA v RMA Watanya SA* [2016] EWHC 2110 (Comm), [2017] 1 All ER (Comm) 438; see also *Harada Ltd (t/a Chequerpoint UK) v Turner (No 2)* [2003] EWCA Civ 1695.

[97] [2011] EWCA Civ 647, [2012] 1 WLR 920.

[98] The *Desarrollo Immobiliario* case at [66].

submission,[99] and will normally amount to submission to the judgment of the court of first instance.[100] However, an appeal, or application for leave to appeal, merely as to a jurisdictional issue would not constitute submission.[101]

(v) Taking procedural steps in the foreign country[102]

In *Adams v Cape Industries plc*[103] Scott J held that the defendants' participation in a consent order given by the Federal District judge extinguishing the cause of action against them as part of a settlement of the litigation in the Tyler 1 actions amounted to submission to the jurisdiction of the Federal District Court in Texas, in relation to those proceedings. In the opinion of Scott J, the defendants had thereby waived the jurisdictional objections that they had raised earlier. However, for such a waiver the defendants must have "taken some step which is only necessary or only useful if the objection has been actually waived, or if the objection has never been entertained at all".[104] There was no such step where a defendant entered a conditional appearance and sought to set aside leave to serve out of the jurisdiction.[105] In the *Adams* case, the argument that submission to the Tyler 1 actions was also submission to the Tyler 2 actions (in respect of which the enforcement proceedings were brought), on the ground that there was just one unit of litigation, was rejected. The basis of submission is consent and participation in the order in relation to the Tyler 1 actions was no evidence of consent to the trial of future actions not yet started (the Tyler 2 actions). More generally, it was said[106] that:

> If the [procedural] steps would not have been regarded by the domestic law of the foreign court as a submission to the jurisdiction, they ought not, in my view, to be so regarded here.

In *Rubin v Eurofinance SA*[107] Lord Collins revisited the principles and the approach to be taken. When determining whether there has been a submission in the context of recognition and enforcement of a foreign judgment in England, the court will not simply consider whether the steps taken abroad would have amounted to a submission in English proceedings. The international context requires a broader approach. Nor does it follow from the fact that the foreign court would have regarded steps taken in the foreign proceedings as a

---

[99] *SA Consortium General Textiles v Sun and Sand Agencies Ltd* [1978] QB 279 at 299, 304, 308–9, CA, discussed infra, p 596; and see *Guiard v De Clermont* [1914] 3 KB 145; *Karafarin Bank v Mansoury-Dara* [2009] EWHC 1217 (Comm) at [28]–[29], [2009] 2 Lloyd's Rep 289.

[100] The *SA Consortium General Textiles* case at 299, 304, CA; cf the *Guiard v De Clermont* case at 155. In so far as these cases discuss appeals on jurisdictional issues they must now be read in the light of s 33 of the 1982 Act, discussed supra, pp 534–7.

[101] The *SA Consortium General Textiles* case at 305, 308–9, CA; s 33 of the 1982 Act. It seems that, in two of the Canadian cases where recognition was denied to a default judgment even though the defendant had moved to set it aside, namely *McLean v Shields* (1885) 9 OR 699, Ont CA and *Esdale v Bank of Ottawa* (1920) 51 DLR 485, Alta CA, the ground on which the defendant moved to set aside the original judgment was want of jurisdiction; see Read, *Recognition and Enforcement of Foreign Judgments* (1938), pp 168–70. In the third it was not clear what the basis for seeking to set aside the original judgment was: *Carrick Estates Ltd v Young* (1988) 43 DLR (4th) 161, Sask CA.

[102] See generally Briggs 2015, para 7.56.

[103] [1990] Ch 433, supra, pp 530–1. See also *The Eastern Trader* [1996] 2 Lloyd's Rep 585 at 600; *Starlight International Inc v AJ Bruce* [2002] EWHC 374 at [41], [2002] IL Pr 35; *Von Wyl v Engeler* [1998] 3 NZLR 416.

[104] The *Adams* case at 459. See also *Akai Pty Ltd v People's Insurance Co Ltd* [1998] 1 Lloyd's Rep 90 at 96, 97. Cf the *Starlight International Inc v AJ Bruce* case at [41]—waiver according to US Federal Law.

[105] *Akande v Balfour Beatty Construction Ltd* [1998] IL Pr 110 at 114–16.

[106] The *Adams* case at 461.

[107] [2012] UKSC 46 at [156]–[167], [2013] 1 AC 236; Aitken (2013) 129 LQR 147; Briggs [2013] LMCLQ 26; Chong [2014] LMCLQ 241; Handley (2013) 129 LQR 144; Kirshner [2013] CLJ 27; Rushworth and Scott (2012) 83 BYBIL 271. See also *Service Temps Inc v MacLeod* [2013] CSOH 162 at [18]-[20], 2014 SLT 375; *Swiss Life AG v Kraus* [2015] EWHC 2133 (QB).

submission that the English court will so regard them. The question whether there has been a submission is to be inferred from all the facts. Lord Collins approved the following statement of Thomas J in *Akai Pty Ltd v People's Insurance Co Ltd*:[108]

> The court must consider the matter objectively; it must have regard to the general framework of its own procedural rules, but also to the domestic law of the court where the steps were taken. This is because the significance of those steps can only be understood by reference to that law. If a step taken by a person in a foreign jurisdiction, such as making a counterclaim, might well be regarded by English law as amounting to a submission to its jurisdiction, but would not be regarded by that foreign court as a submission to its jurisdiction, an English court will take into account the position under foreign law.

It is on this basis that the Supreme Court found in *Rubin* that submitting proofs of debt in a liquidation in Australia and attending and participating in creditors' meetings amounted to submission to the insolvency jurisdiction of the Australian court for the purposes of the enforcement of the judgment of that court in England.[109] This was notwithstanding that these procedural steps would not be regarded either by the Australian court or by the English court as a submission and that, under Australian law, the defendant was not to be taken to have waived its right to object to the court's jurisdiction. According to Lord Collins, the defendant "should not be allowed to benefit from the insolvency proceedings without the burden of complying with the orders made in that proceeding".[110]

(iii) Nothing else founds jurisdiction

The results so far of our inquiry into the international competence of foreign courts is that jurisdiction sufficient to render a judgment effective in England exists in two cases, namely, where the defendant was resident or present in the country of the forum at the time of the action, or where he submitted to the jurisdiction. The question now is whether there are any other grounds of competency.[111]

(a) Political nationality

Is the fact that the defendant is a national of the foreign country where the judgment has been obtained sufficient to render him amenable to the jurisdiction of the local courts? There is no English authority that contains an actual decision to this effect, but the suggestion that this is enough has been affirmed obiter in several cases.[112] It is also adopted by certain textbook writers.[113] It has been rejected by the Irish High Court.[114]

---

[108] [1998] 1 Lloyd's Rep 90 at 97.

[109] See also *Stichting Shell Pensioenfonds v Krys* [2014] UKPC 41 at [30]–[32], [2015] AC 616. Criticised by Briggs 2014, para 6.171; Briggs 2015, para 7.53.

[110] The *Rubin* case at [167].

[111] See generally *Adams v Cape Industries plc* [1990] Ch 433 at 515, CA; and also *Schibsby v Westenholz* (1870) LR 6 QB 155 at 161; *Rousillon v Rousillon* (1880) 14 Ch D 351 at 371; *Emanuel v Symon* [1908] 1 KB 302 at 309, CA. See also *State of New York v Fitzgerald* (1983) 148 DLR (3d) 176, British Columbia Sup Ct.

[112] *Douglas v Forrest* (1828) 4 Bing 686, 130 ER 933; *Schibsby v Westenholz* (1870) LR 6 QB 155 at 161; the *Rousillon v Rousillon* case at 371; the *Emanuel v Symon* case at 309; *Harris v Taylor* [1915] 2 KB 580 at 591, CA; *Forsyth v Forsyth* [1948] P 125 at 132, CA. See also *Gavin Gibson & Co v Gibson* [1913] 3 KB 379 at 388.

[113] Westlake, p 399; Foote, p 398; Schmitthoff, *The English Conflict of Laws* (1954) 3rd edn, p 465. It is rejected by Wolff, p 126; Graveson, pp 621–2 (though he suggests exceptions); Briggs 2014, para 6.173; Briggs 2015, para 7.60; Dicey, Morris and Collins, para 14-085; Fentiman, para 18.25; Hill and Chong, para 12.2.23. But see Read, *Recognition and Enforcement of Foreign Judgments* (1938), pp 151–5.

[114] *Rainford v Newell Roberts* [1962] IR 95; Jackson (1963) 26 MLR 563. Contrast *Independent Trustee Services Ltd v Morris* [2010] NSWSC 1218.

It is submitted that nationality per se is not, and has been rejected as, a reason which, on any principle of private international law, can justify the exercise of jurisdiction.[115] The argument advanced in its favour, namely that "a subject is bound to obey the commands of his Sovereign, and, therefore, the judgments of his sovereign courts",[116] is no doubt true, but, as Wolff pointed out, it is not the duty of another sovereign to aid the enforcement of the obligation.[117] Indeed the undesirability of such a rule becomes abundantly clear when it is remembered that it is essentially within the competence of a state to decide who are and who are not its nationals. The granting or withholding of nationality is sometimes an instrument of political policy. Even if this is not the case, the legal tie of nationality may have an extremely slender factual basis. If a Japanese court were to give judgment in personam against a person who, though born in Japan, had left that country in his infancy and acquired a domicile in England without taking out letters of naturalisation, it is difficult to appreciate the justification for holding the judgment effective in England. Again, to make nationality the basis of jurisdiction is scarcely practicable in the case of states, such as the United Kingdom,[118] the USA,[119] Canada or Australia, which contain several separate law districts. Finally, there is no question of reciprocal recognition, for the British nationality of a defendant does not suffice to found the jurisdiction of the English court.

(b) Domicile

If mere allegiance suffices to give jurisdiction, so also, it might be presumed, does domicile. The connection between a person and the country in which he is domiciled is generally a very real one, but the tie of allegiance may be of the loosest description. An ineffective exercise of jurisdiction ought not to be tolerated, and it is undeniable that a judgment based on domicile is superior on the score of effectiveness to one based merely on allegiance. Yet the curious thing is that those writers who are content to make political allegiance a ground of jurisdiction deny without hesitation the sufficiency of domicile. It is suggested that on this point at least they must be right and that domicile alone will not suffice as a ground of jurisdiction.[120]

(c) Locality of cause of action

According to the decisions that have dealt with the matter up to the present, it is undoubted that the various circumstances considered above exhaust the possible cases in which a foreign court possesses international competence. Thus it is not sufficient that the cause of action, as, for instance, a breach of contract or the commission of a tort,[121] occurred in a foreign country.[122]

---

[115] *Blohn v Desser* [1962] 2 QB 116 at 123; and see *Rossano v Manufacturers' Life Insurance Co Ltd* [1963] 2 QB 352 at 382–3; *Vogel v R and A Kohnstamm Ltd* [1973] QB 133 at 141; *Adams v Cape Industries plc* [1990] Ch 433 at 515, CA.

[116] Dicey (1949) 6th edn, p 357.

[117] Wolff, p 126. He further points out that allegiance is not sufficient even in those civil law countries where nationality is the criterion of the personal law.

[118] See *Patterson v D'Agostino* (1975) 58 DLR (3d) 63, Ont Co Ct.

[119] See *Dakota Lumber Co v Rinderknecht* (1905) 6 Terr LR 210 at 221–4, Sup Ct of the NW Territories.

[120] Read, *Recognition and Enforcement of Foreign Judgments* (1938), p 160.

[121] Eg *Gyonyor v Sanjenko* [1971] 5 WWR 381, Alb Sup Ct.

[122] *Sirdar Gurdyal Singh v Faridkote* [1894] AC 670 at 684, PC; *Phillips v Batho* [1913] 3 KB 25 at 30; *Wendel v Moran* 1993 SLT 44; cf *Schibsby v Westenholz* (1870) LR 6 QB 155 at 161.

(d) Choice of governing law

It has been held that an agreement to submit to the jurisdiction of the Florida's courts is not to be inferred from an agreement to make Florida law the governing law of a contract.[123]

(e) Possession of property

It was once thought, on the authority of *Becquet v MacCarthy*,[124] that the possession of immovable property within the foreign country was sufficient to found jurisdiction. It is safe to conclude that this decision would not be followed now for it has since been decided by the Court of Appeal in *Emanuel v Symon*[125] that neither the fact of possessing property in a foreign country nor the fact of making a partnership contract there relating to the property is sufficient to render the possessor amenable to the local jurisdiction.

(f) Foreign judgment based on service out of the jurisdiction

The practice, illustrated by rule 6.36 of the Civil Procedure Rules and para 3.1 of the Civil Procedure Rules Practice Direction 6B,[126] under which the courts of a country assume jurisdiction over absentees, raises the question whether a foreign judgment given in these circumstances will be recognised in England.[127] The authorities, so far as they go, are against recognition. The question arose in *Buchanan v Rucker*[128] where it was disclosed that, by the law of Tobago, service of process might be effected on an absent defendant by nailing a copy of the summons on the door of the court house. It was held that a judgment given against an absentee after service in this manner was an international nullity having no extra-territorial effect. Indeed, the suggestion that it should be actionable in England prompted Lord Ellenborough to ask with some disdain: "Can the island of Tobago pass a law to bind the rights of the whole world? Would the world submit to such an assumed jurisdiction?"[129]

A less fanciful process again raised the question in *Schibsby v Westenholz*,[130] where a judgment had been given by a French court against Danish subjects resident in England. The defendants were notified of the proceedings in the customary manner, which involved forwarding the summons to the consulate of the country where the defendant resided, with instructions to deliver it to him if practicable. The defendants failed to appear and judgment was given against them. It was held that no action lay on the judgment. Had the principle on which judgments are enforceable been comity, the Court of Queen's Bench intimated that having regard to the English practice of service out of the jurisdiction it would have reached a different conclusion. Since, however, the basis of enforcement is that a judgment imposes an obligation on the defendant, it followed that there must be a connection between him and the forum sufficiently close to make it his duty to perform that obligation. No such duty could be spelt out of the inactivity of the defendants, who were aliens resident in a foreign country. Wright J reached the same conclusion in a later case where a New Zealand judgment

---

[123] *US Mortgage Finance II LLC v Dew* [2015] EWHC 3621 (Comm), affd without discussing this point by the Court of Appeal in an unreported judgment of 1 March 2017. See also *Vizcaya Partners Ltd v Picard* [2016] UKPC 5, [2016] 3 All ER 181; *Dunbee Ltd v Gilman & Co (Australia) Pty Ltd* [1968] 2 Lloyd's Rep 394, NSW CA; *Mattar and Saba v Public Trustee* [1952] 3 DLR 399, Alta CA.

[124] (1831) 2 B & Ad 951, 109 ER 1396.

[125] [1908] 1 KB 302, CA; and see *Schibsby v Westenholz* (1870) LR 6 QB 155 at 163; *Sirdar Gurdyal Singh v Faridkote* [1894] AC 670 at 685, PC.

[126] Supra, pp 334–81.

[127] See Clarence Smith (1953) 2 ICLQ 510, 524–6.

[128] (1808) 9 East 192, 103 ER 546.

[129] Ibid, at 194.

[130] (1870) LR 6 QB 155.

had been given against an absentee under an assumed jurisdiction substantially similar to that countenanced by the English rules on service out of the jurisdiction.[131]

It is not without significance, however, that in this general context the Court of Appeal in *Travers v Holley*[132] acted on the basis of reciprocity and held that what entitles an English court to assume divorce jurisdiction is equally effective in the case of a foreign court. In a later case, however, Hodson LJ observed that *Travers v Holley* was: "a decision limited to a judgment *in rem* in a matter affecting matrimonial status, and it has not been followed, so far as I am aware, in any case except a matrimonial case".[133] Thus, any suggestion that the advance towards "internationalism"[134] made by that decision should be extended to jurisdiction assumed under provisions substantially similar to those contained in the English rules on service out of the jurisdiction has so far not been accepted, and the present position is that the rules set out above remain intact.[135]

(iv) *The real and substantial connection test*

The Supreme Court of Canada in *Morguard Investments Ltd v De Savoye*[136] has adopted a radically different approach towards the recognition and enforcement of foreign judgments at common law in inter-provincial cases. The concern is to produce a greater degree of recognition and enforcement within the Canadian federation than has hitherto been the case under the English-based common law rules. A judgment granted in another province is entitled to recognition and enforcement provided that the judgment granting court "properly, or appropriately, exercised jurisdiction in the action". This requirement is satisfied where the forum that had assumed jurisdiction and given judgment has "a real and substantial connection with the action".[137] This is a more flexible test than that under the English common law and may be satisfied in the situation where the defendant was neither present in the judgment granting state nor submitted to its courts.[138] This approach is not concerned solely with Canadian federalism but also more widely with "the need in modern times to facilitate the flow of wealth, skills and people across state lines in a fair and orderly manner".[139] It is not surprising therefore that the Supreme Court of Canada in *Beals v Saldanha* has extended this approach to the recognition and enforcement at common law of judgments granted outside Canada.[140] It is for the recognising and enforcing court to decide whether there is the

---

[131] *Turnbull v Walker* (1892) 67 LT 767.

[132] [1953] P 246, CA; see also *Re Dulles' Settlement (No 2)* [1951] Ch 842 at 851, CA. For the current law on recognition of foreign divorces, etc see *infra*, p 1000 et seq.

[133] *Re Trepca Mines Ltd* [1960] 1 WLR 1273 at 1281–2, CA; and see *Société Cooperative Sidmetal v Titan International Ltd* [1966] 1 QB 828 at 841; *Schemmer v Property Resources Ltd* [1975] Ch 273 at 287; *Henry v Geoprosco International Ltd* [1976] QB 726 at 745, CA; *Felixstowe Dock and Rly Co v United States Lines Inc* [1989] QB 360; *Murthy v Sivajothi* [1999] 1 All ER 721 at 730, CA; *Crick v Hennessy* [1973] WAR 74; *Gordon Pacific Developments Pty Ltd v Conlon* [1993] 3 NZLR 760. See also *Morguard Investments Ltd v De Savoye* [1990] 3 SCR 1077, (1991) 76 DLR (4th) 256.

[134] Kahn-Freund, *The Growth of Internationalism in English Private International Law* (1960), p 30 et seq.

[135] *Rubin v Eurofinance SA* [2012] UKSC 46 at [126], [127], [2013] 1 AC 236.

[136] [1990] 3 SCR 1077, (1991) 76 DLR (4th) 256; Castel and Walker, *Canadian Conflict of Laws* (2006) 6th edn, para 14.5d; Blom (1991) 70 Can Bar Rev 733; Glenn (1992) 37 McGill LJ 537; confirmed in *Hunt v T & N plc* [1993] 4 SCR 289, (1993) 109 DLR (4th) 16; Walsh (1994) 73 Can Bar Rev 304.

[137] For some of the factors relevant to determining this, see *Bank of Credit and Commerce International (Overseas) Ltd v Gokal* [1995] IL Pr 316 at 319, British Columbia Sup Ct; *Moses v Shore Boat Builders Ltd* (1993) 106 DLR (4th) 654 at 667, British Columbia CA; *Muscutt v Courcelles* (2002) 213 DLR (4th) 577 at [76]–[111], Ont CA. This requirement is also satisfied if the defendant was in the jurisdiction at the time of the action or submitted to the jurisdiction. The new rule can therefore be regarded as adding to the existing common law rules.

[138] As in the *Morguard* case itself.

[139] La Forest J in the *Morguard* case at 269.

[140] [2003] 3 SCR 416, (2003) 234 DLR (4th) 1; criticised by Atrill [2004] CLJ 574, Pitel [2004] LMCLQ 289, Walker (2004) 120 LQR 365. The parties remain free to submit or agree to the jurisdiction in which the dispute is to be resolved, at [34] and [37]. The real and substantial connection test is subject to a different

requisite real and substantial connection. However, it would be "odd indeed if a Canadian court would refuse to recognise and enforce a judgment of a foreign court in a situation where the foreign court assumed jurisdiction on the same basis on which Canadian courts assume jurisdiction".[141] There is much to be said for adopting the real and substantial connection test, or something similar, in England.[142] Indeed, its origin is to be found in a decision of the House of Lords on the recognition of foreign divorces at common law.[143] However, the introduction of any such wider test for the international jurisdiction of a foreign court for recognition and enforcement purposes would need to be accompanied by a re-examination of the natural justice and public policy defences so as to protect defendants who have been subject to injustice abroad.[144]

(b) Judgments in rem

(i) *The definition of a judgment in rem*

The jurisdictional elements that must exist before a foreign judgment in rem can be given effect in England are not difficult to specify, but it is first necessary to appreciate the correct meaning of this species of judgment. It has been defined as:

> a judgment of a court of competent jurisdiction determining the status of a person or thing (as distinct from the particular interest in it of a party to the litigation); and such a judgment is conclusive evidence for and against all persons whether parties, privies or strangers of the matters actually decided.[145]

More recently, a judgment in rem has been defined as the judicial determination of the existence of rights over property.[146] In contrast, a judgment in personam determines the existence of rights against a person.[147] There is no reason why a judgment should be characterised as either wholly in rem or wholly in personam.[148] This is not a matter of severance, rather it is a matter of analysis of the extent to which a judgment operates in part in rem and in part in

---

statutory approach, see at [28]–[29]; *Hull v Wilson* [1996] IL Pr 307, Alta CA. See also *Canada Post Corp v Lépine* 2009 SCC 16, [2009] 1 SCR 549; *Chevron Corp v Yaiguaje* 2015 SCC 42, [2015] 3 SCR 69.

[141] *Moses v Shore Boat Builders Ltd* (1993) 106 DLR (4th) 654 at 667, British Columbia CA. See also *Beals v Saldanha* [2003] 3 SCR 416 at [29], (2003) 234 DLR (4th) 1. For enforcement of a judgment of a foreign state where jurisdiction was based on service out of the jurisdiction see *Frymer v Brettschneider* [1996] IL Pr 138, Ont CA—the subject matter of the litigation must have a real connection with that state.

[142] See Briggs (1987) 36 ICLQ 240 and (1992) 109 LQR 549, who favoured recognition and enforcement where the foreign court is the natural forum; contrast Briggs 2014, paras 6.174–6.175, 6.225; Briggs 2015, paras 6.60–6.61. See also Rogerson [1998] CJQ 91, 102. Cf Harris (1997) 17 OJLS 477, who would base recognition and enforcement on whether or not the English courts are willing to restrain the foreign proceedings by anti-suit injunction. The Supreme Court of Ireland has refused to follow the real and substantial connection test: *Re Flightlease* [2012] IESC 12; Kenny (2014) 63 ICLQ 197.

[143] *Indyka v Indyka* [1969] 1 AC 33, HL. For the present rules, which are statutory, see infra, p 1000 et seq.

[144] See Walker (2004) 120 LQR 365; the dissenting judgments of Binnie, Iacobucci and LeBel JJ in the *Beals* case.

[145] *Lazarus-Barlow v Regent Estates Co Ltd* [1949] 2 KB 465 at 475, CA. And see *Fracis Times & Co v Carr* (1900) 82 LT 698 at 701, CA; *Pattni v Ali and Dinky International SA* [2006] UKPC 51 at [19]–[23], [2007] 2 AC 85; *Serious Fraud Office v Saleh* [2017] EWCA Civ 18 at [48]; Spencer Bower, Turner and Handley, *The Doctrine of Res Judicata* (1996) 3rd edn, paras 234–5.

[146] *Cambridge Gas Transportation Corpn v Official Committee of Unsecured Creditors of Navigator Holdings plc* [2006] UKPC 26 at [13], [2007] 1 AC 508; Briggs [2007] LMCLQ 129 and (2006) 77 BYBIL 575; Ho Tham [2007] LMCLQ 129.

[147] The *Cambridge Gas Transportation* case at [13].

[148] *Pattni v Ali and Dinky International SA* [2006] UKPC 51 at [37], [2007] 2 AC 85; Briggs [2007] LMCLQ 129 and (2006) 77 BYBIL 575; Tham [2007] LMCLQ 129.

personam. An order of a bankruptcy court in the USA during bankruptcy proceedings there has been held to be neither a judgment in rem nor one in personam since such proceedings are not concerned with the determination of the existence of rights.[149] In order for a foreign judgment to be given effect in England as a judgment in rem, it should be characterised as such by the foreign court.[150] The two parts of the above-quoted definition will now be considered.

(a) The subject matter of a judgment in rem

The *res* which may form the subject matter of a judgment in rem is not confined to physical things. If the essence of such a judgment is that it constitutes an adjudication on status, it follows that certain decrees declaring the status of persons must also be classed as operating in rem.[151] Thus, the word *res* as used in this context includes those human relationships, such as marriage, which do not originate merely in contract, but which constitute what may be called institutions recognised by the state.[152] A foreign court which issues, for instance, a decree of divorce or nullity of marriage will, if competent in respect of jurisdiction, be deemed to have pronounced a judgment in rem that is conclusive in England and binding on all persons.[153]

There is some authority for the view that judgments in personam that are ancillary to such judgments in rem are equally conclusive and binding in England. An illustration of this is afforded by *Phillips v Batho*[154] where the facts were as follows:

> The plaintiff, domiciled in India, obtained a divorce from his wife in an Indian court, and was awarded damages against the defendant, as co-respondent. The defendant was not present in India at the time of the suit, nor did he submit to the jurisdiction. The plaintiff then sued him in England to recover the damages awarded by the Indian judgment.

This judgment, if treated as one in personam, was not actionable in England, since the Indian court had no jurisdiction in personam over the defendant. Neither, in the opinion of the judge, could the plaintiff sue in England on the original cause of action, for the English court had divorce jurisdiction, at that time, only where the parties were domiciled in England. Scrutton J avoided the difficulties by holding that the judgment awarding damages was ancillary to the judgment in rem dissolving the marriage and, as such, was probably conclusive everywhere, and at any rate was conclusive in another part of the Commonwealth.[155] This decision has been subjected to devastating criticism;[156] it has been disapproved in New

---

[149] The *Cambridge Gas Transportation* case. According to Lord Hoffmann, at [14], "The purpose of bankruptcy proceedings . . . is not to determine or establish the existence of rights, but to provide a mechanism for collective execution against the property of the debtor by creditors whose rights are admitted or established." The decision in the *Cambridge Gas Transportation* case has been disapproved in *Rubin v Eurofinance SA* [2012] UKSC 46 at [103], [132] (per Lord Collins), [2013] 1 AC 236.

[150] *Air Foyle Ltd v Center Capital Ltd* [2002] EWHC 2535 (Comm), [2003] 2 Lloyd's Rep 753; see also *Serious Fraud Office v Saleh* [2017] EWCA Civ 18 at [48]; *United States of America v Abacha* [2014] EWCA Civ 1291 at [65]–[72], [2015] 1 WLR 1917.

[151] *Salvesen v Administrator of Austrian Property* [1927] AC 641 at 662 (per Lord Dunedin), and see per Lord Haldane at 652–3, HL.

[152] Cf Lord Haldane in the *Salvesen* case at 652–3.

[153] For the estoppel effect of foreign nullity decrees, see *Vervaeke v Smith* [1983] 1 AC 145, HL; discussed infra, pp 582–3.

[154] [1913] 3 KB 25.

[155] "A holding which created a new type of judgment—a hybrid obtained by crossing an action *in rem* with an action *in personam*, with the dominant jurisdictional characteristics being possessed by the former." Read, *Recognition and Enforcement of Foreign Judgments* (1938), p 264.

[156] Ibid, pp 264–7.

Zealand,[157] ignored in Canada[158] and is probably wrong. The judgment should be treated as one in personam whose recognition should be denied on the ground of lack of jurisdiction.

(b) The effect of a judgment in rem

The effect, for instance, of a condemnation in the Admiralty court in prize proceedings is to vest the ship in the captors and thus to alter its status. Such a judgment differs fundamentally from one in personam. A judgment in rem settles the destiny of the res itself "and binds all persons claiming an interest in the property inconsistent with the judgment even though pronounced in their absence";[159] a judgment in personam, although it may concern a res, merely determines the rights of the litigants *inter se* to the res. The former looks beyond the individual rights of the parties, the latter is directed solely to those rights.[160] Thus a judgment of a Kenyan court that two defendants "do transfer all the 100% shares in the 3rd defendant [World Duty] to the plaintiff as per the said sale and purchase agreement . . ." was held to be a judgment in personam, rather than one in rem.[161] It did not constitute or involve any form of adjudication or purported adjudication in rem relating to the shares in World Duty. Nor did it even purport actually to transfer or deal with the shares. Rather, what it did was to determine the parties' rights and duties relating to them.

(ii) Recognition of judgments in rem: the jurisdictional requirements

A foreign judgment which purports to operate in rem will not attract extra-territorial recognition unless it has been given by a court internationally competent in this respect. In the eyes of English law, the adjudicating court must have jurisdiction to give a judgment binding all persons generally.

(a) Judgments relating to immovables

If the judgment relates to immovables, it is clear that only the court of the situs is competent.[162] So English courts will not recognise foreign judgments concerning title under a will to land in England,[163] even though our courts might take jurisdiction to determine the validity of wills as to foreign land.[164] Similarly, though jurisdiction is taken here over actions in personam concerning foreign land,[165] foreign judgments in personam concerning English land are unlikely to be recognised here.[166]

(b) Judgments relating to movables

In the case of movables, however, the question of competence is not so simple, since there would appear to be at least three classes of judgments in rem.[167]

---

[157] *Redhead v Redhead and Crothers* [1926] NZLR 131; see Webb & Davis, *A Casebook on the Conflict of Laws of New Zealand* (1970), pp 182–3.

[158] *Patterson v D'Agostino* (1975) 58 DLR (3d) 63, Ont Co Ct.

[159] *Dollfus Mieg et Compagnie SA v Bank of England* [1949] Ch 369 at 383.

[160] *Castrique v Imrie* (1870) LR 4 HL 414 at 427, HL.

[161] *Pattni v Ali and Dinky International SA* [2006] UKPC 51 at [39], [2007] 2 AC 85.

[162] *Re Trepca Mines Ltd* [1960] 1 WLR 1273 at 1277, CA.

[163] *Boyse v Colclough* (1854) 1 K & J 124, 69 ER 396; and see *Re Hoyles* [1911] 1 Ch 179 at 185–6, CA.

[164] Supra, p 491.

[165] Supra, pp 485–91.

[166] See *Duke v Andler* [1932] SCR 734, [1932] 4 DLR 529, supra, pp 490–1; see also White (1982) 9 Sydney LR 630. Cf *Shami v Shami* [2012] EWHC 664 (Ch) at [30]–[35], affd without discussing this point [2013] EWCA Civ 227; *Chapman Estate v O'Hara* [1988] 2 WWR 275, Sask CA; Briggs 2014, paras 9.57, 9.58. In the USA, although the Supreme Court in *Fall v Eastin* 215 US 1 (1909) held that recognition need not be given to judgments in personam concerning land, most states are prepared to recognise such judgments: Scoles, Hay, Borchers, Symeonides, para 24.10; Restatement 2d § 102, comment d.

[167] Westlake, s 149.

(i) Judgments that immediately vest the property in a certain person as against the whole world
These occur, for instance, where a foreign court of Admiralty condemns a vessel in prize proceedings. The Privy Council has said, obiter, that a judgment in rem of a Kenyan court transferring Isle of Man shares (as required by a sale and purchase agreement) cannot be recognised as having in rem effect.[168] However, it will not be ignored for all purposes. It could arguably operate to create an issue estoppel abroad preventing the defendants from arguing they were not in breach of the sale and purchase agreement.[169] In *United States of America v Abacha*[170] the Court of Appeal held that a judgment in rem in proceedings brought by the US authorities in the USA to forfeit assets located abroad which had allegedly been involved in money laundering offences within its jurisdiction would not be enforceable in England.

(ii) Judgments that decree the sale of a thing in satisfaction of a claim against the thing itself
A judgment which orders a chattel to be sold is a judgment in rem if the object of the sale is to afford a remedy, not by execution against the general estate of the defendant, but by appropriating the chattel in satisfaction of the claimant's claim. Such a judgment is not the same as the sentence of an Admiralty court in a prize case which immediately vests the property in the claimant, but it is analogous thereto if the money demand of the claimant in respect of which it is given is a demand against the chattel and not against the owner personally.[171] In all cases, therefore, the nature of a foreign judgment that has ordered the sale of some chattel must be determined by ascertaining whether, according to the foreign law, the original action was a suit against the chattel. The subject was elaborately considered by fourteen judges in the leading case of *Castrique v Imrie*:[172]

> The owner of a British ship mortgaged her to X while she was on a voyage. During the voyage the master drew a bill of exchange on the owner for the cost of certain repairs and indorsed it to a Frenchman at Le Havre. The indorsee brought an action on the bill against the master at Le Havre, and obtained a judgment which declared as follows: "The Tribunal condemns Benson in his quality (capacity) of captain of the vessel *Ann Martin*, and *by privilege on that vessel* to pay to the plaintiff" the amount of the bill. The court declared the master to be free from arrest to which otherwise he would have been liable. A higher court, though having an opinion from the Attorney-General that by English law the mortgagee had a better right than the indorsee, affirmed the decision and ordered the ship to be sold. The ship, having been sold, ultimately arrived in England, and the mortgagee brought an action in the Court of Common Pleas to recover her, on the ground that the sale in France was illegal and void.

The decision necessarily depended on the nature of the French judgment. If it was in rem, then the plaintiff must fail, since the ship was in France at the time of the proceedings. If the judgment was in personam, it was not binding on the mortgagee, since he had been absent from the French proceedings. The Court of Common Pleas held the judgment to be in personam, but the Exchequer Chamber and the House of Lords reversed this decision.

The "privilege" which the judgment created on the ship was, according to French law, a species of lien, and although the proceedings were started against the master as well as against the ship, the sale was ordered not in execution of the judgment debt, but in enforcement of the

---

[168] *Pattni v Ali and Dinky International SA* [2006] UKPC 51 at [38], [2007] 2 AC 85.
[169] Ibid.
[170] [2014] EWCA Civ 1291, [2015] 1 WLR 1917.
[171] *Imrie v Castrique* (1860) 8 CBNS 405 at 411, 412, 141 ER 1222.
[172] (1860) 8 CBNS 405; revsd, ibid, p 405, reversal affd (1870) LR 4 HL 414, HL. See also *BCEN-Eurobank v Vostokrybprom Co Ltd (The Phoenix)* [2014] 1 Lloyd's Rep 449, E Caribbean CA, concerning the judicial sale of a ship by North Korean and Chinese courts.

lien. A more striking example of the manner in which English courts pay recognition to foreign judgments in rem is afforded by *Minna Craig Steamship Co v Chartered Bank of India*,[173] for there the lien that had been declared by a German court was one which conflicted with the principles of English internal law. In this type of case, the only court competent to give a judgment affecting the status of a res that will command general recognition is the court of the country where the res was situated at the time of the action.

(iii) Judgments that order movables to be sold by way of administration

If, in the course of administering an estate in bankruptcy or on death, a foreign court orders the sale of chattels, the sale will be regarded as conferring a title on the purchaser valid in England. In the case of succession on death, jurisdiction to make such an order resides in the court of the country where the deceased died domiciled.[174] Subject to the European Union Insolvency Regulation,[175] the English courts will recognise the bankruptcy jurisdiction of a foreign court if the debtor was domiciled (or, in the case of corporation, if the debtor was incorporated) in the foreign country or submitted to the jurisdiction of the foreign court.[176]

(iv) Enforcement of judgments in rem

Whilst recognition of a foreign judgment in rem may be fairly common and relatively straightforward, enforcement of such judgments in England raises different issues. No foreign judgment relating to immovables abroad can be enforced in England. If the judgment relates to movables, the real issue is whether it was sufficient to pass title to the property, ie a question of recognition rather than enforcement.[177] A rare example of enforcement of a foreign judgment by an action in rem in England is provided by *The City of Mecca*.[178] Sir Robert Phillimore held that a Portuguese judgment for damages for the loss caused by a collision on the high seas between a Spanish ship and a British ship was a judgment in rem which could be enforced in England by an action in rem against the ship. Although on appeal this decision was set aside on the ground that the Portuguese judgment was, in fact, a judgment in personam,[179] the first instance decision is still of good authority and has been applied by Sheen J in *The Despina GK*.[180]

(c) Final and conclusive judgment

A foreign judgment will not be given effect in England unless it is *res judicata* by the law of the country where it was given.[181] It must be final and conclusive in the sense that it must have determined all controversies between the parties. If it may be altered in later proceedings between the same parties *in the same court*, it will not be effective in England.[182] These principles will now be examined.

---

[173] [1897] 1 QB 55, affd, ibid, 460.

[174] See *Re Trufort, Trafford v Blanc* (1887) 36 Ch D 600.

[175] Regulation (EU) 2015/848 of the European Parliament and of the Council on insolvency proceedings OJ 2015 L 141/19.

[176] Cross-border insolvency is dealt with in Chapter 34 of this book.

[177] *Castrique v Imrie* (1870) LR 4 HL 414 at 429, HL.

[178] (1879) 5 PD 28.

[179] (1881) 6 PD 106.

[180] [1983] 1 QB 214; see also *SS Pacific Star v Bank of America National Trust and Savings Association* [1965] WAR 159.

[181] For the relevance of the law of the county where the judgment is given see *Joint Stock Co 'Aeroflot-Russian Airlines' v Berezovsky* [2014] EWCA Civ 20, [2014] 1 CLC 53; Scott (2014) 85 BYBIL (evidence of Russian law insufficient for summary determination).

[182] *Nouvion v Freeman* (1889) 15 App Cas 1, PC; *Re Riddell* (1888) 20 QBD 512 at 516, CA; *Blohn v Desser* [1962] 2 QB 116. Interim payments are now enforceable under the Foreign Judgments (Reciprocal Enforcement) Act 1933, see infra, p 594.

A provisional judgment is not *res judicata* if it contemplates that a fuller investigation leading to a final decision may later be held. This aspect of the meaning of finality and conclusiveness is illustrated by the leading case of *Nouvion v Freeman*.[183]

> X, who had sold certain land in Seville to Y, brought an "executive" action in Spain against Y and obtained a "remate" judgment for a large sum of money. There were two kinds of proceedings under Spanish law: executive or summary proceedings, and "plenary" or ordinary proceedings. In an executive action, on proof of a prima facie case, the judge without notice to the defendant made an order for the attachment of his property. Notice of the attachment was given to the defendant and he was at liberty to appear and defend the action. But the defences open to him were limited in number, and in particular he could not set up any defence that denied the validity of the transaction upon which he was sued. Either party who failed in executive proceedings could institute plenary proceedings before the same judge, and in these could set up every defence that was known to the law.

It was held by the House of Lords, affirming the Court of Appeal, that no action lay on the remate judgment. Since it was liable to be abrogated by the adjudicating court, it was not *res judicata* with regard to either party, neither did it extinguish the original cause of action.

A more modern illustration is afforded by *Blohn v Desser*.[184] In that case, an action was brought against the defendant personally on an Austrian judgment that had been given not against her individually, but against a firm of which she was a member. To have rendered her personally liable under Austrian law would have necessitated a separate action against her individually, but in this event certain defences would have been available to her that could not have been raised in the proceedings against the firm. Therefore, even if the judgment could be regarded as given against her personally, it was not final and conclusive. Again, to take another important example, a judgment in default of appearance, whilst it can be final and conclusive,[185] does not satisfy the condition of finality and conclusiveness if it is given in a country where the defendant is allowed to apply within a limited time for its rescission by the adjudicating court.[186]

The necessity for finality and conclusiveness appears in a slightly different aspect in the cases dealing with foreign maintenance orders. As is the case in England, foreign courts usually have power to vary the amount of maintenance orders. Thus in *Harrop v Harrop*[187] the issue was the recognition of an order for maintenance made in Perak. A magistrate could order a person to pay a monthly allowance for maintenance of his wife, and, if such order was disregarded, could direct the amount due to be levied in the manner in which fines were levied. On application by the husband or wife and on proof of a change in the circumstances of the parties, the magistrate could vary the amount to be paid. In the present case a magistrate had ordered the payment of a monthly sum, and later, when this fell into arrears, had ordered that payment of the arrears should be enforced by the appropriate method. The wife failed in the action which she brought in England on these orders. Sankey J, in the course of his judgment, put the gist of the matter in these words: "In my view a judgment or order cannot be said to be final and conclusive if (1) an order has to be obtained for its enforcement,

---

[183] (1889) 15 App Cas 1, PC; applied in *Colt Industries Inc v Sarlie (No 2)* [1966] 1 WLR 1287, CA; *Berliner Industriebank AG v Jost* [1971] 2 QB 463, CA; distinguished in *Audrain v Aero Photo Inc* (1983) 138 DLR (3d) 177, Que CA.

[184] [1962] 2 QB 116.

[185] *Starlight International Inc v A J Bruce* [2002] EWHC 374 at [17], [2002] IL Pr 35—it must be *res judicata* in the foreign legal system; *Schnabel v Yung Lui* [2002] NSWSC 15.

[186] Wolff, pp 264, 265. Cf *Barclays Bank Ltd v Piacun* [1984] 2 Qd R 476; *Re Dooney* [1993] 2 Qd R 362.

[187] [1920] 3 KB 386; and see *Re Macartney* [1921] 1 Ch 522. But cf *McC v McC* [1994] 1 IR 293.

and (2) on application for such an order the original judgment is liable to be abrogated or varied."[188]

If a court is empowered to vary the amount of future payments of maintenance but cannot alter its order as to accrued instalments, then instalments that are already due under the foreign judgment may be recovered by action in England.[189] *Harrop v Harrop* is not inconsistent with this rule, for in that case no evidence was given to show that the amount of accrued instalments was unalterable.

A decision that is final and conclusive is not provisional. As regards an interlocutory decision or order, decisions that are interlocutory in the sense of being made pending final determination of the case, such as an interlocutory injunction pending trial, are not final and conclusive.[190] But where a case is *res judicata*, has been decided on a full consideration of the merits, and the matter cannot be challenged or reheard by the same court it will be final and conclusive, even though it remains possible that an adjustment may be made to the damages by the same court on the application of either party (but which does not challenge the existence of the debt).[191]

The requirement of finality means that the judgment must be final in the particular court in which it was pronounced.[192] It does not mean that there must be no right of appeal. Neither the fact that the judgment may be reversed on appeal, nor even the stronger fact that an actual appeal is pending in the foreign country, is a bar to the effectiveness of the judgment in England;[193] though where an appeal is pending the English court has an equitable jurisdiction to stay execution, which it will generally exercise.[194] If, however, the effect under the foreign law of a pending appeal is to stay execution of the judgment, it would seem that, in the interim, the judgment is not effective in England.[195] A foreign judgment that is final in the particular court in which it was pronounced, but which is later set aside by an appeal court, may be effective in England if the foreign setting aside is contrary to public policy

---

[188] [1920] 3 KB 386 at 399. Provision for reciprocal enforcement of foreign maintenance orders is now made by statute, infra, pp 1078–86.

[189] *Beatty v Beatty* [1924] 1 KB 807, CA; and see *Patton v Reed* (1972) 30 DLR (3d) 494, British Columbia Sup Ct; *Lear v Lear* (1974) 51 DLR (3d) 56, Ont CA; *Stark v Stark* (1979) 94 DLR (3d) 556, Alb CA; *McLean v McLean* [1979] 1 NSWLR 620.

[190] *Desert Sun Loan Corpn v Hill* [1996] 2 All ER 847 at 863 (per Stuart-Smith LJ), at 856 (per Evans LJ), CA.

[191] *Lewis v Eliades* [2003] EWHC 368 (QB) at [54]–[56], [2003] 1 All ER (Comm) 850; appeal allowed in part without discussion of this point [2003] EWCA Civ 1758, [2004] 1 WLR 692. The adjustment to the damages arose out of the fact that there was an application for a separate judgment from the same court trebling the damages because of racketeering contrary to the US RICO Act. See also *Schnabel v Yung Lui* [2002] NRWSC 15.

[192] The *Beatty v Beatty* case at 815, 816.

[193] *Scott v Pilkington* (1862) 2 B & S 11, 121 ER 978; *Colt Industries Inc v Sarlie (No 2)* [1966] 1 WLR 1287, CA; *Lewis v Eliades* [2003] EWCA Civ 1758 at [18], [2004] 1 WLR 692; *Malicorp Ltd v Egypt* [2015] EWHC 361 (Comm) at [20], [2015] 1 Lloyd's Rep 423; *Enercon GmbH v Enercon (India) Ltd* [2012] EWHC 689 (Comm) at [51], [2012] 1 Lloyd's Rep 519; *Midtown Acquisitions LP v Essar Global Fund Ltd* [2017] EWHC 519 (Comm). See also *Four Embarcadero Center Venture v Mr Greenjeans Corpn* (1988) 64 OR (2d) 746, affd 65 OR (2d) 160. A judgment enforcing a foreign judgment, which is then overturned, will in principle be set aside (unless the foreign overturning judgment is refused recognition in England): see *Merchant International Co Ltd v Natsionalna Aktsionerna Kompaniya Naftogaz Ukrayiny* [2012] EWCA Civ 196, [2012] 1 WLR 3036; *Benefit Strategies Group Inc v Prider* [2007] SASC 250.

[194] The *Scott v Pilkington* case; the *Nouvion v Freeman* case at 13; the *Colt Industries Inc v Sarlie (No 2)* case; *Four Embarcadero Center Venture v Mr Greenjeans* (1988) 64 OR (2d) 746, affd 65 OR (2d) 160; *Arrowmaster Inc v Unique Forming Ltd* [1995] IL Pr 505, Ont Ct of Justice; *Old North State Brewing Co v Newlands Service Inc* (1998) 155 DLR (4th) 250, British Columbia CA.

[195] *Patrick v Shedden* (1853) 2 E & B 14, 118 ER 674; *Enercon GmbH v Enercon (India) Ltd* [2012] EWHC 689 (Comm) at [51], [2012] 1 Lloyd's Rep 519; cf *Berliner Industriebank AG v Jost* [1971] 2 QB 463 at 470–1, CA.

or for another reason (eg violation of the principles of natural justice or violation of the standards of Article 6 of the European Convention on Human Rights) refused recognition in England.[196]

(d) Enforcement of foreign judgments in personam[197]

(i) Enforcement by institution of fresh legal proceedings

The common law doctrine is that a foreign judgment, though creating an obligation that is actionable in England, cannot be enforced in England without the institution of fresh legal proceedings. If a fresh action is brought in England on the foreign judgment, that action is subject to the Civil Procedure Rules and, for example, the claimant may apply for summary judgment under Part 24 on the basis that the defendant has no real prospect of successfully defending the claim and there is no other compelling reason why the case should be disposed of at a trial.[198] But a summary judgment will not be given where the application of the rules on recognition and enforcement can only be done at trial, for example where the court must decide whether as a matter of foreign law a foreign judgment is final and conclusive and there is conflicting expert evidence on this issue.[199] A foreign judgment cannot be enforced by, for example, the appointment of a receiver without a fresh action in England. Furthermore, any action in England will require the English rules as to jurisdiction and service of claim forms to be satisfied.[200] The claimant's action is barred under section 24(1) of the Limitation Act 1980 after six years.[201] Following the same provision, once an English judgment is given on an action on a foreign judgment, the judgment creditor will have six years to enforce the English judgment.

(ii) Judgment for a fixed sum

As we have seen, the ground on which a foreign judgment is enforceable in England is that the defendant has implicitly promised to pay the amount due under the judgment.[202] It follows that there can be no question of enforcing a foreign decree for specific performance or for the specific delivery or restitution of chattels. Moreover, the law implies a promise to pay a definite, not an indefinite, sum.[203] Unless in an action in personam the foreign court has definitely and finally determined the amount to be paid, no action is maintainable in

---

[196] See *Merchant International Co Ltd v Natsionalna Aktsionerna Kompaniya Naftogaz Ukrayiny* [2011] EWHC 1820 (Comm), [2011] 2 All ER (Comm) 75, affd on a narrower point concerning the exercise of discretion to set aside a default judgment under CPR r 13.3 in [2012] EWCA Civ 196, [2012] 1 WLR 3036; Ahmed (2012) 31 CJQ 417; Harder (2012/13) 14 YBPIL 103; Rushworth and Scott (2012) 83 BYBIL 294; *Joint Stock Co 'Aeroflot-Russian Airlines' v Berezovsky* [2014] EWCA Civ 20, [2014] 1 CLC 53.

[197] For enforcement of judgments in rem see supra, p 548.

[198] *Grant v Easton* (1883) 13 QBD 302, CA; see also *JSC VTB Bank v Skurikhin* [2014] EWHC 271 (Comm) at [14], [15]. On security for costs see *Relational LLC v Hodges* [2011] EWCA Civ 774, [2012] IL Pr 4; Rushworth and Scott (2011) 82 BYBIL 659.

[199] *Joint Stock Co 'Aeroflot-Russian Airlines' v Berezovsky* [2014] EWCA Civ 20, [2014] 1 CLC 53; see also *Seven Arts Entertainment Ltd v Content Media Corp Plc* [2013] EWHC 588 (Ch).

[200] *Perry v Zissis* [1977] 1 Lloyd's Rep 607, CA. Amendments to the rules on service out of the jurisdiction have made this easier: see now CPR, r 6.36 and CPR PD 6B, para 3.1(10), supra, pp 355–6. It is not necessary for the claimant to show that the defendant has assets in England: *Tasarruf Mevduati Sigorta Fonu v Demirel* [2007] EWCA Civ 799, [2007] 1 WLR 2508; *Habib Bank Ltd v Central Bank of Sudan* [2014] EWHC 2288 (Comm); see also *Chevron Corp v Yaiguaje* 2015 SCC 42, [2015] 3 SCR 69; cf *Linsen International Ltd v Humpuss Sea Transport Pte Ltd* [2011] EWCA Civ 1042.

[201] *Re Flynn (No 2)* [1969] 2 Ch 403; *Berliner Industriebank AG v Jost* [1971] 2 QB 463, CA; *Duer v Frazer* [2001] 1 WLR 919; *Society of Lloyd's v Longtin* [2005] EWHC 2491 (Comm), [2005] 2 CLC 774.

[202] *Grant v Easton* (1883) 13 QBD 302, CA. See also *Williams v Jones* (1845) 13 M & W 628 at 630, 153 ER 262.

[203] *Sadler v Robins* (1808) 1 Camp 253 at 256, 170 ER 948. But see White (1982) 9 Sydney LR 630.

England.[204] In *Sadler v Robins*[205] a court in Jamaica had decreed that the defendant should pay to the plaintiff £3,670 9s 1/4d, first deducting therefrom the full costs expended by the defendant, such costs to be taxed by a master of the court. It was held that until taxation the plaintiff had no cause of action in England, since the sum due on the Jamaican decree was indefinite. A sum, however, satisfies the requirement of certainty if it can be ascertained by a simple arithmetical process.[206]

This is the position in England.[207] In contrast, the Supreme Court of Canada in *Pro Swing Inc v Elta Golf Inc*[208] has held that the traditional common law rule that limits enforcement to fixed sum judgments should be revised so as to open the door to equitable orders, such as injunctions, which are key to an effective modern-day remedy. However, this change must be accompanied by a judicial discretion enabling the Canadian court to consider relevant factors, including the criteria that guide Canadian courts when crafting domestic equitable orders, such as the territorial scope of an injunction being specific and clear.[209]

(iii) Non-enforcement of foreign revenue, penal or other public laws

English courts will not enforce foreign revenue, penal or other public laws either directly[210] or through the enforcement of a foreign judgment.[211] Thus in *USA v Inkley*[212] the Court of Appeal refused to enforce a judgment granted in Florida relating to a bail appearance bond, where the purpose of the enforcement action was the execution of a foreign public law/penal process. In *United States of America v Abacha*[213] the Court of Appeal held that a judgment in proceedings brought by the US authorities in the USA to forfeit assets located abroad which had allegedly been involved in money laundering offences within its jurisdiction would not be enforceable in England because, inter alia, it would amount to the enforcement of a foreign penal law. A penalty in this sense normally means a sum payable to the state, and not to a private claimant.[214] However, the foreign judgment will be denied enforcement only if it falls

---

[204] The *Sadler v Robins* case; *Henderson v Henderson* (1844) 6 QB 288, 115 ER 111. For enforcement of judgments expressed in a foreign currency and charging orders see *Carnegie v Giessen* [2005] EWCA Civ 191, [2005] 1 WLR 2510; see also *Miliangos v George Frank (Textiles) Ltd* [1976] AC 443, HL.

[205] (1808) 1 Camp 253, 170 ER 948.

[206] *Beatty v Beatty* [1924] 1 KB 807, CA.

[207] But see Briggs 2014, paras 6.128–6.220; Briggs 2015, para 7.76.

[208] [2006] SCR 612, (2007) 273 DLR (4th) 663; Pitel (2007) 3 J Priv Int L 241; Oppong (2007) 70 MLR 670. See also the decisions of the Grand Court of the Cayman Islands in *Miller v Gianne* [2007] Cayman Islands LR 18 and of the Royal Court of Jersey in *Brunei Investment Agency v Fidelis Nominees Ltd* [2008] JRC 152, [2008] Jersey LR 337; Briggs (2009) 80 BYBIL 583. See also *Independent Trustee Services Ltd v Morris* [2010] NSWSC 1218 at [30]–[37], (2010) 79 NSWLR 425, where the court ordered an account of administration on the basis of wilful default, mirroring an order made in England.

[209] [2006] SCR 612, at [15], [30]–[31], (2007) 273 DLR (4th) 663. The uncertain territorial scope of the injunction in question led to it not being enforced in Canada.

[210] Supra, pp 114–26.

[211] *USA v Harden Huntington v Attrill* [1893] AC 150, PC; *A-G of New Zealand v Ortiz* [1984] AC 1 at 31–5, CA; *USA v Harden* [1963] SCR 366, (1963) 41 DLR (2d) 721. See, however, as exceptions the Criminal Justice Act 1988, s 97 (foreign confiscation orders); *Government of the USA v Montgomery (No 2)* [2004] UKHL 37, [2004] 1 WLR 2241; discussed infra, p 581, and Art 2(12) EU Regulation on Insolvency Proceedings; discussed supra, p 126.

[212] [1989] QB 255, CA; Carter (1988) 59 BYBIL 347.

[213] [2014] EWCA Civ 1291, [2015] 1 WLR 1917; see also *Pocket Kings Ltd v Safenames Ltd* [2009] EWHC 2529 (Ch), [2010] Ch 438 (concerning an order in proceedings brought by a US state in the USA for the seizure or forfeiture of a domain name used for online gambling purposes; the order was categorised as a civil remedy under US law).

[214] See *SA Consortium General Textiles v Sun and Sand Agencies Ltd* [1978] QB 279 at 299–300, CA—an award of exemplary damages or damages for "resistance abusive" under French law not penal. In *Lewis v Eliades* [2003] EWCA Civ 1758 at [50], [2004] 1 WLR 692, this point was not regarded as clear. See also *Pencil Hill Ltd v US Citta Di Palermo SpA*, 19 January 2016, HC—foreign arbitration award enforced where

directly within the area of revenue, penal or other public laws, strictly construed. So, when a public or regulatory body brings civil proceedings on behalf of a group of class of victims, it is not seeking to enforce a foreign penal or other public law.[215] A foreign judgment for costs may be enforced even though the costs would be payable into a foreign legal aid fund.[216] A foreign judgment in respect of an action brought by the USA for compensation under a US statute for the cost of clearing up environmental damage in the USA has been held to be enforceable, the action being regarded as close to one for nuisance.[217]

A civil judgment, though combined with a penal judgment, may be actionable in England as creating a separate and independent cause of action, despite the general principle[218] that penalties imposed abroad are disregarded. Thus in *Raulin v Fischer*:[219]

> The defendant, a young American lady, while recklessly galloping her horse in the Bois de Boulogne, ran into the plaintiff, a French officer, and seriously injured him. She was prosecuted by the French State for her act of criminal negligence. By French law a person who is injured by a crime may intervene in the prosecution and make a claim for damages, whereupon his civil action is tried together with the prosecution and one judgment is pronounced on both matters. The plaintiff did so intervene. The defendant was convicted of the crime and ordered to pay a fine of 100 francs to the State and 15,917 francs by way of damages and costs to the plaintiff.

It was held on these facts, in an action brought by the plaintiff in England to recover the sterling equivalent of 15,917 francs, that the French judgment was severable. That part of it which awarded the plaintiff damages was not tainted with the penal character of the rest of the proceedings, and therefore might be recovered in England without involving enforcement of a penal judgment.

(iv) Non-enforcement of judgments for multiple damages under the Protection of Trading Interests Act 1980[220]

The background to this Act is the United Kingdom resentment[221] at the extra-territorial application of anti-trust laws by the USA. Diplomatic attempts at solving what is a political

---

the arbitrators awarded the claimant a reduced additional sum in place of a contractual penalty, representing 25 per cent of the penalty claimed and *JSC VTB Bank v Skurikhin* [2014] EWHC 271 (Comm) at [94]—arguable that an excessive award of interest is not recoverable on the ground that it is punitive in effect. Compare *Old North State Brewing Co v Newlands Services Inc* [1999] 4 WWR 573, British Columbia Court of Appeal (the judgment for treble damages not regarded as penal), *Benefit Strategies Group Inc v Prider* [2005] SASC 194 at [74]–[75], (2005) 91 SASR 544 and *Doe v Howard* [2015] VSC 75 (punitive damages not penal) with *Schnabel v Yung Lui* [2002] NSWSC 15 (punitive damages with a public element for failing to comply with an order of a US court regarded as penal).

[215] *United States Securities and Exchange Commission v Manterfield* [2009] EWCA Civ 27, [2010] 1 WLR 172; *Robb Evans v European Bank Ltd* (2004) 61 NSWLR 75.

[216] *Connor v Connor* [1974] 1 NZLR 632.

[217] *United States of America v Ivey* (1996) 139 DLR (4th) 570, Ont CA.

[218] Supra, pp 118–22.

[219] [1911] 2 KB 93; and see *Lewis v Eliades* [2003] EWCA Civ 1758, [2004] 1 WLR 692, discussed infra, pp 554–5; *United States Securities and Exchange Commission v Manterfield* [2009] EWCA Civ 27 at [24], [2010] 1 WLR 172; *Pace Europe v Dunham* [2012] EWHC 852 (Ch) at [12]–[15]. See also *Benefit Strategies Group Inc v Prider* [2005] SASC 194 at [74]–[75], (2005) 91 SASR 544; *Schnabel v Yung Lui* [2002] NSWSC 15.

[220] See Huntley (1981) 30 ICLQ 213, 229–33; Jones [1981] CLJ 41; AV Lowe (1981) 75 AJIL 257; Blythe (1983) 31 AJCL 99; Bridge (1984) 4 Legal Studies 2. For analogous statutes in Australia and Canada, see the Foreign Anti-Trust Judgments (Restriction of Enforcement) Act 1979 (Cth) and the Foreign Extraterritorial Measures Act 1985; see generally Patchett, *Recognition of Commercial Judgments and Awards in the Commonwealth* (1984), para 3.24; Castel and Walker, *Canadian Conflicts of Laws* (2006) 6th edn, para 14.29b; Castel (1983) I Hague Recueil 9, 79–92; Collins [1986] JBL 372 and 452.

[221] See *British Nylon Spinners Ltd v ICI Ltd* [1953] Ch 19, CA; *Re Westinghouse Electric Corpn Uranium Contract Litigation NDLMDL Docket No 235* [1978] AC 547, HL. The resentment is also shared by Australia and Canada, see supra, n 220.

as well as an economic and legal problem failed and led to legal warfare. Under the Act, the Secretary of State is given wide powers to counter foreign measures for regulating international trade which affect the trading interests of persons in the United Kingdom.[222]

Alongside this, there are restrictions on the enforcement of certain overseas judgments. Section 5(2) provides that a court in the United Kingdom cannot enforce:[223]

(a) a judgment for multiple damages, ie one "for an amount arrived at by doubling, trebling or otherwise multiplying a sum assessed as compensation for the loss or damage sustained by the person in whose favour the judgment is given";[224]

(b) a judgment based on a competition law which is specified in an order made by the Secretary of State;[225]

(c) where a judgment coming within (a) or (b) has been given against a third party, a judgment on a claim for contribution.

Three points should be noted about section 5. First, although the Act does not mention any specific foreign country, the reference to multiple damages shows beyond any doubt that the target at which the Act is aimed is US anti-trust laws,[226] although it operates against multiple damages in other contexts as well.[227] Secondly, the prohibition on the enforcement of a judgment for multiple damages applies to all of the multiplied award and not merely to the non-compensatory part.[228] However, where a foreign court gives a composite judgment comprising both a multiplied award and ordinary compensatory damages for separate private causes of action similar to those available under English law, it is possible to separate the different parts and enforce the latter but not the former. This is what happened in *Lewis v Eliades*.[229]

---

[222] See ss 1–4. See also the Protection of Trading Interests (US Antitrust Measures) Order, SI 1983/900; the Protection of Trading Interests (Australian Trade Practices) Order, SI 1988/569, on which see *Trade Practices Commission v Australian Meat Holdings Pty Ltd* (1988) 83 ALR 299, Australian HC; Protection of Trading Interests (Hong Kong) Order, SI 1990/2291; US Reexport Control Order, SI 1982/885; and Protection of Trading Interests (US Cuban Assets Control Regulations) Order, SI 1992/2449.

[223] Either at common law or by statute under Part II of the Administration of Justice Act 1920, discussed infra, p 591 et seq, or the Foreign Judgments (Reciprocal Enforcement) Act 1933, discussed infra, p 593 et seq, see s 5(1) and *Service Temps Inc v MacLeod* [2013] CSOH 162 at [31]–[38], 2014 SLT 375; Scott (2013) 84 BYBIL 523. S 5 will not, however, apply to cases coming within the Brussels/Lugano system, discussed infra, pp 608–55, but see especially p 625. For the significance of s 5 in relation to restraining foreign proceedings, see *Simon Engineering plc v Butte Mining plc* [1996] 1 Lloyd's Rep 104 n; *SCOR v Eras EIL (No 2)* [1995] 2 All ER 278 at 308–12.

[224] S 5(3). Foreign laws imposing multiple damages have been described as penal at common law: *British Airways Board v Laker Airways Ltd* [1984] QB 142 at 163 (per Parker J), and in the Court of Appeal at 201 (per Donaldson MR); cf *Old North State Brewing Co v Newlands Services Inc* (1998) 155 DLR (4th) 250, BC CA (treble damages based on an unfair and deceptive trade practice statute not anti-trust). More recently, the Court of Appeal has accepted, obiter, that this is arguable but found it unnecessary to decide the point: *Lewis v Eliades* [2003] EWCA Civ 1758 at [50], [2004] 1 WLR 692; see also *Service Temps Inc v MacLeod* [2013] CSOH 162 at [39]–[41], 2014 SLT 375.

[225] S 5(2)(b) and (4).

[226] See *British Airways Board v Laker Airways Ltd* [1985] AC 58 at 89 (per Lord Diplock), HL.

[227] See *Lewis v Eliades* [2003] EWCA Civ 1758, [2004] 1 WLR 692; discussed infra. Cf the position in Canada, on which see *Old North State Brewing Co v Newlands Services Inc* [1999] 4 WWR 573, British Columbia CA.

[228] *Lewis v Eliades* [2003] EWCA Civ 1758 at [41] (per Potter LJ), [55] (per Carnwath LJ), but cf at [62] (Jacob LJ), [2004] 1 WLR 692; *Service Temps Inc v MacLeod* [2013] CSOH 162 at [38], 2014 SLT 375. Cf *Lucasfilm Ltd v Ainsworth* [2008] EWHC 1878 (Ch) at [230]–[231], [2009] FSR 2; *Pace Europe v Dunham* [2012] EWHC 852 (Ch) at [14], [17]–[20]; Fentiman, para 18.19.

[229] [2003] EWCA Civ 1758, [2004] 1 WLR 692; leave to appeal to the House of Lords refused [2004] 1 WLR 1393; Briggs (2003) 74 BYBIL 549; Kellman (2004) 53 ICLQ 1025. See also the *Pace Europe v Dunham* case at [12]–[15].

A court in the USA gave a composite judgment for over $8 million, which included over $1.1 million damages for racketeering contrary to the RICO Act ($396,000 basic damages trebled up[230]) plus over $6.8 million damages in respect of separate causes of action for breach of fiduciary duty and fraud. Counsel for the claimant conceded that the whole of the $1.1 million racketeering damages (ie including the basic damages of $396,000) was irrecoverable but sought enforcement of $6.8 million damages for breach of fiduciary duty and fraud.

The Court of Appeal enforced that latter part of the judgment. Thirdly, the prohibition on enforcement does not depend on whether the overseas court applied its anti-trust laws extra-territorially. It has been pointed out[231] that section 5 can apply to the enforcement of a judgment in an anti-trust suit brought by one US corporation against another US corporation, which has assets in the United Kingdom, following anti-trust infringements which took place wholly within the USA. The rationale of this section is not, therefore, that there has been an invasion of United Kingdom sovereignty; instead, it is more akin to that underlying the prohibition of enforcement in cases of foreign penal laws or in cases where enforcement would be against public policy.[232]

Section 5 is a negative provision. More controversial is the accompanying positive provision contained in section 6. This gives a "qualifying"[233] defendant, who has actually paid some or all of the multiple damages, the right to recover in the United Kingdom the non-compensatory part of the payment. This claw-back provision is no doubt designed to discourage private litigants from instigating civil proceedings for multiple damages and to persuade the USA to alter its anti-trust stance in respect of United Kingdom defendants.[234] Section 6 provides a unique cause of action; for this to be of any assistance to a claimant in England jurisdictional and enforcement problems have also to be overcome. The 1980 Act helps with both problems. Section 6(5) provides that "a court in the United Kingdom may entertain proceedings on a claim under this section notwithstanding that the person against whom the proceedings are brought is not within the jurisdiction of the court". A claim form will still have to be served on the defendant, but the leave of the court is not required for service out of the jurisdiction.[235] Section 7[236] allows for Orders in Council to be made providing for the enforcement in the United Kingdom of foreign judgments clawing-back sums paid pursuant to an award of multiple damages. This is done on a reciprocal basis[237] so that an overseas country must provide for the enforcement in that country of judgments given in the United Kingdom under section 6. Section 7 applies regardless of whether or not the foreign claw-back provision corresponds to section 6.[238] It follows that an Order in Council could specify that the whole of a foreign judgment, including the claw-back of the compensatory part of an award of multiple damages, is to be enforced in the United Kingdom, even though section 6 does not allow the claw-back of this compensatory part in proceedings in the United Kingdom.[239]

---

[230] Prior to the order abroad to treble the damages there is no judgment for multiple damages and the basic damages can be enforced, see *Lewis v Eliades* [2003] EWHC 368 (QB), [2003] 1 All ER (Comm) 850. By the time the appeal was heard the damages had been trebled and so this situation was not discussed.

[231] See *British Airways Board v Laker Airways Ltd* [1984] QB 142 at 161–2 (Parker J), CA.

[232] Ibid, at 162–3; Blythe (1983) 31 AJCL 99, 123.

[233] Ie a citizen of the United Kingdom, or a body incorporated in the United Kingdom, or a person carrying on business in the United Kingdom, s 6(1). See also s 6(3) and (4).

[234] Blythe (1983) 31 AJCL 99, 126–7.

[235] CPR, r 6.33(3), see supra, pp 379–80. S 6(5) will not apply in the unlikely event of the jurisdiction rules under the Brussels/Lugano system, discussed supra, p 191 et seq, being applicable (European Union and EFTA States are not likely to give judgments for multiple damages).

[236] As amended by s 38 of the Civil Jurisdiction and Judgments Act 1982.

[237] See, eg, the United Kingdom-Australia Agreement (1991) Cmnd 1394, Art 2(2).

[238] This is the effect of the amendment introduced by s 38 of the 1982 Act.

[239] See Anton and Beaumont's *Civil Jurisdiction in Scotland* (1984), paras 11–15.

(e) Recognition of foreign judgments

(i) Estoppel per rem judicatam[240]

A cause of action, once it has been adjudicated by a court of competent jurisdiction, becomes *res judicata*, and as such it raises an estoppel against the unsuccessful party.

> The rule of estoppel by *res judicata*, which is a rule of evidence, is that where a final decision has been pronounced by a judicial tribunal of competent jurisdiction over the parties to and the subject-matter of the litigation, any party or privy to such litigation as against any other party or privy is estopped in any subsequent litigation from disputing or questioning such decision on the merits.[241]

(a) Estoppel as a defence[242]

According to the doctrine of *res judicata*, at common law, a foreign judgment was conclusive in two respects in favour of the defendant in England.

First, in the situation where the claimant lost abroad, the judgment provided the successful defendant in the foreign proceedings with an effective defence if he was sued by the other party in England on the original cause of action. The claimant was estopped from denying the conclusiveness of the judgment.[243]

Secondly, in the situation where the claimant won abroad, but had not been awarded full compensation, the common law rule was that the satisfied judgment of the foreign court provided a good defence to an action brought by the claimant in England for the residue of his claim.[244]

This common law rule has now been superseded by the much wider statutory rule in section 34 of the Civil Jurisdiction and Judgments Act 1982.[245] This provides that:

> No proceedings may be brought by a person in England and Wales . . . on a cause of action in respect of which a judgment has been given in his favour in proceedings between the same parties, or their privies, in a court in another part of the United Kingdom or in a court of an overseas country, unless that judgment is not enforceable or entitled to recognition in England and Wales . . .[246]

The effect of this provision is that, if the judgment is enforceable or entitled to recognition in England and Wales, the claimant has to sue on the judgment obtained[247] and cannot bring fresh proceedings based on the original cause of action.[248] To allow the claimant to bring fresh

---

[240] See generally Barnett, *Res Judicata, Estoppel, and Foreign Judgments* (2001).

[241] *Carl Zeiss Stiftung v Rayner and Keeler Ltd (No 2)* [1967] 1 AC 853 at 933, HL, citing Spencer Bower, *The Doctrine of Res Judicata* (1924), p 3.

[242] See, however, for an example of a claimant who wished to enforce a foreign judgment (using issue estoppel to prevent the defendant from denying that he had authorised a lawyer to act on his behalf, and had accordingly submitted to the foreign court's jurisdiction) *Desert Sun Loan Corpn v Hill* [1996] 2 All ER 847, CA. See also *The Varna (No 2)* [1994] 2 Lloyd's Rep 41 at 48.

[243] *Ricardo v Garcias* (1845) 12 Cl & Fin 368, 8 ER 1450.

[244] *Taylor v Hollard* [1902] 1 KB 676; *Barber v Lamb* (1860) 8 CBNS 95 at 100, 141 ER 1100.

[245] The section applies also in Northern Ireland, but not in Scotland.

[246] For the situation where the foreign judgment is not enforceable or entitled to recognition in England and Wales see *Karafarin Bank v Mansoury-Dara* [2009] EWHC 1217 (Comm), [2009] 2 Lloyd's Rep 289.

[247] In this situation the claimant will be able to ask for service of a claim form out of the jurisdiction under CPR, r 6.36 and CPR PD 6B, para 3.1(10), discussed supra, pp 355–6.

[248] The section applies regardless of whether the judgment is enforceable or entitled to recognition at common law, by statute, or under the Brussels/Lugano system; in the case of the latter, s 34 merely confirms the existing rule under that system, see Case 42/76 *De Wolf v Harry Cox BV* [1976] ECR 1759, discussed infra, pp 649–50.

proceedings in England would be unjust.[249] There is no requirement that the foreign judgment has been satisfied; it must merely have been "given". The operation of this provision has been examined by the House of Lords in *Republic of India v India Steamship Co Ltd*[250] and in *Republic of India v India Steamship Co Ltd (No 2)*.[251]

> Following a fire on board the defendant's ship, a small number of the cargo of artillery shells were jettisoned and the remainder were damaged. In 1988, the plaintiff, a cargo owner, commenced proceedings in personam against the shipowner in India for short delivery and obtained a judgment in its favour in December 1989. Previously, in August 1989, the plaintiff had launched proceedings in rem in England in respect of damage to the whole of the cargo.

The House of Lords in *Republic of India v India Steamship Co Ltd (No 2)* held that the plaintiffs' action in England was barred by section 34. A number of important points emerge from this litigation. First, it did not matter that the English proceedings were launched before the Indian judgment was obtained. Section 34 prohibits proceedings being "brought" in England and this is wide enough to prevent proceedings being continued.[252] Secondly, according to the House of Lords in *Republic of India v India Steamship Co Ltd* the cause of action in the Indian proceedings (for short delivery) and the English proceedings (for damage to the whole of the cargo) was the same. This was despite the fact that the Indian judgment was for only the rupee equivalent of £7,200, whereas the English claim was for the equivalent of £2.6 million. In both sets of proceedings the cause of action came under the same contract of carriage and depended on the same breach of that contract. Moreover, both actions were concerned with a single incident, ie the fire. There may have been a breach of more than one term of the contract but it was not necessary to distinguish these breaches because the factual basis giving rise to the breaches was the same. Thirdly, according to *Republic of India v India Steamship Co Ltd (No 2)* the parties were the same even though one action was in personam and the other in rem. For the purposes of section 34 an action in rem is an action against the shipowners from the moment that the Admiralty Court is seized with jurisdiction.[253] Fourthly, section 34 does not use the idea that a cause of action is lost by its merger in the judgment. It creates a bar against proceedings by the claimant, rather than excluding the jurisdiction of the court.[254] Accordingly, this defence can be defeated by waiver, estoppel or contrary agreement.[255]

It is not required that the claimant should have been the original party in the overseas proceedings or that such proceedings be exclusively civil in character, provided that the judgment

---

[249] *Republic of India v India Steamship Co Ltd* [1993] AC 410 at 422, HL; *Republic of India v India Steamship Co Ltd (No 2)* [1998] AC 878 at 910, HL.

[250] [1993] AC 410, HL; Beckwith (1994) 43 ICLQ 185; Briggs [1993] LMCLQ 451; Carter (1993) 64 BYBIL 470; Davenport (1994) 110 LQR 25. This reversed the decision of the Court of Appeal [1992] 1 Lloyd's Rep 124; Collins (1992) 108 LQR 393.

[251] [1998] AC 878, HL; Briggs (1997) 68 BYBIL 355.

[252] The *Republic of India (No 2)* case at 912. But what if the English proceedings had been commenced before those in India?

[253] Ibid, at 913. This moment is when the claim form is served or deemed to have been served.

[254] See Collins (1992) 108 LQR 393. See *Messer Griersheim GmbH v Goyal MG Gases PVT Ltd* [2006] EWHC 79 (Comm), [2006] 1 CLC 283, setting aside default judgment and granting summary judgment on the merits.

[255] The *Republic of India v India Steamship Co Ltd* case at 424. On the facts there was no estoppel by convention or acquiescence: the *Republic of India v India Steamship Co Ltd (No 2)* case at 914–16. The House of Lords in *(No 2)* found it unnecessary to decide whether the wider principle in *Henderson v Henderson* (1843) 3 Hare 100, 67 ER 313, which prevents points being raised in subsequent proceedings and which could and should have been raised in earlier proceedings (see infra, pp 562–3), applied in cases where s 34 did not do so. Clarke J, at first instance, thought that in principle it could apply: [1994] 2 Lloyd's Rep 331 at 356–7, as did the Court of Appeal [1998] AC 878 at 897–8.

is enforceable or entitled to recognition in England.[256] However, the stronger domestic policy of protecting the interests of minors has meant that this provision may not operate to prevent them from bringing fresh proceedings, when the foreign proceedings were not in their interests and there are questions over their consent to the foreign proceedings.[257]

It must still be the case, though, that if the claimant has two causes of action founded on the same damage against separate defendants, as where the drivers of two vehicles have collided and caused him injury, a judgment of a foreign court against one of them does not bar him from suing the other in England.[258] He cannot, however, sustain such an action if the amount awarded him by the foreign judgment is sufficient to compensate him fully for the damage suffered, for English law does not tolerate double satisfaction.[259]

(b) Cause of action and issue estoppel

So far as English judgments are concerned, estoppel *per rem judicatam* is a generic term which comprises two species.

The first, called *cause of action estoppel*, "is that which prevents a party to an action from asserting or denying, as against the other party, the existence of a particular cause of action, the non-existence or the existence of which has been determined by a court of competent jurisdiction in previous litigation between the same parties".[260] In such a case, a further action for the same cause can never succeed.

The second species, called *issue estoppel*, becomes relevant where the determination of a cause of action has necessitated the determination of a number of different issues.[261] In the case of an English judgment, the rule then is that the parties to an action are estopped from contesting a particular issue which has already been determined in previous proceedings to which they were also parties.[262] It is immaterial that the cause of action is not the same in both proceedings.[263]

There is abundant authority that cause of action estoppel applies to foreign judgments,[264] and it is now clear that issue estoppel also applies to foreign judgments.[265] In *Carl Zeiss Stiftung v Rayner and Keeler Ltd*[266] a majority of the Law Lords[267] were of the opinion that there can be an issue estoppel in respect of a foreign judgment. However, the doctrine was not applied in that particular case since the essentials for the application of the doctrine[268] were not satisfied. Since then a number of cases have accepted that issue estoppel applies in respect of foreign judgments,[269] and the matter was put beyond any doubt by the House of Lords' decision in

---

[256] *Black v Yates* [1992] QB 526; Carter (1991) 62 BYBIL 458.

[257] *Black v Yates* [1992] QB 526.

[258] See *Kohnke v Karger* [1951] 2 KB 670.

[259] Ibid.

[260] *Thoday v Thoday* [1964] P 181 at 197, CA.

[261] The expression "issue estoppel" was coined by Higgins J in the Australian case of *Hoystead v Taxation Comr* (1921) 29 CLR 537, 561, Australian High Ct; on appeal, [1926] AC 155, PC and adopted by Diplock LJ in the *Thoday v Thoday* case at 197–8.

[262] *Fidelitas Shipping Co Ltd v V/O Exporteklab* [1966] 1 QB 630 at 640, 642, CA; *Carl Zeiss Stiftung v Rayner and Keeler Ltd (No 2)* [1967] 1 AC 853 at 913–17, 933–5, 964–5, HL.

[263] *Marginson v Blackburn Borough Council* [1939] 2 KB 426, CA.

[264] Supra, pp 556–8.

[265] See generally Campbell (1994) 16 Sydney LR 311; Rogerson [1998] CJQ 91.

[266] [1967] 1 AC 853, HL.

[267] Contra Lord Guest.

[268] Discussed infra.

[269] *Westfal-Larsen and Co A/S v Ikerigi Compañia Naviera SA* [1983] 1 All ER 382; *Tracomin SA v Sudan Oil Seeds Co Ltd* [1983] 1 WLR 662 (Staughton J), affd by the Court of Appeal [1983] 1 WLR 1026; *The Jocelyne* [1984] 2 Lloyd's Rep 569 (Lloyd J); *Vervaeke v Smith* [1983] 1 AC 145 at 156, 160, 162, HL,

The Sennar (No 2),[270] in which issue estoppel was applied to a Dutch judgment. Lord Diplock said that "it is far too late, at this stage of the development of the doctrine, to question that issue estoppel can be created by the judgment of a foreign court".[271]

(c) Prerequisites of estoppel

The same prerequisites apply for a cause of action and an issue estoppel. In both cases an estoppel will not apply unless three conditions are satisfied.[272]

First, the previous decision must have been final and conclusive[273] on the merits,[274] and must have been given by a court of competent jurisdiction.[275] Generally, a foreign judgment will not be given greater preclusive effect in England than it has in the country where it was given.[276] The requirement that the decision is on the merits has been relaxed by the Court of Appeal, which has accepted that, in principle, an issue estoppel can arise from a judgment of a foreign court on a procedural, ie non-substantive, issue.[277] Seemingly, this would include a

---

discussed infra, pp 582–3, a case of an English judgment creating an issue estoppel; *The European Gateway* [1987] QB 206.

[270] [1985] 1 WLR 490, HL.

[271] At 493; the other Law Lords agreed; the case is discussed infra, pp 561–2.

[272] *Carl Zeiss Stiftung v Rayner and Keeler Ltd (No 2)* [1967] 1 AC 853 at 909–10, 935, 942, 967–71, HL; *The Sennar (No 2)* [1985] 1 WLR 490 at 493–4, 499, HL. On the application of these prerequisites to US judgments approving the settlement of class actions, see Fairclough and Lein (eds), *Extraterritoriality and Collective Redress* (2012); Dixon (1997) 46 ICLQ 134; Stiggelbout (2011) 52 Harvard Int L J 433; Mulheron (2012) 75 MLR 180.

[273] See *Desert Sun Loan Corpn v Hill* [1996] 2 All ER 847 at 855 et seq, 863 (per Stuart-Smith LJ), CA; *Boss Group Ltd v Boss France SA* [1997] 1 WLR 351 at 359, CA; *Kirin-Amgen Inc v Boehringer Mannheim GmbH* [1997] FSR 289, CA; *Buehler AG v Chronos Richardson Ltd* [1998] 2 All ER 960, CA; *The Irini A (No 2)* [1999] 1 Lloyd's Rep 189; *Svenska Petroleum Exploration AB v Government of the Republic of Lithuania* [2005] EWHC 9 (Comm) at [35]–[38], [2005] 1 Lloyd's Rep 515; *Leibinger v Stryker Trauma GmbH* [2006] EWHC 690 (Comm); *Svenska Petroleum Exploration AB v Government of the Republic of Lithuania (No 2)* [2006] EWCA Civ 1529 at [91]–[104], [2007] QB 886; *Barrett v Universal-Island Records Ltd* [2006] EWHC 1009 (Ch) at [176]–[190]; see also *First Laser Ltd v Fujian Enterprises (Holdings) Co Ltd* [2012] HKCU 1397 at [43]-[49]. An issue estoppel may arise out of a judgment which is subject to appeal, see *Hawke Bay Shipping Co Ltd v The First National Bank of Chicago, The Efthimis* [1986] 1 Lloyd's Rep 244 at 247, CA; *Good Challenger Navegante SA v Metalexportimport SA (The Good Challenger)* [2003] EWCA Civ 1668, [2004] 1 Lloyd's Rep 67. A judgment for enforcement of a foreign judgment is not conclusive: *Cortes v Yorkton Securities Inc* (2007) 278 DLR (4th) 740, British Columbia Sup Ct; cf *Morgan Stanley & Co International Ltd v Pilot Lead Investments Ltd* [2006] 4 HKC 93, criticised by Smart (2007) 81 ALJ 349.

[274] The *Carl Zeiss Stiftung v Rayner and Keeler Ltd (No 2)* case at 918–19, 926, 936, 949, 969–70; *Tracomin SA v Sudan Oil Seeds Co Ltd* [1983] 1 WLR 662 (Staughton J); *The Sennar (No 2)* case at 494, 499; *Charm Maritime Inc v Kyriakou and Mathias* [1987] 1 Lloyd's Rep 433, CA; *Naraji v Shelbourne* [2011] EWHC 3298 (QB); *Diag Human SE v Czech Republic* [2014] EWHC 1639 (Comm), [2014] 2 Lloyd's Rep 244; *Midtown Acquisitions LP v Essar Global Fund Ltd* [2017] EWHC 519 (Comm); see also *First Laser Ltd v Fujian Enterprises (Holdings) Co Ltd* [2012] HKCU 1397 at [43]–[49]; *Celtic Salmon Atlantic (Killary) v Aller Acqua (Ireland) Ltd* [2014] IEHC 421. The judgment on the merits can be implicit: *The Republic of Kazakhstan v Istil Group Inc* [2006] EWHC 448 (Comm), [2006] 2 Lloyd's Rep 370, affd without discussing this point [2007] EWCA Civ 471, [2008] 1 All ER (Comm) 88.

[275] The *Carl Zeiss Stiftung v Rayner and Keeler Ltd (No 2)* case at 942; the *Tracomin SA v Sudan Oil Seeds Co Ltd* case (Staughton J); *The Sennar (No 2)* case at 499; *The Good Challenger Navegante SA v Metalexportimport SA (The Good Challenger)* [2003] EWCA Civ 1668, [2004] 1 Lloyd's Rep 67.

[276] The *Carl Zeiss Stiftung v Rayner and Keeler Ltd (No 2)* case at 919, 970; *The Jocelyne* [1984] 2 Lloyd's Rep 569 at 573; *ABCI v BFT* [2002] 1 Lloyd's Rep 511 at 538; *Air Foyle Ltd v Center Capital Ltd* [2002] EWHC 2535 (Comm) at [44], [2003] 2 Lloyd's Rep 753; *Yukos Capital Sarl v OJSC Rosneft Oil Co (No 2)* [2011] EWHC 1461 (Comm) at [56]–[58], [2011] 2 Lloyd's Rep 443; *Joint Stock Co 'Aeroflot-Russian Airlines' v Berezovsky* [2014] EWCA Civ 20, [2014] 1 CLC 53; see also Harder (2013) 62 ICLQ 441; van de Velden (2012) 61 ICLQ 519.

[277] *Desert Sun Loan Corpn v Hill* [1996] 2 All ER 847, CA; Briggs (1996) 67 BYBIL 596. Cf *Relfo Ltd v Varsani* [2009] EWHC 2297 (Ch)—a decision by a Singapore court to decline to exercise jurisdiction to

finding by the foreign court that the defendant had authorised a lawyer to act on his behalf and had accordingly submitted to the jurisdiction.[278] But it would not seem to include an order dismissing a case for want of prosecution, a technical objection, or a default of pleading, nor an order made by consent, because such orders are not the product of a decision-making process.[279]

Secondly, there must be identity of parties,[280] that is to say, the parties to the previous decision or their privies must be the same persons as the parties to the later action or their privies.

Thirdly, the cause of action or issue before the court must be identical with that previously determined.[281]

Nonetheless, when it comes to applying these common rules there is an important difference between cases involving a cause of action estoppel and those involving issue estoppel. When applying the doctrine of issue estoppel the need for caution has been stressed.[282] There are good reasons for adopting this attitude. Confronted with an unfamiliar procedure, it may be difficult for an English judge to ascertain, for instance, the exact issues that have been determined by the foreign court and whether each of them has been determined beyond the possibility of further litigation. Issues may not be fully argued abroad because, in cases of a trivial nature, the defendant may have regarded it as impracticable, in terms of time and expense, to defend fully. It may then be unjust to estop the defendant from raising these issues in England. The application of the principles of issue estoppel is subject to the

---

enforce, directly or indirectly, the revenue laws of another country is not a determination of the cause of action on the merits.

[278] The foreign court made no such specific finding in the *Desert Sun Loan Corpn* case at 860 (per Evans LJ) and 863 (per Stuart-Smith LJ); cf *A/S D/S Svendborg v Wansa* [1997] 2 Lloyd's Rep 183, CA.

[279] *Serious Fraud Office v Saleh* [2015] EWHC 2119 (QB) at [79], [98], [99], [2015] Lloyd's Rep FC 629; affd [2017] EWCA Civ 18 at [50]–[54].

[280] The *Carl Zeiss Stiftung v Rayner and Keeler Ltd (No 2)* case at 910–13, 928–36, 937, 943–6, 968 et seq; *The Sennar (No 2)* case at 499; *House of Spring Gardens Ltd v Waite* [1991] 1 QB 241 at 252–4, CA; *Republic of India v India Steamship Co Ltd (No 2)* [1998] AC 878, HL; discussed supra, pp 557–8; *Kirin-Amgen Inc v Boehringer Mannheim GmbH* [1997] FSR 289, CA; *Baker v Ian McCall International Ltd* [2000] CLC 189; *The Good Challenger Navegante SA v Metalexportimport SA* [2003] EWCA Civ 1668, [2004] 1 Lloyd's Rep 67; *Seven Arts Entertainment Ltd v Content Media Corp Plc* [2013] EWHC 588 (Ch). See generally Handley (2000) 116 LQR 191.

[281] The *Carl Zeiss Stiftung v Rayner and Keeler Ltd (No 2)* case at 913, 935, 942–4, 967–8; *The Sennar (No 2)* case at 494–5, 498–500; *The Efthimis* [1986] 1 Lloyd's Rep 244 at 247, CA; *Siporex Trade SA v Comdel Commodities Ltd* [1986] 2 Lloyd's Rep 428; *Black v Yates* [1992] QB 526; *Republic of India v India Steamship Co Ltd* [1993] AC 410, HL, discussed supra, pp 557–8; *Desert Sun Loan Corpn v Hill* [1996] 2 All ER 847, CA; *Buehler AG v Chronos Richardson Ltd* [1998] 2 All ER 960, CA; *Kirin-Amgen Inc v Boehringer Mannheim GmbH* [1997] FSR 289, CA; *Baker v Ian McCall International Ltd* [2000] CLC 189; *Air Foyle Ltd v Center Capital Ltd* [2002] EWHC 2535 (Comm), [2003] 2 Lloyd's Rep 753; *Masters v Leaver* [2000] IL Pr 387; *Good Challenger Navegante SA v Metalexportimport SA (The Good Challenger)* [2003] EWCA Civ 1668, [2004] 1 Lloyd's Rep 67; *Chantier de l'Atlantique SA v Gaztransport & Technigaz SAS* [2011] EWHC 3383 (Comm); *Yukos Capital Sarl v OJSC Rosneft Oil Co (No 2)* [2012] EWCA Civ 1668, [2014] QB 458; *Seven Arts Entertainment Ltd v Content Media Corp Plc* [2013] EWHC 588 (Ch); *Diag Human SE v Czech Republic* [2014] EWHC 1639 (Comm), [2014] 2 Lloyd's Rep 244; *Chai v Peng* [2014] EWHC 3518 (Fam), [2015] 2 FLR 424. See also Hill (2012) 8 J Priv Int L 159; Scherer (2013) 4 J Int Disputes Settlement 587.

[282] *Carl Zeiss Stiftung v Rayner and Keeler Ltd (No 2)* [1967] 1 AC 853 at 917, 918 (Lord Reid), 925–6 (Lord Hodson), 947 (Lord Upjohn), 967 (Lord Wilberforce); *Westfal-Larsen & Co A/S v Ikerigi Compañia Naviera SA* [1983] 1 All ER 382 at 388–9. See also *The Sennar (No 2)* [1985] 1 WLR 490 at 500; *Owens Bank Ltd v Bracco* [1991] 4 All ER 833 at 856, CA; affd [1992] 2 AC 443, HL; *Desert Sun Loan Corpn v Hill* [1996] 2 All ER 847, CA; *Good Challenger Navegante SA v Metalexportimport SA (The Good Challenger)* [2003] EWCA Civ 1668, [2004] 1 Lloyd's Rep 67; *HJ Heinz Co Ltd v EFL Inc* [2010] EWHC 1203 (Comm), [2010] 1 CLC 868; *Naraji v Shelbourne* [2011] EWHC 3298 (QB).

overriding consideration that it must work justice and not injustice.[283] Issue estoppel is a rule of evidence and, as such, is no doubt governed by the law of the forum, but this is a case where the law of the forum ought to be applied "in a manner consistent with good sense".[284] Three further points to note are that determination of the issue said to give rise to the issue estoppel must have been necessary for the decision of the foreign court;[285] it is irrelevant that the English court may form the view that the decision of the foreign court was wrong either on the facts or as a matter of English law;[286] and an issue estoppel is only created by a decision against an unsuccessful party and not against a successful party on an issue the latter party lost.[287]

The requirements for an estoppel were discussed by the House of Lords in *The Sennar (No 2)*.[288]

> A bill of lading presented by the original sellers of groundnuts to the original buyers contained an exclusive jurisdiction clause, providing that all actions under the contract of carriage should be brought only before the court of Khartoum or Port Sudan and that the law of the Sudan should apply. Nonetheless, GfG, a German company which was the subsequent buyer, brought an action in the Netherlands against the defendant shipowners for damages for the equivalent of a tort, claiming that a false date had been put on the bill of lading by the master of the defendant's ship, *The Sennar*, as a result of which it had incurred liabilities. The Dutch court declined jurisdiction, reasoning that GfG could only found a claim on the contract contained in the bill of lading and the contract had in it the Sudanese exclusive jurisdiction clause. The plaintiff, another German company, which was successor in title to GfG, brought an action in England against the defendant for damages in tort for deceit/negligence in respect of the same cause of action. One of the issues that had to be decided was whether the plaintiff was estopped by the Dutch decision from asserting that its claim did not fall within the exclusive jurisdiction clause, which only dealt with claims under the contract.

The House of Lords unanimously held that the plaintiff was estopped from asserting this; the Sudanese exclusive jurisdiction clause applied with the result that the English proceedings were stayed.[289] Since the substance of the claim had not been decided by the Dutch court, this was not a case of cause of action estoppel but one of issue estoppel. There were, however, problems in the instant case in satisfying two of the prerequisites for an estoppel.

First, was the Dutch decision, which only concerned a preliminary matter of jurisdiction and did not raise the substance of the dispute, decided "on the merits"? Lord Brandon gave a wide definition to this concept thus:

> Looking at the matter negatively a decision on procedure alone is not a decision on the merits. Looking at the matter positively a decision on the merits is a decision which establishes certain facts as proved or not in dispute; states what are the relevant principles of law applicable to such facts; and expresses a conclusion with regard to the effect of applying those principles to the factual situation concerned.[290]

---

[283] *The Good Challenger* case at [54], [75]–[78].
[284] *Carl Zeiss Stiftung v Rayner and Keeler Ltd (No 2)* [1967] 1 AC 853 at 919.
[285] *The Good Challenger* case at [58]–[74].
[286] Ibid, at [55]–[57].
[287] *Joint Stock Asset Management Co Ingosstrakh-Investments v BNP Paribas SA* [2012] EWCA Civ 644 at [61], [2012] 2 CLC 312.
[288] [1985] 1 WLR 490, HL. Only Lords Diplock and Brandon gave detailed judgments. Lords Fraser, Roskill and Bridge concurred with these two Law Lords.
[289] The discretionary power to stay proceedings in this type of case is discussed supra, pp 410–4.
[290] [1985] 1 WLR 490 at 499; see also 494 (per Lord Diplock), HL.

Lord Brandon concluded that the Dutch decision was not a procedural one[291] and therefore came with the above definition.[292] Lord Diplock agreed that the Dutch decision was as to the merits. He held that the Dutch court did not simply decide that it did not have jurisdiction; it decided, first, that the only claim against the shipowners was for breach of contract, and, second, that as a result of the Sudanese exclusive jurisdiction clause that claim was enforceable only in the courts of the Sudan. There was, therefore, a judgment on the merits in respect of these two issues.[293]

Secondly, was the issue the same in the Dutch and English courts? In the Dutch court, although the action was framed in tort, the issue was whether it could be founded in tort or only on the contract (in the latter eventuality, the issue was whether the exclusive jurisdiction clause applied). However, in the English court, the action was framed in tort and undeniably could be founded in tort and the issue was whether the action would come within the exclusive jurisdiction clause. Nevertheless, the basic issue was held to be the same, ie whether, even though the claim was framed in tort rather than in contract, the exclusive jurisdiction clause applied to such a claim.[294]

There was no need for the exercise of caution in the use of issue estoppel in the instant case[295] since all the issues decided in the Netherlands had been fully litigated. Also the reason why caution is needed is so that issue estoppel does not unjustly prevent *defendants* from raising issues in England. In the instant case, it was being used to prevent claimants from relitigating the same claim on another basis in a different jurisdiction.[296] Indeed, there are strong policy reasons why a court should be very willing to use issue estoppel in a case like *The Sennar (No 2)*:[297] shipowners are vulnerable to having their ships arrested and to forum shopping by claimants; exclusive jurisdiction clauses are designed to fix the place of trial and therefore claimants should not be able to avoid such clauses by going from one country to another seeking a classification of the cause of action which achieves this objective; having tried this once abroad, a claimant should not be able to have another bite of the cherry in England.

(ii) The rule in Henderson v Henderson

A related rule is laid down in *Henderson v Henderson*,[298] according to which a party is precluded from raising causes of action and issues which might have been, but were not, raised and decided in the earlier proceedings. In the words of Wigram V-C:

> The plea of res judicata applies, except in special cases, not only to points upon which the court was actually required by the parties to form an opinion and pronounce a judgment, but to every point which properly belonged to the subject of litigation, and which the parties, exercising reasonable diligence, might have brought forward at the time.[299]

Thus if a professional negligence claim is pursued in foreign proceedings solely in tort, a subsequent claim for the same negligence brought in contract in England would be barred;

---

[291] Ibid, at 499. Cf *Harris v Quine* (1869) LR 4 QB 653. That case is now affected by s 3 of the Foreign Limitation Periods Act 1984, discussed infra, p 600.

[292] See also *Tracomin SA v Sudan Oil Seeds Co Ltd* [1983] 1 WLR 662 (Staughton J).

[293] [1985] 1 WLR 490 at 494–5, HL.

[294] Ibid, at 499–500 (per Lord Brandon).

[295] Ibid, at 500 (per Lord Brandon).

[296] See Kerr LJ in the Court of Appeal [1984] 2 Lloyd's Rep 142 at 152–3.

[297] See generally, Lord Diplock at 493, Lord Brandon at 501; Kerr LJ in the Court of Appeal, supra, [1984] 2 Lloyd's Rep 142 at 149–54.

[298] (1843) 3 Hare 100, 67 ER 313. See also *Vervaeke v Smith* [1983] 1 AC 145 at 163, HL; *Fennoscandia Ltd v Clarke* [1999] 1 All ER (Comm) 365 at 372–4, CA.

[299] (1843) 3 Hare 100 at 115.

but if no contract claim could not be pursued in the foreign proceedings because of a foreign procedural rule, the rule in *Henderson v Henderson* is not engaged.[300]

(iii) Abuse of process

Quite apart from estoppel *per rem judicatam*, the courts have an inherent power to prevent any abuse of process which may be involved in an attempt to litigate matters for a second time.[301] This doctrine has been used by the Privy Council to strike out a defence of fraud (in respect of which there was no prima facie evidence), thereby avoiding re-opening this issue when it had been determined abroad.[302] According to Lord Templeman:[303]

> No strict rule can be laid down; in every case the court must decide whether justice requires the further investigation of alleged fraud or requires that the plaintiff having obtained a foreign judgment, shall no longer be frustrated in enforcing that judgment.

Recourse to what justice requires makes it difficult to predict when this doctrine will operate.[304] What is clear, though, is that it is not confined to cases where the issue is that of fraud,[305] and it avoids having to determine whether the prerequisites of estoppel have been met.[306] It is an alternative to estoppel *per rem judicatam* but also involves some overlap with that doctrine in that an attempt to litigate a matter for a second time may fall foul of both doctrines.[307]

(iv) Judgments in personam and in rem

The principle of *res judicata* applies both to actions in personam and actions in rem,[308] for as regards their degree of conclusiveness these actions differ from each other only in the number of persons who are bound by the judgment. A judgment in personam binds the parties and their privies if they litigate the same issue in England. A judgment in rem has a wider operation, since it is conclusive against all the world.[309] Both judgments in rem and judgments in personam are conclusive upon the point decided, but in the former "the point", since it is the determination of status, is conclusive against the whole world, while in the latter, since it is unconcerned with status, is conclusive only between parties and privies.[310]

---

[300] *Naraji v Shelbourne* [2011] EWHC 3298 (QB).
[301] *Desert Sun Corpn v Hill* [1996] 2 All ER 847 at 859 (per Evans LJ), 864 (per Stuart-Smith LJ), CA. See on abuse by not bringing forward the full case in earlier proceedings, *Baker v Ian McCall International Ltd* [2000] CLC 189; *Air Foyle Ltd v Center Capital Ltd* [2002] EWHC 2535 (Comm), [2003] 2 Lloyd's Rep 753; *Good Challenger Navegante SA v Metalexportimport SA (The Good Challenger)* [2003] EWCA Civ 1668 at [100]–[101], [2004] 1 Lloyd's Rep 67; cf *Karafarin Bank v Mansoury-Dara* [2009] EWHC 1217 (Comm) at [20]–[24], [2009] 2 Lloyd's Rep 289.
[302] *Owens Bank Ltd v Etoile Commerciale SA* [1995] 1 WLR 44, PC; discussed infra, p 573. See also *House of Spring Gardens Ltd v Waite* [1991] 1 QB 241 at 254–5, CA.
[303] The *Owens Bank Ltd v Etoile Commerciale SA* case at 51.
[304] See generally Rogerson [1998] CJQ 91, 100–2.
[305] See the *Desert Sun Loan Corpn v Hill* case. See also *J H Rayner (Mincing Lane) Ltd v Bank für Gemainwirtschaft AG* [1983] 1 Lloyd's Rep 462, CA; *Dallal v Bank Mellat* [1986] QB 441; *Kirin-Amgen Inc v Boehringer Mannheim GmbH* [1997] FSR 289, CA.
[306] See the *Owens Bank* case.
[307] See *House of Spring Gardens Ltd v Waite* [1991] 1 QB 241, CA; the *Desert Sun Loan Corpn v Hill* case at 864 (per Stuart-Smith LJ); *Virgin Atlantic Airways Ltd v Zodiac Seats UK Ltd (formerly Contour Aerospace Ltd)* [2013] UKSC 46 at [17]–[26], [2013] 3 WLR 299.
[308] *Serious Fraud Office v Saleh* [2017] EWCA Civ 18.
[309] Supra, p 544. Estoppel in divorce, etc cases is discussed, infra, pp 1025–6.
[310] *Ballantyne v Mackinnon* [1896] 2 QB 455 at 462, CA.

(f) Defences to recognition and enforcement

Despite the fact that the foreign judgment that is relied upon in England is given by a court of competent jurisdiction and is final and conclusive, it is still open to the party against whom the judgment is invoked to show why he should not be bound by the obligation created by the judgment by pleading any one of the available defences. Two situations in which the enforcement of a foreign judgment will be refused, namely non-enforcement of foreign revenue, penal and other public laws and non-enforcement of judgments for multiple damages under the Protection of Trading Interests Act 1980, have already been discussed.[311] The seven defences set out below may be pleaded not only by a defendant resisting an action in England on a foreign judgment in favour of the claimant, but also by a party (eg claimant suing in England on the original cause of action) who is met by the defence of estoppel *per rem judicatam* in favour of the other party.[312] But first the matters that cannot be pleaded as a defence will be mentioned.

(i) Conclusiveness of foreign judgments

It is well established that when deciding whether to give an effect to a foreign judgment the English court is not entitled to investigate the propriety of the proceedings in the foreign court.[313] Erroneous judgments delivered by a foreign court are not void in England.[314] The merits of the case have been argued and determined, and if one of the parties is discontented with the decision his proper course is to take appellate proceedings in the forum of the judgment. The English tribunal, in other words, cannot sit as a court of appeal against a judgment pronounced by a court which was competent to exercise jurisdiction over the parties.[315]

(a) Mistakes by the foreign court
(i) Mistakes as to facts or as to law

The defendant in England may show that the foreign court had no jurisdiction to try the case or that the foreign judgment is not final and conclusive, or he may plead a limited number of defences, such as fraud, but he is not at liberty to show that the court mistook either the facts or the law on which its judgment was founded.[316]

A more difficult question is whether a foreign judgment can be impeached on the ground that the court made an obvious mistake with regard to English law when purporting to give a decision according to that law. It has been decided that such a mistake does not excuse the defendant from performing the obligation that has been laid upon him by the judgment.[317]

---

[311] Supra, 552–5.

[312] *Jacobson v Frachon* (1927) 138 LT 386 (natural justice), CA; *Manolopoulos v Pnaiffe* [1930] 2 DLR 169, Nova Scotia Sup Ct (fraud). The act of state doctrine does not prevent examination of the conduct of the courts of a foreign state, since judicial acts are not acts of state for the purposes of the doctrine: *Yukos Capital Sarl v OJSC Rosneft Oil Co (No 2)* [2012] EWCA Civ 855, [2014] QB 458; Mills [2012] CLJ 465.

[313] *Henderson v Henderson* (1844) 6 QB 288, 115 ER 111; *Bank of Australasia v Harding* (1850) 9 CB 661, 137 ER 1052; *Bank of Australasia v Nias* (1851) 16 QB 717, 117 ER 1055; *Vanquelin v Bouard* (1863) 15 CBNS 341, 143 ER 817; *Godard v Gray* (1870) LR 6 QB 139; *Messina v Petrocacchino* (1872) LR 4 PC 144, PC; *Vadala v Lawes* (1890) 25 QBD 310 at 316, CA; *Pemberton v Hughes* [1899] 1 Ch 781 at 790, CA; *Merker v Merker* [1963] P 283. For earlier doubts, see *Smith v Nicolls* (1839) 5 Bing NC 208 at 221, 132 ER 1084.

[314] *Imrie v Castrique* (1860) 8 CBNS 405 at 428, 141 ER 1222.

[315] *Dent v Smith* (1869) LR 4 QB 414 at 446; *Imrie v Castrique* (1860) 8 CBNS 405, 141 ER 1222; *Ferdinand Wagner v Laubscher Bros & Co* [1970] 2 QB 313 at 318, CA.

[316] The *Bank of Australasia v Nias* case at 735; the *Godard v Gray* case at 150; *Malicorp Ltd v Egypt* [2015] EWHC 361 (Comm) at [25], [2015] 1 Lloyd's Rep 423.

[317] *Castrique v Imrie* (1870) LR 4 HL 414, HL; *Godard v Gray* (1870) LR 6 QB 139; *Good Challenger Navegante SA v Metalexportimport SA (The Good Challenger)* [2003] EWCA Civ 1668 at [56], [2004] 1 Lloyd's Rep 67; cf *Simpson v Fogo* (1863) 1 H & M 195, 71 ER 85.

The doctrine that a foreign judgment cannot be impeached as to merits has been carried to its logical conclusion. Thus in *Godard v Gray*:[318]

> The plaintiffs, who were Frenchmen, sued the defendants (Englishmen) in France on a charter-party, the proper law of which was English law. The charter-party contained the clause: "Penalty for non-performance of this agreement estimated amount of freight." The effect of such a clause under English law was not to quantify the damages exactly, but to leave them to be assessed according to the actual loss suffered; but the French court, believing that the language of the charter-party was to be understood in its natural sense, fixed the damages payable by the defendant at the exact amount of freight.

When sued on the judgment in England, the defendants pleaded this mistaken view of English law in defence. The plea failed. The court held that there could be no difference between a mistake as to English law and any other mistake.

(ii) A mistake as to its own jurisdiction

What, for many years, has been less certain is whether the foreign court must have had internal competence, ie jurisdiction under its own law. Lindley LJ once said that the jurisdiction which alone is important in connection with a foreign judgment is the competence of the foreign court in the international sense. "Its competence or jurisdiction in any other sense is not regarded as material by the courts of this country."[319] According to this view, action will lie in England on a foreign judgment although delivered by a court that, according to its own internal law, had no jurisdiction whatsoever over the cause of action. If, for instance, the foreign court has adjudicated on a claim in excess of the legally permitted amount, is it to be no answer to an action on the judgment in England that the court lacked internal jurisdiction? To admit this would be inconsistent with principle. According at any rate to the English rule, a judgment delivered by a court with no jurisdiction is a complete nullity, and it seems curious that what was null and void in the foreign country can be regarded as valid for the purposes of an English action. Such a foreign judgment creates no rights whatsoever in favour of the claimant, yet it is because a right has been vested in him that, according to the doctrine of obligation, he may sue on the judgment in England. The dictum of Lindley LJ, for it was nothing more, was not applied in *Papadopoulos v Papadopoulos*,[320] where one of the grounds on which the Cypriot decree of nullity was held to be ineffective was that the court had no power by the law of Cyprus to declare the marriage null and void. Similarly, in *Adams v Adams*[321] recognition was refused to a Rhodesian divorce decree because, under Rhodesian law as interpreted in England, the decree was invalid as it had been pronounced by a judge who was not a judge *de jure* of the High Court of Rhodesia.[322]

(iii) A procedural mistake

It is essential to observe that if the foreign court is internally competent the fact that it has erred in its own rules of procedure is no answer to an action in England. This is the

---

[318] (1870) LR 6 QB 139. Approved by Lord Simon in *Vervaeke v Smith* [1983] 1 AC 145 at 162, HL. See also *Tracomin SA v Sudan Oil Seeds Co Ltd* [1983] 1 WLR 662 at 674 (Staughton J); *Tracomin SA v Sudan Oil Seeds Co Ltd* [1983] 1 Lloyd's Rep 560 at 577 (Leggatt J); *Benefit Strategies Group Inc v Prider* [2005] SASC 194 at [76]–[80], (2005) 91 SASR 544.

[319] *Pemberton v Hughes* [1899] 1 Ch 781, CA. See also *Adams v Cape Industries plc* [1990] Ch 433 at 549–50, CA; cf the judgment at first instance, at 492.

[320] [1930] P 55.

[321] [1971] P 188.

[322] Cf *Re James (An Insolvent)* [1977] Ch 41 at 65–6, 77–8, CA; see now the requirement of effectiveness for the recognition of foreign divorces, etc, infra, pp 1008–9.

explanation of *Pemberton v Hughes*,[323] the case in which Lindley LJ delivered his dictum. In that case:

> A decree for divorce had been pronounced by the competent court in Florida in an unde-fended suit brought by a husband against his wife, both parties being domiciled and resident in Florida. It appeared that she had received only nine days' notice of the proceedings instead of ten days as required by the law of Florida.

It was held by the Court of Appeal that the decree was final and was binding in England. Lindley LJ in the course of his judgment said:

> All that the English courts look to are the finality of the judgment and the jurisdiction of the court, in this sense and to this extent—namely its competence to deal with the sort of case that it did deal with, and its competence to require the defendant to appear before it.[324]

In other words, the Florida court was not only internally competent to deal with a case of divorce, but also internationally competent, since the defendant was domiciled in Florida. The judge then concluded as follows:

> If the court had jurisdiction in this sense, and to this extent, the courts of this country never inquire whether the jurisdiction has been properly or improperly exercised, provided that no substantial injustice, according to English notions has been committed.[325]

At first sight the decision of the Court of Common Pleas in *Vanquelin v Bouard*[326] may seem difficult to reconcile with this statement of the law.

> This was an action in England on a judgment obtained in France on a bill of exchange. The defendant pleaded that by French law the French court had no jurisdiction, since the defendant was not a trader and was not resident at Orleans where the bills were drawn. The plea was disallowed.

If the plea meant that the French action had been brought in the wrong court[327] and if this were so, it is arguable that the judgment was a nullity. Erle CJ denied, however, that the court lacked internal jurisdiction. Thus, to repeat the words of Lindley LJ, the French tribunal was competent "to deal with the sort of case that it did deal with", though perhaps the defendant might have pleaded in defence that he personally was not within that competence. In expla-nation of both *Pemberton v Hughes* and *Vanquelin v Bouard* it has been said that:

> The court had competence in the sort of case involved, but there was a mistake or irregular-ity of procedure in the exercise of that competence which rendered the right created by the judgment merely voidable, capable of being made void by subsequent proceedings.[328]

A significant feature of *Vanquelin v Bouard* is that the defendant let the French proceedings go by default. Further, he did not plead in the English action that the French judgment was a complete nullity.

A more recent example of these rules in operation is provided by *Merker v Merker*.[329] A German court had annulled a marriage, declaring it to be "null and void" in circumstances where, under German law, it should have been declared to be "a non-existent marriage". Although the German court had jurisdiction, its decree would be regarded as a complete

---

[323] [1899] 1 Ch 781, CA.
[324] Ibid, at 790.
[325] Ibid, at 790–1.
[326] (1863) 15 CBNS 341, 143 ER 817.
[327] See the *Pemberton v Hughes* case at 791.
[328] Read, *Recognition and Enforcement of Foreign Judgments* (1938), p 100.
[329] [1963] P 283, infra, p 1009.

nullity by other German courts. Nevertheless, the decree was recognised in England. As the German court had jurisdiction, the English court "must accept the actual decision and exclude any evidence impugning it which falls short of showing that it was obtained by fraud or is contrary to natural justice".[330]

(b) Raising defences available abroad

A closely related rule is that defences that were available before the foreign court cannot be raised in England. In such a case the defendant should have raised the defence in the foreign proceedings. Thus in *Ellis v M'Henry*:[331]

> Judgment had been given in Canada in an action that would have failed had the defendant pleaded a certain composition deed. The plaintiff sued on this judgment in England, and the question was whether the defendant was entitled at that stage to set up the deed as a defence.

Bovill CJ dismissed the contention on the basis that this "would go to impeach the propriety and correctness of the judgment, and is a matter which cannot be gone into after the judgment has been obtained".[332]

This doctrine was applied more recently by the Court of Appeal in *Israel Discount Bank of New York v Hadjipateras*:[333]

> A judgment was granted in New York against two defendants in respect of guarantees given by them to the plaintiff bank. The guarantees provided that the defendants submitted to the jurisdiction of the New York courts. The second defendant, who was aged 21 when he entered into his guarantee, alleged that he only did so under the undue influence of his father, the first defendant. He raised this issue for the first time when enforcement of the New York judgment was sought in England, although he could have raised it during the New York proceedings.

The Court of Appeal accepted that, in principle, undue influence could come within the ambit of the defence that enforcement of the judgment would be against public policy, as could duress and coercion.[334] However, since the defence of undue influence was "available" to him in New York (New York law on this defence being the same as English law), he could not now raise it in England. Stephenson LJ, relying on *Ellis v M'Henry*, said that "a defendant must take all available defences in a foreign country"[335] and is at fault if he does not do so. Underlying this principle were considerations of "comity and the duty of the courts to put an end to litigation".

Whilst the principle is undeniably a sound one, the question that arises in the instant case is whether an exception should be made to it in cases involving the defence of public policy. Public policy is treated as an exception to normal private international law rules in other areas[336] and could be treated in the same way in this context. It has to be seriously questioned whether it is right to recognise and enforce a judgment when an allegation of a matter as

---

[330] Ibid, at 298–9.

[331] (1871) LR 6 CP 228. See also *Henderson v Henderson* (1844) 6 QB 288, 115 ER 111, discussed supra, pp 562–3; *Martelli v Martelli* (1983) 148 DLR (3d) 746, British Columbia CA; *Dallal v Bank Mellat* [1986] QB 441.

[332] The *Ellis v M'Henry* case at 238–9.

[333] [1984] 1 WLR 137, CA; Collier [1984] CLJ 47. See also *Tracomin SA v Sudan Oil Seeds Co Ltd* [1983] 1 Lloyd's Rep 560 (Leggatt J), reversed on another point, [1983] 1 WLR 1026, CA; *E D & F Mann (Sugar) Ltd v Yani Haryanto (No 2)* [1991] 1 Lloyd's Rep 429, CA; *Superior Composite Structures LLC v Parrish* [2015] EWHC 3688 (QB).

[334] Per Stephenson LJ at 143; Goff LJ at 147 concurring.

[335] At 144, see also O'Connor LJ at 146.

[336] Supra, pp 132–43.

serious as undue influence has not been considered in either the foreign or the English proceedings. Moreover, as will shortly be seen, where the defendant is relying on the analogous defences of fraud and natural justice, he is allowed to raise these defences in England even though they were available to him abroad, and were not raised there.[337] There are therefore weighty arguments against the decision. In *Yukos Capital Sarl v OJSC Rosneft Oil Co (No 2)*[338] the Court of Appeal refused to apply the principles of issue estoppel to a Dutch judgment refusing recognition to a Russian judgment setting aside an arbitral award made in Russia on the ground that the Russian judgment was contrary to Dutch public policy. The reason for this was that the issues decided in the Dutch judgment were different from ones raised in the English court, since English public policy is not the same as Dutch public policy. In the light of this decision, *Israel Discount Bank of New York v Hadjipateras*[339] should be considered as wrongly decided to the extent that it supports the proposition that a party cannot raise the public policy defence in England where that defence could have been raised in the country of origin.

The possibility that a defendant may be precluded from raising defences that were available before the foreign court inevitably raises the question of what is meant by a defence being "available" to a defendant abroad. In *Israel Discount Bank of New York v Hadjipateras* it was shown that New York law had a defence of undue influence and it was accepted that this was the same as the English defence.[340] Presumably, if New York law had been different from English law and did not have a defence of undue influence, or had a narrower concept of undue influence which did not allow the defence to operate in a situation where the English defence would operate, the defence would not be "available" abroad and the second defendant would have been able to raise the issue in England. What is not clear is whether the concept of availability of a defence abroad is referring solely to the existence of a rule which allows a particular defence, or whether it is also referring to the existence of evidence which goes to establish the defence. If new factual existence of undue influence had only come to light after the New York proceedings had ended, it cannot be said, except in the most limited sense, that the defence was "available" to the defendant abroad. Neither can it be said that the defendant was at fault in failing to raise the defence. In this situation the defendant should be allowed to raise the defence in England.

What if the defendant has raised a defence during the foreign proceedings and this defence has failed; can he re-raise the defence in England? The conclusiveness principle in *Ellis v M'Henry*,[341] which was quoted with approval in *Israel Discount Bank of New York v Hadjipateras*,[342] prevents the defendant from doing so.

(ii) Foreign judgment obtained by fraud

If we omit all reference to private international law for the moment, we find a well-established rule that a domestic judgment may be impeached on the ground that it was obtained by fraud.[343] The unsuccessful party, instead of appealing or applying for a new

---

[337] See *Syal v Heyward* [1948] 2 KB 443, CA, discussed infra, p 573; *Adams v Cape Industries plc* [1990] Ch 433 at 568 et seq, CA; *Jet Holdings Inc v Patel* [1990] 1 QB 335 at 345, CA, discussed infra, pp 570–1. Cf the fraud/public policy and natural justice defences under the Brussels/Lugano system, infra, pp 626–39.

[338] [2012] EWCA Civ 855, [2014] QB 458.

[339] [1984] 1 WLR 137, CA.

[340] Because of the presumption that foreign law is the same as English law unless the contrary is proved, see [1984] 1 WLR 137 at 140, 146, CA and generally on the presumption, supra, pp 105–6.

[341] (1871) LR 6 CP 228, 238; supra, p 567.

[342] [1984] 1 WLR 137 at 144 (Stephenson LJ), CA.

[343] *Duchess of Kingston's Case* (1776) Smith LC 644, 168 ER 175; *R v Humphrys* [1977] AC 1 at 21, 30, HL; Gordon (1961) 77 LQR 358, 533; Garnett (2002) 1 JICL 161.

trial, may bring an independent action to set aside the judgment.[344] It is not a method that is encouraged,[345] or one which, owing to the strict burden of proof imposed on the claimant, easily succeeds. It will not succeed unless he alleges and proves that new facts, evidential of fraud, have been discovered since the judgment and that they were not reasonably discoverable at the time of the trial. He must further prove that this new evidence, had it been adduced in the original action, would in all probability have had a material effect on the decision.[346]

Turning now to private international law, it is firmly established that a foreign judgment is impeachable for fraud in the sense that upon proof of "operative"[347] fraud without which the judgment would not have been obtained to a high degree of probability by the person alleging it[348] the judgment cannot be given effect in England.[349]

Fraud includes "every variety of mala fides and mala praxis whereby one of the parties misleads and deceives the judicial tribunal".[350] Conscious and deliberate dishonesty is required.[351]

(a) Types of fraud

It is clear that, as in domestic law,[352] a judgment will be denied recognition and enforcement if the court had been imposed upon by a trick not apparent at the time of the trial, but discovered later. Thus in *Ochsenbein v Papelier*:[353]

> A French seller, in the course of a dispute in Paris with an English buyer, produced a writ showing that he had begun an action to recover the price of the goods. When remonstrated with, however, he burnt the writ then and there and agreed to refer the dispute to arbitration in London. He nevertheless proceeded with the action behind the buyer's back and obtained judgment by default. The seller brought an action in the Court of Queen's Bench on this judgment, and the Court of Chancery, when asked by the buyer to restrain the action, refused an injunction as being unnecessary. It was unnecessary because the above facts, if proved, would afford a good defence to the common law action. The fraud may consist of perjury by the successful party or witnesses.[354]

The rule that a judgment is impeachable for fraud applies in those rare cases where the foreign court itself has acted in a fraudulent manner. This occurred in *Price v Dewhurst*[355] where, acting under Danish law, certain persons formed themselves into a court for the purpose of administering the property of a deceased testator. On proof that they, or some of them, were interested parties, their decision was treated by Shadwell V-C as fraudulent and void in so far as it favoured the judges themselves.[356]

---

[344] *Flower v Lloyd* (1877) 6 Ch D 297, CA; *Jonesco v Beard* [1930] AC 298, HL.

[345] *Flower v Lloyd (No 2)* (1879) 10 Ch D 327 at 333–4, per James LJ, though Bagallay LJ dissented, CA.

[346] *Boswell v Coaks (No 2)* (1894) 86 LT 365 n, HL; *Falcke v Scottish Imperial Insurance Co* (1887) 57 LT 39; *Birch v Birch* [1902] P 130, CA.

[347] *Gelley v Shepherd* [2013] EWCA Civ 1172.

[348] *Bater v Bater* [1951] P 35, CA; *Ahmed v Habib Bank Ltd* [2001] EWCA Civ 1270 at [32], [2002] 1 Lloyd's Rep 444. See also *Benefit Strategies Group Inc v Prider* [2005] SASC 194, (2005) 91 SASR 544.

[349] *Vadala v Lawes* (1890) 25 QBD 310 at 316, CA; *Ellerman Lines Ltd v Read* [1928] 2 KB 144, CA.

[350] *Jet Holdings Inc v Patel* [1990] 1 QB 335 at 347, CA, citing with approval Spencer Bower and Turner, *The Doctrine of Res Judicata* (1969) 2nd edn, p 323.

[351] *Midtown Acquisitions LP v Essar Global Fund Ltd* [2017] EWHC 519 (Comm).

[352] *Duchess of Kingston's Case* (1776) Smith LC 644, 168 ER 175.

[353] (1873) 8 Ch App 695.

[354] *Benefit Strategies Group Inc v Prider* [2005] SASC 194, (2005) 91 SASR 544—allegation of perjury by process servers abroad.

[355] (1837) 8 Sim 279, 59 ER 111. See also *Korea National Insurance Corp v Allianz Global Corporate & Specialty AG* [2008] EWCA Civ 1355, [2008] 2 CLC 837.

[356] For the effect of fraud on the recognition of foreign divorces and annulments, see the 14th edn of this book, pp 1018–23.

(b) Fraud and going into the merits of the foreign judgment

When fraud is alleged English courts have gone into the merits of the foreign judgment. This has happened both in the situation where the allegation of fraud has been raised and dismissed abroad, and in the situation where the defendant failed to raise this defence abroad, although it was available to him.

(i) Fraud has been raised abroad

The authorities In the case of foreign as distinct from domestic judgments, the English appeal courts have, on no fewer than four occasions, proceeded on the same evidence that was given at the original trial and have sustained a charge of fraud that had been investigated and dismissed by the foreign court. The first of these cases is *Abouloff v Oppenheimer*:[357]

> This was an action brought on a Russian judgment which ordered the return of certain goods unlawfully detained by the defendant or, alternatively, the payment of their value. One defence was that the judgment had been obtained by fraud in that the plaintiff had falsely represented to the Russian court that the defendant was in possession of the goods, the truth being that the plaintiff himself continued in possession of them throughout. It was demurred that this was an insufficient answer in point of law, since the plea was one which the Russian court could, and as a matter of fact did, consider, and that to examine it again would mean a new trial on the merits. The demurrer was overruled.[358]

Lord Esher, at any rate, had no inhibitions. He said:

> I will assume that in the suit in the Russian courts the plaintiff's fraud was alleged by the defendants and that they gave evidence in support of the charge: I will assume even that the defendants gave the very same evidence which they propose to adduce in this action; nevertheless the defendants will not be debarred at the trial of this action from making the same charge of fraud and from adducing the same evidence in support of it.[359]

The next case is *Vadala v Lawes*,[360] which raised the simple point whether an allegation of fraud which has already been fully investigated by a foreign court can once more be investigated in England. The Court of Appeal unanimously answered the question in the affirmative, and ordered a new trial with a view to discovering whether there had been fraud in relation to certain bills of exchange.

These two cases were followed in the third case, *Jet Holdings Inc v Patel*.[361]

> The plaintiffs brought an action in California to recover money allegedly misappropriated by the defendant. The defendant appeared and claimed that he had suffered and been threatened with violence by or on behalf of the president of the plaintiff companies. A default judgment was awarded against the defendant after he failed to attend for a medical examination in California. An action was brought in England to enforce the judgment. This action failed.

The Court of Appeal held that the plaintiffs had implicitly, and even to some extent expressly, asserted to the Californian court that the defendant's account of violence and threats was untrue. If it was true, this, together with the actual incidents of violence relied upon, was capable of amounting to fraud. On the other hand, fraud cannot be a defence if the foreign

---

[357] (1882) 10 QBD 295, CA. See also *Baden v Société Générale SA* [1993] 1 WLR 509 n.

[358] It should be noticed, of course, that by demurring to the plea the plaintiff admitted the truth of the facts it alleged.

[359] The *Abouloff* case at 306.

[360] (1890) 25 QBD 310, CA. See also *Norman v Norman (No 2)* (1968) 12 FLR 39.

[361] [1990] 1 QB 335, CA; Carter (1988) 59 BYBIL 360.

court has not been deceived,[362] or if what the defendant alleges is plainly untrue.[363] The fraud alleged did not relate, as in the previous two cases, to the cause of action (here, the issue of whether the defendant had misappropriated the money); it was instead an example of what was described as being "collateral" fraud. However, this made no difference to the principles to be applied. In either case, "the foreign courts' views on fraud are neither conclusive nor relevant".[364] The issue of fraud had to go on trial in England, where the facts would be considered afresh to see whether the defendant was entitled to resist enforcement on this basis.

Finally, in *Owens Bank Ltd v Bracco*[365] the House of Lords has affirmed the common law rule as set out in *Abouloff* and *Vadala*. The case involved statutory enforcement under the Administration of Justice Act 1920. It was held that the defence of fraud under that Act uses the term "fraud" in the common law (ie *Abouloff* and *Vadala*) sense. Accordingly, the defendants were entitled to show that a St Vincent judgment had been obtained by fraud irrespective of whether they could produce fresh evidence not available to them, or reasonably discoverable by them, before the judgment was delivered. The statutory concept of fraud was settled and could not be altered except by further legislation. Lord Bridge, giving the unanimous decision of the Law Lords, went on to say,[366] obiter, that, whilst there might be strong policy arguments for giving a foreign judgment the same finality as an English judgment, it was out of the question to alter the common law rule so that it was different from the statutory rule; to do so would lead to absurdity.

The effect of these decisions is that the doctrine as to the conclusiveness of foreign judgments is materially prejudiced. The Privy Council, in a subsequent case, has said that it does not regard the decision in the *Abouloff* case with enthusiasm, especially in its application to countries whose judgments the United Kingdom has agreed to register and enforce.[367] Nevertheless the Privy Council has recently refused, on an interlocutory hearing on jurisdiction, to change the *Abouloff* rule,[368] and stated that "a nuanced approach might be required, depending on the reliability of the foreign legal system, the scope for challenge in the foreign court and the type of fraud alleged".[369] The Supreme Court of Canada in *Beals v Saldanha* has adopted a very different rule whereby the merits of a foreign judgment can be challenged for fraud only where the allegations are new and not the subject of prior adjudication.[370] If the Supreme Court were to be faced with a case of fraud arising

---

[362] If a foreign court still gives judgment for a claimant, despite being aware of attempts to mislead that court and of violence against the defendant, recognition and enforcement in England would no doubt be against public policy, discussed infra, pp 573–6.

[363] [1990] 1 QB 335 at 346, CA.

[364] Ibid, at 345.

[365] [1992] 2 AC 443, HL; Briggs (1992) 109 LQR 549; Carter (1992) 63 BYBIL 522; Collier [1992] CLJ 441. The issue of fraud was also raised in Italian proceedings for enforcement of the St Vincent judgment. This raised questions under the Brussels Convention, which the House of Lords referred to the Court of Justice, see Case C-129/92 *Owens Bank Ltd v Bracco (No 2)* [1994] ECR I-117; discussed supra, p 204, which held that the Convention was inapplicable.

[366] The *Owens Bank v Bracco* case at 489.

[367] *Owens Bank Ltd v Etoile Commerciale SA* [1995] 1 WLR 44 at 50, PC.

[368] *Altimo Holdings and Investments Ltd v Kyrgiz Mobil Tel Ltd* [2011] UKPC 7 at [109]–[116], [2012] 1 WLR 1804. See also *Yukos Capital Sarl v OJSC Rosneft Oil Co (No 2)* [2012] EWCA Civ 855 at [154], [2014] QB 458.

[369] Ibid, at [116].

[370] [2003] 3 SCR 416 at [51], (2003) 234 DLR (4th) 1. The defendant has to show the facts raised could not have been discovered by due diligence prior to the judgment, at [52]. This does not apply to fraud going to jurisdiction. See also *Lapp v Lapp* 2010 BCCA 517, [2011] 3 WWR 694. *Abouloff* was rejected by the New South Wales Supreme Court in *Keele v Findley* (1991) 21 NSWLR 444, which case was, however, held to be wrongly decided in *Ki Won Yoon v Young Dung Song* [2000] NSWSC 1147, (2000) 158 FLR 295. In *Quarter Enterprises Pty Ltd v Allardyce Lumber Company Pty Ltd* [2014] NSWCA 3, (2014) 85 NSWLR

in the context of recognition and enforcement at common law, it could overrule the common law rule as set out in *Abouloff*, although this would lead to the absurdity mentioned in *Owens Bank Ltd v Bracco*.[371] In the meantime, it is necessary to find ways of avoiding the *Abouloff* rule.

Ways of avoiding the *Abouloff* rule There are two ways[372] of so doing: the first is to distinguish this rule; the second is to use the court's inherent power to prevent misuse of its process.

The first way was adopted by the Court of Appeal in *House of Spring Gardens Ltd v Waite*,[373] where the fact that the issue of fraud had already been litigated in Ireland estopped defendants from alleging, at the enforcement stage, that the prior Irish judgment had been obtained by fraud. What differentiated this case from the first three decisions[374] mentioned above was said to be that the issue of fraud had been examined in Ireland in a second action (in 1987) separate from the original one (in 1983) in respect of which enforcement was sought.[375] It was the judgment in this second action which created the estoppel. The result would have been different and the question of whether there had been fraud re-examined if it had been possible either to impeach the 1987 judgment on the basis that this judgment had itself been obtained by fraud or to produce new evidence of fraud in relation to the 1983 judgment.[376]

The crucial distinction that has to be drawn is between those foreign judgments which create an estoppel in relation to the issue of fraud and those that do not.[377] It is doubtless easier to satisfy the requirements for an estoppel[378] if there has been a separate action abroad dealing solely with the issue of fraud, but it may be possible to satisfy these requirements without this. Furthermore the foreign judgment creating the estoppel does not have to have been obtained in the country which granted the original judgment for which recognition and enforcement is now sought.[379] The English courts have a discretion to stay the English trial determining whether a foreign judgment was obtained by fraud, pending trial of the same issue in another country.[380]

404, Bathurst CJ found, at [137], that "[t]here are powerful reasons for preferring the views in *Keele*." The Supreme Court of Victoria recently reviewed the relevant authorities and followed *Keele* in *Doe v Howard* [2015] VSC 75. *Keele* was also followed by the Singapore Court of Appeal in *Hong Pian Tee v Les Placements Germain Gauthier Inc* [2002] 2 Sing LR 81. The Irish courts continue to follow the traditional approach: *Bussoleno Ltd v Kelly* [2011] IEHC 220. For the attitude towards fraud in the cases concerning the Recast of the Brussels I Regulation see *Interdesco SA v Nullifire Ltd* [1992] 1 Lloyd's Rep 180; discussed infra, pp 627–8. *Abouloff* has not been extended to enforcement of foreign arbitration awards, see *Westacre v Jugoimport* [2000] 1 QB 288 at 309–10, 316–17, CA; petition for leave to appeal to House of Lords dismissed [1999] 1 WLR 1999.

[371] See *Clarke v Fennoscandia Ltd* (No 2) 2001 SLT 1311 at [28]—inconceivable that the *Owens Bank v Bracco* case would not be followed at common law; this point was not discussed in the House of Lords decision [2007] UKHL 56, 2008 SC (HL) 122.

[372] There is in addition a possible exception to the rule in cases where it is unconscionable for the claimant to assert that the judgment was fraudulent having regard to his subsequent conduct, as where the claimant had previously relied on a fraudulent judgment, knowing of the fraud: *Baden v Société Générale SA* [1993] 1 WLR 509 at 596–7.

[373] [1991] 1 QB 241, CA; Carter (1990) 61 BYBIL 405.

[374] The *Owens Bank Ltd v Bracco* case had not yet been decided.

[375] [1991] 1 QB 241 at 251, CA.

[376] Ibid.

[377] *Owens Bank Ltd v Bracco* [1991] 4 All ER 833 at 855–7, CA, affd without discussing this point [1992] 2 AC 443, HL. See also *Owens Bank Ltd v Etoile Commerciale SA* [1995] 1 WLR 44 at 50, PC.

[378] Supra, pp 559–62.

[379] The *Owens Bank Ltd v Bracco* case at 857, CA, affd without discussing this point [1992] 2 AC 443, HL.

[380] Ibid.

The second way was adopted by the Privy Council in *Owens Bank Ltd v Etoile Commerciale SA*.[381] Lord Templeman, giving the decision of the Privy Council, pointed out that every court has an inherent power to prevent misuse of its process,[382] whether by a claimant or a defendant, and that:

> Where allegations of fraud have been made and determined abroad, summary judgment or striking out in subsequent proceedings are appropriate remedies in the absence of plausible evidence disclosing at least a prima facie case of fraud.[383] No strict rule can be laid down; in every case the court must decide whether justice requires the further investigation of alleged fraud or requires that the plaintiff, having obtained a foreign judgment, shall no longer be frustrated in enforcing that judgment.[384]

(ii) Fraud has not been raised abroad

The decision of the Court of Appeal in *Syal v Heyward*[385] takes matters even further, for it allows retrial in England notwithstanding that the claimant deliberately refrained from raising in the original trial the facts upon which the allegation of fraud is based. The strange result appears to follow that an English defendant to a foreign action may reserve a defence of fraud available to him with the intention of raising it if the judgment is invoked against him in England.[386] There can also be a retrial in England even though there had been an attempt to raise the defence of fraud abroad at a late stage and this had not been allowed.[387]

(iii) Foreign judgment contrary to public policy

No effect can be given to a foreign judgment which is contrary to the English principles of public policy.[388] There is no need to add anything here to what has already been said about the subject of general public policy,[389] except to give some examples of the application of the doctrine to the particular case of a foreign judgment.[390]

---

[381] [1995] 1 WLR 44, PC. This was the alternative ground used by the Court of Appeal in the *House of Spring Gardens Ltd v Waite* case. See generally Briggs 2015, para 7.70.

[382] Supra, p 563.

[383] See also *Commercial Innovation Bank Alfa Bank v Kozeny* [2002] UKPC 66—a triable issue of fraud; *JSC VTB Bank v Skurikhin* [2014] EWHC 271 (Comm); *Open Joint Stock Co Alfa-Bank v Trefilov* [2014] EWHC 1806 (Comm)—no triable issue of fraud. See also *Clarke v Fennoscandia (No 3)* [2007] UKHL 56, 2008 SC (HL) 122, where the House of Lords refused to consider an allegation of fraud whose purpose was not to oppose the recognition or enforcement of a foreign judgment but to undermine the judgment of a competent court, which was the product of a fair hearing.

[384] The *Owens Bank Ltd v Etoile Commerciale SA* at 51.

[385] [1948] 2 KB 443, CA; approved obiter in *Owens Bank Ltd v Bracco* [1992] 2 AC 443 at 487, HL. See also *Adams v Cape Industries plc* [1990] Ch 433 at 568–9, CA; *A/S D/S Svendborg v Wansa* [1997] 2 Lloyd's Rep 183 at 189, CA.

[386] Cowen (1949) 65 LQR 82, 84; though see *Svirskis v Gibson* [1977] 2 NZLR 4 at 10.

[387] The *Owens Bank Ltd v Bracco* case.

[388] *Re Macartney* [1921] 1 Ch 522 at 527; and see *Dalmia Dairy Industries v National Bank of Pakistan* [1978] 2 Lloyd's Rep 223 at 299–301, CA. The same principle applies in Canada, see, eg, *Bank of Montreal v Snoxell* (1982) 143 DLR (3d) 349, Alb Ct of QB.

[389] Supra, pp 132–44.

[390] An early example is the *Re Macartney* case; distinguished *Stark v Stark* (1979) 94 DLR (3d) 556, Alb CA. There were two other grounds on which the *Re Macartney* case was based. The first was that the judgment was not final and conclusive, supra, pp 548–51. The second was that the cause of action was unknown in England, a ground which is supported by *De Brimont v Penniman* (1873) 10 Blatch 437; *Mayo-Perrott v Mayo-Perrott* [1958] IR 336; but Read, *Recognition and Enforcement of Foreign Judgments* (1938), pp 293–5, suggests that such a ground is of dubious merit, on the authority of *Burchell v Burchell* (1928) 58 QLR 527. See also *Phrantzes v Argenti* [1960] 2 QB 19, supra, p 139; *Cablevision Systems Development Co v Shoupe* (1986) 39 WIR 1; Anderson (1993) 42 ICLQ 697. Cf *Telnikoff v*

(a) Application of general principles of public policy to recognition and enforcement of foreign judgments

Israel Discount Bank of New York v Hadjipateras[391] shows that undue influence, duress and coercion can come within the ambit of the public policy defence.[392] The public policy defence also guards against the effectiveness of a judgment given by a court that is biased or corrupt.[393] The defence of public policy can be raised in England in this situation even if it was available in the original proceedings but was not put forward there.[394]

In *Phillip Alexander Securities and Futures Ltd v Bamberger*[395] the Court of Appeal indicated that a foreign judgment obtained in defiance of an anti-suit injunction may not be recognised or enforced in England.

In *Vervaeke v Smith*[396] the House of Lords held that recognition of a Belgian judgment invalidating a sham marriage (ie where the parties had no intention of living together as husband and wife) would be against public policy.[397]

In *Soleimany v Soleimany*, there are obiter dicta in the Court of Appeal to the effect that it would be against public policy to enforce a foreign judgment enforcing a contract in the situation where the foreign court has found as a fact that it was the common intention of the parties to commit an illegal act in a state which England regards as a foreign and friendly state.[398] As an example going the other way, courts in Canada have enforced foreign judgments for gambling debts even though such debts are not recoverable under the law of the province where enforcement was sought and the activity giving rise to the debt would be criminal.[399]

Matusevitch 702 A2d 230 (Md CA 1997)—refusal to enforce English libel judgment; Kyu Ho Youm (2000) 49 ICLQ 131.

[391] [1984] 1 WLR 137, CA, discussed supra, pp 567–8.

[392] The *Israel Discount Bank of New York v Hadjipateras* case was subject to criticism by Collier in [1984] CLJ 47 on the ground that a foreign judgment will be refused recognition or enforcement in England if the recognition or enforcement of the judgment is contrary to English public policy, not the underlying contract on which the cause of action is based.

[393] See *Korea National Insurance Corp v Allianz Global Corporate & Specialty AG* [2008] EWCA Civ 1355, [2008] 2 CLC 837; any claim of bias of corruption cannot be accepted without positive and cogent evidence: *Altimo Holdings and Investments Ltd v Kyrgiz Mobil Tel Ltd* [2011] UKPC 7 at [97], [101], [2012] 1 WLR 1804; *Yukos Capital Sarl v OJSC Rosneft Oil Co (No 2)* [2012] EWCA Civ 855 at [73], [151], [153], [2014] QB 458; *Malicorp Ltd v Egypt* [2015] EWHC 361 (Comm) at [26], [2015] 1 Lloyd's Rep 423. See also *Beals v Saldanha* [2003] 3 SCR 416 at [72], (2003) 234 DLR (4th) 1.

[394] See the *Yukos* case—Dutch public policy not the same as English public policy; cf the *Israel Discount Bank of New York v Hadjipateras* case.

[395] [1997] IL Pr 73 at [112], CA; *Altimo Holdings and Investments Ltd v Kyrgiz Mobil Tel Ltd* [2011] UKPC 7 at [121], [2012] 1 WLR 1804; *A v L* [2010] EWHC 460 (Fam), [2010] 2 FLR 1418; cf *Golubovich v Golubovich* [2010] EWCA Civ 810, [2011] Fam 88; Rushworth and Scott (2010) 81 BYBIL 449; *Spliethoff's Bevrachtingskantoor BV v Bank of China Ltd* [2015] EWHC 999 (Comm) at [129]–[138], [2016] 1 All ER (Comm) 1034.

[396] [1983] 1 AC 145, HL.

[397] Both at common law and under the Foreign Judgments (Reciprocal Enforcement) Act 1933, on which see infra, p 598. See also *E D & F Mann (Sugar) Ltd v Yani Haryanto (No 2)* [1991] 1 Lloyd's Rep 161 at 167, affd by the Court of Appeal but on the basis that there had been a prior English judgment [1991] 1 Lloyd's Rep 429, infra, pp 582–3. The *Vervaeke* case was also decided on an estoppel point, discussed infra, pp 582–3.

[398] [1998] 3 WLR 811 at 821, CA. See also *Society of Lloyd's v Saunders* (2001) 210 DLR (4th) 519, Ont CA. Cf *Westacre v Jugoimport* [2000] 1 QB 288, CA; petition for leave to appeal to House of Lords dismissed [1999] 1 WLR 1999; discussed infra, p 674.

[399] *Boardwalk Regency Corpn v Maalouf* (1992) 88 DLR (4th) 612, Ont CA; *Auerbach v Resorts International Hotel Inc* (1991) 89 DLR (4th) 688, Que CA. For other examples: see *Bolton v Marine Services Ltd* [1996] 2 NZLR 15, CA—irregularly obtained foreign judgment enforced against a defendant in contempt of the

One particularly difficult question that arises is whether the enforcement of a foreign judgment for exemplary or punitive damages would be against public policy.[400] It has been said in the Court of Appeal that there is:

nothing contrary to English public policy in enforcing a claim for exemplary damages, which is still considered to be in accord with the public policy in the United States and many of the great countries of the Commonwealth.[401]

The British Columbia Court of Appeal[402] and the Supreme Court of South Australia (Full Court)[403] have held that the enforcement of a judgment for punitive damages was not against public policy. The former court held that the enforcement of a judgment for treble damages was akin to one for exemplary damages and was not against public policy.[404] Damages awarded, even though not punitive damages, may appear to be excessive. Nonetheless, the Supreme Court of Canada has held that, although the sums awarded by a jury in Florida were considerably larger than those that would be granted as damages in a comparable case in Canada (and indeed appeared disproportionate to the original value of the land in question), this in itself would not bar enforcement under the public policy defence.[405] It did not violate Canadian principles of morality.

In contrast, the German Federal Supreme Court has refused on public policy grounds to enforce that part of a Californian judgment which was in respect of exemplary and punitive damages.[406] However, no objection was made to the fact that under the judgment 40 per cent of the money received was to be handed over to the plaintiff's lawyer under a contingency fee agreement. Nor was any objection made to the fact that the damages for pain and suffering were more than twenty times what a German court would award.

---

foreign court; *Reeves v One World Challenge LLC* [2006] 2 NZLR 184, CA, enforcement of judgment upholding a contract which would not be enforced by a New Zealand court not against public policy.

[400] See Brand (1996) 43 NILR 143 and (2005) 24 J L and Comm 181.

[401] *SA Consortium General Textiles v Sun and Sand Agencies Ltd* [1978] QB 279 at 300, CA, concerning an award of exemplary damages or damages for "resistance abusive" under French law. See also *Pencil Hill Ltd v US Citta Di Palermo SpA*, 19 January 2016, HC—foreign arbitration award enforced where the arbitrators awarded the claimant a reduced additional sum in place of a contractual penalty, representing 25 per cent of the penalty claimed; cf *JSC VTB Bank v Skurikhin* [2014] EWHC 271 (Comm) at [42], concerning an excessive award of interest; *Service Temps Inc v MacLeod* [2013] CSOH 162 at [39]–[41], 2014 SLT 375, concerning an action at common law for the recovery of sums payable under a judgment for multiple damages.

[402] *Old North State Brewing Co v Newlands Services Inc* [1999] 4 WWR 573. See also *Beals v Saldanha* [2003] 3 SCR 416, (2003) 234 DLR (4th) 1—no public policy objection made to damages which included punitive damages.

[403] *Benefit Strategies Group Inc v Prider* [2005] SASC 194 at [60]–[75], (2005) 91 SASR 544. See also *Doe v Howard* [2015] VSC 75 at [182]; cf *Schnabel v Yung Lui* [2002] NSWSC 15—punitive damages with a public element for failing to comply with an order of a US court regarded as penal.

[404] *Old North State Brewing Co v Newlands Services Inc* [1999] 4 WWR 573, British Columbia CA. The Court also held that the judgment for treble damages was not penal. On whether exemplary or punitive damages would be regarded as penal in England see supra pp 119–20. A foreign judgment for treble damages cannot be enforced in England, see the Protection of Trading Interests Act 1980; discussed supra, pp 553–5.

[405] *Beals v Saldanha* [2003] 3 SCR 416, (2003) 234 DLR (4th) 1.

[406] *Re the Enforcement of a United States Judgment for Damages* (Case IX ZR 149/91) [1994] IL Pr 602; Bungert [1993] Int Lawyer 1075; Hay (1992) 40 AJCL 729; Zekoll (1992) 30 Col J Trans L 641. For the position in France see *X v Fountaine Pajot (Societe)* [2011] IL Pr 21, French Cour de cassation—although punitive damages are not, as a matter of principle, contrary to French public policy, the compensation ordered by a Californian court was so disproportionate to the damage suffered and the judgment debtor's breach of his contractual obligations that the foreign judgment was not recognised and enforced in France. See also Art 11 of the Hague Convention on Choice of Court Agreements 2005, which allows the refusal of recognition or enforcement of a judgment that awards damages, including exemplary or punitive damages, that do not compensate a party for actual loss or harm suffered. Similarly, Art 33 of the preliminary draft Hague Judgments Convention, Interim Text of 20 June 2001, which was eventually abandoned. This allowed

(b) Using human rights law to cast light on the public policy defence

The public policy defence is informed by the requirements under Article 6 of the European Convention on Human Rights (ECHR). It sheds light on when there would be a denial of a fair trial abroad. This is the position under the Brussels/Lugano system[407] and it applies equally to recognition and enforcement under the traditional rules. The Court of Appeal in *Al-Bassam v Al-Bassam*[408] said that Lewison J, at first instance, was correct to voice his concern that the judgment of a foreign court given in proceedings which, in the eyes of English law, had failed to meet the requirements of a fair trial, would not be recognised in England.[409] This was because an English court when applying its rules on recognition of foreign judgments "will have regard to its own obligation to act in a manner which is not inconsistent with the Convention right to a fair trial".[410] The English rule on the recognition of foreign judgments that would have to be applied to prevent recognition would be the public policy defence.

(iv) Foreign judgment contrary to natural justice

(a) The meaning of contrary to natural justice

Although the judges have frequently asserted that a foreign judgment obtained in proceedings which contravene the principles of natural justice cannot be given effect in England, it is extremely difficult to fix with precision the exact cases in which the contravention is sufficiently serious to justify a refusal of recognition and enforcement. Shadwell V-C once said that "whenever it is manifest that justice has been disregarded, the court is bound to treat the decision as a matter of no value and no substance".[411] But this goes too far. As we have already seen, a foreign judgment is effective notwithstanding that it patently proceeded upon a wrong view of the evidence or of the foreign law, or even of English law, but it would not be extravagant to suggest that this is a questionable application of natural justice. Such a judgment is in a wide sense unjust, but it is difficult to trace delicate gradations of injustice so as to reach a definite point at which it deserves to be called the negation of natural justice. It is therefore not enough to allege that the decision is very wrong or works injustice in the particular case.[412]

The expression "contrary to natural justice" has, however, figured so prominently in judicial statements that it is essential to fix, if possible, its exact scope. When applied to foreign judgments it relates merely to alleged irregularities in the procedure adopted by the adjudicating court, and has nothing to do with the merits of the case. For many years the courts have been vigilant to ensure that the defendant has been given due notice and a proper opportunity to be heard,[413] and natural justice was regarded as being confined to these two requirements. However, there is more recent authority to the effect that these are merely instances of a wider principle of natural justice, according to which the court has to consider whether there has been a procedural defect such as to constitute a breach of an English court's views of substantial justice.[414]

---

non-compensatory damages (including punitive or exemplary damages), which are grossly excessive, to be enforced to a lesser amount.

[407] *Maronier v Larmer* [2002] EWCA Civ 774, [2003] QB 620; discussed infra, p 629.

[408] [2004] EWCA Civ 857. See also *Service Temps Inc v MacLeod* [2013] CSOH 162 at [39]–[41], 2014 SLT 375 and, more generally, Fawcett, Ní Shúilleabháin and Shah, *Human Rights and Private International Law* (2016), paras 7.29-7.44.

[409] [2004] EWCA Civ 857, at [45].

[410] Ibid.

[411] *Price v Dewhurst* (1837) 8 Sim 279 at 302, 59 ER 111.

[412] *Robinson v Fenner* [1913] 3 KB 835 at 842.

[413] *Jacobson v Frachon* (1927) 138 LT 386 at 390 (Lord Hanworth), 392, (Atkin LJ); *Buchanan v Rucker* (1808) 9 East 192, 103 ER 546; *Rudd v Rudd* [1924] P 72.

[414] *Adams v Cape Industries plc* [1990] Ch 433, CA.

(b) Due notice and proper opportunity to be heard

Concern over due notice has arisen in the situation where jurisdiction has been exercised over absent defendants.[415] The English courts are reluctant to criticise the procedural rules of foreign countries on this matter and will not measure their fairness by reference to the English equivalents but, if the mode of citation has been manifestly insufficient as judged by any civilised standard, they will not hesitate to stigmatise the judgment as repugnant to natural justice and for that reason to treat it as a nullity. The relevant cases in modern times have dealt largely with foreign divorces and annulments, and want of notice or of an opportunity to be heard are now dealt with specifically in the Family Law Act 1986.[416] Due notice is concerned with notice of the proceedings[417] and not of the steps necessary to defend those proceedings.[418] If the defendant had knowledge of the foreign proceedings the lack of due notice defence cannot be used.[419] If the defendant has agreed to a particular method of service, and service has been effected in accordance with that method, it is immaterial that the defendant did not receive actual notice.[420] If the defendant has confessed to judgment and a judgment by confession has been entered against the defendant without notice of proceedings in accordance with foreign procedural rules, the lack of due notice cannot be used.[421]

As regards the requirement of a proper opportunity to be heard, it is a violation of natural justice if a litigant, though present at the proceedings, was unfairly prejudiced in the presentation of his case to the court. A clear example of this would be if he were totally denied a right to plead, but the defence of unfair prejudice is not one that is lightly admitted.[422] It is not sufficient, for instance, that his personal evidence was excluded, if the procedural rule of the forum is that parties may not give evidence on their own behalf.[423] On the other hand, granting judgment against an unrepresented litigant, who had attended with documents, without hearing the litigant or adjourning to allow the material to be put into proper form, was effectively a denial of a hearing on the merits and thus against natural justice.[424] It is a breach of the ECHR to deny the defendant's lawyers permission to put forward the defence case in relation to a civil claim as a penalty for non-appearance by the defendant at a criminal trial[425] and when it comes to recognition and enforcement of a foreign judgment given in such circumstances the natural justice defence should apply. The question whether the defendant had a proper opportunity to present his side of the case arose in *Jacobson v Frachon*.[426]

---

[415] See, eg, *Angba v Marie* (2006) 263 DLR (4th) 562, Federal Ct.

[416] Infra, pp 1027–30.

[417] See, eg, *Cortes v Yorkton Securities Inc* (2007) 278 DLR (4th) 740, British Columbia Sup Ct. The proceedings could refer to appellate proceedings: *Boele v Norsemeter Holding AS* [2002] NSWCA 363 (notice to former foreign lawyer not enough).

[418] *Beals v Saldanha* [2003] 3 SCR 416 at [68], (2003) 234 DLR (4th) 1.

[419] *Commercial Innovation Bank Alfa Bank v Kozeny* [2002] UKPC 66. See also *Re Cavell Insurance Co Ltd* (2006) 269 DLR (4th) 679, Ont CA.

[420] *Vallée v Dumergue* (1849) 4 Ex 290 at 303, 154 ER 1221; *Copin v Adamson* (1874) LR 9 Ex 345, affd (1875) 1 Ex D 17.

[421] *Midtown Acquisitions LP v Essar Global Fund Ltd* [2017] EWHC 519 (Comm).

[422] See *Altimo Holdings and Investments Ltd v Kyrgiz Mobil Tel Ltd* [2011] UKPC 7 at [97], [101], [2012] 1 WLR 1804; *Malicorp Ltd v Egypt* [2015] EWHC 361 (Comm) at [26], [2015] 1 Lloyd's Rep 423—any claim of bias cannot be accepted without positive and cogent evidence.

[423] *Scarpetta v Lowenfeld* (1911) 27 TLR 509; *Robinson v Fenner* [1913] 3 KB 835.

[424] *Leaton Leather & Trading Co v Ngai Tak Kong* (1997) 147 DLR (4th) 377, British Columbia Sup Ct. See also *Kidron v Green* (2000) 48 OR 3rd 775, Ont Sup Ct of Justice—breach of natural justice where jury awarded damages for emotional distress without substantial evidence of condition of plaintiff.

[425] *Krombach v France* Application no 29731/96 (ECtHR) at paras [90]–[91]. See also *Motorola Credit Corpn v Uzan* [2003] EWCA Civ 752 at [54]–[58], [2004] 1 WLR 113.

[426] (1928) 138 LT 386, CA. See also *Society of Lloyd's v Saunders* (2001) 210 DLR (4th) 519, Ont CA.

A French court, before giving judgment in an action brought by an English buyer of goods, alleged to be of inferior quality, against a French seller, appointed an expert to examine the goods in London. The expert, who was a relative of the defendant, made no proper examination, and, though deputed by the court to take evidence, refused to hear the evidence of the plaintiffs and their witnesses. He ultimately made a report adverse to the plaintiffs which was found by Roche J to be the uncandid production of a biased and prejudiced mind. Judgment for the defendant was given by the French court. The plaintiffs then sued the defendant in England for breach of the original contract. The defendant pleaded the French judgment in bar of action, but the plaintiffs replied that this judgment was contrary to natural justice.

The Court of Appeal held that the judgment was not void as contravening the requirements of natural justice, since the plaintiffs had not been prevented from presenting their case to the court. It appeared that by French law the court was not bound by the expert's report, but could reject it if satisfied of its inaccuracy. The plaintiffs therefore were at liberty to produce witnesses to the court and to attack the report. It further appeared that the plaintiffs had taken this course, although without success. It could not, therefore, be said that the court had refused to hear the evidence of the litigant.

(c) Substantial justice

Normally, an allegation that there has been a lack of natural justice will involve either or both of the requirements of due notice and a proper opportunity to be heard. However, the Court of Appeal in *Adams v Cape Industries plc*[427] did not regard the defence as being restricted to these two instances.[428] The ultimate question was whether there was a procedural defect which constituted "a breach of an English court's views of substantial justice".[429] The defendants in the present case had proper notice of the proceedings but chose not to contest them. Nevertheless, it was said, obiter, that there was a breach of natural justice in the way that the Federal District Court judge in Texas had assessed damages in favour of the 206 plaintiffs; this was fixed between the plaintiffs and judge on an average basis per plaintiff rather than on the basis of their individual entitlement according to the evidence.[430] The conclusion of the Court of Appeal that, in such circumstances, a judgment should not be enforced in England is no doubt correct. But it is questionable whether the use of a wide definition of the concept of natural justice was the best way of achieving this result. It opens up a gap between, on the one hand, commercial cases and, on the other hand, cases of recognition of foreign divorces and annulments, where the natural justice defence is expressly confined to instances of want of due notice and opportunity to be heard.[431] Want of substantial justice was a much criticised concept, and is no longer a basis for the refusal of recognition of foreign divorces, etc.[432] The use of the concept of substantial injustice in relation to the recognition and enforcement of foreign judgments creates new uncertainty over the ambit of the defence of natural justice. Cases of procedural unfairness which do not involve a lack of due notice or opportunity to be heard would be better dealt with under the defence of public policy.[433]

---

[427] [1990] Ch 433 at 557 et seq, CA. For the facts of the case see supra, pp 530–1. Followed in *Masters v Leaver* [2000] IL Pr 387, CA. See also *Merchant International Co Ltd v Natsionalna Aktsionerna Kompaniya Naftogaz Ukrayiny* [2012] EWCA Civ 196, [2012] 1 WLR 3036.

[428] See also the position in Canada: *Beals v Saldanha* [2003] 3 SCR 416 at [59]–[70], (2003) 234 DLR (4th) 1, defendant must have been given a fair process abroad, which includes judicial independence.

[429] [1990] Ch 433 at 564, CA.

[430] See also the *Masters v Leaver* case at [39]—failure abroad to use the procedure required by the original decision on liability by which quantum is to be assessed.

[431] Infra, pp 1027–30.

[432] Supra, pp 141–2.

[433] Supra, pp 573–6.

If a foreign judgment, which otherwise satisfies the requirements for recognition and enforcement in England, is set aside in the country of origin by a judgment which does not accord with the principles of natural or substantial justice, the setting aside may be refused recognition and the lower instance judgment may be recognised and enforced in England.[434]

(d) The availability of a remedy in the judgment-granting country

The question was raised in the *Adams* case of whether the defendants should have sought a remedy in Texas in respect of the lack of natural justice. The Court of Appeal said,[435] using the analogy of fraud,[436] that in cases involving lack of due process and opportunity to be heard it may well be that the defendant does not have to show that he has sought to take advantage of any available remedy in the foreign courts before he can raise the defence of lack of natural justice in England at the enforcement stage. However, in cases involving a lack of substantial justice other than the two primary kinds the position is different; here it is relevant to consider the fact that there is the possibility of the correction of error in the country where the judgment was obtained. Nonetheless, this was not fatal to the use of the defence on the facts of the case, since there was no evidence that the defendants had any knowledge of the method used for the assessment of the damages in the USA until the stage when enforcement of the judgment was sought in England. Likewise the exhaustion of appeal procedures in the judgment-granting state cannot be a prerequisite in the situation where the possible ground of appeal is not apparent to the defendant in adequate time to pursue this course.[437] But in a case where the defendant argued that the damages awarded in a foreign judgment were incorrect because there had been double counting, the court did not refuse enforcement on the basis that the judgment might have been appealed successfully abroad.[438]

What happens if the defendant actually raised the issue of natural justice in the foreign judgment-granting court, and the issue was determined by that court? The *Jacobson* case suggests that in such a case the defence of lack of natural justice (at least when referring to a lack of due notice and opportunity to be heard) is no longer available. However, this proposition was doubted in *Jet Holdings Inc v Patel*,[439] a case decided on the basis of fraud which also raised the issue of a lack of natural justice. In fraud cases the normal rule is that an English court at the recognition and enforcement stage can go into this issue, even though it has previously been litigated in the judgment-granting country.[440] The Court of Appeal expected that the same rule would apply in cases involving a lack of natural justice, although it did not finally decide this point.

(e) The relationship with human rights law

The defence of lack of natural justice overlaps to a great extent with the defence established by Article 6 of the ECHR. Although it has been argued that Article 6 may now have taken over the role of the common law defence of lack of natural justice,[441] it appears that the overlap is

---

[434] See *Merchant International Co Ltd v Natsionalna Aktsionerna Kompaniya Naftogaz Ukrayiny* [2012] EWCA Civ 196, [2012] 1 WLR 3036—a foreign judgment violated the principles of substantial or natural justice by setting aside in its entirety the final judgment of a lower court on the basis of partial evidence previously available through the exercise of due diligence. See also *Joint Stock Co 'Aeroflot-Russian Airlines' v Berezovsky* [2014] EWCA Civ 20, [2014] 1 CLC 53.

[435] At 568 et seq.

[436] Supra, pp 568–73.

[437] *Masters v Leaver* [2000] IL Pr 387, CA.

[438] *Superior Composite Structures LLC v Parrish* [2015] EWHC 3688 (QB).

[439] [1990] 1 QB 335 at 345, CA.

[440] Supra, pp 570–3.

[441] Briggs 2014, para 6.188; Briggs 2015, para 7.71.

not complete. As will be discussed next, Article 6 of the ECHR, as interpreted by the House of Lords in *Government of the United States of America v Montgomery (No 2)*,[442] precludes the recognition and enforcement of a foreign judgment only if there is a flagrant breach of the Article 6 standards by the court of origin. An analogous flagrancy requirement does not exist under the common law defence of lack of natural justice, so it seems that this defence can apply in cases in which Article 6 of the ECHR is not engaged.

(v) A breach of Article 6 of the ECHR[443]

There is a separate defence, the source of which is Article 6 of the ECHR,[444] implemented in the United Kingdom by the Human Rights Act 1998, and the jurisprudence of the European Court of Human Rights (ECtHR), rather than the English rules on recognition and enforcement of foreign judgments. Judge Matscher in the ECtHR in *Drozd and Janousek v France and Spain*[445] said that an ECHR Contracting State may incur responsibility by reason of assisting in the enforcement of a foreign judgment, originating from a Contracting State or a non-Contracting State, which has been obtained in conditions which constitute a flagrant breach of Article 6, whether it is a civil or criminal judgment.[446] This is an example of how the ECHR has indirect effect. It means that an English court which enforces a foreign judgment which has been obtained in such circumstances will itself be in breach of Article 6. The ECtHR in *Pellegrini v Italy*[447] adopted a wider principle than this by not requiring the breach to be "flagrant". It held that the Italian courts, before authorising the enforcement of a decision of the Vatican courts, should have satisfied themselves that the Vatican court proceedings fulfilled the guarantees of Article 6 and that "A review of that kind is required where a decision in respect of which enforcement is requested emanates from the courts of a country which does not apply the Convention."[448]

The Court of Appeal in *Al-Bassam v Al-Bassam*[449] refused to accept that the ECHR has this indirect effect, even though the decision of the ECtHR in *Pellegrini v Italy* was cited to it. It accepted that a foreign judgment, granted in circumstances where a fair trial had been denied abroad, would not be recognised. But the reason for this was because the English rules on recognition say it should not be, not because human rights law says it should not.[450] Nonetheless, as has been seen,[451] the human rights position was not irrelevant. When operating the private international law rules on recognition and enforcement of foreign judgments, account would be taken of the human rights position. In other words human rights law is used to cast light upon private international law concepts.

---

[442] [2004] UKHL 37, [2004] 1 WLR 2241.
[443] See Fawcett, Ní Shúilleabháin and Shah, *Human Rights and Private International Law* (2016), Chapter 7; Fawcett (2007) 56 ICLQ 1; Kinsch, in Einhorn and Siehr (eds), *International Cooperation Through Private International Law* (2004) 197.
[444] Supra, p 13.
[445] Judgment of 26 June 1992, (1992) 14 EHRR 745, 749; see also *Lindberg v Sweden*, judgment of 15 January 2004; (2004) 38 EHRR CD 239.
[446] There is no breach of the Canadian Charter of Rights and Freedoms in such a case, see *Beals v Saldanha* [2003] 3 SCR 416 at [78], (2003) 234 DLR (4th) 1, Sup Ct of Canada.
[447] Judgment of 20 July 2001; (2001) 35 EHRR 44.
[448] At [40]. *Pellegrini v Italy* appears to apply where the judgment was granted in an ECHR Contracting State, see Fawcett, Ní Shúilleabháin and Shah, *Human Rights and Private International Law* (2016), paras 5.68–5.83.
[449] [2004] EWCA Civ 857.
[450] Ibid, at [35], [45].
[451] Supra, p 576.

However, in a case decided a few weeks after *Al-Bassam*, the House of Lords in *Government of the United States of America v Montgomery (No 2)*[452] accepted that Article 6 can have indirect effect in cases of enforcement of foreign judgments. The case concerned the registration in England under section 97 of the Criminal Justice Act 1988 of a confiscation order made in the USA in circumstances where the fugitive disentitlement doctrine, under which a court does not have to hear or decide the appeal of a fugitive, was applied. Registration requires the High Court to be "of the opinion that enforcing the order in England and Wales would not be contrary to the interests of justice".[453] Burnton J, at first instance, had decided that it would not be contrary to the interests of justice to do so, even though the order would have been made in breach of the requirements of Article 6 of the ECHR if that Article had applied to the making of that order (which it did not because it was made in the USA). On appeal to the Court of Appeal,[454] it was argued that: (i) if the ECHR had applied in the USA, the confiscation order would have been made in contravention of Article 6 and of Article 1 of Protocol 1 in the ECHR; (ii) this being the case, if the courts registered the order, they would be contravening section 6 of the Human Rights Act 1998. The Court of Appeal did not accept that there had been a breach by the US courts of the standards required by Article 6. But even if there had been such a breach, it could not be said that the decision to register gave rise to any breach of Article 6 of the Convention by the English court. The House of Lords affirmed the decision of the Court of Appeal. However, Lord Carswell, who delivered the unanimous judgment of the House of Lords, followed the dictum of Judge Matscher in the *Drozd* case and accepted that enforcement of a foreign judgment might in principle give rise to responsibility on the part of a Convention State.[455] Under this principle there must be a flagrant breach of Article 6[456] and on the facts of the instant case there was no such breach. The fugitive disentitlement doctrine applied in the USA, although it failed to secure all of the protection required by Article 6, was said to be a rational approach which had commended itself to the federal jurisdiction in the USA. As such, it could not be described as a flagrant breach. The House of Lords refused to accept that *Pellegrini v Italy* gave rise to a wider principle under which it was not necessary to show that there had been a flagrant breach abroad. The *Pellegrini* case was distinguished on the basis that it turned on the relationship between the Italian civil courts and the Vatican court. This confines the *Pellegrini* case to its facts, ie the enforcement of Vatican court judgments in Italy. According to this view, it is therefore not an authority in the private international law situation where the courts in one state are being asked to recognise and enforce the judgment granted in another state. This is an example of the English courts getting human rights law wrong.[457]

In *Maronier v Larmer*[458] the Court of Appeal held that there is a strong presumption that the procedures of other signatories of the ECHR are Article 6 compliant. In *Joint Stock Co 'Aeroflot-Russian Airlines' v Berezovsky*, Arden LJ stated *obiter* that this principle is not limited

---

[452] [2004] UKHL 37, [2004] 1 WLR 2241; Briggs (2004) 75 BYBIL 537.

[453] S 97(1)(c) of the Criminal Justice Act 1988.

[454] [2003] EWCA Civ 392, [2003] 1 WLR 1916; criticised by Hartley (2004) 120 LQR 211, Briggs (2003) 74 BYBIL 553.

[455] At [27]; criticised by Briggs, (2004) 75 BYBIL 537.

[456] See *Joint Stock Co 'Aeroflot-Russian Airlines' v Berezovsky* [2014] EWCA Civ 20 at [51]–[52], [2014] 1 CLC 53; Scott (2014) 85 BYBIL—the violation of the finality principle by the foreign court, if proved, would be a fragrant breach of the Art 6 standards. This judgment further suggests that breaches "which are not serious" or which do not substantially affect the defendant's liability may not be flagrant. See also *Ismail v Secretary of State for the Home Department* [2013] EWHC 663 (Admin), [2013] ACD 76.

[457] Fawcett (2007) 56 ICLQ 1, 35–6.

[458] [2002] EWCA Civ 774 at [25], [2003] QB 620.

to states bound by the Brussels/Lugano system.[459] This is not an irrebuttable presumption. When an English court is asked to enforce a foreign judgment, it need not actively inquire whether the foreign court violated the standards of Article 6, but is entitled to assume that the foreign court acted in a proper way unless the contrary was proved.[460]

If a foreign judgment, which otherwise satisfies the requirements for recognition and enforcement in England, is set aside in the country of origin by a judgment which does not accord with the safeguards of Article 6, the setting aside may be refused recognition and the lower instance judgment may be recognised and enforced in England.[461]

(vi) A foreign judgment on a matter previously determined by an English court[462]

A foreign judgment will not be recognised if there has been a prior English judgment in respect of the same matter. The House of Lords so held in *Vervaeke v Smith*:[463]

> In 1954, the appellant, a Belgian domiciled woman, entered into a sham marriage (ie the parties did not intend to live as husband and wife thereafter) with an Englishman (Smith) in order to avoid deportation. In 1970 the appellant married in Italy, Messina, who died on the day of the ceremony. The appellant wished to inherit Messina's property as his "wife". An obvious obstacle to this was her earlier marriage to Smith. She, therefore, sought a decree of nullity in England in respect of her first marriage on the ground of lack of consent. This petition was dismissed;[464] the marriage was not invalidated, even though it was a sham marriage. Later, the appellant went to Belgium and obtained a nullity decree on the ground that the marriage was a sham. Armed with this decree, the appellant returned to England and sought a declaration that the Belgian decree was entitled to recognition here (the first petition), and a declaration that, this being so, the marriage between the appellant and Messina was valid (the second petition).

Waterhouse J dismissed both petitions and an appeal to the Court of Appeal was dismissed. The appellant then appealed to the House of Lords.

The House of Lords unanimously dismissed both petitions, thereby refusing recognition of the Belgian judgment.[465] The earlier English judgment, which determined the validity of the marriage, meant that the matter was *res judicata*.[466] As far as the appellant's first petition was concerned, the English judgment operated as a cause of action estoppel preventing the same matter from being raised before the English courts. It would prevent the appellant from directly seeking a nullity decree in England, and it was said that she should be in no better position by virtue of proceeding indirectly by obtaining a judgment

---

[459] [2014] EWCA Civ 20 at [55], [2014] 1 CLC 53. This is without a doubt correct, since not all signatories of the ECHR are bound by the Brussels/Lugano system. It is questionable, however, if this principle extends to states that are not parties to the ECHR (see ibid, [58], which seems to indicate that Arden LJ thought that this principle extends also to non-ECHR states).

[460] The *Joint Stock Co 'Aeroflot-Russian Airlines' v Berezovsky* case at [58].

[461] *Merchant International Co Ltd v Natsionalna Aktsionerna Kompaniya Naftogaz Ukrayiny* [2012] EWCA Civ 196, [2012] 1 WLR 3036—a foreign judgment violated Art 6 by setting aside in its entirety the final judgment of a lower court on the basis of partial evidence previously available through the exercise of due diligence.

[462] There is substantially the same defence in cases of recognition under the Brussels/Lugano system see infra, pp 639–41 and 653.

[463] [1983] 1 AC 145, HL; Lipstein [1981] CLJ 20 (on the Court of Appeal's decision); Carter (1982) 53 BYBIL 302; Jaffey (1983) 32 ICLQ 500; Smart (1983) 99 LQR 24; Jaffey (1986) CJQ 35.

[464] *Messina v Smith* [1971] P 322.

[465] The case was also decided on the basis of public policy, discussed supra, p 574. It raised problems of recognition under the Foreign Judgments (Reciprocal Enforcement) Act 1933, discussed infra, p 598.

[466] At 156–7 (per Lord Hailsham), 158–60 (per Lord Diplock).

abroad and then seeking recognition of this judgment.[467] The Belgian judgment was in respect of the very matter, ie the validity of the marriage, which had previously been determined in the English judgment. As regards the second petition, the English judgment operated as an issue estoppel preventing the granting of the declaration which the appellant sought.[468] Although the English judgment did not actually determine the validity of the appellant's second marriage, it did decide the issue upon which this was dependent, the validity of the appellant's first marriage.

Vervaeke leaves open two questions.[469] First, what would happen if the English judgment in respect of the same matter is given *after* the foreign judgment for which recognition is sought.[470] The reasoning of the House of Lords could apply equally well to prevent recognition of the foreign judgment in this situation. Secondly, what would happen where there are two inconsistent foreign judgments given in different states in respect of the same matter, both of which are required to be recognised at common law? This presents more of a problem since the principles in *Vervaeke* do not provide an answer. However, the Privy Council in *Showlag v Mansour*[471] has now provided an answer to the question, which is examined below.[472]

One final observation should be made in connection with *Vervaeke*. The specific question raised in that case of recognition of a foreign nullity decree following an earlier English decision in the same matter is now dealt with by Brussels II *bis*[473] and the Family Law Act 1986.[474] However, *Vervaeke* still remains a good authority on the general principles to be applied in cases involving recognition of foreign judgments (other than divorces, annulments or judicial separations)[475] on matters previously determined by an English court, and has been applied subsequently in a commercial context.[476]

(vii) A foreign judgment on a matter previously determined by a court in another foreign state
We are concerned here with the situation where there are two irreconcilable foreign judgments, each pronounced by a court of competent jurisdiction and both being final and not open to impeachment on any ground. This situation arose in *Showlag v Mansour*.[477]

> The legal representatives of a deceased businessman, believing that money deposited in London banks had been stolen by the defendant employee of the deceased, instituted proceedings against him in various jurisdictions. In 1990 an English court held that this money had been stolen by the defendant. In 1991 an Egyptian appeal court dismissed the legal representatives' civil claim on the ground that the money had been a gift to the defendant. Some of the money was held in Jersey and actions were brought there for its return. It was

---

[467] Per Lord Diplock, at 160. There is, however, a question as to whether the issue was the same in the earlier English judgment and in the present proceedings for recognition of the Belgian judgment, see Jaffey (1983) 32 ICLQ 500.

[468] At 156 (per Lord Hailsham), at 160 (per Lord Diplock).

[469] See generally Stone [1983] LMCLQ 1, 22–3. For the solution to these questions where recognition and enforcement comes within the Brussels/Lugano system, see infra, pp 639–41.

[470] This situation is unlikely to arise because the foreign judgment would normally operate to prevent the English action, see supra, pp 556–8.

[471] [1995] 1 AC 431, PC.

[472] Infra.

[473] Art 22.

[474] S 51(1); Law Com No 137, para 6.65; see the criticisms of Jaffey (1986) CJQ 35; infra, p 1026.

[475] These are dealt with by Art 22 of Brussels II *bis*; s 51(1) of the Family Law Act 1986.

[476] *E D & F Mann (Sugar) Ltd v Yani Haryanto (No 2)* [1991] 1 Lloyd's Rep 429, CA; Carter (1991) 62 BYBIL 461.

[477] [1995] 1 AC 431, PC; Morgan (1995) 33 Can YBIL 3; followed in *The Joanna V* [2003] EWHC 1655 (Comm), [2003] 2 Lloyd's Rep 617.

argued before the Jersey courts that the question of whether the money was a gift was *res judicata* following the English judgment. The Court of Appeal of Jersey held that the legal representatives could not insist on the English judgment being applied in their favour and suggested to the parties that they might prefer to relitigate in Jersey the issue of whether there had been a gift. The legal representatives appealed to the Privy Council.

The Privy Council held that it was necessary to determine which of the two conflicting judgments should be given priority and that the earlier of the two judgments (ie the English judgment) must be recognised and given effect to the exclusion of the other.[478] In coming to this conclusion the Privy Council was influenced by the fact that the same solution was adopted by the Brussels Convention in the situation where there are two irreconcilable judgments; one granted in a Contracting State, the other in a non-Contracting State.[479]

(viii) *An overseas judgment given in proceedings brought in breach of agreement for settlement of disputes*

Section 32 of the Civil Jurisdiction and Judgments Act 1982 provides an important defence which is that:

> a judgment given by a court of an overseas country in any proceedings shall not be recognised or enforced in the United Kingdom if—
>
> (a) the bringing of those proceedings in that court was contrary to an agreement under which the dispute in question was to be settled otherwise than by proceedings in the courts of that country; and
>
> (b) those proceedings were not brought in that court by, or with the agreement of, the person against whom the judgment was given; and
>
> (c) that person did not counterclaim in the proceedings or otherwise submit to the jurisdiction of that court.[480]

The background to section 32[481] is that some legal systems are much stricter than others in their requirements as to when an arbitration or choice of court agreement is incorporated into a contract. A party who wants to avoid such an agreement may be able to do so by seeking trial in a country which does not accept the agreement as being effective. He may then obtain a judgment as to substance in his favour. If the English courts recognise the agreement, section 32 provides that they shall not recognise and enforce this foreign judgment.

Within a short time of section 32 coming into force, the English courts had to consider the operation of this section in *Tracomin SA v Sudan Oil Seeds Co Ltd (Nos 1 and 2)*.[482] A dispute arose between the Sudanese sellers of peanuts and the Swiss buyers. The contracts between the parties

---

[478] This is subject to a proviso, which is part of the law of *res judicata*, see supra, p 556 et seq, that there may be circumstances under which the person holding the earlier judgment may be estopped from relying on it (following *Republic of India v India Steamship Co Ltd* [1993] AC 410, HL—a case of estoppel by representation), ibid, at 440–1.

[479] See Art 27(5) of the Brussels Convention (Art 45(1)(d) of the Recast of the Brussels I Regulation) discussed infra, pp 641–2. See also Art 22 of Brussels II *bis* and s 51(1) of the Family Law Act 1986, discussed infra, pp 1004 and 1026.

[480] The proposition advanced by the Court of Appeal in *AES Ust-Kamenogorsk Hydropower Plant LLP v AES Ust-Kamenogorsk Hydropower Plant JSC* [2011] EWCA Civ 647 at [149]–[150], [2012] 1 WLR 920, discussed supra, p 538, that, where a defendant has submitted to the jurisdiction of a foreign court, the English court is not *required* to recognise or enforce the foreign judgment which would have otherwise breached a dispute resolution agreement, but should carry out an evaluative exercise, is questionable; *Spliethoff's Bevrachtingskantoor BV v Bank of China Ltd* [2015] EWHC 999 (Comm) at [126]–[128], [2016] 1 All ER (Comm) 1034; cf *Ecobank Transnational Incorporated v Mr Thierry Tanoh* [2015] EWHC 1874 (Comm) at [27].

[481] See Collins, *The Civil Jurisdiction and Judgments Act 1982* (1983), pp 141–3.

[482] [1983] 1 WLR 1026, CA.

contained a clause providing for the settlement of disputes by arbitration in London. Despite this, the buyers brought an action for damages before the Swiss courts. The sellers unsuccessfully sought a stay of those proceedings, relying on the arbitration clause. The Swiss courts decided that the arbitration clause was invalid because it had not been properly incorporated into the contracts under Swiss law—no evidence of English law, which governed the contracts, having been given. Under English law the arbitration clause had been incorporated into the contracts.

In *Tracomin (No 1)* the buyers sought an injunction in England restraining the arbitration in London, on the basis that the Swiss judgment created an estoppel in relation to the issue of the validity of the arbitration clause. The Court of Appeal applied section 32 and refused to recognise the Swiss judgment.[483] Sir John Donaldson MR (Ackner and Fox LJJ concurring) confined his comments to the precise point of the appeal, whether sections 32 and 33 applied to a foreign judgment granted before those provisions had come into force.[484] Having decided that in the circumstances of the case[485] they did, it was accepted without argument that the requirements for non-recognition under section 32 were satisfied. This is clearly right. The reasons were explained by Staughton J at first instance. There was an agreement under which the dispute was to be settled otherwise than by proceedings in Switzerland, since the arbitration clause had been validly incorporated into the contracts according to the governing law. The decision of the Swiss court that there was no valid arbitration agreement was immaterial because of section 32(3),[486] which provides[487] that a court in the United Kingdom is not bound by any decision of the overseas court relating to any of the matters in, inter alia, section 32(1). The first requirement under section 32(1)(a) was, therefore, satisfied. These Swiss proceedings were not brought with the agreement of the sellers; the second requirement under section 32(1)(b) was, therefore, also satisfied. The sellers, although they appeared, did not, according to section 33(1)(b) of the 1982 Act, submit to the jurisdiction of the Swiss courts since they only appeared in order to ask the court to stay the proceedings on the ground that the dispute should be submitted to arbitration. The third requirement under section 32(1)(c) was, therefore, also satisfied.

In *Tracomin (No 2)*, which was decided on the next day, the Court of Appeal used their discretionary powers to grant the sellers an injunction restraining the buyers from litigating in Switzerland.[488] The jurisdictional basis for granting this was the existence of the agreement to submit disputes to English arbitration.[489]

(a) The scope of the section

Section 32 only applies to a judgment given by a court of an "overseas country", ie any country or territory outside the United Kingdom.[490] This means that it does not apply to the judgments of Scottish or Northern Ireland courts.[491]

---

[483] Affirming the decision of Staughton J [1983] 1 WLR 662.

[484] See Sch 13, Part 1, para 2, and Pt II, paras 8(1) and 9(1).

[485] The reasoning of the Court of Appeal (at 1029–30) was that Sch 13, Part II, para 8 lists the judgments on which s 32 is not to have retrospective effect; since this judgment did not come within the categories specified therein, s 32 could apply retrospectively to it.

[486] See the decision of Staughton J, *Tracomin (No 1)* [1983] 1 WLR 662 at 670.

[487] Infra, pp 587–8.

[488] Reversing the decision of Leggatt J [1983] 1 Lloyd's Rep 571 on the exercise of this discretion. See generally on injunctions restraining a party from litigating abroad, supra, pp 422–42.

[489] See Leggatt J [1983] 1 Lloyd's Rep 571 at 576 and the Court of Appeal [1983] 1 WLR 1026 at 1035. See also *The Angelic Grace* [1995] 1 Lloyd's Rep 87, CA.

[490] See s 50 of the 1982 Act.

[491] For recognition and enforcement of these, see infra, pp 588–91.

Section 32(1) does not distinguish between recognition and enforcement at common law and by statute and, as will be seen, the defence can operate in respect of at least some of the forms of statutory recognition and enforcement.[492] However, its impact will be felt most at common law because there was already a similarly worded provision to section 32 under the Foreign Judgments (Reciprocal Enforcement) Act 1933,[493] which it replaces.[494]

(b) The three requirements for the operation of section 32

(i) There must be an agreement under which the dispute was to be settled otherwise than by proceedings in the courts of the country where the proceedings were brought, and the bringing of the proceedings in that country must be contrary to that agreement (section 32(1)(a)).[495] This requirement would be satisfied in the following examples: proceedings were brought in Japan when an agreement provided that all disputes were to be settled by trial in England; proceedings were brought in New York when an agreement provided that all disputes were to be settled by arbitration in Switzerland;[496] proceedings were brought in Brazil when an agreement provided that all disputes were to be settled by arbitration in Brazil. The agreement for settlement of disputes will normally take the form of a choice of jurisdiction clause or an arbitration clause contained in a written contract between the parties. It could, however, take the form of an agreement made after the dispute had arisen and could, whenever it was made, be an oral agreement.

The party seeking recognition or enforcement of the overseas judgment can, however, challenge the agreement. Section 32(2) provides that the defence under section 32(1) does not apply where the agreement was "illegal, void or unenforceable or was incapable of being performed for reasons not attributable to the fault of the party bringing the proceedings in which the judgment was given". In the absence of a foreign decision creating an issue estoppel,[497] an English court will have to determine these matters itself. A decision on whether an agreement is illegal, void or unenforceable raises a problem of the applicable law. This will be solved by applying the law governing the agreement as identified using traditional English choice of law principles.[498] In *Tracomin SA v Sudan Oil Seeds Co Ltd*,[499] it will be recalled that

---

[492] It applies to judgments recognised and enforced under Part II of the Administration of Justice Act 1920 and to most judgments coming under the Foreign Judgments (Reciprocal Enforcement) Act 1933. However, it does not affect judgments given in proceedings which arise under a number of international conventions and which are recognised or enforced under the 1933 Act (see s 32(4)(b) of the 1982 Act, as amended by the Statute Law (Repeals) Act 2004, Sch 1(14), para 1), see infra, p 593. It does not affect judgments required to be recognised or enforced under the Hague Convention on Choice of Court Agreements 2005, the Brussels/Lugano system, the Council Regulation No 4/2009 on jurisdiction, applicable law, recognition and enforcement of decisions and cooperation in matters relating to maintenance obligations, and the Hague Convention on International Recovery of Maintenance 2007 (s 32(4), as amended by the Civil Jurisdiction and Judgments (Hague Convention on Choice of Court Agreements 2005) Regulations, SI 2015/1644, reg.16, Civil Jurisdiction and Judgments Act 1991, Sch 2, para 14, the Civil Jurisdiction and Judgments Order, SI 2001/3929, Sch 2(IV), para 14, the Civil Jurisdiction and Judgments (Maintenance) Regulations, SI 2011/1484, Sch 4, para 9 and the International Recovery of Maintenance (Hague Convention 2007 etc.) Regulations, SI 2012/2814, Sch 4, para 5(3)); *The Atlantic Emperor (No 2)* [1992] 1 Lloyd's Rep 624 at 632, CA; *The Heidberg* [1994] 2 Lloyd's Rep 287 at 297; see infra, pp 644–5.

[493] S 4(3)(b) of the 1933 Act, see infra, pp 597–8.

[494] S 54 of the 1982 Act and Sch 14.

[495] For an agreement by the parties that a judgment is to only have local effect, see *Black Gold Potato Sales Inc v Joseph Garibaldi* [1996] IL Pr 171, Ont Ct of Justice.

[496] See *Deutsche Schachtbau-und Tiefbohrgesellschaft mbH v Shell International Petroleum Co Ltd* [1990] 1 AC 295 at 311, CA; the case went to the House of Lords on a garnishment (third party debt order) point, ibid, at 323.

[497] Supra, pp 556–62 and infra.

[498] See Art 1(2)(e) of the Rome I Regulation, infra, pp 700–1.

[499] [1983] 1 WLR 662, affd by the Court of Appeal [1983] 1 WLR 1026; discussed supra, pp 536–7.

the question arose of whether an arbitration clause had been validly incorporated into the contracts. By English law the arbitration clause had been incorporated into the contracts but by Swiss law it had not. Staughton J accepted that English law, as the governing law, should be applied on this question, and that the arbitration clause was validly incorporated into the contracts.[500]

(ii) It must be shown that the person against whom the judgment was given neither brought the proceedings in the first place nor agreed to the proceedings being brought in that court by the other party (section 32(1)(b)). This is a negative requirement and is concerned to ensure that the agreement for settlement of disputes has not been overridden by either of the above two types of conduct.

(iii) It must be shown that the person against whom the judgment was given did not counterclaim or otherwise submit to the jurisdiction of that court (section 32(1)(c)). This shows a similar concern to that shown under section 32(1)(b), but is dealing with the conduct of the party against whom the judgment was given *after* the proceedings have been brought. The losing party abroad must not have submitted to the jurisdiction by putting in a counterclaim or in any other way (eg by fighting the action on its merits). Only such counterclaims as amount to a submission count for these purposes.[501] It is important to note that, in deciding whether there has been submission, section 33 of the 1982 Act will apply.[502] Thus a counterclaim to obtain the release of property threatened with seizure does not amount to a submission and, accordingly, section 32 will operate.[503] Nor does an alternative defence on the merits amount to a submission where the defendant makes it abundantly clear that his primary purpose is to challenge the jurisdiction of the foreign court.[504] Nor does a defendant, who is a company incorporated and operating in the territory of the foreign court, submit to the jurisdiction of the foreign court if it had no other choice than to defend the merits of the case, having lost the jurisdictional argument, pending renewing his jurisdictional challenge at the appeal stage.[505]

(c) Decisions of foreign courts in respect of the above matters

Section 32(3) provides that "a court in the United Kingdom shall not be bound by any decision of the overseas court relating to any of the matters mentioned in subsection (1) and (2)". Thus, as has already been mentioned, in *Tracomin SA v Sudan Oil Seeds Co Ltd*[506] a Swiss court, applying Swiss law, had held that the English arbitration clause was not validly incorporated into the contracts. When the question of recognition of the judgment arose in England, section 32 was raised as a defence. In deciding that there was a valid agreement on arbitration, Staughton J held that the decision of the Swiss court was immaterial, according to section 32(3).

---

[500] [1983] 1 WLR 662 at 668; the point was not argued before him. The Court of Appeal also implicitly accepted this point [1983] 1 WLR 1026. This has now to be read in the light of the introduction of the Rome I Regulation and *Egon Oldendorff v Liberia Corpn* [1995] 2 Lloyd's Rep 64, where Mance J held that the issue of incorporation of an arbitration agreement into a contract was one for the law governing the contract (as identified using Art 10 of the Rome I Regulation) rather than one for the law governing the arbitration agreement (to be identified using traditional English choice of law rules), see infra, p 756.

[501] *The Eastern Trader* [1996] 2 Lloyd's Rep 585 at 600.

[502] See *Tracomin SA v Sudan Oil Seeds Co Ltd* [1983] 1 WLR 1026, CA; *The Atlantic Emperor (No 2)* [1992] 1 Lloyd's Rep 624 at 633, CA.

[503] *The Eastern Trader* case at 600.

[504] *The Atlantic Emperor (No 2)* case at 633.

[505] *AES Ust-Kamenogorsk Hydropower Plant LLP v AES Ust-Kamenogorsk Hydropower Plant JSC* [2011] EWCA Civ 647, [2012] 1 WLR 920, discussed supra, p 538.

[506] [1983] 1 WLR 662 at 670, affirmed by the Court of Appeal in this case without argument on the point.

Section 32(3) does not apply to the decision of a court other than the overseas court which gave the judgment. Instead, the normal principles of issue estoppel[507] will apply, and, according to these principles, issues relating to an agreement on jurisdiction may have to be regarded as being settled by the decision of a foreign court.[508] To take an example:

> Section 32 is raised as a defence to a judgment given in State A and an English court has to decide whether an agreement providing for jurisdiction in State B is valid. The overseas court in State A decided that it was not. The English court is not bound by this decision because section 32(3) applies. However, a court in State C had decided that the agreement was valid. If this judgment is recognised it may create an estoppel in England which prevents any denial that the agreement is valid.

3. DIRECT ENFORCEMENT OF FOREIGN JUDGMENTS BY STATUTE

The common law doctrine that a foreign judgment, though creating an obligation that is actionable in England, cannot be enforced in England except by the institution of fresh legal proceedings is subject to important exceptions introduced by a number of statutes, the most important of which are the Civil Jurisdiction and Judgments Act 1982, as amended by the Civil Jurisdiction and Judgments Act 1991 (which deals with both recognition and enforcement within the United Kingdom and under the Brussels Convention (replaced in virtually all cases by the Recast of the Brussels I Regulation), the Lugano Convention and the Hague Convention on Choice of Court Agreements 2005); the Administration of Justice Act 1920, Part II; the Foreign Judgments (Reciprocal Enforcement) Act 1933 and the European Communities Act 1972. Another important statute in this field is the State Immunity Act 1978. We will deal with these statutes separately. As far as the Civil Jurisdiction and Judgments Act 1982, as amended, is concerned, the provisions therein on recognition and enforcement within the United Kingdom and under the Brussels, Lugano and Hague Conventions will also be dealt with separately. Recognition and enforcement under the Recast of the Brussels I Regulation also constitutes an exception to the common law doctrine but is not a statutory exception and will therefore be considered briefly in another part of this chapter and in more detail in the next chapter.

(a) The Civil Jurisdiction and Judgments Act 1982: Recognition and enforcement within the United Kingdom[509]

(i) Enforcement of United Kingdom judgments in other parts of the United Kingdom

Where a judgment is given in one part of the United Kingdom (ie England and Wales, Scotland and Northern Ireland), section 18 of the 1982 Act provides for its enforcement in another part of the United Kingdom by way of registration under Schedules 6 (money provisions) or 7 (non-money provisions). A judgment to which section 18 applies can be enforced in another part of the United Kingdom only in this way,[510] ie the common law rules on

---

[507] Supra, pp 556–62.

[508] See *The Sennar (No 2)* [1985] 1 WLR 490, HL, discussed supra, pp 561–2.

[509] See generally Beaumont and McEleavy, *Anton's Private International Law* (2011) 3rd edn, paras 9.138–9.148; Collins, *The Civil Jurisdiction and Judgments Act 1982* (1983), pp 131–5; Dicey, Morris and Collins, para 14R-258; Hartley, *Civil Jurisdiction and Judgments* (1984), pp 100–1.

[510] S 18(8). There is an exception in respect of arbitration awards within s 18(2)(e).

enforcement cannot be used. Schedules 6 and 7 will only apply where there is a "judgment" as defined under section 18.

Section 18 initially gives a wide definition to the concept of a judgment.[511] It means, inter alia, "any judgment or order . . . given or made by a court of law in the United Kingdom". A judgment of an inferior court is therefore covered, as is a judgment in rem. It also includes "any award or order made by a tribunal" and "an arbitration award".[512] The section then gives a detailed list of judgments which it does not cover.[513] To take some examples, it does not apply to: (i) a judgment given in a magistrates' court; (ii) a judgment given in proceedings other than civil proceedings; (iii) a judgment given in the exercise of jurisdiction in relation to insolvency law, within the meaning of section 426 of the Insolvency Act 1986;[514] (iv) so much of a judgment as concerns the status or legal capacity of an individual;[515] (v) so much of a judgment as is a provisional measure other than an interim payment; (vi) a maintenance order which is enforceable under the separate statutory provisions dealing with enforcement of maintenance orders in another part of the United Kingdom;[516] (vii) a judgment of a court outside the United Kingdom which falls to be treated for the purposes of its enforcement as a judgment of a court of law in the United Kingdom by virtue of registration under one of the statutory schemes of enforcement of overseas judgments. Finally, to further complicate matters, section 18 contains a few limited specific inclusions within its scope,[517] eg fines for contempt of court.

(a) Enforcement of money provisions

In cases where there is a judgment as defined under section 18, the procedure under Schedule 6 for enforcement of money judgments is as follows.[518]

A certificate in respect of the judgment is obtained in the original court, whether it is a judgment of a superior or inferior court. This is then registered, within six months, in the prescribed manner in the superior court of the other part of the United Kingdom in which enforcement is sought—in England and Wales or Northern Ireland the High Court, in Scotland the Court of Session. A registered certificate is, for the purposes of its enforcement, of the same force and effect as a judgment of the registering court, which has the same powers in relation to enforcement as if it had given the original judgment.[519]

There are few defences to enforcement under Schedule 6. A defendant cannot impeach the judgment on its merits and, unlike at common law, cannot plead that the court in the other part of the United Kingdom lacked jurisdiction. Moreover, the defences available at common law cannot be used,[520] and section 32 of the 1982 Act cannot apply because the judgment is not given by a court of an "overseas" country.

---

[511] S 18(2). The Proceeds of Crime Act 2002 (Investigations in different parts of the United Kingdom) Order, SI 2003/425 Part 6, art 34 adds to this definition.

[512] Cf the position under the Brussels/Lugano system, infra, pp 611–13.

[513] See s 18(3), (4A), (5), (6), (7).

[514] S 18(3)(ba). Under s 426 "insolvency law" means a provision under the Insolvency Act 1986 and accordingly does not include the power to grant an extra-territorial injunction; see *Hughes v Hannover* [1997] 1 BCLC 497, CA; Smart [1998] CJQ 149 at 160–3; (1998) 114 LQR 46. S 426(1) deals with enforcement within the United Kingdom of a judgment or order in the exercise of jurisdiction in relation to insolvency. For general discussion of s 426, see Woloniecki (1986) 35 ICLQ 644.

[515] S 18(5)(b) and (6), as amended by the Courts and Legal Services Act 1990, Sch 16, para 41.

[516] S 18 (5)(a); see also s 18(7). The statute in question is the Maintenance Orders Act 1950 (see s 16 of that Act), as amended by the Courts and Legal Services Act 1990, Sch 20.

[517] S 18(4).

[518] Sch 6, paras 2–6; see also CPR, Part 74, paras 74.14–74.18.

[519] Sch 6, para 6.

[520] See *Clarke v Fennoscandia Ltd* 1998 SLT 1014—interim interdict against the enforcement of an English order for costs on the ground that it had been obtained by fraud refused; see also *Parkes v MacGregor* [2011] CSIH 69.

The only defences to enforcement under Schedule 6 that a defendant is allowed under the 1982 Act are to be raised after registration and are as follows: first, the registering court *must* set aside the registration if the procedure in the Schedule has not been complied with; secondly, it *may* set aside the registration if satisfied that there was an earlier judgment dealing with the matter in dispute given by another court having jurisdiction in the matter.[521] The limited nature of the defences means that the party who objects to the judgment given in the original court has to go there and appeal against it, rather than raise his objections when enforcement of the judgment is sought in another part of the United Kingdom.

This, however, raises the problem of an appeal against the original judgment overturning or amending that judgment. This is met in Schedule 6 by providing that a certificate shall not be issued unless, under the law of the part of the United Kingdom in which the judgment was given: "(a) either the time for bringing an appeal against the judgment has expired . . . or such an appeal . . . has finally been disposed of; and (b) enforcement of the judgment is not for the time being stayed or suspended, and the time available for its enforcement has not expired".[522]

Even after registration there is a power given to the registering court to stay proceedings for enforcement pending the outcome of an application, under the law of the part of the United Kingdom in which the judgment was given, to set aside or quash the judgment.[523]

There are special provisions on costs and interest.[524]

(b) Enforcement of non-money provisions

The 1982 Act extends the previous statutory law by providing in Schedule 7 for the enforcement of non-money provisions. A non-money provision is defined as "any relief or remedy not requiring payment of a sum of money";[525] this would include an injunction, a decree of specific performance and a declaration as to title. The provisions in this Schedule are very similar to those in Schedule 6. There are, however, some minor procedural differences,[526] and, more importantly, there is a major difference of substance. It is stated that "a judgment shall not be registered . . . if compliance with the non-money provisions contained in the judgment would involve a breach of the law of that part of the United Kingdom".[527]

(ii) Recognition of United Kingdom judgments in other parts of the United Kingdom

Section 19(1) simply states that:

> a judgment to which this section applies given in one part of the United Kingdom shall not be refused recognition in another part of the United Kingdom solely on the ground that, in relation to that judgment, the court which gave it was not a court of competent jurisdiction according to the rules of private international law in force in that other part.

With a few exceptions, section 19 applies to the same judgments as section 18.[528] It is a curiously worded provision in that it is phrased in negative terms and does not impose a positive duty to recognise judgments.[529] It could be read literally so as to infer that there are defences

---

[521] Sch 6, para 10.
[522] Sch 6, para 3; criticised by Stone (1983) 32 ICLQ 477, 487–8.
[523] Sch 6, para 9.
[524] Sch 6, paras 7 and 8.
[525] Sch 7, para 1.
[526] See Sch 7, paras 2–5; CPR, Part 74, para 74.16.
[527] Sch 7, para 5(5). See *G v Caledonian Newspapers Ltd* 1995 SLT 559. Obviously there is no provision on interest as such, but costs carry interest, Sch 7, para 7(2).
[528] S 19(2); for exclusions from s 19 that are included within s 18, see s 19(3).
[529] See generally, Anton and Beaumont's *Civil Jurisdiction in Scotland* (1995), para 9.34.

available to prevent recognition[530] and that included in these is a defence of lack of jurisdictional competence, provided that this allegation is combined with another defence.

(iii) *The effect of a judgment given in another part of the United Kingdom*

This is dealt with by section 34 of the 1982 Act, which, it will be recalled,[531] abolishes the non-merger rule in respect of foreign judgments. Once a judgment has been given in another part of the United Kingdom, the claimant may not bring proceedings in England and Wales on the same cause of action unless that judgment is not enforceable or entitled to recognition in England and Wales.

(b) Administration of Justice Act 1920[532]

This Act makes provision for the enforcement within the United Kingdom of judgments obtained in a superior court of any part of the Commonwealth.[533]

(i) *When registration of Commonwealth judgments is allowed*

A person who has obtained a judgment in a superior court in a country or territory forming part of the Commonwealth to which the provisions of the Act have been extended may within twelve months after the date of the judgment[534] apply to the High Court in England or Northern Ireland or to the Court of Session in Scotland for its registration, whereupon the court may, if in all the circumstances of the case they think it is just and convenient that the judgment should be enforced in the United Kingdom, order the judgment to be registered.[535] Thus, registration is not a right, as it is in cases of recognition and enforcement within the United Kingdom, but lies wholly within the discretion of the court. A judgment cannot be registered, however, unless it is given in civil proceedings and is one under which a sum of money is made payable.[536] A "judgment" includes arbitration award.[537]

(ii) *When registration is not allowed*

Under section 9(2) of the 1920 Act registration is not allowed if the original court acted without jurisdiction or if the judgment debtor did not voluntarily submit to the jurisdiction of the court, unless he was carrying on business[538] or was ordinarily resident within that jurisdiction.[539] It is assumed that questions of jurisdiction are to be determined by reference

---

[530] Ie the defences at common law, see Stone [1983] LMCLQ 1; Lane (1986) 35 ICLQ 629; Layton and Mercer, para 39.041. Cf Anton and Beaumont's *Civil Jurisdiction in Scotland* (1995), para 9.34; Hill and Chong, para 13.6.4–13.6.5.

[531] Supra, p 556.

[532] Some minor amendments have been made to this Act by the Civil Jurisdiction and Judgments Act 1982, s 35; ss 10 and 14 of the 1920 Act are amended.

[533] S 13. See generally, Patchett, *Recognition of Commercial Judgments and Awards in the Commonwealth* (1984), Chapters 1–4. See also Sumner Committee Report, 1919, Cmd 251.

[534] This period may be extended by the court: *Ogelegbanwei v Nigeria* [2016] EWHC 8 (QB).

[535] S 9(1); *Akande v Balfour Beatty Construction Ltd* [1998] IL Pr 110 at 123. The registration of a judgment against a state and state officials and agents can attract state immunity: *AIC Ltd v Federal Government of Nigeria* [2003] EWHC 1357 (QB), [2003] All ER (D) 190; *Ogelegbanwei v Nigeria* [2016] EWHC 8 (QB). It has been held in Scotland that a notarial certificate given by an ecclesiastical court called the Court of Faculties from the Territory of Norfolk Island was not a judgment given by a superior court, see *Ivory Petitioner* 2006 SLT 758.

[536] S 12(1). *Platt v Platt* 1957 SLT (Notes) 25; the *Akande* case; *Standard Chartered Bank v Zungeru Power Ltd* [2014] EWHC 4714 (QB).

[537] S 12(1).

[538] See *Sfeir & Co v National Insurance Co of New Zealand* [1964] 1 Lloyd's Rep 330; the *Akande* case; the *Standard Chartered Bank v Zungeru Power Ltd* case. The meaning of this is the same as at common law—the *Akande* case at 119.

[539] See *Brower v Sunview Solariums Ltd* (1998) 156 DLR (4th) 752, Sask Ct of QB.

to the common law rules as to the jurisdiction of the foreign court.[540] The other defences available under section 9(2) are also similar to those available at common law,[541] namely that the judgment debtor was not served and did not appear in the original proceedings, that the judgment was obtained by fraud,[542] and that the original cause of action was one which, for reasons of public policy or for some other similar reason, could not have been entertained in England. A judgment will not be registered if the judgment debtor satisfies the English court either that an appeal is pending or that he is entitled and intends to appeal against the judgment.[543] The defences mentioned so far are ones laid down by the 1920 Act itself. In addition, the defences laid down by s 5 of the Protection of Trading Interests Act 1980, in respect of judgments for multiple damages,[544] and s 32 of the Civil Jurisdiction and Judgments Act 1982, in respect of an overseas judgment given in proceedings brought in breach of an agreement for settlement of disputes,[545] will apply to cases coming within the 1920 Act. A judgment given in a foreign state against that state cannot be registered under the 1920 Act.[546]

(iii) The effect of registration

A judgment registered under the Act is of the same force and effect, and it may be followed by the same proceedings, as if it had originally been obtained in the registering court.[547] A claimant is in no way deprived of his right to sue at common law upon the obligation created by a foreign judgment,[548] but if he sues on a judgment that is registrable under the Act he is not entitled to the costs of the action unless registration has been refused or unless the court otherwise orders.[549]

(iv) Reciprocity

The Act, however, does not render a judgment registrable within the United Kingdom unless its provisions have been extended by Order in Council to the country or territory in which the judgment has been obtained. Reciprocity is essential. When reciprocal provisions have been made by a Commonwealth country or territory for the enforcement of English, Scottish and Northern Ireland judgments, an Order in Council may be made extending the Act to the country or territory in question.[550] The Act has been extended to a substantial number of Commonwealth jurisdictions.[551]

---

[540] Supra, pp 528–40.

[541] Supra, p 564 et seq. The common law cases must be referred to for the meaning of these defences: *Owens Bank Ltd v Bracco* [1992] 2 AC 443, HL.

[542] This term is used in the common law sense, the *Owens Bank Ltd v Bracco* case; supra, p 571.

[543] S 9(2)(e). There is no such common law defence, see supra, pp 550–1.

[544] Supra, pp 553–5.

[545] Supra, pp 584–8. It is suggested that if there are irreconcilable judgments or if the foreign judgment is in the nature of a fine or other penalty, it would not be regarded as just and convenient to enforce the judgment, see Hill and Chong, para 12.6.6.

[546] *AIC Ltd v Federal Government of Nigeria* [2003] EWHC 1357 (QB), [2003] All ER (D) 190 (s 1 of the State Immunity Act 1978 applies).

[547] S 9(3)(a), (b); as amended by the Administration of Justice Act 1956, s 40(b). See *Michael Wilson and Partners Ltd v Sinclair* [2017] EWCA Civ 55, concerning the stay of execution of a Bahamian costs orders registered in England under the 1920 Act.

[548] *Yukon Consolidated Gold Corpn v Clark* [1938] 2 KB 241 at 252, CA.

[549] S 9(5).

[550] S 14; as amended by the Civil Jurisdiction and Judgments Act 1982, s 35(3). The reciprocity is no longer exact in the case of some Commonwealth jurisdictions which now make United Kingdom judgments registrable under their counterparts, not of the 1920 Act, but of the Foreign Judgments (Reciprocal Enforcement) Act 1933.

[551] Supra, pp 521–2.

(c) Foreign Judgments (Reciprocal Enforcement) Act 1933[552]

(i) The object of the Act

The policy of facilitating the direct enforcement of foreign judgments in England, and of ensuring that English judgments are enforced abroad,[553] received a further impulse from the Foreign Judgments (Reciprocal Enforcement) Act 1933, which applies the principle of registration, not only to the Commonwealth, but also to foreign countries.

(ii) The countries to which the provisions of the Act are extended

The provisions made by the Act for the registration of foreign judgments in England may be extended by Order in Council to any country which is prepared to afford substantial reciprocity of treatment to judgments obtained in the United Kingdom.[554] It is undesirable that there should be two systems of registration, one for the Commonwealth, the other for countries outside the Commonwealth, and therefore a policy of the gradual supersession of the 1920 Act has been adopted. With this object in view power is given to render the 1933 Act applicable by Order in Council to countries forming part of the Commonwealth, and it is provided that the 1920 Act shall cease to apply to any such country except those to which it extended at the date of the Order in Council,[555] which was introduced in 1933.[556] However, in order for the 1933 Act to be applied to any particular Commonwealth country, a further specific Order in Council is required, both in the case of a jurisdiction to which the 1920 Act had never been applicable[557] and of one to which it had.[558] Orders to this effect have been made for Pakistan,[559] India,[560] Australia and the Australian states and territories,[561] Jersey, Guernsey, the Isle of Man, and Tonga. The Act has also been extended to Canada (except Quebec).[562] As regards countries outside the Commonwealth, orders have been made extending the provisions of the Act to Austria, Belgium, France, Israel, Italy, the Netherlands, Norway, the Federal Republic of Germany and Suriname.[563] These orders are based on bilateral treaties that the United Kingdom has entered into with these countries and provide that certain judgments in civil and commercial matters

---

[552] The 1933 Act is amended by the Civil Jurisdiction and Judgments Act 1982, s 35(1) and Sch 10. The 1933 Act must also now be read in the light of ss 32 and 33 of the 1982 Act, discussed, generally, supra, pp 584–8 and 533–7 and, more particularly in this context, infra, pp 595–6 and 598. See generally on the 1933 Act, Vallat, *International Law and the Practitioner* (1966), Chapter V; Patchett, *Recognition of Commercial Judgments and Awards in the Commonwealth* (1984), Chapters 1–4; Report of the Foreign Judgments (Reciprocal Enforcement) Committee, 1932, Cmd 4213.

[553] *Yukon Consolidated Gold Corpn v Clark* [1938] 2 KB 241 at 253, CA; and see *Ferdinand Wagner v Laubscher Bros & Co* [1970] 2 QB 313 at 319–20, CA.

[554] S 1; as amended by s 35(1) and Sch 10 of the 1982 Act. Enforcement of a judgment abroad may affect whether security for costs is given in England: *Compagnie Française v Thorn Electrics* [1981] FSR 306; *Porzelack KG v Porzelack (UK) Ltd* [1987] 1 WLR 420.

[555] S 7.

[556] SR & O 1933 No 1073.

[557] The *Yukon Consolidated Gold Corpn v Clark* case (Ontario).

[558] *Jamieson v Northern Electricity Supply Corpn (Private) Ltd* 1970 SLT 113 (Zambia). If an order is made under the 1933 Act applicable to a country to which there is already an Order in force made under the 1920 Act, then the latter ceases to apply: 1933 Act, s 7(2).

[559] See SI 1958/141; Pakistan Act 1990, Sch, para 8.

[560] SI 1958/425.

[561] SI 1994/1901, infra, pp 603–4.

[562] SI 1987/468, infra, pp 603–4.

[563] Judgments given in Austria, Belgium, France, Italy, the Netherlands, Norway and Germany will usually come within the Brussels/Lugano system and will be recognised and enforced under this system rather than under the 1933 Act, see infra, p 608 et seq. The 1933 Act does not extend to the USA and this has been the source of judicial comment, eg *Perry v Zissis* [1977] 1 Lloyd's Rep 607 at 614, 617, CA. A draft bilateral UK/US recognition convention, quite independent of the 1933 Act, was prepared: (1976) Cmnd 6771; but it was never agreed, see infra, pp 603–4.

shall be mutually recognised and enforced, notwithstanding that the adjudicating court followed rules for the choice of law different from those that would have been followed in the country where enforcement is sought. The provisions of the Act apply also to foreign judgments given in proceedings which arise under a number of international conventions.[564]

(iii) Prerequisites of registration

The successful party to proceedings in a foreign country to which the Act has been extended may apply to the High Court at any time within six years[565] for registration of the judgment[566] in England.[567] A "judgment" now includes arbitration awards.[568] It does not, however, include a judgment on a judgment,[569] eg a judgment given in State A providing for the enforcement of a judgment given in State B. The judgment no longer has to be delivered by a superior court.[570] It is, however, required that the judgment was delivered by a recognised court[571] (which refers to the identity of the court and not the capacity in which it is acting)[572] or tribunal;[573] the judgment is given in any civil proceedings[574] or any criminal proceedings for the payment of a sum of money in respect of compensation or damages to an injured party; the judgment is final and conclusive or requires an interim payment to be made;[575] a sum of money is adjudged to be payable to the applicant, other than a sum in respect of taxes or in respect of a fine or other penalty.[576] This latter phrase does not include an award of exemplary damages or damages for "resistance abusive" under French law.[577] A judgment is also not to be registered if it has been wholly satisfied or if it cannot be enforced by execution in the foreign country.[578] A judgment, however, is to be deemed final and conclusive, notwithstanding that an appeal may be pending against it or that it

---

[564] Eg Carriage of Goods by Road Act 1965, s 4, Sch, Art 31(3). See generally, Dicey, Morris and Collins, paras 15R-053–15-071. The provisions of the 1933 Act may also apply to foreign judgments clawing back sums paid pursuant to an award of multiple damages: Protection of Trading Interests Act 1980, s 7, discussed supra, pp 553–5.

[565] S 2. The time runs from the date of the judgment. But if there have been proceedings by way of appeal against the judgment, the time runs from the date of the last judgment given in those proceedings.

[566] Or part of the judgment, see s 2(5); *Ahmed v Habib Bank Ltd* [2001] EWCA Civ 1270 at [55]–[58], [2002] 1 Lloyd's Rep 444.

[567] The judgment can be registered in foreign currency: Administration of Justice Act 1977, s 4(2)(b), supra, pp 100–1; and see *Batavia Times Publishing Co v Davis* (1978) 88 DLR (3d) 144, Ont Sup Ct of Justice; *Principality of Monaco v Project Planning* (1980) 32 OR (2d) 438, Ont Sup Ct of Justice; *Clinton v Ford* (1982) 137 DLR (3d) 281, Ont CA.

[568] S 10A; added by s 35(1) and Sch 10, para 4 of the 1982 Act. See *ABCI v BFT* [1996] 1 Lloyd's Rep 485 at 489.

[569] S 1(2A); added by s 35(1) and Sch 10, para 1 of the 1982 Act. For the position under the Recast of the Brussels I Regulation, see infra, p 613.

[570] Cf the original s 1(1) with the amended version introduced by s 35(1) and Sch 10, paras 1 and 2 of the 1982 Act. See also s 54 and Sch 14 of the 1982 Act.

[571] S 1; as amended by s 35(1) and Sch 10, para 1 of the 1982 Act. For the problems in relation to County Court judgments, see Matthews (1996) 112 LQR 221. Order in Council can specify the courts from a specific foreign country to whose judgments the Act applies, see s 1(1).

[572] *Ahmed v Habib Bank Ltd* [2001] EWCA Civ 1270, [2002] 1 Lloyd's Rep 444.

[573] S11(1); as amended by s 35(1) and Sch 10, para 5 of the 1982 Act.

[574] S 11(1). This includes judgments in insolvency proceedings, see *Rubin v Eurofinance SA* [2012] UKSC 46 at [170]–[176], [2013] 1 AC 236. Order in Council can specify the class of judgments from a specific foreign country to which the Act applies, see s 1(1).

[575] S1(2); as amended by s 35(1) and Sch 10, para 1 of the 1982 Act.

[576] S 1(2); as amended by s 35(1) and Sch 10, para 1 of the 1982 Act. See *Patterson v Vacation Brokers Inc* [1998] IL Pr 482, Ont CA—an order for costs on an indemnity basis not a penalty.

[577] *SA Consortium General Textiles v Sun and Sand Agencies Ltd* [1978] QB 279 at 299–300, 305–6, CA.

[578] S 2(1); and see the *SA Consortium General Textiles v Sun and Sand Agencies Ltd* case at 297, 300–2.

may still be subject to appeal in the foreign courts.[579] The Act differs from the earlier Act of 1920 in that no discretion is left to the High Court. It is expressly provided that: "On any such application the court shall, subject to proof of the prescribed matters and to the other provisions of this Act, order the judgment to be registered."[580]

(iv) Setting aside of registration

There are, however, certain circumstances in which, on the application of the party against whom the registered judgment is enforceable, the registration *must* be set aside and other circumstances in which it *may* be set aside.

(a) When registration *must* be set aside

(i) Lack of jurisdiction

The first case in which the registration must be set aside is if the foreign court acted without jurisdiction.[581] The rules by which the 1933 Act specifies the circumstances in which a foreign court shall be deemed to have had jurisdiction are very similar to the common law rules[582] and vary according to whether the original action was in personam or in rem. But if the original action was neither in personam nor in rem, the foreign court shall be deemed to have jurisdiction if its jurisdiction is recognised at common law.[583]

Bases of jurisdiction in personam   In the case of a judgment given in an action in personam the original court is deemed to have had jurisdiction on three main bases: residence, submission and having an office or place of business within the foreign jurisdiction.

(1) Residence   In the case of residence, the 1933 Act provides that there is jurisdiction "if the judgment debtor, being a defendant in the original court, was at the time when the proceedings were instituted resident in, or being a body corporate had its principal place of business in, the country of that court".[584] As residence is required, temporary presence would appear to be excluded.[585] In the case of corporations, the requirement is not just the one at common law or under the 1920 Act of carrying on business,[586] but rather that the principal place of business be in the foreign country.

(2) Submission   The second basis of jurisdiction is submission and three instances of this are provided in section 4(2)(a) of the 1933 Act:[587]

(i)   if the judgment debtor, being a defendant in the original court, submitted to the jurisdiction of that court by voluntarily appearing in the proceedings;[588] or

---

[579]   S 1(3). But it is provided by s 5(1) that on an application to set aside registration the court may do so or may adjourn the application if satisfied that an appeal is pending or that the defendant is entitled and intends to appeal; see, for examples where such an application was refused: *Re A Debtor (No 11 of 1939)* [1939] 2 All ER 400, CA; the *SA Consortium General Textiles v Sun and Sand Agencies Ltd* case at 297, 298, 306, 307; *Walton, Petitioner* [2012] CSIH 54. See also *Hunt v BP Exploration Co (Libya) Ltd* [1980] 1 NZLR 104. Under the Act of 1920 the fact that an appeal is pending is a bar to registration, supra, p 592.

[580]   S 2.

[581]   Cf the Australian position, on which see *Hunt v BP Exploration Co (Libya) Ltd* (1979) 144 CLR 565, Australian High Ct, and in New Zealand, *Hunt v BP Exploration Co (Libya) Ltd* [1980] I NZLR 104.

[582]   Supra, p 528 et seq.

[583]   *Rubin v Eurofinance SA* [2012] UKSC 46 at [171], [2013] 1 AC 236.

[584]   S 4(2)(a)(iv).

[585]   Cf the common law position, supra, pp 529–30.

[586]   Supra, pp 530–1 and 591.

[587]   As amended by s 54 and Sch 14 of the Civil Jurisdiction and Judgments Act 1982.

[588]   Including an appeal, see *SA Consortium General Textiles v Sun and Sand Agencies Ltd* [1978] QB 279 at 309, CA.

(ii) if the judgment debtor was plaintiff in, or counter-claimed in, the proceedings of the original court; or

(iii) if the judgment debtor, being a defendant in the original court, had before the commencement of the proceedings agreed, in respect of the subject matter of the proceedings, to submit to the jurisdiction of that court or of the courts of the country of that court.

What in general constitutes submission through a voluntary appearance to contest the jurisdiction of the court is likely to be determined in the same way as at common law.[589] The likelihood of this being the case is strengthened by the fact that section 33 of the Civil Jurisdiction and Judgments Act 1982, which provides that in three situations there is no submission by voluntary appearance, applies to recognition or enforcement under the 1933 Act as well as to recognition or enforcement at common law.[590] It will be recalled that under section 33 there is no submission where the appearance is to contest the jurisdiction of the court, to seek a stay of proceedings on the ground that there should be an arbitration or trial in another country, or to protect property.

Whilst there is no doubt that an express agreement to submit would fall within section 4(2) (a)(iii), there remains the problem of an implied agreement to submit. It is suggested that, as at common law,[591] an implied agreement will suffice.[592]

The operation of some of these provisions on submission was considered in *SA Consortium General Textiles v Sun and Sand Agencies Ltd*:[593]

> The plaintiff, a French textile company, sold clothing to the defendant, an English company. The goods came from the plaintiff's branches in Lille and Paris and the invoice from Lille provided that all disputes were to be referred to the commercial court there, whilst the other invoice gave exclusive jurisdiction to the Seine commercial court. The plaintiff claimed the sums due under both invoices and damages for "resistance abusive" in proceedings before the Lille commercial court. Judgment was given for the plaintiff in default of appearance, though the defendant had been served with notice of the proceedings. The defendant failed to appeal within the three-month period allowed under French law. The plaintiff then sought enforcement of the Lille judgment in England, whereupon the defendant applied to the President of the Court of Appeal in Douai for leave to appeal, and then in fact appealed to the full Court of Appeal. The defendant sought, unsuccessfully, to resist the enforcement of the default judgment of the Lille court on a variety of grounds, such as that it could not be enforced by execution in France,[594] or that damages for "resistance abusive" were penal.[595] The main issue, however, was whether the defendant could be taken to have submitted to the jurisdiction of the French courts in respect of both claims.

Section 4(2)(a)(iii) of the 1933 Act was interpreted by a majority in the Court of Appeal as not covering an agreement to submit to all the courts of the foreign country by agreeing to submit to one, so that agreement to submit the issues arising under one invoice to the Seine

---

[589] *Henry v Geoprosco International Ltd* [1976] QB 726, CA, supra, p 534 et seq.

[590] Supra, p 535. S 33 of the 1982 Act replaces a similarly worded provision contained in the end part of s 4(2)(a)(i), see s 54 and Sch 14 of the 1982 Act.

[591] Supra, pp 532–3.

[592] See also *Jamieson v Northern Electricity Supply Corpn (Private) Ltd* 1970 SLT 113 at 116.

[593] [1978] QB 279, CA; Carter (1979) 50 BYBIL 252. The points raised in the case in respect of the 1933 Act are not affected by the alterations made to that Act by s 35(1) of the 1982 Act.

[594] 1933 Act, s 2(1)(b), supra, p 594.

[595] Ibid, s 1(2)(b), supra, p 594.

court did not amount to agreement to submit that issue to any other of the courts of France, including the Lille court.[596] However, the appeal to the Court of Appeal in Douai on the merits of the claim did amount to submission as to both claims,[597] as did a statement by the defendant's English solicitors, when proceedings against the defendant were contemplated in England, that *all* disputes must be brought before the Lille court.[598]

(3) Jurisdiction based on having a place of business The third basis of jurisdiction and one not to be found at common law is provided by section 4(2)(a)(v) of the 1933 Act, namely "if the judgment debtor, being a defendant in the original court, had an office or place of business in the country of that court and the proceedings in that court were in respect of the transaction effected through or at that office or place".

Limitations on jurisdiction The three bases of jurisdiction are subject to qualification in that, notwithstanding them, the foreign court shall not be deemed to have had jurisdiction if the case concerned immovables outside the country of the foreign court or if the defendant was under the rules of public international law entitled to immunity from the jurisdiction of the foreign court and did not submit thereto.[599]

Special statutory grounds of jurisdiction Where a foreign judgment is registered under the 1933 Act pursuant to one of the various statutory provisions[600] embodying international conventions, the different statutes provide that the jurisdictional grounds in the 1933 Act shall all be replaced by special jurisdictional grounds relevant to the particular convention in question.[601]

Statutory grounds of jurisdiction are exclusive In the case of an action in personam, no other ground of jurisdiction will render a foreign judgment registrable under the Act. The fact, for instance, that the claimant has obtained leave from the foreign court to serve process on the defendant in England does not per se generate jurisdiction for the purposes of registration.[602]

Meaning of action in personam It is expressly enacted that the expression "action in personam" shall not include any matrimonial cause,[603] or any proceedings connected with matrimonial matters, the administration of the estates of deceased persons, bankruptcy, winding up of companies, lunacy or guardianship of infants.[604]

Jurisdiction over action in rem The original court is deemed to have had jurisdiction over an action in rem if the subject matter of the action, whether movable or immovable, was situated in the foreign country at the time of the proceedings.[605]

---

[596] [1978] QB 279 at 302–4, 309; cf Lord Denning MR at 298–9, CA.

[597] Ibid at 299, 308–9; see supra, pp 538–9.

[598] Ibid at 299, 307–8; cf Goff LJ at 303–4.

[599] S 4(3); as amended by s 54 and Sch 14 of the Act. On s 4(3)(a) see *Shami v Shami* [2012] EWHC 664 (Ch) at [29], affd without discussing this point [2013] EWCA Civ 227—an Israeli judgment declaring the existence of a trust relating to land outside Israel falls within this exclusion. S 4(3)(b) of the 1933 Act has been repealed and has been replaced, in effect, by s 32 of the 1982 Act, see supra, p 584 et seq.

[600] Supra, p 593.

[601] Eg Carriage of Goods by Road Act 1965, s 4, Sch, Art 31(1). The defence under s 32 of the 1982 Act will not apply: s 32(4)(b).

[602] *Société Cooperative Sidmetal v Titan International Ltd* [1966] 1 QB 828, infra, pp 605–6; *Coast Lines Ltd v Hudig and Veder Chartering NV* [1972] 2 QB 34 at 45, CA.

[603] But see *Vervaeke v Smith* [1983] 1 AC 145, HL, discussed infra, p 599.

[604] S 11(2).

[605] Section 4(2)(b), subject to the qualifications provided by s 4(3) as amended by s 54 and Sch 14 of the 1982 Act, discussed, supra.

(ii) Other circumstances where registration must be set aside

There are a number of circumstances in addition to want of jurisdiction[606] where, according to the 1933 Act,[607] registration must be set aside, most of which are very similar to the common law defences:[608]

(i)   if the judgment is not one to which the Act applies or if the procedure in the Act has not been complied with;

(ii) if the judgment debtor, being the defendant in the original proceedings, did not (despite service of process in accordance with the foreign law) receive notice of the proceedings in sufficient time to enable him to defend them and did not appear;[609]

(iii) if the judgment was obtained by fraud;[610]

(iv) if the enforcement of the judgment would be contrary to public policy in England;[611]

(v)   if the rights under the judgment are not vested in the applicant.

Two further instances of where registration *must* be set aside are provided by section 5 of the Protection of Trading Interests Act 1980 and section 32 of the Civil Jurisdiction and Judgments Act 1982:

(vi) if the judgment is one for multiple damages;[612]

(vii) if the judgment was given in proceedings brought in breach of an agreement for the settlement of disputes.[613]

(b) When registration *may* be set aside

Registration *may* be set aside if the registering court is satisfied that the matter adjudicated upon had already been the subject of a final and conclusive judgment by a court having jurisdiction in that matter.[614]

(v) The effect of a foreign judgment

(a) A judgment which has been registered

A judgment registered under the Act is, for the purposes of execution, of the same force and effect and subject to the same control over the execution as if it had originally been given

---

[606] S 4(1)(a)(ii).

[607] S 4(1)(a).

[608] Supra, pp 564–88. It is arguable that, as a foreign judgment once registered under the 1933 Act shall be of the same force and effect as if it had been a judgment of the English court (s 2(2)), it is open to all defences available under English domestic law.

[609] This is similar to, but narrower than, the common law defence that the foreign proceedings were contrary to natural justice, supra, pp 576–9; and see *Brockley Cabinet Co Ltd v Pears* (1972) 20 FLR 333; *Barclays Bank Ltd v Piacun* [1984] 2 Qd R 476; *Bank of Scotland Plc v Wilson* (2008) 295 DLR (4th) 128, British Columbia Sup Ct. Instances of a lack of natural justice falling outside this narrow provision could be treated as coming within the public policy provision, *Society of Lloyd's v Saunders* (2001) 210 DLR (4th) 519, Ont CA.

[610] When an application is made on this ground, the same rules apply as where the defence of fraud is raised at common law in relation to a foreign judgment, supra, pp 568–73; *Syal v Heyward* [1948] 2 KB 443, CA; *Owens Bank Ltd v Bracco* [1992] 2 AC 443 at 489, HL. See also *Ahmed v Habib Bank Ltd* [2001] EWCA Civ 1270, [2002] 1 Lloyd's Rep 444.

[611] For a recognition case where this applied, see *Vervaeke v Smith* [1983] 1 AC 145 at 156 (per Lord Hailsham) and 159 (per Lord Diplock), HL. This provision does not preclude the recognition of a judgment for exemplary damages or damages for "resistance abusive" under French law: *SA Consortium General Textiles v Sun and Sand Agencies Ltd* [1978] QB 279 at 299, 300, 305, 306, CA.

[612] Supra, pp 553–5.

[613] Supra, pp 584–8.

[614] S 4(1)(b); *Vervaeke v Smith* [1983] 1 AC 145, HL at 156 (per Lord Hailsham) and 159 (per Lord Diplock), HL.

in the registering court.[615] One significance of this provision would appear to be that the grounds on which registration may or must be set aside may be different from those on which enforcement will be refused. Once the foreign judgment is registered, then it would appear that not only may the registration be set aside for failure to satisfy section 4 of the 1933 Act, but also the registered judgment may be set aside and enforcement refused for any one of the various reasons for setting aside English judgments[616] which may be appropriate to a foreign judgment.

(b) A judgment which is capable of registration

Section 6 of the 1933 Act provides that: "No proceedings for the recovery of a sum payable under a foreign judgment, being a judgment to which this Part of this Act applies, other than proceedings by way of registration of the judgment, shall be entertained by any court in the United Kingdom." This clearly means that no action for enforcement at common law can be brought on a judgment that is registrable,[617] but, seemingly, *this provision* did not prevent the claimant from suing on the original cause of action. However, the claimant is now prevented from doing so by section 34 of the Civil Jurisdiction and Judgments Act 1982 which, as has been seen,[618] abolishes the non-merger rule.

(vi) Conclusiveness of foreign judgments

Section 8[619] of the 1933 Act preserves the common law[620] rules as to the conclusiveness of foreign judgments, but it also provides[621] that a judgment to which the registration provisions of the Act apply, or would apply had a sum of money been payable thereunder, whether or not it can be or is registered, is to be recognised in England as conclusive between the parties in all proceedings founded on the same cause of action.

(a) An exception to the conclusiveness rule

However, a foreign judgment is not recognised as conclusive under the Act if the registration has been set aside or, where the judgment has not been registered, it would have been set aside if it had been registered.[622] The grounds on which registered judgments are set aside are contained in section 4 of the Act.[623] The operation of this proviso was considered in *Vervaeke v Smith*,[624] where it was held that a Belgian judgment in respect of the validity of a marriage[625] would not be entitled to recognition under section 8 of the 1933 Act because the matter in dispute had previously been the subject of a final and conclusive judgment in England[626] and also because recognition would be against public policy.[627]

---

[615] S 2(2). So a foreign judgment, registered in England, will, for the purposes of the exercise of the discretion whether to grant a stay of execution, be treated as if it were an English judgment: *Ferdinand Wagner v Laubscher Bros & Co* [1970] 2 QB 313, CA. See also *Susin v Delazzer* (1998) 155 DLR (4th) 170, Nova Scotia CA.

[616] See, eg, Gordon (1961) 77 LQR 358, 533.

[617] See *Rubin v Eurofinance SA* [2012] UKSC 46 at [170]–[176], [2013] 1 AC 236.

[618] Supra, p 556.

[619] S 8(3).

[620] Supra, pp 556–63.

[621] S 8(1).

[622] S 8(2). See *Barclays Bank Ltd v Piacun* [1984] 2 Qd R 476.

[623] Discussed supra, pp 595–8.

[624] [1983] 1 AC 145, HL.

[625] On the question of whether the judgment (a nullity decree) came within the 1933 Act, see infra, p 600. See also *Maples v Maples* [1988] Fam 14.

[626] Per Lord Diplock at 159–60, Lord Hailsham at 156, Lords Brandon and Keith concurring at 167. Registration *may* be set aside in such a case according to s 4(1)(b).

[627] Per Lord Hailsham at 156; Lord Brandon concurring at 167; Lord Diplock at 159 and 161. Registration *must* be set aside in such a case according to s 4(1)(a)(v).

(b) A prerequisite for recognition: the judgment must have been given on the merits

The rule in section 8, unlike the general registration provisions, applies to a judgment in favour of a defendant; ie a foreign judgment to which the Act applies in which the claimant's claim is dismissed will be recognised in England as conclusive between the parties. However, as with the common law rule on conclusiveness,[628] the judgment must have been given on the merits. Thus in *Black-Clawson International Ltd v Papierwerke Waldhof-Aschaffenburg AG*:[629]

> Just within the six-year limitation period under English law, the English plaintiff began pro-ceedings, on bills of exchange which had been dishonoured, in England and in Germany. The limitation period under German law was three years and had expired, and the German trial court dismissed the action on that ground.[630] In the English proceedings, the German defendant argued that the German judgment should be recognised in England under the 1933 Act and, relying on section 8(1), that it was conclusive between the parties as the English and German proceedings were both founded on the same cause of action.

A majority of the House of Lords held that section 8(1), unlike the main provisions of the 1933 Act, applied to judgments in favour of a defendant as well as of a plaintiff. However, the German judgment, dismissing the action because it was time-barred under the German law as to limitation which merely barred the remedy and did not extinguish the right, was not a decision on the merits even though regarded, in Germany, as a decision on substance. The German judgment was not therefore conclusive, though the English proceedings were stayed until the outcome of a final German appeal was known.

The *Black-Clawson* case remains good authority on the general point that a foreign judgment must be given on the merits in order to come within section 8 of the Act. It is, however, no longer good authority on the specific point of the effect of a foreign judgment involving a limitation period. This is because of section 3 of the Foreign Limitation Periods Act 1984,[631] which treats a foreign judgment on a limitation matter as being conclusive "on its merits". Section 3 applies regardless of whether the foreign court has applied its own law on limitation periods or that of any other country, including England and Wales. It also applies regardless of whether recognition is sought under statutory rules or at common law, and therefore, overturns the common law decision in *Harris v Quine*.[632]

(c) The scope of section 8: matrimonial causes

The provisions on recognition (section 8), unlike those on enforcement, are not confined to cases where there is a money judgment. This raises the major question of whether section 8 can apply to matrimonial causes, for example foreign decrees of divorce or nullity. For many years this question remained unanswered. However, it is now clear that an overseas divorce, etc can-not be recognised under the 1933 Act.[633] The 1933 Act is concerned with "actions",[634] whether in personam or in rem.[635] In matrimonial causes, "proceedings" are brought before the English

---

[628] *The Sennar (No 2)* [1985] 1 WLR 490, HL, discussed supra, pp 561–2.

[629] [1975] AC 591, HL; Jaffey (1975) 38 MLR 585; Carter (1974–1975) 47 BYBIL 381.

[630] The analysis of the trial court was that the issue of limitation was one of substance, to be referred to English law as the law governing the contract. English law would classify the issue as procedural to be referred to German law as the law of the forum and German law would accept the renvoi and apply its own law. The effect of German law (though regarded as substantive) was to bar the remedy but not extinguish the right. A German appellate court then decided that the English six-year period applied. A final appeal to the Federal Supreme Court was pending at the time of the English proceedings.

[631] See Law Com No 114 (1982), paras 4.58–4.71; Stone [1985] LMCLQ 497; Carter (1985) 101 LQR 68; supra, pp 78–9.

[632] (1869) LR 4 QB 653, supra, p 562.

[633] *Maples v Maples* [1988] Fam 14. For recognition of overseas divorces, etc, see infra, p 1000 et seq.

[634] See s 4(2); s 4(1)(a)(ii); s 8(2)(b).

[635] These terms are defined supra, pp 323 and 382.

courts rather than "actions". Moreover, section 8(1) is concerned with judgments which affect "the parties thereto". A judgment of marital status has a wider significance and can affect others, such as the state and children of the marriage.

(d) European Union judgments

As a result of the European Communities (Enforcement of Community Judgments) Order 1972[636] any "Community judgment"[637] to which the Secretary of State has appended an order for enforcement shall be registered by the High Court if application is made by the person entitled to enforce it. The judgments to which the Order applies are not those of the national courts of the Member States of the European Union[638] but rather judgments of the courts and institutions of the European Union itself, ie judgments of the Court of Justice of the European Union, and decisions of the Arbitration Committee of the European Atomic Energy Community, of the High Authority of the European Coal and Steel Community which impose a pecuniary obligation, and of the Council and of the Commission of the European Union which impose a pecuniary obligation on persons other than states.

The effect of registration is that such European Union judgments and decisions shall, for all purposes of execution, have the same force and effect as if they were judgments of the High Court. The High Court would appear to have no discretion as to whether to register such judgments;[639] but the Court of Justice of the European Union may order that enforcement of such a registered judgment shall be suspended. Such order then must be registered by the High Court and when registered shall have effect as if it were an order of the High Court staying the execution of the judgment and no steps to enforce the judgment may be taken while the order remains in force.

The judgments which may be registered are not restricted to those under which a sum of money is payable.[640] If, in the case of a European Union money judgment,[641] it has been partly satisfied at the date of registration, then it is to be registered only in respect of the sum outstanding; and if the judgment is satisfied in whole or in part after registration, then the registration shall be appropriately cancelled or varied.

(e) Judgments against states

(i) Judgments against the United Kingdom: The State Immunity Act 1978

It will be recalled that the State Immunity Act 1978 implements the European Convention on State Immunity (1972). The major significance of the Convention and of the 1978 Act is to provide for the circumstances when a sovereign state is to be immune from the jurisdiction of our courts.[642] However, provision is also made for the recognition here of judgments given against the United Kingdom by a court in another state which is a party to the 1972

---

[636] SI 1982/1590, made under s 2(2) of the European Communities Act 1972; amended by SI 1998/1259 (to make provision for Council Regulation (EC) 40/94 on the Community trade mark), SI 2003/3204 (to make provision for Council Regulation (EC) 6/2002 on Community designs), SI 2011/1435 (to make provision for Regulation (EC) 1060/2009 of the Parliament and of the Council on credit rating agencies) and SI 2013/504 (to make provision for Regulation (EU) No 648/2012 of the Parliament and of the Council on OTC derivatives, central counterparts and trade repositories).

[637] S(2)(1); there are similar rules for the registration and enforcement of Euratom inspection orders.

[638] As to recognition and enforcement of which, see infra, p 608 et seq.

[639] Also the defence under s 32 of the Civil Jurisdiction and Judgments Act 1982 will not apply because there is no judgment of a court "of an overseas country" (as defined under s 50).

[640] SI 1972/1590, para 2(1): and see *Re Westinghouse Electric Corpn Uranium Contract* [1978] AC 547 at 636, HL.

[641] A judgment can be registered in a foreign currency: Administration of Justice Act 1977, s 4(2)(b).

[642] Supra, p 497 et seq.

Convention.[643] Recognition must be given to such a judgment if it was a final judgment and if the United Kingdom was not entitled to immunity under the Convention.[644] Such a judgment, and any settlement before a court in a Convention State which is treated under the law of that state as equivalent to a judgment,[645] shall be regarded here as conclusive between the parties.[646] Recognition may, however, be denied on a number of grounds:[647] that recognition would be manifestly contrary to public policy; that a party to the proceedings had no adequate opportunity to present his case; that the procedural requirements of the Convention had not been complied with; if prior similar proceedings between the same parties are pending before a court in the United Kingdom, or before a court in a Convention State whose judgment would be required to be recognised; if there are prior inconsistent judgments of a United Kingdom court or a court in a Convention State; in the case of a judgment concerning the interest of the United Kingdom in movable or immovable property by way of succession, gift or *bona vacantia*, if the foreign court would not have had jurisdiction under rules equivalent to the English rules appropriate to such a claim, or if the foreign court applied a law other than that which would have been applied by an English court and would have reached a different conclusion had it applied that latter law.

(ii) Judgments against other states: the Civil Jurisdiction and Judgments Act 1982

The 1978 Act did not deal with the recognition of foreign judgments against states other than the United Kingdom. These are now dealt with by the Civil Jurisdiction and Judgments Act 1982, section 31(1) of which provides that:

> A judgment given by a court of an overseas country against a State other than the United Kingdom or the State to which that court belongs[648] shall be recognised and enforced in the United Kingdom, if and only if—
>
> (a) it would be so recognised and enforced if it had not been given against a State; and
> (b) that court would have had jurisdiction in the matter if it had applied rules corresponding to those applicable to such matters in the United Kingdom in accordance with sections 2 to 11 of the State Immunity Act 1978.[649]

The concept of "a judgment given against a State" is defined under the 1982 Act,[650] as is the concept of a "State" (ie to include the constituent territories in a federal state).[651] Section 31(1) will not affect judgments given in proceedings which arise under a number of international conventions, and which are recognised and enforced under the 1933 Act.[652]

---

[643] 1978 Act, ss 18, 19; and see Sinclair (1973) 22 ICLQ 254, 266–7, 273–6.

[644] S 18(1).

[645] S 18(3).

[646] S 18(2).

[647] S 19. S 32 of the Civil Jurisdiction and Judgments Act 1982 will not apply, since it only concerns judgments against persons.

[648] A foreign judgment against a state given in that state cannot be registered under the 1920 Act or seemingly the 1933 Act because it attracts immunity under Art 1 of the 1978 Act: *AIC Ltd v Federal Government of Nigeria* [2003] EWHC 1357 (QB), [2003] All ER (D) 190. For a rule preventing enforcement under the 1933 Act of judgments against persons, such as diplomats, entitled to immunity from jurisdiction, see s 4(3)(c) of the 1933 Act.

[649] See *NML Capital Ltd v Argentina* [2011] UKSC 31, [2011] 2 AC 495 dealing with waiver of immunity and submission to the court's jurisdiction; Dickinson [2011] LMCLQ 581; Fox (2012) 128 LQR 10 and, on the High Court judgment, (2009) 125 LQR 544; *Heiser v Iran* [2012] EWHC 2938 (QB) and *Ben-Rafael v Iran* [2015] EWHC 3203 (QB) dealing with actions to enforce US judgments against the defendant state for damages with regard to death or personal injury suffered after terrorist attacks and whether s 5 of the State Immunity Act 1978, discussed supra, p 505, would have applied had the case arisen in the UK.

[650] S 31(2).

[651] S 31(5).

[652] S 31(3); as amended by the Statute Law (Repeals) Act 2004, Sch 1(14), para 1.

(f) The Brussels and Lugano Conventions

The Brussels Convention, which is implemented by the Civil Jurisdiction and Judgments Act 1982, was replaced in virtually all cases by the Brussels I Regulation, which has now been repealed and replaced by the Recast of the Brussels I Regulation. One has to say "virtually" because the Brussels Convention continued to apply and still applies in relation to the territories of the Contracting States[653] which fall within the territorial scope of the Brussels Convention and are excluded from the Brussels I Recast.[654] The territories in question are (in relation to France) the French overseas territories, such as New Caledonia and Mayotte, and (in relation to the Netherlands) Aruba.[655] Judgments from Gibraltar are also recognised and enforced in accordance with the provisions of the Civil Jurisdiction and Judgments Act 1982 that implement the Brussels Convention.[656] The free circulation of judgments within the European Union, which was originally provided by the Brussels Convention, was extended to what was left of the EFTA bloc[657] by the 1988 Lugano Convention.[658] This Convention, which was implemented by the Civil Jurisdiction and Judgments Act 1991 (amending the 1982 Act), was a parallel one to the Brussels Convention, closely based on the latter, but not identical to it. The 1988 Convention has been replaced by the 2007 Lugano Convention, which aligned the Convention with the Brussels I Regulation. Recognition and enforcement under the Brussels and Lugano Conventions is considered in Chapter 17, as is the Recast of the Brussels I Regulation. The rules on recognition and enforcement under the Brussels and Lugano Conventions are significantly different from those of the Brussels I Recast. The biggest difference is the system of exequatur that exists under the two Conventions.

The Brussels Convention provided a new impetus for other countries to enter into bilateral recognition and enforcement conventions with the United Kingdom.[659] The requirement that English courts must recognise all judgments of the courts of other Contracting States, even where jurisdiction was taken against a defendant domiciled in a non-Contracting State under an exorbitant basis of jurisdiction, caused considerable anxiety in, for example, the USA[660] and Australia.[661] However, Article 59 of the Brussels Convention[662] allowed[663] a Contracting State to conclude conventions with other countries under which judgments of the courts of other Contracting States[664] against persons described as habitually resident in such other countries shall not be recognised in the first Contracting State. This was the genesis of a

---

[653] At the moment the Contracting States to the Brussels Convention are the original fifteen Member States.

[654] Art 68(1). Territories are excluded from the Regulation pursuant to Art 355 of the Treaty on the Functioning of the European Union.

[655] See Layton and Mercer, paras 11.061–11.071. See also Kruger, paras 1.026–1.037.

[656] SI 1997/2601 and SI 1997/2602.

[657] Ie Iceland, Norway, and Switzerland.

[658] Infra, p 653 et seq.

[659] It has also led in part to the reconsideration of common law rules and the adoption of a principle of full faith and credit for cases of recognition and enforcement within Canada: *Morguard Investments Ltd v De Savoye* [1990] 3 SCR 1077, (1991) 76 DLR (4th) 256 at 272; discussed supra, pp 543–4.

[660] Von Mehren (1981) 81 Col LR 1044; von Mehren (1980) II Hague Recueil 9, 95 et seq; Nadelmann (1967) 67 Col LR 995, reprinted in *Conflict of Laws: International and Interstate* (1972), p 238; Nadelmann (1967) 5 CML Rev 409; Nadelmann (1977) 41 Law and Contemporary Problems 54, 58–62, and see infra, pp 650–2.

[661] Pryles and Trindade (1974) 42 ALJ 185, 192–5; McEvoy (1994) 68 ALJ 576, 582.

[662] Discussed infra, pp 650–2.

[663] And still allows in the few cases where the Brussels Convention still applies.

[664] And those granted in Gibraltar: SI 1997/2602, para 5.

draft UK/US Judgments Convention.[665] However, this Convention was never implemented because of United Kingdom alarm at the prospect of having to enforce American judgments for large awards of damages. Negotiations with Canada and Australia were more successful, with agreement being reached on a UK/Canada Convention[666] and a UK/Australia Convention.[667] As previously mentioned, the Brussels Convention has been replaced in virtually all cases and the Recast of the Brussels I Regulation contains no equivalent of Article 59.[668] However, bilateral agreements containing the Article 59 let-out entered into prior to the entry into force of the Regulation are still honoured. The 2007 Lugano Convention, like the earlier 1988 Convention, contains an equivalent of Article 59 so that bilateral agreements containing the Article 59 let-out entered into prior to the entry into force of the 2007 Convention are honoured, as are conventions entered into in the future.[669]

(g) The Hague Convention on Choice of Court Agreements 2005

Work carried out at the Hague Conference on Private International Law on a multilateral convention on jurisdiction, recognition and enforcement of foreign judgments in civil and commercial matters ended in failure.[670] However, in 2005, a Convention on Choice of Court Agreements was adopted.[671] This Convention entered into force in 2015. The European Union has ratified the Convention, both in its own right and and on behalf of all the Member States (excluding Denmark). At present, the only other Contracting Parties are Mexico and Singapore, while the USA and Ukraine have signed but not yet ratified. The Convention has been implemented in the United Kingdom by the Civil Jurisdiction and Judgments Act 1982.[672]

The Convention is concerned to ensure the effectiveness of exclusive choice of court agreements.[673] The provisions on jurisdiction have already been discussed.[674] A judgment given by a court of a Contracting State designated in the agreement will be recognised in other Contracting States,[675] subject to a number of grounds of refusal.[676] Where one of these grounds is established,

---

[665] (1976) Cmnd 6771; see Hay and Walker (1976) 11 Texas Int LJ 421; Smit (1977) 17 VA J Int L 443; Mathers (1977) 127 NLJ 777; North (1978) 128 NLJ 315; Alford (1979) 18 Colum J Transnat L 119; North, *Essays*, Chapter 8; Kerr (1980) Europarecht 353, 356–7.

[666] See the Schedule to SI 1987/468. See also Patchett, *Recognition of Commercial Judgments and Awards in the Commonwealth* (1984), pp 32–5; Castel and Walker, *Canadian Conflict of Laws* (2006) 6th edn, para 14.27; SI 1987/468, amended by SI 1987/2211, SI 1988/1304 and 1853, SI 1989/987, SI 1991/1724, SI 1992/1731 and SI 1995/2708 extends the Foreign Judgments (Reciprocal Enforcement) Act 1933 to designated Provinces of Canada (Alberta, British Columbia, Manitoba, New Brunswick, Newfoundland, Nova Scotia, Ontario, Prince Edward Island, the Yukon Territory, Saskatchewan, Northwest Territories): supra, p 593.

[667] See the Schedule to SI 1994/1901. This Order extends the 1933 Act, supra, p 593, to the judgments of designated courts of Australia. Before this, the 1920 Act was extended to Australian states and territories.

[668] See infra, p 643.

[669] Infra, p 654.

[670] See McClean, in Fawcett (ed), *Reform and Development of Private International Law* (2002), Chapter 11; O'Brian (2003) 66 MLR 491; Schulz (2006) 2 J Priv Int L 243. But the attempts at a much wider Hague jurisdiction and judgments convention have since been revived: see https://www.hcch.net/en/projects/legislative-projects/judgments. See also supra, p 315.

[671] See <https://www.hcch.net/en/instruments/conventions/specialised-sections/choice-of-court>. See the Explanatory Report (2007) by Hartley and Dogauchi, available on this website; Hartley, *Choice of Court Agreements Under the European and International Instruments* (2013); Fentiman, para 2.29; Kruger (2006) 55 ICLQ 447; Teitz (2005) 53 AJCL 543; Tu (2007) 55 AJCL 347; Beaumont (2009) 5 J Priv Int L 125; Garnett (2009) 5 J Priv Intl L 161; Keyes and Marshall (2015) 11 J Priv Int L 345.

[672] Amended by Civil Jurisdiction and Judgments (Hague Convention on Choice of Court Agreements 2005) Regulations, SI 2015/1644.

[673] As defined in Art 3.

[674] Supra, pp 315–17.

[675] Art 8.

[676] Art 9.

recognition or enforcement *may* be refused, rather than must be. The court addressed is not precluded from recognition or enforcement and Contracting States will be able to lay down criteria for recognition of judgments where one of these grounds applies.[677] The grounds include where: the agreement was null and void under the law of the state of the chosen court (including its choice of law rules), unless the chosen court has determined that the agreement is valid;[678] a party lacked the capacity to conclude the agreement under the law of the requested state;[679] the document which instituted the proceedings was not notified to the defendant in sufficient time and in such a way as to enable him to arrange for his defence, unless the defendant entered an appearance and presented his case without contesting notification in the court of origin or was notified to the defendant in the requested state in a manner that is incompatible with fundamental principles of the requested state concerning service of documents;[680] the judgment was obtained by fraud in connection with a matter of procedure;[681] recognition or enforcement would be manifestly incompatible with the public policy of the requested state;[682] the judgment is inconsistent with a judgment given in the requested state in a dispute between the same parties;[683] the judgment is inconsistent with an earlier judgment given in another state between the same parties on the same cause of action, provided that the earlier judgment fulfils the conditions necessary for its recognition in the requested state.[684] These last five grounds are very similar to, and at times identical with, those found in the defences to recognition of judgments within the European Union under the Recast of the Brussels I Regulation.[685] The Convention also provides that recognition or enforcement of a judgment may be refused if, and to the extent that, the judgment awards damages, including exemplary or punitive damages, that do not compensate a party for actual loss or harm suffered.[686] Overall, the Convention has a dramatic effect on cases where there is a jurisdiction agreement providing for trial in another Contracting State. Thus, for example, recognition and enforcement of judgments granted in Mexico or Singapore, consequent on a jurisdiction agreement, is dealt with, not under the common law rules, but under the very different rules under the Convention.[687]

4. INTER-RELATION OF THE COMMON LAW AND STATUTES

One problem which has been touched on already[688] and might usefully be examined a little more fully is that of the inter-relation of the common law rules of recognition and those provided by statute (other than the Civil Jurisdiction and Judgments Act 1982[689]), especially in the fields of jurisdiction and defences. It will be recalled[690] that at common law the grounds of jurisdiction of the foreign court which will be recognised in England are based on residence and submission.

---

[677] The Hartley and Dogauchi Report, <http://www.hcch.net>, paras 125 and 183.

[678] Art 9(a).

[679] Art 9(b).

[680] Art 9(c).

[681] Art 9(d).

[682] Art 9(e).

[683] Art 9(f).

[684] Art 9(g).

[685] See Art 45 of the Regulation, discussed infra, pp 625–43.

[686] Art 11(1).

[687] The impact of the Hague Convention on Choice of Court Agreements on recognition and enforcement under the Recast of the Brussels I Regulation is considered infra, p 652.

[688] Supra, pp 593–8.

[689] For the very different rules for recognition and enforcement under the Brussels/Lugano system, see infra, pp 608–55.

[690] Supra, p 525 et seq.

Under section 4(2)(a) of the Foreign Judgments (Reciprocal Enforcement) Act 1933,[691] there are listed five grounds of jurisdiction in actions in personam,[692] the underlying bases of which are residence, submission and having an office or place of business within the country. The problems to be examined are whether the statutory regime is to be regarded merely as a codification of the common law principles and, if not, whether in a case which falls outside the statute, the basis of statutory recognition should affect common law recognition.

Just such issues arose in *Société Coopérative Sidmetal v Tital International Ltd.*[693]

> The defendant, an English company, had agreed to sell steel to the plaintiff, a Belgian company, and to ship the steel direct to an Italian company which had bought the steel from the plaintiff. Dissatisfied with the steel, the Italian company sued the plaintiff in Belgium and the plaintiff sought to join the defendant as a third party and a Belgian writ was served on it in England. The defendant took no part in the Belgian proceedings, but judgment was given against the defendant and in favour of the plaintiff. The plaintiff had the Belgian judgment registered in England under the Foreign Judgments (Reciprocal Enforcement) Act 1933 and the defendant sought to have the registration set aside.

The real issue was whether the Belgian court had jurisdiction such as to permit an English court to recognise and enforce the Belgian judgment. None of the jurisdictional requirements listed in section 4(2) of the 1933 Act was satisfied, nor were any of the heads of jurisdiction laid down at common law in *Emanuel v Symon*.[694] Nevertheless, it was argued for the plaintiff that the effect of the 1933 Act was fundamentally to change the basis on which foreign judgments are recognised in England, namely that the 1933 Act approaches the question of recognition "on the principle that, if there is reciprocity between the courts of this country and the courts of the country in which the judgment was obtained, then comity of nations requires that the jurisdiction of the courts of that country should be recognised for the purposes of the Act".[695] On such a basis, a Belgian judgment should be recognised either if an English court would have had jurisdiction in similar circumstances, ie service of the claim form out of the jurisdiction,[696] or if a Belgian court would have recognised the jurisdiction of the English court in a similar case, mutatis mutandis.

Whilst Widgery J accepted that the 1933 Act did not constitute a codification of the common law principles,[697] he was not prepared to accept that this Act had reintroduced comity or reciprocity as the underlying basis for the recognition of foreign judgments either at common law, or under the 1933 Act.[698] The bases of jurisdiction laid down in section 4(2)(a) of the 1933 Act are exclusive.[699]

A different question is whether, in so far as the provisions of the 1933 Act are broader than those of the common law, the 1933 Act could influence the development of the common law recognition and enforcement rules. It is suggested that it could, and should, as in the case of

---

[691] As amended by s 54 of and Sch 14 to the Civil Jurisdiction and Judgments Act 1982.

[692] Supra, pp 595–6.

[693] [1966] 1 QB 828; Webb (1966) 15 ICLQ 269; followed in *Gordon Pacific Developments Pty Ltd v Conlon* [1993] 3 NZLR 760; *Re Word Publishing Co Ltd* [1992] 2 Qd R 336.

[694] [1908] 1 KB 302 at 309, CA.

[695] [1966] 1 QB 828 at 845.

[696] Cf supra, pp 542–3.

[697] [1966] 1 QB 828 at 841, 846. See for the Australian position, *Hunt v BP Exploration Co (Libya) Ltd* (1979) 144 CLR 565, Australian High Ct and for New Zealand, *Hunt v BP Exploration (Libya) Ltd* [1980] 1 NZLR 104. Cf *Re Trepca Mines Ltd* [1960] 1 WLR 1273 at 1281–2, CA; *Rossano v Manufacturers' Life Insurance Co* [1963] 2 QB 352 at 383.

[698] [1966] 1 QB 828 at 841, 847; and see *Blohn v Desser* [1962] 2 QB 116 at 123; *Vogel v R and A Kohnstamm Ltd* [1973] QB 133 at 134; *Henry v Geoprosco International Ltd* [1976] QB 726 at 751, CA.

[699] And see *Sharps Commercials Ltd v Gas Turbines Ltd* [1956] NZLR 819.

jurisdiction based on having an office or place of business in the foreign country.[700] Certainly it is true in the case of the defence of fraud, illustrated by *Syal v Heyward*,[701] that decisions on recognition at common law may be relied upon for the purposes of the application of the 1933 Act. What one cannot do is to determine the present common law rules by reference to the 1933 Act, for one "cannot ascertain what the common law is by arguing backwards from the provisions of the statute".[702]

5. THE RECAST OF THE BRUSSELS I REGULATION

The jurisdictional provisions of the Recast of the Brussels I Regulation have already been considered,[703] but the Recast provides also for the recognition and enforcement in this country of judgments given in civil and commercial matters in European Union Member States, with the exception of Denmark. Under the EC/Denmark Agreement the provisions of the Recast are applied by international law to the relations between the European Union and Denmark. This means that judgments given in another European Union State[704] that are within the scope of the Recast must be recognised and enforced under this scheme rather than under the 1920 Act,[705] the 1933 Act[706] or the common law rules.[707] There is no implementing legislation in the United Kingdom for the Recast of the Brussels I Regulation. It is directly applicable in Member States, with the exception of Denmark, and cannot therefore be regarded as a United Kingdom statutory scheme of enforcement.[708] The provisions on recognition and enforcement under the Recast are complex, despite the Recast's aim of simplifying this area of law. Moreover, these provisions are markedly different from the rules on recognition and enforcement at common law or under the 1933 Act.[709] For these reasons, it has been thought best to deal with recognition and enforcement under the Recast of the Brussels I Regulation in a separate chapter.[710] That chapter will also consider three related Regulations: the European Enforcement Order Regulation, which applies where there is a judgment on an uncontested claim; the European Order for Payment Procedure Regulation; and the European Small Claims Procedure Regulation.

---

[700] 1933 Act, s 4(2)(a)(v), supra, p 597.

[701] [1948] 2 KB 443, CA, supra, p 573. See also *Owens Bank Ltd v Bracco* [1992] 2 AC 443 at 489, HL; supra, p 571. This is also true in relation to the 1920 Act.

[702] The *Henry v Geoprosco* case at 751.

[703] Supra, p 191 et seq.

[704] Ie in Austria, Belgium, Bulgaria, Croatia, Cyprus, the Czech Republic, Estonia, Finland, France, Germany, Greece, Hungary, Ireland, Italy, Latvia, Lithuania, Luxembourg, Malta, Netherlands, Poland, Portugal, Romania, Slovakia, Slovenia, Spain and Sweden. For the territories covered see Layton and Mercer, paras 11.061–11.071. See the statement by the United Kingdom in relation to Gibraltar attached to the Regulation, whereby other Member States are to enforce Gibraltar judgments as if they are United Kingdom judgments.

[705] Orders were made extending the 1920 Act to Cyprus and Malta.

[706] Orders were made extending the 1933 Act to Austria, Belgium, France, Italy, the Netherlands and Germany. See supra, p 593. For the relationship between the 1933 Act and the Recast see infra, p 611.

[707] The common law rules were used for Bulgaria, Croatia, the Czech Republic, Luxembourg, Denmark, Estonia, Finland, Ireland, Greece, Hungary, Latvia, Lithuania, Poland, Romania, Slovakia, Slovenia, Spain, Portugal, and Sweden; supra, p 525 et seq. For the relationship between the common law rules and the Regulation see infra, p 611.

[708] There are, however, United Kingdom provisions in support of the Regulation contained in the Civil Jurisdiction and Judgments Regulations, SI 2014/2947, which amends the Civil Jurisdiction and Judgments Order, SI 2001/3929.

[709] This is a relevant consideration when deciding whether to award security for costs: *Porzelack KG v Porzelack (UK) Ltd* [1987] 1 WLR 420.

[710] Infra, p 608 et seq.

17

RECOGNITION AND ENFORCEMENT OF JUDGMENTS UNDER THE BRUSSELS/LUGANO SYSTEM

1. The Brussels I Recast	608		(b) Differences between the Lugano	
(a) Introduction	608		Convention and the Brussels I Recast	654
(b) When do the rules on recognition and			5. The European Enforcement Order	
enforcement under the Brussels I Recast			Regulation	656
apply?	611		(a) Subject matter, scope and definitions	656
(c) Problems of interpretation	617		(b) European enforcement order	657
(d) Recognition	617		(c) Minimum standards for uncontested	
(e) Enforcement	619		claims procedures	658
(f) Grounds for refusal of recognition and			(d) Enforcement	659
enforcement	625		6. The European Order for Payment	
(g) Non-grounds for refusal of recognition			Procedure Regulation	660
and enforcement	643		(a) Scope and definitions	660
(h) Appeals in the Member State of origin	646		(b) The European order for payment	
(i) The estoppel effect of a judgment			procedure	661
obtained in a Member State	649		(c) Recognition and enforcement in other	
(j) Foreign reaction	650		Member States	662
(k) The impact of the Hague Convention			7. The European Small Claims Procedure	
on Choice of Court Agreements	652		Regulation	663
2. The EC/Denmark Agreement	652		(a) Scope and definitions	663
3. The Brussels Convention	652		(b) The European small claims procedure	664
4. The Lugano Convention	653		(c) Recognition and enforcement in other	
(a) When do the rules on recognition			Member States	664
and enforcement under the Lugano				
Convention apply?	653			

1. THE BRUSSELS I RECAST[1]

(a) Introduction

The Brussels I Recast[2] aims to achieve rapid and simple recognition and enforcement of judgments given in the Member States of the European

---

[1] For commentaries on recognition and enforcement under the Brussels I Recast, see Briggs 2014, paras 6.08–6.18 and 6.31–6.108; Briggs 2015, paras 7.03–7.45; Dickinson and Lein (eds), *Brussels I Regulation Recast* (2015); Fentiman, *International Commercial Litigation* (2015) 2nd edn, paras 18.70–18.105; Hovaguimian (2015) 11 J Priv Int L 212; Magnus and Mankowski (eds), *Brussels Ibis Regulation* (2015) 3rd edn; Schramm (2013) 15 YPIL 143; Wilke (2015) 11 J Priv Int L 128. See also Dicey, Morris and Collins, paras 14R-197–14-246; Layton and Mercer, Vol 1, Chapters 24–29.

[2] Regulation (EU) No 1215/2012 of the European Parliament and of the Council of 12 December 2012 on jurisdiction and the recognition and enforcement of judgments in civil and commercial matters OJ 2012 L 351/1, amended by Regulation (EU) No 542/2014 of the European Parliament and of the Council of 15 May 2014 as regards the rules to be applied with respect to the Unified Patent Court and the Benelux Court

Union.[3] This is seen as being essential for the sound operation of the internal market.[4] The objective is to have free movement of judgments within the Member States in civil and commercial matters.[5] In order to achieve this, the Recast provides that: first, the recognition of judgments is automatic, in the sense that none of the usual conditions found in cases of recognition and enforcement at common law or under the Foreign Judgments (Reciprocal Enforcement) Act 1933[6] have to be satisfied before recognition can take place; secondly, enforcement is also automatic, in the sense that the Recast abolishes all intermediate measures (exequatur) to be taken prior to enforcement in the Member State in which enforcement is sought and allows the party seeking enforcement to request directly enforcement measures in that Member State;[7] and thirdly, it is left to those who oppose recognition or enforcement to commence proceedings for refusal of recognition or enforcement by invoking the grounds for refusal available under the Recast; such grounds are limited and interpreted strictly—in particular, a court or another competent authority in another Member State is under a duty to recognise and enforce a judgment even though the court which granted it misapplied the rules on jurisdiction under the Recast.

Such liberal provisions on recognition and enforcement can only work where there is mutual trust among the Member States. This requires safeguards to be built into the system.[8] The first, and most obvious, one is that the Recast is a double instrument; ie it contains direct rules both on jurisdiction and on recognition and enforcement.[9] The two sets of rules on jurisdiction and on recognition and enforcement are each part of a single scheme. In order to achieve the objective of the free movement of judgments it is necessary that the rules on jurisdiction are unified.[10] The fact that the Member States share the same rules on jurisdiction means that, when it comes to recognition and enforcement, the Recast does not need to impose a requirement that the court or another competent authority in the second Member State, in which recognition and enforcement is sought, should have to check the basis on which the court in the first Member State, which gave judgment, took jurisdiction. Moreover, the bases of jurisdiction under the Recast are narrow; exorbitant bases are prohibited and there are special provisions on natural justice designed to protect the defendant where he has not entered an appearance at the trial.[11] The second safeguard is that there are still grounds for refusal of

---

of Justice OJ 2014 L 163/1, and Commission Delegated Regulation (EU) No 2015/281 of 26 November 2014 replacing Annexes I and II OJ 2015 L 54/1. The background to the Recast and its provisions on jurisdiction are discussed supra, pp 191–312. The Recast entered into force on 10 January 2013 and applies from 10 January 2015, with the exception of Arts 75 and 76, which apply from 10 January 2014: Art 81.

[3] Recital (4) of the Recast. The Member States in respect of which the Recast is directly applicable are the European Union Member States, with the exception of Denmark (ie Austria, Belgium, Bulgaria, Croatia, Cyprus, the Czech Republic, Estonia, Finland, France, Germany, Greece, Hungary, Ireland, Italy, Latvia, Lithuania, Luxembourg, Malta, the Netherlands, Poland, Portugal, Romania, Slovakia, Slovenia, Spain, Sweden and the United Kingdom). Under the EC/Denmark Agreement, discussed infra, p 652, the provisions of the Recast are applied, with minor amendments, by international law to the relations between the European Union and Denmark. The Lugano Convention extends the Brussels regime to three EFTA countries, namely Iceland, Norway and Switzerland, discussed infra, pp 653–5.

[4] Recitals (3) and (4) of the Recast. For the legal basis for the Recast, see Arts 67(4) and 81 of the Treaty on the Functioning of the European Union.

[5] Recital (6).

[6] Supra.

[7] Critical of this development Timmer (2013) 9 J Priv Int L 129.

[8] See the Jenard Report OJ 1979 C 59/1, p 42; Case 125/79 *Denilauler SNC v Couchet Frères* [1980] ECR 1553.

[9] For the rules on jurisdiction, see supra, pp 191–312.

[10] Recital (6) of the Recast.

[11] See Arts 5, 27 and 28, discussed supra, pp 213, 218 and 310–11; the Jenard Report, p 46.

recognition and enforcement which can be considered by the court in the Member State in which recognition and enforcement of the judgment is sought.[12]

The emphasis under the Recast is away from litigation at the stage of recognition and enforcement (and in the country where this is sought); instead, any disputes as to jurisdiction should be dealt with in the Member State in which the trial of the substantive issue takes place. A defendant can no longer ignore the original action and decide instead to defend by challenging the recognition and enforcement of the judgment when this is sought in another Member State. A defendant is virtually forced to defend the original action; once the judgment is given, there will often be nothing he can do to stop its recognition and enforcement in other Member States. This is not unfair to a defendant who is domiciled in a Member State: the Recast's rules on jurisdiction will frequently mean that the trial takes place in the Member State of his domicile anyway. Even when he has to go to another Member State to defend the action, this will still be within the European Union. It is more questionable, however, whether the Recast is fair in its treatment of defendants domiciled in non-Member States. As will shortly be shown, any judgment given against them in a Member State is to be recognised and enforced under the Recast.[13] This is despite the fact that defendants domiciled in non-Member States are denied the jurisdictional safeguards available to defendants domiciled in Member States; in particular, they are subject to the exorbitant bases of jurisdiction used in Member States. These defendants will have to defend away from home and may have to travel long distances in order to do so.

The Brussels I Recast repeals and replaces the earlier Brussels I Regulation. The Recast applies to legal proceedings instituted, to documents formally drawn up or registered as authentic, and to court settlements approved or concluded on or after its entry into force on 10 January 2015.[14] Judgments given in legal proceedings instituted before this date fall within the temporal scope of the Brussels I Regulation; so do authentic instruments formally drawn up or registered and court settlements approved or concluded before this date.[15] The rules on recognition and enforcement of the Recast, and in particular its rules on the enforcement procedure, are significantly different from those of its predecessor. The biggest change brought about by the Recast is the abolition of exequatur. Since the Recast repeals and replaces the Brussels I Regulation, the rules of the latter instrument are not described in this book. Nevertheless, the rules of the Brussels I Regulation do retain some and diminishing relevance under the transitional rules of the Recast and the reader is referred for further details to what is said in the previous edition of this book where the rules of the Brussels I Regulation were fully described.[16] The Brussels I Regulation, in turn, was based on and updated the Brussels Convention, which it replaced in virtually all cases after its entry into force in March 2002. The exception being that the Brussels Convention continued to apply and still applies in relation to certain overseas territories of some Member States.[17]

---

[12] Discussed infra, pp 625–43.

[13] See infra. For non-EU reaction to the Brussels Convention (now in virtually all cases replaced by the Recast), see infra, pp 650–1.

[14] Art 66(1). When the recognition or enforcement of a judgment is sought either from or in a state that joins the European Union after the entry into force of the Recast, the Recast will apply only if the original proceedings were instituted after its entry into force in both the Member State of origin and the Member State addressed: see Case C-514/10 *Wolf Naturprodukte GmbH v SEWAR spol sro* EU:C:2012:367, [2012] IL Pr 37—a Brussels I Regulation case.

[15] Art 66(2).

[16] See the 14th edn (2008) of this book, pp 596–637. See also the works cited supra, in fn 1.

[17] Infra, pp 652–3.

Before proceeding further, a brief note on terminology should be made. Article 2 of the Recast sets out a number of definitions. For the purposes of the Recast, "Member State of origin" means the Member State in which the judgment is given, the court settlement has been approved or concluded, or the authentic instrument has been formally drawn up or registered.[18] "Court of origin" means the court which has given the judgment.[19] "Member State addressed" means the Member State in which the recognition of a judgment is invoked or in which the enforcement of a judgment, a court settlement or an authentic instrument is sought.[20] This terminology is used in the rest of this chapter.

(b) When do the rules on recognition and enforcement under the Brussels I Recast apply?

Chapter III (Articles 36 to 57) of the Recast deals with the recognition and enforcement of judgments. In cases coming within this chapter traditional national rules cannot be used.[21] Chapter III applies, regardless of which rules on jurisdiction have been applied in the court of origin, to the situation where recognition and enforcement is sought in one Member State of a judgment given in another Member State in respect of a matter coming within the material scope of the Recast. As will be seen, there are special requirements concerning recognition and enforcement of provisional, including protective, measures.

(i) *Regardless of which rules on jurisdiction have been applied*

Chapter III of the Recast applies equally to judgments given by the courts of Member States granted after jurisdiction was taken under the Recast's rules (contained in Chapter II) and to judgments granted after jurisdiction was taken under traditional national rules.[22] It would even apply to the situation where a court has relied upon an exorbitant basis of jurisdiction, eg a French court takes jurisdiction over an American on the basis of the claimant's French nationality.[23] It also applies to judgments granted after jurisdiction was taken under other conventions, eg in cases of admiralty jurisdiction.[24] The basic distinction drawn for jurisdictional purposes between situations where the defendant is and is not domiciled in a Member State does not apply when it comes to recognition and enforcement of judgments. At this stage, any judgment is entitled to recognition irrespective of the domicile of the defendant.

(ii) *There must be a judgment given in a Member State*[25]

"Judgment" is widely defined under Article 2(a) of the Recast as "any judgment given by a court or tribunal of a Member State".[26] There is no limitation on the type of court and,

---

[18] Art 2(d).

[19] Art 2(f). In Croatia, notaries acting within the framework of the powers conferred on them by national law in enforcement proceedings based on an "authentic document" do not fall within the concept of "court": Case C-551/15 *Pula Parking doo v Tederahn* EU:C:2017:193, [2017] IL Pr 15. This is because such enforcement proceedings are not court proceedings which offer the necessary guarantees of independence and impartiality and are delivered in compliance with the principle of *audi alteram partem*. See also Case C-484/15 *Zulfikarpašić v Gajer* EU:C:2017:199, [2017] IL Pr 16.

[20] Art 2(e).

[21] The English rules are set out supra, p 525 et seq.

[22] Recital (27). For an example, see Case 178/83 *Firma P v Firma K* [1984] ECR 3033. For the rules as to when traditional bases of jurisdiction apply, see supra, pp 214–15.

[23] Art 14 of the French Civil Code. The effect of the Recast on exorbitant bases of jurisdiction is discussed supra, p 213.

[24] Of course, if the particular convention also has rules on recognition and enforcement, these will apply rather than the recognition and enforcement rules under the Recast, see infra, p 613.

[25] See Arts 36 and 39. See also Case C-129/92 *Owens Bank Ltd v Bracco (No 2)* [1994] ECR I-117; Briggs (1994) 14 YEL 557; Fentiman (1994) 53 CLJ 239; Hartley (1994) 19 ELR 545; Peel (1994) 110 LQR 386.

[26] This includes courts or tribunals common to several Member States, such as the Benelux Court of Justice when it exercises jurisdiction on matters falling within the scope of the Recast: Recital (11). Judgments

therefore, the judgments of inferior as well as of superior courts are covered. The awards of tribunals are also included, provided that the tribunal is of a Member State. In other words, the tribunal must be a state rather than a private body. The fact that this requirement would exclude most arbitration awards from Article 2(a) is of no practical importance since Article 1 excludes arbitration from the scope of the Recast anyway.[27] Neither does it matter what the judgment is called; it includes "a decree, order, decision or writ of execution, as well as the determination of costs or expenses by an officer of the court".[28] This is a very wide definition, which, for example, includes judgments declining jurisdiction on the basis of a jurisdiction agreement in favour of a foreign court,[29] judgments on preliminary issues[30] and provisional or interlocutory decisions.[31] The Recast applies even if the judgment concerns land situated in an area of the Member State of origin over which its government does not exercise effective control and where the application of the *acquis commuautaire* is suspended.[32] A "judgment" must be distinguished, though, from a court settlement. The former is a decision which emanates from a judicial body deciding on its own authority on the issues between the parties,[33] whereas the latter is essentially contractual, its terms depending first and foremost on the parties' intentions.[34] Similarly, a judgment entered in the terms of an award under 66 of the Arbitration Act 1996 is not a "judgment" for the purposes of Article 2(a).[35]

There is no requirement that the judgment must be a final one and provisional, including protective, measures are covered.[36] This contrasts with the requirement that the judgment be "final and conclusive" under the traditional English rules.[37] Furthermore, in contrast to

---

by the courts of Gibraltar are regarded as UK judgments and, accordingly, can be enforced in other Member States; judgments from Channel Islands and the Isle of Man do not enjoy the same treatment: Art 355(3) and (5)(c) of the Treaty on the Functioning of the European Union.

[27] See supra, pp 208–11.

[28] Art 2(a). Orders of a procedural nature are not, however, included, see the Schlosser Report OJ 1979 C 59/1, paras 184–7.

[29] Case C-456/11 *Gothaer Allgemeine Versicherung AG v Samskip GmbH* EU:C:2012:719, [2013] QB 548. See also *St Vincent European General Partner Ltd v Robinson* [2016] EWHC 2920 (Comm)—a judgment of the Cypriot courts that the dispute falls outside the scope of an exclusive Cypriot jurisdiction agreement binding on the English courts.

[30] *The Heidberg* [1994] 2 Lloyd's Rep 287 at 297.

[31] Case 143/78 *De Cavel v De Cavel* [1979] ECR 1055; Case 120/79 *De Cavel v De Cavel (No 2)* [1980] ECR 731; Case C-39/02 *Maersk Olie and Gas AS v Firma M de Haan en W de Boer* [2004] ECR I-9657 at [46]; *CFEM Facades SA v Bovis Construction Ltd* [1992] IL Pr 561.

[32] Case C-420/07 *Apostolides v Orams* [2009] ECR I-3571 at [39]; De Baere (2010) 47 CML Rev 1123; Hartley (2009) 58 ICLQ 1013.

[33] Case C-414/92 *Solo Kleinmotoren GmbH v Boch* [1994] ECR I-2237; Briggs (1994) 14 YEL 568.

[34] The *Solo Kleinmotoren* case. For special rules on the enforcement of authentic instruments (on which see Case C-260/97 *Unibank A/S v Christensen* [1999] ECR I-3715, Peel (2001) 21 YEL 363) and court settlements, see Art 2(b) and (c) and Chapter IV of the Recast (Art 58, on which see *S & T Bautrading v Bertil Nordling* [1997] 3 All ER 718, CA and Art 59), and CPR, r 74.11. A "consent judgment", which can be obtained from the English courts, is within what is now Art 2(a): the opinion of AG Gulmann in the *Solo Kleinmotoren* case at [29]; *Landhurst Leasing plc v Marcq* [1998] IL Pr 822, CA. So is a default judgment given after the defendant was excluded from the proceedings for being in contempt of court for failure to comply with a disclosure order: Case C-394/07 *Gambazzi v DaimlerChrysler Canada Inc and CIBC Mellon Trust Co* [2009] ECR I-2563 at [23].

[35] Another reason for refusing recognition and enforcement of such judgment under the Recast is that it falls within the arbitration exclusion in Art 1(1)(d): *ABCI v BFT* [1996] 1 Lloyd's Rep 485. But such judgment can engage the ground for refusal of recognition in Art 45(1)(c): see pp 645–6 below.

[36] Art 2(a).

[37] See supra, pp 548–51. However, provisional orders without notice are not included under Chapter III; nor are provisional measures that are not ordered by a court which has jurisdiction as to the substance of the matter, see infra, pp 615–17. Moreover, under Art 39 the judgment must be enforceable in the state in which it was given before it can be enforced, see infra, p 621. There may, therefore, be problems even with provisional orders which satisfy the requirements of Art 2(a).

the position in respect of recognition and enforcement in England, at common law or under existing bilateral treaties, the Recast is not limited to money judgments, and can, therefore, include an order for specific performance or an injunction.[38] The Schlosser Report, when discussing the Brussels Convention, envisaged that, on enforcement of a foreign judgment for specific performance, the same penalties for contempt of court should be imposed as if it were an English judgment.[39] It also envisaged that a foreign judgment imposing a penalty for disregarding a court order can come within what is now the Recast,[40] although it is not clear whether it will do so when it is a fine which accrues to the state rather than to a judgment creditor.[41] A court order in one Member State for the enforcement of a judgment given in another state, whether a Member or a non-Member State, falls outside Chapter III of the Recast.[42] To decide otherwise would mean, in effect, that a court or another competent authority in Member State A would have to recognise a judgment given in a non-Member State (X) simply because a court in Member State B had recognised the judgment given in State X and had granted an enforcement order in respect of it.[43] This would be contrary to one of the basic principles of the Recast, which is only concerned with recognition and enforcement of judgments *given in Member States* and is not intended to affect the recognition and enforcement of judgments given in non-Member States.

(iii) In respect of a matter coming within the material scope of the Recast

Two preliminary points must be made before looking at the scope of the Recast as defined by Article 1. First, Chapter III is only concerned with the *international* recognition and enforcement of judgments;[44] it will not apply to an internal United Kingdom case as, for example, where an English court is asked to recognise a Scottish judgment.[45] Secondly, Article 71 provides that the Recast "shall not affect any conventions to which the Member States are parties and which, in relation to particular matters, govern jurisdiction or the recognition or enforcement of judgments". The effect of this is to preserve a number of conventions dealing with jurisdiction or recognition and enforcement in respect of certain specific matters, such as the international carriage of goods by road.[46] It follows that, if another convention is applicable and has rules on recognition and enforcement, these rules will apply and not those contained in Chapter III of the Brussels I Recast. This can be justified on the ground that these other conventions usually involve obligations towards non-Member States and should not therefore be altered by a European Union Regulation which is confined to Member States.[47] In a field covered by the Recast, however, the rules on recognition and enforcement that are set out in a specialised convention apply only if they ensure, under conditions at least

---

[38] See *Barratt International Resorts Ltd v Martin* 1994 SLT 434; *Berkeley Administration Inc v McClelland* [1995] IL Pr 201 at 220 (per Hobhouse LJ), CA.

[39] The Schlosser Report, para 212.

[40] Ibid, para 213. It is implicit from Art 55 that penalties are included in some circumstances. See also Case C-406/09 *Realchemie Nederland BV v Bayer CropScience AG* [2011] ECR I-9773, concerning the recognition and enforcement of an order to pay a fine in order to ensure compliance with a judgment given in a civil and commercial matter.

[41] See the Schlosser Report, para 213.

[42] See the opinion of AG Lenz in Case C-129/92 *Owens Bank Ltd v Bracco (No 2)* [1994] QB 509 at [22]–[23].

[43] See Briggs 2014, paras 6.45 and 6.46; Briggs 2015, para 7.07; Dicey, Morris and Collins, para 14.205; Fentiman, para 18.82; Hartley, pp 84–5; Collins, p 106; Anton and Beaumont's *Civil Jurisdiction in Scotland* (1995), para 8.05; Layton and Mercer, paras 24.037–24.042. But cf McEvoy (1994) 68 ALJ 576, 580.

[44] See Arts 36 and 39, and more generally on the international scope of the Recast, supra, pp 202–3.

[45] For rules on this, see ss 18 and 19 of the 1982 Act, discussed supra, pp 588–91.

[46] Case C-533/08 *TNT Express Nederland BV v AXA Versicherung AG* [2010] ECR I-4107; Mariani (2012) 8 J Priv Int L 17; Case C-452/12 *Nipponkoa Insurance Co (Europe) Ltd v Inter-Zuid Transport BV* EU:C:2013:858, [2014] 1 All ER (Comm) 288.

[47] See the Jenard Report, pp 59–61.

as favourable as those provided by the Recast, the free movement of judgments and mutual trust in the European Union.[48] Article 71 is only concerned with conventions which Member States have entered into *in the past* (ie prior to the Recast coming into force on 10 January 2015). There is no provision, as there is under the Brussels Convention,[49] for conventions entered into by Member States in the future.[50]

What has already been said in the context of jurisdiction[51] about the meaning of civil and commercial matters under Article 1 need not be repeated. It is, however, important to realise that the interpretation of Article 1 can arise at two stages in the litigation process and in the courts of two Member States.[52] Where a court of a Member State has taken jurisdiction under the rules set out in the Recast, the question of the scope of the Recast may arise both at that stage and at the recognition and enforcement stage in the Member State in which recognition or enforcement is sought. Even where the court of origin decided after full argument that the matter came within the scope of the Recast, the court in the Member State addressed may have to decide the matter afresh, if necessary by referring any question of interpretation to the Court of Justice of the European Union.[53] If the court in the Member State addressed considers that the matter does not come within the scope of the Recast, the Recast is being interpreted differently in the Member States and a reference to the Court of Justice is desirable. Indeed, many of the cases on the interpretation of Article 1 discussed earlier in Chapter 11 are ones where the reference to the Court of Justice came from the court in which recognition and enforcement was sought.[54] In contrast to this, where jurisdiction has been taken under national rules, the first time that the scope of the Recast is considered may well be at the recognition and enforcement stage.

Where the matter is not within the scope of the Recast, judgments given in other Member States will be recognised and enforced in the United Kingdom at common law or under existing bilateral treaties.[55] The Recast and its predecessors have superseded the bilateral treaties previously entered into by the United Kingdom with many European Union States.[56] These earlier arrangements will, however, still operate where the United Kingdom is asked to recognise and enforce a judgment given in one of these states which is in respect of a matter to which the Recast does not apply.[57] It is for national courts to interpret the scope of these bilateral agreements and this may lead to the concept of civil and commercial matters in the Recast and in a bilateral agreement being interpreted differently.

---

[48] Case C-533/08 *TNT Express Nederland BV v AXA Versicherung AG* [2010] ECR I-4107.

[49] Art 57 of the Brussels Convention.

[50] The conclusion of treaties with non-Member States on matters covered by the Recast falls within the exclusive external competence of the European Union: see Opinion 1/03 of the Court of Justice Competence of the Community to conclude the new Lugano Convention [2006] ECR I-1145.

[51] Supra, pp 204–12.

[52] See Giardina (1978) 27 ICLQ 263, 275.

[53] Cf Briggs 2015, para 7.08 (for a different view by the same author see Briggs 2014, para 6.33).

[54] See, eg, Case 29/76 *LTU v Eurocontrol* [1976] ECR 1541; Case 143/78 *De Cavel v De Cavel* [1979] ECR 1055; Case 120/79 *De Cavel v De Cavel (No 2)* [1980] ECR 731; Case C-172/91 *Sonntag v Waidmann* [1993] ECR I-1963.

[55] See Art 70. See Cases 9 and 10/77 *Bavaria Fluggesellschaft Schwabe and Co KG v Eurocontrol* [1977] ECR 1517; Hartley (1977) 2 ELR 461. For the English rules on enforcement at common law and by statute, see supra, pp 527–605.

[56] The United Kingdom has bilateral treaties with Austria, France, Belgium, the Federal Republic of Germany, Italy and the Netherlands.

[57] Art 70. See also Cases 9 and 10/77 *Bavaria Fluggesellschaft Schwabe and Co KG v Eurocontrol* [1977] ECR 1517. The bilateral treaties also apply to judgments given before the entry into force of the Brussels I Regulation: Art 70(2). For transitional provisions generally, see Art 66.

Where a judgment is in respect of several matters, some of which are enforceable under the Recast and others are not, the judgment is split and recognised and enforced to the extent it concerns matters within the scope of the Recast.[58] If the excluded matter is only incidentally raised, the recognition rules under the Recast will still apply.[59]

(iv) Special requirements concerning provisional, including protective, measures

The Recast introduces special requirements that provisional, including protective, measures need to satisfy in order to qualify as judgments that can be recognised and enforced under the Recast. According to Article 2(a), "judgment includes provisional, including protective, measures ordered by a court or tribunal which by virtue of this Regulation has jurisdiction as to the substance of the matter". This Article further provides that "judgment does not include a provisional, including protective, measure which is ordered without the defendant being summoned to appear, unless the judgment containing the measure is served on the defendant prior to enforcement". The second sentence of Article 2(a) represents a partial codification of the decision of the Court of Justice in *Denilauler v SNC Couchet Frères*, whereas the first sentence of this Article represents a partial departure from this decision.[60]

> In *Denilauer* the question arose of whether an order from a French court, during the course of proceedings for payment under a contract (the main action), for a *saisie conservatoire* freezing certain of the German defendant's assets in Germany, thereby preventing the defendant from thwarting enforcement of the judgment in the main action, was enforceable in Germany under the Brussels Convention.

With provisional and protective measures without notice,[61] such as the English freezing injunction (formerly Mareva injunction) or the Continental *saisie conservatoire*, the defendant is not summoned to appear and it is intended that there should be enforcement without prior service. The Court of Justice held that what is now Chapter III does not cover decisions resulting from proceedings which by their very nature neither allow the defendant to state his case nor give him an opportunity to do so. However, if an English freezing injunction is made after notice has been served on the defendant or after the defendant had an opportunity to resist the claimant's application for the order, it is entitled to recognition and enforcement under the Recast,[62] provided of course that the injunction is in aid of substantive proceedings in England. This will be so even if the order relates to assets in another Member State.

In deciding to exclude decisions which were not based on adversary proceedings the Court of Justice was influenced by two considerations. First, there are a number of important provisions in what is now Chapter III which are concerned with whether there has been service of process and compliance with basic requirements of natural justice in the court of origin.[63] These presuppose that, in principle, both parties can participate in the proceedings, although it may be the case that the defendant, having been summoned, does not actually appear.[64]

---

[58] This rule was expressly laid down in Art 48 of the Brussels I Regulation. Although it is omitted in the Brussels I Recast, the objective of the free movement of judgments indicates that it should continue to be applied. Similarly, Briggs 2014, paras 6.34 and 6.35; Dickinson and Lein (eds), paras 13.14 and 13.15.

[59] There is no ground for refusal of recognition under the Recast in this situation; cf Art 27(4) of the Brussels Convention.

[60] Case 125/79 [1980] ECR 1553; Hartley (1981) 6 ELR 59.

[61] See generally on protective measures and what is now the Recast: Collins (1981) 1 European Year Book of International Law 249; Lipstein (1987) 36 ICLQ 873; Hogan (1989) 14 ELR 191.

[62] See *Babanaft International Co SA v Bassatne* [1990] Ch 13 at 31–2 (per Kerr LJ, who was referring obiter to a pre-judgment freezing injunction), CA, followed in *Normaco v Lundman* [1999] IL Pr 381—Brussels Convention cases.

[63] See Arts 45(1)(b) and 53 and Annex I. These provisions are discussed infra, pp 632–9.

[64] See Case C-474/93 *Hengst Import BV v Campese* [1995] ECR I-2113 at [14]. A provisional decision taken without both sides being heard but capable of being challenged is covered: Case C-39/02 *Maersk Olie*

They are not designed, and by inference neither is what is now Chapter III, to deal with the situation where the defendant has not even been summoned to appear. Secondly, the defendant is denied a fundamental right by not being able to put his side of the case in the original proceedings;[65] yet, this is one of the safeguards which is used to justify the liberal provisions on recognition and enforcement under what is now Chapter III.

This principle in the *Denilauler* case, now codified in the second sentence of Article 2(a), equally excludes a permanent injunction without notice if the defendant has not been served with process in the judgment-granting state and has not been given an opportunity to be heard before the order was made.[66]

Given that protective measures without notice cannot be recognised and enforced in other Member States under the Recast, what the claimant has to do is either to wait until the judgment containing the measure is served on the defendant prior to enforcement and then seek enforcement of the measure under the Recast, or to apply under Article 35[67] for a protective measure in the courts of each of the Member States in which the defendant has assets, or to seek enforcement of the measure under national law.[68] Where the defendant has assets in several Member States this involves considerable inconvenience to the claimant. On the other hand, it leaves the decision on the granting of the protective measure to the court in the state where the assets are situated, which is the court best able to decide the issue. It also means that there will be a full examination of all the relevant considerations before an order is granted. In certain circumstances an English court may grant a world-wide freezing injunction (ie over assets abroad).[69] In theory this avoids problems of enforcement of the measure abroad or the need for an application for a protective measure in another Member State. In practice it will normally be followed up with one of these steps.

In *Denilauer* the Court of Justice accepted that a provisional or protective measure can be recognised and enforced irrespective of the basis on which the court of origin assumed jurisdiction, including what is now Article 35 of the Recast.[70] In contrast, in providing that "judgment includes provisional, including protective, measures ordered by a court or tribunal which by virtue of this Regulation has jurisdiction as to the substance of the matter", the Recast departs from this aspect of the *Denilauer* case. The court with jurisdiction as to the

---

and Gas AS v Firma M de Haan en W de Boer [2004] ECR I-9657 at [50]–[52]. So is a default judgment given after the defendant was excluded from the proceedings for being in contempt of court for failure to comply with a disclosure order: Case C-394/07 *Gambazzi v DaimlerChrysler Canada Inc and CIBC Mellon Trust Co* [2009] ECR I-2563 at [23].

[65] The party against whom the order is directed would know nothing about this in the original state, or in the state where enforcement was sought, until after the certificate issued by the court of origin pursuant to Art 53 has been served prior to the first enforcement measure. The Advocate General in the *Denilauler* case gave his opinion that courts in some Member States might use the public policy defence to avoid enforcing *ex parte* (ie without notice) protective measures if these were within what is now Chapter III.

[66] *EMI Records Ltd v Modern Music Karl-Ulrich Waltebach GmbH* [1992] QB 115—a Brussels Convention case.

[67] Discussed supra, pp 303–5. Under Art 35 a court in a Member State can grant a provisional measure even if it does not have jurisdiction under the Recast in respect of the substance of the matter. For doubts on whether the English procedure for providing security for costs comes within Art 24 of the Brussels Convention (Art 35 of the Recast), see *Bank Mellat v Helliniki Techniki SA* [1983] 3 All ER 428 at 434, CA.

[68] Recital (33).

[69] See *Babanaft International Co SA v Bassatne* [1990] Ch 13, CA; Collins (1989) 105 LQR 262; supra, pp 305–7.

[70] Case 125/79 *Denilauler v SNC Couchet Frères* [1980] ECR 1553 at [17]; see also Case C-99/96 *Mietz v Intership Yachting Sneek BV* [1999] ECR I-2277; Case C-80/00 *Italian Leather SpA v WECO Polstermobel GmbH & Co* [2002] ECR I-4995 at [41]. For Art 35, see supra, pp 303–5.

substance of the matter is the court whose jurisdiction is founded on Articles 4 and 7 to 26.[71] Article 2(a) does not require that that court is actually seised of the substantive proceedings, but only that that court can, under the Regulation, be seised of the substantive proceedings.[72]

(c) Problems of interpretation

The points made in the context of jurisdiction in relation to interpretation of the Recast and in relation to referrals to the Court of Justice[73] are equally applicable here. The biggest changes brought about by the Recast are in the area of recognition and enforcement of judgments. Recital (34) emphasises the need to ensure continuity between the Recast and its predecessors, the Brussels Convention and the Brussels I Regulation. Accordingly, the case law of the Court of Justice under the latter two instruments retains relevance. However, because of the significant changes brought about by the Recast, that case law should be read with caution.

(d) Recognition[74]

The issue of recognition can arise in three different ways: (i) in order for a judgment to be enforced under the Recast, it must first be recognised;[75] (ii) recognition will apply on its own, without any question of enforcement, eg where a judgment is used as a defence to a new action;[76] and (iii) recognition can operate on its own in a more positive way, eg in order to establish a title to property or by way of a set-off.[77]

Article 36(1) provides that "a judgment given in a Member State shall be recognised in the other Member States without any special procedure being required".[78] The Recast makes recognition of judgments mandatory between Member States and does so without any conditions having to be satisfied. In contrast to the rules on recognition at common law and under the Foreign Judgments (Reciprocal Enforcement) Act 1933, it does not have to be shown that the judgment is final and conclusive,[79] or that the foreign court had jurisdiction in an international sense;[80] nor is it required that the foreign judgment was on the merits.[81] The Jenard Report, when discussing the Brussels Convention, emphasised the point by describing recognition as being automatic under the Convention.[82] This must be qualified by pointing out that there are grounds for refusal of recognition;[83] and a better way of putting it is to say

---

[71] See Case C-391/95 *Van Uden Maritime BV (t/a Van Uden Africa Line) v Kommanditgesellschaft in Firma Deco-Line* [1998] ECR I-7091.

[72] See Dickinson and Lein (eds), para 2.115 and 2.116; cf Briggs 2015, para 7.36.

[73] Supra, pp 194–8.

[74] See Section 1 of Chapter III (Arts 36–38).

[75] See generally Droz, *Compétence Judicaire et Effets des Jugements dans le Marché Commun* (1972), p 273; the opinion of the Advocate General in Case 42/76 *De Wolf v Cox* [1976] ECR 1759.

[76] See, eg, the *De Wolf v Cox* case, discussed infra, pp 649–50; *Berkeley Administration Inc v McClelland* [1995] IL Pr 201 at 221 (per Hobhouse LJ), CA.

[77] See Anton and Beaumont's *Civil Jurisdiction in Scotland* (1995), para 8.09; cf *Caylon v Michailidis* [2009] UKPC 34; Briggs (2010) 81 BYBIL 583; Briggs (2010) 126 LQR 20. For the position in respect of counterclaims, see Hartley, p 83.

[78] English law has never required any special procedure for recognition. This aspect of Art 36, therefore, represents no change in the law of England.

[79] For the traditional English rules requiring this see supra, pp 548–51. However, the Recast allows the court or authority before which a judgment given in another Member State is invoked to suspend the proceedings where there is a challenge in the Member State of origin: Art 38(a). See infra, pp 647–9.

[80] Cf the traditional English rules, supra, pp 528–40. For the problem of whether the court has international jurisdiction, see Art 45(3), discussed infra, pp 643–4.

[81] Cf the traditional English rules, supra, pp 559–60.

[82] At p 43.

[83] See infra, pp 625–43.

that there is a rebuttable presumption that judgments are to be recognised.[84] Certain documents must, nonetheless, be produced by the party seeking recognition, namely a copy of the judgment which satisfies the conditions necessary to establish its authenticity,[85] a certificate issued by the court of origin pursuant to Article 53 using the form set out in Annex I and, in certain circumstances, the translation or transliteration of these documents.[86] A foreign judgment recognised by virtue of Article 36 in principle has the same effects in the Member State addressed as it does in the state in which it was given.[87] There is, however, no reason for granting a judgment, when it is enforced (as opposed to when it is merely sought to be recognised), effects that a similar judgment given directly in the Member State addressed would not have.[88] The Recast also provides that where a judgment contains a measure or order which is not known in the law of the Member State addressed, that measure or order, including any right indicated therein, will, to the extent possible, be adapted to one which is known in the law of that Member State which has equivalent effects attached to it and pursues similar aims and interests.[89] Such adaptation will not result in effects going beyond those provided for in the law of the Member State of origin.[90] The Recast leaves it to Member States to determine how, and by whom, the adaptation is to be carried out.[91] Member States may confer jurisdiction on authorities other than courts to carry out the adaptation, but the Regulation provides for a safeguard by prescribing that any party may challenge the adaption of the measure or order before a court.[92] Article 36 will not apply to a decision of a court of a Member State on an issue arising in proceedings to enforce a judgment given in a non-Member State, such as the question whether the judgment in question was obtained by fraud.[93] This is dictated by the principle that if a dispute falls outside the scope of the Recast the existence of a preliminary issue which the court must resolve in order to determine the dispute cannot justify application of the Recast.[94]

Section 1 of Chapter III (Articles 36 to 38) contains no procedural provisions in respect of recognition. In the situation where recognition is merely a first step towards enforcement, the enforcement procedure under Section 2 (Articles 39 to 44)[95] will obviously be used. If recognition is used merely as a defence to an action, no procedure is necessary; but this still leaves a minority of cases where there is a need for some procedural rules. Article 36(2) provides that any interested party[96] may, in accordance with the procedure in Subsection 2 of Section 3

---

[84] See the opinion of the Advocate General in Case 42/76 *De Wolf v Cox* [1976] ECR 1759; also the Jenard Report, p 43.

[85] Legalisation cannot be required: Art 61.

[86] Art 37; see also Art 57. A translation or transliteration of the contents of the certificate may be requested "where necessary". A translation of the judgment may be requested "only if [the court or authority] is unable to proceed without such a translation". A document, duly authenticated, which purports to be a copy of a judgment given by a court of a Member State other than the UK is without further proof deemed to be a true copy, unless the contrary is shown: Civil Jurisdiction and Judgments Order, SI 2001/3929 (as amended by SI 2014/2947), Art 3 and Sch 1, para 8(1)(a).

[87] Case 145/86 *Hoffmann v Krieg* [1988] ECR 645; see also Art 65(2); the Jenard Report, p 43; cf Dicey, Morris and Collins, para 14-220; *Caylon v Michailidis* [2009] UKPC 34.

[88] Case C-420/07 *Apostolides v Orams* [2009] ECR I-3571 at [66]. See generally Harder (2013) 62 ICLQ 441.

[89] Art 54(1). See also Recital 28.

[90] Art 54(1).

[91] Recital 28. For English procedural rules on adaptation, see CPR, r 74.11A.

[92] Art 54(2).

[93] Case C-129/92 *Owens Bank Ltd v Bracco (No 2)* [1994] ECR I-117 at [26] and [28].

[94] Ibid, at [34], following Case C-190/89 *Marc Rich and Co AG v Società Italiana Impianti PA* [1991] ECR I-3855.

[95] Infra, pp 619–25.

[96] A party seeking recognition—*Re an Application by National Organisation Systems SA* (Decision 3265/ 2003) [2005] IL Pr 52, the One Member First Instance Court of Athens. On whether the heirs of an intestate

(dealing with refusal of enforcement), apply for a decision that there are no grounds for refusal of recognition of a judgment.[97] For example,[98] if a negotiable instrument declared to be invalid in Italy is presented to a bank in Belgium, the bank can apply for a decision that there are no grounds for refusal of recognition of the judgment in Belgium in accordance with the procedure in Subsection 2 of Section 3. Similarly, Article 45 provides that any interested party may apply to have the recognition of a judgment refused[99] in accordance with the procedures provided for in Subsection 2 of Section 3.[100] If an application under either Article 36(2) or Article 45(4) has been made, the court or another competent authority before which a judgment given in another Member State is invoked may suspend its proceedings.[101] If the outcome of proceedings in a court of a Member State depends on the determination of an incidental question of refusal of recognition, that court shall have jurisdiction over that question.[102]

(e) Enforcement[103]

The Court of Justice decided in *De Wolf v Cox*[104] that, in situations where what is now Chapter III applies, the enforcement procedure in those sections *must* be used. National rules cannot be used as an alternative. With the aim of making international litigation less time-consuming and costly, the Recast abolishes the system of exequatur that existed under the Brussels I Regulation and the Brussels Convention, under which the court in the Member State in which enforcement was sought was required to make a declaration of enforceability prior to enforcement (or, in the UK, to register the judgment for enforcement).[105] As a result, a judgment given in one Member State should now be treated "as if it had been given in the Member State addressed".[106] The party against whom enforcement is sought, however, is informed of the enforcement in reasonable time before the first enforcement measure.[107] This is to allow him to apply for refusal of enforcement if he considers one of the grounds for refusal of recognition to be present. Before considering the details of this procedure, the underlying policy considerations should be examined.

(i) Policy matters

The Recast seeks to improve the sound operation of the internal market by ensuring rapid and simple enforcement of judgments within the European Union.[108] At the same time, it seeks to provide safeguards for both parties.[109]

---

judgment creditor were interested parties for the purposes of applying for a declaration of enforceability under the Brussels I Regulation see *Re Haji-Ioannou (Deceased)* [2009] EWHC 2310 (QB), [2009] Il Pr 56; Briggs (2010) 81 BYBIL 583.

[97] The provisions under Section 4 (Arts 52–57) must also be complied with.
[98] See the Jenard Report, p 43.
[99] Art 45(1).
[100] Art 45(4). The provisions under Section 4 (Arts 52–57) must also be complied with.
[101] Art 38(b). For English procedural rules on suspension of proceedings, see CPR, r 74.7C.
[102] Art 36(3).
[103] See Section 2 of Chapter III (Arts 39–52). See also CPR, Part 74.
[104] Case 42/76 [1976] ECR 1759; Hartley (1977) 2 ELR 146. For further discussion of the case, see infra, pp 649–50.
[105] The procedure for enforcement under the Brussels I Regulation involved making a without notice application in the Member State in which enforcement was sought. The judgment was declared enforceable (or, in the UK, registered for enforcement) on completion of certain formalities. The other party was informed of this and had rights of appeal and, if that party did appeal, the proceedings then became contentious. This procedure is described fully in the 14th edn (2008) of this book, pp 605–10. The Brussels Convention lays down a similar procedure.
[106] Recital (26) of the Recast.
[107] Recital (32).
[108] See Recital (4).
[109] See Recitals (2) and (29).

(a) A rapid and simple procedure

The Recast abolishes exequatur. This means that the judgment given in the Member State of origin, together with a certificate issued by the court of origin, is a sufficient basis for requesting directly enforcement measures in other Member States. The only documents that the party seeking enforcement has to provide to the competent enforcement authority are a copy of the judgment which satisfies the conditions necessary to establish its authenticity,[110] a certificate issued by the court of origin using the form set out in Annex I[111] and, in certain circumstances, the translation or transliteration of these documents.[112] The certificate established under the Recast is aimed to facilitate the enforcement of judgments, in particular where interest and costs have to be calculated and by reducing the need for translation.[113] The enforcement authority cannot raise of its own motion any of the grounds for refusal of recognition (and hence refusal of enforcement) provided by the Recast under Article 45. These grounds may be reviewed only in the course of an application for refusal of enforcement by the party against whom enforcement is sought.

(b) Safeguarding the interests of the party seeking enforcement

The interests of the party seeking enforcement are protected in five ways:

(i) Enforcement is automatic, in the sense that the Recast abolishes all intermediate measures to be taken prior to enforcement in the Member State in which enforcement is sought. By allowing the party seeking enforcement to request directly enforcement measures in the Member State addressed, the party against whom enforcement is sought is prevented from removing assets out of the jurisdiction in order to thwart the enforcement.[114]

(ii) Simplifying the procedural requirements incumbent on the party seeking enforcement.

(iii) An enforceable judgment carries with it by operation of law the power to proceed to any protective measures which exist under the law of the Member State in which enforcement is sought.[115] The party seeking enforcement is thus entitled as of right to protective measures, such as a freezing injunction preventing the other party from removing assets. That party cannot be denied the right to a protective measure by being required, for example, to obtain a court order authorising this, even though this is required by national law.[116] But there is nothing incompatible with the Recast in requiring an applicant for an English freezing injunction to provide the usual undertaking to protect third parties, this being a feature of the English measure.[117] Additionally, an English court which has given the original judgment may safeguard the judgment creditor's interests by

---

[110] Legalisation cannot be required: Art 61.

[111] This certificate is issued pursuant to Art 53. It confirms that the judgment is enforceable under the law of the Member State of origin, the time and fact of service having been made on the defendant, and contains an extract of the judgment, in particular a short description of the subject matter and the order, and, where appropriate, relevant information on the recoverable costs of the proceedings and the calculation of interest.

[112] Art 42(1), (3) and (4); see also Art 57. A translation or transliteration of the contents of the certificate may be requested "where necessary". A translation of the judgment may be requested "only if [the competent enforcement authority] is unable to proceed without such a translation". For documents that need not be provided for the enforcement of a judgment ordering a provisional or protective measure see Art 42(2).

[113] Proposal for the Brussels I Regulation Recast, Brussels 14 December 2010, COM (2010) 748 final, p 6.

[114] See the Schlosser Report, para 219; Case 125/79 *Denilauler v SNC Couchet Frères* [1980] ECR 1553; Case 178/83 *Firma P v Firma K* [1984] ECR 3033; Hartley (1985) 10 ELR 233.

[115] Art 40.

[116] See Case 119/84 *Capelloni v Pelkmans* [1985] ECR 3147; Hartley (1986) 11 ELR 96; *Elwyn (Cottons) Ltd v Pearle Designs Ltd* [1989] IR 9, Irish High Court—both cases were decided under the Brussels Convention.

[117] See *Banco Nacional de Comercio Exterior SNC v Empresa de Telecommunicaciones de Cuba SA* [2007] EWCA Civ 662 at [44]–[46], [2008] 1 WLR 1936.

granting a world-wide freezing injunction over assets in another Member State, pending the enforcement of the judgment under the Recast.[118]

(iv) The party against whom enforcement is sought is not given an excessive number of avenues for resisting enforcement, which could be used as delaying tactics.[119]

(v) If the enforcement of a judgment has been refused, the party seeking enforcement can appeal against this.[120]

(c) Safeguarding the interests of the party against whom enforcement is sought
This party is protected in two ways:

(i) In order to be enforceable in other Member States, a judgment must be "enforceable" in the Member State in which it was granted.[121] The Court of Justice has held that the term "enforceable" is referring solely to the enforceability, in formal terms, of foreign decisions and not to the circumstances in which such decisions may be executed in the state of origin.[122] Moreover, "the question whether a decision is, in formal terms, enforceable in character must be distinguished from the question whether that decision can any longer be enforced by reason of payment of the debt or some other cause". This is a very narrow view of the term "enforceable", and it cast doubt on whether the enforceability requirement would operate in two situations in which it had been previously thought that it would do so. The first was where an appeal was pending in the Member State of origin, and the effect of this was to suspend enforcement in that state.[123] The second was where the judgment had already been complied with in the Member State of origin. The enforceability requirement would, it was thought,[124] prevent the claimant from recovering twice. With regard to the first situation, the Recast now provides that the competent authority in the Member State addressed will, on the application of the person against whom enforcement is sought, suspend the enforcement proceedings where the enforceability of the judgment is suspended in the Member State of origin.[125] With regard to the second situation, the fact that the judgment has already been complied with can be raised as a ground for refusal of enforcement under the law of the Member State addressed.[126] In any event, the fact that a judgment creditor might encounter practical difficulties in having the judgment enforced in the Member State of origin (eg because the judgment concerns land situated in an area over which the government of that state does not exercise effective control) does not deprive the judgment of its enforceability.[127]

---

[118] See *Babanaft International Co SA v Bassatne* [1990] Ch 13, CA; criticised by Hogan (1989) 14 ELR 191, p 197 et seq. See supra, p 306.

[119] See Case C-432/93 *Société d'Informatique Service Réalisation Organisation (SISRO) v Ampersand Software BV* [1995] ECR I-2269 at [28].

[120] See infra, p 624.

[121] Arts 39, 42(1)(b) and 53 and Annex I. A certificate obtained in accordance with these provisions is evidence that the judgment is enforceable in the Member State of origin, see the Civil Jurisdiction and Judgments Order, SI 2001/3929 (as amended by SI 2014/2947), Art 3 and Sch 1, para 8(1)(b).

[122] Case C-267/97 *Coursier v Fortis Bank* [1999] ECR I-2543; Peel (2001) 21 YEL 352. It may be clear that a judgment is enforceable but not clear what is enforceable (a judgment fixing the amount payable by reference to insolvency law or one ordering payment). Proceedings in England can be adjourned so that further evidence on whether and to what extent the foreign judgment is enforceable can be obtained from the foreign court: *La Caisse Régional du Crédit Agricole Nord de France v Ashdown* [2007] EWCA Civ 574—a Brussels I Regulation case.

[123] See the Schlosser Report, para 204.

[124] Ibid, para 220.

[125] Art 44(2).

[126] Art 41(2). This reverses Case C-139/10 *Prism Investment BV v Jaap Anne van der Meer* [2011] ECR I-9511, decided under the Brussels I Regulation.

[127] Case C-420/07 *Apostolides v Orams* [2009] ECR I-3571 at [71].

(ii) In reasonable time prior to the first enforcement measure, the party against whom enforcement is sought must be informed of this through service of the certificate issued by the court of origin established under the Recast and, where necessary, the judgment.[128] This is to enable him to apply for refusal of enforcement of the judgment on the basis that one of the grounds under Article 45 applies.[129] The principle of effective judicial protection, enshrined in Article 47 of the Charter of Fundamental Rights of the European Union, may cover the right to be exonerated from payment of legal costs and fees payable to obtain the assistance of a lawyer in respect of an application for refusal of enforcement.[130]

(ii) Procedural rules

These are derived from the Recast, the Civil Jurisdiction and Judgments Order 2001 and the Civil Procedure Rules.[131] The enforcement procedure under the Recast comprises two elements: enforcement and application for refusal of enforcement.

(a) Enforcement

The basic provision is Article 39 which provides that: "A judgment given in a Member State which is enforceable in that Member State shall be enforceable in the other Member States without any declaration of enforceability being required."

The procedure for the enforcement of judgments given in another Member State, ie their execution, is governed by the domestic law of the Member State addressed.[132] A judgment given in a Member State which is enforceable in the Member State addressed will be enforced there under the same conditions as a local judgment.[133] The Recast merely lays down requirements as to the documents to be provided to the competent enforcement authority[134] and certain limitations regarding the representation of the party seeking enforcement[135] and provision of security in the Member State addressed.[136] The Recast also provides that where a judgment contains a measure or order which is not known in the law of the Member State addressed, that measure or order, including any right indicated therein, will, to the extent possible, be adapted to one which is known in the law of that Member State which has equivalent effects attached to it and pursues similar aims and interests.[137] Such adaptation will not result in effects going beyond those provided for in the law of the Member State of origin.[138] The Recast leaves it to Member States to determine how, and by whom, the adaptation is to be carried out.[139] Member States may confer jurisdiction on authorities other than courts to

---

[128] Art 43(1) and (2) and Recital (32).

[129] Art 46. Art 45 is discussed infra, pp 625–43. A foreign judgment may not be reviewed as to its substance: Art 52.

[130] Case C-156/12 *GREP GmbH v Freistaat Bayern* EU:C:2012:342, [2015] IL Pr 29—a Brussels I Regulation case.

[131] See Sections 2, 3 and 4 of Chapter III of the Recast, the Civil Jurisdiction and Judgments Order, SI 2001/3929 (as amended by SI 2014/2947), Art 3 and sch 1, paras 2–6 and CPR, Part 74.

[132] Art 41(1) of the Recast; 145/86 *Hoffmann v Krieg* [1988] ECR 645.

[133] Art 41(1).

[134] Arts 42 and 53 and Annex I. For provisions on translation and transliteration of documents, see Art 57.

[135] The party seeking enforcement cannot be required to have an authorised representative in the Member State addressed unless such a representative is mandatory irrespective of the nationality or domicile of the parties (for conditions that any sanction for breach of this requirement has to meet see Case 198/85 *Carron v Germany* [1986] ECR 2437, in particular [14]; Hartley (1987) 12 ELR 64); nor can that party be required to have a postal address in that Member State: Art 41(3).

[136] No security, bond or deposit can be required of the party seeking enforcement on the ground that he is a foreign national or that he is not domiciled or resident in the Member State addressed: Art 56.

[137] Art 54(1). See also Recital 28.

[138] Art 54(1).

[139] Recital 28.

carry out the adaptation, but the Regulation provides for a safeguard by providing that any party may challenge the adaption of the measure or order before a court.[140]

In England, a judgment to be enforced under the Recast is, for the purposes of its enforcement, of the same force and effect, and the enforcing court has in relation to enforcement the same powers, and proceedings for or with respect to its enforcement may be taken, as if the judgment had been originally given by the enforcing court.[141] The reasonable costs or expenses of and incidental to its enforcement are recoverable as if they were sums recoverable under the judgment.[142] The debt resulting from enforcement of a judgment under the Recast carries interest if the judgment provides for the payment of a sum of money and interest on that sum is recoverable at a particular rate and from a particular date or time in accordance with the law of the Member State of origin and the terms of the judgment.[143] With regard to adaptation, the court may make an adaptation order on its own initiative or on an application by any party.[144] The application or a challenge to the adaptation of any measure without an adaptation order is to be made to the High Court.[145]

(b) Application for refusal of enforcement

Prior to the first enforcement measure, the certificate of the court of origin established under the Recast will be served on the person against whom enforcement is sought, accompanied by the judgment, if not already served on that person.[146] These documents are to be served "in reasonable time" before the first enforcement measure.[147] The service must be made in accordance with the procedural rules of the Member State addressed.[148] Where the person against whom enforcement is sought is domiciled in a Member State other than the Member State of origin, he has the right to request a translation of the judgment in order to contest its enforcement if it is not written in or accompanied by a translation into a language which he understands or the official language of the place where he is domiciled.[149] No measures of enforcement may be taken other than protective measures until that translation has been provided.[150] In order not to undermine protective measures, the provisions regarding service and translation do not apply to the enforcement of a protective measure in a judgment or where the person seeking enforcement proceeds to protective measures.[151]

An application for refusal of enforcement is submitted to the court which the Member State concerned has communicated to the Commission as the court being competent for this.[152] In England, this is the court in which the judgment is being enforced or, if the judgment

---

[140] Art 54(2).

[141] See the Civil Jurisdiction and Judgments Order, SI 2001/3929 (as amended by SI 2014/2947), Art 3 and Sch 1, para 2(2). See *Noirhomme v Walklate* [1992] 1 Lloyd's Rep 427 at 431—on the equivalent provision in relation to the Brussels Convention (s 4(3) of the Civil Jurisdiction and Judgments Act 1982) and which suggests that there is a discretionary power to order a stay.

[142] See the Civil Jurisdiction and Judgments Order, SI 2001/3929 (as amended by SI 2014/2947), Art 3 and Sch 1, para 2(1).

[143] See the Civil Jurisdiction and Judgments Order, SI 2001/3929 (as amended by SI 2014/2947), Art 3 and Sch 1, para 5.

[144] CPR, r 74.11A(2).

[145] CPR, r 74.11A(4).

[146] Art 43(1) of the Recast.

[147] Recital (32).

[148] See Case C-3/05 *Verdoliva v JM Van der Hoeven BV* [2006] ECR I-1579—a Brussels Convention case.

[149] Art 43(2).

[150] Ibid.

[151] Art 43(3). But a protective measure that has been granted in *ex parte* proceedings and where the judgment has not been served on the defendant cannot be recognised and enforced under the Recast: see Art 2(a).

[152] Art 47(1). The communication is made pursuant to Art 75(a). The relevant information is published on the website of the European Judicial Network: <https://e-justice.europa.eu>.

debtor is not aware of any proceedings relating to enforcement, the High Court.[153] The procedure, in so far as it is not covered by the Recast, is governed by the law of the Member State addressed.[154] The Recast lays down requirements as to the documents to be provided to the court[155] and certain limitations regarding the representation of the party seeking refusal of enforcement.[156] No time limit is laid down for the application for refusal of enforcement to be submitted. The court will decide on the application for refusal of enforcement without delay.[157] The party seeking refusal of enforcement may also apply to have the enforcement proceedings stayed, limited to protective measures, or to have the enforcement made conditional on the provision of security pending the challenge.[158]

The decision on an application for refusal of enforcement[159] may be appealed against by either party.[160] The appeal is lodged with the court which the Member State concerned has communicated to the Commission as being competent for this.[161] In England, the appeal must be made to the High Court in accordance with its rules of procedure.[162] The decision given on appeal[163] may only be contested by a further appeal where the courts with which any such further appeal is to be lodged have been communicated to the Commission as being competent for this.[164] In England, such further appeal is possible on a point of law to the Court of Appeal or to the Supreme Court (if there is an appeal direct from the High Court to the Supreme Court under the leap-frog procedure in the Administration of Justice Act 1969).[165] The Recast does not impose a requirement that the court will decide on an appeal or further appeal without delay.

An application for refusal of enforcement can be submitted only by the person against whom enforcement is sought and not by an interested third party.[166] In *Deutsche Genossenschaftsbank*

---

[153] See CPR, r 74.7A(1).

[154] Art 47(2) of the Recast.

[155] The applicant must provide a copy of the judgment and, where necessary, its translation or transliteration. The court may dispense with the production of those documents if it already possesses them or if it considers it unreasonable to require the applicant to provide them, in which case it may require the other party to provide them: Art 47(3).

[156] The party seeking refusal of enforcement cannot be required to have an authorised representative in the Member State addressed unless such a representative is mandatory irrespective of the nationality or domicile of the parties (for conditions that any sanction for breach of this requirement has to meet see Case 198/85 *Carron v Germany* [1986] ECR 2437, in particular [14]; Hartley (1987) 12 ELR 64); nor can that party be required to have a postal address in that Member State: Art 47(3).

[157] Art 48.

[158] Art 44(1) and Recital (31). For English procedural rules on relief against enforcement under the Recast, see CPR, r 74.7B.

[159] This decision does not include a preliminary or interlocutory order (see Case 258/83 *Brennero v Wendel GmbH* [1984] ECR 3971; Hartley (1986) 11 ELR 95—a Brussels Convention case). Nor does it include a decision under Art 51(1), infra, pp 647–9, relating to a stay of proceedings or provision of security on the ground that an ordinary appeal has been lodged against the judgment in the Member State of origin or that the time for such an appeal has not yet expired (see Case C-183/90 *BJ Van Dalfsen v B Van Loon* [1991] ECR I-4743; Briggs (1991) 11 YEL 530; Case C-432/93 *Société d'Informatique Service Réalisation Organisation (SISRO) v Ampersand Software BV* [1995] ECR I-2269; Briggs (1995) 15 YEL 506; Collier [1996] CLJ 8; Hartley (1996) ELR 169—Brussels Convention cases).

[160] Art 49(1).

[161] Art 49(2). The communication is made pursuant to Art 75(b). The relevant information is published on the website of the European Judicial Network: <https://e-justice.europa.eu>.

[162] For English procedural rules on appeal against a decision on an application for refusal of enforcement, see CPR, r 74.7A(2)–(5).

[163] See supra, fn 159.

[164] Art 50 of the Recast. The communication is made pursuant to Art 75(c). The relevant information is published on the website of the European Judicial Network: <https://e-justice.europa.eu>.

[165] See Civil Jurisdiction and Judgments Order, SI 2001/3929 (as amended by SI 2014/2947), Art 3 and Sch 1, para 4.

[166] Art 46 of the Recast.

v Brasserie du Pêcheur SA, a case decided under the Brussels Convention, the Court of Justice held that the right to appeal against an enforcement order under Art 36 of the Convention was only given to the party against whom enforcement was sought and any procedure whereby interested third parties might challenge the enforcement order was excluded, even where such a procedure was available to such third parties under the national law of the Member State in which the enforcement order was granted.[167] But the Court also held that the Convention governed only the procedure for obtaining an enforcement order, not execution itself; accordingly, interested third parties could contest execution by means of the procedures available to them under the law of the state in which execution was levied. Since the Recast only gives the party against whom enforcement is sought the right to commence proceedings for refusal of enforcement, such right is not conferred on interested third parties. But the Recast also provides that the grounds for refusal or of suspension of enforcement under the law of the Member State addressed will apply in so far as they are not incompatible with the grounds for refusing recognition under Article 45.[168] This provision could potentially be relied on to safeguard the interests of third parties in certain cases. An appeal against a decision on an application for refusal of enforcement and a further appeal also cannot be brought by interested third parties.[169]

(f) Grounds for refusal of recognition and enforcement

It is part of the claimant's case when seeking recognition or enforcement to show that the Recast applies, and, in a case of enforcement, that the judgment is enforceable in the Member State of origin. The court or another competent authority in the Member State addressed will check that the documents supplied by the claimant are correct and these documents include evidence that the judgment is indeed enforceable in the Member State in which it was given.[170] The direct enforcement in the Member State addressed of a judgment given in another Member State without a declaration of enforceability (or registration of the judgment) should not jeopardise respect for the rights of the defence. Therefore, the person against whom enforcement is sought can apply for refusal of recognition or enforcement if he considers one of the grounds for refusal of recognition specified in Article 45 to be present.[171] Another ground for refusal of recognition is laid down in Article 72, which safeguards the application of agreements entered into by Member States pursuant to Article 59 of the Brussels Convention. It would be extraordinary if the defendant cannot also raise the question of whether the Recast applies,[172] and whether the judgment is indeed enforceable in the Member State of origin. Articles 45 and 72 set out exhaustively the grounds for refusal of recognition,[173] but since there can be no enforcement without recognition, they are also implicitly grounds for refusal of enforcement. Article 46 spells this out by providing expressly that the grounds specified in Article 45 operate as reasons for refusing enforcement.

---

[167] Case 148/84 [1985] ECR 1981; see also Case C-167/08 *Draka NK Cables Ltd v Omnipol Ltd* [2009] ECR I-3477—a Brussels I Regulation case.

[168] Art 41(2).

[169] Case C-172/91 *Sonntag v Waidmann* [1993] ECR I-1963 at [35]—a Brussels Convention case.

[170] Arts 42(1)(b) and 53 and Annex I. A certificate obtained in accordance with these provisions is evidence that the judgment is enforceable in the Member State of origin, see the Civil Jurisdiction and Judgments Order, SI 2001/3929 (as amended by SI 2014/2947), Art 3 and Sch 1, para 8(1)(b).

[171] Arts 45 and 46 and Recital (29).

[172] See Dicey, Morris and Collins, para 14-240, which regards this as being a drafting error. The defendant can do so under the Brussels Convention, which has a different enforcement procedure, see the Schlosser Report, p 134. The defendant can also raise under the Brussels Convention the issue whether the proper formalities for presenting an application were observed (see *Artic Fish Sales Co Ltd v Adam (No 2)* 1996 SLT 970). This appears to be not possible under the Recast.

[173] See infra, pp 626–43.

A party challenging the enforcement of a foreign judgment is able to invoke, in the same procedure, in addition to the grounds for refusal of recognition provided for in Articles 45 and 72, the grounds for refusal or suspension of enforcement available under the national law of the Member State addressed and within the time-limits laid down in that law; but those grounds will apply in so far as they are not incompatible with the grounds referred to in Article 45.[174] For example, a party challenging enforcement can invoke a national ground for refusal of enforcement that the judgment has been complied with abroad.[175] A national ground for refusal of enforcement is incompatible with the grounds referred to in Article 45 if, for example, it results in a review of the substance of the judgment or of the jurisdiction of the court of origin.

Where a ground for refusal of recognition is established, the judgment will not be recognised or enforced in the Member State addressed. Some of the grounds for refusal of recognition, eg public policy, have a strictly territorial effect. Other grounds, eg lack of natural justice or, where available, lack of jurisdiction by the court of origin, are of general importance and a refusal of recognition of a judgment from another Member State on these grounds should also preclude the recognition or enforcement of that judgment in other Member States. A judgment will not be recognised or enforced in other Member States if it is not enforceable in the Member State of origin. In contrast to this, where the Recast does not apply, it may still be possible for a judgment to be recognised and enforced in another Member State under an existing bilateral treaty or at common law.[176]

Articles 45 and 72 are an obstacle to the free movement of judgments and should, accordingly, be interpreted strictly.[177]

(i) Grounds under Article 45

Article 45 sets out five grounds for refusal of recognition: (i) public policy; (ii) natural justice; (iii) a conflict with a judgment given in the Member State addressed; (iv) a conflict with an earlier judgment given in another Member State or in a non-Member State; (v) a conflict with the jurisdictional provisions in Sections 3, 4, 5 or 6 of Chapter II of the Recast.

(a) Public policy

Article 45(1)(a) provides that the recognition of a judgment shall be refused "if such recognition is manifestly contrary to public policy (ordre public) in the Member State addressed".

(i) Whose definition of the concept of public policy is to be applied?

The wording of Article 45(1)(a) strongly suggests that the court in the Member State addressed is to apply its own concept of public policy when considering this ground for refusal of recognition. Consequently, the decision of the court of one Member State to refuse recognition or enforcement of a judgment from another Member State on the ground of public policy is not binding on the courts of other Member States.[178] However, because of the differences

---

[174] Art 41(2). See also Recital (30).

[175] Cf Case C-139/10 *Prism Investment BV v Jaap Anne van der Meer* [2011] ECR I-9511—a Brussels I Regulation case.

[176] Supra, pp 527–601.

[177] Case C-414/92 *Solo Kleinmotoren GmbH v Boch* [1994] ECR I-2237 at [20], discussed infra, p 639.

[178] See Case C-394/07 *Gambazzi v DaimlerChrysler Canada Inc and CIBC Mellon Trust Co* [2009] ECR I-2563 at [38] (an Italian enforcing court is not bound by a decision of a Swiss court refusing to enforce an English default judgment on the ground of violation of Swiss public policy). But the findings on facts and matters which make the recognition or enforcement of a judgment in a Member State contrary to that state's public policy may give rise to issue estoppel in another Member State: see infra, pp 649–50.

in the meaning of public policy in the separate Member States,[179] it would be most undesirable for national courts to apply their own concept of public policy automatically. National courts are undoubtedly left with some latitude in deciding on the meaning of the concept, but they must give it a meaning which is appropriate in the context of the Recast, and the Court of Justice may intervene if they fail to do so. Thus we are left with the position whereby the court in the Member State addressed determines, according to its own conceptions, what public policy requires, but there are limits to that concept which are subject to review by the Court of Justice.[180] These limits are a matter for interpretation of the Recast.[181]

(ii) What public policy includes

Public policy should only be used in exceptional cases.[182] The word "manifestly" has been added by the Brussels I Regulation, the predecessor of the Recast, to underscore the exceptional nature of this ground for refusal of recognition.[183] The Jenard Report states that public policy should not be used to criticise the *decision* of the court of origin. It is the *recognition* of the judgment rather than the judgment itself which must be contrary to public policy.[184] This negative approach is not particularly helpful in understanding what is included within the concept.[185]

The Schlosser Report envisages that fraud in the proceedings in the Member State of origin can, in some circumstances, come within the public policy exception.[186] However, it also accepts that there are some situations involving allegations of fraud where it would not be appropriate to use public policy as a ground for refusal of recognition. Two situations come to mind. First, where the allegation of fraud has been raised and dismissed in the court of origin, to reopen the matter at the recognition and enforcement stage, in the absence of new evidence, involves both an implicit criticism of the original judgment and going into the substance of the matter. This is prohibited by Article 52.[187] Secondly, where the issue of

---

[179] See generally Lloyd, *Public Policy: A Comparative Study in English and French Law* (1953).

[180] Case C-7/98 *Krombach v Bamberski* [2000] ECR I-1935 at [22]–[23]; Case C-38/98 *Régie Nationale des Usines Renault SA v Maxicar SpA* [2000] ECR I-2973 at [27]–[28]; Case C-394/07 *Gambazzi v DaimlerChrysler Canada Inc and CIBC Mellon Trust Co* [2009] ECR I-2563 at [26]; Case C-420/07 *Apostolides v Orams* [2009] ECR I-3571 at [56]–[57].

[181] Case C-7/98 *Krombach v Bamberski* [2000] ECR I-1935 at [22]–[23].

[182] The Jenard Report, p 44; Case 145/86 *Hoffmann v Krieg* [1988] ECR 645 at [21]; Case C-78/95 *Hendrikman v Magenta Druck & Verlag GmbH* [1996] ECR I-4943 at [23]; the *Krombach* case at [21]; the *Renault* case at [26]; the *Apostolides* case at [55].

[183] See the Explanatory Memorandum in the Proposal for the Brussels I Regulation, Brussels 14 July 1999, COM (1999) 348 final, p 23. The same word was introduced in the earlier Brussels II Convention and then Regulation (Art 15(1)(a) of Council Regulation (EC) No 1347/2000 of 29 May 2000 on jurisdiction and the recognition and enforcement of judgments in matrimonial matters and in matters of parental responsibility for children of both spouses OJ 2000 L 160/19, replaced by Council Regulation (EC) No 2201/2003 of 27 November 2003 concerning jurisdiction and the recognition and enforcement of judgments in matrimonial matters and the matters of parental responsibility OJ 2003 L 338/1 (Brussels II *bis*)).

[184] See the Jenard Report, p 44. In Case 27/81 *Röhr v Ossberger* [1981] ECR 2431, public policy was raised as a defence but the Court of Justice interpreted Art 18 of the Brussels Convention (Art 26 of the Recast) dealing with submission to jurisdiction in such a way that the defence collapsed.

[185] It is, however, useful in ascertaining what is not included, see infra, pp 631–2.

[186] See the Schlosser Report, p 128. There is no provision in the Recast dealing expressly with fraud; it would, therefore, have to come within Art 45(1)(a) if it is to provide a ground for refusal of recognition; cf the English common law rules, supra, pp 568–73. For fraud and public policy in the area of recognition of foreign divorces, see infra, pp 1004 and 1030–3. An example coming within the public policy exception suggested by English lawyers is multiple damages under the Protection of Trading Interests Act 1980, discussed supra, pp 553–5; see Beaumont and McEleavy, *Anton's Private International Law*, paras 9.45–9.49; Briggs 2014, para 6.66; Briggs 2015, para 7.12, fn 131; Dickinson and Lein (eds), para 13.296, fn 432; Hartley, p 89; Stone (1983) 32 ICLQ 477, 480–1.

[187] *Interdesco SA v Nullifire Ltd* [1992] 1 Lloyd's Rep 180 at 187. Cf the English common law decisions on fraud discussed supra, pp 568–73. On Art 52 see infra, p 644.

fraud *could* have been raised in the Member State of origin, or can still be raised there, it is questionable whether fraud should be available as a ground for refusal of recognition under Article 45(1)(a). Indeed, Phillips J in *Interdesco SA v Nullifire Ltd*,[188] a case decided under the Brussels Convention, refused to allow the defence of fraud in this situation. To deny a party a right to invoke fraud as a ground for refusal of recognition in these circumstances encourages persons who want to raise the question of fraud to do so in the Member State of origin,[189] which is the best place for deciding the issue. It is best to confine public policy in cases of fraud to the situation in which (i) there is evidence of fraud which was unavailable and unexamined earlier on in the proceedings, and (ii) the evidence arises at such a late stage that it cannot be raised on appeal in the Member State of origin, and the only court in which the fraud can be considered is the court in the Member State addressed.[190] However, since all the Member States of the European Union are also parties to the European Convention on Human Rights, whose Article 6 guarantees the right to a fair trial, it seems unlikely that these requirements will often, if ever, be met in practice.

Moving beyond the issue of fraud, in *Krombach v Bamberski*[191] the Court of Justice held that recourse to public policy can be envisaged only where recognition or enforcement would be at variance to an unacceptable degree with the legal order of the Member State addressed by infringing a fundamental principle. The infringement would have to constitute a manifest breach of a rule of law regarded as essential in the legal order of the state in which enforcement is sought or a right recognised as being fundamental within that legal order.[192] In determining whether rights are fundamental the Court of Justice took into account the constitutional traditions common to the Member States and the case law of the European Court of Human Rights.[193] It followed that a German enforcing court was entitled to hold that a refusal by a French judgment-granting court to hear the defence by counsel of an accused person, who was not present at the hearing of a civil claim based on a criminal offence, constituted a manifest breach of a fundamental right.[194] In *Gambazzi v DaimlerChrysler Canada Inc and CIBC Mellon Trust Co*[195] the Court of Justice was concerned with the enforcement in Italy of an English default judgment given after the defendant had been excluded from the proceedings for failure to comply with freezing and disclosure injunctions. The Court held that the

---

[188] [1992] 1 Lloyd's Rep 180; approved by the Court of Appeal in *Société d'Informatique Service Réalisation Organisation v Ampersand Software BV* [1994] IL Pr 55 at 60, CA; *Artic Fish Sales Co Ltd v Adam (No 2)* 1996 SLT 970; *Banco Nacional de Comercio Exterior SNC v Empresa de Telecomunicaciones de Cuba SA* [2007] EWHC 2322 (Comm) at [19], [2007] IL Pr 59. See also *Turczynski v Wilde and Partners* [2003] IL Pr 64, French cour de cassation.

[189] See the Schlosser Report, p 128.

[190] See Case C-681/13 *Diageo Brands BV v Simiramida-04 EOOD* EU:C:2015:471 at [64] and [68], [2016] Ch 147, according to which the requirement to use the legal remedies in the Member State of origin would not apply where specific circumstances make this too difficult or impossible.

[191] Case C-7/98 [2000] ECR I-1935; Lowenfeld, in Einhorn and Siehr (eds), *International Cooperation Through Private International Law: Essays in Memory of Peter E Nygh* (2004) 229; Peel (2001) 20 YEL 347; van Hoek (2001) 38 CML Rev 1011; followed in Case C-341/04 *Eurofood IFSC Ltd* [2006] ECR I-3813. See generally on human rights and public policy Fawcett, Ní Shúilleabháin and Shah, *Human Rights and Private International Law* (2016), paras 5.112–5.198.

[192] The *Krombach* case at [37]; Case C-38/98 *Régie Nationale des Usines Renault SA v Maxicar SpA* [2000] ECR I-2973 at [30]; Case C-394/07 *Gambazzi v DaimlerChrysler Canada Inc and CIBC Mellon Trust Co* [2009] ECR I-2563 at [27]; Case C-420/07 *Apostolides v Orams* [2009] ECR I-3571 at [59].

[193] The *Krombach* case at [25] and [39]; Case C-394/07 *Gambazzi v DaimlerChrysler Canada Inc and CIBC Mellon Trust Co* [2009] ECR I-2563 at [28]. See also Art 47 of the Charter of Fundamental Rights of the European Union, which is addressed to the Member States when they are implementing EU law, including by applying the Brussels I Recast: see Case C-112/13 *A v B* EU:C:2014:2195 at [51].

[194] The *Krombach* case at [40]. The European Court of Human Rights found that the French proceedings had violated the defendant's right to a fair trial: *Krombach v France*, 13 February 2001.

[195] Case C-394/07 [2009] ECR I-2563.

court of the Member State in which enforcement was sought could refuse enforcement on the ground of public policy if, following a comprehensive assessment of the proceedings as a whole and in the light of all the circumstances, it appeared that the exclusion measure constituted a manifest and disproportionate infringement of the defendant's right to be heard.[196] Similarly, in *Trade Agency Ltd v Seramico Investments Ltd*,[197] a case that concerned the enforcement in Latvia of an English default judgment that did not contain judicial reasoning, that is, an assessment of the subject-matter, of the basis of the action and an argument of its merits, the Court of Justice held that enforcement could be refused if it appeared that the judgment is a manifest and disproportionate breach of the defendant's right to a fair trial, in particular in the light of whether the defendant was able to bring an appropriate and effective appeal.[198] The judgment in the *Trade Agency* case can be criticised on the basis that it allows a defendant who has no defence to advance and who chooses not to contest the original English proceedings and, therefore, has a default judgment rendered against him, to resist the recognition and enforcement of the judgment in other Member States rather than to seek to set it aside in the country of origin. This also runs contrary to the policy that uncontested judgments should be enforceable more easily than other judgments.[199] Claimants are therefore advised to invite the court to conduct a trial of the claim before giving a default judgment, so that the court can give a judgment on the merits, or to apply for summary, rather than default, judgment.[200] Finally, in *Meroni v Recoletos Ltd*[201] the Court of Justice held that the recognition and enforcement, in Latvia, of a freezing order issued in England without a prior hearing of a third party whose rights might be affected was not to be refused in so far as that third party was entitled to assert his rights before the court of origin.

Turning to the decisions of national courts on the use of public policy in the context of the right to a fair trial, the Court of Appeal has held that a defendant, who was unaware that Dutch proceedings that had been stayed for twelve years had been reactivated until after the time for an appeal had passed, had manifestly not received the fair trial that Article 6 of the European Convention on Human Rights required. Accordingly, recognition of the Dutch judgment would be contrary to the public policy of England.[202] However, this was an exceptional case. The English courts apply a strong but not irrebuttable presumption that the procedures of other signatories to the Convention are compliant with Article 6.[203] The constitution, procedures and conduct of a court of another Member State may involve the infringement of the defendant's rights under Article 6 but it is necessary to look at the foreign proceedings as a whole, including any appeals by way of a rehearing before courts which are

---

[196] Ibid, at [48]. The Court of Appeal in Milan, by a decision of 24 November 2010, found that the English judgment was not contrary to Italian public policy: see Cuniberti, 'Gambazzi Looses [sic] in Milan', available at <http://conflictoflaws.net/2011/gambazzi-looses-in-milan/>; the Swiss Federal Supreme Court, on the other hand, refused enforcement of the English judgment on the ground of violation of Swiss public policy by a decision of 9 November 2004 (Case 4P082/2004).

[197] Case C-619/10 EU:C:2012:531.

[198] The Latvian Supreme Court found that the English judgment was not contrary to Latvian public policy: see Rudevska (2014) 34 IPRax 85. See also Case C-302/13 *flyLAL—Lithuanian Airlines AS v Starptautiskā Lidosta Rīga VAS and Air Baltic Corp AS* EU:C:2014:2319, [2015] IL Pr 2.

[199] See the European Enforcement Order Regulation, discussed infra, pp 656–9.

[200] See *Berliner Bank v Karageorgis* [1996] 1 Lloyd's Rep 426; *Messer Griesheim GmbH v Goyal MG Gases Pvt Ltd* [2006] EWHC 79 (Comm), [2006] 1 CLC 283.

[201] Case C-559/14 EU:C:2016:349, [2017] QB 85.

[202] *Maronier v Larmer* [2002] EWCA Civ 774 at [37]–[38], [2003] QB 620; Briggs (2002) 73 BYBIL 468; similarly, *Laserpoint Ltd v Prime Minister of Malta* [2016] EWHC 1820 (QB). Cf *Citibank NA v Rafidian Bank* [2003] EWHC 1950, [2003] 2 All ER (Comm) 1054. For France, see *Stolzenberg v Daimler Chrysler Canada Inc* [2005] IL Pr 24, French cour de cassation.

[203] *Maronier v Larmer* [2002] EWCA Civ 774 at [25], [2003] QB 620.

compliant with Article 6.[204] This would mean that the earlier infringement has been rectified or that it could be said that no infringement has ever occurred.[205] Where the factors relied on as being contrary to public policy (including bias, long duration of the trial and various procedural inadequacies) are factors which the foreign court has already considered, or which could have been raised there, then the foreign court must be treated as the best place for them to be raised and determined.[206] To do otherwise would be contrary to the spirit of the Brussels regime and, where issues of unfairness are raised which are capable of being the subject of appeal in the foreign jurisdiction, an enforcing court is much less able to assess them than the original court which is familiar with its own forms of procedure.[207] There is moreover a highly unattractive element in a defendant not raising points which he could have raised in the original jurisdiction, by way of appeal against the judgment and only seeking to raise those matters on enforcement.[208]

The Court of Appeal has also held that if a defendant, after receiving notice of an anti-suit injunction granted by an English court restraining proceedings in another Member State, nevertheless continues with those proceedings and obtains a judgment on the merits in his favour, this will be refused recognition in England on the ground of public policy.[209] However, it is strongly arguable that this is raising the question of the jurisdiction of the court of origin and public policy cannot be used in this situation.[210] Perhaps more importantly, the practical significance of this use of public policy has been much reduced by the fact that it is now clear that the grant of such an injunction will be incompatible with the Recast.[211] The High Court held that it would be contrary to public policy to recognise an order of a foreign court which was no longer in force in its original form in the country of origin and which deprives the judgment debtor resident in England of the ability to spend any money for any purpose.[212] French courts have held that it is contrary to the French concept of public policy to recognise a foreign judgment which does not state the reasoning on which it is based[213] or an English judgment for costs set at a disproportionately high level.[214] German courts have refused the enforcement of an Italian judgment ordering a school teacher to pay damages to the family members of a pupil who suffered a fatal accident during a school trip to Italy on the ground that under German law the social security system replaces the personal liability

---

[204] *SA Marie Brizzard et Roger International v William Grant & Sons Ltd (No 2)* 2002 SLT 1365 at [67].
[205] Ibid.
[206] *Smith v Huertas* [2015] EWHC 3745 (Comm) at [21].
[207] Ibid.
[208] Ibid.
[209] *Philip Alexander Securities and Futures Ltd v Bamberger* [1997] IL Pr 73 at 115, CA; *Through Transport Mutual Insurance Association (Eurasia) Ltd v New India Assurance Co Ltd (The "Hari Bhum")* [2003] EWHC 3158 (Comm) at [42], [2004] 1 Lloyd's Rep 206; appeal allowed in part but without discussion of the recognition and enforcement point [2004] EWCA (Civ) 1598, [2005] 1 All ER (Comm) 715.
[210] See the opinion of AG Ruiz-Jarabo Colomer in Case C-159/02 *Turner v Grovit* [2004] ECR I-0365 at [36], who was clearly of the view that public policy could not be used; *National Navigation Co v Endesa Generacion SA (The Wadi Sudr)* [2009] EWCA Civ 1397 at [60]–[61], [2010] 2 All ER (Comm) 1243.
[211] Supra, pp 475–82.
[212] *D'Hoker v Tritan Enterprises* [2009] EWHC 949 (QB) at [12]–[15]; Briggs (2009) 80 BYBIL 583.
[213] *Sàrl Polypetrol v Société Générale Routière* [1993] IL Pr 107 (it is necessary for the claimant to produce documents which are equivalent to the missing reasoning), French cour de cassation; *Société de Transports Internationaux Dehbashi v Gerling Konzern* [1996] IL Pr 104, CA Poitiers; *Pordea v Times Newspapers Ltd* [2000] IL Pr 763, French cour de cassation; *Society of Lloyd's v X* [2009] IL Pr 12, French cour de cassation. But cf *Materiel Auxiliaire d'Informatique v Printed Forms Equipment Ltd* [2006] IL Pr 803, French cour de cassation and see Cuniberti (2008) 57 ICLQ 25 and Dicey, Morris and Collins, para 14-226. See also Case C-619/10 *Trade Agency Ltd v Seramico Investments Ltd* EU:C:2012:531, discussed supra, p 629.
[214] *Pordea v Times Newspapers Ltd* [2000] IL Pr 763, French cour de cassation; see also *Coburn v The Auxiliary Insurance Fund for Covering Liability Arising from Car Accidents* [2008] IL Pr 9, Greek Supreme Court.

of a teacher at a state school for injuries suffered by students.[215] In a recent decision, the Irish High Court invoked public policy to refuse the enforcement of an English judgment in respect of a gambling debt.[216]

(iii) What public policy does not include

It is easier to say what public policy does not encompass than what it does. Since the concept of public policy seeks to protect legal interests that are expressed through a rule of law and not purely economic interests, the mere invocation of serious economic consequences of the recognition or enforcement of a foreign judgment in the Member State addressed cannot constitute an infringement of public policy.[217] As has already been mentioned, the Jenard Report states that public policy should not be used to criticise the decision of the court which gave the judgment.[218] Neither can it be applied to review the jurisdiction of the court of origin.[219] This prevents it being used to criticise exorbitant jurisdiction taken against defendants domiciled in non-Member States,[220] or even in Member States.[221] The court in the Member State addressed cannot refuse recognition solely on the ground that there is a discrepancy between the legal rule applied in the Member State of origin and that which would have been applied by the court in the Member State addressed if it had been seised of the matter.[222] This is because Article 52 prohibits a foreign judgment being reviewed as to its substance. It would be different if recognition would involve the infringement of a fundamental principle as explained in the *Krombach* case. But this will only happen in the most exceptional cases of error.[223] There was no such infringement in *Régie Nationale des Usines Renault SA v Maxicar SpA*.[224] It was alleged that the judgment-granting court made an error of European Union law by recognising the existence of certain intellectual property rights, rights which would not be recognised in the judgment-recognising state. The question then arose as to whether recognition of the judgment would be against public policy. The Court of Justice held that, in this situation, there was no manifest breach of a rule of law regarded as essential in the legal order of the state in which recognition was sought.[225] A similar decision was reached in *Diageo Brands BV v Simiramida-04 EOOD*,[226] in which case the judgment-debtor argued that the enforcement of a judgment should be refused because the court of origin allegedly misapplied EU law on trade marks. The Court of Justice held that the alleged

---

[215] German Federal Supreme Court (BGH), 16 September 1993, IX ZB 82/90 BGHZ 123, 226, a case decided following the decision of the Court of Justice in Case C-172/91 *Sonntag v Waidmann* [1993] ECR I-1963.

[216] *Sporting Index Ltd v O'Shea* [2015] IEHC 407. The court relied on s 36 of the Irish Gambling and Lotteries Act 1956, which prohibits the enforcement of any gambling contract in Ireland.

[217] Case C-302/13 *flyLAL—Lithuanian Airlines AS v Starptautiskā Lidosta Rīga VAS and Air Baltic Corp AS* EU:C:2014:2319, [2015] IL Pr 2.

[218] At p 44. This prevents an examination of the law and procedure of the court of origin; it surely does not prevent the court in the Member State addressed from considering new evidence as to, for example, an allegation that the trial judge was bribed.

[219] Art 45(3); see the opinion of the Advocate General in Case 27/81 *Röhr v Ossberger* [1981] ECR 2431 at [3].

[220] The Jenard Report, p 44.

[221] Case C-7/98 *Krombach v Bamberski* [2000] ECR I-1935 at [34].

[222] Ibid, at [36]; Case C-38/98 *Régie Nationale des Usines Renault SA v Maxicar SpA* [2000] ECR I-2973 at [29]; Case C-420/07 *Apostolides v Orams* [2009] ECR I-3571 at [58].

[223] See the opinion of AG Alber in Case C-38/98 *Régie Nationale des Usines Renault SA v Maxicar SpA* [2000] ECR I-2973 at [67].

[224] Case C-38/98 [2000] ECR I-2973; Peel (2001) 20 YEL 347. See *Viking Line ABP v The International Transport Workers' Federation* [2005] EWHC 1222 (Comm), [2006] IL Pr 4 at [78]–[81].

[225] The *Renault* case at [34].

[226] Case C-681/13 EU:C:2015:471, [2016] Ch 147.

violation of the provisions of Directive 89/104[227] did not represent a manifest breach of a rule of law regarded as being essential in the EU legal order and therefore in the legal order of the Member State addressed.[228] In such cases, it must be considered that the system of legal remedies in the Member State of origin, together with the preliminary ruling procedure provided for in Article 267 of the Treaty on the Functioning of the European Union, affords a sufficient guarantee to individuals against misapplication of EU law or national law.[229] Furthermore, recognition and enforcement cannot be refused on the ground that a judgment concerning land situated in an area of the Member State of origin over which its government does not exercise effective control cannot, as a practical matter, be enforced where the land is situated.[230] Public policy cannot be used in situations covered elsewhere in Article 45.[231] Accordingly, this ground for refusal of recognition will not protect a defendant whose rights have been infringed by a lack of natural justice as dealt with under Article 45(1)(b) (and therefore that ground applies).[232] But public policy may be used where the requirements of natural justice as laid down in Article 45(1)(b) have been met in circumstances where there has been interference with the defendant's ability to arrange his defence.[233] Nor can public policy be used when the issue is whether a foreign judgment is compatible with a judgment given in the Member State addressed.[234]

In some of the above situations the concept of public policy used in civil law systems would apply,[235] as would the concept of public policy used in common law systems.[236] The fact that Article 45(1)(a) is not intended to apply in these same situations shows the limited nature of public policy as a ground for refusal of recognition under the Recast.

(b) Natural justice

Article 45(1)(b) provides that the recognition of a judgment shall be refused:

> Where the judgment was given in default of appearance, if the defendant was not served with the document which instituted the proceedings or with an equivalent document in sufficient time and in such a way as to enable him to arrange for his defence, unless the defendant failed to commence proceedings to challenge the judgment when it was possible for him to do so.[237]

There is concern that the rights of the defendant should be fully protected by the Recast. When a judgment has been given in default of appearance there is a particular concern as to whether the service on the defendant was such as to give him the opportunity to defend himself properly.[238] Article 45(1)(b) is intended to ensure that a judgment is not

---

[227] First Council Directive 89/104/EEC of 21 December 1988 to approximate the laws of the Member States relating to trade marks OJ 1989 L 40/1, repealed by Directive 2008/95/EC of the European Parliament and of the Council of 22 October 2008 to approximate the laws of the Member States relating to trade marks (codified version) OJ 2008 L 299/25.

[228] The *Diageo Brands* case at [51]–[52] and [68].

[229] Ibid, at [49] and [63]; Case C-38/98 *Régie Nationale des Usines Renault SA v Maxicar SpA* [2000] ECR I-2973 at [33].

[230] Case C-420/07 *Apostolides v Orams* [2009] ECR I-3571 at [62]. See also *Orams v Apostolides* [2010] EWCA Civ 9, [2011] QB 519.

[231] Case C-78/95 *Hendrikman v Magenta Druck & Verlag GmbH* [1996] ECR I-4943 at [23]. See also *Artic Fish Sales Co Ltd v Adam (No 2)* 1996 SLT 970 at 973.

[232] The *Hendrikman* case. See also the opinion of the Advocate General in Case 27/81 *Röhr v Ossberger* [1981] ECR 2431 at [3].

[233] *Re Enforcement of a Judgment (Date Error in Translated Summons)* (Case IX ZB 14/00) [2003] IL Pr 32, German Federal Supreme Court.

[234] Case 145/86 *Hoffmann v Krieg* [1988] ECR 645 at [21]. Art 45(1)(c) deals with this, infra, pp 639–41.

[235] See Forde (1980) 29 ICLQ 259, 272–3.

[236] See supra, pp 132–43 and 573–6.

[237] See generally, the Jenard Report, pp 44–5; Hunnings [1985] JBL 303; Kennett [1992] CJQ 115.

[238] See Art 28(2), discussed supra, pp 309–11. For the position where there is a default judgment, see Art 53 and Annex I at 4.3.

recognised or enforced under the Recast if the defendant has not been given such an opportunity.[239]

(i) The interaction with jurisdictional provisions on natural justice

Where the natural justice safeguards at the jurisdictional stage of proceedings apply under Article 28,[240] Article 45(1)(b) operates as a double check on natural justice, with the court in the Member State addressed examining the same issue that has been examined and decided upon by the court of origin.[241] In this situation, the ground for refusal of recognition under Article 45(1)(b) is only likely to be used in exceptional cases.[242]

Where Article 28 does not apply, eg because the defendant is domiciled in a non-Member State, or is sued in the Member State in which he is domiciled, Article 45(1)(b) provides a check on whether basic requirements of natural justice have been satisfied in the Member State of origin. It is more important to have a check in this situation than in the situation where Article 28 applies, and the ground for refusal of recognition under Article 45(1)(b) is correspondingly more likely to be used. The court of origin may not have even examined the issue of natural justice, and, if it has done so, may only have inadequate procedural safeguards.

(ii) Establishing a lack of natural justice

Article 45(1)(b) has not infrequently been invoked by parties against whom recognition or enforcement has been sought. It comprises the following elements:

(a) The judgment was given in default of appearance

Article 45(1)(b) applies only where the defendant was in default of appearance in the original proceedings. Consequently, it may not be relied upon where the defendant appeared.[243] Appearance should be given an autonomous meaning.[244] But, whatever the definition, if a defendant has neither lodged any formal document with the foreign court (once the proceedings were begun) nor was present when the proceedings came to trial, he cannot be regarded as having appeared.[245] Appearances after the judgment has been given raise particularly difficult problems.

In *Klomps v Michel*[246] a judgment which was treated as being in default of appearance was given in Germany.[247] Subsequently, the defendant raised an objection (based on the service

---

[239] Case 166/80 *Klomps v Michel* [1981] ECR 1593 at [7] and [9]; Case C-123/91 *Minalmet v Brandeis* [1992] ECR 1-5661 at [18]; Case C-172/91 *Sonntag v Waidmann* [1993] ECR I-1963 at [38]; Case C-474/93 *Hengst Import BV v Campese* [1995] ECR I-2113 at [17]; Case C-78/95 *Hendrikman v Magenta Druck v Verlag GmbH* [1996] ECR I-4943 at [15]; Case C-39/02 *Maersk Olie & Gas v Firma Mm de Haan en W de Boer* [2004] ECR I-9657 at [55].

[240] Supra, pp 309–11.

[241] Case 228/81 *Pendy Plastic Products v Pluspunkt* [1982] ECR 2723; Case 166/80 *Klomps v Michel* [1981] ECR 1593; Case C-522/03 *Scania Finance SA v Rockinger Spezialfabrik für Anhängerkupplungen GmbH & Co* [2005] ECR I-8639; Case C-283/05 *ASML Netherlands BV v Semiconductor Industry Services GmbH (SEMIS)* [2006] ECR I-12041; Case C-619/10 *Trade Agency Ltd v Seramico Investments Ltd* EU:C:2012:531. See also Hartley, pp 90–2; Hill and Chong, para 13.3.19.

[242] See infra.

[243] Case C-172/91 *Sonntag v Waidmann* [1993] ECR I-1963 at [39]. Art 45(1)(b) does not apply to a case like Case C-394/07 *Gambazzi v DaimlerChrysler Canada Inc and CIBC Mellon Trust Co* [2009] ECR I-2563, where the court enters a judgment as if the defendant, who has entered appearance, was in default.

[244] Case C-78/95 *Hendrikman v Magenta Druck & Verlag GmbH* [1996] ECR I-4943; Briggs (1996) 16 YEL 606; Hartley (1997) 22 ELR 364.

[245] *Tavoulareas v Tsavliris (No 2)* [2006] EWCA Civ 1772 at [11]–[16], [2007] 1 WLR 1573.

[246] Case 166/80 [1981] ECR 1593; Hartley (1982) 7 ELR 419.

[247] The case involved a German order said to be equivalent to one given in default.

of documents) to this judgment before the same German court which had given the judgment in default. This was held to be inadmissible because the time for lodging objections had expired. A Dutch court which was asked to enforce the German judgment referred a number of issues of interpretation of Article 27(2) of the Brussels Convention (equivalent of Article 45(1)(b) of the Recast) to the Court of Justice, including whether, in these circumstances, a judgment is to be regarded as given in default.

The Court of Justice held, inter alia, that the judgment was given in default of appearance, despite the fact that the defendant had appeared to have it set aside. The reasoning of the Court was that the defendant had not submitted a defence as to substance, and since the objection he did raise was held to be inadmissible, this left the original decision in default intact. In *Maersk Olie and Gas AS v Firma M de Haan en W de Boer*[248] the defendant "appeared" to appeal against a judgment given in default of appearance in order to challenge the jurisdiction of the court but without objecting to default of service of the document instituting the proceedings. The Court of Justice held that this cannot be treated as equivalent to an appearance by the defendant for the purposes of Article 45(1)(b).[249]

There can also be problems where a claim for compensation is joined to criminal proceedings. In *Sonntag v Waidmann*[250] the Court of Justice, adopting an autonomous interpretation of the concept of appearance, held that a defendant is deemed to have appeared if he answered at the trial, through counsel of his own choice, to the criminal charges but did not express a view on the civil claim, on which oral argument was also submitted in the presence of his counsel. It is possible, though, for the defendant to decline to appear in the civil action when answering the criminal charges. Technically there may be an appearance by the defendant according to the law of the Member State of origin in that lawyers purporting to represent the defendant appeared before the court. Nonetheless, Article 45(1)(b) still applies if the proceedings were instituted without the defendant's knowledge and lawyers appeared on his behalf but without his authority (eg having been appointed by business associates of the defendant), since, in such circumstances, the defendant is powerless to defend himself.[251]

(b) The defendant was not served

This is a vital question and one that cannot pass unnoticed at the time when recognition or enforcement is sought. Article 53[252] requires the party seeking recognition or enforcement to produce a certificate issued by the court of origin which contains information on whether and, if so, when the party in default was served with the document instituting the proceedings or an equivalent document. The court in the Member State addressed, however, has jurisdiction to verify whether this information is consistent with the evidence presented to it.[253]

The Brussels I Regulation, the predecessor of the Recast, altered the natural justice defence so as to no longer require that the defendant was "duly" served.[254] This required reference to the legislation of the state in which the judgment was given and to its conventions on

---

[248] Case C-39/02 [2004] ECR I-9657.

[249] Ibid, at [53]–[57]; cf *Tavoulareas v Tsavliris (No 2)* [2006] EWCA Civ 1772 at [12], [2007] 1 WLR 1573; Briggs (2006) 77 BYBIL 593.

[250] Case C-172/91 [1993] ECR I-1963; Briggs (1993) 13 YEL 517; Hartley (1994) 19 ELR 538; Plender (1993) 64 BYBIL 555.

[251] Case C-78/95 *Hendrikman v Magenta Druck & Verlag GmbH* [1996] ECR I-4943. See also Case C-112/13 *A v B* EU:C:2014:2195; *Re Enforcement of a Guarantee* [2001] IL Pr 29, German Federal Supreme Court.

[252] See also Annex I, 4.3.

[253] Case C-619/10 *Trade Agency Ltd v Seramico Investments Ltd* EU:C:2012:531—a Brussels I Regulation case.

[254] This is still required under Art 27(2) of the Brussels Convention, see infra, pp 652–3.

service.[255] The requirements of due service and service in sufficient time constituted two separate and concurrent safeguards for a defendant who failed to appear. If a document was not duly served, this in itself triggered the operation of the natural justice defence, even if the defendant had sufficient time to arrange for his defence.[256] The intention under the Brussels I Regulation, and now the Recast, was that this should no longer be so. It is enough for the defendant in the Member State of origin to have been served with notice in sufficient time and in such a way as to enable him to arrange for his defence.[257] In other words, it is required that the rights of the defendant are effectively respected.[258] This means, for example, that a mere formal irregularity in the service procedure, as where it is not accompanied by a required translation, will not debar recognition or enforcement under the Recast,[259] provided the service was in sufficient time and in such a way as to enable the defendant to arrange his defence. A formal irregularity, which does not affect the capacity of the defendant to understand the elements of the claim and his capacity to defend his rights, can be ignored.[260]

Article 45(1)(b) requires that the defendant was "served" and it is not enough that he was merely notified of the proceedings.[261] This raises the difficult question of what constitutes "service" in the present context. This could be referring to service according to the procedures of the Member State of origin. However, certain irregularities in these procedures will not be fatal.[262] An alternative view, which has found favour with the Court of Appeal, is that this refers to service according to the European Union Service Regulation.[263] But given the purpose of the rewording of Article 45(1)(b), a mere formal irregularity in compliance with that Regulation should not be enough to deny that there has been service. "Service" should be widely construed and the really important question is whether this was in sufficient time and in such a way as to enable the defendant to arrange his defence.

In *Klomps v Michel*[264] the Court of Justice held that Article 27(2) of the Brussels Convention does not require proof that the document instituting the proceedings was actually brought to the knowledge of the defendant. No objection was made to the method of notice employed in that case, although it did not involve personal service on the defendant. The same must be true under the Recast.

---

[255] See the Jenard Report, p 44; Case 166/80 *Klomps v Michel* [1981] ECR 1593 at [15]; Case C-305/88 *Lancray v Peters* [1990] ECR I-2725 at [29]; Case C-39/02 *Maersk Olie & Gas v Firma Mm de Haan en W de Boer* [2004] ECR I-9657 at [60]; Case C-522/03 *Scania Finance SA v Rockinger Spezialfabrik für Anhängerkupplungen GmbH & Co* [2005] ECR I-8639 at [30]—where there is a service convention between the granting and enforcing state due service is determined solely in the light of this.

[256] See Case C-305/88 *Lancray v Peters* [1990] ECR I-2725.

[257] See the Explanatory Memorandum in the Proposal for the Brussels I Regulation, p 23.

[258] Case C-283/05 *ASML Netherlands BV v Semiconductor Industry Services GmbH (SEMIS)* [2006] ECR I-12041 at [20].

[259] See the Explanatory Memorandum in the Proposal for the Brussels I Regulation, p 23; Case C-283/05 *ASML Netherlands BV v Semiconductor Industry Services GmbH (SEMIS)* [2006] ECR I-12041 at [41]–[47]. But it will do so under the Brussels Convention, see Case C-305/88 *Lancray v Peters* [1990] ECR I-2725.

[260] AG Ruiz-Jarabo Colomer in Case C-283/05 *ASML Netherlands BV v Semiconductor Industry Services GmbH (SEMIS)* [2006] ECR I-12041 at [69].

[261] Ibid, the decision of the Court of Justice at [41]–[47]; ibid, the opinion of AG Ruiz-Jarabo Colomer at [65]; *Tavoulareas v Tsavliris (No 2)* [2006] EWCA Civ 1772, [2007] 1 WLR 1573. See Dicey, Morris and Collins, para 14-232; Dickinson and Lein (eds), para 13.328; Layton and Mercer, para 26.026. See also *Re the Enforcement of an Austrian Judgment* (Case 3 W 91/03) [2005] IL Pr 29, Oberlandesgericht (Appeal Court), Düsseldorf.

[262] Layton and Mercer, para 26.052.

[263] Regulation (EC) No 1393/2007 of the European Parliament and of the Council of 13 November 2007 on the service in the Member States of judicial and extrajudicial documents in civil and commercial matters (service of documents) OJ 2007 L 324/79. See *Tavoulareas v Tsavliris (No 2)* [2006] EWCA Civ 1772 at [8], [2007] 1 WLR 1573.

[264] Case 166/80 [1981] ECR 1593.

(c) With the document which instituted the proceedings or with an equivalent document

In *Klomps v Michel*, which was a case decided under the Brussels Convention, it was held that this was referring to "any document . . . service of which enables the plaintiff, under the law of the State of the court in which the judgment was given to obtain, in default of appropriate action taken by the defendant, a decision capable of being recognised and enforced under the provisions of the Convention".[265] This included an order for payment under German law (*Zahlungsbefehl*), but not a subsequent German enforcement order (*Vollstreckungsbefehl*); the latter was the judgment that was enforceable under the Convention and therefore could not be the document which instituted the proceedings. A different and rather better definition, in that it relates to the purpose of what is now Article 45(1)(b), was adopted by the Court of Justice in the subsequent case of *Hengst Import BV v Campese*,[266] which referred to "the document or documents which must be duly and timeously served on the defendant in order to enable him to assert his rights before an enforceable judgment is given in the State of origin".[267] The document in this case encompassed a summary order for the payment of money under Italian law (*decreto ingiuntivo*), which, together with the application instituting the proceedings, was served on the defendant.[268] This started time running for the defendant to oppose the order, which was not enforceable before the expiry of the time limit. The question of how much detail the document must contain, eg whether it must mention the amount of a claim, has been raised before the Court of Justice but left unanswered.[269] It is necessary to look at the procedural law of the Member State of origin to determine whether the proceedings before the court of first instance and the proceedings on appeal are separate proceedings; the High Court has held that, under Italian law, proceedings on appeal should be regarded as separate proceedings and the document instituting the proceedings was the notice of appeal, not the writ of summons.[270] The reference to "an equivalent document" encompasses the situation where an order provisionally determining the maximum amount of liability has at first been provisionally adopted by the court at the conclusion of a unilateral procedure, which was then followed by reasoned submissions by both parties.[271]

(d) In sufficient time and in such a way as to enable him to arrange for his defence

It is for the court in the Member State addressed to determine whether service was effected in sufficient time and in such a way as to enable the defendant to arrange for his defence, account being taken of all the facts of the case.[272] The concepts of sufficiency of time and the "way" in which service is effected are dealing with different situations and problems.

In sufficient time   We are concerned here with the situation where there has been service and the defendant has notice which enables him from that point onwards to defend. Where there has been service, it can usually be assumed that the defendant is able to defend from that moment onwards; this can be assumed even though there was no personal service on the defendant (Article 45(1)(b) does not require actual knowledge of the document instituting the proceedings). The question then arises of whether the defendant has *sufficient time*

---

[265] Ibid, at [11].

[266] Case C-474/93 [1995] ECR I-2113; Briggs (1995) 15 YEL 502.

[267] The *Hengst Import BV v Campese* case at [19]. For yet another definition, see Case C-14/07 *Ingenierbüro Weiss & Partner GbR v Industrie-und Handelskammer Berlin* [2008] ECR I-3367 at [64]–[65] and [68].

[268] The Court of Justice would not go into the question of whether the Italian court had made an error of law in granting the order, see infra, p 644.

[269] Case C-172/91 *Sonntag v Waidmann* [1993] ECR I-1963 at [36] and [43].

[270] *Hasberry v Steele*, 25 November 2011, HC.

[271] Case C-39/02 *Maersk Olie & Gas v Firma Mm de Haan en W de Boer* [2004] ECR I-9657 at [59].

[272] See Case 166/80 *Klomps v Michel* [1981] ECR 1593 at [20]; Case 49/84 *Debaecker and Plouvier v Bouwman* [1985] ECR 1779 at [21]; Case C-39/02 *Maersk Olie & Gas v Firma Mm de Haan en W de Boer* [2004] ECR I-9657 at [61].

in which to defend himself. The *time* in question is that available to the defendant for the purposes of preventing the issue of a judgment in default enforceable under the Recast.[273] This involves looking at the procedural law in the Member State of origin. Under German procedural law a valid notice of appearance entered at any time prior to the issue of a default judgment will prevent its issue.[274] The period in question therefore goes right up to the date of issue of the default judgment. In *Klomps v Michel* the judgment in question was the German enforcement order; this meant that the period after it was granted, during which objections could be made, was disregarded. Time will begin to run from the date on which the service of the document instituting the proceedings is effected.

A more difficult question is whether the time available is *sufficient* to prevent the judgment in default being issued. The court in the Member State addressed will have to look at all the circumstances of the case. Of importance in this regard are the method of service used (eg whether there was personal service or substituted service), availability of legal advice, language obstacle etc. In *Klomps v Michel* the Court of Justice seemed to regard sufficiency of time as being solely a question of fact.[275] But it is hard to see how a court could answer the question without having some yardstick to which the facts could be related. The criterion for sufficiency of time could be left to the law of the Member State of origin, or to the law of the Member State addressed, or by having regard to both of these,[276] or it could be left to be determined by an autonomous meaning to be given to the concept. It would be wrong to leave the matter to the law of the Member State of origin, since this would not provide the check on abuse of natural justice which Article 45(1)(b) was designed to achieve. The most effective way of achieving this objective would be to give an autonomous definition to the concept of sufficiency of time rather than leaving it to the court of the Member State addressed to fall back on its own idea what is sufficient time.[277]

And in such a way   This wording was introduced by the Brussels I Regulation, the predecessor of the Recast, and is not to be found in the Brussels Convention. It is concerned with the manner of service and the effect that this has on the defendant's ability to arrange for his defence. It deals with the problem of inadequate service. That is the situation where, although there was service, there may have been inadequate notice to enable the defendant to defend himself from that point onwards. This will only occur in exceptional cases. Under the Brussels Convention this problem had to be dealt with within the context of sufficiency of time by the rather unsatisfactory device of holding that time has not yet begun to run, with the result that the defence applies.[278] Now it can be dealt with by holding that the defendant was not served "in such a way" as to enable him to arrange for his defence.

In determining whether service has been adequate to enable the defendant to prepare his defence, all the circumstances have to be considered, "including the means employed for effecting service, the relations between the plaintiff and the defendant or the nature of the steps which had to be taken in order to prevent judgment being given in default".[279] It means

---

[273]   *TSN Kunststoffrecycling GmbH v Jurgens* [2002] EWCA Civ 11 at [49], [2002] 1 WLR 2459; Briggs (2002) 73 BYBIL 468.

[274]   The *TSN Kunststoffrecycling GmbH v Jurgens* case.

[275]   Case 166/80 *Klomps v Michel* [1981] ECR 1593 at [15]; See also Case 49/84 *Debaecker and Plouvier v Bouwman* [1985] ECR 1779 at [27]; Case C-619/10 *Trade Agency Ltd v Seramico Investments Ltd* EU:C:2012:531 at [33]; the Pocar Report OJ 2009 C 319/1, paras 134 and 135.

[276]   See *Re Recognition of a Default Judgment* (Case 16 W 12/02) [2005] IL Pr 23 at [5], Oberlandesgericht (Court of Appeal), Cologne.

[277]   Case 49/84 *Debaecker and Plouvier v Bouwman* [1985] ECR 1779 at [27].

[278]   Case 166/80 *Klomps v Michel* [1981] ECR 1593; Case 49/84 *Debaecker and Plouvier v Bouwman* [1985] ECR 1779; applied in *Artic Fish Sales Co Ltd v Adam (No 2)* 1996 SLT 970.

[279]   Case 166/80 *Klomps v Michel* [1981] ECR 1593 at [20].

that, sometimes, personal service will be required and merely serving process at the defendant's address, although in accordance with the law of the Member State of origin, would not be enough. The Advocate General in the *Klomps* case gave as an example the situation where the defendant was in hospital.[280] The English High Court has held that a fictitious service effected by providing a copy of the originating summons to the Belgian public prosecutor did not enable the defendants to arrange for their defence.[281]

The court in the Member State addressed may take into account exceptional circumstances which have arisen after service has been effected. The Court of Justice so decided in *Debaecker and Plouvier v Bouwman*,[282] where it was said that, in deciding whether there had been a breach of the natural justice defence under Article 27(2) of the Brussels Convention, it was relevant to consider the fact that after fictitious service had been made on the defendant—at a police station in Antwerp—the plaintiff had become apprised of the defendant's post office box address in Essen, but had made no effort to contact him there. However, it was also relevant to consider the fact that the defendant was responsible for the earlier failure of the served document to reach him by leaving premises without giving notice and without leaving a forwarding address.

The question of adequacy of service was regarded by the Court of Justice in *Klomps v Michel* and *Debaecker and Plouvier v Bouwman* as being solely one of fact.[283] As with the question of sufficiency of time, it would be better to fix some yardstick to which the facts can be related. If this is to be done, it would be desirable to have an autonomous meaning.

Giving the court in the Member State addressed the power to consider the adequacy of service is an important measure. Without it there would be no substantial check by that court on whether the defendant was able to prepare his defence in the Member State of origin. It is a necessary measure in view of the fact that the concept of "service" does not itself provide a proper check on natural justice by the court in the Member State addressed.

(e) Unless the defendant failed to commence proceedings to challenge the judgment when it was possible for him to do so

This proviso was introduced by the Brussels I Regulation, the predecessor of the Recast. If the defendant was in a position to appeal[284] on grounds of procedural irregularity in the Member State of origin and has not done so,[285] he is not entitled to invoke that procedural irregularity as a ground for refusal of recognition in the Member State addressed.[286] A fortiori, there is no ground for refusal of recognition where the defendant did in fact commence proceedings to challenge the default judgment in the Member State of origin and those proceedings enabled him to argue that his rights of the defence had not been respected.[287] It is unclear whether this requirement comes into play in cases where service has not been effected in the first place and whether it can be satisfied by an appeal in the Member State of origin after the application for

---

[280] Ibid, opinion of AG Reischl at 1622.

[281] *Reeve v Plummer* [2014] EWHC 4695 (QB), [2015] IL Pr 19 at [30]. See also *Laserpoint Ltd v Prime Minister of Malta* [2016] EWHC 1820 (QB); *Corcoz v Molina*, 9 July 2015, HC; *British Seafood Ltd v Kruk* [2008] EWHC 1528 (QB).

[282] Case 49/84 [1985] ECR 1779; Hartley (1987) 27 ELR 220.

[283] See also the Pocar Report, para 135.

[284] This includes applications for relief when the period for bringing an ordinary challenge has expired: Case C-70/15 *Lebek v Domino* EU:C:2016:524, [2016] 1 WLR 4221.

[285] See, eg, Case C-123/91 *Minalmet GmbH v Brandeis Ltd* [1992] ECR I-5661; Case C-78/95 *Hendrikman v Magenta Druck & Verlag GmbH* [1996] ECR I-4943.

[286] The Explanatory Memorandum in the Proposal for the Brussels I Regulation, p 23. See also *Reeve v Plummer* [2014] EWHC 4695 (QB), [2015] IL Pr 19; *Re the Enforcement of a Portuguese Judgment* (Case IX ZB 2/03) [2005] IL Pr 28, German Federal Supreme Court.

[287] Case C-420/07 *Apostolides v Orams* [2009] ECR I-3571.

refusing recognition or enforcement has been made.[288] It is only "possible" for the defendant to challenge the default judgment in the Member State of origin if he has knowledge of its contents.[289] Due service (ie compliance with all the formal rules applicable to service) of the default judgment is not required. A parallel is drawn with service of the document instituting the proceedings so that the default judgment must have been served on the defendant in sufficient time and in such a way as to enable him to arrange for his defence before the courts of the Member State of origin.[290] Where this is not the case, the proviso will not apply.

(iii) Interaction with the public policy defence

There are circumstances where there has been an interference with the defendant's ability to arrange his defence but the ground for refusal of recognition under Article 45(1)(b) does not operate. To take some examples: the judgment was not given in default of appearance but the judge was biased; the service on the defendant was unobjectionable but the court refused to hear counsel for the defendant;[291] the original service was unobjectionable but the defendant was unaware that proceedings were reactivated after a long period during which they had been stayed, without any re-service.[292] In such circumstances the public policy defence can operate.[293]

(c) A conflict with a judgment given in the Member State addressed

Article 45(1)(c) provides that a judgment shall be refused recognition "if the judgment is irreconcilable with a judgment given between the same parties in the Member State addressed". Where there are contemporaneous proceedings between the same parties in two Member States, in respect of the same or a related cause of action, the Recast requires one court to decline jurisdiction in favour of the other.[294] The position is more difficult where the cause of action in the two Member States is neither the same nor related. There is no provision requiring one of the courts to decline jurisdiction in favour of the other, and there can be conflicting judgments in two Member States. Article 45(1)(c) solves this problem, in so far as the conflict is between a judgment given in the Member State addressed and a judgment given in another Member State, by providing that the judgment given in the Member State addressed takes priority.[295] The court of the Member State addressed must refuse recognition; it has no discretionary power to authorise recognition on the basis that the foreign judgment does not sufficiently disturb the rule of law.[296]

All that is required for this ground for refusal of recognition to operate is that: (i) a judgment[297] has been given in the Member State addressed—this can be before or after the

---

[288] See *Tavoulareas v Tsavliris (No 2)* [2006] EWCA Civ 1772 at [17], [2007] 1 WLR 1573—a Brussels I Regulation case.

[289] Case C-283/05 *ASML Netherlands BV v Semiconductor Industry Services GmbH (SEMIS)* [2006] ECR I-12041 at [49].

[290] Ibid, at [41]–[47].

[291] See Case C-7/98 *Krombach v Bamberski* [2000] ECR I-1935.

[292] See *Maronier v Larmer* [2002] EWCA Civ 774, [2003] QB 620.

[293] See supra, p 626.

[294] See Section 9, Chapter II (Arts 29–32) of the Recast, discussed supra, pp 443–57.

[295] See the Jenard Report, p 45.

[296] Case C-80/00 *Italian Leather SpA v WECO Polstermobel GmbH & Co* [2002] ECR I-4995 at [50]–[52]; Kramer (2003) 40 CML Rev 953.

[297] An enforceable settlement reached before a court does not constitute a "judgment" under Art 2(a), supra, p 612, and hence under this provision: Case C-414/92 *Solo Kleinmotoren GmbH v Boch* [1994] ECR I-2237. The existence of a judgment entered in the terms of an arbitral award under s 66 of the Arbitration Act 1996 represents a ground for refusal of recognition: *West Tankers Inc v Allianz SpA* [2011] EWHC 829 (Comm), [2011] 2 All ER (Comm) 1, affd [2012] EWCA Civ 27, [2012] 2 All ER (Comm) 113; *African Fertilizers and Chemicals NIG Ltd (Nigeria) v BD Shipsnavo GmbH & Co Reederei KG* [2011] EWHC 2452 (Comm), [2011] 2 Lloyd's Rep 531; *London Steam-Ship Owners' Mutual Insurance Association Ltd v The Kingdom of Spain* [2013] EWHC 3188 (Comm), [2014] 1 Lloyd's Rep 309; see also *Toyota Tsusho Sugar*

judgment is given in the other Member State;[298] (ii) it is given between the same parties; (iii) this judgment is irreconcilable with the judgment given in the other Member State. In order to ascertain this, the Court of Justice in *Hoffmann v Krieg*[299] has said that the two judgments should be examined to see whether they entail legal consequences that are mutually exclusive. Applying this test, it was held that a German judgment ordering a husband to pay maintenance to his wife as part of his conjugal obligations was irreconcilable with a subsequent Dutch judgment pronouncing a divorce. "Judgment" has the same meaning as under Article 2(a) and therefore includes interim measures.[300] A foreign decision on interim measures ordering an obligor not to carry out certain acts is irreconcilable with a decision on interim measures refusing to grant such an order.[301] The fact that the irreconcilability arose from different procedural requirements in the two states, rather than from legal reasons, is irrelevant.[302] Irreconcilability lies in the *effects* of judgments, it does not concern the requirements governing admissibility and procedure that determine whether judgment can be given and which differ from Member State to Member State.[303] It is left to the court in the Member State addressed to decide whether a judgment has been *given* in that Member State.[304] Where only an interim judgment (as to substance) has been given or where the judgment is subject to an appeal, this may be a difficult decision. Moreover, because the defence does not apply in the situation where proceedings are merely pending in the Member State addressed, the effect of Article 45(1)(c) will be to induce applicants to race to seek recognition before a conflicting judgment is actually given.

When recognition is sought in England, as far as Article 45(1)(c) is concerned the Member State addressed must be the United Kingdom (ie the Member State of the European Union) rather than the individual countries within the United Kingdom. This means that a French judgment will not be recognised in England if it is irreconcilable with a Scottish or Northern Ireland judgment.

It has been suggested[305] that a judgment *given* in the Member State addressed (State A) can include the situation where the judgment has in fact been delivered in another state (State B) but is entitled to recognition in Member State A. The wording of Article 45(1)(c) does not support this wide interpretation. However, in its favour it has to be pointed out that in certain cases it would be a way of resolving the problem of giving priority to one of the conflicting judgments. The first such case would be where the conflicting judgments are both granted in Member States other than the one in which recognition is sought.[306] Article 45(1)

Trading v Prolat SRL [2014] EWHC 3649 (Comm), [2015] 1 Lloyd's Rep 344. The mere fact that there are *proceedings* in the Member State addressed is not a ground for refusing recognition: *Landhurst Leasing plc v Marcq* [1998] IL Pr 822, CA.

[298] See the opinion of AG Gulmann in the *Solo Kleinmotoren* case at [24].

[299] Case 145/86 [1988] ECR 645; Hartley (1991) 16 ELR 64; Briggs (1988) 8 YEL 265; Stone [1988] LMCLQ 393. Followed in *Macaulay v Macaulay* [1991] 1 WLR 179, infra, pp 1082–3. See also *DT v FL* [2006] IEHC 98 at [75]–[76], [2007] IL Pr 56, Irish High Court; *Commune De Macot La Plagne v SA Sebluxl* [2007] IL Pr 12, French cour de cassation; *Materiel Auxiliaire D'Informatique v Printed Forms Equipment Ltd* [2006] IL Pr 44, French cour de cassation.

[300] Case C-80/00 *Italian Leather SpA v WECO Polstermobel GmbH & Co* [2002] ECR I-4995 at [41]. See also *AGF Kosmos Assurances Générales v Surgil Trans Express* [2007] IL Pr 24, French cour de cassation.

[301] The *Italian Leather* case at [47].

[302] Ibid, opinion of AG Leger at [61].

[303] Ibid, judgment of the Court of Justice at [44].

[304] See the Jenard Report, p 45.

[305] Ibid; Collins, p 110; see also the Jenard and Möller Report OJ 1990 C 189/57, para 66. Cf Anton and Beaumont's *Civil Jurisdiction in Scotland* (1995), para 8.19; the Pocar Report, para 138.

[306] See generally, Hartley, p 93; Anton and Beaumont's *Civil Jurisdiction in Scotland* (1995), para 8.20; Layton and Mercer, para 26.081. Art 29 of the Recast (*lis pendens*) will often prevent this situation from

(d) of the Recast is intended to deal with this situation but it may not apply (eg because the judgments involve a related, not the same, cause of action).[307] Article 45(1)(c) will not apply unless this wide interpretation of the word *given* is adopted. The second case is where one of the conflicting judgments is granted in a non-Member State. Article 45(1)(d), which is designed to deal with this situation, may not apply.[308] Again, Article 45(1)(c) will only apply if the wide interpretation of the word *given* is adopted. An alternative way of dealing with these two cases would be by invoking the public policy defence and then giving priority to the earlier judgment.[309]

(d) A conflicting judgment given in another Member State or in a third State

Article 45(1)(d) provides that a judgment shall be refused recognition "if the judgment is irreconcilable with an earlier judgment given in another Member State or in a third State involving the same cause of action and between the same parties, provided that the earlier judgment fulfils the conditions necessary for its recognition in the Member State addressed".

This provision, like Article 45(1)(c), is concerned with the situation where there are two irreconcilable judgments and with ensuring that priority is given to one of them.[310] Where there are contemporaneous proceedings between the same parties in a Member State and a non-Member State, in respect of the same or a related cause of action, the Recast provides for the possibility of staying the proceedings in the Member State in favour of the proceedings in the third state, provided that the third state court has been seised first.[311] These provisions cannot eliminate the possibility of irreconcilable judgments being given because they do not impose an obligation, but confer a discretion, on Member State courts to stay their proceedings in favour of the first seised third state court. Where the proceedings are in a Member State and a third state, there is, therefore, a real possibility of two judgments being given, both of which have to be recognised. This is a serious situation which could give rise to diplomatic problems with non-Member States. To avoid this, Article 45(1)(d) gives priority to the earlier judgment given in the non-Member State, and the judgment given in the Member State is not recognised.

There was a gap in the Brussels Convention in that it did not deal with the situation where the earlier judgment was in another Member State.[312] The *lis pendens* provisions will normally prevent a judgment being given in the court second seised but it will not do so if that court does not accept that the parties or the cause of action are the same or related. The Brussels I Regulation, the predecessor of the Brussels I Recast, closed this gap by extending its Article 34(4) (now Article 45(1)(d) of the Recast) to cover this situation.

For Article 45(1)(d) of the Recast to operate it must be shown that: (i) the judgment given in a non-Member State or in a Member State other than the Member State of origin of the judgment in respect of which an application for refusal of recognition or enforcement has been made[313] is the earlier one; (ii) it is entitled to recognition in the Member State addressed;[314]

---

arising, see supra, pp 443–54, but will not do so where the cause of action is not the same in the actions in the two Member States.

[307] See infra.

[308] See infra.

[309] Hill, *International Commercial Disputes* (2005) 3rd edn, para 13.3.37, fn 152.

[310] See the Schlosser Report, para 205; cf the Jenard Report, p 45.

[311] See Section 9, Chapter II (Arts 33 and 34) of the Recast, discussed supra, pp 457–9.

[312] See the Explanatory Memorandum in the Proposal for the Brussels I Regulation, p 23.

[313] Art 45(1)(d) does not apply where there are irreconcilable judgments from the same Member State: Case C-157/12 *Salzgitter Mannesmann Handel GmbH v SC Laminorul SA* EU:C:2013:597, [2014] 1 WLR 904.

[314] In England this would be at common law or by statute; see *Owens Bank Ltd v Bracco* [1991] 4 All ER 833 at 841, CA, affd by the House of Lords [1992] 2 AC 443, and generally supra, pp 527–601. It is not

(iii) it is irreconcilable with the later judgment given in another Member State; (iv) it involves the same cause of action and the same parties.[315]

There is still a problem where one of these requirements is not satisfied, with the result that Article 45(1)(d) does not apply. If faced with conflicting judgments given in a Member State (A) and in another Member State (B) or a third state (C), it is possible to solve the conflict by applying the wide interpretation of Article 45(1)(c) set out above.[316]

(e) The judgment conflicts with Sections 3, 4, 5 or 6 of Chapter II of the Recast[317]

Article 45(1)(e) provides that the recognition of a judgment shall be refused if it conflicts with the jurisdictional provisions in Section 3 (insurance matters, Articles 10 to 16), Section 4 (consumer contracts, Articles 17 to 19),[318] Section 4 (individual contracts of employment, Articles 20 to 23)[319] or Section 6 (exclusive jurisdiction, Article 24)[320] of Chapter II of the Recast. This ground for refusal of recognition, in so far as it concerns the rules of protective jurisdiction, is applicable only where the defendant was the weaker party (ie the policyholder, the insured, a beneficiary of the insurance contract, the injured party, the consumer or the employee).[321] The weaker party, however, can waive the protection offered by Article 45(1)(e) by submitting to the jurisdiction of the court of origin.[322] Normally, the court in the Member State addressed cannot review the jurisdiction of the court of origin.[323] Article 45(1)(e) provides an exception to this which can be justified because Sections 3, 4, 5 and 6 depart from the normal rules of jurisdiction. In examining jurisdiction, the court in the Member State addressed is bound by the findings of fact on which the court of origin based its jurisdiction;[324] this avoids unnecessary duplication of effort. The court in the Member State addressed will, however, examine whether these special rules on jurisdiction were correctly applied by the court which gave the judgment. It appears to be irrelevant whether jurisdiction has been challenged in the court which gave the judgment. Sections 3, 4, 5 and 6 are complex provisions; there is every likelihood of the court in the Member State addressed interpreting these provisions differently from the way in which they have been interpreted by the court which gave the judgment and holding that the latter court did not have jurisdiction. In order to avoid conflicting interpretations, wherever possible, there should be a referral to the Court of Justice for a definitive interpretation.

---

required that special proceedings to obtain the recognition of the third state judgment are instituted: see the Schlosser Report, para 205; Briggs 2014, para 6.75; cf Dickinson and Lein (eds), para 13.371.

[315] This is assessed by the court in the Member State addressed.

[316] Supra, pp 640–1. Cf the Pocar Report, para 138.

[317] See *Berkeley Administration Inc v McClelland* [1995] IL Pr 201 at 213 (per Dillon LJ), CA.

[318] See Case C-99/96 *Mietz v Intership Yachting Sneek BV* [1999] ECR I-2277; Case C-111/09 *Česká podnikatelská pojišťovna as, Vienna Insurance Group v Bilas* [2010] ECR I-4545; Grušić (2011) 48 CML Rev 947.

[319] Curiously, neither the Brussels Convention nor the Brussels I Regulation included in the list Section 5 (individual contracts of employment): see Art 28 of the Brussels Convention and Art 35 of the Brussels I Regulation. See Grušić (2016) 12 J Priv Int L 521.

[320] See *Prudential Assurance Co Ltd v Prudential Insurance Co of America* [2003] EWCA Civ 327, [2003] 1 WLR 2295. Art 45(1)(e) does not authorise the refusal of recognition or enforcement of a judgment concerning land situated in an area of the Member State of origin over which its government does not exercise effective control: Case C-420/07 *Apostolides v Orams* [2009] ECR I-3571 at [52].

[321] Art 45(1)(e)(i).

[322] Case C-111/09 *Česká podnikatelská pojišťovna as, Vienna Insurance Group v Bilas* [2010] ECR I-4545.

[323] Art 45(3). The test of public policy may not be applied to the rules relating to jurisdiction: Case C-7/98 *Krombach v Bamberski* [2000] ECR I-1935.

[324] Art 45(2); the Jenard Report, p 46.

(ii) The case is provided for under Article 72

A judgment will not be recognised in a case provided for under Article 72. This is concerned with agreements entered into by Member States, prior to the Brussels I Regulation entering into force in March 2002, pursuant to Article 59 of the Brussels Convention,[325] whereby a Contracting State has agreed with a non-Contracting State that, in certain circumstances, it will not recognise judgments given in other Contracting States against defendants from that non-Contracting State. The United Kingdom had entered into conventions with Canada and Australia incorporating the obligation under Article 59.[326] This means that, to take an example, a French judgment will not be recognised in England if jurisdiction could only have been taken in France against a person domiciled or habitually resident in Canada or Australia on one of the exorbitant bases of jurisdiction referred to in Article 3(2)[327] of Title II of the Brussels Convention. This means that the English court would have to examine the jurisdiction of the French court to see whether it could *only* have been founded on one of the specified exorbitant bases. When examining jurisdiction, it is not clear whether the court in the Member State addressed is bound by the findings of fact of the court in which the judgment was given.[328] There is no equivalent of Article 59 in the Brussels I Regulation or the Brussels I Recast. Once the Brussels I Regulation came into force no new agreements of that kind could be entered into by virtue of that Regulation. Neither is this possible under the Brussels I Recast. The defence in relation to Article 59 agreements is therefore confined to agreements entered into prior to the entry into force of the Brussels I Regulation.

(g) Non-grounds for refusal of recognition and enforcement

(i) Other grounds for refusal of recognition are not available

The duty to recognise a judgment under the Recast applies unless one of the grounds for refusal of recognition under Article 45 or 72 is available. It follows that all other grounds for refusal of recognition are implicitly rejected. The Recast reinforces this point by expressly providing that two very important matters may not be raised in the Member State addressed, namely the review of the jurisdiction of the court of origin and of the substance of the judgment.

With regard to refusal of enforcement, Article 41(2) provides that a party challenging enforcement is able to invoke, in the same procedure, in addition to the grounds for refusal provided for in Article 45, the grounds for refusal or suspension of enforcement available under the national law of the Member State addressed and within the time-limits available under that law. Those grounds, however, will apply in so far as they are not incompatible with the grounds referred to in Article 45.[329] For example, a party challenging enforcement can invoke a national ground for refusal of enforcement that the judgment has been complied with abroad.

(a) A review of jurisdiction

Article 45(3) provides that "the jurisdiction of the court of origin may not be reviewed". Strictly speaking, it was not necessary to exclude expressly the review of jurisdiction since the Recast implicitly does so by providing for recognition and enforcement without any reference to the jurisdiction of the court of origin.[330] This provision is wide enough to exclude

---

[325] Discussed infra, pp 650–2.
[326] Reciprocal Enforcement of Foreign Judgments (Australia) Order 1994, SI 1994/1901, Sch, Art 3; Reciprocal Enforcement of Foreign Judgments (Canada) Order 1987, SI 1987/468, Sch, Art IX.
[327] See supra, pp 213–14.
[328] Hartley thinks that it is bound, p 87.
[329] See also Recital (30).
[330] See supra, pp 617–18 and 622–3.

two arguments in respect of jurisdiction.[331] First, it cannot be argued that the court of origin misapplied the jurisdictional rules under the Recast[332] Secondly, it cannot be argued that the court of origin misapplied its traditional national rules on jurisdiction. The prohibition against examining jurisdiction cannot be evaded by using the public policy defence,[333] even where an exorbitant basis of jurisdiction has been used against a defendant domiciled in another Member State.[334]

It is questionable whether it was right to exclude a defence of lack of jurisdiction. It would have been possible under the Recast to lay down a double check on jurisdiction, the court granting the judgment making sure that it has jurisdiction under the Recast, and the court in the Member State addressed checking this. The Recast sets up a system of double checks in respect of natural justice but not in respect of jurisdiction, presumably because it is satisfied that a court will only take jurisdiction under the Recast's rules when it ought to. Despite the safeguards built into the rules on jurisdiction in the Recast, this may be unduly optimistic. It also makes no allowance for the fact that jurisdiction may be taken in a Member State under traditional national rules, some of which are exorbitant and may be misapplied.

(b) A review of substance

Article 52 provides that "under no circumstances may a judgment given in a Member State be reviewed as to its substance". Recognition cannot be refused solely on the ground that there is a discrepancy between the legal rule applied by the court of origin from that which would have been applied by the court in the Member State addressed if it had been seised of the dispute.[335] It cannot be alleged that the foreign court made a mistake of fact or a mistake of law.[336] Even though a defence based on an allegation that there has been a mistake of law is not expressly excluded by Article 52, it is implicitly excluded by the terms of Articles 45 and 72, which provide the *only* grounds for refusal of recognition.[337] Thus, in *Hengst Import BV v Campese*[338] the Court of Justice refused to go into an allegation that the Italian court had made an error of law in granting the order in question. The "substance" of a judgment applies to a legal rule allowing judgment without hearing defence counsel, which is a procedural rule.[339] Procedural irregularities in the judgment-granting state can be examined in order to establish one of the grounds for refusal of recognition under Article 45.[340]

(ii) *The special problem where there is a breach of an agreement for the settlement of disputes*

From an English lawyer's viewpoint the most noticeable omission from the grounds for refusal of recognition under Article 45 is that of a provision equivalent to section 32 of the Civil Jurisdiction and Judgments Act 1982, which, it will be recalled,[341] provides that an

---

[331] For the position where a national court acts in breach of Art 45(3), see Kohler (1985) 34 ICLQ 563 at, pp 578–80.

[332] See Case 7/98 *Krombach v Bamberski* [2000] ECR I-1935 at [31]–[32]. This is subject to the defences under Art 45(1)(e), discussed supra, p 642.

[333] Art 45(3).

[334] See Case 7/98 *Krombach v Bamberski* [2000] ECR I-1935 at [34], discussed supra, p 628.

[335] See Case C-7/98 *Krombach v Bamberski* [2000] ECR I-1935 at [36]; Case C-38/98 *Régie Nationale des Usines Renault SA v Maxicar SpA* [2000] ECR I-2973 at [29]. The question of when public policy can be used in cases of discrepancy is discussed supra, pp 631–2.

[336] See the *Krombach* case at [36]; the *Renault* case at [29].

[337] It does not appear to be a matter of public policy, see supra, pp 631–2.

[338] Case C-474/93 [1995] ECR I-2113 at [24]; discussed supra, p 636. See also *Westpac Banking Corpn v Dempsey* [1993] 3 IR 331 at 340.

[339] See Case 7/98 *Krombach v Bamberski* [2000] ECR I-1935 at [36]–[37]. Cf the opinion of AG Jacobs in Case C-78/95 *Hendrikman v Magenta Druck & Verlag GmbH* [1996] ECR I-4943 at [42]–[54].

[340] The opinion of AG Jacobs in the *Hendrikman* case.

[341] See supra, pp 584–8.

overseas judgment shall not be recognised or enforced in the United Kingdom if it was given in proceedings brought in breach of an agreement for settlement of disputes otherwise than by proceedings in the courts of that country.

(a) A breach of an agreement providing for trial in a particular state

Under the Recast there is a duty to recognise and enforce a judgment obtained in another Member State, despite the fact that there was an agreement between the parties providing for the trial of disputes in a state (whether a Member or non-Member State) other than the one in which trial took place. Following on from this, because the judgment is required to be recognised or enforced under the Recast, section 32 of the 1982 Act will not apply.[342]

The reason for the absence of a ground under the Recast to deal with this situation is not entirely clear. Admittedly, Article 25[343] will operate in many cases and thereby prevent a court in another Member State from taking jurisdiction in defiance of the agreement. But this is not a complete answer. Article 25 will not always apply; eg it will not do so where the agreement on jurisdiction provides for trial in a non-Member State. Even where Article 25 ought to have been applied, there is always the possibility that a court in a Member State might misconstrue its provisions and fail to apply them.

(b) A breach of an agreement to go to arbitration

There is no specific ground for refusal of recognition where recognition or enforcement is sought of a judgment granted by a court in a Member State which has taken jurisdiction despite an agreement by the parties to go to arbitration in that or some other state.

However, the more basic question arises as to whether there is a duty to recognise or enforce a judgment in the first place in these circumstances. This question has to be asked because Article 1 excludes arbitration from the scope of the Recast.[344] Recital (12) answers this question by providing that "where a court of a Member State, exercising jurisdiction under this Regulation or under national law, has determined that an arbitration agreement is null and void, inoperative or incapable of being performed, this should not preclude that court's judgment on the substance of the matter from being recognised or, as the case may be, enforced in accordance with this Regulation". Accordingly, a judgment given by a court of a Member State whose principal subject-matter concerns a civil or commercial nature is within the scope of the Recast and the normal duty to recognise and enforce the judgment in other Member States will apply, even if the court has found, as an incidental question, that there is no valid and binding arbitration agreement between the parties and even if this conclusion was wrong from the standpoint of the defendant and English law. However, if a Member State court has found, as a main question, that there is or that there is no valid and binding arbitration agreement, that judgment is not within the scope of the Recast.[345]

A different question is whether any of the grounds for refusal of recognition under the Recast can be raised to preclude the recognition or enforcement of a judgment given by a court in a Member State in violation of an arbitration agreement. Public policy cannot be used in this situation, since section 32 of the 1982 Act will not apply[346] and a refusal of recognition on this basis would go against the prohibition on the review of the jurisdiction of the court

---

[342] Supra, pp 585–6. See *Marc Rich & Co AG v Società Italiana Impianti PA (The Atlantic Emperor) (No 2)* [1992] 1 Lloyd's Rep 624 at 632, CA; *The Heidberg* [1994] 2 Lloyd's Rep 287 at 297.

[343] See supra, pp 229–43.

[344] Supra, pp 208–11.

[345] This reverses in part the decision in *National Navigation Co v Endesa Generacion SA (The Wadi Sudr)* [2009] EWCA Civ 1397, [2010] 2 All ER (Comm) 1243.

[346] Supra, pp 585–6.

of origin.[347] However, where an arbitral award has been rendered, the award creditor may enforce the award by obtaining a judgment from an English court entered in the terms of the award under 66 of the Arbitration Act 1996 and thereby preclude the recognition of irreconcilable judgments from other Member States under Article 45(1)(c) of the Recast.[348] Finally, a question arises whether a party against whom a judgment has been given in a Member State in violation of an arbitration agreement can rely on Article 73(2) of the Recast which states that this Regulation shall not affect the application of the 1958 New York Convention on the Recognition and Enforcement of Foreign Arbitral Award. The arguments are finely balanced on this point. On one side is the argument that the respect for arbitration agreements and arbitral awards, which policy is enshrined in the New York Convention, should enable the court in the Member State addressed to examine whether or not there is a valid and binding arbitration agreement between the parties and, if so, to refuse the recognition and enforcement of a judgment given in violation of the arbitration agreement. Only this approach, the argument goes, would ensure the effectiveness of the New York Convention. On the other side are the following three arguments: first, the court in the Member State addressed may not review the jurisdiction of the court of origin; second, the New York Convention does not deal with the recognition and enforcement of foreign judgments, but only with the recognition and enforcement of arbitration agreements (by means of stay of court proceedings under Article II(3) of the Convention) and foreign arbitral awards; third, the ruling in *TNT Express Nederland BV v AXA Versicherung AG*[349] that the rules on recognition and enforcement that are set out in a specialised convention apply only if they ensure, under conditions at least as favourable as those provided by the Recast, the free movement of judgments and mutual trust in the European Union. Given that the Recast itself confirms that the New York Convention "takes precedence" and that it is "without prejudice" to the competence of the courts of Member States to decide on the recognition and enforcement of arbitral awards under the Convention, the former line of arguments appears more persuasive.[350] In other words, this would mean that the Brussels I Recast does not prevent an English court to enforce the pro-arbitration policy of the New York Convention by refusing the recognition and enforcement of a judgment from another Member State given in violation of an arbitration agreement. A definitive view, however, cannot be made until the Court of Justice has had an opportunity to decide on the issue.

(h) Appeals in the Member State of origin

It is unfair to the judgment debtor for a judgment to be recognised or enforced where there is a possibility of it being altered subsequently on appeal in the Member State of origin.[351] Articles 39, 44(2), 38(a) and 51 of the Recast may prevent recognition or enforcement in this situation.

---

[347] Art 45(3); cf Briggs 2015, para 7.16; Dickinson and Lein (eds), paras 2.66.

[348] *West Tankers Inc v Allianz SpA* [2011] EWHC 829 (Comm), [2011] 2 All ER (Comm) 1, affd [2012] EWCA Civ 27, [2012] 2 All ER (Comm) 113; *African Fertilizers and Chemicals NIG Ltd (Nigeria) v BD Shipsnavo GmbH & Co Reederei KG* [2011] EWHC 2452 (Comm), [2011] 2 Lloyd's Rep 531; *London Steam-Ship Owners' Mutual Insurance Association Ltd v The Kingdom of Spain* [2013] EWHC 3188 (Comm), [2014] 1 Lloyd's Rep 309. A judgment entered in the terms of an award, however, falls within the arbitration exclusion in Art 1(1)(d) of the Recast and cannot be recognised and enforced in other Member States: *ABCI v BFT* [1996] 1 Lloyd's Rep 485.

[349] Case C-533/08 [2010] ECR I-4107.

[350] Similarly, Briggs 2015, paras 7.38 and 8.17; cf Briggs 2014, para 14.29; Dickinson and Lein (eds), paras 2.69.

[351] See the Jenard Report, p 52; the opinion of the Advocate General in Case 43/77 *Industrial Diamond Supplies v Riva* [1977] ECR 2175. It is equally unfair to the claimant in the original proceedings, who has lost his action, for the judgment to be recognised in other Member States when this judgment is subject to an appeal.

(i) Articles 39 and 44(2)

Article 39 contains a requirement that before enforcement can take place it must be shown that the judgment is enforceable in the Member State in which it was given.[352] This requirement is not specifically designed to deal with appeals. However, the effect of an appeal in the Member State of origin may be to prevent the judgment from being enforceable there, with the result that the judgment is not enforceable in other Member States. A provision specifically designed to deal with this kind of situation is Article 44(2). It provides that the competent authority in the Member State addressed shall, on the application of the person against whom enforcement is sought, suspend the enforcement proceedings where the enforceability of the judgment is suspended in the Member State of origin. The competent authority in the Member State addressed has no discretion and must suspend enforcement upon request by the judgment debtor. This still leaves a problem in other cases where the appeal does not have this effect or where recognition alone, and not enforcement, is sought.

(ii) Articles 38(a) and 51

Article 38(a) applies to cases where recognition alone is sought. It gives the recognising court or another competent authority a power to suspend its proceedings, in whole or in part, if the judgment is challenged in the Member State of origin. The idea is that there should be a suspension of proceedings until the challenge is finally disposed of.

Article 51 is specifically designed to deal with cases where an appeal in the Member State of origin does not lead to the suspension of the enforceability of a judgment. It gives the court to which an application for refusal of enforcement is submitted or the court which hears an appeal lodged against a decision on an application for refusal of enforcement under Article 49 (in England this is the High Court) or Article 50 (in England this is concerned with a single further appeal on a point of law) power, in certain circumstances, to stay the proceedings. If a stay is refused,[353] or a stay previously ordered is lifted,[354] this is not subject to an appeal or a further appeal. Article 51 is a similar provision to that contained in Article 38(a), but with the following important differences. First, the power to stay under Article 51 applies to cases where an "ordinary" appeal has been lodged against the judgment in the Member State of origin and to cases where an ordinary appeal has not been lodged, if the time for such an appeal has not yet expired.[355] In this case, the court may specify the time within which such an appeal is to be lodged. Secondly, pending a challenge to the enforcement of a judgment, the courts in the Member State addressed, during the entire proceedings relating to such a challenge, including any appeal, have power to allow the enforcement to proceed subject to a limitation of the enforcement or to the provision of security.[356]

There are two particular problems concerning Articles 38(a) and 51: (i) Article 51 is only concerned with "ordinary" appeals; and (ii) the power to stay proceedings under the two Articles is a discretionary one.

(a) An ordinary appeal

Under Article 51, an "ordinary" appeal must have been lodged against the judgment in the Member State of origin or the time for an "ordinary" appeal must not yet have expired. In

---

[352] Supra, p 621.
[353] See Case 183/90 *BJ Van Dalfsen v B Van Loon* [1991] ECR I-4743.
[354] See Case C-432/93 *Société d'Informatique Service Réalisation Organisation (SISRO) v Ampersand Software BV* [1995] ECR I-2269.
[355] See *Noirhomme v Walklate* [1992] 1 Lloyd's Rep 427 at 431.
[356] Recital (31).

civil law systems, an "ordinary" appeal is often contrasted with an "extra-ordinary" appeal. The English legal system has no such distinction and this may cause difficulty for both foreign and English courts.

It would be particularly hard for a foreign court, which has been asked to refuse enforcement under the Recast of an English judgment subject to an appeal, to determine whether this was an "ordinary" appeal when there is no such concept under English law.[357] Article 51(2) therefore provides that, where the judgment was given in the United Kingdom, "any form of appeal available in the Member State of origin shall be treated as an ordinary appeal".

This still leaves a problem for English courts; they will have to grapple with an unfamiliar concept when determining whether an "ordinary" appeal has been lodged in the foreign Member State in which the judgment was given. An "ordinary" appeal is, however, a concept that has been defined by the Court of Justice.

In *Industrial Diamond Supplies v Riva*,[358] a case decided under the Brussels Convention, the Court of Justice gave an autonomous meaning to the concept of an ordinary appeal. This was necessary because some Member States do not have the concept, and those that do have it do not always define it in the same way. In deciding what this autonomous definition should be, the Court of Justice was concerned to ensure that the recognising and enforcing court was able to stay the proceedings "whenever reasonable doubt arises with regard to the fate of the decision in the State in which it was given".[359] The Court held that an ordinary appeal is any appeal which: (a) may result in the annulment or amendment of the original judgment, and (b) for which there is a specific time for appealing which starts to run by virtue of the judgment. It is not an ordinary appeal if it is one which is either dependent on events unforeseeable at the time of the original trial or on action taken by persons extraneous to the case who are not bound by the period for making an appeal. However, adopting this two-part definition produces curious results. Where an appeal has been lodged the first part of the definition would be satisfied, since the danger of the original judgment being altered exists. But, if this lodged appeal is of a type for which there is no time limit on when it can be brought, the second part of the definition would not be satisfied. It does not seem right to exclude an appeal which has actually been lodged because it was of a type for which there was no time limit as to when it could have been lodged.[360]

In contrast, Article 38(a) does not make a distinction between "ordinary" and "extra-ordinary" appeals and allows the recognising court or another competent authority to suspend its proceedings whenever the judgment is "challenged" in the Member State of origin. The term "challenge" should be given an autonomous and wide interpretation.[361]

(b) A discretionary power

The court or another competent authority in the Member State addressed has a discretion to stay the proceedings; it is under no duty to grant a stay and one can be refused even though the judgment is challenged in the Member State of origin or, under Article 51, an ordinary appeal has been lodged or the time for such an appeal has not yet expired.[362] The criteria on

---

[357] Since an autonomous meaning is given to the concept, see infra, this would not be an impossible task.

[358] Case 43/77 [1977] ECR 2175; Hartley (1978) 3 ELR 160, and generally Hartley, p 94. See also the Schlosser Report, p 130. Cf *Interdesco SA v Nullifire Ltd* [1992] 1 Lloyd's Rep 180.

[359] At [33].

[360] Hartley interprets the decision in *Industrial Diamond Suppliers v Riva* in such a way as to avoid this, p 94.

[361] See Dickinson and Lein (eds), paras 13.141–13.147.

[362] See *DHL GBS (UK) Ltd v Fallimento Finmatica SpA* [2009] EWHC 291 (Comm), [2009] 1 Lloyd's Rep 430.

which this discretion is to be exercised have not as yet been fully developed by the Court of Justice. The Court of Justice has, however, held that a court, when deciding whether to grant a stay of proceedings, may take into account only such submissions as the party requesting the stay was unable to make before the court of origin.[363] According to Advocate General Leger, the refusal in the Member State of origin to stay the enforcement of the judgment may be a relevant factor when making an assessment of the appeal's chances of success, but is never decisive.[364] Advocate General Leger is clearly of the view that the court in the Member State addressed can consider the likelihood of the appeal's chances of success.[365] However, the Court of Justice in an earlier case has said that this is not something that can be considered.[366] There is English authority on the exercise of the discretion in *Petereit v Babcock International Holdings Ltd*.[367] The court laid down a general principle that prima facie a foreign judgment should be enforced. In deciding whether to grant a stay pending the result of the appeal abroad the court considered the economic consequences to the parties of, on the one hand, granting a stay and, on the other hand, enforcing the judgment; for what is being decided is which party is to have the use of the judgment money during the period up to the result of the appeal being known. In deciding to grant a stay[368] the judge was influenced by the prospect of the defendant suffering potential losses, in terms of cash flow problems and currency exchange losses, which could not be adequately dealt with by the provision of security by the plaintiff. The most likely situation for the exercise of the discretion against a stay is going to arise before courts in other Member States which are asked to recognise or enforce judgments given in the United Kingdom and which are subject to an appeal. The extreme width of Article 51(2), which is not limited to "ordinary" appeals,[369] needs to be countered by the use of the discretion to refuse a stay.[370]

(i) The estoppel effect of a judgment obtained in a Member State

In *De Wolf v Cox*,[371] a case decided under the Brussels Convention, the Court of Justice held that, once a judgment which is enforceable under the Convention has been obtained in one Contracting State, the party who has obtained the judgment in his favour is prevented from bringing a new action before a court in another Contracting State for a judgment in the same terms. The Court came to this conclusion because it foresaw a number of problems that could arise if bringing a new action was allowed. First, it could involve the courts of another Contracting State going into the substance of the dispute when this is a matter for the courts of the Contracting State in which the original judgment was given.[372] Secondly, if a judgment is given in the second Contracting State which conflicts with that given in the first, it means that the court in the second has failed in its duty to recognise the first judgment.[373] Thirdly, the *lis pendens* provisions under the Convention show the general desire to avoid having two

---

[363] Case C-183/90 *BJ Van Dalfsen v B Van Loon* [1991] ECR I-4743.

[364] See the opinion of AG Leger in Case C-432/93 *Société d'Informatique Service Réalisation Organisation (SISRO) v Ampersand Software BV* [1995] ECR I-2269 at [53].

[365] Ibid, at [55]. See also *Petereit v Babcock International Holdings Ltd* [1990] 1 WLR 350 at 355.

[366] Case C-183/90 *BJ Van Dalfsen v B Van Loon* [1991] ECR I-4743 at [32]–[33]. Applied in *Banco Nacional de Comercio Exterior SNC v Empresa de Telecomunicaciones de Cuba SA* [2007] EWHC 2322 (Comm) at [10]–[11], [2007] IL Pr 59.

[367] [1990] 1 WLR 350; Kaye [1991] JBL 261. See also *Banco Nacional de Comercio Exterior SNC v Empresa de Telecomunicaciones de Cuba SA* [2007] EWHC 2322 (Comm) at [12]–[13], [2007] IL Pr 59.

[368] Conditional on the defendant providing adequate security to protect the plaintiff's position.

[369] Discussed supra, pp 647–8.

[370] See the Schlosser Report, para 204.

[371] Case 42/76 [1976] ECR 1759; Hartley (1977) 2 ELR 146.

[372] See Art 52 of the Recast.

[373] See Art 36 of the Recast, discussed supra, pp 617–19.

sets of proceedings and two judgments in respect of the same cause of action and between the same parties.[374] Fourthly, allowing a new action could result in a creditor possessing two orders for enforcement in respect of the same debt.

On the facts of the case, whilst there were two sets of proceedings there were not two inconsistent judgments, since the Dutch court, before which a new action was brought, recognised the judgment granted earlier in Belgium. The Court of Justice was therefore reacting more against potential problems than actual ones and, by forcing the parties to use the enforcement procedure under the Convention, imposed greater expense upon the parties than would have been the case if the plaintiff had been allowed to bring fresh proceedings in the Netherlands.

The effect of the decision in the *De Wolf* case is that a judgment given in a Member State which is to be recognised under the Recast creates what in English law is regarded as a cause of action estoppel from the moment that it has been given.[375] The facts of *De Wolf* only concerned the situation where the estoppel principle prevents the claimant, having obtained a judgment in his favour, from obtaining another judgment against the same defendant in new proceedings involving the same cause of action and subject matter in a different Member State. However, this principle applies equally to prevent a claimant who has lost his action from obtaining a judgment against the same defendant in new proceedings in a different Member State.[376] Where, for the purposes of Article 29 of the Recast, the parties, cause of action and subject matter are the same, a foreign judgment will be recognised as binding between all those parties.[377] A foreign judgment which is recognised under Article 36 may also lead to what in English law is regarded as an issue estoppel. In *Gothaer Allgemeine Versicherung AG v Samskip GmbH*[378] the Court of Justice held that the obligation to recognise a judgment of another Member State court declining jurisdiction on the basis that the parties were bound by a jurisdiction agreement in favour of a court in a Lugano state carried with it also an obligation to recognise as binding the reasons for the judgment. If the judgment of the court of origin was not on the application of the uniform jurisdictional rules of the Brussels/Lugano system, the judgment which is to be recognised under Article 36 may create an issue estoppel in England, provided that the normal requirements at common law for this are satisfied.[379]

(j) Foreign reaction

(i) *The automatic recognition of judgments without jurisdictional safeguards*

American lawyers have been outspoken in their criticism of the Brussels Convention[380] and their criticism is equally applicable to the Recast. The basis of their objection is that what is now the Recast provides for the automatic recognition and enforcement of judgments against defendants domiciled in non-Member States,[381] despite the absence of the jurisdictional

---

[374] See Art 29 of the Recast, discussed supra, pp 443–54.

[375] See supra, p 556.

[376] *Berkeley Administration Inc v McClelland* [1995] IL Pr 201, CA.

[377] Ibid, at 211 (per Dillon LJ).

[378] Case C-456/11 EU:C:2012:719, [2013] QB 548; Torralba-Mendiola and Rodriguez-Pineau (2014) 10 J Priv Int L 403.

[379] See supra, pp 556–62. See also *Berkeley Administration Inc v McClelland* [1996] IL Pr 772 at 787 (per Sir Richard Scott V-C), CA; cf *Boss Group Ltd v Boss France SA* [1997] 1 WLR 351 at 359 (per Saville LJ), CA.

[380] Von Mehren (1981) 81 Col LR 1044; Von Mehren (1980) II Hague Recueil 9, 95 et seq; Nadelmann (1967) 67 Col LR 995, reprinted in *Conflict of Laws: International and Interstate* (1972), p 238; Nadelmann (1967) 5 CML Rev 409; Nadelmann (1977) 41 Law and Contemporary Problems 54, 58–62. For Australian reaction, see Pryles and Trindale (1974) 42 ALJ 185; McEvoy (1994) 68 ALJ 576, 582.

[381] Supra, p 611.

safeguards provided for defendants domiciled in Member States. Minimum standards in relation to natural justice[382] do not have to be complied with. The Recast also recognises the use of exorbitant bases of jurisdiction against defendants domiciled in non-Member States (but not those domiciled in Member States[383]), and under Article 6(2) even extends their use. This provision, to take an example, allows a French domiciliary to use Article 14 of the French Civil Code, under which jurisdiction is based on the claimant's French nationality, to found jurisdiction against a defendant from a non-Member State and to have that judgment recognised and enforced throughout the European Union.

From a European Union point of view there is as great a need for the free circulation of judgments where defendants are domiciled in non-Member States as there is where they are domiciled in Member States,[384] since there is the same risk of a defendant thwarting the claimant by moving his assets from one Member State to another. It is also understandable that the jurisdictional rules in the Recast, since they are only concerned with allocating jurisdiction to Member States, should involve a basic distinction between the situation where the defendant is and is not domiciled in a Member State. But, when you add these two elements together, the result is that defendants domiciled in non-Member States are treated unfairly.[385] This whole problem was, seemingly, only recognised at a late stage by the drafters of the Brussels Convention who, almost as an afterthought, introduced Article 59 to deal with it.[386]

(ii) Article 59 of the Brussels Convention

Article 59 allowed a Contracting State to the Brussels Convention to enter into a convention with a third state (ie a non-Contracting State), under which the former agrees not to recognise judgments given against defendants domiciled or habitually resident in the latter where the judgment could only be founded on an exorbitant basis of jurisdiction specified in Article 3(2) of the Brussels Convention. It was never a satisfactory solution to the problem of unfairness to defendants domiciled in non-Contracting States.[387] But it did at least have the great merit for European Community States of putting them in a very strong bargaining position when it came to negotiating bilateral treaties with third states. The free circulation of judgments founded on exorbitant bases of jurisdiction acted as the stick and the let-out allowed by Article 59 as the carrot to bring third states to the negotiating table.[388] This was the genesis of a draft UK/US Judgments Convention.[389] However, this Convention was never implemented because of United Kingdom alarm at the prospect of having to enforce American judgments for large awards of damages. Negotiations with Canada and Australia were more successful, with agreement being reached on a UK/Canada Convention[390] and a UK/Australia Convention.[391] That is all now in the past. There is no equivalent of Article 59 in the Recast;

---

[382] See Art 28, discussed supra, pp 310–11. The safeguards at the recognition and enforcement stage will, however, apply, see supra, pp 632–9.

[383] Supra, pp 213–14.

[384] See the Jenard Report, p 20.

[385] For an attempt to justify the Brussels Convention's treatment of defendants domiciled in non-Contracting States, see Hauschild, in Goode and Simmonds (eds), *Commercial Operations in Europe* (1978), pp 57–8; see also Kohler (1985) 35 ICLQ 563, 580–1. Cf Nadelmann, *Conflict of Laws: International and Interstate* (1972), pp 246–8; (1967) 5 CML Rev 409, 414–19.

[386] For the origins of Art 59, see Nadelmann (1967) 5 CML Rev 409.

[387] See the 13th edn of this book (1999), p 516.

[388] Nadelmann advocated US retaliation against this: *Conflict of Laws: International and Interstate* (1972), pp 267–8.

[389] (1976) Cmnd 6771; see Hay and Walker (1976) 11 Texas Int LJ 421; Smit (1977) 17 VA J Int L 443; Mathers (1977) 127 NLJ 777; North (1978) 128 NLJ 315; Alford (1979) 18 Colum J Transnat L 119; North, *Essays*, Chapter 8; Kerr (1980) Europarecht 353, 356–7.

[390] See the Schedule to SI 1987/468.

[391] See the Schedule to SI 1994/1901.

nor was it to be found in the Brussels I Regulation.[392] The European Commission explained this by saying that it would be out of place to have such a provision in a European Union Regulation.[393] The Commission has exclusive external competence in matters covered by the Recast.[394] The notion of Member States negotiating and entering into bilateral agreements, which affect the European Union rules on recognition, with non-Member States is seen as being inappropriate. However, the Council and Commission can negotiate international agreements that would mitigate the consequences of Chapter III of the Recast for persons domiciled in third states.[395] Moreover, bilateral agreements containing the Article 59 let-out entered into prior to the entry into force of the Brussels I Regulation are still honoured.[396]

(k) The impact of the Hague Convention on Choice of Court Agreements[397]

In 2015, the Hague Convention on Choice of Court Agreements 2005 entered into force. The European Union ratified this Convention, both in its own right and on behalf of each of the Member States (excluding Denmark). At present, the only other Contracting Parties are Mexico and Singapore, while the USA and Ukraine have signed but not yet ratified. Under this Convention a judgment given by a court of a Contracting State designated in an exclusive choice of court agreement will be recognised and enforced in other Contracting States,[398] subject to limited grounds of refusal.[399] The Brussels I Recast continues to apply in relation to the recognition or enforcement of judgments as between European Union Member States.[400]

2. THE EC/DENMARK AGREEMENT

Under an Agreement between the European Community and Denmark[401] the provisions of the Brussels I Regulation, with minor modifications, were applied by international law to the relations between the European Union and Denmark. Pursuant to the Agreement, Denmark has now agreed to apply the Brussels I Recast.[402] In matters of recognition and enforcement, the Agreement applies where Denmark is either the state of origin or the state addressed.[403]

3. THE BRUSSELS CONVENTION[404]

The Brussels Convention was replaced in virtually all cases by the Brussels I Regulation, which has now been repealed and replaced by the Brussels I Recast. However, one has to say

---

[392] Art 59 still exists under the Brussels Convention, see infra, pp 652–3.
[393] The Explanatory Memorandum in the Proposal for the Brussels I Regulation, pp 7–8.
[394] See Opinion 1/03 of the Court of Justice Competence of the Community to conclude the new Lugano Convention [2006] ECR I-1145 holding that conclusion of a new Lugano Convention fell within the exclusive competence of the European Union.
[395] See the Joint Statement of 14 December 2000 by the Council and the Commission on Arts 71 and 72 of the Brussels I Regulation (Doc Consilium No 14139/00).
[396] Art 72 of the Recast; discussed supra, p 643.
[397] Discussed supra, pp 315–17.
[398] Art 8.
[399] Art 9.
[400] Art 26(6)(b).
[401] OJ 2005 L 299/61. For consequential amendments in the UK see SI 2007/1655. Prior to the entry into force of this Agreement, the Brussels Convention applied in relation to Denmark.
[402] OJ 2013 L 79/4. See generally the discussion in the context of jurisdiction, supra, p 192.
[403] See Art 10(2)(c) of the 2005 Agreement.
[404] See s 4 of the Civil Jurisdiction and Judgments Act 1982.

"virtually" because the Brussels Convention continued to apply and still applies in relation to the territories of the Contracting States[405] which fall within the territorial scope of the Brussels Convention and are excluded from the Recast.[406] The territories in question are (in relation to France) the French overseas territories, such as New Caledonia, and Mayotte, and (in relation to the Netherlands) Aruba.[407] It follows that the rules on recognition and enforcement under the Brussels Convention are still applied in the United Kingdom and in the other Contracting States where, for example, a judgment was given in New Caledonia in respect of a matter within the scope of the Convention. The rules on recognition and enforcement under the Brussels Convention are significantly different from those of the Brussels I Recast. The biggest difference is the system of exequatur that exists under the Brussels Convention. This instrument is described fully in a previous edition of this book[408] and the reader is referred to what is said there for further details.

4. THE LUGANO CONVENTION[409]

The 1988 Lugano Convention extended the free circulation of judgments beyond the European Union to three countries of the EFTA bloc (Iceland, Norway and Switzerland). It did this by means of a parallel Convention to the Brussels Convention, based closely on that Convention, albeit not identical to it. The 1988 Lugano Convention has been replaced by the 2007 Lugano Convention,[410] the terms of which have been aligned with the Brussels I Regulation. The states bound by the Convention are the twenty-eight European Union Member States and the three EFTA States. The Lugano Convention has been examined earlier in the context of jurisdiction.[411] Some of the same issues that were discussed there need to be addressed now in relation to the recognition and enforcement of foreign judgments: when do the rules on recognition and enforcement under the Lugano Convention apply? What are the differences between the Lugano Convention and the Brussels I Recast?

(a) When do the rules on recognition and enforcement under the Lugano Convention apply?[412]

The Lugano Convention applies in matters of recognition and enforcement, where either the state of origin or the state addressed is not applying the Brussels I Recast, the Brussels Convention or the EC/Denmark Agreement,[413] but is, of course, bound by the Lugano Convention. Thus if a United Kingdom court is asked to recognise a Swiss, Norwegian or Icelandic judgment, or vice versa, the Lugano Convention will apply. If both states are members of EFTA, the Lugano Convention will also apply. The Lugano Convention provides that

---

[405] At the moment the Contracting States to the Brussels Convention are the original fifteen Member States.

[406] Art 68(1). Territories are excluded from the Recast pursuant to Art 355 of the Treaty on the Functioning of the European Union.

[407] See Layton and Mercer, paras 11.061–11.071. See also Kruger, paras 1.026–1.037.

[408] See the 13th edn of this book (1999), pp 480–516. See also Dicey and Morris (1999) 13th edn, paras 14R-183–14-229.

[409] See s 4A of the Civil Jurisdiction and Judgments Act 1982, inserted by SI 2009/3131.

[410] OJ 2007 L 339/3, Art 69(6).

[411] Supra, pp 313–14.

[412] Where recognition or enforcement is sought, the Convention applies only to proceedings instituted after its entry into force in the state of origin and in the state addressed: Art 63(1). However, if proceedings in the state of origin were instituted before this date, judgments given after that date will still be recognised under the Convention if certain conditions are met: Art 63(2).

[413] Art 64(2)(c) of the Lugano Convention.

the Brussels I Recast, the Brussels Convention and the EC/Denmark Agreement continue to apply, unaffected by the Convention.[414] Thus if a United Kingdom court is asked to recognise a French judgment, the Brussels I Recast will apply.

(b) Differences between the Lugano Convention and the Brussels I Recast

The alignment of the Lugano Convention with the Brussels I Regulation has resulted in a close similarity between the two. Nonetheless, there are a number of differences in substance between the two instruments, most of which can be traced back to provisions in the 1988 Lugano Convention. Accordingly, the rules on recognition and enforcement under the Lugano Convention are significantly different from those of the Brussels I Recast. The biggest difference is the system of exequatur that exists under the Lugano Convention. The rules of the Brussels I Regulation, on which the Lugano Convention is based, are not described in this book, since they have been repealed and replaced by the Brussels I Recast. The former are described fully in a previous edition of this book[415] and the reader is referred to what is said there for further details. What follows is a list of differences in substance between the Lugano Convention and the Brussels I Regulation, which are also some of the differences between the former instrument and the Brussels I Recast.

First, the Lugano Convention provides that Contracting Parties can enter into Conventions with third states incorporating Article 59 of the Brussels Convention type obligation.[416] There is no such provision in either the Brussels I Regulation or the Recast.[417] The power to enter into the let-out in the future was present in the 1988 Lugano Convention,[418] which was based on the Brussels Convention, and is retained in the 2007 Lugano Convention. This is not as big a difference as it might appear. The Contracting Parties to the Convention are the three EFTA States, Denmark and the European Union, not the individual European Union Member States. Moreover, the European Council and Commission can negotiate international agreements that would mitigate the consequences of Chapter III (Recognition and Enforcement) of the Brussels I Recast in third states.[419] The let-out allowed in the Lugano Convention is a narrow one. It only applies to the exorbitant bases of jurisdiction listed in the Convention. This does not include jurisdiction under rule 6.36 of the Civil Procedure Rules and paragraph 3.1 of the CPR Practice Direction 6B. Moreover, there is an additional limitation on its use. In broad terms, it cannot apply where jurisdiction is based on the presence of the defendant's property in the forum and the action relates to this property.[420]

Secondly, there is an additional defence in Article 64(3) of the Lugano Convention.[421] This was introduced in the 1988 Convention[422] and arose because of a concern raised by EFTA States. It has then been repeated in the 2007 Convention. Article 64(3), contains a discretionary power[423] to refuse to recognise or enforce a judgment "if the ground of jurisdiction on which the judgment has been made differs from that resulting from this Convention". This is designed to deal with the situation where a European Union State takes jurisdiction

---

[414] Art 64(1) of the Lugano Convention.

[415] See the 14th edn (2008) of this book, pp 596–637.

[416] Art 68(1) of the Lugano Convention. Art 59 of the Brussels Convention is discussed supra, pp 651–2.

[417] Art 72 of the Recast; discussed supra, p 643.

[418] Art 59 of the 1988 Lugano Convention.

[419] See the Joint Statement by the Council and the Commission on Arts 71 and 72 of the Brussels I Regulation; supra, pp 651–2.

[420] Art 68(2) of the Lugano Convention.

[421] See generally Art 35(1) of the Lugano Convention.

[422] Art 54(B)(3) of the 1988 Lugano Convention. It was not in the Brussels Convention.

[423] See Case C-80/00 *Italian Leather SpA v WECO Polstermobel GmbH & Co* [2002] ECR I-4995 at [50].

under a differently worded provision of the Brussels I Recast, Brussels Convention or Danish Agreement, when it should have taken jurisdiction under the Lugano Convention.[424] With the alignment of the Lugano Convention with the Brussels I Regulation this will very seldom happen. The defence only applies where recognition or enforcement is sought against a party domiciled in a state where the Lugano Convention applies but not the Brussels I Recast, Brussels Convention or Danish Agreement; ie an Icelandic, Norwegian or Swiss domiciliary. The defence will not apply if the judgment "may otherwise be recognised or enforced under any rule of law in the State addressed", ie under its common law rules.

Thirdly, there is a further additional defence under Article 67(4),[425] which is concerned with the situation where jurisdiction has been taken under a convention on a particular matter, eg the Warsaw Convention on international carriage by air of 1929. When negotiating the 1988 Lugano Convention, the EFTA States would not agree to the open system that then operated under Article 57 of the Brussels Convention[426] (the predecessor of Article 71 of the Brussels I Recast[427]). A safeguard was accordingly introduced and this has been repeated in the 2007 Lugano Convention. Article 67(4) of the 2007 Convention provides a discretionary power to refuse to recognise or enforce a judgment if the state addressed is not bound by the convention under which jurisdiction is asserted and the person against whom recognition or enforcement is sought is domiciled in that state. This defence does not operate solely for the benefit of domiciliaries of the EFTA States; a judgment granted in an EFTA State could be denied recognition in a European Union State on this ground. The 2007 Lugano Convention has introduced additional wording, not to be found in the 1988 Convention, to deal with the situation where the convention on a particular matter is one which would have to be concluded by the European Union.[428] In this situation, the defence applies where the state addressed is a Member State of the European Union, is not bound by the convention which would have to be concluded by the European Union, and the defendant is domiciled in any European Union Member State. Again, the defence will not apply if the judgment may otherwise be recognised or enforced under any rule of law in the state addressed.

Fourthly,[429] Switzerland reserves the right to declare upon ratification that it will not apply the proviso in the natural justice defence in Article 34(2) of the Convention, which says "unless the defendant failed to commence proceedings to challenge the judgment when it was possible for him to do so".[430] Switzerland has made such a declaration, so the other Contracting Parties must apply the same reservation in respect of judgments granted in Switzerland.[431]

---

[424] See the Jenard and Moller Report, p 68, for the purpose of the predecessor provision in the 1988 Lugano Convention (Art 54B(3) of that Convention).

[425] See generally Art 35(1) of the Lugano Convention.

[426] See the Jenard and Moller Report, p 92.

[427] Discussed supra, p 613.

[428] The individual European Union Member States no longer have power to conclude conventions which in particular matters govern jurisdiction or the recognition or enforcement of judgments, see supra, pp 613–14.

[429] There is a fifth difference which concerns decisions in Denmark, Iceland or Norway in respect of maintenance and legal aid: Art 50(2) of the Lugano Convention. There was a similar provision in the 1988 Lugano Convention.

[430] Protocol 1, Art III(1) attached to the Lugano Convention. Art 34(2) of Lugano follows Art 45(1)(b) of the Brussels I Recast discussed supra, pp 632–9. This proviso was not in the 1988 Lugano Convention (Art 27(2)). Other Contracting Parties can make the same reservation in respect of judgments granted in non-European Union/EFTA States which have acceded to the Lugano Convention: Protocol 1, Art III(2).

[431] Protocol 1, Art III(1).

5. THE EUROPEAN ENFORCEMENT ORDER REGULATION

Where there is a judgment, court settlement or authentic instrument on an uncontested claim, the creditor, as an alternative to seeking recognition and enforcement under the Brussels I Recast,[432] can seek this under Regulation (EC) No 805/2004 of the European Parliament and of the Council of 21 April 2004 creating a European Enforcement Order for uncontested claims,[433] which applies[434] in all the European Union Member States with the exception of Denmark.[435] The Regulation, like the Brussels I Recast, is one of the measures[436] relating to judicial co-operation in civil and commercial matters that are regarded as being necessary for the proper functioning of the internal market.[437] The Regulation, like the Brussels I Recast, permits the free circulation of judgments, etc throughout the Member States without any intermediate proceedings needing to be brought prior to enforcement in the Member State where enforcement is sought. The main advantage in using the former instrument as compared with the latter is that the number of defences to enforcement is reduced to only one (irreconcilability). The creation of a European Enforcement Order for uncontested claims was the first stage in a programme[438] of measures for implementation of the principle of mutual recognition of decisions in civil and commercial matters.[439]

(a) Subject matter, scope and definitions

The purpose of the Regulation is to create a European Enforcement Order for uncontested claims[440] to permit, by laying down minimum standards, the free circulation of judgments,[441] court settlements and authentic instruments[442] throughout all Member States without any intermediate proceedings needing to be brought in the Member State of enforcement[443] prior to recognition and enforcement.[444] The material scope of the Regulation is virtually the same as that of the Brussels I Recast[445] The concept of "uncontested claims" covers all situations in which a creditor, given the verified absence of any dispute by the debtor as to the nature or extent of a pecuniary claim, has obtained either a court decision against the debtor or an enforceable document that requires the debtor's express consent.[446] More specifically, a claim

---

[432] Art 27 of the European Enforcement Order Regulation provides that this Regulation will not affect the possibility of seeking recognition and enforcement under the Brussels I Regulation, which has been superseded by the Brussels I Recast.

[433] OJ 2004 L 143/15. See also the Commission's Proposal for the Regulation: Brussels, 18 April 2002 COM (2002) 159 final. For commentaries, see Briggs 2014, paras 6.109–6.112; Briggs 2015, paras 7.31–7.34; Dicey, Morris and Collins, paras 14-247–14-252. For English procedural rules see CPR, Part 74, Section V and CPR, PD 74B.

[434] The Regulation entered into force on 21 January 2004 and applies from 21 October 2005: Art 33. For a transitional provision see Art 26.

[435] Art 2(3).

[436] See for these measures supra, p 193.

[437] Recital (1) of the Regulation. See also Arts 67(4) and 81 of the Treaty on the Functioning of the European Union.

[438] Adopted by the European Council on 30 November 2000 OJ 2001 C 12/1.

[439] Recital (4).

[440] "Claim" is defined in Art 4(2).

[441] As defined in Art 4(1).

[442] As defined in Art 4(3).

[443] As defined in Art 4(5).

[444] Art 1.

[445] Art 2. For the scope of the Brussels I Recast see supra, pp 202–12.

[446] Recital (5).

is regarded as uncontested in four alternative situations:[447] the debtor has expressly agreed to it by admission or by a settlement which has been approved by a court or concluded before a court in the course of proceedings;[448] or the debtor has never objected to the claim in the course of the court proceedings;[449] or the debtor has not appeared or been represented at a court hearing regarding that claim after having initially objected to the claim in the course of the court proceedings, provided that such conduct amounts to a tacit admission of the claim or of the facts alleged by the creditor under the law of the Member State of origin;[450] or the debtor has expressly agreed to the claim in an authentic instrument.[451]

(b) European enforcement order

The Regulation is concerned that a judgment that has been certified as a European Enforcement Order by the court of origin[452] should, for enforcement purposes, be treated as if it had been delivered in the Member State in which enforcement is sought.[453] Article 5 is headed "Abolition of exequatur" and provides that: "A judgment which has been certified as a European Enforcement Order in the Member State of origin shall be recognised and enforced in the other Member States without the need for a declaration of enforceability and without any possibility of opposing its recognition."

Article 6 then sets out the requirements for certification as a European Enforcement Order.[454] It states that a judgment on an uncontested claim delivered in a Member State shall, upon application at any time to the court of origin, be certified as a European Enforcement Order provided that certain conditions are met.[455] First, the judgment is enforceable in the Member State of origin. Secondly, the judgment does not conflict with the rules on jurisdiction in Sections 3 (matters relating to insurance)[456] and 6 (exclusive jurisdiction under Article 24)[457] of Chapter II of the Brussels I Recast. Thirdly, the court proceedings in the Member State of origin met the minimum standards for uncontested claims procedures as set out in Chapter III of the Regulation.[458] Fourthly, in cases where the claim relates

---

[447] Art 3(1). A writ of execution adopted by a notary, in Croatia, based on an "authentic document", namely an invoice unilaterally drawn up by the claimant, and which has not been contested does not relate to an uncontested claim: Case C-484/15 *Zulfikarpašić v Gajer* EU:C:2017:199, [2017] IL Pr 16.

[448] Art 3(1)(a).

[449] Art 3(1)(b). This can take the shape of default of appearance at a court hearing or of failure to comply with an invitation by the court to give written notice of an intention to defend the case: Recital (6). The concept of "uncontested claim" is autonomous and the fact that in the Member State of origin a default judgment is not regarded as a judgment for an uncontested claim is irrelevant: Case C-511/14 *Pebros Servizi Srl v Aston Martin Lagonda Ltd* EU:C:2016:448, [2016] 4 WLR 138.

[450] Art 3(1)(c). "Member State of origin" is defined in Art 4(4).

[451] Art 3(1)(d).

[452] As defined in Art 4(6). In Croatia, notaries, acting within the framework of the powers conferred on them by national law in enforcement proceedings based on an "authentic document", do not fall within the concept of "court": Case C-484/15 *Zulfikarpašić v Gajer* EU:C:2017:199, [2017] IL Pr 16. This is because such enforcement proceedings are not court proceedings which offer the necessary guarantees of independence and impartiality and are delivered in compliance with the principle of *audi alteram partem*. See also Case C-551/15 *Pula Parking doo v Tederahn* EU:C:2017:193, [2017] IL Pr 15.

[453] Recital (8).

[454] For issue of the European Enforcement Order Certificate see Art 9. For its rectification or withdrawal see Art 10.

[455] Art 6(1). The certification of a judgment as a European Enforcement Order requires a judicial examination of the conditions laid down by the European Enforcement Order Regulation and can be carried out only by a judge: Case C-300/14 *Imtech Marine Belgium NV v Radio Hellenic SA* EU:C:2015:825, [2016] 1 WLR 1625.

[456] Discussed supra, pp 289–91.

[457] Discussed supra, pp 217–26.

[458] This requirement only applies where the claim is uncontested within the meaning of Art 3(1)(b) (debtor has never objected to the claim) or (c) (debtor has not appeared or been represented).

to a consumer contract[459] and the debtor is the consumer, the judgment was given in the Member State of the debtor's domicile.[460] Certification is carried out by means of a standard form which is set out in an Annex to the Regulation.

(c) Minimum standards for uncontested claims procedures

Where a court in a Member State has given judgment on an uncontested claim in the absence of participation of the debtor in the proceedings, there is an obvious concern that the debtor was not informed of the proceedings, the requirements for his active participation in the proceedings to contest the claim and the consequences of his non-participation in sufficient time and in such a way as to enable him to arrange for his defence.[461] Chapter III therefore lays down minimum standards in relation to these matters. These procedural requirements apply[462] where there is a judgment on a claim that is uncontested in the sense that the debtor has never objected to the claim in the course of the court proceedings[463] or has not appeared or been represented at a court hearing regarding that claim after having initially objected to the claim in the course of the court proceedings.[464] A judgment on a claim that is uncontested within either of the above two meanings can be certified as a European Enforcement Order only if the court proceedings in the Member State of origin met the procedural requirements as set out in Chapter III.[465] The court in the Member State of enforcement has no power to check that the procedural requirements in Chapter III have been met.[466] The check is carried out by the court of origin before certifying the judgment as a European Enforcement Order. Since there are differences between the Member States as regards the service of documents, Chapter III sets out detailed provisions for the minimum standards for this.[467] The document instituting the proceedings may be served on the debtor by various methods where there is proof of receipt by the debtor.[468] This includes personal service attested either by an acknowledgment of receipt, including the date of receipt, which is signed by the debtor[469] or by a document signed by the competent person who effected the service stating that the debtor has received the document or refused to receive it without any legal justification, and the date of the service.[470] Postal service[471] and service by electronic means such as fax or e-mail[472] is also permissible provided that, in both cases, it is attested by an acknowledgment of receipt. Any summons to a court hearing may be served on the debtor by the above methods or orally in a previous court hearing on the same claim and stated in the minutes

---

[459] Ie it relates to a contract concluded by a person, the consumer, for a purpose which can be regarded as being outside his trade or profession: Art 6(1)(d). The other party must be engaged in commercial or professional activities: Case C-508/12 *Vapenik v Thurner* EU:C:2013:790, [2014] 1 WLR 2486.

[460] It is also required that the claim is uncontested within the meaning of Art 3(1)(b) or (c). Domicile is defined according to Art 62 of the Brussels I Regulation Recast, discussed supra, p 213. This repeats Art 18(2) of the Brussels I Recast. Under the latter Regulation, Art 18(2) can be departed from by an agreement on jurisdiction. This would not appear to be possible under Art 6(1)(d) of the European Enforcement Order Regulation.

[461] Recitals (10)–(13).

[462] Art 12(1).

[463] Art 3(1)(b).

[464] Art 3(1)(c).

[465] Art 12(1).

[466] Recital (18); *SCET v Extrucable (Societe)* [2013] IL Pr 25, French cour de cassation.

[467] Recital (13). See also *Re Confirmation of a European Enforcement Order (Case 5 W 29/07)* [2010] IL Pr 44, Oberlandesgericht (Court of Appeal) Stuttgart.

[468] Art 13.

[469] Art 13(1)(a).

[470] Art 13(1)(b).

[471] Art 13(1)(c).

[472] Art 13(1)(d).

of that previous court hearing.[473] Service of the document instituting the proceedings and any summons to a court hearing without proof of receipt by the debtor is also permissible in certain circumstances.[474] Service may also be effected on a debtor's representative.[475] In order to ensure that the debtor was provided with due information about the claim, the document instituting the proceedings must have contained: the names and addresses of the parties; the amount of the claim; if interest is sought, the interest rate and period for which it is sought; a statement of the reason for the claim.[476] Certain specified information must also have been provided about the procedural steps necessary to contest the claim.[477] Non-compliance with all the minimum standards mentioned above can be cured and the judgment certified as a European Enforcement Order in certain circumstances.[478] The judgment can only be certified as a European Enforcement Order if the law of the Member State of origin has minimum standards for review of the judgment in specified exceptional cases.[479]

(d) Enforcement

Enforcement procedures are governed by the law of the Member State of enforcement.[480] A judgment certified as a European Enforcement Order is enforced under the same conditions as a judgment handed down in the Member State of enforcement.[481] The creditor must provide the competent enforcement authorities with copies of the judgment and the European Enforcement Order certificate, both of which must satisfy the conditions necessary to establish their authenticity, and, where necessary, a transcription or translation of the certificate.[482] There is, though, a defence to enforcement. Enforcement will, upon application by the debtor, be refused if the judgment certified as a European Enforcement Order is irreconcilable with an earlier judgment given in any Member State or in a third country.[483] This is subject to a number of provisos. First, the earlier judgment involved the same cause of action and was between the same parties. Secondly, the earlier judgment was given in the Member State of enforcement or fulfils the conditions necessary for its recognition in that state. Thirdly, the irreconcilability was not and could not have been raised as an objection in the court proceedings in the Member State of origin. Under no circumstances may the judgment or its certification as a European Enforcement Order be reviewed as to their substance in the Member State of enforcement.[484] The Regulation does not affect agreements entered into pursuant to Article 59 of the Brussels Convention.[485] There are powers in certain limited circumstances to stay the enforcement proceedings, limit them to protective measures or make enforcement conditional on the provision of security.[486]

---

[473] Art 13(2).

[474] Art 14. Service is not admissible if a debtor's address is not known with certainty: Art 14(2); see Case C-292/10 *G v De Visser* EU:C:2012:142, [2013] QB 168 (service on a debtor whose address was not known was effected by affixing a notice of that service to the court's bulletin board).

[475] Art 15.

[476] Art 16.

[477] Art 17.

[478] Art 18.

[479] Art 19. See also Recital (14). A member state is not required by Art 19 to establish in its national law a review procedure such as that referred to in Art 19 and is not in breach of Art 288 TFEU if it chooses not to do so; it is for the court hearing an application for certification to examine whether the minimum standards for review of the judgment in the law of the Member State of the court exist: Case C-300/14 *Imtech Marine Belgium NV v Radio Hellenic SA* EU:C:2015:825, [2016] 1 WLR 1625.

[480] Art 20(1).

[481] Ibid.

[482] Art 20(2).

[483] Art 21(1).

[484] Art 21(2). See also *Lothschutz v Vogel* [2014] EWHC 473 (QB) at [21].

[485] Art 22. Such agreements are discussed supra, pp 651–2.

[486] Art 23.

6. THE EUROPEAN ORDER FOR PAYMENT PROCEDURE REGULATION

Regulation (EC) No 1896/2006[487] establishes a procedure for European orders for payment. It is intended to simplify, speed up and reduce the costs of litigation in cross-border cases concerning uncontested pecuniary claims, and to permit the free circulation of European orders for payment throughout the European Union by laying down minimum standards, compliance with which renders unnecessary any intermediate proceedings in the Member State of enforcement prior to recognition and enforcement.[488] The Regulation applies[489] in all the Member States with the exception of Denmark.[490] The Regulation is one of the measures[491] relating to judicial co-operation in civil and commercial matters that are regarded as being necessary for the proper functioning of the internal market.[492] The European order for payment procedure is available to a claimant as an alternative to other procedures existing under the laws of the Member States or under European Union law.[493] The main advantage in using the European Order for Payment Procedure Regulation lies in the ease of obtaining an order under this instrument and in the fact is that the number of defences to enforcement is reduced to only one (irreconcilability).

(a) Scope and definitions

The Regulation applies to civil and commercial matters[494] in cross-border cases.[495] A cross-border case is defined as one in which at least one of the parties is domiciled[496] or habitually resident in a Member State other than the Member State of the court seised.[497] A number of matters are excluded from the material scope of the Regulation. These include some of the matters excluded from the scope of the Brussels I Recast, namely rights in property arising out of a matrimonial relationship,[498] wills and succession,[499] bankruptcy, etc[500] and social security.[501] In addition, there is the exclusion of one matter

---

[487] Regulation (EC) No 1896/2006 of the European Parliament and of the Council of 12 December 2006 creating a European order for payment procedure OJ 2006 L 399/1, amended by Regulation (EU) 2015/2421 OJ 2015 L 341. See also the Commission's Report on the application of Regulation (EC) 1896/2006, 13 October 2015, COM (2015) 495 final; Commission's Proposal for the Regulation: Brussels, 19 March 2004, COM (2004) 173 final; Fiorini (2008) 57 ICLQ 449. For English procedural rules see CPR, Part 78, Section I.

[488] Art 1(1).

[489] The Regulation entered into force on 31 December 2006 and applies from 12 December 2008: Art 33.

[490] Art 2(3).

[491] See for these measures supra, p 193.

[492] Recital (1) of the Regulation. See also Arts 67(4) and 81 of the Treaty on the Functioning of the European Union.

[493] Art 1(2).

[494] For the meaning of this concept see supra, pp 204–12.

[495] Art 2(1).

[496] To be determined in accordance with Arts 62 and 63 of the Brussels I Recast, supra, pp 213–14: Art 3(2).

[497] Art 3(1).

[498] Art 2(2)(a), for the meaning of this exclusion see Art 1(2)(a) of the Brussels I Recast, discussed supra, pp 206–7.

[499] Art 2(2)(a), for the meaning of this exclusion see Art 1(2)(f) of the Brussels I Recast, discussed supra, p 212.

[500] Art 2(2)(b), for the meaning of this exclusion see Art 1(2)(b) of the Brussels I Recast, discussed supra, pp 207–8.

[501] Art 2(2)(c), for the meaning of this exclusion see Art 1(2)(c) of the Brussels I Recast, discussed supra, p 208.

that is not excluded from the scope of the Brussels I Recast, namely claims arising from non-contractual obligations.[502]

(b) The European order for payment procedure

The European order for payment procedure has been "established for the collection of pecuniary claims for a specific amount that have fallen due at the time when the application for a European order for payment is submitted".[503] For the purposes of applying the Regulation, jurisdiction is to be determined in accordance with the relevant rules of European Union law, in particular the Brussels I Recast.[504] In the situation where a claim is brought against a consumer, only the courts of the Member State where the defendant is domiciled have jurisdiction.[505]

The European order for payment procedure is based, to the largest extent possible, on the use of standard forms in any communication between the court and the parties.[506] An application for a European order for payment is made using standard form A as set out in Annex I.[507] The court seised of the application must examine, as soon as possible and on the basis of the information provided in the application form,[508] whether the requirements set out in the Regulation have been met and whether the claim appears to be founded.[509] If the answer is in the negative, the application will be rejected.[510] If, on the other hand, these requirements are met, the court will issue, as soon as possible and normally within thirty days of the lodging of the application, a European order for payment using standard form E as set out in Annex V.[511] The order will inform the defendant, among others, of his options to pay or to oppose the order.[512] The court will ensure that the order is served on the defendant in accordance with national law by a method that meets the minimum standards laid down in the Regulation.[513] The defendant may lodge a statement of opposition to the European order for payment with the court of origin using standard form F as set out in Annex VI.[514] This must be sent within thirty days of service of the order on the defendant.[515] The defendant will indicate in the statement of opposition that he contests the claim, without having to specify

---

[502] Art 2(2)(d). The exclusion applies unless: (i) the claims have been the subject of an agreement between the parties or there has been an admission of debt, or (ii) they relate to liquidated debts arising from joint ownership of property.

[503] Art 4.

[504] Art 6(1).

[505] Art 6(2). This repeats Art 18(2) of the Brussels I Recast. Under the latter Regulation, Art 18(2) can be departed from by an agreement on jurisdiction. This would not appear to be possible under Art 6.

[506] Recital (13).

[507] Art 7(1).

[508] Recital (16).

[509] Art 8. Member States cannot impose additional requirements: Case C-215/11 *Iwona Szyrocka v SiGer Technologie GmbH* EU:C:2012:794. For completion, rectification and modification of the application see Arts 9 and 10.

[510] Art 11.

[511] Art 12(1).

[512] Art 12(3).

[513] Art 12(5). These minimum standards are laid down in Arts 13, 14 and 15 of the Regulation and are virtually identical to the minimum standards laid down in Arts 13, 14 and 15 of the European Enforcement Order Regulation, discussed supra, pp 658–9. See Joined Cases C-119/13 and C-120/13 *Eco Cosmetics GmbH & Co KG v Dupuy and Raiffeisenbank St Georgen reg, Gen mbH v Bonchyk* EU:C:2014:2144, [2015] 1 WLR 678 (the procedures laid down in Arts 16-20 of the Regulation, discussed infra, are not applicable where a European order for payment has not been served in a manner consistent with these minimum standards; if an order has been declared enforceable, the defendant must have the opportunity to raise that irregularity under national law which, if established, will invalidate the declaration of enforceability).

[514] Art 16(1).

[515] Art 16(2).

the reasons for this.[516] A statement of opposition that does not contain any challenge to the jurisdiction of the court of origin is not regarded as constituting the entering of an appearance within the meaning of Article 26 of the Brussels I Recast; the fact that the defendant has put forward argument relating to the substance of the case is irrelevant in that regard.[517] If a statement of opposition is lodged within the thirty-day time limit, the proceedings will continue before the competent courts of the Member State of origin unless the claimant has explicitly requested that the proceedings be terminated in that event.[518] The proceedings shall continue in accordance with the rules of: a) the European Small Claims Procedure laid down in Regulation (EC) No 861/2007, if applicable; or b) any appropriate national civil procedure.[519] If no statement of opposition is lodged within the time limit with the court of origin, that court will without delay declare the order enforceable using standard form G as set out in Annex VII.[520] After the expiry of the thirty-day time limit, the defendant is entitled only in exceptional cases to apply for a review of the order before the competent court in the Member State of origin.[521]

(c) Recognition and enforcement in other Member States

A European order for payment which has become enforceable in the Member State of origin will be recognised and enforced in the other Member States without the need for a declaration of enforceability and without any possibility of opposing its recognition.[522] In other words, exequatur is abolished. Enforcement procedures are governed by the law of the Member State of enforcement.[523] A European order for payment which has become enforceable is enforced under the same conditions as an enforceable decision issued in the Member State of enforcement.[524] The claimant must provide the competent enforcement authorities with a copy of the European order for payment, as declared enforceable by the court of origin, which satisfies the conditions necessary to establish its authenticity, and, where necessary, a translation of the order.[525] There is, though, a defence to enforcement.[526] This is substantially the same as the irreconcilable judgments defence that is to be found in the European Enforcement Order Regulation.[527] Enforcement will, upon application by the defendant, also be refused if and to the extent that the defendant has paid the claimant the amount awarded in the order.[528] Where the defendant has applied for a review,[529] there are powers to

---

[516] Art 16(3).

[517] Case C-144/12 *Goldbet Sportwetten GmbH v Massimo Sperindeo* EU:C:2013:393, [2014] IL Pr 1.

[518] Art 17(1).

[519] Ibid. See also paras 2 to 5 of Article 17(1). See also Case C-94/14 *Flight Refund Ltd v Deutsche Lufthansa AG* EU:C:2016:148, [2016] 1 WLR 3567, concerning the examination of the jurisdiction of the courts of the Member State of origin to hear the contentious proceedings following the lodging of a statement of opposition.

[520] Art 18(1).

[521] Art 20. See C-324/12 *Novontech-Zala kft v Logicdata Electronic and Software Entwicklungs GmbH* EU:C:2013:205 (the failure to observe the time-limit for lodging a statement of opposition to a European order for payment by reason of the negligence of the defendant's legal adviser does not justify a review); Case C-245/14 *Thomas Cook Belgium NV v Thurner Hotel GmbH* EU:C:2015:715, [2016] 1 WLR 878 (a defendant on whom a European order for payment has been served in accordance with the European Order for Payment Procedure Regulation and who failed to observe the time-limit for lodging a statement of opposition is not entitled to apply for a review by claiming that the court of origin incorrectly held that it had jurisdiction on the basis of allegedly false information provided by the claimant in the application form).

[522] Art 19.

[523] Art 21(1).

[524] Ibid.

[525] Art 21(2).

[526] Art 22(1).

[527] See Art 21(1) of the European Enforcement Order Regulation; discussed supra, p 659.

[528] Art 22(2).

[529] Under Art 20, supra.

stay the enforcement proceedings, limit them to protective measures or make enforcement conditional on the provision of security.[530]

7. THE EUROPEAN SMALL CLAIMS PROCEDURE REGULATION

Regulation (EC) No 861/2007[531] establishes a European procedure for small claims, which is intended to simplify and speed up litigation in cross-border cases and to reduce costs.[532] The Regulation applies[533] in all the European Union Member States with the exception of Denmark.[534] The Regulation is one of the measures[535] relating to judicial co-operation in civil and commercial matters that are regarded as being necessary for the proper functioning of the internal market.[536] The European small claims procedure is available to litigants as an alternative to the procedures existing under the laws of the Member States.[537] The main advantage in using the European Small Claims Procedure Regulation lies in the ease of obtaining an order under this instrument and in the fact is that the number of defences to enforcement is reduced to only one (irreconcilability).

(a) Scope and definitions

The Regulation applies, in cross-border cases, to civil and commercial matters.[538] A cross-border case is defined as one in which at least one of the parties is domiciled[539] or habitually resident in a Member State other than the Member State of the court or tribunal seised.[540] The Regulation applies only where the value of the claim does not exceed 5,000 Euros.[541] However, it is not confined to consumer claims and can include commercial claims.[542] A number of matters are excluded from the scope of the Regulation. These are the same matters as are excluded from the scope of the Brussels I Recast[543] plus three additional matters which are not excluded from the latter. These are as follows: employment law;[544] tenancies of immovable property, with the exception of actions on monetary claims;[545] violations of privacy and of rights relating to personality, including defamation.[546]

---

[530] Art 23.

[531] Regulation (EC) No 861/2007 of the European Parliament and of the Council of 11 July 2007 establishing a European Small Claims Procedure OJ 2007 L 199/1, amended by Regulation (EU) 2015/2421 OJ 2015 L 341. See also the Commission's Report on the application of Regulation (EC) 861/2007, 19 October 2015, COM (2015) 795 final; Commission's Proposal for the Regulation: Brussels, 15 March 2005, COM (2005) 87 final; Fiorini (2008) 57 ICLQ 449. For English procedural rules see CPR, Part 78, Section II.

[532] Art 1.

[533] The Regulation entered into force on 1 August 2007 and applies from 1 January 2009: Art 29.

[534] Recital (26) of the Regulation (EU) 2015/2421, amending the European Small Claims Procedure Regulation.

[535] See for these measures supra, p 193.

[536] Recital (1) of the Regulation. See also Arts 67(4) and 81 of the Treaty on the Functioning of the European Union.

[537] Art 1.

[538] Art 2. For the meaning of this concept see supra, pp 204–12.

[539] To be determined in accordance with Arts 62 and 63 of the Brussels I Recast, supra, pp 213–14: Art 3(2) of the European Small Claims Procedure Regulation.

[540] Art 3(1).

[541] Art 2(1).

[542] See Recital (4).

[543] See Art 2(2)(a)–(g) of the European Small Claims Procedure Regulation, for the meaning of these exclusions see Art 1(2) of the Brussels I Recast, discussed supra, p 206 et seq.

[544] Art 2(2)(h).

[545] Art 2(2)(i).

[546] Art 2(j). The meaning of this phrase is examined infra, pp 797–9.

(b) The European small claims procedure

A claimant commences the European small claims procedure by filling in a standard claim form (form A), which is set out in Annex I to the Regulation, and lodging it with the court or tribunal with jurisdiction[547] directly, by post or by any other means of communication, such as fax or e-mail, acceptable to the Member State in which the procedure is commenced.[548] The court or tribunal with jurisdiction must have jurisdiction "in accordance with the rules" in the Brussels I Recast.[549] It is contemplated that, normally, this will be one of the bases of jurisdiction set out in that Regulation[550] but it could presumably also include a case where jurisdiction is taken under traditional national rules of jurisdiction, which Article 6 of the Brussels I Recast instructs the courts of Member States to apply in the situation where the defendant is not domiciled in a Member State (and Articles 18(1), 21(2), 24 and 25 of that Regulation do not apply).[551] The European small claims procedure is a written one.[552] But the court or tribunal will hold an oral hearing only if it considers that it is not possible to give the judgment on the basis of the written evidence or if a party so requests.[553] A copy of the claim form is served on the defendant who must respond within thirty days of service by filling in standard answer form C, as set out in Annex III.[554] Within fourteen days a copy of this response is dispatched to the claimant.[555] The claimant has thirty days to respond to any counterclaim.[556] Within thirty days of the receipt of the response from the defendant or the claimant, the court or tribunal will give a judgment.[557] Member States must inform the Commission whether an appeal is available under their procedural law against a judgment given in the European small claims procedure and within what time limit it must be lodged.[558] A judgment is enforceable in the state in which it was given notwithstanding any possible appeal.[559] There are in any event minimum standards for the review of a judgment in specified situations where the defendant was not able to contest the claim.[560] Where a party has challenged a judgment or where such a challenge is still possible, or where a party has made an application for review, the court or tribunal with jurisdiction may stay or limit the enforcement.[561]

(c) Recognition and enforcement in other Member States

A judgment given in a Member State in the European small claims procedure will be recognised and enforced in other Member States without the need for a declaration of enforceability and without any possibility of opposing its recognition.[562] Thus exequatur is abolished. Enforcement procedures are governed by the law of the Member State of enforcement.[563]

---

[547] Member States must inform the Commission which courts or tribunals have jurisdiction to give a judgment in the European Small Claims Procedure: Art 25(1)(a).

[548] Art 4(1). Member States must inform the Commission which means are acceptable to them: Art 4(2).

[549] Annex I, form A, guideline 4.

[550] See box 4 in form A, which, in effect, sets out the bases of jurisdiction under the Brussels I Recast.

[551] The list of bases of jurisdiction in box 4 includes "Other" (than those under the Recast).

[552] Art 5(1).

[553] Ibid.

[554] Art 5(2) and (3).

[555] Art 5(4).

[556] Art 5(6).

[557] Art 7(1). Alternatively the court or tribunal can (a) demand further details or (b) take evidence or (c) summon the parties to an oral hearing.

[558] Art 17.

[559] Art 15(1).

[560] See Art 18.

[561] Arts 15(2) and 23.

[562] Art 20(1).

[563] Art 21(1).

Any judgment given in the European small claims procedure will be enforced under the same conditions as a judgment given in the Member State of enforcement.[564] The party seeking enforcement must produce a copy of the judgment which satisfies the conditions necessary to establish its authenticity and a certificate and, where necessary, the translation thereof issued by the court or tribunal giving the judgment using standard form D, as set out as Annex IV.[565] There is, though, a defence to enforcement,[566] which is in substance the irreconcilable judgments defence that is to be found in the European Enforcement Order Regulation.[567] Where a party has challenged a judgment given in the European small claims procedure or where such a challenge is still possible, or where a party has made an application for review, the court or tribunal with jurisdiction in the Member State of enforcement may stay or limit the enforcement.[568]

---

[564] Ibid.
[565] Art 21(2).
[566] Art 22(1).
[567] See Art 21(1) of the European Enforcement Order Regulation; discussed supra, p 659.
[568] Art 23.

18

FOREIGN ARBITRAL AWARDS[1]

1. Enforcement At Common Law   667
2. Enforcement Under the Civil Jurisdiction and Judgments Act 1982   669
3. Enforcement Under the Arbitration Act 1950   670
4. Enforcement Under the Arbitration Act 1996   670
5. Enforcement Under the Administration of Justice Act 1920 and the Foreign Judgments (Reciprocal Enforcement) Act 1933   677
6. Enforcement Under the Arbitration (International Investment Disputes) Act 1966   677

A foreign arbitral award is similar to a foreign judgment in that it may be enforced in England in a variety of ways. An action may be brought at common law to recover the sum awarded. Statutory provision is also made for the enforcement of foreign arbitral awards. Before looking at the various methods of enforcement in detail,[2] one general point should be made. The Limitation Act 1980 provides that an action to enforce an award "shall not be brought after the expiration of six years from the date on which the cause of action accrued".[3] This provision applies regardless of the method of enforcement.[4] It has been held that an action to enforce an arbitration award is an independent cause of action, arising from the breach of an implied term in the arbitration agreement that the award would be honoured.[5] Accordingly, time runs not from the date of the original breach of contract which had been the subject of the arbitration or from the date upon which the arbitration award was made or published, but from the date of the failure to honour the award.[6]

Also, if a foreign award has been entered as a judgment abroad, it seems that this not only can[7] but must be enforced under the rules on enforcement of judgments (provided it is

---

[1] Blackaby and Partasides, *Redfern and Hunter on International Commercial Arbitration* (2015) 6th edn, Chapter 11; Briggs 2014, paras 14.81–14.107; Briggs 2015, paras 8.29–8.31 and 8.36–8.39; Lew and others (eds), *Arbitration in England with Chapters on Scotland and Northern Ireland* (2013), Chapter 26; Mustill and Boyd, *Commercial Arbitration* (1989) 2nd edn, pp 421–7 and Companion Volume 2001; Hill and Chong, Chapter 24; Dicey, Morris and Collins, paras 16-099–16-189.

[2] Enforcement procedure is governed by Part 62 of the CPR.

[3] S 7. This section does not apply where the submission is by an instrument under seal.

[4] *Minister of Public Works of the Government of the State of Kuwait v Sir Frederick Snow & Partners* [1983] 1 WLR 818 at 823–4, CA (*per* Kerr LJ); the House of Lords affirmed this decision, without discussing this point [1984] 1 AC 426.

[5] *Agromet Motoimport v Maulden Engineering Co (Beds) Ltd* [1985] 1 WLR 762.

[6] The *Agromet Motoimport* case. See also *Good Challenger Navegante SA v Metalexportimport SA (The Good Challenger)* [2003] EWCA Civ 1668, [2004] 1 Lloyd's Rep 67.

[7] See, eg, *East India Trading Co Inc v Carmel Exporters and Importers Ltd* [1952] 2 QB 439; *L R Avionics Technologies Ltd v Nigeria* [2016] EWHC 1761 (Comm), [2016] 4 WLR 120; *International Alltex Corp v Lawler Creations Ltd* [1965] IR 264.

capable of being so enforced) and not as an award.[8] But this rule does not apply when a foreign award is enforced under an international convention as it would undermine the regime established by the convention.[9]

1. ENFORCEMENT AT COMMON LAW

The basic elements for the successful enforcement of a foreign arbitration award in England are that the parties submitted to arbitration, that the arbitration was conducted in accordance with the submission and that the award is valid by the law of the country in which it was made.[10] A foreign award that satisfies these conditions may also produce an issue estoppel or a cause of action estoppel.[11]

There must be a valid submission to arbitration,[12] either in the form of an arbitration clause contained in a substantive contract or a free-standing agreement to arbitrate. The material validity,[13] scope, interpretation and effect of an arbitration agreement are determined by its proper law.[14] The proper law of the arbitration agreement may not be the same as the law applicable to the substantive contract in which it is contained because of the doctrine of separability.[15] The proper law of the arbitration agreement is the law chosen by the parties, expressly or impliedly; in the absence of choice, it is the system of law with which the arbitration agreement has the closest and most real connection.[16] It often happens that the parties fail to expressly choose the law governing the arbitration agreement, while making an express choice of the law governing the substantive contract in which the arbitration agreement is contained and of the arbitral seat. The question then arises whether any of these is an indication of an implied choice of law governing the arbitration agreement. The natural inference is that the parties intended that the law expressly chosen to govern the substantive contract should govern the arbitration agreement as well.[17] But the law expressly chosen by the parties to govern the substantive contract may be found not to govern the arbitration agreement where there are indications that the parties cannot have intended that law to govern, eg if that law would render the arbitration agreement invalid or ineffective and there is a choice of another country as the seat of arbitration.[18] If the parties fail to choose the law governing the

---

[8] S 34 of the Civil Jurisdiction and Judgments Act 1982, abolishing the doctrine of non-merger in relation to foreign judgments; supra, p 556.

[9] See Briggs 2014, paras 14.91, 14.107; Dicey, Morris and Collins, paras 16-109, 16-110; Hill (2012) 8 J Priv Int L 159; Hill and Chong, paras 24.6.8–24.6.12; Scherer (2013) 4 J Int Dispute Settlement 587, 600–1.

[10] *Norske Atlas Insurance Co Ltd v London General Insurance Co Ltd* (1927) 28 Lloyd's Rep 104.

[11] See *Good Challenger Navegante SA v Metalexportimport SA (The Good Challenger)* [2003] EWCA Civ 1668, [2004] 1 Lloyd's Rep 67.

[12] See *Kruppa v Benedetti* [2014] EWHC 1887 (Comm), [2014] 2 All ER (Comm) 617.

[13] Including the question of whether the arbitration agreement has been rendered void by subsequent illegality, see *Dalmia Dairy Industries Ltd v National Bank of Pakistan* [1978] 2 Lloyd's Rep 223, CA.

[14] This is not affected by the Rome I Regulation, see Art 1(2)(e), infra, pp 700–1.

[15] See the Arbitration Act 1996, s 7; *Fiona Trust & Holding Corp v Privalov* [2007] UKHL 40, [2007] 4 All ER 951.

[16] *Sulamérica Cia Nacional de Seguros SA v Enesa Engelharia SA* [2012] EWCA Civ 638 at [9] and [25], [2013] 1 WLR 102 (*per* Moore-Bick LJ); *Arsanovia Ltd v Cruz City 1 Mauritius Holdings* [2012] EWHC 3702 (Comm), [2013] 2 All ER (Comm) 1; *Habaş Sinai ve Tibbi Gazlar Istihsal Endüstrisi AŞ v VSC Steel Co Ltd* [2013] EWHC 4071 (Comm), [2014] 1 Lloyd's Rep 479.

[17] The *Sulamérica* case at [11] and [26] (*per* Moore-Bick LJ). See also *Arsanovia Ltd v Cruz City 1 Mauritius Holdings* [2012] EWHC 3702 (Comm), [2013] 2 All ER (Comm) 1. Cf *XL Insurance Ltd v Owens Corning* [2001] 1 All ER (Comm) 530; *C v D* [2007] EWCA Civ 1282, [2008] 1 All ER (Comm) 1001. For the law governing substantive contract reference has to be made to the Rome I Regulation, infra, pp 686–775.

[18] The *Sulamérica* case at [26] and [29]–[31] (*per* Moore-Bick LJ).

arbitration agreement, the agreement will have the closest and most real connection with the law of the country where the arbitration is to take place.[19]

The actual arbitration proceedings, in the absence of an express choice by the parties of the law to govern the arbitration proceedings,[20] will be governed by the law of the place of arbitration.[21] That law will determine whether the award is valid;[22] though whether the arbitrator has jurisdiction is a matter for the arbitration agreement and its proper law.[23] The award, to be enforceable in England, must, like a foreign judgment, be final and binding according to the law governing the arbitration proceedings.[24] But the fact that the foreign award, under that law, is not enforceable until it has been confirmed by a court does not prevent its enforcement in England.[25] One justification for this conclusion is that the action in England to enforce the award is an action on the award and not on either the contract to which the award gives effect[26] or on a foreign judgment. If the foreign arbitral award includes an award of interest, the English court in an action on the award will not make a further award of interest at a higher rate.[27]

The recognition and enforcement of a foreign arbitral award seem to be subject to the obvious defences that the arbitrator lacked jurisdiction,[28] that the award was obtained by fraud,[29] that its recognition and enforcement would be contrary to English public policy,[30] and that it was obtained in proceedings which contravene the rules of natural justice.[31] Recognition and enforcement will also be refused if the foreign award has been set aside by the courts of the seat of arbitration, unless the foreign setting aside itself is not given effect in England.[32]

A foreign arbitral award which does not fall within the various statutory provisions for recognition and enforcement based on international conventions[33] may be enforced either by an action on the award at common law,[34] or by recourse to section 66 of the Arbitration Act 1996, which provides that, with leave of the court, an award may be enforced in the same manner as a judgment or order of the court to the same effect. This discretionary procedure is not restricted to domestic English awards but is available for the enforcement of foreign awards,[35] though the award will have to satisfy the other requirements for enforcement in

---

[19] Ibid, at [26] and [32] (*per* Moore-Bick LJ); *Habaş Sinai ve Tibbi Gazlar Istihsal Endüstrisi AŞ v VSC Steel Co Ltd* [2013] EWHC 4071 (Comm), [2014] 1 Lloyd's Rep 479.

[20] *International Tank and Pipe SAK v Kuwait Aviation Fuelling Co KSC* [1975] 1 QB 224 at 232–3, CA. See also *Naviera Amazonica Peruana SA v Cia Internacional de Seguros del Peru* [1988] 1 Lloyd's Rep 116 at 119–20, CA.

[21] *James Miller & Partners Ltd v Whitworth Street Estates (Manchester) Ltd* [1970] AC 583, HL; the *Dalmia Dairy Industries* case.

[22] *Norske Atlas Insurance Co Ltd v London General Insurance Co Ltd* (1927) 28 Lloyd's Rep 104.

[23] The *Dalmia Dairy Industries* case.

[24] Ibid, at 246–50.

[25] *Union Nationale des Cooperatives Agricoles de Céréales v R Catterall & Co Ltd* [1959] 2 QB 44, CA; the *Dalmia Dairy Industries* case at 249–50.

[26] *Norske Atlas Insurance Co Ltd v London General Insurance Co Ltd* (1927) 28 Lloyd's Rep 104.

[27] The *Dalmia Dairy Industries* case at 272–5, 301–3.

[28] The *Dalmia Dairy Industries* case; and see *Kianta Osakeyhtio v Britain and Overseas Trading Co Ltd* [1954] 1 Lloyd's Rep 247, CA.

[29] *Oppenheim & Co v Mahomed Haneef* [1922] 1 AC 482 at 487, PC.

[30] *Hamlyn & Co v Talisker Distillery* [1894] AC 202 at 209, 214, HL; the *Dalmia Dairy Industries* case at 267–9, 299–301.

[31] The *Dalmia Dairy Industries* case at 269–70.

[32] *Yukos Capital Sarl v OJSC Rosneft Oil Co* [2014] EWHC 2188 (Comm), [2014] 2 Lloyd's Rep 435.

[33] Infra, pp 669–77.

[34] CPR Practice Direction 6B, r 3.1(10) (formerly CPR, r 6.20(9), replacing Ord 11, r 1(1)(m) RSC) was introduced, inter alia, to provide jurisdiction in such cases, see supra, pp 355–6.

[35] *Dalmia Cement Ltd v National Bank of Pakistan* [1975] QB 9.

the 1996 Act.[36] Leave to enforce an award will not be given where, or to the extent that, the tribunal lacked substantive jurisdiction to make the award.[37] It will also have to be enforceable here in the same manner as a judgment and, whilst it is possible for an award in foreign currency to be enforced in England,[38] it is not possible for an award for a sum to be paid in a foreign country to be enforced here under section 66 of the 1996 Act, though such an award will still be enforceable by action at common law.[39] The court has the power to grant enforcement of a declaratory award under section 66 where there is a real advantage in doing so, eg to establish the primacy of a declaratory award over an inconsistent judgment.[40] In the case of a purely domestic award it has been suggested that the discretion under section 66 should be exercised to allow enforcement in nearly all cases, ie unless there is real ground for doubting the validity of the award.[41] Where enforcement of a foreign arbitral award is in issue, the discretion is likely to be exercised with considerably more caution.[42]

2. ENFORCEMENT UNDER THE CIVIL JURISDICTION AND JUDGMENTS ACT 1982

Foreign arbitral awards and judgments of courts incorporating such awards are not enforceable under the Brussels/Lugano system.[43] Thus, to take an example, an arbitral award granted in France cannot be enforced in the United Kingdom under the Recast of the Brussels I Regulation. However, an arbitration award granted in one part of the United Kingdom can be enforced in another part under the Civil Jurisdiction and Judgments Act 1982. As has already been seen,[44] enforcement in one part of the United Kingdom of a judgment[45] obtained in another part of the United Kingdom is dealt with by section 18 of the 1982 Act, which provides for a system of registration of United Kingdom judgments and allows very few defences to enforcement. Section 18 defines a "judgment" very widely and includes "an arbitration award which has become enforceable in the part of the United Kingdom in which it was given in the same manner as a judgment given by a court of law in that part".[46] It should, however, be noted that, unlike other forms of judgment, an arbitration award obtained in the United Kingdom does not have to be enforced under section 18.[47] It is still possible for a claimant, if he so chooses, to seek enforcement of the arbitration award

---

[36] Such as the arbitration agreement being in writing; 1996 Act, s 5; on which see infra, p 671, n 59.

[37] S 66(3). The defences of public policy and that the matter is not capable of settlement by arbitration apply to s 66, see s 81(1)(a) and (c).

[38] *Jugoslavenska Oceanska Plovidba v Castle Investment Co Inc* [1974] QB 292, CA; the *Dalmia Cement* case at 24–6; and see *Miliangos v George Frank (Textiles) Ltd* [1976] AC 443, HL; Law Com No 124 (1983) at paras 2.44–2.47, makes no recommendations for change in the law on this point.

[39] See the *Dalmia Cement* case at 23–7; cf *Bank Mellat v GAA Development and Construction Co* [1988] 2 Lloyd's Rep 44.

[40] *West Tankers Inc v Allianz SpA (The Front Comor)* [2011] EWHC 829 (Comm), [2011] 2 All ER (Comm) 1.

[41] *Middlemiss and Gould v Hartlepool Corpn* [1972] 1 WLR 1643 at 1647, CA; cf *Re Boks & Co and Peters, Rushton & Co Ltd* [1919] 1 KB 491 at 497, CA.

[42] The *Dalmia Cement* case at 14–15, 23; and see *Union Nationale des Cooperatives Agricoles de Céréales v Catterall* [1959] 2 QB 44 at 52, CA (an award enforceable under Part II of the 1950 Act, infra).

[43] Supra, p 208. See generally Hascher (1996) 12 Arb Int 233. As regards judgments incorporating awards (as under s 66 of the 1996 Act) see *ABCI v BFT* [1996] 1 Lloyd's Rep 485; affd [1997] 1 Lloyd's Rep 531, CA; Schlosser Report, OJ 1979, C 59/1, para 65.

[44] Supra, pp 588–91.

[45] The judgment may concern money provisions (Sch 6 of the 1982 Act) or non-money provisions (Sch 7 to the 1982 Act).

[46] S 18(2)(e).

[47] See s 18(8).

at common law or by recourse to section 66 of the Arbitration Act 1996.[48] It should also be noted that section 19 of the 1982 Act, which deals with recognition of United Kingdom judgments, does not apply to arbitration awards.[49]

3. ENFORCEMENT UNDER THE ARBITRATION ACT 1950

Provision is made for the enforcement of certain foreign arbitral awards by Part II of the Arbitration Act 1950, which Act consolidates the Arbitration Acts 1889 to 1934. The background to this provision is afforded by a Protocol of 1923 and a Convention of 1927, both of which were signed by the United Kingdom at Geneva. The former deals with the international validity of arbitration agreements, the latter with the enforcement in one country of arbitral awards made in another. Part II of the Arbitration Act 1950 applies to foreign arbitral awards[50] made in pursuance of an arbitration agreement to which the 1923 Protocol applies[51] and made between persons who are subject to the jurisdiction of different countries, both of which, by reason of their reciprocal provisions, have been declared by Order in Council to be parties to the 1927 Convention; the award must also have been made in such a country.[52] Part II of the 1950 Act will seldom operate because it does not apply to New York Convention awards.[53] Most states which were parties to the Geneva Convention subsequently became parties to the New York Convention,[54] and enforcement is then dealt with under the latter. Moreover, the application of Part II of the 1950 Act is not mandatory; an award creditor may seek enforcement at common law.[55]

4. ENFORCEMENT UNDER THE ARBITRATION ACT 1996

The Arbitration Act 1975[56] enabled the United Kingdom to accede to the New York Convention on the Recognition and Enforcement of Foreign Arbitral Awards 1958. The 1975 Act has been repealed and replaced by Part III of the Arbitration Act 1996 which, by and large, is to the same effect.[57] The 1996 Act provides for the recognition and enforcement in England and Wales and Northern Ireland of "New York Convention awards", ie awards[58]

---

[48] Supra, pp 668–9.

[49] S 19(3)(b).

[50] But not to awards made under an arbitration agreement governed by English law: s 40(b).

[51] Sch 1, para 1.

[52] S 35(1).

[53] Arbitration Act 1996, s 99.

[54] For the few states which are parties to the Geneva Convention but not to the New York Convention see Dicey, Morris and Collins, para 16-100. The New York Convention is discussed infra, pp 670–6.

[55] S 40.

[56] See Lew (1975) 24 ICLQ 870; Thomas [1992] CJQ 352. The 1975 Act applied to awards made before the Act came into force: *Minister of Public Works of the Government of the State of Kuwait v Sir Frederick Snow & Partners* [1984] AC 426, HL.

[57] See the Departmental Advisory Committee (DAC) Report on the Arbitration Bill (1996).

[58] This does not include a preliminary award on jurisdiction (in the absence of any agreement to submit the question of jurisdiction itself to arbitration): *Dallah Real Estate and Tourism Co v Ministry of Religious Affairs of the Government of Pakistan* [2010] UKSC 46 at [22], [2011] 1 AC 763; nor an interlocutory order: *Svenska Petroleum Exploration AB v Republic of Lithuania (No 2)* [2005] EWHC 2437 (Comm), [2006] 1 All ER (Comm) 731; nor a judgment of the Sharia Council of Great Britain: *Al Midani v Al Midani* [1999] 1 Lloyd's Rep 923. An award can be enforced in part: *IPCO (Nigeria) Ltd v Nigerian National Petroleum Corpn* [2008] EWCA Civ 1157, [2009] 1 All ER (Comm) 611. If the award includes an order for costs, this is also enforceable under the Convention, see *Bank Mellat v Helliniki Techniki SA* [1984] QB 291 at 308, CA.

made, in pursuance of a written[59] arbitration agreement,[60] in a foreign country which is a party to the New York Convention.[61] If it is declared by Order in Council[62] that a state is a party to the New York Convention, or is a party in respect of any territory so specified, this is to be conclusive evidence of that fact.[63] The relevant date for ascertaining whether a foreign state is a party to the Convention is the date when proceedings to enforce an arbitration award are begun, regardless of whether that state was a party to the Convention at the date when the award was made.[64] An award is treated as "made" at the seat of the arbitration, regardless of where it was signed, despatched or delivered to any of the parties.[65] Moreover, unless otherwise agreed by the parties, where the seat of the arbitration is in England and Wales or Northern Ireland, any award in the proceedings shall be treated as made there, regardless of where it was signed, despatched or delivered to any of the parties.[66] The "seat of the arbitration" means the juridical seat of the arbitration.[67] This can be designated by the parties to the arbitration agreement, any institution or person authorised by the parties, or the arbitral tribunal if authorised by the parties.[68] In the absence of any such designations, it is determined having regard to the parties' agreement and all the relevant circumstances.[69] This ensures that, as far as English law is concerned, every arbitration has a seat.[70]

A New York Convention award may, by leave of the court, be enforced in the same manner as a judgment or order of the court[71] to the same effect.[72] Where leave is so given,[73] judgment may be entered in terms of the award.[74] The granting of leave is subject to

---

[59] The requirement of writing is satisfied if the agreement is made in writing, by exchange of communications in writing, evidenced in writing, or the parties agree by reference to terms which are in writing, or if there is an exchange of written submissions in arbitral or legal proceedings in which the existence of the agreement is alleged by one party and not denied by the other: s 5 of the 1996 Act.

[60] S 100(2). See *Dardana Ltd v Yukos Oil Co* [2002] EWCA Civ 543, [2002] 2 Lloyd's Rep 326.

[61] S 100(1). There are currently 157 state parties to the Convention: <http://www.uncitral.org/uncitral/en/uncitral_texts/arbitration/NYConvention_status.html>.

[62] See SI 1984/1168; SI 1989/1348; SI 1993/1256.

[63] S 100(3); other evidence may be given to show that a state is a party to the Convention, see *Government of the State of Kuwait v Sir Frederick Snow & Partners* [1981] 1 Lloyd's Rep 656 at 666; overruled by the Court of Appeal and House of Lords on another point [1984] AC 426, HL. Cf the 1950 Act which only applies if persons are "subject to the jurisdiction" of different states, supra.

[64] *Minister of Public Works of the Government of the State of Kuwait v Sir Frederick Snow & Partners* [1984] AC 426, HL. Cf the position under the Arbitration Act 1950, s 35; the Foreign Judgments (Reciprocal Enforcement) Act 1933, s 1(2)(c) (as amended by the Civil Jurisdiction and Judgments Act 1982, Sch 10, para 1(2)).

[65] 1996 Act, s 100(2)(b); overturning the principle in *Hiscox v Outhwaite* [1992] 1 AC 562, HL; Davidson (1992) 41 ICLQ 637; Reymond (1992) 108 LQR 1; Mann (1992) 108 LQR 6.

[66] S 53, dealing specifically with the situation that arose in the *Hiscox* case. The result would now be different if the facts of that case arose.

[67] S 3.

[68] Ibid.

[69] Ibid.

[70] According to Kerr LJ, "Despite suggestions to the contrary by some learned writers under other systems, our jurisprudence does not recognise the concept of arbitral procedures floating in the transnational firmament, unconnected with any municipal system of law." *Bank Mellat v Helliniki Techniki SA* [1984] QB 291 at 301, CA.

[71] S 105.

[72] S 101(2). For security for costs in enforcement proceedings, see *Gater Assets Ltd v Nak Naftogaz Ukrainiy* [2007] EWCA Civ 988, [2008] 1 All ER (Comm) 209. See also *Dardana Ltd v Yukos Oil Co* [2002] 2 Lloyd's Rep 261; *Diag Human SE v Czech Republic* [2013] EWHC 3190 (Comm), [2014] 1 All ER (Comm) 605.

[73] For the principles on extension of time to challenge the granting of leave, see *Soinco SACI v Novokuznetsk Aluminium Plant* [1998] 2 Lloyd's Rep 337, CA.

[74] S 101(3). The judgment is treated like any other judgment; in principle the court can grant a stay of execution but in practice will rarely if ever do so: *Far Eastern Shipping Co v AKP Sovcomflot* [1995] 1 Lloyd's Rep 520; *H & C S Holdings PTE Ltd v RBRG Trading (UK) Ltd* [2015] EWHC 1665 (Comm).

the discretion of the court, which may be exercised with caution in the case of foreign awards.[75]

A New York Convention award is recognised as binding on the persons as between whom it was made, and may accordingly be relied on by these persons by way of defence, set off or otherwise in any legal proceedings in the United Kingdom.[76] In order for an award to be recognised or enforced the person wishing to do so merely has to produce the originals of the award and the arbitration agreement, or certified copies, and a certified translation if either is in a foreign language.[77]

There are, however, a number of grounds on which recognition or enforcement may be refused.[78] The court has a discretion[79] to refuse recognition or enforcement if the defendant raises and proves any of the following:[80]

(a) that a party to the arbitration agreement was under some incapacity.[81] The question of capacity is governed by the law applicable to that party under English contract choice of law rules.[82] Furthermore, enforcement of the award can be refused whichever party to the arbitration agreement lacked capacity;

(b) that the arbitration agreement was invalid[83] under the law to which the parties subjected it, ie the law chosen by the parties. Failing any indication of such law, validity is to be determined by the substantive law (and not choice-of-law) rules of the law of the country where the award was made.[84] The defendant has no obligation to participate in the arbitration or to take any steps in the country of the seat of what he maintains to be an invalid arbitration leading to an invalid award against him.[85]

(c) that the defendant was not given proper notice of the appointment of the arbitrator or of the arbitration proceedings or was otherwise unable to present his case;[86]

---

[75] See the *Dalmia Cement* case at 23, supra, pp 668–9.

[76] S 101(1).

[77] S 102. See *Lombard-Knight v Rainstorm Pictures Inc* [2014] EWCA Civ 356, [2014] 2 Lloyd's Rep 74.

[78] The grounds listed in s 103 are the only ones available: s 103(1). The test for determining whether the grounds are met is the usual test on summary judgments, namely whether there is a real prospect of successfully establishing the ground alleged: *Honeywell International Middle East Ltd v Meydan Group LLC* [2014] EWHC 1344 (TCC), [2014] 2 Lloyd's Rep 133.

[79] See *China Agribusiness Development Corpn v Balli Trading* [1998] 2 Lloyd's Rep 76; *Dardana Ltd v Yukos Oil Co* [2002] EWCA Civ 543 at [8] and [18], [2002] 1 All ER (Comm) 819; *Svenska Petroleum Exploration AB v Republic of Lithuania* [2005] EWHC 9 (Comm) at [27], [2005] 1 All ER (Comm) 515; the *Dallah* case at [67]–[69], [126]–[128], [131]. See also Hill (2015) 25 OJLS.

[80] S 103(2); the reasons for an award can be referred to in order to ascertain whether any of the circumstances under this section apply, see *Mutual Shipping Corpn of New York v Bayshore Shipping Co of Monrovia (The Montan)* [1985] 1 WLR 625 at 631, CA; the *Dallah* case at [30]–[31] and [160]. As to the burden of proof, see the *Dallah* case at [12], [28], [30] and [101].

[81] *Irvani v Irvani* [2000] 1 Lloyd's Rep 412 at 423–5, CA.

[82] Infra, pp 761–3.

[83] See *Dallal v Bank Mellat* [1986] QB 441 at 455–6; Kunzlik [1986] CLJ 377; *Irvani v Irvani* [2000] 1 Lloyd's Rep 412 at 425, CA. Proof that a person against whom recognition is invoked was not a party to the arbitration agreement falls within this provision: *Dardana Ltd v Yukos Oil Co* [2002] EWCA Civ 543 at [8], [2002] 1 All ER (Comm) 819; *Svenska Petroleum Exploration AB v Republic of Lithuania* [2005] EWHC 9 (Comm) at [7], [2005] 1 All ER (Comm) 515; the *Dallah* case at [11]–[12] and [77]. This may include continuing, as well as initial, validity: the *Dalmia Dairy Industries* case at 238.

[84] See the *Dallah* case at [14]–[16] and [123].

[85] The *Dallah* case at [23], [28]–[29] and [102]–[104].

[86] *Minmetals Germany GmbH v Ferco Steel Ltd* [1999] CLC 647; *Irvani v Irvani* [2000] 1 Lloyd's Rep 412 at 426–7, CA; *Kanoria v Guinness* [2006] EWCA Civ 222, [2006] 2 All ER (Comm) 413; *Malicorp Ltd v Government of the Arab Republic of Egypt* [2015] EWHC 361 (Comm), [2015] 1 Lloyd's Rep 423. See also *Cukurova Holding SA v Sonera Holding BV* [2014] UKPC 15, [2015] 2 All ER 1061 (a case decided under the British Virgin Islands Arbitration Ordinance).

(d) that the award deals with a difference not contemplated by or not falling within the terms of the submission to arbitration or contains decisions on matters beyond the scope of the submission to arbitration;[87]

(e) that the composition of the arbitral tribunal or the arbitral procedure was not in accordance with the agreement of the parties or, failing such agreement, with the law of the country where the arbitration took place.[88] It is clear from this defence that the parties are free to choose the procedural law to govern the arbitration and that, in the absence of choice, the curial law will be that of the country where the arbitration took place;

(f) that the award has not yet become binding on the parties,[89] or has been set aside or suspended by a competent authority of the country in which, or under the law of which, it was made.[90] This provision recognises the jurisdiction of the courts of the country whose law the parties have chosen to govern their arbitration or, in the absence of choice, of the country of the arbitral seat to conduct setting aside proceedings or suspend the award. This setting aside or suspension may be recognised in England unless the judgment by which the foreign court did so would itself not be given effect in England based on ordinary principles applying to the recognition of foreign judgments.[91] By way of comparison, under the 1950 Act an award is unenforceable, as at common law, if it is not "final",[92] rather than if it is "not yet binding".

There is a further discretion to refuse recognition or enforcement of the award which may be exercised by the court either of its own motion or on the application of a party to the arbitration agreement. Recognition or enforcement may be refused if the award is in respect of a matter which is not capable of settlement by arbitration, or if it would be contrary to public policy to recognise or enforce the award.[93] Whether a matter is capable of settlement by arbitration is determined by English law as the law of the country where recognition or enforcement is sought.[94] Denial of recognition or enforcement of an award as being contrary to English public policy is less extensive than the equivalent provision under the 1950 Act[95]

---

[87] Subject to the proviso in s 103(4) that an award containing decisions on matters not submitted to arbitration may be recognised or enforced to the extent that it contains decisions on separate matters which were so submitted. See, on s 103(2)(d), *Agromet Motoimport v Maulden Engineering Co (Beds) Ltd* [1985] 1 WLR 762 at 775–6—a case on the same provision under the 1975 Act. See also *Cukurova Holding SA v Sonera Holding BV* [2014] UKPC 15, [2015] 2 All ER 1061.

[88] *China Agribusiness Development Corpn v Balli Trading* [1998] 2 Lloyd's Rep 76; *Minmetals Germany GmbH v Ferco Steel Ltd* [1999] CLC 647 at 658–9.

[89] *Diag Human SE v Czech Republic* [2014] EWHC 1639 (Comm), [2014] 2 Lloyd's Rep 283; *Dowans Holding SA v Tanzania Electric Supply Co Ltd* [2011] EWHC 1957 (Comm), [2011] 2 Lloyd's Rep 275.

[90] *Malicorp Ltd v Government of the Arab Republic of Egypt* [2015] EWHC 361 (Comm), [2015] 1 Lloyd's Rep 423. See generally Petrochilos [1999] 48 ICLQ 856. If an application has been made to a competent authority to set aside or suspend a New York Convention award, the English court has a discretion to adjourn the decision on the recognition or enforcement of the award and to order security to be given: s 103(5). On the former see *IPCO (Nigeria) Ltd v Nigerian National Petroleum Corpn* [2017] UKSC 16, [2017] 1 WLR 970. On the latter, see *Soleh Boneh International Ltd v Government of the Republic of Uganda and National Housing Corpn* [1993] 2 Lloyd's Rep 208, CA; *Apis AS v Fantazia Kereskedelmi* [2001] 1 All ER (Comm) 348; *Dardana Ltd v Yukos Oil Co* [2002] EWCA Civ 543, [2002] 1 All ER (Comm) 819; *Dardana Ltd v Yukos Oil Co* [2002] 2 Lloyd's Rep 261; *IPCO (Nigeria) Ltd v Nigerian National Petroleum Corpn* [2005] EWHC 726 (Comm), [2005] 2 Lloyd's Rep 326; *Thai-Lao Lignite (Thailand) and Hongsa Lignite (Lao PDR) v Government of the Lao People's Democratic Republic* [2012] EWHC 3381 (Comm).

[91] See *Yukos Capital Sarl v OJSC Rosneft Oil Co* [2014] EWHC 2188 (Comm), [2014] 2 Lloyd's Rep 435; *Malicorp Ltd v Government of the Arab Republic of Egypt* [2015] EWHC 361 (Comm), [2015] 1 Lloyd's Rep 423. See also *Diag Human SE v Czech Republic* [2014] EWHC 1639 (Comm), [2014] 2 Lloyd's Rep 283.

[92] Supra, pp 548–51.

[93] S 103(3). An enforcing court cannot make the decision of an issue raised under s 103(3) conditional on the provision of security in respect of the award: *IPCO (Nigeria) Ltd v Nigerian National Petroleum Corpn* [2017] UKSC 16, [2017] 1 WLR 970.

[94] See Lew (1975) 24 ICLQ 870 at 876.

[95] The 1950 Act, s 37(1).

in that recognition or enforcement cannot be denied under the 1996 Act on the ground that it would be contrary to the law of England. What has to be shown is that "there is some element of illegality or that the enforcement of the award would be clearly injurious to the public good or, possibly, that enforcement would be wholly offensive to the ordinary reasonable and fully informed member of the public on whose behalf the powers of the state is exercised".[96] Applying this definition, the enforcement of an award arrived at after arbitrators had applied "internationally accepted principles of law governing contractual relations" (the *lex mercatoria)* has been held not to be against public policy.[97] Nor was it against public policy where the arbitrators awarded the claimant a reduced additional sum in place of a contractual penalty, representing 25 per cent of the penalty claimed.[98]

It is consistent with this definition that, in the decision of the Court of Appeal in *Soleimany v Soleimany*,[99] an award was refused enforcement on public policy grounds where it referred on its face to an illegal enterprise under which it was the joint intention that carpets would be exported illegally out of Iran. But Waller LJ in obiter dicta went further. An award will not be enforced where the underlying contract is governed by the law of a foreign and friendly country, or which requires performance in such a country, if performance is illegal by the law of that country.[100] This was distinguished by the Court of Appeal in *Westacre Investments Inc v Jugoimport-SDPR Holding Co Ltd,* a case concerning a contract for the purchase of personal influence (lobbying rather than corruption), which, looking at the award and the reasons stated, was not illegal (or against public policy) by the law of the place of performance or under the governing law and curial law.[101] Whilst the award is not isolated from the underlying contract, it is relevant that the English court is considering the enforcement of an award, and not the underlying contract.[102] The underlying contract, on the facts as they appeared from the award and its reasons, did not infringe one of those rules of public policy where the English court would not enforce it whatever its governing law or place of performance.[103] There is nothing which offends English public policy if a foreign arbitral tribunal enforces a contract for the purchase of personal influence which does not offend the domestic public policy under either the governing law of the contract or the curial law, even if English public policy might have taken a different view.[104] What if there is illegality by the foreign place of performance? In the case of a contract for the purchase of personal influence, that in itself

---

[96] *Deutsche Schachtbau- und Tiefborhgesellschaft MBH v Shell International Petroleum Co Ltd (t/a Shell International Trading Co)* [1990] 1 AC 295 at 316, CA. The case went to the House of Lords (ibid, at 323) on a separate Third Party Debt Order (garnishment) point, discussed infra, pp 1292–4. See also *IPCO (Nigeria) Ltd v Nigerian National Petroleum Corpn* [2005] EWHC 726 (Comm) at [22]–[24], [2005] 2 Lloyd's Rep 326; *Amaltal Corpn Ltd v Maruha (NZ) Corpn Ltd* [2004] 2 NZLR 614, CA. Cf *Resort Condominiums International Inc v Bolwell* (1994) 118 ALR 655.

[97] The *Deutsche Schachtbau- und Tiefborhgesellschaft MBH* case. See Rivkin (1993) 9 Arb Int 67. By way of comparison, the parties cannot choose the *lex mercatoria* as the governing law under the Rome I Regulation, see infra, pp 715–16.

[98] *Pencil Hill Ltd v US Citta Di Palermo SpA,* 19 January 2016, HC.

[99] [1999] QB 785, CA; Harris and Meisel [1998] LMCLQ 568; Enonchong [1999] LMCLQ 495.

[100] [1999] QB 785, CA. The *Soleimany* case has been subsequently reinterpreted by Waller LJ as being decided on the basis that it was plain on the face of the award that the enterprise was unlawful under the law of the place of performance: *Westacre Investments Inc v Jugoimport-SDPR Holding Co Ltd* [2000] 1 QB 288 at 302, CA. Moreover, an award will not be enforced where the underlying contract, which is governed by English law or is to be performed in England, is illegal by English domestic law, the *Soleimany* case at 803.

[101] [2000] 1 QB 288 at 301–5, CA. The *Westacre* case was followed in *OTV v Hilmarton* [1999] 2 Lloyd's Rep 222.

[102] The *Westacre* case at 305.

[103] Following *Lemenda Trading Co Ltd v African Middle East Petroleum Co Ltd* [1988] QB 448—a case on enforcement of the contract rather than an award. The former point is discussed infra, p 752.

[104] The *Westacre* case at 305.

is not enough to lead to non-enforcement of the contract or the subsequent award.[105] This represents a retreat by Waller LJ from his earlier wide obiter dicta in the *Soleimany* case.[106] Subsequently, in *OTV v Hilmarton*,[107] a case of a contract to lobby public servants, an award has been enforced even though there was a finding by the arbitrator of illegality under the law of the place of performance. The *Soleimany* case was distinguished on the basis that, unlike in that case, the illegality fell short of corruption or illicit practice.[108]

A party who had knowledge of the alleged bribery at the time of the arbitration, but failed to use the opportunity to raise it before the arbitrator, will be precluded from doing so as a defence to enforcement.[109] It is more difficult where the arbitrator has considered an allegation of illegality or of bribery and corruption and has rejected it. Where the allegation was a central one, was made, entertained and rejected at the arbitration and, on appeal, before a court in the setting aside proceedings in which the *lex fori* was both the law governing the substantive contract and the curial law, authority apart and in the absence of new evidence, there can be no justification for refusing to enforce the award.[110] Obiter dicta supporting the idea of some kind of a preliminary inquiry[111] have been doubted.[112] Moreover, according to these obiter dicta, in determining whether the case at hand is appropriate for making such a preliminary inquiry, the court will consider whether: there was evidence before the tribunal that this was a straightforward, commercial contract; the arbitrator made a specific finding that the underlying contract was not illegal; there was anything to suggest incompetence on the part of the arbitrators; there was any reason to suggest collusion or bad faith in the obtaining of the award.[113] The application of these criteria may well lead to the rejection of reopening the facts.[114]

Enforcement will be refused on public policy grounds if the award was obtained by fraud, such as perjured evidence[115] or suppression of relevant evidence.[116] However, the principle that enforcement of a foreign judgment can be attacked on the ground of fraud without any requirement that the evidence must not have been available at the trial[117] has not been extended to foreign arbitration awards, which, because the tribunal has been chosen by the parties, should be put into the same category as domestic arbitration awards and not into the same category as foreign judgments.[118] With foreign arbitration awards, normally the conditions to be fulfilled for re-opening the issue of fraud will be (a) that the evidence to establish the fraud was not available to the party alleging the fraud at the time of the hearing before the arbitrators; and (b) where perjury is the fraud alleged, ie where the very issue

---

[105] The *Westacre* case at 304–5 (per Waller LJ); following the *Lemenda* case.

[106] The *Soleimany* case at 803.

[107] [1999] 2 Lloyd's Rep 222; criticised by Hill [2000] LMCLQ 311.

[108] *OTV v Hilmarton* [1999] 2 Lloyd's Rep 222 at 225.

[109] *Honeywell International Middle East Ltd v Meydan Group LLC* [2014] EWHC 1344 (TCC), [2014] 2 Lloyd's Rep 133.

[110] The *Westacre* case at 316–17 (per Mantell and Hirst LJJ); cf the dissent of Waller LJ at 310–16.

[111] The *Soleimany* case at 800–3. See also *Soinco SACI v Novokuznetsk Aluminium Plant* [1998] 2 Lloyd's Rep 337, CA.

[112] The *Westacre* case at 316–17 (per Mantell and Hirst LJJ); cf the dissent of Waller LJ at 310–16.

[113] The *Westacre* case at 316–17; the *Soleimany* case at 800.

[114] The *Westacre* case.

[115] Ibid.

[116] *Gater Assets Ltd v Nak Naftogaz Ukrainiy (No 2)* [2008] EWHC 237 (Comm), [2008] 1 Lloyd's Rep 479.

[117] Supra, pp 568–72.

[118] The *Westacre* case at 309. See also *Re Schreter and Gasmac Inc* (1992) 89 DLR (4th) 365 at 379. See generally Harris and Meisel [1998] LMCLQ 568, on the question of whether public policy in the context of enforcement of arbitration awards raises the same issues as in cases of enforcement of foreign judgments.

before the arbitrators was whether the witnesses were lying, the evidence must be so strong that it would reasonably be expected to be decisive at a hearing, and if unanswered would have that result.[119] The fraud must also be operative in obtaining the award. The enforcement of an award will not be refused merely on the basis that the parties' transaction was "tainted" by fraud.[120] It is also contrary to public policy to enforce a foreign arbitral award where the arbitral proceedings violated English principles of natural justice; but the public policy exception is unlikely to be applied if more specific grounds for refusing recognition and enforcement, such as the one in s 103(2)(c), are not met.[121] Normally, an English court will not reinvestigate allegations of procedural defects, which have already been considered by the supervisory court abroad.[122] It must be noted that recognition or enforcement cannot be refused on the basis that the arbitrator made an error of fact or law.[123] Nor can recognition or enforcement be refused on the basis that there was a subsequent inconsistent decision from a court in another country.[124] Where there are conflicting final decisions each pronounced by a body of competent jurisdiction, the earlier in time is to be recognised and given effect.[125]

An important source of public policy in the United Kingdom is European Union law. In *Eco Swiss China Time Ltd v Benetton International NV*,[126] a case on the setting aside in the Netherlands of a Dutch arbitration award made contrary to the competition law provisions of the EC Treaty, the Court of Justice held that such provisions of the Treaty may be regarded as a matter of public policy within the meaning of the New York Convention.[127] Thus, a foreign arbitral award that violates mandatory EU law may be refused recognition and enforcement in the United Kingdom on public policy grounds.

The 1996 Act contains two provisions which interrelate with other bases for enforcement. If a New York Convention award would also be a foreign award within the meaning of the 1950 Act, the award's recognition or enforcement shall be governed by the 1996 Act only.[128] Secondly, nothing in the 1996 Act prejudices the right to enforce or rely on a New York Convention award at common law,[129] ie by an action on the award, or under section 66 of the 1996 Act[130] (by leave of the court, enforcement in the same manner as a judgment or order of the court to the same effect).

---

[119] The *Westacre* case at 309.

[120] *Sinocore International Co Ltd v RBRG Trading (UK) Ltd* [2017] EWHC 251 (Comm), [2017] 1 Lloyd's Rep 375—a party who presented forged bills of lading in order to obtain payment could enforce an award in its favour where the award was not based on the defendant's failure to pay against the presentation of the forged documents, but on a prior breach of contract by the defendant.

[121] See *Cukurova Holding SA v Sonera Holding BV* [2014] UKPC 15 at [32]–[33], [2015] 2 All ER 1061, referring to *Adams v Cape Industries* [1990] Ch 333, HL.

[122] *Minmetals Germany GmbH v Ferco Steel Ltd* [1999] CLC 647 at 659–62.

[123] *Mutual Shipping Corpn of New York v Bayshore Shipping Co of Monrovia (The Montan)* [1985] 1 WLR 625 at 631, CA.

[124] *The Joanna V* [2003] EWHC 1655 (Comm), [2003] 2 Lloyd's Rep 617.

[125] *The Joanna V* case at 628, following *Showlag v Mansour* [1995] 1 AC 431, PC.

[126] Case C-126/97 [1999] ECR I-3055. See also Case C-168/05 *Claro v Centro Móvil Milenium* [2006] ECR I-10421; *Accentuate Ltd v Asigra Inc* [2009] EWHC 2655 (QB), [2010] 2 All ER (Comm) 738.

[127] The *Eco Swiss* case at [38].

[128] S 99.

[129] S 104; in *Minister of Public Works of the Government of the State of Kuwait v Sir Frederick Snow & Partners* [1984] AC 426, HL, the defences under the 1975 Act were said to cover the whole field of the defences which would be available in a common law action, see supra, p 668.

[130] S 104.

5. ENFORCEMENT UNDER THE ADMINISTRATION OF JUSTICE ACT 1920 AND THE FOREIGN JUDGMENTS (RECIPROCAL ENFORCEMENT) ACT 1933

The provisions of the Administration of Justice Act 1920 whereby judgments given in Commonwealth countries may be registered and enforced in England[131] apply equally to arbitral awards.[132] The Foreign Judgments (Reciprocal Enforcement) Act 1933[133] now also extends to foreign arbitral awards.[134] However, a foreign arbitral award, which is registrable under the Act, unlike other judgments, does not have to be enforced under the Act.[135] The claimant, if he so chooses, can, instead, seek enforcement of the arbitration award at common law or by recourse to section 66 of the Arbitration Act 1996.[136]

6. ENFORCEMENT UNDER THE ARBITRATION (INTERNATIONAL INVESTMENT DISPUTES) ACT 1966

The Arbitration (International Investment Disputes) Act 1966 implements a convention made at Washington, DC in 1965 which established the International Centre for the Settlement of Investment Disputes between Contracting States and the nationals of other Contracting States.[137] Subject to the written consent of the parties to the arbitration, the Centre's arbitration tribunal has jurisdiction to settle any legal dispute arising directly out of such an investment.[138] An arbitral award made by the Centre's tribunal, if registered in the High Court, has, as respects the pecuniary obligations which it imposes, the same force and effect as if it had been a judgment of the High Court.[139] There are no grounds for refusing recognition and enforcement of such an award, although execution of the award may be resisted on grounds of state immunity.[140] The ICSID Convention provides, however, certain grounds for annulment of awards, which can be pursued before an ad hoc committee established in accordance with the Convention. There is a discretion to stay English proceedings in breach of an agreement to submit to the Centre's arbitration.[141]

---

[131] Supra, pp 591–2.
[132] S 12(1) of the 1920 Act.
[133] Supra, pp 592–601.
[134] S 10A of the 1933 Act, added by Sch 10, para 4 of the Civil Jurisdiction and Judgments Act 1982.
[135] See ss 10A and 6 of the 1933 Act.
[136] Supra, pp 668–9.
[137] 1966 Act, Sch, Art 1.
[138] 1966 Act, Sch, Art 25.
[139] 1966 Act, ss 1 and 2. The award may be registered in foreign currency: Administration of Justice Act 1977, s 4(2)(a) and (b); see also Law Com No 124 (1983), paras 2.44–2.47.
[140] 1966 Act, Sch, Art 55. See also *Micula v Romania* [2017] EWHC 31 (Comm)—the court upheld the registration of an ICSID award against Romania, but stayed enforcement on the basis that the European Commission had prohibited Romania under European Union state aid law from making any payment under that award, and a challenge to that decision was pending before the General Court of European Union.
[141] 1966 Act, s 3(2), applying the Arbitration Act 1996, s 9, supra, pp 416–21.

PART IV

THE LAW OF OBLIGATIONS

19.	Contracts	681
20.	Non-Contractual Obligations	776

19

CONTRACTS

1 Introduction	681	(b) When does the Regulation apply?	691
(a) The nature of the problem	681	(c) The applicable law	706
(b) Various solutions to the problem	681	(d) Limitations on the dominance of the applicable law	743
2 The Rome Convention	683	(e) Particular issues	754
(a) The history and purpose of the Convention	683	(f) Relationship with other provisions of EU law	772
(b) The Contracts (Applicable Law) Act 1990	684	(g) Relationship with other conventions	774
3 The Rome I Regulation	686		
(a) Preliminary remarks	686		

1. INTRODUCTION

(a) The nature of the problem

The problem of ascertaining the applicable law is more perplexing in the case of contracts than in almost any other area. There are three reasons for this. First, there is the diversity of connecting factors that can be raised by the facts of the case: the place where the contract is made; the place of performance; the domicile, nationality or place of business of the parties; the situation of the subject matter and so on. In most areas of private international law the decisive connecting factor on which ascertainment of the applicable law depends is reasonably clear. There is general agreement, for instance, that it is the place of celebration which indicates the law to govern the formal validity of a marriage. But with contracts the sheer multiplicity of connecting factors makes it hard to identify one single connecting factor as the determinant of the applicable law. Secondly, contracts are planned transactions and the parties may well have considered the question of what law should govern the contract in the event of a dispute arising between them. They may have made provision in the contract, choosing the applicable law. Thirdly, a wide variety of different contractual issues can arise. For example, there can be a problem over whether a contract has been validly created, concerning how it should be interpreted, about whether it has been discharged. This raises the question whether the same law should govern all of these issues. Moreover, there are many different types of contract. A sale of goods contract has different features from an insurance contract or a contract for carriage of goods by sea. Should the same law govern regardless of the type of contract involved, or do the special features of particular contracts necessitate special choice of law rules?

(b) Various solutions to the problem[1]

As one would expect from the complex nature of the problem, a wide variety of different solutions have been tried in different countries over the years. In the USA a preference was

---

[1] See generally Lando, *International Encyclopedia of Comparative Law*, vol III, Chapter 24; North, *Private International Law Problems in Common Law Jurisdictions* (1993), Chapter V.

formerly shown for a rigid and inflexible test, represented by the place of contracting in some of the states but by the place of performance in others. However, the choice of law revolution in that country[2] has affected not only tort cases but also contract cases, and a wide range of modern approaches is now used in this area.[3] Most of the countries of the European Continent rejected a rigid test and, instead, adopted the doctrine of autonomy under which the parties were free to choose the governing law, though divergent views obtained on the question whether their freedom was absolute or was restricted to the choice of a law with which the contract was factually connected.[4] In the absence of choice by the parties, most of these countries adopted a flexible approach, leaving the judge to select the decisive connecting factors from the various elements of the contract and the circumstances of the case.[5]

English law formerly applied the "proper law of the contract",[6] which was a succinct expression to describe the law governing many of the matters affecting a contract. The doctrine of the proper law was of common law origin and a vast case law developed to take account of the difficulties outlined above. It was both sophisticated and flexible in its approach. The key features of the doctrine were as follows. The parties could choose the proper law, with very little restriction on this right. If the parties did not express a choice, and one could not be inferred by the courts, an objective test was applied. This sought to localise the contract by looking for the system of law with which the transaction was most closely connected. The twin theories which underlay the proper law were therefore the subjective theory, which looked to the intentions of the parties, and the objective theory, which sought to localise the contract. Special rules were adopted for particular issues. The proper law was usually relevant, but the court was required to go beyond the proper law when considering certain issues. Thus, for example, with the issue of illegality the courts were concerned not only with illegality by the proper law but also with illegality by the law of the place of performance. There were also special rules for particular contracts, such as insurance contracts. These rules either made special provision for ascertaining the proper law or departed from the proper law altogether.

Choice of law in contract was later put on a statutory footing. The Contracts (Applicable Law) Act 1990 largely replaced the common law rules and the doctrine of the proper law of the contract. The Act implemented the EEC Convention on the law applicable to contractual obligations of 1980 (the Rome Convention).[7] For contracts concluded since 17 December 2009,[8] the Rome Convention has been replaced by the Rome I Regulation,[9] and any reference

---

[2] Supra, pp 24–33.

[3] *Auten v Auten* 308 NY 155, 124 NE 2d 99 (1954)—grouping of contacts; Restatement, 2d, §§ 187, 188; *Lilienthal v Kaufman* 395 P 2d 543 (1964)—governmental interest analysis; *Haines v Mid-Century Insurance Co* 177 NW 2d 328 (1970)—choice influencing considerations. See generally Weintraub (1984) IV Hague Recueil 239; Penn and Cashel [1986] JBL 333, 497; Nygh (1995) 251 Hague Recueil 281–92; Hay, Borchers and Symeonides, Chapter 18, especially at para 18.21.

[4] For a detailed account, see Rabel, ii 370 et seq.; Basedow, *The Law of Open Societies: Private Ordering and Public Regulation in the Conflict of Laws* (2015), paras 185–98.

[5] See Lando (1987) 24 CMLR 159, 188–99.

[6] For a detailed analysis see the 11th edn (1987) of this book, Chapter 18; Dicey and Morris, (1987) 11th edn, Chapters 32 and 33; Anton, (2011) 3rd edn, Chapter 10. For a recent summary see *Merck KGaA v Merck Sharp & Dohme Corp* [2014] EWHC 3867 (Ch) at [9]; *First Laser Ltd v Fujian Enterprises (Holdings) Co* [2012] HKCU 1397, (2012) 15 HKFCAR 154 at [53]: "the law applicable to a contract is the system of law by which the parties intended the contract to be governed, or, where their intention is neither expressed nor to be inferred from the circumstances, the system of law with which the transaction has its closest and most real connection".

[7] OJ 1980 L 266/1; see also the consolidated version OJ 1998 C 27/34.

[8] Art 28 as amended by OJ 2009 L 307/87. For the temporal scope see infra pp 686–7.

[9] Regulation (EC) No 593/2008 of 17 June 2008 on the law applicable to contractual obligations (Rome I), OJ 2008 L 177/6.

to the Convention shall be understood as a reference to the Regulation.[10] However, in relation to Denmark and those territories of the Member States to which the Rome I Regulation does not apply, the Rome Convention remains in force.[11] The Regulation builds on the *acquis* of the Rome Convention, with some important modernisations and amendments. The future of the Rome I Regulation after Brexit—as that of all other EU regulations—is uncertain. However, as lawyers and courts in England and elsewhere have grown familiar with the Rome Regulations, which also served as a model for law reform outside the EU, there are good reasons to preserve these Regulations as part of domestic UK law in order to enhance legal certainty after Brexit.[12]

2. THE ROME CONVENTION[13]

(a) The history and purpose of the Convention

As early as 1967 there was a proposal from the governments of the Benelux countries to the Commission of the European Communities for the unification of private international law rules, particularly in the field of contract law. Experts from the then six Member States of the Community prepared a preliminary draft Convention before the United Kingdom, Ireland and Denmark joined the European Community. At that time, this draft also covered non-contractual obligations. In negotiations between experts from the then nine Member States of the European Community there was extensive revision of the draft Convention, culminating in a final Convention (the Rome Convention) in 1980.[14] This was only concerned with contractual obligations. By the end of 1981 the Convention had been signed by all of the then Member States.[15] However, ratification of the Rome Convention was delayed whilst

---

[10] Art 24 Rome I.

[11] For Denmark see Art 1(4) Rome I, for the other territories see Art 24(1) Rome I and (now) Art 355(2) and Annex II of the Treaty on the Functioning of the European Union (TFEU). According to Annex II, the Regulation (as other EU law) does not apply to Aruba and the Netherlands Antilles (Kingdom of the Netherlands), French Polynesia, Mayotte, New Caledonia, Saint-Pierre and Miquelon, Wallis and Futuna Islands and the French Southern Antarctic Territories (France) to which the 1980 Rome Convention still applies. For a detailed analysis of the territorial scope of the Regulation, see Magnus in *European Commentaries on Private International Law*, Introduction paras 48–67, pp 26–31.

[12] Financial Markets Law Committee, 'Issues of Legal Uncertainty Arising in the Context of the Withdrawal of the UK from the EU—The Application of English Law, the Jurisdiction of English Courts and the Enforcement of English Judgments' (December 2016), <http://www.fmlc.org/uploads/2/6/5/8/26584807/brexit_-_english_law_and_jurisdiction_paper.pdf>, para 3.4; House of Commons Justice Committee, 'Implications of Brexit for the Justice System' (22 March 2017), HC 750, <https://www.publications.parliament.uk/pa/cm201617/cmselect/cmjust/750/750.pdf> at [32]: "Rome I and II should be brought into domestic law".

[13] Kaye, *The New Private International Law of Contract of the European Community* (1993); Hill, *International Commercial Disputes* (3rd edn, 2005), Chapter 14; Plender, *The European Contracts Convention* (2nd edn, 2001); North (ed), *Contract Conflicts—The EEC Convention on the Law Applicable to Contractual Obligations: A Comparative Study* (1982); Fletcher, *Conflict of Laws and European Community Law* (1982), Chapter 5; Lasok and Stone, *Conflict of Laws in the European Community* (1987), pp 340–87; North [1980] JBL 382; Bennett (1980) 17 CMLR 269; Williams [1981] LMCLQ 250; note (1981) 2 VA J IntL 91; Morse (1982) 2 YEL 107; Weintraub (1984) IV Hague Recueil 239, at 278–90; Williams (1986) 35 ICLQ 1; Lando (1987) 24 CMLR 159; RMM [1991] JBL 205; Young [1991] LMCLQ 314. The Rome Convention served as the model for the Inter-American Convention on the Law Applicable to International Contracts (the Mexico Convention): see (1994) 33 ILM 733; Juenger (1994) 42 AJCL 381. It has also influenced law reform proposals in Australia; see ALRC Rep No 58 (1992); Kincaid (1995) 8 Jo Contract Law 231.

[14] OJ 1980 L 266.

[15] In 1984, the Greek Accession Convention (the Luxembourg Convention) was concluded. This did not alter the substance of the Rome Convention. The Rome Convention is not open to signature by non-Member States, Art 28(1). However, there is nothing to stop other countries incorporating the rules contained in the Rome Convention into their domestic private international law, such as Belgium, Luxembourg, Denmark,

problems in relation to what powers, if any, the European Court of Justice should have as regards interpretation of the Convention were resolved. In 1988, two protocols on inter-pretation of the Convention were signed,[16] which did not enter into force until 2004.[17] The Convention eventually received the requisite number of ratifications and came into force on 1 April 1991.[18]

In general terms, the Convention has been seen as a continuation of the work on unifica-tion begun by the Brussels Convention on jurisdiction and the enforcement of judgments in civil and commercial matters (replaced by the Brussels I Regulation and now the Brussels I Recast).[19] More particularly, since the law would be the same wherever trial takes place in the Community, it inhibited the forum shopping that the Brussels Convention (now Brussels I Recast) allowed.[20] It was also said that such a Convention would increase legal certainty and make it easier to anticipate the law to be applied.[21]

(b) The Contracts (Applicable Law) Act 1990

The introduction of the Rome Convention into English law was a matter of considerable controversy with enthusiasts[22] and critics[23] taking polarised positions. The controversy ranged

the Netherlands and Germany did prior to the Convention itself coming into force in 1991. See generally Lando (1987) 24 CMLR 159; Triebel (1988) 37 ICLQ 935; De Boer (1990) 54 Rabels Zeitschrift 24, 40 et seq.

[16] OJ 1989 L 48; see also OJ 1998 C 27/47 and C 27/52. There is a report by Professor Tizzano on the Protocols: OJ 1990 C 219. See Kaye, pp 415–30. The first Protocol defined the scope of the jurisdiction of the Court of Justice and the conditions under which that jurisdiction is to be exercised. States accept the jurisdiction of the Court of Justice under this Protocol. The second Protocol conferred powers on the Court of Justice to interpret the Rome Convention. The two-Protocol system allowed some Member States to pro-ceed with allowing referrals to the Court of Justice ahead of other Member States, such as Ireland, which had internal problems relating to allowing such a reference.

[17] The commencement of the first Protocol became possible following the ratification of the second Protocol by all fifteen Contracting States and it came into force for the United Kingdom on 1 March 2005, see The Contracts (Applicable Law) Act 1990 (Commencement No 2) Order, SI 2004/3448. The first Protocol came into force internationally on 1 August 2004, see Case C-133/08 *Intercontainer Interfrigo SC (ICF) v Balkenende Oosthuizen BV and MIC Operations BV* [2009] ECR I-9687 at [20]; Case C-29/10 *Heiko Koelzsch v État du Grand Duchy of Luxemburg* [2011] ECR I-1595 at [30].

[18] At first, it only applied to the then ten Member States of the European Community (Belgium, Denmark, France, Germany, Greece, Ireland, Italy, Luxembourg, the Netherlands and the United Kingdom), but subsequently there have been Accession Conventions, see OJ 1992 L 333/1 (Spain and Portugal), OJ 1997 C 15/10 with Explanatory Report in OJ 1997 C 191/11 (Austria, Finland, Sweden) with only minor alterations to the original Convention. For the version of the Rome Convention after these alterations see OJ 1998 C 27/34 and OJ 1998 C 27/47. From henceforth, in this chapter, all references to "the Rome Convention" or "the Convention" are to this version, ie as amended by these two Accession Conventions. The ten 2004 new EU Member States (Cyprus, Czech Republic, Estonia, Hungary, Latvia, Lithuania, Malta, Poland, Slovakia, Slovenia) and the fifteen old Member States have all signed an Accession Convention, OJ 2005 C 169/01.

[19] Para 2 of the Preamble; Case C-133/08 *Intercontainer Interfrigo SC (ICF) v Balkenende Oosthuizen BV and MIC Operations BV* [2009] ECR I-9687 at [22]. However, there is nothing in Art 220 of the Treaty of Rome about contract choice of law.

[20] See the Giuliano and Lagarde Report OJ 1980 C 282 of 31 October, at pp 4–5 which quotes from the address by Vogelaar at the meeting of government experts in 1969; Case C-133/08 *Intercontainer Interfrigo SC (ICF) v Balkenende Oosthuizen BV and MIC Operations BV* [2009] ECR I-9687 at [23]: "The function of the Convention is to raise the level of legal certainty by fortifying confidence in the stability of legal relationships and the protection of rights acquired over the whole field of private law".

[21] The Giuliano and Lagarde Report, ibid.

[22] North, *Contract Conflicts*, p 23; Jaffey (1984) 33 ICLQ 531 and *Topics in Choice of Law* (1996), Chapter 2.

[23] See Mann (1983) 32 ICLQ 265; (1989) 38 ICLQ 715; Briggs [1990] LMCLQ 192.

over both the need for harmonisation of contract choice of law rules and the nature and form of the new law. Nonetheless, when the 1990 Act was presented to Parliament it was said[24] that the Convention would produce benefits in terms both of harmonisation and improved certainty in the law.

The Contracts (Applicable Law) Act 1990[25] provided that the Rome Convention and the different Accession Conventions plus the first Protocol shall have the force of law in the United Kingdom.[26] There was a provision dealing with interpretation of the Conventions and Protocol,[27] and the Act reserved the right not to apply Articles 7(1) (mandatory rules of foreign countries) and 10(1)(e) (the consequences of nullity of a contract) of the Rome Convention.[28] Moreover, for intra-United Kingdom disputes, for which the Convention did not apply,[29] section 2(3) provided that "the Convention shall apply in the case of conflicts between the laws of different parts of the United Kingdom".

The effect of implementation of the Rome Convention was that, for contracts made after the Convention came into force, the traditional common law rules on contract choice of law were largely replaced by the rules contained in the Convention.[30] It was not possible for the parties to contract out of the Convention, for this would have defeated its purpose.[31] Nevertheless, the traditional common law rules continued to be applied to contracts made after the Convention came into force in situations which fell outside the (substantive) scope of the Convention;[32] and the same holds true for situations which fall outside the scope of the Rome I Regulation.[33] English courts therefore still have to operate two different regimes for contract choice of law: for Convention (now Regulation) cases (ie cases coming within the scope of the Convention or Regulation) there are the Convention/Regulation rules; for non-Convention cases (ie cases outside the scope of the Convention, now Regulation) there are the traditional common law rules.[34] This undoubted complication in the law could have been avoided if the 1990 Act had provided that the rules in the Rome Convention were to be applied to all contracts made after the Convention came into force, even in non-Convention cases, thereby assimilating the two sets of rules.[35]

---

[24] See the Lord-Advocate, Hansard, (HL) 12 December 1989 vol 513, cols 1258–60; Lord Chancellor, (HL) 24 April 1990, vol 518, col 439; Solicitor-General, (HC) Second Reading Committee 20 June 1990, cols 3–6.

[25] As amended by SI 1994/1900, in the light of the Spanish/Portuguese Accession Convention to the Rome Convention and by SI 2000/1825 in the light of the Austrian, Finnish and Swedish Accession Convention. From henceforth in this chapter all references to the Contracts (Applicable Law) Act 1990 or to "the 1990 Act" are to this amended version.

[26] S 2(1). The Accession Conventions and the first Protocol are set out in Schedules to the Act, s 3.

[27] S 3.

[28] S 2(2); for this possibility see Art 22 of the Rome Convention.

[29] Art 19(2).

[30] Choice of law rules in statutes may exceptionally be applied under Art 9 and Art 23 of the Regulation, see infra, pp 746–50, 772–4.

[31] North, *Essays*, pp 185–7; Kaye, p 120; Fentiman, *Foreign Law in English Courts* (1998), p 83; Hogan (1992) 108 LQR 12; Rinze [1994] JBL 412 at 417. Cf Mann (1991) 107 LQR 353.

[32] Art 1(2)–(4) Rome Convention.

[33] Art 1(2) Rome I.

[34] See the 11th edn (1987), of this book, Chapter 18. The common law rules were subject to a small number of statutory provisions, ibid.

[35] See North in *Contract Conflicts*, p 12; Fletcher, *Conflict of Laws and European Community Law* (1982), p 155.

3. THE ROME I REGULATION[36]

(a) Preliminary remarks

(i) History

After a consultation process started by a Green Paper in 2002,[37] the European Commission put forward in 2005 a proposal that the Rome Convention should be converted to the Rome I Regulation and its provisions modernised.[38] Harmonisation of choice of law rules was regarded as helping to facilitate the mutual recognition of judgments,[39] and the proper functioning of the internal market was said to create a need for such harmonisation.[40] For the same reason there was said to be a need to achieve harmony between three key instruments: the Brussels I Regulation (now Brussels I Recast) on jurisdiction; the Rome I Regulation on contractual obligations and the Rome II Regulation on non-contractual obligations.[41] The legal basis for the Regulation was Title IV, in particular Article 61(c), of the Treaty on European Union (now Title V, in particular Article 81(2)(c) of the Treaty on the Functioning of the European Union [TFEU]), which authorised the adoption of measures aimed at ensuring the compatibility of the rules applicable in Member States concerning the conflict of laws. The final version of the Regulation is based on a proposal contained in a European Parliament legislative resolution of 29 November 2007.[42] Prior to this there were informal contacts between the Council, the European Parliament and the Commission with a view to avoiding the need for a second reading and conciliation. The Council formally adopted the Regulation on 6 June 2008.[43] The Regulation applies to contracts concluded as from 17 December 2009.[44] Thus, contracts concluded before that date continue to be governed by the Rome Convention, even if the parties agree after 17 December 2009 on a (minor) variation of this contract. The Rome I Regulation applies only to a contract concluded before 17 December

---

[36] Leible and Ferrari (eds), *Rome I Regulation: The Law Applicable to Contractual Obligations in Europe* (2009), Hill and Chong, *International Commercial Disputes* (4th edn, 2010), Chapter 14; Anton, Chapter 10; Dicey, Morris and Collins, Chapter 32; Collier, *Conflict of Laws* (4th edn, 2013), Chapter 10; Briggs, *Private International Law in the English Courts* (2014), Chapter 7; Calliess (ed), *Rome Regulations: Commentary* (2nd edn, 2015), Part One; Crawford and Carruthers, *International Private Law: A Scots Perspective* (4th edn, 2015), Chapter 15; Fentiman, *International Commercial Litigation* (2nd edn, 2015), Chapter 5; Ferrari, *Rome I Regulation* (2015); McParland, *The Rome I Regulation on the Law Applicable to Contractual Obligations* (2015); Hartley, *International Commercial Litigation* (2nd edn, 2015), Chapters 24–25; Plender and Wilderspin, *European Private International Law of Obligations* (4th edn, 2015), Chapters 4–15; Clarkson and Hill, *Conflict of Laws* (5th edn, 2016), Chapter 4; Magnus and Mankowski (eds), *European Commentaries on Private International Law*, vol II (2017).

[37] Green paper on the conversion of the Rome Convention of 1980 on the law applicable to contractual obligations into a Community instrument and its modernisation COM (2002) 654 final; on which see Carruthers and Crawford 2003 SLT 137; Max Planck Institute (2004) 68 Rabels Zeitschrift 1. The contributions to the consultation can be found under <http://ec.europa.eu/justice/newsroom/civil/opinion/040127_en.htm>.

[38] Proposal for a Regulation of the European Parliament and the Council on the law applicable to contractual obligations (Rome I) COM (2005) 650 final. See Dutson (2006) 122 LQR 374 and (2006) IFL 36; Lando and Nielson (2007) 3 J Priv Int L 29; Dickinson (2007) 3 J Priv Int L 53; Gillies (2007) 3 J Priv Int L 89; Crawford and Carruthers, para 15-02; Max Planck Institute (2007) 71 Rabels Zeitschrift 225.

[39] Recital (3) of the Proposal, Recitals (4) and (6) of the final version of Rome I.

[40] Recital (4) of the Proposal, Recital (6) of the final version of Rome I.

[41] Recital (4) of the Proposal. This is not mentioned in the Recitals in the final version of the Regulation.

[42] COM (2005) 0650–C6-0441/2005–2005/0261(COD), A6-0450/2007 (hereinafter referred to as "proposal for a Rome I Regulation EP (first reading)").

[43] The Rome Convention will remain in force in relation to Denmark and for certain territories of Member States, Arts 1(4), 24 of the Regulation.

[44] Art 28 Rome I. Art 28 was amended by OJ 2009 L 309/87 from "contracts concluded *after* 17 December 2009" to "contracts concluded *as from* 17 December 2009".

2009 where this contract is subject, on or after that date, to a variation of such magnitude that it gives rise not to the mere updating or amendment of the contract but to the creation of a new legal relationship between the contracting parties, so that the initial contract should be regarded as having been replaced by a new contract.[45]

The United Kingdom, after stakeholder consultations, elected initially in 2006 not to opt in to the proposed Rome I Regulation.[46] Among the critics of the proposed Regulation[47] was the Financial Markets Law Committee, which took the view that it would cause significant uncertainty in the financial markets.[48] The prospect of having to consider giving effect to overriding mandatory provisions of foreign countries generated the greatest concern in this regard, although other provisions also caused concern. Nonetheless, the United Kingdom government saw clear benefits in a coherent European Union choice of law regime and attended the subsequent negotiations, without voting rights. After the negotiations on Rome I were complete, the United Kingdom has conducted a full public consultation before deciding whether to opt in or not. In its Consultation Paper,[49] the Ministry of Justice has taken the view that the Articles that were of greatest concern to the United Kingdom stakeholders during negotiations have either been removed, substantially revised or returned to their Convention form subject to later review. The Ministry of Justice has also argued that the Regulation improves upon the Convention in a number of respects, in particular in terms of improved drafting. All of this has led to its conclusion that the United Kingdom should opt in to the Rome I Regulation. In July 2008 the United Kingdom government expressed the wish to opt in to the Rome I Regulation and sought the consent of the Council of the European Union and of the European Commission to the United Kingdom's participation which was duly granted.[50]

(ii) Interpretation[51]

(a) Referrals to the Court of Justice

Under Article 267 of the Treaty on Functioning of the European Union (TFEU), the Court of Justice may give preliminary rulings on the validity and interpretation of acts of the institutions of the Union, including Regulations and thus the Rome I Regulation. National courts normally have discretion whether or not to request a preliminary ruling on interpretation from the Court of Justice.[52] However, where the question of interpretation is raised in a case pending before a national court against whose decisions there is no judicial remedy under national law and the question cannot be regarded as *acte clair*,[53] that court or tribunal must bring the matter before the Court of Justice.[54]

---

[45] Case C-135/15 *Republik Griechenland v Grigorios Nikiforidis* ECLI:EU:C:2016:774 at [35], [37].

[46] The Republic of Ireland has elected to opt in, see Recital (44) Rome I Regulation.

[47] See Dutson (2006) 122 LQR 374, [2006] JBL 608 and (2006) IFLR 36; Dickinson (2007) 3 J Priv Int L 53; Gillies (2007) 3 J Priv Int L 89.

[48] See para 17.1 of the Committee's Legal assessment of the conversion of the Rome Convention to a Community instrument and the provisions of the proposed Rome I Regulation, available at <http://www. fmlc.org>.

[49] CP 05/08.

[50] See Decision 2009/26/EC, OJ 2009 L 10/22. The United Kingdom would not have to apply the Regulation in intra-United Kingdom cases, Art 22(2) of the Regulation. However, the Rome I Regulation is applicable as between the different parts of the United Kingdom under the Law Applicable to Contractual Obligations (England and Wales and Northern Ireland) Regulations 2009 (SI 2009/3064) and the Financial Services and Markets Act 2000 (Law Applicable to Contracts of Insurance) Regulations 2009 (SI 2009/3075). For Scotland see SSI 2009/410.

[51] On the interpretation of the Rome Convention and the possibility to refer cases to the Court of Justice under that Convention see the 14th edn of this book (2008), pp 672–6.

[52] Art 267(2) TFEU.

[53] For the (narrow) definition of *acte claire*, see Case 283/81 *Srl CILFIT und Lanificio di Gavardo SpA gegen Ministero della Sanità* [1982] ECR 3415 at [16]–[20].

[54] Art 267(3) TFEU.

(b) The principles and decisions laid down by the Court of Justice[55]

Where the meaning of the Regulation is not referred to the Court of Justice, it should be determined in accordance with the principles laid down by, and any relevant decision of, that Court.[56] This means that the English courts have to act in accordance with two different types of authority: first, any relevant decisions of the Court of Justice; secondly, the principles laid down by the Court of Justice. If the Court of Justice has previously given a decision on the provision in issue, this must be followed. A relevant decision for these purposes could include one of the decisions of the Court of Justice discussing the Rome Convention[57] in a jurisdiction case on the Brussels Convention or the Brussels I Regulation. However, the provision which is in issue may not have been previously discussed by the Court of Justice. In this situation, the English courts must act in accordance with the principles of interpretation laid down by the Court of Justice. In this respect, the Court is likely to apply the same general principles of interpretation to the Rome I Regulation as it applies to other areas of EU law. Thus, in particular three factors should be considered for interpretation: first, the wording of the provision, secondly, the systematic context in which the provision is found, including its relation to other provisions in the Regulation or in other EU instruments, in particular the Brussels I Regulation (now Recast) and the Rome II Regulation,[58] and thirdly, as a very important factor,[59] the objectives of the provision in question and the objectives and scheme of the overall Regulation.[60] These objectives are, in particular, the predictability of the outcome of litigation, legal certainty and foreseeability as to the law applicable and the uniform application in all Member States.[61] In ascertaining the meaning of concepts used in the Regulation, regard should be had to the meaning of cognate concepts to be found in the European Union Treaties or in secondary legislation (in particular in neighbouring instruments such as Brussels I or Rome II), unless the European Union legislature has, in a specific legislative context, expressed a different intention.[62] It is encouraging to note that English judges when construing the Rome Convention have adopted a purposive approach[63] and have given the scope of the Convention an autonomous meaning.[64]

---

[55] For the—very similar—position under the Rome Convention, see s 3(1) Contracts (Applicable Law) Act 1990 and the 14th edn of this book (2008), pp 673–4.

[56] This is the same position in relation to the Brussels system, supra, pp 195–7, the Rome II Regulation, supra, pp 783–4, and the Rome Convention, see the 14th edn of this book (2008), pp 673–4.

[57] See, eg, Case 133/81 *Ivenel v Schwab* [1982] ECR 1891 at [13]–[14]; Case 9/87 *SPRL Arcado v SA Haviland* [1988] ECR 1539 at [15]; Case C-29/10 *Heiko Koelzsch v État du Grand Duchy of Luxemburg* [2011] ECR I-1595 at [45].

[58] Recital 7 Rome I.

[59] Case C-191/15 *Verein für Konsumenteninformation v Amazon EU Sàrl* ECLI:EU:C:2016:612 at [36]: "must be interpreted independently by reference primarily to the regulations' scheme and purpose".

[60] Cf Case C-350/14 *Florin Lazar, représenté légalement par Luigi Erculeo v Allianz SpA* ECLI:EU:C:2015:802 at [21].

[61] See Recital (6) of the Rome I Regulation.

[62] Case C-271/00 *Gemeente Steenbergen v Baten* [2002] ECR I-10489, [2003] 1 WLR 1996, at [43]; Joined Cases C-585/08 and C-144/09 *Peter Pammer v Reederei Karl Schlüter GmbH & Co. KG and Hotel Alpenhof GesmbH v Oliver Hellerat* [2010] ECR I-12527 at [43]; see also Joined Cases C-403/08 and C-429/08 *Football Association Premier League Ltd and Others v QC Leisure and Others and Karen Murphy v Media Protection Services Ltd* [2011] ECR I-9083 at [188].

[63] *Ennstone Building Products Ltd v Stanger Ltd* [2002] EWCA Civ 916 at [26], [2002] 1 WLR 3059; *Egon Oldendorff v Liberia Corpn* [1996] 1 Lloyd's Rep 380 at 387 (Clarke J).

[64] *Raiffeisen Zentralbank Osterreich AG v Five Star Trading LLC* [2001] EWCA Civ 68 at [33], [2001] QB 825.

(c) The principle of uniform and autonomous interpretation

One principle that the Court of Justice and national courts are bound to follow is the principle of uniform interpretation, which was set out in the Rome Convention itself. Article 18[65] provided that "In the interpretation and application of the preceding uniform rules, regard shall be had to their international character and to the desirability of achieving uniformity in their interpretation and application."[66] The same concept applies also to the Rome I Regulation: It follows from the need for uniform application of EU law and from the principle of equality that the terms used in the Regulation which make no express reference to the law of the Member States must normally be given an autonomous (independent) and uniform meaning by reference to their wording, scheme and purpose, rather than being understood as a reference to national law.[67] This means that courts should not define concepts by reference to their national law, but instead give independent EU meanings to the terms used in the Convention and now the Regulation. This also has important consequences when it comes to aids to interpretation, which will now be considered.

(d) Aids to interpretation[68]

(i) The Giuliano and Lagarde Report[69] and other legislative materials

The Rome Convention was accompanied by the Giuliano and Lagarde Report, which is a commentary by members of the Working Group responsible for drafting the Convention. Section 3(3) of the Contracts (Applicable Law) Act 1990 allowed this Report, and the Tizzano Report on the 1988 Protocols on interpretation,[70] to be considered by the English courts in ascertaining the meaning or effect of any provisions in the Rome Convention or first Protocol on interpretation. This follows the pattern of the Civil Jurisdiction and Judgments Act 1982, which allowed the Jenard and Schlosser Reports to be considered by English courts when interpreting the EU law on jurisdiction and enforcement of judgments.[71] The latter Reports have been constantly referred to by the Court of Justice and national courts when interpreting the Brussels Convention and also the Brussels Regulation (where the Regulation builds on the Convention). As many of the provisions of the Rome I Regulation are derived from the Rome Convention, the Giuliano and Lagarde Report is likely to be treated as being of the same high authority when it comes to interpretation of the Rome I Regulation.[72] Also the other legislative materials of the Rome I Regulation[73] should be consulted, even if their contents are not strictly binding for the interpretation of the Regulation.[74] In particular the Explanatory Memorandum contained in the Commission Proposal of 2005[75] may provide helpful insights in interpreting the Rome I Regulation.

---

[65] The same provision is to be found in Art 7 of the United Nations Convention on Contracts for the International Sale of Goods of 1980.

[66] For the principle of autonomous interpretation of the Rome Convention see also Case C-29/10 *Heiko Koelzsch v État du Grand Duchy of Luxemburg* [2011] ECR I-1595 at [32].

[67] Joined Cases C-359/14 and C-475/14 *ERGO Insurance SE v If P&C Insurance AS and Gjensidige Baltic AAS v PZU Lietuva UAB DK* ECLI:EU:C:2016:40 at [43]; Case C-135/15 *Republik Griechenland v Grigorios Nikiforidis* ECLI:EU:C:2016:774 at [28].

[68] See generally Kaye, pp 78–81.

[69] OJ 1980 C 282.

[70] OJ 1990 C 219.

[71] Supra, p 198.

[72] For the Rome Convention see Case C-29/10 *Heiko Koelzsch v État du Grand Duchy of Luxemburg* [2011] ECR I-1595 at [40].

[73] Supra, p 686.

[74] For an example of recourse to legislative materials see Case C-135/15 *Republik Griechenland v Grigorios Nikiforidis* ECLI:EU:C:2016:774 at [35].

[75] COM (2005) 650 final, pp 1–9.

(ii) The decisions of other European courts

Whatever the normal attitude of English judges towards the decisions of Continental courts, in this context foreign decisions on interpretation of the Rome Convention and the Rome I Regulation are of persuasive authority. Article 18 Rome Convention (uniformity of interpretation) enabled parties to rely on foreign decisions.[76] This included the decisions of Continental courts in Member States which have applied the Convention in anticipation of its coming into effect, as well as decisions subsequent to this. The same holds true under the Rome I Regulation, where national courts should strive for an autonomous EU interpretation and thus take the views of other EU courts into consideration.[77]

(iii) Texts in other languages

The 1990 Act gave the force of law[78] to the Convention in its different language texts, all of which are equally authentic,[79] rather than just to the English text, which is merely set out in the Act for ease of reference. Moreover, there is Court of Justice authority to the effect that courts of Member States should always be prepared to consider the texts of EU legislation in other languages.[80] As a consequence, the Rome I Regulation has to be interpreted also in the light of the versions existing in the other official languages. Any divergences between the different languages are to be resolved by reference to the purpose and general scheme of the Regulation.

(iv) The Brussels I and Rome II Regulations

It has already been mentioned[81] that English courts should follow decisions on interpretation of the Brussels Convention and the subsequent Brussels I Regulation which are relevant to interpretation of the Rome Convention[82] and the Rome I Regulation.[83] Going beyond this, some of the provisions in the Rome I Regulation use the same concepts as,[84] or are even lifted word for word from,[85] the Brussels Convention (now the Brussels I Recast). In such a situation, it is only right and proper that the earlier interpretation of this concept or term under the Brussels Convention and recast Regulation should be looked at, and, unless there is a good reason to the contrary, followed.[86] More generally, Recital (7) Rome I states that "[t]he substantive scope and the provisions of this Regulation should be consistent" with the Brussels I Regulation and the Rome II Regulation.[87] As a consequence, it seems safe to assume that the interpretation of parallel terms and concepts

---

[76] The Giuliano and Lagarde Report, p 38. See, eg, *Raiffeisen Zentralbank Osterreich AG v Five Star Trading LLC* [2001] EWCA Civ 68 at [49]–[52], [2001] QB 825.

[77] See, eg, the EUPillar database at <https://w3.abdn.ac.uk/clsm/eupillar/#/home>.

[78] S 2.

[79] See Art 33. See *Ennstone Building Products Ltd v Stanger Ltd* [2002] EWCA Civ 916 at [28]–[29], [2002] 1 WLR 3059—looking at the French version of the Convention.

[80] For the Brussels Regulation (and EU law in general) Case C-347/08 *Vorarlberger Gebietskrankenkasse v WGV-Schwäbische Allgemeine Versicherungs AG* [2009] ECR I-8661 at [26]. For the Brussels Convention Case 150/80 *Elefanten Schuh GmbH v Jacqmain* [1981] ECR 1671. See also *Newtherapeutics Ltd v Katz* [1991] Ch 226 at 243–5.

[81] Supra, p 688.

[82] Case C-29/10 *Heiko Koelzsch v État du Grand Duchy of Luxemburg* [2011] ECR I-1595 at [33], [41].

[83] Recital (7) Rome I. An early example is Case 133/81 *Ivenel v Schwab* [1982] ECR 1891.

[84] See, eg, the concept of a contractual obligation used in Art 1(1) of the Rome Convention, Art 1(1) Rome I Regulation and Art 5(1) of the Brussels Convention and Brussels I Regulation (now Art 7(1) Brussels I Recast); discussed supra, pp 245–50.

[85] See, eg, the concept of "provision of services" and "sale of goods" in Art 4(1)(a), (b) Rome I Regulation which is lifted from (what is now) Art 7(1) Brussels I, see Recital (17) Rome I.

[86] See, eg, *Base Metal Trading Ltd v Shamurin* [2004] EWCA Civ 1316, [2005] 1 WLR 1157.

[87] Joined Cases C-359/14 and C-475/14 *ERGO Insurance SE v If P&C Insurance AS and Gjensidige Baltic AAS v PZU Lietuva UAB DK* ECLI:EU:C:2016:40 at [43].

under these Regulations is to be applied also to the Rome I Regulation, unless there are cogent reasons not to do so.

(v) The traditional common law rules

Much of the Convention appears familiar to English lawyers and there may be a temptation to resort to the old common law rules when interpreting the Convention[88] or the Rome I Regulation. However, this is not usually justified and would be a dangerous habit to get into.[89] The provisions in the Convention and Regulation are not normally based on English law or on that of any other country's national law but on a common core of ideas used in EU countries.[90] A rule which may appear at first sight to be the same as the common law rule it has replaced may turn out, on closer examination, to be different in some respect.[91] The aim of uniformity of interpretation throughout the EU will not be achieved if English courts interpret the Convention or Regulation as a codification of the proper law of the contract. Article 18 (uniform interpretation) served as a reminder that national courts should not act in this way;[92] and the same holds true under the Rome I Regulation as a consequence of the principle of uniform and autonomous interpretation of EU law.[93]

(b) When does the Regulation apply?

The Regulation applies to matters coming within its scope, and it has universal application, ie it applies equally to contracts having no connection with a European Union State and to contracts with such a connection. Before turning to examine in detail these two aspects of the application of the Regulation, four general points need to be made. First, neither the Rome Convention nor the Rome I Regulation have retrospective effect.[94] The Rome Convention only applies in a Contracting State to contracts made after the Convention has entered into force in that state (1 April 1991 in the case of the United Kingdom), and the Rome I Regulation applies only to contracts concluded as from 17 December 2009; the traditional common law rules will continue to apply to contracts made before the Convention has entered into force. Secondly, neither the Rome Convention nor the Rome I Regulation prejudice the application of other international conventions to which a Contracting or Member State is a party.[95] This means, for example, that, as far as the United Kingdom is concerned, carriage of goods by sea will still be dealt with by the Hague-Visby Rules, implemented by the Carriage of Goods by Sea Act 1971, and not by the Rome Convention or Rome I Regulation.[96] Thirdly, acts of the institutions of the European Union, namely Regulations and Directives, and national laws implementing such acts, laying down choice of law rules relating to contractual obligations in relation to particular matters, take precedence

---

[88] This was advocated by the Lord Chancellor, Hansard (HL) 15 February 1990, vol 515, col 1489.

[89] See in relation to Art 4, *Iran Continental Shelf Oil Co v IRI International Corp* [2002] EWCA 1024 at [16], [2004] 2 CLC 696. But cf *Marconi Communications International Ltd v PT Pan Indonesia Bank Ltd TBK* [2005] EWCA Civ 422, [2007] 2 Lloyd's Rep 72.

[90] See *Raiffeisen Zentralbank Osterreich AG v Five Star Trading LLC* [2001] EWCA Civ 68 at [33]–[34], [2001] QB 825.

[91] See, eg, inferred choice of the applicable law, discussed infra, pp 718–23.

[92] See the Giuliano and Lagarde Report, p 38.

[93] See supra p 689.

[94] Art 28 Rome I Regulation, see supra pp 686–7; Art 17 Rome Convention.

[95] Art 25 Rome I Regulation; Art 21 Rome Convention, discussed infra, p 774. An important difference between Convention and Regulation is that the Rome I Regulation gives precedence only to existing international conventions, whereas the Rome Convention preserved the competence of Contracting States to conclude future international conventions.

[96] See Dicey, Morris and Collins, para 33-111, where the Hague-Visby-Rules are understood as overriding mandatory provisions in the sense of Art 9(2) Rome I Regulation. The same result can be achieved by applying Art 25 Rome I Regulation, without relying on the concept of overriding mandatory provisions, see infra, p 750.

over both the Convention and the Regulation.[97] Fourthly, the possibility under the Rome Convention for Contracting States to unilaterally introduce choice of law rules inconsistent with those contained in the Convention[98] has been abolished under the Rome I Regulation.

(i) The scope of the Regulation

(a) Contractual obligations in situations involving a conflict of laws

Article 1(1) Rome I states that: "This Regulation shall apply, in situations involving a conflict of laws, to contractual obligations in civil and commercial matters."[99] There are three separate requirements under this provision. First, the obligation must be contractual. Secondly, there must be a conflict of law problem. And thirdly, the obligation must concern a civil and commercial matter and not, in particular, a revenue, customs or administrative matter. While the meaning of the third requirement is identical to the parallel exclusion under the Brussels I Recast to which may be referred here,[100] the other two requirements deserve closer consideration.

(i) A contractual obligation

This concept should be given a European autonomous meaning that is not blinkered by national conceptions such as consideration[101] or even privity.[102] As the Rome I Regulation does not contain a definition of a "contractual obligation", but requires consistency with the Brussels I Recast and Rome II Regulation,[103] the case law of the Court of Justice on Article 7(1) Brussels I Recast can give guidance to define the "contractual obligation" and to draw the line between contractual and non-contractual obligations.[104] Drawing from an analogy to the meaning of "matter relating to a contract" in Article 7(1) Brussels I Regulation, the Court has held that the concept of "contractual obligation" within the meaning of Article 1 Rome I Regulation "designates a legal obligation freely consented to by one person towards another".[105] Recently, the Court of Justice added that the mere fact that one contracting party brings a civil liability claim against the other is not sufficient to consider that the claim concerns "matters relating to a contract" within the meaning of Article 7(1) Brussels I Recast. Rather, that is the case only where the "conduct complained of may be considered a breach of contract", which will be the case "where the interpretation of the contract which links the defendant to the applicant is indispensable to establish the lawful or, on the contrary,

---

[97] Art 20 Rome Convention; Art 23 and Recital (40) Rome I Regulation, discussed infra, p 772.

[98] Arts 23 and 24 Rome Convention.

[99] This adopts the wording on the scope of the Rome II Regulation on non-contractual obligations, Art 1(1) of Rome II, see infra, pp 792–3. Art 1(1) Rome II also expressly excludes "the liability of the State for acts and omissions in the exercise of State authority (*acta iure imperii*)".

[100] Art 1(1) Brussels I Recast, see supra pp 204–6.

[101] For the application of the Rome I Regulation to *inter vivos* gifts, see the Giuliano and Lagarde Report, pp 10–11; *Gorjat v Gorjat* [2010] EWHC 1537 (Ch) at [10].

[102] *Raiffeisen Zentralbank Osterreich AG v Five Star Trading LLC* [2001] EWCA Civ 68 at [33], [2001] QB 825; contra *Atlantic Telecom GmbH, Noter* 2004 SLT 1031. Cf the 14th edn of this book (2008), pp 677–8: the issue in question must be characterised according to English principles of characterisation to see whether it is contractual or, for example, proprietary or tortious or otherwise non-contractual. See also Case C-292/14 *Elliniko Dimosio v Stefanos Stroumpoulis and Others* ECLI:EU:C:2016:116 at [45]–[46]: request to a guarantee institution for payment of outstanding wages following the insolvency of an employer is not a contractual matter.

[103] Recital (7) Rome I.

[104] Joined Cases C-359/14 and C-475/14 *ERGO Insurance SE v If P&C Insurance AS and Gjensidige Baltic AAS v PZU Lietuva UAB DK* ECLI:EU:C:2016:40 at [43]. See also ibid at [47]: no contractual relationship between the insurers of vehicles which were involved in a traffic accident.

[105] Joined Cases C-359/14 and C-475/14 *ERGO Insurance SE v If P&C Insurance AS and Gjensidige Baltic AAS v PZU Lietuva UAB DK* ECLI:EU:C:2016:40 at [44].

unlawful nature of the conduct complained of against the former by the latter".[106] A non-contractual obligation, on the other hand, can be defined as a claim which seeks to establish the liability of a defendant and which is not related to a "contract" within the meaning of Article 7(1) Brussels I Recast.[107] For the purposes of the Rome II Regulation, such a non-contractual obligation "must be understood as meaning an obligation which derives from one of the events listed in Article 2 Rome II Regulation (tort/delict, unjust enrichment, *negotiorum gestio* or *culpa in contrahendo*)".[108]

Moreover, the process of characterisation can be guided by the subject matter and wording of the Rome I Regulation itself. A provision in the Regulation, such as Article 12 on the scope of the law applicable or Article 14 on voluntary assignment, may show a clear intention to embrace a particular issue.[109] Applying these principles it has been held[110] that the issue of whether, following an assignment (of the benefit of an insurance policy), the obligor (the insurer) had to pay (the proceeds of the insurance policy) to the assignee (a bank) rather than the assignor (a vessel owner) fell within the contractual rather than the proprietary umbrella.[111] Also falling within this contractual umbrella are such issues as whether a contract has been novated, and whether a third party may enforce a right conferred on him from the outset under a contract.[112] Novation and making new contracts with third parties are instances of the parties' freedom to contract and it is this party autonomy that is the dominant theme influencing the modern international view of contract.[113] A contractual obligation "is by its very nature one which is voluntarily assumed by agreement".[114] Where, on the other hand, a tortious or equitable duty of care is imposed entirely independent from the existence of a contract, this arises not from agreement and therefore the Regulation will not apply.[115] Not only do tortious obligations and property rights[116] fall outside the scope of the Regulation but so also do intellectual property rights[117] and claims that arise as a matter of

---

[106] Case C-548/12 *Marc Brogsitter v Fabrication de Montres Normandes EURL and Karsten Fräßdorf* ECLI:EU:C:2014:148 at [23]–[25].

[107] Joined Cases C-359/14 and C-475/14 *ERGO Insurance SE v If P&C Insurance AS and Gjensidige Baltic AAS v PZU Lietuva UAB DK* ECLI:EU:C:2016:40 at [45].

[108] Joined Cases C-359/14 and C-475/14 *ERGO Insurance SE v If P&C Insurance AS and Gjensidige Baltic AAS v PZU Lietuva UAB DK* ECLI:EU:C:2016:40 at [46]. For a detailed definition of non-contractual obligations, see infra, pp 788–92.

[109] The *Raiffeisen* case, supra, at [43]. Art 12 Rome I mentions interpretation, performance, the consequences of a breach of obligations, the various ways of extinguishing obligations, and the consequences of nullity of a contract, see infra, pp 764–9.

[110] The *Raiffeisen* case, supra.

[111] The *Raiffeisen* case, supra. Accordingly Art 14 Rome I (Art 12 Rome Convention), discussed infra, pp 1290–1, applied.

[112] The *Raiffeisen* case, supra, at [43].

[113] Ibid.

[114] *Base Metal Trading Ltd v Shamurin* [2004] EWCA Civ 1316 at [28], [2005] 1 WLR 1157; Briggs (2004) BYBIL 572. This definition raises a difficulty where a contractual obligation is imposed by law as under s 2 of the Carriage of Goods by Sea Act 1992, see generally Fawcett, Harris and Bridge, paras 14.02–14.06.

[115] Where an equitable duty depends on the existence, terms or interpretation of a contract, such an equitable duty can be regarded as contractual, for example a fiduciary relationship between solicitor and client, Dicey, Morris and Collins, paras 34-087, 36-070; but see ibid, para 32-018. For a potentially wider understanding of the exclusion of equitable duties of care in pre-Regulation case law see the *Base Metal* case, supra, at [28].

[116] Subject to Art 14 on assignment of claims, see Recital (38) Rome I Regulation, on assignment, infra, pp 1285–91.

[117] See the Giuliano and Lagarde Report, p 10. See also the special rules for in Arts 16-24a of the EU Trade Mark Regulation 207/2009, OJ 2009 L 78/1, and Arts 27–34 of the EU Design Regulation 6/2002, OJ 2002 L 3/1. However, a *contractual obligation* in respect of an intellectual property right, eg a licensing agreement, would come within the scope of the Regulation. There was an unsuccessful attempt in the House of Lords to

company law and company regulation.[118] The same holds true for obligations directly linked to dealings prior to the conclusion of a contract (*culpa in contrahendo*; eg violation of the duty of disclosure and the breakdown of contractual negotiations) which fall in the scope of the Rome II Regulation,[119] unless a tacit contractual relationship existed between the parties.[120]

The position in relation to quasi-contract, ie the consequences of an invalid contract, and other restitutionary remedies is more complicated. Both the Rome Convention and the Rome I Regulation contain a provision dealing with "the consequences of nullity of the contract",[121] which under English law is regarded as being a quasi-contractual issue.[122] However, the Convention allowed a reservation not to apply this provision of which the United Kingdom made use.[123] Under the Rome I Regulation, this reservation has been abolished. Thus, the consequences of nullity of a contract and any (restitutionary) remedies arising from this situation are to be classified as a contractual matter to be governed by the Rome I Regulation. For other restitutionary remedies, the Rome II Regulation on the law applicable to non-contractual obligations establishes separate provisions for two different types of restitutionary claim, which supports a classification as non-contractual for these types of claims.[124] One provision deals with non-contractual obligations arising out of unjust enrichment, the other with non-contractual obligations arising out of an act performed without due authority (*negotiorum gestio*). Moreover, in the context of jurisdiction, a claim in restitution has not been regarded as a matter relating to a contract.[125] Issues in restitution should therefore be regarded as being outside the scope of the Rome I Regulation and falling in the scope of the Rome II Regulation, unless they concern the consequences of nullity of a contract. In practice, however, it will not make a huge difference whether to apply Rome I or Rome II: Where a non-contractual obligation arising out of unjust enrichment or *negotiorum gestio* concerns a relationship existing between the parties, such as a contract, that is closely connected with that unjust enrichment, it shall be governed by the law that governs that relationship.[126] Therefore the law governing the contract will normally prevail both under Rome I and Rome II.

In cases where there is concurrent liability in contract and tort, the position prior to the introduction of the Rome II Regulation was very favourable to the claimant. As under English domestic law, the claimant was, for choice of law purposes, free to frame the action in tort, in contract, or both.[127] The introduction of the Rome II Regulation means that this

---

amend the 1990 Act to exclude this: Hansard (HL) 5 April 1990, vol 517, cols 1544–7. See generally Fawcett and Torremans, para 14.26; Wadlow [1997] 1 EIPR 11, at 11–12.

[118] Art 1(2)(e) Rome Convention; Art 1(2)(f) Rome I Regulation; *Atlantic Telecom GmbH, Noter* 2004 SLT 1031; see infra, p 701.

[119] See Art 1(2)(i) Rome I and Art 12, Recital (30) Rome II Regulation.

[120] See Case C-196/15 *Granarolo v Ambrosi Emmi France SA* ECLI:EU:C:2016:559 at [23]–[27]: an action for damages founded on an abrupt termination of a long-standing business relationship can be contractual if a tacit contractual relationship existed between the parties.

[121] Art 10(1)(e) Rome Convention; Art 12(1)(e) Rome I Regulation; discussed infra, pp 768–9, and supra, p 685.

[122] Art 13 of the preliminary draft of the Convention which dealt with both contractual and non-contractual obligations included in its provisions on non-contractual obligations a provision dealing with restitution; see generally, Collier in Lipstein (ed), *Harmonization of Private International Law by the E.E.C.*, 81 et seq.

[123] Art 22(1)(b) Rome Convention; s 2(2) Contracts (Applicable Law) Act 1990.

[124] Infra, pp 836–7.

[125] See *Kleinwort Benson Ltd v Glasgow City Council* [1999] 1 AC 153, HL; discussed supra, pp 247–8. It is disputed whether a claim for restitution falls under Art 7(2) Brussels I Regulation, see the discussion in Case C-102/15, *Gazdasági Versenyhivatal v Siemens Aktiengesellschaft Österreich*, Opinion of AG Wahl ECLI:EU:C:2016:225 at [55]–[75].

[126] Art 10(1), Art 11(1) Rome II Regulation.

[127] *Base Metal Trading Ltd v Shamurin* [2004] EWCA Civ 1316 at [31]–[35], [2005] 1 WLR 1157. See generally on choice of law and concurrent claims arising out of the international sale of goods, Fawcett, Harris and Bridge, Chapter 20.

needs rethinking. The analogy should be drawn with jurisdiction under Article 7(1) and (2) of the Brussels I Regulation[128] and each obligation should be classified as contractual or non-contractual but not both, so that there would be no question of the claimant being able to choose.[129]

(ii) A conflict of laws[130]

A preliminary draft of the Rome Convention stated that it only applied "in situations of an international character".[131] This requirement was criticised[132] for the definitional problems it created, and it was replaced by the more straightforward requirement that there be a situation involving a choice between the laws of different countries (Rome Convention), or, respectively, a conflict of laws (Rome I Regulation). As far as the United Kingdom is concerned this merely makes explicit what was implicit under the traditional common law rules on contract choice of law. However, the fact that this is now spelt out in statutory form means that some attention needs to be given to this point. Under English private international law a conflict of laws problem exists whenever the court is faced with a dispute that contains a foreign element.[133] With a contractual dispute, typical examples of a foreign element are as follows: one of the parties to the contract is a foreign national or is habitually resident abroad; the contract is concluded abroad; the contract is to be performed by one of the parties abroad. In such cases the foreign country has a claim to have its law applied, and the uniform rules in the Regulation are intended to apply.

The position is more difficult if the court is faced with a dispute involving a foreign element, but in respect of what is an essentially domestic contract. This can arise in two different types of case. The first is where, for example, there is a purely German contract, which is the subject of trial in England, subsequent to the defendant having moved his business to England after concluding the contract. The situation involves a foreign element in that one of the parties now carries on his business in England. However, what is lacking is any relevant connection with a country other than Germany of the sort which would give that other country's law a claim to be applied.[134] Nonetheless, it is desirable that such cases come within the Regulation.[135] The object of the Regulation of achieving harmonisation of choice of law rules in contract is most likely to be attained if the scope of the Regulation is given as wide an interpretation as possible. The above example should therefore be regarded as one involving a conflict between the laws of different countries. The second type of case is where there is, for example, a purely English contract, but the parties have agreed that French law shall govern the contract. It is implicit from the terms of Article 3(3)[136] that the Regulation will apply in this situation.[137] However, the Regulation will not apply if there is a purely English contract

---

[128] Supra, pp 268–70.

[129] This was advocated by Briggs [2003] LMCLQ 12 even before the introduction of Rome II. For more detail see infra, pp 791–2.

[130] Art 1(1) Rome Convention referred to "a choice between the laws of different countries". See generally Lando in Lipstein (ed), *Harmonization of Private International Law by the E.E.C.*, p 15; (1987) 24 CMLR 159 at 163–4; Diamond (1986) IV Hague Recueil 236 at 248–51; Kaye, pp 107–11. A special problem arises where substantive law has been harmonised by an international convention applicable in the UK, see infra, p 750.

[131] Art 1 of the preliminary draft Convention.

[132] See, eg, Collins (1976) 25 ICLQ 35, 41. But see the definition of "international" in Art 1 of the Inter-American Convention on the Law Applicable to International Contracts of 1994.

[133] Supra, p 3 et seq.

[134] See the Giuliano and Lagarde Report, p 10, which presupposes the existence of such a claim.

[135] See Lando, op cit, pp 15–17. Diamond had no doubts that such cases came within the Rome Convention: ibid, pp 250–1.

[136] Discussed infra, pp 711–13.

[137] See generally Nygh, *Autonomy in International Contracts* (1999), pp 52–5.

which merely incorporates French law by, for example, setting out verbatim a provision of French law as a term of the contract.[138]

There is another problem in relation to the requirement that there is "conflict of laws" which is less easily solved. Under English law, if foreign law is not pleaded or proved, the court gives a decision according to English law.[139] The courts are free to apply this rule in relation to the Rome Regulation because matters of evidence and procedure are excluded from the scope of the Regulation.[140] If the English court is going automatically to apply English law it is arguable that this is not a situation involving a conflict between the laws of different countries. However, the purpose of the Regulation is not going to be met if the English courts allow the parties to side-step the uniform rules contained therein by a simple omission to plead and prove foreign law. It would therefore be better if this sort of case was regarded as coming within the Regulation.[141]

Although it is not stated explicitly in Article 1(1) Rome I Regulation, the conflict must be between the laws of different *countries*,[142] which includes the laws of non-EU Member States.[143] A country is defined under the Regulation in the normal private international law sense as a territorial unit with its own rules of law, in this case relating to contractual obligations.[144] A French court, for example, will have to apply English law, or Scottish, or Northern Irish law under the Regulation, even though the United Kingdom is a Member State in the sense of the Regulation. Similarly, an English court may have to apply, for example, Ontario or New South Wales law under the Regulation. Indeed, the Regulation can apply to an interstate dispute involving connections with the "countries" of California and New York, provided that trial takes place in an EU Member State. However, the Regulation makes it clear that it is for the United Kingdom to decide whether it wants to apply the rules in the Regulation to intra-United Kingdom disputes. It is certainly not bound to do so,[145] but the obvious inconvenience of having a different regime for intra-United Kingdom contractual disputes from all other cases has led to the decision by the UK legislator to apply the Rome Convention and the Rome I Regulation to such disputes.[146] The upshot is that England, Scotland and Northern Ireland are separate countries for the purposes of the Regulation, even in intra-United Kingdom disputes.

---

[138] Incorporation of foreign law is discussed infra, p 717.

[139] Supra, p 105 et seq.

[140] Art 1(3), see infra, pp 704–5.

[141] There are problems then of whether the parties have made a (possibly implicit) choice of the applicable law, infra, p 711.

[142] This was made clear in Art 1(1) Rome Convention: "choice between the laws of different countries". Under the Regulation, Recital (13) states that the parties may include a non-State body of law or an international convention (not applicable under Art 25) (only) by incorporation by reference into their contract. Thus, such rules cannot be chosen as the law governing the contract, but only as contractual terms incorporated by reference within the law of a country applicable to their contract. Art 3(2) of the original Proposal for a Rome I Regulation permitted the parties to choose as the applicable law a non-State body of law, Explanatory Memorandum, COM (2005) 650 final, p 5.

[143] On the universal application of the Regulation see Art 2 Rome I and infra, pp 695–6.

[144] Art 22(1) Rome I Regulation; see also Art 19(1) Rome Convention.

[145] Art 22(2) Rome I Regulation; Art 19(2) Rome Convention.

[146] For the Rome Convention, see s 2(3) Contracts (Applicable Law) Act 1990. For the Rome I Regulation, see the Law Applicable to Contractual Obligations (England and Wales and Northern Ireland) Regulations 2009 (SI 2009/3064), Reg 5; for Scotland see the Law Applicable to Contractual Obligations (Scotland), Reg 4 (SSI 2009/410). For the exception for insurance contracts, see the Financial Services and Markets Act 2000 (Law Applicable to Contracts of Insurance) Regulations 2009 (SI 2009/3075).

(b) Exclusions[147]

Article 1(2) to (3) excludes a wide variety of matters from the scope of the Regulation. These matters can be put into three main categories. First and foremost, it excludes certain commercial contracts such as arbitration agreements and certain contracts of insurance. Secondly, it excludes non-commercial contracts, such as agreements to make wills and agreements to pay maintenance. Thirdly, it excludes certain matters which do not involve contract choice of law, such as evidence and procedure, or which under the laws of some Member States do not involve contract choice of law, such as negotiable instruments and the issue of capacity to contract. The matters excluded from the scope of the Regulation, and the reasons for their exclusion, will now be examined, in the order in which they are set out in the Regulation. These are as follows:

(i) *Questions involving the status or legal capacity of natural persons, without prejudice to Article 13*[148]

This phrase is a familiar one, and is to be found in the list of exclusions from the Rome Convention and Brussels I Recast.[149] Questions of status are clearly outside the scope of a Regulation concerned with contract choice of law, and do not need expressly to be excluded. The exclusion of legal capacity is more controversial. To common lawyers capacity to contract is a matter falling squarely within the ambit of rules on contract choice of law. But to civil lawyers this is regarded as a matter relating to status, hence its exclusion from the Regulation.[150] This particular exclusion only relates to natural persons. The exclusion of the legal capacity of corporations is dealt with under a separate provision.[151] The result of the exclusion is that national courts are left to apply their traditional rules of private international law to the issue of capacity to contract; in England's case this will be the traditional common law rules. However, there is one exception to this. The exclusion of capacity to contract is subject to Article 13 of the Regulation, which is a fairly narrow rule designed to protect a party who contracts with a natural person under an incapacity from being caught unawares by this. The English common law rules on capacity to contract, and Article 13, will be examined later on in this chapter in the section on particular issues.[152]

(ii) *Obligations arising out of family or succession law*

Article 1(2)(b) and (c), which adopt the wording of the Rome II Regulation on non-contractual obligations,[153] are concerned with non-commercial contracts. They exclude

> obligations arising out of family relationships and relationships deemed by the law applicable to such relationships to have comparable effects, including maintenance obligations, [and]

> obligations arising out of matrimonial property regimes, property regimes of relationships deemed by the law applicable to such relationships to have comparable effects to marriage, and wills and succession.[154]

---

[147] See Plender and Wilderspin, paras 5-001–5-005; for the Rome Convention see Kaye, pp 111–42.

[148] Art 1(2)(a) of the Rome I Regulation.

[149] Art 1(2)(a) Rome Convention; Art 1(2)(a) Brussels I Recast.

[150] See North in *Contract Conflicts*, p 10.

[151] Art 1(2)(f), discussed infra, p 701.

[152] Infra, pp 761–4.

[153] Art 1(2)(a) and (b) Rome II Regulation, see infra, pp 793–5. See also the comparable provisions in Art 1(2)(a), (e) and (f) Brussels I Regulation.

[154] Art 1(2)(b) and (c) of the Rome I Regulation. A similar exclusion can be found in Art 1(2)(b) of the Rome II Regulation.

Indeed, many disputes relating to the matters listed above will not even involve contractual obligations. For example, disputes in relation to succession are not normally contractual, but are concerned with issues such as the validity of the will, or concern obligations imposed by law and not by agreement. This provision makes it clear that, in the rare cases which raise contractual obligations, for example an agreement to make a will, the Regulation will not apply.

Family relationships in the sense of Article 1(2)(b) shall include "parentage, marriage, affinity and collateral relatives".[155] Under the Rome Convention, the comparable exclusion of "rights and duties arising out of a family relationship" was intended to ensure that contractual obligations relating to any family law matter were excluded from the Convention.[156] In particular, it was intended to exclude maintenance obligations. However, the exclusion of maintenance was not all-embracing. The Giuliano and Lagarde Report[157] distinguished between, on the one hand, obligations to pay maintenance which are imposed by law in respect of which there is also an agreement to pay (these were excluded from the scope of the Convention) and, on the other hand, purely contractual obligations to do so (these were within the scope of the Convention). This distinction can also be applied under the Regulation. Thus the case of a father who is under a legal obligation to maintain his children after a divorce, but who also agrees to maintain them, although involving a contractual obligation, is excluded from the scope of the Regulation.[158] In contrast to this, if a person who is not under a legal obligation to provide maintenance for a member of the family, nonetheless agrees to do so, as where a child agrees to maintain a parent, this would fall within the scope of the Regulation.

The phrases "wills and succession" and "matrimonial property regime" are to be found among the list of exclusions from the scope of the Brussels I Recast,[159] and their meaning has been discussed in that context. Moreover, the EU has now adopted specific instruments for these matters which may be consulted to interpret the scope of the respective exclusions in Rome I.[160] What deserves to be mentioned, however, is that the exclusion in Article 1(2)(b) goes further than that in the Rome Convention in that it extends also to "relationships deemed by the law applicable to such relationships to have comparable effects". According to Recital (8), the term "relationships having comparable effects to marriage and other family relationships" (such as registered partnerships) "should be interpreted in accordance with the law of the Member State in which the court is seised". This clarifies that the definition of "relationships having comparable effects" is to be determined by the national (choice of law) rules of

---

[155] Recital (8) Rome I Regulation.

[156] The Giuliano and Lagarde Report, p 10.

[157] At p 10.

[158] For "maintenance obligations arising from a family relationship, parentage, marriage or affinity", Regulation (EC) No 4/2009 on jurisdiction, applicable law, recognition and enforcement of decisions and cooperation in matters relating to maintenance obligations (OJ 2009 L 7/1) has been adopted which refers for the applicable law to the Hague Protocol of 23 November 2007 on the law applicable to maintenance obligations (Art 15 of that Regulation). The UK and Ireland chose not to ratify this Protocol. For the English rules in this field, see infra pp 1078–86.

[159] Art 1(2)(a), (f) of the Brussels I Recast; discussed supra, pp 206–7, 212.

[160] For wills and succession, see Regulation (EU) No 650/2012 on jurisdiction, applicable law, recognition and enforcement of decisions and acceptance and enforcement of authentic instruments in matters of succession and on the creation of a European Certificate of Succession (OJ 2012 L 201/107). For matrimonial property, see Regulation (EU) 2016/1103 implementing enhanced cooperation in the area of jurisdiction, applicable law and the recognition and enforcement of decisions in matters of matrimonial property regimes (OJ 2016 L 183/1), for the property consequences of registered partnerships see Regulation (EU) 2016/1104 (OJ 2016 L 183/30). Even if none of these Regulations applies to the UK, they may be helpful in informing about the European understanding of "wills and succession" or "matrimonial property regimes".

the forum in order to respect the traditional national boundaries of what is considered to be part of family law.

(iii) Obligations arising under bills of exchange, cheques and promissory notes and other negotiable instruments to the extent that the obligations under such other negotiable instruments arise out of their negotiable character[161]

The identical exclusion but in respect of non-contractual obligations is to be found in the Rome II Regulation.[162] The reason for the incorporation of the exclusion in Rome I is the same as the reason for its incorporation in the Rome Convention and Rome II Regulation, namely that "the Regulation is not the proper instrument for such obligations, that the Geneva Conventions of 7 June 1930 and 19 March 1931 regulate much of this matter and that these obligations are not dealt with uniformly in the Member States".[163]

Under English law, negotiable instruments involve contractual obligations, but have long been subject to special rules, including those contained in the Bills of Exchange Act 1882, rather than being governed by the proper law of the contract.[164] The effect of the exclusion of negotiable instruments from the Rome I Regulation is to preserve these special rules. The exclusion applies to bills of exchange, cheques and promissory notes, each of which category is well known to English lawyers. It also applies to "other negotiable instruments to the extent that the obligations under such other negotiable instruments arise out of their negotiable character".[165] "Other negotiable instruments" is not defined under the Regulation, and Member States may have different ideas on whether an instrument is negotiable. However, the Giuliano and Lagarde Report on the Rome Convention[166] stated that it is for the private international law of the forum to determine whether a document is to be characterised as being negotiable. If the transfer takes place in England, the instrument is negotiable if English mercantile custom or a statute so provides. Examples of instruments which are negotiable in England include bonds issued by foreign governments and debentures issued to bearer by English companies. On the other hand, a bill of lading which is transferred in England is not negotiable, and is therefore within the scope of the Regulation.

Even if it can be shown that what is involved is a negotiable instrument other than a bill of exchange, cheque or promissory note, the exclusion is limited to cases in which the obligation arises out of the negotiable character of the instrument. This would cover a dispute where, for example, an acceptor of the instrument wants payment but the other party refuses, alleging that the acceptor is not a holder in due course of the instrument. Such a dispute would be outside the scope of the Regulation. On the other hand, contracts for the issue of, for example, Government bonds or for purchase/sale of such bonds are not concerned with the negotiable character of the instrument, and are thus within the scope of the Regulation.[167]

---

[161] Art 1(2)(d) Rome I Regulation; Art 1(2)(c) of the Rome Convention. See the Giuliano and Lagarde Report, p 11; Kaye, pp 116–18.

[162] Art 1(2)(c) of the Rome II Regulation, discussed infra, p 795.

[163] The Explanatory Memorandum on the Rome II Proposal, COM (2003) 427 final of 22 July 2003, OJ 2004 C 96/8, p 9.

[164] Dicey, Morris and Collins, paras 33R-327–33-375.

[165] Recital (9) adds that "obligations under bills of exchange, cheques and promissory notes and other negotiable instruments should also cover bills of lading to the extent that the obligations under the bill of lading arise out of its negotiable character".

[166] At p 11.

[167] Ibid.

(iv) Arbitration agreements and agreements on the choice of court[168]

The exclusion of arbitration agreements and agreements on the choice of court—which is identical in the Rome I Regulation and the Rome Convention—was probably the most controversial of the exclusions from the Rome Convention, with the United Kingdom delegation arguing unsuccessfully that such agreements should be subject to the rules contained in the Convention.[169] The exclusion applies not only to separate arbitration or choice of jurisdiction agreements, ie agreements whose sole or main purpose is to provide for arbitration or a place of trial for a particular dispute, but also to arbitration or choice of jurisdiction clauses contained within a contract, which under English law are themselves regarded as separate agreements. However, when an arbitration or choice of jurisdiction clause is excluded,[170] this only affects the clause itself; the remaining clauses in the contract will be within the scope of the Regulation and judges will have to apply the rules under the Regulation to them. This is uncertain for arbitration tribunals, for which it is disputed whether they are bound by the Rome I Regulation at all (and EU conflict of law rules in general).[171]

The exclusion in Article 1(2)(e) obviously relates to any choice of law issues that arise with regard to arbitration agreements and agreements on the choice of court, such as the formation, validity[172] and effects of such agreements. It is also said to relate to any procedural questions that arise in relation to the arbitration.[173] The result of the exclusion is that national courts will continue to apply their own rules of private international law to arbitration agreements and agreements on the choice of court. In England's case this means the traditional common law rules.[174] Contracts will have to be split up so that a question, for example, of interpretation of a choice of jurisdiction clause will have to be determined under the traditional common law rules, whereas the rest of the contract will be governed by the rules applicable under the Regulation. This can lead to different laws governing the agreement on arbitration/choice of court and the rest of the contract.[175] One could end up with a contract

---

[168] Art 1(2)(e) Rome I Regulation; Art 1(2)(d) of the Rome Convention.

[169] For the reasons for this see infra, p 701. To support the exclusion of choice of court and arbitration agreements, it was pointed out that arbitration agreements were already covered by satisfactory international regulation (see, in particular, the 1958 New York Convention on the recognition and enforcement of foreign arbitral awards) and that the question of the law applicable to the choice-of-forum clause should ultimately be settled by the Brussels I Regulation (now Recast), see the Explanatory Memorandum, p 5. However, the Brussels I Recast does not address the substantive validity of choice-of-court agreements, which is to be decided in accordance with the law of the Member State of the court or courts designated in the agreement, including the conflict-of-laws rules of that Member State (Recital (20) Brussels I).

[170] Nonetheless, according to the Giuliano and Lagarde Report, p 12 and Recital (12) Rome I Regulation, the jurisdiction clause remains relevant to the ascertainment of the applicable law under Art 3(1), see infra, pp 718–20.

[171] See generally Yuksel (2011) 7 J Priv Int L 149, who argues that arbitration tribunals are bound by Rome I, cf Dicey, Morris and Collins, paras 16-010, 32-021 and Arbitration Act 1996, s 46.

[172] *Akai Pty Ltd v People's Insurance Co Ltd* [1998] 1 Lloyd's Rep 90 at 98. Some issues which may appear to be ones of validity of the jurisdiction agreement end up being regarded as ones of validity of the contract as a whole see *Egon Oldendorff v Liberia Corpn* [1995] 2 Lloyd's Rep 64 (Mance J). For cases where it appears to have been accepted that the issue was as to validity of the jurisdiction clause but that the law governing this issue was the law governing the contract as a whole (ie the Rome Convention) see *OT Africa Line Ltd v Magic Sportswear Corpn* [2005] EWCA Civ 710 at [1]–[2], [22] (per Longmore LJ), [2005] 2 Lloyd's Rep 170 (but cf Rix LJ at [60]); *Horn Linie GmbH & Co v Panamericana Formas E Impresos SA (The Hornbay)* [2006] EWHC 373 (Comm) at [20], [2006] 2 Lloyd's Rep 44.

[173] The Giuliano and Lagarde Report, p 12.

[174] The *Akai* case, supra. The test has been summarised in *Sulamérica Cia Nacional de Seguros SA v Enesa Engenharia SA* [2012] EWCA Civ 638 at [25]: "the proper law is to be determined by undertaking a three-stage enquiry into (i) express choice, (ii) implied choice and (iii) closest and most real connection", see also [26]–[32] and *Habas Sinai Ve Tibbi Gazlar Istihsal Endustrisi AS v VSC Steel Co Ltd* [2013] EWHC 4071 (Comm) at [100]–[101].

[175] See *Sulamérica Cia Nacional de Seguros SA v Enesa Engenharia SA* [2012] EWCA Civ 638 at [25]; Lipstein in Lipstein (ed), *Harmonization of Private International Law by the E.E.C.*, p 3. The law chosen in the

which is void according to the rules on the applicable law contained in the Regulation, but which contains an arbitration agreement which is valid according to its proper law. It was in order to avoid such splitting of the contract that the United Kingdom argued that arbitration and choice of jurisdiction agreements should not be excluded from the scope of the Convention (and now Regulation).

*(v) Questions governed by the law of companies and other bodies, corporate or unincorporated,
    such as the creation, by registration or otherwise, legal capacity, internal organisation or
    winding up of companies and other bodies, corporate or unincorporated, and the personal
    liability of officers and members as such for the obligations of the company or body*[176]

This provision—almost identical in the Rome Convention and the Rome I Regulation—clarifies the point that, if contractual matters are raised in a company law context,[177] they fall outside the scope of the Regulation. Examples of matters excluded by this provision are the contract which, under English law, is contained in the memorandum and articles of association of a company, and a contract to wind up a company, including mergers or grouping of companies.[178] The legal capacity of a company to contract is also excluded from the scope of the Regulation.[179] On the other hand, an agreement by promoters to form a company is apparently not excluded from the scope of the Regulation.[180] This is presumably on the basis that this is a purely contractual matter and is not governed by company law. Moreover, the merger of a company under which it loses its legal capacity does not affect the law applicable to contracts taken out by the acquired company with third parties.[181]

*(vi) The question whether an agent is able to bind a principal, or an organ to bind a company
    or other body corporate or unincorporated, in relation to a third party*[182]

The question whether an agent is able to bind a principal is also excluded from the scope of the Rome I Regulation.[183] The original proposal for a Regulation did not exclude this question and contained a proposed new choice of law rule dealing with this issue and other issues arising where a contract is concluded by an agent.[184] However, this special rule was subsequently deleted and the original exclusion in the Rome Convention was restored, albeit with slightly modified wording.

---

main contract is not necessarily the same as that which governs an arbitration agreement within that contract, see the *Sulamérica* case, supra, at [25]–[32].

[176] Art 1(2)(f) Rome I Regulation; Art 1(2)(e) of the Rome Convention; the Giuliano and Lagarde Report, p 12.

[177] For the distinction between company law and employment law in the case of a company director's contract, see Case C-47/14 *Holterman Ferho Exploitatie BV and Others v F.L.F. Spies von Büllesheim* ECLI:EU:C:2015:574 at [45]–[47].

[178] For the exclusion of merger contracts, see Case C-483/14 *KA Finanz AG v Sparkassen Versicherung AG Vienna Insurance Group* ECLI:EU:C:2016:205 at [52].

[179] *Continental Enterprises Ltd v Shandong Zhucheng Foreign Trade Group Co* [2005] EWHC 92 (Comm). This is a total exclusion. For an example of a case raising this issue, see *Janred Properties Ltd v Ente Nazionale Italiano per il Turismo* [1989] 2 All ER 444. Cf the position of natural persons under an incapacity—Art 13 may apply, on which see infra, pp 763–4.

[180] The Giuliano and Lagarde Report, p 12. See also *Base Metal Trading Ltd v Shamurin* [2003] EWHC 2419 (Comm) at [42], [2004] IL Pr 5; respondent's notice rejected without discussing this point [2004] EWCA Civ 1316, [2005] 1 WLR 1157.

[181] For a merger by acquisition, see Case C-483/14 *KA Finanz AG v Sparkassen Versicherung AG Vienna Insurance Group* ECLI:EU:C:2016:205 at [58]–[59].

[182] Art 1(2)(g) of the Rome I Regulation; Art 1(2)(f) of the Rome Convention. For criticism see Lasok and Stone, *Conflict of Laws in the European Community* (1987), p 354.

[183] Art 1(2)(g) of the Regulation.

[184] Art 7 of the Proposal for a Regulation of the European Parliament and the Council on the law applicable to contractual obligations (Rome I) COM (2005) 650 final.

The exclusion is only concerned with the relationship between a principal and a third party, and is confined to the specific question of whether the principal is bound vis à vis third parties by the acts of the agent.[185] It follows that, for example, a contractual dispute between the principal and agent arising out of the contract of agency is not excluded. The exclusion is therefore a narrow one. However, it does encompass the question whether an organ of a company can bind the company. This raises the question of ultra vires, which under English law is a question of company law. The exclusion has been explained[186] on the basis that the principle of freedom of contract, which is deeply enshrined in the Convention's (and Regulation's) rules on the applicable law,[187] is difficult to accept in relation to the matter excluded. As far as English law is concerned, the effect of the exclusion is the retention of the common law rule under which the proper law of the contract concluded between the agent and third party governs the question of whether the principal is bound vis à vis third parties by the acts of the agent.[188]

(vii) *The constitution of trusts and the relationship between settlors, trustees and beneficiaries*[189]

The English concept of a trust is said to define the subject matter of this exception.[190] This raises the question of why this exclusion of the common law trust was introduced. It is presumably because, under English law, the constitution of trusts and the relationship between trustee/beneficiary and settlor/trustee are not based on contract. The exclusion is for the sake of clarity. There are Continental equivalents of a trust which are contractual in origin and thus appear to come within the Regulation. However, these will also be excluded if they exhibit the same characteristics as a common law trust.[191] It is noticeable that the exclusion does not extend to trust property, although this can in fact raise contractual problems. For example, a trustee could invest in property abroad and could then be sued in contract by the vendor of the property. This situation appears to come within the scope of the Regulation.

(viii) *Obligations arising out of dealings prior to the conclusion of a contract*[192]

The Rome I Regulation differs from the Convention by expressly excluding obligations arising out of dealings prior to the conclusion of a contract (*culpa in contrahendo,* eg violation of the duty of disclosure and the breakdown of contractual negotiations) on the basis that these fall within the scope of the Rome II Regulation,[193] which has a separate free-standing provision dealing with non-contractual obligations arising out of dealings prior to the conclusion of a contract.[194] If, however, the breach concerns an obligation arising from a tacit contractual

---

[185] The Giuliano and Lagarde Report, p 13.
[186] Ibid.
[187] Infra, p 706.
[188] See *Marubeni Hong Kong and South China Ltd v Government of Mongolia* [2004] EWHC 472 (Comm) at [105]–[110], [2004] 2 Lloyd's Rep 198; *PEC Ltd v Golden Asia Rice Co Ltd* [2014] EWHC 1583 (Comm) at [74]–[75] (with the exception that the proper law of the contract may not be applied if it resulted in distinct unfairness or there were other strong reason for modifying it). The applicable law to actual (instead of ostensible) authority is less clear, see *Excalibur Ventures LLC v Texas Keystone Inc* [2013] EWHC 2767 (Comm) at [256]–[259] (law of the main contract between principal and third party or law of the relationship between principal and agent).
[189] Art 1(2)(h) Rome I Regulation; Art 1(2)(g) of the Rome Convention. See Morse [1993] JBL 168, 180. For trusts generally in private international law see infra, Chapter 38.
[190] The Giuliano and Lagarde Report, p 13.
[191] Ibid.
[192] Art 1(2)(i) of the Regulation; on the definition of culpa in contrahendo see Recital (30) Rome II Regulation. There was no such express exclusion in the Convention but the Convention should not apply because obligations arising out of a pre-contractual relationship should be regarded as non-contractual.
[193] See Recital (10) of the Rome I Regulation and the Explanatory Memorandum, COM (2005) 650 final, p 5. For the classification of such obligations in the context of the Brussels I Regulation, supra, p 265.
[194] Art 12 and Recital (30) of Rome II; discussed infra, pp 849–54.

relationship existing between the parties, such a dispute may be classified as contractual (and thus fall in the scope of Rome I).[195]

(ix) Insurance[196]

Unlike the Rome Convention,[197] the Rome I Regulation covers most (private[198]) insurance contracts, irrespective of whether an intra-EU or a third-state case is concerned.[199] The inclusion of insurance contracts and the adoption of a special conflict rule for these contracts[200] is a result of a controversial discussion in the legislative process. Despite a specific question in the green paper[201] and academic proposals to include insurance contracts in Rome I,[202] the initial proposal of the Commission excluded them from the scope of the Regulation.[203] The debate continued[204] and soon became one of the most controversial questions of the whole project, prompting a consultation of stakeholders from the United Kingdom[205] which opposed a proposal[206] for extending choice of law restrictions to the insurance of (third-country) mass (non-consumer) risks.[207] As a compromise,[208] insurance contracts were included, but any substantial change in critical points was avoided by merely reflecting in Article 7 Rome I Regulation the conflict-of-law rules which were previously spread over several Directives.[209] This has led to a consolidation of all insurance conflict rules in one instrument which is probably one of the greatest achievements of the new Regulation.[210] Still, a few aspects of insurance contracts are not covered by the Regulation.

First, Article 1(2)(j) Rome I Regulation excludes insurance contracts arising out of operations carried out by organisations other than undertakings referred to in Article 2 of the consolidated life assurance Directive[211] "the object of which is to provide benefits for employed or

---

[195] See Case C-196/15 *Granarolo v Ambrosi Emmi France SA* ECLI:EU:C:2016:559 at [23]–[27]: an action for damages founded on an abrupt termination of a long-standing business relationship can be contractual if a tacit contractual relationship existed between the parties.

[196] Art 1(3) of the Rome Convention. For details see Heinze [2009] Nederlands Internationaal Privaatrecht 445.

[197] The Rome Convention did not apply to contracts of insurance which cover risks situated in the territories of the Member States of the European Economic Community, Art 1(3) Rome Convention. It also excluded contract of re-insurance, Art 1(4) Rome Convention.

[198] Social security systems and other forms of insurance organised in public law form are excluded, Article 1(1) Rome I ("civil and commercial matters").

[199] Art 2 Rome I.

[200] Art 7 of the Regulation, considered infra, pp 742–3.

[201] Green Paper, COM(2002) 654 final, pp 25–6.

[202] Eg by the Max Planck Institute (2004) 68 Rabels Zeitschrift 1, 25.

[203] COM(2005) 650 final.

[204] See the proposals in Council document No 13853/06 of 12 October 2006; Council document No 16353/06 of 12 December 2006; Council document No 8935/07 of 26 April 2007; Council Document No 11150/07 of 25 June 2007; Council document No 13441/07 of 4 October 2007; Council document No 13977/06 of 25 October 2007.

[205] HM Treasury, *Insurance in Rome I: A Consultation* (2007).

[206] Council document No. 11150/07 of 25 June 2007.

[207] Council document No 12521/07 of 31 August 2007, in particular points 10, 11, 17, 18.

[208] Council document No 15316/07 of 19 November 2007; Garcimartín-Alférez [2008] *The European Legal Forum* I-61, I-74.

[209] Declaration by the Council and the Commission relating to the law applicable to insurance contracts, Council document No 7689/08 ADD 1 of 7 April 2008, 1. The relevant provisions were found in Art 7, 8 Second Non-Life Insurance Directive 88/357/EEC, Art 32 Life Insurance Directive 2002/83/EC, and Art 3-5 Rome Convention (for those insurance contracts which fell into the Convention).

[210] The choice-of-law rules of the insurance Directives do not prevail over Article 7 Rome I because the preservation of special EU conflict-of-law rules for contractual obligations does not apply to Article 7 (Article 23 Rome I). For criticism see Opinion of the European Economic and Social Committee, OJ 2006 C 318/56 at 61, para. 3.5.1; Heiss (2008) 10 Yb PIL 261, 262; less critical Merrett (2009) 5 J Priv Int L 49 at 66.

[211] Directive (EC) No 2002/83 of 5 November 2002, OJ 2002 L 345/1. The Directive is amended by Directive (EC) No 2007/44.

self-employed persons belonging to an undertaking or group of undertakings, or a trade or group of trades, in the event of death or survival or of discontinuance or curtailment of activity, or of sickness related to work or accidents at work". This exclusion—modelled on Article 3(3) Life Assurance Directive 2002/83/EC[212]—has been justified by the proximity of such insurance contracts to the social security system of the country where the insurer is established. Its practical relevance is limited because the exclusion applies only to undertakings established in a third country (non-EU/EEA State)[213] which would normally be required to establish an agency or branch in the respective Member State to provide insurance services in that state[214] and thus fall under EU law.[215]

A further exclusion which may be relevant for insurance is Article 1(2)(f) concerning "questions governed by the law of companies and other bodies, corporate or incorporate". This provision might become relevant if insurance is organised in the form of a mutual association membership such as the German "Versicherungsverein auf Gegenseitigkeit". Even if the membership in such an association and the contract of insurance are normally regarded as inextricably linked, it may be appropriate to apply Rome I to those questions of the insurance relationship which are not specific to the membership in the organisation, i.e. which could arise in a similar manner if the insurer was not organised as a mutual association and the insurance was based on an insurance contract alone.

Finally, Article 1(2)(i) excludes obligations arising out of dealings prior to the conclusion of a contract (*culpa in contrahendo*) from the scope of Rome I. Such obligations—eg the obligation to inform or advise the insured—are covered by Article 12 Rome II Regulation. Still, as Article 12(1) Rome II refers back to the law that applies to the contract, which is again determined by the rules of Rome I, a synchronisation of contractual and pre-contractual obligations will normally be achieved despite Article 1(2)(i) Rome I.[216] Beyond specific exclusions, some aspects of insurance contracts fall outside Rome I because they have been considered to be non-contractual in nature: According to Article 18 Rome II Regulation, a direct action against the insurer is possible if either the law applicable to the non-contractual obligation or the law applicable to the insurance contract (as determined by the Rome I Regulation) so provides. Article 19 Rome II Regulation refers the question of subrogation to the law which governs the third person's (i.e. insurer's) duty to satisfy the creditor, i.e. for the case of insurance to the law governing the insurance contract which is determined by Rome I.[217]

(x) Evidence and procedure, without prejudice to Article 18[218]
This provision excludes two matters, procedure and evidence. The exclusion of evidence is not total, but is subject to Article 18,[219] which subjects three specific evidential matters, namely presumptions of law, the burden of proof (in so far as this raises rules of substance) and proving a contract, to the rules of the Regulation. The exclusion of evidence and procedure was said by the Giuliano and Lagarde Report to require no comment.[220] Nonetheless, two

---

[212] Supra previous fn.

[213] Art 2 of the Life Assurance Directive 2002/83/EC covers any "activity of direct insurance carried on by undertakings which are established in a Member State or wish to become established there", thus leaving third-state insurers outside of its scope.

[214] Art 51(1), (2)(b) Life Assurance Directive 2002/83/EC.

[215] Green Paper COM(2002) 654 final, p 22.

[216] Heiss (2008) 10 Yb PIL 261, 264.

[217] Ibid.

[218] Art 1(3) Rome I Regulation; Art 1(2)(h) of the Rome Convention. For the corresponding provision of the Rome II Regulation, see infra pp 799–801.

[219] Discussed supra, pp 80 and 85.

[220] At p 38.

obvious questions need to be asked. First, why were these matters expressly excluded from the scope of the Regulation? Presumably, this is just for the sake of clarity. Procedural and evidential matters would not appear to come within the scope of a Regulation which is concerned with contract choice of law (a matter of substance) and therefore do not need expressly to be excluded. Secondly, there is the vital question of when a matter is to be classified as being one of procedure. Procedure is a very different matter from the other matters excluded in that it involves a potential escape device, ie if you classify a matter as being purely procedural you escape from the choice of law rules under the Regulation. National courts are likely to resort to their own traditional ideas of what is a procedural matter. However, English courts cannot automatically assume that the classifications which they have adopted in the past will continue to be appropriate under the Regulation. For example, the question of whether a contract has to be in writing was classified at common law as being one of procedure. Under the Regulation, seemingly, it is to be regarded as a matter of substance raising an issue of formal validity of the contract.[221] Moreover, certain remedies[222] and the rules on prescription and limitation of actions[223] are classified as substantive and not procedural, thereby falling within the scope of the Regulation. The danger of different states classifying the same matter differently can be avoided by adherence to the principle of uniform interpretation. Once it has been decided that the issue is one of evidence or procedure, the effect of the exclusion is that this issue is left to be governed by the forum's rules on private international law. Under English private international law all procedural matters (including evidence) are automatically a matter for the law of the forum.[224]

(ii) The universal application of the Regulation

The Rome I Regulation is intended to be of universal or world-wide application, ie it applies in any EU Member State forum,[225] regardless of whether the contract has any connection with an EU Member State.[226] In particular, there is no need for either party to the contract to be domiciled or resident in a Member State. The only thing that matters is that the dispute is tried in an EU Member State bound by the Regulation. Thus a contractual dispute between a New York resident and an Ontario resident which is tried before the Commercial Court in England will be subject to the Regulation. This avoids the need to distinguish for choice of law purposes between EU Member States and third States, a distinction which would be particularly difficult to apply to contracts which involve connections with both a Member and a non-Member State.[227]

Article 2[228] provides that: "Any law specified by this Regulation shall be applied whether or not it is the law of a Member State." This provision makes it clear that if the uniform rules under the Regulation point, for example, to Japanese law as the law governing the contract, the courts of Member States will apply that country's law, even though Japan is not an EU Member State. However, Article 2 only deals with one aspect of the universal application of the rules in the Regulation. It says nothing about whether the situation or the parties must have a connection with a Member State. It is the Giuliano and Lagarde Report[229] which makes it clear that the Rome Convention (and now the Rome I Regulation) is intended to

---

[221] Ibid, p 31; infra, p 758.
[222] Art 12(1)(c) Rome I Regulation, see infra pp 766–8.
[223] Art 12(1)(d) Rome I Regulation, see infra p 768.
[224] Supra, pp 73–4.
[225] With the exception of Denmark, Recital (46) and Art 1(4) Rome I.
[226] See the Solicitor-General in Hansard (HC) Second Reading Committee 20 June 1990, col 4.
[227] Lagarde (1981) 22 VA J Int L 91, 93.
[228] See the Giuliano and Lagarde Report, p 13.
[229] Ibid, pp 8, 13.

have universal application and, in particular, will apply to nationals of third states and to persons domiciled or resident therein.[230]

(c) The applicable law

The provisions on the applicable law are at the heart of the Regulation. Two basic distinctions have to be made: First, it needs to be considered whether one of the special rules in Articles 5–8 applies, which is the case for contracts of carriage, consumer contracts, insurance contracts, and individual employment contracts.[231] Then, a distinction is drawn between the situation where the law is chosen by the parties and the situation where the applicable law is ascertained in the absence of choice. Choice is concerned with the actual intentions of the parties (either expressed by the parties or inferred by the court) and absence of choice requires reference to objective connections localising the contract. The applicable law under the Regulation, whether chosen or not, refers to the domestic law of the country in question, and there is no place for the doctrine of renvoi.[232] It is presupposed that there has to be an applicable law at the time when the contract is concluded.[233] It follows that the choice of a "floating" proper law, ie a proper law which was non-existent at the time when the contract was made but which was crystallised later on by the unilateral act of one of the parties, will be ineffective at the time when the contract is made. However, the Regulation does allow the parties to vary the applicable law during the subsequent life of the contract.[234]

(i) The law is chosen by the parties

Any reference to choice of the applicable law raises a number of points which will be examined under the following headings: freedom of choice; limitations on choice; express choice; inferred choice; consent to choice. Before doing so, it must be pointed out that there are no formalities to be satisfied in relation to the parties' choice.[235]

(a) Freedom of choice[236]
(i) The basic principle

Article 3 Rome I Regulation[237] is entitled "Freedom of choice", and paragraph (1) sets out the basic principle[238] that "a contract shall be governed by the law chosen by the parties". The parties' freedom to choose the governing law had been accepted in all the Member States of the European Union already before the Convention for many years.[239] In the United Kingdom

---

[230] See the unsuccessful attempt to amend the 1990 Act so as to limit it to parties habitually resident in a Contracting State: Hansard (HL), 15 February 1990, vol 515, cols 1474–90. See also Case C-281/02 *Owusu v Jackson* [2005] ECR I-1383 at [26] on the universal application of the Brussels I Regulation (now Recast).

[231] The reason for this order is that the special conflict of laws provisions may limit the scope of the freedom of choice of law for the parties, see Art 5(2), 6(2), 7(3) and 8(1) Rome I Regulation.

[232] Art 20 Rome I Regulation; Art 15 Rome Convention; Kaye, pp 343–4. Obiter dicta in *Caterpillar Financial Services Corpn v SNC Passion* [2004] EWHC 569 (Comm) at [31]–[44], [2004] 2 Lloyd's Rep 99.

[233] See Art 3(2).

[234] Art 3(2); discussed infra, pp 709–11. See also the discussion of a "floating" applicable law, infra, p 716.

[235] *Oakley v Ultra Vehicle Design Ltd (In Liquidation)* [2005] EWHC (Ch) at [61], [2005] IL Pr 55. Cf Art 25 of the Brussels I Recast, supra, pp 237–41.

[236] See generally Briggs, *Agreements on Jurisdiction and Choice of Law* (2008), Chapters 10–11; Mankowski in *European Commentaries on Private International Law*, Art 3, pp 87 et seq.; for the theoretical justification of party autonomy and possible objections see Basedow, *The Law of Open Societies: Private Ordering and Public Regulation in the Conflict of Laws* (2015), paras 199–255.

[237] As Art 3 Rome Convention.

[238] Case C-133/08 *Intercontainer Interfrigo SC (SCF) v Balkenende Oosthuizen BV* [2009] ECR I-9687 at [24]: "priority is given to the intention of the parties"; Case C-184/12 *United Antwerp Maritime Agencies (Unamar) NV v Navigation Maritime Bulgare* ECLI:EU:C:2013:663 at [49]: freedom of choice "is the cornerstone of the Rome Convention, reiterated in the Rome I Regulation".

[239] See the Giuliano and Lagarde Report, pp 15–16; Lando (1987) 24 CMLR 159, 171–9. It has also been accepted outside the Community, see Nygh (1995) 251 Hague Recueil Ch II and *Autonomy in International*

the philosophical origin of this freedom is to be found in the fidelity of the Victorian judges to the Benthamite dogma of laissez-faire,[240] although authority for allowing the parties expressly to select the governing law pre-dates this.[241] In more modern policy terms, party autonomy provides the certainty and predictability which are essential in commercial matters.[242] The philosophy of freedom of choice underlies not only the basic principle of allowing the parties to choose the law governing the contract but also some of the more detailed provisions relating to choice. Parties are given the freedom to pick and choose the applicable law so that it governs the whole or merely part of the contract. The parties are free to exercise their choice at any time and to vary their choice. These freedoms will now be examined.

(ii) Chosen law may be unconnected with the contract

As can be seen from Article 3(3), the Regulation permits the choice of the law of another country even where all elements relevant to the situation are located in a country other than the country whose law has been chosen. Therefore, the parties are free to choose any law they desire, even if it may be wholly unconnected with their contract.

(iii) Dépeçage[243]

The last sentence of Article 3(1) provides that: "By their choice the parties can select the law applicable to the whole or to part only of the contract."[244] The parties are given the freedom to pick and choose the applicable law and thereby sever the contract (dépeçage).[245] The parties can choose different laws for different parts of the contract. Thus there could be an express choice of French law to govern one part, but an express choice of German law to govern the rest of the contract. The choice can be expressed by the parties or inferred by the court. If the parties choose different laws for different parts of the contract the choices must be logically consistent, ie they "must relate to elements in the contract which can be governed by different laws without giving rise to contradiction".[246] The Giuliano and Lagarde Report gives two contrasting examples.[247] An index linking clause may be made subject to a law different from the rest of the contract. On the other hand, it was thought unlikely that repudiation of the contract for non-performance could be subjected to two different laws, one for the vendor and the other for the purchaser. If the chosen laws cannot be reconciled, both choices fail and the rules on the applicable law in the absence of choice[248] have to be used. The "general obligation" under a contract (ie the contractual obligations governing the core of the parties' relationship, such issues as whether the contract is discharged by frustration or the innocent

---

Contracts (1999), Chapters 1 and 2. See more generally Harris (2000) 20 OJLS 247; Hartley (2006) 319 Hague Recueil Ch XII.

[240] Graveson, *Lectures on the Conflict of Laws and International Contracts* (1951), pp 6–8.

[241] See *Gienar v Meyer* (1796) 2 Hy Bl 603.

[242] For a comprehensive summary of the theoretical discussion see Mankowski in *European Commentaries on Private International Law*, Art 3 paras 1–12, pp 103–8, and paras 23–47, pp 112–21 (on economic justifications); on economic justifications see also Rühl (2010) 6 J Priv Int L 59.

[243] See generally supra, pp 55–6. See in relation to the Rome Convention: Morse (1982) 2 YEL 107, 117–19.

[244] An almost identical provision was found in Art 3(1) Rome Convention. The Rome Convention reiterated the possibility of dépeçage also in the absence of choice, see Art 4(1) Rome Convention. In Case C-133/08 *Intercontainer Interfrigo SC (SCF) v Balkenende Oosthuizen BV* [2009] ECR I-9687 at [43], [45] the CJEU held that the rule providing for the severance of a contract in absence of choice (Art 4(1) Rome Convention) is of "an exceptional nature" and "must be allowed only where there are a number of parts to the contract who may be regarded as independent of each other".

[245] The same freedom is to be found in relation to trusts under Art 9 of the Hague Convention on the law applicable to trusts and on their recognition, implemented by the Recognition of Trusts Act 1987; see infra, pp 1382–3.

[246] The Giuliano and Lagarde Report, p 17.

[247] Ibid.

[248] See Art 4, discussed infra, pp 724–40.

party can terminate the contract on account of the other party's breach) can only be governed by one law.[249] But it is possible for the general obligation under an agreement to be governed by New York law whilst payment instruments (ie cheques) and their validity, etc are governed by the drawee's law (with drawees from many different jurisdictions).[250] A breach of an insurance policy condition precluding the insured from making recovery from the insurer under a particular part of the policy can be severed from the insured's rights under other parts of the policy.[251] But the words of the policy defining the insured cannot be severed so as to be interpreted by different laws and given possibly different meanings, depending on the part of the globe in which events may occur giving rise to the claim.[252] The parties can choose a law to govern part of the contract but exercise no choice in respect of the remainder of the contract. In this situation the applicable law for the remainder of the contract must be ascertained, again, by the rules on the applicable law in the absence of choice. The Working Group on the Rome Convention rejected the notion of a presumption that the law chosen for one part of the contract should govern the entirety.[253]

What is meant by *part* of the contract? Obviously, this covers parts of the contract that may be regarded as independent of each other. The Giuliano and Lagarde Report seemed to go further and permitted the parties to choose one law to govern a particular clause,[254] and a different law to govern other clauses. From the example given above relating to repudiation of the contract, it can also be deduced that *part* can include a particular issue[255] relating to the contract. Accordingly, the parties could choose one law to govern the interpretation of the contract and a different law to govern its discharge. On the other hand, it seems from the same example that the parties are not free to take a single issue, such as repudiation of the contract, and to split this so that one law governs one party's rights and a different law governs the other party's rights. This is regarded as involving two choices which are logically inconsistent. Moreover, the Court of Justice has held for dépeçage in the absence of choice under Article 4 of the Convention that a part of a contract may be made subject to a different law only where the object of that part is independent in relation to the rest of the contract.[256] In particular, the Court has found that the rules relating to the prescription of a right must fall under the same legal system as that applied to the corresponding obligation.[257] While dépeçage as a consequence of the parties' choice of law under Article 3 could be permitted more liberally than in the absence of choice under Article 4,[258] it cannot be overlooked that both provisions use the words "part of the contract" which have been interpreted narrowly by the Court of Justice. Therefore, it can be accepted that the parties choose different laws to govern particular issues, provided that the issues are independent from each other.[259] Some contracts are, by their very nature, severable, for example a contract which turns out to consist of several independent

---

[249] *Centrax v Citibank NA* [1999] 1 All ER (Comm) 557 at 562 (per Ward LJ), 569 (Waller LJ), CA—citing Dicey and Morris (12th edn, 1993), p 1207.

[250] The *Centrax* case, supra.

[251] *CGU International Insurance plc v Szabo* [2002] 1 All ER (Comm) 83 at [39].

[252] Ibid.

[253] The Giuliano and Lagarde Report, p 17.

[254] Ibid.

[255] This is the type of severing of the contract that "dépeçage" usually refers to: see supra, pp 55–6. For a broader definition of dépeçage, see Plender and Wilderspin, para 6-048.

[256] Case C-133/08 *Intercontainer Interfrigo SC (ICF) v Balkenende Oosthuizen BV and MIC Operations BV* [2009] ECR I-9687 at [45]–[46].

[257] Case C-133/08 *Intercontainer Interfrigo SC (ICF) v Balkenende Oosthuizen BV and MIC Operations BV* [2009] ECR I-9687 at [47].

[258] Mankowski in *European Commentaries on Private International Law*, Art 3 para 317, p 211: "rather generously". Art 4 Rome I Regulation does no longer mention the possibility of dépeçage, see infra, p 740.

[259] As it seems to be the case between interpretation and discharge of a contract.

contracts. Different laws can clearly be applied to these different contracts, without having to resort to the dépeçage provision.

(iv) Timing of choice

The first sentence of Article 3(2) provides that: "The parties may at any time agree to subject the contract to a law other than that which previously governed it, whether as a result of an earlier choice under this Article or of other provisions of this Regulation." The policy underlying this provision[260] is that of providing maximum freedom as to when the parties can make their choice.[261] It can be made before the contract is concluded, at the time of or even after the conclusion of the contract. If the parties' choice is made for the first time after the conclusion of the contract, then the applicable law at the time of the conclusion of the contract will have to be determined by reference to the rules determining the applicable law in the absence of choice (Article 4). This law will apply until the parties subsequently exercise their choice, which may involve a variation in the applicable law.

(v) Variation of choice[262]

The parties' freedom to vary the applicable law follows on logically from their right to choose the applicable law at any time.[263] For example, the parties may have agreed at the time of contracting that Californian law shall govern the contract. They have the freedom under Article 3(2) to agree subsequently[264] that, instead, Japanese law shall govern the contract.[265] It is irrelevant that Californian or Japanese law might not allow variation.[266] Equally, at the time the contract is made Luxembourg law may be applicable by virtue of the rules on the applicable law in the absence of choice (Article 4). The parties may subsequently agree that New York law shall govern. This subsequent agreement involves an exercise of the parties' freedom of choice under Article 3(1) and so can be expressed or inferred.[267] In *The Aeolian*[268] the Court of Appeal held that a supply contract, which was governed by Japanese law, had not been varied by a subsequent undertaking (governed by English law) in relation to a claim for payment under a separate spares contract, even though both parties must be taken to have had in mind that the defence would rely, as a set-off to the claim for payment, on a cross-claim for breach of the supply contract. The agreement in the undertaking was confined to the claim for payment and did not extend to the cross-claim arising out of the supply contract.[269] The undertaking made no reference to the supply contract and no inference could be

---

[260] See the Giuliano and Lagarde Report, p 17.

[261] This is referring to the parties' choice under Art 3(1), discussed infra, pp 717–23.

[262] See North, *Essays*, Chapter 3; Dicey, Morris and Collins, para 32-053; Plender and Wilderspin, paras 6-050–6-058.

[263] *Mauritius Commercial Bank Ltd v Hestia Holdings Ltd* [2013] EWHC 1328 (Comm) at [30].

[264] For the situation where there is an agreement at the time the contract is made to vary the applicable law in the future, see infra, p 716.

[265] See generally Diamond (1986) IV Hague Recueil 236, 262–4.

[266] For criticism of this aspect of Art 3(2), see Diamond [1979] Current Legal Problems 155, 162–5, who argues that variation should be a matter for the original governing law; Fletcher in *Conflict of Laws and European Community Law* (1982), at p 160, argues it should be for both the original and the substitute governing laws. This is supported by Kaye, p 156. Nygh argues it should be for the new law chosen, *Autonomy in International Contracts* (1999), p 101. Cf *Re Apcoa Parking (UK) Ltd* [2014] EWHC 997 (Ch) at [26], [35], where the parties seemed to agree (wrongly, in light of Art 3(2)) that the possibility to change the governing law is determined by the law which previously governed the contract.

[267] See *ISS Machinery Services Ltd v Aeolian Shipping SA (the Aeolian)* [2001] EWCA Civ 1162 at [15] (per Potter LJ), [27] (per Mance LJ), [2001] 2 Lloyd's Rep 641; the Giuliano and Lagarde Report, p 18; cf Morse, op cit, p 120.

[268] *ISS Machinery Services Ltd v Aeolian Shipping SA (the Aeolian)* [2001] EWCA Civ 1162, [2001] 2 Lloyd's Rep 641.

[269] Ibid at [31] (per Mance LJ).

drawn from the circumstances of the case that English law should govern the cross-claim.[270] If the variation is made during the course of legal proceedings, it is for the forum's law of procedure to decide the extent to which this is effective.[271]

The Working Group on the Rome Convention recognised that there were certain dangers in allowing a variation of the applicable law by the parties. The second sentence of Article 3(2) Rome I Regulation[272] provides a safeguard in the following terms: "Any change in the law to be applied that is made after the conclusion of the contract shall not prejudice its formal validity under Article 11 or adversely affect the rights of third parties."

As regards formal validity, the concern was that the new law chosen by the parties might contain formal requirements which were not known under the law originally applicable. This could create doubts as to the validity of the contract during the period preceding the new agreement between the parties;[273] hence the rule that any variation by the parties is not to prejudice the formal validity of the contract under Article 11. The other danger recognised by the Working Group is in relation to third parties, who may have already acquired rights at the time of the conclusion of the contract between the original contracting parties. These rights cannot be affected by a subsequent change in the choice of the applicable law.

There are two other potential dangers that can arise from the parties' variation of the applicable law. First, the parties might thereby evade the mandatory rules (eg controls on exemption clauses) of the country whose law was originally applicable.[274] However, the normal limitations on the right to choose the applicable law will doubtless apply to a subsequent choice of the governing law in the same way that they apply to an initial choice. As will shortly be seen,[275] there are limitations on choice which deal to some extent with this problem of evasion. Secondly, the parties might choose a new law which invalidates the contract. Logically, the contract appears to be rendered invalid. This presupposes, however, that the new choice of the applicable law is itself valid. This is a matter for the new law that has been chosen.[276] Thus the validity of a New York choice of law clause (which operates as a subsequent choice) is a matter for New York law.

(vi) Choice and the English rules on pleading and proof of foreign law[277]

What happens if the parties choose Utopian law to apply but subsequently neither party pleads Utopian law? The Regulation does not provide an answer to this. On the one hand, the English procedural rule preserved by the Regulation[278] indicates that English law must be applied automatically.[279] This would suggest that you can have a procedural variation of the applicable law.[280] On the other hand, Article 3(1) is phrased in strong terms: the "contract

---

[270] Ibid at [15]–[16] (per Potter LJ).

[271] The Giuliano and Lagarde Report, p 18.

[272] An almost identical provision is found in Art 3(2) Rome Convention.

[273] The Giuliano and Lagarde Report, p 18.

[274] See Collins (1976) 25 ICLQ 35, 44; cf North, *Essays*, pp 60–1.

[275] Infra, pp 711–16.

[276] See Art 10(1), infra, pp 755–6.

[277] See generally Fentiman, *Foreign Law in English Courts* (1998), pp 87 et seq.

[278] Art 1(3), supra, p 704.

[279] See, on the Rome II Regulation, *OPO v (1) MLA (2) SLT* [2014] EWCA Civ 1277 at [111], on appeal *James Rhodes v OPO* [2015] UKSC at [121]; see also *Brownlie v Four Seasons Holdings Inc* [2015] EWCA Civ 665 at [89]. But see Fentiman, *Foreign Law in English Courts* (1998), p 93 who suggests that how foreign law is pleaded is for English law but whether it should be pleaded is for the Rome Convention (the predecessor of the Rome Regulation).

[280] See North, op cit, p 61; Diamond, op cit, p 262. See also Hartley (1996) 45 ICLQ 271 at 290–1; Dicey, Morris and Collins, para 9-011.

shall be governed by the law chosen by the parties".[281] But if foreign law has to be applied, this leads on to a practical problem of what an English judge is to do if the parties fail to plead and prove foreign law.[282] In view of this difficulty, English courts are likely to take a pragmatic line and simply apply English law under the English procedural rule.[283] There would be no problem if it could be said that the failure to plead foreign law operates as a new agreement as to the applicable law by the parties replacing the original choice.[284] However, the parties' choice of the applicable law (whether an original or a later choice) must be made expressly or clearly demonstrated by the terms of the contract or the circumstances of the case.[285] A mere omission to plead and prove foreign law would not appear to satisfy this requirement.[286]

(b) Limitations on choice

Any discussion of freedom of choice inevitably leads on to the question of whether there is any restriction on the parties' freedom to choose the governing law.[287] The Regulation also lays down restrictions on the parties' right to choose the governing law,[288] which will now be examined.

(i) Article 3(3)[289]

A first limitation is contained in Article 3(3) which provides that:

> Where all other elements relevant to the situation at the time of the choice are located in a country other than the country whose law has been chosen, the choice of the parties shall not prejudice the application of provisions of the law of that other country which cannot be derogated from by agreement.

The Rome I Regulation retained Article 3(3) Rome Convention in substance, but adopted a slightly different wording so as to align the provision as far as possible with the Rome II Regulation on non-contractual obligations.[290] The most obvious change in wording is that the definition of "mandatory rules" is no longer used.[291]

Article 3(3) is concerned with the situation where there is an essentially domestic contract which is turned into a conflict of laws case by virtue simply of the parties' choice of a foreign applicable law. The provision establishes a limitation on the right to choose in this situation, but only to the extent of preserving the rules which cannot be derogated from by agreement of the country where all the other relevant connections are situated. Such provisions "which cannot be derogated from by agreement" are sometimes referred to as (simple) mandatory rules.[292] They have to be distinguished from overriding mandatory provisions in the sense of Article 9 which not only cannot be derogated from by agreement, but—in

---

[281] Authors' emphasis. See also Fentiman (1992) 108 LQR 142, 144; Kaye, p 98.

[282] See Kaye, p 98.

[283] See, on the Rome II Regulation, *OPO v (1) MLA (2) SLT* [2014] EWCA Civ 1277 at [111]; *Brownlie v Four Seasons Holdings Inc* [2015] EWCA Civ 665 at [89].

[284] Fentiman, *Foreign Law in English Courts* (1998); Dicey, Morris and Collins, para 9-011.

[285] Art 3(1).

[286] Cf Hartley, op cit, p 291 n 101. See Lando (1987) 24 CMLR 159, 186–8 who suggests that the parties, in cases where the expense of proving foreign law is justified, are to be asked whether they intend to submit their contract to the law of the forum.

[287] See generally Nygh, *Autonomy in International Contracts* (1999), Chapter 3.

[288] Rinze [1994] JBL 412.

[289] Hartley (1997) 266 Hague Recueil 341, 366–8; Kaye, pp 159–68.

[290] Recital (15) of the Regulation clarifies that no substantial change is intended as compared with Article 3(3) of the Rome Convention, but the wording of the Regulation is aligned as far as possible with Article 14 of the Rome II Regulation, discussed infra, pp 854–8.

[291] See the discussion of Art 9 of the Regulation (overriding mandatory provisions), infra, pp 744–6.

[292] This means that in a domestic context the rule cannot be contracted out of, see infra, pp 744–6. But see the obiter dicta on Art 3(3) in *Caterpillar Financial Services Corpn v SNC Passion* [2004] EWHC 569 (Comm) at [31]–[44], [2004] 2 Lloyd's Rep 99, which should be regarded as wrong.

addition—"respect for which is regarded as crucial by a country for safeguarding its public interests".[293] As an example of English rules which cannot be derogated from by agreement in the sense of Article 3(3), there are the rules providing controls on exemption clauses or other standard terms such as contained in the Unfair Contract Terms Act 1977 and comparable laws in other countries.[294] This Act makes it clear that these controls will, in certain circumstances, apply despite the parties' choice of a foreign law to govern the contract.[295] The effect of Article 3(3) is that if the parties to an entirely German contract, which contains an exemption clause, choose, for example, French law to govern, the court of any Member State which tries the case will have to apply any controls on exemption clauses contained in a German equivalent of the 1977 Act. The parties' choice of French law would appear to have been made with a view to evading the German controls on exemption clauses. Article 3(3) will stop many cases of evasion of the law,[296] although it goes wider than this and it will ensure that any German controls on exemption clauses apply even if the parties have chosen French law for some perfectly legitimate reason, such as the fact that this is the applicable law under some related contract between the parties.

There are a number of points that can be made in relation to Article 3(3). First, it requires the parties to have chosen a "foreign" law. This raises a problem in the following type of case:

> Two Californian residents enter into an essentially Californian contract but choose English law to govern the contract. Trial of a subsequent dispute takes place in England. English law is "foreign" to the parties and the contract, but not "foreign" to the forum. Article 3(3) is concerned with the choice of a foreign law and with the situation at the time of the choice. At that time, English law was a foreign law, ie was foreign to the parties and the contract.

The result is that Article 3(3) operates and Californian mandatory rules are applicable.[297]

Secondly, Article 3(3) requires "all the other elements relevant to the situation"[298] to be connected with a country in order that its provisions which cannot be derogated from by agreement are to be applied. But when is an element *relevant* to the situation? Take the facts of the well-known case of *Golden Acres Ltd v Queensland Estates Pty Ltd.*[299]

> The case concerned the rate of commission to be paid to an estate agent. Many of the connections were with Queensland, but the plaintiff company was incorporated in Hong Kong. Was the place of incorporation a relevant element, or was the only relevant thing about the company the fact that it acted as an estate agent in Queensland?

Under the common law this case was decided on the basis that the choice of Hong Kong law to govern the contract was not made in good faith. Under the Regulation the parties' motives

---

[293] Art 9(1) Rome I Regulation.

[294] For unfair terms in consumer contracts, the Unfair Contract Terms Act 1977 has been superseded by the Consumer Rights Act 2015, Part 2. However, in the field of consumer contracts, Art 3(3) will probably not be of relevance because Art 6(2) will apply.

[295] S 27(2); discussed infra, p 747.

[296] See the Explanatory Memorandum, COM (2005) 650 final, p 5, according to which Art 3(3) "addresses the issue of fraudulent evasion of the law". But not necessarily all cases, see the discussion, infra, p 712, in relation to *Golden Acres Ltd v Queensland Estates Pty Ltd* [1969] Qd R 378; affd sub nom *Freehold Land Investments v Queensland Estates Ltd* 123 CLR 418. See Lando (1987) 24 CMLR 159, 182–3; Fawcett [1990] CLJ 44.

[297] Where neither party pleads and proves Californian law, English law is likely to be applied either because of Art 1(3) or for pragmatic reasons (see supra, p 711). But see Hartley, op cit, p 291; Fentiman, *Foreign Law in English Courts* (1998), pp 93–5. What is clear is that the failure to plead cannot operate in the context of mandatory rules as a new agreement.

[298] As opposed to relevant to the *contract*.

[299] [1969] Qd R 378; affd sub nom *Freehold Land Investments v Queensland Estates Ltd* 123 CLR 418.

are immaterial, but whilst one problem (ascertaining motives) has now disappeared, another problem (ascertaining whether all the relevant elements are with one country) has sprung up in its place.[300] In *Caterpillar Financial Services Corp v SNC Passion*:[301]

> A loan transaction had a number of connections with France: the borrower was a French company; the loan transaction was originally set up by French companies; it was argued that the loan agreement was made in France; the loan was for building a ship which would fly the French flag with a charter-party subject to French law. But the loan agreement was expressly governed by English law.

It was held that Article 3(3) had no application[302] because significant elements of the loan transaction involved a connection with a jurisdiction other than France. The most important of these was that the lender bank was a Delaware bank which acted through its office in Tennessee. Moreover, the loan agreement was intimately connected with a shipbuilding contract with advances being made directly to the shipbuilder in Singapore. This was a clear-cut case and it would have been astonishing if the opposite conclusion had been reached.

Thirdly, the structure of the Regulation suggests that the country whose rules which cannot be derogated from by agreement have to be applied will be a foreign country and not the forum. However, there is nothing to say that mandatory rules of the forum are excluded under Article 3(3). Indeed, it is important that Article 3(3) should encompass the mandatory rules of the forum, since Article 9(2), although specifically designed to cover the overriding mandatory rules of the forum, is concerned with a different and narrower type of mandatory rule.[303]

Fourthly, you have to look to the law of the country with which there are all the other relevant connections to see whether under *that country's law* the domestic rule is one which cannot be derogated from by contract.

Fifthly, the effect of applying a rule which cannot be derogated from by agreement is to override the parties' choice of law, rather than to destroy it. Reverting to the earlier example, the German controls on exemption clauses will apply despite a French choice of law clause. Nonetheless, the choice of French law will still operate to govern other issues, such as interpretation of the contract, provided that this is an area where German law does not have mandatory rules.

The sixth and final point about Article 3(3) is that it tells us something, by implication, about freedom of choice. Article 3(3) is only concerned with provisions which cannot be derogated from by agreement. It follows that, even if all the other relevant connections are with Country X, the choice of law of Country Y will still apply as far as non-mandatory rules are concerned. This means that the parties can choose, as the applicable law, the law of a country with which there is no relevant connection.[304]

(ii)   Article 3(4): Mandatory rules of EU law

Article 3(4) of the Rome I Regulation introduces an additional limitation on the parties' freedom to choose the applicable law. This provides that:

> Where all other elements relevant to the situation at the time of the choice are located in one or more Member States, the parties' choice of applicable law other than that of a Member

---

[300]   However, there is no such problem in relation to connections if Art 9(2) is used. This is—as Art 7(2) of the Convention—concerned only with the overriding mandatory rules of the forum; infra, pp 746–51. See also Fawcett [1990] CLJ 44, 58–60.

[301]   [2004] EWHC 569 (Comm) at [21]–[30], [2004] 2 Lloyd's Rep 99.

[302]   For another example, see *Bankers Trust International plc v RCS Editori SpA* [1996] CLC 899 at 905. See also *Shell International Petroleum Co Ltd v Coral Oil Co Ltd* [1999] 1 Lloyd's Rep 72 at 78–9.

[303]   Infra, pp 745–6.

[304]   Supra, p 707.

State shall not prejudice the application of provisions of Community law, where appropriate as implemented in the Member State of the forum, which cannot be derogated from by agreement.[305]

This follows an almost identically worded limitation in the Rome II Regulation on non-contractual obligations.[306] The provision treats the European Union as effectively one country and highlights the importance of EU rules which cannot be derogated from by agreement. Given that national law includes EU law, *prima facie* it may seem to be an open question whether Article 3(4) will in fact add anything to what is already provided for by Article 3(3). However, the difference is not the "quality" of law since both Article 3(3) and Article 3(4) address provisions "which cannot be derogated from by agreement" but the extension of the area from one state to the European Union being *treated as one state*. In other words: While Article 3(3) does not capture cases where the relevant elements are located in two EU Member States, Article 3(4) preserves mandatory EU law in such circumstances.

(iii) Other provisions on mandatory rules,[307] public policy[308]
These limitations are more appropriately dealt with later on, where they will be looked at in some detail.

We have dealt with the limitations on choice specifically set out in the Regulation itself. Nonetheless, there are a number of other possible limitations which have to be considered.

(iv) Logically consistent choices
As has already been seen,[309] if the parties are choosing two different laws for different parts of the contract, these choices must be logically consistent.

(v) A meaningless choice of law
In keeping with the above limitation, a meaningless choice of law will be ignored. This was established by the Court of Appeal in *Shamil Bank of Bahrain v Beximco Pharmaceuticals Ltd*:[310]

> A choice of law clause provided that the contract was governed by English law "subject to the principles of the Glorious Sharia'a". It was common ground that only the law of a country[311] can be chosen and therefore it was argued that incorporated into English law were specific principles of Sharia law. But there was no reference to or identification of those aspects of Sharia law which were intended to be incorporated into the contract. The principles of Sharia law were therefore repugnant to the choice of English law and rendered the clause self-contradictory and meaningless.

The construction adopted of the clause by the Court was that English law governed and the additional wording merely reflected the Islamic religious principles according to which the bank held itself out as doing business rather than a system of law intended to trump the application of English law. In contrast, at common law mere difficulty in ascertaining the governing law did not render the choice ineffective.[312]

---

[305] Art 3(4) of the Regulation.

[306] Art 14(3) of Rome II is discussed infra, p 857.

[307] Art 5(2), infra, p 742; Art 6(2), infra, pp 741–2; Art 7(3), infra, pp 742–3; Art 8(1), infra pp 741–2; Art 9, infra, pp 743–52; Art 11(5), infra, pp 760–1.

[308] Art 21, infra, pp 752–4.

[309] Supra, pp 707–9.

[310] [2004] EWCA Civ 19, [2004] 1 WLR 1784. The decision was made on the Rome Convention, but would also apply to the Rome I Regulation.

[311] As defined in Art 22(1) Rome I Regulation; Art 19(1) Rome Convention.

[312] See *The Blue Wave* [1982] 1 Lloyd's Rep 151.

(vi) Choice of the law of a country

The original proposal for a Rome I Regulation intended to give a boost to the principle of freedom of choice by allowing the parties to choose as the applicable law the law of a non-state.[313] Under this provision the parties were able to choose "the principles and rules of the substantive law of contract recognised internationally or in the Community".[314] This would include UNIDROIT principles, the UN Convention on the International Sale of Goods (the Vienna Convention) and the Principles of European Contract Law.[315] It was not intended to cover the *lex mercatoria*, which was regarded as not being precise enough, or private codifications not adequately recognised by the international community.[316] It has been questioned whether such a change in the law would do more than assist in interpretation of the contract since remedies, if they are to be effective, would have to flow from the law of a country.[317] The provision allowing a choice of non-state law was subsequently deleted.[318]

As a consequence, under Article 3(1) of the final text of the Regulation, as under the Rome Convention, the parties' right to choose the applicable *law* refers to the law of a *country*.[319] The Regulation does not sanction the choice of a non-national system of law such as the *lex mercatoria*.[320] Such a choice refers not to the national law of any country but rather to a kind of transnational law consisting of internationally accepted principles of trade law, to be ascertained by arbitrators. Other examples of the choice of a non-national system of law are "general principles of law," the rules of law in the UN Convention on the International Sale of Goods 1980 (where they do not apply as part of a Contracting State's law, but by abstract choice by the parties),[321] the law of Sharia[322] and Jewish law.[323] Such a reference is outside the parties' freedom to choose the applicable law.[324]

However, the parties are free to incorporate by reference into their contract a non-state body of law or an international Convention,[325] such as the UN Convention on the International

---

[313] See the Explanatory Memorandum, COM (2005) 650 final, p 6.

[314] Art 3(2) of the original Proposal for a Regulation, COM (2005) 650 final.

[315] See the Explanatory Memorandum, p 6. For a comprehensive analysis of the potential "non-state laws" to be chosen see Mankowski in *European Commentaries on Private International Law*, Art 3, paras 266–307, pp 190–207.

[316] The Explanatory Memorandum, p 6. For criticism of this see Lando and Nielson (2007) 3 J Priv Int L 29, 30–4.

[317] *Halpern v Halpern* [2007] EWCA Civ 291 at [39], [2007] 2 Lloyd's Rep 56.

[318] Art 3 of the Regulation. It was deleted in the April 2007 compromise package from the Presidency, agreed by the Council, 8022/07 JUSTCIV 73 CODEC 306 of 13 April 2007.

[319] *Shamil Bank of Bahrain v Beximco Pharmaceuticals Ltd* [2004] EWCA Civ 19 at [48], [2004] 1 WLR 1784. But cf *Samcrete Egypt Engineers and Contractors SAE v Land Rover Exports Ltd* [2001] EWCA Civ 2019 at [39] (per Potter LJ), [2002] CLC 533. See Art 3(3) which specifically refers to the law of a "country", and Recital (13). For the meaning of country see Art 22(1) and supra, p 696.

[320] See generally Lando (1985) 34 ICLQ 747; Lord Justice Mustill in Bos and Brownlie (eds), *Liber Amicorum for Lord Wilberforce* (1987), p 149; the symposium in (1989) 63 Tul L R, articles by Delaume at 575, Highet at 613; Smit at 631, Park at 647; North, *Private International Law Problems in Common Law Jurisdictions* (1993), pp 109–111; Chukwumerije [1994] Anglo-Am LR 265, 269 et seq; Nygh (1995) 251 Hague Recueil 269, 308–309; *Autonomy in International Contracts* (1999), Chapter 8.

[321] See Fawcett, Harris and Bridge, paras 13.86–13.94.

[322] The *Shamil Bank of Bahrain* case, supra, at [48]; *Dubai Islamic Bank PJSC Energy Holding BSC* [2013] EWHC 3186 (Comm) at [11]: a proviso in the choice of English law "save insofar as inconsistent with the principles of Sharia law" was held to be ineffective.

[323] *Halpern v Halpern* [2007] EWCA Civ 291 at [19]–[29], [2007] 2 Lloyd's Rep 56.

[324] If the parties agree on the application of the *lex mercatoria*, or of "other considerations" an arbitral tribunal will apply this, see s 46(1)(b) of the Arbitration Act 1996. It is implicit in the Inter-American Convention on the Law Applicable to International Contracts of 1994 that a choice of the *lex mercatoria* is permissible: see Arts 3, 9 and 10.

[325] Recital (13) of the Regulation.

Sale of Goods 1980, or even provisions of religious law such as the Sharia, provided that the parties in their contract have sufficiently identified the specific provisions.[326] It is also possible to incorporate "Jewish law", without any such proviso, at least where the dispute is between Orthodox Jews who are agreed there is such a distinct body of law.[327] Such an incorporation by reference is no choice of law, but only an agreement of the parties about the terms of their contract. As a consequence, the provisions incorporated by reference must comply with the law of the country which is applicable to the contract under the Regulation. Where this law includes provisions which cannot be derogated from by agreement, the incorporation by reference, as a simple contractual term, is ineffective. Finally, should the EU adopt in an appropriate legal instrument rules of substantive contract law, including standard terms and conditions, that instrument may provide that the parties may choose to apply those rules.[328]

(vii) A "floating" applicable law

The parties cannot choose a "floating" applicable law to govern the contract. The applicable law must exist and be identifiable at the time when the contract is made.[329] It follows that a clause which, for example, gives one party the option to determine the applicable law in the future by selecting the law to govern from a list of possible alternatives, will be ineffective at the time when the contract is made, and at this stage the applicable law will be determined objectively under Article 4 of the Regulation.[330] But what happens if one party makes the selection at some future date?[331] This subsequent choice may have been ineffective under the common law rules,[332] but the choice at this future date will be given retrospective effect both under the Convention[333] and the Regulation,[334] since variation of the applicable law is permissible.[335] The form of the variation is just rather unusual in this situation, in that the agreement is from the outset for a change of the applicable law in the future.

---

[326] The *Shamil Bank of Bahrain* case, supra, at [49]–[52].

[327] *Halpern v Halpern* [2007] EWCA Civ 291 at [33], [2007] 2 Lloyd's Rep 56.

[328] Recital (14) of the Regulation.

[329] *CGU International Insurance plc v Szabo* [2002] 1 All ER (Comm) 83 at [37].

[330] Mankowski in *European Commentaries on Private International Law*, Art 3 para 348, p 221. The common law found "floating choice of law clauses" ineffective, see *Dubai Electricity Co v Islamic Republic of Iran Shipping Lines, The Iran Vojdan* [1984] 2 Lloyd's Rep 380 at 385; *Cantieri Navali Riuniti SpA v NV Omne Justitia, The Stolt Marmaro* [1985] 2 Lloyd's Rep 428 at 435; cf *Astro Venturoso Compañia Naviera v Hellenic Shipyards SA, The Mariannina* [1983] 1 Lloyd's Rep 12 at 15; see the summary in *Mauritius Commercial Bank Ltd v Hestia Holdings Ltd* [2013] EWHC 1328 (Comm) at [23]–[27]. But see *King v Brandywine Reinsurance Co (UK) Ltd* [2004] EWHC 1033 (Comm) at [45], [2004] 2 Lloyd's Rep 670; appeal dismissed without discussion of this point [2005] EWCA Civ 235, [2005] 1 Lloyd's 655. See in relation to an implied floating applicable law, *The Star Texas* [1993] 2 Lloyd's Rep 445, CA (no implied choice). These common law cases are still relevant to the law governing a jurisdiction or arbitration agreement, see *Sonatrach Petroleum Corpn v Ferrell International Ltd* [2002] 1 All ER (Comm) 627.

[331] It is very doubtful whether a selection can be made many years after a contract has expired: *Heath Lambert Ltd v Sociedad de Corretaje de Seguros* [2003] EWHC 2269 (Comm) at [18]–[19].

[332] See *Armar Shipping Co Ltd v Caisse Algérienne* [1981] 1 WLR 207 at 216; cf *Black Clawson International Ltd v Papierwerke Waldhof-Aschaffenburg AG* [1981] 2 Lloyd's Rep 446 at 456; *E I Du Pont de Nemours & Co v Agnew and Kerr* [1987] 2 Lloyd's Rep 585 at 592. See generally Beck [1987] LMCLQ 523.

[333] *CGU International Insurance plc v Szabo*, supra, at [37]—rejecting the idea of a "harlequin" proper law so that an insurance policy means different things according to the country of the person claiming under it. See also *Bhatia Shipping v Alcobex Metals* [2004] EWHC 2323 (Comm) at [16], [2005] 2 Lloyd's Rep 336.

[334] Dicey, Morris and Collins, para 32-055.

[335] Art 3(2), discussed supra, pp 709–10; *King v Brandywine Reinsurance Co (UK) Ltd* [2004] EWHC 1033 (Comm) at [45], [2004] 2 Lloyd's Rep 670; appeal dismissed without discussion of this point [2005] EWCA Civ 235, [2005] 1 Lloyd's 655; Nygh (1995) 251 Hague Recueil 269, 320–321; *Autonomy in International Contracts* (1999), p 99; Kaye, p 148. But cf Howard [1995] LMCLQ 1 at 7. Steyn LJ in *The Star Texas*, supra, at 450, left this point open.

(c) An express choice; mere incorporation

The parties can express a choice simply by including a choice of law clause in the contract stating that, for example, all disputes shall be governed by English law.[336] Any question as to the validity or existence of this choice is governed by the rules on consent to choice, which will be examined later.[337] Parties may choose a particular law for a variety of reasons.[338] It is usually convenient for a party to have the familiar law of their home state apply. One country's law may be more developed than another's in technical commercial areas such as banking and insurance, when English law is commonly chosen by the parties. It may have become standard practice for a particular country's law to apply to certain transactions. The content of one country's law may be more favourable to one of the parties than that of another. Whatever the law chosen, it is important that the parties should make an express choice, for without this there is considerable uncertainty as to the applicable law.

The express selection of the proper law (which is a choice of law issue) must be distinguished from the quite different process of the incorporation in the contract of certain domestic provisions of a foreign law, which thereupon became terms of the contract (and which is an issue of the applicable substantive law).[339] Article 3 is only concerned with selection of the applicable law. While contractual reference to specific articles of a foreign law may be interpreted as an inferred choice of law,[340] this is not necessarily the case. It may also be understood as a mere incorporation in the contract of certain provisions of a foreign law as terms of the contract. Such incorporation may be effected either by a verbatim transcription of the relevant provisions or by a general statement that the rights and liabilities shall in certain respects be subject to these provisions. The latter is only a shorthand method of expressing the agreed terms. Thus the parties to an English contract may expressly provide that their duties with regard to performance shall be regulated by certain specific rules contained in the French Civil Code. English law is then applied as the governing law to a contract into which the foreign rules have been incorporated.[341] It is possible to incorporate by reference the terms of the Sharia or of an international code. However, the doctrine of incorporation can only sensibly operate where the parties have, by the terms of their contract, sufficiently identified specific "black letter" provisions of the foreign law or international code.[342] It is common in cases involving carriage of goods by sea to incorporate the Hague Rules. It is possible to incorporate all of the Hague Rules or merely specific provisions. Whether a particular term incorporated in this manner is valid and effective is a matter for determination by the law applicable under the Regulation.[343] At common law, once a foreign law was incorporated into the contract as a term it remained constant in the sense that it was static, ie unaffected by any change in the relevant foreign law occurring after the date of the contract.[344] Under the Regulation, the question of a static or dynamic reference to foreign law incorporated as

---

[336] See Briggs [2003] LMCLQ 389. See on the battle of the forms, Dannemann in Rose (ed), *Lex Mercatoria: Essays in Honour of Francis Reynolds* (2000), Chapter 11; Fawcett, Harris and Bridge, paras 13.57–13.61.

[337] Art 3(5) discussed infra, pp 723–4.

[338] See Collins in *Contract Conflicts*, p 215.

[339] *Shamil Bank of Bahrain v Beximco Pharmaceuticals Ltd* [2004] EWCA Civ 19 at [48]–[52], [2004] 1 WLR 1784; for incorporation of non-State rules supra, p 715.

[340] The Giuliano and Lagarde Report, p 17; infra, p 719.

[341] *Shamil Bank of Bahrain v Beximco Pharmaceuticals Ltd* [2004] EWCA Civ 19 at [51], [2004] 1 WLR 1784.

[342] Ibid.

[343] Art 10(1); discussed infra, p 756.

[344] This is different from a choice of law: any changes of the applicable law will also apply to the contract between the parties, whereas foreign law incorporated by reference remains unaffected.

a contractual term will be decided by the applicable law, as it is a matter of interpretation of the contract.[345]

(d) An inferred choice

Article 3(1) provides, as an alternative to an express choice, that there can be a choice "clearly demonstrated by the terms of the contract or the circumstances of the case." This provision is concerned with a real choice by the parties, the court inferring what the parties' actual intentions[346] were from the terms of the contract or the circumstances of the case. This concept of an inferred or implied choice is well known in English law, and is to be found in civil law countries as well.[347] Inferred choice under the Regulation appears at first sight to be very close to the English law in this area. Nonetheless, there are differences, and cases decided at common law should be treated with caution: "It would be a mistake to attempt to apply article 3 through the prism of the preceding common law."[348] Different from the wording of Article 3(1) of the Rome Convention, which required such a choice to be demonstrated with "reasonable certainty", the Regulation provides now that an inferred choice has to be "clearly demonstrated".[349] It is not entirely clear whether this represents a change in substance, requiring a higher standard to be demonstrated. Against a change from Convention to Regulation, it has been argued that the wording in the Regulation merely brings the English and German texts in line with the French text of the Convention.[350] On the other hand, the fact that the more stringent French wording prevailed could, together with a remark in the Explanatory Memorandum,[351] hint towards a stricter test for inferred choice of law.[352] Even if one finds the latter position more convincing, the effect of this change is likely to be negligible, because a court prepared to find an inferred choice "demonstrated with reasonable certainty" is likely to arrive at the same result also under the "clearly demonstrated"—test. Therefore, it is submitted that the examples discussed under the Rome Convention are still equally relevant under the Regulation.

(i) Drawing the inference

An inference as to the parties' intentions can be drawn from either the terms of the contract or the circumstances of the case. The test whether an implied choice of law has been established is objective:[353] A party asserting an implied choice of law has to establish that, on an objective view,

---

[345] Art 12(1)(a) Rome I Regulation.

[346] See *Hellenic Steel Co v Svolamar Shipping Co Ltd; The Komninos S* [1991] 1 Lloyd's Rep 370 at 374, CA; Reynolds (1992) 108 LQR 395.

[347] The Giuliano and Lagarde Report, pp 15–17; Lando (1987) 24 CMLR 171–9. For inferred choice under German law, see Von Hoffmann in *Contract Conflicts*, pp 221, 224–5. See generally Nygh, *Autonomy in International Contracts* (1999), Chapter 5.

[348] *Lawlor v Sandvik Mining and Construction Mobile Crushers and Screens Ltd* [2013] EWCA Civ 365 at [30]. In older case law, the Court of Appeal had more sympathy to draw an analogy with the common law concept of an implied term, see *American Motorists Insurance Co (Amico) v Cellstar Corpn* [2003] EWCA Civ 206 at [44], [2003] IL Pr 22.

[349] Art 3(3) of the Regulation.

[350] Dicey, Morris and Collins, para 32-059 n 217; Plender and Wilderspin, para 6-026. The wording might be borrowed from some of the Hague Conventions, see Art 7(1) Hague Convention of 22 December 1986 on the Law Applicable to the International Sale of Goods and Art 4 Hague Convention of 5 July 2006 on intermediary-held securities, Mankowski in *European Commentaries on Private International Law*, Art 3, para 105, p 138.

[351] See also Explanatory Memorandum, COM (2005) 650 final, p 5: the proposed changes in Article 3 "require the courts to ascertain the true tacit will of the parties rather than a purely hypothetical will". However, the Commission's proposed wording was changed in the legislative process.

[352] Mankowski in *European Commentaries on Private International Law*, Art 3, para 108, p 140: "tentatively more restrictive".

[353] *Lawlor v Sandvik Mining and Construction Mobile Crushers and Screens Ltd* [2013] EWCA Civ 365 at [31].

the parties must have taken it without saying that their contract should be governed by that law. The party does not have to prove that there was in fact a subjective conscious choice, but it has to satisfy the court that the only reasonable conclusion to be drawn from the circumstances is that the parties should be taken to have intended the putative law to apply.[354]

The terms of the contract   The Giuliano and Lagarde Report[355] on the Rome Convention provides a number of examples of situations where a court may draw an inference as to the parties' intentions. In most of these examples the inference is being drawn from the terms of the contract. Thus an inference can be drawn in cases where the contract is in a standard form known to be governed by a particular system of law, such as a Lloyd's policy of Marine Insurance; the contract contains an exclusive choice of forum clause[356] or an arbitration clause naming the place of arbitration (at least in circumstances indicating that the arbitrator should apply the law of that place); or there is a reference to specific articles of the French Civil Code.[357] The reasoning in such cases is that if, for example, the parties intended that trial should take place in England they must also have intended that English law should apply, it being inconvenient and expensive for a foreign law to be applied.

The interesting thing about these examples, from an English point of view, is that the first three are the standard examples of an inferred choice under the common law rules. Thus in *Amin Rasheed Shipping Corpn v Kuwait Insurance Co*[358] Lord Diplock[359] said that the terms of a standard Lloyd's SG form of policy showed by necessary implication that the parties (a Liberian company and a Kuwaiti insurance company) intended that the English law of marine insurance should apply. Kuwait had no law of marine insurance at that time, and the parties could not have intended Kuwaiti law to apply. The House of Lords unanimously held that the proper law of the contract was English law. This sort of case will be decided in exactly the same way under the Convention[360] and under the Regulation. Similarly, where a reinsurance contract was placed in London on the London market, it was held that the terms of the slip (referring to standard form clauses used in England where they were developed) pointed to an implied choice of English law under the Convention.[361] If, on the other hand, a contractual clause is universal in international trade, such as "cif UK port", this cannot support an inferred choice of law.[362]

---

[354] *Lawlor v Sandvik Mining and Construction Mobile Crushers and Screens Ltd* [2013] EWCA Civ 365 at [33].

[355] At p 17.

[356] See Recital (12) of the Regulation, which provides that (only) an agreement to confer "exclusive jurisdiction" should be one of the factors to be taken into account whether a choice of law has been clearly demonstrated. A non-exclusive jurisdiction clause may support other inferences as to the applicable law, but cannot on its own support an inferred choice, cf *EI Du Pont de Nemours & Co v Agnew* [1987] 2 Lloyd's Rep 585, 592; *King v Brandywine Reinsurance Co (UK) Ltd* [2005] EWCA Civ 235, [2005] 1 Lloyd's 655 at [48].

[357] Instead of a choice of French law this may also, depending on the terms of the contract and the circumstances of the case, be understood as a mere incorporation by reference without a choice of law, supra, p 717.

[358] [1984] AC 50. The case involved service out of the jurisdiction.

[359] At 64–7; Lords Roskill, Brightman and Brandon concurred. Lord Wilberforce reached the same result by applying the objective proper law of the contract.

[360] *Gan Insurance Co Ltd v Tai Ping Insurance Co Ltd* [1999] IL Pr 729 at [31] and [36], CA.

[361] Ibid. See also *Tiernan v The Magen Insurance Co Ltd* [2000] IL Pr 517 at 522–3; *Tryg Baltica International (UK)) Ltd v Boston Compañía de Seguros SA* [2004] EWHC 1186 (Comm) at [8], [2005] Lloyd's Rep IR 40; *Markel International Insurance Co Ltd v La República Compañía Argentina de Seguros Generales SA* [2004] EWHC 1826 (Comm) at [37], [2005] Lloyd's Rep IR 90; *Cadre SA v Astra Asigurari* [2004] EWHC 2504 (QB); *Dornach Ltd v Mauritius Union Assurance Co Ltd* [2006] EWCA Civ 389 at [43], [2006] 2 Lloyd's Rep 475. Cf *Evialis SA v SIAT* [2003] EWHC 863, [2003] 2 Lloyd's Rep 377.

[362] *Lupofresh Ltd v Sapporo Breweries* [2013] EWCA Civ 948 at [15].

Similarly, as at common law, a choice can be inferred from an arbitration clause indicating the place of arbitration or a choice of (exclusive) jurisdiction clause.[363] Thus in *Egon Oldendorff v Liberia Corpn*,[364] a clause providing for arbitration in London[365] was treated as an inferred choice of English law to govern the contract by virtue of Article 3(1). It was also relevant in this case when inferring intention that the parties used a well-known English language form of charter-party containing standard clauses with well-known meanings in English law. The case for an inferred choice is even stronger if the arbitration clause not only provides for arbitration in England but also expressly refers to the English Arbitration Act.[366] Likewise an (exclusive) jurisdiction clause providing for trial in England has been treated as an inferred choice of English law under the Convention.[367] For exclusive jurisdiction clauses, Recital (12) of the Regulation now provides that: "An agreement between the parties to confer on one or more courts or tribunals of a Member State exclusive jurisdiction to determine disputes under the contract should be one of the factors to be taken into account in determining whether a choice of law has been clearly demonstrated." The background to this Recital is that a choice of jurisdiction agreement is an example of an inferred choice under the Rome Convention, but courts in some Contracting States have been more reluctant than the English courts have been to draw the inference in such a case.[368] The original proposal for a Regulation therefore provided that if the parties have agreed to confer jurisdiction on one or more courts or tribunals of a Member State to hear and determine disputes that have arisen or may arise out of the contract, they shall be presumed to have chosen the law of that Member State.[369] But this provision was subsequently deleted. Recital (12) in its final wording does not go as far as the presumption would have done in terms of the impact of a choice of jurisdiction agreement. As far as England is concerned, it will make no difference to drawing an inference. But it is possible that it might prompt the courts in other Member States to draw the inference when they would not have done so otherwise.

These are only examples of situations where it is possible to infer a choice from the terms of the contract, albeit particularly good ones. Could such an inference be drawn, for example, from the fact that the currency in which payment is to be made is that of a particular country? At common law the English courts drew inferences as to parties' intentions from a wide variety of factors relating to the terms of the contract, including this very factor. However, a note of caution should be struck when it comes to inferring a choice under the Regulation. First, the inferred choice must be "clearly demonstrated". If it is not, you move on to the provisions on the applicable law in the absence of choice (Article 4) to decide the case. Secondly, you are looking, on the basis of an objective test, for the actual or real intentions of the parties.[370] It is just about credible to say in a case like *Amin Rasheed* (or in cases involving arbitration or

---

[363] Courts in some other Contracting States have been more reluctant to draw the inference, see the Green Paper of 14 January 2003 on the conversion of the Rome Convention, COM (2002) 654 final, pp 23–5.

[364] [1996] 1 Lloyd's Rep 380 (Clarke J)—determining whether English law governed; [1995] 2 Lloyd's Rep 64 (Mance J)—earlier on determining for the purposes of service out of the jurisdiction whether English law governed. See also *JSC Zestafoni v Ronly Holdings Ltd* [2004] EWHC 245 (Comm) at [75], [2004] 2 Lloyd's Rep 335; *Habas Sinai Ve Tibbi Gazlar Istihsal Endustrisi AS v VSC Steel Co Ltd* [2013] EWHC 4071 (Comm) at [102].

[365] At common law, a clause providing for arbitration in Beijing or London at the defendant's option did not give rise to an implied choice: *The Star Texas* [1993] 2 Lloyd's Rep 445 at 448, 452, CA. The position would be the same under the Rome Convention and Regulation.

[366] *American International Specialty Lines Insurance Co v Abbott Laboratories* [2002] EWHC 2714 (Comm), [2003] 1 Lloyd's Rep 267 at 272.

[367] *Marubeni Hong Kong and South China Ltd v Mongolian Government* [2002] 2 All ER (Comm) 873.

[368] See the Green Paper of 14 January 2003 on the conversion of the Rome Convention, COM (2002) 654 final, pp 23–5.

[369] Art 3(1) of the original Proposal for a Regulation, COM (2005) 650 final.

[370] *Egon Oldendorff v Liberia Corpn* (Clarke J), supra, at 387–8.

choice of jurisdiction clauses) that the parties had real intentions, but the same cannot be said in a case where all that can be shown is that, for example, there is a clause in the contract relating to the currency in which payment is to be made, or where a specific language is used.[371] In the common law cases, although the language of inferred intent was often used it was by no means clear that the courts were looking for a real or actual intention on the parties' part.[372] The upshot is that it may be harder to draw an inference of intention under the Regulation than it was under the common law rules.[373]

The circumstances of the case[374] The inference can be drawn not only from the terms of the contract, but also from the circumstances of the case.[375] The Giuliano and Lagarde Report[376] gives two examples of inferred choice which would seem to fit within this category. The first is the situation where there is an express choice in a *related transaction*. The second is the situation where there is a *previous course of dealing* under contracts containing an express choice of the applicable law and this choice of law clause has been omitted in circumstances which do not indicate a deliberate change of policy by the parties.

However, whether the inference can be drawn will depend very much on the facts of the case. It will be recalled that in *The Aeolian*[377] the Court of Appeal held that an inference as to the law governing a supply contract, out of which a counterclaim arose, could not be drawn from the fact that the parties agreed that English law governed an undertaking in relation to a claim for payment under a separate spares contract. On the other hand, an inference could be drawn from the fact that an excess insurance policy followed the choice of law in the primary reinsurance policy.[378] An inference is likely to be drawn where the parties made a choice of the governing law for a main contract and later conclude a contract ancillary to that main contract, such as a guarantee,[379] or a collateral contract such as a contractual indemnity,[380] or an agency contract,[381] or an implied contract of warranty of authority:[382] If the rights and obligations under the main contract are governed by a chosen system of law it would be incongruous for the ancillary contract to be governed by a different system of law because

---

[371] *Lupofresh Ltd v Sapporo Breweries* [2013] EWCA Civ 948 at [17].

[372] In *Coast Lines Ltd v Hudig and Veder Chartering NV* [1972] 2 QB 34 at 50 it was clear that Stephenson LJ in the Court of Appeal was not. There was much confusion at common law over the meaning of intention, and between the intentions of the parties and objective factors, infra, pp 724–5.

[373] See Morse, (1982) 2 YEL 107, 116–17. The same will be true in Germany, see Triebel (1988) 37 ICLQ 935 at 942.

[374] Cf Art 2 of the 1955 Hague Convention on the law applicable to international sales of goods. Under the Convention and Regulation, the "circumstances of the case" can include subsequent conduct which shows the parties' earlier intentions at the time of conclusion of the contract, see Plender and Wilderspin, paras 6-043–6-045; Dicey, Morris and Collins, para 32-037.

[375] It is a moot point whether this means that the test for an inferred choice is wider than the test for an implied choice at common law. Cp Potter LJ in *ISS Machinery Services Ltd v Aeolian Shipping SA (the Aeolian)* [2001] EWCA Civ 1162 at [16], [2001] 2 Lloyd's Rep 641 and *Samcrete Egypt Engineers and Contractors SAE v Land Rover Exports Ltd* [2001] EWCA Civ 2019 at [28], [2002] CLC 533 with Mance LJ in *American Motorists Insurance Co (Amico) v Cellstar Corpn* [2003] EWCA Civ 206 at [44], [2003] IL Pr 22.

[376] At p 17.

[377] *ISS Machinery Services Ltd v Aeolian Shipping SA (the Aeolian)* [2001] EWCA Civ 1162, [2001] 2 Lloyd's Rep 641; discussed supra, p 709.

[378] *Dornach Ltd v Mauritius Union Assurance Co Ltd* [2006] EWCA Civ 389 at [41], [2006] 2 Lloyd's Rep 475.

[379] *Aquavita International SA v Ashapura Minecham Ltd* [2014] EWHC 2806 (Comm) at [23]: "presumption, in the absence of countervailing indications, that they have impliedly chosen the same system of law".

[380] *Alliance Bank JSC v Aquanta Corp* [2012] EWCA Civ 1588 at [54].

[381] *Lawlor v Sandvik Mining and Construction Mobile Crushers and Screens Ltd* [2013] EWCA Civ 365 at [35].

[382] *Golden Ocean Group Ltd v Salgaocar Mining Industries PVT Ltd* [2012] EWCA Civ 265 at [45].

this could potentially result in a mismatch between the obligations of the party to the main contract and the obligations of the ancillary contract to fulfil those obligations.

The English courts, under the common law rules, also inferred an intent from purely objective factors, such as the residence of the parties[383] or the nature and location of the subject of the contract.[384] This approach has continued to be used in relation to the Rome Convention. In *American Motorists Insurance Co (Amico) v Cellstar Corp*[385] the Court of Appeal inferred a choice of Texas law from the fact that a company from its base in Texas chose on behalf of its whole group of companies to negotiate world-wide cover in Texas with insurers also based in Texas. Whatever the position was at common law, it is submitted that it is inappropriate to infer an actual intention as required under the Convention and Regulation from purely objective factors such as residence of the parties or location of the subject of the contract. The same—no inference—holds true for the mere fact that a contract was written in a particular language or for ritual conduct out of mere politeness, such as a handshake.[386]

The circumstances of the case can also be taken into account to show that no inference can be drawn as to the governing law. This was the situation in *Samcrete Egypt Engineers and Contractors SAE v Land Rover Exports Ltd*[387] where the fact that one party put forward a choice of law clause and the other party deleted it from the draft contract was a positive indication that the parties made no choice as to the applicable law under Article 3(1).[388] The result was that no choice of English law could be inferred from the fact that this was a guarantee contract which was dependant on a principal contract which was governed by English law. Without taking into account the circumstances of the case, there would have been a strong argument for drawing such an inference.[389]

(ii) Conflicting inferences

The Giuliano and Lagarde Report on the Rome Convention states[390] that any inference which arises from a choice of jurisdiction clause "must always be subject to the other terms of the contract and all the circumstances of the case" (ie the very matters from which an inference can be drawn). For example, a choice of exclusive jurisdiction clause may point to an intention that the law of Country A shall apply, whereas a previous course of dealing may point to an intention that the law of Country B shall apply. However, no conflicting inference could be drawn from the fact that an earlier draft of the contract contained an express choice of law clause (providing that English law governed) and this clause was deleted.[391] This notion of conflicting inferences is not confined to the situation where an inferred choice is being drawn from the presence of a choice of jurisdiction clause in the contract. Thus with an excess reinsurance contract, the inference to be drawn from the fact that the primary reinsurance was governed by Mauritian law conflicted with the inference to be drawn from the fact that the excess reinsurance was written on a Lloyd's slip in the London market on London market

---

383 *Jacobs v Crédit Lyonnais* (1884) 12 QBD 589.

384 *Lloyd v Guibert* (1865) LR 1 QB 115 at 122–3.

385 [2003] EWCA Civ 206, [2003] IL Pr 22.

386 *Lupofresh Ltd v Sapporo Breweries* [2013] EWCA Civ 948 at [17], [23].

387 [2001] EWCA Civ 2019, [2002] CLC 533.

388 Ibid, at [28].

389 Ibid, at [23].

390 At p 17. See also *Marubeni Hong Kong and South China Ltd v Mongolian Government* [2002] 2 All ER (Comm) 873 at [35].

391 *Marubeni Hong Kong and South China Ltd v Mongolian Government* [2002] 2 All ER (Comm) 873 at [42]–[43]; distinguishing *Samcrete Egypt Engineers and Contractors SAE v Land Rover Exports Ltd* [2001] EWCA Civ 2019, [2002] CLC 533. There were subsequent proceedings dealing with other issues.

terms.[392] There was a stalemate.[393] If there are conflicting inferences it cannot be said that the choice has been "clearly" demonstrated, and Article 3(1) does not permit the court to infer a choice of law that the parties might have made if they had no clear intention of making a choice.[394] The result is that you have to turn to the rules on the applicable law in the absence of choice[395] to determine the governing law.[396]

What is less clear is how the inference to be drawn from the terms of the contract and the circumstances of the case stands in relation to the objective connections that the contract has with different countries. For example, a previous course of dealing may raise the inference that English law governs, but many of the objective connections, such as the residence of the parties and the place of performance, could be with France. Under the Regulation there is, quite properly, a rigid separation of intention (dealt with under Article 3) from objective connecting factors (dealt with under Article 4). The inference that the parties intended English law to govern can only be challenged by a conflicting inference, ie by evidence showing a real intention that French law should govern. It has been considered as possible, though, to take a robust view that such an inference can be drawn also from the factual connections with France. These could be considered on the basis that they constitute the surrounding circumstances.[397]

This robust view was discussed by Mance J in *Egon Oldendorff v Liberia Corpn.*[398]

> In this case the plaintiff company was German, the defendant Japanese, and the contract provided for arbitration in London. It was argued that the arbitration clause was a minor factor and that other factors pointed objectively to Japanese law. Not only was the defendant corporation Japanese but also a Japanese shipbroker acted as intermediary between the parties, and the ships chartered were to be delivered and redelivered in Japan.

Mance J rejected this argument, saying that these matters were inadequate to lead him to conclude that the parties intended London arbitration under Japanese law,[399] and held that there was a good arguable case for the purposes of service out of the jurisdiction that English law governed. Thus, although it may not be entirely excluded to draw a conflicting inference from objective factors, it seems that the circumstances where it will be right to do so may be relatively rare. Once it had been decided that there was jurisdiction, the issue arose of whether English law did in fact govern. Clarke J held that it did.[400] Having agreed a "neutral forum", the reasonable inference is that the parties intended that forum to apply a "neutral" law, namely English law. In the circumstances, the arbitration clause was a strong indication of the parties' intention to choose English law. Clarke J thought that the approach towards arbitration clauses under Article 3 was little or any different from that at common law.[401]

(e) Consent to choice

There can be a dispute as to whether one of the parties has consented to the choice. Article 3(5) provides that issues in relation to the validity and existence of consent are determined in

---

[392] *Dornach Ltd v Mauritius Union Assurance Co Ltd* [2006] EWCA Civ 389 at [43], [2006] 2 Lloyd's Rep 475.
[393] Ibid.
[394] The Giuliano and Lagarde Report, p 17; the *Dornach* case, supra, at [43].
[395] Arts 4, 5–8.
[396] The *Dornach* case, supra, at [43].
[397] See the *Marubeni* case, supra, at [35].
[398] [1995] 2 Lloyd's Rep 64.
[399] Ibid, at 69.
[400] *Egon Oldendorff v Liberia Corpn* [1996] 1 Lloyd's Rep 380 (Clarke J).
[401] The result would have been the same under the proper law of the contract in a three-country case like this. See *Compañía Naviera Micro SA v Shipley International Inc, The Parouth* [1982] 2 Lloyd's Rep 351, CA.

accordance with the special rules in the Regulation relating to material validity (Article 10), formal validity (Article 11) and incapacity (Article 13).[402] These provisions will be discussed later in this chapter.[403] If there is no valid consent to the choice, the applicable law must be determined under the rules on the applicable law in the absence of choice.[404]

(ii) The applicable law in the absence of choice

In a surprising number of cases the parties fail to choose the applicable law. This may be because they have contracted without first consulting lawyers, or they cannot agree on the applicable law, or because the parties' choice has been ineffective.[405] Today, the determination of the applicable law in the absence of choice is governed by Article 4 of the Regulation which applies a purely objective test. Therefore, it is inappropriate to talk in this context about the intentions of the parties.[406]

(a) The applicable law in the absence of choice under the common law

Under the traditional proper law of the contract approach, in the absence of an express or inferred choice, the court looked for the system of law with which the transaction was most closely connected. This took into account such factors as the place of residence[407] or business[408] of the parties, the place where the relationship between the parties was centred,[409] the place where the contract was made[410] or was to be performed,[411] or the nature and subject matter[412] of the contract. Nonetheless, the common law rule was not as open ended and flexible as might at first appear. In order to promote certainty in the law the courts identified specific factors as having great weight in identifying the closest connection in relation to certain contracts. For example, for insurance contracts the objective proper law would normally be the law of the state where the insurer carried on business.[413] There can be little doubt that when the English courts set out to ascertain the objective proper law of the contract they also sought to achieve certain underlying policy objectives, such as giving business efficacy to the contract.[414]

(b) The applicable law in the absence of choice under the Rome Convention

After the implementation of the Rome Convention[415] into English law, the determination of the applicable law in the absence of choice was dealt with under Article 4 of this Convention,

---

Cf *Compagnie d'Armement Maritime SA v Cie Tunisienne de Navigation SA* [1971] AC 572, HL, treated as a two-country case.

[402] For criticism of the corresponding provision of Art 3(4) Rome Convention see Cavers (1975) 48 So Cal L R 603 at 609; Nadelmann (1976) 24 AJCL 1, 8–9; Kaye, pp 168–70; cf Morse, op cit, at 119.

[403] See infra, pp 754–64.

[404] Art 4. Cf the 1985 Hague Convention on the law applicable to contracts for the international sale of goods, Art 10(1) which spells this out.

[405] Eg, there are two inconsistent choices, see supra, p 714; see the Giuliano and Lagarde Report, p 20.

[406] See *Crédit Lyonnais v New Hampshire Insurance Co* [1997] 2 Lloyd's Rep 1 at 5, CA. Under the objective proper law approach the courts have often referred to the parties' intentions, in the sense of the intentions that they would have had if they had considered the matter, or ought to have had as reasonable persons, see the 11th edn of this book (1987), pp 461–2. It follows that the fact that the contract would be valid under one country's law but not under another's cannot be considered under Article 4, since this factor is only relevant to the determination of the parties' intentions (ie the parties would expect the contract to be valid).

[407] *Jacobs v Crédit Lyonnais* (1884) 12 QBD 589 at 600, 602.

[408] *Re Anglo-Austrian Bank* [1920] 1 Ch 69.

[409] *XAG v A Bank* [1983] 2 Lloyd's Rep 535 at 543—banker and customer.

[410] *Lloyd v Guibert* (1865) LR 1 QB 115 at 122; *Cantieri Navali Riuniti SpA v N V Omne Justitia, The Stolt Marmaro* [1985] 2 Lloyd's Rep 428 at 433–5.

[411] *The Assunzione* [1954] P 150.

[412] *British South Africa Co v De Beers Consolidated Mines Ltd* [1910] 1 Ch 354 at 383, revsd on another point, [1912] AC 52.

[413] See Dicey, Morris and Collins, paras 33-185–33-186.

[414] Wyatt (1974) 37 MLR 399; Jaffey, *Topics in Choice of Law* (1996), p 32.

[415] For a detailed presentation, see the 14th edn of this book (2008), pp 707–22.

which consisted of three main parts. First, there was the basic rule that the contract shall be governed by the law of the country with which it is most closely connected.[416] Secondly, there was a general presumption, based on the concept of characteristic performance, designed to identify the country with which the contract is most closely connected,[417] together with special presumptions[418] for two particular types of contract.[419] Thirdly, there was a provision which, inter alia, stated that the presumptions shall be disregarded if the contract appeared to be more closely connected with another country.[420] These provisions sought to combine certainty, provided by the presumptions, with flexibility, provided by the more closely connected test and the power to rebut the presumptions. Nonetheless, the scheme of Article 4 of the Convention raised an initial dilemma: It was not clear whether what was intended is a three-, two- or even one-stage process.[421] The sequence in which the provisions were set out in Article 4 pointed to a three-stage process.[422] However, the Giuliano and Lagarde Report[423] contemplated that the applicable law can be determined solely by applying the presumptions, without searching for the country with the closest connection: it thus envisaged, at least in many cases, a one-stage process which starts and finishes with the presumptions. This view was supported by Continental case law.[424] Against this, it was hard to see how a court can decide whether it is appropriate to rebut a presumption unless it has first applied the more closely connected test. This would suggest a two-stage process, which starts with a presumption, but then moves on[425] to consider the more closely connected test in order to see whether this presumption can be rebutted. This view was supported by English case law[426] and, arguably, by a decision of the Court of Justice which was rendered after the adoption of the Rome I Regulation.[427] The question of whether it was normally a one-stage or two-stage process became particularly important when it came to the question of how easy it is to displace the general presumption.

After the adoption of the Convention, some of the factors relevant under the proper law of the contract approach remained relevant under Article 4,[428] while the relevance of others, such as the place of performance, declined.[429] Also, in contrast to the proper law approach,

---

[416] Art 4(1). According to the Giuliano and Lagarde Report, pp 19–20, this rule was based on the common core of the law in Member States, where the same sort of flexible approach has been commonly used. A similar approach is found in the US under the American Restatement, Second, see Lando (1982) 30 AJCL 19, 31.

[417] Art 4(2).

[418] Art 4(3) and (4).

[419] The introduction of presumptions turned the clock back as far as English law was concerned. Although popular at one time, presumptions went out of fashion and were rejected, one criticism being the very point that they diverted attention from the necessity to consider every single factor under the objective test, see *Coast Lines Ltd v Hudig and Veder Chartering NV* [1972] 2 QB 34 at 47, 50.

[420] Art 4(5).

[421] Going into this question has been described as being unhelpful, *Definitely Maybe (Touring) Ltd v Marek Lieberberg Konzertagentur GmbH* [2001] 1 WLR 1745 at [15].

[422] See generally Collins (1976) 25 ICLQ 35, 48.

[423] At p 21. The use of presumptions, it is said, "greatly simplifies the problem of determining the law applicable in the absence of choice . . . There is no longer any need to determine where the contract was concluded . . . Seeking the place of performance becomes superfluous".

[424] See infra, pp 736–7; and generally Nygh (1995) 251 Hague Recueil 269, at 332–4.

[425] At least where a party seeks to rely on Art 4(5), see infra, pp 736–7.

[426] See *Samcrete Egypt Engineers and Contractors SAE v Land Rover Exports Ltd* [2001] EWCA Civ 2019 at [37], [2002] CLC 533.

[427] Case C-133/08 *Intercontainer Interfrigo SC (ICF) v Balkenende Oosthuizen BV and MIC Operations BV* [2009] ECR I-9687 at [62]–[63].

[428] See *CGU International Insurance plc v Szabo* [2002] 1 All ER (Comm) 83 at [22].

[429] See *First Laser Ltd v Fujian Enterprises (Holdings) Co* [2012] HKCU 1397, (2012) HKFCAR 154 at [55]–[56].

it was possible to take account of factors which have supervened after the conclusion of the contract.[430] Moreover, the presence of the presumptions and the fact that the law was codified reduced the flexibility, and thus the room for manoeuvre, for a court that wants to achieve certain policy objectives under the Convention. The system of presumptions under the Convention was also criticised for its complexity, which compromised the desired certainty, and for the fact that it elevated one connection (combination of habitual residence and characteristic performance) to a position of importance above all others.[431]

(c) The applicable law in the absence of choice under the Rome I Regulation[432]
Article 4 of the Rome I Regulation sets out one of the most radical departures from the position under the Convention.

(i) Article 4(1): Fixed rules for specific contracts
In order to promote legal certainty and foreseeability of the applicable law, it is provided in Article 4(1) that, where the law applicable to the contract has not been chosen by the parties, there should be a list of eight fixed rules dealing with many of the most commonly encountered contracts.[433] Together with the special provisions for contracts of carriage, insurance contracts, consumer contracts and employment contracts in Articles 5 to 8, the Regulation is much more specific than the Convention, where only two special presumptions[434] and two specific rules for consumer and employment contracts existed.[435] Some of the fixed rules of Article 4(1) of the Regulation, in particular (a) and (b) on sale of goods and provision of services, can be understood as expressions of the principle of characteristic performance. Moreover, the principle of characteristic performance is preserved, as a general principle, (only) for those cases where the contract cannot be categorised as being one of the specified types of Article 4(1) or where its elements fall within more than one of the specified types covered by Article 4(1).[436] Other of the rules in Article 4(1) deviate from the concept of characteristic performance, either because the place of performance prevails over the habitual residence of the party effecting such performance (as in the case of immovable property, (c) and (d)),[437] or in order to favour a party to a complex agreement (as in the case of distribution and franchising, (e) and (f)),[438] or in order to let the law at the market prevail (as in the case of auctions and multilateral settlement systems, (g) and (h)). Still, under many of the fixed

---

[430] The Giuliano and Lagarde Report, p 20; *Caledonia Subsea Ltd v Micoperi SRL* 2002 SLT 1022, where Lord Cameron said that supervening factors refers to ones not existing at the time of conclusion of the contract and which could not have been reasonably contemplated. For criticism, see Lasok and Stone, *Conflict of Laws in the European Community*, p 363; cf Nygh (1995) 251 Hague Recueil 269, 346–7.

[431] For criticism, see the 14th edn of this book (2008), p 716. See also Jaffey, *Topics in Choice of Law* (1996), pp 32 et seq, who argues that the presumption of characteristic performance will often achieve the desired business efficacy and certainty. See on achieving the latter, Atrill (2004) 53 ICLQ 549. See generally Lando, op cit, p 203.

[432] See generally Magnus in *European Commentaries on Private International Law*, Art 4, pp 263 et seq.

[433] See Recital (16) of the Regulation and the Explanatory Memorandum accompanying the Proposal for a Regulation of the European Parliament and the Council on the law applicable to contractual obligations (Rome I) COM (2005) 650 final, at pp 6–7. The European Parliament in its draft Report (PE 374.427v01-00 of 22 August 2006 and 7 December 2006) originally proposed a closest connection rule with a series of presumptions for particular types of contract.

[434] See Art 4(3) (immovable property) and Art 4(4) (carriage of goods) Rome Convention.

[435] See Art 5 (certain consumer contracts) and Art 6 (individual employment contracts) Rome Convention.

[436] Recital (19) of the Regulation. On Art 4(2) infra, pp 731–5.

[437] For immovable property, a comparable—albeit narrower—provision was found in Art 4(3) Rome Convention.

[438] Cf Dicey, Morris and Collins, para 32-075, who consider Art 4(1)(e) and (f) as an emanation of the principle of characteristic performance.

rules of Article 4(1) of the Regulation[439] the result will be the same as that obtained applying the characteristic performance presumptions under Article 4(2) and (3) of the Rome Convention. But under Article 4(1) of the Regulation the route to the result is more direct in that it is no longer necessary to identify what the characteristic performance of a particular contract is.

Sale of goods   Under the Regulation, a contract for the sale of goods[440] shall be governed by the law of the country where the seller has his habitual residence.[441] The same result was reached by English and Scottish courts under Article 4(2) of the Rome Convention, holding that the characteristic performance of a contract for the sale of goods is that of the seller delivering the goods.[442] Article 4(1)(a) covers also contracts where the purchaser of the goods had specified certain requirements for the goods which have yet to be produced, provided that the purchaser did not provide the raw materials.[443] It does not cover the sale of land,[444] the hire of goods,[445] the barter of goods,[446] or a pledge.[447] It is noticeable that there is no attempt made to co-ordinate choice of law and jurisdiction.[448] This is understandable. With a contract for the sale of goods, jurisdiction in some cases will be allocated to the buyer's home state (as the place of delivery),[449] the courts of which will apply the law of the seller's home state. But in other cases it will be allocated to the seller's home state (as the place of delivery). In other words, the jurisdiction is not geared to the buyer's or seller's home state but to the more complex concept of place of delivery (place of performance), which in some cases will be the seller's home state and in others the buyer's.

Provision of services   A contract for the provision of services—a concept to be defined in the same way as in Article 7(1)(b) Brussels I Recast,[450] except distribution and franchising for which there are special rules[451]—shall be governed, under the Regulation, by the law of the country where the service provider has his habitual residence.[452] Here again, courts arrived at the same result under Article 4(2) the Rome Convention by identifying the characteristic performance of a service contract as being the performance of the service provider, eg the

---

[439] But not for distribution contracts (on which see *Print Concept GmbH v GEW (EC) Ltd* [2001] EWCA Civ 352 at [35], [2002] CLC 352; discussed infra, pp 729–30), auctions and, arguably, franchise contracts (the characteristic performance could be regarded as that of the person granting the franchise for which the franchised person pays).

[440] "Sale of goods" should be defined in the same way as when applying Art 7(1)(b) of the Brussels I Recast (discussed supra, p 255): Recital (17) of the Regulation.

[441] Art 4(1)(a) of the Regulation.

[442] *Iran Continental Shelf Oil Co v IRI International Corpn* [2002] EWCA Civ 1024 at [19], [2004] 2 CLC 696; *Ferguson Shipbuilders Ltd v Voith Hydro GmbH & Co KG* 2000 SLT 229 at 232, (OH); *William Grant & Sons International Ltd v Marie Brizard España SA* 1998 SC 536. See also *Machinale Glasfabriek De Maas BV v Emaillerie Alsacienne SA* [1985] 2 CMLR 281, [1984] ECC 123—a Dutch Supreme Court case applying the Convention as part of its private international law prior to the Convention coming into force.

[443] On the parallel provision of Art 7(1)(b) Brussels I Regulation, see Case C-381/08 *Car Trim GmbH v KeySafety Systems Srl* [2010] ECR I-1255 at [38]. If the purchaser provided the raw materials, the contract should be classified as a contract for the provision of services, ibid at [40].

[444] Which falls under Art 4(1)(c) of the Regulation.

[445] Which is likely to fall under Art 4(1)(b), as a service, or Art 4(2) of the Regulation.

[446] Which will normally fall under Art 4(4) of the Regulation.

[447] Which will fall under Art 4(2) of the Regulation, with the pledgor effecting the characteristic performance.

[448] Except in respect of the definition of "sale of goods" and "provision of services", Recital (17) of the Regulation.

[449] See Art 7(1)(b) of the Brussels I Regulation, discussed supra, pp 255–6.

[450] Recital (17) of the Regulation. Art 7(1)(b) is discussed supra, pp 255–6.

[451] Art 4(1)(e) and (f) of the Regulation, see infra, pp 729–30.

[452] Art 4(1)(b) of the Regulation.

insurance[453] or reinsurance[454] provided by the insurer, the services of a pop group,[455] the provision of testing and consultancy services,[456] the provision of architectural[457] or diving[458] services, the service of a commercial agent,[459] the development of a website,[460] or the service of a broker.[461] All of these examples would today be considered as contracts for the provision of services under Article 4(1)(b), leading to the application of the law where the service provider has his habitual residence. Under the Regulation, the concept of service implies, at the least, that the party who provides the service carries out a particular activity in return for remuneration.[462] Therefore, a license contract under which the owner of an intellectual property right grants its contractual partner the right to use that right in return for remuneration is not a contract for the provision of services, even if the licensee is obliged to use the intellectual property right.[463] Under the Convention, the courts encountered some difficulty in identifying the characteristic performance of a loan contract. In most cases this will be the provision of funds by the lender, not the repayment (normally with interest) by the borrower; thus the provision of funds can be considered as the equivalent of a provision of services under Article 4(1)(b) of the Regulation.[464]

Immovable property   While Article 4(1)(a) and (b) of the Regulation opt for the law of the country where the seller or service provider is habitually resident, a contract relating to a right *in rem* in immovable property or to a tenancy of immovable property shall be governed by the law of the country where the property, ie the object of the contract, is situated, not where one party, ie the seller or landlord resides.[465] Examples of contracts governed by the law of the country where the property is situated are contracts for the sale of property[466] or for the rental of a holiday home.[467] On the other hand, a contract for construction or repair would not fall under Article 4(1)(c) because the main subject matter of the contract is not the immovable property itself.[468] The provision in Article 4(1)(c) of the Regulation on immovable property is similar to the presumption of Article

---

[453] *Crédit Lyonnais v New Hampshire Insurance Co* [1997] 2 Lloyd's Rep 1 at 6, CA; *American Motorists Insurance Co (Amico) v Cellstar Corpn* [2003] EWCA Civ 206 at [47], [2003] IL PR 22. Most insurance contracts fall today under Art 7, not Art 3 or 4 of the Regulation.

[454] *AIG Group (UK) Ltd v The Ethniki* [1998] 4 All ER 301 at 310; *Tiernan v The Magen Insurance Co Ltd* [2000] IL Pr 517; *Tryg Baltica International (UK) Ltd v Boston Compania De Seguros SA* [2004] EWHC 1186 (Comm), [2005] Lloyd's Rep IR 40; but cf *Dornach Ltd v Mauritius Union Assurance Co Ltd* [2006] EWCA Civ 389 at [41], [2006] 2 Lloyd's Rep 475—payment in the event of a claim as characteristic performance.

[455] *Definitely Maybe (Touring) Ltd v Marek Lieberberg Konzertagentur GmbH* [2001] 1 WLR 1745 at [5].

[456] *Ennstone Building Products Ltd v Stanger Ltd* [2002] EWCA Civ 916 at [13], [2002] 1 WLR 3059.

[457] *Latchin (t/a Dinkha Latchin Associates) v General Mediterranean Holdings SA* [2002] CLC 330 at [65].

[458] *Caledonia Subsea Ltd v Micoperi SRL* 2002 SLT 1022 at [21].

[459] *Albon v Naza Motor Trading* [2007] EWHC 9 (Ch), [2007] 1 Lloyd's Rep 297 for the relationship between principal and agent. For distribution contracts see Art 4(1)(f) of the Regulation.

[460] *1st Mover APS v Direct Hedge SA* [2003] IL Pr 31 at [11]–[12], Eastern Court of Appeal, Denmark.

[461] *HIB v Guardian Insurance Co* [1997] 1 Lloyd's Rep 412.

[462] On the parallel provision of Art 7(1)(b) Brussels I Recast, see Case C-533/07 *Falco Privatstiftung and Thomas Rabitsch v Gisela Weller-Lindhorst* [2009] ECR I-3327 at [29].

[463] Case C-533/07 *Falco Privatstiftung and Thomas Rabitsch v Gisela Weller-Lindhorst* [2009] ECR I-3327 at [30], [32].

[464] *Atlantic Telecom GmbH, Noter* 2004 SLT 1031 at 1051–2, where a preference was shown for the lender effecting the characteristic performance. But cf *Mirchandai v Somaia* [2001] WL 239782; *Tavoulareas v Tsavliris* [2005] EWHC 2140 (Comm) at [51], [2006] 1 All ER (Comm), 109: repayment of loan as characteristic performance. However, a different classification could be adopted where the consideration for the loan is the issue of shares or other facilities such as a seat on the company's board.

[465] Art 4(1)(c) of the Regulation.

[466] For doubts, see Plender and Wilderspin, para 7-039.

[467] The Giuliano and Lagarde Report, p 21 (on Art 4(3) Rome Convention).

[468] Ibid. Instead, it will fall under Art 4(1)(b) (provision of services).

4(3) Rome Convention,[469] with some changes. Under the Convention, it was considered unfortunate that short term leases fell under the presumption, a problem which could only be solved by applying the exception clause.[470] This weakness is now remedied by Article 4(1)(d), which states that a tenancy of immovable property concluded for temporary private use for a period of no more than six consecutive months shall be governed by the law of the country where the landlord has his habitual residence, provided that the tenant is a natural person and has his habitual residence in the same country.[471] Moreover, Art 4(1)(c) has been aligned with Article 24(1) of the Brussels I Recast, thus replacing the words "right to use property" by "tenancy". This has led to doubts whether rights to use property on a different basis than a tenancy, eg usufructuary leases or agreements giving rise to equitable rights in immovable property, fall under Article 4(1)(c).[472] While it may be right that such rights are no "tenancy",[473] they relate to a right *in rem* in the property, as both an usufruct or an equitable right to use property are effective not only against the other party to the contract, but also against third parties. They thus fall under Article 4(1) (c) of the Regulation.

Franchise and distribution contracts   Although franchise and distribution contracts are contracts for services,[474] they are the subject of specific rules:[475] A franchise contract shall be governed by the law of the country where the franchisee has his habitual residence,[476] a distribution contract[477] by the law of the country where the distributor has his habitual residence.[478] These rules are based on the consideration that EU law seeks to protect the franchisee and the distributor as the weaker parties.[479] Thus, these rules do not reflect the principle of characteristic performance, as can be seen from the case *Print Concept GmbH v GEW (EC) Ltd*[480] which involved an oral distributorship agreement:

> Print Concept (the distributor) was under an implied obligation to maximise sales in the German-speaking marketplace and GEW was under an implied obligation to supply its products to Print Concept which the latter would purchase.

Applying the Rome Convention, the Court of Appeal held that it was the supply of the products that was characteristic of the distribution agreement, for the penetration of the German

---

[469] Art 4(3) Rome Convention stated that "to the extent that the subject matter of the contract is a right in immovable property or a right to use immovable property it shall be presumed that the contract is most closely connected with the country where the immovable property is situated".

[470] The Giuliano and Lagarde Report, p 21 gave the example of a contract between two Belgians for the rental of an Italian holiday home, for which Belgian law should be applied by operation of the exception clause in Art 4(5).

[471] Art 4(1)(d) of the Regulation. For criticism see Plender and Wilderspin, para 7-042, who regards Art 4(1)(d) as "unobjectionable", but "unnecessarily rigid".

[472] For timeshare agreements, see Case C-73/04 *Brigitte and Marcus Klein v Rhodos Management Ltd* [2005] ECR I-8667 at [26]–[27]; Dicey, Morris and Collins, para 33-044: timeshare agreements which are not consumer contracts in the sense of Art 6(1) fall under Art 4(1)(c) and (d).

[473] Plender and Wilderspin, para 7-039.

[474] For distribution contracts see, in the context of Art 7(1)(b) Brussels I Recast, Case C-9/12 *Corman-Collins SA v La Maison du Whisky SA* ECLI:EU:C:2013:860 at [41].

[475] Recital (17) of the Regulation.

[476] Art 4(1)(e) of the Regulation.

[477] For a definition of distribution contract, see Case C-9/12 *Corman-Collins SA v La Maison du Whisky SA* ECLI:EU:C:2013:860 at [27]–[28]: "the grantor undertakes to sell to the distributor, which it has chosen for that purpose, the goods to be ordered by the distributor in order to satisfy the requirements of its clients, while the distributor undertakes to purchase from the grantor the goods he needs".

[478] Art 4(1)(f) of the Regulation.

[479] Explanatory Memorandum COM (2005) 650 final, p 6.

[480] [2001] EWCA Civ 352, [2002] CLC 352.

market could not take place without the supply and purchase of the products.[481] Therefore, according to Article 4(2) of the Rome Convention, the law of the supplier governed the contract. Under Article 4(1)(f) of the Regulation, the opposite result would be reached, as the contract would be governed by the law of the distributor.[482] Likewise, for franchise contracts the characteristic performance could be regarded as that of the person granting the franchise for which the franchised person pays, leading to the application of the law of the franchisor under the characteristic performance test of Article 4(2) Rome Convention. Under Article 4(1)(e) of the Regulation, however, the law of the franchisee will apply.

Auction sales and multilateral trading systems A contract for the sale of goods by auction shall be governed by the law of the country where the auction takes place, if such a place can be determined.[483] Finally, a contract concluded within a multilateral system which brings together or facilitates the bringing together of multiple third-party buying and selling interests in financial instruments,[484] in accordance with non-discretionary rules and governed by a single law, shall be governed by that law.[485] Both provisions provide for the application of the law which governs the marketplace in which the contracts are concluded.

Intellectual property rights The original proposal for a Regulation contained a rule for contracts relating to intellectual or industrial property rights, but the compromise package of the Presidency of April 2007, agreed by the Council, deleted this rule and it is not present in the final version of the Regulation. The reason for this was probably that the original proposal—general application of the law of habitual residence of the party granting the license—was considered as inappropriate in light of the diversity of license contracts, some of which might rather justify the application of the law of the licensee, or even of the country in which the intellectual property right is protected. After deletion of the special rule, license contracts—which cannot be regarded as service contracts[486]—will now fall under the characteristic performance test of Article 4(2), or, if no characteristic performance can be identified, under the closest connection rule of Article 4(4).

Contracts of carriage Under the Rome Convention, contracts for the carriage of goods[487] were regarded by the Working Group as having peculiarities which merited a separate special rebuttable presumption, which referred to the principal place of business of the carrier at the time the contract was concluded, provided that one of a number of alternative connections with that country must also be satisfied, eg that it is also the place of loading or discharge. If not, no presumption operated and the applicable law had to be ascertained using the closest connection test under Article 4(1) of the Convention.[488] The original proposal for a

---

[481] Ibid, at [34]. See also *Optelec v Midtronics* [2003] IL Pr 4, French Cour De Cassation. The opposite result was reached by Dutch courts, *Elinga BV v British Wool International Ltd* (Hoge Raad), Nederlands International Privaatrecht 1998, No 288. See also Case C-9/12 *Corman-Collins SA v La Maison du Whisky SA* ECLI:EU:C:2013:860 at [38].

[482] With only very limited space for the escape clause of Article 4(3) of the Regulation, which probably could not be invoked in this case.

[483] Art 4(1)(g) of the Regulation.

[484] As defined by Art 4(1), point (17) of Directive (EC) No 2004/39. See also Recital (18) of the Regulation.

[485] Art 4(1)(h) of the Regulation.

[486] Case C-533/07 *Falco Privatstiftung and Thomas Rabitsch v Gisela Weller-Lindhorst* [2009] ECR I-3327 at [30], [32]; supra, p 728.

[487] According to Art 4(4) of the Convention, "carriage of goods" encompasses "single voyage charterparties and other contracts the main purpose of which is the carriage of goods". See generally Schultz in *Contract Conflicts*, pp 185 et seq; Fletcher, op cit, pp 164–5; Plender and Wilderspin, paras 8-011–8-017; Kaye, pp 197–202.

[488] Case C-440/97 *GIE Groupe Concorde v The Master of the vessel Suhadiwarno Panjan* [1999] ECR I-6307 at [41] (Opinion of AG Ruiz-Jarabo Colomer).

Regulation also contained a rule under Article 4(1) for contracts of carriage,[489] but this rule did not form part of the compromise package of the Presidency of April 2007 agreed by the Council, and there is no such rule under Article 4 of the final version of the Regulation. However, there is a separate Article 5 setting out a special regime for contracts of carriage. This provision distinguishes between contracts for the carriage of goods[490] and contracts for the carriage of passengers.[491] Article 5(1) on the carriage of goods provides a special rule only for the law applicable in the absence of choice and is thus comparable to the rules of Article 4(1), whereas Article 5(2) on the carriage of passengers also limits the choice of law.[492] According to Article 5(1), the law applicable to a contract of carriage of goods in the absence of choice shall be the law of the country of habitual residence of the carrier, provided that the place of receipt or the place of delivery or the habitual residence of the consignor is also situated in that country. If those requirements are not met, the law of the country where the place of delivery as agreed by the parties is situated shall apply.[493] As regards the interpretation of contracts for the carriage of goods, no change in substance is intended with respect to Article 4(4), third sentence, of the Rome Convention.[494] Therefore, single-voyage charter parties and other contracts the main purpose of which is the carriage of goods should be treated as contracts for the carriage of goods. For the purposes of the Regulation, the term 'consignor' should refer to any person who enters into a contract of carriage with the carrier and the term 'the carrier' should refer to the party to the contract who undertakes to carry the goods, whether or not he performs the carriage himself.[495] With contracts of carriage international conventions may apply, and these take precedence over the Regulation.[496]

(ii) Article 4(2): The characteristic performance test

Article 4(2) of the Regulation retains the characteristic performance criterion of the Rome Convention[497] for contracts for which Article 4(1) lays down no special rule, such as complex contracts that are not easy to categorise or contracts involving mutual performance by the parties in terms that can be regarded as characteristic on both sides.[498] Article 4(2) deals thus with two situations: first, where the contract is not covered by Article 4(1); and, secondly, where the elements of the contract would be covered by more than one of the fixed rules in Article 4(1). In both situations, Article 4(2) provides that the contract shall be governed by the law of the country where the party required to effect the characteristic performance of the contract has his habitual residence.

---

[489] Art 4(1)(c) of the original Proposal for a Regulation, COM (2005) 650 final read: "a contract of carriage shall be governed by the law of the country in which the carrier has his habitual residence".

[490] Art 5(1) of the Regulation.

[491] Art 5(2) of the Regulation.

[492] Art 5(2) on contracts for the carriage of passengers is similar to the other rules for special contracts and thus presented infra, p 742.

[493] Art 5(3) adds an escape clause which also applies to Art 5(1) on contracts for carriage of goods. This clause is almost identical to Art 4(3), on this infra, p 742.

[494] Recital (22) of the Regulation. The case law of the CJEU on Art 4(4) of the Rome Convention thus continues to be relevant for Art 5(1), see Case C-133/08 *Intercontainer Interfrigo SC (ICF) v Balkenende Oosthuizen BV and MIC Operations BV* [2009] ECR I-9687 at [35] (only contracts the main purpose of which is the actual carriage of goods, not only the provision of a means of transport, fall under Art 4(4) of the Convention); Case C-305/13 *Haeger & Schmidt GmbH v Mutuelles du Mans assurances IARD (MMA IARD)* ECLI:EU:C:2014:2320 at [25]–[31].

[495] Recital (22) of the Rome I Regulation.

[496] Art 25, discussed infra, p 774.

[497] So the criterion of characteristic performance is retained but what was a presumption under Article 4(2) of the Convention becomes a rule under the Regulation.

[498] Explanatory Memorandum COM (2005) 650 final, p 6.

The concept of characteristic performance[499]   The origins of the concept of characteristic performance, which is defined neither in the Convention nor in the Regulation, are to be found in Swiss private international law.[500] As far as English law is concerned, the place of performance is well known as a connecting factor, but it suffers from the obvious defect that in a typical contract both parties have to perform and may have to do so in different states. The concept of characteristic performance seeks to avoid this difficulty by concentrating on just one performance, the one which is characteristic of the contract as a whole—ie the one which constitutes the essence of the contract. It is this feature of characteristic performance which was used by the Working Group on the Rome Convention to justify its elevation, above all other connections, to the position of becoming a presumption.[501] More grandiosely, it was said that "the concept of characteristic performance essentially links the contract to the social and economic environment of which it will form a part".[502]

Identifying the characteristic performance   This leaves the problem of identifying the characteristic performance. There is no difficulty if only one party has to perform as, for example, in the case of a contract of gift, or a unilateral contract involving payment of a termination fee on discontinuance of a project.[503] But more typically, one party will perform services or provide goods, and the other will pay money for these. It is not immediately obvious which of these performances constitutes the essence of the contract. As far as each party is concerned what is important to them is the counter-performance by the other party. However, the Giuliano and Lagarde Report states[504] that the characteristic performance is "of course" the performance for which the payment is due; eg the delivery of goods, the granting of a right to make use of property, the provision of a service, transport, insurance, banking operations, security, "which usually constitutes the centre of gravity and the socio-economic function of the contractual transaction".[505] Thus, for example, in an agency contract concluded in France between a Belgian commercial agent and a French company, the characteristic performance being that of the agent, the contract will be governed by Belgian law if the agent has his place of business in Belgium.[506]

Examples   Many of the examples discussed in the Giuliano and Lagarde Report and in the case law on the Rome Convention (sale, provision of services) fall today under Article 4(1) of the Regulation which directly determines the applicable law. The criterion of characteristic performance remains relevant only for contracts which are either not covered by Article 4(1), or where the elements of the contract would be covered by more than one of the points of Article 4(1). In both cases, in ascertaining the characteristic performance, one is not confined

---

[499] For criticism of the concept, see generally: Collins (1976) 25 ICLQ 35, 44 et seq; D'Oliveira (1977) 25 AJCL 303; Kaye, pp 187–91; Dicey, Morris and Collins, para 32-076; Hill and Chong, paras 14.2.41–14.2.48; Juenger in *Contract Conflicts*, pp 300–302; Schultz ibid, pp 186–7; Morse, op cit, pp 126–32; Fletcher, op cit, pp 161–5; Lasok and Stone, op cit, pp 362–3. Cf Lipstein (1981) 3 Northwestern J of Int L and Bus 402; Blaikie 1983 SLT 241; Jaffey, *Topics in Choice of Law* (1996), pp 32 et seq.

[500] For the position in Switzerland, see the Swiss Federal Statute on Private International Law of 18 December 1987, Art 117. The statute is set out in (1989) 37 AJCL 193. For the history in Switzerland, see Schnitzer (1968) *Recueil des Cours* I 541, 562–77.

[501] The Giuliano and Lagarde Report, p 20.

[502] Ibid.

[503] *Ark Therapeutics plc v True North Capital Ltd* [2005] EWHC 1585 (Comm) at [55], [2006] 1 All ER (Comm) 138. See also *Armstrong International Ltd v Deutsche Bank Securities Inc* QBD 11 July 2003—payment of a fee allegedly due to a recruitment agency which had no contractual obligation to make an introduction.

[504] At p 20. See also Forsyth and Moser (1996) 45 ICLQ 190, at 193–4.

[505] For these examples see the Giuliano and Lagarde Report, pp 20–1.

[506] Ibid, p 21.

to the terms of the contract.[507] The global picture must be assessed[508] and the background to the contract may be of particular importance.[509]

An example for a *contract not covered by Article 4(1)* is a contract of guarantee.[510] With a contract of guarantee, the characteristic performance is that of payment of money by the guarantor, whether in relation to the principal debtor or the creditor.[511] Likewise, in an indemnification agreement the characteristic performance is the promise of indemnity.[512] In *Bank of Baroda v Vysya Bank*[513] Mance J regarded the position of a bank confirming a letter of credit as being analogous to that of a guarantor. The characteristic performance of the contract between the confirming bank and the issuing bank was the honouring by the confirming bank of its confirmation of credit in favour of the beneficiary.[514] The characteristic performance of the contract between the issuing bank and the beneficiary was the issue of the letter of credit[515] and that between the confirming bank and the beneficiary was that of the bank providing the banking service of payment under the letter of credit.[516]

This leaves the second category of contracts, contracts that would be *covered by more than one of the points of Article 4(1)*. As a first observation, it should be noted that Article 4(1) is not excluded only because the contract includes a minor part which falls under another point of paragraph 1.[517] If, for example, the parties agree on a lease of immovable property, and in the same contract agree that the tenant buys furniture from the landlord the value of which is minor in relation to the value of the lease, this should not lead to a disapplication of Article 4(1)(c) in favour of Article 4(2).

If the second element of the contract is not minor and entirely subordinate in relation to the first, the applicable law is determined by Article 4(2). A rather easy example is a contract where one party provides both goods and services, ie a contract where the fixed rules of Article 4(1), even if more than one applies, point in the same direction. Even if such a contract is considered to fall under Article 4(2) and not under a combination of Article 4(1)(a) and (b), the characteristic performance is effected by the party providing the goods and services, leading to the same result as a combined application of Article 4(1)(a) and (b) would.[518] More difficult is the case where the different points of Article 4(1) point in different directions. In the case of such a contract consisting of a bundle of rights and obligations capable of being characterised as falling within more than one of the specified types of

---

[507] *Apple Corps Ltd v Apple Computer Inc* [2004] EWHC 768 (Ch) at [50]–[51], [2004] IL Pr 34.

[508] *Print Concept GmbH v GEW (EC) Ltd* [2001] EWCA Civ 352 at [34], [2002] CLC 352.

[509] *Iran Continental Shelf Oil Co v IRI International Corpn* [2002] EWCA Civ 1024 at [24], [2004] 2 CLC 696.

[510] Unless one wants to apply Art 4(1)(b) on provision of services.

[511] *Samcrete Egypt Engineers and Contractors SAE v Land Rover Exports Ltd* [2001] EWCA Civ 2019 at [38], [2002] CLC 533. See also the Giuliano and Lagarde Report, p 21; *Bloch v Soc Lima* (Versailles 14e ch, Feb 6 1991) [1992] JCP 21972. See also *RZB v NBG* [1999] 1 Lloyd's Rep 408 at 413—breach of a warranty.

[512] *Opthalmic Innovations International (United Kingdom) Ltd v Opthalmic Innovations International Inc* [2004] EWHC 2948 Ch at [53], [2005] IL Pr 109.

[513] [1994] 2 Lloyd's Rep 87.

[514] Ibid, at 92. For the characteristic performance in relation to a bank account, see *Sierra Leone Telecommunications Co Ltd v Barclays Bank plc* [1998] 2 All ER 821; discussed infra, p 739.

[515] Supra, at 93.

[516] *Marconi Communications International Ltd v PT Pan Indonesia Bank Ltd TBK* [2005] EWCA Civ 422 at [54] and [59], [2007] 2 Lloyd's Rep 72; *Taurus Petroleum Ltd v State Oil Marketing Co of the Ministry of Oil, Republic of Iraq* [2013] EWHC 33494 (Comm) at [16]–[18], [2015] EWCA Civ 835 at [35].

[517] Magnus in *European Commentaries on Private International Law*, Art 4 para 161, p 310.

[518] See (on the Rome Convention) *Iran Continental Shelf Oil Co v IRI International Corpn* [2002] EWCA Civ 1024 at [19], [2004] 2 CLC 696.

contract, the characteristic performance of the contract should be determined having regard to its centre of gravity.[519]

Criticism   A number of criticisms can be levelled at the concept of characteristic performance and at the way it has been defined in the Giuliano and Lagarde Report. This criticism is also relevant for the Regulation's combination of fixed rules for specific contracts and the general characteristic performance rule, as the rules of the Regulation are less flexible than the presumptions found in the Convention, which amplifies any deficiencies in the design of these provisions.

First, there are some contracts which cannot be fitted easily within the concept. Letters of credit are an example. Article 4(2) assumes the ability to identify a single party charged with the single performance characteristic of the contract.[520] But with a letter of credit there are a number of autonomous bilateral contracts and it is desirable that each contractual relationship arising in the course of the transaction has the same governing law.[521] Even worse, there are some contracts that cannot be fitted at all within the concept. With a contract of barter it is difficult, if not impossible, to say that one party's performance is more characteristic of the contract than the other's.[522] The same is true with complex contracts for the commercial exploitation of intellectual property rights.[523] It was not possible to identify the characteristic performance of a trade mark agreement under which each party had to do (or refrain from doing) the same acts vis à vis the other (ie using their marks in their respective defined fields of use).[524] However, the Regulation allows for this by providing in Article 4(4) that, if neither a fixed rule applies nor the characteristic performance can be determined, the law of the country with which the contract is most closely connected shall apply.

Secondly, the definition of characteristic performance in terms of the performance for which payment is due does not stand up well to close scrutiny. The payment of money was presumably rejected as the characteristic performance because this is a common feature of many contracts and therefore fails to distinguish between different types of contract. Nonetheless, there are some contracts where the payment of money is arguably the essence of the obligation, for example contracts of pledge or hire-purchase.[525] The Working Group qualified their statement about the payment of money by saying that this is not *usually*[526] the essence of the obligation. The payment of money can thus, in unusual cases, constitute the characteristic performance. For example, the characteristic performance of a reinsurance contract has been described as being the making of payment in the event of a claim.[527]

Thirdly, the effect of generally denying that the payment of money constitutes the essence of the contract is to favour the seller of goods over the buyer. This has been justified on the basis

---

[519] Recital (19) of the Regulation.

[520] The *Marconi* case, supra, at [61].

[521] Ibid.

[522] *Caledonia Subsea Ltd v Micoperi SRL* 2002 SLT 1022 at [21]; *Apple Corps Ltd v Apple Computer Inc* [2004] EWHC 768 (Ch) at [54], [2004] IL Pr 34. See the representations of the German Government in Case 266/85 *Shenavai v Kreischer* [1987] ECR 239 at 255.

[523] Wadlow [1997] 1 EIPR 11 at 14; see generally Fawcett and Torremans, paras 14.61–14.66, 14.100– 14.101, 14.110–14.115.

[524] *Apple Corps Ltd v Apple Computer Inc* [2004] EWHC 768 (Ch) at [52]–[55], [2004] IL Pr 34.

[525] Collins (1976) 25 ICLQ 35 at 48; see also Diamond, op cit, p 274. But see the Giuliano and Lagarde Report, p 21. See also *Halpern v Halpern* [2007] EWCA Civ 291 at [28], [2007] 2 Lloyd's Rep 56—action to enforce compromise agreement allegedly entered into by executors.

[526] At p 20.

[527] *Dornach Ltd v Mauritius Union Assurance Co Ltd* [2006] EWCA Civ 389 at [41], [2006] 2 Lloyd's Rep 475. For another example see *Ark Therapeutics plc v True North Capital Ltd* [2005] EWHC 1585 (Comm) at [55], [2006] 1 All ER (Comm) 138.

that the seller's performance is generally more complicated and to a greater extent regulated by rules of law than that of the buyer.[528] However, it is questionable whether this is sufficient to justify completely ignoring the buyer's performance in most cases.

Fourthly, in terms of economic strength, the large enterprise, the manufacturer of goods, the provider of services (such as banks and insurance companies) and the professional is favoured against the other party who may well be in a weaker economic position.[529] It is curious to find a pro-manufacturer stance being taken in a Regulation which is sufficiently concerned about protecting weaker parties to have special rules for passengers, consumers, employees and policyholders of insurance.

(iii) Article 4(4): Closest connection as a residual rule
The criticism of Articles 4(1) and (2) reveals a possible problem in those cases where the law applicable cannot be determined under Article 4(1) or (2). This problem arises where the contract is none of those for which there is a fixed rule under Article 4(1) or where the elements of the contract would be covered by more than one of points (a) to (h) of Article 4(1)—so that Article 4(1) does not apply—*and* the performance of the contract which is characteristic of the contract cannot be identified under Article 4(2), so that Article 4(2) does not apply.[530] The same problem arose under Article 4 of the Convention and the solution adopted under the Regulation[531] is the same one, namely that the contract shall be governed by the law of the country with which it is most closely connected. In such cases there will be the usual problems that arise under an objective approach which seeks to localise the contract. The court will have to ascertain all the connections with the different countries, give weight to these, and, if they are evenly balanced between two countries, find one especially important connection which tips the balance in favour of one country.[532] In order to determine that country, account should be taken, inter alia, of whether the contract in question has a very close relationship with another contract or contracts.[533] Under Article 4(4) the court has to ascertain the law of the country,[534] rather than the system of law with which the contract is most closely connected,[535] but in most cases the difference between these two formulations will not be significant.[536]

(iv) Article 4(3): Escape clause
The escape clause under the Rome Convention   Under the Rome Convention, there were different views concerning the relationship of the general presumption in Article 4(2) and

---

[528] See Fletcher, op cit, p 163.
[529] For attempts to justify this, see Lagarde (1981) 22 VAJ Int L 91 at 97 n 32. See also Vischer in Lipstein (ed), *Harmonization of Private International Law by the E.E.C.* p 28; Lando (1987) 24 CMLR 159, at 202 et seq.
[530] For examples see supra, pp 732–4.
[531] Art 4(4) of the Regulation.
[532] See *Apple Corps Ltd v Apple Computer Inc* [2004] EWHC 768 (Ch) at [61]–[64], [2004] IL Pr 34 (on Art 4(1) of the Rome Convention). For a list of indicators of the closest connection, see Magnus in *European Commentaries on Private International Law*, Art 4 paras 205–28, pp 325–31.
[533] Recital (21) of the Regulation.
[534] For the definition of country see Art 22, discussed supra, p 696.
[535] See North, *Private International Law Problems in Common Law Jurisdictions* (1993), p 127, who suggests that the word "country" instead of "system of law" in the closest connection test under the Convention may make the terminology of a contract a less important factor; cf Dicey, Morris and Collins, para 32-073: "distinction made little practical difference".
[536] In a case such as *James Miller & Partners Ltd v Whitworth Street Estates (Manchester) Ltd* [1970] AC 583, the distinction between "country" and "system of law" may be relevant. In this case, the form, style and legal language of the contract (use of a standard form provided by the Royal Institute of British Architects) pointed towards English law. If the formulation of the test referred to the system of law you would expect

the escape clause in Article 4(5).[537] These differences related to the weight to be given to the presumption and to the significance of the place of performance by the characteristic performer when it came to evidence in favour of displacement. On one end of the scale, the attitude in some English cases was that the escape clause of Article 4(5) "formally makes the presumption very weak".[538] The presumption was displaced already if the court considered that it was not appropriate to apply it in the circumstances of the case, in particular where the place of performance differed from the place of business of the party whose performance is characteristic of the contract.[539] In this situation, displacement in practice meant applying the law of the place of performance by the characteristic performer, rather than the law of the place of business of the characteristic performer.[540] This struck at the heart of Article 4(2) because it favoured the place of performance over the place of business. While other decisions have given more weight to the presumption and less to the place of performance,[541] English courts have been regarded as those most ready to apply the escape clause of Article 4(5). On the other end of the scale, the Dutch Supreme Court in *Société Nouvelle des Papeteries de l'Aa v Machinefabriek BOA*[542] held that the presumption is of great weight and should only be rebutted in exceptional cases, that Article 4(2) was the main rule not Article 4(1), and that the law identified by the presumption prevailed unless it had no real significance as a connecting factor.[543] The Dutch approach has been rejected by the Court of Appeal in England

---

English law to be the applicable law. However, all other factors in the case (such as the place of performance for both parties) pointed strongly towards Scotland. This would appear to be the "country" with which the contract had the closest connections. Under the proper law of the contract approach, connection with the system of law was more commonly required, although two Law Lords in the *James Miller* case combined the two tests.

[537] See *Definitely Maybe (Touring) Ltd v Marek Lieberberg Konzertagentur GmbH* [2001] 1 WLR 1745 at [9]–[15]; *Caledonia Subsea Ltd v Micoperi SRL* 2002 SLT 1022 and Hill (2004) 53 ICLQ 325, 339–50; Atrill (2004) 53 ICLQ 549; the case notes by Briggs in (2001) 72 BYBIL 465 and (2002) 73 BYBIL 473.

[538] *Crédit Lyonnais v New Hampshire Insurance Co* [1997] 2 Lloyd's Rep 1 at 5, CA. See also *Bank of Baroda v Vysya Bank* [1994] 2 Lloyd's Rep 87, 93.

[539] The courts followed the proposition in Dicey and Morris (12th edn, 1993), pp 1137–8, now Dicey, Morris and Collins, para 32-080 in that respect.

[540] This is what happened in *Bank of Baroda v Vysya Bank* [1994] 2 Lloyd's Rep 87, 93. Similarly, in *Definitely Maybe (Touring) Ltd v Marek Lieberberg Konzertagentur GmbH* [2001] 1 WLR 1745 at [12], [15], Fentiman [2002] CLJ 50, Article 4(5) was applied where the claimant characteristic performer, which provided the services of the pop group Oasis, was located in England whereas the place of characteristic performance was in Germany (where Oasis were to perform). See also on letters of credit *Trafigura Beheer BV v Kookmin Bank Co* [2005] EWHC 2350 (Comm); *Trafigura Beheer BV v Kookmin Bank Co* [2006] EWHC 1921 (Comm) at [48]; *Marconi Communications International Ltd v PT Pan Indonesia Bank Ltd TBK* [2005] EWCA Civ 422 at [44], [61], [63], [66], [2005] 2 All ER (Comm) 325. For a common law case following *Bank of Baroda* see *Habib Bank Ltd v Central Bank of Sudan* [2006] EWHC 1767 (Comm), [2006] 2 Lloyd's Rep 412. For an example of displacement which was regarded as obvious, see *American Motorists Insurance Co (Amico) v Cellstar Corpn* [2003] EWCA Civ 206 at [47], [2003] IL Pr 22.

[541] *Samcrete Egypt Engineers and Contractors SAE v Land Rover Exports Ltd* [2001] EWCA Civ 2019, [2002] CLC 533 at [41], [45]. Followed in *Marconi Communications International Ltd v PT Pan Indonesia Bank Ltd TBK* [2005] EWCA Civ 422 at [44], [2005] 2 All ER (Comm) 325; *Caledonia Subsea Ltd v Micoperi SRL* 2002 SLT 1022 (per Lord President Cullen), but cf the support for the Dutch approach by Lords Cameron and Marnoch (infra, pp 736–7). For a narrower understanding of Art 4(5) of the Convention see also *Ennstone Building Products Ltd v Stanger Ltd* [2002] EWCA Civ 916, [2002] 1 WLR 3059 at [42]. See also *Opthalmic Innovations International (United Kingdom) Ltd v Opthalmic Innovations International Inc* [2004] EWHC 2948 Ch at [53], [2005] IL Pr 109; *Armstrong International Ltd v Deutsche Bank Securities Inc* QBD, 11 July 2003 (unreported) at [20]; *Iran Continental Shelf Oil Co v IRI International Corpn* [2002] EWCA Civ 1024 at [90], [2004] 2 CLC 696.

[542] 25 September, NJ (1992) No 750, RvdW (1992) No 207; translated into English by Struycken [1996] LMCLQ 18. For French discussion of Art 4(5) see *Bloch v Soc Lima SpA* (Versailles 14e ch, 6 February 1991) [1992] JCP 21972.

[543] The Dutch Supreme Court refused to apply Article 4(5) to rebut the presumption that Dutch law applied, even though the only connection with the Netherlands was that it was the place of business of the

as being too rigid.[544] However, it has been approved by a majority (Lords Cameron and Marnoch) in the First Division of the Court of Session in Scotland in *Caledonia Subsea Ltd v Micoperi SRL*.[545] The presumption in Article 4(2) was said to be a strong one,[546] which could only be displaced in *exceptional* cases.[547] The place of performance was regarded as only one of a number of factors to be assessed in the exercise of Article 4(5),[548] playing a subordinate role as a circumstance in fixing the applicable law.[549]

After the adoption of the Rome I Regulation, the Court of Justice held that the presumptions may be disregarded not only where they do not have any genuine connecting value. In view of the primary objective of Article 4 of the Convention to apply the law of the country with which it is most closely connected,[550] the Court of Justice advocated a two-step approach: In the interest of foreseeability and legal certainty, the court must always start to determine the applicable law on the basis of the presumptions.[551] In a second step, the court may refrain from application of the presumptions where it is clear from the circumstances as a whole that the contract is more closely connected with a country other than that identified on the basis of the presumptions.[552] In this second step, the court must compare the connections existing between the contract and, on the one hand, the country in which the party who effects the characteristic performance has his or its habitual residence at the time of conclusion of the contract and, on the other, another country with which the contract is closely connected.[553] In other words, the court must conduct an overall assessment of all the objective factors characterising the contractual relationship and determine which of those factors are, in its view, most significant. Significant connecting factors to be taken into account include the presence of a close connection between the contract in question with another contract or contracts which are, as the case may be, part of the same chain of contracts, and the place of delivery of the goods, being the place of performance of the obligation characteristic for the transport contract in question.[554]

---

person whose performance was characteristic of the contract, whereas many elements of the case linked the contract to France, including the fact that performance of the contract took place there.

[544] The *Samcrete* case, supra, at [42]; the *Marconi* case, supra, at [48].

[545] 2002 SLT 1022 (per Lords Cameron and Marnoch). Lord President Cullen approved the approach in the *Sancrete* case, supra, at [41]. But see the analysis of Lord Cameron's judgment by the Court of Appeal in *Marconi Communications International Ltd v PT Pan Indonesia Bank Limited TBK* [2005] EWCA Civ 422 at [48], [2005] 2 All ER (Comm) 325. See also *William Grant v Marie Brizard et Roger International SA* 1998 SC 536; *Krupp Uhde GmbH v Weir Westgarth Ltd*, 31 May 2002 (unreported) (Lord Eassie).

[546] The *Caledonia Subsea* case, supra, (per Lord Marnoch). See also Lord Cameron.

[547] Ibid (per Lord Cameron). See also Lord Marnoch—"very special circumstances".

[548] Ibid.

[549] Ibid (per Lord Cameron). Cf *Ferguson Shipbuilders Ltd v Voith Hydro GmbH & Co AG* 2000 SLT 229 at 232.

[550] Case C-133/08 *Intercontainer Interfrigo SC (ICF) v Balkenende Oosthuizen BV and MIC Operations BV* [2009] ECR I-9687 at [60].

[551] Case C-133/08 *Intercontainer Interfrigo SC (ICF) v Balkenende Oosthuizen BV and MIC Operations BV* [2009] ECR I-9687 at [62]; Case C-305/13 *Haeger & Schmidt GmbH v Mutuelles du Mans assurances IARD* ECLI:EU:C:2014:2320 at [46].

[552] Case C-133/08 *Intercontainer Interfrigo SC (ICF) v Balkenende Oosthuizen BV and MIC Operations BV* [2009] ECR I-9687 at [62]–[63]. On the parallel escape clause for employment contracts in Art 6(2) of the Convention, see also Case C-64/12 *Anton Schlecker v Melitta Josefa Boedeker* ECLI:EU:C:2013:551 at [39]–[42].

[553] Case C-305/13 *Haeger & Schmidt GmbH v Mutuelles du Mans assurances IARD* ECLI:EU:C:2014:2320 at [48].

[554] Case C-305/13 *Haeger & Schmidt GmbH v Mutuelles du Mans assurances IARD* ECLI:EU:C:2014:2320 at [49] with reference to Recital (20) of the Rome I Regulation.

The escape clause under the Rome Regulation The diverging views under the Rome Convention, in particular the little weight given to the presumption of Article 4(2) were a concern also for the Commission in the preparation of the Rome I Regulation.[555] They prompted the pendulum to swing in the opposite direction: Under the original proposal for a Regulation the rules in Article 4(1) and (2) were fixed ones with no exception which would allow the rules to be disregarded if it appears from the circumstances as a whole that the contract was more closely connected with another country. The desirability of achieving certainty in the law was given overriding importance, at the price of total inflexibility. This was subject to criticism,[556] and it is welcome to see that Article 4(3) of the final Regulation contains a flexible let-out[557] stating that "Where it is clear from all the circumstances of the case that the contract is manifestly more closely connected with a country other than that indicated in paragraphs 1 or 2, the law of that other country shall apply." When applying this escape clause, account should be taken, inter alia, of whether the contract in question has a very close relationship with another contract or contracts.[558] The onus is on the party relying on Article 4(3) to establish that it is a proper case for disregarding Article 4(1) or (2).[559] It is not enough to show that the contract is more closely connected, it has to be "manifestly" more closely connected. The addition of the word "manifestly" (and the elevation of the criteria in Articles 4(1) and (2) to tests from mere presumptions) is doubtless designed to underscore the exceptional nature of this escape clause,[560] which is intended to be a narrower one than that under Article 4(5) of the Rome Convention. This can be regarded as an acceptable compromise which reconciles the needs of certainty and flexibility.[561] The English courts have thus rightly concluded that the "new language and structure suggests a higher threshold, which requires that the cumulative weight of the factors connecting the contract to another country must clearly and decisively outweigh the desideratum of certainty in applying the relevant test in Article 4.1 or 4.2".[562] In view of the difference between Convention and Regulation, the case law on the escape clause of the Rome Convention must be used with caution. What may be applicable from the earlier case law is the requirement of an overall assessment of all the objective factors characterising the contractual relationship.[563] However,

---

[555] See Green paper on the conversion of the Rome Convention of 1980 on the law applicable to contractual obligations into a Community instrument and its modernisation COM (2002) 654 final, pp 25–6; on the legislative history see Magnus in *European Commentaries on Private International Law*, Art 4 paras 8–14, pp 270–2.

[556] See Dutson (2006) 122 LQR 374 and (2006) IFLR 36; Max Planck Institute (2007) 71 Rabels Zeitschrift 225, 258.

[557] Originally introduced in the compromise package of the Presidency of 13 April 2007, agreed by the Council, 8022/07 JUSTCIV 73 CODEC 306. See also Recital (16): The courts should, however, retain a degree of discretion to determine the law that is most closely connected to the situation.

[558] Recital (20) of the Regulation. See *Molton Street Capital LLP v Shooters Hill Capital Partners LLP* [2015] EWHC 3419 (Comm) at [105(2)]: proper law above and below a contract in a chain of contracts of sale "is not a strong connecting factor to the proper law of that contract, at least where the proper law of those other contracts is based on the location of the seller or closest connection of those contracts with England (different considerations might apply in the case of an express choice of law known to the parties)".

[559] *Definitely Maybe (Touring) Ltd v Marek Lieberberg Konzertagentur GmbH* [2001] 1 WLR 1745 at [15]; *Caledonia Subsea Ltd v Micoperi SRL* 2002 SLT 1022 (per Lord Cameron) (both on Art 4(5) of the Rome Convention).

[560] See Max Planck Institute (2007) 71 Rabels Zeitschrift 225, 258; *Molton Street Capital LLP v Shooters Hill Capital Partners LLP* [2015] EWHC 3419 (Comm) at [94].

[561] See Lando and Nielsen (2007) 3 J Priv Int L 29 at 38.

[562] *Molton Street Capital LLP v Shooters Hill Capital Partners LLP* [2015] EWHC 3419 (Comm) at [94]; see also *BNP Paribas SA v Anchorage Capital Europe LLP* [2013] EWHC 3073 (Comm) at [64]: "deliberately places a high hurdle in the way of the party seeking to displace the primary rule". The threshold was not met in either of these cases, nor in *Brownlie v Four Seasons Holdings Inc* [2015] EWCA Civ 665.

[563] On this Case C-305/13 *Haeger & Schmidt GmbH v Mutuelles du Mans assurances IARD* ECLI:EU:C:2014:2320 at [48]–[49].

the threshold to overcome the rules of Article 4(1) and (2) of the Regulation is significantly higher than it was under the Convention.

(v) Habitual residence

Despite the emphasis placed on the nature of the contract or the characteristic performance of it, Article 4(1) and (2) do not apply the law of the place of performance. Instead, these Articles, as other provisions in the Regulation,[564] refer to the law of the country where the party who is to effect a certain performance of the contract has his habitual residence, or, in the case of a company, its central administration. Article 19(1) of the Regulation introduces a definition of habitual residence for a company. This provides that, for the purposes of the Regulation, "the habitual residence of companies and other bodies, corporate or unincorporated, shall be the place of central administration". Provision is then made for the situations where the contract is concluded in the course of the operations of a branch, agency or any other establishment, or if, under the contract, performance is the responsibility of such a branch, agency or establishment. In these situations, the place where the branch, agency or any other establishment is located shall be treated as the place of habitual residence.[565] Thus in a contract in relation to a bank account, performance by way of repayment of the sum deposited is effected through the branch where the account is kept. If the account is kept in England, English law will govern.[566] In a contract between a bank issuing a letter of credit and another bank confirming this, if the performance characteristic of the contract (honouring the confirmation) is effected through the confirming bank's London office, English law will govern the contract.[567] In determining whether the principal place of business is to be displaced by some other place of business, it is necessary to ascertain whether "under the contract" the characteristic performance is to be effected through that other place of business. An express or implied term must require performance in this other place so that that there would be a breach of contract if it were performed through another place.[568] It is not enough that the parties anticipated that performance would be effected through a place of business other than the principal place of business.[569] The question whether the "performance is the responsibility" of that other place of business involves looking at the type of contract involved and if the obligation of the performer is, for example, to ship the goods then the question will be whether this is arranged by that place of business.[570]

There is no definition of the habitual residence of a natural person, except for the situation where such a person is acting in the course of his business activity.[571] Article 19(1) provides

---

[564] Art 5(1), (2); Art 6(1); Art 7(2), (3)(b), (e); Art 10(2); Art 11(2), (3); (4) of the Regulation.

[565] Art 19(2) of the Regulation. For a comparable provision, see Art 4(2) Rome Convention. This approach has been criticised as a dilution of the concept of characteristic performance. It has also been questioned whether reference to a personal connecting factor such as a habitual residence is appropriate in the context of commercial contracts. See Collins (1976) 25 ICLQ 35, 45–6; cf the Giuliano and Lagarde Report, at pp 20–1; Jaffey, *Topics in Choice of Law* (1996), p 35.

[566] *Sierra Leone Telecommunications Co Ltd v Barclays Bank plc* [1998] 2 All ER 821. See also the Giuliano and Lagarde Report, p 21.

[567] *Bank of Baroda v Vysya Bank* [1994] 2 Lloyd's Rep 87 at 92. But where an Indian bank issued a letter of credit in London through an English bank, the law of India, as the place of central administration of the Indian bank, was applied under Art 4(2): ibid at 93.

[568] *Ennstone Building Products Ltd v Stanger Ltd* [2002] EWCA Civ 916 at [24]–[36], [2002] 1 WLR 3059. But cf the obiter dicta of Clarke LJ in *Iran Continental Shelf Oil Co v IRI International Corpn* [2002] EWCA Civ 1024 at [65], [2004] 2 CLC 696.

[569] The *Ennstone* case, supra, at [24]–[36].

[570] *Iran Continental Shelf Oil Co v IRI International Corpn* [2002] EWCA Civ 1024 at [64]–[76], [2004] 2 CLC 696.

[571] As under the Convention, there is no guidance as to when a contract is entered into in the course of the business activity (under the Convention: "trade or profession", Art 4(2)) of that party. See also Art 17 of the Brussels I Recast, supra, p 292, for the phrase "outside his trade or profession".

that, in this situation, the habitual residence of a natural person shall be his principal place of business. The idea of giving also an autonomous definition to the concept of the habitual residence of a company echoes the defining of the domicile of a company under the Brussels I Recast. The intention is to produce certainty in the law. It was not possible to adopt the same definition for contract choice of law as has been adopted for jurisdiction. It will be recalled that the latter definition is in terms of three alternatives.[572] Whilst it is fine for jurisdictional purposes for a company to be located in three different states, for choice of law purposes the company must be located in just one state; there cannot be three different laws applying.[573] The definition of the habitual residence of a company in terms of its place of central administration follows that contained in the Rome II Regulation on non-contractual obligations which again builds on the concept of central administration found in the Brussels I Recast.[574] When determining habitual residence, the relevant point in time is that of the conclusion of the contract,[575] because of the possibility of changes in this connecting factor. It is noticeable that, whilst provision is made for the situation where characteristic performance cannot be ascertained, there is no corresponding provision dealing with the situation where the habitual residence, etc cannot be ascertained.[576]

(vi) Severing the contract[577]

As has been seen,[578] the parties have the freedom to sever the contract when exercising their choice as to the applicable law. Under the Convention, Article 4(1) last sentence stated that the courts have the same power when determining the applicable law in the absence of choice. However, the power of severance was to be exercised by the courts "as seldom as possible".[579] The Giuliano and Lagarde Report gave, as examples, joint ventures and complex contracts.[580] Under the Regulation, Article 4—in contrast to Article 3—no longer contemplates that different parts of the contract may be governed by different laws, which seems to suggest that severance is no longer possible in the absence of choice of law.

(iii) Special contracts

In general, the Regulation applies the same rules regardless of the type of contract involved. Nonetheless, it acknowledges that particular contracts can produce special problems. More particularly, there are two groups of special rules in the Regulation. As has been seen,[581] the special rules in Article 4(1) for sale of goods, provision of services, immovable property,[582] franchise and distribution contracts, sale of goods by auction, and contracts concluded in a multilateral trading

---

[572] See Art 63(1) of the Brussels I Recast, discussed supra, pp 200–2.

[573] Recital (39) of the Regulation.

[574] Art 23 of Rome II; discussed infra, p 802; the concept of central administration in Art 63(1) Brussels I Recast is discussed supra, p 201.

[575] Art 19(3) of the Regulation; Art 4(2) Rome Convention.

[576] The preliminary draft Convention contained such a provision in Art 4.

[577] See generally, Diamond (1986) IV Hague Recueil 236, 285–7; Pryles in *Contract Conflicts*, pp 323, 334 et seq; Nygh (1995) 251 Hague Recueil 269, 347–8; Kaye, pp 475–7.

[578] Supra, pp 707–9.

[579] The Giuliano and Lagarde Report, at p 23; Case C-133/08 *Intercontainer Interfrigo SC (ICF) v Balkenende Oosthuizen BV and MIC Operations BV* [2009] ECR I-9687 at [43]. Severance was only permitted where there were a number of parts to the contract, which could be regarded as independent of each other, ibid at [45]. For example, the rules relating to the prescription of a right must fall under the same legal system as that applied to the corresponding obligation, ibid at [47].

[580] The Giuliano and Lagarde Report, at p 23. An English example was *Libyan Arab Foreign Bank v Bankers Trust Co* [1989] QB 728; Carter (1989) 60 BYBIL 502 (a pre-Convention case): Staughton J held that a single banking contract relating to bank accounts in New York and London was governed in part by New York law and in part by English law (as regards the plaintiff's London account).

[581] Supra, pp 724–31.

[582] See also Art 11(5) concerning form.

system and in Article 5(1) for carriage of goods are only concerned with ascertaining the applicable law in the absence of choice. When it comes to carriage of passengers,[583] consumer contracts,[584] insurance contracts,[585] and individual employment contracts,[586] the Regulation goes further and, in Articles 5(2)–8, introduces special choice of law rules which are concerned with both choice of law and the applicable law in the absence of choice.

(a) Consumer and employment contracts

The aim of the special rules for consumer[587] and employment contracts[588] is to provide protection for the consumer and the employee.[589] The way this is done is by, first, ensuring that the protection given to the consumer or employee by provisions in domestic law that cannot be derogated from by agreement[590] is not thwarted by the parties' choice of the applicable law.[591] Secondly, in the absence of choice pre-eminence is given to the law of the consumer's habitual residence and the employee's habitual place for carrying out work in performance of the contract.[592] Finally, the rules in the Regulation dealing with the issue of formal validity make special provision for consumer contracts[593] and contracts for immovable property.[594] In general, the Rome I Regulation retained the means for providing protection

---

[583] Art 5(2). See Schulze in *Rome Regulations: Commentary*, Art 5, pp 127 et seq.

[584] Art 6; see also Art 11(4) concerning form. The definition of a consumer contract is similar to that in Art 17 of the Brussels I Recast (discussed supra, pp 292–3), see Recital (24) of the Rome I Regulation; *Rayner v Davies* [2002] EWCA Civ 1880, [2003] IL Pr 15. See Hartley in *Contract Conflicts*, pp 111 et seq; (1997) 266 Hague Recueil 341, 370–3; Morse (1992) 41 ICLQ 1, 2–11; Kaye, pp 203–20; Hill, *Cross-Border Consumer Contracts* (2008), Chapter 12; Plender and Wilderspin, Chapter 9; Calliess in *Rome Regulations: Commentary*, Art 6, pp 154 et seq. See generally on choice of law, consumers and e-commerce: Tang (2007) 3 J Priv Int L 113; Gillies (2007) 3 J Priv Int L 89; Tang, *Electronic Consumer Contracts in the Conflict of Laws* (2nd ed, 2015).

[585] Art 7. See Heiss (2008) 10 Yb PIL 261; Gruber in *Rome I Regulation: The Law Applicable to Contractual Obligations in Europe*, pp 109 et seq; Heinze [2009] Nederlands Internationaal Privaatrecht 445; Merrett (2009) 5 J Priv Int L 49; Gruber in *Rome Regulations: Commentary*, Art 7, pp 194 et seq. On reinsurance, see Merkin (2009) 5 J Priv Int L 69.

[586] Art 8. See Plender and Wilderspin, Chapter 11; Franzen and Gröner in *Rome Regulations: Commentary*, Art 8, pp 218 et seq; Morse in *Contract Conflicts*, at pp 143 et seq; (1992) 41 ICLQ 1, 11–21; Hartley (1997) 266 Hague Recueil 341, 373–8; Kaye, pp 221–38; Smith and Cromack (1993) 22 Industrial LJ 1; Smith and Villiers [1996] Jur Rev 167; Hoey and McArdie [2008] Jur Rev 291; Barnard (2009) 38 ILJ 122; Merrett (2010) 39 Industrial LJ 355; Scott [2010] LMCLQ 640; Merrett, *Employment Contracts in Private International Law* (2011), Chapters 3, 6–9; Grušić (2012) 75 MLR 722, *The European Private International Law of Employment* (2015), Chapters 5–8; Piñeiro, *International Maritime Labour Law* (2015), Chapter 4.

[587] Art 6. On the combination of Rome I and Rome II to define the law applicable to a consumer contract in the context of an action brought by a consumer association, see Case C-191/15 *Verein für Konsumenteninformation v Amazon EU Sàrl* ECLI:EU:C:2016:612 and infra, pp 825–6.

[588] Art 8.

[589] Recitals (23), (25), (35) of the Regulation; Case C-508/12 *Walter Vapenik v Josef Thurner* ECLI:EU:C:2013:790 at [29]. See generally on weaker parties, Nygh, *Autonomy in International Contracts* (1999), Chapter 7; for a critical assessment Rühl (2014) 10 J Priv Int L 335.

[590] An example of non-derogable rules in English law can be found in the Consumer Rights Act 2015. The provisions of Part 1 of that Act, as specified in ss 31, 47 and 57, and of Part 2 cannot be excluded or restricted in English domestic law and are thus non-derogable provisions in the sense of Art 6(2) of the Regulation. Arts 5, 6 of the Rome Convention made instead reference to "mandatory rules". The change to "provisions that cannot be derogated from by contract" avoids confusion with the concept of overriding mandatory provisions under Art 9 of the Regulation, which is narrower, cp ss 31, 47 and 57 (non-derogable provisions) with ss 32 and 74 (overriding mandatory provisions) of the Consumer Rights Act 2015.

[591] Arts 6(2), 8(1).

[592] Arts 6(1), 8(2). On the interpretation of the criterion of the country in which the employee "habitually carries out his work", see Case C-29/10 *Heiko Koelzsch v État du Grand Duchy of Luxemburg* [2011] ECR I-1595; Case C-384/10 *Jan Voogsgeerd v Navimer SA* ECLI:EU:C:2011:842; for the application of the escape clause in an employment case see Case C-64/12 *Anton Schlecker v Melitta Josefa Boedeker* ECLI:EU:C:2013:551.

[593] Art 11(4).

[594] Art 11(5).

for consumers and employees which were found in the Rome Convention.[595] Some of the terminology in relation to consumer contracts has been altered to bring this into line with the consumer jurisdiction agreement rules under the Brussels I Recast, the idea being that this is better suited to e-commerce.[596] The Regulation also excludes a number of additional contracts from the consumer protection provisions.[597] As regards individual employment contracts, the law has been amplified to deal with personnel working on-board aircraft[598] and to provide guidance as to whether an employee posted abroad is temporarily employed there.[599]

(b) Contracts of carriage and insurance contracts

More radically, Article 5 of the Rome I Regulation introduces special rules for contracts of carriage. The provision has separate rules for carriage of goods and for carriage of passengers. The choice of law rule for contracts for the carriage of goods (Article 5(1)) is in substance very similar to that contained in Article 4(4) of the Rome Convention;[600] as its predecessor, it applies only in the absence of choice of law by the parties.[601] What is new is the introduction of a special choice of law rule for carriage of passengers (Article 5(2)).[602] This restricts the parties' freedom to choose the applicable law to five designated countries, one of which is the country where the passenger has his habitual residence. In the absence of choice, the applicable law will normally be the law of the country where the passenger has his habitual residence. Where it is clear from all the circumstances of the case that the contract, in the absence of a choice of law, is manifestly more closely connected with a country other than that indicated in paragraphs 1 or 2, the law of that other country will apply.[603]

The most radical feature of the Regulation,[604] at least as regards special rules, is the introduction in Article 7[605] of special rules for insurance contracts. These special rules are intended to replace those in various insurance directives[606] and essentially reflect the position under those directives. This has the advantage of the relevant choice of law rules being contained in one instrument. Article 7 applies to insurance contracts covering large risks, whether or not the risk covered is situated in a Member State, and to all other insurance contracts covering risks situated inside the territory of the Member States; it does not apply to reinsurance

---

[595] See Arts 6 (consumer contracts) and 8 (individual employment contracts) of the Rome I Regulation which correspond to Arts 5 (certain consumer contracts) and 6 (individual employment contracts) of the Rome Convention.

[596] Art 6(1) of the Regulation. See Recitals (24) and (25) of the Regulation. But for a denial of this, see Gillies (2007) 3 J Priv Int L 89.

[597] Art 6(4)(d) and (e). Difficult definitional problems are raised in relation to exclusions for which guidance is provided by Recitals (26)–(31).

[598] Art 8(2) of the Rome I Regulation.

[599] Recital (36) of the Regulation; The Explanatory Memorandum, p 8. Further clarification of Art 8 is provided in Recitals (34) and (35).

[600] The definition of "contracts of carriage of goods" is the same as that under Art 4(4) of the Convention, see Recital (22) of the Rome I Regulation.

[601] It is therefore discussed in the context of Art 4, supra, pp 730–1.

[602] Under the Convention, contracts for the carriage of passengers were subject to the general characteristic performance presumption under Art 4(2), the Giuliano and Lagarde Report, p 22.

[603] Art 5(3) of the Rome I Regulation.

[604] A revised Rome I text, presented by the Finnish and German Presidencies on 12 December 2006, proposed bringing insurance generally within Rome I. This was not part of the original proposal for a Regulation of 2005.

[605] For further detail see Recital (33) of the Regulation.

[606] See supra, pp 703–4.

contracts.[607] Insurance contracts falling outside the special rules of Article 7 which are not excluded from the scope of the Regulation[608] will be governed by the general choice of law rules under Articles 3 and 4 of the Regulation. The general choice of law rules will also apply to reinsurance. The choice of law rules in Article 7 are complex and fall outside the scope of this book, which has previously left insurance to more specialised works.

(d) Limitations on the dominance of the applicable law

(i) Mandatory rules[609]

The concept of mandatory rules was one of the key concepts under the Convention, with no fewer than six different provisions using it.[610] Under the Regulation, the terminology has been changed to distinguish between "provisions that cannot be derogated from by agreement" in Articles 3(3), 3(4), 6(2) and 8(1) of the Regulation and "overriding mandatory provisions" under Article 9 of the Regulation,[611] a distinction which existed in substance already under the Convention. The concept of mandatory rules is a particularly difficult concept for English lawyers to apply because it is not known under English law, at least not under that name. Before turning to look at the definition of the concept and at the provisions in which the concept is used, it is important to look at the background to its introduction into the Convention.

(a) The background to the concept

In domestic contract law there are now two very different sorts of rules.[612] There are the traditional rules which are concerned with settling disputes between parties, such as the rules on consideration. There are then the more modern rules which are concerned with protecting a group of persons or the national economic system—rules that arise as the result of state interference with contracts. The concept of mandatory rules only deals with this second class of rules. Consumers and employees provide good examples of groups of persons who are given special protection under the law. There are rules controlling exemption clauses and laying down requirements in relation to hire purchase and consumer credit transactions which are designed to protect consumers. There are also rules on industrial safety and hygiene and in relation to periods of notice for dismissal which are designed to protect employees. When it comes to protecting the national economic system, rules on monopolies, anti-trust, import and export prohibitions, price controls, exchange control legislation,[613] and the regulation of estate agents[614] are all designed to serve this purpose.

---

[607] Art 7(1) of the Rome I Regulation. For the definition of large risks, see Art 7(2). See also Recital (33). For its application, see Joined Cases C-359/14 and C-475/14 *ERGO Insurance SE v If P&C Insurance AS and Gjensidige Baltic AAS v PZU Lietuva UAB DK* ECLI:EU:C:2016:40 at [58].

[608] Art 1(2)(j) of the Rome I Regulation, discussed supra, pp 703–4.

[609] See generally Hartley (1997) 266 Hague Recueil 341; (1979) 4 ELR 236; (2006) 319 Hague Recueil Ch XIII; Diamond (1986) IV Hague Recueil Ch IV; Nygh (1995) 251 Hague Recueil, Ch V; *Autonomy in International Contracts* (1999), Chapter 9; Guedj (1991) 39 AJCL 661; Kaye, Chapter 12; Knofel [1999] JBL 239; Tillman [2002] JBL 45; Wojewoda (2000) 7 Maastricht Journal of European and Comparative Law 183; Renner in *Rome Regulations: Commentary*, Art 9, pp 242 et seq; Plender and Wilderspin, Chapter 12. See in relation to international commercial arbitration: Zhilsov [1995] NILR 91; Hochistrassen [1994] J Int Arb 57. See also ALRC Rep No 58 (1992), Draft Bill, s 9(9).

[610] Arts 3(3) (the limitation on freedom of choice); 5(2) (consumer contracts); 6(1) (individual employment contracts); 7(1) (mandatory rules of another country than the forum), 7(2) (mandatory rules of the forum), and 9(6) (mandatory requirements of form for contracts on immovable property).

[611] Art 9 adopts the heading used in Art 16 of the Rome II Regulation.

[612] Vischer (1974) II Hague Recueil Ch 2; Jaffey (1984) 33 ICLQ 531 at 538 et seq.

[613] See the Giuliano and Lagarde Report, p 28; Art 9(2) infra, pp 746–51.

[614] Hartley (1997) 266 Hague Recueil 341, 404–10.

A state's interest in upholding protectionist laws may be so strong that it prohibits the parties from contracting out of such rules in a domestic situation. Going beyond this and into the realms of private international law, the state's interest in upholding certain laws may dictate that those laws must apply even though the issue is, in principle, governed by a different law selected by contract choice of law rules. An exception to the normal choice of law rules is thereby created. This sort of exception was well known in a number of Member States before the Rome Convention. The Giuliano and Lagarde Report[615] referred to the Dutch decision in the *Alnati* case[616] which is a predecessor of Article 7(1) of the Convention (the general provision dealing with mandatory rules of a foreign country).[617] In *Alnati*, the Dutch Supreme Court said that there could be cases when the interest of a foreign state in having its law applied outside its territory was so great that the Dutch courts should take this into account and give priority to the application of such provisions in preference to the law of another state chosen by the parties. In England, the Unfair Contract Terms Act 1977 with its provisions restricting the parties' freedom to choose the applicable law[618] was considered as an example of what in English law is called an overriding statute,[619] ie a statute that overrides normal choice of law rules so as to apply the rules in the statute, even though the contract is not governed by English law. Thus the parties may have chosen French law to govern the contract, but in certain circumstances the controls on exemption clauses contained in the 1977 Act will still apply. The Working Group was concerned to retain this sort of exception in the Rome Convention.

(b) The definition of (overriding) mandatory rules

(i) The definition of mandatory rules under the Rome Convention[620]

Under the Rome Convention, mandatory rules were defined in Article 3(3) as rules "which cannot be derogated from by contract". At first sight, this definition seemed to apply universally to all of the Convention's six provisions on mandatory rules,[621] an impression that was in fact untrue, because in substance there were two different forms of mandatory rules found in the Convention.[622]

First, there was the basic wide type of mandatory rule, where all that has to be shown is that the definition of a mandatory rule is satisfied, ie under the law of the country with whose rule one is concerned, the rule cannot be derogated from by contract.[623] Articles 3(3),[624] 5(2),[625] and 6(1)[626] of the Convention were all concerned with this basic wide type of mandatory rule. These mandatory rules operated merely as a limitation on the freedom to choose

---

[615] At p 26.

[616] Nederlandse Jurisprudentie 1967, p 3; Rev Crit 1967, p 522; though later Dutch decisions seem to have resiled from this approach. See generally Schultsz (1983) 47 Rabels Zeitschrift 267; Hartley, op cit, at 356–9.

[617] Now Art 9(3) of the Regulation.

[618] S 27(2). For consumer contracts, the Unfair Contract Terms Act has been superseded by the Consumer Rights Act 2015, s 74.

[619] See the 11th edn of this book (1987), pp 466–71. See also *DR Insurance Co v Central National Insurance Co* [1996] 1 Lloyd's Rep 74 at 82—Insurance Companies Acts regarded as overriding statutes.

[620] Criticised by Dickinson (2007) 3 J Priv Int L 53, 66–8.

[621] Arts 3(3) (the limitation on freedom of choice); 5(2) (consumer contracts); 6(1) (individual employment contracts); 7(1) (mandatory rules of another country than the forum), 7(2) (mandatory rules of the forum), and 9(6) (mandatory requirements of form for contracts on immovable property).

[622] The French version of the Convention referred to "dispositions impératives" (see Art 3(3)) and to "Lois de police" (see the heading to Art 7). See generally Kaye, pp 72 et seq.

[623] But see the obiter dicta in *Caterpillar Financial Services Corpn v SNC Passion* [2004] EWHC 569 (Comm) at [31]–[44], [2004] 2 Lloyd's Rep 99, which should be regarded as wrong.

[624] Today Arts 3(3), (4) of the Regulation; supra, pp 711–14.

[625] Today Art 6(2) of the Regulation.

[626] Today Art 8(1) of the Regulation.

the applicable law, namely in purely internal (domestic) cases, as well as in consumer and employment contracts. Here, the effect given to the mandatory rule under the Convention was merely to override the parties' freedom to choose the applicable law.

Secondly, there were the narrower overriding mandatory rules. With these, it must not only be shown that the rule is a mandatory one, within the above definition of being non-derogable, but also that under the law of the country with whose rules you are concerned, the mandatory rule overrides the applicable law. Articles 7(1), 7(2)[627] and 9(6)[628] all required this additional element.[629] Naturally, a rule falling within this narrower type of mandatory rule will automatically come within the wider type as well. If the parties' right expressly to choose the governing law is taken away, it follows that the domestic rule is one that cannot be contracted out of. With mandatory rules under Articles 7(1), 7(2) and 9(6) the effect given to the rule under the Convention was much greater: the mandatory rule was able to override all of the rules on the applicable law under the Convention (including the rules on the applicable law in the absence of choice).

(ii) The definition under the Rome I Regulation
Using the same expression for two very different concepts caused confusion. In order to avoid such confusion, the Rome I Regulation abandoned the term "mandatory rules" altogether. Instead, different terms were introduced for the two different types of "mandatory rules". For the first category, Article 3(3) of the Regulation (as do Articles 3(4), 6(2), 8(1), 11(5) of the Regulation)[630] refers now merely "to provisions which cannot be derogated from by agreement".[631] In order to determine whether rules of a particular country are "provisions which cannot be derogated from by agreement", reference must be made to the law of that country. For example, if an English court is concerned to ascertain whether a French domestic rule is a mandatory one, it has to ask whether under French law that particular rule cannot be derogated from by contract. This definition is asking simply whether the parties can agree to depart from the rule in *domestic* cases.

For the second category, which is relevant only for the purposes of Article 9, Article 9(1) of the Regulation introduces the term "overriding mandatory provisions". This term has to be distinguished from the expression "provisions which cannot be derogated from by agreement" in that it should be construed more restrictively.[632] Thus, all "overriding mandatory

---

[627] Art 7(2) dealt with the mandatory rules of the forum; today Art 9(2) of the Regulation, infra, pp 746–51. Art 7(1) was concerned with the mandatory rules of a foreign country; today Art 9(3) of the Regulation, infra, pp 751–2. Section 2(2) of the Contracts (Applicable Law) Act 1990 provided that Article 7(1) should not have the force of law in the United Kingdom. See the Solicitor-General, HC Second Reading Committee, 20 June 1990, col 4; Lord-Advocate, HL 12 December 1989, vol 513, cols 1258, 1271. See earlier Collins (1976) 25 ICLQ 35, 49–51; for a more extreme criticism in terms of disapproval of statutory regulation of contracts, see Mann in Lipstein (ed), *Harmonization of Private International Law by the E.E.C.*, p 31. Germany also has not included Art 7(1) in its legislation incorporating the Convention into its private international law. Reservations have also been entered by Ireland, Latvia, Luxembourg, Portugal and Slovenia. Cf ALRC Rep No 58 (1992), Draft Bill, s 9(9).

[628] Art 11(5) of the Regulation.

[629] Thus under Article 7(2) mandatory rules were applied in "a situation where they are mandatory irrespective of the law otherwise applicable to the contract". Under Article 7(1) it had to be shown that "those [mandatory] rules must be applied whatever the law applicable to the contract". Under Article 9(6) the mandatory requirements had to be "imposed irrespective of the country where the contract is concluded and irrespective of the law governing the contract".

[630] Supra, pp 711–13.

[631] Art 11(5) of the Regulation also refers to "requirements imposed irrespective of the country where the contract is concluded and irrespective of the law governing the contract". Art 11(5) is discussed infra, pp 760–1.

[632] Recital (37).

provisions" will be "provisions which cannot be derogated from by agreement", but it requires something more to qualify as "overriding mandatory": the provision must not only be non-derogable under a country's law, but also be regarded as crucial by that country for safeguarding its public interests. Article 9(1) of the Regulation defines overriding mandatory provisions as "provisions the respect for which is regarded as crucial by a country for safeguarding its public interests, such as its political, social or economic organisation, to such an extent that they are applicable to any situation falling within their scope, irrespective of the law otherwise applicable to the contract under this Regulation". This definition is inspired by the decision of the Court of Justice in *Arblade*,[633] which was concerned with the relationship between national mandatory provisions of Member States and the EC Treaty. In order to respect the choice of law made by the parties under Article 3, the concept of "overriding mandatory provision" in Article 9 must be interpreted strictly.[634] It is thus the task of the national court, in the course of its assessment of whether the national law in question is an "overriding mandatory provision", to take account not only of the exact terms of that law, but also of its general structure and of all the circumstances in which that law was adopted in order to determine whether it is mandatory in nature in so far as it appears that the legislature adopted it in order to protect an interest judged to be essential by the Member State concerned.[635] The definition in Article 9(1) brings out the protectionist nature of overriding mandatory provisions. The danger of defining what these provisions are protecting is that this may restrict the use of the concept. In particular, the definition will exclude provisions which aim to protect purely private interests. The other feature that is brought out in Article 9(1) is the overriding nature of such provisions. They are applicable "irrespective of the law otherwise applicable to the contract under this Regulation" because the country regarding them as crucial requires them to be applied. This underlines the private international question of whether the rule is intended, according to the law of its country of origin, to apply regardless of the otherwise governing law.

(c) The mandatory rules of the forum

Article 9(2) states that: "Nothing in this Regulation shall restrict the application of the overriding mandatory rules of the law of the forum".[636] The opening words of Article 9(2) make it clear that this provision was inserted so that the forum could continue to apply its own mandatory rules to override contract choice of law rules even after the new regime under the Rome Convention (now Rome I Regulation) entered into force.[637] The Giuliano and Lagarde Report[638] gives some examples of the sort of protectionist domestic rules which Contracting States were anxious to preserve as overriding rules: rules on cartels, competition and restrictive practices, consumer protection and certain rules concerning carriage. Article 9(2) leads to no difficulty in identifying the country whose mandatory rules are in issue: they are solely the mandatory rules of the forum. However, it is not enough merely to show that the forum has a mandatory rule (ie a rule which cannot be derogated from by contract). It has to be shown that what is involved is an overriding mandatory provision in the narrow meaning of Article 9(1).[639]

---

[633] Case C-369/96 [1999] ECR I-8453 at [31].

[634] Case C-184/12 *United Antwerp Maritime Agencies (Unamar) NV v Navigation Maritime Bulgare* ECLI:EU:C:2013:663 at [49].

[635] Ibid, at [50].

[636] This is in substance the same as Art 7(2) of the Convention.

[637] See the Giuliano and Lagarde Report, p 28. See also the Lord Advocate, Hansard (HL) 12 December 1989, vol 513, col 1260. An analogous provision is to be found in the Hague Convention on the Law applicable to Trusts and on their Recognition: Art 16, infra, pp 1392–3.

[638] At p 28.

[639] Supra, pp 745–6 and Case C-184/12 *United Antwerp Maritime Agencies (Unamar) NV v Navigation Maritime Bulgare* ECLI:EU:C:2013:663 at [46]–[51].

(i) Mandatory statutory rules

Assuming that England is the forum, English rules expressing a strong socio-economic policy are more likely to be contained in statutes than in common law rules. Moreover, when it comes to identifying such rules this may be much easier with statutory rules than with common law rules. Unlike a common law rule, a statute may state whether it is intended to have overriding effect.[640] The statute could expressly provide that in certain situations it is to have complete overriding effect,[641] it is to have limited overriding effect, or it is to have no overriding effect. An example for a statute with limited overriding effect is—arguably[642]—the Consumer Rights Act 2015.[643] Pursuant to sections 32(1) and 74(1), most provisions of Chapter 2 of Part 1 (on contracts to supply goods to a consumer) and those of Part 2 (on unfair terms in consumer contracts) of this Act must be applied by an English court, irrespective of the parties' choice of law, if the law of a country or territory other than an EEA State is chosen by the parties to be applicable to a consumer contract, but the consumer contract has a close connection with the United Kingdom.[644] Thus, the overriding effect is limited to scenarios where the parties have made a choice of law; it does not apply where the applicable law is determined in the absence of choice. Alternatively, the statute may say nothing about its overriding effect, in which case it is a matter of statutory construction as to whether, in particular situations, it is intended to have overriding effect. This latter, most difficult possibility will now be examined.

The statute has no express provision on its overriding effect but has a provision on its territorial scope   In cases where a statute says nothing about its overriding effect it is a matter of construction of the statute to ascertain whether it is intended to have overriding effect in a particular situation.[645] Drawing this inference is much easier if the statute has a provision dealing with its territorial scope, albeit whilst not spelling out explicitly whether it is intended to have overriding effect. This can be illustrated by *Boissevain v Weil*.[646] The case concerned a Defence Regulation made under the powers conferred by the Emergency Powers (Defence) Act 1939. This regulation made it an offence, subject to severe penalties, for a *British subject*[647] to carry out certain currency transactions. In the House of Lords, Lord Radcliffe declared that whether such an offence was committed could not depend on whether the law governing a loan contract was English or foreign. In other words, it was a regulation which, in the situation in the case, was construed as being of complete overriding effect. Article

---

[640] See generally on the problems of the interaction between English statutes and the Convention, Morse in *Contract Conflicts*, pp 143, 163 et seq; Collins (1976) 25 ICLQ 35, 37–8. See also Jaffey, *Topics in Choice of Law* (1996), pp 57 et seq; Dutson (1997) 60 MLR 668, 686 et seq; Reynolds [1997] LMCLQ 177; ALRC Rep No 58 (1992), pp 32–9.

[641] An example quoted for this group is the Employment Rights Act 1996, s 204, see the 14th edn of this book (2008), p 732.

[642] Where the Consumer Rights Act 2015 gives effect to provisions in EU directives which limit choice of law which disfavours the consumer, this could also be regarded as falling under Art 23, not Art 9, see infra, pp 773–4. Moreover, it could be argued that the special provision in Art 6 on consumer contracts defines under which circumstances the Member States may disregard the parties' choice of law to protect the consumer, thus ruling out any application of Art 9 for provisions which aim at protecting individual consumers.

[643] Another example is the Unfair Contract Terms Act 1977, s 27(2), see the 14th edn of this book (2008), pp 732–5. For consumer contracts, the Unfair Contract Terms Act 1977, s 27(2) has been superseded by the Consumer Rights Act 2015, s 74.

[644] Moreover, the provisions of Part 1 of that Act, as specified in ss 31, 47 and 57, and of Part 2 will be non-derogable provisions in the sense of Art 6(2) of the Regulation.

[645] See Pryles in *Contract Conflicts*, pp 331 et seq.

[646] [1949] 1 KB 482, CA; affd [1950] AC 327. See also *The Hollandia* [1983] 1 AC 565—a case on the Carriage of Goods by Sea Act 1971; cf *Mediterranean Shipping Co SA v Trafigura Beheer BV* [2007] EWCA Civ 794. The position is different in respect of the Carriage of Goods by Sea Act 1992, on which see Sing [1994] LMCLQ 280.

[647] Defence (Finance) Regulations 1939, reg 2, as amended; Emergency Powers (Defence) Act 1939, s 3(1).

9(2) would now apply, and the result would be the same under the Regulation. Similarly, in *Chiron Corpn v Organon Teknika (No 2)*,[648] the Court of Appeal held that (former) section 44 of the Patents Act 1977, sub-section (1) of which stroke down certain provisions (constituting an abuse of patent rights) in contracts relating to patents, applied regardless of whether English law governed the contract.[649] Section 44 was territorially limited to United Kingdom patents. The court was not prepared, in the light of this important restriction, to add on a further requirement that the contract had to be governed by English law.[650] Again, the result would be the same under the Regulation by virtue of Article 9(2).

The statute has no express provision as to its overriding effect and no provision on its territorial scope Many statutes say nothing about their extra-territorial scope or their overriding effect. The construction of such a statute to ascertain whether it is intended to have an overriding effect in a particular situation is especially difficult. In *English v Donnelly*[651] a Scottish court gave at least limited overriding effect to Scottish mandatory hire purchase requirements, with the result that the parties were not allowed to contract out of the statute in question by an express choice of law clause. In *Irish Shipping Ltd v Commercial Union Assurance Co plc*[652] Staughton LJ showed some concern that "The intention of Parliament could be frustrated if it were open to the parties to a contract of insurance to exclude the operation of section 1 [of the Third Parties (Rights against Insurers) Act 1930] by choosing a foreign proper law". On the other hand, in *Sayers v International Drilling Co NV*[653] the Court of Appeal did not give overriding effect to the Law Reform (Personal Injuries) Act 1948, which is concerned to protect injured employees from clauses exempting the employer from liability.[654] A majority of the Court of Appeal held that the objectively determined proper law of the contract—Dutch law—applied, according to which the exemption clause was valid.

(ii) Mandatory common law rules

Whilst in principle it is possible to have mandatory common law rules, examples are likely to be very rare because of the difficulty in identifying such rules.[655] It has been suggested[656] that in some of the cases decided at common law where the English courts have refused to apply a foreign law on grounds of public policy and have instead applied English law, eg in those where the fundamental concepts of English justice were disregarded,[657] public policy operates in a positive way, the concern being to apply English law, and, accordingly such cases should be regarded as involving an overriding mandatory provision of the forum. In other cases, it is admitted that public policy operates in a negative way, the concern being not to apply an objectionable foreign law (the effect is then that English law will apply), and it is rightly said that in such cases Article 21 of the Regulation[658] will apply rather than Article 9(2). However, it is submitted that public policy primarily operates in a negative way[659] and

---

[648] [1993] FSR 567, CA.

[649] The case concerned a contractual defence to a tort action, see infra, pp 880–3.

[650] The *Chiron Corpn* case, supra, at 572.

[651] 1958 SC 494; see also the High Court of Australia's decision in *Kay's Leasing Corpn Pty Ltd v Fletcher* (1964) 116 CLR 124.

[652] [1991] 2 QB 206.

[653] [1971] 1 WLR 1176, infra, pp 879–83. Cf *Brodin v A R Seljan* 1973 SC 213.

[654] However, the case was argued by counsel on the narrow point as to what the proper law of the contract was.

[655] See the discussion in relation to tort, infra, pp 866–8.

[656] Hartley (1997) 266 Hague Recueil 341, 351–3; Kaye, pp 245–7; Jaffey, *Topics in Choice of Law* (1996), pp 54–6.

[657] See *Kaufman v Gerson* [1904] 1 KB 591; discussed supra, p 134. For a Canadian example, see *Society of Lloyd's v Saunders* (2002) 210 DLR (4th) 519, CA (Ont).

[658] Discussed infra, pp 752–4.

[659] See Nygh (1995) 251 Hague Recueil 269, 379–80; Vischer (1992) I Hague Recueil 9, 165.

it is extremely difficult to identify with any precision cases where public policy operates in a positive way,[660] given that the consequence is that the foreign proper law was not applied. In truth, each case of public policy has a positive and negative aspect but the latter dominates. The better approach is to treat all of these cases of public policy at common law, where the foreign proper law has not been applied and instead English law has been applied, as operating in a negative way and therefore coming not within Article 9(2) but within Article 21.[661]

(iii) Mandatory rules in EU legislation and international conventions

It is not only national rules that can be mandatory. So can provisions of EU legislation.[662] This was established in *Ingmar GB Ltd v Eaton Leonard Technologies Inc*,[663] where the Court of Justice held that Articles 17 and 18 of the self-employed commercial agents Directive, which guarantee certain rights to commercial agents after termination of agency contracts,[664] were overriding mandatory provisions[665] in the sense used in Article 9(2).[666] These Articles applied even though the expressly chosen applicable law was that of California. The Court reached this conclusion in the light of the purpose of the Directive and of these Articles and in the light of Article 19, which provides that the parties may not derogate from Articles 17 and 18 to the detriment of the commercial agent. There was no express provision in the Directive on the territorial scope of these two provisions. However, looking at their purpose the Court held that Articles 17 and 18 applied where the situation was closely connected with the EU, in particular where the commercial agent carries on his activity in the territory of a Member State. These Articles would therefore apply even though the principal was established in a non-Member State country, California. On the facts, the Rome Convention did not come into play because the contract was concluded in 1989. However, it seems that the result would have been the same if the contract had been made after the Convention (and now the Regulation) came into force. The mandatory rules in the Directive[667] would then presumably have applied by virtue of Article 9(2) of the Regulation.[668] Another example of overriding mandatory provisions are the provisions of EU competition law.[669]

---

[660] Note the lack of agreement between Hartley, op cit, Kaye, op cit, and Jaffey, op cit, over examples where public policy operates in this way.

[661] See Dicey, Morris and Collins, paras 32-190–32-193.

[662] In the context of employment, see Recital (34) of the Rome I Regulation, referring to the (implementing) provisions of the posted workers Directive 96/71/EC as "overriding mandatory provisions". If EU legislation contains a choice of law rule, Art 23 Rome I Regulation will apply, see infra, pp 772–4 for examples.

[663] Case C-381/98 [2000] ECR I-9305 at [25]: "essential for the Community legal order"; Verhagen (2002) 51 ICLQ 135.

[664] Council Directive (EEC) No 86/653 of 18 December 1986 on the coordination of the laws of the Member States relating to self-employed commercial agents, OJ 1986 L 382/17; implemented in the United Kingdom by the Commercial Agents (Council Directive) Regulations 1993.

[665] Cf the position in relation to rules such as Arts 6(1) and 13 of the Directive which can be derogated from by a Member State, see the Opinion of AG Leger at [81]–[85]. It is suggested that the E-Commerce Directive also contains mandatory rules, see Fawcett, Harris and Bridge, para 21.110.

[666] See the Opinion of AG Leger at [87]–[89]. See also Art 68(6) of Directive (EU) No 2014/59 of 15 May 2014 establishing a framework for the recovery and resolution of credit institutions and investment firms, OJ 2014 L 173/190, which expressly defines its provisions as overriding mandatory provisions in the sense of Art 9.

[667] Strictly speaking the United Kingdom implementing legislation would have applied, rather than the Directive itself.

[668] See the Opinion of AG Leger at [87]–[89] and now Case C-184/12 *United Antwerp Maritime Agencies (Unamar) NV v Navigation Maritime Bulgare* ECLI:EU:C:2013:663 at [40]–[41]. This will be subject to the point that if a Directive contains choice of law rules then Art 23 of the Regulation will take it outside the Rome I Regulation.

[669] Case C-126/97 *Eco Swiss China Time Ltd v Benetton International NV* [1999] ECR I-3055 at [36]. For the impact on contract law, see the consequence of nullity under Art 101(2) TFEU.

It should be noted that Member States may also go beyond an EU directive and enact over-riding mandatory provisions by extending the scope of a directive or by choosing to make wider use of the discretion afforded by a directive, eg by offering greater protection to commercial agents than the commercial agents Directive provides for.[670] However, in deciding whether such a national extension of a directive qualifies as an overriding mandatory provision in the sense of Article 9(1) of the Regulation, the court must take into account that the law which is to be rejected in favour of the law of the forum is the law of a Member State which had transposed the underlying directive, so that a certain level of protection is already guaranteed.[671]

Finally, international conventions may also include overriding mandatory provisions. For example, the United Kingdom has entered into a number of conventions in relation to carriage. It is believed that the uniform rules which these conventions contain will, in general, be regarded as overriding mandatory provisions of the law of the forum and take effect under Article 9(2) of the Regulation.[672] However, the precedence of the uniform rules contained in these conventions over the law applicable under the Regulation could better be justified by applying Article 25 of the Regulation. While it is true that Article 25 refers only to international conventions "which lay down conflict-of-law rules relating to contractual obligations", the rules of the conventions which define their substantive, personal and territorial scope could be regarded as conflict-of-law rules in a wide sense. Such an approach would avoid applying the narrow definition of Article 9(1) to all mandatory rules in international conventions. The true reason for giving precedence to such rules is to safeguard the uniform application of the convention in all Contracting States, and this would be reflected by applying Article 25, not Article 9 of the Regulation.[673]

(iv) The effect given to mandatory rules under Article 9(2)[674]

Article 9(2) operates as an exception to the normal choice of law rules under the Regulation by giving overriding effect to mandatory rules. Obviously it overrides the rules on the applicable law under Article 3 (choice) and Article 4 (the applicable law in the absence of choice). But Article 9(2) probably has an even wider effect than this. The opening wording of Article 9(2) is that: "Nothing in this Regulation shall restrict the application of the rules of the law of the forum." This suggests that Article 9(2) should be regarded as a general exception to *all* the choice of law rules contained in the Regulation, in the same way that public policy, which is more clearly worded in this respect, provides such an exception.[675] This means that the special rules for particular issues, such as formal validity, and for special contracts will also be overriden.[676] However, there is a particular problem in relation to consumer contracts and individual employment contracts, in that there are provisions on mandatory rules contained in the special regimes set out in Articles 6 and 8. Nevertheless, Article 9(2) should be regarded as overriding the other provisions in the Regulation on mandatory rules. The result

---

[670] Case C-184/12 *United Antwerp Maritime Agencies (Unamar) NV v Navigation Maritime Bulgare* ECLI:EU:C:2013:663 at [50].

[671] Ibid, at [51].

[672] Dicey, Morris and Collins, paras 33-110–33-120.

[673] Sometimes it is also argued that international conventions aiming at substantive law harmonisation (as concluded by the Member States in the realm of their competences) generally define their own scope of application. In relation to the Rome II Regulation see Basedow (2010) 74 Rabels Zeitschrift 118, 127–8, stating that where a uniform substantive law convention applies, no "situation involving a conflict of laws" in the sense of Art 1(1) Rome II Regulation arises, which makes the EU conflict rules inapplicable.

[674] The same question of effect of mandatory provisions arises in relation to Art 9(3).

[675] See the Giuliano and Lagarde Report, p 31; infra, pp 752–4.

[676] Cf Lasok and Stone, pp 378, 383–4. See also Williams (1986) 35 ICLQ 1, 24.

is that English mandatory rules would take priority over foreign mandatory rules. This has wide implications. For example, in a case where the applicable law under Article 4 of the Regulation may be French and English law has mandatory rules, then, in principle, Article 9(2) should operate so that the English mandatory rules override the French ones. However, it must be for English law to decide whether its own mandatory rules are of such importance that they should exceptionally apply in such a case. In all cases, the overriding effect is limited to the extent required by the mandatory provision. Thus, those aspects of the contract which have nothing to do with the mandatory provision, or areas of the law in which the mandatory provision does not purport to intrude, remain to be governed by the law as determined under Articles 3 to 8 of the Regulation.[677]

(d) The mandatory rules of other countries[678]

Article 9(3) of the Regulation[679] provides that:

> Effect may be given to the overriding mandatory provisions of the law of the country where the obligations arising out of the contract have to be or have been performed, in so far as those overriding mandatory provisions render the performance of the contract unlawful. In considering whether to give effect to those provisions, regard shall be had to their nature and purpose and to the consequences of their application or non-application.

The background to this rule is that reservations by Member States in relation to particular Articles, which existed in relation to the corresponding Article 7(1) of the Convention, are in principle incompatible with a Regulation.[680] This means that if the United Kingdom were to opt in to the Regulation, its courts would for the first time have to consider giving effect to the mandatory provisions of other countries in an Article 9(3) situation. This was the most important single objection that the United Kingdom had to opting in to the Regulation. It was objected that the introduction in the United Kingdom of an Article 7(1) of the Rome Convention type of rule would create uncertainty,[681] in particular in the financial markets.[682] There has been an attempt to meet such concern by limiting the new rule in the final version of the Regulation in two major respects. First, Article 9(3) of the Regulation is only concerned with the overriding mandatory provisions of the law of "the country where the obligations arising out of the contract have to be or have been performed". This was perceived as being much more certain than the wording of Article 7(1) of the Rome Convention, with its reference to the mandatory rules of law of another country with which the situation has a close connection. And indeed, the Court of Justice has confirmed that the list, in Article 9(2) and (3) of the Rome I Regulation, of the overriding mandatory provisions to which the court of the forum may give effect is exhaustive.[683] As a consequence, overriding mandatory provisions of another country than the forum state (Article 9(2)) or the state where the obligations have to be or have been performed (Article 9(3)) cannot be applied under the Regulation.

---

[677] *Fern Computer Consultancy v Intergraph Cadworx & Analysis Solutions Inc* [2014] EWCA 2908 (Ch) at [34]; Dicey, Morris and Collins, para 32-092.

[678] See generally, Kaye, pp 248–61; note (2001) 114 Harv LR 2462; Chong (2006) 2 J Priv Int L 27; Dickinson (2007) 3 J Priv Int L 53.

[679] The original proposal for a Rome I Regulation contained the same provision as Art 7(1) of the Rome Convention which is not limited to the mandatory provisions at the place of performance.

[680] It might have been possible for the United Kingdom to negotiate a reservation to Art 9(3) but this might only have been for a limited period.

[681] See Dickinson (2007) 3 J Priv Int L 53; Dutson (2006) 122 LQR 374.

[682] See para 17.1 of the Financial Markets Law Committee's Legal assessment of the conversion of the Rome Convention to a Community instrument and the provisions of the proposed Rome I Regulation, available at <http://www.fmlc.org>.

[683] Case C-135/15 *Republik Griechenland v Grigorios Nikiforidis* ECLI:EU:C:2016:774 at [49].

What remains possible is to take into account overriding mandatory provisions of a state (other than the forum state or the state of performance) as a matter of fact, in so far as this is provided for by a substantive rule of the law that is applicable to the contract pursuant to the Regulation.[684] For example, it may be taken into account on the level of substantive contract law, eg under the doctrine of illegality or the doctrine of impossibility, that the contract violates an overriding mandatory provision of the law of a country other than the forum state or the state where performance is to take place. This, as a matter of the applicable substantive law, is not precluded by the Regulation. Secondly, Article 9(3) is only concerned with that country's overriding mandatory provisions in so far as they render the performance of the contract unlawful. Article 9(3) thus enables the English courts to deal with cases of illegality by the foreign place of performance. Such cases were a concern at common law and, because of the absence in the United Kingdom of a provision on foreign mandatory rules, were not effectively dealt with by the Rome Convention.[685]

(ii) Public policy[686]

Article 21 of the Regulation[687] is entitled "Public policy of the forum" and provides that the "application of a provision of the law of any country specified by this Regulation may be refused only if such application is manifestly incompatible with the public policy (*ordre public*) of the forum". In civil law countries *ordre public* operates as a well-established exception to normal choice of law rules, as does public policy in common law jurisdictions. Any clash between the civil and common law concepts of public policy is resolved by the reference to the application of a rule of law being "manifestly" incompatible with the public policy of the forum. This word has been regularly used in Hague Conventions on private international law in an attempt to restrain the use of the doctrine. This adds nothing as far as English law is concerned since there has long been a reluctance to invoke the public policy doctrine in this country.[688] However, for civil lawyers it makes clear that what is in issue is the narrow concept of international ordre public as opposed to the wide concept of domestic ordre public. It has to be shown that the *application* of a foreign rule of law is against the forum's public policy. The circumstances of the case have to be considered. If, for example, a contract governed by French law restrains a party from competing in *England* then the application of a French rule allowing restraint of trade would appear to be contrary to the well-known English public policy against restraint of trade because of the involvement of England. This limitation is entirely consistent with common law decisions on public policy, which normally have required some relevant connection with England which justifies English courts in invoking the public policy exception.[689] The intention then is that Article 21 will only be used in exceptional circumstances.[690] The forum's public policy includes also the fundamental rules

---

[684] Ibid, at [51]–[52].

[685] See Chong (2006) 2 J Priv Int L 27 and more generally infra, pp 770–1.

[686] See Philip (1978) II Hague Recueil 1, 55 et seq; Diamond, op cit, at 292 et seq; Moscani (1989) V Hague Recueil 9; Plender and Wilderspin, paras 12-070–12-076; Kaye, pp 345–50; Dicey, Morris and Collins, paras 32R-181–32-195. See more generally, Enonchong (1996) 45 ICLQ 633, 634–6. Public policy includes EU public policy: the Giuliano and Lagarde Report, p 38.

[687] Art 21 substitutes provision of law for rule of law, but is in substance the same as Art 16 of the Convention. The position in relation to objectionable foreign laws will therefore be the same.

[688] See the discussion of the public policy defence in relation to the recognition of foreign divorces, etc, infra, pp 1030–3.

[689] Supra, pp 134–5. The fact that an agreement also offended the public policy of the foreign place of performance could provide justification: *Lemenda Trading Co Ltd v African Middle East Petroleum Co Ltd* [1988] QB 448; Carter (1988) 59 BYBIL 356; Collier [1988] CLJ 169; *Apple Corps Ltd v Apple Computer Inc* [1992] FSR 431; *Westacre Investments Inc v Jugoimport-SPDR Holding Co Ltd* [2000] 1 QB 288, CA.

[690] The Giuliano and Lagarde Report, p 38; see also the United Kingdom submission in Case 150/80 *Elefanten Schuh GmbH v Jacqmain* [1981] ECR 1671, [1982] 3 CMLR 1.

of EU law, such as the European human rights.[691] Where the alleged offense to public policy concerns rules of EU law, this does not alter the conditions for being able to rely on the clause on public policy: It is for the national court to ensure with equal diligence the protection of rights established in national law and rights conferred by EU law.[692]

When Article 21 does apply, it provides an exception to all of the preceding choice of law rules contained in the Regulation. Presumably, it can even operate to override the provisions on mandatory rules which are themselves an exception to normal choice of law principles.[693] Thus, an English court could refuse to apply the mandatory rules of a foreign country on the basis that the application of that mandatory rule would be against English public policy. It is possible to envisage this happening in cases where a foreign mandatory rule is in conflict with an English mandatory rule.

Common law cases[694] which involved the consideration of an objectionable foreign law which was held to be contrary to our distinctive English public policy will doubtless be decided in the same way under the Regulation, using Article 21.[695] Thus the English court will continue not to enforce such contracts as those in restraint of trade, assigning a cause of action, involving a certain type of duress,[696] or contracts for prostitution, provided normally[697] that the circumstances involve a sufficient connection with England to justify this.[698] However, there was a very different category of public policy cases at common law based on the notion of the comity of nations. Thus, in one case[699] the Court of Appeal held that it would be against the comity of nations to enforce a contract, the whole object of which was to import whisky into the USA contrary to the prohibition laws of that country.[700] Such cases do not appear to fit within Article 21.[701] This is a negative provision, being concerned with a refusal to apply

---

[691] Case C-7/98 *Dieter Krombach v André Bamberski* [2000] ECR I-1935 at [25] (on the concept of public policy in the Brussels Convention, now Brussels I Recast).

[692] Case C-38/98 *Régie nationale des usines Renault SA v Maxicar SpA and Orazio Formento* [2000] ECR I-2973 at [32] (on the concept of public policy in the Brussels Convention, now Brussels I Recast).

[693] See Fletcher, *Conflict of Laws and European Community Law*, p 172.

[694] Supra, pp 135–9.

[695] But see the argument, discussed supra, p 143, that some common law cases of public policy involve mandatory rules of the forum.

[696] Normally the effect of duress depends on the law governing the contract, but acts of duress or coercion or fraud may be so outrageous that the court refuses to enforce the contract on the basis of public policy, irrespective of the governing law, *Royal Boskalis Westminster NV v Mountain* [1999] QB 674, 689, 729 (CA).

[697] For exceptions see Dicey, Morris and Collins, para 32-185.

[698] Cf *Re Colt Telecom Group plc (No 2)* [2002] EWHC 2815 (Ch), [2003] BPIR 324—no-action clause enforced.

[699] *Foster v Driscoll* [1929] 1 KB 470. English law governed the contract. However, the result doubtless would have been the same if the contract had been governed by a foreign law, according to which the contract had been enforceable. See also *Regazzoni v K C Sethia (1944) Ltd* [1956] 2 QB 490; affd [1958] AC 301; *Euro-Diam Ltd v Bathurst* [1990] 1 QB 1 at 40; *Royal Boskalis Westminster NV v Mountain* [1998] 2 WLR 538 at 555, 565; Briggs (1997) 68 BYBIL 364; *Ispahani v Bank Melli Iran* [1998] Lloyd's Rep Bank 133, (1997) Times, 29 December, CA; *Westacre Investments Inc v Jugoimport-SDPR Holding Co Ltd* [2000] 1 QB 288, CA; *Tekron Resources Ltd v Guinea Investment Co Ltd* [2003] EWHC 2577 (QB), [2004] 2 Lloyd's Rep 26; Enonchong (1996) 45 ICLQ 633 at 649–50. For continuing use of the common law comity principle: in arbitration cases, *JSC Zestafoni v Ronty Holdings Ltd* [2004] EWHC 245 (Comm), [2004] 2 Lloyd's Rep 335; where English law was applied, *Society of Lloyd's v Fraser* [1999] Lloyd's IR 156, CA; *Tekron Resources* supra, *Mahonia Ltd v JP Morgan Chase Bank* [2003] EWHC 1927 (Comm), [2003] 2 Lloyd's Rep 911; and in the context of restitution, *Barros Mattos Junior v General Securities and Finance Ltd* [2004] EWHC 1188 (Ch), [2004] 2 Lloyd's Rep 475.

[700] Distinguished in the *JSC Zestafoni* case, supra—illegality in a foreign court but performance in England where there was no illegality. See also *Ryder Industries Ltd v Chan* [2015] HKCFA 32 (Hong Kong Court of Final Appeal) at [57]: not every breach of foreign law makes enforcement of a contract contrary to public policy.

[701] Hartley, op cit, 353; (1996) 45 ICLQ 271, 289 n 87; Kaye, p 69. Cf Lasok and Stone, op cit, pp 372–4.

some objectionable foreign rule.[702] If the English forum's concern, as appears to be the case in the above example, is to uphold a foreign law[703] on a matter of great importance to that foreign country, this does not look to come within either the wording or purpose of Article 21. The appropriate provision to refer to under the Regulation is Article 9(3).[704] Under this provision, effect may be given to the overriding mandatory provisions of the place of performance in the situation where performance is rendered unlawful in that country. If, however, the place of performance is not in the country of prohibition, Article 9(3) will not apply.[705] What remains possible is to take into account overriding mandatory provisions of a state other than the state of the forum or the state of performance as a matter of fact, in so far as this is provided for by a substantive rule of the law that is applicable to the contract pursuant to the Regulation.[706] Therefore, the foreign prohibition could be taken into account in the context of the English domestic rule on the invalidity of contracts made with the object of breaking the laws of a foreign country. This leaves a gap only for the scenario where the contract is governed not by English, but by a foreign law different from the law which provides for the overriding mandatory provision. Is it possible to use Article 9(2) then? It has been suggested that such cases involve a domestic rule of English law which can be regarded as an overriding mandatory rule of English law within this provision.[707] However, to regard a common law rule of public policy based on the comity of nations, and which therefore only applies in international cases, as a provision the respect for which is regarded as crucial by England for safeguarding its public interests would appear to be a fiction. It looks more like the enforcement of a third country's overriding mandatory provision, and, as such, is implicitly abolished by the Rome Regulation in all cases where the latter applies and does not allow such enforcement.[708]

(e) Particular issues

The scheme of the Regulation is that, having set out the rules on the applicable law, there are then special rules dealing with the particular issues of consent and material validity,[709] formal

---

[702] The Giuliano and Lagarde Report, at p 38; Philip, op cit, 57.

[703] But see Kaye, p 347 and Hill and Chong, para 14.3.20. English courts are not always so concerned. Cf *Akai Pty Ltd v People's Insurance Co Ltd* [1998] 1 Lloyd's Rep 90; Reynolds [1998] LMCLQ 1; where Thomas J, applying the traditional contract choice of law rules, which include the doctrine of public policy, gave effect to the agreement of the parties, rather than to an Australian mandatory rule rendering void a clause choosing English as the applicable law and conferring jurisdiction on the English courts; approved in *OT Africa Line Ltd v Magic Sportswear Corpn* [2005] EWCA Civ 710, [2005] 2 Lloyd's 170. See also *Beijing Jianlong Heavy Industry Group v Golden Ocean Group Ltd* [2013] EWHC 1063 (Comm) at [40]–[47]: arbitration agreement in a contract allegedly illegal under foreign law not unenforceable.

[704] Supra, pp 751–2.

[705] See Case C-135/15 *Republik Griechenland v Grigorios Nikiforidis* ECLI:EU:C:2016:774 at [49]: list, in Article 9(2) and (3) of the Rome I Regulation, of the overriding mandatory provisions to which the court of the forum may give effect is exhaustive. In *Foster v Driscoll* [1929] 1 KB 470 there was no illegality in the foreign place of performance (which was not in the USA). However, the objective of the scheme was that the whisky would end up eventually in the USA, hence the concern with the comity of nations.

[706] Case C-135/15 *Republik Griechenland v Grigorios Nikiforidis* ECLI:EU:C:2016:774 at [51]–[52].

[707] Hartley (1997) 266 Hague Recueil 341, 403, 388–91 (on Art 7(2) of the Rome Convention); see also Dicey, Morris and Collins, para 32-193, who suggest that the English domestic law on the invalidity of contracts made with the object of breaking the laws of a foreign country applies even if the contract is governed by foreign law. Admittedly, *Foster v Driscoll* appears as an example of contracts illegal at common law on grounds of public policy in Cheshire, Fifoot and Furmston's *Law of Contract* (16th edn, 2012), p 468.

[708] Ie in all cases which do not fall under Art 9(2) or (3). What remains possible is to take the prohibition into account on the level of the applicable (foreign) substantive contract law, if the foreign law so provides, Case C-135/15 *Republik Griechenland v Grigorios Nikiforidis* ECLI:EU:C:2016:774 at [51]–[52].

[709] Art 10.

validity,[710] incapacity[711] and a number of other matters.[712] By implication, all other issues must be governed by the rules on the applicable law set out earlier in the Regulation. The point is spelt out by a provision on the scope of the applicable law[713] which gives particular instances of issues governed by the rules on the applicable law. With special rules for particular issues, a problem of classification inevitably arises. Under the common law rules, the English courts adopted the system of classification employed in the domestic law of contract. However, under the Regulation it is important that the classification of issues is made in accordance with the principle of uniform interpretation[714] and in the light of the intentions of the drafters of the Convention (as predecessor of the Regulation) and Regulation.[715] For example, the issue of whether a contract has to be in writing is intended to come within the category of formal validity[716] under the Regulation, whereas this was classified as a procedural issue under the common law rules. The provisions in the Regulation relating to particular issues will now be examined,[717] after which one issue that causes a special problem for the United Kingdom, that of illegality, will be considered.

(i) Consent and material validity

Article 10 of the Regulation—which[718] is virtually identical in wording to Article 8 of the Convention—is entitled "Material Validity" and contains two provisions.[719] Before examining these provisions it is necessary to see what is encompassed within the concept of material validity.

(a) What is meant by consent and material validity?

Material validity under the Regulation covers a wide variety of different issues. This is apparent from both Article 10(1), which is concerned with "the existence and validity of a contract", and Article 10(2), which deals with the existence of consent. The intention is that not only are issues of material validity in the English sense covered (eg the issue of illegality), but also issues relating to formation of the contract[720] (eg offer and acceptance, and consideration). The validity of consent to the contract (eg issues of mistake, misrepresentation and duress) is doubtless also covered under Article 10(1). Issues relating to the existence and validity of the contract itself are obviously covered, but so also are such issues in relation to the terms of the contract.[721] As has already been mentioned,[722] the existence and validity of consent to a choice of the applicable law are to be referred to Article 10.[723] Nonetheless, not

---

[710] Art 11.

[711] Art 13.

[712] Arts 14, 15, 16.

[713] Art 12.

[714] Supra, p 689.

[715] The Giuliano and Lagarde Report, p 38.

[716] Art 11, infra, p 758; see the Giuliano and Lagarde Report, p 31.

[717] Ie apart from Art 14 (voluntary assignment and contractual subrogation), Art 15 (legal subrogation), Art 16 (multiple liability), and Art 18 (burden of proof, proving the contract). These matters are more appropriately dealt with elsewhere in the book, see supra, p 85, infra, pp 1285–94.

[718] This provision remains in substance unaltered from the original 2005 proposal for a Rome I Regulation.

[719] Art 10(1) and (2).

[720] The Giuliano and Lagarde Report, p 28. See *Continental Enterprises Ltd v Shandong Zhucheng Foreign Trade Group Co* [2005] EWHC 92 (Comm) in relation to illegality. Art 10(1) has been applied to determine *where* a contract was made for the purposes of service out of the jurisdiction: *Marconi Communications International Ltd v PT Indonesia Bank Ltd TBK* [2004] EWHC 129 (Comm) at [32]–[33], [2004] 1 Lloyd's Rep 594; appeal dismissed [2005] EWCA Civ 422, [2005] 2 All ER (Comm) 325.

[721] *Thierry Morin v Bonhams & Brooks Ltd* [2003] EWHC 467 (Comm), [2003] IL Pr 25; affd [2003] EWCA Civ 1802 at [21]–[23], [2004] IL Pr 24—upholding the decision at first instance as to the law governing the tort.

[722] See the discussion on Art 3(5), supra, pp 723–4.

[723] The Giuliano and Lagarde Report, p 28. See generally Hill and Chong, para 14.4.5.

all issues of validity are dealt with under Article 10; formal validity has a special rule to itself under Article 11.[724]

(b) The putative applicable law[725]

Article 10(1) states that: "The existence and validity of a contract, or of any term of a contract, shall be determined by the law which would govern it under this Regulation if the contract or term were valid." This means that the normal rules on the applicable law under the Regulation are applied to the issue of material validity. The only gloss on this is that with material validity one has to assume that the contract or term is valid in the first place before ascertaining the applicable law. In the terminology of the common law rules, the "putative" governing law is applied.[726] As the Giuliano and Lagarde Report explains: "This is to avoid the circular argument that where there is a choice of the applicable law no law can be said to be applicable until the contract is found to be valid."[727] The important point of substance is that the parties are free to choose the governing law under Article 3 of the Regulation, eg by putting a choice of law clause in the contract, even though the issue in the case is whether a valid contract exists between them. When it comes to validity of terms of the contract it means that the validity of a New York choice of law clause is governed by substantive New York law, excluding its conflict of laws rules.[728] Similarly, the question whether a clause providing for arbitration in England is validly incorporated into a contract is governed by English law (the arbitration clause being an inferred choice of the governing law).[729] In other words, the parties are able to pull themselves up by their own bootstraps. The principle has much to commend it.[730] Businessmen use choice of law clauses in order to avoid the problems of ascertaining the objective governing law and their wishes should be respected whatever the issue.[731] However, this can lead to unfairness to one of the parties. The Working Group acknowledged this particular problem and included a safeguard in relation to consent to the contract.

---

[724] Capacity is dealt with under Art 13.

[725] See Crawford (2005) 54 ICLQ 829; Harris (2004) 57 CLP 305, 316–21.

[726] *Kingspan Environmental Ltd v Borealis A/s* [2012] EWHC 1147 (Comm) at [559]–[568].

[727] At p 30.

[728] Exclusion of renvoi, Art 20.

[729] *Egon Oldendorff v Liberia Corpn* [1995] 2 Lloyd's Rep 64 (Mance J)—the issue was one for the law governing the *contract* rather than one of material validity of the arbitration agreement. Where the issue is one of material validity of an arbitration or choice of jurisdiction agreement this is a matter for the law governing the arbitration or choice of jurisdiction agreement. But see cases treating it as a matter for the law governing the contract: *OT Africa Line Ltd v Magic Sportswear Corpn* [2005] EWCA Civ 710 at [1]–[2], [22] (per Longmore LJ), [2005] 2 Lloyd's Rep 170 (but cf Rix LJ at [60]); *Horn Linie GmbH & Co v Panamericana Formas e Impresos SA (The Hornbay)* [2006] EWHC 373 (Comm) at [20], [2006] 2 Lloyd's Rep 44. The law governing the arbitration or choice of jurisdiction agreement is identified using traditional English choice of law rules (see Art 1(2)(e) supra, pp 700–1). See also *Egon Oldendorff v Liberia Corpn* [1996] 1 Lloyd's Rep 380 at 385 (Clarke J); *Welex AG v Rosa Maritime Ltd (The Epsilon Rosa) (No 1)* [2002] EWHC 762 (Comm), [2002] 2 Lloyd's Rep 81; an appeal on the issues of incorporation in and grant of an anti-suit injunction was dismissed [2003] EWCA Civ 938, [2003] 2 Lloyd's Rep 509. This did not challenge the Art 10(1) point.

[730] Art 10 does not provide an answer where there are choice of law clauses in conflicting contractual standard forms. In these circumstances, the answer should be sought in the law which would govern the contract in the absence of choice, *Evialis SA v SIAT* [2003] EWHC 863 (Comm). The alternative would be to apply the law of the forum.

[731] See the common law cases of *Compañia Naviera Micro SA v Shipley International Inc, The Parouth* [1982] 2 Lloyd's Rep 351; *The Heidberg* [1994] 2 Lloyd's Rep 287 at 303 et seq.; *Habas Sinai Ve Tibbi Gazlar Istihsal Endustrisi AS v VSC Steel Co Ltd* [2013] EWHC 4071 (Comm) at [109], [116]–[117]. Cf Briggs [1990] LMCLQ 192; Jaffey, *Topics in Choice of Law*, pp 62 et seq; Kaye, pp 270–4. For Australian authority applying the law of the forum to the issue of formation of the contract, see *Oceanic Sun Line Special Shipping*

(c) The safeguard in relation to consent[732]

This is contained in Article 10(2) which provides that: "Nevertheless, a party, in order to establish that he did not consent, may rely upon the law of the country in which he has his habitual residence if it appears from the circumstances that it would not be reasonable to determine the effect of his conduct in accordance with the law specified in paragraph 1." This is designed[733] to cater for the following sort of example:

> A makes an offer to B, and inserts a choice of law clause in the contract stating that the law of Utopia will govern all disputes between the parties. B remains silent, neither expressly accepting nor rejecting the offer. Under the law of Utopia silence can constitute an acceptance. It would be manifestly unfair for B to be contractually bound. The effect of Article 10(2) is that B can assert that he did not consent to the contract according to the law of his habitual residence.

The major proviso is that it would have to appear from the circumstances that it would not be reasonable to determine the effect of his conduct under Utopian law. On the above facts, doubtless it would not be. The circumstances to be taken into account include the parties' previous practices inter se and their business relationship[734] and whether the transaction is a conventional one.[735]

The burden is on the party who wishes to displace Article 10(1) to show that the terms of Article 10(2) have been met.[736] Article 10(2) allows a party to rely on the law of his habitual residence to deny the existence of a contract. It cannot be used in a positive way to create a contract which did not exist under the applicable law. It was specifically devised with the question of silence constituting acceptance of an offer in mind. Nonetheless, it is wide enough to cover any issue of offer and acceptance. It is, though, only concerned with the *existence* of consent, not with the *validity* of consent (eg with duress, mistake, misrepresentation).[737] In cases raising these issues Article 10(1) will no doubt apply; but, on its own, without the safeguard contained in Article 10(2). As far as the issue of consent is concerned, the combined effect of Article 10(1) and (2) is that the contract can be invalidated either by reference to the applicable law or by reference to the law of the habitual residence of the party denying that he consented.

There was an unsuccessful attempt in *Egon Oldendorff v Liberia Corpn*[738] to use Article 10(2) in a very different situation from that for which it was designed. The Japanese defendants sought to rely on Japanese law, which allegedly requires (in an agreement "subject to details") recapitulation and confirmation of contractual details by both parties, to establish that they

---

Co Inc v Fay (1988) 165 CLR 197, HC of Australia; *Jasmin Solar Pty Ltd v Trina Solar Australia Pty Ltd* [2015] FCA 1453 at [86], Federal Court of Australia.

[732] Criticised by Carter (1986) 57 BYBIL 1, 26, n 108. See generally Jaffey, op cit, pp 70–1.

[733] See the Giuliano and Lagarde Report, p 28.

[734] Ibid.

[735] *Welex AG v Rosa Maritime Ltd (The Epsilon Rosa) (No 2)* [2002] EWHC 2035 (Comm) at [11]–[12], [2002] 2 Lloyd's Rep 701; an appeal on the issues of incorporation in and the grant of an anti-suit injunction was dismissed [2003] EWCA Civ 938, [2003] 2 Lloyd's Rep 509. This did not challenge the Art 10(2) point.

[736] *The Epsilon Rosa (No 2)*, supra, at [11].

[737] See the Giuliano and Lagarde Report, p 28; *Lupofresh Ltd v Sapporo Breweries Ltd* [2013] EWCA Civ 948 at [29].

[738] [1995] 2 Lloyd's Rep 64 (Mance J) who had to determine for the purposes of service out of the jurisdiction whether English law governed. Once it had been decided that there was jurisdiction Clarke J had to decide whether English law did in fact govern: [1996] 1 Lloyd's Rep 380. See also *The Epsilon Rosa (No 2)*, supra, at [11]–[12]; the *Thierry Morin* case, supra, at [24]. The approach of Mance J was followed in *Horn Linie GmbH & Co v Panamericana Formas e Impresos SA (The Hornbay)* [2006] EWHC 373 (Comm) at [19]–[21], [2006] 2 Lloyd's Rep 44—involving validity of a choice of law clause in a contract of carriage.

did not consent to the incorporation of an arbitration clause into the contract. Mance J held that the onus was on the party who sought to invoke Article 10(2) to negative consent, and that reliance could only be placed on Japanese law if it was not reasonable to determine the effect of the defendants' conduct in accordance with English law. It was unreasonable to determine consent in accordance with Japanese law because this would mean ignoring the English arbitration clause and to do this would appear to be contrary to ordinary commercial expectations when everything suggested that the defendants must already have considered and accepted the clause. The issue of consent raised by Japanese law looks to have more to do with the validity of consent than with its existence.[739] Accordingly, the case could have been decided on the basis that this issue fell outside the scope of Article 10(2), without going on to apply the "reasonableness" test.

(ii) Formal validity[740]

Article 11 of the Regulation deals with this issue. It contains general rules relating to the formal validity of contracts, a rule for unilateral acts intended to have legal effect (such as notice of termination of a contract), and special rules for consumer contracts and contracts in respect of immovable property. Article 11 of the Regulation is by and large the same in substance as Article 9 of the Convention.[741] There is, though, one significant difference. The rules in the Convention on formal validity were regarded as being too restrictive in the light of the growing frequency of contracts made at a distance.[742] In order to facilitate the formal validation of contracts, a third alternative connecting factor has been introduced in Article 11(2) and (3), namely the law of the country where either of the parties had his habitual residence at the time of conclusion.

(a) What is meant by formal validity?

It is not always easy to decide whether a matter is one of form or substance. English lawyers have particular difficulty with the classification of issues as ones of form because of the relative dearth of formal requirements under English law. This has meant that issues have sometimes been given a surprising classification. For example, the issue of whether a contract has to be in writing looks to be one of form, yet traditionally this has been classified under English law as one of procedure, and thus to be determined by the law of the forum.[743] However, it now appears that under the Regulation this issue should be classified as one of form. The Giuliano and Lagarde Report gives welcome guidance as to what formal validity encompasses. It includes "every external manifestation required on the part of a person expressing the will to be legally bound, and in the absence of which such expression of will would not be regarded as fully effective".[744] The following were given as examples of formal requirements:[745] the requirement that there must be two signatures to the contract;[746] that the contract must be made in duplicate; and, of most interest to English lawyers, that a

---

[739] See likewise the *Horn Linie* case, supra.

[740] See Kaye, pp 281–95; Loacker in *Rome Regulations: Commentary*, Art 11, pp 275 et seq.

[741] Art 9(3) of the Convention (contracts concluded by an agent) has been integrated in Art 11(1) and (2), without any change in substance. More radical changes under the original proposal were dropped.

[742] Explanatory Memorandum, p 9.

[743] *Leroux v Brown* (1852) 12 CB 801; supra, pp 74–7. See also *G & H Montage GmbH v Irvani* [1990] 1 WLR 667 at 684, 690; *Rothwells v Connell* (1993) 119 ALR 538—a requirement that a deed be stamped for it to be admissible in evidence held to be procedural.

[744] At p 29.

[745] At p 31.

[746] But see *Integral Petroleum SA v SCU-Finanz AG* [2015] EWCA Civ 144 at [39]–[47] (requirement that a contract be signed jointly by the two officers authorised to represent a Swiss company not matter of form, but a question of company law, excluded under Art 1(2)(f)).

non-competition clause in a contract of employment must be in writing. On the other hand, it was said[747] that it did not include the special requirements which have to be fulfilled where an act is to be valid against third parties, eg the need in English law for a notice of a statutory assignment of a chose in action. It would be best if the concept of formal validity were to be given an independent European meaning, under which the English courts will need to take a broader view of the concept than they have in the past.

(b) The general rules

(i) The contract is concluded between persons who are in the same country

The first of the general rules on formal validity is contained in Article 11(1) which provides that: "A contract concluded between persons who, or whose agents, are in the same country at the time of its conclusion is formally valid if it satisfies the formal requirements of the law which governs it in substance under this Regulation or of the law of the country where it is concluded." The policy underlying this provision is clear: to avoid the invalidation of contracts on the basis of formal defects. It does this by a validating rule of alternative reference. The normal rules on the applicable law under the Regulation are applied, but if the contract is formally invalid under those rules, as an alternative, recourse can be had to the law of the country where the contract was concluded in order to validate it.

The Working Group[748] justified the reference to the law of the place where the contract was concluded on the basis of the historical importance of this law. A modern policy justification would be that disputes as to form arise at the time when and in the country where the contract is concluded. It is therefore convenient that that country's law should be applied to resolve the dispute. There is no problem in determining where a contract was concluded because of the limitation of Article 11(1) to contracts concluded between parties who are in the same country.

When it comes to applying, as an alternative, the law that governs the contract, there are a number of difficulties. The first is that this law can be varied by the parties after the contract has been concluded. However, Article 3(2)[749] provides that a subsequent variation will not prejudice the formal validity of the contract. A subsequent variation of the governing law will not be allowed to invalidate the contract. On the other hand, a subsequent variation of the governing law which has the effect of formally validating a contract, invalid at its inception, will presumably be allowed,[750] validating the contract from that date. The second difficulty stems from the fact that different laws may govern different parts of the contract. Which of these governing laws is to determine its formal validity? According to the Giuliano and Lagarde Report "it would seem reasonable to apply the law applicable to the part of the contract most closely connected with the disputed condition on which its formal validity depends".[751] Thirdly, when Article 11 refers to the law that governs the contract, apparently this means the *putative* governing law, ie the law which would govern the contract if it were formally valid.[752]

(ii) The contract is concluded between persons who are not in the same country

If the parties are not in the same country at the time of the conclusion of the contract, the second general rule, which is contained in Article 11(2), applies. According to this: "A contract concluded between persons who, or whose agents, are in different countries at the time

---

[747] At p 29.
[748] At p 30.
[749] Supra, pp 709–10.
[750] The Giuliano and Lagarde Report, p 30.
[751] Ibid.
[752] Ibid.

of its conclusion is formally valid if it satisfies the formal requirements of the law which governs it in substance under this Regulation, or of the law of either of the countries where either of the parties or their agent is present at the time of conclusion, or of the law of the country where either of the parties had his habitual residence at that time." Thus, under Article 11(2), a contract is formally valid if it satisfies the formal requirements of: (i) the law which governs it in substance under the Regulation, or (ii) the law of either of the countries where either of the parties or their agent is present at the time of conclusion, or (iii) the law of the country where either of the parties had his habitual residence at that time. This means that recourse may be had to the law of up to five[753] different countries in order to validate the contract. The third alternative connecting factor, the law of the country where either of the parties had his habitual residence at the time of conclusion, has been introduced by the Rome I Regulation to facilitate the formal validation of contracts because the rules in the Convention on formal validity had been regarded as being too restrictive in the light of the growing frequency of contracts made at a distance.[754] In the situation where offer and acceptance has been made by an exchange of e-mails, it is not easy to determine when the contract is concluded, and hence the place where each party is at that time.[755] The rules in Article 11(1) and (2) set out alternatives for validating the contract, rightly without giving a priority to any one alternative.

(iii) Acts intended to have legal effect

The third and last part of the general rules[756] is concerned with formal requirements in respect of acts[757] intended to have legal effect, such as an offer or notice of termination, and is analogous to Article 11(2) in that it refers, as alternatives, to the law applicable to the contract in substance under the Regulation, or the law of the country where the act was done, or the law of the country where the person by whom it was done had his habitual residence at that time. Here again the third alternative was introduced by the Rome I Regulation to facilitate the formal validation of unilateral acts.

(c) The special rules for particular contracts

(i) Consumer contracts

The first of the special rules is concerned with consumer contracts. The formal validity of a consumer contract is governed by the law of the country in which the consumer has his habitual residence.[758] This means that, for consumer contracts,[759] formal validity is governed by the law that governs the substance of the contract in the absence of choice, and the consumer is protected by having the law of his habitual residence applied.[760]

(ii) Immovable property

The second special rule is concerned with contracts relating to immovable property. Article 11(5) states that:

> Notwithstanding paragraphs 1 to 4, a contract the subject matter of which is a right *in rem* in immovable property or a tenancy of immovable property shall be subject to the requirements of form of the law of the country where the property is situated if by that law

---

[753] Seven, if agents acted on both sides and these were in different countries than the parties.

[754] Explanatory Memorandum, p 9.

[755] Green Paper of 14 January 2003 on the conversion of the Rome Convention, COM (2002) 654 final, pp 38–9.

[756] Art 11(3), replacing Art 9(4) of the Convention.

[757] The act must relate to an existing or contemplated contract: the Giuliano and Lagarde Report, p 29.

[758] Art 11(4); see the Giuliano and Lagarde Report, pp 31–2.

[759] Ie ones to which Art 6 applies. The contract must be concluded in the circumstances mentioned in Art 6(1).

[760] Morse in *Contract Conflicts*, pp 143, 151 criticises this for erring in favour of the consumer.

(a) those requirements are imposed irrespective of the country where the contract is concluded and irrespective of the law governing the contract; and

(b) those requirements cannot be derogated from by agreement.

This provision shows a concern to give effect to the rules of form of the law of the situs in cases involving immovable property.[761] It is not enough to show simply that these rules cannot be derogated from by contract. It must also be shown that the requirement of form is imposed "irrespective of the country where the contract is concluded and irrespective of the law governing the contract". In other words, according to the law of the situs the mandatory rule has to have overriding effect.[762] Different from Article 9(6) of the Convention, albeit not in substance, Article 11(5) of the Regulation no longer uses the confusing term "mandatory" requirements. Instead it spells out that in the present context we are concerned with requirements which (a) are imposed irrespective of the country where the contract is concluded and irrespective of the law governing the contracts and (b) cannot be derogated from by agreement.

(iii) Capacity

As has already been seen, questions involving the capacity of corporations are excluded altogether from the scope of the Rome I Regulation.[763] When it comes to natural persons the position is more complex. The status or legal capacity of natural persons is, in general, excluded from the scope of the Regulation.[764] Member States are therefore left to apply their traditional private international law rules to the issue of capacity to contract. However, this is subject to Article 13 of the Regulation. This is a narrow rule concerned with protecting parties who have contracted with a natural person under an incapacity from being caught unawares by this. The traditional English common law rules on capacity will now be examined, and then Article 13 of the Regulation.

(a) The traditional common law rules

What law governs capacity to make a commercial contract is a matter of speculation so far as the English common law authorities are concerned. There is no clear decision and the dicta are not very helpful. It is clear, though, that the choice lies between the law of the domicile,[765] the law of the place where the contract was made[766] and the proper law in the objective sense.[767]

It may be conceded that in modern conditions of trade domicile alone is not a satisfactory test. It is incompatible with justice and with the trust that lies at the basis of commercial dealing that, for instance, a person over eighteen years of age should be able to escape liability for the price of goods sold or delivered to him in a London shop on the ground that he is still a minor by the law of his domicile abroad.[768] Indeed, under civil law systems the rule that

---

[761] See the Giuliano and Lagarde Report, p 31.

[762] See ibid, p 32, which makes this clear.

[763] Art 1(2)(f) of the Rome I Regulation, supra, p 701.

[764] Art 1(2)(a), supra, p 697.

[765] *Sottomayor v De Barros* (1877) 3 PD 1 at 5. Although this was a marriage case, Cotton LJ applied his statement in support of the law of the domicile to any contract. He was severely criticised in *Sottomayor v De Barros (No 2)* (1879) 5 PD 94 at 100; but see *Re Cooke's Trusts* (1887) 56 LJ Ch 637 at 639; *Cooper v Cooper* (1888) 13 App Cas 88 at 99, 100, 108.

[766] *Baindail v Baindail* [1946] P 122 at 128; and see *Simonin v Mallac* (1860) 2 Sw & Tr 67; *Republica de Guatemala v Nunez* [1927] 1 KB 669 at 689.

[767] See *Gorjat v Gorjat* [2010] EWHC 1537 (Ch) at [13]–[14], reiterating rule 228 from Dicey, Morris and Collins, para 32R-168: capacity of an individual to enter into a contract is governed by the law of the country of his domicile and residence or with which the contract is most closely connected.

[768] See Morris, para 15–051.

capacity is governed by the personal law cannot be relied on by a person who, though lacking capacity by his personal law, has capacity according to the law of the place where the contract was made.[769] Under English law, in many cases, contracts by persons under eighteen years of age are not enforceable against them,[770] but the court might well restrict this rule (and it would be reasonable for it to do so) to contracts in respect of which the objective proper law is English law.[771] It is also argued that, in the converse case, capacity conferred by the law of the domicile should not be invalidated by the proper law, ie a person should be regarded as capable if capable by the law of his domicile.[772] So far, however, English courts have not been pressed to adopt such attitudes.

Not only has it been advocated frequently that the law of the place where the contract was made governs the question of capacity,[773] but there is also one old English decision to this effect.[774] This view, if it implies that the law of that place exclusively governs the matter, is clearly untenable, for it would enable a party to evade an incapacity imposed upon him by the law that governs the contract in other respects by the simple device of concluding the contract in a country where the law is more favourable. Moreover, the law of the place of contracting is ill adapted to govern the matter if, as may well happen, the parties conclude the contract in a place where they are only transiently present.

Such modern authority as there is would indicate that capacity to conclude a commercial contract is regulated by the proper law of the contract objectively ascertained. This is supported by the Canadian decision in *Charron v Montreal Trust Co*.[775] It was held there that capacity to enter a separation agreement is to be determined by the law of the country with which the contract is most substantially connected,[776] ie the proper law; though in the actual case this was also the law of the place where the contract was made.

More recently, the issue of capacity arose in *Bodley Head Ltd v Flegon*:[777]

> The defendant argued, inter alia, that an agreement between the Russian author, Alexander Solzhenitsyn, and H, a Swiss lawyer, was invalid as Solzhenitsyn had no capacity under Russian law, which was both the law of the domicile and the law of the place where the contract was made, to enter a contract to appoint an agent to contract abroad on his behalf.

Whilst doubting the correctness of the allegation that Solzhenitsyn was incapable under Russian law, Brightman J had no doubt that the question of his capacity was to be decided by Swiss law as the proper law of the contract. Although the point was not discussed, the facts of this case did raise the issue that, in stating that capacity is governed by the proper law of the contract, this expression must be taken to mean the law of the country with which the contract is most substantially connected. Intention cannot here be allowed free play.[778] A person cannot confer capacity upon himself by deliberately submitting himself to a law to which factually the contract is unrelated.

---

[769] Wolff, pp 281–2.

[770] See Law Com No 134; the Minors' Contracts Act 1987.

[771] See Morris, para 15–051.

[772] Dicey, Morris and Collins, para 32-177; Restatement, 2d § 198.

[773] *Baindail v Baindail* [1946] P 122 at 128; Anton, para 10-209.

[774] *Male v Roberts* (1790) 3 Esp 163; and see *Bondholders Securities Corpn v Manville* [1933] 4 DLR 699.

[775] (1958) 15 DLR (2d) 240.

[776] Ibid, at 244–5.

[777] [1972] 1 WLR 680.

[778] *Cooper v Cooper* (1888) 13 App Cas 88 at 108. This was accepted by counsel in *Marubeni Hong Kong and South China Ltd v Mongolian Government* [2002] 2 All ER (Comm) 873 at [19].

In light of the uncertain state of the common law, it has most recently been suggested to combine the law of the domicile and the proper law of the contract in an objective sense. Under this approach, "a contract will be valid if a party has capacity either under the law with which the contract is most closely connected[779] or under his personal law", ie the law of the country of his domicile.[780]

(b) Article 13

Article 13 of the Rome I Regulation is entitled "Incapacity"[781] and states that:

> In a contract concluded between persons who are in the same country, a natural person who would have capacity under the law of that country may invoke his incapacity resulting from another law only if the other party to the contract was aware of this incapacity at the time of the conclusion of the contract or was not aware thereof as a result of negligence.

This is an unusual article in that it grafts a specific rule dealing with one aspect of capacity onto national rules of private international law on this topic. The aspect it is concerned with is the position of a party who contracts with a natural person who is under an incapacity but where the first party is unaware of this incapacity. In certain circumstances it protects such a party by imposing a limitation on the right of the natural person under the incapacity to invoke his own incapacity. This idea has its origin in the law of certain civil law countries. In order for this limitation to apply, certain stringent conditions have to be satisfied.[782]

First, there must be a contract concluded between persons who are in the same country. The Working Group did not want to prejudice the protection of, for example, minors when a contract was made at a distance. The person under an incapacity must be a natural person. However, there is no such requirement as regards the other party, and this could presumably be a corporation. In cases where the incapacity of a corporation is at issue the traditional common law rules will apply, and in such cases this is not subject to Article 13. Secondly, it must be a situation where, according to the traditional private international law rules applicable in the forum, a natural person has capacity under the law of the country where the contract was concluded, but lacks capacity under another law. For example, a Member State under its traditional private international law rules may apply the proper law (as— probably—in the case of England) or the law of the domicile or nationality (as in the case of some civil law countries) to the issue of capacity, and under that law a person lacks capacity. Under Article 13 it is then necessary to turn to the law of the place where the contract was concluded in order to see if there is capacity by that law. There is no difficulty in identifying the country where the contract was concluded in cases where (as will always be the case under Article 13) both parties are in the same country at the time of the conclusion of the contract. On the other hand, if a Member State applies the law of the place of contracting to the issue of capacity under its traditional private international law rules, Article 13 will not operate.

If these requirements are met, the limitation on the right of an incapacitated person to invoke his own incapacity applies. The person under the incapacity can only invoke his own incapacity if the other party was aware of this incapacity or was not aware thereof as a result of negligence. The burden of proof as to this lies on the incapacitated party.[783] If satisfied, the

---

[779] In an objective sense, ie without considering a possible choice of law.

[780] Dicey, Morris and Collins, paras 32-175 and 32R-168, cited with approval in *Gorjat v Gorjat* [2010] EWHC 1537 (Ch) at [13]–[14].

[781] This includes incapacity in relation to consent to choice: Art 3(5), supra, pp 723–4.

[782] The Giuliano and Lagarde Report, p 34. See generally Kaye, pp 312–19; Loacker in *Rome Regulations: Commentary*, Art 13, pp 321 et seq.

[783] The Giuliano and Lagarde Report, p 34. See generally Kaye, pp 312–19.

incapacitated party lacks capacity to contract. On the other hand, if the incapacitated party does not satisfy the burden of proof he will have capacity to contract. The limitation is a narrow one. It only affects the rights of the person acting under the incapacity. The other party can raise an incapacity that exists according to the law applied by the traditional private international law rules of the forum even though he or she knew of the incapacity at the time of contracting. Furthermore, it only affects the rights of the person acting under the incapacity when that person is seeking to invoke his own incapacity. It does not prevent, for example, a minor from seeking to uphold a contract, and the other party cannot escape from a contract (valid by the applicable law) by saying that he was unaware that he was contracting with a minor.

(iv) Scope of the applicable law[784]

Article 12 of the Rome I Regulation is entitled "Scope of the law applicable" and in paragraph (1) gives a number of examples of issues coming within the scope of the law applicable to the contract by virtue of Articles 3 to 8.[785] This is not intended to be an exhaustive list,[786] and it is implicit that all other issues are governed by the rules on the applicable law. The only exceptions are issues classified as ones of formal validity[787] or incapacity[788]. Material validity is, of course, governed by the rules on the applicable law because of Article 10(1). Article 12 of the Rome I Regulation leaves the terms of its predecessor in Article 10 of the Convention largely unaltered.[789] The examples provided by Article 12 are as follows:

(a) Interpretation

Under the common law rules the province of interpretation was to discover the true intent and meaning of the parties as expressed by the language of the contract. This was a question of fact. Nevertheless, a question of choice of law could arise for, if an expression was ambiguous and if it bore different meanings in different legal systems, its interpretation had to be determined by reference to one only of those systems. This distinction between fact and law is still valid under the Regulation, since the Regulation is only concerned with choice of law. When a choice of law problem arises, the Regulation adopts the simple solution that the law applicable to the contract will govern the issue of interpretation.[790] A problem which arises from this approach can be illustrated by the situation where the contract is governed by Utopian law, but the parties have expressly provided that the contract is to be interpreted according to the law of Ruritania.[791] At common law it seems that Ruritanian law would govern the interpretation of the contract. Under the Regulation it appears, at first glance, that Utopian law has to be applied, since this is the law applicable to *the contract*. However, Article 12(1) refers to the law applicable to the contract "by virtue of this Regulation". Under Article 3(1) the parties are able to choose a law for *part* of the contract which may include a specific issue such as interpretation. The law applicable to the issue of interpretation in the

---

[784] See Plender and Wilderspin, paras 14-001–14-058; Kaye, pp 297–310; Lagarde in *Contract Conflicts*, pp 49 et seq.

[785] In cases of dépeçage the law applicable will be that governing the relevant part of the contract; cf Anton, paras 10.244–10.247.

[786] "The law applicable to a contract . . . shall govern in particular", Art 12(1). See Plender and Wilderspin, para 14-056, where it is suggested that "effects of a contract" are omitted from the list.

[787] Governed by Art 11.

[788] Mainly excluded from the Regulation, with the exception of Art 13.

[789] Art 12(1)(c) refers to the consequences of the "total or partial" breach "of obligations", rather than to the consequences of breach.

[790] Art 12(1)(a).

[791] For this possibility, see supra, pp 707–9.

above example would accordingly be Ruritanian law, which has been expressly chosen to govern that part of the contract.

(b) Performance

(i) What is encompassed within the concept of performance?

Whilst interpretation of a contract is a fairly self-explanatory category, some explanation is needed of what is encompassed within the concept of performance under Article 12(1)(b). The Giuliano and Lagarde Report gives helpful examples of issues coming within Article 12:

> The diligence with which the obligation must be performed; conditions relating to the place and time of performance; the extent to which the obligation can be performed by a person other than the party liable; the conditions as to performance of the obligation both in general and in relation to certain categories of obligation (joint and several obligations, alternative obligations, divisible and indivisible obligations, pecuniary obligations); where performance consists of the payment of a sum of money, the conditions relating to the discharge of the debtor who has made the payment, the appropriation of the payment, the receipt, etc.[792]

It is not clear whether all of these examples come within Article 12(1)(b) or whether some of them are intended to come within Article 12(1)(c) (failure to perform) or (d) (the various ways of extinguishing obligations). However, it is not necessary to decide this since the position is the same under each of the sub-paragraphs of Article 12(1): the law applicable by virtue of the Regulation governs. Nonetheless, it is important to distinguish all of these cases relating to the substance of performance from "the manner of performance and the steps to be taken in the event of defective performance" because of the special provision in Article 12(2), which deals with the latter.

(ii) The manner of performance: a special rule

Article 12(2) provides that: "In relation to the manner of performance and the steps to be taken in the event of defective performance, regard shall be had to the law of the country in which performance takes place." This provision deals with the situation where the law of the country of the place of performance is different from the law of the country whose law is applicable under the Regulation.[793] Two questions arise in relation to Article 12(2). The first is a question of definition: what matters fall within the concept of manner of performance? The second is a question of substance: what is a court supposed to do if it is faced with a matter of the manner of performance?

The definitional question   The Working Group[794] said that they did not want to give a strict definition to the concept of manner of performance. However, they have provided examples of matters normally falling within this category: rules governing public holidays, the manner in which goods are to be examined, and the steps to be taken if they are refused. Ultimately, the Report suggests that it is for the law of the forum to decide if the issue is one relating to the manner of performance.[795] At least under the Regulation, it seems more convincing to apply an autonomous interpretation.[796] An example of this concept from the English courts is the rule under Chilean law that goods must be delivered to a customs warehouse.[797] The following have been held to be matters relating to the manner of performance under the old

---

[792] At pp 32–3.
[793] If the two are the same the court would have to apply that country's law as the applicable law.
[794] The Giuliano and Lagarde Report, at p 33.
[795] Ibid.
[796] Dicey, Morris and Collins, para 32-149.
[797] *East West Corpn v DKBS 1912* [2002] EWHC 83 (Comm) at [131], [2002] 2 Lloyd's Rep 182; appeals on other issues dismissed [2003] EWCA Civ 83, [2003] 1 Lloyd's Rep 239. The issue was whether this

common law rules: questions over the money of payment, ie the currency in which a debt is dischargeable,[798] the date at which lay days begin to run,[799] the hours during which delivery may be tendered,[800] and the meaning to be attributed to the word "alongside" in a stipulation providing that the cargo is "to be taken from alongside the steamer".[801] In all of these examples what is really being talked about are the minor details of performance. These examples would doubtless be classified in the same way under the Regulation, for they are entirely compatible with the examples of manner of performance given in the Giuliano and Lagarde Report.[802] The big difference between the Regulation and the common law rules is in respect of the rule to be applied to the issue of manner of performance.

The question of substance This brings us on to the second question in relation to Article 12(2). What is a court supposed to do if it is faced with a matter of the manner of performance? The court does not have to apply the law of the country in which performance takes place. It is merely required to have regard to that law. The court is thus given a discretion as to whether to apply that law or not, as it so chooses.[803] If it does apply that law it can do so in whole or in part. At common law there was no such discretion; if the issue was one relating to the mode and manner of performance, the law of the place of performance was applied.[804] It may well be that the English courts will do as they used to do and simply apply the law of the place of performance.[805] The adoption of a discretion under the Regulation introduces new and unwelcome uncertainty into this area. Obvious questions are raised. How much regard is to be given to this law? What are to be the criteria for the exercise of the discretion? The only guidance given on this by the Working Group is a reference to the court doing justice between the parties. It is surprising to find a discretion, particularly one to be exercised on such a vague criterion, in a Regulation which places such emphasis on achieving uniformity and certainty in the law.

(c) Within the limits of the powers conferred on the court by its procedural law, the consequences of a total or partial breach of obligations, including the assessment of damages in so far as it is governed by rules of law[806]

(i) What is encompassed within the concept of consequences of breach?
According to the Giuliano and Lagarde Report,[807] "the consequences of breach" encompass such matters as the liability of the party to whom the breach is attributable, claims to terminate the contract for breach, and any "requirement of service of notice on the party to assume his liability". There is also guidance to be found in the European Court of Justice's decision in *SPRL Arcado v SA Haviland*.[808] This case involved, inter alia, an action for damages for wrongful repudiation of an independent commercial agency agreement. A jurisdictional question arose, namely whether the proceedings related to a contract under Article 5(1) of the Brussels Convention (now Article 7(1) Brussels I Recast). In deciding that they did, the Court of Justice was influenced by the fact that any choice of law problem in relation to this claim was

---

discharged the carrier's delivery obligations. See also *Import Export Metro Ltd v Compañía Sud Americana de Vapores SA* [2003] EWHC 11 (Comm) at [20], [2003] 1 All ER (Comm) 703.

[798] *Temperance and General Mount Albert Borough Council v Australasian Mutual Life Assurance Society* [1938] AC 224 at 241.

[799] *Norden Steamship Co v Dempsey* (1876) 1 CPD 654.

[800] Dicey, Morris and Collins, para 32-151; see *Robertson v Jackson* (1845) 2 CB 412.

[801] Mann (1937) 18 BYBIL 97, 108, citing *Pulgrave, Brown & Son Ltd v SS Turid* [1922] 1 AC 397.

[802] Cf Kaye, pp 301–3. For a not very convincing suggestion that manner of performance can include exchange control regulations which make payment illegal, see Diamond, op cit, at 296; discussed infra, p 771.

[803] The Giuliano and Lagarde Report, p 33.

[804] The 11th edn of this book (1987), pp 492–5.

[805] See, eg, *East West Corpn v DKBS 1912*, supra.

[806] Art 12(1)(c). On the parallel provisions in Art 15(c) and (d) Rome II Regulation, see infra, pp 861–4.

[807] At p 33.

[808] Case 9/87 [1988] ECR 1539.

regarded as being contractual according to (then) Article 10 of the Rome Convention (today Article 12 of the Regulation). It was said that this Article "governs the consequence of total or partial failure to comply with obligations arising under it and consequently the contractual liability of the party responsible for such breach".[809] Finally, a Dutch court,[810] discussing the Convention before it came into effect, has said that "the consequences of breach" must be construed widely and can therefore include strikes. The court ordered striking crew members of a Saudi Arabian ship lying at Rotterdam to return to work on the basis that the strike was unlawful under Philippines law, which was the expressly chosen applicable law.[811] The issues raised by the case were held to fall within Article 10(1)(c) (today Article 12(1)(c)). Arguably, the "consequences of breach" could also encompass the issue of whether specific performance is available as a remedy.[812]

(ii) Assessment of damages

Article 12(1)(c) provides that the consequences of breach include the issue of assessment of damages, but this is only in so far as the assessment is "governed by rules of law". This draws a distinction between circumstances when assessment of damages raises questions of fact and those when it raises questions of law. If the question in relation to assessment is only one of fact (eg a judge is to calculate the amount of damages on the basis of facts presented by the parties), this is a matter purely for the court hearing the action and the applicable law under the Regulation will not govern the issue. On the other hand, if the question raised is one of law (the Giuliano and Lagarde Report[813] gives as examples cases where the contract prescribes the amount of damages in cases of non-performance or there is an international convention fixing a limit to the right to compensation), then Article 12(1)(c) will apply. Under the English common law the assessment or quantification of damages is a procedural matter for the law of the forum,[814] whereas the questions of heads of damage available and of remoteness of damage are ones of substance for the applicable law. The effect of Article 12(1)(c) is therefore that English courts will now have to apply the law applicable to the contract to the issue of assessment of damages in so far as this raises questions of law.[815]

(iii) The procedural limitation

The scope of Article 12(1)(c) is limited by its opening words: "within the limits of the powers conferred on the court by its procedural law". It has been suggested[816] that this would, for example, allow an English court to refuse to award damages in the form of periodical payments (as required by the foreign applicable law) on the basis that there is no procedural mechanism under English law for the award of damages in this form. It may also allow a

---

[809] At p 1555.

[810] *Buenaventura v Ocean Trade Co* [1984] ECC 183 at 186.

[811] Today, the legality of a strike would be governed by the law of the country where the action is to be, or has been, taken, see Art 9 of the Rome II Regulation, infra, pp 835–6. What is uncertain is whether the law applicable under Art 9 Rome II would also be applied to decide about the legality of a strike where this issue comes up in a contractual dispute as an incidental question (because the Rome II Regulation applies only to non-contractual obligations). The better view seems to be to apply Art 9 Rome II in all contexts where the legality of the strike is of relevance, whether in a contractual or a non-contractual claim, to avoid contradictory results for the individual workers participating in the strike and the union starting it.

[812] But see the procedural limitation in relation to Art 12(1)(c), infra, pp 767–8; Lasok and Stone, p 370.

[813] At p 33.

[814] Supra, pp 94–6.

[815] See *Excalibur Ventures LLC v Texas Keystone Inc* [2013] EWHC 2767 (Comm) at [1422]–[1423] (date and principles by which damages are to be calculated are determined by the law applicable to the contract).

[816] See Morse's comments on Art 10(1)(c) in his annotations to the 1990 Act in Current Law Statutes; Plender and Wilderspin, para 14-044.

let-out to an English court which is reluctant to grant specific performance, as required by a foreign applicable law.[817]

(d) The various ways of extinguishing obligations, and prescription and limitation of actions[818]

This provision[819] brings together what are, to English eyes, two very different sorts of issue. The first of these is the various ways of extinguishing obligations, of which there is a wide variety: eg by performance; by bankruptcy; by legislation;[820] by a moratorium; by subsequent impossibility; by novation, ie by a new contract which substitutes an existing obligation for another obligation, as, for example, by changing debtors. Any choice of law problems that arise in relation to these situations are a matter for the applicable law under the Regulation, including the provisions on severing the contract.

The second issue covered is prescription and limitation of actions, which is likewise subject to the applicable law as determined by the Regulation. This provision was, in part, responsible for the changes in the English law on limitation of actions. At one time the matter of limitation was regarded under English law as being a procedural one for the law of the forum. However, as has been seen,[821] the Foreign Limitation Periods Act 1984 changed this rule by adopting the principle that the English court is to apply to the issue of limitation the law which governs the substantive issue according to the English choice of law rules. Thus, even before the Rome Convention came into force, the English law on limitation produced the same effect in contract cases as that now produced by Article 12(1)(d) of the Regulation. However, it was an awareness of the corresponding provision in the (then) Rome Convention which helped to lead to the 1984 Act.[822]

(e) The consequences of nullity of the contract

This provision,[823] which was added at a very late stage of the negotiation of the Rome Convention, was designed to make it clear that the issue of whether money paid under a void contract is recoverable is to be subject to the rules on the applicable law under the Convention (now Regulation).[824] In some Member States the consequences of nullity are regarded as being non-contractual in nature. Indeed, under English and Scots law the right to recover money paid under a void contract forms part of the law of restitution, not of contract.[825] Because of this, Contracting States of the Rome Convention were allowed to enter a reservation, reserving the right not to apply Article 10(1)(e) of the Convention, of which the United Kingdom made use.[826] Under the Rome I Regulation, this reservation has been abolished. Thus, the consequences of nullity of a contract and any (restitutionary or other) remedies arising from this situation are to be classified as a contractual matter which are governed by the applicable law as determined by the Rome I Regulation. The same applies for

---

[817] Lasok and Stone, p 370. For a broad understanding of Art 12(1)(c) and a narrow reading of the procedural caveat, see *OJSC TNK-BP Holding v Lazurenko* [2012] EWHC 2781 (Ch) at [20] (availability of a quia timet injunction a matter for the law applicable to the contract).

[818] On the parallel provision in Art 15(h) Rome II Regulation, see infra, p 865.

[819] Art 12(1)(d).

[820] See *Wight v Eckhardt Marine GmbH* [2003] UKPC 37, [2004] 1 AC 147—discussing the borderline between discharge by government act and expropriation. See also *Re Magyar BV* [2013] EWHC 3800 (Ch) at [15].

[821] Supra, pp 78–9.

[822] See Law Com No 114 (1982), para 3.9.

[823] Art 12(1)(e) of the Regulation; Art 10(1)(e) of the Convention.

[824] The Giuliano and Lagarde Report, p 33; North in *Contract Conflicts*, pp 16–17.

[825] For choice of law in relation to restitution, see infra, Chapter 20.

[826] Art 22(1)(b) Rome Convention; s 2(2) Contracts (Applicable Law) Act 1990. See the Lord Advocate, Hansard (HL) 12 December 1989, col 1271.

restitutionary claims between the parties following the discharge of a contract for breach or frustration, or arising from the rescission of a contract.[827]

(v) The special problem of illegality

Article 10(1)[828] subjects illegality[829] to the normal rules under the Regulation. Thus, a court will not enforce a contract which is illegal by the law applicable to the contract. This was equally true under the traditional common law rules.[830]

This still leaves the problem of the effect of illegality under a law which is not the law applicable to the contract. There are no special rules under the Regulation to deal with this problem. This contrasts with the position under the traditional common law rules, under which there were special rules to deal with issues of illegality.[831] In particular, Article 9(3) (the discretion to give effect to the overriding mandatory provisions of a foreign country) is limited to mandatory provisions of the law of the country where the obligations arising out of the contract have to be or have been performed, in so far as those overriding mandatory provisions render the performance of the contract unlawful. It can thus only be used if performance is to be effected in the country which considers the contract as illegal.

In the absence of a general provision, the only way to deal with the problem of the effect of illegality under a law which is not the applicable law is for English courts to use other rules in the Regulation, in particular those contained in Article 12(2) (manner of performance), Article 9(2) (mandatory rules of the forum) and Article 21 (public policy). Four situations involving illegality, which have been much discussed under the common law rules, will now be examined to ascertain what the position is under the Regulation.

(a) An agreement to break a foreign law

At common law such an agreement, even though subject to a foreign law, was probably against the English doctrine of public policy and the comity of nations, and was not enforceable. As has already been seen,[832] cases decided on this basis appear to fall more appropriately within Article 9(3) than within the public policy provision in Article 21. Nonetheless, because of the limitations of the former provision, courts may be inclined to consider this type of case under Article 21.

(b) Illegality by the law of the foreign place of performance in cases where the applicable law is English law

This situation arose in the well-known case under the common law of *Ralli Bros v Cia Naviera Sota y Aznar*.[833] This case was concerned not with illegality from the outset of the contract but with the rather different situation of supervening illegality, ie the illegality in the place of performance only arose after the contract had been made. A simple example would be a contract, made in January, the performance of which is rendered illegal by a statute passed in June. The facts of the *Ralli* case were as follows:

---

[827] See Art 12(1)(c) and (d) Rome I Regulation; Dicey, Morris and Collins, para 32-162.

[828] Supra, pp 755–8.

[829] On what constitutes illegality see *Continental Enterprises Ltd v Shandong Zhucheng Foreign Trade Group Co* [2005] EWHC 92 (Comm) at [48]–[49]. For proof of foreign law in relation to illegality, see Fentiman, *Foreign Law in English Courts*, pp 137, 255–6.

[830] See *Kahler v Midland Bank Ltd* [1950] AC 24. See generally on illegality at common law, Hartley (2006) 319 Hague Recueil Ch XIV.

[831] See the 11th edn of this book (1987) pp 482–9. See also Hartley (1997) 266 Hague Recueil 341 at 385–95, 401–3.

[832] Supra, pp 753–4.

[833] [1920] 2 KB 287. For continuing use of the common law illegality principle in the context of restitution, see *Barros Mattos Junior v General Securities and Finance Ltd* [2004] EWHC 1188 (Ch), [2004] 2 Lloyd's

An English firm chartered a Spanish ship from a Spanish firm to carry jute from Calcutta to Barcelona at a freight of £50 per ton. At the time when payment had fallen due the Spanish government had issued a decree ordaining that freight on jute must not exceed a figure considerably lower than the contractual freight. Freight was tendered at the rate allowed by Spanish law but the receivers of the cargo refused to pay the excess amount.

An action was brought in England to recover freight at the contractual rate. The action failed. The vital point in the case was that the proper law of the contract was English law. The court, therefore, was bound to apply and did in fact apply the internal law, not the private international law, of England. The familiar English cases dealing with impossibility of performance were cited and Scrutton LJ summed up their effect on the instant facts in the following words: "Where a contract requires an act to be done in a foreign country, it is, in the absence of very special circumstances, an implied term of the continuing validity of such a provision that the act to be done in the foreign country shall not be illegal by the law of that State."[834]

The position under the Regulation with regard to such a case would appear to be as follows. The normal rules for the determination of the applicable law would apply to the issue of illegality by virtue of Article 10(1). The applicable law was English. Under the English domestic law of contract's doctrine of frustration, an agreement to perform that later becomes illegal to perform is unenforceable.[835] Moreover, under the Rome I Regulation, Article 9(3) allows a court of a Member State to give effect to the overriding mandatory provisions of the place of performance in so far as those provisions render performance of the contract unlawful already at the level of choice of law.[836] By application of Article 9(3), the result in the case would therefore be the same under the Regulation as under the common law rules it replaces (apart from the discretion available under Article 9(3) of the Regulation), and the action to recover the freight would fail.[837] Only the way to arrive at this result would be different: while the Regulation would solve this case already at the level of choice of law by application of Article 9(3), it is unclear whether the traditional English solution can be regarded as a substantive or a choice of law approach.[838]

(c) Illegality by the law of the foreign place of performance in cases where the applicable law is foreign

No case arose at common law which required the court to consider the effect of illegality at the foreign place of performance on a contract the proper law of which was the law of yet another foreign country; in other words, a case like the *Ralli* case, but now involving a foreign proper law under which there was no illegality. There have been frequent dicta attributing decisive effect to illegality by the law of the place of performance,[839] although it has been

---

Rep 475 and in the context of arbitration, see *Tamil Nadu Electricity Board v ST-CMS Electric Co Private Ltd* [2007] EWHC 1713 (Comm), [2007] 2 All ER (Comm) 701.

[834] The *Ralli* case, supra, at 304.

[835] See Cheshire, Fifoot and Furmston's *Law of Contract* (16th edn, 2012), p 715. If the performance takes place abroad, the domestic rule on frustration is then phrased in terms of illegality by the law of the foreign place of performance: *Bangladesh Export Import Co Ltd v Sucden Kerry SA* [1995] 2 Lloyd's Rep 1 at 5–6, CA. The Law Commission has declined to express a view on whether *Ralli Bros* was truly a case of frustration, Consultation Paper No 154 (1999): Illegal Transactions, para 1.15.

[836] See the discussion, supra, pp 751 and 754.

[837] On the Rome Convention, see Hartley (1997) 266 Hague Recueil 341, 392.

[838] On the question whether the Ralli rule is a conflict rule (and thus superseded by Article 9) or a substantive rule, see *Eurobank Ergasias SA v Kalliroi Navigation Company Ltd* [2015] EWHC 2377 (Comm) at [36], in favour of the latter view. It makes a difference only in very rare cases, see Dicey, Morris and Collins, para 32-102.

[839] *Toprak v Finagrain* [1979] 2 Lloyd's Rep 98 at 114; *United City Merchants (Investments) Ltd v Royal Bank of Canada* [1982] QB 208 at 228; revsd by the House of Lords on other points [1983] 1 AC 168; *XAG*

consistently argued in this book[840] that such an approach is contrary to principle, and not dictated by the authorities.

Turning to the Regulation, a solution can now be found again in Article 9(3). This provision allows to give effect to the overriding mandatory provisions of the law of the country where the obligations arising out of the contract have to be or have been performed, in so far as those overriding mandatory provisions render the performance of the contract unlawful. When a foreign country makes conduct illegal this may well involve a foreign overriding mandatory provision in the sense of Article 9(3).

Where the illegality does not arise from an overriding mandatory provision of the country of performance, but merely from a "simple" prohibition, Article 9(3) does not apply. However, if the issue is classified as one relating to the manner of performance under Article 12(2), then it may be appropriate to apply the law, including any (not only overriding mandatory) rules on illegality, of the country in which performance takes place. The "manner of performance" is, however, a fairly narrow category[841] and it would not be possible to regard the *Ralli* case as one relating to this issue. It has, nevertheless, been suggested[842] that the concept of manner of performance could include the question of whether payment is illegal because of exchange control regulations; and if these regulations are contained in the law of the place of performance it would then be appropriate to apply that country's law under Article 12(2).

Consideration needs also to be given, in the context of illegality by the foreign law of the place of performance, to the public policy provision of Article 21. The first problem with its application in this context is that the suspect English common law rule whereby a contract will not be enforced if it is to be performed in a foreign country where its performance is illegal by the law of that country, seeks to uphold a foreign law and thus appears to fall outside the negative concept of public policy used in Article 21.[843] The second problem is whether a case involving illegality by the law of a foreign place of performance can be regarded as raising public policy considerations for the forum. There was a tendency in the more recent common law decisions discussing the principle of illegality by the law of the place of performance, to describe this principle as being rooted in the notion of not acting against the comity of nations.[844] It is, however, submitted that the comity of nations aspect is much more important in cases where the parties, from the outset, set out to break a foreign law than it is in cases where the parties act in good faith, but find subsequently that performance becomes impossible because of a change in the law of the place of performance. The upshot is that it is very doubtful whether cases of illegality by the foreign law of the place of performance can be regarded as falling within Article 21.[845] This argument is reinforced by the situation under

---

v A Bank [1983] 2 Lloyd's Rep 535 at 543; *Euro-Diam Ltd v Bathurst* [1990] 1 QB 1 at 15, affd by CA at 30; *Libyan Arab Foreign Bank v Bankers Trust Co* [1989] QB 728; *Apple Corps Ltd v Apple Computers Ltd* [1992] FSR 431 at 442. For an attempt to codify this rule see ALRC Rep No 58 (1998), Draft Bill, s 9(10).

[840] See the 11th edn of this book (1987), pp 486–8. See also Reynolds (1992) 109 LQR 553; Hill and Chong, para 14.4.42.

[841] Supra, pp 765–6.

[842] Diamond, op cit, at 296.

[843] Supra, pp 752–4.

[844] *Toprak v Finagrain* [1979] 2 Lloyd's Rep 98 at 107; affd by the Court of Appeal at 112, without mentioning this specific point; *United City Merchants (Investments) Ltd v Royal Bank of Canada* [1982] QB 208 at 228, 242, revsd by the House of Lords on other points [1983] AC 168; *Euro-Diam Ltd v Bathurst* [1987] 1 Lloyd's Rep 178 at 187. See also *Lemenda Trading Co Ltd v African Middle East Petroleum Co Ltd* [1988] QB 448 discussed supra, p 752, n 689. See generally Kincaid (1995) 8 Jo Contract Law 231, 239–40. For the application of Art 21 in cases involving the comity of nations, see supra, pp 753–4.

[845] Dicey, Morris and Collins, para 32-103; Kaye, p 260; Hill, para 14.4.42. Cf Leslie [1995] Jur Rev 477, 483. See also *Ryder Industries Ltd v Chan* [2015] HKCFA 32 (Hong Kong Court of Final Appeal) at

the Regulation: If the prohibition in the state of performance does not qualify as an overriding mandatory provision in the sense of Article 9(3)—otherwise there appears to be no need to invoke Article 21, because the problem can be solved by applying Article 9(3)—, it seems highly doubtful to consider a breach of an apparently "minor" foreign prohibition as being contrary to English public policy.

Finally, can Article 9(2) be used? At least under the Regulation, it can no longer be seriously suggested that the suspect common law rule in relation to illegality by the law of the foreign place of performance is a domestic rule of English law.[846] As Article 9(3) of the Regulation makes clear, it is a rule of private international law, and, as such, is implicitly abolished by the Rome I Regulation in all cases where the latter applies. If the prohibition in the state of performance does not qualify as an overriding mandatory provision in the sense of Article 9(3), the last resort would then be to take illegality in the state of performance into account, as a matter of fact, under the substantive law applicable to the contract pursuant to the Regulation.[847] Thus, where the foreign prohibition does not fall under Article 9(3), the consequences of illegality in the country of performance would depend on the applicable foreign contract law.

(d) Illegality by the law of the English place of performance in cases where the applicable law is foreign

At common law such a contract would not be enforced, and this situation provided an exception to the normal rules on the application of the proper law of the contract.[848] Under the Regulation this situation will arguably involve an overriding mandatory rule of the forum; if so, Article 9(2) will lead to the application of English law and the contract will be unenforceable.

(vi) Set-off under the Rome I Regulation

The Rome I Regulation introduces a rule for set-off, which aims to make set-off easier whilst respecting the legitimate concerns of the person who did not take the initiative.[849] Article 17 provides that: "Where the right to set-off is not agreed by the parties, set-off shall be governed by the law applicable to the claim against which the right to set-off is asserted."[850] This will cover cases of statutory offsetting. Where the right to set-off is agreed by the parties (contractual set-off), the set-off is subject to the general rules in Articles 3 and 4.[851]

(f) Relationship with other provisions of EU law[852]

Under the Rome Convention acts of the institutions of the European Communities, eg Community Regulations and Directives, and national laws implementing such acts,[853]

---

[57]–[58]: not every breach of foreign law (here: in the performance of the contract) makes enforcement of a contract contrary to public policy.

[846] But see Kaye, pp 260–1. Cf the suggestion in respect of the common law public policy/comity of nations rule, supra, pp 753–4.

[847] This is not excluded by Article 9 of the Regulation, see Case C-135/15 *Republik Griechenland v Grigorios Nikiforidis* ECLI:EU:C:2016:774 at [51]–[52].

[848] Dicey and Morris (11th edn, 1987), pp 1218–19. At common law if there was no illegality by the law of the English place of performance, it mattered not that there was a breach of some other country's law: *Fox v Henderson Investment Fund Ltd* [1999] 2 Lloyd's Rep 303.

[849] The Explanatory Memorandum, p 9.

[850] Art 17 of the Regulation.

[851] The Explanatory Memorandum, p 9.

[852] See generally Weller in *Rome Regulations: Commentary*, Art 23, pp 416 et seq.; Magnus in *European Commentaries on Private International Law*, Introduction paras 32–43, pp 21–44.

[853] See, eg, Reg 9 of the Unfair Terms in Consumer Contracts Regulations 1999; now Consumer Rights Act 2015, s 74.

laying down choice of law rules relating to contractual obligations, took precedence over the Convention.[854] The Rome I Regulation is to the same effect. Article 23 provides that: "With the exception of Article 7, this Regulation shall not prejudice the application of provisions of Community law which, in relation to particular matters, lay down conflict-of-law rules relating to contractual obligations." Article 23 is closely modelled on a parallel provision of the Rome II Regulation on non-contractual obligations.[855] Both the legislative history[856] and the wording of Article 23[857] suggest that the provision gives precedence only to special EU *conflict-of-law* rules in relation to *particular matters*. An example[858] of such conflict-of-law rules in relation to particular matters are the provisions of the EU Insolvency Regulation.[859] Other examples are found in a number of consumer directives that provide that, if the contract has a direct link to the territory of one or more Member States, EU law will apply, even if the parties have chosen the law of a third country.[860] However, the classification of these rules is not undisputed. Sometimes they are not regarded as choice of law rules, with the consequence that Article 23 does not apply, and rather Article 9 of the Regulation.[861] Finally, one might consider the provisions of certain transport law regulations to fall under Article

---

[854] Art 20 of the Convention.

[855] Art 27 of Rome II, discussed infra, p 873.

[856] The initial text in Art 22 of the Commission's Proposal was broader. It gave also precedence to a possible optional instrument in the context of the European Contract Law project and to "other instruments laying down provisions designed to contribute to the proper functioning of the internal market" (the latter are now found only in Recital (40)), see Explanatory Memorandum, COM (2005) 650 final, p 9. Council (Document No 14708/06) and European Parliament (EP Amendment 58, A6-0450/2007) favoured to align Art 23 and Recital (40) Rome I with the corresponding provisions in Art 27 and Recital (35) Rome II Regulation. However, it was controversial whether the "internal market rules" should generally be given precedence or not (as in the final text), see Council Document 8408/07 and COM(2006) 566, p 4: "In view of the recent developments in the European Parliament and the Council in the context of negotiations of other proposals such specifically tailored provision in this instrument seems no longer necessary".

[857] Together with Recital (40) first paragraph.

[858] Other examples explicitly acknowledged by the original proposal for a Rome I Regulation (Art 22(a) and Annex I) were: (EC) No Directive 1993/7 of 15 March 1993 on the return of cultural objects; Directive (EC) No 96/71 of the European Parliament and the Council of 16 December 1996 concerning the posting of workers in the framework of the provision of services OJ 1997 L 18/1; and certain insurance directives. All examples were not really helpful: Directive 93/7/EC on the return of cultural objects does not deal with contractual claims, but rather gives a Member State a right of action to secure a return of cultural objects, irrespective of any contract (Art 5 Directive 93/7/EC). Directive 96/71/EC concerning the posting of workers is mentioned in Recital 34 Rome as an example of an "overriding mandatory provisions" and will thus apply via Art 9 Rome I. And the insurance directives are now consolidated in Art 7, see Art 23 Rome I: "With the exception of Article 7".

[859] Case C-557/13 *Hermann Lutz v Elke Bäuerle* ECLI:EU:C:2015:227 at [46], [55] for Arts 4, 13 of Regulation (EC) No 1346/2000 (now Art 7, 16 Regulation (EU) 2015/848, OJ 2015 L 141/19). No special choice of law rule in the sense of Art 23 Rome I is found in Art 14(b) of Directive 2009/103 relating to insurance against civil liability in respect of the use of motor vehicles (OJ 2009 L 263/11), Joined Cases C-359/14 and C-475/14 *ERGO Insurance SE v If P&C Insurance AS and Gjensidige Baltic AAS v PZU Lietuva UAB DK* ECLI:EU:C:2016:40 at [38].

[860] These are: Art 6(2) of Directive 93/13/EEC of 5 April 1993 on unfair terms in consumer contracts, OJ 1993 L 95/29; Art 7(2) of Directive 1999/44/EC of 25 May 1999 on certain aspects of the sale of consumer goods and associated guarantees, OJ 1999 L 171/12; Art 12(2) of Directive 2002/65/EC of 23 September 2002 concerning the distance marketing of consumer financial services, OJ 2002 L 271/16; Art 22(4) of Directive 2008/48/EC of 23 April 2008 on credit agreements for consumers, OJ 2008 L 133/66; and (broader than the other provisions) Art 12(2) of Directive 2008/122/EC of 14 January 2009 on the protection of consumers in respect of certain aspects of timeshare, long-term holiday product, resale and exchange contracts, OJ 2009 L 33/10.

[861] Discussed supra, pp 743–52 and particularly at p 749 (mandatory rules in EU legislation). See generally Knöfel (1998) 47 ICLQ 439; Jayme and Kohler (1995) 84 RCDIP 1. The Green Paper of 14 January 2003 on the conversion of the Rome Convention of 1980 into a community instrument and its modernisation COM (2002) 654 final, pp 17–18 discusses the issue of the proliferation of directives having an impact on the applicable law.

23,[862] unless one does not regard these provisions as conflict-of-law rules, but rather as rules defining unilaterally the scope of application of the respective transport regulation.

Article 23 does not give general precedence to all provisions of EU internal market law, but is limited to conflict-of-law rules. For internal market provisions in general, Recital (40) second paragraph states only that the Rome I Regulation "should not prejudice the application of other instruments laying down provisions designed to contribute to the proper functioning of the internal market in so far as they cannot be applied in conjunction with the law designated by the rules of this Regulation". Moreover, the Rome I Regulation follows the Rome II Regulation in stating that it should not restrict the free movement of goods and services as regulated by the E-Commerce Directive.[863] While the Court of Justice has now shed light on the difficult relationship between that Directive and Rome II,[864] the more general reference in Recital (40) to "other instruments" designed to contribute to the proper functioning of the internal market is unclear.[865] It is probably not much more than a reminder that the European Parliament lost the battle for a general precedence of all EU internal market law. Finally, the opening words in Article 23 make it clear that the special choice of law rules for insurance contracts in Rome I take precedence over the existing choice of law rules contained in various EU directives; a logical consequence because the very purpose of Article 7 was to consolidate all the conflict rules from the different insurance directives.[866]

(g) Relationship with other conventions

Article 25(1) of the Rome I Regulation adopts the wording of Article 28 of the Rome II Regulation[867] and provides that the Regulation "shall not prejudice the application of international conventions to which one or more Member States are parties at the time when this Regulation is adopted and which lay down conflict-of-law rules relating to contractual obligations".[868] This makes it clear that *existing* conventions covering some of the same ground as the Rome I Regulation are preserved. The United Kingdom has entered into a number of such Conventions in relation to carriage.[869] Cases which fell within one of these Conventions

---

[862] See, eg, Art 3(1) of Regulation (EC) No 261/2004 of 11 February 2004 establishing common rules on compensation and assistance to passengers in the event of denied boarding and of cancellation or long delay of flights, OJ 2004 L 46/1; Art 2 of Regulation (EU) No 1177/2010 of 24 November 2010 concerning the rights of passengers when travelling by sea and inland waterway, OJ 2010, L 334/1; see also the EU regulations on cabotage (non-resident carrier) transport operations, eg Art 6(1) of Regulation (EEC) No 3118/93 of 25 October 1993 laying down the conditions under which non-resident carriers may operate national road haulage services within a Member State, OJ 1993 L 279/1.

[863] Directive (EC) No 2000/31 of 8 June 2000, OJ 2000 L178/1.

[864] Infra, p 873. For the "freedom of the parties to choose the law applicable to their contract" and "contractual obligations concerning consumer contracts", the country of origin principle of the E-Commerce-Directive does not apply; see Art 3(3) and the Annex to that Directive. It is therefore predominantly relevant in the field of torts.

[865] Other internal market directives do not seem to impact on the choice of law for contracts. For example, Art 3(2) and Art 17 No 15 of Directive 2006/123/EC of 12 December 2006 on services in the internal market, OJ 2006 L 376/36 exclude rules of private international law, in particular rules governing the law applicable to contractual and non contractual obligations, from the scope of that Directive; see also Recital (90) of that Directive.

[866] See supra, p 703.

[867] Discussed infra, pp 873–5. The only difference between the two provisions is that Rome I refers to contractual obligations and Rome II to non-contractual obligations.

[868] Art 25(1) of the Rome I Regulation. Art 26(1) of the Rome I Regulation imposes an obligation on Member States to notify the Commission of the list of such multilateral conventions to which they are a party.

[869] See the Law Commission Consultative Document (August 1974) on the preliminary draft Convention, pp 93–5. Dicey, Morris and Collins, paras 33-110–33-120 suggest that the provisions of these conventions are overriding mandatory provisions of the law of the forum in the sense of Art 9(2) of the Regulation. It seems more convincing to justify their precedence over the law applicable under the Regulation by Article 25, discussed supra, p 750.

were governed by the rules in the particular carriage Convention (once implemented by legislation) and not by the proper law of the contract.[870] The rules in these carriage Conventions will continue to apply, unaffected by the Rome Convention[871] or the Rome I Regulation.

The original proposal for a Regulation went on to suggest an exception to this principle so that the Regulation would take precedence over two multilateral conventions that have been entered into by a number of Member States, namely the Hague Convention of 15 June 1955 on the law applicable to international sales of goods and the Hague Convention of 14 March 1978 on the law applicable to agency.[872] But this proposal was dropped. The final version of the Regulation therefore has no exception for these multilateral conventions. However, the Regulation does have an exception in respect of conventions concluded exclusively between two or more Member States. The Regulation takes precedence over such conventions in so far as they concern matters governed by the Regulation.[873]

However, the position with regard to *future* conventions will be very different under the Rome I Regulation from that under the Convention. The Convention allowed Contracting States to enter into new conventions covering some of the same ground as the Rome Convention.[874] This is no longer permitted by Article 25 of the Regulation, with the result that Member States will no longer be able to enter into any multilateral conventions as from the date that the Regulation enters into force.[875] The EU, though, does have power to enter into international agreements.[876] Moreover, the EU Council can authorise Member States' accession to international conventions.[877] It is envisaged that Member States will be able to negotiate and conclude on their own behalf agreements with third countries "in individual and exceptional cases, concerning sectoral matters", containing provisions on the law applicable to contractual obligations.[878]

---

[870] *The Hollandia* [1983] 1 AC 565. See also *Kenya Railways v Antares Co Pte Ltd, The Antares (Nos 1 and 2)* [1987] 1 Lloyd's Rep 424.

[871] Which included a similar rule in Art 21.

[872] Art 23(2) of the original proposal for a Regulation.

[873] Art 25(2) of the Regulation.

[874] Art 21 of the Convention. If a Contracting State wished to do so, it had to follow the consultation procedure set out in Arts 23 and 24.

[875] See the analogous position under the Brussels I Regulation, supra, p 203.

[876] See the Opinion of the Court of Justice 1/03 *Competence of the Community to conclude the new Lugano Convention* [2006] ECR-I 1145 at [148]; see also Opinion of the Court of Justice 1/13 *Convention on the civil aspects of international child abduction* ECLI:EU:C:2014:2303 at [67]–[88].

[877] See, eg, Council Decision (EC) No 2002/762 of 19 September 2002 in relation to the Bunkers Convention, OJ 2002 L 256/7.

[878] Recital (42) of the Rome I Regulation, which also provides that the Commission will make a proposal to the European Parliament and the Council concerning the procedures and conditions for this.

20

NON-CONTRACTUAL OBLIGATIONS

1. Introduction	776	3.	Maritime Non-Contractual Obligations	875
(a) Torts	776		(a) Maritime torts	875
(b) Restitution	778		(b) Maritime non-contractual obligations	
(c) Equitable obligations	779		(other than torts)	878
2. The Rome II Regulation	780	4.	Mixed Issues Relating to	
(a) Preliminary remarks	780		Non-Contractual Obligations	
(b) When does the Regulation apply?	786		and Contract	879
(c) The applicable law: preliminary remarks	802		(a) The nature of the problem	879
(d) The applicable law for torts/delicts	804		(b) The nature of the obligation	880
(e) The applicable law for unjust			(c) A contractual obligation to which	
enrichment, *negotiorum gestio* and			there is a contractual defence	880
culpa in contrahendo	836		(d) A non-contractual obligation to which	
(f) Choice of the applicable law	854		there is a contractual defence	880
(g) Scope of the law applicable	858	5.	Non-Contractual Obligations	
(h) Limitations on the dominance of the			Outside the Scope of the Rome II	
law applicable	866		Regulation	883
(i) Rules of safety and conduct	871		(a) Violations of privacy and rights	
(j) Special rules for particular issues	872		relating to personality (excluding	
(k) Relationship with EU law and existing			defamation)	884
international conventions	873		(b) Defamation	885

1. INTRODUCTION

English law has traditionally had separate choice of law rules for torts, restitution and equitable obligations. Since 11 January 2009, these rules have been largely replaced by Regulation (EC) No 864/2007 on the law applicable to non-contractual obligations (the Rome II Regulation).[1] This chapter is primarily concerned with the Regulation but, before turning to examine this in detail, it is useful to say something about the problems involved in ascertaining the applicable law for non-contractual obligations and how English law solved these problems prior to the introduction of the Regulation.

(a) Torts

The problem of ascertaining the applicable law in the case of torts is scarcely less perplexing than that in the case of contract. The reasons for this are as follows. First, there is a variety of different connecting factors that can be raised by the facts of the case: the place where the tort was committed; the residence, habitual residence, domicile, or nationality of the parties; the place where the parties' relationship was centred. Secondly, in the situation where, for example, a wrongful act takes place in one country and the consequent injury in another, there is a serious definitional problem in determining the place where the tort

---

[1] OJ 2007 L 199/40.

was committed. Thirdly, a wide variety of tortious issues may arise. For example, there can be issues of capacity, vicarious liability, defences and immunities, damages, limitations on recovery, wrongful death, or intra-family immunities. Should the same law govern all of these issues? Furthermore, there are many different types of tort or delict, ranging from negligent driving, nuisance, defamation, and fraudulent misrepresentation, to infringement of intellectual property rights and torts involving ships or aircraft. Should the same rule apply, regardless of the type of tort involved? Fourthly, if a foreign tort law is to be applied, this could lead to liability being imposed for torts unknown to English law, such as invasion of privacy or unfair competition, torts which may reflect radically different views and protect radically different interests from those recognised under English law.[2] Fifthly, the question arises of whether the parties should be allowed to choose the law applicable to a tort, and if so, what safeguards are needed.

Since 1996 the English tort choice of law rules[3] have been a combination of common law and statutory rules.[4] These rules continue to apply in relation to those torts (including invasion of privacy and defamation) falling outside the scope of Rome II.[5] The common law rules in respect of foreign torts are derived from *Phillips v Eyre*,[6] as modified by the House of Lords in *Chaplin v Boys*[7] and the Privy Council in *Red Sea Insurance Co Ltd v Bouygues SA*.[8] There is a general rule of double actionability (ie there must be actionability by the law of the forum and the law of the place of the tort), with a flexible exception to this introduced by *Chaplin v Boys*, seemingly based on the concept of the most significant relationship.[9] The exception has been applied in the situation where the parties are from the same country, this also being the forum,[10] and has been extended to enable a claimant to rely exclusively on the foreign law of the place where the tort was committed, even if his claim would not be actionable under the law of the forum.[11] Where a tort is alleged to have been committed in England, the English courts have always applied English law to such a claim.[12] It is doubtful whether the "flexibility" introduced by *Boys v Chaplin* would permit English law to be displaced in favour of the application of some more appropriate law.[13] The place where a tort is committed is to be

---

[2] Briggs (1989) 105 LQR 359, 362.

[3] For the very different common law tort choice of law rules in Australia, Canada and the USA see (for Australia) *John Pfeiffer Pty Ltd v Rogerson* (2002) 203 CLR 503; *Régie Nationale des Usines Renault SA v Zhang* [2002] HCA 10, (2003) 210 CLR 491; *Neilson v Overseas Projects Corpn of Victoria Ltd* [2005] HCA 54, (2005) 221 ALR; (for Canada) *Tolofson v Jensen* (1994) 120 DLR (4th) 289; (for the USA) the conflicts revolution, discussed supra, pp 24–33.

[4] See further the 13th edn of this book (1999), Chapter 19; Dicey, Morris and Collins, Chapter 35.

[5] Infra, pp 883–8.

[6] (1870) LR 6 QB 1 at 18–19 (per Willes J).

[7] [1971] AC 356.

[8] [1995] 1 AC 190.

[9] This seems to be an influence of the flexible approach under the Restatement 2d, Conflict of Laws, § 145(1); for the theory of the 'proper law of the tort' see Morris (1951) 64 Harv L R 881, 888.

[10] *Chaplin v Boys* [1971] AC 356 at 378 (per Lord Hodson), 389–93 (per Lord Wilberforce); *Church of Scientology of California v Metropolitan Police Comr* (1976) 120 Sol Jo 690; *Johnson v Coventry Churchill International Ltd* [1992] 3 All ER 14.

[11] The *Red Sea* case, supra, distinguished in *Ennstone Building Products Ltd v Stanger Ltd* [2002] EWCA Civ 916, [2002] 1 WLR 3059.

[12] See, eg, *Szalatnay-Stacho v Fink* [1947] KB 1.

[13] *Metall und Rohstoff AG v Donaldson Lufkin & Jenrette Inc* [1990] 1 QB 391, CA; overruled on a different point in *Lonrho plc v Fayed* [1992] 1 AC 448, HL. See also *Connelly v RTZ Corpn plc* [1999] CLC 533 at 545. However, the *Red Sea* case, supra, accepted that (with a tort committed abroad) English law could be displaced by a foreign law. Numerous cases proceed on the basis that there is no exception, without the point being raised by counsel. But on their facts, if there was an exception, it would not have applied anyway. See, eg, *Ennstone Building Products Ltd v Stanger Ltd* [2002] EWCA Civ 916 at [48], [2002] 1 WLR 3059; *King v Lewis* [2004] EWCA (Civ) 1329, [2005] IL Pr 16.

determined by asking the following question: "where in substance did this cause of action arise?"[14] There is a considerable body of case law applying this test to particular torts.

Part III of the Private International Law (Miscellaneous Provisions) Act 1995 put tort choice of law rules largely on a statutory basis by abolishing these common law rules and by introducing new statutory rules. There is a general rule, which applies the law of the country in which the events constituting the tort or delict in question occur.[15] Where the elements of these events occur in different countries, there is a series of rules to identify the applicable law.[16] Thus, for example, for a cause of action in respect of personal injury the applicable law is that of the country where an individual sustained the injury.[17] There is also a displacement rule, which applies a flexible exception.[18] This provides that where it is substantially more appropriate for the applicable law for determining the issues arising in the case to be the law of some other country (than that provided for under the general rule), the general rule will be displaced and the law of that other country will apply.[19] There are no special rules for particular torts, with the exception of defamation, which is excluded from the scope of Part III of the 1995 Act.[20] The common law rules therefore continue to apply in defamation cases. There are also no special rules for particular issues.[21] The choice of law rules in Part III apply equally to events occurring in England as they apply to events occurring abroad.[22] Overall the 1995 Act has the effect of getting rid of the idiosyncrasies of the common law and bringing English rules closer to those in other European countries.

(b) Restitution

The problem of ascertaining the applicable law in cases of restitution is arguably more difficult than in respect of other obligations. First, there is a problem of terminology. At the heart of restitution lies the principle of unjust enrichment, which is concerned with reversing a defendant's enrichment at the claimant's expense. There is a view among common lawyers that restitution and unjust enrichment cover the same area of law, restitution being the response to unjust enrichment.[23] Some continental lawyers, though, whilst accepting a principle of unjustifiable enrichment, would also include within the ambit of restitution or

---

[14] *Metall und Rohstoff AG v Donaldson Lufkin & Jenrette Inc* [1990] 1 QB 391; overruled on a different point in *Lonrho plc v Fayed* [1992] 1 AC 448, HL.

[15] S 11(1).

[16] S 11(2).

[17] S 11(2)(a).

[18] S 12.

[19] For cases applying the displacement rule, see *Edmunds v Simmonds* [2001] 1 WLR 1003 (both parties normally resident in England); *Dawson v Broughton*, 31 July 2007 (unreported), Manchester County Court (both parties English but settled in France, English law applied under displacement rule). For cases rejecting the application of the displacement rule see: *Roerig v Valiant Trawlers Ltd* [2002] EWCA Civ 21, [2002] 1 WLR 2304 (one party Dutch, the other English); *Harding v Wealands* [2004] EWCA Civ 1735, [2005] 1 WLR 1539; overruled by the House of Lords without discussion of this point, [2006] UKHL 32, [2007] 2 AC 1 (one party a national of the state whose law applied under the general rule); *Regina (Al-Jedda) v Secretary of State for Defence* [2006] EWCA Civ 327, [2007] QB 621, affd [2007] UKHL 58 (a claim by a British citizen against the British government but the issue was the legality of detention in Iraq, whose law applied under the general rule).

[20] S 13, which defines defamation widely to include malicious falsehood.

[21] Though the displacement rule in s 12 of the 1995 Act is concerned with the issues arising in the case, on which see *Regina (Al-Jedda) v Secretary of State for Defence* [2006] EWCA Civ 327, [2007] QB 621, affd [2007] UKHL 58.

[22] S 9(6).

[23] Birks, *Introduction to the Law of Restitution*, pp 16–22; Burrows, *The Law of Restitution* (3rd edn 2010), Chapter 1. See also the Restatement 2d, Conflict of Laws, para 221 comment a.

quasi-contract the principle of *negotiorum gestio*.[24] Secondly, the English substantive law of restitution, although rapidly developing, is not as well developed as that of contract or tort. Moreover, it is an area where there is much theoretical discussion of what comes within the ambit of restitution and, within this topic, what the different categories of restitution are. All of this raises particularly acute problems of characterisation in private international law. Thirdly, restitutionary claims can arise in an exceptionally wide variety of different situations: for example, where money has been paid under a void contract; or by way of a bribe; or where a person has voluntarily intervened to pay a debt. This raises an important question: should the same choice of law rule apply to all of these different situations? Fourthly, as in tort cases, the English courts may be faced with a restitutionary claim in respect of a cause of action that is unknown to English law, eg for *negotiorum gestio* (the voluntary bestowal of a benefit).[25] This raises the question whether the English courts should allow recovery in respect of such a cause of action.

It can be stated with some confidence that in English cases of unjust enrichment decided under the pre-Rome II Regulation law, the obligation to make restoration is governed by the proper law of the obligation.[26] Dicey, Morris and Collins identified the proper law by means of three sub-rules, each one dealing with a different type of claim to restitution.[27] Thus it seems that, if the obligation arises in connection with a contract, its proper law is the law applicable to the contract. If it arises in connection with a transaction concerning an immovable (land), its proper law is the law of the country where the immovable is situated. If it arises in any other circumstances, its proper law is the law of the country where the enrichment occurs. Although there has been a tendency for the courts to apply these sub-rules,[28] some cases have preferred to adopt a flexible solution, according to which the closest and most real connection is identified in the light of the whole facts and circumstances, without the use of sub-rules.[29]

(c) Equitable obligations[30]

The forms of liability which may arise from a breach of an equitable obligation are very varied. Such breaches may give rise to liability not only under the law of trusts but also in contract or tort, under the law of restitution, under the law of property or in the context of succession. There is a basic problem regarding whether separate choice of law rules for equitable obligations are needed, at least for some equitable obligations, or whether such obligations should always be fitted within the existing well-recognised choice of law categories. The problem is particularly acute where there is an equitable obligation whose domestic classification is uncertain, an obvious example being breach of confidence. There is a further problem in that any attempt to use existing choice of law categories raises the obvious question: which of the existing categories should be used in a particular case?

---

[24] For the restitutionary function of *negotiorum gestio*, see Jansen in Basedow, Hopt and Zimmermann (eds), *The Max Planck Encyclopedia of European Private Law*, Vol II, 2012, pp 1114, 1115.

[25] Infra, pp 848–9.

[26] Dicey, Morris and Collins, para 36-008; the 13th edn of this book (1999), pp 682–3.

[27] Ibid.

[28] See Dicey, Morris and Collins, para 36-009.

[29] *Arab Monetary Fund v Hashim* [1996] 1 Lloyd's Rep 589 at 597, CA, following Evans J [1993] Lloyd's Rep 543 at 566; *Baring Bros & Co Ltd v Cunninghame District Council* [1997] CLC 108, (1996) The Times, 30 September.

[30] See, generally, Yeo (2004); Dicey, Morris and Collins, paras 34-083–34-093 and 36-057–36-100; the 13th edn of this book (1999), p 1044.

Authority on these questions is sparse.[31] Academic opinion is divided on whether separate choice of law rules should be adopted for at least some equitable obligations.[32] The most appropriate separate choice of law rule would be the application of the proper law of the equitable obligation, this being "the legal system governing the relationship in terms of which general access was gained to the beneficiary's assets".[33] When it comes to deciding which of the existing categories of choice of law a case should fall within, it appears that, if an equitable claim is to disgorge an unjust enrichment, this will fall within the unjust enrichment choice of law rules.[34] As far as breach of confidence is concerned, there is authority for this falling within the unjust enrichment choice of law rules, even where there was no element of disgorgement.[35] This observation, however, has now been considered as mere *dictum*, preferring to characterise the misuse of private information as a tort for the purpose of service out of the jurisdiction.[36]

2. THE ROME II REGULATION[37]

(a) Preliminary remarks

As from 11 January 2009,[38] the Rome II Regulation (Regulation (EC) No 864/2007) on the law applicable to non-contractual obligations directly applies in all the European Union Member States,[39] with the exception of Denmark.[40] So far the European Union and Denmark

---

[31] There is some authority which tends to support the application of the law of the forum, *United States Surgical Co v Hospital Products International Pty Ltd* [1982] 2 NSWLR 766 at 796–9; *A-G (UK) v Heinemann Publishers Australia Pty Ltd* (1987) 75 ALR 353 at 414–15. In other cases, an established choice of law category (such as tort or unjust enrichment/restitution) has been applied depending on the equitable obligation in question, see *OJSC Oil Company Yugraneft v Abramovich* [2008] EWHC 2613 (Comm) at [171]–[223] and [237]–[247]; *Fiona Trust & Holding Corp v Privalov* [2010] EWHC 3199 (Comm) at [142]–[148], [149]–[154] and [159]–[162].

[32] Cf (in favour of separate equitable choice of law rules) Barnard [1992] CLJ 474; the 13th edn of this book (1999), p 1044 (for some equitable wrongs) with (against separate rules) Dicey, Morris and Collins, paras 34-083–34-093; Yeo (2004).

[33] Barnard, p 507. See also *Grupo Torras SA v Al-Sabah (No 5)* [2001] Lloyd's Rep Bank 36.

[34] See Dicey, Morris and Collins, paras 34-084–34-085.

[35] *Douglas v Hello! Ltd (No 3)* [2005] EWCA Civ 595 at [97], [2006] QB 125; discussed infra, p 806.

[36] *Vidal-Hall v Google Inc* [2015] EWCA Civ 311 at [38]–[39], [43]. For service out of the jurisdiction in this context, see also the new Civil Procedure Rules Practice Direction 6b, para 3.1(21).

[37] Regulation (EC) No 864/2007, OJ 2007 L 199/40. See the collected papers in (2007) 9 Yb PIL; Ahern & Binchy, *The Rome II Regulation on the Law Applicable to Non-Contractual Obligations* (2008); Dickinson, *The Rome II Regulation: The Law Applicable to Non-Contractual Obligations* (with updating supplement 2010); Anton, *Private International Law* (3rd edn, 2011), Chapter 14; Huber (ed), *Rome II Regulation, Pocket Commentary* (2011); Collier, *Conflict of Laws* (4th edn, 2013), Chapter 11; Briggs, *Private International Law in the English Courts* (2014), Chapter 8; Calliess (ed), *Rome Regulations: Commentary on the European Rules of the Conflict of Laws* (2nd edn, 2015), Part Two; Crawford and Carruthers, *International Private Law: A Scots Perspective* (4th edn, 2015), Chapter 16; Fentiman, *International Commercial Litigation* (2nd edn, 2015), Chapter 6; Plender and Wilderspin, *The European Private International Law of Obligations* (4th edn, 2015), Chapters 16–29; Clarkson and Hill, *Conflict of Laws* (5th edn, 2016), Chapter 5.

[38] Art 32. Except for Art 29 (notification of international conventions entered into by Member States), which applies from 11 July 2008.

[39] The United Kingdom and Ireland "opted in" to the Regulation, in accordance with the Protocol (No 21) on the position of the United Kingdom and Ireland in respect of the area of freedom, security and justice annexed to the Treaty on the Functioning of the European Union, see Recital (39) of the Regulation. The United Kingdom Government's decision to opt in was criticised by the House of Lords EU Committee, HL Paper 66 (2004), paras 80–82. Cf the United Kingdom original position in relation to Rome I, supra, p 687.

[40] See Art 1(4) and Recital (40) of the Regulation and the Protocol (No 22) on the position of Denmark annexed to the Treaty on the Functioning of the European Union.

have not entered into an Agreement,[41] under which the provisions of the Regulation, with minor modifications, are applied by international law to the relations between the Union and Denmark.

(i) *The history, legal basis and justification of the Regulation*

(a) History of the Regulation

In 1972 the original six Member States of the European Community prepared a preliminary draft Convention on the Law Applicable to Contractual and Non-Contractual Obligations.[42] However, in 1978 attention focused on contractual obligations, culminating in the Rome Convention in 1980 which was later replaced by the Rome I Regulation.[43] After years without any progress being made on the harmonisation of choice of law rules in relation to non-contractual obligations, this project was back on the agenda in 1996[44] and a working party was set up by the Council of the European Union.[45] A Green Paper was produced in 2002 with a preliminary draft proposal[46] and, after consultation on this,[47] there was a proposal for a Regulation in 2003 (the Proposal).[48] The European Parliament sought fifty-four amendments, some of major importance.[49] This led to an amended proposal from the Commission in 2006 (the Amended Proposal)[50] which accepted in whole or part some of the European Parliament's amendments but rejected others.[51] After that, the Council adopted its common position in September 2006 (the Common Position).[52] The European Parliament proposed nineteen amendments to the Common Position.[53] The main issues at stake related to: violation of personality rights (including defamation); road traffic accidents; unfair competition; the definition of "environmental damage"; the relationship with other EU instruments; the treatment of foreign law; the review clause. The Council could not accept all of these amendments and recourse had to be had to the conciliation procedure, which produced the present Regulation. This was regarded as a satisfactory compromise by the relevant parties.[54]

---

[41] Along the lines of the EU/Denmark Agreement in relation to the Brussels I Regulation, discussed supra, p 192.

[42] See the Law Commissions' Consultative Document of 1974. The provisions on non-contractual obligations are set out in Law Commission Working Paper No 87 (1984), Appendix; see also Nadelmann (1973) 21 Am J Comp L 584.

[43] Supra, pp 683–4.

[44] See the Council Resolution of 14 Oct 1996, OJ 1996 C 319/1.

[45] The European Group for Private International Law, a private body but whose project was financed by the Commission, adopted a Proposal for a European Convention on the law applicable to non-contractual obligations which was sent to the Council's General Secretariat to assist the working party, see [1998] NILR 465.

[46] Criticised by Dickinson [2002] EBLR 369; Roebuck and Mason (2003) 9 CTLR 1. The text of the preliminary draft proposal can be found in the synopsis by the Max Planck Institute, <http://ec.europa.eu/justice/news/consulting_public/rome_ii/contributions/max_planck_en.pdf>, (2003) 67 RabelsZ 1.

[47] Many of the responses can be found in the news archive of the Directorate Justice, <http://ec.europa.eu/justice/newsroom/news/index-archives_en.htm> (search for "rome ii" and limit the time period from 1 November to 30 November 2002).

[48] COM (2003) 427 final of 22 July 2003, OJ 2004 C 96/8. For United Kingdom reaction, see House of Lords, European Union Committee, 8th Report of Session 2003–4, HL Paper 66, published 7 April 2004; Carruthers and Crawford 2004 SLT 19, (2005) Edin LR 65 and 239; Fawcett, Harris and Bridge, paras 17.165–17.182, 19.98–19.100; Stone (2006), Chapters 14 and 15. The Hague Programme, adopted by the Council on 5 November 2004, OJ 2004 C 53/1, called for work to be pursued actively on Rome II.

[49] See the European Parliament Report on the proposal A66-0211/2005 final of 27 June 2005 (the Wallis Report). This was at the first reading stage before the European Parliament.

[50] COM (2006) 83 final of 21 February 2006.

[51] See the Explanatory Memorandum accompanying the Amended Proposal.

[52] Council's Common Position of 25 September, OJ 2006 C 289/68.

[53] This was at the second reading stage before the European Parliament, concluded on 18 January 2007.

[54] See the Report to the European Parliament of its delegation to the Conciliation Committee A6-0257/2007 of 28 June 2007, Explanatory Statement, at pp 6–9, recommending approval by the European Parliament at the third reading.

Three of the most contentious issues (namely: the choice of law rules that should apply to non-contractual obligations arising out of violations of privacy and rights relating to personality, including defamation; the position of cross-border victims of road traffic accidents; the way in which foreign law is treated in different Member States) were resolved by the Commission undertaking to produce reports on these issues as part of the process of review of the Regulation.[55] The Regulation was adopted in July 2007.

(b) The legal basis and justification of the Regulation
The legal basis for the Regulation was Title IV, in particular Article 61(c), of the Treaty on the European Union (now Title V, Article 81(2)(c) of the Treaty on the Functioning of the European Union [TFEU]),[56] which authorises the adoption of measures promoting the compatibility of the rules applicable in the Member States concerning conflict of laws (ie the applicable law). Such measures are authorised "particularly when necessary for the proper functioning of the internal market".[57] They fall within the wider objective the Union has set itself[58] of establishing an area of freedom, security and justice, in which the free movement of persons is ensured.[59] Rome II is one of a number of measures[60] relating to judicial co-operation in civil matters.

Harmonisation of choice of law rules ensures that the same substantive national law applies, irrespective of the Member State in which the action is brought. Recital (6) of the Regulation states that the proper functioning of the internal market creates a need for this. It goes on to say that this is in order "to improve the predictability of the outcome of litigation, certainty as to the law applicable and the free movement of judgments". The first two of these advantages were already used to justify the Rome Convention (now Rome I Regulation). As regards the third advantage, harmonisation of choice of law rules has been regarded as facilitating the mutual recognition of judgments.[61] At first sight, this line of argument is hard to understand since there is semi-automatic recognition and enforcement of judgments within the European Union, regardless of the law applied in the judgment-granting Member State.[62] However, the harmonisation of the conflict rules may prevent distortions of competition between litigants in the EU by ensuring that each competent court will, within the scope of the Regulation, apply the same substantive law.[63] Even if one does not agree that such distortions exist or may be prevented,[64] a clear advantage gained from harmonisation is mitigating the effects of the forum shopping that the Brussels I Recast allows. It is surprising that this advantage is not expressly mentioned in the Regulation, given that this was used to justify the introduction of the Rome Convention.[65] The most convincing justification for Rome II is

---

[55] See Art 30.

[56] OJ 2012 C 326/47.

[57] Art 81(2) TFEU. The former Art 65 TEU permitted measures only "in so far as necessary for the proper functioning of the internal market". On that basis, the EU Committee of the House of Lords concluded that the Commission had not shown a convincing case of necessity, HL Paper 66 (2004), para 184. See also Dickinson [2002] EBLR 369.

[58] See Art 3(2) of the Treaty on European Union.

[59] See Art 3(2) of the Treaty on European Union and Art 67(1), (4), 81 of the Treaty on the Functioning of the European Union.

[60] For the general context, see supra, pp 33–6.

[61] See the joint Commission and Council programme of measures for implementation of the principle of mutual recognition of decisions in civil and commercial matters adopted by the Council on 30 November 2000, OJ 2001 C 12/1.

[62] See the Brussels I Recast, supra, Chapter 17. See also HL Paper 66 (2004), paras 55–56, referring to the evidence of North and Fentiman.

[63] Recital (13).

[64] For criticism of this argument see HL Paper 66 (2004), paras 57–59, referring to the evidence of Collins.

[65] See the Giuliano and Lagarde Report (1980) OJ 1980 C 282/4–5.

thus that it is an extension of the Brussels I Recast (which deals with jurisdiction in relation to both contractual and non-contractual obligations) and the Rome I Regulation (which deals with the law applicable to contractual obligations).[66]

(ii) Interpretation

(a) Referrals to the Court of Justice
Article 267 of the Treaty on Functioning of the European Union authorises the Court of Justice to give preliminary rulings on the validity and interpretation of acts of the institutions of the Union. Such acts include regulations and thus the Rome II Regulation. National courts normally have discretion whether or not to request a preliminary ruling on interpretation from the Court of Justice.[67] However, where the question of interpretation is raised in a case pending before a national court against whose decisions there is no judicial remedy under national law, that court or tribunal is under an obligation to bring the matter before the Court of Justice.[68]

(b) The principles and decisions laid down by the Court of Justice
Where the meaning of the Regulation is not referred to the Court of Justice, it should be determined in accordance with the principles laid down by, and any relevant decision of, that Court.[69] This means that the English courts should act in accordance with two different types of authority: first, any relevant decisions of the Court of Justice; secondly, the principles laid down by the Court of Justice.

If the Court of Justice has previously given a decision on the provision in issue, this must be followed. However, the provision which is in issue may not have been previously discussed by the Court of Justice. In this situation, the English courts should act in accordance with the principles of interpretation previously laid down by the Court of Justice,which are the following:[70]

(i)   In interpreting a provision of the Regulation, it is necessary to consider not only its wording but also the context and scheme in which it occurs and, in particular, the purpose pursued by the Regulation and the respective provision to be interpreted.[71]
(ii) The need for a uniform application of EU law and the principle of equality require that the terms used in the Regulation which make no express reference to the law of the Member States should be given an autonomous (independent) and uniform meaning by reference to their wording, scheme and purpose, rather than being understood as a reference to national law.[72] This is confirmed in relation to Rome II by its Recitals[73] which provide definitions for certain terms.[74]

---

[66] See the Explanatory Memorandum from the Commission, accompanying the Proposal for Rome II, COM (2003) 427 final of 22 July 2003, OJ 2004 C 96/8 (hereinafter "the Explanatory Memorandum"), p 3. But cf Fentiman, Written Evidence, HL Report 66 (2004), 110.

[67] Art 267(2) of the Treaty on the Functioning of the European Union.

[68] Art 267(3) of the Treaty on the Functioning of the European Union.

[69] This is the same position in relation to the Brussels system, supra, pp 195–7, and Rome I Regulation, supra, pp 688–9.

[70] See also the parallel approach for the Brussels I Recast, supra, pp 196–7.

[71] Case C-350/14 *Florin Lazar, représenté légalement par Luigi Erculeo v Allianz SpA* ECLI:EU:C:2015:802 at [21]; Case C-191/15 *Verein für Konsumenteninformation v Amazon EU Sàrl* ECLI:EU:C:2016:612 at [36]: "must be interpreted independently by reference primarily to the regulations' scheme and purpose".

[72] Case C-412/10 *Deo Antoine Homawoo v GMF Assurances SA* ECLI:EU:C:2011:747 at [28]; Case C-350/14 *Florin Lazar, représenté légalement par Luigi Erculeo v Allianz SpA* ECLI:EU:C:2015:802 at [21]; Joined Cases C-359/14 and C-475/14 *ERGO Insurance SE v If P&C Insurance AS and Gjensidige Baltic AAS v PZU Lietuva UAB DK* ECLI:EU:C:2016:40 at [43].

[73] Recital (11) (non-contractual obligations), Recital (30) (*culpa in contrahendo*).

[74] See Recitals (23), (24), (26).

(iii) When deciding upon what the independent EU meaning should be, three factors should be considered: first, the wording of the provision, secondly, the systematic context in which the provision is found, including its relation to other provisions in the Regulation or in other EU instruments, and thirdly, the objectives of the provision in question and the objectives and scheme of the overall Regulation.[75] These objectives are in particular the predictability of the outcome of litigation, legal certainty and foreseeability as to the law applicable and the uniform application in all Member States.[76]

(iv) In ascertaining the meaning of concepts used in the Regulation, regard should be had to the meaning of cognate concepts to be found in the European Union Treaties or in secondary legislation (in particular in neighbouring instruments such as Brussels I or Rome I), unless the European Union legislature has, in a specific legislative context, expressed a different intention.[77]

(c) Aids to interpretation

(i) Recitals

In the process of interpretation, recourse can be had to the forty Recitals at the beginning of the Regulation,[78] even if the operative part of the Regulation (the articles) takes precedence in case of doubt.[79] Although Rome II has fewer Articles than the Brussels I Recast, it has roughly the some number of Recitals. This is the consequence of a recent tendency to put in the Recitals not just explanations but also a number of amplifications[80] and definitions[81] that could, and perhaps should, have gone in the text.

(ii) The Explanatory Memorandum

There is an Explanatory Memorandum from the Commission of the European Communities on the Proposal for a Rome II Regulation.[82] Both the Court of Justice and English courts have used the Explanatory Memorandum accompanying the Brussels I Regulation (and the former versions of the Brussels Convention) to interpret it.[83] The Explanatory Memorandum on the Proposal for Rome II is reasonably detailed and, although it just sets out the view of the Commission, this view sometimes repeats also the comments in earlier expert reports, what can be described as earlier influences. Also the other legislative materials[84] should be consulted, even if their instructions are not binding for the interpretation of the Regulation.[85]

---

[75] See Case C-350/14 *Florin Lazar, représenté légalement par Luigi Erculeo v Allianz SpA* ECLI:EU:C:2015:802 at [21].

[76] See Recitals (6), (13), (14) and (16) of the Rome II Regulation and Case C-412/10 *Deo Antoine Homawoo v GMF Assurances SA* ECLI:EU:C:2011:747 at [34].

[77] Case C-271/00 *Gemeente Steenbergen v Baten* [2002] ECR I-10489, [2003] 1 WLR 1996, at [43]; see also Joined Cases C-403/08 and C-429/08 *Football Association Premier League Ltd and Others v QC Leisure and Others and Karen Murphy v Media Protection Services Ltd* [2011] ECR I-9083 at [188].

[78] Case C-429/07 *Inspecteur van De Belastingdienst v XBV* [2009] ECR I-403 at [31].

[79] Case C-344/04 *The Queen, on the application of International Air Transport Association and European Low Fares Airline Association v Department for Transport* [2006] ECR I-403 at [76]; for the relevance of recitals in interpreting Rome II see also *Jacobs v Motor Insurers Bureau* [2010] EWHC 231 (QB) at [22].

[80] See Recital (8).

[81] See Recitals (9), (10).

[82] COM (2003) 427 final of 22 July 2003, OJ 2004 C 96/8.

[83] For cases using the Explanatory Memorandum on the proposal for the Brussels I Regulation see supra, p 198.

[84] For a summary see supra, p 781.

[85] For a detailed analysis of the legislative materials of the Rome II Regulation see Dickinson, *The Rome II Regulation: The Law Applicable to Non-Contractual Obligations* (with updating Supplement 2010).

(iii) Earlier influences

The Regulation adopts a substantial number of the provisions in the preliminary draft Convention on the Law Applicable to Contractual and Non-Contractual Obligations of 1972.[86] This was accompanied by the Giuliano, Lagarde and Van Sasse Van Ysselt Report[87] which acknowledged that the 1972 draft was in turn influenced by the Hague Convention on the law applicable to Traffic Accidents of 1971 and the Hague Convention on the law applicable to Products Liability of 1973. The former was accompanied by the Essen Report and the latter by the Von Mehren Report. In so far as provisions in Rome II can be traced back to these Hague Conventions and Reports,[88] the latter may be relevant to the interpretation of the former. The 1972 draft was the subject of a Law Commission Consultative Document which contains interesting comment and criticism but does not set out the views of the two Law Commissions.

(iv) The Brussels I Regulation/Recast and the instruments dealing with the law applicable to contractual obligations (Rome I Regulation)

Recital (7) of Rome II says that the substantive scope and the provisions of the Regulation "should be consistent with the Brussels I Regulation and the instruments dealing with the law applicable to contractual obligations". The instruments referred to are today the Brussels I Recast and the Rome I Regulation.[89] At first sight, Recital (7) could be read as simply an explanation that concepts and terminology used in Rome II have in some cases been lifted from the Brussels I Regulation[90] (today Brussels I Recast) and the Rome Convention (today Rome I Regulation).[91] However, Recital (7) has important implications for the interpretation of Rome II. The need for consistency means that borrowed concepts and terminology should be interpreted in the light of the meaning given to them, in the past and in the future, in these other instruments. In particular the distinction in Art 7(1) and (2) Brussels I Recast between contractual jurisdiction and jurisdiction based on tort/delict can be applied by analogy to the categories of contractual and non-contractual obligations in Rome I and Rome II.[92] Moreover, the need for consistency could in principle come into play even where there is no borrowed concept or terminology. On the other hand, the objective of consistency cannot lead to the provisions of Rome II being interpreted in a manner which is unconnected to the scheme and objectives pursued by that Regulation.[93]

(v) The views of the European Parliament

The Regulation is significantly different in places from the Proposal because of amendments sought by the European Parliament. The history of the Regulation as it progressed through the European Parliament provides an invaluable insight into the thinking underlying these changes.

---

[86] See Arts 15 and 17 of Rome II.

[87] Commission Doc XIV/408/72-E.

[88] See Arts 15 and 17 of Rome II.

[89] Joined Cases C-359/14 and C-475/14 *ERGO Insurance SE v If P&C Insurance AS and Gjensidige Baltic AAS v PZU Lietuva UAB DK* ECLI:EU:C:2016:40 at [43].

[90] See Art 4(1) of Rome II and its reference to direct damage and the discussion of Art 5(3) of the Brussels I Regulation (today Art 7(2) Brussels I Recast Regulation), supra, pp 276–7.

[91] See, eg, Art 14(2) of Rome II, which is virtually the same as Art 3(3) of the Rome Convention and Art 3(3) Rome I Regulation.

[92] Joined Cases C-359/14 and C-475/14 *ERGO Insurance SE v If P&C Insurance AS and Gjensidige Baltic AAS v PZU Lietuva UAB DK* ECLI:EU:C:2016:40 at [43]–[45].

[93] For this limitation in the context of the Brussels I Regulation, see Case C-45/13 *Andreas Kainz v Pantherwerke AG* ECLI:EU:C:2014:7 at [20]. For a discussion of the link between Brussels I, Rome I and Rome II see Crawford and Carruthers (2014) 63 ICLQ 1.

(b) When does the Regulation apply?

The Regulation applies to matters coming within its scope,[94] and it has universal application, ie it applies equally to cases having no connection with a European Union State and to cases with such a connection.[95] Before turning to examine in detail these two aspects of the application of the Regulation, three general points need to be made. First, the Regulation does not have retrospective effect. It only applies in a Member State to events giving rise to damage which occurred after its entry into force.[96] But when does the Regulation enter into force? The obvious answer would be on the date of its application (from 11 January 2009).[97] However, the European legislator normally distinguishes between the date of entry into force and the date of application of an act to allow for sufficient time to prepare for application of the new law.[98] As the Rome II Regulation only provides for a date of application (11 January 2009),[99] the Court of Justice has applied the general rule of Article 297(1) third subparagraph of the Treaty on the Functioning of the European Union to determine the date of entry into force of the Rome II Regulation on the twentieth day following its publication in the Official Journal of the European Union (which is 20 August 2007).[100] This date, however, is only relevant for the administrative obligations of the Member States.[101] The relevant date for the application of the conflict rules of the Regulation is the date of application as defined by Article 31 (11 January 2009), meaning that the Rome II Regulation applies only to events giving rise to damage occurring after that date.[102] Thus, the only time to be taken into account is when the event causing the damage occurred; it does not matter when court proceedings were brought or when the court determined the applicable law.[103] The traditional English statutory and common law rules[104] will continue to apply to events giving rise to damage which occurred before that date. Secondly, the Regulation does not prejudice the application of international conventions to which a Member State was a party at the date when the Regulation was adopted.[105] Thirdly, the Regulation does not prejudice the application of provisions of EU law which, in relation to particular matters, lay down conflict of law (ie choice of law) rules relating to non-contractual obligations.[106]

(i) The scope of the Regulation

(a) Application, in situations involving a conflict of laws, to non-contractual obligations in civil and commercial matters

Article 1(1) states that "This Regulation shall apply, in situations involving a conflict of laws, to non-contractual obligations in civil and commercial matters." There are three separate requirements under this provision. First, the situation must involve a conflict of laws. Secondly, there must be a non-contractual obligation. Thirdly, there must be a civil and commercial matter.

---

[94] Art 1.

[95] Art 3.

[96] Art 31.

[97] Art 32.

[98] See Art 29 Rome I Regulation.

[99] Art 31, 32.

[100] Case C-412/10 *Deo Antoine Homawoo v GMF Assurances SA* ECLI:EU:C:2011:747 at [30]. *Homawoo v GMF Assurance SA* [2010] EWHC 1941 brought the matter before the CJEU.

[101] See Art 29, 30(2).

[102] Case C-412/10 *Deo Antoine Homawoo v GMF Assurances SA* ECLI:EU:C:2011:747 at [33]; see also *Cox v Ergo Versicherung AG* [2014] UKSC 22 at [13, 40]; same view taken by the German Bundesgerichtshof [2009] Neue Juristische Wochenschrift 3371, 3372 at [17].

[103] Case C-412/10 *Deo Antoine Homawoo v GMF Assurances SA* ECLI:EU:C:2011:747 at [36].

[104] Supra, pp 776–80.

[105] Art 28, discussed infra, pp 873–5.

[106] Art 27, discussed infra, p 873.

(i) A conflict of laws

The situation must involve a "conflict of laws". The Regulation frequently uses this term; it is also found in the Rome I Regulation.[107] Conflict of laws is a confusing term for common lawyers since it is used to cover not just choice of law but also jurisdiction and the enforcement of foreign judgments. Nevertheless, the Regulation is undoubtedly concerned only with the question of the applicable law, as its full title and its contents makes clear. In other words, it is concerned with situations involving a choice of law, ie a choice between the laws of different countries. This is clear from the Explanatory Memorandum, which explains that a conflict of laws situation is one where "there are one or more elements that are alien to the domestic social life of a country that entail applying several systems of law".[108]

This brings out the point that there must be a foreign element, not a purely domestic situation. This idea is familiar to English lawyers. Under English private international law a choice of law problem exists whenever the court is faced with a dispute that contains a foreign element.[109] With a non-contractual dispute, typical examples of a foreign element are as follows: one of the parties to the tort is a foreign national or is habitually resident abroad; the harmful event or the damage occurred abroad. In such cases the foreign country has a claim to have its law applied, and the uniform rules in the Regulation are intended to apply.

The position is more difficult if the court is faced with a dispute involving a foreign element, but in respect of what is an essentially domestic non-contractual obligation. This can arise in two different types of case. The first is where, for example, there is a purely German tort, which is the subject of trial in England, subsequent to the defendant having moved his business to England after the tort was committed. The situation involves a foreign element in that one of the parties now carries on his business here. However, what is lacking is any relevant connection with a country other than Germany of the sort which would give that other country's law a claim to be applied. Nonetheless, it is desirable that such cases come within the Regulation.[110] The object of the Regulation of achieving harmonisation of choice of law rules for non-contractual obligations is most likely to be attained if the scope of the Regulation is given as wide an interpretation as possible. The above example should therefore be regarded as one involving a choice between the laws of different countries. The second type of case is where there is, for example, a purely English tort or unjust enrichment, but the parties have agreed that French law shall govern this non-contractual obligation. It is implicit from the terms of Article 14(2)[111] that the Regulation will apply in this situation.[112]

There is another problem which is less easily solved. This relates to the requirement that the foreign element must entail applying several different systems of law, in other words there must be a choice between different laws. Under English law, if foreign law is not pleaded or proved the court gives a decision according to English law.[113] The courts are free to apply this rule in relation to the Regulation because matters of evidence and procedure are excluded from its scope.[114] If the English court is going automatically to apply English law, it is arguable that there is no element of choice between different laws. However, the purpose of the

---

[107] Art 1(1) Rome I Regulation, see supra, pp 695–6. The older 1980 Rome Convention refers to a choice between the laws of different countries.

[108] At p 8.

[109] Supra, p 4 et seq.

[110] See the parallel problem in contract cases, supra, p 695.

[111] Discussed infra, p 857.

[112] See the parallel problem in contract cases, supra, p 696.

[113] Supra, p 105 et seq.

[114] Art 1(3), see infra, pp 799–801.

Regulation is not going to be met if the English courts allow the parties to side-step the uniform rules contained therein by a simple omission to plead and prove foreign law. It would therefore be better if this sort of case was regarded as coming within the Regulation.[115]

The Explanatory Memorandum refers to applying several *systems of law*. Nonetheless, the choice of law rules in the Regulation consistently refer to the application of the law of a *country*. It is clear therefore that, for the purposes of the scope of the Regulation, the choice must be between the laws of different *countries*. A country is defined under the Regulation in the normal private international law sense as a territorial unit with its own rules of law, in this case relating to non-contractual obligations.[116] A German court, for example, will have to apply English law, or Scottish, or Northern Ireland law under the Regulation, even though the United Kingdom is the Member State under the Regulation. Similarly, an English court will have to apply, for example, Ontario or New South Wales law under the Regulation. Indeed, the Regulation will apply to an inter-state dispute involving connections with the "countries" of California and New York, provided that trial takes place in a European Union Member State.

However, the Regulation makes it clear that it is for the United Kingdom to decide whether it wants to apply the rules in the Regulation to intra-United Kingdom disputes.[117] It is certainly not bound to do so,[118] but the obvious inconvenience of having a different regime for intra-United Kingdom non-contractual disputes from all other cases lead to legislation applying the Regulation to such disputes.[119] This is what happened in relation to contract choice of law as well.[120] England, Scotland and Northern Ireland are thus treated as separate countries for the purposes of the Regulation, even in intra-United Kingdom disputes.

(ii) Non-contractual obligations

The Regulation applies to "non-contractual obligations". This concept varies in meaning from one Member State to another and therefore, for the purposes of the Regulation, it should be given an autonomous definition.[121] Unfortunately the Regulation gives only very limited guidance on what this definition should be. We are only told that the choice of law rules in the Regulation should also cover non-contractual obligations arising out of strict liability[122] and that the Regulation also applies to non-contractual obligations that are likely to arise.[123]

Non-contractual The word "non-contractual" does not tell us expressly what obligations are covered. Rather, we are told what is not covered, namely "contractual obligations". Contractual obligations in any situation involving a choice between the laws of different countries fall within the scope of the Rome I Regulation. For the distinction between contractual and non-contractual obligations, the Court of Justice has referred to the distinction in (what is now) Article 7(1) and (2) Brussels I Recast between matters relating to contract and matters relating to tort, delict and quasi-delict. By analogy to the Brussels I case-law, the concept of "contractual obligation" in Art 1(1) Rome I designates a legal obligation freely

---

[115] There are problems then of whether the parties have made a choice of the applicable law, infra, p 856.
[116] Art 25(1).
[117] See generally Carruthers and Crawford (2005) Edin LR 65, 70–6.
[118] Art 25(2).
[119] See the Law Applicable to Non-Contractual Obligations (England and Wales and Northern Ireland) Regulations 2008 (SI 2008/2986) and the Law Applicable to Non-Contractual Obligations (Scotland) Regulations 2008 (SSI 2008/404).
[120] Supra, p 696.
[121] Recital (11); Joined Cases C-359/14 and C-475/14 *ERGO Insurance SE v If P&C Insurance AS and Gjensidige Baltic AAS v PZU Lietuva UAB* DK ECLI:EU:C:2016:40 at [43].
[122] Recital (11).
[123] Art 2(2). Arguably, one could also refer to the definition of "damage" in Art 2(1).

consented to by one person towards another.[124] The concept of "non-contractual obligation" in Article 1(1) Rome II, on the other hand, defines an obligation which derives from one of the events listed in Article 2 of that Regulation, that is to say, any consequence arising out of tort/delict, unjust enrichment, *negotiorum gestio* or *culpa in contrahendo*.[125] The word "non-contractual" obligations literally covers *all obligations* which are not contractual, at least as long as they fall into one of the four categories of tort/delict, unjust enrichment, *negotiorum gestio* or *culpa in contrahendo*.[126] This encompasses not only tortious/delictual and restitution-ary obligations but also (certain) equitable obligations.[127] The Explanatory Memorandum confirms that the inclusion of all obligations, except those expressly excluded under Article 1(2), is what is intended.[128] The text of the Regulation also supports this interpretation. The fact that it was thought necessary expressly to exclude from the scope of the Regulation non-contractual obligations arising out of wills and succession[129] suggests that, without this, they would have come within the Regulation.

Obligations   In private international law there is a fundamental distinction between property, which has its own choice of law rules, and obligations, to which separate choice of law rules apply.[130] The Regulation is only concerned with obligations and leaves choice of law for property untouched.[131] As will be seen, difficult questions arise as to whether a tort (within the meaning of Chapter II of the Regulation) or property classification should be adopted.[132] Equally, the question can arise as to whether an unjust enrichment or property classification should be adopted.[133]

Statutory obligations   The source of non-contractual obligations is often not the common law, but rather statutes or civil codes. These provisions form part of the applicable law under the Rome II Regulation, provided that they can be characterised as non-contractual,[134] are not

---

[124] Joined Cases C-359/14 and C-475/14 *ERGO Insurance SE v If P&C Insurance AS and Gjensidige Baltic AAS v PZU Lietuva UAB DK* ECLI:EU:C:2016:40 at [44]. More precisely, it is relevant whether "the inter-pretation of the contract which links the defendant to the applicant is indispensable to establish the lawful or, on the contrary, unlawful nature of the conduct complained of against the former by the latter", Case C-548/12 *Marc Brogsitter v Fabrication de Montres Normandes EURL and Karsten Fräßdorf* ECLI:EU:C:2014:148 at [25]. On the Rome I Regulation, supra, pp 692–5.

[125] Joined Cases C-359/14 and C-475/14 *ERGO Insurance SE v If P&C Insurance AS and Gjensidige Baltic AAS v PZU Lietuva UAB DK* ECLI:EU:C:2016:40 at [45]–[46].

[126] Collier, p 339: "extremely wide". This is in line with the understanding of Art 7(2) Brussels I Recast, see Joined Cases C-359/14 and C-475/14 *ERGO Insurance SE v If P&C Insurance AS and Gjensidige Baltic AAS v PZU Lietuva UAB DK* ECLI:EU:C:2016:40 at [45]; Case C-191/15 *Verein für Konsumenteninformation v Amazon EU Sàrl* ECLI:EU:C:2016:612 at [37]: "all actions which seek to establish the liability of a defendant and are not related to a 'contract' within the meaning of Article 5(1) thereof" (ibid at [39]: "non-contractual liability extends also to the undermining of legal stability by the use of unfair terms which it is the task of consumer protection associations to prevent"). It is not fully clear whether the reference of the CJEU to "any consequence arising out of tort/delict, unjust enrichment, 'negotiorum gestio' or 'culpa in contrahendo'" in paragraph [45] of the *ERGO* judgment is meant as a limitation which excludes non-contractual obligations not arising from tort/delict, unjust enrichment, *negotiorum gestio* or *culpa in contrahendo*. Arguably, the aim of Rome I and Rome II to catch all contractual and non-contractual obligations not specifically excluded (see *ERGO*, ibid, at [37]) justifies the broad understanding as proposed here.

[127] But see the remark in the preceding footnote and the exclusion for certain equitable obligations dis-cussed infra, pp 805–6.

[128] See the Explanatory Memorandum, p 8. See also HL Paper 66 (2004), para 9.

[129] Art 1(2)(b); discussed infra, pp 794–5.

[130] See generally Yeo, *Choice of Law for Equitable Doctrines*, Chapter 5.

[131] The Regulation does, though, contain choice of law rules for subrogation (Art 19) and multiple liabil-ity (Art 20), which are best discussed infra, Chapter 32, pp 1291–2.

[132] Infra, pp 808–9.

[133] Infra, pp 838–9.

[134] If a statutory duty arises only in the context of a contract between the parties, such mandatory provi-sions or implied terms (even if not freely assumed by the parties in a strict sense) are to be regarded as con-tractual in nature.

excluded from the Regulation's scope[135] and do not violate English public policy.[136] Recital (11) Rome II clarifies that the rules of the Regulation should also cover non-contractual obligations arising out of strict liability.

Non-contractual obligations and the scope of the choice of law rules We must now examine the relationship between the scope of the Regulation (non-contractual obligations) and the scope of the separate choice of law rules contained in Chapters II and III of the Regulation. Chapter II is headed "Torts/Delicts". Its scope is limited to where there is "a non-contractual obligation arising out of a tort/delict". Chapter III is headed "Unjust enrichment, *negotiorum gestio* and *culpa in contrahendo*". Its scope is limited to where there is "a non-contractual obligation arising out of unjust enrichment, *negotiorum gestio* and *culpa in contrahendo*". At first sight it might be thought that these provisions on the scope of Chapters II and III cut back the width of the concept of "non-contractual obligations" so as to exclude equitable obligations.[137] There is no mention of equitable obligations in Chapters II and III and no separate Chapter IV headed "equitable obligations". However, no separate mention of equitable obligations is necessary.[138] For the breach of equitable obligations which are not entered into voluntarily[139] (otherwise they are likely to be characterised as contractual obligations), "Torts/Delicts" should be regarded as a suitable residual category that covers all non-contractual obligations other than those expressly excluded under Article 1(2) and those covered in Chapter III.[140] In distinguishing between Chapters II and III, it seems appropriate to look both at the nature of the obligation and the measure of recovery. Non-contractual obligations (including equitable obligations) which seek to establish the liability of the defendant on the basis of a causal connection between damage to the claimant and a "harmful event" to be imputed to the defendant in which the damage originates may be classified as a tort/delict in the sense of Chapter II, whereas non-contractual obligations which require proof of enrichment on the part of the defendant for which there is no valid legal basis and of impoverishment on the part of the applicant which is linked to that enrichment may be classified as unjust enrichment in the sense of Chapter III.[141] Moreover, it can be asked whether the measure of recovery is determined by reference to the loss to the claimant (Chapter II) or by reference to the enrichment of the defendant (Chapter III).[142] For equitable obligations

---

[135] Art 1(2), (3) Rome II.

[136] For a statutory claim to equitable remuneration in copyright law see Case C-572/14 *Austro-Mechana Gesellschaft zur Wahrnehmung mechanisch-musikalischer Urheberrechte Gesellschaft mbH v Amazon EU Sàrl and Others* ECLI:EU:C:2016:286 at [39]–[51].

[137] On the impact of the definition of damage in Art 2(1), supra, p 126 fn 126.

[138] Collier, p 340.

[139] See Case C-572/14 *Austro-Mechana Gesellschaft zur Wahrnehmung mechanisch-musikalischer Urheberrechte Gesellschaft mbH v Amazon EU Sàrl and Others* ECLI:EU:C:2016:286 at [35]–[36]. More precisely, it is relevant whether "the interpretation of the contract which links the defendant to the applicant is indispensable to establish the lawful or, on the contrary, unlawful nature of the conduct complained of against the former by the latter", Case C-548/12 *Marc Brogsitter v Fabrication de Montres Normandes EURL and Karsten Fräßdorf* ECLI:EU:C:2014:148 at [25].

[140] The Proposal for a Regulation was worded differently, having one section for non-contractual obligations arising out of a tort or delict and another section for non-contractual obligations arising out of an act other than a tort or delict. This made it more obvious that an equitable obligation would be covered. However, the change in wording should not be regarded as being significant. Indeed, the original wording was adopted simply to avoid technical language, see the Explanatory Memorandum, pp 8 and 21.

[141] For these criteria see Case C-47/07 P *Masdar (UK) Ltd v Commission of the European Communities* [2008] ECR I-9761 at [49]; Case C-572/14 *Austro-Mechana Gesellschaft zur Wahrnehmung mechanisch-musikalischer Urheberrechte Gesellschaft mbH v Amazon EU Sàrl and Others* ECLI:EU:C:2016:286 at [39]–[42]. See also Dicey, Morris and Collins, para 34-086.

[142] For the distinction between unjust enrichment and "non-contractual liability in the strict sense" (tort) in Art 340 Treaty on the Functioning of the European Union see Case C-47/07 P *Masdar (UK) Ltd v Commission of the European Communities* [2008] ECR I-9761 at [49].

which do not result from a relationship entered into voluntarily,[143] such a distinction leads to some being classified as tortious,[144] others as belonging to the law of unjust enrichment,[145] and still others as falling outside the scope of Rome II as being proprietary in nature.[146]

This examination of the scope of Chapters II and III enables us to describe "non-contractual obligations" in a positive way as obligations arising out of tort/delict, unjust enrichment, *negotiorum gestio* or *culpa in contrahendo*.[147] The link between non-contractual obligations and these four concepts is shown by the fact that Article 2, which "defines" non-contractual obligations, in fact defines damage which is a requirement in relation to the scope of torts/delicts under Chapter II, rather than non-contractual obligations as such.[148] It will be necessary later on to examine the meaning of the four concepts of tort/delict, unjust enrichment, *negotiorum gestio* and *culpa in contrahendo*.[149] This is because there can be questions as to whether, for example, an obligation arises out of tort or contract, out of contract or unjust enrichment, out of tort or unjust enrichment.

Concurrent liability   In cases where there is concurrent liability in contract and tort, the position prior to the introduction of the Rome II Regulation was very favourable to the claimant. The claimant was, for choice of law purposes, free to frame the action in tort rather than contract.[150] Indeed, the position was the same as under English domestic law and the claimant had the option of framing his claim in contract, or tort, or both.[151] The introduction of the Rome II Regulation means that this needs rethinking. The analogy should be drawn with jurisdiction under Article 7(1) and (2) of the Brussels I Recast[152] and the obligation should be classified as contractual or non-contractual but not both, so that there would be no question of the claimant being able to choose.[153] This leaves the question of how concurrent liability should be classified for the purposes of the Regulation. The first alternative is to say that where there is concurrent liability in contract and tort, the latter should also be regarded as being contractual and therefore cannot be tortious. An English court has adopted this contractual classification of concurrent liability for the purposes of jurisdiction.[154] The second alternative is to say that a tortious classification should be

---

[143] If the relationship is entered into voluntarily, the obligation would be either contractual (and thus fall in the scope of Rome I) or be excluded altogether as an obligation arising from a trust created voluntarily (Art 1(2)(e)). The liability of directors for breach of equitable obligations towards the company could also be regarded as a voluntarily created equitable obligation. In any event, it is excluded from Rome II under Art 1(2)(d).

[144] Such as breach of confidence (in so far as it does not refer to violations of privacy and is excluded under Art 1(2)(g)), or dishonestly procuring or assisting a breach of fiduciary duty, discussed infra, pp 806–7.

[145] Such as constructive trusts imposed where there is unjust enrichment by subtraction or restitution for wrongdoing, discussed infra, pp 840–1.

[146] Such as resulting trusts and certain forms of proprietary restitution, discussed infra, pp 841–3.

[147] It is unclear whether these four categories are meant as a limitation of the "non-contractual obligations" which fall under the Rome II Regulation, supra, p 789 fn 126.

[148] Indeed, damage is defined as covering "any consequence arising out of tort/delict, unjust enrichment, *negotiorum gestio* or *culpa in contrahendo*".

[149] Infra, pp 804–9, pp 836–43, pp 848–9, pp 849–52.

[150] *Base Metal Trading Ltd v Shamurin* [2004] EWCA Civ 1316, [2005] 1 WLR 1157, at [31]–[35].

[151] The *Base Metal* case, supra, at [35]. See also Dicey, Morris and Collins, paras 34-016–34-017. Cf Briggs [2003] LMCLQ 12 and the position in respect of jurisdiction under the Brussels I Recast, supra, pp 268–70. See generally on choice law and concurrent claims arising out of the international sale of goods, Fawcett, Harris and Bridge, Chapter 20.

[152] Supra, pp 268–70.

[153] This was advocated by Briggs even before the introduction of Rome II.

[154] See *Source Ltd v TUV Rheinland Holding AG* [1998] QB 54; discussed supra, p 268. According to *Source*, this would be unaffected by the fact that the claim was only brought in tort or only brought in contract.

adopted for the purposes of the Regulation.[155] Both alternatives, however, go too far in that they change the classification of a claim (from tortious to contractual or vice versa) only because it is factually related to another claim (either in tort or in contract). The better view is to accept that a single factual scenario may generate two (or more) claims, one to be classified as contractual (and thus governed by Rome I), and another to be classified as non-contractual (and thus governed by Rome II).[156] The Rome II Regulation itself envisages that there can be a tortious obligation in the situation where the parties have a pre-existing contractual relationship[157] and that there can be a tortious obligation to which there is a contractual defence.[158] Moreover, in the context of the Brussels I jurisdiction rules it is accepted that contractual and non-contractual obligations may arise from the same set of facts and still be governed by different jurisdictional rules.[159] In such a scenario (as in general), a claim is to be considered as contractual (and thus falling under Rome I) if its legal basis "can reasonably be regarded as a breach of the rights and obligations set out in the contract which binds the parties (. . .), which would make its taking into account indispensable in deciding the action".[160] If, on the other hand, the claimant's action is based on an obligation not deriving from a contract freely consented to by one person towards another, this action is to be regarded as non-contractual and thus falling under Rome II.[161] This distinction should also be applied to concurrent liability in the choice of law context, where the doctrine of secondary (accessory) connection under Art 4(3) of the Rome II Regulation mitigates the problem of distinction between Rome I and Rome II anyway.[162] Finally, there may be claims in tort and contract which do not involve concurrent liability because the claims are not parallel ones, being based on separate lines of argument.[163] In this situation, Rome II will apply in relation to the claim in tort.

(iii) A civil and commercial matter

Rome II applies in civil and commercial matters,[164] irrespective of the nature of the court or tribunal seised.[165] The concept of civil and commercial matters has also been used to limit the scope of the Brussels I Regulation and Recast (and previously the Brussels Convention). It has been borrowed from Brussels I so as to achieve consistency between these two instruments.[166] The meaning of "civil and commercial matters" has been extensively explored by the Court of Justice and by national courts in the context of the Brussels system, and the reader is referred to that discussion for its meaning in the present context.[167] Article 1(1) also goes on to provide that the Regulation shall not apply, in particular, to revenue, customs or administrative matters or to the liability of the state for acts or omissions in the exercise of state authority ("*acta iure imperii*"). These specifically excluded matters were also specifically excluded from the scope of the Brussels I Regulation and have also been borrowed from that

---

[155] See the 14th edn of this book (2008), p 779; see also Collier, p 363.

[156] See Dicey, Morris and Collins, para 34-016.

[157] Art 4(3), discussed infra, pp 814–19.

[158] Art 15(b), discussed infra, pp 859–60. See also the Explanatory Memorandum, pp 12–13.

[159] Art 7(1) and Art 7(2) Brussels Recast, see supra, pp 268–70.

[160] Case C-548/12 *Marc Brogsitter v Fabrication de Montres Normandes EURL and Karsten Fräßdorf* ECLI:EU:C:2014:148 at [26].

[161] See Case C-572/14 *Austro-Mechana Gesellschaft zur Wahrnehmung mechanisch-musikalischer Urheberrechte Gesellschaft mbH v Amazon EU Sàrl and Others* ECLI:EU:C:2016:286 at [36] –[37].

[162] See infra, pp 817–18.

[163] See *Domicrest v Swiss Bank Corpn* [1999] QB 548.

[164] Art 1(1).

[165] Recital (8). Cf the Brussels I Recast, where Art 1(1) makes this point, rather than a Recital.

[166] See Recital (7).

[167] Supra, pp 204–6.

Regulation.[168] For the exclusion of *"acta iure imperii"*, Recital (9) clarifies that this phrase "should include claims against officials who act on behalf of the State and liability for acts of public authorities, including liability of publicly appointed office-holders". These are just examples of *acta iure imperii* and are not intended as a complete definition. *Acta iure imperii* are now specifically excluded also from the scope of the Brussels I Recast. Before, there was Court of Justice authority suggesting that such claims fall outside the scope of Brussels I.[169]

(b) Exclusions

Article 1(2) and (3) expressly excludes a wide variety of matters from the scope of the Regulation. These matters can be put into two categories. First and foremost, Article 1 excludes certain non-contractual obligations. Secondly, it excludes certain matters which do not involve the law applicable to non-contractual obligations, namely evidence and procedure. Most of these exclusions are also exclusions from the scope of the Rome I Regulation. The Commission has asserted that, as exceptions, these exclusions should be interpreted strictly.[170]

(i) The exclusion of certain non-contractual obligations
The matters excluded from the scope of the Regulation, and the reasons for their exclusion, will now be examined. These are as follows:

(a) non-contractual obligations arising out of family relationships and relationships deemed by the law applicable to such relationships to have comparable effects including maintenance obligations[171]
Family relationships are defined as covering "parentage, marriage, affinity and collateral relatives".[172] There is a similar exclusion of family relationships under the Rome I Regulation.[173] The provision of Article 4(3) Rome II Regulation[174] under which the law governing a pre-existing relationship (such as a family relationship) may also govern a non-contractual obligation closely connected with it led some to argue that the family relationship exclusion should be removed from the Regulation. However, at the time the Rome II Regulation was adopted, there were no harmonised choice of law rules for determining the governing law for family relationships.[175] In such circumstances it was thought better to keep the family relationship exclusion.[176]

The exclusion in Article 1(2)(a) Rome II (and Article 1(2)(b) Rome I) goes further than that in the 1980 Rome Convention and extends to "relationships deemed by the law applicable to such relationships to have comparable effects". According to Recital (10), the term "relationships having comparable effects to marriage and other family relationships" should be interpreted in accordance with the law of the Member State in which the court is seised. This

---

[168] For the meaning of "revenue, customs or administrative matters", see the discussion of the scope of the Brussels I Recast Regulation, supra, p 204.

[169] *Lechouritou v Germany* Case C-292/05 [2007] ECR I-1519; discussed supra, p 205.

[170] The Explanatory Memorandum, p 9; criticised by Briggs, Written Evidence, HL Report 66 (2004), 95.

[171] Art 1(2)(a).

[172] Recital (10) of the Regulation.

[173] Art 1(2)(b) of the Rome I Regulation, discussed supra, pp 697–9.

[174] While Art 4(3) applies to torts/delicts only, Art 10(1) and Art 11(1) provide similar rules for unjust enrichment and *negotiorum gestio*.

[175] This has partially changed in the meantime: For maintenance obligations, Regulation (EC) No 4/2009 has been adopted (OJ 2009 L 7/1) which refers (Art 15) for the applicable law to the Hague Protocol of 23 November 2007 on the law applicable to maintenance obligations, see infra, p 1078. The UK and Ireland chose not to ratify this Protocol. On the basis of enhanced cooperation between some Member States (not the UK), Regulation (EU) No 1259/2010 (OJ 2010 L 343/10) has been adopted which deals with the law applicable to divorce and legal separation.

[176] See the Explanatory Memorandum, p 8.

does not suggest that the forum automatically applies its own substantive domestic law to determine the law applicable to "relationships having comparable effects".[177] Rather, it is only meant as a clarification that the definition of "relationships having comparable effects"[178] and thus the scope of the exception in Article 1(2)(a) Rome II for such relationships is to be determined by the national law of the forum in order to respect traditional national boundaries between family law obligations and non-contractual obligations in general. Non-contractual obligations arising out of family relationships, etc are said to include "maintenance obligations" for which now Regulation (EC) No 4/2009[179] has been adopted.[180]

Non-contractual obligations are seldom going *to arise out of* a family relationship. However, an example would be where there is an action for compensation for damage caused by the late payment of maintenance.[181] In contrast, an action by a wife, who has suffered personal injury, against her husband following his negligent driving does not *arise out of* their family relationship but out of his negligent driving. Accordingly, it is not excluded from the scope of the Regulation.

(b) non-contractual obligations arising out of matrimonial property regimes, property
     regimes of relationships deemed by the law applicable to such relationships
     to have comparable effects to marriage, and wills and succession[182]

This exclusion covers two rather different things: first, non-contractual obligations arising out of matrimonial property regimes (and comparable regimes); and secondly, non-contractual obligations arising out of wills and succession. The phrase "matrimonial property regimes" is not defined in Rome II. However, there is Regulation (EU) 2016/1103 implementing enhanced cooperation in the area of jurisdiction, applicable law and the recognition and enforcement of decisions in matters of matrimonial property regimes,[183] which defines such regimes as "a set of rules concerning the property relationships between the spouses and in their relations with third parties, as a result of marriage or its dissolution".[184] The Brussels system (including the Brussels I Recast) and the Rome Convention, all of which pre-date Rome II, exclude "rights in property arising out of a matrimonial relationship".[185] It is not obvious what difference, if any, there is between "rights in property arising out of a matrimonial relationship" and "matrimonial property regimes". There is no need under Rome II to distinguish between non-contractual obligations arising out of matrimonial property regimes and those arising out of maintenance since, as has been seen, the latter are also excluded from the scope of the Regulation.

The exclusion covers not just matrimonial property regimes but also "property regimes of relationships deemed by the law applicable to such relationships to have comparable effects to marriage". Again, Recital (10) provides that relationships having comparable effects to

---

[177] For a possibly different view see the 14th edn of this book (2008), p 781.

[178] Which might be politically sensitive in the case of same sex relationships, which some countries and also EU Member States refuse to regard as family law relationships.

[179] OJ 2009 L 7/1.

[180] Which refers for the applicable law to the Hague Protocol of 23 November 2007 on the law applicable to maintenance obligations (Art 15 of that Regulation), but the UK and Ireland chose not to ratify this Protocol.

[181] The Explanatory Memorandum, p 8.

[182] Art 1(2)(b).

[183] OJ 2016 L 183/1.

[184] Ibid, Art 3(1)(a). See also the additional explanation in Recital (18) of Regulation (EU) 2016/1103.

[185] Art 1(1) of the Brussels I Recast; Art 1(2)(b) of the Rome Convention. Art 1(2)(c) Rome I uses the same wording as Art 1(2)(b) Rome II.

marriage "should be interpreted in accordance with the law of the Member State in which the court is seised" which is not meant as a reference to the forum's substantive law, but rather a clarification that the exact scope of the exception in Article 1(2)(b) Rome II is to be defined by national law.[186] For registered partnerships,[187] Regulation (EU) 2016/1104 implementing enhanced cooperation in the area of jurisdiction, applicable law and the recognition and enforcement of decisions in matters of the property consequences of registered partnerships[188] gives a parallel definition of partnership property regime as Regulation (EU) 2016/1103 does for marriage.[189]

The phrase "wills and succession" is to be found among the list of exclusions from the scope of the Brussels Convention and Brussels I Recast;[190] and its meaning has been fully discussed in that context. "Wills and succession" are also excluded from the scope of the Rome I Regulation.[191] In the European Union, the conflict rules for succession have been harmonised by Regulation (EU) No 650/2012 on jurisdiction, applicable law, recognition and enforcement of decisions and acceptance and enforcement of authentic instruments in matters of succession and on the creation of a European Certificate of Succession.[192] Most disputes in relation to wills and succession will not involve non-contractual obligations but are concerned with issues such as the validity of the will. The exception of Article 1(2)(b) Rome II makes it clear that, in the rare cases which involve non-contractual obligations, the Regulation will not apply.

(c) non-contractual obligations arising under bills of exchange, cheques and promissory notes and other negotiable instruments to the extent that the obligations under such other negotiable instruments arise out of their negotiable character[193]

The identical exclusion in respect of contractual obligations is to be found in the Rome Convention and Rome I Regulation.[194] The reason for the incorporation of the same exclusion in Rome II is the same as the reason for its incorporation in the Rome Convention and Rome I Regulation, namely that "the Regulation is not the proper instrument for such obligations, that the Geneva Conventions of 7 June 1930 and 19 March 1931 regulate much of this matter and that these obligations are not dealt with uniformly in the Member States".[195] The exclusion applies to bills of exchange, cheques and promissory notes, each of which category is well known to English lawyers. It also applies to "other negotiable instruments to the extent that the obligations under such other negotiable instruments arise out of their negotiable character". The meaning of this phrase has already been examined in the context of the Rome I Regulation[196] and the reader is referred to what is said there on this.

---

[186] For the parallel problem in Art 1(2)(a) Rome II, see supra, pp 793–4.

[187] Art 3(1)(a) Regulation (EU) 2016/1104 defines "registered partnership" as "the regime governing the shared life of two people which is provided for in law, the registration of which is mandatory under that law and which fulfils the legal formalities required by that law for its creation".

[188] OJ 2016 L 183/30.

[189] Art 3(1)(b) Regulation (EU) 2016/1104.

[190] Art 1(2)(f) of the Brussels I Regulation, discussed supra, p 212.

[191] Art 1(2)(c) of the Rome I Regulation, discussed supra, p 698.

[192] OJ 2012 L 201/107. The United Kingdom and Ireland chose not to opt into the application of this Regulation, see Recital (82) of that Regulation.

[193] Art 1(2)(c).

[194] Art 1(2)(c) of the Rome Convention, Art 1(2)(d) Rome I Regulation, discussed supra, p 699.

[195] The Explanatory Memorandum, p 9. It may be added that the Geneva Conventions are mostly dealing with contractual obligations only.

[196] Supra, p 699.

(d) *non-contractual obligations arising out of the law of companies and other bodies corporate or unincorporated regarding matters such as the creation, by registration or otherwise, legal capacity, internal organisation or winding up of companies and other bodies corporate or unincorporated, the personal liability of officers and members as such for the obligations of the company or body and the personal liability of auditors to a company or its members in the statutory audits of accounting documents[197]*

This provision clarifies the point that, if non-contractual obligations arise in a company law context, they fall outside the scope of the Regulation. A very similarly worded exclusion was already found in the Rome Convention and still exists in the Rome I Regulation.[198] But the Rome II exclusion gives an additional example of the matters with regard to the law of companies that the exclusion is concerned with, namely "the personal liability of auditors to a company or its members in the statutory audits of accounting documents". The latter would encompass an action for negligence brought by a company or a member[199] against the auditor of a company. The Proposal for a Rome II Regulation contained a much narrower and very specific exclusion which was confined to the personal liability of officers and members as such for the debts of a company and the personal liability of auditors, etc. It was explained in relation to the former that the question of the personal liability of officers could not be separated from the law governing companies (applicable to the company in connection with whose management the question of liability arose).[200] An example of where the exclusion would operate can be seen in a pre-Regulation case, where a claim was brought by a company against one of its directors based on a breach of his equitable duty of care to the company.[201] That duty was held to have arisen only from the director's relationship with the company.[202] If it did not relate to the constitution of the company, it related to its internal management.[203] It was held that the equitable duty was governed by the law of the company's place of incorporation. Under the Regulation the non-contractual obligation (ie the equitable duty) should be regarded, as it is under English law, as arising out of the law of companies (being concerned with the internal organisation of the company) and, accordingly, outside the scope of the Regulation.[204] The English court would apply its domestic private international law rules according to which the director's equitable duty to his company is governed by the law of the company's place of incorporation. While Article 1(2)(d) Rome II excludes non-contractual obligations arising in a company law context, it does not exclude the capacity of a company or other legal body to incur liability in tort/delict, which is governed by the applicable law as determined by the Rome II Regulation.[205] Finally, Article 1(2)(d) Rome II does not apply to non-contractual liability as a consequence of transactions on stock exchanges or related to financial instruments.[206]

(e) *non-contractual obligations arising out of the relations between the settlors, trustees and beneficiaries of a trust created voluntarily[207]*

This exclusion is explained on the simple basis that "trusts are a sui generis institution" and that they are also excluded from the Rome Convention.[208] The latter contains a wider

---

[197] Art 1(2)(d).
[198] Art 1(2)(e) 1980 Rome Convention; Art 1(2)(f) Rome I Regulation, supra p 701.
[199] But an action by a buyer of a company against its auditors would not be excluded.
[200] The Explanatory Memorandum, p 9.
[201] *Base Metal Trading Ltd v Shamurin* [2004] EWCA Civ 1316, [2005] 1 WLR 1157.
[202] Ibid, at [56]. On the scope of the company law exclusion for contractual obligations, see supra, p 701.
[203] Ibid.
[204] Dicey, Morris and Collins, para 36-073.
[205] See Recital (12) and Art 15(1)(a): "determination of persons who may be held liable".
[206] Such an exception was proposed during the legislative process, but not adopted, HM Treasury, Davies Review of Issuer Liability: Final Report (June 2007), para 63.
[207] Art 1(2)(e).
[208] The Explanatory Memorandum, p 9.

exclusion—as now does the Rome I Regulation.[209] First, it also excludes the constitution of trusts; secondly, the Rome Convention exclusion is not confined to trusts created voluntarily.[210] Thus non-contractual obligations arising out of the relations between trustees and beneficiaries of a constructive trust are not excluded from Rome II.[211]

(f) non-contractual obligations arising out of nuclear damage[212]

This exclusion, which is not to be found in the Rome Convention nor the Rome I Regulation, has been explained[213] by "the importance of the economic and State interests at stake and the Member States' contribution to measures to compensate for nuclear damage in the international scheme of liability" established by various international Conventions.[214]

(g) non-contractual obligations arising out of violations of privacy and rights relating to personality, including defamation[215]

The Proposal for a Regulation did not exclude violations of privacy and rights relating to personality. However, it was recognised that there were constitutional concerns over violation of freedom of the press and that the normal tort choice of law rules set out in the Regulation could not apply on their own.[216] A special choice of law rule was therefore proposed which made it explicit that the law designated under the normal tort choice of law rules must be disapplied in favour of the law of the forum if it was incompatible with the public policy of the forum in relation to freedom of the press.[217] The European Parliament wanted a different rule[218] and sought amendments, which were unacceptable to the Commission as being too favourable to editors. The European Parliament withdrew its amendments on the inclusion of these rules as part of the overall compromise on the Regulation. These matters were regarded as being left over to be dealt with in the future. The Commission was required to produce a study on the situation where a non-contractual obligation arises out of violations of privacy and rights relating to personality, including defamation.[219] On that basis, a first comparative study has been published.[220] Moreover, the European Parliament produced two reports,[221] one of them proposing a

---

[209] Art 1(2)(g) 1980 Rome Convention; Art 1(2)(h) Rome I Regulation.

[210] The Proposal for Rome II followed the Rome Convention in not confining the exclusion to trusts created voluntarily.

[211] Art 28(1) Rome II provides that the application of Rome II to trusts is subject to the 1985 Hague Convention on the law applicable to trusts and their recognition which is given effect by the Recognition of Trusts Act 1987.

[212] Art 1(2)(f).

[213] The Explanatory Memorandum, p 9.

[214] Namely, the Paris Convention of 29 July 1960 and the Additional Convention of Brussels of 31 January 1963, the Vienna Convention of 21 May 1963, the Convention on Supplementary Compensation of 12 September 1997 and the Protocol of 21 September 1988. See Council Decision 2013/434/EU authorising certain Member States to ratify, or to accede to, the Protocol amending the Vienna Convention on Civil Liability for Nuclear Damage of 21 May 1963, in the interest of the European Union, and to make a declaration on the application of the relevant internal rules of Union law, OJ 2013 L 220/1.

[215] Art 1(2)(g).

[216] See the Explanatory Memorandum, p 18. This rule was dropped in the amended Proposal.

[217] See Art 6(1) of the Proposal for a Regulation; the Explanatory Memorandum, pp 17–18. A special provision was also needed on the law governing the right of reply, see Art 6(2) of the Proposal for a Regulation.

[218] As did the House of Lords EU Committee, see HL Paper 66 (2004), para 130, which wanted a country of origin rule.

[219] Art 30(2).

[220] Comparative study on the situation in the 27 Member States as regards the law applicable to non-contractual obligations arising out of violations of privacy and rights relating to personality, JLS/2007/C4/028, <http://ec.europa.eu/justice/civil/files/study_privacy_en.pdf>.

[221] Working Document on the amendment of Regulation (EC) No 864/2007 on the law applicable to non-contractual obligations (Rome II), Committee on Legal Affairs, Rapporteur: Diana Wallis, PE443.025v01-00; Draft Report with recommendations to the Commission on the amendment of Regulation (EC) No

conflict rule.[222] Whether and when this proposal might be taken into account in a reform of Rome II is completely uncertain.

Article 1(2)(g) Rome II as it stands today excludes two matters: violations of privacy and rights relating to personality, the latter includes defamation.[223] As regards violations of privacy, many civil law countries have laws on invasion of privacy. Traditionally there was no such cause of action under English law. However, English law has expanded the wrong of breach of confidence to cover cases involving misuse (by publication) of private information.[224] This protects one aspect of privacy.[225] These cases of misuse of private information borne out of non-contractual breach of confidence would undoubtedly be regarded in civil law jurisdictions as instances of invasion of privacy or injury to rights of personality. Accordingly they should fall within the exclusion.

"Rights relating to personality" goes much wider than defamation and may cover, *inter alia*, rights related to the name, to one's image and voice, or the right to one's honour. Broad as it may be, the exclusion in Article 1(2)(g) Rome II does not extend to personality rights violations which are related to physical harm (such as injuries to the physical integrity of a person),[226] as it was motivated by the concerns to protect the freedom of speech, in particular the freedom of the press. The exclusion does however extend to violations of data protection laws.[227]

864/2007 on the law applicable to non-contractual obligations (Rome II) (2009/2170(INI)), Committee on Legal Affairs Rapporteur: Diana Wallis (Initiative—Rule 42 of the Rules of Procedure), PE469.993v02-00.

[222] PE469.993v02-00, p 8 = OJ 2012 C 261E/1: "Article 5a—Privacy and rights relating to personality:

(1) Without prejudice to Article 4(2) and (3), the law applicable to a non-contractual obligation arising out of violations of privacy and rights relating to personality, including defamation, shall be the law of the country in which the rights of the person seeking compensation for damage are, or are likely to be, directly and substantially affected. However, the law applicable shall be the law of the country in which the person claimed to be liable is habitually resident if he or she could not reasonably have foreseen substantial consequences of his or her act occurring in the country designated by the first sentence.

(2) When the rights of the person seeking compensation for damage are, or are likely to be, affected in more than one country, and that person sues in the court of the domicile of the defendant, the claimant may instead choose to base his or her claim on the law of the court seised.

(3) The law applicable to the right of reply or equivalent measures shall be the law of the country in which the broadcaster or publisher has its habitual residence.

(4) The law applicable under this Article may be derogated from by an agreement pursuant to Article 14."

[223] In some countries, there is a cause of action for loss of self-esteem, for bringing a president or the government into disrepute by undermining public confidence in its capacity to govern, and for insult. With these three causes of action there may be liability under the foreign law even though the statement is true. It was suggested that these causes of action did not constitute defamation for the purposes of the defamation exclusion under the English statutory tort choice of law rules, see the 13th edn of this book (1999), pp 654–6. In the 14th edn of this book (2008), p 785, these causes of action were considered to be so far removed from the idea of defamation that they should not be classified as defamation for the purposes of the defamation exclusion. In view of the autonomous interpretation of the exception in Art 1(2)(g), the better view is probably that these causes of action fall under the exception and are thus governed by national conflict rules.

[224] *Campbell v MGN Ltd* [2004] UKHL Ltd, [2002] 2 AC 457; *Douglas v Hello!* [2007] UKHL 21, [2008] 1 AC. Breach of confidence traditionally covers secret (ie confidential) information. See also the suggestion in *Vidal-Hall v Google Inc* [2014] EWHC 13 (QB) at [66]–[68] that the non-existence of a tort of invasion of privacy in English law needs to be revisited in light of the acknowledgement of a "tort" of misuse of private information.

[225] *Campbell v MGN Ltd*, supra, at [15] (per Lord Nicholls); *Douglas v Hello!*, supra, at [255].

[226] In some countries, the right to personality may encompass (certain elements) of the right to physical integrity, the right to move, to sexual freedom, etc.

[227] For harmonisation on the level of substantive law see Art 82 of Regulation (EU) 2016/679 on the protection of natural persons with regard to the processing of personal data and on the free movement of such data, OJ 2016 L 119/1.

A question arises of whether the exclusion of defamation can be avoided by re-labelling the tort as unfair competition, which is within the scope of the Regulation.[228] Under English law, if a business rival disparages the business reputation of a competitor, recourse can be had to the law of defamation. In some other countries the same act of disparagement would allow recourse to the law of unfair competition. The terms "defamation" and "unfair competition" should be defined for the purposes of the Regulation in the light of their meaning in Member States generally. This would suggest that this act should be regarded as one of unfair competition and hence within the Regulation.[229]

(ii) Evidence and procedure, without prejudice to Articles 21 and 22[230]

Article 1(3) provides that the Regulation "shall not apply to evidence and procedure, without prejudice to Articles 21 and 22". The same exclusion is to be found in the Rome I Regulation.[231] The exclusion is justified by the consideration that procedural matters such as the constitution and powers of courts and the mode of trial are an integral feature of the forum's organisation of the judicial process.[232] Requiring the judge to apply foreign procedural or evidential practices would be unrealistic and inefficient, as the judge would have to consult foreign law before being able to proceed with the steps of the court's procedure.[233] Another argument for the exception is the principle "that a litigant resorting to a domestic court cannot expect to occupy a different procedural position from that of a domestic litigant" and thus "cannot expect to take advantage of some procedural rule of his own country to enjoy greater advantage than other litigants here".[234]

Evidence The exclusion of evidence is not total, but is subject to Article 21,[235] which contains a rule on the formal validity of a unilateral act intended to have legal effect and relating to a non-contractual obligation, and Article 22,[236] which subjects two specific evidential matters, rules which raise presumptions of law or determine the burden of proof and proving acts intended to have legal effect, to the rules of the Regulation. Article 22 covers only the burden, not the standard of proof, the latter as a procedural matter falling outside the scope of the Regulation.[237] Another matter of evidence (and procedure) in the sense of Article 1(3) which falls outside the Regulation are methods of proving recoverable loss, for example what (expert) evidence is available or required to prove a claimant's injuries.[238]

---

[228] See Art 6(1), (2).

[229] Art 6(1), (2) Rome II.

[230] Art 1(3).

[231] Art 1(3) of the Rome I Regulation; discussed supra, p 704; see also Art 1(2)(h) of the Rome Convention. The Proposal for a Regulation did not provide for the exclusion, see the Explanatory Memorandum accompanying the Proposal, p 9. Arguably this was the case because matters of evidence and procedure would not appear to come within the scope of a Regulation which is concerned with the law applicable to non-contractual obligations (a matter of substance). On the other hand, there is some overlap in the field of remedies (Art 15) which justifies at least a clarification.

[232] Dicey, Morris and Collins, para 34-036 (proposing a narrow interpretation of Art 1(3)); for a comparable argument in a pre-Regulation case see *Harding v Wealands* [2004] EWCA Civ 1735 at [52]–[54] (per Arden LJ).

[233] See *Wall v Mutuelle de Poitiers Assurances* [2014] EWCA Civ 138 at [43]: "it is unrealistic and inefficient to expect courts to adopt the evidential practices of a different jurisdiction when determining questions of fact".

[234] *Actavis UK Ltd v Eli Lilly & Co* [2015] EWCA Civ 555 at [136].

[235] Discussed infra, pp 872–3.

[236] Discussed supra, p 85. This is lifted from Art 14 of the Rome Convention. See also Art 18 Rome I Regulation.

[237] *Marshall v Motor Insurers Bureau* [2015] EWHC 3421 (QB) at [24]–[25].

[238] *Wall v Mutuelle de Poitiers Assurances* [2014] EWCA Civ 138 at [12], [20], [41]–[45], [48].

Procedure When it comes to procedure there is the vital question of when a matter is to be classified as being one of procedure, rather than one of substance. Procedure is a very different matter from the other matters excluded in that it involves a potential escape device, ie if you classify a matter as being purely procedural you escape from the choice of law rules under the Regulation. In the absence of guidance from the Court of Justice, national courts are likely to resort to their own traditional ideas of what is a procedural matter. However, the concept of procedure must be given an autonomous EU definition,[239] and English courts cannot automatically assume that the classifications which they have adopted in the past will continue to be appropriate under the Regulation.

The terms of the Regulation, in particular the non-exhaustive list of Article 15, make it clear that a different classification should be adopted from that under English law.[240] Three examples can be given to illustrate this. The first example is concerned with damages. The issue of assessment or quantification of damages was classified at common law as being one of procedure, whereas the issue of heads of liability for which damages could be recovered was one of substance.[241] The position was the same under the statutory tort choice of law rules. In that context, it was held that the issue of whether accrued benefits (state benefits, employment pension, personal pension) had to be deducted when assessing damages was a procedural one.[242] Similarly, a statutory ceiling on damages was held to be a matter of assessment of damages and therefore procedural.[243] However, under the Regulation it is expressly stated that the issue of assessment of damage falls within the scope of the law applicable under the Regulation.[244] This includes not only the rules on the applicable law in so far as assessment is prescribed by a black-letter rule of law, but also in so far as it is prescribed by judicial conventions and practices (such as particular tariffs, guidelines or formulae to calculate damages under the applicable law[245]).[246] Also foreign case law on the appropriate level of damages is to be applied.[247] Rules on the deduction of accrued benefits and a statutory ceiling on damages are thus, for the purposes of the Regulation, to be regarded as part of the applicable law defined by the Regulation and not a procedural matter.[248] However, applying foreign substantive law on the assessment of damages does not mean that an English court must adopt also foreign procedures to decide the case in the exact same manner as the foreign court would. Mere methods of proving recoverable loss, in particular what (expert) evidence is required to prove the claimant's injuries and losses is a matter of evidence and procedure in the sense of Article 1(3) Rome II and thus governed by English procedural rules.[249]

---

[239] *Actavis UK Ltd v Eli Lilly & Co* [2015] EWCA Civ 555 at [137].

[240] Ibid, at [144].

[241] Supra, pp 93–6. Contributory negligence, which may reduce damages under the law of some countries, was regarded as being substantive: *Dawson v Broughton*, 31 July 2007 (unreported), Manchester County Court. Contributory negligence falls clearly within the scope of the choice of law rules under the Rome II Regulation, see Art 15(b), discussed infra, pp 859–60.

[242] *Roerig v Valiant Trawlers* [2002] EWCA Civ 21, [2002] 1 WLR 2304. See also *Edmunds v Simmonds* [2001] 1 WLR 1003.

[243] *Harding v Wealands* [2006] UKHL 32, [2007] 2 AC 1; following *Stevens v Head* (1993) 176 CLR 433, HC of Australia. Cf *McNeilly v Imbree* [2007] NSWCA 156.

[244] Art 15(c); discussed infra, pp 861–3.

[245] Such as the foreign equivalent to the Judicial College Guidelines for the Assessment of General Damages in Personal Injury Cases (13th edn, 2015).

[246] *Wall v Mutuelle de Poitiers Assurances* [2014] EWCA Civ 138 at [23]–[24], [34], [51]. In the 14th edn of this book (2008), pp 844–6, it was proposed that Art 15(c) should be interpreted as being implicitly limited to the assessment of damages "in so far as prescribed by law". The reason given for this view was that the words "in so far as prescribed by law" should be read into Art 15(c), as they are included in Art 10(1)(c) of the Rome Convention.

[247] *Wall v Mutuelle de Poitiers Assurances* [2014] EWCA Civ 138 at [53].

[248] Collier, p 344.

[249] *Wall v Mutuelle de Poitiers Assurances* [2014] EWCA Civ 138 at [12], [20], [41]–[45], [48].

The second example of a different delineation between procedure and substance under the Regulation is that of the issue of limitation of liability. In the past, this has been classified as procedural.[250] Again, under the Regulation it is expressly stated that this issue falls within the scope of the law applicable under the Regulation.[251]

A third example are the rules of prescription and limitation. While there is some debate whether these are to be classified as substantive or procedural outside the Regulation,[252] the Regulation makes clear that these issues are not questions of "evidence or procedure", but rather fall within the scope of the law applicable defined by Rome II.[253]

Finally, it deserves to be mentioned that Article 15 does not require all aspects of remedies to be classified as substantive (and thus falling in the scope of Rome II). Article 15(d) provides a counter-exception for "the limits of powers conferred on the court by its procedural law", and the conditions of admissibility of actions, such as the conditions of applying for a declaration of non-infringement, are not to be classified as substantive, but rather as procedural in nature.[254]

Once it has been decided that the issue is one of evidence or procedure, the effect of the exclusion is that this issue is left to be governed by the forum's rules on private international law. Under English private international law all procedural matters (including evidence) are automatically a matter for the law of the forum (*lex fori*).[255]

(ii) *The universal application of the Regulation*

The Rome II Regulation is intended to be of universal or world-wide application, ie it applies regardless of whether the situation giving rise to the non-contractual obligation and the obligation itself has any connection with a European Union Member State. In particular, there is no need for either party to the dispute to be domiciled or resident in a Member State. The only thing that matters is that the dispute is tried in a Member State. Thus a tortious dispute between a New York resident and an Ontario resident which is tried before the High Court in England will be subject to the Regulation.

Article 3 provides that: "Any law specified by this Regulation shall be applied whether or not it is the law of a Member State." This provision makes it clear that, if the uniform rules under the Regulation point, for example, to Russian law as the law governing the non-contractual obligation, the courts of Member States will apply that country's law, even though Russia is not a European Union Member State. However, Article 3 only deals with one aspect of the universal application of the rules in the Regulation. It says nothing about whether the situation giving rise to the non-contractual obligation, including the residence of the parties, must have a connection with a Member State. It is the Explanatory Memorandum[256] which makes it clear that the Regulation is intended to have universal application and will apply to situations giving rise to a non-contractual obligation which have no connection with a Member State. This principle of universal application is well established and is also

---

[250] *Caltex Singapore Pte Ltd and Ors v BP Shipping Ltd* [1996] 1 Lloyd's Rep 86, concerned with limitation of liability in maritime cases under the Merchant Shipping Act 1995; approved in *Harding v Wealands*, supra, at [47] (per Lord Hoffmann), [2] (per Lord Woolf), [78] (per Lord Rodger), [79] (per Lord Carswell). See also *Seismic Shipping Inc v Total E & P UK plc (The Western Regent)* [2005] EWCA Civ 985 at [52], [2005] 2 Lloyd's Rep 359.

[251] Art 15(b), discussed infra, pp 859–60.

[252] See supra, pp 78–9.

[253] Art 15(h); discussed infra, p 865.

[254] *Actavis UK Ltd v Eli Lilly & Co* [2015] EWCA Civ 555 at [137]–[149].

[255] Supra, pp 73–4.

[256] At pp 9–10.

to be found in the Rome I Regulation[257] and in the Brussels I Recast (in the sense that that Regulation governs both purely "intra-EU" situations and certain situations involving a non-Member State).[258] It avoids the need to distinguish for choice of law purposes between intra-EU cases and extra-EU cases, a distinction which is both highly artificial and difficult to draw.[259] It also avoids the complexity of Member States having two sets of choice of law rules and the distortions in competition that would result if Member States applied their own national choice of law rules to extra-EU cases.[260]

(c) The applicable law: preliminary remarks

At the heart of the Regulation lie the rules on the applicable law. There are separate sets of rules for torts/delicts (in Chapter II) and unjust enrichment, *negotiorum gestio* and *culpa in contrahendo* (collectively referred to as unjust enrichment, etc) (in Chapter III). There is then a series of rules (in Chapter IV) allowing the parties to submit non-contractual obligations to the law of their choice.

(i) Exclusion of renvoi

The applicable law under the Regulation, whether chosen or not, refers to the substantive rules of the domestic law of the country in question, and there is no place for application of that country's rules of private international law under the doctrine of renvoi.[261]

(ii) Definition of habitual residence

A number of the rules on the applicable law, in the absence of choice, provide for the application of the law of the country of the parties' habitual residence.[262] The Regulation defines the habitual residence of companies but, apart from in one specific situation, not that of natural persons (ie individuals).[263] For companies, Article 23(1) of Rome II provides that "For the purposes of this Regulation, the habitual residence of companies and other bodies, corporate or unincorporated, shall be the place of central administration.[264] The same term "central administration" is used to define the domicile of companies under the Brussels I Recast,[265] and the same autonomous EU meaning should be given to the concept in both contexts.[266] The place of central administration rule is qualified by a special rule in Article 23(1) to deal with the situation where the event giving rise to the damage occurs, or the damage arises, in the course of operation of a branch, agency or other establishment. In this situation, the place where the branch, etc is located is treated as the place of habitual residence of the company. The terms "branch, agency or other establishment" in the context of the Rome II Regulation can be understood in the same way as they have been understood by the Court of Justice for the purposes of what is now Article 7(5) Brussels I Recast. In this context, the Court of Justice has also defined the concept of "a dispute arising out of the operations of a branch". The requirement under Article 23(1) that the event or damage arises "in the course

---

[257] Art 2 Rome I.

[258] Supra, pp 202–3.

[259] The Explanatory Memorandum, p 10.

[260] Ibid.

[261] Art 24. The position is the same for contract choice of law under the Rome I Regulation, Art 20 Rome I.

[262] Arts 4, 5, 10, 11, 12.

[263] *Winrow v Hemphill & Anor* [2014] EWHC 3164 (QB) at [11].

[264] The same provision is found in Art 19(1) first paragraph Rome I.

[265] Art 63(1)(b) Brussels I Recast. Under Art 63 of the Brussels I Recast domicile is defined in terms of three alternatives and so a company can be domiciled in three different states; this would not work for choice of law purposes hence the use of habitual residence as the connecting factor, rather than domicile.

[266] For the meaning given to the concept in the context of the Brussels I Recast, see supra, pp 201–2.

of operation of a branch", etc looks to be in substance the same, so that recourse can again be had to the case law under Article 7(5).[267]

The one situation where Article 23 defines the meaning of the habitual residence of a natural person is where such a person is "acting in the course of his or her business activity". In this situation, the habitual residence of the natural person is his or her principal place of business.[268] The term "principal place of business" is also used to define the domicile of companies under the Brussels I Recast,[269] so that the same autonomous Community meaning can be given to the concept in both contexts.[270] In all other situations, the English courts will have to have recourse to the meaning of habitual residence of a natural person who is not acting in the course of a business activity. In due course, it is to be hoped that there will be guidance from the Court of Justice on the meaning of the habitual residence of a natural person in the present context, as there has been in the context of income support for employed persons.[271] In the meantime, any guidance on the meaning of the concept from that Court in other contexts[272] should be borne in mind.[273]

(iii) Definition of damage

Many of the choice of law rules use the concept of damage. Damage covers any (direct or indirect) consequence arising out of tort/delict, unjust enrichment, *negotiorum gestio* or *culpa in contrahendo*[274] and also damage that is likely to occur.[275]

(iv) Proof of foreign law

The normal English rules on proof of foreign law apply in relation to the Regulation. However, it is an open question how long this will remain the case. Different practices are followed in different Member States in relation to the treatment of foreign law.[276] The European Parliament unsuccessfully sought an amendment to the Regulation that would have required the court seised to establish the content of the foreign law of its own motion[277] so as to ensure a more uniform approach to the application of foreign law by courts throughout the European Union. The European Parliament dropped this amendment as part of the overall compromise on the Regulation. The matter was settled by the Commission undertaking to produce a study on the effects of the way in which foreign law is treated in the different jurisdictions and on the extent to which courts in the Member States apply foreign law in practice pursuant to the Rome II Regulation.[278] The Commission has made a statement which suggests that the study will not be confined to just the application of foreign law in Rome II cases but more generally in civil and commercial matters.[279] This study shall be included in a more

---

[267] Supra, pp 279–83.

[268] The same provision is found in Art 19(1) second paragraph Rome I.

[269] Art 63(1)(c) Brussels I Recast.

[270] For the meaning given to the concept in the context of the Brussels I Recast, see supra, pp 201–2.

[271] Case C-90/97 *Swaddling v Adjudication Officer* [1999] ECR I-1075.

[272] Guidance may also arise in the context of Council Regulation (EC) No 2201/2003 of 27 November 2003 concerning jurisdiction and the recognition and enforcement of judgments in matrimonial matters and the matters of parental responsibility, known as Brussels II *bis*; discussed infra, pp 954–64.

[273] See *Winrow v Hemphill & Anor* [2014] EWHC 3164 (QB) at [40]–[41], referring to the test of Case C-497/10 *Mercredi v Chaffe* [2010] ECR I-14309 at [47]. For the habitual residence of deceased persons, see also Recitals (23) and (24) of Regulation (EU) No 650/2012 on succession, OJ 2012 L 201/107.

[274] Art 2(1).

[275] Art 2(3)(b).

[276] See supra, pp 105–11.

[277] See EP Report A6-0211/2005 of 27 June 2005 (the Wallis Report), Amendment 43, Art 11 b (new), para 1. According to para 2 of this proposal, if it is impossible to establish the content of the foreign law and the parties agree, the law of the court seised shall be applied. But what if they do not agree?

[278] Art 30(1)(i).

[279] See, attached to the Regulation, the Commission statement on the treatment of foreign law.

general report on the application of the Regulation, accompanied, if necessary, by proposals to adapt the Regulation.[280] This report was to be submitted by 20 August 2011, but apparently has not yet been produced.

(d) The applicable law for torts/delicts

(i) The scope of Chapter II

In order to define the scope of Chapter II, a process of characterisation has to be gone through. If the obligation arises out of tort/delict it is a non-contractual obligation that falls within Chapter II. If the obligation arises out of unjust enrichment, *negotiorum gestio* or *culpa in contrahendo* it is a non-contractual obligation that falls within Chapter III. If the obligation arises out of contract it is a contractual obligation and falls outside the scope of the Regulation altogether (and into that of the Rome I Regulation instead).

How is this process of characterisation to be carried out? If English judges apply the same approach as they have applied in relation to the Rome Convention, this would be according to English principles of characterisation.[281] However, the process of characterisation should be guided by the subject matter and wording of the Regulation itself—as characterisation involves an element of interpretation, it is to be done in an EU autonomous way.[282] Moreover, it is subject to the implicit instruction in Recital (7) of the Regulation that "torts/delicts", being concerned with scope, should be interpreted in a way that is consistent with the meaning attached to this concept under Article 7(2) of the Brussels I Recast (matters relating to tort, delict or quasi-delict). Applying these principles we can examine what is covered by "torts/delicts" and what is not.

(a) What is covered

It will be recalled that "matters relating to tort, delict or quasi-delict" under Article 7(2) Brussels I Recast has been widely interpreted by the Court of Justice to cover all actions which seek to establish the liability of a defendant and which are not related to a contract within Article 7(1) of that Regulation.[283] This definition covers (most) matters which are tortious according to the domestic substantive law of Member States. Thus it has been held to cover negligence, conversion, negligent misstatement, negligent and fraudulent misrepresentation.[284] Torts/delicts for the purposes of Chapter II of Rome II should thus also cover negligence and negligent misstatement, unless the misstatement is made during dealings prior to the conclusion of a contract.[285] We further know from the terms of the Rome II Regulation that the concept of torts/delicts encompasses also product liability, unfair competition, acts restricting free competition, environmental damage, infringement of intellectual property rights, and industrial action because there are separate specific rules for all of these in Articles 5 to 9 of Chapter II. The Regulation applies also to non-contractual obligations that are likely to arise[286] and thus would cover the threat of a tort. This is consistent with the Brussels I Recast which specifically applies to threatened wrongs.[287]

---

[280] Art 30(1).

[281] Supra, p 692 (proposing a different approach under Rome I).

[282] Supra, p 783.

[283] Case C-191/15 *Verein für Konsumenteninformation v Amazon EU Sàrl* ECLI:EU:C:2016:612 at [37]; supra, p 264.

[284] Supra, p 263.

[285] This would constitute *culpa in contrahendo*, discussed infra, pp 850–2.

[286] Art 2(2) Rome II.

[287] Art 7(2) Brussels I Recast: "place where the harmful event occurred or may occur".

But Article 7(2) Brussels I Recast goes beyond this. It is a residual category which covers matters which are not in a strict sense tortious, ie they are not classified as tortious under domestic substantive law. For example, Article 7(2) has been held by an English court to cover a constructive trust claim based on dishonestly assisting a breach of fiduciary duty[288] and has been assumed to cover a claim for breach of fiduciary duty.[289] In both cases, under English substantive law what is involved is a breach of an equitable obligation. Torts/delicts for the purposes of Chapter II should therefore be regarded as a residual category,[290] as it is in jurisdictional cases, that covers, subject to the special rules of Chapter III, all non-contractual obligations (including equitable obligations) which seek to establish the liability of the defendant on the basis of a causal connection between a damage of the claimant and a "harmful event" to be imputed to the defendant in which the damage originates.[291] In distinguishing between tort and unjust enrichment (Chapters II and III), it seems also appropriate to ask whether the measure of recovery is determined by reference to the loss to the claimant (tort) or by reference to the enrichment of the defendant (unjust enrichment).[292] In principle therefore Chapter II is capable of covering equitable obligations where the obligation is not entered into voluntarily[293] (otherwise it is to be characterised as a contractual obligation) and does not fall under Chapter III,[294] such as breach of a fiduciary duty and dishonestly procuring or assisting a breach of fiduciary duty,[295] On this basis, non-contractual breach of confidence, when it is concerned with protecting secret information,[296] should also come within Chapter II.[297] Where a breach of an equitable obligation gives rise to liability under the law

---

[288] *Casio Computer Co Ltd v Sayo* [2001] IL PR 164, CA.

[289] *Benatti v WPP Holdings Italy SRL* [2007] EWCA Civ 263 at [58] (per Toulson LJ), [2007] 1 WLR 2316.

[290] See also the opening words of Art 4: "Unless otherwise provided for in this Regulation"; see also supra, pp 789–90.

[291] For these criteria see Case C-572/14 *Austro-Mechana Gesellschaft zur Wahrnehmung mechanisch-musikalischer Urheberrechte Gesellschaft mbH v Amazon EU Sàrl and Others* ECLI:EU:C:2016:286 at [39]–[42]. The Proposal for a Regulation was worded differently, having one section for non-contractual obligations arising out of a tort or delict and another section for non-contractual obligations arising out of an act other than a tort or delict. This made it more obvious that an equitable obligation would be covered. However, the change in wording should not be regarded as being significant. Indeed, the original wording was adopted simply to avoid technical language, see the Explanatory Memorandum, pp 8 and 21.

[292] For the distinction between unjust enrichment and "non-contractual liability in the strict sense" (tort) in Art 340 TFEU see Case C-47/07 P *Masdar (UK) Ltd v Commission of the European Communities* [2008] ECR I-9761 at [49]: "They [actions for unjust enrichment] differ from actions brought under those rules [tort actions] in that they do not require proof of unlawful conduct—indeed, of any form of conduct at all—on the part of the defendant, but merely proof of enrichment on the part of the defendant for which there is no valid legal basis and of impoverishment on the part of the applicant which is linked to that enrichment." The scope of Chapter III for equitable obligations is discussed infra, pp 806–7; see also supra, pp 788–91.

[293] More precisely, it is relevant whether "the interpretation of the contract which links the defendant to the applicant is indispensable to establish the lawful or, on the contrary, unlawful nature of the conduct complained of against the former by the latter", Case C-548/12 *Marc Brogsitter v Fabrication de Montres Normandes EURL and Karsten Fräßdorf* ECLI:EU:C:2014:148 at [25].

[294] See Case C-572/14 *Austro-Mechana Gesellschaft zur Wahrnehmung mechanisch-musikalischer Urheberrechte Gesellschaft mbH v Amazon EU Sàrl and Others* ECLI:EU:C:2016:286 at [35]–[36].

[295] See Yeo, *Choice of Law for Equitable Doctrines*, para 8.58.

[296] When it is concerned with protecting privacy it is submitted that it is excluded from the scope of the Regulation, supra, pp 797–8.

[297] Usually this will be within Art 4 but for the purposes of the Regulation targeting a competitor by the disclosure of business secrets, which would be regarded under English law as a breach of confidence, should be regarded as an act of unfair competition within Art 6, see infra, p 824 and now *Innovia Films Ltd v Frito-Lay North America, Inc* [2012] EWHC 790 (Pat) at [109]: "common ground that claims for breach of an equitable obligation of confidence fall within Article 6 of the Rome II Directive [Regulation]". In *Kitechnology BV and Ors v Unicor GMBH Plastmaschinen and Ors* [1994] IL Pr 568, the Court of Appeal found it impossible to express a concluded view on whether such a claim came within Art 5(3) of the Brussels Convention. *Vidal-Hall v Google Inc* [2015] EWCA Civ 311 at [38]–[39], [43] has now qualified the observation in *Douglas v Hello! Ltd (No 3)*, supra as mere *dictum* and characterised the misuse of private information as a tort for the

of trusts this will often come within the Hague Convention on the Law Applicable to Trusts and on their Recognition 1985, and recourse must then be had to the choice of law rules in that Convention,[298] rather than those in the Regulation.[299]

In some respects, however, tort/delict for the purpose of Chapter II is a narrower residual category than Article 7(2) of the Brussels I Recast in that Chapter II of Rome II does not include unjust enrichment, *negotiorum gestio* and *culpa in contrahendo* (because they fall within Chapter III), whereas an instance of *culpa in contrahendo* has been held to come within Article 7(2).[300] Moreover, Article 7(2) may encompass certain property matters,[301] whereas the law of property is not part of the law of obligations and therefore falls outside the scope of the Rome II Regulation altogether.[302]

(b) What is not covered

Chapter II does not apply to non-contractual obligations arising out of unjust enrichment, *negotiorum gestio* and *culpa in contrahendo*. These are subject to the choice of law rules in Chapter III.

(i) Tort or unjust enrichment

Equitable obligations   Equitable obligations which are not entered into in the context of a voluntarily assumed obligation[303] will fall within the tort choice of law rules in Chapter II, unless they are classified as unjust enrichment (within the meaning of Article 10 of the Regulation). Under the pre-Regulation classification for choice of law purposes the Court of Appeal found persuasive the argument that a claim for breach of confidence[304] fell to be categorised as a restitutionary claim for unjust enrichment.[305] The case in question involved a claim for damages,[306] rather than for an account for profits, and so made no sense as a matter of domestic classification. Under domestic English law this would not constitute unjust enrichment or restitution for wrongdoing. It would be very odd to adopt, for the purposes of the Regulation, a classification that is not followed as a matter of English substantive law or under the law of any other Member State. It is submitted therefore, as the Court of Appeal has decided now for service out of jurisdiction,[307] that such a case should be classified as

---

purposes of service out of jurisdiction. See also the new Civil Procedure Rules Practice Direction 6b, para 3.1(21) for service out of the jurisdiction in case of claims for breach of confidence and misuse of private information.

[298] Discussed infra, pp 1383–91.

[299] Art 28 of the Regulation; discussed infra, pp 873–5.

[300] Case C-334/00 *Fonderie Officine Meccaniche Tacconi SpA v Heinrich Wagner Sinto Maschinenfabrik GmbH (HWS)* [2002] ECR I-7357; but see also Case C-196/15 *Granarolo v Ambrosi Emmi France SA* ECLI:EU:C:2016:559 at [23]–[27]: an action for damages founded on an abrupt termination of a long-standing business relationship can be contractual if a tacit contractual relationship existed between the parties. The difficulties over whether unjust enrichment falls within Art 7(2) Brussels I Recast are discussed supra, pp 265–6, see also pp 247–8.

[301] Where the action seeks to establish the liability of the defendant, see supra, pp 266–7.

[302] See the discussion of conversion, infra, pp 808–9.

[303] Otherwise they are contractual in nature if "the interpretation of the contract which links the defendant to the applicant is indispensable to establish the lawful or, on the contrary, unlawful nature of the conduct complained of against the former by the latter", Case C-548/12 *Marc Brogsitter v Fabrication de Montres Normandes EURL and Karsten Fräßdorf* ECLI:EU:C:2014:148 at [25]. Alternatively, they may arise from a trust created voluntarily and thus be excluded under Art 1(2)(e).

[304] It was in fact a case of breach of confidence involving invasion of privacy and so would be outside the scope of the Regulation, supra, pp 797–8. But what was said in the case is relevant for the discussion of the other type of breach of confidence involving confidential information.

[305] See *Douglas v Hello! Ltd (No 3)* [2005] EWCA Civ 595 at [97], [2006] QB 125.

[306] For distress and for having to deal hurriedly with the selection of photos.

[307] *Vidal-Hall v Google Inc* [2015] EWCA Civ 311 at [38]–[39], [43] has now qualified the observation in *Douglas v Hello! Ltd (No 3)*, supra as mere *dictum* and characterised the misuse of private information as a

tortious (within the wide meaning to be given to that phrase under Chapter II). However, if the disgorgement of profits was sought from the defendant (an account of profits) this would be regarded under English law as an example of restitution for equitable wrongdoing. It is argued below[308] that such cases fall within the meaning of unjust enrichment under the Regulation, and, accordingly, the choice of law rules in Chapter III (Article 10) would have to be applied. The same principles should apply to other instances of breach of equitable obligations,[309] such as breach of a fiduciary duty.[310]

Contribution and indemnity   A difficult question of classification arises also where a tortfeasor seeks a contribution or indemnity from another tortfeasor. Where the contribution or indemnity does not arise out of a contractual relationship (and the Rome I Regulation therefore does not apply),[311] the Rome II Regulation tells us that the "debtor's right to demand compensation from the other debtors shall be governed by the law applicable to that debtor's non-contractual obligation towards the creditor".[312] For the case of an insurer of a vehicle involved in an accident seeking compensation from the insurer of another vehicle involved in the same accident, the CJEU has held that the applicable law is determined in two steps: (1) the division of liability between the drivers of the vehicles is to be determined under the law applicable according to Article 4 Rome II, (2) the law applicable to the insurance contract between the insurer and the driver of the vehicle seeking compensation must be determined under Article 7 Rome I in order to ascertain whether and to what extent those insurers may (by subrogation) exercise the driver's rights against the insurer of the other vehicle.[313] As the difference in wording between Article 20 Rome II Regulation and its predecessor in Article 13(2) 1980 Rome Convention makes clear, Article 20 covers all possible forms of contribution between jointly liable debtors ("debtor's right to demand"), irrespective of their legal basis (such as *cessio legis*,[314] subrogation, separate cause of action, restitution or *negotiorum gestio*).[315] Therefore, Article 20 Rome II[316] is *lex specialis*[317] to Articles 10, 11 Rome II for compensation claims based on restitution or *negotiorum gestio*.[318] It therefore does not matter that contribution and indemnity might not be regarded as tortious in nature in the strict

---

tort for the purposes of service out of jurisdiction. See also the new Civil Procedure Rules Practice Direction 6b, para 3.1(21) for service out of the jurisdiction in case of claims for breach of confidence and misuse of private information.

[308] Infra, pp 841–3.

[309] See generally Dicey, Morris and Collins, paras 36-057–36-100.

[310] This accords with the pre-Regulation classification of accounting for breach of fiduciary duty for choice of law purposes, see *Kuwait Oil Tanker Co SAK v Al-Bader* [2000] 2 All ER (Comm) 271, CA; approved by *Jacob Engineering Group Inc v Matthew* [2014] CSIH 18, 2014 SC 579 at [105]. The case also concerned a constructive trust, see generally infra, p 840.

[311] Joined Cases C-359/14 and C-475/14 *ERGO Insurance SE v If P&C Insurance AS and Gjensidige Baltic AAS v PZU Lietuva UAB DK* ECLI:EU:C:2016:40 at [61]–[62].

[312] Art 20 Rome II (=Art 16 Rome I). While Art 20 governs the internal relationship between several debtors (eg joint tortfeasors), Art 15(a) Rome II makes clear that the law applicable to the external relationship between each debtor (typically each co-tortfeasor) and the creditor (typically the victim) is the law applicable under the general conflict rules of Arts 4-14 Rome II Regulation. The phrase "extent of liability" in Art 15(a) Rome II "also includes division of liability between joint perpetrators", Explanatory Memorandum p 23; see also Art 15(b) Rome II "division of liability".

[313] Joined Cases C-359/14 and C-475/14 *ERGO Insurance SE v If P&C Insurance AS and Gjensidige Baltic AAS v PZU Lietuva UAB DK* ECLI:EU:C:2016:40 at [61]–[62].

[314] Which is a form of "assignment by operation of law".

[315] And not only—as under Art 19 Rome II—those "rights which the creditor had against the debtor", see the clarifying proposal by the Hamburg Group for Private International Law (2003) 67 RabelsZ 1, 49–50.

[316] Article 16 Rome I.

[317] In the sense of a law governing a specific subject matter (lex specialis) that will override a law which governs general broader matters (lex generalis) that include the specific subject matter concerned.

[318] Dornis (2008) 4 J Priv Int L 237, 244.

sense,[319] but rather as being based on unjust enrichment,[320] or even a *sui generis* claim[321] as has been the classification favoured by the Law Commissions[322] in a pre-Regulation context.

(ii) *Tort or* culpa in contrahendo

A negligent misstatement that is made during dealings prior to the conclusion of a contract where no tacit contractual relationship existed between the parties[323] will fall within the concept of *culpa in contrahendo* and, accordingly, the choice of law rules in Chapter III will apply.[324] If it is not made with a direct link with the dealings prior to the conclusion of a contract, it will fall within the concept of tort/delict.[325] The English law of fraudulent and negligent misrepresentation and duress is a form of pre-contractual liability and will fall within *culpa in contrahendo*.[326]

(iii) *Tort or property*

The common law is unusual in treating claims for interference with property rights as part of the law of tort. With the common law tort of conversion, the claimant seeks damages. In contrast, civil law countries treat interference with property as part of the law of property. The claimant does not seek damages, but rather recovery of an item solely on the basis that he is the rightful owner and the defendant has no right to possession.[327] Such a claim (*rei vindicatio*) should be regarded as falling outside the scope of the Regulation altogether. But what of a claim for damages for conversion under English law or that of some other common law country? The English courts have held that conversion falls within Article 7(2) of the Brussels I Recast[328] but that Regulation encompasses property matters, whereas such matters fall outside the scope of the Rome II Regulation, not being part of the law of obligations. When it comes to choice of law, the Court of Justice, looking at how civil law jurisdictions classify the matter, is likely to decide that a claim for interference with property solely based

---

[319] Law Com No 193 (1990), para 3.48.

[320] See generally Takahashi, *Claims for Contribution and Reimbursement in an International Context*, pp 7–18; Yeo, paras 9.34–9.41. The English statutory rules on contribution have been regarded as being what we now call under the Regulation an overriding mandatory rule of the forum: *Arab Monetary Fund v Hashim (No 9)* (1994) Times, 11 October, see infra, pp 866–8.

[321] *Borg-Warner (Australia) Ltd v Zupan* [1982] VR 437; Law Com No 193 (1990), para 3.48.

[322] Law Com No 193 (1990), paras 3.47–3.48. A claim between joint tortfeasors has been classified by the Australian courts as quasi-contractual and thus governed by the law governing the obligation: *Plozza v South Australian Insurance Co Ltd*, supra, at 127; *Stewart v Honey*, supra, at 592; and see *Nominal Defendant v Bagot's Executor and Trustee Co Ltd* [1971] SASR 347 at 365–7; revsd on other grounds (1971) 124 CLR 179; but see *Baldry v Jackson* [1977] 1 NSWLR 494. Contribution has, however, been held to fall within Art 7(2) (tort, delict or quasi-delict) of the Brussels I Regulation: *Hewden Tower Cranes Ltd v Wolffkran GmbH* [2007] EWHC 857 (TCC), [2007] 2 Lloyd's Rep 138; supra, p 265. A claim for contribution has been regarded as being founded upon a tort for the purpose of service out of the jurisdiction but not as a cause of action in tort: *FFSB Ltd v Seward & Kissel LLP* [2007] UKPC 16 at [22].

[323] If such a tacit contractual relationship existed, it will be a contractual obligation, Case C-196/15 *Granarolo v Ambrosi Emmi France SA* ECLI:EU:C:2016:559 at [23]–[27].

[324] See infra, p 850 and Recital (30) Rome II: *culpa in contrahendo* "should include the violation of the duty of disclosure and the breakdown of contractual negotiations"; but see also Case C-196/15 *Granarolo v Ambrosi Emmi France SA* ECLI:EU:C:2016:559 at [23]–[27]: an action for damages founded on an abrupt termination of a long-standing business relationship can be contractual if a tacit contractual relationship existed between the parties.

[325] See Recital (30) Rome II: "Article 12 covers only non-contractual obligations presenting a direct link with the dealings prior to the conclusion of a contract."

[326] See infra, pp 850–1 and Dicey, Morris and Collins, paras 35-093.

[327] See Fawcett, Harris and Bridge, paras 6.33–6.41. For an example see § 985 of the German *Bürgerliches Gesetzbuch*.

[328] Supra, p 263. An action claiming ownership of a painting and for conversion has been classified by an English court in a pre-Regulation case as a restitutionary proprietary claim and not as one in tort in the strict sense, *Gotha City v Sotheby's (No 2)* (1998) Times, 8 October.

on the claimant's proprietary right, including for conversion, is to be classified as part of the law of property and thus falls outside the scope of the Regulation.[329] Such a classification presents the English courts with a problem: what choice of law rules are they then to apply? There are no English property choice of law rules that would deal with a case of conversion. Such a case would fall naturally within the statutory tort choice of law rules[330] that applied prior to the introduction of the Rome II Regulation and still apply to torts falling outside the scope of the Regulation. It is to these statutory tort choice of law rules that the English courts should have recourse.

Questions of scope also arise in relation to the separate choice of law rules in Chapter II. These questions of scope will be considered below.[331]

(ii) The structure of Chapter II

Chapter II creates a flexible framework of choice of law rules, which seek to reconcile the requirement of legal certainty with the need to do justice in the individual case.[332] Article 4 is entitled the "General rule". Articles 5 to 9 then set out a number of specific rules for special torts "where the general rule does not allow a reasonable balance to be struck between the interests at stake".[333] The "general rule" applies for all other torts/delicts and the term must be understood as contrasting with the specific rules for special torts. For certain provisions there is a let-out which allows for a departure from fixed rules where it is clear from all the circumstances of the case that the tort/delict is manifestly more closely connected with another country.[334]

(iii) Article 4: General rule

The so-called general rule comprises three separate rules: first, a general principle; secondly, an exception to this; thirdly, an escape clause, which operates as a let-out in relation to both the general principle and its exception.[335] It is noticeable that the general principle and the exception to it are rules and not presumptions.

(a) The scope of Article 4

Article 4 applies to "a non-contractual obligation arising out of a tort/delict". Despite the all-embracing language, Article 4 does not encompass the following torts/delicts: product liability; unfair competition; acts restricting free competition; environmental damage; infringement of intellectual property rights; industrial action, as there are separate rules for these in Articles 5 to 9 of the Regulation. The scope of each of these special rules for specific torts will be examined later. Suffice it to say at this stage that difficult problems can arise as to whether the general rule under Article 4 should apply or one of the specific rules for special torts. For example, non-contractual breach of confidence should normally come within Article 4. However, for the purposes of the Regulation, targeting a competitor by the disclosure of business secrets, which would be regarded under English

---

[329] But see Dicey, Morris and Collins, para 34-021 arguing for a classification as a tort/delict. The CJEU tends to define a proprietary action as an action based on a right *in rem* and not on a right *in personam*, see, in the context of Art 24(1) Brussels I Recast, Case C-417/15 *Wolfgang Schmidt v Christiane Schmidt* ECLI:EU:C:2016:881 at [34]. For the incidental question of ownership and acquisition of property, it seems undisputed that these fall outside the scope of Rome II and are governed by the law of the *situs*, see Dicey, Morris and Collins, para 34-022.

[330] Discussed supra, pp 777–8.

[331] Infra, pp 819–36.

[332] Recital (14).

[333] Recital (19).

[334] Recital (14).

[335] See Recital (18).

law as a breach of confidence, should be regarded as an act of unfair competition within Article 6.[336]

(b) Article 4(1): a place of damage general principle

Article 4(1) provides that:

> Unless otherwise provided for in this Regulation, the law applicable to a non-contractual obligation arising out of a tort/delict shall be the law of the country in which the damage occurs irrespective of the country in which the event giving rise to the damage occurred and irrespective of the country or countries in which the indirect consequences of that event occur.

(i) Unless otherwise provided for

The opening words, "Unless otherwise provided for in this Regulation", make it clear that this provision is subject to other provisions in the Regulation. Article 4(1) is subject to the exception in Article 4(2) and the escape clause in Article 4(3), to the specific rules for special torts (Articles 5 to 9), to the right of the parties to choose the applicable law (Article 14), and to the limitations on the applicable law, namely overriding mandatory provisions of the forum (Article 16) and public policy (Article 26).

(ii) The definitional problem and adoption of a place of damage rule

Prior to Rome II, virtually all the Member States agreed on the application of the law of the place where the tort was committed (*lex loci delicti commissi*) as the basic rule for tort/delict choice of law.[337] However, a definitional problem arose where the component factors of the case were spread over several countries. There was no agreement among the Member States on the definition of this place.[338] The basic choice was between the law of the country in which the damage occurs (*lex damni*) and that of the country in which the event giving rise to the damage occurred. In the Regulation, the former was preferred to the latter for two reasons. First it is said that a connection with the country where the direct damage occurred "strikes a fair balance between the interests of the person claimed to be liable and the person sustaining the damage".[339] Secondly, it is said to "reflect the modern approach to civil liability and the development of systems of strict liability".[340] Still, in some cases, there will be very little connection with the country in which the damage occurred. The classic example is that of a car journey from Country A to Country E via Countries B, C and D. The driver drives negligently in Country D and injures his passenger. Both parties are from Country A. The fact that the damage occurred in Country D is fortuitous. Hence the need for the exception in Article 4(2) and the escape clause in Article 4(3).

Article 4(1) not only makes it clear that the law of the country in which the damage occurs is applicable but also spells out that one must not apply the law of the country in which the event giving rise to the damage occurred[341] or is likely to occur.[342] This has been inserted because of the position under the Brussels I Recast in relation to jurisdiction in cases of tort/delict. It will be recalled that Article 7(2) has been interpreted by the Court of Justice to

---

[336] Supra, p 799.

[337] See Collier, p 347: "accords with the parties expectations".

[338] Some applied a place of acting rule (Austria), others a place of damage rule (the Netherlands, France, Switzerland), yet others an alternative reference rule (Germany, Poland), in some it was not clear (Spain). The Explanatory Memorandum, at p 11, says that recent codifications in Member States have adopted a place of damage rule.

[339] Recital (16).

[340] Ibid.

[341] Art 4(1).

[342] Art 2(3)(a).

allocate jurisdiction to both the place of the event giving rise to damage and to the place of damage. But for choice of law purposes it cannot cover both because this would lead to two laws being applicable in cases where the two occurred in different countries.[343]

(iii) Identification of the country in which the damage occurs
Article 4(1) presupposes that it is always possible to identify the country where the damage occurs.[344] Identification of this country is normally easy in cases of *personal injury* or *damage to tangible property*. In a case of personal injury the country in which the damage occurs should be the country where the injury was sustained,[345] not where the payment of compensation was refused.[346] In a case of damage to property the country in which the damage occurs should be the country where the property was damaged.[347] The place where property was damaged is usually easy to identify. However, it may be more difficult in a situation where a damage gradually develops so that it is unknown, at the time of discovery, when and where exactly the damage occurred. Image a scenario where perishable goods are carried across Europe in a refrigerated truck and at some unknown point the refrigeration breaks down and the goods gradually rot. For jurisdictional purposes the place where the damage is discovered does not constitute the place of damage, but rather the place where the actual carrier was to deliver the goods.[348] It may be that, for reasons of foreseeability, legal certainty and coherence between Rome II and the Brussels I Recast the CJEU will adopt a similar approach for choice of law. The position is more straightforward in cases where the damage occurred in several countries and it is possible to identify these countries.[349] In principle, in this situation the laws of all of these countries will have to be applied on a distributive basis,[350] with a different law governing each instance of damage.

Where the action seeks to recover *pure financial loss* not arising from personal injury or damage to (tangible) property, the place of damage will depend on the nature and structure of the action. The location of the bank account in which the damage materialises or the place where the injured party is domiciled and where his assets are concentrated will normally not be the (relevant) place of (direct) damage.[351] Rather, it is to be asked where the direct (first) consequences of the alleged unlawful conduct or the first loss of assets

---

[343] See *Erste Group Bank AG v JSC "VMZ Red October"* [2015] EWCA Civ 379 at [91]: "the purpose of Rome II is to identify a single applicable law rather than a choice".
[344] For torts happening outside territorial waters, see infra, pp 877–8.
[345] See Recital (17) and Case C-350/14 *Florin Lazar, représenté légalement par Luigi Erculeo v Allianz SpA* ECLI:EU:C:2015:802 at [24].
[346] See *Jacobs v Motor Insurers Bureau* [2010] EWHC 231 (QB) at [32]–[40].
[347] Ibid.
[348] Case C-51/97 *Réunion Européenne v Spliethoff's Bevrachtingskantoor BV* [1998] ECR I-6511 at [35].
[349] See, eg, the pre-Regulation case of *Protea Leasing Ltd v Royal Air Cambodge* [2002] 2 All ER 224, damage was failure to pay for aircraft under leases (in a bank account outside Cambodia) and failure to maintain aircraft (in Cambodia). See also the pre-Regulation case of *Morin v Bonhams & Brooks Ltd* [2003] EWCA Civ 1802, [2004] 1 Lloyd's Rep 702, discussed infra, p 854 as an example of *culpa in contrahendo*.
[350] See Explanatory Memorandum, p 11. This is known as "Mosaikbetrachtung" (mosaic principle) in German law, von Hein in Calliess (ed), *Rome Regulations: Commentary*, Art 4 para 15, p 504. Where the fragmented application of several laws is impossible or exceedingly difficult, courts might resort to identifying a "direct" damage in a single State, see Dicey, Morris and Collins, para 35-028, or alternatively to applying the law of the country where the damage predominantly occurred, considered in *Hillside (New Media) Ltd v Baasland & Ors* [2010] EWHC 3336 (Comm) at [37].
[351] See (in the context of Art 7(2) Brussels I Recast) Case C-12/15 *Universal Music International Holding BV v Michael Tétreault Schilling and Others* ECLI:EU:C:2016:449 at [32], [35]; von Hein in Calliess (ed), *Rome Regulations: Commentary*, Art 4 para 23, p 507. This is not called into question by the decision in Case C-352/13 *Cartel Damage Claims (CDC) Hydrogen Peroxide SA v Evonik Degussa GmbH and Others* ECLI:EU:C:2015:335 where the CJEU located the place of damage at the victim's registered office (at [52]) because the *CDC* decision concerns the special scenario of cartel damages which, under Rome II, are governed by Art 6(3) and not Art 4.

occurred.[352] If, however, the alleged unlawful conduct consists of a breach of information duties (or possibly also in inducing the injured party into a transaction by means of fraud), the place of damage may be localised at the place of the account where the financial loss materialises.[353] In recent case law, it seems that the CJEU takes also substantive law considerations (such as protection of consumers or small investors or of cartel victims) into account in localising the place of damage, being more likely to allow for a place of damage at the place of the injured party's account or domicile where this supports a specific substantive law policy. Finally, another problem is identifying the place where damage results in cases where torts are committed via the internet.[354] As defamation is outside the scope of Rome II, such torts will often involve pure financial loss, so that the criteria for localisation of such loss are likely to be applied. In cases where the country has to be artificially fixed or is particularly difficult to identify, it will be easier to show that the tort is manifestly more closely connected with another country under the escape clause in Article 4(3).

(iv) Direct damage

Article 2(1) provides that damage covers "any consequence arising out of tort/delict". This is potentially very wide and could cover indirect consequences as well as direct consequences. However, Article 4(1) limits the meaning of damage by confining it to direct damage and excluding indirect damage. It does this by adding, after the instruction to apply the law of the country in which the damage occurs, the words "irrespective of the country or countries in which the indirect consequences of that event occur". If damage had included both direct and indirect damage this could have led to two or more countries' laws being applicable, which would be unworkable. Moreover, limiting damage to direct damage is consistent with Article 7(2) of the Brussels I Recast, as interpreted by the Court of Justice. We can now look at some examples—drawn from the context of jurisdiction under Article 7(2) Brussels I Recast—of how the direct damage rule will operate. Where an Italian domiciled plaintiff is arrested in England (and promissory notes are sequestrated) and the plaintiff subsequently brings an action in Italy, inter alia, for compensation for the damage he claims to have suffered as a result of his arrest, the breach of several contracts and injury to his reputation, the damage occurs in England, not in Italy.[355] Likewise where initial damage has been suffered by the claimant in a road traffic accident in France but his medical condition has deteriorated whilst living in England, the damage occurs in France.[356] This is unaffected by the fact that under French law deterioration constitutes a separate cause of action from the original injury. Article 4(1) does not explain what happens where direct harm is suffered by an indirect victim,[357] as where, for example, A is injured in State X but B as a consequence suffers nervous shock witnessing this (say on the television) in State Y. As regards the claim by B, does the damage occur in X or Y? Article 4(1) does not specify that the damage is referring to the damage to the claimant. The CJEU has held that where it is possible to identify the occurrence of direct damage, which is usually the case with personal injury or damage to tangible property, the place where the direct damage occurred is the relevant connecting factor for the determination of the applicable law, regardless of the indirect consequences of

---

[352] See Dicey, Morris and Collins, para 35-026 (with examples) and (in the context of Art 7(2) Brussels I Recast) Case C-12/15 *Universal Music International Holding BV v Michael Tétreault Schilling and Others* ECLI:EU:C:2016:449 at [32].

[353] See (in the context of Art 7(2) Brussels I Recast) Case C-375/13 *Harald Kolassa v Barclays Bank plc* ECLI:EU:C:2015:37 at [55].

[354] *Hillside (New Media) Ltd v Baasland & Ors* [2010] EWHC 3336 (Comm) at [28]–[37].

[355] See Case C-364/93 *Marinari v Lloyds Bank plc (Zubaidi Trading Co Intervener)*, [1996] QB 217. See also Case 220/88 *Dumez France and Tracoba v Hessische Landesbank* [1990] ECR 49.

[356] See *Henderson v Jaouen* [2002] EWCA Civ 75, [2002] 1 WLR 2971.

[357] HL Paper 66 (2004), para 98, referring to the Written Evidence by Briggs at 95.

that accident.[358] The damage related to the death of a person in an accident which took place in Member State X sustained by close relatives of that person who reside in Member State Y (eg pain and suffering, psychological damage, loss of maintenance) will thus be regarded as indirect consequences within the meaning of Article 4(1),[359] with the consequence of the law of X applying. According to the CJEU, the application of the law of the place where the direct damage was suffered contributes to the objective set out in Recital (16), seeking to ensure the foreseeability of the applicable law, while avoiding the risk that the tort or delict is broken up in to several elements, each subject to a different law according to the places or the persons other than the direct victim who sustain damage.[360] However, it is yet unclear whether the same analysis applies where uninvolved third parties on the spot of an accident (such as rescue workers) or even relatives claim damages caused by shock (eg for witnessing the accident). In such a scenario, it could be argued that the damage caused by shock is an independent second damage which occurs directly at the place where the shock is felt.

(v) Threatened damage
Damage includes damage that is likely to occur.[361]

(c) Article 4(2): the common habitual residence exception
Article 4(2) sets out an exception to Article 4(1). This provides that "where the person claimed to be liable and the person sustaining damage both have their habitual residence in the same country at the time when the damage occurs, the law of that country shall apply". Article 4(2) is a strict rule, but subject to the narrow exception under Article 4(3). The "person sustaining damage" is the person who suffered direct damage in the sense of Article 4(1). Habitual residence is at least partially defined under Article 23.[362] While the habitual residence of one or both parties can change during the course of events, Article 4(2) is concerned with habitual residence at the time when the damage occurs. Article 4(2) applies also in cases where there are several claimants and/or defendants.[363] In order to avoid manipulation by adding further parties in such a scenario, Article 4(2) is to be applied as between each pair of claimants and defendants. The habitual residence of the other parties and the consequences of a fragmentation of the applicable law may be taken into account under the escape clause of Article 4(3).[364]

Already before Rome II many Member States applied the law of the parties' common residence or habitual residence in a tort choice of law case.[365] Under the English pre-Regulation choice of law rules there was a flexible exception and the personal connecting factor was one important factor to be taken into account. Indeed, English law has been applied under both the common law and statutory rules exception in circumstances where the parties were

---

[358] Case C-350/14 *Florin Lazar, représenté légalement par Luigi Erculeo v Allianz SpA* ECLI:EU:C:2015:802 at [25].

[359] Case C-350/14 *Florin Lazar, représenté légalement par Luigi Erculeo v Allianz SpA* ECLI:EU:C:2015:802 at [27] and Art 15(f) Rome II: the designated law also determines the persons entitled to compensation for damage they have sustained personally which covers, in particular, whether a person other than the "direct victim" may obtain compensation following damage sustained by the victim.

[360] Case C-350/14 *Florin Lazar, représenté légalement par Luigi Erculeo v Allianz SpA* ECLI:EU:C:2015:802 at [29].

[361] Art 2(3)(b).

[362] Discussed supra, pp 802–3.

[363] *Marshall v Motors Insurers Bureau* [2015] EWHC 3241 (QB) at [17].

[364] An example suggested of where Article 4(3) should operate is that of a single defendant being sued by numerous claimants, who have been injured in different countries, see Briggs, Written Evidence, HL Report 66 (2004), 95.

[365] See, eg, Switzerland and Germany (common habitual residence), the Netherlands (common residence) and Italy (common residence and nationality). See the Explanatory Memorandum, p 12.

normally resident in England[366] or resident in England.[367] The same result will apply under the Regulation, but now by virtue of a much stricter rule[368] that only looks at the common habitual residence, rather than as the result of a wider flexible exception. Thus, the rigidity of the Regulation and the flexibility of the traditional English rule can lead to a difference in result. Under the pre-Regulation law there were instances of the English courts not applying the flexible exception, even though both of the parties appeared to be habitually resident in England.[369] In contrast, under the Regulation the habitual residence exception would operate in such a case.[370]

(d) Article 4(3): the manifestly more closely connected escape clause

(i) The escape clause

Article 4(3) is an escape clause.[371] It provides that: "Where it is clear from all the circumstances of the case that the tort/delict is manifestly more closely connected with a country other than that indicated in paragraphs 1 or 2, the law of that other country shall apply." The purpose of this provision is to produce flexibility so that individual circumstances can be taken into account in order as to apply the law that reflects the centre of gravity of the situation.[372] It is the *tort* that must be manifestly more closely connected; it appears not to be sufficient that only a specific issue that arises in the particular case is manifestly more closely connected.[373] It is not enough to show that the tort/delict is more closely connected with a country other than that indicated in paragraphs 1 or 2, it has to be "manifestly" more closely connected. The addition of the word "manifestly" is designed to underscore the exceptional nature of this escape clause.[374] The use of rules in Article 4(1) and (2), rather than presumptions, is also designed to make clear that the exception really is exceptional.[375] The requisite connection under Article 4(3) can be shown from all the circumstances of the case.[376] A particular example is given, namely where there is a pre-existing relationship between the parties. But this is only an example and, in principle, there may be other situations where it is clear from all the circumstances of the case that the tort/delict may be shown to be manifestly more closely connected with another country.[377]

(ii) A pre-existing relationship

Article 4(3) provides an example of a manifestly closer connection: "A manifestly closer connection with another country might be based in particular on a pre-existing relationship

---

[366] *Chaplin v Boys* [1971] AC 356 at 378 (per Lord Hodson), 389–93 (per Lord Wilberforce). The parties were servicemen temporarily stationed in Malta. See in relation to the statutory rules, *Edmunds v Simmonds* [2001] 1 WLR 1003.

[367] *Church of Scientology of California v Metropolitan Police Comr* (1976) 120 Sol Jo 690; *Johnson v Coventry Churchill International Ltd* [1992] 3 All ER 14.

[368] However, this can be escaped from by recourse to Art 4(3).

[369] *Regina (Al-Jedda) v Secretary of State for Defence* [2006] EWCA Civ 327, [2007] QB 621—a claim by a British citizen, who appears to have been habitually resident in England, against the British government where the issue was the legality of detention in Iraq, whose law applied under the general rule.

[370] An English court may then be tempted to apply the escape clause in Art 4(3) in such a case. But the issue in the case does not appear to have any relevance under Art 4(3), see infra.

[371] Recital (18).

[372] See the Explanatory Memorandum, p 12.

[373] Criticised by Morse, Written Evidence, HL Paper 66 (2004), 126. Contrast s 12(1) of the Private International Law (Miscellaneous Provisions) Act 1995.

[374] The Explanatory Memorandum, p 12. See also *Winrow v Hemphill & Anor* [2014] EWHC 3164 (QB) at [42], [63]: "high hurdle"; *Marshall v Motor Insurers Bureau* [2015] EWHC 3421 (QB) at [20].

[375] See the Explanatory Memorandum, p 12.

[376] On the potential relevance of the place where insurance was taken out, Collier, p 353 n 107.

[377] For possible factors to be considered see *Winrow v Hemphill & Anor* [2014] EWHC 3164 (QB) at [47]–[50]; *Marshall v Motor Insurers Bureau* [2015] EWHC 3421 (QB) at [20]–[22]; von Hein in Calliess (ed), *Rome Regulations: Commentary*, Art 4 paras 53–6, pp 524–6.

between the parties, such as a contract, that is closely connected with the tort/delict in question." A very similar example is given under pre-Regulation German private international law.[378] The pre-existing relationship is referred to as a secondary connection.[379] The idea is that the law of the country governing the secondary connection will also govern the non-contractual obligation.[380] This rule has been justified on the basis that by "having the same law apply to all their relationships, this solution respects the parties' legitimate expectations and meets the need for the sound administration of justice".[381] Under the English statutory tort choice of law rules it was possible to take into account a pre-existing relationship and the law governing that relationship when operating the displacement rule.[382] However, the governing law would just be one factor amongst a number of factors. The Regulation gives more significance to this factor by providing that the manifestly closer connection with another country might be *based on* a pre-existing relationship between the parties. In other words, this on its own might be enough for Article 4(3) to operate. It is unclear what significance should be attached to a choice of jurisdiction clause in the parties' contract. In so far as it determines the governing law, the same significance should be attached to it as to a choice of law clause. But if the governing law is different, the choice of jurisdiction clause should just be treated as one factual connection amongst many other factual connections.[383]

The example given in Article 4(3) of a pre-existing relationship is that of a contract. It is not uncommon for the parties to a claim in tort to have a contractual relationship. In cases of concurrent liability, this will be the case.[384] It could also arise where there is a claim based on a non-contractual obligation and where, although there is a contract between the parties, there is no contractual liability.[385] This pre-existing contractual relationship could presumably cover a contract that has been annulled,[386] certainly after the tort was committed. The position is more uncertain in relation to a contract annulled before the tort was committed. In such a case, there may be little connection between the contract and the tort in question and the exception would not operate.[387] Where the contract that constitutes the pre-existing relationship is a consumer contract or an employment contract the consumer and the employee are protected in relation to contractual obligations by special contract choice of law rules under the Rome I Regulation. Thus if an employee habitually carries out his work in State A but the contract of employment has a choice of law clause providing for the application of the law of State B, the employee can still rely on the mandatory (protectionist) rules of State A. But as far as non-contractual obligations are concerned it would appear that the law applicable would be that of State B.

The Commission has foreseen this problem and has said that the secondary connection mechanism cannot have the effect of depriving the weaker party of the protection of the law otherwise applicable (State A in our example).[388] But what is there in the Regulation to stop

---

[378] Art 41(2) of the German Introductory Law to the Civil Code 1999. The German law is still applicable outside the scope of Rome II, in particular for personality rights infringements.

[379] See the Explanatory Memorandum, pp 8 and 12–13.

[380] Ibid.

[381] The Explanatory Memorandum, p 13.

[382] *Trafigura Beheer BV v Kookmin Bank Co* [2006] EWHC 1450 (Comm) at [103]–[104], [2006] 2 Lloyd's Rep 455. Cf Mance LJ in *Morin v Bonham & Brooks Ltd* [2003] EWCA Civ 1802 at [23], [2004] 1 Lloyd's Rep 702, who left the matter open.

[383] This was the position under the statutory tort choice of law rules, see *Trafigura*, supra, at [104].

[384] See the discussion supra, pp 791–2.

[385] See the facts of the pre-Regulation case of *Trafigura Beheer BV v Kookmin Bank Co* [2006] EWHC 1450 (Comm), [2006] 2 Lloyd's Rep 455.

[386] The Explanatory Memorandum, p 13.

[387] See infra, p 816.

[388] The Explanatory Memorandum, p 13.

this? There is no express provision to deal with this situation. The Commission has said this is implicit in the protective rules in the Rome I Regulation but this looks to be an inadequate response and it would have been better to incorporate into the Regulation a restriction of the secondary connection rule.

In principle, a pre-existing relationship could include a pre-contractual relationship where a contract has not been entered into.[389] The relationship between a guest passenger and a host driver who subsequently injures the passenger by his negligent driving is another example of a pre-existing relationship.[390] In this example the pre-existing relationship is undeniably closely connected with the tort/delict in question. The pre-existing relationship could in principle be a family relationship.[391] In practice this scenario is normally not going to face the courts as the Regulation excludes from its scope non-contractual obligations arising out of family relationships.[392] However, it is possible to have a family relationship in respect of which the exclusion does not operate because the non-contractual obligation does not arise out of this, as where, for example, a husband negligently injures his wife in a car crash. In this situation the question is whether the relationship of husband and wife is closely connected with the tort of negligent driving. A family relationship can include an annulled relationship.[393]

Closely connected with the tort/delict in question The pre-existing relationship must be closely connected with the tort/delict in question.

Application of the law governing the pre-existing relationship Let us assume that there is a pre-existing relationship between the parties that is closely connected with the tort/delict in question. A manifestly closer connection with another country might be based on this relationship. But which country does this point to? Take the example of where there is a contractual relationship. The Explanatory Memorandum envisages that the law of the country governing the contract will also govern the non-contractual obligation.[394] Likewise the law of the country governing the family relationship would govern the non-contractual obligation.[395] But what law governs the relationship of husband and wife? There are no harmonised rules of choice of law for marriage in the European Union so this would be a matter to be determined by the national choice of law rules of the forum. At common law the law of the domicile would govern the relationship of husband and wife. Indeed, it is possible at common law to classify the question whether one spouse is liable to the other in tort as a matter of status to be referred to the law of the domicile.[396] Similarly, whether a child can sue his parents may be similarly so classified.[397] The Rome II Regulation would produce the same

---

[389] Ibid.

[390] See, eg, *Babcock v Jackson* [1963] 2 Lloyd's Rep 286, 12 NY 2d 473, 240 NYS 2d 743, New York Court of Appeals.

[391] The Explanatory Memorandum, pp 8 and 13.

[392] Art 1(2)(a), discussed supra, pp 793–4. Moreover, most family member will have the same habitual residence, so that Art 4(2) applies.

[393] The Explanatory Memorandum, p 13. But the same question arises as with an annulled contract (discussed supra, p 815) as to whether this would include a relationship annulled after the tort.

[394] At p 8.

[395] Ibid.

[396] This is the general view in the USA: *Haumschild v Continental Casualty Co* 7 Wis 2d 130, 95 NW 2d 814 (1959); cf *Schwartz v Schwartz* 103 Ariz 562, 447 P 2d 254 (1968) where the same conclusion was reached applying the choice of law rule of the Restatement 2d § 145. Australian courts have taken different views on this matter. Cf *Warren v Warren* [1972] Qd R 386 at 390–1 (application of the law of the domicile) with *Schmidt v Government Insurance Office of New South Wales* [1973] 1 NSWLR 59 and *Corcoran v Corcoran* [1974] VR 164 (application of tort choice of law rules). The Law Commissions reached no conclusion on the characterisation of intra-family immunities: Law Com No 193 (1990), paras 3.45–3.46.

[397] *Balts v Balts* 273 Minn 419, 142 NW 2d 6 (1966); and see *Emery v Emery* 45 Cal 2d 421, 289 P 2d 218 (1955); cf *Pierce v Helz* 314 NYS 2d 453 (1970).

result albeit by a different route. Rather than classifying the claim as family law it is classified as tort but to be governed by the law governing the family relationship.

The lack of harmonisation of choice of law rules for marriage means that different substantive domestic laws would apply to the family relationship depending on which Member State the trial was held in.[398] But what law governs a guest host relationship? Ultimately the search is for a manifestly closer connection with another country. This could be based on where the guest host relationship is centred. Thus if this relationship starts and is to end in New York, New York law should apply, rather than the law of Ontario where the car crash occurred and the guest was injured by the host.[399]

A discretion? The wording of the pre-existing relationship example in Article 4(3) ("might be based") makes clear that even if there is a pre-existing relationship between the parties, such as a contract, which is closely connected with the tort/delict in question, there will not automatically be a manifestly closer connection with another country. The court is said to have a degree of discretion to decide whether there is a significant connection between the non-contractual obligation and the law applicable to the relationship.[400] This is not a discretion in the sense that the term is used under English private international law in, for example, *forum conveniens* cases. Instead it is just making the point that a fine judgment may have to be made as to whether the secondary connection will apply. The question ultimately is whether there is a manifestly closer connection with another country.

(iii) The effect of the secondary connection rule: mitigating problems of classification

The secondary connection rule has the effect of mitigating problems of classification. There are two particular areas where this is particularly noticeable. The first area is that of concurrent liability. The secondary connection rule has considerable implications for such cases.[401] Until the Court of Justice has determined the classification of such liability there is a danger of different national courts adopting different classifications. However, the undesirable lack of uniformity that this would entail is said to be mitigated by the secondary connection rule.[402] This needs a few words of explanation. Let us assume that a French court has adopted a contractual classification and applies French law as the law governing the contract. If an English court adopted a tortious classification it could also apply French law to govern the non-contractual obligation on the basis that the pre-existing contractual relationship between the parties is governed by French law.

The second area where problems of classification arose is that of the consequences of nullity of a contract. The 1980 Rome Convention allowed Member States to enter a reservation against the application of the Convention to this issue because some Member States regarded this issue as non-contractual.[403] The effect of the secondary connection rule was that Member States which had adopted such a reservation would apply, via Article 4(3) Rome II, the same (contractual) law as the Member States which directly applied the Rome Convention.[404]

---

[398] See the Explanatory Memorandum, p 8. This unfortunate result helped prompt the desire by some to exclude family relationships from the scope of the Regulation.

[399] These are the facts of *Babcock v Jackson*, supra.

[400] The Explanatory Memorandum, p 12.

[401] Ibid, pp 12–13. The secondary connection rule applies to any cases of concurrent liability but in particular to those cases where a contractual defence is raised to a claim.

[402] Ibid.

[403] See Art 22(1)(b) 1980 Rome Convention.

[404] The Explanatory Memorandum, p 13. This assumes that, in states which have entered a reservation, the issue in classified as tortious/delictual and therefore Chapter II of the Rome II Regulation will apply. If the issue is regarded as a matter of unjust enrichment, the same result can be achieved via Art 10(1) Rome II.

Under the Rome I Regulation, the reservation was abolished, and the consequences of nullity of a contract are generally regarded as a contractual matter.[405]

(iv) An escape from Article 4(1) and (2)
Article 4(3) operates as an escape from both Article 4(1) and Article 4(2).

An exception to Article 4(1)   Apart from cases where there is a pre-existing relationship between the parties, situations where Article 4(3) would operate as an exception to Article 4(1) are likely to be relatively rare.[406] At common law the flexible exception operated where the parties had the same normal residence. This situation would now involve Article 4(2) (common habitual residence), rather than Article 4(1). Another situation where the common law flexible exception operated was where there were strong connections with the country where the tort was committed (eg Saudi Arabia) with the result that Saudi Arabian law governed. In contrast, Article 4(3) operates to displace the law of the country where damage occurred and so could not operate in such a case.

An exception to Article 4(2)   The scenario we are concerned with here is as follows:

> The law of country A is applicable under Article 4(1), the exception under Article 4(2) then leads to the application of the law of Country B. The question then is whether there is a manifestly closer connection with Country C with the result that under Article 4(3) the law of that country will apply to displace that of Country B.

In the absence of a pre-existing relationship between the parties, it is hard to envisage Article 4(3) operating in a three-country case. The parties' common habitual residence constitutes a strong connection with Country B, as does the occurrence of damage with Country A. If there are strong connections with two countries, it is unlikely that there is a manifestly closer connection with a third country, Country C. So displacement of Article 4(2) by Article 4(3) is likely to be even harder than displacement of Article 4(1) by Article 4(3), at least in a three-country case.

However, there is another possibility that needs to be considered. This involves a two country scenario.

> Let us assume that there are strong connections with the country of damage (Country A), quite apart from the fact that damage occurred there. The parties have a common habitual residence in Country B so that the exception under Article 4(2) will apply. But can the law of Country A be applied by virtue of Article 4(3)?

This raises a question of principle. Can Article 4(3) be used to displace the law applicable under Article 4(2) by the law applicable under Article 4(1)? The wording of Article 4(3) suggests that it can. Article 4(3) refers to the tort being manifestly more closely connected with a country other than that indicated in paragraph 1 *or* 2. The applicable law under Article 4(3) does not have to displace that indicated in both paragraph 1 and 2. Thus Article 4(3) could operate in a two-country situation. In terms of the balance of connections, the fact that damage occurred in Country A is a strong connection and if there are other weighty connections this could outweigh the common habitual residence connection. This would appeal to the English courts which, in a case decided under the common law tort choice of law rules, have used the flexible exception to apply the law of the country where the tort was committed.[407] More significantly, the English courts have, under the statutory tort choice of law rules,

---

[405] Art 12(1)(e) Rome I.
[406] For possible factors to be considered see *Winrow v Hemphill & Anor* [2014] EWHC 3164 (QB) at [47]–[50]; *Marshall v Motor Insurers Bureau* [2015] EWHC 3421 (QB) at [20]–[22].
[407] *Red Sea Insurance Co Ltd v Bouygues SA* [1995] 1 AC 190.

applied Iraqi law under the general rule and refused to apply the displacement rule, despite the fact that both parties appeared to be habitually resident in England.[408] The same result could be reached under the Regulation by applying Iraqi law by virtue of Article 4(3).[409]

(e) Article 4 and road traffic accidents

The choice of law rules in Article 4 apply to the issue of the assessment of damages.[410] So damages are assessed according to the law of the place of damage. This can be unsatisfactory in road traffic accident cases. The victim may be injured in a country other than the one in which he habitually resides. After the accident he will return to his home country and will have to live with the consequences of his injury in that state. It would be better for assessment to be determined by the law of the country in which the victim habitually resides. The European Parliament suggested an amendment to the Regulation to what is now Article 4 to produce this effect. This was not accepted but the European Parliament was able to secure the introduction in the recitals of a statement which ensures that the victim's actual circumstances will be taken into account when damages are quantified.[411] This is seen as a short-term solution. As regards a long-term solution, the European Parliament has managed to secure a commitment by the Commission to examine the problems arising where European Union residents are involved in a road traffic accident in a Member State other than the Member State of their habitual residence and to produce a study on this before the end of 2008.[412] This study shall look at all options, including insurance aspects, for improving the position of cross-border victims from the European Union, which would pave the way for a Green Paper. There is a further problem in relation to road traffic accidents, namely that many Member States (but not the United Kingdom) have entered into the Hague Convention on the Law Applicable to Traffic Accidents of 1971.[413] These states will continue to apply the choice of law rules in the Convention, rather than those in Article 4.[414] The Commission was required to produce, by 20 August 2011, a report on the application of the Regulation, which will include a study on the effects of the 1971 Hague Convention.[415] Both studies have not yet been produced by the Commission.

(iv) Specific rules for special torts

Articles 5 to 9 set out what are described as specific rules for special torts,[416] namely for product liability, unfair competition, acts restricting competition, environmental damage, infringement of intellectual property rights and industrial action. Some of these (product liability, acts restricting competition and infringement of intellectual property rights) are recognisable to common lawyers as torts. Others (unfair competition, environmental damage and industrial action) are broad concepts which are more familiar to civil lawyers than common lawyers but encompass what common lawyers would regard as a number of different torts. According to Recital (19) specific rules should be laid down "where the general

---

[408] *Regina (Al-Jedda) v Secretary of State for Defence* [2006] EWCA Civ 327, [2007] QB 621.

[409] But the decision in *Regina (Al-Jedda)* was influenced by the issue in the case, namely whether the detention in Iraq was lawful. Under Art 4(3) the issue in the case does not appear to be relevant.

[410] Art 15(c), discussed infra, pp 861–3.

[411] Recital (33), discussed further when Art 15(c) is discussed infra, p 863.

[412] See the Commission Statement on road accidents attached to the Regulation.

[413] The participating Member States are Austria, Belgium, Croatia (was not a Member State when Rome II was adopted, but already at that time party to the 1971 Hague Convention), the Czech Republic, France, Latvia, Lithuania, Luxembourg, the Netherlands, Poland, Slovakia, Slovenia, and Spain. Moreover, the following third states have ratified the 1971 Hague Convention: Belarus, Bosnia, Macedonia, Serbia, and Switzerland.

[414] Art 28(1), discussed infra, pp 873–5.

[415] Art 30(1)(ii).

[416] See Recital (19).

rule does not allow a reasonable balance to be struck between the interests at stake". The introduction of specific rules for special torts follows the model adopted in a number of European civil law jurisdictions[417] and in relation to contract choice of law under the 1980 Rome Convention (now the Rome I Regulation) but rejected in England under its choice of law rules in tort[418] on the ground that any special rule might be difficult to put into statutory language and would make the position more complex.[419] In the United Kingdom, the case for having in the Regulation some of these specific rules was not thought to have been made out.[420] The European Parliament was also unconvinced and unsuccessfully sought the deletion of some of these rules.[421]

(a) Product liability[422]

Within the European Union, much of the substantive law of product liability has been harmonised by the EC Product Liability Directive.[423] Nonetheless, choice of law problems still arise,[424] in particular because liability based on fault is not covered by the Directive. Article 5 sets out a special choice of law rule to solve these problems. According to Recital (20), the special rule of Article 5 "should meet the objectives of fairly spreading the risks inherent in a modern high-technology society, protecting consumers' health, stimulating innovation, securing undistorted competition and facilitating trade" by creating "a cascade system of connecting factors, together with a foreseeability clause", as a "balanced solution in regard to these objectives". Product liability has long been regarded as a special tort that requires specific choice of law rules. This was recognised at the Hague Conference on Private International Law, which in 1973 concluded the Hague Convention on the law applicable to products liability which entered into force in seven EU Member States.[425] These Member States will continue to apply the 1973 Hague Convention, rather than Article 5 of Rome II.[426]

(i) The scope of Article 5

Article 5 applies where there is "a non-contractual obligation arising out of damage caused by a product". While "damage" is defined by Article 2 Rome II as any consequence arising out of a tort/delict,[427] "product" is defined under the European Community Product Liability Directive[428] and the intention is that recourse should be had to this definition when deciding whether Article 5 applies.[429] Under the Directive, " 'product' means all movables even if incorporated into another movable or into an immovable", including electricity.[430]

---

[417] And in the USA under the Restatement of the Conflict of Laws 2d.

[418] Apart from defamation, discussed infra, pp 885–8.

[419] Law Commission Working Paper No 87 (1984), paras 5.1–5.70.

[420] HL Paper 66 (2004), paras 106 (referring to product liability), 109 (unfair competition), 134 (violation of the environment).

[421] Ie the specific rules for unfair competition and acts restricting free competition.

[422] For a comparative study of different choice of law solutions in Europe and a discussion of the Proposal and the European Parliament's response see Graziano (2005) 54 ICLQ 475. For comment on Art 5 Rome II Huber & Illmer (2007) 9 Yb PIL 31; Symeonides (2008) 56 Am J Comp L 173 at 207; Koziris (2008) 56 Am J Comp L 471 at 485; Dickinson, Chapter 5; Illmer (2009) 73 RabelsZ 271; Marengi (2014/15) 16 Yb PIL 511; Plender and Wilderspin, Chapter 19.

[423] Council Directive (EEC) No 85/374 of 25 July 1985, OJ 1985 L 210/29.

[424] The harmonisation within Europe has only been partial and there is no world-wide harmonisation; see generally Fawcett (1993-I) 238 Hague Recueil des cours, Chapter II.

[425] Croatia, Finland, France, Luxembourg, the Netherlands, Slovenia, and Spain. It was signed but not ratified in Belgium, Italy and Portugal.

[426] Art 28, discussed infra, pp 873–5.

[427] This definition is broader than the definition of damage in Art 9 Product Liability Directive, which excludes non-material damage.

[428] See Arts 2 and 6 of the Directive. The Proposal for the Rome II Regulation in Art 4 referred to a "defective" product. But this requirement was dropped.

[429] See the Explanatory Memorandum, p 13.

[430] Art 2 Product Liability Directive.

Different from the Directive, Article 5 is not confined to claims brought under the strict liability regime of the Directive (or to be more accurate, under national laws implementing the Directive).[431] In England, claims which could have been brought under the Directive are sometimes brought in negligence, which is more familiar. Such a claim literally falls within the scope of Article 5. Moreover, it would be most undesirable for the claimant to be allowed to avoid the application of Article 5 (with the aim of getting a different law to apply under Article 4) by suing in negligence. Once it has been decided that there is damage caused by a product within the meaning of Article 5, it follows that there is a tort and the obligation that arises out of this tort must be regarded as non-contractual. Article 5 presupposes that damage[432] occurs. This will necessarily be the case because damage is one of the elements of the tort of product liability.

(ii) The law applicable to product liability

Article 5 has two paragraphs. The first paragraph is undeniably complicated, reflecting the wide range of possible connecting factors.[433] It sets out a "cascading" series of rules to which there is a lack of foreseeability exception. All of this is subject to Article 4(2) (the common habitual residence exception). The second paragraph of Article 5 provides an escape from paragraph 1, based on a manifestly closer connection with another country.

A "cascading" series of rules[434]   The first of these is Article 5(1)(a), which provides that the law applicable is "the law of the country in which the person sustaining the damage[435] had his or her habitual residence[436] when the damage occurred, if the product was marketed in that country". The victim will normally have acquired the product and been injured in the state of his habitual residence (and would expect the law of that state to apply) but even if he acquires it abroad (perhaps whilst travelling) and is injured in a state other than his habitual residence, the law of his habitual residence will still apply (provided the product or a product of the same type was marketed there). The requirement that the product was marketed in that country is designed to protect the interests of the producer. The latter normally controls its sales network and should thus, if the product is marketed in a certain state, be able to foresee that the law of that state will be applied. This holds true also if not the producer, but rather a supplier further down the line of distribution is responsible for marketing the product in the respective state.[437] The reference to "the product" being marketed in the country of habitual residence does not make clear whether it is referring to the actual product that caused the injury or to the line of product from which the injuring product came, which seems to be what was intended.[438]

If the product is not marketed in the country in which the person sustaining the damage had his or her habitual residence, paragraph (a) does not apply and one moves on to paragraph (b). This provides that the law applicable is "the law of the country in which the product was acquired, if the product was marketed in that country". The provision does not say who the

---

[431] Explanatory Memorandum, p 13.

[432] As defined in Art 2(1) and 2(3)(b).

[433] Cf Art 4 of the Proposal for a Regulation.

[434] See Recital (20).

[435] So if the right to sue is assigned, the habitual residence of the person sustaining the damage will apply, not that of the assignee.

[436] The meaning of habitual residence is discussed supra, pp 802–3.

[437] Dicey, Morris and Collins, para 35-044. The "foreseeability"-proviso at the end of Article 5(1) would be useless if only the marketing by the producer was relevant.

[438] See the Explanatory Memorandum, p 14; see also the words "product of the same type" in the proviso in Art 5(1). This would be important in a case of travelling abroad and acquiring a product. If the line was marketed in the habitual residence it would be foreseeable to the producer that that country's law would apply.

product must have been acquired by, in particular it does not say that this must have been the victim.[439] Failing paragraph (b), one moves on to paragraph (c). This provides that the law applicable is "the law of the country in which the damage occurred, if the product was marketed in that country".

There is no fall back rule for cases that do not fall within paragraph (a), (b) or (c). Yet this is possible.[440] Rules (a), (b) and (c) all require the product to have been marketed in the country whose law is applicable. But this may not have happened. If the case does not fall within (a), (b) or (c), the specific rules for product liability in Article 5 are inapplicable and one could have to go back to the "general rule" in Article 4. It is perfectly possible to apply those rules to the special tort of product liability.[441] Indeed, the English courts have traditionally applied rules of general application to product liability cases. However, the foreseeability proviso in Article 5(1) last sentence provides for the application of the law of the country in which the person claimed to be liable is habitually resident if he or she could not reasonably foresee the marketing of the product, or a product of the same type, in the country the law of which is applicable under (a), (b) or (c). In light of the overarching aim of foreseeability, the scenario where the person claimed to be liable could not foresee the marketing of the product in a country seems to be comparable with the scenario where no such marketing occurred. Therefore, it appears preferable to apply the law of the country in which the person claimed to be liable is habitually resident to cases where paragraphs (a), (b) and (c) do not apply.[442]

Article 5(1)(a) requires the moment when the damage occurred to be identified (at least when a person is in the process of changing their habitual residence) and Article 5(1)(c) requires the country in which the damage occurred to be ascertained. This country will normally be easy to ascertain but not always. What of the situation where pills are taken as a person moves across Europe and these have a cumulative effect? The country in which the individual sustained damage will have to be artificially fixed, the best solution probably being to fix it where the first impact was felt.[443]

A lack of foreseeability exception   Article 5(1) provides an exception to (a), (b) and (c) in the situation where the person claimed to be liable "could not reasonably foresee the marketing of the product, or a product of the same type, in the country the law of which is applicable under (a), (b) or (c)". This could happen where a product is marketed in a country against the will of the person claimed to be liable. In this situation, the law applicable is that of the country in which the person claimed to be liable[444] is habitually resident. As concerns the timing of the acts of marketing by the person claimed to be liable, it should not be possible to invoke the foreseeability defense if a product has been marketed in a country any time before the date of damage (for paragraphs (a) and (c)) or before the date of acquisition of the

---

[439] Against an application of Art 5(1)(b) to claims by "bystanders" Dickinson, para 5.40; Stone, in Ahern and Binchy, The Rome II Regulation on the Law Applicable to Non-Contractual Obligations, p 189.

[440] The common habitual residence rule of Art 4(2) will in some, but not all cases provide an answer.

[441] The Commission regarded the "country in which the damage occurs" rule as unsatisfactory in that it could be unrelated to the situation, unforeseeable to the producer and no source of protection to the victim, see the Explanatory Memorandum, pp 13–14.

[442] Dickinson, para 5.45; Illmer (2009) 73 RabelsZ 271, 296–7; Dicey, Morris and Collins, para 35-045.

[443] When applying the place of damage rule under Art 4(1), where damage is sustained in different countries the laws of all the countries will normally apply on a distributive basis. This solution will not work in the present context. As an alternative to the "first impact" rule as proposed here, it has been suggested not to apply the relevant subrule and move to the next step in the cascade, Dickinson, paras 5.31-5.33.

[444] Under the Product Liability Directive liability is imposed on the producer proper (as widely defined to extend beyond the manufacturer of the finished product) but also on the importer into the Community and in some circumstances the supplier, see Art 3.

product (for paragraph (b)).[445] Such an interpretation avoids the defendant later terminating the marketing of the product in a specific area in order to rely on the foreseeability defense and thus his own law. The non-foreseeability exception appears to have been influenced by the 1973 Hague Convention, which contains a non-foreseeability rule.[446]

A common habitual residence exception   Article 5(1) is without prejudice to Article 4(2), which provides that "where the person claimed to be liable and the person sustaining the damage both have their habitual residence in the same country at the time when the damage occurs, the law of that country shall apply". Starting Article 5(1) with the words "Without prejudice to Article 4(2)" makes it clear that this common habitual residence exception operates not only as an exception to the law applicable under paragraph 1(a), (b) and (c) but also to the law applicable under the lack of foreseeability exception set out in the last sentence of Article 5(1).

The manifestly more closely connected escape clause   Paragraph (2) provides an escape from the law "indicated in paragraph 1", based on a manifestly closer connection with another country. This provision is identical in wording to Article 4(3). The structure and wording of Article 5 would suggest that the Article 5(2) escape clause will not only override the law applicable under the cascading rules and the lack of foreseeability exception but also the law applicable under Article 4(2). Application of the law of the country of common habitual residence under Article 4(2) is "indicated in paragraph 1". Moreover, this interpretation is consistent with Article 4 where the manifestly more closely connected escape clause operates as an escape also from the common habitual residence exception.[447]

(b) Unfair competition[448]

Article 6 is concerned with two different torts, unfair competition (paragraphs 1 and 2) and acts restricting free competition (paragraph 3). The former will be considered in this section and the latter under the heading "Restricting free competition" in (c) below.

(i) *The scope of the unfair competition choice of law rules*

Article 6 is headed, inter alia, "Unfair competition" and paragraph 1 goes on to provide that the rules on the applicable law apply to "a non-contractual obligation arising out of an act of unfair competition". According to Recital (21), the special rule on Article 6 "is not an exception to the general rule in Article 4(1) but rather a clarification of it". The purpose of rules against unfair competition is to protect competition by obliging all participants to play the game by the same rules.[449] Thus, "the conflict-of-law rule should protect competitors, consumers and the general public and ensure that the market economy functions properly".[450] The understanding of the European legislator is that the "connection to the law of the country where competitive relations or the collective interests of consumers are, or are likely to be, affected generally satisfies these objectives".[451]

---

[445] Dicey, Morris and Collins, para 35-048.

[446] Art 7 of the Hague Products Liability Convention uses the language "his own products of the same type".

[447] Cf Dicey, Morris and Collins, para 35-049.

[448] See generally Augenhofer in Calliess (ed), *Rome Regulations: Commentary*, Art 6, pp 569 et seq. At one time the Hague Conference on private international law had on its agenda for future work the law applicable to unfair competition (see the note drawn up by the permanent Bureau, Prel Doc No 5 of April 2000) but this was dropped in 2006, Prel Doc No 11 of June 2006.

[449] The Explanatory Memorandum, p 15.

[450] Recital (21).

[451] Recital (21).

The definition of "unfair competition" is particularly problematic. Although most civil law systems have a substantive law of unfair competition, there are huge differences over what is covered by these laws. The intention of the Commission was that an autonomous concept of unfair competition for the purposes of Article 6 Rome II should cover, among other things, "acts calculated to influence demand (misleading advertising, forced sales, etc), acts that impede competing supplies (disruption of deliveries by competitors, enticing away a competitor's staff, boycotts), and acts that exploit a competitor's value (passing off and the like)".[452] It was also intended to encompass industrial espionage, disclosure of business secrets and inducing breach of contract.[453] Moreover, unfair competition covers the "use of unfair terms inserted into general terms and conditions, as this is likely to affect the collective interests of consumers as a group and hence to influence the conditions of competition on the market."[454]

There is no tort of unfair competition under English law[455] but there are specific torts of passing off, malicious falsehood, breach of confidence,[456] interference with contractual relations, and defamation (which can be used in a business context). Passing off is clearly an act of unfair competition. Where malicious falsehood and defamation are used in a business context and involve a competitor's goods or business, they should be regarded as coming within the ambit of unfair competition under Article 6.[457] Under English law, disclosure of business secrets would be regarded as coming within breach of confidence. But for the purposes of Article 6 this should be regarded as an act of unfair competition. The specific tort of inducing breach of contract should likewise be so regarded. Once it has been decided that there is an act of unfair competition within the meaning of Article 6(1) it follows that this is a tort and the obligation that arises out of this tort must be regarded as non-contractual.

(ii) The law applicable to unfair competition

There are two different choice of law rules in relation to unfair competition. The two separate rules reflect the fact that unfair competition law seeks to protect not only the market, competitors interests overall, consumers and the public in general but also specific competitors.[458]

Article 6(1) The first and general choice of law rule for unfair competition provides that the "law applicable to a non-contractual obligation arising out of an act of unfair competition shall be the law of the country where competitive relations or the collective interests of consumers are, or are likely to be, affected" (Article 6(1)). According to Recital (21), the legislator considers this rule as an expression of the general *lex loci damni* (law of the place of damage) principle laid down in Article 4(1) to the field of unfair competition. Article 6(1)

---

[452] The Explanatory Memorandum, p 15.

[453] Ibid, at p 16. See also the general definition of unfair competition in Art 10*bis* of the Paris Convention for the Protection of Industrial Property and the examples mentioned there. However, Art 10*bis* provides only very general contours and is incomplete as it does not include many acts of unfair competition which affect consumers. On the level of EU substantive law, the Unfair Commercial Practices Directive (EC) No 2005/29 of 11 May 2005, OJ 2005 L 149/22, the Directive (EC) No 2006/114 of 12 December 2006 concerning misleading and comparative advertising, OJ 2006 L 376/21, and the Directive (EU) 2016/943 of 8 June 2016 on the protection of undisclosed know-how and business information (trade secrets) against their unlawful acquisition, use and disclosure, OJ 2016 L 157/1 deserve to be mentioned. Art 39 TRIPS provides for the protection of confidential information.

[454] Case C-191/15 *Verein für Konsumenteninformation v Amazon EU Sàrl* ECLI:EU:C:2016:612 at [42].

[455] See *L'Oréal SA v Bellure NV* [2007] EWCA Civ 968 at [135]–[161].

[456] See *Innovia Films Ltd v Frito-Lay North America, Inc* [2012] EWHC 790 (Pat) at [109]: breach of an equitable obligation of confidence falls within Art 6.

[457] For why defamation in the business context should be regarded as unfair competition (within the scope of the Regulation) and not defamation (excluded from the scope of the Regulation), see supra, p 799.

[458] Recital (21) and Explanatory Memorandum, p 15.

is concerned with the effect on the market in general, on competitors' interests in general and the effect on the interests of consumers generally.[459] This would cover also an action for an injunction based on unfair competition brought by a consumer association against the defendant, eg to enjoin the use of unfair terms inserted into general terms and conditions.[460]

Under Article 6(1), the law applicable is that of the country where competitive relations or the collective interests of consumers are, or are likely to be, affected. This is the market where competitors are seeking to gain the customers' favour.[461] In determining which markets are likely to be affected, the Commission's original proposal provided that "only the direct substantial effects of an act of unfair competition should be taken into account".[462] However, different from the initial proposal (and from Article 6(3)(b)), Article 6(1) no longer includes the words "directly and substantial" which excludes a requirement of "substantial effect" to be read into Article 6(1).[463] Rather, Article 6(1) is meant to be applied also to unsubstantial effects, since also for these effects a conflict rule on the applicable unfair competition law is required. Still, a limitation of Article 6(1)[464] is to be accepted for mere unintended spill-over effects: such effects can be regarded as an (irrelevant) indirect damage,[465] and the application of the law of a country which has not been targeted would run counter to the overarching principle of foreseeability of the applicable law under Rome II. However, an act of unfair competition affecting more than one country's market, without this being a mere unintended spill-over effect, "gives rise to the distributive application of the laws involved".[466] In such a multi-state scenario, the legality of an act of unfair competition which affects several countries' markets is to be assessed by the law of each of the countries affected, with the consequence that it might be lawful in some and unlawful in other jurisdictions.[467]

When it comes to the second element of Article 6(1), that is the country in which the *collective interests of consumers* are affected, this refers to the country of residence of the consumers to whom the undertaking directs its activities and whose interests are defended by the relevant consumer protection association by means of an action for an injunction.[468] Often the place where the collective interests of consumers are affected will coincide with the place where competitive relations are affected. However, where the collective interests of consumers are affected by the use of unfair terms in general terms and conditions, the unfairness of the

---

[459] On the concept of collective interests of consumers, see Art 1 Directive (EC) No 2009/22 of 23 April 2009 on injunctions for the protection of consumers' interests, OJ 2009 L 110/30.

[460] The Explanatory Memorandum, p 15; Case C-191/15 *Verein für Konsumenteninformation v Amazon EU Sàrl* ECLI:EU:C:2016:612 at [39], [42]. This is consistent with the jurisdictional position, see Case C-167/2000 *Verein Für Konsumenteninformation v K H Henkel* [2002] ECR I-8111 at [42].

[461] The Explanatory Memorandum, p 16.

[462] Ibid.

[463] Dicey, Morris and Collins, para 35-057; Augenhofer in Calliess (ed), *Rome Regulations: Commentary*, Art 6 para 47, p 586. In the 14th edn of this book (2008), pp 844–6, an implicit requirement of direct and substantial effect was read into Article 6(1).

[464] Which is understood as an expression of the general law of the place of damage principle of Article 4(1), Recital (21).

[465] See Dicey, Morris and Collins, para 35-057 who propose that indirect (spill-over) effects can be excluded by analogy with Article 4(1) as an "indirect damage"; cf Augenhofer in Calliess (ed), *Rome Regulations: Commentary*, Art 6 para 47, p 586: Recital (17) cannot be applied to Art 6 because the "indirect" damage is understood to be limited to a scenario where the same person suffers both direct and indirect damage, while under Art 6, the direct and the indirect effects will concern different people.

[466] Explanatory Memorandum, p 16; cf Dicey, Morris and Collins, para 35-057 who remark that it is "wholly unclear how the relevant laws are to be combined in such circumstances".

[467] If this is the case, a possible remedy will have to make sure that only the unlawful conduct is prohibited, eg by effective geo-blocking or denial of delivery to specific countries.

[468] See Case C-191/15 *Verein für Konsumenteninformation v Amazon EU Sàrl* ECLI:EU:C:2016:612 at [43] for a case of an injunction referred to in Directive 2009/22.

terms in consumer contracts which are the subject of an action for an injunction must, as an incidental question, be determined independently. Thus, where the action for an injunction aims to prevent such terms from being included in consumer contracts, the law applicable to the assessment of the terms must be determined in accordance with the Rome I Regulation, in particular Article 6 Rome I.[469] This distinction is necessary to ensure that the same law applies to the unfairness of the terms, whether raised in a collective action by a consumer association or in an individual action raised by a consumer.[470] Finally, Article 6(1), unlike Article 4(1), has no common habitual residence exception or manifestly more closely connected escape clause. The reason for this is that these exceptions are not suited to the matter of unfair competition, since Article 6(1) aims to protect collective interests—more extensive than the relations between the parties to the dispute—by providing for a rule specifically suited to that purpose. That aim would not be achieved if it were permissible to block the rule on the basis of personal connections between those parties.[471]

Article 6(2) The second choice of law rule is concerned with where "an act of unfair competition affects exclusively the interests of a specific competitor" (Article 6(2)). In other words, a specific competitor is targeted. This would, for example, encompass enticing away a competitor's staff, corruption, industrial espionage, disclosure of business secrets or inducing breach of contract.[472] As the word "exclusively" makes clear, Article 6(2) does not apply to acts of unfair competition such as passing-off or misleading advertisement which, while targeting a specific competitor, also affect the market as a whole, in particular the decisions of the other side of the market.[473]

Under Article 6(2) it is provided that Article 4 will apply. In other words, the law of the country applies where the direct damage was sustained, which will normally be the country where the specific competitor affected by the act of unfair competition has his/her habitual residence (ie his/her central administration, unless the damage arises in the operation of a branch, agency or other establishment, Article 23(1)). It is to be noted that the whole of Article 4 will apply, not just the country of damage rule but also the common habitual residence exception and the manifestly more closely connected escape clause. The underlying philosophy is that where a specific competitor has been targeted, that person should enjoy the benefit of the flexibility in Article 4(2) and (3).[474]

Article 6(4) This provides that the law applicable under Article 6 cannot be derogated from by an agreement of the parties as to the governing law pursuant to Article 14. This limitation rule was not in the Proposal for a Regulation and so there is no explanation for it in the Explanatory Memorandum. For the general rule of Article 6(1), the limitation of the parties' autonomy can be justified by the same reasons which are brought forward against applying the exceptions of Article 4(2) and (3), namely that Article 6(1) aims to protect collective interests by providing for a rule specifically suited to that purpose; an aim that would not be

---

[469] Ibid, at [49].

[470] Ibid, at [53]–[58].

[471] For Article 4(3), see ibid, at [45]. The same argument can be made for Article 4(2). Articles 4(2) and 4(3) are said to be "not adapted to this matter in general", the Explanatory Memorandum, p 16.

[472] The Explanatory Memorandum, p 16. See *Innovia Films Ltd v Frito-Lay North America, Inc* [2012] EWHC 790 (Pat) at [110] where it was undisputed that the breach of an equitable obligation of confidence falls under Art 6(2). The same view was taken in *Conductive Inkjet Technology Ltd v Uni-Pixel Displays Inc* [2013] EWHC 2968 (Ch) at [125 ii]. Augenhofer in Calliess (ed), *Rome Regulations: Commentary*, Art 6 para 63, p 590 suggests that Art 6(2) ought to be limited to the acts mentioned in the Explanatory Memorandum.

[473] In the 14th edn of this book (2008), p 810, it was argued that Art 6(2) would also cover passing off and those instances of malicious falsehood and defamation that come within the concept of unfair competition.

[474] The Explanatory Memorandum, p 16.

achieved if it were permissible to block the rule on the basis of an agreement between those parties. It is more surprising to find this limitation on the parties' normal freedom to choose the law applicable to a non-contractual obligation in Article 6(2) cases. After all, the choice of law rule is the flexible one set out in Article 4.[475] So why not allow flexibility in the form of a choice of the applicable law by the parties? A possible justification for this could be that a denial of the freedom to choose also applies to infringements of intellectual property rights.[476] Sometimes a claim for infringement is accompanied by one for disclosure of business secrets, a tort which would fall within Article 6(2). It might be considered undesirable for one part of the claim to be governed by the parties' choice and the other part not so governed.

(c) Restricting free competition

Article 6(3) sets out a choice of law rule for acts restricting free competition.[477] The substantive law background to this rule is Articles 101 and 102 of the Treaty on Functioning of the European Union (TFEU), which deal with competition law within the European Union. In addition, individual Member States have their own competition laws. Any actionable breach of EU law which gives rise to a claim in damages should be categorised as a tort/delict, being a breach of statutory duty.[478] An action for damages based on the breach of competition rules has been held to come within the scope of Article 7(2) of the Brussels I Recast.[479]

(i) The scope of Article 6(3)

Article 6 is headed, inter alia, "acts restricting free competition" and Article 6(3) applies to "a non-contractual obligation arising out of a restriction of competition". Recital (23) explains that the concept of restrictions of competition covers "prohibitions on agreements between undertakings, decisions by associations of undertakings and concerted practices which have as their object or effect the prevention, restriction or distortion of competition within a Member State or within the internal market, as well as prohibitions on the abuse of a dominant position within a Member State or within the internal market, where such agreements, decisions, concerted practices or abuses are prohibited by Articles 81 and 82 of the Treaty or by the law of a Member State". This definition is taken almost verbatim from (now) Articles 101 and 102 TFEU, and those Articles can be consulted for particular instances of such agreements, decisions, concerted practices and abuses. Recital (22) adds that non-contractual obligations arising out of restrictions of competition cover infringements of both EU and national competition law, which includes the national competition law of non-EU Member States. Because of the limitation of the Rome II Regulation to non-contractual obligations, it is uncertain whether the law applicable under Article 6(3) covers also the infringement of competition law as such.[480] Even if it does not, at least for EU competition law this will not make a large difference, as the European courts define the international scope of application of substantive EU competition rules either by reference to the implementation of the practices at issue in the European Economic Area or by demonstrating effects within this territory.[481] If one of this requirements is met, the market in the respective territory is also very

---

[475] Dicey, Morris and Collins, para 35-062 argue that Article 6(4) does not apply to Article 6(2) cases, as Article 6(2) refers to Article 4 which may be displaced under Article 14.

[476] Art 8(3).

[477] There was no such rule in the Proposal for a Regulation.

[478] *Garden Cottage Foods v Milk Marketing Board* [1984] AC 130.

[479] Case C-302/13 *flyLAL-Lithuanian Airlines AS v Starptautiskā lidosta Rīga VAS and Air Baltic Corporation AS* ECLI:EU:C:2014:2319 at [28]; Case C-352/13 *Cartel Damage Claims (CDC) Hydrogen Peroxide SA v Evonik Degussa GmbH and Others* ECLI:EU:C:2015:335 at [34]–[56].

[480] Such an argument could be based on Art 15(a): "basis (. . .) of liability". Against this, it could be argued that Art 6(3), as secondary law, cannot define the scope of application of primary EU rules such as Arts 101, 102 TFEU, see Augenhofer in Calliess (ed), *Rome Regulations: Commentary*, Art 6 para 77, p 595.

[481] See Case T-296/09 Intel Corp. v European Commission ECLI:EU:T:2014:547 at [236] with further references.

likely to be affected, with the consequence that the criteria of Article 6(3) would be met and the law of the respective territory to be applied. Many actions for breach of competition law are brought by the Commission or national competition authorities in administrative proceedings. Such actions fall outside the scope of the Regulation on the basis that they are not civil and commercial matters.[482] In contrast, an action by an individual (or company) who has suffered damage would clearly satisfy this requirement.[483]

(ii) The law applicable to acts restricting free competition

Article 6(3) sets out two choice of law rules. As the general rule, Article 6(3)(a) provides that the law applicable to a non-contractual obligation arising out of a restriction of competition shall be the law of the country where the market is, or is likely to be, affected. Being the general rule, Article 6(3)(a) is not limited to a scenario where the market is affected in just one country. Rather, the principle applies also to cases where markets in two or more states are affected, with the consequence of a distributive application of the law of each country in which the market was affected. As can be seen from the different wording in Article 6(3)(b), Article 6(3)(a) does not require direct or substantial effect on the market. However, as in the field of unfair competition, it appears reasonable to exclude spill-over effects, either as indirect damage by analogy to Article 4(1)[484] or for a lack of foreseeability of the law of mere "spill-over states" being applied.

Article 6(3)(b) applies where the market is, or is likely to be, affected in more than one country. In this situation, the person seeking compensation for damage who sues in the court of the domicile of the defendant may choose to base his claim on the law of the court seised, provided that the market in that Member State is amongst those directly and substantially affected by the restriction of competition out of which the non-contractual obligation on which the claim is based arises.[485] The purpose of this choice is to make competition law enforcement easier by allowing a concentration on one law in case of a multi-state infringement. The law applicable under Article 6(3) may not be derogated from by an agreement pursuant to Article 14.[486]

(d) Environmental damage

Although there has been a gradual harmonisation within the European Union of the substantive law in relation to environmental damage,[487] choice of law problems remain in the world-wide context and even within the European Union.[488] So it is not surprising to find a specific rule in Article 7 of the Regulation for this situation.

---

[482] Case C-102/15 *Gazdasági Versenyhivatal v Siemens Aktiengesellschaft Österreich* ECLI:EU:CU:2016:607 at [34].

[483] Case C-302/13 *flyLAL-Lithuanian Airlines AS v Starptautiskā lidosta Rīga VAS and Air Baltic Corporation AS* ECLI:EU:C:2014:2319 at [28]; Case C-352/13 *Cartel Damage Claims (CDC) Hydrogen Peroxide SA v Evonik Degussa GmbH and Others* ECLI:EU:C:2015:335 at [56]. See now Directive (EU) No 2014/104 of 26 November 2014 on certain rules governing actions for damages under national law for infringements of the competition law provisions of the Member States and of the European Union, OJ L 349/1.

[484] Dicey, Morris and Collins, para 35-060.

[485] Where the claimant sues, in accordance with the applicable rules on jurisdiction, more than one defendant in that court, he or she can only choose to base his or her claim on the law of that court if the restriction of competition on which the claim against each of these defendants relies directly and substantially affects also the market in the Member State of that court (Art 6(3)(b)).

[486] Art 6(4).

[487] See Directive (EC) No 2004/35 of 21 April 2004 on environmental liability with regard to the prevention and remedying of environmental damage, OJ 2004 L 143/56. According to its Art 3(3), this Directive does not give private parties a right of compensation.

[488] The Explanatory Memorandum, p 19.

(i) The scope of Article 7

Article 7 is headed "environmental damage". Recital (24) explains that "environmental damage" means "adverse change in a natural resource, such as water, land or air, impairment of a function performed by that resource for the benefit of another natural resource or the public, or impairment of the variability among living organisms".[489] Article 7 applies to "a non-contractual obligation arising out of environmental damage or damage sustained by persons or property as a result of such damage". It is thus designed to cover two sorts of damage. First, it covers damage to the environment itself. Some civil law states have introduced special rules dealing with the protection of the environment. For example, it is conceivable that somebody who nonchalantly violates environmental law must compensate the state for the damage caused. However, many of such claims, including those introduced to implement Directive 2004/35 on Environmental Liability, will not qualify as civil and commercial matters, but rather as administrative actions. Secondly, it covers damage to persons or property which is a result of environmental damage. This would cover cases brought under the English law of nuisance, trespass and negligence as well as the rule in *Rylands v Fletcher*.[490] With both types of damage, the damage must be the result of human activity.[491] In light of the limitation to "environmental damage" and "damage sustained by persons or property as a result of such damage", it is unclear whether Article 7 covers also pure financial loss as a consequence of environmental damage. The more convincing view is that such loss falls under Article 7, but does not—unlike environmental damage as such and damage sustained by persons or property—constitute direct damage, but rather an "indirect consequence" in the sense of Article 4(1). As a consequence, the location of financial loss is not to be taken into account when the applicable law is identified under Article 7.

(ii) The law applicable to environmental damage

In cases coming within the scope of Article 7 the law applicable "shall be the law determined pursuant to Article 4(1), unless the person seeking compensation for damage chooses to base his claim on the law of the country in which the event giving rise to the damage occurred". This provides for the application of the law of the country in which the damage occurs, but with the claimant having the option of choosing the application of the law of the country in which the event giving rise to the damage occurred.

The place of damage rule   The starting point under Article 7 is the application of the law determined under Article 4(1), which provides for the application of the law of the country in which the damage occurs. The applicable law will thus be the law of the country where the environmental damage occurs, or, if that damage leads to damage sustained by persons or property, the law of the country where this damage is sustained (which will in most places be the same country where the environmental damage occurred). Financial losses resulting from environmental damage are not relevant damage, but only an indirect consequence of environmental damage. Article 7 has been justified on the basis that it conforms to "recent objectives of environmental protection policy, which tends to support strict liability".[492] Moreover, it obliges operators established in low protection countries to abide by the greater protection afforded in neighbouring countries, removing the incentive to establish in low protection countries. This is said to be "conducive to a policy of prevention".[493] No recourse can be had to the Article 4(2) common habitual residence exception or the Article 4(3) manifestly

---

[489] For a more extensive definition, see Art 2(1) of Directive 2004/35 on Environmental Liability.
[490] (1868) LR 3 HL 330.
[491] See the Explanatory Memorandum, p 19.
[492] Ibid.
[493] Ibid.

more closely connected escape clause. This is probably because the place of damage rule provides for the application of the liability rules of the place where the environmental damage occurred to foster the preventive policies of that place so that the use of an exception and a let-out is regarded as being inappropriate. The place of damage rule is the default rule that operates unless the claimant exercises the option to base his or her claim on the law of the country in which the event giving rise to the damage occurred.

The option   This allows the person seeking compensation for damage to base his or her claim on the law of the country in which the event giving rise to the damage occurs, rather than on the law of the country in which the damage occurs. If the claimant exercises this option, the applicable law is that of the country in which the event giving rise to the damage occurred.[494] The claimant can therefore choose the applicable law from two alternatives. This is a one-sided rule, with no such option given to the defendant. Article 7 can therefore be seen to be a pro-claimant rule which is justified by the desired high level of protection in environmental law, based on the precautionary principle and the principle that preventive action should be taken, the principle of priority for corrective action at source and the principle that the polluter pays.[495] The claimant victim is given this option so as to provide him or her with greater protection than is afforded by a place of damage rule. The victim should get the same protection as victims in neighbouring countries.[496] This can be illustrated by taking the following example:

> A polluter establishes its facilities in Country A by a river which flows into the neighbouring Country B, a low protection country. The victim should get the same protection as victims in Country A.[497]

If the victim could only rely on the law of the place of damage this would encourage businesses to establish their facilities on the border of low protection countries. So overall the option should raise the level of environmental protection. The stage at which the victim must exercise this option is for the procedural law of the forum to determine.[498] Giving the person seeking compensation the option of choosing to base his claim on the law of the country where damage was sustained or the law of the country in which the event giving rise to the damage occurred ties in with the jurisdictional choice of the same two countries given to the claimant under Article 7(2) of the Brussels I Recast.[499]

Rules of safety and conduct   Article 17 contains a general limitation on the law applicable under the Regulation, which is concerned with rules of safety and conduct in force at the place of the event giving rise to liability. Environmental damage is an area where this rule may come into play. Operators are required to comply with public law rules as to safety and conduct.

> Let us assume that an operator complies with the rules, eg in relation to the level of toxic emissions, in the country in which it operates (Country A). Nonetheless, it causes damage in the adjacent Country B. The level of emissions exceeds those allowed under the rules of that

---

[494] This is not expressly stated in Art 7 but is implicit. It is also clearly the intention of the provision, see the Explanatory Memorandum, pp 19–20.

[495] For the justification see Recital (25), which refers to Art 174 of the Treaty (now Art 191 TFEU).

[496] The Explanatory Memorandum, pp 19–20.

[497] Ibid.

[498] The Explanatory Memorandum, p 20; Recital (25). Under English law, the claimant may (with permission of the court) amend his pleading any time before the judgment, Civil Procedure Rules 1998, Part 17. For amendment of pleadings after expiry of a limitation period see Limitation Act 1980, s 35; Civil Procedure Rules 1998, r 17.4; *Berezosky v Abramovich* [2011] EWCA Civ 153 at [59]–[72].

[499] Case 21/76 *Handelskwekerij G J Bier BV gegen Mines de potasse d'Alsace SA* [1976] ECR 1735 at [15/19].

country. Under the place of damage rule, the law of Country B will apply and the operator will be liable to the victim.

The effect of Article 17 is that the forum, in assessing the conduct of the operator, must take account "as a matter of fact and in so far as is appropriate, of the rules of safety and conduct" which were in force in Country A. This does not mean applying the law of Country A, rather it is a matter of taking account of its rules of conduct and safety to determine questions of fact, eg when assessing the seriousness of fault.[500]

(e) Infringement of intellectual property rights

Article 8 provides specific rules for infringement of intellectual property rights. Such rules were considered necessary because of the significance given under intellectual property conventions[501] to the territoriality principle which attaches great importance to the law of the country in which protection is claimed.[502] Unfortunately, the Explanatory Memorandum seems to confuse the law of the country for which protection is sought (*lex loci protectionis*) principle (which is now enshrined in Article 8(1) and is a choice of law rule) and the territoriality principle (which is a substantive law rule providing that substantive intellectual property law covers only acts of infringement within the territory of the state granting the intellectual property right).[503] As concerns the former, it is doubtful whether there are indeed specific and clear-cut choice of law rules in these conventions.[504]

(i) *The scope of Article 8*

Article 8 is headed infringement of intellectual property rights and this provision applies to "a non-contractual obligation arising from an infringement of an intellectual property right".[505] Article 13 adds that Article 8 applies also to non-contractual obligations falling within Chapter III of the Regulation. Thus, an obligation based on unjust enrichment arising from an infringement of an intellectual property right is accordingly governed by the same law as the infringement itself.[506] For the purposes of the Regulation the term "intellectual property rights" is to "be interpreted as meaning, for instance, copyright, related rights, the *sui generis* right for the protection of databases and industrial property rights".[507] "Industrial property rights" is a term used in the Paris Convention and in some civil law jurisdictions to encompass patents, utility models, trade marks and registered designs. These are only instances of intellectual property rights. There can be other instances such as plant variety rights.[508] Outside the scope of Article 8 are claims for unfair competition (eg passing off, breach of confidence) which fall under Article 6 and non-contractual obligations based on a person's personality rights (eg in a name or an image) which are excluded from the Regulation under Article 1(2)(g). Moreover, all

---

[500] See further infra, p 871.

[501] See Art 5(2) second sentence of the Berne Convention for the Protection of Literary and Artistic Works and Art 2 of the Paris Convention for the Protection of Industrial Property. Some mention also Art 3, 4 TRIPS and Art 64(3) European Patent Convention in this context.

[502] The Explanatory Memorandum, p 20 and Recital (26).

[503] See the Explanatory Memorandum, p 20: "This rule [principle of lex loci protectionis], also known as the 'territoriality principle'".

[504] See Case C-28/04 *Tod's SpA and Tod's France SARL v Heyraud SA* [2005] ECR I-5781 at [32]; Fawcett and Torremans, Chapter 12; de la Durantaye in Calliess (ed), *Rome Regulations: Commentary*, Art 8 para 2, p 627. Rules referring to the law of the country in which protection is claimed could be regarded as unilateral rules explaining when substantive law applies.

[505] Art 8(1).

[506] The Explanatory Memorandum, p 22.

[507] Recital (26).

[508] Collier, p 358.

questions which are regarded as procedural and not substantive fall, as always, outside the scope of Rome II.[509]

In intellectual property cases, the non-contractual obligations arising from infringement (which fall in the scope of the Rome II Regulation) are often closely linked with the creation, registration, validity, (first) ownership or transfer of the intellectual property right. While (first) ownership and transfer can be regarded as preliminary or incidental questions of a proprietary character which do not fall under Rome II,[510] this is much more difficult to say for the creation, registration and validity of intellectual property rights, as these questions are often closely related to the extent and limitations of such rights which makes a separation between the two for choice of law purposes artificial.[511] In many countries including the UK, this question can be left open in practice, as the choice of law rule for the creation, registration and validity of intellectual property rights under domestic law is the same rule as enshrined in Article 8(1), namely the law of the country for which protection is sought (*lex loci protectionis*).[512]

(ii) The law applicable to intellectual property rights

Article 8 sets out two separate choice of law rules. The first rule is set out in Article 8(1), the second in Article 8(2).

Article 8(1) This is concerned with infringements of intellectual property rights conferred under national legislation or international conventions, such as a United Kingdom patent or a European patent. Article 8(1) provides that: "The law applicable to a non-contractual obligation arising from an infringement of an intellectual property right shall be the law of the country for which protection is claimed." The country (or countries) for which protection is claimed will be determined by the claimant's presentation of his or her claim. It is in the claimant's discretion to seek protection under the intellectual property laws of any country (or countries); this choice is not limited to countries where actual infringement occurred or damage was caused.[513] The question whether or not an infringement actually occurred in that country is a matter for the applicable substantive law (ie the law of the country for which protection is sought, *lex loci protectionis*)[514] of this country to decide. In so deciding, it will be relevant to know whether the allegedly infringing act(s) actually took place in the country for which the claimant has claimed protection under a certain intellectual property right; ie a localisation of the alleged act of infringement under the claimed substantive law becomes necessary.[515] If, under the applicable substantive law, the alleged acts of infringement did not occur in the claimed country of

---

[509] Art 1(3). See *Actavis UK Ltd v Eli Lilly & Co* [2014] EWHC 1511 (Pat) at [210]–[236]: conditions which must be satisfied by a claimant in order to obtain a declaration of non-infringement procedural and not substantive.

[510] Dicey, Morris and Collins, para 34-026 (who also regard creation, registration and validity as proprietary matters outside Rome II); same view: de la Durantaye in Calliess (ed), *Rome Regulations: Commentary*, Art 8 para 37, p 639.

[511] See also Art 15(a) ("basis of liability") which might cover, in an infringement context, the existence of the right which is claimed to be infringed. For a detailed analysis see Fawcett and Torremans, Chapter 13.

[512] See Fawcett and Torremans, Chapter 13; Dicey, Morris and Collins, para 34-026.

[513] De la Durantaye in Calliess (ed), *Rome Regulations: Commentary*, Art 8 para 18, p 633; see also Dicey, Morris and Collins, para 35-078 who argue for an "apparent limitation" to the claimant's discretion from the words "country *for which protection* is claimed" which shall require "some genuine link connection between the acts complained of and their consequences and the country whose laws are relied on". In particular, Art 8 should not permit the wholly extra-territorial application of intellectual property legislation.

[514] Recital (26).

[515] For this analysis see Case C-173/11 *Football Dataco Ltd and Others v Sportradar GmbH and Sportradar AG* ECLI:EU:C:2012:642 at [32]–[33]. See also ibid [34]–[47] for the localisation of an act of infringement in the context of an Internet scenario; for localisation of trade mark infringement Case C-324/09 *L'Oréal v eBay* [2011] ECR I-6011 at [65]; for copyright Case C-5/11 *Criminal Proceedings against Titus Alexander*

protection, there will be no infringement of that country's substantive intellectual property law, as this is limited under the principle of territoriality to "conduct engaged in within national territory";[516] the claim will then fail on the level of substantive law. To take an example of the operation of this rule, let us assume that a patent has been registered in the United Kingdom. It is claimed that this UK patent has been infringed. If, as is usually the case, validity is raised as a defence to the infringement, the UK courts will have exclusive jurisdiction[517] and, by virtue of Article 8(1),[518] will apply UK law to determine whether the defendant is liable for infringement and what (substantive law) remedies are available As there is a single patent for the whole country and a single patent law that applies in the whole of the country, patent judges have stopped referring to English or Scots law on this point and instead refer to UK law, with *Actavis UK Ltd v Eli Lilly & Co* being as case in point.[519] UK law also governs the validity point.[520] Let us now assume that the patent has been registered in ten different European countries. If validity is raised as a defence, each of the ten European countries will have exclusive jurisdiction in relation to the patent that is registered in its country.[521] The claimant would have to bring ten actions in ten different Member States. Under Article 8(1) each Member State would then apply its own law to determine whether there has been infringement.[522] Article 8(1) therefore builds on the territorial principle that is found in intellectual property conventions and adopts a corresponding choice of law rule.[523] This principle is regarded as being so important that there is no common habitual residence exception or "manifestly more closely connected" escape clause from the "country for which protection is claimed" rule.

Article 8(2) The second choice of law rule is concerned with infringements of unitary Community (EU) rights, ie a European Union trade mark,[524] a Community design,[525] a Community plant variety right[526] or (in the future) a European patent with unitary effect.[527]

Jochen Donner ECLI:EU:C:2012:370 at [28]; for both in online sales Case C-98/13 *Martin Blomqvist v Rolex SA and Manufacture des Montres Rolex SA* ECLI:EU:C:2014:55 at [32]. See also Case C-170/12 *Peter Pinckney v KDG Mediatech AG*, Opinion of AG Jääskinen ECLI:EU:C:2013:400 at [47]: Art 8(1) "based on a subjective connection which initially leaves the choice of applicable law to the claimant."

[516] Case C-192/04 *Lagardère Active Broadcast v Société pour la perception de la rémunération équitable (SPRE) and Gesellschaft zur Verwertung von Leistungsschutzrechten mbH (GVL)* [2005] ECR I-7199 at [46].

[517] Case C-4/03 *Gesellschaft für Antriebstechnik mbH & Co KG (GAT) v Luk Lamellen und Kupplungsbau Beteiligungs KG* [2006] ECR I-6509 at [25]. There are specialist IP courts in England, whilst there are no such specialist courts in Scotland and Northern Ireland. This explains why the majority of cases is handled in England, as there is a single patent (and patent law) for the whole country.

[518] Because the claimant, by claiming infringement of a UK patent, implicitly also claims protection for the UK, so that the UK is the country for which protection is sought.

[519] [2014] EWHC 1511 (Pat) at [205], per Arnold J.

[520] The relevant substantive law as law of the country for which protection is sought (*lex loci protectionis*) for patents is UK law and in this case governed the issues of infringement and validity. The law of the forum would however be English law, and in this case that law applied to the question whether Actavis was entitled to a declaration of non-infringement. *Actavis UK Ltd v Eli Lilly & Co* [2014] EWHC 1511 (Pat) at [205].

[521] If validity is not raised as a defence, the defendant can be sued in its domicile (Art 4 Brussels I Recast) or in another Member State under Art 7(2) of the Brussels I Recast. However, validity can be raised at any stage, in which eventuality the exclusive jurisdiction provision will kick in.

[522] *Actavis UK Ltd v Eli Lilly & Co* [2014] EWHC 1511 (Pat) at [204].

[523] See the Explanatory Memorandum, p 20.

[524] See Regulation (EC) No 207/2009 of 26 February 2009 on the Community trade mark, OJ 2009 L 78/1, as amended by Regulation (EU) No 2015/2424 of 16 December 2015, OJ 2015 L 341/21.

[525] See Regulation (EC) No 6/2002 of 12 December 2001 on Community designs, OJ 2002 L 3/1.

[526] See Regulation (EC) No 2100/94 of 1 September 1994 on Community plant variety rights, OJ 1994 L 227/1.

[527] See Regulation (EU) No 1257/2012 of 17 December 2012 implementing enhanced cooperation in the area of the creation of unitary patent protection, OJ 2012 L 361/1. Arguably, registered names etc as protected under Regulation (EU) No 1151/2012 of 21 November 2012 on quality schemes for agricultural products and foodstuffs, OJ 2012 L 343/1 could also be considered as a unitary EU intellectual property right, see Recital (24) of that Regulation.

A unitary Community (EU) right provides protection in every Member State.[528] Article 8(1) works only as a starting point in this situation in that it identifies the entire European Union as the country for which protection is claimed.[529] As the relevant EU instruments do not provide for a complete set of rules for infringement, in particular a complete set of remedies, a supplementary choice of law rule was needed which is provided by Article 8(2): "In the case of a non-contractual obligation arising from an infringement of a unitary Community intellectual property right, the law applicable shall, for any question that is not governed by the relevant Community instrument, be the law of the country in which the act of infringement was committed." Article 8(2) only applies to questions that are not governed by the relevant EU instrument.[530] For example, the EU Trade Mark Regulation harmonises the basic rules on infringement so the question of infringement itself is governed by the EU instrument.[531] However, the EU Trade Mark Regulation has only very limited rules on sanctions. Many issues in relation to sanctions (what are available, in what circumstances, etc, but also issues such as prescription) are left to be dealt with by national substantive law. The resulting choice of law question will be determined in the first instance by the choice of law rules of the respective EU instruments.[532] However, these rules[533] refer, for non-procedural issues,[534] back to the national law of the seised EU Trade Mark court, including its private international law, ie to the choice of law rules of the law of the forum,[535] which is for unitary EU rights Article 8(2). Article 8(2) provides then for the application of the law of the country in which the act of infringement was committed.[536] A particular complexity arises where an EU unitary right has been infringed by several acts in different EU Member States (eg production, advertisement, sale), which from an economic point of view cause a single damage. In order to avoid a mosaic of several national laws being applicable due to the different acts of infringement in different countries, a potential concentration on a single law could be achieved by focusing only on the last act of infringement directly causing the damage for which compensation is claimed, which will normally be the act of distribution.[537] Article 8(2) does not provide for a common habitual residence exception or manifestly more closely connected escape clause.

Article 8(3) provides that the law applicable under Article 8 cannot be derogated from by an agreement of the parties as to the governing law pursuant to Article 14. This is the same as with unfair competition, which can operate as a complementary tort to infringement of intellectual property rights. The only "explanation" given for this limitation in the case of

---

[528] With the exception of European patent with unitary effect, which provides protection only in the participating Member States.

[529] The Explanatory Memorandum, p 21 (with the exception of non-participating Member States in the case of the European patent with unitary effect).

[530] Art 8(2): "for any question that is not governed by the relevant Community instrument".

[531] See Art 9–13 EU Trade Mark Regulation No 207/2009.

[532] These are conflict of law rules in relation to particular matters in the sense of Art 27 Rome II which take precedence over the general Rome II rules (including Article 8(2)).

[533] The relevant choice of law rules in the Regulations are Arts 101, 102(2) EU Trade Mark Regulation No 207/2009; Arts 88(2), (3), 89(1)(d), (2) Community Design Regulation No 6/2002; Arts 97(2), (3), 103 Plant Variety Regulation No 2100/94; see Fawcett and Torremans, paras 15.36–15.41.

[534] Procedural issues are governed by the law of the forum, as under Art 1(3) Rome II.

[535] Case C-479/12 *H Gautzsch Großhandel GmbH & Co KG v Münchener Boulevard Möbel Joseph Duna GmbH* ECLI:EU:C:2014:75 at [49].

[536] In Case C-360/12 *Coty Germany GmbH v First Note Perfumes NV* ECLI:EU:C:2014:1318 at [34], the CJEU has held that the term "act of infringement" in Art 97(5) EU Trade Mark Regulation No 207/2009 refers to "active conduct on the part of the person causing that infringement". It is unclear whether the same meaning would apply to Art 8(2).

[537] For injunctions, the problem is less relevant as Art 102(1) EU Trade Mark Regulation and Art 89(1) Community Design Regulation already provide EU unitary remedies.

infringement of intellectual property rights is that freedom of choice in this area would not be "appropriate", which is no real explanation at all.[538] The actual reason is presumably that the territorial principle that underlies the special choice of law rules for infringements is regarded as being so important that the parties should not be allowed to choose the law of a country other than the one arrived at by the application of that principle.

(f) Industrial action
Article 9 provides that:

> Without prejudice to Article 4(2), the law applicable to a non-contractual obligation in respect of the liability of a person in the capacity of a worker or an employer or the organisations representing their professional interests for damages caused by an industrial action, pending or carried out, shall be the law of the country where the action is to be, or has been, taken.[539]

(i) *The scope of Article 9*
Article 9 is entitled "Industrial action" and the choice of law rule is concerned with the law applicable to "a non-contractual obligation in respect of the liability of a person in the capacity of a worker or an employer or the organisations representing their professional interests for damages caused by an industrial action, pending or carried out". No definition of industrial action is provided. However, Recital (27) gives two examples of such action, namely strike action and lock-outs. More cryptically, Recital (27) points out that the exact concept of industrial action varies from one Member State to another "and is governed by each Member State's internal rules". As a consequence of the great diversity between Member States in this political sensitive subject, "industrial action" is one of the few cases where there shall be no EU autonomous definition of a concept. The reference to national law raises the question which Member State's internal rules should provide the definition. The obvious answer would be the forum. But Recital (27) goes on to say: "Therefore, this regulation assumes as a general principle that the law of the country where the industrial action was taken should apply." This and the purpose of Article 9, namely the preservation of different national concepts of industrial action at the place where such action is taken suggests that the law of the country where the action was taken should determine whether it is industrial action.[540] In English and other common law jurisdictions, there is no tort of industrial action as such. However, a number of torts can arise out of strikes and lockouts: namely, inducement of breach of contract; causing loss by unlawful means; intimidation and unlawful conspiracy.

(ii) *The law applicable to industrial action*
In cases coming within the scope of Article 9, the law applicable is "the law of the country where the [industrial] action is to be, or has been, taken". This rule is designed to protect

---

[538] The Explanatory Memorandum, p 22.

[539] There was no such rule in the Proposal for a Regulation. The Explanatory Memorandum is therefore no guidance as to its meaning. The provision was inserted as a reaction to Case C-18/02 *Danmarks Rederiforening, acting on behalf of DFDS Torline A/S v LO Landsorganisationen i Sverige, acting on behalf of SEKO Sjöfolk Facket för Service och Kommunikation* [2004] ECR I-1417 at [42]–[45] where the Court of Justice had not ruled out that the place of damage (in the sense of Art 7(2) Brussels I Recast) of an industrial action could lie elsewhere than in the country where the action has been carried out. This finding, if applied to choice of law (Art 4(1) Rome II), could expose workers and unions to liability under foreign law which was considered undesirable by most Member States, see the proposal by the Swedish government, Council document No 9009/04 ADD 8 of 15 May 2004, pp 12–13.

[540] There is some debate whether political strikes are excluded from this definition, see Dicey, Morris and Collins, para 35-086. Given the purpose of Art 9 to preserve national concepts of industrial action and the acceptance of political strikes in some EU Member States, such forms of industrial actions should not be generally excluded from Art 9.

the rights of workers and employers.[541] It has been justified on the basis of the difficulty in defining "industrial action".[542] Some Member States were not happy with this rule because it means that vessels would be exposed to substantive law rules which varied according to the laws of the states of their ports of call, irrespective of whether those vessels were in full conformity with the laws of the flag state.[543] The general rule of Article 9 is without prejudice to Article 4(2), the common habitual residence exception. However, the manifestly more closely connected escape clause in Article 4(3) does not apply. Finally, the specific rule on industrial action is "without prejudice to the conditions relating to the exercise of such action in accordance with national law and without prejudice to the legal status of trade unions or of the representative organisations of workers as provided for in the law of the Member States".[544]

(e) The applicable law for unjust enrichment, *negotiorum gestio* and *culpa in contrahendo*

Chapter III is concerned with obligations that arise neither out of a contract nor out of a tort/delict within the meaning of Chapter II.[545] More specifically it is concerned with obligations that arise out of unjust enrichment, *negotiorum gestio* and *culpa in contrahendo*. Obligations arising out of these three concepts are necessarily non-contractual obligations.[546] The first two concepts are concerned with the law of restitution. The third is concerned with the very different matter of pre-contractual obligations. The Commission, in the Proposal for a Regulation, acknowledged the difficulty in devising choice of law rules for these areas. It accepted that the substantive law and the choice of law rules were still evolving rapidly in most of the Member States, which meant that the law was far from certain.[547] The answer in the Proposal was to avoid technical terms and to provide a mixture of specific rules, whilst leaving sufficient flexibility to Member States to adapt the rules to their national system.[548] The final version of the Regulation is markedly different from the Proposal. It is much clearer in that it adopts separate regimes of specific rules for each of the three concepts dealt with in Chapter III, rather than a confusing combination of general rules and specific rules for particular concepts.[549] But this development has necessitated the use of technical terms with attendant definitional problems.

Before turning to examine these special rules, it should be noted that there is one exception to the principle that non-contractual obligations that arise out of unjust enrichment, *negotiorum gestio* and *culpa in contrahendo* are dealt with by the special choice of law rules in Chapter III. This exception is concerned with non-contractual obligations that arise from the infringement of intellectual property rights. For example, a non-contractual obligation may be based on unjust enrichment arising from an infringement of intellectual property rights. In theory two sets of special choice of law rules under the Regulation could come into play in

---

[541] Recital (27).

[542] Ibid.

[543] See the Statement by the Cypriot and Greek Delegations on Art 9, CODEC 838 JUSTCIV 181 of 14 September 2006. See also, at the same reference, the Joint Declaration of Latvia and Estonia, that Art 9 should only apply to cases which arise directly from exercise of the essential right to industrial action.

[544] Recital (28).

[545] The Explanatory Memorandum, p 21. See also Recital (29): "Provision should be made for special rules where damage is caused by an act other than a tort/delict, such as unjust enrichment, *negotiorum gestio* and *culpa in contrahendo*."

[546] See supra, pp 789–91.

[547] See the Explanatory Memorandum, p 21.

[548] Ibid. The UK government and the House of Lords EU Committee preferred confining the Regulation solely to torts/delicts, see United Kingdom Response (2002), para 20; HL Paper No 66 (2004), para 144, and the Written Evidence of Crawford, 100, Fentiman, 112, and Morse, 126.

[549] See Art 9 of the Proposal for a Regulation.

respect of the same dispute, namely the infringement of intellectual property rules in Article 8 of Chapter II and the unjust enrichment rules in Article 10 of Chapter III. To avoid this, Article 13 provides that Article 8 shall apply to non-contractual obligations arising from an infringement of an intellectual property right.[550] This means that the non-contractual obligation based on unjust enrichment is governed by the same law as the infringement itself.[551]

(i) Unjust enrichment

Article 10 sets out the special choice of law rules for unjust enrichment.

(a) The scope of Article 10

Article 10 is headed "Unjust enrichment" and applies where there is "a non-contractual obligation arising out of unjust enrichment".[552] Unjust enrichment includes "payment of amounts wrongly received"[553] which would cover a claim for restitution of an overpayment of money. This gives an example of unjust enrichment but there is no attempt to go further and to define "unjust enrichment".

(i) Characterisation as unjust enrichment

The nature of the problem   Difficult problems of classification arise in relation to unjust enrichment. It is not always clear whether an obligation arises out of unjust enrichment, contract, tort, or equity. If the obligation arises out of unjust enrichment it will fall within Article 10. If the obligation arises out of contract it will fall outside the scope of the Regulation altogether, but within the Rome I Regulation. If the obligation arises out of tort it will fall within Chapter II of the Regulation. If the obligation arises out of equity, it depends on the nature of the obligation.[554] If the matter is essentially proprietary, it will fall outside the Regulation and instead come within the property choice of law rules.

Does it make any practical difference which set of choice of law rules is applied?   In many cases it will make no practical difference whether the contract or unjust enrichment choice of law rules are applied. This is because under Article 10 of the Regulation, normally, the law governing the contractual relationship will also govern the non-contractual obligation arising out of unjust enrichment.[555] Nonetheless, in a minority of cases the effect of Article 10(4) is that the law of some country other than that whose law is applicable to the contract will apply. It is therefore crucial to decide whether the contract choice of law rules or the unjust enrichment choice of law rules should be applied. The same is true in relation to whether the tort choice of law rules[556] or the unjust enrichment choice of law rules are applied. The difference between the unjust enrichment choice of law rule under Article 10 and the English choice of law rules for property is much more marked and makes the question of characterisation on this borderline particularly important.

The approach to be adopted towards characterisation   At common law the English courts characterised the cause of action and the issue. The leading pre-Regulation case on characterisation in the context of restitution is *Macmillan Inc v Bishopsgate Investment Trust plc (No 3)*,[557] which concerned the developing notion of a receipt-based restitutionary claim. In this case, the Court of Appeal accepted that the claim was one in restitution, but characterised

---

[550] See the Explanatory Memorandum, p 22.
[551] Ibid.
[552] Art 10(1).
[553] Ibid.
[554] See supra, pp 790–1 and infra, pp 840–3.
[555] Art 10(1).
[556] These will govern not just obligations characterised as tortious but also those characterised as equitable.
[557] [1996] 1 WLR 387; Forsyth (1998) 114 LQR 141.

the issue as being proprietary with the result that the property choice of law rules applied. Auld LJ referred to the danger of looking at characterisation through domestic eyes, and said that "the 'receipt-based restitutionary claim' is a notion of English domestic law that may not have a counterpart in many other legal systems and is one that it may not be appropriate to translate into the English law of conflict".[558] In the absence of an issue whose characterisation is so clear-cut, it will be the characterisation of the cause of action that matters. This is what will happen in many cases.

Under the Regulation, it has to be decided whether there is a non-contractual obligation and, if there is, whether this arises out of unjust enrichment. This does not tell us precisely what is being characterised. If the facts of *Macmillan* were to arise under the Regulation, is one supposed to characterise the issue or the cause of action? In the context of the Regulation the process of characterisation should not be carried out through English eyes. The approach adopted in *Macmillan* is designed to ensure that this does not happen. Ultimately the question is which set of choice of law rules in the Regulation should you apply and the flexible approach adopted in *Macmillan* is particularly well suited to answering this.

(ii) Specific problems

Property or unjust enrichment? Under English substantive law it is unclear to what extent proprietary claims should be characterised as restitutionary.[559] At first sight, this produces a considerable dilemma for the private international lawyer. However, under the pre-Regulation law it appeared that, regardless of the characterisation of the cause of action, where the issue in the case was essentially a proprietary one, recourse had to be had to the choice of law rules in relation to property issues.[560] The leading pre-Regulation case is *Macmillan Inc v Bishopsgate Investment Trust plc (No 3)*.[561]

> The plaintiff, a Delaware corporation, brought an action against a number of banks claiming that it was beneficially entitled to shares in a New York corporation, that these were held on constructive trust by the defendants for the benefit of the plaintiff, and seeking their return or compensation for their loss. The question arose of the applicable law. This in turn raised a question of characterisation: was the issue in the case restitutionary, in which case the restitution choice of law rules would apply, or proprietary, in which case the property choice of law rules would apply?

The Court of Appeal held that the issue in the case, namely whether the defendants could defeat the plaintiff's interest by establishing that they were bona fide transferees for value without notice, was essentially a proprietary one. Turning therefore to the choice of law rules in relation to property issues, it was held that the law applicable to questions of title to shares in a company was that of the place where the shares were situated, which in the ordinary way was that where the company was incorporated. Accordingly, New York law applied.

It has earlier been submitted that the *Macmillan* approach towards characterisation should be adopted in Regulation cases. This means that, if the facts of *Macmillan* were to arise now, the result should be the same, namely the property choice of law rules should apply, rather than the Regulation.

---

[558] At 604. See also Briggs [1995] Rest LR 94, at 97.

[559] See R Stevens in Rose (ed), *Restitution and the Conflict of Laws* (1995), pp 182–3.

[560] See generally on the extent to which proprietary claims should be regarded as being restitutionary, R Stevens, op cit, pp 182–4.

[561] [1996] 1 WLR 387; Bird [1996] LMCLQ 57; Briggs (1996) 67 BYBIL 604; Swadling [1996] LMCLQ 63; R Stevens (1996) 112 LQR 198; J Stevens (1996) 59 MLR 741; Grantham and Rickett [1996] LMCLQ 463.

The question of characterisation as unjust enrichment or property also arises in relation to proprietary restitution.[562] A claim for proprietary restitution would arise where, for example, a seller delivers goods to the buyer and the latter fails to pay. The seller wants the goods themselves back. If title has passed to the buyer the seller would ask that the goods revest in him. The question is whether such a claim is based on unjust enrichment (and thus falls within Article 10 in Chapter III) or is based on the law of property (and thus falls outside the scope of the Regulation altogether). Under English substantive law there is considerable controversy over the classification of such claims.[563] While there is certainly much force in the argument that claims for proprietary restitution should be regarded as being based on property, since property rights are ultimately at stake,[564] the claim itself is not necessarily based on property (as title has already passed).[565] In order to be classified as proprietary, however, it should be decisive whether the claim to return the goods is based on property, because under the law governing property in the goods (normally the law of the *situs* where the property is located), the claimant preserved some form of (legal or equitable) ownership in them. If, on the other hand, the claim is not based on any form of ownership, because the claimant has lost any form of ownership, it should be classified as a "mere" obligation. Provided that this obligation is not contractual in nature,[566] it would qualify as a form of unjust enrichment in the sense of Article 10 Rome II.

Contract or unjust enrichment? A claim by a buyer of goods for restitution of an overpayment of money to the seller arises out of unjust enrichment, rather than contract. This can be said with confidence because Article 10(1) provides that unjust enrichment includes "payment of amounts wrongly received".[567] If however, a contract is void *ab initio* and one of the parties seeks return of money paid in advance, Article 12(1)(e) of the Rome I Regulation[568] makes it clear that "the consequences of nullity" are to be characterised as contractual for the purposes of EU private international law of obligations. Thus, courts in the United Kingdom will apply the contract choice of law rules under the Rome I Regulation.

A restitutionary obligation may also arise out of discharge of a contract. This does not relate to "the consequences of nullity".[569] Under English law this would probably be regarded as restitutionary rather than contractual[570] and, if this classification is adopted for the purposes of the Rome II Regulation, recourse has to be had to Article 10. However, in some civil law countries, eg Germany, the right to have a contract unwound, and obtain restitution,

---

[562] *Macmillan* was not a case of proprietary restitution; it was one of a restitutionary claim to which there was a proprietary defence (Panagopoulos, *Restitution in Private International Law* (2000), pp 44–5) or better analysed as a direct assertion of a proprietary right (Burrows, *The Law of Restitution* (3rd edn, 2010), p 169 fn 3: "*vindicatio* claim"). We are concerned here with proprietary restitution without a trust. For the situation where there is a trust, see Chong (2005) 54 ICLQ 855 and, in the context of international sale of goods, Fawcett, Harris and Bridge, paras 19.74–19.87.

[563] Cf Birks, *Unjust Enrichment* (2nd edn, 2005), pp 32–8; Burrows, *The Law of Restitution* (3rd edn, 2010), Chapter 8 (unjust enrichment) with Virgo, *The Principles of the Law of Restitution* (2nd edn, 2006), pp 11–17, Chapter 20 (a proprietary claim).

[564] See Fawcett, Harris and Bridge, paras 19.69–19.73 and the 14th edn of this book (2008), p 821.

[565] See Dicey, Morris and Collins, para 36-078, who suggest a classification as non-contractual in the sense of Art 10 Rome II.

[566] See Art 12(1)(e) Rome I.

[567] Art 10(1).

[568] Discussed supra, pp 768–9. The possibility of a reservation in respect of Art 10(1)(e) of the 1980 Rome Convention under Art 7(1)(e) of the Convention (which the UK had entered because it regarded the consequences of nullity of a contract not as contractual, but rather as concerning restitution or unjust enrichment, s 2(2) of the Contracts (Applicable Law) Act 1990) has been abolished by the Rome I Regulation. For the situation before Rome I, see the 14th edn of this book (2008), p 822.

[569] Brereton in Rose (ed), *Restitution and the Conflict of Laws* (1995), pp 166–7.

[570] Ibid.

following a serious breach of contract is regarded as contractual.[571] Moreover, if even the consequences of nullity of a contract are deemed to be contractual under Article 12(1)(e) Rome I, the same should be true for claims arising out of the discharge of a contract, or upon a breach of contract, where even a valid contract has existed. These cases would thus fall within the Rome I Regulation.[572]

Tort or unjust enrichment?   The borderline between unjust enrichment and tort has previously been examined when discussing the scope of Chapter II.[573]

Equity and unjust enrichment   Prior to the Rome II Regulation it was suggested that the equitable parts of the law of restitution, such as the restitutionary *remedy of rescission for common mistake* in equity, should be characterised as restitutionary (unjust enrichment) rather than as equitable.[574] The question now is whether this should be regarded as falling within the meaning of unjust enrichment under the Regulation. As the remedy of rescission seems to allow escape from a contract, it is probably best regarded as contractual and thus falling in the scope of the Rome I Regulation.[575] This is not called into question by the observation that such a remedy may also reverse unjust enrichment where a contract has been wholly or partly executed, because these consequences can also be considered, like the consequences of nullity or avoidance of a contract, as being contractual in nature.[576]

It was also suggested that the question whether a person holds on *constructive trust* is best regarded as coming within the restitution choice of law rules.[577] It is no doubt true that constructive trusts are restitutionary in cases where the constructive trust is imposed where there is unjust enrichment by subtraction or restitution for wrongdoing.[578] With the introduction of the Regulation, such cases would fall within Article 10.[579] But there are other cases where a constructive trust is held to exist where there is no unjust enrichment by subtraction or restitution for wrongdoing.[580] A claim may assert that property is held on constructive trust because the transferee has equitable title to the property. The basis of such a claim is proprietary.[581] The appropriate choice of law rule to be applied will depend on whether the constructive trust falls within the Recognition of Trusts Act 1987,[582] which gives effect to

---

[571] See §§ 323, 326, 346 of the German Bürgerliches Gesetzbuch.

[572] See Art 12(1)(c) (consequences of breach) of the Rome I Regulation.

[573] Supra, pp 806–8.

[574] Bird in Rose (ed), *Restitution and the Conflict of Laws* (1995), pp 77–9.

[575] See Art 10(1) Rome I. Arguably, the equitable doctrine of common mistake has been abolished by *Great Peace Shipping Ltd v Tsavliris Salvage (Int) Ltd* [2002] EWCA Civ 1407 at [157]: "there is no jurisdiction to grant rescission of a contract on the ground of common mistake where that contract is valid and enforceable on ordinary principles of contract law". However, rescission remains possible for misrepresentation and for non-disclosure.

[576] See Art 12(1)(e) Rome I and supra, pp 839–40.

[577] Bird, op cit, pp 82–3. See also the pre-Regulation case of *Kuwait Oil Tanker Co SAK v Al Bader* [2000] 2 All ER (Comm) 271 (this involved a claim for breach of fiduciary duty and thus liability to account as constructive trustees). Cf Barnard (1992) 51 CLJ 474, 479–80.

[578] These terms are explained infra, pp 841–3. This situation is more accurately known as constructive trusteeship, see *Paragon Finance v DB Thakerar and Co* [1999] 1 All ER 400 at 409.

[579] See also Dicey, Morris and Collins, para 36-084, who see the central question as being "whether the trust arises in response to an obligation, or pursuant to the law of property". They propose to apply Rome II "where a [constructive] trust genuinely arises *de novo* in response to the breach of a non-contractual obligation according to the law applicable to that obligation".

[580] R Stevens, in Rose (ed), *Restitution and the Conflict of Laws* (1995), pp 215–18.

[581] See Chong (2005) 54 ICLQ 855. For the jurisdictional position, see *NABB Brothers Ltd v Lloyds Bank International* [2005] EWHC 405 (Ch), [2005] IL Pr 37.

[582] R Stevens ibid n 582. There are different views on the applicability of the Act to constructive trusts, cf Fawcett, Harris and Bridge, para 19.76–19.80 (most constructive trusts will be covered) with Dicey, Morris and Collins, para 36-092 (operation of the Act confined to the situation once a constructive trust has arisen:

the Hague Convention on the Law Applicable to Trusts and on their Recognition. If it does, then the choice of law rules in the Act will apply. This is unaffected by the advent of the Regulation, which does not prejudice the application of this Hague Convention.[583] If the constructive trust does not fall within the 1987 Act, the property choice of law rules should apply.[584]

The position is equally unsettled when it comes to *resulting trusts*. Although it has been argued that, in principle, there are restitutionary resulting trusts and that these should be characterised as restitutionary,[585] the better view is that, as a matter of substantive law, resulting trusts should be regarded as proprietary.[586] This would suggest a proprietary characterisation for the purposes of choice of law. The property choice of law rules would then apply[587] (rather than those in the Regulation), except to the extent, and this is unclear,[588] that resulting trusts fall to be dealt with by the choice of law rules contained in the Recognition of Trusts Act 1987,[589] in which case the choice of law rules in the Act would apply, unaffected by the Regulation.

Finally, it was suggested that, in the situation where the cause of action is in unjust enrichment, the *right to trace* should be determined by the unjust enrichment choice of law rules.[590] This is on the basis that tracing is a process of identification. With the introduction of the Regulation this would mean that Article 10 would apply.

Restitution for wrongdoing and unjust enrichment   Under English substantive law there is a concept of restitution for wrongdoing. The wrongdoing which must be established may be contractual or tortious or an equitable wrong. An example of restitution for contractual wrongdoing would be where a seller breaks his contract with the buyer and sells goods for £1,000 more to a third party. The original buyer seeks restitutionary damages of £1,000. An example of restitution for tortious wrongdoing would be where A wrongfully sells goods belonging to B (the tort of conversion) and B claims for the value of the sale, rather than the loss caused to him. An example of restitution for equitable wrongdoing would be where a person in a fiduciary position (such as a company director) makes an unauthorised profit and a claim is made for him to disgorge it by way of an account of profits. Under English

---

"the Convention prevails in respect of trusts created voluntarily and evidenced in writing; and also in respect of trusts declared by judicial decisions"). Chong, op cit, argues that the Act does not apply to constructive trusts governed by a foreign law. The Act is discussed infra, p 1384.

[583] Art 28(1).

[584] See Stevens, op cit; Chong (2005) 54 ICLQ 855. Stevens argues that the choice of law rules for equitable wrongs (restitution for equitable wrongdoing is now encompassed within Art 10 of the Regulation) should apply where the trust arises by virtue of such a wrong.

[585] Bird, op cit, p 83; R Stevens, op cit, p 218. See also Millett (1998) 114 LQR 399, 415.

[586] *Westdeutsche Landesbank Girozentrade v Islington Borough Council* [1996] AC 669, HL; for choice of law see Dicey, Morris and Collins, para 36-085.

[587] See Chong, op cit.

[588] See Dicey, Morris and Collins, para 29-007; Hayton (1987) 36 ICLQ 260, 263–4; infra, p 1384. Cf Fawcett, Harris and Bridge, para 19.77 for an assertion that most resulting trusts will fall within the Act. See also Chong, op cit, who argues that the Act does not apply to constructive trusts governed by a foreign law.

[589] Bird, op cit, p 83. See also Stevens, op cit. See also Fawcett, Harris and Bridge, para 19.77.

[590] Panagopoulos (1998) 6 Rest LR 73; Fawcett, Harris and Bridge, para 19.96; see also Dicey, Morris and Collins, paras 36-096–36-100. There is a question whether a procedural classification should be adopted. Millett J in *El Ajou v Dollar Land Holdings plc* [1993] 3 All ER 717 at 736 found it unnecessary to decide this point since on the facts English law applied in either eventuality. However, the same judge has said in a conference paper that he inclines to the view that the matter is one of substance to be governed by the law of the restitutionary obligation, 8th Singapore Conference on International Business Law 30 October–1 November 1996. For tracing of trust property generally, see Harris (2002) 73 BYBIL 65; Fawcett, Harris and Bridge, paras 19.90–19.95.

substantive law the classification of restitution for wrongdoing is particularly difficult. A number of different views have been expressed on this.[591] Some leading common law commentators regard this category as coming within the category of unjust enrichment, but consider that unjust enrichment by wrongdoing (or dependent unjust enrichment) is different from the more usual unjust enrichment by subtraction (or autonomous unjust enrichment).[592] With unjust enrichment by wrongdoing, the defendant's gain has been acquired by committing a wrong against the claimant. So the enrichment results from the wrongful act of the person enriched. However, the better view, which enjoys the greatest academic support, is that the cause of action is in tort, contract or equity, and this triggers a restitutionary remedy.[593] Under English law, then, restitution for wrongdoing exists and it is almost universally agreed that it is very different from unjust enrichment by subtraction.[594]

In civil law jurisdictions the position is entirely different. The concept of restitution for wrongdoing is not known as such.[595] Civil law jurisdictions such as Germany, Greece[596] and France[597] tend to classify such actions under unjust enrichment by subtraction.[598] In the light of this, it is not surprising to find that the Regulation does not contain a special choice of law rule for restitution for wrongdoing or explain which of the choice of law rules it falls within. However, the failure to provide an explanation under the Regulation leaves uncertainty in relation to claims based on restitution for wrongdoing.

One possibility would be to adopt the English substantive law classification. Lack of agreement on this classification makes this a rather unattractive proposition. But if one adopts, for the purposes of the Regulation,[599] the most commonly held view, namely that the cause of action is in tort, contract or equity, and this triggers a restitutionary remedy,[600] the result is as follows. Where the obligation is tortious, Chapter II (Article 4) will apply.[601] Where the restitution is sought for breach of a fiduciary duty, this approach would apply the law governing the fiduciary duty. But where the obligation is contractual, this will be excluded from the scope of the Regulation altogether and rather fall within the scope of the Rome I Regulation.[602]

A better alternative would be to adopt the civil law classification, namely that situations falling within the common law concept of restitution for wrongdoing simply come under unjust enrichment by subtraction.[603] Article 10 would then apply. This is supported by the wording of Article 10(1), which envisages that there can be unjust enrichment where the parties do not have just a contractual relationship but also have a tortious or other relationship that is

---

[591] See generally Bird, op cit, pp 72–6; Fawcett, Harris and Bridge, para 8.89; Rotherham (2007) 66 CLJ 172.

[592] Burrows, *The Law of Restitution* (3rd edn, 2010), Part 4; Birks, *An Introduction to the Law of Restitution*, Chapters I and X. Birks later changed his mind, see in Cornish, Nolan, O'Sullivan and Virgo (eds) *Restitution: Past, Present and Future*, pp 14–15.

[593] Virgo, op cit, pp 445–8; Panagopoulos, op cit, pp 16–17, 81–4, 228; Bird, op cit, p 74.

[594] But see Beatson, *The Use and Abuse of Unjust Enrichment* (1991), pp 25–8, who regards restitution for wrongdoing as falling within unjust enrichment by subtraction.

[595] See Beatson and Schrage (eds), *Cases, Materials and Texts on Unjustified Enrichment* (2003), p 523.

[596] Panagopoulos, op cit, 228.

[597] See Beatson and Schrage (eds), *Cases, Materials and Texts on Unjustified Enrichment* (2003), p 543.

[598] It is debatable whether restitution for breach of contract also classifies as restitution, because some might consider this action as contractual in nature.

[599] See Virgo, Written Evidence, HL Paper 66 (2004), 134.

[600] Virgo, op cit, 425–8; Panagopoulos, op cit, 16–17, 81–4, 228; Bird, op cit, 74.

[601] Dicey, Morris and Collins, paras 36-053, 36-055–36.056.

[602] See Art 12(1)(c) Rome I, the restitution being one of the "consequences of a total or partial breach of obligations".

[603] Collier, p 346.

closely connected with the unjust enrichment. The most obvious example of this situation is where there is what common lawyers would call restitution for tortious or equitable wrong-doing. As the legislative history and the difference in wording to Article 4(3) suggests, the relationship in Article 10(1) need not be "pre-existing", but it is sufficient that it is "existing between the parties", which means that it may arise at the same time as the claim for restitution (eg by commission of a tort).[604] As a consequence, most restitutions for wrongdoing, while being classified as unjust enrichment, will be governed by the same law which governs the existing relationship with which they are closely connected (eg contract, tort, or a fiduciary duty). The result would therefore be very similar to the first approach, with the main difference being that it is reached via Article 10 and not by directly applying the law which governs the relationship as such.

(iii) Other aspects of scope
Once it has been decided that there is unjust enrichment within the meaning of Article 10 it follows that the obligation that arises out of this unjust enrichment must be regarded as non-contractual.[605] Article 10 does not presuppose that there is damage. This is not surprising given that damage is not one of the essential elements of unjust enrichment.

(b) The law applicable to unjust enrichment
Article 10 contains four rules, with a separate paragraph for each rule. The first paragraph is concerned with the specific situation where there is a relationship existing between the parties. The second paragraph is a fall-back provision which deals with the situation where the applicable law cannot be determined on the basis of the first paragraph. The third paragraph is a further fall-back provision now dealing with the situation where the applicable law cannot be determined on the basis of the first and second paragraphs. The fourth paragraph contains a manifestly more closely connected escape clause, which allows an escape from the first three paragraphs. Article 10 is very similar to the position under German law.[606]

(i) Where there is a relationship existing between the parties
Article 10(1) provides that:

> If a non-contractual obligation arising out of unjust enrichment, including payment of amounts wrongly received, concerns a relationship existing between the parties, such as one arising out of a contract or a tort/delict, that is closely connected with that unjust enrichment, it shall be governed by the law that governs that relationship.

This rule adopts the philosophy of secondary connection that is also to be found in Article 4(3).[607] The justification for the rule is that the non-contractual obligation arising out of unjust enrichment is so closely connected with the pre-existing relationship between the parties that it is preferable for the entire legal situation to be governed by the same law.[608] The same approach had its advocates in England.[609]

---

[604] It is remarkable that the initial proposal by the Commission limited Art 10(1) (Art 9(1) as it then was) to a "relationship previously existing between the parties", see Explanatory Memorandum p 35, whereas Art 10(1) of the final Regulation speaks only of a "relationship existing between the parties". Moreover, "tort/delict" is expressly mentioned in Art 10(1). But see *Banque Cantonale de Geneve v Polevent Ltd* [2015] EWHC 1968 (Comm) at [16]–[17]: Art 10(1) does not apply to a relationship created merely by the commission of a tort.

[605] Supra, pp 789–91.

[606] Introductory Law to the Civil Code, the 1999 Codification, Arts 38 and 41. See also Swiss law, the Swiss PIL Statute 1987, Arts 128 and 15.

[607] The Explanatory Memorandum, p 21. Art 4(3) is discussed supra, pp 814–19.

[608] Ibid.

[609] On the common law before Rome II Dicey, Morris and Collins, para 36-008 under (a) (for contracts).

When does Article 10(1) apply? In order for Article 10(1) to apply, the following must be shown:

First, there must be a non-contractual obligation arising out of unjust enrichment. In other words, the obligation must come within the scope of Article 10, examined above.

Secondly, the non-contractual obligation must concern a relationship existing between the parties. Article 10(1) goes on to give two examples of such a relationship, namely "one arising out of a contract or a tort/delict". Unjust enrichment most commonly arises out of the situation where the parties have a contractual relationship.[610] But the relationship between the parties can also arise out of a tort/delict.[611] Where there is such a relationship, it may be that the obligation arises out of tort, rather than unjust enrichment and therefore Chapter II will apply, rather than Chapter III. So what is envisaged here is that there is a relationship existing between the parties arising out of a tort but that, nevertheless, the obligation arises out of unjust enrichment. The most obvious example of this situation is where there is what common lawyers would call restitution for tortious wrongdoing (assuming that this falls within Article 10 in the first place).[612] The wording of Article 10(1) makes it clear that the relationship between the parties can arise out of something other than a contract or tort. This would include a relationship based on equity, such as a fiduciary relationship. The relationship must be implicitly limited by the need to fall within a category that has choice of law rules governing that relationship.

Article 10(1) refers to a relationship "existing" between the parties, "such as one arising out of a contract or a tort/delict". A relationship "arising out of" a contract would obviously encompass the relationship between the two parties to that contract. However, the use of the present tense ("existing") in Article 10(1) raises the question whether a past relationship that has subsequently ceased, such as where a contract has been avoided, would come within this provision.[613] While the legislative history sheds doubt on the inclusion of past relationships, it could be argued that an "existing" relationship is sufficiently wide to include mere pre-contractual relationships or void contracts. On the other hand, the systematic context of Article 10(1) has to be observed. Where, for example, a party seeks the return of money paid in advance under a contract that is void *ab initio*, this will fall outside the scope of the Rome II Regulation and thus also Article 10 altogether.[614] But would it cover a pre-contractual relationship, which can give rise to pre-contractual obligations and where there may be no contract entered into by the parties? Article 12 deals with these cases and so Article 10 should be interpreted as not covering them. Finally, as the legislative history and the difference in wording to Article 4(3) suggests, the relationship in Article 10(1) need not be "pre-existing", but it is sufficient that it is "existing between the parties", which means that it may arise at the same time as the claim for restitution (eg by commission of a tort).[615] While it may be true

---

[610] The Rome I Regulation will apply to determine whether there is a contract between the parties and which law applies to it.

[611] The Rome II Regulation will apply to determine whether the parties have a tortious relationship.

[612] Supra, pp 841–3.

[613] Art 9(1) of the Proposal for a Regulation referred to a pre-existing relationship so as to cover void contracts and pre-contractual relationships (see the Explanatory Memorandum, p 21), but Art 9 was replaced by Arts 10(1) and 11(1) of the final version of the Regulation, which refer only to a "relationship existing between the parties".

[614] And rather in the scope of the Rome I Regulation as a consequence of the nullity of the contract, Art 12(1)(e) Rome I.

[615] See Rushworth and Scott [2008] LMCLQ 274, 286. It is remarkable that the initial proposal by the Commission limited Art 10(1) (Art 9(1) as it then was) to a "relationship previously existing between the parties", see Explanatory Memorandum p 35, whereas Art 10(1) of the final Regulation speaks only of a "relationship existing between the parties". Moreover, "tort/delict" is expressly mentioned in Art 10(1). For

that Article 10(1) is to a certain extent rooted in the legitimate expectations of the parties, this is not its only justification. Another important justification is to avoid an unnecessary application of different laws to obligations which are closely connected, which justifies applying Article 10(1) also to cases where the relationship arises at the same time as the claim for restitution.[616] Thirdly, the relationship existing between the parties must be closely connected with that unjust enrichment.

Application of the law that governs the relationship between the parties   Where the parties have a contractual relationship, the law governing that contract will also govern the non-contractual obligation arising out of unjust enrichment. An example of the operation of this rule where there is a tortious relationship between the parties is as follows. A wrongfully sells goods belonging to B (the tort of conversion) and B claims for the value of the sale, rather than the loss caused to him. This is an example of tortious wrongdoing. Under Article 10(1) the law governing the tort of conversion will also govern the obligation to pay the value of the goods. In a case of restitution for equitable wrongdoing the law governing the fiduciary relationship would also govern the obligation to restore the benefit obtained by the defendant by his wrongdoing.

(ii) Where the law applicable cannot be determined on the basis of paragraph (1)
Article 10(2) provides that: "Where the law applicable cannot be determined on the basis of paragraph 1 and the parties have their habitual residence in the same country when the event giving rise to unjust enrichment occurs, the law of that country shall apply."

When does Article 10(2) apply?   There are two requirements for this provision to apply. First, the law applicable cannot be determined on the basis of paragraph 1, so this is a fall-back provision. We are familiar with the idea of a choice of law rule based on the parties' habitual residence from Article 4 but that operates as an exception to the general principle in Article 4(1), rather than as a fall-back where the law applicable cannot be determined on the basis of that provision. The law applicable cannot be determined on the basis of Article 10(1) where the non-contractual obligation arising out of unjust enrichment does not concern a relationship existing between the parties that is closely connected with that unjust enrichment. This could be because there is no relationship existing between the parties, eg a seller delivers goods to the wrong person with whom it has no contractual or other relationship and seeks restitutionary damages equivalent to the value of the goods,[617] or there may be such a relationship but it is not closely connected with that unjust enrichment. If the law can be determined on the basis of paragraph 1, then that provision will apply, not Article 10(2). This will be the case even though the parties have a common habitual residence in some other country, which is different from Article 4(2) where the common habitual residence rule operates as an exception to Article 4(1), applying it to trump that provision. However, it is important to bear in mind that Article 10(4) operates as an escape from paragraph 1 (as well as paragraphs 2 and 3) and where the parties have a common habitual residence this can be one factor to argue that the non-contractual obligation is more closely connected with a country, ie the common habitual residence, other than that indicated in paragraph 1.

---

a different view see Dicey, Morris and Collins, para 36-031 and *Banque Cantonale de Geneve v Polevent Ltd* [2015] EWHC 1968 (Comm) at [16]–[17]: Art 10(1) does not apply to a relationship created merely by the commission of a tort.

[616] In the Explanatory Memorandum p 21, the "legitimate expectations of the parties" are mentioned as a justification of the common habitual residence rule in Art 10(2), not of the rule in Art 10(1).

[617] Neither would there appear to be a tortious relationship. Under English law the mere unauthorised retention of another's goods is not conversion of them: *Kuwait Airways Corpn v Iraqi Airways Co (Nos 4 and 5)* [2002] 2 AC 883 at 1084 (per Lord Nicholls).

The second requirement for Article 10(2) to apply is that the parties must have their habitual residence in the same country. The meaning of habitual residence has previously been examined.[618] The habitual residence of a party can change as events unfold. Article 10(2) is concerned with habitual residence at the time when the event giving rise to unjust enrichment occurs. For example, in a case of payment of amounts wrongly received it would be when the money is received.

Application of the law of the country of common habitual residence   This common habitual residence rule is familiar to us from Article 4(2). However, as has been seen, the place of the rule within the scheme of the Article as a whole is much reduced in Article 10 from that in Article 4. The common habitual residence rule has been justified on the basis that it reflects the legitimate expectations of the parties where they are habitually resident in the same country.[619]

(iii) Where the law applicable cannot be determined on the basis of paragraph 1 or 2
"Where the law applicable cannot be determined on the basis of paragraphs 1 or 2, it shall be the law of the country in which the unjust enrichment took place."

When does Article 10(3) apply?   Paragraph 3 requires that the law applicable cannot be determined on the basis of paragraph 1 or 2. In other words, this is a further fall-back provision to that in Article 10(2). We are therefore dealing with a situation where there is no relationship between the parties that is closely connected with that unjust enrichment (and thus paragraph 1 does not apply) and, where that is the case, there is no common habitual residence (and thus paragraph 2 does not apply).

Application of the law of the country in which the unjust enrichment took place   Where paragraph 3 applies, the applicable law is that of the country in which the unjust enrichment took place. The only explanation of the adoption of this fall-back rule[620] is that it is found in Swiss law[621] and in the European Group for Private International Law's Proposal for a European Convention on the law applicable to non-contractual obligations.[622] The major problem with this rule is the definitional one. Which is the country in which the unjust enrichment took place?[623] This could be referring to: the place where the legal event giving rise to the claim occurred (the *lex loci condictionis*); the place in which the act was committed responsible for conferring the benefit or enrichment (the *lex loci actus*); the place where the impoverishment occurs;[624] or the place where the enrichment occurs. Deciding on the place does not end the definitional problem. Whichever solution is adopted, there is an attendant definitional problem under that solution.[625]

The Swiss choice of law rule for unjust enrichment refers directly to the law of the State in which the enrichment occurred,[626] rather than the more ambiguous law of the country in which the unjust enrichment took place. The position is the same under German law[627] and under the Proposal of the European Group for Private International

---

618   See Art 23 Rome II and supra, pp 802–3.
619   The Explanatory Memorandum, p 21.
620   Ibid, at p 22.
621   See Art 128(2) of the Swiss Federal Statute on Private International Law of 1987. And in German law, see Introductory Law to the Civil Code, the 1999 Codification, Art 38(3).
622   Art 7(3).
623   See Gutteridge and Lipstein (1939) 7 CLJ 80, 89–90; Collier in Lipstein (ed), *Harmonization of Private International Law by the E.E.C.*, pp 81, 85–6; Blaikie [1984] Jur Rev 112, 118–22; Bennett (1990) 39 ICLQ 136, 146–50.
624   See Cohen (1956) 31 LA Bar Bull 71; Bird, op cit, pp 112–13.
625   Bird, op cit, pp 110–16.
626   See Art 128(2) of the Swiss Federal Statute on Private International Law of 1987.
627   Introductory Law to the Civil Code, the 1999 Codification, Art 38(3).

Law.[628] Common lawyers have also directly applied the law of a country in which the enrichment occurred rule.[629] Dicey, Morris and Collins sets out a sub-rule using this point of contact.[630] Given the popularity in the European Union of reference to a country in which the enrichment occurred rule, particularly in Germany whose law appears to have been influential in the development of Article 10, it is submitted that the country in which the unjust enrichment took place should be defined in terms of the country in which the enrichment occurred.[631]

However, the concept of the country in which the enrichment occurs itself involves a definitional problem: is this the place where the benefit accrues to the person who is enriched; or where the loss to the person who is impoverished occurs; or does it vary, depending on the particular situation? The best solution looks to be where the benefit occurs,[632] but is this where it first occurs or, if goods or money are moved to another country, where the person continues to benefit?[633] If money is paid into a branch in Country A to be transferred to an account in a branch of the same bank in Country B does the benefit accrue where the immediate benefit occurred (A) or in the country of ultimate enrichment (B)?[634] What if money is paid mistakenly into bank accounts in a number of different countries?[635] Rather than applying a series of different laws as determined under Article 10(3), it would be better to apply the escape clause under Article 10(4). The place where the benefit occurs will be difficult to ascertain where this consists in saving the defendant from expenditure; presumably it is where the expenditure would have been incurred.[636]

The other problem with a country in which the enrichment occurred rule is that this may be in a country with which the facts have little real connection, for example money may have merely been paid into a bank account there.[637] However, in such a case recourse can be had to the manifestly more closely connected escape clause in Article 10(4).

(iv) The manifestly more closely connected escape clause
Article 10(4) contains an escape clause, which provides that: "Where it is clear from all the circumstances of the case that the non-contractual obligation arising out of unjust enrichment is manifestly more closely connected with a country other than that indicated in paragraphs 1, 2 and 3, the law of that other country shall apply." This adopts the manifestly more closely connected escape clause that is used in Article 4(3) of the Regulation, subject to one difference. Article 4(3) goes on to give an example of a manifestly closer connection,

---

[628] See Art 7(3) of the EGPIL Proposal for a European Convention on the law applicable to non-contractual obligations.

[629] See the American Restatement, First, para 453. For academic support in favour of a place where the enrichment occurred rule see, eg, Gutteridge and Lipstein, op cit, 89–90; Leslie (1998) Edin LR 233 (with a closest connection exception).

[630] On the common law before Rome II see para 36-008 under (c). This rule is merely the starting point for the identification of the proper law of the obligation to make restitution.

[631] Moreover, the proposal by the Parliament to rely on the "law of the country in which the event giving rise to unjust enrichment occurred" (OJ 2005 C 157E/371 in Art 9(3)) was rejected in the Council's Common Position (OJ 2006 C289E/68).

[632] Virgo, Written Evidence, HL Paper 66 (2004), p 135.

[633] Blaikie, op cit, pp 121–2.

[634] The example is given by Dicey, Morris and Collins, para 36-038.

[635] See Virgo, Written Evidence, HL Paper 66 (2004), p 135.

[636] Ibid.

[637] See under the pre-Regulation law, *Baring Bros & Co Ltd v Cunninghame District Council* [1997] CLC 108, (1996) Times, 30 September; *Barros Mattos Junior v Macdaniels* [2005] EWHC 1323 at [118], [2005] IL Pr 630. Under the Regulation see *OJSC TNK-BP Holding v Lazurenko* [2012] EWHC 3286 (Ch) at [103.3].

explaining that this might be based in particular on a pre-existing relationship between the parties, such as a contract. Article 10(4) omits this example. This is because a scenario whereby basing Article 10(4) on a pre-existing relationship would produce a different result from that produced by Article 10, paragraph (1) (which is itself based on the parties' pre-existing relationship), (2) or (3) is not going to arise. The absence of any example as to what might constitute a manifestly closer connection under Article 10(4) means that it is going to be more uncertain as to when the escape clause operates here than under Article 4(3).

Article 10(4) operates as an escape from paragraphs (1), (2) and (3).[638] In determining whether the escape clause should operate as an escape from paragraph (1), it needs to be remembered that that paragraph adopts the secondary connection principle, which is one that is strongly held under the Regulation. The position here is therefore very different from that of Article 4(3) where it is a strongly held principle that forms the basis of the escape clause. Nevertheless, we have already seen a situation where it can at least plausibly be argued that Article 10(4) could operate as an escape from paragraph (1), namely where there is a relationship existing between the parties who have a common habitual residence.

Escaping from paragraph (2) is harder to envisage. Where the applicable law is that of the common habitual residence under paragraph (2) it may be difficult to show that the non-contractual obligation is manifestly more closely connected with some other country. If Article 10(2) applies, this necessarily means that paragraph (1) does not apply so there is no relationship between the parties that is closely connected with that unjust enrichment. So the classic case for the application of the escape clause in Article 4(3), namely where there is a pre-existing relationship between the parties, is not going to arise.

When it comes to escaping from paragraph (3), one is dealing with a situation where there is no relationship between the parties that is closely connected with that unjust enrichment (and thus paragraph (1) does not apply) and there is no common habitual residence (and thus paragraph (2) does not apply). As has been seen, the place in which the unjust enrichment took place may have little connection with the facts, eg money is simply paid into a bank account in that country. In such a case, it may be easier to show that the non-contractual obligation is manifestly more closely connected with some other country.

Until there is guidance from the Court of Justice on the interaction of paragraphs (1) and (4) there is a risk that courts in Member States will be influenced by their traditional national choice of law rules for unjust enrichment. Thus in England, where there has been strong support for the secondary connection principle without any escape clause, there may well be an unwillingness to use the paragraph (4) escape clause. On the other hand, in Scotland, where there has been support for a flexible solution,[639] the courts may be much more willing to be persuaded that paragraph (4) should apply.

(ii) Negotiorum gestio

There is a special provision in Article 11 dealing with *negotiorum gestio*, which has been referred to as agency without authority.[640] The technical definition of this concept is, according to Article 11, "an act performed without due authority in connection with the affairs of another person". *Negotiorum gestio* is concerned with the situation where services are rendered by a person that

---

[638] On a literal reading, Art 10(4) seems to exclude the application of any of the laws which would be applicable under Art 10(1)–(3) ("with a country other than that indicated in paragraphs 1, 2 and 3"). However, such a limitation was probably not meant, see Dicey, Morris and Collins, para 36-042.

[639] *Baring Bros & Co Ltd v Cunninghame District Council* [1997] CLC 108, (1996) Times, 30 September.

[640] See the Explanatory Memorandum, p 22.

enable another person to avoid personal injury or loss of assets.[641] The idea is that there has been the voluntary bestowal of a benefit entitling the intervenor (gestor) to a measure of recovery. Civil law jurisdictions recognise this concept, whereas there is no such recognised concept or cause of action in common law systems.[642] Still, claims under English law which fit into the definition of *negotiorum gestio* fall under Article 11, even if English law does not describe them as such.[643]

Trans-border cases involving *negotiorum gestio* have been rare in the past.[644] The classic case where this has arisen has been that of salvage, ie one ship rendering help to another ship.[645] Continental writers regard *negotiorum gestio* as coming within the broad ambit of restitution or quasi-contract, albeit distinct from unjustifiable enrichment. The Regulation follows this classification by placing *negotiorum gestio* in Chapter III, which is concerned with obligations that arise neither out of a contract nor out of a tort/delict within the meaning of Chapter II. Having a separate provision for *negotiorum gestio* recognises that it is different from unjust enrichment.

(a) The scope of Article 11

Article 11 applies where there is a non-contractual obligation arising out of an act performed without due authority in connection with the affairs of another person. Some cases involve acts of assistance, meaning one-off initiatives taken on an exceptional basis by the "agent", who acted in order to preserve the interests of the "principal". Some cases instead involve measures of interference in the assets of another person, as in the case of payment of a third-party debt. The choice of law rules do not distinguish between these two situations.[646] Article 11(2) (the common habitual residence rule) presupposes that damage occurs.

(b) The rules on the applicable law

These are in substance the same as those in Article 10.[647] There are obviously, though, some differences in language to reflect the fact that concern is now with "an act performed without due authority in connection with the affairs of another person", rather than with unjust enrichment. The use of the same choice of law rules in each article is not surprising when one bears in mind that both articles are concerned with the law of restitution.

(iii) Culpa in contrahendo

Article 12 is headed "*Culpa in contrahendo*" and sets out special choice of law rules for a non-contractual obligation arising out of dealings prior to the conclusion of a contract.[648] Such liability[649] raises difficult problems of classification both under substantive domestic law and under private international law. Some Member States may regard the obligation that arises out of pre-contractual dealings as contractual, others as tortious, yet others as *sui generis*.[650] The Rome II Regulation introduces a special rule for such cases in order to avoid

---

[641] Ibid.

[642] See *Stovin v Wise* [1996] 3 All ER 801 at 819. But see Sheehan (2006) 55 ICLQ 253.

[643] Dickinson, para 11.14 notes that agency of necessity outside contract, involuntary bailment, the trustee *de son tort*, and shadow directors may fall under Art 11. See also ibid, para 11.13, where the consequences of a wider understanding for English law are discussed.

[644] See the Hamburg Group for Private International Law's Comments on the Proposal for a Rome II Regulation, (2003) 67 RabelsZ 1, 34.

[645] The fact that salvage involves a *maritime* non-contractual obligation raises a particular difficulty, see infra, p 878.

[646] Cf Art 9(4) of the Proposal for a Regulation, on which see the Explanatory Memorandum, p 22.

[647] Supra, pp 843–8.

[648] German lawyers use the term *culpa in contrahendo* when referring to pre-contractual liability (see the German national Report by Lorenz in Hondius, *Pre-Contractual Liability: Reports to the XIIIth Congress International Academy of Comparative Law Montreal Canada 18–24 August 1990* (1991)).

[649] For a valuable comparative study of the substantive law see ibid.

[650] See the Explanatory Memorandum, p 8.

the danger of different classifications being adopted in different Member States. It is thereby adopting a *sui generis* classification. The fact that obligations arising out of dealings prior to the conclusion of a contract are placed within the Rome II Regulation has in turn led to its express exclusion from the Rome I Regulation.[651] According to the Commission, *culpa in contrahendo* does not arise out of tort/delict as understood in Chapter II,[652] so it cannot fall within that Chapter. It is therefore placed in Chapter III, even though it is very different from unjust enrichment and *negotiorum gestio*.

Under English substantive domestic law there are no general principles of *culpa in contrahendo*.[653] However, a wide range of claims can arise "as a result of negotiations failing or an argument that a concluded contract is the result of untruths made in the course of the negotiations that preceded it".[654] Not surprisingly, prior to the Rome II Regulation, under English law there were no special choice of law rules for *culpa in contrahendo*. A difficult question of classification would arise as to whether the pre-contractual obligation on which the cause of action was based was contractual, tortious, restitutionary or equitable. Different causes of action could well involve a different classification and different choice of law rules.

(a) The scope of Article 12

(i) Culpa in contrahendo

Article 12 applies to "a non-contractual obligation arising out of dealings prior to the conclusion of a contract".[655] According to Recital (30), *culpa in contrahendo* for the purposes of the Regulation "is an autonomous concept and should not necessarily be interpreted within the meaning of national law". Recital (30) goes on to give two examples of what this concept includes, namely the violation of the duty of disclosure and the breakdown of contractual negotiations. These two situations reflect the two different types of pre-contractual liability under the substantive law.

First, there is pre-contractual liability where *no contract ensues*. This includes duties in negotiation of a contract. For example, under Italian law[656] there is a requirement to act in good faith during the negotiation of a contract.[657] There is no such requirement or cause of action under English law but there may be liability in tort[658] under *Hedley Byrne v Heller*[659] for negligent misstatements made during the course of negotiations or liability in tort for fraudulent misrepresentation. However, in the context of jurisdiction, the Court of Justice has accepted that an action for damages founded on an abrupt termination of a long-standing business relationship can be contractual if a tacit contractual relationship existed between the

---

[651] Art 1(2)(i) of the Rome I Regulation, discussed supra, pp 702–3. See the Explanatory Memorandum from the Commission accompanying the Proposal for the Rome I Regulation, para 4.2.

[652] But see the Explanatory Memorandum from the Commission accompanying the Proposal for the Rome I Regulation, para 4.2, which says that pre-contractual obligations should be treated for the purposes of private international law as a matter of tort/delict.

[653] See Allen, "The English National Report" in Hondius, op cit, p 143, and more generally for a discussion of pre-contractual liability under English law.

[654] Ibid.

[655] Art 12(1).

[656] Article 1337 of the Italian Civil Code. For the position under French law see Giliker (2003) 52 ICLQ 970, 979–85.

[657] Case C-334/00 *Fonderie Officine Meccaniche Tacconi SpA v Heinrich Wagner Sinto Maschinenfabrik GmbH (HWS)* [2002] ECR I-7357 at [25]–[26], where such a claim was held to fall within Art 5(3) of the Brussels Convention. But see also Case C-196/15 *Granarolo v Ambrosi Emmi France SA* ECLI:EU:C:2016:559 at [23]–[27]: an action for damages founded on an abrupt termination of a long-standing business relationship can be contractual if a tacit contractual relationship existed between the parties.

[658] See Giliker, op cit, 974–8.

[659] [1964] AC 465.

parties.[660] If the same applies to choice of law, then there is apparently a further distinction to be added between a general duty to negotiate in good faith (falling under Article 12 Rome II) and a specific (tacit) duty not to abruptly terminate a long-standing business relationship (arising from a contract and falling under Rome I).

Secondly, there is pre-contractual liability where *a contract ensues*. In most countries, once a contract ensues there is no need for pre-contractual liability. Nonetheless, most countries have duties of disclosure. Under English law there can be an action to avoid (ie rescind) an insurance contract on the basis of non-disclosure prior to entering the contract.[661] The English law of misrepresentation also constitutes a form of pre-contractual liability. This would cover liability for fraudulent misrepresentation (such as a claim under the tort of deceit),[662] negligent misrepresentation (such as a claim for damages under the Misrepresentation Act 1967[663] or, more rarely, in tort for negligent misstatement) and innocent misrepresentation (such as a claim for damages in lieu of rescission under the Misrepresentation Act 1967).[664]

The problem of characterisation   The introduction of the special category of *culpa in contrahendo* does not avoid the question of characterisation altogether. This question of characterisation will still arise as to whether the non-contractual obligation arises out of dealings prior to the conclusion of a contract or out of contract, in particular where a contract has later been concluded. While Art 1(2)(i) Rome I excludes "obligations arising out of dealings prior to the conclusion of a contract" from the scope of the Rome I Regulation (and thus mirrors Article 12(1) Rome II), it seems difficult to regard any effects of the parties' dealings prior to the conclusion of a contract as non-contractual, as these dealings may impact on the interpretation, validity and enforceability of the contract. An example is the situation where a claim is made for rescission of a contract induced by mistake or misrepresentation.[665] Arguably such a claim could be regarded as being based on contract, rather than unjust enrichment.[666] But a further possibility is that it should be regarded as arising out of dealings prior to the conclusion of the contract. The result, though, would be the same, regardless of whether a contractual or *culpa in contrahendo* characterisation is adopted. In both cases, the law applicable to the contract would govern the non-contractual obligation.[667]

(ii) A non-contractual obligation

Article 12 is concerned with "a non-contractual obligation" arising out of dealings prior to the conclusion of a contract. Once it has been decided that there is *culpa in contrahendo* within the meaning of Article 12 it follows that the obligation that arises out of this must be regarded as non-contractual.[668] If one were to say that there was a contractual obligation arising out of *culpa in contrahendo* this would open up a gap in the law since such an obligation would fall not only outside the Rome II Regulation but also outside the Rome I Regulation.

---

[660] Case C-196/15 *Granarolo v Ambrosi Emmi France SA* ECLI:EU:C:2016:559 at [23]–[27].

[661] See *Agnew v Lansforsakringsbolagens AB* [2001] 1 AC 223, where the House of Lords held that such a claim fell within Art 5(1) of the Lugano Convention.

[662] Or a claim for rescission of a contract. This could be on the basis not only of a fraudulent misrepresentation but also a negligent or innocent one.

[663] S 2(1).

[664] S 2(2).

[665] See Dicey, Morris and Collins, para 35-094: availability of the remedy of rescission, or damages *in lieu* of rescission, falls under Rome I. See also *Kingspan Environmental Ltd v Borealis A/S* [2012] EWHC 1147 (Comm) at [612]: "Misrepresentation, despite its tortious and statutory parentage, is, in a sense, part of, or at least appurtenant to, the law of contract since it may give rise to a right to rescission."

[666] See Art 10(1), 12(1)(e) Rome I: "existence and validity of a contract" and "consequences of nullity of the contract" to be regarded as contractual.

[667] See the Rome I Regulation, and Art 12(1) of the Rome II Regulation.

[668] Supra, pp 789–91.

(iii) Arising out of dealings

The non-contractual obligation must *arise out of* dealings prior to the conclusion of the contract. There must be a direct link between the non-contractual obligation and the dealings.[669] This means that if, while a contract is being negotiated, a party suffers personal injury, Article 4 or another relevant provision of the Regulation will apply, rather than Article 12.[670] Another example where no direct link exists are cases where a third party relies on a representation made during pre-contractual dealings between different parties, or where a party provides services in anticipation of a contract.[671]

(iv) Prior to the conclusion of the contract

The non-contractual obligation must arise out of dealings *prior to* the conclusion of a contract. It follows that a negligent misrepresentation/negligent misstatement made at the pre-contractual stage will come within Article 12 and Chapter III, whereas a negligent misstatement made after a contract has been entered into will come within Chapter II (or be regarded as contractual and thus fall under the Rome I Regulation).

(v) Regardless of whether the contract was actually concluded or not

Article 12(1) provides that Article 12 applies "regardless of whether the contract was actually concluded or not". This reflects the two types of pre-contractual liability under the substantive law, namely pre-contractual liability where no contract ensues and pre-contractual liability where a contract ensues.

(vi) Damage

Article 12 presupposes that there is damage.[672]

(b) The rules on the applicable law

Culpa in contrahendo is a very different concept and cause of action from unjust enrichment and *negotiorum gestio*. It is not surprising to find that the rules on the applicable law are also different. Article 12(1) sets out a primary rule. There is then in Article 12(2) a fall-back position to deal with the situation where the law applicable cannot be determined on the basis of paragraph 1.

(i) The primary rule

Article 12(1) provides that: "The law applicable to a non-contractual obligation arising out of dealings prior to the conclusion of a contract, regardless of whether the contract was actually concluded or not, shall be the law that applies to the contract or that would have been applicable to it had it been entered into."

It will be recalled that Article 12 applies regardless of whether the contract was actually concluded or not. If it was concluded the law applicable to the non-contractual obligation will be the law that applies to the contract. Identification of this law presents no particular difficulty, or at least no more difficulty than any other case where the law applicable to a contract has to be determined.[673] If a contract was not actually concluded, the law applicable to the non-contractual obligation will be the law that would have been applicable to the contract had it been entered into. This presents particular difficulties. First, there is a difficulty over choice of the applicable law. Let us assume that the parties were negotiating over the terms of the

---

[669] Recital (30) of the Regulation.

[670] Ibid.

[671] Dicey, Morris and Collins, para 35-093. The first case will normally fall directly under tort/delict (Art 4), the latter under restitution (Art 10). However, the latter case may fall under *culpa in contrahendo* if the other party, in the pre-contractual dealings, misrepresented its intentions to enter into a contract.

[672] As defined in Art 2(1) and (3)(b).

[673] The law applicable to the contract will be determined by the Rome I Regulation.

contract, with each party trying to impose its preferred choice of law or choice of jurisdiction clause on the other. However, the parties had not agreed on these terms. In determining which law would have been applicable had the contract been entered into, is the court supposed to speculate on which party was likely to win in this battle of the terms? This would be absurd and an agreement on the applicable law could only operate if the parties have actually agreed those terms, even if they have not entered into a contract.[674] In other words, the parties may have agreed on a choice of law clause providing for the application of English law but have never agreed, for example, on the contract price. Secondly, what happens where the contractual negotiations are broken off at a very early stage? It may be impossible to ascertain the applicable law in any meaningful way.[675] Where it is impossible to determine the law applicable to the contract, as opposed to being merely difficult to do so, the fall-back position under Article 12(2) will come into play and provide an answer as to the law applicable to the non-contractual obligation.

Article 12(1) is a rigid rule that has no exception, for example for cases where the parties have a common habitual residence, and no escape clause for cases where the non-contractual obligation is manifestly more closely connected with another country. It is only when one moves on to the fall-back position in Article 12(2) where the law applicable cannot be determined on the basis of paragraph 1 that familiar rules based on the common habitual residence of the parties and a manifestly more closely connected escape clause come into play. The lack of an exception or escape from Article 12(1) means that it is very different therefore from Article 4(1). Perhaps more interestingly it is also different from Articles 10 and 11. We are familiar with a fall-back position under those Articles where the law applicable cannot be determined under the primary rule in the first paragraph of those Articles but they at least have a manifestly more closely connected escape clause that allows escape from the primary rule. Article 12 does not. The reason for this is probably the interest to align contractual and pre-contractual duties as closely as possible.[676]

(ii) The fall-back position

Article 12(2) sets out the fall-back position. This only comes into play in the situation where the law applicable cannot be determined on the basis of paragraph 1. That would be the case where it is impossible to identify the law applicable to the contract. It is hard to see this operating in the situation where a contract has been concluded, but it is possible to envisage this operating in the situation where the contract was not actually concluded. The contractual negotiations may have been at such an early stage that it is impossible to identify the law that would have been applicable to the contract. At the same time, though, for Article 12 to apply in the first place there must have been sufficient dealings between the parties to give rise to an obligation. This scenario is likely to be rare.

The rules on the applicable law in Article 12(2) are very similar to those in Article 4. So, where contract choice of law does not provide an answer, tort choice of law has to do so. Recourse to tort choice of law rules may appear at first sight to be rather unprincipled but can be forgiven when one bears in mind that there is a case for classifying *culpa in contrahendo*

---

[674] Where the parties have not yet agreed on a choice of law, the law applicable to the putative contract is to be determined by Arts 4–8 Rome I Regulation. If it is impossible to classify the putative contract in any of these categories, Art 12(2) will apply.

[675] It may be easier to come to a finding under the Rome I Regulation, with its emphasis on types of contract, than under the Rome Convention, with its use of connections.

[676] Moreover, by reference in Art 12(1) to the law applicable to the contract, the escape clauses of the Rome I Regulation may be applied (Art 4(3), Art 5(3), Art 8(4) Rome I), but only to the contract as a whole, not only to the pre-contractual obligation in question.

as tortious.[677] Familiar rules are used in Article 12(2), ie country of damage rule, a common habitual residence rule and a manifestly more closely connected rule but all within a limited fall-back framework. Article 12(2), like Article 4, contains three provisions: a general rule; an exception; and a manifestly more closely connected escape clause.

The general rule   Article 12(2)(a) provides that the applicable law is "the law of the country in which the damage occurs, irrespective of the country in which the event giving rise to the damage occurred and irrespective of the country or countries in which the indirect consequences of that event occurred". This is virtually identical to Article 4(1).[678] In a case of negligent misstatement, or negligent or fraudulent misrepresentation, identification of the country in which the damage occurs can be problematic.[679] There can also be losses incurred in more than one country. For example, as a result of a negligent misstatement concerning the mileage of a classic car in an auction catalogue in England, a claimant may incur loss in England in the form of the cost of an airline ticket to go to an auction in Monaco, where there is further loss in the form of entering into an adverse contractual commitment to pay an excessive amount for the car.[680] Under the mosaic principle,[681] English law will apply to the damage occurring in England and the law of Monaco to that occurring in Monaco.

The exception   Article 12(2)(b) provides that "where the parties have their habitual residence in the same country at the time when the event giving rise to the damage occurs, the law of that country" shall apply. This is the same as Article 4(2) except that under Article 12(2)(b) one is concerned with the habitual residence at the time when the event giving rise to the damage occurs, whereas with Article 4(2) one is concerned with habitual residence at the later time when the damage occurs.

The manifestly more closely connected escape clause   Article 12(2)(c) provides that "where it is clear from all the circumstances of the case that the non-contractual obligation arising out of dealings prior to the conclusion of a contract is manifestly more closely connected with a country other than that indicated in points (a) and (b), the law of that other country" shall apply. This is identical to Article 4(3). However, that provision goes on to provide that a manifestly closer connection with another country might be based in particular on a pre-existing relationship between the parties. Article 12(2)(c) has no such provision.[682] This is because a scenario whereby basing paragraph 12(2)(c) on a pre-existing relationship would produce a different result from that produced by paragraph (1), (2)(a) or (b) is not going to arise.[683]

(f) Choice of the applicable law

(i) Freedom of choice

Chapter IV is entitled "Freedom of choice" and contains just one Article, Article 14. This is also headed "Freedom of choice" and sets out the basic principle that: "The parties may agree to submit non-contractual obligations to the law of their choice." Recital (31) gives two justifications for allowing the parties to choose the law applicable to a non-contractual obligation:

---

[677] Supra, p 849.

[678] Discussed supra, pp 810–13. The only difference is a change of tense from the present (occurs) under Art 4 to the past (occurred) under Art 12(2)(a).

[679] See, eg, *Raiffeisen Zentral Bank Osterreich AG v Alexander Tranos* [2001] IL Pr 85—a jurisdiction case involving misrepresentations made during pre-contractual dealings.

[680] These are the facts of the pre-Regulation case of *Morin v Bonhams & Brooks Ltd* [2003] EWCA Civ 1802, [2004] 1 Lloyd's Rep 702.

[681] Supra, p 811, n 350.

[682] This is the same as the manifestly more closely connected escape clause in Arts 10 and 11.

[683] This is explained by the fact that Art 12(1) is based on the parties' existing relationship and by the interaction of the different paragraphs in Art 12.

first, the principle of party autonomy; secondly, the enhancement of legal certainty. This freedom of choice applies to all non-contractual obligations, except for those arising from an act of unfair competition,[684] a restriction of competition[685] or an infringement of an intellectual property right.[686] The extension of freedom of choice to non-contractual obligations follows the national private international law rules in a number of European states[687] and makes clear what was previously unclear under English law.[688] By an analogy to Article 3(2) Rome I Regulation, the freedom to choose should extend to allowing the parties to vary the governing law, subject to the rights of third parties (Article 14(1) final sentence).

(ii) Conditions imposed on the choice

In order to protect the weaker party, certain conditions are imposed on the choice.[689] The agreement must satisfy one of two alternatives. It must have been entered into after the event giving rise to the damage occurred[690] or, where all the parties are pursuing a commercial activity, also by an agreement "freely negotiated" before the event giving rise to the damage.[691]

An agreement entered into after the event giving rise to the damage occurred is less problematic than one entered into before that event. Once a dispute has arisen, it is assumed that the weaker party is not going to agree to the application of a foreign law that adversely affects him. The situation where there is an obvious need for protection of the weaker party is that where the agreement was entered into before the event giving rise to the damage.[692] The requirement that this agreement was "freely negotiated" is designed to provide this protection.[693] There is no explanation of what precisely is meant by these words. Inspiration might be drawn from the similar term "(not) individually negotiated" in Directive (EC) No 93/13 of 5 April 1993 on unfair terms in consumer contracts.[694] According to Article 3(2) of this Directive, a pre-formulated standard contract clause (such as a standard choice of law clause) is to be regarded as not individually negotiated where the other party has not been able to influence the substance of the term. Even if we allow for more flexibility outside the consumer context, it will be difficult for the party relying on a choice of law clause to prove that the other party has been able to influence the clause, making enforceable choice of law agreements before the event likely to be rare in practice.

Let us assume, then, that the agreement was not freely negotiated. In this situation, the parties' choice of the law to govern non-contractual obligations will not take effect under Article 14. Curiously, though, the parties' agreement on the law applicable to their contractual obligations, which may not have been freely negotiated, will operate indirectly to fix the law applicable to

---

[684] Art 6(4).

[685] Ibid.

[686] Art 8(3).

[687] See the Swiss Private International Law statute, Art 132; the German Introductory Law to the Civil Code, the 1999 Codification, Art 42. This is also allowed by the law of Austria, Liechtenstein and the Netherlands.

[688] See Law Commission Working Paper No 87 (1984), p 265 and para 4.21, which recommended that this should be allowed, but the Law Commissions' Report was silent on this. See generally at common law, North, *Essays*, pp 85–6, 187–91. See also *Morin v Bonhams & Brooks Ltd* [2003] IL Pr 25 at [33], no right to choose; affd without discussion of this point [2003] EWCA Civ 1802, [2004] 1 Lloyd's Rep 702.

[689] Recital (31).

[690] Art 14(1)(a).

[691] Art 14(1)(b).

[692] The Proposal for the Regulation did not allow for such an agreement, see Art 10(1) and the Explanatory Memorandum, p 22.

[693] Cf the technique for protecting weaker parties under the Brussels I Recast, Arts 15, 19 and 23 (agreement must be entered into after dispute has arisen).

[694] OJ 1993 L 95/29, implemented in the United Kingdom by the Consumer Rights Acts 2015, Part 2.

non-contractual obligations by virtue of Article 4(3).[695] Thus, it will in practice very often not matter whether the strict requirements of Article 14 are met, as the secondary connection under Article 4(3) will lead to the application of the same law which governs the contract, which is much easier to choose under the Rome I Regulation.[696]

(iii) An express or inferred choice

The choice must be "expressed or demonstrated with reasonable certainty by the circumstances of the case".[697] This phrase has been taken from the Rome Convention.[698] Suffice it to say in the present context that an express choice refers to a choice of law clause. A choice demonstrated with reasonable certainty by the circumstances of the case refers to an inferred choice, two examples of which are a choice of jurisdiction clause and an arbitration clause.[699] One issue that will arise in the context of the Rome II Regulation is whether a choice of law clause or a jurisdiction clause in a contract between the parties is wide enough in its scope to cover a dispute in relation not to contract, but to a non-contractual obligation.[700] This issue has arisen before the English courts in relation to choice of jurisdiction clauses (in the context of jurisdiction)[701] but not choice of law clauses because of the lack of freedom to choose the governing law under the English traditional tort and restitution choice of law rules. Questions concerning the existence and validity of the parties' choice of law agreement are, by analogy to Article 3(5) and Article 10(1) Rome I, to be determined by the law which would apply if the choice of law was valid.

(iv) Choice and the English rules on pleading and proof of foreign law[702]

The same problem arises under the Rome II Regulation as arises under the Rome I Regulation,[703] namely what happens if the parties choose Utopian law to apply but subsequently neither party pleads Utopian law? The Regulation does not provide an answer to this. It is suggested that the English courts should take a pragmatic line and simply apply English law under the English procedural rule that is preserved by Article 1(3) of the Regulation, which provides that the Regulation shall not apply to evidence and procedure.[704]

(v) Choice and third parties

The parties' choice will not prejudice the rights of third parties.[705] The typical example of this is said to be the insurer's obligation to reimburse damages payable by the insured.[706]

---

[695] Or Art 10(1), Art 11(1) and Art 12(1) (for matters other than tort/delict).

[696] See Art 3, 10 Rome I.

[697] Art 14(1).

[698] Art 3(1) 1980 Rome Convention. Art 3(1) Rome I provides that "The choice shall be made expressly or clearly demonstrated by the terms of the contract or the circumstances of the case".

[699] According to Recital (12) Rome I, "an agreement between the parties to confer on one or more courts or tribunals of a Member State exclusive jurisdiction to determine disputes under the contract should be one of the factors to be taken into account in determining whether a choice of law has been clearly demonstrated". The same can probably be said for a choice under Art 14 Rome II.

[700] For example, a clause such as "This contract shall be governed by English law" will raise the question whether it also covers non-contractual obligations between the parties to the contract. For a related discussion on the inclusion of cartel damages claims in jurisdiction agreements, see Case C-352/13 *Cartel Damage Claims (CDC) Hydrogen Peroxide SA v Evonik Degussa GmbH and Others* ECLI:EU:C:2015:335 a [68]–[71].

[701] Supra, pp 236–7.

[702] See generally Fentiman, *Foreign Law in English Courts* (1998), p 87 et seq.

[703] Supra, pp 710–11.

[704] See *OPO v (1) MLA (2) SLT* [2014] EWCA Civ 1277 at [111], on appeal *James Rhodes v OPO* [2015] UKSC at [121]; see also *Brownlie v Four Seasons Holdings Inc* [2015] EWCA Civ 665 at [89].

[705] Art 14(1). Art 3(2) of the Rome I Regulation provides that variation of choice shall not prejudice the rights of third parties.

[706] The Explanatory Memorandum, p 22.

(vi) Limitations on choice

The Regulation lays down restrictions on the parties' right to choose the governing law which will now be examined. Article 14 itself sets out two such limitations. The first of these (Article 14(2)) is concerned with provisions of law that cannot be derogated from by agreement in a domestic context; the second (Article 14(3)) with provisions of EU law that cannot be derogated from by agreement. More generally, the Regulation imposes limitations on the dominance of the applicable law.

(a) Article 14(2): Provisions that cannot be derogated from by agreement

Article 14(2) provides that:

> Where all the elements relevant to the situation at the time when the event giving rise to the damage occurs are located in a country other than the country whose law has been chosen, the choice of the parties shall not prejudice the application of provisions of the law of that other country which cannot be derogated from by agreement.

This provision is in substance the same as Article 3(3) of the Rome I Regulation[707] and is concerned with rules which cannot be departed from in a domestic context (*dispositions impera-tives*). The most noticeable difference between Article 3(3) of the 1980 Rome Convention and Article 14(2) of the Rome II Regulation[708] is that the latter wisely does not use the term mandatory rules to describe provisions which cannot be derogated from by agreement.[709] In accordance with the principle of consistency between these two instruments,[710] Article 14(2) of the Rome II Regulation should be interpreted in the light of the interpretation of Article 3(3) Rome I Regulation.

(b) Article 14(3): Provisions of EU law that cannot be derogated from by agreement

Article 14(3) provides that:

> Where all the elements relevant to the situation at the time when the event giving rise to the damage occurs are located in one or more of the Member States, the parties' choice of the law applicable other than that of a Member State shall not prejudice the application of provisions of Community law, where appropriate as implemented in the Member State of the forum, which cannot be derogated from by agreement.

This provision treats the European Union as effectively one country and highlights the importance of EU mandatory rules. It adds to Article 14(2) that in an international, but purely intra-EU case mandatory provisions of EU law may not be derogated from, which would arguably be possible under Article 14(2) as not all the elements relevant to the situation at the time when the event giving rise to the damage occurs are located in a single country (but rather in at least two countries, namely two Member States).

(c) Overriding mandatory provisions[711] and public policy[712]

These limitations are more appropriately dealt with later on, where they will be looked at in detail.

---

[707] And Art 3(3) of the 1980 Rome Convention.

[708] The same holds true for Art 3(3) Rome I Regulation.

[709] The use of the term mandatory rules in Art 3(3) of the 1980 Rome Convention caused confusion with a different type of mandatory rule, overriding mandatory rules, under Art 7 of the 1980 Rome Convention (Art 16 of the Rome II Regulation); supra, pp 744–6.

[710] Recital (7).

[711] Discussed infra, pp 866–8.

[712] Discussed infra, pp 868–71.

(d) Certain special torts

The law applicable to a non-contractual obligation arising out of an act of unfair competition or a restriction of competition cannot be derogated from by an agreement under Article 14.[713] Likewise, the law applicable to a non-contractual obligation arising from an infringement of an intellectual property right cannot be derogated from by an agreement under Article 14.[714] No other torts are singled out for their own special limitation on the right to choose the applicable law.

(g) Scope of the law applicable

Chapter V is entitled "Common rules", ie rules common to Chapters II, III and IV. The first of these is Article 15, which is entitled "Scope of the law applicable" and in paragraphs (a) to (h) gives a number of examples of issues coming within the scope of the law applicable to non-contractual obligations by virtue of Chapters II, III and IV.[715] Giving examples helps to clarify the position in relation to certain issues, such as limitation periods and assessment of damage, in respect of which different Member States have traditionally adopted a different classification, some regarding the issue as one of substance to be determined by the applicable law, others as procedural to be determined by the law of the forum.[716] In line with the general concern for certainty in the law, Article 15 confers a very wide function on the law designated.[717] Moreover, in contrast to the 1995 Act,[718] the Regulation does not provide for the application of different laws to different issues of the case (*dépeçage*), so that in most cases a single substantive law governs the entire non-contractual obligation.[719]

Paragraphs (a) to (h) are not intended to be an exhaustive list,[720] and it is implicit that there are other issues that are governed by the rules on the applicable law. At the same time it is important to bear in mind that the Regulation in Articles 18 to 22[721] contains some special rules for particular issues and for those issues it is to these special rules that one must turn, rather than to the rules on the applicable law in Chapters II, III and IV. For example, Article 15 does not cover the issue of the burden of proof,[722] which is dealt with in Article 22. Moreover, Art 1(3) excludes evidence and procedure from the scope of the Regulation altogether.

The examples provided by Article 15 are broadly drawn from the 1980 Rome Convention.[723] In addition, also the Hague Convention on the Law Applicable to Traffic Accidents of 1971 and the Hague Convention on the Law Applicable to Products Liability of 1973 appear to have been influential. The striking similarity between the provisions on the scope of the law applicable in these two Conventions[724] and the provisions on scope of the law applicable

---

[713] Art 6(4).

[714] Art 8(3).

[715] For parallel provisions see Art 12 Rome I Regulation and Art 10 1980 Rome Convention.

[716] The Explanatory Memorandum, p 23. See also *Actavis UK Ltd v Eli Lilly & Co* [2015] EWCA Civ 555 at [131], arguing that Art 15 is not itself directly concerned with clarifying the distinction between substance and procedure, but merely gives answers for certain issues.

[717] The Explanatory Memorandum, p 23.

[718] Private International Law (Miscellaneous Provisions) Act 1995, s 12.

[719] For exceptions see Art 17, 21 Rome II.

[720] Art 15: "The law applicable to non-contractual obligations . . . shall govern in particular".

[721] Discussed infra, pp 872–3.

[722] Cf Art 8(8) on the scope of the Hague Convention on the Law Applicable to Products Liability of 1973.

[723] The Explanatory Memorandum, p 23.

[724] See Art 8 of the 1971 Convention and Art 8 of the 1973 Convention.

in Article 15 of the Rome II Regulation means that the Reports accompanying the two Conventions[725] are a valuable source on the meaning of the terms used in Article 15. The examples listed in Article 15 are as follows.

(i) The basis and extent of liability, including the determination of persons who may be held liable for acts performed by them[726]

The basis of liability is concerned with intrinsic factors of liability[727] and encompasses such matters as: "the nature of liability (strict or fault based); the definition of fault, including the question whether an omission can constitute fault; the causal link between the event giving rise to the damage and the damage; the persons potentially liable".[728]

The "extent of liability" encompasses the maximum extent of liability laid down by law,[729] such as a ceiling on liability, and the contribution to be made by each of the persons liable for the damage which is to be compensated.[730] It also includes "the determination of persons who may be held liable for acts performed by them". This is designed to cover also the division of liability between joint perpetrators in the external relationship as towards the victim.[731] The law governing actions for contribution or indemnity between persons jointly liable (eg joint tortfeasors), ie the internal relationship between them, is determined by Article 20.[732]

(ii) The grounds for exemption from liability, any limitation of liability and any division of liability[733]

This provision is concerned with three issues relating to liability. All three can be regarded as extrinsic factors of liability,[734] ie conditions for exoneration from liability.[735] First, there is the issue of grounds for exemption from liability. This would cover acts of God and supervening acts of a third party,[736] as well as such well-known (at least in common law jurisdictions) phenomena as guest statutes (preventing a guest passenger suing a host driver), interspousal immunity laws (preventing a wife from suing her husband and vice versa),[737]

---

[725] See the Essen Report on the Road Traffic Convention and the Reese Report on the Products Liability Convention.

[726] Art 15(a).

[727] The Explanatory Memorandum, p 23. Extrinsic factors of liability are dealt with under Art 15(b).

[728] The Explanatory Memorandum, p 23. Art 15(a) does not cover the procedural admissibility of a positive action or an action for a declaration of non-infringement, *Actavis UK Ltd v Eli Lilly & Co* [2015] EWCA Civ 555 at [145].

[729] The Explanatory Memorandum, p 23.

[730] Ibid.

[731] Ibid and Joined Cases C-359/14 and C-475/14 *ERGO Insurance SE v If P&C Insurance AS and Gjensidige Baltic AAS v PZU Lietuva UAB DK* ECLI:EU:C:2016:40 at [52]–[53], [61], [59]: "the law applicable to the determination of the persons who may be held liable and the allocation of responsibility between them and their respective insurers remains subject, in accordance with Article 19, to Article 4 et seq of the Rome II Regulation".

[732] This provision covers all possible forms of contribution between jointly liable debtors ("debtor's right to demand"), irrespective of their legal basis (eg *cessio legis* = assignment by operation of law, subrogation, separate cause of action, restitution or *negotiorum gestio*), and not only—as under Art 19 Rome II (Art 15 Rome I)—those "rights which the creditor had against the debtor". For the approach under the Hague Convention on Products Liability see the Reese Report on the Hague Convention on the Law Applicable to Products Liability 1973 (Art 8(1) of which also refers to "the basis and extent of liability"), 21. See also the Essen Report on the Hague Traffic Accidents Convention 1971 at p 28, para 4.3, which makes clear that extent of liability does not cover recourse actions between tortfeasors. But this is explained by the fact that this Convention expressly excludes such actions: Art 2(5).

[733] Art 15(b).

[734] Explanatory Memorandum, p 23.

[735] See the Giuliano, Lagarde and Van Sasse Van Ysselt Report, p 58.

[736] See the Reese Report, p 21.

[737] Ibid.

or intra-family immunity laws (preventing children suing their parents and vice versa). It would also cover "*force majeure*, necessity, third-party fault and fault by the victim".[738] Under English law the fault of a victim is known as contributory negligence and operates to reduce damages rather than as an exemption of liability. As both the exemption and any limitation or division of liability fall under Article 15(b), contributory negligence reducing damages falls in any event under this provision.[739] Grounds for exemption from liability would also cover laws which exclude the perpetrator's liability in relation to certain categories of persons.[740] Any limitation of liability would cover provisions on limitation of liability for maritime claims as provided for by international convention.[741] It seems that grounds for exemption from liability and any limitation of liability is intended to cover an exemption or limitation clause in a contract, which is used as a defence to a claim in respect of a non-contractual obligation. Admittedly, although the Explanatory Memorandum mentions a significant number of examples of exemption from liability,[742] it does not mention exemption or limitation clauses in contracts. But the Essen Report on the Hague Convention on the Law Applicable to Traffic Accidents of 1971, which was the template for Article 15 of the Regulation, explains that grounds for exemption and limitation of liability (in Article 8(2) of that Convention) seemingly encompass contractual exemption or limitation clauses.[743] Under the Hague Convention the validity of such clauses falls within the scope of the law applicable to liability in that Convention.[744] Under the system of the Rome Regulations, however, the scope of the Rome II Regulation is to be interpreted consistently with the Rome I Regulation.[745] This suggests that the law governing the non-contractual obligation will decide whether a contractual limitation clause is permissible as a defence. The existence and scope of such a clause, however, will be regarded as a contractual matter to be judged by the rules of Rome I. The significance of this will be examined in more detail below[746] when the topic of contractual defences to an action in tort is considered more fully.[747] Article 15(b) does not seem to effect any change in English private international law since the issues coming within it would all be regarded as ones of substance and accordingly governed by the applicable law.

---

[738] Explanatory Memorandum, p 23.

[739] The Hague Traffic Accidents Convention 1971 understood "fault of the victim" as the situation where the injury is entirely the fault of the victim, see the Essen Report, p 29, para 5.1. As regards division of liability, this would cover contributory negligence on the part of the victim, The Essen Report, p 29, para 5.2.

[740] Explanatory Memorandum, p 23.

[741] The English rules contained in the Merchant Shipping Act 1995, s 185 and Sch 7, have in the past been given a procedural classification: *Caltex Singapore Pte Ltd and Ors v BP Shipping Ltd* [1996] 1 Lloyd's Rep 286; approved in *Harding v Wealands* [2006] UKHL 32, [2007] 2 AC 1; *Seismic Shipping Inc v Total E & P UK plc (The Western Regent)* [2005] EWCA Civ 985 at [52], [2005] 2 Lloyd's Rep 359. Under the Regulation, this looks to be wrong. It has been suggested, though, that these English provisions are overriding mandatory rules of the forum, discussed infra, p 867. As an alternative, it is arguable that provisions of international conventions take precedence over the Regulation under Art 28 Rome II, so that there would be no need to resort to the concept of overriding mandatory provisions, infra, pp 873–4 (it is debatable, however, whether this provision applies only to conventions harmonising conflict of law-rules or also to conventions harmonising substantive rules on liability).

[742] At p 23. As does the Giuliano, Lagarde and Van Sasse Van Ysselt Report, p 53.

[743] At p 29, para 5.1. See also the Law Commissions' Consultative Document 1974, para 11.2.2. The Reese Report, at p 21, suggests it covers non-contractual as well as contractual limitations in adverts and in documents accompanying a product.

[744] The Essen Report, p 29, para 5.1.

[745] Recital (7).

[746] Infra, pp 881–3.

[747] Infra, pp 880–3.

(iii) The existence, the nature and the assessment of damage or the remedy[748] *claimed*[749]

(a) The existence and the nature of damage

This is concerned with determining the damage for which compensation may be due; eg whether this includes for personal injury, damage to property, moral damage, environmental damage, financial loss or loss of an opportunity[750] and whether loss of profits can be recovered.[751] Existence of damage would no doubt cover the issue of remoteness of damage.[752] Article 15(c) should also include the question whether compensation can be recovered for pain and suffering or loss of amenity, ie the question of recovery of heads of damage. Under the English common law the issues of heads of damage available and of remoteness of damage are ones of substance for the applicable law, so the Rome II Regulation does not effect a change in English private international law on this point. The issue may arise of recovery of punitive and exemplary damages. This too should be determined by the law applicable to the non-contractual obligation, on the basis that it falls within the concept of the existence and nature of damage. If it falls outside that concept it should still be a matter to be determined by the law applicable to the non-contractual obligation, because Article 15 only provides examples of matters falling within the scope of the applicable law. There can be other examples which do not fall within Article 15(a) to (h) but which, nonetheless, are within the scope of the applicable law, and this would be one such example. In the case of punitive or exemplary damages, the question arises of whether the application of a law providing for such damages is manifestly incompatible with the public policy of the forum. This question will be examined below when discussing more generally the public policy limitation on the applicable law.[753]

(b) Assessment of damage

Article 15(c) provides that the assessment of damage is a matter to be determined by the law applicable to the non-contractual obligation. This adopts the position taken in most Member States, which regard assessment of damages as a substantive matter to be determined by the applicable law. It also broadly follows Article 10(1)(c) of the 1980 Rome Convention,[754] although there are some noticeable differences in the wording of the two provisions which will be examined below. In contrast, English private international law has traditionally regarded the assessment or quantification of damages as a procedural matter for the law of the forum.[755] Article 15(c) therefore represents a major change in English private international law. Subjecting this issue to the law governing the non-contractual obligation has the virtue of preventing forum shopping within the European Union for an assessment of damages advantage.

In so far as the foreign applicable law has legal rules in relation to assessment of damage, the effect of Article 15(c) is clear enough. The English court must apply these rules. This includes

---

[748] It is remarkable to note that other language versions do not use the general word "remedy" in Art 15(c), but rather a term closer to financial compensation ("la reparation demandée", "l'indennizo chiesto", "la indemnización solicitada", "der geforderten Wiedergutmachung"), which led the Court of Appeal to conclude (*obiter*) that Art 15(c) is limited to financial remedies and does not encompass negative declaratory relief, *Actavis UK Ltd v Eli Lilly & Co* [2015] EWCA Civ 555 at [146].

[749] Art 15(c).

[750] The Explanatory Memorandum, p 23. This refers to the Proposal for a Rome II Regulation which was more clearly worded. Art 11(c) of the Proposal referred to "the existence and kinds of injury or damage for which compensation may be due".

[751] See the Reese Report, p 21.

[752] Alternatively, this could be regarded as an issue of causation, thus falling under Art 15(a), which makes no difference in result.

[753] Infra, pp 868–71.

[754] Now Art 12(1)(c) Rome I.

[755] *Boys v Chaplin* [1971] AC 356; *Harding v Wealands* [2006] UKHL 32.

not only the rules on the applicable law in so far as assessment is prescribed by a black-letter rule of law, but also—which is less clear—in so far as it is prescribed by judicial conventions and practices (such as particular tariffs, guidelines or formulae to calculate damages under the applicable law[756]).[757] Also foreign case law on the appropriate level of damages is to be applied: "in assessing damages in accordance with French law the English judge should endeavour to decide how, in practice, a French judge would assess damages".[758] However, applying foreign substantive law on the assessment of damages does not mean that an English court must adopt also foreign procedures to decide the case in the exact same manner as the foreign court would. Mere methods of proving recoverable loss, in particular what (expert) evidence is required to prove the claimant's injuries and losses is a matter of evidence and procedure in the sense of Article 1(3) Rome II and thus governed by English procedural rules.[759] Moreover, the assessment of damage can involve questions of fact as the amount of damages may be influenced by the specific needs of the victim which depend on the social and economic conditions in his domicile.[760]

This leaves the difficulty of determining whether there is a rule of law, convention or practice in relation to assessment or whether it is a question of evidence or facts of the case. A ceiling on damages in a statute or an international convention clearly involves a rule of law[761] and is subject to the applicable law.[762] With a ceiling on damages it could be argued that this is concerned with limiting liability (in which case it would fall within Article 15(b)), rather than with assessment of damages. In either event, the law governing the non-contractual obligation would apply to determine this issue. Similarly, a rule which requires accrued benefits (state benefits, employment pension, personal pension) to be deducted when assessing damages is subject to the applicable law.[763] The more difficult thing to classify is the calculation of

---

[756] Such as the foreign equivalent to the Judicial College Guidelines for the Assessment of General Damages in Personal Injury Cases (13th edn, 2015).

[757] *Wall v Mutuelle de Poitiers Assurances* [2014] EWCA Civ 138 at [23]–[24], [34], [51]. In the 14th edn of this book (2008), pp 844–6, it was proposed that Art 15(c) should be interpreted as being implicitly limited to the assessment of damages "in so far as prescribed by law". The reason given for this view was that the words "in so far as prescribed by law" (as in Art 10(1)(c) 1980 Rome Convention and Art 12(1)(c) Rome I, see generally the Giuliano and Lagarde Report, p 33) should be read into Art 15(c) Rome II to draw a distinction between circumstances when assessment of damages raises questions of fact and those when it raises questions of law. The Proposal for a Rome II Regulation had followed Art 10(1)(c) Rome Convention (Art 11(e) of the Proposal for a Regulation and The Explanatory Memorandum, p 24). "In so far as prescribed by law" was dropped when assessment of damage was added to Art 15(c), rather than being a separate rule (as was the case under the proposal for a Regulation), see the Council's Common Position of 11 August 2006 (JUSTCIV 137). The European Parliament had earlier proposed this shift (see the Wallis Report A6-0211/ 2005 of 27 June 2005, Amendment 40). The Commission (see the Explanatory Memorandum, pp 6–7, accompanying the Amended Proposal for a Rome II Regulation of 21 February 2006 2003/0168 (COD)) rejected an amendment proposed by the European Parliament (Amendment 41 in the Wallis Report), providing that the court seised would normally apply its national rules relating to the quantification of damages.

[758] Ibid, at [53].

[759] Ibid, at [12], [20], [41]–[45], [48].

[760] See generally the Giuliano and Lagarde Report, p 33, discussing Art 10(1)(c) of the 1980 Rome Convention.

[761] See the Giuliano and Lagarde Report, p 33.

[762] Collier, p 344. Cf the procedural classification under the English statutory tort choice of law rules, *Caltex Singapore Pte Ltd and Ors v BP Shipping Ltd* [1996] 1 Lloyd's Rep 86, concerned with limitation of liability in maritime cases under the Merchant Shipping Act 1995; approved in *Harding v Wealands*, supra, at [47] (per Lord Hoffmann), [2] (per Lord Woolf), [78] (per Lord Rodger), [79] (per Lord Carswell). See also *Seismic Shipping Inc v Total E & P UK plc (The Western Regent)* [2005] EWCA Civ 985 at [52], [2005] 2 Lloyd's Rep 359.

[763] However, a foreign applicable law may be overridden by English law, which it has been said operates as a mandatory rule of the forum: see the interpretation of *Roerig v Valiant Trawlers Ltd* [2002] EWCA Civ 21, [2002] 1 WLR 2304 by Arden LJ in *Harding v Wealands* [2004] EWCA Civ 1735 at [48], [2005] 1 WLR 1539 (revsd by the House of Lords without discussion of this example [2006] UKHL 32, [2007] 2 AC 1).

damages. Under Article 4(1) and Article 15(c) the amount of compensation will have to be calculated according to the law and standards of the country in which the damage occurred, and not those of the country where the victim habitually resides. The European Parliament regarded this as unsatisfactory and secured the introduction of Recital (33), which ensures that the court seised of the dispute will "take into account all the relevant actual circumstances of the specific victim, including in particular the actual losses and costs of after-care and medical attention." In order to reconcile Article 15(c) with Recital (33), it seems that where the evidence is simply that a foreign court applies a different method of assessment,[764] or would make a lower award of general damages in tort than an English court,[765] this method of calculation is to be applied. In applying the foreign method of assessment, however, Recital (33) seems to suggest that the calculation should take into account as a question of fact the social and economic conditions in the country where the victim habitually resides.

One particular problem that is likely to arise is where in the state whose law is applicable a jury fixes the amount of damages in tort cases.[766] This does not normally happen under English law, so there is no mechanism for adopting this procedure. Is the English court now required to introduce such a mechanism? In the case of contractual obligations the answer is no. It could be argued that this involves a matter of fact rather than a rule of law.[767] More importantly, there is an explicit procedural limitation on the scope of Article 12(1)(c) of the Rome I Regulation from the opening words of that Article. These provide that "within the limits of the powers conferred on the court by its procedural law" the assessment of damages is a matter for the applicable law. If the forum has no mechanism for jury trials to assess damages it cannot be expected to use this method of assessment, even though the applicable law is that of a state which uses this method. However, Article 15(c) of the Rome II Regulation contains no such procedural limitation.[768] Nonetheless, common sense requires that Article 15(c) should be interpreted as being implicitly procedurally limited in the same way as Article 12(1)(c) of the Rome I Regulation is explicitly so limited.[769]

(c) The remedy
This would cover, for example, whether in a case of conversion recovery should take the form of money damages or return of goods.

(iv) Within the limits of powers conferred on the court by its procedural law, the measures which a court may take to prevent or terminate injury or damage or to ensure the provision of compensation[770]

This provision is concerned with two sorts of measures. First, it is concerned with measures which a court may take to prevent or terminate injury or damage. A claimant may seek an (interlocutory or final) injunction to prevent damage occurring or to stop further damage where this has already occurred. This will commonly happen in cases, for example, of infringement of intellectual property rights and nuisance. The applicable law will determine whether a court may take this measure, in other words whether the (substantive law) criteria for the grant of an

---

[764] See the facts of the pre-Regulation case *Edmunds v Simmonds* [2001] 1 WLR 1003.

[765] See the facts of the pre-Regulation case *Hulse v Chambers* [2001] 1 WLR 2386.

[766] This was classified as a procedural matter under the pre-Regulation law: *Harding v Wealands* [2004] EWCA Civ 1735 at [57], [2005] 1 WLR 1539; revsd by the House of Lords without discussion of this example [2006] UKHL 32, [2007] 2 AC 1.

[767] See the Giuliano and Lagarde Report, p 33.

[768] Such a limitation is found in Art 15(d): "within the limits of the powers conferred on the court by its procedural law".

[769] See *Wall v Mutuelle de Poitiers Assurances* [2014] EWCA Civ 138 at [12], [20], [41]–[45], [48].

[770] Art 15(d).

injunction have been met. Secondly, it is concerned with measures which a court may take to ensure the provision of compensation.[771] This refers to forms of compensation, such as the question whether the damage can be repaired by payment of damages,[772] and would cover the issue of whether lump sum compensation is adequate or whether periodic payments of compensation are required or whether interest can be ordered. Where an English court awards a lump sum for special damages whereas a foreign court would only award instalments,[773] the applicable law should determine which of the two is to be used.[774] In both cases, Article 15(d) is concerned only with the availability of the remedies mentioned, not with the conditions which must be satisfied for their (procedural) admissibility.[775] Moreover, the scope of Article 15(d) is limited by its opening words "within the limits of the powers conferred on the court by its procedural law". In other words, the forum is not required to order measures that are unknown in the procedural law of the forum.[776] English law allows for the grant of injunctions in the case of non-contractual obligations and has a mechanism for the grant of periodical payments of compensation.

(v) The question whether a right to claim damages or a remedy may be transferred, including by inheritance[777]

This provision is largely self-explanatory.[778] A right to claim damages may be transferred in various ways, most obviously by assignment or by inheritance. The applicable law will govern the question whether the right to claim damages that the deceased victim would have had if he had survived is capable of being transferred on death to his estate.[779] The question of who will benefit from the survival of the cause of action is a matter governed by the law governing the succession.[780] As far as English private international law is concerned, this provision represents no change in the law.[781] Assignment could be by contract or it could be by a method which is non-contractual, for example by way of gift. The law applicable to the non-contractual obligation will determine whether a claim in respect of this obligation is assignable and the relationship between the assignor and debtor.[782]

(vi) Persons entitled to compensation for damage sustained personally[783]

This is concerned with the issue of whether a person can recover for damage he himself has suffered by reason of injury to another person (the direct victim).[784] For example, this would cover whether a widow and children can recover for financial loss to *them* following the death

---

[771] Art 15(d) does not include a negative declaration, because it is not a measure which the court takes to prevent or terminate injury or damage, or provide compensation, *Actavis UK Ltd v Eli Lilly & Co* [2015] EWCA Civ 555 at [147].

[772] The Explanatory Memorandum, p 24.

[773] See the facts of *Hulse v Chambers* [2001] 1 WLR 2386.

[774] This is the position under the Hague Convention on the Law Applicable to Products Liability, see the Reese Report, p 21.

[775] *Actavis UK Ltd v Eli Lilly & Co* [2015] EWCA Civ 555 at [147].

[776] The Explanatory Memorandum, p 24.

[777] Art 15(e).

[778] See the Explanatory Memorandum, p 24.

[779] For English law, see the Law Reform (Miscellaneous Provisions) Act 1934, s 1(1).

[780] The Explanatory Memorandum, p 24. So the law governing succession will determine who the heir is.

[781] See Law Com Working Paper No 87 Private International Law Tort and Delict, para 2.62.

[782] The Explanatory Memorandum, p 24. While the Explanatory Memorandum refers to Art 12(2) 1980 Rome Convention (now Art 14(2) Rome I) in footnote 37, it could be objected that assignment of a non-contractual claim does not fall under Article 1(1) Rome I. In *Cox v Ergo Versicherung AG* [2012] EWCA Civ 1001 (a pre-Regulation case), the 1980 Rome Convention was applied to assignment. Assignment of non-contractual obligations is discussed infra, p 1287.

[783] Art 15(f).

[784] See the Explanatory Memorandum, p 24; the Reese Report, p 22; Case C-350/14 *Florin Lazar, représenté légalement par Luigi Erculeo v Allianz SpA* ECLI:EU:C:2015:802 at [26]–[27].

of the husband/father[785] and whether a person can recover for emotional distress suffered by having witnessed physical injury being done to another. It would also encompass the issue of whether a person can recover solatium (damages for injury to feelings) in respect of the death of a relative under Scots law. The applicable law will determine the answer to these questions, as was the position at common law.[786]

(vii) Liability for the acts of another person[787]

This is concerned with the issue of vicarious liability.[788] This could be liability of parents for their children, of principals for their agents or of employers for their employees. This represents no change in English private international law, which has traditionally regarded vicarious liability as a matter of substance to be determined by the law applicable to the tort.[789]

(viii) The manner in which an obligation may be extinguished and rules of prescription and limitation, including rules relating to the commencement, interruption and suspension of a period of prescription or limitation[790]

This provision is almost identical with a provision in the 1980 Rome Convention.[791] It brings together what are, to English eyes, two very different sorts of issue. The first of these is the manner in which a non-contractual obligation may be extinguished: eg by payment of compensation or repayment of money in a case of unjust enrichment; by a judgment; by accord and satisfaction; by waiver; by bankruptcy; or by death. Any choice of law problems that arise in relation to these situations are matters for the applicable law under the Regulation.

The second issue covered is prescription and limitation of actions, which is likewise subject to the applicable law as determined by the Regulation. Prescription and limitation includes rules relating to the commencement, interruption and suspension of a period of prescription or limitation. Prescription and limitation involves loss of a right by failure to exercise it[792] and accordingly can be seen to have some similarity to the manner in which an obligation may be extinguished. At one time the matter of limitation was regarded under English law as being a procedural one for the law of the forum. However, the Foreign Limitation Periods Act 1984 changed this rule by adopting the principle that the English court is to apply to the issue of limitation the law which governs the substantive issue according to the English choice of law rules. Thus, even before the Rome II Regulation came into force, the English law on limitation produced the same effect in non-contractual obligation cases as that now produced by Article 15(h).[793]

(ix) Capacity

Article 15 does not mention the issue of capacity to incur liability. This would include the issue of the age at which a person can incur capacity. It would also include the question of whether a company can incur liability on some basis other than vicarious liability, which is

---

[785] Under English law dependants can recover for this loss under the Fatal Accidents Act 1976.

[786] See Law Com Working Paper No 87 Private International Law Tort and Delict, paras 2.67–2.76.

[787] Art 15(g).

[788] See the Explanatory Memorandum, p 24.

[789] See *Church of Scientology of California v Metropolitan Police Comr* (1976) 120 SJ 690, CA.

[790] Art 15(h).

[791] Art 10(1)(d) of the Rome Convention, now Art 12(1)(d) Rome I Regulation. Art 15(h) adds the clarification "including rules relating to the commencement, interruption and suspension of a period of prescription or limitation".

[792] The Explanatory Memorandum, p 24.

[793] For slight differences between Art 15(h) and the Act see Dicey, Morris and Collins, para 34-065. See Collier, p 346, pointing out that the exception in s 2(2) Foreign Limitation Periods Act for "undue hardship" is probably incompatible with the Regulation.

already covered under Article 15(g). However, Recital (12) makes it clear that the law applicable should also govern the question of the capacity to incur liability in tort/delict.[794]

(h) Limitations on the dominance of the law applicable

Considerations of public policy are said to justify giving the courts of Member States the possibility of applying exceptions based on the overriding mandatory provisions of the forum and public policy.[795] It is envisaged that these two exceptions will only apply in exceptional circumstances.[796]

(i) Overriding mandatory provisions of the forum

(a) Article 16

Article 16 is headed "overriding mandatory provisions" and goes on to provide that "Nothing in this Regulation shall restrict the application of the provisions of the law of the forum in a situation where they are mandatory irrespective of the law otherwise applicable to the non-contractual obligation". It makes clear that the forum can continue to apply its own mandatory rules to override the rules on the applicable law under the Regulation, including the rules allowing a choice of the applicable law. Article 16 is in substance worded identically to Article 7(2) of the 1980 Rome Convention, but shorter than Art 9 Rome I. Much has already been said in the context of contract about the concept of (overriding) mandatory rules and about how such rules are to be identified.[797] What is said there is equally relevant in the present context. In particular, the definition of overriding mandatory provisions in Article 9(1) Rome I[798] can be applied by analogy to Rome II.[799] Article 16 is concerned with *overriding* mandatory rules, as contrasted with provisions of the law of a country that cannot be derogated from by agreement, as in Article 14(2) of the Regulation. The addition of the word "Overriding" in the heading to Article 16 is to be welcomed. It is noticeable that under the Rome II Regulation the drafters have been concerned to avoid the confusion caused under the Rome Convention by using the same term "mandatory rules" in two different senses. Under the Regulation not only is Article 16 headed "Overriding mandatory rules" but also Article 14(2) avoids using the term mandatory rules altogether.

(b) English overriding mandatory rules

English law is familiar with the concept of overriding mandatory rules of the forum in tort cases. The statutory tort choice of law rule expressly preserved the mandatory rules of the forum exception that existed at common law.[800]

(i) Examples of statutory mandatory rules of the forum

There is a distinct lack of authority in relation to the application of the mandatory rules of the forum exception in tort cases. This is because, under the common law tort choice of

---

[794] See Briggs, Written Evidence, HL Report 66 (2004), p 96, who suggests Art 15(a) will apply.

[795] Recital (32).

[796] Ibid.

[797] Supra, pp 743–52.

[798] "Overriding mandatory provisions are provisions the respect for which is regarded as crucial by a country for safeguarding its public interests, such as its political, social or economic organisation, to such an extent that they are applicable to any situation falling within their scope, irrespective of the law otherwise applicable to the contract under this Regulation." This definition comes from Joined Cases C-369/96 and C-376/96 *Criminal proceedings against Jean-Claude Arblade and Arblade & Fils SARL* [1999] ECR I-8453 at [30].

[799] This is supported by the fact that the CJEU interpreted Art 7(2) of the 1980 Rome Convention in the same way as Art 9(1) Rome I, see Case C-184/12 *United Antwerp Maritime Agencies (Unamar) NV v Navigation Maritime Bulgare* ECLI:EU:C:2013:663 at [47]–[48].

[800] Private International Law (Miscellaneous Provisions) Act 1995, s 14(4) states that: "This Part has effect without prejudice to the operation of any rule of law which either has effect notwithstanding the rules

law rules, there was an automatic reference to English law anyway. Nonetheless, in a pre-Regulation case, the right to contribution, which can arise between joint tortfeasors under the Civil Liability (Contribution) Act 1978, has been held to be a matter solely of construction of the language of the Act.[801] The argument that the Act was only applicable where the law governing the right to contribution was English law was rejected. The Act is applicable once liability against joint tortfeasors has been established, applying tort choice of law rules. It might also be considered that English statutory rules limiting the effect of certain exclusion clauses in contracts of employment[802] might operate as (overriding) mandatory rules in a negligence action brought by an injured employee against the employer.[803] It could also be argued that the provisions on limitation of liability for maritime claims contained in the Merchant Shipping Act 1995,[804] giving the force of law to an international Convention, should be regarded as mandatory rules.[805] In the past, these provisions have been given a procedural characterisation,[806] and so the question of whether they were mandatory rules did not arise. But the Regulation provides that limitation of liability comes within the scope of the rules on the applicable law.[807] Finally there is judicial authority stating that section 4 of the Fatal Accidents Act 1976[808] is a mandatory rule of English law.[809]

(ii) Common law rules of substantive law

The examples given so far all involve statutory provisions. But much of the English law of tort is of common law origin. In principle, it is possible to have a common law mandatory rule of the forum. But this leaves the practical problem of how such rules are to be identified. With a statutory provision, it may be possible to ascertain that it was Parliament's intention that this provision should apply, regardless of the law applicable to the tort. This can be done by looking at other provisions in the statute expressly stating that the whole or part of it is to have overriding effect or imposing a territorial limit on the scope of the statute. But with a common law rule, how is this intention to be ascertained? Indeed, whose intention are we concerned with? Presumably that of the judges, but which particular judge or judges? The upshot is that it is likely that examples of common law mandatory rules of the forum will be very rare. One possible example, concerned with passing off, has been suggested, namely that English law would apply to an act of passing off that occurred in England where the claimant has goodwill in England, even though the law applicable to the tort is that of a foreign country.[810] After the introduction of the Regulation, the specific choice of law rules for the special torts of unfair competition and infringement of an intellectual property right ensure that

---

of private international law applicable in the particular circumstances or modifies the rules of private international law that would otherwise be so applicable."

[801] *Arab Monetary Fund v Hashim (No 9)* (1994) Times, 11 October; Briggs [1995] LMCLQ 437. In this situation, the mandatory rules of the forum rule is probably best regarded as an exception to unjust enrichment choice of law rules.

[802] See the Law Reform (Personal Injuries) Act 1948, s 1(3).

[803] Infra, pp 882–3.

[804] S 185 and Sch 7.

[805] See, for carriage of goods by sea, *The Hollandia* [1983] 1 AC 565. See also Dicey, Morris and Collins, para 34-081 for the situation under Rome II. As an alternative, it may be considered to give precedence to these rules via Art 28(1) Rome II, infra, pp 873–4, and supra, p 860, n 741.

[806] *Caltex Singapore Pte Ltd and Ors v BP Shipping Ltd* [1996] 1 Lloyd's Rep 286; approved in *Harding v Wealands* [2006] UKHL 32, [2007] 2 AC 1; *Seismic Shipping Inc v Total E & P UK plc (The Western Regent)* [2005] EWCA Civ 985 at [52], [2005] 2 Lloyd's Rep 359.

[807] Art 15(b); discussed supra, pp 859–60.

[808] This provides that in assessing damages in respect of a person's death, accrued benefits are to be ignored.

[809] See under the pre-Regulation law the interpretation of *Roerig v Valiant Trawlers Ltd* [2002] EWCA Civ 21, [2002] 1 WLR 2304 by Arden LJ in *Harding v Wealands* [2004] EWCA Civ 1735 at [48], [2005] 1 WLR 1539 (revsd by the House of Lords without discussion of this example [2006] UKHL 32, [2007] 2 AC 1).

[810] See the 13th edn of this book (1999), p 651.

English law will apply in this situation,[811] and so there seems to be no need to have recourse to the mandatory rules of the forum exception.

(c) No provision on the overriding mandatory rules of foreign countries

It is noticeable that there is no equivalent in the Rome II Regulation of Article 7(1) of the 1980 Rome Convention or Article 9(3) Rome I Regulation, which provide for the application of the overriding mandatory rules of a foreign country with which the situation has a close connection or, respectively, where the obligations arising out of the contract have to be or have been performed.[812] Such a provision proved highly controversial.[813] Under the 1980 Rome Convention, Contracting States were allowed to reserve the right not to apply Article 7(1) and the United Kingdom and six other Contracting States to the Convention have done so. Allowing a Member State to enter a reservation would be incompatible under a Regulation. The upshot is that Member States which do not want to apply the overriding mandatory rules of foreign countries would have been forced to consider giving effect to such rules. This could have jeopardised the willingness of these countries to vote for the Rome II Regulation.[814]

(ii) Public policy of the forum

(a) Article 26: General discussion

Article 26 of the Regulation is entitled "Public policy of the forum" and provides that the "application of a provision of the law of any country specified by this Regulation may be refused only if such application is manifestly incompatible with the public policy ('ordre public') of the forum". Recital (32) helpfully gives an example of a situation which may, depending on the circumstances of the case and the legal order of the Member State of the court seised, be regarded as being contrary to the public policy of the forum, namely where "the application of a provision of the law designated by the Regulation has the effect of causing non-compensatory exemplary or punitive damages of an excessive nature to be awarded".[815] Such a law may, "depending on the circumstances of the case and the legal order of the Member State of the court seised", be regarded as contrary to public policy. The addition of the words "of an excessive nature"[816] appears to be making the point that exemplary or punitive damages are not *ipso facto* excessive.[817] The forum may decide that the exemplary or punitive damages to be awarded will not be excessive, with the result that the public policy exception will not apply.[818] It will then award exemplary or punitive damages, the assessment of which will be a matter for the applicable law.[819] This means that, in a case where the Regulation applies and Ruritanian law is applicable, an English court could apply the Ruritanian law on exemplary or punitive damages. Technically, exemplary and punitive damages do not cover multiple damages for breach of US anti-trust law but nonetheless such

---

[811] Art 6(1) and 8(1).

[812] There was such a provision in the Proposal and Amended Proposal for a Rome II Regulation but it was dropped and did not appear in the Common Position.

[813] The United Kingdom Government Response (2002), para 23, and HL Rep 66 (2004), para 146, proposed deleting this provision.

[814] But see Art 9(3) of the Rome I Regulation, which is more limited than Art 7(1) of the 1980 Rome Convention because it is limited to the foreign mandatory rules at the place of performance.

[815] Recital (32).

[816] Art 24 of the Proposal for a Rome II Regulation did not contain these additional words. Art 24 was a categorical rule with no discretion in the court seised. The European Parliament wanted a more discretionary rule (which again did not contain these additional words), see the Wallis Report, p 33. The Amended Proposal accepted this amendment in part, subject to redrafting.

[817] See the Explanatory Memorandum to the Amended Proposal, p 5.

[818] At common law a foreign law awarding exemplary or punitive damages may well be applied and not regarded as penal, supra, p 119.

[819] Art 15(c); discussed supra, pp 861–3.

damages should be regarded as against English public policy.[820] Recital (32) is only concerned with exemplary and punitive damages and does not include other types of non-compensatory damages, such as restitutionary damages.[821]

Article 26 is virtually identical to Article 21 of the Rome I Regulation. We know from the discussion of the latter,[822] and from the discussion of public policy in the context of the Brussels I Recast,[823] the following. First, in civil law countries *ordre public* operates as a well-established exception to normal choice of law rules, as does public policy in common law jurisdictions. Any clash between the civil and common law concepts of public policy is resolved by the reference to the application of a rule of law being "manifestly" incompatible with the public policy of the forum. This adds nothing as far as English law is concerned since there has long been a reluctance to invoke the public policy doctrine in this country. However, for civil lawyers it makes clear that what is in issue is the narrow concept of international *ordre public* as opposed to the wide concept of domestic *ordre public*. The intention then is that Article 26 will only be used in exceptional circumstances.[824] Secondly, it has to be shown that the *application* of a foreign rule of law is against the forum's public policy. The circumstances of the case have to be considered. This is entirely consistent with common law decisions on public policy, which normally have required some relevant connection with England which justifies English courts in invoking the public policy exception.[825] Thirdly, public policy under the Regulation is a negative concept, involving the *refusal* to apply a foreign law. Article 26 is concerned with an objectionable foreign law that is contrary to the public policy of the forum. Fourthly, when Article 26 does apply, it provides an exception to all of the preceding choice of law rules contained in the Regulation. Presumably, it can even operate to override provisions that cannot be derogated from by agreement under Article 14(2) which are themselves an exception to normal choice of law principles. Thus, an English court could refuse to apply a rule which cannot be derogated from by agreement on the basis that the application of that rule would be against English public policy. It is possible to envisage this happening in cases where a foreign rule that cannot be derogated from by agreement is in conflict with an English rule which cannot be derogated from by agreement. Fifthly, Article 26 operates when the application of a provision of the law of any country specified by the Regulation is manifestly incompatible with the public policy (*ordre public*) of *the forum*. National courts are undoubtedly left with some latitude in deciding on the meaning of the concept, but they must give it a meaning which is appropriate in the context of the Regulation, and the Court of Justice may intervene if they fail to do so. The courts of a Member State determine, according to its own conceptions, what public policy requires, but there are limits to that concept which are subject to review by the Court of Justice.[826] These limits are a matter for interpretation of the Regulation.[827] Sixthly, public policy is concerned with the situation where application of the foreign law would involve a manifest breach of a fundamental right in the Member State seised of the matter.[828] When using the public policy

---

[820] See Protection of Trading Interests Act 1980, s 5(1)–(3); Law Com Working Paper No 87 (1984), para 5.63. See also the discussion of foreign penal laws, supra, pp 118–20.

[821] Cf Art 24 of the Proposal, criticised by Virgo, Written Evidence, HL Paper 66 (2004), pp 135–6.

[822] Supra, pp 752–4.

[823] Supra, pp 626–32.

[824] See *Group Seven Ltd v Allied Investment Corp Ltd* [2014] EWHC 2046 (Ch) at [409]: defense of contributory negligence being open to a fraudster to reduce his liability not contrary to English public policy.

[825] Supra, pp 134–5.

[826] Case C-7/98 *Krombach v Bamberski* [2001] QB 709 at [22]; Case C-38/98 *Régie Nationale des Usines Renault SA v Maxicar SpA* [2000] ECR I-2973 at [27].

[827] See the *Krombach* and *Renault* cases, supra.

[828] This applies the analogy of recognition of judgments granted in another Member State, on which see Case C-7/98 *Krombach v Bamberski* [2001] QB 709.

exception a court can be guided by the case law of the European Court of Human Rights.[829] It is submitted that it would be against public policy to apply a foreign law in circumstances where that law operates to deny rights guaranteed by the European Convention on Human Rights. It has also been suggested that a foreign law that provides that torture is lawful would be against public policy, and even a foreign law which provides inadequate redress by domestic standards might be contrary to public policy.[830]

We must now consider when Article 26 would operate in cases where the forum is England. In other words, when is the application of a provision of the law of a foreign country specified by this Regulation manifestly incompatible with the public policy of England?

<u>(b) Against the public policy of England</u>
It is a well-established principle of English private international law that the English courts will not apply a foreign law when to do so would be inconsistent with the fundamental public policy of English law.[831] There are numerous examples of the operation of this doctrine in choice of law cases in contract,[832] but there was a distinct shortage of authority in England in relation to torts under the common law choice of law rules. The reason for this is easily explained. The requirement under the first limb of the double actionability rule of actionability according to English law meant that the English courts seldom got as far as applying a foreign law. The English courts would not be faced with the situation where an objectionable foreign law imposed liability in circumstances where English law would not do so. With the introduction of the statutory tort choice of law rules, abolishing the first limb of the double actionability rule and setting out an explicit public policy exception to the statutory rules,[833] this was due to change and it is likely that a body of case law would have developed on the operation of the doctrine of public policy in the context of statutory tort choice of law.

Under the Regulation, English courts will not infrequently be faced with causes of action that are unknown to English law. If these were to be routinely struck down as being manifestly incompatible with English public policy it could seem as if the common law rules had never been abolished. This would defeat the purpose of the Regulation. To take a practical example, it would be inappropriate for an English court, when faced with a claim for unfair competition based on Swiss law, to say that the application of such a law is against England's distinctive public policy. The Regulation envisages that Member States will apply the unfair competition law of other states, indeed the Regulation has special choice of law rules for unfair competition. Whilst no such cause of action exists under English law, there is nothing so extreme or objectionable about this Swiss law as to justify not applying it. Moreover, there is authority, in the different context of an action in relation to a dowry, to the effect that public policy cannot be invoked simply on the basis that the foreign cause of action is unknown in England.[834]

The situation at common law where public policy did operate was where there was actionability under English law but no actionability under the second limb of the double actionability

---

[829] Ibid.

[830] See HL Paper 66 (2004), para 153 referring to the evidence of Sir Lawrence Collins. See also the Written Evidence of the AIRE centre, JUSTICE and Redress, p 89. An alternative way of dealing with such cases would be by applying English law as a mandatory rule of the forum under Art 16, discussed supra, pp 866–7. But because the content of the foreign law is being considered, such cases are best regarded as coming within public policy.

[831] Supra, pp 132–9.

[832] Supra, pp 753–4.

[833] Private International Law (Miscellaneous Provisions) Act 1995, s 14(3)(a)(i) sets out a public policy exception to the statutory tort choice of law rules.

[834] See *Phrantzes v Argenti* [1960] 2 QB 19.

rule because of an objectionable law. Thus, in a tort choice of law case at common law, the House of Lords refused to apply an Iraqi law providing for the expropriation of Kuwaiti assets following the invasion of that country on the basis that this law involved a breach of international law.[835] Enforcement or recognition of that law would be manifestly contrary to the public policy of English law.[836] The position would doubtless be the same under the Regulation.

(i) Rules of safety and conduct

Article 17 provides that: "In assessing the conduct of the person claimed to be liable, account shall be taken, as a matter of fact and insofar as is appropriate, of the rules of safety and conduct which were in force at the place and time of the event giving rise to the liability." This provision, sometimes also referred to as "local data rule",[837] is derived from the Hague Convention on the Law Applicable to Traffic Accidents of 1971, the Hague Convention on the Law Applicable to Products Liability of 1973[838] and the national choice of law rules of certain Member States.[839] The effect of Article 17 is that, although the law governing the non-contractual obligation is that of Country A, account must be taken of the rules of safety and conduct in operation in the country in which the harmful act was committed (Country B).[840] The rule is said to strike a reasonable balance between the parties.[841] The perpetrator will have to comply with the rules of safety and conduct in the country in which it operates. The phrase "rules of safety and conduct" should be interpreted as referring to "all regulations having any relation to safety and conduct, including, for example, road safety rules in the case of an accident".[842]

But "account" is only required to be taken of rules of safety and conduct. "Taking account of" is not the same as applying the law of the place of the event giving rise to liability.[843] The law applicable under the rules in the Regulation will still govern. Moreover, account is only to be taken of such rules "as a matter of fact and insofar as is appropriate". The rules of safety and conduct of the place of the event giving rise to liability will only be taken account of *as a point of fact*, eg "when assessing the seriousness of the fault or the author's good or bad faith for the purposes of the measure of damages".[844] It is not clear what, if anything, taking account of rules *insofar as is appropriate* adds to what comes before.

To take an example of the operation of Article 17, the parties may have their common habitual residence in Country A but one injures the other in a road traffic accident in Country B. The issue is whether the defendant was, as a question of fact, driving negligently. In order to determine this, account must be taken of the road safety rules in Country B. A further example was given in the context of environmental damage.[845]

---

[835] *Kuwait Airways Corpn v Iraqi Airways Co (Nos 4 and 5)* [2002] 2 AC 883, HL.

[836] No connection with England is needed in such a case because public policy is not based on a principle of English public policy, which is domestic in character.

[837] On the local data theory, see Currie, *Selected Essays on the Conflict of Laws* (1963), 58–61, 67–71, 178; Ehrenzweig Buffalo L Rev 16 (1966-67), 55, 56–8.

[838] Art 7 of the former and Art 9 of the latter.

[839] The Explanatory Memorandum, p 25.

[840] Recital (34).

[841] Ibid.

[842] Ibid.

[843] The Explanatory Memorandum, p 25.

[844] Ibid.

[845] Supra, pp 830–1.

(j) Special rules for particular issues

Rome II contains a number of special rules for particular issues. Most of these are more appropriately discussed elsewhere in this book.[846] The two remaining issues, namely, direct action against the insurer of the person liable and formal validity, will be discussed here.

(i) Direct action against the insurer of the person liable

In common law jurisdictions the classification of a claim by a victim of a road accident under legislation permitting a direct action against the wrongdoer's insurance company has proved to be particularly difficult. The claim has been classified as tortious, as a *sui generis* statutory extension of contractual liability or as quasi-contractual, to be governed by the law governing the insurance contract.[847]

Article 18 of the Regulation adopts a different approach by providing that the person having suffered damage may bring his or her claim directly against the insurer of the person liable to provide compensation if the law applicable to the non-contractual obligation[848] or the law applicable to the insurance contract[849] so provides. This rule—which is not a conflict-of-laws rule[850]—is designed to strike a balance between the interests of the victim and the insurance company.[851] It gives the victim two bites of the cherry when it comes to proceeding directly against the insurer:[852] It is possible to bring a direct action where the law applicable to the non-contractual obligation *or* the law applicable to the insurance contract so provides.[853] As a consequence, the law applicable to the insurance contract cannot be a bar to a direct action being brought on the basis of the law applicable to the non-contractual obligation.[854] At the same time Article 18 limits the laws applicable to the two that the insurer can legitimately expect to be applied, namely the law applicable to the non-contractual obligation and the law applicable to the insurance contract. If several tortfeasors are liable to the victim and the insurance of one of these tortfeasors has compensated the victim, Article 19 Rome II Regulation deals with the recourse of the paying insurance company against the other tortfeasors and their insurances. This will be governed by the law "which governs the third person's duty to satisfy the creditor", ie the duty of the insurance to satisfy the creditor, which will be the law applicable to the insurance contract as determined by Article 7 Rome I.[855]

(ii) Formal validity

The issue of formal validity will seldom arise in the creation of non-contractual obligations but could do so in the context of a unilateral act by one or other of the parties.[856] The

---

[846] For Arts 19 (subrogation) and 20 (multiple liability), see infra, pp 1291–2; Art 22 (burden of proof), supra, p 85.

[847] See 13th edn of this book (1999), p 665.

[848] Determined in accordance with Art 4 Rome II.

[849] Determined in accordance with Art 7 Rome I.

[850] Case C-240/14 *Eleonore Prüller-Frey v Norbert Brodnig and Axa Versicherung AG* ECLI:EU:C:2015:567 at [40]–[41]. Rather, Art 18 makes it possible to bring a direct action where one of the laws to which it refers provides for such a possibility.

[851] See the Explanatory Memorandum, pp 25–6.

[852] Doctrinally, the obligation for an insurer to compensate the damage caused to a victim arises not from the damage caused to the latter but from the contract between it and the insured party who is liable, Joined Cases C-359/14 and C-475/14, *ERGO Insurance SE v If P&C Insurance AS and Gjensidige Baltic AAS v PZU Lietuva UAB DKat* ECLI:EU:C:2016:40 at [54]–[55].

[853] Case C-240/14 *Eleonore Prüller-Frey v Norbert Brodnig and Axa Versicherung AG* ECLI:EU:C:2015:567 at [39], [41].

[854] Ibid, at [44].

[855] Joined Cases C-359/14 and C-475/14, *ERGO Insurance SE v If P&C Insurance AS and Gjensidige Baltic AAS v PZU Lietuva UAB DK* ECLI:EU:C:2016:40 at [58].

[856] The Explanatory Memorandum, p 26. See also Art 11(3) Rome I.

Regulation adopts a rule modelled on Article 9(1) of the 1980 Rome Convention.[857] Article 21 of the Regulation provides that: "A unilateral act intended to have legal effect and relating to a non-contractual obligation shall be formally valid if it satisfies the formal requirements of the law governing the non-contractual obligation in question or the law of the country in which the act is performed."

(k) Relationship with EU law and existing international conventions

(i) Relationship with EU law

When discussing the law applicable to contractual obligations it was seen that there has been a growing problem of the insertion in EU instruments of provisions which have an impact on private international law.[858] In some cases the instrument undeniably contains a choice of law rule, but in other cases it can be a moot point whether the provision is in truth a choice of law rule. It may merely explain when an instrument applies, but not explain what law governs in the event that the instrument does not apply (which a choice of law rule would do). The possibility cannot be excluded that there may be choice of law rules relating to non-contractual obligations in EU instruments dealing with particular matters and that these are inconsistent with the rules in the Rome II Regulation.[859] There is a particular concern that the provisions on the applicable law in the Rome II Regulation should not restrict the free movement of goods and services as regulated by Community instruments.[860] Article 27 therefore provides that the Regulation "shall not prejudice the application of provisions of Community law which, in relation to particular matters, lay down conflict of law [ie choice of law] rules relating to non-contractual obligations". Unlike with contracts, though, it is difficult to find clear examples of choice of law rules relating to non-contractual obligations in Community instruments. In the past, it has been suggested that the E-Commerce Directive[861] is one such instrument.[862] The Court of Justice has now decided that the country of origin rule in this Directive[863] does not require transposition in the form of a specific conflict-of-laws rule, but only precludes[864] a provider of an electronic commerce service from being made subject to stricter requirements than those provided for by the substantive law in force in the Member State in which that service provider is established.[865] In spite of this clarification, the impact of the Directive and of its country of origin rule on internet torts is still significant.[866]

(ii) Relationship with existing international conventions

Article 28 states: "This Regulation shall not prejudice the application of international conventions to which one or more Member States are parties at the time when this Regulation

---

[857] Now Art 11(1) Rome I Regulation; supra, pp 758–61.

[858] Supra, pp 772–4.

[859] Recital (35), para 1.

[860] Recital (35), para 2.

[861] Directive (EC) No 2000/31 of 8 June 2000, OJ 2000 L 178/1; implemented in the United Kingdom by the Electronic Commerce (EC Directive) Regulations 2002, SI 2002/2013.

[862] Recital (35), para 2.

[863] Art 3(1) and (2).

[864] Subject to derogations authorised in accordance with the conditions set out in Art 3(4).

[865] Joined Cases C-509/09 and C-161/10 *eDate Advertising GmbH and Others v X and Société MGN Limited* [2011] ECR I-10269 at [63], [67]. It has also been argued that the provisions in the Directive should apply as mandatory rules of the forum, see Fawcett, Harris and Bridge, paras 21.15–21.20, 21.110. There is a further possibility, Recital (35), para 2 could be interpreted as giving priority to the country of origin rule, even if it does not lay down a choice of law rule.

[866] See Dicey, Morris and Collins, paras 34-012, 35-153–35-162; for the earlier discussion see HL Paper 66 (2004), paras 158–62; Fawcett, Harris and Bridge, paras 21.01–21.19, 21.120–21.210; Law Commission, *Defamation and the Internet: A Preliminary Investigation*, Scoping Study No 2, December 2002.

is adopted and which lay down conflict-of-law rules relating to non-contractual obligations." This provision makes it clear that existing conventions covering some of the same ground as the Rome II Regulation are preserved. Many Member States have entered into the Hague Convention on the Law Applicable to Traffic Accidents of 1971, which determines the law applicable to civil non-contractual liability arising from traffic accidents, and the Hague Convention on the Law Applicable to Products Liability of 1973, which determines the law applicable, in international cases, to products liability. For these Member States the rules in these Conventions will continue to apply, unaffected by the Rome II Regulation. However, the United Kingdom has entered into neither Convention and will accordingly apply the provisions in the Regulation in road traffic and products liability cases. The upshot is a lack of harmonised tort choice of law rules in the European Union in these two areas.[867] The United Kingdom, like only a small number of other Member States,[868] has entered into the Hague Convention on the Law Applicable to Trusts and on their Recognition of 1985 which lays down choice of law rules relating to non-contractual obligations (equitable obligations). So, again, there will be a lack of harmonisation in this area also. Member States are required to notify[869] the Commission of the conventions referred to in Article 28(1).[870]

As under the Rome I Regulation,[871] it is not entirely clear whether Article 28(1) applies only to international conventions "which lay down conflict-of-law rules relating to non-contractual obligations" in a narrow sense (ie to choice of law conventions), or whether it covers also the rules of conventions harmonising substantive law. Arguably, the provisions which define the substantive, personal and territorial scope of such substantive uniform law conventions could be regarded as conflict-of-law rules in a wide sense, allowing to give precedence to such conventions via Article 28. Such an approach would avoid applying Article 16 on overriding mandatory provisions to give precedence to mandatory rules of uniform law. Moreover, the true reason for giving precedence to such rules is to safeguard the uniform application of the respective convention in all Contracting States, and this would be reflected by applying Article 28, not Article 16 of the Regulation.

Article 28 preserves the application of *existing* international conventions, ie conventions to which a Member State is a party at the time when the Regulation is adopted. It has no provision allowing Member States to enter into conventions *in the future* covering some of the same ground as the Regulation. This contrasts with the position under the 1980 Rome Convention, which allowed for this.[872] It would be out of place to have in a Regulation a provision which allows Member States to negotiate and enter into bilateral agreements which affect the EU rules.[873] However, the European Union does have power to enter into

---

[867] For the concern that this has given rise to in road traffic accident cases, see supra, p 819.

[868] Italy, Luxembourg and the Netherlands, see <http://www.hcch.net>.

[869] By 11 July 2008.

[870] Art 29(1). After 11 July 2008, the Member States are required to notify the Commission of denunciations. The Commission has published in the Official Journal lists of notifications and denunciations: Art 28(2), see Notifications under Article 29(1) of Regulation (EC) No 864/2007 on the law applicable to non-contractual obligations (Rome II), OJ 2010 C 343/7.

[871] Supra, pp 774–5. Sometimes it is also argued that international conventions aiming at substantive law harmonisation (as concluded by the Member States in the realm of their competences) generally define their own scope of application. In relation to the Rome II Regulation see Basedow (2010) 74 RabelsZ 118, 127–8, stating that where a uniform substantive law convention applies, no "situation involving a conflict of laws" in the sense of Art 1(1) Rome II Regulation arises, which makes the EU conflict rules inapplicable.

[872] Art 21 of the 1980 Rome Convention.

[873] Likewise the Rome I Regulation (Art 25(1)) only allows for the preservation of existing international conventions.

international agreements.[874] Moreover, the EU Council can authorise Member States' accession to international conventions.[875] It is envisaged that Member States will be able to negotiate and conclude on their own behalf agreements with third countries "in individual and exceptional cases, concerning sectoral matters", containing provisions on the law applicable to non-contractual obligations.[876] Article 28(2) qualifies the preservation of existing international conventions by providing that the Rome II Regulation "shall, as between Member States, take precedence over conventions concluded exclusively between two or more of them insofar as such conventions concern matters governed by this Regulation".

3. MARITIME NON-CONTRACTUAL OBLIGATIONS

(a) Maritime torts

The effect of the introduction of the Regulation in cases involving maritime torts is a matter of considerable difficulty. The Regulation has no specific choice of law rules for maritime torts.[877] So the only rules that can possibly apply are those in Chapter II (normally Article 4 but Article 9 (industrial action) could apply also).[878] However, Chapter II provides for the application of the law of a "country". The scope of that chapter is thus implicitly limited by the need for the identification of a "country", for it cannot operate without this. As has been seen, country is defined under the Regulation in the normal private international law sense as a territorial unit with its own rules of law.[879] Article 4(1) applies the law of the country in which damage occurs. How should the country in which damage occurs be defined in relation to maritime torts? If one looks literally at where damage occurs, ie identifying the waters in which it occurs, it follows that if damage occurs within territorial waters, Chapter II will operate as usual.[880] In contrast, if damage occurs on the high seas, Chapter II would appear not to apply.

An alternative approach would be to say that damage occurs in the country of the flag of the ship.[881] A law of the flag rule has the advantage that Chapter II would apply, regardless of the waters in which the damage occurs. There was a provision in the Proposal for a Regulation that in effect adopted a law of the flag rule[882] but this was deleted in the Amended Proposal.[883] As the reasons for deletion of the special provision are not known, this fact appears to be inconclusive for interpreting the Regulation. A strong argument in favour of the flag rule is

---

[874] See the Opinion of the Court of Justice 1/03 Competence of the Community to conclude the new Lugano Convention [2006] ECR I-1145 at [148].

[875] See, eg, Council Decision (EC) No 2002/762 of 19 September 2002 in relation to the Bunkers Convention, OJ 2002 L 256/7.

[876] Recital (37), which also provides that the Commission will make a proposal to the European Parliament and the Council concerning the procedures and conditions for this.

[877] For a discussion of the impact of Rome II, see Basedow (2010) 74 RabelsZ 118; Siehr (2010) 74 RabelsZ 139.

[878] See the Statement by the Cypriot and Greek Delegations on Art 9, supra, p 836.

[879] Art 25 of the Regulation.

[880] The Cypriot and Greek Delegations in their Statement on Art 9, supra, p 836, assume that it will apply to industrial action in territorial waters.

[881] See generally George (2007) 3 J Priv Int L 137, 168–71.

[882] Art 18 of the Proposal. This showed an intention to bring torts committed on the high seas within the tort choice of law rules.

[883] It is not clear why this provision was deleted. It has been accepted in the past that, in the absence of a special provision dealing with torts committed on the high seas, the EU tort choice of law rules cannot operate, see the Giuliano, Lagarde and Van Sasse Van Ysselt Report, p 50, referring to the 1972 preliminary draft convention which contained no such special provision.

that the Court of Justice has held, in the context of Article 7(2) Brussels Recast, that where damage arose on board, "the flag State must necessarily be regarded as the place where the harmful event caused damage".[884] For damage occurring on board of a single vessel, the country in which the damage occurs can thus be regarded as the flag state, ie the country to which the ship belongs.[885] This corresponds both to the common law and the 1995 Act under which the law of the flag was the decisive factor whenever the acts complained of had all occurred on board a single vessel, for a ship was regarded for certain purposes as a floating island over which the national law prevailed.[886] Where a flag is common to a political unit containing several different systems of law, as in the case of Canada or the USA, the law of the flag means the law of the port at which the ship is registered.[887]

However, the flag state rule is subject to certain limitations. First, a law of the flag rule does not work if there is a collision between two ships flying different flags or damage is caused outside the ship (eg to the environment).[888] Probably for this reason, the Court of Justice[889] has held the "nationality of the ship can play a decisive role only if the national court reaches the conclusion that the damage arose on board".[890] Secondly, ships frequently fly a flag of convenience so that the applicable law could be that of Panama, even though the parties and events have no connection with that country. However, there is under Article 4(2) the common habitual residence exception and under Article 4(3) the manifestly more closely connected escape clause. While the spread of connections in maritime cases will often make it difficult to apply these provisions,[891] the application of the law of the country through which territorial waters (or even continental shelf waters) the ship is passing may be even more fortuitous and unforeseeable than the flag she flies.[892]

---

[884] Case C-18/02 *Danmarks Rederiforening, acting on behalf of DFDS Torline A/S v LO Landsorganisationen i Sverige, acting on behalf of SEKO Sjöfolk Facket för Service och Kommunikation* [2004] ECR I-1417 at [44]; see Basedow (2010) 74 RabelsZ 118, 132–3. For the application of the flag state rule on an activity performed on a vessel by the crew on board the vessel see Case C-286/90 *Anklagemyndigheden v Peter Michael Poulsen and Diva Navigation Corp* [1992] ECR I-6019 at [13], [18], [26]–[29]. The non-application of the law of the flag state in Case C-292/14 *Elliniko Dimosio v Stefanos Stroumpoulis and Others* ECLI:EU:C:2016:116 at [61]–[71] seems to be motivated by the specific purpose of the relevant Directive 80/987, namely to protect employees against insolvency by their employer, even if they work regularly on ships flying the flag of non-EU Member States.

[885] See Law Commission Working Paper No 87 (1984), para 5.84. Cf the 14th edn of this book (2008), pp 859–60 which argued against the application of the flag state rule under Rome II.

[886] For the common law see *R v Anderson* (1868) LR 1 CCR 161 at 168; *R v Keyn* (1876) 2 Ex D 63 at 94. But not for the purpose of jurisdiction, *Chung Chi Cheung v R* [1939] AC 160; *O'Daly v Gulf Oil Terminals (Ireland) Ltd* [1983] ILRM 163. For the situation under the 1995 Act see *Roerig v Valiant Trawlers Ltd* [2002] EWCA Civ 21 at [7], [2002] 1 WLR 2304. See also Law Com No 193 (1990), para 3.27 74 and Law Commission Working Paper No 87 (1984), para 2.110 and para 5.77 (law of the flag even if the ship is passing through territorial waters). But see also *The Arum* [1921] P 12; *The Mary Moxham* (1876) 1 PD 107; *The Waziristan* [1953] 1 WLR 1446; *Mackinnon v Iberia Shipping Co Ltd* [1954] 2 Lloyd's Rep 372, 1955 SLT 49; Carter (1957) 33 BYBIL 342–3 (flag principle does not apply where damage occurs in territorial waters). Cf *Sayers v International Drilling Co NV* [1971] 1 WLR 1176.

[887] For the position under common law see *Canadian National Steamship Co v Watson* [1939] 1 DLR 273; *Gronlund v Hansen* (1969) 4 DLR (3d) 435. See also Law Commission Working Paper No 87 (1984), paras 2.110 and 5.85.

[888] Law Commission Working Paper 87 (1984), paras 5.79–5.81.

[889] As before the common law.

[890] Case C-18/02 *Danmarks Rederiforening, acting on behalf of DFDS Torline A/S v LO Landsorganisationen i Sverige, acting on behalf of SEKO Sjöfolk Facket för Service och Kommunikation* [2004] ECR I-1417 at [44].

[891] Possible other connecting factors are the central administration of the shipowner, the place of registration, the homeport and the nationality of the master, the officers or the parties to the dispute, see Basedow (2010) 74 RabelsZ 118, 133.

[892] See also Case C-286/90 *Anklagemyndigheden v Peter Michael Poulsen and Diva Navigation Corp* [1992] ECR I-6019 at [26]–[29] which limits the application of EU law to vessels from third states which sail only in the exclusive economic zone of an EU Member State.

For those cases where the flag state rule does not apply, ie where damage is caused to persons or property not on board, it is necessary to distinguish between two different situations: first where damage occurs in territorial waters, secondly where it occurs on the high seas.[893]

(i) Damage occurs within territorial waters

In this situation, Article 4 will apply. The place where damage occurs points to a country, namely the country in whose territorial waters the damage occurs. Applying Article 4(1), it may be entirely fortuitous that damage occurs in the country in question. For example, a ship may just be passing through or at anchor in a particular country's territorial waters when the damage occurs. It is possible that the common habitual residence exception (Article 4(2)) will apply or the manifestly more closely connected escape clause (Article 4(3)) but the spread of connections in maritime cases will often mean that these provisions are inapplicable.

(ii) Damage occurs on the high seas

The English High Court has jurisdiction to entertain an action in respect of injurious acts done on the high seas,[894] even though both the litigants are foreigners,[895] unless the restrictions under the Brussels I Recast apply. When it comes to determining the applicable law, Article 4(1) of the Regulation will not apply because damage does not occur in a "country", and the flag state rule does not help because damage did not occur on board. Article 4(2) cannot then apply because that is an exception to Article 4(1).[896] Neither can Article 4(3) apply because that displaces the law applicable under Article 4(1) and (2). In the absence of a binding conflict rule under the Rome II Regulation, Member States are therefore free to apply their national choice of law rules to identify the applicable law for those damages which occur not on board of a single vessel.[897] In the case of England, it is necessary to distinguish between collisions and other external acts.

(a) Collisions

There is no doubt that, prior to the introduction of the statutory tort choice of law rules, the commonest kind of external act, namely, one that causes a collision, was governed solely by the general maritime law as administered in England, and not by that combination of English and foreign law which is required by the double actionability rule as laid down in *Phillips v Eyre*, as amended by *Boys v Chaplin* and the *Red Sea* case.[898] It was said that: "All

---

[893] Arguably between these two scenarios lies the case where damage occurs outside territorial waters, but inside an area over which a State enjoys rights under the United Nations Convention on the Law of the Sea (UNCLOS), see, in particular, Art 33 (contiguous zone), Arts 55–75 (exclusive economic zone), Arts 76–85 (continental shelf) and Dicey, Morris and Collins, para 35-033. The Court of Justice has held in Case C-37/00 *Herbert Weber v Universal Ogden Services Ltd* [2002] ECR I-2013 at [36] "that work carried out by an employee on fixed or floating installations positioned on or above the part of the continental shelf adjacent to a Contracting State, in the context of the prospecting and/or exploitation of its natural resources, is to be regarded as work carried out in the territory of that State for the purposes of applying Article 5(1) of the Brussels Convention". Where damage arises in connection with activities which justify an extension of jurisdiction by coastal states, see UNCLOS, Art 56(1), the Weber judgment may be a basis to localise this damage in the coastal state whose jurisdiction is extended and apply Art 4(1) Rome II, Basedow (2010) 74 RabelsZ 118, 134. However, where no such activity on installations is concerned, as in the case of ordinary shipping, the Weber judgment appears not to apply.

[894] *The Tubantia* [1924] P 78.

[895] *Chartered Mercantile Bank of India v Netherlands India Steam Navigation Co* (1883) 10 QBD 521 at 536–7.

[896] Arguably Art 4(2) could apply by analogy if both colliding ships fly the same flag.

[897] Basedow (2010) 74 RabelsZ 118, 137. For acts which occur on board of a single vessel, the flag state rule applies.

[898] However, in *Gronlund v Hansen* (1969) 4 DLR (3d) 435, a Canadian court seemed prepared to apply the original *Phillips v Eyre* rule to a claim arising from a death resulting from a collision on the high seas.

questions of collision are questions *communis iuris*"[899] and must be decided by the law maritime.[900]

This special tort choice of law rule is preserved, and the statutory tort choice of law rules will not apply to collisions on the high seas. This raises the question of what is meant by "general maritime law". The natural inference to draw from this expression is that there exists a body of law which is universally recognised as binding on all nations in respect of acts occurring at sea. There is, however, no such body of law.[901] The expression, in truth, means nothing more than that part of English law which, either by statute or by reiterated decisions, has been evolved for the determination of maritime disputes.[902] It is the law which, despite the views of Westlake,[903] must be applied to all questions of collision unless international regulations have been laid down by a convention between states.[904]

(b) Other external acts

The question that now arises is whether this maritime law applied to all external acts, ie to all cases where the alleged wrong consists of some act, other than a collision, done by a foreign ship to the property of another, as, for example, where a submarine cable is fouled[905] or where possession is seised of a wreck that is being salvaged by a third party.[906] Prior to the introduction of the statutory tort choice of law rules, it was strongly argued that the law maritime should apply to all external acts.[907] Moreover, the sphere of authority possessed by the general maritime law has been described in such comprehensive terms by the judges that it would appear to cover all torts committed on the high seas,[908] including an action under the Fatal Accidents Acts arising from a collision between a Latvian trawler and a Panamanian tanker off the coast of the USA.[909] It can be confidently stated, therefore, that the law maritime applied to all external acts. This was also the view of the Law Commissions.[910] The law maritime will continue to apply to all such acts, and the statutory tort choice of law rules will not apply.

(b) Maritime non-contractual obligations (other than torts)

Other non-contractual obligations can arise in the maritime context. For example, it has been seen earlier that a common example of *negotiorum gestio* is salvage, ie one vessel renders service to another. Looking at the choice of law rules on *negotiorum gestio*, Article 11(1) and (2) do not refer

---

[899] *The Johann Friedrich* (1839) 1 Wm Rob 36 at 37.

[900] *The Wild Ranger* (1862) Lush 553; *The Zollverein* (1856) Sw 96; *The Leon* (1881) 6 PD 148; *Chartered Mercantile Bank of India, London and China v Netherlands Steam Navigation Co Ltd* (1883) 10 QBD 521; Foote, pp 524–5. Cf the position in Australia, see *Blunden v Commonwealth* (2004) 218 CLR 330, HC of Australia.

[901] *Lloyd v Guibert* (1865) LR 1 QB 115 at 123–5.

[902] *The Gaetano and Maria* (1882) 7 PD 137 at 143.

[903] Westlake, pp 290–1.

[904] The collision regulations at present in force are those which are laid down by various international conventions and given effect by the Merchant Shipping Act 1995. Damage to structures erected for the exploitation of the sea-bed of the Continental Shelf over which the United Kingdom exercises rights falls under the Continental Shelf Act 1964, as amended by the Oil and Gas (Enterprise) Act 1982, see the Informal Briefing by the draftsman HL Paper 36 (1995), pp 65–8.

[905] *Submarine Telegraph Co v Dickson* (1864) 15 CBNS 759.

[906] *The Tubantia* [1924] P 78.

[907] See the 12th edn of this book (1992), pp 559–60.

[908] *Chartered Mercantile Bank of India v Netherlands India Steam Navigation Co* (1883) 10 QBD 521 at 536–7; and see *Lloyd v Guibert* (1865) LR 1 QB 115 at 125; *The Gaetano and Maria* (1882) 7 PD 37; *Davidsson v Hill* [1901] 2 KB 606; *The Esso Malaysia* [1975] QB 198.

[909] *The Esso Malaysia*, supra.

[910] Law Com No 193 (1990), para 3.27 74.

to the place of damage or the place where the act performed without authority occurred, and can therefore be applied to a case of maritime *negotiorum gestio*. However, Article 11(3) applies the law of the country in which the act was performed and the search for the manifestly more closely connected country under Article 11(4) should include the connection with this country. It is easy enough to identify the country where the act occurred if this is in territorial waters but this is problematic if the act occurs on the high seas.

The pragmatic approach would be to start by trying to apply Article 11(1) and (2) and if the circumstances are such that they provide an answer then that is the law that is applied. It would still be possible to go on to apply Article 11(3) and (4) in cases where the act took place in territorial waters. A more principled approach would be to say that Article 11 cannot be split up into its separate components in this way and therefore none of it can apply to maritime *negotiorum gestio* outside territorial waters. In other words, one should treat maritime *negotiorum gestio* like maritime torts on the high seas. This would leave Member States to apply their national choice of law rules on *negotiorum gestio*, as modified where necessary to take into account the maritime element, to solve the problem. This looks, as a matter of principle, to be the better approach. However, there is a practical problem in that English law has never articulated such choice of law rules.

4. MIXED ISSUES RELATING TO NON-CONTRACTUAL OBLIGATIONS AND CONTRACT

The problem of contractual defences to tort claims is one of the most intractable in private international law. This was the case under the English pre-Regulation choice of law rules[911] and remains the case under the Regulation.

(a) The nature of the problem

The leading English case at common law is the pre-Regulation case of *Sayers v International Drilling Co NV*.[912] The facts neatly illustrate the nature of the problem that faces the courts when mixed questions of tort and contract arise.

> The plaintiff was an Englishman who entered a contract of employment with a Dutch company, the defendants, to work on their oil rigs. The plaintiff was sent to work on a rig in Nigerian territorial waters and was injured by the alleged negligence of his fellow employees. He brought an action for damages in England. It was not clear whether this was in tort or contract or both.[913] The contract contained a clause excluding all remedies for such injuries, other than those expressly provided by the contract. Such a clause was valid under Dutch law in the case of international contracts, but void under English domestic law by reason of the Law Reform (Personal Injuries) Act 1948.[914]
>
> The Court of Appeal held unanimously that the plaintiff's claim for damages for his personal injuries should fail. A majority,[915] applying common law contract choice of law rules,[916] without

---

[911] See the 13th edn of this book (1999), pp 666–9.

[912] [1971] 1 WLR 1176; see Collins (1972) 21 ICLQ 320; Carter (1971) 45 BYBIL 404.

[913] The plaintiff sought damages for the negligence of his fellow employees.

[914] S 1(3). See also the Unfair Contract Terms Act 1977, s 2(1) and the Consumer Rights Act 2015, s 65(1).

[915] Salmon and Stamp LJJ. See generally, Morse in Contract Conflicts, p 158 et seq; Morse (1982) 2 YEL 107, 141–2; Lasok and Stone, Conflict of Laws in the European Community, pp 375–6; Hartley (1997) 266 Hague Recueil 341, at 413–16; see also Law Com No 193 (1990), para 3.50.

[916] The case went on appeal to the Court of Appeal on the question of what the proper law of the contract was.

considering the tortious aspect of the case,[917] decided that the proper law of the contract was Dutch law. Applying that law, the majority held that the exemption clause was valid and any claim in tort was defeated thereby.[918]

Which law would govern the issue of validity of the clause under the Rome Regulations? This raises the question of whether this is to be determined by the application of the contract choice of law rules under the Rome I Regulation, or the tort choice of law rules under the Rome II Regulation, or some *sui generis* approach, or by some combination of both tort and contract rules.

(b) The nature of the obligation

The starting point under the Regulations is to determine the nature of the obligation on which the claim is based. Is this a contractual obligation or a non-contractual obligation? Where an employee is suing the employer this will raise the problem of concurrent liability in tort and contract.[919] It has been seen that in such a case, in the absence of a ruling from the Court of Justice, different Member States may well adopt different classifications, some opting for a contractual classification of the obligation, whilst others adopt a tortious classification. It has also been seen that there is a strong argument for adopting a classification which distinguishes between the actions brought. After determining the classification of the obligation, the next question is how this obligation interacts with the contractual defence provided by the exemption clause. To answer this, it is necessary to look separately at, on the one hand, the situation where the obligation is contractual and, on the other hand, where it is non-contractual.

(c) A contractual obligation to which there is a contractual defence

In this situation, there is no problem of a clash between tort choice of law rules and contract choice of law rules. The law governing the contract will determine the validity of the exemption clause, subject to the application of the provisions that cannot be derogated from by agreement according to Article 6(2) and Article 8(1) Rome I, and to overriding mandatory provisions under Article 9(2) Rome I. In *Sayers*, it would thus be necessary to determine the country in which or, failing that, from which the employee habitually carried out his work in performance of the contract.[920] If this was in the case the Netherlands, Dutch law would determine the validity of the exemption clause.[921]

(d) A non-contractual obligation to which there is a contractual defence

This situation would arise where there is only liability in tort; where there are claims in tort and contract and it is the tort claim that is in issue; or where, although there is concurrent liability, the courts regard the obligation as being non-contractual. There is, then, a contractual defence to this claim.[922] This is conceptually the most difficult situation to deal with

---

[917] A similar approach to that of the majority in *Sayers* would appear to have been adopted by the High Court of Australia in *Oceanic Sun Line Special Shipping Co Inc v Fay* (1988) 165 CLR 197; North [1990] I Hague Recueil 9, 228–9. Though see Gaudron J, (1988) 165 CLR 197 at 266.

[918] Lord Denning also applied Dutch law but on a different basis. He regarded the claim as one in tort to which there was a contractual defence. He adopted a proper law of the issue approach, combining elements of the common law proper law of the tort and proper law of the contract approaches.

[919] Discussed supra, pp 791–2.

[920] Article 8(1) second sentence, Article 8(2) Rome I.

[921] Arguably, it is doubtful whether to apply the provisions of the Law Reform (Personal Injuries) Act 1948 or other English law as overriding mandatory provisions in the sense of Article 9(2) Rome I (even if they qualified as such) in this case, because Article 8 Rome I could be considered as a conclusive provision for rules concerning the protection of employees.

[922] If the contract between the parties does not contain any clause which provides a defence, the contract choice of law rules have no role to play and recourse must be had solely to the tort choice of law rules in the

because it involves an interaction of tortious and contractual elements. In determining the validity of the exemption clause there are in theory four different approaches that could be applied:[923] the exclusive application of contract choice of law rules; the exclusive application of tort choice of law rules; a *sui generis* approach; or an approach where choice of law rules in both contract and tort have roles to play, but different roles. The Regulation seemingly provides an answer in Article 15(b).

(i) Article 15(b): Application of tort choice of law rules

Article 15(b) provides that the law applicable to non-contractual obligations under the Regulation governs in particular "the grounds for exemption from liability, [and] any limitation of liability". This phrase could be understood to cover an exemption or limitation clause in a contract, which is used as a defence to a claim in respect of a non-contractual obligation.[924] Such an interpretation could also be justified by the desire to preserve the policies of the law governing the non-contractual obligation.[925] On the other hand, the principle of consistent interpretation of Rome I and Rome II[926] suggests that a contractual exemption or limitation clause constitutes an obligation freely assumed by one party towards the other and thus a contractual matter. In order to reconcile both positions, it seems appropriate to first consult the law applicable to the non-contractual obligation, as determined by the Rome II Regulation, whether it accepts a limitation or exemption clauses as a defence. If this is the case, the validity, interpretation and scope of such a clause is to be determined under the law applicable to the contract as determined by the Rome I Regulation.

(a) Whether a valid exemption clause can provide an effective defence

If the facts of *Sayers* arose now (and the obligation on which the claim was based was classified as tortious), the tort choice of law rules under Article 4 of the Regulation would have to be applied to determine whether an exemption clause is at all accepted as a defence. On the facts of the *Sayers* case there is some difficulty in identifying the country in which the damage occurred for the purposes of Article 4(1). The accident took place on a Dutch rig in Nigerian territorial waters and it is arguable that, in the case of matters purely internal to the rig, Dutch, rather than Nigerian, law should be regarded as the law of the country in which the damage occurred. However, as the case concerned not a ship, but a rig as a fixed installation, the better view is that, the country in which damage occurs should be defined in a literal sense in terms of the waters in which damage occurs, ie Nigeria.[927] Under Article 4(1) therefore, it is for Nigerian law as the law of the country in which the damage occurs to decide whether the exemption clause is valid and can therefore provide a defence. However, there is a pre-existing contractual relationship between the parties. This means that it is likely that Article 4(3) will apply, with the result that the law of the country that governs the contract (Dutch law) will also govern the obligation in tort. This illustrates how the secondary connection rule in Article 4(3) can take the sting out of different classifications being adopted for the obligation in a case like *Sayers*. The result will be the same regardless of whether a contractual or tortious classification is adopted.

Regulation. This is the explanation of the pre-Regulation common law case of *Coupland v Arabian Gulf Oil Co* [1983] 1 WLR 1136.

[923] See Law Com No 193 (1990), para 3.50.

[924] See the 14th edn of this book (2008), p 865; see also the criticism by Briggs, Written Evidence, HL Report 66 (2004), 96.

[925] Which might be intended to be non-waivable to protect public or private interests.

[926] Recital (7).

[927] See the Weber judgment, supra p 877 n 893.

Moreover, "exemption from liability" in Art 15(b) Rome II would cover not just the issue of admissibility of the exemption clause as a defence to the non-contractual obligation. It would also cover the issue that arose in the pre-Regulation case of *Canadian Pacific Railway v Parent*.[928]

> A widow sued her late husband's employers after he was killed in the course of his employment. The employer sought to rely on an exemption clause in the husband's contract of employment. There was no question raised as to the validity of the exemption clause. However, if the widow was suing in her own right as a dependent,[929] the exemption clause would not be effective to provide a defence. In contrast, if she could only sue for rights her husband would have had if he had lived,[930] the exemption clause would have been effective to provide a defence.

The different countries involved took different views of the basis of the widow's right to sue. Under the Regulation, the law governing the tort would determine the basis of the widow's right to sue and hence whether the exemption clause was an effective defence. The application of tort choice of law rules looks to be particularly appropriate.[931]

(b) Overriding mandatory rules of the forum?

The discussion of the *Sayers* case has proceeded so far on the basis that Dutch law will apply by virtue of Article 4(3) of the Rome II Regulation. However, there is an important further possibility to be considered. This is that English law[932] could apply by virtue of Article 16,[933] ie as an overriding mandatory rule of the forum, to deny effect to the exemption clause as a defence to an action in tort. There is a precedent for doing so under the pre-Regulation law. The Court of Session in a very similar pre-Regulation case to *Sayers*, *Brodin v A/R Seljan*,[934] insisted on the application of the statutory prohibition against exemption clauses.

> The deceased, a Norwegian, domiciled in Scotland, was injured on board an oil tanker as it was docking in Scotland. He later died. The law of the forum and the law of the place of the tort were, therefore, Scottish. The proper law of the deceased's contract of employment was Norwegian and it contained an express choice of law clause which also excluded liability for personal injuries. Such an exemption is void under Scots domestic law by reason of the Law Reform (Personal Injuries) Act 1948.[935]

The Court of Session held that Scots law alone was applicable to a claim for damages by the deceased's widow and that no defence based on such an exemption clause was available, irrespective of its effects under Norwegian law. The court was applying what we would now describe as an overriding mandatory rule of the forum.[936] Under the Rome Regulations, such an approach might be questioned if the widow's claim is based on her deceased husband's right and not her own right to damages, because Article 8 Rome I could be regarded as a conclusive provision for the protection of employees. If the law of the country which governs the husband's employment contract according to Article 8 Rome I[937] allows the exclusion

---

[928] [1917] AC 195.

[929] In England, see the Fatal Accidents Act 1976.

[930] For survival of causes of action under English law, see the Law Reform (Miscellaneous Provisions) Act 1934.

[931] In *CPR v Parent*, the common law tort choice of law rules were applied to determine whether exemption clause provided a defence. There is no contractual relationship between the parties (the widow and employer) and so Art 4(3) of the Regulation would not apply.

[932] Law Reform (Personal Injuries) Act 1948, s 1(3).

[933] Discussed supra, pp 866–8.

[934] 1973 SC 213.

[935] S 1(3).

[936] Law Com No 193 (1990), para 3.50. See Art 16 Rome II.

[937] The provisions of which cannot be displaced under a choice of law, Art 8(1) Rome I.

of liability for personal injuries and the tort is governed by this law,[938] it seems doubtful to elevate the law of the forum and domicile of the victim into the status of an overriding mandatory provision in the sense of Article 16 Rome II.

(ii) Existence, validity and scope of the exemption clause

Provided that the law applicable to the non-contractual obligation accepts an exemption clause as a defence to liability, the issue can arise as to whether the exemption clause has been validly agreed in a contract and whether it is worded adequately to exclude liability in tort. Under a literal reading of Article 15(b) Rome II, the tort choice of law rules would have to be applied to determine this question. In principle, this does not make much sense. It would surely be better if the law governing the contract were to be applied to determine the existence, validity and scope of a contractual clause, as it concerns a contractual matter in the sense of Article 1 of the Rome I Regulation. Again, in practice, the secondary connection rule under Article 4(3) Rome II will ensure that the law of the country that governs the contract will also determine the scope of the contractual clause, even if this matter is to be classified as falling under Rome II.

(iii) Other contractual defences

There are contractual defences to actions in tort, other than an exemption clause. "Grounds for exemption from liability, [and] any limitation of liability" under Article 15(b) will cover any such other contractual defence. An example of such a defence can be seen in the pre-Regulation case of *Chiron Corpn v Organon Teknika Ltd (No 2)*.[939] The defendants pleaded section 44(3) of the Patents Act 1977 as a defence to an infringement action. This provided a defence where there was a contract relating to the patent containing a term or condition which had been rendered void under section 44(1) of the 1977 Act on the basis that the patentee had abused his monopoly of power. It was held that section 44(1) applied, regardless of whether English law governed the contract. For the present purpose, what is important is that at common law the question of the applicable law in respect of this contractual defence to an infringement action was treated as a contractual matter, to which English rules on the law governing the contract applied. There was, though, no discussion of the problem raised by the fact that this was an action in tort. Under the Regulation the section 44(3) defence is an example of a ground for exemption from liability. The law applicable to this defence would therefore be the law governing the tort of infringement of the intellectual property right,[940] or, if the defence is based on competition law, the law governing the abuse of monopoly as an act to restrict competition.[941]

5. NON-CONTRACTUAL OBLIGATIONS OUTSIDE THE SCOPE OF THE ROME II REGULATION

The Regulation expressly excludes from its scope "non-contractual obligations arising out of violations of privacy and rights relating to personality, including defamation".[942] Member

---

[938] Under Art 4(3) Rome II, which would not apply to the widow's own damages claim, supra p 882 n 931.

[939] [1993] FSR 567.

[940] See Art 8 of the Regulation.

[941] See Art 6(3) of the Regulation. In practice the law applicable under Art 8 and Art 6(3) will often be the same in such cases.

[942] Art 1(2)(g); discussed supra, pp 797–9. See in particular the meaning of defamation for the purposes of this exclusion. It is argued above that defamation arising in the business context should be regarded as coming within the unfair competition choice of law rules set out in Art 6 of the Regulation.

States must apply their traditional national choice of law rules for these matters. In the case of England, the statutory tort choice of law rules in Part III of the Private International Law (Miscellaneous Provisions) Act 1995 have largely replaced the common law tort choice of law rules. However, section 13 of the 1995 Act excludes defamation claims from Part III.[943] "Defamation" is widely defined in section 13(2)(a) to cover any claim under the law of any part of the United Kingdom for libel or slander and any claim under the law of Scotland for verbal injury. Section 13(2)(b) goes further and covers "any claim under the law of any other country corresponding to or otherwise in the nature of a claim mentioned in paragraph (a) above". This would encompass, for example, a claim for libel under Ontario law. Section 13 went even further and included malicious falsehood. However, it is submitted that this tort—in a business context—does not fall within the defamation exclusion under the Regulation and therefore the choice of law rules in the Regulation will apply.[944] As was seen earlier, under English law there are separate common law choice of law rules for restitution and breach of equitable obligations.

We must now examine the matters expressly excluded from the scope of the Regulation and determine whether the statutory tort choice of law rules or the common law tort choice of law rules apply, or indeed the choice of law rules for restitution or equitable obligations, and then comment on the application of these rules.

(a) Violations of privacy and rights relating to personality (excluding defamation)

The statutory tort choice of law[945] rules will apply to violations of privacy which are tortious, such as an action brought in England for invasion of privacy under Swiss law. In cases of misuse of private information borne out of non-contractual breach of confidence, the position is more difficult. It has been argued above that such cases fall within the exclusion from the Regulation of violations of privacy and rights relating to personality. But it is unclear how such an action should then be classified for the purposes of application of English national choice of law rules. As a matter of substantive law classification, there is support for the view that the expanded wrong of breach of confidence involving publication of private information is a tort.[946] This would mean that the statutory tort choice of law rules would apply. It could, though, be argued that, because of the use of the concept of breach of confidence, recourse should be had to the common law choice of law rules for equitable obligations. The counter-argument is that the misuse of private information is to be regarded as a cause of action separate from misuse of confidential information (even though both fall within the category of breach of confidence),[947] which might suggest a different classification for misuse of private information from that for misuse of confidential information. Finally, in the choice of law context the Court of Appeal has found persuasive the tentative suggestion[948] that a claim for expanded breach of confidence should be classified as a restitutionary claim for unjust enrichment.[949] This would mean that the common law choice of law rules for unjust enrichment would apply. However, most recently the Court of Appeal considered the

---

[943] For the reasons for this see the 13th edn of this book (1999), pp 656–7.

[944] See Art 6, discussed supra, p 824.

[945] Discussed in outline, supra, pp 777–8, and more fully in the 13th edn of this book (1999), pp 614–54.

[946] *Campbell v MGN Ltd* [2004] UKHL 22 at [14]–[15], [2004] 2 AC 457; *McKennitt v Ash* [2006] EWCA Civ 1714 at [8], [2007] 3 WLR 194.

[947] *Douglas v Hello! Ltd* [2007] UKHL 21 at [255], [2007] 2 WLR 920.

[948] In Dicey and Morris, 13th edn, para 34-029. See now Dicey, Morris and Collins, para 34-09–34-092.

[949] *Douglas v Hello! Ltd (No 3)* [2005] EWCA Civ 595 at [97]; [2006] QB 125.

restitutionary classification as obiter and regarded the misuse of private information as a tort for the purposes of service out of the jurisdiction.[950]

The statutory tort choice of law rules will also apply to rights relating to personality (excluding defamation), such as the right to the use of a name. The application of these rules to invasion of privacy and the right to the use of a name is particularly problematic because these are causes of action that are unknown to English law.[951]

(b) Defamation

The consequence of the exclusion of defamation claims—as widely defined by section 13(2)—from the scope of Part III is that the common law tort choice of law rules[952] will continue to be applied to such claims. They are rules which, as regards torts committed abroad, are anomalous, unjust and uncertain, and will discourage claimants in an international defamation case from bringing the action in England.

(i) Defamation committed abroad

The general rule of double actionability (ie there must be actionability by the law of the forum and the law of the place of the tort[953]) will apply to claims in respect of defamation committed abroad.[954] This means that the claimant will be subject to injustice in having a double hurdle to surmount. There is, then, the possibility of the flexible exception (seemingly based on the concept of the most significant relationship) being applied,[955] with all the uncertainty involved in the operation of this exception. The application of these rules in cases of libel and slander will now be considered.

Application of the general rule of double actionability means that a defendant will be able to rely on defences available under English law, such as absolute and qualified privilege, even though the publication was abroad and such a defence is not available under the law of the foreign country where the tort was committed. Even if there is actionability under English law, the claim may fail because there is no actionability under the law of the foreign country where the tort was committed. In many foreign countries, particularly those that have a tort of invasion of privacy, it is much harder to establish defamation than it is under English law. Nonetheless, it may be possible to satisfy both limbs of the rule. An example of where this happened is *Church of Scientology of California v Metropolitan Police Comr*.[956] The claim concerned an alleged libel committed in Germany. There was actionability under both English and German law and the claim succeeded. When it comes to the application of the flexible exception to this general rule, there is one obvious situation where this may come into play. This is where both parties are resident in the same country and this is a country other than the one in which the tort was committed.[957]

---

[950] *Vidal-Hall v Google Inc* [2015] EWCA Civ 311 at [38]–[39], [43].

[951] See the 13th edn of this book (1999), p 619 (misguided attempts to exclude such causes of action from the scope of Part III), pp 646–7 (misguided attempts to use the public policy defence).

[952] See in relation to defamation Prosser (1953) 51 Mich LR 959; Handford (1983) 32 ICLQ 452; Castel (1990) 28 Osgoode Hall LJ 153; Reed (1996) 15 CJQ 305, 306–9.

[953] Supra, pp 777–8.

[954] See *Ontulmus v Collett* [2013] EWHC 980 (QB).

[955] Supra, p 777.

[956] (1976) 120 Sol Jo 690.

[957] See the defamation example discussed by the Law Commissions in Working Paper No 87 (1984), para 5.91.

(ii) Defamation committed in England

The leading authority on the rule that, if a tort is committed in England, the English courts will apply English law, is a defamation case, *Szalatnay-Stacho v Fink*.[958]

> The defendant, an official of the Czech government, then in exile in England during the Second World War, sent to the President of the Czech Republic, also in England, documents alleging misconduct by the plaintiff, the Czech Acting Minister in Egypt. These documents which were published in England were clearly defamatory of the plaintiff. Under Czech law the documents were absolutely privileged, but under English law only the defence of qualified privilege was available.

The Court of Appeal decided that English law was applicable to this tort committed in England, but that the conduct of the defendant fell within the defence of qualified privilege. Indeed, it was suggested that foreign law could only be applied in a case such as this if it was expressly provided for by legislation.[959]

This case was decided before the introduction of the flexible exception to the general rule of double actionability in the case of foreign torts. It is doubtful whether there is likewise a flexible exception in the case of torts committed in England.[960] But if, for the sake of argument, it is assumed that there is such an exception, when will this come into play? The Law Commissions gave the facts of *Fink's* case as an example of circumstances which might justify the application of a foreign law, ie Czech law.[961] This was because of the strong personal connection of the parties with Czechoslovakia.

(iii) Where is defamation committed?

It is well established that the tort of libel is committed where the libel is published. In *Bata v Bata*,[962] where defamatory letters had been written by the defendant in Zurich and posted to certain addresses in London, it was argued on the basis of the private international law rule, which at that time applied to cases of negligence, that the tort had been committed in Switzerland where the letters had been written and that, therefore, leave to serve the defendant out of the jurisdiction should not be granted. The Court of Appeal, however, held that, since publication is the material element that completes the tort of libel, the cause of action had arisen in England.[963] This was a case decided in the context of jurisdiction. However, the same reasoning was seemingly applied by the Court of Appeal in the choice of law context in *Church of Scientology v Metropolitan Police Comr*.[964] English police officers published an allegedly libelous report to a German Police Authority. The court acted on the basis that the tort was committed in Germany.

Furthermore, in *Jenner v Sun Oil Co*[965] an action was brought against the owners of a radio station who were alleged to have defamed the plaintiff by remarks broadcast in the USA and heard in Ontario. The Ontario High Court granted leave for service out of the jurisdiction, holding that the alleged tort had been committed in Ontario.[966]

---

[958] [1947] KB 1.
[959] Ibid, at 13.
[960] See supra, p 777.
[961] Law Commission Working Paper No 87 (1984), para 5.91.
[962] [1948] WN 366; 92 Sol Jo 574.
[963] See also *Kroch v Rossell et Cie* [1937] 1 All ER 725 where it was enough for publication that a few copies of a foreign newspaper had been sold in England.
[964] (1976) 120 Sol Jo 690.
[965] [1952] 2 DLR 526; see also *Pindling v National Broadcasting Corpn* (1984) 14 DLR (4th) 391.
[966] See also *Gordon v Australian Broadcasting Commission* (1973) 22 FLR 181.

The identification of the place where the tort of defamation is committed when this has occurred over the internet is particularly problematic. The Court of Justice of the European Union defined the place of damage under Art 7(2) Brussels I Recast as the place where the alleged victim has his centre of interests and each place where content placed online is or has been accessible.[967] But there is a further problem with internet defamation, namely the impact of the E-Commerce Directive on the law applicable to this tort.[968] The Court of Justice has now clarified that the country of origin principle of Article 3 of the Directive[969] does not require transposition in the form of a specific conflict-of-laws rule. However, it does preclude a provider of an electronic commerce service from being made subject to stricter requirements than those provided for by the substantive law in force in the Member State in which that service provider is established.[970] Turning to a common law environment, in *Dow Jones & Co Inc v Gutnick*[971] the High Court of Australia had to determine the place where the tort of defamation was committed[972] in the situation where the alleged defamatory material was contained in an online journal. It held that, in this situation, ordinarily the place where the tort of defamation is committed is where the material alleged to be defamatory is downloaded on to the computer of a person who has used a web-browser to pull the material from the web-server. This was preferred to the place of uploading (ie the place where information is made available over the internet by placing it in a storage area managed by a web-server). In England, it is well established that a libel is committed where publication takes place and that a text on the internet is published at the place where it is downloaded.[973] The authorities on this have arisen largely in the jurisdictional context of *forum conveniens* where, in order to determine whether England is the natural forum for trial, it has to be decided whether English law is applicable.[974]

(iv) Multi-state defamation

One edition of a newspaper may be read in numerous countries around the world. A radio broadcast may also be heard in numerous countries. Defamation over the Internet inevitably involves multi-state defamation. Under English law, each publication is regarded as a separate publication and gives rise to a separate cause of action. If a text is downloaded in a hundred countries, there are a hundred publications and the tort is committed in

---

[967] Joined Cases C-509/09 and C-161/10 *eDate Advertising GmbH and Others v X and Société MGN Limited* [2011] ECR I-10269 at [48], [51].

[968] Directive (EC) No 2000/31 of 8 June 2000, OJ 2000 L 178/1 (implemented in the United Kingdom by the Electronic Commerce (EC Directive) Regulations 2002, SI 2002/2013). See Law Commission, Defamation and the Internet: a Preliminary Investigation, Scoping Study No 2, December 2002; Fawcett, Harris and Bridge, paras 21.01–21.19 and 21.120–21.134.

[969] Whereby a service provider established on the territory of a Member State merely has to comply with the national provisions applicable in that Member State.

[970] Joined Cases C-509/09 and C-161/10 *eDate Advertising GmbH and Others v X and Société MGN Limited* [2011] ECR I-10269 at [63], [67]. Still, the impact of this Directive is not always clear, see Dicey, Morris and Collins, paras 35-153–35-162. See also *Payam Tamiz v Google Inc* [2013] EWCA Civ 68.

[971] (2002) 210 CLR 575, HC of Australia; discussed supra, p 353.

[972] This was in the context of *forum non conveniens*. If forum law is applicable this is likely to be decisive.

[973] *Godfrey v Demon Internet Ltd* [2001] QB 201, 208–9; *Loutchansky v Times Newspapers Ltd* [2002] QB 783 at [58], CA; *Harrods Ltd v Dow Jones & Co Inc* [2003] EWHC 1162 (QB) at [36]; *King v Lewis* [2004] EWCA (Civ) 1329 at [26], [2005] IL Pr 16 (this was accepted by the parties); *Richardson v Schwarzenegger* [2004] EWHC 2422 (QB) at [19]; *Dow Jones & Co Inc v Jameel* [2005] EWCA (Civ) 75 at [48]–[49], [2005] QB 946; *Al Amoudi v Brisard* [2006] EWHC 1062 (QB) (the claimant must prove that the information was accessed and downloaded, there is no presumption of law that availability means substantial publication). See also Lord Hoffmann in *Berezovsky v Michaels* [2001] 1 WLR 1004 at 1024 and *Payam Tamiz v Google Inc* [2013] EWCA Civ 68.

[974] See *Harrods Ltd v Dow Jones & Co Inc*, supra; *King v Lewis*, supra.

a hundred countries. If the claimant were to bring a claim based on a hundred separate publications this would not only give rise to choice of law problems (the obvious inconvenience of having to apply a hundred different laws[975]) but also to jurisdictional problems. However, a claimant can base a claim solely on publication in England.[976] If this is established, the English courts will have jurisdiction[977] and will apply the English law of defamation.[978]

---

[975] This has led to various suggestions for a separate choice of law rule for multi-state defamation not based on the place of publication. See Castel (1990) 28 Osgoode Hall LJ 153; the Restatement 2d, Conflict of Laws, § 150(2); *Australian Broadcasting Corpn v Waterhouse* (1991) 25 NSWLR 519 at 539; ALRC No 58 1992, Draft Choice of Law Bill, cl 6(5) applying a claimant's residence rule for all cases of defamation. Application of the flexible exception could result in just one law being applicable, thereby avoiding this difficulty, see *Woodger v Federal Capital Press of Australia Pty Ltd* (1996) 107 ACTR 1 at 36.

[976] This is what happened in *Berezovsky*, supra, and in the internet cases of *Harrods Ltd v Dow Jones & Co Inc*, supra; *King v Lewis*, supra; *Dow Jones & Co Inc v Jameel*, supra; *Richardson v Schwarzenegger*, supra. For jurisdictional purposes it is important that the claimant does so, see supra, p 351.

[977] Under both the Brussels I Recast, Joined Cases C-509/09 and C-161/10 *eDate Advertising GmbH and Others v X and Société MGN Limited* [2011] ECR I-10269 at [48], [51] (in Internet cases, an action at the victim's "centre of interest", normally the habitual residence, can be brought even in respect of all the damage caused, ibid, at [48]), and the traditional English rules (there must be *substantial* publication in England), supra, p 351.

[978] See the discussion, supra, pp 886–7, of defamation committed in England. In EU cases, this would be subject to the country of origin principle in Art 3 Directive 2000/31, Joined Cases C-509/09 and C-161/10 *eDate Advertising GmbH and Others v X and Société MGN Limited* [2011] ECR I-10269 at [63], [67], supra, p 887.

PART V

FAMILY LAW

21. Marriage and Other Adult Relationships	891
22. Matrimonial and Related Causes	951
23. Declarations	1049
24. Financial Relief	1059
25. Children	1087
26. Cross-border Surrogacy	1179
27. Legitimacy, Legitimation and Adoption	1193
28. Mental Incapacity	1232

21

MARRIAGE AND OTHER ADULT RELATIONSHIPS[1]

1. The Meaning of "Marriage"	891		(b) Nature of a polygamous marriage	929
2. Formalities of Marriage	893		(c) What law determines the nature of a	
(a) The general rule	893		marriage?	930
(b) Exceptions to the general rule	901		(d) Can the nature of a marriage change?	933
3. Capacity to Marry	909		(e) Capacity to contract a polygamous	
(a) Introduction	909		marriage	936
(b) The two main theories	910		(f) Recognition of polygamous marriages	
(c) Further issues	918		in England	941
(d) Alternative approaches	924		6. Same Sex Relationships: Civil	
(e) Capacity and recognition of foreign			Partnership and Same Sex Marriage	946
divorces or annulments	925		(a) Introduction	946
4. Reform of General Rules	927		(b) Civil partnership	946
5. Polygamous Marriages	928		(c) Same sex marriage	948
(a) Introduction	928		7. De Facto Cohabitation	949

1. THE MEANING OF "MARRIAGE"

A contract to marry differs fundamentally from a commercial contract,[2] since it creates a status that affects both the parties themselves and the society to which they belong. It is *sui generis*. It is fulfilled on the solemnisation of the marriage ceremony, and thereafter there is a change in the law that governs the relationship between the parties.

There are many different situations in which the existence of a marriage must be established as a preliminary to legal proceedings. The matter may concern many different parts of the law. Thus the institution of a matrimonial cause, such as a petition for divorce or judicial separation, implies that the parties are married to each other. If a person claims an inheritance or money due under an insurance policy as the widow or widower of the deceased; if a beneficiary under a will claims to be free from liability to inheritance tax as being the surviving spouse of the testator; in each case a preliminary to success is proof that a regularly constituted marriage exists. The existence of a marriage tie is equally essential in several departments of criminal law, as, for instance, where a person is prosecuted for bigamy. Again, social security benefits and the operation of the immigration laws may depend on the existence of a valid marriage. All these matters, and indeed many others, may raise a problem of private international law, since the parties in question may, for instance, have gone through

---

[1] Maddaugh (1973) 23 U Tor LJ 117; Swan (1974) 24 U Tor LJ 17, 18–41; Jaffey (1978) 41 MLR 38; North (1980) I Hague Recueil 9; Jaffey (1982) 2 OJLS 368, 369–73; North (1990) I Hague Recueil 9, 49–96 and see Audit, *La Fraude à la Loi*, pp 308–23.

[2] Under the Law Reform (Miscellaneous Provisions) Act 1970, s 1, an agreement to marry does not have effect as a contract.

a marriage ceremony abroad which, though valid by the law of the place of celebration or by the law of the domicile, does not create the status of marriage according to English law.

Each legal system must determine the attributes of marriage. Traditionally, in the eyes of English law, the common factor of every marriage was that of a consensual union between a man and a woman.[3] Indeed, in 1866 Lord Penzance defined marriage "as the voluntary union for life of one man and one woman to the exclusion of all others".[4] Although this definition was long accepted as the standard for marriage, it became largely obsolete following the adoption of the Marriage (Same Sex Couples) Act 2013, which removed the requirement that the union must be heterosexual.[5] Nevertheless, putting aside the gender aspect of the definition, and despite the fact that in the intervening years English law has come to accept as valid for many purposes marriages which are polygamous in nature or in fact[6], the requirement of a life long union (despite the prevalence of divorce) is still a necessary characteristic of marriage in the eyes of English law.[7] Similarly, the requirement that marriage be entered into voluntarily continues to form the basis of this institution in English law.[8]

Until the middle of the nineteenth century, English choice of law rules relating to marriage were undeveloped and simple. All matters were to be referred to the law of the country where the marriage was celebrated. However, in 1861, the House of Lords in *Brook v Brook*[9] drew a distinction between the rules governing formalities and those governing capacity to marry. The facts were these:

> A marriage was celebrated in Denmark between a domiciled Englishman and his deceased wife's sister, also domiciled in England. The marriage was legal by Danish law, but illegal at that date (1850) by English law.

Although the marriage was valid by Danish law, the place where it was celebrated, the House of Lords was unwilling to allow the man to evade the prohibitions of English law, the law of his domicile. In applying English law and holding that the marriage was void, Lord Campbell LC drew the following distinction:

> But while the forms of entering into the contract of marriage are to be regulated by the *lex loci contractus*, the law of the country in which it is celebrated, the essentials of the marriage depend upon the *lex domicilii*, the law of the country in which the parties are domiciled at the time of the marriage, and in which the matrimonial residence is contemplated.[10]

In the light of this decision, two major choice of law issues have to be examined: the choice of law rules governing the formal validity of a marriage and those rules governing its essential validity or capacity to marry, and it is necessary in addition to consider the special problems posed by polygamous marriages, and same sex unions.

---

[3] *Corbett v Corbett (otherwise Ashley)* [1971] P 83; *Bellinger v Bellinger* [2003] UKHL 21; *J v C (Void Marriage: Status of Children)* [2006] EWCA Civ 551, [2006] 2 FLR 1098; *Wilkinson v Kitzinger and Ors* [2006] EWHC 2022 (Fam); Matrimonial Causes Act 1973, s 11(c); Norrie (1994) 43 I CLQ 757, 766–75; and see *Re North and Matheson* (1974) 52 DLR (3d) 280.

[4] *Hyde v Hyde* (1866) LR 1 P & D 130 at 133.

[5] For a more detailed analysis of the Marriage (Same Sex Couples) Act 2013, including the private international law aspects of same sex marriage in England & Wales, see infra p 946 et seq.

[6] Infra, p 928 et seq.

[7] This requirement does not mean that a marriage must be indissoluble, but that in the eyes of the law of the place of celebration it must be potentially indefinite in duration. *Nachimson v Nachimson* [1930] P 217. For a detailed analysis of this case see the 14th edition of this book, pp 876–7.

[8] See Lowe and Douglas, p 38.

[9] (1861) 9 HL Cas 193.

[10] Ibid, at 207.

2. FORMALITIES OF MARRIAGE[11]

(a) The general rule

(i) The rule

There is no rule more firmly established in private international law than that which applies the maxim *locus regit actum* to the formalities of a marriage, ie that an act is governed by the law of the place where it is done. Whether any particular ceremony constitutes a formally valid marriage depends solely on the law of the country where the ceremony takes place.[12] Courts have frequently stressed the absolute nature of both the positive and negative aspects of this principle. "Every marriage must be tried according to the law of the country in which it took place",[13] and if it is good by that law, then, so far as its formal validity alone is concerned "it is good all the world over, no matter whether the proceedings or ceremony which constituted marriage according to the law of the place would or would not constitute marriage in the country of the domicile of one or other of the spouses".[14] The reverse is equally true. "If the so-called marriage is no marriage in the place where it is celebrated, there is no marriage anywhere, although the ceremony or proceedings if conducted in the place of the parties' domicile would be considered a good marriage."[15]

It is also important to note that the application of the law of the place of celebration to the formalities of a marriage is not disturbed even though the sole object of the parties in celebrating their marriage abroad is to evade some irksome requirement of the law of their domicile.[16] Thus in *Simonin v Mallac*:[17]

Two persons, French by domicile, contracted a marriage in London which, though formally valid according to English law, would have been void if tested by French law since

---

[11] See Sykes (1952) 2 ICLQ 78; Mendes da Costa (1958) 7 ICLQ 217; Parry, 8 *British Digest of International Law*, pp 513 et seq; Palsson, *Marriage and Divorce in Comparative Conflict of Laws*, Chapter 6; North (1980) I Hague Recueil 9, 69–77.

[12] *Scrimshire v Scrimshire* (1752) 2 Hag Con 395; *Dalrymple v Dalrymple* (1811) 2 Hag Con 54; *Warrender v Warrender* (1835) 2 Cl & Fin 488 at 530; *Harvey v Farnie* (1882) 8 App Cas 43 at 50; *Berthiaume v Dastous* [1930] AC 79, PC; *Kenward v Kenward* [1951] P 124; and see *R v Bham* [1966] 1 QB 159; *Re X's Marriage* (1983) 65 FLR 132; *Burke v Burke* 1983 SLT 331; *McCabe v McCabe* [1994] 1 FCR 257; *Wicken v Wicken* [1999] 1 FLR 293; *Vuong v Hoang* [1999] CLY 3734; *Chief Adjudication Officer v Bath* [2000] 1 FLR 8; *M v M (Divorce: Jurisdiction: Validity of Marriage)* [2001] 2 FLR 6; *Gandhi v Patel* [2002] 1 FLR 603; *Alfonso-Brown v Milwood* [2006] EWHC 642; *AH v Secretary of State for the Home Department* [2006] UKIAT 38, [2006] INLR 517; *Hudson v Leigh* [2009] EWHC 1306 (Fam), per Bodey J at [34]; *R v M (Validity of Foreign Marriage)* [2011] EWHC 2132 (Fam), per Hullparker J at [19]; *Dukali v Lamrani (Attorney-General Intervening)* [2012] EWHC 1748 (Fam), per Holman J at [23] ; *Asaad v Kurter* [2013] EWHC 3852 (Fam), per Moylan J at [72]; *Khan v Ahmad* [2014] EWHC 3850 (Fam), per Roberts J at [42]; and *N v D (Customary Marriage)* [2015] EWFC 28 per Jackson J at [3] See now, in Scots law, Family Law (Scotland) Act 2006, s 38(1). As to the method of proving a foreign marriage in English proceedings, see Dicey, Morris and Collins, paras 17-039 et seq; and *Wicken v Wicken* [1999] 1 FLR 293, per Holman J, at 228. If there is no ceremony and the courts of the country where the parties are domiciled and resident recognise a marriage by repute, then so will the English courts: *Re Green* (1909) 25 TLR 222. Cf in Scotland *Walker v Roberts* 1998 SLT 1133; and *Ackerman v Logan's Executor (No 1)* 2002 SLT 37.

[13] *Herbert (Lady) v Herbert (Lord)* (1819) 3 Phillim 58 at 63.

[14] *Berthiaume v Dastous* [1930] AC 79 at 83. Cf, in USA, Symeonides (2003) 51 AJCL 82, citing *Xiong v Xiong* 648 NW 2d 900; *Donlam v Maggurn* 55 P 3d 74; and *Hudson Trail Outfitters v District of Columbia Department of Employment Services* 801 A 2d 987.

[15] *Berthiaume v Dastous* [1930] AC 79 at 83. This general rule is subject to certain exceptions, discussed, infra, p 901 et seq.

[16] Eg *Scrimshire v Scrimshire* (1752) 2 Hag Con 395; *Ogden v Ogden* [1908] P 46.

[17] (1860) 2 Sw & Tr 67.

the parental consent required by the Code Napoleon had not been obtained. The wife later petitioned for a decree of nullity.

The court dismissed the petition, for, since the necessary consent, as we have seen,[18] was nothing more than a formality, its absence could not affect a marriage celebrated in England.[19] If, however, a marriage, valid as to form under the law of the place of celebration, but formally void according to the personal law of the parties is later annulled in the courts of their domicile, the decree of nullity will be recognised as effective by an English court even if the marriage was celebrated in England.[20]

One conclusion to be drawn from the rule that the law of the place of celebration governs the formal validity of a marriage is that no marriage in England is formally valid unless it complies with the requirements of English law as laid down, primarily,[21] in the Marriage Act 1949 (as amended).[22] Therefore a marriage according to Romany custom,[23] a marriage in polygamous form,[24] a marriage in an unregistered building,[25] for example a private flat,[26] a consulate[27] or a hotel,[28] or a marriage by an unauthorised celebrant[29] are, in the absence of any further civil ceremony, void. Indeed such a marriage is regarded not so much as a void marriage but as no marriage at all.[30] If there is a civil ceremony as well, it is this alone which

---

[18] Supra, pp 48–9. As regards third party consent to a marriage, see also *M v M (Divorce: Jurisdiction: Validity of Marriage)* [2001] 2 FLR 6, per Hughes J, at para 14 (permission of the government of Saudi Arabia required where the intended wife was a national of that country and the intended husband was not).

[19] And see *Ramos v Ramos* (1911) 27 TLR 515 where failure to register a marriage as required by the law of the domicile did not affect the validity of the marriage.

[20] Infra, p 1005 et seq; see *Salvesen v Administrator of Austrian Property* [1927] AC 641; *De Massa v De Massa* [1939] 2 All ER 150 n; *Galene v Galene* [1939] P 237; *Merker v Merker* [1963] P 283.

[21] There are additional requirements imposed on couples where one is subject to immigration control. See, eg, the Immigration (Procedure for Marriage) Regulations 2011/2678, as amended, and the Asylum and Immigration (Treatment of Claimants, etc) Act 2004, as amended by the Asylum and Immigration (Treatment of Claimants, etc) Act 2004 (Remedial) Order, SI 2011/1158.

[22] See, eg, *Gandhi v Patel* [2002] 1 FLR 603. The parties, in marrying at an Indian restaurant in London in a Hindu ceremony presided over by a Brahmin priest acted in knowing and wilful disregard of English law ([16], [40] and [45]). Per Park J, at [45]: "In the present case the Hindu ceremony . . . purported to be a marriage according to a foreign religion, and it made no attempt to be an English marriage within the Marriage Acts." See also *Gereis v Yagoub* [1997] 1 FLR 854 (Coptic Orthodox Christians married in England according to the rites of their church without any civil formalities required under the 1949 Act); despite the religious ceremony being followed by consummation and a period of cohabitation, Aglionby J granted a nullity decree on the basis that the parties had knowingly and wilfully intermarried in England in disregard of the requirements of English law.

[23] National Insurance Decision No R (S) 4/59.

[24] Cf *R v Ali Mohamed* [1964] 2 QB 350 n; *R v Bham* [1966] 1 QB 159.

[25] Marriage Act 1949, s 41; *Gereis v Yagoub* [1997] 1 FLR 854; and *M v M (Divorce: Jurisdiction: Validity of Marriage)* [2001] 2 FLR 6, per Hughes J, at [39]. There is special provision for the marriage of Quakers and Jews and for the marriage by Registrar General's licence and by Archbishop's licence.

[26] *El Gamal v Al Maktoum* [2011] EWHC B27 (Fam).

[27] *Dukali v Lamrani (Attorney-General Intervening)* [2012] EWHC 1748 (Fam) (the Moroccan consulate in London).

[28] *Sharbatly v Shagroon* [2012] EWCA Civ 1507.

[29] *Gereis v Yagoub* [1997] 1 FLR 854.

[30] On the distinction between a void marriage and a "non-marriage", see *Gereis v Yagoub* [1997] 1 FLR 854, per Aglionby J, at 857 (a void marriage case); *M v M (Divorce: Jurisdiction: Validity of Marriage)* [2001] 2 FLR 6, per Hughes J, at [23]; *Gandhi v Patel* [2002] 1 FLR 603, per Park J, at paras [31], [37], [45]–[47] (a non-marriage case); *Burns v Burns* [2007] EWHC 2492 (Fam), per Coleridge J, at [48] and [49] (a void marriage case); and, in particular, *Hudson v Leigh* [2009] EWHC 1306 (Fam), per Bodey J, in particular at [70] and [79] (a non-marriage case). *Hudson v Leigh* was followed in *Al-Saedy v Musawi* [2010] EWHC 3293 (Fam), per Bodey J, at [66] and [68] (a non-marriage case); *El Gamal v Al-Maktoum* [2011] EWHC B27 (Fam), per Bodey J, at [86] and [87] (a non-marriage case); *Galloway v Goldstein* [2012] EWHC 60 (Fam), per Mostyn J, at [13]–[15] (a non-marriage case); and *Dukali v Lamrani (Attorney-General Intervening)* [2012] EWHC 1748 (Fam), per Holman J, at [36]–[37] (a non-marriage case), and cited with approval

the law recognises.[31] Where, however, parties marry in England without acting "knowingly and wilfully" in breach of the provisions of the Marriage Act 1949,[32] the marriage is not necessarily denied effect. This point arose in *Chief Adjudication Officer v Bath*:[33]

> A couple went through a Sikh marriage ceremony conducted by a Sikh priest in accordance with Sikh custom and religion at a Sikh temple in London which, at the material time, was not registered.[34] The marriage was not registered in a register office. The result was that there had not been a valid ceremony in accordance with the Marriage Act 1949. However, it could not be inferred that the couple had "knowingly and wilfully" failed to comply with the relevant statutory provisions.

The court relied on the common law presumption that when there is evidence of a ceremony of marriage having been gone through, followed by the cohabitation of the parties, everything necessary for the validity of the marriage will be presumed in the absence of evidence to the contrary. Having established that the couple was unaware of the fact of the temple's non-registered status, Evans LJ stated:

> There is no statutory provision that a marriage otherwise carried out in proper form, by an authorised celebrant and at a place of worship eligible to be registered under the [1949] Act, is invalid merely on the ground that the building was not registered for whatever reason.[35]

The marriage was not rendered void by section 49 of the 1949 Act. Robert Walker LJ reached the same decision by reference to the presumption of marriage arising from long cohabitation, and the absence of compelling evidence to rebut that presumption:[36] The High Court subsequently held that the presumption would be rebutted where the purported wedding ceremony failed to comply with the Marriage Act 1949 (as amended) to the extent that it did not attain the status of marriage in English law, ie it was neither a valid nor a void marriage but rather a non-marriage.[37] Indeed, "[w]ere it otherwise, it would be tantamount to elevating a presumption born of common-sense into the status of a rule of substance, whereby long cohabitation plus a reputation of marriage would establish marriage, even when all the identified evidence showed that no valid or even void marriage ever took place".[38] No guidance has been given by the High Court in relation to the required length of cohabitation;[39] nevertheless, the period of fourteen years was held to be insufficiently long to give rise to the presumption of marriage.[40] In *Al-Saedy v Musawi*[41] the petitioner "wife" asserted that the parties had been married in a ceremony in Damascus in March 2006. This claim

---

in *Asaad v Kurter* [2013] EWHC 3852 (Fam), per Moylan J, at [100] (a void marriage case). The Court of Appeal confirmed the existence of the concept of 'non-marriage' in *Sharbatly v Shagroon* [2012] EWCA Civ 1507, per Hedley J at [40] (a non-marriage case). See also Probert (2002) 22 Legal Studies 398, and [2013] CFLQ 314. For declarations in non-marriage cases see Chapter 23.

[31] *Qureshi v Qureshi* [1972] Fam 173 at 186.

[32] Pt III, s 49.

[33] [2000] 1 FLR 8. Regrettably the court did not hear any submissions on *Gereis v Yagoub* [1997] 1 FLR 854; see Robert Walker LJ in *Chief Adjudication Officer v Bath*, at [8].

[34] Subsequently it became registered.

[35] At [33].

[36] *M v M (Divorce: Jurisdiction: Validity of Marriage)* [2001] 2 FLR 6, per Hughes J, at [34] et seq (a period of cohabitation of nearly twenty years was held as sufficient to establish the presumption of marriage).

[37] See *Al-Saedy v Musawi* [2010] EWHC 3293 (Fam) and *Dukali v Lamrani (Attorney-General Intervening)* [2012] EWHC 1748 (Fam). See n 39.

[38] *Al-Saedy v Musawi* [2010] EWHC 3293 (Fam), per Bodey J at [71].

[39] In *Dukali v Lamrani (Attorney-General Intervening)* [2012] EWHC 1748 (Fam), Holman J expressly refused to give any guidance on how long the parties should have lived together, however, he opined that "a longer period of seven or eight years must be required", at [33].

[40] *Al-Saedy v Musawi* [2010] EWHC 3293 (Fam), per Bodey J at [72].

[41] [2010] EWHC 3293 (Fam).

was denied by the respondent. The court found that what in fact took place in March 1996 was a family gathering in the respondent's flat in London, which contained multiple failures to comply with the English law of formalities. Unlike the ceremony in *Chief Adjudication Officer v Bath*,[42] the family gathering in the present case suffered from defects which were not "trivial" and the event could not be considered as a "bona fide ceremony" in terms of complying with the Marriage Act 1949.[43] Hence, Bodey J held that the ceremony amounted to a non-marriage, allowing the "husband" to succeed in rebutting the presumption of marriage. Moreover, a cohabitation period of fourteen years was not regarded as sufficiently long to give rise to the presumption of marriage. The length of cohabitation and the nature of the purported marriage ceremony prevented the application of the presumption of marriage also in *Dukali v Lamrani (Attorney-General Intervening)*.[44] In this case, the parties went through a Moroccan civil marriage ceremony at the consulate in London. As foreign consulates and embassies are not approved or registered buildings under the Marriage Act, the ceremony was not effective as a valid or at least a void marriage in English law. Consequently, there was "simply no room for applying the presumption".[45] Moreover, the period of cohabitation (seven years) was deemed too short to establish the presumption.

A presumption of formal validity of marriage arising from long cohabitation operates also when the marriage ceremony took place abroad.[46] For example, in *Vuong v Hoang*[47] the parties went through a marriage ceremony before ancestral stones in China. The ceremony was not registered under Chinese law. Nevertheless, Curl J held that the strong presumption of a valid marriage arising when a marriage ceremony is followed by cohabitation had not been diminished by increasingly liberal social attitudes. Similarly, in *Pazpena de Vire v Pazpena de Vire*[48] where the parties lived together as husband and wife for thirty-five years following a proxy marriage ceremony in Uruguay, Mark Harrison QC held that where there had been a lengthy cohabitation, the presumption of marriage could be rebutted only by clear evidence that there had been no marriage ceremony or that formalities had not been complied with. There was no such evidence in the instant case, and therefore the presumption was not rebutted. In several more recent authorities, the presumption was mentioned but eventually not relied on. In particular, in *R v M (Validity of Foreign Marriage)*[49] a marriage ceremony took place in Pakistan between two members of the Pakistani Ahmadi community. The ceremony was eventually recognized as having effected a valid marriage, without the need to rely on the presumption of marriage based on cohabitation and repute. Nevertheless, Parker J impliedly considered the presumption as an alternative avenue to uphold the validity of the marriage as he explored the existence of the presumption under Pakistani law. He concluded that there was a strong evidential presumption of a marriage based upon cohabitation and reputation in Pakistani law. Similarly, in *N v D (Customary Marriage)*[50] the presumption of marriage based on cohabitation and repute was mentioned, although eventually it was not relied on as there was "abundant actual evidence" relating to the marriage.[51] The presumption was considered briefly also in *Asaad v Kurter*[52]—a case where the parties went through a ceremony in a Syriac

---

[42] [2000] 1 FLR 8, discussed supra.
[43] [2010] EWHC 3293 (Fam), at [66].
[44] [2012] EWHC 1748 (Fam).
[45] Ibid, at [35].
[46] Eg *Mahadervan v Mahadervan* [1964] P 233 (marriage in Ceylon); and *Wicken v Wicken* [1999] 1 FLR 293 (civil marriage ceremony in England followed by Muslim marriage ceremony in the Gambia).
[47] [1999] CLY 3734.
[48] [2001] 1 FLR 460.
[49] [2011] EWHC 2132 (Fam).
[50] [2015] EWFC 28.
[51] Ibid, per Jackson J, at [69].
[52] [2013] EWHC 3852 (Fam).

Orthodox Church in Syria. The presumption was, however, "clearly rebutted" as "the requirements necessary to effect a valid marriage under Syrian law were not fulfilled".[53]

(ii) Retrospectivity

It seems almost axiomatic that the question whether the status of husband and wife has been acquired must be determined once and for all by reference to the law of the place of celebration as it stood at the time when the parties went through the ceremony of marriage. According to this view, the verdict of that law at that time, whether in favour of, or adverse to, the acquisition of a married status, will be unaffected by a later change in its provisions. Otherwise the relationship between the parties will remain insecure. In *Starkowski v A-G*,[54] however, this conclusion was not fully accepted by the House of Lords, which held that a marriage void at the time of its celebration may be validated by a subsequent and retroactive change in the law of the place of celebration.[55]

> H and W, Polish both by nationality and domicile, were married in Austria on 19 May 1945. The marriage was void by Austrian law since the ceremony was religious. On 12 June, a daughter, Barbara, was born to them. As from 30 June, Austrian legislation retrospectively validated such religious marriages, subject to their registration in a public register. In 1949, by which time H and W had both acquired a domicile in England, their marriage was registered in Austria, so that, by Austrian law, the parties were then regarded as having been lawfully married since 19 May 1945. In 1950 W and X went through a ceremony of marriage at Croydon. They had a son, Christopher, born before this marriage.

As indicated earlier, the existence of a marriage may be called into question in many different situations, and here the House of Lords was concerned with the question of Christopher's legitimacy.[56] If the marriage between H and W was still valid in 1950, W and X were bigamously married, Barbara was legitimate, and Christopher illegitimate. On the other hand, if it was void, Barbara was illegitimate, but Christopher had been legitimated by the ceremony of 1950. Thus the crucial question was whether the validity of the marriage between H and W was determinable according to the state of Austrian law on 19 May or on 30 June, when the retrospective legislation came into force. It was held that the latter was the appropriate date.

The answers to the two main arguments against this solution were not altogether convincing. The objection that the status of parties domiciled in England can scarcely be altered by the law of the country with which they are no longer connected was ruled out on the ground that the Austrian legislation dealt with formalities rather than with status. The further objection, that the parties to a void marriage will be unable to rely on their unmarried status if the ceremony remains liable to validation, was met by the reflection that validation will normally not be long delayed.

If the marriage between W and X had preceded the retrospective validation of the marriage between W and H, then it is suggested that the validation would not be recognised so as to nullify the second marriage which was wholly valid when entered into.[57] Similarly, if an English court had granted a decree of nullity in relation to the first marriage, the validity of

---

[53] Ibid, per Moylan J, at [50].

[54] [1954] AC 155; and see *Re Howe Louis* (1970) 14 DLR (3d) 49.

[55] If an act such as registration is required for the retrospective validation of a marriage, then the marriage remains invalid until that act is done: *Pilinski v Pilinska* [1955] 1 All ER 631; see Thomas (1954) 3 ICLQ 353; Mendes da Costa (1958) 7 ICLQ 217, 251–60; Sinclair (1952) 29 BYBIL 479, (1953) 30 BYBIL 523.

[56] Cf *Azad v Entry Clearance Officer (Dhaka)* [2001] Imm AR 318, [2001] INLR 109; and *R (Shamsun Nahar) v The Social Security Commissioners* [2002] 1 FLR 670.

[57] This point is left open by the House of Lords in *Starkowski v A-G* [1954] AC 155 at 168, 171–2, 176, 182; but support for this conclusion is provided by *Ambrose v Ambrose* (1961) 25 DLR (2d) 1.

that decree ought not to be affected by any later act of registration.[58] If the marriage between W and X came after the retrospective validation of the earlier marriage, but W was domiciled at the time of her second marriage in a country which did not recognise the effect of the validation, then the second marriage ought to be regarded in England as valid.[59]

(iii) What are matters of form?

The statement that a marriage good by the law of the place of celebration is good all the world over is accurate only if confined to the question of formal validity. Essential validity is, as we shall see,[60] a matter for the personal law of the parties. This distinction may raise the question whether a particular rule obtaining in the place of the ceremony affects form or essence. Some matters seem clearly to be formal in character,[61] such as whether a religious or civil ceremony is required, the time and place of the ceremony, the persons by whom marriage ceremonies may be conducted, the need for witnesses, registration of the marriage,[62] prior notification of the ceremony or a requirement of premarital blood tests. It has been established, for instance, that a rule which permits a marriage by proxy must be classified as formal since it is concerned with the manner in which the marriage ceremony may be performed.[63] Thus, if a woman, domiciled and resident in England, executes a power of attorney appointing X to act as her representative in the celebration of a marriage between her and Y in a country where marriage by proxy is recognised,[64] and the ceremony is in fact performed, the formal validity of the marriage cannot be impugned. A marriage ceremony solemnised in such a manner, though not possible in England, is not regarded as contrary to English public policy.[65] Indeed, the Court of Appeal has upheld the formal validity of a foreign marriage under customary law where neither spouse was present, both being in England at the time of the foreign ceremony.[66] A variation of this factual scenario occurred in *Westminster City Council v IC (A Protected Party by His Litigation Friend) and Ors*,[67] where an Islamic marriage ceremony was conducted over the telephone between a woman located in Bangladesh and a man located in England. No argument was raised regarding the place of celebration of the marriage as the parties had agreed that the *locus celebrationis* was Bangladesh. Thorpe LJ noted that English courts had not previously been presented with the problem of a marriage by telephone with one spouse in country A and the other in country B. His Lordship, however, accepted the

---

[58] *Salvesen v Administrator of Austrian Property* [1927] AC 641 at 651.

[59] See Law Commission Working Paper No 89 (1985), para 2.11. The Commission recommended, at paras 4.1–4.13, that there should be no legislative reform of the rules on retrospectivity, a view adopted in Law Com No 165 (1987), para 2.13. The rule now contained in the Family Law (Scotland) Act 2006, s 38(1) does not specify the time at which the formal validity of a marriage should be determined.

[60] Infra, p 909 et seq.

[61] See, eg, *Gandhi v Patel* [2002] 1 FLR 603, per Park J, at [34].

[62] *R v M (Validity of Foreign Marriage)* [2011] EWHC 2132 (Fam)—a marriage entered into in Pakistan between two members of the Pakistani Ahmadi community was recognised as valid, although it had not been registered in Pakistan. On the facts of the case, it was the ceremony and not any form of registration that created validity. Ahmadis, even though they were not recognised as Muslims, were not in any different position from adherents to other religious groups who also could not register their marriages in Pakistan.

[63] *Apt v Apt* [1948] P 83; *Ponticelli v Ponticelli* [1958] P 204; *Birang v Birang* (1977) 7 Fam Law 172; and *Pazpena de Vire v Pazpena de Vire* [2001] 1 FLR 460. Nevertheless, in the specific context of immigration for the purposes of EU law it has recently been held that the marriage must be valid also under the national law of the qualifying EEA national. *Kareem v Secretary of State for the Home Department* [2014] UKUT 00024 (IAC).

[64] Cf National Insurance Decision No R (G) 3/74.

[65] *Apt v Apt*, supra; *Ponticelli v Ponticelli*, supra; *Pazpena de Vire v Pazpena de Vire*, supra.

[66] *McCabe v McCabe* [1994] 1 FCR 257. Cf *Alfonso-Brown v Milwood* [2006] EWHC 642.

[67] [2008] EWCA Civ 198. See Probert (2008) FLQ 395. On the problem of a marriage entered into over the telephone see also the Scottish case of *A v K* [2011] CSOH 101. For a detailed analysis of this case see Crawford & Carruthers 11-21.

agreement that had been reached between the parties in the present case, although without endorsing it. Nevertheless, he expressed regret over the fact that in the present case this vital issue was dealt with "without the investigation it required" but concluded that the problem was to be left for a decision in an appropriate future case.[68]

The other important area where the issue of the classification of a particular rule as one of capacity or form has arisen is that of parental consent to marry. It has been seen[69] that English law classifies this as a question of form in relation to consent both under English and under foreign law.[70]

(iv) Marriages in foreign consulates and embassies

It is not wholly clear what the present law is as to celebration of marriages in consulates and embassies. The question of the formal validity of a marriage celebrated in a foreign consulate abroad was considered in *Radwan v Radwan (No 2)*:[71]

> In 1951, the husband, domiciled in Egypt, married Ikbal in Egypt in polygamous form. In 1952, he married the petitioner, Mary, a domiciled Englishwoman, in the Egyptian Consulate General in Paris, in polygamous form, and their matrimonial home was established in Egypt. In 1953, the husband divorced Ikbal by *talak*. In 1956, the husband and Mary came to live in England, where they acquired a domicile. In 1970, the husband obtained a *talak* divorce from Mary in the Egyptian Consulate General in London and then Mary petitioned the English courts for divorce.

This matrimonial saga raises a number of separate issues, not all of which were considered in a logical sequence in the proceedings and some of which must be dealt with at greater length elsewhere. First, it was held that the *talak* divorce in the Egyptian Consulate General could not be recognised in England because the diplomatic premises were to be regarded as English and not Egyptian territory.[72] There was, however, the logically anterior question of the validity of the marriage in the Egyptian Consulate General in Paris and this was considered in the later proceedings in the case.[73] Two questions had to be examined—whether the parties had capacity and whether the marriage was formally valid. Cumming-Bruce J decided that, although Mary was incapable by English law of entering a polygamous marriage, she was capable by Egyptian law, the law of the intended matrimonial home.[74] As to formal validity, the court held that the Egyptian Consulate General in Paris was to be regarded as French, and not Egyptian, territory.[75] French law, as the law of the place of celebration, had to be applied to questions of formal validity. The court presumed the marriage to be formally valid in the absence of decisive evidence of French law to rebut this presumption.

Whilst this case provides clear authority for the view that a marriage abroad in a foreign embassy or consulate[76] must comply with the formalities of the receiving state, there remains

---

[68] Ibid, at [39]. Wall LJ expressed a similar view as he noted that in another case he would "welcome the point being fully argued", at [50].

[69] Supra, pp 47–9.

[70] *Simonin v Mallac* (1860) 2 Sw & Tr 67; *Ogden v Ogden* [1908] P 46; *Lodge v Lodge* (1963) 107 Sol Jo 437; see also *Bliersbach v McEwen* 1959 SC 43; Anton and Francescakis [1958] Jur Rev 253. In Scots law, s 38(5) of the Family Law (Scotland) Act 2006 classifies the requirement of a third party's consent to marry as a rule of essential validity. Crawford and Carruthers, para 11-32.

[71] [1973] Fam 35.

[72] *Radwan v Radwan* [1973] Fam 24; Polonsky (1973) 22 ICLQ 343. The divorce recognition aspect of the case is considered infra, p 1017.

[73] [1973] Fam 35.

[74] This aspect of the case is discussed infra, p 914.

[75] See also *R v Turnbull, ex p Petroff* (1971) 17 FLR 438.

[76] Marriages abroad in British consulates are discussed infra, pp 901–2.

the problem of marriages in England in foreign diplomatic premises.[77] There is some authority for the view that such marriages are formally valid if both parties are nationals and, perhaps, domiciliaries of the foreign state.[78] The opinion has been expressed at the diplomatic, rather than judicial, level that marriages in a foreign embassy between nationals of the sending state will be regarded as valid, but that, apart from diplomatic convention, consular marriages must comply with the formalities of English law.[79] The rejection of the idea of extra-territoriality is certainly consistent with the reasoning in *Radwan v Radwan (No 2)*[80] where the decision that the marriage in Paris must comply with French law was supported by reference to the earlier conclusion[81] that the divorce in London must be regarded as an English and not an Egyptian divorce.

(v) Renvoi

It has been assumed up to this point that formalities are to be governed by the internal law of the place of celebration; but there is some authority that the doctrine of renvoi[82] applies in this area with the result that a marriage will be formally valid if it complies with the formal requirements of whatever law is selected by the choice of law rules of the place of celebration.[83] In *Taczanowska v Taczanowski*:[84]

> Two Polish nationals, domiciled in Poland, were married in Italy in 1946 in a military camp, the husband being a member of the Allied occupation forces in Italy. The ceremony did not comply with the formal requirements of Italian law, but the court considered[85] the rule of Italian law that the marriage would be regarded as valid by the Italian courts if it complied with the formal requirements of Polish law, the law of the parties' common nationality.

In fact the marriage was not formally valid under Polish law, though it was held valid in England as an exception to the general rule of reference to the law of the place of celebration.[86] Nevertheless, it seems to have been assumed that the English courts would have regarded the marriage as formally valid had Polish law so regarded it, applying the renvoi doctrine of transmission from Italian law.

What is the position if a marriage satisfies the formal requirements of the domestic law of the place of celebration, but not those of the country referred to by its choice of law rules? Although there is no direct authority on this issue,[87] it has been suggested that, in the interests

---

[77] And see *Khan v Khan* (1959) 21 DLR (2d) 171 at 176.

[78] *Bailet v Bailet* (1901) 17 TLR 317; and see *Pertreis v Tondear* (1790) 1 Hag Con 136; *Ruding v Smith* (1821) 2 Hag Con 371 at 386.

[79] Parry, 8 *British Digest of International Law*, pp 631–45.

[80] [1973] Fam 35.

[81] *Radwan v Radwan* [1973] Fam 24 (followed eg in *Dukali v Lamrani (Attorney-General Intervening)* [2012] EWHC 1748 (Fam) (a marriage between two English domiciliaries of Moroccan origin at the Moroccan Consulate in London).

[82] Supra, pp 71–2.

[83] The Family Law (Scotland) Act 2006 is silent on the subject of renvoi. Since the Act does not expressly exclude the operation of renvoi, a Scottish court may be open to applying the *lex loci celebrationis* in its entirety; see Crawford and Carruthers, para 11-24. The doctrine of renvoi has been explicitly adopted by the Civil Partnership Act 2004 in respect of the formal validity of a civil partnership formed overseas. In particular, the parties must comply with the formalities of the *lex loci registrationis* "including its rules of private international law": ss 215(1) and 212(3), see infra, n 536 (civil partnership). (Note that in the context of civil partnerships renvoi applies also to capacity to enter into an overseas civil partnership, see infra, n 293.

[84] [1957] P 301, and see *Hooper v Hooper* [1959] 1 WLR 1021.

[85] Ibid, at 305, 318.

[86] Infra, p 905 et seq.

[87] In *Hooper v Hooper* [1959] 1 WLR 1021 a marriage in Baghdad was held formally invalid for failure to comply with the requirements of English law, which law was to be applied under Iraqi choice of law rules; but it does not appear from the brief report whether the domestic law of Iraq had been satisfied.

of upholding the validity of marriage, the English courts should regard the marriage as valid if it complies either with the domestic law of the place of celebration or with the system of law which would be applied by that country's choice of law rules. The Law Commission,[88] whilst supporting generally the application of the doctrine of renvoi in the case of formal validity of marriage in the interests of upholding the validity of marriages and promoting uniformity of status,[89] rejected such an alternative reference rule, despite its convenience, on the ground that it would lead to the marriage being regarded in England as formally valid, though not so regarded in the place of celebration.

(b) Exceptions to the general rule

There are two statutory exceptions and one common law exception to the rule that the law of the place of celebration governs formalities.

(i) The two statutory exceptions

Prior to the adoption of the Marriage (Same Sex Couples) Act 2013, the two statutory exceptions to the *lex loci celebrationis* rule were contained in the Foreign Marriage Act 1892 (as amended). The 1892 Act was repealed by the Section 13(2) of the 2013 Act, and in its place Schedule 6 to the 2013 Act has effect.[90] Schedule 6 is titled "Marriage overseas", and deals with marriages in British consulates overseas;[91] certificates of no impediment issued to facilitate overseas marriages and civil partnerships carried out under local laws;[92] and marriages on armed forces bases overseas.[93] This statutory framework provides uniform rules for opposite sex and same sex couples. A consular marriage or a marriage of a member of British forces serving abroad contracted under these statutory provisions is necessarily formally valid in England, regardless of whether it complies with the law of the country where the marriage was celebrated.[94] However, any real danger that a marriage solemnised under the 2013 Act may be regarded as void under the law of the country where it took place has been virtually eliminated by the provisions of Schedule 6 to the Act (see below).

(a) Consular marriage under UK law[95]

What is generally called a "consular marriage" is the first exception. Schedule 6 to the 2013 Act contains conditions that must be met before a consular marriage can take place: (a) at least one of the persons proposing to marry must be a United Kingdom national; (b) the persons proposing to marry would have been eligible to marry each other in a specified part of the United Kingdom; (c) the authorities of the country or territory in which the consulate is located will not object; and (d) there are insufficient facilities for them to marry under the law of that country or territory.[96]

---

[88] Law Commission Working Paper No 89 (1985), paras 2.39–2.42; and see the views of the Irish Law Reform Commission: LRC 19–1985, p 152.

[89] A view not broadly supported on consultation: Law Com No 165 (1987), para 2.5.

[90] Section 13 of the Marriage (Same Sex Couples) Act 2013 extends also to Scotland. See Crawford and Carruthers, para 11-24.

[91] Schedule 6, Part 1. See also Consular Marriages and Marriages under Foreign Law (No 2) Order 2014, SI 2014/3265.

[92] Schedule 6, Part 2. See also Consular Marriages and Marriages under Foreign Law (No 2) Order 2014, SI 2014/3265.

[93] Schedule 6, Part 3. See also Overseas Marriage (Armed Forces) Order 2014, SI 2014/1108.

[94] Schedule 6, Part 1, s 5; and Schedule 6, Part 3, s 11.

[95] See Civil Partnership Act 2004, s 210 and Civil Partnership (Registration Abroad and Certificates) Order, SI 2005/2761 for corresponding provisions regarding the registration of civil partnerships by a British Consular Officer.

[96] Schedule 6, Part 1, s 1. In relation to same sex couples, sub-paragraph 1(d) covers also situations where same sex marriage is not permitted under the law of that country or territory (Explanatory Note).

A registration officer is not required to solemnise a marriage if to do so "would be inconsistent with international law or the comity of nations".[97]

(b) Marriage[98] of forces personnel under UK law

Schedule 6 to the Marriage (Same Sex Couples) Act 2013 provides also for the marriage of members of British forces serving abroad.[99] A marriage can be solemnised in accordance with these provisions only if the following conditions are met:

(a)   at least one of the people proposing to marry is—
  (i)   a member of Her Majesty's forces serving in the country or territory in which it is proposed that they marry,
  (ii) a relevant civilian who is employed in that country or territory,[100] or
  (iii) a child of a person falling within sub-paragraph (i) or (ii) whose home is with that person in that country or territory,[101] and
(b)   the people proposing to marry would have been eligible to marry each other in such part of the United Kingdom as is determined in accordance with the Order.[102]

"The country or territory" includes the waters of the country or territory.[103] It follows that the term "Her Majesty's forces" covers forces serving in a ship in the waters of the country or territory.[104]

(ii) The common law exception

There are certain exceptional circumstances in which a marriage may be recognised even though it has not been solemnised according to the law of the place of celebration, provided it satisfies the form required by the common law of England. Before discussing the nature of these exceptional circumstances, the meaning of a "common law marriage" must be clarified.

(a) Meaning of "common law marriage"[105]

It has long been admitted that there may be peculiar circumstances which allow a marriage not solemnised according to the law of the place of celebration to be recognised as valid if it satisfies the forms required by the common law of England. Before discussing the nature of these circumstances, it must be made clear what is meant by a "common law marriage", or, as it is better called, a "canon law marriage", since it emerged at a time when the canon law governed the matrimonial affairs of Christians throughout Western Europe.[106]

The only essential to the formal validity of a marriage required by the original common law was that the parties should take each other as husband and wife. In 1843, however, the

---

[97] Schedule 6, Part 1, s 2.

[98] See Civil Partnership Act 2004, s 211 and The Civil Partnership (Armed Forces) Order, SI 2005/3188 for corresponding provisions regarding the registration of a civil partnership in respect of a member of Her Majesty's armed forces serving abroad.

[99] Schedule 6, Part 3.

[100] "A relevant civilian" is a civilian subject to service discipline within the meaning of the Armed Forces Act 2006. Schedule 6, Part 3, s 12(2). The term includes a civilian employed in a ship in the waters of a country or territory. S 12(1)(c).

[101] Where one person ("P") treats, or has treated, another person ("C"), as a child of the family in relation to a marriage or civil partnership to which P is or was a party, C is to regarded for the purposes of this provision as the child of "P". Schedule 6, Part 3, s 3.

[102] Ibid, s 2.

[103] Ibid, s 12(1)(a).

[104] Ibid, s 12(1)(b).

[105] Hall [1987] CLJ 106.

[106] There is Irish authority that a potentially polygamous marriage is excluded: *Conlon v Mohamed* [1989] ILRM 523.

further common law condition was added that an episcopally ordained priest or deacon, whether of the English or Roman Catholic Church, should perform the ceremony. This was decided by the House of Lords in *R v Millis*,[107] where it was held, though in a rather unsatisfactory manner,[108] that a marriage celebrated in Ireland by a Presbyterian minister according to the rites of the Presbyterian Church[109] was invalid. Lord Hardwicke's Marriage Act[110] did not extend to Ireland, and therefore marriages in that country were governed by the common law. This rule, that no common law marriage is valid without the intervention of an episcopally ordained priest, is one that almost certainly lacks historical justification;[111] but its applicability to English common law marriages seems clear, although it may well be thought undesirable.[112]

There are several situations in which a marriage may be celebrated out of England and we shall have to consider them in turn to determine whether the marriage is formally valid if it satisfies the requirements of the common law.

(b) Where the common law is in force in the foreign country
The first situation is where the common law of England continues to govern the parties even in the foreign country where they take each other as husband and wife. This can be illustrated by the early days of colonialism. It was consistently recognised as a matter of constitutional law that the British settlers in such countries as Australia took English common law with them, but only so much of it as was suitable to the local conditions.[113] Tested by this principle, it seems clear that the rule of the common law requiring the intervention of an episcopally ordained priest could scarcely be extended to a marriage contracted in a colony during the early days of the colonisation when there was no Church establishment and no division of the country into parishes.[114] The weight of judicial opinion was for many years in favour of treating the rule in *R v Millis* as being confined to marriages in England and Ireland;[115] and in *Catterall v Catterall*[116] Dr Lushington held that a marriage which had been celebrated in Sydney in 1835 by a Presbyterian minister was valid at common law.

The position may be illustrated by two cases from a rather more modern setting. In *Wolfenden v Wolfenden*:[117]

> A Canadian, whose domicile of choice appears to have been English, went through a ceremony of marriage with a Canadian woman in China. The ceremony was performed, not by an episcopally ordained priest, but by the local minister of the Church of Scotland Mission. A Chinese Order in Council was in force which, after reciting that a treaty had given His

---

[107] (1844) 10 Cl & Fin 534.

[108] The four judges of the Irish Court of Queen's Bench were equally divided, and Perrin J, who had held the marriage valid, formally withdrew his judgment in order that an appeal might be taken to the House of Lords. The case was there argued before six Law Lords and ten judges. A unanimous opinion of all the judges in favour of the invalidity of the marriage was read by Tindal CJ, who explained, however, that lack of time had prevented a proper investigation of the case. The Law Lords, were, however, equally divided.

[109] Whose ministers are not episcopally ordained.

[110] Of 1753.

[111] The majority of canonists and historians consider the decision in *R v Millis* to be wrong; see Pollock and Maitland, *History of English Law*, Vol II, pp 370–2; *Merker v Merker* [1963] P 283 at 293–4; and see Lucas [1990] CLJ 117.

[112] Hall [1987] CLJ 106, 120.

[113] Blackstone, *Commentaries on the Laws of England*, i, 108.

[114] *Maclean v Cristall* (1849) Perry's Oriental Cases 75.

[115] *Beamish v Beamish* (1861) 9 HL Cas 274 at 348, 352; *Lightbody v West* (1903) 18 TLR 526.

[116] (1847) 1 Rob Eccl 580. There was in fact a local marriage statute which had not been observed, but Dr Lushington had already held in *Catterall v Sweetman* (1845) 1 Rob Eccl 304 that the statute did not avoid all marriages failing to satisfy its requirements.

[117] [1946] P 61. A similar case was *Phillips v Phillips* (1921) 38 TLR 150.

Majesty the King jurisdiction in the Republic of China, proceeded to establish a system of judicature there and provided that the civil jurisdiction of every court acting under the Order should "as far as circumstances permit be exercised on the principle of and in conformity with English law for the time being in force".

Lord Merriman P held that the marriage was valid at common law. The parties had freely consented to it and the circumstances precluded the presence of an episcopally ordained priest.

A similar decision was reached in *Penhas v Tan Soo Eng*.[118] Certain charters of justice issued in the first half of the nineteenth century introduced English law into Singapore, but provided that it should be administered in such manner as the religions, manners and customs of the inhabitants would admit. Therefore, a marriage ceremony in 1937 between a Jew and a Chinese woman, both British subjects domiciled in Singapore, at which the man observed the Jewish custom but the woman followed the Chinese rites, was held to be valid at common law. The parties intended the composite ceremony to record that they took each other as man and wife. The rule in *R v Millis* was inapplicable.

It has never been doubted that a marriage in a foreign country, where local formalities are non-existent or where those that exist are inapplicable to an English marriage, is valid if it is contracted in the presence of an episcopally ordained priest.[119] What is not clear is whether the requirement of celebration by an episcopally ordained priest can be ignored even if there is no difficulty in obtaining such services. In such a case, the weight of authority favours compliance with the requirement.[120] Strictly speaking, a marriage held to be valid in the types of case just considered is not a true exception to the doctrine *locus regit actum* for, so far as the parties are concerned, the law of the place of celebration is none other than the common law.[121]

(c) Insuperable difficulty

The second exceptional situation is where the parties, though not subject to the common law in the foreign place of celebration have, nevertheless, without regard to the local formalities, taken each other as husband and wife at a ceremony performed, usually, by an episcopally ordained priest. In such a case the marriage will be regarded as valid if compliance with the local formalities had been prevented by some insuperable difficulty.[122] What is meant by insuperable difficulty has been expressed in various ways. Lord Stowell considered that "legal or religious difficulties" might justify a relaxation of the principle *locus regit actum*.[123] Lord Eldon was clear that the parties might invoke the common law if they could not avail themselves of the law of the place of celebration or if there was no local law. He accordingly held that a marriage between Protestants at Rome solemnised by a Protestant priest was valid, since no Catholic priest would be allowed to perform the ceremony.[124] The parties have to have found it impossible, or virtually impossible,[125] to comply with the local law. It is not enough that they found it inconvenient, embarrassing or distasteful so to comply, as in *Kent*

---

[118] [1953] AC 304.

[119] *Limerick v Limerick* (1863) 32 LJPM & A 92; *Phillips v Phillips* (1921) 38 TLR 150.

[120] *Taczanowska v Taczanowski* [1957] P 301 at 326; *Collett v Collett* [1968] P 482 at 487; *Kuklycz v Kuklycz* [1972] VR 50; cf *Preston v Preston* [1963] P 411 at 436.

[121] *Taczanowska v Taczanowski* [1957] P 301 at 327, 328.

[122] *Kent v Burgess* (1840) 11 Sim 361.

[123] *Ruding v Smith* (1821) 2 Hag Con 371.

[124] *Lord Cloncurry's Case* (1811), cited by Cruise, *Dignities and Titles of Honour*, 276; and see the *Sussex Peerage Case* (1844) 11 Cl & Fin 85 at 92, 102.

[125] *Preston v Preston* [1963] P 411 at 432; or perhaps where conformity with the local law would be contrary to conscience: *Kochanski v Kochanska* [1958] P 147 at 151–2.

v Burgess[126] where a marriage in Belgium was held void for non-compliance with Belgian residence requirements there being no insuperable difficulty in the parties waiting the prescribed six-month period.

Australian courts have considered that "insuperable difficulty" existed in Germany in 1945 at a time when no register offices were open and the registrars had left their posts,[127] and in the Ukraine in 1942 as the German army advanced,[128] but not in Saigon in 1978.[129] The marriages in the first two cases were upheld as valid according to the common law.[130]

Although it has usually been the case that, when a marriage has been upheld under this exceptional head of insuperable difficulty, it has been celebrated by an episcopally ordained priest,[131] it is suggested that this is not a necessary requirement and that celebration by some other minister or even by none at all will suffice.[132]

(d) Marriages of military forces in belligerent occupation[133]

Circumstances can be envisaged where, although compliance with the local law is not impossible, it might be thought unreasonable. Such a problem arose in Europe at the end and in the aftermath of the Second World War, when many people married without recourse to the civilian, often Nazi, authorities. The problem is illustrated by the leading decision in *Taczanowska v Taczanowski*:[134]

> Two Polish nationals, domiciled in Poland, were married in Italy in 1946 by a Polish Army Chaplain, an episcopally ordained priest of the Roman Catholic Church, and therefore their marriage was valid according to the English common law. The husband was serving in the Polish 2nd Corps, an independent command in belligerent occupation in Italy. The ceremony did not comply with the local forms and was therefore void by Italian domestic law, but it would be recognised as valid by that country's private international law if it was valid by the national law of the parties. It was, however, not valid by Polish law. The parties came to England in 1947 and, in 1955, the wife petitioned for a decree of nullity on the ground that the marriage was void for non-compliance with the local forms.

The Court of Appeal felt that, since the parties were presumed not to have submitted themselves to the Italian law of the place of celebration, that law did not have to be applied. It was considered that there will often be no submission by a member of the military forces in occupation of a country, and such was held to be the case here. As Italian law was not applicable and the law of the parties' domicile was considered irrelevant,[135] English common law was applied and the validity of the marriage upheld.[136] The result was that the Court of Appeal, animated perhaps by a desire to save other similar marriages, said to number between three

---

[126] (1840) 11 Sim 361.

[127] *Savenis v Savenis* [1950] SASR 309.

[128] *Kuklycz v Kuklycz* [1972] VR 50; cf *Persian v Persian* [1970] 2 NSWR 538.

[129] *Re X's Marriage* (1983) 65 FLR 132.

[130] It is an interesting question whether laws prohibiting inter-racial marriages could be regarded as creating insuperable difficulty: cf *Conlon v Mohamed* [1989] ILRM 523.

[131] Eg *Savenis v Savenis* [1950] SASR 309 (Roman Catholic priest); *Kuklycz v Kuklycz* [1972] VR 50 (Greek Orthodox priest).

[132] As in the first common law marriage exception, discussed supra, p 887.

[133] See Mendes da Costa (1958) 7 ICLQ 217; Andrews (1959) 22 MLR 396; Brownlie and Webb (1963) 39 BYBIL 457.

[134] [1957] P 301.

[135] As the court was not concerned with a question of capacity; see also *Kochanski v Kochanska* [1958] P 147 at 154–5; *Kuklycz v Kuklycz* [1972] VR 50 at 52; cf *Maksymec v Maksymec* (1955) 72 WNNSW 522.

[136] The argument of the husband that the marriage was valid by virtue of the Foreign Marriage Act 1892, s 22 failed, since the Polish army chaplain was not officiating under the orders of a commanding officer of the British army serving abroad.

and four thousand, recognised as valid at common law a marriage void both by the law of the place of celebration and by the personal law of the parties.

A further step was taken in *Kochanski v Kochanska*.[137]

> Here, two Polish nationals, occupants of a displaced persons' camp in Germany, to whom everything German was anathema, were married by a Catholic priest without compliance with the local forms.

Although this case was distinguishable from previous decisions in that neither party to the marriage could be described as a member of the armed forces of occupation, Sachs J upheld the validity of the marriage. He concluded that there was no submission to the local law; and having thus eliminated German law, the judge held the marriage to be valid on the ground that the ceremony satisfied the common law; though he would have preferred to fall back on the Polish law of the domicile had authority justified that course.

In moving beyond the narrow category of members of the armed forces of occupation, Sachs J gave support to the general idea that the requirement of compliance with the law of the place of celebration is based on submission thereto by the parties. In the case before him there was no submission and so the common law was applied. Such a general principle of submission underlies the decision in *Lazarewicz v Lazarewicz*,[138] where a Polish corporal, serving with the Polish army in Italy, was married in 1946 at Barletta in Italy to an Italian national. The ceremony, performed at a Polish refugee camp by a Catholic priest, did not comply with Italian law. Phillimore J distinguished the case before him from the two earlier cases on the ground that there was evidence of the parties' intention to submit to Italian law: the husband had married not as a member or within the lines of the army of occupation, but as an ordinary sojourner in and subject to the laws of the foreign state.[139] Reliance on the common law was, therefore, precluded and the marriage was void.

This decision adds further support to a general theory that the basis of the rule *locus regit actum* is the presumed intention of the parties to submit themselves to the law of the place of celebration. It is suggested, however, that this theory of submission, if it purports to represent a general principle applicable to marriages other than those in an occupied country or in a country where it is insuperably difficult to comply with the local law, is neither supported by previous authority nor free from other objections. Clear authority against such a general rule is provided by the statement of the Privy Council in 1930 that: "If the so-called marriage is no marriage in the place where it is celebrated it is no marriage anywhere, although the ceremony or proceeding if conducted in the place of the parties' domicile would be considered a good marriage."[140]

If this rule stated in such categorical terms by the Privy Council is to give way to the presumed intention of the parties, certainty will be displaced by uncertainty, unless it is made clear what evidence suffices to establish an intention not to submit to the law of the place of celebration.[141] It will be seen[142] that evidence that the parties did not wish to observe the local law obviously cannot suffice.[143] In the result, the suggestion that the control of the law of the

---

137 [1958] P 147; followed in *Jaroszonek v Jaroszonek* [1962] SASR 157; cf *Fokas v Fokas* [1952] SASR 152; *Grzybowicz v Grzybowicz* [1963] SASR 62.
138 [1962] P 171; and see *Dukov v Dukov* (1968) 13 FLR 149.
139 *Merker v Merker* [1963] P 283 at 295.
140 *Berthiaume v Dastous* [1930] AC 79 at 83. Cf *Gandhi v Patel* [2002] 1 FLR 603, per Park J, at [34].
141 Carter (1957) 33 BYBIL 335.
142 *Merker v Merker* [1963] P 283 at 295; *Preston v Preston* [1963] P 411 at 427.
143 See, eg, *Gandhi v Patel* [2002] 1 FLR 603, per Park J, at [16] and [45].

place of celebration depends on the intention of the parties, whatever its future fate may be, confused what was formerly reasonably clear.

Later decisions have not relied on the dangerous concept of submission. In *Merker v Merker*,[144] Sir Jocelyn Simon P was faced with another marriage in occupied enemy territory:

> The parties were Polish domiciliaries who were serving in the Polish Armoured Division, part of the allied forces occupying Germany. They were married in a local German church by a Roman Catholic priest, a Polish army chaplain. German local law was not complied with. Later a German court granted a decree declaring the marriage to be null and void. After the wife had become resident in England, she petitioned for a declaration as to her status.

The first issue before the court was that of the validity of her marriage.[145] One of the arguments put to the court was that a person marrying in a foreign country could elect whether or not to submit to the local law, and, if he did not submit, then English common law, as the law of the forum, should determine the validity of his marriage. Such a general principle was emphatically rejected, for its effect "would be to leave the rule in *Berthiaume v Dastous*[146] in tatters and to introduce anarchy in a field where order and comity are particularly required".[147] Sir Jocelyn Simon P confined the principle of *Taczanowska's* case to cases of: "Marriages within the lines of a foreign army of occupation (which constitute, so to speak, an enclave within which it is reasonable to hold that the local law has no application), or of persons in a strictly analogous situation to the members of such an army, such as members of an organised body of escaped prisoners of war."[148] Applying such a narrow principle, the marriage before him was, nevertheless, valid according to English common law.

This more restrictive decision was followed by that of the Court of Appeal in *Preston v Preston*[149] where the court had to consider the validity at common law of a marriage, in the same camp as that of *Kochanski v Kochanska*,[150] which had failed to comply with the law of the place of celebration. On the evidence before it, the court considered that the camp in question was part of the organisation of the allied forces in occupation. Ormerod LJ interpreted *Taczanowska's* case as deciding that persons who marry in a foreign country are assumed to have submitted to the local law except in the case of the members of forces in belligerent occupation.[151] The general rule that persons are deemed to submit to the marriage laws of the place of celebration cannot be evaded merely because the parties claim that they did not intend to submit to that law. The circumstances where this general rule is inapplicable were narrowly, though not explicitly, defined.[152]

The conclusion to be drawn is that the principle of submission canvassed in the *Taczanowska* case and other decisions is very limited. It is relevant only to marriages contracted by a member of a conquering force in the conquered country.[153] This is the one type of case in which it is not unreasonable to offer the parties an alternative to the law of the place of celebration, for the incongruity of compelling a conqueror to submit to the conquered is obvious.[154]

---

[144] [1963] P 283.

[145] The problems stemming from recognition of the German decree are considered infra, pp 1008–9.

[146] Supra, p 893.

[147] [1963] P 283 at 295; see also *Milder v Milder* [1959] VR 95.

[148] [1963] P 283 at 295.

[149] [1963] P 411.

[150] Supra, p 906.

[151] This casts doubt on the decision in *Kochanski v Kochanska*, supra, and also on *Oleszko v Pietrucha* (1963) Times, 22 March, where the parties were members of what was considered to be a displaced persons' camp.

[152] [1963] P 411 at 427–8.

[153] Eg *Rosenthal v Rosenthal* (1967) 111 Sol Jo 475; cf *Dukov v Dukov* (1968) 13 FLR 149.

[154] As, perhaps, also with members of an organised body of escaped prisoners of war: *Merker v Merker* [1963] P 283 at 295.

(e) Marriages on the high seas

There is little authority as to what constitutes a valid marriage solemnised in a merchant ship while on the high seas.[155] The general principle is that the law of the flag governs transactions on board a vessel, for, as Byles J once said, a British ship is regarded as a floating island on which British law prevails.[156] This raises two difficulties in the case of British ships.

First, since there is no one system of law common to all the countries that employ the British flag, it is difficult to decide which particular legal system constitutes the law of the flag. The alternative seems to lie between English law and the municipal law of the country in which the ship is registered. The latter is the more reasonable rule and the one that is generally advocated.[157]

Presuming this view to be correct, the second difficulty is to discover from the authorities what part of English law governs a marriage on a ship that is registered in England. Is it the common law or the common law as regulated by statute? The latter alternative appears clearly to be excluded. There is no statute that deals particularly with marriages at sea[158] and the "floating island" theory can scarcely be pressed so far as to suggest that the Marriage Acts are applicable.[159] Thus, the common law is in force on a ship, as in the analogous case of a colony, except where the common law has been modified by statute. To make the analogy complete it must also be conceded that only so much of the law is imported into the ship as is suitable to the local conditions. That raises the further question whether it suffices that the parties have freely taken each other as husband and wife, or whether, in accordance with *R v Millis*,[160] it is necessary that the ceremony should have been performed by an episcopally ordained priest. That the presence of an episcopally ordained priest is sufficient for validity seems generally to be admitted,[161] but that it is essential appears unwarranted.[162] The impossibility of procuring a priest on the high seas is even more apparent than in the case of a remote part of China, and it is difficult to resist the conclusion that the rule laid down in *Wolfenden v Wolfenden*[163] applies equally to a ship. The argument sometimes advanced, that a ship must sooner or later put into a port where advantage may be taken of the facilities offered by the local law or by the Foreign Marriage Acts, is of little weight. It can be countered by the reflection that the same facilities were open to parties in a remote part of China if they were prepared to make the necessary journey.

It has been sometimes suggested that the absence of a priest is fatal to the validity of a marriage at sea, unless it is a *marriage of necessity*. What this ambiguous expression means is not clear but there is little doubt that it is taken from the Irish case of *Du Moulin v Druitt*[164] in 1860, which is no longer a safe guide. In that case:

> A woman stowaway was discovered on a troopship during a voyage to Australia. The commanding officer ordered that she and one of the soldiers on board should immediately be

---

[155] White (1901) 17 LQR 283; Charteris [1907] Jur Rev 178.

[156] *R v Anderson* (1868) LR 1 CCR 161 at 168; but see *R v Carr* (1882) 10 QBD 76 at 85.

[157] Dicey, Morris and Collins, para 17-027; and see *Bolmer v Edsell* 90 NJ Eq 299 (1919); cf *Fisher v Fisher* 250 NY 313 (1929). Cf the rule relating to torts committed on board a ship, supra, p 875.

[158] The provisions of the Merchant Shipping Act 1894, ss 240(6) and 253(1)(viii), requiring particulars of marriages celebrated at sea to be entered in the ship's log were repealed without replacement by the Merchant Shipping Act 1970, ss 100(3), 101(4), Sch 5.

[159] Indeed the theory itself is now hard to sustain: *R v Gordon-Finlayson, ex p an Officer* [1941] 1 KB 171 at 178–9; *Oteri v R* [1976] 1 WLR 1272 at 1276.

[160] (1844) 10 Cl & Fin 534; supra, p 903.

[161] Elphinstone (1889) 5 LQR 44, 53.

[162] *Merker v Merker* [1963] P 283 at 294.

[163] [1946] P 61; supra, pp 903–4.

[164] (1860) 13 ICLR 212.

married, and the marriage was celebrated in his presence. In fact, as soon as the ship arrived in Sydney, the woman left her "husband" and went to live with the officer who had acted as clerk in the marriage ceremony. Later they married, in the lifetime of the soldier, and the issue arose as to the validity of her ship-board marriage.

The court held that the rule in *R v Millis*[165] applied and that the ship-board marriage was void on the ground that the marriage was not one "of necessity", since the vessel would touch at places where a priest would be obtainable.[166] Having regard to *Wolfenden v Wolfenden*,[167] it would seem that this peculiar reasoning need no longer be considered seriously.

It is submitted, then, that if parties, whatever their domicile or nationality, voluntarily take each other as husband and wife while at sea in a vessel registered at an English port, the marriage is formally valid in the eyes of English law provided, probably, that there is some element of urgency about their marriage.[168]

3. CAPACITY TO MARRY[169]

(a) Introduction

We turn now to consider the second major issue relating to choice of law in the context of marriage, namely, the law to govern capacity or, as it is sometimes described, essential validity. There is general agreement that this terminology includes matters of legal capacity[170] such as consanguinity and affinity, bigamy and lack of age. Consideration is given later to the law to govern matters of consent[171] and physical incapacity.[172] The fact that capacity as a term encompasses a wide range of matters does not necessitate the conclusion that all matters of capacity should be subject to the same choice of law rule—a matter to which we shall return.[173] A further preliminary point which ought to be borne in mind is that, provided that

---

[165] (1844) 10 Cl & Fin 534.

[166] Cf *Maclean v Cristall* (1849) Perry's Ori Cas 75; and also *Culling v Culling* [1896] P 116—where the validity of a marriage before the ship's captain on board a warship was upheld; see now the Marriage (Same Sex Couples) Act 2013, Schedule 6, Part 3, s 12(1)(b).

[167] [1946] P 61, supra, pp 903–4.

[168] Dicey, Morris and Collins, para 17-027.

[169] See Jaffey (1978) 41 MLR 38; (1982) 2 OJLS 368; North (1980) I Hague Recueil 9, 53–69; Fentiman [1985] CLJ 256.

[170] With regard to mental capacity, see *Sheffield City Council v E* [2004] EWHC 2808, [2005] 1 FLR 965, per Munby J at [141], to the effect that the test in relation to mental capacity is whether an individual has capacity to understand the nature of the marriage contract, and the duties and responsibilities that normally attach to marriage. See also *M v B* [2005] EWHC 1681, [2006] 1 FLR 117—twenty-three-year-old woman with severe learning disability at risk of parents arranging her marriage overseas, in particular Sumner J, at [36]; *Re SA (Vulnerable Adult with Capacity: Marriage)* [2005] EWHC 2942 (Fam), [2006] 1 FLR 867—eighteen-year-old woman, vulnerable adult, deaf and mute, at risk of unsuitable arranged marriage overseas; *X City Council v MB* [2006] EWHC 168— twenty-three -year-old man with severe autistic spectrum disorder at risk of parents arranging his marriage overseas; *Westminster City Council v IC (A Protected Party by His Litigation Friend) and Ors* [2008] EWCA Civ 198, [2008] WCR (D) 92—twenty-six-year-old man with severe impairment of intellectual functioning and autism married in a Muslim ceremony via a telephone link between England and Bangladesh where the bride lived; *XCC v AA* [2012] EWHC 2183 (COP)—young British woman of a Bangladeshi origin with a very high degree of learning disability, little language and almost no comprehension of anything other than simple matters married to her cousin in a ceremony in Bangladesh; and *Luton Borough Council v SB and another* [2015] EWHC 3534 (Fam) —eighteen-year-old man with intellectual disabilities and autism spectrum disorder married in a ceremony in Pakistan.

[171] Infra, p 986 et seq.

[172] Infra, p 993 et seq.

[173] See *Radwan v Radwan (No 2)* [1973] Fam 35 at 51, infra, p 923.

a person has capacity under the relevant law,[174] the fact that he is, for example, under age according to English law will not invalidate the marriage in the eyes of English law as the law of the forum—at least if the marriage does not take place in England.[175]

There are two main views as to the law which should govern capacity to marry—the dual domicile doctrine, and the intended matrimonial home doctrine.[176] These must now be examined more closely.

(b) The two main theories

(i) The theories stated

The traditional and still prevalent view is that capacity to marry is governed by what may conveniently be called the *dual domicile doctrine*.[177] This prescribes that a marriage is invalid unless, according to the law of the domicile of both contracting parties at the time of the marriage, they each have capacity to contract that particular marriage.[178] This is said to be true whether the incapacity is "absolute", ie one which forbids a person, such as a child below a particular age, to marry anyone;[179] or "relative", ie one which forbids two individual persons, such as an uncle and niece, to marry each other.[180] Under this doctrine, a marriage, for instance, between a man of the Jewish faith domiciled in Egypt and a woman of the same faith domiciled in England, the latter being his niece, is invalid, since a marriage between persons so related, though permissible in Egypt,[181] is prohibited by English law.

The alternative doctrine, and the one which has been supported strongly in earlier editions of the book,[182] is that which submits the question of capacity to what may briefly be termed the law of the *intended matrimonial home*. More fully stated, the doctrine is this:

> The basic presumption is that capacity to marry is governed by the law of the husband's domicile at the time of the marriage, for normally it is in the country of that domicile that the parties intend to establish their permanent home. This presumption, however, is rebutted if it can be inferred that the parties at the time of the marriage intended to establish their home in a certain country and that they did in fact establish it there within a reasonable time.

(ii) Evaluation of the two theories

Postponing for the moment a consideration of the actual decisions, the question must now be asked—what are the respective merits and demerits of the two rival doctrines?

(a) The intended matrimonial home doctrine

On social grounds it can be argued that the doctrine of the dual domicile is inferior to that of the intended matrimonial home. Marriage is an institution that closely concerns the public policy and the social morality of the state. The general laws which dictate its incidents, however, vary considerably between different countries, and where a woman domiciled in one country marries a man domiciled in another the question naturally arises—what state is to

---

[174] In relation to capacity to marry, the standard of proof required to rebut the presumption of a valid matrimonial union is the normal civil standard of a balance of probabilities: *Wicken v Wicken* [1999] Fam 224, per Holman J, at 229.

[175] Eg *Mohamed v Knott* [1969] 1 QB 1, infra, p 945.

[176] Some more recently developed alternative approaches are examined, infra, pp 924–5.

[177] See, in Scots law, a statutory version of the rule: Family Law (Scotland) Act 2006, s 38(2)(a). See Crawford and Carruthers, para 11-28.

[178] Dicey, Morris and Collins, paras 17R-057 et seq; Wolff, pp 332–7.

[179] Eg *A Local Authority v X* [2013] EWHC 3274 (Fam).

[180] Westlake, s 21, p 57.

[181] Cf *Cheni v Cheni* [1965] P 85.

[182] Eg 7th edn of this book (1965), pp 276 et seq.

control the incident of capacity? Which state is in the nature of things entitled to demand pre-eminent consideration for its code of social morality? One clear answer might be—the state in which the parties set up their home.

A choice of law rule commands little respect if it is framed without regard to its impact on the social life of the community that will be most intimately affected by its operation. It seems reasonably clear that whether the inter-marriage of two persons should be prohibited for social, religious, eugenic or other like reason is a question that affects the community in which the parties live together as man and wife.[183]

In support of the argument that it is the law which is in force there which should be allowed to assess the propriety or impropriety of the marriage one might take the example of the extreme case of an absolute incapacity. If an English girl, aged fifteen and a half, contrary to the law of England, marries a foreigner domiciled in a country whose law permits marriage at this early age, it might be doubted whether it is justifiable to regard the marriage as void, for the social life of England is unaffected if the girl goes to live with him in his country, as the girl proposes to sever her connection with England. As against that, however, it is arguable that rules as to the age of marriage are designed to protect minors whether they intend to live abroad or not. It is also arguable that a matter so important as capacity to marry should not be determined by the intentions of the parties.[184]

Apart from social considerations, principle might seem to support the view that, where the parties are domiciled in different countries before their marriage, questions of the essential validity of the marriage, including their personal capacity, should be governed by the law of the place where they establish their joint home.[185] This is at least compatible with the rule that capacity to enter into a commercial contract is governed by the law of the country with which the contract has the closest connection.[186] Broadly speaking, domicile signifies the country with which the *propositus* is most closely connected since it is there that he has established his home.[187]

But owing to the peculiar reverence that English law still pays to the domicile of origin, it may well happen that the country in which a party is technically domiciled immediately prior to marriage in no sense represents his or her home, whether actual or contemplated. Could it be said, for instance, that George Bowie, the work-shy Scotsman in *Bowie (Ramsay) v Liverpool Royal Infirmary*,[188] had his home in, or any substantial connection with, Scotland? Finally, not only is just one law to be applied under the intended matrimonial home theory, but it may be more effective than the dual domicile test in supporting a policy of upholding the validity of marriages and of giving effect to the legitimate expectations of the parties.[189]

When one turns to the disadvantages of the intended matrimonial home theory, then several objections of a practical matter may be advanced against it.[190] It may be objected that any rule is undesirable which renders it impossible to decide whether a marriage is valid or void

---

[183] Report of the Royal Commission on Marriage and Divorce (1956) Cmnd 9678, para 889; and see *Bliersbach v McEwan* 1959 SLT 81 at 89.

[184] Anton, (2nd edn), p 429; and see *Cooper v Cooper* (1888) 13 App Cas 88 at 108; *Muhammad v Suna* 1956 SC 366 at 370. But see Shakargy (2013) 9 J Priv Int L 499 (arguing for the introduction of party autonomy in the area of choice of law in marriage).

[185] *Lawrence v Lawrence* [1985] Fam 106 at 127.

[186] Supra, pp 761–4.

[187] *Warrender v Warrender* (1835) 2 Cl & Fin 488 at 536.

[188] [1930] AC 588, supra, p 153.

[189] Law Commission Working Paper No 89 (1985), para 3.34; and see Jaffey (1978) 41 MLR 38; (1982) 2 OJLS 368.

[190] Law Commission Working Paper No 89 (1985), para 3.35; and see Glenn (1977) 4 Dalh LR 157.

at the time of its celebration.[191] Such may be the case if it is doubtful whether the parties genuinely intend to establish their home in the alleged country. Again, it may be asked what is the position if they delay unreasonably in going to the chosen country or never go there at all, or intend never to set up a matrimonial home?[192] Answers to these criticisms have been propounded. First, the question whether a marriage is void for incapacity, unless it arises incidentally in the course of some other proceedings, will require the institution of a nullity suit for its answer, by which time it will be known whether the alleged intention of the parties was in fact fulfilled. The difficulty with such an answer is that it ignores the fact that a marriage which is *void ab initio* does not require a decision of a court to determine the parties' status. If it is void, it is void. If the parties have to wait and see what law is to govern their capacity, then their marital status remains in doubt. The second suggested answer is that it is not true that the status of the parties will remain indeterminate, for if the place of their future home is doubtful it is presumed to be in the domicile of the husband at the date of their marriage. However, in that case it is not easy to find merit in a discriminatory solution which refers the issue of a wife's capacity to marry to the law of the husband's ante-nuptial domicile.

It is also the case that arguments of principle have been advanced against the intended matrimonial home theory, it being suggested that post-nuptial intentions should be irrelevant when determining ante-nuptial capacity, and that it enables rules which are the legitimate concern of the domiciliary law to be evaded by an intention to set up home elsewhere.

(b) The dual domicile theory

The greatest merit of the dual domicile theory is that it refers capacity to marry to that law which, up to that time, has governed the status of each party.[193] The law of the domicile is the law of the country to which a person "belongs".[194] Furthermore, it preserves equality of the sexes by looking to the law of each party's domicile.[195] This is of added weight since a wife no longer automatically takes her husband's domicile on marriage.[196]

Varied criticisms have been made of the dual domicile theory, eg it tends towards the invalidity of marriages.[197] This is because, where the domiciliary laws differ as to the validity of the marriage, the marriage will be regarded as invalid. It is also said to be inefficacious as a practical working rule, in that it is a rule which admits of its own evasion. Suppose, for instance, that a woman domiciled in England wishes to marry her uncle who lives and is domiciled in Egypt. English internal law would prohibit the marriage. Being properly advised, however, she travels to Cairo for the marriage ceremony with the intention of remaining there for the rest of her married life, and thus acquires a domicile of choice, the law of which permits a marriage between an uncle and a niece. She is now of full capacity in the eyes of English private international law. Thus, it is said that the protection supposedly afforded to an Englishwoman by the dual domicile rule is somewhat illusory. The evasion involved here amounts to as substantial a step as deciding to establish a matrimonial home in Egypt.

Another criticism which might be voiced is that, because of the inflexibility of many of the rules relating to acquisition and loss of a domicile, a person's capacity to marry may be determined by the law of a country he has never visited. Such criticism, however, may provide a

---

191 Dicey, Morris and Collins, para 17-063; and see *Lawrence v Lawrence* [1985] Fam 106 at 127–8.
192 Eg *Vervaeke v Smith* [1983] 1 AC 145.
193 *Lawrence v Lawrence* [1985] Fam 106 at 127.
194 Hartley (1972) 35 MLR 571, 576.
195 Morris, p 199.
196 Domicile and Matrimonial Proceedings Act 1973, s 1.
197 Hartley (1972) 35 MLR 571, 578.

reason for changing the rules relating to domicile,[198] rather than those concerning capacity to marry.

(iii) The rule as deducible from the English decisions[199]

We must turn now from theory and attempt to ascertain whether judicial authority in England supports the view that capacity to marry is governed by the law of the ante-nuptial domicile of each party, or by the law of the intended matrimonial home. It is submitted that many of the relevant decisions[200] are rather inconclusive. It will be seen that in such cases the decision would have been the same whether it had been based on the application of the law of the matrimonial home or on the dual domicile theory.

(a) Inconclusive decisions

For example, in *Brook v Brook*,[201] where, it will be recalled,[202] a Danish marriage was held void because both spouses lacked capacity under English law, the law of their domicile and of the intended matrimonial home, Lord Campbell LC had this to say:

> But I am by no means prepared to say, that the marriage now in question ought to be or would be held valid in the Danish courts, proof being given that the parties were British subjects domiciled in England, that England was to be their matrimonial residence, and that by the law of England such a marriage is prohibited. The doctrine being established that the incidents of the contract of marriage celebrated in a foreign country are to be determined according to the law of the country in which the parties are domiciled and mean to reside, the consequence seems to follow that by this law must its validity or invalidity be determined.[203]

It is not possible to conclude in favour of one theory or the other on the basis of this case.[204]

Mette v Mette[205] is the earliest decision on this matter in which the parties were domiciled in different countries prior to their marriage:

> A domiciled Englishman contracted a marriage in Frankfurt with his deceased wife's half-sister, a domiciled German woman. This marriage, then prohibited by English law but valid by German law, was held to be void.

This decision does not conclude the controversy, since it is again compatible both with the dual domicile doctrine and the doctrine of the intended matrimonial home. The man was domiciled in England until his death; both parties contemplated a matrimonial residence in England; and therefore English law, as being the law of the matrimonial home, was the appropriate legal system to determine the matter. In the words of the judge, the husband "remained domiciled in this country".[206] The ratio decidendi is in fact rather doubtful. After remarking that "there could be no valid contract unless each was competent to contract with the other", words which suggest a preference for the dual domicile doctrine, Sir Cresswell

---

[198] Supra, p 172.

[199] And see North, *Private International Law of Matrimonial Causes*, pp 119 et seq.

[200] *Mette v Mette* (1859) 1 Sw & Tr 416; *Brook v Brook* (1861) 9 HL Cas 193; *Re De Wilton* [1900] 2 Ch 481; *Re Paine* [1940] Ch 46; *Pugh v Pugh* [1951] P 482; and see *In the Will of Swan* (1871) 2 VR (IE & M) 47. In *Ali v Ali* [1968] P 564 infra, p 926, Cumming-Bruce J at 576–7, suggested that both views were tenable and neither concluded by authority. On the facts of the case, the law of the domicile and the law of the intended matrimonial home were both English law.

[201] (1861) 9 HL Cas 193.

[202] Supra, p 892.

[203] (1861) 9 HL Cas 193 at 213; see also at 224, 230–1, 239.

[204] Though see, at 212, Lord Campbell's explanation of *Warrender v Warrender* (1835) 2 Cl & Fin 488. See also *Sottomayor v de Barros* (1877) 3 PD 1, infra, p 918.

[205] (1859) 1 Sw & Tr 416.

[206] Ibid, at 424.

finally concluded that, since the husband had remained domiciled in England, and the marriage was with a view to subsequent residence here, the English prohibition was necessarily operative.[207]

(b) Support for the intended matrimonial home theory

Having considered and discarded such rather inconclusive decisions, one must turn to those which provide more specific support for one theory or the other, starting with those in favour of the intended matrimonial home view. The most persuasive early decision is that in the Australian case of *In the Will of Swan*,[208] where the issue was whether a marriage, which was celebrated on a temporary visit to Scotland between parties domiciled in the State of Victoria, could be held to revoke a will made by the husband before marriage. The wife was the niece of the husband's deceased wife and it was assumed that the marriage, though voidable by Victorian law, was void by Scots law. In upholding the validity of the marriage and thus of the revocation of the will, Molesworth J said:

> The validity of marriages as to ceremonial and so forth depends upon the law of the place of the marriage, but . . . the policy of the occurrence of such marriages and their results, should depend, I think, upon the laws of the country of the parties in which they are afterwards probably to live.[209] No doubt, however, a similar result would have been achieved through the dual domicile test.

There are, moreover, judicial pronouncements which refer the question of the legality of a marriage to the law of the matrimonial domicile, though in all these cases the remarks are made obiter as no issue of capacity to marry was directly involved. In the first of these, *De Reneville v De Reneville*,[210] Lord GREENE MR had this to say:

> The validity of a marriage so far as regards the observance of formalities is a matter for the *lex loci celebrationis*. But this[211] is not a case of forms. It is a case of essential validity. By what law is that to be decided? In my opinion by the law of France, either because that is the law of the husband's domicile at the date of the marriage or (preferably, in my view) because at that date it was the law of the matrimonial domicile in reference to which the parties may have been supposed to enter into the bonds of marriage.[212]

A further judgment which shows a similar trend is that of Denning LJ in *Kenward v Kenward*,[213] where he affirmed, with no ambiguity, that the "substantial validity" of a marriage contracted between persons domiciled in different countries is governed by the law of the country where they intend to live and on the basis of which they agreed to marry.

In *Radwan v Radwan (No 2)*[214] Cumming-Bruce J, after a careful review of the authorities, held that capacity to contract a polygamous marriage is governed by the law of the intended matrimonial home,[215] a conclusion of some significance, for the wife was domiciled in England whilst the husband's domicile and the law of the intended matrimonial

---

[207] Ibid, at 423–4.

[208] (1871) 2 VR (IE & M) 47; Fleming (1951) 4 ILQ 389, 392–3.

[209] *In the Will of Swan*, supra, at 50. This latter law was presumed to be Victorian.

[210] [1948] P 100. See also a similar statement by Bucknill LJ in *Casey v Casey* [1949] P 420 at 429, 430.

[211] Ie the effect on the marriage of the impotence and wilful refusal of one of the parties, see infra, p 985 et seq.

[212] [1948] P 100 at 114, and see Bucknill LJ, at 121–2. In *Ponticelli v Ponticelli* [1958] P 204 at 214, Sachs J assumed that the personal capacity of a spouse is governed by "the *lex domicilii* which normally coincides with the law pertaining to the country of the husband's domicile at the time of the marriage".

[213] [1951] P 124 at 144, 146; see also *Bliersbach v McEwan* 1959 SC 43 at 55.

[214] [1973] Fam 35, supra, pp 899–900.

[215] The whole question of capacity to enter a polygamous marriage is considered in more detail, infra, p 936 et seq.

home was Egyptian. However, he did not maintain that the matrimonial home view provides the universal test, for he said that "Nothing in this judgment bears upon the capacity of minors, the law of affinity, or the effect of bigamy upon capacity to enter into a monogamous marriage."[216]

Support for an approach at least similar to the intended matrimonial home test has been voiced more recently in two decisions where the major issue was the recognition of foreign decrees. In *Vervaeke v Smith*,[217] where the main issue was the recognition of a foreign nullity decree relating to a sham marriage, Lord Simon Glaisdale gave support to a choice of law rule which amounted to applying the law of the country with which the marriage has the most real and substantial connection.[218] Similar support is found for such an approach in the judgment of Lincoln J, at first instance, in *Lawrence v Lawrence*,[219] a decision on the effect of the recognition of a foreign divorce on capacity to remarry,[220] but which also provides a rare example of a case where the dual domicile test would mean that the marriage was void, whilst the application of the intended matrimonial home/real and substantial connection test had the result that the marriage was valid.[221] Although both judges formulated their real and substantial connection test as an application of the "intended matrimonial domicile" doctrine, it is more convenient to consider a real and substantial connection test separately and more fully below.[222]

(c) Support for the dual domicile theory

We must now turn to those decisions which can be said to support the dual domicile theory, and which, it is submitted, are of greater weight than those cited in favour of the opposite theory.[223] There was clear reliance on the dual domicile theory in *Re Paine*:[224]

> An English testatrix left a sum of money on trust for her daughter, W, for life, and, if she died leaving any child or children surviving, then on trust for her absolutely. W was a British subject domiciled in England. In 1875 she travelled to Germany and married H, her deceased sister's husband, a German subject. H had lived in England for some time shortly before the marriage,[225] and he and his wife continued to live there until their respective deaths. H died in 1919, W died some twenty years later. One daughter of the marriage survived W.

In these circumstances the legacy to W would not become absolute unless the surviving daughter was her legitimate child, for the law then was that a reference in a will to a "child" meant a legitimate child only, unless a different intention could be determined from the context.[226] Whether the daughter was legitimate depended on whether the marriage in 1875 was valid. At that time a marriage between a woman and her deceased sister's husband was prohibited in English law, but allowed by German law. Bennett J adopted the dual domicile

---

[216] [1973] Fam 35 at 54. For discussion of whether different rules should apply to different forms of incapacity, see infra, p 923.

[217] [1983] 1 AC 145, infra, pp 1025–6.

[218] Ibid, at 166.

[219] [1985] Fam 106 at 112, 115. The Court of Appeal did not think that the case raised general issues relating to the law governing capacity to marry.

[220] Infra, pp 925–6.

[221] [1985] Fam 106 at 112.

[222] Infra, p 924.

[223] See *Lawrence v Lawrence* [1985] Fam 106 at 122.

[224] [1940] Ch 46. This decision is at first sight difficult to reconcile with that of Romer J in *Re Bischoffsheim* [1948] Ch 79, infra, p 1198, where, however, the question of the legitimacy of the children was held not to depend on the validity of their parents' marriage.

[225] See the facts as reported in (1940) 161 LT 266 at 267.

[226] See now the Family Law Reform Act 1987, s 19, as amended by the Adoption and Children Act 2002, Sch 3, para 52. See *Upton v National Westminster Bank plc* [2004] EWHC 1962, [2004] WTLR 1339.

doctrine and held the marriage to be void because of the incapacity attaching to W under the law of her ante-nuptial domicile. However, the result was exactly what it would have been had he applied the doctrine of the intended matrimonial home.[227] Since England was the country where the woman was domiciled, where the man was resident before the marriage, where they intended to reside together and where in fact they resided throughout their married lives, the decision that English law must prevail could scarcely have been different.

A later case, which raised a question of capacity in the narrow sense of the term, is *Pugh v Pugh*,[228] where the facts were these:

> A British officer, domiciled in England but stationed in Austria, married a Hungarian girl in Austria in 1946. The girl, whose domicile of origin was Hungarian, had gone to Austria with her parents to escape from the Russian advance. She was only fifteen years of age and therefore, if her capacity had been governed by English domestic law, the marriage would undoubtedly have been rendered void by the Age of Marriage Act 1929 which prohibited a marriage "between persons either of whom is under the age of sixteen".[229] By Austrian law the marriage was valid, and by Hungarian law it had become valid in that it had not been avoided before she had attained the age of seventeen.

The wife submitted that the marriage was void for want of capacity, first because the husband was a British subject with an English domicile and therefore bound by the 1929 Act; secondly, and alternatively, because the essential validity of the marriage was determinable by English law as being either the law of the husband's domicile or the law of the country of the proposed matrimonial home. Pearce J granted a decree of nullity, holding that the wife was entitled to succeed on both submissions. The 1929 Act, he said, was intended to affect "all persons domiciled in the United Kingdom wherever the marriage might be celebrated".[230] He also agreed with the second submission, "since by the law of the husband's domicil it was a marriage into which he could not lawfully enter".[231] This passage, coupled with the citation of *Re Paine*,[232] undoubtedly suggests that the judge applied English law as being the law of the husband's domicile before marriage, though the fact remains that the decision is compatible with the doctrine of the intended matrimonial domicile.

Recently, the lack of age as a ground of incapacity arose in the case of *A Local Authority v X*.[233] Unlike in *Pugh*, the party who lacked capacity was an English domiciliary; the marriage having been entered into in Pakistan between a girl of only fourteen years of age, domiciled in England, and a twenty-four year old man, domiciled in Pakistan. Holman J noted the extra territorial effect of the statutory provisions as to minimum age, tracing this feature of the legislation to the decision in *Pugh*. This led his Lordship to the conclusion that "if either party was domiciled here on the date of the marriage (as she was) and one of them was still under the age of sixteen (as she was), it makes no difference that both parties may have been of sufficient minimum age and had capacity under the law of the domicile of the other party or under the law of the place where the marriage was contracted". It was unclear from the factual matrix whether the intended matrimonial home was in England or Pakistan, and no reference was made in the decision to the intended matrimonial home test.

---

[227] *Radwan v Radwan (No 2)* [1973] Fam 35 at 50.
[228] [1951] P 482; cf *Vida v Vida* (1961) 105 Sol Jo 913; and see North, *Private International Law of Matrimonial Causes*, p 120; (1980) I Hague Recueil 9, 57–69.
[229] See now the Marriage Act 1949, s 2.
[230] [1951] P 482 at 493.
[231] Ibid, at 494.
[232] Supra, p 915.
[233] [2013] EWHC 3274 (Fam).

There has been further express approval of the dual domicile theory, though again in circumstances where a similar result would have been achieved by the intended matrimonial home test.[234] However, a more significant decision is that of Sir Jocelyn Simon P in *Padolecchia v Padolecchia*.[235] The facts were as follows:

> The husband, at all times domiciled in Italy, married there in 1953. He was later granted a divorce decree, by proxy, by a Mexican court, which decree would not be recognised in Italy. He went to live in Denmark and, on a one-day visit to England in 1964, he "married" the respondent who was resident and domiciled in Denmark. They both returned to Denmark to live and then the husband petitioned the English court for a decree of nullity on the ground that he was already married when he "married" the respondent.

Having decided that the court had jurisdiction,[236] Sir Jocelyn Simon P had to determine by what law to test the petitioner's capacity to marry the respondent.[237] There was no doubt that, by Italian law, the law of the domicile, the divorce would not be recognised and hence that he had no capacity to marry. The position was probably the same under Danish law, though the evidence of Danish law was not wholly satisfactory. Had the case turned on Danish law, which would seem certain to be classed as the law of the intended matrimonial home, then further investigation of that law would have been necessary. However, the judge had no doubts that the capacity of the petitioner had to be referred to Italian law, the law of the domicile. His examination of the position under other possibly relevant laws seems to have been on the hypothesis that one of them might have been considered to be the law of the domicile.[238]

This decision would seem to provide a clear and explicit authority for the dual domicile theory.[239] Further support for this view may be drawn from two statutory provisions.[240] The first is the Marriage (Enabling) Act 1960, which modified the former rules of affinity. It has long been the rule that, after the death of his wife, a man may marry her sister, aunt or niece; and may also marry the wife of his brother, uncle or nephew after her husband is dead. The Act of 1960 eliminated the condition that the wife, brother, uncle or nephew must be dead at the time of the proposed marriage.[241] Thus, for example, it is now permissible for a man to marry the sister of his divorced wife while the latter is still alive. Having made this change in English internal law, the Act lays down a rule for the choice of law by providing that no such marriage shall be valid "if either party to it is at the time of the marriage domiciled in a country outside Great Britain, and under the law of that country there cannot be a valid marriage between the parties".[242] Despite the argument that this choice of law provision was not discussed in Parliament,[243] it does provide a clear statutory reference to the dual domicile theory, though in admittedly limited circumstances.[244]

---

[234] Eg *R v Brentwood Superintendent Registrar of Marriages, ex p Arias* [1968] 2 QB 956; *Crickmay v Crickmay* (1967) 60 DLR (2d) 734.

[235] [1968] P 314; and see *Szechter v Szechter* [1971] P 286 at 295.

[236] This aspect of the case is considered, infra, Chapter 22.

[237] Had the issue been classified as one concerned with the recognition of foreign divorces the outcome would have been the same, as the petitioner was domiciled at all material times in Italy, by whose law the Mexican decree was not recognised: [1968] P 314 at 338. It also seems most unlikely that the Mexican decree would be recognised under the Family Law Act 1986, infra, p 1005 et seq.

[238] Further support for the approach in this case may be drawn from *Shaw v Gould* (1868) LR 3 HL 55; *Schwebel v Ungar* (1963) 42 DLR (2d) 622; affd (1964) 48 DLR (2d) 644, supra, p 53; Lysyk (1965) 43 Can BR 363, 368–70; and see *Ungar v Ungar* [1967] 2 NSWR 618.

[239] See also National Insurance Decision No R (G) 3/75.

[240] The Marriage (Scotland) Act 1977, ss 1(1), 2(1), specifically refer to persons domiciled in Scotland in relation to the questions of lack of age and consanguinity and affinity; and see also ss 3(5), 5(4).

[241] Marriage (Enabling) Act 1960, s 1(1).

[242] Ibid, s 1(3); see *Crickmay v Crickmay* (1967) 60 DLR (2d) 734.

[243] See 7th edn of this book (1965), p 288.

[244] See *Radwan v Radwan (No 2)* [1973] Fam 35 at 51.

The second statutory provision is section 11(d) of the Matrimonial Causes Act 1973[245] which stipulates that an actually polygamous marriage celebrated abroad is void if either party was domiciled in England at the time of the marriage.[246]

In Scots law, the statutory crystallisation of the dual domicile theory in section 38(2) of the Family Law (Scotland) Act 2006 is thought to have foreclosed any possibility of seeking to persuade a Scots court to apply the intended matrimonial home doctrine.[247]

(c) Further issues

It is now necessary to consider a number of further issues related to the operation of either the dual domicile or the intended matrimonial home approaches.

(i) *The rule in* Sottomayor v De Barros (No 2)[248]

The rule in *Sottomayor v De Barros (No 2)*[249] provides what may appear to be an exception to the two choice of law theories which have just been examined. Two related decisions need to be considered together here:

> The husband and wife were first cousins. They were presumed to be domiciled in Portugal by whose law marriage between first cousins was prohibited in the absence of a Papal dispensation. They married in England and lived together in the same house, though without consummating the marriage, for six years.

The Court of Appeal held[250] that the question of capacity must depend on the law of the domicile. If they were both domiciled in Portugal, the marriage would be void. This decision provides some further support for the dual domicile theory, though it is not conclusive for it appears that the parties never intended to live together as husband and wife, never really had a matrimonial home, and so reference to the law of Portugal as the law of the husband's domicile is compatible with the statement of the intended matrimonial home doctrine.[251]

The actual determination of the parties' domicile fell to be considered in later proceedings,[252] where it was decided that the husband was domiciled in England but the wife in Portugal. What effect, then, did this conclusion have on the validity of the marriage? If it is true to say that a marriage is invalid where either party is incapacitated by his or her personal law, the decision in this case should have been adverse to the legality of the marriage, but Sir James Hannen P held that it constituted a valid marriage. It must be admitted that he did not base his decision on the matrimonial residence of the parties in England, but on the fact that the law of the place of celebration was English. Impressed by the "injustice which might be caused to our own subjects if a marriage were declared invalid on the ground that it was forbidden by the law of the domicile of one of the parties",[253] he refused to give effect to the prohibition imposed on the wife by Portuguese law. The decision has never been overruled. How, then, is it to be rendered compatible with the dual domicile doctrine? The difficulty is usually surmounted by framing an exception to that doctrine. It has been formulated as follows:

---

[245] As amended by the Private International Law (Miscellaneous Provisions) Act 1995, Sch, para 2.
[246] The provision is discussed more fully, infra, p 938 et seq.
[247] See Crawford and Carruthers, para 11-28.
[248] See Clarkson (1990) 10 Legal Studies 80, 84 et seq.
[249] (1879) 5 PD 94; see also *Ogden v Ogden* [1908] P 46.
[250] *Sottomayor v De Barros* (1877) 3 PD 1.
[251] Supra, p 910. It should be mentioned, however, that in the lower court the Queen's Proctor had argued, unsuccessfully, for the application of English law as that of the intended matrimonial home: (1877) 2 PD 81 at 82.
[252] *Sottomayor v De Barros (No 2)* (1879) 5 PD 94.
[253] (1879) 5 PD 94 at 104.

The validity of a marriage celebrated in England between persons of whom the one has an English, and the other a foreign, domicile is not affected by an incapacity which, though existing under the law of such foreign domicile, does not exist under the law of England.[254]

In other words, capacity must be tested by the law of the domicile of each party, but, when one of them has an English domicile, a foreign incapacity affecting the other and unknown to English law must be utterly disregarded if the marriage takes place in England. This suggested rule has been stigmatised as "anomalous"[255] and as "unworthy of a place in a respectable system of the conflict of laws",[256] as well as being criticised by the Law Commission.[257] It is xenophobic in that it gives preference to the law of the place of celebration of the marriage if that is English, but not if it is foreign. It is likely to lead to "limping" marriages, valid in England but not in the country of the domicile of one spouse. Thus, the case for the abandonment of the rule seems clear.

The *Sottomayor* decision could, on the facts, though not on the reasoning, be regarded as supporting the intended matrimonial home theory. A better view would be to regard this decision as an inelegant exception to the dual domicile theory and, if it is to remain, one to be interpreted as restrictively as possible by confining it, for example, "to a condition imposed by the law of the domicile that a specified consent or consents should be given".[258] Even if such restrictive interpretation is not accepted, there has been a narrowing of the scope of the rule by reason of the Marriage (Enabling) Act 1960,[259] for a marriage covered by that Act is not validated if either party is domiciled in a country under whose law there cannot be a valid marriage between the parties. Furthermore, to apply *Sottomayor v De Barros (No 2)* other than to cases of invalidity caused through want of consents would mean that its application would depend on the particular degree of affinity in question.

(ii) The role of the law of the place of celebration[260]

How far is the law of the place of celebration relevant to capacity to marry? This issue has arisen in two contexts. The first is whether there are issues as to essential validity which should be referred exclusively to the law of the place of celebration. Some support for such an approach is to be found in the speech of Lord Simon of Glaisdale in *Vervaeke v Smith*[261] where he suggested that matters of "quintessential validity", such as whether, as in the case before him, a sham marriage could constitute a marriage at all, might be referred to the law of the place of celebration. It seems hard to justify such an approach in the case of matters going to the fundamental nature of marriage, especially as the parties may have had only a limited connection with the

---

[254] Dicey, Morris and Collins, para 17E-107. In addition to *Sottomayor v De Barros (No 2)* (1879) 5 PD 94, the exception is supported by dicta: *Ogden v Ogden* [1908] P 46 at 74–7; *Chetti v Chetti* [1909] P 67 at 81–8; *Vervaeke v Smith* [1981] Fam 77 at 122 (the point was not referred to in the House of Lords: [1981] 1 AC 145); and see *R v Brentwood Superintendent Registrar of Marriages, ex p Arias* [1968] 2 QB 956 at 968–9; see also *MacDougall v Chitnavis* 1937 SC 390; cf Anton, para 15.26. The exception can also be relied on to justify the decision in *Perrini v Perrini* [1979] Fam 84.

[255] *Radwan v Radwan (No 2)* [1973] Fam 35 at 50.

[256] Falconbridge, *Conflict of Laws*, p 711.

[257] Law Commission Working Paper No 89 (1985), para 3.17; and see paras 3.45–3.48. See also Law Com No 165 (1987), paras 2.7–2.8, 2.15.

[258] As can be implied from *Miller v Teale* (1954) 92 CLR 406 at 414.

[259] Supra, p 917.

[260] Clarkson (1990) 10 Legal Studies 80, 81–4. See, in relation to Scots law, Family Law (Scotland) Act 2006, s 38(3). See also Crawford and Carruthers, para 11-29; the Family Law (Scotland) Act 2006 is silent on the question of the requirement of capacity by the law of the country where the marriage was celebrated where that law is other than Scottish. See, however, the role of the law of the country of registration in the context of civil partnerships formed overseas, ie an overseas civil partnership will be recognised in England only if the parties had capacity to enter into the relationship under the law of the country where the relationship is registered: Civil Partnership Act 2004, s 215(1)(a).

[261] [1983] 1 AC 145 at 165–6.

place of celebration.[262] Furthermore, the authorities on which the judge relied either ante-date the distinction which has been maintained since the mid-nineteenth century between form and essential validity[263] or were primarily concerned with formal validity.[264]

The second context in which the application of the law of the place of celebration has arisen is in deciding whether the rules of that law relating to essential validity must be satisfied *in addition* to those of the parties' personal law.[265] Clear authority for the rejection of any reference to the law of the place of celebration is found in *In the Will of Swan*.[266] However, in more recent years, there have been dicta[267] and the decision in *Breen v Breen*[268] which have indicated that the law of the place of celebration is relevant and should be considered in addition to the personal law, so that a marriage will be regarded as invalid if the parties lack capacity by the law of the place of celebration, even though they are capable under their personal law.

In *Breen v Breen*[269] the parties were at all relevant times domiciled in England. They married in Ireland during the lifetime of the husband's former wife, that first marriage having been dissolved by an English court. The second wife petitioned for a decree of nullity on the grounds that the divorce decree would not be recognised in Ireland and that, therefore, her "husband" lacked capacity to marry by Irish law. Karminski J concluded, after examination of the Constitution of Ireland, that since the English divorce decree would be recognised in Ireland the second marriage was valid. However, the only connection with Ireland that this marriage had was that it was celebrated there, yet reference was made to Irish law on an issue of capacity. One can conclude that as an authority for referring issues of capacity to the law of the place of celebration, this case is "a sorry and inarticulate precedent [which] should be considered insufficient to establish a rule of very doubtful merit".[270]

While it is true that the law of the place of celebration cannot always be disregarded,[271] a distinction should be drawn between cases where the law of the place of celebration is that of the forum and other cases. An English registrar, for instance, cannot be required to sanction a marriage if it would be void for incapacity under an English statute and an English court is unlikely, for policy reasons, to uphold such a marriage.[272] It is probably true to say that all marriages celebrated in England must comply with English law, not only as to formal validity but also as to matters of essential validity.[273]

---

[262] For a detailed rejection of the law of the place of celebration as the law generally to be applied to issues of essential validity, see Law Commission Working Paper No 89 (1985), paras 3.21–3.23. Contrast the approach in South Africa: *Phelan v Phelan* 2007 (1) SA 483 (C).

[263] *Warrender v Warrender* (1835) 2 Cl & Fin 488 at 530.

[264] *Berthiaume v Dastous* [1930] AC 79 at 83.

[265] Bradshaw (1986) 15 Anglo-Am LR 112; and see Law Com No 165 (1987), para 2.6.

[266] (1871) 2 VR (IE & M) 47.

[267] Eg *Lendrum v Chakravarti* 1929 SLT 96 at 103. It is not clear why reference was made in *Schwebel v Ungar* (1963) 42 DLR (2d) 622 at 633–4 to the proposition that the law of the place of celebration might be relevant to capacity to marry but without applying it. In that case an incapacity did exist by the law of the place of celebration, which was also the law of the forum, but the marriage in question was upheld; see Lysyk (1965) 43 Can Bar Rev 363, 369–70.

[268] [1964] P 144; Unger (1961) 24 MLR 784.

[269] [1964] P 144.

[270] Unger (1961) 24 MLR 784, 787.

[271] And see the Marriage (Scotland) Act 1977, s 2(3)(a), and Family Law (Scotland) Act 2006, s 38(3).

[272] Support might be inferred from *Padolecchia v Padolecchia* [1968] P 314 at 335; *Vervaeke v Smith* [1983] 1 AC 145 at 152; and also from *Pugh v Pugh* [1951] P 482 at 491–2.

[273] The Marriage (Scotland) Act 1977, ss 1(2) and 2(1)(a) provide expressly that a marriage celebrated in Scotland is void if the requirements as to age or consanguinity and affinity are not satisfied. See also s 38(3) of the Family Law (Scotland) Act 2006 (to which s 38(2)—the dual domicile rule—is expressly subject), which states that: "If a marriage entered into in Scotland is void under a rule of Scots internal law, then, notwithstanding subsection (2), that rule shall prevail over any law under which the marriage would be valid."

On the other hand, incapacity by the law of a foreign place of celebration should be ignored, as is illustrated by the Canadian decision in *Reed v Reed*:[274]

> The husband and wife were first cousins domiciled in British Columbia. The wife was aged eighteen and could not marry in British Columbia without parental consent, which was refused. As a consequence, the parties were married in the State of Washington where all the necessary formal requirements were satisfied, but under whose law first cousins lacked capacity to marry. The wife petitioned, unsuccessfully, in British Columbia for a nullity decree.

Lack of parental consent was characterised as an issue of form to be referred to the law of the place of celebration, Washington, by which law the marriage was formally valid. Consanguinity was a matter of capacity to be referred to the law of the domicile, British Columbia, by which law the parties were capable. The court declined to apply the law of the place of celebration to the issue of capacity.

(iii) Public policy

Where a foreign domiciliary law governs the capacity of the parties to a marriage, it will not be recognised if it is repugnant to public policy.[275] The court has a discretionary power to repudiate a capacity or an incapacity on the ground that to give effect to it would be unconscionable.[276] This discretion, however, is to be exercised sparingly.[277] Thus, so far as repudiation of capacity is concerned, in *Cheni v Cheni*,[278] a case which is considered later in another context,[279] it was argued that a marriage celebrated in Cairo between an uncle and a niece, both domiciled in Egypt, was incestuous by the general consent of Christendom or at least by the general consent of civilised nations. Sir Jocelyn Simon P disagreed. He insisted that a reasonable tolerance must be shown in applying the doctrine of public policy.[280] Marriages between uncle and niece were accepted by general Jewish law and by many Lutheran churches, and were not totally condemned even by the Catholic Church. It would, therefore, be unjustifiable to stigmatise as unconscionable a capacity acceptable "to many people of deep religious convictions, lofty ethical standards and high civilisation".[281]

It does seem clear, however, that the courts would be prepared, albeit with caution, to deny recognition to a wide variety of incapacities imposed by the law of the domicile such as incapacity to marry at all,[282] or inability to marry other than according to the tenets of a particular faith,[283] or incapacity to marry outside one's caste[284] or race.[285]

---

[274] (1969) 6 DLR (3d) 617.

[275] Cf, in Scots law, the Family Law (Scotland) Act 2006, s 38(4). See Crawford and Carruthers, para 11-29. There is also a minor statutory restriction, namely that imposed on descendants of George II by the Royal Marriages Act 1772; see Dicey, Morris and Collins, paras 17E-093–17-098; MacNeill (1922) 38 LQR 74; Parry (1956) 5 ICLQ 61.

[276] *Cheni v Cheni* [1965] P 85 at 98.

[277] *Vervaeke v Smith* [1983] 1 AC 145 at 164.

[278] Supra.

[279] Infra, pp 933–4.

[280] And in *Mohamed v Knott* [1969] 1 QB 1, infra, p 945, the validity of the foreign marriage of a thirteen-year-old Nigerian girl was upheld.

[281] [1965] P 85 at 99.

[282] Eg because the person is a monk or a nun: *Sottomayor v De Barros (No 2)* (1879) 5 PD 94 at 104.

[283] Cf *Gray (otherwise Formosa) v Formosa* [1963] P 259; *Lepre v Lepre* [1965] P 52; and see *Papadopoulas v Papadopoulas* [1930] P 55 at 64; cf *Corbett v Corbett* [1957] 1 All ER 621, where incapacity to marry outside the Jewish faith was recognised. See also *Khan v Ahmad* [2014] EWHC 3850 (Fam) where, however, reliance on the presumption of marriage arising from cohabitation and repute meant that the question of any incapacity in foreign law not recognized by the law of England and Wales—such as religion—did not need to be resolved. The case concerned an inter-faith marriage entered into in Pakistan between a Sunni Muslim and a member of the Ahmadi faith, both domiciled in Pakistan.

[284] *Chetti v Chetti* [1909] P 67.

[285] *Sottomayor v De Barros (No 2)*, supra, at 104; cf *Conlon v Mohamed* [1989] ILRM 523.

Prior to the adoption of the Marriage (Same Sex Couples) Act 2013, a subject which had given rise to some controversy was whether, and if so what, recognition should be afforded in England to same sex or transsexual relationships.[286] The current legislative framework regarding same sex relationships, including the problem of recognition of overseas same sex relationships is examined fully below.[287]

As regards transsexual persons, the Gender Recognition Act 2004 makes it possible for transsexual people to change their legal gender by applying for a gender recognition certificate.[288] Previously, transsexual people who were married or in a civil partnership had to end their marriage or civil partnership before a full gender recognition certificate could be issued. This is, however, no longer the case. The Marriage (Same Sex Couples) Act 2013 amends the 2004 Act to enable an existing marriage registered in England and Wales or outside the UK[289] to continue where one or both parties change their legal gender and both parties wish to remain married. Importantly, where the marriage was entered into under a foreign law,[290] the continuity of the marriage is not affected by any impediment under the proper law of the marriage.[291] Nevertheless, a protected marriage registered under a foreign law is still subject to the law of the country in which it is registered, despite being recognized by English law whilst the couple are resident there.[292]

(iv) Renvoi

There is some authority that a reference to the personal law as governing issues of capacity should include a reference to its rules of private international law, ie that the doctrine of renvoi applies in this context.[293] In *R v Brentwood Superintendent Registrar of Marriages, ex p Arias*[294] the facts were these:

> The husband, an Italian national domiciled in Switzerland, was married to a Swiss wife. He obtained a divorce in Switzerland. His wife remarried. He wished to remarry in England, but his Swiss divorce was not recognised in Italy.

The court upheld the Registrar's objections to the marriage. The husband's capacity to marry was referred to the law of Switzerland, his ante-nuptial domicile and the intended matrimonial home. It was agreed on the facts that Swiss law would refer the issue of his capacity to Italian law. This seems clearly to be an application of the doctrine of renvoi, though the matter is not discussed by the court; and it had the consequence that the husband was incapable

---

[286] See the 14th edition of this book, pp 908–10.

[287] See pp 946–8 (civil partnership) and pp 948–9 (same sex marriage).

[288] Gender Recognition Act 2004, s 1.

[289] Termed "protected marriage" and defined as a marriage under the law of England and Wales, or under the law of a country or territory outside the UK: s 25(1) of the Gender Recognition Act 2004.

[290] Ie where the proper law of the marriage is the law of a country or territory outside the UK ("foreign marriage"). Gender Recognition Act 2004, s 11A (4).

[291] Gender Recognition Act 2004, s 11A (3)(a)). It appears that the effect of this provision is that the continuity of the marriage would not be prejudiced even if the proper law of the marriage recognized only a heterosexual marriage.

[292] Gender Recognition Act 2004, s 11A (3)(b).

[293] The doctrine of renvoi has been explicitly adopted by the Civil Partnership Act 2004 in respect of capacity to enter into a civil partnership overseas. In particular, the parties must have capacity to enter into the relationship under the law of the country where the civil partnership was registered, "including its rules of private international law": ss 215(1) and 212(3), see infra, n 536. (Note that in the context of civil partnerships renvoi applies also to formal validity, see supra n 83).

[294] [1968] 2 QB 956; and see the Marriage (Scotland) Act 1977, s 3(5).

of remarrying even in the country of his domicile and notwithstanding the remarriage in the same country of his first wife.[295]

(v) Should the same rule apply to all issues of capacity?

The discussion of the law governing capacity to marry has, so far, proceeded on the assumption that all incapacitating factors give rise to the same problems and are susceptible of the same solution in choice of law terms. Whilst it is true that, on the balance of the authorities, the ante-nuptial domiciliary law determines issues of capacity[296] such as consanguinity and affinity,[297] lack of age[298] and, indeed, bigamy,[299] it has been suggested that:

> It is an over-simplification of the common law to assume that the same test for purposes of choice of law applies to every kind of incapacity—non age, affinity, prohibition of monogamous contract by virtue of an existing spouse, and capacity for polygamy. Different public and social factors are relevant to each of these types of incapacity.[300]

There is no doubt that there are issues relating to capacity which are governed by special rules. For example, the rules governing capacity to marry following a divorce are now governed by specific statutory provisions,[301] and, as the passage just quoted illustrates, there is some authority for saying that, even though the dual domicile test applies to many forms of incapacity, the intended matrimonial home test ought to apply to capacity to enter a polygamous marriage.[302] It has also been suggested that different rules should apply to matters of "quintessential validity" as compared with other issues of essential validity.[303]

The virtue of a situation in which different choice of law rules may be applied to different issues of essential validity is that it enables the courts to retain the flexibility necessary to reach just results in difficult cases. It is hard to argue against a desire for justice but, in fact, that way lies uncertainty, anarchy and ultimately injustice. Whilst a limited number of exceptions from a general choice of law rule may be justifiable, it is not acceptable to permit the judge to decide which rule to apply essentially by reference to the factual circumstances of a particular case. It is suggested, for example, that there is no justification for applying the intended matrimonial home test to determine whether a man may marry polygamously[304] but the dual domicile test to determine whether he may marry his niece[305]—especially if she is to be his second wife! There would appear to be no social or policy factors justifying a different approach to the two types of case.

---

[295] The Law Commission has supported the application of renvoi to capacity to marry; see Working Paper No 89 (1985), para 3.39, Law Com No 165 (1987), para 2.6; and so has the Irish Law Reform Commission: LRC 19-1985, p 153. The decision in the *Brentwood* case would now be different by reason of the Family Law Act 1986, s 50, infra, pp 925–6.

[296] The questions whether consent and physical incapacities, such as impotence or willful refusal to consummate, are to be regarded as matters of essential validity governed by the law of the domicile are considered, infra, p 984 et seq, as these issues will tend normally to arise in the context of nullity petitions.

[297] Eg *Mette v Mette* (1859) 1 Sw & Tr 416; *Brook v Brook* (1861) 9 HL Cas 193; *Sottomayor v De Barros* (1877) 3 PD 1; *Re Paine* [1940] Ch 46. The effect of the Marriage (Enabling) Act 1960, s 1(3) has already been considered supra, p 917.

[298] *Pugh v Pugh* [1951] P 482. Also *A Local Authority v X* [2013] EWHC 3274 (Fam).

[299] *Padolecchia v Padolecchia* [1968] P 314.

[300] *Radwan v Radwan (No 2)* [1973] Fam 35 at 51; and see Jaffey (1978) 41 MLR 38; Downes (1986) 35 ICLQ 170. See also Clarkson and Hill, at 362–4 (proposing "a variable test or, a functional approach").

[301] Family Law Act 1986, s 50, infra, pp 925–6. The courts have also been prepared to accept the need for a special rule as to capacity in this context, see *Lawrence v Lawrence* [1985] Fam 106 at 114–15, 134.

[302] Discussed more fully, infra, p 936 et seq.

[303] *Vervaeke v Smith* [1983] 1 AC 145 at 165–6.

[304] *Radwan v Radwan (No 2)* [1973] Fam 35.

[305] Eg *Cheni v Cheni* [1965] P 85.

(d) Alternative approaches

It has been assumed so far that, in determining the general choice of law rule to select the law to govern the essential validity of marriage, the choice lies between the dual domicile or the intended matrimonial home approaches. Whilst it is true that the case law overwhelmingly supports one or other of these approaches, consideration has been given in more recent years to other ways of determining the applicable law, some of which will be examined here.

(i) Real and substantial connection[306]

In *Vervaeke v Smith*,[307] Lord Simon of Glaisdale suggested that the "quintessential validity" of a marriage, this being in the case before him the validity of a "sham" marriage, should be governed by the law of the country "with which the marriage has the most real and substantial connection". A similar test was applied by Lincoln J in *Lawrence v Lawrence*[308] to the issue of capacity to marry after a foreign divorce.[309] This approach had received some academic support in the past[310] and these two decisions have prompted further support.[311] It has, however, been vigorously rejected by the Law Commission:

> It is an inherently vague and unpredictable test which would introduce an unacceptable degree of uncertainty into the law. It is a test which is difficult to apply other than through the courtroom process and it is therefore unsuitable in an area where the law's function is essentially prospective, ie a yardstick for future planning.[312]

It does seem to be a retrograde step to introduce into the field of validity of marriage a test which, because of its inherent uncertainty, was abandoned in the field of divorce recognition in 1971.[313] It also seems unworkable where there is a real and substantial connection with more than one country.[314]

(ii) Alternative reference

A criticism that can be advanced against the dual domicile approach is that it favours invalidity, because the marriage will be invalid if either party lacks capacity by their ante-nuptial domiciliary law. To counter this disadvantage, and in order to differentiate between rules designed to protect the public interest and those designed to protect the parties, it has been suggested[315] that, in cases other than those such as non-age, impotence or wilful refusal, where the purpose of the rule is to protect the parties, the marriage should be regarded as valid if either the dual domicile or the intended matrimonial home test is satisfied. This embodies a clear policy in favour of upholding the validity of marriages, and this is a policy

---

[306] See, supra, p 915.

[307] [1983] 1 AC 145 at 165–6.

[308] [1985] Fam 106 at 112–15; though no specific support for this approach is to be found in the judgments in the Court of Appeal. See also *Entry Clearance Officer, Dhaka v Ranu Begum* [1986] Imm AR 461 at 464–5, 466–7; *R v Immigration Appeal Tribunal, ex p Rafika Bibi* [1989] Imm AR 1.

[309] Infra, p 925 et seq.

[310] Sykes suggested that essential validity should be governed by the proper law of the contract to marry, ie the law of that country with which the contract has the most real connection: (1955) 4 ICLQ 159, 168; and see supra, p 761 et seq, for the application of such a test to general contractual capacity.

[311] Fentiman [1985] CLJ 256; Smart (1985) 14 Anglo-Am LR 225; Fentiman (1986) 6 OJLS 353, 354–60.

[312] Working Paper No 89 (1985), para 3.20. This approach (and the next two examined here) were not discussed further in Law Com No 165 (1987).

[313] By the Recognition of Divorces and Legal Separations Act 1971, abrogating the decision in *Indyka v Indyka* [1969] 1 AC 33; see now the Family Law Act 1986, Part II, infra, p 1000 et seq.

[314] *R v Immigration Appeal Tribunal, ex p Rafika Bibi* [1989] Imm AR 1 at 4–5.

[315] Primarily by Jaffey (1978) 41 MLR 38; (1982) 2 OJLS 368; and see Royal Commission on Marriage and Divorce (1956) Cmd 9678, para 891.

which has, in the present context, attracted some judicial support.[316] There are, however, major disadvantages with such an alternative reference approach which led to its rejection by the Law Commission.[317] Not only does it suffer from many of the disadvantages of the intended matrimonial home test, it may also require the substantive marriage laws of three different legal systems to be investigated. Furthermore, it does seem to depend on a distinction being made between grounds of invalidity on the basis of some form of assessment of the purpose of individual invalidating rules, thus introducing into the field of family law many of the problems of American "interest analysis".[318] Finally, it seems unwarranted to give such prominence to a policy in favour of the upholding of marriages that it becomes the fundamental basis of the choice of law rule.

(iii) Elective dual domicile test

Concern for upholding the validity of a marriage has led to the suggestion[319] that, instead of declaring a marriage invalid if either party lacks capacity under his or her ante-nuptial domiciliary law, the marriage should be valid if it is so regarded under either law. Where, however, the issue arises prior to the celebration of the marriage, as where a registrar refuses a licence, it is suggested that the orthodox dual domicile test be applied.[320] This approach also was provisionally rejected by the Law Commission[321] for much the same reasons as the alternative reference test was rejected. It does not appear justified to prefer the rules of one party's domiciliary law to those of the other—to do so could lead to evasion and limping marriages. This approach would, again, give undue prominence to a domestic policy in favour of upholding the validity of marriages.

(e) Capacity and recognition of foreign divorces or annulments

(i) Effect of valid divorce or annulment on capacity to remarry[322]

An allegation of incapacity to marry on the grounds of bigamy involves most frequently in private international law a question of the recognition of a foreign divorce or annulment. In such a case the marriage will be bigamous only if the English courts decline to recognise the foreign divorce or annulment. Whilst the whole general question of the rules for the recognition of foreign divorces or annulments is considered later,[323] it is necessary at this point to examine the effect of such recognition on capacity to remarry. The relevant rule is embodied in section 50 of the Family Law Act 1986 which states:[324]

Where, in any part of the United Kingdom—

(a) a divorce or annulment has been granted by a court of civil jurisdiction, or
(b) the validity of a divorce or annulment is recognised by virtue of this Part,[325] the fact that the divorce or annulment would not be recognised elsewhere shall not preclude either party to the marriage from forming a subsequent marriage or civil partnership in that

---

[316] *Lawrence v Lawrence* [1985] Fam 106 at 115, 134; and see *Minister of Employment and Immigration v Narwal* (1990) 26 RFL (3d) 95.

[317] Working Paper No 89 (1985), para 3.27.

[318] See North (1980) I Hague Recueil 9.

[319] Hartley (1972) 35 MLR 571, 576–8.

[320] Ibid, at p 578.

[321] Working Paper No 89 (1985), para 3.38.

[322] See Law Com No 137; Scot Law Com No 88 (1984), paras 2.35, 6.49–6.60.

[323] Infra, p 1000 et seq.

[324] As amended by the Civil Partnership Act 2004, Sch 27, para 125. There is no provision equivalent to s 50 in the Brussels II *bis* Regulation, presumably because in the light of virtually automatic recognition of European divorces, etc among Member States, such a provision would be largely unnecessary. But see Crawford and Carruthers, para 12-42.

[325] Infra, p 1005 et seq.

part of the United Kingdom or cause the subsequent remarriage or civil partnership of either party (wherever it takes place) to be treated as invalid in that part.

The effect of this provision is to provide one clear straightforward rule that applies to both divorces and annulments, whether granted in England or obtained elsewhere and recognised in England, and whether followed by a marriage in the United Kingdom or abroad. In all cases the fact that the divorce or annulment was not recognised in the country of the domicile or anywhere else should not affect the validity of a later marriage.[326]

(ii) Effect on capacity to marry of non-recognition of a divorce or annulment

Section 50 of the 1986 Act only applies where a foreign divorce or annulment is recognised in England. There can be a similarly difficult, but converse, case where a foreign divorce or annulment is recognised by the law of the domicile, or of the country of the intended matrimonial home at the time of the remarriage, but not in England. There is Canadian authority in *Schwebel v Ungar*[327] for resolving this incidental question in a converse way to that to be found in section 50, ie by regarding the main question as that of capacity to marry, holding the spouse capable notwithstanding the non-recognition of the divorce under the forum's divorce recognition rules. The Law Commission examined this problem but concluded that no legislative provision should be made for it.[328] The Commission's reasons were essentially practical ones—there is no point in introducing legislation to resolve a problem unlikely to arise in real life. In the case of remarriage in England, conflict between the recognition and capacity rules is not likely to arise given that capacity by English law will be required.[329] In the case of remarriage abroad, there is the further factor that English recognition rules are so broad that conflict with the law governing capacity is unlikely, except where recognition is denied in England on grounds of public policy. In such a case recognition of the later re-marriage might well be justified.

(iii) Prohibitions against remarriage

There is one final problem which relates to foreign divorces and capacity to marry. Some foreign divorce decrees, though purporting to dissolve the marriage, provide restrictions or prohibitions on remarriage by one or both of the parties. Restrictions of this kind appear to fall roughly into two classes, namely, those that are directed against the "guilty" party and those that postpone the date at which either party may contract a further marriage.[330]

To take the latter class first, it may be said that a foreign decree which forbids the parties to remarry before a certain period has elapsed has not finally and conclusively restored the parties to the unmarried status. This view was adopted for English law in *Warter v Warter*,[331] where the parties, who had been divorced in Calcutta, were prohibited by the Indian law of their domicile from marrying again before six months. It was held that a marriage in England contracted by the wife within six months with a domiciled Englishman was invalid.[332]

---

[326] The rule embodies a principle which might have already been the law before it was put on a statutory footing by the 1986 Family Law Act. See, eg Lipstein (1986) 35 ICLQ 178; cf *Lawrence v Lawrence* [1985] Fam 106 at 131–2 per Purchas LJ; Carter (1986) 57 BYBIL 441, 444. For a detailed analysis of the common law position see the 14th edition of this book, pp 913–15.

[327] (1963) 42 DLR (2d) 622; affd 48 DLR (2d) 644, supra, p 53.

[328] Law Com No 137; Scot Law Com No 88 (1984), para 6.60; cf Jaffey (1985) 48 MLR 465, 469; Briggs (1989) 9 OJLS 251, 258.

[329] Supra, pp 919–21.

[330] On this subject, see M Mann (1952) 42 Transactions of the Grotius Society 133, 138–41; Hartley (1967) 16 ICLQ 680, 694–9.

[331] (1890) 15 PD 152; but see now *Boettcher v Boettcher* [1949] WN 83; *Buckle v Buckle* [1956] P 181. See the Australian case, *Miller v Teale* (1954) 92 CLR 406; Webb (1956) 5 ICLQ 137.

[332] But why was it not held valid under the exceptional rule in *Sottomayor v De Barros (No 2)* (1879) 5 PD 94, supra, pp 918–19.

On the other hand, a decree which finally dissolves the marriage, but which by way, presumably, of punishment, imposes a restriction on the "guilty" party, is regarded by English law as imposing a penalty. We have already seen that the penal laws of foreign countries may be disregarded in England.[333] Thus in *Scott v A-G*:[334]

> Two persons domiciled in South Africa were divorced in that country, and thereupon became subject to a rule of South African law which provided that the guilty party could not remarry as long as the other party remained unmarried. The wife, who was the guilty party, remarried in England, her former husband being still unmarried.

This second marriage was upheld by the English court on the ground that the restriction on remarriage was a penalty, and therefore inoperative out of the jurisdiction under which it was inflicted.[335] The correctness of this decision would seem, indeed, to rest on an even simpler reason. Since the divorce decree had effected a complete dissolution of the marriage according to South African law, the woman, being no longer a wife, was free to acquire her own separate domicile.[336] She had in fact acquired a new domicile in England at the time of her remarriage, and therefore there was no possible ground on which her capacity to marry could be referred to South African law.[337]

4. REFORM OF GENERAL RULES

There have been various initiatives for reform of the choice of law rules relating to marriage. None has borne significant fruit.[338] On the broader international scene, the Hague Conference on Private International Law in 1978 agreed a Convention on Celebration and Recognition of the Validity of Marriage, but few states have ratified it.[339] The United Kingdom has rejected it,[340] rightly so because the Convention rules are both unacceptable and incomplete.[341]

Closer to home, the Irish Law Reform Commission[342] had no doubt that, in the absence of effective international agreement, reform of the Irish choice of law rules was needed to eradicate uncertainty and complexity and to ensure that practical difficulties for the non-lawyers who have to apply them are avoided. In the Commission's view, this was a task requiring legislative reform and restatement. In making a wide range of recommendations, heavy reliance was placed on Working Paper (No 89) produced in 1985 by the English and Scottish Law Commissions on the same topic.[343] This examined both the desirability of reform of particular rules and, where appropriate, what specific changes might be made. The Commissions' provisional proposals were primarily concerned to produce clarity and certainty and few, if

---

[333] Supra, p 118 et seq.

[334] (1886) 11 PD 128.

[335] As explained in *Warter v Warter* (1890) 15 PD 152 at 155.

[336] She would now, of course, always be free to acquire a separate domicile, supra, p 168 et seq.

[337] (1886) 11 PD 128 at 131; and see Wolff, p 379.

[338] Except in Scotland, where the rules now rest on a statutory footing: s 38 of the Family Law (Scotland) Act 2006.

[339] Australia, Luxembourg and the Netherlands. Interestingly, in Australia the Convention was implemented in the Marriage Amendment Act 1985, see Neave (1990) 4 Aus J Fam Law 190; Nygh in Borras (ed), *E Pluribus Unum* (1996), pp 253–67.

[340] Law Com No 165 (1987), para 1.2.

[341] For a range of criticisms of the Convention, see Batiffol (1977) 66 Rev crit dr int pr 451; Glenn (1977) 55 Can Bar Rev 586; Reese (1977) 25 AJCL 393; (1979) 20 Va J Int L 25; Lalive (1978) 34 *Annuaire suisse de droit international* 31; North (1981) 6 Dalh LJ 417, 430–3; (1990) I Hague Recueil 9, 74–81.

[342] LRC 19–1985.

[343] For criticisms, see Fentiman (1986) 6 OJLS 353, 354–60.

any, proposed radical change. Confirmation that the law of the place of celebration should govern formal validity amounted to nothing new, nor did the idea that there should be some exception founded on the lines of the present common law marriage exception.[344] Again, the provisional proposals that essential validity should be governed by the dual domicile test, that renvoi should apply to the law governing both formal and essential validity and that there should be a public policy safeguard to enable a foreign law not to be applied, either confirmed existing law or did little more than resolve matters of current debate.[345] More substantial were the suggestions that the rule in *Sottomayor v De Barros (No 2)*[346] be abolished and that, in determining essential validity, reference should be made in all cases to the law of the place of celebration as well as to that of the domicile.[347] There were also detailed proposals for minor reforms of the Foreign Marriage Act 1892 and its related delegated legislation.

The Irish recommendations have not been implemented and the provisional proposals in England and Wales have, with the exception of the reform of the Foreign Marriage Act 1892,[348] been abandoned.[349] The Law Commissions decided against recommending comprehensive legislation primarily because, in their view, there were no major areas "where, in practice, the law seems to go wrong, ie to lead to an undesirable result",[350] because satisfactory resolution of uncertainties in the law would require complex legislation, and because statutory intervention was thought undesirable whilst the law is still in a state of development. These reasons for doing nothing are not convincing. The solution of complex problems does not necessarily lead to complex legislation.[351] Aspects of the current law are undoubtedly undesirable; nor can there be doubt that other elements of the marriage choice of law rules are uncertain or unclear. It is perverse then to rely, as in effect the Commissions did, on that uncertainty as a reason for doing nothing, in the hope that the courts will in due course provide the appropriate new, clear rules.[352] The experience of the last hundred years is unlikely to convince those varied officials who have to advise on and apply marriage choice of law rules that the much needed clarification will in fact be forthcoming through judicial decisions.[353]

5. POLYGAMOUS MARRIAGES[354]

(a) Introduction

Since the middle of the nineteenth century, it has been the case that a marriage which was both formally and essentially valid under the laws to be applied under English rules of private

---

[344] Supra, p 902 et seq.

[345] Supra, p 909.

[346] (1879) 5 PD 94, supra, p 918.

[347] This view was, rightly, abandoned in the Law Commissions' Report: Law Com No 165 (1987), para 2.6.

[348] See the Foreign Marriage (Amendment) Act 1988. The Foreign Marriage Act 1892 is no longer in force; it was repealed by the Marriage (Same Sex Couples) Act 2013, s 13(2).

[349] Law Com No 165 (1987), paras 2.13–2.14.

[350] Ibid, para 2.13.

[351] The statutory solution adopted in Scotland (s 38 of the Family Law (Scotland) Act 2006) can be accused of being simplistic, or at least silent on certain important topics, such as renvoi.

[352] Law Com No 165 (1987), para 2.14.

[353] In April 2015, the Law Commission announced plans to carry out a review of the law of marriage. The scoping phase of the project was concluded with the publication of "Getting Married: A Scoping Paper", on 17 December 2015. It has, however, been made clear that the question of how English law deals with marriages that have taken place overseas will, unfortunately, fall outside the scope of the review.

[354] Beckett (1932) 48 LQR 341; Morris (1953) 66 Harv LR 961; Hartley (1969) 32 MLR 155; Poulter (1976) 25 ICLQ 475; Jaffey (1978) 41 MLR 38; James (1979) 42 MLR 533; Shah (2003) 52 ICLQ 369; Rehman (2007) 21 International Journal of Law, Policy and the Family 108; Beilfuss, "Islamic Family Law in

international law could still be regarded as invalid—or as a marriage to which no effect will be given—if it was actually or potentially polygamous. There was a steady erosion, during the twentieth century, of the circumstances in which a different attitude was taken by the law to polygamous marriages from that taken to monogamous marriages. Although differences still remain, they are now for all practical purposes limited to marriages which are actually, rather than potentially, polygamous.[355]

The high water mark of the antipathy to polygamy is to be seen in the judgment of Lord Penzance in *Hyde v Hyde*:[356] an Englishman, who had embraced the Mormon faith, married a Mormon lady in Utah according to the Mormon rites. After cohabiting with her for three years and having children by her, he renounced his faith and soon afterwards became the minister of a dissenting chapel in England. He petitioned for a decree of divorce after his wife had contracted another marriage in Utah according to the Mormon faith. Lord Penzance assumed that a Mormon marriage was potentially polygamous, and he refused to dissolve the marriage. He defined "marriage, as understood in Christendom . . . as the voluntary union for life of one man and one woman to the exclusion of all others".[357] The matrimonial laws of England are adapted to the Christian marriage, he thought, and are wholly inapplicable to polygamy. Parties to a polygamous marriage, therefore, "are not entitled to the remedies, the adjudication, or the relief of the matrimonial law of England".[358] Although the determination of the nature of the marriage is no longer of importance in deciding whether the parties are entitled to matrimonial relief from the English courts,[359] it is still, as will be seen,[360] of some importance in other areas of the law, such as its effect on succession, a later re-marriage, or social security entitlement.

(b) Nature of a polygamous marriage

Some further consideration must be given to Lord Penzance's definition. Although the form of marriage recognised by English law is generally described as a "Christian marriage",[361] this reference to religion is misleading. Whatever may be the religion of the parties or of the country in which they marry, their union is a marriage in the English sense provided that, in the eyes of the relevant law, it possesses the two attributes of indefinite duration and the exclusion of all other persons. Monogamy, for instance, is not and never has been the monopoly of Christianity. Given these two attributes, the union constitutes an English marriage notwithstanding that it may have been contracted in what mid-Victorian judges called an "infidel country", or contracted between non-Christians.[362]

---

the EU", Chapter 13 in Meeusen, Pertegas, Straetmans and Swennen (eds), *International Family Law for the European Union* (2007); and Gaffney-Rhys [2011] IFL 319.

[355] Infra, p 941 et seq.

[356] (1866) LR 1 P & D 130.

[357] Ibid, at 133. For a more recent assessment, see Poulter (1979) 42 MLR 409.

[358] Ibid, at 138.

[359] Matrimonial Causes Act 1973, s 47, replacing with minor amendments, s 1 of the Matrimonial Proceedings (Polygamous Marriages) Act 1972, and amended by the Private International Law (Miscellaneous Provisions) Act 1995, s 8(2), Sch, para 2, discussed infra, p 952 et seq. See also *M v M (Divorce: Jurisdiction: Validity of Marriage)* [2001] 2 FLR 6 at paras 48 et seq.

[360] Infra, p 941 et seq.

[361] Eg *Warrender v Warrender* (1835) 2 Cl & Fin 488 at 532.

[362] *Brinkley v A-G* (1890) 15 PD 76—marriage in Japan between an Englishman domiciled in Ireland and a Japanese woman; *Spivack v Spivack* (1930) 99 LJP 52—Jewish marriage; *Penhas v Tan Soo Eng* [1953] AC 304—marriage between a Jew and a non-Christian solemnised according to mixed Chinese and Jewish rites; and see *Ali v Ali* [1968] P 564 at 576.

The exclusion of polygamy from the English concept of marriage has been held to extend to a marriage that, although actually monogamous, is potentially polygamous.[363] If a husband has been entitled by the law that determined the nature of his marriage to take a plurality of wives, his marriage was considered to be polygamous notwithstanding that at the time when the question was raised he had not exercised that right nor ever intended to.[364] If the marriage was potentially polygamous at its inception then, though it might be possible to change it into a monogamous marriage, it retained its polygamous nature until such change was actually made.

Thus in *Sowa v Sowa*:[365]

> A polygamous marriage was celebrated in Ghana where the parties were domiciled. Prior to the ceremony the husband promised the wife that he would go through a later ceremony which, according to the law of Ghana, would convert the union into a monogamous marriage. He failed to carry out his promise.

It was held that, despite his promise and despite the fact that the husband had not taken an additional wife, the marriage continued to be regarded as polygamous. In conformity with this reasoning, *Mehta v Mehta*[366] indicates that a marriage that is monogamous at its inception is not to be regarded as potentially polygamous merely because the husband is free later to change his religion and join a polygamous sect.[367] It should also be noted that the suggestion in this case that the inception of the marriage is the only time for determining its nature has been disapproved.[368] Such a marriage will remain monogamous until there has been the requisite change.

The border-line between polygamy and concubinage presents a problem in determining the nature of a marriage. In *Lee v Lau*,[369] a marriage in Hong Kong in which the husband, under Chinese customary law, though not permitted to remarry during the lifetime of his first wife, could take "*tsipsis*", ie concubines or secondary wives, was held to be potentially polygamous. In the words of the judge:

> Under a Chinese customary marriage, even if the title of "wife" is given only to the woman who was joined to the man at the marriage ceremony, that ceremony cannot be said to bring about a union to the exclusion of all others, since the husband can take fresh partners to whose status some legal recognition is given.[370]

(c) What law determines the nature of a marriage?

In effect, the inquiry here is to identify the law that determines whether the union conforms to the English concept of marriage. As we have seen, two requirements must be satisfied, the first of which is that the union is potentially for an indefinite period. The relevant law to govern this question is clear beyond all doubt, namely that of the place of celebration.[371]

---

[363] This is now only of practical importance once the marriage becomes actually polygamous, infra, p 941 et seq.
[364] *Hyde v Hyde* (1866) LR 1 P & D 130; *Sowa v Sowa* [1961] P 70; *Cheni v Cheni* [1965] P 85 at 88–9. What law determines the nature of his marriage is discussed infra.
[365] [1961] P 70.
[366] [1945] 2 All ER 690.
[367] But contrast *M v M (Divorce: Jurisdiction: Validity of Marriage)* [2001] 2 FLR 6, per Hughes J, at [54].
[368] Infra, p 933 et seq.
[369] [1967] P 14; cf *Ng Ping On v Ng Choy Fund Kam* [1963] SRNSW 782; and see *Re Ah Chong* (1913) 33 NZLR 384; *Yuen Tse v Minister of Employment* (1983) 32 RFL (2d) 274; *Tang Lai Saukiu v Tang Loi* [1987] HKLR 85 at 90.
[370] *Lee v Lau* [1967] P 14 at 20.
[371] *Nachimson v Nachimson* [1930] P 217.

On the other hand, the law that determines whether the marriage is monogamous or polyga-mous has not yet been settled beyond all doubt.

> If, for instance, a woman domiciled in England marries a Muslim in London and then cohabits with him in Pakistan where he is domiciled, what law determines whether her mar-riage is monogamous or polygamous in nature?[372]

The choice lies between English law as the law of the place of celebration and the law of her ante-nuptial domicile, and Pakistani law as the law of his ante-nuptial domicile and, pre-sumably, of both their post-nuptial domiciles. There is, unfortunately, no case in which this issue has been squarely raised and fully discussed. Whichever be the law, there is much to be said for the view that its function is to determine the nature and incidents of the marriage according to its own view, but not necessarily to impose that classification on the court of the forum. This approach may be seen from *Lee v Lau*[373] where Chinese customary law, being the law to which it was considered that reference should be made to determine the nature of the marriage, regarded the marriage as monogamous. Nevertheless, Cairns J considered that, although reference should be made to the law of the place of celebration to determine the nature and incidents of the union by that law, the ultimate decision on the classification of the nature of the marriage, as with issues of classification generally, must be made by the law of the forum.

There is much to be said in favour of the view that the appropriate law by which to test the monogamous or polygamous character of a marriage is the law of the domicile. To apply the law of the place of celebration runs against the fundamental principle that matters of status, especially the status of husband and wife, are regulated by the law of the domicile. The propo-sition that the nature of a marriage should be determined by the law of the domicile, not by the law of the place of celebration, is certainly not devoid of judicial support.[374]

Determination of the nature of a marriage by reference to the law of the domicile does, how-ever, create a number of real difficulties. Given that a married woman may have a domicile separate from her husband,[375] the problem would arise of deciding whether the domicile of the husband or of the wife, if different, should determine the nature of the marriage. If such a difficulty is to be avoided, and surely it should be, then the nature of a marriage ought to be determined by the law of the place of celebration. Furthermore, to do otherwise would mean acceptance of the fact that a marriage in an English register office could be a polyg-amous marriage. Such a conclusion should be reached only on the clearest authority. There is a further argument against reference to the law of the domicile. In some jurisdictions, both monogamous and polygamous marriages are recognised and therefore the nature of a particular marriage in such a country depends on the form of the ceremony by which it is celebrated. This, as has been seen,[376] indicates a matter to be considered by the law of the place of celebration.[377]

---

[372] The question whether it is a *valid* marriage, of whatever nature, is discussed, infra, p 933 et seq.

[373] Supra; and see *Hassan v Hassan* [1978] 1 NZLR 385 at 390.

[374] *Warrender v Warrender* (1835) 2 Cl & Fin 488 at 535; *Kenward v Kenward* [1951] P 124 at 145; *Russ v Russ* [1964] P 315 at 326; *Ali v Ali* [1968] P 564 at 576–7; *Hussain v Hussain* [1983] Fam 26, infra, p 939, Carter (1982) 53 BYBIL 298; and see Briggs (1983) 31 ICLQ 737, 738. It seems also to have been assumed in *Radwan v Radwan (No 2)* [1973] Fam 35 that the law of the domicile or of the intended matrimonial home determined that the marriage in question was polygamous, because the place of celebration was held (at pp 42–3) to be France.

[375] Domicile and Matrimonial Proceedings Act 1973, s 1.

[376] Supra, p 893.

[377] Eg *Sowa v Sowa* [1961] P 70; *Kassim v Kassim* [1962] P 224; and see *Mohamed v Knott* [1969] 1 QB 1; Mendes da Costa (1966) 44 Can Bar Rev 293, 302.

When one turns to consider what authority there is for reference to the law of the place of celebration, it is true that one will find that a number of the cases often cited in favour of this view[378] have, as the result of careful analysis, been properly described as "either irrelevant or ambiguous".[379] *Hyde v Hyde*[380] itself is not clear on this matter for it is not certain whether the husband was domiciled in Utah where the marriage was celebrated, and so there may have been no conflict between the law of the domicile and of the place of celebration.

It is clear that the crucial case for the determination of this issue is one where the law of the place of celebration is different from that of the domicile.[381] Such a case was *Re Bethell*:[382]

> The deceased had "married" a native girl in Bechuanaland (now Botswana) at a ceremony in accordance with the custom of her tribe, the Barolong tribe, by whose custom marriage was considered to be potentially polygamous. Just after his death, a child was born and a question arose as to whether the child was legitimate for the purposes of an English will.

Having accepted the uncontroverted evidence that the deceased was domiciled in England at the time of his marriage, Stirling J nevertheless concluded that the marriage was a Barolong marriage and thus polygamous. It is clear that the deceased's domiciliary law did not determine the nature of the marriage; though whether, in considering Barolong custom, Stirling J can be said to be referring to the law of the place of celebration is a little doubtful without evidence of the law prevailing in Bechuanaland at that time.[383]

Reference to the law of the place of celebration was assumed to be beyond doubt in *Qureshi v Qureshi*:[384]

> The parties were both Moslems. The husband was domiciled at all material times in Pakistan. The wife was apparently domiciled before her marriage in India and, after her marriage, she assumed her husband's domicile in Pakistan. By both personal laws the marriage was potentially polygamous. They married in an English register office, followed by a religious ceremony. The question arose of recognition in England of an extra-judicial divorce by *talak*.[385]

Although not essential to his decision, Sir Jocelyn Simon P had no doubt that this was a monogamous marriage, for the marriage "having taken place in England, where monogamy is the rule, must be regarded as monogamous for the purpose of invoking the jurisdiction of the court".[386]

More recently, in *M v M (Divorce: Jurisdiction: Validity of Marriage)*,[387] a question arose, in the context of divorce proceedings:

---

[378] *Hyde v Hyde* (1866) LR 1 P & D 130; *Chetti v Chetti* [1909] P 67; *R v Hammersmith Marriage Registrar* [1917] 1 KB 634, CA; *R v Naguib* [1917] 1 KB 359; *Maher v Maher* [1951] P 342 (this last case was overruled as regards another point by *Russ v Russ* [1964] P 315, CA); *Risk v Risk* [1951] P 50. The Scottish decision in *Lendrum v Chakravati* 1929 SLT 96 favours the law of the place of celebration (overruled on another point by *MacDougall v Chitnavis* 1937 SC 390).
[379] Bartholomew (1964) 13 ICLQ 1022, 1058.
[380] (1866) LR 1 P & D 130.
[381] In *Iman Din v National Assistance Board* [1967] 2 QB 213 at 218–19, Salmon LJ went so far as to infer that whether a marriage is polygamous is determined by reference to both the personal law of the parties and the law of the country in which it was celebrated, but this seems to be a doubtful proposition.
[382] (1888) 38 Ch D 220.
[383] Bartholomew (1964) 13 ICLQ 1022, 1052–3.
[384] [1972] Fam 173; and see *Chetti v Chetti* [1909] P 67; *Ohochuku v Ohochuku* [1960] 1 All ER 253.
[385] Discussed, infra, p 1012 et seq.
[386] [1972] Fam 173 at 182.
[387] [2001] 2 FLR 6.

A couple married in 1980 in an Islamic ceremony in a flat in London. At the time of the ceremony, the husband was still married to an existing wife under the civil law of Egypt, which accorded with Islamic religious law and which permitted polygamy. The husband retained an Iraqi domicile throughout. The second wife had been domiciled in several Middle Eastern states before acquiring an English domicile of choice in 1992.

The court held that the ceremony was not a valid marriage under section 11 of the Matrimonial Causes Act 1973. Hughes J stated that:

> When a marriage is characterised as monogamous or polygamous it is often, for convenience, referred to as a marriage in monogamous or polygamous form. That does not mean that a marriage derives its character from the contents of the ceremony. Some ceremonies plainly do refer either to the monogamous, or to the polygamous, rules under which they are conducted . . . But the marriage ceremony need not refer to the question at all . . . What characterises a valid marriage, at any rate at its inception, as monogamous or polygamous is the law of the country in which it is conducted . . . English law contemplates that a marriage will be monogamous.[388]

His Lordship continued:

> A valid English marriage may thus properly be described as monogamous. It may be entered into by persons whose personal laws would allow them to contract polygamous unions, but it remains, if a valid English marriage, a monogamous one.[389] . . . There is neither room for, nor occasion for, any category of potentially polygamous marriage contracted in England.[390]

Thus, the character of a marriage is determined not by the form of the ceremony, but by the law of the country in which it takes place.

One may conclude that, other than on the issue of capacity to marry,[391] all marriages in England are to be characterised as monogamous and that all marriages of English domiciliaries in a foreign country, according to polygamous forms or custom, will be regarded as polygamous. If there is a civil ceremony in England, followed by a religious one, it is the former which constitutes the legal monogamous marriage.[392]

(d) Can the nature of a marriage change?

One issue which has caused difficulty in the past is whether the nature of a marriage as monogamous or polygamous is to be determined as at the date of the marriage or of later legal proceedings. In other words, can the nature of a marriage change? This issue has usually arisen in the context of a claimed change in character from potentially polygamous to monogamous and has diminished in importance as the differences between the two kinds of marriage have narrowed.[393] Earlier cases rejected any possibility of change,[394] but it is now apparent from more recent decisions that English courts will recognise a change in the nature of a marriage after its inception. This is seen quite clearly from *Cheni v Cheni*,[395] where the facts were these:

> Two Sephardic Jews, uncle and niece domiciled in Egypt, were married in Cairo and a child was born to them two years later. By Jewish and Egyptian law the marriage was potentially polygamous in the sense that if no child was born within ten years the husband might take another wife subject to the approval both of his first wife and of the Rabbinical court. Five years after

---

[388] Ibid, at [50].
[389] Ibid, at [51].
[390] Ibid, at [53].
[391] Infra, p 936 et seq.
[392] *Qureshi v Qureshi* [1972] Fam 173 at 186.
[393] Infra, p 941.
[394] See *Hyde v Hyde* (1866) LR 1 P & D 130; *Mehta v Mehta* [1945] 2 All ER 690; *Sowa v Sowa* [1961] P 70.
[395] [1965] P 85.

the parties had acquired an English domicile, the wife petitioned for a decree of nullity on the ground that she and her husband were within the prohibited degrees of consanguinity.

The court had no jurisdiction at the time[396] to entertain this suit if the marriage was potentially polygamous. Sir Jocelyn Simon P was satisfied that at its inception it was undoubtedly of that nature, because of the remote possibility of an additional wife being taken, but he then held that the decisive date for considering its polygamous potential was the start of the instant proceedings. By that date the birth of the child had rendered the marriage monogamous, and the court assumed jurisdiction.

It is now accepted that there is a variety of ways in which the nature of a marriage may be changed from polygamous to monogamous. Furthermore, given that the nature of the marriage can change, then a corollary is that the relevant time for determining the nature of the marriage is that of the commencement of the proceedings in question.[397] Various examples of change from potentially polygamous to monogamous can be given, but it must always be remembered that the marriage must initially be regarded as valid. So a purported change in the nature of a *void* polygamous marriage will not turn it into a *valid* monogamous marriage. If the personal law of the parties refers the nature of their marriage to their religious law, then a change of religion may be held to alter the nature of the marriage.[398] If the law under which the marriage was celebrated later forbids polygamy, then such legislative action will render the marriage monogamous from henceforth,[399] and it has been seen that the birth of a child to the spouses can change the nature of their marriage under the relevant religious law.[400]

There is some authority that, where there is a marriage in polygamous form followed by a later marriage between the same parties in monogamous form, the parties are to be regarded as monogamously married. In *Ohochuku v Ohochuku*[401] a potentially polygamous marriage in Nigeria was followed four years later by a ceremony of marriage in monogamous form, in England, between the same parties. Unable to grant a divorce dissolving the first marriage, the court dissolved the later marriage, thus apparently ignoring the polygamous nature of the union ascribed to the parties at the date of their first marriage. It is suggested that this decision is out of harmony with *Baindail v Baindail*[402] and *Thynne v Thynne*,[403] both decided by the Court of Appeal. As we shall see, it was held in the former case that a polygamous marriage valid according to the law of the parties' domicile is valid in the eyes of English law and therefore that it is an effective bar to a subsequent marriage with a third person in England.[404] *Thynne v Thynne* decided that what a decree of divorce dissolves is not any particular ceremony, but rather the existing status of the parties as husband and wife.[405] The

---

[396] See now Matrimonial Causes Act 1973, s 47 as amended by the Private International Law (Miscellaneous Provisions) Act 1995, s 8(2), Sch, para 2.

[397] *Cheni v Cheni* [1965] P 85 at 92; *Parkasho v Singh* [1968] P 233 at 254–5.

[398] *Sinha Peerage Claim* (1939) 171 Lords Journals 350, [1946] 1 All ER 348 n. See also *Cheni v Cheni* [1965] P 85 at 90–1. An interesting, though undecided, issue is whether the change of religion of only one of the spouses has this effect: *A-G of Ceylon v Reid* [1965] AC 720 suggests that it might. See Webb (1965) 14 ICLQ 992, 996–7.

[399] *Parkasho v Singh* [1968] P 233, a decision on the effect of the Hindu Marriage Act 1955 prohibiting polygamy for Hindus in India, as to which the National Insurance Commissioners had much earlier reached the same conclusion: Decision No R (G) 2/56; and see *Poon v Tan* (1973) 4 Fam Law 161; *R v Sagoo* [1975] QB 885.

[400] *Cheni v Cheni*, supra.

[401] [1960] 1 All ER 253; cf National Insurance Decision No R (G) 11/53; *Sowa v Sowa* [1961] P 70, supra, p 930.

[402] [1946] P 122.

[403] [1955] P 272.

[404] Infra, p 941.

[405] And see *Peters v Peters* (1968) 112 Sol Jo 311.

parties in the *Ohochuku* case possessed a polygamous status according to the law of Nigeria where they were still domiciled and where the first marriage was celebrated. The parties could not be transformed from polygamists to monogamists simply by the nullifying of the English ceremony, because this would not affect their status under the still subsisting Nigerian marriage.[406] It is only if it can be said that the later English marriage altered the character of the first Nigerian marriage that the parties could claim to have acquired a monogamous status.[407]

Finally, *Ali v Ali*[408] provides authority for the proposition that, if a husband changes his domicile from a country which permits polygamy to one which does not, this change of domicile renders the marriage monogamous. The facts were these:

> The parties, both domiciled in India, entered into a valid potentially polygamous marriage there. Later they came to England and the wife left the husband. The husband acquired an English domicile in 1963 and petitioned for divorce on the ground of his wife's desertion. She cross-petitioned on the grounds of the husband's cruelty until she left him, and his adultery in 1964. The court's jurisdiction depended at that time on whether the marriage, at the time of the proceedings, was to be regarded as polygamous or monogamous.

Cumming-Bruce J concluded that the husband's acquisition of an English domicile and continued residence in England precluded him, apart from obtaining a divorce, from marrying a second wife in the lifetime of the first. This prohibition on remarriage was considered to have impressed a monogamous character on his previously polygamous marriage, even though there was no conscious act on the part of the parties directed to this end. Furthermore, the court rejected the argument that the mutability of a marriage depends on whether the facts relied upon to effect the change are capable of taking place in the place of celebration, or probably, according to its law.[409] In other words, although the nature of the marriage is decided by the law of the place of celebration, the issue of mutability is not determined at the time of the marriage.

Now that the main raison d'être for the decision in *Ali v Ali*, namely the rule denying English matrimonial relief to the parties to an actually or potentially polygamous marriage, has disappeared,[410] both the decision and the difficulties posed by it[411] may, one hopes, be regarded as of little more than academic interest.

A marriage that is in fact polygamous cannot be changed to a monogamous one by, for example, a change of domicile by one[412] of the wives or by both;[413] but the problem might arise in the case of a marriage which, though once in fact polygamous, has ceased to be so, eg by divorce or by the death of a wife before the change. If, after the acquisition of an English

---

[406] The decision may perhaps be supported on the ground that the Nigerian law of the subsisting domicile would regard the decree as effective to dissolve the polygamous marriage, a question which the judge was not prepared to consider.

[407] *Cheni v Cheni* [1965] P 85 at 91; *Ali v Ali* [1968] P 564 at 578; *Parkasho v Singh* [1968] P 233 at 242; cf Carter (1965–1966) 41 BYBIL 443. Even so, if the Nigerian marriage was valid, how could they be married again in England? See *Ali v Ali*, supra.

[408] [1968] P 564; and see *R v Sagoo* [1975] QB 885; National Insurance Decision No R (G) 3/75; *Re Hassan v Hassan* (1976) 69 DLR (3d) 224; Social Security Decision No R (G) 1/95. A similar conclusion had been reached much earlier by the National Insurance Commissioners, see Decision No R (G) 12/56.

[409] [1968] P 564 at 575; cf Carter (1963) 39 BYBIL 474, 478. See the rejection of a similar argument in *Parkasho v Singh* [1968] P 233 at 244–5; cf Carter (1967) 42 BYBIL 300–1; and see the slight doubts of Cumming-Bruce J in *Radwan v Radwan* [1973] Fam 24 at 27.

[410] Infra, p 952.

[411] Carter (1965–1966) 41 BYBIL 442–4; Mendes da Costa (1966) 44 Can Bar Rev 293, 307–10; Tolstoy (1968) 17 ICLQ 721; cf Morris (1968) 17 ICLQ 1014.

[412] Eg *Onobrauche v Onobrauche* (1978) 8 Fam Law 107.

[413] Eg *Re Sehota* [1978] 1 WLR 1506.

domicile, the marriage ceased to be in fact polygamous, then that fact combined with the acquisition of an English domicile might well render the marriage monogamous.[414]

The discussion of mutability has centred so far on the change from a polygamous to a monogamous nature. Some consideration must be given to the possibility of change from monogamy to polygamy. If a marriage may be changed from polygamy to monogamy then it might seem logical to recognise a change the other way, based on similar circumstances, eg change of religion or change of law.[415] It has, however, been suggested that a marriage has the benefit of any doubt as to monogamy, ie that "it is sufficient that it is either monogamous in its inception or has become so by the time of the proceedings".[416] This would mean that even though it might be possible to change the nature of a marriage from monogamous to polygamous such change would not affect the attitude of English law towards it. Such an approach would afford a convenient way of dissipating the force of the argument that all monogamous marriages are potentially polygamous in that the spouses are free to change their religion or domicile and thus the nature of their marriage.[417]

There are very real difficulties with a view that, if parties marry in monogamous form, eg in England, one party (normally the husband) may change the whole nature of their marriage by changing his religion or domicile and thereby rendering the marriage potentially polygamous. To deny these difficulties would be to deny that polygamy is a different social and legal institution from monogamy.[418] The problem is seen most sharply where there is a possibility of a man being monogamously married to his first wife and polygamously married to his second, as where a husband domiciled in England marries his first wife, an English domiciliary, in England in a monogamous form and then, having acquired a domicile in Pakistan, marries a second wife, a Pakistan domiciliary, in Pakistan in polygamous form.[419] It would seem most unfair to the first wife that her marriage should, by the unilateral act of her husband, be changed in nature from monogamous to polygamous. This raises two issues—whether the second marriage is valid and, if so, what effect it has on the first marriage and on the rights of the first wife. Such authority as there is points in favour of the validity of the second marriage, which would satisfy general English choice of law rules.[420] It also appears that the fact that the husband has entered a second valid polygamous marriage does not change the nature of the first marriage as monogamous, leaving the first wife free, for example, to petition for divorce on the basis of adultery by the husband in taking a second wife.[421]

(e) Capacity to contract a polygamous marriage

(i) Common law choice of law rules

There has long been controversy in identifying the law that governs capacity in the case of a polygamous union, and the present law on this issue is a confusing mixture of common law and

---

[414] Law Com No 42 (1971), para 13.

[415] See *A-G of Ceylon v Reid* [1965] AC 720 for consideration of this problem under the law of Ceylon; but their Lordships, at 734, declined to express any opinion on "the situation in a purely Christian country"; and see Pearl [1972 A] CLJ 120, 139–42; cf *PP v White* (1940) 9 MLJ 214; and *M v M (Divorce: Jurisdiction: Validity of Marriage)* [2001] 2 FLR 6, per Hughes J, at [53] and [54].

[416] *Cheni v Cheni* [1965] P 85 at 90. This is supported, further, by *Mehta v Mehta* [1945] 2 All ER 690 at 693; *Parkasho v Singh* [1968] P 233 at 243–4.

[417] See *Cheni v Cheni* [1965] P 85 at 90; *Parkasho v Singh* [1968] P 233 at 244.

[418] See Carter (1982) 53 BYBIL 298, 299–300.

[419] The problem is the same if the husband was, at all times, domiciled in Pakistan.

[420] *Drammeh v Drammeh* (1970) 78 Ceylon Law Weekly 55, PC, infra, pp 943–4; *A-G of Ceylon v Reid* [1965] AC 720. In *Nabi v Heaton* [1981] 1 WLR 1052 at 1056–1057, Vinelott J declined to decide the question; and see infra, pp 944–5.

[421] See infra, pp 953–4, and see Law Com No 146; Scot Law Com No 98 (1985), paras 4.10–4.24.

statute. There is support at common law for this issue to be referred to the ante-nuptial domicile of both parties,[422] the law of the intended matrimonial home[423] or the law of the place of celebration.[424] One argument in favour of the last view was that it is that law which determines whether a marriage is polygamous or monogamous[425] but this is not sufficient to outweigh the view that issues of marital status are to be referred to the law of the domicile and it was suggested that capacity to marry more than one spouse is an issue affecting status.[426] Indeed, there was a clear rejection of reference to the law of the place of celebration by Cumming-Bruce J in *Ali v Ali*.[427] He concluded that a husband domiciled in England and intending to reside there[428] did not have capacity to confer the status of "wife" on anyone else, no matter where he purported to "marry" a second wife.[429]

If the law of the place of celebration is rejected, the choice used to lie between the law of the intended matrimonial home and the law of the domicile, and, as has been seen, there was authority in support of both. The fullest fairly recent discussion of the choice of law issue is to be found in *Radwan v Radwan (No 2)*[430] which supports the intended matrimonial home approach. Here, Cumming-Bruce J applied the law of Egypt to determine the issue of capacity to enter an actually polygamous marriage celebrated in the Egyptian Consulate General in Paris between a domiciled Egyptian and a domiciled Englishwoman, the parties intending to live in Egypt, which in fact they did. It was the judge's considered view that the law to determine capacity to enter a polygamous marriage, if no other question of capacity, should be that of the intended matrimonial home.

This decision was greeted with widespread,[431] though not unanimous,[432] criticism—primarily for its rejection of the dual domicile approach and for indicating that a special capacity rule in the case of polygamous marriages can be justified.[433] There is certainly a weight of authority supporting the view that capacity to contract a polygamous marriage is to be determined by the law of the ante-nuptial domicile,[434] whether the marriage is actually[435] or potentially[436] polygamous. Two further factors support this approach. In a number

---

[422] Eg *Re Ullee* (1885) 53 LT 711 at 712; *Lendrum v Chakravarti* 1929 SLT 96 at 99 (overruled on another point by *Lendrum v Chakravarti* 1937 SC 390).

[423] *Kenward v Kenward* [1951] P 124 at 145; *Radwan v Radwan (No 2)* [1973] Fam 35, [1972] 3 All ER 1026.

[424] *Kaur v Ginder* (1958) 13 DLR (2d) 465. In *Sara v Sara* (1962) 31 DLR (2d) 566, varied on other grounds 36 DLR (2d) 499, it seems to have been assumed that capacity by the law of the place of celebration is all that is required.

[425] Supra, p 930 et seq.

[426] The reference in *Kaur v Ginder*, supra, to the law of the place of celebration was on the basis that power to enter a polygamous marriage was more an issue of form than capacity.

[427] [1968] P 564, supra, p 935.

[428] Thus avoiding a choice on the general question of capacity to marry between the ante-nuptial domiciliary laws of both parties and the law of the intended matrimonial home; see supra, p 910.

[429] [1968] P 564 at 576–7; but cf *A-G of Ceylon v Reid* [1965] AC 720.

[430] [1973] Fam 35.

[431] Karsten (1973) 36 MLR 291; Pearl [1973] CLJ 43; Wade (1973) 22 ICLQ 571.

[432] See Jaffey (1978) 41 MLR 38; Stone [1983] Fam Law 76; *Hassan v Hassan* [1978] 1 NZLR 385 at 389–90.

[433] This opposition was not unexpected; see [1973] Fam 35 at 54, and see supra, pp 914–15.

[434] It may well be that the decision in *Re Bethell* (1888) 38 Ch D 220 can only be justified on the ground that the "husband" had no capacity by English law, the law of the domicile, to enter into a polygamous marriage. In *Risk v Risk* [1951] P 50, the court declined jurisdiction to consider this issue on the ground that the marriage, whether valid or not, was polygamous.

[435] *Crowe v Kader* [1968] WAR 122; *Ishiodu v Entry Clearance Officer, Lagos* [1975] Imm AR 56; *R v Immigration Appeal Tribunal, ex p Asfar Jan* [1995] Imm AR 440; Social Security Decisions Nos R (S) 2/92; R (G) 4/93.

[436] *Ali v Ali* [1968] P 564 at 576–7; *Afza Mussarat v Secretary of State for the Home Department* [1972] Imm AR 45; cf Hartley (1969) 32 MLR 155, 158–60.

of cases since 1973 in which the validity of a polygamous marriage has arisen, the court or tribunal has simply applied the law of the domicile without any consideration of whether that country was the same as that of the intended matrimonial home.[437] The second factor is that Parliament seems also to have assumed that the dual domicile test was the law.[438] It is necessary now to look more closely at the current statutory provisions.

(ii) Statutory provisions

In the context of capacity to enter a polygamous marriage, it is necessary first to consider sections 11 and 14 of the Matrimonial Causes Act 1973, which in their original form provided as follows:

11 A marriage celebrated after 31 July 1971 shall be void on the following grounds only, that is to say . . .

(b) that at the time of the marriage either party was already lawfully married . . .

(d) in the case of a polygamous marriage entered into outside England and Wales, that either party was at the time of the marriage domiciled in England and Wales.

For the purposes of paragraph (d) of this subsection a marriage may be polygamous although at its inception neither party has any spouse additional to the other.

. . .

14 Where, apart from this Act, any matter affecting the validity of a marriage would fall to be determined (in accordance with the rules of private international law) by reference to the law of a country outside England and Wales, nothing in section 11 . . . above shall—

(a) preclude the determination of that matter as aforesaid; or

(b) require the application to the marriage of the grounds . . . there mentioned except so far as applicable in accordance with those rules.

Two rather different issues arise. The first is whether, in relation to marriages celebrated after 31 July 1971, these provisions embody a choice of law rule; and the second is to determine the effect of the provisions in cases to which they apply. As to the first issue, although as has been seen[439] some recent decisions have proceeded on the basis that section 11 of the 1973 Act applies whenever one party is domiciled in England, that approach was specifically rejected by Cumming-Bruce J in *Radwan v Radwan (No 2)*.[440] In considering the statutory predecessors of sections 11 and 14,[441] the judge concluded that the Law Commission,[442] the government and Parliament had laboured under a misapprehension as to the common law rules on capacity.[443] His conclusion that the choice of law rule is that the law of the intended matrimonial home should apply has the following effect. Section 11 would not apply in those cases where the parties did not intend to set up a matrimonial home in England, as was the position in *Radwan* itself. This was because section 14 of the 1973 Act expressly preserved the application of the substantive law of another country held to be applicable under our rules of private international law.[444] Put

---

[437] Eg *Hussain v Hussain* [1983] Fam 26; *Zahra v Visa Officer, Islamabad* [1979–80] Imm AR 48; *Rokeya Begum v Entry Clearance Officer, Dacca* [1983] Imm AR 163; National Insurance Decision No R (G) 3/75; and see Social Security Decision No R (G) 1/95.

[438] Matrimonial Causes Act 1973, s 11(d); Private International Law (Miscellaneous Provisions) Act 1995, s 5; and s 8(2), Sch, para 2 of the 1995 Act also amends the 1973 Act.

[439] Supra, pp 937–8.

[440] [1973] Fam 35.

[441] Namely, s 4 of the Matrimonial Proceedings (Polygamous Marriages) Act 1972 and s 4 of the Nullity of Marriage Act 1971.

[442] The predecessor of s 11 is based on Law Com No 42 (1971).

[443] [1973] Fam 35 at 52.

[444] And see the Private International Law (Miscellaneous Provisions) Act 1995, s 5(2).

another way, section 11(d) could only apply to invalidate a marriage if one party was domiciled in England *and* the parties intended to live in England. Of course, if *Radwan* was not followed, section 11(d) would apply whenever one party was domiciled in England, irrespective of the intended matrimonial home.

We must now turn to examine the second issue, namely the effect of section 11 in those polygamous marriage cases where validity *is* governed by English law. From 1973 until 1983, anxiety had been expressed over the impact of section 11(d) in the following type of circumstance.

> An immigrant to the United Kingdom from Pakistan becomes domiciled in England and then returns to Pakistan to marry, for the first time, in Moslem form bringing his new wife back to England with him. This marriage was regarded as potentially polygamous with the result, so it was thought, that the marriage was void under section 11(d)—a conclusion which was much criticised.[445]

Had the Pakistani man been only resident, and not domiciled, in England, his marriage would have been valid[446] and, indeed, would become monogamous in character on his acquisition of an English domicile.[447] Furthermore, if the marriage had taken place in England, being monogamous in fact and in character, it would also have been valid.

Sustained criticism of the effect of section 11(d) in the case of a potentially polygamous marriage prompted the Law Commission to consider the case for reform. The day that its Working Paper was due to be sent for printing,[448] the Court of Appeal in *Hussain v Hussain*[449] cast a wholly new light on the effect of section 11 of the 1973 Act. The facts were as follows:

> The husband and wife married in Pakistan in 1979. They were Moslems and they married in a form appropriate for polygamous marriages. At all times the marriage was in fact monogamous. At the time of the marriage the husband was domiciled in England and the wife in Pakistan. When, on the subsequent breakdown of the marriage, the wife petitioned in England for judicial separation, the husband argued that the marriage was void by reason of section 11(d) in that it was polygamous in nature and that he was domiciled in England at the relevant time.

The Court of Appeal rejected the husband's argument and held the marriage to be valid. In so doing, it met many of the criticisms of section 11(d) and achieved a good deal, though not all, of the reform sought by the Law Commission; but the Court also created a range of further problems and turned on its head the law as it had been assumed to be for a decade by lawyers, immigrants and government officials alike.[450]

The reasoning of the Court of Appeal was as follows. Section 11(d) prevented an English domiciliary from entering a polygamous marriage, whether actually or potentially polygamous, but "a marriage can only be potentially polygamous if at least one of the spouses has the capacity to marry a second spouse".[451] However, in the case of a person domiciled in England, there was no capacity to enter an actually polygamous marriage because section 11(b) of the 1973 Act rendered a person who is actually married incapable of marrying a

---

[445] See Hartley (1971) 34 MLR 305, 306–7; Cretney (1972) 116 Sol Jo 654; Poulter (1976) 25 ICLQ 475, 503–8; James (1979) 42 MLR 533, 536.
[446] Eg *Ishiodu v Entry Clearance Officer, Lagos* [1975] Imm AR 56.
[447] Supra, p 933 et seq.
[448] Working Paper No 83 (1982), para 1.3.
[449] [1983] Fam 26.
[450] Law Commission Working Paper No 83 (1982), paras 4.3–4.39.
[451] [1983] Fam 26 at 32.

second spouse.[452] On this reasoning, the marriage in question was valid. It was not to be regarded as potentially polygamous, and thus falling within section 11(d), because the wife was incapable, under the Moslem law of Pakistan, of marrying a second husband, and the husband was incapable under English law, namely section 11(b) of the 1973 Act, of marrying a second wife.

Whilst the actual decision of the Court of Appeal was welcomed, the process of reasoning by which it was reached and the implications to be drawn from it were widely criticised.[453] It only applied to marriages celebrated after 31 July 1971 because that was the limit of the scope of section 11. This meant that the validity of earlier polygamous marriages was governed by the common law under which a marriage in circumstances similar to *Hussain* would be void. Furthermore, even in the case of a marriage after 31 July 1971, it would be void if the position of the parties in *Hussain* had been reversed, ie the wife was domiciled in England and the husband in Pakistan. This was because the marriage would then be regarded as polygamous in nature, and thus within section 11(d), as the husband was capable under his personal law of marrying a second wife.[454]

This unsatisfactory state of the law on capacity to enter a polygamous marriage led the Law Commission to recommend[455] further reform in the wake of *Hussain*. These proposals were implemented by Part II of the Private International Law (Miscellaneous Provisions) Act 1995. The result is that section 11 of the Matrimonial Causes Act 1973 is amended so as to limit its operation to actually polygamous marriages.[456] Furthermore, section 5(1) of the 1995 Act provides that:

> A marriage entered into outside England and Wales between parties neither of whom is already married is not void under the law of England and Wales on the ground that it is entered into under a law which permits polygamy and that either party is domiciled in England and Wales.

The impact of these changes is that both men and women domiciled in England have capacity under English law to enter a marriage abroad which, though polygamous in form, is in fact monogamous. Two caveats must be expressed. The first is that these changes do not affect the determination of the validity of a marriage to which the law of another country is to be applied under English rules of private international law.[457] The second is that there is no change in the rule that there is no capacity under English law to enter an actually polygamous marriage.[458] The changes are also subject to a number of limitations. Although the changes have retrospective effect[459] and will, therefore, retrospectively validate some marriages thought to be invalid, there will be no such validation where a party to the marriage in question has entered a later marriage which was valid under the law as it was at the time it was celebrated,[460] or which is validated by the changes in the 1995 Act.[461] The retrospective

---

[452] The Court of Appeal assumed that s 11(d) of the 1973 Act applies to all English domiciliaries, without examining the claims of the intended matrimonial home rule laid down in *Radwan v Radwan (No 2)* [1973] Fam 35; and see *R v Junaid Khan* (1987) 84 Cr App Rep 44.

[453] Carter (1982) 53 BYBIL 298; Briggs (1983) 32 ICLQ 737; Pearl [1983] CLJ 26; Schuz (1983) 46 MLR 653; Poulter (1983) 13 Fam Law 72.

[454] Eg Social Security Decision No R (SB) 17/84.

[455] Law Com No 146; Scot Law Com No 96 (1985), Pt II.

[456] 1995 Act, Sch, para 2(2).

[457] Ibid, s 5(2); and see Law Com No 146; Scot Law Com No 96 (1985), paras 2.1–2.3.

[458] See Law Com No 146; Scot Law Com No 96 (1985), paras 4.2–4.8. Cf *Azad v Entry Clearance Officer, Dhaka* [2001] Imm AR 318, per Jacob J, at [4].

[459] 1995 Act, s 6(1).

[460] Ibid, s 6(2).

[461] Ibid, s 6(3)–(5).

effect of section 5 is also limited so as not to affect entitlement under the will or intestacy of a person dying before the provision came into effect, nor similarly to affect benefits, pensions, allowances, or tax, or succession to a dignity or title of honour.[462]

(f) Recognition of polygamous marriages in England

Although it is not possible to enter into a valid polygamous marriage in England, such a marriage abroad can be regarded as valid provided it has been validly created in the eyes of English private international law.[463] In short it must have been contracted between parties of full capacity and in accordance with the formal requirements of the law of the place of celebration.[464] The issue then arises as to the degree of recognition to be afforded by an English court to such a valid polygamous marriage.

Polygamous marriages are now recognised for a wide variety of purposes. In *Baindail v Baindail*,[465] Lord Greene MR stressed that, since the status of a person depends on his personal law, the status of husband and wife conferred on the parties to a polygamous marriage by the law of their domicile must be accepted and acted on in other countries. Although he was careful to add that it must be accepted for certain purposes only, and not for all, the present state of the law is that a polygamous marriage is recognised for most purposes. The balance of definition has tipped from defining those instances where, exceptionally, such a marriage will be recognised to defining those few instances where it may not. A variety of situations needs to be considered.

The position used to be that neither party to a polygamous marriage could invoke "the remedies, the adjudication or the relief" given either by the High Court,[466] or by magistrates' courts,[467] in the exercise of their matrimonial jurisdiction. However, such matrimonial or declaratory relief may now be granted, under section 47 of the Matrimonial Causes Act 1973,[468] whether the marriage is actually or potentially polygamous.[469] The English courts are prepared to recognise the validity of a polygamous marriage[470] as being a later marriage. This means that the second "spouse" is entitled to a nullity decree on the grounds of bigamy.[471] It might be thought that, in such a case, the spouse who "married" twice would also be guilty of the crime of bigamy. It has now been decided, however, in a lower court,[472] and approved by the Court of Appeal,[473] that a party to an existing polygamous marriage is not

---

[462] Ibid, s 6(6).

[463] See now the Private International Law (Miscellaneous Provisions) Act 1995, s 5(2).

[464] Proper investigation ought to be made by the court as to the validity of a particular marriage, and as to the status of an alleged second wife: *Ramsamy v Babar* [2003] EWCA Civ 1252, [2005] 1 FLR 113 (regarding the alleged second wife's occupation of property, as trespasser or spouse occupying the matrimonial home).

[465] [1946] P 122 at 127–8.

[466] *Hyde v Hyde* (1866) LR 1 P & D 130.

[467] *Sowa v Sowa* [1961] P 70.

[468] As amended by the Private International Law (Miscellaneous Provisions) Act 1995, s 8(2), Sch, para 2. See, eg, *El Fadl v El Fadl* [2000] 1 FLR 175; and *M v M (Divorce: Jurisdiction: Validity of Marriage)* [2001] 2 FLR 6.

[469] Infra, p 952.

[470] But the Irish courts have held that it cannot constitute a "common law" marriage: *Conlon v Mohamed* [1989] ILRM 523.

[471] [1946] P 122; and see *Srini Vasan v Srini Vasan* [1946] P 67; *Hashmi v Hashmi* [1972] Fam 36; *Alfonso-Brown v Milwood* [2006] EWHC 642, [2006] 2 FLR 265, per Singer J, at [3]; Hartley (1967) 16 ICLQ 680, 691–4.

[472] *R v Sarwan Singh* [1962] 3 All ER 612; Polonsky [1971] Crim LR 401.

[473] *R v Sagoo* [1975] QB 885; Carter (1974–1975) 47 BYBIL 374; Morse (1976) 25 ICLQ 229. The Court of Appeal held that *R v Sarwan Singh*, supra, was wrongly decided, but only on the ground that no consideration had been given as to whether the marriage had become monogamous. The general principle was approved that "the marriage which is to be the foundation for a prosecution for bigamy must be a monogamous marriage": [1975] QB 885 at 889.

"married" for the purpose of founding a criminal charge of bigamy against him. These decisions create an unfortunate distinction between the civil and the criminal law conceptions of bigamy.[474]

Turning to succession,[475] it seems fairly clear that the children of both a potentially and an actually polygamous marriage can succeed to property in England.[476] The only real doubt[477] on the issue of succession by children concerns whether a child of a polygamous marriage can succeed to a title of honour, or as an "heir" to real property or to an entailed interest.[478] This problem was discussed by Lord Maugham in *The Sinha Peerage Claim*,[479] which concerned succession to a title of honour. In fact, the marriage of the claimant's father, celebrated in polygamous form, was held to have become monogamous by change of religion.[480] In holding that the claimant could succeed to the title, Lord Maugham declined to express a view on succession as "heir" or to entails. It seems, however, that he was primarily concerned with problems which could arise in the case of an actually polygamous marriage: "If there were several wives, the son of a second or third wife might be the claimant to a dignity to the exclusion of a later born son of the first wife. Our law as to heirship has provided no means of settling such questions as these."[481] These problems relate only to actually polygamous marriages and it seems safe to assume, with the Law Commission,[482] that although a child of an actually polygamous marriage cannot succeed as "heir", no such disability attaches to the child of a potentially polygamous marriage.[483]

In the case of intestate succession by the widow of a potentially polygamous marriage, there is Privy Council authority in favour of her being able to succeed.[484] Such English authority as there is supports the view that such a widow would also be able to succeed under the Administration of Estates Act 1925.[485] There appears to be no good reason for not applying a

---

[474] Celebration of a "marriage" in England in polygamous form, in a private house, is not considered to be a celebration of a "marriage" within the meaning of s 75(2) of the Marriage Act 1949, under which it is an offence knowingly and willingly to solemnise a marriage in an unregistered building: *R v Bham* [1966] 1 QB 159; and see *R v Ali Mohamed* [1964] 2 QB 350 n. On the other hand, it might be noted that the parties to a valid polygamous marriage are married for the purposes of the crime of conspiracy so that the spouses are unable to conspire together: *Mawji v R* [1957] AC 126. If it is invalid it is of no effect in the law of evidence: *R v Junaid Khan* (1987) 84 Cr App Rep 44.

[475] Though the determination of legitimacy is now of very limited relevance (infra, Chapter 27), it might be noted that children of a valid potentially polygamous marriage are to be regarded as legitimate: *Sinha Peerage Claim* (1939) 171 Lords Journal 350, [1946] 1 All ER 348 n; *Baindail v Baindail* [1946] P 122 at 127–8. It would also appear that children of an actually polygamous marriage are to be regarded as legitimate: *Hashmi v Hashmi* [1972] Fam 36; and see *Yuen Tse v Minister of Employment and Immigration* (1983) 32 RFL (2d) 274. For criticism of *Hashmi*, see Goldberg and Lowe (1972) 35 MLR 430; Carter (1971) 45 BYBIL 413, 414.

[476] Cf *Bamgbose v Daniel* [1955] AC 107; and see National Insurance Decision No R (G) 11/53. In *Re Bethell* (1888) 38 Ch D 220, such a child was unable to succeed, but this is probably because the polygamous marriage there would not be regarded in England as a valid marriage, given the husband's incapacity by his domiciliary law, supra, p 932; cf Hartley (1969) 32 MLR 155, 171–2.

[477] See Law Commission Working Paper No 83 (1982), para 4.42.

[478] Cf Dicey, Morris and Collins, para 17-195.

[479] [1946] 1 All ER 348 n.

[480] Supra, p 933 et seq.

[481] [1946] 1 All ER 348 n at 349.

[482] Law Com No 146, Scot Law Com No 96 (1985), paras 3.5–3.6.

[483] It should be noted that, under s 6(6) of the Private International Law (Miscellaneous Provisions) Act 1995, the changes introduced by section 5, supra, p 940 do not, in the case of marriages entered into before that section came into force, affect succession rights, including succession to any dignity or title of honour.

[484] *Coleman v Shang* [1961] AC 481.

[485] In *Re Sehota* [1978] 1 WLR 1506, it was suggested (at 1511) that questions of succession had never fallen within the ambit of the rule in *Hyde v Hyde* (1866) LR 1 P & D 130; and see *Chaudhry v Chaudhry* [1976] Fam 148 at 152.

similar rule in the case of succession by the wives of an actually polygamous marriage,[486] and this approach is supported by *Re Sehota*.[487] Here the deceased husband was validly polygamously married to two wives. He left the whole of his estate to the second wife and the first wife applied successfully for reasonable provision as a "wife" out of the estate, under the Inheritance (Provision for Family and Dependants) Act 1975.[488] Indeed, in *Official Solicitor v Yemoh and others*[489] the High Court confirmed that a polygamously married wife (or wives, as in this case) should not be precluded from succeeding to a portion of the estate where she was lawfully married under the law of her domicile and the deceased was married in accordance with the law of his domicile. Consequently, such a wife constituted a surviving spouse for the purposes of intestate succession under the Administration of Estates Act 1925.

Polygamous marriages are recognised for the purpose of determining other property rights. In *Shahnaz v Rizwan*[490] a Moslem woman, whose potentially polygamous marriage celebrated in India had been validly dissolved, was held entitled to recover deferred dower from her former husband. The agreement recorded in the marriage certificate placed the husband under a contractual obligation to pay a certain sum by way of dower in the event of a divorce. Winn J was careful to emphasise[491] that the wife's right arose not out of the relationship of husband and wife, but out of a contract made in contemplation and in consideration of a marriage that was lawful in the eyes of English law. There is statutory recognition of actually and potentially polygamous marriages for the purposes of the protection granted to a spouse by Part IV of the Family Law Act 1996;[492] and it has been held that the summary procedure, under section 17 of the Married Women's Property Act 1882, for determining property disputes between husband and wife extends to polygamous marriages.[493]

Statutory recognition of polygamy is also provided by social security legislation. Regulations made under or preserved by the Social Security Contributions and Benefits Act 1992[494] now govern the present position in relation to benefits falling within these Acts, eg widow's benefit, maternity benefit and child benefit. They allow a valid polygamous marriage to be treated as a monogamous marriage if it has either always been actually monogamous or for any day throughout which it was, in fact, monogamous.[495] This means that when a marriage becomes monogamous through death or divorce or until it ceases to be monogamous by reason of

---

[486] See *Cheang Thye Phin v Tan Ah Loy* [1920] AC 369; cf *The Six Widows' Case* (1908) 12 Straits Settlements LR 120; though it must be admitted that there might be difficulty with distribution of the personal chattels.

[487] [1978] 1 WLR 1506.

[488] Contrast the result in *Gandhi v Patel* [2002] 1 FLR 603—a Hindu marriage ceremony in London amounted to a "non-marriage", and the parties thereto had not entered into it in good faith with regard to the need to satisfy English law, in particular s 25(4) of the Inheritance (Provision for Family and Dependants) Act 1975; see Park J, at [28].

[489] [2010] EWHC 3727 (Ch).

[490] [1965] 1 QB 390; and see *Qureshi v Qureshi* [1972] Fam 173.

[491] Because of the then existing inability of the court to grant matrimonial relief in the case of polygamous marriages.

[492] S 63(5).

[493] *Chaudhry v Chaudhry* [1976] Fam 148—a case of a potentially polygamous marriage.

[494] Ss 121 (1)(b), 147(5), as amended by the Private International Law (Miscellaneous Provisions) Act 1995, s 8(2), Sch, para 4, and the Civil Partnership Act 2004, Sch 24(3), para 40. The 1992 Act is a consolidation statute and regulations made under its forerunners, the Social Security Act 1975 and the Child Benefit Act 1976, continue in effect. See also State Pension Credit Act 2002, s 12; Tax Credits Act 2002, s 43; Age-Related Payments Act 2004, s 8(2); Welfare Reform Act 2007, Sch 1, para 6(7); SI 2006/213, reg 74(3); SI 2006/215, Pt 1, reg 2; SI 2015/457; and SI 2007/719, reg 2(7).

[495] SI 1975/561, regs 1(2), 2(2); and SI 2006/223, reg 35; and see National Insurance Decision Nos R (G) 2/75; R (G) 3/75; Social Security Decision Nos R (S) 2/92; R (G) 4/93; R (G) 1/95; *R v Department of Health, ex p Misra* [1996] 1 FLR 129. A similar approach is taken in the area of immigration control: *R v Immigration Appeal Tribunal, ex p Hasna Begum* [1995] Imm AR 249.

a second valid marriage there is a right to qualification for these social security benefits. If the marriage is actually polygamous at the relevant times no widowed mother's allowance is payable.[496] In the case of income support, however, a crucial factor is the nature of the relationship between a man and a woman who are members of the same household, rather than whether they are validly married. The result is that the relevant legislation[497] extends to cases of actually polygamous marriages.[498]

An issue arose in *Azad v Entry Clearance Officer, Dhaka*[499] concerning the status of a child of an actually polygamous marriage in the context of an application for a right of abode under the British Nationality Act 1981.[500]

> The appellant asserted that he had acquired British citizenship as a result of the polygamous marriage in Bangladesh of his father, a British citizen and English domiciliary, and mother (the third wife of his father), resident in Bangladesh. The claim to British citizenship depended upon the applicant being the legitimate son of his father, which, in turn, rested upon the meaning and application of section 1(1) of the Legitimacy Act 1976.[501]

The Court of Appeal concluded that it was clear that the validity of the (third) marriage, for the purposes of the 1976 Act, was to be measured by English law alone (by which it was void, the father, as an English domiciliary, lacking capacity to contract such a marriage), and not by the Bangladeshi law of the place where the marriage was celebrated (according to which the marriage was valid).

The question of the application of tax legislation to polygamous marriages came before the courts in *Nabi v Heaton*[502] where the facts were these:

> The taxpayer claimed relief on the ground that his wife was wholly maintained by him[503] from 1970 to 1976. He had come to England from Pakistan in 1965 and married his first wife in England in 1968. They soon separated and in 1969, whilst still domiciled in Pakistan, he there married his second wife. She lived in Pakistan, maintained by him from England, until she came to join him here in 1975 when he divorced his first wife. The allowance was claimed in respect of the second wife.

Although logically the first question to ask was whether the second marriage was to be regarded in England as valid,[504] Vinelott J felt it unnecessary to answer it because he concluded that the taxpayer failed whether or not the second marriage was a valid actually polygamous marriage.[505] The reason for his conclusion was that he decided that reference to "his wife" in the Income and Corporation Taxes Act 1970 had to be construed in the singular.[506] Although it

---

[496] *Bibi v Chief Adjudication Officer* [1998] 1 FLR 375. Cf *R (Shamsun Nahar) v The Social Security Commissioners* [2001] EWHC Admin 1049, [2002] 1 FLR 670.

[497] Social Security Act 1986.

[498] See generally Wikeley, Ogus and Barendt, *The Law of Social Security* (2002) 5th edn; and see *Iman Din v National Assistance Board* [1967] 2 QB 213.

[499] [2001] Imm AR 318.

[500] Cf *R (Shamsun Nahar) v The Social Security Commissioners* [2001] EWHC Admin 1049, [2002] 1 FLR 670; and *SB (Bangladesh) v Secretary of State for the Home Department* [2007] EWCA Civ 28, [2007] Fam Law 494—concerning a polygamously married spouse's application for indefinite leave to remain in the United Kingdom as a dependent relative of a person present and settled in the United Kingdom.

[501] As amended by the Family Law Reform Act 1987, s 28.

[502] [1981] 1 WLR 1052, appeal allowed by consent [1983] 1 WLR 626; see Carter (1981) 52 BYBIL 322.

[503] Income and Corporation Taxes Act 1970, s 8(1). Note that non-residents' personal reliefs in relation to income tax have now been abolished. See the Finance Act 2009, Sch 1, paras 1, and 2(d).

[504] Supra, p 936 et seq.

[505] [1981] 1 WLR 1052 at 1056-7.

[506] Ibid at 1057-9.

was the practice of the Revenue to grant the relief claimed in the case of potentially polygamous marriages,[507] Vinelott J's decision would deny the relief in respect of any wife in the case of a valid actually polygamous marriage. When the taxpayer appealed, the Crown obviously had second thoughts, accepting that the appeal should be allowed by consent.[508] From this, one may conclude that, in practice, the relief will now be extended to all wives.

Other illustrations can be provided of the acceptance of polygamous marriages in English law. For example, it seems generally agreed[509] that a wife, or wives, of a polygamous marriage should be able to claim under the Fatal Accidents Act 1976 on the basis of dependence on the deceased husband. Finally, one of the most striking examples of recognition of the marital status conferred by a polygamous marriage is provided by *Mohamed v Knott*:[510]

> A Nigerian domiciled in Nigeria married a thirteen-year-old girl there according to Moslem law. This marriage was potentially polygamous and was valid under Nigerian law. Three months later they both came to England and a complaint was made against the husband that the girl was in need of care and protection within the meaning of section 2 of the Children and Young Persons Act 1963. The justices refused to recognise the marriage and concluded that a thirteen-year-old girl living with a man twice her age was in need of care and protection.

The Divisional Court differed and decided that this was a valid though potentially polygamous marriage, which should be recognised as conferring the status of a "wife" on the girl.[511]

A number of general conclusions may now be drawn as to the recognition afforded today by English law to polygamous marriages. The wheel has almost come full circle since 1866.[512] Instead of such marriages, whether actually or potentially polygamous, being denied recognition for all purposes, they are now widely recognised. The general pattern of legislative interpretation over the last few decades has been a liberal one, so that the term "wife" is generally taken to include the wives of an actually polygamous marriage. There is now a presumption in favour of the recognition of a polygamous marriage unless a good contrary reason can be shown. This has led to the suggestion that the rule in *Hyde v Hyde* has been entirely abolished.[513] If that is to be taken to mean that all *actually* polygamous marriages have the same effect and recognition as monogamous ones, it is too extravagant a statement. Obvious continuing areas of difference are capacity to marry[514] and the rules as to social security benefits.

The final issue is whether there are, or should be, any differences between monogamous and *potentially* polygamous marriages. The Law Commission identified[515] only two possible differences—the then rules on capacity to marry and on succession as an "heir" to real property, an entailed interest or a title of honour. The first difference has disappeared with the implementation of the Law Commission's recommendations in the Private International Law (Miscellaneous Provisions) Act 1995.[516] The second difference is more apparent than real because the restrictions on succession would seem to be limited to the children of actually

---

[507] Ibid at 1059.

[508] [1983] 1 WLR 626.

[509] Law Com No 42 (1971), para 124; Hartley (1969) 32 MLR 155, 169–70.

[510] [1969] 1 QB 1; Karsten (1969) 32 MLR 212.

[511] Whilst the court considered that an order under the 1963 Act could be made in respect of a married woman, it declined to make one in this case.

[512] *Hyde v Hyde* (1866) LR 1 P & D 130.

[513] *Re Sehota* [1978] 1 WLR 1506 at 1511.

[514] English domiciliaries continue to be incapable of contracting actually polygamous marriages, supra, p 940.

[515] Law Com No 146, Scot Law Com No 96 (1985), para 3.5.

[516] Ss 5, 6, supra, p 940.

polygamous marriages.[517] We can agree with the conclusion of the Law Commission that, provided a marriage remains actually monogamous, there should be no difference between a marriage celebrated in a monogamous form and a potentially polygamous one. The recent statutory changes now mean that this is, in fact, the law with the consequence that all references to potentially polygamous marriages can safely be removed from the statute book.[518] The concept is dead.[519]

6. SAME SEX RELATIONSHIPS: CIVIL PARTNERSHIP AND SAME SEX MARRIAGE[520]

(a) Introduction

In England & Wales, same sex couples seeking to formalize their relationship have the option of either registering as civil partners or entering into marriage.[521] Since 21 December 2005, by virtue of the Civil Partnership Act 2004, same sex partners[522] have been able to register their relationship, in England and Wales, Scotland and Northern Ireland, as a civil partnership, a form of regulated relationship bearing specified legal and personal consequences.[523] The Marriage (Same Sex Couples) Act 2013 received Royal Assent on 17 July 2013 and extends marriage to same sex couples. The Act provides also for the possibility of the conversion of a qualifying civil partnership into a same sex marriage.[524] The 2004 Act and the 2013 Act both contain not only substantive, but also relevant conflict of laws rules. There follows, in this chapter, consideration of the private international law aspects of formation of civil partnerships, eligibility to register a partnership, recognition of overseas relationships akin to civil partnership, and recognition of same sex marriages in England celebrated under the law of any part of the UK other than England and Wales or overseas. Other relevant topics, including the dissolution and annulment of civil partnerships and same sex marriages, will be addressed at relevant points throughout the book.

(b) Civil partnership

The 2004 Civil Partnership Act is divided into eight Parts and has thirty Schedules. Part 1, section 1, describes a civil partnership as a relationship between two people of the same sex

---

[517] Supra, p 942.

[518] Law Com No 145, Scot Law Com No 96 (1985), paras 3.6–3.10.

[519] As it seems to be in the USA: *Royal v Cudahy Packing Co* (1922) 190 NW 427 at 428.

[520] See Swennen, "Atypical Families in EU (Private International) Family Law", Chapter 12 in Meeusen, Pertegas, Straetmans and Swennen (eds), *International Family Law for the European Union* (2007).

[521] See the Civil Partnership Act 2004 and the Marriage (Same Sex Couples) Act 2013 respectively.

[522] It has been suggested that the right to form a civil partnership as an alternative to marriage should be extended to opposite-sex couples. See Lowe and Douglas, p 61 and R Gaffney-Rhys, 'Same-Sex Marriage but not Mixed-Sex Partnerships: Should the Civil Partnership Act 2004 Be Extended to Opposite-Sex Couples?' (2014) 26 Child & Family Law Quarterly 173–94. Some countries permit registered or civil partnerships between persons of the opposite sex which potentially raises the question of the recognition of such relationships in England. See K Norrie, 'Recognition of Foreign Relationships under the Civil Partnership Act 2004' (2006) 2 J Priv Int L 137, for an argument in favour of such a recognition. However, it appears that, as the law currently stands, such relationships would be regarded in England as mere cohabitations.

[523] Civil partnership is defined in s 1 of the 2004 Act as a legal relationship between two people of the same sex which is formed when they register as civil partners of each other in accordance with the Act, and which ends only on death, dissolution or annulment, or (since the availability in the UK of same sex marriage) conversion of the civil partnership into marriage.

[524] Marriage (Same Sex Couples) Act 2013, s 9(1). See also the Marriage (Same Sex Couples) Act 2013 (Conversion of Civil Partnership) Regulations 2014, SI 2014/3181. Section 9(6) contains a rare rule which has a retrospective effect, ie the resulting marriage is to be regarded as having subsisted since the date of the formation of the civil partnership.

which is formed when they register as civil partners of each other in England and Wales under Part 2 of the Act; in Scotland under Part 3; in Northern Ireland under Part 4; outside the United Kingdom under an Order in Council made under Chapter 1 of Part 5 (registration at British consulates etc, or by armed forces personnel); or which is registered as an equivalent overseas relationship in accordance with Chapter 2 of Part 5. Section 1(3) provides that a civil partnership ends only on death, dissolution or annulment, or as a result of the conversion of the civil partnership into a marriage.[525]

(i) Civil partnerships registered in England

A civil partnership registered in England must comply with the registration provisions (including provisions concerning formation, eligibility and parental, etc consent) set out in Chapter 1 of Part 2 of the Act.[526] Two people are to be regarded as having registered as civil partners of each other once each party has signed the civil partnership document at the invitation of, and in the presence of, a civil partnership registrar, and in the presence of each other and two witnesses.[527] No religious procedure is to be used during the officiation by the civil partnership registrar at the signing of the civil partnership document.[528] There are four procedures by which a civil partnership may be registered in England, each having its own particular rules.[529] Section 20 provides modified procedures for use in cases where a party who is resident in England intends to register a civil partnership in England with another party who is not so resident.[530]

As regards eligibility, two people are not eligible to register in England as civil partners of each other if (a) they are not of the same sex; (b) either of them is already a civil partner or lawfully married; (c) either of them is aged under sixteen; or (d) they are within the prohibited degrees of relationship.[531] The consent of appropriate persons[532] is required before a person under eighteen years of age and another person may register in England as civil partners of each other.[533]

(ii) Overseas relationships treated as civil partnerships

Chapter 2 of Part 5 of the Act concerns overseas relationships which are treated in the United Kingdom as equivalent to civil partnership. An overseas relationship is defined as one which (a) is either a specified relationship[534] or a relationship which meets the general conditions[535] laid down in the Act, and (b) is registered (whether before or after the passing of the Act) with a responsible authority in a country or territory outside the United

---

[525] The Marriage (Same Sex Couples Act) 2013, s 9(1). See supra, n 523.

[526] As amended by SI 2005/2000 and SI 2011/1171. See also SI 2005/3176, as amended by SI 2015/177.

[527] S 2(1).

[528] S 2(5).

[529] S 5(1): the standard procedure (s 8); the procedure for house-bound persons (s 18); the procedure for detained persons (s 19); and the special procedure (for cases where a person is seriously ill and not expected to recover: s 21).

[530] S 20(2) where the other party resides in Scotland; and (4) where s/he is "an officer, seaman, or marine borne on the books of her Majesty's ships at sea". See also ss 97 and 239.

[531] S 3(1), and Sch 1. See *M v Secretary of State for Work and Pensions* [2006] 2 AC 91.

[532] See Sch 2, Pt 1.

[533] S 4 and Sch 2.

[534] S 213(1); and see Sch 20, as amended by SI 2005/3135, SI 2005/3129 and SI 2976/2012.

[535] S 214: that, under the relevant law, being the law of the country or territory in which the relationship is registered (*lex loci registrationis*), including its rules of private international law, (a) the relationship may not be entered into if either of the parties is already a party to a relationship of that kind or lawfully married; (b) the relationship is of indeterminate duration; and (c) the effect of entering into it is that the parties are (i) treated as a couple either generally or for specified purposes, or (ii) treated as married.

Kingdom, by two people (i) who under the relevant law[536] are of the same sex at the time of registration of the relationship;[537] and (ii) neither of whom is already a civil partner or lawfully married.[538]

As a general rule, two people are to be treated as having formed a civil partnership as a result of having registered an overseas relationship if, under the law of the country or territory where the relationship is registered,[539] they (a) had capacity to enter into the relationship,[540] and (b) met all requirements necessary to ensure the formal validity of the relationship. If an overseas relationship has been registered by a person who was, at the relevant time,[541] domiciled in England and Wales, the two people concerned are not to be treated as having formed a civil partnership if, at that time, (a) either of them was under sixteen years of age; or they would have been within the prohibited degrees of relationship under Part 1 of Schedule 1 to the Act had they been intending to register their relationship in England.[542] Accordingly, an English domiciliary cannot evade the provisions of his/her personal law as to eligibility by registering an overseas relationship. Moreover, two people are not to be treated as having formed a civil partnership as a result of entering into an overseas relationship if it would be manifestly contrary to public policy to recognise the capacity, under the law of the country or territory where the relationship is registered,[543] of one or both of them to enter into the relationship.[544]

(c) Same sex marriage

Section 1(1) of the Marriage (Same Sex Couples) Act 2013 states that "Marriage of same sex couples is lawful". By Section 11(1), in English law marriage is to have the same effect in relation to same sex couples as it has in relation to opposite sex couples. Schedule 3 para 1 provides that "In existing England and Wales legislation—(a) a reference to marriage is to be read as including a reference to marriage of a same sex couple [. . .]". It follows that the rules that apply to formal validity of marriage and capacity to marry, as explained above, apply also to same sex marriage.

---

[536] Meaning the law of the country or territory where the relationship is registered (*lex loci registrationis*), including its rules of private international law: s 212(2). See, on renvoi, supra, Chapter 5.

[537] However, two people are not to be treated as having formed a civil partnership as a result of having registered an overseas relationship if, at the critical time, they were not of the same sex under United Kingdom law: s 216. See also Gender Recognition Act 2004.

[538] S 212. For the purposes of the 2004 Act, marriage is not an overseas relationship: s 212(1A).

[539] Including its rules of private international law: s 212(2). Cf *Taczanowska v Taczanowski* [1957] P 301. See supra, pp 905–6.

[540] See also ss 240 and 241 (certificates of no impediment to overseas relationships). The requirement of capacity according to the law of the country or territory where the relationship is registered is notably different from the current choice of law rule regarding capacity to marry, which, being characterised as a matter of essential validity, is governed by the dual domicile theory. See supra, p 912. See also Crawford and Carruthers, para 11-37.

[541] S 215(2): the time when the overseas relationship is registered under the relevant law as having been entered into; except where the overseas relationship is registered under the relevant law as having been entered into before 5 December 2005, in which case, the relevant time is 5 December 2005 (SI 2005/3175).

[542] S 217(2).

[543] Including its rules of private international law: s 212(2).

[544] S 218.

(i) Same sex marriage celebrated under the law of any part of the UK other than England and Wales

Pursuant to Section 10(1)(a), a marriage celebrated under the law of any part of the UK other than England and Wales is not precluded from being recognized under English law only because it is the marriage of a same sex couple.[545]

(ii) Same sex marriage celebrated under the law of a country or territory outside the UK

By Section 10(1)(b), overseas marriages of same sex couples which are valid as to capacity and form according to the relevant law will be recognized in England.

7. DE FACTO COHABITATION[546]

During the passage through Parliament of the Civil Partnership Act 2004, the House of Lords noted the lack of legal remedies under English law for couples who live together but do not marry or register a civil partnership (in the case of same sex couples). This subject was addressed by the Law Commission in 2006.[547] In July 2007, following consultation, the Law Commission published a report which recommended the introduction of a new scheme of financial remedies for cohabitants on separation.[548] The Government, however, announced that no action would be taken to implement the Law Commission's recommendations until research on the cost and effectiveness of the scheme recently implemented in Scotland could be studied. In September 2011, the Government declared that, having carefully considered the Law Commission's recommendations, together with the outcomes of research on the Family Law (Scotland) Act 2006, it did not intend to reform the law relating to cohabitation during the 2010–2015 parliamentary term.[549]

In the main, disputes arising in connection with *de facto* cohabitation concern matters of financial/proprietary relief rather than personal status.[550] It may be the case, however, that

---

[545] This applies regardless of whether the other jurisdiction provides for same sex marriage at the time of the entry into force of s 10(1) of the 2013 Act or from a later time. S 10(2).

[546] Ie Cohabiting relationships (usually of a sexual rather than platonic nature, where the parties are living together "as if they were husband and wife", meaning that shared living arrangements between parent and adult child, or between siblings, or among friends, for economic or other reasons, are not generally to be included in this category), established otherwise than by means of formal registration and/or legal ceremony.

[547] Law Commission Consultation Paper No 179, "Cohabitation: The Financial Consequences of Relationship Breakdown—A Consultation Paper" (2006). In July 2007, following consultation, the Law Commission published a report which recommended the introduction of a new scheme of financial remedies for cohabitants on separation ("Cohabitation: the Financial Consequences of Relationship Breakdown" Cm 7182, LAW COM No 307). The Government, however, announced that no action would be taken to implement the Law Commission's recommendations until research on the cost and effectiveness of the scheme recently implemented in Scotland could be studied. In September 2011, the Government declared that, having carefully considered the Law Commission's recommendations, together with the outcomes of research on the Family Law (Scotland) Act 2006, it did not intend to reform the law relating to cohabitation during the 2010-2015 parliamentary term. See the House of Commons Library Briefing Paper No 03372, "'Common Law Marriage' and Cohabitation" (2016).

[548] "Cohabitation: The Financial Consequences of Relationship Breakdown" Cm 7182, Law Com No 307.

[549] See the House of Commons Library Briefing Paper No 03372, "'Common Law Marriage' and Cohabitation" (2016).

[550] See infra, p 1309; also Carruthers (2008) Edin LR 1.

in order to qualify for financial/proprietary relief under a given system of law, an individual will require first to establish his/her status as "cohabitant".[551] Establishing qualifying status, it is submitted, is a matter to be determined by the law under which the relief and/or rights in question is/are claimed. There is currently no instrument at the global or regional level dealing with the private international law aspects of cohabitation outside marriage in a comprehensive way.[552]

---

[551] Eg in order to apply for financial/proprietary relief under the Family Law (Scotland) Act 2006, ss 25–30, an individual must establish that s/he is a "cohabitant", defined in s 25(1) of that Act as follows: "either member of a couple consisting of (a) a man and a woman who are (or were) living together as if they were husband and wife; or (b) two persons of the same sex who are (or were) living together as if they were civil partners". By s 4(2) and (3) of the Marriage and Civil Partnership (Scotland) Act 2014, s 25(1)(a) of the 2006 Act must be read as applying also to two people of the same sex who are (or were) living together as if they were married to each other. See Crawford and Carruthers, para 11-39. Cf. Schedule 3, Part 1 of the Marriage (Same Sex Couples) Act 2013.

[552] Nevertheless, the topic is on the agenda of the Hague Conference for Private International Law. See Hague Conference on Private International Law, "Update on the Developments in Internal Law and Private International Law Concerning Cohabitation Outside Marriage, Including Registered Partnerships" (Prel Doc No 5 of March 2015). The Permanent Bureau is to present a report on the topic to the Council on General Affairs and Policy in 2017. See "Conclusions and Recommendations of the Council on General Affairs and Policy" (Prel Doc No 1 of March 2016) at para [22].

22

MATRIMONIAL AND RELATED CAUSES[1]

1. Introduction	951	(a) Jurisdiction	1038
2. Polygamous Marriages and		(b) Choice of law	1038
Matrimonial Relief	952	(c) Recognition	1038
(a) At common law	952	5. Dissolution, Nullity and Separation	
(b) Matrimonial Causes Act 1973,		of Civil Partnerships	1039
section 47	952	(a) Jurisdiction	1039
(c) Remaining problems	953	(b) Choice of law	1042
3. Divorce, Nullity and Judicial		(c) Recognition of dissolution, annulment	
Separation	954	and separation	1043
(a) Jurisdiction	954	6. Divorce, Nullity and Separation of	
(b) Choice of law	979	Same Sex Marriages	1045
(c) Recognition	1000	(a) Jurisdiction	1045
4. Presumption of Death and		(b) Choice of law	1047
Dissolution of Marriage	1037	(c) Recognition of dissolution, annulment	
		and separation	1048

1. INTRODUCTION

Matrimonial causes are now generally taken to include petitions for divorce, nullity of marriage, judicial separation, and presumption of death and dissolution of marriage, as well as similar foreign proceedings which may fall for recognition in England.

The rules relating to the jurisdiction of the courts and to the recognition of foreign divorces, annulments and judicial separations are, in essence, the same for all three matrimonial causes, and will therefore be examined together, identifying where appropriate any rules which do not apply to all three. It will be seen that the one major area of difference remaining concerns the determination of the law to be applied by the English courts.[2] We shall then go on to examine, separately, proceedings for presumption of death and dissolution of marriage. Thereafter, consideration will be given separately to conflict rules concerning the dissolution, nullity and separation of civil partnerships and same sex marriage.

Before these various matrimonial and related causes are considered, it is necessary to discuss a further preliminary issue, namely whether an English court will assume jurisdiction to grant matrimonial relief in the case of a polygamous marriage.

---

[1] See North, *Private International Law of Matrimonial Causes*; (1990) I Hague Recueil 9, 97–126; Boele-Woelki (ed), *Perspectives for the Unification and Harmonisation of Family Law in Europe* (2003); Stark, *International Family Law* (2005), Chapters 3–6; Meeusen, Pertegas, Straetmans and Swennen (eds), *International Family Law for the European Union* (2007); and Ní Shúilleabháin, *Cross-Border Divorce Law* (2010).

[2] Infra, p 979.

2. POLYGAMOUS MARRIAGES AND MATRIMONIAL RELIEF[3]

(a) At common law

Until 1972, the rule of English law was that the parties to a polygamous marriage were "not entitled to the remedies, the adjudication, or the relief of the matrimonial law of England".[4] It meant that, in the case of a polygamous marriage, the courts would decline to grant a divorce,[5] a decree of nullity even where the petitioner claimed lack of capacity to enter a polygamous marriage,[6] or a decree of judicial separation.[7] It came to be realised, however, that fundamental reform was called for in view of the number of immigrants from jurisdictions where they had contracted valid marriages in polygamous form. A substantial number of people, permanently resident though not domiciled in England, were denied all matrimonial relief.

(b) Matrimonial Causes Act 1973, section 47

All this has now changed. Section 47(1) of the Matrimonial Causes Act 1973[8] provides that: "A court in England and Wales shall not be precluded from granting matrimonial relief or making a declaration concerning the validity of a marriage by reason only that either party to the marriage is, or has during the subsistence of the marriage been, married to more than one person."

This section makes available to the parties to an actually polygamous marriage[9] a wide range of matrimonial relief,[10] namely decrees of divorce, nullity, judicial separation, presumption of death and dissolution of marriage, orders for financial provision in the cases of neglect to maintain, variation of maintenance agreements, orders for financial relief or relating to children which are ancillary to any of the preceding decrees or orders,[11] orders made under Part I of the Domestic Proceedings and Magistrates' Courts Act 1978,[12] orders for financial relief after a foreign divorce, annulment or legal separation,[13] and any declaration under Part III of the Family Law Act 1986 involving a determination as to the validity of a marriage.[14] Indeed it has been said that the effect of section 47 of the 1973 Act is to abolish entirely the old rule, so that all forms of relief which can be classed as matrimonial are now available in the case of polygamous marriages.[15]

---

[3] See North, op cit, Chapter 7.

[4] *Hyde v Hyde* (1866) LR 1 P & D 130 at 138.

[5] *Hyde v Hyde*, supra; *Muhammad v Suna* 1956 SC 366.

[6] *Risk v Risk* [1951] P 50.

[7] Cf *Nachimson v Nachimson* [1930] P 217.

[8] As amended by the Private International Law (Miscellaneous Provisions) Act 1995, Sch, para 2(3). This amendment removes reference to potentially polygamous marriages which reference the Law Commission concluded was no longer necessary, given the absence of any difference between such marriages and monogamous ones: Law Com No 146 (1985), para 3.10; and see, supra, p 940.

[9] And see Matrimonial Causes Act 1973, s 47(4), as amended by the Private International Law (Miscellaneous Provisions) Act 1995, Sch, para 2(3); see, eg, *Onobrauche v Onobrauche* (1978) 8 Fam Law 107; *Quoraishi v Quoraishi* [1985] FLR 780, CA.

[10] Matrimonial Causes Act 1973, s 47(2).

[11] *Chaudhary v Chaudhary* [1976] Fam 148 at 151.

[12] See 1978 Act, Sch 2, para 39.

[13] Matrimonial and Family Proceedings Act 1984 Sch 1, para 15, infra, p 1072 et seq.

[14] Matrimonial Causes Act 1973, s 47(3), as substituted by the Family Law Act 1986, Sch 1, para 14.

[15] *Re Sehota* [1978] 1 WLR 1506 at 1511. Supra, p 945.

(c) Remaining problems

Whilst polygamous marriages will, for the purposes of such relief, normally be treated just as if they were monogamous marriages, they do pose certain peculiar problems in the, albeit rare, cases of actually polygamous marriages. Indeed, in such cases the 1973 Act makes specific provision for the making of rules of court to require notice of the proceedings to be served on any spouse other than one who is party to the proceedings and to confer on such a spouse a right to be heard.[16]

Where a party to an actually polygamous marriage brings proceedings for divorce alleging irretrievable breakdown of the marriage,[17] difficulties may arise over adultery, unreasonable behaviour or desertion as proof of breakdown.[18] If a wife alleges that her husband has committed adultery with another wife, such a claim will usually fail because "it is an essential element of adultery that intercourse has taken place outside the marriage relationship ie between persons not married to each other. This being so, intercourse with a wife could not be adultery".[19] In terms of policy, this conclusion seems right if both marriages were entered into in polygamous form. It has been said[20] that in such a case there has been no breach of the obligation of fidelity imposed by the law governing the marriage. Difficulties arise, however, in the case of a valid monogamous marriage, followed by a valid polygamous one,[21] as in the decision of the Privy Council in *Drammeh v Drammeh*:[22]

> H, domiciled in The Gambia, married W1 in England in monogamous form. Both professed the Christian faith. H then returned to The Gambia, reverted to his Moslem faith and married W2 in polygamous form. W1 petitioned for divorce, before the courts of The Gambia, alleging adultery by H and W2.

The Privy Council upheld the decision that W1 was entitled to a divorce, holding that even if the marriage to W2 was a valid polygamous marriage under the law of The Gambia, this should not affect the rights of W1 stemming from her valid English monogamous marriage. The nature of her marriage was not changed by H's unilateral change of faith. So far as W1's marriage was concerned, H had committed adultery with W2.[23] Had W1 chosen, as well she might, to have petitioned for divorce in England, it seems likely that an English court would have reached the same conclusion as the Privy Council.[24] When the Law Commission considered the effect of a later polygamous marriage on an earlier marriage, whether in monogamous or polygamous form, it concluded that legislative intervention was neither necessary nor desirable.[25]

If a wife's divorce petition is based on the husband's unreasonable behaviour,[26] the court will have to examine all the circumstances of the marriage.[27] It has been held that the taking by the husband of a second wife is unreasonable behaviour towards the first.[28] Similarly, if a

---

[16] Matrimonial Causes Act 1973, s 47(4); see Family Procedure Rules 2010, Pt 7 and Practice Direction 7C.
[17] Ibid, s 1.
[18] Ibid, s 1(2)(a), (b) and (c).
[19] Law Com No 42 (1971), para 50; and see *Onobrauche v Onobrauche* (1978) 8 Fam Law 107.
[20] Clive, *The Law of Husband and Wife in Scotland* (1997) 4th edn, pp 109–10.
[21] The question of the validity of the second marriage where the first was monogamous is discussed supra, p 933 et seq.
[22] (1970) 78 Ceylon Law Weekly 55.
[23] See also *A-G of Ceylon v Reid* [1965] AC 720 at 729; *Lendrum v Chakravarti* 1929 SLT 96 at 99.
[24] Law Com No 146 (1985), para 4.16.
[25] Ibid, para 4.23.
[26] Matrimonial Causes Act 1973, s 1(2)(b).
[27] *Gollins v Gollins* [1964] AC 644.
[28] *Poon v Tan* (1973) 4 Fam Law 161.

husband's petition is based on desertion by the first wife,[29] the fact that he has validly married a second wife has been held to give the first wife reasonable grounds for leaving him.[30]

3. DIVORCE, NULLITY AND JUDICIAL SEPARATION

(a) Jurisdiction

(i) Bases of jurisdiction

The Domicile and Matrimonial Proceedings Act 1973, Part II, lays down, in section 5, rules of jurisdiction for proceedings for divorce, judicial separation and nullity of marriage.[31] The rules contained in Part II of the 1973 Act were significantly changed, with effect from 1 March 2001, to take account of European harmonisation in the form of Council Regulation (EC) No 1347/2000 of 29 May 2000 on jurisdiction and the recognition and enforcement of judgments in matrimonial matters and in matters of parental responsibility for children of both spouses (known colloquially as "Brussels II").[32] Brussels II, in turn, was repealed, with effect from 1 March 2005, by Council Regulation (EC) No 2201/2003 of 27 November 2003 concerning jurisdiction and the recognition and enforcement of judgments in matrimonial matters and matters of parental responsibility ("Brussels II *bis*").[33] The rules of jurisdiction in matrimonial matters contained in Brussels II *bis* were taken substantially from Brussels II, which, in turn, were taken[34] from the Brussels II Convention of 28 May 1998 (never implemented) on the same subject.[35]

(a) Divorce or judicial separation

Section 5(2) of the Domicile and Matrimonial Proceedings Act 1973 provides that the High Court or a divorce county court shall have jurisdiction to entertain proceedings if, and only if: (a) the court has jurisdiction under Brussels II *bis*; or (b) no court of a Contracting State[36] has jurisdiction under Brussels II *bis*, and either of the parties to the marriage is domiciled in England on the date when the proceedings are begun. In other words, pre-eminent jurisdiction lies with the courts of a country which has jurisdiction in terms of Brussels II *bis*.

---

[29] Matrimonial Causes Act 1973, s 1(2)(b).

[30] *Quoraishi v Quoraishi* [1985] FLR 780, CA.

[31] S 5(1)(a). S 5(1)(b), which set out jurisdiction of the English court to entertain proceedings for death to be presumed and a marriage to be dissolved, was repealed by the Presumption of Death Act 2013, Sch 2, para 2(a). The 2013 Act, ss 1(3) and (4), lay down rules of jurisdiction for proceedings for a declaration of presumed death, the effect of which is the ending of a marriage to which the missing person is a party (s 3(2)(b)). See infra, pp 1037–9 and Chapter 23, p 1058.

[32] OJ 2000 L 160/19. See also the European Communities (Matrimonial Jurisdiction and Judgments) Regulations, SI 2001/310. For details of the rules of jurisdiction applying prior to 1 March 2001, see the 13th edition of this book (1999), p 764 et seq.

[33] OJ 2003 L 338/1; and The *Practice Guide for the Application of the Brussels IIa Regulation* (2014), at <http://ec.europa.eu/justice/civil/files/brussels_ii_practice_guide_en.pdf>. See generally Boele-Woelki and Beilfuss (eds), *Brussels II bis: Its Impact and Application in the Member States* (2007); McEleavy (2002) 51 ICLQ 883, and (2004) 53 ICLQ 503; and Ní Shúilleabháin, *Cross-Border Divorce Law* (2010) Ch 4.

[34] See Brussels II, Recital (6).

[35] See Borras, "Explanatory Report on the Convention on Jurisdiction and the Recognition and Enforcement of Judgments in Matrimonial Matters" OJ 1998 C 221/27.

[36] The expression "Contracting State" is defined in s 5(1A) as Belgium, Cyprus, Czech Republic, Germany, Greece, Spain, Estonia, France, Hungary, Ireland, Italy, Latvia, Lithuania, Luxembourg, Malta, Netherlands, Austria, Poland, Portugal, Slovakia, Slovenia, Finland, Sweden, the UK, and any party which subsequently has adopted Council Regulation (EC) No 2201/2003 of 27 November 2003. Denmark is not a Contracting State to this instrument (Brussels II *bis*, Recital (31)), and there has been no suggestion to date of the EU entering into an agreement with Denmark pursuant to Brussels II *bis*, akin to the EC/Denmark Agreement which operates pursuant to the Brussels I (Recast) Regulation (in respect of which, see supra, p 192).

(i) Jurisdiction under Domicile and Matrimonial Proceedings Act 1973, section 5(2)(a)

Article 3[37] of Brussels II *bis* states the principles of general jurisdiction. Jurisdiction shall lie with the courts of the Member State:

(a) in whose territory:
 —the spouses are habitually resident,[38] or
 —the spouses were last habitually resident, insofar as one[39] of them still resides[40] there, or
 —the respondent is habitually resident,[41] or
 —in the event of a joint application, either of the spouses is habitually resident, or
 —the applicant is habitually resident if s/he resided[42] there for at least a year immediately before the application was made,[43] or
 —the applicant is habitually resident if s/he resided there for at least six months immediately before the application was made and is either a national of the Member State in question or, in the case of the United Kingdom and Ireland, has his/her domicile there;[44]

(b) of the nationality[45] of both[46] spouses or, in the case of the United Kingdom and Ireland, of the domicile[47] of both spouses.

The grounds of jurisdiction in Article 3 are set out as alternatives, and not in any order of precedence.[48] It is apparent that there is some overlap in the provisions of Article 3; there is no need for a basis of jurisdiction on the ground of the spouses' common habitual residence (indent 1), if jurisdiction can be founded upon the respondent's habitual residence alone (indent 3). This overlap is a result of political compromise: "The grounds adopted are based on the principle of genuine connection between the person and a Member State. The decision to include particular grounds reflects their existence in various national legal systems

---

[37] See generally Borras, *Explanatory Report*, paras 27–34. See also Ní Shúilleabháin, *Cross-Border Divorce Law* (2010); Hodson [2014] IFL 170–4; and Beaumont, Trimmings, Danov and Yüksel (eds), *Cross-Border Litigation in Europe* (2017, forthcoming).

[38] Eg *L-K v K (Brussels II Revised: Maintenance Pending Suit)* [2006] EWHC 153 (Fam), [2006] 2 FLR 1113; and *Z v Z (Divorce: Jurisdiction)* [2009] EWHC 2626 (Fam).

[39] The claimant or the defendant.

[40] See infra, pp 956–60.

[41] Eg *Armstrong v Armstrong* [2003] EWHC 777, [2003] 2 FLR 375; *L-K v K (No 2)* [2006] EWHC 3280 (Fam); and *Tan v Choy* [2014] EWCA Civ 251.

[42] See infra, pp 956–60.

[43] Eg *Sulaiman v Juffali* [2002] 1 FLR 479—applicant's Saudi Arabian nationality considered irrelevant; *Olafisoye v Olafisoye* [2010] EWHC 3539 (Fam)—alternatively, jurisdiction was based on section 5(2) of the Domicile and Matrimonial Proceedings Act 1973, ie the applicant wife's domicile in England and Wales; *V v V (Divorce: Jurisdiction)* [2011] EWHC 1190 (Fam); *Vardinoyannis v Vardinoyannis* [2011] EWCA Civ 1369; *Chai v Peng (Jurisdiction: Forum Conveniens)* (No 2) [2014] EWHC 3518 (Fam); and *Tan v Choy* [2014] EWCA Civ 251.

[44] See *Marinos v Marinos* [2007] EWHC 2047 (Fam). *C v S* [2010] EWHC 2676 (Fam)—alternatively, if the conclusion regarding the habitual residence of the applicant was incorrect, jurisdiction was engaged under Art 3(1)(a) indent 3.

[45] Eg *L-K v K (Brussels II Revised: Maintenance Pending Suit)* [2006] EWHC 153 (Fam), [2006] 2 FLR 1113.

[46] Some states had wanted the condition to attach to one spouse only, but that was rejected on the ground that it would amount to pure "*forum actoris*": Borras, *Explanatory Report*, para 33. Where nationality is the relevant connecting factor and spouses have dual nationality of the same Member States, the courts of either of those States have jurisdiction to hear matrimonial proceedings and the spouses can seise the court of the Member State of their choice—*Hadadi v Mesko* (Case C-168/08) [2009] ECR I-6871.

[47] For the purposes of Brussels II *bis*, "domicile" has the same meaning it has under English law. See supra, p 145 et seq. See also *Re N (Jurisdiction)* [2007] EWHC 1274 (Fam Div), discussed by Douglas (2007) 37 Fam Law 901; *Chandler v Chandler* [2011] EWCA Civ 143; *Ray v Sekhri* [2014] EWCA Civ 119; and *Divall v Divall* [2014] EWHC 95 (Fam).

[48] See Borras, *Explanatory Report*, paras 28 and 44.

and their acceptance by the other Member States or the effort to find points of agreement acceptable to all".[49]

"Habitual residence"[50] It can be seen that the principal connecting factor is habitual residence. This factor is nowhere defined in the instrument,[51] and it is not easy to define.[52] It has been held that the term "habitual residence" has an autonomous meaning for the purposes of the Brussels II *bis* Regulation.[53] The autonomous EU interpretation of habitual residence (as opposed to the domestic interpretation) does not accord decisive importance to the length of time a person spends in or out of a country; instead, the focus is on the centre of interests, whereas account must be taken of all relevant factors, including both intention and relevant objective factors. It is not required that the centre of interests be permanent; it need only be habitual.[54] Chapter 9, above, contains a full analysis of the concept of habitual residence, and so reference should be made to that treatment of the subject. In the context of jurisdiction in divorce, judicial separation and nullity of marriage, it suffices to make the following remarks.

With regard to the 1973 Act, the House of Lords held in *Mark v Mark*[55] that there was no reason for the word "lawfully" to be implied into section 5(2) of the Act: residence for the purpose of section 5(2) need not be lawful residence,[56] for the purpose of section 5(2) is to provide an answer to the question whether the parties and their marriage have a sufficiently close connection to the United Kingdom to make it desirable that English courts should have jurisdiction to dissolve the marriage.

A difficulty of interpretation has arisen in relation to the text of indents 5 and 6 of Art 1(3) (a) of Brussels II *bis*. In both indents the connecting factor of "habitual residence" is coupled with the connecting factor of "residence",[57] and it is disputed whether, in this context,

---

[49] Ibid, para 30.

[50] See, for detailed examination, supra, p 175 et seq. Also Bogdan, "The EC treaty and the Use of Nationality and Habitual Residence as Connecting Factors in International Family Law", and Pertegas, "Nationality and Habitual Residence: Other Connecting Factors in European Private International Law", both in Meeusen, Pertegas, Straetmans and Swennen (eds), *International Family Law for the European Union* (2007).

[51] See, for background, Borras, *Explanatory Report*, para 32. To date, there is no CJEU decision on the interpretation of habitual residence for the purposes of Article 3. The CJEU authorities on the interpretation of habitual residence for the purposes of Article 8 (ie *Re A (Area of Freedom, Security and Justice)*, Case C-523/07, and *Mercredi v Chaffe*, Case C-497/10, infra, pp 1094–5) need to be distinguished on the basis of their different context. *Z v Z (Divorce Jurisdiction)* [2009] EWHC 2626 (Fam), at [31].

[52] Though see suggested definition in Borras, *Explanatory Report*, para 32 ("the place where the person had established, on a fixed basis, his permanent or habitual centre of interests, with all the relevant facts being taken into account for the purpose of determining such residence"), cited with approval in *Marinos v Marinos* [2007] EWHC 2047 (Fam), per Munby J, at [33]; and confirmed by the Court Appeal in *Tan v Choy* [2014] EWCA Civ 251, per Aikens LJ, at [31] and per Macur LJ, at [11]. See also *Munro v Munro* [2007] EWHC 3315 (Fam), per Bennett J, at [46]; *Z v Z (Divorce: Jurisdiction)* [2009] EWHC 2626 (Fam), per Ryder J, at [35]; *Olafisoye v Olafisoye* [2010] EWHC 3539 (Fam), per Holman J, at [20]; *C v S* [2010] EWHC 2676 (Fam), per Hedley J; and *V v V (Divorce Jurisdiction)* [2011] EWHC 1190 (Fam), per Jackson J, at [35].

[53] *Marinos v Marinos* [2007] EWHC 2047 (Fam), per Munby J, at [17]–[18]; *L-K v K (No 2)* [2006] EWHC 3280 (Fam), per Singer J, at [35]; *Munro v Munro* [2007] EWHC 3315 (Fam), per Bennett J at [45]; and *Z v Z (Divorce Jurisdiction)* [2009] EWHC 2626 (Fam), per Ryder J, at [32]–[34].

[54] *Z v Z*, supra, at [40]–[41]. See also *V v V (Divorce: Jurisdiction)* [2011] EWHC 1190 (Fam), per Jackson J, at [38]—Jackson J concurred with Ryder J in *Z v Z*, supra, that intention formed part of the court's overall assessment of the facts and that it took its place as one of the facts in the case.

[55] [2005] UKHL 42, [2006] 1 AC 98. Cf *Witkowska v Kaminski* [2006] EWHC 1940 (Ch), [2007] 1 FLR 1547.

[56] For relevance of lawfulness of residence in relation to domicile, see supra, pp 160–1.

[57] For the purposes of indent 6, the two connecting factors are further supplemented by either "domicile" (in relation to the UK and Ireland), or "nationality" (in relation to the other Contracting States, see supra n 46).

the two terms are to be interpreted as two distinct concepts, or whether "residence" is to be interpreted as meaning "habitual residence". In *Marinos v Marinos*,[58] Munby J (as he then was) took the view that there were two elements to the sixth indent (and thus also to the fifth indent). What appears, therefore, to be required for the purpose of these two indents is: "(i) habitual residence on a particular day and (ii) residence, though not necessarily habitual residence, during the relevant immediately preceding period".[59] In the words of Munby J, " 'Resided' means just that. It refers to residence; it does not connote habitual residence".[60] In *Munro v Munro*,[61] Bennett J took the opposite view and considered that the fifth and sixth indents were to be read as imposing a single requirement of habitual residence of at least one year or six months, as the case may be, at the date of the presentation of the petition.[62] In both judgments, the views expressed were *obiter dicta*.[63] In *V v V (Divorce: Jurisdiction)*,[64] Jackson J preferred the approach taken by Munby J in *Marinos* to the analysis of Bennett J in *Munro*.[65] The learned judge preferred the interpretation in *Marinos* because it "reflected a plain reading" of Art 3(1)(a).[66] Jackson J submitted that "habitual residence is a term of art, while residence is not. Residence [. . .] is simply where a person lives".[67] He referred to the fact that Brussels II *bis* differentiated between the two concepts and, as Munby J said in *Marinos*, "if it had been intended to refer just to the one concept the regulation could, for example, very easily have used [other] words".[68] In 2014, the ambiguity in the wording of indent 5 of Art 3(1)(a) was addressed by the Court of Appeal. In *Tan v Choy*[69] , Aikens LJ suggested that there were (at least) three possible constructions of the provision,[70] proposing thus an interpretation additional to the two approaches that had been put forward by the first instance authorities. First, that the person seeking to establish jurisdiction shows that he was "habitually resident" in the territory concerned at the date the proceedings began and that he had "resided" there for at least a year before the relevant proceedings started. Secondly, that he was "habitually resident" there for one year prior to the start of the proceedings. Thirdly, that "habitual residence" is proved by establishing that he had resided in the territory for at least a year immediately before the proceedings started. His Lordship, however, concluded that in the present case, it was not necessary to resolve this "doctrinal dispute" as the finding that the husband was 'habitually resident' in England for the relevant period, satisfied any of the three possible constructions of the provision.[71]

Of the contradictory interpretations, the reasoning of Munby J in *Marinos* appears to be the most convincing. Such a literal interpretation of Art 3(1)(a), indent 6 as advocated in *Marinos*, can be justified by reference to the precise language of the text. It would be illogical

---

[58] [2007] EWHC 2047 (Fam).

[59] At [46]. Contra Dicey, Morris and Collins, para 18-006. Dr Borras' Explanatory Report lends no assistance on this point of interpretation.

[60] At [49].

[61] [2007] EWHC 3315 (Fam).

[62] At [45]–[53].

[63] The decision in *Munro* was determined by a finding that both spouses had been domiciled in England and the jurisdiction existed under Article 3(1)(b).

[64] [2011] EWHC 1190 (Fam).

[65] At [47].

[66] The judge also suggested, although rather unconvincingly, that the approach taken in *Marinos* was supported by the Borras Report. Ibid.

[67] Ibid.

[68] Ibid, at [46].

[69] [2014] EWCA Civ 251.

[70] At [30].

[71] At [31]. On the findings of fact, the trial judge had correctly decided that it was not necessary to make a reference to the CJEU to resolve the question of the interpretation of indent five of Art 3(1)(a)—per Aikens LJ at [36].

and inconsistent to take a different approach to the interpretation of "resided" where it appears in the similarly worded Art 3(1)(a), indent 5. Munby J's interpretation of "resided" would be more strained, however, if it were applied to Art 3(1)(a), indent 2, for that provision would appear to require, extending his Lordship's reasoning: (i) common habitual residence on the last day on which the parties cohabited and (ii) residence, though not necessarily habitual residence, on a subsequent day, namely, that on which proceedings are commenced. A requirement only of "residence" on the date on which proceedings are commenced would seem to be at odds with the importance otherwise attributed by Art 3(1)(a) to "habitual residence" as at the date of commencement of proceedings. However, as a matter of fact, it is unlikely, for the purposes of indent 2, that the "residence" of the "remaining" spouse, having regard to its continuing nature, would be other than "habitual".

Stipulation of a one-year period of residence for the purposes of habitual residence in Article 3, indent 5 of Brussels II *bis* should not be taken to be a definition of habitual residence for the purposes of the other indents in that provision. Indents 5 and 6 allow *forum actoris*[72] in exceptional cases, on the basis of habitual residence coupled with another connection.[73]

It has been explained in Chapter 9[74] that a degree of continuity of residence is required: "a residence must be more than transient or casual; once established, however, it is not necessarily broken by a temporary absence".[75] Indeed, in the context of divorce jurisdiction, a respondent has been held to be habitually resident in England even though she spent one-third of the relevant year either on holiday in Spain or visiting her children in the USA and Canada.[76] The Court of Appeal in *Ikimi v Ikimi*[77] had to consider whether a Nigerian wife who filed a petition for dissolution of marriage in England on the basis of habitual residence had two such residences. The family had two matrimonial homes, of equal status, in Nigeria and in England, and the wife had spent 161 days of the year in England. The submission that it was not possible to be habitually resident in two places simultaneously was firmly rejected by the Court of Appeal,[78] but the Court took the view that the bodily presence required to form a basis for habitual residence had to be more than merely token in duration, probably amounting to residence for "an appreciable part of the relevant year".[79] Subsequently, in *Armstrong v Armstrong*,[80] Dame Elizabeth Butler-Sloss concluded that the correct approach

---

[72] Ie a rule that links the exercise of jurisdiction to certain characteristics of the plaintiff, such as his domicile, (habitual) residence or nationality.

[73] Borras, *Explanatory Report*, para 32. See also *Marinos v Marinos* [2007] EWHC 2047 (Fam); infra, p 959; and *V v V (Divorce Jurisdiction)* [2011] EWHC 1190 (Fam), at [40].

[74] Supra, p 145 et seq. See, in particular, *Armstrong v Armstrong* [2003] EWHC 777, [2003] 2 FLR 375, at [29].

[75] Law Com No 48 (1972), para 42. See also *V v V (Divorce Jurisdiction)* [2011] EWHC 1190 (Fam)—a four-month absence in Switzerland did not affect the applicant wife's residence in England. However, context was important, meaning in particular that this case concerned a "multinational family" whose way of life made temporary absences from England less significant than in many other cases. Nevertheless, alternatively, even if the wife was resident in Switzerland during the four-month period, she was simultaneously resident in England. In any case, the wife's stay in Switzerland had no effect on her habitual residence in England. Cf *Breuning v Breuning* [2002] EWHC 236, [2002] 1 FLR 888 (presence in England for medical treatment was not enough to establish habitual residence in England).

[76] *Oundjian v Oundjian* (1979) 1 FLR 198. See also comment of Ryder J in *Z v Z (Divorce Jurisdiction)* [2009] EWHC 2626 (Fam): "Habitual residence in one country may not be lost despite a lengthy period in another", at [40].

[77] [2001] EWCA Civ 873, [2001] 2 FLR 1288.

[78] Cf *Mark v Mark* [2005] UKHL 42, [2006] 1 AC 98.

[79] *Ikimi v Ikimi*, above, per Thorpe LJ, at [35]. His Lordship favoured a liberal rather than restrictive approach to the determination of habitual residence, whilst noting that one consequence of liberality might be forum shopping.

[80] [2003] EWHC 777, [2003] 2 FLR 375.

to the degree of continuity required to establish habitual residence in a country "cannot just be a counting of the days spent in the country. There has to be an element of quality of residence."[81]

In *Marinos v Marinos*[82] it fell to be decided whether, for the purposes of Brussels II *bis*, a person can be habitually resident in two different countries at the same time. Munby J considered that while it was clear that, for the purposes of English domestic law, one could be habitually resident contemporaneously in two different countries,[83] "the same is not necessarily true of the law laid down by the ECJ nor, specifically, for the purposes of the Regulation".[84] His Lordship suggested that the point of interpretation of Article 3 of the relevant Regulation (Brussels II) in *Armstrong* was inadequately argued and addressed, and that the decision of Dame Elizabeth Butler-Sloss P, therefore, rests on a "frail foundation".[85] Munby J concluded in *Marinos*[86] that, "the language of Article 3(1) (a) of the Regulation [Brussels II *bis*[87]] is clear, as is the ECJ case-law. For the purposes of the Regulation, one cannot be habitually resident in more than one country at the same time."[88] Of the two conflicting interpretations in *Armstrong* and *Marinos*, respectively, the latter commends itself as being technically more accurate,[89] whereas the former has the advantage of flexibility. Even adopting the strict interpretation of Munby J, however, to the effect that, for the purposes of the Brussels II *bis* Regulation, a party has only one habitual residence at any given time, there is room for disagreement[90] between the courts of different Member States on the question, where a party is habitually resident, particularly in cases such as these, where residence is divided. By reason of Article 19 (lis pendens),[91] however, such disagreement will emerge only consecutively, and not contemporaneously.

The concept of alternating, or consecutive, habitual residences has been accepted in relation to a family that spends six continuous months in one home, followed by six continuous months in another.[92]

---

[81] *Armstrong v Armstrong*, ibid, at [30]—pattern of respondent's visits to England, together with the number of days spent in the country—one-fifth of the year—did not demonstrate sufficient residence to meet the statutory requirement of habitual residence in the 1973 Act and Brussels II. The significance of the quality of residence as opposed to solely the length of time spent in the given jurisdiction was highlighted also in *Z v Z (Divorce Jurisdiction)* [2009] EWHC 2626 (Fam), at [37]—"the interpretation of habitual residence involves not a purely quantitative evaluation of the time spent by a person in a particular place, but, rather, a qualitative evaluation of all the facts pertaining to an individual's links with a place"; and *Chai v Peng (No 2)* [2014] EWHC 3518 (Fam), at [23]—"Habitual residence does not depend critically on the length of residence, but on the 'centre of interest' and on the intention and motive element behind living in the particular jurisdiction."

[82] [2007] EWHC 2047 (Fam).

[83] At [38].

[84] Ibid.

[85] At [42].

[86] At [43].

[87] Art 3 of which is in identical terms to Art 3 of Brussels II.

[88] This view has been reiterated in a number of first instance decisions: *Munro v Munro* [2007] EWHC 3315 (Fam), per Bennett J, at [47]; *Z v Z (Divorce Jurisdiction)* [2009] EWHC 2626 (Fam), per Ryder J, at [41]; *Olafisoye v Olafisoye* [2010] EWHC 3539 (Fam), per Holman J, at [21]; *C v S* [2010] EWHC 2676 (Fam), per Hedley J; and *V v V (Divorce: Jurisdiction)* [2011] EWHC 1190 (Fam), per Jackson J, at [50]; as well as in the Court of Appeal judgment in *Tan v Choy* [2014] EWCA Civ 251, per Aikens LJ at [29]. See also Crawford and Carruthers 12-07.

[89] *Marinos*, supra, [40].

[90] Cf Munby J in *Marinos v Marinos* [2007] EWHC 2047 (Fam), at [17]–[18], and Singer J in *L-K v K (No 2)* [2006] EWHC 3280 at [35].

[91] Infra, pp 968–71.

[92] *Re V (Abduction: Habitual Residence)* [1995] 2 FLR 992. The concept breaks down, however, in the instance of a family moving between two jurisdictions on a weekly basis: *Ikimi v Ikimi* supra, per Thorpe LJ at [32]. See also *In the Marriage of Hanbury Brown* (1996) FLC 92-671.

The time at which the personal law connecting factor (habitual residence or domicile, as the case may be) is to be determined is, as at common law and under the 1973 Act prior to 1 March 2001,[93] the time when proceedings are commenced, and not at the later time when the case is actually tried.[94] If the rule were otherwise, a respondent habitually resident in England could frustrate a petition brought by the other spouse, domiciled and resident abroad, by changing his residence between the presentation of the petition and the hearing of the case. The rule is "once competent, always competent"[95] and this will be so even if the party habitually resident in England at the time of the English proceedings has since changed his residence and disassociated himself from the determination of his status by an English court.

Counterclaims   In terms of Article 4 of Brussels II *bis*, a court which has jurisdiction on the basis of Article 3, and in which proceedings are pending, also has jurisdiction to examine a counterclaim, insofar as the counterclaim falls within the scope of the Regulation.[96]

Conversion of legal separation into divorce   A Member State court which has given a judgment[97] on a legal separation has jurisdiction, by virtue of Article 5 of the Regulation, to convert that judgment into a divorce, if the law of that Member State so provides.[98] In some countries, legal separation is a necessary step prior to divorce, and so the conversion of legal separations into divorces is not infrequent in certain States.

Exclusive nature of jurisdiction under Articles 3, 4 and 5 and residual jurisdiction   By virtue of Article 6 of Brussels II *bis*, a spouse who (a) is habitually resident in a Member State; or (b) is a national of a Member State,[99] or, in the case of the United Kingdom, has his/her "domicile" in that state, may be sued in another Member State only in accordance with Article 3, 4 or 5. In other words, national rules of residual jurisdiction, set out, for England, in section 5(2)(b) of the Domicile and Matrimonial Proceedings Act 1973, considered below, cannot be relied upon in respect of such a person.

Article 7(1) of Brussels II *bis* provides that, where no court of a Member State has jurisdiction pursuant to Article 3, 4 or 5 of the Regulation, jurisdiction shall be determined in each Member State by the laws of that state.[100] The European Court of Justice (ECJ) has stated that the application of Article 7(1) does not depend on the "position"[101] of the respondent,

---

[93] *Leon v Leon* [1967] P 275; and see 13th edn of this book (1999), p 765.

[94] Eg *Olafisoye v Olafisoye* [2010] EWHC 3539 (Fam), per Holman J at [9].

[95] *Leon v Leon*, supra, at 284.

[96] Art 1(1) provides that Brussels II *bis* shall apply, whatever the nature of the court or tribunal, in civil matters relating to (a) divorce, legal separation or marriage annulment (but only to the dissolution of matrimonial ties, and not to issues such as the grounds for divorce, property consequences of marriage, or other ancillary measures: recital (8)); and (b) the attribution, exercise, delegation, restriction or termination of parental responsibility. The Regulation does not apply to: (a) the establishment or contesting of a parent-child relationship; (b) decisions on adoption, measures preparatory to adoption, or the annulment or revocation of adoption; (c) the name and forenames of a child; (d) emancipation; (e) maintenance obligations; (f) trusts or succession; (g) measures taken as a result of criminal offences committed by children.

[97] Defined in Brussels II *bis*, Art 2(4).

[98] Art 5. See *Ville De Bauge v China* [2014] EWHC 3975 (Fam).

[99] See discussion regarding non-Member State nationals in *Sulaiman v Juffali* [2002] 1 FLR 479, and conclusion of Munby J, at para 24, that Art 2 of Brussels II (Art 3 of Brussels II *bis*) is founded simply and solely on the habitual residence of one or other or both of the spouses, not on their nationality, rendering the Saudi Arabian nationality of both spouses, in the instant case, irrelevant. Cf *Singh v Singh* 2005 SLT 749, per Judge R F Macdonald QC, at [12].

[100] See McEleavy (2004) 53 ICLQ 605, at 614. *F v F (Divorce: Jurisdiction)* [2009] EWHC 1448 (Fam)—jurisdiction fell to be determined by English law as no court of any Member State had jurisdiction under Brussels II *bis*.

[101] *Sundelind Lopez v Lopez Lizazo* (Case C-68/07) [2008] IL Pr 4 at [25].

but solely on the question whether the court of a Member State has jurisdiction pursuant to Articles 3 to 5 of the Regulation.[102] By way of rationalisation of this statement, it should be noted that the rules for allocation of jurisdiction under Articles 3 to 5 envisage that jurisdiction can be established without reference to the "position" of the respondent as at the date of commencement of proceedings. This is true, however, only in respect of Article 3(1)(a), indents 5 and 6, based as they are upon principles of *forum actoris*,[103] and potentially also in respect of indent 2.

By Article 7(2), as against a respondent who is not habitually resident and is not either a national of a Member State or, in the case of the United Kingdom and Ireland, does not have his domicile within the territory of one of the latter Member States, any national of a Member State who is habitually resident within the territory of another Member State may, like the nationals of that state, avail himself of the rules of jurisdiction applicable in that state.[104] For Article 7(2) to apply, the applicant must be a national of a Member State habitually resident in another Member State. Moreover, the respondent must satisfy two conditions: he must be habitually resident in a non-Member State country, and he must not be a citizen of a Member State (or, in the case of the United Kingdom and Ireland, must not be domiciled there).[105]

A question existed as to the extent to which the national rules of residual jurisdiction of one Member State could be used to trump the (putative) exercise by another Member State of jurisdiction under Article 3 of the Regulation. This very issue arose in Sweden, in the case of *Sundelind Lopez v Lopez Lizazo*.[106]

> The case concerned the commencement of divorce proceedings in the District Court of Stockholm by the female petitioner, a Swedish national, against her respondent husband, a Cuban national. The couple had lived together in France. At the date of commencement of proceedings, the petitioner continued to reside in France, whereas her husband, by then, was resident in Cuba.

The Swedish court dismissed the petition on the ground that, under Article 3(1)(a)[107] of Brussels II *bis*, only the French courts had jurisdiction and that, accordingly, Article 7 of the Regulation precluded Swedish rules on jurisdiction from applying. The Swedish Court of Appeal dismissed the appeal brought by the petitioner against that judgment. In a further appeal to the Swedish Supreme Court, the petitioner submitted that Article 6 of Brussels II *bis* implies that the courts of Member States do not have exclusive jurisdiction where the respondent neither has his habitual residence in, nor is a national of, a Member State. In February 2007, the Swedish Supreme Court referred the following question[108] to the ECJ for a preliminary ruling on the matter, namely:

> The respondent in a case concerning divorce is neither resident in a Member State nor a citizen of a Member State. May the case be heard by a court in a Member State which does not have jurisdiction under Article 3 [of Brussels II *bis*], even though a court in another Member State may have jurisdiction by application of one of the rules on jurisdiction set out in Article 3?

---

[102] Ibid.
[103] See supra n 57.
[104] Art 7(2).
[105] See *Singh v Singh* 2005 SLT 749, per Judge R F Macdonald QC, at [12].
[106] *Sundelind Lopez v Lopez Lizazo* (Case C-68/07) [2008] IL Pr 4.
[107] Indent 2 or indent 5; supra, p 955.
[108] *Kerstin Sundelind Lopez v Miquel Enrique Lopez Lizazo* (Case C-68/07).

In November 2007, the ECJ delivered its judgment,[109] ruling as follows:

> Articles 6 and 7 of the Regulation are to be interpreted as meaning that where, in divorce proceedings, a respondent is not habitually resident in a Member State and is not a national of a Member State, the courts of a Member State cannot base their jurisdiction to hear the petition on their national law, if the courts of another Member State have jurisdiction under Article 3 of the Regulation.

The Court held that, according to Article 7(1), it is only where no court of a Member State has jurisdiction pursuant to Articles 3 to 5 of the Regulation that jurisdiction is to be governed, in each Member State, by the laws of that state. Moreover, according to Article 17 of the Regulation, where a court of one Member State is seised of a case over which it has no jurisdiction under the Regulation, and a court of another Member State has jurisdiction pursuant to the Regulation, the former is to declare of its own motion that it has no jurisdiction. Finally, the ECJ made clear that Article 6 does *not* lay down a general rule that the jurisdiction of the courts of a Member State to hear questions relating to a divorce in respect of a respondent who does *not* have his habitual residence in a Member State and is *not* a national of a Member State is to be determined, in all cases, under national law.[110]

The consequence, in *Sundelind Lopez v Lopez Lizazo*, was that since the French courts had jurisdiction to hear the divorce petition pursuant to Article 3(1)(a), the Swedish courts could not base their jurisdiction to hear that petition upon rules of their national law, pursuant to Article 7(1), but were required, in accordance with Article 17, to declare of their own motion that they had no jurisdiction, in favour of the French courts.[111]

(ii) Jurisdiction under Domicile and Matrimonial Proceedings Act 1973, section 5(2)(b)
For England,[112] the national rules of residual jurisdiction are to be found in section 5(2)(b) of the 1973 Act, ie: "the High Court or a divorce county court shall have jurisdiction to entertain proceedings if, and only if no court of a Contracting State[113] has jurisdiction under Brussels II *bis*, and either of the parties to the marriage is domiciled in England on the date when the proceedings are begun".[114]

(iii) Reform of rules of matrimonial jurisdiction in Brussels II bis[115]
In July 2006, the European Commission published a Proposal for a Council Regulation amending Regulation (EC) No 2201/2003 as regards jurisdiction and introducing rules concerning applicable law in matrimonial matters (known colloquially as "Rome III").[116] The Proposal had a dual objective: to amend Brussels II *bis* as regards jurisdiction in matrimonial matters, and to introduce harmonized choice of law rules in matrimonial matters. In relation to jurisdiction, the following four objectives were to be attained: (i) to strengthen legal certainty and

---

[109] *Sundelind Lopez v Lopez Lizazo* (Case C-68/07) [2008] IL Pr 4.

[110] Ibid, at [24].

[111] Ibid, at [20].

[112] Cf residual rules of other Member States: Borras, *Explanatory Report*, para 47.

[113] See supra, p 954, n 36.

[114] Eg *Kearly v Kearly* [2009] EWHC 1876 (Fam)—the Australian wife succeeded in obtaining a decree nisi on the jurisdictional basis of her British husband's domicile of origin in England, notwithstanding that the couple had not lived in England since 1987; *M v M (Domicile: Divorce)* [2010] EWHC 982 (Fam)— despite the couples' strong connection with Denmark, the English court had jurisdiction based on applicant wife's domicile of origin. Cf *Olafisoye v Olafisoye* [2010] EWHC 3539 (Fam)—see supra, p 955, n 43.

[115] Kruger (2016) 12 J Priv Int L 132.

[116] COM (2006) 399 final, and Document 5274/07 LIMITE JUSTCIV 4, 12 January 2007. See also Green Paper on applicable law and jurisdiction in divorce matters (COM (2005) 82 final 14 March 2005); Commission Staff Working Paper, Annex to the Green Paper on applicable law and jurisdiction in divorce matters (SEC (2005) 331) 14 March 2005; and House of Lords EU Committee, 52nd Report, Session 2005/06, "Rome III—Choice of Law in Divorce" (2006).

predictability; (ii) to increase flexibility by introducing limited party autonomy; (iii) to ensure access to court; and (iv) to prevent a "rush to court" by one spouse.[117] In detail, it was proposed to insert a choice of court clause into Brussels II *bis*, to permit spouses in proceedings for divorce or legal separation (but not marriage annulment) to choose the jurisdiction of a "substantially connected"[118] Member State court.[119] This clearly could be advantageous to "international" couples. Additionally, it was proposed to introduce a new Article 7, providing a uniform and exhaustive rule on residual jurisdiction to replace national rules of residual jurisdiction. The concern was to ensure access to a Member State court for spouses who live in a non-Member State country but who retain strong links with a Member State of which they are nationals or in which they have resided for a certain period. On a point of the EU competence, however, it is highly questionable what interest the EU has in residual cases such as these, which, by definition, fall outside the jurisdictional boundaries of Article 3 of Brussels II *bis*.[120] The United Kingdom government decided not to opt into a resulting EU instrument.[121]

The provisions on applicable law contained in the Proposal, however, proved problematic, and no unanimity could be reached within the Council with regard to these rules.[122] The Commission therefore withdrew the Proposal.[123]

As a part of the ongoing review of the Brussels II *bis* Regulation,[124] in April 2014, the Commission adopted a Report on the on the application of Council Regulation (EC) No 2201/2003 concerning jurisdiction and the recognition and enforcement of judgments in matrimonial matters and the matters of parental responsibility, repealing Regulation (EC) No 1347/2000.[125] The Report identified three underlying shortcomings of the jurisdictional rules of the Regulation in relation to matrimonial matters. First, the alternative (as opposed to hierarchical) grounds of jurisdiction encourage the "rush to court" behavior, which goes against the culture of reconciliation and mediation.[126] Second, the Regulation lacks provision for at least a limited party autonomy in matrimonial matters.[127] By not allowing spouses to agree on the competent court, Brussels II *bis* fails to follow the trend in recent EU regulations in civil matters to permit at least a certain level of party autonomy, and hinders the objectives of legal certainty and predictability. Finally, Article 6 which reiterates the exclusive nature of the jurisdiction determined under Articles 3, 4 and 5 of Brussels II *bis* can "create confusion" and is "superfluous" as Articles 3, 4 and 5 state when a court has exclusive jurisdiction.[128]

---

[117] Proposal for a Council Regulation, Explanatory Memorandum, pp 2–3.

[118] See Proposal for a Council Regulation, Art 1(2).

[119] Party freedom of choice of court in relation to matrimonial matters presently is restricted in Brussels II *bis* to Art 3.1(a), indent 4 (joint application). See, however, Brussels II *bis*, Art 12, which permits parties, subject to certain conditions, to agree the competent court in matters of parental responsibility. See infra, p 1098.

[120] The label "extra-Community disputes", which, at one point, was considered as an alternative to the term "residual jurisdiction", perhaps better reveals the absence of EU interest in such cases. See Borras, *Explanatory Report*, para 47.

[121] See House of Lords, Written Statements, 18 April 2007: Column WS 7, per Baroness Ashton of Upholland; and in Scotland, Report of the Justice I Committee of the Scottish Parliament, CJ1004/2005, 7 October 2005. Ireland also has decided not to opt into Rome III: Press Release 10 October 2006, at <http://www.justice.ie/en/JELR/Pages/Government-rejects-EU-divorce-proposals>.

[122] See 2873rd Council Meeting Justice and Home Affairs, Luxembourg, 5–6 June 2008, C/08/146, 9956/08 (Presse 146), p 22. For analysis of subsequent developments in the area of choice of law see infra, pp 982–4.

[123] OJ 2013 C 109/04.

[124] See, eg, European Parliament, "Jurisdiction in matrimonial matters—Reflections for the review of the Brussels IIa Regulation", 2016, at <http://www.europarl.europa.eu/RegData/etudes/STUD/2016/571361/IPOL_STU(2016)571361_EN.pdf>.

[125] COM (2014) 225 final.

[126] Ibid, p 5.

[127] Ibid.

[128] Ibid.

On 30 June 2016, the Commission published a Proposal for a Council Regulation on jurisdiction, the recognition and enforcement of decisions in matrimonial matters and the matters of parental responsibility, and on international child abduction (recast).[129] Very surprisingly, however, as regards matrimonial matters, the Proposal departs entirely from the 2014 Report. It claims that due to "limited evidence of existing problems" it was not possible to identify the scale of the issues or to establish "the need to intervene".[130]

This failure to act is highly regrettable. Indeed, it means that the Brussels II *bis* recast will become a missed opportunity to rectify at least some of the issues that were justifiably highlighted in the 2014 Report, in particular the "race to court" problem,[131] and the lack of party autonomy in relation to jurisdiction in matrimonial matters. The "race to court" problem could have been resolved either through establishing a hierarchy of jurisdiction, or through a transfer provision which would have allowed a Member State to transfer proceedings to the court of a Member State with the closer connection.[132] With regard to party autonomy, as a minimum, spouses should have been allowed to enter into a choice of court agreement opting for either the courts of the Member State of their habitual residence, at the time the agreement is concluded; the courts of the Member State of their last habitual residence, provided that one of them still resides there at the time of the agreement; or the courts of the Member State of the nationality of either spouse at the time of the agreement.

(b) Nullity of marriage

Section 5(3) of the 1973 Act provides that the High Court or a divorce county court shall have jurisdiction to entertain proceedings if, and only if: (a) the court has jurisdiction under Brussels II *bis*,[133] or (b) no court of a Contracting State[134] has jurisdiction under Brussels II *bis*, and either of the parties to the marriage (i) is domiciled in England on the date when the proceedings are begun,[135] or (ii) died before that date and either was domiciled at death in England or had been habitually resident there for one year immediately prior to the date of death.

(i) *Jurisdiction under Domicile and Matrimonial Proceedings Act 1973, section 5(3)(a)*

Section 5(3)(a) refers to the rules of jurisdiction contained in Brussels II *bis* which, in relation to petitions for nullity of marriage, are the same as those discussed above in relation to divorce and judicial separation.[136]

---

[129] COM (2016) 411 final. See also Commission Staff Working Document, Impact Assessment Accompanying the Document Proposal for a Council Regulation on jurisdiction, the recognition and enforcement of decisions in matrimonial matters and the matters of parental responsibility, and on international child abduction (recast) (SWD (2016) 207 final, 30 June 2016).

[130] COM (2016) 411 final, p 3.

[131] The Commission believes that the "rush to court" problem was already addressed by the harmonisation of the rules on the law applicable to divorce in the Rome III Regulation, discussed infra, pp 982–4. SWD (2016) 207 final, Part II.

[132] See, eg, Hedley J's comments in *S v S (Brussels II Revised: Articles 19(1) and (3): Reference to ECJ)* [2014] EWHC 3613 (Fam), where he expressed a strong criticism about the Brussels II *bis* "seemingly inflexible jurisdiction rules in relation to divorce", which may lead parties to engage in "extensive, expensive and futile manoeuvres", at [17]. His Lordship rightly suggested that such undesirable situation could be prevented if powers were available to achieve a transfer of jurisdiction to a "court which is better placed to hear the case or otherwise is a more convenient forum", as available with regard to parental responsibility cases by virtue of Art 15 of the Regulation. Ibid. For a detailed analysis of the policy options that were considered by the Commission see SWD (2016) 207 final, section II.

[133] As above.

[134] See supra, p 954, n 36.

[135] See, eg, *Singh v Singh* 2005 SLT 749—Scottish case under the equivalent rules of jurisdiction for Scotland, contained in Part III of the 1973 Act, s 7(3A) and (3B).

[136] Supra, p 954 et seq.

(ii) Jurisdiction under Domicile and Matrimonial Proceedings Act 1973, section 5(3)(b)

As with proceedings for divorce and judicial separation, Article 7 of Brussels II *bis* provides that where no court of a Member State has jurisdiction in annulment proceedings pursuant to Article 3, 4 or 5 of Brussels II *bis*, jurisdiction shall be determined in each Member State by the laws of that state. For England, the residual rules of jurisdiction for proceedings for nullity of marriage are to be found in section 5(3)(b): either of the parties to the marriage (i) is domiciled in England on the date when the proceedings are begun, or (ii) died before that date and either was domiciled at death in England or had been habitually resident there for one year immediately prior to the date of death.

The basis of jurisdiction in section 5(3)(b)(ii) is peculiar to nullity petitions, and is available only where either party to the marriage has died before the date when the proceedings for nullity were begun. The reason for this special jurisdictional rule is that, whilst divorce and judicial separation petitions can be brought only if both spouses are alive, the validity of a marriage may need to be tested in a nullity petition notwithstanding the death of one spouse, or even after the death of both, as where succession issues are involved.

(c) Jurisdiction to entertain other matrimonial proceedings in respect of the same marriage

By virtue of section 5(5) of the Domicile and Matrimonial Proceedings Act 1973, the High Court or a divorce county court shall, at any time when proceedings are pending in respect of which it has jurisdiction by virtue of section 5(2) or (3), discussed above, also have jurisdiction to entertain other proceedings, in respect of the same marriage, for divorce, judicial separation or nullity of marriage, notwithstanding that jurisdiction would not be exercisable under section 5(2) or (3). The purpose of this somewhat cryptic provision seems to be to deal with two jurisdictional problems. For example, let us assume that a husband, habitually resident in France at the date the proceedings are begun, petitions for nullity in England on the basis of his wife's habitual residence in England, but, before the petition is heard, she abandons her English residence. The wife, domiciled and resident abroad, wishes to cross-petition for divorce in England. At that time, there is no apparent jurisdictional basis for her petition; but section 5(5) confers jurisdiction because proceedings for nullity are pending in respect of which the court does have jurisdiction. Secondly, the English court appears also to have jurisdiction where the petitioner changes his mind, as in the case where a spouse petitions for judicial separation, jurisdiction being based on the respondent's habitual residence, and then, before the petition is heard but after the respondent has lost her English habitual residence, the petitioner amends his petition to one for divorce. Finally, there is one further complication in that section 5(5) applies to cases where jurisdiction is conferred by reason of that sub-section itself. For example, proceedings are pending for divorce, jurisdiction being based on habitual residence; then a cross-petition is brought for divorce even though the original jurisdictional grounds no longer exist, jurisdiction being conferred by section 5(5); the original proceedings are abandoned; the cross-petitioner then wishes to amend the petition to one for nullity. The court has jurisdiction, again under section 5(5), to hear the final nullity petition so long as the cross-petition is still pending.

(ii) Impact of the statutory bases

If the statutory bases of jurisdiction are satisfied, the court does not have a general discretion to refuse to hear the petition. We shall see[137] that there is a discretion to stay the proceedings in cases where to proceed would lead to a clash with foreign proceedings in a non-EU Member State or in Denmark, but there is no other discretion. For instance, leave is not required to serve a petition on a respondent overseas.[138] The position has been summed up

---

[137] Infra, p 972 et seq.
[138] Family Procedure Rules 2010, r 6.41.

by Bush J in a case where the respondent wife was resident in Ireland and could not afford to contest the English divorce proceedings: "If a court has jurisdiction . . . there is no way in which the court could decline jurisdiction on the ground of hardship, apparent unfairness or any other ground."[139]

(iii) Procedural issues

(a) Service of the petition[140]

A copy of every petition for divorce, nullity or judicial separation must be served on the respondent and every co-respondent,[141] and there is no need to obtain the leave of the court for service out of the jurisdiction.[142] An order for service by an alternative method may be made in appropriate circumstances,[143] and service may even be dispensed with altogether in any case in which service is impracticable.[144] This discretion is unfettered, but it will be exercised in favour of the petitioner only in exceptional cases,[145] as, for instance, when the possible methods of substituted service are likely to be ineffective.[146] Where the service of an application for a matrimonial order[147] or other document is to be effected within the EU, the Service Regulation[148] applies.[149] Where the service is to be effected in a country which is a party to the 1965 Hague Convention,[150] and the Service Regulation does not apply,[151] the following rules are applicable.[152] The application may be served "(a) through the authority designated under the Hague Convention in respect of that country; or (b) if the law of that country permits—(i) through the judicial authorities of that country; or (ii) through a British Consular authority in that country".[153] Where the service is to be effected in a country which is not a party to the 1965 Convention, the application and associated documents may be served, if permitted by the law of that country, "(a) through the government of that

---

[139] *Kapur v Kapur* [1984] FLR 920 at 922.

[140] See generally Family Procedure Rules 2010, Part 6, Chapter 4; and Practice Direction 6B.

[141] Family Procedure Rules 2010, r 7.8(1).

[142] Ibid, r 6.41.

[143] Ibid, r 6(19). Eg *W v W (Preliminary Issue: Stay of Petition)* [2002] EWHC 3049, [2003] 1 FLR 1022; and *Bentinck v Bentinck* [2007] EWCA Civ 175, at [49].

[144] Ibid, r 6.20.

[145] See *Akhtar v Rafiq* [2006] 1 FLR 27—no proper service on respondent wife; cogent evidence that the respondent was aware that divorce proceedings were under way might satisfy the judge prior to the issue of a special procedure certificate, but could not save the situation after the event, unless the circumstances were exceptional; *Ali Ebrahim v Ali Ebrahim* [1983] 1 WLR 1336 applied.

[146] *Luccioni v Luccioni* [1943] P 49 (no dispensation); *Weighman v Weighman* [1947] 2 All ER 852 (dispensation); *Paolantonio v Paolantonio* [1950] 2 All ER 404 (dispensation); *Spalenkova v Spalenkova* [1954] P 141 (no dispensation); and see *Whitehead v Whitehead* [1963] P 117 at 138. Different considerations are relevant in the case of a petition for presumption of death and dissolution of marriage: *N v N* [1957] P 385; infra, p 1038.

[147] Or a civil partnership order.

[148] Regulation (EC) No. 1393/2007 of the European Parliament and of the Council of 13 November 2007 on the service in the Member States of judicial and extrajudicial documents in civil or commercial matters (service of documents), and repealing Council Regulation (EC) No. 1348/2000. The Regulation applies between all Member States of the European Union including Denmark (see [2009] OJ L 331, 10 December 2008, p 21). Service of a document in Scotland or Northern Ireland is to be effected by any method that is applicable to service within England and Wales. Family Procedure Rules 2010, r 6.43(2).

[149] Family Procedure Rules 2010, r 6.44.

[150] The 1965 Hague Convention on the service abroad of judicial and extrajudicial documents in civil or commercial matters (15 November 1965).

[151] The Service Regulation prevails over the provisions of the 1965 Hague Convention (as well as over other provisions contained in bilateral or multilateral agreements or arrangements concluded by the Member States) (Art 20(1) of the Service Regulation). Consequently, if the service is to be effected in a Regulation State, the 1965 Convention does not apply.

[152] Family Procedure Rules 2010, rr 6.45(1) and 6.46.

[153] Ibid, r 6.45(1).

country, where that government is willing to serve it; or (b) through a British Consular authority in that country".[154] Additionally, there are special rules applicable to service in a Commonwealth country which is not a party to the 1965 Convention; the Isle of Man or the Channel Islands; or a British Overseas Territory.[155]

(b) Staying proceedings[156]

The breadth of the English jurisdictional rules set out in the Domicile and Matrimonial Proceedings Act 1973 has the consequence that there is a greater risk of divorce and other matrimonial proceedings in respect of the same marriage being pursued in England and in some other country simultaneously. Indeed, there could be several jurisdictions potentially in conflict, as where a wife habitually resident in England, but domiciled in Ireland, petitions for divorce from a husband habitually resident in Ontario, but domiciled in New York. There are related problems in that the concurrent matrimonial proceedings[157] may either be in some other part of the British Isles or in some politically foreign country. The provisions in Schedule 1 of the Domicile and Matrimonial Proceedings Act 1973 for the staying of the English proceedings vary according to the identity of the country in which the concurrent proceedings are taking place, ie: (i) a related jurisdiction in the British Isles; (ii) another EU Member State, except Denmark; or (iii) a non-EU Member State, or in Denmark. The rules are set out in section 5(5A) and (6) and Schedule 1 to the 1973 Act, and are subject, by virtue of section 5(6A), to Article 19 of Brussels II *bis*. In every instance, however, there is an obligation on the petitioner, or a cross-petitioner, when proceedings are pending before the English court to furnish particulars of any proceedings[158] in respect of that marriage, or affecting its validity, which he knows are continuing in another jurisdiction.[159]

(i) Concurrent proceedings in a related jurisdiction—obligatory stays

Paragraph 8 of Schedule 1 to the 1973 Act provides for obligatory stays. Where it appears before the beginning of the trial[160] of proceedings for divorce, and only divorce,[161] that proceedings for divorce or nullity are continuing in a related jurisdiction elsewhere in the British Isles;[162] that the parties of the marriage have resided together after they entered into the marriage; that the place where they resided together when those proceedings began or where they last resided together before those proceedings began is that other related jurisdiction in the British Isles; and that either of the parties was habitually resident there throughout the year ending with the date on which they last resided there together, the English court must, on the application of one of the spouses,[163] order the English proceedings to be stayed.[164]

---

[154] Ibid, r 6.45(2).

[155] Ibid, r 6.45(3).

[156] Schuz (1987) 17 Fam Law 438; (1989) 38 ICLQ 946.

[157] Defined in the 1973 Act, Sch 1(2) as proceedings for divorce, judicial separation, nullity of marriage, a declaration as to the validity of a marriage of the petitioner, and a declaration as to the subsistence of such a marriage.

[158] Including non-judicial proceedings of a description prescribed by rules of court: Sch 1, paras 5 and 6; see Family Proceedure Rules 2010, r 7.27 (Stay of proceedings). See *Trussler v Trussler* [2003] EWCA Civ 1830.

[159] Domicile and Matrimonial Proceedings Act 1973, s 5(6), Sch 1, para 7; see *Krenge v Krenge* [1999] 1 FLR 969 at 974–5.

[160] Trial of a preliminary issue of jurisdiction does not constitute trial of the proceedings for this purpose: Sch 1, para 4(1). Nor does trial of an issue as to custody or financial relief: *Thyssen-Bornemisza v Thyssen-Bornemisza* [1986] Fam 1.

[161] Where the proceedings are not only proceedings for divorce, then references to divorce apply only to the extent to which the proceedings are for divorce: Sch 1, para 8(2).

[162] Defined by Sch 1, para 3(2), to mean Scotland, Northern Ireland, Jersey, Guernsey and the Isle of Man.

[163] But not by the court's acting of its own motion, see Law Com No 48 (1972), paras 90–3. See Family Procedure Rules 2010, r 7.27(1).

[164] Sch 1, para 8(1); see *T v T (Custody: Jurisdiction)* [1992] 1 FLR 43. There are similar provisions requiring divorce proceedings in Scotland or Northern Ireland to be stayed when proceedings for divorce or

The salient features of this obligatory stay are that it only applies to English divorce proceedings and then only when the parties to the marriage are closely and clearly connected with the other jurisdiction in the British Isles. If the English proceedings are other than for divorce, or if the other British proceedings are other than for divorce or nullity, or if the residential connections with the other British jurisdiction are not all satisfied, this does not mean that the other proceedings cannot be stayed. It means, merely, that there will be no obligatory stay and that the question must be considered instead in the context of the court's *discretion* to stay the other proceedings. The object of the fairly elaborate criteria as to obligatory stays is to ensure that the proceedings are heard in the more appropriate forum; though it is possible to point to cases where the criteria produce the less appropriate forum.[165]

(ii) Concurrent proceedings in another EU Member State, except Denmark—Brussels II bis, Article 19

Article 19 (Lis pendens and dependent actions) provides that:

1. Where proceedings relating to divorce, legal separation or marriage annulment between the same parties are brought before courts of different Member States, the court second seised shall of its own motion stay its proceedings until such time as the jurisdiction of the court first seised is established. . . .
3. Where the jurisdiction of the court first seised is established, the court second seised shall decline jurisdiction in favour of that court. In that case, the party who brought the relevant action before the court second seised may bring that action before the court first seised.

Article 3 of Brussels II *bis*, by its nature, often will confer jurisdiction on the courts of more than one Member State in respect of a single dispute, and so there is a clear need for a provision to deal with the problem of concurrent proceedings and conflicting judgments in the courts of different Member States.[166] Article 3 is limited to concurrent proceedings[167] in Member States, but it is not limited to proceedings under the bases of jurisdiction set out in the Regulation. Article 19 will apply equally where proceedings relating to divorce, legal separation or marriage annulment[168] between the same parties have been commenced in two Member States under their national rules of residual jurisdiction[169] (the bases of jurisdiction under Brussels II *bis* being inapplicable).[170]

Article 19, like Article 29 of the Brussels I (Recast) Regulation, is a purely mechanical rule, which could lead to a race between the parties and which, arguably, is at odds with the prevailing culture of encouraging parties to attempt to engage in reconciliation and/or mediation processes rather than rushing to litigate.[171] Against that, however, the need for expensive litigation, generally conducted concurrently in two jurisdictions, as each party

---

nullity are continuing elsewhere in the British Isles: Sch 3, para 8. of the 1973 Act; and Matrimonial Causes (Northern Ireland) Order, SI 1978/1045, Sch 1, para 8.

[165] North, op cit, pp 37–8.

[166] Cf in relation to civil and commercial matters, the Brussels I (Recast) Regulation, Art 29. See supra, pp 311–12.

[167] Pending not concluded. See, in relation to civil and commercial matters, supra, pp 443–4.

[168] Art 11 of Brussels II comprised two separate clauses dealing, respectively, with proceedings involving the same cause of action (Art 11.1), and proceedings not involving the same cause of action (Art 11.2) (see Borras, *Explanatory Report*, para 54), but the two clauses have been collapsed into a unitary clause in Art 19 of Brussels II *bis*.

[169] Sch 1(9)(1) of the 1973 Act supports this interpretation.

[170] See supra, p 962.

[171] See possible objections to the *lis pendens* doctrine in *Wermuth v Wermuth* [2003] EWCA Civ 50, [2003] 1 WLR 942, at [3].

endeavours to establish that his/her favoured jurisdiction is the more appropriate, has been eliminated.[172] The court of the Member State first seised of the matter takes priority, and any court of another Member State must of its own motion decline jurisdiction,[173] once the jurisdiction of the court first seised is established in that state. The winner of the race to litigation is the spouse who can show that the court where s/he brought the action is first seised of jurisdiction.[174]

The rule as to the time at which a court is seised is set out in Article 16 (Seising of a Court), which provides two alternatives,[175] namely:

1. A court shall be deemed to be seised:
    (a) at the time[176] when the document instituting the proceedings or an equivalent document is lodged with the court, provided that the applicant has not subsequently failed to take the steps he was required to take to have service effected on the respondent;[177] or
    (b) if the document has to be served before being lodged with the court, at the time when it is received by the authority responsible for service, provided that the applicant has not subsequently failed to take the steps he was required to take to have the document lodged with the court.

The steps which the petitioner is required to take to effect service will depend on the legal system in question. As with the seising of a court in civil and commercial matters, the fact that Member States will not all be applying the same definition runs the risk that the race to become first seised will be run on unequal terms.[178] Additionally, the time zone offset may be a further reason why the "race to court" is run on unequal terms.[179] Such scenario was outlined in *S v S (Brussels II Revised: Articles 19(1) and (3): Reference to ECJ)*[180] where following the lapse of judicial separation proceedings in France, at midnight 17 June 2014, the husband—being well aware of the advantage of the French time-zone—filed his divorce petition at 8.20 am local time (ie a time of day when it would have been impossible for the wife to issue divorce proceedings in England).[181]

---

[172] *Wermuth v Wermuth* [2003] EWCA Civ 50, [2003] 1 WLR 942, per Thorpe LJ, at [3].

[173] Art 17 (Examination as to jurisdiction) provides that, "Where a court of a Member State is seised of a case over which it has no jurisdiction under this Regulation and over which a court of another Member State has jurisdiction by virtue of this Regulation, it shall declare of its own motion that it has no jurisdiction." See, eg, *W v W (Preliminary Issue: Stay of Petition)* [2002] EWHC 3049, [2003] 1 FLR 1022; *Rogers-Headicar v Rogers-Headicar* [2004] EWCA Civ 1867, [2005] 2 FCR 1; *L-K v K (Brussels II Revised: Maintenance Pending Suit)* [2006] EWHC 153 (Fam), [2006] 2 FLR 1113; and *Moore v Moore* [2007] EWCA Civ 361, [2007] IL Pr 36.

[174] *Jefferson v O'Connor* [2014] EWCA Civ 38—neither a jurisdictional agreement or an estoppel (ie the petitioner's promise to discontinue the earlier English proceedings) can defeat the effect of Art 19 of Brussels II *bis*.

[175] Cf in relation to civil and commercial matters, the Brussels I (Recast) Regulation, Art 32. See supra, pp 448–9.

[176] The French language version of the instrument refers not to the "time", but to the date (*"la date à laquelle"*) on which the court is seised; a verbal inconsistency noted, but not emphasised, by Singer J in *L-K v K (Brussels II Revised: Maintenance Pending Suit)* [2006] EWHC 153 (Fam), [2006] 2 FLR 1113 at [15].

[177] Eg *W v W (Preliminary Issue: Stay of Petition)* [2002] EWHC 3049, [2003] 1 FLR 1022; and *L-K v K (Brussels II Revised: Maintenance Pending Suit)* [2006] EWHC 153 (Fam), [2006] 2 FLR 1113.

[178] Cf Brussels I Regulation, Art 32. See supra, pp 448–9.

[179] See *S v S (Brussels II Revised: Articles 19(1) and (3): Reference to ECJ)* [2014] EWHC 3613 (Fam), at [15].

[180] [2014] EWHC 3613 (Fam).

[181] Ibid, at [15]. See infra, pp 970–1.

An English court may have to determine whether, and when, a foreign court has been seised; this should be a matter for the national law of that foreign Member State to determine.[182] In this regard, problems have arisen in relation to the temporal extent of the seisin under Articles 16 and 19 especially regarding Italy where judicial separation is a necessary precursor to divorce. In particular, in *C v S*[183] the wife's petition for judicial separation in Italy was declared void by the Italian court due to a non-appearance of the petitioner. The petition was then archived but remained revivable. Hedley J held that the Italian decision had brought the matrimonial proceedings in Italy to an end, with the effect that the Italian court could no longer be regarded as being seised under Articles 16 and 19 of Brussels II *bis*. His Lordship rightly suggested that Article 19 had to be read purposively, meaning that for a court to remain seised, there must be existing proceedings before it. Any other interpretation would "make a nonsense" of the provision by a "court being seised of a matter about which it can do nothing unless a party revives it".[184] In contrast, however, in *Ville De Bauge v China*,[185] it was held that the Italian court that had been seised of separation proceedings did not lose the seisin after the ending of the separation proceedings but before the expiry of a thirty-day appeal period. As the Italian court remained seised of the matter during the appeal period, both parties were precluded from issuing Italian or English divorce proceedings until the expiration of the appeal period at which the husband issued formal divorce proceedings in Italy.[186] An English court will determine whether and, if so, when it has been seised.[187] The court seised second cannot examine the jurisdiction of the court first seised. It was held in *Trussler v Trussler*[188] that "any litigant who asserts that there is a *lis alibi pendens* undertakes an obligation to prove the issue of the *lis* and the fact that it is still pending as at the date of issue of the proceedings in [England]".[189]

Once the jurisdiction of the court first seised has been established, the court second seised must then decline jurisdiction. This avoids the danger of the court second seised declining jurisdiction in favour of the court first seised, and that first court subsequently deciding that it has no jurisdiction.[190] There is no discretion given to the courts of either Member State as to whether they should take jurisdiction.

The meaning of the verb "established" for the purposes of Art 19 arose as the central issue in the case of *S v S (Brussels II Revised: Articles 19(1) and (3): Reference to ECJ)*.[191] The conflict resulted in Hedley J staying the proceedings and making a reference for a preliminary ruling to the Court of Justic of the European Union (CJEU). The factual scenario was as follows:

---

[182] *W v W (Preliminary Issue: Stay of Petition)* [2002] EWHC 3049, [2003] 1 FLR 1022, citing *Overseas Union Ltd v New Hampshire Co* [1992] 1 QB 434; *C v C (Brussels II: French Conciliation and Divorce Proceedings)* [2005] EWCA Civ 68, [2005] 1 WLR 469; and *L-K v K (Brussels II Revised: Maintenance Pending Suit)* [2006] EWHC 153 (Fam), [2006] 2 FLR 1113.

[183] [2010] EWHC 2676 (Fam).

[184] Ibid, at [20].

[185] [2014] EWHC 3975 (Fam).

[186] Ibid, per Nicholas Cusworth QC, at [17].

[187] *Rogers-Headicar v Rogers-Headicar* [2004] EWCA Civ 1867, [2005] 2 FCR 1—the state of the pleadings cannot qualify the existence or otherwise of a court's jurisdiction to hear a suit; W's being given permission to amend her pleaded case was held to be only a case management decision which had no impact on the time at which the court was seised; and *Weiner v Weiner* [2010] EWHC 1843 (Fam)—the fact that the wife had effected service of the divorce petition on a Sunday was a minor and unintentional violation of an "archaic, anomalous, technical rule" which the English court would disregard for all purposes. Accordingly, the jurisdiction of the English court, as the court first seised, was established.

[188] [2003] EWCA Civ 1830.

[189] Ibid, per Thorpe LJ, at [8].

[190] See *Wermuth v Wermuth* [2003] EWCA Civ 50, [2003] 1 WLR 942, per Thorpe LJ, at [34]; and *L-K v K (Brussels II Revised: Maintenance Pending Suit)* [2006] EWHC 153 (Fam), [2006] 2 FLR 1113.

[191] [2014] EWHC 3613 (Fam).

The husband issued judicial separation proceedings in France. The wife then filed for divorce in England but her application was dismissed by consent on the basis that the jurisdiction of the French courts had been established under the Brussels II *bis* Regulation. Later, the husband filed a divorce petition in France but this was also dismissed, because the French judicial separation proceedings were still alive. The husband, however, took virtually no steps to progress those proceedings. Under French law, the judicial separation suit would lapse after thirty months following the first court appointment and whilst these proceedings were ongoing, neither spouse could initiate divorce proceedings. In the present case, the judicial separation proceedings lapsed at midnight on 16 June 2014. Nevertheless, prior to that, on 13 June 2014, the wife had again seised the English court of divorce proceedings.

Hedley J asked the CJEU whether in the case of judicial separation and divorce proceedings brought between parties before the courts of two Member States, Article 19 of Brussels II *bis* should be interpreted to mean that where proceedings before the court first seised had expired after the second court in the second Member State has been seised, the jurisdiction of the court first seised should be regarded as not being established.[192]

The CJEU held that once the judicial separation proceedings before the French court lapsed as a result of the expiry of the legal time-limit, the jurisdiction of the French court was no longer established, and, accordingly, criteria for *lis pendens* were no longer fulfilled.[193] Consequently, since the proceedings before the French court first seised lapsed, only the English court remained seised of the dispute.

Article 19 is limited to concurrent proceedings in different Member States. It does not apply to concurrent actions in England and a non-Member State country, such as South Africa. In such cases, an English court will continue to employ traditional rules based upon the doctrine of *forum conveniens*, and given statutory expression in Schedule 1, paragraph 9 of the Domicile and Matrimonial Proceedings Act 1973, discussed later in this chapter.[194]

Brussels II *bis*, Article 20 (Provisional, including protective, measures) Article 20 provides that:

1. In urgent cases, the provisions of this Regulation shall not prevent the courts of a Member State from taking such provisional, including protective, measures in respect of persons or assets in that State as may be available under the law of that Member State, even if, under this Regulation, the court of another Member State has jurisdiction as to the substance of the matter.
2. The measures referred to in paragraph 1 shall cease to apply when the court of the Member State having jurisdiction under this Regulation as to the substance of the matter has taken the measures it considers appropriate.[195]

The rule on provisional and protective measures is not subject to the jurisdictional rules of Brussels II *bis*. It does not require provisional measures to be taken, but rather gives a discretion to a court which has no jurisdiction over the substance of the dispute if four conditions are satisfied:[196] (a) the measures are provisional within the meaning of the Regulation; (b) the court has power to grant the measures under national law; (c) the court considers that in the circumstances of the case it is appropriate to grant them; and (d) the case is urgent. In applying to "persons or assets", Article 20 affects matters outside the scope of the instrument, and

---

[192] *A v B* (Case C-489/14, OJ 2015 C 389/12), at [26].
[193] Ibid, at [45].
[194] Infra, p 972 et seq.
[195] See also Brussels II *bis*, Recital (16).
[196] Articulated in *Wermuth v Wermuth* [2003] EWCA Civ 50, [2003] 1 WLR 942, per Lawrence Collins J, at [40].

is silent not only on the types of measures which may be taken, but also regarding the extent of their necessary connection with the matrimonial proceedings. The significance lies in the fact that the measures may be adopted by the court of one Member State even though the court of another Member State has jurisdiction over the main dispute. In invoking Article 20, the court of one Member State plays a supporting role to the court of another. The measures terminate, however, when a court in the Member State having jurisdiction over the main dispute delivers a judgment on the basis of Article 3 of the Regulation.

In *Wermuth v Wermuth*,[197] the Court of Appeal was required to consider whether an English order for maintenance pending suit in the sum of £12,500 per month, two-thirds of which was intended to provide the respondent wife with funds with which to litigate, was a protective measure in terms of Brussels II. It had been envisaged by the judge at first instance that the maintenance would run indefinitely. There was no realistic prospect of repayment by the wife, should that have been required by the substantive judgment of the German court in which the divorce proceedings were taking place. The Court of Appeal concluded that, in the light of the substance and duration of the maintenance order, it was neither a protective nor a provisional measure under Article 12 of Brussels II (Article 20 of Brussels II *bis*), for the maintenance order had not been urgent or protective in accordance with established principles, and it amounted to an unwarranted invasion of the proper function of the German court. Article 12 (Article 20, Brussels II *bis*) was to be narrowly construed since to do otherwise would be to usurp the power of the court first seised. Lawrence Collins J sounded a word of caution regarding the use of Article 12 (Article 20, Brussels II *bis*):

> Provisional measures vary from one context to another, and from one country to another, but what they have in common is that their object is to ensure that the rights of parties and the ultimate effectiveness of a judgment are not frustrated by the actions of one party pending resolution of their respective rights. In the international context it is vitally important to ensure that provisional measures are not used to frustrate internationally agreed principles of jurisdiction.[198]

(iii) Concurrent proceedings in a non-EU Member State, or in Denmark—discretionary stays
As stated above, Article 19 of Brussels II *bis* is limited to concurrent proceedings in different Member States. It does not apply to concurrent actions in England and a non-EU Member State country, such as South Africa. In such cases, an English court will continue to employ traditional rules based upon the doctrine of *forum non conveniens*, and given statutory expression in paragraph 9 of Schedule 1 to the Domicile and Matrimonial Proceedings Act 1973. Where, before the beginning of the trial of any matrimonial proceedings[199] (other than proceedings governed by Brussels II *bis*)[200] which are continuing before the English courts, it appears that any proceedings[201] are pending in another jurisdiction[202] in respect of, or capable of affecting, the validity or subsistence of the marriage in question, then the English court has a discretion to stay its own proceedings. It has been held that proceedings in India

---

[197] Ibid.
[198] At [38].
[199] These are defined as proceedings for divorce, judicial separation, nullity, and declarations as to the validity or subsistence of the petitioner's marriage: Sch 1, para 2. Proceedings for a declaration of presumed death, the effect of which is the termination of the missing person's marriage, and for declarations of legitimacy or parentage are not included. Trial of an ancillary issue as to custody or financial relief is not trial of the matrimonial proceedings: *Thyssen-Bornemisza v Thyssen-Bornemisza* [1986] Fam 1.
[200] In respect of which, see supra, pp 968–71.
[201] The foreign proceedings may be of any kind, both as to the relief sought and the nature of the proceedings, including presumably administrative proceedings, so long as they are of a description prescribed by rules of court: Sch 1, paras 5 and 6.
[202] Ie a non-EU Member State, or in Denmark.

for maintenance and for an injunction to allow the wife to reoccupy the matrimonial home do not affect the validity or subsistence of the marriage.[203] This discretion is wider than in the case of the obligatory staying provisions in that it applies to proceedings before other foreign[204] courts and it also applies to a much wider range of proceedings before the other courts.[205] In this case, the court may act not only on the application of a spouse but also of its own motion, and so it might exercise its discretion to stay proceedings in circumstances covered by the mandatory staying provisions where a spouse has not sought such a stay.

The basis on which the court's discretion is to be exercised is stated to be that the balance of fairness and convenience between the parties, having regard to all relevant factors, including the convenience of witnesses and delay or expense likely to result from a decision whether or not to stay the proceedings, is such that it is appropriate for the proceedings before the other court to be disposed of first.[206] It will depend on the facts of each case as to how the judge will draw this balance, but some guidance has emerged from the small number of reported cases directly concerned with the exercise of the discretion. What is clear is that, in determining the principles for the exercise of the discretion under the 1973 Act, the courts are to apply the general approach to the operation of the doctrine of *forum non conveniens* under the inherent jurisdiction which was developed in the context of commercial cases.[207] This means that the discretion under paragraph 9 of Schedule 1 to the 1973 Act ought to be exercised to grant a stay if the defendant can point to another forum which is the appropriate one for trial of the proceedings, provided that the petitioner does not show that justice cannot be done there.[208] However, it does not seem that it has to be shown that the foreign forum is clearly or distinctly more appropriate than the English one.[209]

The drawing together of the statutory and common law approaches was achieved by the House of Lords in *De Dampierre v De Dampierre*:[210]

> The husband and wife were both French nationals who married in France in 1977. Two years later they moved to London. Then, in 1984, the wife established an antiques business in New York and in 1985 she took their child to live there with her. The wife refused to return and the husband started divorce proceedings in France, whereupon the wife then petitioned for divorce in England.[211] The husband sought to have the English proceedings stayed. This was resisted by the wife who claimed that, if she was found to be solely responsible for the breakdown of the marriage, she would receive less financial support from a French court than from an English one.

The House of Lords granted a stay, having little doubt that France was the more appropriate forum, given the wife's tenuous links with England and that "she voluntarily severed all connections with England before instituting her English divorce proceedings".[212] If France was

---

[203] *Kapur v Kapur* [1984] FLR 920 at 922.

[204] Ie a non-EU Member State, or in Denmark.

[205] In so far as it applies also to cases covered by the mandatory staying provisions, the court shall not exercise its discretionary power whilst an application for a mandatory stay is pending: Sch 1, para 9(3).

[206] Sch 1, paras 9(1) and (2).

[207] *Spiliada Maritime Corpn v Cansulex Ltd* [1987] AC 460, supra, p 393 et seq.

[208] See *T v T (Jurisdiction: Forum Conveniens)* [1995] 2 FLR 660—English proceedings stayed in favour of those in Kenya, despite the absence of legal aid there.

[209] *Butler v Butler* [1997] 2 All ER 822; cf *S v S* [1997] 2 FLR 100.

[210] [1988] AC 92, especially at pp 102, 108–9; and see *Gadd v Gadd* [1984] 1 WLR 1435; *K v K* [1986] 2 FLR 411; *Mitchell v Mitchell* 1993 SLT 123; see also *Kornberg v Kornberg* (1991) 76 DLR (4th) 379.

[211] Being pre-Brussels II, the English court had jurisdiction to entertain the wife's petition on the basis of the husband's habitual residence in England.

[212] [1988] AC 92 at 102. Cf *Breuning v Breuning* [2002] EWHC 236, [2002] 1 FLR 888; and *Armstrong v Armstrong* [2003] EWHC 777, [2003] 2 FLR 375. Another factor as to the appropriateness of the forum might be the language in which the proceedings are to be conducted and the availability of witnesses: *Shemshadfard*

the natural forum, then the issue had to be addressed as to whether substantial justice could be done there. In particular, what weight was to be given to the fact that the wife was likely to receive a lower level of financial support from a French than from an English court? In earlier decisions, this had proved to be a factor of considerable significance. For example, in *Gadd v Gadd*,[213] the fact that a wife would receive no financial support in divorce proceedings in Monaco tipped the scales in favour of refusing a stay. Courts should be less influenced by the issue of whether or not financial relief is available in a foreign court, given that the factor of advantage to the petitioner is of less significance since the *Spiliada* case,[214] and that the English courts now have power to grant such relief after a foreign divorce.[215] Certainly, in *De Dampierre*, the House of Lords did not find the difference between French and English matrimonial relief a convincing reason for refusing a stay of the English proceedings.[216] In other cases, as well as the availability of remedies,[217] other factors existing at the time of the application for a stay[218] which have been taken into account are whether any English decree or financial provision order will be recognised in the other country,[219] whether continuation of the English proceedings will lead to a speedier outcome of the issue,[220] the location of family property and the matrimonial home,[221] in the case of proceedings where the main issue relates to the children, their links with the jurisdiction in question,[222] and the costs of litigation.[223]

Finally, it should be mentioned that the English proceedings cannot be stayed once the trial of the main issues has begun, save that the court may stay the proceedings at a later time if the petitioner has failed to furnish particulars of concurrent proceedings in another jurisdiction.[224]

Implications of *Owusu v Jackson*[225] A question arises in this connection regarding the potential implications for matrimonial proceedings of the ECJ ruling in *Owusu v Jackson*.

---

v Shemshadfard [1981] 1 All ER 726 at 734–5; *C v C (Divorce: Stay of English Proceedings)* [2001] 1 FLR 624; and *O v O (Appeal against Stay: Divorce Petition)* [2002] EWCA Civ 949, [2003] 1 FLR 192.

[213] [1984] 1 WLR 1435.

[214] [1987] AC 460 at 482–4, supra, p 393 et seq.

[215] Matrimonial and Family Proceedings Act 1984, Part III, infra, p 1072 et seq; referred to in *Gadd v Gadd* [1984] 1 WLR 1435 at 1442.

[216] [1988] AC 92 at 102, 110; cf *Armstrong v Armstrong* [2003] EWHC 777, [2003] 2 FLR 375. Contrast *R v R (Divorce: Stay of Proceedings)* [1994] 2 FLR 1036; *S v S* [1997] 2 FLR 100; and *O v O (Appeal against Stay: Divorce Petition)* [2002] EWCA Civ 949, [2003] 1 FLR 192.

[217] And see *Mytton v Mytton* (1977) 7 Fam Law 244; *Thyssen-Bornemisza v Thyssen-Bornemisza* [1985] FLR 670. The existence of a pre-nuptial agreement and mutual wills created by the spouses under French law was relevant in the decision to allow the application for stay of the English proceedings in *C v C (Divorce: Stay of English Proceedings)* [2001] 1 FLR 624.

[218] *Shemshadfard v Shemshadfard* [1981] 1 All ER 726 at 735.

[219] *Thyssen-Bornemisza v Thyssen-Bornemisza* [1985] FLR 670 at 687; and *Armstrong v Armstrong* [2003] EWHC 777, [2003] 2 FLR 375. See, however, *O v O (Appeal against Stay: Divorce Petition)* [2002] EWCA Civ 949, [2003] 1 FLR 192, per Thorpe LJ, at [60] et seq, criticising the reasoning of the judge at first instance, who attached significant weight to doubts about whether an English decree would be recognised in Nigeria.

[220] Ibid.

[221] *Armstrong v Armstrong* [2003] EWHC 777, [2003] 2 FLR 375.

[222] *A v A (Forum Conveniens)* [1999] 1 FLR 1; *Armstrong v Armstrong* [2003] EWHC 777, [2003] 2 FLR 375; and *O v O (Appeal against Stay: Divorce Petition)* [2002] EWCA Civ 949, [2003] 1 FLR 192 (the Nigerian cultural background of the family was a factor put on the scales in favour of a stay of the English proceedings).

[223] *O v O (Appeal against Stay: Divorce Petition)* [2002] EWCA Civ 949, [2003] 1 FLR 192; and *Armstrong v Armstrong* [2003] EWHC 777, [2003] 2 FLR 375.

[224] Sch 1, para 9(4). Trial of a preliminary issue of jurisdiction will, also, not terminate the power to order a stay: Sch 1, para 4(1).

[225] Case C-281-02, [2005] ECR I-1383, [2005] QB 801; supra, Chapter 13.

Is it competent for an English court to accede to the plea of *forum non conveniens* (ie in this context, to grant a discretionary stay under the Domicile and Matrimonial Proceedings Act 1973),[226] in circumstances where a defendant, having been sued in a Member State court on the basis of jurisdiction under Article 3 of Brussels II *bis*, nevertheless argues that the balance of fairness, including convenience, is such that it is appropriate that the English proceedings be stayed in favour of another non-Member State court, which constitutes a competent forum in which the case might be tried more suitably for the interests of all the parties and the ends of justice? In other words, would it be consistent with the Brussels II *bis* Regulation, in a case where a claimant has commenced proceedings on the basis of Article 3, for a court of a Member State to exercise its discretionary power, available under its national law, to decline to hear proceedings brought against a person who is habitually resident in the territory of a Member State, or is a national of a Member State (or, in the case of the United Kingdom and of Ireland, has his domicile there), in favour of the courts of a non-Member State?

In light of the judgment in *Owusu v Jackson*, and by analogy with the Court's reasoning in that case, one might speculate that the ECJ would consider Article 3 of Brussels II *bis* to be mandatory[227] in nature, meaning that an English judge, being persuaded that another, non-Member State forum is appropriate, would *not* be permitted to stay proceedings against a defendant sued in England on the basis of Article 3. The likelihood is that the ECJ, if asked by means of a preliminary reference to give an interpretative ruling on the point, would deny the possibility of any derogation from the principles enshrined in Article 3, except such as is expressly provided for by Article 7 (residual jurisdiction). The Regulation provides no exception in relation to *forum non conveniens*, at least in relation to matrimonial proceedings.[228] It is highly probable that application, in a case such as has been conjectured, of the doctrine of *forum non conveniens* by means of the operation of a discretionary stay, would be deemed to undermine the desired objectives of certainty and predictability, which are inherent in the Regulation, as well as to jeopardise the legal protection of persons established in the EU. Thus, by analogous reasoning, it is suggested that the decision in *Owusu* would be likely to preclude a court in a Member State from declining jurisdiction conferred upon it by Article 3 of Brussels II *bis*, on the ground that the court of another, non-Member State constitutes an appropriate forum for trial of the proceedings.[229]

In *JKN v JCN*,[230] however, the High Court held the opposite view, ie that the *Owusu* principle does not apply to Brussels II *bis*. The case concerned a couple who married in New York, however, lived in London for most of their marriage. Nevertheless, by the time they separated, they were both living in New York. The wife, after having been advised that she did not satisfy the residence requirement for New York jurisdiction, issued divorce proceedings in England, relying on Article 3 of the Brussels II *bis* Regulation. The husband filed an acknowledgement of service confirming that he did not intend to defend the proceedings in England but stated that New York was the appropriate forum. He then issued divorce proceedings in New York, and sought to stay the wife's English proceedings. The wife argued that it was not open to the court to grant a stay of her English petition since, by analogy with the decision in *Owusu*, where jurisdiction was founded on Article 3 of Brussels II *bis*, there was no power to grant a stay of English proceedings under the Domicile and Matrimonial Proceedings Act 1973. Theis J held that it was "neither necessary nor desirable

---

[226] Sch 1, paras 9(1) and (2); supra, pp 972–3.

[227] Cf reasoning of ECJ in *Owusu*, supra, at [32].

[228] See, however, the transfer mechanism in Art 15, in relation to proceedings concerning matters of parental responsibility.

[229] See also Crawford and Carruthers, para 12-16, and Karsten, [2009] IFL 35.

[230] [2010] EWHC 843.

to extend the *Owusu* principle in cases where there were parallel proceedings in a non-member state".[231] If the *Owusu* principle applied to Brussels II *bis*, there would be a risk of irreconcilable judgments as both sets of proceedings would continue.[232] Alternatively, the principle was inapplicable to Brussels II bis as there was no "direction connection" between the Brussels I and the Brussels II *bis* Regulations, and although it was possible to refer to Brussels I in interpreting Brussels II *bis* where the language was identical, the respective provisions of the Regulations were different in several material respects.[233] The court's discretion to stay under paragraph 9 of Schedule 1 to the Domicile and Matrimonial Proceedings Act 1973 remained in place where the competing proceedings were in a non-Member State.[234] Accordingly, the English court retained discretion to stay its proceedings where there were proceedings pending in a non-EU Member State,[235] and, as New York was the more appropriate forum,[236] the wife's English proceedings were stayed in favour of the husband's proceedings in New York on the ground of *forum non conveniens*. The dicta of Theis J in *JKN v JCN* was approved by the Court of Appeal in the case of *Mittal v Mittal*.[237] Lewison LJ, with whom Rimer and Jackson LLJ agreed, confirmed the first instance decision of Bodey J that the English court had jurisdiction to stay the wife's English divorce proceedings on the ground of *forum non conveniens*, in favour of divorce proceedings commenced earlier by the husband in India. His Lordship held that the dicta in *Owusu* had "little to do" with the present case, and did not apply to Brussels II *bis* for six reasons:[238] 1) *Owusu* was concerned with a different instrument regulating jurisdiction in the commercial, rather than family law sphere; 2) The legislative language under Brussels I is very different from the language of Brussels II *bis*; the former being "mandatory, transitive, and prescriptive", whereas the language of Article 3(1) of Brussels II *bis* being "intransitive and facilitative"; 3) *Owusu* did not answer the question whether proceedings should be stayed in favour of competing prior proceedings in a non-Member State, and therefore cannot be regarded as a precedent on that issue; 4) The policy objectives of the two Regulations are dissimilar; 5) Brussels II *bis* recognises diversity in the legal systems of different Member States, which was one of the objections in *Owusu* where the ECJ held that the discretionary power to stay proceedings was not recognised in all Member States. As such, the objective of uniformity of procedure would be undermined if only some Member States were to exercise discretion. On the contrary, Article 3 of Brussels II *bis* recognises different jurisdictional basis in the UK and Ireland to other Member States, implying that complete uniformity of treatment is not inevitable; and 6) The policy underlying Brussels I has itself changed: the Brussels I (Recast) Regulation recognises a discretionary power to stay proceedings where there are parallel proceedings in a non-Member State. Accordingly, if the revised Brussels I Regulation had applied to the present case, the English court would have been permitted to stay the English proceedings.[239]

---

[231] Ibid, at [149].

[232] Ibid. This point is not very persuasive. Indeed, the risk of irreconcilable judgments is equally undesirable in the context of matrimonial proceedings as it is in the commercial law context. See also Crawford and Carruthers, para 12-16.

[233] Ibid.

[234] Ibid.

[235] See, ibid, at [150].

[236] Ibid, at [158].

[237] [2013] EWCA Civ 1255 (also known as *AB v CB (Divorce and Maintenance: Discretion to Stay)*). The decision was welcomed by the legal profession—see, eg, Frankle [2014] IFL 17; and Sanders [2013] Fam Law 1618. See also Bantekas [2014] IFL 30.

[238] [2013] EWCA Civ 1255, at [37].

[239] Ibid, at [40]. See Brussels I (Recast) Regulation, Arts 33 and 34 and Recitals 23 and 24. Discussed supra, Chapter 13.

The approach adopted by the High Court in *JKN v JCN* and the Court of Appeal in *Mittal v Mittal* seems to be at odds with the latest European developments. The recently published Proposal for a Council Regulation on jurisdiction, the recognition and enforcement of decisions in matrimonial matters and the matters of parental responsibility, and on international child abduction (recast)[240] makes it clear that no changes to Article 19 of the Regulation are contemplated as a part of the ongoing Brussels II *bis* review process.[241] This means that, in respect of parallel proceedings, the Brussels II *bis* (Recast) Regulation will not be following the Brussels I (Recast) Regulation.[242] To confirm this, in a document accompanying the Proposal,[243] the Commission expressly refers to the judgment in *Owusu* by stating: "As the Court of Justice has ruled that Member States are not allowed to use any discretion which may exist under their national law to transfer jurisdiction established by EU Regulations, the transfer mechanism could only be created by including it into the Regulation."[244] Contrary to the reasoning of Lewison LJ in *Mittal v Mittal*, the Commission adds that, although *Owusu* concerned the Brussels I Convention, "the overwhelming majority of courts and academics applies this statement also to other EU instruments such as the Brussels I Regulation and the Brussels IIa Regulation, as far as matrimonial matters are concerned".[245] This is in line with the view advocated earlier in this Chapter.[246]

A related question which arises is whether the plea of *forum non conveniens* might be sustained (ie in this context, whether a discretionary stay might be granted in terms of the Domicile and Matrimonial Proceedings Act 1973),[247] in cases where jurisdiction is exercised by a Member State court on the basis of Article 7 (residual jurisdiction)[248] of Brussels II *bis*.[249] The situation envisaged here is where the proceedings in question are within the subject matter scope of Brussels II *bis*, but where none of the bases of jurisdiction set out in Article 3 comes into operation in a given case. According to Article 7 of the Regulation, jurisdiction in this situation is determined by the laws of each Member State.

Despite *Owusu*, it might be speculated that, where the jurisdiction of a court of a Member State is established pursuant to Article 7, the court in question would *not* be prevented from declining to exercise its jurisdiction, in accordance with the doctrine of *forum non conveniens* (ie in this context, on the basis of a discretionary stay under the 1973 Act), on the ground that the court of a *non-Member State* would be an appropriate forum for trial of the proceedings.[250] Where the alternative forum is a non-Member State, it may be assumed, with some confidence, that the exercise of a *forum non conveniens* discretion still would be available. Where, however, the alternative forum is another Member State, it seems most unlikely that the CJEU would interpret the provisions of the Regulation in such a manner as would sanction the continuing exercise of a *forum non conveniens* discretion.[251] A further consideration in support of this view, and a practical danger, corresponding to that mentioned previously

---

[240] COM (2016) 411 final. See supra, p 242.
[241] Ibid, p 42.
[242] See supra.
[243] SWD (2016) 207 final. See supra, p 242.
[244] Ibid, Part II.
[245] Ibid, fn 49.
[246] See supra, p 975.
[247] Sch 1, paras 9(1) and (2); supra, pp 972–3.
[248] For England, under s 5(2)(b) of the Domicile and Matrimonial Proceedings Act 1973; supra, p 962.
[249] Cf, in civil and commercial matters, supra, pp 443–4.
[250] Cf reasoning in relation to matrimonial anti-suit injunctions, discussed, infra, pp 978–9.
[251] Irrespective, it is submitted, of the position which currently pertains with regard to civil and commercial matters, per *Sarrio SA v Kuwait Investment Authority* [1997] 1 Lloyd's Rep 113; supra, p 469 et seq.

in relation to civil and commercial matters,[252] is that even if an English court, the jurisdiction of which has been "established", should attempt to exercise its discretion and to stay English proceedings in favour of an alternative Member State forum, the court "second seised" would be bound to decline jurisdiction on the basis of Article 19 (lis pendens) of Brussels II *bis*.[253] The risk, therefore, would be that no court would exercise jurisdiction in the given case to hear the proceedings.

(iv) General matters

In the case of both obligatory and discretionary stays, the English court has a power, on application by one of the parties to the proceedings, to discharge the order staying any proceedings if the other proceedings are stayed or concluded, or if there has been unreasonable delay in prosecuting them.[254] Once an obligatory stay has been discharged the proceedings cannot again be obligatorily stayed;[255] though a discretion to stay remains but cannot normally be exercised once the trial of the English proceedings has begun. Special provision is made for the granting of ancillary relief in the case where English proceedings are stayed because proceedings are pending in another British jurisdiction.[256] It should be mentioned that the staying provisions contained in the Domicile and Matrimonial Proceedings Act 1973 are in addition to, and not in substitution for, any other power to stay proceedings.[257] The inherent power to stay was rarely used in matrimonial proceedings,[258] but, as we have seen, there is now little difference between the statutory power to stay and the developed common law doctrine of *forum non conveniens*.[259]

(c) Restraining foreign proceedings (anti-suit injunctions)

The English court has long had the inherent power, in matrimonial proceedings, to restrain by injunction a party who wished to pursue foreign matrimonial proceedings;[260] but it is a power which has been sparingly and carefully exercised. Lord Goff in the Privy Council[261] and in the House of Lords[262] has laid down the principles on which this inherent power is to be exercised in the commercial context, and the Court of Appeal has made clear in *Hemain v Hemain*[263] that such principles are to be applied in matrimonial cases.[264]

---

[252] See supra, p 470, regarding the operation of Art 29 of the Brussels I (Recast) Regulation (previously Art 27 of the Brussels I Regulation).

[253] Supra, pp 469–70.

[254] Sch 1, para 10(1).

[255] Sch 1, para 10(2).

[256] Sch 1, para 11. These provisions are considered more fully in the context of jurisdiction to grant ancillary relief, infra, p 1059 et seq.

[257] S 5(6)(b). This seems to have been overlooked by Dunn LJ in *Gadd v Gadd* [1984] 1 WLR 1435 at 1438.

[258] *Sealey (otherwise Callan) v Callan* [1953] P 135—a divorce case where the court, in fact, declined to stay the English proceedings; and see *Baroness von Eckhardstein v Baron von Eckhardstein* (1907) 23 TLR 539 and 593 (judicial separation).

[259] But see *W v W (Financial Relief: Appropriate Forum)* [1997] 1 FLR 257; *Krenge v Krenge* [1999] 1 FLR 969.

[260] See *Orr-Lewis v Orr-Lewis* [1949] P 347, where, in the exercise of its discretion, the divorce court declined to issue an injunction; contrast *Bryant v Bryant* (1980) 11 Fam Law 85 where an injunction was issued restraining a husband from taking steps to have a Canadian divorce decree nisi made absolute in order to protect the wife's position in seeking relief from the English courts. In *Christian v Christian* (1897) 78 LT 86 the English courts hearing judicial separation proceedings did restrain the husband from pursuing divorce proceedings in Scotland.

[261] *Société National Industrielle Aérospatiale v Lee Kui Jak* [1987] AC 871 supra, p 427.

[262] *Airbus Industrie GIE v Patel* [1999] 1 AC 119, HL. See supra, p 431.

[263] [1988] 2 FLR 388.

[264] See also *Kornberg v Kornberg* (1991) 76 DLR (4th) 379; *Harris v Murray* (1995) 11 RFL (4th) 450; *B v B (Divorce: Stay of Foreign Proceedings)* [2002] EWHC 1711, [2003] 1 FLR 1 (injunction refused); *R v R (Divorce: Hemain Injunction)* [2003] EWHC 2113, [2005] 1 FLR 386 (injunction granted); *S v S (Hemain*

In the commercial context, the decision in *Turner v Grovit*[265] made plain that the use by one EU Member State forum of an anti-suit injunction to seek to restrain a party from litigating in the court of another Member State is not acceptable, as being tantamount to interference with the jurisdiction of the foreign court, and in breach of the obligation on the courts of Member States to refrain from acting in a manner that is incompatible with the Brussels I Regulation. Whether, in a family law context, the Brussels II *bis* Regulation would be construed in like manner, as precluding the grant by a court in one Member State of an injunction prohibiting a party to proceedings before it from commencing or continuing proceedings in the court of another Member State, is a matter of speculation. It is not clear whether it would be deemed inconsistent with the Brussels II *bis* Regulation for one Member State court to grant an injunction against a defendant who is threatening to commence or continue matrimonial proceedings in a "foreign" court.

In the light of the decision in *Turner v Grovit*, and by analogy with the Court's reasoning in that case, it might be thought likely that the ECJ, if asked by means of a preliminary reference to give an interpretative ruling on the point, would deny the availability of an injunction restraining foreign proceedings as a remedy in a matrimonial case, at least in the situation where it is sought to restrain proceedings in *another Member State*. This, it is suggested, would probably be the decision, regardless of whether the court exercising jurisdiction were doing so on the basis of Article 3 (general jurisdiction), or Article 7 (residual jurisdiction) of Brussels II *bis*. It is submitted that an injunction in these circumstances would be very likely to be judged incompatible with the regime put in place by Brussels II *bis*.

Where, however, the proceedings sought to be restrained are in a *non-Member State*, the position would be less clear. This would be the situation where an English court has jurisdiction under one of the bases set out in Article 3 of Brussels II *bis*, and the claimant in those proceedings seeks to restrain a party from commencing or continuing proceedings in a non-Member State. The injunction, if granted, would constitute, in effect, an interference with the jurisdiction of a non-Member State court only. In this situation, it could plausibly be argued that this would not be incompatible with the Brussels II *bis* regime. Indeed, as previously stated in relation to civil and commercial matters, in these circumstances the injunction, if anything, would be being utilised to uphold the jurisdiction allocated under Brussels II *bis*, and so its grant ought not to be viewed as being incompatible with the Regulation. Likewise, where the jurisdiction of a Member State court is established pursuant to Article 7 of the Regulation, this, it is submitted, should not prevent the court from granting an injunction prohibiting a party to proceedings before it from commencing or continuing proceedings in the court of a *non-Member State*.

(b) Choice of law

(i) Divorce and judicial separation[266]

At common law, the sole basis of the jurisdiction of the English courts in divorce was domicile[267] and no choice of law problem arose. English law was applied and this could be justified either as the application of the law of the domicile[268] to issues affecting status or as the application of the law of the forum on the basis that dissolution of a marriage is a matter which

---

Injunction) [2009] EWHC 3224 (Fam) (injunction refused); and *T v T (Hemain Injunction)* [2012] EWHC 3462 (Fam) (injunction refused).

[265] Case C-159/02, [2005] 1 AC 101; supra, p 477.

[266] North, op cit, pp 146–51; North (1980) I Hague Recueil 9, 77–88; and see for separation Grodecki (1957) 42 Transactions of the Grotius Society 23, 41–3.

[267] *Le Mesurier v Le Mesurier* [1895] AC 517.

[268] *Lord Advocate v Jaffrey* [1921] 1 AC 146 at 152.

"touches fundamental English conceptions of morality, religion and public policy",[269] and one which is governed exclusively by rules and conditions imposed by the English legislature.

The need for a choice of law rule arises when the court possesses jurisdiction on some basis other than domicile, as may be illustrated by *Zanelli v Zanelli*:[270]

> An Italian national, domiciled in England, married an Englishwoman in England in 1948. Later he was deported from England and thereupon reverted to his Italian domicile. The Matrimonial Causes Act 1937, which was then in force, had given the English court jurisdiction in divorce (and also judicial separation) in such a case,[271] but it did not impose a rule for the choice of law.

The court, applying English domestic law but without any consideration of the choice of law issue, granted the wife a decree of divorce, despite the rule of the Italian law of her domicile at that time that divorce was not permissible. A similar approach, namely the uniform application of English law, was seen in the case of judicial separation not only where, at common law, jurisdiction was taken on the basis of domicile,[272] but also on the basis of residence[273] or of a matrimonial home within the jurisdiction,[274] even though the parties were domiciled elsewhere.

The English common law rules were later extended to permit divorce and nullity (but not judicial separation) decrees to be granted on the basis of three years' residence in England by a wife,[275] and at that point a statutory choice of law rule was introduced both for this case and for that exemplified in *Zanelli v Zanelli*, ie the domicile of the wife in England immediately prior to the husband's desertion or deportation. This choice of law rule provided that the court should apply "the law which would be applicable thereto if both parties were domiciled in England at the time of the proceedings".[276]

Strangely, this rule was cast in terms which pointed more to the law of the domicile than to the law of the forum. The latter approach could have been expressed far more simply by just saying that English law was applicable. Whilst the two statutory jurisdictional grounds available to the wife prevented considerable hardship in the case of divorce, they did not provide nearly so far-reaching an inroad into the basic jurisdictional rule dependent on domicile as was made by the Domicile and Matrimonial Proceedings Act 1973, and subsequently by the Brussels II and II *bis* Regulations.[277] Habitual residence is now, in practice, the main jurisdictional basis. The two statutory grounds available to a wife, and the attendant choice of law provision, have been abolished.[278] There is now no statutory choice of law rule. It was undoubtedly the intention of the Law Commission, in proposing the reforms which led to the 1973 Act, that English law should be applied,[279] but this does raise the issue whether such a rule is desirable.

---

[269] Wolff, p 374; and see *Holland v Holland* 1973 (1) SA 897 (T) at 902.

[270] (1948) 64 TLR 556; see also *Niboyet v Niboyet* (1878) 4 PD 1 at 9.

[271] S13 (re-enacted in the Matrimonial Causes Act 1973, s 46(1)(a), itself repealed by the Domicile and Matrimonial Proceedings Act 1973). Jurisdiction could be assumed, in the case of a petition by a wife, on the basis of the husband's domicile in England prior to his desertion or deportation.

[272] *Eustace v Eustace* [1924] P 45.

[273] *Armytage v Armytage* [1898] P 178; *Ward v Ward* (1923) 39 TLR 440.

[274] *Wells v Wells* [1960] NI 122.

[275] Law Reform (Miscellaneous Provisions) Act 1949, s 1(1), re-enacted in the Matrimonial Causes Act 1973, s 46(1)(b), and repealed by the Domicile and Matrimonial Proceedings Act 1973.

[276] Ibid, s 1(4), re-enacted in the Matrimonial Causes Act 1973, s 46(2).

[277] Supra, p 1039 et seq.

[278] Domicile and Matrimonial Proceedings Act 1973, s 17(2).

[279] Law Com No 48, paras 103–8.

Whilst some civil law jurisdictions are prepared to consider the relevance of the divorce law of countries other than the forum,[280] the general approach of the common law is to apply the law of the forum.[281] It is not self-evidently correct that this should be so. One argument in favour of the law of the forum is that divorce law may be regarded as part of the public law of the forum and so should be applied as part of that country's mandatory laws governing the continuance of a marital relationship within that particular society.[282] This argument is strongest in a jurisdiction, like many in the USA, with narrow rules for both jurisdiction and the recognition of foreign divorces. In England—where both sets of rules are broader—it may be much less obvious that parties have a close connection with the forum, especially if they can obtain a divorce abroad and readily have it recognised in England even though obtained on grounds unavailable under English law.[283] A further argument in favour of the law of the forum is that it would cause delay and create expense to apply foreign law to English petitions for divorce or judicial separation, most of which are undefended; and it has also been suggested that to "require English courts to dissolve marriages on exotic foreign grounds would be distasteful to the judges and unacceptable to public opinion".[284] These are dangerous arguments if carried too far. It is always easier and cheaper to apply the law of the forum, but nowhere else in English choice of law rules do we generally apply the law of the forum as such. If we are prepared to take jurisdiction over "exotic foreigners", under broad jurisdictional rules, it is arguably no more distasteful to apply their personal law to the dissolution than to apply it, as we do,[285] to the creation of their marriage.

There are certainly those who advocate the application of the party's personal law, ie the law of their domicile, to divorce and judicial separation—that being the law which should govern matters of status. The main argument in favour of applying the law of the domicile is that dissolution of the marriage affects the status of the parties no less than does the creation of the marriage and is a substantive, not just a procedural, matter. Whilst the public policy of the forum may have a role to play, as elsewhere in choice of law matters,[286] this should not, it is said, be to the exclusion of other laws. There is, however, a practical difficulty with the application of the law of the domicile. Since a wife may acquire a separate domicile, and this is more likely to have occurred if the marriage has broken down and one spouse is petitioning for a divorce, it would have to be determined which spouse's domicile is to be regarded as the relevant one for choice of law purposes. The answer to such a question can be little more than arbitrary and militates against the application of the law of the domicile.

The arguments on choice of law in divorce and judicial separation have been summed up thus:

> The decision on choice of law rules in divorce must depend upon a balance between principle, which undoubtedly points to the application of the personal law, and pragmatism which favours the *lex fori*. It is no surprise that the civil law supports the former and the common law the latter. What is worrying about the common law approach is that a rule which was historically justified by its jurisdictional link has been maintained with little real consideration of the implications of breaking that jurisdictional link.[287]

---

[280] Eg France, see Batiffol and Lagarde, *Droit International Privé* (1983) 7th edn, Vol II, pp 79–82; and see Palsson, *International Encyclopaedia of Comparative Law* Vol III, Chapter 16, p 129 et seq.

[281] Palsson, op cit, pp 126–9; though see *Alton v Alton* 207 F 2d 667 at 684–5 (1953).

[282] Wolff, *Private International Law* (1950) 2nd edn, 373–4; Cavers (1970) III Hague Recueil 75, 245–6.

[283] See infra, p 1000 et seq.

[284] Morris, para 9-027.

[285] Supra, p 910 et seq.

[286] Supra, p 132 et seq.

[287] North (1980) I Hague Recueil 9, 87–8.

The Matrimonial Causes Act 1973, unlike its predecessors, is silent on choice of law matters relating to divorce and judicial separation, though the fact that there is no express saving for the rules of private international law in the case of divorce and judicial separation, such as there is in the case of nullity,[288] provides some tacit support for the application of the law of the forum. There is no doubt, however, that in practice English law is applied to all petitions for divorce or judicial separation which come before the English courts.[289] The rules of English law existing at the time of the proceedings are applied and they will decide whether there is a good cause for divorce or judicial separation, and will determine the form of relief and the conditions on which the decree will be granted. Any other legal system, such as the law under which the parties married, the law(s) of their domiciles or nationalities, or the law of the place where the facts on which the petition is based took place, is completely irrelevant.[290] It should be mentioned that under English law it does not matter that the facts evidencing breakdown of the marriage did not constitute a basis for divorce in the country where they took place,[291] or in the country of the parties' domiciles.[292] Nor does it matter that the ground for divorce was not a ground under English law at the time that the cause arose.[293]

Rome III[294] As stated above,[295] in July 2006, the European Commission published a Proposal for a Council Regulation amending Regulation (EC) No 2201/2003 as regards jurisdiction and introducing rules concerning applicable law in matrimonial matters.[296] The United Kingdom government decided not to opt into a resulting instrument due to the "legal and practical issues relating to application of foreign law in this sensitive area".[297] Other Member States also found the provisions on applicable law contained in the Proposal to be problematic. This resulted in the Proposal being eventually withdrawn by the Commission.[298] In July 2008, 14 Member States presented the Commission with a request in which they sought to establish enhanced cooperation[299] among themselves in the area of applicable law in divorce and legal separation. The Commission's response to the petition was positive.[300] On 12 July 2010, the Council adopted a decision authorizing enhanced cooperation in the area of the law applicable to divorce and legal separation between the participating Member States.[301]

---

[288] Matrimonial Causes Act 1973, s 14, infra, pp 996–7.

[289] *Quoraishi v Quoraishi* [1985] FLR 780, especially at 783.

[290] *Czepek v Czepek* [1962] 3 All ER 990.

[291] Eg *Czepek v Czepek*, supra; and see *Holland v Holland* 1973 (1) SA 897 (T).

[292] See *Quoraishi v Quoraishi* [1985] FLR 780, [1985] Fam Law 308, CA; *Grummett v Grummett* (1965) 7 FLR 415.

[293] Eg *Pratt v Pratt* [1939] AC 417.

[294] See Calliess (ed), *Rome Regulations: Commentary* (2015), Part Three; Fiorini (2008) 22 International Journal of Law, Policy and Family 178; Fiorini (2010) 59 ICLQ 1143; Pocar [2012] IFL 24–6; and Viarengo (2014) 15 ERA Forum 547.

[295] Supra, p 962.

[296] COM (2006) 399 final, and Document 5274/07 LIMITE JUSTCIV 4, 12 January 2007. See also Green Paper on applicable law and jurisdiction in divorce matters (COM (2005) 82 final) 14 March 2005; Commission Staff Working Paper, Annex to the Green Paper on applicable law and jurisdiction in divorce matters (SEC (2005) 331) 14 March 2005; and House of Lords EU Committee, 52nd Report, Session 2005/06, "Rome III—Choice of Law in Divorce" (2006).

[297] See House of Lords, Written Statements, 18 Apr 2007: column WS7, per Baroness Ashton of Upholland; and in Scotland, Report of the Justice I Committee of the Scottish Parliament (CJ1004/2005, 7 October 2005).

[298] See 2873rd Council Meeting Justice and Home Affairs, Luxembourg, 5–6 June 2008, C/08/146, 9956/08 (Presse 146), p 22, and OJ 2013 C 109/04.

[299] See Art 20(2) of the TEU and Arts 326–334 of the TFEU. Fiorini (2010) 59 ICLQ 1143.

[300] See Proposal for a Council Regulation implementing enhanced cooperation in the area of the law applicable to divorce and legal separation (COM (2010) 105 final). See also COM (2010) 104 final/2.

[301] 2010/405/EU.

Consequently, the participating Member States adopted Council Regulation (EU) No 1259/ 2010 implementing enhanced cooperation in the area of the law applicable to divorce and legal separation ("Rome III"), which became applicable on 21 June 2012.[302] The Regulation is intended to operate in tandem with the Brussels II *bis* Regulation.[303] Rome III applies in relation to the dissolution of matrimonial ties, and the law determined by the Regulation applies solely to the grounds for divorce and legal separation.[304] The Regulation enhances the parties' autonomy in matrimonial matters[305] as the rule contained therein is based, in the first instance, on the possibility of choice of law by the spouses.[306] The choice is confined to either the law of the forum or laws with which the spouses are deemed to have a close connection.[307] This close connection is to be demonstrated by the chosen law being either the law of the State: (a) where the spouses are habitually resident at the time the agreement is concluded, or (b) where the spouses were last habitually resident, in so far as one of them still resides there at the time the agreement is concluded; or (c) of the nationality of either spouse at the time the agreement is concluded.[308]

In the absence of choice of the applicable law, a hierarchical rule applies whereby the governing law is the law of the state (a) where the spouses have their common habitual residence at the time the court is seised; or failing that (b) where the spouses had their last common habitual residence, as long as the period of residence did not end more than 1 year before the court was seised, and in so far as one of them still resides there at the time the court is seised; or failing that (c) of which both spouses are nationals at the time the court is seised; or failing that (d) where the application is lodged.[309] Commendably, the Regulation sets out clear rules in relation to *renvoi*,[310] material and formal validity of the parties' choice of law agreement,[311] the conversion of a legal separation into divorce,[312] and territorial[313] and inter-personal[314] conflict of laws. The worrying aspect of the Regulation, however, is that the instrument is of universal application, ie the parties' choice of law, and the applicable law in the absence of choice of law, is not restricted to the law of a European Union Member State.[315] Although the principle of universal application is familiar in choice of law in contract[316] and has been adopted in relation to choice of law concerning non-contractual obligations,[317] its appropriateness in the context of family law is questionable. Indeed, how desirable would it be for an

---

[302] The original 14 participating Member States are Belgium, Bulgaria, Germany, Spain, France, Italy, Latvia, Luxembourg, Hungary, Malta, Austria, Portugal, Romania and Slovenia (see Rome III, Recital 6). Lithuania and Greece joined later (May 2014 and July 2015 respectively: see Commission decisions 2012/ 714/EU and 2014/39/EU); and Estonia will join as of 11 February 2018 (see Commission decision 2016/ 1366/EU).

[303] The substantive scope of Rome III is intended to be consistent with Brussels II *bis*, (although the former does not apply to marriage annulment) (see Recital 10 and Arts 1(1) and 1(2)(c)). Also, a court in Rome III proceedings should be deemed to be seized in accordance with the Brussels II *bis* Regulation (see Recital 13 and Art 2).

[304] Recital 10. Preliminary questions such as legal capacity and the validity of the marriage, and matters such as the effects of divorce or legal separation on property, name, parental responsibility, maintenance obligations, and trusts or succession are outside the scope of the Regulation. Recital 10 and Art 1(2).

[305] Recital 15.

[306] Ibid.

[307] Recital 16 and Art 5(1).

[308] Art 5(1).

[309] Art 8.

[310] By virtue of Art 11, *renvoi* is excluded.

[311] Recital 19, Arts 6 and 7.

[312] Recital 23 and Art 9.

[313] Recitals 27, 28 and Art 14.

[314] Recital 27 and Art 15.

[315] Recital 12 and Art 4.

[316] 1980 Rome Convention, Art 2. See also Rome I, Art 2.

[317] Rome II, Art 3.

English court to be required to apply for example the provisions of the Muslim Family Law Ordinance of Pakistan, were spouses to agree upon the application of the law of Pakistan? Even though the drafters of the Regulation sought to alleviate the concerns over the potential application of the law of a non-EU Member State through the inclusion of a number of safeguards,[318] these did not suffice to persuade the UK to take part in the enhanced cooperation measure.

Whilst a harmonised choice of law rule in itself might be an attractive prospect,[319] and would help to offset any tactical advantage which a party intent on forum shopping (aided by the operation of the *lis pendens* doctrine) might enjoy,[320] opting into the Regulation would override the certainty and ease of application afforded by the choice of law rule currently applied by the legal systems of the United Kingdom, in terms of which the applicable law is the domestic law of the forum.[321]

(ii) Nullity[322]

(a) Introduction

Whilst divorce gives rise to few choice of law problems, the same cannot be said for nullity. The reasons for this are varied. A nullity decree is concerned with the validity of the creation of a marriage, unlike divorce which dissolves a marriage which is admittedly validly created. This means that the choice of law issues in nullity are essentially the same as those already examined in the context of marriage. The question to be asked is the same—is the marriage valid or invalid? General issues of formal and essential validity have already been examined[323] as matters relating to marriage. But others, such as lack of consent and physical defects, are considered here because they tend to arise in nullity petitions. Another reason why choice of law in nullity is a more difficult area than divorce is that the effects of annulment vary according to the particular ground in issue and they vary in relation to the same ground even within the United Kingdom. Some defects avoid a marriage *ab initio*, ie render it void, whilst others merely render it voidable.[324] These distinctions can readily be exemplified. If one party is below the minimum age of marriage or is already married, English law regards the marriage

---

[318] Firstly, the law chosen by the parties must be compatible with the fundamental rights recognised by the Treaties and the Charter of Fundamental Rights of the European Union (Recital 16). See also Recital 30 which requires that the Regulation be applied in observance of fundamental rights and principles recognized by the EU Charter, in particular Art 21 (the principle of non-discrimination); secondly, the applicable law is subject to the public policy of the forum (Recital 25 and Art 12); and thirdly, where the applicable law makes no provision for divorce or does not grant one of the spouses equal access to divorce or legal separation on gender grounds, the law of the forum shall apply (Recital 24 and Art 10). Additionally, the Regulation seeks to safeguard the position of the forum more generally—in relation to cases where the law of the forum does not know the institute of divorce or does not deem the marriage in question valid. In such circumstances, the court of the forum is not obliged to pronounce a divorce or a legal separation by virtue of the Regulation. Recital 26 and Art 13. See Möller (2014) 10 J Priv Int L 461.

[319] The objectives of the Regulation being "the enhancement of legal certainty, predictability in international matrimonial proceedings". Recital 29.

[320] See, eg, *Rapisarda v Colladon (Irregular Divorces)* [2014] EWFC 35—in each of the 180 divorce petitions concerned, the Italian petitioner or respondent fraudulently asserted that they were habitually resident in England for the purposes of Brussels II *bis*. See Herring (2014) 164 NLJ 12–13.

[321] Although the Regulation suggests that the network created by Council Decision 2001/470/EC of 28 May 2001 establishing a European Judicial Network in civil and commercial matters could be utilised in assisting the courts with regard to the content of foreign law. Recital 18.

[322] North, op cit, chapter 8; Law Commission Working Paper No 89 (1985), Pt V.

[323] Supra, p 893 et seq.

[324] Additionally, where there has been a complete non-compliance with the requirements, the "marriage" cannot even be classified as a "void marriage". It will instead be termed as a "non-marriage". The appropriate remedy in such circumstances is a declaration of non-recognition as opposed to a decree of nullity (see supra, p 894, n 30 and infra, pp 998–9. See also Chapter 23.

as void.[325] If, however, a decree is granted in England on the ground of lack of consent, the marriage will be regarded as voidable.[326] In Scotland, on the other hand, lack of consent renders the marriage void *ab initio*.[327] Again, impotence or wilful refusal to consummate the marriage renders it voidable under English law;[328] whereas in Scotland, although impotence also renders the marriage voidable, wilful refusal has no effect on its validity.

The difference between void and voidable marriages is significant.[329] "A void marriage is no marriage. Considered literally the expression is self-destructive and contradictory. But without misleading anyone it serves to denote the situation where a ceremony of marriage does not bring about a marriage."[330] No proceedings are necessary to establish the fact of its nullity, though it may in practice be wise to take them, eg to obtain maintenance for the "wife" and any child of the "marriage" or to still doubts as to one's status where the position is disputed. Moreover, any member of the public may treat the marriage as void, notwithstanding the absence of a decree, as, for instance, by withholding payment of money that is due to the woman conditionally on her being the wife of the man.

On the other hand: "A voidable marriage is one that will be regarded by every court as a valid subsisting marriage until a decree annulling it has been pronounced by a court of competent jurisdiction."[331] So the effect of a defect, like impotence, that renders a marriage voidable in England is such that the status of the parties as husband and wife, having sprung from a contract free from imperfection, cannot be affected until the existence of the defect has been proved, and therefore the rule is that the marriage is valid and must be treated as such by every court and every person until it has been judicially declared void. No one but the parties themselves can be heard to deny that they are married or can challenge, by nullity proceedings or otherwise, the validity of their marriage. Until either of them obtains a decree of nullity, all the normal consequences of the married status ensue, both *inter se* and as regards third parties.

There are also further differences in relation to the effects of an annulment. The annulment of a void marriage has retrospective effect; it declares the marriage never to have existed. However, the position is different in England in the case of a voidable marriage. Although the annulment of such a marriage had retrospective effect at common law, the position in the case of nullity decrees granted after 31 July 1971 is that the decree operates to annul the marriage prospectively only from the date of the decree absolute. Until that time the marriage must be treated as subsisting.[332]

A further difficulty in nullity cases is the all too common disregard of the elementary and primary distinction between jurisdiction and choice of law. The tendency of the judges, in cases involving lack of consent or physical incapacities, after surmounting the problem of jurisdiction, has been to apply the internal law of England as a matter of course.[333] Not only does this mean that the principles on which the choice of law depends are undeveloped, but

---

[325] Matrimonial Causes Act 1973, s 11.

[326] Ibid, s 12.

[327] See Bromley, pp 63–86. See, however, Family Law (Scotland) Act 2006, s 2, inserting s 20A into the Marriage (Scotland) Act 1977.

[328] Matrimonial Causes Act 1973, s 12.

[329] On the differences between void marriages and "non-marriages", see, eg, *Gereis v Yagoub* [1997] 1 FLR 854, at 857; *Gandhi v Patel* [2002] 1 FLR 603, at [31] and [37]; *Hudson v Leigh* [2009] EWHC 1306 (Fam), at [70] and [79]; and *Sharbatly v Shagroon* [2012] EWCA Civ 1507, at [40]. Supra, p 894, n 30.

[330] *Ross Smith v Ross Smith* [1963] AC 280 at 314.

[331] *De Reneville v De Reneville* [1948] P 100 at 111.

[332] Matrimonial Causes Act 1973, s 16.

[333] Eg *Easterbrook v Easterbrook* [1944] 1 All ER 90; *Hunter v Hunter* [1944] P 95; *Buckland v Buckland* [1968] P 296.

it is particularly regrettable that the personal law should be deprived of its control over the married status.

(b) Classification of the nature of the defect

The ascertainment of the proper law in a nullity suit depends on analysing the various defects that may constitute cause for annulment, in order to determine their intrinsic nature. Once this is done, the legal system to which a particular defect is subject should become apparent. The consequence of this analysis is that, once the court has jurisdiction, then, in order to determine the law applicable to some alleged defect, it applies its own characterisation to decide whether the defect is as to form or essential validity. If, for example, it is the former, then it applies the rules of the law of the place of celebration to the issue in question. This may be illustrated by the British Columbia decision in *Solomon v Walters*,[334] where the facts were these:

> A marriage had been celebrated in Nevada between the husband, domiciled in British Columbia, and the wife, apparently domiciled in Alberta. The wife petitioned in British Columbia for a nullity decree on the ground of lack of parental consent as required by Nevada law, though by the domestic law of British Columbia the marriage was unaffected by the defect; by Nevada law it was rendered voidable.

The judge, having classified the defect as one of form, applied Nevada law and granted a decree of nullity. If the defect is as to capacity, then as has been seen,[335] the court should apply the ante-nuptial domiciliary law of the party alleged incapable.

It remains to consider other, more problematical, choice of law areas, namely lack of consent and personal physical defects.

(c) Lack of consent: is it formal or essential?

There is no settled authority as to whether defects affecting consent to marry are to be classified as akin to form, and thus to be governed by the law of the place of celebration, or as personal defects, thus raising questions of essential validity to be referred to the personal law of the parties.[336] There is a variety of different grounds on which an allegation of lack of consent can be based,[337] not all of which are sufficient in English domestic law. It may be argued that one party was mistaken as to the identity of the other party[338] or as to the marriage ceremony,[339] or that the marriage was entered into as the result of fraud[340] or fear caused by duress or coercion,[341] or during mental illness,[342] or there may have been a mistake as to the legal effects

---

[334] (1956) 3 DLR (2d) 78; and see *Lepre v Lepre* [1965] P 52 at 60, where the law of the place of celebration considered the marriage to be valid rather than voidable or void.

[335] Supra, p 910.

[336] Woodhouse (1954) 3 ICLQ 454.

[337] Neville Brown (1968) 42 Tul LR 837.

[338] Cf *C v C* [1942] NZLR 356.

[339] *Valier v Valier* (1925) 133 LT 830; *Parojcic v Parojcic* [1958] 1 WLR 1280; and see *Ford v Stier* [1896] P 1; and similarly *Mehta v Mehta* [1945] 2 All ER 690—belief that the marriage ceremony was merely one of conversion to Hinduism. See also *Alfonso-Brown v Millwood* [2006] EWHC 642 (Fam)—belief by the respondent that the ceremony was merely an engagement ceremony.

[340] *Johnson v Smith* (1968) 70 DLR (2d) 374.

[341] Either external pressure, such as political oppression, or for humanitarian reasons (*H v H* [1954] P 258; *Szechter v Szechter* [1971] P 286); or family/community pressure in respect of a forced marriage (*Hussein v Hussein* [1938] P 159; *Parojcic v Parojcic* [1958] 1 WLR 1280; *Buckland v Buckland* [1968] P 296; *Mahmood v Mahmood* 1993 SLT 589; *Mahmud v Mahmud* 1994 SLT 559; *Sohrab v Kahn* 2002 SLT 1255; *Hakeem v Hussain* 2003 SLT 515, and on appeal, *H v H* 2005 SLT 1025; *P v R (Forced Marriage: Annulment: Procedure)* [2003] 1 FLR 661; *Singh v Singh* 2005 SLT 749; *NS v MI* [2006] EWHC 1646 (Fam); *SL v MJ* [2006] EWHC 3743 (Fam); *SH v NB* [2009] EWHC 3274 (Fam); *B v I (Forced Marriage)* [2010] FLR 1721; *Re P (Forced Marriage)* [2010] EWHC 3467 (Fam); and *A Local Authority v X* [2013] EWHC 3274 (Fam)).

[342] *Westminster City Council v IC (A Protected Party by His Litigation Friend) and Ors* [2008] EWCA Civ 198; *XCC v AA* [2012] EWHC 2183 (COP); *Luton Borough Council v SB and another* [2015] EWHC 3534

of the ceremony,[343] or as to the attributes of the other party,[344] or cases where one or both parties has/have made mental reservations as to the effect of the ceremony.[345] What is remarkable is that the English courts for many years failed to realise that a choice of law problem existed in such cases and invariably applied English law. It is a masterly understatement to say that, "there has been some difference of opinion as to what law applies".[346] Indeed, virtually the only cases in which there has been any discussion of the issue have been those where it was not necessary for the decision.

(i) Application of the law of the forum

The only solution supported by all the direct authorities is reference to English law as the law of the forum in "consent" cases, but this is, in truth, an abdication from the problem. The decisions can be explained as having been reached *per incuriam*, and so reference to the law of the forum should only be accepted on such merits of principle as it may have. It has been suggested[347] that the law of the forum can be applied to cases of mistake as to the legal nature of the ceremony and to sham marriages, but not to cases of mistake as to the legal effects of the marriage which should be referred to the law of the mistaken party's ante-nuptial domicile.[348] The justification that the former concern issues of fact more appropriate for the forum than the issues raised in the latter case is not convincing, because the determination of a factual question, such as whether or not duress existed, does not of itself resolve the problem of the effect of such duress on the validity of the marriage.

The common judicial attitude of ignoring choice of law issues so far as the parties' consent is concerned may be illustrated by *Buckland v Buckland*.[349] Here a marriage celebrated in Malta between two Maltese domiciliaries was declared a nullity by an English court on the ground that the petitioner had gone through the ceremony because of fear of an unjust prosecution if he did not. Only English law was referred to, and yet the only connection with England was that, by the date of the proceedings, the petitioner had become domiciled in England. Determination of the applicable law could have been referred to other legal systems, whose varied claims we must now examine.

(ii) Application of the law of the place of celebration

In *Parojcic v Parojcic*,[350] Davies J referred the question of the effect of duress to English law as the law of the place of celebration. Despite this dictum, the view that that law should govern only "the method of giving consent as distinct from the fact of consent"[351] seems preferable. This is because, even in the sphere of commercial contracts, the issue of the parties' consent is not referred to the law of the place of contracting.[352] Indeed, it would seem that a marriage may comply with all the formal requirements of the law of the place of celebration and yet

---

(Fam); and *Sandwell Metropolitan Borough Council v RG* [2013] EWHC 2373 (COP). Cf *Re Park's Estate* [1954] P 89; affd [1953] 2 All ER 1411.

[343] *Way v Way* [1950] P 71 at 79–80, approved [1951] P 124 at 133–4; *Kassim v Kassim* [1962] P 224.
[344] Cf *Mitford v Mitford* [1923] P 130.
[345] *Bell v Graham* (1859) 13 Moo PCC 242; *Silver v Silver* [1955] 1 WLR 728; cf *Johnson v Smith* (1968) 70 DLR (2d) 374. In Scotland, see *Akram v Akram* 1979 SLT (Notes) 87; *Hakeem v Hussain* 2003 SLT 515, and on appeal, *H v H* 2005 SLT 1025; and Family Law (Scotland) Act 2006, s 2, discussed infra, p 992.
[346] *Mahadervan v Mahadervan* [1962] 3 All ER 1108 at 111. This is omitted from the report in [1964] P 233.
[347] Webb (1959) 22 MLR 198, 202–4.
[348] Cf *Kassim v Kassim*, supra.
[349] [1968] P 296; see also *Kassim v Kassim*, supra; *Kelly v Ireland* [1996] 2 ILRM 364.
[350] [1958] 1 WLR 1280 at 1283.
[351] *Apt v Apt* [1948] P 83 at 88.
[352] Supra, pp 755–6.

lack essential validity because of lack of consent.[353] Thus, even though reference to the law of the place of celebration is in accordance with many of the cases, there are certainly others which militate against it.[354]

(iii) Application of the law of the domicile

The same can also be said of the opinion that "no marriage is (*semble*) valid if by the law of either party's domicile he or she does not consent to marry the other".[355] There are at least three English decisions[356] in which the validity of a marriage, so far as consent is concerned, has been considered without reference to the domiciliary law of one or both of the parties. The weight of opinion does, however, favour reference of the issue of consent to the law of the domicile. The view that lack of consent is a personal defect was accepted by Hodson J in *Way v Way*:[357]

> The petitioner, a British subject domiciled in England, went through a ceremony of marriage at Archangel with the respondent, domiciled in Russia, as the result of which he believed that he had been legally married. He later claimed annulment on the grounds (1) that certain formalities required by Russian law had been omitted and (2) that the marriage was void for want of consent, since he believed at the time of the ceremony that his wife would be allowed to accompany him to England (which was not permitted by the Soviet authorities) and also that it was the duty of both parties to live together. According to Russian law he was mistaken in both respects.

Hodson J began by finding that there had been no neglect of Russian formalities. He went on to propound the doctrine that "questions of consent are to be dealt with by reference to the personal law of the parties rather than by reference to the law of the place where the contract was made", with the result that "the matrimonial law of each of the parties" had to be applied.[358] He then held that, by English law, which was the personal law of the petitioner, consent is not nullified by a mistake of the kind pleaded, ie mistake as to attributes, a finding with which it is impossible to disagree.

The Court of Appeal[359] held the marriage to be void on the ground that the Russian formalities had not, in fact, been observed, and therefore anything that was said about the law to govern the question of consent was obiter. However, Sir Raymond Evershed MR was "prepared to assume" that Hodson J was correct in referring the question to the personal law of the parties.[360]

This decision to refer issues of consent to the law of the domicile was followed in *Szechter v Szechter*:[361]

> The husband, his first wife and his secretary, Nina, all were domiciled in Poland. The secretary was imprisoned for "anti-state activities" and her health deteriorated rapidly. In order to obtain her release from prison, the husband secretly divorced his first wife and in 1968 married Nina in prison. Shortly thereafter she was released from prison and all three came to

---

[353] *Nane v Sykiotis* (1966) 57 DLR (2d) 118 at 122.

[354] *Bell v Graham*, supra; *Mehta v Mehta*, supra; *Apt v Apt* [1948] P 83 at 88; and see *H v H* [1954] P 258; *Silver v Silver*, supra; *Kassim v Kassim*, supra; *Buckland v Buckland*, supra.

[355] Dicey, Morris and Collins, para 17R-119.

[356] *Silver v Silver*, supra; *Kassim v Kassim*, supra; *Buckland v Buckland*, supra; and see *Cooper v Crane* [1891] P 369; *H v H*, supra; and see also *Parojcic v Parojcic* [1958] 1 WLR 1280 at 1283.

[357] [1950] P 71.

[358] Ibid, at 78.

[359] *Kenward v Kenward* [1951] P 124.

[360] Ibid, at 133.

[361] [1971] P 286; cf *Feiner v Demkowicz* (1973) 42 DLR (3d) 165; *Re Suria's Marriage* (1977) 29 FLR 308.

England, where they acquired a domicile. Nina petitioned for the annulment of her marriage on the grounds of duress, so that the husband and first wife could resume their married life.

These facts undoubtedly raised an issue of choice of law. Polish law was the law of the place of celebration and the law of the domicile of both parties at the time of the marriage. English law was the law of the forum and the law of the domicile at the time of the proceedings. Both legal systems agreed that the marriage was void for duress. However, Sir Jocelyn Simon P concluded that it was for Polish law, as the law of the domicile of the parties at the time of the marriage, to determine the validity of the marriage.[362] In so doing, he approved the proposition in Dicey and Morris[363] that "no marriage is valid if by the law of either party's domicile one party does not consent to marry the other".[364] The editors of that work have, however, accepted[365] the suggestion made in these pages[366] that the issue of a party's alleged lack of consent to marry should be determined by reference to that person's ante-nuptial domiciliary law, and not to the law of both parties' ante-nuptial domiciles.[367]

It seems adequate to analyse the issue of consent as a personal issue to be referred to the law governing capacity, without requiring a wife to have consented not only according to her own law but also according to her husband's, or vice versa. This was the approach taken in Scotland in *Singh v Singh*.[368] The case concerned a United Kingdom citizen, domiciled in Scotland, who sought declaration of nullity of her marriage, celebrated in India, in 2001, to an Indian national, on the grounds of her lack of consent and that the marriage had been entered into under duress. The judge, RF Macdonald QC, declining to follow the obiter dictum of Lord Guthrie in *Di Rollo v Di Rollo*[369] that the question of consent should be decided by the law of the place where the marriage was celebrated,[370] held that the law governing the issue of consent to marriage was the law of the domicile of the party claiming lack of consent.[371] In the instant case, by the law of the petitioner's Scottish domicile, the threats from her mother were deemed to be of a serious nature, amounting to threats of immediate danger to her liberty, which caused her will to be overborne, and vitiated her consent to marry. Declarator of nullity of marriage was granted.

Application of the law of the domicile to issues of consent was supported by the Court of Appeal in *Vervaeke v Smith*.[372] A major issue in this case was whether the English courts would recognise the validity of a Belgian nullity decree;[373] but the Court of Appeal also gave some consideration to the original validity of the marriage in question. The marriage had taken place in England between a woman domiciled in Belgium and a man domiciled in

---

[362] Nevertheless, he satisfied himself that the marriage was also invalid under English domestic law. Indeed so extensive was his examination of English law, that, had the marriage been valid by Polish law, the impression is given that he would, nevertheless, have held it to be void as contrary to English public policy; see Hartley (1972) 35 MLR 571, 580; cf Carter (1971) 45 BYBIL 406, 409.

[363] Dicey and Morris (1967) 8th edn, p 271. The proposition in the (2012) 15th edn, para 17R-119 is in substantially the same terms.

[364] [1971] P 286 at 294–5.

[365] See now Dicey, Morris and Collins (2012) 15th edn, para 17-122.

[366] 8th edn of this book, p 396.

[367] This view was taken recently by Moylan J in *SH v NB* [2009] EWHC 3274 (Fam).

[368] 2005 SLT 749. See now s 38(1)(b) of the Family Law (Scotland) Act 2006 which makes it clear that consent is related to matters of capacity and is governed by the law of the ante-nuptial domicile of the person concerned.

[369] 1959 SLT 278.

[370] RF Macdonald QC judged Lord Guthrie's approach to be "unsupported by reasoning and unvouched by authority" (at [22]).

[371] At [22].

[372] [1981] Fam 77 at 122.

[373] Infra, pp 1025–6.

England. This was essentially a sham marriage whose purpose was to give the woman British nationality. Such a marriage, though valid under English law, was void under Belgian law. Nevertheless, its validity was upheld under the exception to the dual domicile rule provided by *Sottomayor v De Barros (No 2)*[374] in that the marriage was valid by English law, that of the domicile of one party and the place of celebration.[375]

(iv) Reform

In their examination of the choice of law rules relating to marriage, the Law Commission considered the issue of the law to be applied to matters of consent.[376] They suggested that, although some arguments can be advanced in favour of the application of the law of the forum, issues of consent are concerned with the essential or substantive validity of a marriage and that "it would be contrary to principle and inconvenient in practice to fragment the question of essential validity".[377] This led to the conclusion that the law of the domicile should govern issues of consent, as it probably does already; and the Law Commission favoured reference to the domiciliary law of the person whose consent is alleged to be defective, rather than the formulation approved in *Szechter v Szechter*.[378] Certain other piecemeal measures have been implemented concerning consent to marriage:

Forced Marriage (Civil Protection) Act 2007 Royal Assent was given on 26 July 2007 to the Forced Marriage (Civil Protection) Act 2007. The Act, which was introduced by Lord Lester of Herne Hill as a Private Member's Bill,[379] applies to England and Wales, and Northern Ireland. The aim of the Act, which inserts a new Part 4A into the Family Law Act 1996, is to provide civil protection against forced marriage[380] in England and Wales, and Northern Ireland.[381] Forced marriage is defined in the Act as a situation in which one person, "A", is forced, by means of coercion by threats or other psychological means,[382] by another person, "B", into a marriage,[383] with B or another person, without A's free and full consent.[384] It is irrelevant whether B's conduct is directed against A, B, or another person.[385] The Act empowers the High Court or the family court[386] to make a forced marriage protection order, ie an order for the purposes of protecting (i) a person from being forced into a marriage or

---

[374] (1879) 5 PD 94, supra, pp 918–19.

[375] The House of Lords did not discuss the application of the *Sottomayor* rule; though Lord Simon of Glaisdale was prepared to regard this issue of reality of consent as one of "quintessential validity" to be governed by the law of the country with which the marriage had the most real and substantial connection: [1983] 1 AC 145 at 166, supra, p 924.

[376] Law Commission Working Paper No 89 (1985), paras 5.6–5.24. Their Report, Law Com No 165 (1987), adds little to this discussion, see paras 2.4, 2.8.

[377] Ibid, para 5.18.

[378] [1971] P 286, supra.

[379] It is the first House of Lords Private Member's Bill to become legislation since 2002 (House of Commons Library Research Paper 07/56, 28 June 2007, p 26).

[380] Distinguished from arranged marriages, where both parties fully and freely consent to the marriage.

[381] For Scotland, see Forced Marriage etc. (Protection and Jurisdiction) (Scotland) Act 2011.

[382] Ibid, s 63A(6). See also *XCC v AA* [2012] EWHC 2183 (COP)—where the victim is a vulnerable adult who lacks capacity, no compulsion or coercion is required. In this context, "force" includes inducing or arranging for such a person to undergo a ceremony of marriage. It follows that a marriage with an incapacitated person who is unable to consent is a forced marriage within the meaning of the Forced Marriage Act 2007; and s 121(2) of the Anti-Social Behaviour, Crime and Policing Act 2014 (in relation to a victim who lacks capacity to consent to marriage, the offence of forced marriage can be committed by any conduct carried out for the purpose of causing the victim to enter into a marriage, whether or not coercion is used).

[383] Any religious or civil ceremony of marriage, whether or not legally binding: ibid, s 63S. "Although in the Western world, forced marriage is sometimes discussed as a religious practice, no major faith condones forced marriage." (House of Commons Library Research Paper 07/56, 28 June 2007, Summary).

[384] Family Law Act 1996, s 63A(4).

[385] S 63A(5).

[386] S 63M(1).

from any attempt to be forced into a marriage; or (ii) a person who has been forced into a marriage.[387] An application may be made for an order by the person who is to be protected by the order, or by certain third parties.[388] A forced marriage protection order may contain such prohibitions, restrictions, requirements, or other terms as the court considers appropriate for the purposes of the order.[389] In deciding whether to exercise its powers, the court must have regard to all the circumstances, including the need to secure the health, safety and well-being of the person to be protected.[390] In ascertaining that person's well-being, the court must have regard, in particular, to his/her wishes and feelings, so far as they are reasonably ascertainable, and as the court considers appropriate in the light of the person's age and understanding.[391] Breach of a forced marriage protection order is a criminal offence with a maximum penalty of five years' imprisonment.[392] Alternatively, a protected person who does not want to pursue criminal proceedings, can apply for an arrest warrant for breach of a forced marriage protection order in the civil court.[393] The 2007 Act does not affect any other protection or assistance which currently is available to victims of forced marriage, such as the inherent jurisdiction of the High Court, criminal liability, civil remedies under the Protection from Harassment Act 1997, or the law of marriage.[394]

Although the Act contains no conflict of laws provisions as such, it is intended to have extra-territorial import in so far as the terms of a forced marriage protection order may relate not only to conduct within England and Wales, but also (or instead of) to conduct outside England and Wales.[395] Thus, for example, a forced marriage protection order may be sought in England by a young girl living there who fears that she may be taken by her parents from the United Kingdom, against her will, for the purpose of forced marriage abroad.[396] An order

---

[387] S 63A(1).

[388] Ss 63C.

[389] S 63B(1).

[390] S 63A(2).

[391] S 63A(3).

[392] S 63CA, inserted by the Anti-Social Behaviour, Crime and Policing Act 2014, s 120. See also s 121 of the 2014 Act which makes forced marriage itself a criminal offence. The criminal legislation has extra-territorial jurisdiction (s 121(7)).

[393] However, there cannot be double jeopardy. Thus, where a person has been convicted of a breach of a forced marriage protection order, that person cannot be punished subsequently for contempt in relation to the same conduct, and vice versa. S 63CA(3) and (4).

[394] Family Law Act 1996, s 63R. The appropriate remedy in cases of forced marriage is a decree of nullity rather than a divorce decree, due to the stigma that can attach to victims of forced marriage within their communities as a result of divorce. Where nullity is not available due to lapse of time (note that s 13(2) of the Matrimonial Causes Act 1973 places a three-year time limit on bringing petitions for nullity on the basis of lack of consent), courts have utilized the emerging concept of "non-marriage" (see Chapter 21) to provide another type of remedy, pursuant to its inherent jurisdiction, in the form of a declaration denying the marriage recognition in England and Wales (see Chapter 23). See *NS v MI* [2006] EWHC 1646 (Fam); *SL v MJ* [2006] EWHC 3743 (Fam) (nullity decrees); *B v I (Forced Marriage)* [2010] FLR 1721; *Re P (Forced Marriage)* [2010] EWHC 3467 (Fam); and *SH v NB* [2009] EWHC 3274 (Fam) (declarations of non-recognition). Cf *A Local Authority v X* [2013] EWHC 3274 (Fam) (a declaration of non-recognition refused as an application for a nullity decree based on the alternative ground of age (the victim being 16 at the time of the marriage) was available). In relation to the specific category of forced marriage involving incapacitated individuals (supra) see *Westminster City Council v IC (A Protected Party by His Litigation Friend) and Ors* [2008] EWCA Civ 198 (a declaration of non-recognition); *XCC v AA* [2012] EWHC 2183 (COP), and *Luton Borough Council v SB and another* [2015] EWHC 3534 (Fam) (declarations of non-recognition as a precursor to the initiation of the formal proceedings to annul the marriage); and *Sandwell Metropolitan Borough Council v RG* [2013] EWHC 2373 (COP) (a nullity decree refused as such a decree was not in the incapacitated person's best interests). See also Gaffney-Rhys [2010] IFL 336.

[395] S 63B(2)(a). Cf, for Northern Ireland, Forced Marriage (Civil Protection) Act 2007, Sch 1, para 2(2)(a).

[396] Cf *NS v MI* [2006] EWHC 1646 (Fam), [2007] 1 FLR 444.

may affect respondents who force, or attempt to force, a person to enter a marriage, as well as persons who aid, abet, counsel, procure, encourage or assist the forcing, or attempted forcing, of a marriage.[397]

Asylum and Immigration (Treatment of Claimants, etc) Act 2004 Sections 19 to 24 of the 2004 Act[398] establish a regime, for England and Wales, Scotland and Northern Ireland, the aim of which is to prevent the abuse of immigration rights by means of sham marriages. The procedure is applicable where a marriage is to be solemnized in the UK and a party to the marriage is subject to immigration control.[399]

The position in Scots law The subject of sham marriages and marriages of convenience has provoked considerable interest in recent years in Scots law.[400] The outcome has been a statutory response, in sections 2 and 38 of the Family Law (Scotland) Act 2006. Section 38, in the part of the Act headed "private international law", provides in sub-section (2) that the question whether a person who enters into a marriage (a) had capacity;[401] or (b) consented, to enter into it shall be determined[402] by the law of the place where, immediately before the marriage, that person was domiciled. This provision makes it clear, therefore, that consent to marry is a matter to be determined by a person's ante-nuptial domicile. Section 2 of the Act inserts a new section 20A (Grounds on which marriage void) into the Marriage (Scotland) Act 1977. Separate provision is made for marriages solemnised in Scotland where (a) at the time of the marriage ceremony a party to the marriage who was capable of consenting to the marriage purported to give consent, but did so by reason only of duress[403] or error;[404] and (b) at the time of the marriage ceremony a party to the marriage was incapable of (i) understanding the nature of the marriage; and (ii) consenting to the marriage. In each case, the marriage shall be void.[405] In contrast, if a party purported to give consent to the marriage other than by reason only of duress or error, the marriage shall not be void by reason only of that party's having tacitly withheld consent to the marriage at the time when it was solemnised.[406] The latter provision, which is aimed at tackling the problem of sham marriages, is a

---

[397] S 63B(2)(b) and (3).

[398] See the Asylum and Immigration (Treatment of Claimants, etc) Act 2004, as amended by the Asylum and Immigration (Treatment of Claimants, etc) Act 2004 (Remedial) Order, SI 2011/1158. The Order has removed the incompatibility of section 19 of the 2004 Act with Arts 12 and 14 of the ECHR. Section 19 created a Certificate of Approval Scheme, which prohibited people subject to immigration control from marrying without authorization, other than in a Church of England religious ceremony. See the 14th edition of this book, pp 977–8. The scheme had been declared incompatible with the Convention by the High Court in *R (on the application of Baiai) v Secretary of State for the Home Department* [2006] EWHC 823, [2006] 2 FLR 645; and the House of Lords in *R (Baiai and others) v Secretary of State for the Home Department* [2008] UKHL 53, [2009] AC 287. The UK courts' view that the Certificate of Approval Scheme had operated in violation of Convention rights was confirmed by the European Court of Human Rights (ECtHR) in *O'Donoghue and Others v. the United Kingdom*, Application no. 34848/07, 14 November 2010. See also the Immigration (Procedure for Marriage) Regulations 2011/2678, as amended, and *Aguilar Quila v Secretary of State for the Home Department* [2011] UKSC 45.

[399] Defined in s 19(4) as a person who is not a national of a state which is a party to the Agreement on the European Economic Area signed at Oporto on 2 May 1992, and who, under the Immigration Act 1971, requires leave to enter or remain in the United Kingdom.

[400] See Crawford and Carruthers, para 12-53.

[401] See supra, p 909 et seq.

[402] Subject to s 38(3) and (4) of the Act, and s 50 of the Family Law Act 1986, supra, p 926.

[403] Eg *Mahmood v Mahmood* 1993 SLT 589; *Mahmud v Mahmud* 1994 SLT 559; *Sohrab v Kahn* 2002 SLT 1255; and *Singh v Singh* 2005 SLT 749.

[404] Error as to the nature of the ceremony, or error as to identity: s 20A(5).

[405] S 20A(1), (2) and (3).

[406] S 20A(4). Contrast *Akram v Akram* 1979 SLT (Notes) 87; and the Inner House decision in *H v H* 2005 SLT 1025.

legislative answer to difficulties encountered by the Scottish courts, and "establishes a criterion of consent, objectively construed, to marriage".[407]

Rome III   As stated above,[408] on 21 June 2012, the Council Regulation (EU) No. 1259/2010 implementing enhanced cooperation in the area of the law applicable to divorce and legal separation ("Rome III") came into effect. Unlike the Brussels II *bis* Regulation in respect of jurisdiction in matrimonial matters,[409] the Rome III Regulation extends only to divorce and judicial separation.[410] Indeed, the Regulation does not apply to marriage annulment, even if the issue arises "merely as a preliminary question within the context of divorce or legal separation proceedings".[411]

(d) Physical defects[412]

It remains to identify the law which governs other personal physical defects. These can encompass a wide range of grounds of invalidity, as is illustrated by those which render a marriage voidable under section 12 of the Matrimonial Causes Act 1973: impotence, wilful refusal to consummate the marriage, mental disorder such as to render the person unfitted for marriage, venereal disease, that the woman was pregnant by another man, that, after the time of the marriage, an interim gender recognition certificate has been issued to either party to the marriage under the Gender Recognition Act 2004, or the respondent is a person whose gender at the time of the marriage had become the acquired gender under that Act. In the context of English law, a nullity petition on the ground of the respondent's pregnancy or suffering from venereal disease may only be brought if the petitioner is unaware of this fact and so such grounds could be regarded more properly as relating to the reality of the petitioner's consent and thus to be governed by the law appropriate to that issue.[413] However, other legal systems do not necessarily take the same approach and, in any event, the consent classification cannot so readily be applied to issues such as wilful refusal or impotence. Two issues are raised: what are the current choice of law rules to govern these personal physical defects, and are the rules appropriate and adequate?

(i) What is the present law?

It is not easy to resolve the first issue and state the current law with any confidence. The main defects to consider are impotence and wilful refusal, but the authorities are far from clear as to what law is to govern these defects. There is some authority to support the application of the law of the domicile, of the place of celebration or of the forum. The difficulty with the decisions is that in all but one of the cases[414] English law has been applied, often with little or no consideration of the choice of law issue. Even when that issue is considered, the varied dicta seem to be at odds with the facts of the reported decisions. For instance, in *Robert v Robert*[415] wilful refusal is characterised as an "error in the quality of the respondent"[416] to which the

---

[407] Crawford and Carruthers, 3rd edn, para 12-38.

[408] Supra, p 983.

[409] The Brussels II *bis* Regulation covers divorce, legal separation and marriage annulment: Art 1(1)(a).

[410] Art 1(1).

[411] Art (1)(2)(c). See also Recital (10). Marriage annulment appears to be excluded partly on the ground that it raises specific issues, closely connected to the validity of marriage. See COM (2006) 399 final, and Document 5274/07 LIMITE JUSTCIV 4, 12 January 2007.

[412] Bishop (1978) 41 MLR 512; Law Commission Working Paper No 89 (1985), paras 5.25–5.43; Law Com No 165 (1987), para 2.9.

[413] Supra, pp 986–7.

[414] *Robert v Robert* [1947] P 164.

[415] Ibid.

[416] Ibid, at 167–8. This is criticised by Morris, para 8-032.

law of the place of celebration should be applied.[417] Against such classification may be cited *Way v Way*,[418] where English law was applied to a nullity petition based on wilful refusal arising from a marriage celebrated in Russia; and *Ponticelli v Ponticelli*,[419] where English law was applied though the place of celebration was Italy.

The confused state of the cases can be further illustrated by the fact that application of the law of the husband's domicile at the time of the marriage is supported by some decisions[420] on impotence and wilful refusal but is inconsistent with others.[421] Again, application of English law as the law of the forum finds support in some cases,[422] but not in all.[423]

(ii) What ought the law to be?

If the cases provide no clear guide to the law to govern nullity petitions based on personal physical defects, are there obvious principles which might guide courts in the future? Application of the law of the place of celebration can be rejected. The defects in question cannot be classified as relating to formalities of marriage. Support can be found in principle for the application of both the law of the domicile and the law of the forum. If one regards defects such as impotence, pregnancy by another man, mental disorder, and the fact that the respondent was suffering from venereal disease, as matters of essential validity akin to capacity, then the relevant law to determine the effect of such alleged invalidity is that of the domicile.[424] It is, however, more difficult to adopt that approach in the case of wilful refusal to consummate the marriage. It is a post-nuptial defect and it might be thought inappropriate to apply the law of the domicile existing at the time of the marriage to a ground of annulment more akin to evidence of irretrievable breakdown of the marriage justifying divorce. Indeed, the divorce analogy would provide support for applying the law of the forum.[425]

It might seem that the easy answer would be to have different choice of law rules for defects which are ante-nuptial, eg impotence, as opposed to those which are post-nuptial, eg wilful refusal. This is, however, an impracticable solution because the two grounds are frequently pleaded in the alternative and, as the Law Commission has pointed out, "it would be undesirable and inconvenient if different choice of law rules were to apply, depending on whether non-consummation was due to inability to consummate or unwillingness to do so".[426] This means that either the law of the domicile or the law of the forum must apply to both impotence and wilful refusal.

Although arguments in favour of the law of the forum are good, they are not good enough. It is easier, and cheaper, to apply the law of the forum than any other law; but that argument

---

[417] Though the court did consider that, if the defect was to be classified as a question affecting the capacity of one of the parties to contract a marriage, then the law of the domicile was applicable and this is supported by the citing of *Sottomayor v De Barros* (1877) 3 PD 1, and see *Addison v Addison* [1955] NI 1 at 30.

[418] [1950] P 71 at 80.

[419] [1958] P 204.

[420] *Way v Way*, supra; *Ponticelli v Ponticelli*, supra.

[421] *Easterbrook v Easterbrook* [1944] P 10; *Hutter v Hutter* [1944] P 95, unless one can explain them on the ground that, when the foreign law is not pleaded, it is the same as English law. In so far as *Ramsay-Fairfax v Ramsay-Fairfax* [1956] P 115 at 125 can be considered an authority on choice of law, it militates against this view, unless Scots law, the law of the husband's domicile, is not only considered to be the same as English law (which is not the case), but it is accepted that this is a reason for applying English law as such.

[422] *Easterbrook v Easterbrook*, supra; *Hutter v Hutter*, supra; *Magnier v Magnier* (1968) 112 Sol Jo 233.

[423] *Robert v Robert* [1947] P 164; and see *Ponticelli v Ponticelli* [1958] P 204 at 214–16; *Sangha v Mander* (1985) 47 RFL (2d) 212 at 216.

[424] See *Robert v Robert* [1947] P 164 at 168; and see *Ramsay-Fairfax v Ramsay-Fairfax* [1956] P 115 at 125.

[425] Supra, p 979 et seq; for rejection of the analogy, see *Sangha v Mander* (1985) 47 RFL (2d) 212 at 216–17.

[426] Law Commission Working Paper No 89 (1985), para 5.30.

can be used in relation to choice of law in any context, yet it is not generally accepted, save in the case of divorce. Wilful refusal may be like divorce in its post-nuptial character, but it is significant that English law has chosen to regard it as a ground of annulment. That being so, to apply the law of the domicile will ensure consistency with the treatment of all grounds of invalidity. It will also confirm the view that these personal defects go to the essential validity of a marriage and that all aspects of essential validity are to be governed by the law of the domicile.[427] Finally, it is hard to disagree with Lord Reid when he pointed out that application of the law of the forum is wrong in principle, saying: "Suppose a case where the law of the parties' domicile gives no relief on this ground [ie wilful refusal],[428] it seems to me quite contrary to principle that the wife should be able to come here and seek relief on that ground."[429]

Returning to the authorities, the most persuasive decision in favour of the application of the law of the domicile is *Ponticelli v Ponticelli*,[430] where the facts were these:

> The parties married by proxy in Italy. The wife was domiciled in Italy and the husband was domiciled in England. When the husband petitioned for a nullity decree on the ground of wilful refusal, the court had to face the choice of law issue, for wilful refusal was not in the circumstances a ground for annulment in Italian law.

Sachs J rejected a classification of wilful refusal as akin to an issue of form and so he rejected the law of the place of celebration, here Italian law, as the appropriate law.[431] He did not favour the analogy of wilful refusal with divorce, and so his arguments militated against the application of the law of the forum.[432] Although he applied English law, he did so rather because it was the law of the husband's domicile[433] at the time of the marriage and of the petition,[434] and it was also the law of the intended matrimonial home. Furthermore, he rejected any attempt to distinguish between the choice of law rules for wilful refusal and for impotence. He considered they should both be regarded as matters of personal capacity,[435] to be governed by the law of the domicile, for "it is surely a matter of some importance that the initial validity of a marriage should, in relation to all matters except form and ceremony . . . be consistently decided according to the law of one country alone . . . and that consistency cannot be attained if the test is *lex fori*".[436]

Agreeing that physical personal defects are to be governed by the law of the domicile does not, however, solve all problems in this area. It remains to decide which spouse's domiciliary law is to be applied and whether the domicile, and thus the applicable law, is to be determined at the date of the marriage or at the date of the nullity petition. Although in *Ponticelli* reference was made to the law of the husband's domicile, there seems little doubt that, since a married woman is now capable of acquiring a separate domicile, reference must be made to her domicile where appropriate. Various ways have been suggested to decide which domiciliary law should be applied. One approach is to look at the law of each spouse's domicile and to annul the marriage if there are grounds for so doing under either law.[437] This tips the scales firmly in

---

[427] *De Reneville v De Reneville* [1948] P 100 at 114; *Szechter v Szechter* [1971] P 286 at 295; *Sangha v Mander* (1985) 47 RFL (2d) 212 at 217–18.
[428] As is the case in Scotland.
[429] *Ross Smith v Ross Smith* [1963] AC 280 at 306; and see *Ponticelli v Ponticelli* [1958] P 204 at 215.
[430] [1958] P 204; and see more recently *Sangha v Mander* (1985) 47 RFL (2d) 212.
[431] Thereby rejecting *Robert v Robert* [1947] P 164.
[432] He regarded *De Reneville v De Reneville*, supra, as supporting his view.
[433] The question of which spouse's domiciliary law should be applied is discussed infra.
[434] [1958] P 204 at 216; though reference to domicile at the time of the petition seems hard to justify.
[435] See *Ramsay-Fairfax v Ramsay-Fairfax* [1956] P 115 at 133.
[436] [1958] P 204 at 215–16.
[437] Palsson, *Marriage in Comparative Conflict of Laws* (1981), pp 314–15.

favour of annulling a marriage, with the result that the petitioner would succeed even though there were no grounds for annulment under the law of the domicile and even though he was the person alleged to lack capacity. The balance can be redressed by always applying the law of the petitioner's domicile.[438] Under this approach, however, a nullity decree will be denied in, say, a case of wilful refusal if that does not constitute a ground of annulment under the law of the petitioner's domicile even though it is a ground under that of the respondent, the respondent being the person who has refused. A third approach, which avoids this difficulty, is to apply the law of the domicile of the spouse who is alleged to be incapable, taking that in the case of non-consummation to be the spouse who is unable, or refuses, to consummate the marriage. In its turn, this approach would deny annulment in the case where wilful refusal was a ground for nullity under the law of the petitioner's, but not the respondent's domicile, assuming the refusal to be by the respondent.

No answer is perfect; but it is suggested that the third approach is the most appropriate in that it accords with the general choice of law rule relating to matters of essential validity, ie the application of the ground of invalidity under the domiciliary law of the person alleged to be incapable. This would still leave it open to a court to conclude that, in the special circumstances of non-consummation, it would be right to apply the law of the person who is rendered unable to consummate the marriage by reason of the conduct of the other party.

Finally, there is the question of the time at which the law of the domicile is to be determined. The general rule applicable to matters of essential validity is that the applicable law is that of the domicile immediately preceding the marriage—the ante-nuptial domicile.[439] There should be no doubt that this is the relevant time in all cases of alleged invalidity except wilful refusal.[440] The more doubtful case is that of wilful refusal. If it is also to be regarded as a straightforward issue of capacity, then the relevant time is again that of the marriage.[441] If, however, it is regarded more properly as an anomalous ground of nullity more like a basis for divorce, since it is post-nuptial, then the relevant date for determining domicile might be thought to be that of the proceedings.[442] However, the Law Commission would seem to be right in indicating that, if domicile is to be the test for determining the governing law in all issues of essential validity, consistency requires the domicile to be determined at the same time in all cases, ie immediately before the marriage, especially as wilful refusal and impotence are often pleaded in the alternative.[443]

(e) Annulment on grounds unknown to English law

There is a further issue, closely connected with the question whether English law as the law of the forum should be applied to cases of impotence and wilful refusal. This is whether the English courts will annul a marriage on grounds unknown to English law. There is clear statutory provision for the application of foreign law to any question affecting the validity of a marriage. Section 14(1) of the Matrimonial Causes Act 1973 qualifies the grounds of annulment of void and voidable marriages laid down by that Act[444] by stating that, where

---

[438] Jaffey (1978) 41 MLR 38; Bishop (1978) 41 MLR 512.

[439] Supra, p 910.

[440] *De Reneville v De Reneville* [1948] P 100 at 114. This may have been lost sight of in *Savelieff v Glouchkoff* (1964) 45 DLR (2d) 520; Lysyk (1965) 43 Can Bar Rev 107, 121.

[441] Cf *Robert v Robert* [1947] P 164 at 167–8.

[442] Such a view might be supported by *Way v Way* [1950] P 71 at 80. In *Ponticelli v Ponticelli* [1958] P 204 it is expressly stated, at 216, that the husband was domiciled in England both at the date of the marriage and of the petition; cf *De Reneville v De Reneville* [1948] P 100 at 114 where Lord Greene's reference to the date of the marriage is made without qualification of the case of wilful refusal.

[443] Law Commission Working Paper No 89 (1985), para 5.41.

[444] Ss 11–13.

any matter affecting the validity of a marriage would, in accordance with the rules of private international law, fall to be determined by a foreign law, nothing in the nullity provisions of the 1973 Act should preclude the application of the foreign law or require the application of the English law of nullity.[445]

There is no doubt that this provision contemplates that English courts will apply foreign law to nullity petitions in appropriate circumstances and, equally, there is no doubt that English courts will annul marriages on the basis of foreign rules as to invalidity. As has been seen when considering the validity of a marriage,[446] the English courts will annul a marriage celebrated in a foreign country if the formalities of the law of the place of celebration are not complied with, irrespective of the English law on such matters.[447] Similarly, the English courts will annul a marriage, even if celebrated in England, on a ground laid down by the parties' ante-nuptial domiciliary laws, whether or not that ground is co-extensive with a similar English ground. For instance, a marriage has been treated as void because the parties were within the prohibited degrees of relationship under their foreign domiciliary law, though not under English law.[448]

There appears to be no authority on whether an English court will annul a marriage on a ground which, under the law of the domicile, renders the marriage voidable but which falls quite outside the grounds on which a marriage might be declared voidable under English domestic law. Any determination of the question whether English courts would annul a marriage in such circumstances is speculative.[449] It is suggested, however, that an English court should be prepared fully to accept the general principle that questions as to the essential validity of the marriage are to be referred to the law of the domicile. In that event, it is submitted that it does not matter whether the English court applies foreign grounds verbally similar to English grounds, such as consanguinity or non-age, even though the substance of the rule is different. Similarly, it should make no difference if a foreign ground is applied which is a variant of the English ground, such as declaring a marriage voidable on the ground that at the time of the marriage another woman was pregnant by the husband,[450] or a foreign ground substantially different from any under English law, such as the incapacity of a person of one religion to marry a member of another[451] or annulment on the ground of a mistake as to the attributes of the other spouse.[452] It must not be forgotten that the English courts would always retain the power, as in the case of other issues of validity,[453] to refuse to apply a foreign provision laying down a rule of invalidity where the application of that rule would be contrary to English public policy.[454]

---

[445] S 14(2) also provides that the grounds on which a marriage is to be declared void, laid down in s 11, are without prejudice to other grounds under which a marriage celebrated under the Foreign Marriage Acts 1892–1947 or a common law marriage celebrated abroad might be declared void. See also the Marriage (Prohibited Degrees of Relationship) Act 1986, s 1(7).

[446] Supra, p 893.

[447] *Berthiaume v Dastous* [1930] AC 79—marriage with religious, but no civil, ceremony; *Kenward v Kenward* [1951] P 124—failure to comply with the Russian Marriage Code.

[448] *Sottomayor v De Barros* (1877) 3 PD 1.

[449] Morris, para 9-027.

[450] This used to be a ground in New Zealand. The English rule is limited to the case of a wife being pregnant by another man: Matrimonial Causes Act 1973, s 12(1)(f).

[451] Eg *Lendrum v Chakravarti* 1929 SLT 96; though see *MacDougall v Chitnavis* 1937 SC 390; cf *Corbett v Corbett* [1957] 1 WLR 486, a decision on recognition of a foreign decree.

[452] Cf *Mitford v Mitford* [1923] P 130, also a decision on recognition.

[453] Supra, p 921.

[454] *Vervaeke v Smith* [1983] 1 AC 145 provides some support for the view that English courts might not apply foreign rules invalidating sham marriages.

(f) What law determines whether a marriage is void or voidable?

It has been suggested[455] that, as the annulment of a voidable marriage and a divorce decree both only have prospective effect, the law of the forum should be applied to the former as to the latter. This would have the disadvantage of requiring the choice of law rule to depend on whether the marriage was void or voidable, and of deciding by what law that issue is to be determined—a difficult problem to which we must now turn.

It has been seen that different legal systems attribute different effects to invalidating factors. A clear example is provided by lack of consent, which renders a marriage void under Scots law[456] but voidable under English law.[457] This poses a problem. If an English court annuls the marriage of parties both domiciled in Scotland, applying the Scottish law on consent, is the marriage to be regarded in England as void or merely as voidable? In other words, is the English court to apply its own criteria for determining whether the problem is one of alleged voidness or of alleged voidability? The previous edition of this book[458] advocated the view that whether a marriage was void or voidable was merely a facet of the question whether it was valid or invalid. It followed that the proper law, whether it was the law of the place of celebration or the law of the parties' domiciles, also determined what was meant by invalidity, ie whether it meant voidness or voidability. It was suggested that any other approach would be highly unsatisfactory where the marriage was void under the governing law, but entirely valid under the law of the forum. Indeed, "to give the marriage full effect under the law of the forum notwithstanding its invalidity under the governing law would be to deprive the choice of law rule of any real impact".[459]

Recent developments, however, appear to justify a shift from the originally advocated approach towards the opposite proposition, i.e. that once English law as the law of the forum has classified the type of defect as one of formalities (governed by the law of the place of celebration) or as a personal defect (governed by the law of the domicile), the effect of the defect on the validity of the marriage should be determined by the law of the forum.[460] This departure is warranted in particular by the emergence of the concept of "non-marriage" in English law, and by the recognition of the fact that there may be situations where the classification employed by the proper law differs significantly from the terminology used in English law. Thus, for example, the governing law may not recognise terms such as "void" or "voidable" but simply characterise a marriage as "invalid" or "non-existent", with the meaning of these words corresponding variably to a "void" marriage, "voidable" marriage or even a "non-marriage" in English law terms.[461] The point is well illustrated by the decisions in *Burns v Burns*[462] and *Asaad v Kurter*.[463] Both cases concerned the formal validity of marriage. In *Burns v Burns*, a "marriage" ceremony took place in a hot air balloon in California. As a result of the failure to comply with the formal requirements of Californian law, the marriage was regarded as "invalid" under the law of the place of celebration. Such a marriage might give

---

[455] Law Commission Working Paper No 89 (1985), para 5.47.

[456] But see, with regard to sham marriages, *Hakeem v Hussain* 2003 SLT 515, and on appeal, *H v H* 2005 SLT 1025 (especially per Lord Penrose, at [28] and [35]); Clive, *Husband and Wife*, para 07-047; and Family Law (Scotland) Act 2006, ss 2 and 38, supra, p 992.

[457] Supra, pp 984–5.

[458] The 14th edition of this book, p 984. See also *De Reneville v De Reneville* [1948] P 100 at 114; *Casey v Casey* [1949] P 420 at 429–30; *Merker v Merker* [1963] P 283 at 297; *Szechter v Szechter* [1971] P 286 at 294; and Law Commission Working Paper No 89 (1985), para 5.53.

[459] See the 14th edition of this book, p 984.

[460] Cf Morris (1970) 19 ICLQ 424, 427–8.

[461] See *Burns v Burns* [2007] EWHC 2492 (Fam), and *Asaad v Kurter* [2013] EWHC 3852 (Fam) at [84].

[462] [2007] EWHC 2492 (Fam).

[463] [2013] EWHC 3852 (Fam).

rise to remedies under the concept of "putative marriage"; however, it was clear that the marriage was neither void nor voidable, both of which were specifically defined in Californian law. It was argued that, as the law of the place of celebration did not categorise the marriage as void or voidable, the English court could not grant a decree of nullity. Coleridge J, however, rejected this argument and held that "once the foreign law had determined whether it is or is not a valid marriage, it is for the *lex fori* to decide its implications and what remedies are available to the petitioning spouse".[464] He then awarded a decree of nullity, making it clear that the English court was not precluded from granting a decree of nullity solely on the ground that the governing law did not categorise the marriage as void under its own terminology. This approach was approved and refined by Moylan J in *Asaad v Kurter*. Here the marriage celebrated in Syria had failed to comply with the formal requirements of Syrian law. As a result, it was not a valid marriage under the law of the place of celebration; which, however, had no separate concepts of a marriage being void, voidable or a non-marriage. In these circumstances, was the English court to categorise the marriage as a void marriage or a non-marriage? To answer this question, Moylan J proposed the following test: "(a) whether the defect makes the marriage valid or invalid is a matter to be determined by the applicable law, being in the case of the formalities of marriage the law of the place where the marriage was celebrated; (b) the English court must determine the effect of the foreign law by reference to English law concepts; if the applicable foreign law determines the effect of the defect by reference to concepts which clearly (or sufficiently) equate to the same concepts in English law then the English court is likely to apply those concepts; if the foreign law does not, then it is for the English court to decide which English law concept applies; and (c) in any event, it is for the English court to decide what remedy under English law, if any, is available."[465] In applying the above test to the facts of the present case, Moylan J concluded that the ceremony in Syria had not been "so deficient" that it could be characterised in English law terms as a non-marriage. Instead, it amounted to a void a marriage in English law terms and, as such, entitled the petitioner to a decree of nullity.

The test suggested by Moylan J can be seen as a compromise between the approach originally advocated in this book and the view that it is for English law as the law of the forum and not for the foreign governing law to determine the effect of the defect on the validity of the marriage. It is a very sensible approach. Indeed, it appears entirely appropriate to employ a functional method in determining the effect of the defect on the validity of the marriage. Where the applicable law uses the same or sufficiently similar concepts and ascribes them the same meaning as English law, the English court is presumed to apply those concepts. In such circumstances, characterisation by the law of the forum will lead to the same result as characterisation by the foreign governing law, and, from the practical perspective, it is not strictly necessary to establish which approach is being followed. However, in all other situations, including those where an identical expression has a different meaning in English law terms, the English court ought to apply English law to determine which concept is applicable.

(g) The law to govern the effect of a nullity decree[466]

The effect of any decree of nullity is a matter for the law of the forum which granted it.[467] So, if an English court grants a decree annulling a marriage, it is for English law, as the law of the forum governing procedure, to determine the effect of its own decree. That being so, the law of the domicile or of the place of celebration, depending on the type of defect in question,

---

[464] *Burns v Burns* [2007] EWHC 2492 (Fam) at [45].
[465] *Asaad v Kurter* [2013] EWHC 3852 (Fam) at [97].
[466] North, op cit, p 135; Law Commission Working Paper No 89 (1985), paras 5.54–5.55.
[467] For the effect of a foreign decree, see infra, pp 1035–6.

will decide whether the marriage is void or voidable, but English law will decide whether, in the light of that classification, the decree should have retrospective effect.

(c) Recognition[468]

(i) Introduction

Until 1972, recognition of foreign divorces and legal separations was governed by common law rules. These rules were substantially, but not wholly, replaced by statutory grounds of recognition in the Recognition of Divorces and Legal Separations Act 1971, which was passed to implement the Convention on the Recognition of Divorces and Legal Separations adopted in 1970 by the Hague Conference on Private International Law. There had previously been criticism of the common law rules, and the implementation of the Convention in the 1971 Act provided an opportunity to introduce reforms rather broader in scope than the Convention required. However, the 1971 Act did not extend to the recognition of foreign annulments, which continued to be governed by common law recognition rules. The uncertainty of those rules and the fact that different regimes applied to divorce and nullity recognition was a source of criticism[469] which led the Law Commission, in 1984, to examine the varied rules for the recognition of divorces, annulments and legal separations and to propose that essentially the same statutory rules should apply in the case of all three matrimonial causes, and that those rules should be based on the Recognition of Divorces and Legal Separations Act 1971, subject to a number of amendments.[470] These recommendations were substantially carried into effect by Part II of the Family Law Act 1986.[471]

The general effect of the statutory rules in the 1986 Act is that, subject to a few minor exceptions mentioned later,[472] the same recognition rules apply to all three matrimonial causes. Furthermore, the common law rules of nullity recognition,[473] and those common law rules relating to the recognition of divorces and legal separations which survived the 1971 Act,[474] were replaced by the statutory regime of the 1986 Act, irrespective of where the divorce, annulment or legal separation was obtained and of whether it was obtained before or after the 1986 Act came into force.[475]

Different rules were provided in the 1986 Act for the recognition of divorces, annulments and judicial separations granted in other jurisdictions within the British Isles[476] and of divorces, annulments and legal separations[477] obtained in politically foreign countries. The 1986 Act governed the recognition of all overseas divorces, annulments and legal separations until 1 March 2001, when, as has been explained above,[478] the Brussels II Regulation took

---

[468] McClean, *Recognition of Family Judgments in the Commonwealth* (1983), Chapters 2 and 3; Gordon, *Foreign Divorces: English Law and Practice* (1988).

[469] Eg Carter (1979) 50 BYBIL 250, 252; Collier [1979] CLJ 289, 290.

[470] Law Com No 137 (1984).

[471] For discussion of Part II of the 1986 Act, see Pearl [1987] CLJ 35. The major difference between the Law Commission proposals and the 1986 Act is that the latter introduces separate, and more restrictive, recognition rules for foreign extra-judicial divorces obtained where there have been no judicial or other proceedings, discussed infra, p 1012 et seq.

[472] Infra, p 1005 et seq.

[473] See 10th edn of this book, pp 406–16; and see Law Com No 137 (1984), Pt II.

[474] Ibid, pp 366–9.

[475] This is subject to rules preserving the effect of common law recognition in very limited circumstances, infra, p 1034.

[476] This means the United Kingdom, the Channel Islands and the Isle of Man: see Interpretation Act 1978, Sch 1.

[477] The differing use of "judicial separation" and "legal separation" in the 1986 Act is discussed infra, p 1011.

[478] Supra, p 954.

effect. With effect from 1 March 2005, account has had to be taken of the Brussels II *bis* Regulation.[479] Now, the rules for recognition of divorces, annulments and legal separations differ according to the identity of the state (the court of origin) in which the decree or judgment was issued: (i) a court elsewhere in the British Isles; (ii) a court or other authority in another EU Member State, except Denmark; or (iii) a court or other authority in a non-EU Member State, or in Denmark. These three situations must be considered separately.

(ii) Divorces, annulments and judicial separations granted elsewhere in the British Isles

Any decree of divorce, nullity, or judicial separation granted by a court of civil jurisdiction[480] in any part of the British Isles must be recognised in any part of the United Kingdom,[481] irrespective of when it was granted.[482] So, the English courts must[483] recognise any divorce, etc granted elsewhere in the British Isles and, similarly, such divorces, etc must be recognised in Scotland and Northern Ireland.[484]

Although such divorces, etc cannot be denied recognition on jurisdictional grounds,[485] two qualifications to recognition are provided. First, an English court can refuse recognition to a divorce or a judicial separation granted elsewhere in the British Isles at a time when there was no subsisting marriage between the parties, according to English law, including English rules of private international law.[486] This would cover such situations as where a marriage in England was invalid under English domestic law or a marriage abroad failed to satisfy English rules of private international law. In such circumstances, the English court has a discretion[487] to refuse recognition to, say, a Scottish divorce decree dissolving that marriage. It may be noted that this provision does not apply to recognition of nullity decrees for which, given the invalidity of the marriage, it might be thought inappropriate. However, the second qualification does extend to other British nullity decrees, as well as to divorces and judicial

---

[479] Ibid.

[480] The significance of this is that extra-judicial divorces, etc are excluded: see Family Law Act 1986, s 44(1); Law Com No 137 (1984), para 4.14, and infra, p 1012 et seq. There is one minor exception to the denial of recognition to extra-judicial divorces obtained in England, relating to those obtained before 1974, see infra, p 1034. See *Solovyev v Solovyeva* [2014] EWFC 1546—divorce obtained through an administrative procedure at the Russian Consulate in London could not be regarded as having been granted by "a court of civil jurisdiction", and had to be viewed as an English divorce because the Consulate of a foreign state is to be treated as English and not foreign territory. Supra, p 896.

[481] Family Law Act 1986, ss 44(2), 54(1). S 44 apparently has not been affected by the introduction of Brussels II *bis* (see SI 2005/265, reg 8), in spite of Art 66 (Member States with two or more legal systems) of that Regulation (see Crawford and Carruthers, para 12-28; Morris, para 9-035; and McEleavy (2004) 53 ICLQ 605, 615).

[482] Family Law Act 1986, s 52(1)(a), (3). This marks a change from the Recognition of Divorces and Legal Separations Act 1971 which only applied to the recognition of British divorces granted after the Act came into force. There are a number of transitional provisions which apply both to the recognition of other British and overseas divorces, etc, and which are discussed in the 13th edn of this book (1999), p 820.

[483] Subject to s 51 of the 1986 Act, infra, p 1024 et seq.

[484] The Isle of Man has enacted legislation similar to Part II of the 1986 Act: the Recognition of Divorces etc Act 1987; and there is also legislation, based on similar rules in the Recognition of Divorces and Legal Separations Act 1971, s 1, in the Channel Islands, see North, op cit, pp 309–10, 324–6, 343–6.

[485] Since 1974, the bases of divorce jurisdiction have been the same in England, Scotland and Northern Ireland: Domicile and Matrimonial Proceedings Act 1973, Parts II and III, as amended, and Matrimonial Causes (Northern Ireland) Order, SI 1978/1045, as amended. However, until 1974, there were significant differences between England and Scotland. The Scottish courts, but not the English, would grant a decree of divorce where a respondent was domiciled within the jurisdiction at the time of his adultery but not at the time of the proceedings: *Clark v Clark* 1967 SC 269; North, op cit, pp 26–7, 167–8. So a Scottish divorce granted in such circumstances before 1974 will be recognised in England.

[486] 1986 Act, s 51(2)(a).

[487] Under the 1971 Act, s 8(1)(a) refusal of recognition was mandatory. For the reasons for the change to a discretionary rule, see Law Com No 137 (1984) paras 4.6 and 6.66, and infra, p 1026.

separations.[488] It gives the English court a discretion to deny recognition on a *res judicata* basis, ie if the other British decree was granted at a time when it was irreconcilable with a decision on the validity of the marriage previously given either by an English court or given elsewhere and entitled to be recognised in England. So a Scottish decree annulling or dissolving an English marriage can be denied recognition if there is already an English decree, or a South African decree recognised in England, to similar effect. In the case of a divorce or judicial separation, if there is a previous decision ending the marriage, the court's discretion can be exercised under either of the two heads just mentioned.[489]

Because of the mandatory wording of section 44(2) of the Family Law Act 1986, which states that divorce, etc decrees granted by a court of civil jurisdiction elsewhere in the British Isles *shall be recognised* in England, such other British decisions cannot be denied recognition in England even though they may contravene the rules of natural justice or be manifestly contrary to English public policy.[490] The justification for this is that it was "thought that in such circumstances the complaining party should seek to have the decree set aside by the court which granted it,[491] or an appeal from that court, and that it would be objectionable to allow a court in another part of the British Isles[492] to refuse to recognise the decree".[493] However, an English court is not required under Part II of the 1986 Act to recognise any findings of fault or any maintenance, custody or other ancillary order made in the other British proceedings.[494]

(iii) Divorces, annulments and legal separations obtained in another EU Member State, except Denmark

(a) Introduction
As has been stated previously in this book, the principle of mutual recognition of judgments has been fixed as the cornerstone for the creation of a European judicial area.[495] Alongside the objective of the free movement of judgments within the Member States in civil and commercial matters, the EU has set the objective of creating an area of freedom, security and justice, in which the free movement of persons is ensured. "To this end, the Community is to adopt, among others, measures in the field of judicial co-operation in civil matters that are necessary for the proper functioning of the internal market."[496]

Article 1 (scope) of the Brussels II *bis* Regulation provides that, "1. This Regulation shall apply, whatever the nature of the court or tribunal, in civil matters relating to: (a) divorce, legal separation or marriage annulment."[497] It is interesting to compare this wording with that in Recital (9) of Brussels II, ie: "The scope of this Regulation should cover civil proceedings and non-judicial proceedings in matrimonial matters in certain States, and exclude purely religious procedures. It should therefore be provided that the reference to 'courts'

---

[488] S 51(1)(a).

[489] The two grounds for denying recognition are examined more fully in the context of the recognition of overseas divorces, etc, infra, p 1024 et seq.

[490] These are reasons for denying recognition to divorces, etc obtained in other, foreign countries: Brussels II *bis*, Art 22(a) (infra, pp 1004–5), and 1986 Act, s 51(3), infra, p 1025 et seq.

[491] See *Gaffney v Gaffney* [1975] IR 133.

[492] This must mean "the United Kingdom".

[493] Law Com No 34 (1970), p 43; and see Law Com No 137 (1984), para 4.7.

[494] 1986 Act, s 51(5); for recognition of maintenance and custody orders generally, see infra, p 1078 et seq, p 1126 et seq.

[495] See generally supra, Chapter 17.

[496] Brussels II *bis*, Recital (1).

[497] Cf Recital (7): "The scope of this Regulation covers civil matters, whatever the nature of the court or tribunal."

includes all the authorities, judicial or otherwise, with jurisdiction in matrimonial matters."[498] According to the Explanatory Report on the Brussels II Convention, the term "civil" was to be understood not only as a means of including administrative (ie non-judicial) proceedings, but also as a means of excluding all merely religious proceedings.[499] The Report expressly states that: "The Convention excludes from its scope religious proceedings, which may become more frequent as a result of immigration (Muslim and Hindu marriages, for instance)."[500] Therefore, Brussels II *bis*, in covering civil matters, should be construed as applying to judicial or non-judicial (ie administrative) proceedings, but not to religious proceedings. All religious divorces, regardless of the country in which they are obtained, should be treated as falling under the scheme of recognition in Part II of the Family Law Act 1986.[501]

(b) General principle of recognition

It is stated in Brussels II *bis* that: "The recognition and enforcement of judgments given in a Member State should be based on the principle of mutual trust and the grounds for non-recognition should be kept to the minimum necessary."[502] Accordingly, Article 21 of the Regulation[503] states that;

1. A judgment[504] given in a Member State shall be recognised in the other Member States without any special procedure being required.
2. In particular, and without prejudice to paragraph 3, no special procedure shall be required for updating the civil-status records of a Member State on the basis of a judgment relating to divorce, legal separation or marriage annulment given in another Member State, and against which no further appeal lies under the law of that Member State.[505]
3. Without prejudice to Section 4[506] of this Chapter, any interested party[507] may, in accordance with the procedures provided for in Section 2[508] of this Chapter, apply for a decision that the judgment be or not be recognised . . .
4. When the recognition of a judgment is raised as an incidental question in a court of a Member State, that court may determine that issue.

---

[498] Cf Art 1, Brussels II: "This Regulation shall apply to: (a) civil proceedings relating to divorce, legal separation or marriage annulment; . . ."

[499] Borras, *Explanatory Report*, para 20.

[500] Ibid, para 20B.

[501] Infra, p 1012. Cf Dicey, Morris and Collins, para 18-101; and Crawford and Carruthers, para 12-41.

[502] Recital (21).

[503] Applicable only to legal proceedings instituted, to documents formally drawn up or registered as authentic instruments and to agreements concluded between the parties after 1 March 2005: Arts 64 and 72. Transitional provisions are set out in Art 64.

[504] Meaning a divorce, legal separation or marriage annulment pronounced by a court of a Member State (including all the authorities in a Member State with jurisdiction in the matters falling within the scope of the Regulation pursuant to Art 1), whatever the judgment may be called, including a decree, order or decision: Art 2(1) and (4). Documents which have been formally drawn up or registered as authentic instruments and are enforceable in one Member State and also agreements between the parties that are enforceable in the Member State in which they were concluded shall be recognised and declared enforceable under the same conditions as judgments: Art 46. See Borras, *Explanatory Report*, paras 60 and 61.

[505] Article 27 (Stay of proceedings) provides that: "1. A court of a Member State in which recognition is sought of a judgment given in another Member State may stay the proceedings if an ordinary appeal against the judgment has been lodged. 2. A court of a Member State in which recognition is sought of a judgment given in Ireland or the United Kingdom may stay the proceedings if enforcement is suspended in the Member State of origin by reason of an appeal." Cf Brussels I (Recast) Regulation, Art 38(a).

[506] Enforceability of certain judgments concerning rights of access and of certain judgments which require the return of the child.

[507] See Borras, *Explanatory Report*, para 65: the concept of interested party is to be interpreted "in the broad sense under the national law applicable and may include the public prosecutor or other similar bodies where permitted in the State in which the judgment is to be recognised or contested".

[508] Application for a declaration of enforceability.

(c) Grounds of non-recognition

Article 22[509] provides that a judgment relating to a divorce, legal separation or marriage annulment shall not be recognised:

(a) if such recognition is manifestly contrary to the public policy of the Member State in which recognition is sought;[510]

(b) where it was given in default of appearance, if the respondent was not served with the document which instituted the proceedings or with an equivalent document in sufficient time and in such a way as to enable the respondent to arrange for his or her defence[511] unless it is determined that the respondent has accepted the judgment unequivocally;[512]

(c) if it is irreconcilable with a judgment[513] given in proceedings between the same parties in the Member State in which recognition is sought;[514] or

(d) if it is irreconcilable with an earlier judgment given in another Member State[515] or in a non-Member State between the same parties, provided that the earlier judgment fulfils the conditions necessary for its recognition in the Member State in which recognition is sought.[516]

These grounds for non-recognition are very similar to those contained in Article 45(1)(a)-(d) of the Brussels I (Recast) Regulation.[517]

Perhaps the most controversial of the Article 22 defences is that of public policy.[518] As with the Brussels I (Recast) Regulation, the wording of Article 22(a) strongly suggests that the recognising court is to apply its own concept of public policy when considering this defence. National courts have a degree of latitude in determining the meaning of the concept, but it is to be expected that they will give it an interpretation which is appropriate in the context and spirit of the Regulation. The public policy defence should be used only sparingly, in exceptional cases, as is underscored by use of the word "manifestly".[519] It is recognition of the judgment, rather than the judgment itself, which must be contrary to public policy.

One possible challenge to recognition under Article 22(a) is in relation to the divorce, legal separation or annulment of a same sex marriage.[520] Neither "marriage" nor "divorce" is defined in Brussels II *bis*,[521] however, there is nothing in the Regulation to suggest that it applies to

---

[509] By implication, Art 22 provides the only defences to recognition.

[510] See also Arts 24, 25 and 26, infra, p 1005. Cf Brussels I (Recast) Regulation, Art 45(1)(a), discussed supra, p 626 et seq.

[511] Cf Brussels I (Recast) Regulation, Art 45(1)(b), discussed supra, p 632 et seq.

[512] Eg by remarrying.

[513] Regardless of whether the judgment in the Member State in which recognition is sought pre- or post-dates the judgment given in the Member State of origin; *contra* Art 22(d).

[514] Cf Brussels I (Recast) Regulation, Art 45(1)(c), discussed supra, p 639 et seq. The situation envisaged here is, eg, where the Member State in which recognition is sought, having already issued a divorce decree in respect of a couple, subsequently is asked to recognise a legal separation in respect of the same couple granted by a court or other authority in another Member State (Borras, *Explanatory Report*, para 71).

[515] The *lis pendens* provision in Art 19 normally will prevent a judgment being given in the court second seised, but it will not do so if that court does not accept that the parties are the same.

[516] Cf Brussels I (Recast) Regulation, Art 45(1)(d), discussed supra, pp 641–2.

[517] Supra, p 625 et seq.

[518] See Peruzzetto, "The Exception of Public Policy in Family Law within the European Legal System" in Meeusen, Pertegas, Straetmans and Swennen (eds), *International Family Law for the European Union* (2007).

[519] Unfortunately, the Borras *Explanatory Report* provides no examples of what might be a reasonable use of the public policy defence. It is stated, however, that, "the States are extremely sensitive on this issue on account of the major discrepancies between their laws on divorce. Those Member States in which dissolution of the marriage bond is easiest fear that their judgments may not be recognised in Member States with more stringent rules" (para 69).

[520] See supra, p 1045 et seq.

[521] McEleavy (2004) 53 ICLQ 605, at 607, refers to the "gender neutral terminology" of the Regulation.

the divorce, etc of a marriage of a same sex couple. Academic opinion on this issue appears to be divided, with some authors suggesting that same sex marriage is covered by Brussels II *bis*,[522] whilst others arguing that it is not.[523] Were the former view to be correct, it would be unclear to what extent the courts of the Member States that do not formally recognize same sex relationships would have discretion to refuse recognition under Article 22 (bearing in mind the terms of Articles 24 and 25, discussed below). Although there is clearly potential for a reference to be made to the CJEU for a preliminary ruling on this point of interpretation, the English legislator seems to have taken a clear view on the matter, namely, that the divorce, etc of a same sex relationship does not fall within the scope of Brussels II *bis*.[524]

(d) Prohibition of review of jurisdiction of the court of origin

Article 24 of Brussels II *bis* narrates the important principle that: "The jurisdiction of the court of the Member State of origin may not be reviewed.[525] The test of public policy referred to in [Article 22(a)] may not be applied to the rules relating to jurisdiction set out in Articles [3 to 7]." It cannot be argued that the court of origin misapplied the jurisdictional rules in Brussels II *bis*, or its national rules of residual jurisdiction. In particular, this prohibition cannot be evaded by using the public policy defence.

(e) Differences in applicable law

By virtue of Article 25: "The recognition of a judgment may not be refused because the law[526] of the Member State in which recognition is sought would not allow divorce, legal separation or marriage annulment on the same facts." This provision is the counterbalance to Article 22(a), and is:

> designed to meet the concerns of States with more tolerant internal provisions on divorce who fear that the judgments given by their courts might not be recognised in another State because they are based on grounds unknown in the legislation of the State in which recognition is sought. The provision therefore limits indiscriminate use of public policy.[527]

(f) Non-review as to substance

Article 26 lays down the classic rule that under no circumstances may a judgment be reviewed as to its substance.[528] This buttresses the principle stated in Article 25, to the effect that recognition cannot be refused solely on the ground that there is a discrepancy between the legal rules applied, respectively, by the court of origin and by the recognising court. It cannot be alleged that the court of origin made a mistake of fact or of law. Procedural irregularities in the court of origin, however, can be examined in order to establish a defence under Article 22.

(iv) Divorces, annulments and legal separations obtained in a non-EU Member State, or in Denmark

(a) Introduction

Part II of the Family Law Act 1986 deals with a range of matters relating to the recognition in England of divorces, annulments and legal separations which have been obtained in a

---

[522] See, eg, Martiny, The impact of the EU private international law instruments on European Family Law, in Scherpe (ed), *European Family Law: Volume I* (2016), pp 262–92, 269.

[523] Eg Dicey, Morris and Collins, para 18-027 and Clarkson and Hill, para 8.54.

[524] See, respectively, separate provisions in domestic law for recognition in England of a judgment on dissolution, annulment or separation of a civil partnership or a same sex marriage granted in an EU Member State: SI 2005/3334, rr 6–12, and SI 2014/543, rr 3–9. Discussed infra, pp 1044–5 and 1048 respectively.

[525] Cf Brussels I (Recast) Regulation, Art 45(3), discussed supra, p 643 et seq.

[526] Including its rules of private international law: Borras, *Explanatory Report*, para 76.

[527] Borras, *Explanatory Report*, para 76.

[528] Cf Brussels I (Recast) Regulation, Art 52, discussed supra, p 644.

country[529] outside the British Isles, other than those in respect of which provision as to recognition is made by Brussels II *bis*. Essentially, Part II applies to divorces, etc obtained in a state which is not an EU Member State, or in Denmark; these are referred to in the 1986 Act as "overseas divorces", etc,[530] and references in this section of the chapter to "overseas divorces" or "foreign divorces" should be construed in like manner. No distinction is drawn in the 1986 Act, as there was in the 1971 Act,[531] between different kinds of foreign divorce, etc dependent on whether their recognition fell within or outside the Hague Convention of 1970. The consequence, as recommended by the Law Commission,[532] is a less complex set of recognition rules, especially in relation to issues of jurisdiction.[533] The areas to be examined here include the jurisdictional bases for recognition, the requirement of effectiveness of the divorce, etc in the country where it was obtained, the grounds on which recognition may be denied and the special problems and rules relating to different kinds of extra-judicial divorce.

(b) General matters

The recognition rules laid down in Part II are exclusive.[534] It is not possible for the recognition of a foreign divorce, annulment or legal separation to be governed by common law recognition rules, whether or not it was obtained[535] before or after the 1986 Act came into effect.[536] As a result, the extension of the statutory regime for recognition to foreign annulments has the effect that it is now clear that an annulment of a void marriage will not be recognised on the basis that it was obtained in the country where the marriage was celebrated.[537] Furthermore, the general rule is that recognition is mandatory,[538] provided that the requirements of Part II (as to jurisdiction, etc) are satisfied and that one of the statutory grounds for denying recognition[539] is not relevant.

(c) Jurisdictional rules

Section 46(1) of the 1986 Act provides a number of jurisdictional grounds for the recognition of overseas divorces, annulments and legal separations which have been obtained by judicial or other proceedings.[540]

(i) Domicile

An overseas divorce, etc will be recognised if either party, whether petitioner or respondent, to the marriage was domiciled in the country where it was obtained[541] at the date of the commencement of the foreign proceedings.[542] In the case of the recognition of foreign divorces and legal separations, this involves a very slight limitation on the recognition rules available under the 1971 Act where it was possible for a divorce, etc to be recognised in England if its validity was recognised in the country of each spouse's domicile, though obtained in

---

[529] The meaning of "country" is discussed more fully, infra, pp 1009–10.

[530] S 45, as amended by SI 2005/265, reg 17. Recognition by virtue of any other statute is preserved: s 45(1)(b), discussed infra, p 1012.

[531] Contrast ss 2–5 with s 6 of the 1971 Act; and see North, op cit, pp 172–6.

[532] Law Com No 137 (1984), paras 6.3–6.6.

[533] Though the eradication of complexity has been somewhat offset by the decision, not recommended by the Law Commission, to have special rules for the recognition of some extra-judicial divorces, infra, p 1012 et seq.

[534] S 45.

[535] S 52, subject to certain saving provisions, discussed infra, p 1034.

[536] S 52(1).

[537] As in *Merker v Merker* [1963] P 283; Law Com No 137 (1984), paras 6.33–6.34.

[538] S 45.

[539] S 51, infra, p 1024 et seq.

[540] See the definition of "proceedings" in s 54. The jurisdictional rules relevant to extra-judicial divorces obtained without proceedings are discussed infra, p 1012 et seq.

[541] S 46(1)(b)(ii).

[542] S 46(3)(a).

neither.[543] The Law Commission[544] concluded that there was no case for the retention of such an extended rule relating to domicile, given that there is no equivalent rule in relation to the other jurisdictional heads of habitual residence and nationality,[545] and that the old rule was inequitable if one of the spouses was domiciled in England and the other abroad. In such a case the divorce, etc would only be recognised if recognised in England, which was the very matter in issue; so recognition would have to be refused.[546] There is, therefore, no counterpart of such an extended domiciliary rule in the 1986 Act[547] where there are foreign proceedings.[548]

It has been assumed so far, as is usual in private international law, that domicile means domicile in the English sense. However, section 46(1)(b) requires an overseas divorce, etc to be recognised if either party is domiciled in the foreign country in either the English or the foreign sense of domicile,[549] this latter being a ground of jurisdiction provided in the 1970 Hague Convention and in the 1971 Act. Hence an overseas divorce may have to be recognised on the basis of such foreign concept of domicile,[550] even though neither spouse was domiciled in the foreign country in the English sense of the term.[551]

It is possible that a country may have different concepts of domicile for different purposes;[552] and so section 46(5) of the 1986 Act makes clear that the concept of domicile relevant for recognition purposes is that used in the foreign country "in family matters".[553]

(ii) Habitual residence
An overseas divorce will be recognised if it was obtained in a country in which, at the time of the commencement of the proceedings,[554] either spouse was habitually resident as determined under English law.[555] No length of period of residence is specified or required;[556] and jurisdiction may be founded on the habitual residence of either spouse, whether petitioner or respondent.

---

[543] Recognition of Divorces and Legal Separations Act 1971, s 6(3)(b); based on the common law decision in *Armitage v A-G* [1906] P 135.

[544] Law Com No 137 (1984), paras 6.27–6.30.

[545] Infra. Though the rules in the 1986 Act in relation to domicile are in other respects much wider than those in s 6 of the 1971 Act, where the domicile connection had to be satisfied in relation to both parties: see Law Com No 137 (1984), paras 6.21–6.26.

[546] See North, op cit, p 185.

[547] Though there are saving provisions which preserve the validity of divorces and legal separations obtained before the 1986 Act came into effect and which would have been recognised under the now abandoned rule: s 52(5)(b), (e), infra, p 1034.

[548] The common law rule is retained in cases where there are no proceedings: s 46(2), infra, p 1021 et seq.

[549] S 46(5). The same applies where there are no proceedings, infra, p 1021 et seq.

[550] See *Lawrence v Lawrence* [1985] Fam 106 at 121.

[551] Recognition does not depend, under the 1986 Act, on the foreign court having assumed jurisdiction on the basis of domicile.

[552] Indeed, England has a special concept of domicile for the purposes of the Civil Jurisdiction and Judgments Acts 1982 and 1991, supra, p 198 et seq.

[553] This is consistent with Art 3 of the 1970 Hague Convention. It also involves dropping the requirement, to be found in s 3(2) of the 1971 Act, that the foreign country uses its concept of domicile as a ground of jurisdiction in divorce, etc. The Law Commission considered such a limitation to be ineffective, unnecessary and illogical, especially in the case of extra-judicial divorces: Law Com No 137 (1984), para 6.18.

[554] This head is inapplicable if there are no proceedings, infra, p 1021 et seq.

[555] S 46(1)(b)(i), (3)(a). See, eg, *Cruse v Chittum* [1974] 2 All ER 940; *Kendall v Kendall* [1977] Fam 208; *Joyce v Joyce* [1979] Fam 93 at 105; *Quazi v Quazi* [1980] AC 744 at 788, 821; Social Security Decision No R (P) 2/90.

[556] Cf the jurisdictional test in Pt II of the Domicile and Matrimonial Proceedings Act 1973, supra, pp 956–60, where the meaning of "habitual residence" is discussed.

(iii) Nationality

A similar rule applies in the case of nationality, so that divorces, etc obtained in a country of which, at the time of the proceedings,[557] either party was a national will be recognised in England.[558] No definition of nationality is provided,[559] but there seems little doubt that, in the case of a person with dual nationality, recognition will be given to divorces, etc obtained in either country of the nationality.[560]

(d) The time at which the jurisdictional rules must be satisfied

As we have seen, the general rule is that the jurisdictional connection must be satisfied at the date of the commencement of the foreign proceedings by which the divorce, etc was obtained.[561] There are, however, two exceptions to this. The first is relevant only to the recognition of foreign annulments. It is possible both in England, and elsewhere, for an annulment of a void marriage to be obtained by a person other than a spouse and for that to be done after the death of either or both spouses. English jurisdictional rules make special provision for such a case,[562] as does section 46(4) of the 1986 Act in the case of recognition of an overseas annulment. If the annulment was obtained after the death of a party to the marriage, the jurisdictional requirements of domicile, habitual residence or nationality are satisfied if the appropriate connection existed at the date of the death.[563]

The second exception concerns cross-proceedings, where it is sufficient if the jurisdictional grounds of habitual residence, nationality and domicile in the English or the foreign sense existed either at the date of the original proceedings or of the cross-proceedings.[564] This applies irrespective of which proceedings led to the foreign divorce, etc. Of course, even if this special jurisdictional provision is satisfied, it is necessary to satisfy all the other requirements of Part II of the 1986 Act for the divorce, etc to be recognised.[565]

(e) Effectiveness

Not only must one of the various jurisdictional requirements be satisfied at the relevant time, but it is also necessary that the overseas divorce, etc be "effective under the law of the country in which it was obtained".[566] This requirement of effectiveness was also to be found in the 1971 Act[567] but did not there extend to recognition on the jurisdictional basis of domicile in the English sense. Following the recommendations of the Law Commission,[568] this requirement applies, under the 1986 Act, also to the domicile basis[569] and is extended, as is the whole of Part II of the 1986 Act, to the recognition of overseas annulments. This marks a change from the common law rules as to nullity recognition where, for example, a German

---

[557] Again, this head is inapplicable if there are no proceedings, infra, p 1022.

[558] S 46(1)(b)(iii), 3(a); see, eg, *Broit v Broit* 1972 SLT (Notes) 32; *Quazi v Quazi* [1980] AC 744 at 805, 813, 821; *Lawrence v Lawrence* [1985] Fam 106 at 121.

[559] Though see s 54(2).

[560] *Torok v Torok* [1973] 1 WLR 1066 at 1069.

[561] S 46(3)(a).

[562] Domicile and Matrimonial Proceedings Act 1973, s 5(3)(b), supra, p 965.

[563] See Law Com No 137 (1984), para 6.32; s 46(4).

[564] S 47(1)(a).

[565] S 47 (1)(b); and see Law Com No 137 (1984), para 6.39.

[566] S 46(1)(a). See *Kellman v Kellman* [2000] 1 FLR 785; and *Duhur-Johnson v Duhur-Johnson* [2005] 2 FLR 1042.

[567] S 2(b).

[568] Law Com No 137 (1984), paras 6.12–6.13.

[569] An example of a divorce recognised under common law domicile rules where the effectiveness requirement would not have been satisfied is provided by *Har-Shefi v Har-Shefi (No 2)* [1953] P 220; though see now the 1986 Act, ss 44(1), 52(5), infra, pp 1019–20.

decree was recognised in England even though it was regarded in Germany as invalid and of no effect there.[570]

Various examples of legal ineffectiveness might be provided, as, for instance, where a foreign divorce does not, in the foreign country, dissolve a marriage until a specified period has elapsed,[571] or whilst an appeal is pending,[572] or until a decree absolute is pronounced.[573] It is also possible[574] that, under the law of the foreign country, the divorce, etc might be regarded as ineffective there because that country's rules as to service on the parties or as to the jurisdiction of its courts had not been satisfied, even though the jurisdictional requirements of the 1986 Act[575] had been. This might be so even if the procedural defects did not fall within the heads listed in the 1986 Act[576] as grounds for denying recognition.[577]

(f) Meaning of "country"

So far, in examining the jurisdictional and other rules of Part II of the 1986 Act, it has been assumed that the requirement of a connection with the "country" in which the divorce, etc was obtained causes no difficulty.[578] There are, however, political countries which comprise different territories[579] and those territories may have different substantive or jurisdictional rules for obtaining divorces, etc. There were problems with the 1971 Act in deciding whether some or all of the references in that Act to "country" meant the political state or the individual territory.[580] In order to try to resolve these difficulties, section 49 of the 1986 Act[581] provides express modifications of the provisions of Part II of that Act in those cases where, in a country comprising different territories, there are different systems of law in force in relation to divorce, annulment or legal separation.[582] The general approach is to say that, in such cases, any requirement of domicile (in the English or foreign senses) or habitual residence in a country, and indeed effectiveness under the law of that country, means domicile or habitual residence in an individual territory.[583] This means that, as each American state has its own divorce, etc laws, New York or California is to be treated as a separate country for the purposes of determining domicile or habitual residence. On the other hand, Canada

---

[570] *Merker v Merker* [1963] P 283. It might be argued that a foreign decree, though invalid in the country where granted, is effective there until actually set aside: *Kendall v Kendall* [1977] Fam 208 at 214.

[571] Eg *Martin v Buret* 1938 SLT 479.

[572] Eg *Torok v Torok* [1973] 1 WLR 1066; cf Social Security Decision R (P) 2/90, p 6.

[573] Eg *De Thoren v Wall* (1876) 3 R (HL) 28. A further example in the case of an extra-judicial divorce by *talak* might be a delay whilst conciliation proceedings are continuing: National Insurance Decision Nos R(G) 5/74; R(G) 2/75.

[574] North, op cit, pp 175–6.

[575] S 46(1)(b), supra, p 1006 et seq; see, eg, *Papadopoulos v Papadopoulos* [1930] P 55.

[576] S 51, infra, p 1024 et seq; see, eg, *Pemberton v Hughes* [1899] 1 Ch 781.

[577] Particular problems of effectiveness relating to extra-judicial divorces are discussed, infra, p 1020 et seq.

[578] Part II of the 1986 Act does not define "country" apart from saying that it includes a colony or other dependent territory of the United Kingdom, but that a person is to be treated as a national of such a territory only if it has a law of citizenship or nationality separate from that of the United Kingdom and he is a citizen or national of that territory under that law: s 54(2).

[579] Eg the USA, Canada, Australia, the United Kingdom.

[580] North, op cit, pp 173–5, 177, 179, 181; Law Com No 137 (1984), para 6.15.

[581] Following recommendations made in Law Com No 137 (1984), para 6.16.

[582] S 49(1). See *Kellman v Kellman* [2000] 1 FLR 785; and *Emin v Yeldag* [2002] 1 FLR 956.

[583] S 49(2), (4), (5), amending where appropriate the main jurisdictional rules in s 46(1)(b), and also the special jurisdictional rules where there are no proceedings, in s 46(2)(b); as well as the rules for the conversion of a legal separation into a divorce (s 47(2), infra, p 1010) and relating to proof of finding of facts in the foreign proceedings (s 48, infra, pp 1010–11). Also amended are the provisions of s 52(3) and (4); but this appears to be a slip, as the appropriate provisions to be amended appear to be those in s 51(3) and (4). None of the provisions mentioned above are amended in relation to nationality, which is dealt with by s 49(3), infra.

and Australia, both also federal states, have federal divorce laws;[584] so one must ask whether in divorce proceedings a spouse was habitually resident or domiciled in Canada or Australia, rather than in an individual province or state.

Nationality as a connecting factor poses rather different problems. Federal and other non-unitary states do not have different nationality rules, depending on a person's connection with a particular territory within the state. This would suggest that a connection with a territory is satisfied for jurisdictional purposes if either party is a national of the political state as a whole. This means that if a divorce, etc is obtained in New York, it will be recognised in England even though the only relevant connection for the purposes of the 1986 Act is that one spouse is a US citizen.[585] The provisions which state that connection by domicile or habitual residence with a territory will suffice[586] do not extend to connection by nationality.

It is necessary in the case of connection by nationality, as in other cases, not only that the divorce, etc was obtained in the country of the nationality but also that it was effective "under the law of the country in which it was obtained".[587] This raises the issue as to the meaning of "country" in this latter context. If, for instance, a divorce is obtained in California by an American citizen, and the only jurisdictional test which is satisfied is that of nationality, does the divorce have to be effective in California or throughout the USA? The 1971 Act was unclear on this question and academic views differed as to the answer; but section 49(3)(a) of the 1986 Act now makes it clear that, in such a case, effectiveness "throughout the country in which [the divorce] was obtained" is necessary.[588] So, in the example just given, the Californian divorce will only be recognised in England if it is recognised throughout the USA. Indeed, it has been thought to be "absurd" to recognise a divorce obtained in one American state which would not be recognised elsewhere in the USA.[589]

(g) Two procedural issues

(i) Conversion of legal separation into divorce

Some jurisdictions permit a legal separation automatically to be converted into a divorce at the end of a prescribed period. If the legal separation would be recognised on the jurisdictional grounds[590] of habitual residence, nationality, or domicile in the English or the foreign sense, then the later divorce will be recognised even though the jurisdictional criteria cannot be satisfied at that later date.[591] The conversion must, however, be in the country where the legal separation was obtained and the new divorce must be effective under the law of that country.

(ii) Findings of fact

If any finding of fact on the basis of which jurisdiction was assumed, such as to the domicile in the foreign sense,[592] habitual residence,[593] or nationality[594] of the parties,[595] is made in

---

[584] The position would be different in Canada with regard to legal separation which, unlike divorce, is a provincial rather than a federal matter.

[585] S 46(1)(b)(iii).

[586] S 49(2), (4), (5).

[587] S 46(1)(a).

[588] There is a similar provision in s 49(3)(b) in relation to the effectiveness of the conversion into a divorce of a legal separation obtained in a country of which one party was a national.

[589] Morris (1975) 24 ICLQ 635, 641; and see Law Com No 137 (1984), para 6.16.

[590] Including the provisions as to cross-proceedings in s 47(1).

[591] S 47(2).

[592] It is not appropriate for a finding by a foreign court as to domicile in the English sense to be binding on an English court: see Law Com No 137 (1984), para 6.40.

[593] Eg *Cruse v Chittum* [1974] 2 All ER 940; cf Social Security Decision R (P) 2/90.

[594] Eg *Torok v Torok* [1973] 1 WLR 1066 at 1069.

[595] S 48(2).

the foreign divorce, etc proceedings, it shall be conclusive evidence of the fact found if both spouses took part in the proceedings.[596] In any other case, eg an *ex parte* divorce, it shall be sufficient proof of that fact unless it is challenged and the contrary is shown.[597]

(h) Meaning of divorce, annulment or legal separation

As foreign matrimonial proceedings may differ markedly from English ones, it is necessary for the English court to decide whether the foreign proceedings come within one of the categories of divorce, annulment[598] or legal separation within the meaning of Part II of the 1986 Act. It has been held, for example, that the termination of a marriage by the husband's unilateral decision to change his religion and become a Moslem, which was evidenced by a declaration before witnesses in Malaysia, could not be regarded here as either a divorce or an annulment.[599] In the case of legal separations, it should be noted that, although the rules for the recognition of other British decrees refer to decrees of "judicial separation",[600] those for recognition of separations obtained outside the British Isles refer to "legal separations".[601] A legal separation is not defined in the 1986 Act, nor indeed in the 1970 Hague Convention on which the Act is based. It must be assumed that the Act extends to all foreign decrees or orders which are similar in character to an English decree of judicial separation and, indeed, to any order or decree made by a foreign court which has the effect that the parties are no longer obliged to live together, but not the effect of dissolving the marriage. The consequence of the use of different terminology is that, for example, a non-cohabitation order made in Northern Ireland will not be recognised in England because it is not a decree of judicial separation.[602] On the other hand, had it been made outside the British Isles, it is likely to be recognised as a legal separation.[603]

(i) Irrelevance of the foreign jurisdictional rules or of the grounds for granting the divorce, etc

It should be pointed out that, as was the case at common law,[604] the grounds on which the foreign divorce, etc were obtained are irrelevant to the question of recognition.[605] It is immaterial that the divorce, etc was obtained on a ground unknown to English law. This is illustrated clearly by the fact that, at common law, a foreign nullity decree has been recognised

---

[596] S 48(1)(a), as in *Lawrence v Lawrence* [1985] Fam 106 at 121; and appearance is to be treated as taking part in proceedings: s 48(3). See *A v L (Overseas Divorce)* [2010] EWHC 460 (Fam)—for a party to a marriage to have "appeared" in judicial proceedings, for the purposes of s 48(3), there must have been "something more than mere proof of service upon him or her. There must be active participation in the proceedings by the party concerned, either in person or through a representative, or at the very least by means of some formal steps taken, at least equivalent to the entry of an appearance in English proceedings." Per Sir Mark Potter P, at [70].

[597] S 48 (1)(b); eg *Mandani v Mandani* [1984] FLR 699 at 700; *A v L (Overseas Divorce)* [2010] EWHC 460 (Fam) at [70]; and *Ivleva v Yates* [2014] EWHC 554 (Fam) at [65]. The court is not required under Part II of the 1986 Act to recognise any findings of fault made in any divorce, nullity or separation proceedings or any maintenance, custody or other ancillary order made in such proceedings: s 51(5); see *Sabbagh v Sabbagh* [1985] FLR 29. For recognition of maintenance and custody orders generally, see infra, p 1078 et seq and p 1126 et seq.

[598] A non-exclusive definition of annulment is provided in s 54(1) to include "any decree or declaration of nullity of marriage, however expressed".

[599] *Viswalingham v Viswalingham* (1979) 1 FLR 15. As the marriage was held to be ended under the law of Malaysia, the common domicile of the parties, prima facie this would be recognised in England; but recognition was in fact denied on public policy grounds.

[600] 1986 Act, s 44(2).

[601] Ibid, ss 46–52.

[602] North, op cit, pp 278–80.

[603] Ibid, pp 286–7.

[604] *Indyka v Indyka* [1969] 1 AC 33 at 66.

[605] Subject to any public policy factor, infra, p 1030 et seq. Cf Brussels II *bis*, Art 25, discussed supra, p 1005.

as annulling a marriage, validly celebrated in England, on the ground of what English courts would class as formal invalidity.[606] A corollary of this is that a foreign divorce or annulment will be recognised though granted on grounds unknown to English law,[607] even where one spouse was domiciled in England.[608]

Furthermore, again as at common law, the jurisdictional basis assumed by a foreign court is similarly irrelevant. The English court is concerned only with the factual jurisdictional circumstances in the foreign country when the divorce, etc was obtained.

(j) Other statutory grounds of recognition

Section 45(1)(b) of the 1986 Act preserves the rules for the recognition of overseas divorces, annulments and legal separations which exist by virtue of any other enactment. However, at the same time, the 1986 Act repeals[609] as spent legislation most, if not all, of the other statutory provisions[610] under which overseas divorces, etc might be recognised, whilst also preserving the validity of past divorces, etc which would be recognised under that spent legislation, and might not be recognised under the 1986 Act.[611] Furthermore, it has been made clear[612] that an overseas divorce, etc not recognised under the 1986 Act cannot be recognised under the Foreign Judgments (Reciprocal Enforcement) Act 1933.[613]

(v) Extra-judicial divorces, annulments and legal separations[614]

(a) Introduction

Divorces may be obtained not only in judicial proceedings but also extra-judicially in a variety of ways. These include divorce by mutual consent,[615] by administrative process[616] or, more commonly, under religious laws.[617] For instance, a Jewish Rabbinical law allows a husband to dissolve his marriage by delivering to his wife a letter of divorce, called a *gett* and, though this necessitates his appearance before a Rabbinical court, the proceeding is a formality and is not accompanied by a judicial finding and pronouncement.[618] Under Moslem law,[619] a husband is permitted to divorce his wife without any reference to a court. Such a divorce, by

---

[606] *De Massa v De Massa* (1931), reported in [1939] 2 All ER 150 n; *Galene v Galene (otherwise Galice)* [1939] P 237.

[607] *Corbett v Corbett* [1957] 1 WLR 486 at 490.

[608] *Mitford v Mitford* [1923] P 130.

[609] S 68(2) and Sch 2.

[610] The main ones are the Colonial and Other Territories (Divorce Jurisdiction) Acts 1926 and 1950 and the Matrimonial Causes (War Marriages) Act 1944, s 4; see Law Com No 137 (1984), paras 6.44–6.48.

[611] S 52(5)(c), (d); and see Law Com No 137 (1984), pp 115–16.

[612] *Maples v Maples* [1988] Fam 14.

[613] Supra, p 593.

[614] North, op cit, Chapter 11; (1975) 91 LQR 36; Young (1987) 7 Legal Studies 78; Edwards (1988) 18 Fam Law 419; Pilkington (1988) 37 ICLQ 131.

[615] National Insurance Decision No R(G) 1/72; and *H v H (Validity of Japanese Divorce)* [2006] EWHC 2989 (Fam), [2007] 1 FLR 1318 (divorce by "*kyogi rikon*", ie by agreement, under Art 763 of the Japanese Civil Code).

[616] *Manning v Manning* [1958] P 112.

[617] Gordon, *Foreign Divorces: English Law and Practice* (1988), Chapters 1–3.

[618] Eg *Har-Shefi v Har-Shefi (No 2)* [1953] P 220; *Broit v Broit* 1972 SLT (Notes) 32; *Maples v Maples* [1988] Fam 14; *Berkovits v Grinberg* [1995] Fam 142; and *O v O (Jurisdiction: Jewish Divorce)* [2000] 2 FLR 147; and see Berkovits (1988) 104 LQR 60, 81–93. See now Divorce (Religious Marriages) Act 2002 (and SI 2003/186), by which the English court may order that a decree of divorce is not to be made absolute until a declaration made by both parties that they have taken such steps as are required to dissolve the marriage in accordance with the usages of the Jews, or any other prescribed religious usages, is produced to the court. Cf in Scotland, Family Law (Scotland) Act 2006, s 15 (inserting s 3A into the Divorce (Scotland) Act 1976) and SSI 2006/253, discussed by Crawford and Carruthers, at para 12-34.

[619] See generally Rehman (2007) 21 International Journal of Law, Policy and the Family 108, 118 et seq; and *El Fadl v El Fadl* [2000] 1 FCR 685, per Hughes J at 694 et seq.

talak, merely requires him to state unequivocally three times his intention to repudiate the marriage. In some countries, no further formality is required than this—what is often called a "bare" *talak*.[620] In other jurisdictions where Moslem law is applied, it is necessary also either to register such a divorce with a court or administrative body[621] or, as under the Pakistan Muslim Family Laws Ordinance 1961,[622] to go through procedures giving the opportunity of conciliation proceedings.[623] Moslem law also provides other forms of divorce, such as by *khula*, a form of divorce by agreement on the suggestion of the wife.[624]

Examples of extra-judicial annulments are very much less easy to provide,[625] not least because few countries recognise religious or administrative annulment of marriage. However, examples can be provided of annulment by an ecclesiastical rather than civil tribunal.[626]

At common law, English courts were originally very reluctant to recognise the effectiveness and validity of extra-judicial divorces;[627] but attitudes have changed and it has come to be accepted that they should normally be recognised if the general jurisdictional criteria for recognition have been established.[628] Indeed, in 1970 recognition was given to a *talak* divorce pronounced in England, dissolving the marriage celebrated in England of spouses domiciled in Pakistan.[629]

The rules for the recognition of foreign extra-judicial divorces and legal separations were placed by the Recognition of Divorces and Legal Separations Act 1971 on the same general statutory basis as the rules for the recognition of foreign divorces and legal separations obtained by court order; though the grounds for recognising extra-judicial divorces and legal separations obtained without there having been any proceedings (such as a bare *talak*) were narrower[630] than for those which involved some form of proceedings as in the case of a *gett*.[631] There were also special rules generally denying recognition to extra-judicial divorces and separations obtained in the British Isles but recognised as valid elsewhere.[632] This pattern has substantially been retained in Part II of the Family Law Act 1986, with the addition that the recognition rules now extend to the recognition of extrajudicial annulments.[633] The Law Commission[634] had proposed a more liberal approach[635] so that, for

---

[620] Eg *Sharif v Sharif* (1980) 10 Fam Law 216 (Iraq); *Zaal v Zaal* (1982) 4 FLR 284 (Dubai); *Chaudhary v Chaudhary* [1985] Fam 19 (Kashmir).

[621] Eg *Russ v Russ* [1964] P 315 (Egypt).

[622] See *Qureshi v Qureshi* [1972] Fam 173; *R v Registrar General of Births, Deaths and Marriages, ex p Minhas* [1977] QB 1; *Quazi v Quazi* [1980] AC 744; *R v Secretary of State for the Home Department, ex p Fatima* [1986] AC 527.

[623] See *Radwan v Radwan* [1973] Fam 24 (Egypt).

[624] *Quazi v Quazi* [1980] AC 744.

[625] Cases of extra-judicial separation have not come before the courts for many years: *Connelly v Connelly* (1851) 7 Moo PCC 438; North, op cit, p 280.

[626] *Di Rollo v Di Rollo* 1959 SC 75; *Butterley v Butterley* (1974) 48 DLR (3d) 351; see North, op cit, pp 264–6.

[627] Eg *R v Hammersmith Superintendent Registrar of Marriages, ex p Mir-Anwarrudin* [1917] 1 KB 634.

[628] Though the extra-judicial annulment in *Di Rollo v Di Rollo*, supra, was denied recognition on grounds of public policy.

[629] *Qureshi v Qureshi* [1972] Fam 173. Recognition was denied at common law if the spouses were domiciled in England, [1972] Fam 173 at 199; *Radwan v Radwan* [1973] Fam 24.

[630] Jurisdiction could only be based on domicile in the English sense under s 6 of the 1971 Act.

[631] Jurisdiction could also be based on habitual residence, nationality or domicile in the foreign sense under ss 2–5 of the 1971 Act.

[632] See the 1971 Act, ss 1, 6: Domicile and Matrimonial Proceedings Act 1973, s 16 (repealed by Family Law Act 1986, ss 68(2), 69, and Sch 2).

[633] Ss 44, 45; following the recommendations of the Law Commission: Law Com No 137 (1984), para 6.9.

[634] Law Com No 137 (1984), para 6.11.

[635] Similar to that in Australia (eg Family Law Act 1975, s 104).

example, "bare" *talaks* would fall within the broader recognition rules applicable where there had been some proceedings. On the other hand, they also proposed that the requirement of some form of proceedings, albeit more liberally interpreted,[636] should apply to all divorces, etc irrespective of the jurisdictional basis of recognition. This would have had the effect that an entirely informal divorce could no longer be generally recognised[637] even though obtained in the country of the spouses' common domicile. This essentially more liberal approach was rejected[638] for three reasons, namely because of problems of proof in the case of informal divorces, because such divorces tend to discriminate against women (being usually obtained by men) and because they often provide little or no financial protection for the wife and family. These arguments are not wholly convincing. The last is met by the provisions in Part III of the Matrimonial and Family Proceedings Act 1984 allowing the courts to grant financial relief even though a foreign divorce is recognised in England.[639] If there is force in the first two arguments they militate against any recognition of such informal divorces, but in fact they continue to be recognised, provided they are obtained or recognised in the country of the domicile in the English sense.[640] It is not easy to see why a domicile connection provides any greater protection than one based, say, on habitual residence.[641]

The result is that, in relation to extra-judicial divorces, etc, Part II of the 1986 Act still follows very much the approach of the 1971 Act. We shall have to consider, therefore, the rules relating to extra-judicial divorces, etc obtained in the British Isles separately from those obtained overseas, and to determine where a divorce, etc is obtained, given that the recognition rules depend on this factor even though, because of the very informality of many of the divorces, etc under consideration, the parties may regard the place where it takes place as totally unimportant. In the context of overseas divorces, etc, it is also necessary to look separately at those obtained by some form of proceedings and, indeed, to consider what constitutes "proceedings".

Before turning to examine the detail of the 1986 Act, it should be borne in mind that the approach of English law and the attitude of English courts in this regard is one of tolerance, as is clear from the words of Munby J in *Sulaiman v Juffali*:[642]

> Although historically [England] is part of the Christian west, and although it has an established church which is Christian, I sit as a secular judge serving a multi-cultural community of many faiths in which all of us can now take some pride, sworn to do justice "to all manner of people". Religion—whatever the particular believer's faith—is no doubt something to be encouraged but it is not the business of government or of the secular courts. So the starting point of the law is an essentially agnostic view of religious beliefs and a tolerant indulgence to religious and cultural diversity. A secular judge must be wary of straying across the well-recognised divide between church and state. It is not for a judge to weigh one religion against another. All are entitled to equal respect, whether in times of peace or, as at present, amidst the clash of arms.

---

[636] It was suggested that the statutory phrase "judicial or other proceedings" should include acts which constitute the means by which the divorce, etc may be obtained and which are done in compliance with the procedures required in the country where it was obtained.

[637] Under s 6 of the 1971 Act.

[638] 473 HL Official Report, cols 1082, 1103 (1986); see Young (1987) 7 Legal Studies 78, 81–3.

[639] Infra, p 1072 et seq.

[640] S 46(2).

[641] S 46(1).

[642] [2002] 2 FCR 427, at 439.

(b) General issues

Before examining the particular rules relating to the recognition of extra-judicial divorces, etc, it is necessary to examine, first, two of those inter-related general issues. As there are different rules for extra-judicial divorces, etc obtained in the British Isles and overseas, and for overseas divorces, etc depending on whether or not they were obtained by "proceedings", we shall consider here the two questions: where is an extra-judicial divorce, etc obtained and what constitutes proceedings?

(i) Where is an extra-judicial divorce, etc obtained?

This question may be asked in two main contexts. First, it is necessary that an overseas divorce, etc be effective in the country where it was obtained and that one of the relevant jurisdictional links with that country is satisfied.[643] The second context, which has proved in practice to be the more important, is to determine whether the divorce, etc was obtained in the British Isles or overseas. The significance of this is that the divorce, etc will normally be denied recognition if obtained in the British Isles.[644]

It might be thought that the proceedings or act[645] by which an extra-judicial divorce, etc is obtained could only occur in one country. Whilst this is usually true, particular difficulty has been caused by Moslem divorces by *talak*, especially where this religious requirement is also combined with a need for some further type of proceedings. This is illustrated by a decision under the Recognition of Divorces and Legal Separations Act 1971, *R v Secretary of State for the Home Department, ex parte Fatima*:[646]

> The husband was a Pakistan national who married there in 1968, but had lived in England ever since. In 1978, he purported to divorce his wife by *talak* and in 1982 wished to marry Ghulam Fatima; but she was refused entry to England by an immigration officer at Heathrow Airport. This was because the officer concluded that the husband's *talak* divorce would not be recognised in England and so the husband was not free to marry again here.

The crucial issue with which the House of Lords was faced was to determine where the *talak* divorce in 1978 was obtained. If it was obtained in Pakistan, where it was effective, it would be recognised in England as a divorce obtained in the country of the nationality.[647] If it was obtained in England, it would be denied recognition.[648] The circumstances were that it was a "transnational" divorce:[649] some proceedings took place in England, others in Pakistan under the Muslim Family Laws Ordinance 1961 in force there. The husband had pronounced the *talak* in England and made a statutory declaration to that effect to an English solicitor. Copies of this were sent to Pakistan both to the wife and, as required by the Ordinance, to the chairman of the relevant local union council; and it would appear that all the necessary conciliation procedures in Pakistan were complied with. The effect of this was that the divorce became effective there ninety days after receipt of notice of the *talak* by the chairman. Lord Ackner concluded that the divorce was not obtained by proceedings wholly in Pakistan because the pronouncement of the *talak* in England was an essential part of the proceedings.[650] This led him to the conclusion that the divorce was obtained by proceedings which took place in both countries and that recognition must be denied, because section 2 of the

---

[643] 1986 Act, s 46.

[644] Ibid, s 44, infra, p 1016.

[645] The need to decide where a divorce, etc was obtained arises whether or not it was obtained by judicial or other proceedings.

[646] [1986] AC 527; affirming the CA, [1985] QB 190; Berkovits (1988) 104 LQR 60.

[647] Supra, p 1008.

[648] Infra, p 1016.

[649] [1985] QB 190 at 197, 207.

[650] [1986] AC 527 at 533–4; and see *Quazi v Quazi* [1980] AC 744 at 817, 826.

1971 Act required an overseas divorce to be obtained by means of judicial or other proceedings in a country outside the British Isles and to be effective under the law of that country. Similarly, in *Sulaiman v Juffali*,[651] a bare *talak* pronounced by the husband in England, and registered with the Sharia Court in Saudi Arabia three days later was "obtained" in England for the purposes of the 1986 Act, since its effect was to dissolve the marriage as soon as it had been pronounced; the validity of this *talak* was in no way dependent upon the participation or authorisation of judicial authorities, and so, having been obtained in England other than through a court of civil jurisdiction, the divorce fell foul of section 44(1).

Such a result is wholly consistent with the policy of denying recognition to extra-judicial divorces, etc which have been obtained by proceedings in England,[652] but it does highlight the particular weight which the legislation places on where a divorce, etc is obtained. If the husband in this case had had the advice, or the funds, to go to Pakistan to pronounce the *talak*, it would have been recognised in England.[653]

There is a difficult question as to whether the same result is compelled under the 1986 Act which is worded slightly differently. Section 46(1) requires an overseas divorce obtained by proceedings to be effective in the country where it was obtained but does not, in so many words, require the proceedings to be in that country. This led to the suggestion[654] that where the proceedings take place in more than one country, as in *Ex p Fatima*, the divorce may still be recognised if that element of the proceedings which renders the divorce effective takes place in the overseas country with which the necessary jurisdictional links may be established. So, it is argued,[655] a *talak* pronounced in England by a Pakistan national but perfected by proceedings in Pakistan is obtained (and effective) in Pakistan and should be recognised in England.

Whilst there is undoubted force in the argument both from the point of view of policy and on construction of the statutory provisions, it was rejected by Wall J in *Berkovits v Grinberg*.[656] In that case, a *gett* had been written in England but was delivered in Israel. Although it was effective under the law of Israel to dissolve the marriage, it was denied recognition in England. The judge accepted the argument that there was no evidence that the 1986 Act was intended to change the law and that it should be so construed.[657] Furthermore, other provisions of the 1986 Act, like their predecessors in the 1971 Act, are drafted on the basis that the divorce was obtained in the foreign proceedings.[658] This is particularly true of those provisions concerned with the giving of notice of the proceedings to the parties.[659] It is nonetheless undesirable to say, as was said by Lord Ackner in *Ex p Fatima*, that there "must be a single set of proceedings which have to be instituted in the same country as that in which the relevant divorce was ultimately obtained".[660] This may

---

[651] [2002] 2 FCR 427.

[652] 1986 Act, s 44(1).

[653] See [1985] QB 190 at 199–200.

[654] Pilkington (1988) 37 ICLQ 130, 132–6; and see Young (1987) 7 Legal Studies 78, 87; Berkovits (1988) 104 LQR 60, 79–80; Gordon, op cit, pp 101–4.

[655] Pilkington (1988) 37 ICLQ 130, 135.

[656] [1995] Fam 142. McClean (1996) 112 LQR 230.

[657] Section 46(1) is essentially to the same effect as clause 3(1)(a) of the Law Commission's draft Bill on which the 1986 Act is based and the Commission expressed itself content with the decision in *Ex p Fatima*: see Law Com No 137 (1984), para 6.11 and p 94.

[658] Eg ss 47(1), 48(1).

[659] S 51(3), infra, p 1027 et seq. Had the 1986 Act changed the law, it would have been necessary also to amend Part III of the Matrimonial and Family Proceedings Act 1984, infra, p 1072; see *Berkovits v Grinberg* [1995] Fam 142 at 157–8.

[660] [1986] AC 527 at 534.

be too sweeping a statement.[661] It is surely understandable to deny recognition to a divorce obtained by proceedings partly in England and partly abroad, given the prohibition on recognition of extra-judicial divorces, etc obtained in the British Isles.[662] It is less justifiable to deny recognition to, say, a *talak* pronounced in Dubai followed by conciliation proceedings in Pakistan, given that the divorce is effective in each of the countries where some of the proceedings took place.

If a divorce, etc is obtained in a consulate or embassy, it is to be taken to be obtained in the country where the consulate or embassy is situated, not in the country of the sending state. So it has been held that an extra-judicial divorce obtained in the Consulate-General of the United Arab Republic in London was obtained in England and was not an overseas divorce.[663]

(ii) What constitutes proceedings?

The significance of this question is that, where the divorce, etc is obtained by judicial or other proceedings,[664] the jurisdictional bases of recognition are much wider than if there are no proceedings[665]—being limited in the latter case to domicile.[666] This is much the same as the position under the 1971 Act[667] in which context the courts had to consider the same question. Whilst there is no definition of "judicial or other proceedings" in the 1986 Act,[668] it has been suggested[669] that the phrase is limited to cases involving some act external to the parties themselves, such as registration, conciliation proceedings or some other form of approval.[670] The House of Lords has held in *Quazi v Quazi*[671] that a divorce obtained in Pakistan by *talak* and which then involved the procedures of the Pakistan Muslim Family Laws Ordinance 1961—namely the giving of notice to the wife and to the chairman of the local union council, with the prospect of conciliation proceedings—had been obtained by means of judicial or other proceedings. On the other hand, after a period of uncertainty, the Court of Appeal[672] has concluded that a "bare" *talak*, ie where there is no more than an oral pronouncement by the husband three times, whether or not before witnesses, that he divorces his wife, does not constitute proceedings.[673]

It has been suggested by Oliver LJ that proceedings "must impart a degree of formality and at least the involvement of some agency, whether lay or religious, of or recognised by the state

---

[661] Indeed, it was made in answer to a question posed by Lord Ackner which was restricted to proceedings which took place both in the British Isles and overseas: [1986] AC 527 at 533. See also Crawford and Carruthers, para 12-34.

[662] 1986 Act, s 44(1).

[663] *Radwan v Radwan* [1973] Fam 24, supra, pp 914–15; and see *Chaudhry v Chaudhry* [1976] Fam 148.

[664] To be distinguished from "procedure": *H v H (Validity of Japanese Divorce)* [2006] EWHC 2989 (Fam), [2007] 1 FLR 1318, per S Wildblood QC, sitting as Deputy Judge of the High Court, at [101].

[665] 1986 Act, s 46(1).

[666] S 46(2). See *M v M (Divorce: Jurisdiction: Validity of Marriage)* [2001] 2 FLR 6 at [42].

[667] Contrast the broad recognition rules of ss 2–5 with the more limited domicile ground of s 6 which was the only ground of recognition if there were no proceedings.

[668] S 54(1), and nor was there in the 1971 Act; and see *Quazi v Quazi* [1980] AC 744 at 788–9. Contrast the proposed definition in Law Com No 137 (1984), pp 122–3.

[669] North, op cit, pp 225–30; Polonsky (1973) 22 ICLQ 343, 345.

[670] Including the delivery of a *gett* before a Rabbinical court, even though there is no judicial investigation: *Broit v Broit* 1972 SLT (Notes) 32; *Berkovits v Grinberg* [1995] Fam 142 and see Gordon, *Foreign Divorces: English Law and Practice* (1988) pp 96–7.

[671] [1980] AC 744; Karsten (1980) 43 MLR 202.

[672] This point had been left open by the House of Lords in *Quazi v Quazi* [1980] AC 744 at 817.

[673] *Chaudhary v Chaudhary* [1985] Fam 19; Canton (1985) 48 MLR 212. This confirms the view of Wood J in *Sharif v Sharif* (1980) 10 Fam Law 216 in contrast to those of Bush J in *Zaal v Zaal* (1982) 4 FLR 284 at 286–8 and Taylor J in *R v Secretary of State for the Home Department, ex p Ghulam Fatima* [1985] QB 190 at 195.

having a function that is more than simply probative",[674] and would exclude "a private act conducted entirely by parties *inter se* or by one party alone, as a proceeding, even though the party performing it may give it an additional solemnity or even an efficacy by performing it in the presence of other persons whose only involvement is that they witness the perform-ance".[675] On this approach, it can be concluded that a divorce in Thailand by mutual consent based simply on an agreement signed by the spouses;[676] a divorce by consent under Chinese customary law, even if the agreement is presented to, and authenticated by, a local body;[677] or a divorce by "divorce letter" in The Gambia[678] will not be regarded as having been obtained by proceedings.[679] In taking this approach, the Court of Appeal does seem to have rejected the more liberal line of Lord Scarman in *Quazi v Quazi*.[680] He defined "proceedings" as "any act or acts officially recognised as leading to divorce in the country where the divorce was obtained and which itself is recognised by the law of the country as an effective divorce". On this basis, he was prepared to recognise, as obtained by proceedings, a divorce by *khula* in Thailand which involved no more than a written agreement witnessed by two persons.[681] The problem with Lord Scarman's approach is that it is so wide that it would include virtually every kind of effective divorce, etc and thus deprive of any content the special rules in Part II of the 1986 Act governing divorces, etc obtained where there are no proceedings.[682] Finally, there seems little doubt that, if the termination of a marriage by one spouse's unilateral dec-laration of his change of religion could be regarded as a divorce,[683] it is certainly not obtained by proceedings.[684]

In *El Fadl v El Fadl*,[685] Hughes J recognised that the rules applicable to *talak* procedures differ to some extent from country to country, and that different varieties of *talak* may coexist within a single country, and so his Lordship viewed it as important to confine himself to the circum-stances of the particular case, and to refrain from generalisation.[686] With regard to a *talak* divorce pronounced by a husband (a Lebanese national, habitually resident in the Lebanon), in front of two witnesses, and registered with the Sharia court in the Lebanon, as required by Lebanese law,[687] Hughes J, in concluding that the divorce was a "proceedings divorce" was swayed by the requirement of registration:

> If . . . this had been a talaq which depended for its effectiveness solely upon the pro-nouncement in front of witnesses I should have held . . . that it was not a proceedings divorce[688] . . . Although the Sharia court has no judicial decision to make whether there is to be divorce or no, what occurred before it with the assembly of the court, judge and clerk, and the duty to record into the register, having taken formal declarations, is properly described

---

674 [1985] Fam 19 at 41.
675 Ibid. Cf *Baig v Entry Clearance Officer, Islamabad* [2002] INLR 117—*talak* divorce did not amount to "proceedings" as it was a personal act lacking formality other than ritual performance, and lacking the involvement or any contact with the state.
676 Eg *Ratanachai v Ratanachai* [1960] CLY 480; *Varanand v Varanand* (1964) 108 Sol Jo 693.
677 Eg *Lee v Lau* [1967] P 14.
678 *Wicken v Wicken* [1999] Fam 224.
679 *Chaudhary v Chaudhary* [1985] Fam 19 at 42, 47.
680 [1980] AC 744 at 824.
681 Ibid.
682 S 46(2).
683 Supra, p 1012 et seq.
684 *Viswalingham v Viswalingham* (1979) 1 FLR 15 at 19.
685 [2000] 1 FCR 685.
686 Ibid, at 694. Cf *Sulaiman v Juffali* [2002] 2 FCR 427, per Munby J, at [37].
687 Without any requirement, however, that notice be given to the wife: ibid, at 696.
688 As required by *Chaudhary v Chaudhary* [1985] Fam 19 at 42.

as "proceedings" and the local law explicitly requires such proceedings as an integral part of the divorce process.[689]

Similarly, the following circumstances have been found to amount to "proceedings" under s 46(1): the giving notice of the talaq to the relevant chairman of the union council;[690] a talaq pronounced under Libyan law and confirmed by an Egyptian judgment to meet the requirement of Libyan law that proof of the talaq to be confirmed by the judgment of a competent court;[691] a talaq pronounced in Saudi Arabia and certified by a Saudi religious court as required by Saudi Sharia law; and a customary "panchayat" divorce registered in Gujarat, India.[692] In *H v H (Validity of Japanese Divorce)*,[693] the court held that a form of consensual divorce under Japanese law ("*kyogi rikon*"), which required the parties to sign a form called a *rikon todoke* and which became effective only upon registration of the form in the manner prescribed by Japanese law, was within the ambit of "other proceedings". The involvement of the state in the form of requiring registration of a divorce by consent was more than "simply probative" and certainly was not to be regarded as "mere surplusage"; the state did not simply prove the divorce that the parties had achieved by their prior act of consent, for the consent of itself created nothing. Although the state exercised no discretionary power of veto, the formalities of registration by the state were essential to the divorce; no registration, no divorce.[694] The fact that the state employee who effected the registration played no more than an administrative role did not make the procedure as a whole purely administrative.

(c) Extra-judicial divorces and annulments obtained in the British Isles
The type of situation with which we are concerned here is illustrated by the case of the pronouncement of a *talak* in England,[695] whether it is a "bare" *talak* or one followed by further procedures in, say, Pakistan.[696] The common law position was that, if such divorces were recognised as valid under the common law recognition rules, ie if recognised by the law of the domicile,[697] then they would be recognised in England, notwithstanding the fact that the *talak* was pronounced in England.[698] The Recognition of Divorces and Legal Separations Act 1971 left this position unaffected;[699] but two years later section 16(1) of the Domicile and Matrimonial Proceedings Act 1973 denied recognition to any such divorces obtained after 1973. It provided that "no proceedings" in the British Isles "shall be regarded as validly dissolving a marriage unless instituted in the courts of law" there. This general approach is maintained in section 44(1) of the Family Law Act 1986, but with rather different wording:[700] "No divorce or annulment obtained in any part of the British Isles shall be regarded as effective in any part of the United Kingdom unless granted by a court of civil jurisdiction." This means that extra-judicial divorces and annulments wholly obtained in any part of the British Isles will not be valid in England, including of course such divorces and annulments

---

[689] [2000] 1 FCR 685, at 700.

[690] *H v H (Talaq Divorce)* [2007] EWHC 2945 (Fam).

[691] *A v L (Overseas Divorce)* [2010] EWHC 460 (Fam)—it was irrelevant that the law applicable to the talaq was that of Libya (the husband being a Libyan citizen), whereas the law of the forum was Egyptian law.

[692] *NP v KRP (Recognition of Foreign Divorce)* [2013] EWHC 694 (Fam).

[693] [2006] EWHC 2989 (Fam), [2007] 1 FLR 1318.

[694] Ibid, para 85.

[695] Including a consulate or embassy in England.

[696] A trans-national divorce, supra, p 1015.

[697] Under the rule in *Armitage v A-G* [1906] P 135.

[698] *Har-Shefi v Har-Shefi(No 2)* [1953] P 220; *Qureshi v Qureshi* [1972] Fam 173; provided in fact the law of the domicile regarded it as effective; National Insurance Decisions No R(G) 5/74, No R(G) 2/75.

[699] Such divorces fell through the provisions of the Act: North, op cit, p 223.

[700] The Law Commission's draft Bill followed the wording of s 16(1) of the 1973 Act: Law Com No 137 (1984), p 90.

obtained in England.[701] Nor will they be valid where some part of the proceedings takes place in England and others abroad.[702]

The inclusion of annulments marks an extension from the 1971 Act; but in the absence of evidence of extra-judicial separations in the British Isles it was not felt necessary to provide for denial of their recognition.[703] What now seems clear is that any form of extra-judicial divorce or annulment obtained in the British Isles will be denied effect in England. Finally, the 1986 Act follows the pattern of the earlier legislation[704] and preserves the effect of an extra-judicial divorce obtained in the British Isles before 1974 and which would be recognised under the common law rules then applicable.[705] This saving provision is limited to divorces and does not apply to extra-judicial annulments.

(d) Recognition of extra-judicial divorces, etc obtained overseas

It is necessary to examine separately the recognition rules for extra-judicial divorces, etc obtained overseas depending on whether or not there are "judicial or other proceedings".[706]

(i) Where there are proceedings

The basic approach where there are proceedings is that recognition of the divorce, etc is governed by the general rules as to recognition already discussed in relation to judicial divorces, etc. So, the divorce, etc must have been obtained in a country where one party to the marriage was domiciled (in the English or the foreign sense) or habitually resident or of which one party was a national,[707] and it must have been effective under the law of that country.[708] All the other provisions of Part II of the 1986 Act applicable to judicial divorces, etc apply to divorces, etc obtained by other types of proceedings.[709] It might be noted that, as at common law,[710] an extra-judicial divorce, etc obtained by proceedings can be recognised in England despite the fact that both spouses are domiciled in England. So, a *talak* obtained in Pakistan by a husband who is a Pakistan national can be recognised in England, notwithstanding the English domicile of both spouses.[711]

The application of these general rules as to recognition in the context of divorces, etc obtained by extra-judicial proceedings does raise a number of special problems. The jurisdictional rules assume that the divorce, etc is *obtained* by the particular proceedings,[712] that the divorce, etc is effective under the law of *the country* where it was obtained[713] and that the connecting factors of habitual residence, domicile or nationality in the country where it was obtained are satisfied at the date of the commencement of the proceedings.[714] These requirements mean

---

[701] Eg *Chaudhary v Chaudhary* [1985] Fam 19 at 28; *Maples v Maples* [1988] Fam 14; and see Young (1987) 7 Legal Studies 78, 84, 86. A difficult "incidental question" (supra, Chapter 4) will arise if the spouses are domiciled in a country where the extra-judicial divorce in England is recognised and one of them remarries either there or in England. Does that spouse have capacity to remarry? See North, op cit, pp 224–5.

[702] Supra, p 1002 et seq.

[703] Law Com No 137 (1984), p 91.

[704] Domicile and Matrimonial Proceedings Act 1973, s 16(3).

[705] Family Law Act 1986, s 52(4), (5)(a); see, eg, *Chaudhry v Chaudhry* [1976] Fam 148.

[706] 1986 Act, s 54(1). The meaning of this phrase has been discussed, supra, p 1017 et seq.

[707] S 46(1)(b).

[708] S 46(1)(a).

[709] Ss 46(4), 47(1)—supplementary rules on jurisdiction; s 48 on proof of facts; s 49—the meaning of "country"; s 51—the grounds for refusing recognition; and s 52—transitional provisions.

[710] Eg *Manning v Manning* [1958] P 112.

[711] See 1986 Act, s 46(1)(b)(iii). It might, however, be denied recognition on the ground of public policy, infra, p 1030 et seq.

[712] S 46(1).

[713] S 46(1)(a).

[714] S 46(1)(b), (3)(a).

that it is necessary to determine whether a divorce, etc is obtained by going through all, or only part of, the proceedings and to identify the date of the commencement of the proceedings by which it was obtained. These issues have arisen in the context of "transnational" *talak* divorces[715] where it has been held that, though conciliation proceedings are required, and have taken place, in Pakistan, the earlier pronouncement of the *talak* in England constituted the commencement of the proceedings by which the divorce was obtained.[716]

Particular concerns arise, in the context of the recognition of extra-judicial divorces, etc in relation to the requirement that the divorce be effective "under the law of" the country where it was obtained.[717] The effectiveness of a divorce, nullity or legal separation decree will be tested in terms of its validity in the courts which granted it, but it will often be necessary to determine in the case of an extra-judicial divorce, etc whether it satisfies the domestic law requirements of the country where it was obtained.[718] For example, the House of Lords in *Quazi v Quazi*,[719] whilst satisfied that the *talak* divorce obtained in Pakistan had satisfied the procedural requirements of that country's Muslim Family Laws Ordinance 1961 (and thus was effective there),[720] expressed much greater doubt as to the effectiveness under Thai law of the divorce by *khula* obtained in that country.[721] It may also be the case that the country where the extra-judicial divorce, etc was obtained requires the parties to go through civil judicial proceedings, and the courts in Ontario have denied recognition on this basis to an extra-judicial annulment.[722] However, the validity of an extra-judicial divorce can be tested not simply according to the domestic law of the country where it was obtained but also according to that country's rules of private international law. Take the following example:

> The husband and wife are Jews, both Israeli nationals domiciled in Israel, but habitually resident in British Columbia in Canada. They are divorced by *gett* before a Rabbinical court in British Columbia.

The requirements of the 1986 Act that there be judicial or other proceedings if recognition is to be based jurisdictionally on habitual residence are satisfied.[723] The extra-judicial divorce is not valid under the domestic law of British Columbia but it will be recognised there under that province's divorce recognition rules.[724] On that basis it should be considered to be "effective" under the law of British Columbia and thus be recognised in England.[725]

(ii) Where there are no proceedings

We are concerned here with the special recognition rules for extra-judicial divorces, etc obtained overseas without any proceedings.[726] This type of case can best be illustrated by such Moslem religious divorces as consensual divorce by *khula*[727] or divorce by "bare" *talak*.[728]

---

[715] Supra, p 1015 et seq.

[716] *R v Secretary of State for the Home Department, ex p Fatima* [1986] AC 527 at 533; *Berkovits v Grinberg* [1995] Fam 142 at 147.

[717] North, op cit, pp 231–2.

[718] See *D v D* [1994] 1 FLR 38.

[719] [1980] AC 744.

[720] Ibid, at 805, 818, 824–6.

[721] Ibid at 824; and see Carroll (1985) 48 MLR 434, 437–8.

[722] *Butterley v Butterley* (1974) 48 DLR (3d) 351.

[723] S 46(1).

[724] Because it was recognised in Israel: see *Walker v Walker* [1950] 4 DLR 253; *Viccari v Viccari* (1972) 7 RFL 241, applying *Armitage v A-G* [1906] P 135.

[725] Indeed, a divorce obtained in England in similar circumstances before 1974 was recognised here: *Qureshi v Qureshi* [1972] Fam 173; and see the 1986 Act, s 52(5)(a).

[726] As to what constitutes "proceedings", see supra, p 1017 et seq. *El Fadl v El Fadl* [2000] 1 FCR 685, per Hughes J, at 698: ". . . it is not every form of activity by which legal divorce is achieved which can qualify as proceedings".

[727] See *Quazi v Quazi* [1980] AC 744 at 824; and see *Wicken v Wicken* [1999] Fam 224.

[728] *Chaudhary v Chaudhary* [1985] Fam 19.

Under the Recognition of Divorces and Legal Separations Act 1971, such a divorce could only be recognised if the spouses were domiciled (in the English sense) in the country where it was obtained, or if it was recognised in the country or countries of their domicile.[729] It was not enough that one spouse was habitually resident[730] in, or a national of,[731] the country where the divorce was obtained. It was not, however, a specific statutory requirement that the divorce should be effective in the country in which it was obtained.[732]

As has been indicated earlier,[733] the Law Commission's proposals[734] to have one set of recognition rules for all overseas divorces, etc, coupled with a broadening of the concept of proceedings, was not accepted. Part II of the Family Law Act 1986 follows the general approach of the 1971 Act and provides special, and limited, recognition rules for overseas divorces, etc obtained where there are no proceedings. The central provision is section 46(2):

> The validity of an overseas divorce, annulment or legal separation obtained otherwise than by means of proceedings shall be recognised if—
>
> (a) the divorce, annulment or legal separation is effective under the law of the country[735] in which it was obtained;
> (b) at the relevant date[736]—
>   (i) each party to the marriage was domiciled in that country; or
>   (ii) either party to the marriage was domiciled in that country and the other party was domiciled in a country under whose law the divorce, annulment or legal separation is recognised as valid; and
> (c) neither party to the marriage was habitually resident in the United Kingdom throughout the period of one year immediately preceding that date.

It will be seen that the divorce, etc must be obtained in one country and be effective there. This can raise the same type of problem as has been discussed in relation to divorces obtained by proceedings in the case of a transnational divorce.[737] It will be necessary to decide where, in the case of a divorce by mutual agreement, as in the Moslem *khula*, the divorce is obtained if the spouses are in different countries. It is also necessary that the divorce, etc be "obtained" in the country of the domicile. Where there are no proceedings, a divorce is not obtained in the sense of being granted or approved by a third party; it is only obtained in the sense of being obtained by reason of legal provision made for it.

The rules laid down in section 46(2) of the 1986 Act reveal three particular changes from the rules applicable under the 1971 Act, in addition to their extension to extra-judicial annulments.

---

[729] 1971 Act, s 6, as substituted by the Domicile and Matrimonial Proceedings Act 1973, s 2.

[730] Eg *Chaudhary v Chaudhary* [1985] Fam 19.

[731] Eg *Sharif v Sharif* (1980) 10 Fam Law 216; *Chaudhary v Chaudhary* [1985] Fam 19.

[732] This was because the requirement of effectiveness in s 2 of the 1971 Act did not apply to recognition on the domicile basis under s 6 of the Act.

[733] Supra, p 1014.

[734] Law Com No 137 (1984), para 6.11.

[735] "Country" in s 46(2) means territory within a political state if each territory has different laws on divorce, etc: s 49(1), (4), supra, pp 1009–10.

[736] This means the date on which the divorce, etc was obtained: s 46(3)(b), with appropriate amendments in the rare case of an extra-judicial annulment without proceedings after the death of one spouse (s 46(4)). Although the special rules on cross-proceedings (s 47(1)) and proof of facts made in foreign proceedings (s 48) cannot apply where there are no proceedings, the special jurisdictional rule on conversion of a legal separation into a divorce (ss 47(2), 49(4)) does, in theory at least, apply to an extra-judicial divorce, etc obtained without proceedings.

[737] Supra, p 1015 et seq.

The first is that there is an express statutory requirement that the divorce, etc be effective in the country in which it was obtained[738] and, indeed, recognition may be refused if no official documents can be produced certifying that effectiveness.[739]

The second change concerns the jurisdictional test. Section 46(2) follows the pattern of the 1971 Act in limiting the jurisdictional basis to domicile. It also provides, as did the 1971 Act,[740] that such a divorce, etc will be recognised not only if it was obtained in the overseas country in which both spouses were domiciled, but also if it was obtained in the overseas country in which one spouse was domiciled and was recognised in the country of the domicile of the other spouse.[741] So, if a husband domiciled in Dubai obtains a "bare" *talak* there which is recognised in Pakistan, where the wife is domiciled, the essential requirements of section 46(2) are satisfied.[742] There is no express requirement that the country of one spouse's domicile in which the divorce, etc is recognised is an overseas country, to the exclusion of a part of the British Isles, including even England. Nevertheless, if one spouse was domiciled in England, recognition would be refused. There is here a circular problem, which also arose under the 1971 Act.[743] The divorce will be recognised only if recognised in England and that is the very matter at issue. That being so, recognition must be refused.[744] However, the domicile test under section 46(2) is more narrowly drawn than under the 1971 Act. Under that Act, recognition was allowed even though the overseas divorce, etc was obtained in a country in which neither spouse was domiciled, provided it was recognised either in their common domicile or in the countries of their separate domiciles.[745] The 1986 Act, however, contains no such jurisdictional basis of recognition.

The third change from the jurisdictional rules under the 1971 Act is that, under those provisions, the reference to domicile was to domicile in the English sense. However, domicile under section 46(2) of the 1986 Act includes, rather surprisingly, domicile in both the English sense and that of the country where the divorce was obtained or recognised.[746] So a "bare" *talak* obtained in, say, Dubai will be recognised in England if the spouses were domiciled in Dubai according to the law of Dubai on domicile in family matters, even though not so domiciled according to English law.

There is one major limitation on the recognition of overseas divorces, etc obtained where there are no proceedings, and that is the provision in section 46(2)(c) that recognition will be denied, despite the validity of the divorce, etc under the law of the domicile, if either party had been habitually resident in the United Kingdom for a year immediately preceding the date on which the divorce was obtained.[747] The major purpose of this provision, like its

---

[738] S 46(2)(a); see *Wicken v Wicken* [1999] Fam 224.

[739] S 51(3)(b)(i).

[740] S 6(3)(a).

[741] This is a statutory perpetuation of the common law recognition rule in *Armitage v A-G* [1906] P 135. Recognition may be refused if no official document certifying effectiveness in the country of the domicile of the second spouse can be produced: s 51(3)(b)(ii).

[742] The result would be the same if the situations were reversed, ie if the husband, domiciled in Pakistan, obtained the divorce in Dubai—provided it is valid in both countries. It does not matter with which of the spouses the two jurisdictional links are established.

[743] S 6; see North, op cit, p 185.

[744] As was probably the case in *R v Secretary of State for the Home Department, ex p Fatima* [1986] AC 527, especially at 535.

[745] S 6(3)(b). An overseas divorce or legal separation which would have been recognised under this provision and which was obtained before Part II of the 1986 Act came into force will continue to be recognised: Family Law Act 1986, s 52(5)(b), (e).

[746] S 46(5).

[747] See *R v Immigration Appeal Tribunal, ex p Asfar Jan* [1995] Imm AR 440.

predecessor in the earlier legislation,[748] is to prevent circumvention of the rule that, in the case of British divorces, etc, recognition will only be given to those "granted by a court of civil jurisdiction".[749] It is not possible for the ban on extra-judicial divorces in the British Isles to be evaded by one spouse going to the country of his domicile to pronounce a "bare" *talak*, relying on the fact that it will be recognised in England if recognised in the country of the other spouse's domicile, if either spouse has been habitually resident for one year anywhere in the United Kingdom, not just in England. In fact this type of anti-evasion provision is actually less necessary under the 1986 Act than under the previous legislation, because, under the old law, without such a prohibition, a "bare" *talak* pronounced in, for example, France by a husband on a day trip there would have been recognised in England if recognised in the domicile of both spouses.[750] This cannot happen under the 1986 Act because the divorce, etc has to be obtained in the country of the domicile of one spouse and be effective under that law. It is, therefore, rather surprising to find that the anti-evasion provision in section 46 of the 1986 Act applies if *either* spouse had been habitually resident in the United Kingdom for one year, whereas the old law required them *both* to have been.[751] Finally, it should be emphasised that this limitation on recognition of divorces, etc obtained in, or recognised under the law of, the spouses' domiciles applies only to extra-judicial divorces, etc obtained "otherwise than by means of proceedings". There is no general prohibition on the recognition in England of a divorce obtained in, for example, Pakistan, under the Muslim Family Laws Ordinance 1961, even if the spouses have both been habitually resident in England for years and even if they are both domiciled here, provided one of them is a Pakistan national.[752]

(vi) Grounds for non-recognition of divorces, annulments and legal separations

(a) Introduction

Not only does Part II of the 1986 Act provide an exclusive list of the jurisdictional bases on which overseas divorces, etc may be recognised in England,[753] it also provides, in section 51, an exclusive list of the grounds on which recognition may be denied both to other British[754] and to overseas divorces, etc.[755] There are only two discretionary grounds on which another British divorce, etc may be denied recognition: *res judicata* and that there was no subsisting marriage between the parties at the time of the divorce, etc.[756] On the other hand, an over-seas divorce, etc may be denied recognition, not only on these grounds but also, if there have been judicial or other proceedings, on the grounds of want of notice of, or opportunity to take part in, the proceedings. Where there were no proceedings, recognition may be denied to an overseas divorce, etc if there is no certificate as to its effectiveness where it was obtained or, when recognition depends on reference to the law of the domicile of one of the parties in another country, if there is no certificate as to its validity under the law of that country. Finally, recognition will be denied to all overseas divorces if it would be manifestly contrary to public policy. It was thought to be inappropriate to allow a court in the United Kingdom

---

[748] Domicile and Matrimonial Proceedings Act 1973, s 16; *Sharif v Sharif* (1980) 10 Fam Law 216.

[749] 1986 Act, s 44(1); see Law Com No 137 (1984), para 6.30.

[750] 1971 Act, s 6(3)(b).

[751] Domicile and Matrimonial Proceedings Act 1973, s 16(2).

[752] 1986 Act, s 46(1); see *R v Secretary of State for the Home Department, ex p Fatima* [1985] QB 190 at 199–200. If recognition is to be denied in such a case, it would have to be on one of the discretionary grounds in s 51, most probably the public policy ground, infra, p 1030 et seq.

[753] It being borne in mind that recognition of other British divorces, etc is automatic so far as jurisdiction is concerned.

[754] *Eroglü v Eroglü* [1994] 2 FLR 287.

[755] The limiting of the grounds for non-recognition to those provided by the 1986 Act is effected by s 45. For non-recognition of European divorces etc, see supra, pp 1004–5.

[756] Supra, pp 1001–2.

to deny recognition to another British decree, etc on any of these further grounds. If it is felt necessary to attack a British decree on one of those bases, that should be done in the court which granted it.[757] All the grounds of non-recognition mentioned so far are discretionary.[758] There are, however, two further circumstances in which an overseas divorce, etc *must* be denied recognition, both of which have already been fully considered, namely if the jurisdictional requirements for recognition under the 1986 Act are not satisfied,[759] or if the divorce, etc is not effective in the country where it was obtained.[760] There is nothing in Part II of the 1986 Act to indicate that the right to challenge the recognition of a divorce, etc is confined to a party to the marriage. Such a restriction does not seem to have existed at common law,[761] and Part III of the 1986 Act contemplates the making of declarations as to the validity or invalidity of a divorce, etc obtained outside England and Wales on the application by a person other than a party to the marriage.[762]

The various grounds for non-recognition laid down in section 51 of the 1986 Act must now be considered in more detail.

(b) *Res judicata*

In the 1971 Act there was no ground of non-recognition based specifically on *res judicata*. Instead, another British or a foreign divorce or legal separation would be denied recognition if it was obtained at a time when there was no subsisting marriage between the parties.[763] One purpose of this provision was, however, to deal with issues of *res judicata*,[764] as where the marriage has already been brought to an end by either an English divorce or nullity decree or a foreign one which was recognised in England. Whilst such an approach may be appropriate for the recognition of divorces and legal separations, it is not appropriate in the case of annulments where the whole issue in the foreign nullity proceedings for which recognition is now sought in England may be to declare that the marriage was void *ab initio*. On the other hand, there is common law authority that a foreign nullity decree may be denied recognition on the basis of *res judicata*, as in *Vervaeke v Smith*:[765] in 1970, the wife sought to have her English marriage in 1954 annulled on the ground that her husband was already married at the time, even though he had gone through divorce proceedings in Nevada in 1946, and that it was a "sham" marriage, being celebrated simply to enable her to acquire British nationality. The English court refused to grant her a nullity decree—because the Nevada divorce was recognised in England and the fact her marriage was a "sham" was no ground for annulling it.[766] Then, in 1972, the wife obtained a nullity decree from a Belgian court on the ground, considered but rejected in England, that the marriage was a "sham". It was held, in the lower courts,[767] that the Belgian decree satisfied the common law jurisdictional rules for the

---

[757] Supra, pp 1001–2.

[758] See *Duhur-Johnson v Duhur-Johnson* [2005] 2 FLR 1042, per Jeremy Richardson QC, at [44], "The provisions [of s 51(3)] need not be exercised if the interests of the respondent spouses (as opposed to the petitioning spouse) are met by other means . . . The important point to note is that the judicial discretion is wide and the applicability of the section will vary depending on the many and varied circumstances of each case."

[759] S 46(1), (2).

[760] Ibid, supra, pp 1008–9.

[761] Eg *Pemberton v Hughes* [1899] 1 Ch 781; *Powell v Cockburn* (1976) 68 DLR (3d) 700.

[762] S 55, infra, pp 1051–2.

[763] 1971 Act, s 8(1), and there is a similar ground of non-recognition in s 51(2) of the 1986 Act, infra, pp 1026–7.

[764] Implementing Art 9 of the 1970 Hague Convention: see Law Com No 34 (1970), para 16 and App B (notes on clause 8); Law Com No 137 (1984), paras 4.66, 6.64.

[765] [1983] 1 AC 145; Carter (1982) 53 BYBIL 302; Jaffey (1983) 32 ICLQ 500, [1986] Civil Justice Quarterly 35.

[766] *Messina v Smith* [1971] P 322.

[767] [1981] Fam 77.

recognition of foreign annulments.[768] Nevertheless, recognition was denied, on the basis of the doctrine of *res judicata*.[769] The House of Lords had no doubt that the issue before the Belgian courts was the very point earlier decided in the English courts.[770]

It was thought that it would be desirable to retain the effect of this decision in any statutory regime for recognition of annulments, but that it would be inappropriate to extend the existing statutory rule from divorces to annulments. So, a new head of non-recognition based more specifically on *res judicata* had to be introduced.[771] To this end, section 51(1) of the 1986 Act[772] provides:

Subject to section 52 of this Act, recognition of the validity of—

(a) a divorce, annulment or judicial separation granted by a court of civil jurisdiction in any part of the British Islands, or
(b) an overseas divorce, annulment or legal separation, may be refused in any part of the United Kingdom if the divorce, annulment or separation was granted or obtained at a time when it was irreconcilable with a decision determining the question of the subsistence or validity of the marriage of the parties previously given (whether before or after the commencement of this Part) by a court of civil jurisdiction in that part of the United Kingdom or by a court elsewhere and recognised or entitled to be recognised in that part of the United Kingdom.

It is important to emphasise a number of points. Like the common law rule and the other statutory heads under section 51, this ground for non-recognition is discretionary. It applies to the recognition in England of divorces, annulments and legal separations whether they were granted elsewhere in the British Isles or obtained in some other foreign country. Furthermore, the earlier irreconcilable decision which brings the provision into play may be either an earlier English decision, as was the case in *Vervaeke v Smith*, or it could be an earlier decision from a court elsewhere but which is recognised in England under Part II of the 1986 Act. This statutory head does, however, only apply to an earlier decision of a court, and so the fact that there had been an earlier extra-judicial divorce which was recognised in England would not bring the provision into play.[773] Since the earlier decision must relate to the "subsistence or validity" of the marriage, the provision would seem inapplicable where there has been an earlier decision refusing to grant a divorce or legal separation unless that was because there was held to be no marriage between the parties.[774]

(c) No subsisting marriage

The English court has a discretion to refuse recognition to a divorce or legal separation, whether granted elsewhere in the British Isles, or obtained overseas, if it was obtained at a time when, according to English law, there was no subsisting marriage between the parties.[775] Under the 1971 Act, denial of recognition on this ground was mandatory[776] but, because of the possible overlap with the *res judicata* ground, it was thought more appropriate that this head also should become discretionary.[777] This head is limited to the recognition of divorces

---

[768] The wife had a real and substantial connection with Belgium at the relevant time: *Indyka v Indyka* [1969] 1 AC 33; *Law v Gustin* [1976] Fam 155.

[769] And also on more general public policy grounds, see, infra, p 1030, n 821. Estoppel is discussed generally, supra, p 556 et seq.

[770] [1983] 1 AC 145 at 156, 160, 161–3.

[771] See Law Com No 137 (1984), paras 4.6, 6.65–6.66.

[772] See the critical discussion in Jaffey [1986] Civil Justice Quarterly 35, 44–5, 47–9.

[773] Though it would be relevant under s 51(2).

[774] See Jaffey [1986] Civil Justice Quarterly 35, 47–8.

[775] S 51(2). Cf *Dukali v Lamrani (Attorney-General Intervening)* [2012] EWHC 1748 (Fam).

[776] 1971 Act, s 8(1).

[777] Law Com No 137 (1984), para 6.66.

and legal separations because it is inappropriate in the case of annulments whose purpose is to declare that the marriage is invalid. Whilst there is some overlap with section 51(1), as where there is a prior "decision" dissolving or annulling the marriage, there are other cases for which this further provision is required. It may be, for example, that the marriage in question is regarded by English law (and this includes English rules of private international law) as void *ab initio*, even though there has been no annulment of it. Furthermore, the *res judicata* provisions of section 51(1) would not apply where the marriage is terminated by an extra-judicial annulment which is recognised in England.

(d) Want of notice of the proceedings

Recognition may[778] be refused to an overseas[779] divorce, etc which has been obtained by judicial or other proceedings if it was obtained without such steps having been taken for giving notice[780] of the proceedings to a party to the marriage as, having regard to the nature of the proceedings and all the circumstances, should reasonably have been taken.[781] Recent examples of the recognition of the resulting divorce being refused include situations where the husband had acted contrary to an injunction restraining him from pursuing a divorce in Egypt and the wife had no notice or knowledge of the proceedings;[782] or where, in divorce proceedings instigated by the wife in Ukraine, she falsely claimed that no address for service for the husband was available.[783] Service by advertisement in a Ukrainian newspaper was therefore authorized by the Ukrainian court, although the husband had no opportunity whatever of coming across the advertisement.[784] This provision would seem to embody the common law rules for denying recognition to a divorce or annulment on the ground of want of notice of the proceedings;[785] so lack of notice will not normally affect the recognition of a foreign divorce, etc if the foreign court's rules as to service or dispensation therefrom had been complied with.[786] This is subject to the qualification that such rules are themselves not unreasonable.[787] Indeed, "it cannot be sufficient merely to comply with local procedure, otherwise the provisions of the Act would be nugatory".[788] Recognition should still be denied where the lack of notice is consequent upon the petitioner's fraud.[789] In determining whether to deny recognition because of want of notice, the court will have to examine a wide range of factors, including whether one party has already decided not to take part in the foreign proceedings.[790] In *Duhur-Johnson v Duhur-Johnson*,[791] Jeremy Richardson QC concluded

---

[778] *El Fadl v El Fadl* [2000] 1 FCR 685, at 700—emphasis on discretion to refuse recognition; and *Duhur-Johnson v Duhur-Johnson* [2005] 2 FLR 1042.

[779] This does not apply to the recognition of other British divorces, etc, supra, pp 1001–2.

[780] Ie advance notice: *El Fadl v El Fadl* [2000] 1 FCR 685, at 700.

[781] S 51(3)(a)(i). This marks a slight, but possibly significant, change in approach from its predecessor, s 8(2) of the 1971 Act.

[782] *A v L (Overseas Divorce)* [2010] EWHC 460 (Fam)—Alternatively, if s 51(3)(a)(i) was sufficiently satisfied by the fact that the wife had had notice of the original institution of the proceedings, the wife could still rely on s 51(3)(a)(ii) (infra, p 1029) as she was deprived of an opportunity to take part in the proceedings which she should reasonably have been given, having regard to the nature of the proceedings and all the circumstances, per Sir Mark Potter P, at [78].

[783] *Ivleva v Yates* [2014] EWHC 554 (Fam).

[784] Ibid, per Jackson J, at [71]. See also *Olafisoye v Olafisoye* [2010] EWHC 3540 (Fam); and *Liaw v Lee* [2015] EWHC 1462 (Fam).

[785] *Kendall v Kendall* [1977] Fam 208, infra, p 1031.

[786] *Igra v Igra* [1951] P 404; *Hornett v Hornett* [1971] P 255.

[787] *Macalpine v Macalpine* [1958] P 35 at 45; *Sabbagh v Sabbagh* [1985] FLR 29 at 33–4.

[788] *Sabbagh v Sabbagh* [1985] FLR 29 at 33; and see *Joyce v Joyce* [1979] Fam 93 at 111.

[789] *Macalpine v Macalpine* [1958] P 35. Cf *Duhur-Johnson v Duhur-Johnson* [2005] 2 FLR 1042, at [44]; *Abbassi v Abbassi* [2006] EWCA Civ 355, [2006] 2 FLR 415, per Thorpe LJ, at [18]; *Ivleva v Yates* [2014] EWHC 554 (Fam), at [64] and [66]; and *Liaw v Lee* [2015] EWHC 1462 (Fam), at [30].

[790] Eg *Sabbagh v Sabbagh* [1985] FLR 29.

[791] [2005] 2 FLR 1042 at [44].

that, in determining whether reasonable steps have been taken by the petitioning spouse to notify the respondent spouse of the divorce proceedings in advance of their taking place, a judge should look at all the circumstances of the case, and the nature of the proceedings in the overseas jurisdiction. Whether reasonable steps have been taken is a question of fact in each case, to be judged by English standards. It has been held that the reference to "English standards" in this proposition should be taken to include "European standards applicable in the UK".[792] In particular, in interpreting the want of notice provision of s 51(3), reference should also be made to the corresponding provision of Article 22(b) of Brussels II *bis*. This will ensure that the same rules apply to an application seeking non-recognition of a divorce granted in an EU Member State and to an application concerning a divorce granted outside of the EU or in Denmark.[793] Importantly, "whether the respondent spouse has notice of the proceedings is not the issue. It is whether the petitioner spouse has taken reasonable steps to notify the other party. The focus of inquiry is upon the actions of the petitioning spouse not simply a question of whether the respondent spouse knew about the proceedings."[794] Importantly, when exercising discretion, the court should be "very slow" to refuse recognition of the decision of the foreign court, especially where the order was made by an "independent, properly constituted court" applying procedural and substantive law that largely corresponds with the law of the forum.[795]

The application of this ground of non-recognition may not prove to be easy in the case of extra-judicial divorces, etc. It is only relevant to those cases of extra-judicial divorce, etc which have been obtained by means of judicial or other proceedings. So there must have been sufficient formality for these to be considered to be "proceedings",[796] but recognition may only be denied if the steps taken to give notice are inadequate with regard, inter alia, to the nature of the proceedings.[797] It may be, therefore, that it is thought unreasonable to have to give notice of exiguous proceedings. This would certainly be compatible with the approach to the recognition of extra-judicial divorces at common law where recognition was given to informal divorces in the absence of any notice to the other spouse.[798] Indeed, it has been suggested that the requirement, in what is now the 1986 Act, to have regard to the nature of the proceedings in deciding whether to deny recognition must "contemplate the possibility of proceedings which preclude the possibility of notice or participation".[799] In *El Fadl v El Fadl*,[800] Hughes J declined to exercise his discretion to refuse recognition of a *talak* divorce on the ground of want of notice, for four reasons: first, advance notice could avail the wife nothing, the nature of the proceedings being such as to render notice of practically no value; secondly, the proceedings in question were the prescribed form of divorce in the Lebanon, where both parties were domiciled and in which they had been married, and both parties were taken to have known what the procedure was there and to which they were both subject by their personal law; thirdly, the divorce was accomplished in the forum (the Lebanon) which was the natural forum for both parties; and fourthly, the divorce was obtained in 1981, and it was not a proper exercise of discretion to refuse to recognise a divorce which is valid by the personal laws of both parties and of which they have both had knowledge for such a long

---

[792] *Liaw v Lee* [2015] EWHC 1462 (Fam), per Mostyn J, at [8].
[793] Ibid.
[794] Ibid. The above propositions as formulated by Jeremy Richardson QC were adopted and applied in *Olafisoye v Olafisoye* [2010] EWHC 3540 (Fam); and *Ivleva v Yates* [2014] EWHC 554 (Fam).
[795] *Olafisoye v Olafisoye* [2010] EWHC 3540 (Fam), at [35].
[796] Supra, pp 1017–19.
[797] *D v D* [1994] 1 FLR 38.
[798] Eg *Maher v Maher* [1951] P 342 at 344–5.
[799] *Chaudhary v Chaudhary* [1985] Fam 19 at 44; and see at 48.
[800] [2000] 1 FCR 685, at 701.

period.[801] Tellingly, his Lordship remarked: "I am certainly satisfied that it is not in the public interest to disturb a status which has existed according to the personal law of both parties for 17 years and on the basis of which I am satisfied that both parties have conducted themselves for at any rate two thirds of that period."[802] Similarly, in *H v H (Talaq Divorce)*,[803] Sumner J did not deny recognition to a Pakistani talaq divorce where the wife was not given notice or the opportunity to take part. In this case, the decision was based primarily on considerations of comity and international mobility. His Lordship noted that many people moved freely between the UK and Pakistan, and where there were close links between each country, it was vital that "marriages and divorces recognised by the country where they take place should be recognised in the other country unless there are good reasons for not doing so".[804] The fact that the wife was domiciled in England was not a good reason to refuse the recognition as she had been brought up and married in Pakistan to someone of the same background and neither party wished the marriage to continue.[805]

(e) Want of opportunity to take part in the proceedings

Recognition of an overseas[806] divorce, etc obtained by proceedings may be refused if it was obtained without a party to the marriage having been given (for any reason other than lack of notice) such opportunity to take part in the proceedings as, having regard to the nature of the proceedings and all the circumstances, he should have been given.[807] There may be cases where a party is prevented by external events from taking part in the proceedings, as in time of war; but even then an English court has recognised a German nullity decree obtained in wartime despite the fact that the English respondent was unable to go to Germany.[808] The courts have examined a range of matters as relevant to the issue of opportunity to take part in the proceedings. These include the failure of lawyers in the foreign country to comply with the respondent's instructions,[809] whether the respondent has the financial resources and time to attend or be represented in the foreign proceedings,[810] or even the fact that the husband has the wife's passport.[811] The "opportunity" is not to be limited to the mere taking part in the proceedings; it must be an effective opportunity to place views before the court.[812] However, the opportunity to take part in the proceedings does not necessarily require the spouse to attend the proceedings,[813] and it has been held in one case that five days' notice of foreign nullity proceedings was sufficient.[814] In the case of an extra-judicial divorce, etc the exiguous

---

[801] His Lordship noted, ibid, that even if he were wrong in his classification of the divorce as a "proceedings" divorce, nonetheless, if it were a "non-proceedings" divorce, it would qualify for recognition since both parties were domiciled in the Lebanon (where the divorce was obtained) at the material time, and in that event, questions of notice and participation would not arise.

[802] Ibid, 703. Cf *H v H (Validity of Japanese Divorce)* [2006] EWHC 2989 (Fam), [2007] 1 FLR 1318, per S Wildblood QC, sitting as Deputy Judge of the High Court, at [183] (Japanese divorce obtained twenty years earlier); and *H v H (Talaq Divorce)* [2007] EWHC 2945 (Fam), per Sumner J, at [87] (Pakistani *talaq* divorce obtained in 1987).

[803] [2007] EWHC 2945 (Fam).

[804] At [85].

[805] At [84]–[86].

[806] But not a British divorce, etc, supra, pp 1001–2.

[807] S 51(3)(a)(ii). See *A v L (Overseas Divorce)* [2010] EWHC 460 (Fam) at [78], supra p 1027. Cf *Olafisoye v Olafisoye* [2010] EWHC 3540 (Fam) at [69].

[808] *Mitford v Mitford* [1923] P 130.

[809] *Newmarch v Newmarch* [1978] Fam 79 at 90–4.

[810] *Joyce v Joyce* [1979] Fam 93; *Quazi v Quazi* [1980] AC 744 at 780; *Sabbagh v Sabbagh* [1985] FLR 29 at 34; *Mamdani v Mamdani* [1984] FLR 699.

[811] *Sharif v Sharif* (1980) 10 Fam Law 216 at 217.

[812] *Joyce v Joyce* [1979] Fam 93 at 111–12.

[813] *Sabbagh v Sabbagh* [1985] FLR 29 at 34; cf *Joyce v Joyce* [1979] Fam 93 at 113.

[814] *Law v Gustin* [1976] Fam 155.

nature of the proceedings will not, as in the case of lack of notice,[815] necessarily constitute grounds for denial of recognition. Finally, the discretionary nature of the power to refuse recognition must be stressed.[816] Even if the necessary opportunity is lacking, the court may still recognise the foreign divorce, etc.[817]

(f) Public policy[818]

Denial of recognition to an overseas[819] divorce, etc on public policy grounds is specifically provided for in section 51(3)(c) of the 1986 Act.[820] In particular, the provision states that recognition of the validity of an overseas divorce, etc may be refused if such recognition would be manifestly contrary to public policy. It seems very likely that the courts will, in applying this provision, seek guidance from relevant common law decisions.[821] It should be emphasised that, again, the court has a discretion;[822] there is no requirement that recognition be refused on this basis and there is some authority for the unusual view that the discretion would be exercised in favour of recognition even if such recognition would be manifestly contrary to public policy.[823]

It is suggested that Thorpe LJ was not correct, in *Golubovich v Golubovich*[824] to submit that if the court has formed an opinion that recognition would be "manifestly contrary to public policy", the exercise of any residual discretion could only be one direction, ie "refusal of recognition must follow".[825] The statute clearly leaves the decision on recognition to the discretion of the court, as s 51(3)(c) of the 1986 Act states that recognition of the validity of an overseas divorce, etc *may* be refused if such recognition would be manifestly contrary to public policy (emphasis added).

Section 51(3)(c) refers to recognition being "manifestly"[826] contrary to public policy. This does no more than confirm the stated attitude at common law that the discretion is one to be exercised sparingly.[827] Indeed "manifestly" has been held to add nothing to the common law rule;[828] but the courts may prove to be willing to maintain the breadth which the common law rule had reached, and there is some evidence that the courts will deny recognition where

---

[815] Supra, pp 1027–9.

[816] *Chaudhary v Chaudhary* [1985] Fam 19 at 43–4, 48.

[817] As in *Newmarch v Newmarch* [1978] Fam 79, where the factors relevant to the exercise of the discretion are discussed; and see Dickson (1979) 28 ICLQ 132.

[818] Carter (1984) 55 BYBIL 111, 127–30; (1993) 42 ICLQ 1, 5–10.

[819] But not a British divorce, etc, supra, pp 1001–2.

[820] See *Golubovich v Golubovich* [2010] EWCA Civ 810; *Olafisoye v Olafisoye* [2010] EWHC 3540 (Fam) [17]–[31] and [89]; and *NP v KRP (Foreign Divorce)* [2013] EWHC 694 (Fam). See also obiter comments of Sir Mark Potter P in *A v L (Overseas Divorce)* [2010] EWHC 460 (Fam), to the effect that had his Lordship been satisfied that the husband had obtained the divorce decree in Egypt by falsely claiming that he had pronounced a *talaq* over the telephone, the President would have been prepared to accept the plea that recognition should be refused under section 51(3)(c), at [79].

[821] Discussed in detail in the 14th edition of this book, pp 1018–20. It is suggested that Wood J was wrong, in *Chaudhary v Chaudhary* [1985] Fam 19 at 29, to indicate that there also coexisted a common law basis for denial of recognition on public policy grounds. Recognition is exclusively governed by what is now Part II of the 1986 Act, and the grounds for denying recognition are limited to those in the Act: s 45.

[822] See *H v H (Validity of Japanese Divorce)* [2006] EWHC 2989 (Fam), [2007] 1 FLR 1318 at [182].

[823] *Newmarch v Newmarch* [1978] Fam 79 at 97.

[824] [2010] EWCA Civ 810.

[825] Ibid, at [69].

[826] The term is only in the statute in order to conform to Art 10 of the 1970 Hague Convention: Law Com No 34 (1970), p 43.

[827] *Eroglü v Eroglü* [1994] 2 FLR 287 at 289; *Tahir v Tahir* 1993 SLT 194; *El Fadl v El Fadl* [2000] 1 FCR 685, per Hughes J, at 702; and *B v B (Divorce: Northern Cyprus)* [2001] 3 FCR 331 at 340. Cf the position under Brussels II *bis*, supra, p 1004.

[828] *Sharif v Sharif* (1980) 10 Fam Law 216 at 217–18; *Chaudhary v Chaudhary* [1985] Fam 19 at 28–9.

the application of the foreign rule is, in the particular circumstances, felt to be contrary to public policy.[829]

The principles on which the statutory discretion should be exercised have been stated thus:

> In exercising its discretion . . . this court should have regard to all the surrounding circum-
> stances which would include a full investigation of the facts relied upon to support a refusal
> of recognition; the likely consequences if the petitioning spouse had been given the oppor-
> tunity to take part in the proceedings; an assessment of what the legitimate objectives of the
> petitioning spouse are, and to what extent those objectives can be achieved if the foreign
> decree remains valid, and what the likely consequences to the spouses and any children of
> the family would be if recognition were refused.[830]

Further, it has been stated[831] that the principle of comity is a relevant consideration;[832] the conduct of the parties leading up to the divorce may be a relevant factor; and motivation may be relevant. In *Golubovich v Golubovich*,[833] Thorpe LJ accentuated the gravity and undesir-ability of refusal to recognise a divorce granted by a foreign court of competent jurisdiction, particularly if the foreign state is a member of the Council of Europe, and in the situation where the other party was entitled in England to a remedy under Part III of the Matrimonial and Family Proceedings Act 1984.

In applying such principles, it has been held that the fact that a foreign decree has a different effect from an English one is not, as such, grounds of public policy for denying recognition to the former.[834] The operation of such principles might be illustrated by *Kendall v Kendall*:[835]

> H and W lived together in Bolivia. W decided to leave Bolivia, with their children, in
> 1974. Before leaving she signed documents, in Spanish (a language of which she had little
> understanding), which H told her were documents to permit her to take the children out
> of the country. In 1975 the Bolivian courts granted a decree of divorce, purporting to be a
> decree granted to W as petitioner. It was probably the case that the documents W signed
> constituted a power of attorney enabling a decree to be granted without W's presence before
> the court.

As H was habitually resident in Bolivia at the time of the decree it ought, prima facie, to be recognised in England.[836] It could not be denied recognition for want of notice under the relevant provisions of the Recognition of Divorces and Legal Separations Act 1971[837] because they only related to lack of notice of, or want of opportunity to take part in, the proceed-ings in the case of the respondent.[838] Here, the party disadvantaged was W, the apparent petitioner. However, Hollins J concluded that recognition of the decree would manifestly be contrary to public policy as the Bolivian court had been deceived, not just as to facts alleged in the petition, but as to the fundamental issue of whether W was petitioning at all.[839]

---

[829] Eg *Newmarch v Newmarch* [1978] Fam 79; Carter (1978) 49 BYBIL 295, 297; *Joyce v Joyce* [1979] Fam 93 at 114; Dickson (1980) 43 MLR 81, 84–5; *Chaudhary v Chaudhary* [1985] Fam 19 at 39–40, 43–5.

[830] *Newmarch v Newmarch* [1978] Fam 79 at 95.

[831] *H v H (Validity of Japanese Divorce)* [2006] EWHC 2989 (Fam), [2007] 1 FLR 1318, per S Wildblood QC, sitting as Deputy Judge of the High Court, at [182].

[832] *El Fadl v El Fadl* [2000] 1 FCR 685; and *NP v KRP (Foreign Divorce)* [2013] EWHC 694 (Fam), per Parker J, at [129].

[833] [2010] EWCA Civ 810, at [78] and [81].

[834] Social Security Decision No R(G) 1/85.

[835] [1977] Fam 208.

[836] See now the 1986 Act, s 46(a)(i).

[837] S 8(2)(a).

[838] There is no such restriction in s 51(3)(a) of the 1986 Act, supra, pp 1027–30.

[839] Contrast *Eroglü v Eroglü* [1994] 2 FLR 287, where both spouses were party to the deception of a Turkish court whose divorce decree was recognised.

Finally, particular problems in relation to public policy may arise in the context of the recognition of extra-judicial divorces, etc. The recognition of extra-judicial divorces as such is not contrary to public policy.[840] However, when it was thought[841] that recognition of a "bare" *talak*, ie one delivered without any further proceedings, fell within the broad recognition rules of the Recognition of Divorces and Legal Separations Act 1971,[842] it was suggested that, though it would not be right to lay down a general rule for "bare" *talaks*, such a divorce could be denied recognition on the public policy grounds that it was done in secrecy and without the wife being in any way aware that it was about to happen.[843] It is now the case that specific provision is made in the 1986 Act for the recognition of "bare" *talaks* and other divorces, etc where there are no proceedings, but only on the limited jurisdictional basis of domicile.[844] "Bare" *talaks* cannot, therefore, be denied recognition, as such, on public policy grounds, because Parliament has provided clearly for their recognition. The courts will remain free, however, to take account of the particular circumstances of a case as justifying denial of recognition. In *El Fadl v El Fadl*,[845] Hughes J remarked: "I am satisfied that however much a unilateral divorce without notice may offend English sensibilities comity between nations and belief systems requires at any rate this much, that one country should accept the conscientiously held but very different standards of another where they are applied to those who are domiciled in it."

It has also been suggested that recognition should be denied on public policy grounds to an extra-judicial divorce, etc if both parties were domiciled in England when it was obtained:

> It must plainly be contrary to the public policy of the law in a case where both parties to the marriage are domiciled in this country to permit one of them, whilst continuing his English domicile, to avoid the incidents of his domiciliary law and to deprive the other party to the marriage of her rights under that law[846] by the simple process of taking advantage of his financial ability to travel to a country whose laws appear temporarily to be more favourable to him.[847]

This suggestion was made in the context of the recognition of a "bare" *talak* and the problem cannot in fact now arise in that context because recognition is based on the domicile of the parties.[848] This approach has, however, been welcomed[849] as more widely appropriate to the case of extra-judicial divorces, etc where there are proceedings which could be recognised, even though both spouses are domiciled in England, because they have been obtained, for example, in the country of which one spouse was a national.[850] There are difficulties with so broad an approach. Why should such a rule be limited to extra-judicial divorces, etc as there may well be judicial divorces, etc where a spouse domiciled in England takes advantage of his financial resources to obtain a valid divorce abroad, to the disadvantage of the other spouse,

---

[840] *Quazi v Quazi* [1980] AC 744 at 781–2.

[841] That was shown to be incorrect in *Chaudhary v Chaudhary* [1985] Fam 19.

[842] Ie those based on nationality, habitual residence and domicile in the foreign sense, under ss 2–5 of the 1971 Act.

[843] *Zaal v Zaal* (1982) 4 FLR 284 at 288–9; and see *Quazi v Quazi* [1980] AC 744 at 783; *Chaudhary v Chaudhary* [1985] Fam 19 at 28–9, 39–41, 43–5.

[844] S 46(2)(b).

[845] [2000] 1 FCR 685 at 702–3.

[846] *Tahir v Tahir* 1993 SLT 194 makes clear that, in the light of the financial provisions for the benefit of a divorced spouse, contained in the Matrimonial and Family Proceedings Act 1984, Part III, infra, p 1072 et seq, recognition will not be denied on financial grounds alone.

[847] *Chaudhary v Chaudhary* [1985] Fam 19 at 45.

[848] 1986 Act, s 46(2).

[849] Carroll (1985) 101 LQR 175, 177; for a markedly different approach, see Gordon (1986) 16 Fam Law 169.

[850] 1986 Act, s 46(1).

also domiciled in England? If all divorces, etc obtained in such circumstances are to be denied recognition on public policy grounds, this seems to run counter to the policy of Parliament, for the legislation does not in terms preclude their recognition nor could it under the 1970 Hague Convention on which the 1986 Act is still based.[851]

(g) Special rules for extra-judicial divorces, etc where there are no proceedings

It will be recalled[852] that where a divorce, etc is obtained overseas but there are no judicial or other proceedings, eg a "bare" *talak*, the only jurisdictional basis for recognition is domicile in the English sense. However, even if the overseas divorce, etc satisfies that jurisdictional test and is effective in the relevant country of the domicile,[853] it may be denied recognition on any one of the following three bases for non-recognition already discussed: *res judicata*, no subsisting marriage or that recognition would manifestly be contrary to public policy.[854] However, the two bases concerned with notice of, or opportunity to take part in, the proceedings[855] are not applicable, for obvious reasons, where there are no proceedings. Instead, a foreign divorce, etc obtained without proceedings may be refused recognition if "there is no official document certifying that the divorce, annulment or legal separation is effective under the law of the country where it was obtained".[856] The purpose of this provision seems to be evidential, rather than going to issues of justice between the parties. An official document is defined as one "issued by a person or body[857] appointed or recognised for the purpose"[858] in the foreign country. So the operation of the provision will depend on whether court or other officials in the country where a bare *talak* or the like is obtained are prepared to provide such certification for the purposes of English proceedings, and certificates may not be easy to obtain.[859] Whilst proof of effectiveness of such divorces has been shown on occasions to be a problem,[860] one would hope that an English court is unlikely to deny recognition if it is satisfied as to the effectiveness of the divorce, etc even though no certificate is forthcoming. If that is so, it is hard to see what real purpose this provision serves.[861]

This provision on certification assumes that the divorce, etc is obtained in the country where both parties were domiciled at that time,[862] but there is a variant of it to deal with the case where the divorce, etc is obtained in the country where one spouse was domiciled and is recognised in the country of the domicile of the other spouse.[863] In such a case, recognition may be denied not only if there is no official certificate as to the effectiveness of the divorce where it was obtained, but also if there is no "official document" certifying that it is recognised as valid in the country of the domicile of the other spouse.[864] So, if a husband domiciled in

---

[851] Art 1 of the Hague Convention envisages the recognition of at least some extra-judicial divorces and legal separations.

[852] Supra, p 1021 et seq.

[853] Supra, pp 1006–7.

[854] S 51(1), (2), (3)(c).

[855] S 51(3)(a).

[856] S 51(3)(b)(i). See, eg, *Wicken v Wicken* [1999] 2 WLR 1166 (no justification for refusing recognition under s 51(3)(b)(i)).

[857] See *El Fadl v El Fadl* [2000] 1 FCR 685, per Hughes J, at 702: "Many states will have more than one person or body capable of certifying officially and authoritatively."

[858] S 51(4).

[859] See Lord Meston, 473 HL Official Report, col 1094 (1986).

[860] *Quazi v Quazi* [1980] AC 744 at 824.

[861] No guidance can be found from Law Com No 137 (1984) because this basis of non-recognition is not one recommended by the Law Commission, who did not propose special rules for divorces, etc obtained where there were no proceedings; see *Wicken v Wicken* [1999] 2 WLR 1166 at 1180.

[862] S 46(2)(b)(i).

[863] S 46(2)(b)(ii).

[864] S 51(3)(b)(ii).

Dubai obtains a "bare" *talak* there,[865] his wife being domiciled in Pakistan, the divorce may be denied recognition if there is no official certificate as to its effectiveness in Dubai or that it will be recognised in Pakistan.

(vii) Retrospectivity

The general rule in Part II of the 1986 Act is that its provisions govern the recognition of both British and overseas divorces, annulments and legal separations, whether they were obtained before or after the 1986 Act came into force.[866] There are two kinds of limitation on this general retrospective effect, both of which are fully explained in the 13th edition of this book.[867]

(viii) Effect of a foreign divorce, annulment or legal separation[868]

One problem which is untouched by the 1986 Act and by Brussels II *bis* is as to the effect to be given in England to a divorce, annulment or legal separation obtained outside England (described in this section of the chapter as a "foreign" divorce, etc)[869] and whose recognition is governed by Part II of that Act, or by Brussels II *bis*. This is left to the common law and it is convenient to consider the three matrimonial causes separately.

(a) Divorce

The effect of a foreign divorce on the married status of the parties is obvious. If, in the eyes of English law, the divorce is valid, it effectively terminates that status;[870] if it is void for want of jurisdiction, the status remains unchanged. Nevertheless, the divorce may have an effect with regard to certain subsidiary purposes other than the assessment of status. The question of the effect of a foreign divorce seldom arises in practice, but three situations merit some discussion.

First, although a valid divorce terminates the married status of the parties, it does not automatically terminate a maintenance order in favour of the wife made by an English court at a time when they were living permanently in England.[871] The court has discretion to retain, vary or discharge it, and in exercising this discretion it is relevant to consider whether the wife participated in the divorce proceedings, whether the question of maintenance was raised in the foreign court and whether the basis for the divorce was insufficient by English law.[872]

It is rare that a foreign divorce will be denied recognition in England for want of jurisdiction, given the breadth of English recognition rules under the 1986 Act, and the prohibition upon review of jurisdiction of the court of origin under Article 24 of Brussels II *bis*. If, however, lack of jurisdiction were to render the foreign divorce invalid in England, it would not be altogether devoid of effect even though it leaves the married status of the parties undisturbed.[873] It may at least require consideration in the context of desertion and estoppel. There is little authority on the question whether the effect of an invalid divorce is to exclude from consideration the period during which the respondent may have been in desertion prior to the divorce. This may be a critical factor if the petitioner later institutes divorce proceedings in England on the ground that the marriage has broken down in that the respondent has

---

[865] Cf *Zaal v Zaal* (1982) 4 FLR 284.

[866] 1986 Act, s 51(1), (2), (3).

[867] See 13th edn of this book (1999), p 820.

[868] North, op cit, pp 135, 191–201, 266–8, 287–92.

[869] Including both those granted elsewhere in the British Isles and those obtained overseas.

[870] For discussion of its effect on capacity to remarry, see supra, p 926.

[871] See infra, p 1071.

[872] *Wood v Wood* [1957] P 254; Carter (1957) 33 BYBIL 336; *Qureshi v Qureshi* [1972] Fam 173 at 200–1; *Newmarch v Newmarch* [1978] Fam 79.

[873] Subject to problems of the "incidental question", discussed, supra, Chapter 4, and see North, op cit, pp 199–200.

deserted the petitioner for a period of at least two years immediately preceding the presentation of the petition.[874] Although the answer no doubt depends on the conduct of the parties, it would appear from the two relevant decisions, both concerned with a Jewish divorce by delivery of a *gett*, that the desertion is not terminated unless the respondent initiated or instigated the foreign suit or at least freely consented to its institution.[875]

Another question is whether a foreign divorce, invalid for want of jurisdiction, is affected by the doctrine of estoppel. It is clear that there is no estoppel so far as the married status of the parties is concerned. Neither party is precluded from denying that in the eyes of English law the parties are still husband and wife.[876] It is, however, unclear whether the doctrine of estoppel can be invoked for other purposes. Can, for instance, a woman who has obtained an invalid divorce in a foreign country claim a widow's share of her deceased husband's estate? To succeed, she must show that she was the "wife" of her late husband at the time of his death, which involves relying on the invalidity of the divorce. But can it not be maintained that she is estopped from impugning the decision of the court whose jurisdiction she herself invoked? This question has met with conflicting answers in Canada, though the Supreme Court of Canada[877] has expressed itself in favour of there being no conclusive overriding principle of estoppel, and certainly there is no estoppel in the case of a person not a party to the foreign divorce.[878] So far as English courts are concerned, there is in principle no room for estoppel, since the paramount issue from which all else flows is the marital status of the parties at the time of the husband's death, and of that there can be no doubt.[879]

(b) Annulment[880]

In considering the effect in England of a foreign annulment which is recognised in England, it is necessary to investigate what effect the annulment has in the country where it was obtained and compare that effect with the effect of an English nullity decree. Where the foreign annulment has the same effect on the status of the parties as an equivalent English decree, there will be little difficulty in giving full effect to it.[881] Difficulty may arise where, for example, a decree annulling a voidable marriage is retrospective in effect, whilst an equivalent English decree is only prospective in effect.[882] This problem has arisen in a decision concerned with the recognition in Scotland of a Northern Ireland nullity decree. It concerned a claim to social security: Social Security Decision No R (G) 1/85 where the facts were these:

> The wife lived in Scotland. Her first husband died in 1966 and she had received a widow's pension ever since. In 1980, in Northern Ireland, she went through a ceremony of marriage with M with whom she lived for just seven weeks before returning to Scotland. As soon as she married, her widow's pension ceased to be paid. In 1982, she obtained a decree absolute from the Northern Ireland court declaring her second marriage void on the ground of

---

[874] Matrimonial Causes Act 1973, s 1(2)(c).

[875] *Joseph v Joseph* [1953] 1 WLR 1182 (desertion terminated); *Corbett v Corbett* [1957] 1 WLR 486.

[876] *Travers v Holley* [1953] P 246 at 254; and see *Bonaparte v Bonaparte* [1892] P 402; *Schwebel v Schwebel* (1970) 10 DLR (3d) 742; *Gaffney v Gaffney* [1975] IR 133. Indeed, it has been said, in *Hornett v Hornett* [1971] P 255 at 261, that "there are great difficulties about applying a doctrine of estoppel to a legal decree affecting status"; and see Carter (1971) 45 BYBIL 410.

[877] *Downtown v Royal Trust Co* (1972) 34 DLR (3d) 403.

[878] *Fromovitz v Fromovitz* (1977) 79 DLR (3d) 148; cf *Knight v Knight* (1995) 16 RFL (4th) 48.

[879] And see *Gaffney v Gaffney* [1975] IR 133; *PK v TK* [2002] IR 186 (Sup Ct); and *CK v JK* [2004] IR 224, referred to by Dicey, Morris and Collins, para 18-149.

[880] See Law Com No 137 (1984), paras 2.32–2.38. The Law Commission recommended (at para 6.60) that the effect in this country of a foreign annulment should not be the subject of legislation; and see Jaffey (1983) 32 ICLQ 500.

[881] *Von Lorang v Administrator of Austrian Property* [1927] AC 641 at 654–5. For its effect on capacity to marry, see supra, p 926.

[882] Matrimonial Causes Act 1973, s 16, supra, p 985.

non-consummation because of M's impotence. In the light of that, she sought, in Scotland, to have her widow's pension reinstated retrospectively. The effect in Northern Ireland of the nullity decree was that the marriage was voidable, and the decree had only prospective effect.[883] However, an equivalent decree in Scotland would render the marriage void and have retrospective effect.

The two issues for the Social Security Commissioner were whether the Northern Ireland nullity decree should be recognised in Scotland and, if so, whether it should be given prospective or retrospective effect. If the former, the wife would lose; if it had the Scottish retrospective effect, she would succeed. The Commissioner had no hesitation in holding that the Northern Ireland nullity decree should be recognised in Scotland.[884] Having rejected arguments that to recognise the Northern Ireland effect of the decree as prospective only would be contrary to Scottish public policy or that the effect was simply a matter of procedure to be ignored in Scotland,[885] he followed the approach recommended by the Law Commission[886] that the foreign effects of the annulment should normally be recognised and gave the Northern Ireland decree only prospective effect. To do otherwise would have given the decree greater effect in Scotland than it had in Northern Ireland as well as differing effects as between the two "spouses" who were domiciled in different countries.

Where the foreign annulment is not recognised, it should be treated in the same way as a foreign divorce that is not recognised.[887] There is Canadian authority[888] for the application of the doctrine of estoppel; but it is suggested that an English court should deny operation to the doctrine, whether the matter at issue is the direct one of marital status or a less central question, such as succession.

(c) Legal separation

An English decree of judicial separation entitles the petitioner to live apart from the respondent,[889] but does not dissolve the married status of the parties.[890] It is permanent in the sense that it remains in operation unless and until a discharge of the decree is ordered. The effect to be given to a foreign legal separation which is recognised in England was considered at common law in *Tursi v Tursi*:[891]

> Two Italian subjects, domiciled in Italy, married there in 1942. The husband deserted the wife and never returned to her. In 1947, the wife obtained in Rome a decree of judicial separation, substantially similar in effect to an English decree, on the ground of the husband's desertion. In 1955, the wife, who had been resident in England since 1949, petitioned for divorce on the ground of the husband's desertion for three years,[892] he being still domiciled and resident in Italy.

In deciding to recognise the foreign decree granted by the law of the domicile, Sachs J had to consider its effect under English law. He held that it should have the same effect with respect to desertion as an English decree of judicial separation, namely that a decree of judicial

---

[883] Matrimonial Causes (Northern Ireland) Order 1978, Art 18.

[884] Applying common law recognition rules, based on the fact that M, though not the wife, was domiciled in Northern Ireland.

[885] Social Security Decision No R(G) 1/85, 8–10.

[886] Law Com No 137 (1984), para 2.33; North, op cit, p 267; cf Smith (1980) 96 LQR 380, 390–3.

[887] Supra, p 1034 et seq.

[888] *Re Capon* (1965) 49 DLR (2d) 675; *Schwebel v Schwebel* (1970) 10 DLR (3d) 742.

[889] Matrimonial Causes Act 1973, s 18(1).

[890] Though if a spouse dies intestate whilst such a decree is in force, his property will devolve as if the other spouse was dead: Matrimonial Causes Act 1973, s 18(2).

[891] [1958] P 54.

[892] The equivalent ground of divorce under the Matrimonial Causes Act 1973, s 1(1) and (2)(c) is breakdown of marriage as evidenced by two years' desertion immediately preceding the petition.

separation did not put an end to desertion, as at common law,[893] but that the wife could treat any period of desertion occurring before the decree as occurring immediately before the petition for divorce.[894] There seems no reason why the same conclusion should not be reached, under the Matrimonial Causes Act 1973, in respect of a petition for divorce on the ground of breakdown of marriage being evidenced by two years' desertion, so that a period of desertion preceding a foreign legal separation may be deemed to precede the English petition.[895] Similarly, it may be argued that the provision barring one spouse, judicially separated from the other, from succeeding to the latter's estate on intestacy[896] applies equally to foreign legal separations.[897]

More recent discussion of the effect to be given to a foreign legal separation which is recognised in England is found in *Sabbagh v Sabbagh*:[898]

> The spouses were married in Brazil in 1965, where they were domiciled. Shortly thereafter they came to England and acquired a domicile in England; but in 1980 the marriage broke up. The husband returned to Brazil and became domiciled and habitually resident there, whilst the wife remained in England. In 1983 the husband obtained a decree of judicial separation in Brazil, the effect of which was to freeze the proprietary rights of the parties, without dissolving the marriage. The wife then petitioned for divorce in England and two issues arose: should the Brazilian decree be recognised and, if so, what effect did recognition have on the rights of the English court to grant the wife financial and other relief on her divorce petition?

There was no doubt in the mind of Balcombe J that the Brazilian decree, being a decree of the country of the petitioner's domicile and habitual residence,[899] should be recognised.[900] The question remained, however, as to what effect was to be given to it. If its effect was the same as that of an English decree of judicial separation, it would prevent the English court from itself making a decree.[901] However, the effects of the Brazilian decree on the property rights of the parties were not to be recognised in England. This was not required by the statute[902] and "there is no basis here for the contention that the Brazilian decree of judicial separation will have the effect of excluding the English court's powers to deal with the wife's financial application once she has been granted a decree of divorce in England".[903]

4. PRESUMPTION OF DEATH AND DISSOLUTION OF MARRIAGE[904]

Section 1 of the Presumption of Death Act 2013[905] provides that the High Court can, on application of a person with sufficient interest, make a declaration that a missing person is to

---

[893] *Harriman v Harriman* [1909] P 123.
[894] Under the Matrimonial Causes Act 1950, s 7(3).
[895] Matrimonial Causes Act 1973, s 4(3).
[896] Ibid, s 18(2).
[897] Dicey, Morris and Collins, para 18-152.
[898] [1985] FLR 29.
[899] Applying s 3 of the Recognition of Divorces and Legal Separations Act 1971; see now s 46(1) of the 1986 Act.
[900] None of the grounds for non-recognition in s 8 of the 1971 Act (s 51 of the 1986 Act) were made out.
[901] [1985] FLR 29 at 35.
[902] S 8(3) of the 1971 Act; now s 51(5) of the 1986 Act.
[903] [1985] FLR 29 at 36. The availability of financial relief after foreign divorces, etc is discussed generally infra, p 1071 et seq.
[904] North, op cit, pp 68, 71, 151, 297–9; and see Kelly and Varsanyi (1971) 20 ICLQ 535.
[905] The procedure for a declaration of death under the Presumption of Death Act 2013 has replaced some of the procedures by virtue of which a person might be presumed dead under the law of England and Wales,

be presumed dead. One of the effects of such a declaration is that it ends the missing person's marriage.[906] Strictly speaking, once a person is dead in the eyes of the law, it is superfluous to talk about the dissolution of his marriage. Nevertheless, it is desirable that a declaration of presumed death has this effect in order to meet the contingency of the presumption being proved wrong.[907] Such decrees are, therefore, *sui generis*, because in the case of divorce the court proceeds on the assumption that the respondent is alive, whilst here the opposite is assumed.[908]

(a) Jurisdiction[909]

The jurisdiction of the English court for granting a declaration that a missing person is to be presumed dead is provided for in sections 1(3) and (4) of the Presumption of Death Act 2013.[910] The jurisdictional grounds are examined in Chapter 23 ("Declarations").[911]

(b) Choice of law

So far as choice of law is concerned, the problem is similar to that in divorce.[912] The courts appear consistently to have applied English law, even though the petitioner was domiciled elsewhere,[913] but their statutory obligation to do so[914] has been repealed.[915]

(c) Recognition

The rules as to recognition of foreign decrees of presumption of death and dissolution of marriage are not wholly clear, for no statutory provision has expressly been made for them.[916] If such a foreign decree is granted in circumstances which, *mutatis mutandis*, would have conferred jurisdiction on an English court, then it will be recognised in England.[917] It is quite possible that the common law rules for the recognition of divorces might be applied by analogy so as to permit recognition in England of a decree granted in a jurisdiction with which the petitioner had a "real and substantial connection".[918] If the foreign decree can, properly, be classed as a decree of divorce[919] then it may be recognised under the rules laid down in Part

---

including the declaration of presumption of death and dissolution of marriage under the Matrimonial Causes Act 1973. See the 14th edition of this book (2008), p 953 for the jurisdictional rules as they stood under s 5(4) of the 1973 Act. For Scotland, see the Presumption of Death (Scotland) Act 1977, s 1(3) (jurisdiction of the Court of Session to entertain an "action of declarator"), and for Northern Ireland see the Presumption of Death Act (Northern Ireland) 2009, s 1(2) (jurisdiction of the High Court to entertain proceedings for a declaration of presumed death).

[906] S 3(2)(b). The same effect ensues in relation to the missing person's civil partnership. Ibid. See infra, pp 1041–2.

[907] The court may order the variation or revocation of a declaration of presumed death (s 5(1)); however, such an order does not revive any marriage (or civil partnership) ended by the declaration (s 6(2)). This is to ensure that subsequent marriages (or civil partnerships) of the missing person's spouse or civil partner are not invalidated.

[908] *Wall v Wall* [1950] P 112 at 122–3, 125; *N v N* [1957] P 385 at 391.

[909] Presumption of death does not fall within the scope of Brussels II *bis*.

[910] In relation to civil partnerships, see Civil Partnership Act 2004, s 222, discussed infra, p 1041. In relation to same sex marriage, see Domicile and Matrimonial Proceedings Act 1973, Sch A1, para 3, discussed infra, p 1047.

[911] Infra, p 1058.

[912] Discussed, supra, p 979 et seq; see North, op cit, p 151.

[913] *Wall v Wall* [1950] P 112.

[914] Matrimonial Causes Act 1973, s 19(5).

[915] Domicile and Matrimonial Proceedings Act 1973, s 17(2).

[916] See North, op cit, pp 297–9.

[917] *Szemik v Gryla* (1965) 109 Sol Jo 175.

[918] Cf *Indyka v Indyka* [1969] 1 AC 33, [1967] 2 All ER 689; North (1968) 31 MLR 257, 281.

[919] On the question of classification, see North, op cit, p 203.

II of the Family Law Act 1986.[920] Neither that Act nor the Convention on which it is based defines what is meant by a "divorce". However, a foreign decree of presumption of death not coupled with one for dissolution of marriage might well not be recognised in England, on the ground that it was merely a matter of procedure and not of substantive law.[921] Matters relating to the presumption of death were not within the contemplation of the drafters of Brussels II *bis*. As mentioned previously, the term "divorce" is not defined in the Regulation, but the recognition rules contained in Chapter III of the instrument[922] should not be construed as applying to matters concerning the presumption of death, since such matters go beyond the "dissolution of matrimonial ties".[923]

5. DISSOLUTION, NULLITY AND SEPARATION OF CIVIL PARTNERSHIPS

(a) Jurisdiction

(i) Bases of jurisdiction

(a) Introduction

Chapter 2 (Dissolution, nullity and other proceedings)[924] of Part 2[925] of the Civil Partnership Act 2004 sets out the orders that an English court can make to bring a civil partnership to an end, or to provide for the separation of the parties. In particular, by virtue of section 37(1), the High Court or the family court[926] has power to make four orders: (a) a dissolution order, which dissolves a civil partnership on the ground that it has broken down irretrievably;[927] (b) a nullity order, which annuls a void or voidable civil partnership;[928] (c) a presumption of death order, which dissolves a civil partnership on the ground that one of the civil partners is presumed to be dead;[929] and (d) a separation order, providing for the separation of civil partners.[930] The power which is conferred on English courts by Chapter 2 of Part 2 of the Act, to grant orders of a type specified in section 37(1), is expressly subject[931] to sections 219 to 224 of the Act, discussed below. If, by virtue of sections 219 to 224 (jurisdiction of the court), an English court has jurisdiction in respect of a civil partnership, then the court is empowered to make an order under section 37.

(b) Civil Partnership (Jurisdiction and Recognition of Judgments) Regulations 2005 ("section 219 regulations")[932]

Chapter 3 (Dissolution etc: jurisdiction and recognition)[933] of Part 5[934] of the Civil Partnership Act 2004 makes provision concerning the exercise of jurisdiction by courts in England and Wales for the dissolution or annulment of a civil partnership, or for the legal

---

[920] Supra, p 1005 et seq; and see Law Com No 48 (1972) para 74 n 21.
[921] *Re Wolf's Goods* [1948] P 66, [1947] 2 All ER 841; though see *In the Goods of Schlesinger* [1950] CLY 1549.
[922] Supra, p 1002 et seq.
[923] Brussels II *bis*, Recital (8).
[924] Ss 37–64.
[925] Headed "Civil Partnership: England and Wales".
[926] S 37(4)(b).
[927] S 44 provides that an application may be made to the court by either civil partner on the ground that the civil partnership has broken down irretrievably.
[928] Ss 49 and 50, respectively, state the grounds on which, by English law, a civil partnership is void or voidable. See special provision for civil partnerships registered in Scotland, in Northern Ireland, at British consulates abroad, etc by members of armed forces serving abroad, or overseas: s 54.
[929] S 55 states the grounds on which, by English law, a presumption of death order may be granted.
[930] S 56 narrates the bases on which, by English law, an application for a separation order may be made.
[931] S 37(5).
[932] SI 2005/3334. See, for Scotland, SSI 2005/629.
[933] Ss 219–38.
[934] Headed "Civil partnership formed or dissolved abroad etc".

separation of civil partners. Section 219 of the Act empowers the Lord Chancellor to make provision as to the jurisdiction of courts in England and Wales[935] in respect of civil partnerships, corresponding to the Brussels II *bis* Regulation,[936] for cases where one partner is, or has been, habitually resident in a Member State, or is a national of a Member State, or is domiciled in a part of the United Kingdom.

The regulations made by virtue of section 219 are the Civil Partnership (Jurisdiction and Recognition of Judgments) Regulations 2005[937] (known as the "section 219 regulations"), which apply to proceedings for the dissolution, annulment or legal separation of all civil partnerships, including overseas relationships entitled to be treated as civil partnerships by virtue of the 2004 Act.[938]

(c) Proceedings for dissolution or separation

Section 221(1) of the 2004 Act provides that the English court[939] has jurisdiction to entertain proceedings for a dissolution order or a separation order in three situations. First, under section 221(1)(a), if the court has jurisdiction under the section 219 regulations.[940] Regulation 4[941] of the section 219 regulations provides that the courts in England shall have jurisdiction in relation to proceedings for the dissolution or annulment of a civil partnership or for the legal separation of civil partners where:[942] (a) both civil partners are habitually resident in England; (b) both civil partners were last habitually resident in England and one of the civil partners continues to reside there; (c) the respondent is habitually resident in England; (d) the petitioner is habitually resident in England and has resided there for at least one year immediately preceding the presentation of the petition;[943] or (e) the petitioner is domiciled and habitually resident in England and has resided there for at least six months preceding the presentation of the petition.[944]

Secondly, section 221(1)(b) of the 2004 Act provides that the English court has jurisdiction to entertain proceedings for a dissolution order or a separation order if no court has, or is recognised as having, jurisdiction under the section 219 regulations, and either civil partner is domiciled in England on the date when the proceedings are begun.[945]

Thirdly, section 221(1)(c) of the 2004 Act provides that the English court has jurisdiction to entertain proceedings for a dissolution order or a separation order if the following conditions are met: (i) the parties registered as civil partners in England or Wales; (ii) no court has, or is recognised as having, jurisdiction under the section 219 regulations; and (iii) it appears to the court to be in the interests of justice to assume jurisdiction in the case.[946] The rationale behind this discretionary *"forum necessitatis"* rule of jurisdiction is to acknowledge the fact

---

[935] S 219(a).

[936] S 219(3).

[937] SI 2005/3334.

[938] Rule 3.

[939] High Court or the family court: s 220.

[940] SI 2005/3334.

[941] Rule 5 makes corresponding provision for Northern Ireland.

[942] Cf SI 2014/543, r 2 (same sex marriage), discussed infra, p 1046, and generally Art 3, Brussels II *bis*, discussed supra, pp 955–6. However, there is no ground of jurisdiction in the s 219 regulations equivalent to Brussels II *bis*, Art 3, indent 4 (joint applications).

[943] This wording is slightly different from that in Brussels II *bis*, Art 3, indent 5, on which the provision is based.

[944] This wording is slightly different from that in Brussels II *bis*, Art 3, indent 6, on which the provision is based.

[945] Cf Domicile and Matrimonial Proceedings Act 1973, Sch A1, para 2(1)(b) (same sex marriage), discussed infra, p 1046.

[946] Cf Domicile and Matrimonial Proceedings Act 1973, Sch A1, para 2(1)(c) (same sex marriage), discussed infra, p 1046.

that many legal systems do not recognise the institution of civil partnership. The rule therefore provides protection to parties who registered as civil partners in England or Wales but are unable to obtain a dissolution or separation in the country of their residence and, at the same time, do not meet the jurisdictional requirements laid down by the section 219 regulations.

(d) Proceedings for nullity

Section 221(2) of the 2004 Act provides that the English court[947] has jurisdiction to entertain proceedings for a nullity order in three situations. First, under s 221(2)(a), if the court has jurisdiction under the section 219 regulations.[948] Secondly, section 221(2)(b) of the Act provides that the English court has jurisdiction, if no court has, or is recognised as having, jurisdiction under the section 219 regulations and either civil partner (i) is domiciled in England on the date when the proceedings are begun, or (ii) died before proceedings were begun and was at death domiciled in England or had been, for one year immediately preceding death, habitually resident in England.[949] Thirdly, section 221(2)(c) of the Act provides that the English court has jurisdiction, if the following conditions are met: (i) the parties registered as civil partners in England or Wales; (ii) no court has, or is recognised as having, jurisdiction under the section 219 regulations; and (iii) it appears to the court to be in the interests of justice to assume jurisdiction in the case.[950] Like the equivalent *"forum necessitatis"* rule provided for in relation to dissolution and separation of a civil partnership,[951] this provision facilitates access to court for civil partners who registered their partnership in England or Wales but can neither obtain an annulment in the country where they reside nor are able to demonstrate a close connection with England by meeting the jurisdictional requirements set out in the section 219 regulations.

(e) Other proceedings in relation to the same civil partnership

Section 221(3) of the 2004 Act provides that when proceedings are pending in respect of which the court has jurisdiction by virtue of section 221(1) or (2), it also has jurisdiction to entertain other proceedings for dissolution, separation or nullity in respect of the same civil partnership, notwithstanding that jurisdiction would not be exercisable in those proceedings under section 221(1) or (2).[952]

(f) Presumption of death and dissolution of civil partnership

By section 222 of the 2004 Act, the English court has jurisdiction to entertain proceedings for a presumption of death order, on an application made by a civil partner, if: (a) at the time the application is made, the High Court does not have jurisdiction to entertain an application by that civil partner under section 1 of the Presumption of Death Act 2013 for a declaration that the other civil partner is presumed to be dead,[953] and (b) the parties registered as civil partners of each other in England and it appears to the court to be in the interests of justice to assume jurisdiction in the case. This *"forum necessitatis"* rule of jurisdiction provides a safeguard to civil partners who registered their partnership in England but, at the time of the application for a presumption of death order, do not meet the jurisdictional criteria for

---

[947] High court or the family court: s 220.

[948] Detailed supra. Cf SI 2014/543, r 2 (same sex marriage), discussed infra, p 1046.

[949] Cf Domicile and Matrimonial Proceedings Act 1973, Sch A1, para 2(1)(b) (same sex marriage), discussed infra, pp 1046–7.

[950] Cf Domicile and Matrimonial Proceedings Act 1973, Sch A1, para 2(1)(b) (same sex marriage), discussed infra, pp 1046–7.

[951] Civil Partnership Act 2004, s 221(1)(c) (discussed supra).

[952] Cf Domicile and Matrimonial Proceedings Act 1973 (marriage), s 5(5), supra, p 965, and Domicile and Matrimonial Proceedings Act 1973, Sch A1, para 3 (same sex marriage), infra, p 1047.

[953] See Chapter 23, p 1058.

proceedings for a declaration of presumed death under section 1 of the Presumption of Death Act 2013.[954]

(ii) Procedural issues

(a) Service of the petition

The rules on service of a petition for dissolution, etc are the same as those concerning petitions for divorce, etc.[955]

(b) Staying proceedings

The Family Procedure (Civil Partnership: Staying of Proceedings) Rules 2010,[956] made under section 223 of the 2004 Act, make provision for civil partnerships corresponding to that which is made for marriages in Schedule 1 to the Domicile and Matrimonial Proceedings Act 1973.[957] The Rules make equivalent provision, *mutatis mutandis*, for obligatory[958] and discretionary[959] stays of civil partnership proceedings in England for cases where civil partnership proceedings[960] are continuing in another jurisdiction outside England.[961] Given the close similarity between the regime set out in the 2010 Rules and that which applies to concurrent matrimonial proceedings, it is not proposed to examine the Rules in detail. In outline, however, rule 2 requires a party who is seeking an order in civil partnership proceedings to furnish the court with particulars of relevant civil partnership proceedings in another jurisdiction. Rule 3 provides for obligatory stays in relation to proceedings in a related jurisdiction.[962] Rule 4 concerns discretionary stays of civil partnership proceedings in a non-related jurisdiction.[963] Rule 5 relates to discharge of orders staying proceedings under rules 3 and 4. Rule 7 concerns the court's power to make ancillary relief orders where a stay is imposed, and rule 8 deals with the effect of orders already made in civil partnership proceedings which have been stayed.

(b) Choice of law

(i) Dissolution, separation orders and presumption of death orders

There is no direct reference in the Civil Partnership Act 2004 to choice of law. In the case of proceedings for dissolution of a civil partnership in England, a decree of dissolution will be granted only in accordance with sections 44 to 48 of the 2004 Act (ie English domestic law provisions on dissolution). Similarly, as regards proceedings for separation orders, such an order will be granted only in accordance with sections 56 and 57 of that Act (ie English domestic law provisions on separation). Finally, the court may make a presumption of death order only if the provisions of section 55 are satisfied (ie English domestic law provisions on presumption of death orders).

---

[954] Cf Domicile and Matrimonial Proceedings Act 1973, Sch A1, para 3 (same sex marriage).
[955] Supra, pp 966–7.
[956] SI 2010/2986.
[957] Discussed supra, p 972 et seq.
[958] Rule 3.
[959] Rule 4.
[960] Defined in r 1(2) as proceedings for one or more of: a dissolution order; a separation order; a nullity order; a declaration as to the validity of a civil partnership of the petitioner; or a declaration as to the subsistence of such a civil partnership.
[961] Cf Domicile and Matrimonial Proceedings Act 1973, s 5(6), infra, p 1047 (same sex marriage).
[962] Defined in r 1(2)(c) as Scotland, Northern Ireland, Jersey, Guernsey and the Isle of Man.
[963] Any state, European Union or non-European Union; Brussels II *bis* does not apply to civil partnerships, and so Art 19 (lis pendens) has no application here.

(ii) Nullity

The position is more complicated in relation to nullity. In the case of civil partnerships registered in England, a decree of nullity will be granted by an English court only in accordance with sections 49 to 53 of the 2004 Act.[964]

Section 54 of the Act lays down special rules as to the validity of civil partnerships registered *outside* England and Wales, to be used by the English court (having jurisdiction under section 221(2) of the Act)[965] when determining whether, under English law, a civil partnership is void or voidable where the parties did not register as civil partners in England and Wales.[966] As far as an apparent or alleged overseas relationship[967] is concerned, it will be held to be void[968] if (a) the relationship is not an overseas relationship,[969] or (b) even though the relationship is an overseas relationship, the parties are not treated as having formed a civil partnership under Chapter 2 of Part 5 of the Act.[970] A civil partnership registered overseas is voidable[971] if: (a) it is voidable under the law of the country where the relationship was registered, including its rules of private international law;[972] (b) the circumstances fall within section 50(1)(d)[973] of the Act; or (c) where either party was domiciled in England or in Northern Ireland at the time of registration of the relationship, the circumstances fall within section 50(1)(a), (b), (c) or (e).[974] The Explanatory Notes to the Act make clear that where a civil partnership is voidable under section 54, the provisions of section 51 (bars to relief where civil partnership is voidable) are applicable. Where, however, a civil partnership is voidable by virtue of application of foreign law, the bars to relief will apply only to the extent that they are applicable under the foreign law.[975]

(c) Recognition of dissolution, annulment and separation

(i) Introduction

Chapter 3 (Dissolution etc: jurisdiction and recognition)[976] of Part 5[977] of the Civil Partnership Act 2004 makes provision in sections 233 to 238 concerning recognition of the dissolution or annulment of a civil partnership or the legal separation of civil partners.

(ii) Effect of dissolution, annulment or separation obtained in the United Kingdom

Section 233[978] of the 2004 Act states that no dissolution or annulment obtained in one part of the United Kingdom is effective in any part of the United Kingdom, unless obtained from

---

[964] Having, in the case of a voidable civil partnership, only prospective effect: s 37(3).

[965] Supra, p 1041.

[966] Explanatory Notes, para 104. For civil partnerships registered: in Scotland, see s 54(1); in Northern Ireland, s 54(2); at British consulates, etc or by armed forces personnel, s 54(3) and (4); overseas, s 54(7), (8) and (10).

[967] S 54(6).

[968] S 54(7).

[969] Defined in ss 212–14, discussed supra, pp 947–8.

[970] Eg if, under the law of the country in which the relationship was registered, the necessary formalities were not complied with, or there was no capacity to enter the relationship.

[971] S 54(8).

[972] S 54(8) and (10).

[973] An interim gender recognition certificate under the Gender Recognition Act 2004 has, after the time of formation of the civil partnership, been issued to either civil partner.

[974] Grounds on which a civil partnership registered in England (and, by virtue of s 174, in Northern Ireland) is voidable.

[975] Explanatory Notes, para 111. See ss 51 and 54(9).

[976] Ss 219–38.

[977] Headed "Civil partnership formed or dissolved abroad etc".

[978] Cf Family Law Act 1986, s 44(1).

a court of civil jurisdiction. The validity of a dissolution, etc which has been obtained from a court of civil jurisdiction elsewhere in the United Kingdom shall be recognised in England, subject only to limited defences, namely: (a) if the dissolution, etc was obtained at a time when it was irreconcilable with a decision determining the question of the subsistence or validity of the civil partnership previously given by a court in England, or entitled to be recognised in England;[979] or (b) if the dissolution, etc was obtained at a time when, according to English law, there was no subsisting civil partnership.[980]

(iii) Recognition in the United Kingdom of dissolution, annulment or separation granted in a Member State[981]

Section 234 of the 2004 Act provides that the validity of an overseas dissolution, etc is to be recognised in the United Kingdom only by virtue of the scheme of recognition imposed by sections 235 to 237 of the Act, which, in turn, are subject to the recognition rules set out in the section 219 regulations.[982] Section 219 of the Act empowers the Lord Chancellor to make provision as to the recognition in England and Wales of any judgment of a court of another Member State which orders the dissolution or annulment of a civil partnership, or the legal separation of civil partners.[983] Part 2[984] of the section 219 regulations lays down rules concerning the recognition and refusal of recognition of judgments[985] made by a court[986] in another Member State.[987] The scheme[988] of recognition of overseas judgments is a peculiar conglomerate of provisions, partly modelled upon the provisions of Chapter III, Section 1 of Brussels II *bis*, and partly upon Part II of the Family Law Act 1986.[989] Whilst it was no doubt convenient to draft the regulations in this manner, the wisdom of so doing is far from clear.[990] The overall policy has been to provide, where possible, parity of treatment between civil partners and spouses.

Given the close similarity between the rules for recognition of judgments set out in the section 219 regulations and those which have been examined in the context of Brussels II *bis* and the Family Law Act 1986,[991] it is not proposed to examine the former in detail. In

---

[979] S 233(3).

[980] S 233(4).

[981] Defined in r 6(3) of the section 219 regulations: see infra, n 987.

[982] Civil Partnership (Jurisdiction and Recognition of Judgments) Regulations, SI 2005/3334; supra, p 1040. Cf Marriage (Same Sex Couples) (Jurisdiction and Recognition of Judgments) Regulations, SI 2014/543, rr 3–9, infra, p 1048 (same sex marriage). See, for Scotland, SSI 2005/629.

[983] S 219(1)(b).

[984] Rules 6–12.

[985] Defined in r 6(1) as an order for the dissolution or annulment of a civil partnership or the legal separation of civil partners, pronounced by a court of a Member State, however termed by that state.

[986] Defined in r 6(2) as meaning all authorities, whether judicial or administrative, having jurisdiction in matters falling within the scope of the s 219 regulations.

[987] Defined in r 6(3): Belgium, Cyprus, Czech Republic, Germany, Greece, Spain, Estonia, France, Hungary, Ireland, Italy, Latvia, Lithuania, Luxembourg, Malta, Netherlands, Austria, Poland, Portugal, Slovakia, Slovenia, Finland, Sweden, and, notably, Denmark.

[988] See also SI 2005/3104, which includes provisions to deal with countries which comprise territories having different systems of law (r 2); cross-proceedings (r 4); the recognition of dissolutions obtained following the conversion of legal separations (r 5); and the facilitation of the proof of certain facts relevant to recognition and established in proceedings abroad (r 6), analogous to the rules found in ss 47, 48 and 49 of the Family Law Act 1986, discussed, supra, pp 1010–11.

[989] Supra, p 1005 et seq.

[990] Commentators have rightly pointed out that imitating the rules applicable to opposite-sex couples has led to "some odd results". See Clarkson and Hill, para 8.148. For example, the reference to a dissolution, legal separation or annulment of a civil partnership obtained "otherwise than by means of proceedings" (see r 8(3)(b) of the section 219 regulations in relation to judgments granted in a Member State, and ss 235(2) and 236(3)(b) of the 2004 Act in relation to judgments granted other than in a Member State) has been appropriately described as "fanciful" or "absurd". Dicey, Morris and Collins, para 18-136.

[991] See, in relation to Family Law Act 1986, s 46, supra, p 1005 et seq.

outline, regulation 7 states that an overseas judgment shall be recognised in England without any special formalities. Regulation 8 sets out criteria for refusal of recognition of a judgment, adopting,[992] peculiarly, the bifurcated scheme contained in Part II of the 1986 Act, according to whether or not the judgment has been obtained by means of proceedings. Regulations 9, 10 and 11, based on Brussels II *bis*,[993] prevent the court from reviewing the jurisdiction of the Member State of origin, and from reviewing the substance of that judgment, and ensure that a judgment is recognised notwithstanding that there might have been a different result if English law had been applied to the facts of the case. Regulation 12 allows the court to stay proceedings for recognition when there is an appeal outstanding against that judgment.[994]

(iv) Recognition in the United Kingdom of dissolution,
       annulment or separation granted other than in a Member State[995]

Section 234 states that the validity of an overseas (ie non-Member State)[996] dissolution, etc is to be recognised in the United Kingdom only by virtue of the scheme of recognition imposed by sections 235 to 237 of the 2004 Act. The grounds for recognition are set out in section 235(1) and (2), and for refusal of recognition in section 236, and essentially mirror the terms of sections 46(1) and (2) and 51 of the Family Law Act 1986. Given the close similarity of wording, it is not proposed to examine sections 235 and 236 in detail.[997] Two provisions which merit comment, however, are section 235 (1A) and (2A), which were inserted[998] to deal with situations where section 235 would be insufficient to ensure proper recognition of the validity of certain overseas dissolutions, etc because one or both of the civil partners is either habitually resident or domiciled in a country whose law does not recognise legal relationships between persons of the same sex. The need for this provision is said to rest on the fact that there are many countries where the legal status of civil partnership is not established, and where, therefore, foreign dissolution of that status may not be recognised.[999]

The remaining provisions in Chapter 3 of Part 5 of the 2004 Act are based upon provisions in the Family Law Act 1986, including, in particular, those concerning the meaning of "domicile",[1000] and the fact of non-recognition elsewhere of a decree of dissolution, etc being no bar to remarriage.[1001]

6. DIVORCE, NULLITY AND SEPARATION
OF SAME SEX MARRIAGES

(a) Jurisdiction[1002]

(i) Bases of jurisdiction

There is nothing in the Brussels II *bis* Regulation to suggest that it applies to the termination of same sex marriages.[1003] English law therefore makes special provision for

---

[992] Reg 8(3).
[993] Arts 24, 26 and 25 (in that order), discussed supra, p 1005.
[994] Cf Brussels II *bis*, Art 27.
[995] For list of Member States, see supra, p 1044, n 987.
[996] Member State judgments are governed by the s 219 regulations: s 234(2). For Member States, see SI 2005/3334, r 6(3).
[997] See, in relation to ss 46 and 51 of the Family Law Act 1986, supra, p 1005 et seq and p 1024 et seq.
[998] By SI 2005/3104, r 3.
[999] Explanatory Memorandum to SI 2005/3104, para 7.3.
[1000] S 237(1); cf 1986 Act, s 46(5), supra, pp 1006–7.
[1001] S 238; cf 1986 Act, s 50, supra, p 926.
[1002] See, for Scotland, Domicile and Matrimonial Proceedings Act 1973, Sch 1B, and Marriage (Same Sex Couples) (Jurisdiction and Recognition of Judgments) (Scotland) Regulations, SSI 2104/362.
[1003] See also Dicey, Morris and Collins, para 18-027, and Clarkson and Hill, para 8.54.

jurisdiction of the English courts to entertain, in relation to same sex marriages, proceedings for divorce, judicial separation and nullity.[1004] Additionally, jurisdictional provision is made for proceedings for an order which ends a same sex marriage on the ground that one of the couple is dead, and proceedings for a declaration of validity of a same sex marriage.[1005]

(a) Proceedings for divorce and separation
The domestic law lays down, for divorce and separation of marriages of same sex couples, jurisdictional grounds that are very similar to those set out in Article 3 of the Regulation.[1006] In particular, the English court has jurisdiction in proceedings for the divorce or judicial separation of a married same sex couple where: (a) both spouses are habitually resident in England; (b) both spouses were last habitually resident in England and one of them continues to reside there; (c) the respondent is habitually resident in England; (d) the petitioner is habitually resident in England and has resided there for at least one year immediately preceding the presentation of the petition; (e) the petitioner is domiciled and habitually resident in England and has resided there for at least six months immediately preceding the presentation of the petition; or (f) both spouses are domiciled in England.[1007] If none of these jurisdictional criteria is met, the English court may still have jurisdiction under Schedule A1 to the Domicile and Matrimonial Proceedings Act 1973[1008] if: (a) either party is domiciled in England on the day the proceedings are begun;[1009] or (b) the parties married each other under the law of England, and it appears to the court to be in the interests of justice to assume jurisdiction in the case.[1010] Perhaps not surprisingly, the above rules mirror the jurisdictional provisions set out in the Civil Partnership Act 2004 and the section 219 regulations in the context of civil partnership.[1011]

(b) Proceedings for nullity
The rules of jurisdiction in relation to proceedings for nullity of a marriage of a same sex couple follow the same pattern as the corresponding rules for jurisdiction in divorce and separation of a same sex marriage.[1012] Therefore, in the first instance, the English court has jurisdiction to entertain proceedings for nullity of a same sex marriage on the basis of the alternative Brussels II *bis*-inspired grounds of jurisdiction, set out in the Marriage (Same Sex Couples) (Jurisdiction and Recognition of Judgments) Regulations.[1013]

If no court has, or is recognised as having jurisdiction under the Regulations, the English court can still entertain jurisdiction for the proceedings if: (a) either of the parties is domiciled in England on the date when the proceedings are begun, or died before that date and either was at death domiciled in England or had been habitually resident in England for one

---

[1004] Domicile and Matrimonial Proceedings Act 1973, Sch A1, para 1(a).
[1005] Ibid, para 1(b) and (c) respectively, discussed in Chapter 23, pp 1057–8.
[1006] Ibid, para 5. Marriage (Same Sex Couples) (Jurisdiction and Recognition of Judgments) Regulations, SI 2014/543. The Regulations apply to all same sex marriages, including those registered outside England and Wales (SI 2014/543, Explanatory Note).
[1007] SI 2014/543, r 2. Cf generally Art 3, Brussels II *bis*, discussed supra, pp 955–6; and SI 2005/3334, r 4 (civil partnership), supra, p 1041.
[1008] Inserted by Marriage (Same Sex Couples) Act 2013, Sch 4(4), para 8.
[1009] Domicile and Matrimonial Proceedings Act 1973, Sch A1, para 2(1)(b). Cf Civil Partnership Act 2004, s 221(1)(b), supra, p 1040.
[1010] Domicile and Matrimonial Proceedings Act 1973, Sch A1, para 2(1)(c). Cf Civil Partnership Act 2004, s 221(1)(c), supra, p 1040.
[1011] Discussed supra, pp 1040–1 (the commentary is equally applicable to same sex marriage).
[1012] See supra.
[1013] SI 2014/543, r 2, see supra.

year immediately preceding death,[1014] or (b) the parties married each other under the law of England, and it appears to the court to be in the interests of justice to assume jurisdiction in the case.[1015]

As with jurisdiction in divorce and separation, the above provisions replicate the rules on jurisdiction for proceedings for nullity of a civil partnership.[1016]

(c) Other matrimonial proceedings in relation to the same marriage

When proceedings are pending in respect of which the court has jurisdiction by virtue of paras 2(1) or 2(2) of Schedule A1 to the Domicile and Matrimonial Proceedings Act 1973, it also has jurisdiction to entertain other proceedings for divorce, judicial separation or nullity in respect of the same marriage, notwithstanding that jurisdiction would not be exercisable under sub-paragraph (1) or (2).[1017]

(f) Presumption of death and dissolution of same sex marriage

By virtue of the Domicile and Matrimonial Proceedings Act 1973, Sch A1, para 3, the English court has jurisdiction to entertain proceedings for a presumption of death order, on an application made by a civil partner, if (a) at the time the application is made, the High Court does not have jurisdiction to entertain an application by the applicant under section 1 of the Presumption of Death Act 2013 for a declaration that the applicant's spouse is presumed to be dead,[1018] and (b) the parties married each other under the law of England and Wales, and it appears to the court to be in the interests of justice to assume jurisdiction in the case.[1019]

(ii) Procedural issues

(a) Service of the petition

The rules on service of a petition for dissolution, etc are the same as those concerning petitions for divorce, etc. of a marriage of an opposite sex couple.[1020]

(b) Staying proceedings

Schedule 1 to the Domicile and Matrimonial Proceedings Act 1973 has been extended to same sex marriage.[1021] Accordingly, provisions concerning the grant of obligatory and discretionary stays of matrimonial proceedings in England where matrimonial proceedings are pending in another jurisdiction outside England set out in Schedule 1, apply also to same sex couples.[1022]

(b) Choice of law

It appears sensible to follow, in matrimonial proceedings concerning a marriage of a same sex couple, the same choice of law approach as in relation to a marriage of an opposite

---

[1014] Domicile and Matrimonial Proceedings Act 1973, Sch A1, para 2(2)(b). Cf Civil and Partnership Act 2004, s 221(2)(b), supra, p 1041.

[1015] Ibid, Sch A1, para 2(2)(c). Cf Civil and Partnership Act 2004, s 221(2)(c), supra, p 1041.

[1016] Discussed supra, p 1041 (the commentary is equally applicable to same sex marriage).

[1017] Domicile and Matrimonial Proceedings Act 1973, Sch A1, para 3. Cf Civil and Partnership Act 2004, s 221(3), supra, p 1041.

[1018] See Chapter 23, p 1058.

[1019] Cf Civil and Partnership Act 2004, s 222, supra, pp 1041. Discussed supra, pp 1041–2 (the commentary is equally applicable to same sex marriage).

[1020] Supra, pp 966–7.

[1021] Domicile and Matrimonial Proceedings Act 1973, s 5(6), as amended by the Marriage (Same Sex Couples) Act 2013, Sch 4(4), para 6(4). Cf Civil Partnership Act, s 223 and Family Procedure (Civil Partnership: Staying of Proceedings) Rules, SI 2010/2986, supra, p 1042.

[1022] See supra, p 972 et seq.

sex couple.[1023] Accordingly, the English law of the forum approach should extend, *mutatis mutandis*, to same sex marriage.

(c) Recognition of dissolution, annulment and separation[1024]

The recognition provisions of the Family Law Act 1986 would seem to apply to same sex marriages.[1025] As these provisions are analysed in detail elsewhere in this Chapter,[1026] it is not proposed to examine them here.[1027]

Separate provisions have been adopted for recognition in England of a judgment on dissolution, annulment or separation of a same sex marriage granted in an EU Member State.[1028] These rules, which represent a combination of the recognition schemes contained in the Brussels II *bis* Regulation and the Family Law Act 1986, reproduce the terms of the section 219 regulations in relation to civil partnership,[1029] which have been examined earlier in this Chapter. The reader is therefore referred to the appropriate section.[1030]

Potentially, a question may arise as to by which law the relationship is to be classified as "marriage" or "civil partnership", and, consequently, where the demarcation should lie between the recognition rules contained in the Family Law Act 1986 and the Civil Partnership Act 2004,[1031] and the Family Law Marriage (Same Sex Couples) (Jurisdiction and Recognition of Judgments) Regulations and the section 219 regulations[1032] respectively. It is submitted that the English court would employ the law of the forum approach to classification and, accordingly, characterise the relationship pursuant to English law. Nevertheless, given that the recognition rules pertaining to same sex marriage and civil partnership respectively are nearly identical, this problem appears to be of a theoretical importance only.

[1023] See supra, p 979 et seq.

[1024] See, for Scotland, Domicile and Matrimonial Proceedings Act 1973, Sch 1B, and Marriage (Same Sex Couples) (Jurisdiction and Recognition of Judgments) (Scotland) Regulations, SSI 2104/362.

[1025] The Marriage (Same Sex Couples) Act 2013, Sch 3(1), para 1 ("Interpretation of existing England and Wales legislation") states that references to a marriage, a married couple or married person in existing legislation in England and Wales are to be read as also referring to a marriage of a same sex couple, married same sex couples or to a person married to someone of the same sex.

[1026] See supra, p 1000 et seq.

[1027] For equivalent recognition rules pertaining to civil partnership, see Civil Partnership Act 2004, ss 233–8, discussed supra, pp 1043–5.

[1028] Marriage (Same Sex Couples) (Jurisdiction and Recognition of Judgments) Regulations, SI 2014/543, rr 3–9.

[1029] Civil Partnership (Jurisdiction and Recognition of Judgments) Regulations, SI 2005/3334, rr 6–12.

[1030] Supra, pp 1044–5.

[1031] In respect of dissolutions, etc of same sex marriages and civil partnerships granted other than in a Member State.

[1032] In respect of dissolutions, etc of same sex marriages and civil partnerships granted in an EU Member State.

23

DECLARATIONS

1. Introduction	1049		(e) Limits on the courts' powers	1054
2. Family Law Act 1986, Part III	1050		(f) Safeguards and other procedural matters	1055
(a) Declarations as to marital status	1051		3. Child Abduction and Custody Act 1985	1056
(b) Declarations of parentage	1052		4. Civil Partnership Act 2004	1057
(c) Declarations of parentage, legitimacy			5. Marriage (Same Sex Couples) Act 2013	1057
or legitimation	1053		6. Presumption of Death Act 2013	1058
(d) Declarations as to adoptions effected				
overseas	1054			

1. INTRODUCTION

For many years, the courts had power, both under their inherent jurisdiction[1] and by statute,[2] to make declarations as to status. The purpose of such a declaratory judgment is not to determine the rights of the parties and to grant the appropriate relief but merely to affirm what their rights are without any reference to the enforcement of such rights. For many years, the courts had statutory power[3] to grant declarations of legitimacy,[4] of legitimation, of the validity of a marriage or that the petitioner is a British subject. They have exercised their inherent powers to declare that a foreign divorce or annulment should, or should not, be recognised in England.[5] There was no power, however, to declare the invalidity of a marriage by declaration: that had to be done in nullity proceedings.[6] Whether a marriage could be declared valid under the inherent jurisdiction was a matter of doubt and uncertainty.[7] Certainly declarations were made as to the subsisting validity of a marriage;[8] but it has also been said[9] that declarations as to the initial validity of a marriage could only be made in the exercise of the statutory powers. The significance of this was that the jurisdictional grounds varied as between the two heads of jurisdiction and, furthermore, various procedural safeguards were available under the statutory jurisdiction but not in the exercise of the inherent powers.

In 1984, the Law Commission expressed concern as to the general state of the law on declarations in family matters, identifying a number of major defects.[10] They proposed a clean sweep

---

[1] Under RSC Ord 15, r 16.
[2] Matrimonial Causes Act 1974, s 45 (repealed by Family Law Act 1986, ss 68(2), 69 and Sch 2).
[3] Ibid.
[4] But not of illegitimacy: *Mansel v A-G* (1877) 2 PD 265; affd 4 PD 232; *B v A-G* [1967] 1 WLR 776.
[5] *Har-Shefi v Har-Shefi*[1953] P 161; *Law v Gustin* [1976] Fam 155; *Kendall v Kendall* [1977] Fam 208; *Lepre v Lepre* [1965] P 52 at 57; *Lawrence v Lawrence* [1985] Fam 106.
[6] *Kassim v Kassim* [1962] P 224.
[7] See Law Com No 132 (1984), paras 2.7–2.8; North, op cit, Chapter 6.
[8] Eg *Garthwaite v Garthwaite* [1964] P 356; *Re Meyer* [1971] P 298.
[9] *Collett v Collett* [1968] P 482; *Aldrich v A-G* [1968] P 281; *Vervaeke v Smith* [1981] Fam 77; affd [1981] Fam 77, CA, [1983] 1 AC 145; *Williams v A-G* [1987] 1 FLR 501; though this was actually done in *Woyno v Woyno* [1960] 1 WLR 986.
[10] Law Com No 132 (1984), para 2.12.

and a fresh start, recommending "a new legislative code, based on consistent principles [to] replace the existing hotchpotch of statutory and discretionary relief".[11] That was achieved in Part III of the Family Law Act 1986. In that year, the Law Commission also recommended that there should be a power to grant declarations of parentage and that such declarations should be governed by essentially the same rules as those contained in the 1986 Act for other declarations, particularly those of legitimacy.[12] That particular recommendation was implemented by amendments to Part II of the 1986 Act, as introduced by the Family Law Reform Act 1987.[13]

2. FAMILY LAW ACT 1986, PART III

Part III of the 1986 Act states what kinds of declaration may be granted under the Act and what are the relevant jurisdictional rules for each class of declaration. The four classes of declaration, ie declarations as to marital status, of parentage, as to parentage, legitimacy or legitimation, and as to adoptions effected overseas will be considered separately. A number of matters which are common to all four classes will then be examined. It ought to be noted at the outset that the various types of declaration listed in Part III may only be granted by the court[14] on the basis of the rules there laid down; section 45 of the Matrimonial Causes Act 1973 has been repealed[15] and the inherent jurisdiction of the High Court is inapplicable to matters falling within Part III.[16] On the other hand, however, on the basis of their inherent jurisdiction, courts have recently been willing to grant other types of declarations as to status. For example, the following types of declarations have been made: a) that there never had been a marriage between the parties as the alleged "marriage ceremony" fell within the category of a "non-marriage"; b) that the foreign marriage was not capable of recognition in England and Wales for want of consent, and amounted to a "non-marriage" (implicitly or explicitly);[17] and c) that a vulnerable adult who was at risk of being taken abroad for the purpose of marriage did not have the capacity to marry.[18] The first type of declarations, as set out above, may concern either a "marriage ceremony" conducted abroad,[19] or a "marriage ceremony" that

---

[11] Ibid, para 2.13.

[12] Law Com No 156 (1986), para 3.14.

[13] S 22.

[14] The High Court or the family court.

[15] This means that there is no longer a statutory power to grant a declaration that the applicant is a British citizen. Any inherent power to make a declaration that a person is a British citizen is unaffected, as in *Bulmer v A-G* [1955] Ch 558; *A-G v Prince Ernest Augustus of Hanover* [1957] AC 436; *Motala v A-G* [1990] 2 FLR 261, revsd on another point [1992] 1 AC 281, infra, pp 1198–9.

[16] S 58(4). It is unlikely that foreign declaratory judgments in personam would be recognised in England— and no rules have been devised for the recognition of foreign declarations in rem. This is probably because it would usually require an English declaration to recognise the foreign one: see North, *Private International Law of Matrimonial Causes*, p 300.

[17] Either on account of a mental impairment of one of the parties to the marriage— *Westminster City Council v IC (A Protected Party by His Litigation Friend) and Ors* [2008] EWCA Civ 198; *XCC v AA* [2012] EWHC 2183 (COP); and *Luton Borough Council v SB and another* [2015] EWHC 3534 (Fam); or on account of duress in cases involving a forced marriage—*SH v NB* [2009] EWHC 3274 (Fam); *B v I (Forced Marriage)* [2010] FLR 1721; and *Re P (Forced Marriage)* [2010] EWHC 3467 (Fam). Cf *A Local Authority v X* [2013] EWHC 3274 (Fam)—declaration of non-recognition refused in relation to a marriage which had taken place between a fourteen-year-old girl and a twenty-four-year-old-man in Pakistan and under duress, as the girl could issue a petition for a decree of nullity on the ground that the marriage was void by virtue of her age.

[18] Eg *X City Council v MB* [2006] EWHC 168 (Fam).

[19] Eg *Hudson v Leigh* [2009] EWHC 1306 (Fam)—South Africa.

took place in England.[20] In either case the ceremony is characterised by a wholesale failure to comply with the formal requirements of the law of the place of celebration; the failure being of such a severity that the ceremony is incapable of creating a marriage (not even a void one) under the applicable law. With regard to the second type of declarations, the lack of consent can arise either on account of a mental impairment of one of the parties to the marriage,[21] or on account of duress in cases involving a forced marriage.[22]

(a) Declarations as to marital status

There are five declarations which the court may make in this category,[23] all of which had been made under the old law, ie:

(i)   that the marriage[24] was valid at its inception;[25]
(ii) that it did subsist on a date specified in the application;[26]
(iii) that it did not so subsist on a date so specified;
(iv) that the validity of a divorce, annulment or legal separation obtained outside England and Wales is entitled to recognition in England and Wales;[27] and
(v)   that the validity of such a divorce, etc so obtained is not entitled to recognition in England and Wales.

The jurisdictional rules for granting any of those five types of declaration are as follows:[28] that either party to the marriage is domiciled in England and Wales on the date of the application, or has been habitually resident in England and Wales throughout the period of one year ending with that date. If a party to the marriage is dead then the jurisdictional requirements of domicile or one year's habitual residence in England and Wales have to be satisfied at the date of death.[29] The jurisdictional connection is not with the applicant but rather with a party

---

[20] Eg *Galloway v Goldstein* [2012] EWHC 60 (Fam)—the deficient ceremony in England followed a valid marriage ceremony in Connecticut.

[21] Eg *Westminster City Council v IC (A Protected Party by His Litigation Friend) and Ors* [2008] EWCA Civ 198; *XCC v AA* [2012] EWHC 2183 (COP); and *Luton Borough Council v SB and another* [2015] EWHC 3534 (Fam).

[22] *SH v NB* [2009] EWHC 3274 (Fam); *B v I (Forced Marriage)* [2010] FLR 1721; and *Re P (Forced Marriage)* [2010] EWHC 3467 (Fam). Cf *A Local Authority v X* [2013] EWHC 3274 (Fam)—declaration of non-recognition refused in relation to a marriage which had taken place between a fourteen-year-old girl and a twenty-four-year-old-man in Pakistan and under duress, as the girl could issue a petition for a decree of nullity on the ground that the marriage was void by virtue of her age.

[23] S 55(1). See also the Family Procedure Rules 2010, rr 8.18–8.21. Additionally, the court may, on application of a person with sufficient interest, make a declaration that a missing person is to be presumed dead. One of the effects of such a declaration is that it ends the missing person's marriage. See Presumption of Death Act 2013, s 3(2)(b). The procedure is applicable also in relation to civil partnership (ibid. See infra, p 1058), and same sex marriage (see Domicile and Matrimonial Proceedings Act 1973, Sch A1, para 3(a)).

[24] For equivalent rules pertaining to civil partnership, see infra, p 1057.

[25] Eg *Bellinger v Bellinger* [2003] 2 AC 467; *A v A (Attorney General Intervening)* [2012] EWHC 2219 (Fam); *Khan v Ahmad* [2014] EWHC 3850 (Fam); and *N v D (Customary Marriage)* [2015] EWFC 28. Cf *MO v RO* [2013] EWHC 392 (Fam). See also *Westminster City Council v IC (A Protected Part by His Litigation Friend) and Ors* [2008] EWCA Civ 198, [2008] WCR (D) 92—the only route to a judicial conclusion that a marriage was void at its inception is a petition for nullity.

[26] Eg *Khan v Ahmad* [2014] EWHC 3850 (Fam); *GE v KE and AE (Nigerian Customary Marriage and Divorce)* [2013] EWHC 1938; and *Galloway v Goldstein* [2012] EWHC 60 (Fam).

[27] Eg *Berkovits v Grinberg* [1995] Fam 142; *Abbassi v Abbassi* [2006] EWCA Civ 355; [2006] 2 FLR 648.

[28] S 55(2). The rules are modelled on those which applied to nullity decrees prior to the entry into force of Council Regulation (EC) No 1337/2000 of 29 May 2000 on jurisdiction and the recognition and enforcement of judgments in matrimonial matters and in matters of parental responsibility for children of both spouses. Cf Domicile and Matrimonial Proceedings Act 1973, s 5(3). Supra, p 954 et seq.

[29] S 55(2)(c). The effect of these rules is to abolish the common law ground of jurisdiction that a declaration could be granted as to the validity of a foreign divorce if that was a necessary step in adjudicating

to the marriage and this accounts for the need for a rule, as in nullity, dealing with the case where a party to the marriage had died.[30] The reason for the connection being with the party to the marriage is because section 55 of the 1986 Act allows anyone to apply for one of the five listed declarations. If, however, the applicant is not a party to the marriage, the court has a discretion to refuse to hear the application if it considers that the applicant does not have a sufficient interest in the determination of the application.[31] As under the old law, a declaration may not be made that a marriage was void at its inception.[32] That is to be determined by means of a nullity petition, the powers to grant which are unaffected by Part III of the 1986 Act.[33] In this way, a party will be unable to avoid the ancillary relief powers of the court available on a nullity petition, by seeking instead a declaration where such powers are unavailable.[34] The Domicile and Matrimonial Proceedings Act 1973 provides[35] that, in the case of any proceedings[36] for a declaration as to the validity of a marriage of the petitioner or as to the subsistence of such a marriage, the court has a discretion to stay the English proceedings before the beginning of the trial thereof. This would seem to cover all five declarations as to marital status falling within section 55 of the 1986 Act. The statutory discretion is the same as that in divorce proceedings and has been fully discussed in that context.[37]

(b) Declarations of parentage

Section 55A of the 1986 Act,[38] inserted by section 83(2) of the Child Support, Pensions and Social Security Act 2000, introduced a new, wider power whereby any person[39] may apply to a civil court[40] for a declaration as to whether or not a person named in the application is or was the parent of another person so named. Section 55A is intended to provide a single procedure for obtaining a declaration of parentage to replace the two discrete provisions contained in the 1986 Act and in section 27 of the Child Support Act 1991 (effective only for the purposes of child support and maintenance proceedings). The court can entertain an application only if either of the persons named therein is domiciled in England on the date of the application, or has been habitually resident in England throughout the period of one year

---

on a matter within the jurisdiction of the court: *Lepre v Lepre* [1965] P 52; see Law Com No 132 (1984), para 3.45.

[30] This can be very useful, as in *Re Meyer* [1971] P 298.

[31] S 55(3); see *Berkovits v Grinberg* supra—application by Jewish ecclesiastical judge. See Law Com No 132 (1984), paras 3.29–3.33 for discussion of the issue of who should be able to apply for these declarations.

[32] S 58(5)(a).

[33] S 58(6).

[34] *Kassim v Kassim* [1962] P 224. It will, however, be possible for a petitioner to seek in the alternative a nullity decree or a declaration as to the validity of the marriage: Law Com No 132 (1984), paras 3.26–3.27.

[35] Sch I, para 9.

[36] Other than proceedings governed by Council Regulation (EC) No 2201/2003 of 27 November 2003 concerning jurisdiction and the recognition and enforcement of judgments in matrimonial matters and matters of parental responsibility, repealing Regulation (EC) No 1347/2000. Supra, p 968 et seq.

[37] Supra, p 972 et seq.

[38] See also Family Procedure Rules 2010, rr 8.18–8.22.

[39] The power is wider than that in s 56 (discussed, infra, p 1053). Subject to s 55A(3) and (4), *any* person may apply under s 55A(1) for a declaration of parentage of a person named in the application, whereas application may be made under s 56 only by an applicant in respect of his own parentage/status. See *Leeds Teaching Hospital NHS Trust v A and Ors* [2003] EWHC 259 (QB); [2003] All ER (D) 374; *Secretary of State for Work and Pensions v Jones* (2003) Times, 13 August; *Re B (A Child) (Parentage: Knowledge of Proceedings)* [2003] EWCA Civ 1842; [2004] 1 FLR 473; *Re F (Children) (Paternity: Registration)* [2011] EWCA Civ 1765; *Re A (Children)* [2015] EWCA Civ 133; *D v D (Fertility Treatment: Paperwork Error)* [2016] EWHC 2112 (Fam); *Re L (A Child) (Human Fertilisation and Embryology Act 2008: Declaration of Non-parentage)* [2016] EWHC 2266 (Fam); and *Re N (Human Fertilisation and Embryology Act 2008)* [2016] EWHC 1329 (Fam).

[40] The High Court or the family court: s 55A(1).

ending with that date; or if either of the persons named in the application died before the date of application, and was at death domiciled in England, or had been habitually resident in England for one year preceding his/her death.[41]

If the applicant is not the child or one of the alleged parents concerned, then the court shall refuse to hear the application unless it considers that the applicant has a sufficient personal interest in the determination of the application.[42] Additionally, the court may refuse to hear the application if one of the persons named in it is a child, and it considers that the determination would not be in the best interests of that child.[43]

(c) Declarations of parentage, legitimacy or legitimation

Section 56 of the 1986 Act[44] retains and slightly extends the previous statutory power[45] to make declarations as to legitimacy and legitimation,[46] and introduces a new power to make declarations of parentage.[47] The court[48] may make four kinds of declaration in this category:

(i)   that a person is or was the applicant's parent;
(ii) that the applicant is the legitimate child of his parents; and
(iii) that the applicant has, or has not, become a legitimated person.[49]

Declarations as to legitimation[50] may relate to legitimation by statute, or to foreign legitimations which are recognised in England either under statutory provisions or at common law.[51] Declarations may be sought, for example, to acquire nationality, to establish rights of inheritance or to amend a birth certification. Only a person alleging that he is the child of someone may apply for a parentage declaration; and an application for a declaration as to legitimacy or legitimation may be made only by the person whose status is in issue.[52]

The jurisdictional rules for granting any of these declarations are the simple and familiar ones that the applicant is, at the time of the application, domiciled in England or has been habitually resident in England for one year immediately preceding that date.[53]

---

[41] S 55A(2).

[42] S 55A(3) and (4).

[43] S 55(A)(5); *Re R (A Child)* [2003] EWCA Civ 182; [2003] Fam 129 per Hale LJ at [32].

[44] As substituted by s 22 of the Family Law Reform Act 1987; and see Family Procedure Rules 2010, rr 8.18, 8.20 and 8.21.

[45] See the Matrimonial Causes Act 1973, s 45; and see *Motala v A-G* [1990] 2 FLR 261; revsd on another point [1992] 1 AC 281, infra, pp 1198–9.

[46] Such declarations are still needed notwithstanding the major reforms of the law relating to legitimacy contained in the Family Law Reform Act 1987, infra, p 1194, see Law Com No 118 (1982), para 10.2; Law Com No 157 (1986), para 3.14.

[47] See Norrie (1994) 43 ICLQ 757.

[48] The High Court or the family court.

[49] These may be sought in the alternative: s 56(2).

[50] S 58(5)(b) (prohibition of declaration of illegitimacy) has been excised from the Act by virtue of s 83(3) of the Child Support, Pensions and Social Security Act 2000. The reason for this is that the effect of a declaration of parentage under s 55A could be that a child is or was illegitimate, which is inconsistent with s 58(5)(b) as was.

[51] S 56(5). Recognition of foreign legitimations is discussed infra, p 1202 et seq.

[52] Contrast applications for declaration of parentage under s 55A, discussed, supra, p 1052.

[53] S 56(3); and see Law Com No 132 (1984), paras 3.34–3.36; *Motala v A-G* [1990] 2 FLR 261; revsd on another point [1992] 1 AC 281.

(d) Declarations as to adoptions effected overseas

Whilst recognition in England of adoption orders made elsewhere in the British Isles is automatic,[54] this is not true of foreign adoptions.[55] Although there is no reported case of an application for a declaration as to the validity of a foreign adoption,[56] the Law Commission concluded[57] that it would be desirable to take the opportunity to make clear provision for such declarations and to provide appropriate procedural safeguards.[58] Under section 57(2) of the Family Law Act 1986[59] the court[60] may grant a declaration that the applicant either is[61] or is not the adopted child of a particular person.[62] The only person who can apply for a declaration as to the validity of a foreign adoption is the child himself, and he can apply whether he has been adopted by a Convention adoption, or an overseas adoption, within the meaning of the Adoption and Children Act 2002,[63] or an adoption recognised by English law and effected under the law of any country outside the British Islands.[64] The specific terms of section 57(1)(b) denote the discrete two stage character of the process of recognition and then declaration. In particular, before an application can be made for a declaration, the applicant must be able to demonstrate that the adoption is "recognised by the law of England and Wales".[65] Again the jurisdiction of the court is based on the domicile of the applicant in England on the date of the application or his habitual residence in England for one year immediately preceding that date.[66]

(e) Limits on the courts' powers

The basic approach of Part III of the 1986 Act is that the court may make the declarations listed there in family matters but may make no others.[67] Thus, as was mentioned earlier, there is express provision that no court may make a declaration as to the initial invalidity of a marriage,[68] and that the declarations available under Part III of the 1986 Act may only be made under that Part.[69] This latter provision excludes any possibility of the exercise of an overlapping jurisdiction under the inherent powers of the court.[70] It is also not possible for a

---

[54] Adoption Act 1976, s 38(1)(c); Adoption and Children Act 2002, ss 66(1) and 105–8.

[55] Infra, p 1222 et seq; and see Law Com No 132 (1984), para 3.15.

[56] The issue of the validity of a foreign adoption has always arisen in the course of other proceedings such as entitlement under a settlement (*Re Valentine's Settlement* [1965] Ch 831), a will (*Re Marshall* [1957] Ch 507), or an intestacy (*Re Wilson* [1954] Ch 733).

[57] Law Com No 132 (1984), paras 3.15–3.16.

[58] Infra, p 1222 et seq.

[59] See, eg, *D v D* [2008] EWHC 403 (Fam); *Re B (Children) (Foreign Adoption: Refusal of Recognition)* [2013] EWHC 1501 (Fam); *Z v Z (Recognition of Brazilian Adoption Order)* [2013] EWHC 747 (Fam); *Re G (Children) (Recognition of Brazilian Adoption)* [2014] EWHC 2605 (Fam); and *QS v RS* [2016] EWHC 2470 (Fam). And see the Family Procedure Rules 2010, rr 8.18, 8.20 and 8.21.

[60] The High Court or the family court.

[61] For the purposes of s 39 of the Adoption Act 1976, or s 67 of the Adoption and Children Act 2002, in respect of which, see infra, p 1229.

[62] These declarations may be sought in the alternative: s 57(1).

[63] S 57(1)(a).

[64] S 57(1)(b). See, for detailed consideration of adoption, infra, Chapter 27.

[65] *Re G (Children) (Recognition of Brazilian Adoption)* [2014] EWHC 2605 (Fam), at [30].

[66] S 57(3).

[67] It might also be noted that the power to grant declarations under the Greek Marriages Act 1884 has been abolished as has the right to petition for jactitation of marriage: ss 61, 62: and see Law Com No 132 (1984), paras 4.1–4.13.

[68] S 58(5).

[69] S 58(4).

[70] S 58(3); and see Law Com No 132 (1984), para 3.28. Note, however, the willingness of the courts in the recent years to grant, on the basis of their inherent jurisdiction, other types of declarations as to status, discussed supra p 1050.

court to make a "negative declaration", ie to declare the opposite of what is sought,[71] eg that a marriage was not subsisting on a particular date when a declaration is sought that it was.[72] There is nothing, however, to prevent a petitioner in that case from petitioning for the two declarations in the alternative, and indeed the Act expressly refers to this possibility in relation to declarations as to legitimation and adoption.[73]

(f) Safeguards and other procedural matters

All declarations made under Part III of the 1986 Act are binding in rem, ie they bind not only the parties but all other persons including the Crown.[74] It is important that in matters of personal status some finality is brought to the proceedings in order to still any doubts on the issue, and declarations as to the validity of a marriage, for example, are very close in nature to decrees of divorce or nullity which do operate in rem. Although it is always possible for a declaration, like any other judgment, to be rescinded for fraud, the binding nature conferred on declarations under Part III does call for a number of procedural safeguards to protect the interests of third parties and of the public.

The first concern is that a declaration should only be granted on convincing evidence, and it is provided that the truth of the proposition to be declared has to be proved "to the satisfaction of the court".[75] A further safeguard is provided by involvement of the Attorney-General to enable him to protect the public interest.[76] The outcome of a petition for a declaration could be highly relevant, for example, on issues of nationality[77] or immigration.[78] To meet these concerns, it is provided that the court may at any stage of the proceedings, either of its own motion or on the application of a party to the proceedings, direct that all papers be sent to the Attorney-General who may, whether or not he has been sent the papers, intervene in the proceedings in such manner as he thinks necessary or expedient.[79] It is also desirable that adequate provision be made for giving notice of the proceedings to all interested parties and to the Attorney-General, and power is given to make rules of court for that purpose.[80]

Finally, there is the issue of whether declarations under Part III should be available as of right, or only within the discretion of the court. The power of the court to grant a nullity decree is not discretionary,[81] and it has been said that "the right to obtain a declaration of status is a human right which should not be subject to the court's discretion".[82] Consequently, section 58(1) of the 1986 Act requires the court to make a declaration if the truth of the proposition to be declared is proved to the satisfaction of the court. There is, however, one exception to this in that the court may refuse to grant a declaration if to do so "would manifestly be contrary to public policy".[83] This follows the approach of the earlier law, when courts were

---

[71] S 58(3); and see Law Com No 132 (1984), paras 3.24–3.27.

[72] Under s 55(1).

[73] Ss 56(2), 57(1). As has been mentioned, supra, p 1051, it is also possible to petition for a nullity decree and a declaration of initial validity in the alternative.

[74] S 58(2).

[75] S 58(1).

[76] S 59.

[77] Eg *Puttick v A-G* [1980] Fam 1; *D v D* [2008] EWHC 403 (Fam), at [17]; and *Re G (Children) (Recognition of Brazilian Adoption)* [2014] EWHC 2605 (Fam), at [53]–[55].

[78] Eg *D v D* [2008] EWHC 403 (Fam), at [18]–[22]; and *Re G (Children) (Recognition of Brazilian Adoption)* [2014] EWHC 2605 (Fam), at [46]–[52].

[79] S 59(2).

[80] S 60; and see Law Com No 132 (1984), paras 3.60–3.63. In the case of declarations of parentage under s 55A, and of parentage and of legitimacy under s 56, if a declaration is made the Registrar General must be notified: Family Law Act 1986, ss 55A(7) and 56(4), respectively.

[81] *Kassim v Kassim* [1962] P 224 at 234.

[82] Law Com No 132 (1984), para 3.39.

[83] Eg *Re B (Children) (Foreign Adoption: Refusal of Recognition)* [2013] EWHC 1501 (Fam).

prepared to refuse a declaration as to the subsisting validity of a marriage, under section 45 of the Matrimonial Causes Act 1973, on grounds of public policy:

> It cannot be the intention of the statute that a decree must be pronounced (to the permanent prejudice of the Crown) when, although there has been no fraud at the hearing, the whole history is of fraud and perjury and the facts to found a decree have been brought about by criminal acts and offences and a fraudulent, deceitful course of conduct.[84]

3. CHILD ABDUCTION AND CUSTODY ACT 1985

In terms of Article 15 of the 1980 Hague Convention on the Civil Aspects of International Child Abduction,[85] the judicial or administrative authorities of a Contracting State may, prior to the making of an order for the return of the child, request that the applicant obtain from the authorities of the state of the habitual residence of the child a decision or other determination that the removal or retention was wrongful within the meaning of Article 3 of the Convention, where such a decision or determination may be obtained in that state. The Central Authorities of the Contracting States shall, so far as practicable, assist applicants to obtain such a decision or determination.

Section 8 of the Child Abduction and Custody Act 1985, which gives effect to the Convention in the United Kingdom, provides that the High Court[86] may, on an application made for the purposes of Article 15 of the Convention[87] by any person[88] appearing to the court to have an interest in the matter, make a declaration that the removal of any child from, or his retention outside, the United Kingdom was wrongful within the meaning of Article 3 of the Convention.[89]

A declaration should not be sought in a case where it is likely unnecessarily to delay or hamper the application for a return order.[90] This may occur, for example, where the requesting State has either not incorporated Article 15 into its domestic law or, alternatively, has

---

[84] *Puttick v A-G* [1980] Fam 1 at 22.

[85] See generally infra, Chapter 25. Also Family Procedure Rules 2010, Part 12.

[86] In Scotland, the Court of Session.

[87] Though see *Re D (A Child) (Abduction: Rights of Custody)* [2007] 1 AC 619, per Lord Brown of Eaton-under-Heywood, at [79]: the terms of s 8 of the 1985 Act "contemplate and empower [the English court] to make . . . a declaration even before there are any proceedings in, or any request from, a foreign contracting state".

[88] Not only persons having rights of custody or rights of access. *Re P (A Minor) (Child Abduction: Declaration)* [1995] 1 FLR 831; [1995] Fam Law 398.

[89] *Re D (A Child) (Abduction: Rights of Custody)* [2007] 1 AC 619; *Hunter v Murrow (Abduction: Rights of Custody)* [2005] EWCA Civ 976; [2005] 2 FLR 1119; *Re H (Child Abduction) (Unmarried Father: Rights of Custody)* [2003] EWHC 492; [2003] 2 FLR 153; *Re G (Abduction: Rights of Custody)* [2002] 2 FLR 703; [2002] Fam Law 732 (Fam Div); *Re L (Children) (Abduction: Declaration)* [2001] FCR 1; *Re J (Abduction: Rights of Custody)* [1999] 3 FCR 577; *Re P (Abduction: Declaration)* [1995] 1 FLR 831; *Re J (A Minor) (Abduction: Ward of Court)* [1989] Fam 85; [1990] Fam Law 177; *Re T (Abduction: Rights of Custody)* [2008] EWHC 809 (Fam); *A v B (Abduction: Rights of Custody: Declaration of Wrongful Removal)* [2008] EWHC 2524 (Fam); *A v H* [2009] EWHC 636 (Fam); and *X County Council v B (Abduction: Rights of Custody in the Court)* [2009] EWHC 2635 (Fam). See also *Re A (Abduction: Declaration of Wrongful Removal)* [2002] NI 114.

[90] *Re P (Diplomatic Immunity: Jurisdiction)* [1998] 1 FLR 1026; *Hunter v Murrow (Abduction: Rights of Custody)* [2005] EWCA Civ 976; [2005] 2 FLR 1119, per Thorpe LJ at [40]–[41] (eg where the question for determination in the requested state turns on a point of autonomous (ie Hague Convention) law); and Dyson LJ, at [50]–[51]; and *Re D (A Child) (Abduction: Rights of Custody)* [2007] 1 AC 619, per Lord Hope of Craighead, at [6]. See also *Re A (Abduction: Declaration of Wrongful Removal)* [2002] NI 114, per Gillen J at [120].

no experience of its operation.[91] It has therefore been suggested that, as an alternative to a request for an Article 15 declaration, the court might consider soliciting an opinion from a single joint expert[92] or the relevant liaison judge, whilst making use of the European Judicial Network.[93] A declaration made for the purposes of Article 15 is not binding on the requesting authority or the Courts of that country, but is designed to be of assistance. Although, strictly, a declaration so obtained is no more than persuasive,[94] it has recently been held by the House of Lords that a determination under Article 15 should be treated as determinative unless clearly out of line with the international understanding of the Convention's terms.[95]

4. CIVIL PARTNERSHIP ACT 2004

Section 58 of the Civil Partnership Act 2004 provides that any person may apply to the High Court or the family court for one or more of the following five[96] declarations in relation to a specified civil partnership:

(i)   that the civil partnership was valid at its inception;
(ii) that it subsisted on a date specified in the application;
(iii) that it did not so subsist on a date so specified;
(iv) that the validity of a dissolution, annulment or legal separation obtained outside England and Wales is entitled to recognition in England and Wales; and
(v)   that the validity of such a dissolution, etc so obtained is not entitled to recognition in England and Wales.

Sections 59 (general provisions as to making and effect of declarations), 60 (the Attorney General and proceedings for declarations) and 61 (supplementary provisions as to declarations) of the 2004 Act reproduce the terms of sections 58, 59 and 60 of the Family Law Act 1986,[97] *mutatis mutandis*, with regard to declarations in relation to civil partnerships.

5. MARRIAGE (SAME SEX COUPLES) ACT 2013

The Marriage (Same Sex Couples) Act 2013 has inserted a new Schedule A1 into the Domicile and Matrimonial Proceedings Act 1973. Para 4 of the Schedule sets out jurisdictional grounds

---

[91]   *Re F (A Child) (Abduction: Refusal to Order Summary Return)* [2009] EWCA Civ 416, per Thorpe LJ, at [12]. For example, an application under Art 15 is unusual if not unprecedented in Spain and it might well take up to a year to resolve. *Kennedy v Kennedy* [2009] EWCA Civ 986, per Thorpe LJ, at [3].

[92]   Eg *Kennedy v Kennedy* [2009] EWCA Civ 986—instead of seeking an Art 15 declaration, it was pragmatically decided that the extent of the unmarried father's rights of custody in Spain should be determined as a preliminary issue by a judge in England, guided by expert evidence as to the law of Spain. Ibid, per Thorpe LJ, at [3].

[93]   *Re F (A Child) (Abduction: Refusal to Order Summary Return)* [2009] EWCA Civ 416, per Thorpe LJ, at [12].

[94]   *Hunter v Murrow (Abduction: Rights of Custody)* [2005] EWCA Civ 976; [2005] 2 FLR 1119, per Thorpe LJ, at [27]; and *Re D (A Child) (Abduction: Rights of Custody)* [2007] 1 AC 619, per Lord Carswell at [71]; and Lord Brown of Eaton-under-Heywood, at [82]–[83].

[95]   *Re D (A Child) (Abduction: Rights of Custody)* [2007] 1 AC 619, per Baroness Hale of Richmond, at [43] and [44] (eg where the ruling was obtained by fraud or in breach of the rules of natural justice); Lord Carswell at [71]; and Lord Brown of Eaton-under-Heywood, at [81] (eg where there was a manifest misdirection as to the autonomous meaning of the Convention term "rights of custody"). See also *Re F (A Child) (Abduction: Refusal to Order Summary Return)* [2009] EWCA Civ 416, per Thorpe LJ, at [12]—in practice, in most cases, a ruling from the court of the requesting State under Art 15 will be determinative of the issue.

[96]   Cf declarations as to marital status: s 55, Family Law Act 1986. Supra, p 1051.

[97]   Supra, pp 1051–2.

for proceedings for a declaration of validity of a same sex marriage. The first part of this provision[98] replicates the terms of s 55(2) of the Family Law Act 1986, with regard to jurisdiction for granting declarations as to marital status in respect of opposite sex couples.[99] It states that the English court has jurisdiction to entertain an application for a declaration of validity of a same sex marriage if either of the parties to the marriage (a) is domiciled in England on the date of the application, or has been habitually resident there throughout the period of one year ending with that date, or (b) died before that date and either was at death domiciled in England or had been habitually resident there throughout the period of one year ending with the date of death.

The second part of para 4 of the Schedule[100] embodies a special *"forum necessitatis"* rule to enable the exercise of jurisdiction, on a discretionary basis, in exceptional cases where otherwise the parties would have no access to the English court. By this provision, the English court has jurisdiction to entertain an application for a declaration of validity if the parties married each other under the law of England and Wales, and it appears to the court to be in the interests of justice to assume jurisdiction in the case.[101]

6. PRESUMPTION OF DEATH ACT 2013

The Presumption of Death Act 2013 states that the court may, on application of a person with sufficient interest, make a declaration that a missing person is to be presumed dead.[102] One of the effects of a declaration of presumed death is that it ends the missing person's marriage or civil partnership.[103] Under the 2013 Act, the English court has jurisdiction for proceedings for a declaration that a missing person is presumed to be dead if: (a) either the missing person was domiciled in England and Wales at the date on which he or she was last known to be alive or had been habitually resident there for the whole of the year ending with that date;[104] or, (b) if the application was made by the spouse or civil partner of the missing person, the spouse or civil partner was domiciled in England and Wales when the application was made or had been, for one year immediately preceding the application, habitually resident there.[105]

---

[98] Domicile and Matrimonial Proceedings Act 1973, Sch A1, para 4(a).

[99] See supra, p 1051.

[100] Domicile and Matrimonial Proceedings Act 1973, Sch A1, para 4(b).

[101] A similar discretionary *"forum necessitatis"* rule in relation to same sex marriage can be found also in the Domicile and Matrimonial Proceedings Act 1973, Sch A1, paras 2(1)(b) (divorce and legal separation); 2(2)(c) (nullity); and 3 (presumption of death), discussed in Chapter 22, pp 1046–7. Cf Civil Partnership Act 2004, ss 221(1)(c), 221(2)(c), and 222, discussed in Chapter 22, pp 1040–2.

[102] See Chapter 22, pp 1037–9 (marriage), pp 1041–2 (civil partnership) and p 1047 (same sex marriage).

[103] Presumption of Death Act 2013, s 3(2)(b).

[104] S 1(3).

[105] S 1(4).

24

FINANCIAL RELIEF

1. **Jurisdiction of the English Court**	1059	3. **Choice of Law**	1078
(a) General jurisdictional rules	1060	4. **Recognition and Enforcement of**	
(b) Jurisdiction under the Maintenance		**Foreign Orders**	1078
Regulation	1064	(a) Relief ancillary to a foreign divorce,	
(c) Jurisdiction under the Lugano		annulment or legal separation	1078
Convention	1069	(b) Maintenance orders made elsewhere in	
(d) Inter-relation of the Maintenance		the United Kingdom	1079
Regulation and the Lugano Convention		(c) Recognition under the Maintenance	
with other bases of jurisdiction	1070	Orders (Facilities for Enforcement)	
2. **Financial Relief After a Foreign**		Act 1920	1079
Divorce/Dissolution, Annulment or		(d) Recognition under the Maintenance	
Legal Separation	1071	Orders (Reciprocal Enforcement)	
(a) Effect of foreign divorce, etc on		Act 1972	1080
financial relief already granted in		(e) Recognition and enforcement under	
England	1071	the Maintenance Regulation	1081
(b) Powers of English court to grant		(f) Recognition and enforcement under	
financial relief, despite an earlier		the 2007 Hague Convention	1084
foreign divorce/dissolution, annulment			
or legal separation	1071		

In many petitions for financial relief, the parties are not only, or indeed primarily, concerned with the determination of their personal status, but are also concerned with the powers of the court to make orders as to financial support, rights to the family home and property, and the like.[1] These forms of relief, often ancillary to that obtained in the main proceedings, give rise to three main questions of private international law—the jurisdiction of the English court; the power to order relief after a foreign divorce/dissolution, annulment or legal separation; and the recognition and enforcement of foreign decrees or orders in relation to financial relief.[2]

1. JURISDICTION OF THE ENGLISH COURT

As the types of relief available to the parties to a marriage or civil partnership are varied, the jurisdictional issues raised thereby must be considered separately. The position is complicated by the fact that general jurisdiction over claims for maintenance is conferred by the Maintenance Regulation,[3] the Lugano Convention and indirectly by the 2007

---

[1] Their other main concern is with orders concerning the welfare of the children, infra, p 1087 et seq.

[2] See Martiny (1994) III Hague Recueil 131.

[3] Council Regulation (EC) 4/2009 of 18 December 2008 on jurisdiction, applicable law, recognition and enforcement of decisions and cooperation in matters relating to maintenance obligations [2009] OJ L7/1. The Regulation entered into force on 18 June 2011, replacing the system under Brussels I. It applies in all Member States, but in Denmark it is only implemented to the extent that it amends Brussels I (OJ L 149/80).

Hague Convention.[4] There are also special rules for married couples under Part III of the Matrimonial and Family Proceedings Act 1984, and corresponding rules for civil partners in terms of section 72(4) and Schedule 7 to the Civil Partnership Act 2004,[5] as to the powers and jurisdiction of the English courts to grant financial relief following the obtaining of a foreign divorce/dissolution, annulment or legal separation. It is necessary, therefore, to examine separately the jurisdictional rules governing the various heads of English financial relief, those which are uniform within the European Union and the EFTA States under the Maintenance Regulation and Lugano Convention, before considering the position under Part III of the 1984 Act.

(a) General jurisdictional rules

(i) *Relief ancillary to an English decree of divorce, nullity or judicial separation*

On granting a decree of divorce, nullity or judicial separation,[6] or at any time thereafter, the English court may make a variety of financial provision orders,[7] eg an order for the payment of periodical payments, which may be ordered to be secured, or that a lump sum shall be paid by one spouse to the other, or that similar payments may be made by one spouse to or for the benefit of a child of the family,[8] or that a spouse shall transfer to or settle property on the other spouse or a child or for the benefit of a child,[9] or the court may order the variation of any settlement made on the parties to the marriage or order the extinction or reduction of the interest of either party thereunder.[10] The court also has power[11] to restrain or set aside transactions intended to prevent or reduce relief and will, in appropriate circumstances, exercise this power in relation to immovables abroad.[12]

The court has jurisdiction to make such orders and grant such ancillary relief whenever it has jurisdiction in the main proceedings for divorce, nullity or judicial separation.[13] This means, primarily, when the court has jurisdiction under Article 3 of the Brussels II *bis* Regulation,[14] ie where:

(a) both parties are habitually resident in England and Wales;

(b) both parties were last habitually resident in England and Wales and one of them still resides there;

(c) the respondent is habitually resident in England and Wales;

(d) in the event of a joint application, either party is habitually resident in England and Wales;

---

[4] Hague Convention of 23 November 2007 on the International Recovery of Child Support and other Forms of Family Maintenance. The Convention entered into force on 1 January 2013 and the EU approved the Convention as a regional economic integration organisation (REIO) on 9 April 2014.

[5] The rules which apply to civil partners under the 2004 Act are based upon those which apply to married couples, and so all references in this chapter to "marriage" and "married persons" should be construed as including civil partnership and civil partners.

[6] Provision is also made for the payment of maintenance pending suit: Matrimonial Causes Act 1973, s 22. See *Harb v Aziz (No 1)* [2005] EWCA Civ 632, [2005] 2 FLR 1108.

[7] Matrimonial Causes Act 1973, s 23(1)(a)–(c).

[8] Ibid, s 23(1)(d)–(f). This relief may be ordered before a decree is granted, or if the proceedings are dismissed: ibid, s 23(2).

[9] Ibid, s 24(1)(a), (b).

[10] Ibid, s 24(1)(c), (d). For consent orders, see the Matrimonial and Family Proceedings Act 1984, s 7.

[11] Matrimonial Causes Act 1973, s 37.

[12] *Hamlin v Hamlin* [1986] Fam 11 (subject always to exclusive jurisdiction under the Brussels I recast, Art 24 and the Lugano Convention).

[13] *Cammell v Cammell* [1965] P 467 and the Maintenance Regulation, Art 3(c).

[14] Domicile and Matrimonial Proceedings Act 1973, s 5(2)(a) and (3)(a). Residual national rules of jurisdiction apply if no court of a Member State has jurisdiction under the Regulation (s 5(2)(b) and (3)(b)). See p 962, supra.

(e) the applicant is habitually resident in England and Wales if s/he resided there for at least a year immediately before the application was made;

(f) the applicant is habitually resident in England and Wales if s/he resided there for at least six months immediately before the application was made and s/he has his/her domicile there; or

(g) both parties are domiciled in England and Wales.[15]

On the basis of jurisdiction in the main suit, an order for periodical payments has been made against a husband domiciled and resident in France and with no assets in England but where there was a real probability of his appearing before the English courts.[16] As the power to make orders for ancillary relief is discretionary,[17] the court will decline to make such an order where to do so would be quite ineffective.[18] The fact that there has been a legal separation abroad which is recognised in England does not prevent the English court from granting relief ancillary to a later English divorce petition.[19]

The power to make orders for ancillary relief may be exercised at any time after the granting of the main decree,[20] and there is authority for the opinion that, so long as there was jurisdiction in the main suit, ancillary relief may still be granted notwithstanding that the jurisdictional ground in the main suit no longer exists.[21]

It will be recalled that the jurisdiction of the English courts to grant decrees of divorce, nullity and judicial separation is subject to a discretionary power in the court to stay the proceedings if similar proceedings are continuing in another, non-European Union jurisdiction.[22] If English proceedings are stayed because similar proceedings are continuing in another jurisdiction in the British Isles,[23] the English court does not have power to make, inter alia, orders for periodical payments or the payment of lump sums, except in circumstances of urgency.[24] Furthermore, any order, other than a lump sum order, already made in connection with the stayed proceedings ceases to have effect three months after the proceedings were stayed.[25] If an order for periodical payments or any provision relating to a child has been made in the other British proceedings, then any English order made in connection with the stayed English proceedings in relation to the same matters shall cease to have effect and no such order may be made.[26]

---

[15] Notably, the Brussels II *bis* Regulation (Recital (8)), like its predecessor, the Brussels II Regulation (Recital (10)), applies only to the dissolution of matrimonial ties; it does not deal with issues such as the property consequences of marriage or any other ancillary measures.

[16] *Cammell v Cammell*, supra (preceding the Brussels II *bis* Regulation); and see the power to vary a marriage settlement exercised over foreign settlements in *Nunneley v Nunneley* (1890) 15 PD 186; *Forsyth v Forsyth* [1891] P 363; and see *Hunter v Hunter and Waddington* [1962] P 1, infra, pp 1394–6. See now Matrimonial Causes Act 1973, s 23.

[17] Eg, the Matrimonial Causes Act 1973, ss 23, 24.

[18] *Tallack v Tallack* [1927] P 211; *Goff v Goff* [1934] P 107; *Wyler v Lyons* [1963] P 274.

[19] *Sabbagh v Sabbagh* [1985] FLR 29. Relief after a foreign divorce, etc is discussed more fully, infra, p 1071 et seq.

[20] Matrimonial Causes Act 1973, ss 23(1), 24(1).

[21] *Moss v Moss* [1937] QSR 1. However this common law authority is now subject to Art 8 of the Maintenance Regulation and Art 18 of the 2007 Hague Convention, on modification, where applicable.

[22] The discretionary power does not exist in the case of competing proceedings in another European Union Member State: Brussels II *bis* Regulation, Art 19. See p 967 et seq, supra.

[23] A "related jurisdiction", per Domicile and Matrimonial Proceedings Act 1973, Sch 1, para 3.

[24] Domicile and Matrimonial Proceedings Act 1973, Sch 1, para 11(2)(c).

[25] Ibid, Sch 1, para 11(2)(b).

[26] Ibid, Sch 1 para 11(3), as amended by the Children Act 1989, Sch 13, para 33, Sch 15.

(ii) Failure to provide reasonable maintenance

The court has power to order periodical payments, which may be ordered to be secured, or lump sum payments to be made to a spouse or to or for the benefit of a child if the other spouse has failed to provide reasonable maintenance.[27] This relief may be sought during the continuance of the marriage, during the joint lives of the spouses,[28] and is not ancillary to a petition for divorce, nullity or judicial separation. Indeed it assumes that the spouses are still married, though such relief may be granted after there has been a decree of judicial separation.[29] The court can only consider applications under this section if it has jurisdiction under the Maintenance Regulation and Schedule 6 to the Civil Jurisdiction and Judgments (Maintenance) Regulations 2011.[30]

(iii) Alteration of maintenance agreements

The court has power to order alterations, by variation or revocation, to a maintenance agreement on application by either of the parties thereto.[31] The court must be satisfied that the financial circumstances of the parties have changed or that the agreement fails to make proper arrangements for a child of the family. Jurisdiction is generally based on the domicile or residence in England of each party to the agreement at the time of the application.[32] However if an application, or part of an application, relates to a matter where jurisdiction falls to be determined by the requirements under the Maintenance Regulation then the requirement as to domicile or residence does not apply to that matter.[33] Where the Maintenance Regulation applies the court may not hear an application unless it has jurisdiction to do so under that Regulation.[34]

(iv) Financial provision in the family court

(a) Under the Domestic Proceedings and Magistrates' Courts Act 1978

The family court has power under Part I of the Domestic Proceedings and Magistrates' Courts Act 1978 to order either party to a marriage to make financial provision for the other spouse or for a child of the family.[35] The domicile of the parties is irrelevant to the jurisdiction of the family court.[36] All other issues remain to be determined, as they were with the forerunners of this Act, by the common law, subject to the Maintenance Regulation where applicable.

---

[27] Matrimonial Causes Act 1973, s 27. The differing obligations of maintenance on a husband and a wife are laid down in s 27(1), as substituted by s 63 of the Domestic Proceedings and Magistrates' Courts Act 1978; and see the Matrimonial and Family Proceedings Act 1984, s 4; Family Law Reform Act 1987, Sch 2, para 52.

[28] *Harb v Aziz (No 2)* [2005] EWCA Civ 1324, [2005] 1 FLR 825.

[29] *King v King* [1954] P 55.

[30] Matrimonial Causes Act 1973, s 27(2), as substituted by the Civil Jurisdiction and Judgments (Maintenance) Regulations 2011, Sch 7, para 6(2). For the jurisdictional requirements under the Maintenance Regulation, see infra, p 1064 et seq.

[31] Matrimonial Causes Act 1973, s 35.

[32] Ibid, s 35(1). For the meaning of "residence", see *Sinclair v Sinclair* [1968] P 189 and cases there cited. Also *Harb v Aziz (No 1)* [2005] EWCA Civ 632, [2005] 2 FLR 1108; and *Harb v Aziz (No 2)* [2005] EWCA Civ 1324, [2005] 1 FLR 825. If an agreement provides for the continuation of payment after the death of one party, and that party died domiciled in England, the court has jurisdiction over any application by the survivor or the personal representatives of the deceased: s 36.

[33] Matrimonial Causes Act 1973, s 35 (1A)(a), as added by the Civil Jurisdiction and Judgments (Maintenance) Regulations 2011, Sch 7, para 6(3)(b).

[34] Ibid, s 35 (1A)(b).

[35] Ss 1 and 2, as substituted by the Crime and Courts Act 2013, Sch 11(1) para 68.

[36] S 30(5), as substituted by the Crime and Courts Act 2013, Sch 11(1) para 81(3).

(b) Under the Maintenance Orders (Facilities for Enforcement) Act 1920 and the Maintenance Orders (Reciprocal Enforcement) Act 1972

If the defendant resides in a country outside the United Kingdom, the English courts may have jurisdiction to make a maintenance order against him if the circumstances are such that either the Maintenance Orders (Facilities for Enforcement) Act 1920[37] or the Maintenance Orders (Reciprocal Enforcement) Act 1972[38] is applicable.[39] Both these statutes deal with the problem of reciprocal enforcement of maintenance orders. As the basis of the operation of both statutes is reciprocity, they both deal with the recognition of foreign maintenance orders as well as the jurisdiction of the English court, but only the latter aspect is considered here.[40]

The 1920 Act applies only to those Commonwealth countries to which it has been extended by Order in Council. If a defendant is resident in such a country, then the English family court may make a provisional order against him in his absence,[41] as if that person had been habitually resident in England and he had received reasonable notice of the date of the hearing of the application, even though the applicant's basis of complaint did not arise in England.[42] A copy of such an order is then sent by diplomatic channels to the Commonwealth country where the defendant resides with a view to its being confirmed by the courts of that country. In other words, there are proceedings in England for a provisional order, followed by proceedings in the foreign country for confirmation thereof.

Part I of the 1972 Act establishes a similar procedure but it is wider in scope. It applies to all countries with whom reciprocal agreements have been reached and not just Commonwealth countries,[43] and it contains a wider definition of the type of orders to which it applies than does the 1920 Act.[44] Furthermore, the "shuttlecock" procedure of provisional order in one country followed by confirmation in the other also applies to variation and revocation of maintenance orders.[45] Such variation or revocation may be made either by the court which made the original provisional order or the court which confirmed it.

Part II of the 1972 Act gives effect in the United Kingdom to the United Nations Convention on the Recovery Abroad of Maintenance (1956). If a person, usually the wife, in the United Kingdom claims maintenance from a person "subject to the jurisdiction" of a convention country,[46] she makes an application through an officer of the family court.[47] This application

---

[37] As amended by the Maintenance Orders (Reciprocal Enforcement) Act 1992, Sch 1, Part I; SI 1992/709, Art 4; Access to Justice Act 1999, Sch 15, Pt V; and the Courts Act 2003, Sch 8, para 68 and Sch 10. See McClean, *Recognition of Family Judgments in the Commonwealth* (1983), Chapter 5.

[38] As amended by the Domestic Proceedings and Magistrates' Courts Act 1978, ss 54–61, and by the Maintenance Orders (Reciprocal Enforcement) Act 1992, Sch 1, Part II. See McClean, op cit, Chapters 6 and 7.

[39] Dicey, Morris and Collins, paras 18–216–18–222.

[40] Recognition is discussed, infra, p 1079 et seq.

[41] S 3, as amended by the Crime and Courts Act 2013, Sch 11(1) para 68.

[42] *Collister v Collister* [1972] 1 WLR 54.

[43] Indeed the 1920 Act is being replaced in the case of Commonwealth countries by new Orders made under the 1972 Act; see, eg, SIs 1983/1124, 1983/1125, 2002/788 and 2002/789.

[44] S 21, as amended by Courts Act 2003, Sch 10, para 1.

[45] 1972 Act, ss 5, 9, as amended by the Domestic Proceedings and Magistrates' Courts Act 1978, s 54; the Civil Jurisdiction and Judgments Act 1982, Sch 11, para 12; the Maintenance Enforcement Act 1991, Sch 1, para 14; the Maintenance Orders (Reciprocal Enforcement) Act 1992, Sch I, Part II; Access to Justice Act 1999, Sch 13, para 71; and the Courts Act 2003, Sch 8, para 153. For an example, see *Killen v Killen* 1981 SLT (Sh Ct) 77.

[46] By s 25(1) the Crown, by Order in Council, may declare that any country or territory specified in the Order, being a country or territory outside the United Kingdom to which the 1956 Maintenance Convention extends, is a Convention country for the purposes of Part II of the 1972 Act. See SIs 1975/423, 1978/279, 1982/1530, 1996/1925, and 2002/2839.

[47] S 26(3) and (6), as substituted by the Access to Justice Act 1999, Sch 13, paras 71, 76, the Crime and Courts Act 2013, Sch 11(1) para 42, and as amended by the Courts Act 2003, Sch 8, para 158. In Scotland, the application is submitted to the sheriff clerk for the sheriffdom in which the applicant resides.

is forwarded through diplomatic channels to that foreign country and there are no judicial proceedings in England. In the converse case, where a foreign application is received in England by the family court,[48] the court proceeds just as if the complainant was before the English court.[49]

Under section 40 of the 1972 Act,[50] special recognition arrangements may be made with countries designated by Order in Council, applying modified versions of either Part I or Part II to such countries. Under this provision, there are, for example, reciprocal arrangements applying an amended version of Part I[51] to the Republic of Ireland,[52] to a majority of the states in the USA,[53] and to countries which are parties to the 1973 Hague Convention on the Recognition and Enforcement of Decisions Relating to Maintenance Obligations.[54] A modified version of Part II has also been applied to certain states in the USA.[55]

(b) Jurisdiction under the Maintenance Regulation

Prior to June 2011 the recovery of maintenance within the EU was regulated by the Brussels/Lugano system.[56] The jurisdictional rules under the Maintenance Regulation differ from those under the previous system, therefore the Regulation and the Lugano Convention will be dealt with separately. Denmark is not officially party to the Maintenance Regulation but has agreed to implement the Regulation to the extent that it amends Brussels I.[57]

(i) What are maintenance orders?

Article 1 of the Maintenance Regulation declares that: "This Regulation shall apply to maintenance obligations arising from a family relationship, parentage, marriage or affinity." In order to determine whether a 'family relationship' exists English courts should apply the common law, which may include private international law rules.[58] The concept of maintenance is not defined in the Regulation, nor was it defined in Brussels I.[59] Whether an application is to be regarded as a "maintenance obligation" depends on an autonomous interpretation of the term,[60] derived from the judgments of the CJEU: "the label given to the claim by national law is not decisive".[61] "Whether a claim relates to maintenance will depend on its purpose, and in particular whether it is designed to enable one spouse to provide for himself or herself or if

---

[48] S 27B, as substituted by the Crime and Courts Act 2013, Sch 11(1) para 43(a).

[49] Under s 28A of the 1972 Act (as substituted by the Maintenance Orders (Reciprocal Enforcement) Act 1992, Sch 1, Part II, para 13 and the Crime and Courts Act 2013, Sch 11(1) para 46(a)) the English family court can entertain an application for maintenance from a person who is residing in England, even though the spouses' marriage had been dissolved or annulled by an overseas decree which is recognised as valid in England.

[50] As amended by the Civil Jurisdiction and Judgments Act 1982, Sch 11, para 17.

[51] See SI 2001/410.

[52] SI 1993/594; see *Macaulay v Macaulay* [1991] 1 WLR 179; *R v West London Magistrates' Court, ex p Emmett* [1993] 2 FLR 663; and see *Sachs v Standard Chartered Bank (Ireland) Ltd* [1987] ILRM 297. Since June 2011 the Maintenance Regulation applies to all disputes involving England and the Republic of Ireland, infra p 1070.

[53] SI 1995/2709, as amended by SI 2003/776.

[54] SI 1993/593, SI 1994/1902, SI 1999/1318, SI 2001/2567, SI 2002/2838; and see *Armitage v Nanchen* (1983) 4 FLR 293.

[55] SI 1993/591.

[56] See the 14th edition of this book (2008).

[57] Agreement OJ L149/80, 12 June 2009.

[58] The English courts will apply the law of the forum for all elements of the maintenance case, because England is not party to the Hague Protocol, see infra at p 1078. The Hague Protocol States should also apply national law to determine whether a family relationship exists, Rec 21 Maintenance Regulation.

[59] Art 5(2) and see Schlosser Report, pp 101–5.

[60] See Rec 11.

[61] *Moore v Moore* [2007] EWCA Civ 361, [2007] IL Pr 36, (Thorpe LJ) [80].

the needs and resources of each spouse are taken into consideration in the determination of its amount, or where the capital sum set is designed to ensure a predetermined level of income."[62] Some assistance may be derived from *De Cavel v De Cavel*[63] which illustrates that financial relief in its common form of periodical payments falls within the meaning of maintenance. There an order was made in the course of divorce proceedings for interim payments to be paid on a monthly basis. This was held to be within the Brussels Convention, but the court stressed that the payments were designed to support the spouse and were based on need. It has also been authoritatively stated that maintenance can include lump sum orders or transfers of property, if these are intended to ensure the support of a spouse.[64] The fact that a financial relief order is ancillary to a divorce order or decree or other judgment (such as parental responsibility) outside the Maintenance Regulation[65] does not mean that the financial relief order is excluded. Indeed, specific mention is made of such a case in Articles 3(c) and (d), and 4(c)(i).

Applying these criteria to the various financial orders that can be made by English courts, it is clear that financial orders (periodical or lump sum) made during the subsistence of a marriage, both for a spouse and for children being designed for support, must rank as maintenance orders within the Maintenance Regulation. The position where there is a divorce, or annulment, is more difficult. Financial orders for periodical payments to be made to a child or spouse are designed to support that person and must, therefore, be within the Regulation. The position in respect of lump sum payments is more problematical. Sometimes these are undoubtedly concerned with the support of a spouse, and will constitute "maintenance";[66] whereas other lump sum payments may be more in the nature of compensation for non-material damage or a division of matrimonial property[67] and will fall outside the meaning of maintenance.[68] Consequently, the latter will fall outside the special jurisdictional rules for "maintenance".[69] In *Kremen v Agrest*, where a lump sum payment was awarded, the High Court stated that £8.3 million of that sum was to be "certified as "constituting maintenance".[70] The remainder of the award was left undefined. Such non-maintenance lump sum payments are likely to fall outside the scope of the Maintenance Regulation altogether because they might not be considered to be "maintenance" for the purposes of the Regulation.

(ii) Jurisdictional rules

(a) General rules

A person who is seeking an order for financial relief which falls within the Maintenance Regulation has a number of jurisdictional options open to him. First, he can sue under

---

[62] Ibid.

[63] Case 120/79 [1980] ECR 731, [1980] 3 CMLR 1. It does not matter whether the order is interim or final: *De Cavel v De Cavel* Case 143/78 [1979] ECR 1055, [1979] 2 CMLR 547.

[64] Schlosser Report, p 102, C-220/95 *Van den Boogard v Laumen* [1997] QB 759 and *Moore v Moore* [2007] EWCA Civ 361, [2007] IL Pr 36, (Thorpe LJ) [76] and [80].

[65] Divorce, being a matter of status, is outside the scope of the Maintenance Regulation, the Lugano Convention and the Hague Convention.

[66] Case C-220/95 *Van den Boogard v Laumen* [1997] QB 759.

[67] *Moore v Moore* [2007] EWCA Civ 361, [2007] IL Pr 36, (Thorpe LJ) [80]: "Where the provision is solely concerned with dividing property between the spouses, the decision will be concerned with rights in property arising out of a matrimonial relationship and will not therefore be enforceable under Brussels I."

[68] Eg *Moore v Moore* [2007] EWCA Civ 361, [2007] IL Pr 36, (Thorpe LJ) [76] and [80]. The essential object of H's application was to achieve sharing of the property on his terms (cf *Miller v Miller, McFarlane v McFarlane* [2006] UKHL 24, [2006] 2 AC 618, [16] and [141]), rather than an order based on financial needs, and so there was no scope for application of Art 5(2) of the Brussels I Regulation.

[69] The English courts have a wide range of orders available to them, and the discretionary powers conferred on the court by ss 23–25 of the Matrimonial Causes Act 1973 have been described as limitless, see *NR v AB* [2016] EWHC 277 (Fam) [175].

[70] *Kremen v Agrest* [2012] EWHC 45 (Fam) (Mostyn J) [91].

any of the general jurisdiction provisions provided by the Regulation.[71] This means that the English courts can have jurisdiction if the defendant,[72] or the creditor is habitually resident in England.[73] These provisions are pro-claimant, as the creditor can sue in either the state of their habitual residence or the state of the defendant's habitual residence, whereas the defendant can only sue in the state of the creditor's habitual residence.[74] This is designed to protect the weaker party the maintenance creditor. The claimant's habitual residence is an appropriate forum for trial, since a court situated there is best able to gauge the claimant's needs.

There are two other general provisions and these relate to ancillary proceedings. Firstly, the court, which according to its own law, has jurisdiction to hear proceedings on the status of the person has jurisdiction for maintenance proceedings if the matter relating to maintenance is ancillary to those proceedings, unless that jurisdiction is based solely on the domicile or nationality of one of the parties.[75] This provision is important because, as we have seen, many applications for financial relief are made in conjunction with divorce proceedings, and there is a recognised practice of combining maintenance claims (which on their own are within the scope of the Maintenance Regulation) with main proceedings for divorce (which on their own are outside the scope of that Regulation). Whilst no definition is provided in the Maintenance Regulation of proceedings concerning status, there seems little doubt that the term will cover proceedings for divorce, nullity or judicial separation. So, an English court will be able to make a maintenance order in such proceedings against a respondent habitually resident in another Member State if the court has jurisdiction over the main proceedings on the basis of, inter alia, both spouses being domiciled in England.[76] Secondly, the court, which according to its own law, has jurisdiction to hear proceedings on parental responsibility also has jurisdiction for maintenance proceedings if the matter relating to maintenance is ancillary to those proceedings, unless that jurisdiction is based solely on the domicile or nationality of one of the parties.[77] In most, if not all, cases this ancillary jurisdiction will be determined by the jurisdiction rules in Brussels II *bis*, which focus on the habitual residence of the child.[78]

A question that has been raised is whether the two ancillary provisions are mutually exclusive, in disputes where spouses are divorcing and making applications for child maintenance and spousal maintenance, or whether they are two separate and independent ancillary claims. This problem arose in an English-Italian case, where the spouses were Italian nationals who had lived in England for the majority of their married life and the children had been born and raised in England.[79] The father initiated divorce proceedings in Italy on the basis of the parties' common nationality,[80] but it was clear that questions relating to parental responsibility had to be decided by the English courts.[81] The question therefore was which court should deal with the maintenance dispute.[82] The CJEU considered that the scope of the

---

[71] Art 3.
[72] Art 3(a).
[73] Art 3(b).
[74] Subject to the special rule on modification in Art 8.
[75] Art 3(c) and Art 2(3).
[76] Brussels II *bis* Regulation, Art 3(b).
[77] Art 3(d) and Art 2(3).
[78] Brussels II *bis* Regulation, Art 8.
[79] *EA v AP* [2013] EWHC 2344 (Fam).
[80] Brussels II *bis* Regulation, Art 3(b).
[81] Brussels II *bis* Regulation, Art 8. Parental responsibility is the generic term used by the Regulation, for proceedings relating to the care and / or upbringing of the child. Under English law the father automatically had parental responsibility, so any proceedings would be for a child arrangements order under s 8 of the Children Act 1989.
[82] C-184/14 *A v B*, 16 July 2015, ECLI:EU:C:2015:479.

concept of ancillary matter could not be left to the discretion of national courts, and instead an autonomous and uniform application was required.[83] The court pointed out that a literal interpretation of the Maintenance Regulation indicated that proceedings on status and parental responsibility were to be distinguished from one another,[84] and that Brussels II *bis* also separates parental responsibility proceedings from divorce proceedings.[85] The purpose of this separation was to ensure the protection of the best interests of the child on the basis of proximity.[86] The court also considered that the valuation of child maintenance was intrinsically linked to parental responsibility,[87] therefore decisions on child maintenance could only be ancillary to parental responsibility proceedings and not divorce proceedings where the two provisions resulted in conflicting jurisdictions.[88]

(b) Special rules

In addition to the general provisions, there are several special jurisdictional rules found in the Maintenance Regulation. Article 4 provides a choice of court clause, but the provision limits the parties' choice. Under Article 4 the parties can select a court, or courts, in a Member State where one of the parties is habitually resident,[89] or court(s) in a Member State where one of the parties is domiciled or a national.[90] Where the maintenance obligation relates to spouses or former spouses, they can also designate the court which has jurisdiction to determine their matrimonial disputes, or the court of the Member State where they had their last common habitual residence, provided that that residence lasted for at least a year.[91] Any agreement must be in writing,[92] however in *B v B* Parker J held that a choice of court agreement does not have to be explicitly stated and it can be inferred.[93] In *B* it was held that the agreement was clearly inferred from the prayers in the divorce petition.[94] A choice of court clause does not apply to maintenance proceedings concerning children under the age of eighteen.[95] Article 4 departs from the previous system where the provisions on prorogation of jurisdiction permitted the parties to select any court and covered child maintenance.[96] Where the parties have attributed exclusive jurisdiction under the Lugano Convention, to a court of a Lugano Contracting State that is not an EU Member State, such as Switzerland, then the Lugano Convention will apply, except in cases where the maintenance obligation concerns a child under the age of eighteen years.[97]

Jurisdiction can also be based on the defendant's submission. Article 5 provides that if "the defendant enters an appearance before a court, and the appearance is not to contest jurisdiction, then that court will be considered to have jurisdiction for the purposes of the Regulation".[98] The provision prevents the defendant from contesting jurisdiction at a later

---

[83] Ibid, [30]–[31].
[84] Ibid, [32].
[85] Ibid, [36].
[86] Ibid, [37].
[87] Ibid, [40].
[88] Ibid, [48].
[89] Art 4 (1)(a).
[90] Arts 4(1)(b) and 2(3).
[91] Art 4(1)(c).
[92] Art 4(2).
[93] *B v B* [2014] EWHC 4857 (Fam) [45].
[94] Ibid. The prayers are the term used for the section at the end of the divorce petition where the applicant indicates whether financial provision or property adjustment orders will be sought.
[95] Art 4(3) and see *B v B* [2014] EWHC 4857 (Fam) [62], where the choice of court agreement could not apply to child maintenance.
[96] Art 23 Brussels I and see *M v V* [2010] EWHC 1453 (Fam) where a jurisdiction agreement in relation to a child was upheld by the High Court.
[97] Art 4 (4) Maintenance Regulation.
[98] Art 5.

date, thus preventing delays, in cases where it appears that the defendant has already accepted the jurisdiction. In *B v B* the husband acceded to a maintenance pending suite order which required him to file a record of his means for the purpose of a maintenance hearing. This was deemed sufficient to meet the requirements in Article 5.[99] The policy behind this basis of jurisdiction is party autonomy, as it is effectively "consent based jurisdiction".[100] Unfortunately this can disadvantage weaker parties, such as litigants in person, who do not consult a legal professional before entering an appearance.[101] Where courts in more than one Member State have jurisdiction to hear the dispute under the rules in Articles 3 to 5, and multiple courts are seised, then the court first seised will have jurisdiction.[102]

The remaining two provisions extend the scope of the Regulation so it can apply to parties not habitually resident in the EU, and there is no geographic limitation in the Maintenance Regulation. Where no court has jurisdiction under Articles 3, 4 and 5 (so neither the defendant nor the creditor is habitually resident in the EU, and there is no ancillary jurisdiction) and no court of a Lugano Contracting State, that is not a Member State, such as Switzerland, has jurisdiction under the Lugano Convention the courts of the Member State of the common domicile of the parties shall have jurisdiction.[103] There is also a forum necessitatis rule, which applies, on an exceptional basis, where there is no jurisdiction under Articles 3, 4, 5 and 6, and if proceedings cannot be brought in a third state with which the dispute has a closer connection.[104] The provision is only applicable where the dispute has a sufficient connection with the Member State of the court seised.[105]

In *B v B* the court considered Article 7 as an alternative jurisdiction and held that it would be applicable if Articles 4 and 5 were not applicable.[106] The English court was seised for divorce on the basis of the husband's domicile which was considered to be a "sufficient connection".[107] The husband also intended to seek a residence order, in relation to his child,[108] in England which would create an even closer connection.[109] Parker J suggested that "exceptional" means by way of exception, rather than extraordinary.[110] She concluded that proceedings could not be brought in Dubai, as Mrs B no longer had a residence visa, and could not obtain entry without one,[111] and there was not a sufficient connection with Indonesia so proceedings could not be brought there.[112] There was a connection with Ethiopia, but the connection was no closer than the connection with England, and as the wife had already committed herself to the proceedings in England it would not have been reasonable for her

---

[99] *B v B* [2014] EWHC 4857 (Fam) [53]–[54].

[100] P Beaumont, 'International Family Law in Europe—the Maintenance Project, the Hague Conference and the EC: A Triumph of Reverse Subsidiarity' (2009) *Rabels Zeitschrift* 509, 534.

[101] This is in contrast to the general approach of the Regulation which is designed to protect the weaker party, allowing for creditor based jurisdiction under Art 3. See Art 26(2) Brussels I recast, which is a more nuanced submission provision designed to protect weaker parties and requires that the defendant is informed of the consequences of entering an appearance.

[102] Arts 12 and 13, and see Art 9. The rules on *lis pendens* and related actions are the same as the main rules (excluding the exceptions for choice of court agreements and exclusive jurisdiction) in Brussels I in Arts 29 and 30 discussed supra Chapter 11(3)(f) and Chapter 13(4)(a). See also supra, pp 968–71.

[103] Art 6 and Art 2(3).

[104] Art 7.

[105] Ibid.

[106] *B v B* [2014] EWHC 4857 (Fam).

[107] However, because this was based on the husband's domicile only (Domicile and Matrimonial Proceedings Act 1973, s 5(2)(b)), Art 3(c) could not apply as the wife was not domiciled in England and Wales.

[108] Under s 8 of the Children Act 1989, now known as a child arrangements order.

[109] *B v B* [2014] EWHC 4857 (Fam) [59].

[110] Ibid, [55].

[111] Ibid, [57].

[112] Ibid, [58].

to be compelled to re-litigate in another jurisdiction.[113] Parker J held that jurisdiction was established under Article 7 because proceedings could not reasonably be brought in a third State for the reasons outlined above. So the interpretation was based on the expectations of the parties in light of the husband's behaviour, at least in relation to Ethiopia,[114] rather than whether or not it was possible to bring proceedings. However even if Mrs B gained an order from the English Courts, she would have difficulty enforcing that order in the State where the husband is living (Indonesia at the time of the hearing) as the recognition and enforcement provisions in the Regulation will not apply.[115]

Maintenance orders are often varied and sometimes revoked. A court which made the original order may only vary or revoke it, at a later date, if it still has jurisdiction under the Maintenance Regulation. The Maintenance Regulation seeks to limit the jurisdiction of debtors when they bring proceedings to modify a decision.[116] The general rule, when a maintenance decision has been given by the Courts in the state of the habitual residence of the creditor, is that modification proceedings cannot be brought in another state by the debtor for as long as the creditor remains habitually resident in the state where the decision was given.[117] This rule does not apply where: the parties have designated a court in accordance with Article 4,[118] or the creditor submits to an alternative jurisdiction meeting the requirements in Article 5.[119] There are two further exceptions to the general rule and these apply where the state of origin is a Contracting State to the Hague 2007 Convention, but not an EU Member State. Jurisdiction will not be limited where the competent authority in the 2007 Hague Convention Contracting State of origin cannot, or refuses to, exercise jurisdiction to modify the decision.[120] The final exception is where the decision given in the Hague Contracting State cannot be recognised or declared enforceable in the Member State where proceedings to modify the decision or have a new decision given are contemplated.[121] However an English court will be unable to vary or revoke its own order if the maintenance creditor is not habitually resident in England at the time of the later proceedings, assuming that the maintenance debtor is still habitually resident in a Member State.[122]

(c) Jurisdiction under the Lugano Convention

As far as jurisdiction under the Lugano Convention is concerned,[123] there are some differences between the Maintenance Regulation and the Lugano Convention. Jurisdiction under the Lugano Convention can be based on the domicile of the defendant if that person is domiciled in a Lugano Contracting State.[124] Jurisdiction can also be based on the domicile or the habitual residence of the maintenance creditor.[125] The Convention also has two provisions on ancillary proceedings, equivalent to those in the Maintenance Regulation.[126] The

---

[113] Ibid, [59].

[114] Ibid, [60]–[61]. The husband chose to seise the English court for divorce and child arrangements. He should not be able to avoid that jurisdiction for maintenance, given that it was not possible to bring proceedings in Dubai the country with the closest connection to the marriage.

[115] Unless the husband subsequently moves to a EU Member State.

[116] Art 8 and Recital 17. This provision was taken from Art 18 of the 2007 Hague Convention, and the Regulation makes reference to the Contracting States to the Hague Convention in this provision.

[117] Art 8(1).

[118] Art 8(2)(a).

[119] Art 8(2)(b).

[120] Art 8(2)(c).

[121] Art 8(2)(d).

[122] And will have to recognise a variation or revocation made by a court in another Member State.

[123] Title 2, Arts 2–31. See, eg, *Bentinck v Bentinck* [2007] EWCA Civ 175 (CA (Civ Div)).

[124] Art 2.

[125] Art 5(2)(a).

[126] Art 5(2)(b) and (c).

choice of court provision applies where one of the parties to the agreement is domiciled in a Contracting State and the court designated is in one of the Contracting States bound by the Convention.[127] The parties can select a court in any Contracting State, so the provision is broader than the equivalent provision in the Maintenance Regulation, as long as the maintenance dispute does not concern a child under eighteen years old.[128]

(d) Inter-relation of the Maintenance Regulation and the Lugano Convention with other bases of jurisdiction

Finally, there is the question of the inter-relation of jurisdiction under the Maintenance Regulation and the Lugano Convention with the other jurisdictional bases already discussed. Difficulty arises from the fact that, for example, the jurisdictional rules of the Maintenance Regulation provide that only the courts given jurisdiction under the Maintenance Regulation or the Lugano Convention, as appropriate, may exercise it. This means that, in the case of a defendant who is habitually resident in another part of the United Kingdom or in another Member State and the proceedings concern "maintenance" in the Regulation sense, there may be circumstances in which an English court is deprived of jurisdiction.

Where the Maintenance Regulation applies then the jurisdictional grounds provided by the Regulation will generally have precedence.[129] If the creditor, or the debtor, is habitually resident in a Member State then the Regulation will almost always apply, apart from where there is a valid choice of court agreement under the Lugano Convention.[130] However, if the creditor seises the court in the state of their habitual residence under Article 3(a) of the Maintenance Regulation and the debtor submits to the jurisdiction, then the court in the state of the creditors habitual residence will still have jurisdiction regardless of the choice of court agreement by virtue of Articles 3 and 5.

The Regulation also provides that it "shall not affect the application of bilateral or multilateral conventions and agreements to which one or more Member States are party at the time of adoption of this Regulation, without prejudice to the obligations of Member States under Article 307 of the Treaty".[131] Despite this, in all applications between Member States the Regulation shall take precedence over other conventions and agreements.[132] Article 69(1) is relevant in disputes where one party is habitually resident in England and the other party is habitually resident in a 2007 Hague Contracting State (that is not an EU nor Lugano State) such as Ukraine. The 2007 Hague Convention provides that it shall not affect any international agreement, particularly those created by a Regional Economic Integration Organisation (REIO) and it cannot affect the recognition and enforcement provisions of the REIO, whether they were adopted before or after the conclusion of the instrument.[133] However the Convention also states that it "shall not prevent the application of an agreement, arrangement or international instrument in force between the requesting State and the requested State, or a reciprocity arrangement in force in the requested State".[134] As this refers

---

[127] Art 23.

[128] Art 4(4) Maintenance Regulation.

[129] Particularly where jurisdiction is found on Arts 3, 5 and in most cases Art 4. Arts 4 and 6 give precedence to the Lugano Convention in certain circumstances, and because Art 7 is an exceptional ground it should really only apply where jurisdiction cannot be found via a different mechanism.

[130] Art 4(d).

[131] Art 69(1).

[132] Art 69(2). So in a dispute where one party is habitually resident in Ireland and the other party is habitually resident in England the Maintenance Regulation would apply rather than the Maintenance Orders (Reciprocal Enforcement) Act 1972.

[133] Art 51.

[134] Art 52.

specifically to agreements or instruments in force between the two states in question then this would not provide for the application of the Maintenance Regulation, rather than the Hague Convention, where one party is habitually resident in England and the other the Ukraine. In light of the broad approach taken by the Maintenance Regulation the best option is to select the most effective rule available. If the maintenance debtor is habitually resident in England and the creditor is habitually resident in a 2007 Hague Contacting State, such as the USA, the most effective method would be for the creditor to sue in England, under the rules of the Maintenance Regulation,[135] because the decision would also be enforced in England. Where the facts are reversed the creditor would be better to sue on the basis of one of the indirect grounds in the 2007 Hague Convention[136] because that person would have to get the decision recognised and enforced in the non-EU state under the relevant recognition and enforcement rules in the Convention which permit a review of the jurisdictional bases.[137]

2. FINANCIAL RELIEF AFTER A FOREIGN DIVORCE/ DISSOLUTION, ANNULMENT OR LEGAL SEPARATION

There are two issues to be examined in this context: the effect of a foreign divorce, annulment or legal separation on a pre-existing English order for financial relief, and the powers of the English court to grant such relief notwithstanding a prior foreign divorce, etc.

(a) Effect of foreign divorce, etc on financial relief already granted in England

Under English domestic law, a maintenance order granted by the family court could be continued in the discretion of the family court even after the marriage had been dissolved in England.[138] The Court of Appeal has decided that the position is the same if the marriage is dissolved by a foreign divorce recognised in England;[139] and the same principle has been applied to an interim order for maintenance made by a divorce county court, notwithstanding a later foreign divorce recognised in England.[140] The English court retains its discretion to continue, vary or discharge the English maintenance order, but the changed marital circumstances of the parties may well affect their financial position and the view taken thereof by the court, as where dower became payable on the termination of a marriage by *talak*.[141]

(b) Powers of English court to grant financial relief, despite an earlier foreign divorce/dissolution, annulment or legal separation

(i) The common law position

Until Part III of the Matrimonial and Family Proceedings Act 1984 came into force, the general rule was that, once a marriage had been dissolved or annulled, the English court's power to grant financial relief came to an end.[142] No ancillary relief could be granted on the basis of a foreign divorce. The more liberal the English rules for the recognition of foreign divorces, etc, the greater the problem for spouses who wished to seek financial relief in England.[143] Various devices were utilised by the courts to minimise the difficulties of those

---

[135] Art 3(a).
[136] This is permitted by Art 69(1) Maintenance Regulation.
[137] See infra p 1084 et seq.
[138] *Bragg v Bragg* [1925] P 20; and see Matrimonial Causes Act 1973, s 28; Domestic Proceedings and Magistrates' Courts Act 1978, s 4.
[139] *Wood v Wood* [1957] P 254.
[140] *Newmarch v Newmarch* [1978] Fam 79.
[141] *Qureshi v Qureshi* [1972] Fam 173, 200–1.
[142] *Moore v Bull* [1891] P 279.
[143] Eg *Turczak v Turczak* [1970] P 198.

who sought financial relief in England, such as expediting English proceedings if there were parallel foreign ones,[144] or granting relief in favour of a child though none could be granted to a parent.[145] Useful though these devices were, the law was undoubtedly unsatisfactory in that, if the foreign proceedings had included no, or inadequate, financial provision for an English spouse (usually the wife) she could find herself destitute in England with social security as her only source of financial support. This could be so even though her husband lived in England and had substantial assets in England. Furthermore, the inability of the English courts to grant relief if a foreign divorce was recognised in England led regularly to challenges to the validity of such divorces for recognition purposes. This problem[146] led to proposals for reform being made by the Law Commission[147] which were carried into effect by Part III of the Matrimonial and Family Proceedings Act 1984; and this applies whether the foreign divorce was obtained before or after Part III came into effect.[148]

(ii) Part III of the Matrimonial and Family Proceedings Act 1984[149]

In considering the powers of the English court[150] to grant matrimonial relief after a foreign divorce, etc, it is necessary to consider the orders which the court may make, the bases of jurisdiction available for the making of such orders and certain limitations or controls on the courts' powers.

Powers equivalent to those set out in Part III of the 1984 Act operate in respect of civil partners by virtue of section 72(4) of the Civil Partnership Act 2004. Schedule 7 to the 2004 Act makes provision for financial relief in England after a civil partnership has been dissolved or annulled, or civil partners have been legally separated, in a country outside the British Islands. The following commentary on Part III of the 1984 Act should be read as applying, *mutatis mutandis*, to the grant of financial relief in respect of civil partnerships, in terms of the 2004 Act.

(a) Orders which the court can make

The powers conferred by Part III of the 1984 Act apply to the High Court and the family court.[151] The general approach is that the court can make any of the orders which it could make on granting an English decree of divorce, annulment or judicial separation,[152] including consent orders,[153] orders for the transfer of tenancies[154] and orders relating to children.[155] So, notwithstanding a foreign divorce, the English court will, for example, be able to make periodical payments orders lump sum orders, property adjustment orders, and pension sharing orders.[156] In deciding whether to make any of the orders which it could make on granting

---

[144] Eg *Torok v Torok* [1973] 1 WLR 1066; *Bryant v Bryant* (1980) 11 Fam Law 85.

[145] See *P (LE) v P (JM)* [1971] P 318; *Hack v Hack* (1976) 6 Fam Law 177.

[146] Exemplified by *Quazi v Quazi* [1980] AC 744.

[147] Law Com No 117 (1982).

[148] *Chebaro v Chebaro* [1987] Fam 127.

[149] See the Family Proceedings Rules, 1991, rr 3.17–3.19; and see Gordon, *Foreign Divorces: English Law and Practice*, Chapter 11.

[150] Part IV of the 1984 Act confers similar, but more limited, powers on the Scottish courts, following the report of the Scottish Law Commission in Scot Law Com No 72 (1982). See Crawford and Carruthers, para 13–43.

[151] S 27, as substituted by the Crime and Courts Act 2013, sch 11(1) para 88.

[152] Matrimonial Causes Act 1973 ss 22–24.

[153] S 19.

[154] Ss 17, 19, 21–2. There are also provisions similar to those in the Matrimonial Causes Act 1973 for avoiding transactions designed to defeat applications for financial relief (s 23) and, for preventing transactions intended to defeat prospective applications (s 24). The court's powers are limited to orders relating to the matrimonial home (s 20) in cases when jurisdiction is taken solely on the basis of the presence of that home in England.

[155] Children Act 1989, s 8(4)(g).

[156] S 17, as amended by the Welfare Reform and Pensions Act 1999.

a decree, the court must have regard to a range of matters[157] which are essentially the same as if it were granting a decree itself.[158] In addition, section 18(6) provides as follows:

> Where an order has been made by a court outside England and Wales for the making of payments or the transfer of property by a party to the marriage, the court in considering in accordance with this section the financial resources of the other party to the marriage or a child of the family shall have regard to the extent to which that order has been complied with or is likely to be complied with.

The purpose of this provision is to enable the court to take account of any foreign order which has been made and of its likely effectiveness.[159] Furthermore, the English court may, if it thinks it appropriate, make an order in relation to matrimonial assets which are abroad, just as would seem to be the case in normal English matrimonial proceedings.[160]

(b) Jurisdiction of the English courts

There are three main bases of jurisdiction laid down by section 15(1) of the 1984 Act,[161] ie:

(a) the domicile in England and Wales of either party to the marriage—this can be at one of two dates: either the start of the English proceedings for relief[162] or the date when the foreign divorce, etc took effect in the foreign country;[163]

(b) the habitual residence in England and Wales of either party to the marriage for one year ending on either of the two dates relevant to domicile, ie the date of application for leave to bring the English proceedings or the date on which the foreign divorce, etc took effect in the country in which it was obtained;

(c) either or both of the parties to the marriage had at the date of application for leave to bring the English proceedings a beneficial interest in possession in a dwelling-house[164] in England and Wales which was at some time during the marriage a matrimonial home of the parties to the marriage.

These grounds are now subject to those under the Maintenance Regulation, where applicable.[165] In the Law Commission's view, the use of the same jurisdictional criteria of domicile and habitual residence as then[166] applied to divorce petitions struck the proper balance of formulating "jurisdictional rules strict enough to prevent persons, whose marriage is insufficiently connected with this country to make it appropriate for the English court to adjudicate on financial matters, from invoking the court's powers; but not so strict as to exclude meritorious cases".[167] The third head of jurisdiction, that there had been a matrimonial home

---

[157] S 18, as amended by the Welfare Reform and Pensions Act 1999.

[158] See Matrimonial Causes Act 1973, ss 25, 25A.

[159] Eg *M v M (Financial Provision After Foreign Divorce)* [1994] 1 FLR 399.

[160] *Razelos v Razelos (No 2)* [1970] 1 WLR 392 at 400, 401; and see *Hunter v Hunter* [1962] P 1; *Tallack v Tallack* [1927] P 211; *Hamlin v Hamlin* [1986] Fam 11.

[161] Cf, for civil partnerships, Civil Partnership Act 2004, Sch 7, para 7.

[162] Technically, the date of the application for leave, under s 13 of the 1984 Act.

[163] For detailed discussion of the reasons for selecting these alternative dates, see Law Commission Working Paper No 77 (1980), paras 33, 38.

[164] Defined in s 27 and see *MA v SK* [2015] EWHC 887 (Fam) [39]–[42].

[165] S 15(1A), as amended by the Civil Jurisdiction and Judgments (Maintenance) Regulations 2011/1484 Sch7 para 10(2)(b). Where the dispute is considered to be a "maintenance" dispute for the purposes of the Maintenance Regulation, then the jurisdictional bases in the Regulation are always applicable, regardless of the parties' residence and domicile, because there is no residual jurisdiction. (Cf Brussels II *bis* Art 7). However, although the bases in (a) and (c) of the 1984 Act are technically not available under the Maintenance Regulation, if one party seises the English court on either basis and the other party submits to the jurisdiction, then the English court will have jurisdiction by virtue of Art 5.

[166] See now Domicile and Matrimonial Proceedings Act 1973, s 5, referring primarily to the rules of jurisdiction contained in the Brussels II *bis* Regulation.

[167] Law Commission Working Paper No 77 (1980), para 31, and see Law Com No 117 (1982), paras 2.7–2.8.

in England, might be thought to cause more problems in terms of striking the correct balance and, indeed, was provisionally rejected by the Law Commission at one stage.[168] It was, however, felt necessary[169] to give the court power to deal with the quite common situation where the parties, though living abroad at the date of the divorce, had lived previously in England and where their only substantial asset was the former matrimonial home. The danger perceived by the Law Commission[170] that this head of jurisdiction could be too wide, in giving the court power to make orders in relation to all the property of persons who had left England long ago, has been met by limiting the orders which the court may make, when exercising this head of jurisdiction alone, to orders relating to the former matrimonial home.[171]

Part III of the Matrimonial and Family Proceedings Act 1984 also provides for dovetailing these rules of jurisdiction into the structure of the Maintenance Regulation, Lugano Convention and Hague Convention.[172] It will be recalled that the Maintenance Regulation extends the jurisdiction to grant all maintenance obligations, arising out of a family relationship, parentage, marriage or affinity. There is no definition of maintenance obligation, but the Regulation requires an autonomous interpretation.[173] Therefore the CJEU might hold that an order made under Part III of the 1984 Act is not within that Regulation because it is first granted after the spouses' marriage has come to an end, however this seems unlikely. The Maintenance Regulation provides a variety of jurisdictional bases, one of these is the court that has jurisdiction to deal with status, which includes divorce.[174] There is no requirement to apply for maintenance in the state in which the divorce was granted, this is just a possibility, suggesting that the Regulation envisages a scenario where a divorce is granted in one Member State and maintenance is then granted in another state following the divorce, particularly where the parties are habitually resident in the latter State and divorce jurisdiction was based on common domicile or nationality.[175] The English courts have found that the 1984 Act can apply,[176] and held that creditor in Article 3 of the Regulation includes potential creditor.[177] Where the Regulation is applicable, it will not apply to those orders under the 1984 Act which concern "rights in property arising out of a matrimonial relationship".[178] In order to deal with the possibility of clashes between the jurisdictional rules of the European system and of the 1984 Act, section 15(2) of the 1984 Act provides that where the jurisdiction of the court to entertain proceedings under Part III of the 1984 Act would fall to be determined by reference to the jurisdictional requirements imposed by virtue of Part I of the Civil Jurisdiction and Judgments Act 1982, then (a) satisfaction of the jurisdiction provisions laid

---

[168] Ibid, para 44.

[169] Law Com No 117 (1982), paras 2.8–2.9.

[170] Ibid, para 2.10.

[171] 1984 Act, s 20; and there is in such cases no power to make interim maintenance orders under s 14 (s 14(2)).

[172] 1984 Act, s 15 as substituted, repealed and added by Civil Jurisdiction and Judgments (Maintenance) Regulations 2011/1484 Sch 7, para 10 and Civil Jurisdiction and Judgments Act, s 1 as amended.

[173] Recital 11. The reference to 'all' maintenance obligations suggests a broad interpretation of the term maintenance obligations.

[174] Art 3(c) Maintenance Regulation. See also C-184/14 *A v B*, 16 July 2015, ECLI:EU:C:2015:479.

[175] The grounds for jurisdiction in the Maintenance Regulation do not align with those in Brussels II *bis* Art 3, and see L Walker, *Maintenance and Child Support in Private International Law* (2015) 55–65.

[176] See *AA v BB* [2015] EWCA Civ 1138, where the wife applied for maintenance in England following a divorce in Slovenia.

[177] *M v W (Application after New Zealand Financial Agreement)* [2014] EWHC [39].

[178] In *Van den Boogaard* the CJEU referred to maintenance as an award that is designed to enable one spouse to provide for them self and should take account of the needs and resources of each of the spouses. A right in property on the other hand should be solely concerned with dividing property (C-220/95 *Van den Boogard v Laumen* [1997] I-01147 [22]). This definition creates some grey areas and the label given to a payment by national law will not necessarily be definitive. See *Moore v Moore* [2007] EWCA Civ 361 [80].

down in section 15(1) of the 1984 Act shall not obviate the need to satisfy the requirements imposed by the Regulation or the 1982 Act; and (b) satisfaction of the requirements imposed by virtue of Part I of the 1982 Act shall obviate the need to satisfy the requirements of section 15(1) of the 1984 Act.[179] Assuming that some orders, at least, made under Part III of the 1984 Act fall within the Maintenance Regulation, the jurisdictional rules in the Regulation shall apply to such orders.[180]

(c) "Filter" mechanisms

In making proposals for giving the courts power to make financial relief orders after foreign divorces, etc the Law Commission was much concerned that the relief should be "confined to those cases in which it is appropriate for the English court to intervene".[181] In addition to rules as to jurisdiction, Part III of the 1984 Act contains two further means[182] for limiting relief to appropriate cases.[183] The first is a filter mechanism for applications to the court. Under section 13 of the 1984 Act no application for a financial relief order can be made unless the leave of the court has been obtained, and "the court shall not grant leave unless it considers that there is substantial ground for the making of an application".[184] The paradigm case creating the need for the legislation is one where the foreign court offered no rights to financial provision,[185] but the existence of a foreign financial provision order is no bar as such to the English application.[186] This is because the foreign order may be inadequate or inappropriate.[187] A mere disparity between the foreign award and what would be awarded by the English court would be insufficient in itself to trigger Part III.[188] However where there is a large disparity between the two jurisdictions and also a very large disparity between what each party received then that will create a real hardship and serious injustice, so Part III will be triggered.[189] It is important to note, however, that in intra-EU cases where a court in another EU Member State has also been seised for the "maintenance dispute" only the court first validly seised will have jurisdiction.[190] Where a party is unhappy with a maintenance order made by a court in another Member State, it might be possible to seek modification of that order in England, subject to Articles 3 to 8. Where the proceedings in the court of the Member State first seised were withdrawn, or expired, then an applicant can bring proceedings in England for maintenance following an overseas divorce. In *AA v BB*,[191] the wife successfully applied

---

[179] S 15(2), as amended by Sch 1(1), para 13 of the Civil Jurisdiction and Judgments Regulations, SI 2007/1655 and repealed by Civil Jurisdiction and Judgments (Maintenance) Regulations 2011/1484 Sch.7 para 10(2)(c).

[180] Matrimonial and Family Proceedings Act 1984, s 15(1A) as added by Civil Jurisdiction and Judgments (Maintenance) Regulations 2011/1484, Sch 7, para 10(2)(b).

[181] Law Com No 117 (1982), para 2.1.

[182] To be read in conjunction: *Holmes v Holmes* [1989] Fam 47, (Purchas LJ), 53; *Jordan v Jordan* [2000] 1 WLR 210, (Thorpe LJ), 218; *Moore v Moore* [2007] EWCA Civ 361, [2007] IL Pr 36, (Thorpe LJ), [107] and *Agbaje v Akinnoye-Agbaje* [2010] UKSC 13.

[183] To block unmeritorious applications under the Act and to avoid abuse of its underlying purpose: *M v L (Financial Relief after Overseas Divorce)* [2003] EWHC 328, [2003] 2 FLR 425.

[184] *Jordan v Jordan* [2000] 1 WLR 210, (Thorpe LJ), 220; and *Ella v Ella* [2007] EWCA Civ 99, (Charles J) [62]. It is necessary for the applicant to place all the material facts before the court: *W v W* [1989] 1 FLR 22; *M v M (Financial Provision After Foreign Divorce)* [1994] 1 FLR 399. Cf, for civil partnerships, Civil Partnership Act 2004, Sch 7, para 4.

[185] *Jordan v Jordan* [2000] 1 WLR 210, (Thorpe LJ), 219.

[186] S 13(2). *Jordan v Jordan* [2000] 1 WLR 210, (Thorpe LJ), 219: "after Parliament had provided the remedies for the paradigm case, attempts were repeatedly made to extend the statutory provisions to obtain for the applicant some specific outcome or target which she had failed to achieve in the jurisdiction where the marriage had been dissolved".

[187] *Agbaje v Akinnoye-Agbaje* [2010] UKSC 13.

[188] Ibid, [72].

[189] Ibid, [76].

[190] Maintenance Regulation, Art 12.

[191] [2015] EWCA Civ 1138.

for maintenance in England after the proceedings in Slovenia were withdrawn. In cases where the English courts and the courts in a non-EU/ Lugano State are seised of the same proceedings, the English court can hear the case because the lis pendens provisions do not apply.[192] Leave may also be granted subject to such conditions as the court thinks fit,[193] such as an undertaking not to enforce a foreign order. If, however, the court concludes that it would not be appropriate (under the second filter mechanism) for an order to be made because, for example, the matter of financial relief is properly before or has been appropriately decided by a foreign court, it should refuse leave.[194] It will be unusual for Part III to apply "where the wife had a right to apply for financial relief under the foreign law, and an award was made in a foreign country."[195] It is not necessary[196] in order to obtain the court's leave for the applicant to prove some hardship or injustice: "A case in which the applicant crosses the barriers contained in sections 13 and 16 without proving some specific hardship or injustice is perfectly conceivable."[197] If leave is to be granted, the jurisdiction should be tailored to the individual needs of the case "so that the grant of leave does not inevitably trigger a full blown claim for all forms of ancillary relief".[198]

The second control or filter mechanism operates at the time of the actual hearing of the application, ie once leave to apply has been given[199] and even if the jurisdictional rules are satisfied. Under section 16 the court has to be satisfied that in all the circumstances of the case it is appropriate for a court in England and Wales to make the order and the court is directed to consider a wide range of matters in determining the appropriateness of the venue.[200] These include[201] the connection of the parties with England, with the country where the divorce, etc was obtained or with any other country, the relief ordered in a foreign country and the likely effectiveness of that order,[202] whether there is a right to apply for relief abroad, the existence of property in England in respect of which an order under Part III could be made,

---

[192] See Art 12.

[193] S 13(3).

[194] *Holmes v Holmes* [1989] Fam 47; *M v M (Financial Provision After Foreign Divorce)* [1994] 1 FLR 399; *Hewitson v Hewitson* [1995] Fam 100, CA; *N v N (Foreign Divorce: Financial Relief)* [1997] 1 FLR 900. *Jordan v Jordan* [2000] 1 WLR 210, (Thorpe LJ), 219: "*Holmes v Holmes* and the subsequent cases are in the main restrictive and negative in conclusion, defining and policing the boundary between relieving hardship in the paradigm case and disqualifying the forum shopper for the applicant seeking a second bite of the cherry". Cf *A v S (Financial Relief after Overseas US Divorce)* [2002] EWHC 1157, [2003] 1 FLR 431, (Bodey J) [76]; and *M v L (Financial Relief after Overseas Divorce)* [2003] EWHC 328, [2003] 2 FLR 425, (Coleridge J) [37] and [54].

[195] *Agbaje v Akinnoye-Agbaje* [2010] UKSC 13, (Collins LJ) [72].

[196] *Jordan v Jordan* [2000] 1 WLR 210, (Thorpe LJ), 221: "Parliament might have so legislated, but it did not. The statutory criteria are fully expressed." Also *Moore v Moore* [2007] EWCA Civ 361, [2007] IL Pr 36, (Thorpe LJ) [108]; and *A v S (Financial Relief after Overseas US Divorce)* [2002] EWHC 1157, [2003] 1 FLR 431, (Bodey J) [75]: it is not necessary to look for financial hardship or injustice "although an applicant's case is stronger if such exist".

[197] *Jordan v Jordan* [2000] 1 WLR 210, (Thorpe LJ), 221. This interpretation was held to be correct by the Supreme Court in *Agbaje v Akinnoye-Agbaje* [2010] UKSC 13 [60].

[198] *Agbaje v Akinnoye-Agbaje* [2010] UKSC 13 [73] and see *M v V* [2014] EWHC 925 (Fam) [37]–[39].

[199] The court has power to make interim orders between the granting of leave to apply and the full hearing of the application: ss 14, 21.

[200] *Jordan v Jordan* [2000] 1 WLR 210, (Thorpe LJ), 221–8; and *A v S (Financial Relief after Overseas US Divorce)* [2002] EWHC 1157, [2003] 1 FLR 431, (Bodey J) [74]–[75]. Cf, for civil partnerships, Civil Partnership Act 2004, Sch 7, para 8.

[201] S 16(2); see *Z v Z (Financial Provision: Overseas Divorce)* [1992] 2 FLR 291; *A v S (Financial Relief after Overseas US Divorce)* [2002] EWHC 1157, [2003] 1 FLR 431; and *M v L (Financial Relief after Overseas Divorce)* [2003] EWHC 328, [2003] 2 FLR 425, (Coleridge J) [32].

[202] *Jordan v Jordan* [2000] 1 WLR 210, (Thorpe LJ), 220: "Prima facie, the primary jurisdiction offering comparable rights of equitable redistribution will also offer comparable powers of implementation and enforcement."

the likelihood of any order made under Part III of the 1984 Act being enforceable, and the length of time which has elapsed since the date of the foreign decree.[203] In determining the appropriateness of the English court granting relief,[204] the court will have regard, where there are proceedings in a foreign country, to questions of comity.[205]

(d) Other matters

Part III of the 1984 Act gives the English court power to make orders for financial relief not only when a foreign divorce, but also when a foreign annulment or legal separation,[206] is recognised in England.[207] The case for having the same powers in the case of divorce and annulment is strong. In both cases the marriage is at an end[208] and the rules for the recognition of foreign divorces and annulments are now the same.[209] They are also the same in the case of legal separations but in that case the marriage still subsists and there would be no bar to taking divorce proceedings in England and seeking the usual ancillary relief in England.[210] If, however, a divorce decree was not sought, proceedings could be brought on the ground of failure to provide maintenance.[211] The powers of the English court are less extensive in such a case than those provided in Part III of the 1984 Act, and so it was felt desirable[212] to make the latter powers available also in the case of legal separations.

The powers of the court under Part III of the 1984 Act depend not only on there having been a foreign divorce, annulment or legal separation but also on its being entitled to recognition in England.[213] However, the powers are limited to divorces, etc obtained in an "overseas country" which is defined as a country or territory outside the British Islands.[214] This means that the English court has no power to make an order under Part III following, for example, a Scottish divorce or Northern Ireland annulment. It was thought more appropriate, and not too inconvenient, in such a case for the party seeking relief to return to the court which granted the original decree.[215] Furthermore, the powers are limited to divorces obtained "by means of judicial or other proceedings",[216] thus excluding informal divorces despite the fact that they will be recognised in England by virtue of section 46(2) of the Family Law Act 1986.[217]

---

[203] *N v N (Foreign Divorce: Financial Relief)* [1997] 1 FLR 900; cf *Lamagni v Lamagni* [1995] 2 FLR 452, CA; and *M v L (Financial Relief after Overseas Divorce)* [2003] EWHC 328, [2003] 2 FLR 425.

[204] It is inappropriate to apply the traditional *forum non conveniens* test, because the Court is not necessarily determining which of the two jurisdictions is the most appropriate, *Agbaje v Akinnoye-Agbaje* [2010] UKSC 13 [49]–[50].

[205] *Moore v Moore* [2007] EWCA Civ 361, [2007] IL Pr 36, (Thorpe LJ) [109].

[206] S 12(1).

[207] For an application under Part III, not only does there have to be a valid divorce, or legal separation, but the divorce has to be based upon a marriage which was recognised under English law as a valid or at least a void marriage, *Shagroon v Shabartly* [2012] EWCA Civ 1507.

[208] If a party remarries or forms a civil partnership, then he or she loses the right to apply for relief under the 1984 Act: s 12(2), (3).

[209] Brussels II *bis* Regulation, Ch III; and Family Law Act 1986, Part II, supra, p 1002 et seq.

[210] *Sabbagh v Sabbagh* [1985] FLR 29.

[211] Matrimonial Causes Act 1973, s 27.

[212] See Law Commission Working Paper No 77 (1980), para 64.

[213] S 12(1)(b); *B v B (Divorce: Northern Cyrus)* [2002] 2 FLR 707; and *Emin v Yeldag* [2002] 1 FLR 956—application for leave granted on the basis of recognition of divorce granted by Turkish Republic of Northern Cyprus, notwithstanding non-recognition by the United Kingdom Government of Northern Cyprus as a country. See Law Commission Working Paper No 77 (1980), para 59. The rules for recognition are discussed supra, p 1000 et seq.

[214] S 27.

[215] Law Commission Working Paper No 77 (1980), paras 65–6.

[216] S 12(1)(a).

[217] Supra, p 1017.

3. CHOICE OF LAW

There is little doubt that, when an English court is considering an application for maintenance or similar relief, it applies English domestic law,[218] irrespective of the domicile of the parties or any other factors connecting them with some other jurisdiction.[219] The English court also applies domestic law when considering an application under the Maintenance Regulation. It should be noted however that the courts in all other EU Member States, excluding Denmark, now apply the Hague Protocol on Applicable Law (Hague Protocol)[220] to maintenance obligations. This distinction is important because any decision given in accordance with the Hague Protocol is automatically enforceable in another Member State irrespective of public policy considerations.[221] Where the 2007 Hague Convention applies the English court will also apply domestic law.

In cases to which the Maintenance Orders (Facilities for Enforcement) Act 1920 or the Maintenance Orders (Reciprocal Enforcement) Act 1972 apply, there may be a limited number of circumstances where foreign law is relevant by reason of the reciprocal provisions.[222]

4. RECOGNITION AND ENFORCEMENT OF FOREIGN ORDERS

All forms of financial relief, such as orders for periodical payments, the payment of lump sums or maintenance orders granted by a foreign court, may be regarded as foreign judgments in personam.[223] Usually, the foreign court has a power to vary the amount of such payments, in which event the order will not be recognised in England as it is not "final or conclusive".[224] Where the power to vary is only prospective, any arrears of past payments may be recovered in England.[225] This is an atypical situation and the rules for the recognition and enforcement of foreign orders have not been left to the common law but are essentially statutory in formulation.

(a) Relief ancillary to a foreign divorce, annulment or legal separation

The main legislative provisions in this area are negative in effect. Article 1(3)(e) of the Brussels II *bis* Regulation states that it shall not apply to maintenance proceedings.[226] However the Maintenance Regulation does now provide for the enforcement of maintenance obligations

---

[218] 1984 Act, s 18. Eg *A v S (Financial Relief after Overseas US Divorce)* [2002] EWHC 1157, [2003] 1 FLR 431, (Bodey J) [78]–[80]; and *M v L (Financial Relief after Overseas Divorce)* [2003] EWHC 328, [2003] 2 FLR 425, (Coleridge J) [39] et seq.

[219] Eg *Sealey v Callan* [1953] P 135; and see Law Commission Working Paper No 77 (1980), para 56.

[220] Hague Protocol of 23 November 2007 on the Law Applicable to Maintenance Obligations. The EU signed and ratified the agreement as an REIO on 8 April 2010. The Protocol applied provisionally within the EU from the date of application of the Maintenance Regulation, 18 June 2011. The Protocol entered into force officially, on 1 August 2013. See also A Bonomi, 'The Hague Protocol of 23 November 2007 on the Law Applicable to Maintenance Obligations' (2008) 10 *Yearbook of Private International Law* 333.

[221] Art 17, Maintenance Regulation.

[222] See Dicey, Morris and Collins, para 18–232.

[223] Discussed supra, p 528 et seq, and see especially the critical discussion of *Phillips v Batho* [1913] 3 KB 25, supra, p 545. See McClean, *Recognition of Family Judgments in the Commonwealth* (1983), Chapter 4.

[224] Supra, p 548 et seq; contrast *McC v McC* [1994] 1 IR 293.

[225] *Beatty v Beatty* [1924] 1 KB 807; and see *G v G* [1984] IR 368; *Sachs v Standard Chartered Bank (Ireland) Ltd* [1987] ILRM 297.

[226] See also Recitals (8) and (11).

ancillary to a foreign divorce, where jurisdiction is based on Article 3(c). The Family Law Act 1986 provides that nothing in that Act shall be construed as requiring the recognition in England of any maintenance, custody or other ancillary order made in any foreign proceedings for divorce, annulment or legal separation.[227] In such cases, recognition depends on the common law rules for the recognition of foreign judgments,[228] unless covered by any of the statutory provisions considered below. An English court will not recognise a foreign maintenance order ancillary to a foreign divorce, etc where it considers, under the English rules for the recognition of foreign divorces, etc, that the foreign court lacked jurisdiction.[229] For "if the main order goes, then any order which is merely ancillary to that order should go with it".[230]

(b) Maintenance orders made elsewhere in the United Kingdom

A maintenance order made elsewhere in the United Kingdom may, under Part II of the Maintenance Orders Act 1950,[231] be registered in an English court if the person liable to make the payments resides in England and it is regarded as convenient that the order should be enforceable in England.[232]

This procedure applies to a wide range of orders, including those for periodical payments ancillary to decrees of divorce, nullity or judicial separation, or for failure to provide reasonable maintenance. Registration is in the discretion of the court making the original order and not the court which is asked to register it, as is also normally the case with variation or discharge of a registered order; but once registered, the order may be enforced as if an order of the registering court.[233]

(c) Recognition under the Maintenance Orders (Facilities for Enforcement) Act 1920

Under the Maintenance Orders (Facilities for Enforcement) Act 1920, provision is made for the reciprocal enforcement of maintenance orders between England, on the one hand, and, on the other, those Commonwealth countries to which the Act has been extended by Order in Council. The "shuttlecock" procedure applicable to English proceedings is equally applicable to foreign proceedings, so that if a provisional order is made in a Commonwealth country in the absence of the defendant, it may be confirmed by the English magistrates' court in the

---

[227] S 51(5) and see *Liaw v Lee* [2015] EWHC 1462 (Fam).

[228] Supra, p 528 et seq.

[229] *Simons v Simons* [1939] 1 KB 490, [1938] 4 All ER 436; and see *Papadopoulos v Papadopoulos* [1930] P 55. This is subject to the rules in the Maintenance Regulation and the 2007 Hague Convention. Where the Maintenance Regulation applies, jurisdiction cannot be reviewed. Minimal review is permitted under the 2007 Hague Convention, infra p 1084 et seq.

[230] *Simons v Simons* [1939] 1 KB 490.

[231] By virtue of the Civil Jurisdiction and Judgments Act 1982, s 18(5)(a), the enforcement of a maintenance order made elsewhere in the United Kingdom continues to be governed by the Maintenance Orders Act 1950.

[232] S 18(1), as amended by the Courts Act 2003, Sch 8, para 88(2). Such orders are brought within the provisions of the Maintenance Orders Act 1958 as to registration and enforcement by reason of the amendments to that Act contained in the Administration of Justice Act 1977, s 3, Sch 3; Civil Jurisdiction and Judgments Act 1982, Sch 11, para 2; and the Matrimonial and Family Proceedings Act 1984, s 46(1), Sch 1, paras 4 and 5.

[233] Recognition of liability orders, made elsewhere in the United Kingdom under the Child Support Act 1991, is governed by regulations made by the Secretary of State: Child Support Act 1991, s 39. The jurisdiction of a child support officer to make an original maintenance assessment is based on the relevant person's habitual residence in the United Kingdom: 1991 Act, s 44, as amended by the Child Support, Pensions and Social Security Act 2000, Sch 3, para 11(2).

area where the defendant resides.[234] The defendant may raise any defence which he might have raised in the foreign proceedings and the English court has a discretion whether or not to confirm the foreign provisional order.

There are further reciprocal provisions in the 1920 Act whereby an English maintenance order may be registered in the Commonwealth country[235] or a Commonwealth order may be registered in England.[236] These provisions assume that the court making the original order had jurisdiction to make it but that there is difficulty in enforcing it in that jurisdiction, as where the defendant was resident in the Commonwealth country when the order was made, but is resident in England when enforcement is sought. Registration is mandatory if a certified copy of the maintenance order is sent from the Commonwealth court to the designated officers of the English court. The order also has the same effect as if it were an English order, though there is no power to rescind or vary such an order.[237]

(d) Recognition under the Maintenance Orders (Reciprocal Enforcement) Act 1972

There is reciprocal machinery in the 1972 Act, similar to that contained in the 1920 Act, for the recognition of maintenance orders made in any foreign reciprocating country.[238] A foreign provisional order made in the absence of the defendant may be sent to the English court within whose jurisdiction the defendant resides and that court has a discretion as to whether or not to confirm the order.[239] The defendant may raise any defences open to him in the original proceedings; but, once confirmed, the order is registered and has effect as if made by the English court. Variation or revocation of such orders may normally be made by either the English or the foreign court.[240]

As with the 1920 Act, there is also provision for the registration of a foreign order in an English court[241] and vice versa.[242] Again, it is assumed that the original court had jurisdiction to make the order, but it is more convenient for it to be enforced in the other country. If a certified copy of a foreign order is sent to the designated officer of the magistrates' court where the defendant resides, registration is mandatory and the order has effect as if made by the English court.

We have seen that section 40 of the 1972 Act allows Part I of the Act to be applied, by Order in Council, in amended form to specified countries. These amended versions extend to recognition as well as to jurisdiction.[243] The variations can be illustrated by the fact that, although registration (and thus recognition) of a certified foreign order is mandatory under the 1972 Act itself,[244] there are a number of grounds on which it can be refused under the version

---

[234] S 4 of the 1920 Act, amended by the Maintenance Enforcement Act 1991, Sch 1, para 1; the Maintenance Orders (Reciprocal Enforcement) Act 1992, Sch 1, Part I, para 2; and the Courts Act 2003, Sch 8, para 69(3)(b).

[235] S 2.

[236] S 1.

[237] *Pilcher v Pilcher* [1955] P 318; and see *Sethi v Sethi* 1995 SLT 104.

[238] S 1.

[239] S 5(5), including a foreign provisional order varying an original English order: *Horn v Horn* [1985] FLR 984.

[240] Eg *Hinkley v Hinkley* (1984) 38 RFL (2d) 337.

[241] S 6.

[242] S 2.

[243] Eg *R v West London Magistrates' Court, ex p Emmett* [1993] 2 FLR 663.

[244] S 6; though it has been suggested that it might be possible to challenge the validity of the order itself: *Sethi v Sethi* 1995 SLT 104.

implementing the 1973 Hague Convention on the recognition of maintenance orders,[245] including that "registration is manifestly contrary to public policy".[246]

(e) Recognition and Enforcement under the Maintenance Regulation

The Maintenance Regulation requires that maintenance orders, provided they fall within the meaning of "maintenance" under the Regulation,[247] given in one Member State are recognised in another Member State without any special procedure being required.[248] There are two systems for enforceability, depending on whether the decision originated in Member State bound by the Hague Protocol or not. Where the decision originated in a Member State bound by the Hague Protocol, such as France, it is not possible to oppose the recognition of the decision,[249] and the decision is automatically enforceable,[250] in the same manner as a national order given in the state of enforcement.[251] There is a very limited right to apply for a review, "in order to guarantee compliance with the requirements of a fair trial".[252] A defendant who did not enter into an appearance in the Member State of origin can apply for a review, in that state, where it was not possible for him to challenge the decision, because either he did not have sufficient time to arrange a defence or he was prevented from contesting the claim due to extraordinary circumstances without any fault on his part.[253] If it was possible for the defendant to challenge the decision and he did not do so, then the defence is unavailable.[254] The ground for review is time barred,[255] represents a minimum standard and may not guarantee a fair trial in all circumstances.[256]

The authorities in the Member State of enforcement can refuse to enforce a maintenance decision, or suspend enforcement, on the grounds of refusal of enforcement under the law of that Member State.[257] Enforcement can also be refused if the right to enforce the decision is extinguished by the effect of prescription or limitation, under either the law of the Member State of origin or enforcement. The law which provides the longer limitation period should be applied.[258] On the application of the debtor, the Member State can refuse enforcement where the decision is irreconcilable with a decision given in that state, another Member State or a third state (if it is enforceable in the state where enforcement is requested),[259] and where the competent court in the state of origin has been seised for an application for review under Article 19.[260] The English courts will have to apply this procedure to all maintenance orders made in another Member State, apart from those originating in Denmark. However the English implementing legislation has created some uncertainty in this area.[261] The

---

[245] SI 1993/593, para 6(6).

[246] Ibid, para 6(6)(a); *Armitage v Nanchen* (1983) 4 FLR 293.

[247] Supra, pp 1064–5.

[248] Ch IV Maintenance Regulation. This applies to all maintenance orders given after 18 June 2011. Orders established before that date can, in some circumstances, be recognised and enforced in accordance with Brussels I (Art 75 Maintenance Regulation).

[249] Art 17(1).

[250] Art 17(2). It is possible to request a declaration of enforceability, but this is not required.

[251] Art 41.

[252] Rec 29.

[253] Art 19 (1) Maintenance Regulation.

[254] Ibid.

[255] Art 19(2), the defendant has a maximum of forty-five days to apply for the review.

[256] G Cuniberti and I Reuda, 'Abolition of Exequatur—Addressing the Commissions Concerns' (2011) 75 *Rabels Zeichshrift* 286, 298–9.

[257] Art 21(1).

[258] Art 21(2).

[259] Ibid. For more on irreconcilable judgments in this context see infra pp 1082–3.

[260] Art 21(3).

[261] See *MS v PS* [2016] EWHC 88 (Fam), *EDG v RR* [2014] EWHC 816 (Fam) and *AB v JJB* [2015] EWHC 192 (Fam).

implementing legislation states that an application should be made to the family court,[262] but this is subject to para 4(2), which indicates that the application should be transferred to the family court by the Lord Chancellor.[263] It has been argued that the effect of this provision is that "all applications for enforcement under the Maintenance Regulation have to be presented to the Family Court by REMO".[264] It is unlikely that this procedure constitutes a simplified mechanism for enforcement as envisaged by the Maintenance Regulation, nor does it mean that intra-EU orders are treated in the same way as national orders.[265] In *EDG* Mostyn J considered that the provision was ambiguous and argued that there was a mistake in the provisions and individuals should have a right to direct enforcement.[266] In *MS* Roberts J decided to request a ruling from the CJEU in order to determine in which circumstances a direct right to enforcement is necessary, and if each Member State must provide a direct right to enforcement.[267] It seemed inconceivable that the CJEU would not insist on a direct right to enforcement, and in February 2017 the CJEU confirmed that a direct right to enforcement was required.[268] However, this step should provide more certainty for applicants seeking to enforce a decision in England.[269] It is important to note that enforcement of a decision made in accordance with the Maintenance Regulation and the Hague Protocol does not imply the recognition of the family relationship that gave rise to the order.[270] As there is no review on grounds of public policy at the enforcement stage the maintenance decision will have to be enforced regardless of whether the Member State of enforcement recognises the relationship that the obligation arose from.

In contrast, all outgoing orders from England are subject to a different procedure in the receiving Member State. Maintenance orders established by a court in England, or Denmark, can be refused recognition if an interested party makes an application for recognition.[271] Recognition shall be refused where the recognition would be manifestly contrary to the public policy of the state addressed,[272] where it was given in default of appearance and it was not possible for the defendant to challenge the decision,[273] if the decision is irreconcilable with a decision given in a dispute between the same parties in the state where the recognition is sought,[274] or if the dispute is irreconcilable with a decision given in another Member State or a third state, involving the same cause of action and the same parties.[275] Irreconcilable

---

[262] Civil Jurisdiction and Judgments (Maintenance) Regulations 2011/1484, Sch 1, para 4(1)(a), as substituted by Crime and Courts Act 2013 (Family Court: Consequential Provision) (No 2) Order 2014/879 Pt 2, Art 128(a).

[263] Civil Jurisdiction and Judgments (Maintenance) Regulations 2011/1484, Sch 1, para 4(2)(a), as inserted by Crime and Courts Act 2013 (Family Court: Consequential Provision) (No 2) Order 2014/879 Pt 2, Art 128(b).

[264] *MS v PS* [2016] EWHC 88 (Fam) [34]. REMO is the designated Central Authority for England and Wales.

[265] See *MS v PS* [2016] EWHC 88 (Fam) and *EDG v RR* [2014] EWHC 816 (Fam).

[266] *EDG v RR* [2014] EWHC 816 (Fam) [15]–[16].

[267] *MS v PS* [2016] EWHC 88 (Fam), Annex.

[268] Case C-283/16 *MS v PS* ECLI:EU:C:2017:104.

[269] The Scottish legislation, correctly, provides for direct enforcement (*MS v PS* [2016] EWHC 88 (Fam) [25]).

[270] Art 22.

[271] Arts 23 and 24. Such an application is not necessary.

[272] Art 24(a) and see (C-7/98) *Krombach v Bamberski* ECLI:EU:C:2000:164, for the application of this provision under Brussels I. Certain Member States may refuse recognition of, or refuse to grant a declaration of enforceability to, a maintenance obligation arising from a same-sex marriage or civil partnership on grounds of public policy.

[273] Art 24(b) and see (C-283/05) *ASML Netherlands BV v Semiconductor Industry Services GmbH* ECLI:EU:C:2006:787.

[274] Art 24(c).

[275] Art 24(d).

judgments could be problematic in this area mainly because there is no clear definition of "maintenance". This could be particularly problematic in the context of spousal maintenance on divorce where there are a number of alternative bases of jurisdiction available and parties could select different courts to deal with divorce,[276] maintenance and matrimonial property.[277] It could also be the case that different courts are dealing with spousal maintenance and child maintenance.[278] Irreconcilable judgments could arise where one court characterises a payment as maintenance and another as matrimonial property, particularly in relation to lump sum payments. If money has already been allocated in relation to property, in one state, then it could be difficult to enforce a lump sum maintenance order made in a different Member State. A decision awarding an interim payment on divorce could also conflict with a final maintenance order. Irreconcilable judgments could also arise in relation to maintenance decisions given in third states, because the lis pendens and related actions provisions only cover proceedings in another Member State.[279] In *Hoffmann v Kreig* it was held that a German award for spousal maintenance was irreconcilable with a later decision on divorce, between the same parties, given in the Netherlands.[280]

Under this non-Hague Protocol track it is essential that a declaration of enforceability is granted before the decision can be enforced. In England this is known as registration for enforcement.[281] The application for registration, in respect of judgments originating in Denmark, is to be made to the family court.[282] The application is to be transmitted to the family court by the Lord Chancellor.[283] Once it is registered, the order is treated for enforcement purposes as if it were an English order made by the court and the methods of enforcement are the same as for an English order.[284]

Although the main enforcement route is by way of the Maintenance Regulation, there is scope also for enforcing a claim for maintenance payment using the European Enforcement Order for Uncontested Claims.[285] Like the route for maintenance decisions originating in

---

[276] Under Brussels II *bis*.

[277] The proposal on Matrimonial Property was rejected by Council on 3 December 2015. On 2 March 2016 the European Commission adopted a proposal for a Council decision authorising enhanced cooperation in the area of jurisdiction, applicable law and the recognition and enforcement of decisions on the property regimes of international couples, covering both matters of matrimonial property regimes and the property consequences of registered partnerships (COM (2016) 108 final). Seventeen Member States wish to participate in the enhanced cooperation regime, if it is authorised.

[278] See C-1845/14 *A v B*, 16 July 2015, ECLI:EU:C:2015:479.

[279] Maintenance Regulation, Arts 12 and 13. If the proceedings are caught by Art 12, lis pendens, (both proceedings have the same cause of action) the Court second seised must stay proceedings. Where the actions are related actions, caught by Art 13, the court second seised has discretion to stay proceedings.

[280] C-145/86 *Hoffmann v Kreig* [1988] ECR 645, this decision has been criticised by Martiny D Martiny, 'Maintenance Obligations in the Conflicts of Laws' (1994) 247 Recueil des Cours 131, 270–1). See also *R v West London Magistrates' Court* [1994] 1 FCR 421 and *Macaulay v Macaulay* [1991] 1 WLR 179.

[281] Civil Jurisdiction and Judgments (Maintenance) Regulations 2011/1484, Sch 1, para 6(3).

[282] Civil Jurisdiction and Judgments (Maintenance) Regulations 2011/1484, Sch 1, para 6(1)(a), as substituted by the Crime and Courts Act 2013 (Family Court: Consequential Provision) (No 2) Order 2014/879 Pt 2, Art 129(a).

[283] Civil Jurisdiction and Judgments (Maintenance) Regulations 2011/1484, Sch 1, para 6(2)(a) as inserted by Crime and Courts Act 2013 (Family Court: Consequential Provision) (No 2) Order 2014/879 Pt 2, Art 129(b).

[284] Civil Jurisdiction and Judgments (Maintenance) Regulations 2011/1484, Sch 1, para 7, as substituted and revoked by the Crime and Courts Act 2013 (Family Court: Consequential Provision) (No 2) Order 2014/879 Pt 2, Art 129(c)(i)(aa) and (bb). Interest is payable on the order according to the law of the country making the order (Maintenance Regulations, Sch 1, para 8). Sums payable in England under the foreign order are to be paid in sterling, converted as at the date of registration (Sch 1, para 9).

[285] Regulation (EC) No 805/2004 creating a European Enforcement Order for Uncontested Claims, which applies in all the Member States with the exception of Denmark. See generally supra, p 656 et seq.

a Hague Protocol State, this procedure permits the free circulation of judgments,[286] court settlements and authentic instruments[287] throughout the Member States without the need for intermediate proceedings being brought in the Member State of enforcement[288] prior to recognition and enforcement.[289]

Orders made under the Lugano Convention can be refused recognition and enforceability on the same grounds as a judgment from a non-Hague Protocol State, under the Maintenance Regulation.[290] In England and Wales the application for recognition or enforceability shall be transmitted to the appropriate court by the Lord Chancellor.[291] Once the order has been registered, for the purposes of enforcement, it will have the same force and effect as a national decision and the same enforcement powers are available.[292]

(f) Recognition and Enforcement under the 2007 Hague Convention

A Maintenance decision given in one Contracting State, the UK, can only be recognised and enforced in another Contracting State, such as Bosnia and Herzegovina, if certain jurisdictional requirements are complied with.[293] There are six bases listed, but Contracting States are permitted to make a reservation in respect of three of these.[294] The jurisdictional bases for recognition and enforcement in the Maintenance Convention are that the respondent was habitually resident in the state of origin at the time the proceedings were instituted;[295] the respondent submitted to the jurisdiction, either expressly or by defending the case on the merits without contesting the jurisdiction at the first available opportunity;[296] the creditor was habitually resident in the state of origin at the time the proceedings were instituted;[297] or the child for whom maintenance was ordered was habitually resident in the state of origin at the time the proceedings were instituted, provided that the respondent has lived with the child in that state and provided support for the child there.[298] The Convention also provides for indirect jurisdiction on the basis of a choice of court agreement, where the dispute does not relate to children,[299] and the final bases are where the decision was made by an authority exercising jurisdiction on either a matter of personal status or parental responsibility, as long as that jurisdiction was not based on the nationality of one of the parties.[300]

Contracting States can make reservations in regard to Article 20(1)(c), the habitual residence of the creditor, (e) jurisdiction agreements and (f) jurisdiction linked to personal status or

---

[286] Defined in Art 4(1).
[287] Defined in Art 4(3).
[288] Defined in Art 4(5).
[289] Recital (9) and Art 1.
[290] Lugano Convention 2007, Art 34.
[291] Civil Jurisdiction and Judgments Act 1982, s 5A(1).
[292] Ibid, s 5A(3). Interest is recoverable in accordance of the law of the Contracting State in which the order was given (s 7(1)) and sums payable in England under the foreign order are to be paid in sterling, converted as at the date of registration (s 8).
[293] Hague 2007 Convention, Art 20. The Contracting States to the 2007 Convention are: the EU Member States (bound as a result of an approval by the EU), Albania, Bosnia and Herzegovina, Montenegro, Norway, Turkey, Ukraine and the USA.
[294] Art 20(2). The USA has made a reservation in respect of each. None of the other Contracting States have made a reservation in this context, as of October 2016.
[295] Art 20(1)(a).
[296] Art 20(1)(b).
[297] Art 20(1)(c).
[298] Art 20(1)(d).
[299] Art 20(1)(e).
[300] Art 20(1)(f).

parental responsibility.[301] However even where a Contracting State, such as the USA, has made a reservation, the court in the USA may be required to recognise a decision that was based on that ground of jurisdiction in certain circumstances. The Contracting State should still recognise the decision if under its own law, in similar factual circumstances, an order would have been made.[302] Where it is not possible to recognise the order, the court should take all appropriate measures to establish a decision for the creditor, if the debtor is habitually resident in that state.[303] Finally where a decision in respect of a child cannot be recognised only because of a reservation in regards to (c), (e) or (f), the decision must be accepted as establishing that the child is eligible for maintenance in the state addressed.[304]

Where jurisdiction is based on one of the grounds listed above then the order should be recognised and enforced. However the court may still refuse recognition, or registration in England, if the order is manifestly contrary to public policy.[305] The Convention allows for ex officio review of public policy, so a court can review this ground regardless of whether an objection is raised by the parties. After the order has been registered by the authorities the parties can challenge this on either the grounds for refusal of recognition under Article 22, the bases of jurisdiction in Article 20 or the authenticity or the integrity of the document.[306]

The grounds for refusal of recognition and enforcement are: that the recognition and enforcement of the decision would be manifestly contrary to the public policy of the state addressed;[307] the decision was obtained by fraud in connection with a matter of procedure;[308] proceedings between the same parties and having the same purpose are pending before an authority of the state addressed and those proceedings were the first to be instituted;[309] the decision is incompatible with a decision rendered between the same parties and having the same purpose, either in the state addressed or in another state, provided that the latter decision fulfills the conditions necessary for its recognition and enforcement in the state addressed;[310] where the decision was given in default of appearance and the defendant was not served with sufficient notice, or was not given an opportunity to challenge or appeal the decision;[311] or the decision was made in violation of Article 18.[312] Article 18 places constraints on the jurisdiction of debtors when they are attempting to modify a decision. If the debtor attempts to modify a decision in a different Contracting State from the one designated by Article 18, then the creditor can challenge the recognition and enforcement of the modification decision.

The courts of England and Wales will have jurisdiction for the recognition and enforcement of judgments made under the Hague Convention if the person against whom enforcement is sought is habitually resident in England and Wales, or that person has assets in England

---

[301] Art 20(2). The UK is bound by the Convention as a result of an approval by the EU as a REIO, and no reservations were made in relation to jurisdiction. However where English courts are making an order on the basis of one of these grounds of indirect jurisdiction, and that order is to be enforced in another Hague 2007 Contracting State, such as the USA, the judge should be aware of any reservations made by that state when making their order.

[302] Art 20(3).

[303] Art 20(4).

[304] Art 20(5).

[305] Art 23(4).

[306] Art 23(7). There is an alternative procedure for recognition and enforcement in Art 24 of the Convention but this does not apply in England and Wales.

[307] Art 22(a).

[308] Art 22(b).

[309] Art 22(c).

[310] Art 22(d).

[311] Art 22(e).

[312] Art 22(f).

and Wales.[313] An application for registration should be made to the family court by the Lord Chancellor.[314] An application for registration should be determined at first instance by the prescribed officer of the registering court.[315] This decision can be appealed to the registering court in accordance with the rules of court.[316] Once the decision has been registered it shall have the same force and effect as a national decision and shall be enforceable in the family court in the same way as an order made by that court.[317] Maintenance arrangements shall be recognised and enforced in the same way as maintenance decisions.[318] Interest is payable in accordance with the law of the Contracting State, in which the decision was given, only if the date from which interest as payable and the rate at which it is payable is registered with the judgment.[319] Sums payable under a maintenance decision registered in England and Wales, including any arrears, are payable in sterling.[320]

---

[313] International Recovery of Maintenance (Hague Convention 2007 etc) Regulations 2012/2814, Sch 1, para 2(3).

[314] International Recovery of Maintenance (Hague Convention 2007 etc) Regulations 2012/2814, Sch 1, para 2(1) and (2), as substituted by Crime and Courts Act 2013 (Family Court: Consequential Provision) (No 2) Order 2014/879 Pt 2, Art 138(a) and (b).

[315] International Recovery of Maintenance (Hague Convention 2007 etc) Regulations 2012/2814, Sch 1, para 2(4). This is equivalent to ex officio review under Art 23(4) of the Hague Convention.

[316] International Recovery of Maintenance (Hague Convention 2007 etc) Regulations 2012/2814, Sch 1, para 2(5).

[317] International Recovery of Maintenance (Hague Convention 2007 etc) Regulations 2012/2814, Sch, 1 para 2(6)-(8), as substituted and revoked by Crime and Courts Act 2013 (Family Court: Consequential Provision) (No 2) Order 2014/879 Pt 2, Art 138(c)(i) and (ii).

[318] International Recovery of Maintenance (Hague Convention 2007 etc) Regulations 2012/2814, Sch 1, para 6.

[319] International Recovery of Maintenance (Hague Convention 2007 etc) Regulations 2012/2814, Sch 1, para 3.

[320] International Recovery of Maintenance (Hague Convention 2007 etc) Regulations 2012/2814, Sch 1, para 4.

25

CHILDREN[1]

1. Introduction	1087	(b)	Orders granted in another European Union Member State, except Denmark	1127
2. Jurisdiction in Matters of Parental Responsibility	1089	(c)	Orders granted in another Contracting State to the 1996 Hague Protection Convention	1131
(a) Background	1089			
(b) Bases of jurisdiction	1091			
(c) Variation and duration of Part I orders	1112	(d)	Orders granted in Scotland and Northern Ireland	1132
(d) Refusal of application and stay of proceedings	1113	(e)	Child Abduction and Custody Act 1985	1134
3. Choice of Law	1125	(f)	Common law rules	1172
4. Recognition and Enforcement	1126	5. Other Developments		1177
(a) Introduction	1126	Council of Europe Convention on Contact concerning Children		1177

1. INTRODUCTION

We are concerned in this chapter with the private international law rules regulating orders concerning children. The most important of these, so far as English law is concerned, are orders determining with whom a child shall live or with whom he may have contact.[2]

Until the late 1980s, many of the private international law rules in this field were provided by an unclear and inconsistent mixture of statutory provision and common law decisions.[3] Indeed, the English jurisdictional rules to make orders concerning the welfare of children were a mixture of very broad and very narrow rules, statutes and common law, detail and vagueness, clarity and confusion, and the rules were, above all, bewilderingly complex.[4] By contrast, the rules for the recognition or enforcement of orders made outside England, whether elsewhere in the British Isles or overseas, were simple. Whilst such orders would be given "grave consideration",[5] they had no direct effect in England and their relevance lay only in assisting an English court in deciding whether to exercise its own discretion to make an order and, if so, to what effect.

It came increasingly to be realised that, in an age of great mobility, a situation in which there are no rules for the recognition of other countries' parental responsibility and similar orders, at least on a reciprocal basis, was capable of engendering great anguish for parents and for children who might be shuttled from country to country. The legal position was in danger of

---

[1] See North (1990) I Hague Recueil 9, 127 et seq; and Lowe and Nicholls, *International Movement of Children: Law, Practice and Procedure* (2016).

[2] So called "child arrangements order"; Children Act 1989, s 8, as amended by the Children and Families Act 2014, Sch 2(1), para 3, and Pt 2, s 12(3).

[3] See Law Com No 138 (1985), Part II.

[4] Ibid, paras 2.5, 2.32, 2.48, 2.52.

[5] *McKee v McKee* [1951] AC 352 at 365.

verging on anarchy; indeed, the Law Commission described the position as a "state of legal disorder".[6] It was the source of potential and, sometimes, actual conflict between the courts in England and Scotland, with each claiming jurisdiction, making conflicting orders and not recognising orders made in the other country.[7] On the broader international scene, child abduction by, or on behalf of, one parent often unsuccessful in custody proceedings became so serious an international issue that action at last was taken.

This area of law has been characterised, since 1980, by a proliferation of legislative intervention on a national, regional and global scale.[8] Nationally, the Child Abduction Act 1984[9] introduced criminal offences governing the taking of a child under sixteen out of the United Kingdom without consent. The statute covers abduction both by a parent and by others. Secondly, more effective powers have been given to the courts to order the disclosure of the whereabouts of a child, to order its recovery, to order the surrender of the child's passport and to prohibit the removal of the child from the United Kingdom.[10] The administrative procedures to prevent children being removed by stopping them at airports or ports have also been improved.[11] On the civil side, Part I of the Family Law Act 1986[12] was introduced to amend the law relating to the jurisdiction of courts in the United Kingdom to make orders with regard to the custody of children; to make provision as to the recognition and enforcement of such orders throughout the United Kingdom; and to make further provision as to the imposition, effect and enforcement of restrictions on the removal of children from the United Kingdom. The Law Commission and the Scottish Law Commission, on whose recommendations[13] Part I of the 1986 Act is based, concluded that, if there was to be a scheme for intra-United Kingdom recognition of such orders, the acceptability of such a scheme would be advanced by uniform jurisdictional rules throughout the United Kingdom for the making of the orders—a step which would also provide the opportunity of curing the varied defects in the then English rules. The statutory jurisdictional rules, however, are limited to the making of such orders as are defined by section 1 of the Act (ie Part I orders).

At a regional level, with effect from 1 March 2001, Council Regulation (EC) No 1347/2000 of 29 May 2000 on jurisdiction and the recognition and enforcement of judgments in matrimonial matters and in matters of parental responsibility for children of both spouses[14] (known colloquially as "Brussels II"),[15] came into operation. Brussels II, in turn, was repealed, with effect from 1 March 2005, by Council Regulation (EC) No 2201/2003 of 27 November 2003 concerning jurisdiction and the recognition and enforcement of judgments in matrimonial

---

[6] Law Com No 138 (1985), para 1.9.

[7] Eg *Johnstone v Beattie* (1843) 10 Cl & Fin 42; *Babington v Babington* 1955 SC 115; *Hoy v Hoy* 1968 SC 179; though courts later tried to avoid such conflicts: *Re H* [1966] 1 WLR 381; *Re L* [1974] 1 WLR 250; *Campbell v Campbell* 1977 SLT 125; *Thomson, Petitioner* 1980 SLT (Notes) 29; *Girven, Petitioner* 1985 SLT 92.

[8] See de Boer [2002] XLIX NILR 307.

[9] Amended by the Family Law Act 1986, s 65, the Children Act 1989, Sch 12, paras 37–40, Sch 15, the Adoption and Children Act 2002, Sch 3, para 42, and the Children and Families Act 2014, Sch 2, Pt 2, para 47.

[10] Family Law Act 1986, ss 33–37 (in respect of s 33, *Re G (Children) (Residence: Same Sex Partner)* [2006] EWCA Civ 372, [2006] 2 FLR 614); Children Act 1989, s 13; *Practice Direction (Disclosure of Addresses: 1989)* [1989] 1 WLR 219.

[11] *Practice Direction (Minor: Preventing Removal Abroad)* [1986] 1 WLR 475.

[12] References to the 1986 Act are to the Act as later amended, most significantly by the Children Act 1989, Schs 13, 15 and by SI 1991/1723.

[13] Law Com No 138 (1985).

[14] OJ 2000 L 160/19.

[15] Based upon the Brussels II Convention of 28 May 1998 (never implemented) on the same subject, in respect of which, see Borras, "Explanatory Report on the Convention on Jurisdiction and the Recognition and Enforcement of Judgments in Matrimonial Matters" (OJ 1998 C 221/27).

matters and matters of parental responsibility ("Brussels II *bis*").[16] This Europeanisation of rules relating to parental responsibility matters resulted in significant changes being made to the Family Law Act 1986, to ensure compliance with the Brussels regime.[17]

On a global platform, two organisations, the Hague Conference on Private International Law and the Council of Europe, have been responsible for the introduction of various instruments concerning children. Work at The Hague has resulted in, among other conventions,[18] the 1980 Hague Convention on the Civil Aspects of International Child Abduction (the "1980 Hague (Abduction) Convention"),[19] and the 1996 Hague Convention on Jurisdiction, Applicable Law, Recognition, Enforcement and Co-operation in respect of Parental Responsibility and Measures for the Protection of Children (the "1996 Hague (Protection) Convention").[20] The Council of Europe, meanwhile, has produced the 1980 European Convention on Recognition and Enforcement of Decisions concerning Custody of Children and on the Restoration of Custody of Children,[21] and the 2003 Convention on Contact concerning Children.[22]

Unfortunately, the scope of application of each instrument, national and international, and the manner of their interlocking is not always as clear as might be hoped or expected.[23] We must now turn to consider the instruments in detail, examining, in turn, the rules governing the jurisdiction of the English courts as regards parental responsibility matters, the choice of law rules applied, and, finally, the varied provisions for the recognition and enforcement of parental responsibility and related orders made elsewhere.

2. JURISDICTION IN MATTERS OF PARENTAL RESPONSIBILITY

(a) Background

The Children Act 1989 introduced major changes in the law relating to children and, in particular, as to the orders which the English courts may make concerning them. Out went the old terminology of custody and custodianship orders; indeed the wardship jurisdiction is now described as the inherent jurisdiction. Instead the court may make orders under section

---

[16] OJ 2003 L 338/1. See also *Practice Guide for the Application of the Brussels IIa Regulation* (2014) ("*Practice Guide*").

[17] See The European Communities (Matrimonial Jurisdiction and Judgments) Regulations, SI 2001/310; and The European Communities (Jurisdiction and Judgments in Matrimonial and Parental Responsibility Matters) Regulations, SI 2005/265.

[18] Eg 1961 Hague Convention concerning the Powers of Authorities and the Law Applicable in respect of the Protection of Minors (to which the United Kingdom is not a party) and 1993 Hague Convention on Protection of Children and Co-operation in respect of Intercountry Adoption (to which the United Kingdom is a party: infra, p 1206).

[19] Given force of law in the United Kingdom by the Child Abduction and Custody Act 1985, Sch 1; infra, p 1134.

[20] In the United Kingdom, the Convention entered into force on 1 November 2012; infra, p 1102. See also Lagarde, *Explanatory Report on the 1996 Hague Child Protection Convention* (1996) ("Lagarde, *Explanatory Report*"); and *Practical Handbook on the Operation of the 1996 Hague Child Protection Convention* (2014) ("*Practical Handbook*").

[21] Otherwise known as the "Luxembourg Convention", and given force of law in the United Kingdom by the Child Abduction and Custody Act 1985, Sch 2.

[22] The United Kingdom is not yet a party to this Convention; infra, p 1176.

[23] The area has been described by Thorpe LJ as a "treaty jungle": *Re G (Children) (Foreign Contact Order: Enforcement)* [2003] All ER (D) 144 at [32].

8 of the Children Act 1989 which are child arrangements,[24] prohibited steps, or specific issue orders—generally described as "section 8 orders". The powers of the court to make such orders[25] may be exercised in a range of "family proceedings"[26] which include both proceedings under the statutory jurisdiction[27] and under the inherent jurisdiction of the High Court in relation to children.[28] The court also has power to make orders for the appointment of a guardian of a child[29] which, again, are regarded as orders made in family proceedings.[30]

Part I of the Family Law Act 1986[31] establishes the jurisdictional rules of the English courts to make "Part I orders" in relation to children under the age of 18.[32] The principles on which the jurisdictional rules under Part I of the 1986 Act are founded are that they should be: clear, systematic and uniform throughout the United Kingdom; designed to reduce the likelihood of courts in more than one part of the United Kingdom having concurrent jurisdiction; and normally result in the case being heard in the country with which the child has the closest long-term connection.[33] These objectives are achieved in the following ways. First, Part I of the 1986 Act contains essentially identical jurisdictional rules for England and Wales, Scotland, and Northern Ireland.[34] Secondly, these rules in places interlock, with the result that a court in one country usually will not have jurisdiction if jurisdiction lies with a court elsewhere. Thirdly, the rules are exclusive. Part I orders falling within the 1986 Act may be made only if the jurisdictional provisions of that Act are satisfied.[35]

The rules contained in Part I of the 1986 Act were significantly changed, with effect from 1 March 2001, to take account of European harmonisation in the form of the Brussels II Regulation.[36] Brussels II, in turn, was repealed, with effect from 1 March 2005, by the Brussels II *bis* Regulation.[37] Although the rules of jurisdiction in matrimonial matters contained in

---

[24] The "child arrangement orders" have replaced the "residence" and "contact" orders. See the Children Act 1989, s 8(1), as amended by the Children and Families Act 2014, Pt 2, s 12.

[25] Under the Children Act 1989, ss 9–11.

[26] 1989 Act, s 8(3), (4). The term "family proceedings" refers to both private and public law proceedings. Lowe and Douglas, *Bromley's Family Law*, p 480.

[27] The Children Act 1989, s 8(3)(b), (4); namely Parts I, II, IV; Matrimonial Causes Act 1973; Schs 5 and 6 to the Civil Partnership Act 2004; Adoption and Children Act 2002; Domestic Proceedings and Magistrates' Courts Act 1978; Matrimonial and Family Proceedings Act 1984, Part III; Family Law Act 1996; and ss 11 and 12 of the Crime and Disorder Act 1998.

[28] The Children Act 1989, s 8(3)(a).

[29] Ibid, ss 5, 6.

[30] Because made under Part I of the 1989 Act.

[31] As amended in particular by the Children Act 1989, and by the European Communities (Jurisdiction and Judgments in Matrimonial and Parental Responsibility Matters) Regulations, SI 2005/265, regs 8–18.

[32] Family Law Act 1986, s 7(a); though under the Children Act 1989, s 9(7) such orders (other than one varying or discharging an existing order) will only be made in relation to children of 16 or over in exceptional cases.

[33] Law Com No 138 (1985), para 3.10.

[34] Chapters II, III and IV respectively of Part I. There is also power under s 43 of the 1986 Act to extend Part I by Order in Council to the rest of the British Isles and to any colony and, as has been seen, this has been done in the case of the Isle of Man: SI 1991/1723.

[35] Ss 2, 2A and 3.

[36] Council Regulation (EC) No 1347/2000 of 29 May 2000 on jurisdiction and the recognition and enforcement of judgments in matrimonial matters and in matters of parental responsibility for children of both spouses (OJ 2000 L 160/19). See The European Communities (Matrimonial Jurisdiction and Judgments) Regulations, SI 2001/310. For detail on the origins of Brussels II, see McEleavy (2002) 51 ICLQ 883 at 888, and Crawford and Carruthers, paras 14-09–14-10. On the impact of Brussels II on the 1986 Act, see Lowe [2002] Fam Law 39.

[37] Council Regulation (EC) No 2201/2003 of 27 November 2003 concerning jurisdiction and the recognition and enforcement of judgments in matrimonial matters and matters of parental responsibility (OJ 2003 L 338/1). See The European Communities (Jurisdiction and Judgments in Matrimonial and Parental Responsibility Matters) Regulations, SI 2005/265. See also *Practice Guide* (the *Practice Guide* is not legally binding and does not prejudice any opinion given by the CJEU or decision issued by national courts

Brussels II *bis* were taken substantially from Brussels II, which, in turn, were taken[38] from the Brussels II Convention of 28 May 1998 (never implemented) on the same subject,[39] more significant changes were wrought by Brussels II *bis* in relation to matters of parental responsibility.[40] Another important milestone in this area of private international law was the entry into force in the UK of the 1996 Hague Protection Convention on the 1 November 2012.[41]

The recent European and global developments in this field have had the unwelcome consequence of the operation of one regime for intra-United Kingdom cases; another for intra-European Union cases; still another for 1996 Hague Convention cases; and of residual common law rules for such cases as fall outside the scope of application of the various instruments. Such a multiplicity of regimes is unnecessarily complicated and so, for the sake of clarity and simplicity, determined efforts should be made to streamline the rules.

In examining the jurisdictional rules for making parental responsibility orders, it is necessary to look separately at the harmonised rules of jurisdiction which apply throughout the European Union Member States (except Denmark) by virtue of Brussels II *bis*, the rules of jurisdiction embodied in the 1996 Hague Convention, and the residual national rules of jurisdiction contained, for the United Kingdom, in the Family Law Act 1986.

(b) Bases of jurisdiction[42]

(i) Introduction

Section 2 of the Family Law Act 1986 deals with the jurisdiction of courts in England and Wales to make a "Part I order", ie, an order to which Part I of the 1986 Act applies,[43] namely: (a) an order made under section 8 of the Children Act 1989, other than an order varying or discharging such an order;[44] (b) a special guardianship order made under the Children Act 1989;[45] (c) an order made under section 26 of the Adoption and Children Act 2002, other than an order varying or discharging such an order;[46] (d) an order made under section 51A of the Adoption and Children Act 2002, other than an order varying or revoking such an order;[47] or (e) an order in the exercise of the inherent jurisdiction of the High Court with respect to children.[48]

---

concerning interpretation of the Regulation); Boele-Woelki and Beilfuss (eds), *Brussels II bis: Its Impact and Application in the Member States* (2007); McEleavy (2002) 51 ICLQ 883, and (2004) 53 ICLQ 503; Magnus and Mankowski (eds), *European Commentaries on Private International Law: Brussels II bis Regulation* (2012); Kruger and Samyn (2016) 12 J Priv Int L 132; Commission Proposal for a Council Regulation on jurisdiction, the recognition and enforcement of decisions in matrimonial matters and the matters of parental responsibility, and on international child abduction (recast) (COM (2016) 411 final 30 June 2016) ("Commission Proposal for the Recast of Brussels II *bis*, COM (2016) 411 final 30 June 2016"); and Beaumont, Trimmings, Danov and Yüksel (eds), *Cross-Border Litigation in Europe* (2017, forthcoming). With regard to transitional provisions, see Art 64, *M v H (Custody: Residence Order)*, 27 July 2005 (unreported) (Fam Div), and *W v W (Foreign Custody Order: Enforcement)* [2005] EWHC 1811.

[38] See Brussels II, Recital (6).

[39] See Borras, "Explanatory Report on the Convention on jurisdiction and the recognition and enforcement of judgments in matrimonial matters" (OJ 1998 C 221/27).

[40] See *Practice Guide*, para 3.1.

[41] For a detailed analysis of the 1996 Hague Convention, see infra.

[42] For details of the rules of jurisdiction applying prior to 1 March 2001, see the 13th edn of this book (1999) p 858 et seq.

[43] As regards courts in England and Wales. See s 1(1)(b) as regards orders made by a court in Scotland, and s 1(1)(c) and (e) as regards orders made in Northern Ireland.

[44] 1986 Act, s 1(1)(a).

[45] Ibid, s 1(1)(aa).

[46] Ibid, s 1(1)(ab).

[47] Ibid, s 1(1)(ac).

[48] Ibid, s 1(1)(d).

(ii) Jurisdiction to make "section 8 orders"

Section 2(1) of the 1986 Act provides that a court in England and Wales shall not make a "section 8 order"[49] with respect to a child unless (a) it has jurisdiction under Brussels II *bis* or the 1996 Hague Convention; or (b) neither Brussels II *bis* nor the 1996 Hague Convention applies but (i) the question of making the order arises in, or in connection with, matrimonial proceedings or civil partnership proceedings and the condition in section 2A[50] of the 1986 Act is satisfied, or (ii) the condition in section 3[51] of the Act is satisfied. In other words, pre-eminent jurisdiction lies with the courts of the country which has jurisdiction in terms of Brussels II *bis* or the 1996 Hague Convention. The way the Regulation and the Convention interact with each other is rather complex.[52] Article 61 of the Regulation specifically deals with the relationship between the two instruments.[53] It provides that the Regulation shall apply (a) where the child concerned has his habitual residence on the territory of a Member State; and (b) as concerns the recognition and enforcement of a judgment given in a court of one Member State in the territory of another Member State, even if the child is habitually resident in a third state which is a Contracting State to the 1996 Convention. By virtue of Article 61, however, the 1996 Hague Convention shall have effect in relation to matters not governed by the Regulation; principally, and most significantly, applicable law.[54] If a case were to arise concerning a matter covered by the Regulation (on a point of jurisdiction, or recognition and enforcement), and the child in question was habitually resident in a European Union Member State, Brussels II *bis* would take priority. If a case were to arise concerning the recognition and enforcement of a judgment issued by a court in another EU Member State, Brussels II *bis* would apply, even if the child in question lives in a third state which is a Contracting Party to the 1996 Hague Convention.[55]

(a) Jurisdiction under the 1986 Act, s 2(1)(a)

Section 2(1)(a) of the 1986 Act provides that a court in England and Wales shall not make a "section 8 order"[56] with respect to a child unless it has jurisdiction under Brussels II *bis* or the 1996 Hague Convention. The sections that follow will examine respectively the relevant provisions of these two instruments.

Brussels II *bis*[57]

(i) Scope of Brussels II bis

In order to ensure equality for all children, the ambit of Brussels II *bis* is more extensive than was that of Brussels II, which applied only to matters of parental responsibility for children of both spouses on issues that were closely linked to proceedings for divorce, legal separation or marriage annulment.[58] Brussels II *bis* covers all decisions on parental responsibility, including measures for the protection of children, independently of any link with matrimonial proceedings.[59] Parental responsibility is defined in the Regulation as meaning, "all rights

---

[49] An order made by a court in England under the Children Act 1989, s 8, other than an order varying or discharging such an order: 1986 Act, s 1(1)(a).

[50] Infra, p 1106.

[51] Infra, p 1107.

[52] See *Re J (A Child) (1996 Hague Convention: Morocco)* [2015] EWCA Civ 329, per Black LJ, at [37]–[40] (overturned on appeal on other points: *Re J (A Child) (1996 Hague Convention: Morocco)* [2015] UKSC 70). See also Gration *et al*, paras 1.28–1.36.

[53] See *Practice Guide*, para 8. See also the 1996 Hague Convention, Art 52 which deals with the relationship between the 1996 Convention and other instruments; and *Practical Handbook*, para 12.7.

[54] See infra, pp 1125–6.

[55] See *Practice Guide,* para 8.3.3.

[56] See supra, n 49.

[57] See also Commission Proposal for the Recast of Brussels II *bis*, COM (2016) 411 final 30 June 2016.

[58] Brussels II, Recital (11).

[59] Brussels II *bis*, Recital (5).

and duties relating to the person or the property of a child which are given to a natural or legal person by judgment, by operation of law or by an agreement having legal effect".[60] In particular, Brussels II *bis* shall apply,[61] whatever the nature of the court or tribunal, in civil matters[62] relating to the attribution, exercise, delegation, restriction or termination of parental responsibility.[63] Specifically included are: (a) rights of custody[64] and rights of access;[65] (b) guardianship, curatorship and similar institutions; (c) the designation and functions of any person or body having charge of the child's person or property, representing or assisting the child; (d) the placement of the child in a foster family or in institutional care; (e) and measures for the protection of the child relating to the administration, conservation or disposal of the child's property.[66] A decision ordering a child to be taken into care and placed in a foster family is covered by the term "civil matters" even if the decision was made in the context of public law proceedings relating to child protection.[67] Notably, the placement of the child in institutional care covers placement in a secure care institution.[68] As regards the property of a child, it is important to point out that the Regulation applies only to protective measures.[69] The need to obtain approval from the court dealing with guardianship matters is a direct consequence of the status and capacity of the minor children and constitutes a protective measure for the child relating to the administration, conservation or disposal of the child's property in the exercise of parental responsibility within the meaning of Article 1(1) (b) and 1(2)(e) of the Regulation.[70] Brussels II *bis* does not apply to[71] (a) the establishment or contesting of a parent-child relationship;[72] (b) decisions on adoption, measures preparatory to adoption, or the annulment or revocation of adoption;[73] (c) the name and forenames of the child; (d) emancipation; (e) maintenance obligations;[74] (f) trusts or succession;[75] or (g) measures taken as a result of criminal offences committed by children.[76] Not specifically mentioned in Article 1, but excluded from the scope of the Regulation by virtue of Recital (10), are other questions linked to the status of persons, matters relating to social security, public measures of a general nature in matters of education or health, and decisions on the right of asylum and on immigration.

---

[60] Ibid, Art 2(7). Cf 1996 Hague Convention, Art 1(2), infra, pp 1102–3.

[61] Cf 1996 Hague Convention, Art 3, infra, pp 1102–3.

[62] To be interpreted autonomously: *Re C* (Case C-435/06) [2007] ECR I-10141.

[63] Brussels II *bis*, Art 1(1)(b).

[64] Defined in Art 2(9) as rights and duties relating to the care of the person of a child, and in particular the right to determine the child's place of residence. See Case C-400/10 PPU, *J McB v LE* [2010] ECR I-08965—rights of custody of an unmarried father, see infra, p 1138.

[65] Defined in Art 2(10) as including in particular the right to take a child to a place other than his habitual residence for a limited period of time.

[66] Art 1(2)(e).

[67] See Case C-435/06, *C* [2007] ECR I-10141, at [34] and [50]; Case C-523/07, *Proceedings Brought by A* [2009] ECR I-02805, at [24] and [27]–[29]; Case C-92/12, *Health Service Executive v SC and AC*, [2012] 2 FLR 1040, at [60] and [61]; and Case C-428/15, *Child and Family Agency v J. D.*, [2016] All ER (D) 24 (Nov), at [33].

[68] Case C-92/12, *Health Service Executive v SC and AC*, [2012] 2 FLR 1040.

[69] Brussels II *bis*, Recital (9). Eg, the Regulation applies in all cases where a child's parents are in dispute as regards the administration of his property. Measures relating to the child's property which do not concern the protection of the child continue to be governed by the Brussels I (Recast) Regulation, supra, Chapter 11.

[70] Case C-92/12, *Health Service Executive v SC and AC*, [2012] 2 FLR 1040.

[71] Cf 1996 Hague Convention, Art 4, infra, p 1103.

[72] The establishment of parenthood is a different matter from the attribution of parental responsibility: Recital (10). See *L v C (Applications by a Non-Biological Mother)* [2014] EWFC 1280.

[73] See infra, Chapter 27.

[74] See supra, Chapter 24.

[75] See infra, Chapters 38 and 36 respectively.

[76] Brussels II *bis*, Art 1(3).

Unlike most other instruments concerning children, Brussels II *bis* does not define "child", or set a maximum age regarding the children who are affected by its provisions.[77] This question is left to be determined by national law.

(ii) Rules of jurisdiction in Brussels II bis

The rules of jurisdiction in matters of parental responsibility are set out in Chapter II, section 2 of the Regulation. Unlike the grounds of jurisdiction set out in Article 3 in relation to divorce, legal separation and marriage annulment, which are set out as alternatives, and not in any order of precedence,[78] the rules of jurisdiction in relation to parental responsibility are set out in quasi-hierarchical form. The general rule is set out in Article 8, and the exceptions to that rule are to be found in Articles 9, 10, 12 and 13.

General jurisdiction—Article 8[79] Article 8(1) provides that, subject to Articles 9, 10 and 12,[80] examined below, the courts of a Member State shall have jurisdiction in matters of parental responsibility over a child who is habitually resident in that Member State at the time the court is seised. The grounds of jurisdiction established in the Regulation are said to have been:

> shaped in light of the best interests of the child, in particular on the criterion of proximity. This means that jurisdiction should lie in the first place with the Member State of the child's habitual residence, except for certain cases of a change in the child's residence or pursuant to an agreement between the holders of parental responsibility.[81]

The fundamental principle of the Regulation is that the court of the Member State in which the child is habitually resident is best placed to determine matters of parental responsibility.

"Habitual residence"[82] The connecting factor of habitual residence is nowhere defined in Brussels II *bis*.[83] The meaning of habitual residence for the purposes of Article 8 is to be determined not by recourse to any particular national law, but by reference to the "autonomous" EU law meaning of the concept,[84] having regard to the context and the objective pursued by the Regulation.[85] Recital 12 to Brussels II *bis* states that the grounds of jurisdiction established in the Regulation were shaped in the light of the best interests of the child, in particular, on the criterion of proximity. Accordingly, habitual residence in Article 8 must be interpreted as meaning that it corresponds to the place which reflects some degree of integration by the child in a social and family environment.[86] In this respect, the age of the child is of particular importance.[87] As a general rule, the environment of a very young child

---

[77] Cf 1996 Hague Convention, Art 2. See, infra n 168. But see Commission Proposal for the Recast of Brussels II *bis*, COM (2016) 411 final 30 June 2016, p 21.

[78] Supra, pp 955–6.

[79] Cf 1996 Hague Convention, Art 5, infra, pp 1103–4.

[80] Art 9 (continuing jurisdiction of the child's former habitual residence); Art 10 (jurisdiction in cases of child abduction); and Art 12 (prorogation of jurisdiction).

[81] Brussels II *bis*, Recital (12).

[82] See, for detailed examination, supra, p 175 et seq. Also Bogdan, "The EC Treaty and the Use of Nationality and Habitual Residence as Connecting Factors in International Family Law", Pertegas, "Nationality and Habitual Residence: Other Connecting Factors in European Private International Law" in Meeusen, Pertegas, Straetmans and Swennen (eds), *International Family Law for the European Union* (2007); and Lowe and Douglas, *Bromley's Family Law*, pp 1040–5.

[83] See, for background, Borras, *Explanatory Report*, para 32.

[84] *Practice Guide*, para 3.2.3.1.

[85] Case C-523/07, *Proceedings Brought by A* [2009] ECR I-02805, at [35]; Case C-497/10 PPU, *Mercredi v Chaffe* [2010] ECR I-14309, at [45]; and Case C-376/14 PPU *C v M* [2014] All ER (D) 160 (Oct), at [50].

[86] Case C-523/07, *Proceedings Brought by A*, at [44]; Case C-497/10 PPU, *Mercredi v Chaffe*, at [47]; and Case C-376/14 PPU *C v M*, at [51].

[87] Case C-497/10 PPU, *Mercredi v Chaffe*, at [52].

is essentially a family environment determined by reference to the person(s) on whom the child is dependent, ie the child's primary carer(s).[88] The determination of the child's social and family environment requires consideration of a range of factors beyond the physical presence of the child in a Member State; in particular, the duration, regularity, conditions and reasons for the stay on the territory of that Member State and the family's move to that State, the child's nationality, the place and conditions of attendance at school, linguistic knowledge and the family and social relationships of the child in that State.[89] The respective importance of these factors, however, varies according to the age of the child. It follows that, where a very young child is involved, the factors which are to be taken into consideration include, first, the duration, regularity, conditions and reasons for the stay in the territory of that Member State and for the child's primary carer's move to that State and, second, the child's primary carer's geographic and family origins and the family and social connections which the primary carer and child have with that Member State.[90] Where the intention of the parent(s) to settle permanently with the child in another Member State is evidenced by certain tangible steps such as the purchase or lease of a residence in that Member State, it may constitute an indicator of the transfer of the child's habitual residence.[91] It is for the national court to establish the habitual residence of the child, taking into account all the circumstances specific to each individual case.[92]

The CJEU jurisprudence has to be applied in conjunction with domestic authority on the topic. In the past few years, the concept of habitual residence has developed significantly through a sequence of decisions of the Supreme Court.[93] The first of these authorities was the case of *In the Matter of A (Children)*,[94] in which Lady Hale summarized the proper approach to habitual residence as follows:[95]

i) . . . habitual residence is a question of fact and not a legal concept such as domicile. There is no legal rule akin to that whereby a child automatically takes the domicile of his parents.

ii) It was the purpose of the 1986 Act to adopt a concept which was the same as that adopted in the Hague and European Conventions. The Regulation must also be interpreted consistently with those Conventions.

iii) The test adopted by the European Court is "the place which reflects some degree of integration by the child in a social and family environment" in the country concerned. This depends upon numerous factors, including the reasons for the family's stay in the country in question.

iv) It is now unlikely that that test would produce any different results from that hitherto adopted in the English courts under the 1986 Act and the Hague Child Abduction Convention.

---

[88] Ibid, at [55].

[89] Case C-523/07, *Proceedings Brought by A*, at [44]; and Case C-376/14 PPU *C v M*, at [52].

[90] Case C-497/10 PPU, *Mercredi v Chaffe*, at [56].

[91] Case C-523/07, *Proceedings Brought by A*, at [40]; Case C-497/10 PPU, *Mercredi v Chaffe*, at [50]; and Case C-376/14 PPU *C v M*, at [52].

[92] Case C-523/07, *Proceedings Brought by A*, at [37] and [42]; Case C-497/10 PPU, *Mercredi v Chaffe*, at [47]; and Case C-376/14 PPU *C v M*, at [51].

[93] *In the Matter of A (Children)* [2013] UKSC 60; *Re KL (Abduction: Habitual Residence: Inherent Jurisdiction)* [2013] UKSC 75; *In the Matter of LC (Children)* [2014] UKSC 1; *AR v RN* [2015] UKSC 35; and *In the Matter of B (A Child)* [2016] UKSC 4. See also *Re H (Children) (Jurisdiction: Habitual Residence)* [2014] EWCA Civ 1101. See eg Schuz (2014) 26 CFLQ 342; Williams [2014] IFL 84; Blackburn [2014] IFL 8; Walsh [2016] Fam Law 143; and Williams *et al* [2016] IFL 239.

[94] [2013] UKSC 60.

[95] Ibid, at [54]. (Lords Wilson, Reed and Toulson agreed with Lady Hale. Lord Hughes, who dissented in part, nevertheless, agreed with this passage, at [81]).

v)   In my view, the test adopted by the European Court is preferable to that earlier adopted by the English courts, being focussed on the situation of the child, with the purposes and intentions of the parents being merely one of the relevant factors. The test derived *from R v Barnet London Borough Council, ex p Shah* should be abandoned when deciding the habitual residence of a child.

vi)   The social and family environment of an infant or young child is shared with those (whether parents or others) upon whom he is dependent. Hence it is necessary to assess the integration of that person or persons in the social and family environment of the country concerned.

vii)   The essentially factual and individual nature of the inquiry should not be glossed with legal concepts which would produce a different result from that which the factual inquiry would produce.

viii)   As the Advocate General pointed out in para AG45 and the court confirmed in para 43 of *Proceedings brought by A*, it is possible that a child may have no country of habitual residence at a particular point in time.

In addition to the above guidance, the following key principles can be extracted from the other recent authorities cited above:

(a)   The test for habitual residence of children is the same for all purposes (ie in the context of Brussels II *bis*, the Family Law Act 1986 or the 1980 Hague Abduction Convention).[96]

(b)   Parental intent in relation to the reasons for a child's leaving one country and going to stay in another[97] does play a role in establishing or changing the habitual residence of a child. This will have to be taken into account, along with all the other relevant factors, in deciding whether a move from one country to another has a sufficient degree of stability to amount to a change of habitual residence.[98]

(c)   The "rule" advocated by Lord Scarman in *Shah* that habitual residence is to be determined by objective factors is to be consigned to legal history.[99] The integration of the child should be judged by objective as well as subjective factors.[100]

(d)   The state of mind of an adolescent child may be relevant in determining whether he has achieved a sufficient degree of integration.[101]

(e)   The old rule that habitual residence cannot be changed without the consent of all holders of parental responsibility is to be discarded.[102]

(f)   The absence of a joint parental intention to live permanently in a country is not a bar to acquiring habitual residence in a country.[103] Neither is an intention to live in a country for a limited period inconsistent with becoming habitually resident there.[104] It is the stability of the residence what matters, not whether the residence is of a permanent character.[105]

(g)   It is not clear whether a child can be habitually resident in a country which he has never visited; this question might need to be referred to the CJEU.[106]

(h)   A child will not lose his habitual residence immediately upon removal from a jurisdiction, even where there was a settled intention that the child would no longer live in that

---

[96]   *Re KL (Abduction: Habitual Residence: Inherent Jurisdiction)* [2013] UKSC 75, at [19].
[97]   As opposed to a parental intent in relation to habitual residence as a legal concept. Ibid, at [23].
[98]   Ibid.
[99]   *In the Matter of LC (Children)* [2014] UKSC 1, at [37].
[100]   Ibid, at [60].
[101]   Ibid, at [37] and [61].
[102]   *Re H (Children) (Jurisdiction: Habitual Residence)* [2014] EWCA Civ 1101, at [34].
[103]   *AR v RN* [2015] UKSC 35, at [21].
[104]   Ibid.
[105]   Ibid, at [16] and [21].
[106]   *In the Matter of A (Children)* [2013] UKSC 60, at [58].

jurisdiction. The child can only lose his habitual residence when he has achieved the requisite degree of disengagement from that jurisdiction.[107] In this respect, the following considerations are to apply: (a) the deeper the child's integration in the old state, the slower the expected degree of integration in the new state; (b) the greater the adult pre-planning of the move, the faster the child's integration in the new state; and (c) were all the key members of the child's life in the old state have moved with him, the faster the child's integration will be.[108]

(i) It is possible that, exceptionally, a child may have no habitual residence for a period of time.[109]

It has been thought that a child can have only one habitual residence at any one time,[110] though may have more than one during a year.[111] In the context of divorce proceedings, however, the submission that it is not possible to be habitually resident in two places simultaneously was firmly rejected by the Court of Appeal in *Ikimi v Ikimi*.[112] The Court took the view that the bodily presence required to form a basis for habitual residence had to be more than merely token in duration, probably amounting to residence for "an appreciable part of the relevant year".[113] If an adult is capable of being habitually resident in two places simultaneously, it is difficult to see why the same should not be true also of a child. Doubt has been cast, however, on whether, *for the purpose of the Brussels II bis Regulation*, an adult can be habitually resident in more than one country at the same time.[114] The wording of the *Practice Guide*,[115] coupled with the approach in *Marinos v Marinos*,[116] would appear to indicate that, at least for the purpose of Brussels II *bis*, a child may have only one habitual residence at any given time. It is apparent from the *Practice Guide* that if a competent court is seised, in principle it retains jurisdiction under Article 8, even if the child subsequently should acquire a new habitual residence in another Member State; this is the principle of *perpetuatio fori*.[117]

Continuing jurisdiction of the child's former habitual residence—Article 9[118]
Where a child moves lawfully from one Member State to another and acquires a new habitual residence there,[119] the courts of the Member State of the child's former habitual residence shall, by way of exception to Article 8, retain jurisdiction during a three-month period following the move for the purpose of modifying a judgment on access rights issued in that Member State before the child moved, where the holder of access rights pursuant to the

---

[107] *In the Matter of B (A Child)* [2016] UKSC 4, at [45].

[108] Ibid, at [46].

[109] Ibid, at [45].

[110] *Re V (Abduction: Habitual Residence)* [1995] 2 FLR 992; *In the Marriage of R and S S Hanbury-Brown* (1996) 20 Fam LR 334; *Cameron v Cameron* 1996 SLT 306. Rarely will a child be without an habitual residence, though see the unusual circumstances of *W v H (Child Abduction: Surrogacy) (No 1)* [2002] 1 FLR 1008.

[111] *Re A (Abduction: Habitual Residence)* [1998] 1 FLR 497.

[112] [2001] EWCA Civ 873, [2001] 2 FLR 1288, considered supra, p 958. But contra *Marinos v Marinos* [2007] EWHC 2047 (Fam), per Munby J, at [43].

[113] *Ikimi v Ikimi*, above, per Thorpe LJ, at [35]. His Lordship favoured a liberal rather than restrictive approach to the determination of habitual residence, whilst noting that one consequence of liberality might be forum shopping.

[114] *Marinos v Marinos* [2007] EWHC 2047 (Fam), per Munby J, at [43]; supra, p 959.

[115] *Practice Guide*, para 3.2.3.3.

[116] [2007] EWHC 2047 (Fam).

[117] *Practice Guide*, para 3.2.3.3. Cf 1996 Hague Convention, infra, p 1104. See also Commission Proposal for the Recast of Brussels II *bis*, COM (2016) 411 final 30 June 2016, pp 22 and 36—proposal for the abandonment of the principle of *perpetuatio fori* in the context of Brussels II *bis*.

[118] There is no equivalent provision in the 1996 Convention.

[119] Art 9 presupposes that the child in question has attained a new habitual residence within only three months of arriving in the new Member State. See criticism by McEleavy (2004) 53 ICLQ 503 at 508.

judgment continues to have his habitual residence in the Member State of the child's former habitual residence.[120] This does not apply, however, if the holder of access rights has accepted the jurisdiction of the courts of the Member State of the child's new habitual residence by participating in proceedings before those courts without contesting their jurisdiction.[121] It may be that the holder of the access rights wishes to seise the courts of the new Member State for the purpose of having those rights reviewed.

Article 9, which is limited to jurisdiction in respect of access rights:

> provides a guarantee that the person who can no longer exercise access rights as before does not have to seise the courts of the new Member State, but can apply for an appropriate adjustment of access rights before the court that granted them during a period of three months following the move. The courts of the new Member State do not have jurisdiction in matters of access rights during this period.[122]

It is important to recognise that Article 9 applies only in cases where a child has been moved lawfully from one Member State to another; the lawfulness of the removal is a matter to be determined by the law (including private international law) of the Member State of origin. Cases of wrongful removal or retention are dealt with according to Article 10.

Jurisdiction in cases of child abduction—Article 10[123] Special rules apply in cases of child abduction, and will be considered in that context, below.[124]

Prorogation of jurisdiction—Article 12 Article 12(1)[125] provides that the courts of a Member State exercising jurisdiction by virtue of Article 3[126] of Brussels II *bis* on an application for divorce, legal separation or marriage annulment shall have jurisdiction in any matter relating to parental responsibility connected with that application where two conditions are satisfied: (a) at least one of the spouses has parental responsibility in relation to the child; and (b) the jurisdiction of the courts has been accepted expressly or otherwise in an unequivocal manner by the spouses and by the holders of parental responsibility, at the time the court is seised,[127] and is in the superior[128] interests of the child.[129] Jurisdiction under Article 12(1)

---

[120] See also Arts 40 and 41, infra, pp 1129–30.

[121] Art 9(2).

[122] *Practice Guide*, para 3.2.4.1. However, "Article 9 does not prevent a holder of parental responsibility who has moved with the child to the 'new' Member State, from seising the courts of that Member State on any other question of parental responsibility during the three-month period following the move." Ibid, para 3.2.4.2.7.

[123] Cf 1996 Hague Convention, Art 7, infra, pp 1104–5.

[124] Infra, pp 1157–8.

[125] Cf 1996 Hague Convention, Art 10, infra, p 1105. See Commission Proposal for the Recast of Brussels II *bis*, COM (2016) 411 final 30 June 2016, p 22.

[126] Supra, pp 955–6. See *C v FC (Brussels II: Freestanding Application for Parental Responsibility)* [2001] 1 FLR 317.

[127] Cf *Re I (A Child) (Contact Application: Jurisdiction)* [2009] UKSC 10—the Court was divided as to whether acceptance of jurisdiction had to take place at the commencement of the proceedings, or could take place at any time thereafter providing that the court was already seised. This issue, however, did not need to be resolved as all parties accepted that there had been unequivocal acceptance both before and after the proceedings began.

[128] The *Practice Guide* explains that: "No distinction was intended by the drafters between the term 'superior interests of the child' [Art 12(1)(b)] . . . and the term 'best interests of the child' [Art 12(3) (b)] . . . Versions of the Regulation in other languages employ an identical wording in both paragraphs." (para 3.2.6.2). See *also Re I (A Child) (Contact Application: Jurisdiction)* [2009] UKSC 10, per Lady Hale, at [36] and Lord Collins, at [50].

[129] Eg *Re ML and AL (Children) (Contact Order: Brussels II Regulation) (No 1)* [2006] EWHC 2385 (Fam), [2007] 1 FCR 475; *Bush v Bush* [2008] EWCA Civ 865; *R-S (Contact: Jurisdiction)* [2008] 2 FLR 1741; and *AP v TD (Relocation: Retention of Jurisdiction)* [2010] EWHC 2040 (Fam). Cf *VC v GC (Jurisdiction: Brussels II Revised Art 12)* [2012] EWHC 1246 (Fam).

shall cease as soon as (a) the judgment allowing or refusing the application for divorce, legal separation or marriage annulment has become final;[130] (b) a final judgment is issued in parental responsibility proceedings which were still pending on the date when the divorce, etc proceedings became final; or (c) the divorce, etc proceedings referred to in (a) and the parental responsibility proceedings referred to in (b) have come to an end for another reason.[131]

The courts of a Member State shall also have jurisdiction[132] in relation to parental responsibility in proceedings other than matrimonial proceedings where: (a) the child has a substantial connection with that Member State,[133] in particular by virtue of the fact that one of the holders of parental responsibility is habitually resident in that Member State or that the child is a national of that Member State; and (b) the jurisdiction of the courts has been accepted expressly or otherwise in an unequivocal manner by all the parties to the proceedings at the time the court is seised and is in the best[134] interests of the child.[135] Article 12(3) has to be interpreted as establishing jurisdiction over proceedings in matters of parental responsibility even where no other related proceedings are pending before the court chosen.[136] For the purposes of this provision, it cannot be considered that the jurisdiction of the court seised by one party of proceedings in matters of parental responsibility has been "accepted expressly or otherwise in an unequivocal manner by all the parties to the proceedings" where the defendant in those first proceedings subsequently brings a second set of proceedings before the same court and, on taking the first step required of him in the first proceedings, pleads the lack of jurisdiction of that court.[137] Jurisdiction in matters of parental responsibility which has been prorogued under Article 12(3) ceases following a final judgment in the parental responsibility proceedings.[138]

Where the child is habitually resident in a non-Member State which is not a contracting party to the 1996 Hague Convention,[139] jurisdiction in a Member State under Article 12 shall be deemed to be in the child's interest, in particular if it is found impossible to hold proceedings in the third State in question.[140] In *Re I (A Child) (Contact Application: Jurisdiction)*[141] the Supreme Court held that Article 12 was not limited to situations where the child was habitually resident within the European Union.[142] Hence, in referring to a "third state", Article 12(4) denoted a non-Member State.[143] In the present case, the non-Member State in question was Pakistan. The father had been permitted to take the child to live in Pakistan with his mother and sister on condition that the child would be returned if requested by the court. The order also provided for interim contact with the mother who, like the father, was

---

[130] See, in relation to Brussels II, Art 3(3), *Re A (A Child) (Foreign Contact Order: Jurisdiction)* [2003] EWHC 2911, [2004] 1 FLR 641.

[131] Eg the application for divorce, etc has been withdrawn.

[132] Art 12(3).

[133] See, in relation to operation of Art 66, infra, pp 1100–1.

[134] See supra, n 128, regarding the difference in wording between Art 12(1)(b) and (3)(b).

[135] Eg *Re W (Jurisdiction: Mirror Order)* [2011] EWCA Civ 703; *Re C* [2012] EWHC 907 (Fam); *Re ED (Jurisdiction: Undertaking to Return)* [2014] EWHC 2731 (Fam); and *Re Z (A Child)* [2014] EWHC 2147 (Fam). Cf *B v B (Relinquishment of Jurisdiction: Brussels II Revised Art 12)* [2012] EWHC 1924 (Fam); and *Re LR (A Child)* [2014] EWCA Civ 1624.

[136] Case C-656/13, *L v M*, at [52].

[137] Ibid, at [59].

[138] Case C-436/13, *E v B*, at [50]. See Pedreno *et al* [2015] IFL 35. See also *Re S (Jurisdiction: Prorogation)* [2013] EWHC 647 (Fam), at [45].

[139] Ie a "third State".

[140] Art 12(4).

[141] [2009] UKSC 10. See also *Re Z (A Child)* [2014] EWHC 2147 (Fam).

[142] *Re I (A Child) (Contact Application: Jurisdiction)* [2009] UKSC 10, per Lady Hale, at [20].

[143] Ibid, at [18].

resident in England. The mother subsequently brought proceedings in England to vary and enforce the existing contact arrangements. The court held that the criteria in Article 12(3) had been met as, by virtue of the child's British nationality and the parents' habitual residence in England, the child had a substantial connection with the jurisdiction, and the father had expressly accepted jurisdiction. It followed that English courts had jurisdiction to hear the case on the basis of Article 12(3) and (4).

Jurisdiction based on child's presence—Article 13[144] Where a child's habitual residence cannot be established, and jurisdiction cannot be determined on the basis of Article 12, the courts of the Member State where the child is present shall have jurisdiction.[145] This provision also applies to refugee children or children internationally displaced because of disturbances occurring in their country.[146]

Transfer to a court better placed to hear the case—Article 15[147]

(iii) Allocation of jurisdiction within the United Kingdom

Article 66 of Brussels II *bis* applies to Member States in which two or more systems of law apply. The precise meaning of Article 66 is not clear.[148] It mentions only references to (a) the "habitual residence" of a person in a Member State; (b) the "nationality" or "domicile" of a person in a Member State; (c) the "authority" of a Member State"; and (d) "the rules of the requested Member State". The references to a Member State are to be interpreted as references to the relevant territorial unit within that state. Article 66 does not mention the "courts of a Member State", referred to in Articles 12 and 15; "presence in a Member State", which is the connecting factor relied upon in Article 13; or the "courts of different Member States" referred to in Article 19.[149] The question arises whether the jurisdiction provisions of Brussels II *bis* operate so as to allocate jurisdiction among the territorial units of the United Kingdom. Chapter II of Part I of the Family Law Act 1986, dealing with the jurisdiction of courts in England and Wales, gives priority to the rules of jurisdiction contained in Brussels II *bis* (and the 1996 Hague Convention), but does not expressly state whether those rules are intended to allocate jurisdiction as between the different territorial units of the United Kingdom. In contrast, Chapter III of Part I of the Act, dealing with the jurisdiction of courts in Scotland, in section 17A,[150] provides that the provisions of Chapter III are subject to sections 2 and 3 of Chapter II of Brussels II *bis*, ie Articles 8 to 20, (and the 1996 Hague Convention). By inference, it seems that the jurisdiction provisions in Articles 8, 9 and 10, all of which rely upon personal law connecting factors mentioned in Article 66, should operate to allocate jurisdiction within the United Kingdom. However, the extent of application of Article 12, as well as of Articles 13, 15 and 19, is more difficult, since those provisions refer to the "courts of a Member State", "substantial connection with a Member State", "presence in a Member State" or the "courts of different Member States", expressions to which no reference is made in Article 66. As regards Article 12(3), it was held in *S v D*[151] that a proper interpretation of Article 66 requires that the child in question has a "substantial connection" with the relevant territorial unit of the United Kingdom, and not generally with the United Kingdom as a

---

[144] Cf 1996 Hague Convention, Art 6, infra, p 1105.

[145] Eg *Bridgend CBC v GM* [2012] EWHC 3118 (Fam); and *Re F (Habitual Residence: Peripatetic Existence)* [2014] EWFC 26. Cf *Coventry City Council v A* [2014] EWHC 2033 (Fam).

[146] Art 13(2).

[147] Discussed infra, pp 1113–16.

[148] Eg *S v D* 2007 SLT (Sh Ct) 37; and *Re ESJ* [2008] NI Fam 6, at [9]; and *Re PC (A Child) (Brussels II Revised: Jurisdiction within United Kingdom)* [2013] EWHC 2336 (Fam), at [16].

[149] Infra, pp 1117–19.

[150] Added by SSI 2005/42, reg 4(3) and amended by SSI 2010/213, Sch 1, para 4.

[151] 2007 SLT (Sh Ct) 37, criticised by Maher 2007 SLT (News) 117.

Member State.[152] For reasons of clarity and simplicity, it is submitted that it is preferable to construe Articles 8, 9, 10 and 12 of the Regulation as applying to the allocation of jurisdiction intra-United Kingdom in parental responsibility disputes,[153] but strictly, and bearing in mind issues of European Union competence, this expansive interpretation of Articles 12 and 66 may be open to challenge.[154] At any rate, however: "To assume the operation of Regulation 2201 in intra-UK cases is the less complex interpretative option."[155]

First instance courts in the UK have reached differing conclusions as to the applicability of Brussels II *bis* to jurisdictional disputes involving the different territorial units of the UK. For example, in the Scottish case of *S v D*[156] it was held that Brussels II *bis* applied when determining jurisdictional disputes between Scotland and England,[157] however, in *Re ESJ* [158] Morgan J took the opposite view as to a jurisdictional dispute between Northern Ireland and England. The English Court of Appeal, in *Re W-B (Family Jurisdiction: Appropriate Jurisdiction within the UK)*,[159] concluded that Brussels II *bis* did not apply to the determination of jurisdiction between the different units of the UK, on the basis that they were all part of one Member State.[160]

The 1996 Hague Convention

In 1996, the Hague Conference concluded a Convention on Jurisdiction, Applicable Law, Recognition, Enforcement and Co-operation in Respect of Parental Responsibility and Measures for the Protection of Children.[161] The Convention was designed to replace the 1961 Hague Convention concerning the Powers of Authorities and the Law Applicable in Respect of the Protection of Minors, to which the United Kingdom was not a party, mainly because of the role given to the authorities of the state of the child's nationality. The 1996 Convention was signed on 1 April 2003 by the then fourteen European Union Member States, including the United Kingdom.[162] It entered into force on 1 January 2002 and as

---

[152] Since, in the instant case, the child no longer had a substantial connection with Scotland, the "robust conditions" of Art 12(3) were not satisfied.

[153] See, eg, Lowe [2004] IFLJ 205; Morris, p 293; and Crawford and Carruthers, para 14–36. This is in line with the Scottish position, in terms of the Family Law Act 1986, s 17A, added by SSI 2005/42, in respect of Chapter III of the 1986 Act (Jurisdiction of Courts in Scotland).

[154] Maher 2007 SLT (News) 117.

[155] Crawford and Carruthers, para 14–36.

[156] 2007 SLT (Sh Ct) 37.

[157] See also *T v T (Jurisdiction)* [2012] EWHC 2877 (Fam)—Brussels II *bis*, Arts 8, 12(3) and 15, considered as applicable *prima facie*.

[158] [2008] NI Fam 6.

[159] [2012] EWCA Civ 592.

[160] Ibid, per McFarlane LJ, at [10]. *Re W-B* was followed in *Re PC (A Child) (Brussels II Revised: Jurisdiction within United Kingdom)* [2013] EWHC 2336 (Fam)—transfer of jurisdiction from England to Scotland; and *Re C (Children)* [2015] EWHC 2082 (Fam)—recognition and enforcement of a Scottish judgment in England.

[161] See generally Lagarde, *Explanatory Report* (1996); and *Practical Handbook*. Also Detrich [1996] Hague Yearbook of Int L 77; Lagarde (1997) 86 Rev Crit Dr Int Priv 217; Clive [1998] Jur Rev 169; Nygh (1998) 45 Neth Int L R 1; Clive [2002] Fam Law 131; Lowe and Nicholls, *The 1996 Hague Convention on the Protection of Children* (2012); Pirrung [2012] IFL 70; and Gration *et al, International Issues in Family Law: The 1996 Hague Convention on the Protection of Children and Brussels IIa* (2015).

[162] See Council Decision of 19 December 2002 authorising the Member States in the interest of the Community to sign the Convention (OJ 2003 L 48/1); and Council Decision of 5 June 2008 authorising certain Member States to ratify, or accede to, in the interest of the European Community, the 1996 Hague Convention on Jurisdiction, Applicable Law, Recognition, Enforcement and Cooperation in Respect of Parental Responsibility and Measures for the Protection of Children and authorising certain Member States to make a declaration on the application of the relevant internal rules of Community law—Convention on Jurisdiction, Applicable Law, Recognition, Enforcement and Cooperation in respect of Parental Responsibility and Measures for the Protection of Children (OJ 2008 L 151/36).

of March 2017 has forty-six Contracting States. The UK's ratification came into force in November 2012. The Convention is directly effective as a matter of EU law[163] and therefore did not require formal transposition into domestic law. Instead, the necessary changes to relevant primary legislation were brought about through secondary legislation.[164]

(i) Scope of the 1996 Hague Convention

The 1996 Convention is the broadest in scope of the Hague Conference's children conventions.[165] As its name indicates, not only does it contain rules on jurisdiction,[166] applicable law,[167] recognition and enforcement of measures on parental responsibility and protection of children,[168] it also establishes a framework for co-operation among Contracting States.[169] The scope of application of the Convention is very similar to that of Brussels II *bis*, although the latter, as has been seen, does not deal with choice of law. Parental responsibility is defined in the Convention as including "parental authority, or any analogous relationship of authority determining the rights, powers and responsibilities of parents, guardians or other legal representatives in relation to the person or the property of the child".[170] Article 3 of the Convention[171] contains a non-exhaustive list of the types of matters that are covered by the Convention: (a) the attribution, exercise, termination and delegation of parental responsibility; (b) rights of custody[172] and access;[173] (c) guardianship, curatorship and analogous institutions; (d) the designation and functions of any person or body having charge of the child's person or property, representing or assisting the child; (e) the placing a child in foster or institutional care[174] or the provision of care by kafala or an analogous institution; (f) the supervision by a public authority of the care of a child by any person having charge of the child; and (g) the administration, conservation or disposal of the child's property. The English courts have expanded the interpretation of the scope of the Convention by holding that undertakings given in the course of return proceedings under the 1980 Hague Convention fall within Article 3 of the 1996 Convention.[175] Similarly, an order for the return of a child to the country of his or her habitual residence is a "measure of protection" falling within the scope of the

---

[163] The European Communities Act 1972, s 2(2). See the European Communities (Definition of Treaties) (1996 Hague Convention on Protection of Children etc) Order 2010, SI 2010/232. See also Ministry of Justice, Explanatory Memorandum to the Parental Responsibility and Measures for the Protection of Children (International Obligations) (England and Wales and Northern Ireland) Regulations 2010, 2010, No 1898, Annex A, para 4.

[164] See the Parental Responsibility and Measures for the Protection of Children (International Obligations) (England and Wales and Northern Ireland) Regulations 2010, SI 2010/1898. For Scotland, see, SI 2010/213.

[165] Cf 1980 Convention on Civil Aspects of International Child Abduction, supra, p 1134 et seq; and 1993 Convention on Protection of Children and Co-operation in Respect of Intercountry Adoption, infra, p 1205.

[166] Chapter II.

[167] Chapter III.

[168] Applying to children from the moment of their birth until they reach eighteen years: Art 2. There is no definition of a "child" in Brussels II *bis*. Provisions on recognition and enforcement are set out in Chapter IV.

[169] Chapter V.

[170] Art 1(2). Cf Brussels II *bis*, Art 2(7).

[171] Cf Brussels II *bis*, Art 1.

[172] Defined in Art 3(b) as "rights relating to the care of the person of the child and, in particular, the right to determine the child's place of residence". Cf Brussels II *bis*, Art 2(9) and 1980 Hague Convention, Art 5(b), supra, p 1093 and infra, p 1136 et seq respectively.

[173] Defined in Art 3(b) as "including the right to take a child for a limited period of time to a place other than the child's habitual residence". Cf Brussels II *bis*, Art 2(10) and 1980 Hague Convention, Art 5(b), supra, p 1093 and infra, p 1136 et seq respectively.

[174] See, in the context of Brussels II bis, Case C-435/06, *C* [2007] ECR I-10141, and Case C-523/07, *Proceedings Brought by A* [2009] ECR I-02805, see, supra p 1093, n 67.

[175] See *Re Y (Abduction: Undertakings Given for Return of Child)* [2013] EWCA Civ 129, applied by Mostyn J in *B v B* [2014] EWHC 1804 (Fam); and *RB v DB* [2015] EWHC 1817 (Fam).

Convention.[176] Article 4, in contrast to Article 3, sets out in a comprehensive manner matters which are expressly excluded from the scope of the Convention. These are: (a) the establishment or contesting of a parent-child relationship; (b) decisions on adoption, measures preparatory to adoption, or the annulment or revocation of adoption; (c) the name and forenames of the child; (d) emancipation; (e) maintenance obligations; (f) trusts or succession; (g) social security; (h) public measures of a general nature in matters of education or health; (i) measures taken as a result of penal offences committed by children; and (j) decisions on the right of asylum and on immigration. The Convention applies only to measures which are taken in a Contracting State after the entry into force of the Convention in that State.[177]

(ii) Rules of jurisdiction in the 1996 Hague Convention

Chapter II (Articles 5 to 14) of the Convention contains rules of jurisdiction. The jurisdictional provisions are similar to those in Brussels II *bis*—the primary ground of jurisdiction is the country of the habitual residence of the child, whilst a departure from the general rule is justified if one of the exceptions specified in the instrument applies. Accordingly, Article 5 sets of the general rule that jurisdiction is vested in the authorities of the Contracting State in which the child is habitually resident. By way of exception, Article 10 permits the authorities of a Contracting State exercising jurisdiction in respect of the divorce, legal separation or annulment of marriage of a child's parents, also to take measures for the protection of the child.[178] A special rule for cases of wrong removal or retention of the child is laid down in Article 7,[179] and there exists also an emergency jurisdiction based upon presence of the child in the jurisdiction of a Contracting State.[180] A mechanism for the transfer of jurisdiction, akin to that contained in Article 15 of Brussels II *bis*,[181] is set out in Articles 8 and 9, and operates by way of exception and in the best interests of the child. Like Brussels II *bis*, the Convention adopts a principle of priority of process (*lis pendens*) to resolve problems of conflicting jurisdiction.[182]

General jurisdiction—Article 5   Article 5 provides that jurisdiction in respect of the person and property of the child rests principally with the authorities of the Contracting State in which the child is habitually resident.[183] "Habitual residence" is not defined in the Convention, however, the concept should be interpreted autonomously and in the light of the objectives of the Convention.[184] It has also been suggested[185] that, for the purposes of the

---

[176] *Re J (A Child) (1996 Hague Convention: Morocco)* [2015] UKSC 70, per Lady Hale, at [23] (circumstances where the 1980 Hague Abduction Convention did not apply).

[177] Art 53(1). *Practice Guide*, para 3.1.

[178] Cf Brussels II *bis*, Art 12, supra, p 1098 et seq.

[179] Cf Brussels II *bis*, Art 10, supra, p 1098.

[180] Art 11; see also Art 12 with regard to jurisdiction to take provisional protective measures. Cf Brussels II *bis*, Arts 13 and 20, supra, p 1100 and infra, pp 1119–20.

[181] Supra, pp 1113–16.

[182] Art 13. Cf Brussels II *bis*, Art 19, supra, pp 1117–19.

[183] Art 5. Eg *Rotherham Metropolitan Borough Council v J and others* [2016] EWHC 1844 (Fam). Cf Brussels II *bis*, Art 8, supra, p 1094 et seq. "Article 5 is based on the supposition that the child has his or her habitual residence in a Contracting State. In the contrary case, Article 5 is not applicable and the authorities of the Contracting States have jurisdiction under the Convention only on the basis of provisions other than this one (Art 11 and 12). But nothing prevents these authorities from finding themselves to have jurisdiction, outside of the Convention, on the basis of the rules of private international law of the State to which they belong." (Lagarde, *Explanatory Report*, para 39).

[184] *Practical Handbook*, para 4.5.

[185] *In the Matter of A (Children)* [2013] UKSC 60—the fact that the 1996 Hague Convention (and the 1980 Hague Convention) "formed part of the legislative history" of Brussels II *bis* presumes a "uniform understanding of the concept of habitual residence", at [35]. See also *DL v EL* [2013] EWCA Civ 865 at [48] where the Court of Appeal expressed the view that "there is now no distinction to be drawn" between the test adopted in the context of Brussels II *bis*, the 1980 Hague Convention and the 1996 Hague Convention.

1996 Convention, the concept be interpreted in the same way as construed by the CJEU for the purposes of Brussels II *bis*.[186] It may be thought that, on this point, there is a discrepancy between the approach endorsed by the Supreme Court and the intention of the drafters of the 1996 Convention.[187] Indeed, the *Practical Handbook* cautions against an automatic transposition of the concept of habitual residence, in particular from the child abduction context, as "there may be different considerations to be taken into account when determining the habitual residence of a child for the purposes of this Convention".[188] Admittedly, in the process of interpreting habitual residence, account must be taken, among other factors, of the purpose of the instrument in question. This requirement, nevertheless, does not seem to contradict the pragmatic approach proposed by the Supreme Court, which endorses the application in the context of the 1996 Convention of the habitual residence test set out by the CJEU for the purposes of Brussels II *bis*. Indeed, in its jurisprudence, the CJEU acknowledged that determination of habitual residence for the purposes of Article 8(1) of Brussels II *bis* "must be made in the light of the context of the provisions and the objective of the Regulation".[189] By analogy, determination of habitual residence for the purposes of the 1996 Convention must be made in the light of the context of the provisions and the objective of the Convention. This means that, in establishing habitual residence for the purposes of the 1996 Convention, the context and the objective of the Convention have to be taken into account in conjunction with the factors set out in the jurisprudence of the CJEU,[190] and in consideration of the principles propounded by the Supreme Court.[191] The trend towards a uniform understanding of habitual residence appears to be a highly sensible one. It serves the goals of increased predictability and legal certainty in cross-border cases involving children, with the ultimate objective of achieving consistency in the interpretation of the concept of habitual residence of a child in cross-border scenarios.

Importantly, unlike under Brussels II *bis*,[192] the principle of *perpetuatio fori* does not apply under the 1996 Convention. This means that where, in the course of the proceedings, the child's habitual residence changes from one Contracting State to another, jurisdiction will move to the courts of the Contracting States of the child's new habitual residence.[193]

Jurisdiction in cases of child abduction—Article 7[194]   Special rules apply in cases of child abduction, and these rules correspond to Article 10 of Brussels II *bis*, which is considered in the context of child abduction, below.[195] In summary, Article 7 provides that jurisdiction in respect of a child will be retained by the Contracting State in which the child was

---

[186] *In the Matter of A (Children)* [2013] UKSC 60; *Re KL (Abduction: Habitual Residence: Inherent Jurisdiction)* [2013] UKSC 75; Case C-523/07, *Proceedings Brought by A* [2009] ECR I-02805; Case C-497/10 PPU, *Mercredi v Chaffe* [2010] ECR I-14309; and Case C-376/14 PPU *C v M* [2014] All ER (D) 160 (Oct). See supra, p 1094 et seq and Chapter 9, p 175 et seq.

[187] See Gration *et al*, para 3.17.

[188] *Practical Handbook*, para 4.6.

[189] Case C-523/07, *Proceedings Brought by A* [2009] ECR I-02805, at [35].

[190] See supra, pp 1094–5.

[191] See supra, pp 1095–7.

[192] See supra, p 1097, and note Commission Proposal for the Recast of Brussels II *bis*, COM (2016) 411 final 30 June 2016, pp 22 and 36.

[193] See Lagarde, *Explanatory Report*, para 42 and *Practical Handbook*, para 4.10. Where appropriate, the rigidity of this rule can be mitigated by the provisions of either Art 9 (transfer of jurisdiction) or Art 10 (prorogation). See infra. Where the child acquires habitual residence in a non-Contracting State, Art 5 ceases to be applicable; however, the Contracting State originally seised of the matter can retain jurisdiction under its residual (ie non-Convention) rules of jurisdiction. Nevertheless, this will have implications at the recognition stage, as the decision will not be covered by the recognition rules set out in the Convention. *Practical Handbook*, [4.11]. See infra, pp 1130–2.

[194] Cf Brussels II *bis*, Art 10.

[195] Infra, pp 1157–8.

habitually resident immediately before the removal or retention until such time that the child has acquired habitual residence in another Contracting State and one of the requirements set out in Article 7 has been met.[196]

Prorogation of jurisdiction—Article 10[197] The 1996 Hague Convention adopts a narrower approach to prorogation than Brussels II *bis*.[198] Under Article 10, jurisdiction can be prorogued only if there are divorce, legal separation or marriage annulment proceedings of the parents of the child pending in a Contracting State, and the following requirements are met: (a) the child is habitually resident in another Contracting State; (b) the domestic law of the Contracting State seised with the divorce, etc proceedings so permits; (c) the jurisdiction of that Contracting State in relation to the child has been accepted by parents, as well as by any other person who has parental responsibility in relation to the child; (d) at the time of the commencement of the proceedings, at least one of the parents is habitually resident in that Contracting State, and at least one of them has parental responsibility in relation to the child; and (e) it is in the best interests of the child that jurisdiction be exercised on this basis. Unlike under Brussels II *bis*, the jurisdiction conferred by prorogation ceases when the divorce, etc. proceedings come to an end, either because the decision allowing or refusing the application for divorce, etc. has become final, or the divorce, etc. proceedings ended for another reason.[199]

Jurisdiction based on child's presence—Article 6[200] Similar to Brussels II *bis*, the 1996 Hague Convention provides for jurisdiction in cases of refugee children and children internationally displaced as a result of disturbances occurring in their country.[201] In such circumstances, by virtue of Article 6(1), jurisdiction is vested with the authorities of the Contracting State on the territory of which the child is present. The same rule applies to children whose habitual residence cannot be established.[202]

Transfer to a court better placed to hear the case—Articles 8 and 9[203]

(b) Jurisdiction under the 1986 Act, Section 2(1)(b)

By virtue of Article 14 of Brussels II *bis*,[204] where no court of a Member State has jurisdiction pursuant to Articles 8 to 13 (either because of the factual circumstances of the case, ie the matter in dispute falls outside the subject matter scope of the Regulation;[205] or by reason of a lack of relevant geographical connecting factor),[206] jurisdiction shall be determined, in each

---

[196] See Gration *et al*, paras 9.23–9.60.

[197] Cf Brussels II *bis*, Art 12, supra, p 1098 et seq.

[198] Cf Brussels II *bis*, Art 12(1), supra, pp 1098–9. Unlike Brussels II *bis*, the Convention does not provide for prorogation on basis of a "substantial connection" between the child and the jurisdiction in question. See Brussels II *bis*, Art 12(3), supra, p 1099.

[199] Eg Upon a withdrawal or lapse of the application, or the death of a party. *Practical Handbook*, para 4.27. There is no such limitation in Brussels II *bis*. Under Art 12(2), where the proceedings in relation to parental responsibility are still pending on the date when the judgment in relation to divorce, etc. becomes final, the jurisdiction conferred by prorogation will continue until the conclusion of the proceedings concerning matters of parental responsibility.

[200] Cf Brussels II *bis*, Art 13, supra, p 1100.

[201] But not runaway or abandoned children. Lagarde, *Explanatory Report*, para 44.

[202] Art 6(2). The jurisdiction based on the presence of the child will, however, cease once the habitual residence of the child has been established. Lagarde, *Explanatory Report*, para 44. See *Re NH (1996 Child Protection Convention: Habitual Residence)* [2015] EWHC 2299 (Fam).

[203] Discussed infra, pp 1116–17.

[204] There is no equivalent provision in the 1996 Convention.

[205] Supra, pp 1092–4.

[206] Art 14(1) is in the same terms, mutatis mutandis, as Art 7(1) (residual jurisdiction in divorce, etc). Notably, however, there is no provision in Art 14 which corresponds to Art 7(2), discussed, supra, pp 961–2.

Member State, by the laws of that state. The residual rules of jurisdiction are to be found, for England and Wales, in section 2(1)(b) of the 1986 Act.[207]

Section 2(1)(b) provides that a court in England and Wales shall not make a "section 8 order"[208] with respect to a child unless neither Brussels II *bis* nor the 1996 Hague Convention applies,[209] but (i) the question of making the order arises in, or in connection with, matrimonial proceedings or civil partnership proceedings and the condition in section 2A[210] of the 1986 Act is satisfied,[211] (ii) or the condition in section 3[212] of the 1986 Act is satisfied.

(i) Jurisdiction in or in connection with matrimonial proceedings or civil partnership proceedings

A court may make a "section 8 order" if the question of making the order arises in, or in connection with,[213] matrimonial proceedings or civil partnership proceedings[214] in respect of the marriage or civil partnership of the parents of the child concerned, and (a) the proceedings, being ones for divorce or nullity of marriage,[215] or dissolution or annulment of civil partnership, are continuing;[216] or (b) the proceedings, being ones for judicial separation or legal separation, are continuing, and no proceedings for divorce or nullity proceedings, or dissolution or annulment proceedings, are continuing in Scotland or Northern Ireland.[217] The jurisdictional basis for so doing is that the court has jurisdiction over the matrimonial proceedings or civil partnership proceedings.[218]

The rules are dovetailed with those applicable in the other parts of the United Kingdom in two respects. First, if the English proceedings are merely for judicial separation or legal separation, the English court will lose its power to make a section 8 order therein if, after the granting of the decree of judicial separation and at the date of the application,[219] divorce or nullity, or dissolution or annulment proceedings are continuing in Scotland or Northern Ireland.[220] It seems right that the court dealing with the continued existence of the marriage should assume the position of primacy. Secondly, an English court in which the appropriate matrimonial proceedings or civil partnership proceedings are continuing may conclude that it is more appropriate for an application for a Part I order to be determined outside England.[221] In that

---

[207] For Scotland, see Family Law Act 1986, ss 8–18.

[208] A section 8 order made by a court in England under the Children Act 1989, other than an order varying or discharging such an order: 1986 Act, s 1(1)(a). See, eg, *Re H (Residence Order: Placement out of Jurisdiction)* [2004] EWHC 3243, [2006] 1 FLR 1140.

[209] See Gration *et al*, paras 2.29–2.32.

[210] Infra.

[211] Cf *AP v TD (Relocation: Retention of Jurisdiction)* [2010] EWHC 2040 (Fam), at [110]–[126].

[212] Infra, pp 1107–8.

[213] The mere existence of the matrimonial proceedings is insufficient. There must be "some nexus" between these proceedings and the "section 8 proceedings". Any other interpretation would "drive a coach and horses" through the generally accepted approach to jurisdiction based on the habitual residence of the child. *J v U* [2016] EWHC 2481 (Fam), at [16]–[17]. See also *AP v TD (Relocation: Retention of Jurisdiction)* [2010] EWHC 2040 (Fam), at [123] (obiter).

[214] Defined in Family Law Act 1986, s 7(aa) as proceedings for the dissolution or annulment of a civil partnership or for legal separation of the civil partners.

[215] The English courts have power in proceedings under the Matrimonial Causes Act 1973 for divorce, nullity and judicial separation to make section 8 orders relating to children. See *T v T (Custody: Jurisdiction)* [1992] 1 FLR 43.

[216] See *V v V* [2006] EWHC 3374 (Fam), [2007] Fam Law 304.

[217] 1986 Act, ss 2A(1) and (2).

[218] Supra, pp 954 and 1039.

[219] Or when the court is considering making the order if no application is made: 1986 Act, s 7(c).

[220] S 2A(1), (2).

[221] In *J v U* [2016] EWHC 2481 (Fam), Bodey J remarked, although obiter, that this was a *forum conveniens* exercise, at [20].

event it may direct that no section 8 order may be made by an English court in those matrimonial or civil partnership proceedings.[222] The need for this provision is caused by the fact
that matrimonial/civil partnership proceedings once begun, and not dismissed, may continue
indefinitely[223] even though, for instance, a divorce has been granted. This could have the result
that the English divorce court retains its prime jurisdiction to make a section 8 order long after
all the parties have ceased to have a close, or any, connection with England. Therefore, a power
to decline jurisdiction where appropriate is desirable.[224]

(ii) Habitual residence or presence of the child
Alternatively, a court may make a "section 8 order" if, on the date of the application for an
order,[225] the child concerned is (a) habitually resident in England and Wales,[226] or (b) is present
in England and Wales and is not habitually resident in any part of the United Kingdom,[227]
and, in either case, so long as matrimonial proceedings or civil partnership proceedings are not
continuing in respect of the marriage or civil partnership of the child's parents in Scotland or
Northern Ireland.[228] If matrimonial proceedings or civil partnership proceedings are continuing elsewhere in the United Kingdom,[229] then the English court must not exercise jurisdiction
to make a section 8 order, despite the habitual residence or presence of the child in England.
English jurisdiction must yield to the primacy of the courts of the country of the matrimonial/
civil partnership proceedings.[230]

Habitual residence[231]   No period of habitual residence is specified.[232] This is hardly surprising, given that Part I orders may be made in relation to very young children. There is, however, a danger that one parent, by taking the child to another jurisdiction, often wrongfully,
could change his habitual residence and thus deprive the English court of its jurisdictional
power to make a Part I order.[233] To combat this, section 41 of the 1986 Act[234] provides that,
if a child under sixteen who is habitually resident in a part of the United Kingdom is removed
from or leaves that part[235] and becomes habitually resident outside that part,[236] either in
contravention of an English court order[237] or without the consent of anyone having the right
to determine where he resides,[238] then he is still treated as continuing to be habitually resident

---

[222] S 2A(4); see *R S (A Minor) (Jurisdiction to Stay Application)* [1995] 1 FLR 1093. It can always reinstate
the basis of jurisdiction by revoking such direction.

[223] English proceedings may be treated by s 42(2) of the 1986 Act as continuing until the child is eighteen.

[224] Law Com No 138 (1985), para 4.97.

[225] 1986 Act, s 7(c). It is irrelevant that the jurisdictional link is later broken.

[226] Eg *JK v KC* [2011] EWHC 1284 (Fam).

[227] Eg *SF v HL* [2015] EWHC 2891 (Fam).

[228] 1986 Act, s 3.

[229] Eg *B v B (Scottish Contact Order: Jurisdiction to Vary)* [1996] 1 FLR 688.

[230] See *Dorward v Dorward* 1994 SCCR 928.

[231] See, for detailed examination, supra, p 175 and p 182 et seq.

[232] See *F v S (Wardship: Jurisdiction)* [1993] 2 FLR 686.

[233] Cf *Re A (A Minor) (Wardship: Jurisdiction)* [1995] 1 FLR 767.

[234] Cf *Scullion v Scullion* 1990 SCLR 577.

[235] S 41 also covers the case where the child was temporarily out of England, eg on holiday or at school,
and is not returned when he should have been.

[236] *Re M (Minors) (Residence Order: Jurisdiction)* [1993] 1 FLR 495, the Court of Appeal concluded that
a child who never in his life had left the United Kingdom, having always lived in England or Scotland, was
not habitually resident in either country. The result was that s 41 could not apply and jurisdiction was based
on presence in England. The criticism of this decision seems fully justified: Cretney (1993) 109 LQR 538.
Contrast *Morris v Morris* 1993 SCLR 144.

[237] The English order must precede the removal: *Re E (Child: Abduction)* [1991] FCR 631 at 636; revsd
on other grounds: [1992] 1 FCR 541.

[238] In relation to acquisition of parental responsibility by unmarried fathers and by step-parents, see
Children Act 1989, ss 4 and 4A.

in England for a year from the date he left,[239] or until he becomes sixteen or there is agreement to his living elsewhere.[240] In *Re S (A Child) (Abduction: Residence Order)*[241] the Court of Appeal held that section 41 of the 1986 Act is a deeming provision to resolve conflicts between the constituent parts of the United Kingdom, and not between the United Kingdom and any jurisdiction that is not a constituent part.

Presence This basis of jurisdiction operates, irrespective of the child's nationality,[242] if the child is present in England at the date of the application for the Part I order. The retention of presence as a residual basis of jurisdiction is desirable in order to ensure that a range of appropriate cases may be entertained by the English courts. For example, if a child habitually resident abroad is brought to England against the wishes of the person entitled to exercise parental responsibilities in relation to the child[243] in the country of habitual residence, that person would be deprived of any effective remedy[244] unless the English court took jurisdiction on the basis of the presence of the child in England.[245]

(iii) Jurisdiction to make special guardianship orders, and orders under Adoption and Children Act 2002, section 26

Section 2(2A) of the 1986 Act provides that a court in England and Wales shall not have jurisdiction to make a special guardianship order under the Children Act 1989 unless the condition in section 3 of the 1986 Act is satisfied, ie the child concerned is (a) habitually resident in England and Wales, or (b) is present in England and Wales and is not habitually resident in any part of the United Kingdom, and, in either case, so long as matrimonial proceedings or civil partnership proceedings are not continuing in respect of the marriage or civil partnership of the child's parents in Scotland or Northern Ireland. The same condition applies, by virtue of section 2(2B) of the 1986 Act, to jurisdiction in respect of orders for contact under section 26 of the Adoption and Children Act 2002.

(iv) Jurisdiction to make orders under Adoption and Children Act 2002, section 51(A)

Section 2(2C) of the 1986 Act provides that a court in England and Wales shall not have jurisdiction to make an order under section 51A of the Adoption and Children Act 2002 unless: (a) it has jurisdiction under Brussels II *bis*[246] or the 1996 Hague Convention,[247] or (b) neither Brussels II *bis* nor the 1996 Hague Convention applies but the condition in section 3 is satisfied.[248]

(v) Jurisdiction to make orders in the exercise of the inherent jurisdiction of the High Court[249]

Section 2(3) of the 1986 Act provides that a court in England and Wales shall not have jurisdiction to make an order under section 1(1)(d) of the Family Law Act 1986 (ie, an order in the exercise of the inherent jurisdiction of the High Court so far as it gives care of a child to any person or provides for contact with, or the education of, a child)[250] unless: (a) it has

---

[239] Eg *D v D (Custody: Jurisdiction)* [1996] 1 FLR 574.

[240] Provided in this last case, there has been no contravention of a court order.

[241] [2002] EWCA Civ 1949, [2003] 1 FLR 1008.

[242] *Findlay v Matondo and Secretary of State for the Home Department* [1993] Imm AR 541.

[243] Cf Children Act 1989, ss 2, 3, 4, 4ZA and 4A.

[244] Unless the child could be returned under the provisions of the Child Abduction and Custody Act 1985, infra, p 1134 et seq.

[245] For other examples, see Law Com No 138 (1985), para 4.25. See also *Re P (A Child) (Mirror Orders)* [2000] 1 FLR 435—as a matter of comity and common sense it is desirable to continue the practice of making mirror orders so that the court in one jurisdiction can be confident that there will be redress in another jurisdiction should the parent refuse to comply.

[246] See supra, p 1094 et seq.

[247] See supra, p 1103 et seq.

[248] See supra.

[249] See eg Jones [2015] Fam Law 1371; and Williams *et al* [2016] IFL 239.

[250] Excluding an order varying or revoking such an order: 1986 Act, s 1(1)(d)(ii).

jurisdiction under Brussels II *bis*[251] or the 1996 Hague Convention,[252] or (b) neither Brussels II *bis* nor the 1996 Hague Convention applies but (i) the condition in section 3 of the Act is satisfied,[253] or (ii) the child concerned is present in England on the relevant date,[254] and the court considers that the immediate exercise of its powers is necessary for his protection.[255]

Whilst there is much to be said for a carefully constructed, interlocking set of jurisdictional rules, there is a danger that a hierarchy of jurisdictions may provide too cumbersome a set of rules to deal with those not infrequent, cases, where courts are called upon to act very quickly in matters concerning the welfare of children. To address this difficulty, section 2(3) (b)(ii) of the 1986 Act confers an emergency basis of jurisdiction on a court to make an order in exercise of the inherent jurisdiction of the High Court with regard to children. As the Law Commission noted: "Where a child is in immediate danger, his protection must take precedence over procedural considerations."[256] The effect of section 2(3)(b)(ii) is to allow the inherent jurisdiction of the High Court to be exercised to make such "emergency orders" even though, for example, the child is habitually resident elsewhere in the United Kingdom, or matrimonial proceedings between its parents are continuing in Scotland or Northern Ireland. The exercise of the inherent jurisdiction to make such orders is described as that of the High Court and would seem to be limited to that jurisdiction.[257] The English "emergency order" can be superseded at any time by an order of a court in the country with primacy of jurisdiction.

In relation to wardship proceedings,[258] it is necessary to distinguish between the jurisdictional rules for making orders under the inherent jurisdiction of the High Court giving the care of a child to any person, or providing for contact with, or the education of, a child, which are governed by the Family Law Act 1986,[259] and the jurisdictional rules governing the exercise of the inherent jurisdiction making a child a ward of court. The difference is important because the High Court[260] may make orders under the inherent jurisdiction in wardship proceedings relating to matters other than the care of the child, such as orders as to his property;[261] and, indeed, the jurisdictional rules of the 1986 Act concerning orders as to the care of the child will apply only if the court had had jurisdiction to entertain the original wardship application.[262] Although a child becomes a ward of court on the making of the application,

---

[251] See supra, p 1094.

[252] See supra, p 1103 et seq.

[253] See supra.

[254] The date of application for an order or variation thereof or, where no such application is made, the date on which the court is considering whether to make or, as the case may be, vary the order: 1986 Act, s 7(c). It is irrelevant that the jurisdictional link is later broken.

[255] *H v D* [2007] EWHC 802 (Fam). See also Brussels II *bis*, Art 20, infra, pp 1119–20; and the 1996 Hague Convention, Arts 11 and 12, infra, pp 1121–3.

[256] Law Com No 138 (1985), para 4.19.

[257] 1989 Act, s 8(3)(a). The power to transfer family proceedings from the High Court to the family court, though it includes wardship proceedings, excludes applications for a child to be or cease to be a ward of court and "any proceedings which relate to the exercise of the inherent jurisdiction of the High Court with respect to minors": Matrimonial and Family Proceedings Act 1984, s 38(2)(b).

[258] See Law Com No 138 (1985), para 1.25.

[259] 1986 Act, s 1(1)(d).

[260] Wardship jurisdiction is limited to the High Court. See Senior Courts Act 1981, s 41(1)(1)—subject to the provisions of the Act, no minor can be made a ward of court except by virtue of an order to that effect made by the High Court.

[261] Lowe and Douglas, *Bromley's Family Law*, p 743.

[262] Because s 1(1)(d) refers to orders made in the exercise of the inherent jurisdiction, which latter must be validly established.

the wardship lapses unless a wardship order is made within the prescribed period.[263] After the making of a wardship order the High Court can subsequently order that the child ceases to be a ward of court.[264] The making of a care order, or the child attaining the age of eighteen automatically brings wardship to an end.[265]

The inherent jurisdiction of the High Court to make a child a ward of court is founded on the prerogative power of the Crown acting in its capacity as *parens patriae* to do what is necessary for the welfare of children. It has long been held that this royal prerogative delegated to the courts should benefit those who owe allegiance to the Crown. It has been well established, therefore, that the High Court may exercise this jurisdiction in respect of any British subject[266] aged under eighteen, even though he possesses no property in England and even if he is out of the country at the time of the proceedings.[267] This includes situations where it is necessary to order the return of a British child to the United Kingdom[268] but the 1980 Hague Abduction Convention cannot be utilized, either because the jurisdiction to which the child has been removed, or within which the child is retained, is not a party to the Convention,[269] or because the child has been removed or retained lawfully.[270] The child's interests are likely to require the powers to be invoked in particular where the respondent is in breach of an English court order.[271] Jurisdiction has also been extended to an alien child who, at the time of the proceedings, is either (i) physically present though not domiciled in England,[272] or (ii) ordinarily resident, though not in fact present, in England.[273] The continued existence of inherent jurisdiction was confirmed recently by the Supreme Court, in *In the Matter of A (Children)*.[274] The key issue was whether English courts had jurisdiction to order the return of a British child from Pakistan in circumstances where the child had never lived or even been to the United Kingdom. The Court found that a return order was not a "Part 1 order" within the meaning of the Family Law Act 1986. It fell neither within section 1(1)(a) nor section 1(1)(d) of the 1986 Act, and was therefore not covered by the jurisdictional restrictions in section 2 of that Act, which prohibited the making of an order in wardship proceedings for the care of, or contact with a child.[275] The order was one that related to parental responsibility within the scope of

---

[263] Senior Courts Act 1981, s 41(2). This provision, however, does not apply to a child who is the subject of a care order. Ibid, s 41(2A).

[264] Senior Courts Act 1981, s 41(3).

[265] Children Act 1989, s 91(4) and Family Law Reform Act 1969, Sch 3, para 3 respectively.

[266] Which would probably now mean a "British citizen" within the meaning of the British Nationality Act 1981.

[267] *Hope v Hope* (1854) 4 De G M & G 328; *Re Willoughby* (1885) 30 Ch D 324; *Harben v Harben* [1957] 1 WLR 261; *Re P (GE)* [1965] Ch 568 at 582, 587, 592; *McM v C (No 2)* [1980] 1 NSWLR 27; *Romeyko v Whackett (No 2)* (1980) 25 SASR 531; *Brown v Kalal* (1986) 7 NSWLR 423; *Re B (A Child) (Forced Marriage: Wardship: Jurisdiction)* [2008] EWHC 1436 (Fam); *Re T (A Child)* [2015] EWHC 4050 (Fam); *H v H (Protective Order: Exercise of Jurisdiction)* [2016] EWHC 1252 (Fam); and *JB v D* [2016] EWHC 1607 (Fam). Cf *McM v C* [1980] 1 NSWLR 1; and *Re N (A Child) (Abduction: Appeal)* [2012] EWCA Civ 1086.

[268] *In the Matter of A (Children)* [2013] UKSC 60, at [28]; and *In the Matter of B (A Child)* [2016] UKSC 4, at [58].

[269] *Re H (A Child)* [2013] EWCA Civ 148, per Thorpe LJ, at [8].

[270] *In the Matter of S (A Child)* [2010] EWCA Civ 465, per Wall LJ, at [14].

[271] *JB v D* [2016] EWHC 1607 (Fam), per Hayden J, at [20].

[272] *Re D* [1943] Ch 305; *Re P (GE)* [1965] Ch 568 at 582, 588, 592; *J v C* [1970] AC 668 at 700–701, 720; *Re A* [1970] Ch 665.

[273] *Re P (GE)* [1965] Ch 568 at 584–6; and see *Scheffer v Scheffer* [1967] NZLR 466; *Holden v Holden* [1968] VR 334; *Nielsen v Nielsen* (1970) 16 DLR (3d) 33; *Glasson v Scott* [1973] 1 NSWLR 689; *Re Allison* (1979) 96 DLR (3d) 342; and *Re A (A Child) (Wardship: Habitual Residence)* [2006] EWHC 3338 (Fam), [2007] 1 FCR 390.

[274] [2013] UKSC 60, per Lady Hale, at [60]–[63]. See also *Re KL (Abduction: Habitual Residence: Inherent Jurisdiction)* [2013] UKSC 75, at [28]. Cf *SH v HH* [2011] EWCA Civ 796, per Thorpe LJ, at [52].

[275] *In the Matter of A (Children)* [2013] UKSC 60, at [25]–[28].

Brussels II *bis*,[276] which extended to cases where there was a rival jurisdiction in a non-Member State.[277] Pursuant to Article 14 of Brussels II *bis*, where no court of a Member State has jurisdiction under Articles 8 to 13, jurisdiction should be determined, in each Member State, by the laws of that state. In that respect, the inherent jurisdiction of the High Court could be exercised if the child was a British national.[278] Lady Hale, however, made it clear that there was a difference between the availability of the inherent jurisdiction and its exercise.[279] The case was therefore remitted to the High Court for consideration whether it was appropriate to exercise the jurisdiction in the particular circumstances of the case.[280]

In *Al-H v F*,[281] Lord Justice Thorpe opined that English courts should be extremely circumspect in assuming jurisdiction in relation to children physically present in some other jurisdiction founded only on the basis of nationality, explaining that:

> In order to achieve essential collaboration internationally it has been necessary to relax reliance upon concepts understood only in common law circles. Thus our historic emphasis on the somewhat artificial concept of domicile has had to cede to an acknowledgement that the simpler fact based concept of habitual residence must be the currency of international exchange. The *parens patriae* concept must seem even more esoteric to other jurisdictions than the concept of domicile. If we are to look for reciprocal understanding and co-operation . . . we must refrain from exorbitant jurisdictional claims founded on nationality.[282]

The requirement of "extreme circumspection" in deciding whether to exercise the jurisdiction was quoted with approval by Lady Hale in *In the Matter of A (Children)*.[283] By way of an example, her Ladyship mentioned the following reasons which "may militate against" the exercise of the inherent jurisdiction: 1) inconsistency with the modern trend towards habitual residence as the principal jurisdictional ground; 2) potential for conflicting decisions in competing jurisdictions; 3) disruption of the jurisdictional scheme of the Family Law Act 1986 as the child could be ordered to return to England and then courts would be able to make a variety of orders on the basis of the child's presence; and 4) interference with the rules of public international law concerning the determination of the effective nationality in cases where a person holds dual nationality.[284] All must, however, depend on the circumstances of the particular case.[285] More recently, in *In the Matter of B (A Child)*,[286] the Supreme Court reiterated that the use of the jurisdiction had to be approached with "great caution or circumspection", however, held that its exercise was not restricted to "dire and exceptional" cases[287] or cases which are "at the extreme end

---

[276] Ibid, at [29]. Furthermore, an order warding a child places the child in the guardianship of the High Court and is therefore one of the examples expressly referred to in Art 1(2) of Brussels II *bis*. Ibid.

[277] Ibid, at [30]–[33]. See *Re I (A Child) (Contact Application: Jurisdiction)* [2009] UKSC 10, which concerned a rival jurisdiction in a non-Member State in relation to Art 12 of the Regulation. In the present case, Lady Hale held that there was no reason to distinguish Art 12 from other bases of jurisdiction in Brussels II *bis*. At [30].

[278] *In the Matter of A (Children)* [2013] UKSC 60, at [59].

[279] Ibid, at [63].

[280] Ibid.

[281] [2001] EWCA Civ 186, [2001] 1 FLR 951.

[282] Ibid, at [42].

[283] [2013] UKSC 60, at [65].

[284] Ibid, at [64].

[285] Ibid, at [65].

[286] [2016] UKSC 4.

[287] Ibid, per Lady Hale and Lord Toulson, at [59] (obiter). See *Re B (A Child) (Forced Marriage: Wardship : Jurisdiction)* [2008] EWHC 1436 (Fam), per Hogg J, at [10].

of the spectrum".[288] The real issue was whether the British child required protection.[289]

In the past, orders made by the High Court under the inherent jurisdiction in wardship proceedings were quite often for the appointment of a guardian to a child.[290] The Children Act 1989[291] abolished this power and introduced, both in its place and in place of the previous statutory rules[292] relating to the making of guardianship orders, a statutory regime for the appointment of a guardian under that Act.[293] Guardianship falls now within the scope of both Brussels II *bis*[294] and the 1996 Hague Convention.[295]

(c) Variation and duration of Part I orders

One characteristic of orders relating to the welfare of children is that parents may well return to the courts to claim that their circumstances, or those of the child, have changed and to seek the variation of the order. Such applications inevitably pose jurisdictional problems, such as whether the court which made the original order should retain jurisdiction to vary it, even though in the meantime its jurisdictional link with the child has been broken.[296] The general approach of Part I of the 1986 Act is that the power to vary[297] continues, despite the loss of the jurisdictional link.[298] If, however, a Part I order (or a variation of such an order) made by a court in Scotland or Northern Ireland comes into force with respect to a child at a time when an English Part I order has effect, the original English order shall cease to have effect so far as it makes provision for any matter for which the same or different provision is made by the Scottish or Irish order.[299] Where the original English order ceases to have effect, an English court shall not have jurisdiction to vary that order.[300] Further, an English court shall not have jurisdiction to vary a Part I order if, on the date of application for variation of the order, matrimonial proceedings or civil partnership proceedings are continuing in Scotland or Northern Ireland in respect of the marriage or civil partnership of the parents of the child concerned, unless the original English order was made (a) in connection with divorce or nullity proceedings, or dissolution or annulment proceedings, in respect of the marriage or civil partnership of the parents of the child concerned, and those proceedings are continuing; or (b) in connection with proceedings for a judicial separation or legal separation in respect of the marriage or civil partnership of the parents of the child concerned, and those proceedings are continuing and the decree has not yet been granted.[301] The English court will not lose its

---

[288] *In the Matter of B (A Child)* [2016] UKSC 4, at [60]. See *Re N (A Child) (Abduction: Appeal)* [2012] EWCA Civ 1086, per McFarlane LJ, at [29].

[289] *In the Matter of B (A Child)* [2016] UKSC 4, at [60]. See eg *H v H (Protective Order: Exercise of Jurisdiction)* [2016] EWHC 1252 (Fam); and *JB v D* [2016] EWHC 1607 (Fam). Cf *J v U* [2016] EWHC 2481.

[290] Eg *Hope v Hope* (1854) 4 De G M & G 328; *Re Willoughby* (1885) 30 Ch D 324.

[291] S 5(13). The appointment of a guardian of the estate of a child may be made under the inherent jurisdiction, if so provided by rules of court: Children Act 1989, s 5(11), (12).

[292] Eg the Guardianship of Minors Act 1971.

[293] S 5.

[294] See, eg, *In the Matter of A (Children)* [2013] UKSC 60, at [29].

[295] Art 1(2)(b) and Art 3 *c*) respectively.

[296] The answer in the past was unclear: see Law Com No 138 (1985), para 2.33.

[297] As to what constitutes a variation, see the 1986 Act, ss 6, 42 (5), (6).

[298] Eg *Re S (Residence Order: Forum Conveniens)* [1995] 1 FLR 314.

[299] 1986 Act, s 6(1).

[300] Ibid, s 6(2). See *Re K (A Minor: Wardship: Jurisdiction: Interim Order)* [1991] 2 FLR 104, [1991] Fam Law 226: *T v T (Custody: Jurisdiction)* [1992] 1 FLR 43; *S v S (Custody: Jurisdiction)* [1995] 1 FLR 155; and *A v A (Forum Conveniens)* [1999] 1 FLR 1.

[301] Ibid, s 6(3).

power, in proceedings under the inherent jurisdiction of the High Court, in an emergency to vary a Part I order relating to a child then present in England.[302]

(d) Refusal of application and stay of proceedings

The two main principles underlying the jurisdictional rules—a clear hierarchy of jurisdictional rules, coupled with a desire that an application for an order relating to the welfare of a child is to be heard by the court with the most appropriate links with the issue—are bound at times to come into conflict.

(i) Refusal of application

The power of the English court to refuse an application or to stay proceedings is set out in section 5 of the Family Law Act 1986. Section 5(1) provides that a court in England and Wales which has jurisdiction to make a Part I order may refuse an application for the order in any case where the matter in question has already been determined in proceedings outside England and Wales. This provision is concerned with the case where the issue in question had already been determined in proceedings elsewhere. This situation is separate from that of recognition of any other order. No matter where the other order has been made and irrespective of whether or not it may be recognised and enforced in England, the English court may decline jurisdiction, on any basis, to make a Part I order.[303] The English court is free to take the view that it does not wish to interfere with a decision as to the child's welfare which has already been made.[304]

(ii) Transfer to a court better placed to hear the case—Brussels II bis, Article 15 and the 1996 Hague Convention, Articles 8 and 9[305]

Where, at any stage of the proceedings on an application to a court in England and Wales for a Part I order, or for variation of such an order, it appears to the court that it should exercise its powers under Article 15 of Brussels II *bis* or Articles 8 and 9 of the 1996 Hague Convention, the court may proceed accordingly.

Brussels II *bis*—Article 15[306]

Uniquely in a European private international law Regulation, Brussels II *bis* incorporates what is, in effect, a *forum conveniens* rule.[307] "It is a provision negotiated for the comfort of those jurisdictions who have reservations about the introduction of a strict *lis alibi pendens* rule into family litigation."[308] Article 15(1) provides, by way of exception,[309] and only if it is in the best interests of the child, that the courts of a Member State having jurisdiction as to the substance of the matter may, if they consider that a court of another Member State,

---

[302] Ibid, s 6(5).

[303] S 5(1). This may be very significant where the child has been "kidnapped" from another jurisdiction. The difficulties arising in such cases are discussed more fully, infra, p 1134 et seq.

[304] This general system of interlocking rules makes it very important for the court to be aware of other proceedings which relate to the child, whether in the United Kingdom or elsewhere, including administrative proceedings; see 1986 Act, ss 39, 42(7).

[305] See Gration *et al*, Chapter 5; and Family Procedure Rules 2010, rr 12.66–12.67.

[306] See Family Procedure Rules 2010, rr 12.61–12.66.

[307] This, however, does not mean that traditional *forum conveniens* considerations as known in English law should be imported into the determination of Article 15. Such approach would undermine the objective of a uniform construction of Article 15 throughout the courts of the Member States. *Re T (A Child) (Care Proceedings: Request to Assume Jurisdiction)* [2013] EWCA Civ 895, per Thorpe LJ, at [19].

[308] *Re Clark (A Child)* [2006] EWCA Civ 1115, per Thorpe LJ, at [18].

[309] As regards civil law jurisdictions, "truly exceptional" cases (Thorpe LJ, ibid).

with which the child has a particular connection, would be better placed to hear the case, or a specific part of it:[310] (a) stay the case, or the part in question, and invite the parties to introduce a request before the court of that other Member State, in accordance with Article 15(4); or (b) request a court of another Member State to assume jurisdiction, in accordance with Article 15(5). The court of the other Member State shall be regarded as being better placed to hear the case where the transfer will provide genuine and specific added value to the examination of the case, taking account of, among other factors, the rules of procedure applicable in that State.[311]

The operation of Article 15 may be triggered in one of three ways: by application from a party;[312] of the court's own motion;[313] or upon application from a court of another Member State with which the child has a particular connection,[314] in accordance with Article 15(3). In the case of a transfer made of the court's own motion, or by application of a court of another Member State, the transfer must be accepted by at least one of the parties.[315] In order for a transfer to take place, the child must have a "particular connection" with the "receiving State". By Article 15(3), a child shall be considered to have such a connection if the receiving state: (a) has become the habitual residence of the child after the court of the state of origin was seised; (b) is the former habitual residence of the child; (c) is the place of the child's nationality;[316] (d) is the habitual residence of a holder of parental responsibility;[317] or (e) is the place where the child's property is located and the case concerns measures for the protection of the child relating to the administration, conservation or disposal of this property.

If the court of the state of origin stays the case, or part thereof, and invites the parties to introduce a request before the court of another Member State, Article 15(4) provides that the first court must set a time limit[318] by which the courts of the other Member State shall be seised. If the courts of another Member State have not been seised by that time, the first court shall continue to exercise jurisdiction in accordance with Articles 8 to 14. The courts of the "receiving State" may, where due to the specific circumstances of the case, this is in the best interests of the child, accept jurisdiction within six weeks of their seizure. In this event, the court first seised shall decline jurisdiction. Otherwise, the court first seised shall continue to exercise jurisdiction in accordance with Articles 8 to 14.

---

[310] The transfer of a specific part of a case may be considered in particular where the proximity criterion contained in Art 15(3)(d) applies. Case C-428/15, *Child and Family Agency v J. D.*, [2016] All ER (D) 24 (Nov), at [60].

[311] Case C-428/15, *Child and Family Agency v J. D.*, [2016] All ER (D) 24 (Nov).

[312] See Family Procedure Rules 2010, r 12.62. Eg *Walsall MBC v K* [2013] EWHC 3192 (Fam)—request for a transfer to Slovakia refused; *Re J and S (Care Proceedings: Appeal)* [2014] EWFC 4—request for a transfer to Slovakia refused; *Re A (Children) (Brussels II Revised: Article 15)* [2014] EWFC 40—request for a transfer to the Czech Republic granted; and *Medway Council v JB and others* [2015] EWHC 3064 (Fam)—request for a transfer to Slovakia granted in respect of five out of seven siblings.

[313] Family Procedure Rules 2010, r 12.64. Eg *Bristol City Council v AA and HA* [2014] EWHC 1022 (Fam)—decision to request the transfer of proceedings to Lithuania; and *Barking and Dagenham LBC v C* [2014] EWHC 2472 (Fam)—decision to request the transfer of proceedings to Romania.

[314] Family Procedure Rules, r 12.63. Eg *Re HJ (Transfer of Proceedings)* [2013] EWHC 1867 (Fam)—transfer request from Ireland granted.

[315] Brussels II *bis*, Art 15(2).

[316] Nationality is only one of the "gateways" to establishing the court's jurisdiction to consider making an order under Article 15. Therefore, nationality alone cannot determine whether an order under Article 15 should be made. *Re M (Brussels II Revised: Art 15)* [2014] EWCA Civ 152, per Munby P, at [55].

[317] In circumstances where the relation of proximity between the case and the other Member State does not directly concern the child as such, but one of the holders of parental responsibility, as envisaged in Art 15(3)(d), the court having jurisdiction may consider to request the transfer of a specific part of a case only. See Art 15(1), and Case C-428/15, *Child and Family Agency v J. D.*, [2016] All ER (D) 24 (Nov), at [60].

[318] The Regulation does not prescribe a specific limit.

English courts have highlighted the practical advantages of Article 15 by holding that in every case with a European dimension, the judge must consider whether to exercise powers under this provision to request the court of another Member State to assume jurisdiction where the child has a particular connection with the other Member State as defined in Article 15(3); the other court would be better placed to hear the case; and this is in the child's best interests.[319]

Although an Article 15 request may be made at any stage of the proceedings, from the child welfare perspective it is highly desirable that transfer of jurisdiction be considered and determined at the earliest opportunity during the initial stages of the proceedings.[320]

In order for the transfer mechanism to operate effectively, the courts shall co-operate either directly,[321] or through the Central Authorities designated pursuant to Article 53 of the Regulation.[322] In the event of a transfer under Article 15, the court in the "receiving State" is not allowed to make a further transfer of the case to a third court.[323]

The principles for the interpretation of Article 15 were first set out by English courts in *AB v JLB (Brussels IIR: Art 15)*[324] where Munby J suggested that Article 15 required consideration of three separate questions: (1) whether the child has a particular connection with the other Member State; (2) whether the other court is better placed to hear the case; and (3) whether the transfer is in the child's best interests, the best interests' evaluation being limited to matters of forum. These principles were expressly endorsed by the Court of Appeal in *Re M (Brussels II Revised: Art 15)*.[325] In this decision, the Court also analysed the relationship between Article 15 and Article 12 of the Brussels II *bis*, holding that the scope of any best interests' enquiry when deciding whether to make a transfer request under Article 15 should be the same as when determining jurisdiction under Article 12. Importantly, such inquiry should not involve any in-depth investigation of the child's situation and upbringing but rather should be an "attenuated"[326] one with focus on the considerations relevant to the choice of the forum, which informed the considerations that came into play when deciding upon the most appropriate forum.

In *Re N (Children) (Adoption: Jurisdiction) (AIRE Centre and others intervening)*,[327] the traditional approach to Article 15 applications as outlined above was rejected by the Supreme

---

[319] *Re J (A Child: Brussels II Revised: Art 15: Practice and Procedure)* [2014] EWFC 41, at [1]; and *Re E (A Child) (Care Proceedings: Jurisdiction)* [2014] EWHC 6 (Fam), at [31].

[320] See *Re M (Brussels II Revised: Art 15)* [2014] EWCA Civ 152, per Ryder LJ, at [32] and Munby P, at [58]. This was reiterated in *Re J (A Child: Brussels II Revised: Art 15: Practice and Procedure)* [2014] EWFC 41, per Pauffley J, at [36]; and noted and applied in a number of first instance decisions eg *Leicester City Council v S* [2014] EWHC 1575 (Fam); *Re J and S (Care Proceedings: Appeal)* [2014] EWFC 4; and *Bristol City Council v AA and HA* [2014] EWHC 1022 (Fam).

[321] See, on the practicalities, *Practice Guide*, para 3.3.4. See eg *Re S (Jurisdiction: Prorogation)* [2013] EWHC 647 (Fam), at [38]–[39]; *Re B (A Child) (Care Proceedings: Jurisdiction)* [2013] EWCA Civ 1434, at [34]–[35] (international judicial co-operation); and *Re E (A Child) (Care Proceedings: Jurisdiction)* [2014] EWHC 6 (Fam), at [38]–[41] (the role of the Vienna Convention in public proceedings involving Article 15).

[322] Brussels II *bis*, Art 15(6).

[323] Ibid, Recital (13).

[324] [2008] EWHC 2965 (Fam).

[325] [2014] EWCA Civ 152. See also *Re T (Brussels II Revised: Art 15)* [2013] EWCA Civ 895; *A v D* [2014] EWHC 3851 (Fam); *Re J (A Child: Brussels II Revised: Art 15: Practice and Procedure)* [2014] EWFC 41; *A Local Authority v MGM* [2014] EWHC 1221 (Fam); *Bristol City Council v AA and HA* [2014] EWHC 1022 (Fam); *Norfolk CC v VE* [2015] EWFC 30; *Hertfordshire CC v LC* [2015] EWHC 1617 (Fam); *Re N (Children) (Adoption: Jurisdiction)* [2014] EWFC 45; and *Medway Council v JB and others* [2015] EWHC 3064 (Fam).

[326] This term was originally used by Mostyn J in his judgment in *Re T (A Child: Art 15, Brussels II Revised)* [2013] EWHC 521 (Fam), at [21].

[327] [2016] UKSC 15. See Trimmings (2016) 75 Cambridge Law Journal 471–4.

Court. In particular, Lady Hale held that the best interests' assessment should not be "attenuated" but rather it should involve an inquiry into important welfare factors. In particular, as a part of the best interests' assessment, the court should take account of the long as well as short-term consequences for the child of transferring the proceedings, and the impact of the transfer on the choices that would be available to the court reaching the eventual substantive outcome in the case. Importantly, it is to be noted that the proposed approach does not advocate a full welfare enquiry in transfer proceedings.[328] It strikes a sensible balance between a plain forum-type assessment and a full welfare enquiry in transfer proceedings, guarding wisely against a full welfare inquiry at the jurisdiction stage of the proceedings, whilst providing safeguards against "inappropriate" transfers, for example in situations where the court of the other Member State would not be able to consider one of the possible outcomes for the child.

The CJEU has clarified that in determining that a transfer is in the best interests of the child, the court having jurisdiction must be satisfied, especially, that the transfer is not likely to be detrimental to the situation of the child.[329] The effect of a transfer on the right of freedom of movement of persons concerned other than the child is irrelevant, unless disregarding such considerations may have adverse repercussions on the situation of the child.[330]

The transfer of jurisdiction under Article 15 is confined to specific "live" proceedings before a court of a Member State, not to its jurisdiction in respect of parental responsibility for the child generally.[331]

As evidenced by recent Article 15 jurisprudence,[332] the provision is often triggered in public law proceedings. In such circumstances, Article 15 exercise does not allow an evaluation of the child protection services of the other Member State, which are presumed to be equally competent.[333]

The 1996 Hague Convention—Articles 8 and 9

A mechanism for the transfer of jurisdiction, akin to that contained in Article 15 of Brussels II *bis*,[334] is set out in Articles 8 and 9, and operates by way of exception and in the best interests of the child.[335] The Explanatory Report to the Convention explains that "[t]hese Articles introduce into the Convention a reversible mechanism for forum non conveniens and forum conveniens, where it appears that the child's best interest is that his or her protection be ensured by authorities other than those of the State of the habitual residence".[336] The transfer of jurisdiction under the Convention can be initiated either by an authority of a Contracting State having general jurisdiction under the Convention, if this authority considers that an authority of a Contracting State which does not have jurisdiction would be better

---

[328] See *Re N (Children) (Adoption: Jurisdiction) (AIRE Centre and others intervening* [2016] UKSC 15, per Lady Hale, at [57]—the best interests' exercise for the purposes of Article 15 is a "different question from what eventual outcome to the case will be in the child's best interests".

[329] Case C-428/15, *Child and Family Agency v J. D.*, [2016] All ER (D) 24 (Nov).

[330] Ibid.

[331] *Re S (Jurisdiction: Prorogation)* [2013] EWHC 647 (Fam), at [36]; and *Re HA (A Child) (Brussels IIA Art 15)* [2015] EWHC 1310 (Fam).

[332] Eg *Walsall MBC v K* [2013] EWHC 3192 (Fam); *Re J and S (Care Proceedings: Appeal)* [2014] EWFC 4; *Re A (Children) (Brussels II Revised: Article 15)* [2014] EWFC 40; *Bristol City Council v AA and HA* [2014] EWHC 1022 (Fam); and *Barking and Dagenham LBC v C* [2014] EWHC 2472 (Fam).

[333] See *Re K (A Child)* [2013] EWCA Civ 895, per Thorpe LJ, at [24]; and *Re M (Brussels II Revised: Art 15)* [2014] EWCA Civ 152, per Ryder LJ, at [19].

[334] Supra.

[335] Eg *JA v TH* [2016] EWHC 2535 (Fam).

[336] Lagarde, *Explanatory Report*, para 52.

placed in the particular case to assess the best interests of the child;[337] or by an authority of a Contracting State which does not have jurisdiction but believes that it is better placed in the particular case to assess the best interests of the child.[338] In either scenario, the following conditions have to be met before the transfer can take place: 1) Connection between the child and the Contracting State to which jurisdiction is to be transferred;[339] 2) The authority of the other Contracting State would be better placed in the particular case to assess the best interests of the child;[340] and 3) Both authorities agree to the transfer.[341] The transfer of jurisdiction can be for an entire case or for a specific part of a case,[342] and does not institute a permanent transfer.[343]

Given the close similarities between the transfer provisions of the Brussels II *bis* and the 1996 Convention, it may be expected that English courts will approach the interpretation of the two sets of provisions in a comparable way.

(iii) Concurrent proceedings in another European Union Member State, except Denmark—Brussels II bis, Article 19[344]

Article 15 of Brussels II *bis* concerns "consecutive" rather than "concurrent" proceedings. The rule in respect of concurrent, or parallel, proceedings in two or more European Union Member States is contained in Article 19[345] (lis pendens and dependent actions), which provides that:

2. Where proceedings relating to parental responsibility relating to the same child[346] and involving the same cause of action are brought before courts of different Member States, the court second seised shall of its own motion stay its proceedings until such time as the jurisdiction of the court first seised is established . . ..
3. Where the jurisdiction of the court first seised is established, the court second seised shall decline jurisdiction in favour of that court. In that case, the party who brought the relevant action before the court second seised may bring that action before the court first seised.

Articles 8 to 14 of Brussels II *bis*, by nature, may confer jurisdiction on the courts of more than one Member State in respect of the same child and the same cause of action, and so there is a need for a provision dealing with the problem of concurrent proceedings and conflicting judgments in the courts of different Member States.[347] Article 19, like Article 29 of the Brussels I Recast, but unlike Article 15 of Brussels II *bis*, is a purely mechanical rule. The court of the Member State first seised of the matter takes priority, and any court of another

---

[337] Art 8.

[338] Art 9.

[339] Arts 8(2) and 9(1). The Contracting State must be one of the following: a State of which the child is a national; a State in which property of the child is located; a State whose authorities are seised of an application for divorce or legal separation of the child's parents, or for an annulment of their marriage; a State with which the child has a substantial connection. Cf Brussels II *bis*, Art 15(3).

[340] Arts 8(1) and 9(1). Cf Brussels II *bis*, Art 15(1).

[341] Arts 8(4) and 9(3).

[342] *Practical Handbook*, para 5.5. Cf Brussels II *bis*, Art 15(1).

[343] *Practical Handbook*, para 5.7, and Lagarde, *Explanatory Report*, para 56.

[344] Cf 1996 Hague Convention, Art 13, infra, pp 1120–1. See Family Procedure Rules 2010, r 12.68.

[345] See eg *A v B (Jurisdiction)* [2011] EWHC 2752 (Fam); *Re C* [2012] EWHC 907 (Fam); and *Re G (Jurisdiction: Art 19 BIIR)* [2014] EWCA Civ 680.

[346] Perhaps surprisingly, there is no requirement in Art 19 that parental responsibility matters in respect of two or more children of the same family are to be determined in the same proceedings in the same Member State.

[347] Cf in relation to civil and commercial matters, Brussels I Recast, Art 29. See supra, p 443 et seq.

Member State must of its own motion decline jurisdiction, once the jurisdiction of the court first seised is established in that state. The rule as to the time at which a court is seised is set out in Article 16 (Seising of a Court), examined earlier in relation to concurrent matrimonial proceedings.[348] Although the court second seised must decline jurisdiction, there is scope, nonetheless, in a suitable case,[349] for application to be made by that court to the court first seised for a transfer in terms of Article 15.[350]

By Article 17 where a court of a Member State is seised of a case over which it has no jurisdiction and over which a court of another Member State has jurisdiction by virtue of Brussels II *bis*, then it shall declare of its own motion that it has no jurisdiction.[351] Although Article 17 does not impose a consequential obligation on the original court to transfer the case to another court, the original court should, as long as the protection of the best interests of the child so requires, inform directly or through its Central Authority, the court of the Member State having jurisdiction.[352]

Importantly, Article 19(2) is not applicable where a court of a Member State first seised is seised only for the purpose of making provisional measures within the meaning of Article 20 of Brussels II *bis*.[353] In other words, provisional measures made under Article 20, since they are not capable of recognition in another Member State under the Regulation, cannot give rise to *lis pendens* within the meaning of Article 19(2). However, proceedings pending before a court whose jurisdiction is based on Articles 8 to 14, and which is first seised of an action relating to parental responsibility over a child, irrespective of the characterisation of the proceedings according to the national law of that Member State and irrespective of whether the measure is sought on a provisional basis, or whether it is sought for a definite or indefinite period, prevent a court in another Member State from ruling on the same cause of action until the court first seised has established that it has jurisdiction.[354] Nevertheless, the best interests of the child principle requires that there is a limit as to how long the court second seised should be expected to wait for the information from which it can determine whether it can assume jurisdiction.[355] Although this approach enables the court second seised to end the stalemate in the proceedings, there is a risk that, eventually, conflicting judgments emerge from the proceedings.

Article 19 is limited to concurrent proceedings in different Member States. It does not apply to actions proceeding concurrently in England and in a non-Member State country. Where the non-Member State is a Contracting State to the 1996 Hague Protection

---

[348] Supra, pp 969–70.

[349] Ie where the child in question has a "particular connection" with the Member State whose court was second seised: Art 15(2)(c) and (3).

[350] Supra, pp 1113–16. Cf *A v B (Jurisdiction)* [2011] EWHC 2752 (Fam). Nevertheless, there is no obligation to transfer a case following an Article 17 declaration.

[351] See *W v W (Preliminary Issue: Stay of Petition)* [2002] EWHC 3049, [2003] 1 FLR 1022; *Rogers-Headicar v Rogers-Headicar* [2004] EWCA Civ 1867, [2005] 2 FCR 1; *L-K v K (Brussels II Revised: Maintenance Pending Suit)* [2006] EWHC 153 (Fam), [2006] 2 FLR 1113; *Moore v Moore* [2007] EWCA Civ 361, [2007] IL Pr 36; *Re S (A Child) (Care Proceedings: Jurisdiction)* [2008] EWHC 3013 (Fam); *Re B (A Child) (Care Proceedings: Jurisdiction)* [2013] EWCA Civ 1434; *L v C (Applications by a Non-Biological Mother)* [2014] EWFC 1280; and *In the Matter of D (Habitual residence)* 2014 WL 7254970.

[352] Case C-523/07, *Proceedings Brought by A* [2009] ECR I-02805.

[353] Infra, pp 1119–20. Case C-296/10, *Bianca Purrucker v Guillermo Vallés Pérez (No 2)*, [2010] ECR I-11163. The same holds true for return proceedings under the 1980 Hague Abduction Convention as such proceedings do not concern the substantive issue of parental responsibility and hence have "neither the same object nor the same cause of action as an action seeking a ruling on parental responsibility". Case C-376/14 PPU, *C v M*, [2014] All ER (D) 160 (Oct), at [40].

[354] Case C-296/10, *Bianca Purrucker v Guillermo Vallés Pérez (No 2)*, [2010] ECR I-11163.

[355] Ibid.

Convention, Article 13 of the Convention will come into play.[356] In cases involving third States (ie those that are neither EU-Member States nor Contracting States to the 1996 Convention), an English court will continue to employ traditional rules based upon the doctrine of *forum conveniens*, and given statutory expression in section 5 of the Family Law Act 1986.[357]

Brussels II *bis*, Article 20 (provisional, including protective, measures)[358]
Article 20 of Brussels II *bis* provides that:

1. In urgent cases, the provisions of this Regulation shall not prevent the courts of a Member State from taking such provisional, including protective, measures in respect of persons or assets in that State as may be available under the law of that Member State, even if, under this Regulation, the court of another Member State has jurisdiction as to the substance of the matter.
2. The measures referred to in paragraph 1 shall cease to apply when the court of the Member State having jurisdiction under this Regulation as to the substance of the matter has taken the measures it considers appropriate.[359]

This rule, which is not subject to the jurisdictional rules of Brussels II *bis*, and does not require that provisional measures be taken (but rather gives a discretion to certain courts), has been examined already in the context of matrimonial proceedings.[360] The Article provides the courts of all European Union Member States with an emergency jurisdiction. The Practice Guide offers the following example of the utility of Article 20:

> A family is travelling by car from Member State A to Member State B on their summer holiday. Once arrived in Member State B, they are victims of a traffic accident, where they are all injured. This child is only slightly injured, but both parents arrive at the hospital in a state of coma. The authorities of Member State B urgently need to take certain provisional measures to protect the child who has no relatives in Member State B. The fact that the courts of Member State A have jurisdiction under the Regulation as to the substance does not prevent the courts or competent authorities of Member State B from deciding, on a provisional basis, to take measures to protect the child. These measures cease to apply once the courts of Member State A have taken a decision.[361]

Article 20 should not be used illegitimately to seise jurisdiction validly vested in the first court.[362] The CJEU has explained that Article 20 applies to "children who have their habitual residence in one Member State but stay temporarily or intermittently in another Member State and are in a situation likely seriously to endanger their welfare, including their health or their development, thereby justifying the immediate adoption of protective measures".[363] In *Proceedings Brought by A*,[364] the Court clarified the requirements that must

---

[356] Infra, pp 1120–1.
[357] Infra, p 1124.
[358] Cf Hague Protection Convention, Arts 11 and 12, infra, pp 1121–3.
[359] See also Brussels II *bis*, Recital (16).
[360] Supra, pp 971–2.
[361] *Practice Guide*, para 3.1.3. Another instance, suggested by Nicholas Mostyn QC in *Re ML and AL (Children) (Contact Order: Brussels II Regulation) (No 1)* [2006] EWHC 2385 (Fam), [2007] 1 FCR 475, at [35], is where there is evidence that children are about to be removed from the second state in order to frustrate the enforcement of a contact order there; the court of that state would be well justified in making an Art 20 order preventing the removal pending enforcement of the contact order.
[362] *Re ML and AL (Children) (Contact Order: Brussels II Regulation) (No 1)* [2006] EWHC 2385 (Fam), [2007] 1 FCR 475.
[363] Case C-92/12, *Health Service Executive v SC and AC*, [2012] 2 FLR 1040, at [131].
[364] Case C-523/07, *Proceedings Brought by A* [2009] ECR I-02805.

be met before the power under Article 20 can be exercised by national courts: 1) the measure must be urgent;[365] 2) it must be taken in respect of persons or assets in the Member State concerned;[366] and 3) it must be provisional. Article 20 allows courts to take a variety of measures, including an interim order placing a child in an institutional care;[367] and an interim care order.[368] However, Article 20 does not extend to situations where a court purporting to act under Article 20 grants custody to one parent where a court of another Member State, which has jurisdiction under the Regulation as to the substance of the dispute, has already provisionally granted custody of the child to the other parent, and that judgment has been declared enforceable in the territory of the former Member State.[369] Provisional measures made under Article 20 are not capable of recognition in another Member State within the meaning of Article 21 of Brussels II *bis*[370] and, as such, cannot give rise to *lis pendens* within the meaning of Article19(2).[371] The measures cease to apply when the court of the Member State having jurisdiction as to the substance of the matter has taken the measures it considers appropriate.[372] There is no obligation for the national court that has taken the provisional measure to transfer the case to the court of another Member State which has jurisdiction but, as far as required by the child's best interests, it should inform that court.[373]

The emergency jurisdiction can be compared to the making of orders by a court in England and Wales in the exercise of the inherent jurisdiction of the High Court.[374] It has already been noted that the inherent jurisdiction of the High Court can operate in cases where the court has jurisdiction under Brussels II *bis*.[375] In relation to the operation of protective emergency jurisdiction by a court in England, the demarcation between these two bases of jurisdiction is not entirely clear. Arguably, Article 20 of Brussels II *bis* confers wider powers than does section 1(1)(d) of the 1986 Act to protect not only the person, but also the assets, of a child.

---

[365] The concept of urgency relates to the situation of the child and the impossibility in practice of bringing the parental responsibility application before the court with jurisdiction as to the substance. Case C-403/09 PPU, *Detiček v Sgueglia* [2009] ECR I-12193.

[366] A provisional measure ordering a change of custody of a child is a measure taken not only in respect of the child, but also in respect of the left-behind parent. Case C-403/09 PPU, *Detiček v Sgueglia* [2009] ECR I-12193. This interpretation of the geographical element of Art 20 by the Court seems unconvincing as, taking this to the extreme, there could then never be any interim orders in respect of a child where one parent is in another country.

[367] Eg *HSE Ireland v SF* [2012] EWHC 1640 (Fam). See also Case C-92/12, *Health Service Executive v SC and AC*, [2012] 2 FLR 1040, para 132.

[368] Eg *Re S (A Child) (Care Proceedings: Jurisdiction)* [2008] EWHC 3013. See also Case C-523/07, *Proceedings Brought by A* [2009] ECR I-02805.

[369] Case C-403/09 PPU, *Detiček v Sgueglia* [2009] ECR I-12193.

[370] Infra, p 1127. Case C-256/09, *Bianca Purrucker v Guillermo Vallés Pérez*, [2010] ECR I-07353. Cf 1996 Hague Protection Convention, Art 11, infra, pp 1121–3. But see Commission Proposal for the Recast of Brussels II *bis*, COM (2016) 411 final 30 June 2016, p 22—"provisional, including protective measures, in urgent cases, should be recognised and enforced in all other Member States including the Member States having jurisdiction under this Regulation until a competent authority of such a Member State has taken the measures it considers appropriate".

[371] Supra, p 1118. Case C-296/10, *Bianca Purrucker v Guillermo Vallés Pérez (No 2)*, [2010] ECR I-11163.

[372] Case C-523/07, *Proceedings Brought by A* [2009] ECR I-02805, para 48; and Case C-92/12, *Health Service Executive v SC and AC*, [2012] 2 FLR 1040, para 131.

[373] Case C-523/07, *Proceedings Brought by A* [2009] ECR I-02805. See also Commission Proposal for the Recast of Brussels II *bis*, COM (2016) 411 final 30 June 2016, p 39.

[374] Family Law Act 1986, s 2(3).

[375] Ibid, s 2(3)(a).

(iv) Concurrent proceedings in a Contracting State to the 1996 Hague Protection Convention—Article 13[376]

Like Brussels II *bis*, the Convention adopts a principle of priority of process (*lis pendens*) to resolve problems of conflicting jurisdiction.[377] Pursuant to Article 13(1), the authorities of a Contracting State which have jurisdiction under Articles 5–10[378] must refrain from exercising jurisdiction if, at the time of the commencement of the proceedings, corresponding measures[379] have been requested from the authorities of another Contracting State with jurisdiction under Articles 5–10, and these measures are still under consideration. The Explanatory Report to the Convention envisages that the most common concurrent jurisdiction will be the one of the divorce court.[380] By Article 13(2), however, the *lis pendens* provision of Article 13(1) does not apply if the authorities of the Contracting State initially seised have declined jurisdiction, giving thus priority to the authorities of the Contracting State second seised, if it is regarded as a more appropriate forum.[381] The *Practical Handbook* suggests that where the authority first seised is contemplating renouncing jurisdiction under Article 13(2), communication should take place between the two Contracting States in order to ensure that no gap in the protection of the child ensues. Such a gap could result from the refusal of the authority second seised to exercise jurisdiction on the basis of Article 13(1), and a parallel renunciation of jurisdiction under Article 13(2) by the authority first seised.[382]

The renunciation of jurisdiction by the authority first seised may resemble the transfer of jurisdiction pursuant to Articles 8 and 9. The Explanatory Report, however, clarifies that the key difference between the two procedures is that the former results in jurisdiction being eventually assumed by an authority with general jurisdiction under Articles 5–10.[383] In contrast, Articles 8 and 9 envisage the transfer of jurisdiction to authorities which do not themselves have jurisdiction. Unlike the transfer of jurisdiction under Articles 8 ad 9, the renunciation of jurisdiction under Art 13(2) may result from a unilateral decision of the authority first seised.[384] The Explanatory Report states that the possibility envisaged in Article 13(2) "gives to the solution of the conflict a greater flexibility than that which is authorised by the technique of lis pendens".[385]

The 1996 Hague Protection Convention, Articles 11 and 12 (provisional, including protective, measures)[386]

Article 11 represents a derogation from the general rules of jurisdiction under the Convention; and therefore needs to be interpreted "rather strictly".[387] The provision provides for an additional jurisdictional ground[388] which allows the authorities of a Contracting State in whose

---

[376] Cf Brussels II *bis*, Art 19, supra, pp 1117–19. See Family Procedure Rules 2010, r 12.68.

[377] Art 13.

[378] Notably, Article 13(1) does not apply to measures taken under Article 11 (cases of urgency) or Article 12 (provisional measures). See also *Practical Handbook*, para 4.34. Cf Brussels II *bis*, Art 19, supra, pp 1117–19.

[379] The two requests must be "the same or similar in substance". *Practical Handbook*, para 4.31. See also Lagarde, *Explanatory Report*, para 79.

[380] Lagarde, *Explanatory Report*, para 78.

[381] Lagarde, *Explanatory Report*, para 80. See also *Practical Handbook*, para 4.33.

[382] *Practical Handbook*, para 4.33.

[383] Lagarde, *Explanatory Report*, para 80. See also *Practical Handbook*, para 4.33.

[384] Ibid.

[385] Lagarde, *Explanatory Report*, para 80.

[386] Cf Brussels II *bis*, Art 20, supra, pp 1119–20.

[387] Lagarde, *Explanatory Report*, para 68.

[388] In contrast, Brussels to *bis*, Art 20, gives only an "ancillary power". *Re J (A Child) (1996 Hague Convention: Morocco)* [2015] UKSC 70, per Lady Hale, at [29].

territory the child or property belonging to the child[389] is present to take, in cases of urgency, any necessary measures of protection.[390] At first sight, Article 11 resembles Article 6 of the Convention,[391] however, the two provisions differ in at least two significant respects. First, unlike Article 6, Article 11 covers not only refugee/displaced children, or children without a habitual residence; and second, Article 11 jurisdiction is limited to situations of urgency, as opposed to general jurisdiction in respect of refugee/displaced children, or children without a habitual residence under Article 6.[392] "Urgency" in this context is a functional concept[393] and therefore is not defined in the Convention. However, the Explanatory Report suggests that an urgent situation within the meaning of Article 11 arises where "if remedial action were only sought through the normal channels of Articles 5 to 10, might bring about irreparable harm for the child".[394] The *Practical Handbook* provides further guidance, recommending the authorities that contemplate exercising jurisdiction under Article 11 "to consider whether the child is likely to suffer irreparable harm or to have his / her protection or interests compromised if a measure is not taken to protect the child in the period that is likely to elapse before the authorities with general jurisdiction under Articles 5 to 10 can take the necessary measures of protection".[395] There are three elements to Article 11—presence, necessity and urgency. Accordingly, the court is required to ask itself three questions: 1) Is the child here? 2) Are measures of protection necessary? and 3) Are they urgent?[396] The provision is to be applied according to its terms, meaning that the order in which the three questions are asked may differ.[397]

Article 11 can be invoked for example[398] in order to facilitate medical treatment to save the life of the child who is away from his or her habitual residence;[399] to make a speedy sale of perishable goods that belong to the child;[400] to facilitate interim contact between the child and the left-behind parent pending return proceedings under the 1980 Hague Abduction Convention;[401] and to facilitate, through a "safe harbour order", a safe return of the child following the making of a return order under the 1980 Convention, securing thus a valuable "soft landing"[402] for the child upon the return to the country of his or her habitual residence.[403] In *Re J (A Child) (1996 Hague Convention: Morocco)*[404] the Supreme Court held that Article 11 extended to the making of a return order in the situation of a wrongful removal or retention to which the 1980 Convention does not apply.[405]

---

[389] The jurisdictional ground can be relied on even if the child's ownership of the property is being contested. Lagarde, *Explanatory Report*, para 70.

[390] Art 11(1).

[391] See, supra, p 1105.

[392] See Lagarde, *Explanatory Report*, para 69.

[393] Ibid, para 70.

[394] Ibid, para 68.

[395] *Practical Handbook*, para 6.2.

[396] *Re J (A Child) (1996 Hague Convention: Morocco)* [2015] UKSC 70, at [33].

[397] Ibid.

[398] For additional examples see *Practical Handbook*, paras 6.4 and 6.12.

[399] Lagarde, *Explanatory Report*, para 68.

[400] Ibid.

[401] *Practical Handbook*, para 6.12.

[402] *Re J (A Child) (1996 Hague Convention: Morocco)* [2015] UKSC 70, at [31].

[403] See *Practical Handbook*, para 6.4; and *Conclusions and Recommendations and Report of Part I of the Sixth Meeting of the Special Commission on the Practical Operation of the 1980 Hague Child Abduction Convention and the 1996 Hague Child Protection Convention* (1–10 June 2011), Annex 1, para 41. See also *Re Y (Abduction: Undertakings Given for Return of Child)* [2013] EWCA Civ 129; *B v B* [2014] EWHC 1804 (Fam); and *RB v DB* [2015] EWHC 1817 (Fam).

[404] [2015] UKSC 70. See also Devereux [2016] IFL 21.

[405] *Re J (A Child) (1996 Hague Convention: Morocco)* [2015] UKSC 70, at [38]. The 1980 Convention did not apply in the present case as, although Morocco had acceded to the Convention, its accession has not been accepted by the EU on behalf of the Member States (see Opinion 1/13 of the CJEU).

This interpretation finds support in the fact that the Convention provides for wrongful removal and retention in its Article 7.[406] Moreover, the approach adopted by the Supreme Court accords with the general ground of jurisdiction within the Convention as it reinforces the principle that the child's future should be determined by the authorities of the child's state of habitual residence. Indeed, "[f]ar from derogating from the jurisdiction of the home state in these circumstances, the use of article 11 would be supporting it".[407] Although an abduction case which is governed solely by the 1996 Convention will not necessarily be one of "urgency", it is hard to foresee a situation in which the court should not regard it to be so.[408]

The measures of protection taken under Article 11 are entitled to recognition and enforcement in accordance with Chapter IV of the Convention,[409] and lapse as soon as necessary measures have been taken by the authorities of the Contracting State with general jurisdiction.[410] There is no obligation for the authority that has taken the measures under Article 11 to transfer the case to the authorities of a Contracting State with general jurisdiction, however, it is recommended that the authority which has taken the measures communicates and cooperates with any other State it deems necessary in order to safeguard the sustained protection of the child.[411]

Although Article 11 strikingly resembles Article 20 of Brussels II *bis*, it has been held that the CJEU case-law on the interpretation of Article 20 can provide only a limited assistance in the interpretation of Article 11.[412]

By Article 12, authorities of a Contracting State in whose territory the child or property belonging to the child is present can, in non-urgent situations, assume jurisdiction to take measures of a provisional character for the protection of the person or property of the child. Unlike measures taken under Article 11, "Article 12 measures" have a territorial effect limited to the Contracting State in question,[413] and must be compatible with measures taken previously by authorities with general jurisdiction under Articles 5 to 10. The power to act under Article 12 is unavailable in cases of child abduction. In particular, authorities of the Contracting State to which the child has been wrongfully removed, or in which the child has been wrongfully retained, cannot take provisional measures under Article 12 if the Contracting State from which the child was wrongfully removed or retained still has

---

[406] Ibid, at [38].

[407] Ibid.

[408] Ibid, at [39].

[409] *Practical Handbook*, para 6.12, and Lagarde, *Explanatory Report*, para 72. See, in particular, Art 23, infra, pp 1130–1. In this respect Art 11 measures differ from provisional measures taken under Art 20 of Brussels II *bis*. See C-256/09, *Bianca Purrucker v Guillermo Vallés Pérez*, [2010] ECR I-07353, supra, pp 1120. However, see, Commission Proposal for the Recast of Brussels II *bis*, COM (2016) 411 final 30 June 2016, p 22—it is proposed that provisional, including protective measures, be entitled to recognition and enforcement under the Regulation.

[410] Art 11(2). For the position where the child is habitually resident in a non-Contracting State, see Art 11(3), and Lagarde, *Explanatory Report*, para 73. Cf Brussels II *bis*, Case C-523/07, *Proceedings Brought by A* [2009] ECR I-02805, para 48; and Case C-92/12, *Health Service Executive v SC and AC*, [2012] 2 FLR 1040, para 131, supra, p 1120.

[411] *Practical Handbook*, para 6.10. See also Lagarde, *Explanatory Report*, para 72. Cf Brussels II *bis*, Case C-523/07, *Proceedings Brought by A* [2009] ECR I-02805, supra, p 1120.

[412] In *Re J (A Child) (1996 Hague Convention: Morocco)* [2015] UKSC 70, at [28].

[413] As a result, the *lis pendens* rules set out in Art 13 of the Convention do not apply to provisional measures taken under Art 12. In this respect, these measures resemble protective measures under Art 20 of Brussels II *bis*. See C-256/09, *Bianca Purrucker v Guillermo Vallés Pérez*, [2010] ECR I-07353; and Case C-296/10, *Bianca Purrucker v Guillermo Vallés Pérez (No 2)*, [2010] ECR I-11163, supra, p 1118.

jurisdiction.[414] Like Article 11 measures, the measures under Article 12 lapse as soon as the authorities with general jurisdiction under Articles 5 to 10 have taken a decision required by the situation.[415]

(v) Concurrent proceedings in a related United Kingdom jurisdiction

The question whether the jurisdiction provisions of Brussels II *bis* should be interpreted as operating so as to allocate jurisdiction among the territorial units of the United Kingdom has been considered previously in this chapter.[416] A similar interpretative difficulty arises in connection with the manner of treatment of concurrent proceedings in different territorial units of the United Kingdom. Article 19(2) (lis pendens) of Brussels II *bis* refers to the "courts of different Member States", an expression to which no reference is made in Article 66. If, as has been submitted is appropriate, the rules of allocation of jurisdiction contained in Brussels II *bis* are taken to apply so as to allocate jurisdiction to disputes within the United Kingdom, then it would be illogical to provide that concurrent proceedings in a related United Kingdom jurisdiction should be resolved by any means other than by the *lis pendens* rule set out in Article 19. If, however, an expansive interpretation of this sort is to be taken in respect of Article 19, then the same should be true also of Article 15, providing for the availability in such cases of the transfer mechanism,[417] by way of exception and in the best interests of the child.

(vi) Concurrent proceedings outside England and Wales, other than in another European Union Member State (except Denmark) or a Contracting State to the 1996 Hague Protection Convention

Where, at any stage of the proceedings on an application to a court in England and Wales for a Part I order, or for variation of such an order, it appears to the court that proceedings with respect to the same matter are continuing outside England and Wales; or that it would be more appropriate for those matters to be determined outside England and Wales, the court may stay the proceedings.[418] This flexibility is particularly relevant where there are two sets of proceedings continuing simultaneously, but no Part I order has been made in either. This could happen, for example, where proceedings are started in England for a Part I order, in relation to a child who is habitually resident in England, followed by divorce proceedings in a third State (ie a jurisdiction which is neither an EU-Member State nor a Contracting State to the 1996 Hague Convention) where the father is habitually resident. In such a case, the English court has a power to stay its proceedings if it thinks it appropriate to do so. It seems clear that "appropriateness" is not directly concerned with the welfare of the child, but rather with the suitability of the court to entertain the proceedings.[419] This was certainly the view of the Law Commission who gave,[420] as an example of appropriate circumstances for a waiver of jurisdiction, the case where a divorce had been granted in England five years earlier, with no application for an order relating to a child, but where, at the time of the later application

---

[414] See Arts 12(1) and 7(3).

[415] Art 12(2). For the position where the child is habitually resident in a non-Contracting State, see Art 12(3), and Lagarde, *Explanatory Report*, para 77.

[416] Supra, pp 1100–1.

[417] Supra, pp 1113–16.

[418] S 5(2)(b); see, eg, *Hill v Hill* 1990 SCLR 238, OH. It can also lift the stay as appropriate: s 5(3).

[419] See *Spiliada Maritime Corpn v Cansulex Ltd* [1987] AC 460 at 474–5; *A v A (Forum Conveniens)* [1999] 1 FLR 1; and *Re K (A Child)* [2015] EWCA Civ 352. See eg *MB v GK* [2015] EWHC 2192 (Fam); and *SF v HL* [2015] EWHC 2891 (Fam).

[420] Law Com No 138 (1985), para 9.97.

for such an order, the parents and the child were habitually resident in another country. This view has been accepted,[421] despite earlier decisions to the contrary.[422]

3. CHOICE OF LAW

There seems little doubt that, when an English court takes jurisdiction to make orders with respect to children, it will apply English law as the law of the forum.[423] The application of English law is reinforced by the requirement imposed on the court to regard the welfare of the child as the paramount consideration.[424] There are no provisions in Brussels II *bis* concerning applicable law. Nevertheless, unlike the Regulation, the 1996 Hague Protection Convention governs also applicable law.[425] The relevant provisions are set out in Chapter III (Articles 15 to 22). In exercising jurisdiction under Chapter II of the Convention, the authorities of Contracting States shall apply their own law.[426] Since jurisdiction is conferred, as a general rule, on the authorities of the Contracting State in which the child is habitually resident, the law of the forum, in most cases, will be the most appropriate law to apply. By secondary legislation, this rule is applicable also to cases where the court assumes jurisdiction under Brussels II *bis*.[427]

Exceptionally, the forum may apply or take into consideration the law of another state with which the situation has a substantial connection.[428] It is said that this provision is based "not on the principle of proximity (the closest connection), but on the best interests of the child".[429] If the child should become habitually resident in another Contracting State, the law of that state, from the time of the change, will govern the conditions of application of the measures taken in the state of former habitual residence.[430]

The attribution or extinction of parental responsibility by operation of law,[431] without the intervention of a judicial or administrative authority, is governed, by virtue of Article 16 by the law of the state in which the child is habitually resident.[432] Similarly, the attribution or extinction of parental responsibility by agreement or unilateral act (eg a will by which a parent nominates a guardian for the child) is governed by the law of the child's

---

[421] *Re S (Residence Order: Forum Conveniens)* [1995] 1 FLR 314; *M v B (Residence: Forum Conveniens)* [1994] 2 FLR 819; *Re F (Residence Order: Jurisdiction)* [1995] 2 FLR 518; *M v M (Stay of Proceedings: Return of Children)* [2005] EWHC 1159 (Fam), [2006] 1 FLR 138—in the application for a stay of English divorce proceedings, the welfare of the two children of the marriage was important, but not paramount; but in the application for the children's summary return to South Africa, their welfare was paramount; see remarks of Wilson J, at [9]; and *V v V* [2006] EWHC 3374 (Fam), [2007] Fam Law 304.

[422] Eg *Hallam v Hallam (Minors) (Forum Conveniens) (Nos 1 and 2)* [1993] 1 FLR 958; and see *Re S (A Minor) (Stay of Proceedings)* [1993] 2 FLR 912.

[423] Cf Children (Scotland) Act 1995, s 14(3).

[424] Children Act 1989, s 1(1).

[425] See eg Lowe [2010] IFL 51.

[426] Art 15(1). "Law" means the law in force in a state other than its choice of law rules: Art 21 (subject to Art 21(2), which makes special provision for cases where the law applicable according to Art 16 is that of a non-Contracting State). The instrument adopts a principle of universal application, meaning that the law designated by the Convention shall apply, whether or not it is the law of a Contracting State: Art 20.

[427] The Parental Responsibility and Measures for the Protection of Children (International Obligations (England and Wales and Northern Ireland) Regulations 2010, SI 2010/1898, reg 7.

[428] Art 15(2). Eg, in relation to immovable property, where application of the law of the situs might be more appropriate (Lagarde, *Explanatory Report*, para 89).

[429] Lagarde, *Explanatory Report*, para 89.

[430] Art 15(3). See also Art 5(2).

[431] Recognising that most children are not subject to parental responsibility measures.

[432] Art 16(1).

habitual residence at the time when the agreement or act takes effect.[433] Likewise, the exercise of parental responsibility is governed by the law of the state of the child's habitual residence.[434]

The Convention confers a certain degree of third party protection: the validity of a face-to-face[435] transaction entered into between a third party and another person who would be entitled to act as the child's legal representative under the law of the state where the transaction was concluded cannot be contested, and the third party cannot be held liable, on the sole ground that the other person was not entitled to act as the child's legal representative under the law designated by the Convention, unless the third party knew or ought to have known that the parental responsibility was governed by the latter law.[436]

4. RECOGNITION AND ENFORCEMENT

(a) Introduction

The historic attitude of English courts to the recognition of orders relating to children, such as custody, guardianship and wardship orders, made in other countries was simple. Though they might be given careful consideration by an English court in deciding whether and, if so, what order to make, they were never recognised as such. The reasons for this attitude were primarily[437] because the English courts are instructed to regard the welfare of the child as the paramount consideration,[438] and this could conflict with recognition of a foreign order; and because such orders relating to children are never final, being always subject to review by the courts which made them.[439] This attitude contrasted strikingly with that, for example, in Canada, Australia and the USA, where there has for some time been legislation regulating the recognition of such foreign orders. Significant change in the English attitude was apparent with the introduction of legislation governing the recognition and enforcement of orders falling under Part I of the Family Law Act 1986 and made elsewhere in the United Kingdom, and with two international conventions, given the force of law in England by means of the Child Abduction and Custody Act 1985, which provide for the recognition of custody orders granted in, or custody rights under the law of, a number of foreign countries. Most important of all, however, has been the European objective of attaining the free movement of judgments in matrimonial matters and in matters of parental responsibility within the Union, leading ultimately to the implementation of Brussels II *bis*. Similarly, the 1996 Hague Convention sets forth the principle of recognition by each Contracting State of the measures taken in another Contracting State. As a result, the historic denial of recognition now is greatly reduced, affecting only orders granted in those countries not covered by Brussels II *bis*, the 1996 Hague Convention, the Family Law Act 1986, or the Child Abduction and Custody Act 1985. These varied rules must be considered in turn.

---

[433] Art 16(2).

[434] Art 17. This provision, unlike Art 16 (attribution or extinction of parental responsibility), incorporates a mutability principle.

[435] Art 19(2).

[436] Art 19(1). Cf the Rome I Regulation, Art 13, supra, pp 763–4.

[437] See Law Com No 138 (1985), para 2.45.

[438] Children Act 1989, s 1(1).

[439] *McKee v McKee* [1951] AC 352 at 364–5.

(b) Orders granted in another European Union Member State, except Denmark[440]

(i) Principle of recognition

As has been stated already in this book, the principle of mutual recognition of judgments has been fixed as the cornerstone of the European judicial area.[441] Alongside the objective of the free movement of judgments within the Member States in civil and commercial matters, the European Community has set the objective of creating an area of freedom, security and justice, in which the free movement of persons is ensured. "To this end, the Community is to adopt, among others, measures in the field of judicial co-operation in civil matters that are necessary for the proper functioning of the internal market."[442]

It is stated in Brussels II *bis* that: "The recognition and enforcement of judgments given in a Member State should be based on the principle of mutual trust and the grounds for non-recognition should be kept to the minimum necessary."[443] Accordingly, Article 21 of the Regulation[444] states that:

1. A judgment[445] given in a Member State[446] shall be recognised in the other Member States without any special procedure being required.[447]
2. In particular, and without prejudice to paragraph 3, no special procedure shall be required for updating the civil-status records of a Member State on the basis of a judgment relating to divorce, legal separation or marriage annulment given in another Member State, and against which no further appeal lies under the law of that Member State.[448]

---

[440] See the Family Procedure Rules 2010, Pt 31. Lowe [2011] IFL 121.

[441] See generally supra, Chapter 17.

[442] Brussels II *bis*, Recital (1).

[443] Recital (21).

[444] Applicable only to legal proceedings instituted, to documents formally drawn up or registered as authentic instruments, and to agreements concluded between the parties after 1 March 2005: Arts 64 and 72. Transitional provisions are set out in Art 64.

[445] Meaning a divorce, legal separation or marriage annulment, as well as a judgment relating to parental responsibility, pronounced by a court of a Member State (including all the authorities in a Member State with jurisdiction in the matters falling within the scope of the Regulation pursuant to Art 1), whatever the judgment may be called, including a decree, order or decision: Art 2(1) and (4). Documents which have been formally drawn up or registered as authentic instruments and are enforceable in one Member State and also agreements between the parties that are enforceable in the Member State in which they were concluded shall be recognised and declared enforceable under the same conditions as judgments: Art 46. See Borras, *Explanatory Report*, paras 60 and 61. "The aim is to encourage parties to reach agreement on matters of parental responsibility outside court" (*Practice Guide*, para 3.1.3.3).

[446] Whether that Member State was seised of jurisdiction on the basis of Arts 8–13 of Brussels II *bis*, or founded its jurisdiction on the basis of its own residual rules, per Art 14. In the case of the latter: "Such decisions are to be recognised and declared enforceable in other Member States pursuant to the rules of the Regulation" (*Practice Guide*, para 3.2.8). However, provisional measures made on the basis of Art 20 are not covered as they are not capable of recognition in another Member State within the meaning of Art 21: Case C-256/09, *Bianca Purrucker v Guillermo Vallés Pérez*, [2010] ECR I-07353, see supra, p 1120. Nevertheless, see Commission Proposal for the Recast of Brussels II *bis*, COM (2016) 411 final 30 June 2016, p 22, supra, p 1120, n 370.

[447] Cf 1996 Hague Convention, Art 23(1), infra, p 1130.

[448] Article 27 (Stay of proceedings) provides that: "1. A court of a Member State in which recognition is sought of a judgment given in another Member State may stay the proceedings if an ordinary appeal against the judgment has been lodged. 2. A court of a Member State in which recognition is sought of a judgment given in Ireland or the United Kingdom may stay the proceedings if enforcement is suspended in the Member State of origin by reason of an appeal." Cf Brussels I Recast Regulation, Art 38 (a).

3. Without prejudice to Section 4[449] of this Chapter, any interested party[450] may, in accordance with the procedures provided for in Section 2[451] of this Chapter, apply for a decision that the judgment be or not be recognised . . .

4. When the recognition of a judgment is raised as an incidental question in a court of a Member State, that court may determine that issue.

(ii) Grounds of non-recognition

Article 23[452] provides that a judgment relating to parental responsibility shall not be recognised: (a) if such recognition is manifestly contrary to the public policy of the Member State in which recognition is sought taking into account the best interests of the child;[453] (b) if it was given, except in cases of urgency, without the child having been given an opportunity to be heard, in violation of fundamental principles of procedure of the Member State in which recognition is sought;[454] (c) where it was given in default of appearance if the person in default was not served with the document which instituted the proceedings or with an equivalent document in sufficient time and in such a way as to enable that person to arrange for his or her defence[455] unless it is determined that such person has accepted the judgment unequivocally;[456] (d) on the request of any person claiming that the judgment infringes his or her parental responsibility, if it was given without such person having been given an opportunity to be heard; (e) if it is irreconcilable with a later judgment relating to parental responsibility given in the Member State in which recognition is sought;[457] (f) if it is irreconcilable with a later judgment relating to parental responsibility given in another Member State[458] or in the non-Member State of the habitual residence of the child provided that the later judgment fulfils the conditions necessary for its recognition in the Member State in which recognition is sought;[459] or (g) if the procedure laid down in Article 56[460] has not been complied with.

Recital 21 to the Regulation requires that the grounds for non-recognition be kept to a minimum. This means that Article 23 has to be interpreted strictly.[461] Arguably, the public

---

[449] Enforceability of certain judgments concerning rights of access and of certain judgments which require the return of the child.

[450] See Borras, *Explanatory Report*, para 65: the concept of interested party is to be interpreted "in the broad sense under the national law applicable and may include the public prosecutor or other similar bodies where permitted in the State in which the judgment is to be recognised or contested".

[451] Application for a declaration of enforceability.

[452] By implication, Art 23 provides the only defences to recognition. Cf 1996 Hague Convention, Art 23(2), infra, p 1131.

[453] See also Arts 24 and 26, infra, p 1129, and under Brussels II, *Re S (Brussels II: Recognition: Best Interests of Child) (No 1)* [2003] EWHC 2115, [2004] 1 FLR 571, followed in a number of first instance decisions under Brussels II *bis*, eg *W v W (Foreign Custody Order: Enforcement)* [2005] EWHC 1811 (Fam); *LAB v KB (Abduction: Brussels II Revised)* [2009] EWHC 2243 (Fam); and approved by the Court of Appeal in *Re L (A Child) (Recognition of Foreign Order)* [2012] EWCA Civ 1157. Cf Brussels I Recast Regulation, Art 45(1)(a), supra, p 626 et seq.

[454] See eg *Re D (A Child) (Recognition and Enforcement of Romanian Order)* [2016] EWCA Civ 12, at [36]–[46] (appeal to the Supreme Court struck out on the ground of the lack of jurisdiction: *Re D (A Child)* [2016] UKSC 34); and *ET v TZ (Recognition and Enforcement of a Foreign Residence Order)* [2013] EWHC 2621 (Fam), at [31].

[455] Cf Brussels I Recast Regulation, Art 45(1) (b), supra, p 632 et seq.

[456] See eg *Re D (A Child) (Recognition and Enforcement of Romanian Order)* [2016] EWCA Civ 12, at [58]–[108]; and *MD v CT* [2014] EWHC 871 (Fam).

[457] Cf Brussels I Recast Regulation, Art 45(1) (c), supra, p 639 et seq.

[458] The *lis pendens* provision in Art 19 normally will prevent a judgment being given in the court second seised, but it will not do so if that court does not accept that the parties are the same.

[459] Cf Brussels I Regulation, Art 45(1) (d), supra, pp 641–2.

[460] Concerning the placement of a child in institutional care or with a foster family in another Member State.

[461] Case C-455/15 PPU, *P v Q,* [2015] All ER (D) 181 (Nov).

policy exception embodied in Article 23 (a) is potentially the widest, however, the English courts have consistently held that the provision is to be approached restrictively. Indeed, in the words of Munby LJ, the exception is a very narrow one and "sets the bar very high".[462] Accordingly, the test in Article 23 (a) will not be met by virtue of the mental or emotional state of the parent who opposes recognition;[463] or by the passage of time, without substantially more, since the making of the order.[464] Although there is an overlap between public policy and breach of a fundamental principle under Article 23 (b), public policy, being an "exceptional remedy", requires "something more".[465] The public policy of the Member State where recognition is sought cannot be raised as an obstacle to the recognition or enforcement of a judgment given in another Member State solely on the ground that the Member State of origin failed to comply with the rules on jurisdiction contained in Brussels II *bis*.[466]

(iii) Prohibition of review of jurisdiction of the court of origin

Article 24 of Brussels II *bis* narrates the important principle that: "The jurisdiction of the court of the Member State of origin may not be reviewed.[467] The test of public policy referred to in [Article 23(a)] may not be applied to the rules relating to jurisdiction set out in Articles 3 to 14." It cannot be argued that the court of origin misapplied the jurisdictional rules in Brussels II *bis*, or its national rules of residual jurisdiction. In particular, this prohibition cannot be evaded by using the public policy defence.

(iv) Non-review as to substance

Article 26 lays down the classic rule that under no circumstances may a judgment be reviewed as to its substance.[468] It cannot be alleged that the court of origin made a mistake of fact or of law. Procedural irregularities in the court of origin, however, can be examined in order to establish a defence under Article 23. The nature of parental responsibility matters, however, is such that it may be in the best interests of the child for custody and access arrangements to be reviewed by a court having jurisdiction in terms of Articles 8 to 14.

(v) Application for a declaration of enforceability

Article 28(1) provides that a judgment on the exercise of parental responsibility in respect of a child given in a Member State which is enforceable in that Member State and has been served shall be enforced in another Member State when, on the application of any interested party, it has been declared enforceable there ("*exequatur* procedure").[469] Article 28(2) sets out a special rule in respect of the United Kingdom, providing that such a judgment shall be enforced in England and Wales, Scotland or Northern Ireland, only when, on the application of any interested party, it has been registered for enforcement in that part of the United Kingdom.[470]

---

[462] *Re L (A Child) (Recognition of Foreign Order)* [2012] EWCA Civ 1157, per Munby LJ, at [46]. See also *ET v TZ (Recognition and Enforcement of a Foreign Residence Order)* [2013] EWHC 2621 (Fam); and *Re N (A Minor) (Abduction: Brussels II Revised)* [2014] EWHC 749 (Fam).

[463] *Re L (A Child) (Recognition of Foreign Order)* [2012] EWCA Civ 1157.

[464] *Re N (A Minor) (Abduction: Brussels II Revised)* [2014] EWHC 749 (Fam).

[465] See *Re D (A Child) (Recognition and Enforcement of Romanian Order)* [2016] EWCA Civ 12, at [50].

[466] Case C-455/15 PPU, *P v Q*, [2015] All ER (D) 181 (Nov). This is because Art 24 of Brussels II *bis* prohibits the review of the jurisdiction of the court of origin, even if that court relied erroneously on Art 15 (not specifically treated as a non-reviewable ground under Art 24 but deemed by the CJEU to be so), the transfer ground, as the basis of jurisdiction.

[467] Cf Brussels I Recast Regulation, Art 45(3), supra, pp 643–4; and 1996 Hague Convention, Art 25, infra, p 1131.

[468] Cf Brussels I Recast Regulation, Art 52, supra, pp 644–5; and 1996 Hague Convention, Art 27.

[469] Cf 1996 Hague Convention, Art 28, infra, p 1131.

[470] See Family Procedure Rules 2010, r 31.8. See eg *Re S (A Child) (Enforcement of Foreign Judgment)* [2009] EWCA Civ 993. Cf 1996 Hague Convention, Art 28, infra, p 1131.

(vi) Enforceability of certain judgments concerning rights of access

Chapter III, Section 4 of Brussels II *bis* (Articles 40 to 45) concerns rights of access[471] and the return of a child entailed by a judgment given pursuant to Article 11(8).[472] Article 41 provides that the rights of access granted[473] in an enforceable judgment given in a Member State shall be recognised and enforceable in another Member State without the need for a declaration of enforceability and without any possibility of opposing its recognition if the judgment has been certified in the Member State of origin in accordance with Article 41(2),[474] thereby demonstrating that the necessary procedural safeguards have been complied with in that state.[475] The judgment shall be certified in the Member State of origin only if all parties concerned (including the child, if appropriate, having regard to his age and maturity) were given an opportunity to be heard; and where the judgment was given in default, the person defaulting was served with the document which instituted the proceedings or with an equivalent document in sufficient time and in such a way as to enable him to arrange for his defence,[476] unless it is determined that such person has accepted the judgment unequivocally. The *Practice Guide* makes plain that the consequence of this special rule for rights of access is two-fold: "(a) it is no longer necessary to apply for an '*exequatur*' and (b) it is no longer possible to oppose the recognition of the judgment."[477]

(vii) Enforcement procedure

Enforcement procedure is governed, not by the Regulation, but by the law of the Member State of enforcement.[478] However, "it is of the essence that national authorities apply rules which secure efficient and speedy enforcement of decisions issued under the Regulation so as not to undermine its objectives".[479] As regards practical arrangements for the exercise of rights of access, the courts of the Member State of enforcement may make the necessary arrangements if they have not already been made in the judgment delivered by the courts of the Member State having jurisdiction as to the substance of the matter and provided that the essential elements of the judgment are respected.[480]

(viii) Role of Central Authorities

In parental responsibility cases, it is especially important that the designated Central Authorities of Member States cooperate both in general matters and in specific cases,[481] to achieve the purpose of the Regulation. Each Central Authority is required to take all appropriate steps in accordance with the law of its Member State to collect and exchange information concerning the child, to provide information and assistance to holders of parental

---

[471] Art 2(10): "rights of access" shall include in particular the right to take a child to a place other than his or her habitual residence for a limited period of time.

[472] In respect of the latter, see infra, p 1159 et seq.

[473] Art 41 does not apply to judgments which refuse a request for rights of access.

[474] Using the standard form certificate in Annex III to the Regulation. See Family Procedure Rules 2010, r 31.7.

[475] See, however, Austrian court's failure to enforce an English contact order judged by the Deputy Judge of the High Court, relevant experts, and the children's guardian to be in the children's best interests, in *Re ML and AL (Children) (Contact Order: Brussels II Regulation) (No 2)* [2006] EWHC 3631 (Fam), [2007] 1 FCR 496.

[476] Cf Brussels I Recast Regulation, Art 45(1) (b), discussed supra, p 632 et seq.

[477] *Practice Guide*, para 3.6.7. See also Case C-195/08 PPU, *Rinau v Rinau*, [2008] ECR I-05271, supra, p 1162, which concerned the interpretation of Art 41, however, arguably, applies equally to Art 42.

[478] Art 47(1). See Family Procedure Rules 2010, r 31.17. Cf 1996 Hague Convention, Art 28, infra, p 1131.

[479] *Practice Guide*, para 5.1.

[480] Art 48.

[481] Recital (25).

responsibility who are seeking the recognition and enforcement of decisions, to facilitate agreement between holders of parental responsibility through mediation or other means, and to facilitate communications between courts.[482]

(c) Orders granted in another Contracting State to the 1996 Hague Protection Convention[483]

Article 23(1) of the Convention sets out a rule of recognition whereby measures taken by the authorities of a Contracting State must be recognised by operation of law in all other Contracting States.[484] Article 23(2) provides six grounds on which recognition may be refused. These grounds are comparable to those set out in Article 23 of Brussels II *bis*, namely: (a) jurisdiction was not based on one of the grounds provided for in Articles 5 to 14 of the Convention; (b) the child was not given the opportunity to be heard in violation of fundamental principles of procedure of the requested State (except in a case of urgency);[485] (c) a person claiming that the measure infringes his or her parental responsibility has not been given the opportunity to be heard (except in a case of urgency); (d) the recognition is manifestly contrary to public policy of the requested State, taking into account the best interests of the child; (e) the measure is incompatible with a later measure taken in the non-Contracting State of the habitual residence of the child, where this later measure fulfils the requirements for recognition in the requested State; (f) the procedure set out in Article 33 which concerns cross-border placements of children has not been complied with.

Article 24 provides for "advance recognition"[486] or "preventive action for recognition or non-recognition".[487] It states that "any interested person may request from the competent authorities of a Contracting State that they decide on the recognition or non-recognition of a measure taken in another Contracting State. The procedure is governed by the law of the requested State". Article 24 may be utilized, for example, by a father whose child is relocating from State X to State Y with the mother, and who wishes to secure ongoing contact with the child following the move. The father is prepared to consent to the move, however, in order to safeguard his position, seeks a ruling from State Y as to whether a contact order that has been made in State X will be recognised in State Y once the child has relocated.[488] There is no provision for advance recognition in Brussels II *bis*.

Article 25 states that the authority of the requested State is prohibited from reviewing any "findings of fact" on which the authority of the State where the measure was taken based its jurisdiction. This, however, does not prevent the authority of the requested State from refusing to recognise the measure pursuant to Article 23(2)(a), ie where it was taken "by an authority whose jurisdiction was not based on one of the grounds provided for in Chapter II".[489] The combined effect of the two provisions is that, unlike Brussels II *bis*,[490] the Convention does not prohibit review of the jurisdiction of the court of origin.[491]

---

[482] Art 55.
[483] Where the recognition and enforcement of a judgment given in a court of an EU Member State is sought on the territory of another Member State, Brussels II *bis* will apply even if the child concerned is habitually resident on the territory of a third State which is a contracting Party to the Convention: Brussels II *bis*, Art 61(b). See the Family Procedure Rules 2010, Part 31; and *Re P (Recognition and Registration of Orders under the 1996 Hague Child Protection Convention)* [2014] EWHC 2845 (Fam).
[484] Cf Brussels II *bis*, Art 21, supra, p 1127.
[485] Eg *G v G* [2014] EWHC 4182 (Fam).
[486] *Practical Handbook*, para 10.16.
[487] Lagarde, *Explanatory Report*, para 129.
[488] For more examples, see, *Practical Handbook*, para 10.18; and Lagarde, *Explanatory Report*, para 129.
[489] Art 23(2)(a).
[490] Art 24, supra, p 1129.
[491] Case C-256/09, *Bianca Purrucker v Guillermo Vallés Pérez*, [2010] ECR I-07353, at [90].

By Article 26(1), measures taken in one Contracting State and enforceable there must, upon request by an interested party, be declared enforceable or registered for enforcement in another Contracting State.[492] This procedure, which is governed by the law of the State of enforcement,[493] must be "simple and rapid".[494] The declaration of enforceability or registration can only be refused on one of the grounds on which recognition can be denied.[495] Once the measure has been declared enforceable or registered for enforcement, it has to be enforced as if it had been taken by the authorities of the State of enforcement.[496] Enforcement takes place "in accordance with the law of the requested State to the extent provided by such law, taking into consideration the best interests of the child".[497] There is no equivalent to the accelerated procedure set out in Articles 40 to 45 of Brussels II *bis*.[498]

(d) Orders granted in Scotland[499] and Northern Ireland

In 1985 the Law Commissions recommended not only that there should be uniform jurisdictional rules throughout the United Kingdom for the making of "custody orders", but also as a corollary that such orders should be recognised and enforceable elsewhere in the United Kingdom. In this way, protracted, expensive and disruptive proceedings might be avoided. The Commissions said: "In broad terms, our proposals are that the custody orders of the courts of each country [in the United Kingdom] should be recognised in the other countries but should only be enforceable if centrally registered in the courts of the receiving country and should only be enforced through the process of the receiving country."[500] These proposals were carried into effect in that form by Part I of the Family Law Act 1986.[501]

The extent of application of the jurisdiction provisions contained in Brussels II *bis* and of the *lis pendens* provision in Article 19 as regards intra-United Kingdom proceedings has been considered previously in this chapter.[502] The opaque wording of Article 66 of Brussels II *bis* generates a similar interpretative difficulty in relation to the recognition and enforcement of "Part I Orders" as between the territorial units of the United Kingdom. Article 66 of Brussels II *bis* does not refer to "judgments given in a Member State", which is the concern of the Article 21 recognition provisions of the Regulation. It does, however, provide, in Article 66(d), that, "any reference to the rules of the requested Member State shall refer to the rules of the territorial unit in which jurisdiction, recognition or enforcement is invoked". Except for the special Scottish rule of recognition contained in section 26 of the 1986 Act,[503] the recognition and enforcement provisions in Chapter V of the Family Law Act 1986 (sections 25 to 32) appear, from the fact of the Act, to be unaffected by Brussels II *bis*, and untouched by secondary legislation passed subsequent to Brussels II *bis*.[504] The assumption, therefore, is

---

[492] Cf Brussels II *bis*, Art 28, supra, p 1129.

[493] Art 26(1). Cf Brussels II *bis*, Art 30.

[494] Art 26(2).

[495] Art 23(2), supra. Cf Brussels II *bis*, Art 31(2).

[496] Art 28.

[497] Ibid.

[498] See supra, pp 1129–30 (rights of access), and infra, p 1159 et seq (the return of a child entailed by a judgment given pursuant to Article 11(8)).

[499] See Crawford and Carruthers, paras 14–44 et seq.

[500] Law Com No 138 (1985), para 3.19.

[501] See the Family Procedure Rules 2010, Part 32, C. 4. There is power under s 43 of the 1986 Act to extend Part I of the Act by Order in Council to the rest of the British Isles and to any colony, and this power has been exercised in relation to the Isle of Man (with effect from 14 October 1991) and Jersey (with effect from 10 July 2006): SI 1991/1723, as amended by SI 2006/1456.

[502] Supra, pp 1100–1 and 1124.

[503] Which now is subject to Brussels II *bis*.

[504] SI 2005/265 does not purport to amend Pt V (ss 25–33) of the 1986 Act.

that the intra-United Kingdom scheme of recognition and enforcement contained in sections 27 to 29 of the 1986 Act still applies, notwithstanding Chapter III (recognition and enforcement) of Brussels II *bis*.[505] Whether this outcome was intended by Article 66 is not clear. It seems inconsistent and anomalous to apply, in intra-United Kingdom cases, the jurisdiction provisions of the Regulation (or at least some of them), but not to apply the recognition and enforcement provisions in Brussels II *bis*;[506] "picking and choosing" selective parts of the Regulation to operate intra-United Kingdom seems, in principle, surprising and undesirable.

The recognition and enforcement provisions of the 1986 Act apply to exactly the same range and type of orders, ie Part I orders, as do the jurisdictional provisions.[507] However, whilst the English jurisdictional provisions govern all Part I orders made in relation to children under the age of eighteen, the recognition and enforcement provisions are limited to orders applying to children under the age of sixteen, and they cease to have effect when the child reaches this age. There are various reasons for this difference:[508] Scottish orders can only be made up to the age of sixteen; the international conventions are limited to children under sixteen;[509] English orders in relation to sixteen and seventeen-year-olds are rare and their enforcement would be difficult against the wishes of the child.

Part I orders made elsewhere in the United Kingdom and still in force in relation to a child under sixteen must be recognised in England.[510] This will be of practical importance to third parties, such as social workers and school teachers, to know that rights conferred by, say, a Scottish order are to be recognised in England.[511] A Scottish or Northern Ireland order cannot, however, be enforced in England until it has been registered in England,[512] and proceedings have been taken in England for its enforcement.[513] Registration is effected by applying to the court which made the order which, provided the order is still in force, passes a certified copy of the order and other relevant documents to the High Court[514] for registration.[515] If the order ceases to have effect, other than by revocation,[516] as where it is superseded by a later order, its registration will be cancelled by the English court.[517]

Once registered in England, the Scottish and Northern Ireland order can be enforced in exactly the same way as if it was an English Part I order,[518] provided it remains in force where

---

[505] Cf Crawford and Carruthers, para 14–44; and Dicey, Morris and Collins, paras 19R-082–19R-083. In relation to Scotland, although s 17A of the 1986 Act gives priority to the rules of jurisdiction contained in Brussels II *bis*, there is no equivalent provision in relation to the recognition and enforcement provisions of the Regulation.

[506] Particularly when the special United Kingdom provision contained in Art 28(2) and concerning registration for enforcement (supra, p 1129) echoes the registration provisions in s 27 of the 1986 Act.

[507] 1986 Act, s 1, supra, p 1091.

[508] Law Com No 138 (1985), para 1.22.

[509] Infra, p 1134 et seq.

[510] 1986 Act, s 25(1). No recognition is given to parts of the order which may relate to enforcement, such as a requirement to hand over the child at a particular time or place: s 25(2). This is so as to ensure that all matters of enforcement are in the hands of courts in the receiving country.

[511] There is also power, under the Children (Scotland) Act 1995, s 33, for effect to be given in England to prescribed Scottish orders, and vice versa.

[512] Ss 25(3), 27. See Lowe [2002] Fam Law 39, at 54. Also *Re T (A Child) (Application for Parental Responsibility)* [2001] EWCA Civ 1067.

[513] S 29. They will fail if, by then, the order has ceased to have effect where granted: *T v T (Custody: Jurisdiction)* [1992] 1 FLR 43.

[514] S 32(1).

[515] S 27.

[516] If the order is cancelled, this is notified by the court which made the order: s 28(1).

[517] S 28(2).

[518] S 29; and see *Woodcock v Woodcock* 1990 SLT 848.

made.[519] However, enforcement proceedings may be stayed on the application of any interested party on the ground that he has taken or intends to take other proceedings, whether in the United Kingdom or elsewhere, as a result of which the order may cease to have effect or have a different effect.[520] So although the merits of the order cannot be attacked in the country of registration,[521] a parent might convince the English court that he was going to attack them before the Scottish court which made the order, or there argue that that court lacked jurisdiction, or, indeed, that he proposes to apply to another court for a new order.[522] In all such cases, the English court has a discretion to stay the enforcement proceedings and, indeed, to lift any stay.[523] If the English court is satisfied that the original order, now registered in England, has ceased to have effect, it will dismiss the enforcement proceedings.[524]

Whilst it is to be hoped that the system for the recognition and enforcement throughout the United Kingdom of orders made in one part thereof will eradicate the conflicts which arose in the past, particularly between English and Scottish courts,[525] attention has to be drawn to the fact that the recognition and enforcement procedures apply only to orders falling under Part I of the 1986 Act.

(e) Child Abduction and Custody Act 1985[526]

Special rules have been developed to govern cases where a child has been unlawfully removed from the state of his habitual residence and taken to another state. The Child Abduction and Custody Act 1985[527] gives effect to two international conventions relating to the recognition of foreign custody rights and orders, both of which are scheduled to the Act and provide very similar mechanisms for their operation.[528] The first is the Hague Convention on the Civil Aspects of International Child Abduction (1980), in respect of which there are ninety-seven Contracting States,[529] and which is implemented by Part I of the 1985 Act. The second is the Council of Europe Convention on Recognition and Enforcement of Decisions concerning Custody of Children and on the Restoration of Custody of Children (1980). There are currently thirty-seven parties[530] to the European Convention, which is implemented by Part II of the 1985 Act. These two Conventions now must be examined in the light of Brussels II *bis*, which contains special provisions pertaining to international child abduction, and which, by virtue of Article 60

---

[519] *S v S (Custody: Jurisdiction)* [1995] 1 FLR 155.

[520] S 30.

[521] It is suggested that the Court of Session was incorrect in *Woodcock v Woodcock* 1990 SLT 848 at 853 in indicating the contrary; see Edwards (1992) 41 ICLQ 444.

[522] Such an argument failed in *Re M (Minors) (Custody: Jurisdiction)* [1992] 2 FLR 382.

[523] S 30(3).

[524] S 31. It is relevant in the context of enforcement, as of jurisdiction, that the English court knows of similar proceedings elsewhere, including administrative proceedings, ss 39, 42(7).

[525] Contrast the balanced approach under the 1986 Act as evidenced by *Re K (A Minor: Wardship)* [1991] 2 FLR 104, [1991] Fam Law 226.

[526] See the Family Procedure Rules 2010, rr 12.44–12.57.

[527] As amended by the Family Law Act 1986, ss 67, 68, Sch 1, para 28, and by the Children Act 1989, Sch 13, para 57, Sch 15.

[528] In relation to both there is power to order the disclosure of a child's whereabouts: 1985 Act, s 24A. See *Re D (A Minor) (Child Abduction)* [1988] FCR 585, [1989] 1 FLR 97; and *M, Petitioner* 2000 GWD 32–1242.

[529] See SI 2009/702. The above number of Contracting States is valid as of 1 May 2017. See status table at www.hcch.net. Notably, on 1 March 2017, the Convention entered into force in Pakistan. Previously, the relationship between the UK and Pakistan in the area of child abduction was governed by the UK-Pakistan Judicial Protocol on Child Contact and Abduction. For a detailed analysis of the Protocol and related case-law see the 14th edition of this book, pp 1135–6.

[530] See http://conventions.coe.int.

of the Regulation, takes precedence over the Hague Convention[531] and the Council of Europe Convention as regards relations between European Union Member States.

(i) Part I of the 1985 Act: the Hague Convention[532]

(a) Aim of the Convention

The prime concern of the Hague Convention is the restoration of children who have been wrongfully removed or wrongfully retained, whether or not this is in breach of a custody order in one of the Contracting States. Not only does the Convention provide for the recognition and enforcement of custody orders, but it also protects rights of custody even where there has been no order.[533] The Convention does not provide for the enforcement of access rights in the same way as it seeks to uphold custody rights, but an application to make arrangements for organising or securing the effective exercise of rights of access nevertheless may be presented to the Central Authorities[534] of Contracting States.[535]

(b) Wrongful removal and wrongful retention

Essential elements of the Convention are that it applies to a child under the age of sixteen who was habitually resident in a Contracting State at the time when he was wrongfully removed or retained.[536] The House of Lords[537] has made clear that both removal and retention are single events, so that if a child is wrongfully removed before the Convention came into force, but not returned after that date, such latter conduct does not constitute "retention" within the

---

[531] *Re A (A Child)* [2016] EWCA Civ 572.

[532] See Beaumont and McEleavy, *The Hague Convention on International Child Abduction* (1999); Anton (1981) 30 ICLQ 537; Eekelaar (1982) 32 U Tor LJ 281, 305–325; Shapira (1989) II Hague Recueil 127, 189–200; Crawford (1990) 35 JLSS 277; Davis (1990) 4 Aus J Fam L 31; Crawford (1992) 2 JR 192; Silberman (1994) 28 Family LQ 9; Bruch (2004) 38 Fam LQ 529; Schuz (1995) 44 ICLQ 771; McClean and Beevers (1995) 7 Ch FLQ 128; Balfour and Crawford (1996) SLPQ 411; Reddaway and Keating (1997) 5 Int J of Children's Rights 77; Lowe and Pery (1999) 48 ICLQ 127; Armstrong (2002) 51 ICLQ 427; McEleavy (2005) 1.1 J Priv Int L 5; Beevers and Perez Milla (2007) 3.1 J Priv Int Law 201; Kruger, *International Child Abduction* (2011); and Rains (ed), *The 1980 Hague Abduction Convention: Comparative Aspects* (2014); and Schuz, *The Hague Child Abduction Convention: A Critical Analysis* (2013). Conclusions and Recommendations of the Hague Conference Special Commission meetings on the practical operation of the Convention (1989, 1993, 1997, 2001, 2002, 2006 and 2011) can be found on the website of the Hague Conference on Private International Law. For a database of cases on the Convention, see http://www.incadat.com.

[533] See *B v B (Minors: Enforcement of Access Abroad)* [1988] 1 WLR 526; *C v C (Minors) (Child Abduction)* [1992] 1 FLR 163; *Re G (A Minor; Enforcement of Access Abroad)* [1993] Fam 216; *Re T (Minors) (Hague Convention: Access)* [1993] 2 FLR 617; and see [1993] 1 WLR 1461; cf *S v H (Abduction: Access Rights)* [1997] 1 FLR 970.

[534] S 3 of the Child Abduction and Custody Act 1985 establishes that the functions of the Central Authority in England and Wales and in Northern Ireland shall be discharged by the Lord Chancellor, and in Scotland, by the Secretary of State. No obligation is imposed, however, upon judicial authorities: *Donofrio v Burrell* 1999 GWD 12–528, aff d 2000 SLT 1051.

[535] Art 21. See *B v B (Minors: Enforcement of Access Abroad)* [1988] 1 WLR 526; *C v C (Minors) (Child Abduction)* [1992] 1 FLR 163; *Re G (A Minor: Enforcement of Access Abroad)* [1993] Fam 216; *Re T (Minors) (Hague Convention: Access)* [1993] 2 FLR 617; and see [1993] 1 WLR 1461; cf *S v H (Abduction: Access Rights)* [1997] 1 FLR 970. See, for Scottish cases, Crawford and Carruthers, para 14–21. See access provisions of Brussels II *bis*, supra, pp 1129–30, and Council of Europe Convention on Contact concerning Children, infra, pp 1176–8.

[536] Art 4. The Convention ceases to apply when the child attains the age of sixteen years: *Re H (Abduction: Child of 16)* [2000] 2 FLR 51.

[537] *Re H (Minors) (Abduction: Custody Rights)* [1991] 2 AC 476; and see *Kilgour v Kilgour* 1987 SLT 568; *B v B (Minors: Enforcement of Access Abroad)* [1988] 1 WLR 526; *Re S (Minors) (Abduction: Wrongful Retention)* [1994] Fam 70; *Re S (Child Abduction: Delay)* [1998] 1 FLR 651; *Findlay v Findlay* 1994 SLT 709; *Findlay v Findlay (No 2)* 1995 SLT 492; *Re Gollogly and Owen's Marriage* (1989) 13 Fam LR 622; *In the Marriage of Murray and Tam* (1993) 16 Fam LR 982; *BP v DP (Children: Habitual Residence)* [2016] EWHC 633 (Fam) ("anticipatory breach"). Cf *S v S (Abduction: Wrongful Retention)* [2009] EWHC 1494 (Fam).

meaning of the Convention[538] and section 2 of the Act. This means that, for those purposes, removal and retention[539] are mutually exclusive concepts: "Removal occurs when a child, which has previously been in the state of its habitual residence, is taken across the frontier of that state;[540] whereas retention occurs where a child, which has previously been for a limited period outside the state of its habitual residence,[541] is not returned to that state on the expiry of such limited period."[542] Furthermore, the wrongful removal or retention under the Convention must be "international" in nature,[543] ie the child must have been taken from, or retained outside, the country of his habitual residence in which the custody or access rights existed.[544] In other words, what is involved is wrongful removal from, or retention out of, that country, rather than just from or out of the care of the parent having custody rights.

(i) Habitual residence

The habitual residence of the child is the crucial connecting factor[545] and it is not defined in the Convention. The concept of habitual residence has been examined in detail in Chapter 9 and earlier in this Chapter in the context of Brussels II *bis*.[546]

(ii) Rights of custody

"The world would be a simpler place if the Convention had provided that all removal or retention of a child outside the country where he or she is habitually resident without the consent of the other parent or the authority of a court is wrongful. But it does not."[547] Removal or retention is wrongful if it is, at that time,[548] in breach of custody rights under the law of the child's habitual residence which were being exercised.[549] Therefore, when determining whether removal or retention is wrongful within the meaning of Article 3 of the Convention, the first task for the court to which the application is made[550] is to establish what rights, if any, the left-behind parent

---

[538] [1991] 2 AC 476 at 499. Cf *Re J (A Minor) (Abduction: Custody Rights)* [1990] 2 AC 562 at 578–9.

[539] Retention may be evidenced by the institution of proceedings for a court order preventing the return of the child: *Re AZ (A Minor) (Abduction: Acquiescence)* [1993] 1 FLR 682; *Re B (Minors) (Abduction) (No 2)* [1993] 1 FLR 993; and *Re S (A Minor) (Abduction: European Convention)* [1998] AC 750.

[540] *Re L (Abduction: Pending Criminal Proceedings)* [1999] 1 FLR 433; *Re L (Children) (Abduction: Declaration)* [2001] 2 FCR 1.

[541] *Re D (Abduction: Discretionary Return)* [2000] 1 FLR 24; *Re H (A Child) (Abduction: Habitual Residence: Consent)* [2000] 2 FLR 294; *Re M (Abduction: Conflict of Jurisdiction)* [2000] 2 FLR 372; *H v H* [2004] EWHC 2111; and *Re C (A Child) (Abduction: Residence and Contact)* [2005] EWHC 2205, [2006] 2 FLR 277.

[542] [1991] 2 AC 476 at 500. Retention may be wrongful where a parent decides not to return a child, even though the period for which the child is lawfully with that parent has not yet expired: *Re S (Minors) (Abduction: Wrongful Retention)* [1994] Fam 70. Cf *D v S (Abduction: Acquiescence)* [2008] EWHC 363 (Fam), per Charles J, at [179]; and *S v S (Abduction: Wrongful Retention)* [2009] EWHC 1494 (Fam), per Macur J, at [37]–[38]—the relevant date for determining when a wrongful retention occurs is that of the child's intended return.

[543] *Re H (Minors) (Abduction: Custody Rights)* [1991] 2 AC 476; *In the Marriage of R and S S Hanbury-Brown* (1996) 20 Fam LR 334.

[544] *B v B (Minors: Enforcement of Access Abroad)* [1988] 1 WLR 526 at 532.

[545] Eg *V v B (A Minor) (Abduction)* [1991] FCR 451, [1991] 1 FLR 266.

[546] See supra, pp 1094–7.

[547] *Re D (A Child) (Abduction: Rights of Custody)* [2006] UKHL 51, [2007] 1 AC 619, per Baroness Hale of Richmond, at [24].

[548] *Re S (A Minor) (Abduction)* [1991] FCR 656, [1991] 2 FLR 1; *Re H (Minors) (Abduction: Custody Rights)* [1991] 2 AC 476 at 484–5, CA, affd, ibid, at 491, HL; *S v S (Child Abduction: Custody Rights: Acquiescence)* 2003 SLT 344 (father considered not to have abandoned the exercise of legal rights, or ceased exercising rights of custody while mentally ill and compulsorily detained in hospital); *Re A (A Child) (Abduction: Rights of Custody: Imprisonment)* [2004] 1 FLR 1; *Re L (A Child)* [2005] EWHC 1237, [2006] 1 FLR 843 (incarceration in a Spanish prison did not preclude child's father from exercising rights of custody).

[549] Art 3; *Re W (Abduction: Procedure)* [1995] 1 FLR 878.

[550] Not the authorities of the requesting State: *Re D (A Child) (Abduction: Rights of Custody)* [2006] UKHL 51, [2007] 1 AC 619, per Lord Hope of Craighead, at [7]. See *Re M (Abduction: Paternity: DNA*

had under the law of the state in which the child was habitually resident immediately prior to his removal,[551] and whether those rights amount to "rights of custody" for the purpose of Articles 3 and 5(b) of the Convention.

> This is a matter of international law and depends on the application of the autonomous meaning of the phrase "rights of custody".[552] Where . . . an application is made in the courts of England and Wales, the autonomous meaning is determined in accordance with English law as the law of the court whose jurisdiction has been invoked under the Convention.[553]

That said, the Convention cannot be construed differently in different jurisdictions: it must have the same meaning and effect under the laws of all Contracting States.[554] Whilst it is for the law of the country of the habitual residence to determine the nature and extent of the rights,[555] it is for English law to determine whether they amount to "rights of custody" within the Convention;[556] a broad, purposive interpretation has been encouraged.[557]

Custody rights include those which can be attributed to one parent, or to both jointly,[558] and which can arise "by operation of law or by reason of a judicial[559] or administrative decision,[560] or by reason of an agreement having legal effect under the law" of the child's habitual

---

Testing) [2013] EWCA Civ 1131—DNA testing should only be ordered by the requested court as a last resort; ie where the question of custody rights is contingent on a finding of biological fatherhood.

[551] Arts 14, 15; and see 1985 Act, s 8; *C v C (Minors) (Child Abduction)* [1992] 1 FLR 163. An English court can, therefore, make a declaration as to wrongfulness for the benefit of a foreign court considering whether to order the return of a child: eg *Re J (Abduction: Ward of Court)* [1989] Fam 85; *A v B (Abduction: Rights of Custody: Declaration of Wrongful Removal)* [2008] EWHC 2524 (Fam); and *A v H* [2009] EWHC 636 (Fam). There is, however, no absolute guarantee that it will be followed abroad, just as there is no obligation on an English court to follow a foreign court's ruling; see *Re J (A Minor) (Abduction: Custody Rights)* [1990] 2 AC 562 at 577–8. Nor is there a requirement to seek a ruling from a foreign court: *Taylor v Ford* 1993 SLT 654; *Perrin v Perrin* 1994 SC 45. In relation to Art 15 declarations, see supra, pp 1056–7.

[552] See *Re D (A Child) (Abduction: Rights of Custody)* [2006] UKHL 51, [2007] 1 AC 619, per Lord Hope of Craighead, at [8].

[553] *Hunter v Morrow* [2005] EWCA Civ 976, [2005] 2 FLR 1119, per Dyson LJ, at [47]. See also *Kennedy v Kennedy* [2009] EWCA Civ 986, per Thorpe LJ, at [10].

[554] *Re H (Abduction: Acquiescence)* [1998] AC 72 at 87 per Lord Browne-Wilkinson. Though, as noted in *Re D (A Child) (Abduction: Rights of Custody)* [2006] UKHL 51, [2007] 1 AC 619, per Lord Hope of Craighead, at [15], the Convention has not provided any formal mechanisms to ensure that the international legal norms that it has created are applied uniformly and consistently in the numerous Contracting States (cf Baroness Hale of Richmond, at [28]). See also Silberman (2005) 38 U C Davis Law Review 1049, 1057, criticising *Croll v Croll* (2000) 229 F 3 d 133, (2001) 534 US 949.

[555] *Hunter v Morrow* [2005] EWCA Civ 976, [2005] 2 FLR 1119. See also *F v B-F* [2008] EWHC 272 (Fam), at [14]—the court should resist the temptation to make its own findings as to whether the law of the requesting State gives the applicant custody rights or not.

[556] *Re B (A Minor) (Abduction)* [1994] 2 FLR 249; *Re F (A Minor) (Abduction: Custody Rights Abroad)* [1995] Fam 224; *S v H (Abduction: Access Rights)* [1997] 1 FLR 970.

[557] *Re B (A Minor) (Abduction)*, supra; *Re M and J (Children) (Abduction: International Judicial Collaboration)* [2000] 1 FLR 803; *Re H (A Minor) (Abduction: Rights of Custody)* [2000] 2 AC 291; *Re G (Abduction: Rights of Custody)* [2002] 2 FLR 703; *Re D (A Child) (Abduction: Rights of Custody)* [2006] UKHL 51; *Kennedy v Kennedy* [2009] EWCA Civ 986, per Thorpe LJ (obiter), at [20]; and *Re K (Abduction: Inchoate Rights)* [2014] UKSC 29.

[558] Art 3.

[559] See *Re E (A Child) (Abduction: Rights of Custody)* [2005] EWHC 848, [2005] 2 FLR 759, per Sir Mark Potter—in summary proceedings under the Convention it is not appropriate for an English court to go behind the decision of a competent court of another Contracting State dealing with the custody of the child, where the terms of the foreign court's order, relied on as establishing custody rights under the Convention, were clear, apt for the purpose, and had not been appealed.

[560] *Re JS (Private International Adoption)* [2000] 2 FLR 638.

residence.[561] Rights of custody are not defined exclusively but include rights relating to the care of the person of the child and to determine his place of residence.[562] A person with "parental responsibility" has rights of custody[563] and may even have such rights when exercising parental functions short of full parental responsibility.[564] They also include, in England, custody rights attributed to a court when a child is made a ward of court,[565] where the court is exercising its powers to determine the child's place of residence,[566] where a guardianship application is pending,[567] or where a parent awarded an interim custody order is prohibited from removing the child from the jurisdiction;[568] but the rights of the court do not appear to continue once a final custody order has been made.[569]

It has been held[570] that a right of veto (but not a potential right of veto),[571] giving one parent the right to insist that the other parent does not remove the child from the home country without either his consent or a court order, amounts to "rights of custody". It is possible for someone who is not related by blood to the child to fall within a quasi-parental role in relation to the child, and so to acquire inchoate rights of custody, namely, those which are capable of being effected by an application to the court which has a reasonable prospect of success.[572] In *J.McB. v L.E.*,[573] the Irish Supreme Court sought a preliminary ruling from the CJEU as to whether, in the light of Article 24 of the Charter of Fundamental Rights of the European Union, the lack of recognition of the concept of inchoate custody rights in Irish law was compatible with the correct interpretation of Article 2(11) of Brussels II *bis*.[574] The CJEU held that the fact that, under Irish law, an unmarried father did not automatically

---

[561] Art 3. See, *Re K (Abduction: Inchoate Rights)* [2014] UKSC 29, per Lady Hale, at [34]–[42]—discussing the difference between the concepts "an agreement having legal effect" and "inchoate custody rights" (see infra).

[562] Art 5(a). See *C v C (Abduction: Rights of Custody)* [1989] 1 WLR 654; *C v C (Minors) (Child Abduction)* [1992] 1 FLR 163.

[563] *Re M (Minors) (Residence Order: Jurisdiction)* [1993] 1 FLR 495.

[564] *Re B (A Minor) (Abduction)* [1994] 2 FLR 249 at 261; *Re O (Child Abduction: Custody Rights)* [1997] 2 FLR 702. Cf *Re B (Abduction) (Rights of Custody)* [1997] 2 FLR 594. Also *T, Petitioner* 2007 SLT 543, and 2007 GWD 11–240.

[565] *Re J (Abduction: Ward of Court)* [1989] Fam 85. A Canadian court has held that rights of custody may be attributed to a North American Indian Tribe: *S (S M) v A(J)* (1990) 65 DLR (4th) 222. It was left open, in *Re K (Abduction: Consent: Forum Conveniens)* [1995] 2 FLR 211, as to whether a parent may apply for the return of a child wrongfully removed when the rights were attributed to a court rather than to the applicant parent.

[566] *B v B (Abduction: Custody Rights)* [1993] Fam 32; cf *The Ontario Court v M and M (Abduction: Children's Objections)* [1997] 1 FLR 475. Also *Re W (Minors) (Abduction: Father's Rights)* [1998] 2 FLR 146; and *X County Council v B (Abduction: Rights of Custody in the Court)* [2009] EWHC 2635 (Fam).

[567] *Re H (A Minor) (Abduction: Rights of Custody)* [2000] 2 AC 291.

[568] *Thomson v Thomson* (1994) 119 DLR (4th) 253; *W (V) v S (D)* (1996) 134 DLR (4th) 481.

[569] *Seroka v Bellah* 1995 SLT 304; and see *Thomson v Thomson*, supra, at 281.

[570] *Re D (A Child) (Abduction: Rights of Custody)* [2006] UKHL 51, [2007] 1 AC 619 (see especially Baroness Hale of Richmond, at [37]); *Re E (Children) (Abduction: Custody Appeal)* [2011] UKSC 27, per Lady Hale and Lord Wilson, at [6]; and *Re A (A Child) (Abduction: Rights of Custody: Imprisonment)* [2004] 1 FLR 1. See, eg, *P v A* [2015] EWHC 3818 (Fam).

[571] *Re D (A Child) (Abduction: Rights of Custody)*, supra, at [38]. Where, for instance, a parent has the right to go to court to ask for an order regarding the child's upbringing, including relocation abroad. Cf *Re J (A Minor) (Abduction: Custody Rights)* [1990] 2 AC 562; and *Re V-B (Abduction: Rights of Custody)* [1999] 2 FLR 192—distinction must be drawn between rights of custody and rights of access.

[572] *Re F (Abduction: Unmarried Father: Sole Carer)* [2002] EWHC 2896, [2003] 1 FLR 839.

[573] Case C-400/10 PPU, *J.McB. v L.E.* [2010] ECR I-08965. See Blanco (2012) 8 J Priv Int L 135. See also Fawcett, Ní Shúilleabháin and Shah, *Human Rights and Private International Law* (2016), paras 13.97–13.111.

[574] The wording of which is very similar to the wording of Art 3 of the 1980 Convention, see supra, p 1136.

acquire custody rights within the meaning of Article 2 of Brussels II *bis* did not affect his right to private and family life, as long as he had the right to apply to the national court for an order awarding him custody rights. This interpretation applied also in cases where the father did not apply for custody rights prior to the removal of the child by the mother who, at the time of the removal, was alone the legitimate custody rights holder. Hence, to accept the possibility that an unmarried father has rights of custody under Art 2(11) of Brussels II *bis*, although no such rights are conferred on him under national law, would be incompatible with the requirements of legal certainty and with the need to protect the rights of the mother. The implications of this ruling for those Member States that accept the concept of inchoate rights in their national law, including the UK, are ambivalent. Nevertheless, the Supreme Court, in *Re K (Abduction: Inchoate Rights)*,[575] held that the CJEU decision did not represent an "insuperable obstacle" to the continuous acceptance of the concept of inchoate custody rights in UK law.[576] Following on from this statement, Baroness Hale who gave the majority judgment proceeded to set out the requirements which must be satisfied before a person can be held to have had inchoate rights of custody: (a) they are undertaking the responsibilities, and thus enjoying the corresponding rights and powers, entailed in the primary care of the child; (b) they are not sharing these responsibilities with the person having a legally recognised right to determine where the child shall live and how he shall be brought up; (c) that person must have either abandoned the child or delegated his primary care to them; (d) there is some form of legal or official recognition of their position in the country of habitual residence; (e) there is every reason to believe that were they to seek the protection of the courts of that country, the status quo would be preserved for the time being so that the long-term future of the child could be determined in those courts in accordance with his best interests and not by the pre-emptive strike of abduction.[577] On the facts it was held that a maternal grandmother who had been delegated primary care of a child subsequently removed from her care by his mother had "rights of custody" for the purposes of the Convention and the Regulation.[578]

If one parent had no rights of custody under the law of the child's habitual residence at the time of the removal or retention by the other parent, then such conduct is not wrongful and falls outside the Convention even if such rights are acquired later.[579]

(c) Restoration of status quo: return of the child to his habitual residence
The Convention requires administrative structures and procedures to be established, in particular the use of a designated Central Authority for each Contracting State,[580] to enable a child to be returned to the country from which it has been wrongfully removed or outside which it has

---

[575] [2014] UKSC 29.

[576] Per Baroness Hale, at [58].

[577] See [59]. Dissenting, Lord Wilson, although in principle accepting the concept of inchoate custody rights, considered that (d) was unnecessary and (e) "set the bar too low", at [76].

[578] Per Baroness Hale, at [62].

[579] *Re J (A Minor) (Abduction: Custody Rights)* [1990] 2 AC 562; *Re W (Minors) (Abduction: Father's Rights)* [1998] 2 FLR 146; *Re D (Abduction: Custody Rights)* [1999] 2 FLR 626; *B v United Kingdom* [2000] 1 FLR 1; *Re C (Child Abduction) (Unmarried Father: Rights of Custody)* [2002] EWHC 2219, [2003] 1 FLR 252; *Re H (Child Abduction) (Unmarried Father: Rights of Custody)* [2003] EWHC 492, [2003] 2 FLR 153; and *Re JB (Child Abduction: Rights of Custody: Spain)* [2003] EWHC 2130, [2004] 1 FLR 796 (in respect of which see Beevers and Perez Milla (2007) 3.1 J Priv Int L 201, 212 et seq).

[580] See Arts 7–11. S 3 of the Child Abduction and Custody Act 1985 establishes that the functions of the Central Authority shall be discharged as follows: in England and Wales, by the Lord Chancellor, in Scotland, by the Secretary of State, and in Northern Ireland, by the Department of Justice. On the matter of costs, see Arts 22 and 26 and 1985 Act, s 11; also *EC-L v DM (Child Abduction)* [2005] EWHC 588, [2005] 2 FLR 772; and *B v A (Wasted Costs Order)* [2012] EWHC 3127 (Fam).

been wrongfully retained. If we assume that a child has been wrongfully removed from Australia to England, the procedures to ensure its return to Australia are as follows.[581] The parent or other person claiming the child applies to the Central Authority in Australia, or in any other Contracting State, for assistance in securing the return of the child. The application, which has to contain essential particulars of the child, the grounds of the claim and available information as to the child's whereabouts,[582] is sent without delay by the Central Authority which receives it to the Central Authority in the country where the child is thought to be.[583] In the case of a child thought to be in England, the application is sent to the Lord Chancellor,[584] who must then cause all appropriate measures to be taken to discover the whereabouts of the child, to prevent further harm to him and to try to secure the voluntary return of the child.[585] He must also initiate, or facilitate, the institution of judicial or administrative proceedings to secure the return of the child[586] without considering the merits of any custody issue;[587] and any judicial proceedings in England are in the High Court.[588] If less than one year has elapsed between the date of the wrongful removal and the English proceedings, the child must[589] be ordered to be returned forthwith; if more than a year has elapsed, the return of the child must be ordered "unless it is demonstrated that the child is now[590] settled in its new environment".[591]

Settlement of the child in his new environment
Settlement in this context means more than mere adjustment to surroundings. It involves both the physical element of being established in a community and an environment, and an emotional and psychological[592] constituent of security and stability.[593] The concept of "new environment" has been held to encompass place, home, school, people, friends, activities and opportunities, but not, per se, the child's relationship with the abductor.[594] The absence of

---

[581] Similar procedures apply, *mutatis mutandis*, where a parent in England seeks the recovery of a child wrongfully taken or retained abroad; see eg *Re J (Abduction: Ward of Court)* [1989] Fam 85.

[582] Art 8.

[583] Art 9.

[584] 1985 Act, s 3. In fact, the Official Solicitor acts on his behalf: *Re T (Minors) (International Child Abduction: Access)* [1993] 1 WLR 1461, through the International Child Abduction and Contact Unit (ICACU).

[585] Arts 7, 11.

[586] The return of the child is to the country of its habitual residence: *Re A (A Minor) (Abduction)* [1988] 1 FLR 365 at 373. Cf *O v O (Child Abduction: Return to Third Country)* [2013] EWHC 2970 (Fam).

[587] Art 19.

[588] 1985 Act, s 4. Once an application has been made to the court, it may give interim directions to secure the welfare of the child or to prevent a change in circumstances: s 5; see *Re D (A Minor) (Child Abduction)* [1988] FCR 585, [1989] 1 FLR 97 n; *Re N (Child Abduction: Jurisdiction)* [1995] Fam 96.

[589] Subject to the discretionary grounds for refusal of return, infra, p 1143 et seq.

[590] This means the date of the commencement of the proceedings: *Re N (Minors) (Abduction)* [1991] 1 FLR 413 at 417.

[591] Art 12. See eg Schuz (2008) 20 CFLQ 64. There is also power to stay or dismiss the application if it is thought that the child has been taken to another state. The Convention powers are in addition to any other powers to order the return of the child: Art 18.

[592] Though see *Re C (A Child) (Child Abduction: Settlement)* [2006] EWHC 1229 (Fam), [2006] 2 FLR 797—the fact that a child or teenager is "unsettled" in her own emotional or psychological state does not demonstrate that she is not well settled for the purposes of the Convention in the place where she resides.

[593] *Re N (Minors) (Abduction)* [1991] 1 FLR 413, [1991] Fam Law 367; and see eg *Re S (A Minor) (Abduction)* [1991] 2 FLR 1 at 23–24; *Perrin v Perrin* 1994 SC 45; *Soucie v Soucie* 1995 SLT 414; *Graziano v Daniels* (1991) 14 Fam LR 697; and *Re H (Children)* [2011] CLY 1350. It is possible that in certain situations it may be thought appropriate to put to the child, for his view, the hypothetical scenario of return ("what if?"), but this should never be deemed necessary: *Re H (Children) (Child Abduction: Objection to Return)* [2005] EWCA Civ 319, (2005) 149 SJLB 178, per Sedley LJ, at [25].

[594] *Re N (Minors) (Abduction)* [1991] 1 FLR 413. See also *Re C (A Child) (Child Abduction: Settlement)* [2006] EWHC 1229 (Fam), [2006] 2 FLR 797 at [46]; *Re H and L (Abduction: Acquiescence)* [2010] EWHC 652 (Fam); and *Re H (Children)* [2011] CLY 1350.

any meaningful links between the child and the requesting State will be regarded as highly significant as it shows that the child's life in his new environment is subject to no competition.[595] In *Cannon v Cannon*[596] Thorpe LJ identified three different categories of case in which the issue of settlement may arise. First, there are cases which demonstrate a delayed reaction, short of acquiescence, on the part of the bereft parent: "In that category of case the court must weigh whether or not the child is settled and whether nevertheless to order return having regard to all the circumstances, including the extent of the plaintiff's delay and his explanation for the delay."[597] The second category is where concealment or other subterfuge on the part of the abductor has contributed to the period of delay: "In those cases I would not support a tolling rule that the period gained by concealment should be disregarded and therefore subtracted from the total period of delay in order to ascertain whether or not the twelve-month mark has been exceeded."[598] However, an abducting parent who has engaged in such clandestine and deceitful behaviour will find it harder to prove settlement, and the burden of demonstrating the necessary elements of emotional and psychological settlement will be much increased.[599] It is possible, nevertheless, that the turpitude of the abductor's conduct will be outweighed by the quality of the new environment: "the longer the [abductor] persists in her deceit the more likely she is to hold her advantage".[600] Thirdly, there is the category of "manipulative delay", where, by deliberate conduct, the abductor is successful in delaying the issue of proceedings beyond the twelve-month limit. It is not the case that judges should disregard the "settlement" defence altogether in such cases, but they will look critically at any alleged settlement built upon intentional concealment and deceit, especially if the defendant is a fugitive from criminal justice.[601] Neither uncertain immigration status of the child in the requested State[602] nor the deprivation of the child's previously close relationship with the bereft parent[603] will necessarily prevent the finding of settlement. It is not unusual that considerations pertaining to the settlement of the child in his new environment are merged with considerations related to defences to return under Article 13 of the Convention.[604] Indeed, as the House of Lords has held, "settlement" cases are the most "child-centric" of

---

[595] *Re H (Children)* [2011] CLY 1350.

[596] [2004] EWCA Civ 1330, [2005] 1 FLR 169 at [50] et seq. See also *Re C (Abduction: Settlement) (No 2)* [2005] 1 FLR 938; and *Re M (Children) (Abduction)* [2007] UKHL 55, [2007] 3 WLR 975.

[597] *Cannon v Cannon*, supra, at [50].

[598] Ibid, at [51].

[599] Ibid, at [54]–[58]. See also *Re L (Abduction: Pending Criminal Proceedings)* [1999] 1 FLR 433—hiding children in England for ten months unlikely to constitute settlement; *Re B (Abduction: False Immigration Information)* [2000] 2 FLR 835—due administration of justice requires the courts to be intolerant of attempts to deceive other bodies operating legal functions, such as immigration authorities; and *Re C (A Child) (Child Abduction: Settlement)* [2006] EWHC 1229 (Fam), [2006] 2 FLR 797.

[600] *Cannon v Cannon*, at [58]. Eg *Re C (A Child) (Abduction: Residence and Contact)* [2005] EWHC 2205, [2006] 2 FLR 277.

[601] *Cannon v Cannon*, at [61]. See *M v M (Abduction: Settlement)* [2008] EWHC 2049 (Fam), per Black J, at [35]–[36]. Cf *P v S (Child Abduction: Wrongful Removal)* [2002] Fam LR 2—Lord Ordinary entitled to find child not settled in new environment given circumstances of mother who had moved around Europe for several years, who only recently moved to current location with child and who, upon receiving warning of impending arrest, undoubtedly would have taken steps to evade the authorities further.

[602] *Re E (Abduction: Intolerable Situation)* [2008] EWHC 2112 (Fam). See also *Re H and L (Abduction: Acquiescence)* [2010] EWHC 652 (Fam); and *Re H (Children)* [2011] CLY 1350—in both cases the impact of immigration issues on settlement was commented on by the court in the situation where the child had indefinite leave to remain in the UK.

[603] *F v M and N (Abduction: Acquiescence: Settlement)* [2008] EWHC 1525 (Fam).

[604] Infra. Eg *S v S (Abduction: Wrongful Retention)* [2009] EWHC 1494 (Fam)—twelve months not elapsed, however, return would expose the child to an intolerable situation, under Art 13(b), given his settlement in the UK; and *W v W* [2010] EWHC 332 (Fam)—children objecting to return under Art 13 were found to be settled in the UK.

all child abduction cases and very likely to be combined with the child's objections.[605] Even if settlement is established on the facts, the court retains a residual discretion to order the return of the child.[606] At one time, it was considered that the discretion was specifically conferred by Article 18 of the Convention.[607] However, in *Re M (Children) (Abduction)*,[608] the House of Lords held that Article 18 did not confer any new power to order the return of the child; instead it only contemplated powers conferred by the ordinary domestic law.[609] On the court's view, the discretion to return is implicit in the wording of Article 12 itself.[610] This reading of Article 12 is consistent with Articles 13[611] and 20,[612] both of which expressly confers a discretion on the court.[613] Indeed, the wording of Article 12 "shall also order the return of the child, unless . . ." appears to be just as capable of importing a discretionary power of return into the provision as is the wording "is not bound" in Article 13 and "may also refuse" or "may be refused" in Articles 13 and 20 respectively. Accordingly, the principles for the exercise of discretion as set out by the House of Lords in *Re M*, and outlined below apply equally in the context of all three provisions.[614]

Where the terms of the Convention give rise to discretion, the discretion is at large.[615] Significantly, the Convention objectives should not always be given more weight than the other considerations: "[s]ometimes they should and sometimes they should not."[616] Rather, the court exercising discretion is permitted to take account of "the various aspects of the Convention policy, alongside the circumstances which gave the court a discretion in the first place and the wider considerations of the child's rights and welfare".[617] Departing from earlier authorities,[618] Baroness Hale of Richmond suggested that exercise of discretion should now be approached in a more lenient way than it was before. In particular, her Ladyship held:[619]

> [. . .] it is wrong to import any test of exceptionality into the exercise of discretion under the Hague Convention. The circumstances in which return may be refused are themselves

---

[605] *Re M (Children) (Abduction)* [2007] UKHL 55, at [57].

[606] See *Re S (A Minor) (Abduction)* [1991] FCR 656, [1991] 2 FLR 1; *Re L (Abduction: Pending Criminal Proceedings)* [1999] 1 FLR 433; *J v K (Child Abduction: Acquiescence)* 2002 SC 450; *Cannon v Cannon* [2004] EWCA Civ 1330, [2005] 1 FLR 169; *Re C (A Child) (Child Abduction: Settlement)* [2006] EWHC 1229 (Fam), [2006] 2 FLR 797; and *Re M (Children) (Abduction)* [2007] UKHL 55, [2007] 3 WLR 975.

[607] *Cannon v Cannon*, supra.

[608] [2007] UKHL 55. See also *F v M and N (Abduction: Acquiescence: Settlement)* [2008] EWHC 1525 (Fam); *F v B-F* [2008] EWHC 272 (Fam); *In the Matter of Z (Children)* [2008] EWHC 3473 (Fam), at [55] (obiter); *S v S (Abduction: Wrongful Retention)* [2009] EWHC 1494 (Fam); *D v O* [2011] EWCA Civ 128; and *Re K (A Child)* [2014] EWCA Civ 1364. See also Setright [2008] Fam Law 230.

[609] *Re M (Children) (Abduction)* [2007] UKHL 55, per Baroness Hale of Richmond, at [21].

[610] Ibid, at [31]. Lord Rodger of Earlsferry dissented on this point, however, concluded that "it may not make very much difference in practice whether the discretion is exercised under or outside the Convention". At [7].

[611] Infra, pp 1143–56.

[612] Infra, pp 1162–3.

[613] Ibid, per Lord Hope of Craighead, at [5], and Baroness Hale of Richmond, at [31].

[614] See, infra, pp 1147–8, 1150–1 and 1153–6.

[615] *Re M (Children) (Abduction)* [2007] UKHL 55, per Baroness Hale of Richmond, at [43].

[616] Ibid, at [44].

[617] Ibid. In cases involving settlement, the assumption that the requesting State is the better forum for the resolution of the parental dispute is not necessarily valid. Hence, the policy of the Convention will not automatically point towards a return in such cases, "quite apart from the comparative strength of the countervailing factors". At [47].

[618] *Re S (A Minor) (Abduction: Custody Rights)* [1993] Fam 242—return should be ordered unless the discretionary exercise leads to the conclusion that there are exceptional circumstances for ordering otherwise. See also *Z v Z (Abduction: Children's Views)* [2005] EWCA Civ 1012, at [18]; *Re M (A Child) (Abduction: Brussels II Revised)* [2006] EWCA Civ 630; *K v K* [2007] EWCA Civ 533; and *Re M (A Child)* [2007] EWCA Civ 260, at [80].

[619] *Re M (Children) (Abduction)* [2007] UKHL 55, per Baroness Hale of Richmond, at [40].

exceptions to the general rule. That in itself is sufficient exceptionality. It is neither necessary nor desirable to import an additional gloss into the Convention.

The removal by *Re M* of the "gloss" which had been put on the straightforward terms of the Convention[620] by the previous authorities is to be commended, partly on the grounds of simplicity that it implies and partly in acknowledgement of the "child-centric"[621] trend that it sets in relation to the exercise of discretion in return proceedings. This trend is best summed up in the concluding observation of Baroness Hale of Richmond who, on the facts of the present case, aptly remarked: "children should not be made to suffer for the sake of general deterrence of the evil of child abduction worldwide".[622]

Furthermore, if notice of a wrongful removal has been received in England, whether expressly or by inference,[623] the merits of the custody issue cannot be determined in England until a decision has been taken on the return of the child or unless an application for its return is not made within a reasonable time.[624]

(d) Defences

Although the purpose of the Hague Convention and Part I of the 1985 Act is to ensure the summary return of a child without consideration of the merits of the custody issue,[625] there are three grounds in Article 13 of the Convention on which return may be refused. Such refusal is discretionary and, whilst the court must have regard to the welfare of the child, it must do so in the context of "the overall purpose and philosophy of the Convention".[626] The exceptions to the obligation to return are by their very nature limited in their scope. As such, they do not need "any extra interpretation or gloss".[627]

(i) Child's objections

The first ground of refusal is if the child objects at the date of the court hearing[628] to being returned to the country of his habitual residence, rather than objecting simply to living with a particular parent,[629] "and has attained an age and degree of maturity at which it

---

[620] As her Ladyship rightly observed, "[t]he Convention itself has defined when a child must be returned and when she need not be. Thereafter the weight to be given to Convention considerations and to the interests of the child will vary enormously." Ibid, at [44].

[621] Ibid, at [53].

[622] Ibid, at [54].

[623] *R v R (Residence Order: Child Abduction)* [1995] Fam 209, where a parent abroad had not initiated proceedings under the Convention in the case of what the court concluded was wrongful removal. The court sought to have the parent informed of his rights.

[624] Art 16. It seems hard to understand why, in *H v H (Child Abduction: Stay of Domestic Proceedings)* [1994] 1 FLR 530, the court felt able to order the return of the child to France but then allowed English proceedings to go ahead. Issues which in England are held to go to the merits are listed in the 1985 Act, s 9, as amended by the Children Act 1989, Sch 15, and the Children (Scotland) Act 1995, Sch 4. Furthermore, if an order is made by the High Court for the return of the child, any similar English order ceases to have effect: ss 25, 27, Sch 3 (as amended by the Children Act 1989, Sch 13, para 57, Sch 15).

[625] See *Re E (A Minor) (Abduction)* [1989] 1 FLR 135 at 145; *P v P (Minors) (Child Abduction)* [1992] 1 FLR 155; *Re F (A Minor) (Child Abduction)* [1992] 1 FLR 548; *Re K (Abduction: Child's Objections)* [1995] 1 FLR 977; *Re S (Child Abduction: Delay)* [1998] 1 FLR 651. Speed is strikingly illustrated by *Re J (A Minor) (Abduction: Custody Rights)* [1990] 2 AC 562 where less than three months elapsed between a request being made by the Australian Central Authority for the return of a child in England and the House of Lords decision.

[626] *Re A (Minors) (Abduction: Custody Rights) (No 2)* [1993] Fam 1; *A v A (Child Abduction)* [1993] 2 FLR 225; *W v W (Child Abduction: Acquiescence)* [1993] 2 FLR 211; *Re R (Abduction: Consent)* [1999] 1 FLR 828; and *AVH v SI (Abduction: Child's Objection)* [2014] EWHC 2938 (Fam), at [26].

[627] *Re E (Children) (Abduction: Custody Appeal)* [2011] UKSC 27, at [52].

[628] *Cameron v Cameron (No 2)* 1997 SLT 206.

[629] *Re R (Minors: Child Abduction)* [1995] 1 FLR 716.

is appropriate to take account of its views".[630] The defence of child's objections has to be seen in the context of wider developments that reflect the "growing understanding of the importance of listening to the children involved in children's cases".[631] These developments include, in particular, Article 12 of the United Nations Convention on the Rights of the Child (UNCRC),[632] and Article 11(2) of Brussels II *bis*, which imposes on the courts the duty to hear the child in return proceedings under the 1980 Hague Convention, regardless of whether the child's objections defence has been raised.[633] Even though strictly the obligation that arises from Article 11(2) only applies in intra-European Union return proceedings, in *Re D (A Child) (Abduction: Rights of Custody)*,[634] Baroness Hale of Richmond suggested that the principle was of "universal application" and, as such, was applicable in every Hague Convention case.[635] Her Ladyship considered that the principle that emerged from Article 11(2) of Brussels II *bis* erected "a presumption that the child will be heard unless this appears inappropriate",[636] and this aligned with her view that "children should be heard far more frequently in Hague Convention cases than has been the practice hitherto".[637]

In England, the approach to the child's objections defence is broken down into two stages: the "gateway stage" and the discretion stage.[638] At the gateway stage, the court has to assess two elements: first, whether or not the objections to return are made out;[639] and second, whether the age and maturity of the child are such that it is appropriate for the court to take account of the objections (for unless this is so, the defence cannot be established).[640] Only if the gateway elements are established, the court can proceed to considering whether or not it should exercise its discretion in favour of retention or return.[641] The gateway components are both questions of fact within the province of the trial judge.[642] It will usually be necessary for the trial judge to find out why the child objects to being returned. Normally, the judge will

---

[630] Art 13; and see *Re G (A Minor) (Abduction)* [1990] FCR 189, [1989] 2 FLR 475; *Re S (A Minor) (Abduction)* [1991] FCR 656, [1991] 2 FLR 1.

[631] *Re D (A Child) (Abduction: Rights of Custody)* [2006] UKHL 51, per Baroness Hale of Richmond, at [57]. See also *Re G (Children) (Abduction: Children's Objections)* [2010] EWCA Civ 1232, per Thorpe LJ, at [15].

[632] United Nations Convention on the Rights of the Child 1989 (entered into force in the UK on 15 January 1992). Art 12 provides: "States Parties shall assure to the child who is capable of forming his or her own views the right to express those views freely in all matters affecting the child, the views of the child being given due weight in accordance with the age and maturity of the child." See Schuz [2012] IFL 35.

[633] See infra, pp 1158–9. Another notable development is the decision of the Supreme Court in *Re LC (Children) (International Abduction: Child's Objections to Return)* [2014] UKSC 1, the focus of which was on the importance of the child's own state of mind when determining the child's habitual residence; discussed supra, p 1096.

[634] *Re D (A Child) (Abduction: Rights of Custody)* [2006] UKHL 51.

[635] Ibid, per Baroness Hale of Richmond, at [58].

[636] Ibid.

[637] Ibid, per Baroness Hale of Richmond, at [59].

[638] *Re M (Children) (Abduction: Child's Objections: Joinder of Children as Parties to Appeal)* [2015] EWCA Civ 26, per Black LJ, at [18].

[639] Eg *C v B (Abduction: Grave Risk)* [2005] EWHC 2988, [2006] 1 FLR 1095—child's views not strong enough to amount to "objection" for the purposes of Art 13. See also *K v K* [2006] EWHC 2685, [2007] 1 FCR 355, where a nine-year-old child expressed conflicting opinions, the court held insufficient strength and clarity of objections to warrant exercise of Art 13 discretion.

[640] See *Re M (Children) (Abduction)* [2007] UKHL 55, per Baroness Hale of Richmond, at [46].

[641] *Re M (Children) (Abduction: Child's Objections: Joinder of Children as Parties to Appeal)* [2015] EWCA Civ 26, per Black LJ, at [18].

[642] *Re S (A Minor) (Abduction: Custody Rights)* [1993] Fam 242; *The Ontario Court v M and M (Abduction: Children's Objections)* [1997] 1 FLR 475; *Urness v Minto* 1994 SC 249; *De L v Director-General, New South Wales Department of Community Services* (1996) 139 ALR 417; further proceedings (1997) 21 Fam LR 413.

obtain the views of the child through the CAFCASS[643] officer or other professional.[644] In some cases, especially where the child asked to meet the judge,[645] it may be appropriate for the judge to hear the child.[646] A face to face meeting is an opportunity for the judge to hear what the child might wish to say, and to explain to the child the nature of the process and in particular why, despite the child's views, the court's order might direct a different outcome.[647] Very occasionally, the court might order that the child should be separately represented, but only in exceptional circumstances,[648] subject to the child being capable of giving instructions,[649] and under the condition that separate representation adds enough to the court's understanding of the relevant issues to justify "the intrusion, the expense and the delay that might result".[650] Separate representation will be necessary only in a few cases, however, it is imperative that the child be separately represented whenever "it appears likely that the child's views and interests may not be properly presented to the court, and in particular where there are legal arguments which the adult parties are not putting forward".[651] It is vital that the question of joinder of the child as a party and separate representation be considered at the earliest stage of the return proceedings.[652]

Before the child's views can give rise to the Article 13(2) exception, they must amount to objections as opposed to mere "preferences".[653] In relation to the age and degree of maturity

---

[643] Children and Family Court Advisory and Support Service; see www.cafcass.gov.uk/about-cafcass.aspx.

[644] *Re D (A Child) (Abduction: Rights of Custody)* [2006] UKHL 51, per Baroness Hale of Richmond, at [60]. See also *Re G (Children) (Abduction: Children's Objections)* [2010] EWCA Civ 1232, per Thorpe LJ, at [15].

[645] Although there would also be cases where the judge of his or her own motion should attempt to engage the child. *AJ v JJ* [2011] EWCA Civ 1448, per Thorpe LJ, at [31].

[646] *Re D (A Child) (Abduction: Rights of Custody)* [2006] UKHL 51, per Baroness Hale of Richmond, at [60]. See the Family Justice Council, "Guidelines for Judges Meeting Children who are Subject to Family Proceedings", April 2010. See also *C v W* [2007] EWHC 1349 (Fam), per Sir Mark Potter, at [47]; *De L v H* [2009] EWHC 3074 (Fam), per Sir Mark Potter, at [44]–[45] and [65]; *Re G (Children) (Abduction: Children's Objections)* [2010] EWCA Civ 1232, per Thorpe LJ, at [15]; *AJ v JJ* [2011] EWCA Civ 1448; *Re A (Abduction: Child's Objections to Return)* [2014] EWCA Civ 554; and *Re F (Children)* [2016] EWCA Civ 546.

[647] *Re A (Abduction: Child's Objections to Return)* [2014] EWCA Civ 554, per Moore-Bick, at [53]. It is not the purpose of the meeting to obtain evidence.

[648] Eg *Re T (A Child) (Abduction: Appointment of Guardian ad Litem)* [1999] 2 FLR 796—European Convention case; and *Re F (A Child) (Application for Child Party Status)* [2007] EWCA Civ 393—child party status has been granted only in those cases in which there has been some element of state intervention within the affairs of the family. See also *Re H (A Child) (Child Abduction)* [2006] EWCA Civ 1247, [2007] 1 FLR 242, per Thorpe LJ, at [16]: the test for grant of party status, if it is to be revised in any direction in future, should be more, rather than less, stringently applied, especially in view of strict time limits imposed under Brussels II *bis*, Art 11(3), examined infra, p 1158. See also *Re D (A Child) (Abduction: Rights of Custody)* [2006] UKHL 51, per Baroness Hale of Richmond, at [61]; *Re BF (Children) (Abduction: Child's Objections)* [2010] EWHC 2909 (Fam); and *Re M (Republic of Ireland) (Child's Objections) (Joinder of Children as Parties to Appeal)* [2015] EWCA Civ 26.

[649] *Re T (A Child) (Abduction: Appointment of Guardian ad Litem)* [1999] 2 FLR 796; *Re J (Children) (Abduction: Child's Objections to Return)* [2004] EWCA Civ 428, [2004] 2 FLR 64; and *Re F (A Child) (Application for Child Party Status)* [2007] EWCA Civ 393.

[650] *Re M (Children) (Abduction)* [2007] UKHL 55, at [57]. This test should, however, be less stringent in cases where settlement is raised under Art 12 (see supra, pp 1140–3) as in this type of cases the separate point of view is particularly significant and "should not be lost in the competing claims of the adults". Ibid. See also *Re D (A Child) (Abduction: Rights of Custody)* [2006] UKHL 51, per Baroness Hale of Richmond, at [61]; and *Re C (Abduction: Separate Representation of Children)* [2008] EWHC 517 (Fam).

[651] *Re D (A Child) (Abduction: Rights of Custody)* [2006] UKHL 51, per Baroness Hale of Richmond, at [61]. See also *Re N (Children)* [2015] EWCA Civ 1076.

[652] *Re M (Children) (Abduction: Child's Objections: Joinder of Children as Parties to Appeal)* [2015] EWCA Civ 26, per Black LJ, at [140]. See also *Re N (Children)* [2015] EWCA Civ 1076, per Ryder LJ, at [8].

[653] *Re S (A Minor) (Abduction: Custody Rights)* [1993] Fam 242, per Balcombe LJ. See also *Re LC (Children) (International Abduction: Child's Objections to Return)* [2014] UKSC 1, per Lord Wilson, at [8] and [17] (not

of the child, it should be asked whether the child is more mature or less mature or as mature as his chronological age.[654] There is no minimum age below which the child's views are to be discounted,[655] nor has maturity been defined for this purpose. Although it is rare for the courts to take account of the views of a child of seven or younger,[656] in *Re W (Abduction: Child's Objections)*,[657] the Court of Appeal accepted that objections of a child as young as six were capable of justifying a refusal to return under Article 13(2). It is accepted that a child "may be mature enough for it to be appropriate for her view to be taken into account even though she may not have gained that level of maturity that she is fully emancipated from parental dependence and can claim autonomy of decision-making".[658]

Over the years, the approach at the gateway stage was discussed in numerous authorities, with the resulting law being "far from simple".[659] In particular, a highly technical approach emerged from the decision of Ward LJ in *Re T (Children) (Abduction: Child's Objections to Return)*.[660] In that case, after reviewing some of the early authorities,[661] his Lordship drew a number of principles from them, and listed some of the factors which the court should consider at this stage. These included: (a) the child's own perspective of what is in his interests in the short, medium and long term; (b) the extent to which the reasons underpinning the objection are rooted in reality; (c) the extent to which the child's views have been shaped or coloured by undue influence and pressure, directly or indirectly exercised by the abductor;[662] and (d) the extent to which the objections will be mollified upon return and, where relevant, removal from any pernicious influence from the abductor. Despite its complexity, the "*Re T*" approach became accepted as the proper approach at the gateway stage.[663] Recently, however, the "*Re T*" reasoning was doubted by Black LJ in *Re M (Children) (Abduction: Child's Objections: Joinder of Children as Parties to Appeal)*.[664] Her Ladyship expressed preference for "the more basic" approach, embodied in the decision of Wilson LJ, in *Re W (Abduction: Child's Objections)*,[665] advocating hence a much simpler

---

disapproving the terminology); and *Re M (Children) (Abduction: Child's Objections: Joinder of Children as Parties to Appeal)* [2015] EWCA Civ 26, per Black LJ, at [38].

[654] *Re T (Children) (Abduction: Child's Objections to Return)* [2000] 2 FLR 192.

[655] *Re S (A Minor) (Abduction: Custody Rights)* [1993] Fam 242; *Re R (Minors: Child Abduction)* [1995] 1 FLR 716.

[656] *Re R (Minors: Child Abduction)*, supra, at 730; *Re K (Abduction: Child's Objections)* [1995] 1 FLR 977; *Cameron v Cameron (No 2)* 1997 SLT 206. Cf *Re B (Abduction: Children's Objections)* [1998] 1 FLR 667.

[657] [2010] EWCA Civ 520.

[658] *Re T (Children) (Abduction: Child's Objections to Return)* [2000] 2 FLR 192, per Ward LJ.

[659] *Re M (Children) (Abduction: Child's Objections: Joinder of Children as Parties to Appeal)* [2015] EWCA Civ 26, per Black LJ, at [13]. See also *Re M (Republic of Ireland) (Child's Objections) (Joinder of Children as Parties to Appeal)* [2015] EWCA Civ 26.

[660] [2000] 2 FLR 192. See also *Re J (Children) (Abduction: Child's Objections to Return)* [2004] EWCA Civ 428; *De L v H* [2009] EWHC 3074 (Fam); *W v W* [2010] EWHC 332 (Fam); *Re A (Children) (Abduction: Objections: Non-Return)* [2013] EWCA Civ 1256; and *Kinderis v Kineriene (No 2)* [2014] EWHC 693 (Fam).

[661] Eg *Re S (A Minor) (Abduction: Custody Rights)* [1993] Fam 242; and *Re S (Minors) (Abduction: Acquiescence)* [1994] 1 FLR 819.

[662] If it appears that a child has been "coached" by the abducting parent, then it is probable that little or no weight will be attributed to his views.

[663] Eg *Re J (Children) (Abduction: Child's Objections to Return)* [2004] EWCA Civ 428; *Re M (A Child)* [2007] EWCA Civ 260; *De L v H* [2009] EWHC 3074 (Fam); and *W v W* [2010] EWHC 332 (Fam).

[664] [2015] EWCA Civ 26 (Ryder LJ and Richards LJ agreeing). See also *NP v JP* [2015] EWHC 2551 (Fam); *Re F (Child's Objections)* [2015] EWCA Civ 1022; and *C v V* [2016] EWHC 559 (Fam).

[665] [2010] EWCA Civ 520. See *Re BF (Children) (Abduction: Child's Objections)* [2010] EWHC 2909 (Fam); and *Re M (Children) (Abduction: Child's Objections: Joinder of Children as Parties to Appeal)* [2015] EWCA Civ 26, at [50] and [56]. See also *AVH v SI (Abduction: Child's Objection)* [2014] EWHC 2938

exercise at the gateway stage whereby the detail of the case is left to be considered at the discretion stage.[666] Namely, she stated:[667]

> [. . .] the position should now be, in my view, that the gateway stage is confined to a straightforward and fairly robust examination of whether the simple terms of the Convention are satisfied in that the child objects to being returned and has attained an age and degree of maturity at which it is appropriate to take account of his or her views. Sub-tests and technicality of all sorts should be avoided. In particular, the Re T approach to the gateway stage should be abandoned.

Black LJ was careful to point out that she did not intend to develop a new test; quite the contrary, she sought to dissuade "an over-prescriptive or over-intellectualised approach" to the child's objections defence.[668] Nevertheless, she was willing to provide a few examples of situations when the gateway stage assessment will result in the Article 13(2) defence not being established. These include situations where the child is "merely parroting" the views of the abducting parent; lacks the requisite degree of maturity; objects not to the "right thing"; or expresses a preference rather than an objection.[669]

The approach at the gateway stage suggested by Black LJ is to be preferred over the view of Ward LJ in *Re T*. The solution proposed by her Ladyship is simple and straightforward, and avoids the technicalities inherent in the "*Re T*" approach. Not less importantly, by simplifying the gateway stage and moving the assessment of the relevant details to the discretion stage, accord is achieved with the second stage of the process, ie the exercise of discretion.[670]

The exercise of discretion is to be guided by the principles set out by the House of Lords in *Re M (Children) (Abduction)*.[671] These principles were mentioned earlier[672] and can be summarized as follows: (1) the discretion is at large; (2) there is no requirement of exceptionality; and (3) the court is entitled to take into account the various aspects of Convention policy, the circumstances which gave the court discretion in the first place, and wider considerations of the child's rights and welfare.[673] Additionally, specific to the exercise of discretion in relation to the child's objections defence, the court may have to consider "the nature

---

(Fam), at [29]; and *Re M (Republic of Ireland) (Child's Objections) (Joinder of Children as Parties to Appeal)* [2015] EWCA Civ 26.

[666] *Re M (Children) (Abduction: Child's Objections: Joinder of Children as Parties to Appeal)*, [2015] EWCA Civ 26, at [50]. See also *Re W (Abduction: Child's Objections)* [2010] EWCA Civ 520—the gateway stage represents a "fairly low threshold". Per Wilson LJ, at [22].

[667] *Re M (Children) (Abduction: Child's Objections: Joinder of Children as Parties to Appeal)*, [2015] EWCA Civ 26, at [68].

[668] Ibid, at [77].

[669] Ibid.

[670] Infra. See *Re M (Children) (Abduction: Child's Objections: Joinder of Children as Parties to Appeal)* [2015] EWCA Civ 26, at [70]. The "*Re T*" approach is likely to lead to duplication and to strip the discretionary role of its proper function. Ibid, at [65] and [66]. See also *Re U-B (A Child)* [2015] EWCA Civ 60, at [15].

[671] [2007] UKHL 55. See also *S v De P* [2008] EWHC 1798 (Fam); *M v T (Abduction)* [2008] EWHC 1383 (Fam) (obiter); *Re BF (Children) (Abduction: Child's Objections)* [2010] EWHC 2909 (Fam); *CB v CB* [2013] EWHC 2092 (Fam); *AVH v SI (Abduction: Child's Objection)* [2014] EWHC 2938 (Fam); *Kinderis v Kineriene (No 2)* [2014] EWHC 693 (Fam); *Re S (A Child) (Habitual Residence and Child's Objections)(Brazil)* [2015] EWCA Civ 2; *MR v HS* [2015] EWHC 234 (Fam); *NP v JP* [2015] EWHC 2551 (Fam); and *Re F (Child's Objections)* [2015] EWCA Civ 1022.

[672] See supra, p 1142. The same principles apply in relation to the exercise of discretion under Art 12 as well as Art 13.

[673] *Re M (Children) (Abduction)* [2007] UKHL 55, per Baroness Hale of Richmond, at [40], [43] and [47].

and strength of the child's objections, the extent to which they are 'authentically her own' or the product of the influence of the abducting parent, the extent to which they coincide or are at odds with other considerations which are relevant to her welfare,[674] as well as the general Convention considerations".[675] Importantly, regardless of the age of the child,[676] his objections are not determinative of the outcome of the case; rather the objections are merely one of the factors to be considered at the discretion stage.[677] In other words, the child's "right" under Article 13 of the Convention is a right to be heard, not a right to self-determination.[678] Accordingly, "hearing the child is not to be confused with giving effect to his views".[679]

(ii) Consent or acquiescence

The second ground on which return may be refused requires opponents[680] of the child's return to establish that the person, institution or other body in the other country having care of the child was not actually exercising custody rights at the time of removal, or consented to or subsequently acquiesced in the removal or retention. So far as consent is concerned, it does not fall to be considered in order to establish the wrongfulness of a removal or a breach of custody rights pursuant to Article 3, but rather it is to be taken into account for the purpose of invoking the court's discretion pursuant to Article 13.[681] It follows that the burden of proof rests on the abducting parent who has to establish, on a simple balance of probability, that there was, prior to the child's removal, a "positive and unequivocal giving of consent".[682] The most recent authoritative summary of the English courts' approach to consent can be found in the Court of Appeal decision in *Re P-J (Children) (Abduction: Consent)*.[683] Consent to the removal of the child must be clear and unequivocal,[684] and can only be given by the custody holder whose rights are at risk of being breached.[685] Although the inquiry is inevitably fact specific,

---

[674] This does not mean that the discretionary stage is to involve a full-blown welfare enquiry. Such an approach would run contrary to the underlying philosophy of the Convention that return proceedings are of a summary nature and designed to be concluded very quickly. *Re S (A Child)(Habitual Residence and Child's Objections)(Brazil)* [2015] EWCA Civ 2, per Black LJ, at [59]. See also *AVH v SI (Abduction: Child's Objection)* [2014] EWHC 2938 (Fam).

[675] *Re M (Children) (Abduction)* [2007] UKHL 55, per Baroness Hale of Richmond, at [46]. The list is not to be considered as exhaustive. *Re M (Children) (Abduction: Child's Objections: Joinder of Children as Parties to Appeal)* [2015] EWCA Civ 26, per Black LJ, at [71].

[676] Nevertheless, the older the child is, the greater the weight his objections are likely to carry. *Re M (Children) (Abduction)* [2007] UKHL 55, per Baroness Hale of Richmond, at [46].

[677] *Re M (Children) (Abduction)* [2007] UKHL 55, per Baroness Hale of Richmond, at [46]. See also *Re M (Children) (Abduction: Child's Objections: Joinder of Children as Parties to Appeal)* [2015] EWCA Civ 26, per Black LJ, at [46]; [62] and [63].

[678] *C v W* [2007] EWHC 1349 (Fam), per Sir Mark Potter, at [48].

[679] *Re D (A Child) (Abduction: Rights of Custody)* [2006] UKHL 51, per Baroness Hale of Richmond, at [58].

[680] *T v T* 2004 SC 323; and *K v K* [2006] EWHC 2685, [2007] 1 FCR 355. See also *Re P-J (Children) (Abduction: Consent)* [2009] EWCA Civ 588, per Ward LJ, at [48].

[681] *Re P (A Child) (Abduction: Custody Rights)* [2004] EWCA Civ 971, [2004] 2 FLR 1057, per Ward LJ, at [22]. See also *Re P-J (Children) (Abduction: Consent)* [2009] EWCA Civ 588, per Ward LJ, at [38]–[43] and Wilson LJ, at [53]—both Lords Justices touched on the issue, however, neither of them wished to revive that debate. Ward LJ, nevertheless, remarked that it was "much better to deal with consent as a discrete issue being a defence under Article 13(a)". At [43].

[682] *C v H (Abduction: Consent)* [2009] EWHC 2660 (Fam), per Munby J, at [10]. This approach follows the House of Lords decision in *Re B (Children) (Care Proceedings: Standard of Proof)* [2008] UKHL 35.

[683] [2009] EWCA Civ 588. See also *M v M* [2010] EWHC 3350 (Fam); *A v T (Abduction: Consent)* [2011] EWHC 3882 (Fam); *In the Matter of H, R and E (Children)* [2013] EWHC 3857 (Fam); *C v D* [2015] EWHC 3990 (Fam); *IB v MM* 2015 EWHC 1502 (Fam); and *A v B* [2015] EWHC 1562 (Fam).

[684] *Re P-J (Children) (Abduction: Consent)* [2009] EWCA Civ 588, per Ward LJ, at [48].

[685] *C v H (Abduction: Consent)* [2009] EWHC 2660 (Fam)—consent given by the parents of a bereft parent who himself is a minor is irrelevant for the purposes of the Convention. Ibid, per Munby J, at [8].

the ultimate question is whether the bereft parent had clearly and unequivocally consented to the removal.[686] Whilst consent does not have to be in writing,[687] and can be inferred from conduct,[688] there must be firm and unequivocal evidence of it.[689] Furthermore, purported consent obtained by deception or non-disclosure will be disregarded.[690] Similarly, statements made in anger and distress which were not intended by the bereft parent as permission to the removal of the child, will not be considered as amounting to consent.[691] Consent within the meaning of Article 13 is not governed by the law of contract; instead it must be viewed "in the context of the realities of the disintegration of family life".[692] Accordingly, it can be withdrawn any time before actual removal,[693] however, in order for the withdrawal to be effective, it must be objectively plain to the party who would otherwise seek to rely upon it.[694] Nevertheless, once consent has been acted upon it cannot be retracted by the parent who gave it.[695] Reliance can be placed on advance or conditional consent whereby the removal is to occur at some future unspecified time or upon the happening of some future event.[696] Such consent, however, must still be effective at the time of the removal.[697] Where future consent is conditioned by the happening of some future event, this event must be reasonably ascertainable.[698] Fulfilment of the condition must not depend on the subjective determination of one party.[699]

The difference between consent and acquiescence is in the timing.[700] The former must be given before or at the time of removal or retention,[701] whilst the latter can be passive and

---

[686] *Re P-J (Children) (Abduction: Consent)* [2009] EWCA Civ 588, per Ward LJ, at [48]. It is not required that words such as "agree" or "consent" are used: *Re C (Abduction: Consent)* [1996] 1 FLR 414; and *C v H (Abduction: Consent)* [2009] EWHC 2660 (Fam), per Munby J, at [18].

[687] *Re C (Abduction: Consent)* [1996] 1 FLR 414 at 418–19; *Re K (Abduction: Consent)* [1997] 2 FLR 212 at 216–18; *Re R (Minors) (Abduction: Consent)* [1999] 1 FCR 87 at 90; all disapproving *Re W (Abduction: Procedure)* [1995] 1 FLR 878 at 888; but see now *Re M (Abduction: Consent: Acquiescence)* [1999] 1 FLR 171 at 187.

[688] *Zenel v Haddow* 1993 SC 612; *Re C (Abduction: Consent)* [1996] 1 FLR 414; and *Re R (Abduction: Consent)* [1999] 1 FLR 828. However, unlike acquiescence, consent cannot be inferred from inactivity: *Re W (Abduction: Procedure)* [1995] 1 FLR 878; and *C v H (Abduction: Consent)* [2009] EWHC 2660 (Fam), at [15].

[689] *Re C (Abduction: Consent)*, supra, at 419; *Re R (Minors) (Abduction: Consent)*, supra, at 90; *Re M (Abduction: Consent: Acquiescence)* [1999] 1 FLR 171; *C v C* 2003 SLT 793; and *Re A (Abduction: Consent: Habitual Residence: Consent)* [2005] EWHC 2998, [2006] 2 FLR 1.

[690] *Re B (A Minor) (Abduction)* [1994] 2 FLR 249; *Re B (Abduction: Article 13 Defence)* [1997] 2 FLR 573 at 575; *Re M (Abduction) (Consent: Acquiescence)* [1999] 1 FLR 171 at 189; *T v T (Child Abduction: Consent)* [1999] 2 FLR 912; *H v H* [2004] EWHC 2111; and *D v S (Abduction: Acquiescence)* [2008] EWHC 363 (Fam). It has been suggested that this principle is applicable also in the context of acquiescence. *BT v JRT* [2008] EWHC 1169 (Fam), per Sir Christopher Sumner, at [53].

[691] *JPC v SLW and SMW (Abduction)* [2007] EWHC 1349 (Fam); and *C v D* [2015] EWHC 3990 (Fam).

[692] *Re P-J (Children) (Abduction: Consent)* [2009] EWCA Civ 588, per Ward LJ, at [48]. See also *C v D* [2015] EWHC 3990 (Fam).

[693] *Re P-J (Children) (Abduction: Consent)* [2009] EWCA Civ 588, at [48].

[694] *Re Z (Abduction)* [2008] EWHC 3473 (Fam), per Macur J, at [34]. See also *VK v JV (Abduction: Consent)* [2012] EWHC 4033 (Fam)—consent withdrawn successfully in relation to one of the children concerned.

[695] *Re K (Abduction: Consent)* [1997] 2 FLR 212. See also *K v K (Abduction: Consent)* [2009] EWHC 2721 (Fam); and *VK v JV (Abduction: Consent)* [2012] EWHC 4033 (Fam)—consent withdrawn too late in relation to one of the children concerned.

[696] *Re P-J (Children) (Abduction: Consent)* [2009] EWCA Civ 588, per Ward LJ, at [48]. See also *Re L (Abduction: Future Consent)* [2007] EWHC 2181 (Fam); and *C v H (Abduction: Consent)* [2009] EWHC 2660 (Fam).

[697] *Re P-J (Children) (Abduction: Consent)* [2009] EWCA Civ 588, per Ward LJ, at [48].

[698] Ibid. See also *Re L (Abduction: Future Consent)* [2007] EWHC 2181 (Fam).

[699] *Re P-J (Children) (Abduction: Consent)* [2009] EWCA Civ 588, per Ward LJ, at [48].

[700] *Re A (Minors) (Abduction: Custody Rights)* [1992] Fam 106 at 123.

[701] *Re A (Minors) (Abduction: Custody Rights)* [1992] Fam 106 at 115; *Re C (Abduction: Consent)* [1996] 1 FLR 414; and *Re M (Abduction) (Consent: Acquiescence)* [1999] 1 FLR 171.

can be inferred simply from lapse of time after the removal or retention without objection to it,[702] as in the case of a fourteen-month,[703] but not a four-month,[704] delay. Acquiescence may be implied from other circumstances,[705] as well, of course, as being expressly conveyed,[706] but, like consent, it must be unequivocal.[707] It had been thought that, in determining whether a parent had acquiesced, a court was only to consider his actual intentions in a case of passive acquiescence.[708] This approach was rejected by the House of Lords in *Re H (Abduction: Acquiescence)*[709] where Lord Browne-Wilkinson made clear that "acquiescence is a question of the actual subjective intention of the wronged parent, not of the outside world's perception of his intentions".[710] This question is one of fact,[711] not law, and subject to one exception applies to all types of acquiescence. The exception is: "Where the words or actions of the wronged parent clearly and unequivocally show and have led the other parent to believe that the wronged parent is not asserting or going to assert his right to the summary return of the child and are inconsistent with such return, justice requires the wronged parent be held to have acquiesced."[712]

One factor that may be relevant in determining whether in fact there has been acquiescence is the extent to which the wronged parent has received correct legal advice, or is broadly aware of, his position.[713] The court will also be cautious of statements which might appear to amount to acquiescence if they were made when "the parties are in a state of confusion and emotional turmoil",[714] or in the heat of argument.[715] It has been said that "acquiescence is not a continuing state of affairs",[716] which would tend to indicate that acquiescence for however short a period before it is retracted will fall within this second ground. More recently, however, the courts have taken a broader view and discounted a very short period of acquiescence, certainly where it had not been relied on by the other parent.[717] The court will be reluctant to infer acquiescence from

---

[702] *Re A (Minors) (Abduction: Custody Rights)* [1992] Fam 106.

[703] *Re M (Abduction: Acquiescence)* [1996] 1 FLR 315; and see *W v W (Child Abduction: Acquiescence)* [1993] 2 FLR 211. Undue delay could also lead to the proceedings being struck out: *Re G (Abduction: Striking Out Application)* [1995] 2 FLR 410. Cf *Medhurst v Markle* (1995) 17 RFL (4th) 428.

[704] *Re R (Minors) (Abduction)* [1994] 1 FLR 190; and see *Re K (Abduction: Child's Objections)* [1995] 1 FLR 977.

[705] *Re M (Abduction) (Consent: Acquiescence)* [1999] 1 FLR 171; and see *Re D (Abduction: Acquiescence)* [1999] 1 FLR 36.

[706] *A v A (Child Abduction)* [1993] 2 FLR 225; *Re O (Abduction: Consent and Acquiescence)* [1997] 1 FLR 924; and *Re B (A Child) (Abduction: Acquiescence)* [1999] 2 FLR 818.

[707] *T v T (Child Abduction: Consent)* [1999] 2 FLR 912; *Re I (Abduction: Acquiescence)* [1999] 1 FLR 778; *Re H (A Child) (Abduction: Habitual Residence: Consent)* [2000] 2 FLR 294; *Re A (Abduction: Consent: Habitual Residence: Consent)* [2005] EWHC 2998, [2006] 2 FLR 1; and *M v M* [2007] EWHC 1820 (Fam).

[708] Eg *Re A (Minors) (Abduction: Custody Rights)* [1992] Fam 106; and see *Re AZ (A Minor) (Abduction: Acquiescence)* [1993] 1 FLR 682; though doubts were expressed in *Re S (Minors) (Abduction: Acquiescence)* [1994] 1 FLR 819.

[709] [1998] AC 72.

[710] Ibid, at 88. See also *Re H (Abduction: Child of 16)* [2000] 2 FLR 51.

[711] Eg, *Re D (Abduction: Acquiescence)* [1998] 2 FLR 335.

[712] [1998] AC 72 at 90; eg, *Re AZ (A Minor) (Abduction: Acquiescence)* [1993] 1 FLR 682; *D v S (Abduction: Acquiescence)* [2008] EWHC 363 (Fam); *B-G v B-G* [2008] EWHC 688 (Fam); *Re H and L (Abduction: Acquiescence)* [2010] EWHC 652 (Fam); and *Re H (Children)* [2011] CLY 1350.

[713] *Re AZ (A Minor) (Abduction: Acquiescence)*, supra; *Re S (Abduction: Acquiescence)* [1998] 2 FLR 115; *B-G v B-G* [2008] EWHC 688 (Fam); and *D v S (Abduction: Acquiescence)* [2008] EWHC 363 (Fam.

[714] *Department of Health and Community Services v Casse* (1995) 19 Fam LR 474 at 480; and see *Re A (Abduction: Custody Rights)* [1992] Fam 106 at 121.

[715] *C v W* [2007] EWHC 1349 (Fam).

[716] *Re A (Abduction: Custody Rights)* [1992] Fam 106 at 121. See also *De L v H* [2009] EWHC 3074 (Fam), per Sir Mark Potter, at [38].

[717] *Re R (Child Abduction: Acquiescence)* [1995] 1 FLR 716 at 727; and see *Re R (Minors) (Abduction)* [1994] 1 FLR 190 at 200.

attempted reconciliation or efforts to secure a voluntary return of the child.[718] Furthermore, it has been held that "acquiescence shown to have been obtained by fraud, misunderstanding or nondisclosure is unlikely to be effective".[719]

Notwithstanding a finding of consent or acquiescence, the court has discretion to order the child's immediate return,[720] in order that outstanding custody issues might be resolved in the court of the state where the child is habitually resident. Exercise of discretion in this respect is equivalent, in effect, to the court sanctioning a change of mind by the consenting or acquiescing party after the other parent (the "abductor") has acted in reliance upon that consent or acquiescence.[721] When exercising discretion courts are to be guided by the principles set out by the House of Lords in *Re M (Children) (Abduction)*.[722]

(iii) Grave risk of harm

The third ground on which return may be refused is "that there is a grave risk that his or her return would expose the child to physical or psychological harm or otherwise place the child in an intolerable position".[723] The provision is of restricted application and, accordingly, there is no need for it to be "narrowly construed".[724] In other words, the terms of Article 13(b) are unambiguous and, by themselves, demonstrate the restricted availability of the defence.[725] As such, they need no further elaboration or "gloss".[726] The words "physical or psychological harm" are not qualified; however, they "gain colour" from the third limb of the defence.[727] As Ward LJ, in *Re S (A Child) (Abduction: Custody Rights)*,[728] explained:

> To the extent that three risks are named, there are three discrete defences. They are, however, linked by the use of the word "otherwise" . . . The use of the word "otherwise" points inescapably to the conclusion that the physical or psychological harm contemplated by the first clause of Article 13(b) is harm to a degree that also amounts to an intolerable situation.[729]

---

[718] *P v P (Abduction: Acquiescence)* [1998] 2 FLR 835; *Re L (Abduction: Acquiescence)* [1999] 1 FLR 778; and *Re G (Abduction: Withdrawal of Proceedings, Acquiescence, Habitual Residence)* [2007] EWHC 2807 (Fam)—withdrawal of the first return proceedings to attempt reconciliation did not constitute acquiescence for the purposes of subsequent return application; *W v W* [2010] EWHC 332 (Fam); and *Re WA (a Child) (Abduction) (Consent; Acquiescence; Grave Risk of Harm or Intolerability)* [2015] EWHC 3410 (Fam).

[719] *BT v JRT* [2008] EWHC 1169 (Fam), per Sir Christopher Sumner, at [53].

[720] *Re D (Abduction: Discretionary Return)* [2000] 1 FLR 24; and *T v T* 2004 SC 323.

[721] *M v M* [2007] EWHC 1404 (Fam), per Sumner J, at [48]–[49].

[722] [2007] UKHL 55; discussed supra, pp 1142 and 1147–8. See eg *T v T* [2008] EWHC 1169 (Fam); *M v T (Abduction)* [2008] EWHC 1383 (Fam) (obiter); *K v K (Abduction: Consent)* [2009] EWHC 2721 (Fam); *A v T (Abduction: Consent)* [2011] EWHC 3882 (Fam); and *A v B* [2015] EWHC 1562 (Fam). Specifically, in relation to consent and acquiescence cases, the Court noted that general considerations of comity and individual considerations relating to the specific child might point to a speedy return so that the child's future can be decided in his home country. *Re M (Children) (Abduction)* [2007] UKHL 55, at [45].

[723] Art 13(b).

[724] *Re E (Children) (Abduction: Custody Appeal)* [2011] UKSC 27, per Lady Hale and Lord Wilson, at [31]. See also *Re WA (a Child) (Abduction) (Consent; Acquiescence; Grave Risk of Harm or Intolerability)* [2015] EWHC 3410 (Fam), at [57]; *AT v SS* [2015] EWHC 2703 (Fam), at [31]; and *T v E* [2016] EWHC 3148 (Fam), at [34].

[725] *Re S (A Child) (Abduction: Rights of Custody)* [2012] UKSC 10, at [6].

[726] *Re E (Children) (Abduction: Custody Appeal)* [2011] UKSC 27, per Lady Hale and Lord Wilson, at [31]. See eg *F v M* [2015] EWHC 3300 (Fam), at [22]; and *AT v SS* [2015] EWHC 2703 (Fam), at [31].

[727] *Re E (Children) (Abduction: Custody Appeal)* [2011] UKSC 27, per Lady Hale and Lord Wilson, at [34]. See also *IB v MM* 2015 EWHC 1502 (Fam), at [88]; *F v M* [2015] EWHC 3300 (Fam), at [22]; *AT v SS* [2015] EWHC 2703 (Fam), at [31]; and *T v E* [2016] EWHC 3148 (Fam), at [34].

[728] [2002] EWCA Civ 908, [2002] 2 FLR 815.

[729] Ibid, [38]. Cf *Director-General of Family and Community Services v Davis* (1990) 14 Fam LR 381.

An intolerable situation has to be "something extreme and compelling".[730] Put another way, "a very high degree of intolerability must be established".[731] In practical terms, the term "intolerable" in Article 13(b) refers to "a situation which this particular child in these particular circumstances should not be expected to tolerate".[732] Although "every child has to put up with a certain amount of rough and tumble, discomfort and distress", there are certain situations which it is unreasonable to expect a child to tolerate.[733] It has been held that such situations include not only physical or psychological abuse or neglect of the child himself, but also exposure to the harmful effects of witnessing by the child of physical or psychological abuse of his own parent.[734] It is irrelevant whether the risk is the result of objective reality or of the abducting parent's subjective perception of reality.[735] As Lord Wilson, in *Re S (A Child) (Abduction: Rights of Custody)*, observed:[736]

> The critical question is what will happen if, with the mother, the child is returned. If the court concludes that, on return, the mother will suffer such anxieties that their effect on her mental health will create a situation that is intolerable for the child, then the child should not be returned. It matters not whether the mother's anxieties will be reasonable or unreasonable. The extent to which there will, objectively, be good cause for the mother to be anxious on return will nevertheless be relevant to the court's assessment of the mother's mental state if the child is returned.

Whilst it may be clear that a child will suffer psychological harm if its return is ordered, the court has to determine whether that is outweighed by the harm that would ensue if no order was made. It is clear that the harm must be substantial[737] and the risk of it must be "grave".[738] Although "grave" denotes the risk rather than the harm, there is a connection between the two.[739] This means that "a relatively low risk of death or really serious injury might properly be qualified as 'grave' while a higher level of risk might be required for other less serious forms of harm".[740] In assessing the degree of risk, the court may look at the practical

---

[730] *Re N (Minors) (Abduction)* [1991] 1 FLR 413 at 419; *Re R (A Minor: Abduction)* [1992] 1 FLR 105 at 107; *Re C (Abduction: Grave Risk of Psychological Harm)* [1999] 1 FLR 1145.

[731] *B v B (Abduction: Custody Rights)* [1993] Fam 32 at 42; *C (A Child) (Abduction: Grave Risk of Physical or Psychological Harm) (No 1)* [1999] 2 FLR 478; and *Re M (A Child) (Abduction: Intolerable Situation)* [2000] 1 FLR 930.

[732] *Re D (A Child) (Abduction: Rights of Custody)* [2006] UKHL 51, [2007] 1 AC 619, at [52]; and *Re S (A Child) (Abduction: Rights of Custody)* [2012] UKSC 10, at [27]. See also *Re H (Abduction)* [2009] EWHC 1735 (Fam), at [17]; *Re WA (A Child) (Abduction) (Consent; Acquiescence; Grave Risk of Harm or Intolerability)* [2015] EWHC 3410 (Fam), at [57]; *AT v SS* [2015] EWHC 2703 (Fam), at [31]; and *T v E* [2016] EWHC 3148 (Fam), at [34].

[733] *Re E (Children) (Abduction: Custody Appeal)* [2011] UKSC 27, at [34].

[734] Ibid, at [34] and [52].

[735] Ibid, at [34]; and *Re S (A Child) (Abduction: Rights of Custody)* [2012] UKSC 10, at [31]. See also *IB v MM* (2015) EWHC 1502 (Fam), at [89]; *F v M* [2015] EWHC 3300 (Fam), at [31]; and *AT v SS* [2015] EWHC 2703 (Fam), at [31].

[736] [2012] UKSC 10, at [34]. See also *Re E (Children) (Abduction: Custody Appeal)* [2011] UKSC 27, at [34]—in principle, a defence under Art 13(b) can be founded upon the anxieties of the mother about a return with the child to the requesting State not based upon objective risk to her but, nevertheless, of such intensity as to be likely, in the event of a return, to destabilise her mental health and her ability to parent the child to the point at which the child's situation would become intolerable. See eg *T v E* [2016] EWHC 3148 (Fam). Cf *Re F (A Child) (Abduction: Art 13(b): Psychiatric Assessment)* [2014] EWCA Civ 275.

[737] *Re Gsponer's Marriage* (1988) 94 FLR 164 at 177; *Director-General of Family and Community Services v Davis* (1990) 14 Fam LR 381; and *Re L (A Child)* [2005] EWHC 1237, [2006] 1 FLR 843.

[738] It is insufficient, as it is for example in the context of asylum, that the risk be "real". *Re E (Children) (Abduction: Custody Appeal)* [2011] UKSC 27, at [33].

[739] *Re E (Children) (Abduction: Custody Appeal)* [2011] UKSC 27, at [33]. See also *IB v MM* (2015) EWHC 1502 (Fam), at [88]; and *F v M* [2015] EWHC 3300 (Fam), at [22]; and *T v E* [2016] EWHC 3148 (Fam), at [34].

[740] *Re E (Children) (Abduction: Custody Appeal)* [2011] UKSC 27, at [33].

consequences involved in the return of the child, such as financial provision, accommodation, or language.[741]

The burden of proof rests with the person opposing the child's return, and the standard of proof is the simple balance of probabilities.[742] Given the summary nature of return proceedings under the Convention, it will seldom be appropriate to hear oral evidence related to the allegations made under Article 13(b).[743]

The role of the "home country" cannot be thwarted by a parent refusing to return with the child and then arguing that the child will suffer grave psychological harm from being separated from that parent.[744] To accept such an argument would "drive a coach and four through the Convention, at least in respect of applications by young children".[745] However, the notion that a parent cannot be allowed to create a situation and then rely on it to his/her benefit "is not a principle articulated in the Convention or the [1985] Act and should not be applied to the effective exclusion of the very defence itself, which is in terms directed to the question of risk of harm to the child and not the wrongful conduct of the abducting parent".[746] The courts have regularly emphasised that they are concerned here not with the "paramount consideration" of the child's welfare, but rather with whether the child should be returned speedily to the jurisdiction most appropriate for the determination of that issue.[747] "No requested country can be expected to return children to a situation where they will be at serious risk, but this must not be turned into a substitute for the welfare test, usurping the function of the courts of the home country."[748]

Even if the threshold of grave risk is crossed, there still remains a discretion in the court whether to return the child. Traditionally, English courts have taken a good deal of convincing that return should be refused on this ground to which they have given a strict and

---

[741] *Re A (A Minor) (Abduction)* [1988] 1 FLR 365, [1988] Fam Law 54; *Re A (Minors) (Abduction: Custody Rights)* [1992] Fam 106; *B v B (Abduction: Custody Rights)* [1993] Fam 32; *MacMillan v MacMillan* 1989 SLT 350; *C v C* 2003 SLT 793; *Re J (Abduction: Acquiring Custody Rights by Caring for Child)* [2005] 2 FLR 791; and *S v B (Abduction: Human Rights)* [2005] EWHC 733, [2005] 2 FLR 878. See also *Re C (Abduction: Interim Directions: Accommodation by Local Authority)* [2003] EWHC 3065, [2004] 1 FLR 653.

[742] *Re E (Children) (Abduction: Custody Appeal)* [2011] UKSC 27, at [32]. See also *F v M* [2015] EWHC 3300 (Fam), at [22]; *AT v SS* [2015] EWHC 2703 (Fam), at [31]; and *T v E* [2016] EWHC 3148 (Fam), at [34].

[743] *Re E (Children) (Abduction: Custody Appeal)* [2011] UKSC 27, at [32].

[744] *TB v JB (Abduction: Grave Risk of Harm)* [2001] 2 FLR 515, per Arden LJ, at [96]. The situation may be different where it is impossible or impractical for the abductor to return with the child: *C v C* 2003 SLT 793; *Re A (Abduction: Consent: Habitual Residence: Consent)* [2005] EWHC 2998, [2006] 2 FLR 1. But see *AL, Petitioner* [2007] CSOH 55—respondent mother unable to accompany child on flight to Australia due to pregnancy, but other travel options identified by court, and so return ordered.

[745] *C v C (Abduction: Rights of Custody)* [1989] 1 WLR 654 at 661; *V v B (A Minor) (Abduction)* [1991] 1 FLR 266 at 274; *N v N (Abduction: Article 13 Defence)* [1995] 1 FLR 107; *McCarthy v McCarthy* 1994 SLT 743; *Thorne v Dryden-Hall* (1995) 18 RFL (4th) 15; and *S v B (Abduction: Human Rights)* [2005] EWHC 733, [2005] 2 FLR 878 at [49].

[746] *S v B (Abduction: Human Rights)* [2005] EWHC 733, [2005] 2 FLR 878, per Sir Mark Potter, at [49]. See also *AT v SS* [2015] EWHC 2703 (Fam), at [46].

[747] Eg *C v C (Abduction: Rights of Custody)* [1989] 1 WLR 654 at 661; *V v B (A Minor) (Abduction)* [1991] 1 FLR 266 at 273; *Re Gsponer's Marriage* (1988) 94 FLR 164 at 178–80; and *I, Petitioner* [1999] Fam LR 126. See Schuz [2012] IFL 35.

[748] *TB v JB (Abduction: Grave Risk of Harm)* [2001] 2 FLR 515, per Hale LJ, at [38]. On this point, see *Neulinger and Shuruk v Switzerland* (Grand Chamber) [2010] ECHR 41615/07; *X v Latvia* (Grand Chamber) [2013] ECHR 27853/09, [2014] 1 FLR 1135; *Re E (Children) (Abduction: Custody Appeal)* [2011] UKSC 27; and *Re S (A Child) (Abduction: Rights of Custody)* [2012] UKSC 10; discussed infra, p 1156.

narrow interpretation:[749] "for the child's Article 13 defence to prevail over the policy of the Convention, there must be something in the facts of the case which takes it out of the ordinary into the exceptional".[750] So, in the past, English courts ordered the return of a child to Australia even though the mother would have serious accommodation problems there,[751] or would face the prospect of arrest and imprisonment;[752] they ordered return of a child to Israel, in spite of political instability and random, indiscriminate terrorist attacks;[753] and a Scottish court concluded that a child is unlikely to be placed in an intolerable position by being returned to Canada even though a grandparent who was likely to look after the child spoke no English.[754] In only a few cases the high threshold required for the Article 13(b) defence to be established was reached and discretion was exercised in favour of a non-return order. It was held that the kind of risk which would justify a refusal of the return order was return to a war zone, or to a child abuser, or to some other risk of that nature and gravity.[755] So, for example, a Scottish court refused to return a child to Canada in the face of evidence of the Canadian father's depression and alcoholism;[756] and an English court refused to return a child to the USA, given the violence shown by the father both to the child and to his mother.[757]

The approach to the exercise of discretion has, however, changed following the judgment of the House of Lords in *Re M (Children) (Abduction)*.[758] As mentioned earlier,[759] in rejecting the principle of exceptionality, the decision has signaled a shift towards a more "child-centered" approach to the exercise of discretion in return proceedings.[760] As Baroness Hale of Richmond remarked: "It was not the policy of the Convention that children should be put at serious risk of harm or placed in intolerable situations."[761] The correct approach is now to consider the different aspects of the Convention policy in conjunction with the circumstances which gave the court discretion in the first place, and wider considerations of the child's rights and welfare.[762]

---

[749] Eg *P v P (Minors) (Child Abduction)* [1992] 1 FLR 155; *Starr v Starr* 1999 SLT 335; and *Re C (Minors) (Abduction: Grave Risk of Psychological Harm)* [1999] 1 FLR 1145.

[750] *Re M (A Child) (Abduction: Brussels II Revised)* [2006] EWCA Civ 630, [2006] 2 FLR 1180, per Wall LJ, at [75]. Cf *Re S (A Child) (Abduction: Custody Rights)* [2002] EWCA Civ 908, [2002] 2 FLR 815, per Ward LJ, at [49]: "The court must steel itself against too freely allowing this exceptional defence and the defendant must be put to strict proof."

[751] *Re A (A Minor) (Wrongful Removal of Child)* [1988] Fam Law 383; and see *C v C (Abduction: Rights of Custody)* [1989] 1 WLR 654; *Re E (A Minor) (Abduction)* [1989] 1 FLR 135, [1989] Fam Law 105; *Re G (A Minor) (Abduction)* [1989] 2 FLR 475, [1989] Fam Law 473; *V v B (A Minor) (Abduction)* [1991] FCR 451, [1991] 1 FLR 266; *Parsons v Styger* (1989) 67 OR (2d) 1.

[752] *Re L (Abduction: Pending Criminal Proceedings)* [1999] 1 FLR 433.

[753] *Re S (A Child) (Abduction: Custody Rights)* [2002] EWCA Civ 908, [2002] 2 FLR 815. See also *Re M (A Child)* [2007] EWCA Civ 260, (2007) 151 SJLB 434, per Sir Mark Potter, at [84].

[754] *Viola v Viola* 1988 SLT 7.

[755] *M, Petitioner* 2007 SLT 433, per Lord Malcolm, at 436; and *Re L (A Child) (Abduction: Jurisdiction)* [2002] EWHC 1864, [2002] 2 FLR 1042.

[756] *Macmillan v Macmillan* 1989 SLT 350. See also *Q, Petitioner* 2001 SLT 243. Contrast *McCarthy v McCarthy* 1994 SLT 743; *Medhurst v Markle* (1995) 17 RFL (4th) 428.

[757] *Re F (A Minor) (Abduction: Custody Rights Abroad)* [1995] Fam 224; cf *N v N (Abduction: Article 13 Defence)* [1995] 1 FLR 107; *Re M (A Minor) (Abduction: Leave to Appeal)* [1999] 2 FLR 550; and *Re D (Children) (Article 13(b): Non-Return)* [2006] EWCA Civ 146, [2006] 2 FLR 305.

[758] [2007] UKHL 55. See supra, pp 1142 and 1147–8. See eg *M v T (Abduction)* [2008] EWHC 1383 (Fam) (obiter); and *Re H (Abduction)* [2009] EWHC 1735 (Fam).

[759] See supra, pp 1142 and 1147–8.

[760] See supra, p 1142.

[761] *Re M (Children) (Abduction)* [2007] UKHL 55, per Baroness Hale of Richmond, at [45].

[762] Ibid, at [40], [43] and [47].

Usually, it is reasonable to expect the "home country" to be able to provide adequate protection.[763] In intra-EU Hague Convention cases, Article 11(4) of Brussels II *bis* expressly provides that a court cannot refuse to return a child on the basis of the "grave risk of harm" defence "if it is established that adequate arrangements have been made to secure the protection of the child after his or her return".[764] The role of the protective measures is to ensure a "soft landing" for the child's return.[765] The measures of protection can take the form of undertakings offered by the left-behind parent[766] or court orders available from the courts of the requesting State.[767] In either case, it has to be shown that such arrangements will be effective to protect the child.[768] The effectiveness of undertakings in particular is likely to be compromised by their non-enforceability in the requesting State.[769] Indeed, as has been rightly pointed out, there is no coherent mechanism for recognizing and enforcing protective measures.[770]

Reliance is often placed on Article 13(b) where the wrongful removal or retention was prompted by alleged ill-treatment of the abducting parent by the bereft parent.[771] Cases

---

[763] *TB v JB (Abduction: Grave Risk of Harm)*, [2001] 2 FLR 515; *Re M (A Child)(Abduction: Intolerable Situation)* [2000] 1 FLR 930; *Re H (Children) (Child Abduction: Grave Risk)* [2003] EWCA Civ 355, [2003] 2 FLR 141; *Re W (A Child) (Abductions: Conditions for Return)* [2004] EWCA Civ 1366, [2005] 1 FLR 727; *M v T (Abduction)* [2008] EWHC 1383 (Fam); *Re E (Children) (Abduction: Custody Appeal)* [2011] UKSC 27, at [35]; *In the Matter of H, R and E (Children)* [2013] EWHC 3857 (Fam); *AT v SS* [2015] EWHC 2703 (Fam), at [31] and [61]–[63]; *F v M* [2015] EWHC 3300 (Fam), at [22]; and *In the Matter of M (Children)* [2016] EWCA Civ 942. But see *Q, Petitioner* 2001 SLT 243, *Re S (A Child) (Abduction: Custody Rights)* [2002] EWCA Civ 908, [2002] 2 FLR 815, per Ward LJ, at [85]; *MR v HS* [2015] EWHC 234 (Fam), at [46]; and *T v E* [2016] EWHC 3148 (Fam), at [69].

[764] See infra, p 1159.

[765] *Re E (Children) (Abduction: Custody Appeal)* [2011] UKSC 27, at [45].

[766] Undertakings can be described as "promises offered or in certain circumstances imposed upon an applicant to overcome obstacles which may stand in the way of the return of a wrongfully removed or retained child". Beaumont and McEleavy, *The Hague Convention on International Child Abduction*, p 30. See also McClean (1990) 106 LQR 375; and Trimmings, *Child Abduction within the European Union* (2013) pp 155–61. Eg *C v C (Abduction: Rights of Custody)* [1989] 1 WLR 654; *Re G (A Minor) (Wrongful Removal of Child)* [1990] FCR 189, [1989] 2 FLR 475; *Re O (Child Abduction: Undertakings)* [1994] 2 FLR 349; *Re M (Minors) (Child Abduction: Undertakings)* [1995] 1 FLR 1021; *Police Comr of South Australia v Temple* (1993) 17 Fam LR 144; *P v B (Child Abduction: Undertakings)* [1994] 3 IR 507; *Re W (A Child) (Abductions: Conditions for Return)* [2004] EWCA Civ 1366, [2005] 1 FLR 727; *Re R (Abduction: Immigration Concerns)* [2004] EWHC 2042, [2005] 1 FLR 33; *C v W* [2007] EWHC 1349 (Fam); *LL v PL*, 29 March 2007 (unreported) (Fam Div); *PF v EM* [2008] EWHC 1467 (Fam); *In the Matter of H, R and E (Children)* [2013] EWHC 3857 (Fam); *C v D (Abduction: Grave Risk of Harm)* [2013] EWHC 2989 (Fam); *NF v EB* [2014] EWHC 484 (Fam); *AT v SS* [2015] EWHC 2703 (Fam); *MS v PS* [2015] EWHC 2880 (Fam); and *F v M* [2015] EWFC 76.

[767] *Re D (A Child) (Abduction: Rights of Custody)* [2006] UKHL 51, [2007] 1 AC 619, at [52].

[768] Ibid.

[769] *Re E (Children) (Abduction: Custody Appeal)* [2011] UKSC 27, at [7]: "indeed the whole concept of undertakings is not generally understood outside the common law world". Eg *In the Marriage of McOwan* (1993) 17 Fam LR 377—anxieties as to how far undertakings can be enforced in the country to which the child is returned; cf *Re K (Abduction: Psychological Harm)* [1995] 2 FLR 550; and *Walley v Walley* [2005] EWCA Civ 910, [2005] 3 FCR 35, where an order with stringent conditions attached has been breached, the proper course is to apply for the order to be set aside in light of the non-compliance, rather than to appeal. See also *C v D (Abduction: Grave Risk of Harm)* [2013] EWHC 2989 (Fam)—three potential safeguards as regards the enforceability in Spain of undertakings given in England discussed.

[770] *Re E (Children) (Abduction: Custody Appeal)* [2011] UKSC 27, at [37]. Although it has been held that the 1996 Hague Protection Convention could be utilized to ensure enforceability of undertakings (see supra, p 1102; and see also Lowe and Douglas, *Bromley's Family Law*, p 1066), there is a more fundamental problem, namely that "the whole concept of undertakings is not generally understood outside the common law world". See *Re E (Children) (Abduction: Custody Appeal)* [2011] UKSC 27, at [7].

[771] Ibid. For a critical appraisal of the operation of the Convention in the context of domestic violence, see Weiner (2000) 69 Fordham Law Review 593; Kaye (1999) 13 International Journal of Law, Policy and the Family 191; and Bruch (2004) 38 Fam LQ 529.

involving domestic violence are likely to trigger a particular need for protection not only in relation to the child but also the abducting parent, as it is now acknowledged that violence between parents may constitute a grave risk of harm to the child.[772] The summary nature of return proceedings, however, prevents the court of the requested State from fully investigating factual disputes between the parties,[773] and, in effect, establishing with requisite precision the risks that the child will face upon his return should the allegations of domestic abuse be true. In order to alleviate this tension, the following approach has been endorsed by the House of Lords:[774]

> Where allegations of domestic abuse are made, the court should first ask whether, if they are true, there would be a grave risk that the child would be exposed to physical or psychological harm or otherwise placed in an intolerable situation. If so, the court must then ask how the child can be protected against the risk. The appropriate protective measures and their efficacy will obviously vary from case to case and from country to country.

In other words, where there are disputed allegations which cannot be investigated or objectively verified, the inquiry is to be focused on the sufficiency of any protective measures. The logical implication is that the more obvious the need for protection, the more effective the measures will have to be.[775]

In many cases, protective measures will be sufficient to avoid the risk; however, it will not always be the case.[776] In such circumstances, it would be "inconceivable that a court which reached the conclusion that there was a grave risk that the child's return would expose him to physical or psychological harm or otherwise place him in an intolerable situation would nevertheless return him to face that fate".[777]

Sibling solidarity[778] A difficult issue may arise where there appears to be a good case for declining to order the return of one child but not his sibling, as where the former child is older and objects to the return, or indeed vice versa. Courts have concluded that the separation of siblings can amount to intolerability and / or grave risk of psychological harm for the purposes of Article 13(b).[779] In such circumstances, either both[780] or neither[781] of the children have been returned. A Canadian court, on the other hand, has ordered the return of a three-year-old child, but not her fourteen-year-old sister, who objected to her return.[782]

---

[772] *Re E (Children) (Abduction: Custody Appeal)* [2011] UKSC 27, at [34] and [52].

[773] See supra, p 1140.

[774] *Re E (Children) (Abduction: Custody Appeal)* [2011] UKSC 27, at [36]. See eg *Kent CC v C* [2014] EWHC 604 (Fam), at [43]; and *In the Matter of M (Children)* [2016] EWCA Civ 942, per Macur LJ, at [7].

[775] *Re E (Children) (Abduction: Custody Appeal)* [2011] UKSC 27, at [52].

[776] *Re D (A Child) (Abduction: Rights of Custody)* [2006] UKHL 51, [2007] 1 AC 619, at [52].

[777] Ibid, at [55]. See also *Re S (A Child) (Abduction: Rights of Custody)* [2012] UKSC 10, at [5]; and *Re M (Children) (Abduction)* [2007] UKHL 55, per Baroness Hale of Richmond, at [45]. See eg *NP v JP* [2015] EWHC 2551 (Fam), at [36]; and *T v E* [2016] EWHC 3148 (Fam), at [35].

[778] Sometimes, older siblings who are not subject to the return proceedings can be joined as a party. See eg *W v W* [2009] EWHC 3288 (Fam); *Re E (Children) (Abduction: Custody Appeal)* [2011] UKSC 27, at [50]–[51]; and *Re S (Child Abduction: Joinder of Sibling: Child's Objections)* [2016] EWHC 1227 (Fam). See Family Proceedings Rules 2010, r 12.3.

[779] *Re LC (Children) (International Abduction: Child's Objections to Return)* [2013] EWCA Civ 1058 (reversed on other points: *Re LC (Children) (International Abduction: Child's Objections to Return)* [2014] UKSC 1); and *Re WA (a Child) (Abduction) (Consent; Acquiescence; Grave Risk of Harm or Intolerability)* [2015] EWHC 3410 (Fam), at [58]. Cf *F v M* [2015] EWHC 3300 (Fam), per Cobb J, at [31].

[780] *Re HB (Abduction: Children's Objections)* [1997] 1 FLR 392.

[781] *B v K (Child Abduction)* [1993] 1 FCR 382; *Urness v Minto* 1994 SC 249; *The Ontario Court v M and M (Abduction: Children's Objections)* [1997] 1 FLR 475; *Re T (Children) (Abduction: Child's Objections to Return)* [2000] 2 FLR 192; *Q, Petitioner* 2001 SLT 243; *W v W* 2003 SCLR 478; *Re BF (Children) (Abduction: Child's Objections)* [2010] EWHC 2909 (Fam); and *IB v MM* (2015) EWHC 1502 (Fam).

[782] *Chalkley v Chalkley* (1995) 10 RFL (4th) 442.

Importantly, a return order which interferes with the sibling's enjoyment of family life may amount to a violation of that sibling's rights under Article 8 of the European Convention on Human Rights[783] (ECHR), unless it is in accordance with the law, in pursuit of a legitimate aim and proportionate.[784]

(e) Impact of Brussels II *bis*[785]

Recital 17 of Brussels II *bis* narrates that, in cases of wrongful removal or retention[786] of a child, the return of the child should be obtained without delay. To this end, it is said that the 1980 Hague Convention should continue to apply, *as complemented by* the provisions of the Regulation,[787] in particular Article 11. The 1980 Hague Convention has been ratified by all EU Member States, but the provisions of Brussels II *bis* will prevail in relation to "intra-EU" abductions, ie any case where a child is "abducted" from one European Union Member State (except Denmark) (the "Member State of origin") and taken to another European Union Member State (the "requested Member State").

(i) Jurisdiction in cases of child abduction

The 1980 Hague Convention does not lay down rules of jurisdiction, and so to this extent the special rule of jurisdiction contained in Article 10 of Brussels II *bis* complements the Convention. Where a child is abducted from the Member State of origin to the requested Member State, Article 10 ensures that the courts in the first state retain jurisdiction to determine questions of custody.[788] In a case of wrongful removal or retention of a child, the courts of the Member State where the child was habitually resident immediately before the wrongful removal or retention shall retain their jurisdiction until the child has acquired a habitual residence in another Member State and: (a) each person, institution or other body having rights of custody has acquiesced in the removal or retention;[789] or (b) the child has resided in that other Member State for a period of at least one year after the person, institution or other body having rights of custody has had or should have had knowledge of the whereabouts of the child[790] and the child is settled in his new environment and at least one of four conditions is met, namely: (i) within one year after the holder of rights of custody has had or should have had knowledge of the whereabouts of the child, no request for return has been lodged before the competent authorities of the Member State where the child has been removed or is being retained; (ii) a request for return lodged by the holder of rights

---

[783] European Convention for the Protection of Human Rights and Fundamental Freedoms 1950.

[784] See *S v B (Abduction: Human Rights)* [2005] EWHC 733 (Fam); and *Re WA (A Child) (Abduction) (Consent; Acquiescence; Grave Risk of Harm or Intolerability)* [2015] EWHC 3410 (Fam), at [58] and [68].

[785] For background, see McEleavy (2004) 53 ICLQ 503, 509. See also Lowe *et al*, *The New Brussels II Regulation* (2005); Trimmings, *Child Abduction within the European Union* (2013); and Lowe and Nicholls, *International Movement of Children: Law, Practice and Procedure* (2016).

[786] Defined in Art 2(11). Cf definition in 1980 Hague Convention, Art 3. The Regulation expressly states that: "Custody shall be considered to be exercised jointly when, pursuant to a judgment or operation of law, one holder of parental responsibility cannot decide on the child's place of residence without the consent of another holder of parental responsibility." In consequence of this, removal of a child from one European Union Member State to another Member State without the consent of such a person amounts to wrongful removal under Brussels II *bis*. Where the removal is lawful according to the Member State of origin, Art 9 may apply. Supra, pp 1097–8.

[787] Art 60 of the Regulation states that Brussels II *bis* takes precedence over the 1980 Hague Convention as regards relations between European Union Member States. See also Child Abduction and Custody Act, s 1(3). As regards the relationship between Brussels II and the 1980 Hague Convention, see *Re L (A Child) (Abduction: Jurisdiction)* [2002] EWHC 1864, [2002] 2 FLR 1042.

[788] See, eg, *Re A, HA v MB (Brussels II Revised: Article 11(7) Application)* [2007] EWHC 2016 (Fam); *B v D* [2008] EWHC 1246 (Fam); *Re A (Child) (Hague Convention Proceedings)* [2014] EWCA Civ 375; and *Re X, Y and Z (Children) (Retrospective Leave to Remove from the Jurisdiction)* [2016] EWHC 2439 (Fam).

[789] See eg *Tower Hamlets LBC v MK* [2012] EWHC 426 (Fam).

[790] *M v M (Abduction: Settlement)* [2008] EWHC 2049 (Fam).

of custody has been withdrawn and no new request has been lodged within the time limit set in (i); (iii) a case before the court in the Member State where the child was habitually resident immediately before the wrongful removal or retention has been closed pursuant to Article 11(7) because the parties have not made relevant submissions within three months of notification;[791] or (iv) a judgment[792] on custody that does not entail the return of the child has been issued by the courts of the Member State where the child was habitually resident immediately before the wrongful removal or retention. It has been held that, in principle, jurisdiction can be retained by virtue of Article 10 even where the child concerned is presently living in a country which is a non-Member State.[793] The CJEU has clarified that Article 10(b)(iv) is to be construed strictly, and that the judgment referred to in the provision must be a final judgment.[794] Accordingly, a provisional measure does not constitute a judgment for the purposes of Article 10(b)(iv).[795]

(ii) Return of the child

Where the court of a Member State receives a request for return of a child pursuant to the 1980 Hague Convention, it must apply the rules in the Convention as complemented by Brussels II *bis*, in particular Article 11(2) to (8).[796]

(iii) Expeditious procedure[797]

Article 11(3) stipulates that a court to which an application for return of a child is made shall act expeditiously in proceedings on the application, using the most expeditious procedures available in national law. In particular, save where exceptional circumstances render it impossible, the court shall issue its judgment no later than six weeks after the application is lodged.[798] "Article 11(3) does not specify that such decisions . . . shall be enforceable within the same period. However, this is the only interpretation which would effectively guarantee the objective of ensuring the prompt return of the child within the strict time-limit."[799] To this effect, the Court of Appeal has held that the requirement to deal with return proceedings within six weeks extended to appeal hearings.[800] Article 11(3) is designed to eliminate detailed examination of welfare considerations.[801]

---

[791] Infra, p 1159.

[792] See remarks of Singer J in *Re A, HA v MB (Brussels II Revised: Article 11(7) Application)* [2007] EWHC 2016 (Fam) at [122] et seq.

[793] *Re H (Children) (Jurisdiction: Habitual residence)* [2014] EWCA Civ 1101, per Black LJ, at [51]. Cf *Re I (A Child) (Contact Application: Jurisdiction)* [2009] UKSC 10, discussed supra, pp 1099–100; and *A v A and Another (Children: Habitual Residence) (Reunite International Child Abduction Centre and Others Intervening)* [2013] UKSC 60—the jurisdiction rules of the Regulation apply regardless of whether there is an alternative jurisdiction in a non-Member State.

[794] Case C-211/10PPU, *Povse v Alpago* [2010] ECR I–6673, at [45]–[46].

[795] Ibid, at [47].

[796] Art 11(1).

[797] See Commission Proposal for the Recast of Brussels II *bis*, COM (2016) 411 final 30 June 2016, pp 12–13.

[798] It was indicated in *Re M (A Child) (Abduction: Brussels II Revised)* [2006] EWCA Civ 630, [2006] 2 FLR 1180, per Thorpe LJ, at [44], that compliance with this time limit generally will require "queue-jumping" for cases proceeding under Brussels II *bis*. Priority will be given to Brussels II *bis* abduction cases over other cases on the Family Division list, which seems barely justifiable. It may well be necessary to reconsider the six-week target. See also *Re H (A Child) (Child Abduction)* [2006] EWCA Civ 1247, [2007] 1 FLR 242, per Thorpe LJ, at [16]–[18]; *K v K* [2007] EWCA Civ 533, per Thorpe LJ, at [27]–[30]; *Re F (A Child) (Abduction: Obligation to Hear Child)* [2007] EWCA Civ 468, per Thorpe LJ, at [28].

[799] *Practice Guide*, para 4.3.5.

[800] *K v K* [2007] EWCA Civ 533, per Thorpe LJ, at [27]–[30].

[801] See supra, p 1140.

(iv) Child's views[802]

It is expressly stated that, "the hearing of the child plays an important role in the application of this Regulation".[803] This is true generally,[804] and in particular in relation to cases of wrongful removal or retention. Article 11(2) establishes that, when applying the provisions of Articles 12 and 13 of the 1980 Hague Convention, the competent authorities in a Member State shall ensure that the child is given the opportunity to be heard during the proceedings,[805] unless this appears inappropriate having regard to his age or degree of maturity. The principle of a mandatory hearing of the child of an appropriate age and a sufficient degree of maturity established by Article 11(2) represents an expansion on the Hague Convention obligation to hear the child in those abduction cases where the defence of child's objections has been raised by the abducting parent.[806] The child's views may be ascertained for the purposes of the Regulation according to normal procedures.[807] The grant of party status is to be made only in exceptional cases. Although it is vital that the child's voice be heard, "the method by which the voice of the child is heard admits of a wide degree of appreciation in the individual member state",[808] and can be achieved without the child being joined as a party to the proceedings.[809]

(v) Applicant's views

Article 11(5) forbids a Member State court from refusing to return a child unless the person who requested the return of the child has been given an opportunity to be heard.

(vi) Enquiry as to adequate arrangements to secure child's protection[810]

Article 11(4) prevents a Member State court from refusing to return a child on the basis of Article 13(b) of the 1980 Hague Convention if it is established that adequate arrangements have been made to secure the protection of the child after his return. The fact that protective measures[811] are available in the state of the child's habitual residence should nullify an Article 13(b) defence.[812] The Article 13(b) exception to the return of the child is to be kept to a "strict minimum".[813] The court is obliged to return the child where, despite it having been established that return could expose the child to physical or psychological harm or otherwise place him in an intolerable situation, the authorities in the Member State of origin have made adequate arrangements, ie "concrete measures",[814] to secure the protection of the child upon his return.

---

[802] See Trimmings, *Child Abduction within the European Union* (2013) Ch 7; and Commission Proposal for the Recast of Brussels II *bis*, COM (2016) 411 final 30 June 2016, pp 15 and 42.

[803] Recital (19).

[804] Hearing the child's views is a requirement of the abolition of *exequatur* procedure in relation to rights of access (Arts 40 and 41), and also may be a ground for refusing to recognise a judgment relating to parental responsibility (Art 23(b)).

[805] Recital 20 allows the hearing of a child in another Member State to take place under the arrangements laid down in Council Regulation (EC) No 1206/2001 (supra, p 81 et seq).

[806] See supra, p 1143 et seq.

[807] Recital (19). Eg *C v W* [2007] EWHC 1349 (Fam); and *K v K* [2007] EWCA Civ 533. Discussed, supra p 1158.

[808] *Re H (A Child) (Child Abduction)* [2006] EWCA Civ 1247, [2007] 1 FLR 242, per Thorpe LJ, at [16].

[809] *Re F (A Child) (Application for Child Party Status)* [2007] EWCA Civ 393. Supra, p 1145.

[810] See Commission Proposal for the Recast of Brussels II *bis*, COM (2016) 411 final 30 June 2016, pp 43–4.

[811] Discussed supra, pp 1154–6.

[812] *Re M (A Child) (Abduction: Brussels II Revised)* [2006] EWCA Civ 630, [2006] 2 FLR 1180, per Thorpe LJ, at [36]; *Re A (A Child) (Custody Decision after Maltese Non-Return Order)* [2006] EWHC 3397 (Fam), [2007] 1 FCR 402, per Singer J, at [109]; and *K v K* [2007] EWCA Civ 533. See also *PF v EM* [2008] EWHC 1467 (Fam); *Re Y (Abduction: Undertakings Given for Return of Child)* [2013] EWCA Civ 129; *Kinderis v Kineriene (No 2)* [2014] EWHC 693 (Fam), at [46]; *AT v SS* [2015] EWHC 2703 (Fam); and *NP v JP* [2015] EWHC 2551 (Fam).

[813] *Practice Guide*, para 4.3.3.

[814] Ibid.

Article 11(4) clearly envisages that "adequate measures actually be in force."[815] The involvement of relevant Central Authorities is likely to be necessary in order to assist the judge in the receiving Member State to assess the factual circumstances in the Member State of origin.

(vii) Non-return orders[816]

If a Member State court has issued a non-return order pursuant to Article 13(b) of the 1980 Hague Convention, the court must immediately,[817] either directly or through its Central Authority, transmit a copy of that order and relevant documents to the court with jurisdiction or Central Authority in the Member State where the child was habitually resident immediately before the wrongful removal or retention, as determined by national law. Unless the court in that state (the Member State of origin) has already been seised by one of the parties, it must notify the parties of the receipt of information and invite them to make submissions to the court within three months of the date of notification, so that it can examine the question of custody of the child.[818] If no submission is received by the court within the time limit specified, it shall close the case. If the court of the Member State of origin receives submissions, it is competent to deal with the substance of the case in its entirety, eg custody and access rights.

The significance of Brussels II *bis* in this regard concerns Article 11(8), which provides that, notwithstanding a non-return order pursuant to Article 13 of the 1980 Hague Convention,[819] any subsequent judgment which requires the return of the child issued by a court having jurisdiction in terms of Brussels II *bis* shall be enforceable in accordance with Articles 40 to 45 of the Regulation.[820] Recital (17) explains the rationale:

> The courts of the Member State to or in which the child has been wrongfully removed or retained should be able to oppose his or her return in specific, duly justified cases. However, such a decision could be replaced by a subsequent decision by the court of the Member State of habitual residence of the child prior to the wrongful removal or retention. Should that judgment entail the return of the child, the return should take place without any special procedure being required for recognition and enforcement of that judgment in the Member State to or in which the child has been removed or retained.

In other words, the Member State of origin has the final say in the matter.

Recital (17) envisages the situation where a *subsequent* decision by the court of the Member State of habitual residence requires return; it does not deal with the situation where a decision already has been made by that court sanctioning *ex post facto* the removal of a child.[821] In *Re T and J (Children) (Abduction: Recognition of Foreign Judgment)*,[822] Sir Mark Potter stated:

---

[815] *Re E (Children) (Abduction: Custody Appeal)* [2011] UKSC 27, at [37].

[816] See Beaumont *et al* (2016) 12 J Priv Int L 211.

[817] Within 1 month of the date of the non-return order: Art 11(6).

[818] Art 11(7); and Recital (17). See eg *Re A, HA v MB (Brussels II Revised: Article 11(7) Application)* [2007] EWHC 2016 (Fam); *Re H (Abduction: Jurisdiction)* [2009] EWHC 2280 (Fam); *M v T* [2010] EWHC 1479 (Fam); and *AF (Father) v T (Mother)* [2011] EWHC 1315 (Fam).

[819] But not an order under other provisions of the Convention see, eg *Re RD (Child Abduction) (Brussels II Revised: Arts 11(7) and 19)* [2009] 1 FLR 586—Art 12(2); and *Re RC and BC (Child Abduction) (Brussels II Revised: Article 11(7))* [2009] 1 FLR 574—Art 3.

[820] See eg *Re A (A Child) (Custody Decision after Maltese Non-Return Order)* [2006] EWHC 3397 (Fam), [2007] 1 FCR 402; and *R v D* [2016] EWHC 1154 (Fam).

[821] As in *Re T and J (Children) (Abduction: Recognition of Foreign Judgment)* [2006] EWHC 1472, [2006] 2 FLR 1290. See comments of Sir Mark Potter, at [42]: Art 11 of Brussels II *bis* "does not touch on the situation where the court of the State to which the child has been removed has available to it, before its decision is made, a court decision from the State of the child's habitual residence which sanctions the removal of the child". Recognition of judgments is addressed by Arts 21 and 23, examined, supra, p 1126 et seq.

[822] [2006] EWHC 1472, [2006] 2 FLR 1290.

If . . . proceedings under the Hague Convention are commenced at a time when the issue sought to be resolved, namely where and with which parent the child should be residing, is already before the Court of the Member State where the child is habitually resident, and if, prior to the Hague Convention hearing, that issue is resolved in favour of the abducting parent, then the whole thrust and purpose of Brussels II b (as well as in spirit, if not the letter of the Hague Convention itself) operates in favour of an order for non-return.[823]

It has been held[824] that in exercising the jurisdiction under Article 11(7) of Brussels II *bis*, the court is not carrying out an appeal process in respect of a foreign decision but rather is exercising the welfare jurisdiction it has always held under Article10. Accordingly, a welfare approach has to be applied.[825] In *D v N v D (By her Guardian ad Litem)*[826] Theis J summarized the approach to undertaking the examination of the question of the custody of the child pursuant to Article 11(7) as follows: 1) The interrelationship of Articles 10 and Articles 11(7) and (8) permit the Member State of origin to undertake an examination of the question of the custody of the child once a non-return order pursuant to Article 13 has been made by the requested State; 2) Proceedings under Article 11(7) should be carried out as speedily as possible;[827] 3) The judge should be in a position that he or she would have been in if the abducting parent had not abducted the child.[828] Hence, the whole range of orders that would normally be available to a judge should be available also in proceedings under Article 11(7);[829] 4) The child's welfare shall be the court's paramount consideration;[830] 5) It may not be necessary or appropriate to classify the jurisdictional basis for the proceedings as deriving from the inherent jurisdiction. The foundation for any examination of the question of the custody of the child is simply through the gateway of Article 11(7); 6) In proceedings under Article 11(7) the court is able to order the summary return of a child to England to facilitate the decision making process leading to a final judgment;[831] 7) In deciding whether to order a summary return or to carry out a full welfare enquiry, the court exercises a welfare jurisdiction.[832] "It is not altogether clear whether the decision to order a return of the child on a summary basis is more appropriately considered as akin to that which might be ordered under the inherent jurisdiction or whether it is effectively a specific issue order under the Children Act 1989 order: if it is more appropriately considered as akin to the inherent jurisdiction then — at least as to the question of summary return — it may not be necessary for the court mechanistically and slavishly to direct itself to the welfare checklist; that having been said, once the child has returned and the court is considering what order to make the court should direct itself to the welfare checklist;" and 8) The summary return order is directly enforceable in accordance with the relevant provisions of Brussels II *bis*.[833]

---

[823] Ibid, at [52].

[824] *M v T* [2010] EWHC 1479 (Fam), per Charles J, at [17].

[825] Ibid.

[826] [2011] EWHC 471 (Fam), at [39]. See also *Re AJ (A Minor) (Brussels II Revised)* [2011] EWHC 3450 (Fam); *AF (Father) v T (Mother)* [2011] EWHC 1315 (Fam); and *R v D* [2016] EWHC 1154 (Fam).

[827] See also *M v T* [2010] EWHC 1479 (Fam), per Charles J, at [8]—the rationale for speed under Article 11(3) applies also to applications under Article 11(7).

[828] See also *Practice Guide*, para 4.4.4.

[829] See also *Re A (A Child) (Custody Decision after Maltese Non-Return Order)* [2006] EWHC 3397 (Fam), [2007] 1 FCR 402; *Re A, HA v MB (Brussels II Revised: Article 11(7) Application)* [2007] EWHC 2016 (Fam), at [90]; and *M v T* [2010] EWHC 1479 (Fam), at [17].

[830] See Children Act 1989, s 1(1); *Re A, HA v MB (Brussels II Revised: Article 11(7) Application)* [2007] EWHC 2016 (Fam), at [90]; and *M v T* [2010] EWHC 1479 (Fam), at [17].

[831] See also *M v T* [2010] EWHC 1479 (Fam), at [17]; and Case C-211/10 PPU *Povse v Alpago* [2010] ECR I–6673— it is not necessarily required that the proceedings in the Member State of origin should have led to the adoption of a decision on the custody of the child.

[832] See also *M v T* [2010] EWHC 1479 (Fam), at [17].

[833] Arts 42 and 47. See also Case C-211/10 PPU *Povse v Alpago* [2010] ECR I–6673.

(viii) Enforceability of certain judgments requiring return of the child

If return of the child is entailed by a judgment given pursuant to Article 11(8) (ie a judgment by the Member State of origin), that shall be recognised and enforceable in another Member State[834] without the need for a declaration of enforceability (*exequatur*) and without any possibility of opposing its recognition,[835] if the judgment has been certified in the Member State of origin in accordance with Article 42(2),[836] demonstrating that necessary safeguards have been complied with in that state.[837] The judgment shall be certified in the Member State of origin only if: (a) the child, if appropriate having regard to his age and degree of maturity, was given an opportunity to be heard;[838] (b) the parties were given an opportunity to be heard; and (c) the court has taken into account in issuing its judgment the reasons for and evidence underlying the order issued pursuant to Article 13 of the 1980 Hague Convention. It is improbable that the abductor and child will return to the Member State of origin in order to give evidence, and so it is likely that evidence will be taken by means of video-conferencing or tele-conferencing.

The ECJ has clarified that the Articles 11(8) and 42 procedure will be triggered if a non-return order is made in the State where the child is present even though, on appeal, a return order is made by a court in that State.[839] Once a non-return decision had been taken and brought to the attention of the court of origin, it is irrelevant, for the purposes of issuing the certificate pursuant to Article 42, that that decision had been "suspended, overturned, set aside or, in any event, had not become *res judicata* or had been replaced by a decision ordering return, in so far as the return of the child had not actually taken place".[840] Furthermore, once an order implying the return of the child has been issued and certified by the State of origin under Article 42, it is not possible to seek non-recognition of that order in the requested State.[841] Otherwise, the objective of the immediate return of the child would remain subject to the condition that the redress procedures allowed under the domestic law of the Member State in which the child is wrongfully retained have been exhausted. The enforcement of a certified judgment cannot be refused in the Member State of enforcement on the ground that the court of the Member State of origin which handed down that judgment may have infringed Article 42.[842] Similarly, it cannot be refused where, as a result of a subsequent change of circumstances, the enforcement might be detrimental to the best interests of the child.[843] Such issues fall exclusively within the jurisdiction of the courts of the Member State of origin, and as such must be pleaded in the State of origin.

The "overriding mechanism" embodied in Articles 11(6)-(8) and 42 has attracted justifiable criticism.[844] The scheme has proven difficult "because the custody proceedings do not take place in the Member State where the child is present and because the abducting parent is

---

[834] Ie in all Member States, and not just the Member State in which the non-return order was made.

[835] Art 42(1).

[836] Using the standard form certificate in Annex IV to the Regulation. If the court takes measures to ensure the protection of the child after its return to the State of habitual residence, the certificate shall contain details of such measures (Art 42(2)). See Family Procedure Rules 2010, r 12.60. Eg *Re A (A Child) (Custody Decision after Maltese Non-Return Order)* [2006] EWHC 3397 (Fam), [2007] 1 FCR 402.

[837] Cf Arts 40 and 41 regarding rights of access. Supra, pp 1129–30.

[838] See also Commission Proposal for the Recast of Brussels II *bis*, COM (2016) 411 final 30 June 2016, p 4.

[839] Case C-195/08 PPU, *Rinau v Rinau*, [2008] ECR I-05271.

[840] Ibid.

[841] Ibid.

[842] C-491/10 PPU, *Aguirre Zarraga v Simone Pelz* [2010] ECR I-14247. See McEleavy [2013] IFL 172.

[843] Case C-211/10PPU, *Povse v Alpago* [2010] ECR I–6673.

[844] See, in particular, Beaumont *et al* (2016) 12 J Priv Int L 211.

often not cooperative. In particular, it is often difficult to hear the child".[845] In response to these concerns, major changes have been proposed by the European Commission in the ongoing review of Brussels II *bis*, including provisions for hearing the child,[846] the requirement for full welfare inquiry before return orders are made,[847] and the ability for the court in the State where the child is present to refuse enforcement of the return order made by the court of habitual residence, on the basis of public policy if the enforcement of the order is manifestly incompatible with the best interests of the child.[848]

(f) Implications of the Human Rights Act 1998

(i) Article 20 of the 1980 Hague Convention

Article 20 of the 1980 Hague Convention provides that: "The return of the child under the provisions of Article 12 may be refused if this would not be permitted by the fundamental principles of the requested State relating to the protection of human rights and fundamental freedoms."[849] Article 20 was not included in the provisions incorporated into the law of the United Kingdom by virtue of the Child Abduction and Custody Act 1985, for the reason that it would have been difficult to state with certainty at that time what were the fundamental principles of the law relating to the protection of human rights and fundamental freedoms.[850] In the light of the Human Rights Act 1998, however, the position now is clearer. In *Re D (A Child) (Abduction: Rights of Custody)*,[851] the House of Lords pointed out that it was now unlawful for the court to act incompatibly with the human rights and fundamental freedoms guaranteed by the ECHR. Article 20 has thus been given domestic effect by a different route. The provision was, however, intended by the drafters of the Convention to be applied only exceptionally,[852] and the requirement of a strict interpretation of Article 20 has generally been closely followed by the Contracting States.[853]

(ii) European Court of Human Rights (ECtHR) jurisprudence

Since 2000, there has been a growing trend in abduction cases for bereft parents to lodge complaints under the European Convention on Human Rights. Claims typically are based upon alleged violation of the right to a fair trial (Article 6), and/or the right to respect for private and family life (Article 8).[854] Whilst the object of Article 8 is to protect the individual against arbitrary interference by public authorities, there may also be positive obligations[855] inherent in an effective "respect" for family life, which "may involve the adoption

---

[845] Commission Proposal for the Recast of Brussels II *bis*, COM (2016) 411 final 30 June 2016, p 3. See also Beaumont *et al* [2016] IFL 307.

[846] Commission Proposal for the Recast of Brussels II *bis*, COM (2016) 411 final 30 June 2016, p 42.

[847] Ibid, p 45.

[848] Ibid, p 53.

[849] See Trimmings and Beaumont (2014) 9 JCL 66. More generally, see, Fawcett, Ní Shúilleabháin and Shah, *Human Rights and Private International Law* (2016).

[850] *Re J (A Child (Custody Rights: Jurisdiction)* [2005] UKHL 40, [2006] 1 AC 80, at [44].

[851] [2006] UKHL 51, at [65]. See also *Re M (Children) (Abduction)* [2007] UKHL 55, at [19].

[852] Pérez-Vera, *Explanatory Report on the 1980 Hague Child Abduction Convention* (1982), at [31]. For a rare example of a successful Art 20 plea, see *Foyle Health and Social Services Trust v EC & Anor* [2006] IEHC 448—a likely adoption of a child upon the return would breach the respondent parents' and the child's constitutional rights. Cf *Nottingham County Council v KB* [2010 IEHC 9.

[853] See Lowe, *A Statistical Analysis of Applications Made in 2008 under the Hague Convention of 25 October 1980 on the Civil Aspects of International Child Abduction* (2011).

[854] Also, occasionally, on Art 14 (prohibition of discrimination), eg, *Re J (A Child (Custody Rights: Jurisdiction)* [2005] UKHL 40, [2006] 1 AC 80; and *EM (Lebanon) v Secretary of State for the Home Department* [2006] EWCA Civ 1531, [2007] 1 FLR 991.

[855] To be interpreted in the light of the 1980 Hague Convention: *Sylvester v Austria* [2003] 2 FLR 210, (2003) 37 EHRR 17; *Maire v Portugal* [2004] 2 FLR 653, (2006) 43 EHRR 13; and *Iglesias Gil v Spain* [2005] 1FLR 190, (2005) 40 EHRR 3.

of measures designed to secure respect for family life even in the sphere of relations between individuals".[856] Such measures include enforcement mechanisms aimed at protecting individuals' rights, including the right of a parent to have measures taken with a view to his being reunited with the child, and an obligation upon the national authorities to take such measures. However, there is no absolute obligation upon national authorities to ensure contact between a child and his non-custodial parent following divorce.[857] Moreover, any obligation to apply coercion must be limited since the interests, as well as the rights and freedoms, of all concerned must be taken into account, especially those of the child.[858] The key question is whether those authorities have taken all necessary steps to facilitate contact as can reasonably be demanded in the special circumstances of each case.[859] Time is of particular significance as there is always a risk that any procedural delay will result in the *de facto* determination of the issue before the court.[860] The European Court of Human Rights has consistently ruled that once the authorities of a Contracting State to the 1980 Hague Convention have determined that a child has been wrongfully removed or retained, there is a duty incumbent upon them to take adequate and effective measures to secure the return of the child to his/her habitual residence, with due expedition. Reasonableness in terms of length of proceedings will be assessed by reference to the circumstances of the particular case, including its complexity, the conduct of the applicant and the relevant authorities, and what is at stake for the applicant.[861] Failure to make due effort is likely to amount to violation of Articles 6 and/or 8. It was held in *Sylvester v Austria*[862] that a change in the relevant facts exceptionally might justify the non-enforcement of a foreign order, but the court must be satisfied that the change was not brought about by the state's failure to take all measures that reasonably could be expected to facilitate execution of the order.

The following failures on the part of the requested State in particular have been held as having amounted to the violation of the applicant's rights under Article 8 or Article 6:[863] a delay of nine months in enforcing a return order;[864] a failure by domestic authorities to take sanctions against the abducting parent to enforce return of the child;[865] a refusal to issue an international search and arrest warrant;[866] a failure by domestic authorities to make adequate and effective efforts for the child's return;[867] an absence of satisfactory explanation for delay in obtaining expert opinion, or for dormant period during the 3 year proceedings;[868] periods of inactivity by the domestic

---

[856] *G v United Kingdom (Children: Rights of Contact)* [2001] 1 FLR 153, (2001) 33 EHRR 1.

[857] *Sylvester v Austria* [2003] 2 FLR 210, (2003) 37 EHRR 17.

[858] Ibid, at [H6]. But see *Maire v Portugal* [2004] 2 FLR 653, (2006) 43 EHRR 13, where use of coercive measures could not be ruled out in the event of manifestly unlawful behaviour by the abductor parent. See also *S v B (Abduction: Human Rights)* [2005] EWHC 733, [2005] 2 FLR 878; and *Re C (A Child) (Abduction: Residence and Contact)* [2005] EWHC 2205, [2006] 2 FLR 277.

[859] *G v United Kingdom (Children: Rights of Contact)* [2001] 1 FLR 153, (2001) 33 EHRR 1.

[860] Ibid, per Costa J, at [66]. Cf *Sylvester v Austria* [2003] 2 FLR 210, (2003) 37 EHRR 17, per Rozakis J, at [60].

[861] *Monory v Romania* (2005) 41 EHRR 37.

[862] [2003] 2 FLR 210, (2003) 37 EHRR 17.

[863] Cf *Mattenklott v Germany (Admissibility)* (2007) 44 EHRR SE 12—order to return applicant's daughter to USA, if necessary by force, not in violation of Art 8; and *Deak v Romania and United Kingdom* [2008] 2 FLR 994—no breach of Art 8 as both the requesting and the requested States had complied with their obligations under the 1980 Hague Convention.

[864] *Sylvester v Austria* [2003] 2 FLR 210, (2003) 37 EHRR 17 (nine months' delay; Art 8).

[865] *Maire v Portugal* [2004] 2 FLR 653, (2006) 43 EHRR 13 (Art 8).

[866] *Iglesias Gil v Spain* [2005] 1 FLR 190, (2005) 40 EHRR 3 (Art 8).

[867] *Monory v Romania* (2005) 41 EHRR 37 (Art 8).

[868] *HN v Poland* [2005] 3 FCR 85.

authorities;[869] an 18 months' delay between lodging of request for return of child under the 1980 Hague Convention and the final decision;[870] a failure of the domestic authorities to take timely and adequate measure for the applicant father to be reunited with his child;[871] refusal of the domestic courts to grant a return order;[872] the length of the return proceedings (17 months);[873] an inadequate decision-making process under the domestic law;[874] a lack of procedural protection for the applicant before the Constitutional Court in proceedings which led to the quashing of a return order previously issued by the ordinary courts;[875] and a failure of the domestic authorities to act swiftly in return proceedings, combined with a failure of the available procedural framework to facilitate the expeditious and efficient conduct of the return proceedings.[876]

More recently, a number of complaints have been lodged by disconcerted abducting parents arguing that a return order or the enforcement of this order would violate both the abducting parent's and the child's Article 8 rights as it would amount to a disproportionate interference with their rights to respect for private and family life.[877] It was the second of these complaints, *Neulinger and Shuruk v Switzerland*,[878] that attracted significant attention among the commentators.[879] This was not as much due to the decision itself but rather because of the comments made by the ECtHR which appeared to be suggesting that domestic courts should apply the child's best interests analysis in return proceedings under the 1980 Convention—this approach being contrary to the underlying philosophy of the Convention.[880] In particular, the ECtHR, sitting as a Grand Chamber, expressed the view that domestic courts were expected to engage in

> [a]n in-depth examination of the entire family situation and of a whole series of factors, in particular of a factual, emotional, psychological, material and medical nature, and make a balanced and reasonable assessment of the respective interests of each person, with constant concern for determining what the best solution would be for the abducted child in the context of an application for his return to his country of origin . . . .[881]

The Court appeared to say that Hague Convention orders cannot be granted automatically and that the best interests of the child must be considered.[882] A return order where the above procedure was not followed would conflict with Article 3(1) of the UNCRC or violate Article 8 of

---

[869] *Karadzic v Croatia* [2006] 1 FCR 36, (2007) 44 EHRR 45.

[870] *Iosub Caras v Romania* [2007] 1 FLR 661.

[871] *Shaw v Hungary* [2012] 2 FLR 1314, [2011] ECHR 6457/09; *Cavani v Hungary* [2014] ECHR 5493/13; and *GN v Poland* [2016] ECHR 667.

[872] *RS v Poland* [2015] 2 FLR 848; *GS v Georgia* [2015] 2 FLR 647, [2015] ECHR 2361/13; and *KJ v Poland* [2016] 2 FCR 539; [2016] Fam Law 554.

[873] *Ferrari v Romania* [2015] ECHR 1714/10, [2015] 2 FLR 303.

[874] *Blaga v Romania* [2014] ECHR 54443/10.

[875] *Frisancho Perea v Slovakia* [2016] 1 FLR 267; and *Guió v Slovakia* [2014] ECHR 10280/12.

[876] *MA v Austria* [2015] ECHR 4097/13.

[877] *Maumousseau and Washington v France* (2010) 51 EHRR 55; *Neulinger and Shuruk v Switzerland* (Grand Chamber) [2010] ECHR 41615/07; *Raban v Romania* [2011] 1 FLR 1130, [2010] ECHR 1625; *Šneersone and Kampanella v Italy* [2011] 2 FLR 1322; and *X v Latvia* (Grand Chamber) [2013] ECHR 27853/09, [2014] 1 FLR 1135. See also *Povse v Austria* [2014] 1 FLR 944—application inadmissible. See Beaumont *et al* (2015) 64 ICLQ 39.

[878] *Neulinger and Shuruk v Switzerland* [2010] ECHR 41615/07. See eg *DT v LBT (Abduction: Domestic Abuse)* [2010] EWHC 3177 (Fam).

[879] See eg Conclusions and Recommendations of the Sixth Special Commission on the Practical Operation of the 1980 Convention, June 2011, at [47]–[49]; Lowe [2012] IFL 170; Schulz [2012] IFL 43; Walker (2010) 6 J Priv Int L 649; Wheeler [2011] IFL 224; and Paton (2012) 8 J Priv Int L 547.

[880] See also *Raban v Romania* [2011] 1 FLR 1130, [2010] ECHR 1625; and *X v Latvia* (first instance) [2012] 1 FLR 860, [2011] ECHR 27853/09. See Costa [2011] IFL 183; and Schuz [2012] IFL 35.

[881] *Neulinger and Shuruk v Switzerland* [2010] ECHR 41615/07, at [139].

[882] Ibid, at [138].

the ECHR of the child or the abducting parent.[883] Not surprisingly, the decision was greeted with concern as it is unclear how such an "in-depth examination" can truly be consistent with the summary return procedure envisaged by the 1980 Convention. Indeed, in *Neulinger* the ECtHR gave "the appearance of turning the swift, summary decision- making which is envisaged by the Hague Convention into the full-blown examination of the child's future in the requested state which it was the very object of the Hague Convention to avoid".[884] The UK Supreme Court rejected the *Neulinger* test.[885] In *Re E (Children) (Abduction: Custody Appeal)*,[886] the Court held that *Neulinger* had not intended to introduce any revision to well-established Convention principles, and refused to accept that abduction cases should now be approached differently at the domestic level. In particular, Baroness Hale and Lord Wilson opined:[887]

> . . . in every Hague Convention case where the question is raised, the national court does not order return automatically and mechanically but examines the particular circumstances of this particular child in order to ascertain whether a return would be in accordance with the Convention; but that is not the same as a full blown examination of the child's future.

Furthermore, as the Hague Convention was designed with the best interests of the child as a primary consideration, if applied properly, it is unlikely that the Article 8 rights of the child or either of the parents will be violated.[888] Even though it is possible to envisage highly unusual cases where a return order could violate Article 8,[889] it is "a far cry from the suggestion that article 8 'trumps' the Hague Convention: in virtually all cases, as the Strasbourg court has shown, they march hand in hand".[890] The Supreme Court on two occasions called upon the ECtHR to reconsider its dicta in *Neulinger*.[891] An opportunity arose for the Grand Chamber to revisit the requirement set out in *Neulinger* in the rehearing of the chamber judgment in *X v Latvia*.[892] In its decision, the Grand Chamber replaced the requirement of an "in-depth" examination with the concept of an "effective" examination of any allegations made in connection with a refusal to return.[893] The Grand Chamber also helpfully clarified when an examination will be considered "effective". Namely, national courts have to consider any "arguable claims"[894] against a return based on the exceptions to return contained in Articles 12, 13 and 20; and must give a "sufficiently reasoned opinion" regarding those claims to evidence that an effective examination of the issues has been carried out.[895] Furthermore, the consideration must not be "automatic or stereotyped"[896] and the exceptions to return

---

[883] The Court was requested to address the question whether a decision of the Swiss court to order a child to be returned to Israel under the Hague Convention amounted to a violation of Arts 8 and 6 of the ECHR. On the facts, the Court decided that enforcement of the return order five years after the child's removal would violate the Art 8 ECHR rights of the mother and the child. Ibid, at [151].

[884] *Re E (Children) (Abduction: Custody Appeal)* [2011] UKSC 27, at [22].

[885] Ibid, at [19]–[27]. See also *Re S (A Child) (Abduction: Rights of Custody)* [2012] UKSC 10.

[886] [2011] UKSC 27. See also *Re S (A Child) (Abduction: Rights of Custody)* [2012] UKSC 10, at [37].

[887] [2011] UKSC 27, at [26].

[888] *Re E (Children) (Abduction: Custody Appeal)* [2011] UKSC 27, at [26].

[889] For example, where the returning parent would face a real risk of torture or inhuman or degrading treatment or the flagrant denial of a fair trial, and the child could not be safely returned without that parent. In such circumstances, it would be unlawful for the court to act incompatibly with the ECHR by ordering the child's return. *Re E (Children) (Abduction: Custody Appeal)* [2011] UKSC 27, at [27]. See also *Re D (A Child) (Abduction: Rights of Custody)* [2006] UKHL 51, at [65]; and *Re M (Children) (Abduction)* [2007] UKHL 55, at [19].

[890] *Re E (Children) (Abduction: Custody Appeal)* [2011] UKSC 27, at [27].

[891] Ibid, at [22]–[27]; and *Re S (A Child) (Abduction: Rights of Custody)* [2012] UKSC 10, at [37]–[38].

[892] *X v Latvia* [2013] ECHR 27853/09, [2014] 1 FLR 1135..

[893] Ibid, at [118]. See Beaumont *et al* (2015) 64 ICLQ 39.

[894] *X v Latvia* [2013] ECHR 27853/09, [2014] 1 FLR 1135, at [106]. .

[895] Ibid, majority opinion, at [106]–[107] and dissent, at [2].

[896] Ibid, at [107].

"must be interpreted strictly".[897] This new ECtHR approach is much more consistent with the summary return mechanism envisioned by the 1980 Convention, and, arguably, does not alter the way in which the English courts had approached the issue previously.

(ii) Part II of the 1985 Act: the Council of Europe Convention[898]

This Convention governs the recognition and enforcement of decisions relating to custody, whether made by a judicial or administrative authority, in force in relation to children under sixteen.[899] The Council of Europe Convention has not been widely used in the United Kingdom, and so there is very little authority on its construction and ambit.[900] The Convention shall therefore not be recounted in detail in this chapter, and reference is made instead to the 14th edition of this book.[901]

(iii) Permission to remove children from the jurisdiction[902]

Difficult tensions emerge in cases where one parent wishes to relocate with his/her child, against the wishes of another person having parental responsibilities.[903] The proposed relocation might be internal to the United Kingdom, to another European Union Member State, or to a non-Member State country;[904] and it might be temporary or permanent, exposing the child to varying degrees of upheaval and loss of the familiar.[905] Relocation cases often bear common characteristics: "(a) the applicant is invariably the mother and the primary carer; (b) generally the motivation for the move arises out of her remarriage[906] or her urge to return home;[907] and (c) the father's opposition is commonly founded on a resultant reduction in

---

[897] Ibid.

[898] See Jones (1981) 30 ICLQ 467; Shapira (1989) II Hague Recueil 127, 200–6; and Lowe and Douglas, *Bromley's Family Law*, pp 1083–91. The Council of Europe has reviewed the operation of the Convention: DIR/JUR (89) 1.

[899] 1985 Act, Sch 2, Art 1. It does not apply to a child under sixteen if he has the right to decide the place of his residence under the law of his habitual residence, nationality or of the Contracting State where recognition and enforcement is sought.

[900] See, for a rare example, *AA v TT (Recognition and Enforcement)* [2014] EWHC 3488 (Fam).

[901] See pp 1123–7.

[902] See eg Geekie [2008] Fam Law 446; Taylor and Freeman (2010) 44 Fam LQ 317; Roche [2010] Fam Law 978; Eaton [2011] Fam Law 1093; Freeman [2011] IFL 131; Carruthers [2012] Jur Rev 187; George and Cominetti [2013] IFL 149; George, *Relocation Disputes: Law and Practice in England and New Zealand* (2014); and George (2015) 27 CFLQ 377.

[903] Defined in Children Act 1989, s 3.

[904] With "gradations of hurdles" according to the destination: *Re H (Children: Residence Order: Relocation)* [2001] EWCA Civ 1338, [2001] 2 FLR 1277, per Thorpe LJ, at [20].

[905] The considerations relevant to an application for permission to relocate permanently are not automatically, if at all, applicable to an application for temporary relocation: *Re A (A Child) (Temporary Removal from Jurisdiction)* [2004] EWCA Civ 1587, [2005] 1 FLR 639. In applications for a temporary removal to a country which is not a signatory to the 1980 Hague Abduction Convention the court is to consider the magnitude of the risk of breach of the order if permission were given; the magnitude of the consequence of a breach if it occurred; and the level of security that might be achieved by building into the arrangements all of the available safeguards. *Re R (A Child) (Prohibited Steps Order)* [2013] EWCA Civ 1115. See eg *Re R (Children) (Temporary Leave to Remove from Jurisdiction)* [2014] EWHC 643 (Fam); and *C v K (Children: Application for Temporary Removal to Algeria)* [2014] EWHC 4125 (Fam).

[906] Eg *Re B (Children) (Removal from Jurisdiction), Re S (Children) (Removal from Jurisdiction)* [2003] EWCA Civ 1149, [2003] 2 FLR 1043.

[907] Usually following marital breakdown, as in *Payne v Payne* [2001] EWCA Civ 166; *Re S (Children: Application for Removal from Jurisdiction)* [2004] EWCA Civ 1724, [2005] 1 FCR 471—leave to remove children from England to Spain, mother's country of origin, granted on appeal; and *C v S* [2006] EWHC 2891—leave to remove children from England to Australia, mother's country of origin, granted. *Contra Re Y (Leave to Remove from Jurisdiction)* [2004] 2 FLR 330—leave to remove child from Wales to USA, mother's country of origin, refused; *R v R (Leave to Remove)* [2004] EWHC 2572, [2005] 1 FLR 687—leave to remove children from England to Paris refused; *Re G (Removal from Jurisdiction)* [2005] EWCA Civ 170, [2005] 2 FLR 166—leave granted, on appeal, to remove children to Argentina, mother's country of origin;

contact and influence".[908] Section 13 of the Children Act 1989 provides that where a child arrangements order which sets out with whom the child concerned is to live is in force, no person may remove[909] the child from the United Kingdom without either the written consent of every person who has parental responsibility for the child, or the leave of the court. Additionally, under section 8 of the 1989 Act, the English court can make a prohibited steps order, or impose conditions on a child arrangements order under section 11(7).

There is a clear link between relocation cases and abduction cases.[910] In *Payne v Payne*, a case concerning a mother's desire to return to her country of origin following the failure of her marriage, Thorpe LJ opined that, "if individual jurisdictions adopt a chauvinistic approach to applications to relocate then there is a risk that the parent affected will resort to flight".[911] Conversely, an order for return of the child to his habitual residence, following wrongful removal or retention, will not infrequently lead to an application to relocate being issued in that jurisdiction. Thorpe LJ stated that the judge in the second application must be free to carry out a fully independent function unfettered by the conclusion of the judge in the earlier return proceedings, and without any fear of breaching the principle of comity, for the functions of the two judges are quite different and will require an assessment of the circumstances as they are, rather than as they were.[912]

Equally, there is a clear conflict between the desire and ambitions of the relocating parent (recognised in the right of mobility in Article 2 of Protocol 4 to the ECHR),[913] and the right of the other parent to respect for his/her private and family life (Article 8 of the ECHR).[914] As Thorpe LJ remarked in *Payne v Payne*,[915] however: "Once a family unit disintegrates the separating members' separate rights can only be to a fragmented family life . . . the absent parent has the right to participation to the extent and in what manner the complex circumstances of the individual case dictate."

The Court of Appeal, in *Payne*, carried out a review of relocation jurisprudence over a thirty-year period,[916] and concluded that relocation cases have been consistently decided on the basis of two propositions: (a) although each member of the "fractured family" has rights to assert, the welfare of the child is the paramount consideration;[917] and (b) refusing the

---

and *Re J (Children)* [2006] EWCA Civ 1897, [2007] 2 FCR 149—leave granted, on appeal, to remove children to Bulgaria, father's country of origin.

[908] *Payne v Payne* [2001] EWCA Civ 166, [2001] Fam 473, 483–4.

[909] For a period longer than 1 month: 1989 Act, s 13(2).

[910] *Re A (A Child) (Temporary Removal from Jurisdiction)* [2004] EWCA Civ 1587, [2005] 1 FLR 639. See also *Re K (A Minor) (Removal from Jurisdiction: Practice)* [1999] 2 FLR 1084—utmost vigilance is required where a parent seeks to take a child to a country that is not a signatory to the 1980 Hague Convention, infra, p 1171 et seq; *F v R* [2007] EWHC 64 (Fam); and Freeman [2013] IFL 41.

[911] *Payne v Payne* [2001] EWCA Civ 166, [2001] Fam 473 at 484.

[912] Ibid, at 492.

[913] Yet to be ratified by the United Kingdom. But Thorpe LJ, in *Payne*, ibid, at 487, stated that refusal to recognise such a right beyond the jurisdictional boundary "represents a stance of disproportionate parochialism".

[914] *Re A (Permission to Remove Child from Jurisdiction: Human Rights)* [2000] 2 FLR 225.

[915] [2001] EWCA Civ 166, [2001] Fam 473, at 486.

[916] *Poel v Poel* [1970] 1 WLR 1469; *Nash v Nash* [1973] 2 All ER 704; *Re A v A (Child: Removal from Jurisdiction)* [1979] 1 FLR 380; *Moodey v Field*, 13 February 1981 (unreported); *Chamberlain v de la Mare* [1982] 4 FLR 434; *Lonslow v Hennig* [1986] 2 FLR 378; *Belton v Belton* [1987] 2 FLR 343; *Tyler v Tyler* [1989] 2 FLR 158; *MH v GP (Child: Emigration)* [1995] 2 FLR 106; *Re H (Application to Remove from Jurisdiction)* [1998] 1 FLR 848; *Re C (Leave to Remove from Jurisdiction)* [2000] 2 FLR 457; and *Re L (A Child) (Contract: Domestic Violence)* [2001] Fam 260.

[917] Children Act 1989, s 1(1). See also *Re S (Violent Parent: Indirect Contact)* [2000] 1 FLR 481; *Re H (Children: Residence Order: Relocation)* [2001] EWCA Civ 1338, [2001] 2 FLR 1277; *R v R (Leave to Remove)*

primary carer's reasonable proposals for the relocation of her family life is likely to impact detrimentally on the welfare of dependent children,[918] especially in cases where the applicant has forged a new family unit by marriage or other relationship. The court must evaluate factors such as the child's emotional and psychological dependency upon the primary carer; the relationship between the child and the non-respondent parent; the relationship between the child and extended family, including siblings, grandparents and step-parents; the reasonableness of the proposals and motivation of the parent who wishes to relocate; and, perhaps most importantly of all, the likely effect of the refusal of the application upon the psychological and emotional stability of the parent who wishes to relocate. In assessing the reasonableness of the relocation proposal, Thorpe LJ has suggested the following discipline:[919] (a) Is the applicant's proposal genuine, ie not motivated by a selfish desire to reduce or terminate contact between the other parent and the child, and realistic, ie founded upon well conceived and well researched proposals?[920] (b) Is the respondent parent's opposition motivated by genuine concern for the future of the child's welfare or is it driven by an ulterior motive? (c) What would be the impact upon the applicant parent of a refusal of a genuine and realistic proposal? (d) What does an overriding review of the child's welfare as the paramount consideration indicate is best for the child? Whilst there is no presumption in favour of the applicant parent,[921] the reasonable proposals of such a person having a residence order in respect of the child typically will be granted unless the court concludes that this is incompatible with the child's welfare.[922]

The *Payne* principles were articulated with cases of permanent relocation in mind; the more temporary the proposed removal, the less regard should be had to the principles.[923] Moreover, in *Re B (Children)*,[924] a case in which both parents had strong connections with other jurisdictions, the mother with Holland, and the father with Dubai, the judge was required to determine, removal from England being inevitable, which of two jurisdictions would better advance the children's welfare,[925] and so *Payne*, being factually distinct (the respondent in that case having resisted the application for removal of the children to New Zealand in order that they might stay within the jurisdiction of England and Wales) was distinguished.

[2004] EWHC 2572, [2005] 1 FLR 687; and *Re A (Leave to Remove: Cultural and Religious Considerations)* [2006] EWHC 421, [2006] 2 FLR 572.

[918] Eg, *Re B (Children) (Removal from Jurisdiction), Re S (Children) (Removal from Jurisdiction)* [2003] EWCA Civ 1149, [2003] 2 FLR 1043—relocation to South Africa and Australia, respectively, in furtherance of each mother's new relationship; leave granted, on appeal, to remove children; *Re B (Children) (Leave to Remove: Impact of Refusal)* [2004] EWCA Civ 956, [2005] 2 FLR 239—leave granted, on appeal, to remove children to Australia, following mother's remarriage; *Re A (A Child) (Temporary Removal from Jurisdiction)* [2004] EWCA Civ 1587, [2005] 1 FLR 639—leave granted, on appeal, to remove four-year-old child to South Africa for two years, in furtherance of mother's academic career; surprisingly, scant attention was paid to the fact that two years in the life of a four -year-old child is a very substantial period of time; *Re G (Removal from Jurisdiction)* [2005] EWCA Civ 170, [2005] 2 FLR 166; and *C v S* [2006] EWHC 2891.

[919] *Payne v Payne*, [2001] EWCA Civ 166, [2001] Fam 473 at 488. Applied in *R v R (Leave to Remove)* [2004] EWHC 2572, [2005] 1 FLR 687.

[920] *H v F* [2005] EWHC 2705, [2006] 1 FLR 776—leave to remove child from England to Jamaica refused since proposal was ill-conceived, unrealistic and speculative in terms of income and probable benefit to family. *Contra McShane v Duryea* [2006] Fam LR 15; and *Re A (Leave to Remove: Cultural and Religious Considerations)* [2006] EWHC 421, [2006] 2 FLR 572.

[921] *Payne v Payne* [2001] EWCA Civ 166, [2001] Fam 473, at 483, per Butler-Sloss P, at 500.

[922] Ibid.

[923] *Re A (A Child) (Temporary Removal from Jurisdiction)* [2004] EWCA Civ 1587, [2005] 1 FLR 639.

[924] [2005] EWCA Civ 643.

[925] The judge concluded that the children's best interests would be served by relocating with their father to Dubai.

Over the recent years, there has been considerable criticism of Payne in both academic[926] and judicial circles. In *Re D (A Child)*,[927] Wall LJ observed that the English approach to relocation paid too much attention to the wishes and feelings of the relocating parent and gave little consideration to the damage caused to the child by the loss of the relationship with the left-behind parent.[928] Similarly, in *Re AR (A Child: Relocation)*,[929] Mostyn J opined:

> . . . there is a strong view that the heavy emphasis on the emotional reaction of the thwarted primary carer represents an illegitimate gloss on the purity of the paramountcy principle. Moreover, some argue that it promotes selfishness and detracts from the importance of co-parenting. Some argue that on the birth of children parents are indentured to sacrifice throughout their minority, but that the one word that is missing from Payne is, in fact, sacrifice.[930]

Furthermore, in the view of Mostyn J, the *Payne* approach supplied a tendency which was "the almost invariable success of the application, save in those cases where it is demonstrably irrational, absurd or malevolent".[931]

The significance of *Payne* was considered by the Court of Appeal in *K v K (Relocation: Shared Care Arrangement)*[932] which, unlike *Payne*, concerned a shared care arrangement. This decision represented the first shift from the complete reliance on *Payne*. In particular, the Court rejected the view that Payne set out any presumption in deciding relocation cases,[933] and held that the only principle to be extracted from *Payne* was the paramountcy of the child's welfare.[934] All the rest was guidance as to factors to be weighed in search of the welfare paramountcy.[935] Thorpe LJ further highlighted that the *Payne* guidance was based on the premise that the applicant was the primary carer.[936] Where each carer was providing a more or less equal proportion and one sought to relocate externally, the judge should exercise his discretion by applying the statutory checklist in section 1(3) of the Children Act 1989 rather than applying the approach suggested in *Payne*.[937] The proposition to differentiate between relocation cases on the basis of the nature of the care arrangement in place was, however, not accepted by the majority. In the words of Black LJ, relocation cases should not be "bogged down with arguments as to whether the time spent with each of the parents or other aspects of the care arrangements" are such as to amount to a "primary care" or a "shared care" case.[938] This approach was strongly endorsed by Munby LJ in *Re F (A Child) (Permission to Relocate)*[939] where he noted: "The last thing that this very difficult area of family law requires is a satellite jurisprudence generating an ever-more detailed classification of supposedly different types of

---

[926] Eg Roche [2010] Fam Law 978; and Devereux and George [2014] Fam Law 1586.

[927] [2010] EWCA Civ 593.

[928] At [4]. This view was reiterated by Wall LJ in *Re D (Children) (Relocation: Permission)* [2010] EWCA Civ 50, at [33]. See also *Re H (Leave to Remove)* [2010] EWCA Civ 915, per Wilson LJ, at [23].

[929] [2010] EWHC 1346 (Fam).

[930] Ibid, at [8].

[931] Ibid, at [7].

[932] [2011] EWCA Civ 793. See Eaton and Reardon [2011] IFL 308; Gilmore [2011] Fam Law 970; and George (2012) 24 CFLQ 110.

[933] *K v K (Relocation: Shared Care Arrangement)* [2011] EWCA Civ 793, per Black LJ, at [143]: "Even where the case concerns a true primary carer, there is no presumption that the reasonable relocation plans of that carer will be facilitated unless there is some compelling reason to the contrary, nor any similar presumption however it may be expressed."

[934] Ibid, per Thorpe LJ, at [39]; Moore-Bick LJ, at [86]; and Black LJ, at [141]–[142].

[935] *K v K (Relocation: Shared Care Arrangement)* [2011] EWCA Civ 793, per Thorpe LJ, at [39].

[936] Ibid, per Thorpe LJ, at [41].

[937] Ibid, at [57].

[938] Ibid, per Black LJ, at [145].

[939] [2012] EWCA Civ 1364.

relocation cases. Any move in that direction is, in my judgment, to be firmly resisted."[940] His Lordship held that, in every relocation case, the focus must be on the child's best interests as the child's welfare is paramount., though regard must also be had, where relevant and helpful, to the guidance given in *Payne*.[941] In reinforcing the point that there should be no distinction between cases where there is a "primary" and a "shared" care arrangement, Munby LJ held that the *Payne* guidance was not to be confined to cases where the applicant was the primary carer; instead, it can be utilized in other types of relocation cases, if the judge considers it helpful and appropriate to do so.[942] Finally, his Lordship reiterated that there were no presumptions in cases governed by s 1 of the Children Act 1989:[943] "From beginning to end the child's welfare is paramount, and the evaluation of where the child's best interests truly lie is to be determined having regard to the 'welfare checklist' in s 1(3)."[944]

The principles set out in post-*Payne* case-law were helpfully summarized and presented as the presently governing principles for relocation applications by Mostyn J in *Re TC and JC (Children: Relocation)*.[945] Most recently, in *Re F (A Child) (International Relocation Cases)*,[946] the Court of Appeal held that *Payne* had to be read in the context of *K v K (Relocation: Shared Care Arrangement)*[947] and *Re F (A Child) (Permission to Relocate)*,[948] and not instead of or in priority over them.[949] The Court concluded that a "holistic evaluative analysis" was required, with the details of the analysis depending on the facts of the individual case.[950]

The Hague Conference on Private International Law has been involved in a debate about whether international relocation ought to be regulated at the international level;[951] however, decided not to undertake the task as it was considered as a domestic rather than an international law problem.[952] At present, there are two soft law instruments that seek to promote a more informal international approach to relocation: the Washington Declaration[953] and the Council of Europe Recommendation on preventing and resolving disputes on child relocation.[954]

---

[940] Ibid, at [60].

[941] Ibid, at [61].

[942] Ibid, at [37].

[943] However, see s 1(2A) of the Children Act 1989, inserted by the Children and Families Act 2014, which has introduced the presumption that, unless the contrary is shown, the continued involvement of each parent in the child's life will further the child's welfare.

[944] *Re F (A Child) (Permission to Relocate)* [2012] EWCA Civ 1364, per Munby LJ, at [37].

[945] [2013] EWHC 292 (Fam), at [11].

[946] [2015] EWCA Civ 882. See also *Re S (A Child)* [2015] EWFC 86; *Re C (A Child) (Internal Relocation)* [2015] EWCA Civ 1305; *M v F* [2016] EWHC 3194 (Fam); and *Re K (A Child) (External Relocation: Judge's Evaluation)* [2016] EWCA Civ 931.

[947] [2011] EWCA Civ 793. See Eaton and Reardon [2011] IFL 308; Gilmore [2011] Fam Law 970; and George (2012) 24 CFLQ 110.

[948] [2012] EWCA Civ 1364.

[949] *Re F (A Child) (International Relocation Cases)* [2015] EWCA Civ 882, per Ryder LJ, at [20].

[950] Ibid, per Ryder LJ, at [30]; and McFarlane LJ, at [51].

[951] See Permanent Bureau of the Hague Conference on Private International Law, Preliminary Note on International Family Relocation, January 2012.

[952] See Conclusions and Recommendations of Part I and Part II of the Special Commission on the Practical Operation of the 1980 Child Abduction Convention and the 1996 Child Protection Convention and a Report of Part II of the Meeting, April 2012, at [64]–[85].

[953] The text of the Declaration is available on the Hague Conference website; https://assets.hcch.net/upload/decl_washington2010e.pdf.

[954] Recommendation CM/Rec (2015) 4 of the Committee of Ministers to member States on preventing and resolving disputes on child relocation, 11 February 2015. Coenraad [2015] IFL 312.

(f) Common law rules[955]

(i) Recognition of foreign orders

Despite the recent legislative developments, the common law rules as to the recognition of foreign orders continue to be important. This is because the Child Abduction and Custody Act 1985 and its Conventions apply to a relatively restricted (though continually growing) number of countries. Thus the common law rules apply in the case of all orders (whether custody, guardianship or wardship orders) made in other "non-Convention" countries outside the United Kingdom; to any orders made in countries covered by the 1980 Hague Convention or by the European Convention but which do not fall within their definitions of "rights of custody"[956] or "decisions relating to custody";[957] to orders made in a 1996 Hague Convention Contracting State which are outside the scope of the Convention;[958] to orders made in a European Union Member State which are outside the scope of Brussels II *bis*;[959] and to any orders made elsewhere in the United Kingdom which are not "Part I orders" within the meaning of the 1986 Act. The common law position is simple. No automatic recognition or enforcement is given to a foreign custody order.[960] Arguments of comity or reciprocity, however potent they may be, are held to be outweighed by the principle that the welfare of the child is the paramount consideration of the English court in all proceedings concerned with the upbringing of the child or the administration of his property.[961] Even though a custody order has been made by a foreign court, the English judge can still make such order as he thinks is in the best interest of the child;[962] for "national status is merely one of the factors which the judge in exercising his discretion will take into consideration".[963]

The Court of Appeal made it clear in *Re F (A Minor) (Abduction: Custody Rights)*[964] that there are two contexts in which the court must consider the welfare of the child:

> The first is the context of which court shall decide what the child's best interests require. The second context, which only arises if it has first been decided that the welfare of the child requires that the English rather than a foreign court shall decide what are the requirements of the child, is what orders as to custody, care and control and so on should be made.[965]

Although, in deciding whether to order the immediate return of a child abducted from his habitual residence in a non-Convention country, the welfare of the child is the court's paramount consideration, the Court of Appeal in *Osman v Elasha*[966] made clear that the welfare principle is not an absolute standard: "What constitutes the welfare of the child must be subject to the cultural background and expectations of the jurisdiction striving to achieve it."[967] In particular, it is not for an English court to criticise the standards of, or paramount

---

[955] See McClean, *Recognition of Family Judgments in the Commonwealth* (1983), pp 252–62.

[956] Child Abduction and Custody Act 1985, Sch 1, Art 5(a).

[957] Ibid, Sch 2, Art 1(c).

[958] Arts 3 and 4, supra, pp 1102–3.

[959] Art 1(3), supra, pp 1092–4.

[960] For ease of exposition, we shall take recognition of custody orders as the prime example.

[961] See Children Act 1989, s 1; and *Re J (A Child) (Custody Rights: Jurisdiction)* [2005] UKHL 40, [2006] 1 AC 80, in which Baroness Hale of Richmond pointed out, at [20], that application of the welfare principle might be specifically excluded by statute as, for example, by the Child Abduction and Custody Act 1985.

[962] *Re G (JDM)* [1969] 1 WLR 1001 at 1004; *J v C* [1970] AC 668 at 700–1, 714, 720; and *AB v CD* [2000] Fam LR 91.

[963] [1970] AC 668 at 701; cf *Re B (Infants)* [1971] NZLR 143.

[964] [1991] Fam 25.

[965] Ibid, at 31.

[966] [2000] Fam 62.

[967] Ibid, at 69. Cf *B v El-B (Abduction: Sharia Law: Welfare of Child)* [2003] 1 FLR 811; and *Re J (A Child) (Custody Rights: Jurisdiction)* [2005] UKHL 40, [2006] 1 AC 80, per Baroness Hale of Richmond, at [37].

principles applied by, the family justice system in such a country, except in exceptional circumstances, such as persecution or ethnic, sex[968] or other discrimination.[969] With regard to three boys abducted by their mother from the Sudan to England, the welfare principle in *Osman* had to be looked at in the context of Sudanese custom and culture, which applied Islamic law and which was familiar and acceptable to a practising Muslim family. The point was made by Baroness Hale of Richmond in *Re J (A Child (Custody Rights: Jurisdiction)*[970] that: "In a world which values difference, one culture is not inevitably to be preferred to another. Indeed, we do not have any fixed concept of what will be in the best interests of the individual child." It is necessary that this realisation informs judicial policy with regard to the return of children abducted from "non-Convention" countries. If, however, as was the case in *Re J*, there is a genuine issue between the parents as to whether it is in the best interests of the child to live in England or in a non-Convention country, it must be relevant whether that issue is capable of being tried freely and fully in the courts of that country:

> If those courts have no choice but to do as the father wishes, so that the mother cannot ask them to decide, with an open mind, whether the child will be better off living [in England] or there, then our courts must ask themselves whether it will be in the interests of the child to enable that dispute to be heard. The absence of a relocation jurisdiction must do more than give the judge pause . . .; it may be a decisive factor.[971]

A leading common law authority is *McKee v McKee*:[972]

> A husband and wife, American citizens, separated and agreed in writing that neither of them, without the permission of the other, would remove their son out of the USA. A year later the husband obtained a decree of divorce from a Californian court and an order awarding him the custody of the child and confirming the written agreement. About four years later, the same court, on the applications of both parties, awarded custody to the wife, whereupon the husband took his son to Ontario without the leave or knowledge of his wife. The wife thereupon took *habeas corpus* proceedings in Ontario. The trial judge, after a careful review of the circumstances, awarded custody of the child to the husband, but his decision was reversed by the Supreme Court of Canada.

The Privy Council restored the Ontario decision. The two charges levelled against the husband, that he had broken the agreement with his wife and had flouted the order of the Californian court, had been adequately considered by the trial judge, who, in the opinion of the court, was justified in concluding that in the light of the other circumstances the interests of the child would best be served by leaving him in the custody of his father. The order of the Californian court was a factor of great importance, but it was not decisive:

> It is the law . . . that the welfare and happiness of the infant is the paramount consideration in questions of custody . . . To this paramount consideration all others yield. The order of a foreign court of competent jurisdiction is no exception. Such an order has not the force of a foreign judgment: comity demands not its enforcement, but its grave consideration. This distinction . . . rests on the peculiar character of the jurisdiction and on the fact that an order providing for the custody of an infant cannot in its nature be final.[973]

---

[968] See *EM (Lebanon) v Secretary of State for the Home Department* [2008] UKHL 64—the return of a Lebanese asylum seeker and her twelve-year-old son to Lebanon would so flagrantly violate Art 8 of the ECHR as to completely deny or nullify those rights given that the mother would be compelled to transfer custody of her son to his father, who had been violent towards her and who had not seen the son since his birth.

[969] Cf, under 1980 Hague Convention, *Re S (Abduction: Intolerable Situation: Beth Din)* [2000] 1 FLR 454.

[970] [2005] UKHL 40, [2006] 1 AC 80, at [37] and [38].

[971] Ibid, [39].

[972] [1951] AC 352.

[973] [1951] AC 352 at 365; and see *Re B's Settlement* [1940] Ch 54; *Re G (JDM)* [1969] 1 WLR 1001.

Giving a foreign order "grave consideration" certainly does not prevent the English court from making a contrary order if the judge thinks it is in the best interests of the child to do so;[974] but it must not be forgotten that the judge who made the first order will have had the advantage of seeing the parties and hearing cross-examination of witnesses.[975] The court will be influenced by a variety of factors in deciding whether to make an order in terms similar to, or different from, those of the foreign order. If the foreign order was made some years ago, and the family circumstances have changed, the English order may well be in different terms and a further significant time factor is that the children will be older and their views more important.[976]

Attitudes towards the basic common law rule have changed over time,[977] with the acceptance of statutory provisions within the United Kingdom and elsewhere of Conventions providing for the speedy return of children. For a time, there was a view that the principles of the Hague Convention should be applied, by analogy, where there has been wrongful removal of a child from a country not, at the relevant time, a party to that Convention.[978] This approach, however, has been declared wrong by the House of Lords in what now is the leading case on "non-Convention" child abduction, *Re J (A Child) (Custody Rights: Jurisdiction)*.[979] An issue of principle arose in *Re J* regarding the proper approach to be taken in applications for the summary return of children to "non-Convention" countries. Baroness Hale of Richmond directed that there is no warrant, either in statute or authority, for the principles of the Hague Convention to be extended or applied by analogy to countries which are not parties to it.[980] Rather, where a non-Convention country is involved, a trial judge must focus on the individual child in the particular circumstances of the case:

> Hence, in all non-Convention cases, the courts have consistently held that they must act in accordance with the welfare of the individual child. If they do decide to return the child, that is because it is in his best interests to do so, not because the welfare principle has been superseded by some other consideration . . . the child's welfare is paramount and the specialist rules and concepts of the Hague Convention are not to be applied by analogy in a non-Convention case.[981]

---

[974] *McKee v McKee* [1951] AC 352 at 364–5; *J v C* [1970] AC 668 at 700–1, 714, 720, 728; *Re L* [1974] 1 WLR 250 at 264; *Re C* [1978] Fam 105; *Re R* (1981) 2 FLR 416 at 425; *Sinclair v Sinclair* 1988 SLT 87.

[975] *McKee v McKee*, supra, at 360; *Re Kernot* [1965] Ch 217; *Re S(M)* [1971] Ch 621.

[976] *Re T* [1969] 1 WLR 1608, at 1611; and see *E v F* [1974] 2 NZLR 435; and *Re Z (A Child)* [2006] EWCA Civ 1291.

[977] *McKee v McKee*, supra, has been described as "somewhat discredited": *Re Taylor's Marriage* (1988) 92 FLR 172 at 178.

[978] *Re F (A Minor) (Abduction: Custody Rights)* [1991] Fam 25; *G v G (Minors) (Abduction)* [1991] 2 FLR 506; *Re S (Minors) (Abduction)* [1994] 1 FLR 297; *D v D (Child Abduction: Non-Convention Country)* [1994] 1 FLR 137; *Re M (Abduction Non-Convention Country)* [1995] 1 FLR 89; *Re P (Abduction: Non-Convention Country)* [1997] 1 FLR 780; *Re Z (Abduction: Non-Convention Country)* [1999] 1 FLR 1270; *Re Lavitch* (1985) 24 DLR (4th) 248; *Re H's Marriage* (1985) FLC 80, 164; *Re Bannios and Sanchez's Marriage* (1989) 96 FLR 336; *ZP v PS* (1994) 122 CLR 639; *Re Z (Abduction: Non-Convention Country)* [1999] 1 FLR 1270; and *Re Z (A Child)* [2006] EWCA Civ 1219, per Wall LJ, at [14].

[979] [2005] UKHL 40, [2006] 1 AC 80. See also *Re M (Children) (Abduction)* [2007] UKHL 55; *U v U* [2010] EWHC 1179 (Fam); *Re S (Wardship: Summary Return: Non-Convention Country)* [2015] EWHC 176 (Fam); *Re C (A Child); Saudi Arabia* [2015] EWHC 3440 (Fam); *Re S (Wardship: Summary Return: Non-Convention Country)* [2015] EWHC 176 (Fam); and *LM v DR* [2016] EWHC 1943 (Fam).

[980] *Re J (A Child) (Custody Rights: Jurisdiction)* [2005] UKHL 40, at [22]. See also *Re H (Abduction: Dominica: Corporal Punishment)* [2006] EWHC 199 (Fam), [2006] 2 FLR 314—in determining whether the courts of Dominica could offer children the protection they needed, it had to be borne in mind that that jurisdiction condoned treating children with physical violence, and therefore the English court could not contemplate returning the children there (reversed on a different point: *Re H (Abduction: Dominica: Corporal Punishment)* [2006] EWCA Civ 871).

[981] *Re J (A Child) (Custody Rights: Jurisdiction)* [2005] UKHL 40, per Baroness Hale of Richmond, at [25].

There are decisions under the common law rules, just as there are under the 1980 Hague and Council of Europe Conventions, involving cases where children have been brought within the jurisdiction of the English courts by one parent against the wishes of the other, often in flagrant contempt of the order of a foreign court;[982] though in other cases the "kidnapping" has been done before there has been a foreign order,[983] sometimes to frustrate foreign proceedings.[984] These cases raise the issue of whether the English court should, despite any foreign custody order, examine the merits of the case concerning the child or make a summary order and send the child back to the jurisdiction from which he has come. *Re F (A Minor) (Abduction: Custody Rights)*[985] establishes that the first task for the court in assessing the welfare of the child is to decide whether the return of the child to the country from which it has been wrongfully taken should be ordered. It was argued on behalf of the bereft father in *Re J (A Child) (Custody Rights: Jurisdiction)*[986] that there should be a "strong presumption" that it is "highly likely" to be in the best interests of a child, subject to unauthorised removal or retention, to be returned to his country of habitual residence so that any issues which remain can be decided in the courts there.[987] Such an approach, however, is open to the objection that, "it would come so close to applying the Hague Convention principles by analogy that it would be indistinguishable from it in practice".[988] Instead, Baroness Hale of Richmond stated that: "The most one can say . . . is that the judge may find it convenient to start from the proposition that it is likely to be better for a child to return to his home country for any disputes about his future to be decided there. But the weight to be given to that proposition will vary enormously from case to case."[989] Important variables are the degrees of connection of the child with each country (including his nationality, where he has lived for most of his life, his first language, his race or ethnicity, his religion, his culture, and his education), and the length of time he has spent in each country. The extent to which it is relevant that the legal system of the other country differs from that of England will depend on the facts of the particular case.[990] "Our law does not start from any a priori assumptions about what is best for any individual child. It looks at the child and weighs a number of factors in the balance."[991] The evaluation and balancing of these factors is a matter for the trial judge: "only if his decision is so plainly wrong that he must have given far too much weight to a particular factor is the appellate court entitled to interfere".[992] Only in the relatively rare case of immediate return not being ordered, will the English court decide what order, in the best interests of the child, to make under section 8 of the Children Act 1989.[993]

---

[982] Eg *McKee v McKee* [1951] AC 352; *Re H* [1966] 1 WLR 381; *Re E(D)* [1967] Ch 761, [1967] 2 WLR 1370; *Re T* [1968] Ch 704; *Re L* [1974] 1 WLR 250; *Re C* [1978] Fam 105; *Re R* (1981) 2 FLR 416; *Re G* (1983) 5 FLR 268; and *Re S (Children) (Child Abduction: Asylum Appeal)* [2002] EWCA Civ 843; [2002] 2 FLR 465.

[983] Eg *Re T* [1968] Ch 704; *Re L* (1982) 4 FLR 368; and *Re S (Wardship: Summary Return: Non-Convention Country)* [2015] EWHC 176 (Fam).

[984] Eg *Re B* (1982) 4 FLR 492.

[985] [1991] Fam 25. And see *Re P (Abduction: Non-Convention Country)* [1997] 1 FLR 780; cf *Re L* [1974] 1 WLR 250; *Re R* (1981) 2 FLR 416.

[986] [2005] UKHL 40, [2006] 1 AC 80.

[987] Ibid, at [30].

[988] Ibid, per Baroness Hale of Richmond, at [31].

[989] Ibid, at [32].

[990] Ibid, at [36].

[991] Ibid, at [38].

[992] Ibid, at [12]. See eg *Re S (A Child) (Abduction: Hearing the Child)* [2014] EWCA Civ 1557—an order for the summary return of a child to Russia was set aside as no consideration had been given by the trial judge to the child's wishes and feelings.

[993] Taking account of the "check-list" in s 1(3) of the Children Act 1989.

(ii) Effect of a foreign order in England

Foreign custody and guardianship orders may not be devoid of effect in England even though, as we have seen, there are no rules at common law regulating their recognition and enforcement. Whilst there is no clear judicial authority in the case of custody orders, the Law Commission has suggested that "in practice a third person, such as an English headmaster, would be held to have acted properly if he acted on the assumption that a custody order made [elsewhere] was effective in England and Wales".[994]

There is some old authority in relation to foreign guardianship orders which supports the idea that effect will be given to such an order in England as it affects third parties, even though the English courts will remain free to make their own order.[995] A major question which arises is whether the foreign guardian is entitled to exercise, in England, those rights over the person and property of his ward that are recognised by English internal law. It is clear in the first place that, with or without an English order, his powers are limited to those recognised by English internal law.[996] This rule is in sharp contrast to the practice adopted in civil law countries, where it is admitted in general that a tutor appointed under the personal law of the child enjoys the same rights over his ward's movable property in other countries as he possesses in the country of his appointment. The problem, then, is whether a foreign guardian is justified if he acts in England within the limits of English internal law. The answer would appear to be that he occupies in effect the same position as a person appointed in England as the child's guardian. What he does within the limits of English internal law will be recognised as validly done provided that his authority has not been challenged;[997] but if his position or his authority is challenged, then, as in the case of an English guardian, it lies within the discretion of the court to decide whether he should be replaced by another person or whether his acts or proposed acts should be approved. Perhaps the major difference in this respect between a foreign and an English guardian is that the court would be more ready to displace the former than the latter.[998]

So, a foreign guardian whose authority was unchallenged in England would act properly if he took the child abroad, as he would be doing no more than an English guardian could do in exercising parental responsibility for the child.[999] Conversely, the English courts have recognised a foreign guardian and ordered that his ward, the young Prince Rainier of Monaco, at school in England, be delivered up to him.[1000]

With regard to property rights, English practice has also shown a tendency to recognise the right of a foreign guardian to claim movable property in England.[1001] Again, however, if his right is challenged it is at the discretion of the court whether, having regard to the interests of the child, the property shall be delivered to the guardian or to some other person.[1002] The

---

[994] Law Com No 138 (1985), para 5.6.

[995] See Dicey, Morris and Collins, paras 19R-073–19–080.

[996] *Johnstone v Beattie* (1843) 10 Cl & Fin 42 at 114.

[997] *Nugent v Vetzera* (1866) LR 2 Eq 704 at 712.

[998] Old cases in which foreign guardianship orders were recognised without regard to the paramount importance of the welfare of the child would not, in that respect, now be followed, ie *Nugent v Vetzera* (1866) LR 2 Eq 704; *Di Savini, Savini v Lousada* (1870) 18 WR 425; see *Re S (Hospital Patient: Foreign Curator)* [1996] Fam 23 at 30–1.

[999] Children Act 1989, s 5(6); and see *Nugent v Vetzera* (1866) LR 2 Eq 704 at 714; provided removal was done with the appropriate consent required under the Child Abduction Act 1984, s 1.

[1000] *Monaco v Monaco* (1937) 157 LT 231.

[1001] *Mackie v Darling* (1871) LR 12 Eq 319; *Re Crichton's Trust* (1855) 24 LTOS 267; *Re Brown's Trust* (1865) 12 LT 488.

[1002] *Ex p Watkins* (1752) 2 Ves Sen 470; *Re Hellmann's Will* (1866) LR 2 Eq 363; *Re Chatard's Settlement* [1899] 1 Ch 712. Cf *Dharamal v Lord Holm-Patrick* [1935] IR 760: A, domiciled in Indore in India, was not

question generally arises where money is due to a foreign child under an English settlement, will or intestacy. Where the money has not been paid into court, it has been said that the trustees are legally discharged if they make payment to the foreign guardian and take his receipt.[1003] Where the money is in court, then the court is entitled, but not compelled, to order payment to the guardian, and whether it does so or not depends on whether it is satisfied that the property will be properly administered for the child's benefit.[1004]

5. OTHER DEVELOPMENTS

Council of Europe Convention on Contact concerning Children

On 15 May 2003, the Council of Europe Convention on Contact concerning Children[1005] opened for signature. The Convention entered into force on 1 September 2005, and to date there have been nine ratifications.[1006] As it was with the 1996 Hague Convention, European Union Member States are no longer free to conclude the 2003 Convention on their own, since its provisions affect Union rules as contained in Brussels II *bis*, meaning that competence is shared between the Union and the Member States.[1007]

The Convention aims at reinforcing the fundamental right of children and their parents and other persons having family ties with the child to maintain contact on a regular basis, and seeks to "improve the machinery for international co-operation especially as regards transfrontier access to children in order to establish safeguards for the return of children after a period of access".[1008] The risk of unnecessary duplication and overlap with the provisions of Brussels II *bis*, the 1980 Hague Convention, the 1980 Council of Europe Convention and the 1996 Hague Convention, is obvious, but nevertheless the view has been advanced that the 2003 Convention will "contribute to the realisation of the aims underlying existing and future Community rules in the field of recognition and enforcement of judgments in the area of parental responsibility".[1009] The preamble to the 2003 Convention states that, "an additional instrument is necessary to provide solutions relating in particular to transfrontier contact concerning children".[1010] Given the proliferation of instruments in this field of law, it is scarcely possible to justify this statement.

"Contact" is defined in the Convention as including direct and indirect contact with a child.[1011] In particular, it includes "(i) the child staying for a limited period of time with or

---

entitled as of right to the Irish Sweep winnings of his daughter, aged seven, though by the law of Indore he could give a good discharge.

[1003] *Re Chatard's Settlement* [1899] 1 Ch 712 at 716.

[1004] Children Act 1989, s 1.

[1005] CETS No 192. See also *Explanatory Report*, adopted 3 May 2002.

[1006] Albania, Bosnia and Herzegovina, Croatia, Czech Republic, Malta, Romania, San Marino, Turkey and Ukraine.

[1007] Art 22(1) of the 2003 Convention allows for accession by the European Union. In 2002, the Commission presented a Proposal for a Council Decision on the signing by the EC of the Council of Europe Convention on Contact concerning Children (COM 2002/0520 final), OJ 2003 C 20E/369. The Proposal was, however, later withdrawn, see Withdrawal of Obsolete Commission Proposals, OJ 2013 C 109/04. In relation to England and Wales, see Department for Constitutional Affairs Consultation Paper 02/04, 28 May 2004.

[1008] *Explanatory Report*, para I.

[1009] Proposal for a Council Decision on the signing by the EC of the Council of Europe Convention on Contact concerning Children (COM 2002/0520 final), Recital (4).

[1010] Recital (16).

[1011] A person under eighteen years of age in respect of whom a contact order may be made or enforced in a state party to the Convention: Art 2(c).

meeting a person[1012] . . . with whom he or she is not usually living; (ii) any form of communication between the child and such person; (iii) the provision of information to such a person about the child or to the child about such a person".[1013] "Contact", arguably, is broader than "rights of access" referred to in Brussels II *bis*,[1014] and use of the expression is intended to demonstrate that children are the holders of certain rights.[1015]

Article 20(1) of the Convention provides that it shall not prejudice the application of the 1980 Hague Convention, the 1980 Council of Europe Convention[1016] or the 1996 Hague Convention.[1017] Moreover, by virtue of Article 20(3), if the European Union and its Member States should accede to/ratify the 2003 Convention, in their mutual relations those Member States would give preference to the application of Brussels II *bis*, meaning that the 2003 Convention would apply only in so far as there is no Union rule to govern the particular issue arising.

The 2003 Convention is merely a "good practice guide". It does not lay down rules of jurisdiction, or a mechanism for the recognition and enforcement of contact orders. Rather, it is a "medium for promoting co-operation and consistency of practice".[1018] Since the procedure for recognition and enforcement of orders has been laid down already in other instruments operating in the field, the advantages to be gained from ratification of yet another instrument are not obvious. Ratification of the Convention is more likely to confuse than to enhance regulation of contact concerning children.[1019] It is to be hoped, therefore, that political pressure alone will not compel the United Kingdom to become a state party to this Convention.

[1012] A parent (Art 4) or a person other than the parent having family ties with the child (Art 5).
[1013] Art 2(a).
[1014] Art 2(10). Supra, p 1093.
[1015] *Explanatory Report*, para 6.
[1016] Though see special provision in Art 19 of the 2003 Convention.
[1017] *Explanatory Report*, para 11.
[1018] Department for Constitutional Affairs Consultation Paper 02/04 (28 May 2004), para 4.
[1019] Cf remarks of Thorpe LJ in *Re G (Children) (Foreign Contact Order: Enforcement)* [2003] All ER (D) 144 at [32].

26

CROSS-BORDER SURROGACY[1]

1. **Introduction**	1179	2. **UK Approach to Surrogacy**	1183
(a) Background	1179	(a) Background	1183
(b) Legal parenthood	1180	(b) "Section 54" requirements	1184
(c) Diversity in national approaches		(c) Authorisation of payments	1187
to surrogacy	1182	3. **Human Rights Considerations**	1189

1. INTRODUCTION

(a) Background

There is a complete void in the regulation of surrogacy arrangements at the international level, as none of the existing international instruments contains specific provisions designed to regulate this emerging area of international family law. In the absence of a global legislative response, highly complex legal problems arise.[2] Among these problems, the key private international law issue is legal parenthood, with attendant problems of nationality and immigration.[3] In addition to the difficulties concerning legal parenthood and nationality, a number of other legal hurdles can easily be envisaged. For example, what happens if the intending parents[4] refuse to accept the child because it suffers from a serious disability,[5] or because

---

[1] This chapter draws heavily on K Trimmings and P Beaumont 'General Report on Surrogacy' in K Trimmings and P Beaumont (eds), *International Surrogacy Arrangements: Legal Regulation at the International Level* (2013) 439–549; K Trimmings and P Beaumont 'Parentage and Surrogacy in a European Perspective' in Scherpe (ed) *European Family Law, Vol III* (2016) 232–283; and P Beaumont and K Trimmings, 'Recent Jurisprudence of the European Court of Human Rights in the Area of Cross-Border Surrogacy: Is There Still a Need for Global Regulation of Surrogacy?' in G Biagioni and F Ippolito (eds), *Migrant Children in the XXI Century. Selected Issues of Public and Private International Law* (forthcoming). See also Hague Conference on Private International Law, The Parentage / Surrogacy Project, https://www.hcch.net/en/projects/legislative-projects/parentage-surrogacy.

[2] See *X & Y (Foreign Surrogacy)* [2008] EWHC 3030, per Hedley J, at [8]—"many pitfalls confront the couple who consider commissioning foreign surrogacy", and "potentially difficult conflict of law issues arise which may have wholly uncommissioning and unforeseen consequences". See also Theis *et al* (2009) 39 FLJ 239.

[3] Where a parental order is made in the UK and one or both of the intending couple are British citizens, the child—if not already so—will become a British citizen. The Human Fertilization and Embryology (Parental Orders) Regulations 2010, Explanatory Memorandum, at [8.7]. See also Home Office, Inter-country Surrogacy and Immigration Rules, 2009; *Re IJ (A Child)* [2011] EWHC 921 (Fam), at [8]–[11]; *Re Z (Foreign Surrogacy: Allocation of Work: Guidance on Parental Order Reports)* [2015] EWFC 90, at [76], [94]–[97]; *KB v RT* [2016] EWHC 760 (Fam); and *Re X (Foreign Surrogacy: Child's Name)* [2016] EWHC 1068 (Fam), at [6]–[12].

[4] Ie the person(s) who had entered into an agreement with the surrogate mother prior to the conception of the child, with the view that the child should be handed over to them after the birth (the "intended parents").

[5] See eg Hyder, BioNews, 11 October 2010. See also *Farnell & Anor and Chanbua* [2016] FCWA 17—decision of the Family Court of Western Australia in the case of baby Gammy, born to a Thai surrogate mother and abandoned by his Australian parents after they discovered he had Downs syndrome.

their relationship breaks down before the child is born[6] or the transfer of legal parenthood is resolved?[7] What happens if the surrogate mother changes her mind and decides to keep the child?[8] At a later stage, other complications may arise, such as a cross-border custody and access dispute between the intending parents residing in one country and the surrogate mother in another, a dispute over maintenance and financial support,[9] or a dispute over international child abduction.[10]

Legal problems arising from the lack of international regulation of surrogacy arrangements are, however, not the only cause for concern in this respect.[11] Another great worry springing from the unregulated character of "procreative tourism" is the potential for a black market preying on peoples' emotional or economic needs.[12] This concern is particularly legitimate in cases of surrogacy for profit, where the commercial nature of these arrangements renders them akin to child trafficking.

(b) Legal parenthood

Prior to the advent of assisted reproduction, legal parenthood was of little if no concern to private international lawyers. Indeed, legal parenthood was covered by a "common core" of law, which was founded on the recognition of legal motherhood on the basis of gestation and childbirth, and of legal fatherhood on the basis of the father's marriage to the child's mother.[13] Assisted reproductive technology, in particular surrogacy, however, poses a challenge to the traditional rules on legal parenthood, in particular legal motherhood. Indeed, surrogacy completely disrupts these rules as it separates the three principal markers of legal motherhood: gestation, genetics and the intention to parent. Hence, in surrogacy there is the potential for multiple claims of legal parenthood based on biology (ie gestation and birth), genetics (ie by the person who contributes egg or sperm) and intention (ie by the person who initiated the child's conception and intends to raise the child).[14] In recognition of this reality, courts and legislatures in different jurisdictions have developed alternative approaches to legal parenthood in surrogacy arrangements: the "genetics" test[15] and the

---

[6] See eg "Surrogate Mum of Twins Unfazed After Baby Deal Fall Apart", CBC News, New Brunswick, 13 September 2011.

[7] See eg *Re C and D (Children) (Fact finding Hearing)* [2015] EWHC 1059 (Fam).

[8] Eg *CW v NT & Anor* [2011] EWHC 33 (domestic surrogacy case).

[9] See K Trimmings 'The Interface between Maintenance and Cross-Border Surrogacy' in Beaumont *et al* (eds), *The Recovery of Maintenance in the EU and Worldwide* (2014) 261–74.

[10] *W and B v H (Child Abduction: Surrogacy)* [2002] 1 FLR 1008.

[11] Exceptionally, intending parents embarking on a surrogacy arrangement abroad may encounter also difficulties caused by force majeure, as happened in *Re X (Foreign Surrogacy: Child's Name)* [2016] EWHC 1068 (Fam), when a devastating earthquake struck Nepal shortly after the child was born, resulting in a significant delay in the immigration procedure, at [5].

[12] See *X & Y (Foreign Surrogacy)* [2008] EWHC 3030, per Hedley J, at [29]—" . . . the present law might encourage the less scrupulous to take advantage of the more vulnerable, unmarried surrogate mothers and to be less than frank in the arrangements that surround foreign surrogacy".

[13] European Parliament, Directorate General for Internal Policies, "Recognition of Parental Responsibility: Biological Parenthood vs. Legal Parenthood, i.e. Mutual Recognition of Surrogacy Agreements: What is the Current Situation in the MS? Need for EU Action?" 2010, p 16. See also Lowe, "A Study into the Rights and Legal Status of Children Being Brought up in Various Forms of Marital and Nonmarital Partnerships and Cohabitation", Report for the attention of the Committee of Experts on Family Law, September 2009, CJ-FA (2008) 5; and *The Ampthill Peerage* [1977] AC 547.

[14] Ministry of Attorney General Justice Services Branch, Civil and Family Law Policy Office (British Columbia), "Family Relations Act Review: Discussion Paper", August 2007.

[15] Eg *M v An t-Ard-Chláraitheoir* [2013] IEHC 91 (overturned on appeal: *M.R. and D.R.(suing by their father and next friend O.R.) & ors -v- An t-Ard-Chláraitheoir & ors* [2014] IESC 60). See also Caffrey [2013] Medico-Legal Journal of Ireland 34.

"intent" test.[16] Nevertheless, many countries, including the UK,[17] continue to apply in surrogacy cases the traditional rules on legal parenthood, based on the gestational test. As different countries are likely to assign legal parenthood in surrogacy cases differently, there is a potential for conflicting legal statuses across boundaries,[18] resulting in practical problems for children and families such as uncertain paternity or maternity or limping parent-child relationships.[19]

There are two dimensions to the problem of legal parenthood in a cross-border surrogacy case: first, the acquisition of legal parenthood in the country of birth and second, the transfer of the legal parenthood to the intending parents in their home state. Indeed, the fact that the intending parents have been declared the legal parents in the country of birth does not automatically make them the legal parents in their home country. The intending parents will therefore seek to confirm the child's status through the recognition of the legal parenthood established in the country of birth in their "home" jurisdiction. Generally, the problem of transfer of legal parenthood is treated differently in common law jurisdictions and in civil law countries.[20] In most civil law countries the issue of the legal parenthood of a child born abroad will be approached through the application of relevant private international law rules on recognition of foreign judgments, legal facts or juridical acts, or the application of the relevant foreign law where there is no judgment to recognize (the "conflict of laws" or the "recognition" method).

In contrast, in common law countries, the law of the forum will normally be applied to the establishment of legal parenthood where a child is born outside the jurisdiction (the "*lex fori*" method).[21] In some of these jurisdictions, including the UK, the relevant domestic law expressly states that it has an extraterritorial effect, in other words it applies regardless of whether the child was born in the state concerned or abroad.[22] This approach is often re-affirmed through guidance issued by the state authorities for intending parents in cross-border surrogacy cases. For example, guidance issued by the UK Border Agency states that "anyone considering entering into an inter-country surrogacy arrangement must remember that if they reside in the United Kingdom, they are subject to United Kingdom law and the definitions which underlie it".[23]

---

[16] Eg *Johnson v Calvert* Cal Sup Ct, 5 Cal4th 84, 851 P.2d 776 (1993); *Buzzanca v Buzzanca*, 61 Cal App 4th 1410, 72 Cal Rptr 2d 280 (Cal Ct App 1998; and California Family Code, section 7960 (c). See also Horsey (2010) 22 CFLQ 449.

[17] Human Fertilisation and Embryology Act 2008 (HFEA 2008), s 33(1), discussed infra, p 1183.

[18] The problem of private international law rules on parentage (generally or in relation to surrogacy) has not been dealt with in existing Hague Conventions. Hague Conference, Report of the February 2016 Meeting of the Experts' Group on Parentage / Surrogacy, February 2016, at [5].

[19] Ibid, at [4].

[20] See also Hague Conference on Private International Law, "The Private International Law Issues Surrounding the Status of Children, Including Issues Arising from International Surrogacy Arrangements", March 2012, at [35]–[41].

[21] HFEA 2008, discussed infra, p 1183 et seq.

[22] Eg the UK (HFEA 2008, section 33(3)) and New Zealand (the Status of Children Act 1969, section 5(3)).

[23] Home Office, UK Border Agency, "Inter-country Surrogacy and the Immigration Rules". See also Irish Ministry for Justice, Equality and Defence, "Citizenship, Parentage, Guardianship and Travel Document Issues in Relation to Children Born as a Result of Surrogacy Arrangements Entered into Outside the State" S 1—in considering the issue of legal parenthood in relation to children born as a result of a surrogacy arrangement outside Ireland, "the Irish authorities are required to apply Irish law".

(c) Diversity in national approaches to surrogacy[24]

At the regulatory level, countries differ considerably in their legal approaches to surrogacy.[25] Accordingly, the following four categories can be identified: (1) Countries where surrogacy in both its forms (namely, altruistic and commercial)[26] is outlawed;[27] (2) Countries where surrogacy has been ignored by the legislature and remains unregulated;[28] (3) Countries where surrogacy is regulated whilst only an altruistic form of surrogacy is permitted;[29] and (4) Countries where commercial surrogacy is permitted ("surrogacy-friendly" jurisdictions).[30]

The diversity in national approaches to surrogacy as described above has encouraged widespread *forum shopping* where intending parents from all over the world flock to "surrogacy-friendly" jurisdictions with the intention of taking advantage of liberal local commercial surrogacy regimes. Indeed, it is no exaggeration to say that the modern world has already witnessed a development of an extensive international commercial surrogacy market.[31] "Surrogacy-friendly" jurisdictions are particularly attractive to foreign intending parents for the following three reasons: 1) These countries do not impose nationality, domicile or habitual residence prerequisites for the intending parents. 2) Legal parenthood does not follow the general rules but instead is established on the basis of the intent test, often in combination with the genetics test.[32] Consequently, intending parents (or at least one of them) are able to acquire legal parenthood in the country of birth;[33] 3) There is no shortage of willing surrogates given the commercial nature of surrogacy in these jurisdictions.

Although countries with a relatively neutral approach to surrogacy where altruistic surrogacy is permitted and regulated also allow intending parents in surrogacy cases to acquire legal parenthood, either immediately upon the birth of the child (eg Greece) or through a post-birth transfer of legal parenthood (eg the UK),[34] these countries do not generally attract intending parents from abroad. The reason is that these jurisdictions commonly impose stringent requirements on the domicile/habitual residence/residence of the intending parents[35] and/or the surrogate mother. The underlying rationale is to discourage "procreative tourism". An additional deterrent is the ban on commercial surrogacy in these countries as finding an altruistic surrogate is much more difficult than finding a commercial one.

---

[24] For a detailed analysis see Trimmings and Beaumont, "General Report on Surrogacy", in Trimmings and Beaumont (eds), *International Surrogacy Arrangements: Legal Regulation at the International Level* (2013) 443–64. See also Fenton-Glynn and Scherpe (eds), *Eastern and Western Perspectives on Surrogacy* (forthcoming).

[25] *X & Y (Foreign Surrogacy)* [2008] EWHC 3030 (Fam), per Hedley J, at [3].

[26] In commercial surrogacy arrangements, the surrogate mother receives a payment beyond her reasonable pregnancy-related expenses.

[27] Eg France and Germany.

[28] Eg Belgium and Finland.

[29] Eg the UK, South Africa and Israel.

[30] Eg Some US States, such as California, Minnesota and Illinois; Ukraine and Russia.

[31] Permanent Bureau of the Hague Conference, "Private International Law Issues Surrounding the Status of Children, Including Issues Arising From International Surrogacy Arrangements", March 2011, at [11]. See also Smerdon, (2008–2009) 39 Cumberland Law Review 15.

[32] See supra, p 1181, n 16.

[33] See *Re IJ (A Child)* [2011] EWHC 921 (Fam), per Hedley J, at [4]—overseas jurisdictions can confer parental status on the intending couple but that status is not recognised in our domestic law.

[34] See infra, p 1183 et seq.

[35] Eg HFEA 2008, s 54(4)(b). See *Re G (Surrogacy: Foreign Domicile)* [2007] EWHC 2814. Discussed infra, p 1184, n 48.

2. UK APPROACH TO SURROGACY[36]

(a) Background

The underlying policy aim of the regulation of surrogacy in the UK is to prohibit commercial surrogacy arrangements and to limit surrogacy to a relatively small number of altruistic arrangements. Altruistic surrogacy is available in the UK to specific qualified persons, with the eligibility criteria being set out in relevant statutory instruments.[37] The key piece of legislation that sets rules for the establishment of legal parenthood in cases of assisted reproduction, including surrogacy, is the Human Fertilisation and Embryology Act 2008 (HFEA 2008). Although altruistic surrogacy is legal in the UK, the principal aspect of the surrogacy arrangement, namely the obligation of the surrogate mother to hand the child over to the intending parents, is unenforceable.[38]

Upon the birth of the child legal motherhood is established on the basis of the gestational test, with legal paternity depending upon the marital status of the surrogate mother. In particular, section 33(1) of the HFEA 2008 states:

> The woman who is carrying or has carried a child as a result of the placing in her of an embryo or of sperm and eggs, and no other woman, is to be treated as the mother of the child.

Section 35(1) of the same Act further states that if, at the time of the procedure, the woman was a party to marriage and the embryo was not created with the sperm of the other party to the marriage, then the other party to the marriage is to be treated as the father of the child unless it is shown that he did not consent to the procedure. In other words, the surrogate mother is regarded as the legal mother of the child (whether or not she is also the genetic mother) and her husband/partner (if applicable) is presumed to be the legal father of the child. Nevertheless, there is a specific statutory remedy available to the intending parents that allows for a transfer of legal parenthood from the surrogate mother (and her husband/partner as applicable) to the intending parents. In order to extinguish the legal status of the surrogate mother (and her husband/partner as applicable) and reassign legal parenthood to the intending parents, the intending parents must go through a post-birth legal process known as the "parental order application". The effect of a parental order is that it provides for a child to be treated as the legitimate child of the intending parents, with *inter alia* the attendant rights of inheritance from the intending parents and the right to be registered as a British citizen if one of the intending parents is a British citizen.[39] A parental order confers parental responsibility for the child exclusively on the intending parents and extinguishes the parental responsibility of anyone else.[40]

Applications for parental orders are governed by section 54 of the HFEA 2008 and the Human Fertilisation and Embryology (Parental Order) Regulations 2010.[41] Applications

---

[36] See eg Welstead [2014] Fam Law 1299 and [2015] Fam Law 1415; Cabeza [2014] Fam Law 1444; Wells-Greco "National Report on Surrogacy: United Kingdom" in Trimmings and Beaumont (eds), *International Surrogacy Arrangements: Legal Regulation at the International Level* (2013) 367–86; and Wells-Greco, The Status of Children Arising from Inter-Country Surrogacy Arrangements (2016) 149–79.

[37] Surrogacy Arrangements Act 1985; Human Fertilisation and Embryology Act 1990 (HFEA 1990) and Human Fertilisation and Embryology Act 2008 (HFEA 2008).

[38] Surrogacy Arrangements Act (1985), s 1A.

[39] Explanatory Memorandum to the Human Fertilization and Embryology (Parental Orders) Regulations 2010, No 985/2010, at [2.1]. See also Home Office, UK Border Agency, "Inter-country Surrogacy and the Immigration Rules".

[40] Lowe and Douglas, *Bromley's Family Law*, p 281.

[41] See also Family Procedure Rules 2010, Part 13.

involving cross-border surrogacy are to be heard by a judge of High Court level.[42] A parental order will be issued if the court is satisfied that the requirements under section 54 of the HFEA 2008 are met, and, if they are, that it is in the child's lifelong welfare interests for the court to make such an order. Namely, the Human Fertilisation and Embryology (Parental Order) Regulations 2010 apply section 1 of the Children and Adoption Act 2002 to parental order applications so that the child's welfare must be the court's "paramount consideration . . . throughout his lifetime".[43]

(b) "Section 54" requirements

(i) Domicile[44]

A parental order is not a Part 1 Order as defined in Chapter I of the Family Law Act 1986, and therefore jurisdiction to make such an order is not governed by the 1986 Act.[45] Under section 54(4)(b) of the HFEA 2008 the Court's jurisdiction is based on one of the applicants having a domicile in the UK, the Channel Islands or the Isle of Man. The HFEA 2008 does not require that the child who is the subject of a parental order application is to be present or habitually resident in the jurisdiction for the Court to exercise its jurisdiction under section 54. Although section 54(4)(a) requires the child's home to be with the applicants at the time of the application and the making of the order,[46] it does not specify that the child's or the applicants' home must be in the UK. Hence, as long as the domicile requirement is met, a parental order can be granted even if the applicants and the child are resident overseas.[47]

Arguably, English judges have taken a rather liberal approach to the interpretation of domicile for the purposes of section 54.[48] Thus, for example, in a case involving an Israeli same sex couple,[49] Theis J was satisfied that one of the men had abandoned his domicile of origin and acquired an English domicile of choice immediately upon his arrival in England in January 2008.[50] Similarly, a parental order was granted to a Polish-American same sex couple who, having decided to cut all ties with the USA, moved to England in 2008;[51] to a French same sex couple whose domicile of origin was France and who moved to the UK only two months before the birth, albeit with the intention to make their home there permanently and indefinitely;[52] or to a German couple, residing in Germany, on the basis that the intending mother had acquired domicile of choice in England, and did not abandon it, although, due to force of circumstances, she had physically been out of the jurisdiction since 2013.[53] In a different

---

[42] *Re IJ (A Child)* [2011] EWHC 921 (Fam), per Hedley J, at [12]; and *Re Z (Foreign Surrogacy: Allocation of Work: Guidance on Parental Order Reports)* [2015] EWFC 90, per Russell J, at [73].

[43] Human Fertilisation and Embryology (Parental Order) Regulations 2010, at [2] and Schedule 1. See eg *Re WT (A Child)* [2014] EWHC 1303, at [38]–[40]; *Re G (Parental Orders)* [2014] EWHC 1561 (Fam), at [53]-[55]; *Re A* [2015] EWHC 1756 (Fam), at [21]; and *AB and Another v GH* [2016] EWHC 2063 (Fam), at [32]–[33].

[44] See, generally, supra p 145 et seq. See eg *Re Z (Foreign Surrogacy: Allocation of Work: Guidance on Parental Order Reports)* [2015] EWFC 90, at [57]; and *KB v RT* [2016] EWHC 760 (Fam), at [42].

[45] *CC and DD* [2014] EWHC 1307, per Theis J, at [20]. See also *Re Z (Foreign Surrogacy: Allocation of Work: Guidance on Parental Order Reports)* [2015] EWFC 90, per Russell J at [71]. See supra, p 1090.

[46] See infra, p 1186.

[47] *CC and DD* [2014] EWHC 1307; and *Re A* [2015] EWHC 1756 (Fam).

[48] Cf *Re G (Surrogacy: Foreign Domicile)* [2007] EWHC 2814 (in the context of the HFEA 1990)—it was not open to a Turkish couple, domiciled in Turkey, who had entered into a surrogacy arrangement in the UK, to apply for a parental order under s 30 of the HFEA 1990. See Cullen (2008) 32 Adoption & Fostering 1.

[49] *Z and another v C and another* [2011] EWHC 3181 (Fam), per Theis J, at [29]–[31]. In her judgment, her Ladyship also set out "the general principles of domiciliary law", see [12]–[18].

[50] Ibid, at [30]–[31].

[51] *Re A (Parental Order: Domicile)* [2013] EWHC 426 (Fam), per Theis J, at [25]–[27].

[52] *Re G (Parental Orders)* [2014] EWHC 1561 (Fam), per Theis J, at [41]–[51].

[53] *AB and Another v GH* [2016] EWHC 2063 (Fam), per Theis J, at [14]–[31].

set of circumstances, a parental order was made in favour of a British-French couple residing in France, on the basis that the intending mother, who left England in 2006, had retained her domicile of origin in England;[54] and an English-South African same sex couple, on the grounds that the English intending father had not lost his domicile of origin in England by living in South Africa since 2007.[55] Similarly, UK-born male intending parents who had entered into a civil partnership in the UK were held to have retained their domicile of origin in England in circumstances where they had spent periods living in Australia and obtained Australian citizenship, however, always intending to return to live in the UK as they did in 2014.[56]

(ii) Personal status

The provisions of section 54(2) require that the applicants are a married couple,[57] or same sex civil partners[58] or two people who are living as partners in an enduring family relationship.[59] It has been held that a parental order could be made in favour of a single applicant in circumstances where the other applicant had died subsequent to the making of the application.[60] It was not certain whether the intending mother, in favour of which the parental order was made, was genetically linked to the child, although the deceased applicant was clearly the child's genetic father.[61] In her decision, Theis J was careful to point out that the decision was not meant to "pave the way for single intending parents to apply for a parental order".[62] Despite that, in *Re Z (A Child) (Surrogate Father: Parental Order)*,[63] a parental order was sought by a single male applicant who had commissioned a child through a surrogacy arrangement in Minnesota. Although Sir James Munby P found himself unable to make a parental order, in his latter decision in the same case[64] the President acknowledged the potentially discriminatory nature of s 54(2), and made a formal declaration of incompatibility[65] to the effect that the exclusion of single applicants from section 54 was incompatible with the applicant father and the child's rights under Articles 8 and 14 of the European Convention on Human Rights (ECHR).[66]

(iii) Genetic link and minimum age

Section 54(1)(a) and (b) requires that the applicants have attained the age of 18[67] and that there is a genetic link between at least one of the applicants and the child.[68]

---

[54] *CC and DD* [2014] EWHC 1307, per Theis J, at [22]–[27].

[55] *Re B-G (A Child) (Parental Orders: Domicile)* [2014] EWHC 444 (Fam), per Jackson J, at [7]–[11] and [14].

[56] *AB v CD* [2015] EWFC 12, at [26] and [6]:

[57] Eg *Re G (Parental Orders)* [2014] EWHC 1561 (Fam), at [26]; and *AB and Another v GH* [2016] EWHC 2063 (Fam), at [7].

[58] Eg *AB v CD* [2015] EWFC 12, at [24].

[59] See *Re F (Children) (Thai Surrogacy: Enduring Family Relationship)* [2016] EWHC 1594 (Fam). Eg *Re A* [2015] EWHC 1756 (Fam), at [5].

[60] *A v P* [2011] EWHC 1738 (Fam)—a surrogacy arrangement commissioned by a married couple in India.

[61] The surrogate mother was implanted with several embryos, some of which were formed using the intending mother's eggs and some using donor eggs; all had been fertilised with the intending father's sperm.

[62] *A v P* [2011] EWHC 1738 (Fam), at [31].

[63] [2015] EWFC 73.

[64] Re Z (A Child) (Surrogate Father: Parental Order) [2016] EWHC 1191 (Fam).

[65] Human Rights Act 1998, s 4(1).

[66] European Convention for the Protection of Human Rights and Fundamental Freedoms 1950. *Re Z (A Child) (Surrogate Father: Parental Order)* [2016] EWHC 1191 (Fam), at [17]–[19].

[67] See eg *Re WT (A Child)* [2014] EWHC 1303, at [27]; *Re G (Parental Orders)* [2014] EWHC 1561 (Fam), at [31]; *AB v CD* [2015] EWFC 12, at [27]; and *Re A* [2015] EWHC 1756 (Fam), at [9].

[68] See eg *Re WT (A Child)* [2014] EWHC 1303 (Fam), at [24]; *Re G (Parental Orders)* [2014] EWHC 1561 (Fam), at [25]; *AB v CD* [2015] EWFC 12, at [22]; *Re A* [2015] EWHC 1756 (Fam), at [5]; and *AB and Another v GH* [2016] EWHC 2063 (Fam), at [6].

(iv) Child's home

Section 54(4)(a) lays down the requirement that "both at the time of the application and of the making of the order the child's home is with the applicants".[69] The concept of "home" within this requirement has been construed flexibly. In *Re X (A Child) (Surrogacy: Time Limit)*[70] Sir James Munby P held that the child's home was "with the applicants" within the meaning of the provision, even though at the time of the application the intending parents lived in separate homes and the child's living arrangements were split between them. The requirement was found to be satisfied even in circumstances where the child was stranded abroad with extended family and/or one of the intending parents.[71]

(v) Time limit

A purposive interpretation[72] has been taken also in relation to section 54(3) which sets out the requirement that the application is made within six months of the birth of the child.[73] In *Re X (A Child) (Surrogacy: Time Limit)*,[74] a parental order was granted even though the application had been made two years and two months after the birth of the child. Despite the lengthy delay Sir James Munby P reasoned that "to construe section 54(3) as barring forever an application made just one day late is not, in my judgment, sensible. It is the very antithesis of sensible; it is almost nonsensical".

(vi) Consent

Pursuant to section 54(6), the surrogate mother and her husband/partner (if applicable)[75] have to consent to the making of the parental order. The consent, which has to be free and unconditional, must be given not less than six weeks after the child's birth,[76] and with full understanding of what is involved.[77] The six-week requirement parallels the adoption legislation[78] and in the cross-border surrogacy setting means that the surrogate mother will often be required to give consent twice as the overseas law may require consent at or before birth or handing over of the child.[79] It has been suggested that independent legal advice for the surrogate mother (and her husband) to establish their free and unconditional consent should be considered, together with the provision of evidence that any legal documents signed by the surrogate mother had been fully understood by her.[80] Legal costs incurred for

---

[69] See eg *Re WT (A Child)* [2014] EWHC 1303, at [27]; *AB v CD* [2015] EWFC 12, at [26]; *Re A* [2015] EWHC 1756 (Fam), at [5]; and *AB and Another v GH* [2016] EWHC 2063 (Fam), at [9].

[70] [2014] EWHC 3135 (Fam). See also *Re A* [2015] EWHC 2080 (Fam); *AB v CD* [2015] EWFC 12; and *DM v SJ* [2016] EWHC 270 (Fam).

[71] Eg *Re Z (Foreign Surrogacy: Allocation of Work: Guidance on Parental Order Reports)* [2015] EWFC 90, at [57] and [89]–[94]; and *KB v RT* [2016] EWHC 760 (Fam), at [39]–[41].

[72] Cf *X & Y (Foreign Surrogacy)* [2008] EWHC 3030 (Fam), per Hedley J, at [12]; and *Re WT (A Child)* [2014] EWHC 1303, per Theis J, at [42]. Alternatively, the provision can be "read down" in order to give effect to the relevant ECHR rights, in particular Article 8. See *Re X (A Child) (Surrogacy: Time Limit)* [2014] EWHC 3135 (Fam), per Sir James Munby P, at [58].

[73] Eg *Re WT (A Child)* [2014] EWHC 1303, at [26]; *Re G (Parental Orders)* [2014] EWHC 1561 (Fam), per Theis J, at [27]; *Re A* [2015] EWHC 2080 (Fam), per Theis J, at [64]; *Re A* [2015] EWHC 1756 (Fam), per Theis J, at [5]; and *AB and Another v GH* [2016] EWHC 2063 (Fam), per Theis J, at [8].

[74] [2014] EWHC 3135 (Fam). See Trimmings (2015) 37 JSWFL 241–3; and Isaacs [2014] Fam Law 1723. See also *AB v CD* [2015] EWFC 12; *Re A* [2015] EWHC 2080 (Fam); *A and B (Children: Surrogacy: Parental Orders: Time limit)* [2015] EWHC 911 (Fam); *A v C* [2016] EWFC 42; and *KB v RT* [2016] EWHC 760 (Fam).

[75] See *AB v CD* [2015] EWFC 12, at [48]; and *KB v RT* [2016] EWHC 760 (Fam), at [45]–[51].

[76] HFEA 2008, s 54(7).

[77] HFEA 2008, s 54(6).

[78] Adoption and Children Act 2002, s 52(3).

[79] *Re IJ (A Child)* [2011] EWHC 921 (Fam), at [5].

[80] *Re WT (A Child)* [2014] EWHC 1303, at [42].

this should be borne by the intending parents and are likely to be regarded as an expense reasonably incurred.[81] Furthermore, where the intending parents are unable to meet the surrogate mother, they should establish clear lines of communication with her and ensure she is informed during the pregnancy of the need to give consent at least six weeks after the birth.[82]

The consent is not required if the person cannot be found or is incapable of giving agreement.[83] Accordingly, Baker J held in *Re D (Children)(Parental Order: Foreign Surrogacy)*[84] that where the surrogate mother cannot be found and the applicants have taken all reasonable steps to obtain her consent, and further delay in determining the application would be contrary to the child's welfare, the consent can be dispensed with by the court.

(vii) Payments

Section 54(8) sets out the principle that the surrogacy arrangement must not be commercial; ie that the payments to the surrogate mother do not exceed reasonable pregnancy-related expenses, *unless authorised by the court* (emphasis added).[85]

(c) Authorisation of payments

The most controversial aspect of the "section 54 requirements" is the power vested in the court to retrospectively authorise payments to the surrogate mother that exceed the reasonable pregnancy-related expenses. This aspect of section 54 demonstrates itself most obviously in the context of cross-border surrogacy arrangements. Although the term "reasonable pregnancy-related expenses" is defined nowhere in the legislation, courts have been willing to retrospectively approve sums paid to foreign surrogates clearly in excess of such expenses.

The principles that are to guide judges in the exercise of discretion have evolved from case-law. In *X & Y (Foreign Surrogacy)*[86] Hedley J was considering a Ukrainian surrogacy arrangement under the Human Fertilisation and Embryology Act 1990 (HFEA 1990), section 30(7) of which was in similar terms to section 54(8) of HFEA 2008. His Lordship set out three questions that the court should ask itself when faced with a request for a retrospective authorisation of payments in a surrogacy arrangement: 1) Was the sum paid to the surrogate disproportionate to reasonable expenses? 2) Were the applicants acting in good faith and without "moral taint" in their dealings with the surrogate? 3) Were the applicants party to any attempt to defraud the authorities?[87] In *Re S (Parental Order)*[88] Hedley J set out further the approach the court should take. He acknowledged that cross-border commercial surrogacy raised matters of public policy and identified those as follows: 1) To ensure that commercial surrogacy was not used to circumvent childcare laws in the UK in that arrangements would be approved in favour of applicants who "would not have been approved as parents under any set of existing arrangements in this country".[89] 2) The court should be cautious not to get involved in anything that resembles "the simple payment for effectively buying children overseas".[90] 3) The court should be careful to make sure that sums of money which might appear modest in themselves are not in reality "of such a substance that they overbear the will of

---

[81] Ibid.
[82] Ibid.
[83] HFEA 2008, s 54(7).
[84] [2012] EWHC 2631 (Fam). See also *AB v CD* [2015] EWFC 12.
[85] See infra. Eg *AB v CD* [2015] EWFC 12, at [29] and [32]; *KB v RT* [2016] EWHC 760 (Fam), at [55]; and *Re A* [2015] EWHC 1756 (Fam), at [18]—altruistic surrogacy arrangement; only expenses paid.
[86] [2008] EWHC 3030 (Fam).
[87] Ibid, at [24].
[88] [2009] EWHC 2977 (Fam).
[89] Ibid, at [7].
[90] Ibid.

a surrogate".[91] Following these decisions, the legislative framework applicable to parental orders changed under the HFEA 2008, which came into force on 6 April 2010. In particular, under the Human Fertilisation and Embryology (Parental Order) Regulations 2010, which accompany HFEA 2008, the child's welfare throughout the child's lifetime must now be the court's paramount consideration.[92] The impact of this change was highlighted by Hedley J in *Re L (A Minor)*.[93] Namely, his Lordship pointed out that welfare was no longer merely the court's first consideration but became its paramount consideration.[94] Consequently, the balance between public policy considerations and welfare must be weighed "decisively in favour of welfare".[95] It follows that "it will only be in the clearest case of the abuse of public policy that the court will be able to withhold an order if otherwise welfare considerations supports its making".[96] Nevertheless, applications for authorization under section 54(8) should continue be scrutinised carefully on a case by case basis.[97] The approach developed by Hedley J has been expressly endorsed by Sir Nicholas Wall P in *Re X (Children)*,[98] and followed in subsequent cases.[99] The above principles now seem to be firmly established and have been succinctly summarized by Theis J in *Re WT (A Child)*.[100] Payments made to surrogacy agencies or other intermediaries also fall within section 54(8) and, as such, need to be retrospectively authorized by the court,[101] although payments to the egg donor are excluded.[102]

In applying the above principles to concrete cases, the High Court has adopted a very lenient approach towards the enforcement of the public policy against commercial surrogacy.[103] In particular, an extremely liberal interpretation has been adopted in assessing the element of proportionality of the payments received by the surrogate, thus giving effect to arrangements that had been entered into on a purely commercial basis. For example, it has been held that providing a Ukrainian surrogate with a sum of money sufficient for her to put down a deposit on a flat (in addition to covering her expenses and loss of earnings) was "not so disproportionate to 'expenses reasonably incurred' that the granting of an order would be an unacceptable affront to public policy".[104] Similarly, $23,000 paid to a Californian surrogate was considered "not greatly disproportionate to expenses reasonably incurred";[105] and in a case involving a payment of around 2 million rupees or £27,500 to a clinic in India that had provided two surrogates, the intending parents were described by Sir Nicholas Wall P as "entirely genuine".[106] The rationale behind this liberal approach to the authorisation of payments has been explained by Hedley J as follows:

> The difficulty is that it is almost impossible to imagine a set of circumstances in which by the time the case comes to court, the welfare of any child (particularly a foreign child) would

---

[91] Ibid.

[92] See supra, p 1184.

[93] [2010] EWHC 3146 (Fam).

[94] Ibid, at [9].

[95] Ibid, at [10].

[96] Ibid.

[97] Ibid, at [12].

[98] [2011] EWHC 3147 (Fam), at [40].

[99] Eg *D and L (Surrogacy)* [2012] EWHC 2631 (Fam); *Re W* [2013] EWHC 3570 (Fam); *Re C (Parental Order)* [2013] EWHC 2413 (Fam); *J v G (Parental Orders)* [2013] EWHC 1432 (Fam); *Re A (Parental Order: Domicile)* [2013] EWHC 426 (Fam); *Re P-M (Parental Order: Payments to Surrogacy Agency)* [2013] EWHC 2328 (Fam); and *AB and Another v GH* [2016] EWHC 2063 (Fam).

[100] [2014] EWHC 1303 (Fam), at [35].

[101] *Re P-M (Parental Order: Payments to Surrogacy Agency)* [2013] EWHC 2328 (Fam).

[102] *Re C (Parental Order)* [2013] EWHC 2408 (Fam).

[103] See Fenton-Glynn (2015) 27 CFLQ 83.

[104] *X & Y (Foreign Surrogacy)* [2008] EWHC 3030 (Fam), per Hedley J, at [22].

[105] *Re S (Parental Order)* [2009] EWHC 2977 (Fam), per Hedley J, at [8].

[106] *Re X (Children)* [2011] EWHC 3147 (Fam), at [32].

not be gravely compromised (at the very least) by a refusal to make an order . . .. If public policy is truly to be upheld, it would need to be enforced at a much earlier stage than the final hearing of a section 30 application.[107]

Despite the obvious tension between the welfare principle and the public policy against commercial surrogacy, the inclination to favour the former stems from the objective to lessen the detrimental impact of the legal limbo for children born as a result of a cross-border commercial surrogacy. The pragmatic approach that has been adopted by judges in relation to the authorisation of payments is far from ideal as it clearly undermines the domestic policy against commercial surrogacy. Nevertheless, given the *fait accompli* nature of the situation, where the welfare of a very young child is at stake, it appears unrealistic to expect judges to strictly implement the policy considerations against commercial surrogacy at this late stage.

3. HUMAN RIGHTS CONSIDERATIONS[108]

In June 2014, the European Court of Human Rights (ECtHR) delivered two long expected judgments in cross-border surrogacy cases of *Mennesson v France*[109] and *Labassee v France*.[110] The cases concerned the refusal to grant legal recognition in France to parent-child relationships that had been lawfully established in the US between children born as a result of a commercial surrogacy arrangement in circumstances where the intending father was also the genetic father of the child. The applications were lodged with the ECtHR jointly by the intending parents (the Mennessons and the Labassees respectively) and the children born as the result of the surrogacy arrangements. In both cases the respondent was the French Government. The applicants relied on Article 8 of the ECHR which guarantees the right to respect for private and family life. The Court first explored the applicability of Article 8 to the given situation and found that the provision was applicable as "there was no doubt that the Mennessons had cared for the twins as parents since the children's birth and that the four of them lived together in a way that was indistinguishable from 'family life' in the accepted sense of the term".[111] In relation to "private life" the Court found that the right of identity was "an integral part of the concept of private life and there was a direct link between the private life of children born following a surrogacy treatment and the legal determination of their parenthood".[112] The Court noted that France's refusal to recognize the legal parent-child relationship stemmed "from a wish to discourage French nationals from having recourse outside France to a reproductive technique that was prohibited in that country with the aim, as the authorities saw it, of protecting the children and the surrogate mother".[113] The interference pursued two legitimate aims listed in Article 8: the "protection of health" and the "protection

---

[107] *X & Y (Foreign Surrogacy)* [2008] EWHC 3030 (Fam), at [24].

[108] See eg Beaumont and Trimmings, 'Recent Jurisprudence of the European Court of Human Rights in the Area of Cross-Border Surrogacy: Is There Still a Need for Global Regulation of Surrogacy?' in Biagioni and Ippolito (eds), Migrant Children in the XXI Century. Selected Issues of Public and Private International Law (2017); Beaumont and Trimmings, 'The European Court of Human Rights in *Paradiso and Campanelli v Italy* and the Way Forward for Regulating Cross-Border Surrogacy' in Fenton-Glynn and Scherpe (eds), Eastern and Western Perspectives on Surrogacy (forthcoming); Puppinck and de la Hougue [2014] Revue Lamy de Droit Civil 78 (in French; English version available at http://papers.ssrn.com/sol3/papers.cfm?abstract_id=2500075); and Fawcett, Ní Shúilleabháin and Shah, Human Rights and Private International Law (2016), paras 14.36–14.60. 14.95–14.110. See also Smolin (2016) 43 Pepperdine Law Review 265.

[109] *Mennesson v France* [2014] ECHR 185.

[110] *Labassee v France* [2014] ECHR 185. The two cases were conducted simultaneously. *Mennesson*, at [3].

[111] European Court of Human Rights, "Press Release" (185) 2014, 26 June 2014, p 3.

[112] Ibid.

[113] Ibid.

of the rights and freedoms of others". Consequently, the interference had been "in accord-ance with the law" within the meaning of Article 8.

It was noted by the Court that approaches to surrogacy within Europe differed widely and that surrogacy raised "delicate ethical questions".[114] Furthermore, the Court indicated that the prohibition of surrogacy was acceptable in principle; however, this liberty was "mitigated" by the practical need to "take into account the fact that an essential aspect of the identity of individuals is at stake when it comes to kinship".[115] Consequently, the margin of apprecia-tion was narrow when it came to parenthood, which involved a key aspect of an individual's identity.

The Court examined the issues separately from the perspective of the applicant parents and from the perspective of the children. No violation of Article 8 was found in relation to the applicant parents' right to respect for their family life. This was because France enabled the family to settle in the country with the children and to live with them together in circum-stances which were similar to other families. There was no risk of the applicant parents and the children being separated by the authorities. The Court, however, found a violation of Article 8 concerning the children's right to respect for their private life due to the refusal by France to recognise the children's legal relationship with their genetic fathers. In particular, it was held that given the significance of genetic parenthood as an element of a person's identity, it was contrary to the best interests of the children to deprive them of the legal relationship with their genetic fathers. It is not clear if the Court would extend the same rights to the child of an intending mother who is the genetic mother of the child given the existence of a different birth mother.

In January 2015, another important judgment concerning cross-border surrogacy was handed down by the ECtHR, in the case of *Paradiso and Campanelli v Italy*.[116] Unlike the *Mennesson* and *Labassee* cases, the present Article 8 complaint did not concern the registra-tion of a foreign birth certificate and recognition of the legal parent-child relationship in respect of a child born from a gestational surrogacy arrangement. Rather, the issue in the present case was the measures taken by the Italian authorities which resulted in a permanent separation of the child and the applicants, neither of whom had a genetic link with the child. The Chamber held that, despite the lack of a genetic link, there existed a *de facto* family life between the applicants and the child.[117] The decision was, however, reversed by the Grand Chamber which correctly restricted the notion of a *de facto* family life and held, by eleven votes to six, that there had been no violation of Article 8 of the Convention.[118]

The following principles can be deduced from the above decisions:

1) The existence of a genetic link between a child born through surrogacy and the intend-ing parent(s) is a prerequisite for the establishment of "family life" under Article 8 of the ECHR.

2) A child's identity is inherently connected with genetic parenthood (at least with the genetic parenthood of their genetic father). The right to establish the child's identity is in turn interrelated with the right to respect for private life under Article 8 of the ECHR;

3) It is acceptable for States to outlaw the practice of surrogacy on ethical grounds;

---

[114] *Mennesson*, at [79].
[115] Ibid, at [80].
[116] *Paradiso and Campanelli v Italy* ECLI:CE:ECHR:2015:0127JUD002535812.
[117] Ibid, at [69].
[118] *Paradiso and Campanelli v Italy* (Grand Chamber) ECLI:CE:ECHR:2017:0124 JUD002535812.

4) Even where surrogacy is banned domestically, the State is obliged to legally recognise the effects of a cross-border surrogacy agreement executed abroad if the following three conditions are met: a) The recognition concerns the legal parenthood of the genetically-related intending parent (at least where the parent is the genetic father); b) The legal parenthood was established legally in the country of birth; and c) There is no alternative way by which the legal parent-child relationship could be legally established in the receiving State;[119]

5) The above obligation arises even in commercial cross-border surrogacy cases; and

6) The best interests of the child principle prevails over public policy considerations regarding surrogacy.

Admittedly, the above guidance gives some limited direction to national authorities. It is, however, very patchy and leaves too many questions unanswered. For example: To what extent can one disassociate a surrogacy arrangement from its effects? Should the home country of the intending parrents be compelled to recognise the effects of a commercial surrogacy agreement executed abroad? Should the genetically-unrelated intending parent also have the right to have his/her legal parenthood recognised in the receiving country? Should it matter whether the child was born through altruistic or commercial surrogacy? Should it matter whether the child was born through a traditional or gestational surrogacy arrangement? Does the child have a right to his or her genetically related intending mother being recognised as his or her legal mother? What happens if the surrogate mother wishes to be regarded as the child's legal parent and would it make a difference if she had already consented (before or after the birth) to the child being handed over to the intending parents or if she had actually already participated in the handover of the child to the intending parents?

The main drawbacks of the ECtHR's approach are that, like the current UK approach,[120] it offers only an *ex post facto* solution to some of the issues surrounding cross-border surrogacy and that it is based solely on the recognition method. This method, although capable of reducing limping relationships, does not address other serious issues that arise from cross-border commercial surrogacy. Indeed, this approach is not suitable to tackle a complex phenomenon such as surrogacy. Instead, there is a need for a truly multilateral approach whereby an international Convention on surrogacy, which would depart from the traditional method of the unification of the conflicts rules, would be developed.[121] This would help to solve the problem at its source in countries which permit commercial surrogacy and are happy for foreign intending parents to take advantage of this service. Rather than focusing on traditional rules on jurisdiction and applicable law, the Convention should establish a framework for international co-operation with emphasis on the need for substantive safeguards and on procedures for courts, administrative authorities and private intermediaries. The Convention would be based on a pre-approval system and would not only seek to tackle the problem of legal parenthood but also to protect the people involved (notably intending parents, surrogate mothers, and, above all, the putative child(ren)) and to regulate the cross-border surrogacy market. The Convention should draw inspiration from the highly successful Hague Convention on Protection of Children and Co-operation in Respect of Intercountry Adoption, 1993, which is also based on the principle of cooperation between the country of origin and the receiving country and on the need to regulate international adoptions to protect the people involved, especially the children. Regulation has the benefits of reducing the

---

[119] *Mennesson*, at [67].

[120] See supra, p 1183 et seq.

[121] See eg Trimmings and Beaumont 'General Report on Surrogacy' in Trimmings and Beaumont (eds), *International Surrogacy Arrangements: Legal Regulation at the International Level* (2013) 531–49; and Margalit (2016) 24 Brooklyn Journal of Law and Policy 41.

risks of exploitation of surrogate mothers by middlemen (eg those operating fertility clinics) and sometimes by intending parents; creating mechanisms to screen out intending parents who are a potential danger to children; of ensuring that intending mothers, whether genetically linked to the child or not, are treated equally with genetically linked intending fathers as the legal parents; and ensuring that children will be able to trace their surrogate (birth) mother and understand their complex identity when they become adults.

Recent developments at the Hague Conference for Private International Law demonstrate the pressing need for a global regulation of cross-border surrogacy.[122] At the Council on General Affairs and Policy meeting in March 2015, it was decided that an Experts' Group be set up to explore the feasibility of further work in the area of international surrogacy arrangements.[123] The first meeting of the Experts' Group was held in February 2016.[124] The Group concluded that work should continue, whilst its focus should be primarily on recognition of legal parentage.[125] This, however, appears to be a rather narrow approach which does not adequately address the complex nature of a cross-border surrogacy arrangement.[126] It is to be hoped that the Expert Group comes to realise that an *ex post facto* solution based on recognition of parenthood is not a satisfactory way forward for surrogacy and instead press for a regulatory solution in order to protect the rights of the vulnerable, notably the putative child and the surrogate mother.[127]

---

[122] See Hague Conference website, section "Parentage/Surrogacy Project", http://www.hcch.net/index_en.php?act=text.display&tid=178.

[123] Hague Conference on Private International Law, "Council on General Affairs and Policy of the Conference: Conclusions and Recommendations", March 2015, at [5].

[124] See Hague Conference on Private International Law, "Report of the February 2016 Meeting of the Experts' Group on Parentage / Surrogacy", February 2016. See also Hague Conference on Private International Law, "Report of the Experts' Group on the Parentage / Surrogacy Project (Meeting of 31 January - 3 February 2017)", February 2017.

[125] Ibid, at [16].

[126] See also Hague Conference on Private International Law, "The Desirability and Feasibility of Further Work on the Surrogacy / Parentage Project", at [44]–[47] and [52]–[60]— overview of possible future approaches as considered by the Hague Conference prior to the Experts' Group meeting.

[127] The Experts' Group's mandate has been extended until 2017. Hague Conference on Private International Law, "Council on General Affairs and Policy of the Conference: Conclusions & Recommendations", March 2016, at [15]. See supra, n 124.

27

LEGITIMACY, LEGITIMATION AND ADOPTION

1. Introduction	1193	3. Legitimation	1202
2. Legitimacy	1194	(a) Legitimation by subsequent marriage	1202
(a) Legitimacy to be governed by the law		(b) Legitimation by recognition	1204
of the domicile	1194	4. Adoption	1205
(b) *Shaw v Gould*	1195	(a) Adoption proceedings in England	1206
(c) Other authorities	1197	(b) Procedures for taking children into	
(d) Effect of doctrine of putative marriage	1199	and out of the United Kingdom	1219
(e) Meaning of "domicile of origin"	1200	(c) Recognition of foreign adoptions	1222
(f) Relevance of the incidents of status	1201	(d) Effect of foreign adoptions	1229
(g) Where birth to parents who are			
married does not confer legitimacy	1202		

1. INTRODUCTION

The three matters that require consideration in this chapter are legitimacy, legitimation and adoption.[1] None of these topics falls within the scope of the Brussels II *bis* Regulation.[2] Legitimacy ordinarily means the status acquired by a person who is born to parents who are married to one another at the time of the birth. Legitimation means that a person who has not been born to married parents acquires the status of a legitimate person as the result of some act, such as the subsequent marriage of his parents, that occurs after the date of his birth. Adoption, in English law, involves the extinction of the parental links between the child and the biological parents and the creation of similar links between the child and the adoptive parents.

Whether a person is legitimate or has been legitimated or adopted has, in the past, been of considerable importance in the field of succession. If the will of a domiciled Englishman contained a gift to the "children" of a specified person it had to be asked whether this included not only legitimate children but also those who were illegitimate, legitimated or adopted. English domestic law has moved from a position in which it was rare that a will or intestacy applied to other than legitimate children to the situation where, as a consequence of a process culminating in the Family Law Reform Act 1987, there has been a very substantial assimilation of the rights of children, irrespective of the circumstances of their birth.[3] This legislation does not, however, abolish the distinction between legitimacy and illegitimacy, nor the concept of legitimation. Though they have become far less important,[4] it will still

---

[1] For a speculative discussion of private international law problems arising from issues of parentage, see Norrie (1994) 43 ICLQ 757.

[2] Recital (10) and Art 1(3)(a) and (b).

[3] 1987 Act, s 1, as amended by the Adoption and Children Act 2002, Sch 3, para 51.

[4] Eg, regarding citizenship, in respect of which see now the British Nationality Act 1981, ss 1 and 50(9), as substituted by the Nationality, Immigration and Asylum Act 2002, Pt 1, s 9(1); and SI 2015/1615, reg 3. In

be necessary to determine whether or not the parents of a child are married, or whether the child is legitimate, for the purposes, for example, of domicile, as well as in determining the rights of the father.[5]

The general effect of these developments has been to diminish, though not to eradicate,[6] the need for rules of private international law to determine a person's legitimacy or the validity of his legitimation. It might, for example, also be necessary for a child domiciled in England to have his legitimacy determined for the purposes of succession under a foreign law. On the other hand, there has if anything been an increase in the need to determine the validity in England of foreign adoptions, resulting from the increase in the number of foreign children adopted, sometimes abroad, by English parents.

We have examined already[7] the powers and jurisdiction of the English courts to make declarations relating to legitimacy, legitimation and adoption. We have now to consider the choice of law rules relating to legitimacy, legitimation and adoption. It is also necessary, with regard to adoption, to discuss the further questions of the rules for the jurisdiction of the English courts to make adoption orders and for the recognition of foreign adoptions.

2. LEGITIMACY[8]

(a) Legitimacy to be governed by the law of the domicile

Before the passing of the Legitimacy Act 1959, the rule of domestic English law was that no child acquired the status of legitimacy unless he was born in lawful wedlock, ie, born of parents whose marriage was valid at the time of his birth. This exclusive test, however, was exceptional, for most countries, including Scotland,[9] had long recognised the doctrine of the putative marriage, according to which a child even of a void marriage is also legitimate. A common, though not a universal, qualification of this doctrine is that the spouses should have bona fide believed in the validity of their marriage. A question of choice of law might therefore arise if a child were born out of lawful wedlock in the country where X and Y, his parents, were domiciled and where the doctrine of the putative marriage was recognised.

Several writers have expressed the view that in such circumstances the English test of birth in lawful wedlock becomes applicable. This is open to the insuperable objection that it fails to appreciate the true function of English law in such a case. If an English will bequeaths a legacy to the "legitimate children" of parents who were domiciled abroad at the time of their son's birth and if his legitimacy is disputed, there are two separate questions to be resolved. The first is a question of construction—what did the testator intend by his use of the phrase "legitimate children"? This is a matter for English domestic law as the law governing succession. If the answer is that he referred to legitimate children, then the second question, whether the children are in fact legitimate, is a question not of construction, but of status

---

relation to the previous position, see, eg, *R (On the Application of Montana) v Secretary of State for the Home Department* [2001] 1 FLR 449; and *Azad v Entry Clearance Officer (Dhaka)* [2001] Imm A R 318.

[5] Children Act 1989, s 2, as amended by the Adoption and Children Act 2002 and the Human Fertilisation and Embryology Act 2008.

[6] See Law Com No 132 (1984), paras 3.9–3.14; Law Com No 158 (1986), para 3.14.

[7] Supra, p 1053 et seq.

[8] Welsh (1947) 63 LQR 65; Lipstein (1954) *Festschrift für Ernst Rabel*, Vol I, p 611; and Bainham [2009] Fam Law 673.

[9] If by the law of the domicile of the innocent "spouse" he is legitimate: *Smijth v Smijth* (1918) 1 SLR 156. See Crawford (2005) 54 ICLQ 829, 851; and Crawford and Carruthers, para 14-01. See also Family Law (Scotland) Act 2006, ss 21 and 41.

determinable by the law of their domicile.[10] The subject of inquiry is not whether the marriage of the legatee's parents is valid, but whether he is legitimate in the eyes of the law of his domicile—the only law that is entitled to pass upon his status.[11] English law is, indeed, relevant so far as concerns the construction of the will, but as Romer J said in one case: "The only relevant rule of construction is that a bequest in an English will to the children of A means to his legitimate children[12] and that does not carry the matter very far, for the question remains who are his legitimate children, and that is not a question of construction at all, it is a question of law."[13]

(b) *Shaw v Gould*

(i) *The decision*

This principle, that any person legitimate according to the law of his domicile, though not born in lawful wedlock, is legitimate for the purpose of succeeding to movables under an English will or intestacy has been repeatedly affirmed in a stream of cases from at least 1835 onwards;[14] but, with few exceptions,[15] these statements were made in cases concerned with legitimation. It is sometimes said, therefore, that they are of little value having regard to the decision of the House of Lords in *Shaw v Gould*,[16] which raised a question of legitimacy. The facts of this case were as follows:

> Funds were bequeathed by a testator domiciled in England in trust for Elizabeth Hickson for life and after her death in trust for her children. English land was also devised after her death to "her first and other sons *lawfully begotten*". Elizabeth, at the age of sixteen, was induced by fraud, without the knowledge of her family, to marry a domiciled Englishman, named Buxton, at Manchester. Her friends, however, succeeded in taking her away just after the ceremony, and she never lived with her husband. Sixteen years later, Elizabeth, having become engaged to a domiciled Englishman named Shaw, devised a scheme for obtaining a divorce in Scotland from Buxton. Shaw acquired a domicile in Scotland, and Buxton was paid £250 to go to that country for forty days. The marriage was dissolved by the Court of Session. Elizabeth then married Shaw in Edinburgh and had by him two daughters and one son, all of whom were born in the lifetime of Buxton. At the time of the present action Buxton, Elizabeth and Shaw were dead. The questions before the English court were whether the daughters and son were entitled under the will of the testator to the funds as being the "children" of Elizabeth, and also whether the son was entitled to the land as being her "son lawfully begotten". Evidence was given that by Scots law the divorce and second marriage were valid; also, that children born of a putative marriage, ie one regular in point of form but void owing to the prior existing marriage of one of the parties, were regarded as legitimate, provided that the parents were justifiably ignorant of the prior existing marriage.

It was the opinion of the Scottish advocates who gave evidence that justifiable ignorance existed if the parents believed in the validity of the divorce. The House of Lords unanimously

---

[10] See, eg, *Wright's Trs v Callender* 1993 SC (HL) 13; discussed by Crawford 1994 SLT (News) 225, and Leslie 1995 SLT 264.

[11] See, eg, *Re Andros* (1883) 24 Ch D 637 at 639 where the position is stated with great clarity.

[12] Before the operation of what is now the Family Law Reform Act 1987, s 19, as amended by the Adoption and Children Act 2002, Sch 3, para 52.

[13] *Re Bischoffsheim* [1948] Ch 79 at 86.

[14] *Doe and Birtwhistle v Vardill* (1835) 2 Cl & Fin 571 at 573, 574; *Re Don's Estate* (1857) 4 Drew 194 at 197–8; *Re Goodmans' Trusts* (1881) 17 Ch D 266 at 291, 296–7; *Re Andros* (1883) 24 Ch D 637 at 639; and *Re Bischoffsheim* [1948] Ch 79 at 92.

[15] *Re Bischoffsheim*, supra; *Motala v A-G* [1990] 2 FLR 261; revsd on another point [1992] 2 AC 281; and see *Hashmi v Hashmi* [1972] Fam 36; *Re Karnenas* (1978) 3 RFL (2d) 213.

[16] (1868) LR 3 HL 55.

held that the children were not entitled to take under the will.[17] Their Lordships appear to have been impressed by the supposedly logical reason that since Buxton, and therefore Elizabeth, remained domiciled in England, the Scottish divorce was not recognised in England; therefore the union between Elizabeth and Shaw was not a valid marriage according to English law; and that therefore the children were not born to lawfully married parents (being the test of legitimacy according to English domestic law). Lord Colonsay, though impressed with the logic of the reasoning, was perplexed with doubts as to whether the status of legitimacy ought to be denied to the children. He felt that this denial was difficult to reconcile with general principles of jurisprudence or with the generally recognised rules of international law.[18]

(ii) Criticisms

It is difficult to resist the conclusion that the House of Lords lost its direction through its persistent concentration on one general principle to the exclusion of others. It certainly was a general principle that a divorce not recognised as valid by the law of the husband's domicile is invalid in England. But another principle, affirmed many times by the judiciary, is that legitimacy is determined by the law of the father's domicile at the time of the child's birth. Both these principles demanded attention in *Shaw v Gould*. There is nothing inconsistent in them, and they are not mutually antagonistic. It was easy to argue in this manner:

> The father cannot be granted the status of a husband, since the woman whom he purported to marry is, owing to the continuance of her earlier marriage, the wife of another man. Therefore the children of the father by this woman cannot be regarded as legitimate.

Nevertheless, the conclusion is a non sequitur. The issue was the status of the children, not of their parents. The fact that Mrs Buxton could not claim to be Mrs Shaw was not necessarily a bar to the legitimate status of the children. The legitimacy of a child happened at the time of the case to depend according to English domestic law on the validity of the marriage of which he was born; but this is not and was not the case in all legal systems. If the two questions are separable by the law of the child's domicile of origin, they should be kept separate by an English court when dealing with a private international law case. The courts of other countries have found no difficulty in this. Thus in South Africa it was held that the children of a polygamous union, born when the father was domiciled in India, were to be regarded as legitimate in Natal, which was his domicile at death. For the purpose of fixing the rate of succession duty payable on the father's death, the status of the mother as a "wife" was tested by the internal law of Natal; but the status of the children was referred to their domicile of origin.[19] Innes CJ stated that:

> It is essential to bear in mind the distinction between the points to be decided in each instance. With regard to the wife, the issue is the validity of the marriage to which she was a party; with regard to the children, the issue is their right to the status of legitimacy. The wife's position cannot be considered apart from the marriage, but the position of the children may be.[20]

It is submitted that in any event *Shaw v Gould* ought to be regarded as an abnormal decision and one to be interpreted in the light of the exceptional circumstances involved. "My opinion

---

[17] Though see now the Family Law Reform Act 1987, s 19, as amended by the Adoption and Children Act 2002, Sch 3, para 52.

[18] (1868) LR 3 HL 55 at 96–7.

[19] *Seedat's Executors v The Master* 1917 AD 302.

[20] Ibid, at 311–12. In the New York case of *Re Hall* (1901) 61 App D 266, a woman obtained a divorce in Dakota that was not regarded as valid in New York. She then married a man domiciled in Dakota and a child was born of the marriage. It was held that the child was legitimate for the purposes of taking under the will of a testator who died domiciled in New York.

in this case", said Lord Chelmsford, "is founded entirely upon the peculiar circumstances attending it."[21] It was, indeed, distinguished by a number of special features among which may be mentioned the following:

> The Scots divorce was granted in 1846, eleven years before judicial divorce was possible in England and at a time when the prevalent view, in accordance with the unanimous opinion of the judges in *Lolley's* case,[22] was that no foreign proceedings in the nature of a divorce could affect a marriage that had been contracted in England. In fact, in the court of first instance, Kindersley V-C said: "By the English law of marriage, an English marriage is absolutely indissoluble by the sentence of any court (of course I am speaking of the law as it stood at the time of the transactions in question which was long before the Act establishing the Divorce Court). . . . Any decree or judgment or sentence of any foreign court, purporting to dissolve such marriage, is treated as a mere nullity."[23] It must be observed, however, that this view did not appeal to the House of Lords. The conduct of the Shaws was calculated to arouse the suspicion of any court. In the greatest secrecy and with every precaution against discovery, they contrived a scheme to obtain a divorce in a court which, to their knowledge, had no jurisdiction in the eyes of English law.[24]

The children were legitimate by Scots law if either of the Shaws was justifiably ignorant that there was an impediment to their marriage, ie in their case, a prior invalid divorce. After a careful examination of the facts, Kindersley V-C found himself unable to agree that even Mrs Shaw was justifiably ignorant of the true position.

(c) Other authorities

It is significant that, in the much later case of *Re Stirling*,[25] Swinfen Eady J was far from repudiating the suggestion that a child might be legitimate although the previous divorce of one of his parents was invalid. It was not necessary, however, to decide the point, for it was held that the doctrine of putative marriage, on which the argument for the child turned, did not obtain in Scotland unless at least one of the parties was ignorant of the impediment that invalidated the second marriage. The party had to be mistaken as to some fact;[26] but here the ignorance alleged was that the mother of the child was unaware that her divorce from her first husband was invalid, and this was an error of law, not of fact.

Another authority that is sometimes said to support *Shaw v Gould* is *Re Paine*.[27] The question there was whether the children of W were legitimate for the purpose of the effect of a disposition to W contained in an English will:

> In 1875 W, when domiciled in England, was married in Germany to the widower of her deceased sister. At that date a marriage between such persons was prohibited. The husband was held to have been domiciled in Germany at the time of the ceremony. The parties cohabited in England until the husband's death in 1919.

Bennett J adopted the dual domicile doctrine of capacity and held the three children of the union to be illegitimate, since they had sprung from a void marriage. But, as in *Shaw v Gould*, the possibility that the children might be legitimate according to the German law of their domicile of origin, despite the absence of lawful wedlock between their parents, was not canvassed.

---

[21] *Shaw v Gould* (1868) LR 3 HL 55 at 79.
[22] (1812) Russ & Ry 237. The view was finally repudiated in *Harvey v Farnie* (1882) 8 App Cas 43.
[23] *Re Wilson's Trusts* (1865) LR 1 Eq 247 at 257–8.
[24] For the details see ibid, at 260–2.
[25] [1908] 2 Ch 344.
[26] Crawford (2005) 54 ICLQ 829 at 851. See *Smijth v Smijth* (1918) 1 SLT 156.
[27] [1940] Ch 46; supra, p 915.

However, despite all attempts to rationalise *Shaw v Gould* the fact remains that, until the decision of Romer J in *Re Bischoffsheim*,[28] it seemed to provide an embarrassing obstacle to the prevalent judicial view that the legitimacy of a child is a matter for the law of his domicile of origin. This view, however, was translated into action in *Bischoffsheim's* case where the facts were these:

> In 1919 W was married in New York to H, the brother of her deceased husband. It may be taken that at that time both parties were domiciled in England. The marriage was void by English law, but valid by the law of New York. After they had acquired a domicile in New York a son was born to them. The question was whether the son was the legitimate child of his mother so as to entitle him to benefit under the will of a testator who had died domiciled in England.

Romer J found in favour of the son on the following principle:

> Where succession to personal property depends upon the legitimacy of the claimant, the status of legitimacy conferred on him by his domicile of origin (ie the domicile of his parents at birth) will be recognised by our courts; and that, if that legitimacy be established, the validity of his parents' marriage should not be entertained as a relevant subject for investigation.[29]

He distinguished *Shaw v Gould* by showing that, since in that case the House of Lords chose to concentrate their attention on the validity of the divorce, they were bound to find it invalid and consequently to fix the children's domicile of origin in England. This left no room for a claim based on the ground that their legitimacy stood apart from the validity of the divorce and that, if so, their domicile of origin was in Scotland.[30]

It has been argued that this decision should be dismissed as being inconsistent with higher authority, an opinion that has been expressed on several occasions.[31] To do so would have the startling result that in the same context legitimacy is subject to one rule, legitimation to another. Where a question has arisen of succession under an English testacy or intestacy, it has long been settled that, if a claimant has been legitimated by the law of the country where at the time of his birth (and of the subsequent marriage) his father was domiciled, English law "recognises and acts on the status thus declared by the law of the domicil".[32] There is no substantial difference between legitimacy and legitimation[33] and no reason of logic or convenience why the law should relegate them to mutually exclusive categories. If from the date of the act of legitimation the child assumes the status that he would have possessed had he been born legitimate, it is incomprehensible that these two causes of the same result should be subject to divergent rules for the choice of law.

Fortunately, Sir Stephen Brown P in *Motala v A-G*[34] clearly rejected any such divergence of approach:

> H and W, domiciled at all material times in India, went to live in Northern Rhodesia (now Zambia) where in 1950 they went through a ceremony of marriage according to Sunni

---

[28] [1948] Ch 79. Followed in *Green v Montagu* [2011] EWHC 1856 (Ch).

[29] [1948] Ch 79 at 92. Approved by the Privy Council in *Bamgbose v Daniel* [1955] AC 107 at 120; and see *Re Jones* (1961) 25 DLR (2d) 595, and *Re Karnenas* (1978) 3 RFL (2d) 213.

[30] [1948] Ch 79 at 92.

[31] Morris (1948) 12 Conveyancer (NS) 223; F A Mann (1948) 64 LQR 199; Falconbridge, *Conflict of Laws* (2nd edn), p 747 et seq. On the other hand, it is approved by Wolff, p 388.

[32] *Re Goodman's Trusts* (1881) 17 Ch D 266 at 299; and see *Boyes v Bedale* (1863) 1 Hem & M 798; *Re Andros* (1883) 24 Ch D 637; *Re Grey's Trusts* [1892] 3 Ch 88.

[33] *Re Bischoffsheim* [1948] Ch 79 at 92.

[34] [1990] 2 FLR 261; revsd on another point by the House of Lords [1992] 1 AC 281; and see *R v Secretary of State for the Home Department, ex p Brassey* [1989] 2 FLR 486 at 494; *A-G for Victoria v Commonwealth of Australia* (1961–1962) 107 CLR 529 at 596; *Re Sit Woo-tung* [1990] 2 HKLR 410.

Moslem law. The marriage was invalid under the law of Northern Rhodesia and, in 1968, the parties went through another ceremony of marriage there, valid by that law. The first marriage, however, was regarded as valid by Indian law. The question arose of the legitimacy of some of the spouses' children in the context of their claims to British citizenship.

An immediate question to be considered was whether the children had been legitimated by their parents' subsequent marriage. This was referred to Indian law, being that of the domicile of the parents of the children at all material times, and Indian law did not recognise legitimation by subsequent marriage. That left the question of legitimacy which was answered by means of the same process. Legitimacy, being regarded as an issue of status, was referred to the law of the children's domicile of origin, India, which law regarded the children as legitimate because Indian law regarded the parents' first marriage as valid. *Shaw v Gould* was distinguished as being concerned with the validity of the Scottish decree, and the decision in *Re Bischoffsheim* was approved.

What is striking about this decision is that the children were regarded in England as legitimate, notwithstanding the fact that their parents' marriage was, in the eyes of English private international law, invalid. Had the parents petitioned for a declaration as to the validity of their first marriage, it would have been refused on the ground that the marriage was invalid as to form according to the law of the place of celebration.[35] This strengthens the view that a child's legitimacy depends on the law of his domicile of origin.

(d) Effect of doctrine of putative marriage

It is submitted, then, even if there had been no statutory alteration of English domestic law in 1959 the courts would have endorsed the approach to the subject made in *Bischoffsheim's* case and would have restricted the decision in *Shaw v Gould* to the exceptional circumstances of the case. This submission was considerably fortified once the doctrine of putative marriage was accepted in the Legitimacy Act 1959.[36] Birth in lawful wedlock no longer represents the sole test of legitimacy according to English domestic law.

Section 1(1) of the Legitimacy Act 1976 provides as follows:[37]

> The child of a void marriage, whenever born,[38] shall . . . be treated as the legitimate child of his parents if at the time of the insemination resulting in the birth or, where there was no such insemination, the child's conception (or at the time of the celebration of the marriage if later) both or either of the parties reasonably believed that the marriage was valid.[39],[40]

This provision does not apply unless the father of the child was domiciled in England at the time of the birth or, if he died before the birth, was so domiciled immediately before his death.[41] Where this condition is not satisfied, the legitimacy of a child born of a void

---

[35] See *Berthiaume v Dastous* [1930] AC 79, supra, p 893, n 14.

[36] See now Legitimacy Act 1976, infra.

[37] First introduced by the Legitimacy Act 1959, s 2. Special provision is introduced in the Family Law Reform Act 1987, s 27 to deal with the status of a child born to a married couple by artificial insemination, with the semen of a man other than the husband. However, no choice of law rule is laid down, though the provisions are limited to the case of a child born in England. See *J v C (Void Marriage: Status of Children)* [2006] EWCA Civ 551, [2007] Fam 1.

[38] Provided the child was born after the marriage was entered into: *Re Spence* [1989] 2 All ER 679.

[39] According to English law: *Azad v Entry Clearance Officer (Dhaka)* [2001] Imm A R 318, per Jacob J, at p [15]; and *A v H* [2009] EWHC 636 (Fam).

[40] S 1(1) of the Legitimacy Act 1976, amended by the Family Law Reform Act 1987, s 28(1). A presumption of reasonable belief is introduced by s 28(2) of the 1987 Act.

[41] S 1(2) of the 1976 Act, as amended by SI 560/2014, Sch 1, s 15. See *Re Barony of Moynihan* [2000] 1 FLR 113. S 1(2) has been extended to include children conceived by assisted reproduction and born to a same sex female couple who have either entered into a civil partnership or are married. See s 48(6) of the Human Fertilisation and Embryology Act 2008 Act.

marriage must be determined by the law of his domicile of origin. Where the father is domiciled in a foreign country where a similar doctrine is recognised, there would be even less justification than before for denying the legitimate status of a child born of a void marriage.[42]

In a provision that is susceptible of more than one interpretation,[43] a void marriage for the purposes of the Act is defined as "a marriage, not being voidable only, in respect of which the High Court has or had jurisdiction to grant a decree of nullity, or would have or would have had such jurisdiction if the parties were domiciled in England and Wales".[44] Although the meaning of this provision is far from clear, its probable object is to exclude any union which in the eyes of English law has no claim to be a marriage at all, as for example one springing from concubinage.[45]

(e) Meaning of "domicile of origin"

Romer J's statement[46] that the domicile of origin means the country in which the parents are domiciled at the birth of the child is not supported by indisputable authority. Some of the judges have preferred to refer to the domicile of the father,[47] though others, probably having in mind the usual case where the father and mother possess a common domicile, with Romer J, have preferred to speak of "the domicile of the parents", a view which, if adopted, would require the law of each domicile to be satisfied. It is, of course, true that to attribute to the child the domicile of his father where his parents have different domiciles is to beg the question of his legitimacy, for, since the domicile of a child is said to be that of his father if legitimate but of his mother if illegitimate,[48] it would appear to be impossible to fix his domicile until the question of his legitimacy has been settled.

This vicious circle would disappear if it could be said that the legitimacy of a child was to be referred to the domicile of one of his parents, but that his domicile of origin depended on the validity of his parents' marriage. Some nineteenth-century cases[49] on the domicile of origin of a child are compatible with such a view. The present difficulty stems from Lord Westbury's statement that "the law attributes to every individual as soon as he is born the domicil of his father, if the child be legitimate, and the domicil of his mother if illegitimate".[50] As in *Shaw v Gould*, the questions of the legitimacy of a child and of the validity of his parents' marriage seemed to nineteenth-century judges inextricably to be the same. The later acceptance that a child might be legitimate notwithstanding the invalidity of his parents' marriage[51] must inevitably cast doubt on the acceptability of Lord Westbury's views.[52]

---

[42] Jones (1959) 8 ICLQ 722, 725.

[43] For various views on its almost identical predecessor, s 2(5) of the Legitimacy Act 1959, see Jones (1959) 8 ICLQ 725, 726; Tucker (1960) 9 ICLQ 321, 322; and Kahn-Freund (1960) 23 MLR 58, 59.

[44] S 10(1).

[45] It is clear, at least, that the validity of a marriage for the purposes of s 1 of the 1976 Act is to be measured by reference only to English law, and not, eg, the law of the place of celebration: *Azad v Entry Clearance Officer (Dhaka)* [2001] Imm A R 318, per Jacob J, at p [13]–[15].

[46] *Re Bischoffscheim* [1948] Ch 79 at 92.

[47] Eg *Yuen Tse v Minister of Employment and Immigration* (1983) 32 RFL (2d) 274.

[48] Supra, p 165. See Crawford (2005) 54 ICLQ 829, at 852.

[49] Eg, in *Forbes v Forbes* (1854) Kay 341 at 343 it is said that "every person born in wedlock acquires by birth the domicil of its father".

[50] *Udny v Udny* (1869) LR 1 Sc & Div 441 at 457.

[51] Eg putative marriage under the Legitimacy Act 1976, s 1.

[52] The vicious circle also disappears under the view in the Restatement 2d, § 287 that a child's legitimacy may be determined as to one parent only by reference, normally, to the domicile of that parent, so that a child may be legitimate with respect to one parent, but illegitimate with respect to the other.

If one must accept that Lord Westbury's statement has stood the test of time too well and cannot now be confounded, the vicious circle must be broken; for logic must not be allowed to impede the best solution of the problem. It is not easy to determine whether the domicile of the father or of the mother should predominate.[53] In an age of equality of treatment between the sexes, there is no particular reason or justification for preferring the application of the personal law of one parent over that of the other,[54] and so a cumulative test seems appropriate, ie a child not born of a marriage valid by English conflict rules is legitimate only if he is legitimate by the law of the domicile of *each* parent at the date of his birth. Of course, the disadvantage of a cumulative test is that it requires that two legal systems be satisfied, arguably making it more difficult for a child to attain the status of legitimacy, but this is a problem caused by current rules for the ascription of a domicile of origin. The decisive date for fixing the domicile of origin is the birth of the child. A child, no doubt, is for various purposes deemed at birth to have been in existence from the time of conception,[55] and if the parents change their domicile between the time of conception and of birth it is arguable that the law of the father's domicile at the former time deserves consideration.[56] However, despite the lack of authority in point, it is probable that the English courts would regard the domicile at the time of birth as decisive. A somewhat analogous question arises in the case of a posthumous child whose mother has changed her domicile since the death of the father. Is the law of the father's domicile at the time of his death or the law of the mother's domicile at the time of the child's birth to determine the question of legitimacy? The latter is probably the correct solution because the domicile of origin of a posthumous child is that of his mother.[57]

(f) Relevance of the incidents of status

The question whether a child is legitimate or not by the law of the domicile is to be determined by examining the incidents of his status under that law rather than the title used to describe it. Take, for example, the situation where the law of the domicile is that of a country such as New Zealand,[58] where there is no distinction drawn between legitimate and illegitimate children. In such a case, the child would have all the incidents of the status of a legitimate child in England, though only described in New Zealand as a "child",[59] and should therefore be regarded in England as legitimate, even though not born to parents who are married. Indeed, the Supreme Court of Canada[60] has concluded that a child born in Mexico to parents who are not married, who was described by Mexican law as illegitimate, was to be considered

---

[53] Some cases, arbitrarily, favour application of the law of the mother's domicile (eg *Smijth v Smijth* (1918) 1 SLT 156), whereas others favour application of the law of the father's domicile (eg *Re Grove* (1888) 40 Ch D 216; *Re Don's Estate* (1857) 4 Drew 194 at 198; *Re Andros* (1883) 24 Ch D 637 at 642; *R and McDonell v Leong Ba Chai* [1954] 1 DLR 401 at 403; *Perpetual Executors and Trustees Association of Australia Ltd v Roberts* [1970] VR 732 at 756, 575; and *Hashmi v Hashmi* [1972] Fam 36).

[54] Cf the position in Scots law where, by s 22 of the Family Law (Scotland) Act 2006, the domicile of a person under sixteen years of age no longer is tied to the issue of the marital status of his parents. Where the child's parents are not domiciled in the same country as each other, the child shall be domiciled in the country with which he has for the time being the closest connection (s 22(3)). See also s 21 of the 2006 Act (abolition of status of illegitimacy). For criticism of the s 22 rule, see Crawford and Carruthers, paras 6-05 and 14-02.

[55] *Re Salaman* [1908] 1 Ch 4; *Re Callaghan* [1948] NZLR 846. But see *Elliot v Lord Joicey* [1935] AC 209.

[56] Taintor (1940) 18 Can Bar Rev 589, 596, 597.

[57] There seems to be no English authority on the domicile of a posthumous child, but academic opinion favours the view that it is the same as the mother's: Westlake (7th edn), s 250; Dicey, Morris and Collins, para 6-028.

[58] Status of Children Act 1969 (New Zealand). Cf, in Scots law, Family Law (Scotland) Act 2006, ss 21 and 41.

[59] Ibid, s 3.

[60] *Re MacDonald* (1962) 34 DLR (2d) 14; affd 44 DLR (2d) 208; and see *Khoo Hooi Leong v Khoo Hean Kwee* [1926] AC 529 at 543; *Re Sit Woo-tung* [1990] 2 HKLR 410.

to have the status of a legitimate child in Canada. Under Mexican law she had all the capacities and obligations of such a child, though certain social limitations attached to her position in Mexico causing her to be described there as "illegitimate".

(g) Where birth to parents who are married does not confer legitimacy

The rule suggested above[61] allocates a question of legitimacy to the law of the domicile of origin. Principle requires that this personal law should apply exclusively, since it is the only law competent to determine the status of the child. Nevertheless, if a case were to arise in which a child, though born to married parents, was for some reason not regarded as born legitimate, as for example because he was not conceived during the marriage, it is probably a safe assumption that an English court would be satisfied with the practically universal test of birth to parents married to one another.[62] This break with principle might be justified by the paramount importance of communicating to the child the beneficial status of legitimacy if some rational ground for doing so exists.

3. LEGITIMATION[63]

In the various legal systems of the world two main methods are found by which a person, not born with the status of legitimacy, may be later legitimated. These are: subsequent marriage of the parents and recognition of the child by the father. Each of these methods requires separate consideration. Here again, however, it should be emphasised that our concern is to examine the law which should determine the status. It is, for example, for the law governing succession to decide whether a child who has been legitimated may or may not succeed by will or under an intestacy.

(a) Legitimation by subsequent marriage

(i) Introduction

It has been accepted that children born before marriage were made legitimate by the subsequent marriage of their parents. This rule became part of canon law around the twelfth century, and was later adopted by practically all the legal systems on the Continent and in South America. It has received statutory recognition in most of the common law world. Until the Legitimacy Act 1926, however, it formed no part of the law of England and Wales or of Ireland, though it obtained in Scotland, the Isle of Man and the Channel Islands.

(ii) Common law rule

The role of private international law is to choose the system of law which shall determine whether legitimation by this method is effective or not. The rule finally established at common law by *Re Grove*,[64] after some hesitation,[65] is that a foreign legitimation by subsequent marriage is not recognised in England unless the father is domiciled, *both at the time of the*

---

[61] Supra, p 165.

[62] See, for Scotland, the rule in s 41 of the Family Law (Scotland) Act 2006, which states that: "Any question arising as to the effect on a person's status of—(a) the person's parents being, or having been, married to each other; or (b) the person's parents not being, or not having been, married to each other, shall be determined by the law of the country in which the person is domiciled at the time at which the question arises."

[63] On the subject generally see Taintor (1940) 18 Can Bar Rev 589 and 691; F A Mann (1941) 57 LQR 112; Lipstein (1954) *Festschrift für Ernst Rabel*, Vol I, p 611. For problems connected with legitimation under a foreign statute, see Dicey, Morris and Collins, paras 20R041–20-091.

[64] (1888) 40 Ch D 216.

[65] See, eg, *Boyes v Bedale* (1863) 1 Hem & M 798, disapproved in *Re Goodman's Trusts*, infra.

child's birth and also at the time of the subsequent marriage, in a country whose law allows this method of legitimation.[66]

A simple illustration of the working of the rule is afforded by the case of *Re Goodman's Trusts*,[67] where a domiciled Englishwoman had died intestate in respect of a large sum of money, and it was necessary to decide which of her brother's children were entitled to share therein, as being her "next of kin" under the Statutes of Distribution. The relevant events in her brother's life were chronologically as follows.

(a) While domiciled in England he had three children by Charlotte Smith, to whom he was not married.

(b) He acquired a Dutch domicile, and had a fourth child, Hannah, by Charlotte Smith.

(c) He married Charlotte Smith in Amsterdam.

(d) While still domiciled in the Netherlands he had a fifth child, Anne, by Charlotte Smith.

Legitimation by subsequent marriage was part of Dutch law. It was, therefore, held on the above facts that Hannah and Anne alone were legitimate for the purposes of the English intestacy. It was only in their cases that, at the two critical moments, birth and marriage, the law of the father's domicile recognised this particular form of legitimation.

(iii) Under the Legitimacy Act 1976

The operation of the common law rules, though not abrogated, was immensely curtailed by the Legitimacy Act 1926[68] which made legitimation by subsequent marriage part of the law of England. The present law is to be found in section 2 of the Legitimacy Act 1976[69] which provides that, where the mother and father of an illegitimate person marry, the marriage shall, if the father is *at the date of the marriage* domiciled in England and Wales, render that person, if living, legitimate from the date of the marriage.[70]

With regard to persons who are not domiciled in England and Wales, section 3(1) of the Legitimacy Act 1976[71] provides as follows:

> Where the mother and father of an illegitimate person marry one another and the father of the illegitimate person is not at the time of the marriage domiciled in England and Wales but is domiciled in a country by the law of which the illegitimate person became legitimated by virtue of such subsequent marriage, that person, if living, shall in England and Wales be recognised as having been so legitimated from the date of the marriage[72] notwithstanding that, at the time of his birth, his father was domiciled in a country the law of which did not permit legitimation by subsequent marriage.[73]

---

[66] *Re Goodman's Trusts* (1881) 17 Ch D 266; *Re Andros* (1883) 24 Ch D 637; *Re Grove* (1888) 40 Ch D 216; and see *Motala v A-G* [1990] 2 FLR 261 at 267.

[67] (1881) 17 Ch D 266.

[68] S 1; the status of a person legitimated thereunder is preserved by the Legitimacy Act 1976, Sch 1, para 1.

[69] As amended by SI 2014/560, Sch.1 para.15(3).

[70] This provision has been extended to cover children conceived by assisted reproduction and born to a same sex female couple who enter into subsequent civil partnership or marriage. S 2A of the Legitimacy Act 1976 (added by the Human Fertilisation and Embryology Act 2008, Sch.6(1) para.16, and amended by SI 2014/560, Sch.1 para.15(4)).

[71] As amended by SI 2014/560, Sch 1 para 15(5)(a).

[72] This applies even though the father or mother was married to a third person at the time of the child's birth; cf Legitimacy Act 1926, s 1(2) since repealed, but its effect is preserved by Legitimacy Act 1976, s 11 and Sch 1, para 1(1).

[73] This provision has been extended to cover children conceived by assisted reproduction and born to a same sex female couple who enter into subsequent civil partnership or marriage. S 3(2) of the Legitimacy Act 1976 (added by the Human Fertilisation and Embryology Act 2008, Sch 6(1) para 17, and amended by SI 2014/560, Sch 1 para 15(5)).

This section discards the old rule that the law of the father's domicile at the time of the child's birth must be taken into account. The law of the father's domicile at the time of the marriage is the sole decisive factor.[74] It is this law that decides, for instance, whether something more than mere marriage, such as a formal acknowledgment, is necessary to effect legitimation.

(b) Legitimation by recognition

It has been assumed so far that the foreign legitimation is by subsequent marriage. However, in several states in Europe and in North and South America a father is allowed to legitimate his child by formally recognising it as his own. The first question that this raises in private international law is—which legal system will the English courts look to in order to determine the validity of this particular form of legitimation? Is it sufficient that it is valid by the law of the father's domicile at the time of recognition, or, like legitimation by subsequent marriage before the Legitimacy Act 1926, must it also be valid by the law of the father's domicile at the time of the child's birth? The matter has been considered in only one case—*Re Luck's Settlement Trusts*[75]—where the facts were as follows:

> Under the will of George Luck, a British subject domiciled in England, funds were held in trust for all his children attaining twenty-one. Each child was to receive the income of his share for life, and after his death the capital was to be divided equally among his children at twenty-one. The marriage settlement of George limited further sums in the same manner, except that only those grandchildren born within twenty-one years of the death of the survivor of George and his wife were to take a share of the capital. The survivor died in 1896. Therefore, no grandchild was entitled under the settlement trusts unless he was alive and legitimate in 1917 at the latest. Charles was a son of George Luck. He married in 1893, but in 1906, while still married, he became the father of an illegitimate son, David, in California. At this time both he and David's mother were domiciled in England. After the dissolution of his first marriage he married a second wife. In 1925 he signed a formal document with the assent of his second wife by which he acknowledged David to be his legitimate son and adopted him as such.[76] At this time Charles was domiciled in California. It was assumed by the Court of Appeal that David's mother was also domiciled there. By the law of California the acknowledgement in 1925 operated to legitimate David from his birth in 1906.

The question that arose on these facts was whether David was entitled to a share under the will and marriage settlement of his grandfather, George. At that time, to take under the latter he was required to be a legitimate grandchild alive as such in 1917.

The Court of Appeal held that David was entitled neither under the will nor under the settlement. The reasoning was that legitimation by subsequent marriage is disregarded at common law unless allowed by the law of the father's domicile at the time both of the birth and the marriage; that the relevant judgments regard this rule, not as confined to the single case of a subsequent marriage but as applicable to all forms of legitimation; and that in any case both convenience and principle demand the application of a uniform rule to all forms. Therefore David was disqualified, since at the time of his birth his father was subject to English law, by which legitimation by recognition is not allowed.

---

[74] See *Heron v National Trustees Executors and Agency Co of Australasia Ltd* [1976] VR 733.

[75] [1940] Ch 864; and see *R and McDonnell v Leong Ba Chai* [1954] 1 DLR 401.

[76] It is important to notice, as F A Mann has shown ((1941) 57 LQR 112, 119), that the Californian method was not adoption, but legitimation by recognition. The unwary might assume from the judgments in the Court of Appeal that it was equivalent to adoption in the English sense. See Adoption and Children Act 2002, s 55, by which an adoption order may be revoked, upon application, in circumstances where a child is legitimated by the marriage of his natural parents to each other, and s 67.

The common law rule based on capacity at birth was never in fact extended to cases other than legitimation by subsequent marriage. Even in this connection, it was curtailed substantially by the Legitimacy Act 1926.[77] Gratuitously to prolong its life and extend its operation is a retrograde step. In fact the decision has been most generally criticised on the ground that, though it is obviously convenient that one principle should govern all types of legitimation, it is a little eccentric to choose one whose operation has been greatly curtailed by statute.[78]

It is therefore to be hoped that, if the occasion arises, the House of Lords will prefer the dissenting judgment of Scott LJ, who argued in a convincing manner and at no little length that status, the outstanding characteristic of which is its "quality and universality", once determined by the law of the domicile, must be judicially recognised all the world over. At a time when David and his father and mother were domiciled in California, his father made a certain declaration according to Californian law. The effect of this by that law was to clothe David with the status of a legitimate person. Therefore, "that status, established by the law of that foreign country, was under English law one which it was the duty of the English court to recognise, and *prima facie* to enforce in accordance with its nature and attributes as determined by the law of that country".[79] It is the law of the domicile at the time when the legitimation is effected that should alone be considered.

It might also be added that the Legitimacy Act 1976 in referring to the recognition of legitimation at common law talks of a "legitimation (whether or not by virtue of the subsequent marriage of his parents)".[80]

4. ADOPTION

Intercountry adoption is the responsibility of the United Kingdom Government Department for Education. It is recognised that there are many children in the United Kingdom and abroad who are in need of a permanent home and an adoptive family, and for whom intercountry adoption offers the best prospects of stable domestic life.[81] Whilst the United Kingdom government does not actively promote intercountry adoption, it is willing to allow it where a child cannot be cared for in a suitable manner in his country of origin;[82] the adoption would be in his best interests, with respect to the child's fundamental rights as recognised by international law; and the prospective adopter has been assessed by a registered adoption agency as eligible[83] and suitable to adopt a child from abroad.[84]

---

[77] S 8(1).

[78] Beckett (1944) 21 BYBIL 209; Taintor (1940) 18 Can Bar Rev 589, 652; F A Mann (1941) 57 LQR 112, 120.

[79] [1940] Ch 864 at 888.

[80] 1976 Act, s 10(1).

[81] For general information see UK Government, Department for Education website: https://www.gov.uk/child-adoption/adopting-a-child-from-overseas, and Department for Education, "A Guide to Intercountry Adoption for UK Residents", February 2011.

[82] "Intercountry adoption should never be considered as the first or only option for a child": Explanatory Memorandum to the Adoptions with a Foreign Element Regulations 2005 (SI 2005/392), p 14. See also Full Regulatory Impact Assessment for the Adoptions with a Foreign Element Regulations 2005 (SI 2005/392), p 2.

[83] There is no "right" to adopt a child.

[84] See House of Commons Library Research Paper 06/07, 7 February 2006, "Children and Adoption Bill"; and Full Regulatory Impact Assessment for the Adoptions with a Foreign Element Regulations 2005 (SI 2005/392), p 2.

A variety of issues arises from consideration of the private international law rules relating to adoption. There are wide differences among the laws of different countries on a number of matters, such as who can adopt, or be adopted, and the effects of adoption on, for instance, succession rights. For example, the requirements of English law that an adoption order may not be made in relation to a person who has attained the age of nineteen years,[85] or who is or has been married,[86] are not found in all legal systems.

In examining the rules concerning adoption, it is important to consider the jurisdiction of the English courts to make adoption orders; the choice of law rules applied by English courts; and the rules for recognition of foreign adoptions. It is necessary also to distinguish the different types of intercountry adoption, according to the identity of the other country involved in the adoption process: (a) a Hague Convention country, being one which, like the United Kingdom, is a signatory to the 1993 Hague Convention on Protection of Children and Co-operation in respect of Intercountry Adoption;[87] (b) a country[88] on the United Kingdom's list of designated countries, as set out in the Adoption (Designation of Overseas Adoptions) Order 1973;[89] or a country which is neither a Hague Convention country, nor one which features on the United Kingdom's designated list.

(a) Adoption proceedings in England

(i) Introduction

Adoption, the process by which, under English law, a child is brought permanently into the family of the adopter and parental responsibility for the child is transferred to the adopter,[90] was introduced into England by the Adoption of Children Act 1926, which was ultimately replaced by the consolidating legislation of the Adoption Act 1976.[91] Unlike the case in some other countries, adoption can be effected only by the order of a court,[92] after a judicial inquiry directed mainly to ensuring that such an order will be for the welfare of the child. The effect of an order is to take away from the child whatever legal benefits nature conferred upon him and to transfer all obligations towards him to the adoptive parents who, by nature, have no obligation towards him at all.[93] There is a complete and fundamental change in the status of the child. He becomes a child in law of his adoptive parent(s) to the exclusion of his natural parents.

(a) Adoption and Children Act 2002

The 2002 Act modernised the legal framework for domestic and intercountry adoption.[94] It largely replaces the Adoption Act 1976,[95] and incorporates most[96] of the provisions of the

---

[85] Adoption and Children Act 2002, s 47(9).

[86] Ibid, s 47(8).

[87] See Adoption (Intercountry Aspects) Act 1999, supplemented by the Intercountry Adoption (Hague Convention) Regulations, SI 2003/118; and Adoption and Children Act 2002, supplemented by the Adoptions with a Foreign Element Regulations, SI 2005/392, as amended, and the Adoptions with a Foreign Element (Amendment) Regulations, SI 2009/2563.

[88] Which may, or may not, also be a Hague Convention Contracting State.

[89] SI 1973/19, as amended.

[90] 2002 Act, s 46(1).

[91] Only brought into force on 1 January 1988.

[92] This can be the High Court or the family court: 2002 Act, s 144(1).

[93] 2002 Act, s 46.

[94] See also the Family Procedure Rules, SI 2010/2955, Part 14 (In relation to adoption, the 2010 Rules have replaced the Family Procedure (Adoption) Rules, SI 2005/2795). See also Practice Direction 14B.

[95] Except provisions regarding the status of children already adopted. The 2002 Act includes some provisions amending the Adoption Act 1976, which enabled certain important elements of the new adoption framework to be implemented in advance of full implementation of the 2002 Act.

[96] Ss 1 and 2 (regulations to give effect to the 1993 Hague Convention), 7 (amendments to the British Nationality Act 1981), and Sch 1 (the text of the 1993 Hague Convention) continue in force. The remaining

Adoption (Intercountry Aspects) Act 1999 (examined below), providing a statutory basis for the regulation of intercountry adoption, strengthening existing safeguards, introducing some new ones, and enabling the United Kingdom to ratify the 1993 Hague Convention on Protection of Children and Co-operation in respect of Inter-country Adoption. In introducing wide-ranging reform of the rules in England and Wales for domestic and intercountry adoption, it affects all adoptions in England, and all adoption applications from persons resident and settled in England who are seeking to adopt children living abroad. Part 1 of the Act sets out the framework of adoption law for England and Wales, including in Chapter 6 (sections 83 to 91) provision for inter-country adoption; Part 2 makes amendments to the Children Act 1989; and Part 3 makes miscellaneous provision on advertising and the Adoption and Children Act Register.

(b) Adoptions with a Foreign Element Regulations 2005[97]

The Adoptions with a Foreign Element (AFE) Regulations, which are one of a series of statutory instruments implementing the provisions of the Adoption and Children Act 2002,[98] set out safeguards and procedures for intercountry adoption. They apply to England and Wales with effect from 30 December 2005,[99] and are intended to replace the Intercountry Adoption (Hague Convention) Regulations 2003[100] and the Adoption (Bringing Children into the United Kingdom) Regulations 2003,[101] both of which came into force only on 1 June 2003[102] and which were intended to be repealed when the Adoption and Children Act 2002 was fully implemented.

The AFE Regulations underpin a number of policy objectives, ie: to establish safeguards to ensure intercountry adoption takes place in the best interests of the child and with respect for his/her fundamental rights as recognised in international law; to ensure prospective intercountry adopters have been assessed and approved in accordance with the appropriate procedures; and to enable the United Kingdom to continue to meet its duties under international law.[103]

The AFE Regulations set out procedures in relation to incoming adoptions (adoption of children from abroad by British residents) and outgoing adoptions (adoption of children in England and Wales by persons resident abroad), and for Convention adoptions and

---

provisions of the 1999 Act have ceased to apply in England and Wales, and instead are incorporated in the 2002 Act.

[97] SI 2005/392 ("AFE Regulations"); made under powers conferred by ss 83(4)–(6), 84(3) and (6), 140 (7)–(8), 142(4)–(5) of the 2002 Act, and s 1(1) of the 1999 Act.

[98] See generally Explanatory Memorandum to the AFE Regulations, paras 14 and 15. See also the Adoption Agencies Regulations, SI 2005/389 and the Adopted Children and Adoption Contact Register Regulations, SI 2005/924.

[99] Reg 1.

[100] SI 2003/118; made under the Adoption (Intercountry Aspects) Act 1999, and applicable to Convention adoptions.

[101] SI 2003/1173; made under the transitional provisions in the 2002 Act (s 56A of the 1976 Act, as amended by the 2002 Act), and applicable to adoptions from non-Hague Convention countries, or from Contracting States that have acceded to the Convention, but in respect of which the United Kingdom has raised an objection.

[102] The 2003 Regulations put in place the necessary provisions to give effect in England and Wales to the 1993 Convention. See corresponding legislation in Scotland (SSI 2001/236, 2003/19 and 2003/67) and Northern Ireland (SR 2002/144 and 2006/336), which enabled the United Kingdom to ratify the 1993 Convention. Essentially, the 2003 Regulations required anyone habitually resident in England and wishing to adopt a child living in another country to be assessed and approved as suitable to adopt by a local authority or Voluntary Adoption Agency registered to work on intercountry adoption, regardless of the nature of that person's relationship to the child or the country from which they wished to adopt.

[103] Explanatory Memorandum to the AFE Regulations, para 7.

non-Convention adoptions, respectively. The jurisdiction of the English court to make an adoption order and the law to be applied by the court depend on two different sets of legislative rules, namely general rules (for non-Convention adoptions) and Convention rules (for Hague Convention adoptions).

(ii) General rules

(a) Jurisdiction[104]

An application for an adoption order, other than a Convention adoption order, may be made, in terms of the Adoption and Children Act 2002, by a couple,[105] or by one person only, subject to satisfaction of one of two conditions.[106] In the case of adoption by a couple, an order may be made where both have attained twenty-one years,[107] or if one of the couple is the mother or father of the child and is at least eighteen years of age, and the other has attained twenty-one years.[108] In the case of adoption by one person only, an order may be made if he has attained twenty-one years and is not married or a civil partner, or if he is the partner of a parent of the person to be adopted.[109] The two conditions, only one of which must be satisfied, are that (i) at least one of the couple (in the case of a joint application), or the applicant (in the case of a sole applicant) is domiciled in a part of the British Islands;[110] or (ii) both applicants (in the case of a joint application), or the applicant (in the case of a sole applicant) have/has been habitually resident in a part of the British Islands for a period of not less than one year ending with the date of the application.[111] If only the domicile criterion is satisfied, the prospective adopters would not be eligible, in principle, to seek a Hague Convention adoption order,[112] habitual residence on the part of the applicant(s) being a requirement of such adoptions.[113] If, on the other hand, only the habitual residence criterion is satisfied, the applicant(s) can consider adopting a child from any country. It should be borne in mind, however, that even if the applicant is domiciled or habitually resident in England, the court will be unable to make an adoption order if the other conditions set out in the 2002 Act are not satisfied.[114] Importantly, the jurisdictional provisions of the 2002 Act remain unchanged by the Brussels II *bis* Regulation or the 1996 Hague Convention as "decisions on adoption, measures preparatory to adoption, or the annulment or revocation of adoption" fall outside of the scope of the Regulation and the Convention.[115] It has been held that an application for a placement order[116] under section 21 of the 2002 Act is to be regarded as a "measure

---

[104] See the 13th edn of this book (1999), p 903, for an examination of the rules operating prior to the entry into force of the Adoption and Children Act 2002.

[105] Ie a married couple, civil partners or two people (of different sexes or the same sex) living as partners in an enduring family relationship (but not two people one of whom is the other's parent, grandparent, sister, brother, aunt or uncle): 2002 Act, s 144(4), as amended by the Civil Partnership Act 2004, s 79.

[106] Ibid, s 49(1).

[107] Ibid, s 50(1).

[108] Ibid, s 50(2).

[109] Ibid, s 51(1) and (2); also (3), (3A) and (4).

[110] Ibid, s 49(2).

[111] Ibid, s 49(3).

[112] Infra, p 1213 et seq.

[113] See 1993 Hague Convention, Art 2: "The Convention shall apply where a child habitually resident in one Contracting State ('the State of origin') has been, is being, or is to be moved to another Contracting State ('the receiving State') either after his or her adoption in the State of origin by spouses or a person habitually resident in the receiving State, or for the purposes of such an adoption in the receiving State or in the State of origin."

[114] Eg, s 47. See generally the 2002 Act, ss 18–65, especially ss 42–45 (preliminaries to adoption). Rules on service, including service out of the jurisdiction, are set out in the Family Procedure Rules 2010, SI 2010/2955, Pt 6.

[115] Art 1(3)(b) and Art 4 *b)* respectively.

[116] Ie an order that authorises a local authority to place a child for adoption with any prospective adopters who may be chosen by that authority.

preparatory to adoption".[117] Section 21, in conjunction with section 22, implicitly govern the English court's jurisdiction to grant a placement order.[118]

The domicile,[119] habitual residence or nationality of the child to be considered for adoption is not relevant to the matter of allocation of jurisdiction. Indeed, nowhere in the Act is there any requirement relating to these connecting factors; although it ought to be noted that there is a residence-related requirement which in effect supplements the jurisdictional rules. The requirement is that the child must have his home with the applicant(s) at all times during a specified period immediately before the application. This period ranges from ten weeks to three years, depending on the circumstances of the case.[120] The original requirement that the child should be of British nationality, contained in the Adoption and Children Act 1929, was expressly removed after the Second World War by the Adoption of Children Act 1949.[121] The 1949 Act was largely repealed by Schedule 4 to the Adoption Act 1950, which made no reference to the child's nationality at all. It remained the same in consecutive adoption acts, including the current Act of 2002. Against this background, it was rightly remarked by Black LJ, in *Re N (Children) (Adoption: Jurisdiction)*,[122] that "the absence of reference to the child's nationality in the 2002 Act is no accident but rather the product of a deliberate decision not to restrict adoption to children who are British nationals".[123] The 2002 Act is also silent as to the domicile, habitual residence, nationality or presence of the child's biological parents, whose consent can be dispensed with pursuant to the 2002 Act.[124] It follows that the English court has jurisdiction to make an adoption order in respect of a foreign child, i.e. regardless of his/her domicile, habitual residence or nationality, and, similarly, has jurisdiction to dispense with the consent of the biological parent(s)[125] regardless of their domicile, habitual residence, nationality or presence.[126] It has been aptly remarked that the restriction of the jurisdictional requirement in the 2002 Act to the domicile/habitual residence of the adopter(s) was rather arbitrary as "there is no qualitative distinction between the extinction and creation of status: just as the adopting parents gain the status of parent, so do the natural parents revert to the status of non-parent".[127]

---

[117] *Re N (Children) (Adoption: Jurisdiction)* [2015] EWCA Civ 1112, per Munby P, at [72].

[118] Ibid, per Black LJ, at [182]—"the court has jurisdiction to make a placement order on the application of a [domestic] local authority which fulfils the conditions set out in section 22".

[119] See *In re B (S) (An Infant)* [1968] Ch 204, per Goff J (in relation to the Adoption Act 1958 which, like the 2002 Act, contained no reference to the child's domicile): "it is clear that this court has jurisdiction to make an adoption order in respect of an infant domiciled abroad". Ibid, p 208. The reasoning and conclusion of Goff J was approved and held applicable to the 2002 Act by Munby P and Black LJ in *Re N (Children) (Adoption: Jurisdiction)* [2015] EWCA Civ 1112, at [89] and [180] respectively. (The decision was later appealed to the Supreme Court; however, on different points: *Re N (Children) (Adoption: Jurisdiction) (AIRE Centre and others intervening)* [2016] UKSC 15. See Chapter 25, supra, pp 1115–16).

[120] See 2002 Act, s 42(1)–(6).

[121] See 2002 Act, s 1(2)—"An adoption order may be made in respect of an infant resident in England or Wales who is not a British subject."

[122] [2015] EWCA Civ 1112.

[123] Ibid, at [179].

[124] See related discussion on "choice of law", infra, p 1210 et seq.

[125] The question of the parental consent may arise either at the stage of the making of the adoption order, or earlier—i.e. at the stage of an application for a placement order. The relevant jurisdictional provisions are ss 49 and 21 (together with s 22) respectively. (See supra).

[126] *Re N (Children) (Adoption: Jurisdiction)* [2015] EWCA Civ 1112, per Munby P, at [77] and Black LJ at [175]. For a recent discussion of these issues see Laing [2015] Fam Law 565. See also Dicey, Morris and Collins, paras 20-096–20-097.

[127] Laing [2015] Fam Law 703.

(b) Choice of law

The absence of any requirement in the 2002 Act that the child should be domiciled in England raises a question of choice of law. If an applicant, domiciled or habitually resident in England, applies for an adoption order in respect of a child domiciled abroad, will the court have regard to the substantive requirements of the foreign law of the child's domicile, which may differ widely from their English equivalents contained in the 2002 Act in such matters as the age of the respective parties and the required consents? Similarly, should the child be habitually resident abroad or (although domiciled/habitually resident in England) happen be a non-British national, to what extent will the court consider the law of the child's habitual residence/nationality when deciding whether to make an adoption order and, if necessary, whether to dispense with parental consent? The terms of the English legislation are such that an adoption order made by the court would not be vitiated by a failure to take account of the foreign law. It has been suggested that, in England, the law of adoption is viewed as a set of requirements which regulate the procedure of an English court rather than a body of substantive rules, as adoption is seen as the result of an administrative act in judicial form rather than a private law transaction approved by the state. Procedure, as a matter of a basic principle, is governed by the law of the forum, meaning that an adoption in England cannot be governed by foreign law.[128] In the absence of an express choice of law rule in the 2002 Act, the law of the forum must be assumed to apply. However, it is submitted that to refer exclusively to the law of the forum would be contrary to principle and often prejudicial to the well-being of the child. The admitted and basic feature of status as fixed by the law of the domicile is its universality.[129] The status attributed to a child in his domicile of origin is entitled to universal respect. It is, therefore, undesirable for the English court to make an adoption order which claims to destroy that status and to substitute another that is fundamentally different. Moreover, such an order would scarcely be recognised in the domicile of origin,[130] with the result that the child would be the child of X in England, but of Y in all other countries, a situation which seems strangely at odds with the statutory requirement that, in making any decision relating to the adoption of a child, the paramount consideration of the court or adoption agency must be the child's welfare, throughout his life.[131] Certainly, the possibility of taking account of foreign law, whether or not the law of the child's domicile, is envisaged by the Family Procedure Rules 2010,[132] rule 23.7 of which sets out the procedure that must be followed by a party who intends to put in evidence a finding on a question of foreign law by virtue of section 4(2) of the Civil Evidence Act 1972.

It might be extremely difficult to blend two opposing systems of adoption law, but nonetheless the fact remains that to impose a status on a child in conflict with that which he possesses in his domicile of origin, to create as it were a "limping child", would be a doubtful blessing to bestow upon him.

A resolution of the conflict between principle and the then applicable statutory wording[133] was found in *Re B (S) (An Infant)*:[134]

---

[128] Kahn-Freund, *The Growth of Internationalism in English Private International Law* (1960), pp 62–66, per Munby P in *Re N (Children) (Adoption: Jurisdiction)* [2015] EWCA Civ 1112, at [102].

[129] *Re Luck's Settlement Trusts* [1940] Ch 864 at 894. See also the speech of James LJ in *Re Goodmans' Trusts* (1881) 17 Ch D 266 at 297–298.

[130] Masson [2016] Fam Law 1113.

[131] 2002 Act, s 1(2).

[132] SI 2010/2955.

[133] Adoption Act 1958, s 1(1).

[134] [1968] Ch 204; Blom-Cooper (1968) 31 MLR 219; Carter (1967) 42 BYBIL 309–10.

An application was made by proposed adopters for the consent of the natural father to the adoption to be dispensed with. The natural father was domiciled in Spain and the child and the adoptive parents were resident in England where the adoptive parents were domiciled. It was assumed that the child was domiciled in Spain,[135] and this raised the issue of whether Spanish law should be considered relevant to the application.

Goff J decided that the court had jurisdiction to make an adoption order "notwithstanding that by the law of the infant's domicil the court there could not make an order or could only make one having different consequences".[136] Nevertheless, he admitted that the law of the domicile is not to be ignored, for "the true impact of the domiciliary law is purely as a factor—albeit an important one—to be taken into account in considering whether the proposed order will be for the welfare of the infant, a matter upon which the Statute expressly provides[137] that the court must be satisfied before making an order".[138] Moreover, Goff J took the view that "welfare", as used in the statute, "does not mean simple physical or moral well-being, but benefit in the widest sense which must include consideration of the effect the order, if made, will have on the infant's status".[139] If the adoption will not be recognised by such law, though here there was evidence that Spain would recognise the English order, then the court will have to weigh the serious disadvantages of being a "limping child" against the benefits which may accrue from adoption. This balancing process will inevitably result in cases, albeit rare ones, where an English adoption order will be made in circumstances where it will not be recognised by the law of the child's domicile.[140]

Recently, the reasoning and conclusion of Goff J in *Re B (S) (An Infant)* was approved by Munby P and Black LJJ in *Re N (Children) (Adoption: Jurisdiction)*.[141] As a starting point, Munby P agreed that adoption in England was to be governed by English law.[142] He then continued, in line with Goff J's argument, that although English law was the applicable law, "foreign law is an important factor to be taken into account in considering the welfare of the child".[143] This is, however, not "by virtue of the foreign law" but rather because the court is required to do so by English law as a part of the welfare considerations.[144] The President then concurred with Goff J's view that, before making an adoption order, the English court will need to consider whether the order will be recognised elsewhere, especially in the country of the child's domicile, habitual residence or nationality.[145]

---

[135] The natural parents were divorced and the court would not decide whether in such a case a child took the domicile of the mother to whom custody had been awarded.

[136] [1968] Ch 204 at 210.

[137] Adoption Act 1958, s 7(1)(b); see now 2002 Act, s 1(2).

[138] [1968] Ch 204 at 211; approved in *Re G (An Infant)* [1968] 3 NSWR 483 at 485–6.

[139] Ibid.

[140] Eg *Re R (Adoption)* [1967] 1 WLR 34; cf *Re A (An Infant)* [1963] 1 WLR 231. See *also Re N (Children) (Adoption: Jurisdiction)* [2015] EWCA Civ 1112, at [187].

[141] [2015] EWCA Civ 1112.

[142] Ibid, at [102].

[143] Ibid, at [103].

[144] See in particular s 1(2)—the paramount consideration of the court or adoption agency must be the child's welfare, throughout his life; s 1(4)—the "welfare checklist" for courts and adoption agencies when determining the best interests of the child in any decision relating to adoption; and s 52(1)(b)—dispensation with parental consent on the ground that the welfare of the child requires the consent to be dispensed with. The paramountcy of the child's welfare and the welfare checklist apply also to dispensing with consent.

[145] *Re N (Children) (Adoption: Jurisdiction)* [2015] EWCA Civ 1112, at [111]. In order to avoid the possibility of a "limping" adoption order, the English court should follow the guidance set out at para [104] et seq of Munby P's judgment. Throughout this process, particular attention should be paid to the child's national, linguistic, cultural, ethnic and religious background, whilst bearing in mind the requirement to consider "the likely effect on the child *throughout her life* of having ceased to be a member of her original family." Ibid, at [105].

Although jurisdiction can be exercised without reference to the domicile of the biological parents, one might question[146] whether an order which deprives them in England of the status of parent should be made without consideration, not only of their interests in relation to matters such as consent, but also of the effect of the adoption order under the law governing their status.[147] Not only a child but also a parent can "limp". The Supreme Court of Canada, in 1981, decided[148] (though without detailed consideration of the choice of law issues) that the question whether a child was one who could be adopted should be referred not only to the domiciliary law of the applicants and of the child, but also, at least in contested cases, to that of the biological parents. One may, however, argue that there are obvious practical reasons that militate against the application of the domiciliary law of the biological parent(s) such as the necessity to determine the relevant domicile(s) and its laws; and to reconcile several, possibly opposing, systems of adoption law.[149] These arguments apply to a varied extent also in relation to the law of the habitual residence and the law of the nationality of the biological parent(s). Equally, the same concerns may arise when considering the application of the law of the child's domicile/habitual residence/nationality.[150]

More recently, the issue of the effect of the adoption order on the status of the biological parents according to their own personal law(s) was touched on by the Court Appeal in *Re N (Children) (Adoption: Jurisdiction)*.[151] Munby P set out the argument that had been "rumbling around" in the context of the debate on applicable law in adoption "for years": "[. . .] the status of the child's natural parent(s) and their parental rights cannot be extinguished by the English court dispensing with their consent and making an adoption order except in accordance with and as permitted by the law of the state of the parental domicile."[152] Although he did not provide an explicit answer to this problem, it appears that his reasoning in relation to the place of the law of the child's domicile/habitual residence/nationality in English adoption proceedings as outlined above, is intended to apply also to the law with which the biological parents have a particular connection (ie the law of their domicile, (habitual) residence or nationality). The concurring judgment of Black LJ, which seeks to merely draw out from the President's judgment the main points of his reasoning, confirms this presumption. In particular, her Ladyship's summary goes as follows: "[. . .] English law is the applicable law in determining the adoption application, and that includes the provisions of section 52 of the 2002 Act as to dispensing with parental consent. What the English court cannot do, however, is to assume without more that its determination will bind other jurisdictions. They will make their own determination as to the status of the natural parents vis-à-vis the child and vis-à-vis the adopters and the natural parents and it is for that reason that, although foreign connections do not prevent the English court from having jurisdiction and power to grant an adoption order, they are potentially very material in its determination of how to exercise that power."[153] Nevertheless, this does not mean that an adoption order could not be made by the English court if there was evidence that the decision would not be recognised in a country

---

[146] See Blom-Cooper (1968) 31 MLR 219 and Laing [2015] Fam Law 703.

[147] In *J v C* [1970] AC 668, the House of Lords granted custody of a child to foster parents against the desire of the unimpeachable natural parents in Spain. Their Lordships were at pains to indicate they were not considering an application for an adoption order (see at 692, 714, 719), thus suggesting greater weight would be paid to the interests of the natural parents in the case of adoption because of its permanent effect.

[148] *Paquette v Galipean* [1981] 1 SCR 29; and see *Re L (HK)* [1989] 1 WWR 556; *Re S (H)* (1995) 13 RFL (4th) 301.

[149] See Laing [2015] Fam Law 703.

[150] See supra.

[151] [2015] EWCA Civ 1112.

[152] Ibid, at [93].

[153] Ibid, at [181].

with which the child has a particular link, either through his/her own domicile/nationality/ habitual residence or those of his/her parents.[154]

The proposed approach that requires the English court to consider and actively seek to evade the negative consequences for the child of the lack of a universal recognition of the adoption order is highly pragmatic and, on the surface, appears to be eminently sensible. The challenge, however, it to reconcile in practice the opposing and strongly emotional interests that become obvious especially in cases of non-consensual adoption where such adoption orders are unavailable under the foreign law with which the child and/or the biological parents have a particular connection.[155]

(iii) Convention rules

(a) Background

In 1964, the Hague Conference on Private International Law produced a Convention on Adoption, which was signed in 1965.[156] The Convention, which was ratified by the United Kingdom in 1978, related to jurisdiction, choice of law and recognition of foreign adoptions.[157] On 15 April 2003, however, the United Kingdom denounced the 1965 Convention,[158] with effect from 23 October 2003, in order that it could be replaced by the 1993 Hague Convention on Protection of Children and Co-operation in respect of Intercountry Adoption, signed by the United Kingdom on 12 January 1994.[159] With effect from 1 June 2003, in accordance with the Adoption (Intercountry Aspects) Act 1999, supplemented by the Intercountry Adoption (Hague Convention) Regulations 2003,[160] and the Adoption and Children Act 2002, supplemented by the Adoptions with a Foreign Element Regulations 2005,[161] the 1993 Convention came into force in the United Kingdom.

(b) 1993 Hague Convention on Protection of Children and Co-operation in respect of Intercountry Adoption[162]

Preparation of the 1993 Convention involved more than sixty-five countries, including the United Kingdom, as well as non-government organisations and voluntary bodies having an interest in intercountry adoption. The purpose of the Convention is to establish safeguards to ensure that intercountry adoptions take place in the best interests of the child and with

---

[154] Ibid, at [187].

[155] Recently, as a consequence of the EU enlargement process that culminated in the 2000s, a number of care or placement order proceedings potentially leading to adoption, involving in particular children of Eastern/Central European origin, have been brought before the English courts. These cases tend to arise mainly (but not exclusively) in the context of applications under Article 15 of the Brussels II *bis* Regulation. See supra, p 1116.

[156] Cmnd 2615. See Graveson (1965) 13 ICLQ 528; Lipstein [1965] CLJ 224; Unger (1965) 28 MLR 463.

[157] For examination of the 1965 Convention and the Adoption Act 1976, see the 13th edn of this book (1999), p 906 et seq.

[158] As also did Switzerland. Austria, the only other Contracting State to the 1965 Convention, denounced it on 20 April 2004.

[159] See van Loon [1993] VII Hague Recueil 191, [1994] Hague Yearbook of International Law 325–8; Pfund in Borras (ed), *E Pluribus Unum* (1996) 321–36; Hinchliffe [2003] Fam Law 570; Watkins [2012] CFLQ 389; Cabeza *et al, International Adoption* (2012); Fenton-Glynn, *Children's Rights in Intercountry Adoption: A European Perspective* (2014); and Baker and Groff in Scherpe (ed), *European Family Law: Volume I* (2016) 163–77.

[160] SI 2003/118.

[161] SI 2005/392.

[162] As at March 2017, there are 98 Contracting States to the Convention. See Parra-Aranguren, *Explanatory Report on the Convention* (1994) (hereinafter "*Explanatory Report*"); and documents drawn up by the Permanent Bureau of the Hague Conference on Private International Law, regarding the Special Commissions of 2000, 2005, 2010 and 2015 on the practical operation of the 1993 Convention; and the Hague Conference Guides to Good Practice (2008 and 2013) (http://www.hcch.net).

respect for his fundamental rights as recognised in international law; to establish a system of co-operation among Contracting States to ensure that those safeguards are respected, and thereby prevent abduction, the sale of, or traffic in children;[163] and to secure the recognition in Contracting States of adoptions made in accordance with the Convention.[164]

The Convention applies where a child[165] who is habitually resident[166] in one Contracting State (the state of origin)[167] has been, is being, or is to be moved to another Contracting State (the receiving state), either after his adoption in the state of origin by a person or persons habitually resident in the receiving state, or for the purposes of such an adoption in the receiving state or in the state of origin.[168]

There is no express mention of choice of law in the 1993 Hague Convention. Instead, the Convention sets out the reciprocal obligations resting, respectively, upon the authorities in the state of origin and in the receiving state. The successful operation of the Convention depends to a large extent on effective collaboration between the two states.

Article 4 determines the duties of the state of origin.[169] It provides that a Convention adoption can proceed only if the competent authorities in the state of origin have (a) established that the child is adoptable; (b) determined, after possibilities for placement of the child within the state of origin have been given due consideration, that an intercountry adoption is in the child's best interests; (c) ensured that the persons,[170] institutions and authorities[171] whose consent is necessary[172] for adoption have given their informed[173] consent, without coercion or financial incentive, and, in particular, that the consent of the child's biological mother, where required, has been given only after the birth of the child; and (d) ensured, having regard to the age and maturity of the child, that he has been duly counselled and informed of the effects of the adoption, that consideration has been given to his wishes and opinions, and that his consent, where required, was duly informed and freely given, not induced by payment or compensation of any kind. Article 5 determines the duties of the

---

[163] See, regarding breach of procedure, *Re C (A Minor) (Adoption: Illegality)* [1999] 1 FLR 370; and *Re M (Adoption: International Adoption Trade)* [2003] EWHC 219, [2003] 1 FLR 1111.

[164] Art 1.

[165] A person under the age of eighteen on the date when the Central Authorities of the receiving state and the state of origin agree that the adoption may proceed: Art 3.

[166] The Convention does not define when a child or a prospective adopter shall be deemed to be habitually resident in a Contracting State. For an overview of challenges concerning the interpretation of the concept of habitual residence in the context of the Convention see Permanent Bureau of the Hague Conference, Special Commission of June 2015, Prel Doc No 4, April 2015; and Conclusions and Recommendations adopted by the Special Commission of June 2015, paras [22]–[25].

[167] There was some early criticism of this expression, born of fear that it would cause misunderstandings, especially if interpreted as meaning the "State of the nationality". The drafters concluded, however, that the specific meaning for the purpose of the Convention was clear. Parra-Aranguren, *Explanatory Report*, para 73.

[168] Art 2. The Convention applies in every case where an application pursuant to Art 14, infra, has been received after the Convention has entered into force in the receiving state and the state of origin: Art 41.

[169] See Parra-Aranguren, *Explanatory Report*, paras 108–172; and *Pini v Romania* [2005] 2 FLR 596, (2005) 40 EHRR 13.

[170] Eg *Re A (A Child) (Adoption of a Russian Child)* [2000] 1 FLR 539; *Re C (A Child) (Foreign Adoption: Natural Mother's Consent: Service)* [2006] 1 FLR 318; *Re AMR (Adoption: Procedure)* [1999] 2 FLR 807—consent of Polish guardian—child's grandmother.

[171] Eg *Re N (A Child) (Adoption: Foreign Guardianship)* [2000] 2 FLR 431—consent of orphanage *qua* guardian; *Re J (A Child) (Adoption: Consent of Foreign Public Authority)* [2002] EWHC 766, [2002] 2 FLR 618; and *Re D (Adoption: Foreign Guardianship)* [1999] 2 FLR 865—consent of Romanian hospital not required as not guardian appointed in accordance with Children Act 1989.

[172] *Re K (A Minor) (Adoption: Foreign Child)* [1997] 2 FLR 221.

[173] *Re R (A Minor) (Inter-Country Adoptions: Practice) (No 1)* [1999] 1 FLR 1014; and *(No 2)* [1999] 1 FLR 1042.

receiving state,[174] providing that a Convention adoption can proceed only if the competent authorities in that state have determined that the prospective adoptive parents are eligible and suited to adopt, and have been counselled as may be necessary, and that the child is or will be authorised to enter and reside permanently in the receiving state.

The effective operation of the Convention is dependent upon co-operation and coordination among the designated Central Authorities of Contracting States.[175] The procedural requirements of intercountry adoption are detailed in Chapter IV (Articles 14 to 22). Article 14 states that persons habitually resident in a Contracting State, who wish to adopt a child habitually resident in another Contracting State, shall apply to the Central Authority in the state of their habitual residence.[176] The Parra-Aranguren Report makes clear that since Article 14 does not expressly regulate the formal requirements to be fulfilled by the application, these shall be determined by the law of the habitual residence of the prospective adoptive parents, it being understood, however, that they must identify themselves, and give all the necessary information to facilitate the preparation of the report prescribed by Article 15.[177] It follows from Article 14 that prospective adopters are not able to apply directly to the Central Authority or to any other public authority or accredited body of the state of origin of the child.

When the application is presented to the Central Authority of the receiving state (ie the state in which the prospective adopters are habitually resident), the Central Authority must ascertain whether the prospective adopters are eligible and suited to adopt, as is required by Article 5(a) of the Convention. Therefore, "it shall establish their compliance not only with all legal conditions prescribed by the applicable law, as determined by the receiving State, but also with the necessary socio-psychological requirements needed to guarantee the success of the adoption".[178] If the Central Authority of the receiving state is satisfied that the applicants are eligible and suited to adopt, it must prepare a report (an "Article 15 Report"), for transmission to the Central Authority of the state of origin,[179] including information about the applicants' identity, eligibility and suitability to adopt, background, family and medical history, social environment, reasons for adoption, ability to undertake an intercountry adoption, as well as the characteristics of the children for whom they would be qualified to care. The Parra-Aranguren Report explains that this is intended to be an additional safeguard to guarantee the success of the adoption. Preferences of the prospective adopters should be "expressed in general terms, eg age, religion and special needs (disability etc) of a child in accordance with their parenting skills and experiences, children professing a certain religion, and not make reference to a specific child in particular".[180]

If the Central Authority of the state of origin is satisfied that the child is adoptable, it shall prepare a report (an "Article 16 Report"), including information about the child's identity, adoptability, background, social environment, family history, medical history including that

---

[174] Parra-Aranguren, *Explanatory Report*, paras 173–93.

[175] Cf the 1980 Hague Convention on the Civil Aspects of International Child Abduction, supra, p 1134 et seq. Ch III (Arts 6–13) of the 1993 Convention sets out the role and responsibilities of Central Authorities. The Central Authority for England and Wales is the Secretary of State. Chapter III should be read in conjunction with Art 22, which permits, within some limits and under certain conditions, delegation of the functions assigned to the Central Authority by Chapter IV to other public authorities or accredited bodies, or even non-accredited bodies or persons. See Parra-Aranguren, *Explanatory Report*, paras 194–279, especially para 196.

[176] Art 14.

[177] Parra-Aranguren, *Explanatory Report*, para 289.

[178] Ibid, para 294.

[179] Art 15(2).

[180] Para 297.

of his family, and any special needs.[181] The Central Authority of the state of origin must give due consideration to the child's upbringing and to his ethnic, religious and cultural background; ensure that relevant consents have been obtained,[182] and determine, on the basis of the Article 15 and 16 Reports, whether the envisaged placement is in the best interests of the child. Once it has been determined that the child should be entrusted to the prospective adopters,[183] the Central Authorities of both states shall take all necessary steps to obtain permission for the child to leave the state of origin and to enter and reside permanently in the receiving state.[184]

Article 28 makes clear that the Convention does not affect any law of the state of origin which requires that the adoption of a child habitually resident within that state take place in that state, or which prohibits the child's placement in, or transfer to, the receiving state prior to adoption. It is not the aim of the Convention to unify the substantive laws of Contracting States with regard to adoption.

In keeping with the objectives of the Convention, it is expressly stated that no-one shall derive improper financial or other gain from an activity related to an intercountry adoption; only proper costs and expenses, including reasonable professional fees, may be charged or paid.[185]

(c) Adoptions with a Foreign Element Regulations 2005[186]

(i) Convention adoptions where the United Kingdom is the receiving state
Chapter 1 of Part 3 of the Adoptions with a Foreign Element (AFE) Regulations deals with the requirements, procedure, recognition and effect of adoptions where the United Kingdom is the receiving state in relation to a Convention adoption, ie where a couple or a person habitually resident in the British Islands wish(es) to adopt a child who is habitually resident in a Convention country outside the British Islands in accordance with the Convention.

A prospective adopter in these circumstances must apply to an adoption agency for a determination of eligibility and an assessment of his suitability to adopt a child, and must give the agency such information as it may require for the purpose of the assessment.[187] An application will not be considered unless, at the date thereof (a) in the case of an application by a couple, they have both attained twenty-one years and have been habitually resident in the British Islands for a period of not less than one year ending with the date of application; and (b) in the case of an application by one person, he has attained twenty-one years and has been habitually resident in the British Islands for a period of not less than one year ending with the date of application.

An assessment will be carried out by the adoption agency in accordance with regulations 14 to 34.[188] The assessment (or "home-study"), which involves detailed interviews with a social

---

[181] Art 30 imposes a duty on the competent authorities of a Contracting State to ensure that information held by them concerning the child's origin, in particular information concerning the identity of his parents, and medical history, is preserved. See Art 30(2) as regards the child's access to such information.

[182] See Art 4.

[183] Art 17.

[184] Art 18. The actual transfer of the child to the receiving state must be carried out in accordance with Art 19.

[185] Art 32. See, for an example of bad practice and exploitative intercountry adoption, *Re M (Adoption: International Adoption Trade)* [2003] EWHC 219, [2003] 1 FLR 1111.

[186] SI 2005/392, as amended.

[187] AFE Regulations, reg 13, as amended by Adoption Agencies (Miscellaneous Amendments) Regulations, SI 2013/985.

[188] See also Adoption Agencies Regulations, SI 2005/389, as amended by Adoption Agencies (Miscellaneous Amendments) Regulations, SI 2013/985.

worker, as well as medical checks and police checks, will be considered by the agency's adoption panel. A prospective adopter's report must be prepared, including: the state of origin from which the prospective adopter wishes to adopt a child; confirmation that he is eligible to adopt a child under the law of that state; any additional information obtained as a consequence of the requirements of that state; and the agency's assessment of the prospective adopter's suitability to adopt a child who is habitually resident in that state.[189] If the applicant is deemed suitable to adopt, the application will be forwarded to the Department for Education to be processed.[190] At that stage, a Certificate of Eligibility to adopt normally will be issued on behalf of the Secretary of State. Following notarisation and legalisation of documents, the papers will be forwarded to the Central Authority of the state of origin.[191]

Regulations 21 and 22 set out the requirements in respect of a prospective adopter proposing to enter the United Kingdom with a child, and the relevant adoption agency.[192] Regulations 24 to 27 lay down provisions following a child's entry into the United Kingdom where no Convention adoption was made or applied for in the state of origin. Regulation 31 provides that an adoption order shall not be made as a Convention adoption order unless (a) in the case of (i) an application by a couple, both have been habitually resident in the British Islands for a period of not less than one year ending with the date of application; or (ii) on application by one person, he has been habitually resident in the British Islands for a period of not less than one year ending with the date of application; (b) on the date when the Central Authorities of the state of origin and the receiving state agreed that the adoption may proceed,[193] the child was habitually resident in a Convention country outside the British Islands; and (c) in a case where one member of a couple (in the case of an application by a couple) or the applicant (in the case of an application by one person) is not a British citizen, the Home Office has confirmed that the child is authorised to enter and reside permanently in the United Kingdom.

(ii) Convention adoptions where the United Kingdom is the state of origin

Chapter 2 of Part 3 of the AFE Regulations deals with the requirements, procedure, recognition and effect of adoptions in England and Wales where the United Kingdom is the state of origin in respect of a Convention adoption, ie where a couple or a person habitually resident in a Convention country outside the British Islands wish(es) to adopt a child who is habitually resident in the British Islands.[194]

To a large extent, as is to be expected, the provisions of Chapter 2 of Part 3 are the mirror image of those in Chapter 1. Regulation 38 provides that the report which the relevant adoption agency is required to prepare in accordance with regulation 17 of the Adoption Agencies Regulations 2005[195] must include a summary of the possibilities for placement of the child within the United Kingdom, and an assessment of whether an adoption by a person in a particular receiving state is in the child's best interests. The relevant Central Authority in the receiving state, if satisfied that a prospective adopter who is habitually resident in that state is eligible and suited to adopt, will prepare an "Article 15 Report"[196] comprising information about the prospective adopter's identity, eligibility and suitability to adopt, background, family and medical history, social environment, reasons for adoption,

---

[189] Reg 15(4).
[190] Reg 18. See reg 20 for procedure where the proposed adoption is not to proceed.
[191] Reg 19.
[192] Infra, p 1219 et seq.
[193] 1993 Hague Convention, Art 17(c).
[194] Eg *Greenwich LBC v S* [2007] EWHC 820 (Fam).
[195] SI 2005/389.
[196] Supra, p 1215.

ability to undertake an intercountry adoption, and the characteristics of the child for whom they would be qualified to care.[197] The United Kingdom adoption agency, when considering whether a proposed placement for adoption should proceed, must take into account the Article 15 Report[198] and any other information passed to it as a consequence of the AFE Regulations.[199]

Before a child will be placed for adoption with the prospective adopter, the Secretary of State may notify the Central Authority of the receiving state that it is prepared to agree that the adoption may proceed, subject to confirmation that, inter alia,[200] the prospective adopter is aware of the need to make an application under section 84 of the 2002 Act.[201] It has been held that the expression "entrusted to prospective adopters" within the meaning of Article 17 of the 1993 Hague Convention equated to the making of a parental responsibility order under s 84 of the 2002 Act.[202]

Regulation 50 provides that an adoption order shall not be made as a Convention adoption order unless (a) in the case of (i) an application by a couple, both have been habitually resident in a Convention country outside the British Islands for a period of not less than one year ending with the date of application; or (ii) on application by one person, he has been habitually resident in a Convention country outside the British Islands for a period of not less than one year ending with the date of application; (b) on the date when the Central Authorities of the state of origin and the receiving state agreed that the adoption may proceed,[203] the child was habitually resident in any part of the British Islands; and (c) the competent authority has confirmed that the child is authorised to enter and remain permanently in the Convention country in which the applicant is habitually resident.

The meaning and application of regulation 50 was considered recently in *Greenwich LBC v S*:[204]

> The case concerned the intercountry adoption of four siblings. The children had spent what was described as an "extended holiday" with the putative adopter, their maternal great-aunt, at her home in Canada. They had been in Canada, save for two breaks, for a period of one year, and a question arose as to whether they had lost their habitual residence in England. Sumner J concluded[205] that whilst they had been in Canada for what might be described as an "appreciable time", there was no settled intention at that time by the local authority for the children to live in Canada. It was held that the placement of children overseas by a local authority, in the absence of a final plan for them, ought not to run the risk that they would lose their habitual residence after one year or two, unless there is compelling evidence leading to that conclusion. In the instant case, in the absence of such evidence, the children's habitual residence in England continued.

---

[197] Reg 42.
[198] Reg 43.
[199] Reg 44.
[200] Reg 47(1).
[201] Application for an order for transfer of parental responsibility prior to adoption abroad (infra, p 1220). See *Re G (A Child) (Adoption: Placement Outside Jurisdiction)* [2008] EWCA Civ 105, [2008] WLR (D) 56, and the sequel to this decision *Re G (Adoption: Placement Outside Jurisdiction) (No 2)* [2008] EWCA Civ 105 2; and *A LBC v Department for Children, Schools and Families* [2009] EWCA Civ 41. See also reg 47(2).
[202] *Haringey London Borough Council v MA, JN and IA* [2008] EWHC 722 (Fam), Charles J, at [95].
[203] 1993 Hague Convention, Art 17(c).
[204] [2007] EWHC 820 (Fam).
[205] [2007] EWHC 820 (Fam), at [27] et seq. Cf *Re JS (Private International Adoption)* [2000] 2 FLR 638.

(iii) Power to charge

Section 13 of the Children and Adoption Act 2006[206] allows the Secretary of State to charge an administrative fee to adopters for services provided or to be provided by him in relation to intercountry adoptions.

(b) Procedures for taking children into and out of the United Kingdom

(i) Procedures under the AFE Regulations 2005[207]

Perceived deficiencies in the Adoption Act 1976 were intended to be remedied by the Adoption and Children Act 2002, and the Adoption (Bringing Children into the United Kingdom) Regulations 2003,[208] made in accordance with section 56A of the 1976 Act, as amended,[209] which enhanced the sanctions introduced in the Adoption (Intercountry Aspects) Act 1999 in respect of individuals who bring children into the United Kingdom in connection with adoption, without following proper procedures. This has now been replaced by the procedures set out in the AFE Regulations.

(a) Bringing children into the United Kingdom

Chapter 1 of Part 2 of the AFE Regulations deals with bringing children into the United Kingdom, for cases where the United Kingdom is the receiving state. This should be read in conjunction with section 83[210] of the 2002 Act, which imposes restrictions on British residents bringing or causing someone else to bring a child habitually resident outside the British Islands into the United Kingdom with the intention of adopting the child in the United Kingdom, unless the person complies with prescribed requirements and meets prescribed conditions.[211] It also makes it a criminal offence for a British resident to bring or cause someone else to bring a child habitually resident outside the British Islands whom he has adopted within the last twelve months into the United Kingdom, unless the person complies with prescribed requirements and meets prescribed conditions.[212] The restrictions in section 83 do not apply if the child is intended to be adopted under a Convention adoption order, as the provisions in the 1993 Hague Convention will apply in such cases.[213]

By virtue of regulation 3 of the AFE Regulations, a prospective adopter falling within the circumstances described in section 83 of the 2002 Act must apply to an adoption agency for an assessment of his suitability to adopt a child, and must give the agency such information as it may require for the purpose of the assessment. The conditions applicable in respect of a child brought into the United Kingdom are set out in detail in regulation 4 of the AFE Regulations.

---

[206] Inserting s 91A into the Adoption and Children Act 2002.

[207] SI 2005/392, as amended.

[208] SI 2003/1173, revoking (reg 7) the Adoption of Children from Overseas Regulations 2001.

[209] Substituted by the Adoption and Children Act 2002, Sch 4(12).

[210] Replacing and strengthening s 56A of the 1976 Act. See also Children and Adoption Act 2006, s 9(2), infra, p 1222.

[211] 2002 Act, s 83(1) and (5). The conditions are set out in reg 4 of the AFE Regulations. See *Re X (A Child), Northumberland County Council v Z and Others (No 2)* [2008] EWHC 1324 (Fam), and *Northumberland City Council v Z, Y, X* [2009] EWHC 498 (Fam) (illustration of the consequences of illegally bringing a child from a foreign jurisdiction to the UK in connection with adoption). See also *Re IH (A Child) (Permission to Apply for Adoption)* [2013] EWHC 1235 (Fam) (permission to apply for adoption was refused in respect of a fourteen-year-old boy who had been brought to the UK from Pakistan outside the immigration rules and the rules relating to adoption of a foreign child).

[212] Ibid, s 83(7).

[213] Ibid, s 83(2).

(b) Taking children out of the United Kingdom

Chapter 2 of Part 2 of the AFE Regulations applies in a situation where a person or couple wish(es) to remove a child from the United Kingdom for the purposes of adoption under the law of a non-Convention country, for cases where the United Kingdom is the state of origin of the child. This should be read in conjunction with sections 84 and 85 of the 2002 Act.

Section 84 provides that the High Court may make an order for the transfer of parental responsibility for a child to prospective adopters who are not domiciled or habitually resident in England and Wales, but who intend to adopt the child outside the British Islands.[214] Regulation 10 of the AFE Regulations, and regulation 48 in the case of a proposed Convention adoption, respectively set out the prescribed requirements which must be satisfied before an order will be made under section 84.[215] An application for an order may not be made unless at all times during the preceding ten weeks the child's home was with the applicant(s).[216]

Section 85 forbids the removal of a child who is a Commonwealth citizen or habitually resident in the United Kingdom to a place outside the British Islands for the purpose of adoption unless a section 84 order has been made conferring parental responsibility for the child on the prospective adopters.[217] A person who removes a child in contravention of section 85 is guilty of an offence.[218]

(ii) Imposition of temporary suspensions

In June 2004, the then United Kingdom Minister for Children announced the Secretary of State's decision to impose a temporary suspension of adoptions of Cambodian[219] children by United Kingdom residents.[220] The suspension was introduced in response to concerns raised and investigated by United Kingdom officials regarding the Cambodian adoption system, including, in particular, lack of proper consents being given by birth parents,[221] and improper financial gain being made by individuals involved in the adoption process.[222] The Minister announced that: "Only in exceptional circumstances will I consider that the temporary suspension should not apply in a particular case. Any decision relating to a particular case will of course take account of what is in the best interests of the child and all the facts of the particular case."[223] The suspension was reviewed between September 2007 and April 2008. The review work assessed what changes, if any, to adoption practice and legislation had been made in Cambodia in the three years since the temporary suspension was introduced. The review also took account of Cambodia's accession to the 1993 Hague Convention in April 2007.[224] However, evidence from the review demonstrated that adoption legislation, practice and

---

[214] Cf *Re A (Adoption: Placement Outside Jurisdiction)* [2004] EWCA Civ 515, [2004] 2 FLR 337.

[215] The 2002 Act, s 84(3). See *Re G (A Child) (Adoption: Placement Outside Jurisdiction)* [2008] EWCA Civ 105, [2008] WLR (D) 56.

[216] The 2002 Act, s 84(4).

[217] Cf *Re M (A Child) (Adoption: Placement outside Jurisdiction)* [2010] EWHC 1694 (Fam); and *Kent County Council v PA-K and IA (a child)* [2013] EWHC 578 (Fam).

[218] Ibid, s 85(4).

[219] Cambodia acceded to the 1993 Hague Convention on 6 April 2007 and the Convention entered into force in that jurisdiction on 1 August 2007.

[220] Hansard, 22 June 2004, cols WS61 and WS62. Concerns have been widely shared by the international community, leading a number of countries to impose suspensions: see *R (On the Application of Thomson) v Minister of State for Children* [2005] EWHC 1378, [2006] 1 FLR 175, per Munby J, at p [25].

[221] Including evidence of systematic falsification of Cambodian official documents relating to the adoption of children, and evidence relating to the procurement of children by facilitators' use of coercive tactics and financial incentives.

[222] See *R (On the Application of Thomson) v Minister of State for Children* [2005] EWHC 1378, [2006] 1 FLR 175, per Munby J, at p [23] et seq.

[223] Hansard, 22 June 2004, col WS62.

[224] See infra.

procedure in Cambodia remained insufficient to ensure the proper protection of children and their families; and that lifting the suspension would expose Cambodian children and their families to an increased risk of improper practices that are contrary to the principles of the 1993 Hague Convention and the United Nations Convention on the Rights of the Child. It was therefore decided that the suspension would remain in place.[225]

Following the precedent set by the restriction on adoptions from Cambodia, in December 2007, an immediate suspension of adoptions of Guatemalan children by UK residents was announced in response to concerns about adoption practice in Guatemala.[226]

A question of the lawfulness of the Secretary of State's conduct with regard to intercountry adoptions generally, and the Cambodian suspension, in particular, arose in *R (On the Application of Thomson) v Minister of State for Children*:[227]

> The case concerned six couples (the third[228] to fourteenth claimants) who applied for judicial review of the Secretary of State's decision to impose the temporary suspension on intercountry adoptions from Cambodia, and her subsequent decisions in each of their cases not to allow them to proceed under the "exceptional circumstances" exception. The fifteenth claimant was the adopted daughter of one of the couples, whom they had adopted from Cambodia prior to imposition of the suspension.

Munby J noted that the regime prior to 1 June 2003 for adopting children from abroad had been problematic, and sometimes productive of serious concern.[229] His Lordship outlined two notable problems: the lack of effective regulation of intercountry adoptions,[230] and a growing sense that the best interests of children were not always served by such forms of adoption.[231] The claimants did not dispute the serious nature of these concerns, but they challenged the manner in which the problems had been addressed and the decisions taken by the Secretary of State.

The claimants' applications were refused. It was held that the Secretary of State's exercise of discretion in imposing the suspension, and in denying the claimants' adoption applications was consistent with the proper exercise of her powers in the context of the statutory scheme as a whole, and that her refusal to utilise the "exceptional circumstances" procedure met every common law requirement of "fairness" and was not incompatible with Article 6 of the European Convention on Human Rights (right to a fair trial), assuming that Article 6 applied.[232] The judge considered there to be a pressing public interest that justified the introduction of the suspension without prior warning.

Given the nature and extent of the challenges to the exercise of powers by the Secretary of State in *R (On the Application of Thomson) v Minister of State for Children*, it is not surprising that the Children and Adoption Bill introduced in the House of Lords in June 2005[233] included provisions dealing with the suspension of intercountry adoptions.

---

[225] Hansard, 2 April 2008, cols WS49 and WS50.

[226] Hansard, 6 December 2007, col WS215.

[227] [2005] EWHC 1378, [2006] 1 FLR 175. See Cordery [2006] (Mar) IFL 39.

[228] The first and second claimants having withdrawn their applications.

[229] [2005] EWHC 1378, [2006] 1 FLR 175, p at [4].

[230] Criminal prosecutions under ss 11 and 57 of the Adoption Act 1976 were seldom pursued: [2005] EWHC 1378, [2006] 1 FLR 175 p at [7].

[231] Cf Parliamentary Assembly of the Council of Europe, Recommendation 1443 (2000), 26 January 2000; and UN General Assembly, Resolution 41/85, 3 December 1986.

[232] [2005] EWHC 1378, [2006] 1 FLR 175 at [192].

[233] The Children (Contact) and Adoption Bill was published in draft on 2 February 2005 for pre-legislative scrutiny by an ad hoc joint committee of both Houses of Parliament.

(iii) The Children and Adoption Act 2006[234]

Part 2 of the 2006 Act[235] concerns adoptions with a foreign element. It makes express provision for the Secretary of State to suspend intercountry adoptions from a country if he has concerns about the practices there in connection with the adoption of children by British residents[236] in specified cases.[237] If the Secretary of State has reason to believe[238] that, because of practices[239] taking place in a foreign country (whether or not it is a Convention country)[240] in connection with the adoption of children, it would be contrary to public policy to further the bringing of children into the United Kingdom, he may declare, in relation to that country, that special restrictions are to apply.[241] The special restrictions are that the appropriate authority[242] is not to take any step which otherwise might have been taken in connection with furthering the bringing of a child into the United Kingdom.[243] The effect of the imposition of restrictions is that the Secretary of State no longer will process intercountry adoptions to or from a restricted country. There is scope, however, for the restrictions to be waived, exceptionally,[244] in an individual case, if the prospective adopters can satisfy the Secretary of State that the steps in question should be taken, ie that the adoption should proceed.[245] There is an obligation on the Secretary of State to keep the list of restricted countries under review.[246] As of September 2016, there are four countries on the restricted country list: Cambodia, Guatemala, Nepal and Haiti.[247]

(c) Recognition of foreign adoptions

There may be a variety of circumstances in which a court in England is faced with the decision whether to recognise an adoption which has taken place abroad. The issue may arise incidentally in the course of other proceedings and the main examples in the reported cases

---

[234] See [2006] (Sept) IFL 120; Cordery [2006] (Mar) IFL 139; and [2005] (Mar) IFL 51.

[235] Ss 9–14. Part 1 concerns the improved facilitation and enforcement of orders with respect to children in family proceedings.

[236] Ie persons habitually resident in the British Islands: 2006 Act, s 9(10)(a).

[237] 2006 Act, s 9(2): where a British resident (a) wishes to bring, or cause another to bring, a child who is not a British resident into the United Kingdom for the purpose of adoption by the British resident and, in connection with the proposed adoption, there have been, or would have to be, proceedings in the other country or dealings with authorities or agencies there, or (b) wishes to bring, or cause another to bring, into the United Kingdom a child adopted by the British resident under an adoption effected, within the period of twelve months ending with the date of bringing in, under the law of the other country. These cases mirror the cases to which s 83 of the Adoption and Children Act 2002 (restriction on bringing children in) applies, subject to the amendment of that section by s 14 of the 2006 Act.

[238] The Secretary of State must publish reasons for making the declaration in relation to each restricted country: 2006 Act, s 9(7).

[239] Eg child trafficking, or removal of children against their parents' wishes.

[240] 2006 Act, s 9(3).

[241] Ibid, s 9(4).

[242] In a Convention case, the Central Authority (for England and Wales, the Secretary of State), and in any other case, the Secretary of State: ibid, s 11(4).

[243] Ibid, s 11(1).

[244] Eg where the child in question is a relative of the prospective adopter, or the sibling of a child already adopted by that person. See [2005] (Mar) IFL 51.

[245] 2006 Act, s 11(2).

[246] Ibid, s 10.

[247] SI 2008/1808 (Cambodia); SI 2008/1809 (Guatemala); SI 2010/951 (Nepal); and SI 2010/2265 (Haiti). The first two orders place on a statutory footing the suspension of adoptions from Cambodia and Guatemala, where adoptions had already been suspended under existing common law power. See supra pp 1220–1. See Department for Education, Adoptions: restricted list, June 2010; and Department for Education, Post-legislative assessments of the Education and Inspections Act 2006, Childcare Act 2006 and Children and Adoption Act 2006: Memorandum to the Education Committee of the House of Commons, December 2011.

concern property rights—eg whether a child adopted abroad can take under a will,[248] in an intestacy[249] or a settlement,[250] or whether a parent can succeed on his adopted child's intestacy.[251] The recognition of a foreign adoption may also affect the powers of the English court to make an adoption order itself,[252] social security issues,[253] or rights of entry to the United Kingdom as an immigrant.[254] Finally, it is possible that a child might simply wish to seek from the English courts a declaration as to his status, and thus ascertain whether his foreign adoption will be recognised in England.[255]

(i) Recognition of adoptions made elsewhere in the British Isles

Any adoption order made in Scotland,[256] Northern Ireland,[257] the Channel Islands, or the Isle of Man[258] will be recognised and given effect to in England.[259] Further, adoption records from Scotland, Northern Ireland, the Channel Islands or the Isle of Man, are receivable as evidence in England.[260]

(ii) Recognition of adoptions made in Hague Convention countries ("Convention adoptions")

As explained above, with effect from 1 June 2003, the 1993 Hague Convention on Protection of Children and Co-operation in respect of Intercountry Adoption came into force in the United Kingdom. Chapter V (Articles 23 to 27) of the Convention concerns the recognition and effects of the adoption. Recognition of an adoption includes recognition of (a) the legal parent-child relationship between the child and his adoptive parents; (b) the parental responsibility of the adoptive parents for the child; and (c) the termination of a pre-existing legal relationship between the child and his biological parents[261] (if the adoption has this effect in the Contracting State where it was made).[262] By Article 23, an adoption certified by the competent authority of the state of the adoption[263] as having been made in accordance with the Convention shall be recognised by operation of law[264] in the other Contracting States. This is one of the primary benefits of the instrument, thereby "superseding the existing practice that an adoption already granted in the State of origin is to be made anew in the receiving State only in order to produce such effects".[265] Recognition of a Convention adoption may be

---

[248] *Re Marshall* [1957] Ch 507; and see *Perpetual Trustee Co Ltd v Montuori* [1982] 1 NSWLR 710.

[249] *Re Wilson* [1954] Ch 733.

[250] *Re Valentine's Settlement* [1965] Ch 831; *Spencer's Trustees v Ruggles* 1982 SLT 165.

[251] *Re Wilby* [1956] P 174.

[252] *Re H (An Infant)* (1973) 4 Fam Law 77.

[253] Eg National Insurance Decisions Nos R(F) 1/65; R(F) 3/73.

[254] Eg *Mathieu v Entry Clearance Officer, Bridgetown* [1979–1980] Imm AR 157; *Secretary of State for the Home Department v Lofthouse* [1981] Imm AR 166. See infra, pp 1176–7.

[255] The bases on which the court will grant a declaration in relation to a foreign adoption are considered, supra, p 1043.

[256] Adoption and Children Act 2002, s 105.

[257] Ibid, s 106.

[258] Ibid, s 108.

[259] See also Adoption Act 1976, s 38(1)(c).

[260] 2002 Act, s 107 (replacing s 60 of the 1976 Act, which did not extend to the Channel Islands or the Isle of Man).

[261] Art 26.

[262] Art 27 provides that where an adoption granted in the state of origin does not have the effect of terminating a pre-existing legal parent-child relationship, it may, in the receiving state be converted into an adoption having such an effect if the law of the receiving state so permits and if relevant consents have been given. See, for England, infra, pp 1229–30 (status conferred by adoption).

[263] The state of origin, or the receiving state, depending on the circumstances of the case.

[264] Ie automatically, without the need for a procedure for recognition, enforcement or registration: see Parra-Aranguren, *Explanatory Report*, para 409.

[265] Ibid, para 402.

refused in a Contracting State only if the adoption is manifestly contrary to its public policy, taking into account the best interests of the child.[266]

The question as to the persons who could be prospective adoptive parents was discussed at length during negotiations, in particular whether the Convention should cover adoptions applied for by unmarried heterosexual couples, or by same sex persons, living as a couple or individually. The Parra-Aranguren Report states that:

> Notwithstanding the fact that these cases were thoroughly examined, the problems they raise may be qualified as false problems, since the State of origin and the receiving State shall collaborate from the very beginning and they may refuse the agreement for the adoption to continue, for instance, because of the personal conditions of the prospective adoptive parents. Moreover, in case they agree to those specific kinds of adoption, the other Contracting States are entitled to refuse its recognition on public policy grounds, as permitted by Article 24.[267]

Interestingly, the Parra-Aranguren Report notes that:

> The Convention does not specifically answer the question as to whether an adoption granted in a Contracting State and falling within its scope of application, but not in accordance with the Convention's rules, could be recognized by another Contracting State whose internal laws permit such recognition. Undoubtedly, in such a case, the Contracting State granting the adoption is violating the Convention, because its provisions are mandatory and such conduct may give rise to the complaint permitted by Article 33,[268] but the question of the recognition would be outside of the Convention and the answer should depend on the law applicable in the recognizing State, always taking into account the best interests of the child.[269]

Recognition in England of an adoption granted in a Contracting State which falls outside the scope of application of the Convention must be dealt with according to residual national rules.[270]

(iii) Recognition of adoptions made in designated countries ("overseas adoptions")

The adoption of a child[271] effected in a country[272] or territory outside the British Islands which is included in the United Kingdom's list of designated countries, as set out in the Adoption (Recognition of Overseas Adoptions) Order 2013,[273] and which is effected under the law in force in that place,[274] is known as an overseas adoption.[275] Overseas adoptions do not include Convention adoptions.[276] The recognition of this wide range of foreign adoptions is not dependent, in any way, on reciprocity between England and the "overseas adoption" country.

Overseas adoption orders, being those of a description specified in the 2013 Order, are recognised automatically in England, and have the same incidents and effects as if they were

---

[266] Art 24. See also *Singh (Pawandeep) v Entry Clearance Officer (New Delhi)* [2004] EWCA Civ 1075, [2005] QB 608.

[267] Parra-Aranguren, *Explanatory Report*, para 79.

[268] Concerning failure to respect the provisions of the Convention.

[269] Parra-Aranguren, *Explanatory Report*, para 411.

[270] For England, infra, pp 1225–9.

[271] A person who has not attained the age of eighteen years: Adoption and Children Act 2002, s 144(1).

[272] Which may, or may not, also be a Hague Convention Contracting State.

[273] SI 2013/1801, Sch 1, para 1. For Scotland see Adoption (Recognition of Overseas Adoptions) (Scotland) Regulations, SI 2013/310, Sch 1, para 1.

[274] The reference to "law" does not include customary or common law, meaning that the overseas adoption must be effected by means of legislative provision: SI 2013/1801, art 2(2).

[275] SI 2013/1801, art 2(1). Sometimes known also as a "designated country adoption".

[276] 2002 Act, s 87(1)(b).

made in England. Section 87 of the 2002 Act allows the Secretary of State to prescribe the requirements that must be met before a country will be included in the list of designated countries. Curiously, the only requirement for recognition appears to be that the adoption is effected under the law in force in the designated country; there is no scope for reviewing or challenging the jurisdiction of the country which effected the overseas adoption. There is no necessary link, such as is required in English law,[277] between the country where the adoption is effected and the adoptive parents.

Evidence that an overseas order has been effected may be given by the production of a document purporting to be a certified copy of any entry made, in accordance with the law of the country concerned, in a public register of adoptions, or of an adoption certificate signed, or purporting to be signed, by an authorised person.[278]

(iv) Annulment, etc of overseas or Hague Convention adoptions

Section 89 of the 2002 Act provides for the High Court to annul a Convention adoption or Convention adoption order on the ground that the adoption is contrary to public policy.[279] In particular, an intercountry adoption which has come about in circumstances in which little or no regard has been paid to the best interests of the child must be viewed with great caution.[280] Similarly, the High Court, on application, may provide for an overseas adoption or determination under section 91 of the 2002 Act to cease to be valid on the ground that it is contrary to public policy. An application for a section 89 order must be made within two years of the date on which the adoption (Convention or overseas) to which it relates was made.[281] Regulation 34 of the AFE Regulations provides that where a Convention adoption order or a Convention adoption is annulled under section 89, and the Secretary of State receives a copy of the order from the court, it must forward a copy to the Central Authority of the state of origin. The effect of any annulment is that the adoption will cease to have effect in the United Kingdom. Section 89(4) makes clear that except as provided for by section 89, the validity of a Convention adoption or overseas adoption order, or determination under section 91, cannot be called in question in proceedings in any court in England.

(v) Recognition of adoptions made in other foreign countries

The statutory recognition rules considered in relation to Convention adoptions and overseas adoptions are in addition to, and not in substitution for, the common law rules of recognition.[282] If an "overseas adoption" is denied recognition under the statutory rules because, for example, it was made under customary law, it may still be possible for the adoption to be recognised or given effect under the common law rules for recognition. Furthermore, although the list of countries whose adoptions have been included under the definition of

---

[277] Infra, p 1225 et seq.

[278] SI 2013/1801, art 3(1).

[279] See 1993 Convention, Art 24.

[280] Though there may be cases where, although the order in question was made without regard to the best interests of the child, it could be seen, with hindsight, that adoption was in fact in the child's best interests, and that a family relationship sufficient to be recognised as family life had developed: *Singh (Pawandeep) v Entry Clearance Officer (New Delhi)* [2004] EWCA Civ 1075, [2005] QB 608.

[281] Family Procedure Rules, SI 2010/2955, r 14.22.

[282] Adoption and Children Act 2002, s 66(1)(e). For recent examples of foreign adoption orders recognised under the common law rules see *D v D (Foreign Adoption)* [2008] EWHC 403 (Fam); *Re N (Recognition of Foreign Adoption Order)* [2010] 1 FLR. 1102; [2010] Fam. Law 12; *Re T and M (Adoption)* [2010] EWHC 964 (Fam); *Re R (Recognition of Indian Adoption)* [2012] EWHC 2956 (Fam); *Re J (Recognition of Foreign Adoption Order)* [2012] EWHC 3353 (Fam); *Z v Z (Recognition of Brazilian Adoption Order)* [2013] EWHC 747 (Fam); and *Re G (Recognition of Brazilian Adoption)* [2014] EWHC 2605 (Fam). Cf *A County Council v M & Others (No 4) (Foreign Adoption: Refusal of Recognition)* [2013] EWHC 1501 (Fam).

overseas adoptions is extensive, it is not world-wide. In the case of such other countries[283] and "overseas adoptions" which, as has just been seen, fall outside the legislative rules, as well as those adoptions which have been effected in Convention countries but which fall outside the scope of application of the Convention, it is necessary to have resort to the common law recognition rules, to which we now turn.

The question of the extent to which, at common law, the English courts will recognise and give effect to an adoption order made abroad is of much less significance in the light of the statutory recognition provisions. It is still, however, of importance as evidenced also by the recent surge in the reported case-law on the topic.[284] The leading case on this subject is *Re Valentine's Settlement*.[285] The facts were these:

> A British subject, domiciled in what was then Southern Rhodesia, in 1946 made an English settlement of a fund on trust for her son, Alastair, for life and then to his children. Alastair had married only once and had one child, Simon, by the marriage. He and his wife had adopted two other children—Carol in 1939 and Timothy in 1944. These adoptions took place in South Africa where, at the date of their respective adoptions, Carol and Timothy were domiciled. Under the law of Southern Rhodesia an adoption order could not be made in respect of any child who was not resident and domiciled there: so no Southern Rhodesian adoption order was made. Alastair and his wife were themselves domiciled and resident in Southern Rhodesia at all material times, and Alastair died domiciled there in 1962 without having exercised a power of appointment under the settlement. The trustees issued a summons to determine whether the trust fund devolved on Simon or equally among Simon, Carol and Timothy.

The fundamental question was as to whether the two adopted children were "children" of Alastair within the meaning of the settlement. The Court of Appeal by a majority answered this question in the negative. The whole Court was clearly prepared to countenance the recognition of foreign adoptions in some circumstances.[286] Lord Denning MR stated: "But when is the status of adoption duly constituted? Clearly it is so when it is constituted in another country in similar circumstances as we claim for ourselves. Our courts should recognise a jurisdiction which mutatis mutandis they claim for themselves: see Travers v Holley. We claim jurisdiction to make an adoption order when the adopting parents are domiciled in this country and the child is resident here. So also, out of the comity of nations, we should recognise an adoption order made by another country when the adopting parents are domiciled there and the child is resident there."[287] It was held, however, that the South African adoptions could not be recognised in the instant case because the adopting parents were not domiciled in South Africa.[288]

The test for recognition of a foreign adoption at common law set out in *Re Valentine's Settlement* has recently been re-visited and refined by the High Court. In *Re T and M (Adoption)*[289]

---

[283] Cf *Re H (An Infant)* (1973) 4 Fam Law 77.

[284] See supra and infra.

[285] [1965] Ch 831; and see National Insurance Decisions Nos R(F) 1/65; R(F) 3/73.

[286] The earlier contrary decision in *Re Wilby* [1956] P 174 was said to have been wrongly decided.

[287] [1965] Ch 831 at 842; and see National Insurance Decision No R(F) 1/65; *Perpetual Trustee Co Ltd v Montuori* [1982] 1 NSWLR 710; *R v Secretary of State for the Home Department, ex p Brassey* [1989] FCR 423, [1989] 2 FLR 486; *Patel v Visa Officer, Bombay* [1990] Imm AR 297; *MF v An Bord Vehtala* [1991] ILRM 399.

[288] It was further held that, even if the South African adoptions were to be recognised, Carol and Timothy would be treated in English law (the law governing the settlement) as if they had been adopted in England. They would, therefore, be unable to take as the settlement was made before 1 January 1950, and English adopted children by virtue of s 5(2) of the Adoption of Children Act 1926 would have had no rights under it.

[289] [2010] EWHC 964 (Fam), at para [12].

Hedley J set out the test for recognition as follows: First, was the adoption order obtained wholly lawfully in the foreign jurisdiction? Second, if it was, did the concept of adoption in that jurisdiction substantially conform to the English concept of adoption? Third, if so, is there any public policy consideration that should mitigate against recognition? Hedley J reaffirmed these criteria in *Re R (Recognition of Indian Adoption)*[290] while stressing the second condition—ie whether the requirements of adoption law in the foreign jurisdiction were sufficiently similar to those in English adoption law, currently to be found in s 49(2) of the Adoption and Children Act 2002.[291]

In the latter case his Lordship also addressed the jurisdiction requirements for recognition as laid down in *Re Valentine's Settlement*.[292] He noted that the rationale in *Re Valentine* was that an adoption order would be recognised only if the conditions that existed in foreign jurisdiction were such that would permit an English court to make an adoption order. His Lordship highlighted the fact that since *Re Valentine* there had been material changes in English law. Firstly, the Domicile and Matrimonial Proceedings Act 1973[293] has abolished the concept of spousal unity of domicile so it is now possible for married partners to have different domiciles. In contrast, when *Re Valentine* was decided the wife would have had a dependent Southern Rhodesian domicile. Secondly, English domestic law has been changed by the Adoption and Children Act 2002 which does not require both applicants to be domiciled in England; instead, pursuant to section 49(2) of the Act, it suffices if only one of the applicants is domiciled in a part of the British Islands. Alternatively, the qualifying conditions for adoption will be met if both applicants have been habitually resident in a part of the British Islands for a period of not less than one year ending with the date of the application.[294] Equivalent conditions of domicile or twelve-month habitual residence must be met by the applicant in case of adoption by one person.[295] Hedley J then rightly observed that *Re Valentine* had to be interpreted in the light of the aforementioned changes. On the facts of *Re R (Recognition of Indian Adoption)*[296] this meant that the requirement of *Re Valentine* was met even though only the father had been domiciled in the foreign jurisdiction (India). It followed that the court had jurisdiction to recognise the Indian adoption.[297] The second limb of s 49 of the 2002 Act (ie habitual residence as the connecting factor) was relied upon[298] in *Z v Z (Recognition of Brazilian Adoption Order)*.[299] In the instant case, Theis J found that jurisdiction of the English court to recognise a Brazilian adoption order existed on the basis of the sole adopter mother's habitual residence in Brazil during the twelve months preceding the adoption.[300]

---

[290] [2012] EWHC 2956 (Fam), at para [12].

[291] The test was applied in a number of subsequent cases—eg *Re J (Recognition of Foreign Adoption Order)* [2012] EWHC 3353 (Fam); *Z v Z (Recognition of Brazilian Adoption Order)* [2013] EWHC 747 (Fam); and *Re G (Recognition of Brazilian Adoption)* [2014] EWHC 2605 (Fam). In *A County Council v M and Others (No 4) (Foreign Adoption: Refusal of Recognition)* [2013] EWHC 1501 (Fam) Jackson J added a further requirement, ie that the adoption is in the best interests of the child. Ibid, at para [61]. This additional condition is, however, not supported by other authority.

[292] Ie that the minimum requirement for recognition was that both applicants were domiciled in the country in which the order was made and that the child was resident there.

[293] S 1.

[294] Adoption and Children Act 2002, s 49(3).

[295] Ibid, s 49(1) and (2).

[296] [2012] EWHC 2956 (Fam).

[297] Ibid, at para [21].

[298] Although with no reference to the principles set out in *Re Valentine* and re-interpreted by Hedley J in *Re R (Recognition of Indian Adoption)* [2012] EWHC 2956 (Fam).

[299] [2013] EWHC 747 (Fam).

[300] Ibid, at para [38]. See also *Re G (Recognition of Brazilian Adoption)* [2014] EWHC 2605 (Fam) where Cobb J found that both limbs of s 49 were met simultaneously as the sole adopter mother had been domiciled and was also, for the twelve months preceding the adoption, habitually resident in Brazil. Ibid, at para [24].

The recent authorities show that, in line with the jurisdictional requirements contained in s 49 of the 2002 Act, it is no longer required that the child be resident in the country where the adoption was effected.[301] The confirmation that the legal principles for recognition of foreign adoptions as laid down by the Court of Appeal in *Re Valentine* should follow the changes in the jurisdictional rules for adoption is plausible; nevertheless, two issues still warrant a brief comment. The first is whether it is right to concentrate exclusively on the domicile of the adopters and ignore the domicile of the child or of the natural parents. The view was expressed obiter by Lord Denning MR[302] that it would not have been neces- sary to show in addition that the children were domiciled in South Africa at the time of the adoptions.[303] There is no agreement on the question among foreign legal systems. In some, the personal law of the child governs; in others, the personal law of the adopters is preferred; but in many, the doctrine of cumulation prevails by which the personal law of all three parties must be satisfied.[304] Whilst one may argue that the only law to pronounce on status is that of the domicile, the jurisdiction of the English court is based on the domicile or habitual residence of the prospective adopters—that of the child and the bio- logical parents is ignored. It seems reasonable to recognise a foreign jurisdiction exercised in similar circumstances. There is no justification, by analogy with English jurisdictional rules, for looking especially to the domicile of the biological[305] rather than the adoptive parents.[306] If the domicile or habitual residence of the prospective adopters is accepted as the main jurisdictional criterion for recognition, then it is suggested that, on the analogy of the common law rule for divorce recognition in *Armitage v A-G*,[307] an adoption should be recognised in England as conferring the status of child of the adopted person if recognised in the country (or countries) of the adopters' domicile or habitual residence, even though actually effected elsewhere.[308]

Secondly, it is not clear whether the English courts will be prepared to recognise foreign adop- tions in wider circumstances such as those where, *mutatis mutandis*, an English court could not have jurisdiction, but where there was a "real and substantial connection" with the foreign court.[309]

We have seen that the statutory rules relating to the recognition of overseas adoptions and Convention adoptions provide that such adoptions may be denied recognition on grounds of public policy.[310] Public policy is similarly relevant to the recognition of foreign adoptions at common law.[311] Adoption law in other countries may be very different from English law, as,

---

[301] That criterion was relied on in *Re Valentine's Settlement* because at that time there was a similar require- ment for the jurisdiction of the English courts. In particular, it was required that the adoptive parents be resident and domiciled in England and the child be resident in England. See Adoption Act 1950, ss 1(1) and 2(5).

[302] [1965] Ch 831 at 842–3.

[303] Residence would have sufficed. See supra. This was approved in *Re B (S) (An Infant)* [1968] Ch 204 at 209–10.

[304] Mann (1941) 57 LQR 112, 123; Wolff, op cit, 398; Jones (1956) 5 ICLQ 205, 210–219. For a fuller discussion, see de Nova (1961) III Hague Recueil 75, 153; Lipstein (1963) 12 ICLQ 835.

[305] See *Re G (Foreign Adoption: Consent)* [1995] 2 FLR 534.

[306] Cf [1965] Ch 831 at 854.

[307] [1906] P 135, supra, pp 1006–7.

[308] Some support for this may be drawn from *Re Valentine's Settlement* [1965] Ch 226 at 234, at first instance; and see ibid at 855.

[309] Cf *Indyka v Indyka* [1969] 1 AC 33; North (1968) 31 MLR 257, 280–281.

[310] Supra, p 1222 et seq.

[311] See *Re C (A Child) (Foreign Adoption: Natural Mother's Consent: Service)* [2006] 1 FLR 318; and *A County Council v M & Others (No 4) (Foreign Adoption: Refusal of Recognition)* [2013] EWHC 1501 (Fam), at para [83].

for example, with the adoption of adults and married persons.[312] Whilst great caution should be exercised in denying recognition on public policy grounds,[313] the courts have power to do so both in relation to the incidents of the adoption, such as whether the child can succeed to the adoptive parents, and, in an extreme case, to the adoption's effect on the status of the parties, ie as to whether the parent and child relationship has been created at all.[314]

If a child is adopted from a country which is neither a Hague Convention country, nor on the United Kingdom list of designated countries in the 2013 Order, and the English court refuses to recognise the foreign adoption at common law, an adoption order will require to be made in England, under the Adoption and Children Act 2002, following the child's entry to the United Kingdom, ie there must be "re-adoption" in England, dependent upon the prospective adopter satisfying a registered adoption agency that he is eligible and suitable to adopt a child from abroad.

(d) Effect of foreign adoptions

(i) Status conferred by adoption

Section 67 of the Adoption and Children Act 2002 provides that, with effect from the date of adoption,[315] an adopted person is to be treated in law as if born as the child of the adopter. An adopted person is the legitimate child of the adopter and, if adopted by a couple, or one of a couple under section 51(2), is to be treated as the child of the relationship of the couple in question.[316] The effect of the adoption is not determined by the law of the country of adoption.[317] If, for example, a child, adopted in New York, claims to succeed to the movable property of an adoptive parent dying domiciled in England, the adoption will be recognised and the child will, under English law as the law governing succession, have the same rights as an English adopted child.[318] This rule applies to succession, testate and intestate. It is important, however, to distinguish between the question of recognition and the determination of, for example, the succession rights of an adopted child once his status has been recognised. This latter issue should be determined by the appropriate law to govern matters of succession.[319] This means that the provisions of the 2002 Act, giving a child whose foreign adoption is recognised in England the same succession rights as an English adopted child, are relevant only if English law governs the succession. If the law governing the succession is foreign, it will be for that law to decide whether, and if so what, succession rights are given to an adopted child, even though the adoption is recognised in England.

Section 88 of the 2002 Act provides that the operation of section 67 may be modified in relation to Hague Convention adoptions. Where the High Court is satisfied that the conditions in section 88(2) have been met,[320] it may direct that section

---

[312] Eg *Ehrenclou v MacDonald* 12 Cal Rptr 3d 411 (Cal App 2004)—adult adoptees, discussed by Symeonides (2004) 52 AJCL 919, 986.

[313] The European Court of Human Rights has held that the rules on the recognition of foreign adoptions have to be compliant with the European Convention on Human Rights. See *Wagner v Luxembourg* [2007] ECHR 76240/01, and *Negrepontis-Giannisis v Greece* [2011] ECHR 56759/08. See, generally, Fawcett, Ní Shúilleabháin and Shah, *Human Rights and Private International Law* (2016), paras 14.72–14.87.

[314] *Re Valentine's Settlement* [1965] Ch 831 at 842, 854; *Bouton v Labiche* (1994) 33 NSWLR 225.

[315] 2002 Act, s 67(5).

[316] 2002 Act, s 67(2).

[317] *R v Secretary of State for the Home Department, ex p Brassey* [1989] FCR 423, [1989] 2 FLR 486.

[318] See the Family Law Reform Act 1987, ss 1 (as amended by the 2002 Act, Sch 3, para 51), 18 and 19 (as amended by the 2002 Act, Sch 3, para 52). See, in Scotland, *Salvesen's Trs* 1993 SC 14.

[319] See *Re Valentine's Settlement* [1965] Ch 831 at 843–5, rejecting suggestions to the contrary in *Re Marshall* [1957] Ch 507.

[320] Namely, under the law of the country in which the adoption was effected, the adoption is not a full adoption; the consents referred to in Art 4(c) and (d) of the 1993 Convention have not been given for a full

67(3)[321] does not apply or does not apply to any extent specified in the direction, ie that the order does not have the effect of "full adoption".[322] The reason for this provision[323] stems from the fact that the United Kingdom recognises only "full adoption", in terms of which all legal ties between the child and his biological parents are severed, whereas some countries have other forms of adoption, known as "simple adoption" or "limited adoption", whereby not all ties between the child and his/her biological parents are severed. Article 26 of the 1993 Hague Convention provides for recognition of full and simple adoptions, and Article 27 allows a receiving state to convert a simple adoption into a full adoption if its law so permits, and provided the biological parents and relevant parties[324] give their consent to a full adoption.

(ii) British citizenship and immigration

(a) Adoption orders made in the United Kingdom

An adoption order made in a United Kingdom court (including, for this purpose, the Channel Islands and the Isle of Man) automatically confers British citizenship on the child if the adopter, or one of the adopters, is a British citizen on the date on which the adoption order is made.[325]

(b) Convention adoptions

A final adoption order under the Hague Convention, wherever made, will confer British citizenship on the child if the adopter (or one of them in the event of a joint adoption) is a British citizen and if the adopter was habitually resident in the United Kingdom on the date on which the Convention adoption is effected.[326] This ensures, in this respect at least, parity of treatment between Convention adoptions and adoption orders made in the United Kingdom. In *Re B (A Minor) (Adoption Order: Nationality)*[327] the House of Lords held that, in determining an adoption application, the judge was entitled to have regard to all the circumstances of the case, including the views of the Home Office on immigration policy, but that:

> In cases in which it appears to the judge that adoption would confer real benefits upon the child during its childhood, it is very unlikely that general considerations of "maintaining an effective and consistent immigration policy" could justify the refusal of an order. The two kinds of consideration are hardly commensurable so as to be capable of being weighed in the balance against each other.[328]

When a Convention order in consequence of which any person became a British citizen by virtue of section 1(5) of the British Nationality Act 1981 ceases to have effect, whether on

---

adoption or the United Kingdom is not the receiving state; and it would be more favourable to the adopted child for a direction to be given under s 88(1).

[321] Whereby an adopted person is to be treated in law as not being the child of any person other than the adopter(s).

[322] Ie, one by virtue of which the child is to be treated in law as not being the child of any person other than the adopter: s 88(3).

[323] See Explanatory Notes to the 2002 Act, paras 229 and 230.

[324] 1993 Hague Convention, Art 4.

[325] British Nationality Act 1981, s 1(5)(a).

[326] Ibid, ss 1(5)(b) and (5A) ("acquisition by adoption").

[327] [1999] 2 AC 136.

[328] Ibid, per Lord Hoffman, at 141, distinguishing *Re K (A Minor) (Adoption Order: Nationality)* [1995] Fam 38. Cf *D v D (Foreign Adoption)* [2008] EWHC 403 (Fam), at para [17]; *Re G (Recognition of Brazilian Adoption)* [2014] EWHC 2605 (Fam) at paras [50]–[55]; and *ASB and KBS v MQS (Secretary of State for the Home Department Intervening)* [2009] EWHC 2491 (Fam). See also *SK (India) v Secretary of State for the Home Department* [2007] Imm A R 142.

annulment[329] or otherwise, the cesser shall not affect the status of that person as a British citizen.[330]

(c) Overseas adoptions

Overseas adoptions do not result in the automatic granting of British citizenship to the adopted child. An application for British citizenship must be submitted in respect of the child, and registration as such is at the discretion of the Secretary of State.[331]

(d) Immigration[332]

British citizens are not subject to control under United Kingdom immigration legislation, but they must be able to prove their status when seeking admission to the United Kingdom. Except where a child is a British citizen, or is a national of another European Economic Area country, he will require entry clearance under United Kingdom immigration rules before travelling to the United Kingdom.[333] Where a prospective adopter is not a British citizen, he must have indefinite leave to remain in the United Kingdom to be able to sponsor an entry clearance application in respect of a child.

---

[329] Supra, p 1225.

[330] British Nationality Act 1981, s 1(6).

[331] Ibid, s 3(1).

[332] See eg *MN (India) v Entry Clearance Officer (New Delhi)* [2008] EWCA Civ 38 (interrelationship between a refusal of entry to the UK to a child adopted by British residents in India and the child's rights under Article 8 of the ECHR); *D v D (Foreign Adoption)* [2008] EWHC 403 (Fam); *Re IH (A Child) (Permission to Apply for Adoption)* [2013] EWHC 1235 (Fam); and *Re G (Recognition of Brazilian Adoption)* [2014] EWHC 2605 (Fam).

[333] For detailed information, see UK Government, Department for Education, Department for Education, "A Guide to Intercountry Adoption for UK Residents", February 2011.

28

MENTAL INCAPACITY

1. Introduction	1232	(e)	Co-Operation among Hague Convention Contracting States	1244
2. Mental Capacity Act 2005	1233	3.	Cases Outside the Mental Capacity Act	1245
(a) Concept	1233	(a)	Jurisdiction	1245
(b) Jurisdiction	1235	(b)	Choice of law	1246
(c) Choice of law	1238	(c)	Recognition and enforcement of protective measures taken abroad	1246
(d) Recognition and enforcement of protective measures taken abroad	1242			

1. INTRODUCTION

The increased mobility, medical development, lengthening of lifespan and corresponding rise of age-related illness, such as Alzheimer's disease, make the protection of mentally incapacitated adults a special issue in private international law. A mentally incapacitated person may be present in one country but habitually resident in another when measures of protection are needed; this person may own property situated in a country different from his present location or habitual residence that needs to be dealt with; he might have made advanced arrangements for his personal care and it is questionable whether this arrangement will be respected in a different country. All these examples generate private international law problems. It will be necessary to decide when an English court has jurisdiction to order protective measures over a mentally disordered person or over his property, such as the detention of this person or management of his property and affairs, and what law is to be applied in such circumstances. If a person has made an arrangement or medical directive in advance, which law should govern its validity and enforceability. The extent to which the English courts will recognise the measures of protection ordered by a foreign court or under foreign law will also need to be determined.

English private international law in this area was underdeveloped before the enforcement of the Mental Capacity Act 2005.[1] The old system combines common law and statutory supplements of Parts VI and VII of the Mental Health Act 1983 and the Enduring Powers of Attorney Act 1985.[2] The rules, however, are far from comprehensive.[3] The situation is significantly improved by the Mental Capacity Act 2005. Section 63 (international protection of adults) and Schedule 3 to the Act give effect in England and Wales to the Convention on the International Protection of Adults signed at The Hague on 13 January 2000.[4] The Hague Convention protects adults who, as a result of impairment or insufficiency of personal faculties, cannot protect their own interests.[5]

---

[1] The 2005 Act extends only to England and Wales. For Scotland, see the Adults with Incapacity (Scotland) Act 2000, and the Mental Health (Care and Treatment) (Scotland) Act 2003.

[2] 2005 Act, ss 66 and 67; Sch 5, Parts 1 and 2; and Sch 6.

[3] *Dicey, Morris and Collins: Conflict of Laws* (2016) paras 21-002, 21-106.

[4] See generally P Lagarde, *Explanatory Report on the 2000 Hague Protection of Adults Convention.*

[5] Art 1; and 2005 Act, Sch 3, para 4. For history and background of the Hague Convention, see A R Fagan, "An Analysis of the Convention on the International Protection of Adults", (2002) 10 The Elder Law Journal 229, 331–8.

The Convention lays down rules of jurisdiction, for determining the state(s) whose authorities can take measures directed to the protection of the person and/or property of such adults;[6] of applicable law;[7] of recognition and enforcement of measures for the protection of adults;[8] and of co-operation among Contracting States.[9]

The Hague Convention on the International Protection of Adults entered into force from 1 January 2009.[10] It has been ratified by the UK in 2003 but only extends to Scotland.[11] Nevertheless, section 63 and Schedule 3 to the Mental Capacity Act 2005 incorporate the Convention in English domestic law. Both section 63 and Schedule 3 have taken effect from 1 October 2007 save certain provisions which came into effect only after the Convention entered into force.[12] Since the Hague Convention came into force on 1 January 2009, these reserved provisions came into force in England and Wales from the same date. Therefore, although the UK ratification of the Convention does not extend to England and Wales, it now has full effect in England and Wales.[13] Furthermore, since the Convention is incorporated in English law, it applies as part of English domestic law in all cases irrespective of whether the other relevant country is a Convention contracting state.[14] From this perspective, the Convention may have even greater impact in England and Wales than the countries that have ratified it.

After the 2005 Act entered into force, private international law provided in Schedule 3 of the Act applies to most cases concerning protective measures over a person or his property in international situations. However, the old rules prior to the enforcement of the 2005 Act are not completely extinguished and continue to apply in cases falling outside the scope of Schedule 3 of the 2005 Act.

2. MENTAL CAPACITY ACT 2005

(a) Concept

(i) Adult

Schedule 3 of the 2005 Act applies to protect an "adult", which is defined as a person over sixteen who "as a result of an impairment or insufficiency of his personal faculties, cannot protect his interests".[15] This definition directly implements the definition in the Convention.[16] The Convention deliberately avoids the judicial term of "incapacity", but adopts a factual description of the adult that is vulnerable and needs special protection.[17] This definition makes "adult" a question of fact and avoids the applicable law problem.

---

[6] Art 2(a); also Arts 3 and 4. The Convention rules on jurisdiction are laid down in Chapter II (Arts 5–12).

[7] Chapter III (Arts 13–21).

[8] Chapter IV (Arts 22–27).

[9] Chapter V (Arts 28–37).

[10] The Convention has been ratified by Austria, Czech Republic, Estonia, Finland, France, Germany, Monaco, Switzerland and United Kingdom.

[11] The UK has made such declaration under Article 55 of the Convention.

[12] 2005 Act, s 68; Mental Capacity Act 2005 (Commencement No 2) Order, SI 2007/1987, art 2 (1) (b). These provisions are provided in para 35 of Sch 3, including paras 8 (jurisdiction in relation to non resident), 9 (jurisdiction in relation to convention countries), 19(2) and (5)(protective measures made by convention countries), Part 5 (cooperation with convention countries), and para 30 (Article 38 certificates given by convention countries).

[13] See discussion in D Hill, "The Hague Convention on the International Protection of Adults", (2009) 58 ICLQ 469, 473.

[14] *Re M*, [2011] EWHC 3590 (COP), para 2.

[15] Sch 3, para 4.

[16] Sch 3, para 4. Cf. Hague Convention, Arts 1(1) and 2.

[17] Lagarde, *Explanatory Report*, para 9.

Definition of "adult" includes two conditions. Firstly, adults who fall within the scope of Schedule 3 are those suffering from impairment or insufficiency of personal faculties. The Convention does not accept the view that only mental incapacity that hampers decision-making would qualify for protection.[18] Impairment or insufficiency can be physical or mental, as well as age-related diseases, such as Alzheimer's disease.[19] Therefore, the Convention, and Schedule 3 of the Act, protects a broader scope of adults than simply mentally incapacitated adults.[20] There is no consensus as to whether the impairment and insufficiency must fall within the medical concept. Uncertainty might exist concerning gambling or drug addiction, alcoholism, eating disorder, squandering, prodigality and age. It has been argued by some that if these conditions do not fall within medical impairment, they will not usually put a person in the need of the Conventional protection.[21] This opinion may be criticised for being uncertain and restrictive. It is not always easy to determine if certain conditions fall within the medical concept or not. It is also argued that the purpose of the Convention is to protect all vulnerable adults who lack capacity to protect their interests regardless of how the vulnerability is caused.[22] Other commentators argue that the Convention was drafted particularly bearing in mind the need to protect the elderly. It thus should include all elderly who suffer from any impairment and cannot protect their interests, even if these impairments do not result from clear-cut diseases.[23] The requirement of a medical condition, as a result, should not be relevant.

Such impairment and insufficiency must prevent the adult from protecting his interests, including personal, health and physical interests.[24] Ability to protect one's interests is clearly broader than ability to make decisions or communicate.[25]

Both conditions must be present. Therefore, not all disabled persons are qualified "adults" in Schedule 3 if such disability may not hamper their ability to protect their interests. A person may lose a limb or an organ, for example, but is still competent to protect his interests. Equally, not all persons that cannot protect their interests are such "adults", if not caused by impaired faculties, such as vulnerable women facing threat of any kind of violence from society or their family.[26]

The scope of Schedule 3 is broader than the scope of the Mental Capacity Act 2005, which states that "a person lacks capacity in relation to a matter if at the material time he is unable to make a decision for himself in relation to the matter because of an impairment of, or a disturbance in the functioning of, the mind or brain".[27] This definition addresses the nature of incapacity, i.e. unable to make a decision, and the subject of the impairment, i.e. must be the mind or brain. Neither is required for an "adult" protected for the private international law purpose in Schedule 3. Schedule 3, and therefore, covers a wider range of adults not protected under the 2005 Act.

---

[18] Ibid. J Long, "Rethinking Vulnerable Adult's Protection in the Light of the 2000 Hague Convention", (2013) 27 International Journal of Law, Policy and the Family 51, 61–2.

[19] Lagarde, *Explanatory Report,* para 9.

[20] Committee of Ministers of the Council of Europe "On Principles Concerning Legal Protection of Incapable Adults" (adopted on 23 February 1999) para 4.

[21] Long, 62; Report of the Special Commission (3–12 September 1997).

[22] Long, 63; A Borras, "Una nueva etapa en la protecció'n internacional de adultos" (2000) 2 Geriatrianet 3.

[23] Fagan, 339.

[24] Lagarde, *Explanatory Report,* para 10.

[25] Lagarde, *Explanatory Report,* para 9. Long, 61–2.

[26] Lagarde, *Explanatory Report,* paras 9 and 10.

[27] 2005 Act, s 2.

(ii) Protective measures

Schedule 3 addresses private international law questions of issuing and enforcing a protective measure, which is defined as "a measure directed to the protection of the person or property of an adult".[28] Paragraph 5(1) of the Schedule 3 also provides a non-exhaustive list of different types of measures of protection covered in this Schedule. Protective measures may include: (a) the determination of incapacity and the institution of a protective regime; (b) placing an adult under the protection of an appropriate authority; (c) guardianship, curatorship or any corresponding system; (d) the designation and functions of a person having charge of the adult's person or property, or representing or otherwise helping him; (e) placing the adult in a place where protection can be provided; (f) administering, conserving or disposing of the adult's property; and (g) authorising a specific intervention for the protection of the person or property of the adult.[29] Protective measures only cover judicial or administrative measures, and exclude measures imposed by medical professionals or care institutes.

(b) Jurisdiction

Under the 2005 Act,[30] a new Court of Protection, being a superior court of record, replaces the Court of Protection, being an office of the Supreme Court, which operates under the 1983 Act.[31] For England and Wales, Schedule 3 to the 2005 Act, in Part 2, establishes the rules of jurisdiction of the Court of Protection.[32] The Court of Protection may exercise jurisdiction under the Act in six circumstances.[33] These jurisdiction grounds incorporate Articles 5-11 of the Hague Convention and should be interpreted taking into account the Convention and its explanatory report.

(i) Habitual residence in England

Firstly, the English court can take protective measures in relation to an adult habitually resident in England.[34] This is the primary jurisdiction ground and grants the Court of Protection general jurisdiction to take any measures of protection of person and of property.[35] The concept of "habitual residence" under the Act is no different from that in other contexts, in particularly the concept in the Hague Convention on the Civil Aspects of International Child Abduction and Brussels II bis.[36] Two issues, however, need to be addressed. Firstly, where an adult loses capacity to decide where to live, the decision is conferred on his relative or carer under the doctrine of necessity and there is no need for any formal process, judicial or administrative.[37] The doctrine of necessity requires the decision to be reasonable, arrived at in good faith and taken in the best interests of the vulnerable adult.[38] A decision is held wrongful and failing the necessity test if someone abducts the adult; removes him in breach of a court order;[39] or breaches authority granted in the adult's

---

[28] 2005 Act, Sch 3, para 5(1).

[29] Sch 3, para 5(1).

[30] Pt 2.

[31] Ss 45 and 46.

[32] Under s 21 of the 2005 Act, the Lord Chancellor may order the transfer of proceedings relating to a person under 18 years from the Court of Protection to a court having jurisdiction under the Children Act 1989, or vice versa.

[33] Sch 3, para 7(1).

[34] Sch 3, para 7(1)(a).

[35] This effect is not expressly stated in para 7(1)(a) of Schedule 3 but is provided in Art 5 of the Hague Convention.

[36] *An English Local Authority v SW* [2014] EWCOP 43, para 64.

[37] *Re O* [2014] 3 WLR 453, para 18.

[38] *Re O* [2014] 3 WLR 453, para 18; *Re F (Mental Patient: Sterilisation)* [1990] 2 AC 1; *Re S (Adult Patient)(Inherent Jurisdiction: Family Life)* [2003] 1 FLR 292, paras 20–21.

[39] *Re HM (Vulnerable Adult: Abduction)* [2010] 2 FLR 1057.

advanced arrangement.[40] For example, in *Re HM (Vulnerable Adult: Abduction)*,[41] the mentally incapacitated adult was put in the joint care of her divorced parents and ordered to live in a residential care home in England. Her father took her to Israel and refused to return her unless the court made an order for her to stay with him and for him to receive state funding for her welfare. This removal was obviously wrongful and cannot change the adult's habitual residence. In more complicated cases, the court needs to decide the extent of the authority granted to the vulnerable adult's carer and the nature of the decision-making. For example, in *Re MN,* an elderly woman habitually resident in California authorised her niece to make personal care decisions for herself and also expressed her wish to live in her home in California as long as possible. After the woman lost her mental capacity, the niece removed her to the UK. Whether the removal lawfully changes the habitual residence of the elderly woman should be decided by considering all the circumstances of the case, including the interpretation of the terms of the care arrangement under the applicable law, the reason and motive for relocating the elderly woman, the woman's health and financial condition, her link with two countries, her family link, the standard of care in both countries, and her best interests. Finally, if a vulnerable adult is under the care of multiple relatives, the disagreement of the decision by one or a few carers may not make the removal wrongful, as far as the decision is justified by the necessity test.[42]

Secondly, an adult present in England and Wales is to be treated for the purposes of jurisdiction as a habitual resident there if (a) his habitual residence cannot be ascertained; (b) he is a refugee; or (c) he has been displaced as a result of disturbance in his country of habitual residence.[43] This grants the English court jurisdiction over a present adult based on necessity.[44] Ground (a) should be used restrictively. In many adult abduction cases, the habitual residence of an adult is hard to determine. It does not entitle the court of the country, where the adult is present, to take jurisdiction.[45] Grounds (b) and (c) fill the gap where it is practically inappropriate or impossible to have this adult protected in his habitual residence.

(ii) Property situated in England

The English court can take measures directed to the vulnerable adult's property situated in England.[46] The *situs* rule allows the measures to be easily enforced and all extra procedural, judicial or administrative obstacles are avoided.[47]

(iii) Jurisdiction in case of urgency

Paragraph 7(1)(c) states the English court may take protective measures in relation to an adult present in England or who has property there, if the matter is urgent. This provision is not drafted clearly and may be misleading. It should be interpreted according to the text of Article 10 of the Hague Convention and its explanatory report. It is there to protect a vulnerable adult away from his habitual residence and any delay of action may cause irreparable harm to this adult's interests. Jurisdiction of urgency may be exercised if the habitual residence of an adult is in dispute and it takes time before the competent court finally makes the decision and takes jurisdiction; or the court of the adult's habitual residence is not easily

---

[40] *Re MN (Recognition and Enforcement of Foreign Protective Measures)* [2010] COPLR Con Vol 893 (CP); *Re PO* [2013] EWHC 3932 (COP); [2013] WLR (D) 495 (CP).
[41] *Re HM (Vulnerable Adult: Abduction)* [2010] 2 F.L.R. 1057.
[42] *Re O* [2014] Fam. 197, para 26.
[43] Sch 3, para 7(2). Convention, Art 6.
[44] Lagarde, *Explanatory Report,* para 55.
[45] Lagarde, *Explanatory Report,* para 55.
[46] Sch 3, para 7(1)(b). Convention, Art 9.
[47] Lagarde, *Explanatory Report,* para 75.

accessible when the emergency occurs. However, it by no means deprives the court of the country where the adult has his habitual residence of jurisdiction. The jurisdiction of urgency and any measures taken under this jurisdiction ground are temporary and should lapse as soon as the authority of the adult's habitual residence takes necessary protective measures.[48]

This jurisdiction ground can only be exercised in the case of urgency, which should be interpreted restrictively and may include an urgent medical treatment to save the adult's life or an action to stop an immediate threat of damage to the adult's property. The harm must be irreparable or sufficiently serious, as well as imminent.[49] An action, which may be performed within a time scale, would not qualify as a matter of urgency.[50]

A court, when exercising jurisdiction of urgency, would have the power to take any measures of protection, in relation to a person or property. In other words, if an adult's property is situated in England, the English court has jurisdiction of urgency not limited to the protection of this adult's property. For example, the English court, in such circumstances, could appoint guardianship for an adult in another country and use the adult's assets situated in England to pay for the cost of this.[51]

(iv) Jurisdiction to take temporary and limited territorial effect protective measures

The Court of Protection has jurisdiction to take temporary measures of limited territorial effect to protect vulnerable adults present in England. Protective measures taken under this jurisdictional ground can only relate to the person, and should not be extended to his property.[52] The measures must be temporary and only have limited effect within England, for example, by placing the adult under the protection of an authority in England, appointing guardianship, curatorship or any corresponding system which is only valid in England, designating a person in charge of the adult's affairs in England, or placing the adult temporarily in a mental hospital or special care home. Any measures that may have permanent or final effects are not eligible, such as termination of pregnancy, sterilisation, or operation to remove an organ or limb.[53] Protective measures issued under this jurisdiction ground will lapse when the authority of the adult's habitual residence takes jurisdiction to determine the same matter.[54]

(v) Jurisdiction based on nationality

The English court can also exercise jurisdiction over an adult of British nationality, who has a closer connection with England and Wales than with Scotland or Northern Ireland. Article 7 of the Hague Convention is thoroughly complied with.[55] The Convention requires the court to satisfy itself that it is in the better position to assess the interests of an adult, in contrast to the court of the adult's habitual residence.[56] It is not particularly clear how this is assessed, but it is suggested the court should consider the nature of the protective measures, the need for protection and other connecting factors, such as the adult's previous habitual residence, the location of property, and the residence of the adult's relatives or family members.[57]

---

[48] Convention on the International Protection of Adult, Art 10(2).

[49] Fagan, 344.

[50] Lagarde, *Explanatory Report*, para 78 (give example of termination of pregnancy of an incapacitated woman); Fagan, 345–6.

[51] Lagarde, *Explanatory Report*, para 79.

[52] Ibid, para 84.

[53] Ibid, para 84.

[54] Convention, Art 11(2).

[55] Sch 3, para 8(1) and (2).

[56] Convention, Art 7(1).

[57] Lagarde, *Explanatory Report*, para 57.

Furthermore, jurisdiction based on nationality shall not be exercised if the adult is a refugee or internationally displaced in another country.[58] Jurisdiction based on nationality cannot be exercised or shall lapse if the authority of the adult's habitual residence takes jurisdiction.[59]

Since there are multiple legal districts in the UK, British nationality does not directly grant jurisdiction to England. The Court of Protection, before taking jurisdiction, needs to be satisfied that the adult has a closer connection with England and Wales than Scotland and Northern Ireland. Such a connection is determined by examining all factual connecting factors, such as the adult's place of residence, family link and relatives, social link and other personal affairs.

(vi) Jurisdiction upon request

The Lord Chancellor, being the Central Authority for England and Wales,[60] having consulted the adult as he considers appropriate, can agree to a request from the authority of the adult's habitual residence for the Court of Protection to take protective measures under Article 8 of the Convention.[61] However, pursuant to the Convention, such a request can only be addressed to a Contracting State. Since England and Wales is not yet a Contracting State, it will not receive such a request in practice.[62] The text of the Act also implies that the English court will not accept jurisdiction upon a request from a non-Contracting State pursuant to the latter's domestic law, which is not covered by Article 8 of the Convention. This jurisdiction ground may be practically possible only when a non-Contracting State, like England and Wales, give the Convention effect in domestic law and issues the request under Article 8 of the Convention.

(c) Choice of law

(i) General applicable law

In exercising jurisdiction under the 2005 Act, the Court of Protection will apply English law,[63] unless it thinks that the matter has a substantial connection with a country other than England and Wales, in which case it may apply the law of that other country.[64] Allowing the court to apply its own law is efficient and could assist the smooth execution of the protective measures, which usually are executed locally in the forum.[65] Furthermore, since the adult's habitual residence is the primary jurisdiction, the law of the forum rule also allows the application of the law of the habitual residence in most cases, subject the adult to the law that he is presumably most familiar with.[66]

However, flexibility is also introduced in cases where the application of foreign law is more appropriate. This exception applies where the matter has a substantive connection with another country.[67] Regardless of the wording, the exception is not based on proximity but on the best interests of the adult.[68] Therefore, the exception should be interpreted restrictively.

---

[58] Convention, Art 7(1).
[59] Convention, Art 7(2) and (3).
[60] Sch 3, para 6.
[61] Sch 3, para 8(3).
[62] See also D Hill, "The Hague Convention on the Protection of Adults", 473.
[63] Cf Hague Convention, Art 13(1).
[64] Sch 3, para 11; cf Hague Convention, Art 13(2).
[65] Lagarde, *Explanatory Report*, para 91.
[66] P M M Mostermans, "A New Hague Convention on the International Protection of Adults", (2000) 2 International Law FORUM du droit international 10, 12; J Long, "Rethinking Vulnerable Adult's Protection in the Light of the 2000 Hague Convention", (2013) 27 International Journal of Law, Policy and the Family 51, 59–60.
[67] Sch 3, para 11; Hague Convention, Art 13(2).
[68] Lagarde, *Explanatory Report*, para 92. For the principle of the best interests of the adult, see Long, 60–1.

The court should only apply the law of the other country if: (a) the matter has substantially closer connections with the other country; and (b) applying the law of the other country is in the best interests of the vulnerable adult. The best interests is a question of fact and no test or guidance is provided for the court to follow. It is suggested that the court should consider the smooth execution of the protective measures, the physical and psychological health of the adult, the wish of the adult expressed when he has mental capacity, etc.

(ii) Law applicable to implementation of protective measures

Where a protective measure is taken in one country, but implemented in another, the conditions of implementation are governed by the law of that other country.[69] This situation usually arises if the adult changes his habitual residence after the protective measure is issued, or where his representative appointed in relation to the protective measure needs to exercise the power abroad, for example, to sell the adult's property situated abroad. It, however, does not cover the power of a representative appointed by the adult in advance.[70] "Conditions of implementation" is not defined in either the Act or the Convention, but it should broadly cover all formal requirements or official authorisation for executing the protective measures.[71] Thus, the conditions of implementation of any protective measure taken abroad will be governed by English law, if implemented in England.

(iii) Power of attorney

Sections 9 to 14 of the 2005 Act create a statutory form of power of attorney, the "lasting power of attorney", replacing the "enduring power of attorney" provided for by the Enduring Powers of Attorney Act 1985.[72] It encourages autonomy of an adult to make advanced arrangements for someone to manage his affairs once he becomes incapacitated.[73] For example, a competent adult may create this power in his habitual residence. After he retires, he decides to spend his retired life in another country and changes his habitual residence. He then suffers from mental impairment in his new habitual residence and the appointed representative needs to exercise the power in the new country. The court of the new habitual residence of the adult would have to decide whether the arrangement is valid and fully enforceable in this country.

The power of attorney covered in the Act is a mandate conferred by a competent adult that takes effect only after the donor is incapacitated. On the other hand, power granted to take care of an adult's affair when he is competent is not covered. However, there is also a mandate that grants the power to the representative to take care of the adult's affairs through his entire life, both before and after he becomes incapacitated. This mandate, nonetheless, should be covered by the Act.[74] The applicable law provided in the Act applies only to the execution of the power after the date when the adult becomes mentally incapacitated.[75] This may create uncertainty in practice. For example, a competent adult habitually resident abroad has property located in England and his representative could handle his property in England pursuant to the governing law designated by English common law.[76] After the adult becomes incapacitated, the effect of the mandate is then governed by the law designated under the Act.

---

[69] Sch 3, para 12; cf Hague Convention, Art 14. See Lagarde, *Explanatory Report*, para 93.
[70] This is discussed in sub-section (iii) below.
[71] Lagarde, *Explanatory Report*, para 94; Dicey, Morris and Collins, para 21-018.
[72] 2005 Act, ss 66 and 67; Sch 5, Parts 1 and 2; and Sch 6.
[73] Ss 9–14 and Sch 1 of the Act.
[74] Lagarde, *Explanatory Report*, para 97; D Hill, 475.
[75] Lagarde, *Explanatory Report*, para 97.
[76] This is a contract of agency which is excluded from the Rome I Regulation, Art 1(2)(g).

Applying different laws to the same mandate executed at different time may harm the donor's reasonable expectations and increase complexity for the representative in implementation.

The choice of law rule for cross-border enforcement of the power of attorney is designed by taking two interests into account, i.e. promotion of autonomy and protection of policy of the country of implementation. The donor could choose the applicable law to govern the existence, extent, modification and extinction of the power.[77] There are two limitations to this choice. Firstly, the choice is limited to a "connected country" being a country of which the donor is a national; in which he was habitually resident; or in which he has property.[78] The law of the first two countries can govern all aspects of the mandate. The law of the third country, however, can only be designated to govern property situated in that country.[79] The donor has no absolute freedom of choice. This limitation aims to balance the conflicting interests. On the one hand, the adult could have his reasonable wishes respected and, on the other hand, he should not be able to choose any law in the world. In particular, not all countries recognise the advance arrangement of affairs after incapacitation.[80] The Convention does not allow an adult to freely introduce this practice while none of his connected countries allow it.[81] Secondly, in order to avoid uncertainty, the law must be designated "in writing". Besides these two limitations, the choice is flexible. For example, nothing prevents the adult from choosing different laws to govern different issues (*dépeçage*). The adult could decide that the power to arrange his medical care is governed by the law of his previous habitual residence, while the power to handle his property is governed by the law of the place where the property is situated.[82] The Explanatory Report even suggests that the mandate as a whole may be subject to multiple designated laws either alternatively in favour of validity or cumulatively to create a higher standard for implementation.[83]

In the absence of choice, the law of the country where the adult has his habitual residence at the time of granting the power should apply.[84] Since most donors create the power of attorney in their habitual residence, the applicable law has the closest connection with the mandate and is reasonably expected by the donor.

As regards the manner of exercising a lasting power, the applicable law is the law of the country where it is exercised.[85] Autonomy is excluded, which means the donor could not designate the law governing the manner of exercising the power. The manner of exercise of the power is interpreted restrictively and should be much narrower than the "extent" of power'.[86] While the extent of the power includes the act that the representative could carry out and is subject to the law of the adult's habitual residence, the manner of the exercise of the power only covers the detailed way to carry out the above act, such as any local judicial or administrative procedure. The manner of exercise of the power is also narrower than "implementation" of the power in paragraph 12, which covers every matter concerning exercising the power.[87]

---

[77] Convention, Art 15(1) and (2); Act, Sch 3, para 13(1) and (2).
[78] Act, Sch 3 para 13(3); Convention, Art 15(2).
[79] Sch 3, para 13(4).
[80] For a comparative study of national law on this issue, see, in general, Long.
[81] Lagarde, *Explanatory Report*, para 105.
[82] Ibid, para 103.
[83] Ibid, para 103.
[84] Convention, Art 15(1); Act, Sch 3 para 13(1).
[85] Sch 3, para 13(5); cf Hague Convention, Art 15(3). See Lagarde, *Explanatory Report*, paras 106–7. For a power exercised in England and Wales, see the 2005 Act, Sch 1.
[86] Lagarde, *Explanatory Report*, paras 99 and 107.
[87] Lagarde, *Explanatory Report*, paras 99 and 107.

Finally, the Court of Protection is entitled to terminate or modify the power if the lasting power is not exercised in a manner sufficient to guarantee the protection.[88] This rule aims to provide flexibility to balance the protection of the adult's genuine wishes and the need to protect the best interests of the adult. On the one hand, it allows the court of the adult's habitual residence to terminate or modify the power to ensure the adult is actually protected. It is particularly useful in cases where the representative appointed is incompetent or does not act at the interests of the adult. The Court of Protection, in such circumstances, may replace the adult's mandate with protective measures under English law. On the other hand, the court is not permitted to deprive the adult of his wishes too readily. It must be satisfied that the power is exercised in a manner insufficient to protect the adult's interests. For example, the adult is denied necessary medical care or the adult's property is sold at a price much lower than the market value. When deciding whether the exercise of power is insufficient, the Court of Protection must consider the standard applied not in England but under the law governing the mandate. This requirement again assists the promotion of autonomy and prevents easy modification of the mandate by local standards.

(iv) Protection of third parties

Paragraph 16 of Schedule 3 operates to protect third parties who enter into transactions with a person (a "representative") who purports to act in exercise of an authority to act on behalf of a mentally disordered/incapacitated adult.[89] Where the representative and the third party are in England and Wales when entering into the transaction, the validity thereof may not be questioned in proceedings, nor may the third party be held liable, merely because by virtue of some foreign law applicable in terms of Schedule 3, the representative is not entitled to exercise the authority in that/those respect(s).[90] Conversely, where the representative and the third party are in a country other than England and Wales at the time of entering into the transaction, its validity may not be questioned in proceedings, nor may the third party be held liable, merely because by virtue of English law, the law applicable to the authority in terms of Schedule 3, the representative is not entitled to exercise the authority in that/those respect(s).[91]

(v) Mandatory rules and public policy

Regardless of any system of law which otherwise would apply in relation to the matter, the mandatory provisions of English law will apply.[92] Similarly, a provision of the law of another country will not be applied by the English court if its application would be manifestly contrary to public policy.[93] Examples include the adult's representative, who seeks to exercise his power to put the adult in the psychiatric hospital or any confinement, may have to receive judicial authorisation, which is mandatory under the law of the court; the adult's advanced medical directive that denies life-saving treatment, such as blood transfusion, may be valid under the governing law but fall foul of public policy of the forum.[94]

---

[88] Sch 3, para 14(1).

[89] Cf Hague Convention, Art 17. See Lagarde, *Explanatory Report*, paras 109–10.

[90] Sch 3, para 16(2) and (3). If, however, the third party knew or ought to have known that the applicable law was the law of the other foreign country, the para 16 protection is not afforded to him: para 16(5)(a); cf Hague Convention, Art 17. See Lagarde, *Explanatory Report*, paras 109–10.

[91] Sch 3, para 16(2) and (4); unless the third party knew or ought to have known that the applicable law was English law, in which case the para 16 protection is not afforded to him: para 16(5)(b).

[92] Sch 3, para 17; cf Hague Convention, Art 20. See Lagarde, *Explanatory Report*, para 113.

[93] Sch 3, para 18; cf Hague Convention, Art 21.

[94] For using public policy to limit the effect of advanced medical directive, see Fagan, 350–3.

(d) Recognition and enforcement of protective measures taken abroad

(i) Recognition of protective measures

Part 4 of Schedule 3 to the 2005 Act provides for the recognition and enforcement of protective measures[95] taken abroad. A protective measure will be recognised in England if it was taken under the law of the country in which an adult is habitually resident;[96] or under the law of a Contracting State which exercised jurisdiction pursuant to the Convention.[97] The grounds for mandatory recognition of protective measures are based on the Hague Convention. Although the UK ratification of the Convention only applies to Scotland, the 2005 Act implements the Convention rules in domestic law and obliges the Court of Protection in England and Wales to recognise protective measures issued by any foreign court pursuant to the Hague standard and should not take a more cautious approach to measures imposed by a non-Contracting state than a Contracting state.[98]

An interested person may apply to the Court of Protection for a declaration as to whether a protective measure taken under the law of a foreign country is to be recognised in England.[99] Notably, any finding of fact relied on when the measure is taken is conclusive for the purpose of recognition.[100] The Court of Protection may not review the merits of a measure taken outside England except to establish, in so far as it may be necessary so to do, whether the measure complies with Schedule 3.[101] The Court of Protection has the authority to review jurisdiction taken by the Contracting State though.[102] In *Health Service Executive of Ireland v PA*,[103] disputes arose as to whether the Court of Protection could review the Irish court's finding that the individuals were "adults" within Schedule 3 of the 2005 Act and they had their habitual residence in Ireland. The Court of Protection ruled that the definition of "adult" in the 2005 Act was a factual description rather than a legal test.[104] Equally, the finding on habitual residence is also a finding of fact and should not be challenged in the process of recognition and enforcement of protective measures in England.[105]

(ii) Refusal grounds

Recognition of a protective measure taken abroad may be refused under paragraph 19(3) of Schedule 3, if the Court of Protection thinks that (a) the case in which the measure was taken was not urgent, (b) the adult was not given an opportunity to be heard, and (c) that omission amounted to a breach of natural justice.[106] This is a general ground to refuse recognising an order made with procedural irregularity. The word "think", however, does not suggest a relatively low standard is provided. The court still needs to apply the ordinary standard based on the balance of probabilities.[107] The adult is properly heard and represented if he has made an arrangement in advance and his representative represents him or appoints a competent

---

[95] Defined in Sch 3, para 5.

[96] Sch 3, para 19(1).

[97] Sch 3, para 19(2).

[98] *Health Service Executive of Ireland v PA*, [2015] EWCOP 38; [2015] 3 WLR 1923, para 39; *Re M*, para 2.

[99] Sch 3, para 20(1).

[100] Sch 3, para 21.

[101] Sch 3, para 24.

[102] Lagarde, *Explanatory Report*, para 119.

[103] [2015] EWCOP 38; [2015] 3 WLR 1923.

[104] Ibid, para 43–4. The concept is defined in Sch 3, para 4. See discussion in section 2(a) above.

[105] Ibid, para 52–4. See also *A v A (Children: Habitual Residence)(Reunite International Child Abduction Centre Intervening)* [2014] AC 1; Case C-523/07 *Proceedings brought by A* [2010] Fam 42; Case C-497/10PPU *Mercredi v Chaffe* [2012] Fam 22.

[106] Cf Hague Convention, Art 22(2)(b). See Lagarde, *Explanatory Report*, para 120.

[107] *Health Service Executive of Ireland v PA*, para 55.

council to represent him in the court; or he is represented by a guardian *ad litem* and a competent council appointed by the guardian. An adult may be denied the right to be heard, if he was not joined as a party in the proceedings that result in depriving him of his liberty.[108] Furthermore, only when all three conditions are satisfied the court exercise its discretion to refuse recognition. Protective measures may be recognised in urgent cases even if the adult was not heard or represented. Urgent cases include cases where the adult requires immediate medical treatment to save his life, or where injunctions are required to prevent an immediate threat of harm to the adult's property.

Additionally, recognition may be refused, under paragraph 19(4) of Schedule 3, if (a) recognition of the measure would be manifestly contrary to public policy, (b) the measure would be inconsistent with a mandatory provision of English law, or (c) the measure is inconsistent with one subsequently taken or recognised in England in relation to the adult.[109] Public policy and mandatory rules reservation is common to allow a court to protect its fundamental interests. In practice, grounds (a) and (b) may be overlapping because measures in breach of mandatory rules would also be treated as being contrary to public policy of England.[110] But the two concepts are not identical as public policy covers broader circumstances not codified in mandatory rules.

In deciding whether protective measures taken abroad are contrary to mandatory rules or public policy, the Court of Protection will firstly review the compatibility with the Convention for the Protection of Human Rights and Fundamental Freedoms.[111] Protective measures purporting to put the mentally incapacitated adult in detention would have to meet the criteria established by the European Court of Human Rights.[112] It has been established by the ECHR that before depriving liberty of a mentally incapacitated adult the authority must satisfy itself that the adult is mentally incapacitated based on objective medical expertise; the mental disorder is a kind or degree warranting compulsory confinement; and the validity of continued confinement depends on the persistence of mental disorder.[113] Furthermore, the Court of Protection should also satisfy itself that the adult has the right to challenge the detention and the right to regular review.[114] For example, no courts would enforce an oppressive or tyrannical detention order depriving an individual of the liberty on behalf of a foreign court.[115] Protective measures stained by any ideology may also be ruled as being contrary to public policy, such as using psychiatric institutes to enforce ideology in the former Soviet Union.[116] Orders that require the use of certain medical measures that are prohibited or abandoned due to health and safety concerns may also infringe public policy. And permanent confinement without the right to challenge or regular review would fall foul of public policy.

The mandatory rules and public policy defence will not be applied simply where the foreign court makes an order that usually will not be made by an English court; the adult is treated differently from the requirements and procedure under English law; or the foreign court determines protection of a mentally incapacitated adult following a different culture and in an overall different manner. In particular, it cannot conclude that any other provisions in

---

[108] *The Health Service Executive of Ireland v CNWL* [2005] EWCOP 48, paras 33–5; *Re X (Court of Protection Practice)* [2015] EWCA Civ 599, para 86.
[109] Cf Hague Convention, Art 22(2)(c) and (d). See Lagarde, *Explanatory Report*, paras 121–2.
[110] *Health Service Executive of Ireland v PA*, para 62; *Re M*, para 5.
[111] *Health Service Executive of Ireland v PA*, para 63.
[112] Ibid, para 64;
[113] *Winterwerp v The Netherlands* (1979) 2 EHRR 387.
[114] *Health Service Executive of Ireland v PA*, para 96.
[115] *Re M*, para 5.
[116] Ibid.

the 2005 Act are mandatory in nature and any foreign protective measures are contrary to mandatory rules or public policy if they cannot be taken under the 2005 Act. For example, an English court may not include in a welfare order a provision authorising the deprivation of liberty,[117] but this does not prevent an English court from recognising any foreign order of such a nature.[118]

Further, recognition of a protective measure taken by a Convention Contracting State may be refused, under paragraph 19(5) of Schedule 3, if Article 33 of the Convention has not been complied with in a suitable qualifying case. Article 33 of the Convention permits an authority to place an adult in another Contracting State. The authority of the requesting state should consult the competent authority of the requesting state and shall not make such a decision if the latter indicates its opposition within a reasonable time.[119] This provision prevents the authority of a Contracting State from placing an adult in the other Contracting State without proper consultation of the latter. It is hard to see how this provision is relevant to England which is not a Contracting State. The only possible relevance is that the adult is present in England and the order is made by the adult's habitual residence to place the adult in another Contracting State. The English court may refuse to recognise the foreign order and order the adult not to be removed out of England instead.

(iii) Enforcement of protective measures

An interested person may apply to the Court of Protection for a declaration as to whether a protective measure taken under the law of a foreign country, and enforceable there, is enforceable, or to be registered, in England, in accordance with the Court of Protection Rules.[120] A measure to which such a declaration relates is enforceable in England as if it were a measure of like effect taken by the Court of Protection.[121]

With regard to the powers of a foreign curator over the property or affairs in England of a mentally disordered/incapacitated adult, section 18(4) of the 2005 Act, incorporating Schedule 2(7) to the Act, provides for the vesting of stock[122] in a curator appointed outside England and Wales. If the Court of Protection is satisfied that under some foreign law a curator has been appointed to exercise powers in respect of the property and affairs of an adult on the ground that the latter lacks capacity to make decisions with respect to the management and administration of his property and affairs, the Court may, if it considers it expedient so to do, having regard to the nature of the appointment and the circumstances of the case, direct that any stocks standing in the incapable adult's name, or the right to receive dividends therefrom, be transferred into the curator's name, or otherwise be dealt with as required by the curator, and give such directions as it thinks fit for dealing with accrued dividends.[123]

(e) Co-Operation among Hague Convention Contracting States

Chapter V of the Hague Convention facilitates co-operation and information sharing between Contracting States. Co-operation is done by direct communication and request between Central Authorities of Contracting States.[124] Co-operation and information sharing is vital in contributing to jurisdiction, especially where a Contracting State, which is not the

---

[117] S 16A of the Mental Capacity Act.
[118] *Re M,* para 6; *Health Service Executive of Ireland v PA,* para 98.
[119] Art 33 of the Convention.
[120] Sch 3, para 22(1); and ss 50 and 51.
[121] Sch 3, para 22(3).
[122] Defined in Sch 2, para 3.
[123] Sch 2, para 7.
[124] Arts 31–35 of the Convention.

habitual residence of an adult, intends to take jurisdiction under other grounds. It would also encourage recognition and enforcement of protective measures taken in another Contracting State.[125]

Since the UK ratification of the Convention does not extend to England and Wales, most of the Convention rules on co-operation are irrelevant to the Court of Protection. Part 5 of Schedule 3 to the 2005 Act establishes a system of co-operation between public authorities[126] in England and authorities in other Convention countries to operate in two situations. First, as regards proposals for cross-border placements of mentally disordered/incapacitated adults,[127] where a public authority proposes to place an adult in an establishment in a foreign Convention country, it must consult an appropriate authority in that country, and provide it with a report on the adult and a statement of reasons for the proposed placement.[128] If the foreign authority opposes the proposed placement within a reasonable time, it cannot proceed.[129] Secondly, in respect of adults in "serious danger",[130] a public authority which is aware of such a person who is the subject of actual or proposed protective measures and who is, or has become, resident in another Convention country, must tell an appropriate authority in that foreign country of the danger and the measures in question.[131]

3. CASES OUTSIDE THE MENTAL CAPACITY ACT

(a) Jurisdiction

Under the common law, the powers of the English court can be exercised over anyone present in England, irrespective of their domicile or nationality.[132] The jurisdiction is broad and can be exercised over the person or over his property, even if the property is located abroad.[133] In the latter situation, the English court usually would not make an order directly affecting property situated in a country where the authority of the court is not recognised, but the Court achieves its object by directing the receiver to take such steps as may be necessary to effect the purposes of the court, eg by appointing an attorney to act in the name of the patient in selling property and accounting to the receiver for the proceeds. Secondly, the Court acts in accordance with the comity of nations and refrains from making orders that would be regarded as an infringement of a foreign jurisdiction. The English court also has jurisdiction over a person's property if the property is situated in England, even though the person is outside the country.[134] This jurisdiction, however, is narrow and cannot be exercised over the person. If the person is not present in England and has no property situated in this country,

---

[125] Hill, 476; Mostermans, 13.

[126] Having the same meaning as "public authorities" under the Human Rights Act 1998: 2005 Act, s 64(1).

[127] Sch 3, para 26. Cf Sch 3, para 19(5) and Hague Convention, Art 33. As regards the general powers of the Court of Protection concerning an adult's personal welfare, and property and affairs, see 2005 Act, ss 15–21.

[128] Subject to Sch 3, para 29, which provides that no information may be sought or communicated if to do so would be likely to endanger the adult or his property, or would amount to a serious threat to the liberty or life of a member of the adult's family.

[129] Sch 3, para 27.

[130] Eg illness requiring constant treatment, drugs, or influence of a sect: Lagarde, *Explanatory Report*, para 140.

[131] Sch 3, para 28; cf Hague Convention, Art 34. See Lagarde, *Explanatory Report*, para 140.

[132] Eg *Re Sottomaior* (1874) 9 Ch App 677; *Re S (Hospital Patient: Foreign Curator)* [1996] Fam 23.

[133] *Re Houstoun* (1826) 1 Russ 312; *Re Princess Bariatinski* (1843) 1 Ph 375; *Re Burbidge* [1902] 1 Ch 426.

[134] *Ex p Southcote* (1751) 2 Ves Sen 401; *Re Scott* (1874) 22 WR 748.

the English court has no jurisdiction; though the court could order that he be returned within the jurisdiction of the court.[135]

(b) Choice of law

There seems little doubt that, when exercising powers over the person, property or affairs of a mentally disordered or incapacitated person at common law or in terms of the Mental Health Act 1983, the English court will apply English law. The one specific statutory provision relating to choice of law is section 97(4) of the Mental Health Act 1983 which limits the effect of a will which a judge has authorised to be made on behalf of a patient.[136] The will is limited in its effect to matters governed by English law—and so has no effect in relation to foreign immovables or to the movable property of a person domiciled outside England unless the law of his domicile, by renvoi, refers the issue of his testamentary capacity to English law.

(c) Recognition and enforcement of protective measures taken abroad

Before a foreign curator can enforce in England any rights relating to the property or affairs of a mentally disordered or incapacitated person, the English courts must be satisfied, first, that the curator is entitled, according to the law under which he was appointed, to take proceedings in England (ie abroad) to recover the property or manage the affairs of that person.[137] Secondly, the English court must be prepared to recognise that the curator was appointed under the law of a country with which the patient was sufficiently closely connected. Whilst in many cases, the mentally disordered/incapacitated adult will be domiciled and present in, and a national of, the country where the curator was appointed,[138] presence alone will suffice at common law or under the Mental Health Act 1983.[139] The English courts have recognised a curator appointed in New York to manage the affairs of a widow domiciled in England;[140] though the rights of the curator in relation to proceedings in England concerning the patient's property are less extensive than if the patient had been domiciled in New York.[141] The English courts have also recognised a curator appointed in Norway to manage the affairs of a man domiciled in Norway, but present in England.[142] A foreign curator can exercise, as of right, no control in England over the person of the patient;[143] but the English court can authorise the handing over of the mentally disordered or incapacitated person into the care of the foreign curator and the person's removal abroad.[144] Where a person who is neither a British nor Commonwealth citizen with a right of abode in the United Kingdom is detained in hospital as a patient receiving mental treatment, the Secretary of State, subject to the approval of a Mental Health Review Tribunal, can authorise the patient's removal to a country outside the British Isles[145] if he is satisfied as to the arrangements made for such removal, and that it is in the interests of the patient. Provision is also made relating to the removal of patients to and from Scotland, Northern Ireland, the Isle of Man and the Channel Islands on the authority of the Secretary of State or other appropriate authority.[146] With regard to the powers of a

---

[135] See *Re Sykeham* (1823) Turn & R 537.

[136] Mental Health Act 1983, s 96(1)(e).

[137] *Re Barlow's Will* (1887) 36 Ch D 287, on which see *Didisheim v London and Westminster Bank* [1900] 2 Ch 15 at 49–50; and see *Re Piper* [1927] 4 DLR 924.

[138] Eg *Re De Linden* [1897] 1 Ch 453.

[139] *Re De Larragoiti* [1907] 2 Ch 14.

[140] *New York Security and Trust Co v Keyser* [1901] 1 Ch 666.

[141] Infra, p 1247.

[142] *Re S (Hospital Patient: Foreign Curator)* [1996] Fam 23.

[143] *Re Houston* (1826) 1 Russ 312.

[144] Eg *Re S (Hospital Patient: Foreign Curator)* [1996] Fam 23.

[145] Mental Health Act 1983, s 86.

[146] Ibid, ss 80–85; and Mental Health (Care and Treatment) (Scotland) Act 2003, ss 289, 290 and 309.

foreign curator over the property or affairs in England of a mentally disordered or incapacitated person, it must first be observed that the curator has no power to bring an action for
the recovery of immovables.[147] He also has no power in the case of movables if a receiver has
been appointed in England, because in that case all powers to deal with the person's property
and affairs are vested in the Court of Protection.[148] Subject to this, the rule has been established that a foreign curator can sue in England as of right to claim money or property due
to the mentally disordered/incapacitated person and to demand, and to give valid receipts
for, property belonging to the patient which is held by persons in England.[149] This principle
was finally laid down by the Court of Appeal in the leading case of *Didisheim v London and
Westminster Bank*,[150] where the facts were as follows:

> A lady, domiciled and resident in Belgium, had securities of great value deposited with the
> defendant bank in London. She became insane in fact, though without being so found judi-
> cially, and Didisheim, having applied to the bank without success for the securities, brought
> an action for their recovery.

The Court of Appeal held that Didisheim was entitled to call for the securities and to give the
bank a good discharge: "On general principles of private international law, the courts of this
country are bound to recognise the authority conferred on him by the Belgian courts, unless
lunacy proceedings in this country prevent them from doing so."[151] The court, however,
ordered Didisheim to pay all the costs of the action, since the bank was justified in not complying with his demands until he had established his title by a successful action in the High
Court. *Didisheim's* case has definitely established the right of a foreign curator to demand
property, and so if an English debtor insists on proceedings, he acts with an unreasonable
excess of caution and will have to pay his own costs.[152]

Some limitations on the decision in *Didisheim's* case must be noticed. The foreign curator has
no greater rights than his English counterpart. So, if there are funds in court, the payment
out of which is in the discretion of the court, payment to a foreign creditor who claims the
funds will be subject to such discretion.[153] Furthermore, in *Didisheim's* case, the owner of the
property was an alien domiciled abroad over whom the court had no jurisdiction personally.
If the patient is domiciled in England, then the foreign curator does not have a right to claim
property in England, though the court has a discretion to order payment of appropriate
sums.[154]

Although the principle established by *Didisheim's* case is of great benefit to foreign curators,
its usefulness is limited not only by the fact that it has no application to immovable property
but also because it does not enable the foreign curator to reduce into possession stock and
shares registered in the name of the patient. This is because stock and shares can only be
transferred by an instrument of transfer executed by the registered holder or by a person having authority to execute the document on his behalf, and a foreign curator is not recognised
as having this power.

---

[147] *Grimwood v Bartels* (1877) 46 LJ Ch 788.
[148] *Re RSA* [1901] 2 KB 32.
[149] *Didisheim v London and Westminster Bank* [1900] 2 Ch 15; and see *Scott v Bentley* (1855) 1 K & J
281; *Re De Linden* [1897] 1 Ch 453; *Thiery v Chalmers Guthrie & Co* [1900] 1 Ch 80; *Kamouh v Associated
Electrical Industries International Ltd* [1980] QB 199 at 205–206; *Re FN and the Mental Health Act 1958*
[1984] 3 NSWLR 520.
[150] [1900] 2 Ch 15.
[151] Ibid, at 51.
[152] *Pélégrin v Coutts & Co* [1915] 1 Ch 696.
[153] *Re Garnier* (1872) LR 13 Eq 532; *Re De Linden* [1897] 1 Ch 453.
[154] *New York Security and Trust Co v Keyser* [1901] 1 Ch 666.

It is not, however, necessary in every case where stock and shares are concerned to appoint a receiver in England or to have independent medical evidence of mental incapacity. The reason for this is that the Court of Protection is empowered, if satisfied that the foreign curator has been appointed on the ground that the patient is incapable by reason of mental incapacity of managing his property, to direct any stock or shares standing in the name of the patient to be transferred to the curator or otherwise dealt with as he may direct.[155] The power is discretionary, and the court will not direct the capital to be transferred unless satisfied that it is required for the patient's maintenance or that there is other sufficient reason justifying a transfer.[156]

---

[155] Mental Health Act 1983, s 100.
[156] *Re Knight* [1898] 1 Ch 257; *Re De Larragoiti* [1907] 2 Ch 14.

PART VI

THE LAW OF PROPERTY

29. The Distinction Between Movables and Immovables   1251
30. Immovables   1255
31. The Transfer of Tangible Movables   1263
32. The Assignment of Intangible Movables   1280
33. Corporations   1306
34. Insolvency   1312
35. Administration of Estates   1325
36. Succession   1338
37. Matrimonial Property   1365
38. Trusts   1382

29

THE DISTINCTION BETWEEN MOVABLES AND IMMOVABLES

1. Introduction	1251	4. Relevance of Distinction Between	
2. Classification by the Law of the Situs	1252	Realty and Personalty	1254
3. Some Examples	1252	5. Distinction Between Tangible and	
(a) Mortgages	1252	Intangible Movables	1254
(b) Trusts for sale	1252		
(c) Annuities	1254		

1. INTRODUCTION[1]

In order to arrive at a common basis on which to determine questions involving a foreign element, English private international law classifies the subject matter of ownership into movables and immovables, and thus adopts a distinction that is accepted in other legal systems,[2] though even common law jurisdictions cannot agree whether some kinds of property are movable or immovable.[3] The first task of the court in a private international law case when required to decide some question of a proprietary or possessory nature is to decide whether the item of property which is the subject of the dispute is movable or immovable. The legal system that will be applicable to the case depends on this preliminary decision. Rights over immovables are determined by the law of the situs; rights over movables are not necessarily governed by that law. In the sphere of private international law, then, the common law distinction between realty and personalty is abandoned, even though the case concerns a common law country where it is recognised in the sphere of domestic law. The importance of not confusing the domestic distinction between realty and personalty with the private international law distinction between movables and immovables can scarcely be exaggerated. They do not cover the same ground. The one cuts across the other in the sense that personalty includes both movables and immovables. Thus "realty" is not synonymous either with "land" or with "immovables", for though a life tenant, for instance, holds an interest in realty, a leaseholder holds an interest in personalty. For the purpose of private international law, however, a lease creates an interest in an immovable and is subject to the law of the situs.[4]

---

[1] See Carruthers (2005), Chapter 1.

[2] *Re Hoyles* [1911] 1 Ch 179 at 185. For a critical examination of the relevant authorities, see Clarence Smith (1963) 26 MLR 16.

[3] Eg, the right of a mortgagee. England and Ontario consider it to be immovable: *Re Hoyles* [1911] 1 Ch 179; *Re Ritchie* [1942] 3 DLR 330; whereas New Zealand and Australia consider it to be movable: *Re O'Neill* [1922] NZLR 468; *Re Greenfield* [1985] 2 NZLR 662 at 664; Wills Amendment Act 1955, s 14(4); *Haque v Haque (No 2)* (1965) 114 CLR 98; see Sykes and Pryles, pp 648–51, 658–60. There are differing views in Canada as to whether mineral rights are movable or immovable property: *War Eagle Mining Co v Robo Management Co* [1996] 2 WWR 504.

[4] *Freke v Carbery* (1873) LR 16 Eq 461; *Duncan v Lawson* (1889) 41 Ch D 394; *Re Caithness* (1891) 7 TLR 354.

2. CLASSIFICATION BY THE LAW OF THE SITUS

The determination of whether the subject matter of ownership is movable or immovable generally presents no difficulty. English law and most other legal systems accept that interests in land, whether classified according to their nature, such as legal estates and equitable interests; or limited in duration, such as fees simple, entails and terms of years; or independent of the right to possession of the land, such as easements, profits and rent charges, are interests in immovable property. A more complex problem arises in those cases where a right over what is physically movable is regarded by a particular legal system as a right over immovable property. For instance, the owner of such obvious chattels as title-deeds, fixtures, fish in a pond and the key of a house is regarded by English internal law as having an interest in land.[5] Again, it seems obvious at first sight that a building erected for the purposes of an exhibition, and which cannot be removed without losing its identity, must be in the same category as normal buildings, yet in the USA[6] its owner has been deemed to hold an interest in movable property. If, therefore, the subject matter of ownership is regarded as immovable by one system of law but as movable by another, to which law is the decision left? The answer given by English law and by most foreign legal systems is: the law of the situs.[7] If the law of the situs attributes the quality of movability or of immovability to the property in question, the English court which is seised of the matter must proceed on that basis.[8]

3. SOME EXAMPLES

(a) Mortgages

Mortgages provide an important illustration of this classification. It has been held that the right vested in a mortgagee of English land must be regarded by English law, being the law of the situs, as an interest in an immovable. This is notwithstanding that it is classified by English domestic law as personalty and that the debt, not the charge, is the principal characteristic of the transaction.[9]

(b) Trusts for sale

A further and important illustration is provided by *Re Berchtold*.[10] This case turned on the English doctrine of conversion,[11] namely, that: "Money directed to be employed in the purchase of land, and land directed to be sold and turned into money, are to be considered as that species of property into which they are directed to be converted."[12] What this equitable

---

[5] Cf *The Islamic Republic of Iran v Berend* [2007] EWHC 132 (QB), [2007] 2 All ER (Comm) 132, where the parties agreed that a fragment of limestone relief dating from a building in 5th century BC Persepolis should be characterised as movable.

[6] Eg *Public Service Co of New Hampshire v Voudonas* 84 NH 387, 157 A 81 (1930). Cf Germany: BGB, s 95, and Cohn, *Manual of German Law* (2nd edn), Vol 1, p 72.

[7] See Carruthers (2005), paras 1.20–1.46 for full discussion of the meaning of the "law of the situs", and infra, Chapter 31.

[8] *Johnstone v Baker* (1817) 4 Madd 474 n; Westlake, s 160, approved in *Re Hoyles* [1910] 2 Ch 333 at 341; affd [1911] 1 Ch 179; *Macdonald v Macdonald* 1932 SC (HL) 79; *Air Foyle Ltd and Anor v Center Capital Ltd* [2002] EWHC 2535; [2003] 2 Lloyd's Rep 753 at [41].

[9] *Re Hoyles* [1911] 1 Ch 179.

[10] [1923] 1 Ch 192; and see *Philipson-Stow v IRC* [1961] AC 727 at 762.

[11] On the uses to which this doctrine may be put in a conflict of laws situation, see Hancock (1965) 17 Stan LR 1095, and Carruthers (2005), paras 2.87–2.88.

[12] *Fletcher v Ashburner* (1779) 1 Bro CC 497 at 499; Pettit, *Equity and the Law of Trusts* (12th edn), pp 73–4 and 456.

doctrine means in effect is that where there is such a direction the realty is treated as person-alty for certain purposes, or in the reverse case, the personalty is treated as realty for certain purposes. If, for instance, land is conveyed to trustees on trust for sale and payment of the proceeds to A, and A dies before the actual sale, a bequest by him of all his personalty will include the money eventually arising from the sale. This, of course, does not alter the fact that until sold, the land is still immovable. This becomes material if the beneficiary under the trust dies domiciled in a foreign country before the conversion has actually been effected. *Re Berchtold* is just such a case:

> A party died intestate, domiciled in Hungary, and entitled to a freehold interest in English land which though subject to a trust for sale, had not been sold. The English choice of law rule is that intestate succession is governed by the law of the situs in the case of immovables, but by the law of the deceased's last domicile in the case of movables. It was, therefore, vital to decide whether the freehold interest, despite the doctrine of conversion, was still to be regarded as an interest in immovable property.

It was argued with some plausibility that by reason of the trust for sale the land was already money in the eyes of equity, that money is a movable, and that, therefore, the devolution was governed by Hungarian law. The fallacy of this argument, however, was demonstrated by Russell J. The primary question before the court was whether the subject matter in which the deceased was interested was immovable. This had nothing to do with a subsequent question that might arise under the doctrine of conversion, namely, whether realty was to be treated as personalty, or vice versa. It was held that the unsold land was immovable, notwithstanding the binding direction for its conversion into money, and that therefore the appropriate law to govern its devolution on intestacy was the law of the situs.[13]

The decision was distinguished by Morton J in *Re Cutcliffe's Will Trusts*,[14] where the distinc-tion between realty and personalty, and therefore the doctrine of conversion, were not strictly relevant.

> English land that was subject to an English settlement had been sold under the Settled Land Act 1882 and the proceeds had been invested in English debenture stock. The beneficiary under the settlement died intestate in 1897 domiciled in Ontario.

So far it seems obvious that the stock was in fact movable and that therefore under the relevant doctrine of private international law its devolution was governed by the law of the deceased's last domicile. The Settled Land Act 1882, however, provided that: "Capital money arising under this Act while remaining uninvested or unapplied and securities on which an investment of any such capital money is made shall, for all purposes of disposition, transmis-sion and devolution, be considered as land."[15]

Deciding whether the stock was movable or immovable was the primary issue in trying to determine the governing law. It was held that it was immovable and subject as such to the English law of devolution. The decision has been attacked on the ground that the domestic doctrine of conversion was erroneously applied at the stage when the case was being consid-ered internationally.[16] But this is to misinterpret the ratio of the case. How could the decision have been otherwise? The stock was physically situated in England. English law, therefore, had to determine whether it was to be treated as movable or immovable. An English statute

---

[13] Cf *Murray v Champernowne* [1901] 2 IR 232.
[14] [1940] Ch 565.
[15] S 22(5); see now Settled Land Act 1925, s 75(5).
[16] Falconbridge (1940) 18 Can Bar Rev 568.

peremptorily demanded that for all purposes, ie presumably including the choice of the applicable law, it should be regarded as land.

(c) Annuities

The character of annuities and other periodical payments depends on whether they issue out of, or are charged on, land. An annuity in the strict sense represents a right to movable property, but a rent charged on land is an interest in immovable property.[17]

4. RELEVANCE OF DISTINCTION BETWEEN REALTY AND PERSONALTY

Once the choice of law has been made, there may come a stage at which the distinction between realty and personalty then becomes relevant. This occurs where the choice falls on a law that recognises the distinction. The chosen law now has control of the case and it must be allowed to operate in its own way. In *Re Berchtold*,[18] for instance, the effect of deciding that the intestate died entitled to immovable property was to apply English law as the law of the situs, with the result that the immovable, being regarded as money under the domestic doctrine of conversion, devolved as personalty according to the rules of English internal law.

5. DISTINCTION BETWEEN TANGIBLE AND INTANGIBLE MOVABLES[19]

By English domestic law, the subject matter of ownership, if not immovable, is property divisible into choses in possession, ie tangible physical objects, and choses in action, such as debts, patents, copyright, goodwill, shares and securities. Private international lawyers usually prefer, however, to classify movables as either tangible or intangible.[20] This is not only a linguistic solecism, since it is scarcely possible to move a thing that cannot be touched, but it provokes an unfortunate tendency to ascribe to a disembodied thing, such as a debt, the physical attributes of a corporeal object as, for instance, a definite situs. Although Lord Halsbury once remarked that he was "wholly unable to see that goodwill itself is susceptible of having any local situation",[21] it is of course necessary for certain purposes, such as jurisdiction or probate, to assign a situs not only to goodwill, but to choses in action generally.[22] This is not without its dangers. Since the situs principle has furnished a simple and effective rule for questions relating to a physical thing, the natural inclination is to extend it to all questions and to regard it as the general determinant of rules for the choice of law concerning choses in action. This is a false analogy. Moreover, it frequently leads to forcing a rule, eminently adapted to one set of circumstances, to fit circumstances for which it is entirely inappropriate. It is reasonably clear that the appropriate law to govern goodwill or a debt depends on quite different considerations from those that are relevant to a physical thing. One must be aware of the danger of straining rules to fit categories.

---

[17] *Chatfield v Berchtoldt* (1872) 7 Ch App 192.
[18] Supra, pp 1252–3.
[19] See Carruthers (2005), paras 1.13–1.14.
[20] For a criticism of the distinction, see Cook, pp 284 et seq. See also Crawford and Carruthers, Ch 17.
[21] *IRC v Muller & Co's Margarines Ltd* [1901] AC 217 at 240.
[22] See Dicey, Morris and Collins, paras 22R-023–22-053; and Carruthers (2005), paras 1.31–1.42. See also *Perrin v Revenue and Customs Commissioners* [2014] UKFTT 223 (TC), [2014] SFTD 919, paras 34–35.

30

IMMOVABLES

1. Jurisdiction	1255	(a) The law of the situs rule	1255
2. Choice of Law	1255	(b) Specific issues	1258

1. JURISDICTION

An English court, as we have seen earlier,[1] will not generally take jurisdiction to determine the issue of title, or right to possession of, foreign land. This rule stems from two sources. The first is the common law rule in *British South Africa Co v Companhia de Moçambique*.[2] The second, in the case of land within another European Community State or in an EFTA State, is derived from Article 24(1) of the Brussels I Recast and the equivalent rules in the Brussels Convention and Lugano Convention, each of which gives exclusive jurisdiction in proceedings "which have as their object rights in rem in immovable property or tenancies of immovable property" to the courts of the country in which the property is situated.[3]

There are, nevertheless, a range of circumstances in which the English courts may have jurisdiction (either under common law or EU rules) over cases which require the determination of legal issues relating to foreign immovable property. These include cases where the question of title arises incidentally in a personal claim against a defendant, or in the administration of a trust, will or divorce over which the English courts have jurisdiction, or in the context of a claim for trespass over foreign land.[4] The question of choice of law for immovables may thus arise in these contexts, as well as when a dispute involving one or more foreign parties concerns English immovable property.

2. CHOICE OF LAW

(a) The law of the situs rule

In the USA[5] and in most European countries the general rule is that the law of the situs (often referred to as the *lex situs*) is the governing law for all questions that arise with regard

---

[1] Supra, Chapter 14.

[2] [1893] AC 602.

[3] Art 24(1), para 2 of the Brussels I Recast, Art 22(1) of the Brussels I Regulation, Art 16(1)(b) of the Brussels Convention and Art 22(1), para 2 of the Lugano Convention deal with jurisdiction over disputes concerning short-term tenancies, supra, pp 222–4.

[4] Eg *Ashurst v Pollard* [2001] Ch 595; *Webb v Webb* [1994] ECR I 1717; *Reichert v Dresdner Bank* [1990] ECR I 27; *Cook Industries Inc v Galliher* [1979] Ch 439; *Re Duke of Wellington* [1948] Ch 118; Civil Jurisdiction and Judgments Act 1982 s. 30. See further eg Wass (2014) 63 ICLQ 103.

[5] Hay, Borchers and Symeonides, p 1230; and see Restatement 2d, §§ 222, 223.

to immovable property.[6] The same rule was authoritatively stated for English law in *Nelson v Bridport*,[7] where Lord Nelson, in his capacity as Duke of Bronte, had attempted to devise his Sicilian estate in a manner contrary to the law of Sicily. Lord Langdale MR said:[8]

> The incidents to real estate, the right of alienating or limiting it, and the course of succession to it, depend entirely on the law of the country where the estate is situated. Lord Nelson having accepted the Sicilian estate could deal with it only as the Sicilian law allowed; he had a right to appoint a successor, but no right to modify the estate, interest, or powers of disposition to which the successor was entitled by the law of Sicily. The successor became the holder of the estate subject to the incidents annexed to it by the grant and the law of Sicily and no others.

Whilst the situs rule may have been authoritatively stated, it has come under occasional criticism.[9] Indeed the rule has been condemned as a "taboo".[10] There is no doubt, however, that the law of the situs has a powerful interest in its rules being applied to a wide range of matters—essentially "with the manner in which land is used, occupied or developed".[11] This concern is seen at its strongest in the case of the transfer of title to land.[12] At the end of the day, only the law of the situs can control the way in which land, which constitutes part of the situs itself, is transferred. Application of the law of the situs to questions of transfer of title is thus desirable as a matter of comity and also often necessary in terms of effectiveness. In other cases, however, "where the parties are non residents and the policy of the situs does not concern the use, tenure or marketing of its land",[13] the case for the application of the law of the situs is much weaker. Although the courts have been prepared to apply a law other than that of the situs to govern a contract for the sale of land,[14] equitable questions arising under a mortgage of foreign land,[15] a foreign implied marriage settlement,[16] the division of property upon divorce,[17] or the formal validity of a will of immovables,[18] the generality of the situs rule remains in force, as is illustrated by the law on intestate succession to immovables[19] and on the essential validity of a will relating to immovables.[20] It seems unlikely that the entrenched position of the law of the situs as the choice of law rule for immovables is going to be altered other than by legislation.[21]

---

[6] This proposition is so clear as scarcely to require authorities, but see *Birtwistle v Vardill* (1840) 7 Cl & Fin 895; *Coppin v Coppin* (1725) 2 P Wms 291; *Re Duke of Wellington* [1947] Ch 506; affd [1948] Ch 118; Dicey, Morris and Collins, Rule 132, para 23R-062; Westlake, s 156; Story, Chapter X; and Carruthers (2005), Chapter 2. A corollary of this rule is that, under the act of state doctrine, the application of foreign law to property within the territory of the foreign state cannot be disputed: see further *Belhaj v Straw* [2017] UKSC 3, [2017] 2 WLR 456.

[7] (1846) 8 Beav 547.

[8] Ibid, at 570.

[9] Cavers (1970) III Hague Recueil 75, 196 et seq.

[10] Hancock (1964) 15 Stan LR 561; (1965) 17 Stan LR 1095; (1966) 18 Stan LR 1299; (1967) 20 Stan LR 1; Weintraub (1966) 52 Cornell LQ 1; Morris (1969) 85 LQR 339; Alden (1987) 65 Texas LR 585; Anderson (1999) 48 ICLQ 167; and Carruthers (2005), paras 2.01–2.14.

[11] Hay, Borchers and Symeonides, p 1231.

[12] Eg *Re Ross* [1930] 1 Ch 377; *Re Duke of Wellington* [1947] Ch 506.

[13] Hancock (1966) 18 Stan LR 1299, 1321. See also Carruthers (2005), paras 2.51–2.86.

[14] See now supra, p 728.

[15] *British South Africa Co v De Beers Consolidated Mines Ltd* [1910] Ch 502; *Dubai Islamic Bank PJSC v PSI Energy Holding Company BSC* [2013] EWHC 3186 (Comm).

[16] *Re De Nicols (No 2)* [1900] 2 Ch 410, infra, p 1373.

[17] *Hamlin v Hamlin* [1986] Fam 11; *Razelos v Razelos* [1970] 1 WLR 390. Cf *Holmes v Holmes* [1989] Fam 47.

[18] Infra, p 1352.

[19] Infra, pp 1351–2.

[20] Infra, p 1353.

[21] As in the case of the formal validity of wills, infra, p 1352.

(i) Meaning of the "law of the situs"[22]

Before giving specific illustrations of the situs doctrine in operation it is essential that the true meaning of the expression "the law of the situs" should be understood. In general, the term "the law of the situs" is interpreted in its narrow literal sense as meaning that rule which applies to an analogous situation free from all trace of foreign elements. There is a strong argument that this narrow meaning should be adopted when the dispute concerns the legal effects of a conveyance, as, for example, when the question is whether there has been an infringement of the rule against perpetuities or whether the interest created is legally possible.[23] Outside this context, this approach may, however, not necessarily be warranted. It may be that a court at the situs, if required to give a decision, would apply the relevant rule of its own law applicable to a purely domestic situation. This, however, is not necessarily so, and if the foreign court of the situs would not apply its own law, then neither concerns of comity nor effectiveness would suggest that the English court must do so (although this might nevertheless be justified on the basis that English choice of law rules designate the most appropriate law). If consistency with the approach of the courts of the situs is prioritised, there are two methodologies which might be followed. The first, which has the support of some authority, is that the "law of the situs" might be understood to include its rules of private international law, thus potentially applying renvoi.[24] Second, determining the law of the situs might involve an examination of the foreign rule applicable to a domestic situation to see whether it truly extends to a case with international elements. In order to apply this second approach, a court could perhaps draw on US-style interest analysis methodology,[25] examining the relevant rule in the light of its reason, the purpose that it is designed to effect and the policy on which it is based. It does not follow that a rule of land law designed to promote the welfare of persons domiciled in a country or to regulate local transactions should necessarily be extended to transactions completed abroad between domiciled foreigners. This is well brought out by Cook in his discussion of the New Hampshire case of *Proctor v Frost*:[26]

> This concerned a married woman, domiciled in Massachusetts, who, by the statute law of New Hampshire was incapable of becoming surety for her husband, but by the law of Massachusetts was free from this incapacity. By a transaction in Massachusetts she became surety for her husband, and by way of security she executed in that state a mortgage of her land in New Hampshire.

There was no dispute that her capacity to execute the mortgage as a surety fell to be determined by the law of the situs, but that did not inevitably mean that the New Hampshire statute applied to the instant case. A correct decision on that question could scarcely be reached without first considering the purpose of the statute. Was the purpose to regulate the conveyance of New Hampshire land, or to protect wives against the importunities of financially embarrassed husbands? If it was the latter, it would be unseemly and inexpedient to extend this paternal solicitude to wives domiciled in foreign jurisdictions. In the result, the Supreme Court of New Hampshire considered that the object of the statute was to protect married women within the jurisdiction, and they therefore held the mortgage to be valid.[27] This approach has not, however, been greatly influential in English law—it is, instead, choice

---

[22] See Carruthers (2005), paras 1.20–1.21, and 1.43–1.45.

[23] Cook, p 270.

[24] Eg, *Re Ross* [1930] 1 Ch 377; *Re Duke of Wellington* [1947] Ch 506; supra, p 68.

[25] Supra pp 26–7.

[26] 89 NH 304, 197 A 813 (1938); Cook, p 274; and see the articles by Hancock, supra, p 1256, n 10.

[27] Though their decision to apply the law of Massachusetts, essentially by way of renvoi, (see 197 A 813 at 815) as the place of execution of the mortgage, rather than as the place of the wife's domicile, is hard to justify: Cook, p 275.

of law rules themselves which generally determine the scope of application of rules of private law, rather than a policy analysis of the potentially applicable law.[28]

(b) Specific issues

Problems relating to choice of the law applicable to immovables may arise in a variety of contexts. Some of these are considered separately in later chapters, such as the administration of estates of immovables and succession thereto, and the effect of marriage and other adult relationships on property, both movable and immovable. Nevertheless, some of the cases to be discussed in this chapter will be drawn from those fields, especially succession, where they illustrate principles generally applicable to immovables.

(i) Capacity to take and transfer immovables

Unless a person has capacity by the law of the situs to take immovables, he will be excluded from ownership. In *Duncan v Lawson*,[29] for instance, it was admitted that a bequest by a domiciled Scotsman of English leaseholds to trustees on trust for sale, and out of the proceeds to pay certain legacies to charities, was void as infringing the Mortmain and Charitable Uses Act 1888 (since repealed).[30] This was because the question whether a charity was competent to take English freeholds and leaseholds, even under a foreign will, must depend on English law. The same is true of capacity to transfer immovables, whether by sale, gift, mortgage or devise. If full age is attained in Country A at eighteen and in Country B at twenty-five, a person twenty-two years old, domiciled in A, cannot execute a valid conveyance of lands lying in B; whereas a person of the same age, even though domiciled in B, can effectually convey land in A.[31]

Bank of Africa Ltd v Cohen[32] unequivocally established that the situs rule is part of English law in relation to capacity to transfer land abroad. The facts were these:

> The defendant, a married woman domiciled in England, entered into a deed in England by which she agreed to make a mortgage of her land in Johannesburg in favour of the plaintiff. The mortgage was intended to secure money lent to her husband. The Roman-Dutch law prevailing in the Transvaal ordained that a married woman could not be bound as a surety unless she specifically renounced certain rights under that law. This renunciation had not been made in the formal manner required by the local law.

In an action in England for specific performance of the English transaction, judgment was given in favour of the defendant, based on her lack of capacity. In the words of Buckley LJ: "a person's capacity to make a contract with regard to an immovable is governed by the *lex situs*".[33]

This decision is not entirely satisfactory. If the facts raised a true question of capacity, it did not necessarily follow that issues of *contractual* capacity should be governed by the law of the

---

[28] But see eg *Serco v Lawson* [2006] UKHL 3, [2006] 1 All ER 823; *Office of Fair Trading v Lloyds TSB Bank plc* [2007] UKHL 48, [2008] AC 316. These are not property law cases, but they show that exceptionally the courts deal with private law applicable law problems through interpreting the policy and thus scope of the relevant statute, as proposed in the text, rather than a classical choice of law analysis.

[29] (1889) 41 Ch D 394; and see *A-G v Parsons* [1956] AC 421.

[30] *Hewit's Trustees v Lawson* (1891) 18 R 793.

[31] Cf *Sell v Miller* 11 Ohio State 331 (1860); Hay, Borchers and Symeonides, p 1234; Restatement 2d, § 223.

[32] [1909] 2 Ch 129.

[33] Ibid, at 143.

situs (and not the law of the contract),[34] nor (in any case) that the object of the South African rule was to protect married women domiciled in other countries.[35] If a question of form was involved, it is difficult to distinguish the case from that of *Re Courtney*,[36] where a contrary decision was reached.

There is no English authority on the law governing capacity to transfer land in England where the transferor is domiciled abroad. However, there is clear Canadian authority in favour of applying the law of the situs in such a case. In *Landry v Lachapelle*:[37]

> A husband and wife were domiciled in Quebec, the wife owned land in Ontario which she conveyed to her husband, to be owned by them both as joint tenants. As a married woman, she had capacity to do this under the law of Ontario, but not of Quebec.

The Ontario Court of Appeal identified the issue as one relating to title, not to the validity of any contract. "The crucial question . . . may be stated as follows:—Is the law of Ontario inconsistent with the law of Quebec as regards the conveyance to the defendant of the lands in question? If so, the Ontario law must govern."[38]

Although the choice of law rule designates the law of the situs, once again it does not necessarily follow that the substantive rules of law to be applied in the situs in the case of a foreign domiciliary are the same as would be applied to someone domiciled in the situs.[39]

(ii) Formalities of alienation

The formal validity of a transfer of immovables is determined by the law of the situs.[40] This is generally taken to mean that a transfer must comply with the formalities prescribed by the internal law of the situs for a purely domestic transaction containing no foreign element. For example, in *Adams v Clutterbuck*[41] it was held that a conveyance between two domiciled Englishmen of shooting rights in Scotland was valid, notwithstanding the fact that it was not under seal as required by English, but not Scots, law. Similarly it was held that a devise which was valid by the law of the testator's domicile was ineffectual to pass English land, since it was not attested by three witnesses as then required by the Statute of Frauds.[42] Nevertheless, it does not inevitably follow that a local formality must in all circumstances be observed. The law of the situs may regard the formality as essential for every conveyance, no matter where or by whom executed. On the other hand, it may regard the formality as necessary only for conveyances completed within the jurisdiction.[43]

---

[34] See infra, pp 1261–2.

[35] See this aspect of the matter discussed supra, p 1257.

[36] (1840) Mont & Ch 239.

[37] [1937] 2 DLR 504.

[38] Ibid, at 508.

[39] Cf *Proctor v Frost*, supra, p 1257, where, although the New Hampshire court, by a process of renvoi, applied Massachusetts law, it could have achieved the same outcome by determining that the wife had capacity under New Hampshire law, given that the statutory restriction on capacity did not apply to her as a foreign domiciliary.

[40] Dicey, Morris and Collins, para 23-073. On the other hand, a contract to transfer an interest in land does not generally have to satisfy the formal requirements of the law of the situs: *Re Smith, Lawrence v Kitson* [1916] 2 Ch 206; infra, pp 1260–1. But see Rome I Regulation, Art 11(5), discussed supra, pp 760–1.

[41] (1883) 10 QBD 403.

[42] *Coppin v Coppin* (1725) 2 P Wms 291.

[43] In the USA many statutes have expressly provided that a transfer shall be valid if the formalities of the place of execution are observed; see the Uniform Acknowledgement Act 1957; Restatement 2d, § 223, comment e.

(iii) Essential validity of transfers

The general rule laid down in *Nelson v Bridport*,[44] as we have already seen,[45] is that no disposition can create an interest in immovables that is contrary to the law of the situs. The law of the situs must decide whether an interest in land is permissible in nature or extent, and also exclusively governs the tenure, title and descent of immovables.[46] Thus a disposition of English land, whether by will or otherwise, which contains limitations that infringe the rules as to perpetuities and accumulations is void.[47]

A common application of the general principle occurs in the case of those restraints on alienation which are found in many systems of law. Most civil law systems, for example, forbid testators to dispose of more than a certain proportion of their property. When the subject matter of alienation is immovable property, the application of such restraints depends solely on the law of the situs.[48] Similarly, in determining whether a purported testamentary transfer infringes rules against perpetuities and accumulations, the law of the situs governs, and not the law of the testator's domicile.[49]

(iv) Contracts

Recognising the primacy of the law of the situs does not resolve all difficulties. The generality of the rule and the sweeping manner in which it is sometimes stated are apt to lead to error unless we notice the distinction between an actual transfer of land and a contract to transfer.[50] So far as formalities are concerned, for example, any transaction or instrument that purports to change, then and there, the ownership of immovables must satisfy the formal requirements of the law of the situs. But a different position arises where the inquiry relates not to the actual transfer of some interest, but to the rights and liabilities of the parties under a contract relating to immovables. A contract by A that he will transfer some interest in land to B also brings into play the choice of law rules governing the contract, now to be found in the Rome I Regulation.[51]

(a) Form

Under Article 11(1) of the Regulation, a contract is binding, so far as relates to form, if it satisfies the requirements of the law of the place of contracting or of the law applicable to it under the other Regulation rules.[52] So if A and B, two domiciled Englishmen, make a contract relating to foreign land in London in such terms that its governing law is that of England, the formal validity of the contract is generally subject only to English law.

---

[44] (1846) 8 Beav 547.

[45] Supra, p 1256.

[46] *Fenton v Livingstone* (1859) 33 LTOS 335. Contrast the law governing the essential validity of contracts relating to land, infra, p 1261.

[47] *Re Grassi, Stubberfield v Grassi* [1905] 1 Ch 584 at 592; *Freke v Carbery* (1873) LR 16 Eq 461.

[48] *Re Hernando* (1884) 27 Ch D 284 (English land); *Re Ross* [1930] 1 Ch 377 (foreign land).

[49] *Curtis v Hutton* (1808) 14 Ves 537; *Duncan v Lawson* (1889) 41 Ch D 394; *Re Hoyles, Row v Jagg* [1911] 1 Ch 179. Though cf *Re Piercy* [1895] 1 Ch 83 (apparently approved in *Philipson-Stow v IRC* [1961] AC 727 at 744–5), where application of the Italian law of the situs was somewhat limited. Cf *Brown v Gregson* [1920] AC 860 at 886.

[50] See Carruthers (2005), Chapter 4.

[51] See supra, p 706 et seq. Note that the applicable law for contracts concluded before 17 December 2009 may be determined by the Rome Convention or common law. See supra, p 691.

[52] Supra, pp 759–60.

There is, however, a special rule in Article 11(5) of the Regulation which deals with the formal validity of a contract the subject matter of which is a right in immovable property or the right to use immovable property.[53] Such a contract shall:

> be subject to the requirements of form of the law of the country where the property is situated if by that law:
>
> (a) those requirements are imposed irrespective of the country where the contract is concluded and irrespective of the law governing the contract; and
> (b) those requirements cannot be derogated from by agreement.

It has been observed that such mandatory requirements are "probably rather rare",[54] though there may be some such rules under Scots law.[55]

(b) Essential validity

Under Article 10 of the Regulation, the essential validity of a contract is generally determined by the law which would govern the contract if it were valid,[56] and contracts relating to immovables are no exception. Under Article 3(1) of the Regulation, parties are free to choose the law to govern their contract, again including a contract relating to immovables.[57] In the absence of choice, the law governing a contract will be determined by Article 4.[58] Article 4(1)(c) provides that "a contract relating to a right in rem in immovable property or to a tenancy of immovable property shall be governed by the law of the country where the property is situated".[59] This rule is subject to an escape clause under Article 4(3) if "the contract is manifestly more closely connected with a country other than that indicated",[60] as well as the other usual exceptions regarding mandatory rules and public policy.[61] The key point is that the law governing the essential validity of a contract for disposition of immovables will not necessarily be the law of the situs, although that law is likely to apply as a default in the absence of a contrary choice by the parties. Whether the contract is effective to transfer title will, however, always be determined by the law of the situs, as discussed above.

(c) Capacity

It would seem, on principle, that the distinction between an actual transfer and a contract to transfer must also be relevant in a question of capacity. The question of contractual capacity is (largely) excluded from the Rome I Regulation.[62] It might be argued that where a person contracts in one country to transfer land in another country, questions of capacity should be tested by the law governing the essential validity of the contract, which would point in any

---

[53] See supra, p 760–1.
[54] Report on the Rome Convention by Giuliano and Lagarde, OJ 1980 c 282/32.
[55] Eg Requirements of Writing (Scotland) Act 1995, s 1(2)(a)(i).
[56] Supra, p 755 et seq.
[57] Supra, p 705 et seq.
[58] Supra, p 724 et seq.
[59] Supra, pp 428–9. This is subject to an exception under Article 4(1)(d) which provides that "a tenancy of immovable property concluded for temporary private use for a period of no more than six consecutive months shall be governed by the law of the country where the landlord has his habitual residence, provided that the tenant is a natural person and has his habitual residence in the same country".
[60] Supra, p 735 et seq.
[61] Supra, p 711 et seq.
[62] Art 1(2)(a), but see Art 13.

event to the application of Article 10 of the Rome I Regulation.[63] The difficulty, however, of maintaining this view is that, if the contracting party were subject to some incapacity in the true sense, eg nonage, by the law of the situs though not by the governing law, it would be futile to make a decree of specific performance that the local law would forbid the parties to implement.[64] The most that could be done would be to hold the party subject to an incapacity liable in damages; alternatively the contract might be considered void on the grounds of common mistake.

---

[63] See Carruthers (2005), para 4.04.
[64] See supra, p 1258; *Bank of Africa Ltd v Cohen* [1909] 2 Ch 129.

31

THE TRANSFER OF TANGIBLE MOVABLES

1. Introduction	1263	(b) Derivative claims	1271
2. The Various Theories	1264	(c) Retention of title clauses	1272
(a) The law of the domicile	1264	(d) Meaning of "the law of the situs"	1273
(b) The law of the situs	1265	(e) Attachment of movables by creditors	1275
(c) The law of the place of acting	1265	(f) Goods in transit	1275
(d) The proper law of the transfer	1266	(g) Gifts	1276
3. The Modern Law	1267	(h) Cultural property	1277
(a) The general rule	1267	(i) Human rights	1278

1. INTRODUCTION

An assignment of movables can give rise to various problems. This chapter will focus on trying to determine the legal system according to which such matters should be resolved.[1] We are not concerned here with what are usually called general assignments, under which, on the occasion of marriage, death and bankruptcy, the entirety of a person's property may pass to another. Our inquiry is confined to particular assignments *inter vivos* of isolated or individual movables, of which the commonest examples are sales, gifts, mortgages and pledges. Further, the present discussion is limited to tangible movables.[2]

This has traditionally been one of the most intractable topics in English private international law, because many of the few relevant authorities are antiquated and they do not reveal with any certainty what principles govern the subject as a whole. A common but fallacious assumption is that all problems must be referred to one single law. In the course of time varied views on what this is have been advanced. The law of the situs of the property, the law of the place of the parties' domicile or of the transferor, the law of the place of acting, the proper law of the transfer—each of these has had its advocates. The assumption, however, is untenable. It represents an oversimplification of the position, because it is based on the fallacy that the possible questions arising out of a transfer of movables all fall into the same category and are all of the same juridical nature. This is not so. Suppose, for instance, the following facts:

> A, resident and domiciled in England, sells goods lying in a Barcelona warehouse to B, a Dutch businessman. He transmits the bill of exchange and the bill of lading to B to secure acceptance. B fails to accept the bill of exchange but takes the bill of lading to Antwerp and transfers it there to C, a Belgian businessman. Meanwhile, the goods have been shipped from Barcelona en route to Holland. The ship is wrecked off the coast of France, but the goods are salvaged and sold to D by the judicial authorities in Bordeaux.

---

[1] On this subject see especially Carruthers, *The Transfer of Property in the Conflict of Laws* (2005); Lalive, *The Transfer of Chattels in the Conflict of Laws* (1955); Zaphiriou, *The Transfer of Chattels in Private International Law* (1956); North (1990) I Hague Recueil 9, 259 et seq; Prott (1989) V Hague Recueil 215, 262–81; Chesterman (1973) 22 ICLQ 213; Morris (1945) 22 BYBIL 232.

[2] Intangibles are considered in Chapter 30.

A number of questions, some contractual others proprietary, differing fundamentally in character, may arise from these facts, and it does not require much acumen to appreciate that each one of these cannot satisfactorily be submitted to one system of law. Litigation may occur between A and B as to the formal or essential validity of the original transfer. A may claim as against B that he is entitled to stop the goods in transit. C may claim a derivative title from B which he alleges renders stoppage unlawful. D may claim that the effect of the judicial sale in France has been to divest all previous owners, original as well as derivative, of their former titles. If it is true to say that questions arising out of the transfer and acquisition of property in corporeal movables are determinable by one single law, what is that law in the instant case? Is Spanish law, which happened to be the law of the situs at the time of the original transfer, to determine, inter alia, the essential validity of the transaction between A and B, the effect of a failure by a Dutch buyer to accept a bill of exchange received by him from an English seller, and the title of a Frenchman who buys goods in France publicly sold by a French judicial authority? Furthermore, the law of the situs has not remained constant. Is it Spanish law for some questions, French law for others? If so, how are the questions to be classified for this purpose, and resolved? Consideration now will be given to the various theories that have been advanced with regard to the resolution of problems such as these.

2. THE VARIOUS THEORIES[3]

In choosing the proper law to govern the transfer of movable objects, arguments may be advanced in favour of the law of the domicile, the law of the situs, the law of the place of acting, or the proper law of the transfer. It will be well to consider the relative merits of these legal systems before attempting a final statement of the law.

(a) The law of the domicile

Historically, the starting-point was the maxim *mobilia sequuntur personam*—goods follow the person. Sweeping statements to the effect that rights over movables are to be governed by the law of the owner's domicile, on the basis that "personal property has no locality", may be found in the earlier English authorities.[4] Now, however, it is generally agreed that to allow either party to invoke the law of his domicile in the case of a dispute arising out of a transfer of chattels would be commercially impracticable and contrary both to natural justice and to the normal expectations of the parties themselves. Indeed, it has been said by the Privy Council that the maxim *mobilia sequuntur personam* does not mean that movables are deemed to be situated where their owner is domiciled, but merely that their devolution on his death is governed by his personal law.[5] Moreover, the application of the maxim might result in prejudice to innocent third parties, as can be seen from a hypothetical case:

> A, a domiciled Englishman, by a transaction which is valid by English law but void by the law of Illinois, executes a bill of sale in favour of X, another domiciled Englishman, over goods that are situated in Chicago, Illinois. Later, Y, also domiciled in England, causes a writ of attachment to be levied on the goods in Chicago in respect of a debt due to him from A. The attachment action proceeds to judgment and the goods are sold in satisfaction of Y's debt.

The result of holding in such a case that the original transaction conferred a valid and prior title to the goods on X, since it conformed to the law of the common domicile of A and X,

---

[3] Carruthers (2005), paras 3.02–3.10.
[4] *Sill v Worswick* (1791) 1 Hy Bl 665 at 690; *Re Ewin* (1830) 1 Cr & J 151 at 156.
[5] *Alberta Provincial Treasurer v Kerr* [1933] AC 710 at 721. See infra, p 1139.

would be to impose liability for conversion on the sheriff and the officer who conducted the sale in Chicago. Yet it is obvious that, though the sheriff must be presumed to know the law of the place where the goods are situate, he cannot be expected to investigate the law of their owner's domicile.

Again, whose domicile is decisive? Suppose, for instance, that the question is whether goods stored in Rotterdam belong to a domiciled Englishman or to a domiciled Frenchman. In such a case no decision is possible on the basis of the law of the domicile if the laws of France and of England differ, for there is no guide as to which of these laws shall be chosen. If the law of the claimant's domicile is chosen on the ground that the question of his title has been raised, this is a circular argument, since the sole issue is whether he possesses a title. The result is the same if the law of the defendant's domicile is chosen. Moreover, if the decisive factor is the domicile of one of the parties, the governing law would vary according to which of them began proceedings.

(b) The law of the situs[6]

An alternative to the law of the domicile is the law of the situs. This has obvious virtues. Where claimants have different domiciles or where they rely on transactions in different countries, the law of the situs has the great advantage of being a single and exclusive system that can act as an independent arbiter of conflicting claims. Moreover, its right of control satisfies the expectations of the reasonable person, for a party to a transfer naturally concludes that the transaction will be subject to the law of the country in which the subject matter is at present situated.

> If a movable which is vested in A as the result of a transaction with B governed by English law is taken by B to France and there sold to C in circumstances which, by French law but not by English law, confer a valid title on C, it would be a travesty of justice to determine the mutual rights of A and C by English law, the relevancy of which would be entirely unknown to C.

Nevertheless, there may be cases where reference to the law of the situs appears arbitrary. If, for example, goods deposited temporarily in a Hamburg warehouse are sold by their owners, London importers, to another London dealer by a contract effected in England, there may seem to be no obvious reason why any question concerning the title to the goods should be governed by German law. However, there would seem to be good policy reasons to support reference to the law of the situs. "Two decisive considerations are, firstly, that the country of the situs has the effective power over the chattel, secondly that the exclusive application of the law of the situs alone can fulfil the need for security in international property transactions."[7] A further argument is that the situs is generally likely to be objectively ascertainable by the parties to a transaction.

As can be seen from the example suggested earlier,[8] difficulties may arise where the situs of the goods changes during the course of events leading to litigation. If this is so then the problem will be to identify the law of the particular situs that must govern.[9]

(c) The law of the place of acting

There is little to be said in favour of the law of the place of acting, ie the law of the country where the legal act of purported creation/acquisition etc, or the transfer/transaction

---

[6] Carruthers (2005), paras 3.07–3.10, and Chapter 8.
[7] Lalive, op cit, p 115. But see, in contrast, Carruthers (2005), paras 8.16–8.71.
[8] Supra, p 1264.
[9] Morris (1945) 22 BYBIL 232, 233; and Carruthers (2005), paras 1.22–1.30.

took place. Here, as in other areas of law, the mere fact that a transaction is completed in a particular place is no adequate reason for admitting the control of the local law. If, for instance, an Englishman executes a document in Edinburgh granting a lien over his furniture in London to another Englishman it is unthinkable that this slight and perhaps incidental connection with Scotland should require the possessory rights of the parties to be determined by Scots law. Yet, curiously enough, there are decisions, dealing with negotiable instruments, which contain strong dicta in favour of the law of the place of acting. Thus in *Alcock v Smith*, Romer J said:

> Generally, the rights of transferor and transferee, on a transfer in one country of a document of title to a debt or to an interest in personal property, are governed by the law of the country where the transfer takes place, although the debt may be due from persons living in, or the personal property may be situate in, a foreign country.[10]

On appeal, Kay LJ in terms said the same thing,[11] but it seems clear from the illustrations he gave that he had in mind a case where the law of the place of acting and the law of the situs coincided. Since the place of acting and the situs are necessarily the same in the transfer of a negotiable instrument, it is probable that in these cases the judges, despite their reference to the law of the place of acting, were in fact speaking in terms of the law of the situs.[12]

(d) The proper law of the transfer

The last law that may be chosen to govern questions arising out of a transfer of movables is the proper law of the transfer. This might mean one of two things. First, it could simply mean applying the law governing the contract of transfer to proprietary questions.[13] Second, it could mean identifying the law governing proprietary issues using a rule analogous to the choice of law rule for contracts under the common law (the law with which the transfer has the closest and most real connection, perhaps also giving effect to party autonomy). In most cases, these alternatives would be the same, and their ascertainment would cause little difficulty, as for instance where the law of the place of acting and the law of the situs are identical or where two English businessmen meet in Paris and complete a transfer there of goods situated in England. But a more complex problem may arise, as where A, resident and domiciled in England, sells goods lying in a Naples warehouse to B, who is resident and domiciled in the Netherlands. Without more facts it is scarcely possible to say what the proper law would be in such a case. Before it could reach a decision, the court might be required to take into consideration a range of connecting factors, including the location of the transfer, the precise terms under which the transfer was drafted, and whether the goods were only temporarily or permanently in Italy. The danger is that the uncertainty created by a fact-sensitive and flexible approach would not meet commercial needs and could require litigation to resolve, not to mention the difficulties it might create for third parties.

As discussed further below, the law of the situs is the general choice of law rule for tangible movables, not the proper law or the other candidates discussed above. It is, however, important to note that this law will not govern all the issues exclusively, because an assignment or other disposition of property may raise both proprietary and contractual questions.[14] The law

---

[10] [1892] 1 Ch 238 at 255. See also *Embiricos v Anglo-Austrian Bank* [1905] 1 KB 677 at 683, 685.

[11] Ibid, at 267.

[12] Lalive, op cit, p 79.

[13] Cf *Glencore International AG v Metro Trading International Inc* [2001] 1 Lloyd's Rep 284, discussed infra, p 1270.

[14] It has been argued that the application of the law governing the contract might also be appropriate for proprietary questions in two-party cases: Bridge, 'English Conflicts Rules for Transfers of Movables: A Contract-based Approach?', in Bridge and Stevens (eds), *Cross-Border Security and Insolvency* (2001), p 123. However, the courts have repeatedly held that "the proprietary effects of a contractual transfer are governed by the *lex*

governing the latter will not be determined by the law of the situs rule, but rather by contractual choice of law rules, which are now generally set out in the Rome I Regulation (and not the common law 'proper law' approach).[15]

3. THE MODERN LAW

(a) The general rule

The questions which arise in relation to a transfer of tangible movables may include a variety of matters, such as whether the transfer is void for incapacity, whether it is formally or essentially valid, whether it is voidable for misrepresentation or other cause, whether the transferor has a lien on the goods or a right to stop them in transit, and what is the nature of the interest created by the transfer. Some of these questions are of a contractual, others of a proprietary, character.

It is clear that the contractual rights and obligations fall to be determined by the law governing the transfer contract.[16] This category includes such questions as whether there is an implied condition that the subject matter of the transfer is of satisfactory quality or is reasonably fit for a particular purpose, or whether the transfer contract itself is formally valid.

The solution is not so obvious, however, where the question relates not to the purely contractual rights but to claims to some possessory or proprietary right in the chattel itself. If, in such a case, the law of the situs and the law governing the transfer contract do not coincide, which is to prevail? It is now established that the proprietary effect of a particular assignment of movables is governed exclusively by the law of the country where they are situated at the time of the assignment.[17] An owner will be divested of his title to movables if they are taken to a foreign country and there assigned in circumstances sufficient by the local law to pass a valid title to the assignee. The title recognised by the law of the foreign situs overrides earlier and inconsistent titles, no matter by what law they may have been created. As Diplock LJ has said:[18]

> The proper law governing the transfer of corporeal movable property is the lex situs. A contract made in England and governed by English law for the sale of specific goods situated in

---

situs, even in a dispute between only the contracting parties"—*Dornoch Ltd v Westminster International BV* [2009] EWHC 1782 (Admlty) at [5], [2009] 2 Lloyd's Rep 420.

[15] Carruthers (2005), paras 4.05–4.09, 4.16–4.22. See also *Pattni v Ali and Dinky International SA* [2006] UKPC 51, per Lord Mance, at [25].

[16] On this distinction, see, eg, *Dornoch Ltd v Westminster International BV* [2009] EWHC 889 (Admlty), [2009] 2 Lloyd's Rep 191; *Luxe Holding Ltd v Midland Resources Holding Ltd* [2010] EWHC 1908 (Ch).

[17] *Cammell v Sewell* (1858) 3 H & N 617; on appeal 5 H & N 728; *Winkworth v Christie, Manson and Woods Ltd* [1980] Ch 496; *Air Foyle Ltd & Anor v Center Capital Ltd* [2002] EWHC 2535; [2003] 2 Lloyd's Rep 753; *Government of the Islamic Republic of Iran v The Barakat Galleries Ltd* [2007] EWCA Civ 1374; *T Comedy (UK) Ltd v Easy Managed Transport Ltd* [2007] EWHC 611 (Comm), [2007] 2 Lloyd's Rep 397; *Dornoch Ltd v Westminster International BV* [2009] EWHC 1782 (Admlty), [2009] 2 Lloyd's Rep 420; *Bonhams 1793 Ltd v Lawson* [2015] EWHC 3257 (Comm). A corollary of this rule is that, under the act of state doctrine, the application of foreign law to property within the territory of the foreign state cannot be disputed: see further *Belhaj v Straw* [2017] UKSC 3, [2017] 2 WLR 456. On the position in relation to aircraft, however, note the Cape Town Convention on International Interests in Mobile Equipment 2001 and the Protocol on Matters Specific to Aircraft Equipment, given effect through the International Interests in Aircraft Equipment (Cape Town Convention) Regulations 2015 (SI 2015/912).

[18] *Hardwick Game Farm v Suffolk Agricultural Poultry Producers Association* [1966] 1 WLR 287 at 330; affd by the House of Lords [1969] 2 AC 31; and see *Bank voor Handel en Scheepvart NV v Slatford* [1953] 1 QB 248 at 257.

Germany, although it would be effective to pass the property in the goods at the moment the contract was made if the goods were situate in England would not have that effect if under German law . . . delivery of the goods was required in order to transfer the property in them.

The application of the law of the situs rule must prevail on practical grounds of business convenience.[19]

The leading historical authority for the application of the law of the situs is *Cammell v Sewell*,[20] where the facts were these.

> A Russian seller shipped, in Russia, a cargo of timber on a Prussian vessel to English importers in Hull who insured the cargo with the plaintiffs as underwriters. The vessel having been wrecked off the coast of Norway, the timber was sold to X at a public auction held at the instance of the master in Norway. An action, brought by the underwriters in the Norwegian court to set aside the sale, failed. X shipped the timber to England and transferred it to the defendants. The underwriters sued the defendants for its value.

By English law, the auction sale had not affected the title vested in the English importers by the original contract and which was now vested in the claimants. The defendants, however, did not deny the effect of that contract. Their case was that, by virtue of what happened in Norway at the time when the timber was there, they had acquired a title which under Norwegian law overrode that of the earlier English purchaser. The Court of Exchequer gave judgment for the defendants on the ground that the decision of the Norwegian court was a judgment in rem which vested the property in X as against the whole world. On appeal, a majority of the Court of Exchequer Chamber, without giving a definite decision on the point, were of the opinion that the judgment was not a judgment in rem, but they decided that the title conferred on X by Norwegian law must prevail. Crompton J said: "We think the law on this subject was correctly stated by the Lord Chief Baron . . . when he says, 'If personal property is disposed of in a manner binding according to the law of the country where it is that disposition is binding everywhere'."[21]

Exclusive reference to the law of the situs will undoubtedly cause hardship to the previous owner if his movables are dealt with in a foreign country without his knowledge.[22] Thus, Crompton J acknowledged that the English law as to the distraint of a foreigner's goods for rent due from a tenant, or as to the title to stolen property acquired by a purchaser under a sale in market overt,[23] might appear harsh: "But we cannot think that the goods of foreigners would be protected against such laws, or that if the property once passed by virtue of them it would again be changed by being taken by the new owner into the foreigner's own country."[24]

---

[19] *Re Anziani* [1930] 1 Ch 407; see obiter remarks of Maugham J at 420, "I do not think that anybody can doubt that with regard to the transfer of goods the law applicable must be the law of the country where the movable is situate."

[20] (1858) 3 H & N 617; affd 5 H & N 728. In *Air Foyle Ltd and Anor v Center Capital Ltd* [2003] 2 Lloyd's Rep 753, Gross J, at [42], described the *situs* rule, dating back to *Cammell v Sewell*, as "long established beyond challenge".

[21] (1860) 5 H & N 728 at 744–5. See, more recently, *Pattni v Ali and Dinky International SA* [2006] UKPC 51.

[22] Eg *Winkworth v Christie, Manson and Woods Ltd* [1980] Ch 496.

[23] The market overt rule was abolished by the Sale of Goods (Amendment) Act 1994, s 1, but not with retrospective effect.

[24] (1860) 5 H & N 728 at 744; and see at 741, 743. In *Alcock v Smith* [1892] 1 Ch 238 at 267, Kay LJ said: "The goods of a foreigner sold in market overt by one who had no title to them could not be recovered from the purchaser." It seems likely that such a view would also be taken of transfers under such provisions as the Sale of Goods Act 1979, s 25, the Hire Purchase Act 1964, s 27 and the Factors Act 1889, ss 2, 8 and 9 (the 1889 and 1964 Acts as amended by the Consumer Credit Act 1974, s 192, Sch 4, Pt 1).

This approach was applied by Slade J in *Winkworth v Christie, Manson and Woods Ltd*[25] to the converse case of goods stolen in England, sold abroad and brought back to England.

> Works of art were stolen from the plaintiff's house in England. They were taken to Italy and there sold to the second defendant, an Italian, who then sent them back to England to be auctioned by the first defendants. It was agreed that, under Italian law, though probably not under English law,[26] the second defendant acquired a title to the goods, good against the world. It was crucial to decide whether title to the goods was governed by Italian law, as the law of the situs at the time of the transfer to the second defendant.

Slade J upheld the law of the situs rule even though it seemed hard on the plaintiff to see goods which had been stolen from him in England being validly offered for sale in England by the defendants. The judge would not accept that there should be any exception to the rule on the basis that the goods had been returned to England: "Security of title is as important to an innocent purchaser as it is to an innocent owner whose goods have been stolen from him. Commercial convenience may be said imperatively to demand that proprietary rights to movables shall generally be determined by the lex situs."[27] In support of this approach it may be added that the original owner is in a position to take measures to secure the property and prevent its transfer overseas, while the foreign purchaser is unlikely to know the prior location of the property and cannot be expected to do more than satisfy the requirements of the place of purchase.[28] The fact that the goods were wrongfully removed from England to Italy was thus held not to affect the fact that their situs at the time of the transfer to the second defendant was Italian. Slade J was not prepared to attribute a fictional English situs to them: "Intolerable uncertainty in the law would result if the court were to permit the introduction of a wholly fictional English situs when applying the principle to any particular case, merely because the case happened to have a number of other English connecting factors."[29]

The situs rule, though correct in general,[30] is not without its exceptions.[31] It was accepted in *Winkworth*[32] that there are a number of exceptions to the rule such as, for example, the rules applicable to goods in transit with a casual or unknown situs at the relevant time.[33] Again, succession is governed by separate choice of law rules.[34] Further, the law of the situs will not be applied if there is a mandatory statutory provision of English law which the courts are required to apply; though it should be pointed out that it is very rare for an English provision to be so interpreted. However, Slade J was prepared to accept two further exceptions. The first is where the purchaser claiming title did not act bona fide. This is a dubious exception.[35] If good faith is required by the law of the situs, as it was in the present case, this is no exception. It can only be an exception if the English requirement of good faith is to be insisted upon,

---

[25] [1980] Ch 496; Carruthers (2005), paras 3.24–3.30; Carter (1981) 52 BYBIL 329; Knott [1981] Conv 279; and see *Todd v Armour* (1882) 9 R 901.

[26] [1980] Ch 496 at 500.

[27] Ibid, at 512.

[28] *Macmillan v Bishopsgate Investment Trust plc (No 3)* [1996] 1 WLR 387, at 400.

[29] [1980] Ch 496, at 509.

[30] See *Bank voor Handel en Scheepvaart NV v Slatford* [1953] 1 QB 248, per Devlin J, at 257: "There is little doubt that it is the lex situs which as a general rule governs the transfer of movables when effected contractually"; *Kuwait Airways Corpn v Iraq Airways Co* [2002] 2 AC 883, per Lord Nicholls of Birkenhead, at 1077; and *Government of the Islamic Republic of Iran v The Barakat Galleries Ltd* [2007] EWCA Civ 1374, per Lord Phillips of Worth Matravers CJ at [132].

[31] Carruthers (2005), paras 3.23–3.78.

[32] [1980] Ch 496 at 501 and 514. See Carruthers (2005), paras 8.36 et seq.

[33] See infra, pp 1275–6.

[34] See infra, p 1339 et seq.

[35] See Carruthers (2005), paras 8.38–8.46. Also *Glencore International AG v Metro Trading International Inc* [2001] 1 Lloyd's Rep 284, per Moore-Bick, J at 295. Cf Knott (1981) 281.

notwithstanding its absence under the law of the situs. It is suggested that this exception can only be justified, if at all, as an example of the broader public policy exception and that would mean that it would not apply in every case where the English concept of good faith had not been satisfied; but only in the rare case where the application of the law of the situs in the particular circumstances was quite unacceptable to English public policy. Slade J himself described this second public policy exception as applicable to a case "where the content of the particular foreign law on which [the defendant] relied was so outrageous that this court regarded it as wholly contrary to justice and morality".[36] This is no more than the application of a general rule of private international law.[37]

An attempt by counsel for the claimants in *Glencore International AG v Metro Trading International Inc*[38] to have the court expand the categories of permitted exception to the situs rule was not successful. The litigation arose out of the collapse of an oil storage facility operated by the defendant ("MTI") in Fujairah, UAE.

> Each of the five claimants had entered into agreements with MTI, in terms of which they delivered oil products to MTI for storage. When MTI became insolvent the claimants asserted proprietary rights to the oil then held by MTI, and competing claims to the oil were made by several banks, and by the purchasers of various cargo parcels of fuel oil. The primary choice of law issue was this: what system of law governs title to oil delivered by the claimants to MTI, and by MTI to the purchasers, and what system of law governs any non-contractual liabilities which MTI and the purchasers may have incurred to the claimants? MTI and the purchasers alleged that the transfer of title to the oil in Fujairah was governed by the law of Fujairah (in terms of which the property had passed to MTI, and then to the purchasers). The claimants, on the other hand, sought to rely on the law which governed the contracts between themselves and MTI.

The issue was whether:

> as between the immediate parties to a contract under which goods are delivered by one party to the other, the passing of property is governed by the intention of the parties as expressed in the contract (the proper law) or by the law of the place where the property is situated (the lex situs) where these do not coincide in their effect.[39]

In the instant case, counsel for the claimant argued for the application of English law, being the proper law of the contract.[40]

Moore-Bick J, whilst recognising the attractiveness of the claimants' argument, preferred "consistency of principle . . . whether or not third party interests are involved",[41] and applied the law of Fujairah, as the situs of the oil, on the basis that, "it would be highly anomalous if questions of title to the goods were to be governed by English law as the proper law of the contract if the seller had not purported to re-sell the goods to a third party, but by . . . the lex situs if he had".[42]

---

[36] [1980] Ch 496 at 510.
[37] See supra, p 132 et seq. See also Carruthers (2005), paras 8.47–8.50.
[38] [2001] 1 Lloyd's Rep 284. See Carruthers (2005), paras 3.60–3.77, pp 249, 257–72.
[39] [2001] 1 Lloyd's Rep 284, per Moore-Bick, J at 290.
[40] Ibid, at 294.
[41] Ibid, at 295.
[42] Ibid. But see Carruthers (2005), para 3.75.

(b) Derivative claims

The principle of the situs rule is that title to movables acquired in one country by A under a transaction with B is good all over the world,[43] unless and until it is displaced by a new title vested in C as the result of an assignment effective by the law of the country to which the movables have been taken. As has been seen, the principle extends to a case where C claims derivatively from one of the parties to the earlier transaction. This type of problem often arises from the conditional sale.[44]

> Suppose, for instance, that a car is delivered by A to B under a hire-purchase transaction concluded in England. By English law, which is both the law of the situs and the proper law of the transaction, the ownership of the car remains in A until all the instalments of the price have been paid. B takes the car to the Netherlands and sells it to C, a bona fide purchaser. Suppose also that Dutch internal law requires hire-purchase agreements to be recorded in a public register, and holds that whether a sale by the hirer binds the owner depends on whether the agreement has been recorded. Later C brings the car to England in the course of his holiday. A then brings an action against him claiming the return of the car or, alternatively, the payment of damages.

These facts raise the question whether the rights of the parties are determinable by Dutch or by English law. It might be thought that on general principles English law should be preferred, for the alleged derivative title of C should depend on B's title from which its derivation is claimed. However, principle and policy demand that the bona fide assignee of movables should be protected if they act according to the law of their situation, and there can be no doubt that a derivative title to them, recognised as valid by that law, will be recognised as valid by English law. In the present context, this means that, where there have been two transactions relating to the same subject matter, the first in one situs, the second in another situs to which the subject matter has been transferred, it is the law of the second situs that governs the conflicting claims of the parties.[45]

Two North American cases might be discussed as illustrations of the problem where goods are removed from one state to another, there having been a reservation of title in the first state. The first case is the Canadian decision in *Century Credit Corpn v Richard*:[46]

> X sold and delivered a car, in Quebec, to Y under a conditional sale agreement. This agreement reserved title in X, the unpaid seller, until full payment of the purchase price. Under Quebec law this agreement did not have to be, and was not, registered. Y took the car to Ontario and sold it to Z who was unaware of X's reservation of title. Under Ontario law such conditional sale agreements were required to be registered. Furthermore, under Ontario law, Y could pass a good title to Z despite any defects in his own title.

The Ontario court held that Z's title, good under the law of Ontario, prevailed against X. The reasoning was that, so far as the requirement of registration was concerned, X had made a valid reservation of title under Quebec law which was not affected by taking the car to

---

[43] *Simpson v Fogo* (1863) 1 Hem & M 195 at 222 where Page-Wood V-C said: "A good title acquired in one country shall be a good title all over the globe."

[44] See Schilling (1985) 34 ICLQ 86; Fawcett, Harris and Bridge, paras 18.112–18.118; and Carruthers (2005), para 3.59. For a discussion of the relevant authorities in Australia, Canada and the USA, see Davis (1964) 13 ICLQ 53; Ziegel (1967) 45 Can Bar Rev 284; Juenger (1978) 26 AJCL (Supp) 145.

[45] Davis (1964) 13 ICLQ 53, 56. It is, however, possible that the law of the second situs might partially depend on the law of the first situs—if, for example, the rules governing whether C obtained title depended on whether B had good title to pass.

[46] (1962) 34 DLR (2d) 291; and see *Price Mobile Homes Centres Inc v National Trailer Convoy of Canada* (1974) 44 DLR (3d) 443; *Re Delisle* (1988) 52 DLR (4th) 106. For criminal law implications, see *R v Atakpu* [1993] 4 All ER (Ch D) 215, at 217–18.

Ontario. Ontario courts should recognise the validity of X's claim as against Y.[47] However, the sale of the car by Y in Ontario amounted, under Ontario law, to an overriding of X's reservation of title.

The second case is *Goetschius v Brightman*:[48]

> Y obtained possession of a car in California from X under a conditional sale contract by which the title remained in X until the whole price had been paid. The contract expressly provided that the car should not be removed from California. Y, however, took it to New York and there sold it to the defendant. The conditional sale was recorded neither in New York nor in California. By the domestic law of California applicable to a purely domestic case, the title of X would prevail over that of the defendant; by the equivalent domestic law of New York the title of X would only prevail if the conditional sale was registered. The plaintiff was the assignee of X.

Although the New York court applied its own law, as being the law of the situs, it found for the plaintiff. The judgment can be summarised as follows. The law that governs the interpretation and effect of the conditional sale is Californian law; by that law the title of the claimant is superior to that of the defendants; but, since the defendants bought the car while it was present in New York, it does not follow that New York law will recognise the superiority of the claimant's title. "No rule of comity requires this State to subordinate its public policy in regard to transfers made within the State of property situated here to the policy of the State where the owner of the property resides or where he acquired title."[49] The law of New York applies as being the law of the situs. But what is the New York rule applicable to the circumstances of this case? Although by New York statutory law a conditional sale reservation of title could not be enforced against a purchaser unless it were filed, the correct interpretation of this law is that it should be confined to sales effected in New York, not in some other state or country.[50] As a consequence, the failure of the original owner to register their conditional sale agreement in New York should not have precluded protection of their title.

(c) Retention of title clauses[51]

There have been a number of Scottish and Irish decisions in which the effect of retention of title clauses in international contracts has had to be considered.[52] Foreign suppliers of goods have included terms in contracts of sale to Scottish or Irish buyers which purport to incorporate the provisions of the seller's law,[53] allowing him to reserve title to goods which he has

---

[47] See, eg, *Taylor v Lovegrove* (1912) 18 ALR (CN) 22.

[48] 245 NY 186 (1927).

[49] Ibid, at 191.

[50] In cases where title would not appear to have been effectively reserved in one jurisdiction and the chattel is taken to another jurisdiction where the reservation of title was effective, there is a tendency in the courts to protect the original owner's title, either by generous interpretation of the domestic law of the original jurisdiction (eg *A J Smeman Car Sales v Richardsons Pre-Run Cars* (1969) 63 QJPR 150; David (1970) 2 ACLR 50) or, apparently, of its territorial scope (eg *Marvin Safe Co v Norton* 48 NJL 410, 7 A 418 (1886); cf *Charles T Dougherty Co Inc v Krimke* 144 A 617 (1929)).

[51] Dicey, Morris and Collins, paras 33-029–33-031; North (1990) I Hague Recueil 9, 265–73; Fawcett, Harris and Bridge, paras 18.93–18.110; McCormack, *Secured Credit under English and American Law* (2004), Chapter 6; McCormack, *Reservation of Title* (1995) 2nd edn; and Morse [1993] JBL 168. For discussion of Directive (EC) No 2000/35 on Combating Late Payment in Commercial Transactions OJ 2000 L 200/35, Art 4 (now recast as Directive 2011/7/EU, with Art 9 in identical terms as the previous Art 4), see Fawcett, Harris and Bridge, paras 18.104–18.107.

[52] *Hammer and Sohne v HWT Realisations Ltd* 1985 SLT (Sh Ct) 21; *Zahnrad Fabrik Passau GmbH v Terex Ltd* 1986 SLT 84; *Armour v Thyssen Edelstahlwerke AG* [1991] 2 AC 339; *Re Interview Ltd* [1975] IR 382; *Kruppstaal AG v Quitmann Products Ltd* [1982] ILRM 551.

[53] Often the foreign law is not pleaded, eg, *Aluminium Industrie Vaassen BV v Romalpa Aluminium Ltd* [1976] 1 WLR 676; *Emerald Stainless Steel Ltd v South Side Distribution Ltd* 1983 SLT 162; *Deutz Engines Ltd v Terex Ltd* 1984 SLT 273; *Armour v Thyssen Edelstahlwerke AG* [1991] 2 AC 339 at 350; or the parties may

delivered until they have been fully paid for. Almost inevitably in this type of case, the situs of the goods will change with their delivery, raising issues as to what law is to govern the operation of the reservation of title clause. This may be illustrated by *Zahnrad Fabrik Passau GmbH v Terex Ltd*:[54]

> Plaintiffs in Germany agreed to supply vehicle components to a manufacturer in Scotland under a contact containing a reservation of title clause, the law governing the contract appearing to be German law. The components were used in the construction of earth-moving equipment and, when the Scottish buyer became insolvent,[55] the plaintiffs claimed title to the goods supplied by them.

Notwithstanding the fact that German law may have been the law governing the contract, the court concluded that, as the dispute concerned title to the goods, this issue fell to be decided by Scots law as that of the situs of the goods. The reason given for applying Scots law was that title was alleged by the defendants to have been acquired in Scotland by accession once the components were included in the equipment. A fuller analysis might have been to ask whether title was properly reserved in Germany when that was the situs of the goods and then to ask, when the goods were moved to Scotland, whether the reserved title was overridden by accession under the law of the new situs.[56]

(d) Meaning of "the law of the situs"

In determining the meaning and content of the law of the situs, there are two problems to consider. The first is whether, when English law refers to the law of the situs, the doctrine of renvoi[57] applies; ie will the English court apply the law, not of the situs itself, but of whichever country is selected as applicable by the choice of law rules of the law of the situs? Some tentative support for the application of renvoi in this context can be derived from *Winkworth v Christie, Manson and Woods Ltd* where Slade J said: "It is theoretically possible that the evidence as to Italian law would show that the Italian court would itself apply English law. In this event I suppose it would be open to the plaintiff to argue that English law should, in the final result, be applied by the English court by virtue of the doctrine of renvoi."[58]

The question whether renvoi should be applied with regard to movable property arose in *The Islamic Republic of Iran v Berend*,[59] a case concerning the disputed ownership of a fragment of limestone relief believed to originate from fifth century BC Persepolis. The defendant claimed to have acquired title to the fragment when it was delivered to her in Paris in 1974, following purchase at auction in New York. Eady J was required to address the question whether, as a matter of English private international law, in determining the question of title to the fragment as movable property situated in France at the time of the event said to confer title, the English court should apply (as the defendant contended) only the relevant provisions of French domestic law, or (as the claimant contended) the relevant French conflict of laws rules as well as any relevant substantive provisions of French domestic law. His Lordship considered that, in the absence of binding authority to the effect that the renvoi doctrine

---

agree (rightly or wrongly) that the foreign law is the same as that of the forum, as in *E Pfeiffer Weinkellerei-Weineinkauf GmbH & Co v Arbuthnot Factors Ltd* [1988] 1 WLR 150.

[54] 1986 SLT 84.

[55] See now Council Regulation (EC) No 1346/2000 on Insolvency Proceedings, Art 7.

[56] Even without a further act of accession, when the property is delivered in the second situs the question would arise whether title transferred with possession, or whether the law of that situs accepted a reservation of title valid under the law of the first situs: see *Armour v Thyssen Edelstahlwerke AG* [1991] 2 AC 339.

[57] Supra, Chapter 5.

[58] [1980] Ch 496 at 514. See Carruthers (2005), paras 1.43–1.45.

[59] [2007] EWHC 132 (QB).

should apply to such questions: "Whether or not it should apply in any given circumstances is largely a question of policy."[60] As a matter of policy, Eady J saw no room for the introduction of renvoi to problems concerning tangible movable property.[61] Accordingly, title to the fragment was to be determined in accordance with French domestic law, in terms of which the defendant was held to have acquired valid title in 1974. The most recent authorities appear therefore to reject the application of renvoi for tangible movables.[62]

The second problem is illustrated by the reasoning in *Goetschius v Brightman*.[63] It concerns the identification of the substantive rules which are to be applied once the appropriate legal system has been selected. The English judge must apply the law of the situs, but this may not necessarily be the same law as a court at the situs would apply to a domestic case containing no foreign element.[64] This approach, under which the law of the situs means the law that a court at the situs would apply to the case in hand and not necessarily the domestic law applicable to a purely domestic case, would suggest a limited role for private international law so far as individual assignments of movables are concerned. Its role is to choose what law shall determine the conflicting claims of the parties. Its function in this regard is completed as soon as it has ruled that the law of the situs governs. Once this ruling has been given, ie once the choice of law has been made, we pass from the sphere of private international law; and it merely remains for the English court to ascertain as a fact what particular principle a court at the situs would follow in the actual circumstances.[65]

The authorities, so far as they go, appear to support the proposition that the English court, when required to apply English law as being the law of the situs in a case containing a foreign element, does not necessarily apply the ordinary domestic law of England. *Dulaney v Merry & Son*,[66] though it concerned a general assignment, may be given by way of analogy:

> Two domiciled Americans executed a deed in Maryland by which they assigned all their property wherever situate to another domiciled American for the benefit of their creditors. The deed was valid by the law of Maryland, but it was not registered under the English Deeds of Arrangement Act 1887.

The question was whether the assignee was entitled to goods situated in England. This was determinable by the English law of the situs. Had a similar assignment been effected in England between English traders concerning goods situated in England alone, there is no doubt that the deed would have been void. But this was a private international law case, and therefore a necessary inquiry was whether the English statute was designed to strike at all assignments, wherever made, affecting goods in England, or whether its operation was confined to assignments made in England. Channell J said that the question before him reduced itself to the construction of the 1887 Act; he concluded that the policy of the Act was not to bring within its provisions an assignment by foreign debtors affecting goods abroad as well as goods in England. By internal English law, therefore, the Maryland assignment was valid with regard to the English goods.

---

[60] Ibid, at [20] and [31].
[61] Cf, with reference to intangible movable property, *Macmillan v Bishopsgate Investment Trust plc (No 3)* [1995] 1 WLR 978, per Millett J, at 1008. Also Carruthers (2005), para 1.44.
[62] See also *Blue Sky One v Mahan Air* [2010] EWHC 631 (Comm), at [151]–[185]; Forsyth (2010) 6 J Priv Intl L 637.
[63] 245 NY 186 (1927), discussed, supra, p 1272.
[64] Cook, pp 263 et seq.
[65] Eg *The Islamic Republic of Iran v Berend* [2007] EWHC 132 (QB), per Eady J, at [32]–[33], [57]–[58].
[66] [1901] 1 KB 536.

(e) Attachment of movables by creditors

The attachment of movables by a creditor is also controlled by the law of the situs. The creditor enjoys the rights recognised by the law of the country where the movables are situated at the time of the attachment.[67] Those rights prevail against all persons claiming under some other law.[68]

The principle is illustrated by *Inglis v Robertson*,[69] where the facts were these:

> G, a domiciled Englishman, the owner of whisky stored in a warehouse at Glasgow, held delivery warrants issued by the warehouse-keeper stating that the whisky was held to G's order or "assigns by endorsement hereon". In return for a loan, G delivered in London to Inglis, an English merchant, a letter of hypothecation stating that the whisky was deposited with him as security for the loan, with power of sale. He indorsed the warrants and handed them to Inglis. Inglis gave no notice of his right to the warehouse-keeper. Robertson, claiming as personal creditor of G, arrested the whisky in the hands of the warehouse-keeper.

Presuming that by English law Inglis, claiming through G, had a better right to the whisky than Robertson, would that conclude the matter in his favour? It would not do so if Scots law were applicable, for the rule in Scotland was that a pledgee who wished to make his pledges effective in such circumstances had to give notice to the warehouse-keeper, otherwise his right was subordinated to the claims of the pledgor's creditor. The House of Lords gave judgment for Robertson. After stating that Robertson had done what was necessary by Scots law to acquire a real right against the whisky, Lord Watson proceeded as follows:

> It would . . . be contrary to the elementary principles of international law, and . . . without authority, to hold that the right of a Scottish creditor when so perfected can be defeated by a transaction between his debtor and the citizen of a foreign country which would be according to the law of that country, but is not according to the law of Scotland, sufficient to create a real right in the goods.[70]

(f) Goods in transit

The transfer of movables while they are in course of transit raises a difficult question of choice of law.[71] Suppose, for instance, that goods have been dispatched overland from London to Vienna, and that before reaching their destination they have been the subject of a sale or some other commercial transaction. The problems that such circumstances raise become more complex if the parties have different domiciles, or if the transaction is effected in some third country, ie other than Austria or England.

So far, English courts have not had to address the issue of which law should be applied in such a case. The probable explanation is that goods in transit are generally represented by a bill of lading or other documentary symbol of ownership which is capable of an independent dealing.[72] Jurists have advocated several laws, such as the law of the situs, the law of the owner's

---

[67] But, for the distinction between the assignment of a movable and its attachment, see Lalive, op cit, p 156.

[68] *Liverpool Marine Credit Co v Hunter* (1867) LR 4 Eq 62; on appeal 3 Ch App 479; cf Lalive, op cit, p 69. See also Council Regulation (EC) No 1346/2000 on Insolvency Proceedings, Arts 5 (third parties' rights in rem) and 6 (set-off).

[69] [1898] AC 616.

[70] Ibid, at 625.

[71] See *Winkworth v Christie, Manson and Woods Ltd* [1980] 1 Ch 496, per Slade J, at 501. For a fuller discussion see Carruthers (2005), paras 1.27–1.30, and 3.31–3.35; Lalive, op cit, pp 186–93; and Wolff, pp 519–21.

[72] See, eg, the delivery warrants in *Inglis v Robertson*, supra. There is, however, no clear authority on what law governs the transfer of a bill of lading or other document of title to goods. The three possibilities seem to

domicile, the law of the place of ultimate destination, the law of the place of dispatch and the proper law of the particular transfer (meaning generally the law of the contract of transfer).[73] Objections may be raised to each of these. The law of the situs, owing to its inconstancy, is an impracticable choice unless the movables have come to a definite resting-place at the time of the transfer.[74] The domicile of the owner, as well as begging the question potentially in issue (*who* is the owner?), is not a suitable criterion of the law to govern a mercantile transaction.[75] The law of the stipulated place of destination, though an appropriate choice in many circumstances, suffers from the disadvantage that it may be and frequently is altered during the course of the transit. The law of the place of dispatch is not well adapted to govern a transfer effected abroad when the transit is nearing completion. The proper law is, no doubt, suitable to govern some questions dependent upon the effect of a particular transaction, but scarcely apposite to every question, and may be difficult to ascertain, particularly for third parties.

The truth is that no single law can be made the exclusive arbiter of disputes arising out of a transfer of goods in transit. The problems must be broken down. A dispute between the parties to a particular transaction, as, for example, a mortgage of the goods granted by the assignee, will be governed by the proper law of the transaction.[76] If the movables come to rest sufficiently to admit of a dealing with them, as where they are seized by creditors in accordance with the local law or wrongfully sold by the carrier, the question of title must clearly be determined by the law of the situs.[77] Finally, if the transit is by sea in a single ship, there is much to be said for applying the law of the flag.[78]

(g) Gifts

Some special comment should be made on the transfer of movables by gift. The more common context for this issue to arise is that of *donatio mortis causa*—a gift in contemplation of death. Where such a gift has been characterised as a transfer of property,[79] then its validity and effect are governed by the law of the situs.[80] It should however, be noted that Farwell J in *Re Craven's Estate*[81] characterised such a gift as a testamentary disposition and applied the law of the testatrix's domicile, English law, by which law an effective parting with dominion was necessary to make the gift valid. He did not refer to the law of the situs to determine what was sufficient to pass the dominion.[82]

There is very little authority on transfer of movables by gift *inter vivos*, but it has been suggested that the validity of such transfers of property should be governed by the law of the

---

be the proper law of the bill of lading, the law of the situs of the bill at the time of its endorsement, and the law of the situs of the goods at that time. The point is important, since in some other countries the endorsement of a bill of lading does not pass the property in the goods. It is suggested that the correct choice is the law of the situs of the bill of lading at the time of its endorsement; see Zaphirou, op cit, pp 199–209; and Fawcett, Harris and Bridge, paras 18.78–18.92.

[73] See supra, p 1264 et seq.

[74] Eg *Cammell v Sewell* (1858) 3 H & N 617; on appeal 5 H & N 728; and see *Hardwick Game Farm v Suffolk Agricultural Poultry Producers Association* [1966] 1 WLR 287 at 300; affd by the House of Lords [1969] 2 AC 31.

[75] Supra, p 1264.

[76] Cf *North Western Bank v Poynter* [1895] AC 56.

[77] *Cammell v Sewell* (1860) 5 H & N 728.

[78] Cf *Lloyd v Guibert* (1865) LR 1 QB 115.

[79] See Lalive, op cit, pp 26–29.

[80] *Re Korvine's Trust* [1921] 1 Ch 343.

[81] [1937] Ch 423, and see the fuller report in (1937) 53 TLR 694.

[82] [1937] Ch 423 at 430, and see (1937) 53 TLR 694 at 698.

situs.[83] In *Cochrane v Moore*[84] a donor, apparently domiciled and resident in England, purported, by words of gift spoken in England, to give to the defendant a quarter share in a horse at all relevant times stabled in Paris. Later, the plaintiff advanced money on the security of the horse and, when the horse was sold, he claimed that he was entitled to the whole proceeds of the sale. The issue whether any title had passed by the gift was decided solely by reference to English law, under which delivery was held to be necessary. However, as French law was not pleaded or referred to, the case is hardly strong authority against the application of the law of the situs.

The American decision in *Morson v Second National Bank of Boston*[85] is of interest in this context. The donor, whilst travelling in Italy with the donee, handed her an envelope containing shares in a Massachusetts company, thus purporting to transfer to her the title to the shares; later, the donor, whilst still in Italy, signed and delivered the stock certificate to the donee. This was adequate under Massachusetts law, but not under Italian law, to effect transfer of legal title to the shares. It was concluded by the Massachusetts court that the law of the situs should determine whether there had been a completed gift of a tangible chattel and, had the shares been tangible chattels, Italian law, as the law of the situs, would have governed. This rule for the choice of law was, however, inapplicable since a transfer of shares fell to be governed by the law of the country in which the issuing company had been incorporated. On the other hand, the validity of the transfer of the actual certificate was subject to the law of the situs.[86]

(h) Cultural property[87]

Since 1970, there has been a developing landscape of regulation of what may be termed cultural property. The area is dominated by two international conventions, the 1970 UNESCO Convention on the Means of Prohibiting and Preventing the Illicit Import, Export and Transfer of Ownership of Cultural Property, and the 1995 UNIDROIT Convention on Stolen or Illegally Exported Cultural Objects.[88] To complement the United Kingdom's treaty obligations under the 1970 Convention, there has been created in England and Wales, by virtue of the Dealing in Cultural Objects (Offences) Act 2003, the criminal offence of trading in cultural objects in designated categories from designated countries, which have been stolen, illegally excavated, or illegally exported from those countries. Moreover, at a European level, a 1993 Directive on the Return of Cultural Objects Unlawfully Removed from the Territory of a Member State[89] has been implemented in the United Kingdom by means of The Return of Cultural Objects Regulations 1994,[90] and a further EU Regulation restricts the export of European cultural goods outside the EU.[91]

---

[83] Zaphiriou, op cit, pp 57–8. See, however, Carruthers (2005), para 3.12, for a situation where application of the situs rule may be inappropriate.

[84] (1890) 25 QBD 57.

[85] 306 Mass 589, 29 NE 2d 19 (1940).

[86] The rules as to assignment of shares in English private international law are discussed infra, p 1298 et seq.

[87] See, generally, Carruthers (2005), Chapter 5; Frigo (2015) 375 Recueil des cours 89; Roodt (2015).

[88] The 1970 Convention entered into force in the United Kingdom on 1 November 2002. The United Kingdom is not a party to the 1995 Convention. There are, in addition, various instruments concerning the import and export control of cultural objects.

[89] Now recast as Directive 2014/60/EU of 15 May 2014.

[90] SI 1994/501, most recently amended by The Return of Cultural Objects (Amendment) Regulations 2015 SI 2015/1926.

[91] Council Regulation (EC) No 116/2009 of 18 December 2008 on the export of cultural goods.

The 1970 Convention and the 1994 Regulations impose duties only upon states, and not upon individuals. Consequently, recovery of cultural property is dependent upon state intervention, and property must be explicitly designated by a state if it is to warrant protection under either instrument.

In practice, rules of private international law still govern legal questions arising in the United Kingdom concerning title to cultural property,[92] and to date no special choice of law rules have been introduced in the United Kingdom in respect of dealings with such property.[93] The law of the situs rule may assist a foreign state to reclaim cultural property which has been misappropriated and brought to England,[94] but only if the law vested title in the state while the property was in its territory.[95] Anti-seizure legislation, however, was introduced in Part 6 of the Tribunals, Courts and Enforcement Act 2007 (Protection of Cultural Objects on Loan),[96] in terms of which protection from seizure and forfeiture is conferred on certain cultural objects ("protected objects"),[97] which have been brought to the United Kingdom from overseas for public display in a temporary exhibition at a museum or gallery. Protected objects may not be seized or forfeited[98] unless by virtue of an order made by a court in the United Kingdom in circumstances where the court is required to make the order by reason of an EU obligation or any international treaty.[99]

(i) Human rights[100]

Article 1 of Protocol No 1 to the European Convention on Human Rights, implemented in the United Kingdom by means of the Human Rights Act 1998, provides that:

> Every natural or legal person is entitled to the peaceful enjoyment of his possessions. No one shall be deprived of his possessions except in the public interest and subject to the conditions provided for by law and by the general principles of international law.

> The preceding provisions shall not, however, in any way impair the right of a State to enforce such laws as it deems necessary to control the use of property in accordance with the general interest to secure the payment of taxes or other contributions or penalties.[101]

---

[92] See, eg, *Government of the Islamic Republic of Iran v The Barakat Galleries Ltd* [2007] EWCA Civ 1374.

[93] See, in contrast, *The Islamic Republic of Iran v Berend* [2007] EWHC 132 (QB), in which evidence was led regarding a proposed exception (application of the law of the state of origin) to the French choice of law rule (application of the law of the situs). For an example of a special choice of law rule for cultural property, see the Belgian *Code de droit international privé* (16 July 2004), Art 90; cf Carruthers (2005), pp 265–272. Consider also the role and work of the United Kingdom's Spoliation Advisory Panel, created in 2000 to help to resolve claims in respect of cultural objects looted during the Nazi era and now held in national collections; see generally https://www.gov.uk/government/collections/reports-of-the-spoliation-advisory-panel and note also the Holocaust (Return of Cultural Objects) Act 2009.

[94] Note also the Brussels I Recast, Art 7(4), supra p 279.

[95] See, eg, *Attorney General of New Zealand v Ortiz* [1984] AC 1; *Government of the Islamic Republic of Iran v The Barakat Galleries Ltd* [2007] EWCA Civ 1374, [2008] 3 WLR 486.

[96] Ss 134–8.

[97] Ie those which satisfy the conditions set out in the Tribunals, Courts and Enforcement Act 2007, s 134(2).

[98] In respect of which, see s 135(3).

[99] S 135(1). Eg "where . . . the court is asked to enforce an order for the seizure of an object made by the courts of another country to confiscate proceeds of crime" (Explanatory Notes to the Tribunals, Courts and Enforcement Act 2007, para 625).

[100] See, generally, Fawcett, Ni Shuilleabhain and Shah, *Human Rights and Private International Law* (2016), Ch 15 and Carruthers (2005), paras 8.71–8.76.

[101] See, eg, *Scotts of Greenock Ltd and Lithgows Ltd v United Kingdom* (1986) A 102; *Agosi v United Kingdom* (1986) A 108; *National and Provincial Building Society and Ors v United Kingdom* [1997] STC 1466.

It is reasonable to inquire whether an English forum's strict application of the situs rule, where the effect of application is to deprive an "innocent" owner of his right to the peaceful enjoyment of his possessions, might be said to violate Article 1 of Protocol No 1. Where, by virtue of the situs rule, a deprived owner has no right of action or recourse in respect of his property, there might appear to be an *ex facie* violation of his proprietary rights. Arguably, however, the right to peaceful enjoyment does not attach to property which, by application of the situs rule, has been determined to belong to another.

32

THE ASSIGNMENT
OF INTANGIBLE MOVABLES

1. Introduction	1280		(c) The modern law	1284
2. Debts	1280	3. Negotiable Instruments		1294
(a) The situs of a debt	1280	4. Shares and Securities		1298
(b) The various theories on the law		(a) The traditional approach		1298
applicable to assignments of debts	1282	(b) The modern holding system		1301

1. INTRODUCTION[1]

Intangible movables may be divided into rights which are mere rights of action, and rights which are represented by some document or writing that is not only capable of delivery but in the modern commercial world is negotiated as a separate physical entity. A debt, arising from a loan or from an ordinary commercial contract, is an example of the first class; while the second class is chiefly exemplified by negotiable instruments and shares. It is proposed here to keep the two classes separate, and to deal first with debts, secondly with negotiable instruments, and thirdly with shares and securities.[2]

2. DEBTS[3]

(a) The situs of a debt[4]

In previous chapters we have seen that the determination of the situs of immovable and tangible movable property may be necessary in order to determine the applicable law. It is possible also that a debt may be deemed by English law to have a definite locality of its own for several different purposes, such as the exercise of jurisdiction,[5] the payment of taxes, the grant of probate or of letters of administration,[6] or the determination of the location of damage for the purposes of another choice of law rule.[7] The test by which the locality is traditionally determined has been explained by Atkin LJ in the following words:

---

[1] See, generally, Carruthers (2005), Chapter 6; Benjamin (2000), Chapter 1; and Ooi (2003), Chapters 1–5.

[2] On issues relating to intellectual property, see Fawcett and Torremans, *Intellectual Property and Private International Law* (2011) 2nd edn; Bariatti (2010) 6 J Priv Intl L 395.

[3] Moshinsky (1992) 109 LQR 591.

[4] Rogerson [1990] CLJ 441; and Carruthers (2005), paras 1.31–1.42.

[5] Kaye [1989] JBL 449. The place of performance of a payment obligation may also be relevant for jurisdictional purposes, and may be different from the situs of the debt: see eg *Definitely Maybe (Touring) Ltd v Marek Lieberberg Konzertagentur GMBH* [2001] 2 Lloyd's Rep 455.

[6] See, eg, *A-G v Bouvens* (1838) 4 M & W 171 at 191; *Stamps Comrs v Hope* [1891] AC 476 at 481–2; *A-G v Lord Sudeley* [1896] 1 QB 354 at 360–1; *Re Maudslay, Sons and Field* [1900] 1 Ch 602; Falconbridge (1935) 13 Can Bar Rev 265.

[7] See eg *Hillside (New Media) Ltd v Baasland* [2010] EWHC 3336 (Comm), [2010] 2 CLC 986.

The test in respect of simple contracts was: Where was the debtor residing? . . . The reason why the residence of the debtor was adopted as that which determined where the debt was situate was because it was in that place where the debtor was that the creditor could, in fact, enforce payment of the debt.[8]

Thus the traditional rule is that an intangible movable, such as a right to recover a loan[9] or money due under an insurance policy,[10] is situated in the country where the debtor resides (for legal persons, generally understood to be their place of business),[11] because that is where it can be enforced.[12] This rule is, however, far from a complete or clear guide. First, it may not be applicable to every debt—it has been held that a debt which arises under an irrevocable letter of credit is situated in the place where it is in fact payable against the documents,[13] rather than the place of residence of the bank. Second, if the motivation for the general reference to the residence of the debtor is that it is where the debt is enforceable, eg being where the debtor can be found for service,[14] this raises two complexities. First, under modern jurisdictional rules, a company may usually be sued not only where it is 'resident', but also in the place of performance of the contractual obligation in question, which would generally[15] be the place of payment of the debt (although whether the debt is practically enforceable there would depend on whether the company had assets in that location). Second, an individual or company may have more than one 'residence' for jurisdictional purposes—for example, under the Brussels I Recast a company may be subject to the general jurisdiction of the courts of its domicile, meaning its seat/registered office, principal place of business, or central administration,[16] or if the dispute arises out of the activities of a branch office, in the courts of the location of that branch.[17] So if the situs is supposed to be based on enforceability, there may actually be a range of different locations where a debt is potentially enforceable.[18]

One suggested approach is that if the debtor resides in two or more countries, the debt should be situated in the one in which "it is required to be paid by an express or implied provision of the contract or, if there is no such provision, where it would be paid according to the ordinary course of business".[19] If, however, the debtor resides only in one country, the

---

[8] *New York Life Insurance Co v Public Trustee* [1924] 2 Ch 101 at 119; *Kwok Chi Leung Karl v Comr of Estate Duty* [1988] 1 WLR 1035 at 1040. See, however, Carruthers (2005), paras 8.67–8.70.

[9] *Re Helbert Wagg & Co Ltd's Claim* [1956] Ch 323.

[10] *New York Life Insurance Co v Public Trustee* [1924] 2 Ch 101; *Jabbour v Custodian of Israeli Absentee Property* [1954] 1 WLR 139.

[11] *Swiss Bank Corpn v Boehmische Industrial Bank* [1923] 1 KB 673 at 678; *Sutherland v German Property Administrator* (1933) 50 TLR 107.

[12] *Alloway v Phillips* [1980] 1 WLR 888. In *Brooks Associates Inc v Basu* [1983] QB 220, it was held that a debt due from the National Savings Bank could be attached in England even though the head office of the Bank was in Scotland.

[13] *Power Curber International Ltd v National Bank of Kuwait SAK* [1981] 1 WLR 1233 at 1240; see also *Taurus Petroleum Limited v State Oil Company of the Ministry of Oil, Republic of Iraq* [2015] EWCA Civ 835, [2016] 1 Lloyd's Rep 42.

[14] *Kwok Chi Leung Karl v Comr of Estate Duty* [1988] 1 WLR 1035 at 1041.

[15] But note Brussels I Recast, Art 7(1)(b), supra, p 225 et seq.

[16] See supra, p 198 et seq. See discussion in *Hillside (New Media) Ltd v Baasland* [2010] EWHC 3336 (Comm), at [33]–[36], [2010] 2 CLC 986; *Perrin v Revenue and Customs Commissioners* [2014] UKFTT 223 (TC), at [34]–[45].

[17] See supra, p 279 et seq.

[18] See further discussion in Dicey, Morris and Collins, para 22-026 et seq.

[19] *Jabbour v Custodian of Absentee's Property of State of Israel* [1954] 1 WLR 139 at 146; and see *Re Russo-Asiatic Bank* [1934] Ch 720; *Rossano v Manufacturers' Life Insurance Co Ltd* [1963] 2 QB 352 at 378–80. A debt due from a bank to a customer, for instance, is deemed by the general law to be situated at the branch where the account is kept: *Clare & Co v Dresdner Bank* [1915] 2 KB 576; *Joachimson v Swiss Bank Corpn* [1921] 3 KB 110 at 127; *Société Eram Shipping Co Ltd v Cie Internationale de Navigation and Ors* [2004] 1 AC 260, per Lord Hobhouse of Woodborough, at [73]; *Kuwait Oil Tanker Co SAK v Qabazard* [2004] 1 AC 300; and *Wight and Ors v Eckhardt Marine GmbH* [2004] AC 147.

debt is situated there alone, notwithstanding that it may be expressly or implicitly payable elsewhere.[20] An Australian court[21] has suggested that the place of payment in the ordinary course of business should be preferred as a general rule, notwithstanding the fact that the debtor is not resident there. The general view, however, is that the residence of the debtor is "an essential element in deciding the situs of the debt".[22] On this basis, the better approach may be that a debt is located at the place of residence (for companies, place of business) of the debtor, and if there is more than one such place, at the place of residence which is most closely connected to the debt.

(b) The various theories on the law applicable to assignments of debts

The conflict of opinion that impedes the search for the law to govern an assignment of tangible movables[23] has been equally evident in the corresponding case of debts. Various theories have been propounded advocating the following legal systems: the law of the place where the creditor is domiciled; the law of the place where the debt may be said to have an artificial situation (the *lex situs*, which as discussed is traditionally the residence of the debtor); the law of the place where the assignment is made; the proper law of the assignment; and the proper law of the transaction that created the debt.

There appears to be neither authority nor reason for choosing the law of the domicile as such, either of the creditor or the debtor, as the law to govern an assignment of a debt, and in fact cases may be put in which the choice would lead to absurdity.[24]

> If a domiciled Englishman, having acquired a right to receive a sum of money from a Belgian by reason of some commercial transaction governed by the law of France, were to assign that debt first to one man in Italy and then to another in Switzerland, it is difficult to adduce any principle that would justify the settlement of a dispute between the parties according to the law either of England or of Belgium. On the contrary, the assignee of a debt could not reasonably be expected to realise that he was subjecting his rights to the law of the domicile of either the creditor or the debtor, especially as the place of domicile might well be an unknown quantity.

As we have seen, a debt may possess a definite, though artificial, situation for certain purposes. This does not, however, necessarily imply that its assignment should be governed by the law of its situs, and there is authority rejecting reference to the law of the situs, principally because the residence of the debtor may change after the debt has arisen.[25] Another reason given is that in practice a single assignment may cover debts with different locations, and it would be undesirable for the effectiveness of the assignment to be governed by more than one applicable law.[26]

Historically, English judges regularly said that an assignment is to be governed by the law of the place where it is executed.[27] Another theory is that the governing system is the *lex actus*,

---

[20] *Re Helbert Wagg & Co Ltd's Claim* [1956] Ch 323.

[21] *Cambridge Credit Corpn Ltd v Lissenden* (1987) 8 NSWLR 411.

[22] *Deutsche Bank und Gesellschaft v Banque des Marchands de Moscou* (1930) (unreported), CA, cited in *Re Helbert Wagg & Co Ltd's Claim* [1956] Ch 323 at 343.

[23] Supra, p 1264 et seq.

[24] Carruthers (2005), paras 6.19–6.21.

[25] *Re Anziani* [1930] 1 Ch 407; *Macmillan Inc v Bishopsgate Investment Trust plc (No 3)* [1996] 1 WLR 387 at 401; Carruthers (2005), paras 6.24–6.30.

[26] *Raiffeisen Zentralbank Österreich v Five Star General Trading LLC* [2001] EWCA Civ 68; [2001] QB 825, per Mance LJ, at [38].

[27] *Lee v Abdy* (1886) 17 QBD 309; *Alcock v Smith* [1892] 1 Ch 238; *Embiricos v Anglo-Austrian Bank* [1905] 1 KB 677; *Republica de Guatemala v Nunez* [1927] 1 KB 669; *Re Anziani* [1930] 1 Ch 407. But see criticism in *Macmillan Inc v Bishopsgate Investment Trust plc (No 3)* [1996] 1 WLR 387, per Staughton LJ, at 402. See also Carruthers (2005), paras 6.22–6.23.

ie the law of the country with which the assignment is most closely connected.[28] This is preferable to the law of the place of acting, since it does not depend on the chance place of execution, but nevertheless it would seem to be less convenient than still another law which will now be discussed.

It is submitted that there is an obvious answer to the question—What is the most appropriate law to govern proprietary questions arising from the voluntary assignment of a debt as an intangible movable? The appropriate law is not the law governing the validity of the assignment, but the law governing the validity of the original transaction out of which the debt arose.[29] It is reasonable and logical to refer certain questions relating to a debt to the transaction in which it has its source and to the legal system which governs that transaction. If the transaction under which A lends money or sells goods to B is connected with no other country but England, A acquires a right that is admittedly governed by English law. The right thus created under the aegis of English law should, so far as its assignability is concerned, be governed throughout its existence by English law. Again, reference to such law is logical to determine most questions of priorities.[30] This is not to deny that certain (contractual) questions might be determinable by the governing law of the assignment itself, as for example those concerned with the validity of a particular assignment and arising between the parties or their representatives.[31] But when the question travels beyond these boundaries—when, for example, it is denied that the right is capable of assignment—a solution must obviously be sought elsewhere. What is more reasonable than to refer to the law that admittedly continues to govern the subject matter of the assignment? One undeniable merit of this is that, where there have been assignments in different countries, no confusion can arise from a conflict of laws since all questions are referred to a single legal system.[32] The same merit is not shared by the law of the situs, since this follows the residence of the debtor and is not therefore a constant.

An illustration may demonstrate the logic of the application of the law governing the validity of the original transaction out of which the debt arose:

> If an Englishman contracts a debt as a result of the purchase of goods from another Englishman in London, his obligation, if expanded in words, is to pay not only the seller but also an assignee of the seller, provided, however, that the assignment is regarded as good by English law. What governs his liability to the seller must also govern his liability to any person deriving title from the seller.

In such a case the attention of the debtor, when he assumes that role, is confined solely to the legal system under which he contracts the obligation, and the reasonable inference is that any transfer of the obligation made by the creditor shall be governed by the law of England as being the legal system to which the subject matter of the transfer owes its existence—that the law which governs the validity of the contract under which the debt arises ought to also govern its assignability.

---

[28] *Macmillan Inc v Bishopsgate Investment Trust plc (No 3)* [1996] 1 WLR 387, per Staughton LJ, at 399; *Atlantic Telecom GmbH, Noter* 2004 SLT 1031, per Lord Brodie, at 1043. See also Carruthers (2005), paras 6.31–6.32.

[29] *Macmillan Inc v Bishopsgate Investment Trust plc (No 3)* [1996] 1 WLR 387, per Staughton LJ, at 401.

[30] Infra, pp 1288–9.

[31] Carruthers (2005), paras 6.36–6.38, and 6.46–6.48.

[32] It must be admitted, however, that the effectiveness of a single assignment of a group of debts, such as through factoring, may under this approach be subject to a variety of different laws. A special rule may perhaps be justified for this particular context: see eg the UNCITRAL Convention on the Assignment of Receivables in International Trade (2001).

Let us turn from the debtor and contemplate the attitude of mind of an assignee.

> If B, the debtor under the original transaction from which the obligation sprang, takes up residence in Italy, and A, the creditor, makes in France an assignment of the debt to X, it is reasonable to presume that X, as a prudent businessperson, would concentrate his attention on the transaction which gave rise to B's obligation to pay, because X is purchasing the benefit of that obligation and will at least wish to confirm its validity.

It is likely that X would presume that an obligation having its origin in, and drawing its protection from, English law, will in all respects be subject to that law. We should then naturally expect him to inquire what is necessary under English law for the completion of an effective assignment. What would not occur to him would be to consider the law of Italy merely because of the debtor's residence in that country. It would, perhaps, be convenient to allow the law of France, as the law governing the assignment, to govern the rights of A and X *inter se*, but, to take only one example, it cannot solve a question of priorities between X and an assignee claiming under an assignment made in some other country, except in the simplest case.[33]

In conclusion, it is suggested that the most appropriate law to govern the question at any rate of priorities is the law governing the transaction by which the subject matter of the various assignments was created.[34]

(c) The modern law

Leaving theory on one side, we must examine the present state of the law governing the assignment of a debt. An initial distinction has to be drawn, because there are two types of assignment, the voluntary (which may be contractual or non-contractual)[35] and the involuntary. The former occurs where the creditor of his own volition transfers his right to another party; the latter, where his right is transferred against his will by operation of law, as, for example, where in the course of execution the debt is attached as being part of his assets.

Furthermore, the questions in which the issue is the validity or effect of an assignment fall into two classes. The issue may depend solely on the validity and effect of the assignment itself, as, for example, where the dispute relates to capacity, form or essential validity; or it may depend on the validity and effect of the original transaction by which the debt was created, as, for example, where the question is whether the debt is capable of assignment, or to which of two or more competing assignees it is payable.[36]

---

[33] Cf *Bankhaus H Aufhauser v Scotboard Ltd* 1973 SLT (Notes) 87.

[34] Cf Carruthers (2005), paras 6.39–6.40. This principle seems to have been adopted by Warrington J in *Kelly v Selwyn* [1905] 2 Ch 117, infra, p 1289; and see *Banque Paribas v Cargill International SA* [1992] 1 Lloyd's Rep 96 at 100; *Macmillan Inc v Bishopsgate Investment Trust plc (No 3)* [1996] 1 WLR 387 at 401. Contrast Goode, *Commercial Law* (2004) 3rd edn, pp 1128–30 who would apply the law of the situs of the debt; and Moshinsky (1992) 108 LQR 591 at 613.

[35] Carruthers (2005), paras 6.12–6.17.

[36] On the distinction between an "original parties dispute" (where the problem arising stems from the original relationship between the debtor and his creditor) and a "remote parties dispute" (where the problem arising stems from the terms of the contract by which the debt is assigned), see Carruthers (2005), paras 6.41–6.62. The distinction between the two types of dispute is long-standing (*Dinwoodie's Executrix v Carruthers' Executrix* (1895) 23 R 234, at 239; *Scottish Provident Institution v Cohen* (1888) 16 R 112, at 113; *Scottish Provident Institution v Robinson* (1892) 29 SLR 733 at 734; and *Bankhaus H Aufhauser v Scotboard Ltd* 1973 SLT (Notes) 87, at 89), and is affirmed by Art 12 of the Rome Convention and Art 14 of the Rome I Regulation.

(i) Voluntary assignments[37]

The source of the modern law concerning the voluntary, contractual assignment of a right is Article 14 of the Rome I Regulation (2008), which is the successor to Article 12 of the (1980) Rome Convention on the Law Applicable to Contractual Obligations.[38]

(a) Contractual assignments—questions dependent solely on the validity and effect of the assignment[39]

Issues of form and essential validity are governed by Article 14(1) of the Rome I Regulation, which provides:

> The relationship between assignor and assignee under a voluntary assignment[40] . . . of a claim against another person (the debtor) shall be governed by the law that applies to the contract between the assignor and assignee under this Regulation.[41]

The effect of this provision is to require the application, to most questions which arise between assignor and assignee, of the law which governs the validity and effect of the contract between them.[42] So, in the case of essential validity, reference must generally be made (pursuant to Article 10 of the Regulation) to the law which would govern the contract if it were valid.[43] This general approach confirms the view previously adopted by the English courts.[44] Turning to formalities, the assignment will be formally valid, under Article 11 of the Regulation,[45] if it satisfies the formal requirements of the governing law, or of the law of the place where it was concluded if both parties were in the same country, or, if they were in different countries, of the law of one of those countries, or the law of either party's habitual residence.[46]

---

[37] There is a growing literature on this subject; see generally eg Goode [2015] LMCLQ 289; Hartley (2011) 60 ICLQ 29; Verhagen and van Dongen (2010) 6 J Priv Intl L 1; Bridge (2009) 125 LQR 671; Flessner and Verhagen, *Assignment in European Private International Law* (2006); *Guest on the Law of Assignment* (2015) 2nd edn; Plender and Wilderspin, *The European Private International Law of Obligations* (2014) 4th edn, Chapter 13.

[38] The Rome I Regulation only applies to contracts concluded after 17 December 2009 (it is not clear if this requires the underlying contract giving rise to the debt to be concluded after this date, or only the contract of assignment); the applicable law for older contracts may be determined by the Rome Convention or common law. See supra, p 686 et seq. Art 14 of the Rome I Regulation also deals with the related matter of contractual subrogation, and Article 15 with legal subrogation.

[39] Carruthers (2005), paras 6.13–6.16.

[40] Article 14(3) clarifies that "The concept of assignment in this Article includes outright transfers of claims, transfers of claims by way of security and pledges or other security rights over claims."

[41] It might have been thought clearer to deal with the rights as between assignor and assignee after examining, for example, the question of assignability (Art 14(2)); but the reasons for this order are explained in the Report on the Rome Convention by Giuliano and Lagarde, OJ 1980 C 282/31, 34–35. The Rome I Regulation does not make significant changes to the substance of the rule in Art 12(1) of the Rome Convention, although the use of the term "relationship" in the Rome I Regulation instead of "mutual obligations" under the Rome Convention may be significant: see Hartley (2011) 60 ICLQ 29, at 33.

[42] Recital 38 states, with perhaps unclear effect, that "the term 'relationship' should make it clear that Article 14(1) also applies to the property aspects of an assignment, as between assignor and assignee, in legal orders where such aspects are treated separately from the aspects under the law of obligations". Cf approach in Australia: *Pacific Brands Sport Leisure Pty Ltd v Underworks Pty Ltd* (2006) 149 FCR 395; [2006] FCAFC 40; and also (re non-contractual rights), *Salfinger v Niugini Mining (Australia) Pty Ltd (No 3)* [2007] FCA 1532.

[43] Supra, p 755 et seq.

[44] *Trendtex Trading Corpn v Crédit Suisse* [1980] QB 629 at 658; affd on other grounds [1982] AC 679.

[45] Supra, p 758 et seq.

[46] This somewhat complex and anti-formality approach nevertheless marks a distinct improvement on the confused state of the old law on formal validity (prior to the Rome Convention) stemming from *Republica de Guatemala v Nunez* [1927] 1 KB 669.

There remains the issue of capacity[47] which, save in one limited respect,[48] falls outside the ambit of the Rome I Regulation. So here reference must continue to be made to common law rules, under which the issue of capacity should (arguably) be governed by the proper law of the contract, objectively ascertained.[49] This seems correct on principle, but unfortunately, in the few cases that have raised the question, the courts have shown a preference for the law of the place of acting. In *Lee v Abdy*:[50]

> A policy of life insurance issued by an English company was assigned in Cape Colony by a husband to his wife. The assignment was valid by English law, but was invalid by the law of Cape Colony, where the parties were domiciled, because the assignee was the wife of the assignor. The insurance company, when sued by the wife for the recovery of the money, pleaded that the assignment was void.

It was held that the law of Cape Colony governed the assignment. There is much to be said for the view that the proper law of the assignment was the law of the Cape, for it was there that the parties were domiciled and the assignment was effected, but the judgments leave little doubt that the mechanical test of the place of the transaction was applied by the court.

In *Republica de Guatemala v Nunez*,[51] Scrutton LJ said that: "in cases of personal property, the capacity of the parties to a transaction has always been determined either by the *lex domicilii* or the law of the place of the transaction; and where, as here, the two laws are the same it is not necessary to decide between them".[52] It is a little surprising to meet the suggestion that the capacity of a person to enter into a commercial contract is determined by the law of his domicile; little less surprising is the suggestion that the determining law is the law of the place of acting, if that expression is to be taken literally. Assuming the law unchanged from *Lee v Abdy*, should an assignment by an Englishman to his wife of a debt situated in London and governed by English law really be held void, merely because he executes the instrument of transfer in Cape Town while on a short visit to South Africa?

The only question is whether the judges in these two cases meant the idea of the application of the law of the place of acting to be taken literally and rigidly, or whether they intended to indicate the law governing the assignment.[53] The law of the place of contracting historically often constituted the proper law of the contract, so that judges tended to adopt the former expression when their intention seems to have been to refer to the proper law. This was especially true in the late nineteenth century when *Lee v Abdy* was decided. In fact, in that case, Day J stated the rule for contracts in language that was scarcely felicitous, namely: "The general rule, . . . is that the validity and incidence of a contract *must be determined* by the law of the place where it is entered into."[54] Just as there has been a development in the general common law rules of contract in favour of the proper law as the law to govern capacity,[55] so there should also be a similar development in the particular context of assignment.[56]

---

[47] Carruthers (2005), paras 6.34–6.35.
[48] Article 13, supra, pp 763–4.
[49] Supra, pp 761–3.
[50] (1886) 17 QBD 309.
[51] [1927] 1 KB 669.
[52] Ibid, at 689; and see Lawrence LJ at 701.
[53] Cf Morris, *Cases on Private International Law*, (1968) 4th edn, pp 362. See Carruthers (2005), para 6.35.
[54] Emphasis added.
[55] Supra, pp 761–3.
[56] Cf *Lowenstein v Allen* [1958] CLY 491; and Carruthers (2005), para 6.35.

(b) Non-contractual assignments—questions dependent solely on the validity
     and effect of the assignment

It has been assumed, so far, that the assignments under consideration have been effected, as is usually the case,[57] by a 'contract' (in the English law sense) between assignor and assignee. This does not necessarily have to be the case because a voluntary assignment may be effected, for example, by non-gratuitous, unilateral obligation or by outright gift.[58] The contractual or non-contractual character of the intangible right or claim which is the subject of the assignment should not be confused with the contractual or non-contractual character of the assignment; the latter of these is the focus of this discussion. The issue arises of whether *non-contractual assignments* fall within the scope of Article 14 of the Rome I Regulation. It will be recalled[59] that Article 14(1) makes provision for the law applicable to the relationship between assignor and assignee under a voluntary assignment, but without at that point restricting the provision to contractual assignments. However, the law to be applied is that which "applies to the contract between the assignor and assignee". If there is no such contract, then the rule cannot apply. However, the Giuliano and Lagarde Report makes clear that "contractual obligations" for the purposes of the Rome Convention (and presumably now Rome I Regulation[60]) encompasses at least gifts.[61] It is thus arguable that the Rome I Regulation rules apply to all voluntary assignments, classifying them as 'contractual' even if they are not pursuant to a "contract" (in the English law sense).[62] If this is not the case, it is to be hoped that the courts will apply the provisions of Article 14 by analogy to cases of voluntary, non-contractual assignments.[63]

(c) Questions dependent on the nature of the right assigned

The assignment of a debt may raise questions that cannot be answered without considering the legal effect of the transaction to which the debt owes its origin. In such cases it is imperative, if a satisfactory solution is desired, to be guided exclusively by the law governing that transaction. This was the view taken in a number of common law authorities,[64] and it is the view now adopted as English law by reason of Article 14(2) of the Rome I Regulation which provides:

> The law governing the assigned . . . claim shall determine its assignability, the relationship between the assignee and the debtor, the conditions under which the assignment . . . can be invoked against the debtor and whether the debtor's obligations have been discharged.[65]

It will be seen that a number of different types of problem may fall to be governed by the law governing the validity of the debt, the most important of which are whether the debt may be assigned, and the issue of priorities between successive assignments. These issues may be exemplified by common law decisions.

---

[57] Eg *Lee v Abdy* (1886) 17 QBD 309; *Trendtex Trading Corpn v Crédit Suisse* [1980] QB 629.

[58] See *Re Westerton* [1919] 2 Ch 104; *Republica de Guatemala v Nunez* [1927] 1 KB 669; *Re Anziani* [1930] 1 Ch 407.

[59] Supra, p 1285.

[60] Note also Recital 7, and the case law on the Brussels I Recast, Article 7(1): see supra, p 245 et seq.

[61] Giuliano and Lagarde Report, OJ 1980 C 282/10.

[62] But see Giuliano and Lagarde Report, OJ 1980 C 282/29.

[63] Dicey, Morris and Collins, Rule 135(2), and para 24R-050; and Carruthers (2005), para 6.32.

[64] *Compañia Colombiana de Seguros v Pacific Steam Navigation Co* [1965] 1 QB 101 at 128, 129; and see *Pender v Commercial Bank of Scotland* 1940 SLT 306; *Bankhaus H Aufhauser v Scotboard Ltd* 1973 SLT (Notes) 87.

[65] Cf Rome Convention, Art 12(2).

(i) Assignability[66]

The primary question of whether a legal right may be assigned at all may be illustrated by *Trendtex Trading Corpn v Crédit Suisse*:[67]

> A Swiss company sued a Nigerian bank in England for failing to honour a letter of credit. The Swiss company assigned this cause of action to one of its creditors, a Swiss bank, the assignment taking place in Geneva. The Swiss company then later took proceedings in England against the Swiss bank, alleging that the assignment was void, such a right of action being incapable of assignment as it offended against English rules relating to maintenance and champerty.

The Court of Appeal held that the Swiss company's right of action against the Nigerian bank was English, having been reduced into possession by the issue of the writ in England.[68] In examining the nature and attributes of this right of action, it was necessary to refer to the legal system under which it arose, English law.[69] Neither its content nor its characteristics could be altered merely because it had been the subject of a later transaction that in certain respects was subject to a foreign system of law. Such questions as whether the assignment was voidable for fraud or unenforceable for lack of a written memorandum might be determinable by Swiss law, but the primary and fundamental question,[70] whether the subject matter was even capable of assignment, fell to be determined by English law.[71]

(ii) Priorities

The law governing the right to which the assignment relates is the most satisfactory legal system by which to determine the ranking of competing claimants where the creditor has made more than one contractual assignment. One arguable exception to this principle is where there is a competition between two or more assignments which derive from the same creditor and which have the same governing law, in which case the assignees' rights *inter se* may be more appropriately governed by that common governing law, where that law differs from the law governing the right to which the assignment relates.[72] A true question of priorities arises

---

[66] Carruthers (2005), paras 6.06–6.10.

[67] [1980] QB 629. In relation to the assignment of non-contractual obligations in civil and commercial matters falling within the scope of the Rome II Regulation (Art 1), the law applicable to the obligation under the Regulation shall govern the question whether a right to claim damages or a remedy may be transferred, including by inheritance (Art 15(e)). The applicable law under the Rome II Regulation will govern, therefore, the matter of assignability. See *supra*, p 864; and Rome II Explanatory Memorandum, p 24. In relation to the assignment of non-contractual obligations which fall outside the scope of the Rome II Regulation (Art 1), the matter of assignability will be determined by the proper law of the right transferred. Whether a copyright may be assigned has been held to be determined by the law governing the creation of the copyright: *Campbell Connelly & Co Ltd v Noble* [1963] 1 WLR 252; see Wadlow, *Enforcement of Intellectual Property in European and International Law* (1998), pp 441–51; Fawcett and Torremans, *Intellectual Property and Private International Law* (2011) 2nd edn, pp 515–17.

[68] Strictly speaking this was therefore not an assignment of a debt or other contractual right, but of a bare cause of action, but in any case the letter of credit was also governed by English law.

[69] Cf approach in Australia: *Salfinger v Niugini Mining (Australia) Pty Ltd (No 3)* [2007] FCA 1532.

[70] Ibid, at 652.

[71] In the House of Lords ([1982] AC 679) the choice of law issues were not addressed with great clarity. The House of Lords took the view that, under English law, the cause of action could not be assigned, but that nevertheless it was for Swiss law to determine the effect of the invalidity of the assignment on the agreement as a whole between the parties, there being issues involved other than just the validity of the assignment. See also *Grant's Trustees v Ritchie's Executor* (1886) 13 R 646; *Pender v Commercial Bank of Scotland* 1940 SLT 306; *Companhia Colombiana de Seguros v Pacific Steam Navigation Co* [1965] 1 QB 101, per Roskill J, at 128; and *Libertas-Kommerz GmbH v Johnson* 1977 SC 191.

[72] *Scottish Provident Institution v Robinson* (1892) 29 SLR 733. See Crawford and Carruthers (2006), para 17-28; and Carruthers (2005) para 6.39–6.40.

where there have been two or more valid and competing assignments, the ranking of which is doubtful, as may be illustrated by *Kelly v Selwyn*:[73]

> By an assignment executed in 1891 in New York, X (domiciled in New York) assigned to his wife an interest in certain English trust funds. Notice was not given to the trustees until twelve years later, since none was required by the law of New York. In 1894, X assigned the same interest to the plaintiff by a deed executed in England. Immediate notice of this was given to the trustees.

It was held that the plaintiff ranked first, since the rights of the claimant fell to be regulated by English law. Warrington J said:

> The ground on which I decide it is that, the fund here being an English trust fund and this being the Court which the testator may have contemplated as the Court which would have administered that trust fund, the order in which the parties are to be held entitled to the trust fund must be regulated by the law of the Court which is administering that fund.[74]

The judge's language is somewhat ambiguous, leaving it a little doubtful whether he chose English law as that of the forum, the situs or the law governing the validity of the debt.[75] It is suggested, however, that the decisive factor in the mind of the judge, if his language is considered as a whole, was that the subject matter of the assignment consisted of a trust fund, the governing law of which was English law. Such an analysis is supported by *Le Feuvre v Sullivan*[76] where the law of the forum was the law of Jersey, but English law, which would appear to have been the law governing the debt,[77] was relied on to determine priorities. This approach is now apparently confirmed by Article 14(2) of the Rome I Regulation,[78] which also applies the law governing the debt to such questions as whether notice of an assignment must be given to the debtor and whether an assignee takes subject to equities.

(iii) Substance or procedure?

The question whether an assignee must add the assignor as a party to his action raises the distinction between substance and procedure.

> Suppose, for instance, that a Frenchman assigns by way of charge to another Frenchman a sum of money due from a French debtor, the assignment being made in France and according to the law of that country.

According to the rules of private international law, the assignment has universal validity. According to English domestic law, the assignment is valid, but unless the assignee has notified the debtor in writing, the assignee cannot recover the money unless he makes the assignor a party to the action against the debtor.[79] If this rule as to the adding of parties is to be regarded as a procedural rule for the purposes of private international law,[80] it is governed

---

[73] [1905] 2 Ch 117; and see *Le Feuvre v Sullivan* (1855) 10 Moo PCC 1. In *Republica de Guatemala v Nunez* [1927] 1 KB 669, there were successive assignments but they were, for different reasons, held to be invalid.

[74] [1905] 2 Ch 117, at 122.

[75] Cf *Macmillan Inc v Bishopsgate Investment Trust plc (No 3)* [1996] 1 WLR 387; and *Raiffeisen Zentralbank Österreich v Five Star General Trading LLC* [2001] EWCA Civ 68; [2001] QB 825.

[76] (1855) 10 Moo PCC 1.

[77] Ibid, at 13.

[78] The exact scope of what is covered by Article 14(2) is not, however, entirely clear. See *Raiffeisen Zentralbank Österreich v Five Star General Trading LLC* [2001] EWCA Civ 68 at [49], [2001] QB 825; Hartley (2011) 60 ICLQ 29; British Institute of International and Comparative Law, *Study on the Question of Effectiveness of an Assignment or Subrogation of a Claim against Third Parties and the Priority of the Assigned or Subrogated Claim over a Right of Another Person* (2011), available at http://ec.europa.eu/justice/civil/files/report_assignment_en.pdf.

[79] Law of Property Act 1925, s 136. Recovery may, however, be possible in equity even if the notice requirements are not satisfied: *William Brandts Sons & Co v Dunlop Rubber Co* [1905] AC 454.

[80] See supra, p 73 et seq.

by the law of the forum and it must be obeyed in an action brought in England notwithstanding that it is not recognised by French law. Such old authorities as there are would indicate, however, that the rule as to the adding of parties is substantive[81] and, thus, governed by the law governing the debt.[82]

(iv) Characterisation of the issue as contractual or proprietary

The operation of Article 12 of the Rome Convention (the predecessor to Article 14 of the Rome I Regulation) was subjected to close judicial scrutiny in *Raiffeisen Zentralbank Österreich v Five Star General Trading LLC*,[83] a case which reveals that litigants seeking to rely on the prima facie clear direction offered by these provisions may yet stumble on the preceding obstacle of characterisation. The facts of the case were as follows:

> The claimant Austrian bank lent money to the first defendants, Dubai shipowners, to assist them in the purchase of a vessel, the "Mount I". In turn, the owners mortgaged the vessel to the claimants, agreeing to assign to the bank the policy of marine insurance in respect of the vessel. Although the insurers were French, the insurance policy was governed by English law. By deed of assignment (also governed by English law), the owners purported to assign to the claimant "all their right, title and interest in and to the insurances". Two weeks after the assignment, the Mount I collided with a second vessel, causing the latter to sink. The owners of the sunken vessel, together with the Taiwanese owners of its cargo, sought, in France, attachment orders in respect of the Mount I insurance proceeds. Accordingly, the claimant bank commenced proceedings, in England, against the Dubai owner, the French insurers, and the Taiwanese cargo owners, seeking various declarations, including one that, as from the date of the assignment, the owners had no right, title or interest in or to the insurances, or to moneys payable thereunder, and that, as from the same date, the bank was entitled to all such interests and money. The cargo owners, pleading French law, denied that the notice of assignment was valid or binding on them.

The principal issue for decision was whether the assignee of a marine insurance policy, made with French insurers, but governed by English law, was entitled to recover to the extent of his interest. According to French law, the assignment was invalid but, according to English law, it was valid. The choice of law issue was a complex one of characterisation, namely, whether the assignee's claim was to be determined by English law, as the law governing the underlying contract of insurance, or by French law, the law of the situs of the chose in action which had been assigned. Counsel for the claimant argued that the matter should be governed by Article 12(2) of the Rome Convention, whereas counsel for the defendant contended that, since the Convention was applicable only to contractual obligations, it did not apply to the dispute in hand, and advocated the *lex situs* as the common law rule.

In the Court of Appeal, Mance LJ appraised the conflicting contractual and proprietary analyses of the issues in dispute. The respondent bank maintained that the issue in dispute was a contractual one, ie, whether the insurance contract had been validly assigned by the owners to the bank. The appellant cargo owners, with whom the bank had no contractual nexus, maintained that the issue was essentially a proprietary one, concerning the validity against third parties of the assignment of an intangible claim against insurers. His Lordship pointed to the straitened nature of the litigants' respective approaches, stating that: "These opposing analyses both assume that the factual complex raises only one issue and, in their differing identification of that issue, emphasise different aspects of the facts. In my judgment a more nuanced analysis is required."[84] It is of note that Mance LJ took the view that, "there

---

[81] *Innes v Dunlop* (1800) 8 Term Rep 595; *O'Callaghan v Thomond* (1810) 3 Taunt 82; cf *Regas Ltd v Plotkins* (1961) 29 DLR (2d) 282.
[82] Rome I Regulation, Art 14(2).
[83] [2001] EWCA Civ 68, [2001] QB 825, [2001] 1 Lloyd's Rep 597.
[84] [2001] 1 Lloyd's Rep 597 at [20].

is no hint in article 12(2) of any intention to distinguish between contractual and proprietary aspects of assignment. The wording appears to embrace all aspects of assignment".[85] The Court of Appeal concluded that:

> Whatever might be the domestic legal position in any particular country . . . the Rome Convention now views the relevant issue—that is, what steps, by way of notice or otherwise, require to be taken in relation to the debtor for the assignment to take effect as between the assignee and debtor—not as involving any "property right", but as involving—simply—a contractual issue to be determined by the law governing the obligation assigned.[86]

Hence, the issue whether, following assignment to the bank of the benefits under the insurance policy, the French insurer had to pay the insurance proceeds to the bank as assignee, rather than to the vessel owner, was characterised as a contractual, not a proprietary, issue. In consequence, Article 12 was applicable and the tripartite dispute fell to be determined according to English law, the law governing the obligation assigned, under which the assignment was effective.

Although this approach is buttressed by the Giuliano and Lagarde Report,[87] characterisation of notice provisions as contractual, even vis-à-vis the debtor with whom the assignee has no contractual nexus, is a curious and anomalous conclusion. To characterise all the matters arising under Article 12(2) (or 14(2) of the Rome I Regulation) as contractual is rather strained. That said, to provide that the law governing the right to which the assignment relates is, by virtue of that law's relationship with the parties and their circumstances, the law which is appropriate to determine the issue in dispute, is a sensible rule of choice of law; the connecting factor and choice of law rule applied generally will be appropriate, even if characterisation of the issue as a purely contractual matter is not. It may have been better simply to observe that the scope of the Rome Convention and now Rome I Regulation extends to cover proprietary questions to the limited extent set out in Articles 12(2) and 14(2) respectively.[88]

In transactions which concern intangible movable property, the borderland between contract and conveyance is more extensive than typically is the case regarding other types of property. Another reading of this case is that it was the proposed application of the *lex situs* rule as part of the common law, should the issues be determined to be proprietary, which was problematic. If the common law choice of law rule for voluntary assignments adopted were, as advocated above, the law which governs the right to which the assignment relates (the rule in the Rome Convention and Rome I Regulation), then the characterization issue would be almost inconsequential.[89]

(ii) Subrogation

The Rome I Regulation[90] contains two provisions concerning subrogation: Article 14 (voluntary assignment and contractual subrogation) and Article 15 (legal subrogation). Article 14 deals with contractual (ie voluntary) subrogation of claims, subjecting them to the law of the underlying contract in the same way as a voluntary assignment. The Explanatory Memorandum accompanying the Commission Proposal for a Rome I Regulation justified

---

[85] Ibid, [45]. Contrast Giuliano & Lagarde Report (1980), comment 2 on Art 1, which reports that, "since the Convention is concerned only with the law applicable to contractual obligations, property rights. . . are not covered by these provisions".

[86] Ibid, at [48].

[87] At pp 34–5.

[88] Note also Recital 38, relating to the scope of Article 14(1) of the Rome I Regulation: supra, p 692 et seq.

[89] Cf Plender and Wilderspin (2012) 4th edn, para 13-043; and Rogerson [2000] All ER Annual Review 106.

[90] In respect of which, see generally supra, Chapter 19.

the expanded provision by stating that voluntary assignment and contractual subrogation "perform a similar economic function".[91] By contrast, Article 15 provides that:

> Where a person (the creditor) has a contractual claim against another (the debtor) and a third person has a duty to satisfy the creditor, or has in fact satisfied the creditor in discharge of that duty, the law which governs the third person's duty to satisfy the creditor shall determine whether and to what extent the third person is entitled to exercise against the debtor the rights which the creditor had against the debtor under the law governing their relationship.

Thus, for example, where an insurer who has compensated a person who has suffered loss under a contract is subrogated to the victim's rights against the person who caused the loss, the law governing the insurance contract determines whether the insurer can exercise the rights of the person who suffered loss (although the nature of those rights will itself of course be determined by the law of the underlying contract).[92]

It is also worth noting in this regard the subrogation provision contained in the Rome II Regulation.[93] Article 19 of that instrument, which is in virtually identical terms to Article 15 of the Rome I Regulation, applies, *mutatis mutandis*, to the subrogation of non-contractual claims.

Multiple liability

Article 16 of the Rome I Regulation[94] provides that:

> If a creditor has a claim against several debtors who are liable for the same claim, and one of the debtors has already satisfied the claim in whole or in part, the law governing the debtor's obligation towards the creditor also governs the debtor's right to claim recourse from the other debtors. The other debtors may rely on the defences they had against the creditor to the extent allowed by the law governing their obligations towards the creditor.

This is broadly equivalent, *mutatis mutandis*, to Article 20 of the Rome II Regulation, in respect of multiple liability for non-contractual claims.

(iii) Involuntary assignments[95]

The problem that affects private international law in the case of the involuntary assignment of a debt, as for instance where a customer's credit balance at a bank is vested by legislation in a custodian of enemy property,[96] is best illustrated by the process known formerly in England as garnishment and now by the making of a third party debt order, and in Scotland[97] and many other countries as arrestment. This is a process by which a judgment creditor attaches a sum of money that is due to the judgment debtor from a third party (formerly called the garnishee). If the necessary proceedings are taken, the court may order that the third party debtor shall pay the money direct to the judgment creditor.

In purely domestic proceedings, where the parties and the relevant transactions are connected solely with England,[98] the third party debtor is, of course, effectively discharged from further liability once he has paid the judgment creditor. The position, however, is not so

---

[91] Proposal for a Rome I Regulation (Commission version), Explanatory Memorandum, p 8.

[92] Ibid.

[93] In respect of which, see generally supra, Chapter 20.

[94] The equivalent provision under the Rome Convention was Article 13(2).

[95] See Carruthers (2005), paras 6.63–6.66.

[96] See eg *Arab Bank Ltd v Barclays Bank (Dominion, Colonial and Overseas)* [1954] AC 495. Also *Wight and Ors v Eckhardt Marine GmbH* [2004] 1 AC 147, per Lord Hoffmann, at [12].

[97] Eg *Stewart v Royal Bank of Scotland* 1994 SLT (Sh Ct) 27. See Debt Arrangement and Attachment (Scotland) Act 2002.

[98] Cf *Brooks Associates Inc v Basu* [1983] QB 220, supra, p 1281, n 12.

straightforward in a case containing a foreign element. The first problem arises where the third party debtor may be in one country and the debt situated in another. In debt attachment proceedings in England, it is necessary that the third party debtor be within the jurisdiction,[99] albeit temporarily, or have submitted to the jurisdiction.[100] It is not, however, necessary that the judgment debtor be within the jurisdiction nor, strictly speaking, that the debt be situated within the jurisdiction. If the debt is enforceable within the jurisdiction, even though payable elsewhere, the court has jurisdiction to make a third party debt order.[101] There is a risk in the case of a debt that is not situated within the jurisdiction that the third party debtor, having already complied with an order made in one country, will remain liable to pay his debt a second time if he is sued by the judgment debtor in a foreign court which refuses to recognise the validity of the order.[102] It had been thought that that risk was met by the court having a discretion whether or not to assume jurisdiction, being prepared to decline where the risk of the third party debtor being ordered to pay twice was real.[103] It was usually the case that the court would assume jurisdiction to make a third party debt order, confident that no such risk would materialise, as is illustrated by *Swiss Bank Corpn v Boemische Industrial Bank*.[104]

> In that case, the plaintiff had recovered judgment for a large sum of money against the defendant, a company carrying on business exclusively in Czechoslovakia. The defendant kept an account at a London bank where its balance was over £9,000. The plaintiff issued a garnishee summons against the bank. It was objected that to make a garnishee order in these circumstances would be inequitable, since the bank, if sued later in Czechoslovakia, would probably be ordered to pay the sum over again to the defendants.

The Court of Appeal nevertheless made the order in the confident belief that, having been made in the country where the debt was normally and properly recoverable, its validity and effect would not be repudiated in Czechoslovakia.

It must not be assumed, however, that where a debt is situated in England, there will never be a risk of double jeopardy and that jurisdiction always will be assumed, as is illustrated by the unusual decision in *Deutsche Schachtbau v Shell International Petroleum Co Ltd*.[105] The case concerned a garnishee order absolute (termed now a final third party debt order) made in respect of a debt situate in England. Lord Goff, referring[106] to the court's "discretionary power" to make such an order, said[107] that it would be "inequitable" to make an order where there was a "real risk that [the third party] may be held liable in some foreign court to pay a second time." A majority in the House of Lords concluded that, even though the debt was situated in England, the exercise of jurisdiction in garnishment proceedings was discretionary

---

[99] CPR, r 72.1(1).

[100] *Société Eram Shipping Co Ltd v Cie Internationale de Navigation and Ors* [2004] 1 AC 260, per Lord Bingham of Cornhill, at [27]; *SCF Finance Co Ltd v Masri (No 3)* [1987] QB 1028; Kaye [1989] JBL 449, 455–9. See, for consideration of whether a third party debtor might be regarded as being "sued" within the meaning of the Brussels I Recast and the Brussels and Lugano Conventions, supra, Chapter 11, see Dicey, Morris and Collins, paras 24R-080–24-084.

[101] *Deutsche Schachtbau und Tiefbohrgesellschaft GmbH v Shell International Petroleum Co Ltd* [1990] 1 AC 295, CA, revsd in part, ibid, 323, HL; cf *Delaire v Delaire* [1996] 9 WWR 469.

[102] *Martin v Nadel* [1906] 2 KB 26. Such a risk should no longer arise between EU Member States, however, pursuant to the rules on recognition and enforcement of judgments under the Brussels I Recast. See supra, Chapter 17.

[103] *SCF Finance Co Ltd v Masri (No 3)* [1987] QB 1028 at 1044; *Interpool Ltd v Galani* [1988] QB 738 at 741.

[104] [1923] 1 KB 673.

[105] [1990] 1 AC 295; see Briggs [1988] Lloyd's MCLQ 429; see also *Zoneheath Associates Ltd v China Tianjin International Economic and Technical Co-operative Corpn* [1994] CLC 348.

[106] [1990] 1 AC 295 at 350.

[107] Ibid, at 355.

and that it would be inequitable to exercise it in the instant case, bearing in mind that "the garnishee does not have to establish a certainty, or a very high degree of risk, of being compelled to pay the debt twice over; he has only to establish a real risk of being required to do so".[108] There is no doubt that the court's power to make an order in the case of an English debt is discretionary.[109]

Lord Goff in *Deutsche Schachtbau* was not concerned with the court's power to refuse an order in the case of a foreign debt. That, however, was the issue which arose in *Société Eram Shipping Co Ltd v Cie Internationale de Navigation and Ors*,[110] in which the House of Lords was called to consider the power of an English court to make an order in relation to a foreign debt (in the instant case, a debt situated in Hong Kong and governed by the law of Hong Kong) and, if there were such a power, to determine the manner in which it ought to be exercised. Lord Bingham of Cornhill concluded:[111]

> It is not in my opinion open to the court to make an order in a case . . . where it is clear or appears that the making of the order will not discharge the debt of the third party or garnishee to the judgment debtor according to the law which governs that debt. In practical terms, it does not matter very much whether the House rules that the court has no jurisdiction to make an order in such a case or that the court has a discretion which should always be exercised against the making of an order in such a case. But the former seems to me the preferable analysis . . .[112]

The law of the situs of the debt is not only relevant in determining the question of jurisdiction, it is also relevant to the effect of the third party debt order as regards other parties.[113] If, for example, an involuntary assignment occurs after a voluntary assignment has already been made, the law governing the debt determines the effectiveness of the voluntary assignment (pursuant to Article 14(2) of the Rome I Regulation), but the law of the situs of the debt determines whether the rights of the voluntary assignee have been postponed or defeated.

3. NEGOTIABLE INSTRUMENTS[114]

If a transfer of a negotiable instrument has been made abroad and its validity is disputed in an English action, the court is confronted with a problem of choice of law. What the choice should be depends on the manner in which the problem is analysed. It may be regarded as raising a question of form or interpretation to be governed by the Bills of Exchange Act 1882; or as the transfer of a chattel, in which case the law of the situs will be applicable;[115] or as an assignment of a contractual right and therefore subject to the law governing the contract. *Koechlin et Cie v Kestenbaum*,[116] the leading decision on the matter, definitely treats the

---

[108] [1990] 1 AC 295, at 359.

[109] *Société Eram Shipping Co Ltd v Cie Internationale de Navigation and Ors* [2004] 1 AC 260, per Lord Millett, at [105].

[110] Ibid.

[111] Ibid, at [26].

[112] Cf Lord Hoffmann, at [59]; Lord Millett, at [109]. See also *FG Hemisphere Associates LLC v Congo* [2005] EWHC 3103 (QBD); The Times, 27 February 2006; *Kuwait Oil Tanker Co SAK v Qabazard* [2004] 1 AC 300; and *Tasarruf Mevduati Sigorta Fonu (A Firm) v Demirel (Application to Set Aside)* [2006] EWHC 3354 (Ch); [2007] 1 Lloyd's Rep 223.

[113] *Re Queensland Mercantile and Agency Co* [1891] 1 Ch 536; affd [1892] 1 Ch 219.

[114] For a modern, specialised treatment, see Proctor, *International Payment Obligations* (1998), Chapter 27.

[115] Such a classification was supported by Staughton LJ in *Macmillan Inc v Bishopsgate Investment Trust plc (No 3)* [1996] 1 WLR 387 at 400.

[116] [1927] 1 KB 889.

question as one of form or interpretation, although doubt may be expressed as to whether the Court of Appeal reached this conclusion by reading too much into the earlier authorities.

The common law authorities[117] which preceded the Bills of Exchange Act 1882, with one exception,[118] showed a marked tendency to determine the validity of an indorsement by the law which governs the original contract of the acceptor or maker.

The relevant sub-sections of the Bills of Exchange Act 1882 are as follows:

72.—Where a bill drawn in one country is negotiated, accepted or payable in another, the rights, duties and liabilities of the parties thereto are determined as follows:

(1) The validity of a bill as regards requisites in form is determined by the law of the place of issue, and the validity as regards requisites in form of the supervening contracts, such as acceptance, or indorsement, or acceptance supra protest, is determined by the law of the place where such contract was made. Provided that—
   (a) Where a bill is issued out of the United Kingdom it is not invalid by reason only that it is not stamped in accordance with the law of the place of issue.
   (b) Where a bill, issued out of the United Kingdom, conforms asregards requisites in form, to the law of the United Kingdom, itmay, for the purpose of enforcing payment thereof, be treated asvalid as between all persons who negotiate, hold, or become partiesto it in the United Kingdom.
(2) Subject to the provisions of this Act, the interpretation of the drawing, indorsement, acceptance, or acceptance supra protest of a bill, is determined by the law of the place where such contract is made.

The question is whether these sections are concerned with the subject of transfer at all, and whether it is possible to ascertain from them the legal system that determines the validity and effect of an indorsement, or of a delivery, of a negotiable instrument.

There have been only a relatively small number of relevant cases since the 1882 Act.[119] The first of these was *Alcock v Smith*:[120]

A bill of exchange, drawn by and on English firms, and payable in England to the order of X, was indorsed and delivered in Norway by X to Y. While in the hands of Y it was seized by a judgment creditor in Norway, and in the due course of Norwegian law was ultimately sold by public auction to Z. In fact, Z had no title to the bill by English law, but according to Norwegian law the property was duly passed to him as a result of the sale. In the action subsequently brought in England, it was held that the effect of the transactions in Norway must be governed by Norwegian law, and therefore that the title acquired thereunder by Z must prevail over one which by English law would have been stronger.

The judgments paid little heed to the statutory provisions, but in general applied Norwegian law as the law of the place of acting. Romer J, indeed, held that the word "interpretation" in section 72(2) was wide enough to cover the "legal effect" of a contract and that therefore statutory effect had been given to the principle of the application of the law of the place of acting. In the Court of Appeal, however, no reliance was placed on the Act.

---

[117] *Trimby v Vignier* (1834) 1 Bing NC 151; *Lebel v Tucker* (1867) LR 3 QB 77; *Re Marseilles Extension Rly and Land Co* (1885) 30 Ch D 598.

[118] *Bradlaugh v De Rin* (1868) LR 3 CP 538.

[119] *Alcock v Smith* [1892] 1 Ch 238; *Embiricos v Anglo-Austrian Bank* [1904] 2 KB 870; affd [1905] 1 KB 677; *Koechlin v Kestenbaum* [1927] 1 KB 616; revsd [1927] 1 KB 889. Brief reference was made to the 1882 Act in *Zebrarise Ltd and Anor v De Nieffe* [2004] EWCA 1842; [2005] 1 Lloyd's Rep 154—formal validity of a promissory note; and *Aspinall's Club Ltd v Fouad Al-Zayat* [2007] EWHC 362 (Comm)—English law applied qua law of place of issue.

[120] [1892] 1 Ch 238.

In the second case, *Embiricos v Anglo-Austrian Bank*:[121]

> A cheque on a London bank was drawn in Romania in favour of the plaintiffs, who specially indorsed it there to a firm in London and placed it in an envelope addressed to that firm. The cheque was stolen from the envelope in Romania by a clerk of the plaintiffs. Three days later the cheque, bearing an indorsement which purported to be that of the London firm but which was in fact a forgery, was presented for payment at a bank in Vienna. The Vienna bank cashed the cheque in good faith, indorsed it to the defendants, who were their London agents, and the latter collected the amount from the bank on which the cheque was drawn. The plaintiffs then sued the defendants in damages for conversion. Austrian law provided that, notwithstanding the theft and forgery, the Viennese bank acquired good title to the cheque, and judgment was given for the defendants.

In this case the title that was acquired under the law of the country where the instrument was situated at the time of the transaction was upheld by the English court.

Again Austrian law was chosen as being the law of the place of acting (though perhaps what was in the mind of the court was the law of the situs, since this necessarily coincided with the law of the place of acting),[122] and again the judgments attributed only trifling importance to the Bills of Exchange Act 1882. Romer LJ thought that section 72(2) recognised the law of the place of acting as being applicable to the matter, an opinion which Walton J was prepared to share if "interpretation" includes "legal effect". Vaughan Williams LJ was not clear that the sub-section covered the case, but according to Stirling LJ its applicability was worthy of serious consideration.

Section 72, which, it will be observed, was only a secondary consideration in these two decisions, played, however, a decisive part in *Koechlin et Cie v Kestenbaum*:[123]

> A bill of exchange was drawn in France by X on the defendants in London to the order of Y, who was X's father. It was accepted, payable in London, by the defendants. The bill was indorsed not by the payee, Y, but by X, and was then transferred for value to the plaintiffs in France. X's indorsement was affixed on behalf of, and with the authority of, Y. On presentment the defendants refused payment, on the ground that the bill did not bear the signature of Y by way of indorsement. English law requires that a bill payable to order shall be indorsed by the payee, or by an agent who expressly signs per pro the payee. French law, however, permits a valid indorsement to be made by an agent in his own name, provided that he so acts with the authority of the payee. Therefore, whether the plaintiffs were entitled to payment depended on whether the validity of the indorsement was to be determined by English or by French law.

Bankes LJ held that the proper law to govern the validity of a transfer had been definitely settled by section 72 of the Bills of Exchange Act in favour of the law of the place of acting, here French law. In his opinion this legal system was deliberately applied by the Court of Appeal in the *Embiricos* case long after the passing of the Act. The bill, he said, was drawn and indorsed in France in a form recognised by French law, and therefore it became valid in England by virtue of section 72(1).[124]

Sargent LJ agreed, the essence of his judgment being contained in the following words:

---

[121] [1904] 2 KB 870; affd [1905] 1 KB 677.

[122] Supra, pp 1282–3.

[123] [1927] 1 KB 889.

[124] Cf *Aspinall's Club Ltd v Fouad Al-Zayat* [2007] EWHC 362 (Comm), per David Steel J, at [16]; and *Zebrarise Ltd and Anor v De Nieffe* [2004] EWCA 1842; [2005] 1 Lloyd's Rep 154, per Judge Havelock-Allan, QC, at [36].

In my judgment the question whether this bill could properly be indorsed in the name of the payee . . . only or could rightly be indorsed by the son . . . in his own name if he had authority in fact to do so is purely a question of form, and is therefore covered in terms by s 72, sub-s (1); but if it is not covered by that subsection it is covered by sub-s (2), in view of the very wide effect of the decision in *Embiricos v Anglo-Austrian Bank* . . . If the indorsement in fact made is, according to the law of the place where it is made, sufficient to give a title to the indorsee, it appears to me that by the express terms of the Act the indorsee is entitled to sue. The effect is not to increase the liabilities of the acceptor, but merely to enlarge the methods by which the right to enforce those liabilities can be transferred by the person originally entitled to them to some subsequent indorsee.[125]

This case is a definite authority in favour of the law of the place of acting, though it is remarkable that it attributes to the judges who decided *Embiricos v Anglo-Austrian Bank* a confidence in the applicability of the Bills of Exchange Act 1882 that is not very apparent from their judgments.

It is necessary in stating the law with regard to the transfer of negotiable instruments to deal with both inland and foreign bills of exchange. An "inland bill" is one which is both drawn and payable within the British Isles, or one which is drawn within the British Isles upon some person resident there.[126] The Bills of Exchange Act 1882 expressly provides that,[127] when such a bill is indorsed in a foreign country, the indorsement shall, *as regards the payer*, be interpreted according to the law of the United Kingdom. This confirms the decision in *Lebel v Tucker*,[128] and means that the acceptor of an inland, as contrasted with a foreign, bill is liable only to holders who claim under an indorsement valid by English law. The enactment, however, is expressly confined to the liability of the payer.

One must also consider the transfer of a foreign bill, ie one which does not satisfy the definition given in the preceding paragraph. The rule here is that whether a transfer is valid or not is determined by the law of the place where the transfer is effected, ie in the words of the Act, "where such contract is made".[129] This rule applies equally to a promissory note[130] and to a cheque.[131] The position was thus stated by Sargent LJ in *Koechlin v Kestenbaum*:[132]

> The result [of the 1882 Act] was that any one dealing with a foreign bill of exchange was in a less certain position than a person dealing with an inland bill, because in the case of an indorsement abroad on a foreign bill he might find substituted for the person to whom he was originally liable as acceptor not merely a person to whom the transfer would have been good if made in England, but a person to whom the transfer by indorsement would be good if made according to the law of the country in which it was made. That is rendered perfectly clear by s 72, sub-ss 1 and 2, of the Act. The matter was carried probably further than was contemplated by the actual language of the sub-sections by the decision in *Embiricos v Anglo-Austrian Bank*.

The result of this distinction is scarcely satisfactory to the commercial world, but it certainly shows how important it is that as wide a unification as possible of the internal laws relating to negotiable instruments should be effected.

---

[125] [1927] 1 KB 889, at 899.

[126] Bills of Exchange Act 1882, s 4.

[127] S 72(2), proviso.

[128] (1867) LR 3 QB 77.

[129] Bills of Exchange Act 1882, s 72(1), (2); *Embiricos v Anglo-Austrian Bank* [1904] 2 KB 870; affd [1905] 1 KB 677; *Alcock v Smith* [1892] 1 Ch 238; *Koechlin v Kestenbaum* [1927] 1 KB 889.

[130] *Zebrarise Ltd and Anor v De Nieffe* [2004] EWCA 1842; [2005] 1 Lloyd's Rep 154, per Judge Havelock-Allan, QC, at [36].

[131] *Embiricos v Anglo-Austrian Bank*, supra.

[132] [1927] 1 KB 889 at 898–9.

4. SHARES AND SECURITIES

(a) The traditional approach[133]

A share of stock is intimately connected with the place where the issuing company has its residence, since the general rule is that it can be effectively transferred only by a substitution of the name of the transferee for that of the transferor in the register of shareholders. This register is normally kept by the company at its principal place of business, though there may be branch registers in other countries for the purpose of recording transactions that are effected there.[134] Despite the fact that a share, traditionally, is generally represented by a certificate which may be pledged and otherwise dealt with as a document of value, for registered shares it still remains true that by English law entry on the register alone constitutes legal ownership.[135] In the context of private international law, it can be said that, as intangible property, questions relating to title to shares are to be governed by the law of the situs of the shares.[136] That leads to the conclusion that shares are deemed to be situated in the country where they can be effectively dealt with as between the shareholder and the company.[137] In other words, shares that are transferable only by an entry in the register have been deemed to be situated, for tax purposes, in the country where the register or branch register is kept.[138] If a company keeps registers in two or more countries, in any of which transfers may be registered, the question where any particular shares are situated has been held to depend on the country in which according to the ordinary course of business the transfer would be registered.[139] On the other hand, there is Canadian authority in the context of expropriation of enemy property which refers to the place of incorporation.[140]

A question of choice of law may arise with regard to a transfer[141] of shares, as may be illustrated by *Macmillan Inc v Bishopsgate Investment Trust plc (No 3)*,[142] which concerned the issue of priorities:

> The plaintiff, a wholly-owned subsidiary of one of the Robert Maxwell group of companies, owned shares in a company which was incorporated in New York, where the share register

---

[133] See, generally, Carruthers (2005), paras 1.38–1.40, 7.01, 7.08–7.12; Ooi (2003), Chapters 1–5; Benjamin (2001), Chapter 1; Ooi (2016) 12 J Priv Intl L 411.

[134] For instance, the Companies Act 2006, s 129 provides that an English company may keep a branch register (called an overseas branch register) in any of a given list of countries of members there resident. No transaction affecting shares so registered shall be registered in any other register (s 133(2)). An instrument of transfer of a share registered in an overseas branch register is regarded as a transfer of property situated outside the United Kingdom (s 133(3)).

[135] Bearer instruments are treated essentially as tangible property, and thus located at the place of the document and of any transfer in title: supra, Chapter 31; *AG v Bouwens* (1838) 4 M&W 171. Bearer shares have, however, recently been abolished for UK companies under the Small Business, Enterprise and Employment Act 2015, s 84.

[136] Carruthers (2005), paras 7.08–7.09; and *Shahar v Tsitsekkos* [2004] EWHC 2659 (Ch).

[137] On the situs of letters of allotment, see *Young v Phillips* [1984] STC 520.

[138] *Brassard v Smith* [1925] AC 371; *Baelz v Public Trustee* [1926] Ch 863; *London and South American Investment Trust v British Tobacco Co (Australia)* [1927] 1 Ch 107; *Erie Beach Co v A-G for Ontario* [1930] AC 161; *R v Williams* [1942] AC 541.

[139] *R v Williams*, supra; *Treasurer of Ontario v Blonde* [1947] AC 24; *Standard Chartered Bank Ltd v IRC* [1978] 1 WLR 1160. See Ooi (2003), Chapter 2; and Goode, Kanda and Kreuzer, *Explanatory Report on the Hague Convention on the Law Applicable to Certain Rights in Respect of Securities Held with an Intermediary* (2005), Int 36, and para 4.3.

[140] *Braun v Custodian* [1944] 4 DLR 209.

[141] The term is used here for convenience, but see Ooi (2003), paras 4.01–4.15 for legal analysis of the correct terminology.

[142] [1996] 1 WLR 387; see Bird [1996] LMCLQ 57; J Stevens (1996) 59 MLR 541; R Stevens (1996) 112 LQR 198.

was situated. The shares were transferred into the name of the first defendant as nominee and were deposited with the Depository Trust Co (DTC) in New York. Later, without the plaintiff's knowledge, some of the shares were used by Maxwell companies to secure loans from three banks who were further defendants in the proceedings. These loans were secured initially either by deposit of the share certificates in England or by transfer of the shares to the defendant banks through the DTC system in New York, but eventually all the shares were registered in New York in the names of the banks. The plaintiff company sought a declaration that it was beneficially entitled to the shares as being held by the defendants on trust for it.

The crucial issue was whether the plaintiff's claim was governed by New York law, under which it would fail as the defendants were bona fide purchasers without notice of the plaintiff's claim, or by English law under which the plaintiff could rely on constructive notice of its claim. The Court of Appeal rejected the argument that English law applied by reason of the claim being a restitutionary one and classified the particular issue as a proprietary one, namely whether the defendants had a good defence as bona fide purchasers for value without notice of the plaintiff's claim.[143] Given that conclusion, the central issue for the court was to determine the law to be applied to the issue of priority of title to the shares. The Court of Appeal concluded that the applicable law was that of the situs of the shares, ie New York law.[144] Although the determination of the law to govern ownership of shares might be thought to be "a specific case",[145] the members of the Court of Appeal drew support for their conclusion[146] from the fact that the law of the situs also applies to immovable and tangible movable property, though not to debts.

There still remained the issue of determining what was the situs of the shares. On this issue, the Court of Appeal was agreed that the situs was New York, whose law was to be applied, but was less clear as to the basis for that conclusion. The situs of shares was variously described as the place where the company is incorporated, where the share register is kept or in the case of shares which are negotiable the place where the actual documents are at the time of transfer.[147] As to whether the place of incorporation or that where the share register is kept is to be preferred as the situs, there is undoubted support for the latter approach.[148] It has been pointed out,[149] however, that this may be a distinction without a real difference as the law of the place of incorporation may always override the law of another attributed situs.

It is necessary, however, to distinguish the situs of shares from the situs of the actual certificates, at least where the shares are non-negotiable. Indeed, the Court of Appeal in *Macmillan's* case was in agreement[150] that the situs of such share certificates is where the

---

[143] On the classification issue, see Bird [1996] LMCLQ 57, 58–60; Briggs (1996) 67 BYBIL 604; J Stevens (1996) 59 MLR 741, 744–746; Forsyth (1998) 114 LQR 141. Also *Raiffeisen Zentralbank Österreich v Five Star General Trading LLC* [2001] EWCA Civ 68; [2001] QB 825, per Mance LJ, at [27]–[28]; *Atlantic Telecom GmbH, Noter* 2004 SLT 1031, per Lord Brodie, at 1043; and *Wight and Ors v Eckhardt Marine GmbH* [2004] AC 147, per Lord Hoffmann, at [11]. For classification generally, see supra, p 41 et seq.

[144] Rejecting the view of the trial judge, Millett J, ([1995] 1 WLR 978) that the applicable law was that of the country where the transaction had taken place—again New York.

[145] [1996] 1 WLR 387 at 402.

[146] Ibid, pp 399–402, 410–11, 424.

[147] Though Aldous LJ would also determine the situs in this way in the case of non-negotiable shares, at 411.

[148] Supra, p 1298; and see J Stevens (1996) 59 MLR 741, 744. For a preference for the law of the place of incorporation on the ground that there is always only one such place, see Bird [1996] LMCLQ 57, 62; R Stevens (1996) 112 LQR 198, 200.

[149] Dicey, Morris and Collins, para 22–045.

[150] [1996] 1 WLR 387 at 402–4, 412–13, 419–21.

certificates physically are situated at the time of the transfer. This is well illustrated by *Colonial Bank v Cady*:[151]

> The executors of a deceased Englishman, owner of certain New York railroad shares, wanted to be registered as owners in the books of the company. The executors sent the certificates to London brokers for transmission to New York. At the request of the brokers the executors signed the certificates in blank. The brokers deposited the certificates with the Colonial Bank as security for a debt, and later became bankrupt.

The question whether the deposit conferred a legal title on the bank depended on whether the transaction was to be governed by English or by New York law. By English law no title passed, but by New York law the delivery of the certificates operated to vest in the bank both the legal and the equitable ownership of the shares. Since the deposit was made in England, it was held that its effect must be determined by English law. Lord Herschell stated:

> I agree, that the question, what is necessary or effectual to transfer the shares in such a company, or to perfect the title to them, must be answered by a reference to the law of the State of New York. But I think that the rights arising out of a transaction entered into by parties in this country, whether, for example, it operated to effect a binding sale or pledge as against the owner of the shares, must be determined by the law prevailing here.[152]

In the court below, Bowen LJ simplified the problem with terse felicity:

> The key to this case is whether the defendants [the bank] have a right to hold these pieces of paper, these certificates. What the effect upon their ulterior rights in America would be, if we were to declare that they are entitled to these pieces of paper, is another question.[153]

It must be borne in mind that disputes in relation to the transfer of shares may give rise to choice of law issues in a related, but different,[154] context, namely as to the effect of the transfer as regards the parties to the transfer and persons claiming under them. If, for example, as in the *Macmillan* case, the certificates of a company incorporated in New York where the shares are registered have been transferred in England, New York law will decide whether the method by which the transfer has been effected entitles the transferee to be registered as a shareholder. However, the question whether the transferee is, for example, entitled by virtue of the transaction to retain the share certificates as against the transferor is determined by the law governing the transaction, which will normally be determined by choice of law rules in contract, and will often (although not invariably) be the law of the place where the certificates were delivered—in the above example, English law. If English law decides in favour of the transferee, the question whether he can demand to be registered as a shareholder will, as seen above, be a matter for New York law.[155]

This type of issue might be illustrated by *Re Fry*,[156] where the facts were as follows:

> X was resident in New Jersey and domiciled in Florida. Whilst in New Jersey he executed transfers of shares, which he owned in an English company, by way of gift to a private company and to his son. The share certificates were sent to England to be registered but, under the Defence Regulations 1939, the English company could not register the shares without

---

[151] (1890) 15 App Cas 267; in the Court of Appeal, sub nom *Williams v Colonial Bank* (1888) 38 Ch D 388.

[152] (1890) 15 App Cas 267 at 283.

[153] (1888) 38 Ch D 388 at 408.

[154] This distinction was drawn by the Court of Appeal in *Macmillan Inc v Bishopsgate Investment Trust plc (No 3)* [1996] 1 WLR 387 at 404, 409–10, 419, 424.

[155] Falconbridge, pp 590–1.

[156] [1946] Ch 312.

Treasury consent. The necessary forms were sent to X who signed and returned them but died before consent was actually obtained. As English law, the proper law of the transfers, had not been complied with, the transfers were incomplete and invalid.

(b) The modern holding system[157]

Market pressure, linked with technological and electronic advancement, has led to the development of a more efficient system for the holding and transfer of securities, namely, one which permits holding via an intermediary, and which allows for the transfer of interests by means of electronic book-entry to securities accounts. The traditional device of paper-based, materialised securities has been replaced by dematerialised securities, dealings with which are effected by virtue of electronic debit and/or credit book entries. Dematerialisation has been accompanied by immobilisation, which refers to the reduction in circulation of paper certificates as part of the transaction process, by means of their being deposited in a Central Securities Depositary, or International Central Securities Depositary, or other intermediary.

Given the global nature of the financial market, it is increasingly likely that the players in, or the elements of, a securities transaction will be situated in different jurisdictions. Cross-border clearing and settlement processes, by definition, will necessitate the interaction of different legal systems, and a cross-border securities transaction frequently will trigger complex questions of choice of law, including, most importantly, the question, what law should govern all or part(s) of a transaction which is cleared and/or settled in more than one jurisdiction?

Efforts to apply the traditional situs rule to intermediated securities have involved the so-called "look-through" approach: "'looking through' the tiers of intermediaries to the laws of one or more of the following: the jurisdiction of incorporation of the issuer, the location of the issuer's register or the location of the actual underlying securities certificates".[158] This amounts less to an application of the situs rule, than to a distortion of it, for it may be virtually impossible to ascertain the location of securities (materialised or dematerialised) held with an intermediary, particularly where securities are held in a multi-tier holding arrangement. The result is that it is not always clear to, or ascertainable by, market participants, which law is the governing law in relation to core issues such as enforceability, perfection of interests, and priority of interests.[159]

(i) European legislative measures

There have been piecemeal attempts within the European Community to deal with the issue of legal uncertainty in the securities market, principally, Directive (EC) No 98/26 of the European Parliament and of the Council of 19 May 1998 on settlement finality in payment and securities settlement systems (the "Settlement Finality Directive"),[160] and Directive 2002/47/EC of the European Parliament and of the Council of 6 June 2002 on financial collateral arrangements (the "Financial Collateral Directive").[161]

---

[157] See, generally, Carruthers (2005), Chapter 7; Goode, Kanda and Kreuzer, *Explanatory Report on the Hague Convention on the Law Applicable to Certain Rights in Respect of Securities Held with an Intermediary* (2005); Benjamin (2000), Chapter 1; and Ooi (2003), Chapters 1–5.

[158] Goode, Kanda and Kreuzer (2005), Int 37.

[159] Ibid, Int 5.

[160] OJ 1998 L166/45 (since amended by Directive 2009/44/EC, Directive 2010/78/EU, Regulation (EU) No 648/2012 and Regulation (EU) No 909/2014).

[161] OJ 2002 L168/43 (since amended by Directive 2009/44/EC and Directive 2014/59/EU).

The Settlement Finality Directive[162] "aims at contributing to the efficient and cost effective operation of cross-border payment and securities settlement arrangements in the Community, which reinforces the freedom of movement of capital in the internal market . . . ".[163] It addresses the issue of choice of law in relation to the provision of collateral security in cases where the entitlement of the collateral taker is recorded on a register, account or a centralised deposit system (Central Securities Depositary) within a Member State. The choice of law rule favoured by the Directive embodies the place of the relevant intermediary approach (so-called "PRIMA"): the determination of the rights of the collateral holders shall be governed by the law of the Member State where the register, account or centralised deposit system is located.[164]

The Financial Collateral Directive,[165] which is much wider in scope than the Settlement Finality Directive, sought to extend the PRIMA principle incorporated in that instrument, in order to create legal certainty regarding the use of book entry securities held in a cross-border context and used as financial collateral.[166]

From a choice of law perspective, the European instruments are notable, but from an economic perspective, the fragmented nature of the legislative framework means that the securities trading environment is less than ideal. Improvement in the system is not only desirable, but necessary.

(ii) The Hague Securities Convention

(a) Background

To address the demands of the global financial market for legal certainty and predictability as to the law applicable to securities, and conscious of the importance of "reducing legal risk, systemic risk and associated costs in relation to cross-border transactions involving securities held with an intermediary so as to facilitate the international flow of capital and access to capital markets",[167] the Hague Conference on Private International Law commenced work in May 2000 on a project concerning choice of law in relation to securities held with an intermediary. The Conference adopted a "fast-track" procedure which, together with industry involvement in, and transparency of, the negotiations, made it possible for the resulting Convention to be finalised in a remarkably short period of time: on 13 December 2002, the Convention on the Law Applicable to Certain Rights in respect of Securities Held with an Intermediary ("the Hague Securities Convention") was adopted,[168] and opened for signature and ratification by states.[169]

---

[162] Implemented in the United Kingdom by means of the Financial Markets and Insolvency (Settlement Finality) Regulations, SI 1999/2979. See also The Financial Markets and Insolvency (Settlement Finality) (Revocation) Regulations, SI 2001/1349. See Benjamin (2000), paras 7.46–7.51; and Ooi (2003), paras 12.03–12.80.

[163] Settlement Finality Directive, preamble (3).

[164] Art 9(2); and see SI 1999/2979, above, reg 23 (applicable law relating to securities held as collateral security).

[165] Implemented in the United Kingdom by means of The Financial Collateral Arrangements (No 2) Regulations, SI 2003/3226.

[166] Financial Collateral Directive, preamble (6) and (7), and Art 9(1); and see SI 2003/3226, above, reg 19 (standard test regarding the applicable law to book entry securities financial collateral arrangements). See Ooi (2003), paras 12.128–12.160.

[167] Convention on the Law Applicable to Certain Rights in respect of Securities Held with an Intermediary, preamble.

[168] The Convention is accompanied by an Explanatory Report prepared by Professor Roy Goode (United Kingdom), Professor Karl Kreuzer (Germany) and Professor Hideki Kanda (Japan), which, like the final text of the Convention, was reviewed and accepted by the Member States of the Conference. See also Goode (2005) 54 ICLQ 539; and Ooi [2005] LMCLQ 467.

[169] To date, the Convention has been ratified by only two Contracting States (Switzerland and Mauritius), and signed but not ratified by the USA. Under Art 19, the Convention shall enter into force following deposit of the third instrument of ratification, acceptance, approval or accession.

By reason of the adoption of a number of European Community Directives containing choice of law provisions relative to securities accounts, a transfer of competence has been effected by European Community Member States to the Community, in respect of matters covered by the Hague Securities Convention. The European Community qualifies as a Regional Economic Integration Organisation for the purposes of Article 18 of the Convention, but imminent signature and ratification appears unlikely,[170] principally because the regime adopted by the drafters of the Convention departs significantly from the choice of law rules currently applied in the Member States, as based on Community legislation.[171] Further reflection and exploration is needed at a Community level before a decision is taken to replace the European regime with the Convention.[172]

(b) Detail

The purpose of the Convention is to harmonise rules of choice of law, not rules of substantive law, concerning certain rights in respect of securities held with an intermediary. The objective is to achieve certainty as to the applicable law, in order that market participants are capable of knowing in advance what law governs securities transactions,[173] thereby keeping legal risk and, in turn, economic risk, at a minimum.[174]

The Convention applies in all cases where securities are held with an intermediary, ie where the securities are credited to a securities account, "regardless of how the relevant substantive law classifies the nature of the right resulting from the credit of the securities to the securities account",[175] ie as proprietary or contractual.[176] The Convention does not apply to directly held securities.

The preamble to the Convention takes the line that the PRIMA ("place of the relevant intermediary") approach remains the basis of the choice of law rule contained in the Convention, but there is an important modification, in the form of party autonomy.

The primary choice of law rule is contained in Article 4 of the Convention, which recognises the relevance of party choice (albeit restricted choice). The rule settled upon gives effect to an express agreement on governing law[177] between an account holder and its immediate intermediary, subject only to the "qualifying office" requirement. The choice of law may be

---

[170] Serious reservations were expressed by the European Banking Federation (Carruthers (2005), paras 7.46–7.49), and by the European Central Bank (OJ 2005 C 81/10) in response to a Proposal for a Council Decision concerning the signing of the Convention (COM (2003) 783 final). The Proposal was subsequently withdrawn: OJ 2009 C 71/07.

[171] Opinion of the European Central Bank OJ 2005 C 81/10, para 8.

[172] The European Central Bank has stressed the importance of assessing whether the Convention's approach would provide a greater degree of legal certainty and protection against systemic risk compared to the existing Community legislation (ibid, para 9).

[173] See Goode, Kanda and Kreuzer (2005) Int 33.

[174] Ibid, Int 34.

[175] Goode, Kanda and Kreuzer (2005) Int 20, 24, and para 1-16. See Art 2(2).

[176] In terms of Art 2(3), however, the Convention does not determine the law applicable to (a) the rights and duties arising from the credit of securities to a securities account to the extent that such rights or duties are purely contractual or otherwise purely personal; (b) the contractual or other personal rights and duties of parties to a disposition of securities held with an intermediary; or (c) the rights and duties of an issuer of securities . . . whether in relation to the holder of the securities of any other person. See Goode, Kanda and Kreuzer (2005) para 4-2, Int 25; and Int 59, which cites the following examples of rights or duties which are considered purely contractual/personal: the content and frequency of account statements; the intermediary's standard of care in maintaining securities accounts; risk of loss; and deadlines in giving instructions.

[177] Art 9 adopts the principle of universality, according to which the Convention applies regardless of whether the applicable law is the law of a Contracting State. Art 10 excludes operation of the doctrine of renvoi, meaning that reference to the "law of a state" is to its internal law only; see, however, the limited appearance of renvoi in Art 12(2)(b) and (3) regarding multi-legal system states.

expressly agreed in the account agreement[178] between the parties as being the state whose law governs that account agreement,[179] or if the account agreement expressly provides that another law is applicable to the issues specified in Article 2(1) of the Convention,[180] that other law shall govern those issues.[181] In any event, the law chosen will apply only if the relevant intermediary has, at the time of the agreement, a qualifying office[182] in that state.

Article 7 makes special provision for a case where an account agreement is amended so as to change the applicable law regarding Article 2(1) issues. One of the perceived benefits of allowing (limited) party autonomy in this sphere is that, as well as permitting greater legal certainty, it "reflects existing and foreseeable market practice".[183]

The secondary and subsequent choice of law rules (which are applicable either in the event of the parties failing to make an express agreement as to choice of law, or in the event of their choosing the law of a state in which, at the time of the agreement, the intermediary does not have a qualifying office) are narrated in Article 5 of the Convention. In terms of Article 5(1), if the applicable law is not determined under Article 4, but it is expressly and unambiguously stated in a written account agreement that the relevant intermediary entered into the account agreement through a particular office, then the law applicable to all the issues specified in Article 2(1) shall be the law of the state[184] in which that office then was located. However, as with Article 4, the law thus identified will apply only if the relevant intermediary has, at the time of the agreement, a qualifying office in that state.

If the applicable law is not determined under Article 5(1) (ie if there is no express and unambiguous statement in a written account agreement that the relevant intermediary entered into the account agreement through a particular office), then the applicable law, under Article 5(2), shall be the law in force in the state[185] under whose law the relevant intermediary is incorporated or otherwise organised at the time the written agreement is entered into or, if

---

[178] Defined in Art 1(1)(e) as meaning, in relation to a securities account (ie an account maintained by an intermediary to which securities may be credited or debited: Art 1(1)(b)), the agreement with the relevant intermediary governing that securities account.

[179] See Goode, Kanda and Kreuzer (2005), Int 60.

[180] Being the issues which are deemed to fall within the scope of the applicable law under the Convention, namely: (a) the legal nature and effects against the intermediary of the rights resulting from a credit of securities to a securities account; (b) the legal nature and effects against the intermediary and third parties of a disposition of securities held with an intermediary; (c) the requirements, if any, for perfection of a disposition of securities held with an intermediary; (d) whether a person's interests in securities held with an intermediary extinguishes or has priority over another person's interest; (e) the duties, if any, of an intermediary to a person other than the account holder who asserts in competition with the account holder or another person an interest in securities held with that intermediary; (f) the requirements, if any, for the realisation of an interest in securities held with an intermediary; and (g) whether a disposition of securities held with an intermediary extends to entitlements to dividends, income, or other distributions, or to redemption, sale or other proceeds. The list of issues in Art 2(1) is intended to be exhaustive: Goode, Kanda and Kreuzer (2005), Int 54, and para 2-2.

[181] "The parties may expressly agree to have the law of one State govern all the Article 2(1) issues and that of a different State to govern the account agreement." (Goode, Kanda and Kreuzer (2005), Int 60; also Int 47).

[182] Defined in Art 4(1)(a) and (b), and meaning essentially that the intermediary must have in the state the law of which has been chosen by the parties, an office which is engaged in the activity of maintaining securities accounts (though not necessarily the account in question). See Goode, Kanda and Kreuzer (2005), Int 62.

[183] Goode, Kanda and Kreuzer (2005), Int 48; this is true, even though the rule is "counter-intuitive and . . . contrary to a well-established principle that two parties to a contract cannot by their agreement affect the rights of third parties, still less subject those rights to a given law". (Goode, *Commercial Law* (2004) 3rd edn, pp 1111–12). Various protections are, however, set out in Article 7.

[184] Or relevant territorial unit of a multi-unit state.

[185] Or relevant territorial unit of a multi-unit state.

there is no such agreement, at the time the securities account was opened; and, failing which, under Article 5(3), the law in force in the state[186] in which the relevant intermediary has its (principal) place of business.

Article 6 of the Convention lists certain factors of which no account may be taken in determining the applicable law under the Convention: (a) the place where the issuer of the securities is incorporated or otherwise organized; (b) the places where certificates representing or evidencing securities are located; (c) the place where a register of holders of securities maintained by or on behalf of the issuer of the securities is located; and/or (d) the place where any intermediary other than the relevant intermediary (ie an upper-tier intermediary) is located. What is significant is that Article 6, by its terms, deliberately severs any residual link with traditional situs thinking and methodology.

The customarily included public policy exception is to be found in Article 11(1) of the Convention, in terms of which application of the prima facie applicable law may be refused only if the effects of its application would be manifestly contrary to the public policy of the forum. So too, there is a saving provision in Article 11(2) regarding mandatory rules of the forum, according to which application is preserved of those provisions of the law of the forum which, irrespective of rules of conflict of laws, must be applied, even to international situations. Article 11(1) and (2), however, will be strictly construed, and in terms of Article 11(3), will not justify the application of those provisions of the law of the forum which impose requirements with respect to perfection, or relating to priorities between competing interests, *unless* the law of the forum is also the applicable law under the Convention.

---

[186] Or relevant territorial unit of a multi-unit state.

33

CORPORATIONS[1]

1. Domicile	1306	4. Internal Management	1308
2. Residence	1307	5. Winding Up	1309
3. Status and Capacity	1307		

1. DOMICILE

The domicile of a corporation is sometimes used as a connecting factor for corporations in private international law, despite the fact that the concept of domicile applies primarily to natural persons. It is after all not easy to determine an intention to reside and nor is it obvious that one should seek to determine one when a corporation is involved. An example of a statute that nevertheless uses the concept of domicile for corporations is the Income and Corporation Taxes Act 1988.[2] Whereas every natural person gets a domicile of origin upon birth a corporation's domicile is linked to its incorporation. A corporation is therefore domiciled in the country under whose law it was incorporated.[3] Turning to the situation in the UK under the provisions of the Companies Act 2006, that means that a company registered in England will have an English domicile, whereas a company registered in Scotland will have a Scottish domicile. And a company registered in Spain will have a Spanish domicile. Such a corporate domicile is of course independent of the domicile of the persons who are its members.

On the basis of the analogy with a natural person, one would think that a corporation could only have one domicile,[4] ie that of the country in which it was incorporated.[5] Clearly the Companies Act 2006 does not envisage a company being re-incorporated somewhere else. What can be created is a second separate company incorporated abroad in case the company was registered in England or a separate company incorporated in England in case the company was registered abroad.[6] These are then legally distinct from one another. But other legal systems may allow a company to be incorporated in more than one country. The question whether that would give rise to such a corporation having a domicile in each of these

---

[1] S Rameloo, *Corporations in Private International Law* (2001). See also P Paschalidis, *Freedom of Establishment and Private International Law for Corporations* (2012).

[2] S 749(1).

[3] *Gasque v Inland Revenue Commissioners* [1940] KB 80; *The Eskbridge* [1931] P 51; *National Trust Company v Ebro Irrigation and Power Ltd* [1954] 3 DLR 326 (Ont). Domicile has a specific meaning in a Brussels I Regulation context (now the Recast Brussels I), see supra, p 198 et seq.

[4] See supra, p 200 et seq.

[5] *Saccharin Corp Ltd v Chemische Fabrik von Heyden* [1911] 2 KB 516, 527 (CA). See also *Australian Securities and Investment Commission v Medical Defence Association of Western Australia* [2005] FCAFC 173.

[6] *Re Irrigation Company of France Ltd, Ex p Fox* (1871) LR 6 Ch App 176 and *Concept Oil Services Limited (a company incorporated in Hong Kong) v EN-GIN Group LLP (a limited liability partnership under the law of Kazakhstan), EN-GIN Production LLP (a limited liability partnership under the law of Kazakhstan), and others* [2013] EWHC 1897 (Comm), para 72.

countries of incorporation did not receive lot of attention in English private international law.[7] But there is no argument in principle why an English court should not recognize a multiple domicile in cases where that flows from the (legally correct) incorporation is more than one country. Corporations could on this basis change their domicile by being dissolved in one country after having re-incorporated themselves in another country, always subject to the control of the legal systems of the countries involved.[8]

2. RESIDENCE

Residence is not looked at from a jurisdictional perspective here.[9] But tax law for example use the criterion of residence for corporations to determine their tax liability, ie to determine whether English tax law applies to them. As a general rule a corporation is resident in the country where its central management and control are exercised. This rule applies to foreign corporations and needs to be distinguished from the place of incorporation[10] or the place where central management and control ought to be exercised.[11] Instead the focus lies on the place where central management and control are de facto exercised. A company that is incorporated in the United Kingdom is by law to be regarded as resident therein for taxation purposes.[12] The term ordinary residence[13] is also found in legislation and its emphasis on how things are habitually and with a degree of continuity is likely to lead in practice to the application of the central management and control test.

In principle a corporation will exercise its central management and control from a single place and will therefore have a single residence. Exceptionally there could be multiple residences.[14] In those cases there is a division of power over the various residences and one cannot identify a single place of management and control.[15]

3. STATUS AND CAPACITY

The problem of status usually arises in relation to corporations that have purportedly been established under a foreign law. The question whether the English legal system will recognize them as corporations and thereby eg give them the right to sue and be sued can only be answered once the issue of the existence (or dissolution) of the corporation has been dealt with. English law refers in this respect to the creation or dissolution of the corporation under the foreign law and recognizes the latter.[16] The existence of a legal entity, such as a corporation will therefore depend on the law of the country under which it was formed. That law

---

[7] See *Carl Zeiss Stiftung v Rayner & Keeler Ltd (No 3)* [1970] Ch 506.

[8] For the EU position see Case 81/87 *R v HM Treasury and Commissioners of Inland Revenue, ex p Daily Mail and General Trust plc* [1988] ECR 5483; Case C-201/06 *Cortesio Oktaó és Szolgáltató bt* [2008] ECR I-9641 and Case C-378/10 *VALE Építési Kft* ECLI:EU:C:2012:440. See also Rameloo, Chapters 1–3.

[9] See supra, pp 172–5.

[10] Cf *Egyptian Delta Land and Investment Co v Todd* [1929] AC 1.

[11] *Unit Construction Company Ltd v Bullock* [1960] AC 351 and *Re Little Olympian Each Ways Ltd* [1995] 1 WLR 560.

[12] Income and Corporation Taxes Act 1988, s 749.

[13] *Re Little Olympian Each Ways Ltd* [1995] 1 WLR 560.

[14] *Swedish Central Railway v Thompson* [1925] AC 495.

[15] *Unit Construction Company Ltd v Bullock* [1960] AC 351, at 366.

[16] *International Bulk Shipping and Services Ltd v Minerals and Metals Trading Corp of India* [1996] 1 All ER 1017 (CA) and *Re Eurodis Electron plc* [2011] EWHC 1025 (Ch).

will also determine the legal nature of the entity that was created and whether it has a separate legal existence.[17]

This principle of the recognition of the status awarded by the foreign law under which the corporation was created needs to be seen in conjunction with the rules on jurisdiction that apply when such a foreign company establishes a branch or a place of business in the UK. These derive from the Companies Act 2006 and the Civil Procedure Rules 1998.[18]

Whereas status refers to the corporation's right to sue (and be sued) capacity refers to the corporation's ability to enter into legal transactions. A dual track approach applies on this point and highlights the limitations placed on the corporation in this respect. A first set of limitations can be derived from the constitution of the corporation. It is this constitution, as interpreted by the law of the place of incorporation, that defines what kind of transactions the corporation can (and cannot) enter into. The constitution decides in other words which transactions will in the company law jargon be *ultra vires*.[19] The second track follows the law of the country which governs the transaction concerned and further limitations can arise. This applicable law can on the other hand never empower the corporation to conclude a transaction that its constitution holds to be *ultra vires*.[20]

The court of Appeal has however held by a majority that when applying the concept of capacity the court has to give it an "internationalist" meaning. Narrow definitions that flow from English domestic law are to be avoided. From that perspective capacity refers to the legal ability of a corporation to exercise specific rights and more specifically its legal ability to enter into a contract with a third party. In the case at issue a lack of capacity was derived from the lack of substantive power to conclude a contract of a particular type.[21]

In terms of the execution of documents when the corporation enters into a legal transaction there are provisions in the Companies Act that have been amended from the provisions that apply to companies incorporated in England.[22]

4. INTERNAL MANAGEMENT

Leaving the external dealing of corporations there is of course also the issue of their internal management. English courts are reluctant to intervene in the internal management of foreign companies, but the following principles can nevertheless be derived from the case-law. The composition and the powers of the various organs of the corporation are determined by the law of the place of incorporation of the corporation.[23] With that starting point established the same law is then also applied to the question whether the directors have been appointed validly,[24] the question what the nature and extent of their duties to the corporation are,[25] the

---

[17] *Maritime Investment Holdings Inc v Underwriting Members of Syndicate 1183 at Lloyd's* [2015] EWHC 2190 (Comm).

[18] See above p 328 et seq.

[19] See *Sierra Leone Telecommunications Co Ltd v Barclays Bank plc* [1998] 2 All ER 821.

[20] *Haugesund Kommune v Depfa ACS Bank* [2010] EWCA Civ 579 and *Integral Petroleum SA v SCU-Finanz AG* [2015] EWCA Civ 144.

[21] *Haugesund Kommune v Depfa ACS Bank* [2010] EWCA Civ 579.

[22] Companies Act 2006, ss 43, 44 and 46.

[23] *Grupo Torras SA v Al-Sabah* [1996] 1 Lloyd's Rep 7 (CA); *Haugesund Kommune v Depfa ACS Bank* [2010] EWCA Civ 579.

[24] *Sierra Leone Telecommunications Co Ltd v Barclays Bank plc* [1998] 2 All ER 821; *Speed Investments Ltd v Formula One Holdings Ltd* [2004] EWCA Civ 1512.

[25] *Base Metal Trading v Shamurin* [2004] EWCA Civ 1316; *Isis investments Ltd v Oscatello Investments Ltd* [2013] EWHC 7 (Ch). See also *Re Douglas Webber Events Pty Ltd* [2014] NSWSC 1544.

question of which officials can act on behalf of the corporation,[26] the question of individual member's liability for the engagements or debts entered into by the corporation,[27] the question of the ability of the corporation to make a distribution to its members[28] and the question of the validity of a transfer of assets and liabilities by way of amalgamation with another corporation or universal succession.[29] Even the right of a shareholder to bring an action against the corporation has been held to be of a material nature and governed by the law of the place of incorporation of the company.[30]

5. WINDING UP

This area of the law is now dominated by Regulation 2015/848 on insolvency proceedings,[31] which will be analysed in the next chapter. First of all, this dominance comes into play when the issue of jurisdiction arises. In the obvious scenario where an English registered company is insolvent the Regulation limits the jurisdiction of the English courts to wind up the company under the traditional rules to the situation where the company has its centre of main interests in a state which is not a Regulation state for the purposes of the Regulation.[32] The traditional rules use the place of registration, here registration in England, as a hook for jurisdiction.[33] In the most extreme scenario, that jurisdiction will be established on the basis that the company was registered in England even if the company never carried on business in England, never had any property in England and all its directors and shareholders were domiciled and resident abroad in non-Regulation states.[34] As the recast Brussels I Regulation does not apply in such a case the court will however be able to decline jurisdiction on *forum non conveniens* grounds where appropriate.[35]

The Regulation does not apply to solvent companies.[36] These can be wound up by the English courts if they are registered in England. Article 24(2) recast Brussels I Regulation and its counterpart in the Lugano convention even grant the English courts exclusive jurisdiction on this point. The court will have no option but to hear the case, as there is no room for *forum non conveniens*,[37] but the court retains a discretion when deciding whether or not to wind up the company.[38] Outside the recast Brussels I Regulation there is also an option for the Secretary of State to petition the court to wind up a company in the public interest.[39]

---

[26] *Sierra Leone Telecommunications Co Ltd v Barclays Bank plc* [1998] 2 All ER 821; *Isis investments Ltd v Oscatello Investments Ltd* [2013] EWHC 7 (Ch). See also *Re Douglas Webber Events Pty Ltd* [2014] NSWSC 1544.

[27] *Grupo Torras SA v Al-Sabah* [1996] 1 Lloyd's Rep 7 (CA); *Speed Investments Ltd v Formula One Holdings Ltd* [2004] EWCA Civ 1512.

[28] *Base Metal Trading v Shamurin* [2004] EWCA Civ 1316; *Shaker v Al-Bedrawi* [2002] EWCA Civ 1452.

[29] *National Bank of Greece and Athens SA v Metliss* [1958] AC 509; *Eurosteel Ltd v Stinnes AG* [2000] 1 All ER 964 (Comm).

[30] *Base Metal Trading v Shamurin* [2004] EWCA Civ 1316; *Novatrust Ltd v Kea Investments Ltd* [2014] EWHC 4061.

[31] Regulation (EU) 2015/848 of the European Parliament and of the Council of 20 May 2015 on Insolvency Proceedings (Recast) [2015] OJ L 141/19.

[32] Insolvency Act 1986, s 117(7).

[33] Insolvency Act 1986, ss 117(1) and (2). See also the principle in article 24(2) recast Brussels I Regulation.

[34] Cf *Reuss v Bos* (1871) LR 5 HL 176.

[35] See *Re Rodenstock GmbH* [2011] EWHC 1104 (Ch).

[36] Ibid.

[37] Case C-28/02 *Owusu v Jackson* [2005] ECR I-1383.

[38] Insolvency Act 1986, ss 122(g) and 125.

[39] S 124A. This is a discharge of a public duty and thus it is not a civil and commercial matter as required by the Regulation.

So far we dealt with companies that are registered in England.[40] The insolvency act 1986 deals with companies registered outside the United Kingdom as if they are unregistered companies.[41] But once again the Insolvency Regulation limits the jurisdiction of the English courts to wind up the company under the traditional rules when it is insolvent to the case where the company has its centre of main interests in a state which is not a Regulation state for the purposes of the Regulation. And in case the company is solvent the recast Brussels I Regulation and the Lugano Convention limit the jurisdiction of the English courts to the cases where the company does not have its seat in a Member State or in a Convention State. When the limitations do not apply section 221(5) of the Act gives the English courts jurisdiction to wind up such a company:

(a) if the company is dissolved,[42] or has ceased to carry on business, or is carrying on business only for the purpose of winding up its affairs;

(b) if the company is unable to pay its debts;

(c) if the court is of opinion that it is just and equitable that the company should be wound up.

The court retains a discretion whether or not to make an order under any of these grounds.[43] The court is likely to exercise its discretion to make an order if there is a sufficient connection between the company and England, if there are persons who would benefit from the making of a winding up order and if one or more persons who have an interest in the distribution of the assets of the company are persons over whom the court can exercise jurisdiction.[44] Such a link with the jurisdiction, first of all, does not necessarily involve the presence of assets within the jurisdiction. The carrying out of business in the jurisdiction and even the presence of agreements governed by English law can point in that direction.[45] Secondly, the elements of benefits that can be derived or interests in assets that can be distributed is based on common sense and often arises as a result of the company carrying out business in England.

Once the jurisdiction of the English court has been established the issue of choice of law arises. Once again the traditional English rules will only apply in the situation where the rules of the Insolvency Regulation do not apply.[46] The Insolvency Act 1986 takes its property away from the company and entrusts it to the liquidator who is appointed for it to be dealt with for the benefit of the persons who are interested in the winding up.[47] These winding up proceedings are governed by English law.[48]

---

[40] Companies registered in Scotland are to be wound up by the Scottish courts and the English courts lack jurisdiction to do so. In the same way unregistered companies having a principal place of business in Scotland or Northern Ireland that do not have a principal place of business in England fall outside the jurisdiction of the English courts. Insolvency Act 1986, ss 221(1), (2) and (3).

[41] Insolvency Act 1986, s 220.

[42] In the sense of 'has been dissolved', *Banque des Marchants de Moscou v Kindersley* [1951] Ch 112, 125 (CA); cf *Re ARM Asset Backed Securities SA* [2013] EWHC 3351 (Ch); *Re ARM Asset Backed Securities SA (No 2)* [2014] EWHC 1097 (Ch).

[43] *Re Hibernian Merchants Ltd* [1958] Ch 76, 78.

[44] *Stockznia Gdanska SA v Latreefers Inc (No 2)* [2001] BCLC 116, 130 (CA). See also *Re Real Estate Development Co* [1991] BCLC 210, 217 and *Banco Nacional de Cuba v Cosmos Trading Corp* [2000] 1 BCLC 116 (CA).

[45] *In Re A Company (No. 00359 of 1987)* [1988] Ch 210. But the presence of a more appropriate jurisdiction in which to wind up the company can point in the other direction, see *Re Seat Pagine Gialle Spa* [2012] EWHC 3686 (Ch).

[46] See infra, p 1312.

[47] *Re Oriental Inland Steam Co* (1874) LR 9 Ch App 557; *Bloom v Harms Offshore AHT* [2009] EWCA Civ 632; *Singularis Holdings SA v PricewaterhouseCoopers* [2014] UKPC 36; *Stichting Shell Pensioenfonds v Krys* [2014] UKPC 41. See also *PricewaterhouseCoopers v Saad Investments* [2014] UKPC 35.

[48] Re *Bank of Credit and Commerce International SA (No 10)* [1997] Ch 213; *Re HIH Casualty and General Insurance Ltd* [2008] UKHL 21; *Bloom v Harms Offshore AHT* [2009] EWCA Civ 632; *Re Swissair Schweizerische Luftverkehr-Aktiengesellschaft* [2009] EWHC 2099 (Ch).

When proceedings have been brought abroad the authority of the liquidator appointed by the foreign court will be recognized in England if the liquidator was appointed by the court of the place of incorporation of the company being wound up.[49] This rule flows from the basic principle that it is the law of the place of incorporation that decides who can act on behalf of the company.[50] That includes a liquidator who was appointed by the court of the place of incorporation to take charge of the company's affairs in the winding up proceedings. But obviously this rule now only applies in cases that are not covered by the Insolvency Regulation. The recognition of the authority of the liquidator also does not mean that foreign insolvency orders arising from the foreign winding up proceedings will automatically be entitled to enforcement in England. In order to get the foreign orders enforced the foreign liquidator needs to show that the judgment debtor:

1 was present in the foreign jurisdiction at the time of when the proceedings were instituted; and
2 was the claimant or the counter–claimant in the foreign proceedings; and
3 had submitted to the foreign proceedings by appearing voluntarily; or
4 had submitted to the foreign proceedings by agreement.[51]

Finally, receivers can also be appointed and this does not necessarily involve the court. It is arguable that a receiver who was appointed under the law of another part of the United Kingdom can exercise his powers in England. This is envisaged when the appointment was in respect of property of a corporation over which a charge was created that was a floating charge when created.[52] In cases where the receiver was appointed outside the United Kingdom an additional requirement that the exercise of the powers of the receiver was authorized by the law of the country of incorporation applies.[53]

---

[49] *Baden, Delvaux and Lecuit v Société Générale pour Favoriser le Développement du Commerce et de l'Industrie en France SA* [1983] BCLC 325; *Felixtowe Dock and Railway Co v US Lines Inc* [1989] QB 360, 374–5.

[50] *Banco de Bilbao v Sancha and Rey* [1938] 2 KB 176 (CA).

[51] *Rubin v Eurofinance SA* [2012] UKSC 46, reversing *Rubin v Eurofinance SA* [2010] EWCA Civ 895 and affirming *New Cap Reinsurance Corp Ltd v Grant* [2011] EWCA Civ 971.

[52] Cf Insolvency Act 1986, ss 72 and 426 and *Gordon Anderson (Plant) Ltd v Campsie Construction Ltd and Anglo Scottish Plant Ltd* 1977 SLT 7 by way of inspiration. See Dicey, Morris and Collins, 30R-124.

[53] See Dicey, Morris and Collins, 30R-124.

34

INSOLVENCY

1. Scope   1312
2. Jurisdiction   1313
   (a) Main insolvency proceedings
       jurisdiction   1313
   (b) Secondary insolvency proceedings
       jurisdiction   1315
   (c) Checks on jurisdiction   1317
   (d) Extent of jurisdiction   1318

3. Choice of Law   1319
   (a) The general rule   1319
   (b) A list of issues that are covered   1319
   (c) Additional exceptions   1322
4. Recognition of Insolvency Proceedings   1323
5. Groups of Companies and
   Their Members   1324

1. SCOPE

This chapter deals with insolvency in the context of the Regulation on insolvency proceedings (recast).[1] Its impact became already clear in the previous chapter when it was pointed out that it put sever limitations on the scope of the traditional rules on winding up. The recast Regulation will apply to insolvency proceedings opened after 26 June 2017.[2]

The scope of the Regulation is determined in Article 1. In essence it deals with public collective insolvency proceedings. Private proceedings are not included and the proceedings need to have a collective nature, ie bring the different creditors together, all of them or a significant part of them.[3] The proceedings need to be based on insolvency laws and may have as their purpose either the rescue, reorganization or liquidation of the debtor or the adjustment of its debt. The proceeding are then further defined as proceedings in which, for the purpose described above, the debtor is totally or partially divested of its assets and an insolvency practitioner is appointed. Alternatively, the assets and affairs of the debtor are made subject to control or supervision by a court. A temporary stay of individual enforcement proceedings can also be granted by a court or by operation of law, in order to allow for negotiations between the debtor and its creditors. The latter scenario can only unfold on condition that the proceedings in which the stay is granted provide for suitable measures to protect the general body of creditors, and, where no agreement is reached, these proceeding are preliminary to one of the two other types of proceedings.

There are therefore three types of public collective insolvency proceedings that fall within the scope of the Regulation. They are to be based on laws relating to insolvency and when initiated when there is merely a likelihood of insolvency their purpose shall be to avoid the

---

[1] Regulation (EU) 2015/848 of the European Parliament and of the Council of 20 May 2015 on insolvency proceedings (recast)]2015] OJ L 141/19. Denmark is not covered by the Regulation, but it has introduced very similar national legislation.

[2] Earlier proceeding are dealt with under Regulation (EC) 1346/2000 on insolvency proceedings [2000] OJ L 160/1. See I F Fletcher, *Insolvency in Private International Law* (2005), and P Torremans, *Cross Border Insolvencies in EU, English and Belgian Law* (2002).

[3] Article 2(1). The proceedings should not affect the claims of creditors which are not involved in them.

debtor's insolvency or the cessation of the debtor's business activities.[4] All of this presupposes that the debtor is either insolvent or that there is at the very least a likelihood of insolvency. But surprising as it may seem, the Regulation does not define insolvency and leaves that explicitly to the national laws of the Member States. Instead, what the Regulation offers is a list of proceedings that are covered by it. Annex A lists the following for the United Kingdom:

- Winding-up by[5] or subject to the supervision of the court.
- Creditors' voluntary winding-up (with confirmation by the court).[6]
- Administration, including appointments made by filing prescribed documents with the court.[7]
- Voluntary arrangements under insolvency legislation.[8]
- Bankruptcy or sequestration.[9]

Finally, the following are excluded from the scope of the Regulation:

- insurance undertakings;
- credit institutions;
- investment firms and other firms, institutions and undertakings to the extent that they are covered by Directive 2001/24/EC; or
- collective investment undertakings.[10]

2. JURISDICTION

The Regulation distinguishes between main insolvency proceedings and secondary insolvency proceedings when it comes to international jurisdiction to open the proceedings described in Article 1 and listed in Annex A.

(a) Main insolvency proceedings jurisdiction

The connecting factor for jurisdiction in relation to main insolvency proceedings is the centre of the debtor's main interests. The courts of the Member State within which that centre of the debtor's main interests is situated will have jurisdiction to open main insolvency proceedings in respect of the debtor. Helpfully, the Regulation then defines the concept of the centre of the debtor's main interests as the place where the debtor conducts the administration of its interests on a regular basis and which is ascertainable by third parties.[11] Such main insolvency proceedings will have universal effect in the sense that they encompass all assets in any state covered by the Regulation.

For the purposes of this provision, a court is defined in Article 2 as "the judicial body or any other competent body of a Member State empowered to open insolvency proceedings,

---

[4] Article 1(1).

[5] Insolvency Act 1986, Part IV, Chapter VI, extended to winding up insolvent partnerships, s 420 and SI 1994/2421 Insolvent Partnerships Order, as amended by SI 2002/1308.

[6] This new procedure was introduced into the Insolvency Rules 1986, rr 7.62 and 7.63, inserted by SI 2002/1307.

[7] Insolvency Act 1986, Sch B1. There can be no pre-condition of residence in the Member State concerned, Case C-461/11 *Ulf Kazmierz Radziejewski v Kronofogdemyndigheten i Stockholm*, ECLI:EU:C:2012:704.

[8] Solvent schemes of arrangement are excluded, see *Re Rodenstock GmbH* [2011] EWHC 1104 (Ch).

[9] Insolvency Act 1986, s 421 (1A).

[10] Article 1(2). These are governed by separate instrument, due to their special characteristics. In relation to credit institutions see under the EU instruments *Guardians of New Zealand Superannuation Fund & others v Novo Banco SA* [2016] EWCA Civ 1092 and *Tchenguiz & others v Kaupthing Bank hf and Johannas Runar Johannsson* [2017] EWCA Civ 83 and compare under English law *In the matter of International Bank of Azerbaijan OJSC*, Ch D, 6 June 2017 (nyr).

[11] Article 3(1). The emphasis on third parties' perception is also found in Case C-341/04 *Eurofood IFSC Ltd* [2006] ECR I-3813, paras 32–33. The Court set out an autonomous interpretation of the term centre of the debtor's main interests along these lines.

to confirm such opening or to take decisions in the course of such proceedings" and the judgment of such a court opening insolvency proceedings includes both the decision to open insolvency proceedings or to confirm the opening of such proceedings and the decision to appoint an insolvency practitioner.[12] Applying that to winding up or administration proceedings we are talking about the winding up order or the administration order, rather than the presentation of any petition seeking such an order.[13] Finally, Article 2(8) stipulates that "'the time of the opening of proceedings' means the time at which the judgment opening insolvency proceedings becomes effective, regardless of whether the judgment is final or not". Timing can be of the essence if more than one Member State could claim to have jurisdiction to open main insolvency proceedings. The CJEU held that as long as the two key components are present, ie divestment of the debtor and the appointment of a liquidator, proceedings have been opened.[14] The Irish Supreme Court then held this to mean that the appointment of a provisional liquidator was sufficient, as it involved these two elements, even if there was not yet a final decision on a proceeding listed in Annex A.[15]

The Regulation then acknowledges that identifying the centre of the debtor's main interests is not always straightforward despite the emphasis on the dual factors of administration of interests on a regular basis and ascertainable by third parties. The Regulation therefore sets out a series of rebuttable presumptions. It distinguishes in this respect between companies and legal persons, individuals exercising a business or professional activity and any other individual:

> In the case of a company or legal person, the place of the registered office shall be presumed to be the centre of its main interests in the absence of proof to the contrary. That presumption shall only apply if the registered office has not been moved to another Member State within the 3-month period prior to the request for the opening of insolvency proceedings.

> In the case of an individual exercising an independent business or professional activity, the centre of main interests shall be presumed to be that individual's principal place of business in the absence of proof to the contrary. That presumption shall only apply if the individual's principal place of business has not been moved to another Member State within the 3-month period prior to the request for the opening of insolvency proceedings.

> In the case of any other individual, the centre of main interests shall be presumed to be the place of the individual's habitual residence in the absence of proof to the contrary. This presumption shall only apply if the habitual residence has not been moved to another Member State within the 6-month period prior to the request for the opening of insolvency proceedings.[16]

There is therefore a rebuttable presumption in favour of a stable place of the registered office, principal place of business and habitual residence respectively. The exclusion of cases where the relevant location was changed shortly before the opening of the proceedings needs to be seen as a tool to avoid manipulation of the centre of the debtor's main interests in a period where insolvency may already have been on the horizon. The CJEU has also declined to consider transferring a case where the debtor had petitioned the court in order to be made bankrupt to the new centre of main interests to which she had moved her assets before the Court

---

[12] Article 2(7).
[13] This is confirmed by the fact that a request to open proceedings is treated separately in Article 3(4)(b)(i).
[14] Case C-341/04 *Eurofood IFSC Ltd* [2006] ECR I-3813.
[15] *Re Eurofood IFSC Ltd* (No 2) [2006] IESC 41.
[16] Article 3(1).

of Appeal could deal with her case. Once the case was pending legal certainty should prevail, even if handling the case might in practice have been rendered more difficult.[17]

That brings us back to the rebuttable nature of the presumption. In this respect the court will have to look at all possible factors that point away from the jurisdiction identified by the presumption. For companies an important factor will often be the fact that the head office function is exercised somewhere else than at the registered office.[18] But in the light of the way the Regulation conceives the concept of the centre of the debtor's main interests the presumption can only be rebutted if factors which are both objective and at the same time ascertainable by third parties enable the court to establish that an actual situation exists that is different from the situation which the presumption is deemed to reflect.[19] A letterbox company that does not carry on business in its state of registration could be an example of such a situation if all decisions are taken elsewhere and this is ascertainable by third parties. On the other hand the mere fact that the company's economic choices are controlled by a foreign parent company is not sufficient to rebut the presumption if the company carries on business in the country of registration.[20] Immovable property in another country that is exploited by the company may also be a relevant factor for the rebuttal of the presumption, especially as it is also ascertainable by third parties, but, just like any other assets and their presence in another jurisdiction, taken on its own this will not be sufficient to rebut the presumption.[21]

(b) Secondary insolvency proceedings jurisdiction

The Regulation also offers the opportunity to offer another type of insolvency proceedings if the debtor has its centre of main interests in a country covered by the Regulation. The connecting factor in this respect is the existence of an establishment of the debtor in the territory of another country covered by the Regulation. The courts of that other country can then open insolvency proceedings against the debtor, but the effect of those proceedings will be restricted to the assets of the debtor that are situated on the territory of that state.[22]

The key concept in this regard is the concept of an "establishment". The Regulation defines this in an open way[23] as "any place of operations where a debtor carries out or has carried out in the three-month period prior to the request to open main insolvency proceedings a non-transitory economic activity with human means and assets".[24] The key elements are "any place of operations" and the fact that these operations amount to "a non-transitory economic activity with human means and assets". The CJEU has held that this involves a clear abandonment of the mere criterion of the presence of assets or bank accounts in the jurisdiction and that one needs to demonstrate that there exists or existed within the jurisdiction concerned a structure with a minimum of organization and a minimum of stability for the exercise of an economic activity by the debtor.[25] Only in this context does human, in the

---

[17] Case C-1/04 *Staubitz-Schreiber* [2006] ECR I-701, ECLI:EU:C:2006:39. On the change of COMI see also *Trillium (Nelson) Properties Ltd v Office Metro Ltd* [2012] EWHC 1191 (Ch); *Trustees of Olympic Airlines SA Pension and Life Insurance Scheme v Olympic Airlines SA* [2015] UKSC 27.

[18] *Re BRAC Rent-a-Car International Inc* [2003] EWHC 12 (Ch); *Re Daisytek-ISA Ltd* [2003] BCC 562; *Re Sendo Ltd* [2005] EWHC 1604 (Ch); *Re Parkside Flexibles SA* [2006] BCC 589.

[19] Case C-191/10 *Rastelli Davide e C Snc v Jean-Charles Hidoux (qualitate qua)*, ECLI:EU:C:2011:838.

[20] Case C-341/04 *Eurofood IFSC Ltd* [2006] ECR I-3813.

[21] Case C-396/09 *Interedil Srl v Fallimento Interedil Srl en Intesa Gestione Crediti SpA*, ECLI:EU:C:2011:671. The court again emphasized the overall assessment based on objective factors and the ascertainable character for third parties.

[22] Article 3(2).

[23] See also *Shierson v Vlieland-Boddy* [2005] EWCA Civ 974.

[24] Article 2(10). This now effectively reverses on this point *Trustees of Olympic Airlines SA Pension and Life Insurance Scheme v Olympic Airlines SA* [2015] UKSC 27.

[25] Case C-396/09 *Interedil Srl v Fallimento Interedil Srl en Intesa Gestione Crediti SpA*, ECLI:EU:C:2011:671.

sense of employees or agents,[26] and material assets[27] come into the picture. The presence of an establishment must be determined on the basis of objective factors and it must be ascertainable to third parties.[28]

It is clear that on this basis that the debtor can have establishments in many countries and that any of these will have jurisdiction to open this type of territorially limited insolvency proceedings. The exact location of the assets then becomes crucial in order to determine by which territorial proceeding they are covered. Article 2(9) offers a set of definitions to assist on this point:

"the Member State in which assets are situated" means, in the case of:

(i) registered shares in companies other than those referred to in point (ii) the Member State within the territory of which the company having issued the shares has its registered office;

(ii) financial instruments, the title to which is evidenced by entries in a register or account maintained by or on behalf of an intermediary ("book entry securities"), the Member State in which the register or account in which the entries are made is maintained;

(iii) cash held in accounts with a credit institution, the Member State indicated in the account's IBAN,[29] or, for cash held in accounts with a credit institution which does not have an IBAN, the Member State in which the credit institution holding the account has its central administration or, where the account is held with a branch, agency or other establishment, the Member State in which the branch, agency or other establishment is located;

(iv) property and rights, ownership of or entitlement to which is entered in a public register other than those referred to in point (i), the Member State under the authority of which the register is kept;

(v) European patents, the Member State for which the European patent is granted;

(vi) copyright and related rights, the Member State within the territory of which the owner of such rights has its habitual residence or registered office;

(vii) tangible property, other than that referred to in points (i) to (iv), the Member State within the territory of which the property is situated;

(viii) claims against third parties, other than those relating to assets referred to in point (iii), the Member State within the territory of which the third party required to meet the claims has the centre of its main interests, as determined in accordance with Article 3(1).

These definitions are in general terms based on the solutions traditionally adopted in private international law. But they exclude the option to refer back to national (insolvency) law on this point.[30]

This type of proceedings can work very to assist the liquidator in the main insolvency proceedings. Where main insolvency proceedings have been opened the Regulation then deems these new territorial proceedings to be secondary insolvency proceedings.[31] This is even the case if the main proceedings are merely protective in nature and all the assets are located in the territory of the state in which secondary proceedings are opened.[32] The

---

[26] *Shierson v Vlieland-Boddy* [2005] EWCA Civ 974.
[27] Property or assets of any kind.
[28] *Shierson v Vlieland-Boddy* [2005] EWCA Civ 974, at para 63.
[29] The international bank account number.
[30] Case C-649/13 *Comité d'entreprise de Nortel Networks SA and Others v Cosme Rogeau (qualitate qua) and Cosme Rogeau (qualitate qua) v Alan Robert Bloom, Alan Michael Hudson, Stephen John Harris and Christopher John Wilkinson Hill*, ECLI:EU:C:2015:384.
[31] Article 3(3).
[32] Case C-116/11 *Bank Handlowy w Warszawie SA and PPHU "ADAX"/Ryszard Adamiak v Christianapol sp z o o, ECLI*:EU:C:2012:739. The secondary proceedings also need to take the aim of the main proceedings into account.

CJEU in practice applies Article 3(3) as a hard and fast rule. In the context of these secondary insolvency proceedings, the state of insolvency of the debtor cannot be re-examined and the Regulation contains detailed provisions on the interaction between main and secondary insolvency proceedings.[33] It is important to note that the Regulation no longer requires these secondary proceedings to be winding up proceedings (with the proceeds being provided to the main proceedings), as did its 2000 predecessor. The court before which secondary proceedings are pending will have concurrent jurisdiction with the court before which the main insolvency proceedings are pending.[34]

There are also limited circumstances in which territorial insolvency proceedings can be opened prior to the opening of main insolvency proceedings.[35] This can first of all happen when main insolvency proceedings cannot be opened because of the conditions laid down by the law of the Member State within the territory of which the centre of the debtor's main interests is situated, eg because the debtor is not a trader. If universal main proceeding are not possible, then territorial proceedings are the way forward. But this ground does not refer to conditions excluding particular persons, such as a procurator of another state, from the category of persons empowered to request the opening of such proceedings.[36] Secondly, a creditor whose claim arises from or is in connection with the operation of an establishment situated within a territory of the Member State can request the opening of territorial proceedings in that Member State. One does not want to oblige a purely local creditor to bring main proceedings, potentially in a far-away court, in order to recoup his money if the claim is linked merely to the local establishment. Finally, the same applies to a public authority situated in the territory of the Member State concerned.[37] One thinks here about the role of courts or procurators in several Member States who have the right to bring insolvency proceedings and a role to police their jurisdiction and eliminate insolvent companies. In the latter two cases, ie that of the local claim and that of the public authority, the opening of main insolvency proceedings will turn the territorial proceedings into secondary insolvency proceedings.

(c) Checks on jurisdiction

Ensuring that the proceedings are pending in the right court is of vital importance and this is also the case for a number of parties who are not directly involved in bringing the insolvency proceedings, be they the debtor, creditors or third parties. The Regulation addresses this issue by obliging a court before which proceedings are brought to examine its jurisdiction under Article 3 of its own motion. And the judgment opening proceedings needs to mention the exact basis for the jurisdiction of the court.[38] If the national law does not require a court decision for the opening of insolvency proceedings the national law may entrust the task of examining the jurisdiction to the insolvency practitioner who has been appointed.[39]

In addition, the debtor or any creditor has the opportunity to challenge the crucial decision to open main insolvency proceedings on grounds of international jurisdiction before a court.

---

[33] See Chapter III of the Regulation. These are insolvency law provisions and are not discussed in this book.

[34] Case C-649/13 *Comité d'entreprise de Nortel Networks SA and Others v Cosme Rogeau (qualitate qua) and Cosme Rogeau (qualitate qua) v Alan Robert Bloom, Alan Michael Hudson, Stephen John Harris and Christopher John Wilkinson Hill*, ECLI:EU:C:2015:384.

[35] Article 3(4).

[36] Case C-112/10 *Procureur-generaal bij het hof van beroep te Antwerpen V Zaza Retail BV*, ECLI:EU:C:2011:743.

[37] This new addtional rule rectifies the problem identified in Case C-112/10 *Procureur-generaal bij het hof van beroep te Antwerpen V Zaza Retail BV*, ECLI:EU:C:2011:743.

[38] Article 4(1).

[39] Article 4(2).

National law can expand both the parties who can bring judicial review of the decision and the ground that can form the basis of such a review.[40]

(d) Extent of jurisdiction

The core jurisdiction to open insolvency proceedings is relatively clear and straightforward, but in the course of insolvency proceedings ancillary issues arise easily and frequently. That bring with it the question of the extent of the jurisdiction of the insolvency court. The liquidator may for example wish to set aside certain transactions the debtor entered into. The CJEU held in this respect that the insolvency court will have jurisdiction on this point, despite the fact that the setting aside action was brought against a third party that was domiciled in another Member State.[41]

The criterion to extend the jurisdiction of the insolvency court to these ancillary actions is that the action derives directly from the insolvency proceedings and is closely linked with them. The Regulation now spells this out[42] and gives avoidance actions as a clear example.[43] Other examples are an action by a liquidator against the managing director to obtain the reimbursement of payments made once the company was insolvent[44] and a claim to join another company whose registered office is in another Member State to the main insolvency proceedings on the grounds that the property of the companies has been intermixed.[45] However, the CJEU did in this case require that the centre of the debtor's main interests for the second company was found to be in the territory of the court whose jurisdiction was expanded. On the other hand a claim to get payment for services rendered by the insolvent debtor again a third party in another Member State was held to be covered by the Brussels I rules, rather than by the ancillary claim rule.[46]

In addition, if such an ancillary action is related to an action in civil and commercial matters against the same defendant, the insolvency practitioner may bring both actions before the courts of the Member State within the territory of which the defendant is domiciled, or, where the action is brought against several defendants, before the courts of the Member State within the territory of which any of them is domiciled, provided that those courts have jurisdiction pursuant to the recast Brussels I Regulation.[47] This last option requires the actions to be related and actions are deemed to be related where they are so closely connected that it is expedient to hear and determine them together to avoid the risk of irreconcilable judgments resulting from separate proceedings.[48]

There is also no doubt that the court that has jurisdiction to open main insolvency proceedings has jurisdiction to order interim measures, in essence preservation measures. This can be done from the moment the request to open main insolvency proceedings is pending, but it can also be done once the proceedings have been opened. The aim of such measures is of course to guarantee the effectiveness of the insolvency proceedings. Which measures are available will depend on the national law of the court, but clear examples are the appointment of a temporary administrator or provisional liquidator[49] or measures to freeze assets.[50] Such

---

[40] Article 5.
[41] Case C-339/07 *Christopher Seagon (qualitate qua) v Deko Marty Belgium NV*, ECLI:EU:C:2009:83.
[42] Article 6(1).
[43] Case C-328/12 *Ralph Schmid v Lilly Hertel*, ECLI:EU:C:2014:6.
[44] Case C-295/13 *H v HK*, ECLI:EU:C:2014:2410.
[45] Case C-191/10 *Rastelli Davide e C. Snc v Jean-Charles Hidoux (qualitate qua)*, ECLI:EU:C:2011:838.
[46] Case C-157/13 *Nickel & Goeldner Spedition GmbH v "Kintra" UAB*, ECLI:EU:C:2014:2145.
[47] Article 6(2).
[48] Article 6(3).
[49] Case C-1/04 *Staubitz-Schreiber* [2006] ECR I-701, ECLI:EU:C:2006:39; Case C-341/04 *Eurofood IFSC Ltd* [2006] ECR I-3813, ECLI:EU:C:2006:281.
[50] See also *Fairfield Sentry Ltd v Sitco Bank Nederland NV* [2012] IEHC 81.

measures can cover assets located in other Member States, as recognition and enforcement of such measures is explicitly provided in Article 32 of the Regulation. And the temporary administrator is explicitly granted access to seek measures to preserve assets in the courts where the assets are located during the period between the request to open proceedings and the decision to open proceedings.[51] This rule specifically applies to secondary proceedings[52] and one can derive from this that for Member States where there is no establishment the interim measures will be granted by the court that has main insolvency jurisdiction, with recognition and enforcement elsewhere to follow.

3. CHOICE OF LAW

(a) The general rule

The general choice of law rule contained in the Regulation is very straightforward and sees the insolvency court apply its own law, or in the words of Article 7(1):

> [. . .] the law applicable to insolvency proceedings and their effects shall be that of the Member State within the territory of which such proceedings are opened (the "State of the opening of proceedings").

Article 35 contains the same approach for secondary proceedings, so the choice of law rule in favour of the law of the insolvency court applies for main, secondary and territorial insolvency proceedings. It refers to the national law of the state of the court, ie both its procedural and substantive law. An English court will on this basis apply its own procedural law and the Insolvency Act 1986. The Regulation does not exclude renvoi specifically, but there has never been any room for renvoi in the area of insolvency. The doctrine of renvoi can therefore not be applied.

The scope of the choice of law rule is very wide, as the wording "law applicable to insolvency proceedings and their effects" already hints at. The CJEU has eg held that a provision of German law seeking reimbursement of payments made by the managing director before the opening of the insolvency proceedings but after the date on which the insolvency of that company was established came within the scope of the choice of law rule and German law could be applied on this point in insolvency proceedings brought before a German court, even if the company involved had been registered in England.[53]

(b) A list of issues that are covered

The Regulation provides assistance on the issue of the scope of the choice of law rule[54] by setting out a list of specific point that are covered by the rule.[55] The law of the State of the opening of proceedings shall in general terms determine the conditions for the opening of those proceedings, their conduct and their closure. The list that follows is not exhaustive, as demonstrated by the use of the term "in particular".

The first item on the list and therefore covered by the law of the State of the opening of proceedings is that of the debtors against which insolvency proceedings may be brought on account of their capacity.[56] It will therefore eg be up to that law to determine whether

---

[51] Article 52.
[52] As it is found in part III of the Regulation.
[53] Case C-594/14 *Simona Kornhaas v Thomas Dithmar (qualitate qua)*, ECLI:EU:C:2015:806.
[54] See *Syska v Vivendi Universal SA* [2009] EWCA Civ 677.
[55] Article 7(2).
[56] Article 7(2)(a). See *Fondazione Enascarco v Lehman Brothers Finance SA* [2014] EWHC 34 (Ch).

insolvency proceedings can be brought against a private person who is not a trader, irrespective eg of the provisions on this point of the law of the nationality of the person involved.

Secondly, the applicable law covers the determination of "the assets which form part of the insolvency estate and the treatment of assets acquired by or devolving on the debtor after the opening of the insolvency proceedings".[57] This means that it will determine what is eventually comprised in the estate for distribution, how after-acquired property is to be dealt with and whether assets to which a security right, such as a fixed charge, applies can be excluded from the estate.[58]

Thirdly, the applicable law determines the respective powers of the debtor and the insolvency practitioner.[59]

Fourthly, the conditions under which set-offs may be invoked are covered by the applicable law.[60] It does so despite the fact that the laws of the Member States differ substantially on this point.[61] But Article 9 builds in an exception along the lines that the opening of insolvency proceedings shall not affect the right of creditors to demand the set-off of their claims against the claims of a debtor, where such a set-off is permitted by the law applicable to the insolvent debtor's claim. It was clearly felt that the latter law could have created a legitimate expectation and that taking that expectation away would have been unfair. The exception does not preclude actions for voidness, voidability and unenforceability that are themselves governed by the law of the State of the opening of proceedings.[62]

The fifth issue to which the law of the State of the opening of proceedings applies is the effects of insolvency proceedings on current contracts[63] to which the debtor is a party.[64] But there are specific exceptions for contracts relating to immovable property, for which the effects of the insolvency proceeding are governed by the law of the State within the territory of which the immoveable property is situated,[65] and for contracts of employment, for which that role is given to the law of the contract of employment.[66]

The sixth issue in the list of examples is the effects of the insolvency proceedings on proceedings brought by individual creditors, with the exception of pending lawsuits.[67] This includes questions such as whether the opening of insolvency proceedings will lead to a stay on enforcement or the individual collection of debts.[68] Article 18 then picks up the exception that is made for pending lawsuits and stipulates that:

> The effects of insolvency proceedings on a pending lawsuit or pending arbitral proceedings[69] concerning an asset or a right which forms part of a debtor's insolvency estate shall be

---

[57] Article 7(2)(b).

[58] The latter is of course subject to Article 8. See also Case C-292/08 *German Graphics Graphische Maschinen GmbH v Alice van der Schee (qualitate qua)*, ECLI:EU:C:2009:544.

[59] Article 7(2)(c).

[60] Article 7(2)(d). Cf *Joint Administrators of Heritable Bank plc v Winding up Board of Landsbanki Islands hf* [2013] UKSC 13.

[61] See *Re Bank of Credit and Commerce SA (No 10)* [1997] Ch 213.

[62] Article 9(2).

[63] Arbitration clauses were held to be included in this concept in *Syska v Vivendi Universal SA* [2009] EWCA Civ 677.

[64] Article 7(2)(e).

[65] Article 11.

[66] Article 13.

[67] Article 7(2)(f). Cf *Isis Investments Ltd v Oscatello Investments Ltd* [2013] EWCA Civ 1493; *Joint Administrators of Heritable Bank plc v Winding up Board of Landsbanki Islands hf* [2013] UKSC 13.

[68] See *Mazur Media Ltd v Mazur Media GmbH* [2004] EWHC 1566 (Ch).

[69] See *Syska v Vivendi Universal SA* [2009] EWCA Civ 677.

governed solely by the law of the Member State in which that lawsuit is pending or in which the arbitral tribunal has its seat.

A straightforward seventh issue on the list is the question of the claims which are to be lodged against the debtor's insolvency estate and the treatment of claims arising after the opening of insolvency proceedings.[70] This must include the question which debts are provable, and can therefore be lodged.

The eight issue that follows logically in the list and is therefore governed by the law of the State of the opening of proceedings is that concerning the rules governing the lodging, verification and admission of claims.[71] This includes time limits for the lodging of claims and all matters concerned with proof of debt procedure. Chapter IV of the Regulation adds to this specific rules on the provision of information for creditors and lodgement of their claims.

The ninth issue on the list concerns the rules governing the distribution of proceeds from the realisation of assets, the ranking of claims and the rights of creditors who have obtained partial satisfaction after the opening of insolvency proceedings by virtue of a right in rem or through a set-off.[72] This must include also matters such as whether certain categories of preferential debt rank ahead of the holder of a floating charge.[73]

Following on from this is the tenth issue on the list, ie the conditions for, and the effects of closure of, insolvency proceedings, in particular by composition.[74] This includes issues such as whether a discharge of claims of a creditor will be brought about by the closure of the main insolvency proceedings through a company voluntary arrangement.

The eleventh issue on the list is concerned with the creditors' rights after the closure of insolvency proceedings,[75] including the question under which conditions there can be a discharge of the debtor.

The twelfth issue on the list is who is to bear the costs and expenses incurred in the insolvency proceedings. This issue too will be governed by the law of the State of the opening of proceedings.[76]

The final issue on the list is concerned with the rules relating to the voidness, voidability or unenforceability of legal acts detrimental to the general body of creditors.[77] In essence we are concerned with the crucial question whether and to what extent pre-insolvency transactions entered into by the debtor can be struck down and whether acts and proprietary transactions can be impeached. On this point the law of the State of the opening of proceedings takes over and a single law will apply, which is a major advantage. There is however a major limitation on the operation of this provision. It takes the format of Article 16, which provides that the rule shall not apply where the person who benefited from an act detrimental to all the creditors provides proof that:

(a) the act is subject to the law of a Member State other than that of the State of the opening of proceedings; and

---

[70] Article 7(2)(g).

[71] Article 7(2)(h).

[72] Article 7(2)(i).

[73] Insolvency Act 1986, s 175(2)(b).

[74] Article 7(2)(j). Case C-116/11 *Bank Handlowy w Warszawie SA, PPHU "ADAX"/Ryszard Adamiak v Christianapol sp z o o*, ECLI:EU:C:2012:739.

[75] Article 7(2)(k).

[76] Article 7(2)(l).

[77] Article 7(2) (m). Case C-594/14 *Simona Kornhaas v Thomas Dithmar (qualitate qua)*, ECLI:EU:C:2015:806; Case C-339/07 *Christopher Seagon (qualitate qua) v Deko Marty Belgium NV*, ECLI:EU:C:2009:83; See also Case C-111/08 *SCT Industri AB i likvidation v Alpenblume AB*, ECLI:EU:C:2009:419.

(b) the law of that Member State does not allow any means of challenging that act in the relevant case.[78]

These two factors need to be proven by whoever claims the benefit of Article 16, but if they are proven the provision acts as a veto against the law of the State of the opening of proceedings invalidating certain acts.[79] It was eg held that Article 16 applies to a situation in which a payment of a sum of money attached before opening of the insolvency proceedings, but made only after such opening is challenged by the administrator of the insolvency. In that case there were limitation periods or other time-bars relating to actions to set aside transactions under the law governing the act challenged by the liquidator and these were held to be covered by Article 16.[80]

(c) Additional exceptions

The Regulation also contains further exceptions for specific situations. Article 8 deals with third parties' rights in rem and brings in the rule that

> the opening of insolvency proceedings shall not affect the rights in rem of creditors or third parties in respect of tangible or intangible, moveable or immoveable assets, both specific assets and collections of indefinite assets as a whole which change from time to time [such as the floating charge], belonging to the debtor which are situated within the territory of another Member State at the time of the opening of proceedings.

Article 10 in turn deals with reservation of title in the following way:

1. The opening of insolvency proceedings against the purchaser of an asset shall not affect sellers' rights that are based on a reservation of title where at the time of the opening of proceedings the asset is situated within the territory of a Member State other than the State of the opening of proceedings.
2. The opening of insolvency proceedings against the seller of an asset, after delivery of the asset, shall not constitute grounds for rescinding or terminating the sale and shall not prevent the purchaser from acquiring title where at the time of the opening of proceedings the asset sold is situated within the territory of a Member State other than the State of the opening of proceedings.
3. Paragraphs 1 and 2 shall not preclude actions for voidness, voidability or unenforceability as referred to in point (m) of Article 7(2).

Payment systems and financial markets present particular problems and are typically governed by a single law. Article 12 recognises this principle and applies the law of the Member State applicable to such a system or market to the effects of insolvency proceedings on the rights and obligations of the parties to a payment or settlement system or to a financial market, whilst respecting any rights in rem and Article 8. The rule does not preclude any action for voidness, voidability or unenforceability which may be taken to set aside payments or transactions under the law applicable to the relevant payment system or financial market.

Article 14 deals in a similar way with the effects on rights subject to registration and submits the effects of insolvency proceedings on the rights of a debtor in immoveable property, a ship or an aircraft subject to registration in a public register to the law of the Member State under

---

[78] The latter goes beyond the insolvency law and includes the general provisions and principles of that law. Case C-310/14 *Nike European Operations Netherlands BV v Sportland Oy*, ECLI:EU:C:2015:690. See also Case C-54/16 *Vinyls Italia SpA v Mediterranea di Navigazione SpA* ECLI:EU:C:2017:433.

[79] Case C-557/13 *Hermann Lutz v Elke Bäuerle (qualitate qua)*, ECLI:EU:C:2015:227; Case C-310/14 *Nike European Operations Netherlands BV v Sportland Oy*, ECLI:EU:C:2015:690.

[80] Case C-557/13 *Hermann Lutz v Elke Bäuerle (qualitate qua)*, ECLI:EU:C:2015:227.

the authority of which the register is kept. And Article 15 adds that a European patent with unitary effect, a Community trade mark or any other similar right established by Union law may be included only in main insolvency proceedings as this type of (unitary) asset cannot be split up per Member State.

Finally, Article 17 deals with the protection of third-party purchasers:

> Where, by an act concluded after the opening of insolvency proceedings, a debtor disposes, for consideration, of:
>
> (a) an immoveable asset;
> (b) a ship or an aircraft subject to registration in a public register; or
> (c) securities the existence of which requires registration in a register laid down by law;
>
> the validity of that act shall be governed by the law of the State within the territory of which the immoveable asset is situated or under the authority of which the register is kept.

4. RECOGNITION OF INSOLVENCY PROCEEDINGS

The main principle in the area of recognition is that this should be automatic. It is straight-forward if one accepts that main insolvency proceedings are universal in nature, covering all the assets of the debtor irrespective of their location. The judgment then has to cross the border of the territory of the court granting it automatically. Article 19 of the Regulation indeed sets out the principle of automatic recognition of any judgment opening insolvency proceedings from the moment that it becomes effective in the State of the opening of proceedings.[81] There is merely a public policy exception.[82] The principle also applies to territorial and secondary proceedings, even if their impact is limited to the territory in which they are opened. The strength of the principle is demonstrated further by the addition of the rule that it shall also apply where, on account of a debtor's capacity, insolvency proceedings cannot be brought against that debtor in other Member States.

Recognition of the main insolvency proceedings does not on the other hand preclude the opening of territorial/secondary insolvency proceedings by a court in another Member State.[83] This is logical, as the Regulation is based on a mix of both types of proceedings in order to deal successfully with the various insolvency scenarios.

Article 20 then draws the inevitable consequences from this principle when it comes to the effects of the automatic recognition. For main insolvency proceedings this means that:

> The judgment opening insolvency proceedings as referred to in Article 3(1) shall, with no further formalities, produce the same effects in any other Member State as under the law of the State of the opening of proceedings, unless this Regulation provides otherwise and as long as no proceedings referred to in Article 3(2) are opened in that other Member State.[84]

---

[81] Case C-444/07 *MG Probud Gdynia sp z o o*, ECLI:EU:C:2010:24; Case C-341/04 *Eurofood IFSC Ltd* [2006] ECR I-3813, ECLI:EU:C:2006:281. The principle applies even if the main insolvency proceedings are merely protective in nature, see Case C-116/11 *Bank Handlowy w Warszawie SA and PPHU "ADAX"/Ryszard Adamiak v Christianapol sp z o o*, ECLI:EU:C:2012:739.

[82] Article 33.

[83] Case C-444/07 *MG Probud Gdynia sp z o o*, ECLI:EU:C:2010:24; Case C-339/07 *Christopher Seagon (qualitate qua) v Deko Marty Belgium NV*, ECLI:EU:C:2009:83; Case C-341/04 *Eurofood IFSC Ltd* [2006] ECR I-3813, ECLI:EU:C:2006:281.

[84] Article 20(1).

These effects are both procedural and substantive.

Whereas for territorial insolvency proceedings this means that:

The effects of the proceedings referred to in Article 3(2) may not be challenged in other Member States. Any restriction of creditors' rights, in particular a stay or discharge, shall produce effects vis-à-vis assets situated within the territory of another Member State only in the case of those creditors who have given their consent.[85]

5. GROUPS OF COMPANIES AND THEIR MEMBERS

Groups of companies raise particularly tricky issues when they or some of their members become insolvent. The *Eurofood* case[86] made this clear early on. The Regulation now deals with this in a new Chapter V, but these provisions deal mainly with an insolvency point and it is not intended to discuss them here.

---

[85] Article 20(2).
[86] Case C-341/04 *Eurofood IFSC Ltd* [2006] ECR I-3813, ECLI:EU:C:2006:281.

35

ADMINISTRATION OF ESTATES

1. **Introduction** 1325
   (a) Administration of Estates: Difference between common law and civil law jurisdictions 1325
   (b) Hague Convention on Administration of Estates 1326
   (c) EU Succession Regulation 1327
2. **English Grants** 1330
   (a) Jurisdiction of English courts 1330
   (b) Separate wills 1330
   (c) Persons to whom grant will be made 1331
   (d) Consular Grant 1332
   (e) Title of administrator under an English grant 1332
3. **Choice of Law** 1333
   (a) Classification 1333
   (b) Law governing administration 1334
4. **Foreign Administrators** 1335
   (a) Foreign administrators 1335
   (b) Commonwealth grant 1336
   (c) Scotland and Northern Ireland grant 1337

1. INTRODUCTION

(a) Administration of Estates: Difference between common law and civil law jurisdictions

The modern legal systems which have had their origin in English law differ fundamentally from the civil law jurisdictions with regard to the procedure by which property is administered after the death of its owner. In England the only person entitled to deal with the property is the person to whom a grant has been made by the court. When the deceased has appointed an executor by the will, the grant is made to the executor. If the deceased has died intestate, left a will which omitted to appoint an executor, or left a will with a failed appointment, for example, the appointed executor refused to act or died, the grant is made to the administrator. The executors and administrators or, to use a comprehensive expression, the personal representatives, become subject to two distinct duties. First, they must clear the estate of liabilities by the payment of funeral expenses and debts; secondly, they must distribute the residue of the estate among the beneficiaries according to the limitations of the will or the rules of intestacy. These two functions, debt-administration and beneficial distribution, are governed by different principles of private international law.

In the civil law countries, in the rare case where personal representatives are appointed, their duties and functions are generally of a supervisory nature widely different from those of their English counterparts.[1] The general civil law rule is that the entire property of a deceased person passes directly to his heirs, testate or intestate, or to his universal legatee, subject, of course, to their acceptance. These successors, broadly speaking, continue the existence of their predecessor.[2] For instance, unless they accept the inheritance with the benefit of an inventory, their liability for the debts of the deceased is not limited to the assets but is enforceable against their private property.

---

[1] See, eg, *Re Achillopoulos* [1928] Ch 433 at 435.
[2] Distinguish the English personal representative, who, strictly speaking, does not represent the deceased at all.

The striking difference between English and civil law practice is that in the latter case the property passes on death directly to the successor, but in England it cannot be dealt with by anyone without a public grant.[3] The automatic transfer recognised by civil law systems cannot operate on property of the deceased situated in England. Succession to movables is governed by the law of the deceased's domicile,[4] but, no matter what that domicile may be, nobody can rightfully and effectually obtain possession of movable property situated in England unless he gets an English grant of probate or of administration.[5] An English grant is always required in order to provide authority to administer English assets.

(b) Hague Convention on Administration of Estates

The diversity between common law and civil law jurisdictions on administration procedure, the strict territorial limit on the effect of a grant and the lack of cooperation between countries create difficulty in international succession. For example, where a deceased died in country A, was last domiciled in country B, and left assets in multiple states, including countries A, B and C, the personal representative may need to apply for multiple grants to deal with the property in each state, and some courts may refuse the application until the personal representative receives the grant from the deceased's domicile first. This may lead to delay and cost. In order to simplify administration of estates with cross-border implications, both the Hague Conference on Private International Law and the European Union have established international or regional frameworks to facilitate judicial cooperation in administration of estates.

The Hague Conference on Private International Law has adopted the Convention concerning the International Administration of the Estates of Deceased Persons in 1973. This convention establishes an "international certificate" system which allows the international certificate designating the personal representative of a deceased to be recognised in other Contracting States.[6] The "competent authority" of the deceased's habitual residence has the authority to draw up the international certificate.[7] The term "competent authority" is designed to be compatible with both common law jurisdiction, where the court will supervise the probate, and civil law jurisdiction, which largely relies on notaries.[8] A competent authority, in general, is entitled to draw up the certificate according to its own law.[9] Although the general rule seems straightforward, there are a lot of restrictions which make the Convention very complicated. For example, a Contracting State could make a declaration under Article 31 that if the deceased was a national of this state, its domestic law should apply.[10] The unilateral declaration may not be favoured by countries not using nationality as connecting factors for administration of estates and may hamper judicial cooperation. Requiring the issuing country to apply the law of administration of a foreign country could also lead to difficulty; in particular, it requires an authority to be familiar with another country's substantive and procedural law.[11] Furthermore, although the certificate holder's power is derived from the law

---

[3] But the Revenue Act 1889, s 19, provides that where a policy of life insurance has been effected by a person who dies domiciled elsewhere than in the United Kingdom, a grant of representation shall not be necessary to establish the right to receive the money payable; see *Haas v Atlas Assurance Co Ltd* [1913] 2 KB 209, where Scrutton J gives the genesis of the provision. For another case where no grant is necessary, see *Vanquelin v Bouard* (1863) 15 CBNS 341; and see the Administration of Estates (Small Payments) Act 1965.

[4] See infra, p 1339 et seq.

[5] *New York Breweries Co v A-G* [1899] AC 62.

[6] Art 1.

[7] Arts 2.

[8] G M Beckman, "Evolving Role of Executor in International Estates" (1973) 8 Real Property, Probate and Trust Journal 634, 643.

[9] Art 3.

[10] Art 31.

[11] Beckman, 647.

governing the certificate, the court where the certificate is to be recognised has the power to subject the exercise of the certificate to the local supervision and control as applicable to the local representative under its domestic law.[12] Although it is important to respect the law of the country where the estate is located, the relevant rule subjects administration of estates to multiple regulations. Secondly, although the international certificate is meant to be recognised automatically in all Contracting States, there are seven grounds of refusal, ie the authority lacks competence,[13] the state where the deceased has his nationality made the Article 31 declaration to apply its internal law to the designation of the certificate holder and his power and the content of the certificate contradicts that law,[14] the certificate is not authentic or lacks proper form,[15] the decendent's habitual residence is in dispute,[16] the certificate is incompatible with a prior decision on merits,[17] two incompatible certificates are issued,[18] and the certificate is manifestly incompatible with the requested state's public policy.[19] The broad refusal grounds may produce uncertainty. Thirdly, there is no procedure designed to prevent concurrent certificates from being issued in various Contracting States.[20]

The Hague Convention is not very successful due to its complexity. It has been signed by Italy, Luxembourg, Netherlands, Portugal, Turkey, and the United Kingdom, and ratified by Czech Republic, Portugal and Slovakia. Although the United Kingdom has signed the Convention, the Law Commission considers the complexity of the rules makes it impractical and shows no intention to implement this Convention.[21]

(c) EU Succession Regulation

The EU also aims to simplify international succession and administration procedure by adopting the Regulation (EU) No 650/2012 of the European Parliament and of the Council of 4 July 2012 on jurisdiction, applicable law, recognition and enforcement of decisions and acceptance and enforcement of authentic instruments in matters of succession and on the creation of a European Certificate of Succession (Succession Regulation).[22] It applies to estates of individuals dying after 17 August 2015 and applies in all Member States, except Denmark, the UK and Ireland. This Regulation provides the European Certificate of Succession,[23] which modeled the International Certificate from the 1973 Hague Convention.[24] Because national grants or certificates are usually not recognised in other Member States, administrators appointed in one Member State can hardly prove his status and exercise his power in another Member State.[25] The European Certificate of Succession allows the administrators or

---

[12] Art 30.
[13] Art 13(2).
[14] Art 14(2).
[15] Art 13(1).
[16] Art 14(1).
[17] Art 15.
[18] Art 16.
[19] Art 17.
[20] Beckman, 647.
[21] D Hayton, "Cross-Border Estates" (1994) 5 Private Client Business 329, 331.
[22] [2012] OJ L 201/107.
[23] Chapter VI and Recital 67 of the Regulation.
[24] Max Planck Institute for Comparative and International Private Law, "Comments on the European Commission's Proposal for a Regulation of the European Parliament and of the Council on jurisdiction, applicable law, recognition and enforcement of decisions and authentic instruments in matters of succession and creation of a European Certificate of Succession", para 2.
[25] Max Planck, para 264. National certificate of succession or administration varies largely between Member States. In Germany and Austria, judicial certificates of succession naming the heirs to protect third parties, in England, the court grants the letter of administration, in France and Spain, certificates are issued by notaries, Sweden and Finland provide private inventories, and Italy does not provide certificate of succession.

executors to exercise their power in other Member States without any special procedure being required.[26] The European Certificate of Succession shall demonstrate the status and/or rights of each administrator or executor and his powers to administrate the estates.[27] The Certificate will not be an enforceable title but has evidentiary effects by indicating accurate information established under the governing law of succession.[28] The use of the European Certificate is not mandatory and would not exclude the national certificate from being issued.[29] In other words, the competent applicant may, in theory, apply for national certificates or grants of individual Member States instead of a European Certificate. If more than one person is competent, they may apply for both European Certificate and national certificate/grant, or apply for more than one European Certificate from different Member States respectively. Concurrent Certificates may be used at the same time, but problems arise if they conflict between each other and the Regulation does not include proper rules to deal with it.

This Regulation also provides uniform jurisdiction and choice of law rules for administration of estates. The Succession Regulation provides the catch-all private international law rules for both succession and administration of estates.[30] It is no longer necessary to classify administration and succession, which are very different from English practice. As a general principle in the Regulation, the deceased's last habitual residence forms the connecting factor for both jurisdiction and choice of law,[31] subject to certain exceptions.[32] It is, however, recognised that habitual residence, as a connecting factor, may not be easy to determine and cause uncertainty, especially where the deceased had alternative residences simultaneously or lived in another country for economic or professional reasons for a long time while maintaining connections with his previous residence.[33] Besides uncertainty, habitual residence may prove a particularly weak link for administration of estates, as the deceased's estates may be situated out of his habitual residence. It is also likely that the deceased had lived in the previous habitual residence for a very long time and left the whole estate there, while died shortly after he changed his habitual residence. Although Article 21 provides that the general choice of law rule may be departed from if the deceased was manifestly more closely connected with the other country at the time of death, which leads to the application of the law of the deceased's previous habitual residence,[34] the authority of the deceased's last habitual residence, which has a weak connection with the deceased and his assets, would still be competent to appoint personal representatives.

The Regulation also allows limited party autonomy, under which the deceased could choose the law of the Member State of his nationality[35] and the relevant parties could make an exclusive choice of the court of this country to decide any succession issues, including administration of estates.[36] While the deceased has chosen the applicable law, the court of other Member States may decline jurisdiction in favour of the country whose law is chosen.[37] This rule aims to improve certainty and encourage succession planning. It, however, may cause problems in countries like the UK, which include multiple jurisdictions and the choice of law of the deceased's nationality would not help in deciding which part of the UK law/jurisdiction should be relevant. Since there is no relevant internal conflict of laws in the UK,

---

[26] Art 69(1).
[27] Art 63 of the Regulation.
[28] Recital 71.
[29] Recital 69, and Art 62(2) and (3).
[30] Recital 42 and Article 23(2)(f) of the Regulation.
[31] Arts 4 and 21 of the Regulation.
[32] For exceptions in jurisdiction, see Arts 5, 6, 7, 9,10, 11; for exceptions in choice of law, see Art 21.
[33] Recital 25 of the Regulation.
[34] Art 21.
[35] Art 22.
[36] Art 5.
[37] Art 6.

the specific unit should be the one with which the deceased had the closest connection,[38] which is an ambiguous concept. Furthermore, even if party autonomy may help succession, it is questionable whether it could be extended to the administration of estates which largely relates to procedure of the country where the assets of the estate are situated.[39] It is also noted that the deceased could choose the law of any country whose nationality he possessed at the time of making a choice or at the time of death, the choice may refer to the law of a non-EU country, which may provide very different law on administration of estates.

The Regulation claims not to affect national domestic system concerning administration of estates and indeed adjusts the rules to meet the UK administration procedure. For example, Article 29 provides that where the appointment of an administrator is mandatory under the law of the Member State whose courts have jurisdiction and the governing law is a foreign law, the competent court could appoint administrators under its own law.[40] The administrator will administer the estate under the governing foreign law, though the competent court could lay down specific conditions for exercising the power.[41] If the governing foreign law does not provide sufficient power to preserve the assets of the estate or to protect the rights of the creditors, the court could allow the administrator to exercise the power under its own law.[42] The competent court is even allowed to vest in the administrators all the power of the Member State where they are appointed if the applicable law is the law of a third country.[43] These rules aim to assist Member States, like the UK, to reconcile the Regulation conflicts rules with their special domestic administration procedure. Nevertheless, this is deemed not enough to smooth the transition. For example, the eligibility of the appointed personal representatives is still determined by the governing law, and the validly appointed person pursuant to the foreign law may not be qualified in the law of the appointing court.[44] Furthermore, although the Regulation tries to leave domestic procedure alone, influence at a certain level is inevitable. Under English law, the personal representative is not obliged to administrate assets abroad,[45] while one purpose of the Regulation is to require such a person to manage the whole estate.[46] Furthermore, the English personal representative is protected from being personally sued for distribution of assets as far as he advertised his intention in the London Gazette, but this protection is inappropriate in administrating foreign assets because interested parties abroad usually would not consult the London Gazette.[47] More importantly, if the competent court, e.g. the court where the deceased has his habitual residence, is not England, but the deceased left assets in England, the competent court is not obliged to take English law into account, though the power to administrate the assets is exercised in England.

The very different treatment to administration of estates in the EU Succession Regulation from English law is one of the reasons that the UK decided to opt out of the Succession Regulation.[48] Since both international and EU initiatives in administration of estates are not implemented in the UK, England continues to apply its traditional private international law in dealing with cross-border administration of assets.

---

[38] Art 36(2)(b).
[39] Dicey, Morris and Collins, para 26-032.
[40] Art 29(1).
[41] Art 29(1) and (2).
[42] Art 29(2).
[43] Art 29(3).
[44] House of Lords, European Union Committee, "Sixth Report: The EU's Regulation on Succession", para 72.
[45] See section 2 below.
[46] House of Lords, "Sixth Report", para 75.
[47] Ibid.
[48] The other two Member States not participating in the EU Succession Regulation are Denmark and Ireland.

2. ENGLISH GRANTS

(a) Jurisdiction of English courts

One of the cardinal rules of private international law is that the movable property of a deceased person is regulated by the law of that country in which he died domiciled. It might be thought, therefore, that the courts of that domicile have jurisdiction to make a grant of administration, merely on the ground of domicile and regardless of whether there are assets actually within the jurisdiction.[49] Theoretically this principle is tenable, but two facts militate against its application. First, such a grant would be ineffective if there were no assets within the jurisdiction. Secondly, the jurisdiction of the old ecclesiastical courts, of which the High Court exercising jurisdiction in probate matters[50] is the successor, was universally founded on the presence within the jurisdiction of movables belonging to the deceased. In fact, for many years the rule has been that an English court can grant administration only if there is property in England.[51] Probate jurisdiction based solely on the situs of the property could assist enforcement and execution but may lead to difficulty where a deceased English domiciliary left property abroad. The court of the situs may need the English Court, as the court of the deceased domicile, to make a grant before proceeding to grant administration.[52] This justifies extending the jurisdiction of the High Court. Since 1932 the High Court has acquired statutory authority to make a grant of representation of any deceased person, notwithstanding that the deceased left no estate in England.[53] This power, however, is discretionary. A grant probably will be refused if neither the deceased's property nor the deceased's domicile is situated in England.[54]

A case that commonly arises is where a person dies domiciled abroad, leaving the bulk of his property in the foreign country and a smaller amount in England. It is ideal to have one administration in the domicile for the whole of the property, but the principle of unity is only attainable by international agreements, which do not exist in the UK.[55] A separate grant of administration must be obtained from the English court with regard to the property in England. In such a situation, the administration in England is said to be "ancillary", whilst that in the country of the deceased's domicile is the "principal" administration.

(b) Separate wills

Testators quite often have property both in England and abroad and, in such cases, they sometimes make separate wills, one disposing of their English property and the other of the foreign. In such cases, the normal practice is only to admit to probate the English will,[56] but it is also possible to admit to probate in England the foreign will, provided there is

---

[49] Cf *Hindocha and Ors v Gheewala and Ors* [2003] UKPC 77; [2004] 1 CLC 502.

[50] Senior Courts Act 1981, s 25. Under Sch 1, paras 1 and 3, non-contentious or common form probate business is assigned to the Family Division and all other probate business to the Chancery Division. As to what is included in non-contentious business, see *Re Clore* [1982] Fam 113 at 116; affd [1982] Ch 456.

[51] *Evans v Burrell* (1859) 28 LJP & M 82; *In the Goods of Tucker* (1864) 34 LJPM & A 29; Dicey, Morris and Collins, paras 26-001–26-004.

[52] Dicey, Morris and Collins, para 26-004.

[53] Senior Courts Act 1981, s 25(1); see *In the Estate of Wayland* [1951] 2 All ER 1041.

[54] *Aldrich v A-G* [1968] P 281 at 295.

[55] See, eg, both the Hague Convention on the International Administration of the Estates of Deceased Persons (1972), which provides one international initiative, but one with a low success rate and the European Succession Regulation do not apply in the UK. See Law Com No 107 (1981), para 2.45; and also Nadelmann (1973) 21 AJCL 136, 139–49; House of Lords, "Sixth Report".

[56] *Re Western's Goods* (1898) 78 LT 49; *Re Tinkler* [1990] 1 NZLR 621.

some appropriate reason for so doing.[57] In *Re Wayland (Deceased)*,[58] the testator domiciled in England made two wills, one expressly dealt with Belgian property and another exclusively property situated in England. Under the Belgian law, Belgium duty would be payable on the whole estate including property situated in England if a grant of the Belgian will was not obtained in England. A grant was thus made by the English court to obviate injustice in respect of the Belgian property.

(c) Persons to whom grant will be made

Who are the persons in whose favour this jurisdiction ought to be exercised? The general principle applies the law of the country where the deceased has his last domicile. Where the deceased dies domiciled in England, probate of his will is normally granted to the executors named in it.[59] On intestacy, letters of administration are usually granted to a person taking a beneficial interest in the estate.[60]

Where the deceased died domiciled abroad, the English court will normally make a grant to a person who has been entrusted with the administration of the deceased's estate by a court in the country of the deceased's last domicile.[61] However, in some countries, grants of representation, in the English sense, are not made by courts; or it could be that no application may in fact have been made in the country of the domicile. In such cases an English grant may then be made to the person beneficially entitled to the estate by the law of the place where the deceased died domiciled.[62] The making of such a grant is discretionary and the court may make a grant to such persons as it thinks fit, whether or not there is someone who fits into the above categories.[63] For example, in *Re Kaufman's Goods*[64] the deceased died domiciled in the Netherlands and the only person entitled to the estate under Dutch law died before the estate could be administered. The court made a grant, in the interests of convenience, to the deceased's brother who would have been entitled to a grant under English law if the deceased had died domiciled in England.

If the foreign domiciliary has made a will in English or Welsh, names an executor in the will, or in whatever language, describes "the duties of a named person in terms sufficient to constitute him executor according to the tenor of the will",[65] then the court may grant probate to this named person.[66] However, if the court of the country where the deceased has his domicile appoints another person to administer the property, the English court usually will not make a grant conflicting with the foreign appointment.[67] Furthermore, if the law of the foreign domicile restricts the authority of such an executor to a limited period, this rule must be disregarded in the English administration.[68]

---

[57] *Re Wayland's Estate* [1951] 2 All ER 1041; *Re Baldry (Deceased)* [2004] WTLR 609 (Fam Div); and *Lamothe v Lamothe* [2006] EWHC 1387; [2006] WTLR 1431.

[58] [1951] 2 All ER 1041.

[59] Tristram and Coote's *Probate Practice*, (2006) 30th edn, Chapter 4. Under the Senior Courts Act 1981, s 116, the court has a discretion to appoint someone else; see *IRC v Stype Investments (Jersey) Ltd* [1982] Ch 456.

[60] Tristram and Coote's *Probate Practice*, supra, Chapter 6.

[61] Non-Contentious Probate Rules, SI 1987/2024, r 30(1)(a). Rule 31 is amended in minor respects by SI 1991/1876.

[62] Non-Contentious Probate Rules 1987, r 30(1)(b).

[63] Ibid, r 30(1)(c).

[64] [1952] P 325; and see *Bath v British and Malayan Trustees Ltd* [1969] 2 NSWLR 114.

[65] Non-Contentious Probate Rules 1987, r 30(3)(a)(ii).

[66] Ibid, r 30(3)(a)(i).

[67] *In the Estate of Eugene Cocquerel, Deceased*, [1918] P 4.

[68] *Re Goenaga's Estate* [1949] P 367. See Morris (1950) 3 ILQ 243 where it is shown that the decision, though correct in principle, is irreconcilable with *Laneuville v Anderson* (1860) 2 Sw & Tr 24.

When the person who has been authorised to administer the estate in the country of the deceased's domicile seeks a grant of probate in England, the English court does not examine the grounds of his appointment under the foreign law.[69] This does not mean, however, that the domiciliary executor or heir has an absolute right to administer the English assets. The court has discretion, and although there are few cases where it refuses to follow the foreign grant, it will certainly do so if the foreign grantee is disqualified or incompetent according to English law to act as administrator. For example, no grant will be made to a minor.[70] Where a minority or life interest arises in an estate, the grant of probate must normally be made to not fewer than two individuals or to a trust corporation, irrespective of the law of the domicile that may allow one person to administer the estate.[71] In practice, the grant usually is made to the minor's both parents jointly or his guardian.[72]

It might be thought that an English court is justified in following the grant made in the foreign country on the basis of consistency with the rule that succession to a deceased's movable estate is governed by his domicile on death.[73] The logic of such a justification breaks down, however, if the deceased's estate consists of immovables because succession to them is governed by the law of the situs.[74] Indeed the High Court of Australia has refused to follow the law of the domicile, England, and make a grant to the English personal representative in the case of a will of movables and immovables. The court required the title to administer the will, and its validity, to be determined by the law of the situs.[75] English law does not adopt so purist an approach, which is highly inconvenient where, as is often the case, the estate consists of both movables and immovables. The English court will make a grant following the one made in the domicile, even though the estate includes immovables.[76] Where, however, the whole or substantially the whole of the estate in England consists of immovables, the court may make a grant, in respect of the whole estate, in accordance with the law which would have been applicable if the deceased had died domiciled in England,[77] ie English law.

(d) Consular grant

Under the Consular Conventions Act 1949 a grant of administration may be made to the consular officer of a foreign state where the executor or other such person is a national of that state and is not resident in England and where no other application is made by a person duly authorised by power of attorney.[78] A "foreign State" means one with which a Consular Convention has been concluded and so declared by Order in Council.[79]

(e) Title of administrator under an English grant

Although the theory may be that an English grant extends to property no matter where it is situated, it is obviously of no practical importance, because whether the administrator is entitled to the property of the deceased in a foreign country must necessarily depend on the local law. The one certainty is that an administrator acting under an English grant, who does

---

[69] *Re Hill's Goods* (1870) LR 2 P & D 89; *Re Humphries's Estate* [1934] P 78.
[70] *Re D'Orleans's (Duchess) Goods* (1859) 1 Sw & Tr 253; *In the Goods of Meatyard* [1903] P 125.
[71] Senior Courts Act 1981, s 114(2); Non-Contentious Probate Rules 1987, r 30(2).
[72] *In the Goods of the Duchesse D'Orleans* (1859) 1 Sw & Tr 253; *In the Goods or Sartoris* (1838) 1 Curt 910; Non-Contentious Probate Rules 1987, r 32.
[73] Infra, p 1339 et seq.
[74] Infra, p 1351 et seq.
[75] *Lewis v Balshaw* (1935) 54 CLR 188. See, more recently, *Weinstock v Sarnat* [2005] NSWSC 744.
[76] *Re Meatyard's Goods* [1903] p 125.
[77] Non-Contentious Probate Rules 1987, r 30(3)(b).
[78] S 1(1).
[79] For a list of current Orders in Council see Halsbury's *Statutes of England*, 4th edn, Vol 10 (2001 Reissue), p 579.

succeed in obtaining property in a foreign country, is accountable for it as administrator in England.[80]

His title extends not only to property situated in England at the death of the deceased,[81] but also to all property that comes to England thereafter.[82] Property, however, which comes to England after the death of the deceased does not pass to the administrator under an English grant if it has previously been appropriated abroad by an administrator acting under the law of the foreign situs.[83]

3. CHOICE OF LAW

(a) Classification

Succession and administration of estates are closely related, but subject to different private international law rules. The importance of correct classification between administration and succession concerns not only the application of different choice of law rules, but also the application of *renvoi*. Although *renvoi* is available in succession, it is not applicable to administration of estates.[84]

Administration concerns the procedure to deal with the deceased's estates, including grants of representation, the representative's power to collect the deceased's assets and to pay debts,[85] order of priority for the payment of creditors, and the power of the representative to handle the deceased's assets, such as postponing the sale.[86] Succession concerns the substantive rights, such as the beneficial entitlement to the deceased's estates.[87] Under English law, distribution of the deceased's estates to beneficiaries after clearance of debts is classified as succession. Administration, therefore, is usually followed by succession. The personal representative usually exercises his power to collect assets and to clear debts, pursuant to the law of administration, before distributing assets to beneficiaries under the law of succession. It is sometimes difficult to determine, in practice, at what stage administration ends and beneficial distribution begins.[88] It has been held, for instance, that even though all debts have been paid and a net residue ascertained, if the beneficiaries are minors, the administrator under the Administration of Estates Act 1925[89] can still exercise the right to postpone the realisation of the English assets. This is because postponement is a matter of administration.[90]

Disputes on classification may also arise in cases where an heir, to whom the deceased's estates pass directly under the foreign law, applies to enforce foreign judgments concerning the deceased's estate in England,[91] or brings actions in England to recover the deceased's assets.[92] It has been argued that these actions do not concern succession but administration of estates and the foreign heir has no interest to bring any action in relation to the deceased's property

---

[80] *Dowdale's Case* (1604) 6 Co Rep 46b; *Stirling-Maxwell v Cartwright* (1879) 11 Ch D 522.

[81] Administration of Estates Act 1925, s 1; *IRC v Stype Investments (Jersey) Ltd* [1982] Ch 456 at 473.

[82] See, eg, *Whyte v Rose* (1842) 3 QB 493 at 506; *Dicey, Morris and Collins*, paras 26R-022, 26-022, 26-023.

[83] *Currie v Bircham* (1822) 1 Dowl & Ry KB 35; Dicey, Morris and Collins, para 26-024.

[84] *Haji-Ioannou (Deceased) v Frangos* [2009] EWHC 2310 (QB).

[85] Williams, Mortimer and Sunnucks on Executors, Administrators and Probate, para 1-20.

[86] *Dicey, Morris and Collins,* para 26-034; *Re Wilks* [1935] Ch 645.

[87] *Williams, Mortimer and Sunnucks,* para 1-21.

[88] *Re Kehr* [1952] Ch 26.

[89] S 33, as amended by the Trustee Act 2000, Sch 2(II), para 27.

[90] *Re Wilks* [1935] Ch 645; cf *Re Northcote's Will Trusts* [1949] 1 All ER 442; *Re Kehr* [1952] Ch 26.

[91] *Haji-Ioannou (Deceased) v Frangos* [2009] EWHC 2310 (QB).

[92] *Vanquelin v Bouard* (1863) 15 CBNS 341.

in England before obtaining a grant from the English court.[93] The courts, though accepted the classification as a matter of administration, recognised the heir's interest to enforce a personal rights acquired pursuant to the choice of law of succession.[94]

(b) Law governing administration

Administration of estates is exclusively governed by the law of the country where the power of the representative is granted. Thus the duty of an executor who receives a grant of administration from the English court is to pay all debts, whether domestic or foreign, according to the rules of English law. No distinction must be made between English and foreign creditors; no regard must be had to the corresponding rules of the law of the deceased's domicile. A foreign creditor seeking payment in England must take the law of England as he finds it. He can neither claim an advantage which his own or any other foreign law may allow him, nor can he be deprived of an advantage which belongs to him by English law though not by the law of the deceased's domicile. In particular, the priority of debts[95] and their extinction by lapse of time[96] are matters to be governed exclusively by English law.

Where an ancillary administrator has been authorised to deal with the movable English assets of a person dying domiciled abroad, though beneficial distribution is governed by the law of the domicile, the administration of the assets is governed exclusively by English law.[97] If certain foreign debts owed by the deceased are statute-barred by English law but not so barred by the law of the domicile, the principal administrator in the country of the domicile is not entitled as of right to demand that the surplus English assets shall be handed over to him in order to satisfy the claims of the foreign creditors.[98]

Once all debts have been paid by an ancillary administrator according to the law of England, the usual procedure is for him to remit any surplus assets to the principal administrator in the country of the deceased's last domicile. This is to allow them to be distributed among the beneficiaries according to the law of the domicile.[99] But this remission of assets is not a matter of course. It is within the discretion of the English court whether surplus assets shall be remitted to the domicile for purposes of beneficial distribution or whether that distribution shall be made from England. The sole function of the law of the domicile with regard to English assets is to regulate their beneficial distribution, not to allocate them in payment of debts. An immoderate use was made of this rational principle in *Re Lorillard*:[100]

> The testator, domiciled in New York, died leaving assets and creditors both in England and America. Administration proceedings were taken in both countries. The New York assets were exhausted, leaving unpaid certain creditors whose debts were statute-barred by English law but not so by the law of New York. There was a surplus of English assets after all creditors entitled under English law had been paid.

Eve J made an order that, if the American creditors did not within two months establish that their debts were payable by English law, the executor must not remit the assets in England

---

[93] *Haji-loannou (Deceased) v Frangos* [2009] EWHC 2310 (QB).
[94] Ibid. See section 4 below.
[95] *Re Kloebe* (1884) 28 Ch D 175.
[96] *Re Lorillard* [1922] 2 Ch 638.
[97] *Re Kloebe* (1884) 28 Ch D 175; *Re Lorillard* [1922] 2 Ch 638; *Preston v Melville* (1841) 8 Cl & Fin 1 at 12, 13; *Enohin v Wylie* (1862) 10 HL Cas 1 at 13, 14.
[98] Ibid.
[99] *Re Achillopoulos* [1928] Ch 433; *Re Manifold* [1962] Ch 1; *In the Estate of Weiss* [1962] P 136; and see *Scottish National Orchestra Society Ltd v Thomson's Executor* 1969 SLT 325; *Re Lord Cable* [1977] 1 WLR 7 at 25–6.
[100] [1922] 2 Ch 638. The decision has been severely criticised by Nadelmann (1951) 49 Mich LR 1129, 1148–9.

to the New York executor, but must distribute them among the beneficiaries. The Court of Appeal refused to interfere with the exercise by Eve J of his discretion.

It does, however, seem strange to exercise judicial discretion to enrich beneficiaries at the expense of creditors who were entitled to payment in the place of the principal administration.[101] In any event, this attack on the creditors will not always succeed, and only succeeded in the instant case because the beneficiaries were resident in England. Had they resided in New York or, indeed, in any other country where statutes of limitation were not then classified as procedural, they would have been liable at the suit of the creditors to disgorge what they had received.

4. FOREIGN ADMINISTRATORS

(a) Foreign administrators

The status of an administrator appointed by a foreign court is not recognised in England. His title relates only to property that lies within the jurisdiction of the country from which he derives his authority, and therefore he has no right to take or to recover by action property in England without a grant from the English court.[102] If, without the support of a grant, he succeeds in obtaining property in England, he is clearly liable as executor *de son tort* to account for the assets received.[103] Since a foreign administrator has no right to sustain actions or to receive property in England qua representative of the deceased,[104] it would appear clear on principle that a debtor from whom he receives payment is not discharged from liability to an English administrator.[105] However, there is much room for discussion and doubt on this matter.[106] On the one hand, the domestic rule of English law is that "where an executor *de son tort* is really acting as executor, and the party with whom he deals has fair reason for supposing that he has authority to act as such, his acts shall bind the rightful executor, and shall alter the property".[107] On the other hand, there is the undoubted fact that a foreign administrator, as such, has no authority to receive or otherwise deal with English assets. There is no English case directly in point, but, if a debtor had reasonable grounds for believing that the foreign administrator was the bona fide representative of the deceased, it would seem justifiable to depart from strict principle and to regard the payment as a valid discharge. The majority of courts in the USA adopt this view.[108]

Although a foreign administrator is not permitted to sue in England as the representative of the deceased, he may enforce by action a right that is personal to him and which he is entitled to assert in his own individual capacity, even though it is connected with the estate that he is administering.[109] If, for instance, in his official capacity he recovers judgment abroad against

---

[101] But the decision was approved in *Government of India v Taylor* [1955] AC 491 at 509, per Lord Simonds; same case sub nom *Re Delhi Electric Supply and Traction Co Ltd* [1954] Ch 131 at 161, per Evershed MR, and at 165–6, per Jenkins LJ. On this aspect of the case see M Mann (1954) 3 ICLQ 502, 504–6. See also *Re Manifold* [1962] Ch 1; and *Permanent Trustee Co (Canberra) Ltd v Finlayson* (1968) 122 CLR 338.

[102] For discussion generally of the right to sue in a representative capacity, see supra, section 2(a), p 1330.

[103] *New York Breweries Co v A-G* [1899] AC 62; and see *Beavan v Lord Hastings* (1856) 2 K & J 724; and *IRC v Stype Investments (Jersey) Ltd* [1982] Ch 456 at 474.

[104] It even appears that a foreign personal representative cannot sue on behalf of the deceased's dependants under a Fatal Accidents Act claim: *Finnegan v Cementation Co* [1953] 1 QB 688, though see the criticisms at 699–700.

[105] Westlake, s 98; cf Dicey, Morris and Collins, para 26-039.

[106] Story, section 514.

[107] *Thomson v Harding* (1853) 2 E & B 630 at 640.

[108] Restatement 2d, § 322.

[109] *Vanquelin v Bouard* (1863) 15 CBNS 341.

a debtor, he has effectually reduced the debt into his possession, and can sue on the judgment in England without taking out a separate administration.[110] In *Vanquelin v Bouard*:[111]

> A widow in France became donee of the universality of the succession of her deceased husband. By French law she was, as such donee, *personally* liable for her husband's debts and *personally* entitled to his property. She paid to an indorsee the amount of a bill of exchange that her husband had drawn, and later brought an action in England to recover this amount from the acceptor.

It was held that there were two grounds on which the widow must succeed. First, the right that she sought to enforce was one that she had acquired personally since it arose from a payment made by her after her husband's death. Secondly, her position as donee gave her, according to French law, a personal right to recover the sum from the acceptor.

The liabilities to which an administrator is subject are imposed on him in his capacity as the lawful representative of the deceased, and since the status of a representative appointed abroad is not recognised in England, it follows that a foreign administrator as such is not liable to be sued in England.[112] This is so even though he brings foreign assets to England. He cannot sue, neither can he be sued, in his capacity as administrator, but an action might lie, at the suit of a creditor or beneficiary, for the judicial administration of any unappropriated assets.[113]

But just as a foreign administrator can enforce in England a right that attaches to him personally, so he can be sued on a claim that is sustainable against him not in his representative, but in his personal, capacity, eg as trustee for legatees,[114] or as an executor *de son tort*.[115] An action will not lie against an administrator if it is based on a transaction entered into by the deceased, but it will lie on a transaction effected by the administrator after taking office. Thus, for instance, he will be liable on any contract connected with the winding up of the estate that he makes in England.[116] Indeed, the liability in England of a foreign executor would seem to go further than this, for if he has changed his character in any way from that of an executor to that of a trustee he would seem to incur liability within the principle of *Penn v Baltimore*.[117]

(b) Commonwealth grant

A grant of administration made in any country to which the Colonial Probates Act 1892[118] has been extended by Order in Council may be sealed with the seal of the English probate registry, ie "resealed", and thus made effective with regard to English assets. An Order in Council, however, is not made until the country in question has made adequate provision for the recognition of English grants within its territory. The Act has been applied to most

---

[110] *Re Macnichol* (1874) LR 19 Eq 81; *Peterson v Bezold* (1970) 17 DLR (3d) 471; *Haji-loannou (Deceased) v Frangos* [2009] EWHC 2310 (QB).

[111] (1863) 15 CBNS 341.

[112] *Beavan v Lord Hastings* (1856) 2 K & J 724; *Degazon v Barclays Bank International Ltd* [1988] 1 FTLR 17; *Nova v Grove* (1982) 140 DLR (3d) 527; *Canadian Commercial Bank v Belkin* (1990) 73 DLR (4th) 678; Dicey, Morris and Collins, para 26-043.

[113] *Logan v Fairlie* (1825) 2 Sim & St 284; *Tyler v Bell* (1837) 2 My & Cr 89 at 110; Dicey, Morris and Collins, paras 26R-042(1) and 26-044.

[114] Dicey, Morris and Collins, para 26-044.

[115] *New York Breweries v A-G* [1899] AC 62; cf *Charron v Montreal Trust* (1958) 15 DLR (2d) 240; *Re Pemberton* (1966) 59 DLR (2d) 44; *Canadian Commercial Bank v Belkin* (1990) 73 DLR (4th) 678 at 684–5.

[116] See the American case, *Johnson v Wallis* 112 NY 230 (1889); Restatement 2d, § 359.

[117] *Bond v Graham* (1842) 1 Hare 482 at 484; *Ewing v Orr-Ewing* (1885) 10 App Cas 453; *Penn v Baltimore* (1750) 1 Ves Sen 444.

[118] As amended by the Administration of Estates Act 1971, s 11, and the Supreme Court Act 1981, Sch 5.

Commonwealth countries.[119] Resealing is discretionary and the court will not normally reseal a grant unless it was made to the person entitled to an English grant where the deceased died domiciled abroad,[120] eg the person entrusted with the administration of the estate by the court of the deceased's last domicile or the executor named in a will in English or Welsh.[121] Notice of the resealing is sent to the court which made the original grant.[122]

(c) Scotland and Northern Ireland grant

The position in the United Kingdom is that a grant of administration in Scotland or Northern Ireland is directly effective in England without the need for resealing.[123] Similarly, English grants may be directly recognised in Scotland[124] and Northern Ireland;[125] Scottish in Northern Ireland;[126] and vice versa.[127]

---

[119] Colonial Probates Act 1892; extended to protected states and mandated territories by the Colonial Probates (Protected States and Mandated Territories) Act 1927, s 1. For the countries to which the legislation applies, see Halsbury's *Statutes of England*, 4th edn, Vol 17 (2002 Reissue), p 660.

[120] Supra, section 2(c), p 1331.

[121] Non-Contentious Probate Rules 1987, r 39(3).

[122] Ibid, r 39(6).

[123] Administration of Estates Act 1971, s 1 which is retrospective in effect; and see *Practice Direction* [1971] 1 WLR 1790.

[124] Administration of Estates Act 1971, s 3(1).

[125] Ibid, s 2(1).

[126] Ibid, s 2(2).

[127] Ibid, s 3(1).

36

SUCCESSION[1]

1. Introduction	1338	5. Powers of Appointment Exercised		
2. Movables	1339	by Will	1359	
(a) Intestate succession	1339	(a) Special and general powers	1360	
(b) Wills	1339	(b) Capacity	1361	
3. Immovables	1351	(c) Formal validity	1361	
(a) Intestate succession	1351	(d) Essential validity	1362	
(b) Wills	1352	(e) Construction	1363	
4. European Harmonisation Concerning		(f) Revocation	1364	
Succession and Wills	1358			

1. INTRODUCTION

Presuming that the estate of the deceased has been cleared of debts and all taxes and duties paid, the duty of the administrator is to distribute the property among those to whom it beneficially belongs. These persons are to be identified by the choice of law rules relating to succession and these rules may vary according to whether the estate consists of movables or immovables and whether the deceased left a will or died intestate. It is also necessary to examine the rules relating to the exercise of powers of appointment by will.

Most foreign countries have adopted the principle of unity of succession by which questions relating to intestacy or wills are governed by one single law, the personal law of the deceased, irrespective of the nature of the subject matter. The common law of England has consistently adhered to what is called the principle of scission by which the issues are dealt with separately, with the result that the destination of movables on the death of the owner is governed by the law of his domicile, whilst the destination of immovables is governed by the law of the situs.[2] It is for that reason that we have to examine succession to movables separately from succession to immovables.

---

[1] See Miller [1988] Conv 30; (1990) 39 ICLQ 261; Scoles (1988) II Hague Recueil 9, 54–89; North (1990) I Hague Recueil 9, 273–82; Miller, *International Aspects of Succession* (2000); and Hayton, *European Succession Laws* (2002) 2nd edn.

[2] For a fuller account of the opposing principles, see Wolff, p 567 et seq; Cohn (1956) 5 ICLQ 395. For criticism of the idea of scission, see *Re Collens* [1986] Ch 505, 512–13. The Hague Conference on Private International Law concluded, in 1989, a Convention on the Law Applicable to Succession to the Estates of Deceased Persons. This Convention adopts the principle of unity of succession, applying the same rules to movables and immovables, and to testate and intestate succession. In most cases the law to be applied would be that of the deceased's habitual residence at the time of death. The Convention is still not yet in force and has not been signed or ratified by the United Kingdom. For varied assessments of the Convention's merits, see von Overbeck (1989) 46 *Annuaire suisse de droit international* 138; Lagarde (1989) 78 Rev crit dr int privé 249; North (1990) I Hague Recueil 9, 278–82; Schoenblum (1991) 32 Va J Int L 83.

2. MOVABLES

(a) Intestate succession

The rule has been established for over two hundred and fifty years that movable property in the case of intestacy is to be distributed according to the law of the domicile of the intestate at the time of his death.[3] This law determines the class of persons to take, the relative proportions to which the distributees are entitled, the right of representation, the rights of a surviving spouse and all analogous questions.

The fate of movables situated in England and belonging to an intestate who has left no relatives recognised as his successors by the law of the domicile has already been fully discussed.[4] Summarily stated, the rule, which derives from the principle that the authority of the law of the domicile is rigorously confined to questions of succession, is this:

> If, by the law of the domicile, the movables pass to the state or some other body in the domicile by way of succession, English law gives effect to this ruling;[5] if, on the other hand, they are claimed by some body in the domicile as being no-one's property, they pass to the English Crown as *bona vacantia*. In this latter case, there is no question of succession to be referred to the law of the domicile.[6]

(b) Wills

The general rule, established both in England and in the USA, is that testamentary succession to movables is governed exclusively by the law of the domicile of the deceased as it existed at the time of his death.[7] When a testator dies domiciled abroad leaving assets in England, it is true that probate must be taken out in England, and it is also true that the assets must be administered in England according to English law, but nevertheless all questions concerning beneficial succession under a will must be decided in accordance with the law of the domicile. The duty of the executor is to ascertain who, by the law of the domicile, is entitled under the will and, once that is ascertained, to distribute the property accordingly.[8] It is necessary, however, to deal separately with the various questions that arise in the case of wills.

(i) Capacity

The capacity of a testator to make a will is determined by the law of his domicile;[9] and there is no distinction between "lack of capacity due to immaturity or status and incapacity arising from ill health".[10] The meaning of this statement is clear enough if the testator is domiciled in the same country at the time both of his making the will and of his death. If this is a foreign country, his capacity by English law is immaterial. Thus, in a case decided when a married

---

[3] *Pipon v Pipon* (1744) Amb 25. See, more recently, *Re Barton (Deceased), Tod v Barton* [2002] EWHC 264 (Ch); [2002] WTLR 469; *Re Haji-Ioannou (deceased)* [2009] EWHC 2310 (QB).

[4] Supra, pp 49–50.

[5] *In the Estate of Maldonado* [1954] P 223; Lipstein [1954] CLJ 22.

[6] *Re Barnett's Trusts* [1902] 1 Ch 847; *In the Estate of Musurus* [1936] 2 All ER 1666; cf *Re Mitchell, Hatton v Jones* [1954] Ch 525, on which see Ing, *Bona Vacantia*, pp 57–62.

[7] A subsequent change in the law of the domicile is in general of no effect: *Lynch v Provisional Government of Paraguay* (1871) LR 2 P & D 268. See also *Re Aganoor's Trusts* (1895) 64 LJ Ch 521; *Morris v Davies* [2011] EWHC 1773 (Ch); but see the Wills Act 1963, s 6(3), infra, p 1342 et seq; cf succession to immovables where the relevant date is that of the proceedings: *Nelson v Lord Bridport* (1846) 8 Beav 547.

[8] *Enohin v Wylie* (1862) 10 HL Cas 1, 19.

[9] *In the Estate of Fuld (No 3)* [1968] P 675 696. See also *Re Lewal's Settlement Trusts* [1918] 2 Ch 391; *Key v Key* [2010] EWHC 408 (Ch); *Simon v Byford* [2014] EWCA Civ 280.

[10] *In the Estate of Fuld (No 3)*, supra, 696.

woman possessed no testamentary capacity at common law,[11] the English court granted probate of the will of a married woman, a domiciled Spaniard, on proof that by Spanish law a wife was empowered to bequeath her movables.[12]

But what is the position where the testator has changed his domicile after making his will? Is the determinant of the governing law his domicile at death or at the time when he made the will? There is no decision on the matter. Some writers hold that it means the former.[13] This is curious, for by English internal law, and presumably by other legal systems, the decisive moment for testing capacity is the time when the will is made. A will made by a minor or by a person of unsound mind cannot be validated by subsequent events. No will can be valid unless it is valid when made. On principle it makes no difference that the subsequent event consists in a change of domicile to a new country where the law has a more favourable rule for capacity. For instance:

> a domiciled Hungarian, twenty-two years of age, and therefore (it is assumed) lacking testamentary capacity by Hungarian law, makes a will, but ultimately dies domiciled in England.

It is submitted that the will is void. What is invalid for incapacity in its origin can scarcely be automatically validated by the change of domicile. If, on the other hand,

> a domiciled German, sixteen years of age, makes a will, as he is permitted to do by German law, but ultimately dies domiciled in England,[14]

it is submitted that the will is valid. In fact it is difficult to disagree with the view that testamentary capacity, in the sphere of both internal law and private international law, is governed by the law of the testator's domicile at the time when the will is made.[15]

The capacity of a legatee to take a bequest is determined by either the law of his domicile,[16] or the law of the testator's domicile. These determine, for instance, whether he is of full age or whether an unincorporated association is capable of receiving a legacy. Thus, in the case of *Re Hellmann's Will*,[17] the court did not apply the law of the legatee's domicile exclusively, but adopted the principle that, where these two laws as to capacity conflict, the one which is most favourable to the *propositus* is selected.

(ii) Formal validity

According to the common law, domicile was the only connecting factor that determined the law to govern the formal validity of a will of movables. The formal requirements of the law of the country where the testator was domiciled at the time of his death had to be satisfied. His nationality, his domicile at the time of making the will and the place where he executed his will were inadmissible factors. The disadvantages of so rigid a principle were brought to light by the case of *Bremer v Freeman* in 1857,[18] where it was held that a will made in the English

---

[11] Until the Married Women's Property Act 1882, a married woman could dispose by will of her separate estate or exercise a power of appointment, and she could bequeath personalty with the assent of her husband, but otherwise she had no testamentary capacity.

[12] *In the Goods of Maraver* (1828) 1 Hag Ecc 498.

[13] Westlake, s 86.

[14] Cohn, *Manual of German Law* (2nd edn) Vol 1, § 614.

[15] See *Re Lewal's Settlement* [1918] 2 Ch 391; and see Dicey, Morris and Collins, paras 27R-023–27-025; Wolff, pp 581–2.

[16] *Re Hellmann's Will* (1866) LR 2 Eq 363; *Re Schnapper* [1928] Ch 420; and see *Re Pemberton* (1966) 59 DLR (2d) 44.

[17] Supra. By German law the boy's father was entitled as guardian to receive the legacy. Lord Romilly MR, however, refused to permit payment to him and ordered that during the minority the money should be treated as a minor's legacy.

[18] (1857) 10 Moo PCC 306.

form by a British subject who died domiciled in France was invalid, since it neglected the formalities prescribed by French law. This decision led to the passing of the Wills Act 1861, often known as Lord Kingsdown's Act, which was designed to offer testators a wider choice of laws so far as formalities were concerned. Although that Act was a welcome step forward, it was disfigured by several serious blemishes.[19] It was badly drafted and was, for example, confined to the wills of British subjects, differentiating moreover between realty and personalty rather than between movables and immovables.

The 1861 Act was repealed and replaced by the Wills Act 1963[20] which applies to a will, whether of movables or immovables, made by any testator, irrespective of his domicile or nationality, provided that he died on or after 1 January 1964, even though it was executed before that time. A will made before 1964 that satisfies the Wills Act 1861, is, however, admissible to probate notwithstanding the repeal of that Act.[21]

The gist of the Act of 1963 is that it increased the relevant connecting factors by adding nationality and habitual residence to those which were already recognised by common law and the Wills Act 1861, namely domicile and the place of acting. It provides that "a will shall be treated as properly executed" if its execution conforms to the internal law in force in any one of the following territories:[22]

(a) The territory where the will was executed, even if the testator was on a temporary visit.[23]

Where a will is made on board a vessel or aircraft, whether civil or not, the identity of the law of the place of execution receives special statutory treatment. If at the time of execution the aircraft grounded in a particular territory or the vessel is within territorial waters, the testator may comply with the internal law of that territory. Alternatively he may comply with the internal law of the territory with which, having regard to its registration and other relevant circumstances, the vessel or aircraft, whether in course of transit or not, has the closest connection.[24] Judged by this test, the law of the place of acting will normally be the law of the flag, which is represented by the law of the territory where the ship or aircraft is registered if the flag is common to a political unit containing a variety of legal systems.[25]

(b) The territory where the testator was domiciled either at the time of making the will or at death.

(c) The territory where the testator was habitually resident either at the time of making the will or at death.

(d) The state of which the testator, either at the time of making the will or at death, is a national.[26]

This extension of the civil law principle of nationality, though it is a departure from the common law, does at least unify English and continental European rules so far as the formal validity of wills is concerned and will often save a will that under the old law would have failed. For instance, a will made at Zurich in Dutch form by a citizen of the Netherlands, domiciled

---

[19] Morris (1946) 62 LQR 170, 173–176.

[20] This enabled the United Kingdom to ratify the 1961 Hague Convention on the Formal Validity of Wills, Cmnd 1729 (1961).

[21] Wills Act 1963, s 7(1), (2), (3), (4). For notes on the Act, see Morris (1964) 13 ICLQ 684; Kahn-Freund (1964) 27 MLR 55.

[22] S 1.

[23] Eg *Re Wynn* [1984] 1 WLR 237; and see *Re Kanani* (1978) 122 Sol Jo 611.

[24] S 2(1)(a).

[25] Cf supra, p 835 et seq and 875.

[26] *Re Tadros (deceased)* [2014] EWHC 2860 (Ch).

and habitually resident at all material times in France, is properly executed even though it may be formally void in the eyes of French and Swiss law.

Where, however, reliance is placed on the national law of the testator, there are two situations in which it may be difficult to determine the relevant internal law. The first is where he is simultaneously a national of more than one country. The problem then is to decide whether it is necessary to select one particular nationality to denote the internal law or whether the will shall be formally valid if it satisfies the internal law of any of the nationalities. If the former approach is to be adopted, it has been suggested that the court should select either the nationality of the country in which the testator is habitually and principally resident, or the nationality of the country with which in the circumstances he appears to be in fact most closely connected.[27] The other approach, namely of upholding the validity of the will if any of the relevant laws is satisfied, is said to conform more closely with the intentions of those who drafted the 1961 Hague Convention on which the Wills Act 1963 is based.[28]

The second situation that causes difficulty is where the state of which the testator is a national comprises various systems of internal law, as is the case for instance in the United Kingdom or the USA. The 1963 Act solves the problem by providing that the system to be applied shall be ascertained as follows. First, if there is in force throughout the state a rule indicating which of the various systems can properly be applied to the case in question, that rule shall be followed. Failing such a rule, the system shall be that with which the testator was most closely connected at the relevant time.[29] The first of these rules is likely to be of little practical benefit because there will be few composite states which have a unified conflict of laws rule but different domestic rules as to the formal validity of wills. It is reasonable to assume that under the second rule the court, in its search for the country with which the testator was most closely connected at the relevant time, will attribute most importance to his domicile and habitual residence. Where, however, he is domiciled and resident other than in the composite state of which he is a national, as is likely to be the case where he is relying on the law of his nationality as the basis of formal validity, the one remaining factor of significance seems to be the situation of his assets. The relevant time at which the connection must exist is specified in the 1963 Act as "the time of the testator's death where the matter is to be determined by reference to circumstances prevailing at his death, and the time of execution of the will in any other case".[30]

More generally, it will have been observed that the time at which the connecting factors of domicile, habitual residence or nationality may indicate an applicable law is either when the will is executed or when the testator dies. In effect, therefore, there are seven statutory rules for the choice of law.[31] It would seem that if in fact a will satisfies the requirement of any one of these possible laws it is valid as regards form even though the validating law was not deliberately chosen by the testator. This is the reasonable implication of the statutory provision that "a will shall be treated as properly executed if its execution conformed"[32] to one of the prescribed laws.

---

[27] This is the test laid down by the Hague Convention on Conflict of Nationality Laws (1930). If, however, the testator is a national of the forum, it is generally agreed that that nationality prevails; see Rabel, Vol 1, p 120.

[28] Mann (1986) 35 ICLQ 423.

[29] S 6(2).

[30] S 6(2)(b).

[31] In the case of immovables it is also sufficient to comply with the law of the situs: s 2(1)(b), infra, p 1351. The Law Reform Committee of British Columbia, in its Report on the Making and Revocation of Wills (1981), recommended (p 107) that a will should also be formally valid if it complies with the law of the situs of movables either at the time the will was made or at the date of death.

[32] S 1.

A testator, for instance, domiciled in country X makes a will in country Y which is formally valid under the law of X but not under the law of Y. He believes that he has satisfied the requirements of the law of the place of execution.

It might be thought that the will is void, since the intention was to conform to the rules of the law of the place of execution, not of the law of the domicile. But the paramount intention of the testator in such a case is to make a valid will and if he achieves this purpose under one possible law his erroneous belief that he is achieving it under another is immaterial.[33]

The merit of the statutory provision that the legal system to govern formalities (whether it be based on nationality, domicile, habitual residence or place of execution) means the internal law of that system is that the doctrine of renvoi is excluded. This is fortified by the definition of "internal law" as the "law which would apply in a case where no question of the law in force in any other territory or State arose".[34] Nevertheless, for three reasons, this does not mean that renvoi is wholly inapplicable in the case of the formal validity of wills. First, there is the transitional point that the Wills Act 1861 is still applicable to a will made before 1964 and the doctrine of renvoi has been applied under that Act.[35] Secondly, the Wills Act 1963 does not, despite the references to domicile, abolish the old common law rule whereby the formal validity of a will may be referred to the law of the testator's domicile on death,[36] including any further legal system referred to by that law.[37] Thirdly, the Wills Act 1963 does not take away the right to prove in England a will which has been accepted by a court of the deceased's last domicile,[38] even if that acceptance was based other than on that country's internal law.

In considering, under the Wills Act 1963, whether a will has been properly executed, regard must be had to the internal law as it existed at the time of execution. Any later alteration of the law, operating retrospectively to that time, may, however, be taken into account if it validates, but not if it invalidates, the will.[39]

Although it is clear that the capacity of a testator is governed by his personal law, and therefore not necessarily by the law that governs the formal validity of his will, it may sometimes be troublesome to determine whether or not a given rule affects capacity.

> Suppose, for instance, that the testator, Dutch by nationality and by domicile, makes a holograph will in France and leaves assets in England. Both English and French law recognise holograph wills, but the original Article 992 of the Netherlands Civil Code forbade a Dutch national to make such a will abroad.

If the proper execution of the will were to be questioned in England, the court would have to determine the scope of the rule contained in Article 992. If it imposed an incapacity upon the testator, it must be enforced; if it related to formalities, it must be ignored. Such a problem is dealt with by the following section of the Wills Act 1963.[40]

> Where (whether in pursuance of this Act or not) a law in force outside the United Kingdom falls to be applied in relation to a will, any requirement of that law whereby special formalities are to be observed by testators answering a particular description, or witnesses to the

---

[33] Wolff, p 586.
[34] S 6(1).
[35] *In the Goods of Lacroix* (1877) 2 PD 94; *In the Estate of Fuld (No 3)* [1968] P 675.
[36] *In the Goods of Deshais* (1865) 4 Sw & Tr 13, 17.
[37] *Collier v Rivaz* (1841) 2 Curt 855; cf *Bremer v Freeman* (1857) 10 Moo PCC 306; and see Morris, p 351.
[38] *Enohin v Wylie* (1862) 10 HL Cas 1; *Doglioni v Crispin* (1866) LR 1 HL 301.
[39] S 6(3). If this extends to alterations in the law made after the death of the testator, it reverses the effect of *Lynch v Provisional Government of Paraguay* (1871) LR 2 P & D 268, supra, p 1339, n 7.
[40] S 3.

execution of a will are to possess certain qualifications, shall be treated, notwithstanding any rule of that law to the contrary, as a formal requirement.

In the hypothetical case suggested above, therefore, the will made in France would be formally valid in the eyes of English law.

<u>International form of will</u>

Increased mobility has meant an increase in the number of people who make wills in a country in which they are not domiciled or habitually resident or of which they are not nationals. Undoubtedly the Convention which led to the Wills Act 1963 has done much to assist with this problem; but a further step has been taken with the United Kingdom's ratification of the Washington Convention on International Wills (1973).[41] The Annex to the Convention was brought into force by section 27 of the Administration of Justice Act 1982 and is scheduled to that Act. Its essential provision[42] is that a will shall be formally valid in all the Contracting States if it complies with the formalities laid down in the Convention, irrespective of where the will was made, the location of the assets or the nationality, domicile or residence of the testator. The main formalities[43] are that the will be in writing (in any language) and signed or acknowledged by the testator in the presence of two witnesses and an "authorised person" (which in England is a solicitor or a notary public),[44] who have then to attest the will in the presence of the testator. The authorised person has to attach to the will a certificate in the form prescribed by the Convention,[45] authenticating the will and its proper execution.

In essence, the Convention provides a new, additional form for a will which a Contracting State must recognise as formally valid. It may also be recognised in a non-Contracting State under general choice of law rules, as where that state looks to the law of the domicile of the testator and the testator was domiciled in a state which is a party to the Convention and his will had complied with the Convention even though not with the formal requirements of his domiciliary law.[46]

(iii) Essential validity

The essential, or material, validity of a will, and of any particular gift of movables therein is determined by the law of the country in which the testator was domiciled at death.[47] This rule is not affected by the Wills Act 1963. A will may be admitted to probate under that statute as having complied with the formalities of one of the legal systems that it makes available, but the actual effect of its dispositions must be measured by the law of the testator's domicile at death. The grant of probate is conclusive proof that the instrument proved is the will of the testator but it is not conclusive as to the validity of the dispositions.

If, for instance, a British subject dies domiciled in France, having made a will in England according to English law, probate is necessarily granted. But if he has neglected to leave to his

---

[41] Nadelmann (1974) 22 AJCL 365; Brandon (1983) 32 ICLQ 742; Kearney (1984) 18 Int Lawyer 613.

[42] Art 1.

[43] Arts 2–5.

[44] 1982 Act, s 28(1).

[45] Art 10.

[46] The Administration of Justice Act 1982, ss 23–26 (ss 23–25 not yet in force) also implements another international convention, namely the Council of Europe Convention on the Establishment of a Scheme of Registration of Wills (1972) which may also be of practical assistance to the person who makes a will away from home. It provides for the establishment of national registration schemes for wills and access to them from other Contracting States.

[47] *Thornton v Curling* (1824) 8 Sim 310; *Campbell v Beaufoy* (1859) John 320; *Macdonald v Macdonald* (1872) LR 14 Eq 60; *Re Groos, Groos v Groos* [1915] 1 Ch 572; *Philipson-Stow v IRC* [1961] AC 727 at 761; *Re Levick's Will Trusts* [1963] 1 WLR 311; *Re Barton (Deceased), Tod v Barton* [2002] EWHC 264 (Ch); [2002] WTLR 469; *Al-Bassam v Al-Bassam* [2004] EWCA Civ 857, [2004] WTLR 757.

children that portion of the estate required by French law, the English court allows the will to take effect only as it would do in France. If French law regards the testamentary dispositions as ineffective, the court directs the property to be distributed according to the French law of intestacy;[48] if French law requires only part of the estate to go to the children, the will would be valid as to the rest with the bequests proportionately reduced.[49]

The principle that the law of the domicile at death is decisive is well illustrated by the reverse case to that just given. An example is afforded by *Re Groos, Groos v Groos*:[50]

A Dutch woman made her will in the Netherlands constituting her husband heir of her movable property except for the "legitimate portion to which her descendants were entitled". She died domiciled in England, leaving her husband and five children surviving. By Dutch law the "legitimate portion" of the children was three-fourths of the estate, but by English law it was nothing. It was held that, since the will operated under English law, the whole estate passed to the husband.

Whether a beneficiary is entitled to take under a will is determined by the law of the testator's domicile if the question turns on a rule of substantive law, not on procedure. In the case of *Re Cohn*:[51]

A testatrix and her daughter, both domiciled in Germany, were killed in an air raid in London in circumstances which left it uncertain which of them died first. The daughter's estate was entitled to movables under her mother's will, but only if she were the survivor. In such a case the English rule is that the younger person is presumed to have survived the elder,[52] but the presumption by German law was that they died simultaneously.

These presumptions were classified as falling within the sphere of substantive law, and it was held that the German view must be adopted. On the other hand, the English rule relating to the burden of proof of testamentary capacity has been classified as procedural and governed by the law of the forum.[53]

Other examples of questions of substance are whether a gift to an attesting witness, or to the relative of an attesting witness, is valid,[54] whether the testator acted under duress or undue influence,[55] and whether a beneficiary is put to his election.[56] Similarly, legislation empowering the court to make an order for such provision out of the estate as is adequate to support the dependants of the deceased would appear to be a matter of substance applicable only if the testator died domiciled within the jurisdiction.[57]

---

48 *Thornton v Curling*, supra; *Campbell v Beaufoy*, supra.
49 Eg *Re Annesley* [1926] Ch 692; *Re Adams* [1967] IR 424, especially 452–8.
50 [1915] 1 Ch 572.
51 [1945] Ch 5; Morris (1945) 61 LQR 340.
52 Law of Property Act 1925, s 184.
53 *In the Estate of Fuld (No 3)* [1968] P 675, 694–9.
54 *Re Priest* [1944] Ch 58. This case has been much discussed; see RMW (1944) 60 LQR 114; Morris (1945) 61 LQR 124; (1946) 62 LQR 172, 173; Kahn-Freund (1946) 7 MLR 238; Wolff, p 586. See now the Wills Act 1968.
55 *In the Estate of Fuld (No 3)* [1968] P 675, 698–9.
56 See *Re Ogilvie* [1918] 1 Ch 492, 500; *Re Mengel's Will Trust* [1962] Ch 791; Dicey, Morris and Collins, paras 27R-075–27-077. Election is discussed more fully in the context of succession to immovables, infra, p 1355 et seq.
57 *Pain v Holt* (1919) 19 SRNSW 105; *Re Herron* [1941] 4 DLR 203; *Re Terry* [1951] NZLR 30; *Re Greenfield* [1985] 2 NZLR 662. The English legislation is limited in terms to testators dying domiciled in England and Wales: Inheritance (Provision for Family and Dependants) Act 1975, s 1(1), as amended by the Civil Partnership Act 2004, Sch 4(2), para 15(6); and see *Mastaka v Midland Bank Executor and Trustee Co Ltd* [1941] Ch 192; *Wilson v Jones (Preliminary Issue)*, 8 June 2000 (unreported), Ch D; *Cyganik v Agulian* [2006] EWCA Civ 129; [2006] 1 FCR 406.

It should not be assumed that because a testator dies domiciled in England his will is therefore inevitably subject to all the rules of English domestic law concerned with essential validity. This fact has not always been admitted. It has been said,[58] for instance, that whether a restraint on marriage or a gift to a charity is valid, or whether a limitation is void as infringing the rule against perpetuities,[59] must be determined by the law of the testator's domicile no matter what the domicile of the beneficiary may be. It is submitted that this view is neither consonant with principle nor warranted by the authorities. It entirely ignores the essential difference between the right to give and the right to receive. The two are not necessarily analogous. The right of a testator to give, for example as to whether he is free to bequeath the whole of his property as it pleases him or on the contrary whether he must reserve a legitimate portion for his children, is of necessity governed by the English law of succession from which his testamentary power of disposition is derived. But there is no reason why this law should restrict the right of a foreign legatee to enjoy a gift in accordance with the terms of the will, provided that the legacy is valid according to his personal law and provided that the limitations imposed on its enjoyment do not offend some rule of public policy so sacred in English eyes as to demand extra-territorial application.

> Suppose that a testator domiciled in England bequeaths a sum of money to a legatee domiciled in France, and that the legacy, though valid by French law, is void by English internal law as being obnoxious to the perpetuity rule.

If the English policy is to insist on the early vesting of interests regardless of where the property is to be enjoyed and administered then the legacy must be regarded as void. Such a suggestion is, however, untenable. The object of the perpetuity rule is to restrict the withdrawal of property from the channels of commerce, a purpose which is clearly local, and which, therefore, cannot justifiably be invoked to destroy a bequest of money that is to be enjoyed and administered in a foreign country. As Lord Cottenham said in an early case:

> The rules acted upon by the courts in this country with respect to testamentary dispositions tending to perpetuities relate to this country only . . . The fund [given by the English will] being to be administered in a foreign country is payable here though the purpose to which it is to be applied would have been illegal if the administration of the fund had been to take place in this country.[60]

This conclusion has been reached several times by the New York Court of Appeals[61] and on one occasion at least by an Australian court.[62] In the laconic words of one judge: "It is no part of the policy of the State of New York to interdict perpetuities or gifts in mortmain in Pennsylvania or California."[63]

Again:

> Suppose that a testator, domiciled in England, leaves a sum of money in trust that the income thereof shall be used for purposes most conducive to the good of religion in a certain diocese in country X, and that persons domiciled in X are appointed to administer the trust.[64]

---

[58] Westlake, p 154.

[59] Ibid; and Dicey, Morris and Collins, paras 27-048–27-050.

[60] *Fordyce v Bridges* (1848) 2 Ph 497, 515. An English testator gave the residue of his personal estate to trustees to convert it into money and lay it out in the purchase of land in England or Scotland according to the limitations of a Scottish entail. Such limitations infringed the English rule against perpetuities. The trustees were allowed to purchase land in Scotland in accordance with the terms of the will.

[61] Gray, *The Rule against Perpetuities* (1942) 4th edn, § 263.2; Morris and Leach, *The Rule against Perpetuities* (1962) 2nd edn, pp 22–3; and see *Re Chappell's Estate* 124 Wash 128, 213 P 684 (1923).

[62] *Re Mitchner* [1922] St R Qd 252.

[63] *Chamberlain v Chamberlain* 43 NY 424, 434 (1870).

[64] The American position relating to charitable gifts is discussed by Hancock (1964) 16 Stan LR 561.

The trust is invalid by English law as not being charitable;[65] but, if it is valid by the law of X, must the court forbid payment of the money to the trustees? Again, such a ruling would be indefensible. English law confines the definition of a charity within comparatively narrow limits, presumably with the object of restricting the amount of money that may be withdrawn from circulation, but it cannot justifiably claim to impose this policy on foreign countries. The decisive factor is the law of the country where the trust is to be administered, ie its proper law, not the law that governs the instrument of gift.[66] Three conditions must be satisfied before transfer of the money to the foreign country will be authorised. First, the charitable bequest must be valid according to its proper law, the law of the country where it is to be administered. Secondly, there must be persons in that country willing and competent to undertake the task of administration.[67] Thirdly, the purposes for which the bequest is to be employed must not conflict with some rule of English public policy intended to operate extra-territorially. It can scarcely be maintained that a rule which confines within narrow limits the possible beneficiaries of a charitable gift is intended to be anything more than local in its operation.[68]

It would seem, then, that the principle which refers questions of substantial validity to the law of the testator's domicile is not unqualified.

(iv) Construction

The province of construction is to ascertain the expressed intentions of the testator, ie the meaning which the words of the will, when properly interpreted, convey. If the intention is expressed in a manner that leaves no room for doubt, the aid of private international law is unnecessary. This is because the duty of any court, no matter in which country it may sit, is to give effect to expressed intentions and, if these are clear, there can be no occasion to test the language of the will by reference to any particular legal system. If, however, the language of the will leaves the intention doubtful, or if it uses expressions which are ambiguous or equivocal or if the testator has failed to provide for certain events which have not been covered by his dispositions, a problem of choice of law arises, for it is essential that the doubtful intention of the testator should be ascertained by reference to rules of construction obtaining in one particular system of law. The consequences may be serious according to whether this law or that law is chosen, for when it is said that the intention of the testator is the sovereign guide in questions of construction, this does not mean that his language is necessarily to be construed in a manner that would commend itself to an intelligent man, but that it must be read in the light of those technical rules of construction recognised by the governing legal system.

It will be seen, therefore, that in choosing a law to govern construction it is desirable to discover that system with which the testator was most intimately acquainted, and which it is just to presume that he had in mind when drafting his will.[69] Certain expressions, such as "next of kin", bear different meanings in different countries, and it is obvious that the intention of a testator may be defeated unless the legal system with reference to which he wrote his will is correctly ascertained.

---

[65] *Dunne v Byrne* [1912] AC 407.

[66] The majority decision of the Supreme Court of Canada to the contrary: *Jewish National Fund Inc v Royal Trust Co* (1965) 53 DLR (2d) 577, has been strongly criticised: Picarda, *The Law and Practice Relating to Charities* (1995) 2nd edn, pp 783–5; Waters, *Law of Trusts in Canada* (2005) 3rd edn, Chapter 14.

[67] *New v Bonaker* (1867) LR 4 Eq 655.

[68] *Oliphant v Hendrie* (1784) 1 Bro CC 571; *Mackintosh v Townsend* (1809) 16 Ves 330; *A-G v Mill* (1827) 3 Russ 328, 338; affd by the House of Lords 2 Dow and Clark 393; *Fordyce v Bridges* (1848) 2 Ph 497, 515.

[69] See *Re McMorran* [1958] Ch 624, 634; *Durie's Trustees v Osborne* 1960 SC 444, 450–451; *Re Adams* [1967] IR 424, 458, 461.

The law with which the ordinary person is most familiar is the law of his existing domicile, and, despite the fact that certain authorities choose the domicile at death as the controlling factor,[70] it is more consonant with the desire of the court to implement the intention of the testator to say that the law of the domicile at the time when his will is made governs its construction, unless there is evidence indicating that his mind was directed to some other legal system. This approach is supported by section 4 of the Wills Act 1963 which provides that the "construction of a will shall not be altered by reason of any change in the testator's domicile after the execution of the will".[71]

In most cases, of course, the domicile does not change after the will has been made and examples can readily be provided of the application of the law of the domicile being unchanged between the making of the will and death. Where, for instance, a domiciled Englishman bequeathed a legacy to the "next of kin" of a foreigner, it was held that the legatees must be ascertained according to English law.[72] Whether a gift in the will of a domiciled Englishman was a satisfaction of a debt due under a Scottish settlement was tested by reference to English law.[73] Words of value or of quantity or of measurement, which vary in meaning in different countries, have been interpreted according to the law of the testator's domicile.[74]

There is, however, no absolute rule that the interpretation of a will depends on the law of the testator's domicile. It is merely a prima facie rule that is displaced if the testator has manifestly contemplated and intended that his will should be construed according to some other system of law.[75] Thus where a domiciled Frenchwoman left an unattested will valid by the law of France, in which she said that the will was to "be considered in England the same as in France", Stirling J held, on the question whether the document operated as the execution of a power, that the testatrix wrote with reference to English law.[76]

(v) Revocation

Since the rules relating to revocation vary from country to country,[77] the problem is to ascertain the law that determines what suffices to revoke an existing will. According to English internal law, a will may be voluntarily revoked either by a fresh will or by its destruction, or obliteration, with the intention of revoking it, by the testator himself or by some authorised person in his presence. Further, its automatic revocation may result from the later marriage of the testator. These three methods will serve as the basis on which to discuss the problem of the choice of law.

(a) Revocation by later will

A will purporting to revoke an earlier will is formally valid and effective if it satisfies the requirements of any one of the laws by which, under the Wills Act 1963, its formal validity is determinable. Suppose, for instance, that a testator domiciled in England makes a will in

---

[70] *Re Cunnington* [1924] 1 Ch 68; and see *Trotter v Trotter* (1828) 4 Bli NS 502; *Yates v Thompson* (1835) 3 Cl & Fin 544.

[71] And see *Philipson-Stow v IRC* [1961] AC 727, 761. Cf *Re Levick's Will Trusts* [1963] 1 WLR 311.

[72] *Re Fergusson's Will* [1902] 1 Ch 483. But see *Re Goodman's Trusts* (1881) 17 Ch D 266; cf the Scottish view: *Mitchell's Trustee v Rule* 1908 SLT 189; *Smith's Trustees v Macpherson* 1926 SC 983; Anton, para 24.82-24.96.

[73] *Campbell v Campbell* (1866) LR 1 Eq 383.

[74] *Saunders v Drake* (1742) 2 Atk 465.

[75] *Pierson v Garnet* (1786) 2 Bro CC 38; Westlake, s 123; cf *Re Cunnington* [1924] 1 Ch 68.

[76] *Re Price, Tomlin v Latter* [1900] 1 Ch 442. In *Re Wynn* [1984] 1 WLR 237, English law was applied to determine whether a will which revoked previous wills but made no fresh dispositions of the testatrix's property (apparently both movable and immovable) could have the effect of excluding her husband from taking on intestacy, even though it was not decided where the testatrix was domiciled at the material time.

[77] In relation to South Africa, see Neels (2007) 56 ICLQ 613.

the English form revoking an earlier will that he had made when domiciled in France. The revocation is effective even if ineffective according to French law.

The Wills Act 1963, however, goes further. It provides that the revoking will shall be effective if it complies with the requirements of any one of the laws qualified to govern the formal validity of the *earlier* will.[78] The mere fact that, at the time of his death, the testator has become subject to another testamentary law is not to upset what he lawfully and intentionally did according to a law that governed him in the past. Thus, to reverse the illustration suggested above, the revocation would be effective if contained in a will that was formally void by English law but valid according to the law of France.

It should be noted, however, that a testator may make a valid English will which does not revoke an earlier will in foreign form where the latter deals solely with property in a foreign country and the English will deals only with English property, even though it contains a revocation clause.[79]

(b) Revocation by destruction of the will

The Private International Law Committee recommended in 1958 that the effect of the destruction of a will should be determinable by any one of the laws capable of governing the formal validity of the testator's will, had he chosen to make one.[80] This proposal has not been accepted by the legislature. The Wills Act 1963 deals only with a testamentary revocation. Hence, the problem of choice of law in the case of acts such as destruction of the will, or obliteration of some of its provisions, must be solved on the basis of the common law principle of domicile.[81] But what is the decisive domicile in this context? The question is superfluous if the testator has lived in the same country throughout his life, since there is only one possible domiciliary law. It requires an answer, however, if he possessed one domicile at the time of the act of destruction, and another at the time of death, for what is an effective revocation by the earlier law of the domicile, may be ineffective by the later.

> Suppose, for instance, that a testator domiciled in Quebec sent written instructions to his solicitor to destroy his will. The will was accordingly burnt and was thereby revoked in the eyes of Quebec law. The testator died domiciled in England. English internal law would not regard the revocation as effective since the burning was not carried out in the presence of the testator.[82]

Since the testator died subject to English law, could it successfully be contended that his will, presuming its contents to be ascertainable, was still operative? It is submitted that such a contention would be ill-founded. The legal effect of the act of destruction fell to be determined at the time of its performance. The testator intended to revoke his will. He fulfilled his intention by an act that was regarded as final and effective by the law to which he was then subject. There was no other law available to him.[83] The mind recoils from the suggestion that the effect of such an act within the law might be nullified or changed merely because at some later period in his life he happened to be subjected to a different legal system. It requires something more than this to undo what has lawfully and intentionally been done in the past.

---

[78] S 2(1)(c).

[79] *In the Estate of Wayland* [1951] 2 All ER 1041; *Guardian Trust and Executors Co of New Zealand Ltd v Darroch* [1973] 2 NZLR 143. Also *In the Estate of Vickers* (2001-02) 4 ITELR 584; *Re Baldry (Deceased)* [2004] WTLR 609 (Fam Div), in respect of which see Simm 2005 TEL & TJ (65) (Apr) 15; *Lamothe v Lamothe* [2006] EWHC 1387; [2006] WTLR 1431.

[80] (1958) Cmd 491, p 8.

[81] Cf *Velasco v Coney* [1934] P 143.

[82] Wills Act 1837, s 20.

[83] See *Re Traversi's Estate* 189 Misc 251, 64 NYS 2d 453 (1946).

The same reasoning applies to the reverse case. If the act of destruction were sufficient by English law but insufficient by Quebec law, the will would remain unrevoked. A chance change of domicile could scarcely infuse life into an act that was legally stillborn.[84]

(c) Revocation by marriage

The rule of English law is that a will is revoked by marriage unless it is explicitly expressed to be made in contemplation of marriage.[85] Few other legal systems have adopted the rule and so choice of law problems may arise. When a person marries after making a will and then dies leaving movables in some other country, the question may arise as to whether the law of his domicile at the time of marriage or at the time of death determines the effect of the marriage on the will.[86] The answer to this question depends on whether the rule as to revocation by marriage is to be classified as a rule of matrimonial law or of testamentary law. If it is a rule concerning the former, then its effect must be tested by the law of the domicile at the time of marriage; if on the other hand, it has nothing to do with the matrimonial regime at all, its effect is to be measured by the law of the domicile at the date of death. It would seem scarcely open to doubt that it is essentially a doctrine connected with the relationship of marriage, and that this is so was affirmed in the case of *Re Martin, Loustalan v Loustalan*,[87] where a woman, after making a will, married a man domiciled in England and subsequently died domiciled in France. By English internal law a will is revoked by marriage, but this is not so under French law. In order to decide whether the will was revoked it was necessary to decide whether this was a matrimonial question governed by English law or a testamentary question governed by French law. Vaughan-Williams LJ in the Court of Appeal held[88] that the question was one of matrimonial law, English law applied and the will was revoked.

As the relevant domicile is that at the time of the marriage, the effect of a change of domicile may be shown by the following two examples:

> A makes a will while domiciled in England; then he acquires a domicile in Scotland (where marriage does not revoke a will); he later marries in Scotland, and ultimately dies domiciled in England.[89]

In this case the will stands. English law applies only as being the governing testamentary law under which A dies, and therefore its doctrine as to the effect of marriage cannot affect a marriage that took place when the parties had a foreign domicile. The reverse case to that just put is as follows:

> A makes a will while domiciled in Scotland, then acquires an English domicile and later marries in England.

Here the question as to revocation is governed by English law as being the law applicable to all matters concerning the matrimonial regime.

It has been assumed so far that the spouses have a common domicile on marriage. However, this may not always be the case, given that a wife may have a domicile independent from

---

[84] Mann (1954) 31 BYBIL 217, 231.

[85] Wills Act 1837, s 18 (as substituted by the Administration of Justice Act 1982, s 18), and s 18A, as amended by the Law Reform (Succession) Act 1995, s 3 and the Family Law Act 1996, Sch 8). See also s 18B (will to be revoked by civil partnership) and s 18C (effect of dissolution or annulment of civil partnership on wills); *Re Ikin (deceased)* [2009] EWHC 3340 (Ch).

[86] There is also the fundamental question as to whether the relevant marriage was valid; see *Re Fleming* [1987] ILRM 638.

[87] [1900] P 211; and see *Re Micallef's Estate* [1977] 2 NSWLR 929.

[88] Ibid, 240.

[89] *In the Goods of Reid* (1866) LR 1 P & D 74; cf *In the Estate of Groos* [1904] P 269.

that of her husband.[90] As domicile for the purposes of revocation of a will by marriage is to be determined as at the time of marriage, there may be some cases where a wife retains her separate domicile notwithstanding her marriage. If so, the law of that country will determine whether her will is revoked by marriage.

So far as English law is concerned, a marriage which is void under English rules of private international law will have no effect on the will;[91] but a voidable marriage will revoke it.[92]

3. IMMOVABLES

(a) Intestate succession

We have seen earlier[93] that, under the principle of scission, succession to immovables is governed, not by the law of the testator's domicile, but by the law of the situs.[94]

Accordingly, where the owner of immovables dies intestate, the order of descent or distribution prescribed by the law of the situs is applied by the English court no matter what his domicile may have been.[95] This rule can be criticised on a number of grounds.[96] It is an historical anomaly from the time before 1926 when intestate succession to land was subject to rules different from intestate succession to personalty. Domestic legislation on intestate succession would seem to be based on the assumption, erroneous in fact, that succession to all the intestate's property will be governed by the same law. This is particularly striking with regard to the statutory legacies which go to a surviving spouse under the law of England[97] and of Northern Ireland.[98] Can a widow claim two such statutory legacies, one based on land in England and the other on personalty in Northern Ireland?[99] The operation of the rule may be illustrated by two decisions.

The first is an Irish case, *Re Rea*[100] in which:

> A domiciled Irishman died intestate without issue in Ireland, owning land in both Ireland and Victoria. In such circumstances a widow was entitled by a Victorian statute to a charge of £1,000 on land in the colony and by an Irish statute to a charge of £500 payable out of the real and personal estate in Ireland. The land in Victoria having been sold and the proceeds remitted to Ireland, it was held that the widow was entitled to the £1,000 under the Victorian statute, as well as the £500 under the Irish statute, since her rights were those conferred by the law of the situs.

---

[90] Domicile and Matrimonial Proceedings Act 1973, s 1.

[91] *Mette v Mette* (1859) 1 Sw & Tr 416.

[92] *Re Roberts* [1978] 1 WLR 653.

[93] Supra, p 1338.

[94] This would seem to mean the law of the situs at the date of the proceedings, rather than at the time of death: *Nelson v Lord Bridport* (1846) 8 Beav 547.

[95] *Balfour v Scott* (1793) 6 Bro Parl Cas 550; *Duncan v Lawson* (1889) 41 Ch D 394; cf *Re Ralston* [1906] VLR 689. When the immovables are situated in a country that adopts the principle of unity of succession this means that, subject to the acceptance of the renvoi doctrine by the law of the situs, the order of descent may be that of England; cf *Re Duke of Wellington* [1947] Ch 506; supra, pp 68–9.

[96] See Morris (1969) 85 LQR 339, 348–52.

[97] Administration of Estates Act 1925, s 46(1)(i), para (3), as amended.

[98] Administration of Estates Act (Northern Ireland) 1955, s 7, as amended.

[99] Morris and North, p 575. A clear negative answer has been given in Canada: *Re Thom* (1987) 40 DLR (4th) 184; *Vak Estate v Dukelow* (1994) 117 DLR (4th) 122; cf *Train v Train's Executor* (1899) 2 F 146.

[100] [1902] 1 IR 451.

The second, and more recent, decision is *Re Collens*:[101]

> The deceased died in 1966. He was intestate and died domiciled in Trinidad and Tobago, leaving property there, in Barbados and in England. The property in England included immovable property. There was a dispute over succession to the estate and it was agreed that the deceased's second wife should receive $1 million in settlement of any claim to the property in Trinidad and Tobago, but that succession to the estate in Barbados and England should be governed by their respective laws. It was not contested that English law as the law of the situs governed the intestate succession to the English immovables. The question for the court was whether the second wife could take, not only the $1 million agreed under the law of the deceased's domicile, but also the statutory legacy due to a widow under the English law of intestacy.

Sir Nicolas Browne-Wilkinson V-C was reluctant to see the widow succeed both under the law of the domicile and to the statutory legacy under English law, as the law of the situs. Nevertheless he was unable to interpret either the English statutory provisions or the choice of law rules so as to lead to any other result. Although he saw force in the criticisms of this state of the law, he felt obliged to conclude that "my job is to administer the law as it now is".[102]

(b) Wills

The general rule in the case of testamentary succession to immovables is, as with intestate succession, that it is the law of the situs of the immovables which governs.[103] Though there are fewer authorities relating to wills of immovables, it may be helpful to consider the various issues that may arise in the same order as with wills of movables.

(i) Capacity

There seems little doubt that the law of the situs exclusively determines whether the testator has capacity to make a will of immovables,[104] and also probably capacity to take a bequest.

(ii) Formal validity

At common law, a will of immovables had to comply with the formal requirements of the law of the situs.[105] However, as with wills of movables,[106] the common law principles have been much enlarged by the Wills Act 1963. It is sufficient for the will to comply with any one of the seven laws specified in section 1 of the Act in relation to movables, namely the territory where the testator was domiciled or habitually resident or of which he was a national, either when the will was executed or when the testator died, or the territory where the will was executed. Furthermore, the common law rule, ie compliance with the formalities of the law of the situs, is also retained in the case of immovables.[107] However, reference in the Wills Act to the law of the situs is in terms of "the internal law in force in the territory where the property was situated"[108] and the reference to the "internal law" of the situs seems to exclude the doctrine of renvoi.[109]

---

[101] [1986] Ch 505.

[102] Ibid, 513. See Carruthers (2005), paras 2.76–2.86

[103] *Scarfe v Matthews* [2012] EWHC 3071 (Ch).

[104] See *Re Hernando, Hernando v Sawtell* (1884) 27 Ch D 284, where the proposition, so far as related to English land, was undisputed.

[105] *Coppin v Coppin* (1725) 2 P Wms 291, supra, pp 1255–6; *Pepin v Bruyère* [1900] 2 Ch 504.

[106] Supra, p 1339 et seq.

[107] Wills Act 1963, s 2(1)(b).

[108] Ibid.

[109] Cf wills of movables, supra, p 1343.

(iii) *Essential validity*

There is no doubt[110] that the law of the situs, including its choice of law rules (which means that the doctrine of renvoi[111] is applicable), governs matters of essential validity. This rule has been applied to such issues as whether the bequest contravenes the rule against perpetuities or against accumulations,[112] whether gifts to charities are valid,[113] whether a proportion of the estate has to be left to the children or to a surviving spouse,[114] whether a power to assign part of the estate is valid,[115] and, indeed, whether the land can be devised at all.[116]

A matter of considerable practical importance is whether a court can order payment to be made out of the estate for the support of dependants. In the case of movables, we have seen[117] that, under the Inheritance (Provision for Family and Dependants) Act 1975, an English court can make such an order only if the testator died domiciled in England. It might, therefore, have been expected that, in the case of an estate of immovable property, the 1975 Act would have been applicable if England was the law of the situs.[118] Unfortunately the 1975 Act is seriously defective[119] in that the court can only make an order in the case of immovables, as well as movables, if the testator died domiciled in England.[120] This means that, in the case of a testator who dies domiciled in a country which applies the law of the situs rule such as New South Wales[121] or New Zealand,[122] no provision for support can be made out of the English immovable property. The foreign court has no power because of the English situs and the English court has no power because of the foreign domicile.

(iv) *Construction*

A somewhat difficult question arises with regard to the construction of wills of immovables. It has been seen that a bequest of movables is construed according to the law intended by the testator, which is generally the law of his domicile at the time when he prepared his will.[123] The problem is whether the English authorities extend the same rule to wills of immovables, or whether they require that exclusive regard shall be paid to the law of the situs.

It is submitted that there is little difficulty if we resort to first principles, and determine what are the natural provinces of the law of the domicile and of the law of the situs respectively in this matter. The objective of all courts, when dealing with a will, is first to ascertain the intention of the testator and then to give effect to that intention so far as is consonant with the governing law. In the ascertainment of this intention in a case where the will has reference to more than one country, it may be a matter of great moment whether the testator's language is read in the light of this or that legal system. This is because it frequently happens that the

---

[110] Note, however, in the USA, the gradual erosion of the situs rule for testate succession to immovable property: *Saunders v Saunders* 796 So 2d 1253 (Fla App 2001), cited in Symeonides (2002) 50 AJCL 1, 94.

[111] Supra, Chapter 5.

[112] *Freke v Carbery* (1873) LR 16 Eq 461.

[113] *Duncan v Lawson* (1889) 41 Ch D 394; supra, p 1258.

[114] *Re Hernando* (1884) 27 Ch D 284; *Re Ross* [1930] 1 Ch 377. See also *Re Bailey* [1985] 2 NZLR 656; *Hays v Hays* [2015] EWHC 3825 (Ch).

[115] *Public Trustee v Vodjdani* (1988) 49 SASR 236.

[116] *Nelson v Bridport* (1846) 8 Beav 547.

[117] Supra, p 1339.

[118] See eg *Re Paulin* [1950] VLR 462, 465.

[119] Morris (1946) 62 LQR 170, 178–179; cf Law Com No 61 (1974), paras 258–62.

[120] 1975 Act, s 1(1), as amended by the Civil Partnership Act 2004, Sch 4(2), para 15(6). See *Wilson v Jones (Preliminary Issue)*, 8 June 2000 (unreported), Ch D; *Cyganik v Agulian* [2006] EWCA Civ 129; [2006] 1 FCR 406.

[121] *Pain v Holt* (1919) 19 SRNSW 105.

[122] *Re Bailey* [1985] 2 NZLR 656.

[123] Supra, pp 1339–40.

same word or phrase, such as "heirs of the body", bears a different signification in different countries. It follows, therefore, in such a case that the result which the testator intended will not ensue unless we discover the system of law which he had in mind when he wrote the will. The presumption should be in favour of the law of the domicile at the time of the making of the will, for that is the system of law under which he lives and with which he is expected to be familiar.

It may, of course, be some other system, such as the law of the situs, for the inquiry turns wholly on intention, and if there is anything clearly indicative of a desire to exclude the law of the domicile, the will must be construed accordingly.[124] Thus, if a domiciled Englishman, possessing land in Scotland, were to adopt in his will the terms "liferent" and "fee", it would be reasonable to conclude that he wished Scots law to govern his disposition; similarly, if he made one will for the land and a separate will for his English property.[125]

Where a testator is domiciled in one country and has land in another, the fact to be borne in mind, then, is that the law of the situs, as such, has no paramount claim to exclusive recognition.[126] Otherwise the result may be to defeat a testator's intention, for he may leave property, not to named persons, but to those persons who would be entitled were he to die intestate. It is obvious, in such a case, that his intention is to benefit the successors admitted by the law of his domicile, since it is that system with which he is familiar, and it can scarcely be denied that arbitrarily to make a new will for him by admitting a different line of succession imposed by the law of a foreign situs, merely because the will includes a certain amount of land situated abroad, would constitute a departure from principle.

The adoption of this principle does not infringe any local rule of the law of the situs; nor does it derogate from the sovereign power of the country in which the land is situated. All courts, in administering private international law, desire to give effect to expressed intentions, provided that this does not conflict with the public policy of the forum or of the situs, and it is a matter of indifference that A takes land under a will that has been construed according to the law of the testator's domicile, though B would have taken had the construction been that of the law of the situs. This, however, gives us the clue to the limits of the doctrine. If the rules of the law of the situs make it illegal or impossible to give effect to the will as construed by the system of law intended by the testator, the general principle must perforce give way, and the construction adopted must be that of the law of the situs.[127] Or, again, if the interest arising from a will that has been so construed possesses incidents different in the situs from those recognised by the law of the domicile, the law of the situs must prevail, for it is that law which determines the nature and extent of estates and interests in immovables.

The principle may, then, be stated as follows:

A will of immovables must be construed according to the system of law intended by the testator. This is presumed to be the law of the domicile at the time when the will is made, but the presumption will be rebutted if evidence is adduced from the language of the will proving that he made his dispositions with reference to some other legal system. If, however, the interest that arises from such construction is not permitted or not recognised by the law of the situs, the latter law must prevail.

---

[124] *Public Trustee v Vodjdani* (1988) 49 SASR 236.
[125] As in *Re Duke of Wellington* [1947] Ch 506.
[126] Cf *Re Osoba, Osoba v Osoba* [1979] 1 WLR 247, 250.
[127] *Philipson-Stow v IRC* [1961] AC 727, 761.

It was decided in *Studd v Cook*,[128] an appeal to the House of Lords from the Court of Session in Scotland, that the size of estate which a devisee takes depends on the law of the testator's domicile. In that case:

> A domiciled Englishman devised land in both England and Scotland to the use of X for his life, without impeachment of waste, remainder to the use of the first and every other son of X, "successively, according to their respective seniorities, in tail male". By English law X took a mere life interest, but by Scottish law he was entitled to the fee simple. It was held that the testator clearly intended the limitations of his will to be understood in their English sense, since he had used technical language familiar to English conveyancing, and that therefore his intention was effective so far as the law of Scotland permitted.

This case is distinguishable from *Re Miller, Bailie v Miller*,[129] in which:

> By a trust disposition made in Scots form but sufficient to constitute a valid will by English law, A, a domiciled Scotsman, gave his lands in Scotland and England "for behoof of my eldest son, James . . . and the heirs male of his body in fee", with remainders over. James died without issue and without having executed any disentailing assurance of the English land. He made, however, a trust disposition in Scots form, executed in the manner required by English law for the execution of wills, by which he disposed of the whole of his real and personal property. By English law, as it then stood, the will of James was ineffectual to pass the estate tail in the English land. By Scots law the will of A did not create a strict entail but gave James an interest that he could dispose of either *inter vivos* or by will. It was held that the question whether James had power to dispose of his London house by will must be decided according to English law.

It would seem that the decision in *Miller* is not inconsistent with *Studd v Cook*, where it was decided that a will should be construed according to the law of the domicile in order to ascertain the size and nature of the interest that the testator intended to give.

(v) Election

The idea that a will of immovables does not necessarily depend in all matters on the law of the situs may also be illustrated by decisions dealing with the doctrine of election.

> Suppose, for instance, that a domiciled Englishman makes a will by which he devises his son's foreign land to X but gives £50,000 out of his own property to his son. The rule of domestic English law applicable to these circumstances is that, if the testator clearly intended to dispose of the land in favour of X, the son cannot claim the whole of the £50,000 unless he adopts the testamentary disposition of the land. He must elect, ie he must either keep the land and have the legacy correspondingly reduced, or must recognise the whole of the will by taking his legacy in full and abandoning the land to X. Election is based on the presumption that a testator intends his will to take effect in its entirety.

The rule of English private international law is now well settled that, where a testator disposes of property in more countries than one, the question whether a beneficiary is put to his election is governed by the law of the testator's domicile.[130] This is so even though the subject matter of the election is land situated abroad, for, though the courts of the domicile cannot withhold the land from the person to whom it belongs according to the law of the situs, they

---

[128] (1883) 8 App Cas 577.

[129] [1914] 1 Ch 511. See also *Nelson v Bridport* (1846) 8 Beav 547; *Philipson-Stow v IRC* [1961] AC 727, 761.

[130] *Orrell v Orrell* (1871) 6 Ch App 302; *Dewar v Maitland* (1866) LR 2 Eq 834; *Re Ogilvie* [1918] 1 Ch 492. This rule was overlooked by Cohen J in *Re Allen's Estate* [1945] 2 All ER 264, as to which case see *Re Mengel's Will Trusts* [1962] Ch 791; Dicey, Morris and Collins, paras 27R-078–27-085; Morris (1945) 10 Conv (NS) 102; (1946) 24 Can Bar Rev 528.

can, in the administration of the movables which is their particular province, insist that if he retains the land contrary to the will he shall compensate the disappointed beneficiaries by relinquishing the whole or part of the legacy.[131] The English court in adopting this attitude does not interfere with the law of the situs. The foreign heir comes to the court, not as heir to the land, over which the court has no jurisdiction, but as legatee of movable property which is being administered in England. It can thus be said to him: "We have no power to dispense with the provisions of the foreign law relating to wills of land, but you come to us as legatee under the will of a testator domiciled in England; and if you claim the legacy you must also recognise the disposition which the will has purported to make of the land." It is always open to the heir to ignore the English administration and to claim the land under the territorial law.[132]

If a case involving the doctrine of election falls to be considered in England, the court turns to the law of the testator's domicile. That domicile may be English or foreign. If it is English, the court merely considers whether the domestic doctrine of election is applicable to the circumstances in question; if it is foreign, its sole guide is the law of the foreign domicile.[133] In *Balfour v Scott*:[134]

> A person domiciled in England died intestate leaving immovables in Scotland. The heir to the Scottish land was also one of the next of kin, and as such he claimed a share of the English movables. It was objected to this claim that, by the law of Scotland, an heir could not share in movables unless he consented to the immovables being massed with the movables so as to form one common subject of division. This, however, was not the English rule, and it was therefore held that the heir could take his share as one of the next of kin without complying with the rule of the law of the situs.

As far as private international law is concerned, the question of election generally arises where the testator devises his own land away from the heir by a will that is void, either formally or essentially, according to the law of the situs, but bequeaths by a valid will a legacy to the rejected heir. An issue which arises here is whether the heir must elect, ie if he claims the land on the ground that the will is invalid, can he retain the legacy in full or must he make compensation out of it to the disappointed devisee?

This situation was possible in England prior to 1837 *in a purely domestic case*, for, until the law was altered by the Wills Act 1837, the formalities necessary for a valid will varied according to whether the subject matter of the disposition was realty or personalty. In this state of the law it was established as early as 1749 in *Hearle v Greenbank*[135] that, if a testator devised his English freeholds to a stranger and bequeathed legacies to the heir-at-law in a will that was valid as to personalty but void as to realty, the heir was not bound to elect, unless there was an express direction that anyone who disputed any part of the will should forfeit all benefits.[136] He was entitled both to the land and to the legacies. Although this situation can

---

[131] There is a conflict of authority in the USA in the case of immovables as to whether the law of the domicile or the law of the situs applies: Leflar, p 557. The Restatement 2d, § 242 supports the law of the situs. In the case of movables, whilst the predominant view is that expressed in the Restatement 2d, § 265 that the law of the domicile applies, this conclusion has been justified by reference to a balancing of the predominant interests of the jurisdictions involved: *Re Clark's Estate* 21 NY 2d 478, 236 NE 2d 152 (1968); *Re Mulhern's Estate* 297 NYS 2d 485 (1969).

[132] The present account of election is confined to a case where movables are bequeathed to the owner of the foreign land, and in such a case the law of the domicile governs. If English land is left to the foreign heir and foreign land left away from the heir, then English law as that of the situs governs, irrespective of domicile.

[133] *Dundas v Dundas* (1830) 2 Dow & Cl 349.

[134] (1793) 6 Bro Parl Cas 550.

[135] (1749) 1 Ves Sen 298.

[136] *Boughton v Boughton* (1750) 2 Ves Sen 12.

no longer arise in the case of an English will disposing of English property, it may well be so where the testator is domiciled abroad. Suppose that a testator domiciled in Italy makes a will by which he devises his English entailed interests to X and bequeaths a legacy to Y, who is his heir-at-law according to English law. The will is formally valid by Italian law but ineffective by English law. In such a case as this it has been held, following the principle of *Hearle v Greenbank*, that the English heir is not put to his election.[137] He can claim the land as heir against the invalid will of realty, and retain the legacy under the bequest which, since its validity falls to be determined by the law of the domicile, is invulnerable. This is an example of that "special tenderness" which the courts have always shown to the heir-at-law of English land,[138] though given that the heir has been abolished for fee simple estates in England it is doubtful whether a similar indulgence will be extended to those relatives who are entitled to the residuary estate of an intestate person. It is an inequitable privilege established by the courts at a time when they particularly favoured the heir-at-law and frowned on any attempt to defeat his rights.

This tenderness has never been shown to a foreign heir, ie to the heir entitled to take foreign land under the rules of intestate succession recognised by the law of the situs. The attitude of English law with regard to election in a case of this sort can be illustrated by *Re Ogilvie*,[139] where the facts; were as follows:

> A domiciled Englishwoman devised her land in Paraguay to a charity and gave legacies to the persons who were the obligatory heirs of the land according to Paraguayan law. The charitable devise was void by the law of the situs to the extent of four-fifths, which was the portion reserved for the obligatory heirs. Moreover, according to the law of the situs, the right of an heir to his legal portion was not affected by any other benefit that he might have received under the will.

In a case of this description, English law, as being the law of the testator's domicile, determines whether the foreign heir is to be put to his election. This raises the question of construction whether the testator has manifested an intention to pass the foreign land for, if he has, then despite the invalidity of the will by the law of the situs the doctrine of election becomes applicable.[140] The rule evolved by English courts on this matter is that the foreign property must be described either specifically or by necessary implication.[141] Thus, if a testator uses only general descriptive words, as for example where he says, "I devise all my estate, whatsoever or wheresoever, whether in possession or reversion", he is taken to intend that his disposition shall be restricted to such land as he is empowered to pass by a will executed in that particular form.[142] There was no difficulty of this sort in *Re Ogilvie*, since the testatrix had shown a plain intention to pass the Paraguayan property, and therefore it was held that the obligatory heirs must elect between what they took under the law of the situs owing to the invalidity of the charitable devise and what they were given in the shape of legacies by the will.[143]

---

137 *Re De Virte* [1915] 1 Ch 920.
138 *Re Ogilvie* [1918] 1 Ch 492, 496.
139 [1918] 1 Ch 492.
140 *Trotter v Trotter* (1828) 4 Bli NS 502.
141 *Maxwell v Maxwell* (1852) 16 Beav 106; *Orrell v Orrell* (1871) 6 Ch App 302.
142 *Maxwell v Maxwell*, supra.
143 Cf the decision in *Brown v Gregson* [1920] AC 860, where it was held that a foreign heir will not be put to his election if it would be impossible by the law of the situs to give effect to the disposition of the foreign land intended by the testator.

(vi) Revocation

As with the case of a will of movables,[144] a will relating to immovables may be revoked by a later valid will and its validity will depend on the rules discussed earlier.[145] It should be mentioned that the provisions of the Wills Act 1963 relating to the testamentary revocation of an earlier will apply to a will of immovables as to a will of movables.[146] In the case of revocation by destruction or obliteration of the will, there is US authority for referring this issue to the law of the situs, as in *Re Barrie's Estate*[147] where the testatrix, who was domiciled in Illinois, wrote "void" across the will several times. The effect of such an act was determined not by the law of Illinois but by that of Iowa, the situs of her immovable property.

Finally, in the case of revocation by subsequent marriage, we have seen that,[148] in the case of movables, such revocation is generally to be regarded as an aspect of matrimonial law to be governed by the domiciliary law at the time of marriage rather than of death. Such an approach would indicate that, in the case of the revocation of a will of immovables by a subsequent marriage, reference should also be made to the law of the domicile at marriage and not to the law of the situs. Despite one English decision to the contrary,[149] it is suggested that the view just expressed is correct and support for it is to be found in the Australian decision in *Re Micallef's Estate*:[150]

> The testator, who was at all material times domiciled and resident in Malta, owned land in New South Wales. In 1970 he made a valid will disposing of all his property, including the land. He married in Malta in 1972 and died in 1973. Under Maltese law, the marriage did not revoke the will; under New South Wales law it did.

The court could find no policy justifying the imposition of New South Wales law on Maltese parties to a Maltese marriage. Furthermore, there was no justification for departing from the rule applicable to movable property.[151]

4. EUROPEAN HARMONISATION CONCERNING SUCCESSION AND WILLS

Previous harmonisation measures in the field of succession have been of mixed result. The successful harmonisation of choice of law rules in relation to the formal validity of wills[152] is to be contrasted with the disappointing outcome of work at the Hague Conference on Private International Law in producing the 1989 Hague Convention on the Law Applicable to Succession to the Estates of Deceased Persons.[153]

With regard to the European Community, the 1998 Vienna Action Plan[154] placed among its priorities the adoption of a European instrument concerning conflict rules of succession.[155]

---

[144] Supra, pp 1348–51.

[145] Supra, p 1352 et seq; see also *In the Estate of Vickers* (2001-02) 4 ITELR 584; *Re Baldry (Deceased)* [2004] WTLR 609 (Fam Div), in respect of which see Simm 2005 TEL & TJ (65) (Apr) 15; *Lamothe v Lamothe* [2006] EWHC 1387; [2006] WTLR 1431.

[146] 1963 Act, s 2(1)(c), supra, p 1348.

[147] 240 Iowa 431, 35 NW 2d 658 (1949).

[148] Supra, pp 1350–1.

[149] *Re Caithness* (1891) 7 TLR 354. See Dicey, Morris and Collins, para 27-089.

[150] [1977] 2 NSWLR 929; and see *Davies v Davies* (1915) 24 DLR 737, 740.

[151] [1977] 2 NSWLR 929, 933.

[152] 1961 Hague Convention on the Conflicts of Laws Relating to the Form of Testamentary Dispositions, leading in the United Kingdom to the Wills Act 1963.

[153] See supra, p 1326, n 2.

[154] OJ 1999 C 19.

[155] See generally supra, Chapter 1; Crawford and Carruthers [2005] Jur Rev 251.

The Hague Programme[156] called upon the European Commission to present a Green Paper covering jurisdiction, applicable law, and recognition, together with administrative measures relating to wills. The Commission's Green Paper on Succession and Wills was issued in 2006,[157] commencing a broad-based consultation process concerning testate and intestate succession having an international dimension. In October 2009, the European Commission announced the publication of their proposal. The resulting Regulation, the Succession Regulation,[158] was completed in July 2012 and applies to the estates of individuals who die after 17 August 2015.[159] The United Kingdom did not "opt-in" to the Succession Regulation,[160] therefore the common law will continue to apply in England.

The Succession Regulation provides rules relating to jurisdiction, applicable law and the recognition and enforcement of decisions as well as the enforcement of authentic instruments. It also introduces a European Certificate of Succession. The default basis for jurisdiction and applicable law is the habitual residence of the deceased at the time of death.[161] However the Regulation also provides choice of court,[162] and importantly, choice of law clauses.[163] The choice of law provisions have universal application,[164] so they can assist British nationals who are habitually resident in another EU Member State. An individual can select the law of their nationality under Article 22 of the Succession Regulation. If the individual has more than one nationality they can select whichever one they wish.[165] The designated law will apply to the succession as a whole,[166] including the substantive validity of the act (or document) where the choice of law clause was made.[167] Therefore if an English national makes a choice of law clause in favour of English law in a will, the court with jurisdiction will have to apply English law to determine the succession and the substantive validity of the will. This would be English internal law only as the application of renvoi is excluded in relation to choice of law clauses.[168] English nationals living in the EU would be wise to include a choice of law clause in their will, if they want English law to continue to determine their succession.[169]

5. POWERS OF APPOINTMENT EXERCISED BY WILL[170]

Under English law, instead of disposing directly of his property, a person, either in a settlement or in his will, can nominate a person who, in his own

---

[156] OJ 2005 C 53.

[157] COM (2005) 65 final. See also Commission Staff Working Paper, Annex to the Green Paper on Succession and Wills (SEC (2005) 270); Opinion of the European Economic and Social Committee on the Green Paper on Succession and Wills (OJ 2006 C 28); and European Parliament Report with Recommendations to the Commission (A6-0359/2006).

[158] Regulation (EU) No 650/2012 of the European Parliament and of the Council of 4 July 2012 on jurisdiction, applicable law, recognition and enforcement of decisions and enforcement of authentic instruments in matters of succession and on the creation of a European Certificate of Succession OJ L 201/107.

[159] Succession Regulation, Arts 83 and 84.

[160] Hansard, HL Vol 502, Part no 17, col 141 (16 December 2009).

[161] Succession Regulation, Arts 4 and 21.

[162] Arts 5–6.

[163] Arts 22 and Art 7.

[164] Art 20.

[165] Art 22(1).

[166] Art 23.

[167] Art 22(3).

[168] Art 34(2).

[169] For further analysis of the Succession Regulation see, for example, E Crawford and J Carruthers, "Speculation on the Operation of the Succession Regulation 650/2012: Tales of the Unexpected" (2014) 22 *European Review of Private Law* 847.

[170] Fridman (1960) 9 ICLQ 1.

will,[171] shall have the power to specify the ultimate recipient of the property which is the subject matter of the original settlement or will. For example:

> A in his will could leave the property to trustees to pay the income to B and then to transfer the capital to whoever B, in his will, appointed. In this case, A is described as the donor of the power of appointment and B is the donee of the power, or appointor. Whoever B selects as the beneficiary is described as the appointee.

There are two kinds of powers of appointment—general and special—and we shall see that this may be of significance in determining the appropriate choice of law rules. If the donee of the power, B in the above example, can appoint anyone he chooses, including himself, the power is general. If, however, the donor of the power, A, limits, in the instrument creating the power, the people or class of people among whom B can appoint, the power is special. One significance of the difference is that in the case of a special power B, the appointor, is clearly seen to be disposing of A's property, rather than his own, for A, the donee, has determined the class within which B must choose. In the case of a general power, though it may in strict theory still be true that B is disposing of A's property, this is more apparent than real, as B has the same freedom of choice as if the property was his own, including the power to appoint himself.

Choice of law problems may arise from powers of appointment exercised by will in a number of ways. It may be that the donor, the appointor and appointee all have different domiciles. Whilst it might seem logical to refer the essential validity of, for instance, the will of the donor which created the power (the instrument of creation) to the law of his domicile on death and the validity of the exercise of the power by will (the instrument of appointment) to the law of the donee's domicile on death, problems arise if the donee dies domiciled in a civil law country, such as France, where the concept of a power of appointment is unknown. The only practical answer would seem to be to refer to the law governing the instrument of creation. There is the further problem that, in the case of immovables, the law of the situs may be different from that of any of the relevant domiciles, though most of the cases are in fact concerned with movables.[172]

It can readily be argued that the law governing the instrument of creation should govern in the case of a special power, for the donee is manifestly no more than the agent for disposal of the appointor's property. As we have seen, this is less obviously true in the case of a general power which then poses a preliminary choice of law problem. If the main choice of law rule may depend on whether a power is special or general, by what law is that issue to be determined? After examining that question, we shall consider the other more general choice of law matters relating to powers of appointment exercised by will.

(a) Special and general powers

It is not always easy in a domestic system of law to decide whether a power is general or special. Also, more significantly, different legal systems which are familiar with powers of appointment may classify them differently.[173] As a matter of principle, it seems right that the nature of the power, ie as to whether it is special or general, should be determined by the law governing the instrument which created the power.

---

[171] It could also be a further settlement, *inter vivos*, but our concern here is with powers exercised by will.

[172] It should be assumed that the discussion relates to movables, unless immovables are referred to.

[173] See Dicey, Morris and Collins, paras 27R-098–27-101.

(b) Capacity

Considerations different from those relevant to testamentary capacity[174] apply to the question of capacity to exercise a testamentary power of appointment given by an English instrument to an appointor domiciled abroad. The obvious principle here is that, just as in the case where a testator disposes of his own property, capacity must be tested by the law of the appointor's domicile. There is indeed no doubt that, if the domiciliary law's rule on the matter is satisfied, the appointment is good. It is enough, whether the power is general or special, that the appointor is of full capacity by the law of his own domicile, even though he is incapable by the law that governs the instrument by which the power was created, ie the will. For example, in *Re Lewal's Settlement Trusts*,[175] the wife had a general power of appointment under an English marriage settlement. She had originally been domiciled in England but on her marriage had acquired the French domicile of her husband. In her will, made when she was aged nineteen, she appointed her husband her "legataire universel", and ten years later she died domiciled in France. Under English law, she had no capacity to exercise the power, being under twenty-one; under French law, she was capable of disposing of half the property she could have disposed of had she been twenty-one. The court applied French law[176] to the issue of her capacity, with the result that half the property subject to the power went to her husband, and the other half went as in default of appointment.

But this does not conclude the matter. What of the converse case, ie where the appointor has capacity by the law governing the instrument by which the power was created, but not under the law of his domicile? The view taken by English law is that it is the instrument which creates the power, and not the one by which the power is exercised, which is the governing instrument, and that the appointor is a mere agent to carry out the wishes of the donor. The appointee takes under the instrument of creation, not under the will of the appointor. It follows, therefore, that an appointment is valid if the appointor has capacity by the law that governs the instrument of creation, though he may be incapable by the law of his own domicile. It may well be objected that even if the appointor is regarded as merely the agent of the donor he should not be free to do what, according to the law to which he is subject, he is incapable of doing. Nevertheless, to treat him as an agent is not unreasonable in the case of a special power, for here, as has been seen, his function is to select the beneficiaries from the class already designated by the donor. He is in no sense disposing of his own property. But there is little to justify a reference to the law governing the instrument of creation in the case of a general power, for the appointor in such a case can scarcely be regarded as a mere agent to implement the wishes of the donor.

The correct rule probably is, therefore, that the testamentary exercise of a general power is invalid for want of capacity unless the appointor is capable by the law of his domicile; but that in the case of a special power the exercise is valid if he is capable either by the law of his domicile or by the law that governs the instrument of creation.[177]

(c) Formal validity

A power of appointment exercisable by will is frequently given by an English settlement or an English will to a person who ultimately dies domiciled in a foreign country or who makes

---

[174] Supra, pp 1339–40 and 1352.

[175] [1918] 2 Ch 391.

[176] The English marriage settlement also provided that the appointment should be made by will "executed in such manner as to be valid according to the law" of the appointor's domicile.

[177] Cf Fridman (1960) 9 ICLQ, 1, 2–11. For a full discussion of the whole subject see Dicey, Morris and Collins, paras 27-102–27-103.

his will in a foreign country. In such circumstances it is essential to ascertain the legal system that determines whether the formalities attending the testamentary exercise of the power are sufficient. The Wills Act 1963 has extended and amended the previous law. The position now is as follows.

First, a will so far as it exercises a power of appointment is to be treated as properly executed if it complies with the requirements of any one of the legal systems specified in the Act.[178] Thus the connecting factors now qualified to determine the governing law are the place of execution of the will or the nationality, domicile or habitual residence of the testator, or the law of the situs in the case of immovables.

Secondly, the will is to be treated as properly executed if its execution conforms to the law that governs the essential validity of the instrument creating the power.[179] If the power is created by an English instrument, it will be validly executed if it conforms with English law;[180] and if creation is by a foreign instrument, then there should be conformity with that foreign law.[181]

There is a further provision in the 1963 Act, resolving some tiresome problems in the law before 1964,[182] that the testamentary exercise of a power of appointment is not formally invalid by reason only of a failure to observe a formality required by the instrument of creation.[183]

(d) Essential validity

The determination of the law to govern the essential validity of a disposition resulting from the exercise of a power of appointment depends on whether the power is general or special. The effect of the appointment in the case of a special power is determined by the legal system to which the instrument that created the power is subject, for, since the appointor is merely the agent through whom the donor of the power designates the beneficiaries, the latter take under the instrument of creation.[184] Thus, in *Pouey v Hordern*[185] a domiciled Frenchwoman, who had a special power of appointment given by an English settlement, was held capable under English law of exercising it in a manner that was incompatible with the French doctrine of community.

In the case of general powers, the property given thereunder may be treated by the donee either as if it were his own, ie as a mass combined with his own, or quite separately therefrom. It is a question of construction as to how it is to be considered.[186] In the first case, where the donee treats the settled property as his own, the Court of Appeal in *Re Pryce*[187] held that the operation and effect of the donee's appointment must be determined by the law that governs the will by which he exercises the power, ie by the law of his last domicile. Danckwerts J in *Re Waite's Settlement*[188] preferred to apply the law governing the instrument creating the power, rather than the law of the donee's domicile, despite the fact that the case related to a

---

[178] Supra, p 1339.
[179] Wills Act 1963, s 2(1)(d). Essential validity of wills is discussed, supra, pp 1344–7 and 1353.
[180] Eg *Murphy v Deichler* [1909] AC 446.
[181] See (1958) Cmnd 491, para 11(c).
[182] See, eg, *Barretto v Young* [1900] 2 Ch 339.
[183] Wills Act 1963, s 2(2).
[184] See *Pouey v Hordern* [1900] 1 Ch 492, 494.
[185] Ibid.
[186] *Re Pryce* [1911] 2 Ch 286, 295.
[187] Ibid; and see *Re Lewal's Settlement Trusts* [1918] 2 Ch 391.
[188] [1958] Ch 100; and see *Re McMorran* [1958] Ch 624, 633–4; for criticisms, see Dicey, Morris and Collins, paras 27-122–27-124.

general power where the funds were massed, but his decision was disapproved in *Re Khan's Settlement*.[189] In the latter case:

> The testator, the Nawab of Bhopal, domiciled in India, made a settlement in which he reserved to himself a general power of appointment by will. This settlement was to be governed by English law, apart from a clause referring to his heirs under Indian law. His English will gave legacies to three of his seven heirs, in excess of the free estate under the will, and then executed the power of appointment in favour of all his heirs. Under Indian law, the domiciliary law, the consent of all heirs was necessary before payment of legacies to any heirs could be made, and this consent was refused. Thus, if Indian law governed, the legacies could not be paid out of the free estate or the settlement funds, whilst there was no such restriction under English law, the law governing the instrument of creation.

Russell LJ concluded that he was bound to follow *Re Pryce*[190] rather than *Re Waite's Settlement*.[191] He decided that the free estate and the settled fund formed one mass, the distribution of which was to be governed by Indian law, and the legacies could not be paid. He thought "it a logical consequence of the grounds of those decisions in cases of blending or massing . . . that the settled funds are subjected to the whole succession law of the domicile of the appointor, including any restriction on testation".[192]

If, in the case of a general power, the settled funds are not treated as having been taken out of the settlement and massed with the donee's own funds, then, as in *Re Mégret*,[193] the validity of the exercise of the power of appointment is governed, not by the law of the domicile of the donee, but by the law governing the instrument of creation, as in the case of special powers. This can be justified on the ground that in neither of these cases is the donee in reality disposing of his own funds.

All the cases discussed so far concern movable property. In the case of the essential validity of the exercise by will of a general power of appointment over immovables, there is clear authority that this should be governed by the law of the situs of the property.[194]

(e) Construction

In accordance with the principle applicable to wills generally, the construction of a power of appointment is governed by the law intended by the testator (or appointor) which, in the case of movables, is presumed to be that of his domicile when the will was made.[195] This appears to be true whether the power is special[196] or general.[197] If it appears that the testator intended a law other than that of his domicile at the time of making the will to apply, as in *Re Price*,[198] then that other law governs the construction.

But the question has arisen whether the intention of the testator is decisive if it indicates a foreign law that has no knowledge of powers.

> Suppose, for instance, that a testator, domiciled in France and having a general power of appointment by virtue of an English settlement, makes a valid will according to French law. The will does not refer in any way to the power but merely disposes of the property in general

---

189 [1966] Ch 567; cf *Re Fenston's Settlement* [1971] 1 WLR 1640, 1647.
190 [1911] 2 Ch 286.
191 *Supra.*
192 [1966] Ch 567, 578.
193 [1901] 1 Ch 547; and see *Re Pryce* [1911] 2 Ch 286, 296–297; cf Fridman (1960) 9 ICLQ 1, 9–10.
194 *Re Hernando* (1884) 27 Ch D 284; and see *Murray v Champernowne* [1901] 2 IR 232.
195 *Supra*, pp 1339–40.
196 *Re McMorran* [1958] Ch 624; and see *Re Walker* [1908] 1 Ch 560.
197 *Durie's Trustees v Osborne* 1960 SC 444; Gareth Jones (1961) 10 ICLQ 624.
198 [1900] 1 Ch 442; and see *Mitchell and Baxter v Davies* (1875) 3 R 208.

words. A power to dispose of property not belonging to the donor (which is the true nature of a power of appointment) is unknown in French law.[199] The will, therefore, if construed according to French law, can scarcely be said to constitute an execution of the power. Can English law be applied to the issue of construction?

After considerable judicial conflict this question has been answered in the affirmative.[200] The French court, being ignorant of the peculiar power of disposition thus given by an English instrument, would have to turn to English law (with reference to which the testator obviously wrote) in order to ascertain the nature of the right and the manner in which it might be exercised.

A consequence of this conclusion is that section 27 of the Wills Act 1837 may apply to wills of persons who are domiciled other than in England. Under section 27 a general devise or bequest is construed as exercising a general power of appointment unless a contrary intention appears in the will. In the above example, the testator's French will falls to be construed in accordance with section 27 as exercising a general power of appointment.[201] Were the power merely special, it would not be held to be exercised under section 27.

(f) Revocation

A power of appointment over movables exercisable by will may be revoked under the law of the donee's domicile.[202] A power over movables or immovables will be revoked if it is revoked by a later will properly executed under the Wills Act 1963.[203] Under section 2(1)(d) of the 1963 Act, a will so far as it exercises a power of appointment is validly executed if it complies with the law governing the essential validity of the power. This does not apply, however, to a will which merely revokes a power of appointment without providing another power in its place. Finally a power exercisable by will may be revoked by the subsequent marriage of the testator according to the law of his domicile at the time of his marriage, rather than of his death.[204] Where, however, the testator is domiciled in England at the time of his marriage then, under section 18(2) of the Wills Act 1837,[205] an exercise of a power of appointment by will takes effect, "notwithstanding the subsequent marriage unless the property so appointed would in default of appointment pass to his personal representatives".

---

[199] Contrast the position in Scotland: *Re McMorran* [1958] Ch 624, 634–635; *Durie's Trustees v Osborne*, supra.

[200] *Re Simpson* [1916] 1 Ch 502; *Re Wilkinson's Settlement* [1917] 1 Ch 620; *Re Lewal's Settlement* [1918] 2 Ch 391; *Re Waite's Settlement* [1958] Ch 100; *Re Fenston's Settlement* [1971] 3 All ER 1092. Decisions to the contrary are *Re D'Este's Settlement Trusts* [1903] 1 Ch 898; *Re Scholefield* [1905] 2 Ch 408.

[201] Eg *Re Lewal's Settlement*, supra; cf *Re Fenston's Settlement*, supra, where the will, as construed by the law of the domicile, contained no "bequest" to anyone.

[202] *Velasco v Coney* [1934] P 143. Presumably, compliance with the law of the situs is required in the case of immovables.

[203] Ss 1, 2(1)(b), (c).

[204] Supra, pp 1350–1.

[205] As substituted by the Administration of Justice Act 1982, s 18(1).

37

MATRIMONIAL PROPERTY[1]

1. Introduction	1365	(c) Formal validity	1377
2. Assignment Where There is no		(d) Essential validity	1378
Ante-nuptial Contract	1366	4. Matrimonial Property Rights and	
(a) Movables	1366	Divorce	1378
(b) Immovables	1371	5. Property Rights Arising from Other	
3. Assignment Where There is an		Adult Relationships	1379
Ante-nuptial Contract	1372	(a) Civil Partnership Act 2004	1379
(a) The general rule	1372	(b) Cohabitation	1380
(b) Capacity	1375	6. European Proposals for Reform	1380

1. INTRODUCTION

The problem that confronts us in this chapter is how to determine what system of law regulates the rights of a husband and wife in the movable and immovable property which either of them may possess at the time of marriage or may acquire afterwards. Important consequences may ensue depending on which law is chosen. For instance, the result of choosing one particular legal system may be that the property of the wife passes entirely to the husband, as was substantially the case in England prior to 1883. Again, if an Englishwoman marries a Belgian and Belgian law is regarded as the governing system, it may be that the parties become subject to "community of goods" under which everything that belongs to either spouse at the time of marriage or that is acquired by either afterwards is owned by them jointly. They become joint co-owners of everything by the mere fact of marriage.[2]

In determining the choice of law rules for identifying the appropriate matrimonial property regime, it will be necessary to look separately at two types of case—first where the parties have not made an ante-nuptial contract and, secondly, where there is such a contract.

---

[1] Marsh, *Marital Property in the Conflict of Laws* (1952); Goldberg (1970) 19 ICLQ 357; McLachlan (1986) 12 NZUL Rev 66; Scoles (1988) II Hague Recueil 9, 17–53; Davie (1993) 42 ICLQ 855; and Hartley in Fawcett (ed), *Reform and Development of Private International Law* (2002), Chapter 9. There is a Hague Convention on the Law Applicable to Matrimonial Property (1978) but it has not been signed by the United Kingdom: see Philip (1976) 24 AJCL 307; Glenn (1977) 54 Can Bar Rev 586.

[2] For a valuable exposition of the different systems found in the world see Rheinstein and Glendon, *International Encyclopedia of Comparative Law* (1980), Vol iv, Chapter 4, pp 47–118. There is a tendency in civil law countries now to allow the spouses the separate administration of their property during marriage, but to constitute the community of property on death or divorce: "deferred community". See Hartley, op cit, p 231; for France, see Amos and Walton, *Introduction to French Law*, (1966) 3rd edn, pp 379–92; for Germany, see Leyser (1958) 7 AJCL 276.

2. ASSIGNMENT WHERE THERE IS NO ANTE-NUPTIAL CONTRACT[3]

(a) Movables

(i) Application of matrimonial domicile

Until recently the rule,[4] long-prevailing, was that the effect of marriage on the proprietary rights of the parties in movables should be determined by the law of the husband's domicile[5] at the time of the marriage.[6]

Whilst acceptable against the legal background of the unity of domicile principle,[7] it is highly doubtful that the rule in favour of application of the law of the husband's domicile is acceptable in light of the prohibition upon discrimination on the grounds of sex contained in the Article 14 of the European Convention on Human Rights.[8] Since 1974 a wife has been capable of acquiring a domicile independent of her husband.[9] One effect of this is that it is no longer the case that the law of the husband's domicile ought automatically to govern the spouses' rights to movable property.[10] Instead, as a general presumption, the law of the matrimonial domicile ought to apply. The law of the matrimonial domicile should be ascertained thus: in cases where the husband and wife are of the same domicile at the time of the marriage, the law of the common domicile should apply;[11] and in cases where the parties are not of the same domicile at the time of the marriage, the law of the matrimonial domicile should be that of "the country with which the parties and the marriage have the closest connection, equal weight being given to connections with each party".[12] Equal weight, however, should not necessarily be given to each and every connection;[13] the test is a qualitative one, to ascertain the "centre of gravity"[14] of the marriage.

In those cases where the husband and wife are of the same domicile at the time of the marriage, it must be asked whether account should be taken of their intention to set up home soon after marriage in another legal system.[15] Should the presumption in favour of application of the matrimonial domicile at the time of the marriage be rebutted if, in pursuance of

---

[3] Cf Goldberg (1970) 19 ICLQ 557 who maintains that there is always a contract which may be express, implied or presumed.

[4] Or presumption: *Re Egerton's Will Trusts* [1956] Ch 593, 607 (Roxburgh J).

[5] Subject to the application of a foreign law not being contrary to the public policy of the forum: *Vladi v Vladi* (1987) 39 DLR (4th) 563.

[6] Dicey, Morris and Collins, para 28-010; *Welch v Tennent* [1891] AC 639, 644. For a case where a retrospective change in the law to a community regime was accepted, see *Topolski v R* (1978) 90 DLR (3d) 66.

[7] Supra, p 147. As Hartley points out, the "leading cases almost all date from the nineteenth century. They are based on social attitudes so at odds with those of today that the legal rules laid down may no longer be acceptable" (op cit, p 215).

[8] Dicey, Morris and Collins, para 28-011.

[9] Domicile and Matrimonial Proceedings Act 1973, s 1.

[10] Cf Hartley, op cit, pp 226–7; and for Scotland, Crawford and Carruthers, para 13-10.

[11] Dicey, Morris and Collins, para 28-020. Cf, for Scotland, Family Law (Scotland) Act 2006, s 39(2).

[12] Dicey, Morris and Collins, para 28-011. This solution is preferable to that which has been articulated for Scots law in s 39(3) of the Family Law (Scotland) Act 2006, which ignores the very fact of marriage. "If spouses are domiciled in different countries then, for the purposes of any question in relation to the rights of the spouses to each other's moveable property arising by virtue of the marriage, the spouses shall be taken to have the same rights to such property as they had immediately before the marriage."

[13] Eg the situs of the matrimonial home is likely to be more significant than the nationality/ante-nuptial domicile of the parties.

[14] Hartley, op cit, p 226.

[15] *Corbet v Waddell* (1879) 7 R (Ct of Sess) 200, 208; and see Anton, para 20.08; Story, paras 191–9; Westlake, s 36; Crawford and Carruthers, para 13-10.

their previous agreement, the parties in fact acquire a fresh domicile within a reasonable time after the marriage? The merit of this approach is that it meets the not unusual case where the parties intend to settle immediately after marriage in another country and in fact do so.

That a rigid application of the law of the domicile at the time of the marriage[16] has caused hardship can be illustrated by the facts of the South African case, *Frankel's Estate v The Master*.[17]

> H, whose domicile of origin was German, and W, domiciled in Czechoslovakia, were married in Czechoslovakia in 1933. At the time of the marriage the parties had definitely agreed that they would leave Europe for good and settle permanently in Johannesburg. They established their home in that city four months after the marriage. After working there for four years, they moved to Durban with the intention of remaining there permanently. Eleven years later, H died. According to the law of South Africa, the parties had married in community of property, but according to German law the doctrine of community was inapplicable. If South African law applied, as W claimed, death duties were not payable. The Appellate Division of the Supreme Court of South Africa held unanimously that German law applied.

Thus the proprietary rights of the parties were subjected to the law of Germany, a country which the parties had abandoned and which, it may be surmised, they would be little inclined to revisit. To this extent, the civil status of a German was indelibly impressed on the husband against his will and, in turn, on the wife, against her will. Indeed, South African courts have applied the law of the domicile at marriage including retrospective changes in that law effected after the spouses had become domiciled in South Africa.[18] On the other hand, reliance on the intended matrimonial domicile does suffer from the disadvantage, here as elsewhere,[19] that there is no certainty that it will ever be acquired.

Whether the test of the intended matrimonial domicile would be accepted by English law was not squarely raised until the case of *Re Egerton's Will Trusts*,[20] where Roxburgh J stated the law to the effect that there is a presumption that the mutual property rights of spouses are determined by the law of the husband's domicile[21] at the time of the marriage. In his Lordship's view, that presumption was capable of being rebutted by an express contract that some other law should apply,[22] or by a tacit contract inferred from the conduct of the parties.[23] It was judicially admitted that application of the law of the husband's domicile at the time of the marriage would be ousted if the intention to adopt the law of another domicile could be deduced from the facts of the particular case. A tacit agreement would be sufficient to rebut the primary presumption. It has not been judicially tested whether the presumption in favour of applying the matrimonial domicile at the time of the marriage is open to rebuttal in like manner. It is submitted that rebuttal should be available in these circumstances, to be inferred from the conduct of the parties, if the circumstances justify the inference.

But what the judge in *Egerton's* case repudiated is the suggestion that an ante-nuptial agreement to establish the matrimonial home in another country, even though carried out with reasonable promptitude, would be sufficient per se to rebut the presumption and to let in the law of the new domicile. To have this effect, the circumstances must warrant the inference

---

[16] In this case, the law of the husband's domicile, not the matrimonial domicile.
[17] 1950 (1) SA 220 (AD), analysed by Ellison Kahn (1950) 3 ILQ 439; and Hartley, op cit, pp 227–9.
[18] *Sperling v Sperling* 1975 (3) SA 707 (AD).
[19] This is discussed generally, supra, p 910.
[20] [1956] Ch 593; Carter (1957) 33 BYBIL 345.
[21] And now, the matrimonial domicile: see supra, p 1366 et seq.
[22] *Re Martin, Loustalan v Loustalan* [1900] P 211, 240.
[23] [1956] Ch 593, 607.

that the parties intended not merely to acquire a new domicile, but also to subject their proprietary rights to the law of that domicile. The judgment makes it clear that everything must turn on the precise facts of each case, including the reliability of the evidence by which the alleged agreement to change the domicile is supported, the length of time that may have elapsed before the fulfilment of that agreement and even the financial circumstances of the spouses.[24]

In *Egerton's* case itself the particular circumstances did not warrant any such inference. The facts were these:

> In 1932, the testator domiciled in England married a woman domiciled in France. The parties agreed, before the marriage, to settle in France, but the testator did not acquire a French domicile until some time after September 1934, which he retained until his death. The question to be decided was whether his estate should be administered on the footing that he and his wife were subject to the French regime of community of property at the time of the marriage.

Roxburgh J held that the parties' agreement to settle in France did not render their proprietary rights subject to French law. The equivocal nature of the agreement which contemplated no immediate change of home, but only one that should be effected "as soon as possible"; the long period that in fact elapsed before the new domicile was acquired; the lack of any evidence that the parties even appreciated the difference between the property regimes of the two countries: all these precluded the inference that in the minds of the parties the law of England was to be supplanted by that of France. On the other hand, it is submitted that in *Frankel's* case the only reasonable intention to attribute to the parties was to sever all links with the German domicile of origin of the husband as quickly as possible.[25]

(ii) Effect of a change of domicile

A further question may arise—what is the effect of a subsequent change of the matrimonial domicile? Are the mutual proprietary rights of the spouses affected by the change? Many legal systems adopt what has been called the doctrine of immutability,[26] according to which the rights of property in movables as fixed by the law of the matrimonial domicile at the time of the marriage are unaffected by the acquisition of a fresh domicile. Thus the established rule in France is that the law of the matrimonial domicile governs the rights of the spouses in movables, whether existing at the time of the marriage or acquired later, and continues to govern them despite a change of domicile. This is so even with respect to movables acquired in the new domicile.[27] The prevailing rule in the USA is not so comprehensive. The law of the matrimonial domicile at the time of the marriage continues to govern movables owned at that time, but movables acquired later are subject to the law of the parties' domicile at the time of acquisition.[28]

---

[24] [1956] Ch 593, 605.

[25] *Devos v Devos* (1970) 10 DLR (3d) 603 might similarly be criticised, for there the matrimonial domicile was held to be Belgian, where the husband was domiciled at the time of the marriage, even though the parties emigrated to Canada less than three months later. Contrast *Vien Estate v Vien Estate* (1988) 49 DLR (4th) 558.

[26] Wolff, pp 360–1.

[27] Batiffol and Lagarde, *Droit International Privé* (1983) 7th edn, Vol II, pp 356–65; and see Juenger (1981) 81 Col LR 1061, 1062–6.

[28] Scoles, Hay, Borchers and Symeonides, Chapter 14; Juenger, op cit; cf Restatement 2d, § 258 which adopts a "most significant relationship" test, though retaining emphasis on the law of the domicile at the time of acquisition; see *Re Crichton's Estate* 20 NY 2d 124, 228 NE 2d 799 (1967) (the Louisiana courts have been constrained by the US Constitution to uphold this decision despite their clear view that the New York decision was erroneous: *Crichton v Successor of Crichton* 232 So 2d 109 (1970); though see now La Civ Code 2334 (1980)); cf *Wyatt v Fulrath* 16 NY 2d 169, 211 NE 2d 673 (1965).

It has been said that, according to English private international law, if the marriage domicile[29] is abandoned, the proprietary rights of the spouses are governed by the law of the new domicile. It is extremely doubtful, however, whether English law is committed to this doctrine of mutability.[30] The one case invariably cited in support of this doctrine is the Scots decision in *Lashley v Hog*.[31] When analysed, however, this appears to be quite irrelevant to the controversy. The facts were these:

> Hog, a native of Scotland, married an Englishwoman at a time when he was domiciled in England. There was no marriage settlement. After living in England for fifteen years the parties acquired a domicile in Scotland. Hog survived his wife and died in 1789. After his death, his daughter, Mrs Lashley, brought an action in the Scottish court claiming as the representative of her mother a share in her father's movables which, according to the then law of Scotland, were subject to the doctrine of community of goods. The basis of her claim was that, on the change of domicile from England to Scotland, her father's proprietary rights vis-à-vis his wife became restricted by the Scottish rule of community.

The House of Lords held that Scots law governed Mrs Lashley's claim, and that she was entitled in right of her mother to a share of the movables owned by her father at the time of her mother's death.[32]

What was the ratio decidendi? Was it that the rights of the wife with regard to the matrimonial property were enlarged as a result of the change of domicile? It would seem not. The House of Lords took the view that the matter "turned on testamentary and not on matrimonial law".[33] The so-called community of goods did not give the wife on marriage a proprietary interest similar to that recognised, for instance, by Belgian law, but only a hope of succeeding to the property.[34] The question therefore, was not: Were the rights of the wife enlarged by the change of domicile? but: What were the succession rights of the wife or her representative on the death of her husband? Thus Lord Halsbury, speaking of the decision in a later case, said:

> If the wife by the marriage in Scotland[35] acquired no proprietary rights whatever, but only what is called a hope of a certain distribution upon the husband's death, it is intelligible that that right of distribution, or by whatever name it is called, should be dependent upon the husband's domicil as following the ordinary rule that the law of a person's domicil regulates the succession of his movable property. But if by the marriage the wife acquires as part of that contract relation a real proprietary right, it would be quite unintelligible that the husband's act[36] should dispose of what was not his; and herein, I think, is to be found the key to Lord Eldon's judgment.[37]

The last sentence of this statement is a repudiation of the doctrine of mutability, for if the wife's acquired rights cannot be defeated by a change of domicile, neither can they be enlarged.

The position in Scots law now is governed by the Family Law (Scotland) Act 2006, section 39(5) of which provides that: "A change of domicile by a spouse (or both spouses) shall not

---

[29] Formerly the law of the husband's domicile, but now the matrimonial domicile.

[30] Marsh, op cit, pp 103–8.

[31] (1804) 4 Pat 581; analysed by Goldberg (1970) 19 ICLQ 557, 580–4; Crawford and Carruthers, para 13-02; and Hartley, op cit, pp 219–20.

[32] Cf Married Women's Property (Scotland) Act 1920, s 7 of which was repealed by the Family Law (Scotland) Act 1985, Sch 2. See now Succession (Scotland) Act 1964.

[33] Westlake, p 74; Dicey, Morris and Collins, para 28-052-054; and Crawford and Carruthers, paras 13-02 and 13-10.

[34] Falconbridge (1937) 53 LQR 537, 539–40. For the purposes of private international law, it is treated in Scotland as a right of succession; Anton, para 24.20.

[35] The marriage in fact took place in London.

[36] Ie the act of changing his domicile.

[37] *De Nicols v Curlier* [1900] AC 21 at 27.

affect a right in moveable property which, immediately before the change, has vested in either spouse." It is not always clear, however, when or how a right vests. Nor is it clear whether, with regard to what may be termed "non-vested rights", the rights of the spouses will vary according to the content of the "matrimonial property law" of their common domicile from time to time; the inference seemingly is that this should be the case.

In England, a more decisive authority than *Lashley v Hog* must be found, before it can be categorically asserted that the proprietary relations between husband and wife change with a change of their domicile (the doctrine of mutability). It is a strong assertion to make, for, as Westlake says, "justice is shocked by allowing the husband to affect the wife's position by a change for which he does not require her assent",[38] and which, of course, now does not affect her domicile. What is shocking is suspect, and it is in fact doubtful whether English law has adopted the doctrine of mutability to its full extent.

English law, then, is far from certain, but nevertheless an attempt must be made to state the modern rule. The clue to it seems to be the distinction between inchoate and vested rights. Even if the doctrine of mutability is part of English law it can scarcely operate without restriction, for not only justice but principle demands that a spouse shall not, by reason of a change of domicile, be divested of a right of property actually acquired under the law of the matrimonial domicile, even though enjoyment of the right may be postponed until the death of the other spouse. Under the Dutch system of community of goods, for instance, all movables belonging to husband and wife fall on marriage into the common ownership of both. Thus, on marriage, the wife becomes co-owner of movables then belonging to the husband. She also becomes co-owner of future movables when and as they are acquired.[39] If parties domiciled in the Netherlands at the time of marriage acquire a fresh domicile in England where the husband dies, the wife cannot on principle be deprived by her husband's will of what she owned when she reached England. No doubt the will of her husband, since he dies domiciled in England, is governed by English law, and English internal law does not recognise community of goods, but that cannot entitle him to dispose of what is not his. His power of testamentary disposition is limited by the extent of his title. If he dies intestate, his distributable assets are diminished by the rights of property therein owned by his wife.

But vested rights must be distinguished from those that are inchoate. When the Dutch couple change their domicile from the Netherlands to England, it cannot be said that either of them has a vested right of property in movables not yet acquired. At the most they have the hope of acquiring. It is a hope that is not recognised by the law to which they are now subject and which alone can make its voice effective. If, therefore, it should ultimately be decided that the proprietary rights of spouses change with a change in their domicile, this would presumably be subject to the exception that rights vested in either party under the law of some previous domicile remain unaffected. Indeed, this is the approach in Scots law,[40] and this view has been accepted in Canadian courts:

> The law appears to be that the mutual rights of husband and wife as to personal property are governed by the law of the matrimonial domicile, and such rights are not affected by a subsequent change, but rights acquired after such change are, of course, governed by the law of the actual domicile.[41]

---

[38] *Private International Law* (7th edn), p 73.
[39] Rheinstein and Glendon, *International Encyclopedia of Comparative Law* (1980), Vol iv, Chapter 4, pp 52–7.
[40] Family Law (Scotland) Act 2006, s 39(5); see Crawford and Carruthers, para 13-11.
[41] *Pink v Perlin & Co* (1898) 40 NSR 260 at 262; *Re Heung Won Lee* (1963) 36 DLR (2d) 177.

The solution that the rights of the spouses in movable property change with a change of domicile, though leaving acquired rights unaffected, is complicated by the possibility that only one spouse may change his/her domicile.[42] To continue the example of spouses domiciled at marriage in the Netherlands, if only one spouse later becomes domiciled in England, the other remaining domiciled in the Netherlands, the court will be faced with the difficult question whether after-acquired property is governed by English law or by the community rules of Dutch law. It seems wrong that the rights of the spouse domiciled in the Netherlands should be prejudiced by the other spouse's change of domicile. A change of domicile by only one spouse should not affect a right in movable property which, immediately before the change, has vested in either party.[43]

(b) Immovables

Discussion so far has been concerned with the effect of marriage on the spouses' movable property in the absence of a marriage contract. With regard to immovables, the leading decision is *Welch v Tennent*,[44] a Scottish appeal to the House of Lords. The facts were these:

> The husband and wife were domiciled in Scotland. The wife owned land in England which she sold with her husband's agreement and the proceeds of sale were paid to him. Later the parties separated and the wife claimed that the proceeds of sale be paid to her, arguing that under Scots law she was entitled to recall any donation made by her to her husband.

Lord Herschell disposed very rapidly of the argument that Scots law might be applied, saying: "The rights of the spouses as regards movable property must, in the circumstances of this case be regulated by the law of Scotland, but it is equally clear that their rights in relation to heritable estate are governed by the law of the place where it was situate."[45] English law was applied and the husband was entitled to keep the proceeds of sale of the land.

It has been suggested that an English court should refuse to follow *Welch v Tennent*, applying instead, to immovables as well as to movables, the law of the domicile.[46] Whilst this might be acceptable, indeed appropriate, for disputes between husband and wife, on the basis that it would "reflect the values, attitudes and expectations of the parties",[47] it would not be satisfactory in the case of disputes involving third parties.[48]

The choice of law rule now in Scots law rests on a statutory footing. Section 39(1) of the Family Law (Scotland) Act 2006 provides that: "Any question in relation to the rights of spouses to each other's immoveable property arising by virtue of the marriage shall be determined by the law of the place in which the property is situated." Section 39(1), however, is subject to section 39(6)(b), which permits party autonomy to override the choice of law rule set out in section 39(1).[49]

---

[42] Supra, pp 168–9.

[43] Cf Family Law (Scotland) Act 2006, s 39(5).

[44] [1891] AC 639; discussed by Hartley, op cit, p 224; and see *Callwood v Callwood* [1960] AC 659, 683–4; *Tezcan v Tezcan* (1992) 87 DLR (4th) 503, 518–19.

[45] Ibid, 645.

[46] Dicey, Morris and Collins, para 28-028; and Hartley, op cit, p 225. See also Clarkson and Hill, p 491, where a distinction is drawn between the treatment of foreign immovables (to be governed, it is suggested, by the law of the situs) and immovables situated in England (to be governed, it is suggested, by the law of the matrimonial domicile).

[47] Hartley, op cit, p 225.

[48] Cf Hartley, op cit, pp 232–4.

[49] See Crawford and Carruthers, paras 13-10–13-11.

3. ASSIGNMENT WHERE THERE IS AN ANTE-NUPTIAL CONTRACT

(a) The general rule

When we turn to the situation where the parties have entered an ante-nuptial contract, it must be borne in mind that the choice of law issues which may arise are governed by common law rules.[50] This is because the Rome I Regulation on the Law Applicable to Contractual Obligations[51] does not apply to contractual obligations arising out of family relationships, which includes matrimonial property regimes.[52] If the parties have made an ante-nuptial contract to regulate their future proprietary relationship, then the difficulties, just discussed, concerning the identification of the governing laws or the effect of a change of domicile do not arise. The contract continues to govern the proprietary rights of the parties not only in the matrimonial domicile, but also in any other domicile that may later be acquired.[53] It must be recognised no matter where it may be put in suit[54] (subject to any overriding provisions of the law of the forum),[55] and it applies whether the property in question is movable[56] or immovable.[57] It may either define precisely what the rights shall be or state the system of law by which they are to be regulated.[58]

The leading case on ante-nuptial agreements is *Radmacher*.[59] In *Radmacher* the wife was German, the husband was French and they spent most of their married life living in England. The wife came from a wealthy family who encouraged her to enter into a premarital agreement. The agreement was entered into in accordance with German Law, prior to the marriage. The general effect of the agreement, although purporting that German law should apply to all aspects of the marriage, was to exclude certain aspects of German Law.[60] In fact the terms of the agreement in relation to property were very similar to English Law.

The court held that ante-nuptial agreements could be taken into account on divorce, but did not go so far as to hold that they were legally binding and applicable in the sense that a contract would be. This is because section 25 of the Matrimonial Causes Act 1973 is the law that applies following an English divorce. Therefore the court is required to apply the checklist in section 25, which requires that all circumstances are taken into account. Where there is an ante-nuptial agreement this is just one of the factors the court should take into account when making an order for the transfer or the sale of property. This means that some of the wishes of the parties might be upheld, or none at all, depending on the circumstances and whether the agreement is considered to be fair. One reason for not finding ante-nuptial contracts legally binding is because it is necessary to factor in changes that may happen over

---

[50] Though where the marriage contract purports to create a trust, the Recognition of Trusts Act 1987 will apply. Where an ante-nuptial agreement is embodied in a trust, as in *Re Fitzgerald* [1904] 1 Ch 573, the rules relating to the essential validity of trusts fall to be considered; see infra, Chapter 38.

[51] See Chapter 19 for further details.

[52] Art 1(2)(b) and (c), supra pp 697–9. See also Recital 8.

[53] Though the original law governing the contract may allow it to be amended under the law of a new domicile: *Duyvewaardt v Barber* (1992) 43 RFL (3d) 139.

[54] *Anstruther v Adair* (1834) 2 My & K 513: *Montgomery v Zarifi* (1919) 88 LJPC 20; *De Nicols v Curlier* [1900] AC 21 at 46; *Re Hannema's Marriage* (1981) 54 FLR 79.

[55] Eg *Stark v Stark* (1988) 16 RFL (3d) 257.

[56] *De Nicols v Curlier* [1900] AC 21.

[57] *Re De Nicols* [1900] 2 Ch 410. Cf Family Law (Scotland) Act 2006, s 39(6)(b).

[58] *Este v Smyth* (1854) 18 Beav 112.

[59] *Radmacher (formerly Granatino) v Granatino* [2010] UKSC 42.

[60] *Radmacher* [184].

the course of the marriage, particularly children. This is not to say that the ante-nuptial contract will be completely excluded where children are involved, but in such cases the best interests of the child is the key factor and in any decision on the division of property the first consideration must be the welfare of any minor children.[61] In *Radmacher* the ante-nuptial contract was unobjectionable under French and German law. It is not clear whether the result would have been the same if the agreement had been legally invalid or ineffective according to the personal law or laws of the spouses.[62]

No distinction in this respect is made between an express and a tacit contract, as is illustrated by *De Nicols v Curlier*:[63]

> H and W, French both by nationality and by domicile, were married in Paris without making an express contract as to their proprietary rights. Nine years after their marriage, they came to England, acquired an English domicile and prospered as the owners of the Cafe Royal, in Regent Street. The husband died in 1897 leaving a considerable fortune in movable and immovable property. In his will, he disposed of all of his property without taking account of the wife's entitlement to a half share in the property under the French system of community of property. The issue was whether the spouses' change of domicile from French to English affected their legal position in relation to the property.

The position of the movable property was considered first by the House of Lords, and separately from that of the immovables. The expert evidence accepted by the court was that according to French law parties who marry without an express marriage contract are bound by a tacit contract to abide by the system of community. Therefore, said Lord Macnaghten: "if there is a valid compact between spouses as to their property, whether it be constituted by the law of the land or by convention between the parties, it is difficult to see how that compact can be nullified or blotted out merely by a change of domicile".[64]

The question then arose whether the French contract or English law as that of the situs determined the rights of the surviving wife to the English immovables of her deceased husband. Kekewich J held,[65] after further argument, that the French implied contract must operate according to the intention of the parties so as to bind the immovable property of the deceased, unless there was any overriding rule of English law that would render it unenforceable. The only possible rule was the provision of section 4 of the Statute of Frauds 1677, requiring a written memorandum in the case of a contract concerning land;[66] but the judge held that, since this particular contract constituted a partnership between the spouses in the eyes of French law, it fell within the rule of English law that a parol agreement for a partnership was not caught by the statute and was enforceable despite the lack of written evidence. The accuracy of the view expressed by Kekewich J that the contract implied by French law included foreign immovables is open to doubt and impractical.[67] His decision might have been based more surely on counsel's other argument, namely that the land represented the investment of money acquired by the husband during marriage, and that the wife could follow the money, to which she was admittedly entitled, into whatsoever form it had been converted.

---

[61] Matrimonial Causes Act 1973, s 25(1).
[62] Dicey, Morris and Collins 28-005.
[63] [1900] AC 21; and see *Tezcan v Tezcan* (1992) 87 DLR (4th) 503. Hartley, op cit, pp 220 et seq.
[64] Ibid, 33.
[65] *Re De Nicols* [1900] 2 Ch 410.
[66] See now Law of Property (Miscellaneous Provisions) Act 1989, s 2.
[67] Or indeed that French law would today consider there was a tacit contract in such a case; see Dicey, Morris and Collins, paras 28-024–28-025.

Support for the application to immovables of the law governing the ante-nuptial contract is provided by *Chiwell v Carlyon*,[68] a case which appeared before both the English and the South African courts, in which the facts were as follows:

> In 1887 H married W at Kimberley in South Africa. No express ante-nuptial contract was made. The parties were domiciled at the time in South Africa, and while still domiciled there they made a joint will disposing of their joint estate, ie of the movables and immovables that they held in community. In 1892, after the parties had settled in England, certain land in Cornwall was bought by H and conveyed to him. W died in 1893, H in 1895. The question that arose before the Chancery Division was whether the Cornish land passed under the will of the joint estate.

Stirling J felt that the law of the previous domicile at the time of their marriage could not be disregarded and he submitted two questions to the Supreme Court in the Cape of Good Hope. The second[69] question was this:

> Assuming H and W to have been domiciled in South Africa at the time of their marriage, but subsequently to have acquired an English domicile before the purchase of the land, would this change have any effect by South African law on their respective rights in regard to the land?

The Supreme Court held that this question must be answered in the negative. The marriage created a universal partnership between husband and wife in all property, movable and immovable, belonging to either of them before marriage or coming to either during marriage. De Villiers CJ took the view that: "It is competent for the intended spouses, before marriage, to regulate their respective rights by express contract, but in the absence of such an express contract, they are understood to enter into a tacit contract that community of property between them shall prevail."[70] This tacit contract of community extended to foreign land. It was unaffected by a change of domicile.

On receipt of this opinion from the South African court, Stirling J decided that: "in any event the joint estate passing under the said will includes all property which according to the law of the Cape of Good Hope would fall within the community of property which would have been created by the marriage of the testator and testatrix, if they were domiciled at the Cape of Good Hope at the time of their marriage".[71] He thereupon made an order declaring that the Cornish land passed under the will apparently in accordance with the tacit contract, though the decision is perhaps also explicable on other grounds.[72]

It remains now to consider specifically what law governs the three questions of capacity, formal validity and essential validity in the case of marriage contracts.

---

[68] (1897) 14 SC 61 (South Africa); but see *Tezcan v Tezcan* (1992) 87 DLR (4th) 503, 517–18.

[69] The first question was whether the South African community system applied to immovables acquired outside South Africa. The Supreme Court held that it did. Had it decided the opposite, that would have been the end of the claim, as in *Callwood v Callwood* [1960] AC 659.

[70] (1897) 14 SC 61, 65.

[71] This case is not reported in England, but the Public Record Office reference to the Entry Books of Decrees and Orders (Supreme Court of Judicature) is 1897 A 2919.

[72] One possible ground is that the land represented money already owned by the parties in South Africa. Another, that it was merely a question of testamentary construction—what did the parties intend? Being subject to and conversant with South African law at the time of making the will, they would naturally contemplate that the common property would include everything regarded as such by that law.

(b) Capacity[73]

The combination of circumstances which most neatly raises the question of capacity occurs where a woman, being a minor according to the law of her English domicile, makes a marriage contract in England prior to her marriage with a foreigner, by the law of whose domicile the woman is not subject to any incapacity. A variation, which occurred in *Viditz v O'Hagan*,[74] arises if the contract is made in a country which is the domicile neither of the woman nor of the man.

In relation to immovables, it is arguable that capacity to enter into a marriage contract should be governed by the law of the situs.[75] Strictly, however, the law of the situs should govern only capacity to convey immovable property, and not capacity to make a contract with regard to such property.[76] As regards movables, if we reason by analogy to commercial contracts, the proper law of the contract governs,[77] but if by analogy to the contract to marry, then the law of the parties' domicile[78] is the governing system. It is submitted, however, that on principle the proper law of the agreement should govern, and that the proper law is prima facie deemed to be the law of the matrimonial domicile.[79] It is that law which is universally recognised as controlling the personal and proprietary relations of the parties during their marriage.

The relevant cases[80] in chronological order are: *Re Cooke's Trusts*,[81] *Cooper v Cooper*,[82] and *Viditz v O'Hagan*.[83]

The facts of *Re Cooke's Trusts* were as follows:

> A domiciled Englishwoman under married a Frenchman in France. Prior to the marriage, she made a notarial twenty-one contract in France, which excluded the French doctrine of community of goods, and gave her "the entire administration of her property and the free enjoyment of her income". There were three children of the marriage. After having lived in Jersey for eight years separately from her husband, she went through a ceremony of marriage with X in 1853 under the mistaken belief that her husband was dead. She resided with X and with her three children in New South Wales until her death in 1879. Her French husband did not die until 1877. She made a will leaving all her property to X. It was argued that a notarial contract was valid, and that it precluded the testatrix from depriving her children of the vested interests in her property given to them by French law.

Stirling J, after deciding that the woman died domiciled in New South Wales, held that her capacity to make the notarial contract was governed by English law, as being the law of her ante-nuptial domicile. The consequence was that in his opinion her minority rendered the contract "void".[84] The reasoning which led the judge to this conclusion was not impressive.

---

[73] On this difficult subject see Dicey, Morris and Collins, paras 28-039–28-043; Crawford and Carruthers, para 13-05; Morris (1938) 54 LQR 78; cf Goldberg (1970) 19 ICLQ 557, 569–73. Capacity to contract is largely unaffected by the Contracts (Applicable Law) Act 1990, supra, pp 684–5.

[74] [1900] 2 Ch 87. See Dicey, Morris and Collins, para 28-041.

[75] *Black v Black's Trs* 1950 SLT (Notes) 32. See, however, criticism in relation to *Bank of Africa Ltd v Cohen* [1909] 2 Ch 129 (not, however, a matrimonial property case): Morris, *Cases on Private International Law*, (1968) 4th edn, p 350.

[76] Carruthers (2005), para 4.04.

[77] It should be the proper law objectively ascertained, rather than deemed to be chosen by the parties; see supra, p 706 et seq.

[78] As to the law of the parties' domicile, see supra, p 909 et seq.

[79] On the meaning of this, see supra, pp 1366–7.

[80] The practical significance of all three cases is now much less, given that the age of majority has been reduced to 18: Family Law Reform Act 1969, s 1.

[81] (1887) 56 LJ Ch 637.

[82] (1888) 13 App Cas 88.

[83] [1899] 2 Ch 569; revsd [1900] 2 Ch 87.

[84] Though see *Edwards v Carter* [1893] AC 360.

All that he did was to follow *Sottomayor v De Barros*,[85] relying on statements that personal capacity to contract is governed by the law of the domicile.[86] The decision is of little value on the question of capacity, for the right of the Englishwoman to dispose of her property by will was in no way restricted by the French contract on which the children relied. As Morris has said: "If a woman makes an ante-nuptial contract which merely excludes *communauté des biens* [community of goods] and gives her full powers of disposition, it is difficult to see how the children of the marriage can complain if they take nothing under the will."[87] The decision, in other words, would have been the same had she been of full age when she made the contract.

The facts of *Cooper v Cooper*,[88] a Scottish appeal to the House of Lords, were as follows:

> A domiciled Irishwoman of eighteen made an ante-nuptial contract in Dublin with her intended husband, a domiciled Scotsman, by which she purported to relinquish the proprietary rights that she would be entitled to under Scottish law on the death of her husband. Both parties contemplated, in accordance with what proved to be the fact, that the matrimonial home would be established in Scotland. The husband died thirty-five years after his wife attained her majority. On his death she sued to set aside the contract on the ground that at the time of its execution she was a minor by Irish law.

It was held that the woman's capacity must be governed by the law of Ireland, since that country was not only her domicile but also the place where the contract was made. Lord Macnaghten rejected the notion that Scots law, as being the law of the matrimonial domicile, applied, saying: "It is difficult to suppose that Mrs Cooper could confer capacity upon herself by contemplating a different country as the place where the contract was to be fulfilled, if that be the proper expression, or by contracting in view of an alteration of personal status which would bring with it a change of domicil."[89] In any event the decision is not readily explicable. By Irish law, as well as by English law, a marriage contract was voidable, in the sense that it was to be treated as valid unless repudiated by the minor within a reasonable time after the attainment of majority.[90] Since there had been no repudiation within thirty-five years after the event, why was the contract not valid even by the law of the minor's ante-nuptial domicile? The true explanation seems to be that the House of Lords considered Scots law as well as Irish law to be a governing factor. By Irish law she might repudiate the contract or leave it in operation. By Scots law, the law of her new domicile, she could do nothing but repudiate it, since to ratify it or to leave it unrepudiated would constitute a gift that was revocable as being a gift between husband and wife.[91] The decision is far from convincing as an authority in support of the view that capacity to make a marriage settlement depends on the law of the domicile at the time of the contract.

Viditz v O'Hagan[92] is a curious case, in which the facts were these:

> A domiciled Englishwoman, under twenty-one, made a marriage contract at Berne in view of her approaching marriage with a domiciled Austrian. The contract was voidable by English law, ie it could be rescinded by her after she attained majority, though it would become irrevocable if not rescinded within a reasonable time after that event. The rule of Austrian law, the law of the matrimonial domicile, was that the husband and wife might

---

[85] (1877) 3 PD 1.
[86] Ibid, 5. This is no longer regarded as being so, see supra, pp 761–3.
[87] (1938) 54 LQR 78, 81.
[88] (1888) 13 App Cas 88.
[89] (1888) 13 App Cas 88, 108.
[90] *Edwards v Carter* [1893] AC 360.
[91] Morris, p 375, citing Lord Lindley in *Viditz v O'Hagan* [1900] 2 Ch 87, 96, 98.
[92] [1900] 2 Ch 87.

revoke the settlement agreement at any time. Twenty-nine years after the settlement, ie long after it had become irrevocable by English law, the husband and wife executed an instrument in the Austrian form by which they exercised the right of revocation. They then brought the present action against the English trustees claiming a declaration that the agreement had been annulled.

It was held by the Court of Appeal that they were entitled to the declaration, since the power of revoking the settlement agreement was a matter for Austrian law. In other words, by English law the wife could repudiate the contract, provided that she did so within a reasonable time after attaining her majority; by Austrian law, to which she later became subject, she could always repudiate it. Therefore the joint operation of the two laws rendered effective what the parties had done.

Neither *Cooper v Cooper* nor *Viditz v O'Hagan*, then, justifies the view that the law of each party's domicile governs capacity, for if this were the law the contract in each case would have been valid as not having been repudiated within a reasonable time.

(c) Formal validity

What is the appropriate legal system to determine the formalities that must be observed in the case of a marriage contract? If, for instance, an Englishwoman marries a man domiciled in a country in which the couple wishes to settle and where such a contract is void unless made by notarial act, and she wishes to make a settlement agreement with ordinary English limitations, it is important to know whether the English or the foreign form must be followed. The proper course is to execute the settlement as an English deed and then to re-execute it as a notarial act, but if this is not done a difficult question arises. If the deed is executed in the foreign country it neglects the forms required by the law of the place of contracting; if in England, it requires the parties to act under a transaction that is devoid of effect by the law of the matrimonial domicile.

Formerly, the traditional view was that a contract must observe the forms required by the law of the place of contracting. However it has been accepted at common law, as well as under the Contracts (Applicable Law) Act 1990,[93] that formalities, like essential validity, may be governed by the proper law. At common law, the form required by the law of the place of contracting is sufficient[94] but not essential. The English cases clearly show that in the case of marriage contracts relating to property it is sufficient to adopt the formalities of the proper law as an alternative to those of the law of the place of contracting.[95]

The exact point arose in *Van Grutten v Digby*:[96]

Prior to a marriage between an Englishwoman and a domiciled Frenchman, a deed of settlement in the English form and containing the usual English limitations was executed at Dunkirk. The settlement was wholly void by French law, since it had not been executed before a notary public. Five years later the husband claimed that, owing to the formal invalidity of the contract by French law, the settled property was subject to the doctrine of community of goods.

---

[93] Supra, p 684 et seq.

[94] Eg *Guépratte v Young* (1851) 4 De G & Sm 217.

[95] As to what is the proper law see infra, under (D) ESSENTIAL VALIDITY; see also *Ex p Spinazzi* 1985 (3) SA 650.

[96] (1862) 31 Beav 561; see also *Watts v Shrimpton* (1855) 21 Beav 97; *Re Barnard, Barnard v White* (1887) 56 LT 9; *Re Bankes* [1902] 2 Ch 333.

Lord Romilly held, however, that the contract was binding on both parties:

> I hold it to be the law of this country that if a foreigner and an Englishwoman make an express contract previous to marriage, and if on the faith of that contract the marriage afterwards takes place, and if the contract relates to the regulation of property within the jurisdiction and subject to the laws of this country, then, and in that case, this court will administer the law on the subject as if the whole matter were to be regulated by English law.[97]

(d) Essential validity

The essential validity of a marriage contract is governed by its proper law. In relation to immovable property, at least as regards matters in rem, the law of the situs must surely be the proper law.[98] Otherwise, it seems clear that there may be express selection of the governing law, at least if it is connected with the transaction.[99] In the absence of choice, the proper law will be the law of the country with which the contract is most closely connected. In effect, the principles on which the proper law is to be determined are much the same as those relevant at common law to determine the proper law of a commercial contract.[100] However, the nature of the subject matter is such that certain factors may predominate in significance, not least being the matrimonial domicile.[101] Indeed there would appear to be a presumption in favour of the law of the matrimonial domicile, but this may well be rebutted by other circumstances.[102] Other factors to which consideration may be given include: the nature and situation of the property; whether the form and contents of the document are appropriate to one law, but not to another; the place where the accounts, the shares and other indicia of title are kept; the fact that the contract is invalid under the law of the matrimonial domicile.

The proper law, once it has been identified in accordance with these principles, continues to govern the marriage contract even though the interested parties may establish their house in a country where a different law prevails.[103]

Where there is a marriage settlement creating trusts of that settlement, the essential validity of such trusts falls to be governed by the law determined by reference to the Recognition of Trusts Act 1987.[104]

4. MATRIMONIAL PROPERTY RIGHTS AND DIVORCE

Although the law applicable to matrimonial property appears complicated, in reality the law applicable to matrimonial property on divorce will be English law. As a general rule where the English court has jurisdiction for divorce the court will apply English law to the divorce and

---

[97] (1862) 31 Beav 561, 567.

[98] Cf *Teczan v Teczan* (1992) 87 DLR 503 (BCCA). Though see Dicey, Morris and Collins, para 28R-031, which in advocating the law of the matrimonial domicile as the proper law of a marriage contract makes no exception, or special mention, of the position with regard to immovable property.

[99] *Re Fitzgerald, Surman v Fitzgerald* [1904] 1 Ch 573, 587–588; *Montgomery v Zarifi* 1918 SC (HL) 128; Crawford and Carruthers, para 13.07; cf *Re Bowen's Estate* 351 NYS 2d 113 (1973).

[100] Including the possibility that, exceptionally, different proper laws may govern different parts of a contract, eg as regards movable, and immovable, property, respectively: Cheshire, *International Contracts* (1948), p 42.

[101] Supra, p 1366 et seq. See Dicey, Morris and Collins, para 28-033.

[102] *Re Fitzgerald* [1904] 1 Ch 573; and see *Re Hannema's Marriage* (1981) 54 FLR 79, 7 Fam LR 542. Crawford and Carruthers, para 13-08.

[103] *Re Hewitt's Settlement* [1915] 1 Ch 228.

[104] Infra, p 1384 et seq.

its financial consequences. Under the Brussels II *bis* regime a spouse can apply for divorce in England following six months residence there, or on the basis of sole domicile,[105] regardless of a matrimonial domicile in a different state.

Under the Matrimonial Causes Act 1973 the court has a wide discretion to make property adjustment orders on divorce.[106] In exercising this discretion the courts often pay little or no attention to the fact that the parties might be married under some proprietary regime other than separation of property. When deciding whether to exercise its powers under s 24 the court should have regard to all circumstances of the case,[107] but this has not usually meant that the court has had regard to other property regimes and this is not a factor which the court should have particular regard to.[108] For all intents and purposes if the divorce is carried out in England then English law will apply. Usually the only time the court will consider applying a different law is where there is an ante-nuptial agreement which the court considers it would be fair to uphold.[109] In such cases the ante-nuptial contract would be one factor to consider when making the s 25 assessment.[110] Therefore the decision to uphold all or part of the ante-nuptial agreement is at the discretion of the court.[111]

5. PROPERTY RIGHTS ARISING FROM OTHER ADULT RELATIONSHIPS

(a) Civil Partnership Act 2004

The Civil Partnership Act 2004 introduced the status of civil partnership for same sex couples.[112] In the case of civil partnerships registered in England, the property and financial consequences of such relationships are detailed in Chapter 3 of Part 2 of the Act.[113] Provision for recognition in England of civil partnerships formed abroad is set out in Chapter 2 of Part 5 of the Act.[114]

The 2004 Act does not lay down express choice of law rules regarding the property rights of civil partners resulting from civil partnership[115] akin to those rights which apply at common law in relation to the property of married persons resulting from marriage.[116] It is submitted, however, that the property rights of civil partners should be determined under English conflict rules in the same manner as those of married persons.[117] The rules and principles set out

---

[105] Brussels II *bis*, Art 3(1)(a) and Domicile and Matrimonial Proceedings Act 1973 s 5(2). For further information see chapter 22?

[106] Matrimonial Causes Act 1973, s 24.

[107] Ibid, s 25(1).

[108] Ibid, s 25(2).

[109] *Radmacher (formerly Granatino) v Granatino* [2010] UKSC 42.

[110] *Radmacher* [83], supra, pp 1327–30.

[111] See for example *Z v Z (No 2)(Financial Remedy: Marriage Contract)* [2012] 1FLR 1100; *B v S (Financial Remedy: Matrimonial Property Regime)* [2012] 2 FLR 502; *AH v PH (Scandinavian Marriage Settlement)* [2014] 2 FLR 251.

[112] See generally pp 946–8, supra.

[113] Ss 65–72.

[114] See pp 946–8, supra.

[115] See, however, Sch 4 in relation to wills, administration of estates, and family provision; and Sch 7 regarding financial relief in England following the overseas dissolution of a civil partnership.

[116] As described in this chapter.

[117] Dicey, Morris and Collins, para 28-004.

in this chapter, therefore, should be treated as applying, *mutatis mutandis*, to civil partners as well as to married persons.

(b) Cohabitation[118]

Included in the Law Commission's Ninth Programme of Law Reform[119] is a project to consider the financial hardship suffered by cohabitants[120] or their children on the termination of the cohabiting relationship by reason of breakdown or death.[121] It is recognised that, "when cohabitants separate, the courts use a patchwork of statutory and non-statutory rules to determine what should happen to the couple's property".[122] The Law Commission's Consultation Paper, in proposing a new scheme for cohabitants, recognised that account must be taken of the international dimension, and so there were proposed in Part 11 new rules of jurisdiction[123] and applicable law relevant to cohabitation, including rules pertaining to cohabitation contracts and "opt-out agreements".[124] The consultation did not result in amendments to the law and there is still no specific regime that applies to cohabitant's in England and Wales.[125]

6. EUROPEAN PROPOSALS FOR REFORM

In July 2006, the European Commission published a Green Paper on Conflict of Laws in Matrimonial Property Regimes.[126] Accompanying the Green Paper is an Annex,[127] partially comprising the fruits of a European-commissioned study entitled, "Matrimonial Property Regimes and the Property of Unmarried Couples in Private International Law".[128] On 16 March 2011 the Commission adopted a proposal for a Council Regulation on jurisdiction, applicable law and the recognition and enforcement of decisions in matters of matrimonial

---

[118] See generally Carruthers (2008) 12 Edin LR 51.

[119] Law Com No 293 (2005), para 3.6.

[120] "Opposite-sex and same-sex couples in clearly defined relationships." The project excludes relationships between blood relatives and "caring" relationships, as well as "commercial" relationships (eg landlord and tenant/lodger). Law Commission Consultation Paper No 179, "Cohabitation: The Financial Consequences of Relationship Breakdown—A Consultation Paper" (2006), para 1.19. See also Report on Cohabitation: "The Financial Consequences of Relationship Breakdown", Law Com No 307, (2007).

[121] The project is limited in scope. It is not a comprehensive review of all the law that currently applies to cohabitants, but rather deals only with the issue of financial relief between cohabitants upon termination of their relationship. Cf the position in Scotland where statutory rules recently have been introduced pertaining to the financial and proprietary consequences of cohabitation: Family Law (Scotland) Act 2006, ss 25–30. The 2006 Act does not clearly specify, from a conflict of laws perspective, when or in what circumstances the rights established therein should apply: Crawford and Carruthers, paras 13-12–13-15.

[122] Consultation Paper, para 3.3.

[123] See Report on Cohabitation: "The Financial Consequences of Relationship Breakdown", Law Com No 307, (2007), para 7.15.

[124] See Carruthers, (2008) 12 Edin LR 51, 61 et seq.

[125] In contrast Scotland does now have a domestic property regime that applies to cohabitants, Family Law (Scotland) Act 2006 ss 25–30 and see *Gow v Grant* [2012] UKSC 29.

[126] COM (2006) 400 final. See, for comment, Carruthers, op cit, at 72 et seq. Matrimonial property regimes hitherto have been excluded from Community instruments. The Green Paper is one of several initiatives deriving from the Hague Programme, adopted by the European Council in November 2004 (The Hague Programme: Strengthening Freedom, Security and Justice in the European Union, OJ 2005 C 53/ 1; and the Council and Commission Action Plan Implementing the Hague Programme on Strengthening Freedom, Security and Justice in the European Union, OJ 2005 C 198/1) (in respect of which, see generally, supra, Chapter 1).

[127] SEC (2006) 952.

[128] JAI/A3/2001/03.

property regimes,[129] and an equivalent proposal for registered partnerships.[130] Unfortunately on 3 December 2015 the Council concluded that unanimity could not be reached and therefore the proposals could not be adopted by the Union as a whole. Since then 17 Member States have requested the authorisation of enhanced cooperation to continue working in this area.[131] The UK will not be participating in this.

---

[129] COM (2011) 126.
[130] COM (2011) 127.
[131] COM (2016) 106.

38

TRUSTS

1. Introduction	1382		(b) Absence of choice	1387
2. Preliminary Issues	1383		(c) Scope of the applicable law	1389
(a) Definition of a trust	1383		(d) Variation of the applicable law	1390
(b) Types of trust falling within			4. Recognition	1391
the 1987 Act	1384		5. Mandatory Rules and Public Policy	1392
(c) Validity of the instrument of creation			(a) Mandatory rules	1392
of the trust	1385		(b) Public policy	1393
(d) Transfer of trust assets	1385		6. Variation of Trusts and Settlements	1393
3. Choice of Law	1386		(a) Variation of Trusts Act 1958	1393
(a) Choice by the settlor	1386		(b) Variation of marriage settlements	1394

1. INTRODUCTION

The common law rules concerning the validity of trusts in the international context were described in 1951 as "simply specific rules, evolved to meet particular difficulties. They do not reflect, or form part of a fully-developed system, and it is a matter for remark that they deal with so few of the many possible situations which may possibly arise."[1] In the intervening years the case law remained thin, with patchy analysis of the issues and uncertainty as to the relevant rules in a number of areas. It is, therefore, not surprising that the Recognition of Trusts Act was passed in 1987 to enable the United Kingdom to give effect to the Convention, formally concluded in 1985 by the Hague Conference on Private International Law, on the Law Applicable to Trusts and on their Recognition.[2] This Convention is implemented by being scheduled, with some omissions,[3] to the 1987 Act.[4]

It has to be said that the main reason for the initiation of work on this Convention was not the unsatisfactory nature of the private international law of trusts in those countries familiar with the law of trusts, but rather the fact that issues involving the validity of trusts or the powers of trustees may arise in countries where the trust concept is unfamiliar.[5] This accounts for the fact that the Hague Convention and the 1987 Act not only lay down choice of law

---

[1] Keeton (1951) 4 Current Legal Problems 111, 119.

[2] See *Actes et Documents de la Quinzième session*, Vol II, especially the official Explanatory Report, at p 370, by von Overbeck; Harris (2002); Hayton (1987) 36 ICLQ 260; Gaillard and Trautman (1987) 35 AJCL 307; Klein, in *Mélanges Paul Piotet* (1990), p 467; Hayton, in Borras (ed), *E Pluribus Unum* (1996), p 121; Hayton, (2014) 366 Recueil des Cours de l'Académie de droit international de la Haye, pp 58–95; Hayton, (2016) T&T 1002.

[3] It would have been more helpful to have scheduled a fuller version. Indeed reference is made in this chapter to some provisions which have not been scheduled.

[4] 1987 Act, s 1(1).

[5] *Actes et Documents de la Quartorzième* session, Vol I, p 189; see Paton and Grosso (1994) 43 ICLQ 654. The EU Draft Common Frame of Reference, revised outline, published in March 2009, contains a book on trusts, Book X, which provides a set of model rules, aimed at providing Europe with a uniform trust law, see Braun [2011] CLJ 327.

rules but also extend to the question of the recognition of trusts, which is a particular problem if they are unknown in the domestic law.[6]

In considering the private international law rules governing trusts which are laid down in the Recognition of Trusts Act 1987 and its scheduled Convention,[7] it is necessary to examine a range of preliminary issues before turning to the specific rules governing choice of law and the recognition of trusts.

2. PRELIMINARY ISSUES[8]

(a) Definition of a trust

A major objective of the Convention is "to establish common provisions on the law applicable to trusts and to deal with the most important issues concerning the recognition of trusts";[9] but these common provisions are to be applied in countries some of which are familiar with the trust concept and others of which are not. Furthermore, as the Convention is an "open" and not a "reciprocal" Convention, the law to be applied to the validity or recognition of a trust may not be that of a Contracting State.[10] This led to the decision to include, in Article 2 of the Convention, a description, if not a definition, of a trust for the purposes of the Convention:

> For the purposes of this Convention, the term "trust" refers to the legal relationships created—*inter vivos* or on death—by a person, the settlor, when assets[11] have been placed under the control of a trustee for the benefit of a beneficiary or for a specified purpose.
>
> A trust has the following characteristics—
>
> (a) the assets constitute a separate fund and are not a part of the trustee's own estate;
> (b) title to the trust assets stands in the name of the trustee or in the name of another person on behalf of the trustee;
> (c) the trustee has the power and the duty, in respect of which he is accountable, to manage, employ or dispose of the assets in accordance with the terms of the trust and the special duties imposed upon him by law.
>
> The reservation by the settlor of certain rights and powers, and the fact that the trustee may himself have rights as a beneficiary, are not necessarily inconsistent with the existence of a trust.

The effect of this is to include within the Convention the classic concept of trust known to the common law world, whilst also making it possible to extend the Convention to trust-like institutions familiar to other jurisdictions.

---

[6] The Convention rules apply to trusts regardless of the date on which they were created: Art 22; though other states have a power (not exercised by the United Kingdom) to limit the rules to trusts created after the Convention came into force in those states. S 1(5) of the 1987 Act makes clear that Art 22 is not to be construed as affecting the law to be applied to anything done or omitted to be done before the Act came into force, though the combined meaning of these provisions is not without doubt: see *Re Carapiet's Trust, The Armenian Patriarch of Jerusalem v Sonsino* [2002] EWHC 1304 (Ch); [2002] WTLR 989, per Jacob J, at [3]; and Harris (2002), pp 406–8.

[7] The rules apply to conflicts between the laws of parts of the United Kingdom as they do more generally internationally; though there is a power in the Convention (Art 24) which would have allowed the exclusion of intra-United Kingdom conflicts.

[8] See generally Harris (2002), Part One.

[9] Convention, Preamble.

[10] Though there is a power for Contracting States to make a reservation limiting the application of the rules on recognition to a trust the validity of which is governed by the law of a Contracting State: Art 21.

[11] No distinction is drawn between movable and immovable property.

(b) Types of trust falling within the 1987 Act[12]

The definition of a trust in Article 2 ensures that the rules of the Convention apply both to trusts created *inter vivos* and on death, and that they apply both to trusts for the benefit of specific beneficiaries and for "a specified purpose", thus including charitable trusts. Under Article 3, it is stated that: "The Convention only applies to trusts created voluntarily and evidenced in writing." Whilst this does not require the trust to be in writing, merely evidenced in writing, it would appear to exclude purely oral trusts, trusts which are created by judicial decision and trusts created by statute. All three such categories of trust are, however, covered by the 1987 Act, though in differing ways.

The Convention[13] gives Contracting States the power to extend the provisions of the Convention to trusts created by judicial decision and this has, in fact, been done in the 1987 Act.[14] It should be noted that the extension is unlimited in that it applies to trusts created by virtue of a judicial decision whether in the United Kingdom or elsewhere. This means that trusts created by judicial decision elsewhere in the European Community or in the EFTA States will fall to be recognised under the Civil Jurisdiction and Judgments Acts 1982 and 1991 respectively.[15] If the trust is created by judicial decision in some other country its recognition will depend on whether that foreign judgment falls to be recognised under the general rules for the recognition of foreign judgments.[16]

Oral trusts and trusts created by statute fall outside the Convention and there is no express power to extend the Convention provisions to them. Nevertheless, in the interests of ensuring that as many kinds of trust as is appropriate are governed by the same rules, the 1987 Act applies the rules in the Convention on both choice of law and recognition to "any other trusts of property arising under the law of any part of the United Kingdom".[17] There is no doubt that this includes purely oral trusts arising under English law,[18] as well as trusts created by the operation of a statute[19] or by specific action under a statute.[20]

Although the rules of the Convention are to be applied to a wide variety of trusts, not every type of trust is included. For example, the validity of an oral trust which arises under the law of some country outside the United Kingdom will have to be determined by an English court according to the common law rules of private international law, which, notwithstanding the 1987 Act, will remain applicable to such a trust.[21] The extension of the provisions of the Convention to trusts of property created by judicial decision will ensure that many instances of constructive trust are included, but not cases where constructive trusts are created as a form of personal remedy.[22]

---

[12] See Harris (2002), pp 123–38.

[13] Art 20.

[14] S 1(2).

[15] Supra, p 595 et seq.

[16] Supra, p 513 et seq.

[17] S 1(2).

[18] *Berezovsky v Abramovich* [2010] EWHC 647 (Comm), [176] reversed but not on this point [2011] EWCA Civ 153; [2011] 1 WLR 2290.

[19] Eg under the Law of Property Act 1925, ss 34–36; Administration of Estates Act 1925, s 33; Administration of Justice Act 1925, s 42; *Re Kehr* [1952] Ch 26.

[20] Eg under the Mental Health Act 1983, s 96(1)(d), repealed by the Mental Capacity Act 2005, s 67(2) and Sch 7 (see, for transitional provisions, s 66(4) and Sch 5, Pt 1).

[21] Though there are unlikely to be major differences between the two sets of rules, see infra, p 1315 et seq. For the common law rules, see the 11th edn of this book (1987), Chapter 35.

[22] See Chong (2005) 54 ICLQ 855; Hayton (1987) 36 ICLQ 260 at 264; and see Barnard [1992] CLJ 474, 479. See also *Minera Aquiline Argentina SA v IMA Exploration Inc and Inversiones Mineras Argentinas SA* 2006 BCSC 1102. Whether most forms of resulting trust are included is unclear, see Hayton, supra, 263–4.

(c) Validity of the instrument of creation of the trust

In the case of a voluntary testamentary or *inter vivos* trust, there is an important preliminary issue to be faced, namely whether the instrument which creates the trust, ie the will or the settlement, is valid according to the relevant governing law. Article 4 of the Convention makes it quite clear that this preliminary issue as to validity falls outside the scope of the Convention. The relevant choice of law rules will be those governing, for example, the formal or essential validity of wills[23] or, in the fairly rare cases where there is a settlement, those governing the validity of contracts[24] or deeds. In the case of a testamentary trust it will also be for the law governing the validity of the will to determine, for example, whether the testator is required to leave a fixed portion of his estate to his/her spouse or children rather than on trust for other beneficiaries.[25]

(d) Transfer of trust assets

Not only does a voluntary trust depend on there being a valid instrument of creation, it is also necessary that the transfer of the trust assets is valid. This further preliminary issue is also excluded from the Convention by reason of Article 4, as being an act "by virtue of which assets are transferred to the trustee". The choice of law issue as to whether a trustee has effective legal title to the assets to hold them for the beneficiaries will normally be governed by the general rules applicable to the transfer of property, eg the law of the situs in the case of tangible movables[26] and of immovables.[27] If the instrument of creation of the trust is valid under its governing law, the trust will, nevertheless, fail if the law of the situs does not permit the transferee to alienate the property at all, but once the property can be alienated in some way it is for the law applicable to the trust to govern the validity and effect of a declaration of trust.[28] *Re Pearse's Settlement*[29] provides an illustration of this type of problem:

> In 1897, the settlor conveyed property to trustees to hold on the trusts of a marriage settlement. In all respects this was an English settlement. She agreed to settle after-acquired property on the same trusts. In 1901 she became entitled to land in Jersey and the question was whether that land was caught by the covenant to settle after-acquired property. There was no doubt as to the validity under English law of the instrument creating the trust. However, since under the law of Jersey, the settlor could not transfer land in Jersey to trustees, in the absence of adequate pecuniary consideration, the Jersey land was not subject to the covenant to settle after-acquired property.

In the case of a declaration of trust over assets already held by the trustee, the exclusion in Article 4 may not apply as assets are not transferred "to" the trustee.[30] The *lex situs* must govern whether the trustee has capacity to alienate the property at all, but once it is clear that the property can be alienated in some way, the *lex situs* cannot govern the trust or its validity of effect, those matters are for the law applicable to the trust determined in accordance with the Convention.[31]

For discussion of the law applicable to other equitable obligations, see supra, p 769. See further on constructive and resulting trusts Dicey, Morris and Collins, 15th edn, 29R-075.

[23] Supra, p 1264 et seq, p 1279 et seq.
[24] Supra, p 689 et seq.
[25] Eg *Re Hernando* (1884) 27 Ch D 284; *Re Annesley* [1926] Ch 692; *Re Ross* [1930] 1 Ch 377; and see supra, pp 1270–1.
[26] Supra, p 1211 et seq.
[27] Supra, p 1199 et seq.
[28] *Akers v Samba Financial Group* [2014] EWCA Civ 1516, [50].
[29] [1909] 1 Ch 304.
[30] *Akers v Samba Financial Group* [2014] EWCA Civ 1516; [2015] Ch 451, [50].
[31] *Akers v Samba Financial Group* [2014] EWCA Civ 1516, [51] applying and explaining the dictum of Lord Hodge in *Joint Administrators of Rangers Football Club Plc, Notes* 2012 SLT 599. See further Harris, in Hayton (ed) *The International Trust* (2011), Chapter 2.

3. CHOICE OF LAW

(a) Choice by the settlor[32]

Article 6 of the Convention embodies party autonomy by providing:

> A trust shall be governed by the law chosen by the settlor. The choice must be express or be implied in the terms of the instrument creating or the writing evidencing the trust, interpreted, if necessary, in the light of the circumstances of the case.

This makes clear that either an express[33] or an implied choice by the settlor of the governing law is permitted. A choice of law clause can also be incorporated from an underlying agreement.[34] Such a rule confirms what had generally been accepted to be the position at common law in relation both to testamentary[35] and *inter vivos*[36] trusts, and whether the case is one of choice of a foreign law by an English domiciled testator or settlor or of English law by a foreign domiciliary.[37] To be effective the choice must be of the substantive law of the jurisdiction chosen[38] and cannot include its private international law rules; ie the doctrine of renvoi is excluded here as elsewhere in the Convention.[39]

No guidance is provided by the Convention on what will constitute an implied choice of the applicable law. In *Berezovsky v Abramovich*,[40] the Court of Appeal held that it must be arguable that what was said at the time when the trust was set up and the matrix within which that agreement was made are both highly relevant considerations. There is a suggestion at common law in the case of testamentary trusts that the testator was presumed to intend that the law of his domicile governed the validity of such trusts.[41] In *Re Barton (Deceased)*, Lawrence Collins J concluded that, even if there had been no express choice of English law, the terms of the Will by which the trust was created, particularly the reference to charitable trusts under English law, would have pointed to an implied choice of English law.[42] In the case of *inter vivos* trusts there is a degree of common law authority indicating circumstances from which the settlor's intention can be determined.[43] For example, reference has been made to such factors as the place of making the original contract or deed,[44] the situs of the property subject to the trust[45] and the place of registration of the trustee company[46] or the place of

---

[32] See Harris (2002), pp 166–213.

[33] See *Re Barton (Deceased), Tod v Barton* [2002] EWHC 264 (Ch); [2002] WTLR 469, per Lawrence Collins J, at [34] and [35].

[34] *Ackerman v Synergy Capital* [2013] EWHC 887 (Ch).

[35] See, eg, *Re Lord Cable* [1977] 1 WLR 7 at 20; *Re Healy's Will* 125 NYS 2d 486 (1953).

[36] See, eg, *Este v Smith* (1854) 18 Beav 112 at 122; *Re Hernando* (1884) 27 Ch D 284 at 292–293; *Re Fitzgerald* [1904] 1 Ch 573 at 587; *Augustus v Permanent Trustee Co (Canberra) Ltd* (1971) 124 CLR 245; *Re Pratt* 8 NY 2d 855, 168 NE 2d 709 (1960).

[37] Cf *Canterbury Corpn v Wyburn and Melbourne Hospital* [1895] AC 89.

[38] This includes, here as elsewhere in the Convention, the law of a part of a multi-territory state which has its own law of trusts, eg of a part of the United Kingdom or of a state within the USA: 1987 Act, s 1(4), and Art 23 of the Convention (not scheduled to the Act).

[39] Art 17; though see Art 15, discussed infra, p 1393.

[40] [2011] EWCA Civ 153; [2011] 1 WLR 2290 at [108].

[41] Eg *Peillon v Brooking* (1858) 25 Beav 218; *Re Aganoor's Trusts* (1895) 64 LJ Ch 521; *Re Lord Cable* [1977] 1 WLR 7 at 20; though this was not an invariable rule, see *A-G v Campbell* (1872) LR 5 HL 524.

[42] *Re Barton (Deceased), Tod v Barton* [2002] EWHC 264 (Ch); [2002] WTLR 469, per Lawrence Collins J, at [36].

[43] See *Revenue Comrs v Pelly* [1940] IR 122.

[44] *Harris Investments Ltd v Smith* [1934] 1 DLR 748.

[45] Ibid; *Lindsay v Miller* [1949] VLR 13.

[46] *A-G v Jewish Colonization Association* [1901] 1 KB 123.

administration of the trust.[47] In *Gorgeous Beauty Ltd v Liu,* Arnold J, found an implied choice of English law on the basis that (i) the declaration of trust was written in English, (ii) the style of drafting corresponded to the English legal style, and (iii) the sole assets of the trust were shares in a UK LLP.[48]

The Convention allows "a severable aspect of the trust" to be governed by a different law from that otherwise applicable.[49] So, a testator or settlor could choose English law to govern the administration of a trust but New York law to govern all other matters relating to the trust—or he could choose the law to govern just one aspect, leaving the determination of the law to govern the others to be decided by the rules applicable in the absence of choice. Where there are trust assets in different jurisdictions the Convention will have to be construed to decide whether choosing different laws to govern the different assets is permitted as "a severable aspect" of the trust.

There are some limits on the freedom of the settlor to choose the governing law. First, if he chooses the law of a country which "does not provide for trusts or the category of trust involved",[50] then such a meaningless choice is ineffective and the trust is governed by the law applicable in the absence of choice.[51] Although the court will be cautious in concluding that the governing law of a trust is one which does not provide for the trust envisaged, such a conclusion is possible.[52] Secondly, there are certain rules which take precedence over any chosen applicable law, ie mandatory rules of the forum, mandatory rules of other countries applicable by reason of the forum's private international law rules and the forum's rules on public policy.[53] Thirdly, a factor which may inhibit choice of the applicable law is that recognition of a trust may be refused if the significant elements of the trust are, but for the choice of the applicable law, the place of administration and the habitual residence of the trustee, more closely connected with a state or states which do not have the institution of the trust or the category of trust involved.[54] So life may not be breathed into a trust in such circumstances by the choice of the law of a common law country.

(b) Absence of choice[55]

If the settlor has not chosen the law to govern the validity of the trust, or has made an ineffective choice by selecting the law of a country where the trust concept is unknown, then Article 7 provides for the determination of the applicable law as follows:

> Where no applicable law has been chosen, a trust shall be governed by the law with which it is most closely connected. In ascertaining the law with which a trust is most closely connected reference shall be made in particular to—
>
> (a) the place of administration of the trust designated by the settlor;
> (b) the situs of the assets of the trust;
> (c) the place of residence or business of the trustee;
> (d) the objects of the trust and the places where they are to be fulfilled.

---

[47] *Chellaram v Chellaram* [1985] Ch 409 at 424–5.
[48] [2014] EWHC 2952 (Ch), at [309].
[49] Art 9. *Re Barton (Deceased), Tod v Barton* [2002] EWHC 264 (Ch); [2002] WTLR 469 at [35].
[50] Art 6.
[51] Art 7, infra. If that law also does not provide for trusts, then the Convention rules cease to apply: Art 5.
[52] *Akers v Samba Financial Group* [2014] EWCA Civ 1516, [30]: Cp cases on Art 7 implied choice referred to below.
[53] Arts 15, 16, 18, discussed infra, pp 1392–3.
[54] Art 13, infra, p 1392.
[55] See Harris (2002), pp 215–32.

The basic rule that a trust should be governed by the law of the country with which it is most closely connected[56] is in substance the same rule as applied at common law, in the absence of choice, both in the case of testamentary[57] and *inter vivos*[58] trusts.

Although Article 7 provides a list of factors for the court to consider, it is not an exclusive list and a court would remain free to attach importance, for example, to domicile.[59] What is not clear is the relative weight to be given to all the factors, whether or not listed in Article 7. All that can really be said is that it will vary with the circumstances of each individual case.[60] There may be a tendency to favour the application of the law of a country under which the trust is valid.[61] However, in *Gorgeous Beauty Ltd v Liu*, Arnold J held that it was not relevant that the trust would be valid under one law and not another.[62] If the trust assets consist of immovable property, it is likely that greater significance will be afforded to the law of the situs of the property.[63] Direct evidence of the settlor's intention as to governing law is not admissible.[64]

What is not made clear expressly by Article 7 is the time at which the factors determining closeness of connection must be considered. It is suggested, however, that, as express provision is made later in relation to change of the applicable law,[65] the appropriate time to consider the factors should be that of the creation of the trust. This would follow the common law position where changes in the identity, and thus the domicile or residence, of the trustees,[66] or in the place of investment,[67] which took place after the trust was created were to be ignored.

Just as with a choice of the applicable law, there are certain limits on the application of the most closely connected law. The forum's mandatory rules and rules of public policy remain applicable despite the close connection of the trust with another law;[68] the mandatory rules

---

[56] In theory, at least, Art 9 would allow different laws to be applied to different aspects of the trust more closely connected with different jurisdictions. If the court decides, unusually, that the most closely connected law is that of a country which does not provide for trusts or for trusts of this kind, then the Convention is inapplicable: Art 5.

[57] See, in the case of movables, *A-G v Campbell* (1872) LR 5 HL 524; and *Re Carapiet's Trust, The Armenian Patriarch of Jerusalem v Sonsino* [2002] EWHC 1304 (Ch); [2002] WTLR 989, at [3]. The position in relation to immovables was less clear, see the 11th edn of this book (1987), pp 884–5.

[58] Eg *Iveagh v IRC* [1954] Ch 364; *Chellaram v Chellaram* [1985] Ch 409; *Chellaram v Chellaram (No 2)* [2002] EWHC 632 (Ch); [2002] 3 All ER 17, per Lawrence Collins J, at [142] and [166]; *Perpetual Executors and Trustees Association of Australia Ltd v Roberts* [1970] VR 732; *Branco v Veira* (1995) 9 ETR (2d) 49 and *Martin v SOS for Work and Pensions* [2009] EWCA Civ 1289, at [35].

[59] Cf *Iveagh v IRC* [1954] Ch 364; *Re Hewitt's Settlement* [1915] 1 Ch 228; and *Re Lord Cable* [1977] 1 WLR 7 at 20. In contrast, see *Re Barton (Deceased), Tod v Barton* [2002] EWHC 264 (Ch); [2002] WTLR 469, per Lawrence Collins J, at [36]. In *Gorgeous Beauty Ltd v Liu* [2014] EWHC 2952 (Ch) Arnold J also considered the legal style in which the declaration was drafted, at [307] and [314].

[60] See Wallace (1987) 36 ICLQ 455, 468–9.

[61] Hayton (1987) 36 ICLQ 260, 272.

[62] [2014] EWHC 2952 (Ch), at [307]. See also *Martin v SOS for Work and Pensions* [2009] EWCA Civ 1289 and *Berezovsky v Abramovich* [2010] EWHC 647 at [183] (reversed but not on this point [2011] EWCA Civ 153).

[63] Art 7, para (b); and see, eg, *Freke v Lord Carbery* (1873) LR 16 Eq 461; *Peabody v Kent* 153 App Div 286, 13 NYS 32 (1912); affd 213 NY 154, 107 NE 51 (1914).

[64] *Chellaram v Chellaram* [1985] 1 Ch 409 at 425; *Re Carapiet's Trust, The Armenian Patriarch of Jerusalem v Sonsino* [2002] EWHC 1304 (Ch); [2002] WTLR 989 at [5] and [12].

[65] Art 10, infra, pp 1390–1.

[66] *Iveagh v IRC* [1954] Ch 364 at 370; and see *Re Hewitt's Settlement* [1915] 1 Ch 228 at 233–234; *Duke of Marlborough v A-G* [1945] Ch 78 at 85.

[67] *Iveagh v IRC*, supra: and see *Re Fitzgerald* [1904] 1 Ch 573 at 588; *Duke of Marlborough v A-G*, supra.

[68] Arts 16, 18, infra, pp 1392–3.

of other countries which are to be applied by reason of the forum's private international law rules are also applicable.[69]

(c) Scope of the applicable law[70]

Article 8 makes it clear that the applicable law determined by reference to Articles 6 or 7 is to govern "the validity of the trust, its construction, its effects and the administration of the trust". The basic starting point is, therefore, that the same law governs all these issues; though, as has been seen, it is possible for a severable aspect of a trust to be governed by a different law.[71] This generality of approach has the effect that the same law will normally apply to a testamentary or *inter vivos* trust even though the trust property consists of both movable and immovable property.

Article 8 goes on to list a non-exclusive range of matters which are to be governed by the applicable law, namely:

(a) the appointment, resignation and removal of trustees, the capacity to act as a trustee, and the devolution of the office of trustee;

(b) the rights and duties of trustees among themselves;

(c) the right of trustees to delegate in whole or in part the discharge of their duties or the exercise of their powers;

(d) the power of trustees to administer or dispose of trust assets, to create security interests in the trust assets, or to acquire new assets;

(e) the powers of investment of trustees;

(f) restrictions upon the duration of the trust, and upon the power to accumulate the income of the trust;

(g) the relationships between the trustees and the beneficiaries including the personal liability of the trustees to the beneficiaries;[72]

(h) the variation or termination of the trust;[73]

(i) the distribution of the trust assets;

(j) the duty of trustees to account for their administration.

The reference of these matters to the law determined by Articles 6 or 7 very much follows the common law approach in the case of *inter vivos* trusts. This may be illustrated by *Augustus v Permanent Trustee Co (Canberra) Ltd*:[74]

> The settlor executed a voluntary deed of settlement in the Australian Capital Territory. He was resident and domiciled in New South Wales. The trusts were in favour of the settlor's children and grandchildren; and those who were alive at the date of the settlement were also domiciled and resident in New South Wales. The trustee was a corporation registered in Canberra which was where the funds were paid over by the settlor. The trust was void for perpetuity under the law of the Australian Capital Territory, but valid under the law of New South Wales.

In the High Court of Australia, Walsh J held that the issue of validity was to be determined by the proper law of the trust and, there being a clause in the trust deed which was interpreted as a reference to the law of New South Wales, he upheld the validity of the trust, applying the law of that state.

---

[69] Art 15, infra, p 1393.

[70] See Harris (2002), pp 233–80.

[71] Art 9, supra, p 1390.

[72] See Barnard [1992] CLJ 472.

[73] Discussed more fully, infra, p 1323 et seq; see also *Re Barton (Deceased), Tod v Barton* [2002] EWHC 264 (Ch); [2002] WTLR 469.

[74] (1971) 124 CLR 245; and see *Lindsay v Miller* [1949] VLR 13.

Article 8 specifically states that the applicable law is to govern the construction of the trust. Where no view, express or implied, has been indicated by the testator or settlor, no problem arises and the most closely connected law will be applied.[75] It may be, however, that it is possible to determine the law which was intended to govern the construction or interpretation of the trust and it would seem to be the case that, under the Convention, as under the common law, the court's first task is to try to find whether there is any such intention on the part of the testator or settlor.[76] If so, then the intended law should be applied by reason of Article 6 even though it may only be applied to this severable aspect of the trust.[77]

The law to govern the administration of the trust is also specifically included within the terms of Article 8. This means that, where there is a choice, express or implied, of the law to govern the administration of the trust, effect will be given to that choice,[78] even though a different law is held to govern the validity of the trust.[79] Indeed it may also be the case that the closest connection test, in the absence of choice, leads to a different law being applied to administration from that applied to validity.[80] One or two words of caution are, however, necessary here. It may not always be easy to determine the place of administration, as where a testator leaves property in two countries creating separate administrations in each with the trustees' investment powers varying as between the applicable laws of the two separate places of administration.[81] Whilst here it could be argued that there are two separate administrations governed by separate laws, that escape is not available where there are issues which affect the administration of the trust as a whole, such as the appointment of a new trustee. For such an issue the law of just one place of administration needs to be identified; and whilst there is some common law authority supporting reference to the place where the bulk of the assets is held,[82] a better view is to identify the place of administration by reference to the place of residence of all, or a majority, of the trustees.[83] It has been assumed so far that it is easy to decide whether a matter refers to validity or administration but this may not always be the case.[84] Indeed the categorisation may vary between legal systems, thus requiring the choice of a legal system to resolve the issue. Whilst the Convention is silent on this issue, it has been suggested that it is for the law governing validity to determine the matter.[85]

(d) Variation of the applicable law[86]

There is no doubt that a trust must have a law or laws governing its validity, construction and administration from the moment of its creation. If further assets are later transferred to the trustees, that will not, as such, affect the law applicable to the trust. Article 10 of the Convention envisages, however, that as with contracts[87] the law to govern some or all aspects

---

[75] As at common law in *Re Levick's Will Trusts* [1963] 1 WLR 311 at 319; *Philipson-Stow v IRC* [1961] AC 727; *Perpetual Executors and Trustees Association of Australia Ltd v Roberts* [1970] VR 732.

[76] Eg *Re Pilkington's Will Trusts* [1937] Ch 574; *Trustees Executors and Agency Co Ltd v Margottini* [1960] VR 417; *Philipson-Stow v IRC*, supra, at 761.

[77] Eg *Spencer's Trustees v Ruggles* 1982 SLT 165.

[78] As at common law, see *Chelleram v Chelleram* [1985] Ch 409 at 431–2; *In the Estate of Webb* (1992) 57 SASR 193.

[79] Art 9, in allowing a different law to be applied to a severable aspect of a trust, makes specific reference to matters of administration; and see *In the Estate of Webb*, supra, at 204.

[80] Eg *Re Wilks* [1935] Ch 645; *Re Kehr* [1952] Ch 26.

[81] Eg *Re Tyndall* [1913] SASR 39.

[82] *Permanent Trustee Co (Canberra) Ltd v Permanent Trustee Co of New South Wales Ltd* (1969) 14 FLR 246 at 252–3.

[83] *Re Smyth* [1898] 1 Ch 89 at 94.

[84] *Chelleram v Chelleram* [1985] Ch 409; and see Wallace (1987) 36 ICLQ 454, 474–5.

[85] Harris (2002), pp 234, and 283–9.

[86] See Harris (2002), pp 297–308.

[87] Supra, pp 692–4.

of a trust may be varied during the lifetime of the trust, eg by a later express choice of the governing law, the trust up to that point having been governed by the law determined under Article 7. Article 10 does not lay down a substantive rule that such variation is permitted but rather provides a choice of law rule for resolving this issue by stipulating that "the law applicable to the validity of the trust shall determine whether that law or the law governing a severable aspect of the trust may be replaced by another law".[88] So, if English law is the law already applicable to the trust, it will decide whether or not, for example, a provision in the trust allowing the trustees to replace the law governing all or part of the trust shall have effect.[89] It should be noted that Article 10 assumes that one law can be identified as that applicable to the validity of the trust even though different aspects of the trust are expressly governed by different laws. So if validity is expressly governed by English law and administration by New York law, it is for English law to decide whether the law governing the administration of the trust may later be varied.

4. RECOGNITION[90]

Chapter III of the Hague Convention is concerned with the recognition of trusts, and, as such, is of more practical importance for the recognition of trusts in civil law countries where the concept of the trust is unfamiliar—though it is no doubt important that English trusts secure recognition in other Contracting States. The approach of the Convention is, in Article 11, almost to state the obvious by providing that a trust created in accordance with the choice of law rules laid down in the Convention shall be recognised as a trust. It goes on, however, to make provision (really for the benefit of countries where the trust is unfamiliar) for the implications and effects of recognition:

> Such recognition shall imply, as a minimum, that the trust property constitutes a separate fund,[91] that the trustee may sue and be sued in his capacity as trustee, and that he may appear or act in this capacity before a notary or any person acting in an official capacity.
>
> In so far as the law applicable to the trust requires or provides, such recognition shall imply, in particular—
>
> (a) that personal creditors of the trustee shall have no recourse against the trust assets;
> (b) that the trust assets shall not form part of the trustee's estate upon his insolvency or bankruptcy;
> (c) that the trust assets shall not form part of the matrimonial property of the trustee or his spouse nor part of the trustee's estate upon his death;
> (d) that the trust assets may be recovered when the trustee, in breach of trust, has mingled trust assets with his own property or has alienated trust assets. However, the rights and obligations of any third party holder of the assets shall remain subject to the law determined by the choice of law rules of the forum.[92]

It is noticeable that these provisions concentrate, at least on their face, on the position of the trustee though they do by inference provide safeguards for beneficiaries. Attention has been drawn to the fact that the last part of paragraph (d) will restrict the ability of a beneficiary

---

[88] *Chellaram v Chellaram (No 2)* [2002] EWHC 632 (Ch); [2002] 3 All ER 17, at [146] and [160].

[89] Change could also be effected by agreement of the beneficiaries, though this really amounts to the making of a new settlement: *Duke of Marlborough v A-G* [1945] Ch 78 at 85; *Iveagh v IRC* [1954] Ch 364 at 370.

[90] Harris (2002), pp 311–35; Hayton, in Hayton (ed) *The International Trust* (2011), chapter 3.

[91] The trustee is entitled, under Art 12, to register trust assets in his capacity as trustee provided such registration is not prohibited by or inconsistent with the law of the country where registration is sought.

[92] Art 14 permits, also, the application of rules of law more favourable to recognition.

to trace trust assets into the hands of a third party where the assets are situated in a country where the trust concept is unknown.[93]

There are, however, limitations on the recognition to be given to a foreign trust. There are, first, the generally applicable limitations which allow for the application of the public policy or mandatory rules of the forum or those designated by its choice of law rules.[94] If these last rules prevent the recognition of a trust, then Article 15 stipulates that "the court shall try to give effect to the objects of the trust by other means". This is a very vague exhortation and is likely to prove particularly difficult to operate in civil law countries.

A further limitation on recognition is provided by Article 13:

> No State shall be bound to recognise a trust the significant elements of which, except for the choice of the applicable law, the place of administration and the habitual residence of the trustee, are more closely connected with States which do not have the institution of the trust or the category of trust involved.

This is designed to protect the interests of states where the trust concept is unknown and has, therefore, been excluded from the provisions of the Convention scheduled to the 1987 Act.[95] Nevertheless, lawyers in England need to be aware that the provision may limit the recognition abroad of a trust expressed to be governed by English law but which is generally more closely connected with a "non-trust" state.[96]

5. MANDATORY RULES AND PUBLIC POLICY

The provisions of the Convention dealing with mandatory rules and public policy apply, normally, both to the question of the determination of the applicable law and to that of the recognition of a foreign trust.

(a) Mandatory rules[97]

Article 16 embodies the generally accepted private international law provision that, notwithstanding choice of law or recognition rules, the mandatory rules[98] of the forum may continue to be applied.[99] It does so by describing such rules as "provisions of the law of the forum which must be applied even to international situations".[100] Article 16 goes on to allow a court to apply the mandatory rules of another sufficiently closely connected state. Such a provision was no more acceptable to the United Kingdom in the context of trusts than of contract[101] and a power of reservation[102] was exercised to exclude it.

---

[93] Hayton (1987) 36 ICLQ 260, 275–6.
[94] Arts 15, 16 and 18, infra, pp 1392–3.
[95] Harris (2002), pp 341–50.
[96] It is also the case that a Contracting State may reserve the right to apply the recognition provisions only to trusts whose validity is governed by the law of a Contracting State: Art 21 (not included in the provisions scheduled to the 1987 Act as the United Kingdom has not exercised this power of reservation).
[97] Harris (2002), pp 355–85.
[98] Examples that have been given of such rules include those designed to prevent the export of currency or of cultural heritage objects: Hayton (1987) 36 ICLQ 260, 278.
[99] S 1(3) of the 1987 Act makes clear that, if there are such mandatory rules, then an English court must apply them. See, however, Harris (2005) 121 LQR 16, 21; Harris (2002) pp 264–7.
[100] Contrast the rather different description in Art 7(2) of the 1980 Rome Convention on Contractual Obligations, scheduled to the Contracts (Applicable Law) Act 1990, and the definition of overriding mandatory provisions in Art 9(1) of the Rome I Regulation, supra, p 746 et seq.
[101] See Rome Convention, Art 7(1), supra, p 745. A more limited application of third state mandatory rules is provided for in Art 9(3) of the Rome I Regulation, supra, p 751 et seq.
[102] Art 16, third para.

Rather more complex, and loosely drafted, provisions as to mandatory rules are to be found in Article 15 which states that the "Convention does not prevent the application of provisions of the law designated by the conflicts rules of the forum, in so far as those provisions cannot be derogated from by voluntary act". There is a somewhat broader description here than under Article 16 of the rules which the forum may apply, notwithstanding the provisions of the Convention. Although Article 15 merely gives the forum court power to continue to apply those rules, the 1987 Act requires an English court to do so.[103] What is striking is that the mandatory rules in question are not those of the forum but rather of another country (not that governing the trust) the application of whose law has been determined by "the conflicts rules of the forum". Such conflicts rules must be rules other than those contained in the Convention, ie rules applicable to an issue classified as other than one concerning the validity or recognition of a trust.[104] Article 15 then goes on to give a non-exclusive list of such issues:

(a) the protection of minors and incapable parties;
(b) the personal and proprietary effects of marriage;
(c) succession rights, testate and intestate, especially the indefeasible shares of spouses and relatives;
(d) the transfer of title to property and security interests in property;
(e) the protection of creditors in matters of insolvency;
(f) the protection, in other respects, of third parties acting in good faith.

(b) Public policy[105]

Article 18 contains the provision generally to be found in Hague Conventions allowing the forum to disregard the Convention provisions "when their application would be manifestly incompatible with public policy".[106] This would enable an English court to impose some limit on the freedom to choose the applicable law under Article 6 if, for example, there had been an attempt to evade the English rule against perpetuities by the choice of a foreign law to govern what was essentially an English trust.[107]

6. VARIATION OF TRUSTS AND SETTLEMENTS

(a) Variation of Trusts Act 1958[108]

Section 1 of the Variation of Trusts Act 1958 provides that where property, whether movable or immovable, is held on trusts arising under any will, settlement or other disposition, the court may, if it thinks fit, approve any arrangement varying or revoking all or any of the trusts. The courts have held that the power of the English courts to exercise their jurisdiction under this provision is not limited to trusts governed by English law,[109] because to take such a restrictive view would mean "that the court would be unable to vary a settlement made (say) in 1920 and governed by (say) Australian law, even though the beneficiaries, the trustees and

---

[103] S 1(3). See *C v C (Ancillary Relief: Nuptial Settlement)* [2004] EWCA Civ 1030; [2005] Fam 250.

[104] *Re Barton (Deceased), Tod v Barton* [2002] EWHC 264 (Ch); [2002] WTLR 469, per Lawrence Collins J, at [42]. See for a discussion of Art 15(d) *Akers v Samba Financial Group* [2014] EWCA Civ 1516, [62].

[105] Harris (2002), pp 390–5.

[106] Art 19 preserves the powers of states in fiscal matters. It appears not to have been thought necessary to include this in the provisions scheduled to the 1987 Act.

[107] Dicey, Morris and Collins, 15th edn, paras 29-033–29.035.

[108] Harris (2002), pp 261–4.

[109] *Re Kerr's Settlement Trusts* [1963] Ch 553; *Re Paget's Settlement* [1965] 1 WLR 1046.

the trust property had been for many years in this country. It would be unfortunate if the court had no jurisdiction in such a case."[110]

The power under the 1958 Act has to be set against the provision in Article 8 of the Trusts Convention which makes clear that "the variation or termination of the trust"[111] is a matter to be governed by the law applicable to the trust and not, for example, by the law of the forum. In *Re Barton (Deceased)*,[112] in proceedings brought by one of the executors and trustees of Professor Sir Derek Barton, for directions in relation to a Deed of Variation executed by the deceased's beneficiaries, the principal question of law was whether English law (the law expressly chosen in terms of Article 6) or Texas law (the deceased having died domiciled in Texas) should govern the validity and effect of the Deed. The court concluded that Article 8 assigned to English law the question of the ability of the beneficiaries to end or reconstitute the trust.[113]

How does Article 8 inter-relate with the 1958 Act? The 1958 Act, as its long title states, is concerned with the jurisdiction of the courts to vary trusts, whereas Article 8 of the Trusts Convention is concerned with choice of law matters. On that basis the court still retains the power under the 1958 Act to vary a trust governed by foreign law but there would seem to be two limitations on the exercise of that power. The first is that, where there are substantial foreign elements in the case, the court should proceed with caution in deciding whether to assume jurisdiction in such a case, following the advice of Cross J in *Re Paget's Settlement*:

> If, for example, the court were asked to vary a settlement which was plainly a Scottish settlement, it might well hesitate to exercise its jurisdiction to vary the trusts, simply because some, or even all, the trustees and beneficiaries were in this country. It may well be that the judge would say that the Court of Session was the appropriate tribunal to deal with the case.[114]

The second limitation is that, in exercising the jurisdiction under the 1958 Act, the court, in making a variation, should apply the substantive law of the country governing the trust, identified by reference to Articles 6 or 7 of the Convention. If the law governing the trust does not permit variation, then the jurisdiction under the 1958 Act should not be exercised.[115]

(b) Variation of marriage settlements

There is power in the English court when granting a divorce, nullity or judicial separation decree, or at any time after the decree, to vary any settlement of movable and immovable property made on the parties to the marriage, whether by an ante-nuptial or a post-nuptial settlement.[116] The court can also extinguish or reduce the interest of either of the parties to the marriage under such a settlement.[117] Whenever the court has jurisdiction in the main

---

[110] *Re Paget's Settlement*, supra, at 1050.

[111] Art 8, para (h).

[112] *Re Barton (Deceased), Tod v Barton* [2002] EWHC 264 (Ch); [2002] WTLR 469.

[113] Ibid, at [38] and [43].

[114] [1965] 1 WLR 1046 at 1050. It has, however, to be noted that the judge was in fact prepared to vary a trust which may have been governed by New York law.

[115] See further Harris (2007) 11(2) Jersey and Guernsey Law Review 184.

[116] Matrimonial Causes Act 1973, s 24(1)(c) discussed in *Radmacher v Granatino* [2010] UKSC 42. See also the orders which can be made after a foreign decree, under the Matrimonial and Family Proceedings Act 1984, s 17, supra, p 1063 et seq. See *C v C (Ancillary Relief: Nuptial Settlement)* [2004] EWCA Civ 1030; [2005] Fam 250.

[117] Ibid, s 24(1)(d).

proceedings for divorce, nullity or judicial separation, then it also has jurisdiction to order such variations.[118] This application of English law as the law of the forum has not been restricted to settlements governed by English law or of English property. For example, in *Nunneley v Nunneley and Marrian*,[119] the English court varied a settlement made in Scotland and in Scottish form of movables and immovables in Scotland. Is this power now limited by the Recognition of Trusts Act 1987 to settlements governed by English law? It would seem undesirable that the power of the court in such family proceedings should be limited by the choice of law rules in the 1987 Act; and the exclusion of those rules might well be supported by reference to Article 15[120] which allows the English forum still to apply its conflict rules, here in fact leading to the application of the substantive law of the forum, to, inter alia, "the personal and proprietary effects of marriage".

The issue of whether an English court might vary a trust governed by a foreign law in ancillary relief proceedings, and which law it should apply in so doing,[121] was addressed in *C v C (Ancillary Relief: Nuptial Settlement)*.[122] Mr and Mrs Charalambous married in 1984. Before the birth of their second child, Mr Charalambous' mother created a settlement, expressly governed by Jersey law, known as the Hickory Trust. In 2001, by deed of appointment, Mr and Mrs Charalambous ceased to be beneficiaries under the Hickory Trust. Their marriage broke down in 2002. Mrs Charalambous commenced ancillary relief proceedings, including an application under section 24 of the Matrimonial Causes Act 1973 for the variation of the Hickory Trust as a post-nuptial settlement. It is clear from Article 8(2)(h) of the Trusts Convention that, if a foreign law governs the trust, it is that foreign law's substantive provisions on variation of trusts which should be applied. The difficulty arose, however, from the interface between Article 8(2)(h), which would have led to the application of Jersey law, and Article 15(b), which would have secured the operation of English law. The Court of Appeal concluded that the statutory provisions to vary settlements under section 24(1)(c) were provisions which could not be derogated from by voluntary act within the meaning of Article 15. Accordingly, Mrs Charalambous' claim was excepted from the Convention, and governed by English law rather than by the law of Jersey.

It has been pointed out that Article 15 does not expressly mention the effects of divorce as an area of law in which the governing law's mandatory rules are preserved, and further, that even if Article 15 is deemed broad enough to encompass ancillary relief upon divorce, it should not necessarily be invoked to override the general rule in Article 8(2)(h).[123] Harris has argued that it would be better to apply the law applicable to the trust to determine whether to vary the trust upon divorce, subject only to the Article 18 public policy saving.[124] Whilst a restrained approach to the application of Article 15 may be desirable, arguably that is not permitted by the wording of section 1(3) of the 1987 Act;[125] but restraint may be shown, nevertheless, in the exercise of classifying rules as mandatory.[126] The fact that the English court

---

[118] *Cammell v Cammell* [1965] P 467, supra, p 1051.
[119] (1890) 15 PD 186; and see *Forsyth v Forsyth* [1891] P 363.
[120] Supra, p 1393.
[121] Harris (2005) 121 LQR 16.
[122] [2004] EWCA Civ 1030; [2005] Fam 250.
[123] Though see Von Overbeck Report, paras 138 and 139; and *C v C (Ancillary Relief: Nuptial Settlement)* [2004] EWCA Civ 1030; [2005] Fam 250, per Thorpe LJ, at [32].
[124] Harris (2005) 121 LQR 16, 19.
[125] *Pace* Harris (2002), p 266.
[126] Cf Dicey, Morris and Collins, 15th edn, paras 29-029–29-032.

would seem to continue to have power to apply English law to the variation of such marriage settlements does not mean that all foreign elements are to be ignored. The jurisdiction of the court is discretionary and it may well choose not to exercise its power if its order would be ineffective in the foreign country, as where the respondent had no connection with England, no property in England and where any English order would not be recognised in the foreign country.[127] Indeed, such ineffectiveness may justify setting aside service of the claim form on the foreign trustees.[128]

---

[127] *Tallack v Tallack and Broekema* [1927] P 211; cf *Hunter v Hunter and Waddington* [1962] P 1.
[128] *Goff v Goff* [1934] P 107; *Wyler v Lyons* [1963] P 274.

INDEX

Abduction of children *see* child
  abduction
Abuse of process
  recognition of foreign
    judgments 432–3, 563
  residual discretion to decline
    jurisdiction 471–2
  unconscionable
    conduct 432–3
Acquired rights theory 21–3
Actions *in personam*
  enforcement of foreign
    judgments in personam
    fixed sum
      judgments 551–2
    institution of fresh legal
      proceedings 551
    multiple damages
      awards 553–5
    public laws 552–3
  Foreign Judgments
    (Reciprocal
    Enforcement) Act
    1933 595–7
  jurisdiction 6–7
  jurisdiction of English courts
    under traditional rules
    other bases of
      jurisdiction 381–2
    overview 323–4
    service of
      proceedings 324–32
    service out of
      jurisdiction 334–81
    submission to
      jurisdiction 332–4
  limitations on proceedings
    sovereign immunity 504
    statutory limitations 518
  recognition and enforcement
    of foreign judgments at
    common law
    meaning and scope 528
    residence and presence at
      time of suit 529–31
    submission to
      jurisdiction 531–40
  recognition of foreign
    judgments *in
    personam* 563
  scope of PIL 6
Actions *in rem*

Brussels I Recast
  exclusive
    jurisdiction 219–20
  jurisdiction under
    Art 8(4) 288
  Foreign Judgments
    (Reciprocal
    Enforcement) Act
    1933 597
  jurisdiction of English courts
    under traditional rules
    effect of Brussels/Lugano
      system 386–90
    ships as
      defendants 382–4
    ships other than the
      primary ship 384–5
    stays 385
  limitations on proceedings
    sovereign
      immunity 504
    statutory
      limitations 518
  recognition and enforcement
    of foreign judgments at
    common law
    definition of judgment in
      rem 544–6
    enforcement 548
    jurisdictional
      requirements 546–8
  recognition of foreign
    judgments *in rem* 563
Administration of estates
  see also succession; trusts
  bona vacantia 49–50
  choice of law
    classification 1333–4
    governing law 1334–5
  common law and civil
    law jurisdictions
    distinguished 1325–6
  commonwealth
    grants 1336–7
  English grants
    administrator's
      title 1332–3
    consular grants 1332
    jurisdiction 1330
    person to whom grant
      made 1331–2
    separate wills 1330–1

EU Succession
  Regulation 1327–9
  Hague Convention 1326–7
  immovables 1258
  recognition of foreign
    administrators 1335–6
  renvoi 58, 58–9
  Scotland and NI 1337
  sovereign immunity 505
Administration of Justice Act
  1920 677
Admiralty claims *see*
  maritime law
Adoption
  Convention rules
    Adoptions with a Foreign
      Element Regulations
      2005 1216–19
    background 1213
    Hague
      Convention 1213–16
  declarations 1054
  effect of foreign adoptions
    British citizenship and
      immigration 1230–1
    status 1229–30
  English law
    Adoption and Children
      Act 2002 1206–7
    Adoptions with a Foreign
      Element Regulations
      2005 1207–8
    choice of law 1210–13
    jurisdiction 1208–9
    overview 1206
  overview 1193–4, 1205–6
  parental responsibility 1108
  recognition of foreign
    adoptions
    adoptions made elsewhere
      in the British
      Isles 1223
    adoptions made in
      other foreign
      countries 1225–9
    annulment of foreign
      adoptions 1225
    Convention
      adoptions 1223–4
    overseas
      adoptions 1224–5
    overview 1222–3

Adoption (*cont.*):
taking children into and
out of UK
Adoptions with a Foreign
Element Regulations
2005 1219–20
temporary
suspensions 1220–2
Agencies
habitual residence 739, 802
insurance 703
secondary insolvency
jurisdiction 1316
special jurisdiction under
Article 7(2) 279–83
Agents
contractual claims 344
exclusions from Rome
I Regulation 701–2
mandatory rules 749
non-contractual
obligations 849
powers of appointment
capacity 1361
essential validity 1362
service of
proceedings 326, 329
state immunity 498,
511–13, 515
Alien enemies 495–6
Ambassadors 509–10
Ancillary relief *see also*
maintenance
jurisdiction of English
court 1060–1
recognition and
enforcement 1078–9
Annuities
arrears of rent charged on
land abroad 485
movable and immovable
property
distinguished 1254
Annulments
foreign annulments
capacity to
remarry 925–6
effect of
non-recognition 926
prohibitions against
remarriage 926–7
recognition of foreign
annulments
decrees made elsewhere in
British Isles 1001–2
decrees obtained in
EU 1002–5

decrees obtained
outside EU or in
Denmark 1005–12
extra-judicial
annulments 1012–24
grounds for non-
recognition 1024–34
history and development
of rules 1000–1
retrospectivity 1034,
1035–6
Ante-nuptial contracts
capacity 1375–7
essential validity 1378
formal validity 1377–8
general rule 1372–4
Anti-suit injunctions *see*
restraint of foreign
proceedings
Appeals
default judgments 538–9
fling a second
acknowledgement of
service 333
recognition and enforcement
under Brussels I Recast
overview 646–7
requirement for
enforceable
judgment 647
where recognition alone
sought 647–9
Applicable law *see*
governing law
Arbitration
exclusion from Brussels
I Recast 208–11
exclusion from Rome
I Regulation 700–1
no specific ground for refusal
of recognition 645–6
recognition and enforcement
of foreign awards
Administration of Justice
Act 1920 677
Arbitration Act
1950 670
Arbitration Act
1996 670–6
Arbitration (International
Investment
Disputes) Act
1966 677
Civil Jurisdiction and
Judgments Act
1982 669–70
common law rules 667–9

complicated questions of
PIL 520–1
Foreign Judgments
(Reciprocal
Enforcement) Act
1933 677
numerous separate sets of
rules 524
overview 666–7
restraint of foreign
proceedings
Brussels I Recast 478–80
common law rules 441–2
stays of English proceedings
under common
law 416–21
Arbitration Act 1950 670
Arbitration Act 1996
discretion to refuse
recognition or
enforcement 673–6
grounds for refusal of
recognition 672–3
scope 670–2
Arbitration (International
Investment Disputes) Act
1966 677
Armed forces
state immunity 500
valid marriages
ceremonies abroad 902
military forces in
belligerent
occupation 905–7
voluntary residence 160, 181
Arrestment *ad fundandam*
jurisdictionem 381–2
Assessment of damages
applicable law in the absence
of choice under
Rome I 767
non-contractual
obligations 861–3
road traffic accidents 819
scope of PIL 95–6
Assignments *see* **transfers and**
assignments
Asylum seekers *see* **Refugees**
and asylum seekers
Attachment by creditors
competence of English
Courts 382
res judicata 549
tangible movables 1275
Auction sales
applicable law in the absence
of choice 726, 730

effect on title 1268–9
negotiable
    instruments 1295

Bona vacantia 49–50, 505
Branches
    habitual residence 739, 802
    insurance 703
    secondary insolvency
        jurisdiction 1316
    special jurisdiction under
        Article 7(2) 279–83
Breach of obligations
    applicable law in the absence
        of choice under Rome I
        assessment of
            damages 767
        meaning and
            scope 766–7
        procedural
            limitation 767–8
    Brussels/Lugano
        System 253, 277
Brussels Convention 1968
    jurisdiction 312
    recognition and
        enforcement 652–65
Brussels I Recast
    applicability
        civil and commercial
            matters 204–6
        within its scope 202–4
    bases of jurisdiction
        exclusive subject-matter
            jurisdiction 217–26
        overview 216–17
    consumer contracts
        scope 292–5
        special rules 295–6
    employment contracts
        jurisdiction
            agreements 302
        scope 297–9
        special rules 300–2
        submissions 302
    excluded matters
        arbitration 208–11
        domicile 212–15
        insolvency 207–8
        maintenance
            obligations 211–12
        marriage 206–7
        social security 208
        succession 212
    exclusive subject-matter
        jurisdiction
        company law issues 224

enforcement of
    judgments 225–6
intellectual property 225
overview 217–19
public registers 224–5
rights in rem 219–20
short-term holiday
    lets 222–6
tenancies 221–2
general jurisdiction 243–4
interpretation of Rome
    I Regulation 690–1
matters relating to insurance
    jurisdiction
        agreements 290–1
    scope 289–90
    special rules 290
    submissions 290–1
overview 191–4
parallel proceedings
    overview 311–12, 442–3
    proceedings in
        another Member
        State 443–57
    proceedings in
        non-Member
        State 457–9
prorogation of jurisdiction
    overview 226
    submission to
        forum 226–9
provisional measures
    as to the substance 303
    where no jurisdiction as to
        the substance 303–5
    where none were available
        beforehand 305–7
recognition and enforcement
    of foreign judgments
    and awards
    agreements with non-
        Contracting
        States 651–2
    appeals in original
        Member
        State 646–50
    applicability 611–18
    automatic recognition
        without
        jurisdictional
        safeguards 650–1
    difference with Lugano
        Convention
        1988 654–5
    enforcement 619–25
    estoppel effect of
        judgment

in Member
    State 649–50
grounds for
    refusal 625–43
impact of the Hague
    Convention on
    Choice of Court
    Agreements 651
non-grounds for
    refusal 643–6
objectives 608–11
recognition 617–19
restraint of foreign
    proceedings
    discretion to
        restrain 475–6
    traditional English
        powers 476–82
service of proceedings
    practicalities 308–9
    rights of the
        defendant 309–11
    rules 308
special definition of domicile
    companies 200–2
    natural persons 198–200
    trusts 200–2
special jurisdiction
    under Article 7 244–83
    under Article 8 283–8
    under Article 9 288–9
    relevant provisions 244
stays
    discretion to stay 459–60
    forum non
        conveniens 459
    forum non
        conveniens 460–71
    overview 311–12
    "reflexive" effects 471–3
    residual discretion
        to decline
        jurisdiction 471–3
Brussels II
child abduction
    adequate arrangements
        for child
        protection 1159–60
    applicant's views 1159
    child's views 1159
    complementary
        provisions 1157
    enforcement of return
        judgments 1162–3
    expeditious
        procedure 1158
    jurisdiction 1157–8

Brussels II (*cont.*):
child abduction (*cont.*):
non-return
orders 1160–61
return of child 1158
divorce and judicial
separation
application of national
rules 962
principles of general
jurisdiction 955–62
proposals for
reform 962–4
nullity of marriage 964–5
parental responsibility
concurrent proceedings in
EU 1117–20
refusal of applications and
stays 1113–16
rules of
jurisdiction 1094–
101
scope 1092–4
recognition of divorces,
separations and
annulments
applicability 1002–3
differences in applicable
law 1005
general principle of
recognition 1003
grounds for non-
recognition 1004–5
jurisdiction of origin
may not be
reviewed 1005
non-review as to
substance 1005
restraint of foreign
proceedings 979
stays of matrimonial
proceedings
discharge of orders 978
discretionary
stays 972–8
obligatory stays 967–72
overview 967
Brussels/Lugano System
see also **Rome I Regulation**;
Rome II Regulation
actions *in rem* under
traditional English rules
basis of
jurisdiction 386–7
stays 387–90
Brussels Convention 1968
jurisdiction 312

recognition and
enforcement 652–3
Brussels I Recast
applicability 202–15
overview 191–4
special definition of
domicile 198–202
Brussels II
application of national
rules 962
child abduction 1152–63
nullity of
marriage 964–5
parental
responsibility 1092–
101, 1113–16,
1117–20
principles of general
jurisdiction 955–62
proposals for
reform 962–4
restraint of foreign
proceedings 979
stays of matrimonial
proceedings 967–78
Hague Convention
on Choice of
Court Agreements
2005 314–17
jurisdiction
aids to
interpretation 197–8
Brussels
Convention 188–9
Brussels I Recast 191–4
Brussels I Regulation
and Brussels
I Recast 187–8
EC/Denmark
Agreement 188
Lugano Convention
2007 189
Modified Regulation 189
principles and decisions
laid down by
Court 195–7
referrals to the Court of
Justice 194–5
jurisdiction within UK
under Modified
Regulation
applicability 317–19
modifications 319–21
stays 321–2
limitations on proceedings
foreign
immovables 492–4

persons who cannot
invoke the
jurisdiction 495–6
sovereign
immunity 497–518
statutory
limitations 518–19
Lugano Convention 2007
applicability 313–14
financial relief in
the English
courts 1069–70
part of the process of
cooperation 313
stays 314
terminology 314
Modified Regulation
jurisdiction within
UK 317–22
overview 189
recognition and enforcement
of foreign judgments
and awards
Brussels Convention
1968 652–65
Brussels
I Recast 608–52
EC/Denmark
Agreement 652
European Enforcement
Order Regulation
2004 656–9
European Order For
Payment Procedure
Regulation
2006 660–3
European Small
Claims Procedure
Regulation
2007 663–5
Lugano Convention
1988 653–5
overview 522–4
statutory
provisions 603–4
Rome Convention
1980 683–4
Rome III
applicable law in
matrimonial
matters 982
coming into
effect 993
enhanced
cooperation 983
reform proposals 962
Burden of proof *see* **proof**

Capacity
ante-nuptial
    contracts 1375–7
applicable law under Rome
    II 865–6
contracts to transfer
    immovable
    property 1261–2
corporations 1308
domicile 168
exclusion from Rome
    I Regulation 697
family law
    capacity to marry 1050
    to marry 909–27
    rights of custody 1136
    welfare of children 1153
limitations on dominance of
    applicable law
    Article 13 763–4
    common law rules 761–3
to marry
    law of the place of
        celebration 919–21
    major issue relating
        to choice of
        law 909–10
    public policy 921–2
    real and substantial
        connection test 924
    recognition of foreign
        divorces or
        annulments 925–8
    renvoi 922–3
    rule in *Sottomayor v De*
        Barros (No 2) 918–19
    theoretical
        perspectives 910–18
mental incapacity
    common law
        rules 1245–8
    Mental Capacity Act
        2005 1233–45
    overview 1232–3
polygamous marriages
    common law rules 936–8
powers of appointment
    exercised by will 1361
refusal to recognise arbitral
    award 673
wills
    immovable property 1352
    movable
        property 1339–40
Carriage contracts
applicable law in the absence
    of choice

Article 4(1) 730–1
Article 5 742–3
avoiding conflicts 9
Brussels I Recast 613
Brussels I Regulation 257
date for conversion of
    currency 100
limitations on
    jurisdiction 190, 518
relationship between
    Conventions 774–5
Rome I Regulation 706
Causes of action
champerty 135
classification
    correct legal category 42
    difficulties 42–3
    effect on law of
        forum 43–5
issue estoppel 558–9
recognition and enforcement
    of foreign judgments at
    common law 541
tracing 446
Celebration *see* **law of the**
    place of celebration
Champerty 135
Characteristic performance
    test 731–5
Child abduction
application of renvoi 71
defences
    child's objections 1143–8
    consent to
        removal 1148–51
    risk of grave harm if
        returned 1151–7
parental
    responsibility 1104–5
recognition and enforcement
    of orders
    aims of Hague
        Convention 1135
    defences 1143–57
    human rights 1163–71
    impact of Brussels
        II 1152–63
    return of child to habitual
        residence 1139–42
    statutory provisions 1134
    wrongful removal
        and wrongful
        retention 1135–9
Children *see also*
    financial relief
acquisition of new habitual
    residence 182–3

adoption
    Convention rules 1213–19
    declarations 1054
    effect of foreign
        adoptions 1229–31
    English law 1206–13
    overview 1193–4, 1205–6
    parental
        responsibility 1108
    recognition of foreign
        adoptions 1222–9
    taking children into and
        out of UK 1219–22
choice of law 1125–6
contact concerning
    children 1177–8
cross-border surrogacy
    background 1179–80
    diversity of national
        approaches 1182
    human rights 1189–92
    legal parenthood 1180–1
    UK approach 1183–9
declarations
    adoption 1054
    as to parentage 1052–3
domicile
    discriminatory effect 167
    domicile of choice 165
    domicile of origin 165
    effect of change in parental
        domicile 166–7
legitimacy
    declarations 1053
    doctrine of putative
        marriage 1199–200
    governed by law of the
        domicile 1194–9
    incidents of status 1201–2
    total renvoi
        doctrine 67–8
    where birth parent
        married 1202
legitimation
    declarations 1053
    domicile of origin 165
    foreign status 140
    historical development of
        English law 20
    overview 1193–4
    by recognition 1204–5
    by subsequent
        marriage 1202–4
    total renvoi
        doctrine 67–8
Maintenance
    Regulation 1066–7

Children (*cont.*):
overview 1087–9
parental responsibility
   background 1089–91
   bases of
      jurisdiction 1091–112
   refusal or stays 1112–25
   variation and duration of
      Part I orders 1112–13
parenthood
   declarations 1053
recognition and
   enforcement
   Child Abduction and
      Custody Act
      1985 1134–71
   common law
      rules 1172–7
   orders made in
      EU 1127–31
   orders made in Hague
      Convention
      States 1131–2
   orders made in Scotland
      and NI 1132–4
   overview 1126
Choice of court agreements
Brussels I Recast
   consumer
      contracts 296–7
   domicile of parties 230
   employment
      contracts 302
   enforceability by third
      parties 241–2
   form of
      agreement 237–41
   insurance 290–1
   limitations on
      effectiveness 242–3
   overview 229–30
   requirements in
      relation to the
      agreement 230–7
direct enforcement by
   statute 604–5
duty to recognise and
   enforce judgment 645
exclusion from Rome
   I Regulation 700–1
financial relief in the
   English courts
   Lugano Convention
      2007 1069–70
   under Maintenance
      Regulation 1067
Hague Convention 2005

direct enforcement by
   statute 604–5
impact on recognition and
   enforcement 651
part of Brussels/Lugano
   System 314–17
traditional rules on
   jurisdiction 190
service out of jurisdiction
   under English
   traditional rules
   with permission 369–71
   without permission 380
stays of English proceedings
   under common law
   exclusive jurisdiction
      clauses 414–16
   exercise of the discretion
      to stay 410–14
   overview 410
Choice of law
see also **governing law**
acquired rights theory 22
administration of estates
   classification 1333–4
   governing law 1334–5
adoption 1210–13
child issues 1125–6
defamation
   committed abroad 885
   committed in
      England 886
   committed where
      published 886–7
   multi-state
      defamation 887–8
dépeçage 54–5
development of English law
   early history 18–19
   later development 20–1
dissolution, nullity and
   separation of civil
   partners 1042–3
divorce 979–84
divorce, nullity and
   separation of same sex
   marriage 1047–8
express choice 717–18
family law
   divorce and judicial
      separation 979–84
   nullity of
      marriage 984–1000
financial relief 1078
freedom of choice
   basic principle 706–7
   dépeçage 707–9

English rules on pleading
   and proof of foreign
   law 710–11
law unconnected with the
   contract 707
timing 709
variation of
   choice 709–10
immovable property
   capacity to take
      and transfer
      immovables 1258–9
   contractual
      obligations 1260–2
   essential validity of
      transfers 1260
   formal validity of
      transfers 1259
   law of the situs 1255–6
   meaning of situs 1257–8
incidental questions
   rules of law 52
   suggested approach 54
inferred choice
   alternative to an express
      choice 718
   conflicting
      inferences 722–3
   drawing the
      inference 718–22
insolvency
   additional
      exceptions 1322–3
   general rule 1319
   issues covered 1319–22
judicial separation 979–84
law in the absence of choice
   under Rome I
   characteristic performance
      test 731–5
   closest connection 735
   common law rules 724
   escape clause 735–9
   habitual
      residence 739–40
   limitations on dominance
      of applicable
      law 743–54, 743–64
   overview 724–6
   particular issues 754–72
   relationship with
      EU 772–4
   relationship with
      international
      law 774–5
   scope of applicable
      law 764–9

severance of
    contracts 740
special contracts 740–3
specific contracts 726–31
limitations on choice
    conflict of laws
        cases 711–13
    "floating" applicable
        law 716
    logical consistency 714
    mandatory rules 713–14
    meaningless choices 714
    non-state 715–16
marriage
    capacity to marry 909–27
    formal validity 893–909
    reform initiatives 927–8
Mental Capacity Act 2005
    general applicable
        law 1238–41
    mandatory rules 1241
    powers of
        attorney 1239–41
    protective measures 1239
    public policy 1241
    third party
        protection 1241
mental incapacity - common
    law rules 1246
mixed issues under Rome
    II 881–2
movable property
    distinguished 1254
new American revolution
    basic characteristic 24
    choice of law
        factors 29–31
    general approaches 25–6
    principles of
        preference 27–8
non-contractual obligations
    outside Rome II
    defamation 885–8
    overview 883–4
    privacy 884–5
nullity of marriage
    classification of
        defects 986
    consent 986–93
    effect of a nullity
        decree 999–1000
    grounds unknown to
        English law 996–7
    personal physical
        defects 993–6
    underlying
        problems 984–6

void or voidable
    marriages 998–9
presumption of death
    and dissolution of
        marriage 1038
privacy 884–5
Rome II Regulation
    conditions
        imposed 855–6
    English rules on pleading
        and proof of foreign
        law 856
    express or inferred
        choice 856
    freedom of choice 854–5
    limitations on choice of
        law 857–8
    third party rights 856
rules of law
    English rules 46–7
    foreign rules 47–50
    underlying
        problem 45–6
scope of private international
    law 7–8
share transfers 1298–9
tracing 841
transfer of tangible movables
    attachment by
        creditors 1275
    cultural property 1277–8
    derivative claims 1271–2
    general rule 1267–70
    gifts 1276–7
    goods in transit 1275–6
    human rights 1278–9
    law of the
        domicile 1264–5
    law of the place of
        acting 1265–6
    law of the situs 1265
    meaning of the law of the
        situs 1273–4
    proper law of the
        transfer 1266–7
    retention of title
        clauses 1272–3
    underlying
        problems 1263–4
trusts
    absence of
        choice 1387–9
    scope of applicable
        law 1389–90
    by settlor 1386–7
    variation of applicable
        law 1390–1

Civil and commercial matters
    applicability of Brussels
        I Recast 204–6
    defined 126
    effect of EU law on
        PIL 125
    history and development
        of IPL 35
    scope of PIL 13
    scope of Rome II
        Regulation 792–3
    sovereign immunity 504
    taking of evidence outside
        the EU 83–5
Civil Jurisdiction and
    Judgments Act
    1982 669–70
Civil partnership
    see also **marriage; same sex
        marriage**
    declarations 1057
    dissolution, nullity and
        separation
        choice of law 1042–3
        jurisdiction 1039–42
        procedural issues 1042
        recognition 1043–5
    formal validity 947
    matrimonial property
        rights 1379–80
    parental
        responsibility 1106–7
    recognition of overseas
        relationships 947–8
    relationship between two
        people of the same
        sex 946–7
Claimants
    exclusion from Brussels
        I Recast 215
    proper parties 86–7
Classification
    administration of
        estates 1333–4
    assignment of debts 1290–1
    causes of action
        correct legal category 42
        difficulties 42–3
        effect on law of
            forum 43–5
    culpa in contrahendo 849–50
    examination of matters in
        sequence 41–2
    movable and immovable
        property distinguished
        by law of situs 1252
    nullity of marriage 986

Classification (*cont.*):
  restraint of foreign
    proceedings cases
    alternative fora
      abroad 431–42
    overview 425–6
    unconscionable
      conduct 426–31
  rules of law
    English rules 46–7
    foreign rules 47–50
    underlying problem 45–6
  substance or procedure
    evidence 80–5
    time within which an
      action must be
      brought 78–9
  unjust enrichment 837–8
Cohabitation
  de facto cohabitation 948–9
  property rights on
    breakdown of
    relationship 1380
Collective agreements
  choice of court
    agreements 316
  contracts of employment
    distinguished 298
  law governing procedure 75
Collisions at sea 877–8
Comity of nations
  agreements to break foreign
    law 769
  illegality by foreign law 771
  infringements of foreign
    jurisdiction 1245
  objectionable foreign
    law 753
  objections to total renvoi
    doctrine 62
  raison d'être for PIL 4
  recognition of
    adoptions 1226
  recognition of maritime
    liens 90
  registration of marriage 902
Commercial matters *see* **civil**
  and commercial matters
Common law marriages
  compliance prevented
    by insuperable
    difficulties 904–5
  law in force in foreign
    country 903–4
  meaning 902–3
  military forces in belligerent
    occupation 905–7

Common law rules
  see also **rules of law**
  administration of
    estates 1325–6
  ante-nuptial
    contracts 1372–4
  applicable law in the absence
    of choice under
    Rome I 724
  application of renvoi 71
  capacity to contract
    polygamous
    marriage 936–8
  classification 46–7
  damages for pain and
    suffering 94
  early development of
    English law 18
  financial relief after foreign
    decrees 1071–2
  interpretation of Rome
    I Regulation 691
  jurisdiction of English courts
    under traditional rules
    actions *in personam* 323–81
    actions *in rem* 382–90
  legitimation by subsequent
    marriage 1202–3
  limitations 78
  limitations on dominance of
    applicable law
    mental disorder or
      incapacity 761–3
    Rome I Regulation 748–9
    Rome II Regulation 866
  limitations on proceedings
    involving foreign
    immovables
    exceptions to exclusionary
      rule 485–92
    exclusionary rule 484–5
  matrimonial proceedings
    choice of law 980
    relief for polygamous
      marriages 952
  mental incapacity
    choice of law 1246
    jurisdiction 1245–6
    recognition and
      enforcement
      of protective
      measures 1246–8
  objections to total renvoi
    doctrine 62–3
  recognition and enforcement
    of foreign judgments
    and awards

    children 1172–7
    defences 564–88
    enforcement of foreign
      judgments in
      personam 551–6
    final and conclusive
      judgments 548–51
    inter-relation with
      statute 605–7
    judgments in
      personam 528–44
    other grounds of
      competency 540–3
    overview 527–8
    real and substantial
      connection
      test 543–4
    recognition of foreign
      judgments 556–63
    underlying theory 525–7
  recognition of foreign
    adoptions 1225–9
  relationship between
    public and private
    international law 16
  restraint of foreign
    proceedings
    categorization of the
      cases 425–42
    overview 422
    underlying
      principles 423–5
  scope of PIL 6
  service of claims 334
  service out of jurisdiction
    under English
    traditional
    rules 334
  sovereign immunity 497–8
  stays of English proceedings
    arbitration 416–21
    choice of court
      agreements 410–16
    forum non
      conveniens 393–409
    inherent
      jurisdiction 392–3
    pending the
      determination
      of proceedings
      abroad 421
  unification of
    internal laws 9
Commorientes 50
Companies *see* **corporations**
Compensation *see* **damages**
  and compensation

Competition torts
limitations on choice of
law 858
restrictions on free
competition 827–8
unfair competition 823–7
Concurrent proceedings
see **stays**
Conduct *see* **safety and
conduct rules**
Confidentiality
competence of English
Courts 360
exclusion of foreign
law 123–4
jurisdiction 272
violations of privacy 884–5
Conflict of laws
see also **Private
international law**
avoidance
unification of internal
laws 9–10
unification of PIL 10–15
common title to describe
IPL 15–16
limitations on choice of
law 711–13
scope of Rome
I Regulation 692–6
scope of Rome II
Regulation 787–8
Conflicting judgments
family law 969, 1117–18
lis pendens 407, 443
recognition and enforcement
under Brussels
I Recast 639
service of claims out of the
jurisdiction 340
stays 459
Consent
choice of law 723
cross-border
surrogacy 1186–7
limitations on
dominance of
applicable law 757–8
marriage 892
nullity of marriage
classification of
defects 986–7
domicile 988–90
forced marriages 990–1
law of forum 987
law of the place of
celebration 987–8

sham marriages 992–3
to removal of
children 1148–51
underlying safeguard 757–8
Consulates
grants of representation 1332
sovereign immunity 516–18
valid marriages
exceptions to general
rule 901–2
general rule 899–900
Consumer contracts
applicable law in the absence
of choice 741–2
jurisdiction under Brussels
I Recast
jurisdiction
agreements 296–7
scope 292–5
special rules 295–6
submissions 296–7
limitations on dominance of
applicable law 760
service without permission
out of jurisdiction
under English
traditional rules 380
**Consummation of
marriage 993–6**
**Contact concerning
children 1089, 1177–8**
**Contracts (Applicable Law)
Act 1990 684–5**
Contractual obligations
see also **non-contractual
obligations**
ante-nuptial contracts
capacity 1375–7
essential validity 1378
formal validity 1377–8
general rule 1372–4
applicable law in the absence
of choice 768–9
classification of English law
rules 46–7
defined 692–5
development of English
law 19–20
exclusion of foreign law
laws repugnant to
English public
policy 133–5
transactions prejudicial to
UK 136–7
governing law
Rome Convention
1980 683–5

Rome
I Regulation 683–5
solutions to
problems 681–3
underlying problem 681
immovable property
capacity 1261–2
contracts and transfers
distinguished 1260
essential validity 1261
formal validity 1260–1
mandatory rules 143
mixed issues under Rome II
contractual obligations
with contractual
defences 880, 880–3
nature of the
obligation 880
nature of the
problem 879–80
Rome Convention 1980
history and
purpose 683–4
implementation
by Contracts
(Applicable Law) Act
1990 684–5
Rome I Regulation
applicability 691–706
applicable law 706–43
history 686–7
interpretation 687–90
universal and world-wide
application 705–6
service with permission out
of jurisdiction under
English traditional
rules 341–7
special jurisdiction under
Article 7(1)
matters relating to a
contract 245–55
sales and service
contracts 255–63
special jurisdiction under
Article 7(2) 268–70
substance and procedure
distinguished
appropriate currency for
judgment 101–3
execution of
judgments 104
heads of damage 93
law governing
procedure 74
remoteness of
damage 92–3

Contractual obligations
(*cont.*):
substance and procedure
distinguished (*cont.*):
time within which an
action must be
brought 78
whether interest is
payable 96–7
substance or procedure
evidence and
interpretation
distinguished 84
presumptions and burden
of proof 85
unjust enrichment 839–40
Conventions *see*
international law
Corporations
capacity 1308
domicile 1306–7
domicile under Brussels
I Recast 200–2
exclusion from Rome II 796
exclusions from Rome
I Regulation 701
group insolvencies 1324
internal
management 1308–9
recognition and enforcement
of foreign judgments at
common law 530–1
residence 1307
service of proceedings under
English traditional rules
Civil Procedure
Rules 331–2
overseas
companies 329–31
registered in UK 328
sovereign immunity 505
status 1307–8
winding up 1309–11
Costs
competence of English
Courts 360
cross-border disputes 46
cross-border security
transactions 1302
enforcement 590, 611
expert evidence 111
service with permission out
of jurisdiction under
English traditional
rules 360
taking of evidence
abroad 82

Counterclaims
Brussels II 960
competence of English
Courts 237
against non-parties 339
Creditors *see also* **debts**
attachment
competence of English
Courts 382
res judicata 549
tangible movables 1275
fugitive debtors 159
priority
assignment of
debts 1288–9
substance and procedure
distinguished 89–90
substance and procedure
distinguished 89–90
Cross-border litigation
children 1091
substance and procedure
distinguished 79
Cross-border surrogacy
background 1179–80
diversity of national
approaches 1182
human rights 1189–92
legal parenthood 1180–1
UK approach
authorisation
requirements for
payments 1187–9
background 1183–4
child's home 1186
consent 1186–7
domicile 1184–5
genetic link and
minimum age 1185
personal status 1185
time limits 1186
Culpa in contrahendo
exclusion from Rome
I Regulation 702–3
Rome II Regulation
applicable law 852–4
problems of
classification 849–50
scope of Article 12 850–2
Currencies *see* **Foreign
currencies**
Custody rights 1136–9

Damage
maritime torts 877
Rome II Regulation
defined 803

environmental
damage 829–30
general principle 810–13
scope of applicable
law 861–4
Damages and compensation
assessment of damages
applicable law in the
absence of choice
under Rome I 767
non-contractual
obligations 861–3
road traffic accidents 819
scope of PIL 95–6
measure of damages
safety and conduct
rules 871
substance and procedure
distinguished 92
penal laws 119
Rome II Regulation 863–5
substance and procedure
distinguished
heads of damage 93–4
measure of damages 94–6
remoteness of
damage 92–3
underlying problem 91–2
whether interest is
payable 96–7
De facto **cohabitation** 948–9
Death *see* **presumption
of death**
Debts
assignment
involuntary
assignments 1292–4
modern approach 1284
need to determine situs of
debt 1280–2
subrogation 1291–2
theoretical
perspectives 1282–4
voluntary
assignments 1285–91
execution 104
foreign currency
awards 97–8
foreign revenue laws
116–18
fugitive debtors 159
interest on awards 99
personal liability of officers
and member 796
tangible and intangible
movables
distinguished 1254

Declarations
child abduction 1056–7
civil partnership 1057
family law
adoption 1054
limits on powers 1054–5
as to marital
status 1051–2
overview 1049–50
as to parentage 1052–3
presumption of
death 1058
same sex marriage 1057–8
statutory provisions 1050–1
Human Rights Act
1998 503
negative declarations
375–6, 446
procedural matters 1055–6
Defamation
choice of law
committed abroad 885
committed in
England 886
committed where
published 886–7
multi-state
defamation 887–8
exclusion from Rome
II 797–9
jurisdiction issues under the
Brussels I Recast 351–5
proof of foreign law 106
service with permission out
of jurisdiction under
English traditional
rules 353–5
Default judgments
recognition and enforcement
under Brussels
I Recast 633
submission to
jurisdiction 538–9
Defendants
exclusion from Brussels
I Recast
defendant domiciled
in Member
State 213–14
defendant not domiciled
in Member
State 214–15
proper parties 87–8
service of proceedings under
Brussels I Recast
minimum standards of
notice 310–11

practicalities 308–9
rules 308
where no appearance
entered 309
service of proceedings under
English traditional rules
Civil Procedure
Rules 331–2
companies 328–32
individuals 324–7
partnerships 327–8
service out of
jurisdiction 334–81
special jurisdiction under
Art 8 283–8
Denmark Agreement *see* **EC/
Denmark Agreement**
Dépeçage
contractual obligations 764
family law 858, 1240
freedom of choice 707–9
underlying problem 54–5
Derivative claims 1271–2
Diplomatic agents 511–12
Distribution contracts *see*
**franchise and distribution
contracts**
Divorce
see also **judicial separation;
marriage; nullity of
marriage**
Brussels II
application of national
rules 962
principles of general
jurisdiction 955–62
proposals for
reform 962–4
choice of law 979–84
exclusion of foreign
law 141–2
financial relief
after foreign
decrees 1071–7
jurisdiction of English
court 1059–71
recognition and
enforcement 1078–
86
foreign divorces
capacity to
remarry 925–6
effect of
non-recognition 926
prohibitions against
remarriage 926–7
habitual residence 177–8

incidental questions 52–3
jurisdiction
bases of
jurisdiction 954–64
other matrimonial
proceedings for same
marriage 965–7
restraint of foreign
proceedings 978–9
stays 967–78
matrimonial property
rights 1378–9
presumption of death and
dissolution of marriage
choice of law 1038
jurisdiction 1038
recognition 1038–9
statutory
provisions 1037–8
recognition of foreign
divorces
decrees made elsewhere in
British Isles 1001–2
decrees obtained in
EU 1002–5
decrees obtained
outside EU or in
Denmark 1005–12
effect of foreign
decree 1034–5
extra-judicial
divorces 1012–24
grounds for non-
recognition 1024–
34
history and development
of rules 1000–1
retrospectivity 1034
same sex marriage
choice of law 1047–8
jurisdiction 1045–7
recognition 1048
Domicile
administration of
estates 1331–2
assignments of matrimonial
property
applicable law 1366–8
effect of change 1368–71
Brussels I Recast
companies 200–2
general
jurisdiction 243–4
natural persons 198–200
special jurisdiction under
Art 8 283–4
trusts 200–2

Domicile (*cont.*):
children
discriminatory effect 167
domicile of choice 165
domicile of origin 165
effect of change
in parental
domicile 166–7
choice of court
agreements 230
corporations 1306–7
cross-border
surrogacy 1184–5
domicile of choice
acquisition 148–62
domicile of origin
distinguished 162–3
dual domicile doctrine of
marriage
English judicial
authorities 915–18
evaluation of
theory 912–13
prevalent view 910
exclusion from Brussels
I Recast
claimant's domicile 215
defendant domiciled
in Member
State 213–14
defendant not domiciled
in Member
State 214–15
exceptions to general
rule 215
key distinctions 212–13
financial relief in the English
courts 1069–70
general rules 147–8
jurisdiction within UK
under Modified
Regulation 318–19
legitimacy
domicile of origin 1200–1
incidents of status 1201–2
other authorities 1197–9
overview 1194–5
Shaw v Gould 1195–7
where birth parent
married 1202
married women
abolition of dependency
rule 168–9
transitional problems 169
mental disorder or
incapacity 168
merits and demerits 170–1

movable property 1339
nationality
distinguished 170
nullity of marriage 988–90
recognition and enforcement
of foreign judgments at
common law 541
recognition of divorces,
separations and
annulments outside
EU 1006–7
relevance of time 5–6
transfer of tangible
movables 1264–5
underlying problems 146
Domicile of choice
acquisition
burden of proof 161
changes of domicile and
nationality 161
intention 151–7
overview 148–9
precarious
residence 160–1
residence 149–50
voluntary
residence 158–60
children
children under 16 165
effect of change
in parental
domicile 166–7
domicile of origin
distinguished
abandonment 162–3
revival 163–4
tenacity 162
Domicile of origin
abandonment 162–3
children 165
legitimacy 1200–1
revival 163–4
tenacity 162
Double renvoi *see* **total renvoi**
doctrine
Dual domicile doctrine
English judicial
authorities 915–18
evaluation of theory 912–13
prevalent view 910

EC/Denmark Agreement
jurisdiction 188
recognition and
enforcement 652
Embassies
divorce 1017, 1019

employment contracts 280
limitations on
jurisdiction 517
state immunity 501, 503
valid marriages 899–900
Employment contracts
jurisdiction under Brussels
I Recast
scope 297–9
special rules 300–2
mandatory rules 143
service without permission
out of jurisdiction
under English
traditional rules 380
sovereign immunity 504–5
Enforcement *see* **recognition**
and enforcement
English law
see also **common law rules;**
Northern Ireland;
Scotland
administration of estates
administrator's
title 1332–3
consular grants 1332
jurisdiction 1330
person to whom grant
made 1330–1
separate wills 1330–1
adoption
Adoption and Children
Act 2002 1206–7
Adoptions with a Foreign
Element Regulations
2005 1207–8
choice of law 1210–13
jurisdiction 1208–9
overview 1206
classification
causes of action 42–5
rules of law 45–50
cross-border surrogacy
authorisation
requirements for
payments 1187–9
background 1183–4
child's home 1186
consent 1186–7
domicile 1184–5
genetic link and
minimum age 1185
personal status 1185
time limits 1186
development 17–19
early history 17–19
later development 19–21

direct enforcement by
statute
Administration of Justice
Act 1920 591–2
Brussels /Lugano
system 603–4
Civil Jurisdiction and
Judgments Act
1982 588–91
European Union
judgments 601
Foreign Judgments
(Reciprocal
Enforcement) Act
1933 593–600
Hague Convention
on Choice of
Court Agreements
2005 604–5
inter-relation with
common law 605–7
overview 588
sovereign
immunity 601–2
'foreign law' 8
forum non conveniens 393
jurisdiction of English courts
under traditional rules
actions *in*
personam 323–81
actions *in rem* 382–90
jurisdiction over
financial relief
after foreign
decrees 1071–7
general rules 1060–4
inter-relation with
other jurisdictional
bases 1070–1
under Lugano
Convention 1069–70
under Maintenance
Regulation 1064–9
overview 1059–60
jurisdiction within UK
under Modified
Regulation
applicability 317–19
modifications 319–21
stays 321–2
mandatory rules 143–4
power of English courts to
hear case 190
recognition of polygamous
marriages 941–6
theoretical perspectives
law of forum 36–7

principles for construction
of rules 37
Equitable obligations
equitable obligations
violations of
privacy 884–5
forms of liability 779–80
'non-contractual
obligations' 788–90
problem of ascertaining
applicable law 778–9
tort and unjust enrichment
distinguished 806–7
violations of privacy 884–5
Essential validity
ante-nuptial contracts 1378
contracts 37
contracts to transfer
immovable
property 1261
marriages 47–8, 911, 919
personal law of the
parties 898
powers of appointment
exercised by
will 1362–3
scope of PIL 7, 11
transfers of immovable
property 1260
wills 66, 71
immovable property 1353
movable property 1344–7
Estoppel
enforcement of foreign
judgments in personam
as defence 556–8
issue estoppel 558–9
prerequisites 559–63
res judicata 556
law of forum 77
recognition and enforcement
under Brussels
I Recast 649–50
submission to
jurisdiction 534
EU law
see also **Brussels/**
Lugano System
administration of
estates 1327–9
avoidance of conflict
through
unification 11–13
European Enforcement
Order
Regulation 2004
applicability 656

enforcement 659
European Enforcement
Orders 657–8
subject matter and
scope 656–7
uncontested claims
procedures 658–9
European Order For
Payment Procedure
Regulation 2006
collection of specific
pecuniary
claims 661–2
objectives 660
payments in other
Member
States 662–3
scope and
definitions 660–1
European Small
Claims Procedure
Regulation 2007
objectives 663
in other Member
States 664
overview 664
scope and definitions 663
exclusion of foreign
law 125–6
foreign law 8
harmonisation of succession
and wills 1358–9
impact on exclusion
of foreign
law 114–15, 142–3
insolvency
choice of law 1319–23
group companies 1323
jurisdiction 1313–19
scope of
Regulation 1312–13
limitations on dominance of
applicable law 749–50
Maintenance Regulation
inter-relation with
other jurisdictional
bases 1070–1
jurisdictional
rules 1064–9
maintenance orders
defined 1064–5
recognition and
enforcement 1081–4
mandatory rules 143–4
matrimonial property reform
proposals 1380–1
public policy 676

EU law (*cont.*):
  recognition and
    enforcement 1323–4
  relationship with Rome
    I 772–4
  relationship with
    Rome II 873
  share transfers 1301–2
  taking of evidence within
    the EU 81–3
  theoretical evolution
    constitutionalisation 35
    disagreement over extent
      of change 33–4
    federalization 34
    'vertical' and 'horizontal'
      conflicts
      distinguished 35–6
Evidence
  domicile of choice 155–7
  exclusions from Rome
    I Regulation 704–5
  exclusions from Rome
    II 798–9
  proof of foreign law
    appropriate
      evidence 108–9
    expert witnesses 110–13
  substance or procedure
    interpretation and
      proof of document
      distinguished 80–1
    interpretation
      distinguished 84
    law of the forum 80
    presumptions and burden
      of proof 85
    taking of evidence outside
      the EU 83–4
    taking of evidence within
      the EU 81–3
Exclusion of foreign law
  divorce 141–2
  effect of EU law 125–6
  expropriatory legislation
    overview 126–7
    property outside foreign
      jurisdiction at time
      of decree 130–2
    property within foreign
      jurisdiction at time
      of decree 127–30
    requisition of
      property 132
  foreign status 139–41
  impact of
    EU Law 142–3

laws repugnant to
  English public
  policy 136–7, 137
  basic principles of justice
    and fairness 135
  general principles 132–5
  infringements of
    morality 135–6
  transactions prejudicial to
    UK 136–7
  mandatory rules 143–4
  overview 114–15
  public laws
    common thread
      running through
      the exclusionary
      rule 115–16
    other public laws 123–5
    penal laws 118–22
    revenue law 116–19
Exclusive jurisdiction clauses
  arbitration 720
  Brussels I Recast
    consumer
      contracts 296–7
    domicile of parties 230
    employment
      contracts 302
    enforceability by third
      parties 241–2
    form of
      agreement 237–41
    insurance 290–1
    limitations on
      effectiveness 242–3
    overview 229–30
    requirements in
      relation to the
      agreement 230–7
  Brussels II 960
  consolidation of claims 367
  estoppel 562
  restraint of foreign
    proceedings
    cases 436–41
  stays of English proceedings
    under common
    law 414–16
Exclusive subject-matter
  jurisdiction
  company law issues 224
  enforcement of
    judgments 225–6
  intellectual property 225
  overview 217–19
  public registers 224–5
  rights *in rem* 219–20

short-term holiday
  lets 221–2
Execution of judgments 104
Exorbitant basis of jurisdiction
  Brussels Convention
    Art 59 651
  limits on the application of
    Article 26 227
  non-grounds for refusal
    of recognition and
    enforcement 644
  rules on recognition and
    enforcement under
    Brussels I Recast 611
  service with permission out
    of jurisdiction under
    English traditional
    rules 376–8
  stays 405
Expert witnesses
  court controls 111–13
  sufficient
    qualifications 110–11
Expropriatory legislation
  overview 126–7
  property outside foreign
    jurisdiction at time of
    decree 130–2
  property within foreign
    jurisdiction at time of
    decree 127–30
  requisition of property 132

Fair trial (Art 6)
  ECtHR
    jurisprudence 1163–7
  impact of ECHR on
    unification 14
  important role in the field
    of recognition and
    enforcement 35
  issues of justice and juridical
    advantage 372
  Maintenance
    Regulation 1081
  public policy defence 576
  recognition and enforcement
    of foreign judgments
    and awards 580–2
  recognition and enforcement
    under Brussels
    I Recast 629–30
  temporary suspension of
    adoptions 1221
Family law
  see also **mental incapacity**
  adoption

Convention rules 1213–19
declarations 1054
effect of foreign
adoptions 1229–31
English law 1206–13
overview 1193–4, 1205–6
parental
responsibility 1108
recognition of foreign
adoptions 1222–9
taking children into and
out of UK 1219–22
application of renvoi 70–1
bases of jurisdiction 954
children
choice of law 1125–6
contact concerning
children 1177–8
overview 1087–9
parental
responsibility 1089–
124
recognition and
enforcement 1126–
79
choice of law
divorce and judicial
separation 979–84
nullity of
marriage 984–1000
civil partnership
formal validity 947
recognition of overseas
relationships 947–8
relationship between two
people of the same
sex 946–7
cross-border surrogacy
background 1179–80
diversity of national
approaches 1182
human rights 1189–92
legal parenthood 1180–1
UK approach 1183–9
de facto cohabitation 948–9
declarations
adoption 1054
child abduction 1056–7
civil partnership 1057
limits on powers 1054–5
as to marital
status 1051–2
overview 1049–50
as to parentage 1052–3
presumption of
death 1058
same sex marriage 1057–8

statutory
provisions 1050–1
difficulties of
classification 42–3
dissolution, nullity and
separation of civil
partners
choice of law 1042–3
jurisdiction 1039–42
procedural issues 1042
recognition 1043–5
divorce, nullity and
separation of same sex
marriage
choice of law 1047–8
jurisdiction 1045–7
exclusion from Brussels
I Recast
maintenance
obligations 211–12
marital status 206–7
exclusion from Rome
I Regulation 697–9
exclusion from Rome II
maintenance
obligations 793–5
matrimonial
property 794–5
financial relief
after foreign
decrees 1071–7
choice of law 1078
jurisdiction of English
court 1059–71
recognition and
enforcement
1078–86
Foreign Judgments
(Reciprocal
Enforcement) Act
1933 601
judicial separation
bases of
jurisdiction 954–64
other matrimonial
proceedings for same
marriage 965–7
restraint of foreign
proceedings 978–9
stays 967–78
jurisdiction under Lugano
Convention 2007 314
legitimacy
declarations 1053
doctrine of putative
marriage 1199–200
domicile of origin 1200–1

governed by law of the
domicile 1194–9
incidents of status 1201–2
total renvoi
doctrine 67–8
where birth parent
married 1202
legitimation
declarations 1053
domicile of origin 165
foreign status 140
historical development of
English law 20
overview 1193–4
by recognition 1202–4
by subsequent
marriage 1202–4
total renvoi
doctrine 67–8
marriage
capacity to marry 909–27
defined 891–2
formal validity 893–909
polygamous
marriages 928–46
matrimonial property
applicable law on
divorce 1378–9
assignments - ante-
nuptial agreement in
place 1372–8
assignments - no
ante-nuptial
agreement 1366–71
civil partnership 1379–80
cohabitation 1380
European Commission
reform
proposals 1380–1
underlying problem 1365
matrimonial relief
actions *in personam* 323
general relevance 929
polygamous
marriages 943, 951–
4
recognition of foreign
status 140
nullity
bases of jurisdiction 954,
964–5
other matrimonial
proceedings for same
marriage 965–7
restraint of foreign
proceedings 978–9
stays 967–78

Family law (*cont.*):
  presumption of death and
      dissolution of marriage
    choice of law 1038
    jurisdiction 1038
    recognition 1038–9
    statutory
        provisions 1037–8
  recognition and enforcement
      of decrees
    foreign divorces or
        annulments 925–7
    overview 524
  recognition of foreign
      decrees and separations
    decrees made elsewhere in
        British Isles 1001–2
    decrees obtained in
        EU 1002–5
    decrees obtained
        outside EU or in
        Denmark 1005–12
    divorce, nullity and
        separation of civil
        partners 1048
    effect of foreign
        decrees 1034–7
    extra-judicial divorces,
        annulments and legal
        separations 1012–24
    grounds for non-
        recognition 1024–
        34
    history and development
        of rules 1000–1
    retrospectivity 1034
  same sex marriage 948–9
Financial relief
  see also **matrimonial relief**
  after foreign decrees
    powers of English
        court 1071–7
    relief already granted in
        England 1071
  choice of law 1078
  jurisdiction of English court
      after foreign
        decrees 1071–7
    general rules 1060–4
    inter-relation with
        other jurisdictional
        bases 1070–1
    under Lugano
        Convention 1069–70
    under Maintenance
        Regulation 1064–9
    overview 1059–60

recognition and enforcement
    ancillary relief
        abroad 1078–9
    Hague Convention
        2007 1084–6
    Maintenance Orders
        (Facilities for
        Enforcement) Act
        1920 1079–80
    maintenance orders made
        in UK 1079
    Maintenance Orders
        (Reciprocal
        Enforcement) Act
        1972 1080–1
    Maintenance
        Regulation 1081–4
Flag rule 875–7
Forced marriages 990–1
Foreign court theory *see* **total
    renvoi doctrine**
Foreign currencies
  appropriate currency for
      judgment 101–4
  date for conversion 100–1
  interest on judgments 99
  law of forum 100
  Miliangos rule 98–9
  old rule: judgment must be
      in sterling 97
**Foreign Judgments (Reciprocal
    Enforcement) Act
    1933 677**
Foreign law
  agreements to break foreign
      law 769
  choice of law
    Rome
        I Regulation 710–11
    Rome II Regulation 856
    scope of private
        international
        law 7–8
  comity of nations 4
  exclusion
    divorce 141–2
    effect of EU law 125–6
    expropriatory
        legislation 126–32
    foreign status 139–41
    impact of EU Law 142–3
    laws repugnant to
        English public
        policy 132–43
    mandatory rules 143–4
    overview 114–15
    public laws 115–26

incidental questions 52
  meaning 8
  mistakes 108
  objectionable foreign
      law 753
  proof
    appropriate
        evidence 108–9
    expert witnesses 110–13
    question of fact 105–8
    raison d'être for PIL 4
    Rome II Regulation 803–4
Foreign status 139–41
Formal validity
  ante-nuptial
      contracts 1377–8
  civil partnership 947
  defined 758–9
  general rules
    acts intended to have legal
        effect 760
    persons in the same
        country 759
    persons not in the same
        country 759–60
  immovable property 1260–1
  limitations on dominance of
      applicable law 758
  marriage
    dépeçage 54–5
    development of
        English law 20
    exceptions to general
        rule 901–9
    in foreign consulates and
        embassies 899–900
    general rule 893–7
    renvoi 900–1
    retrospectivity 897–9
  non-contractual
      obligations 872–3
  powers of appointment
      exercised by will 1361
  special contracts
    capacity 760–4
    consumer contracts 760
    immovable
        property 760–1
  transfers of immovable
      property 1259
  trusts 1385
  wills
    immovable property 1352
    movable property
        1340–4
Forum *see* **law of forum; law of
    the forum**

Forum conveniens
appropriate forum
applicable law 367–9
burden of proof 365–6
consolidation of claims
and prior foreign
proceedings 366–7
jurisdiction
agreements 368–71
basic principle 365
exorbitant basis of
jurisdiction 376–8
justice and juridical
advantage 372–5
negative declarations 375–6
operation of the
principles 379
Practice Direction
6B 378–9
service of claim
form out of the
jurisdiction 379–81
Forum necessitatis 1040–1,
1058, 1068
Forum non conveniens
actions *in rem* under
traditional English
rules 389
Brussels I Recast
parallel proceedings 458
stays 459
jurisdiction of English
courts under traditional
rules 190
actions *in rem* 388–9
service without permission
out of jurisdiction
under English
traditional rules 372,
373–4, 377
stays of English proceedings
under common law
another appropriate
and available
forum 395–400
lis pendens 407–10
requirements of
justice 400–7
stays under Brussels I Recast
applicability 460–8
application of Art 71 471
general discretion to
stay 321
inapplicability 460
long-running issue 311
multi-defendant
cases 470–1

national rules of
jurisdiction 468–70
Forum shopping
cross-border surrogacy 1182
matrimonial
proceedings 984
new American revolution 29
**Franchise and distribution
contracts**
applicable law in the absence
of choice 729–30
Brussels I Recast 257
special contracts 740
Fraud
recognition and enforcement
under Brussels
I Recast 627–8
recognition and enforcement
under traditional rules
fraud not raised
abroad 573
going into the merits
of the foreign
judgment 570–5
impeachment of
judgment 568–9
types of fraud 569
refusal to recognise arbitral
award 675–6
Freedom of choice
Rome I Regulation
basic principle 706–7
dépeçage 707–9
English rules on pleading
and proof of foreign
law 710–11
law unconnected with the
contract 707
timing 709
variation of
choice 709–10
Rome II Regulation 854–5
Freezing injunctions *see*
provisional measures
Fugitives
debtors 159
from justice 158–9

Gifts
charitable gifts 1353
renvoi 70
Rome I Regulation 692
transfer of tangible
movables 1276–7
Goods in transit 1275–6
Governing law *see also*
choice of law

administration of
estates 1334–5
ante-nuptial contracts
capacity 1375–7
essential validity 1378
formal validity 1377–8
general rule 1372–4
assignment of debts
involuntary
assignments 1292–4
modern approach 1284
need to determine situs of
debt 1280–2
subrogation 1291–2
theoretical
perspectives 1282–4
voluntary
assignments 1285–91
contractual obligations
Rome Convention
1980 683–5
Rome
I Regulation 683–5
solutions to
problems 681–3
underlying problem 681
equitable obligations
forms of liability 779–80
'non-contractual
obligations' 788–90
problem of ascertaining
applicable
law 778–9
tort and unjust
enrichment
distinguished 806–7
law in the absence of choice
under Rome I
characteristic performance
test 731–5
closest connection 735
common law rules 724
escape clause 735–9
habitual
residence 739–40
limitations on dominance
of applicable
law 743–54, 743–64
overview 724–6
particular issues 754–72
relationship with
EU 772–4
relationship with
international
law 774–5
scope of applicable
law 764–9

Governing law (*cont.*):
law in the absence of choice
under Rome I (*cont.*):
severance of
contracts 740
special contracts 740–3
specific contracts 726–31
legal parenthood 1181
matrimonial property
applicable law on
divorce 1378–9
assignments - ante-
nuptial agreement in
place 1372–8
assignments - no
ante-nuptial
agreement 1366–71
civil partnership 1379–80
cohabitation 1380
European Commission
reform
proposals 1380–1
underlying problem 1365
movable property
intestate succession 1339
wills 1340–51
polygamous
marriages 930–3
powers of appointment
exercised by will
capacity 1361
essential validity 1362–3
formal validity 1361
interpretation 1363–4
overview 1359–60
revocation 1364
special and general powers
distinguished 1360
procedure 73–4
recognition and enforcement
of foreign judgments at
common law 542
recognition of divorces,
separations and
annulments 1005
renvoi
possible solutions 58–69
scope of
application 69–72
underlying
problem 57–8
restitution 777–8
Rome I Regulation
in the absence of choice
under Rome
I 724–43
basic distinctions 706

law chosen by
parties 706–24
law in the absence of
choice under
Rome I 724–43
limitations on dominance
of the applicable
law 743–54
relationship with other
Conventions 774–5
relationship with other
EU law 772–4
special rules for particular
issues 754–72
Rome II Regulation
applicability 780–1,
786–802
choice of law 854–8
culpa in
contrahendo 849–54
damage 803
exclusion of renvoi 802
exclusions 793–801
habitual
residence 802–3
limitations on dominance
of the applicable
law 866–71
maritime
obligations 875–9
mixed issues with
contract 880–3
negotiorum gestio 848–9
proof of foreign
law 803–4
relationship with EU
law 873
relationship with
international
law 873–5
safety and conduct
rules 871
scope of applicable
law 858–66
special rules for particular
issues 872–3
torts 804–36
universal
application 801–2
unjust
enrichment 837–48
service with permission out
of jurisdiction under
English traditional
rules 367–9
share transfers
EU law 1301–2

Hague Securities
Convention 1302–5
modern holding
system 1301–5
traditional
approach 1298–301
status 145
torts 776–7
transfers of negotiable
instruments 1294–7
trusts
absence of choice 1387–9
scope of applicable
law 1389–90
variation of applicable
law 1390–1
variation of trusts and
settlements
law of the country
governing trust 1394
marriage
settlements 1394–6
**Governmental interest
analysis 26–7**

Habitual residence
acquisition of new habitual
residence
periods of absence 177–8
requirement for voluntary
residence 181–4
role of intentions 180–1
stability over time 178–80
applicable law in the absence
of choice 739–40
child abduction
declarations 1056
return of child to habitual
residence 1139–42
wrongful removal
and wrongful
retention 1136
divorce jurisdiction 956–60
financial relief
jurisdiction of English
court 1060–1
Lugano Convention
2007 1069–70
under Maintenance
Regulation 1065
judicial separation
jurisdiction 956–60
Mental Capacity Act
2005 1235–6
parental responsibility
Brussels II 1094–100
section 8 orders 1107–8

question of fact 175–6
recognition of divorces,
  separations and
  annulments outside
  EU 1007
Rome II Regulation
  escape clause
  applicable law 813–14
  defined 802–3
  product liability 823
underlying safeguard for
  consent 757–8
**Hague Convention on
  Choice of Court
  Agreements 2005**
direct enforcement by
  statute 604–5
impact on recognition and
  enforcement 651
part of Brussels/Lugano
  System 314–17
traditional rules on
  jurisdiction 190
Heads of damage
applicable law 861
substance and procedure
  distinguished 93–4
Henderson v Henderson, **rule
  in** 562–3
High seas
collisions at sea 877–8
damage occurs on the high
  seas 877
exclusion of foreign
  law 130
judgments *in rem* 548
no appropriate foreign
  forum 400
valid marriages 908–9
Human rights
child abduction
  Council of Europe
    Convention 1167
  ECtHR
    jurisprudence 1163–7
  permission to remove
    children form
    jurisdiction 1167–71
  provisions of Hague
    Convention 1163
cross-border
  surrogacy 1189–92
exclusion of laws repugnant
  to English public
  policy 137
impact of ECHR on
  unification 13–15

important role in the field
  of recognition and
  enforcement 35
issues of justice and juridical
  advantage 372
Maintenance
  Regulation 1081
public policy defence 576
recognition and enforcement
  of foreign judgments
  and awards
  fair trial 580–2
  public policy 576
  relationship with natural
    justice 579–80
sovereign immunity 500–3
temporary suspension of
  adoptions 1221
transfer of tangible
  movables 1278–9

Illegality
applicable law in the absence
  of choice under Rome I
  agreements to break
    foreign law 769
  performance 769–72
  special problem 769
  refusal to recognise arbitral
    award 774–5
Immovable property
applicable law in the absence
  of choice 728–9
assignments of matrimonial
  property
  no ante-nuptial
    agreement 1371
choice of law
  capacity to take
    and transfer
    immovables 1258–9
  contractual
    obligations 1260–2
  essential validity of
    transfers 1260
  formal validity of
    transfers 1259
  law of the situs 1255–6
  meaning of situs 1257–8
contractual obligations
  capacity 1261–2
  contracts and transfers
    distinguished 1260
  essential validity 1261
  formal validity 1260–1
development of
  English law 20

exclusive subject-
  matter jurisdiction
  under Brussels
  I Recast 218, 221–3
immovable property 279
incidental questions 51
jurisdiction 246, 1255
limitations on dominance of
  applicable law 760–1
limitations on proceedings
  involving foreign
  immovables
  common law
    limitation 484–91
  exceptions to exclusionary
    rule 485–92
  exclusionary rule 484–5
  limitation under the
    Brussels/Lugano
    system 492–4
Mental Capacity Act
  2005 1236
movable property
  distinguished
  annuities 1254
  classification by law of
    situs 1252
  mortgages 1252
  overview 1251
  relevance 1254
  trusts for sale 1252–4
renvoi 71
sovereign immunity 505
succession
  intestate
    succession 1351–2
  wills 1352–8
Impotence 993–6
Incidental questions
defined 51
insolvency
  jurisdiction 1318–19
limitations on proceedings
  involving foreign
  immovables 491–2
presumed facts 52
suggested approach 54
underlying
  problem 52–3
Indirect impleading 507–8
Industrial action
exclusive competence of
  individual Member
  States 36
maritime torts 875
Rome II
  Regulation 802, 835–6

Insolvency
choice of law
additional
exceptions 1322–3
general rule 1319
issues covered 1319–22
exclusion from Brussels
I Recast 207–8
fugitive debtors 159
jurisdiction
ancillary actions 1318–19
checks on proper
jurisdiction
1317–18
main
proceedings 1313–15
secondary
proceedings 1315–17
recognition and
enforcement 1323–4
recognition and enforcement
of foreign judgments
and awards
overview 524
scope of Regulation
1312–13
sovereign immunity 505
substance and procedure
distinguished 89–90
winding up of
companies 1309–11
Insurance
applicable law in the absence
of choice 742–3
civil and commercial
matters 205
exclusion from Rome
I Regulation 703–4
governing law 50
jurisdiction under Brussels
I Recast
jurisdiction
agreements 290
scope 289–90
special rules 290
submissions 290–1
Rome II Regulation 872
Intangible movables
assignment of
debts 1280–94
negotiable
instruments 1294–7
rights distinguished 1280
shares and
securities 1298–304
tangible movables
distinguished 1254

Intellectual
property rights
applicable law in the absence
of choice 730
exclusive jurisdiction under
Lugano Convention
2007 314
limitations on choice of
law 858
limitations on
proceedings 494–6
Intended matrimonial
home doctrine
basic presumption 910
English judicial
authorities 914–15
evaluation of theory 910–12
Intention
see also **choice of law**
abandonment of
domicile 162–3
agreements to submit 533
contractual
obligations 719–24
domicile of choice
evidence 155–7
nature of the
intention 151–4
relationship with
residence 149–50
habitual residence 1096
marriage 906
precarious residence 160
repudiate of marriage 1013
revocation of wills 1349
role in determining factual
concept 180–1
wills 1343, 1347–9, 1353
Interest on judgments
damages 96–7
foreign currency
judgments 99
penal laws 119
Interim relief *see* **provisional**
measures
Internal management of
companies 1308–9
International law
exclusion of laws repugnant
to English public
policy 138–9
limitations on dominance of
applicable law 749–50
relationship with Rome
I 774–5
International organizations
sovereign immunity 514–15

Interpretation
applicable law in the absence
of choice under Rome
I 764–5
jurisdiction under Brussels/
Lugano System
aids to
interpretation 197–8
principles and decisions
laid down by
Court 195–7
referrals to the Court of
Justice 194–5
new American
revolution 28–9
powers of appointment
exercised by
will 1363–4
recognition and enforcement
under Brussels
I Recast 617
Rome I Regulation
aids to
interpretation 689–
91
principles laid down by
ECJ 688
referrals to Court of
Justice 687
uniform and autonomous
interpretation 689
Rome II Regulation
aids to
interpretation 784–5
general principles 783–4
referalls to ECJ 783
substance and procedure
distinguished
evidence distinguished 84
proof of document
distinguished 80–1
wills
immovable
property 1357
movable
property 1347–8
Intestate succession
bona vacantia 49–50
classification of cause of
action 43
immovable property 1351
incidental questions 51
movable property 1339
situs rule 1256
Invalids
domicile of choice 159
Ireland *see* **Northern Ireland**

Issue estoppel
exclusive jurisdiction
clauses 415
prerequisites 559–63
recognition of foreign
judgments 558–9

Judicial notice
limitations on
jurisdiction 509
proof of foreign law 105
Judicial separation *see also*
divorce
Brussels II
application of national
rules 962
principles of general
jurisdiction 955–62
proposals for
reform 962–4
choice of law 979–84
civil partnership
choice of law 1042–3
jurisdiction 1039–42
procedural issues 1042
recognition 1043–5
financial relief
after foreign decrees 1071–7
jurisdiction of English
court 1059–71
recognition and
enforcement
1078–86
jurisdiction
bases of
jurisdiction 954–64
other matrimonial
proceedings for same
marriage 965–7
restraint of foreign
proceedings 978–9
stays 967–78
recognition of foreign
separations
decrees made elsewhere in
British Isles 1001–2
decrees obtained in
EU 1002–5
decrees obtained
outside EU or in
Denmark 1005–12
effect of foreign
decree 1036–7
extra-judicial legal
separations 1012–24
grounds for non-
recognition 1024–34

history and development
of rules 1000–1
retrospectivity 1034
same sex marriage
choice of law 1047–8
jurisdiction 1045–7
recognition 1048
Jurisdiction
see also **Brussels I Recast**
administration of
estates 1330
adoption 1208–9
Brussels Convention 312
Brussels/Lugano System
aids to
interpretation 197–8
Brussels
Convention 188–9
Brussels I Recast 191–4,
198–312
Brussels I Regulation
and Brussels
I Recast 187–8
EC/Denmark
Agreement 188
Lugano Convention
2007 189
Modified
Regulation 189
principles and decisions
laid down by
Court 195–7
referrals to the Court of
Justice 194–5
children
choice of law 1125–6
overview 1087–9
parental
responsibility 1089–
124
competence of English
courts under
traditional rules
actions *in*
personam 323–81
actions *in rem* 382–90
corporations
capacity 1308
domicile 1306–7
internal
management 1308–9
residence 1307
status 1307–8
winding up 1309–11
dissolution, nullity and
separation of civil
partners

bases of
jurisdiction 1039–42
procedural issues 1042
divorce
bases of
jurisdiction 954–64
other matrimonial
proceedings for same
marriage 965–7
restraint of foreign
proceedings 978–9
stays 967–78
divorce, nullity and
separation of same sex
marriage
bases of
jurisdiction 1045–7
procedural issues 1047
financial relief after foreign
decrees
powers of English
court 1071–7
relief already granted in
England 1071
financial relief in the
English courts
general rules 1060–4
inter-relation with
other jurisdictional
bases 1070–1
under Lugano
Convention 1069–70
under Maintenance
Regulation 1064–9
overview 1059–60
Hague Convention on
Choice of Court
Agreements 2005 190
immovable property 1255
insolvency
ancillary actions 1318–19
checks on proper
jurisdiction 1317–18
main
proceedings 1313–15
secondary
proceedings 1315–17
judicial separation
bases of
jurisdiction 954–64
other matrimonial
proceedings
for same
marriage 965–7
restraint of foreign
proceedings 978–9
stays 967–78

Jurisdiction (*cont.*):
  limitations
    carriage
        contracts 190, 518
      embassies 517
      foreign
          immovables 484–94
      foreign intellectual
          property
          rights 494–6
      Foreign Judgments
          (Reciprocal
          Enforcement) Act
          1933 597
      judicial notice 509
      law of the situs 489–90
      mortgages 489
      overview 483–4
      parties 495–518
      set-off 497
      statutory
          limitations 518–19
      traditional rules on
          jurisdiction 190
  Lugano
      Convention 2007
      applicability 313–14
      part of the process of
          cooperation 313
      stays 314
      terminology 314
  Mental Capacity Act 2005
      habitual residence in
          England 1235–6
      jurisdiction upon
          request 1238
      nationality 1237–8
      property situated in
          England 1236
      protective measures 1237
      urgent cases 1236–7
  mental incapacity - common
      law rules 1245–6
  mistakes by foreign
      courts 565
  new American
      revolution 25–6
  nullity
      bases of
          jurisdiction 954,
          964–5
      other matrimonial
          proceedings for same
          marriage 965–7
      restraint of foreign
          proceedings 978–9
      stays 967–78

presumption of death
    and dissolution of
    marriage 1038
recognition of divorces,
    separations and
    annulments outside EU
    domicile 1006–7
    habitual residence 1007
    nationality 1008
    time when jurisdictional
        rules must be
        satisfied 1008
refusal of review 643–5
scope of private international
    law 6–7
traditional rules
    applicability 189–90
    decline of jurisdiction 190
    limitations 190
    power of English courts to
        hear case 190
traditional rules on
    jurisdiction
    actions *in personam see*
        Actions in personam
    actions *in rem see*
        Actions *in rem*
    applicability 189–90
    power of English courts to
        hear case 190
variation of trusts and
    settlements
    marriage
        settlements 1394–6
    Variation of Trusts Act
        1958 1393–4
Jurisdiction agreements
    see **choice of court**
    agreements

Law of obligations
  contractual obligations
    mixed issues 879–83
    Rome Convention
        1980 683–5
    Rome I Regulation 686–
        775
    solutions to
        problems 681–3
    underlying problem 681
  limitations on proceedings
    involving foreign
    immovables 485–91
  non-contractual obligations
    maritime
        obligations 875–9
    mixed issues 879–83

obligations outside Rome
    II 883–8
  overview 776–80
  Rome II
      Regulation 780–875
  theory of recognition and
      enforcement 527
Law of the forum
  choice of law 7–8
  classification of causes of
      action 43–5
  English approach 36–7
  estoppel 77
  governing procedure 73–4
  legal parenthood 1181
  limitations on dominance of
      applicable law
      Rome
          I Regulation 746–51
          Rome II Regulation 866
  local law theory 23–4
  new American revolution
      comparative
          impairment 27–8
      governmental interest
          analysis 26–7
      interpretation of forum
          policy 28–9
  nullity of marriage 987
  substance and procedure
      distinguished
      foreign currency
          judgments 100
      measure of damages 94
Law of the place of acting
  formal validity of wills 1341
  property law
      transfer of intangible
          movables 1283,
          1286, 1295–7
      transfer of tangible
          movables 1265–6
Law of the place of celebration
  capacity to marry 919–21
  nullity of marriage 987–8
Law of the situs
  assignment of debts
      need to determine situs of
          debt 1280–2
      theoretical
          perspectives 1282
  assignments of matrimonial
      property 1371
  children 1125
  classification of causes of
      action 43–4
  contractual obligations 761

debts 1294
disputes outside
    Rome II 809
exclusion of foreign law 128
gifts 1277
immovable property
    choice of law 1255–6
    meaning 1257–8
limitations on
    jurisdiction 489–90
movable and immovable
    property
    distinguished 44,
    1252, 1254
renvoi doctrine 67–8
share transfers 1299–300
succession in Scotland 42
transfer of tangible movables
    choice of law 1265
    meaning of the law of the
    situs 1273–4

Legitimacy
declarations 1053
governed by law of the
    domicile
    domicile of origin 1200–1
    incidents of status 1201–2
    other authorities 1197–9
    overview 1194–5
    Shaw v Gould 1195–7
    where birth parent
    married 1202

Legitimation
declarations 1053
domicile of origin 165
foreign status 140
historical development of
    English law 20
overview 1193–4
by recognition 1204–5
by subsequent marriage
    common law rule 1202–3
    Legitimacy Act
    1976 1203–4
    long-standing rule 1202
    total renvoi doctrine 67–8
Lex actus 1282–3
Lex fori *see* **law of forum**
Lex situs *see* **law of the situs**
Libel *see* **defamation**
Limitation of actions
applicable law in the absence
    of choice under
    Rome I 768
exclusion of laws repugnant
    to English public
    policy 135

substance and procedure
    distinguished 78
Limitations on jurisdiction
carriage contracts 190, 518
embassies 517
foreign immovables
    common law
    limitation 484–91
    exceptions to exclusionary
    rule 485–92
    exclusionary rule 484–5
    limitation under the
    Brussels/Lugano
    system 492–4
foreign intellectual property
    rights 494–6
Foreign Judgments (Reciprocal
    Enforcement) Act
    1933 597
judicial notice 509
law of the situs 489–90
mortgages 489
overview 483–4
parties
    persons who cannot
    invoke the
    jurisdiction 495–6
    sovereigns and sovereign
    states 497–518
set-off 497
statutory limitations 518–19
traditional rules 190
Lis pendens
actions *in rem* under
    traditional English
    rules 389
Brussels I Recast
    defendant not domiciled
    in EU 214
    exclusive jurisdiction 218,
    450–3
    insurance jurisdiction 291
    jurisdiction
    agreements 243
    parallel proceedings 311,
    443–53
    service of
    proceedings 308
    submission to
    jurisdiction 226
Hague Convention on
    Choice of Court
    Agreements 2005 316
Lugano Convention
    2007 313
matrimonial proceedings
    forum shopping 984

general principles of
    jurisdiction 959
stays 968, 971
Modified Regulation 321
service without permission
    out of jurisdiction
    under English
    traditional rules 380
stays of English proceedings
    under common
    law 407–10
Local law theory 23–4
Lugano Convention 1988
applicability 653–4
difference with Brussels
    I Recast 654–5
Lugano Convention 2007
financial relief in the
    English courts
    inter-relation with
    other jurisdictional
    bases 1070–1
    jurisdictional
    basis 1069–70
jurisdiction
    applicability 313–14
    part of the process of
    cooperation 313
    stays 314
    terminology 314
terminology 314

Maintenance
see also **ancillary relief**
after foreign decrees
    powers of English
    court 1071–7
    relief already granted in
    England 1071
choice of law 1078
financial relief in the
    English courts
    alteration of maintenance
    agreements 1062
    enforcement of
    orders 1063–4
    failure to provide 1062
under Maintenance
    Regulation
    inter-relation with
    other jurisdictional
    bases 1070–1
    jurisdictional rules 1064–9
    maintenance orders
    defined 1064–5
    recognition and
    enforcement 1081–4

Maintenance (*cont.*):
  recognition and enforcement
    Hague Convention
      2007 1084–6
    Maintenance Orders
      (Facilities for
      Enforcement) Act
      1920 1079–80
    maintenance orders made
      in UK 1079
    Maintenance Orders
      (Reciprocal
      Enforcement) Act
      1972 1080–1
    Maintenance
      Regulation 1081–4
Mandatory rules
  effect on exclusion of foreign
    law 143–4
  limitations on choice of
    law 713–14
  limitations on dominance of
    applicable law
    key concept 743
    Rome II
      Regulation 866–8
  limitations on dominance of
    applicable law (Rome I)
    background 743–4
    mandatory rules
      defined 744–6
    mandatory rules of the
      forum 746–51
    rules of other
      countries 751–2
  Mental Capacity Act
    2005 1241
  mixed issues under Rome
    II 882–3
  trusts 1392–3
**Manifestly more closely
  connected escape clause**
  culpa in contrahendo 854
  product liability 823
  Rome II Regulation escape
    clause 814–19
  unjust enrichment 847–8
Maritime law
  actions *in rem* under
    traditional English rules
  effect of Brussels/Lugano
    system 386–90
  ships as
    defendants 382–4
  ships other than the
    primary ship 384–5
  appropriate defendants 88

evidence and interpretation
  distinguished 84
priority of creditors 89–90
recognition and enforcement
  of foreign judgments at
  common law
  definition of judgment in
    rem 544–6
  enforcement 548
  jurisdictional
    requirements 546–8
Rome II Regulation
  negotiorum gestio 878–9
  torts 875–8
service with permission out
  of jurisdiction under
  English traditional
  rules 361
sovereign immunity 505–6
Marriage *see also* **divorce**
  capacity to marry
    law of the place of
      celebration 919–21
    major issue relating
      to choice of
      law 909–10
    public policy 921–2
    real and substantial
      connection test 924
    recognition of foreign
      divorces or
      annulments 925–8
    renvoi 922–3
    rule in *Sottomayor
      v De Barros
      (No 2)* 918–19
    theoretical
      perspectives 910–18
  choice of law rule 47–9
  declarations as to marital
    status 1051–2
  defined 891–2
  doctrine of putative
    marriage 1199–200
  domicile of married women
    abolition of dependency
      rule 168–9
    transitional problems 169
  exclusion from Brussels
    I Recast
    maintenance
      obligations 211–12
    marital status 206–7
  formal validity
    dépeçage 54–5
    development of
      English law 20

exceptions to general
  rule 901–9
in foreign consulates and
  embassies 899–900
general rule 893–7
renvoi 900–1
retrospectivity 897–9
incidental questions 52–3
legitimation by subsequent
  marriage
  common law rule 1202–3
  Legitimacy Act
    1976 1203–4
  long-standing rule 1202
personal physical
  defects 993–6
polygamous marriages
  capacity to
    contract 936–41
  date when
    determined 933–6
  English approach to
    validity 928–9
  governing law as to
    nature 930–3
  matrimonial
    relief 943, 951–4
  meaning and
    scope 929–30
  recognition in
    England 941–6
presumption of death and
  dissolution of marriage
  choice of law 1038
  jurisdiction 1038
  recognition 1038–9
  statutory
    provisions 1037–8
reform initiatives 927–8
revocation of wills 1350–1
variation of trusts and
  settlements 1394
Material validity
  defined 755–6
  meaning and scope 232
  putative applicable
    law 755–6
Matrimonial property
  applicable law on
    divorce 1378–9
  assignments - no ante-
    nuptial agreement
    immovable property 1371
  movable
    property 1366–71
  civil partnership 1379–80
  cohabitation 1380

European Commission
reform
proposals 1380–1
underlying problem 1365
Matrimonial relief
see also **financial relief**
actions *in personam* 323
general relevance 929
polygamous marriages
common law rules 952
Matrimonial Causes Act
1973 952
previous inability to
grant 943
remaining problems 953–5
recognition of foreign
status 140
Measure of damages
safety and conduct rules 871
substance and procedure
distinguished 92, 94–6
Mental Capacity Act 2005
choice of law
general applicable
law 1238–41
mandatory rules 1241
powers of attorney 1239–41
protective measures 1239
public policy 1241
third party
protection 1241
co-operation by Hague
Contracting
States 1244–5
jurisdiction
habitual residence in
England 1235–6
jurisdiction upon
request 1238
nationality 1237–8
property situated in
England 1236
protective measures 1237
urgent cases 1236–7
recognition and enforcement
of protective measures
enforcement 1244
recognition 1242
refusal grounds 1242–4
Mental incapacity
common law rules
choice of law 1246
jurisdiction 1245–6
recognition and
enforcement
of protective
measures 1246–8

Mental Capacity Act 2005
choice of law 1238–41
jurisdiction 1235–8
recognition and
enforcement
of protective
measures 1242–4
underlying
concepts 1233–5
overview 1232–3
Mistakes
consent to marry 986–8
contractual obligations 757
by foreign courts
as to facts or law 564–5
as to jurisdiction 565
procedure 565–7
as to foreign law 108
material validity 232
non-review as to
substance 1005, 1129
recission as remedy 840
Modified Regulation
jurisdiction within UK
applicability 317–19
modifications 319–21
stays 321–2
overview 189
Mortgages
limitations on
jurisdiction 489
movable and immovable
property
distinguished 1252
Movable property
assignment of intangible
movables
debts 1280–94
negotiable
instruments 1294–7
rights distinguished 1280
shares and
securities 1298–304
assignments of matrimonial
property
no ante-nuptial
agreement 1366–71
exclusion of foreign law 129
immovable property
distinguished
annuities 1254
classification by law of
situs 1252
mortgages 1252
overview 1251
relevance 1254
trusts for sale 1252–4

renvoi 71
sovereign immunity 505
succession
intestate succession 1339
wills 1340–51
tangible and intangible
movables
distinguished 1254
transfer of tangible movables
attachment by
creditors 1275
cultural property 1277–8
derivative claims 1271–2
general rule 1267–70
gifts 1276–7
goods in transit 1275–6
human rights 1278–9
law of the domicile 1264–5
law of the place of
acting 1265–6
law of the situs 1265
meaning of the law of the
situs 1273–4
proper law of the
transfer 1266–7
retention of title
clauses 1272–3
underlying
problems 1263–4
Multilateral trading systems
applicable law in the absence
of choice 730
special contracts 741

Nationality
domicile distinguished 170
domicile of choice 161
Mental Capacity Act
2005 1237–8
merits and demerits 171
recognition and enforcement
of foreign judgments at
common law 540–1
recognition of divorces,
separations and
annulments outside
EU 1008
Natural justice
recognition and enforcement
under Brussels I Recast
default judgments 633
establishing a lack of
natural justice 633–9
interaction with
jurisdictional
provisions 633
overview 632–3

Natural justice (*cont.*):
  recognition and enforcement
      under traditional rules
  due notice and proper
      hearing 577–8
  meaning and scope 576
  relationship with human
      rights 579–80
  substantial justice 578–9
Negative
  declarations 375–6, 446
Negotiable instruments
  application of renvoi 70
  exclusion from Rome
      I Regulation 699
  exclusion from Rome II 795
  transfers 1294–7
Negotiorum gestio
  general principles
      under Rome II
      Regulation 848–9
  maritime obligations 878–9
New American revolution
  basic characteristic 24
  general approaches
      rule or jurisdiction
          selection 25
      true and false
          conflicts 25–6
  limited impact 31–2
  rule-selection techniques
      choice of law
          factors 29–31
      comparative
          impairment 27–8
      governmental interest
          analysis 26–7
      interpretation of forum
          policy 28–9
      principles of
          preference 28
  subsequent
      developments 32–3
Non-consummation of
  marriage 993–6
Non-contractual obligations
  see also **contractual**
      obligations
  appropriate defendants 88
  classification of causes of
      action 43
  meaning and scope of Rome
      II 788–92
  outside Rome II
      defamation 885–8
      overview 883–4
      privacy 884–5

overview
  equitable
      obligations 778–9
  restitution 777–8
  torts 776–7
Rome II Regulation
  applicability 780–1,
      786–802
  choice of law 854–8
  culpa in
      contrahendo 849–54
  damage 803
  exclusion of renvoi 802
  exclusions 793–801
  habitual residence 802–3
  limitations on dominance
      of the applicable
      law 866–71
  maritime
      obligations 875–9
  mixed issues with
      contract 880–3
  negotiorum gestio 848–9
  proof of foreign
      law 803–4
  relationship with EU
      law 873
  relationship with
      international
      law 873–5
  safety and conduct
      rules 871
  scope of applicable
      law 858–66
  special rules for particular
      issues 872–3
  torts 804–36
  universal
      application 801–2
  unjust enrichment 837–48
substance and procedure
  distinguished 85
Northern Ireland
  administration of
      estates 1337
  allocating jurisdiction
      within the United
      Kingdom 236, 317–18
  Brussels I Recast 194
  contractual obligations 696
  custody orders 1132
  estoppel as a defence 556
  foreign law 8
  jurisdiction based on
      nationality 1238
  legitimation by subsequent
      marriage 1202

orders relating to
  children 1132–4
protective measures 1246
recognition and enforcement
  of judgments 524, 588
recognition of
  adoptions 1223
recognition of divorce and
  annulment 1001,
  1035–6
registration of
  companies 328
retention of title
  clauses 1272–3
revenue claims 360
section 8 orders 1106
sham marriages 992
special guardianship
  orders 1108
special jurisdiction 244
Nullity of civil partnership
  choice of law 1042–3
  jurisdiction 1039–42
  procedural issues 1042
  recognition 1043–5
Nullity of marriage *see also*
  divorce
  choice of law
      classification of
          defects 986
      consent 986–93
      effect of a nullity
          decree 999–1000
      grounds unknown to
          English law 996–7
      personal physical
          defects 993–6
      underlying
          problems 984–6
      void or voidable
          marriages 998–9
  exclusion of foreign
      law 141–2
  financial relief
      after foreign
          decrees 1071–7
      jurisdiction of English
          court 1059–71
      recognition and
          enforcement
          1078–86
  jurisdiction
      bases of jurisdiction 954,
          964–5
      other matrimonial
          proceedings for same
          marriage 965–7

restraint of foreign
proceedings 978–9
stays 967–78
lack of consent
classification of
defects 986–7
domicile 988–90
forced marriages 990–1
law of forum 987
law of the place of
celebration 987–8
sham marriages 992–3
Nullity of same sex marriage
choice of law 1047–8
jurisdiction 1045–7
recognition 1048

Obligations *see* **law of**
obligations
Ordinary residence
corporations 1307
meaning and scope 173–5
Ottomayor v De Barros (No 2),
rule in **918–19**

Parallel proceedings
Brussels I Recast
overview 311–12, 442–3
proceedings in
another Member
State 443–57
proceedings in
non-Member
State 457–9
Hague Convention on
Choice of Court
Agreements 2005 316
lis pendens 321
overview 391–2
Parental responsibility
background 1089–91
bases of jurisdiction
adoption 1108
Brussels II 1094–100
inherent jurisdiction of
High Court 1108–12
overview 1091
section 8 orders 1092–108
special guardianship
orders 1108
transfers to better
court 1100–8
refusal of applications
and stays
Brussels II 1113–16
concurrent proceedings in
EU 1117–20

concurrent proceedings
in related UK
jurisdiction 1124
concurrent proceedings
outside EU 1124
Family Law Act 1986 1113
Hague Convention
States 1121–4
transfers under Hague
Convention
1996 1116–17
variation and duration of
Part I orders 1112–13
Parenthood
declarations 1053
diversity of national
approaches 1182
legal parenthood 1180–1
UK approach
authorisation
requirements for
payments 1187–9
background 1183–4
child's home 1186
consent 1186–7
domicile 1184–5
genetic link and
minimum age 1185
personal status 1185
time limits 1186
Parties
appropriate
defendants 87–8
choice of law
consent to choice 723
express choice 717–18
freedom of choice 706–11
inferred choice 718–23
law in the absence of
choice under Rome
I 724–43
limitations on
choice 711–16
scope of private
international
law 7–8
liability under Rome
II 859–60
limitations on proceedings
persons who cannot
invoke the
jurisdiction 495–6
sovereigns and sovereign
states 497–518
matters relating to a contract
under Art 7(1) 245–6
proper claimants 86–7

Partnerships
appropriate
defendants 87–8
service of proceedings under
English traditional
rules 327–8
sovereign immunity 505
Payment procedure *see*
European Order For
Payment Procedure
Regulation2006
under **EU law**
Penal laws
enforcement of foreign
judgments in
personam 552–3
exclusion of foreign law
characterization of foreign
rights 121–2
examples of indirect
enforcement 120
meaning of a
penalty 119–20
recognition of foreign
law 122
settled rule 118–19
Performance
applicable law in the absence
of choice under Rome I
extinguishing of
obligations 768
manner of
performance 765–6
meaning and scope 765
illegality
agreements to break
foreign law 769
illegality by English
law 772
illegality by law of foreign
place 769–72
special problem 769
matters relating to a contract
under Art 7(1)
identifiable place 250
place of performance
defined 254
Place of damage rule
environmental
damage 829–30
general principle 810–13
Polygamous marriages
capacity to contract
common law
rules 936–8
statutory
provisions 938–41

Polygamous marriages (*cont.*):
date when
determined 933–6
English approach to
validity 928–9
governing law as to
nature 930–3
matrimonial relief
common law rules 952
Matrimonial Causes Act
1973 952
previous inability to
grant 943
remaining
problems 953–5
meaning and scope 929–30
recognition in
England 941–6
Powers of appointment
exercised by will
capacity 1361
essential validity 1362–3
formal validity 1361–2
interpretation 1363–4
overview 1359–60
revocation 1364
special and general powers
distinguished 1360
family law 1226
Precarious residence 160–1
Presumption of death
declarations 1058
and dissolution of civil
partnership 1041–2
and dissolution of marriage
choice of law 1038
jurisdiction 1038
recognition 1038–9
statutory
provisions 1037–8
and dissolution of same sex
marriage 1047
Presumptions
proof of foreign law 105–6
substance and procedure
distinguished 85
Priority of creditors
assignment of debts
1288–9
substance and procedure
distinguished 89–90
Prisoners
domicile of choice 158
escaped prisoners of
war 907
State immunity and human
rights 501

Privacy
choice of law 884–5
ECtHR
jurisprudence 1163–7
exclusion from Rome
II 797–9
impact of ECHR on
unification 14–15
Private international law
see also **Conflict of laws**
avoidance of conflict
through unification
Europeanisation 11–13
impact of ECHR 13–15
overview 10–11
common title to describe the
subject 15–16
English law *see* **English law**
functions
space 5
time 5–6
part of English law containing
foreign element 3
raison d'être 3–4
rules voluntarily chosen by
given State 4–5
scope
choice of law 7–8
jurisdiction 6–7
overview 6
recognition 7
separate and distinct unit 6
theoretical perspectives
acquired rights 21–3
assignment of
debts 1282–4
capacity to marry 910–18
English law 36–7
evolution of EU
law 33–6
local law theory 23–4
new American
revolution 24–33
recognition and
enforcement at
common law 525–7
Private international law rules
see **rules of law**
Procedure
assignment of
debts 1289–90
damages 91–7
dissolution, nullity and
separation of civil
partners 1042
enforcement under Brussels
I Recast 622–5

European Enforcement
Order
Regulation 2004
enforcement 659
uncontested claims
procedures 658–9
European Order For
Payment Procedure
Regulation 2006
collection of specific
pecuniary
claims 661–2
objectives 660
payments in other
Member
States 662–3
scope and
definitions 660–1
European Small
Claims Procedure
Regulation 2007
objectives 663
in other Member
States 664
overview 664
scope and definitions 663
evidence
interpretation and
proof of document
distinguished 80–1
interpretation
distinguished 84
law of the forum 80
presumptions and burden
of proof 85
taking of evidence outside
the EU 83–4
taking of evidence within
the EU 81–3
exclusions from Rome
I Regulation 704–5
exclusions from Rome
II 799–801
execution of judgments 104
family law
declarations 1055–6
foreign currency judgments
appropriate currency for
judgment 101–4
date for conversion 100–1
interest on judgments 99
law of forum 100
Miliangos rule 98–9
old rule: judgment must
be in sterling 97
governed by law of the
forum 73–4

mistakes by foreign
    courts 565–7
nature and extent of the
    remedy 89–90
parties
    appropriate
        defendants 87–8
    proper claimants 86–7
priority of creditors 89–90
recognition of divorces,
    separations and
    annulments outside
    EU 1010–11
sovereign immunity 508–9
substance distinguished
    drawing the line 75–7
    importance 74–5
time within which an action
    must be brought 78–9
Product liability
Rome II Regulation
    applicable law 821–3
    overview 820
    scope of Article 5 820–1
Proof
domicile of choice 161
foreign law
    appropriate
        evidence 108–9
    expert witnesses 110–13
    question of fact 105–8
substance or procedure
    interpretation and
        proof of document
        distinguished 80–1
    presumptions and burden
        of proof 85
Property law
assignment of intangible
    movables
    debts 1280–94
    negotiable
        instruments 1294–7
    rights distinguished 1280
    shares and
        securities 1298–304
exclusive subject-matter
    jurisdiction
    short-term holiday
        lets 222–6
    tenancies 221–2
immovable property
    applicable law in
        the absence of
        choice 728–9
    choice of law
        issues 1255–62

jurisdiction 246,
    279, 1255
limitations on dominance
    of applicable
    law 760–1
Mental Capacity Act
    2005 1236
movable property
    distinguished 1251–4
renvoi 71
immovables
development of
    English law 20
exclusive subject-
    matter jurisdiction
    under Brussels
    I Recast 219–23
incidental questions 51
limitations on proceedings
    involving foreign
    immovables
common law
    limitation 484–91
exceptions to exclusionary
    rule 485–92
exclusionary rule 484–5
limitation under the
    Brussels/Lugano
    system 492–4
matrimonial property
applicable law on
    divorce 1378–9
assignments - ante-
    nuptial agreement in
    place 1372–8
assignments - no
    ante-nuptial
    agreement 1366–71
civil partnership 1379–80
cohabitation 1380
European Commission
    reform
    proposals 1380–1
underlying problem 1365
movable property
exclusion of foreign
    law 129
immovable property
    distinguished 1251–4
renvoi 71
sovereign immunity 505
tangible and intangible
    moveables
    distinguished 1254
recognition and enforcement
    of foreign judgments at
    common law 542

service with permission out
    of jurisdiction under
    English traditional
    rules 356–8
sovereign immunity 505
transfer of tangible
    movables
    attachment by
        creditors 1275
    cultural property 1277–8
    derivative claims 1271–2
    general rule 1267–70
    gifts 1276–7
    goods in transit 1275–6
    human rights 1278–9
    law of the
        domicile 1264–5
    law of the place of
        acting 1265–6
    law of the situs 1265
    meaning of the law of the
        situs 1273–4
    proper law of the
        transfer 1266–7
    retention of title
        clauses 1272–3
    underlying
        problems 1263–4
unjust enrichment 838–9
Prorogation of jurisdiction
bases of jurisdiction 216
Brussels I Recast
    choice of court
        agreements 229–44
    submission to
        forum 226–9
family law
    child abduction 1098
    children 1105
Prostitution
exclusion of laws repugnant
    to English public
    policy 135–6
law of obligations 753
Protective measures *see*
    provisional measures
Provisional measures
jurisdiction under Brussels
    I Recast
    as to the substance 303
    where no jurisdiction as to
        the substance 303–5
Mental Capacity Act 2005
    choice of law 1239
    jurisdiction 1237
    recognition and
        enforcement 1242–4

Provisional measures (*cont.*):
mental incapacity - common
law rules 1246–8
parental responsibility
applications 1121–4
recognition and enforcement
under Brussels
I Recast 615–17
service out of jurisdiction
under English
traditional rules
with permission 340–1
without permission 380
Public laws
common thread
running through
the exclusionary
rule 115–16
enforcement of foreign
judgments in
personam 552–3
other public laws 123–5
penal laws 118–22
revenue law 116–19
Public policy
bona vacantia 50
capacity to marry 921–2
defence to recognition and
enforcement 14
development of
English law 19
development of EU law 36
exclusion of foreign law
basic principles of justice
and fairness 135
fundamental breaches
of international
law 138–9
general principles 132–5
gross infringements of
human rights 137
infringements of
morality 135–6
transactions prejudicial to
UK 136–7
fraudulent tax-evasion
schemes 118
limitations on choice of
law 714
limitations on dominance of
applicable law
Rome I Regulation 752–4
Rome II
Regulation 868–71
mandatory rules 143
Mental Capacity Act
2005 1241, 1243

new American revolution 33
non-recognition of
foreign divorces,
annulments and legal
separations 1029–33
proof of foreign law 105
recognition and
enforcement under
Brussels I Recast
excluded matters 631–2
interaction with
lack of natural
justice 639–42
meaning and
scope 626–7
recognition and enforcement
under traditional rules
general principles 574–5
human rights 576
recognition of divorces,
separations and
annulments 1004–5
refusal to recognise arbitral
award 675–6
stays of English proceedings
under common
law 406–7
total renvoi doctrine 62
trusts 1393
**Putative marriage
doctrine 999, 1194–200,
1199–200**

**Real and substantial
connection test**
foreign adoptions 1229
marriage
formal validity 924
recognition of foreign
decrees 1038
recognition and enforcement
of foreign judgments
and awards 349,
397, 543–4
validity of marriage 924
Recognition and enforcement
acquired rights theory 21
administration of estates
commonwealth
grants 1336–7
foreign adminis-
trators 1335–6
annulments
decrees made elsewhere in
British Isles 1001–2
decrees obtained in
EU 1002–5

decrees obtained
outside EU or in
Denmark 1005–12
extra-judicial
annulments 1012–24
grounds for non-
recognition 1024–
34
history and development
of rules 1000–1
retrospectivity 1034,
1035–6
arbitral awards
Administration of Justice
Act 1920 677
Arbitration Act 1950 670
Arbitration Act
1996 670–6
Arbitration (International
Investment
Disputes) Act
1966 677
Civil Jurisdiction and
Judgments Act
1982 669–70
common law
rules 667–9
complicated questions of
PIL 520–1
Foreign Judgments
(Reciprocal
Enforcement) Act
1933 677
numerous separate sets of
rules 524
overview 666–7
Brussels Convention
1968 652–3
Brussels I Recast
agreements with non-
Contracting
States 651–2
appeals in original
Member
State 646–50
applicability 611–18
automatic recognition
without
jurisdictional
safeguards 650–1
difference with Lugano
Convention
1988 654–5
estoppel effect of
judgment
in Member
State 649–50

grounds for
refusal 625–43
non-grounds for
refusal 643–6
objectives 608–11
recognition 617–19
Brussels/Lugano System
Brussels Convention
1968 652–3
Brussels
I Recast 608–52
EC/Denmark
Agreement 652
European Enforcement
Order Regulation
2004 656–9
European Order For
Payment Procedure
Regulation
2006 660–3
European Small
Claims Procedure
Regulation
2007 663–5
Lugano Convention
1988 653–5
overview 522–4
children
Child Abduction and
Custody Act
1985 1134–71
common law
rules 1172–7
orders made in
EU 1127–31
orders made in Hague
Convention
States 1131–2
orders made in Scotland
and NI 1132–4
overview 1126
common law rules
defences 564–88
enforcement of foreign
judgments in
personam 551–6
final and conclusive
judgments 548–51
inter-relation with
statute 605–7
judgments in
personam 528–44
judgments in rem 544–8
other grounds of
competency 540–3
overview 527–8

real and substantial
connection
test 543–4
recognition of foreign
judgments 556–63
complicated questions of
PIL 520–1
differing regimes
family law 524
insolvency 524
judgments from other
parts of the United
Kingdom 524
judgments originating
from European
Union and EFTA
States 522–4
judgments originating
from outside the
European Union and
EFTA 521–2
succession 524
direct enforcement by
statute
Administration of Justice
Act 1920 591–2
Brussels /Lugano
system 603–4
Civil Jurisdiction and
Judgments Act
1982 588–91
European Union
judgments 601
Foreign Judgments
(Reciprocal
Enforcement) Act
1933 593–601
Hague Convention
on Choice of
Court Agreements
2005 604–5
inter-relation with
common law 605–7
overview 588
sovereign
immunity 601–2
dissolution, nullity and
separation of civil
partners
effect of decree from
EU 1044–5
effect of decree from
outside EU 1045
effect of decree in
UK 1043–4
statutory provisions 1043

divorce, nullity and
separation of same sex
marriage 1048
European Enforcement
Order
Regulation 2004
applicability 656
enforcement 659
European Enforcement
Orders 657–8
subject matter and
scope 656–7
uncontested claims
procedures 658–9
European Order For
Payment Procedure
Regulation 2006
collection of specific
pecuniary
claims 661–2
objectives 660
payments in other Member
States 662–3
scope and
definitions 660–1
European Small
Claims Procedure
Regulation 2007
objectives 663
in other Member
States 664
overview 664
scope and definitions 663
financial relief
ancillary relief
abroad 1078–9
Hague Convention
2007 1084–6
maintenance
orders 1063–4
Maintenance Orders
(Facilities for
Enforcement) Act
1920 1079–80
maintenance orders made
in UK 1079
Maintenance Orders
(Reciprocal
Enforcement) Act
1972 1080–1
Maintenance
Regulation 1081–4
foreign adoptions
adoptions made elsewhere
in the British
Isles 1222–3

Recognition and enforcement
  (*cont.*):
  foreign adoptions (*cont.*):
    adoptions made in
      other foreign
      countries 1225–9
    annulment of foreign
      adoptions 1225
    Convention
      adoptions 1223–4
    overseas
      adoptions 1224–5
    overview 1222–3
  foreign annulments
    capacity to
      remarry 925–6
    effect of
      non-recognition 926
    prohibitions against
      remarriage 926–7
  foreign divorces
    capacity to
      remarry 925–6
    decrees made elsewhere in
      British Isles 1001–2
    decrees obtained in
      EU 1002–5
    decrees obtained
      outside EU or in
      Denmark 1005–12
    effect of foreign
      decree 1034–5
    effect of
      non-recognition 926
    extra-judicial
      divorces 1012–24
    grounds for non-
      recognition 1024–
      34
    history and development
      of rules 1000–1
    prohibitions against
      remarriage 926–7
    retrospectivity 1034
  insolvency
    proceedings 1323–4
  judgments from other
    parts of the United
    Kingdom 524
  judgments originating
    from outside the
    European Union and
    EFTA 521–2
  judicial separation
    decrees made elsewhere in
      British Isles 1001–2

decrees obtained in
  EU 1002–5
decrees obtained
  outside EU or in
  Denmark 1005–12
effect of foreign
  decree 1036–7
extra-judicial legal
  separations 1012–24
grounds for non-
  recognition 1024–
  34
history and development
  of rules 1000–1
retrospectivity 1034
legitimation 1204–5
Lugano Convention 1988
  applicability 653–4
  difference with Brussels
    I Recast 654–5
Mental Capacity
  Act 2005
  enforcement 1244
  recognition 1242
  refusal grounds 1242–4
mental incapacity - common
  law rules 1246–8
presumption of death
  and dissolution of
  marriage 1038–9
scope of private
  international law 7
service with permission out
  of jurisdiction under
  English traditional
  rules 355–6
theoretical perspectives
  at common law 525–7
  enforcement by
    statute 527
  trusts 1391–2
Recognition of foreign law
  acquired rights theory 21
  penal laws 122
  raison d'être for PIL 3–4
  revenue law 118
Refugees and asylum seekers
  Area of Freedom, Security
    and Justice 12
  domicile of choice 158
  family law
    habitual residence in
      England 1236
    Hague Protection
      Convention
      1996 1121–2

jurisdiction based
  on child's
  presence 1100, 1103
jurisdiction based on
  nationality 1239
welfare of
  children 1172–3
Remedies *see* **enforcement and
  remedies**
  Rome II Regulation 863–5
  substance and procedure
    distinguished
    damages 91–7
    nature and extent of the
      remedy 90–1
Remoteness of damage
  contractual obligations 767
  non-contractual
    obligations 861
  substance and procedure
    distinguished 92–3
Renvoi
  foreign movable and
    immovable property 71
  marriage
    capacity to marry 922–3
    formal validity 900–1
  possible solutions
    application of internal law
      only 58–9
    single renvoi
      doctrine 59–60
    total renvoi
      doctrine 60–9
  scope of application
    no general
      application 69–71
    succession 70
  underlying problem 57–8
Res judicata
  foreign judgments 564
  non-recognition of
    foreign divorces,
    annulments and legal
    separations 1025–6
  oppression 430
  recognition and enforcement
    of foreign judgments at
    common law 548–51
  rule of estoppel 556
Residence
  see also **habitual residence**
  corporations 1307
  domicile of choice
    precarious
      residence 160–1

relationship with
intention 149–50
voluntary
residence 158–60
habitual residence
acquisition of
new habitual
residence 177–84
question of fact 175–6
ordinary residence 173–5
precarious residence 160–1
recognition and enforcement
of foreign judgments at
common law 529–31
underlying problems with
nationality 172
voluntary residence 158–60
Restitution claims
problem of ascertaining
applicable law 777–8
service with permission out
of jurisdiction under
English traditional
rules 358–60
total renvoi doctrine 70
**Restraint of foreign
proceedings**
see also **stays**
Brussels I Recast
discretion to
restrain 475–6
traditional English
powers 476–82
common law rules
overview 422
underlying
principles 423–5
matrimonial
proceedings 978–9
Retention of title clauses
jurisdiction under Brussels/
Lugano system 208
transfer of tangible
movables 1272–3
Revenue claims
enforcement of foreign
judgments in
personam 552–3
exclusion of foreign law
indirect
enforcement 117–18
prohibition on
enforcement 116–17
recognition of foreign
law 118
service with permission out
of jurisdiction under

English traditional
rules 360
sovereign immunity 505
Revocation of wills
immovable property 1358
movable property
by destruction 1349–50
by later will 1348–9
by marriage 1350–1
overview 1348
powers of appointment
exercised by will 1364
Rights *in rem*
exclusive subject-matter
jurisdiction 219–20
immovable property 1255
insolvency 1275
insurance claims 289
property law 1322–3
Road traffic accidents
direct damage 812
key issue 781–2
Rome II Regulation 819
safety and conduct rules 871
Rome I Regulation
applicability
overview 691–2
scope of the
Regulation 692–705
applicable law
law in the absence of
choice 724–43
assignment of debts
contractual
assignments 1285–6
nature of right
assigned 1287–91
non-contractual
assignments 1287
source of modern
law 1285
subrogation 1291–2
choice of law
consent to choice 723
express choice 717–18
freedom of choice 706–11
inferred choice 718–23
law in the absence of
choice under Rome
I 724–43
limitations on
choice 711–16
scope of private
international
law 7–8
history 686–7
interpretation

aids to
interpretation 689–
91
principles laid down by
ECJ 688
referrals to Court of
Justice 687
uniform and autonomous
interpretation 689
law in the absence of choice
under Rome I
characteristic performance
test 731–5
closest connection 735
common law rules 724
escape clause 735–9
habitual
residence 739–40
limitations on dominance
of applicable
law 743–54, 743–64
overview 724–6
particular issues 754–72
relationship with
EU 772–4
relationship with
international
law 774–5
scope of applicable
law 764–9
severance of
contracts 740
special contracts 740–3
specific contracts 726–31
universal and world-wide
application 705–6
Rome II Regulation
applicability
civil and commercial
matters 792–3
conflict of laws 787–8
matters coming within its
scope 787
non-contractual
obligations 788–92
overview 780–1
Chapter II
scope 802–9
structure 809
choice of law
conditions
imposed 855–6
English rules on pleading
and proof of foreign
law 856
express or inferred
choice 856

Rome II Regulation (*cont.*):
  choice of law (*cont.*):
    freedom of choice 854–5
    limitations on choice of
        law 857–8
    third party rights 856
  culpa in contrahendo
    applicable law 852–4
    problems of
        classification 849–50
    scope of Article 12 850–2
  damage 803
  exclusion of renvoi 802
  exclusions
    companies 796
    evidence 798–9
    family law 793–5
    negotiable
        instruments 795
    privacy and
        defamation 797–9
    procedure 799–801
    trusts 796–7
  habitual residence 802–3
  history 781–2
  interpretation
    aids to
        interpretation 784–5
    general principles 783–4
    referrals to ECJ 783
  interpretation of Rome
      I Regulation 690–1
  legal basis 782–3
  limitations on dominance of
      applicable law
    overriding mandatory
        provisions of the
        forum 866–8
    public policy 868–71
  maritime obligations
    negotiorum gestio 878–9
    torts 875–8
  mixed issues with contract
    contractual obligations
        with contractual
        defences 880
    nature of the
        obligation 880
    nature of the
        problem 879–80
    non-contractual
        obligations with
        contractual
        defences 880–3
  negotiorum gestio 848–9
  proof of foreign
      law 803–4

relationship with EU
    law 873
relationship with
    international
    law 873–5
safety and conduct rules 871
scope of applicable law
  capacity 865–6
  damage 861–4
  liability 859–60
  remedies 863–5
  rules common to
      Chapters II, III and
      IV 858–9
special rules for
    particular issues
  formal validity 872–3
  insurance 872
torts
  borderline with unjust
      enrichment 840
  environmental
      damage 828–31
  escape clause 814–19
  exception to general
      rule 809–14
  general rule 810–13
  industrial action 835–6
  intellectual property
      rights 831–5
  manifestly more closely
      connected escape
      clause 814–19
  maritime
      obligations 875–8
  product liability 819–23
  restrictions on free
      competition 827–8
  road traffic accidents 819
  scope of Chapter
      II 802–9
  specific rules for special
      torts 819–36
  structure of
      Chapter II 809
  unfair competition 823–7
universal application 801–2
unjust enrichment
  applicable law 843–7
  borderline with torts 840
  contractual
      obligations 839–40
  manifestly more closely
      connected escape
      clause 847–8
  problems of
      classification 837–8

problems with
    equity 840–1
  proprietary claims 838–9
  scope of Article 10 837
  wrongdoing 841–3
Rome III
  applicable law in
      matrimonial
      matters 982
  coming into effect 993
  enhanced cooperation 983
  reform proposals 962
Rules of law
  see also **common law rules**
  classification
    English rules 46–7
    foreign rules 47–50
    underlying problem 45–6
  English approach 37
  incidental questions 52
  mandatory rules 143–4
  new American revolution
    comparative
        impairment 27–8
    governmental interest
        analysis 26–7
    interpretation of forum
        policy 28–9
    principles of
        preference 27–8
  proof of foreign law 107
  rules voluntarily chosen by
      given State 4–5
  traditional rules on
      jurisdiction
    applicability 189–90
    decline of jurisdiction 190
    limitations 190
    power of English courts to
        hear case 190
  variety 8

Safety and conduct rules
  general limitation on
      applicable law 830–1
  requirements 871
Sale of goods
  applicable law in the absence
      of choice 727
  Brussels I Recast 727
  Brussels/Lugano
      System 245, 250, 252,
      255–7, 260–2, 293
  unification of
      internal laws 9
Same sex marriage
  see also **civil partnership**

declarations 1057–8
divorce, nullity and
    separation
  choice of law 1047–8
  jurisdiction 1045–7
  recognition 1048
recognition of overseas
    relationships 948–9
recognition under Brussels
    II 1004–5
Scope of private
    international law
  choice of law 7–8
  jurisdiction 6–7
  overview 6
  recognition 7
  separate and distinct unit 6
Scotland
  administration of
    estates 1337
  allocating jurisdiction
    within the United
    Kingdom 236, 317–18
  attachment of
    movables 1275
  Brussels I Recast 194
  change of domicile 161
  contractual obligations 696
  custody orders 1132
  de facto cohabitation 949
  dual domicile theory 918
  estoppel as a defence 556
  forced marriages 990
  foreign law 8
  forum non conveniens 393
  habitual residence 179
  judgments under Brussels I
    Recast 613
  jurisdiction based on
    nationality 1238
  legitimation by subsequent
    marriage 1202
  national law of a British
    subject 64
  orders relating to
    children 1132–4
  proof of Scots law 109
  protective measures 1246
  recognition and enforcement
    of judgments 524, 585
  recognition of
    adoptions 1223
  recognition of divorce and
    annulment 1001,
    1035–6
  recovery under void
    contracts 768

registration of
    Commonwealth
    judgments 591
registration of
    companies 328
retention of title
    clauses 1272–3
revenue claims 360
section 8 orders 1106
sham marriages 992
special guardianship
    orders 1108
special jurisdiction 244
Securities *see* **shares and**
    securities
Service of proceedings
  Brussels I Recast
    practicalities 308–9
    rights of the
      defendant 309–11
    rules 308
  dissolution, nullity and
    separation
    civil partnerships 1042
    same sex marriage 1047
  jurisdiction of English courts
    under traditional rules
    companies 328–32
    individuals 324–7
    partnerships 327–8
  non-recognition of
    foreign divorces,
    annulments and legal
    separations 1027–9
  recognition and
    enforcement at
    common law 542–3
  recognition and enforcement
    under Brussels
    I Recast 634–9
  service out of jurisdiction
    under English
    traditional rules
    with permission of the
      court 334–79
    service in practice 381
    traditional rule at
      common law 334
    without permission of the
      court 379–80
Service provision 727–8
Set-off
  applicable law in the absence
    of choice under
    Rome I 772
  attachment of
    movables 1275

Brussels/Lugano
    System 225, 227, 237
  insolvency 1321
  limitations on
    jurisdiction 497
  property law 1320
  substance and procedure
    distinguished 91
Settlement
    agreements 584–8
Severance of contracts 740
Sham marriages 992–3
Shares and securities
  gifts 1277
  tangible and intangible
    movables
    distinguished 1254
  transfers
    EU law 1301–2
    modern holding
      system 1301–5
    traditional
      approach 1298–301
Shipping *see* **maritime law**
Short-term holiday lets 221–2
Single renvoi doctrine 59–60
Small claims procedure
    see **European Small**
    Claims Procedure
    Regulation 2007
    under **EU law**
Social security
  English exclusionary
    rules 126
  exclusion from Brussels
    I Recast 208
  ordinary residence 173
Sovereign immunity
  administrative and service
    staff 512–13
  ambassadors and
    other diplomatic
    officers 509–10
  basic rule at common
    law 497–8
  cessation of
    immunities 513
  consular
    immunities 516–18
  diplomatic agents 511–12
  direct enforcement by
    statute 601–2
  foreign sovereigns 515–16
  indirect impleading 507–8
  international
    organizations 514–15
  restriction on privileges 514

Sovereign immunity (*cont.*):
State Immunity Act 1978
exceptions 503–7
human rights 500–3
procedure 508–9
scope 498–500
waiver of privileges 513–14
Space 5
Special guardianship orders
Children Act 1989 1091
parental responsibility 1108
Special jurisdiction
under Article 7
Article 7(1) 245–63
Article 7(2) 263–83
importance 244–5
under Article 8 279–83
relevant provisions 244
Status
corporations 1307–8
cross-border surrogacy 1185
effect of foreign
adoptions 1229–30
exclusion from Rome
I Regulation 697
foreign
administrators 1335–6
foreign status 139–41
governing law 145
legitimacy
declarations 1053
governed by law of the
domicile 1194–202
legitimation
declarations 1053
domicile of origin 165
foreign status 140
historical development of
English law 20
overview 1193–4
by recognition 1204–5
by subsequent
marriage 1202–4
total renvoi
doctrine 67–8
Maintenance
Regulation 1066
marital status
declarations 1051–2
exclusion from Brussels
I Recast 206–7
matrimonial relief 140
Stays
see also **restraint of foreign
proceedings**
actions *in rem* under
traditional English rules

effect of Brussels/Lugano
system 387–90
subject to conditions 385
Brussels I Recast
discretion to stay 459–60
*forum non
conveniens* 460–71
overview 311–12
residual discretion
to decline
jurisdiction 471–
3, 473–6
dissolution, nullity and
separation of civil
partners 1042
divorce, nullity and
separation of same sex
marriage 1047
English proceedings under
common law
arbitration 416–21
choice of court
agreements 410–16
forum non
conveniens 393–409
inherent
jurisdiction 392–3
pending the
determination
of proceedings
abroad 421
jurisdiction under Lugano
Convention 2007 314
jurisdiction within UK
under Modified
Regulation 321–2
matrimonial proceedings
see **stays**
discharge of orders 978
discretionary
stays 972–8
obligatory stays 967–72
overview 967
overview 391–2
parental responsibility
applications
Brussels II 1113–16
concurrent proceedings in
EU 1117–20
concurrent proceedings
in related UK
jurisdiction 1124
concurrent proceedings
outside EU 1124–5
Family Law Act 1986 1113
Hague Convention
States 1121–4

transfers under Hague
Convention
1996 1116–17
traditional rules on
jurisdiction 190
Subject matter
European Enforcement
Order Regulation
2004 656–7
exclusive subject-matter
jurisdiction 221–2
overview 217–19
rights in rem 219–20
tenancies 221–2
name of subject 15–16
Submission to jurisdiction
Brussels I Recast 226–9
consumer
contracts 296–7
employment
contracts 302
insurance 290–1
lis pendens 226
jurisdiction of English
courts under traditional
rules 332–4
under Maintenance
Regulation 1067–8
recognition and enforcement
of foreign judgments at
common law
agreements to
submit 532–3
appeals against default
judgments 538–9
arguing in the
alternative 537–8
counterclaims 531
procedural steps 539–40
voluntary
appearances 533–7
sovereign immunity 506
Subrogation
assignment of debts 1291–2
insurers' rights 807
parties 447
Subsidiary issues *see* **incidental
questions**
Substance
damages 91–7
evidence
interpretation and
proof of document
distinguished 80–1
interpretation
distinguished 84
law of the forum 80

presumptions and burden
    of proof 85
taking of evidence outside
    the EU 83–4
taking of evidence within
    the EU 81–3
execution of judgments 104
foreign currency judgments
    appropriate currency for
        judgment 101–4
    date for conversion 100–1
    interest on judgments 99
    law of forum 100
    Miliangos rule 98–9
    old rule: judgment must
        be in sterling 97
jurisdiction within UK
    under Modified
    Regulation 318
nature and extent of the
    remedy 89–90
parties
    appropriate
        defendants 87–8
    proper claimants 86–7
priority of creditors 89–90
procedure distinguished
    drawing the line 75–7
    importance 74–5
provisional measures under
    Brussels I Recast
    jurisdiction as to the
        substance 303
    where no jurisdiction as to
        the substance 303–5
time within which an action
    must be brought 78–9
Succession
    see also **administration of
        estates; trusts**
    application of renvoi 70
    choice of law rule
        bona vacantia 49–50
        commorientes 50
    European
        harmonisation 1358–9
    exclusion from Brussels
        I Recast 212
    exclusion from Rome
        I Regulation 697–9
    immovable property
        intestate
            succession 1351–2
        wills 1352–8
    mandatory rules 143
    movable property
        intestate succession 1339

wills 1340–51
polygamous marriages 943
powers of appointment
    exercised by will
    capacity 1361
    essential validity 1362–3
    formal validity 1361–2
    interpretation 1363–4
    overview 1359–60
    revocation 1364
    special and general powers
        distinguished 1360
recognition and enforcement
    of foreign judgments
    and awards
    overview 524
    sovereign immunity 505
total renvoi doctrine
    essential validity of
        will 66
    essential validity of will
        and codicils 68–9
    excluded
        beneficiaries 66–7
    legitimacy 67–8
    validity of codicils 65
transfer of damages under
    Rome II 864
unity principle 1338
Surrogacy *see* **cross–border
    surrogacy**

Taking of evidence abroad
    taking of evidence outside
        the EU 83–4
    taking of evidence within
        the EU 81–3
Tangible movables
    intangible movables
        distinguished 1254
    transfers
        attachment by
            creditors 1275
        cultural property 1277–8
        derivative claims 1271–2
        general rule 1267–70
        gifts 1276–7
        goods in transit 1275–6
        human rights 1278–9
        law of the
            domicile 1264–5
        law of the place of
            acting 1265–6
        law of the situs 1265
        meaning of the law of the
            situs 1273–4

proper law of the
    transfer 1266–7
retention of title
    clauses 1272–3
underlying
    problems 1263–4
Tenancies 221–2
Territoriality
    acquired rights theory 21–3
    administration of
        estates 1326
    forced marriages 991
    limitations on dominance of
        applicable law 748
    mandatory rules 143
Theoretical perspectives
    acquired rights 21–3
    assignment of
        debts 1282–4
    capacity to marry
        alternative
            approaches 910
        English judicial
            authorities 913–18
        evaluation of
            theories 910–13
    English law
        law of forum 36–7
        principles for construction
            of rules 37
    evolution of EU law
        constitutionalisation 35
        disagreement over extent
            of change 33–4
        federalization 34
        'vertical' and 'horizontal'
            conflicts
            distinguished 35–6
    local law theory 23–4
    new American revolution
        basic characteristic 24
        general approaches 25–6
        limited impact 31–2
        rule-selection
            techniques 26–31
        subsequent
            developments 32–3
    recognition and enforcement
        at common law
        at common law 525–7
        enforcement by
            statute 527
Time 5–6
Torts
    development of
        English law 20
    mandatory rules 143

Torts (*cont.*):
problem of ascertaining
applicable law 776–7
Rome II Regulation
borderline with unjust
enrichment 840
environmental
damage 828–31
escape clause 814–19
exception to general
rule 809–14
general
rule 809–10, 810–13
industrial action 835–6
intellectual property
rights 831–5
manifestly more closely
connected escape
clause 814–19
maritime
obligations 875–8
product liability 819–23
restrictions on free
competition 827–8
road traffic accidents 819
scope of Chapter
II 802–9
specific rules for special
torts 819–36
structure of
Chapter II 809
unfair competition 823–7
service with permission out
of jurisdiction under
English traditional
rules 347–55
sovereign immunity 505
special jurisdiction under
Article 7(2)
branches and
agencies 279–83
concurrent actions
in tort and
contract 268–70
matters relating to
tort, delict or
quasi-delict 263–7
place where harmful event
occurred 270–9
threatened wrongs 270
substance and procedure
distinguished
appropriate currency for
judgment 103–4
heads of damage 93
measure of damages 94–5

time within which an
action must be
brought 79
total renvoi doctrine 69
Total renvoi doctrine
decisions supporting the
doctrine 65–9
key elements 60–1
objections to doctrine
capitulation of English
rules 62–3
difficulties of
application 63–5
lack of international
support 61
uniform decisions 61–2
Tracing
causes of action 446
choice of law 841
substance and procedure
distinguished 77
Transfers and assignments
intangible movables
debts 1280–94
negotiable
instruments 1294–7
rights distinguished 1280
shares and
securities 1298–304
matrimonial property - no
ante-nuptial agreement
immovable property 1371
movable
property 1366–71
name of subject 15–16
proper claimants 86
'provision of services' 256
tangible movables
attachment by
creditors 1275
cultural
property 1277–8
derivative claims 1271–2
general rule 1267–70
gifts 1276–7
goods in transit 1275–6
human rights 1278–9
law of the
domicile 1264–5
law of the place of
acting 1265–6
law of the situs 1265
meaning of the law of the
situs 1273–4
proper law of the
transfer 1266–7

retention of title
clauses 1272–3
underlying
problems 1263–4
Trusts
see also **administration of
estates; succession**
choice of law
absence of choice 1387–9
scope of applicable
law 1389–90
by settlor 1386–7
variation of applicable
law 1390–1
defined 1383
domicile under Brussels
I Recast 200–2
exclusion from
Rome I 702
exclusion from Rome
II 796–7
formal validity 1385
mandatory rules 1392–3
overview 1382–3
public policy 1393
recognition 1391–2
service with permission out
of jurisdiction under
English traditional
rules 358–60
sovereign immunity 505
substance and procedure
distinguished 85
trusts falling within the 1987
Act 1384
validity of transfer of trust
assets 1385
variations
jurisdiction 1393–4
marriage
settlements 1394–6
Trusts for sale
capacity to take and transfer
immovables 1258
English doctrine of
conversion 44
movable and immovable
property
distinguished 1252–4

Unjust enrichment
Rome II Regulation
applicable law 843–7
borderline with torts 840
contractual
obligations 839–40

manifestly more closely
connected escape
clause 847–8
problems of
classification 837–8
problems with
equity 840–1
proprietary claims 838–9
scope of Article 10 837
total renvoi doctrine 70

**Variation of trusts and
settlements**
marriage settlements 1394–6
Variation of Trusts Act
1958 1393–4
Vested rights *see* **Acquired
rights theory**
Voluntary residence 158–60

Wills
see also **administration of
estates**
English grants for separate
wills 1330–1
European
harmonisation 1358–9
immovable property
capacity 1352
essential validity 1353
formal validity 1352
general rule 1352
revocation 1358
movable property
capacity 1339–51
essential validity 1344–7
formal validity 1340–4
general rule 1339
interpretation 1347–8

revocation 1348–51
powers of appointment
exercised by will
capacity 1361
essential validity 1362–3
formal validity 1361–2
interpretation 1363–4
overview 1359–60
revocation 1364
special and general powers
distinguished 1360
Winding up 1309–11
Witnesses
proof of foreign law 110–13
sufficient
qualifications 110–11